October 24–28, 2011
Glasgow, Scotland, UK

Association for
Computing Machinery

Advancing Computing as a Science & Profession

CIKM 2011 GLASGOW

CIKM'11

Proceedings of the 2011 ACM International

Conference on Information and Knowledge Management

Sponsored by:

ACM SIGIR & ACM SIGWEB

Association for
Computing Machinery

Advancing Computing as a Science & Profession

The Association for Computing Machinery
2 Penn Plaza, Suite 701
New York, New York 10121-0701

Notice to Past Authors of ACM-Published Articles
ACM intends to create a complete electronic archive of all articles and/or other material previously published by ACM. If you have written a work that has been previously published by ACM in any journal or conference proceedings prior to 1978, or any SIG Newsletter at any time, and you do NOT want this work to appear in the ACM Digital Library, please inform permissions@acm.org, stating the title of the work, the author(s), and where and when published.

ISBN: 978-1-4503-0717-8 (Digital)

ISBN: 978-1-4503-1353-7 (Print)

Additional copies may be ordered prepaid from:

ACM Order Department
PO Box 30777
New York, NY 10087-0777, USA

Phone: 1-800-342-6626 (USA and Canada)
+1-212-626-0500 (Global)
Fax: +1-212-944-1318
E-mail: acmhelp@acm.org
Hours of Operation: 8:30 am – 4:30 pm ET

ACM Order Number: 605110

Printed in the USA

CIKM 2011 Chairs' Welcome

On behalf of the organizing committee, it is our great pleasure to welcome you to the *20th ACM Conference on Information and Knowledge Management* in Glasgow!

Since its inception, the CIKM conference has provided a unique international forum for the presentation, discussion and dissemination of research findings in data management, information retrieval and knowledge management. The purpose of the conference is to identify challenging problems facing the development of future knowledge and information systems and to shape future research directions through the publication of high quality, applied and theoretical research findings. The conference has been a leading forum in which experts from academic, industry and the public sector gather to exchange ideas, research achievements and technical developments in multidisciplinary research areas.

CIKM is one of the world's most recognized conferences in the field. This year CIKM received 918 full paper submissions, 220 poster submissions, and 56 demonstration submissions. This is a great demonstration of the lively research areas that contribute to the CIKM area. In addition, CIKM 2011 will host 10 tutorials from leading researchers, 15 workshops on cutting-edge areas of research, a panel session on Social and Collaborative Search and a dedicated Industry Day featuring leading industrial practitioners. We are grateful to all authors who chose to submit their research to CIKM 2011 and are very excited by the final program.

CIKM values interdisciplinary research and we are proud to present three keynote speakers, Professor Justin Zobel, Professor Maurizio Lenzerini and Professor David Karger, all of whom will give presentations that cross discipline boundaries.

The program of CIKM 2011 represents a huge amount of effort on behalf of many people. The contributions to the technical program were selected by a large program committee headed by our three program chairs, Arjen de Vries, Bettina Berendt and Wenfei Fan. We are grateful to them for all their hard work in managing such a complex reviewing task and to their senior program committee members, program committee members and additional reviewers who freely gave their time, effort and intelligence to the difficult task of selecting which contributions would form the program. We are also very grateful to Fidel Cacheda, Matt Lease and Sara Hawkins, who monitored and managed the process of editing the proceedings to meet very tight production schedules.

We are also grateful to Gianni Amati who ran CIKM's first dedicated poster submission route; Omar Alonso who managed the demonstrations track and introduced demo boaster sessions into the program; Craig Macdonald who handled the very difficult job of organizing the workshop program; Jaap Kamps and Fabrizio Silvestri who solicited a great range of tutorials; Donald Metzler who was a great publicity chair; Leif Azzopardi for handling the student award scheme and student volunteers; Ryen White and Marius Pasca who were very active sponsorship chairs and whose hard work allowed us to award grants to several student attendees; Daniel Tunkelang and Tony Russell-Rose for organizing such an interesting Industry program; Jeremy Pickens for organizing an exciting panel session; David Carmel for organizing the Best Paper Awards committee. The local arrangements team has been superbly managed by Jon Richie, our local arrangements chair who has made a huge effort into every aspect of the conference. Finally, we value the efforts of Richard McCreadie (invitation letters) and Rodrygo Santos (website & social media).

We would like to express our appreciation to all our sponsors: EMC^2, Microsoft Research, Google, Yahoo! Research, SAP, Yandex, IBM Research, eBay Research Labs, Cambridge University Press, Springer, Taylor & Francis and CrossRef. Google generously provided travel support for East European attendees and Springer kindly sponsored the Best Paper Awards. All their generous sponsorship and support made this conference successful and possible. We would also like to thank the sponsoring SIGs, SIGIR and SIGWEB, and their respective chairs, James Allan (SIGIR), Ethan Munson and Simon Harper (SIGWEB) for their advice and support.

It is a great pleasure to be able to welcome you to CIKM 2011 in Glasgow. We hope that attendees find the technical program of CIKM 2011 to be interesting and productive and you enjoy CIKM 2011 and your stay in Glasgow.

Iadh Ounis
CIKM 2011 General Co-Chair
University of Glasgow

Ian Ruthven
CIKM 2011 General Co-Chair
University of Strathclyde

Message from the Program Committee Chairs

Welcome to the 20th ACM Conference on Information and Knowledge Management. Since 1992, CIKM has been successfully bringing together leading researchers from the database, information retrieval, and knowledge management communities. The purpose of the conference is to identify challenging problems facing the development of future knowledge and information systems, and to shape future research directions through the publication of high-quality research findings, both theoretical and applied. In CIKM 2011, we continued the tradition of promoting collaboration among the general areas of databases, information retrieval, and knowledge management. This year's call for papers attracted 918 submissions from Africa, the Americas, Asia, Australia, Europe, and the Middle East. The program committee accepted 134 submissions as full papers for oral presentation (15%), an additional 93 as short papers for oral presentation and 98 as poster presentations (a cumulative acceptance rate of 35%). We also accepted 21 demonstrations, 10 tutorials and 15 workshops. CIKM 2011 also organized the first direct call for poster submissions, resulting in 220 submissions and 66 poster acceptances.

We'd like to acknowledge everyone who made this technical program possible. First, we would like to thank the authors for providing the contents of the program: the conference would not be possible without your contributions. Our gratitude goes out to the program committee and external reviewers, who worked extremely hard in providing feedback on the submissions. The senior program committees deserve much recognition for shepherding the review process and for helping along the way. A very big "thank you" goes out to all the countless others who have contributed to making CIKM 2011 a success. Finally, we would like to thank all our corporate sponsors for their generous support.

We hope that you will find this program interesting and thought-provoking. Please enjoy the conference and the opportunity to network with friends and colleagues from around the world.

Bettina Berendt
CIKM 2011 KM Chair
Katholieke Universiteit Leuven, Belgium

Arjen de Vries
CIKM 2011 IR Chair
Centrum Wiskunde & Informatica, The Netherlands

Wenfei Fan
CIKM 2011 DB Chair
University of Edinburgh, UK

Table of Contents

VOLUME 1

Keynote Address

Session 1: Retrieval Models

Session 2: Techniques for the Web

Session 5: Type and Structure

Session Chair: Leif Azzopardi *(University of Glasgow)*

Session 6: Machine Learning for Information Retrieval

Session Chair: Stephen Robertson *(Microsoft Research Cambridge)*

Session 7: Information Retrieval Implementation Techniques

Session Chair: Justin Zobel *(The University of Melbourne)*

Session 8: Language Technology and Information Retrieval

Session Chair: Jussi Karlgen *(Swedish Institute of Computer Science)*

Session 9: Results in Context

Session Chair: Noriko Kando *(NII)*

Session 10: Algorithms

Session Chair: Felix Naumann *(Hasso-Plattner-Institute)*

Session 11: Image Retrieval

Session Chair: Yi Chang *(Yahoo! Labs)*

Session 12: Social Media

Session Chair: Jun Wang *(University College London)*

Session 13: Personalization and Advertising

Session Chair: Emine Yilmaz *(Microsoft Research Cambridge)*

Session 14: Evaluation and Analysis

Session Chair: Jaap Kamps *(University of Amsterdam)*

Session 15: Classification and Evaluation

Session Chair: Nicolas Garcia Pedrajas *(University of Córdoba)*

Session 16: Information Filtering

Session Chair: Yan Zhang *(Vermont Information Processing)*

Session 17: Topics and Events

Session Chair: Ram Akella *(Stanford University & University of California)*

Session 18: Temporal, Stream and Spatial Information

Session Chair: Massimo Ruffolo *(ICAR-CNR)*

Session 19: Text Mining

Session Chair: Yunyao Li *(IBM Research)*

Session 25: Link Prediction

Session Chair: B. Barla Cambazoglu *(Yahoo! Research)*

Session 26: Link, Graph and Relation Mining

Session Chair: Roi Blanco *(Yahoo! Research)*

Session 27: Science, the Past, and the Future

Session Chair: Giorgio Orsi *(University of Oxford)*

Session 28: Information Extraction and Entities

Session Chair: Xiaofeng Yu *(The Chinese University of Hong Kong)*

Session 29: Queries, Questions and Tags Mining

Session Chair: Jian-Tao Sun *(Microsoft Research Asia)*

Session 30: Preparing, Mining and Evaluating with and for Different Views

Session Chair: Hwanjo Yu *(POSTECH)*

Session 31: Information Extraction and Semantic Techniques

Session Chair: Marie-Aude Aufaure *(Ecole Centrale Paris)*

Session 32: Data on the Web

Session Chair: K. Selcuk Candan *(Arizona State University)*

Session 33: Query Processing and Optimization

Session Chair: Alberto Laender *(Universidade Federal de Minas Gerais)*

Session 34: Semantic Web and Information Retrieval

Session Chair: Alfredo Cuzzocrea *(University of Calabria)*

Session 35: Query Answering and Social Search

Session Chair: Yuqing Wu *(Indiana University)*

Session 36: Distributed Data Management and Data Integration

Session Chair: Philip Bohannon *(Yahoo! Research)*

Poster Session: Knowledge Management

Poster Session: Databases

Demonstration Session 1

Demonstration Session 2

Demonstration Session 3

Co-located Tutorial Summaries

Co-located Workshop Summaries

Panel

CIKM 2011 Conference Organization

General Conference Chairs:	Iadh Ounis *(University of Glasgow, UK)* Ian Ruthven *(University of Strathclyde, UK)*
Chair-at-Large:	Craig Macdonald *(University of Glasgow, UK)*
DB Track Program Chair:	Wenfei Fan *(University of Edinburgh, UK)*
IR Track Program Chair:	Arjen de Vries *(Centrum Wiskunde & Informatica, The Netherlands)*
KM Track Program Chair:	Bettina Berendt *(Katholieke Universiteit Leuven, Belgium)*
Workshops Chair:	Craig Macdonald *(University of Glasgow, UK)*
Posters Chair:	Gianni Amati *(FUB, Italy)*
Tutorials Chairs:	Jaap Kamps *(University of Amsterdam, The Netherlands)* Fabrizio Silvestri *(ISTI-CNR, Italy)*
Industry Event Chairs:	Daniel Tunkelang *(LinkedIn, US)* Tony Russell-Rose *(UXLabs and City University London, UK)*
Demonstrations Chair:	Omar Alonso *(Microsoft, US)*
Panel Chair:	Jeremy Pickens *(Catalyst Repository Systems, US)*
Proceedings Chairs:	Fidel Cacheda *(University of A Coruña, Spain)* Matt Lease *(University of Texas at Austin, US)*
Local Arrangements Chair:	Jon Ritchie *(University of Glasgow, UK)*
Travel Award Chair:	Leif Azzopardi *(University of Glasgow, UK)*
Publicity Chair:	Donald Metzler *(University of Southern California ,US)*
Sponsorship Chairs:	Marius Pasca *(Google, US)* Ryen White *(Microsoft Research, US)*
Awards Chair:	David Carmel *(IBM Research Lab, Israel)*
Registration Chair:	Richard McCreadie *(University of Glasgow, UK)*,
Steering Committee Chair:	E.K. Park *(City University of New York, US)*

CIKM 2011 DB Track Program Committees

Senior Program Committee:

Marcelo Arenas (*Pontificia Universidad Católica de Chile, Chile)*
Pablo Barcelo (*Universidad de Chile, Chile)*
Philip Bohannon (*Yahoo! Research, US)*
Diego Calvanese (*Free University of Bozen-Bolzano, Italy)*
Chee-Yong Chan (*National University of Singapore, Singapore)*
Lei Chen (*Hong Kong University of Science and Technology, Hong Kong)*
Giuseppe De Giacomo (*University of Rome La Sapienza, Italy)*
Xin (Luna) Dong (*ATT Labs-Research, US)*
Alan Fekete (*University of Sydney, Australia)*
Floris Geerts (*University of Edinburgh, UK)*
Torsten Grust (*Universität Tübingen, Germany)*
Anastasios Kementsietsidis (*IBM T.J. Watson Research Center, US)*
Frank McSherry (*Microsoft Research Silicon Valley, US)*
Divesh Srivastava (*AT&T Labs, US)*
Yufei Tao (*Chinese University of Hong Kong, Hong Kong)*
Jeffrey Yu (*Chinese University of Hong Kong, Hong Kong)*

Program Committee:

Ashraf Aboulnaga (*University of Waterloo, Canada)*
Yanif Ahmad (*Johns Hopkins University, US)*
Denilson Barbosa (*University of Alberta, Canada)*
Zohra Bellahsene (*Université Montpellier, France)*
Michael Benedikt (*Oxford University, UK)*
Leopoldo Bertossi (*Carleton University, Canada)*
Mikolaj Bojanczyk (*Warsaw University, Poland)*
Angela Bonifati (*CNR, Italy)*
Michael Cafarella (*University of Michigan, US)*
Zhipeng Cai (*Mississippi State University, US)*
Kevin C. Chang (*University of Illinois, US)*
Haiming Chen (*Chinese Academy of Sciences, China)*
Wenguang Chen (*Peking University, China)*
Rada Chirkova (*North Carolina State University, US)*
Gao Cong (*NTU, Singapore)*
Richard Connor (*University of Strathclyde, UK)*
Alfredo Cuzzocrea (*University of Calabria, Italy)*
Anish Das Sarma (*Google Research, US)*
Ting Deng (*Beihang University, China)*
Jens Dittrich (*Saarland University, Germany)*
Guozhu Dong (*Wright State University, US)*
Songyun Duan (*IBM T.J. Watson Research Center, US)*
Irini Fundulaki (*Foundation for Research and Technology - Hellas, Greece)*
Avigdor Gal (*Technion - Israel Institute of Technology, Israel)*

Program Committee (continued):

Minos Garofalakis (*Technical University of Crete, Greece)*
Tingjian Ge (*University of Kentucky, US)*
Lukasz Golab (*AT&T Labs Research, US)*
Wook-Shin Han (*Kyungpook National University, Korea)*
Sven Helmer (*Birkbeck, University of London, UK)*
Kien Hua (*University of Central Florida, US)*
Ela Hunt (*ETH Zurich, Switzerland)*
Seung-won Hwang (*POSTECH, Korea)*
Zack Ives (*University of Pennsylvania, US)*
Gao Jun (*Peking University, China)*
Jaewoo Kang (*Korea University, Korea)*
Carl-Christian Kanne (*IBM Almaden Research Center, US)*
Raghav Kaushik (*Microsoft Research, US)*
Eamonn Keogh (*University of California Riverside, US)*
Benny Kimelfeld (*IBM, US)*
Masaru Kitsuregawa (*University of Tokyo, Japan)*
Solmaz Kolahi (*University of British Columbia, Canada)*
Hank Korth (*Lehigh University, Bethlehem, US)*
Maurizio Lenzerini (*Università di Roma La Sapienza, Italy)*
Feifei Li (*Florida State University, US)*
Yingshu Li (*Georgia State University, US)*
Jianzhong Li (*Harbin Institute of Technology, China)*
Xiang Lian (*HKUST, Hong Kong)*
Xuemin Lin (*University of New South Wales, Australia)*
Shuai Ma (*Beihang University, China)*
Jayant Madhavan (*Google, US)*
Ioana Manolescu (*INRIA, France)*
Wim Martens (*Technische Universität Dortmund, Germany)*
Maarten Marx (*University of Amsterdam, The Netherlands)*
Weiyi Meng (*SUNY Binghamton, US)*
Bongki Moon (*University of Arizona, US)*
Filip Murlak (*University of Warsaw, Poland)*
Muthu Muthukrishnan (*Rutgers University, US)*
Rimma Nehme (*Microsoft, US)*
Wolfgang Nejdl (*University of Hannover, Germany)*
Joachim Niehren (*INRIA Lille, France)*
Werner Nutt (*Free University of Bozen-Bolzano, Italy)*
Dan Olteanu (*Oxford University, UK)*
Dimitris Papadias (*HKUST, Hong Kong)*
Mary-Angela Papalaskari (*Villanova University, US)*
Alexandra Poulovassilis (*Birkbeck, University of London, UK)*
Sunil Prabhakar (*Purdue University, US)*
Lu Qin (*CUHK, China)*
Christopher Re (*University of Wisconsin-Madison, US)*
Dimitris Șacharidis (*IMIS "Athena" Research Centre , Greece)*
Arnaud Sahuguet (*Google, US)*
Marc H Scholl (*Universitaet Konstanz, Germany)*
Thomas Schwentick (*TU Dortmund, Germany)*
Jianhua Shao (*Cardiff University, UK)*
Mohamed Sharaf (*University of Queensland, Australia)*
Kian Lee Tan (*National University of Singapore, Singapore)*
Nan Tang (*University of Edinburgh, UK)*
Val Tannen (*University of Pennsylvania, US)*
Evimaria Terzi (*Boston University, US)*
Jens Teubner (*ETH Zurich, Switzerland)*

Program Committee (continued):

Alex Thomo (*University of Victoria, Canada)*
Marcos Vaz Salles (*Cornell University, US)*
Dirk Van Gucht (*Indiana University, US)*
Millist Vincent (*University of South Australia, Australia)*
Wei Wang (*University of North Carolina, US)*
Hongzhi Wang (*Harbin Institute of Technology, China)*
Jianmin Wang (*Tsinghua University, China)*
Junhu Wang (*Griffith University, Australia)*
Wei Wang (*Fudan University, China)*
Haixun Wang (*Microsoft Research Asia, China)*
Jianyong Wang (*Tsinghua University, China)*
Jef Wijsen (*University of Mons, Belgium)*
Ouri E. Wolfson (*University of Illinois at Chicago, US)*
Limsoon Wong (*National University of Singapore, Singapore)*
Peter Wood (*Birkbeck, University of London, UK)*
Yuqing Wu (*Indiana University, US)*
Ming Xiong (*Google, US)*
Fei Xu (*Microsoft, US)*
Ke Yi (*Hong Kong University of Science and Technology, Hong Kong)*
Ken Yocum (*UC San Diego, US)*
Clement Yu (*University of Illinois at Chicago, US)*
Xiaohui Yu (*York University, Canada)*

CIKM 2011 IR Track Program Committees

Senior Program Committee:

James Allan (*University of Massachusetts Amherst, US)*
Javed Aslam (*Northeastern University, US)*
Leif Azzopardi (*University of Glasgow, UK)*
Nicholas Belkin (*Rutgers University, US)*
Paul Bennett (*Microsoft Research, US)*
Wray Buntine (*National ICT Australia Limited, NICTA), Australia)*
Yi Chang (*Yahoo! Labs, US)*
Paul Clough (*University of Sheffield, UK)*
Fabio Crestani (*University of Lugano, Switzerland)*
Maarten de Rijke (*University of Amsterdam, The Netherlands)*
Patrick Gallinari (*University Pierre & Marie Curie, France)*
Bin Gao (*Microsoft Research Asia, China)*
Cathal Gurrin (*Dublin City University, Ireland)*
Djoerd Hiemstra (*University of Twente, The Netherlands)*
Winston Hsu (*National Taiwan University, Taiwan)*
Panos Ipeirotis (*New York University, US)*
Gareth Jones (*Dublin City University, Ireland)*
Jaap Kamps (*University of Amsterdam, The Netherlands)*
Noriko Kando (*NII, Japan)*
Jaana Kekäläinen (*University of Tampere, Finland)*
Oren Kurland (*Technion, Israel)*
Elizabeth Liddy (*Syracuse University, US)*
Mounia Lalmas (*Yahoo! Research, Spain)*
Paul McNamee (*Johns Hopkins University, US)*
Peter Mika (*Yahoo! Research Barcelona, Spain)*
Wolfgang Nejdl (*L3S Research Center, Germany)*
Omar Alonso (*Microsoft Research, US)*
Tetsuya Sakai (*Microsoft Research Asia, China)*
Fabrizio Silvestri (*ISTI - CNR, Italy)*
Torsten Suel (*NYU Poly, US)*
Andrew Trotman (*University of Otago, New Zealand)*
Ellen Voorhees (*National Institute of Standards and Technology, US)*
Jun Wang (*University College London, UK)*
Ji-Rong Wen (*Microsoft Research Asia, China)*
Ryen White (*Microsoft Research, US)*
Emine Yilmaz (*Microsoft Research Cambridge, UK)*
ChengXiang Zhai (*University of Illinois at Urbana-Champaign, US)*
Min Zhang (*Tsinghua University, China)*

Program Committee:

Maristella Agosti (*University of Padua, Italy)*
Robin Aly (*University of Twente, The Netherlands)*
Giambattista Amati (*Fondazione Ugo Bordoni, Italy)*
Marcos Andre Goncalves (*Universidade Federal de Minas Gerais, Brazil)*
Avi Arampatzis (*Democritus University of Thrace, Greece)*
Jaime Arguello (*Carnegie Mellon University, US)*
Hany Azzam (*Queen Mary, University of London, UK)*
Jing Bai (*Microsoft Corporation, US)*
Niranjan Balasubramanian (*University of Massachusetts Amherst, US)*
Krisztian Balog (*Norwegian University of Science and Technolog, Norway)*
Alejandro Bellogín Kouki (*Universidad Autónoma de Madrid, Spain)*
Michael Bendersky (*University of Massachusetts, Amherst, US)*
Paul Bennett (*Microsoft Research, US)*
Pushpak Bhattacharyya (*IIT Bombay, India)*
Jiang Bian (*Yahoo! Labs, US)*
Cui Bin (*Beijing University, China)*
Roi Blanco (*Yahoo! Research Barcelona, Spain)*
Toine Bogers (*RSLIS, Denmark)*
Gloria Bordogna (*CNR IDPA, Italy)*
Corrado Boscarino (*Centrum Wiskunde & Informatica, The Netherlands)*
Mohand Boughanem (*Universite Paul Sabatier, France)*
Sam Brody (*Rutgers, US)*
Wray Buntine (*National ICT Australia Limited, Australia)*
Fidel Cacheda (*University of Coruña, Spain)*
Pavel Calado (*Technical Univ. of Lisbon, Portugal)*
Gilberto Camara (*INPE - National Institute for Space Research, Brazil)*
Guihong Cao (*Microsoft, US)*
Ben Carterette (*University of Delaware, US)*
Marc-Allen Cartright (*University of Massachusetts Amherst, US)*
Pablo Castells (*Universidad Autonoma de Madrid, Spain)*
Carlos Castillo (*Yahoo! Research, Spain)*
Zheng Chen (*Microsoft Research Asia, China)*
Xueqi Cheng (*Institute of Computing Technology, CAS, China)*
Gordon Cormack (*University of Waterloo, Canada)*
Ricardo da Silva Torres (*University of Campinas, Brazil)*
Franciska de Jong (*University of Twente, The Netherlands)*
Gianluca Demartini (*Université de Fribourg, Switzerland)*
Ludovic Denoyer (*LIP6, France)*
Giorgio Maria Di Nunzio (*University of Padova, Italy)*
Fernando Diaz (*Yahoo! Research, US)*
Lan Du (*ANU & NICTA, Australia)*
Carsten Eickhoff (*Delft University of Technology, The Netherlands)*
Li Fan (*Yahoo, US)*
Hui Fang (*University of Delaware, US)*
Ayman Farahat (*Yahoo, US)*
Henry Feild (*University of Massachusetts Amherst, US)*
Juanma Fernández-Luna (*University of Granada, Spain)*
Nicola Ferro (*University of Padova, Italy)*

Program Committee (continued):

Dennis Fetterly (*Microsoft Research, US)*
Boudin Florian (*Université d'Avignon, France)*
Colum Foley (*Dublin City University, Ireland)*
Ingo Frommholz (*University of Bedfordshire, UK)*
Susan Gauch (*University of Arkansas, US)*
Eric Gaussier (*Laboratoire d'Informatique de Grenoble, France)*
Shlomo Geva (*Queensland University of Technology, Australia)*
Fredric Gey (*University of California, Berkeley, US)*
Ayse Goker (*City University London, UK)*
Gregory Grefenstette (*EXALEAD, France)*
Nils Grimsmo (*NTNU, Norway)*
Maxim Gurevich (*Yahoo! Research, US)*
Karl Gyllstrom (*Katholieke Universiteit Leuven, Belgium)*
Harry Halpin (*University of Edinburgh, UK)*
Claudia Hauff (*Delft University of Technology, The Netherlands)*
David Hawking (*Funnelback Ltd and Australian National University, Australia)*
Daqing He (*University of Pittsburgh, US)*
Jiyin He (*Centrum Wiskunde & Informatica, The Netherlands)*
Ben He (*Graduate University of CAS, China)*
Andreas Henrich (*University of Bamberg, Germany)*
Eduard Hoenkamp (*Queensland University of Technology, Australia)*
Katja Hofmann (*University of Amsterdam, The Netherlands)*
Laura Hollink (*Delft University of Technology, The Netherlands)*
Vera Hollink (*Centrum Wiskunde & Informatica, The Netherlands)*
Vivian Hu (*York University, Canada)*
Xuanjing Huang (*Fudan University, China), China)*
Gilles Hubert (*IRIT, University of Toulouse, France)*
Tereza Iofciu (*L3S Research Center, Germany)*
Daxin Jiang (*Microsoft Research Asia, China)*
Hideo Joho (*University of Tsukuba, Japan)*
Joemon Jose (*University of Glasgow, UK)*
Vanja Josifovski (*Yahoo! Research, US)*
Marko Junkkari (*University of Tampere, FI)*
Changsung Kang (*Yahoo! Labs, US)*
Gabriella Kazai (*Microsoft Research, UK)*
Heikki Keskustalo (*University of Tampere, FI)*
Jinyoung Kim (*University of Massachusetts, Amherst, US)*
Sang-Wook Kim (*Hanyang University, Korea)*
Irwin King (*The Chinese University Hong Kong, Hong Kong)*
Marijn Koolen (*University of Amsterdam, The Netherlands)*
Veit Koeppen (*Otto-von-Guericke-Universität Magdeburg, Germany)*
Donald Kraft (*Colorado Technical University, US)*
Raghu Krishnapuram (*IBM India Research Lab, India)*
Jérôme Kunegis (*University of Koblenz-Landau, Germany)*
Monica Landoni (*University of Lugano, Switzerland)*
Birger Larsen (*Royal School of LIS, Denmark)*
Martha Larson (*Delft University of Technology, The Netherlands)*
Hady Lauw (*Institute for Infocomm Research, Singapore)*
Victor Lavrenko (*University of Edinburgh, UK)*
Fotis Lazarinis (*University of Teesside, UK)*
Ronny Lempel (*Yahoo! Labs, Israel)*
Johannes Leveling (*CNGL, Dublin City University, Ireland)*

Program Committee (continued):

Qing Li (*City University of Hong Kong, Hong Kong)*
Huajing Li (*Facebook, US)*
Wen Li (*Delft University of Technology, The Netherlands)*
Xiaoming Li (*Peking University, China)*
Zhoujun Li (*Beihang University, China)*
Xia Lin (*Drexel University, US)*
Chin-Yew Lin (*Microsoft Research Asia, China)*
Hongfei Lin (*Dalian University of Technology, China)*
Yang Liu (*Shandong University, China)*
Alexander Löser (*TU Berlin, Germany)*
Claudio Lucchese (*ISTI-CNR Pisa, Italy)*
Yuanhua Lv (*University of Illinois Urbana-Champaign, US)*
Craig Macdonald (*University of Glasgow, UK)*
Walid Magdy (*Dublin City University, Ireland)*
Marco Maggini (*University of Siena, Italy)*
Yosi Mass (*IBM Research Lab at Haifa, Israel)*
James Mayfield (*Johns Hopkins University, US)*
Richard Mccreadie (*University of Glasgow, UK)*
Edgar Meij (*University of Amsterdam, The Netherlands)*
Dalila Mekhaldi (*University of Wolverhampton, UK)*
Donald Metzler (*University of Southern California, US)*
Jun Miao (*York University, Canada)*
Natasa Milic-Frayling (*Microsoft Research, UK)*
Vibhu Mittal (*Root-1, US)*
Dunja Mladenic (*Jozef Stefan Institute, Slovenia)*
Marie-Francine Moens (*Katholieke Universiteit Leuven, Belgium)*
Josiane Mothe (*Université de Toulouse, France)*
Vanessa Murdock (*Yahoo! Research, Spain)*
Arlindo L. Oliveira (*Instituto Superior Tecnico / INESC-ID, Portugal)*
Sandeep Pandey (*Yahoo Research, US)*
Gabriella Pasi (*Università degli Studi di Milano Bicocca, Italy)*
Raffaele Perego (*ISTI-CNR, Italy)*
Nils Pharo (*Oslo University College, Norway)*
Karen Pinel-Sauvagnat (*IRIT, University of Toulouse, France)*
Benjamin Piwowarski (*University of Glasgow, UK)*
Vassilis Plachouras (*Presans, France)*
Barbara Poblete (*Yahoo! Research, CL)*
Tamara Polajnar (*University of Glasgow, UK)*
Jeffrey Pound (*University of Waterloo, Canada)*
Kunal Punera (*Yahoo! Research, US)*
Tao Qin (*Microsoft Research Asia, China)*
Novi Quadrianto (*ANU & NICTA, Australia)*
Filip Radlinski (*Microsoft, Canada)*
Davood Rafiei (*University of Alberta, Canada)*
Georgina Ramirez (*Universitat Pompeu Fabra, Spain)*
Jan Ramon (*Katholieke Universiteit Leuven, Belgium)*
Edie Rasmussen (*University of British Columbia, Canada)*
Andreas Rauber (*Vienna University of Technology, Austria)*
Stephen Robertson (*Microsoft Research Cambridge, UK)*
Monica Rogati (*LinkedIn, US)*
Stevan Rudinac (*Delft University of Technology, The Netherlands)*
Scott Sanner (*NICTA & ANU, Australia)*

Program Committee (continued):

Rodrygo Santos (*University of Glasgow, UK)*
Ralf Schenkel (*Max-Planck-Institut Informatik, Germany, Germany)*
Falk Scholer (*RMIT University, Australia)*
Pavel Serdyukov (*Yandex, RU)*
James G Shanahan (*Church and Duncan Group, US)*
Milad Shokouhi (*Microsoft Research, UK)*
Wolf Siberski (*L3S Research Center, University of Hannover, Germany)*
Mark Smucker (*University of Waterloo, Canada)*
Cees Snoek (*University of Amsterdam, The Netherlands)*
Dawei Song (*Robert Gordon University, UK)*
Benno Stein (*Bauhaus-Universität Weimar, Germany)*
Venkata Subramaniam (*IBM Research India, India)*
Krysta M. Svore (*Microsoft Research, US)*
Lynda Tamine (*IRIT- Paul Sabatier University, France)*
Paul Thompson (*Dartmouth Medical School, US)*
Nicola Tonellotto (*CNR, Italy)*
Thanh D. Tran (*Institute AIFB, KIT, Germany)*
Dolf Trieschnigg (*University of Twente, The Netherlands)*
Ming-Feng Tsai (*National Chengchi University, Taiwan)*
Theodora Tsikrika (*University of Applied Sciences Western Switzerland, Switzerland)*
David Vallet (*Universidad Autonoma de Madrid, Spain)*
Arthur van Bunningen (*Teezir, The Netherlands)*
Theo P. van der Weide (*Radboud University, The Netherlands)*
Olga Vechtomova (*University of Waterloo, Canada)*
Suzan Verberne (*Radboud University Nijmegen, The Netherlands)*
Jesus Vilares (*University of A Coruña, Spain)*
Robert Villa (*University of Sheffield, UK)*
Vishwa Vinay (*Microsoft Research, UK)*
Stefanos Vrochidis (*CERTH-ITI, Greece)*
Xiaojun Wan (*Peking University, China)*
Bin Wang (*Institute of Computing Technology, CAS, China)*
Christian Wartena (*Novay, The Netherlands)*
Takashi Washio (*ISIR - Osaka University, Japan)*
William Webber (*University of Melbourne, Australia)*
Wouter Weerkamp (*University of Amsterdam, The Netherlands)*
Thijs Westerveld (*Teezir, The Netherlands)*
Yuchen Wu (*Google, US)*
Wensi Xi (*Google, US)*
Christopher C. Yang (*Drexel University, US)*
Shuang-Hong Yang (*Georgia Institute of Technology, US)*
Zheng Ye (*York University, Canada)*
Wai Gen Yee (*Orbitz, LLC, US)*
Xing Yi (*University of Massachusetts, Amherst, US)*
Hwan-Seung Yong (*Ewha Womans University, KR)*
Shichao Zhang (*Guangxi Normal University, China)*
Jun Zhao (*National Laboratory of Pattern Recognition, China)*
Zhaohui Zheng (*Yahoo! Inc, US)*
Ding Zhou (*Facebook, US)*
Nivio Ziviani (*UFMG, Brazil)*

CIKM 2011 KM Track Program Committees

Senior Program Committee:

Sarabjot Anand (*University of Warwick, UK)*
Francesco Bonchi (*Yahoo! Research, Spain)*
Ulrik Brandes (*University of Konstanz, Germany)*
Ronen Feldman (*Hebrew University of Jerusalem, Israel)*
Fosca Giannotti (*CNR, Italy)*
Dunja Mladenic (*Jozef Stefan Institute, Slovenia)*
Bamshad Mobasher (*DePaul University, US)*
Siegfried Nijssen (*Katholieke Universiteit Leuven*, Belgium)
Sanjay Ranka (*University of Florida, US)*
Yucel Saygin (*Sabanci University, Turkey)*
Myra Spiliopoulou (*University of Magdeburg, Germany)*
Xindong Wu (*University of Vermont, US)*
Qiang Yang (*Hong Kong University of Science and Technology, Hong Kong)*
Xingquan Zhu (*University of Technology Sydney, Australia)*

Program Committee:

Ram Akella (Stanford University & University of California)
Rocio Alaiz-Rodriguez (*University of Leon, Spain)*
Reda Alhajj (*University of Calgary, Canada)*
Aijun An (*York University, Canada)*
Shin Ando (*Gunma University, Japan)*
Marie-Aude Aufaure (*Ecole Centrale Paris, France)*
Rina Azoulay (*Jerusalem College of Technology, Israel)*
James Bailey (*University of Melbourne, Australia)*
Farokh Bastani (*University of Texas at Dallas, US)*
Michele Berlingerio (*ISTI-CNR Pisa, Italy)*
Sam Brody (*Rutgers University, US)*
Gilberto Camara (*INPE - National Institute for Space Research, Brazil)*
B. Barla Cambazoglu (*Yahoo! Research, Spain)*
K. Selcuk Candan (*Arizona State University, US)*
James Caverlee (*Texas A&M University, US)*
Chia-Hui Chang (*National Central University, Taiwan)*
Philip Chan (*Florida Institute of Technology, US)*
Sharma Chakravarthy (*University of Texas at Arlington, US)*
Narayanan Chatapuramkrishnan (*Washington State University, US)*
Cindy Chen (*University of Massachusetts Lowell, US)*
Li Chen (*Hong Kong Baptist University, Hong Kong)*
Ming-Syan Chen (*Research Center for Information Technology, Taiwan)*
Shu-Ching Chen (*Florida International University, US)*
Weizhu Chen (*Microsoft Research Asia, China)*
Xue-wen Chen (*Unversity of Kansas, US)*
Hong Cheng (*Chinese University of Hong Kong, Hong Kong)*
Kun-Ta Chuang (*National Cheng Kung University, Taiwan)*
Luísa Coheur (*Instituto Superior Técnico / L2F - INESC-ID, Portugal)*
Carlo Combi (*University of Verona, Italy)*
Manuel Contero (*Universidad Politécnica de Valencia, Spain)*
Francisco Couto (*Universidade de Lisboa, Portugal)*
Alfredo Cuzzocrea (*University of Calabria, Italy)*
Martine De Cock (*Ghent University, Belgium)*
Pablo de la Fuente (*Universidad de Valladolid, Spain)*
Pasquale De Meo (*Università di Messina, Italy)*
Tommaso Di Noia (*Politecnico di Bari, Italy)*
Wei Ding (*University of Massachusetts Boston, US)*
Juergen Dix (*Clausthal University of Technology, Germany)*
Debora Donato (*Yahoo! Labs, US)*
Dejing Dou (*University of Oregon, US)*
Brian Eoff (*Texas A&M University, US)*
Wei Fan (*IBM T.J.Watson, US)*
Olivier Ferret (*CEA LIST, France)*
Blaz Fortuna (*Jozef Stefan Institute, Slovenia)*
Johannes Fuernkranz (*TU Darmstadt, Germany)*

Program Committee (continued):

Tim Furche (*Oxford University, UK)*
Jose Gamez (*University of Castilla-La Mancha, Spain)*
Matjaz Gams (*Jozef Stefan Institute, Slovenia)*
Nicolas Garcia-Pedrajas (*University of Córdoba, Spain)*
Minos Garofalakis (*Technical University of Crete, Greece)*
Bugra Gedik (*IBM Research, US)*
Michael Gertz (*University of Heidelberg, Germany)*
Rayid Ghani (*Accenture Technology Labs, US)*
S.K. Ghosh (*Indian Institute of Technology, Kharagpur, IN)*
Bart Goethals (*University of Antwerp, Belgium)*
Jesus Gonzalez (*National Institute Astrophysics, Optics and Electronics, Mexico)*
Sergio Greco (*University of Calabria, Italy)*
Le Gruenwald (*University of Oklahoma, US)*
Christian Gütl (*Curtin University of Technology, Austria)*
Ido Guy (*IBM Research Haifa, Israel)*
Peng Han (*Chongqing Academy of Science & Technology, China)*
Dan He (*University of California, Los Angeles, US)*
Andreas Hotho (*University of Würzburg, Germany)*
Vagelis Hristidis (*Florida International University, US)*
Kien Hua (*University of Central Florida, US)*
Luke Huan (*University of Kansas, US)*
Jimmy Huang (*York University, Canada)*
Eyke Huellermeier (*Marburg University, Germany)*
Jing Jiang (*Singapore Management University, Singapore)*
Wei Jiang (*Missouri University of Science and Technology, US)*
Ruoming Jin (*Kent state University, US)*
Zhi Jin (*Peking University, China)*
Murat Kantarcioglu (*University of Texas at Dallas, US)*
Hung-Yu Kao (*National Cheng Kung University, Taiwan)*
Shiva Kasiviswanathan (*IBM T.J. Watson Research Center, US)*
Chan Keith (*Hong Kong Polytechnic University, Hong Kong)*
Eamonn Keogh (*University of California Riverside, US)*
Vlado Keselj (*Dalhousie University, Canada)*
Latifur Khan (*University of Texas at Dallas, US)*
Deepak Khemani (*IIT Madras, India)*
Hyerin Kim (*Korea Advanced Institute of Technology, Korea)*
Frank Klawonn (*Ostfalia University of Applied Sciences, Germany)*
Alek Kolcz (*Microsoft Live Labs, US)*
Patty Kostkova (*City eHealth Research Centre, UK)*
Wai Lam (*Chinese University of Hong Kong, Hong Kong)*
Won Suk Lee (*Yonsei University Korea, Korea)*
Young-Koo Lee (*Kyung Hee University, Korea)*
Carson K. Leung (*University of Manitoba, Canada)*
Bin Li (*University of Technology, Sydney, Australia)*

Program Committee (continued):

Jianzhong Li (*Harbin Institute of Technology, China)*
Tao Li (*Florida International University, US)*
Althea Liang (*HP Cloud and Security Lab, Singapore)*
Giuseppe Liotta (*Università di Perugia, Italy)*
Huan Liu (*Arizona State University, US)*
Nathan Liu (*Hong Kong University of Science and Technology, Hong Kong)*
Yan Liu (*IBM Research, US)*
Yang Liu (*Shandong University, China)*
Ying Liu (*KAIST, South Korea)*
Dmitri Loguinov (*Texas A&M University, US)*
Chang-Tien Lu (*Virginia Tech, US)*
Ping Luo (*Hewlett Packard Labs China, China)*
Mondher Maddouri (*URPAH, Tunisia)*
Hiroshi Mamitsuka (*Kyoto University, Japan)*
Bruno Martins (*Instituto Superior Técnico / INESC-ID, Portugal)*
Sergio Mascetti (*Università degli Studi di Milano, Italy)*
Stan Matwin (*University of Ottawa, Canada)*
Guy Melancon (*Université Bordeaux I, France)*
Gabor Melli (*PredictionWorks Inc., Canada)*
Ernestina Menasalvas (*Universidad Politecnica de Madrid, Spain)*
Ralf Moeller (*Hamburg University of Technology, Germany)*
Yang-Sae Moon (*Kangwon National University, Korea)*
Roser Morante (*University of Antwerp, Belgium)*
Ion Muslea (*Language Weaver, US)*
Mirco Nanni (*CNR, Italy)*
Olfa Nasraoui (*University of Louisville, US)*
Roberto Navigli (*Sapienza University of Rome, Italy)*
Tim Oates (*University of Maryland Baltimore County, US)*
Daniel O'Leary (*University of Southern California, US)*
Jonice Oliveira (*Federal University of Rio de Janeiro, Brazil)*
Weike Pan (*HKUST, China)*
Youngja Park (*IBM Research, US)*
Nikos Pelekis (*University of Piraeus, Greece)*
Kumaraguru Ponnurangam (*Indraprastha Institute of Information Technology, India)*
Vikram Pudi (*IIIT Hyderabad, India)*
Naren Ramakrishnan (*Virginia Tech, US)*
Vikas Raykar (*Siemens Healthcare, US)*
Daniele Riboni (*Universita degli Studi di Milano, Italy)*
Rong Pan (*Sun Yat-sen University, China)*
Massimo Ruffolo (*ICAR-CNR, Italy)*
Giovanni Maria Sacco (*Universita di Torino, Italy)*
Kazuhiro Seki (*Kobe University, Japan)*
Yi-dong Shen (*Chinese Academy of Science, China)*
Kyuseok Shim (*Seoul National University, Korea)*
Andrzej Skowron (*University of Warsaw, Poland)*
Dominik Slezak (*University of Warsaw, Poland)*

Program Committee (continued):

Manas Somaiya (*Ebay Inc., US*)
Bingjun Sun (*eBay/Shopping.com, US*)
Xiaoping Sun (*Chinese Academy of Science, China*)
Einoshin Suzuki (*Kyushu University, Japan*)
Keishi Tajima (*Kyoto University, Japan*)
Pang-Ning Tan (*Michigan State University, US*)
Lei Tang (*Yahoo! Labs, US*)
Maguelonne Teisseire (*TETIS, France*)
Konstantinos Tserpes (*National Technical University of Athens, Greece*)
Christopher Thomas (*Kno.e.sis Center, US*)
Agma Traina (*University of Sao Paulo at Sao Carlos, Brazil*)
Celine Vens (*Katholieke Universiteit Leuven, Belgium*)
Maria Virvou (*University of Piraeus, Greece*)
Xiaojun Wan (*Peking University, China*)
Haixun Wang (*Microsoft Research Asia, China*)
Jason Wang (*New Jersey Institute of Technology, US*)
Wei Wang (*University of North Carolina, US*)
Wei Wei (*Norwegian University of Science and Technology, Norway*)
Albert Weichselbraun (*Vienna University of Economics and Busines, Austria*)
Dwi Widyantoro (*STEI - Bandung Institute of Technology, Indonesia*)
Tak-Lam Wong (*The Hong Kong Institute of Education, Hong Kong*)
Bin Wu (*Beijing University of Posts and Telecom, China*)
Hui Xiong (*Rutgers University, US*)
Li Xiong (*Emory University, US*)
Jeonghee Yi (*Yahoo!, US*)
Jin Soung Yoo (*Indiana University - Purdue University, US*)
Hwanjo Yu (*POSTECH, Korea*)
Philip Yu (*University of Illinois at Chicago, US*)
Shipeng Yu (*Siemens Medical Solutions, US*)
Xiaofeng YU (*Chinese University of Hong Kong, China*)
Li Yunyao (*IBM Research, US*)
Markus Zanker (*Alpen-Adria-Universitaet Klagenfurt, Austria*)
Yi Zeng (*Beijing University of Technology China, China*)
Chengqi Zhang (*University of Technology Sydney, Australia*)
Dongsong Zhang (*University of Maryland Baltimore County, US*)
Yan Zhang (*Vermont Information Processing, US*)
Jessie Zhao (*York University, Canada*)
Lina Zhou (*University of Maryland Baltimore County, US*)
Geraldo Zimbrao (*Federal University of Rio de Janeiro, Brazil*)
Albrecht Zimmermann (*Katholieke Universiteit Leuven, Belgium*)

CIKM 2011 Industry Track, Workshop, Tutorial and Demonstration Committees

Industry Track Program Committee:

Steve Beitzel (*Telcordia Technologies, US)*
Jidong Chen (*EMC Research China, China)*
Nikesh Garera (*Kosmix, US)*
David Grossman (*Illinois Institute of Technology, US)*
Yoshinori Hara (*Kyoto University, Japan)*
Arvind Hulgeri (*Persistent Systems, India)*
Mizuho Iwaihara (*Waseda University, Japan)*
Giridhar Kumaran (*Microsoft Corporation, US)*
Ni Lao (*Carnegie Mellon University, US)*
Jonathan Ledlie (*Nokia Research, US)*
Wookey Lee (*Inha University, Korea)*
Wen-Syan Li (*Directorial MTS, China)*
Einat Minkov (*University of Haifa, Israel)*
Fuchun Peng (*Microsoft, US)*
Diego Puppin (*Google, US)*
Prasan Roy (*IBM Research, India)*
Robert Warren (*University of Waterloo, Canada)*

Tutorial Program Committee:

Daniel J. Abadi (*Yale University, US)*
Philip A. Bernstein (*Microsoft, US)*
Albert Bifet (*University of Waikato, New Zealand)*
Francesco Bonchi (*Yahoo!, Spain)*
Gianluca Demartini (*University of Fribourg, Switzerland)*
Thore Graepel (*Microsoft, UK)*
Antonio Gulli (*Microsoft, UK)*
Djoerd Hiemstra (*University of Twente, The Netherlands)*
Rosie Jones (*Akamai, US)*
Jaap Kamps (*University of Amsterdam, The Netherlands)*
Ray R. Larson (*UC Berkeley, US)*
Leonid Libkin (*University of Edinburgh, UK)*
Claudio Lucchese (*ISTI-CNR, Italy)*
Paul Ogilvie (*LinkedIn, US)*
Fabrizio Silvestri (*ISTI-CNR, Italy)*
Trevor Strohman (*Google, US)*
Daniel Tunkelang (*LinkedIn, US)*
Arjen P. de Vries (*CWI & Technical University of Delft, The Netherlands)*
Daniel J. Abadi (*Yale University, US)*
Philip A. Bernstein (*Microsoft, US)*

Demonstration Program Committee:

Enrique Alfonseca (*Google, Switzerland*)
Klaus Berberich (*Max-Planck Institute, Germany*)
Joaquin Delgado (*Yahoo, US*)
Alex Dow (*Microsoft, US*)
Conny Junghans (*University of Heidelberg, Germany*)
Vasilis Kandylas (*Microsoft, US*)
Jussi Karlgren (*SICS, Sweden*)
Dmitry Lenkov (*Oracle, US*)
David Losada (*University of Santiago de Compostela, Spain*)
Bertram Ludaescher (*University of California, Davis, US*)
Gerard de Melo (*Max-Planck Institute, Germany*)
Ullas Nambiar (*IBM Research, India*)
Alexandros Ntoulas (*Zynga, US*)
Ximena Olivares (*eBay, US*)
Cristobal Pedregal-Martin (*Oracle, US*)
Alvaro Pereira (*Federal University of Ouro Preto, Brazil*)
Igor Perisic (*LinkedIn, US*)
Jorge Quiane-Ruiz (*Saarland University, Germany*)
Mandar Rahurkar (*Yahoo!, US*)
Martin Theobald (*Max-Planck, Germany*)

Workshop Program Committee:

Karl Aberer (*EPFL, Switzerland*)
James Allan (*University of Massachusetts, Amherst, US*)
Roi Blanco (*Yahoo! Research, Spain*)
Pia Borlund (*Royal School of Library and Information Science, Denmark*)
Wray Buntine (*NICTA, Australia*)
Marcos Goncalves (*Universidade Federal de Minas Gerais, Brazil*)
Alasdair Gray (*University of Manchester, UK*)
Donna Harman (*NIST, US*)
Bill Hersh (*Oregon Health & Science University, US*)
Noriko Kando (*National Institute of Informatics, Japan*)
Anastasios Kementsietsidis (*IBM Research, US*)
Elizabeth Liddy (*Syracuse University, US*)
Hervé Martin (*Joseph Fourier University (France)*
Mirjam Minor (*University Trier, Germany*)
Pavel Serdyukov (*Yandex LLC, Russia*)
Nicola Tonellotto (*CNR, Italy*)
Rosina Weber (*Drexel University, US*)
Emine Yilmaz (*Microsoft, UK*)
Shichao Zhang (*University of Technology Sydney, Australia*)

Poster Program Committee (continued):

Bill Eberle (*Tennessee Tech University, US)*
Hui Fang (*University of Delaware, US)*
Nicola Ferro (*University of Padova, Italy)*
Boudin Florian (*Université d'Avignon, France)*
Giorgio Gambosi (*University of Rome "Tor Vergata", Italy)*
Giorgos Giannopoulos (*NTU Athens, Greece)*
Jesus Gonzalez (*National Institute of Astrophysics, Optics and Electronics, Mexico)*
Sergio Greco (*University of Calabria, Italy)*
Gregory Grefenstette (*EXALEAD, France)*
Cathal Gurrin (*Dublin City University, Ireland)*
Ido Guy (*IBM Research Haifa, Israel)*
Claudia Hauff (*Delft University of Technology, Netherlands)*
Ben He (*Graduate University of Chinese Academy of Sciences, China)*
Andreas Henrich (*University of Bamberg, Germany)*
Vivian Hu (*York University, Canada)*
Qiang Huang (*University of East Anglia, UK)*
Rong Huang (*NC State University, US)*
Xiaojiang Huang (*Peking University, China)*
Gilles Hubert (*IRIT, University of Toulouse, France)*
Kai Hui (*Graduate University of Chinese Academy of Sciences, China)*
Arvind Hulgeri (*Persistent Systems, India)*
Ela Hunt (*ETH Zurich, Switzerland)*
Seung-won Hwang (*POSTECH, Korea)*
Giacomo Inches (*University of Lugano, Switzerland)*
Jing Jiang (*Singapore Management University, Singapore)*
Hideo Joho (*University of Tsukuba, Japan)*
Gao Jun (*Peking University, China)*
Mouna Kacimi (*Free University of Bozen-Bolzano, Italy)*
Toshihiro Kamishima (*AIST, Japan)*
Jaewoo Kang (*Korea University, Korea)*
Abhijith Kashyap (*Florida International University, US)*
Gabriella Kazai (*Microsoft Research, UK)*
Chan Keith (*The Hong Kong Polytechnic University, Hong Kong)*
Anastasios Kementsietsidis (*IBM T.J. Watson Research Center, US)*
Eamonn Keogh (*University of California Riverside, US)*
Sang-Wook Kim (*Hanyang University, Korea)*
Benny Kimelfeld (*IBM, US)*
Iraklis Klampanos (*University of Glasgow, UK)*
Solmaz Kolahi (*University of British Columbia, Canada)*
Donald Kraft (*Colorado Technical University, US)*
Giridhar Kumaran (*Microsoft Corporation, US)*
Wai Lam (*The Chinese University of Hong Kong, Hong Kong)*
Monica Landoni (*University of Lugano, Switzerland)*
Ni Lao (*Carnegie Mellon University, US)*
Birger Larsen (*Royal School of LIS, Denmark)*
Martha Larson (*Delft University of Technology, Netherlands)*
Hady Lauw (*Institute for Infocomm Research, Singapore)*
Won Suk Lee (*Yonsei University Korea, Korea)*
Maurizio Lenzerini (*Università di Roma La Sapienza, Italy)*
Johannes Leveling (*CNGL, Dublin City University, Ireland)*
Bin Li (*University of Technology, Sydney, Australia)*

Poster Program Committee (continued):

Wei Li (*IBM Silicon Valley Lab, US)*
Huiying Li (*Peking University, China)*
Hongfei Lin (*Dalian Univ. of Technology, China)*
Christina Lioma (*University of Stuttgart, Germany)*
Giuseppe Liotta (*Università di Perugia, Italy)*
Yang Liu (*Shandong University, China)*
David Losada (*University of Santiago de Compostela, Spain)*
Robert Luk (*The Hong Kong Polytechnic University, Hong Kong)*
Ping Luo (*Hewlett Packard Labs China, China)*
Shuai Ma (*Beihang University, China)*
Craig Macdonald (*University of Glasgow, UK)*
Andrew MacFarlane (*City University London, UK)*
Ioana Manolescu (*INRIA, France)*
Maarten Marx (*University of Amsterdam, Netherlands)*
Richard McCreadie (*University of Glasgow, UK)*
Gabor Melli (*PredictionWorks, Canada)*
Umar Minhas (*University of Waterloo, Canada)*
Einat Minkov (*University of Haifa, Israel)*
Vibhu Mittal (*Root-1, US)*
Dunja Mladenic (*Jozef Stefan Institute, Slovenia)*
Marie-Francine Moens (*Katholieke Universiteit Leuven, Belgium)*
Yang-Sae Moon (*Kangwon National University, Korea)*
Alessandro Moschitti (*DISI, University of Trento, Italy)*
Miyuki Nakano (*University of Tokyo, Japan)*
Mirco Nanni (*ISTI-CNR, Italy)*
Dan Olteanu (*Oxford University, UK)*
Iadh Ounis (*University of Glasgow, UK)*
Dimitris Papadias (*HKUST, Hong Kong)*
Mary-Angela Papalaskari (*Villanova University, US)*
Javier Parapar (*University of A Coruña, Spain)*
Pawel Parys (*University of Warsaw, Poland)*
Nikos Pelekis (*University of Piraeus, Greece)*
Benjamin Piwowarski (*University of Glasgow, UK)*
Vassilis Plachouras (*PRESANS, France)*
Barbara Poblete (*Yahoo! Research, Chile)*
Edie Rasmussen (*University of British Columbia, Canada)*
Francisco J. Ribadas-Pena (*University of Vigo, Spain)*
Pan Rong (*Sun Yat-sen University, China)*
Prasan Roy (*IBM Research, India)*
Stefan Rüger (*The Open University, UK)*
Keun Ho Ryu (*Chungbuk National University, Korea)*
Giovanni Maria Sacco (*Università di Torino, Italy)*
Dimitris Sacharidis (*IMIS "Athena" Research Centre , Greece)*

Poster Program Committee (continued):

Rodrygo Santos (*University of Glasgow, UK)*
Ulrike Sattler (*University of Manchester, UK)*
Jacques Savoy (*University of Neuchatel, Switzerland)*
Maximilian Schich (*CCNR, Northeastern University, US)*
Falk Scholer (*RMIT University, Australia)*
Giovanni Semeraro (*University of Bari, Italy)*
Pavel Serdyukov (*Yandex, Russia)*
Yue Shi (*Delft University of Technology, Netherlands)*
Kyuseok Shim (*Seoul National University, Korea)*
Milad Shokouhi (*Microsoft Research, UK)*
Mário J. Silva (*Instituto Superior Técnico/INESC-ID, Portugal)*
Andrzej Skowron (*University of Warsaw, Poland)*
Amanda Spink (*Loughborough University, UK)*
Venkata Subramaniam (*IBM Research India, IN)*
Xiaoping Sun (*ICT, CanadaS, China)*
Bingjun Sun (*eBay/Shopping.com, US)*
Xuning Tang (*Drexel University, US)*
David Taniar (*Monash University, Australia)*
Dacheng Tao (*University Technology Sydney, Australia)*
Jens Teubner (*ETH Zurich, CH)*
Paul Thomas (*CSIRO, Australia)*
Alex Thomo (*University of Victoria, Canada)*
Paul Thompson (*Dartmouth Medical School, US)*
Anastasios Tombros (*Queen Mary University of London, UK)*
Ming-Feng Tsai (*National Chengchi University, Taiwan)*
Ivor Wai-Hung Tsang (*Nanyang Technological University, Singapore)*
David Vallet (*Universidad Autonoma de Madrid, Spain)*
Theo van der Weide (*Radboud University Nijmegen, Netherlands)*
Thanasis Vergoulis (*National Technical University of Athens, Greece)*
Jesus Vilares (*University of A Coruna, Spain)*
Manuel Vilares (*University of Vigo, Spain)*
Vishwa Vinay (*Microsoft Research, UK)*
Xiaojun Wan (*Peking University, China)*
Jianyong Wang (*Tsinghua University, China)*
Hongzhi Wang (*Harbin Institute of Technology, China)*
William Webber (*Computer Science and Software Engineering, Australia)*
Jef Wijsen (*University of Mons, Belgium)*
Peter Wood (*Birkbeck, University of London, UK)*
Yuqing Wu (*Indiana University, Bloomington, US)*
Lei Xie (*NorthWestern Polytechnical University, China)*
Hui Xiong (*Rutgers University, US)*
Hongbo Xu (*Chinese Academy of Sciences Beijing, China)*
Grace Hui Yang (*Institute of Computing Technology, Chinese Academy of Sciences, China)*

Poster Program Committee (continued):

Zheng Ye (*York University, Canada)*
Wai Gen Yee (*Orbitz Worldwide, US)*
Jeonghee Yi (*Yahoo! Inc, US)*
Emine Yilmaz (*Microsoft Research Cambridge, UK)*
Ken Yocum (*University of California, San Diego, US)*
Xiaohui Yu (*York University, Canada)*
Markus Zanker (*Alpen-Adria-Universitaet Klagenfurt, Austria)*
Yi Zeng (*Beijing University Of Technology, China)*
Yan Zhang (*Vermont Information Processing, US)*
Peng Zhang (*The Robert Gordon University, UK)*
Peng Zhang (*Texas State University - San Marcos, US)*
Wei Zhang (*Amazon.com Inc., US)*
Jessie Zhao (*York University, Canada)*
Zhi-Hua Zhou (*Nanjing University, China)*
Dong Zhou (*Trinity College Dublin, Ireland)*
Jianhan Zhu (*University College London, UK)*
Xingquan Zhu (*University of Technology, Australia)*
Guido Zuccon (*University of Glasgow, UK)*

CIKM 2011 Additional Reviewers

Additional reviewers:

Jaafar Ben Abdallah
Joel Barajas
Letizia Bertolaja
Romaric Besançon
Karla Caballero
Weiwei Cheng
Krzysztof Dembczynski
Nurcan Durak
Liyue Fan
Stefan Gindl
Jonatan Gomez
Slawomir Goryczka
Basheer Hawwash
Christian Kop
Elizabeth Leon
Thomas Lukasiewicz
Ana Cristina Mendes
Roberto Mirizzi
Thomas Peetz
Arthur Pitman
Esin Saka
Sofiane Sellah
Christian Sengstock
Jannik Strötgen
Ilija Subasic
Abhradeep Guha Thakurata
Jasna Tusek
Mathias Verbeke
Carmen Ruiz Vicente
Willem Waegeman
Chunye Wang
Xufei Wang
Albert Weichselbraun
Evan Wei Xiang
Yonghui Xiao
Lili Zhao
Erheng Zhong

CIKM 2011 Sponsors & Supporters

Sponsors: SIGIR — Special Interest Group on Information Retrieval; sig web

Platinum Supporter: EMC²

Gold Supporters: Google™; Microsoft® Research

Silver Supporter: SAP®

Bronze Supporters: ebY® Research Labs; YAHOO!® LABS; Yandex

Supporters: crossref; IBM Research

Exhibitors: Cambridge University Press; Springer — the language of science; Taylor & Francis Group — an informa business

Organisations: Glasgow: Scotland with style®; University of Glasgow — Via Veritas Vita; University of Strathclyde Glasgow

Creating User Interfaces that Entice People to Manage Better Information

Keynote Presentation

David R. Karger
Computer Science and Artificial Intelligence Laboratory
Massachusetts Institute of Technology
32 Vassar St.
Cambridge, MA 02139
karger@mit.edu

ABSTRACT

Much research in information management begins by asking how to manage a given information corpus. But information management systems can only be as good as the information they manage. They struggle and often fail to correctly infer meaning from large blobs of text and the mysterious actions and demands of users. And they are useless for managing information that is never captured.

Instead of accepting the existing information as an immutable condition, I will argue that there are significant opportunities to help and motivate people to improve the quality and quantity of information their tools manage, and to exploit that better information to benefit its users.

The greatest challenge in doing so is developing systems, and particularly user interfaces, that overcome humans' perverse reluctance to invest small present-moment effort for large future payoffs. Effective systems must minimize the effort needed to record high-quality information and maximize the perceived future benefits of that information investment.

I will support these ideas with examples covering structured data management [3] and presentation [2], notetaking [5], collaborative filtering [1], and social media [4].

Categories and Subject Descriptors

H.3.3 [**Information Systems**]: Information Storage and Retrieval; H.3.4 [**Information Systems**]: Information Systems and Software; H.5.2 [**Information Interfaces and Presentation**]: User Interfaces

General Terms

Algorithms, Design, Human Factors

Keywords

Personal Information Management, CSCW

BIO

David Karger (Ph.D. Stanford University, 1994) is a Professor of Computer Science and a member of the Computer Science and Artificial Intelligence Laboratory at the Massachusetts Institute of Technology. His work spans many areas of computer science including algorithms, information retrieval, databases, machine learning, natural language processing, distributed systems, coding and communication, networking, and human computer interaction.

His work in Information Management includes document classification and clustering, probabilistic models for information retrieval and extraction, Semantic Web tools, Personal Information Management, the social web, and crowdsourcing. An ongoing interest has been developing tools that give individual users more power to define the way their own information is modeled, organized, visualized, and managed. His group's Haystack system (CIKM '99) was one of the first "Semantic Desktop" applications offering flexible unified management of a personal information repository. He also co-led MIT's SIMILE project, a collaboration with MIT Libraries and the World Wide Web consortium developing Semantic-Web tools to improve the management and retrieval of information at the institutional level.

He received the National Academy of Science's 2004 Award for Initiatives in research and was elected an ACM Fellow in 2009. He was program co-chair for the 2009 International Semantic Web Conference and regularly serves on the program committees for ISWC, WWW and CHI.

CIKM'11, October 24–28, 2011, Glasgow, Scotland, UK.
ACM 978-1-4503-0717-8/11/10.

1. REFERENCES

[1] M. S. Bernstein, A. Marcus, D. R. Karger, and R. C. Miller. Enhancing directed content sharing on the web. In *CHI '10: Proceedings of the 28th international conference on Human factors in computing systems*, pages 971–980, Apr. 2010.

[2] D. Huynh, R. Miller, and D. R. Karger. Exhibit: Lightweight structured data publishing. In *WWW '07: Proceedings of the 16th international World Wide Web conference*, pages 737–746, May 2007.

[3] D. R. Karger, S. Ostler, and R. Lee. The web page as a WYSIWYG end-user customizable database-backed information management application. In *UIST '09: Proceedings of the 22nd annual ACM symposium on User interface software and technology*, pages 257–260, Oct. 2009.

[4] M. Van Kleek, B. Moore, D. R. Karger, P. André, and m. schraefel. Atomate it! end-user context-sensitive automation using heterogeneous information sources on the web. In *WWW '10: Proceedings of the 19th international World Wide Web conference*, pages 951–960, Apr. 2010.

[5] M. G. Van Kleek, W. Styke, m. schraefel, and D. Karger. Finders/keepers: a longitudinal study of people managing information scraps in a micro-note tool. In *CHI '11: Proceedings of the 2011 annual conference on Human factors in computing systems*, pages 2907–2916, May 2011.

Data, Health, and Algorithmics: Computational Challenges for Biomedicine

Justin Zobel
Dept. of Computer Science & Software Engineering, and NICTA
The University of Melbourne, Australia
jzobel@unimelb.edu.au

ABSTRACT

In the decade following the completion of the Human Genome Project in 2000, the cost of sequencing DNA fell by a factor of around a million, and continues to fall. Applications of sequencing in health include precise diagnosis of infection and disease, lifestyle management, and development of highly targeted treatments. However, the volume and complexity of the data produced by these technologies presents a severe computational challenge. Breakthroughs in methods for search, storage, and analysis are required to keep pace with the flow of data, and to make use of the changes in biomedical knowledge that these technologies are creating. This keynote is an overview of some of these technologies and the new computational obstacles they have engendered, and reviews examples of algorithmic innovations and approaches currently being explored. These illustrate both the kinds of solutions that are required and the challenges that must be addressed to allow this data to be fully exploited.

Categories and Subject Descriptors

J.3 [**Computer applications**]: Life and medical sciences—*Biology and genetics*

General Terms

Algorithms, Performance

Overview

Knowledge of DNA and its function is key to the understanding of living organisms. A first step is to read an organism's DNA, which consists of a simple alphabet of four nucleotides, or bases, into a digital form, allowing it to be processed computationally. Such reading is accomplished by sequencing, a technology employing chemistry and visual analysis that is increasingly automated, and is plummeting in cost. Within a year or so the price of reading an individual human genome could easily be less than $1000.

Sequencing is now a standard tool for biomedical research, and the use of sequencing is producing massive quantities of genetic data, and leading to innovations that have the potential to drastically change medicine. This data presents biomedical scientists with opportunities to pursue new approaches to research and practice. For example, such data makes it possible to identify organisms; to examine how bacterial communities respond to stresses such as new drugs; to examine how lifestyle and genetics interact; and to cheaply assemble and annotate of the complete genomic sequence of an individual. Sequencing also has sweeping implications for agriculture, biofuels, and ecology.

However, the raw data produced by sequencing machines cannot be immediately used for these kinds of biomedical investigation. The most successful of the current technologies reads the DNA as fragments of 35-500 bases. The DNA is first replicated many times, as twenty- to thirty-fold redundancy is needed to give a reasonable likelihood of usable data. The fragmentation is highly non-uniform, and the read process introduces errors such as missing or misread bases. Further issues arise from the fact that genome sizes vary greatly, from a few kilobases for a virus to over 100 gigabases for some plants; the human genome is 3 gigabases. Other problems arise from the data volume. For example, on the order of a hundred gigabases of sequencing data is required to construct the genome of a human individual or to quantify activity within a cell. The computational cost of analysis may greatly exceed that of the sequencing that produced the data, and the cost of reliable storage of the raw data for a single year could soon exceed that of production.

There are several elementary computational challenges, including storage, mapping and search, and assembly. Storage can be addressed through compression, but methods are required that take advantage of repetition between genomes rather than within an individual genome. The task of mapping involves identifying the genomic source of a given read. Effective techniques have been developed for this task, but they do not scale well, and it is plausible that genomic repositories will soon be of the same scale as the web. The task of assembly involves finding from amongst a billion reads those that contain substrings that approximately match each other, and then stitching them together in a consistent way.

There are also more sophisticated challenges, including (to take two arbitrary examples) automated interpretation of genetic data in the context of human-curated knowledge such as annotated databases, and linkage of genetic data to outcomes captured in medical records. In the longer term, there is the need to link data at level of gene, molecule, cell, organ, individual, and populations – a task that, computationally, rivals that of climate modelling. But the potential benefits for human health are enormous, and solutions to these problems require widespread involvement of research communities such as that at CIKM.

Acknowledgements. Colleagues in this work include Gad Abraham, Lloyd Allison, James Bailey, Brian Beresford-Smith, Andrew Bromage, Thomas Conway, Izhak Haviv, Kathryn Holt, Mike Inouye, Arun Konagurthu, Adam Kowalczyk, Shanika Kuruppu, Andrew Lonie, Andrew Peel, Simon Puglisi, Jan Schröder, and Anthony Wirth. NICTA is funded by the Australian Government as represented by the Department of Broadband, Communications and the Digital Economy and the Australian Research Council through the ICT Centre of Excellence program.

CIKM'11, October 24–28, 2011, Glasgow, Scotland, UK.
ACM 978-1-4503-0717-8/11/10.

Ontology-based Data Management

Maurizio Lenzerini
Dipartimento di Ingegneria Informatica, Automatica e Gestionale Antonio Ruberti
Università di Roma La Sapienza
lenzerini@dis.uniroma1.it

ABSTRACT

Ontology-based data management aims at accessing and using data by means of an ontology, i.e., a conceptual representation of the domain of interest in the underlying information system. This new paradigm provides several interesting features, many of which have been already proved effective in managing complex information systems. On the other hand, several important issues remain open, and constitute stimulating challenges for the research community. In this talk we first provide an introduction to ontology-based data management, illustrating the main ideas and techniques for using an ontology to access the data layer of an information system, and then we discuss several important issues that are still the subject of extensive investigations, including the need of inconsistency tolerant query answering methods, and the need of supporting update operations expressed over the ontology.

Categories and Subject Descriptors

H.2 [**Database Management**]: Miscellaneous;
I.2.4 [**Knowledge Representation Formalisms and Methods**]: Predicate Logic

General Terms

Theory

1. INTRODUCTION

While the amount of data stored in current information systems and the processes making use of such data continuously grow, turning these data into information, and governing both data and processes are still tremendously challenging tasks for Information Technology. The problem is complicated by the proliferation of data sources and services both within a single organization, and in cooperating environments.

The following factors contribute explaining why such a proliferation constitutes a major problem with respect to the goal of carrying out effective data governance tasks:

1. Although the initial design of a collection of data sources and services might be adequate, corrective maintenance actions tend to re-shape them into a form that often diverges from the original conceptual structure.

2. It is common practice to change a data source (e.g., a database) so as to adapt it both to specific application-dependent needs, and to new requirements. The result is that data sources often become data structures coupled to a specific application (or, a class of applications), rather than application-independent databases.

3. The data stored in different sources and the processes operating over them tend to be redundant, and mutually inconsistent, mainly because of the lack of central, coherent and unified coordination of data management tasks.

The result is that information systems of medium and large organizations are typically structured according to a "sylos"-based architecture, constituted by several, independent, and distributed data sources, each one serving a specific application. This poses great difficulties with respect to the goal of accessing data in a unified and coherent way. Analogously, processes relevant to the organizations are often hidden in software applications, and a formal, up-to-date description of what they do on the data and how they are related with other processes is often missing.

The introduction of service-oriented architectures is not a solution to this problem per se, because the fact that data and processes are packed into services is not sufficient for making the meaning of data and processes explicit. Indeed, services become other artifacts to document and maintain, adding complexity to the governance problem. Analogously, data warehousing techniques and the separation they advocate between the management of data for the operation level, and data for the decision level, do not provide solutions to this challenge. On the contrary, they also add complexity to the system, by replicating data in different layers of the system, and introducing synchronization processes across layers.

2. THE NOTION OF "ONTOLOGY-BASED DATA MANAGEMENT"

All the above observations show that a unified access to data and an effective governance of processes and services are extremely difficult goals to achieve in modern information systems. Yet, both are crucial objectives for getting useful information out of the information system, as well as for taking decisions based on them. This explains why organizations spend a great deal of time and money for the understanding, the governance, the curation, and the integration of data stored in different sources, and of the processes/services that operate on them, and why this problem

CIKM'11, October 24–28, 2011, Glasgow, Scotland, UK.
ACM 978-1-4503-0717-8/11/10.

is often cited as a key and costly Information Technology challenge faced by medium and large organizations today [1].

We argue that ontology-based data management (OBDM) is a promising direction for addressing the above challenges. The key idea of OBDM is to resort to a three-level architecture, constituted by the ontology, the sources, and the mapping between the two, where the ontology is a formal description of the domain of interest, and is the heart of the whole system. In this sense, OBDM can be seen as a form of information integration, where the usual global schema is replaced by the conceptual model of the application domain, formulated as an ontology expressed in a logic-based language. With this approach, the integrated view that the system provides to information consumers is not merely a data structure accommodating the various data at the sources, but a semantically rich description of the relevant concepts in the domain of interest, as well as the relationships between such concepts.

The distinction between the ontology and the data sources reflects the separation between the conceptual level, the one presented to the client, and the logical/physical level of the information system, the one stored in the sources, with the mapping acting as the reconciling structure between the two levels [3]. This sepration brings several potential advantages:

- The ontology layer in the architecture is the obvious mean for pursuing a declarative approach to information integration, and, more generally, to data governance. By making the representation of the domain explicit, we gain re-usability of the acquired knowledge, which is not achieved when the global schema is simply a unified description of the underlying data sources.

- The mapping layer explicitly specifies the relationships between the domain concepts on the one hand and the data sources on the other hand. Such a mapping is not only used for the operation of the information system, but also for documentation purposes. The importance of this aspect clearly emerges when looking at large organisations where the information about data is widespread into separate pieces of documentation that are often difficult to access and rarely conforming to common standards. The ontology and the corresponding mappings to the data sources provide a common ground for the documentation of all the data in the organisation, with obvious advantages for the governance and the managament of the information system.

- A third advantage has to do with the extensibility of the system. One criticism that is often raised to data integration is that it requires merging and integrating the source data in advance, and this merging process can be very costly. However, the ontology-based approach we advocate does not impose to fully integrate the data sources at once. Rather, after building even a rough skeleton of the domain model, one can incrementally add new data sources or new elements therein, when they become available, or when needed, thus amortising the cost of integration. Therefore, the overall design can be regarded as the incremental process of understanding and representing the domain, the available data sources, and the relationships between them. The goal is to support the evolution of both the ontology and the mappings in such a way that the system continues to operate while evolving, along the lines of "pay-as-you-go" data integration pursed in the research on data-spaces [4].

3. CHALLENGES

OBDM is a new paradigm, which provides several interesting features. Many of them have been already proved effective in managing complex information systems. On the other hand, several important issues remain open, and constitute stimulating challenges for the research community. We mention some of them here.

- In OBDM, the client of the information system can interact with the system by means of an abstract representation of the domain. She can ask queries on the basis of the concepts of the domain, rather than the structures of the data sources. By taking into account the ontology and the mappings to the data sources, the OBDM system is in charge of translating all these tasks into correct operations on the resources. How to do this translation efficiently is a fascinating research problem [2].

- Since the ontology should reflect the conceptual model of the domain, and not the information at the sources, it is likely that data at the sources are not fully coherent with the axioms in the ontology. How to design incosistency tolerant query answering methods is one of the most important challenges in OBDM.

- Although in classical data integration the main service to be delivered by the system is query answering, the OBDM should also provide the client with update facilities. Obviously, the updates should be expressed at the level of the ontology, and the main challenge is to design the OBDM system so that the update request is translated into appropriate updates on the source data. How to do this translation is largely open.

4. REFERENCES

[1] Philip A. Bernstein and Laura Haas. Information integration in the enterprise. *Comm. of the ACM*, 51(9):72–79, 2008.

[2] Diego Calvanese, Giuseppe De Giacomo, Domenico Lembo, Maurizio Lenzerini, and Riccardo Rosati. Tractable reasoning and efficient query answering in description logics: The *DL-Lite* family. *J. of Automated Reasoning*, 39(3):385–429, 2007.

[3] Diego Calvanese, Giuseppe De Giacomo, and Maurizio Lenzerini. Answering queries using views in description logics. In *Proc. of KRDB'99*, volume 21 of *CEUR, ceur-ws.org*, 1999.

[4] Anish Das Sarma, Xin Dong, and Alon Y. Halevy. Bootstrapping pay-as-you-go data integration systems. In *Proc. of ACM SIGMOD 2008*, pages 861–874, 2008.

Lower-Bounding Term Frequency Normalization

Yuanhua Lv
Department of Computer Science
University of Illinois at Urbana-Champaign
Urbana, IL 61801
ylv2@uiuc.edu

ChengXiang Zhai
Department of Computer Science
University of Illinois at Urbana-Champaign
Urbana, IL 61801
czhai@cs.uiuc.edu

ABSTRACT

In this paper, we reveal a common deficiency of the current retrieval models: the component of term frequency (TF) normalization by document length is not lower-bounded properly; as a result, very long documents tend to be overly penalized. In order to analytically diagnose this problem, we propose two desirable formal constraints to capture the heuristic of lower-bounding TF, and use constraint analysis to examine several representative retrieval functions. Analysis results show that all these retrieval functions can only satisfy the constraints for a certain range of parameter values and/or for a particular set of query terms. Empirical results further show that the retrieval performance tends to be poor when the parameter is out of the range or the query term is not in the particular set. To solve this common problem, we propose a general and efficient method to introduce a sufficiently large lower bound for TF normalization which can be shown analytically to fix or alleviate the problem. Our experimental results demonstrate that the proposed method, incurring almost no additional computational cost, can be applied to state-of-the-art retrieval functions, such as Okapi BM25, language models, and the divergence from randomness approach, to significantly improve the average precision, especially for verbose queries.

Categories and Subject Descriptors

H.3.3 [**Information Search and Retrieval**]: Retrieval models

General Terms

Algorithms, Theory

Keywords

Term frequency, lower bound, formal constraints, data analysis, document length, BM25+, Dir+, PL2+

1. INTRODUCTION

Optimization of retrieval models is a fundamentally important research problem in information retrieval because an improved retrieval model would lead to improved performance for all search engines. Many effective retrieval models have been proposed and tested, such as vector space models [16, 18], classical probabilistic retrieval models [13, 8, 14, 15], language models [12, 20], and the divergence from randomness approach [1]. However, it remains a significant challenge to further improve these state-of-the-art models and design an ultimately optimal retrieval model.

In order to further develop more effective models, it is necessary to understand the deficiencies of the current retrieval models [4]. For example, in [18], it was revealed that the traditional vector space model retrieves documents with probabilities different from their probabilities of relevance, and the analysis led to the pivoted normalization retrieval function which has been shown to be substantially more effective than the traditional vector space model. In this work, we reveal a common deficiency of existing retrieval models in optimizing the TF normalization component and propose a general way to address this deficiency that can be applied to multiple state-of-the-art retrieval models to improve their retrieval accuracy.

Previous work [4] has shown that all the effective retrieval models tend to rely on a reasonable way to combine multiple retrieval signals, such as term frequency (TF), inverse document frequency (IDF), and document length. A major challenge in developing an effective retrieval model lies in the fact that multiple signals generally interact with each other in a complicated way. For example, document length normalization is to regularize the TF heuristic which, if applied alone, would have a tendency to overly reward long documents due to their high likelihood of matching a query term more times than a short document. On the other hand, document length normalization can also overly penalize long documents [18, 4]. What is the best way of combining multiple signals has been a long-standing open challenge. In particular, a direct application of a sound theoretical framework such as the language modeling approach to retrieval does not automatically ensure that we achieve the optimal combination of necessary retrieval heuristics as shown in [4].

To tackle this challenge, formal constraint analysis was proposed in [4]. The idea is to define a set of formal constraints to capture the desirable properties of a retrieval function related to combining multiple retrieval signals. These constraints can then be used to diagnose the deficiency of an existing model, which in turn provides insight into how to improve an existing model. Such an axiomatic approach has been shown to be useful for motivating and developing more effective retrieval models [6, 7, 2].

CIKM'11, October 24–28, 2011, Glasgow, Scotland, UK.

In this paper, we follow this axiomatic methodology and reveal a common deficiency of the current retrieval models in their TF normalization component and propose a general strategy to fix this deficiency in multiple state-of-the-art retrieval models. Specifically, we show that the normalized TF may approach zero when the document is very long, which often causes a very long document with a non-zero TF (i.e., matching a query term) to receive a score too close to or even lower than the score of a short document with a zero TF (i.e., not matching the corresponding query term). As a result, the occurrence of a query term in a very long document would not ensure that this document be ranked above other documents where the query term does not occur, leading to unfair over-penalization of very long documents.

The root cause for this deficiency is that the component of TF normalization by document length is not lower-bounded properly, i.e., the score "gap" between the presence and absence of a query term could be infinitely close to zero or even negative. In order to diagnose this problem, we first propose two desirable constraints to capture the heuristic of lower-bounding TF in a formal way, so that it is possible to apply them to any retrieval function analytically. We then use constraint analysis to examine several representative retrieval functions and show that all these retrieval functions can only satisfy the constraints for a certain range of parameter values and/or for a particular set of query terms. Empirical results further show that the retrieval performance tends to be poor when the parameter is out of the range or the query term is not in the particular set.

Motivated by this understanding, we propose a general and efficient methodology for introducing a sufficiently large lower bound for TF normalization, which can be applied directly to current retrieval models. Constraint analysis shows analytically that the proposed methodology can successfully fix or alleviate the problem.

Our experimental results on multiple standard collections demonstrate that the proposed methodology, incurring almost no additional computational cost, can be applied to state-of-the-art retrieval functions, such as Okapi BM25 [14, 15], language models [12, 20], and the divergence from randomness approach [1], to significantly improve their average precision, especially when queries are verbose. Due to its effectiveness, efficiency, and generality, the proposed methodology can work as a "patch" to fix or alleviate the problem in current retrieval models, in a plug-and-play way.

2. RELATED WORK

Developing effective retrieval models is a long-standing central challenge in information retrieval. Many different retrieval models have been proposed and tested, such as vector space models [16, 18], classical probabilistic retrieval models [13, 8, 14, 15], language models [12, 20], and the divergence from randomness approach [1]; a few representative retrieval models will be discussed in detail in Section 3.1. In our work, we reveal and address a common "bug" of these retrieval models (i.e., TF normalization is not lower-bounded properly), and develop a general plug-and-play "patch" to fix or alleviate this bug.

Term frequency is the earliest and arguably the most important retrieval signal in retrieval models [15, 18, 12, 20, 17, 1, 4, 10]. The use of TF can be dated back to Luhn's pioneer work on automatic indexing [9]. It is widely recognized that linear scaling in term frequency puts too much weight on repeated occurrences of a term. Thus, TF is often upper-bounded through some sub-linear transformations [15, 18, 12, 20, 1, 2, 10] to prevent the contribution from repeated occurrences from growing too large. Particularly, in Okapi BM25 [14, 15], it is easy to show that there is a strict upper bound ($k_1 + 1$) for TF normalization. However, the other interesting direction, *lower-bounding TF*, has not been well addressed before. Our recent work [11] appears to be the first study that notices the inappropriate lower-bound of TF in BM25 through empirical analysis, but there is no theoretic diagnosis of the problem. Besides, the approach proposed in [11] is not generalizable to lower-bound TF normalization in retrieval models other than BM25. In this paper, we extend [11] to show analytically and empirically that lower-bounding TF is necessary for all representative retrieval models and develop a general approach to effectively lower-bound TF in these retrieval models.

Document length normalization also plays an important role in almost all existing retrieval models to fairly retrieve documents of all lengths [18, 4], since long documents tend to use the same terms repeatedly (higher TF). For example, both Okapi BM25 [14, 15] and the pivoted normalization retrieval model [18] use the pivoted length normalization schema [18], which uses the average document length as the pivoted length to coordinate the normalization effects for documents longer than this pivoted length and documents shorter than it. The PL2 model, a representative of the divergence from randomness models [1], also uses the average document length to control document length normalization. A common deficiency of all these existing length normalization methods is that they tend to force the normalized TF to approach zero when documents are very long. As a result, a very long document with a non-zero TF could receive a score too close to or even lower than the score of a short document with a zero TF, which is clearly unreasonable. Although some exiting studies have attempted to use a sublinear transformation of document length (e.g., the squared root of document length [3]) to heuristically replace the original document length in length normalization, they are not guaranteed to solve the problem and often lose to standard document length normalization such as the pivoted length normalization in terms of retrieval accuracy. Our work aims at addressing this inherent weakness of traditional document length normalization in a more general and effective way.

Constraint analysis has been explored in information retrieval to diagnostically evaluate existing retrieval models [4, 5], introduce novel retrieval signals into existing retrieval models [19], and guide the development of new retrieval models [6, 2]. The constraints in these studies are basic and are designed mostly based on the analysis of some common characteristics of existing retrieval formulas. Although we also use constraint analysis, the proposed constraints are novel and are inspired by our empirical finding of a common deficiency of the existing retrieval models. Moreover, although some existing constraints (e.g., LNCs and TF-LNC in [4, 5]) are also meant to regularize the interactions between TF and document length, they tend to be loose and cannot capture the heuristic of lower-bounding TF normalization. For example, the modified Okapi BM25 satisfies all the constraints proposed in [4, 5], but it still fails to lower-bound TF normalization properly. In this sense, the proposed two new constraints are complimentary to existing constraints [4, 5].

Model	$G(c(t,Q))$	$F(c(t,D), \|D\|, td(t))$
BM25	$\frac{(k_3+1)\cdot c(t,Q)}{k_3+c(t,Q)}$	$\frac{(k_1+1)c(t,D)}{k_1(1-b+b\cdot \|D\|/avdl)+c(t,D)} \cdot \log \frac{N+1}{df(t)}$
PL2	$c(t,Q)$	$\begin{cases} \frac{tfn_t^D \cdot \log_2(tfn_t^D \cdot \lambda_t)+\log_2 e\cdot(1/\lambda_t - tfn_t^D)+0.5\log_2(2\pi\cdot tfn_t^D)}{tfn_t^D+1} & \text{if } tfn_t^D > 0 \text{ and } \lambda_t > 1 \\ 0 & \text{otherwise} \end{cases}$
Dir	$c(t,Q)$	$\log\left(\frac{\mu}{\|D\|+\mu} + \frac{c(t,D)}{(\|D\|+\mu)p(t\|C)}\right)$
Piv	$c(t,Q)$	$\begin{cases} \frac{1+\log(1+\log(c(t,D)))}{1-s+s\cdot \|D\|/avdl} \cdot \log\frac{N+1}{df(t)} & \text{if } c(t,D) > 0 \\ 0 & \text{otherwise} \end{cases}$

Table 1: Document and query term weighting components of representative retrieval functions.

Notation	Description
$c(t,D)$	Frequency of term t in document D
$c(t,Q)$	Frequency of term t in query Q
N	Total number of docs in the collection
$df(t)$	Number of documents containing term t
$td(t)$	Any measure of discrimination value of term t
$\|D\|$	Length of document D
$avdl$	Average document length
$c(t,C)$	Frequency of term t in collection C
$p(t\|C)$	Probability of a term t given by the collection language model [20]

Table 2: Notation

3. MOTIVATION OF LOWER-BOUNDING TF NORMALIZATION

In this section, we discuss and analyze a common deficiency (i.e., lack of appropriate lower bound for TF normalization) of four state-of-the-art retrieval functions, which respectively represent the classical probabilistic retrieval model (Okapi BM25 [14, 15]), the divergence from randomness approach (PL2 [1]), the language modeling approach (Dirichlet prior smoothing [20]), and the vector space model (pivoted normalization [18, 17]).

An effective retrieval function is generally comprised of two basic separable components: a within-query scoring formula for weighting the occurrences of a term in the query and a within-document scoring formula for weighting the occurrences of this term in a document. We will represent each retrieval function in terms of these two separable components to make it easier for us to focus on studying the document side weighting:

$$S(Q,D) = \sum_{t\in Q} G(c(t,Q)) \cdot F(c(t,D), |D|, td(t)) \quad (1)$$

where $S(Q,D)$ is the total relevance score assigned to document D with respect to query Q, and $G(\cdot)$ and $F(\cdot)$ are within-query scoring function and within-document scoring function respectively. In Table 1, we show how this general scheme can be used to represent all the four major retrieval models. Other related notations are listed in Table 2. Note that most of the notations were also used in some previous work, e.g., [4], and will be adopted throughout our paper.

3.1 Deficiency of Existing Retrieval Functions

3.1.1 Okapi BM25 (BM25)

The Okapi BM25 method [14, 15] is a representative retrieval function that represents the classical probabilistic retrieval model. The BM25 retrieval function is summarized in the second row of Table 1. Following work [4], we modify the original IDF formula of BM25 to avoid the problem of possibly negative IDF values. The within-document scoring function of BM25 can be re-written as follows:

$$F_{BM25}(c(t,D), |D|, td(t)) = \frac{(k_1+1)\cdot tfn_t^D}{k_1 + tfn_t^D} \cdot \log\frac{N+1}{df(t)} \quad (2)$$

where k_1 is a parameter, and tfn_t^D is the normalized TF by document length using pivoted length normalization [18].

$$tfn_t^D = \frac{c(t,D)}{1 - b + b\frac{|D|}{avdl}} \quad (3)$$

where b is the slope parameter in pivoted normalization.

When a document is very long (i.e., $|D|$ is much larger than $avdl$), we can see that tfn_t^D could be very small and approach 0. Consequently, F_{BM25} will also approach 0 as if t did not occur in D. It can be seen clearly in Figure 1 (1): when $|D_2|$ becomes very large, the score difference between D_2 and D_1 appears to be very small. This by itself, would not necessarily be a problem, but the problem is that, the occurrence of t in a very long document D fails to ensure D to be ranked above other documents where t does not occur. It suggests that the occurrences of a query term in very long documents may not be rewarded properly by BM25, and thus those very long documents could be overly penalized, which as we will show later, is indeed true.

3.1.2 PL2 Method (PL2)

The PL2 method is a representative retrieval function of the divergence from randomness framework [1]. In this paper, we use the modified PL2 formula derived by Fang et al. [5] instead of the original PL2 formula [1]. The only difference between this modified PL2 function and the original PL2 function is that the former essentially ignores non-discriminative query terms. It has been shown that the modified PL2 is more effective and robust than the original PL2 [5]. The modified PL2 (still called PL2 for convenience in the following sections) is presented in the third row of Table 1, where $\lambda_t = \frac{N}{c(t,C)}$ is the term discrimination value, and tfn_t^D is the normalized TF by document length:

$$tfn_t^D = c(t,D) \cdot \log_2\left(1 + c\cdot\frac{avdl}{|D|}\right) \quad (4)$$

where $c > 0$ is a retrieval parameter.

We can see that, when a document is very long, tfn_t^D could be very small and approach 0, which is very similar to the corresponding component in BM25. What is worse is that, when tfn_t^D is sufficiently small, the within-document score F_{PL2} will be a **negative** number surprisingly. However, as shown in Table 1, even if the term is missing, i.e., $c(t,D) = 0$, F_{PL2} can still receive a default *zero* score. This interesting observation is illustrated in Figure 1 (2). It suggests that a very long document that matches a query term

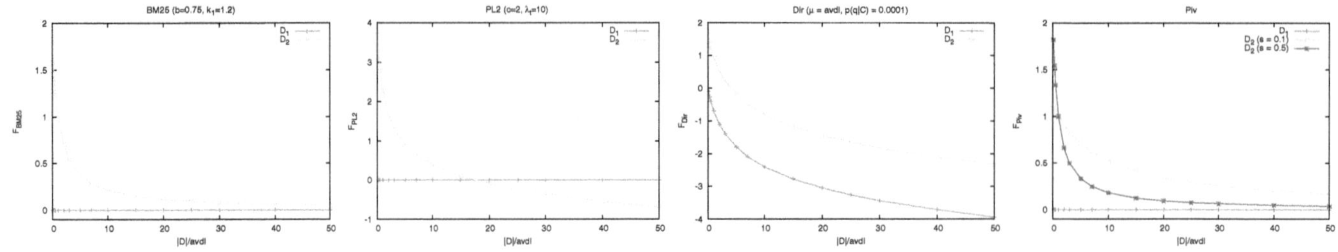

Figure 1: Comparison of the within-document term scores, i.e., $F(\cdot)$, of documents D_1 and D_2 w.r.t. query term t against different document lengths, where we assume $c(t, D_1) = 0$ and $c(t, D_2) = 1$. Here, x-axis and y-axis stand for the length of documents and the within-document term scores respectively.

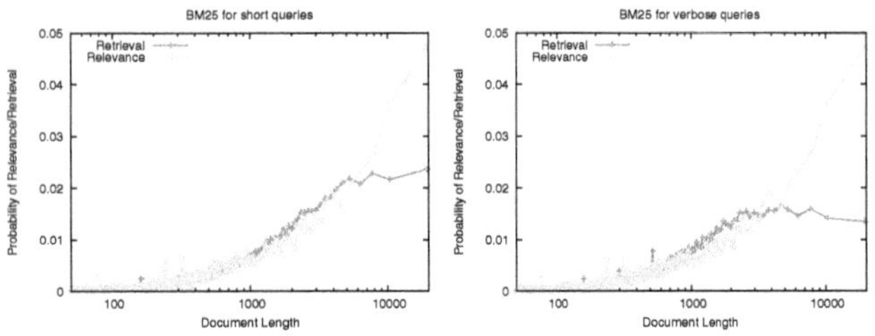

Figure 2: Comparison of retrieval and relevance probabilities against all document lengths when using BM25 on short (left) and verbose (right) queries.

may be penalized even more than another document (the length can be arbitrary) that does not match the term; consequently, those very long documents tend to be overly penalized by PL2.

3.1.3 Dirichlet Prior Method (Dir)

The Dirichlet prior method is one of the best performing language modeling approaches [20]. It is presented in the fourth row of Table 1, where μ is the Dirichlet prior.

It is observed that, the within-document scoring function F_{Dir} is monotonically decreasing with the document length variable. And when a document D_2 is very long, say $50 * avdl$, even if it matches a query term, the within-document score of this term could still be arbitrarily small. And this score could be smaller than that of any average-length document D_1 which does not match the term. This is shown clearly in Figure 1 (3). Thus, the Dirichlet prior method can also overly penalize very long documents.

3.1.4 Pivoted Normalization Method (Piv)

The pivoted normalization retrieval function [17, 4] represents one of the best performing vector space models. The detailed formula is shown in the last row of Table 1, where s is the slope parameter. Similarly, the analysis of the pivoted normalization method also shows that it tends to overly penalize very long documents, as shown in Figure 1 (4).

3.2 Likelihood of Relevance/Retrieval

Our analysis above has shown that, *in principle*, all these retrieval functions tend to overly penalize very long documents. Now we turn to seeking empirical evidence to see if this common deficiency hurts document retrieval *in practice*.

Inspired by Singhal et al.'s finding that a good retrieval function should retrieve documents of all lengths with similar chances as their likelihood of relevance [18], we compare the retrieval pattern of different retrieval functions with the relevance pattern. We follow the binning analysis strategy proposed in [18] and plot the two patterns against all document lengths on WT10G in Figure 2, where the bin size is set to 5000. Due to the space reason, we only plot BM25 as an example. But it is observed that other retrieval functions have similar trends as BM25. The plot shows clearly that BM25 retrieves very long documents with chances much lower than their likelihood of relevance. This empirically confirms our previous analysis that very long documents tend to be overly penalized.

4. FORMAL CONSTRAINTS ON LOWER-BOUNDING TF NORMALIZATION

A critical question is thus how we can regulate the interactions between term frequency and document length when a document is very long so that we can fix this common deficiency of current retrieval models?

To answer this question, we first propose two desirable heuristics that any reasonable retrieval function should implement to properly lower bound TF normalization when documents are very long: (1) there should be a sufficiently large gap between the presence and absence of a query term, i.e., the effect of document length normalization should not cause a very long document with a non-zero TF to receive a score too close to or even lower than a short document with a zero TF; (2) a short document that only covers a very small subset of the query terms should not easily dominate over a very long document that contains many distinct query terms.

Next, in order to analytically diagnose the problem of over-penalizing very long documents, we propose two formal constraints to capture the above two heuristics of lower bounding TF normalization so that it is possible to apply them to any retrieval function analytically. The two constraints are defined as follows:

LB1: Let Q be a query. Assume D_1 and D_2 are two documents such that $S(Q, D_1) = S(Q, D_2)$. If we reformulate the query by adding another term $q \notin Q$ into Q, where $c(q, D_1) = 0$ and $c(q, D_2) > 0$, then $S(Q \cup \{q\}, D_1) < S(Q \cup \{q\}, D_2)$.

LB2: Let $Q = \{q_1, q_2\}$ be a query with two terms q_1 and q_2. Assume $td(q_1) = td(q_2)$, where $td(t)$ can be any reasonable measure of term discrimination value. If D_1 and D_2 are two documents such that $c(q_2, D_1) = c(q_2, D_2) = 0$, $c(q_1, D_1) > 0$, $c(q_1, D_2) > 0$, and $S(Q, D_1) = S(Q, D_2)$, then $S(Q, D_1 \cup \{q_1\} - \{t_1\}) < S(Q, D_2 \cup \{q_2\} - \{t_2\})$, for all t_1 and t_2 such that $t_1 \in D_1$, $t_2 \in D_2$, $t_1 \notin Q$ and $t_2 \notin Q$.

The first constraint LB1 captures the basic heuristic of 0-1 gap in TF normalization, i.e., the gap between presence and absence of a term should not be closed by document length normalization. Specifically, if a query term does not occur in document D_1 but occurs in document D_2, and both documents receive the same relevance score from matching other query terms, then D_1 should be scored lower than D_2, no matter what are the length values of D_1 and D_2. In other words, the occurrence of a query term in a very long document should still be able to differentiate this document from other documents where the query term does not occur.

In fact, when $F(0, |D|, td(t))$ is a document-independent constant, LB1 can be derived from a basic TF constraint, TFC1 [4]. Here, $F(0, |D|, td(t))$ is the document weight for a query term t not present in document D, i.e., $t \in Q$ but $t \notin D$. This property is presented below in Theorem 1.

THEOREM 1. *LB1 is implied by the TFC1 constraint, if the within-document weight for any missing term is a document independent constant.*

Proof: Let Q be a query. Assume D_1 and D_2 are two documents such that $S(Q, D_1) = S(Q, D_2)$. We reformulate query Q by adding another term $q \notin Q$ into the query, where $c(q, D_1) = 0$ and $c(q, D_2) > 0$. If D_2' is another document, which is generated by replacing all the occurrences of q in D_2 with a non-query term $t \notin Q \cup \{q\}$, then $c(q, D_2') = 0$ and $S(Q, D_1) = S(Q, D_2) = S(Q, D_2')$. Due to the assumption that the document weight for the missing term q is a document independent constant, it follows that $S(Q \cup \{q\}, D_1) = S(Q \cup \{q\}, D_2')$. Finally, since $|D_2'| = |D_2|$ and $c(q, D_2') = 0 < c(q, D_2)$, according to TFC1, we get $S(Q \cup \{q\}, D_1) = S(Q \cup \{q\}, D_2') < S(Q \cup \{q\}, D_2)$. □

However, when the document weights for missing terms are document dependent, LB1 will not be redundant in the sense that it cannot be derived from other constraints such as the proposed LB2 and the seven constraints proposed in [4]. For example, the Dirichlet prior retrieval function, as shown in Table 1, has a document-dependent weighting function for a missing term, which is $\log \frac{\mu}{|D|+\mu}$. As will be shown later, the Dirichlet prior method violates LB1, although it satisfies LB2 and most of the constraints proposed in [4].

The second constraint LB2 states that if two terms have the same discrimination value, a repeated occurrence of one term is not as important as the first occurrence of the other. LB2 essentially captures the intuition that covering more *distinct* query terms should be rewarded sufficiently, even if the document is very long. For example, given a query Q = {"computer", "virus"}, if two documents D_1 and D_2 with identical relevance scores with respect to Q both match "computer", but neither matches "virus", then if we add an occurrence of "virus" to D_1 to generate D_1' and add an occurrence of "computer" to D_2 to generate D_2', we should ensure that D_1' has a higher score than D_2'. This intuitively makes sense because D_1' is more likely to be related to computer virus, while D_2' may be just about other aspects of computer.

LB1 and LB2 are two necessary constraints to ensure that very long documents would not be overly penalized. When either is violated, the retrieval function would likely not perform well for very long documents and there should be room to improve the retrieval function through improving its ability of satisfying the corresponding constraint.

5. CONSTRAINT ANALYSIS ON CURRENT RETRIEVAL MODELS

5.1 Okapi BM25 (BM25)

BM25 satisfies TFC1 [4], and the within-document weight for any missing term is always 0. Therefore, BM25 satisfies LB1 unconditionally according to Theorem 1.

We now examine LB2. Due to the sub-linear property of TF normalization, we only need to check LB2 in the case when $c(q_1, D_1) = 1$, since when $c(q_1, D_1) > 1$, it is even harder to violate the constraint. Consider a common case when $|D_1| = avdl$. It can be shown that the LB2 constraint is equivalent to the following constraint on $|D_2|$:

$$|D_2| < \left(\frac{2k_1 + 2}{(k_1)^2 \cdot b} + 1\right) \cdot avdl \quad (5)$$

This means that LB2 is satisfied only if $|D_2|$ is smaller than a certain upper bound. Thus, a sufficiently long document would violate LB2. Note that the upper bound of $|D_2|$ is a monotonically decreasing function with both b and k_1. This suggests that a larger b or k_1 would lead BM25 to violate LB2 more easily, which is confirmed by our experiments.

5.2 PL2 Method (PL2)

In Fang et al.'s work [5], the TFC1 constraint is regarded equivalent to that "the first partial derivative of the formula w.r.t. the TF variable should be positive", which has been shown to be satisfied by the modified PL2 [5]. However, the PL2 function is not continuous when the TF variable is zero, and what is worse is that,

$$\lim_{c(t,D)\to 0} F_{PL2}(c(t, D), |D|, td(t)) < F_{PL2}(0, |D|, td(t)) = 0 \quad (6)$$

which shows that even the modified PL2 still fails to satisfy TFC1. So we cannot use Theorem 1 for PL2.

We thus check both LB1 and LB2 directly. Since the optimal setting of parameter c is usually larger than 1 [4], we consider a common case when $|D_1| = \frac{c}{3} \cdot avdl$. Similar to the analysis on BM25, we only need to examine LB2 for $c(q_1, D_1) = 1$. The LB1 constraint is approximately equivalent to

$$|D_2| < \frac{c}{2^{\exp\left(-\frac{2}{\lambda_t} - 1.84\right)} - 1} \cdot avdl \quad (7)$$

and LB2 is approximately equivalent to

$$|D_2| < \frac{c}{2^{\exp\left(0.27 \log(\lambda_t) - \frac{2.27}{\lambda_t} - 2.26\right)} - 1} \cdot avdl \quad (8)$$

Due to space limit, we cannot show all the derivation details.

We can see that both LB1 and LB2 set an upper bound for document length, suggesting that a very long document would violate both LB1 and LB2. However the upper bound introduced by LB1 is always larger than that introduced by LB2. So we focus on LB2 in the following sections.

The upper bound of document length in LB2 is monotonically increasing with both c and λ_t. It suggests that, when c is very small, there is a serious concern that long documents would be overly penalized. On the other hand, a more discriminative term also violates the constraint more easily. These analyses are confirmed by our experiments.

5.3 Dirichlet Prior Method (Dir)

With Dir, the within-document weight for a missing term is $\log \frac{\mu}{|D|+\mu}$, which is document dependent. So Theorem 1 is not applicable to the Dirichlet method. We thus need to examine LB1 and LB2 directly.

First, we only check LB1 at the point of $c(q, D_2) = 1$, which is the easiest case for LB1 to be violated. By considering the common case that $|D_1| = avdl$, the LB1 constraint is equivalent to the following constraint on $|D_2|$:

$$|D_2| < avdl + \frac{1}{p(q|C)}\left(1 + \frac{avdl}{\mu}\right) \tag{9}$$

It shows that the Dirichlet method can only satisfy LB1 if $|D_2|$ is smaller than a certain upper bound, suggesting again that a very long document would violate LB1. And this upper bound is monotonically decreasing with both $p(q|C)$ and μ. On the one hand, a non-discriminative (i.e., large $p(q|C)$) term q violates LB1 easily; for example, if $\mu \cdot p(q|C) = 1$, the upper bound appears to be as low as $(2 * avdl + \mu)$. Thus, the Dirichlet method would overly penalize very long documents more for verbose queries. On the other hand, a large μ would also worsen the situation according to Formula 9. These are all confirmed by our experimental results.

Next, we turn to check LB2, which is equivalent to

$$\frac{n + 1 + \mu \cdot p(q|C)}{n + \mu \cdot p(q|C)} < \frac{1 + \mu \cdot p(q|C)}{\mu \cdot p(q|C)} \tag{10}$$

where $n \in \{1, 2, \cdots\}$. Interestingly, this inequality is always satisfied, suggesting that the Dirichlet method satisfies LB2 *unconditionally*. We thus expect that the Dirichlet method would have some advantages in the cases when other retrieval functions tend to violate LB2.

5.4 Pivoted Normalization Method (Piv)

It is easy to show that the pivoted normalization method also satisfies LB1 unconditionally.

We now examine LB2. Similar to the analysis on BM25, we only need to check LB2 in the case of $c(q_1, D_1) = 1$. By considering a common case when $|D_1| = avdl$, we see that LB2 is equivalent to the following constraint on $|D_2|$:

$$|D_2| < \left(\frac{0.899}{s} + 1\right) \cdot avdl \tag{11}$$

This means that LB2 is satisfied only if $|D_2|$ is smaller than a certain upper bound. And this upper bound is a monotonically decreasing function with s. So, in principle, a larger s would lead the pivoted normalization method to violate LB2 more easily, which can also explain why the optimal setting of s tends to be small [4]. Of course, if s is set to zero, LB2 would be satisfied, but that would be to turn off document length normalization completely, which would clearly lead to non-optimal retrieval performance.

6. A GENERAL APPROACH FOR LOWER-BOUNDING TF NORMALIZATION

The analysis above shows analytically that all the state-of-the-art retrieval models would tend to overly penalize very long documents. In order to avoid overly penalizing very long documents, we need to lower-bound TF normalization to make sure that the "gap" of the within-document scores $F(c(t, D), |D|, td(t))$ between $c(t, D) = 0$ and $c(t, D) > 0$ is sufficiently large. However, we do not want that the addition of this new constraint changes the implementations of other retrieval heuristics in these state-of-the-art retrieval functions, because the implementations of existing retrieval heuristics in these retrieval functions have been shown to work quite well [4].

We propose a general heuristic approach to achieve this goal by defining an improved within-document scoring formula F' as shown in Equation 12, where δ is a pseudo TF value to control the scale of the TF lower bound, and l is a pseudo document length which is document-independent. In this new formula, a retrieval model-specific, but document-independent value $F(\delta, l, td(t)) - F(0, l, td(t))$ would serve as an ensured "gap" between matching and missing a term: if $c(t, D) > 0$, the component of TF normalization by document length will be lower-bounded by such a document-independent value, no matter how large $|D|$ would be.

$$F'(c(t, D), |D|, td(t)) = \begin{cases} F(c(t, D), |D|, td(t)) + F(0, l, td(t)) & \text{if } c(t, D) = 0 \\ F(c(t, D), |D|, td(t)) + F(\delta, l, td(t)) & \text{otherwise} \end{cases} \tag{12}$$

It is easy to verify that $F'(c(t, D), |D|, td(t))$ is able to satisfy all the basic retrieval heuristics [4] that are satisfied by $F(c(t, D), |D|, td(t))$: first, it is trivial to show that, if $F(c(t, D), |D|, td(t))$ satisfies TFCs, $F'(c(t, D), |D|, td(t))$ will also satisfy them; secondly, $F(\delta, l, td(t))$ and $F(0, l, td(t))$, as two special points of $F(c(t, D), |D|, td(t))$, satisfy the TDC constraint in exactly the same way as $F(c(t, D), |D|, td(t))$, so does $F'(c(t, D), |D|, td(t))$; finally, since the newly introduced components are document-independent, they raise no problem for LNCs and TF-LNC.

The proposed methodology is very efficient, as it only adds a retrieval model specific but document-independent value to those standard retrieval functions. For a query Q, we only need to calculate $|Q|$ such values, which can even be done offline. Therefore, our method incurs almost no additional computational cost.

Finally, we can obtain the corresponding lower-bounded retrieval function through substituting $F'(c(t, D), |D|, td(t))$ for $F(c(t, D), |D|, td(t))$ in each retrieval function,

Take BM25 as an example. Obviously $F'(0, |D|, td(t)) = 0$. In $F(\delta, l, td(t))$, since l is a constant document length variable used for document length normalization, its influence can be absorbed into the TF variable δ, we thus set $l = avdl$ simply. Then, we obtain $F(\delta, avdl, td(t)) = \frac{(k_1+1)\delta}{k_1+\delta} \log \frac{N+1}{df(t)}$. Clearly parameter k_1 can also be absorbed into δ, and the above formula is simplified again as $\delta \log \frac{N+1}{df(t)}$. Finally, we derive a lower-bounded BM25 function, namely **BM25+**, as shown in the following Formula 13.

$$\sum_{t \in Q \cap D} \frac{(k_3 + 1)c(t, Q)}{k_3 + c(t, Q)} \times \left[\frac{(k_1 + 1)c(t, D)}{k_1\left(1 - b + b\frac{|D|}{avdl}\right) + c(t, D)} + \delta\right] \times \log \frac{N + 1}{df(t)} \tag{13}$$

$$\sum_{t \in Q \cap D} c(t, Q)\left[\log\left(1 + \frac{c(t, D)}{\mu \cdot p(t|C)}\right) + \log\left(1 + \frac{\delta}{\mu \cdot p(t|C)}\right)\right] + |Q| \cdot \log \frac{\mu}{|D| + \mu} \tag{14}$$

$$\sum_{t \in Q \cap D} c(t, Q)\left[\frac{1 + \log(1 + \log(c(t, D)))}{1 - s + s\frac{|D|}{avdl}} + \delta\right] \log \frac{N + 1}{df(t)} \tag{15}$$

$$\sum_{t \in Q \cap D, \lambda_t > 1} c(t, Q) \left[\frac{tfn_t^D \log_2 \left(tfn_t^D \cdot \lambda_t \right) + \log_2 e \cdot \left(\frac{1}{\lambda_t} - tfn_t^D \right) + \frac{\log_2 \left(2\pi \cdot tfn_t^D \right)}{2}}{tfn_t^D + 1} + \frac{\delta \log_2 (\delta \cdot \lambda_t) + \log_2 e \cdot \left(\frac{1}{\lambda_t} - \delta \right) + \frac{\log_2 (2\pi\delta)}{2}}{\delta + 1} \right] \tag{16}$$

Similarly, we can derive a lower-bounded Dirichlet prior method (**Dir+**), a lower-bounded pivoted normalization method (**Piv+**), and a lower-bounded PL2 (**PL2+**), which are presented in Formulas 14, 15, and 16 respectively.

Next, we check LB1 and LB2 on these four improved retrieval functions.

6.1 Lower-Bounded BM25 (BM25+)

It is trivial to verify that BM25+ still satisfies LB1 unconditionally. To examine LB2, we apply an analysis method that is consistent with our analysis for BM25 in Section 5.1. The LB2 constraint on BM25+ is equivalent to

$$\frac{k_1}{k_1 + 2} < \frac{(k_1 + 1) \cdot 1}{k_1 \left(1 - b + b \frac{|D_2|}{avdl} \right) + 1} + \delta \tag{17}$$

which can be shown to be satisfied unconditionally if

$$\delta \geq \frac{k_1}{k_1 + 2} \tag{18}$$

Clearly, if we set δ to a sufficiently large value, BM25+ is able to satisfy LB2 unconditionally, which is also confirmed in our experiments that BM25+ works very well when we set $\delta = 1$.

6.2 Lower-Bounded PL2 (PL2+)

We only need to check LB2 on PL2+, since it is easier to violate than LB1. With a similar analysis strategy as used for analyzing PL2, the LB2 constraint on PL2+ is equivalent to

$$|D_2| < \frac{c \cdot avdl}{2^{\exp\left(\left(0.27 - \frac{2\delta}{\delta+1}\right) \log(\lambda_t) - \frac{2.27 - \frac{2}{\delta+1}}{\lambda_t} - 2.26 - g(\delta) \right)} - 1} \tag{19}$$

where $g(\delta) = \frac{(2\delta+1)\log\delta - 2\delta + \log(2\pi)}{\delta+1}$. Due to space limit, we cannot show all the derivation details in this section.

We can see that, given a δ, the right side of the Formula 19 (i.e., the upper bound of $|D_2|$) is minimized when $\lambda_t = \frac{2.27\delta + 0.27}{1.73\delta - 0.27}$. This suggests that, in contrast to PL2, the upper bound of $|D_2|$ is not monotonically decreasing with λ_t. This interesting difference is shown clearly in Figure 3. Thus, if we set δ to an appropriate value to make the minimum upper bound still large enough (e.g., larger than the length of the longest document), PL2+ would not violate LB2.

6.3 Lower-Bounded Dirichlet Method (Dir+)

It is easy to show that Dir+ also satisfies LB2 unconditionally. We analyze Dir+ in the same way as analyzing Dir, and obtain the following equivalent constraint of LB1:

$$|D_2| < avdl + \frac{1 + \delta}{p(t|C)} \left(1 + \frac{avdl}{\mu} \right) + \frac{\delta}{\mu \cdot p^2(t|C)} \left(1 + \frac{avdl}{\mu} \right) \tag{20}$$

We can see that, although Dir+ does not guarantee that LB1 is always satisfied, it indeed enlarges the upper bound of document length as compared to Dir in Section 5.3, and thus makes the constraint harder to violate. Generally, if we set δ to a sufficiently large value, the chance that very long documents are overly penalized would be reduced.

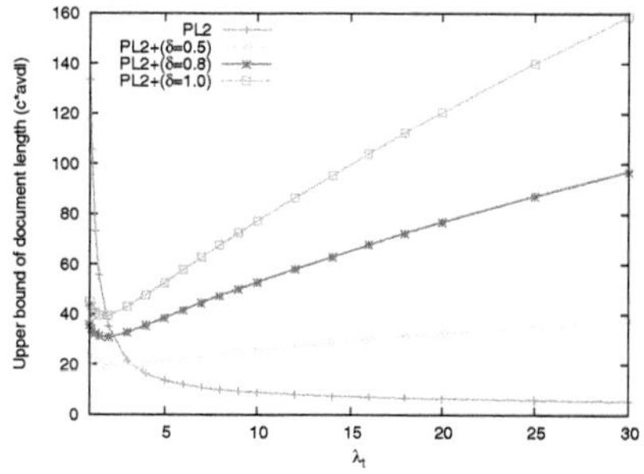

Figure 3: Comparison of upper bounds of document length in PL2 and PL2+ to satisfy LB2.

	Terabyte	WT10G	Robust04	WT2G
queries	701-850	451-550	301-450 601-700	401-450
#qry(with qrel)	149	100	249	50
avg(ql_short)	3.13	4.24	2.74	2.46
avg(ql_verb)	11.55	11.61	15.47	13.86
#total_qrel	28,640	5,981	17,412	2,279
#documents	25205k	1692k	528k	247k
avdl	949	611	481	1056
std(dl)/avdl	2.63	2.31	1.19	2.14

Table 3: Document set characteristic

6.4 Lower-Bounded Pivoted Method (Piv+)

It is easy to verify that Piv+ also satisfies LB1. Regarding LB2, similar to our analysis on Piv, the LB2 constraint on Piv+ is equivalent to

$$\log(1 + \log 2) < \frac{1}{1 - s + s\frac{|D_2|}{avdl}} + \delta \tag{21}$$

which is always satisfied if

$$\delta \geq \log(1 + \log(2)) \approx 0.53 \tag{22}$$

This shows that Piv+ can be able to satisfy LB2 unconditionally with a sufficiently large δ.

7. EXPERIMENTS

7.1 Testing Collections and Evaluation

We use four TREC collections: WT2G, WT10G, Terabyte, and Robust04, which represent different sizes and genre of text collections. WT2G, WT10G, and Terabyte are small, medium, and large Web collections respectively. Robust04 is a representative news dataset. We test two types of queries, short queries and verbose queries, which are taken from the title and the description fields of the TREC topics respectively. We use the Lemur toolkit and the Indri search engine (http://www.lemurproject.org/) to carry out our experiments. For all the datasets, the preprocessing of documents and queries is minimum, involving only Porter's stemming. An overview of the involved query topics, the average length of short/verbose queries, the total number of relevance judgments, the total number of documents, the

Query	Method	WT10G		WT2G		Terabyte		Robust04	
		MAP	P@10	MAP	P@10	MAP	P@10	MAP	P@10
Short	BM25	0.1879	0.2898	0.3104	0.4840	0.2931	0.5785	0.2544	0.4353
	BM25+	**0.1962**^{4}	0.3040	0.3172^{1}	0.4820	**0.3004**^{1}	0.5685	**0.2553**	0.4357
	BM25+ ($\delta = 1.0$)	0.1927^{3}	0.3010	**0.3178**^{1}	0.4840	0.2997^{4}	0.5718	0.2548	0.4349
Verbose	BM25	0.1745	0.3250	0.2484	0.4380	0.2234	0.5221	0.2260	0.4036
	BM25+	**0.1850**^{1}	0.3360	**0.2624**^{3}	0.4400	0.2336^{4}	0.5309	0.2274	0.4056
	BM25+ ($\delta = 1.0$)	0.1841^{1}	0.3340	0.2565^{1}	0.4340	**0.2339**^{4}	0.5329	**0.2275**	0.4052

Table 4: Comparison of BM25 and BM25+ using cross validation. Superscripts 1/2/3/4 indicate that the corresponding MAP improvement is significant at the 0.05/0.02/0.01/0.001 level using the Wilcoxon test.

average document length, and the standard deviation of document length in each collection are shown in Table 3.

We employ a 2-fold cross-validation for parameter tuning, where the query topics are split into even and odd number topics as the two folds. The top-ranked 1000 documents for each run are compared in terms of their mean average precisions (MAP), which also serves as the objective function for parameter training. In addition, the precision at top-10 documents (P@10) is also considered. Our goal is to see if the proposed general heuristic can work well for improving each of the four retrieval functions.

7.2 BM25+ VS. BM25

In both BM25+ and BM25, we train b and k_1 using cross validation, where b is tuned from 0.1 to 0.9 in increments of 0.1, and k_1 is tuned from 0.2 to 4.0 in increments of 0.2. Besides, in BM25+, parameter δ is trained using cross validation, where δ is tuned from 0.0 to 1.5 in increments of 0.1, but we also create a special run in which δ is fixed to 1.0 empirically (labeled as BM25+ ($\delta = 1.0$)). The comparison results of BM25+ and BM25 are presented in Table 4.

The results demonstrate that BM25+ outperforms BM25 consistently in terms of MAP and also achieves P@10 scores better than or comparable to BM25. The MAP improvements of BM25+ over BM25 are much larger on *Web* collections than on the *news* collection. In particular, the MAP improvements on all Web collections are statistically significant. This is likely because there are generally more very long documents in Web data, where the problem of BM25, i.e., overly-penalizing very long documents, would presumably be more severe. For example, Table 3 shows that the standard deviation of the document length is indeed larger on the three Web collections than on Robust04.

Another interesting observation is that, BM25+, even with a fixed $\delta = 1.0$, can still work effectively and stably across collections and outperform BM25 significantly. This empirically confirms the constraint analysis results in Section 6.1 that, when $\delta > \frac{k_1}{k_1+2}$, BM25+ can satisfy LB2 unconditionally. It thus suggests that the proposed constraints can even be used to guide parameter tuning.

We further plot the curves of MAP improvements of BM25+ over BM25 against different δ values in Figure 4, which demonstrates that, when δ is set to a value around 1.0, BM25+ works very well across all collections. Therefore, δ can be safely "eliminated" from BM25+ by setting it to a default value 1.0.

Regarding different query types, we observe that BM25+ improves more on verbose queries than on short queries. For example, the MAP improvements on Web collections are often more than 5% for verbose queries and are around 2% for short queries. We hypothesize that BM25 may overly-penalize very long documents more seriously when queries are verbose, and thus there is more room for BM25+ to boost the performance. To verify our hypothesis, we collect the optimal settings of b and k_1 for BM25 in Table 5, which show that the optimal settings of b and k_1 are clearly *larger* for verbose queries than for short queries. Recall that our constraint analysis in Section 5.1 has shown that the likelihood of BM25 violating LB2 is monotonically increasing with parameters b and k_1. We can now conclude that BM25 indeed tends to overly penalize very long documents more when queries are more verbose.

Query	WT10G		WT2G		Terabyte		Robust04	
	b	k_1	b	k_1	b	k_1	b	k_1
Short	0.3	1.0	0.2	0.8	0.3	1.0	0.4	0.6
Verbose	0.6	2.0	0.6	1.6	0.4	1.8	0.7	1.2

Table 5: Optimal settings of b and k_1 in BM25.

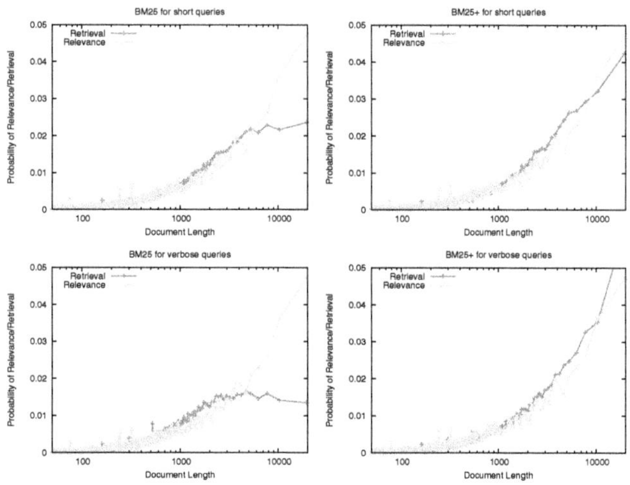

Figure 5: Comparison of retrieval and relevance probabilities against all document lengths when using BM25 (left) and BM25+ (right) for retrieval. It shows that BM25+ alleviates the problem of BM25 that overly penalizes very long documents.

So far we have shown that BM25+ is more effective than BM25, but if it is really because BM25+ has alleviated the problem of overly-penalizing very long documents? To answer this question, we plot the retrieval pattern of BM25+ as compared to the relevance pattern in a similar way as we have done in Section 3.2. The pattern comparison is presented in Figure 5. We can see that the retrieval pattern of BM25+ is more similar to the relevance pattern, especially

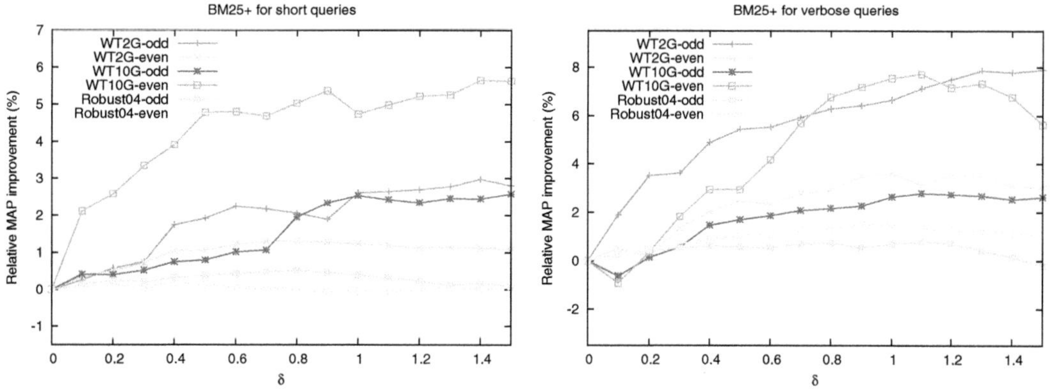

Figure 4: Performance Sensitivity to δ of BM25+, where y-axis shows the relative MAP improvements of BM25+ over BM25, and suffix '-even'/'-odd' indicates that only even/odd-number query topics are used.

Query	Method	WT10G	WT2G	Robust04
Short	PL2	0.1883	0.3231	0.2531
	PL2+	**0.1920**	0.3227	**0.2549**
	PL2+ ($\delta = 0.8$)	0.1912	**0.3255**	0.2540
Verbose	PL2	0.1695	0.2473	0.2185
	PL2+	**0.1886**^{4}	0.2595	**0.2348**^{4}
	PL2+ ($\delta = 0.8$)	**0.1886**^{4}	**0.2639**^{2}	0.2347^{4}

Table 6: Comparison of PL2 and PL2+ using cross validation. Superscripts 1/2/3/4 indicate that the corresponding MAP improvement is significant at the 0.05/0.02/0.01/0.001 level using the Wilcoxon test.

Query	WT10G	WT2G	Robust04
Short	9	23	9
Verbose	2	3	2

Table 7: Optimal settings of c in PL2.

for the retrieval of very long documents. This suggests that BM25+ indeed retrieves very long documents more fairly.

7.3 PL2+ VS. PL2

In both PL2+ and PL2, we train parameter c using cross validation, where c is tuned from 0.5 to 25 (27 values). Besides, in PL2+, parameter δ is also trained using cross validation, where δ is tuned from 0.0 to 1.5 in increments of 0.1. Also we create a special run of PL2+ in which δ is fixed to 0.8 empirically without training. The comparison results of PL2+ and PL2 are presented in Table 6.

The results show that PL2+ outperforms PL2 consistently, and even if we fix $\delta = 0.8$, PL2+ can still achieve stable improvements over PL2. Specifically, PL2+ improves significantly over PL2 for about **10%** on verbose queries, yet it only improves slightly on short queries; PL2+ appears to be less sensitive to the genre of collections, since it also improves significantly over PL2 on *news* data (verbose queries). We hypothesize that, PL2 may overly-penalize very long documents seriously on verbose queries but works well on short queries, and thus there is more room for PL2+ to improve the performance on verbose queries than on short queries. To verify it, we collect the optimal settings of c in PL2 and show them in Table 7. We can see that the optimal settings of c are "huge" for short queries as compared to that for verbose queries, presenting an obvious contrast. As a result, recalling the upper bound of document length in Formula 8,

Query	Method	WT10G	WT2G	Robust04
Short	Dir	0.1930	0.3088	0.2521
	Dir+	0.1961	0.3112^{2}	**0.2530**^{1}
	Dir+ ($\delta = 0.05$)	**0.1967**^{1}	**0.3123**^{3}	0.2525
Verbose	Dir	0.1790	0.2742	0.2329
	Dir+	**0.1874**^{3}	0.2867^{1}	0.2440^{4}
	Dir+ ($\delta = 0.05$)	0.1871^{3}	**0.2871**^{2}	**0.2440**^{4}

Table 8: Comparison of Dir and Dir+ using cross validation. Superscripts 1/2/3/4 indicate that the corresponding MAP improvement is significant at the 0.05/0.02/0.01/0.001 level using the Wilcoxon test.

verbose queries would be more likely to violate LB2 even if a document is not very long (e.g., a news article), while short queries would only have a very small chance to violate LB2 even if a document is very long. Again, we can see that our constraint analysis is consistent with empirical results.

7.4 Dir+ VS. Dir

In both Dir+ and Dir, we train parameter μ using cross validation, where μ is tuned in a parameter space of 12 values from 500 to 10000. Besides, in Dir+, parameter δ is also trained, the candidate values of which are from 0.0 to 0.15 in increments of 0.01. Similarly, we also create a special run in which δ is fixed to 0.05 empirically without training. The comparison of Dir+ and Dir is presented in Table 8.

Overall, we observe that Dir+ improves over Dir consistently and significantly across different collections, and even if we fix $\delta = 0.05$ without training, Dir+ can still outperform Dir significantly in most cases. Note that, similar to BM25+ and PL2+, Dir+ works more effectively on verbose queries, which is consistent with our constraint analysis that Dir is more likely to overly penalize very long documents when a query contains more non-discriminative terms. In addition, we further compare Dir+ and Dir thoroughly by varying μ from 500 to 10000. It shows that Dir+ is consistently better than Dir no matter how we change the μ value.

Moreover, comparing Table 8 with Table 4 and 6, we can see that Dir works clearly better on verbose queries than BM25 and PL2. One possible explanation is that Dir satisfies LB2 unconditionally, but BM25 and PL2 do not.

7.5 Piv+ VS. Piv

In both Piv+ and Piv, we train s using cross-validation, where s is tuned from 0.01 to 0.25 in increments of 0.02.

Query	Method	WT10G	WT2G	Robust04
Short	Piv	0.1870	0.2915	0.2410
	Piv+	0.1869	0.2945^1	0.2455^1
Verbose	Piv	0.1493	0.2148	0.2144
	Piv+	0.1493	0.2154	0.2150

Table 9: Comparison of Piv and Piv+ using cross validation. Superscripts 1 indicates that the corresponding MAP improvement is significant at the 0.05 level using the Wilcoxon test.

Query	WT10G	WT2G	Robust04
Short	0.05	0.01	0.05
Verbose	0.05	0.11	0.19

Table 10: Optimal settings of s in Piv.

Besides, in Piv+, parameter δ is also trained, the candidate values are from 0.0 to 1.5 in increments of 0.1. The comparison results of Piv+ and Piv are presented in Table 9.

Unfortunately, Piv+ does not improve over Piv significantly in most of the cases, which, however, is also as we expected: although there is an upper bound of document length for Piv to satisfy LB2 (as shown in Formula 11), this upper bound is often very large because the optimal setting of parameter s is often very small as presented in Table 10. Nevertheless, Piv+ would work much better than Piv when s is large, as observed in our experiments.

7.6 Summary

Our experiments demonstrate empirically that, the proposed general methodology can be applied to state-of-the-art retrieval functions to successfully fix or alleviate their problem of overly-penalizing very long documents.

We have derived three effective retrieval functions, BM25+ (Formula 13), PL2+ (Formula 16), and Dir+ (Formula 14). All of them are as efficient as but more effective than their corresponding standard retrieval functions, i.e., BM25, PL2, and Dir, respectively. There is an extra parameter δ in the derived formulas, but we can set it to some default values (i.e., $\delta = 1.0$ for BM25+, $\delta = 0.8$ for PL2+, and $\delta = 0.05$ for Dir+), which perform quite well. The proposed retrieval functions can potentially replace its corresponding standard retrieval functions in all retrieval applications.

8. CONCLUSIONS

In this paper, we reveal a common deficiency of the current retrieval models: the component of term frequency (TF) normalization by document length is not lower-bounded properly; as a result, very long documents tend to be overly-penalized. In order to analytically diagnose this problem, we propose two desirable formal constraints to capture the heuristic of lower-bounding TF, and use constraint analysis to examine several representative retrieval functions. We find that all these retrieval functions can only satisfy the constraints for a certain range of parameter values and/or for a particular set of query terms. Empirical results further show that the retrieval performance tends to be poor when the parameter is out of the range or the query term is not in the particular set. To solve this common problem, we propose a general and efficient method to introduce a sufficiently large lower bound for TF normalization which can be shown analytically to fix or alleviate the problem.

Our experimental results on standard collections demonstrate that the proposed methodology, incurring almost no additional computational cost, can be applied to state-of-the-art retrieval functions, such as Okapi BM25 [14, 15], language models [20], and the divergence from randomness approach [1], to significantly improve the average precision, especially for verbose queries. Our work has also helped reveal interesting differences in the behavior of these state-of-the-art retrieval models. Due to its effectiveness, efficiency, and generality, the proposed methodology can work as a "patch" to fix or alleviate the problem in current retrieval models, in a plug-and-play way.

9. ACKNOWLEDGMENTS

We thank the anonymous reviewers for their useful comments. This material is based upon work supported by the National Science Foundation under Grant Numbers IIS-0713581, CNS-0834709, and CNS 1028381, by NIH/NLM grant 1 R01 LM009153-01, a Sloan Research Fellowship, and a Yahoo! Key Scientific Challenge Award.

10. REFERENCES

[1] G. Amati and C. J. Van Rijsbergen. Probabilistic models of information retrieval based on measuring the divergence from randomness. *ACM Trans. Inf. Syst.*, 20:357–389, October 2002.

[2] S. Clinchant and E. Gaussier. Information-based models for ad hoc ir. In *SIGIR '10*, pages 234–241, 2010.

[3] R. Cummins and C. O'Riordan. An axiomatic comparison of learned term-weighting schemes in information retrieval: clarifications and extensions. *Artif. Intell. Rev.*, 28:51–68, June 2007.

[4] H. Fang, T. Tao, and C. Zhai. A formal study of information retrieval heuristics. In *SIGIR '04*, pages 49–56, 2004.

[5] H. Fang, T. Tao, and C. Zhai. Diagnostic evaluation of information retrieval models. *ACM Trans. Inf. Syst.*, 29:7:1–7:42, April 2011.

[6] H. Fang and C. Zhai. An exploration of axiomatic approaches to information retrieval. In *SIGIR '05*, pages 480–487, 2005.

[7] H. Fang and C. Zhai. Semantic term matching in axiomatic approaches to information retrieval. In *SIGIR '06*, pages 115–122, 2006.

[8] N. Fuhr. Probabilistic models in information retrieval. *The Computer Journal*, 35:243–255, 1992.

[9] H. P. Luhn. A statistical approach to mechanized encoding and searching of literary information. *IBM J. Res. Dev.*, 1:309–317, October 1957.

[10] Y. Lv and C. Zhai. Adaptive term frequency normalization for bm25. In *CIKM '11*, 2011.

[11] Y. Lv and C. Zhai. When documents are very long, bm25 fails! In *SIGIR '11*, pages 1103–1104, 2011.

[12] J. M. Ponte and W. B. Croft. A language modeling approach to information retrieval. In *SIGIR '98*, pages 275–281, 1998.

[13] S. E. Robertson and K. S. Jones. Relevance weighting of search terms. *Journal of the American Society of Information Science*, 27(3):129–146, 1976.

[14] S. E. Robertson and S. Walker. Some simple effective approximations to the 2-poisson model for probabilistic weighted retrieval. In *SIGIR '94*, pages 232–241, 1994.

[15] S. E. Robertson, S. Walker, S. Jones, M. Hancock-Beaulieu, and M. Gatford. Okapi at trec-3. In *TREC '94*, pages 109–126, 1994.

[16] G. Salton, A. Wong, and C. S. Yang. A vector space model for automatic indexing. *Commun. ACM*, 18(11):613–620, 1975.

[17] A. Singhal. Modern information retrieval: a brief overview. *Bulletin of the IEEE Computer Society Technical Committee on Data Engineering*, 24:2001, 2001.

[18] A. Singhal, C. Buckley, and M. Mitra. Pivoted document length normalization. In *SIGIR '96*, pages 21–29, 1996.

[19] T. Tao and C. Zhai. An exploration of proximity measures in information retrieval. In *SIGIR '07*, pages 295–302, 2007.

[20] C. Zhai and J. D. Lafferty. A study of smoothing methods for language models applied to ad hoc information retrieval. In *SIGIR '01*, pages 334–342, 2001.

A Quasi-Synchronous Dependence Model for Information Retrieval

Jae-Hyun Park, W. Bruce Croft and David A. Smith
Center for Intelligent Information Retrieval
Department of Computer Science
University of Massachusetts, Amherst, MA 01003
{jhpark,croft,dasmith}@cs.umass.edu

ABSTRACT

Incorporating syntactic features in a retrieval model has had very limited success in the past, with the exception of binary term dependencies. This paper presents a new term dependency modeling approach based on syntactic dependency parsing for both queries and documents. Our model is inspired by a quasi-synchronous stochastic process for machine translation [21]. We model four different types of relationships between syntactically dependent term pairs to perform inexact matching between documents and queries. We also propose a machine learning technique for predicting optimal parameter settings for a retrieval model incorporating syntactic relationships. The results on TREC collections show that the quasi-synchronous dependence model can improve retrieval performance and outperform a strong state-of-art sequential dependence baseline when we use predicted optimal parameters.

Categories and Subject Descriptors

H.3.3 [**Information System**]: Information Search and Retrieval

General Terms

Algorithm, Experimentation, Performance

Keywords

Term Dependency, Quasi-synchronous Grammar, Weighting Retrieval Model

1. INTRODUCTION

Term dependency has been studied for several decades to improve the effectiveness of information retrieval. Although independence assumptions simplify retrieval models, terms are actually dependent upon each other within documents and within queries. Terms are used together to make more specific meanings or, sometimes, totally different meanings. Despite this, it has been difficult to develop retrieval models incorporating term dependence that show consistent improvements over those that assume term independence. One of the challenging issues in modeling term dependence is that a concept can be expressed in different ways syntactically as well as lexically. In describing a concept in their queries, people use different vocabularies than authors use in describing the same concepts in their documents [27]. Query term expansion techniques have been studied to deal with a lexical mismatch between queries and relevant documents.

Similarly, even if the vocabularies in queries and documents are identical to each other, their relationships can differ in various ways: specifically, in order, proximity, and grammatical relation. In order to take account of the variability in relationships of terms between queries and documents, successful term dependence models in previous work allowed inexact matches in the order and proximity of dependent terms [16, 23]. Figure 1 shows example sentences containing the words "chemical" and "weapons". Even though the concept implied by "chemical weapons" is similar, their orders, distances, and syntactic relations vary between the example sentences. If we strictly regulate the order, distance, and syntactic relation of dependent terms, we will miss "chemical weapons" in relevant documents. The sequential dependence model (SDM) can match these important dependent terms by allowing differences in their order and proximity [16].

However, current models typically ignore term dependence based on syntactic relationships in queries and often restrict dependency relations to adjacent term pairs. If the example

> Al-Rabta ***chemical weapons*** plant was uncovered and destroyed in a fire.
>
> ... mentions ricin, sarin, soman, or anthrax as a toxic ***chemical*** used as a ***weapon***.
>
> ... its ***chemical*** and biological ***weapons*** and nuclear program.
>
> He intends to produce not only ***chemical*** but also bacteriological ***weapons***.

Figure 1: Example sentences that show syntactic variations in the term dependency of the concept "chemical weapons"

CIKM'11, October 24–28,2011, Glasgow, Scotland, UK.

sentences in Figure 1 are used in a query, all dependencies except the first will be ignored because they are not adjacent. Gao et al. [7] propose an approach which tries to extract long-distance term dependencies by incorporating information from syntactic dependencies. Song et al. [22] and Lee et al. [12] also propose a model based on linguistic parsing. By choosing syntactically related term pairs in a query as dependent terms, these models attempt to overcome the limitation of sequential dependencies. However, the models are still limited to a head-modifier relation in which two dependent terms are directly linked in a dependency structure. Thus, they would still ignore all dependencies in Figure 1 except the first.

In this paper, we propose a term dependence model inspired by a quasi-synchronous stochastic process developed by Smith and Eisner [21]. Synchronous grammars were proposed for machine translation to generate translated expressions or identify translation examples by aligning a parse tree in a source language to a parse tree in a target language [20]. Because of inherent incompatibility between a source language and target language, syntactic and lexical variations occur during translating from a source sentence to a target sentence. Thus, a synchronous model should be able to align a translation unit in a source language to different forms than that of the original [8]. Smith and Eisner [21] model several different types of syntactic configurations in a target language. A synchronous model allows parent-child words in a source language tree to be associated with words having different syntactic configurations in a target language tree.

This inexact matching process of the quasi-synchronous model has also shown significant improvements for other research tasks such as open domain question-answering(QA) [26] and paraphrasing [6]. The processes of selecting answer sentences and paraphrased sentences are interpreted as a free translation process between sentences in the same language. In a similar way, we adopt the quasi-synchronous stochastic approach and generalize it for information retrieval, where a target sentence (a query) is generated from a set of sentences (a document) instead of a single source sentence. By using the quasi-synchronous stochastic approach, we represent term dependence more flexibly and incorporate transformations of dependence relationships.

The remainder of this paper is organized as follows. Section 2 introduces previous work about term dependence models, syntactic features, and parameter optimization methods for integrating different retrieval models. In Section 3 we explain how our model covers syntactic variations between queries and documents. Next, Section 4 describes a method to predict optimal weights of models for a given query. In Section 5 we evaluate our proposed model. Finally, in Section 6 we conclude and outline future work.

2. RELATED WORK

Term dependency has long been studied in the field of information retrieval and has been based on various features such as co-occurrences of terms, proximities between terms, etc. [5, 7, 12, 16, 23, 25]. Dependence models based on syntactic parsing results have been proposed to capture long-distance term dependencies. Gao et al. [7] proposed a dependence language model in which term dependencies were selected based upon the linkage structure L of queries and documents. The fundamental idea of this model is that

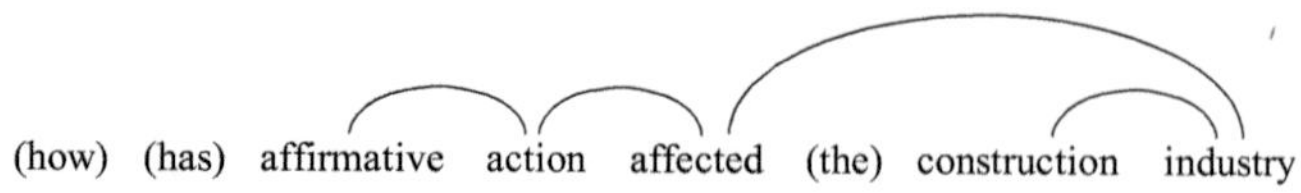

Figure 2: The sample linkage graph L of a query in [7]. They consider only a direct linkage between a word and its head word.

queries and documents are represented in the form of the hidden variable, an acyclic, planar, undirected linkage graph L as shown Figure 2. The dependence language model generates not only a query but also the linkages of the query as follows

$$P(Q|D) = \sum_L P(Q, L|D) = \sum_L P(L|D)P(Q|L, D) \quad (1)$$

Then, dependent terms are defined by the edges in a linkage graph L and $P(Q|L, D)$ is decomposed in the similar way with the bigram model.

$$P(Q|L, D) = P(q_h|D) \prod_{(i,j)\in L} P(q_j|q_i, L, D) \quad (2)$$

in which, q_h is the sentential head word of a query. q_i is the head word of q_j in L.

Maisonnasse et al. [13] extend this dependence language model using a syntactic and semantic analysis model. Lee et al. [12] also suggested a language model which is based on dependency parse trees generated by a linguistic parser. These models aim to solve the limitation of the language model approach in which models fail to detect long-distance dependencies when just replacing the unigram language model with a bigram or biterm language model. However, they still have the limitation that term dependencies are derived only from head-dependent term pairs or directly connected nodes in the linkage structure L. As shown Figure 1, a head-dependent relation of terms can be expressed using indirect relations without changing its meaning.

Song et al. [22] introduced *variability*, which represents the probability that a head-modifier term pair in a query will not have a head-modifier relation in a document. They observe that some head-modifier term pairs in queries have stronger relations with each other than other head-modifier term pairs. If a strongly tied term pair, e.g. "mutual" → "fund", is unseen in a document, it is unlikely to expect the strongly tied term pair be used in a different way. On the other hand, although a weakly tied term pair, e.g. "textile" → "product" is unseen in a document, we can expect that the term pair is used with a transformed relation in the document. Based on this assumption, they use predicted variabilities for an interpolation weight as follows.

$$\begin{aligned} P(w_i \to w_j|w_i, D) =& (1 - v_i) \cdot P(w_i \to w_j|w_i, D) + \\ & v_i \cdot P(w_i \to w_j|w_i, C) \end{aligned} \quad (3)$$

in which, v_i is the variability of a head-modifier q_i and q_j. D and C represent a document and a collection, respectively. Although the variability implies the possibility that there are the transformations of the syntactic relationships of dependent terms between queries and documents, the variability still does not consider the transformed term pairs explicitly.

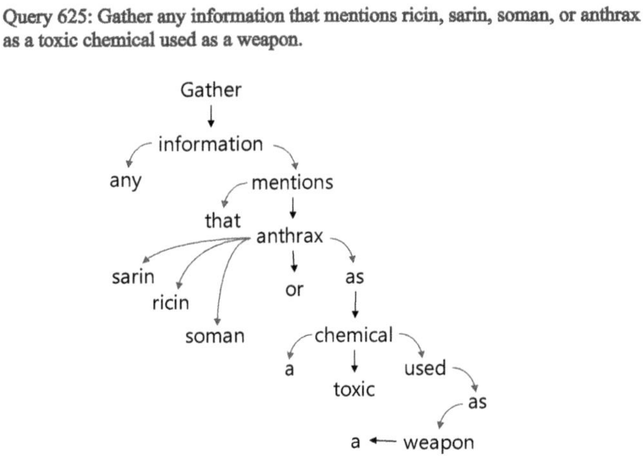

Figure 3: Example of syntactic parsing results (The description query of the TREC topic 625)

To identify dependencies of terms beyond head-modifier in both queries and documents and also to handle variations in dependence relations of terms, we adopt a relaxed alignment approach, specifically a quasi-synchronous grammar developed by Smith and Eisner [21]. As in Berger and Lafferty [3], we view the probability $p(Q|D)$ as the document-to-query translation process. We bring a quasi-synchronous approach to information retrieval and generalize it to adapt it for an alignment between a query and a document. In the next section, we briefly describe dependency parsing technique and then explain the quasi-synchronous model for information retrieval.

3. QUASI-SYNCHRONOUS MODEL

Dependency grammar describes linguistic structures directly in terms of dependencies between words themselves [14]. This is especially useful in information retrieval, where the words themselves, and not additional phrasal or clausal structures, are not our primary concern. Dependency parsers output directed trees over words: each word in the sentence has exactly one incoming edge, which comes from its 'head' or 'parent', with the except of the 'root' word, which has no incoming edges. An example dependency tree for a query is depicted in Figure 3.

In information retrieval, we wish to measure the distance between a query and various candidate documents. By using dependency syntax, we can cast this problem as one of distance between a query tree and document trees. Of especial interest are the many approaches to comparing trees in the machine translation literature. In particular, Smith and Eisner proposed a quasi-synchronous stochastic process [21] to allow parent and child words in a source-language tree to be associated with words having different syntactic relations in a target-language tree.

3.1 Modeling Dependency Transformations

Synchronous grammars, originally proposed for machine translation [20], jointly generate trees of a source and target sentence. Depending on the size and complexity of the rewrite rules in a synchronous grammar—and the computational complexity required for inference—, the source and target trees can diverge more or less in their structures. For information retrieval and other problems, however, we are only interested in the *conditional* probability of one tree given another; moreover, we are usually not interested in the full generative process of either tree but only in the parts of the two trees that match with greater or lesser fidelity. Words in a source tree (e.g., in a document) are not always translated into a target tree (e.g., a query) with the same syntactic structure. Some source words may be translated into one target word, and others may be match more than one word or a phrase. To solve these disagreements in source and target languages, a *quasi-synchronous* model allows words in a target sentence, which are aligned with a words in a parent-child dependency relation in a source sentence, to have a different relationship to each other. In this paper, we consider the four following configurations:

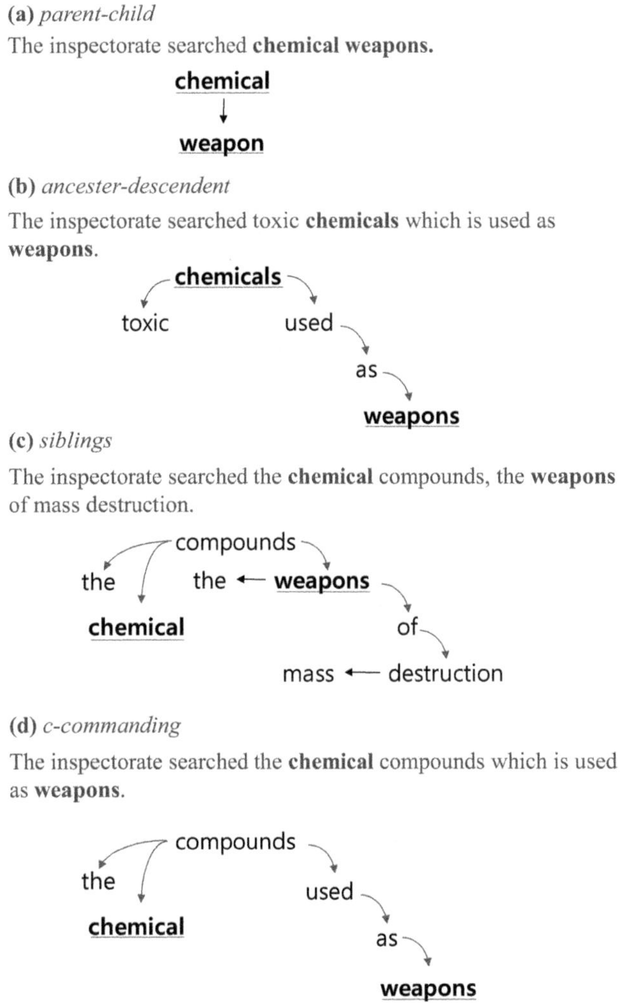

Figure 4: Four types of syntactic dependency configurations for the quasi-synchronous model. The quasi-synchronous model matches terms in queries and documents along with transformations between these dependence relations: (a) parent-child, (b) ascendant-descendant, (c) siblings, and (d) c-commanding.

- Parent-Child
- Ancestor-Descendent
- Siblings
- C-Commanding

Figure 4 shows examples for terms, "chemical" and "weapon".

Like the language model framework, the basic idea of the quasi-synchronous model is to rank a document using the probability that a query is generated by the document model. However, we infer a document model from the dependency tree T_D of a document rather than the raw term sequence D as in the dependence language model [7]. The document model generates not an individual term or a dependent term pair but a fragment of the parsing tree T_Q of a query Q through the loose alignment A.

$$P(Q|D) \approx P(T_Q, A|T_D) = P(A|T_D) \cdot P(T_Q|A, T_D) \quad (4)$$

where T_Q and T_D are the parsing trees of a query and a document, respectively. A is a set of possible combinations of the four syntactic configurations between a query and a document.

In previous work [7, 12, 22], valid alignments A contain only parent-child relations. Our quasi-synchronous approach, on the other hand, allows inexact matching from all four above-listed syntactic configurations to all other. More specifically, when we consider the transformation of the syntactic configurations, being aligned with a parent-child (t_i, t_j) is different from being aligned with a child-parent (t_i, t_j). Parent-child, ancestor-descendent, and c-commanding relations are different according to the order of two terms. Therefore, a dependent term pair in a query can be aligned not to four syntactic configurations but to seven syntactic configurations, and A has 4×7 elements for the combinations of syntactic configurations in a query and a document.

$$P(A|T_D)P(T_Q|A, T_D) = \sum_{(syn_D, syn_Q) \in A} P(syn_D, syn_Q|T_{D,syn_D}) \cdot P(T_{Q,syn_Q}|T_{D,syn_D}) \quad (5)$$

where syn_Q and syn_D are one of the four syntactic configurations and $P(syn_D, syn_Q|T_{D,syn_D})$ is the probability that a syntactic relation syn_D in a document is used in the form of syn_Q in a query. Intuitively, the probability that syn_D is transformed to syn_Q is different according to different terms as pointed out by [22]. For example, two words for a person's name are less likely to be used in the forms of ancestor-descendant, siblings, or c-commanding. However, to estimate the probabilities for a quasi-alignment, the number of parameters becomes impractically large. Therefore, for simplicity, we use a uniform distribution for $P(syn_D, syn_Q|T_{D,syn_D})$.

$$\sum_{(syn_D, syn_Q) \in A} P(syn_D, syn_Q|T_{D,syn_D}) P(T_{Q,syn_Q}|T_{D,syn_D}) = \sum_{(syn_D, syn_Q) \in A} \frac{1}{N} \cdot P(T_{Q,syn_Q}|T_{D,syn_D}) \quad (6)$$

awhere N is the number of elements in the set A.

T_{D,syn_D} and T_{Q,syn_Q} represent a set of dependent terms having syn_D and syn_Q in a document and a query, respectively. For example, $T_{Q,parent-child}$ of the query in Figure 3 are (anthrax,sarin), (anthrax,ricin), (anthrax, soman), and (chemical,toxic). The probability $P(T_{Q,syn_Q}|A, T_{D,syn_D})$ is computed by the non-negative potential function of a term pair that has a syntactic relation syn_Q in a query and syn_D in a document as follows:

$$P(T_{Q,syn_Q}|T_{D,syn_D}) \stackrel{\text{rank}}{=} \sum_{(t_i,t_j) \in T_{Q,syn_Q}} \lambda(t_i, t_j) P(t_i, t_j|T_{D,syn_D}) \quad (7)$$

where t_i and t_j are dependent terms with relations syn_Q in the parse tree of a query. Because the model considers more complex term dependencies, a harmful term dependency is more frequently introduced by unimportant terms in a query. To circumvent this problem, we use the query term ranking score of [18]. $\lambda(t_i, t_j)$ is the mean value of query term ranking scores of t_i and t_j. $P(t_i, t_j|T_{D,syn_D})$ is calculated in the same way of the potential function in [16].

$$P(t_i, t_j|T_{D,syn_D}) = (1 - \alpha_D)\frac{tf_{t_i,t_j,syn_D}}{|D|} + \alpha_D \frac{cf_{t_i,t_j,syn_D}}{|C|} \quad (8)$$

tf_{t_i,t_j,syn_D} is the term frequency of term pairs t_i and t_j with the syntactic relation syn_D in a document D. We smoothed the probability distribution using the Dirichlet smoothing algorithm. cf_{t_i,t_j,syn_D} is the collection frequency of term pairs t_i and t_j with the syntactic relation syn_D in a collection.

Compared to the quasi-synchronous models for machine translation, QA, and paraphrasing in previous work [21, 6, 26], our quasi-synchronous model: (1) aligns single query sentences with entire documents; (2) considers syntactic variations, but not lexical translation, through quasi-synchronous matching; and (3) considers features other than head-modifier matching not only in documents but also in queries. We expand on these characteristics below.

First, basically, our model matches terms of different units: a document and a query. On the other hand, in the previous work, matching is conducted between sentences. Therefore, terms of a query are allowed to match multiple times with terms in a document in information retrieval. As pointed out by Wang et al. [26], we are not interested in actual alignment between a query and a document. Rather, we interpret the process of matching as one in which a term pair with various dependency relations is generated by a document.

Second, our model focuses only on syntactic variations between queries and documents. The original quasi-synchronous grammar is established to consider both syntactic and semantic variations. Smith and Eisner[21] allows the original quasi-synchronous model to have a NULL alignment and a 1-to-2 alignments. Wang et al.[26] extends a term pair in a question to consider $2^{13} - 1$ possible combinations of expanded term pairs by using a thesaurus, WordNet. A quasi-synchronous model for information retrieval must take into account an entire collection while previous work has targeted a relatively small number of sentences. It is impractical to consider these kinds of semantic variations for all

What is the prognosis *for* new drugs?

Find *ways of* measuring creativity.

What are commercial *uses of* Magnetic Levitation?

Mexico City *has the worst* air pollution *in the* world

What are the arguments *for and against* Great Britain's approval *of* women *being* ordained *as* Church *of* England priests?

What are the industrial *or* commercial uses *of* cyanide *or its* derivatives?

Figure 5: Example queries from the Robust 2004 collection that demonstrate better results when more weight is assigned to the query likelihood model, the sequential dependence model and the quasi-synchronous model, respectively.

documents. Therefore, we make the model consider only term pairs which are lexically identical. We also ignore the transformations to a NULL node, an identical node and an arbitrary term pair in a sentence.

Third, most previous work [7, 13, 21, 22] treats only a parent-child relation or a head-modifier dependency in the parse tree of a query. On the other hand, in the quasi-synchronous model, we expect to cover various dependency relations of terms in both a query and a document. As all the four syntactic configurations in a document can have important meanings, dependent terms having the four syntactic configurations in a query would also be important to find relevant documents. Thus, we model the transformation from all the four syntactic configurations to all the four syntactic configurations instead of counting only the direct head-modifier relation.

3.2 Parameter Optimization

Although the quasi-synchronous model is based on the premise that syntactically dependent terms are important for retrieving relevant documents, a retrieval model based on independence assumptions or simpler dependence assumptions can also be effective and may outperform our model for at least some queries. The quasi-synchronous model ranks a document based on complex syntactic term dependencies in a parsing tree, so it is less applicable for a query containing a single important keyword. Figure 5 shows some example queries. In the first group of queries, the important terms are not expected to be used with specific dependencies. Therefore, treating terms individually is sufficient to retrieve relevant documents. Because dependent terms in the second group of queries are placed near each other, the quasi-synchronous model may consider unnecessary dependencies and can assigns inaccurate scores to the documents containing these dependencies. We need to combine the quasi-synchronous model with other retrieval models to address this problem.

When we combine several retrieval models, it is important to assign a proper weight to each retrieval model according to the characteristics of queries. Metzler [15] claimed that applying different types of models to new tasks typically requires an information retrieval expert to modify the underlying model in some way to properly account for the new types of features. He suggests an automatic feature selection model which determines the optimal weight of a linear feature-based model by using a greedy procedure. Zhai and Lafferty [29] also stressed an optimal parameter setting depends upon not only on document collections but also queries. Consider a linear interpolated model of the quasi-synchronous model and the sequential dependence model as follows:

$$P(q, d) = \lambda \cdot SDM(q, d) + (1 - \lambda) \cdot QuasiSync(q, d) \quad (9)$$

where $SDM(q, d)$ and $QuasiSync(q, d)$ represent the log-scores of the document d given a query q measured by the sequential dependence model and quasi-synchronous model, respectively. In this preliminary experiment, we select an optimal parameter λ value which maximizes the overall average precision of the interpolated retrieval model. Figure 6 demonstrates that the distribution of weights according to the length of queries. This result demonstrates that the sequential dependence model and the quasi-synchronous model have their own advantages for different types of queries. If we use a fixed parameter for all queries, the quasi-synchronous model improves the effectiveness for some queries but also adversely affects the performance for other queries.

We can find an optimal parameter setting for a new task and document collection although this may require excessive tuning. On the other hand, it is impossible to optimize a parameter setting for an unseen query. To solve this problem, we exploit a machine learning approach to predict the optimal parameter settings for individual retrieval models based on a given query. Machine learning methods have been intensively studied for query term ranking approaches to predict the importance of an individual term or a set of terms in a given query [1, 2, 10, 11, 18, 28]. We extend this general approach to weighting the combination of different retrieval models.

In training data for training a query term ranking model, each term or the set of terms is labeled by its optimal weights. Similarly, we train a prediction model to measure the im-

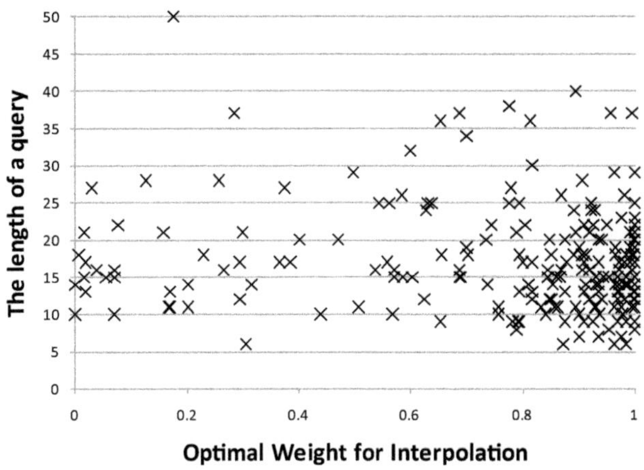

Figure 6: The distribution of optimal weight according to the length of a query from Robust 2004 collection when linear interpolating the sequential dependence model and the quasi-synchronous model.

portance of a individual retrieval model for a given query. Training data for the prediction model consists of a query and the optimal weights of retrieval models,

$$(x_1, w_{i1}), \ldots, (x_n, w_{in})$$

where x_j is a ith query and its feature vector. w_{ij} is the optimal parameter setting of a jth sub retrieval model for the ith query.

A training label w_{ij}, which is the optimal weight for a ith query and a jth retrieval model, are selected empirically. First, we retrieve an initial ranked list of documents for a specific query by using a baseline retrieval model. When we retrieve initial documents, we make the retrieval model retrieve more documents because we wish training data cover documents out of the rank which may be retrieved by different parameter settings. Then, we choose optimal parameter values of retrieval models which maximize the performance of the initial document set. In this paper, we used mean average precision (MAP) as the retrieval metric. The weights in Figure 6 were chosen in this way.

The regression model we adopt in this paper is Support Vector Regression (SVR) [4]. Table 1 shows the list of features. Statistical features are an aggregation of feature values representing the characteristics of an individual term. Syntactic features are derived from the dependency parsing result of a query. These features are used to measure the number of the complex syntactic relations of terms in the query have. The higher the number of noun phrases and the depth of a parsing tree, the more complex the syntactic structure of a query. The quasi-synchronous model aims to capture these complex syntactic relations of terms from both queries and documents. These features also reflect whether we need to consider syntactic variations between a query and a document. For example, if a query is a wh-question such as a factored question, a relevant document contains terms of the query without rephrasing it.

Table 1: A summary of features used to measure importance of models for an individual query.

	Statistical Features
q_len	The length of query
aver_TF/DF/ TFIDF	The average of term frequency, document frequency and TFxIDF of terms in a query
ratio_NOUN/ ADJ/VERB	The ratio of nouns, adjectives and verbs in a query per the query length
KeyConcept	The ratio of terms which is selected by query term ranking methods
mean_score	The average of query term ranking scores
stopwords	The ratio of stopwords in a query
	Syntactic Features
is_question	Is a query a question?
is_wh	Is a query a wh-question?
num_NP	The number of a noun phrases in a query
ratio_NP	The number of a noun phrases in a query per the query length
num_clause	The number of a dependent clauses in a query
ratio_clause	The number of a dependent clauses in a query per the query length
aver_depth	the average depth of Key-Concept terms in a parsing tree of a query
height_tree	The height of a parsing tree of a query
ratio_PC/AD / SB/CC	The ratio of dependent term pairs which have parent-child, ancestor-descendent, siblings and c-commanding relations in a query, respectively.

4. EXPERIMENTS

In this section, we describe experiments to evaluate the quasi-synchronous model. In particular, we aim to compare the effectiveness of the quasi-synchronous approach to models based on the term-independence and sequential dependency assumptions. For this purpose, we interpolated the quasi-synchronous model with the query likelihood model [19] and the sequential dependence model [16] to compare the quasi-synchronous model in different settings.

4.1 Experimental Settings

We made use of the TREC Robust 2004 and Gov2 collections for experiments. Some statistics for these two collections are shown in Table 2. All documents were indexed using the Indri search engine [17]. Terms were stemmed by using the Porter stemmer and were stopped using a standard list of stopwords. Only the description queries were used because our approach targets queries submitted in well-formed sentences[1]. We used Dirichlet smoothing for both the quasi-synchronous model and other retrieval models.

Table 2: The statistics of the TREC Robust 2004 and Gov2 collections

Coll	Description	# Doc.	TREC topics
Ro04	Newwire articles	528,155	301-450, 601-700
Gov2	.gov web collection	25,205,179	701-850

For the Robust 2004 collection, all documents and queries were parsed using the Stanford dependency parser [9]. The Stanford dependency parser internally includes the Stanford Part-of-Speech tagger [24]. Because the quasi-synchronous model needs an acyclic tree structure, we use the basic dependency representation form instead of the Stanford parser's collapsed representation. For the Gov2 collection, it is impractical to parse all documents. Therefore, we retrieve an initial document set using a baseline retrieval model. We then parsed documents in the initial set and evaluate the quasi-synchronous model only on the initial document set. Because the dependency parser accepts raw text format, we used ***lynx***[2] to convert the documents of the Gov2 collection in the TREC web format to raw text format before parsing documents.

To predict optimal weights for the interpolation of retrieval models, we used the support vector regression method

[1]Compared to previous work, we use original description queries instead of refined queries from which command stop phrases are manually deleted.

[2]http://en.wikipedia.org/wiki/Lynx_(web_browser)

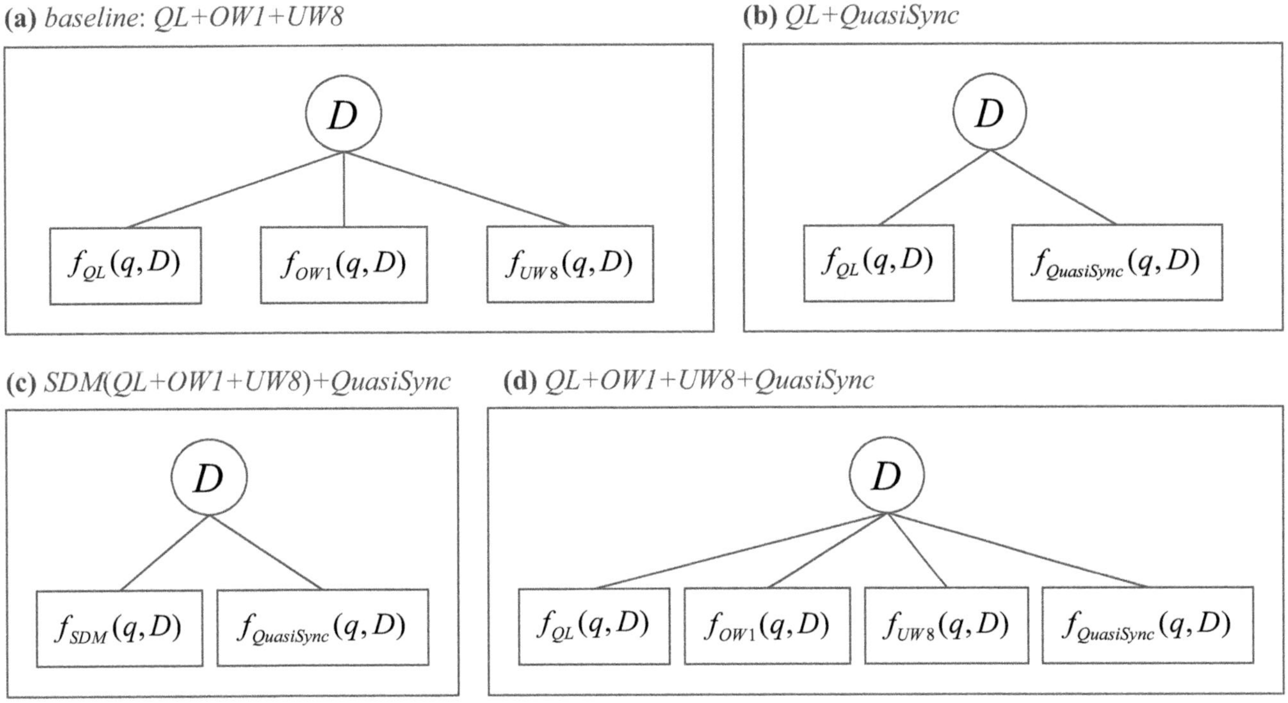

Figure 7: Four strategies of linear interpolation with the query-likelihood model(*QL*), the sequential dependence model(*SDM*), and the quasi-synchronous model(*QM*). The sequential dependence model interpolates three scores with fixed weights: the query-likelihood score f_{QL}, the ordered window score f_{OW1} and the unordered window score f_{UW8} [16].

which predicts the approximate target value based on a given feature vector [4]. We trained the regression model for each query using leave-one-out cross-validation in which one query was used for test data and the others were used for training data. Among the features in Table 1, some features are not appropriate for a certain retrieval model. For example, the number of term pairs having parent-child, ancestor-descendent, siblings and c-commanding in a query may be not discriminative to weight the ordered window function and the unordered window function in the sequential dependence model. Thus, we chose ten features for each interpolation strategy based on an self-evaluation result using the training data.

The dependent term pairs of the quasi-synchronous model include 98.31% of adjacent term pairs (3,365) Among the 3,365 adjacent term pairs, 54.65% $(1,839)$ of them have a parent-child relation. 19.67% (662), 6.03% (203) and 19.64% (661) have ancestor-descendent, siblings and c-commanding relations, respectively.

4.2 Quasi-Synchronous vs. Exact Matching

We combine the quasi-synchronous model with two baseline retrieval models using four different interpolation strategies. Figure 7 shows these four linear interpolation strategies. The first baseline model is the query-likelihood model (QL), a standard bag-of-word retrieval model based on the independent assumption [19]. The other baseline model is the sequential dependence model (SDM), which consists of three factors: a query likelihood factor, an ordered window factor and an unordered window factor [16]. In the four interpolation strategies, the three factors of the sequential dependence model are interpolated in two ways. The "$SDM+QuasiSync$" strategy interpolates three factors using fixed weights–$f_{SDM} = 0.85 \cdot f_{QL} + 0.10 \cdot f_{OW1} + 0.05 \cdot f_{UW8}$–and, then, interpolates f_{SDM} and $f_{QuasiSync}$ using predicted optimal weights. The "$QL+OW1+UW8+QuasiSync$" strategy use predicted weights for all the individual factors: f_{QL}, f_{OW1} and f_{UW8}.

Table 3 shows the experimental results of the four interpolation strategies. The statistical significance of the differences in the performance is determined using a two-sided Wilcoxon sign test, with $\alpha < 0.05$. As described in section 3, compared to the previous work, the quasi-synchronous model is different with respect to allowing inexact matching of syntactic relations between queries and documents. In Table 3, "**Quasi-Synchronous Matching**" represents the experimental results where we allow inexact matching while "**Exact Matching**" shows the experimental results when we align between term pairs having only the same syntactic relation. For all interpolation strategies, the quasi-synchronous approach shows better results than exact matching.

Among the four interpolation strategies in Figure 7, all the strategies with the quasi-synchronous model show significant improvements compared to a stat-of-art baseline model, the sequential dependence model. $SDM + QuasiSync$ achieves the best improvement. On the other hand, predicting the weights for the factors of the sequential dependence model fails to show improvement. The performance of $QL+OW1+UW8$ is similar with that of the sequential dependence model.

Table 3: Experimental results with the Robust 2004 with four interpolation strategies. Numbers in parentheses depict % improvement over the sequential dependence model.

	MAP	nDCG	prec@10
QL	0.2414	0.5061	0.4096
SDM	0.2477	0.5097	0.4217
$QL + OW1 + UW8$	$0.2462^{\dagger}$ (-0.62%)	$0.5067^{\dagger}$ (-0.59%)	0.4177 (-0.95%)
Quasi-Synchronous Matching			
$QL + QuasiSync$	$0.2754^{\dagger}_{\star}$ (11.19%)	$\mathbf{0.5473}^{\dagger}_{\star}$ (7.38%)	$0.4606^{\dagger}_{\star}$ (9.24%)
$SDM + QuasiSync$	$\mathbf{0.2786}^{\dagger}_{\star}$ (12.48%)	$0.5472^{\dagger}_{\star}$ (7.37%)	$\mathbf{0.4614}^{\dagger}_{\star}$ (9.43%)
$QL + OW1 + UW8$ $+QuasiSync$	$0.2765^{\dagger}_{\star}$ (11.61%)	$0.5440^{\dagger}_{\star}$ (6.74%)	$0.4582^{\dagger}_{\star}$ (8.67%)
Exact Matching			
$QL + Exact$	$0.2553_{\star}$ (3.07%)	$0.5231^{\dagger}_{\star}$ (2.63%)	0.4273 (1.33%)
$SDM + Exact$	$0.2590^{\dagger}_{\star}$ (4.54%)	$0.5234^{\dagger}_{\star}$ (2.70%)	$0.4345_{\star}$ (3.05%)
$QL + OW1 + UW8$ $+Exact$	$0.2583^{\dagger}_{\star}$ (4.27%)	$0.5218^{\dagger}_{\star}$ (2.39%)	$0.4361_{\star}$ (3.43%)

$\star$ denotes significantly different with QL
† denotes significantly different with SDM

Table 4: Mean Average Precision of the Robust 2004 collection when we use the four interpolation strategies using the true optimal weights of the training data. ***Matching*** **means "Quasi-Synchronous Matching" or "Exact Matching" in the second and third column, respectively.**

	MAP	
	Quasi	**Exact**
SDM	0.2477	
$QL + OW1 + UW8$	0.2725	
$QL + Matching$	0.3013	0.2699
$SDM + Matching$	0.3022	0.2724
$QL + OW1 + UW8 + Matching$	**0.3165**	0.2936

The performance of $QL + OW1 + UW8 + QuasiSync$ is slightly worse than that of $SDM + QuasiSync$.

4.3 Using True Optimal Parameters

To see the potential of the quasi-synchronous model, we evaluate the four interpolation strategies using the training label as the interpolation weights. Table 4 shows the experimental results with the Robust collection.

When we use the training label or the true optimal weight, the ($QL{+}OW1{+}UW8{+}QuasiSync$) strategy demonstrates the best results. The $QL{+}OW1{+}UW8$ strategy is also better than the baseline. This demonstrates that the sequential dependence model still has a considerable margin for being improved by using a proper parameter setting instead of a fixed parameter setting.

Comparing the MAP value of $QL{+}QuasiSync$ or $SDM{+}$ $QuasiSync$ with $QL{+}OW1{+}UW8$, the quasi-synchronous model has higher potential for taking into an account term dependencies than the sequential dependency model. Meanwhile, ($QL{+}OW1{+}UW8{+}QuasiSync$) shows considerable improvement compared to $SDM + QuasiSync$. $SDM +$ $QuasiSync$ assigns the same weights to adjacent term pairs while ($QL + OW1 + UW8 + QuasiSync$) gives different weights based on the query. It means that certain types of dependency could prove superior for a given query. Thus, we expect further improvement by using a different probability distribution for the alignment $P(syn_D, syn_Q|T_{D,syn_D})$ in Eq. 6.

On the other hand, the exact matching approach fails to show the potential to improve the effectiveness of a retrieval model even though ($QL{+}OW1{+}UW8{+}QuasiSync$) shows a significant improvement over $QL + OW1 + UW8$. The sequential dependence model can take account of long-distance term dependencies on the document side by the unordered window factor $UW8$ [16] and the exact matching approach considers long-distance term dependencies on the query side by extracting dependent terms having a parent-child, ancestor-descendent, siblings or c-commanding relation. Because the exact matching approach does not consider the possibility of the transformation of dependency relations between queries and documents, the gap of MAP values between $QL{+}ExactMatching$ and $SDM{+}ExactMatching$ is bigger than that of $QL + QuasiSync$ and $SDM +$ $QuasiSync$. Only $QL + OW1 + UW8 + ExactMatching$ achieves similar improvement to the quasi-synchronous model.

4.4 Experimental Results with Web Collection

We also applied the quasi-synchronous model to a web collection, the Gov2 collection. For the Gov2 collection, it is impractical to parse all documents. We retrieve an initial document set (1,000 documents) using the sequential dependence model and then run experiments against this initial document set.

Table 5 shows the experimental results for the Gov2 collection. The performances of the interpolation strategies do not show as much improvement as the Robust 2004 collection. Still, $SDM + QuasiSync$ and $QL + OW1 + UW8 +$ $QuasiSync$ interpolation strategies improve the effectiveness significantly.

Table 5: Experimental results with the Gov2 collection based on an initial document set retrieved by the sequential dependence model. Numbers in parentheses depict % improvement in each evaluation measure.

	Gov2		
	MAP	nDCG	P10
SDM	0.2654	0.5234	0.5195
QL+OW1+UW8	0.2674 (0.75%)	0.5246 (0.22%)	0.5228 (0.65%)
$SDM + QuasiSync$	0.2755 † (3.81%)	**0.5352** † (2.25%)	**0.5443** (4.78%)
$QL + OW1 + UW8+$ $QuasiSync$	**0.2764** † (4.14%)	0.5342 † (2.06%)	0.5396 (3.88%)

† means statistically significance difference with SDM

Table 6: Comparison of the MAP of the sequential dependence model, SDM, and $SDM + QuasiSync$. Statistics are collected from the experiments with the Robust 2004 collection. *# queries* is the number of queries belong to each group and *query length* is the average length of queries.

	# queries	query length
$SDM \geq QL + OW1 + UW8$	163	17.12
$SDM < QL + OW1 + UW8$	86	16.78
$SDM \geq SDM + QuasiSync$	98	15.14
$SDM < SDM + QuasiSync$	151	18.21

4.5 Analysis By Query Length

Compared to the sequential dependence model, the quasi-synchronous model aims to capture long distance dependencies in queries. To test the impact of the quasi-synchronous model on long distance dependencies, we analyze queries for which this quasi-synchronous model shows better or worse results. Table 6 demonstrates comparison results between SDM, $QL + OW1 + UW8$ and $SDM + QuasiSync$. The upper two rows are the comparison of the sequential dependence model with fixed and predicted weights. This result demonstrates that the length of queries does not matter for the sequential dependence model itself. On the other hand, the lower two rows are the comparison between the sequential dependence model, SDM, and $SDM + QuasiSync$. It shows that queries improved by the quasi-synchronous model tend to be longer than the other queries.

Based on this observation, we analyze the experimental results of the Robust 2004 collection according to the average length of queries. Table 7 shows an experimental result in which we compared MAP of queries classified according to the length of queries. In this experiment, queries are split into three groups according their length. In the table, the interpolation strategies having the quasi-synchronous model demonstrate a clear tendency to larger improvements for longer queries while the strategy $QL + OW1 + UW8$ does not. The longer a query is, the more long-distance term dependencies the quasi-synchronous model extracts from the query that are not considered by the sequential dependency model. These experimental results show that the quasi-synchronous model can help to capture long-distance term dependencies in not only documents but also queries.

5. CONCLUSIONS

We have proposed a novel term dependence model, the quasi-synchronous model, inspired by a quasi-synchronous stochastic process which constructs an inexact matching of syntactic relations between source and target sentences. As in query term expansion techniques that address lexical variation between query and document, we aim to support syntactic divergence of term dependencies from documents to queries using an inexact matching approach. We generalize these ideas from machine translation to the information retrieval task in which matching occurs between a sentence and an entire document. Experimental results show that the quasi-synchronous model can significantly improve effectiveness compared to a strong state-of-the-art retrieval model.

Table 7: Experimental results with the Robust 2004 according to the length of queries. *Length* is the number of terms in a query and *# queries* is the number of queries belonging to each group. Numbers in parentheses depict % improvement in each evaluation measure.

	Robust 2004 (MAP)		
Length	**∼ 10**	**11 ∼ 20**	**21 ∼**
# queries	**43**	**147**	**59**
SDM	0.3062	0.2398	0.2248
$QL + OW1 + UW8$	0.3056 (-0.19%)	0.2380 (-0.75%)	0.2232 (-0.71%)
$QL + QuasiSync$	0.3268 (6.72%)	0.2613 (8.98%)	0.2731 (21.51%)
$SDM + QuasiSync$	0.3255 (6.29%)	0.2668 (11.27%)	0.2738 (21.81%)
$QL + OW1 + UW8 +$ $QuasiSync$	0.3251 (6.17%)	0.2649 (10.47%)	0.2698 (20.04%)

Each retrieval model, however, has its own strengths and weaknesses, which can differ query by query. A simpler retrieval model may be superior to a more sophisticated model depending on the query. This is why most previous work using term dependencies has had problems showing consistent improvement. To address this issue, we used a machine learning approach to find an optimal parameter setting for a combination of retrieval models. By using a predicated optimal weight, we optimized the overall performance of the interpolation of several retrieval models. This interpolation technique, we found, is necessary for achieving the best results with the quasi-synchronous model.

6. FUTURE WORK

In this paper, we use a uniform distribution over alignments between different syntactic relations in queries and documents. Intuitively, however, dependent terms are expected to be used less frequently in a certain syntactic configurations and more frequently in others. For example, dependent terms in fixed phrases such as technical terminology, proper names, etc., will be used in the same way by both searchers and authors. Moreover, as shown in the experimental results, certain syntactic configurations could prove more important for evaluating the relevance of documents. Thus, instead of a uniform distribution, employing a weighted alignment model could improve the effectiveness of the quasi-synchronous approach.

7. ACKNOWLEDGEMENT

This work was supported in part by the Center for Intelligent Information Retrieval and in part by ARRA NSF IIS-9014442 . Any opinions, findings and conclusions or recommendations expressed in this material are the authors' and do not necessarily reflect those of the sponsor.

8. REFERENCES

[1] M. Bendersky and W. B. Croft. Discovering key concepts in verbose queries. In *Proc. ACM SIGIR*, pages 491–498, 2008.

[2] M. Bendersky, D. Metzler, and W. B. Croft. Learning concept importance using a weighted dependence model. In *Proceedings of the third ACM international conference on Web search and data mining*, pages 31–40, 2010.

[3] A. Berger and J. Lafferty. Information retrieval as statistical translation. In *Proceedings of the 22nd annual international ACM SIGIR conference on Research and development in information retrieval*, pages 222–229, 1999.

[4] C.-C. Chang and C.-J. Lin. *LIBSVM: a library for support vector machines*, 2001. Software available at `http://www.csie.ntu.edu.tw/~cjlin/libsvm`.

[5] W. B. Croft, H. Turtle, and D. Lewis. The use of phrases and structured queries in information retrieval. In *Proceedings of the 14th annual international ACM SIGIR conference on Research and development in information retrieval*, pages 32–45, 1991.

[6] D. Das and N. A. Smith. Paraphrase identification as probabilistic quasi-synchronous recognition. In *Proceedings of the Joint Conference of the 47th Annual Meeting of the ACL and the 4th International Joint Conference on Natural Language Processing of the AFNLP: Volume 1-Volume 1*, pages 468–476, 2009.

[7] J. Gao, J. Y. Nie, G. Wu, and G. Cao. Dependence language model for information retrieval. In *Proceedings of the 27th annual international ACM SIGIR conference on Research and development in information retrieval*, pages 170–177, 2004.

[8] D. Gupta and N. Chatterjee. Study of divergence for example based English-Hindi machine translation. In *Proc. STRANS*, pages 132–140, 2002.

[9] D. Klein and C. D. Manning. Accurate Unlexicalized Parsing. *Proceedings of the 41st Meeting of the Association for Computational Linguistics*, pages 423–430, 2003.

[10] G. Kumaran and V. Carvalho. Reducing long queries using query quality predictors. In *Proceedings of the 32nd international ACM SIGIR conference on Research and development in information retrieval*, pages 564–571, 2009.

[11] C. Lee, R. Chen, S. Kao, and P. Cheng. A term dependency-based approach for query terms ranking. In *Proc. CIKM*, pages 1267–1276, 2009.

[12] C. Lee, G. G. Lee, and M.-G. Jang. Dependency structure applied to language modeling for information retrieval. *ETRI journal*, 28(3):337–346, 2006.

[13] L. Maisonnasse, E. Gaussier, and J. P. Chevallet. Revisiting the dependence language model for information retrieval. In *Proceedings of the 30th annual international ACM SIGIR conference on Research and development in information retrieval*, pages 695–696. ACM, 2007.

[14] C. Manning and H. Schütze. *Foundations of statistical natural language processing*. MIT Press, 1999.

[15] D. Metzler. Automatic feature selection in the markov random field model for information retrieval. In *Proceedings of the sixteenth ACM conference on Conference on information and knowledge management*, pages 253–262, 2007.

[16] D. Metzler and B. W. Croft. A Markov random field model for term dependencies. In *Proceedings of the 28th annual international ACM SIGIR conference on Research and development in information retrieval*, pages 472–479, 2005.

[17] D. Metzler, T. Strohman, H. Turtle, and W. B. Croft. *Indri at TREC 2004: Terabyte track*. 2004.

[18] J. H. Park and W. B. Croft. Query term ranking based on dependency parsing of verbose queries. In *Proceeding of the 33rd international ACM SIGIR conference on Research and development in information retrieval*, pages 829–830, 2010.

[19] J. M. Pont and W. B. Croft. A language modeling approach to information retrieval. In *Proceedings of the 21st annual international ACM SIGIR conference on Research and development in information retrieval*, pages 275–281. ACM, 1998.

[20] S. M. Shieber and Y. Schabes. Synchronous tree-adjoining grammars. In *Proceedings of the 13th conference on Computational linguistics-Volume 3*, pages 253–258, 1990.

[21] D. A. Smith and J. Eisner. Quasi-synchronous grammars: Alignment by soft projection of syntactic dependencies. In *Proceedings of the Workshop on Statistical Machine Translation*, pages 23–30, 2006.

[22] Y. Song, K. Han, S. Kim, S. Park, and H. Rim. A novel retrieval approach reflecting variability of syntactic phrase representation. *Journal of Intelligent Information Systems*, 31(3):265–286, 2008.

[23] M. Srikanth and R. Srihari. Biterm language models for document retrieval. In *Proceedings of the 25th annual international ACM SIGIR conference on Research and development in information retrieval*, pages 425–426, 2002.

[24] K. Toutanova, D. Klein, C. D. Manning, and Y. Singer. Feature-rich part-of-speech tagging with a cyclic dependency network. In *Proceedings of the 2003 Conference of the North American Chapter of the Association for Computational Linguistics on Human Language Technology-Volume 1*, pages 173–180, 2003.

[25] C. Van Rijsbergen. A theoretical basis for the use of co-occurrence data in information retrieval. *Journal of Documentation*, 33(2):106–119, 1993.

[26] M. Wang, N. A. Smith, and T. Mitamura. What is the Jeopardy model? A quasi-synchronous grammar for QA. In *Proceedings of the the 2007 Conference on Empirical Methods in Natural Language Processing and Computational Natural Language Learning*, pages 22–32, 2007.

[27] J. Xu and W. B. Croft. Query expansion using local and global document analysis. In *Proceedings of the 19th annual international ACM SIGIR conference on Research and development in information retrieval*, pages 4–11, 1996.

[28] X. Xue, S. Huston, and W. B. Croft. Improving verbose queries using subset distribution. In *Proc. CIKM*, 2010.

[29] C. Zhai and J. Lafferty. Two-stage language models for information retrieval. In *Proceedings of the 25th annual international ACM SIGIR conference on Research and development in information retrieval*, pages 49–56, 2002.

Improving Retrieval Accuracy of Difficult Queries through Generalizing Negative Document Language Models

Maryam Karimzadehgan
Department of Computer Science
University of Illinois at Urbana-Champaign
Urbana, IL 61801
mkarimz2@illinois.edu

ChengXiang Zhai
Department of Computer Science
University of Illinois at Urbana-Champaign
Urbana, IL 61801
czhai@cs.illinois.edu

ABSTRACT

When a query topic is difficult and the search results are very poor, negative feedback is a very useful method to improve the retrieval accuracy and user experience. One challenge in negative feedback is that negative documents tend to be distracting in different ways, thus as training examples, negative examples are sparse. In this paper, we solve the problem of data sparseness in the language modeling framework. We propose an optimization framework, in which we learn from a few top-ranked non-relevant examples, and search in a large space of all language models to build a more general negative language model. This general negative language model has more power in pruning the non-relevant documents, thus potentially improving the performance for difficult queries. Experiment results on representative TREC collections show that the proposed optimization framework can improve negative feedback performance over the state-of-the-art negative feedback method through generalizing negative language models.

Categories and Subject Descriptors

H.3.3 [**Information Search and Retrieval**]: Retrieval models

General Terms

Algorithms, Experimentation

Keywords

Negative Feedback, Language Models, Difficult topics, Generalizing Language Model, Optimization.

1. INTRODUCTION

When a query is so difficult that a large number of top-ranked documents are non-relevant, a user would have to either reformulate the query or go far down on the ranked list to examine more documents, both may decrease the user satisfaction. As a result, improving the effectiveness of search results for such difficult queries would bring user satisfaction which is the ultimate goal of search engines.

A commonly used strategy to improve search results is through feedback techniques, including relevance feedback (e.g., [29, 30, 31]), pseudo-relevance feedback (e.g., [1, 3, 42]) and implicit feedback [33]. In the case of difficult queries, if we can perform effective negative feedback when a user could not find any relevant document on the first page of the search results, we would be able to improve the ranking of the unseen results in the next few pages. It is clear that in this case of negative relevance feedback, we only have negative (i.e., non-relevant) documents since a query is difficult that none of the top-ranked documents are relevant. When a user is unable to reformulate an effective query (which happens often in informational queries due to insufficient knowledge about the relevant documents), negative feedback can be quite beneficial, and the benefit can be achieved without requiring extra effort from users (e.g., by assuming the skipped documents by a user to be non-relevant).

While relevance feedback has been studied extensively, negative feedback has just attracted attention recently. In [40, 41], the authors studied different methods for negative feedback in both language models and vector space model and concluded that negative feedback for language modeling approaches works better than the vector space model. Negative feedback works by excluding documents that are similar to an example negative document. Previous work [41] has shown MultiNeg strategy is most useful when each individual negative document is considered independently, suggesting that negative documents are distracting in different ways. Thus, as training examples, negative examples are sparse. Intuitively, if we can learn from each single negative example to prune aggressively a lot of non-relevant documents from the top-ranked documents, we should improve the performance more, but in reality there is a risk of over-generalization of a negative example. Thus, an important, yet difficult question is how to appropriately generalize a negative language model; specifically, there are two technical challenges to be solved:

1. What does a general language model mean? How do we formally define generality?
2. Among all the general negative language models of a given negative example, which one should we choose so that we can both maximize its pruning power and avoid over-generalization?

In this paper, we tackle these two challenges in the language modeling framework. To address the first research question, we propose a formal definition of *generality of a*

CIKM'11, October 24–28, 2011, Glasgow, Scotland, UK.

language model to measure if one negative language model is more general than another. For example, if the query is "jaguar" and the user is looking for documents about jaguar animals, a document containing a jaguar car would be a non-relevant example. This document, however, may not mention the word "car" that often, so if we construct a negative document language model based on this document, the high probability words may be words of a particular jaguar car model such as "Alezon" and "Oxford models". While it is safe to use such words to prune non-relevant documents, their pruning power is limited. A more common word like "car" would be able to prune non-relevant documents more effectively. This generalized negative language model is meant to capture this intuition, and it can be expected to be more effective than the original negative document language model in removing other unseen non-relevant documents, thus improving the accuracy of search results.

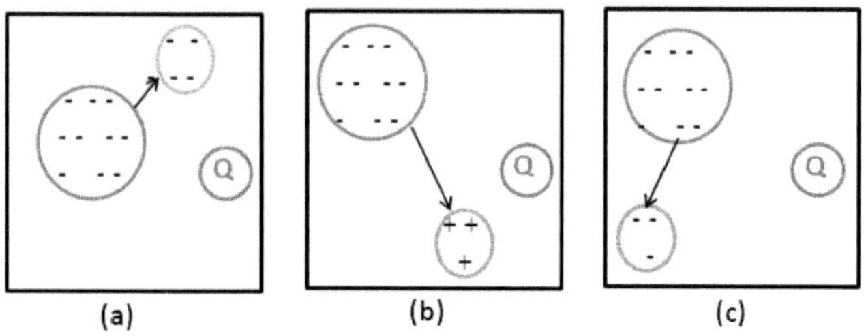

Figure 1: An illustrative example. Only case (a) is desirable.

To address the second research question, we propose an optimization framework where we seek a generalized negative language model that optimizes three criteria: **1)** closeness to the original negative language model, **2)** closeness to the query (if it is far from the query, the pruning power is not very effective), and **3)** a generalization constraint that defines the amount of generalization we would like to achieve. The reason why all these three components are important can be explained in Figure 1, where (a) shows that the general negative language model (i.e., green circle) is safe since it is both close to the original negative language model (thus ensures that the pruned documents to be non-relevant) and reasonably close to the query (thus can make a difference in the top-ranked results through pruning). Figure 1 (b) shows that if we move too far away from the original negative language model and very close to the query, there would be a danger that we would move into the relevant documents zone (red circle). Figure 1 (c) shows another undesirable case where we move too far away from the query and as a result, pruning would only affect the lowly ranked documents, and thus is less effective; specifically, although those documents (shown in red circle) are negative documents, removing those documents does not help improving the retrieval accuracy for the given query since they are not in the query zone. So, it is very important to ensure the generalized negative language model to be close to **both** *the given query* and *the original negative language model.*

Since the space of all possible negative language models is infinite, we propose two instantiations of our proposed optimization framework to search in a finite space of all feasible language models, which is more tractable.

The first instantiation is based on the KL-divergence distance function where we propose two different methods:

1) Perturbation: to remove the terms (based on the generality measure) in the original negative language model that have less power in pruning non-relevant documents.

2) K-nearest neighborhood (KNN): to search in the neighborhood of the original negative language model to find a more general negative language model.

The second instantiation is based on selecting only powerful terms from the original negative language model where we define an optimization formulation and find an exact solution by solving the optimization formulation directly.

We evaluate the proposed methods by comparing them with the best-performing negative feedback method from the existing work (i.e., MultiNeg) [41] on several representative TREC data sets. Experiment results show that our proposed solutions are more effective in removing non-relevant documents, thus improving the accuracy of search results for difficult queries.

The rest of the paper is organized as follows. We first review related work in section 3. We then describe our optimization framework for generalizing negative language models in section 4. In section 5, we describe the generality notion and instantiations of the proposed optimization framework. In sections 6 and 7, we describe our experimental design and results. Finally, we conclude the paper in section 8.

2. RELATED WORK

The study of difficult queries has attracted much attention recently especially with the launch of ROBUST track in TREC conference which aims at studying the robustness of retrieval models [37, 38]. However, the most effective retrieval models that are developed by ROBUST participants relied on external resources (mostly Web) to perform query expansion which has bypassed the difficulty of the problem in reality. Because there are often no such external resources to exploit and indeed the web resources would not help improve the search accuracy for difficult queries on the Web itself. In this work, we aim at exploiting negative feedback information in the target collection through an optimization framework.

There has been some work on understanding why a query is difficult [4, 6, 15] or identifying difficult queries [38] or on predicating query performance [11, 43] but none of this work has addressed how to improve the search accuracy for difficult queries.

Feedback techniques have proven to be very effective for improving retrieval performance (e.g. [1, 14, 18, 20, 29, 30, 31, 33, 42, 44]). Most feedback methods rely on positive documents, i.e., documents that are judged as relevant to provide useful related terms for query expansion. In contrast, negative (non-relevant) documents have not been found to be very useful. However, there have been some attempts to exploit non-relevant documents; query zone [34] appears to be the only major heuristic proposed to effectively exploit non-relevant information for document routing tasks. It showed that using non-relevant documents that are close to the original query is more effective than using all non-relevant documents in the collection. Also, the work in [27] exploits high-scoring documents outside of top N documents (called pseudo-irrelevant documents) to improve the performance of pseudo-relevance feedback. The work in [40] and later extension to that [41] are the first studies of negative relevance feedback that exploit the top non-relevant documents to improve the ranking of documents. Our work defines an important concept called *generalization of a language model* and we propose an optimization framework based on this concept to more aggressively (but carefully) prune non-relevant documents, leading to a more effective negative feedback method.

Since we define an optimization framework for negative feedback, our work is also related to previous optimization techniques for pseudo-relevance feedback [7, 8, 12]. Our work is similar to all this work since we also define an optimization framework for term selection. However, it differs in that 1) our optimization framework is defined based on generalizing a negative language model, an important concept that none of the previous work considered; 2) our optimization framework is for negative feedback not for positive feedback, thus helps improving difficult queries.

Our work is also similar to other previous work that consider co-occurrence thesaurus to improve retrieval ranking(e.g., [2, 16, 21, 24, 26, 32, 35]) or hand-crafted thesaurus [22, 39]. Some other work has considered to combine both approaches [5, 23]. Also, the query expansion work in [9] used a term dependency graph in which word co-occurrence was one of the several dependency types. In this paper, we consider word co-occurrence relationship based on Mutual Information [28] (which has shown to be effective for word-to-word translation probabilities in Statistical Translation Language Model [17]) to find the similarity between words in our optimization framework.

3. NEGATIVE FEEDBACK FOR LANGUAGE MODELS

In the following we review basic retrieval model and feedback methods used throughout this paper.

3.1 The KL-Divergence Retrieval Model:

KL-divergence retrieval model [19] is one of the most effective retrieval models in the language modeling framework. This model is a generalization of the query likelihood retrieval model [25] and would score a document D w.r.t query Q based on the negative Kullback-Leibler divergence between the query language model θ_Q and the document language model θ_D:

$$S_R(D,Q) = -D(\theta_Q||\theta_D) = -\sum_{w\in V} p(w|\theta_Q)\log\frac{p(w|\theta_Q)}{p(w|\theta_D)}$$

where V is the words in the vocabulary.

Clearly, the two main tasks are to estimate the query language model θ_Q and the document language model θ_D. The document language model θ_D is usually smoothed using Dirichlet prior smoothing which is an effective smoothing method [45].

The query model intuitively captures what the user is interested in, thus would affect retrieval accuracy significantly. The query language model, is often estimated (in case of no feedback) based on $p(w|\theta_Q) = \frac{c(w,Q)}{|Q|}$, where $c(w,Q)$ is the count of word w in query Q and $|Q|$ is the total number of words in the query. Such a model, is not very discriminative because a query is typically extremely short. When there is feedback information, the information would be used to improve our estimate of query language model, θ_Q.

3.2 The Negative Feedback Model

Since a query model described above is usually short, the simple estimation method explained before is not discriminative. Several methods have proposed to improve the estimation of θ_Q by exploiting documents terms, i.e., documents that are used for either relevance or pseudo-relevance feedback [19, 20, 36, 44]. In [44], authors have defined a two-component mixture model (i.e., a fixed background language model, $p(w|\mathcal{C})$, estimated using the whole collection and unknown topic language model to be estimated) and assumed that the feedback documents are generated using such a mixture model.

The basic idea in relevance feedback is to extract useful terms from positive documents and use them to expand the original query. When a query is difficult, it is often impossible to obtain positive (or relevant) documents for feedback. Therefore, the best way would be to exploit the negative documents to perform negative feedback [41]. The idea of negative feedback is to identify distracting non-relevant documents and penalize unseen documents containing such information. More formally:

Given a query Q and a document collection $\mathcal{C}$, a retrieval system returns a ranked list of documents $\mathcal{L}$ where l_i is the $i-$th ranked document in the ranked list $\mathcal{L}$. We assume that the query Q is difficult so that the top n ranked documents (seen so far by the user) are non-relevant. The goal is to study how to use these negative examples, i.e., $\mathcal{N} = \{l_1,\ldots,l_f\}$, to re-rank the next r unseen documents in the original ranked list: $\mathcal{U} = \{l_{f+1},\cdots,l_{f+r}\}$. In our experiments we set $f = 10$ to simulate the first-page result and set $r = 1000$ but any other values could be used without loss of generality.

The two negative feedback methods proposed in [41] are *SingleNeg* and *MultiNeg* methods which we briefly describe below:

SingleNeg: This method adjusts the original relevance score of a document with a single negative model. Let θ_Q and θ_D be estimated query model and document model, respectively. Let θ_N be a negative topic model estimated based on negative feedback documents $\mathcal{N} = \{l_1,\ldots,l_f\}$. The new scoring according to this model is:

$$S(Q,D) = -D(\theta_Q||\theta_D) + \beta.D(\theta_N||\theta_D)$$

In order to estimate θ_N, it is assumed that all non-relevant documents are generated from a mixture model of a unigram language model θ_N and a background language model (generating common words). The log-likelihood of the N sample documents is:

$$L(\mathcal{N}|\theta_N) = \sum_{D\in\mathcal{N}}\sum_{w\in D} c(w,d)log[(1-\lambda)p(w|\theta_N) + \lambda p(w|\mathcal{C})]$$

Where λ (=0.9 in our experiments) is a mixture parameter that controls the weight of the background model, i.e., $p(w|\mathcal{C}) = \frac{c(w,\mathcal{C})}{\sum_w c(w,\mathcal{C})}$. A standard EM algorithm is used to estimate parameters $p(w|\theta_N)$.

MultiNeg: This method adjusts the original relevance scores with multiple negative models. Document D w.r.t query Q is scored as follows:

$$\begin{aligned} S(Q,D) &= S_R(Q,D) - \beta\times S(Q_{neg},D) \\ &= S(Q,D) - \beta\times\max(\bigcup_{i=1}^{f}\{S(Q^i_{neg},D)\}) \\ &= -D(\theta_Q||\theta_D) + \beta\times\max(\bigcup_{i=1}^{f}\{D(\theta_i||\theta_D)\}). \end{aligned}$$

where Q_{neg} is a negative query representation and β is a parameter that controls the influence of negative feedback. EM algorithm is used to estimate a negative model θ_i for each individual negative document l_i in $\mathcal{N}$. Then we obtain f negative models and combine them with the above formula in our experiments.

Improving negative document language model: A basic component in both SingleNeg and MultiNeg is a negative document language model (i.e., θ_N in SingleNeg and θ_i in MultiNeg), and the accuracy of the estimate of these negative document models may affect the effectiveness of the negative feedback significantly. A main goal of our study is to improve the estimate of a negative document language model through generalizing a basic negative document language model (estimated with an existing approach) with an optimization framework. The improved negative document language models can then be directly plugged into an existing negative feedback method to replace a current negative document language model. In the next section, we present an optimization framework for improving the estimate of negative document language models.

4. AN OPTIMIZATION FRAMEWORK FOR GENERALIZING NEGATIVE LANGUAGE MODELS

4.1 Problem Formulation

Given a query Q and a document collection $\mathcal{C}$, a retrieval system returns a ranked list of documents $\mathcal{L}$ where l_i is the $i-$th ranked document in the ranked list $\mathcal{L}$. We assume that the query Q is difficult so that the top n ranked documents (seen so far by the user) are non-relevant. The goal of our study is to use these negative examples, i.e., $\mathcal{N} = \{l_1, \ldots, l_f\}$ (with language model θ_N) to build a set of more general negative language models, each corresponding to a negative example, so that these general negative language models are better able to describe other unseen negative documents and improve the ranking of documents by pushing down negative documents in the ranked list. More formally, given

$\theta_N = \{\theta_1, \ldots, \theta_f\}$ which is the original negative language model based on documents in $\mathcal{N}$,
where $\theta_1 = \{w_1 : p_1, \ldots, w_m : p_w\}$ (similarly for $\{\theta_2, \ldots, \theta_f\}$), i.e., each language model consists of words along with their probabilities.

Our goal is to estimate $\theta_{G_N} = \{\theta_{G_1}, \ldots, \theta_{Gf}\}$, a set of more general negative language models than θ_N, where each negative language model θ_{G_i} is more general than its corresponding negative language model, θ_i. The improved negative language models θ_{G_N} can then be plugged into a negative feedback method to improve feedback performance.

4.2 Optimization Framework

In order to build a more general negative language model, we propose an *abstract optimization framework* that given θ_N, searches in the space of all language models and finds a set of more general negative language models, i.e., θ_{G_N}. Note that since there are so many general language models, we make it tractable by searching in a *finite space* of all feasible solutions, S.

The objective function is defined as:

$$\theta_{G_N^*} = arg \min_{\theta_{G_N} \in S} (\alpha.\delta(\theta_{G_N}, \theta_N) + (1-\alpha).\delta'(\theta_{G_N}, Q))$$

Subject to:

$$\mathcal{G}(\theta_{G_N^*}) > \mathcal{G}(\theta_N) + \epsilon.$$

This abstract optimization framework defines that we would like to search in the finite space of all language models S, to find a more general negative language model $\theta_{G_N^*}$, that is **1)** close to the original negative language model θ_N (the first term), **2)** and close to query Q (the second term). The closeness to the query ensures the *pruning* power and the closeness to the original negative language model ensures that the feedback model is indeed *accurate*. The generalization constraint is to avoid *over-generalization*. So, we want the general negative language model to deviate by *only* ϵ from its original negative language model (i.e., $\mathcal{G}(\theta_{G_N^*}) > \mathcal{G}(\theta_N) + \epsilon$).

δ and δ' are distance functions. $\mathcal{G}(\theta)$ is a generality measure defined in the next section. α is a tradeoff between closeness to the query and closeness to the original negative language model. ϵ controls the deviation from the original negative language model. These parameters can be optimized based on training data (i.e., cross validation) as done in our experiments.

In order to use the proposed optimization framework for negative feedback, there are three remaining problems to be solved:

1. Definition of the generality measure, i.e., $\mathcal{G}(\theta)$.
2. Definition of the similarity/distance functions δ and δ'.
3. Definition of a search algorithm to efficiently enumerate the most promising candidate language models. Note that the space of potential language models is infinite, but in order to do effective enumeration, our proposed methods search in the finite space (we discuss how to search in the finite space in the next section).

In the next section, we discuss how we solve these problems.

5. INSTANTIATION OF THE OPTIMIZATION FRAMEWORK

5.1 Generalization of Language Models

In this section, we propose to quantify the generality of a language model by introducing a new notion called **Generality**, which is defined as the *expected number* of documents that hit a word. More Formally:

Generality $\mathcal{G}(\theta)$: A language model θ_{G_K} is more general than language model θ_K iff $\mathcal{G}(\theta_{G_K}) > \mathcal{G}(\theta_K)$ where $\mathcal{G}$ is defined as:

$$\mathcal{G}(\theta) = \sum_{w \in \theta} df(w) \times p(w|\theta) \quad (1)$$

Where $df(w)$ is the number of documents containing word w in collection $\mathcal{C}$ (document frequency) and $p(w|\theta)$ is the probability of word w given language model θ. Intuitively, the generality in this formula is captured through both the probability of the word in the language model and the number of documents containing that word in the collection.

Next, we define the distance functions, δ and δ' in our optimization framework, and discuss how to efficiently solve the optimization problem.

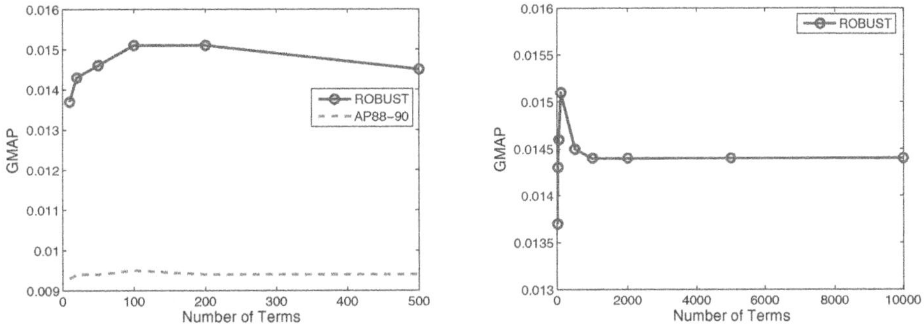

Figure 2: Sensitivity of the number of terms used for negative feedback to GMAP with MultiNeg method.

5.2 Distance Functions δ and δ'

We define two distance functions based on KL-divergence [10] and Term-based-Similarity, respectively. The search strategies vary according to the distance functions.

5.2.1 KL-Divergence

The first instantiation of the abstract optimization framework is to define the distance functions based on KL-divergence. Formally:

$$\delta(\theta_{G_N}, \theta_N) = \frac{1}{2}\left[D_{KL}(\theta_{G_N}||\theta_N) + D_{KL}(\theta_N||\theta_{G_N})\right]$$
$$\delta'(\theta_{G_N}, Q) = D_{KL}(\theta_{G_N}||\theta_Q)$$

where θ_Q is the query language model. Since there might be some terms which are absent in each of those distributions, we use the symmetric version of KL-divergence for the similarity between two distributions θ_N and θ_{G_N}, (i.e. $\delta(\theta_{G_N}, \theta_N)$).

With these instantiations, our objective function is completely defined. So the next challenge is how to efficiently search in the space S to find an optimal solution. Here we propose two strategies:

1. **Perturbation of θ_N**: For each θ_i in the original negative language model, we build a more general negative language model by removing those words w that satisfy $p(w|\theta_i) \times df(w) < \Psi$ and we still ensure that the final negative language model, i.e., θ_{G_i} is still more general than θ_i, i.e., satisfying the generalization constraint and minimizing the objective function. Note that the probabilities are re-normalized to ensure they are comparable.
2. **K-nearest Neighborhood (KNN)**: For this method, we search among the K-neighbors of the negative language model θ_i for those satisfying the generality constraint, and then among the satisfied ones, we select the best one that minimizes our abstract objective function, i.e., it is both close to the original negative language model and query. Then we use the negative language model of that neighbor instead of the original negative language model as a more general negative language model. We denote this as KNN in our experiments.

5.2.2 Term-based Similarity

In this section, we present another instantiation of our abstract optimization framework where we seek an exact solution in a finite space of all language models defined based on term similarity and selection. Specifically, for each top non-relevant document, we get m non-relevant words gained from MultiNeg strategy and feed those terms to the following objective function.

In the abstract optimization framework defined earlier, there are two important components, which we now discuss how to instantiate using term-based similarity. For convenience, in the following we use δ and δ' to denote similarity instead of distance as in the original optimization framework.

1) Closeness to the original negative language model: We instantiate this component as

$$\delta(\theta_{G_N}, \theta_N) = (DF.P)^T \times X$$

where

$DF = [df(w_1), \ldots, df(w_m)]^T$ is a vector of document frequencies (in the collection) for each word w_i (document frequency for word w_i).
$P = [p(w_1|\theta_i), \ldots, p(w_m|\theta_i)]^T$ where i is between zero and 10 for each of the 10 non-relevant documents (e.g., $p(w_1|\theta_i)$ is the probability of word w_1 given the language model θ_i).
$X = [x_1, \ldots, x_m]^T$ is the solution vector, which tells which of the words among m words should be included as final words according to the objective function.

2) Closeness to query:

$$\delta'(\theta_{G_N}, Q) = Sim_Q^T \times X$$

where $Sim_Q = [Sim(w_1, q), \ldots, Sim(w_m, q)]^T$ which is the similarity between each word and query word. In case a query consists of multiple words, we get their average similarity. We define the co-occurrence between two words as their similarity. The co-occurrence similarity is based on Mutual Information [28]. Mutual Information is a good measure to assess how two words are related. We compute the mutual information scores for each pair of two words w and u in the collection. Informally, mutual information compares the probability of observing w and u together (the joint probability) with the probabilities of observing w and u independently. The mutual information between words w and u is calculated as follows:

$$I(w;u) = \sum_{X_w=0,1} \sum_{X_u=0,1} p(X_w, X_u) \log \frac{p(X_w, X_u)}{p(X_w)p(X_u)} \quad (2)$$

where X_u and X_w are binary variables indicating whether u or w is present or absent.

And,

$$
\begin{aligned}
p(X_u = 1) &= \frac{c(X_u = 1)}{N} \\
p(X_u = 0) &= 1 - p(X_u = 1) \\
p(X_w = 0, X_u = 0) &= 1 - p(X_w = 0, X_u = 1) \\
p(X_w = 1, X_u = 1) &= \frac{c(X_w = 1, X_u = 1)}{N} \\
p(X_w = 1, X_u = 0) &= \frac{(c(X_w = 1) - c(X_w = 1, X_u = 1))}{N} \\
p(X_w = 0, X_u = 1) &= \frac{(c(X_u = 1) - c(X_w = 1, X_u = 1))}{N} \\
p(X_w = 0, X_u = 0) &= 1 - p(X_w = 0, X_u = 1) \\
&\quad - p(X_w = 1, X_u = 0) - p(X_w = 1, X_u = 1)
\end{aligned}
$$

The objective function is then defined as follows:

Maximize

$$((DF.P)^T \times X + \gamma.Sim_Q^T \times X)$$

Subject to:

$$\mathbf{C1}{:}0 \leq x_i \leq 1$$
$$\mathbf{C2}{:}\sum_i x_i = 1$$

Figure 3: Optimization Formulation

Since the two components defined in this optimization framework (i.e., closeness to query and closeness to original negative language model) are not really comparable, we re-parameterize it as above, i.e., α in the abstract optimization framework is replaced with γ parameter when we instantiate it as shown in the figure.

Our solution, i.e., X would tell us which terms should be added to the final negative language model. $x_i = 1$, if the word should strongly be selected and zero otherwise. In all other cases, it is between 0 and 1. So, it can serve as our confidence in selecting the terms. We can then recover the θ_{G_N} based on X as follows (re-normalization is done):

$$p(w_i|\theta_{G_N}) = x_i.p(w_i|\theta_N)$$

We denote this method as OptMultiNeg in our experiment results.

6. EXPERIMENT DESIGN

6.1 Data Sets

We experiment with two data sets that are representative of heterogeneous and homogeneous data sets, respectively. Our first data set is ROBUST track of TREC 2004 which has 528,155 news articles [38]. On average, each document has 521.89 words and there are 249 queries[1] in this set. The robust track is a standard ad hoc retrieval with an emphasis on the overall reliability of IR systems which contains difficult queries and is a **heterogeneous** data set. The data set is called "ROBUST".

The second data set is the AP88-90 in ad hoc retrieval which is a **homogeneous** data set. It contains 242,918 documents. On average, each document has about 464.226 terms. We used queries 51−200 for our experiments. The data set is called "AP88-90".

[1]One query was dropped because the evaluators did not provide any relevant documents for it.

For both data sets, preprocessing of documents and queries is minimum and involves only stemming with Porter stemmer but without removing any stopwords. As in some previous work (e.g., [45]), we did not remove stop words for two reasons: (1) A robust model should be able to discount the stop words. (2) Removing stop words would introduce one extra parameter (e.g. the number of stop words) into our experiments.

Since our goal is to study difficult queries, we consider naturally difficult queries from our data sets as follows:

We follow the definition of naturally difficult queries as in [41]. A query is naturally difficult when its P@10=0 given a retrieval model. For language model (LM), we use the standard ranking function (i.e., KL-divergence retrieval model with Dirichlet Prior Smoothing [19]) to select their naturally difficult queries. We first optimize the parameter μ (Dirichlet Prior) for LM on all data sets. The optimal is gained when $\mu = 2000$ for ROBUST data set and $\mu = 3000$ for AP88-90 data set using Lemur toolkit[2]. We then fix these parameters in all the following experiments. Using the optimal parameter setting, we select those queries whose P@10=0 as our naturally difficult queries. 26 queries in ROBUST and 38 queries from AP88-90 are selected as naturally difficult queries and we experiment with these query sets in the rest of the paper.

6.2 Baselines and Experiment Procedure

Since previous work has shown MultiNeg is the most effective negative feedback method [41], we focus on applying the proposed language model generalization method to MultiNeg, and compare our proposed methods (i.e., OptMultiNeg, KNN and Perturbation) with two state of the art methods proposed in [41], i.e., SingleNeg and MultiNeg. All our proposed solutions follow the same scoring as in [41], i.e., each negative document is used to penalize unseen documents, however the language models in our methods are more general. All the experiments are done using Lemur toolkit. The exact solution for OptMultiNeg method is solved using MATLAB.

Our experiment setup is the same as the one adopted in [41]. The goal is to simulate a scenario when a user has found the top-K ranked documents are non-relevant (i.e., these document were skipped by a user without being viewed) and is about to view the rest of the search results. At this point, we can naturally apply negative feedback to re-rank all the *unseen* documents. As in [41], we set $K = 10$, which simulates the scenario of applying negative feedback when a user has not found any relevant document on the first page of search results and is about to view the next page of results (a realistic assumption in the case of difficult topics).

With this setup, the top-ranked 1000 **unseen** documents for all runs were compared in terms of two sets of performance measures: (1) Mean Average Precision (MAP) and Geometric mean Average Precision (GMAP), which serve as good measures for the overall ranking accuracy. (2) Mean Reciprocal Rank (MRR) and Precision at 10 (P@10), which reflect the utility from users perspective who only read the top-ranked documents. Please note that since we are working with difficult queries, GMAP is considered as our **main measure**, however, we show our experimental results based on all measures for the sake of completeness.

In order to set two baseline parameters (i.e., β and ρ), we do cross validation as follows: We fix the number of feedback terms to 100 and learn two baseline parameters, i.e., β (described in section 3, i.e., a parameter to control the in-

[2]http://www.lemurproject.org/

Table 1: **Performance of the Optimization framework on ROBUST data set based on cross validation (left) and Upper bound (right), * and + means improvements over MultiNeg and SingleNeg are statistically significant with Wilcoxon signed-rank test, respectively. We only show the significance tests for GMAP measure since this is our main measure given that we are improving the performance of difficult queries. These results are only based on 100 words extracted from each top non-relevant document.**

Methods	MAP	**GMAP**	MRR	P@10
SingleNeg (baseline)	0.0321	0.0134	0.1775	0.088
MultiNeg (baseline)	0.0318	0.0132	0.2124	0.08
KNN	0.0322	0.0138^{*+}	0.2137	0.084
Perturbation	0.0327	0.0136^{*}	0.2597	0.088
OptMultiNeg	0.0365	$\mathbf{0.0144}^{*+}$	0.2804	0.084
OptMultiNeg/MultiNeg	14.7%	9%	32%	5%
OptMultiNeg/SingleNeg	13.7%	7%	57%	-4.5%
Perturbation/MultiNeg	2.8%	3%	22%	10%
Perturbation/SingleNeg	1.8%	1.5%	46%	0%
KNN/MultiNeg	1.2%	4.5%	0.6%	5%
KNN/SingleNeg	0.31%	3%	20%	-4.5%

Methods	MAP	**GMAP**	MRR	P@10
SingleNeg (baseline)	0.0351	0.0145	0.2195	0.092
MultiNeg (baseline)	0.0361	0.0151	0.2388	0.088
KNN	0.034	0.0154^{*+}	0.2445	0.088
Perturbation	0.0393	$\mathbf{0.0159}^{*+}$	0.3407	0.1
OptMultiNeg	0.0378	$\mathbf{0.0156}^{*+}$	0.3223	0.088

Table 2: **Performance of the Optimization framework on AP88-90 data set based on cross validation (left) and Upper bound (right), * and + means improvements over MultiNeg and SingleNeg are statistically significant with Wilcoxon signed-rank test, respectively. We only show the significance tests for GMAP measure since this is our main measure given that we are improving the performance of difficult queries. These results are only based on 100 words extracted from each top non-relevant document.**

Methods	MAP	**GMAP**	MRR	P@10
SingleNeg (baseline)	0.0377	0.0091	0.1500	0.0631
MultiNeg (baseline)	0.0389	0.0093	0.1521	0.0651
KNN	0.0388	0.0094^{+}	0.1554	0.0657
Perturbation	0.0386	0.0093^{+}	0.1523	0.0631
OptMultiNeg	0.0391	$\mathbf{0.0096}^{*+}$	0.1937	0.0658
OptMultiNeg/MultiNeg	0.5%	3%	27%	1.1%
OptMultiNeg/SingleNeg	3.7%	5.5%	29%	4%
Perturbation/MultiNeg	-0.7%	0%	0.13%	-3%
Perturbation/SingleNeg	2.4%	2%	1.5%	0%
KNN/MultiNeg	-0.25%	1%	2.2%	0.9%
KNN/SingleNeg	2.9%	3%	3.6%	4.1%

Methods	MAP	**GMAP**	MRR	P@10
SingleNeg (baseline)	0.0381	0.0092	0.1517	0.0684
MultiNeg (baseline)	0.0396	0.0094	0.1914	0.0684
KNN	0.0393	0.0095^{+}	0.1755	0.0684
Perturbation	0.0403	0.0096^{*+}	0.197	0.071
OptMultiNeg	0.0392	$\mathbf{0.0097}^{*+}$	0.1950	0.0658

fluence of the negative feedback) and "number of documents to penalize" (ρ in [41]) based on the training data. Since there are not so many naturally difficult queries in TREC data sets, we do leave-one-out cross validation to learn the parameters for the baselines. The parameters of our proposed methods, i.e., γ, α, Ψ and ϵ are also leaned through leave-one-out cross validation. Thus, the parameters of all the methods (i.e., our proposed methods and baseline methods) are optimized in the same way (i.e., leave-one-out cross validation) to have a fair comparison. Please note that the number of feedback terms is chosen to be 100 (for each document) without loss of generality. As shown in Figure 2, when the number of feedback terms are small (smaller than 100), the performance is not good (with MultiNeg baseline method) and when the number of feedback terms are very large (larger than 200), the performance drops. To aid exposition, we increase the number of feedback terms to even 10000 in Figure 2 (right), and as shown, the performance drops when the number of feedback terms increases.

We also experiment to get the optimal performance on test queries. For that, we vary β from 0.1 to 0.9 and ρ from 50 to 1000 on test queries and select the best-performing set of parameters (i.e., one β and one ρ for all test queries) according to GMAP measure as done in [41][3] but our main focus would be on the results gained from cross validation.

[3]The authors only reported the upper bound results (or the optimal results) without reporting the results based on cross validation. However, one should note that parameters should be learned based on training data sets.

We also vary γ, α, Ψ and ϵ in our proposed solutions as shown in Figures 4 and 5 to get the optimal parameters.

7. EXPERIMENT RESULTS

7.1 Effectiveness of our Proposed Solutions

In order to see the effectiveness of our proposed solutions, we compare them with the baselines methods.

The results are shown in Tables 1 and 2 based on both collections ROBUST and AP88-90, respectively. Table 1 (left) shows the cross validation results on ROBUST data set and Table 1 (right) shows the upper bound results. The results in Table 2 (left) and (right) also show cross validation and upper bound results based on AP88-90 data set, respectively. The upper bound baseline results are comparable to their corresponding results reported previously [41] (the authors of [41] did not report the cross validation results). From these two tables, we have the following observations:

(1) The results both based on upper bound and cross validation show that our proposed methods outperform the baselines in terms of GMAP (since this serves as our main measure and we maximize based on this measure when learning the parameters). For example, on ROBUST data set, the OptMultiNeg method can improve GMAP from 0.0132 (in MultiNeg method) to 0.0144, about 9% relative improvement which is a significant improvement given that the difficult queries are harder to be improved. On AP88−90, our proposed methods can also significanlty improve over baseline methods. The results are also statistically significant

Table 3: Performance of the Optimization framework on ROBUST data set based on cross validation (left) and Upper bound (right), * and + means improvements over MultiNeg and SingleNeg are statistically significant with Wilcoxon signed-rank test, respectively. We only show the significance tests for GMAP measure. These results are based on all words extracted from each top non-relevant document.

Methods	MAP	GMAP	MRR	P@10
SingleNeg (baseline)	0.0336	0.0137	0.1861	0.088
MultiNeg (baseline)	0.0287	0.0127	0.1502	0.08
OptMultiNeg	0.0316	**0.0141**$^{*+}$	0.2082	0.08

Methods	MAP	GMAP	MRR	P@10
SingleNeg (baseline)	0.0350	0.0147	0.2119	0.088
MultiNeg (baseline)	0.0318	0.0144	0.2147	0.088
OptMultiNeg	0.0326	**0.0151**$^{*+}$	0.2463	0.088

Table 4: Performance of the Optimization framework on AP88-90 data set based on cross validation (left) and Upper bound (right), * and + means improvements over MultiNeg and SingleNeg are statistically significant with Wilcoxon signed-rank test, respectively. We only show the significance tests for GMAP measure. These results are based on all words extracted from each top non-relevant document.

Methods	MAP	GMAP	MRR	P@10
SingleNeg (baseline)	0.0395	0.0094	0.1702	0.0710
MultiNeg (baseline)	0.0386	0.0091	0.1723	0.0684
OptMultiNeg	0.0389	**0.0096**$^{*+}$	0.1869	0.0710

Methods	MAP	GMAP	MRR	P@10
SingleNeg (baseline)	0.0396	0.0095	0.1752	0.071
MultiNeg (baseline)	0.0401	0.0096	0.1981	0.071
OptMultiNeg	0.0396	**0.0097**$^{*+}$	0.1917	0.0763

based on Wilcoxon signed-rank tests (for GMAP measure) for those cases marked in the tables. We also show the percentage improvement for our methods over the baselines (based on cross validation only) in Tables 1 and 2 (left). For example, OptMultiNeg/MultiNeg means the improvement of OptMultiNeg over MultiNeg baseline method. Please note that we only show the percentage improvement for cross validation results *only* since these are our main results.

(2) Another interesting observation is that although we only maximize based on GMAP, the results of our proposed methods also outperform MAP and MRR measure in most cases (cross validation results).

(3) Comparing our proposed methods shows that the *OptMultiNeg* method outperforms (according to GMAP measure) all the other proposed methods since it finds an exact optimal solution.

Given that these are all very difficult queries where the state of the art retrieval models worked poorly and negative feedback can be done automatically based on implicit feedback information without requiring any additional user effort, these results are quite encouraging.

Table 5 shows some sample words along with their probabilities selected both based on MultiNeg and OptMultiNeg for TREC query 690 (This is an example where our OptMultiNeg outperformed the baselines in terms of GMAP measure a lot). We only show top 10 selected terms and also calculate their generality measures for these two methods. It is shown that our OptMultiNeg method is more general (i.e., $\mathcal{G}_{10}(\theta') > \mathcal{G}_{10}(\theta)$). Please note that the generality values calculated here is based on only 10 shown words; we should also mention that $\mathcal{G}_{100}(\theta') > \mathcal{G}_{100}(\theta)$, i.e., our OptimizeMultiNeg is more general than MultiNeg when top 100 words are selected (this is the number of feedback terms that we experimented with). In addition, we show another example (TREC query 343) where the performance was hurt a lot. The sample words selected are shown in Table 6 which shows the over-generalization both in terms of the words themselves (e.g., words are not specific compared to the original words) and in terms of the generalization value.

Another experiment setup is to give all the words extracted from the original non-relevant documents to the OptMultiNeg method and let the method choose among them (instead of choosing among top 100 words). Our hypothesis is that the results of our OptMultiNeg from this experiment should also be better than that of baselines for the case when we have only 100 terms. The results of such experiments are shown in Tables 3 and 4 for both data sets. As shown in the tables, the results are worse than their corresponding results in Tables 1 and 2 (as we expected from the analyses shown in Figure 2). However, the OptMultiNeg still outperforms the baselines which confirms our hypothesis.

Efficiency of our Proposed Methods: Since we only have 10 negative examples (first-page result simulation), building a language model for each of them can be done efficiently online. Also, since we search in the finite space of all the potential language models, the search is fast enough to be done online, i.e., even for the OptMultiNeg method, search does not take a lot of time to select words since the space of the selection is also finite.

Table 5: 10 Sample word selected from MultiNeg model (left) and OptMultiNeg (right) for Query TREC 690= "colleg educ advantag". Note that words are stemmed.

q	$p(q\|\theta)$
shanghai	0.0512
school	0.0354
we	0.0336
reform	0.0171
teacher	0.0155
system	0.0141
higher	0.0138
establish	0.0125
learn	0.0124
graduat	0.0117
$\mathcal{G}_{10}(\theta) = 32,899$	

q	$p(q\|\theta')$
shanghai	0.275
we	0.1804
reform	0.0921
system	0.0760
establish	0.0672
percent	0.0542
cooper	0.0450
must	0.0444
construct	0.0441
develop	0.0294
$\mathcal{G}_{10}(\theta') = 33,461$	

7.2 Parameter Sensitivity Study

Since there are parameters associated with our proposed methods, in this section, we analyze the sensitivity of the parameters to GMAP measure.

Figure 4 (left) shows sensitivity of γ to GMAP in OptMultiNeg method for both ROBUST and AP88-90 data sets. We first fix β, ρ to their optimal values and vary γ to see how it changes to the GMAP value. As shown in the figure, the two-end points show poor performance of the OptMultiNeg method which indicates that over-generalization hurts the performance.

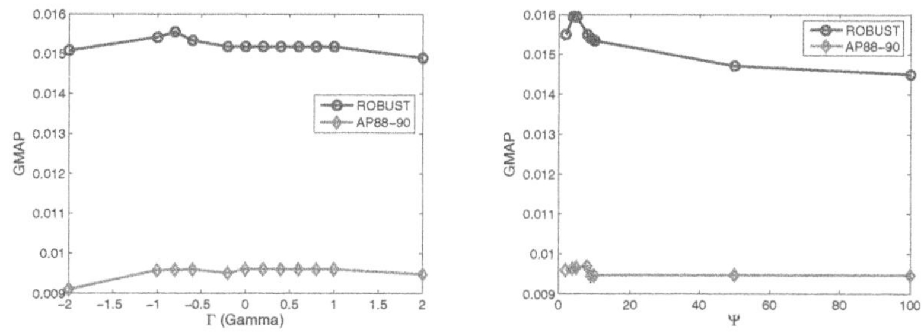

Figure 4: Sensitivity of different parameters to GMAP measure: γ in OptMultiNeg method to GMAP (left), Ψ in Perturbation method to GMAP (right).

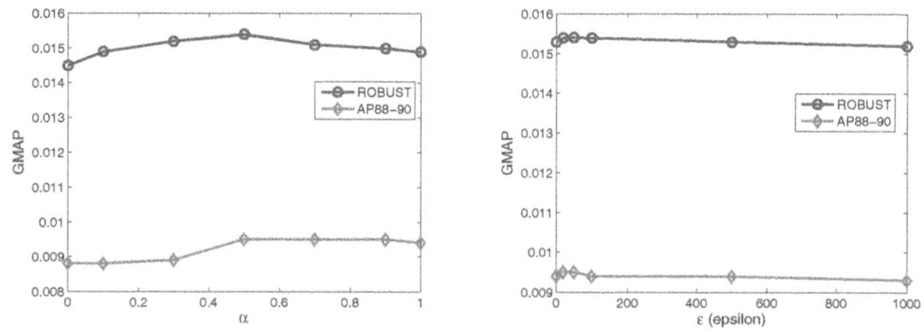

Figure 5: Sensitivity of different parameters to GMAP measure: α in KNN method to GMAP (left), ϵ in KNN method to GMAP (right).

Table 6: 10 Sample word selected from MultiNeg model (left) and OptMultiNeg (right) for Query TREC 343= "polic death". It is an example that over-generalization hurts the performance. Note that words are stemmed.

q	$p(q\|\theta)$
injuri	0.0336332
anc	0.0318221
attack	0.0264466
support	0.0204667
hostel	0.0200951
incid	0.0193305
ifp	0.0180334
allegedli	0.0158444
secur	0.0141943
member	0.0140543
$\mathcal{G}_{10}(\theta) = 10,990$	

q	$p(q\|\theta')$
anc	0.1325
support	0.0852
secur	0.0591
member	0.0585
forc	0.0497
were	0.0479
week	0.0402
sub	0.04023
11	0.0323
region	0.0317
$\mathcal{G}_{10}(\theta') = 20,850$	

Figure 4 (right) shows the sensitivity of Ψ in Perturbation method. As shown in the figure, when we increase the amount of Ψ, it hurts the performance, so it indicates that over-generalization hurts the performance and Ψ should be set to: $1 < \Psi < 5$ to ensure improvement in the performance.

Figure 5 (left) also shows the sensitivity of parameter α in KNN method[4] which is a tradeoff between closeness to query and closeness to negative language model. The best performance is gained when $0.4 < \alpha < 0.6$ which confirms our hypothesis that the general negative language model should be close to both query and original negative language model.

Figure 5 (right) also shows the sensitivity of parameter ϵ in KNN method. As we increase ϵ, the performance hurts indicating that over-generalization hurts the performance and ϵ should be set to: $1 < \epsilon < 50$.

[4]The same pattern can also be seen with Perturbation method.

8. CONCLUSIONS AND FUTURE WORK

How to help users when their queries do not work well with state of the art retrieval methods is a very important, yet difficult challenge. Negative feedback is an important and useful technique for tackling this challenge, and can be done automatically without requiring extra user effort based on implicit feedback information (such as skipping all the results on the first page and attempting to view additional results on the next page). In this paper, we addressed the problem of data sparseness in negative feedback in the language modeling framework by proposing an abstract optimization framework, in which we learn from a few top-ranked non-relevant examples, and search in the space of all candidate language models to build a more general negative language model. This general negative language model has been shown to have more power in pruning the non-relevant documents on two representative TREC data sets, outperforming state of the art negative feedback methods significantly for difficult queries. The proposed method is general and can be potentially implemented in any search engine applications to improve a user's experience in the case of difficult topics.

Our work is only a first step in the exploration of the general idea of generalization of language models. There are many interesting directions to further explore. First, we can relax the feedback condition to include a small number of positive feedback examples, which would lead to the interesting problem of how to generalize both negative and positive language models simultaneously. Second, it would be interesting to apply Explanation-based Learning (EBL) [13] to feedback and construct a generalized language model based on a formal explanation of why a document has been judged as non-relevant (or relevant). Finally, we believe that the idea of generalizing language models can also be potentially applied to many other tasks in interactive retrieval where we need to infer a user's intent based on the user's behavior.

9. ACKNOWLEDGMENTS

This material is based upon work supported by the National Science Foundation under Grant Numbers IIS-0713581, CNS-0834709, and CNS 1028381, by NIH/NLM grant 1 R01 LM009153-01, and by a Sloan Research Fellowship. Maryam Karimzadehgan was supported by the Google PhD fellowship. Any opinions, findings, conclusions, or recommendations expressed in this material are the authors' and do not necessarily reflect those of the sponsors.

10. REFERENCES

[1] R. Attar and A. S. Fraenkel. Local feedback in full-text retrieval systems. *J. ACM*, pages 24(3):397–417, 1977.

[2] J. Bai, D. Song, P. Bruza, J. Y. Nie, and G. Cao. Query expansion using term relationships in language models for information retrieval. *ACM CIKM*, pages 688–695, 2005.

[3] C. Buckeley, G. Salton, J. Allan, and A. Singhal. Automatic query expansion using smart: Trec3. *TREC94*, pages 69–80, 1994.

[4] C. Buckley. Why current ir engines fail. *ACM SIGIR*, pages 584–585, 2004.

[5] G. Cao, J. Y. Nie, and J. Bai. Integrating word relationships into language models. *ACM SIGIR*, pages 298–305, 2005.

[6] D. Carmel, E. Yom-Tov, A. Darlow, and D. Pelleg. What makes a query difficult? *ACM SIGIR*, pages 390–397, 2006.

[7] K. Collins-Thompson. Estimating robust query models using convex optimization. *NIPS*, 2008.

[8] K. Collins-Thompson. Reducing the risk of query expansion via robust constrained optimization. *ACM CIKM*, pages 837–846, 2009.

[9] K. Collins-Thompson and J. Callan. Query expansion using random walk models. *ACM CIKM*, pages 704–711, 2005.

[10] T. Cover and J. Thomas. Elements of information theory. *John Wiley and Sons, New York, USA*, 1991.

[11] S. Cronen-Townsend, Y. Zhou, and W. B. Croft. Predicting query performance. *ACM SIGIR*, pages 299–306, 2002.

[12] J. V. Dillon and K. Collins-Thompson. A unified optimization framework for robust pseudo-relevance feedback algorithms. *ACM CIKM*, pages 1069–1078, 2010.

[13] T. Ellman. Explanation-based learning: a survey of programs and perspectives. *ACM Comput. Surv.*, 21:163–221, June 1989.

[14] D. Harman. Relevance feedback revisited. In *Proceedings of ACM SIGIR 1992*, pages 1–10, 1992.

[15] D. Harman and C. Buckley. Sigir 2004 workshop: Ria and where can ir go from here. *SIGIR Forum*, pages 38(2):45–49, 2004.

[16] Y. Jing and B. Croft. An association thesaurus for information retrieval. *RIAO*, pages 141–160, 1994.

[17] M. Karimzadehgan and C. Zhai. Estimation of statistical translation models based on mutual information for ad hoc information retrieval. *ACM SIGIR*, pages 323–330, 2010.

[18] M. Karimzadehgan and C. Zhai. Exploration-exploitation tradeoff in interactive relevance feedback. *ACM CIKM*, pages 1397–1400, 2010.

[19] J. Laffetry and C. Zhai. Document language models, query models, and risk minimization for information retrieval. *ACM SIGIR*, pages 111–119, 2001.

[20] V. Lavrenko and W. B. Croft. Relevance-based language models. *SIGIR*, pages 120–127, 2001.

[21] M. Lesk and B. Croft. Word-word associations in document retrieval systems. *American Documentation*, 20:20–27, 1969.

[22] S. Liu, F. Lin, C. Yu, and W. Meng. An effective approach to document retrieval via utilizing wordnet and recognizing phrases. *ACM SIGIR*, pages 266–272, 2004.

[23] R. Mandala, T. tokunaga, H. Tanaka, and K. Satoh. Ad hoc retrieval experiments using wordnet and automatically constructed thesauri. *TREC-7*, pages 475–481, 1998.

[24] H. J. Peat and P. Willett. The limitations of term co-occurrence data for query expansion in document retrieval systems. *J. of Information science*, 42(5):378–383, 1991.

[25] J. Ponte and W. Croft. A language modeling approach to information retrieval. *ACM SIGIR*, 1998.

[26] Y. Qiu and H. Frei. Concept based query expansion. *ACM SIGIR*, pages 160–169, 1993.

[27] K. Raman, R. Udupa, P. Bhattacharya, and A. Bhole. On improving pseudo-relevance feedback using pseudo-irrelevant documents. *LNCS*, pages 573–576, 2010.

[28] C. J. V. Rijsbergen. Information retrieval. *Butterworths*, 1979.

[29] S. E. Robertson and K. S. Jones. Relevance weighting of search terms. *Journal of the American Society of Information Science*, pages 27(3):129–146, 1976.

[30] J. Rocchio. Relevance feedback in information retrieval. *In the SMART Retrieval System*, pages 313–323, 1971.

[31] G. Salton and C. Buckley. Improving retrieval performance by relevance feedback. *Journal of Information Science*, pages 41(4):288–297, 1990.

[32] H. Schutze and J. O. Pedersen. A co-occurrence based thesaurus and two applications to information retrieval. *Information and processing management*, 33(3):307–318, 1997.

[33] X. Shen, B. Tan, and C. Zhai. Context-sensitive information retrieval using implicit feedback. *ACM SIGIR*, pages 43–50, 2005.

[34] A. Singhal, M. Mitra, and C. Buckley. Learning routing queries in a query zone. *ACM SIGIR*, pages 25–32, 1997.

[35] A. F. Smeaton and C. J. V. Rijsbergen. The retrieval effects of query expansion on a feedback document retrieval system. *The Computer Journal*, 26(3):239–246, 1983.

[36] T. Tao and C. Zhai. Regularized estimation of mixture models for robust pseudo-relevance feedback. *ACM SIGIR*, pages 162–169, 2006.

[37] E. M. Voorhees. Overview of the trec 2004 robust retrieval track. *TREC*, 2004.

[38] E. M. Voorhees. Draft: Overview of the trec 2005 robust retrieval track. *Notebook of TREC2005*, 2005.

[39] E. M. Voorhess. Query expansion using lexical-semantic relations. *ACM SIGIR*, pages 61–69, 1994.

[40] X. Wang, H. Fang, and C. Zhai. Improve retrieval accuracy for difficult queries using negative feedback. *ACM CIKM*, pages 991–994, 2007.

[41] X. Wang, H. Fang, and C. Zhai. A study of methods for negative relevance feedback. *ACM SIGIR*, pages 219–226, 2008.

[42] J. Xu and W. B. Croft. Query expansion using local and global document analysis. *ACM SIGIR*, pages 4–11, 1996.

[43] E. Yom-Tov, S. Fine, D. Carmel, and A. Darlow. Learning to estimate query difficulty: including applications to missing content detection and distributed information retrieval. *ACM SIGIR*, pages 512–519, 2005.

[44] C. Zhai and J. Lafferty. Model-based feedback in the language modeling approach to information retrieval. *ACM CIKM*, pages 403–410, 2001.

[45] C. Zhai and J. Lafferty. A study of smoothing methods for language models applied to ad hoc information retrieval. *ACM SIGIR*, pages 334–342, 2001.

S3K: Seeking Statement-Supporting top-K Witnesses*

Steffen Metzger
Max Planck Institute for Informatics
Saarbrücken, Germany
smetzger@mpi-inf.mpg.de

Shady Elbassuoni
Max Planck Institute for Informatics
Saarbrücken, Germany
elbass@mpi-inf.mpg.de

Katja Hose
Max Planck Institute for Informatics
Saarbrücken, Germany
hose@mpi-inf.mpg.de

Ralf Schenkel
Saarland University and MPI Informatics
Saarbrücken, Germany
schenkel@mmci.uni-saarland.de

ABSTRACT

Traditional information retrieval techniques based on keyword search help to identify a ranked set of relevant documents, which often contains many documents in the top ranks that do not meet the user's intention. By considering the semantics of the keywords and their relationships, both precision and recall can be improved. Using an ontology and mapping keywords to entities/concepts and identifying the relationship between them that the user is interested in, allows for retrieving documents that actually meet the user's intention. In this paper, we present a framework that enables semantic-aware document retrieval. User queries are mapped to semantic statements based on entities and their relationships. The framework searches for documents expressing these statements in different variations, e.g., synonymous names for entities or different textual expressions for relations between them. The size of potential result sets makes ranking documents according to their relevance to the user an essential component of such a system. The ranking model proposed in this paper is based on statistical language-models and considers aspects such as the authority of a document and the confidence in the textual pattern representing the queried information.

Categories and Subject Descriptors

H.3 [**INFORMATION STORAGE AND RETRIEVAL**]: Information Search and Retrieval

General Terms

Algorithms, Experimentation

Keywords

Information Retrieval, Ranking, Language Models, Information Extraction, Statement Search, Semantic Search, RDF

*This work was partially supported by the BMBF under grant 01IG09008E.

CIKM'11, October 24–28, 2011, Glasgow, Scotland, UK.

1. INTRODUCTION

Information retrieval (IR) is traditionally based on keyword queries and aims at identifying documents containing a set of keywords, which provides a simple human understandable user interface. Semantically aware techniques, as for instance used in information extraction, can be used to enhance this basic paradigm [5, 6, 26, 27]. Query expansion, for instance, may consider the semantics of the given keywords [27]. Thus, the system is looking not only for exact matches of the given keywords but also for semantically similar keywords. Other approaches use information extraction techniques as a filter to rerank retrieved results [5] or to generate keyword queries using an IE framework [26].

Still, these systems have their shortcomings. Assume, for instance, a user is looking for documents that verify if Barack Obama was born in Kenya using "Obama" and "Kenya" as keywords. Although keyword search might consider techniques such as query expansion and alternative keywords for entities, documents are still considered as bag-of-words so that the system might also output documents mentioning that Obama visited Kenya on a diplomatic mission. Although the search result might be improved by adding keywords such as "birthplace" or "born", query results still potentially contain many false positives and documents using alternative formulations are not found. The search can be improved by making use of the full potential that information extraction offers, i.e., by also considering the relationships between entities and the patterns expressing these relationships.

In this paper, we propose a retrieval framework that applies information extraction to transform a user query into RDF statements and retrieves the most relevant witness documents supporting them. For instance, given the phrase query *"Barack Obama was born in Kenya"*, information extraction tools can identify the contained statement in canonic form as the RDF triple (`Barack_Obama,bornIn,Kenya`). Having applied the same extraction tool on the document corpus beforehand allows us to retrieve documents that mention the given statement. Thus, we can find documents expressing the statement in various ways using different representations of the entities and different textual expressions for the relationships between them. For example, the statement (`Barack_Obama,bornIn,Kenya`) can be textually expressed in many different forms: *"Barack Obama was born in Kenya"*, *"Obama's birthplace is Kenya"*, *"Kenya, the birthplace of the first African-American president,... "*, etc. In analogy to the term *keyword search*, we refer to this concept as *statement search*. The user input can either be a phrase (or a set of phrases) that is mapped to RDF statements or an arbitrary set of RDF statements that is selected by the user or corresponds to the result of a SPARQL query evaluated over an RDF knowledge base.

To make this work, our framework requires some information: entity and relation dictionaries. For each entity, an entity dictionary contains a set of possible textual expressions denoting the entity. For instance, for the entity `Barack_Obama` the following expressions are associated: *"Barack Obama"*, *"Obama"*, *"the first African-American president"*. Each of these expressions can be weighted to reflect how likely it represents the entity. This information can easily be obtained from large knowledge bases such as YAGO [33]. A relation dictionary provides a set of textual expressions or patterns for each relation. For instance, the relation `bornIn` can be expressed using the following patterns: *"X was born in Y"*, *"Y, the birthplace of X"*. Each such pattern can be associated with a confidence weight reflecting how well it expresses the corresponding relation. Such patterns for relations can be extracted using an information extraction tool such as [21]. After having applied such information extraction techniques to a corpus of documents, we can derive indexes that relate factual statements, entities, and their relations to documents. And we can use this information to retrieve a set of documents that satisfy the user's information need.

Given a user query, there are two important steps: (i) transform the user query into a set of statements and (ii) ranking matching documents according to their relevance. In this paper, we focus on the second problem and assume that the first one can be solved using information extraction tools [21, 33]. Consider, for example, again our example statement (`Barack_Obama,bornIn, Kenya`). Documents containing this statement multiple times should be ranked higher than documents that only casually mention it. This is similar in spirit to the term frequency in traditional IR models. In addition, an appropriate ranking model also needs to consider how well the statement is expressed in the document. For example, a document containing the sentence *"Barack Obama was born in Kenya"* should be preferred over a document stating *"Obama spent his childhood in Kenya"*. This can be achieved by exploiting confidences associated with the patterns. Another important aspect that an appropriate ranking model needs to consider is the *on-topicness* of a document. Biographical pages about Barack Obama, for instance, are more likely to be relevant than a news article that simply mentions the claim that he was born in Kenya as a side note. Furthermore, authoritative pages such as `http://www.whitehouse.gov/` should be preferred over documents such as blog entries. This is similar to authority-ranking in traditional IR.

In summary, this paper introduces the notion of *statement search* and proposes a framework that enables semantic-aware document retrieval by mapping user queries to semantic statements and retrieving witness documents expressing these statements in different textual forms. We propose an appropriate ranking model based on statistical language-models that considers the following criteria: 1) statement frequency, 2) pattern confidence, 3) entity occurrences, and 4) page authority.

The rest of the paper is organized as follows: we first discuss related work in Section 2 and provide background on information extraction in Section 3. Section 4 gives an overview of statement search. While Section 5 introduces the framework implementing statement search, Section 6 presents the ranking model that the framework relies on. Finally, Section 7 presents evaluation results and Section 8 concludes the paper with an outlook to future work.

2. RELATED WORK

Utilizing information extraction (IE) techniques to support keyword-based document retrieval has been studied in the literature [5, 15, 27]. While applying such techniques can improve the performance of a keyword-based document search engine by providing some understanding of the underlying information need of a user, these approaches usually only use additional techniques extending existing information retrieval (IR) algorithms.

Recently published approaches try to integrate ontological knowledge databases with document retrieval techniques. Pound et al. [26] propose a framework using descriptive structured queries with keywords as basic operators. A query is assumed to describe a set of entities by a set of constraints. After resolving the entities that satisfy the query constraints using an ontological knowledge base, the framework retrieves documents containing references to those entities. However, the retrieved documents do not necessarily contain the relations given as constraints in the query. Hence, looking for a US President born in Hawaii, President Obama would probably satisfy the statement and the retrieved documents would include documents containing Obama and a reference to Hawaii, but the documents are not necessarily talking about the claim that he was born in Hawaii. In contrast, our system also ensures the presence of the relation in retrieved documents. While the proposed framework is similar to ours to some extent, the authors focused on the query language and used an ad hoc tf-idf approach for the ranking whereas our work focuses on the ranking of result documents. Still, the proposed query language could be combined with our ranking mechanism.

Bear et al [5] couple an NLP information extraction tool with an information retrieval engine by using it as a re-ranking filter for result lists obtained from the IR engine. They report only small gains by their technique compared to the results of the IR engine alone. A similar combination is proposed by Hearst [15] for the particular domain of topic based sentiment analysis.

Similarly, Blanco, and Zaragoza [6] examine ranking of support sentences for entities. Given a keyword query, they aim at finding entities in context answering the query, i.e., support sentences that explain why an entity is an answer to the query. The paper compares a number of different ranking approaches for the support sentences. In contrast to our approach, the sentences are ranked based on entities, not on statements.

Fagin et al. [13] investigate how to interpret keyword queries, given an auxiliary database providing semantic concepts for entities and relations. Given a keyword query, their technique can produce various interpretations that (partially) match the given keywords to semantic concepts or relations. For instance, it is not clear whether the keyword query "buzz price" refers to documents containing those words explicitly, documents about the Disney affiliated economist Harrison "Buzz" Price, or documents stating the price of the "Buzz Lightyear" toy. These *parses* of a keyword query – and documents containing expressions of such a parse – can be ranked by their specificity. Using this terminology, our approach is given a specific parse (or a set of parses) as input. Instead of considering different interpretations of the query, the problem we focus on is to rank the documents containing textual manifestations of the given (set of) parse(s).

Sereno et al. [30] as well as Uren et al. [34] propose a set of tools to annotate documents, especially research documents, with ontological expressions (claims) that form a claim network that can be browsed and searched. While claims can be seen as statements, their annotating approach is semi-automatic while our approach tries to automatically annotate documents with contained statements. This kind of search analysis focuses on the claim network, while we investigate document based rankings.

Our ranking model for witness documents is based on language models. Due to their good empirical performance and sound theoretical foundation, approaches based on language models have received much attention in the IR community. Many variations of the basic language model approach have been proposed and studied. Language models have been applied to various retrieval tasks such as cross-lingual retrieval [35], expert finding [2], XML retrieval [17]. In particular, recently Elbassuoni et al. [11] proposed a language-model-based ranking for structured queries over RDF graphs. Also, Nie et al. [22] used language models to retrieve and rank entities given a keyword query. However, our retrieval model is the first to adopt language models for statement search over documents.

An overview of semantic search for textual documents is given in [20], which surveyed 22 systems, none of which providing any document ranking; the authors actually point out the necessity of research in that direction. The Semantic Desktop [29] is a semantic search engine that combines fact retrieval with semantic document retrieval using a triple-based algorithm and graph traversal. Given a natural language query, the approach tries to infer a structured query and retrieve matching triples. If there is no perfect answer, the ontology that the queries are evaluated against is used to expand the user query, and the expanded query is evaluated on a document collection to retrieve matching documents. RankIE [7] is a system for entity-based document search that can exploit structural background knowledge such as ontologies. It includes the ExplainIE tool [4], which was developed to debug IE results in business intelligence applications, mainly by visualizing how entities and documents are related.

Semantic Web search engines try to find RDF content on the Web based on keywords or URIs. To rank the sources of relevant content, they often use variations of the the PageRank algorithm [9, 14] or the tf-idf measure [23]. Semantic Web search engines focus on locating RDF sources and do not consider provenance of RDF data. An important aspect in this context is how to present results to a user, the problem of snippet generation for facts has been studied a lot [1, 24].

3. BACKGROUND ON INFORMATION EXTRACTION

Information Extraction (IE) is the process of automatically extracting structured information such as entities, relationships between entities, and properties of entities from unstructured and semi-structured sources. The process of information extraction typically is a two-fold process. First, the system analyzes documents and extracts *statement candidates* from the text. Second, it integrates these candidates by removing contradictory statements or deriving new ones (through inference for instance).

One common approach to extract statements from text is to use a set of phrase-patterns to match the possible linguistic realizations of the abstract statements. This is usually done by combining natural language processing and statistical inference in order to identify qualifying patterns that are used to extract facts of interest.

Once statements, also referred to as facts, have been extracted, they are stored in a fact repository or a knowledge base. The most common format to store extracted facts is the W3C-endorsed RDF, which is the model adopted in the Semantic Web community. RDF knowledge bases consist of statements in the form of subject-property-object triples. For example, the information that Barack Obama was born in Hawaii can be represented formally as the RDF triple (`Barack_Obama,bornIn,Hawaii`) with subject `Barack_Obama`, property/relation `bornIn`, and object `Hawaii`. An RDF knowledge base can conceptually be regarded as a large graph with nodes corresponding to entities (subjects and objects) and edges denoting relationships or properties, which we refer to as an RDF graph. Search on this kind of ER/RDF data is naturally expressed by means of structured graph-pattern queries using query languages such as the W3C-endorsed query language SPARQL [31]. A result to a query expressed in such a way is a subgraph of the underlying knowledge graph that consists of a set of triples matching the query graph.

In this paper, we assume that our framework is working with named (canonic) relations originating from information extraction tools working with predefined canonic relations [21, 33], i.e., the system is configured to look for patterns for a set of given relations, e.g., `bornIn`. We can easily extend the framework to work with anonymous relations defined by clusters of similar patterns. For a cluster the confidence of each pattern can be defined by the distance to the cluster center. Some systems [3, 12] extract "interesting" patterns from a document corpus without naming them and try to cluster semantically similar patterns. Each obtained cluster represents an anonymous relation.

4. STATEMENT SEARCH

As explained in the introduction, *statement search* aims at retrieving a set of relevant documents to a set of given statements. This type of search can be motivated by two slightly different information needs. First, a user might want to verify whether a certain statement is true. For instance, a user might wonder whether Barack Obama was born in Kenya and seek documents confirming this statement. Second, a user might want to investigate a certain statement, i.e., learn more details about it. For example, the user might know that Osama Bin Laden died on May 2011 but wants to find more details about his death. In both cases, the user is interested in documents referencing the statement in some way. However, with respect to these two user goals, a document is relevant to a statement query if it either verifies the statement *(persuasiveness)* or provides further information about the statement topic *(on-topicness)*. These two main properties might compete with each other in determining the relevance of a given witness document. There might be documents that very clearly and convincingly support the statement (*persuasive*) but only casually mention the statement and are mainly concerned with another topic (not *on-topic*). For instance, the Wikipedia article about the Kapiolani Medical Center in Honolulu might clearly state that Obama was born there but then would provide no further information about Obama's childhood. A blog post discussing Obama's childhood on the other hand could provide more information about the president's youth but might be a less convincing source for the verification of his birthplace. The quality of a witness for a given query therefore depends on the user's preference on these two aspects. Our ranking model tries to incorporate different features estimating a document's *on-topicness* and its *persuasiveness* in a way that allows to adapt the ranking according to a user's preferences. Still, a perfect witness would satisfy both properties to the full, being informative on the topic and persuasive for the statement(s) in the query. Thus, at the core, our ranking model aims at finding the best documents based on the probability that they are a perfect witness for a given set of statements. In our model, the quality of a witness is therefore based on the following aspects:

1. Given a set of statements g, a witness can only be perfect if it covers all statements in g. This affects both properties, as a statement cannot be verified with a document that does not contain the statement, and it is also unlikely that additional information related to the statements can be found there.
2. A document is only informative to a user if she can learn more about the statement(s) of interest. Therefore, the

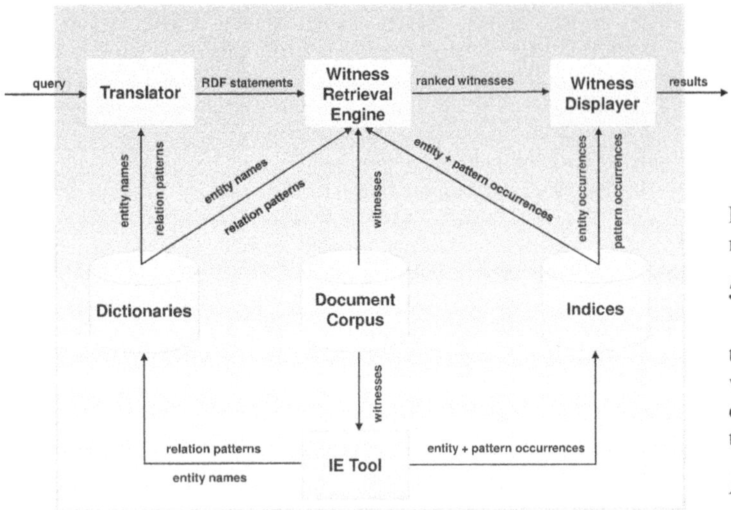

Figure 1: Architecture

document needs to focus on the topic given by the statement(s). This is the main aspect of on-topicness: that more information on the topic needs to be present.

3. Statements can be expressed in various textual forms. Some of these statement representations are more directly associated with the abstract statement than others. A witness can only be used to verify a statement if the statement is expressed clearly within the document's content. A perfect witness will formulate the statement(s) in a way that leaves no room for other interpretations. This is the main aspect of persuasiveness, if the expression of the statement is vague it will not convince a user.
4. In general, we trust information obtained from some documents more than information contained in others. For instance, if the White House website issues a birth certificate for President Obama stating that he was born in Hawaii while a conspiracy blog page states that he was instead born in Kenya, ignoring other factors, most people would rather believe the White House. Both, the statement(s) of interest expressed in the documents (persuasiveness) as well as further information *(on-topicness)* are subjects to trustworthiness.

Our ranking model, introduced in detail in Section 6, tries to take all these considerations into account. Before we dwell into the details of our ranking model and how it achieves the aforementioned goals, we describe our system framework in the next section.

5. SYSTEM OVERVIEW

As explained in the introduction, our system employs an information extraction tool to implement *statement search.* That is, it transforms a user query into RDF statements and retrieves the most relevant witness documents supporting them. Figure 1 gives an overview of our system. In a nutshell, our system works as follows:

1. The document corpus is processed by an information extraction (IE) tool. This process results in two types of information:
   - dictionaires that are used to look up entities based on entity names and textual patterns based on relations, and
   - a set of indices that can be used to find occurrences of a given entity or a statement inside the documents of the corpus.
2. Given a user query, our system utilizes a translation component that transforms the user query into a set of RDF statements referring to entities and relations contained in our dictionaries.
3. The system retrieves the documents that match these statements and ranks them based on how likely they are to be relevant witnesses to the given statements.

In the remainder of this section, we provide more details on the most important components of our framework.

5.1 Dictionaries

The framework uses two types of dictionaries: an entity dictionary and a relation dictionary. With the help of an IE system, we can use these dictionaries to identify statements expressed in documents and to understand user queries and translate them into triple-based statement queries.

Entity Dictionary

Unique entities usually have several non-canonical *names* (Definition 5.1). For instance, the unique entity `Barack_Obama` can be represented by the names *"Obama"*, *"Barack Hussein Obama"*, *"the US President"*, etc. The relationship between entities and their names is an m-to-n relation, i.e., every entity can have many names and every name can refer to different entities. The same entity name could even refer to different entities within the same document. For instance, in a biography about President Obama, the entity name *"Obama"* might refer to President `Barack_Obama` or to his father `Barack_Obama_Sr`. The problem of identifying the right entity for a given name is known as *entity disambiguation* [19] . However, at this point we assume:

1. Each entity name is uniquely addressing exactly one entity within a given document.
2. The disambiguation is solved externally and a mapping from entity names to the entity they refer to is given, e.g., as a side product obtained from information extraction.

DEFINITION 5.1 (ENTITY DISAMBIGUATION). *Given an entity name $\tilde{s}$ that occurs in a document d, the entity it refers to within d is given by: entity ($\tilde{s}$,d).*

The framework makes use of the entity dictionary in three respects: first, when translating user queries into triple form (Section 5.5), second, when matching statements back to their textual occurrences in the document (Section 5.1), and third, when creating the entity occurrence index (Section 5.3).

Relation Dictionary

Similar to the case of entities, a relation can be expressed using various *patterns.* A pattern p is defined as a recurring textual representation of an abstract relation r. For instance, the textual phrase *"was born in"* could correspond to the pattern "X was born in Y" indicating the `bornIn` relation on the subject entity X and the object entity Y. While we assume that the patterns we deal with represent *binary relations* between two arguments, we make no assumptions on the way a pattern is defined. A pattern could, for example, be represented by a textual phrase, an n-gram, or a regular expression. We refer to the occurrence $p(\tilde{s}, \tilde{o})$ of a pattern p with two entity names $\tilde{s}$ and $\tilde{o}$ as a *pattern instance.* If it occurs in document d, we write $p(\tilde{s}, \tilde{o}) \in d$. For example, given the pattern above, the phrase *"Obama was born in Kenya"* would be a pattern instance with X representing the entity name *"Obama"* and Y being instantiated with *"Kenya"*.

Any pattern can indicate multiple relations with varying certainty. For instance, the phrase *"Obama's home country Kenya"* could refer to the fact that Barack Obama has family roots in Kenya (`Barack_Obama,hasAncestorsFrom,Kenya`) or it could indicate that he was born (`bornIn`) in Kenya. Thus, for any relation r that can be expressed by pattern p a confidence value $conf(p,r)$ (Definition 5.2) representing the likelihood that p expresses r is given.

DEFINITION 5.2 (PATTERN CONFIDENCE). *Assume two entity names $\tilde{s}$ and $\tilde{o}$, a pattern p, and a relation r are given. The confidence $conf(p,r)$ represents the probability that given that a pattern instance $p(\tilde{s},\tilde{o})$ appears in a document d, the author wanted to express the relation $r(entity(\tilde{s},d), entity(\tilde{o},d))$. We say p indicates r ($indicates(p,r)$) if and only if $conf(p,r) > 0$.*

Given a query statement (RDF triple), indicative pattern instances can easily be identified by matching the entities and the triple relation to patterns that indicate it. Formally, if D is the document corpus, all indications of a triple statement (s,r,o) are given by $\{p(\tilde{s},\tilde{o}) | indicates(p,r) \wedge \exists d \in D.entity(\tilde{s},d) = s \wedge entity(\tilde{o},d) = o \wedge p(\tilde{s},\tilde{o}) \in d\}$.

For instance, given the statement triple t = (`Barack_Obama`, `bornIn`, `Kenya`), a document where *"Kenya"* is mapped to `Kenya`, *"Obama"* is mapped to `Barack_Obama`, and given that $indicates($"X was born in Y",`bornIn`) holds, then the pattern instance *"Obama was born in Kenya"* is an indicative pattern instance for t.

5.2 Witnesses

Based on the above introduced formalisms, we can now formally define the notion of a witness (document) for a (set of) statement(s).

Whenever a pattern instance $p(\tilde{s},\tilde{o})$ of a pattern indicating a relation r occurs in a document d, d is called a witness for the statement $r(s,o)$ with $s = entity(\tilde{s},d)$ and $o = entity(\tilde{o},d)$. Thus, given a set of statements $g = \{t_1, ...t_n\}$, where $t_i = (s_i, r_i, o_i)$, then d is a witness for g if there is at least one t_i for that a pair $\tilde{s}$,$\tilde{o}$ exists such that:

1. s_i=entity ($\tilde{s}$,d),
2. o_i=entity ($\tilde{o}$,d),
3. $indicates(p, r_i)$, and
4. $p(\tilde{s},\tilde{o})$ occurs in d.

Any witness for g is a candidate considered in our ranking algorithm described in Section 6. In order to efficiently identify documents in which pattern instances matching a given statement occur, we make use of a set of indices (Section 5.3).

5.3 Indices

We have two types of indices in our system. The first one deals with relation patterns and utilizes both the entity and relation dictionaries. For each document, it stores the number of times a certain pattern is instantiated with certain arguments in a document. For example, given the statement (`Barack_Obama,bornIn, Kenya`), and the text snippet *"Obama was born in Kenya"*, the index would store that pattern "X was born in Y" appears with *"Obama"* and *"Kenya"*. In fact, as we assume entity names are disambiguated, the index directly stores the disambiguated entities `Barack_Obama` and `Kenya`. Hence, to identify witness candidates given a statement triple, it suffices to match the pattern instances of all patterns indicating the relation against the arguments of the statement.

The second index deals with entities and stores for each document d the number of times an entity is mentioned in d. Since entities do not directly appear inside the documents but are referred to using different natural language names, this index utilizes the entity dictionary in order to look up the entity corresponding to an entity name (see Definition 5.1).

5.4 IE Tool

The information extraction tool is responsible for processing the documents in our corpus and providing the dictionaries. It is also responsible for generating the necessary indices that our retrieval engine operates on to retrieve and rank the witnesses. Generally speaking, we can use any information extraction tool, e.g., [21], if it provides us with some sort of binary patterns, preferably associated with confidence values, to extract entity occurrences. Since information extraction is not the focus of this paper, we omit the details of the information extraction tool and refer the user to related work [21]. The output of the IE tool that our system uses consists of the dictionaries and indices.

5.5 Query Translator

The query translator is responsible for processing a given user query and transforming it into a set of RDF statements that our system can process. In order to do so, it utilizes the dictionaries and the IE tool to perform the translation of the query into a set of RDF statements using the same vocabulary as our dictionaries and indices. Assume, for instance, a user wants to verify that Obama was born in Kenya, she might provide the phrase query *"Obama was really born in Kenya?"*. It would then be translated into the statement triple (`Barack_Obama,bornIn,Kenya`) and the system would output witnesses containing the statement.

Alternatively, queries might also be given directly as a set of RDF triples, such that our system could, for instance, be used as a verification tool for automatically extracted ontologies. Assume, for instance, a movie knowledge base is generated by an information extraction tool. Then, a user might consider it to be a mistake if she sees four different statements claiming that the role of the character Tony in the movie "The Imaginarium of Dr. Parnassus" was played by four different actors. Using our framework, she could issue the set of all four statements to see which of them is more likely to be true. This might lead her to a document containing expressions of all four statements, which explains that three actors replaced Heath Ledger as he died in the midst of the production.

5.6 Witness Retrieval Engine

The witness retrieval engine is responsible for retrieving *any document that matches the given query* (i.e. at least one statement of the query is indicated in the document) and rank this set of *witnesses* according to the ranking model described in Section 6. It utilizes the entity and relation dictionaries to identify the corresponding possible entity names and relation patterns for the given statements. It uses this information, along with the indices in order to rank the matching witnesses according to the ranking criteria described in Section 4.

Once witnesses are ranked, they are passed to the witness displayer which is responsible for displaying the ranked witnesses to the user. The witness displayer can utilize a variety of techniques to display the witnesses to the user in response to its original query. For instance, the identified statements corresponding to the user query can be highlighted in the returned witnesses, as well as any other automatically extracted information that our IE tool managed to extract from the witnesses. However, this is not the focus of this work, and we thus omit further details about the witness displayer.

6. WITNESS RETRIEVAL AND RANKING

As explained in the previous section, our ranking model is concerned with ranking a set of witnesses that are relevant to a given set of RDF statements. Note that we decouple the problem of transforming the user query into RDF statements from the ranking of witnesses problem since they are basically independent problems. We thus assume that the transformation of queries into RDF statements is deterministic. Our ranking model can easily be extended to handle the case where this transformation process involves inaccuracies. However, in this paper we focus on the problem of ranking the witnesses given a set of RDF statements.

Our ranking model is based on statistical language models (LMs) [16,25]. The witness documents are ranked based on the probability of being relevant to the query statements $\{t_1, t_2, ..., t_n\}$, which we denote as $P(d|t_1, t_2, ..., t_n)$ (here, d is a witness). Applying Bayes' rule, we have:

$$P(d|t_1, t_2, ..., t_n) = \frac{P(t_1, t_2, ..., t_n|d)P(d)}{P(t_1, t_2, ..., t_n)} \quad (1)$$

Since $P(t_1, t_2, ..., t_n)$ does not depend on the witnesses, we can ignore it during the ranking. This implies that

$$P(d|t_1, t_2, ..., t_n) \propto P(t_1, t_2, ..., t_n|d)P(d) \quad (2)$$

$P(d)$ is the prior probability that witness d is relevant to any statement. This probability can be estimated in various ways, and in our case we estimate it using the static authority of the page or pagerank [8]. We do this in order to take into consideration the trustworthiness of the witnesses (i.e., give higher weight to witnesses that are authoritative).

As for the probability $P(t_1, t_2, ..., t_n|d)$, we assume independence between the query statements for computational tractability (in-line with most traditional keyword ranking models). Thus,

$$P(t_1, t_2, ..., t_n|d) = \prod_{i=1}^{n} P(t_i|d) \quad (3)$$

To avoid overfitting and to ensure that the witnesses that do not contain all the query statements do not have a zero probability, we use smoothing:

$$P(t_1, t_2, ..., t_n|d) = \prod_{i=1}^{n} [\alpha P(t_i|d) + (1-\alpha)P(t_i|Col)] \quad (4)$$

The first component is the the probability of the statement t_i being generated by document d and the second component is the probability of generating the statement t_i by the whole collection Col.

We rely on two different methods to estimate the probability $P(t_i|X)$ of generating statement t_i using X, where $X \in \{d, Col\}$:

Unbiased Estimator. Since statements can appear in different forms in witnesses, we need to first fold a statement into all corresponding indicative patterns instances that can be used to represent the statement in order to estimate the probability $P(t_i|X)$. This is similar to translation models [36], when the query is expressed in one language, and the documents retrieved are in a different language. Let the set $Y = \{y_1, y_2, ..., y_m\}$ be the set of all possible pattern instances. The probability $P(t_i|X)$ is then computed as follows:

$$P(t_i|X) = \Sigma_{j=1}^{m} P(t_i|y_j)P(y_j|X) \quad (5)$$

The first component $P(t_i|y_j)$ in Equation 5 is the probability of representing the statement t_i using pattern instance y_j, which is computed as a function of the confidence of representing the relation of t_i using the pattern of y_j, as defined in Definition 5.2. Assuming that the relation of t_i is r_i and the pattern of y_j is p_j, we have: $P(t_i|y_j) = f(conf(p_j, r_i))$. Note that $P(t_i|y_j)$ would be *zero* if r_i cannot be expressed using pattern p_j.

The second component $P(y_j|X)$ in Equation 5 is the probability of generating pattern instance y_j given X where $X \in \{d, Col\}$. This is estimated using a maximum-likelihood estimator as follows:

$$P(y_j|X) = \frac{c(y_j; X)}{\Sigma_{y \in Y} c(y; X)} \quad (6)$$

Here, $c(y; X)$ denotes how often the pattern instance y occurs in X.

Entity-Biased Estimator. The unbiased estimator only takes into consideration the occurrence of the statements in the witnesses. It does not take into consideration what other statements occur in the witness and whether or not they are related to the query statements. For instance, assume the user query consisted of the statement t =*(Barack_Obama, bornIn, Kenya)*. Also assume that witnesses d_1 and d_2 both contain x statements, and that the query statement appears in each witness only once. Thus, $P(t|d_1) = P(t|d_2)$. However, assuming that d_2 contains more statements about Obama than d_1 which is a news directory for instance, we would like to rank d_2 higher than d_1. To this end, let the statement t_i be of the form: *(s, r, o)* with subject s, predicate r and object o. The probability $P(t_i|d)$ is now defined as follows:

$$P(t_i|d) = \beta_s P_e(s|d) + \beta_o P_e(o|d) + (1-\beta_s-\beta_o)P_t(t_i|d) \quad (7)$$

where $P_e(s|d)$ and $P_e(o|d)$ are the probabilities of generating the subject s and object o using witness d respectively, and $P_t(t_i|d)$ is the probability of generating the whole statement t using d. The parameters β_s and β_o control the influence of each component.

The probability $P_t(t_i|d)$ is estimated using the unbiased estimator from Equation 5. The probabilities $P_e(s|d)$ and $P_e(o|d)$ are in turn estimated using the frequency of occurrence of s and o in d, respectively. For instance, $P_e(s|d)$ is computed as follows:

$$P_e(s|d) = \frac{c(s; d)}{\Sigma_{e \in d} c(e; d)} \quad (8)$$

where $c(e; d)$ is the number of times an entity e occurs in document d.

7. EVALUATION

In this section, we discuss a three-fold evaluation of our ranking model. First, we outline the setup of our evaluation environment (Section 7.1). Then, we discuss what effect the parameters in general have (Section 7.2). Afterwards, we analyze the performance of our ranking model (given the set of witnesses is already determined) based on some concrete settings tailored towards different use cases. We use a naive arbitrary ranking and a keyword-based entity-oriented ranking for comparison (Section 7.3). Finally, our retrieval approach is compared to a purely keyword-based retrieval approach, that is not aware of any statement indication found by the extraction engine (Section 7.4).

7.1 Setup

Dataset & Document Pooling. We use the English part of the ClueWeb 09 document corpus[1], a standard IR benchmark collection containing about 500 million English language documents harvested from the Web. As running our extraction system, SOFIE/PROSPERA [21,33], on the whole ClueWeb corpus would have been too expensive with our current setup, we constructed a document topic subset by selecting 43 well-known entities, i.e., politicians (e.g., Barack Obama), actors/directors (e.g., Clint Eastwood), soccer players and clubs (e.g., David Beckham) and scientists (e.g., Albert Einstein), to retrieve the top-1000 documents based on a BM25-based score [28] for different names and spelling variants of these entities taken from the general purpose knowledge base YAGO [32]. This resulted in a pool of 182,139 documents, on

[1]http://boston.lti.cs.cmu.edu/Data/clueweb09/

which a modified version of SOFIE/PROSPERA was run that keeps track of fact provenance information. As SOFIE/PROSPERA iteratively learns new patterns, the extraction process was repeated several times.

Queries. We defined 56 queries in the form of statement sets. For instance, one query with a single statement would be the set $\{(\texttt{Barack\_Obama}, \texttt{isLeaderOf}, \texttt{USA})\}$, while one with multiple statements focussing on JFK's assassination would be given by $\{(\texttt{JFK}, \texttt{diedOn}, \texttt{1963-11-22}), (\texttt{JFK}, \texttt{diedIn}, \texttt{Dallas})\}$. We only considered statements that were supported by at least 10 documents (usually more). For each query, a set of potentially relevant documents was generated by pooling the top-50 rankings using various settings of our ranking mechanism. Remember that this includes a filtering step such that only documents containing an indication for at least one statement of the query were considered for the ranking. This resulted in witness pools of 80 witnesses per query on average with a minimum of 11 documents and a maximum of 435 documents for a single query. For the system comparison (see Section 7.4), additional documents retrieved by the (statement indication unaware) runs based on keyword search were added to each pool.

Human Assessments. As outlined earlier, our framework aims at two different use cases. First, a user might aim to learn more about specific statements; second, she might be interested in verifying the validity of some statements. Reflecting these two use-cases our system aims to support, all documents in the pool were assessed 1) as a whole document on their on-topicness (does it contain more information relevant to the query than the actual statement indication) and 2) separately for each statement on their persuasiveness (how strong is its support for this statement). For both assessment dimensions a graded relevance scale with three grades (*non-relevant, somewhat relevant, highly relevant*) was used. For binary measures such as MAP we project the graded assessments to a binary relevance scale, such that a statement or document is relevant in the binary scale if it is highly relevant in the graded scale. For the parameter and ranking (of prefiltered witnesses), evaluation we will mostly assume that documents can only be judged as being relevant for a statement on the *persuasiveness* scale if the extraction system recognized an appropriate indication of the statement in that document. From a usability point of view this makes sense since a user will usually skip a result for which the system cannot highlight a statement indication. However, if the user considers the document, she may be able to identify support for statements not recognized by the extraction engine. In a more aggressive assessment, we have also considered a document as relevant with regard to persuasiveness if the assessor could find the statement, but the system could not. Note that this only affects multi-statement queries since we require at least one indication of a statement to add a document to the pool. We denote the evaluation ignoring indications not recognized by the extraction system as *machine-ignorant* and the one that is more thorough as *human-aware*. For the system evaluation (Section 7.4), where we compare against purely keyword search approaches without any prior knowledge about statement indications, we solely use the *human-aware* method.

Measures. We apply different measures for result quality that loosely correspond to our two evaluation aspects. First, we compute the mean average precision (MAP) and the normalized discounted cumulative gain (nDCG, [18]) for the top 5,10, and 20 results, averaged over all queries. Second, we compute the mean rank (mr), i.e., the first rank at which at least one convincing (highly relevant) indication has been seen for each statement in the query on average, and related to this the mean reciprocal rank (mrr).

7.2 Parameter Analysis

Our model provides several possibilities to adjust it to a user's needs. The entity bias can be controlled by the β_s, β_o variables (see Equation 7). Similarly the influence of the smoothing versus the main ranking function can be influenced by setting the α parameter (Equation 4). Additionally our implementation allows to switch influence of document trustworthiness (i.e., pagerank) on and off. Similarly, the influence of the pattern confidence for computing $P(t_i|X)$ in Equation 5 can be set to no influence, linear influence or quadratic influence.

We have investigated the effects of different settings of these parameters. The pagerank values, which we use as an approximation of a document's probability to contain accurate and extensive information, do not seem to have a significant impact. This might have several reasons: 1) Our query set did not contain many disputed statements where we saw "untrustworthy" witnesses. 2) SPAM pages were already sorted out using the Waterloo Spam rankings[2]. 3) We use pagerank only as a page trust approximation. Pagerank might not always be a good indicator that the information provided is of high quality, in the end we aim at having user feedback provide the trust values. The other parameters, however, provide the expected effects. For instance, increasing the β values tends to improve results on the on-topicness aspect, but might decrease the precision for the persuasiveness (see Table 1), while a higher confidence influence tends to have the inverse effect. However, those parameters are quite interdependent, so that there is no definite behavior that applies to each setting, e.g., increasing one β value means decreasing either the pattern confidence influence or the other β parameter. If one of the β weights or both together reach 1 they completely dominate the ranking formula which might provoke a stronger negative (or sometimes positive) effect depending on the other settings. Similarly, the initial step from both β values being set to 0 towards having at least one of them at 0.1 has a much larger impact as similar increases on a setting where $\beta_s + \beta_o > 0$ already holds. Table 1 shows one of the more extreme cases clearly outlining the influence of the β_s parameter on the ranking performance. For changes of the α value we could not find a noteworthy overall impact on average. However, we did not look into extreme values (e.g., $\alpha = 1$ or 0). Still, a high value of α can lead to overfitting as the smoothing looses influence.

7.3 Ranking Evaluation

In this section, we analyze the performance of our ranking method, given a set of documents identified as witnesses for (part of) the query, in terms of *on-topicness* and *persuasiveness*. We compare the proposed ranking method to a naive ranking (*naive*), which ranks the witness set randomly, as well as to a keyword-based entity-oriented ranking method (*lucene*) implemented with *Apache Lucene*[3] using its default parameter setting. *Both alternative ranking methods were applied on the prefiltered witness pool generated for each query*, as we only evaluate the ranking of witnesses, not the identification of potential witnesses.

For the Lucene-based rankings, we generated keyword queries based on the entities contained in the statement(s) of the query. The relations are therefore not represented in the Lucene keyword query translations. As keyword engines are specialized in finding documents for a certain topic given by keywords, we expected that this method will have good results in the on-topic evaluation.

[2]http://durum0.uwaterloo.ca/clueweb09spam/

[3]`http://lucene.apache.org/`

relevance type	measure	grading scheme	$\beta_s = 0$	$\beta_s = 0.1$	$\beta_s = 0.3$	$\beta_s = 0.5$	$\beta_s = 0.6$	$\beta_s = 0.8$	$\beta_s = 1$
persuasiveness	Avg MAP	binary	0.898	0.813	0.817	0.826	0.816	0.815	0.79
persuasiveness	Avg nDCG	graded	0.898	0.844	0.82	0.808	0.802	0.8	0.78
persuasiveness	Avg mrr	binary	0.89	0.80	0.78	0.76	0.75	0.747	0.746
on-topicness	Avg MAP	binary	0.673	0.703	0.752	0.759	0.755	0.757	0.777
on-topicness	Avg nDCG	graded	0.61	0.71	0.764	0.781	0.780	0.786	0.79

Table 1: The effects of β_s with $\beta_o = 0$, quadratic pattern confidence influence, pattern weighing on and $\alpha = 0.5$

We were mainly interested in a on-topicness-oriented baseline and whether using the knowledge about relations in the ranking would have a noticeable impact in terms of persuasiveness.

Name	α	β_s	β_o	confidence	pagerank
persuade	0.5	0	0	quadratic	on
topic	0.9	0.5	0.5	no	off
mix	0.9	0.1	0.3	quadratic	off
old	0.7	0	0	linear	on
pr	0.5	0	0	no	on
cf	0.9	0	0	quadratic	off

Table 2: The ranking model configurations

For our own system, we make use of three main example configurations of our ranking model representing different use cases (for details see Table 2). One setting (*persuade*) aims at high persuasiveness by ignoring any entity occurrences, but rather relying on the pattern confidence values. Another one (*topic*) mimics an entity search, aiming at on-topicness by focusing totally on the entity occurrences ($\beta_s = \beta_o$= 0.5, thus in a maximal combination) ignoring any other influence like page rank or pattern confidence. A third configuration tries to achieve a good balanced mix of both goals by applying some entity bias while still considering pattern confidences and applying pattern frequency smoothing (*mix*).

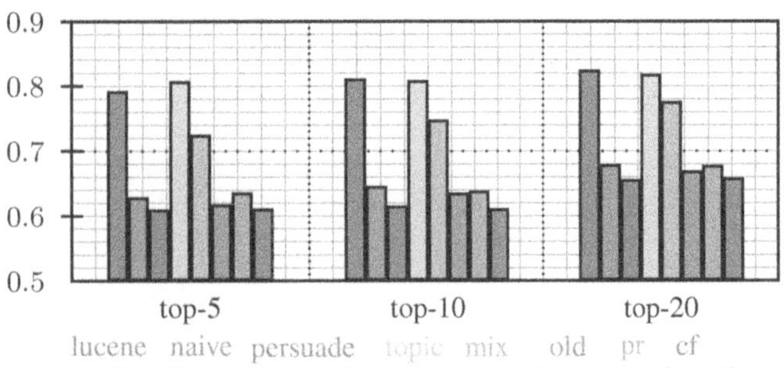

Figure 2: Comparison of *on topic* performance based on *machine-ignorant nDCG* for all queries

Additionally, settings that mainly rely on pattern confidence (*cf*) and respectively pagerank (*pr*) are investigated as well as a setting without any entity bias and with linear confidence influence (*old*) introduced in an earlier demo paper [10].

Fig. 2 shows that *lucene* clearly meets the expectation of performing well in the *on-topic* evaluation in terms of nDCG, and only *topic*, our parameter setting optimized for achieving high on-topicness, can compete with it. Note, however, that the mixed configuration *mix* is not too far behind (~7%), while all other configurations are at the same level as the naive approach.

The picture changes when we look at persuasiveness of statement indications. Fig. 5(a) shows the mean rank for single-statement queries. Here, the statement-oriented rankings (*persuade*, *old*) are notably better than the entity-oriented approaches: using *persuade* a user would on average have to look only at the first result to be convinced that the statement she is interested in holds, while with

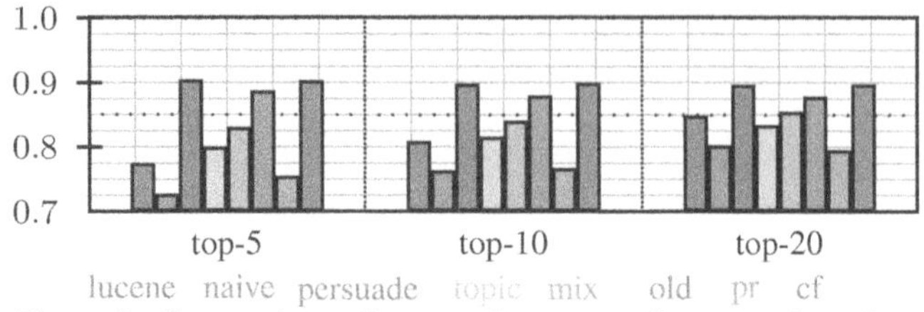

Figure 3: Comparison of persuasiveness performance based on *machine-ignorant nDCG* for all queries

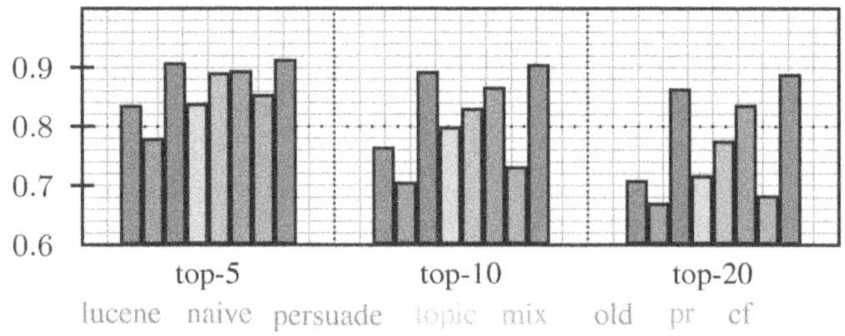

Figure 4: Comparison of persuasiveness performance based on *machine-ignorant MAP* for all queries

lucene she would on average need to look at a second document. Note that *topic* performs similar to *lucene*. The better performance of statement-oriented approaches is reinforced by the mrr values in Fig. 5(b), where *persuade* dominates while pagerank-only ranking is surprisingly good. The reason for the latter might be that those documents with a large pagerank in our corpus are often from Wikipedia. So for most single-statement queries the Wikipedia page of the main entity will be in the top results and would usually contain what we are looking for. The good performance of *pr* breaks down on multiple-statement queries or when we look at the nDCG values in Fig. 3, 6 and 7, as a single good document is not enough for a high nDCG value. For nDCG (Fig. 6) and MAP (Fig. 4), *persuade* is notably ahead of the other approaches.

The advantage of using relation information on persuasiveness becomes even clearer when we look at multi-statement queries (Fig. 5(a), 5(b) and 7). Note that the difference between *persuade*, *cf* and *old* and the topic-oriented approaches *lucene,topic* increases further. You may also note that *cf*, which sometimes outperforms *persuade* falls behind on multi-statement queries (Fig. 7). This is probably due to the higher α value, which may lead to overfitting. Also, pagerank cannot help as a counterweight. It might also be surprising that the naive approach has obviously quite a convincingly small mr value, however, the nDCG is about half that of the better pattern aware settings.

So far we have only considered results from the *machine-ignorant* evaluation. However, results from a *human-aware* evaluation recognizing also statement indications not found by the extraction system as support for the persuasiveness judgements are, in general, not too different as can be seen in Fig. 5(c). While the advantage of *persuade* and *mix* over lucene stays similar for single fact queries, lucene can gain on multi-statement queries.

Finally, in Fig. 8 we investigate a combined relevance measure that only counts documents as being relevant if they are highly

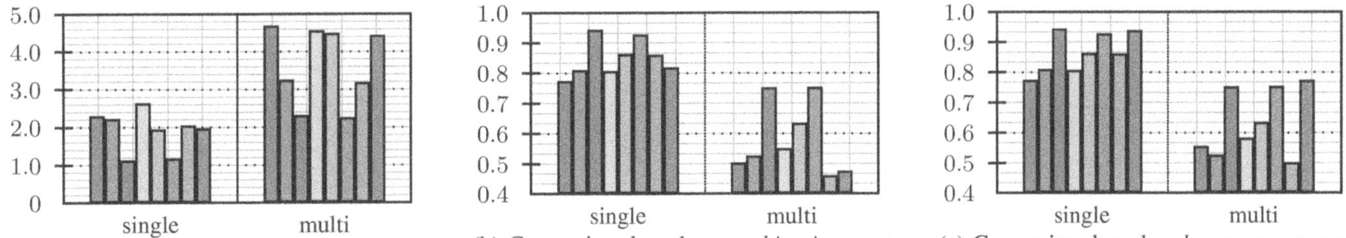

(a) Comparison based on *machine-ignorant mr* for single- and multi-statement queries

(b) Comparison based on *machine-ignorant mrr* for single- and multi-statement queries

(c) Comparison based on *human-aware mrr* for single- and multi-statement queries

Figure 5: Comparison of lucene, naive, persuade, topic, mix, old, pr, cf on persuasiveness performance based on *mrr* and *mr* values

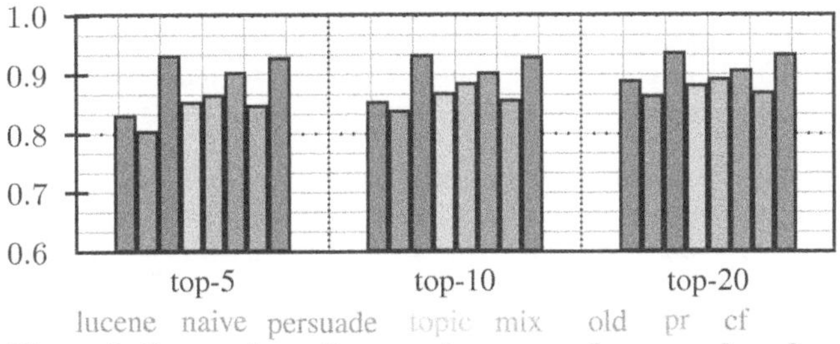

Figure 6: Comparison of persuasiveness performance based on *machine-ignorant nDCG* for single-statement queries

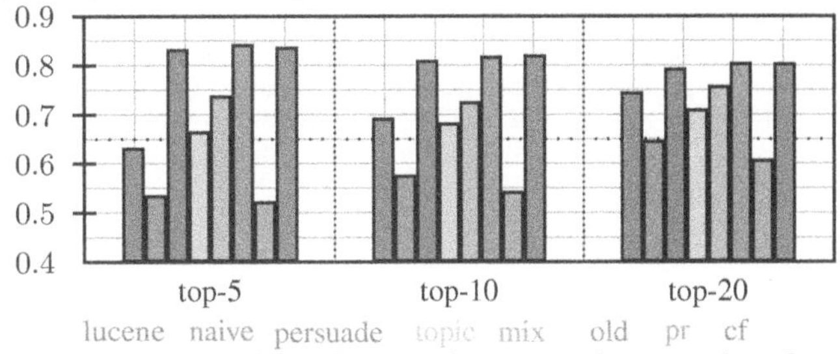

Figure 7: Comparison of persuasiveness performance based on *machine-ignorant nDCG* for multi-statement queries

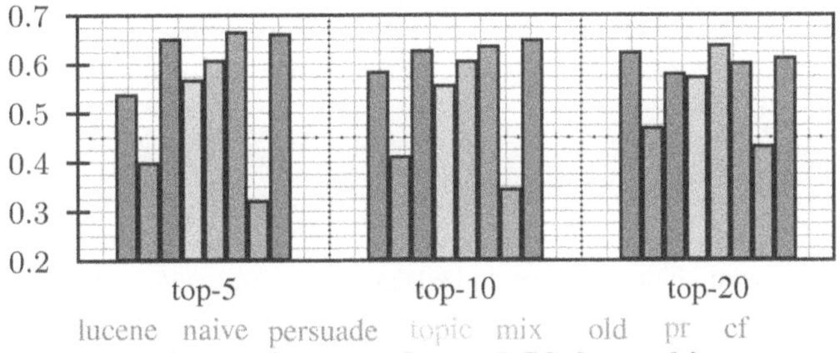

Figure 8: Comparison based on *nDCG* for multi-statement queries in a combined *machine-ignorant* evaluation setup

relevant on exactly one aspect and as being highly relevant if they are highly relevant on both aspects. For instance, a document being relevant in the on-topicness aspect alone is non-relevant, a document being highly relevant in the on-topicness aspect alone is relevant and a document being highly relevant in the on-topicness and persuasiveness aspect is highly relevant. Here we can see that the statement-oriented and mixed settings perform quite well with *mix* being more adept for the long tail while the topic-oriented approach falls behind.

After all, by relying mainly on entity occurrences (*topic*), we can mimic the performance of a state-of-the-art keyword-based ranking system, and this gives good results in terms of on-topicness, while bringing in the relations (*persuade*) will increase the persuasiveness decreasing the on-topicness, but also a balancing is possible with our framework (*mix*). In the next step, we investigate how useful our framework for the overall retrieval task is compared to a keyword query system.

7.4 System Evaluation

The general use case discussed in this paper is end-user statement search, so we also compare against a keyword search retrieval system without any prior knowledge about contained statements. Therefore, we ran Lucene (again with default settings) on the initial set of 182,139 documents retrieved from ClueWeb with three variations of keyword queries. First, each of our queries was translated into a keyword query based only on the involved entities (*fluc:ee*). Second, each query was fully translated with the relations being translated by a manual mapping, e.g., translating the relation `wasBornIn` to "was born in" (*fluc:ere*). Finally, each query was translated fully again but the relations were translated based on the best (highest confidence) pattern known to the extraction system for that particular relation (*fluc:epe*). For each of these variations, we gathered the top-20 documents and assessed them. The results of the evaluation are shown in Fig. 9. As expected, the keyword-based search achieves good results for on-topicness that are competitive to our approach, albeit by comparing *lucene* with *fluc:ee* one can see that the indication-based filtering improves results notably. This becomes even more evident with respect to *persuasiveness*. This can be seen by comparing the keyword-based approaches to the *naive* ranking (with prefiltering) or to the prefilter-supported Lucene run (*lucene*). Our persuasiveness tailored approach stands out prominently: similarly clear as the three measures shown in Fig. 9 are the mr values: using a keyword-based approach, a user would need to look on average at ~4.5 results (*fluc:ee*), ~3.8 results (*fluc:ere*), and ~3.7 results (*fluc:epe*) compared to ~2.9 results with the prefilter supported *lucene* or ~1.5 results with the *persuade* setting. Note that in general the effectiveness of our pattern index based ranking strongly depends on the quality of the extraction system. A keyword search approach has the general advantage that it is independent of the extraction system but vice versa does not gain from the extraction system's knowledge about statement indications.

8. CONCLUSION AND FUTURE WORK

In this paper, we introduced the notion of statement search and presented a framework implementing it. Given a phrase query, the proposed framework maps it to a factual statement (or a set of such statements) and retrieves documents containing textual expressions supporting the queried statement(s). We proposed a configurable ranking model based on language models for ranking witnesses, which can be tuned for favoring either documents with strong statement support or further information related to the given statement(s). Our evaluation results show that our ranking model outperforms term-based document ranking in finding strongly supportive documents.

There are a number of possible directions for future work. An important extension of the ranking model would be to automatically derive optimal tuning parameters based on user preferences. Another aspect in this context is diversification, i.e., given multiple statements and a set of documents that only contain subsets of the statements, adapt the ranking of the results in a way that documents

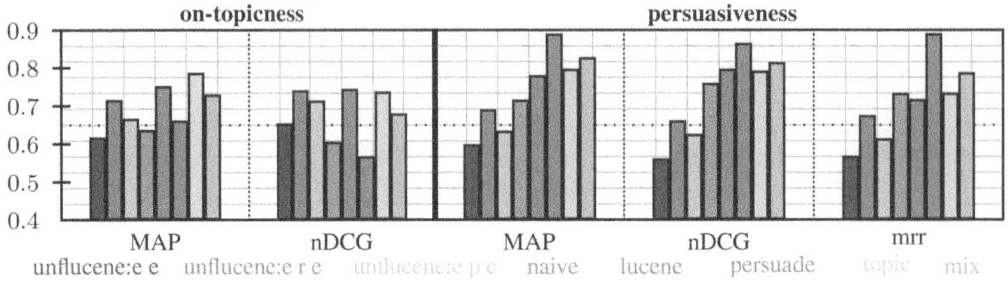

Figure 9: Comparison against pure lucene based approaches with respect to on-topicness and persuasiveness based on the top-10

in the top ranks contain different subsets of the statements. In addition, considering user feedback might help to improve result ranking as well as the precision of the underlying information extraction process, e.g., by exploiting direct feedback on fact quality and counting user clicks to measure the importance of a witness document.

9. REFERENCES

[1] X. Bai, R. Delbru, and G. Tummarello. RDF snippets for Semantic Web search engines. In *OTM Conferences (2)*, pages 1304–1318, 2008.

[2] K. Balog, L. Azzopardi, and M. de Rijke. A language modeling framework for expert finding. *Inf. Process. Manage.*, 45(1):1–19, 2009.

[3] M. Banko and O. Etzioni. The tradeoffs between open and traditional relation extraction. In *ACL*, pages 28–36. The Association for Computer Linguistics, 2008.

[4] W. M. Barczynski, F. Brauer, and A. Mocan. ExplainIE - Explaining Information Extraction Systems. In *ICIQ*, pages 268–269, 2009.

[5] J. Bear, D. J. Israel, J. Petit, and D. L. Martin. Using information extraction to improve document retrieval. In *TREC*, pages 367–377, 1997.

[6] R. Blanco and H. Zaragoza. Finding support sentences for entities. In *SIGIR*, pages 339–346, 2010.

[7] F. Brauer, W. M. Barczynski, G. Hackenbroich, M. Schramm, A. Mocan, and F. Förster. RankIE: Document Retrieval on Ranked Entity Graphs. *PVLDB*, 2(2):1578–1581, 2009.

[8] S. Brin and L. Page. The anatomy of a large-scale hypertextual web search engine. *Computer Networks*, 30(1-7):107–117, 1998.

[9] L. Ding, T. Finin, A. Joshi, R. Pan, R. S. Cost, Y. Peng, P. Reddivari, V. Doshi, and J. Sachs. Swoogle: a search and metadata engine for the semantic web. In *CIKM*, pages 652–659, 2004.

[10] S. Elbassuoni, K. Hose, S. Metzger, and R. Schenkel. ROXXI: Reviving witness dOcuments to eXplore eXtracted Information. *PVLDB*, 3(2):1589–1592, 2010.

[11] S. Elbassuoni, M. Ramanath, R. Schenkel, M. Sydow, and G. Weikum. Language-model-based ranking for queries on RDF-graphs. In *CIKM*, pages 977–986, 2009.

[12] O. Etzioni, M. Banko, S. Soderland, and D. S. Weld. Open information extraction from the web. *Commun. ACM*, 51(12):68–74, 2008.

[13] R. Fagin, B. Kimelfeld, Y. Li, S. Raghavan, and S. Vaithyanathan. Understanding queries in a search database system. In *PODS*, pages 273–284, 2010.

[14] A. Harth, A. Hogan, R. Delbru, J. Umbrich, S. O'Riain, and S. Decker. SWSE: Answers Before Links! In *Semantic Web Challenge*, 2007.

[15] M. Hearst. Direction-based text interpretation as an information access refinement. In *Text-Based Intelligent Systems*, pages 257–274. 1992.

[16] D. Hiemstra. A probabilistic justification for using tf x idf term weighting in information retrieval. *Int. J. on Digital Libraries*, 3(2):131–139, 2000.

[17] D. Hiemstra. Statistical language models for intelligent xml retrieval. In *Intelligent Search on XML Data*, pages 107–118, 2003.

[18] K. Järvelin and J. Kekäläinen. Cumulated gain-based evaluation of ir techniques. *ACM Trans. Inf. Syst.*, 20(4):422–446, 2002.

[19] S. Kulkarni, A. Singh, G. Ramakrishnan, and S. Chakrabarti. Collective annotation of Wikipedia entities in web text. In *KDD*, pages 457–466, 2009.

[20] C. Mangold. A survey and classification of semantic search approaches. *IJMSO*, 2(1):23–34, 2007.

[21] N. Nakashole, M. Theobald, and G. Weikum. Scalable knowledge harvesting with high precision and high recall. In *WSDM*, pages 227–236, 2011.

[22] Z. Nie, Y. Ma, S. Shi, J.-R. Wen, and W.-Y. Ma. Web object retrieval. In *WWW*, pages 81–90, 2007.

[23] E. Oren, R. Delbru, M. Catasta, R. Cyganiak, H. Stenzhorn, and G. Tummarello. Sindice.com: a document-oriented lookup index for open linked data. *Int. J. Metadata Semant. Ontologies*, 3:37–52, November 2008.

[24] T. Penin, H. Wang, T. Tran, and Y. Yu. Snippet Generation for Semantic Web Search Engines. In *ASWC*, pages 493–507, 2008.

[25] J. M. Ponte and W. B. Croft. A language modeling approach to information retrieval. In *SIGIR*, pages 275–281. ACM, 1998.

[26] J. Pound, I. F. Ilyas, and G. Weddell. Expressive and flexible access to web-extracted data: a keyword-based structured query language. In *SIGMOD*, pages 423–434, 2010.

[27] Y. Qiu and H.-P. Frei. Concept based query expansion. In *SIGIR*, pages 160–169, 1993.

[28] S. E. Robertson and H. Zaragoza. The probabilistic relevance framework: Bm25 and beyond. *Foundations and Trends in Information Retrieval*, 3(4):333–389, 2009.

[29] K. Schumacher, M. Sintek, and L. Sauermann. Combining Fact and Document Retrieval with Spreading Activation for Semantic Desktop Search. In *ESWC*, pages 569–583, 2008.

[30] B. Sereno, S. B. Shum, and E. Motta. Claimspotter: an environment to support sensemaking with knowledge triples. In *IUI*, pages 199–206, 2005.

[31] W3c: Sparql query language for rdf. www.w3.org/TR/rdf-sparql-query/.

[32] F. M. Suchanek, G. Kasneci, and G. Weikum. Yago: A Core of Semantic Knowledge. In *WWW*, 2007.

[33] F. M. Suchanek, M. Sozio, and G. Weikum. SOFIE: A Self-Organizing Framework for Information Extraction. In *WWW*, 2009.

[34] V. S. Uren, S. B. Shum, M. Bachler, and G. Li. Sensemaking tools for understanding research literatures: Design, implementation and user evaluation. *International Journal of Man-Machine Studies*, 64(5):420–445, 2006.

[35] J. Xu, R. M. Weischedel, and C. Nguyen. Evaluating a probabilistic model for cross-lingual information retrieval. In *SIGIR*, pages 105–110, 2001.

[36] C. Zhai. Statistical language models for information retrieval a critical review. *Found. Trends Inf. Retr.*, 2, March 2008.

Finding Relevant Information of Certain Types from Enterprise Data

Xitong Liu
Dept of Electrical and Computer Engineering
University of Delaware, DE, USA
xliu@ece.udel.edu

Hui Fang
Dept of Electrical and Computer Engineering
University of Delaware, DE, USA
hfang@ece.udel.edu

Cong-Lei Yao
HP Labs, China
conglei.yao@hp.com

Min Wang
HP Labs, China
min.wang6@hp.com

ABSTRACT

Search over enterprise data is essential to every aspect of an enterprise because it helps users fulfill their information needs. Similar to Web search, most queries in enterprise search are keyword queries. However, enterprise search is a unique research problem because, compared with the data in traditional IR applications (e.g., text data), enterprise data includes information stored in different formats. In particular, enterprise data include both unstructured and structured information, and all the data center around a particular enterprise. As a result, the relevant information from these two data sources could be complementary to each other. Intuitively, such integrated data could be exploited to improve the enterprise search quality. Despite its importance, this problem has received little attention so far. In this paper, we demonstrate the feasibility of leveraging the integrated information in enterprise data to improve search quality through a case study, i.e., *finding relevant information of certain types from enterprise data*. Enterprise search users often look for different types of relevant information other than documents, e.g., the contact information of persons working on a product. When formulating a keyword query, search users may specify both content requirements, i.e., what kind of information is relevant, and type requirements, i.e., what type of information is relevant. Thus, the goal is to find information relevant to both requirements specified in the query. Specifically, we formulate the problem as keyword search over *structured* or *semistructured* data, and then propose to leverage the complementary *unstructured* information in the enterprise data to solve the problem. Experiment results over real world enterprise data and simulated data show that the proposed methods can effectively exploit the unstructured information to find relevant information of certain types from structured and semistructured information in enterprise data.

CIKM'11, October 24–28, 2011, Glasgow, Scotland, UK.

Categories and Subject Descriptors

H.3.3 [**Information Search and Retrieval**]: Retrieval models

General Terms

Algorithms

Keywords

Enterprise search, structured information, unstructured information, retrieval, type requirements

1. INTRODUCTION

Enterprise search allows users to access information from enterprise data to fulfill their information needs such as information seeking and decision making. For example, a customer may need to search for specifications of certain products, and a product manager may need to find persons who have expertise in certain areas. Clearly, enterprise search quality is essential to an enterprise's productivity and customer satisfaction.

Similar to Web search and traditional ad hoc search, queries of enterprise search are often keyword queries. However, enterprise search is different in many aspects [22]. One of the most unique characteristics is that enterprise data include not only *unstructured* information such as documents but also *structured* or *semistructured* information such as relational databases and RDF data. These two types of information are complementary to each other since all the information centers around the enterprise. In particular, *structured* or *semistructured* information has schema which ties a piece of information with its meaning, while *unstructured* information often contains more detailed information described in free text. The different characteristics of these two types of information make it possible to leverage one type of information to help search over the other. Intuitively, the schema of the structured databases or RDF data could be useful for providing domain knowledge in keyword search over unstructured information while the rich content information in free text could be useful for query understanding and term weighting in keyword search over structured information. There have been some previous studies on enterprise search such as document search and expert finding [13, 35, 5, 11], but few of them studied how to leverage *structured* or *semistructured* information to improve search quality over *unstructured* information or vice versa.

In this paper, we study a research problem related to enterprise search, i.e., *finding relevant information of certain types from enterprise data*. The problem is chosen because it can demonstrate the feasibility of leveraging *unstructured* information to improve search over *structured* or *semistructured* data. Instead of finding relevant documents, enterprise search users often want to search for other types of relevant information. When searching for relevant information, a user may specify not only a content requirement, i.e., what kind of information is relevant, but also a type requirement, i.e., what type of information is a user looking for. For example, a user may submit query "John Smith contact information" to find the contact information of John Smith. In this query, "John Smith" is the content requirement while "contact information" is the type requirement. Clearly, the retrieved results should be the contact information of John Smith such as his emails and phone numbers rather than a ranked list of relevant documents. Despite its importance, the problem of finding relevant information of certain types has not received much attention in IR until recently. Related efforts mainly focused on finding a particular type of information such as experts [8] and related entities [10]. It remains unclear how to solve the problem in a more general way.

We formulate the problem as finding the information that is relevant to both content and type requirements specified in keyword queries from semistructured or structured data. The first challenge is to separate the type requirement from content requirement in a keyword query. We propose to utilize term semantic similarities computed from unstructured data and the difference of term distributions in unstructured data and structured data to identify type requirements specified in keyword queries. The second challenge is to rank results based on their relevance to both requirements. We discuss how to compute the relevance scores for each requirement and combine the relevance scores for the two requirements then. Our main contribution is that we proposed methods that can utilize the unique characteristic of enterprise data, i.e., the complementary information in the structured databases and unstructured documents, and use the integrated information to improve the accuracy of enterprise search.

Figure 1 illustrates the main ideas. Give a keyword query, we first identify both the content and type requirements by utilizing the unstructured information. After that, we conduct search over the (semi-)structured information based on both requirements. Note that the semistructured or structured information could be either manually created or automatically extracted from unstructured data.

We evaluate the proposed methods over a real-world enterprise data collection and a simulated collection constructed from standard collections [1, 2]. Both of them contains unstructured documents and structured information such as relational databases or RDF data. Experiment results show that the proposed methods can effectively utilize the integrated enterprise data to find relevant information satisfying both content and type requirements. Our work is the first step towards the goal of leveraging the integrated information to improve enterprise search quality.

The rest of the paper is organized as follows. We discuss the related work in Section 2. Section 3 describes the problem formulation. We discuss how to identify content requirement and type requirement in Section 4 and how to rank results based on both requirements in Section 5. Experiment design and results are discussed in Section 6. Finally, we conclude in Section 7.

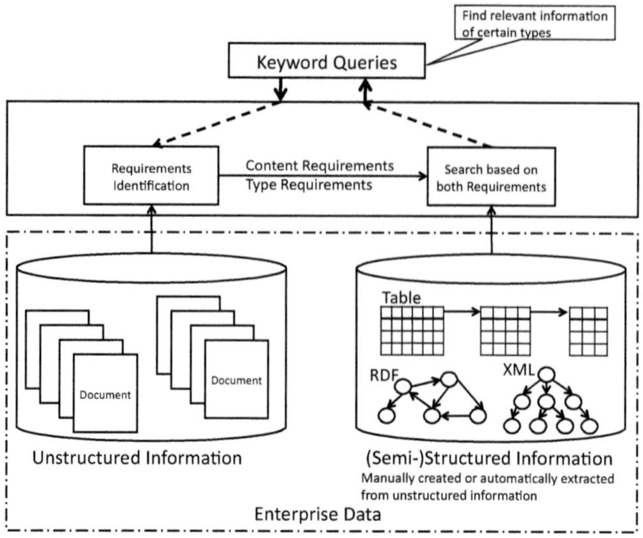

Figure 1: Overview of finding relevant information of certain types from enterprise data.

2. RELATED WORK

Enterprise search is important, but it has not received much attention in the research community until recently. One study suggests that poor search quality within enterprises often causes significant loss of opportunities and productivities [18]. A more recent study takes one step further and discusses several challenges in enterprise search [22], unfortunately, no solution has been presented there. Motivated by the importance of the enterprise search, the enterprise track in TREC has been launched since 2005 [13, 35, 5, 11]. Most research efforts focus on some particular enterprise search problems such as document search [26, 30, 6, 33, 38], expert finding [8, 7, 34, 12, 9], metadata extraction [14] and user behavior in enterprise search [19, 25]. To our best knowledge, few studies looked into how to better leverage the integrated data to improve the enterprise search quality.

One limitation of traditional IR systems is that retrieved information items are limited to documents. However, users may be interested in other types of relevant information such as persons or product prices. Many recent efforts attempted to address this limitation. For example, commercial Web search engines started to direct queries to different vertical search engines based on user intentions and then aggregate the vertical search results [4]. Dalvi et. al. [15] proposed to develop a web of concepts and discussed the importance of concept search, which is in the similar line as the problem we studied in this paper. This work mainly discussed the challenges in Web domain while our work focuses on solving the problem in enterprise search. Li [29] has studied how to better understand the semantic structure of noun phrase queries by formulating them as intent heads and intend modifiers which correspond to type and content requirements in our paper. However, the work does not move further to utilize the semantic structure of query to build a more effective retrieve model. Other research efforts in IR include related entity finding [10] and expert finding [8, 7, 34, 12, 9]. These studies mainly focused on searching over *unstructured* data for a particular type of information such as experts [8] or related entities [10]. On the contrary, we focus on searching over *structured* or *semistructured* data for a broad range of information type specified in keyword queries.

Our work is closely related to semantic data search and keyword search over semistructured or structured data. Semantic data search mainly deals with the retrieval of semantic data [21], but most existing studies focused on the Web domain. DBXplorer [3] and DISCOVER [24] join tuples with primary-foreign key relation from multiple tables as *tuple trees* and rank them solely by the number of joins in the trees. EASE [28] follows the same idea to favor the compact joining graphs by utilizing the proximity between the keyword nodes to model the compactness of the joining graph. Hristidis et al. [23] adopt pivoted normalization methods to rank tuple trees. Koutrika et al. [27] use the IR-standard ranking method to compute the $tf \cdot idf$ weight of any query term in search entity. However, most of them assume that keyword queries only contain content requirement. None of them studied how to return results based on both content and type requirements and how to leverage unstructured information as what we do in this paper.

Compared with existing work, our main contribution is to leverage the unique characteristic of enterprise data, i.e., the integration of unstructured and structured information, to improve the search quality of enterprise search. In particular, we propose methods that can exploit unstructured data to identify the type and content requirements in keyword queries and to bridge the vocabulary gap between query and the structured data. Moreover, to our best knowledge, our work is the first one that studies the problem of finding relevant information of the certain type from structured and semistructured data for enterprise search.

3. PROBLEM FORMULATION

Enterprise search users often look for relevant information other than documents. When formulating a keyword query, search users may specify not only what kind of information is relevant, i.e., *content requirements*, but also what type of information is desirable, i.e., *type requirements*. Without loss of generality, we assume that a query term describes either content or type requirement and we can represent a keyword query as $Q = Q_C \bigcup Q_T$, where Q_C is the set of query terms describing the content requirement and Q_T is the set of query terms describing the type requirement. Given a keyword query and an enterprise data collection, our goal is to retrieve information satisfying both requirements from the collection.

An enterprise data collection contains unstructured, semi-structured as well as structured information. Semistructured and structured data always associate the type or semantic meaning information with a piece of information. For example, the schema of a relational database specify the type of each cell in the database, and the RDF predicates or XML tags specify the semantic meaning of RDF triples or XML elements. On the contrary, unstructured data do not directly provide any information about the type or semantic meanings. A commonly used strategy for dealing with search for information of certain types over unstructured information is to apply natural language processing techniques such as NER to extract information of certain types from the unstructured information [10], and then store the extracted semantic information in structured or semi-structured format. Therefore, the problem can be simplified as finding relevant information of certain types from semistructured or structured collections for keyword queries.

In a structured collection such as a relational database, there are multiple tables and each of them contains a set of attributes. For example, every tuple in the table corresponds to an entity, and every column corresponds to an attribute of the entity. Given the schema of a table, we know the type for each attribute based on the attribute name. Every element in the table contains the value of an attribute (i.e., type) for the corresponding entity. As an example, Figure 2 shows an relational database instance with two tables. The `Employee` table stores the information about the employees, and it has nine attributes: `Employee ID, Name, Department, Email, Phone, Education, Starting Date, Salary` and `Job Description`). The `Department` table stores the information about the departments, and it has five attributes: `Department ID, Name, Address, Phone` and `Contact Person`. Although semi-structured data do not have a strict schema as structured data, predicates or tag names often provide the meaning for corresponding information items in the collection. For example, besides the relational database, Figure 2 also shows two XML documents, one of which stores the employee data such as `name, homepage` and the other stores the department data such as `office location, director`.

An alternative way of looking at the structured or semistructured data is to represent each information item as a two dimensional vector, where one dimension represents the type and the other represents the value. Thus, the problem of finding relevant information of certain type can be reformulated as ranking all the information items in the collections based on their relevance to the query $Q = Q_C \bigcup Q_T$. Let us consider the example shown in Figure 2 again. Given query "John Smith contact information", the system is expected to return his email address and phone number stored in the `Employee` table, the address and phone number stored in the `Department` table, plus the homepage and office location stored in the two XML documents. Note that the relevant information is scattered in multiple tables and XML documents.

It is clear that there are two challenges we need to address. The first one is to separate content and type requirements in a keyword query, and the second one is to rank information based on their relevance to both requirements. We will discuss how to utilize the integrated information of enterprise data to address these two challenges in the next two sections.

4. REQUIREMENTS IDENTIFICATION

Search users may specify both type requirement, i.e., what type of information is desirable, and content requirement, i.e., what kind of information is relevant. Note that, in this paper, we assume that we know whether a query has type requirements and consider only those with both requirements. Deciding whether a query contains type requirements is out of the scope of this paper and could be solve using classification methods, which we plan to study in our future work. We now discuss how to identify these two requirements in a keyword query.

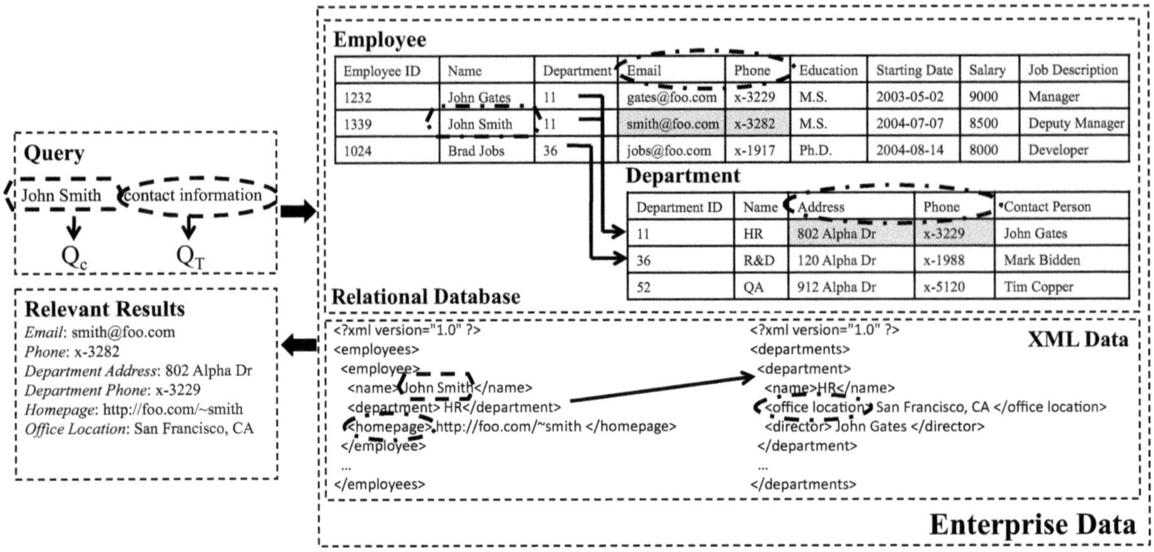

Figure 2: An example of finding relevant information of certain types from enterprise data.

4.1 Similarity based method

Intuitively, terms describing content requirement are semantically related, and those describing type requirement are semantically related. For example, consider query "John Smith contact information", terms "John Smith" are semantically related while "contact information" are semantically related. It is clear that the terms describing these two requirements naturally form two clusters. Thus, to identify requirements, we need to cluster query terms into two clusters and then assign one cluster as type requirement and the other as content requirement.

One deciding factor in clustering algorithm is the term similarity function. Fortunately, in addition to the structured databases, we also have a complementary collection of unstructured documents in enterprise data. Thus, we propose to utilize the *unstructured* information to compute similarities among query terms based on the assumption that the co-occurrences of terms indicate their semantic relations. The term similarity can be computed based on mutual information as follows [37]:

$$sim(t,u) = \sum_{\substack{Occ_t \in \{0,1\} \\ Occ_u \in \{0,1\}}} p(Occ_t, Occ_u) \log \frac{p(Occ_t, Occ_u)}{P(Occ_t)P(Occ_u)} \quad (1)$$

where Occ_t and Occ_u are two binary random variables which represents the presence or absence of two terms t and u.

Note that, unlike previous studies [16], the data collection used for computing term similarities and the collection used for searching are quite different. If these two collections are quite different, this method would not work because related terms on one domain may not be related on another. For example, "jaguar" and "drive" may be related on a set of documents about cars while they would not be related in a document collection about animals. Fortunately, since the two collections we used in this paper, i.e., structured information and unstructured information of one enterprise, are complementary and both about the enterprise, related terms discovered from one data set are likely to be related on another data set as well.

Given the term similarity function, we then cluster query term using *hierarchical agglomerative clustering* [31], which starts by treating each term in the query as one cluster, merges two clusters with highest mutual information at each step and stops when there are only two clusters left. Note that each query is treated as bag of words and terms are assumed to be independent with each other. We plan to consider the order of terms in our future work.

The remaining problem is to identify which term cluster is the content requirement and which is the type requirement. Since the database schema contains the table names as well as attributes names, they provide descriptions of different types. Thus, given a database, we can create a profile about types according to its schema by merging all the table names and attribute names together as one document. We then compute the similarity between our profile about type and each of the clusters. The similarity is computed by taking the average of term semantic similarity as shown in Equation (1). The cluster with higher similarity would be identified as the type requirement while the other corresponds to the content requirement. Similar approaches can also be applied to RDF or XML data collection.

4.2 Language Modeling based Method

We assume that each term in the query Q is independent and terms in content requirement Q_C and type requirement Q_T are generated from two different unigram language models θ_C and θ_T, respectively. The language models can be estimated using maximum likelihood estimation over the enterprise collection. In particular, we estimate $p(w_i|\theta_T)$ over all the attributes of semistructured or structured data while we compute $p(w_i|\theta_C)$ over the unstructured data.

Given a query $Q = \{q_1, q_2, \ldots, q_i, \ldots, q_n\}$, we use $R_{lm}(q_i) \in \{0,1\}$ to denote the requirements identification result for each term using language modeling approach, where $R_{lm}(q_i) = 0$ means q_i is identified as content requirement and $R_{lm}(q_i) = 1$ means q_i is identified as type requirement. Intuitively, the requirements identification for term q_i can be formulated as comparing the language modeling generation probability directly:

$$R_{lm}(q_i) = \begin{cases} 0 & \text{if } p(w_i|\theta_C) > p(w_i|\theta_T) \\ 1 & \text{if } p(w_i|\theta_C) \leq p(w_i|\theta_T) \end{cases} \quad (2)$$

The idea behind this method is that we assume terms from one requirement has higher probability to be generated from the associated language model than the other [32]. However, results show that this method fails to work effectively, since it ignores the similarity between terms. In order to overcome this limitation, we propose to use the language modeling generation probability as prior to adjust the results of similarity-based methods. Similarly, we use $R_{sim}(q_i) \in \{0, 1\}$ to denote the identification results of similarity based method. First, we use the results of language modeling approach to *validate* the results of similarity-based method for each term:

$$R_{sim}(q_i) = \begin{cases} R_{sim}(q_i) & \text{if } R_{sim}(q_i) = R_{lm}(q_i) \\ R_{adjust}(q_i) & \text{if } R_{sim}(q_i) \neq R_{lm}(q_i) \end{cases} \quad (3)$$

The reason of the validation approach is that we think for each term if the identification results from two methods are consistent, it is a strong proof that the term is correctly identified. For terms whose results from two methods differ, we will adjust the identification results to $R_{adjust}(q_i)$, which can be formulated as:

$$R_{adjust}(q_i) = \begin{cases} R_{sim}(q_i) & \text{if } \frac{sim(q_i, O_{q_i})}{sim(q_i, C_{q_i})} > prior_{lm}(q_i) \\ 1 - R_{sim}(q_i) & \text{otherwise} \end{cases} \quad (4)$$

where:

$$prior_{lm}(q_i) = \begin{cases} \frac{p(q_i|\theta_T)}{p(q_i|\theta_C)} & \text{if } Rsim(qi) = 0 \\ \frac{p(q_i|\theta_C)}{p(q_i|\theta_T)} & \text{if } Rsim(qi) = 1 \end{cases} \quad (5)$$

and $O_{q_i} = \{q_j | q_j \in Q, i \neq j, R_{sim}(q_i) = R_{sim}(q_j)\}$ is a set of terms which share the same semantic based identification results with q_i and $C_{q_i} = \{q_j | q_j \in Q, R_{sim}(q_i) \neq R_{sim}(q_j)\}$ is a set of terms whose identification results differ from that of q_i. Here $\frac{sim(q_i, O_{q_i})}{sim(q_i, C_{q_i})}$ is the probability that q_i is correctly identified by the similarity based method and $prior_{lm}(q_i)$ is the prior probability that q_i is incorrectly identified based on the knowledge of language modeling. Based on the comparison of two probabilities, we decide whether we should keep the similarity based identification result or adjust the result to another requirement.

5. RANKING METHODS

After identifying two requirements in a given keyword query, we may formulate a query as $Q = Q_C \bigcup Q_T$, where Q_C is the content requirement and Q_T is the type requirement. The problem is to rank information items such as all the table elements in the database, all the XML elements or all RDF nodes based on their relevance with respect to the query. Recall that every information item in the structured or semistructured information can be represented as a two dimensional tuple, where one dimension corresponds to its type and the other corresponds to its value. Thus, the problem boils down to model the relevance for each two dimensional information item $\mathcal{I}$ with respect to $Q = Q_C \bigcup Q_T$, which is referred to as *2-dimensional search*. The general relevance estimation approach can be formulated as:

$$Score(Q, \mathcal{I}) = \alpha \cdot Score(Q_T, \mathcal{I}) + (1 - \alpha) \cdot Score(Q_C, \mathcal{I}) \quad (6)$$

$\alpha \in [0, 1]$ controls the influence of these two scores. The estimation of $Score(Q_T, \mathcal{I})$ and $Score(Q_C, \mathcal{I})$ varies on structured and semi-structured data due to the different data characteristics.

5.1 Structured Data

In the relational databases, Q_C is used to rank tuples, i.e., rows in the table, while Q_T is used to rank attributes, i.e., columns in the table. Thus, we need to assign a relevance score to each of the table elements and rank them according to their relevance scores.

Let us start with a simple case when there is only one table in the database. For table T, we denote its m attributes as $\mathcal{AS}_T = \{\mathcal{A}_T^1, \mathcal{A}_T^2, ..., \mathcal{A}_T^m\}$. The table has n tuples which are denoted as $T = \{T_1, T_2, \ldots, T_n\}$, each tuple represents one entity with M attribute values and therefore it can be denoted as $T_i = \{T_i^1, T_i^2, \ldots, T_i^m\}$ where T_i^j denotes the jth attribute value of the ith tuple. In order to estimate the relevance score of a table element T_i^j, we can utilize its context information including T_i and $\mathcal{A}_T^j$. Specifically, T_i is the tuple which contains the table element and the values of other attributes in the tuple provide context information that can be exploited to infer the relevance of the tuple with respect to the content requirement, i.e., Q_C. $\mathcal{A}_T^j$ is the attribute name of the table element, and it can provide information related to the type requirement, i.e., Q_T. Therefore, we propose to compute the relevance score of table element T_i^j as follows:

$$\begin{aligned} Score(Q, T_i^j) &= \alpha \cdot Score(Q_T, T_i^j) + (1 - \alpha) \cdot Score(Q_C, T_i^j) \\ &= \alpha \cdot Score(Q_T, \mathcal{A}_T^j) + (1 - \alpha) \cdot Score(Q_C, T_i) \quad (7) \end{aligned}$$

where $Score(Q_T, \mathcal{A}_T^j)$ is the relevance score between the type requirement Q_T and attribute name $\mathcal{A}_T^j$, $Score(Q_C, T_i)$ is the relevance score between the content requirement Q_C and the tuple T_i. When $\alpha = 0$, only the relevance score for content requirement contributes to the final relevance score, which means that every attribute of a tuple would receive the same relevance score. When $\alpha = 1$, only the relevance score for type requirement matters, which means that all the information with the certain type would be relevant.

Let's consider the example in Figure 2. We assume there is only one `Employee` table in the database. $Score(Q_T, \mathcal{A}_T^j)$ will calculate the relevance score between the type requirement "contact information" and all the nine attribute names, and it's expected to give higher rank score to attribute `Email` and `Phone` than others. $Score(Q_C, T_i)$ will calculate the relevance score between the content requirement "John Smith" and all the three tuples, and it's expected to give higher rank score to tuple with `Employee ID` 1339 than others. By combining the results of two ranking scores using Equation (7), we can get the email and phone (i.e. smith@foo.com, x-3282) of John Smith at the top of the ranked list of attribute values.

However, tables in a real database are more complicated. In particular, the information related to an entity might be scattered in multiple tables due to normalization [20]. In the example shown in Figure 2, the address of an employee is stored in the `Department` table rather than the `Employee` table where "John Smith" occurs. Fortunately, these two table can be joined based on the foreign/primary key relationship. For example, `Department` is a foreign key from the `Employee` table to the `Department` table. After joining these two tables, we would be able to know that the attributes in the `Department` table can provide additional information to the tuples in the `Employee` table.

It is clear that, given a tuple in a table, we can find additional information stored in other tables that can be connected to the table through join operations. Let $\mathcal{N}(T)$ denote a set of all the tables that can be either directly or indirectly connected to the table T through join operations. Thus, in order to exploit the additional information, we propose to generalize the ranking function as follows:

$$Score(Q, T_i^j) = \alpha \cdot Score(Q_T, \mathcal{A}_T^j) + (1-\alpha) \cdot \sum_{T' \in \{T_i\} \cup \mathcal{N}(T)} Score(Q_C, T_k') \cdot Proximity(T', T_i) \quad (8)$$

where T_k' corresponds to a tuple in table T' that is connected to the tuple T_i in table T, and $T_k' = T_i$ when $T = T'$.

$Proximity(T', T_i)$ denotes the proximity between the two tables. It intends to assign prior weights to the attributes in connected tables. The intuition is that we need to give more weights to the information stored in a table that is closer to the target table. The closeness between tables is defined by the number of foreign key links used to connect these two tables. There could be different ways of defining such a proximity function, and in this paper, we use the following simple strategy:

$$Proximity(T_1, T_2) = \frac{1}{1 + nl(T_1, T_2)}$$

where $nl(T_1, T_2)$ is the number of foreign key links between table T_1 and T_2. If T_1 is the same as T_2, $nl(T_1, T_2) = 0$. The estimation follows the intuition that the farther a table is from the target table T_i, the less confidence we have to conclude that the additional information in the table is relevant to the one in the target table. Therefore, for the example shown in Figure 2, we will give higher weight to the attributes in table `Employee` (e.g. `Email`, `Phone`) and lower weight to the attribute in table `Department` (e.g. `Address`).

We now describe how we estimate the two score components: $Score(Q_C, T_i)$ and $Score(Q_T, \mathcal{A}_T^j)$. Since Q_C and Q_T are essentially keyword queries, and T_i and $\mathcal{A}_T^j$ can be treated as unstructured document, we may use any retrieval functions to compute them. In this paper, we use F2-EXP, an axiomatic retrieval function [16] because previous study shows that the function is robust and insensitive to parameter settings and a fixed parameter setting can reach comparable performance with other state of the art retrieval functions.

However, the users may not be aware of the schema of the enterprise database, thus if they come up with the type requirement of the query, it may not have any overlapped terms with the target attribute names in the database. In the example shown in Figure 2, the relevant attributes `Email`, `Phone` and `Address` do not have any overlapped term with the type requirement "contact information". The attribute `Contact Person` has one overlapped term, but it's not a relevant attribute with regard to the query. We call this the *vocabulary gap* between database and user queries. Therefore, using ordinary keyword search retrieval models will fail definitely because these models depends on the overlapped terms between the query and document. To bridge the vocabulary gap, we follow the existing work on semantic term matching [17] and utilize the unstructured documents collection to get the K most semantic similar terms of the original type requirement based on the mutual information estimated in Equation (1). This works under the assumption that the type requirement and its target attribute have high semantic similarity. We then expand the original type requirement Q_T with the K weighted terms into $Q_{T_{EXP}}$, which is used to replace Q_T to estimate the relevance score.

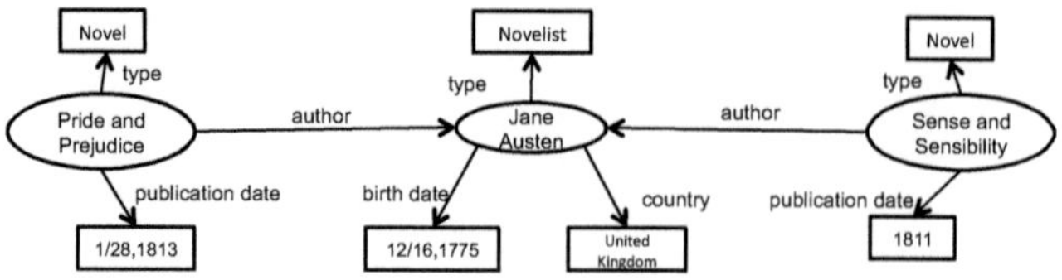

Figure 3: An example RDF graph.

5.2 Semi-Structured Data

Due to space limit, here we only take RDF as example of semi-structured data. Our method is also applicable to other semi-structured data like XML. In RDF graph, each entity is represented as one node, and one entity may have several attributes. Each attribute is a pair of attribute name and attribute value. In the terminology of RDF, each entity and one of its attribute is expressed in one statement called *triple*, in which the entity is subject, attribute name is predicate and attribute value is object. Consider the example shown in Figure 3, there are three entities in total, and entity "Pride and Prejudice" has three attributes (i.e. `type`, `author` and `publication date`). Intuitively, the *type* attribute describes the type information of the entity and the other attributes as well as entity name describes all the other information related to the entity. Therefore, for each entity E_i, we take the `type` attribute as the *type aspect* E_i^T and all the other attributes as *content aspect* E_i^C and eventually each entity can be expressed as 2-dimensional vector $E_i = \{E_i^C, E_i^T\}$. For example, consider the entity $E_i =$ "Pride and Prejudice" in Figure 3, $E_i^C =$ "Pride and Prejudice, 1/28, 1983, Jane Austen". Currently we only consider the type attributes with directly connections to the entities. However, they may also inherit type attributes from others through hierarchical relations. We will take them into consideration in our future work.

To retrieve entities from RDF graph, we need to estimate the relevance between E_i and both the content requirement Q_C and type requirement Q_T. Similar to Equation (7), the relevance score can be formulated as:

$$\begin{aligned} Score(Q, E_i) &= \alpha \cdot Score(Q_T, E_i) + (1-\alpha) \cdot Score(Q_C, E_i) \\ &= \alpha \cdot Score(Q_T, E_i^T) + (1-\alpha) \cdot Score(Q_C, E_i^C) \quad (9) \end{aligned}$$

Note that for one entity not all of the attributes values are plain text. Some of the attribute values may also be other entities in the graph, therefore entities are connected with each other through such attributes as links. In the example shown in Figure 3 both the entity "Pride and Prejudice" and "Sense and Sensibility" share the same attribute "author" with value "Jane Austen" which is also an entity. These three entities are connected through the directed arcs. Therefore, the related information for one entity is scattered into several nodes, similar to the normalization [20] in relational database. Intuitively, to get a more accurate estimation of the content requirement score of each entity, we should not only consider the node itself, but also its neighbors. By leveraging the graph information, after we have done the initial estimation of $Score(Q_C, E_i^C)$, we update it in the following way:

$$Score(Q_C, E_i^C) = (1-\beta)Score(Q_C, E_i^C) + \beta\frac{1}{|\mathcal{N}(E_i)|}\sum_{j\in\mathcal{N}(E_i)} Score(Q_C, E_j^C) \quad (10)$$

where $\mathcal{N}(E_i)$ is the set of all the neighbor nodes of entity E_i, $|\mathcal{N}(E_i)|$ is the size of $\mathcal{N}(E_i)$, $\beta \in [0,1]$ controls the influence of the scores from neighbor nodes.

We now describe how we estimate the two score components: $Score(Q_C, E_i^C)$ and $Score(Q_T, E_i^T)$. Similar to the score component estimation over structured data as described in end of Section 5.1, we may also use any retrieval functions to do so by treating Q_C and Q_T as keyword queries and E_i^C and E_i^T as unstructured documents, respectively. Again, considering the vocabulary gap between the type requirement and the attribute names in the RDF data, we expand the original type requirement Q_T with the K most semantic similar terms into $Q_{T_{EXP}}$ based on the mutual information by utilizing the unstructured documents collection.

6. EXPERIMENTS

We describe the experiment design and results in this section. We choose two data sets for evaluation: one is a real world enterprise data set, and the other one is a simulated data set constructed using standard collections. Over each data set, we conduct two sets of experiments to evaluate the effectiveness of requirement identification methods and ranking methods.

6.1 Real-world Enterprise Data Set

We now describe the enterprise data set used in this paper. The data set contains both *unstructured* and *structured* information about HP, which is referred to as **REAL**.

We first study a query log with queries submitted to the HP web search engine. The log includes 1,060,792 queries in total. The average number of terms in each query is 2.2, which is similar to the observation in web search [36]. After analyzing the query log, we find that the majority of the queries are about product search. Thus, the enterprise data we use for this paper is built around products of HP.

The first part of the data collection includes all the web pages of HP. There are 477,800 web pages, which leads to a total size of 18 GB *unstructured* information. On average each document has 877 terms. The second part of the collection includes a relational database with 25 tables that contain the information about products of HP with a total size of 39,524 KB *structured* information. A table could be either independent or related to other tables. When a table is related to another table, they could be joined together based on their foreign/primary keys.

Specifically, there are five types of tables in the database: *product, product series, product marketing subcategory, product marketing category* and *product type*. A product belongs to one product series, a product series belongs to one product marketing subcategory, a product subcategory belongs to one product category, and a product category belongs to one product type. Clearly, these five types form a concept hierarchy of the products in the databases. The database contains 3,238 products, 983 product series, 134 product marketing subcategories, 54 product marketing categories and 8 product types. Each product table contains information about one type of products. Each product type has its own schema because different types of products may have different specifications. For example, the specification of a printer may include resolution while that of a camera may include storage. Within a product table, each tuple in the table contains the information of a product with the corresponding type. For instance, every tuple in the printer table corresponds to a printer.

Methods	Equation	Prec	Recall	F1
Similarity	(1)	0.752	0.746	0.746
Language Modeling	(4)	0.890	0.887	0.887

Table 1: Performance of type requirement identification over REAL.

Note that although the enterprise data we used center around products, our proposed algorithms are general enough and can be applicable to any enterprise data.

Based on the analysis over the query log, we find that 23.21% queries have mentioned any attribute in the product database, thus these queries have great potential to benefit from our proposed 2-dimensional search methods. Within these queries, we manually select a set of 50 queries which mention both valid product name and attribute in the database. Clearly, all the 50 queries contain both the content and type requirement. The search results of the 2-dimensional search need to follow the format below:

```
<tuple ID, attribute name, attribute value>
```

Each result is specified by the triple of tuple ID (the primary key of the tuple), attribute name and attribute value. Moreover, we create a judgment file which assign relevance labels to table elements for every query by manually retrieving relevant elements from the table. A relevant result should be an exactly same triple in the judgment file. We use MAP (Mean Average Precision) over the 50 queries as the main measurement for the performance. Since each query has 9 relevant results on average, we also use $P@10$ (Precision at rank 10). Besides that, the performance measured with R-precision (R is the number of relevant results for a given topic) is also reported.

We first compare performance of two requirement identification methods proposed in Section 4. To evaluate their performance, we first create judgment files for all the query set by manually identify both content and type requirements for each query. Since the query requirement identification essentially is a classification problem in which each term has to be classified into two classes: either content requirement or type requirement, we evaluate the performance by calculate the macro-average of precision, recall and F1 for each query, and take the average over all the queries then. Table 1 shows the performance of two query requirements identification methods over **REAL**. We can see that both methods can reach reasonable performance, and the language modeling method can reach better performance than similarity based method. In the following experiments, we only report the ranking results using the identification results of

Models	Equation	MAP	P@10	R-Precision
1dBL	(11)	0.0637	0.1466	0.0111
2dBL	(12)	0.5416	0.5640	0.5111
2dRank	(8)	**0.6655***	**0.7139***	**0.6546***

Table 2: Optimal performance comparison on REAL. ⋆ means improvement over 2dBL is statistically significant.

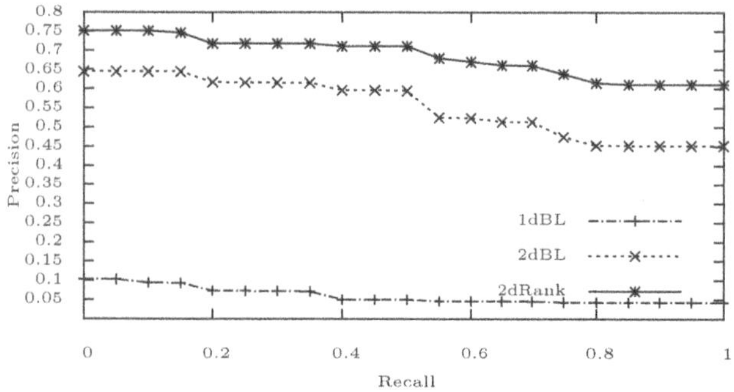

Figure 4: Precision-recall curves over REAL.

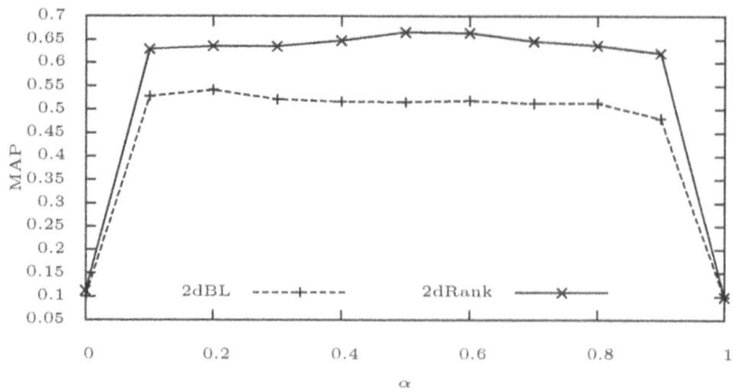

Figure 5: Performance sensitivity of 2dBL and 2dRank over REAL.

Identification Methods	MAP	P@10	R-Precision
Similarity	0.5349	0.5542	0.5170
Language Modeling	0.6655	0.7139	0.6546

Table 3: Optimal performance of ranking based on different type requirement identification results on REAL.

language modeling method because it is expected to lead to better performance.

Baseline Methods: Our work is related to keyword search over structured databases. The main difference is that existing methods only consider ranking joined tuples rather than table elements [23], i.e., attributes. The first baseline method we use is one of the state of the art methods for keyword search over structured databases [23], which is referred to as **1dBL**. In order to apply existing methods to solve our problem, we can use them to rank tuples and then return all the attributes in a random order as follows:

$$Score_{1dBL}(Q, T_i^j) = \frac{1}{|\mathcal{N}(T)|} \sum_{T' \in \{T\} \in \mathcal{N}(T)} Score(Q_C, T_k'), \quad (11)$$

where $\mathcal{N}(T)$ denotes a set of all the tables that can be either directly or indirectly connected to the table T through join operations and $|\mathcal{N}(T)|$ is the size of $\mathcal{N}(T)$.

Moreover, we also implement a stronger baseline where we combine our proposed method by incorporating the relevance score based on the type requirement into the first baseline. This method is referred to as **2dBL**.

$$Score_{2dBL}(Q, T_i^j) = \alpha \cdot Score(Q_{T_{EXP}}, \mathcal{A}_T^j) + (1-\alpha) \cdot \frac{1}{|\mathcal{N}(T)|} \sum_{T' \in \{T\} \in \mathcal{N}(T)} Score(Q_C, T_k') \quad (12)$$

In fact, **1dBL** is a special case of **2dBL** when α is set to 0.

Implementation Details: Our proposed method is referred to as **2dRank**. There are two components in the proposed ranking function and two baseline methods. (Note that Q_T is expanded into $Q_{T_{EXP}}$ as described at the end of Section 5.1.)

Table 2 shows the optimal performance comparison of the three methods measured with three standard evaluation metrics. In addition, we also plot the precision-recall curve for all the three models in Figure 4. It is clear that the **2dRank** performs much better than the two baseline methods. First, we can see that the *2-dimensional search* can clearly yield to better search performance because it can return direct answers. Second, the proximity function in Equation 8 is more effective for 2-dimensional search. Moreover, **1dBL** shows that even without incorporating type constraints into the ranking, our model can still find some relevant information, although with the penalty of great performance loss.

We have manually checked the results of some queries, and found that for some queries whose type requirements have vocabulary gap with the database schema (for example, one such type requirement is "dimension"), some relevant attributes ("width", "depth", "height") are successfully ranked at the top. This proves the effectiveness of our method on bridging the vocabulary gap.

We also examine the performance sensitivity with respect to the parameter α for **2dBL** and **2dRank**, as shown in Figure 5. We find that **2dRank** always performs better than **2dBL** at all α levels. When $\alpha = 1$, both models are essentially the same as their ranking functions regress to $Score(Q_T, \mathcal{A}_T^j)$. For α set to either 0 or 1, both models regress to one-dimensional search, therefore the performance is definitely poor. We also notice that **2dBL** reaches the optimal performance when $\alpha = 0.2$ and **2dRank** reaches the optimal performance when $\alpha = 0.5$.

To verify the correlation between the ranking performance and quality of query requirements identification, we report the optimal performance of the ranking results using different identification methods in Table 3. Connecting with the results in Table 1 we find that that better requirements identification results can lead to better ranking results, as we expected.

6.2 Simulated Data Set

Enterprise data collection is hard to find since most enterprises do not want to publish their internal data for security concerns. In order to evaluate our proposed methods on

Methods	Equation	Prec	Recall	F1
Similarity	(1)	0.771	0.748	0.757
Language Modeling	(4)	0.605	0.618	0.601

Table 4: Performance of type requirement identification over SIMU.

semistructured data, we constructed a simulated data set by choosing the Billion Triple Challenge 2009 dataset [1], which consists of a RDF graph with 1,464,829,200 nodes, as semi-structured data. Beside this, we choose the Category B (first 50 million pages of English part) of ClueWeb09 collection [2] as the complementary unstructured data. The reason that they can serve as complementary to each other is because both data sets contain entity information over the web. The data set is referred to as **SIMU**.

We choose the query set used in the List Search Track of SemSearch 2011 Challenge [21]. The query set consists of 50 queries which are hand-written by the organizing committee. The average number of terms in each query is 5.4. Here are some sample queries:

```
astronauts who walked on the Moon
nations where Portuguese is an official language
```

The reason to choose it is because based on the analysis we find all the queries have mentioned both the content and type requirements. The judgment file, which is created by system pooling from the participants' submissions, is also provided along with the query set. We report the performance evaluation using MAP, P@10 and R-Precision.

We first report the performance of two query requirements identification methods over **SIMU** data set in Table 4. According to the results, we find that the language modeling based method failed to outperform similarity based method. Results analysis shows that the quality of language modeling estimation of θ_C on ClueWeb09 is not as accurate as that on unstructured part of **REAL** data set, since ClueWeb09 has a much wider domain coverage. In the following experiments, we only report the ranking results using the identification results of similarity based method.

Baseline Methods: By treating each entity as an unstructured document by merging all the attributes, we use the whole original query directly to retrieve entities from the data collection directly using the F2-EXP retrieval function. This method essentially performs 1-dimensional retrieval, and is denoted as **1dBL**.

Moreover, we implemented another baseline by estimating $Score(Q_T, E_i^T)$ and $Score(Q_C, E_i^C)$ directly using F2-EXP retrieval function and combine them as shown in Equation (9). As it is essentially 2-dimensional search, we refer it as **2dBL**.

Implementation Details: Based on **2dBL**, we use our proposed graph based method in Equation (10) to estimate $Score(Q_C, E_i^C)$. This method is referred as **2dGraph**.

Moreover, based on **2dBL**, we also implement another ranking method by substituting Q_T with the semantic expanded requirement $Q_{T_{EXP}}$ in the estimation of $Score(Q_T, E_i^T)$. This method is referred as **2dSem**.

Finally, we implement one method by both using the graph based method to estimate $Score(Q_C, E_i^C)$ and substituting Q_T with $Q_{T_{EXP}}$. It is referred to as **2dGraphSem**. The ranking function is:

Method	MAP	P@10	R-Precision
1dBL	0.1542	0.1780	0.1553
2dBL	0.1585	0.1920	0.1767
2dSem	**0.1675***	0.1900	0.1636
2dGraph	0.1659*	0.2120	**0.1835**
2dGraphSem	0.1653	**0.2180**	0.1831

Table 5: Optimal performance comparison on SIMU. $\star$ means improvement over 2dBL is statistically significant.

Identification Methods	MAP	P@10	R-Precision
Similarity	0.1675	0.1900	0.1636
Language Modeling	0.1612	0.1850	0.1609

Table 6: Optimal performance of ranking based on different type requirement identification results on SIMU.

$$Score(Q_C, E_i^C) = \alpha \cdot Score(Q_{T_{EXP}}, E_i^T) + (1-\alpha) \cdot \Big((1-\beta) Score(Q_C, E_i^C) + \beta \frac{1}{|\mathcal{N}(E_i)|} \sum_{j \in \mathcal{N}(E_i)} Score(Q_C, E_j^C)\Big) \quad (13)$$

The optimal performance for the five methods are shown in Table 5. By comparing 1dBL with other methods, we find that 2-dimensional search can always outperforms 1 dimensional search. What's more, both the graph based estimation of the content requirement score and type requirement score using semantic expanded queries can lead to better performance.

Finally, we verify the correlation between the ranking performance and quality of query requirements identification, by reporting the optimal performance of the ranking results using different identification methods in Table 6. It shows again that better requirements identification results can lead to better ranking results.

7. CONCLUSIONS AND FUTURE WORK

The paper aims to demonstrate the feasibility of leveraging unstructured information to improve the search quality over structured and semi-structured information. The problem is to find relevant information of certain types from *structured* and *semi-structured* information. We propose ranking methods that can utilize *unstructured* information to identify type requirement in keyword queries and bridge the vocabulary gap between the query and the data collection. We conduct experiments over one real world enterprise data set and one simulated data set. Experiment results show that our proposed ranking strategy is effective to retrieve relevant information with the type specified in keyword queries.

Enterprise search is important. Our proposed work is only a small step toward improving enterprise search quality. There are many interesting future research directions based on this work. First, it would be interesting to study how to identify queries with type requirements. Second, we would like to extend our query requirements identification model so that it can process queries with multiple content or type requirements. Third, we plan to study how to retrieve information of certain types from unstructured information directly in our future work. Finally, it would be interesting to study how to provide seamless support for search over both unstructured and structured information.

8. ACKNOWLEDGEMENTS

This material is based upon work supported by the HP Labs Innovation Research Program. We thank the anonymous CIKM reviewers for their useful comments.

9. REFERENCES

[1] Billion Triple Challenge 2009 dataset: http://vmlion25.deri.ie/.

[2] The ClueWeb09 Dataset: http://www.lemurproject.org/clueweb09/.

[3] S. Agrawal, S. Chaudhuri, and G. Das. DBXplorer: A System for Keyword-Based Search over Relational Databases. In *ICDE*, pages 5–16, 2002.

[4] J. Arguello, F. Diaz, J. Callan, and J.-F. Crespo. Sources of Evidence for Vertical Selection. In *SIGIR*, pages 315–322, 2009.

[5] P. Bailey, N. Craswell, A. P. de Vries, and I. Soboroff. Overview of the TREC 2007 Enterprise Track. In *Proceedings of TREC'07*, 2007.

[6] P. Bailey, D. Hawking, and B. Matson. Secure Search in Enterprise Webs: Tradeoffs in Efficient Implementation for Document Level Security. In *CIKM*, pages 493–502, 2006.

[7] K. Balog. People Search in the Enterprise. In *SIGIR*, pages 916–916, 2007.

[8] K. Balog, L. Azzopardi, and M. de Rijke. Formal Models for Expert Finding in Enterprise Corpora. In *SIGIR*, pages 43–50, 2006.

[9] K. Balog and M. de Rijke. Non-Local Evidence for Expert Finding. In *CIKM*, pages 489–498, 2008.

[10] K. Balog, A. P. de Vries, P. Serdyukov, P. Thomas, and T. Westerveld. Overview of the TREC 2009 Entity Track. In *Proceedings of TREC'09*, 2009.

[11] K. Balog, I. Soboroff, P. Thomas, P. Bailey, N. Craswell, and A. P. de Vries. Overview of the TREC 2008 Enterprise Track. In *Proceedings of TREC'08*, 2008.

[12] J. Brunnert, O. Alonso, and D. Riehle. Enterprise People and Skill Discovery Using Tolerant Retrieval and Visualization. In *ECIR*, pages 674–677, 2007.

[13] N. Craswell, A. P. de Vries, and I. Soboroff. Overview of the TREC 2005 Enterprise Track. In *Proceedings of TREC'05*, 2005.

[14] M. Şah and V. Wade. Automatic Metadata Extraction from Multilingual Enterprise Content. In *CIKM*, pages 1665–1668, 2010.

[15] N. Dalvi, R. Kumar, B. Pang, R. Ramakrishnan, A. Tomkins, P. Bohannon, S. Keerthi, and S. Merugu. A Web of Concepts. In *PODS*, pages 1–12, 2009.

[16] H. Fang and C. Zhai. An Exploration of Axiomatic Approaches to Information Retrieval. In *SIGIR*, pages 480–487, 2005.

[17] H. Fang and C. Zhai. Semantic Term Matching in Axiomatic Approaches to Information Retrieval. In *SIGIR*, pages 115–122, 2006.

[18] S. Feldman and C. Sherman. The High Cost of Not Finding Information. In *Technical Report No. 29127, IDC*, 2003.

[19] L. Freund and E. G. Toms. Enterprise Search Behaviour of Software Engineers. In *SIGIR*, pages 645–646, 2006.

[20] H. Garcia-Molina, J. Ullman, and J. Widom. *Database Systems: The Complete Book*. Prentice-Hall, 2008.

[21] H. Halpin, D. Herzig, P. Mika, J. Pound, H. Thompson, and T. T. Duc. SemSearch Evaluation 2011: Semantic Search Challenge. In *WWW*, 2011.

[22] D. Hawking. Challenges in Enterprise Search. In *Proceedings of ADC'04*, pages 15–24, 2004.

[23] V. Hristidis, L. Gravano, and Y. Papakonstantinou. Efficient IR-style Keyword Search over Relational Database. In *VLDB*, pages 850–861, 2003.

[24] V. Hristidis and Y. Papakonstantinou. DISCOVER: Keyword Search in Relational Databases. In *VLDB*, pages 670–681, 2002.

[25] A. Kale, T. Burris, B. Shah, T. L. P. Venkatesan, L. Velusamy, M. Gupta, and M. Degerattu. iCollaborate: Harvesting Value from Enterprise Web Usage. In *SIGIR*, pages 699–699, 2010.

[26] M. Kolla and O. Vechtomova. Retrieval of Discussions from Enterprise Mailing Lists. In *SIGIR*, pages 881–882, 2007.

[27] G. Koutrika, Z. M. Zadeh, and H. Garcia-Molina. Data Clouds: Summarizing Keyword Search Results over Structured Data. In *EDBT*, pages 391–402, 2009.

[28] G. Li, B. C. Ooi, J. Feng, J. Wang, and L. Zhou. EASE: an Effective 3-in-1 Keyword Search Method for Unstructured, Semi-structured and Structured Data. In *SIGMOD*, pages 903–914, 2008.

[29] X. Li. Understanding the Semantic Structure of Noun Phrase Queries. In *ACL*, pages 1337–1345, 2010.

[30] C. Macdonald and I. Ounis. Combining Fields in Known-Item Email Search. In *SIGIR*, pages 675–676, 2006.

[31] C. D. Manning, P. Raghavan, and H. Schütze. *Introduction to Information Retrieval*. Cambridge University Press, 2008.

[32] C. D. Manning and H. Schütze. *Foundations of Statistical Natural Language Processing*. The MIT Press, 1999.

[33] J. Peng, C. Macdonald, B. He, and I. Ounis. A Study of Selective Collection Enrichment for Enterprise Search. In *CIKM*, pages 1999–2002, 2009.

[34] P. Serdyukov, H. Rode, and D. Hiemstra. Modeling Multi-step Relevance Propagation for Expert Finding. In *CIKM*, pages 1133–1142, 2008.

[35] I. Soboroff, A. P. de Vries, and N. Craswell. Overview of the TREC 2006 Enterprise Track. In *Proceedings of TREC'06*, 2006.

[36] A. Spink, D. Wolfram, M. Jansen, and T. Saracevic. Searching the Web: The Public and Their Queries. *Journal of the American Society for Information Science and Technology*, pages 226–234, 2001.

[37] C. J. van Rijsbergen. *Information Retrieval*. Butterworths, 1979.

[38] S. Yang, J. Jin, and Y. Xiong. Using Weighted Tagging to Facilitate Enterprise Search. In *ECIR*, pages 590–593, 2010.

Unsupervised Transactional Query Classification Based on Webpage Form Understanding

Yuchen Liu[1]*, Xiaochuan Ni[2], Jian-Tao Sun[2], Zheng Chen[2]

[1]School of Software
Tsinghua University
Beijing 100084, P. R. China
yuchen.liu07@gmail.com

[2]Microsoft Research Asia
No.5 Danling Street, Haidian District
Beijing 100080, P. R. China
{xini, jtsun, zhengc}@microsoft.com

ABSTRACT

Query type classification aims to classify search queries into categories like navigational, informational and transactional, etc., according to the type of information need behind the queries. Although this problem has drawn many research attentions, previous methods usually require editors to label queries as training data or need domain knowledge to edit rules for predicting query type. Also, the existing work has been mainly focusing on the classification of informational and navigational query types. Transactional query classification has not been well addressed. In this work, we propose an unsupervised approach for transactional query classification. This method is based on the observation that, after the transactional queries are issued to a search engine, many users will click the search result pages and then have interactions with Web forms on these pages. The interactions, e.g., typing in text box, making selections from dropdown list, clicking on a button to execute actions, are used to specify detailed information of the transaction. By mining toolbar search log data, which records the associations between queries and Web forms clicked by users, we can get a set of good quality transactional queries without using manual labeling efforts. By matching these automatically acquired transactional queries and their associated Web form contents, we can generalize these queries into patterns. These patterns can be used to classify queries which are not covered by search log. Our experiments indicate that transactional queries produced by this method have good quality. The pattern based classifier achieves 83% F_1 classification result. This is very effective considering the fact that we do not adopt any labeling efforts to train the classifier.

*This work is done when the first author is visiting Microsoft Research Asia.

CIKM'11, October 24–28, 2011, Glasgow, Scotland, UK.

Categories and Subject Descriptors

H.3.3 [**Information Storage and Retrieval**]: Information Search and Retrieval; H.4.m [**Information Systems Applications**]: Miscellaneous

General Terms

Experimentation, Measurement

Keywords

Query Type Classification, Transactional Query, Unsupervised Learning

1. INTRODUCTION

Search engines are widely used to search information on the Web. According to [25], about 70% of web searchers set search engines as their main entry point to the Internet. Popular search engines like Google, Yahoo! and Bing will receive a large number of search queries each day. Due to the fierce competition in search market, it is critical for search engine companies to return desired search result pages to end users.

Search engine users have different types of information needs. In [4], Broder divides queries into three categories based on the type of search intent: navigational, informational and transactional. This classification is also widely used in subsequent research work:

- **Navigational query**: the purpose of navigational query is to reach a particular website that user has in mind. For example, the query "myspace" can be regarded as navigational, because most users may want to visit the `http://www.myspace.com` website.

- **Informational query**: the purpose of informational query is to find information on the web. For example, the query "canon 5d review" can be regarded as informational, since the user may expect to read reviews about Canon 5D product even he or she does not know which website contains such information.

- **Transactional query**: the purpose of transactional query is to conduct transactions on a website. Usually users have some tasks to complete and may have actions or interactions with one or several websites. For

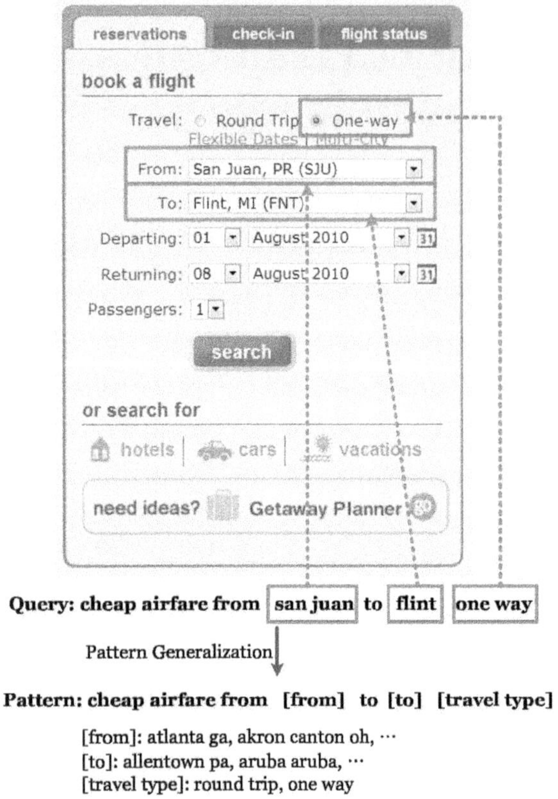

Figure 1: A Query Associated with A Webpage Form and Pattern Generalization Example

example, the query "book Marriott hotel for my Seattle visit" can be regarded as transactional, because the user intent is to complete the task of booking hotel.

Understanding the type of search intent will be helpful for improving search engine relevance. For example, the authors of [5, 19, 2] proposed to optimize search results by adopting specific methods to deal with different types of search queries. However, how to automatically predict query type is challenging and this problem is not well addressed in literature. The authors of previous research work mainly focused on classifying queries into informational and navigational categories. Transactional query classification problem is not well studied. In fact, transactional queries are important for search engine users. According to the studies of Broder [4] and Rose [24], over 25% queries of a commercial search engine are transactional, as shown in Table 1 [1]. In literature, when supervised learning algorithms are used for query type classification [17, 16, 22, 20], human efforts are required for labeling queries to train the classifier, which is usually time-consuming. Some researchers adopted rules to predict query types [13]. The drawback is that compiling rules depends on domain knowledge and it is usually hard to enumerate all feasible rules. The dependencies of existing query type classification methods block them from being widely used in practice.

[1]INF: Informational Query, NAV: Navigational Query, TRA: Transactional Query

Table 1: The Percentage of Queries Belonging to Different Types

Query Type	INF	NAV	TRA
Broder (user survey)	39%	24.5%	36%
Broder (log analysis)	48%	20%	30%
Rose (test set1)	60.9%	14.7%	24.3%
Rose (test set2)	61.3%	11.7%	27%
Rose (test set3)	61.5%	13.5%	25%

In this paper, we will focus on transactional query classification problem and target to reduce the dependency on manual efforts. According to our observation, after the transactional queries are issued to search engine, many users will click the search result links and then have interactions with forms on the corresponding websites. For example, the search engine user may type in text box to fill in the form, select items from the dropdown list and click on a button to execute actions associated with the form. In this way, the information need of the user is satisfied. Such interactions are very common when users have online transactions, e.g., booking hotel, buying movie tickets, or finding dealers of used car. The user clicks can be used to associate search queries with webpage forms. Figure 1 gives an example of a user query with its associated form from the AirTran Airways website (`http://www.airtran.com/`). Therefore it is reasonable to assume that, if a query is frequently associated with many forms of different web sites (i.e., corresponding with many form clicks), most likely the query belongs to transactional type. This assumption is consistent with the transactional query type definition given by [4].

Although many transactional queries are frequently associated with form clicks, not all queries with form clicks belong to transactional type. For example, the user may first input a *navigational* query (e.g., "united airline") to search for the corresponding website (`http://www.united.com`), and then have form clicks on that website. Also, not all forms are designed for users to complete transactions, e.g, the form which only contains a search box. In this work, we first analyze the distribution of form clicks and get a group of high quality transactional queries by mining toolbar log which conveys the relations between queries and their clicked forms. With these transactional queries as training data, we match them with the information contained in forms to help generalize these queries into patterns. A brief illustration of pattern generalization is shown in Figure 1. The patterns will be used to classify the queries which are not covered by log data. Compared with previous methods, our classifier is learnt from user log data instead of manually labeled queries. Experiments show that this unsupervised method achieves 83% F_1 classification result. This is very effective considering it is a fully unsupervised approach, although the performance is slightly worse than a supervised approach which requires many labeled data for training.

According to our knowledge, this is the first work of using form clicks to help transactional query classification. We are also the first to use webpage form information to help understand the structure of associated queries. Besides the direct benefit of classifying transactional queries, we have also identified a list of forms associated with each query. They are useful for simplifying user transactions, for exam-

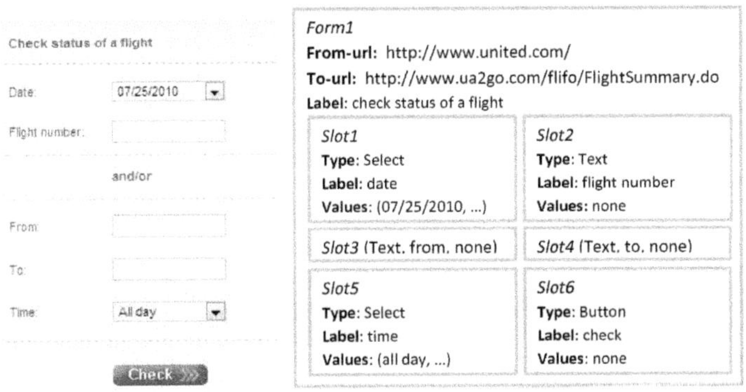

Figure 2: A Web Form Example

ple, the forms can be placed on the search result page thus users can directly finish transactions on them.

The following contents are organized as follows. In Section 2, we introduce the data source used in this work. In Section 3, we give framework of our solution and three key components. Two possible optional solutions to improve the classification performance are given in Section 4. Section 5 gives our experimental results. Section 6 discusses some work related to query type classification and form extraction. We conclude the paper in Section 7.

2. DATA

In this section, we will first introduce the data sources used in this research, including web forms and toolbar log data.

2.1 Web Form

A *form* refers to all contents between the html tags "<form>" and "</form>". In this work, we model a form as the container of *slots*. Each slot corresponds with one component of a *form*, which is provided for users to interact with, e.g. fill in some value or select a value from a given list. A form also contains a button for submission. Figure 2 gives an example form and describes the slots contained by this form.

A *slot* has three properties: label, type and a list of values. The label gives a description of the *slot*. 5 types of slots are used in this research: *text*, *select*, *radio*, *checkbox* and *button*. The *text* type refers to the text input box, *select* refers to a dropdown selection list, *radio* refers to a group of radio buttons, *checkbox* refers to a group of check boxes and *button* refers to a button used for submission. Except for *text* slot, each slot has a list of pre-set values (*none* is used to refer an empty list in this work).

A *form* has four properties: a label to describe the form, a collection of *slots* contained in this *form*, *from-url* which is the URL of the page containing the form, and *to-url* which is the URL where users will visit after the form is submitted.

In the following sections, *slot* is denoted by s. $L(s)$ and $V(s)$ are used to denote the slot label and the set of values of this slot respectively. A *form* is denoted by f. $L(f)$ and $S(f)$ are used to denote the form label and the set of *slots* in this *form* respectively.

2.2 Toolbar Log

Toolbar log is widely used by search engine companies to record the behaviors of users. When a user submits a query to search engine, a list of search result pages will be returned to the user. Then the user may browse one result page of interest and click on hyperlinks contained by that page. The following information recorded by toolbar log will be used in our research: *user id, search query, clicked result page URL, further clicked page URL in result page.*

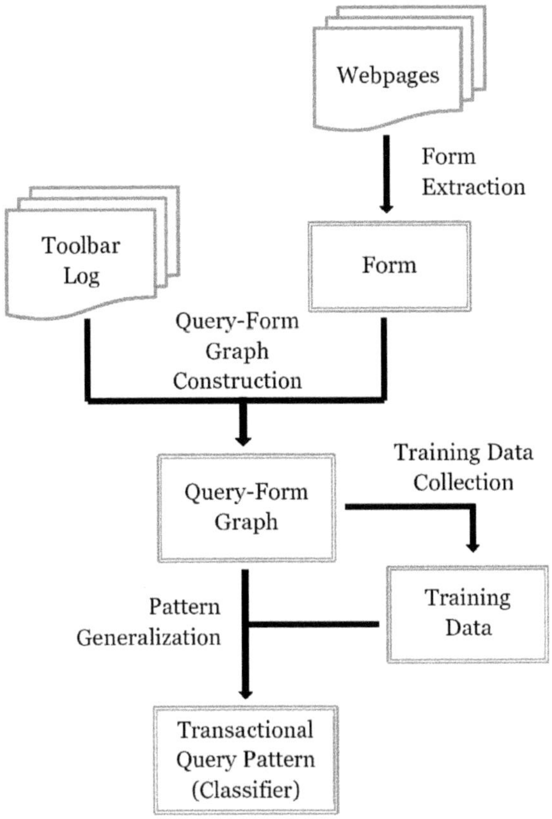

Figure 3: Framework of Our Solution

2.3 Query-Form Virtual Graph

With help of toolbar log, we can construct a virtual bipartite graph with nodes corresponding with query and form respectively. For each query issued by search engine user, we can analyze the contents of its result page. When the result page contains a form, we can use its {*from-url, to-url*} values to match with {*clicked result page url, further clicked page url in result page*} of toolbar log. If the two URL pairs can be successfully matched, we can add one virtual link between the query and form nodes, which means that the query is associated with the corresponding form click. If a query can be matched with a form for several times, the frequency will be used as weight of the virtual link.

3. SOLUTION

The framework of our unsupervised transactional query classification solution is shown in Figure 3. It contains three components:

1) Analyze the query-form graph to get a group of high quality transactional queries and use them as training data.

2) Match training queries with their corresponding form properties to generate transactional query patterns.

3) Adopt transactional query patterns to predict types for new search queries.

3.1 Training Data Collection

With the query-form click graph as input, we propose two score functions to measure how likely a query belongs to transactional type: *click entropy* and *click ratio.*

Considering the click distribution on the query-form bipartite graph, we show three typical types of queries in Figure 4. For query q_a, users usually go to one specific website and have interactions with a fixed form of that website. This query very likely belongs to transactional type. For query q_b, users usually go to the same website but have interactions with many forms of that website. According to our observation, many users usually use a search engine to find the website of interest and then browse different pages on that website. Such query may belong to navigational type although it is associated with many forms. Query "american airlines" belongs to such case. The third type of query, q_c is associated with many forms from different websites. Most likely such query also belongs to transactional type, e.g., "cheap flight".

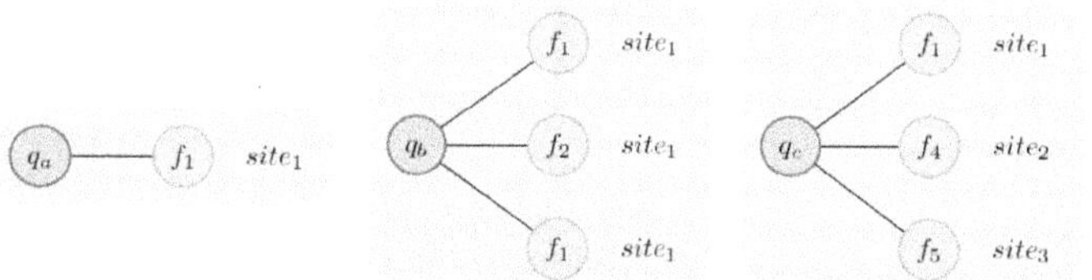

Figure 4: Three Types of Queries in Query-*Form* Graph

We define a **click entropy** score function to measure how likely the query q is transactional:

$$ClickEntropy(q) =$$
$$(1 + E(p_{site})) \sum_{s_i \in Site(q)} \frac{Click(q, s_i)}{Click(q)} \frac{1}{2^{E(p_{s_i})}} \quad (1)$$

In Equation 1, $Site(q)$ denotes the set of URLs which have virtual links with q while s_i is the i-th URL in $Site(q)$. Note that there might be multiple forms in a single webpage s_i. $Click(q, s_i)$ refers to the link frequency between q and s_i, which equals sum of link frequency between q and all forms in s_i. $Click(q)$ is the total link frequency of q. Here we define two kinds of click distribution for query q: p_{site} and p_{s_i}. p_{site} denotes the click distribution for a query at webpage level, where $p_{site}(s_i) \propto Click(q, s_i)$. While p_{s_i} denotes the click distribution of *forms* in specific webpage s_i. $E(p)$ is the *entropy* computed with the distribution p, as shown in the following equation:

$$E(p) = -\sum_{i=1}^{n} p(x_i) \log_2 p(x_i) \quad (2)$$

where distribution p may refer to either p_{site} or p_{s_i}, and x_i denotes a webpage s_i or a form in s_i which has virtual links to q, respectively.

It is apparent that, the bigger $ClickEntropy(q)$ is, the more likely that query q is transactional. We can find queries q_a, q_b, q_c of Figure 4 satisfy

$$ClickEntropy(q_c) > ClickEntropy(q_a) > ClickEntropy(q_b)$$

This is consistent with our observations discussed at the beginning of this sub-section.

Click ratio score function is defined by:

$$ClickRatio(q) = \log_2\left(\frac{Click(q)}{Impression(q)} + 1\right) \quad (3)$$

where $Click(q)$ is the frequency of query q associated with *form* clicks, while $Impression(q)$ is the impression number of q in toolbar log, which is the frequency of q's appearance. The log function is adopted to smooth the distribution. The click ratio score function can be used to distinguish between informational queries and transactional ones.

By combining both click entropy and click ratio functions, we use the following equation to estimate how likely a query is transactional:

$$Score(q) = ClickEntropy(q_i) \times ClickRatio(q_i) \quad (4)$$

In practice, the queries with high score are regarded as transactional. We will discuss an algorithm for improving quality of training data collected in Section 4.1.

3.2 Query Pattern Generalization

In this subsection, we will introduce how to generalize query patterns with the collected training data. The idea is to match query content with properties of clicked forms. Figure 1 gives an example. We first give some definitions related to the process of query pattern generalization:

Attribute: An *attribute* a has a textual description *label* and a list of possible values $V(a)$. In the following sections, we present *attribute* a as "[*label*]". We could easily transform a *slot* s in a *form* to an *attribute* a, where the label of s could be textual description of a and slot values of s could be possible values $V(a)$.

Query Pattern: A *query pattern* p is a sequence of terms $<t_1, \ldots, t_n>$, where each t_i could be a word w or an *attribute* a, such that at least one of the terms is an *attribute*, *i.e.*, $\exists j \in [1, n]$ for which t_j is an *attribute*. An example of *query pattern* is "flights to [city]", where *attribute* "[city]" has possible values $V(a) = \{$ seattle, new york, $\ldots\}$.

Given a list of *attributes* $A = \{a_1, a_2, \ldots, a_m\}$ and a query q, presented by a sequence of words $W = <w_1, \ldots, w_n>$, we aim to generalize q with the help of A in order to generate a candidate pattern p, where $t_i \in W \cup A$ for all terms in p. In the query-form graph, we could use a pair of query and form to generalize query patterns by easily transforming *slots* in the *form* to a list of *attributes*.

Generally, if we could find a possible value of an attribute appearing in a query, we will replace the value with the attribute to generalize the query to a query pattern. In many cases, the query may fail to be exactly matched with attribute values, especially when there exists spelling errors or abbreviations in users' queries. Therefore, we adopt a fuzzy string matching function for comparing a candidate string s with an attribute value v:

$$Match(s, v) = 1 - \frac{EditDistance(s, v)}{|v|} \quad (5)$$

where $EditDistance(s, v)$ measures the edit distances of two strings[21] and $|v|$ is the length of string v.

We adopt a greedy algorithm for matching query contents with attribute values for query pattern generalization. The algorithm is described in Algorithm 1. δ_m is a pre-defined threshold score for fuzzy string matching.

Algorithm 1 Query Pattern Generalization

Input: $A = \{a_1, \ldots, a_m\}, q = \{w_1, \ldots, w_n\}$ where $w_i \in W$.
Output: $p = \{t_1, \ldots, t_k\}$, where $t_i \in W \cup A$.

1: Set $p = q = \{t_1, \ldots, t_n\}$, where $t_i = w_i$.
2: **for** $u = 1$ **to** m **do**
3: compute $Match(p, a_u)$
$= \max_{v \in V(a_u)} Match(p, v)$
$= max_{v \in V(a_u)} \{max_{0 \le i < j \le n} Match(p_{ij}, v)\}$,
where $p_{ij} = t_i, \ldots, t_j$, $s.t.$ $t_l \in W$ for $l \in [i, j]$.
4: **end for**
5: find the most matchable attribute with
$max = \arg\max_{1 \le u \le m} Match(p, a_u)$
6: **if** $Match(p, a_{max}) > \delta_m$ **then**
7: replace $t_i, \ldots, t_j$ in p with a_{max}
8: remove a_{max} from A
9: $m \leftarrow m - 1$
10: $n \leftarrow n - (j - i)$
11: go to step 2
12: **else**
13: **return** p
14: **end if**

We could obtain a list of candidate query patterns through each pair of query and form in the query-form click graph. Finally we count all patterns and calculate a confidence score for each of them:

$$ScoreQP(p) = |Slot(p)| \sum_{q_i \in Q(p)} Score(q_i) \quad (6)$$

where p is a pattern, $Q(p)$ is the set of transactional queries which can be generalized to p, and $Score(q_i)$ is the transaction score of query q_i, which is computed in Section 3.1. $|Slot(p)|$ is the number of slots in pattern p.

Intuitively, if a pattern is generated from transactional queries with high quality, it will also have high quality. Also, if a pattern can be matched with many form slots, it is more likely to be a transactional pattern.

3.3 Transactional Query Classification

Query patterns are put in use for judging if a new query is transactional. Both pattern quality and how well queries fit with patterns are considered in classification process. We find patterns which well match with query q using:

$$p_{fit} = argmax_{p_i \in P} Fit(p_i, q) \quad (7)$$

where p_i is a transactional query pattern and P is the set of all patterns. $Fit(p_i, q)$ indicates how well query q fits pattern p_i. Then we adopt the following equation to calculate transactional score for q:

$$ScoreQ(q) = Fit(p_{fit}, q) \times ScoreQP(p_{fit}) \quad (8)$$

where $ScoreQP(p_i)$ is the transactional score of each pattern computed with Equation 6.

The larger $ScoreQ(q)$ is, the more likely query q is transactional. In practical applications, we will compare this score with a threshold value $\delta_{predict}$ and predict q as transactional or not-transactional. In order to determine the fitness between query and pattern, we use slot values associated with the pattern to match with the query sub-string. If the match is successful, the substring will be removed from the query. Finally, we compute a textual similarity between the pattern and remaining words of the query. The fitness measurement of query q and pattern p will consider both the number of successful matches and the similarity score, as shown in the following equation:

$$Fit(p, q) = \frac{SlotMatch(p, q)}{|Slot(p)|} Cosine(p\prime, q\prime) \quad (9)$$

where $SlotMatch(p, q)$ is the number of slot matches between pattern p and query q. $|Slot(p)|$ is the number of slots in pattern p. $p\prime$ and $q\prime$ refer to the remaining text after the matched slots are removed. The *Cosine* similarity is measured using their *bags-of-words* representations.

4. DISCUSSION

In the previous section, we have described our unsupervised transaction query classification algorithm. In this section, we will discuss two possible solutions to improve the classification performance. Both solutions are optional and we will study their impacts on classification performance in Section 5.

4.1 Improving Training Data Quality

We have defined Equation 4 to measure how likely a query is transactional. Considering the relations between query and form, we can use an iterative algorithm to re-score them according to how likely they are transactional. The idea is based on the *mutual reinforcement principle*[2]:

> A transactional query is usually associated with transactional *forms*. A transactional *form* is usually associated with transactional queries.

Based on the query-form relations encoded by the bipartite graph, the transactional scores for query, $Score(q)$, and *form*, $Score(f)$ are updated iteratively, following equations:

$$Score_{k+1}(q_i) = ClickEntropy(q_i) \times ClickRatio(q_i) \times \sum_{f_j \in F(q_i)} Click(q_i, f_j) Score_k(f_j) \quad (10)$$

$$Score_{k+1}(f_j) = \sum_{q_i \in Q(f_j)} Click(q_i, f_j) Score_k(q_i) \quad (11)$$

where $F(q_j)$ is the set of forms associated with q_j; $Q(f_j)$ is the set of queries associated with f_j. $Click(q_i, f_j)$ is frequency of q_i clicking on f_j. $ClickEntropy(q_i)$ and $ClickRatio(q_i)$ can be calculated using Equation 1 and 3, respectively.

The algorithm terminates when the scores for queries and forms are converged (the property of converging can be proved according to [18]). The queries with high scores will be considered as transactional queries.

4.2 Improving Transactional Pattern Quality

In reality, different websites may contain forms for completing the same transaction. If we can group them together and merge *attributes* transformed from all forms belonging

[2]Similar principles are incorporated in HITS[18].

to the same cluster, it will increase the possibility of successful matches between query and *attributes*. This observation also applies to form slots, since the slots with same functionality may have different names on different websites. Grouping them according to functionalities will increase the amount of possible values for the *attribute* transformed from the slot, thus help pattern generalization.

We adapt the clustering algorithm of [27] to cluster forms and slots in this work. A two-step clustering method is used: first we adopt a hierarchical agglomerative method to cluster all *slots* using their content information (labels and list of values) and the co-occurrence information with other slots. In the second step, the same method is used to cluster *forms* using their labels and *slots*.

The similarity between two *slots*, denoted by $Sim(s_i, s_j)$, is calculated by:

$$Sim(s_i, s_j) = \alpha LSim(s_i, s_j) + \beta VSim(s_i, s_j) + (1 - \alpha - \beta) CoSim(s_i, s_j) \quad (12)$$

where α and β are two weight coefficients, which are used to balance different similarity measures.

The label similarity is calculated with a Cosine function on two term vectors, each of which corresponds with *bags-of-words* representation of the slot label: $LSim(s_i, s_j) = Cosine(L(s_i), L(s_j))$. The value similarity is based on the matching between values in $V(s_i)$ and $V(s_j)$. The value similarity of two *slots* are calculated with Dice's function [6]: $VSim(s_i, s_j) = 2|C|/(|V(s_i)| + |V(s_j)|)$, where C is the set of matching pairs.

The Co-occurrence similarity is proposed by us to consider the co-occurrence information of two *slots*. $P(s_i|s_j)$ denotes the probability of s_i appearing in a *form* if s_j already appears in the same *form*. $P(s_i|s_j)$ can be calculated in the form extraction phase. For each *slot*, we can have a vector to measure the co-occurrence of other slots: $CoV(s_i) = (P(s_1|s_i), P(s_2|s_i), \ldots, P(s_n|s_i))$. The Co-occurrence similarity is computed by Cosine function on co-occurrence vector: $CoSim(s_i, s_j) = Cosine(CoV(s_i), CoV(s_j))$.

The hierarchical agglomerative clustering for *slot* can be depicted in Algorithm 2. A slot cluster merging similarity threshold δ_{slot} is adopted in this algorithm.

Algorithm 2 Pseudo Codes for *Slot* Clustering

```
1: treat each slot as a cluster
2: calculate the similarity of all pairs of clusters
   CSim(c_i, c_j) = max_{1<=u<=m,1<=v<=u} Sim(s_iu, s_jv)
3: if MaxSim(c_i, c_j) > δ_slot then
4:    merge c_i and c_j into a new cluster, go to step 2
5: else
6:    return
7: end if
```

We extend this *slot* clustering algorithm to cluster *forms* using form label and the set of slots contained by the form. The similarity between two forms, f_i and f_j, is calculated by considering both the label similarity and the slot set similarity:

$$Sim(f_i, f_j) = \gamma LSim(f_i, f_j) + (1 - \gamma) SSim(f_i, f_j) \quad (13)$$

After the slot clustering step, each slot will belong to a cluster. We can build a *slot* cluster vector for all *slots* belonging to a form. Assuming there are total n slot clusters (denoted by sc) after previous step, the slot cluster vector of form f_i can be denoted by $ScV(f_i) = (c_1, c_2, \ldots, c_n)$, where c_k is the number of slots in slot cluster sc_k. Therefore, the slot set similarity can be computed by: $SSim(f_i, f_j) = Cosine(ScV(f_i), ScV(f_j))$. The form clustering algorithm is similar to previous one for slot in Algorithm 2 but a different cluster merging similarity threshold δ_{form} is used to decide whether to merge two forms.

Query and User Distribution	
Total # of unique queries	1,965,750
Total # of unique users	1,915,458
Total # of unique webpages	1,684,145
Total # of issuing history	7,773,800
Avg. # of issues per query	3.95
Avg. # of issues per user	4.06
Avg. # of characteristics per query (including blank spaces)	
All queries	15.5
Unique queries	25.7

Table 2: Statistics of Log Data Used in Our Experiments

5. EXPERIMENT

In this section, we will introduce the data set used in our experiments and the effectiveness of our unsupervised transactional query classification approach, including the performances of all three components: training data collection, query pattern generalization, transactional query classification.

5.1 Experimental Settings

We use a set of toolbar log data collected by a commercial search engine company. The log spans a month, from December 1 to 31 of 2009. It contains 100 million log records, 30 million unique queries issued by 7 million unique users. In order to conduct experiments efficiently, we use Bing Local taxonomy[3] to help reduce the experimental scale. We crawl home pages of all Web sites belonging to three categories, "Travel / Airlines & Airline Ticket Agencies", "Travel / Car Rentals" and "Travel / Hotels & Accommodations". Since our transactional query classification approach is category-independent, we merge all the crawled pages together in our experiments. We also filter the toolbar log by only keeping the records which have clicks on these pages. Table 2 shows the details about the data set.

We process HTML codes of each page and extract Web forms. In order to remove obviously non-transactional forms, we apply the following rules in form extraction: 1)The HTML code of a form should be shorter than 75% of the whole page; 2) The number of slots contained in a form is less than 15; 3) A form should contain at least one button for submission; 4) A form should contain an attribute named "action" which is used to declare the submission URL of this form. Finally we build a query-form bipartite graph, consisting of 155 forms and 20,934 queries. The log data of the last 7 days are held out for testing purpose.

5.2 Evaluation of Training Data Collection

[3]http://www.bing.com/local/YPDefault.aspx

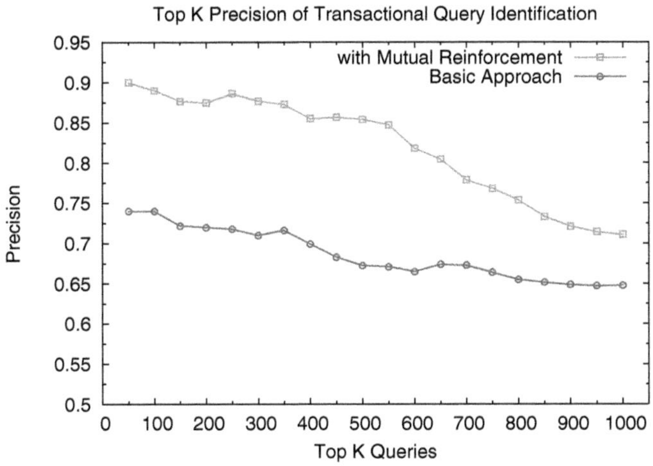

Figure 5: Top K Precision of Transactional Query Identification

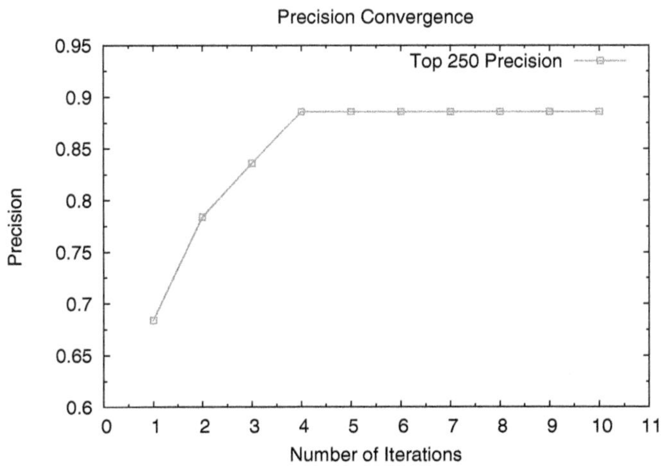

Figure 6: Top 250 Precision with Iteration Number

In order to evaluate the performance of the transactional query collection component, we invited 5 human judges to label the queries produced by this component. We manually labeled about 3,000 queries which are pooled from top-ranked queries by each method. Among them, 1,269 queries are labeled as transactional while the remaining ones are labeled as not-transactional.

As discussed in Section 4.1, the *mutual reinforcement principle* based iterative algorithm can help remove noisy queries. In this section, we will also study the influence of this algorithm.

Since all queries in query-form graph are ranked according to their likelihood of belonging to the transactional type, we can evaluate the result by computing top K precision. The result is shown in Figure 5, where "basic-approach" means the iterative algorithm is not used while "with mutual reinforcement" corresponds with the result of mutual reinforcement approach after the algorithm converges. We can see that the mutual reinforcement approach achieves a precision of 89% at top 100 and maintains a precision of 85% at top 500. In addition, it is better than the basic method for almost all K values. For example, when K is 50, the mutual reinforcement approach can achieve 90% precision while the basic method can only achieve 72% precision. Those results indicate that the iterative algorithm incorporating mutual reinforcement principle is indeed effective to identify high quality transactional queries.

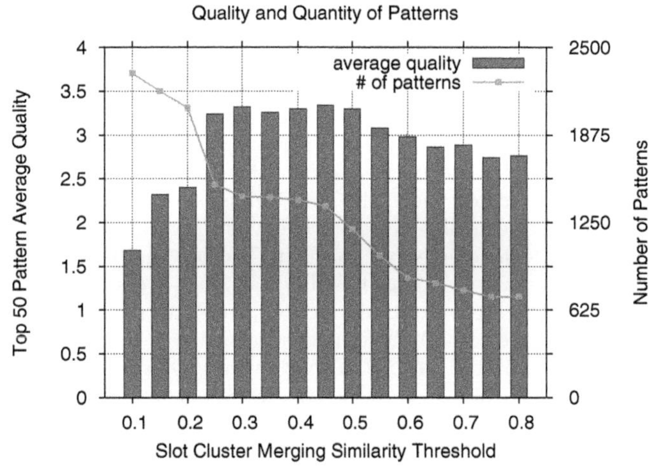

Figure 7: The Number of Patterns Generalized from *slot*-cluster-based Method and the Average Quality of Top 50 Patterns

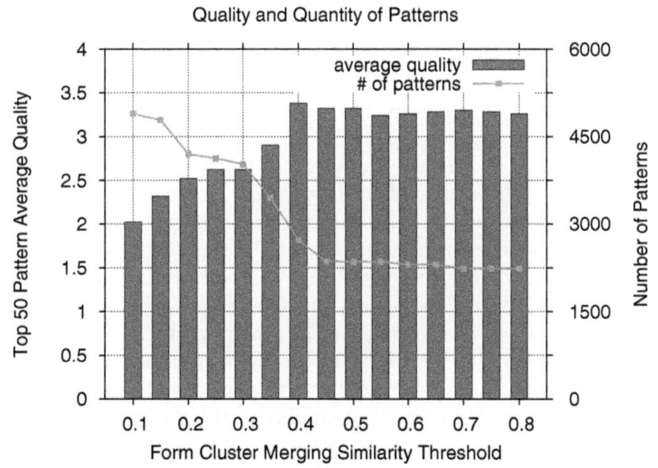

Figure 8: The Number of Patterns Generalized from *form*-cluster-based Method and the Average Quality of Top 50 Patterns

In addition, the mutual reinforcement iterative algorithm can converge quickly. Figure 6 shows the top 250 precision with iteration number. We can see that the result converges to the maximum after only 5 iterations. We have similar observations on the other settings, but we do not report the results due to space limitation.

5.3 Evaluation of Query Pattern Generalization

In this experiment, the top 8,000 queries ranked by the mutual reinforcement approach in last step are used to generalize patterns.

As mentioned in section 3.2, the content in web forms will be used to generate query patterns, and a basic solution is proposed: use slots and values of clicked *forms* (Direct-match). In Section 5.2 we discussed that by clustering slots and forms, the possibility of successful matching between query and form slots will be increased. Thus we can get slots and values of clicked forms, then use slot clustering results to include more slot and value pairs (Slot-cluster-based). We can also get slots and values of clicked forms, then use form clustering results to include more slot and value pairs (Form-cluster-based).

In order to evaluate the quality of query patterns, we manually rate the top 50 patterns generalized by each method. Each pattern is given one of four ratings: 4 (accurate and good generalization), 3 (accurate but bad generalization), 2 (incorrect and good generalization) or 1 (incorrect and bad generalization). We compute an average score for each group of 50 patterns.

There are several parameters in the clustering algorithm. Weight coefficients such as α, β and γ in Equation 12 and 13 are decided based on our experiment experience. Both α and β are set to be 0.33 and γ is set to be 0.5 in our experiment. The threshold score δ_m of fuzzy matching in Section 3.2 is set to be 0.75.

Other parameters which affect clustering results include the threshold score used to merge slot clusters in Algorithm 2, δ_{slot}, and the one used to merge form clusters, δ_{form}. We conduct a study here on the effects of both parameters on the quality and quantity of query patterns.

Figure 7 shows the effect of the *slot* clustering similarity threshold on the number of patterns extracted using *slot*-clusters and the average quality of the top 50 patterns. We can see that as the increase of δ_{slot} the number of extracted patterns tends to decrease. It makes sense since a larger δ_{slot} will produce a smaller number of clusters, i.e. less slot and value pairs will be used for generalizing patterns. We can also see that the quality of patterns varies according to the change of the *slot* clustering similarity threshold. Basically, we can get that the quality of patterns is poor when there are excessive or inadequate patterns extracted. It also makes sense since a large number of patterns may include more noise, while a small number of patterns may cause to lose high quality patterns. According to this experiment, we set δ_{slot} to be 0.3.

After setting a proper δ_{slot}, we continue to study the effect of *form* clustering similarity threshold δ_{form}. Figure 8 shows the number of patterns extracted using form-clusters and the average quality of the top 50 patterns when the threshold of *form* clustering similarity changes. Like the effect of δ_{slot}, similar observations can be made about δ_{form}. We set δ_{form} to be 0.4 in the following experiments.

After choosing the optimal parameters, we compare the pattern generalization approaches using different sets of slot and value pairs, "Direct-match", "Slot-cluster-based" and "Form-cluster-based". Figure 9 shows the comparison results with regard to both pattern number and pattern quality. We can see that, *form*-cluster-based method has the best average pattern quality. As expected, this method also generates more patterns than the other two approaches. According to our observation, *form*-cluster-based method indeed generalizes better patterns. Some values in query cannot be matched by clicked forms. However, in many cases, such

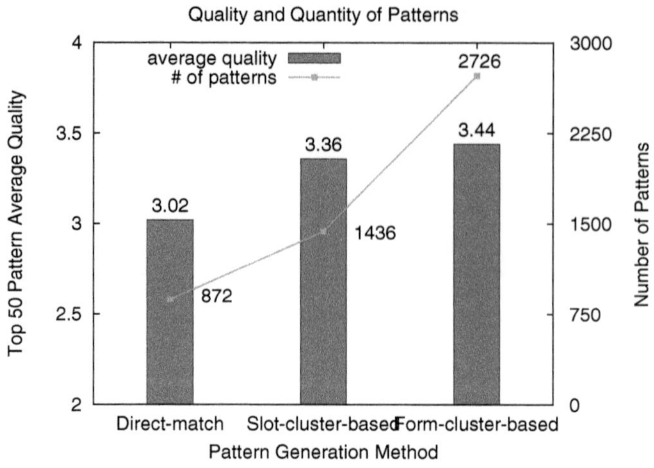

Figure 9: Comparison of Different Methods

mis-match problem can be addressed by *slots* from other *forms* in the same *form* cluster.

We present top query patterns generalized from form-cluster-based method for three domains, flight, car and hotel respectively, in Table 3.

5.4 Evaluation of Transactional Query Prediction

In this section, we evaluate the performance of the pattern based transactional query prediction approach.

The patterns learnt from the previous section by using the *form*-cluster-based method are utilized for prediction here. We construct test data set by randomly sampling some queries from last 7 days' log. After removing the queries which occur in the queries that are used for pattern learning, we get 324 transactional queries and 319 not-transactional queries labeled by human judges. In this experiment, Precision, Recall and F_1 which are frequently used in classification problems are selected as the evaluation measures.

As we mentioned in Section 3.3, in prediction, threshold parameter $\delta_{predict}$ is used to determine whether a query belongs to transactional category or not. In this experiment, we firstly tune $\delta_{predict}$ on a tuning data set (it contains 200 transactional queries and 200 not-transactional queries and there is no overlap between the tuning data set and the test data set). According to our experiment, $\delta_{predict} = 0.5$ produces the highest F_1. Therefore, we set $\delta_{predict}$ to be 0.5 and then do the rest of experiments.

Table 4 (the row named "pattern-based") shows the transactional query classification results of the pattern-based classification approach. 83% F_1 is achieved, which indicates the effectiveness of this approach.

Moreover, we compare the performance of our unsupervised pattern-based method with a supervised learning approach for transactional query classification. We build a training data set for the supervised learning approach: 884 transactional queries and 864 not-transactional queries labeled by human judges. A binary classifier with uni-gram features is trained based on the training set. (We adopt SVM algorithm and use SVM-*Light*[14] in this experiment).

Table 4 (the row named "supervised-approach") shows the transactional query classification results of the supervised

Generalized Query Patterns with High Confidence Score		
Flight Domain	Car Domain	Hotel Domain
flights from [departure] to [destination]	[year] [make] [model]	[city] [state province] hotels
[departure] to [destination]	[make] [model] [year]	[city] hotels
flights to [destination]	[year] [make] [model] reviews	comfort inn [city] [state province]
cheap flights from [departure] to [destination]	[car type] [make] [model]	cheap hotels [state province] [city]
cheap flights to [destination]	[make] [model] for sale	[city] [state province] motels
flights [departure] to [destination]	[year] [make] [model] for sale	downtown [city] hotels
[departure] airport	car rental [pickup location]	[state province] quinta inn [city]
flights to [destination] from [departure]	reviews on [year] [make] [model]	omni hotel [city]
airlines that fly to [destination]	rent [state province] [car type]	hilton [city]
[maximum stops] flights to [destination]	[year] [make] [model] [body style]	hotels [state province] [city] [country]

Table 3: Query Patterns Generalized using Form Clusters

	Precision	Recall	F_1
Pattern-based	0.832	0.830	0.830
Supervised-approach	0.864	0.848	0.847

Table 4: Comparison of Performance with Supervised Approach

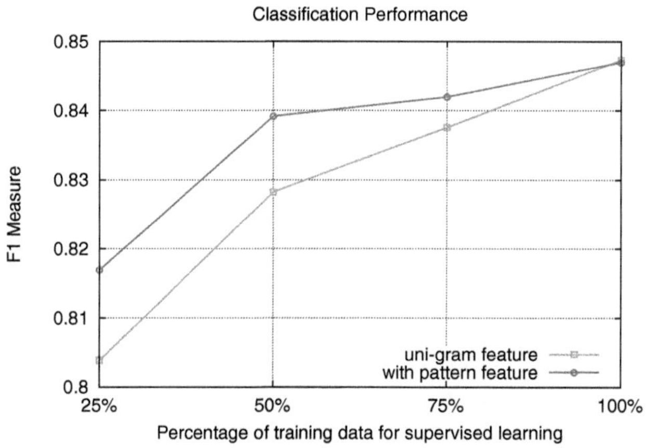

Figure 10: Comparison of Performance for Different Feature Settings

approach. We can see that the supervised approach is slightly better than our approach in terms of F1 measure. We also found that our pattern-based approach has a higher precision (85%) than the supervised approach (79%) on transactional category, but lower recall (80% compared to 95%). This is reasonable, since the performance of pattern-based approach is limited to the coverage of patterns. In this experiment, some queries in test data can not be covered by any pattern, thus the pattern-based approach has a low recall comparing with the supervised approach.

Furthermore, we examine whether our unsupervised pattern-based approach can help supervised learning approach. Besides uni-gram features used in the SVM classifier, we incorporate "pattern matching" as a new feature. Particularly, we add a new feature named "PATTERN". For a query, if it is classified into transactional query by the pattern-based approach, the value of "PATTERN" for this query is set to be 1, otherwise, 0. Figure 10 shows the F_1 values when different percentages of training data are used for two feature settings:only uni-gram features(uni-gram feature) and including pattern as feature (with pattern feature). We can see that including pattern matching feature improves the classification performance, particulary when small amount of training data are used. The improvement becomes larger while less training data are used. This is reasonable, since supervised learning approaches rely on the amount of training data. More training data can produce better result. The smaller the scale of training data is, the more valuable other information is.

6. RELATED WORK

By studying user behavior in search engine logs, Broder [4] and Rose [24] divide user queries into three different categories, informational, navigational and transactional (noted as resource type by Rose). Several previous works [5, 19, 2] show that it is feasible to optimize search engines' performance by adopting specific strategy and ranking method for informational and navigational queries. However, how to predict query type is an open research problem and many researchers have proposed different methods to tackle it. Kang and Kim [17] focus on the classification of informational and navigational queries. They manually separate documents into two sets, content pages and site entry pages. The difference of query term distribution, mutual information, anchor text usage rate and Part of Speech (POS) tagging information over these two document sets are used to predict query type. The authors also extend their method to classify transactional queries in [16]. They use a supervised learning approach with the help of webpages whose title or linked anchor text contains the query. Jansen *et al.* [13] conduct a comprehensive study on query type using different search engines' log. They adopt Broder's classification of query types and further propose a three-level hierarchy classification for user search intents. Furthermore, they manually derive rules for each category to support the automatic query type classification. Lee *et al.* [20] propose two groups of features to predict if the user goal is informational or navigational. They use user-click log to compute the click distribution and the average number of clicks per query. They also use the distribution of anchor text which contains the query to be classified. Later, Liu *et al.* [22] extend Lee's work [20] and extract another two click features from search engine click through log: N Clicks Satisfied evidence and Top n Results Satisfied evidence. A decision tree method is adopted for learning the model and prediction on new queries. As we have mentioned in the previous section, most of the existing methods rely on manual efforts to prepare training data.

In this work, we leverage user clicks on webpage forms to classify transactional queries. In database area, the webpage form is regarded as query interface of *Deep Web* database. There exist some research work of integrating multiple databases, such as WISE [11, 12] and MetaQuerier [10]. In [15, 23], query interface is modeled as a flat collection of fields. Each field is regarded as a triple tuple with a label, field type, and a finite collection of values. Later on, [23] proposes to use *attributes* to group sets of related fields together. [7] uses a hierarchical approach by building a hierarchy tree for each query interface in order to have the structured representation. The matching of Web query interface has also been extensively studied. Generally, there are two kinds of matching methods. [27] uses content information of fields in the query interface, e.g., labels, names and domain values to compute the similarity between two fields. Next, a clustering algorithm is used to group similar fields together. [8, 9] adopt a correlation mining approach to match fields. They calculate the co-occurrence relationship between fields and infer the matching relationship between them.

There are many log mining research works incorporating toolbar log data. For example, [3] mines toolbar log data to suggest authoritative websites for search queries. In this work, we leverage the relationship between search query and online forms clicked by users after they examine the search results. According to our knowledge, we are the first to exploit form click information from tool bar log and use it to do transactional query type classification.

The concept of query pattern, also known as query template, is used in a few recent works. Agarwal *et al.* [1] mines query templates in a specific domain, with domain attributes and seed queries manually provided. In [26], Szpektor *et al.* uses query templates to provide recommendations for long-tail queries. Unlike these works, our work aims to automatically generate query patterns and further use these patterns as a classifier for transactional queries.

7. CONCLUSION AND FUTURE WORK

In this work, we proposed an unsupervised method for transactional query classification. The method is based on the relationship between search queries and online forms on webpages. By mining the query-form click graph which is built from toolbar log data, we were able to identify a set of high quality transactional queries. Also, by leveraging the contents contained by forms, we generalized the identified transactional queries into patterns, which were then used to predict queries not covered by log data. Experiments conducted on real data set showed that our method can identify high quality transactional queries effectively. The patterns extracted from the transactional queries and forms were also promising in predicting the type of unseen queries.

In future, we plan to optimize search engines' performance by considering Web *forms* in search result ranking. We also plan to build a system to help users directly complete their transactions with Web forms, instead of using search engine.

8. REFERENCES

[1] G. Agarwal, G. Kabra, and K. C.-C. Chang. Towards rich query interpretation: walking back and forth for mining query templates. In *WWW '10*, pages 1–10, 2010. ACM.

[2] K. Bharat and M. R. Henzinger. Improved algorithms for topic distillation in a hyperlinked environment. In *SIGIR '98*, pages 104–111, 1998. ACM.

[3] M. Bilenko and R. W. White. Mining the search trails of surfing crowds: identifying relevant websites from user activity. In *WWW '08*, pages 51–60, 2008. ACM.

[4] A. Broder. A taxonomy of web search. *SIGIR Forum*, 36(2):3–10, 2002.

[5] N. Craswell, D. Hawking, and S. Robertson. Effective site finding using link anchor information. In *SIGIR '01*, pages 250–257, 2001. ACM.

[6] L. Dice. Measures of the amount of ecologic association between species. *Ecology*, 26(3), 1945.

[7] E. C. Dragut, T. Kabisch, C. Yu, and U. Leser. A hierarchical approach to model web query interfaces for web source integration. *Proc. VLDB Endow.*, 2(1), 2009.

[8] B. He and K. C.-C. Chang. Automatic complex schema matching across web query interfaces: A correlation mining approach. *ACM Trans. Database Syst.*, 31(1), 2006.

[9] B. He, K. C.-C. Chang, and J. Han. Discovering complex matchings across web query interfaces: a correlation mining approach. In *KDD '04*, pages 148–157, 2004. ACM.

[10] B. He, Z. Zhang, and K. C.-C. Chang. Metaquerier: querying structured web sources on-the-fly. In *SIGMOD '05*, pages 927–929, 2005. ACM.

[11] H. He, W. Meng, C. Yu, and Z. Wu. Wise-integrator: an automatic integrator of web search interfaces for e-commerce. In *VLDB '2003*, pages 357–368, 2003.

[12] H. He, W. Meng, C. Yu, and Z. Wu. Wise-integrator: a system for extracting and integrating complex web search interfaces of the deep web. In *VLDB '05*, pages 1314–1317. VLDB Endowment, 2005.

[13] B. J. Jansen, D. L. Booth, and A. Spink. Determining the informational, navigational, and transactional intent of web queries. *Inf. Process. Manage.*, 44(3):1251–1266, 2008.

[14] T. Joachims. *Making large-Scale SVM Learning Practical. Advances in Kernel Methods - Support Vector Learning, B. Schølkopf and C. Burges and A. Smola (ed.).* MIT-Press, 1999.

[15] O. Kaljuvee, O. Buyukkokten, H. Garcia-Molina, and A. Paepcke. Efficient web form entry on pdas. In *WWW '01*, pages 663–672, 2001. ACM.

[16] I.-H. Kang. Transactional query identification in web search. In *AIRS*, 2005.

[17] I.-H. Kang and G. Kim. Query type classification for web document retrieval. In *SIGIR '03*, pages 64–71, 2003. ACM.

[18] J. M. Kleinberg. Authoritative sources in a hyperlinked environment. *J. ACM*, 46(5):604–632, 1999.

[19] W. Kraaij, T. Westerveld, and D. Hiemstra. The importance of prior probabilities for entry page search. In *SIGIR '02*, pages 27–34, 2002. ACM.

[20] U. Lee, Z. Liu, and J. Cho. Automatic identification of user goals in web search. In *WWW '05*, pages 391–400, 2005.

[21] V. LEVENSHTEIN. Binary codes capable of correcting deletions, insertions and reversals. *Sov. Phys. Dokl.*, 10(8):707–710, 1966.

[22] Y. Liu, M. Zhang, L. Ru, and S. Ma. Automatic query type identification based on click-through information. In *LNCS 4182*, pages 593–600, 2006.

[23] S. Raghavan and H. Garcia-Molina. Crawling the hidden web. In *VLDB '2001*, pages 129–138, 2001.

[24] D. E. Rose and D. Levinson. Understanding user goals in web search. In *WWW '04*, pages 13–19, 2004. ACM.

[25] D. Sullivan. Nielsen/netratings search engine ratings. *Available from http://www.searchenginewatch.com/reports/netratings.html*, 2006.

[26] I. Szpektor, A. Gionis, and Y. Maarek. Improving recommendation for long-tail queries via templates. In *WWW '11*, pages 47–56, 2011. ACM.

[27] W. Wu, C. Yu, A. Doan, and W. Meng. An interactive clustering-based approach to integrating source query interfaces on the deep web. In *SIGMOD '04*, pages 95–106.

Assigning Documents to Master Sites in Distributed Search

Roi Blanco
Yahoo! Research
Barcelona, Spain
roi@yahoo-inc.com

B. Barla Cambazoglu
Yahoo! Research
Barcelona, Spain
barla@yahoo-inc.com

Flavio P. Junqueira
Yahoo! Research
Barcelona, Spain
fpj@yahoo-inc.com

Ivan Kelly
Yahoo! Research
Barcelona, Spain
ivank@yahoo-inc.com

Vincent Leroy
Yahoo! Research
Barcelona, Spain
leroy@yahoo-inc.com

ABSTRACT

An appealing solution to scale Web search with the growth of the Internet is the use of distributed architectures. Distributed search engines rely on multiple sites deployed in distant regions across the world, where each site is specialized to serve queries issued by the users of its region. This paper investigates the problem of assigning each document to a master site. We show that by leveraging similarities between a document and the activity of the users, we can accurately detect which site is the most relevant to place a document. We conduct various experiments using two document assignment approaches, showing performance improvements of up to 20.8% over a baseline technique which assigns the documents to search sites based on their language.

Categories and Subject Descriptors

H.3.3 [**Information Storage Systems**]: Information Retrieval Systems

General Terms

Design, Experimentation, Performance

Keywords

Multi-site web search engine, distributed index, document assignment

1. INTRODUCTION

Web search requires building very large data centers, comprising a large number of computer resources [2]. As the Web grows in size and extent, it becomes necessary for a search engine to increase its capacity, and one typical solution is to rely upon more resources of an existing data center. One important drawback of this solution is requiring larger data centers over time, which presents severe limitations regarding space, energy provision, and connectivity. A viable alternative is to design the search engine to enable new, smaller data centers to be incorporated when more capacity becomes necessary. This design has the advantage of not requiring data centers to grow over time. Designing a search engine to distribute its functionality across multiple data centers, however, is not trivial since most techniques used in commercial search engines to date rely upon tightly coupled computer resources to operate efficiently. Recent work has focused on moving away from this paradigm and devising techniques that enable the design of efficient distributed search engines [1, 6].

A distributed search engine is comprised of geographically distributed data centers (sites), and users submit queries to the closest location, where closest can be either with respect to geographic or network distance. Upon receiving a user query, a site either processes a query locally or forwards it to other sites for processing. Techniques for deciding when to forward a query are consequently critical to the performance of such a distributed search engine [1, 7].

Forwarding queries, however, introduces extra latency to the processing of a query, so ideally a site is able to process many of its received queries locally to avoid the extra latency of processing remotely. To enable sites to process many queries locally, it is necessary to select documents to index in a site that are among the top results of queries that are submitted to the site. At the same time, to avoid replicating all documents across all sites, which leads to sites growing with the Web, it is necessary that we carefully select the documents that a site indexes. Such a mechanism to select documents for a site must use some metric of relevance to determine the importance of documents to a given geographic region. Some previous work has proposed techniques for distributed index construction [12, 14] and partitioning [10, 11, 13, 15] over a cluster of computers within a search site, thus targeting a local setting. The only work we are aware of that targets distributed settings is the one of Brefeld *et al.*, which uses machine-learning techniques to replicate documents across sites and are able to forward only 4% of the queries while indexing in each site 55% of documents, on average [4].

Contributions. We argue for an approach consisting of two steps for the construction of the distributed indexes. The first step is assigning a document to exactly one site,

CIKM'11, October 24–28, 2011, Glasgow, Scotland, UK.

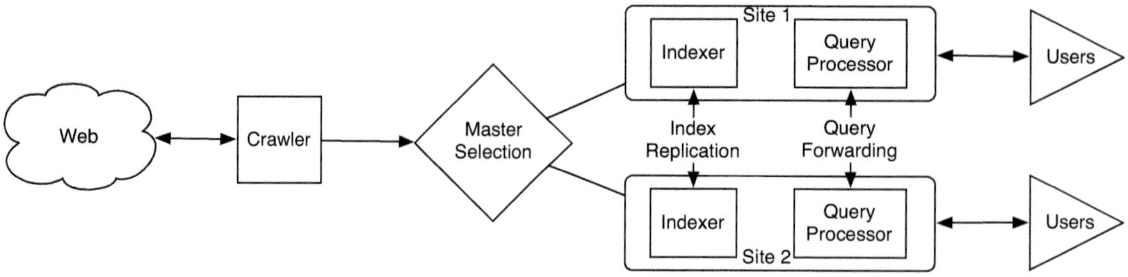

Figure 1: Architecture of a distributed search engine

the document's *master site*. The master site is responsible for indexing the document, which ensures that each crawled document exists in the global search index. The second step consists of enabling sites to replicate documents in a site that is not the master site to enhance the performance of the search engine. Having a master for each document simplifies the design of the replication strategy: each site can make local decisions about replication and document masters guarantee that at least one site indexes a given crawled document. As our experiments show, assigning documents to sites using document content alone is difficult and consequently popularity information is key for efficient replication. Separating mastership and replication, consequently, leads to a more efficient utilization of indexer resources, since sites replicate documents only once they have sufficient evidence of interest from their local users.

This work focuses on the selection of document masters and replication techniques are outside the scope. An efficient master selection strategy assigns documents to sites where users are most likely to access them. Having master sites also enables other sites to arbitrarily add and delete documents for which they are not masters without compromising the coverage of the search engine. Since master sites index the documents assigned to them, we guarantee that every crawled document is indexed by at least one site.

In our evaluation, we consider three approaches to partition the index across master sites. The first one assigns documents to sites using their language, and we use it as a baseline. The second approach uses KL divergence to evaluate the similarity between the distribution of terms in the new document and a description of each site. This description can be either extracted from the queries of the users, or from the documents given as results. Finally, we consider a metric based on cache invalidation to estimate the impact of the document on each site of the search engine. We evaluate these techniques over a large document collection and a query set obtained from a commercial search engine. Our results indicate a 20.8% overall improvement over our baseline, as well as up to 88% of the optimal performance under some document popularity conditions. This result provides evidence that a tight integration with the search engine with access to user feedback significantly improves the accuracy of documents' placement.

Roadmap. The remainder of this paper is organized as follows. Section 2 discusses the high-level architecture we consider for distributed search engines. In Section 3, we present the document assignment techniques we evaluated. We describe the experimental setup in Section 4 and report our results in Section 5. Section 6 contains a discussion of practical implementation aspects. Finally, we discuss related work in Section 7 and conclude the paper in Section 8.

2. ARCHITECTURE

We consider a distributed search engine deployed in several regions across the world. We refer to the sites of a distributed search engine as $\mathcal{S}$, while $\mathcal{D}$ is the set of documents it processes. Fig. 1 presents an overview of the search engine. We now describe the different components of the search engine as well as their interactions.

2.1 Crawler

A search engine discovers and acquires content through a crawler. The main research challenge in multi-site Web crawling is to partition the Web document collection across multiple search sites so that pages can be crawled faster, due to the improved network proximity between the search sites and Web servers. Gao *et al.* formulates this problem as a geographically focused Web crawling problem [8].

In this paper, we do not evaluate crawling performance. Hence, for the sake of simplicity, we consider the case of a single crawler. Once a document has been fetched by the crawler, it is sent to an indexer in order to be added to the inverted index of the search engine. The transition from the crawler to an indexer is the main focus of this paper. The index is divided among the sites of the distributed search engine. Hence, the crawler has to decide which sites should index the document. In Brefeld *et al.*'s work [4], the crawler selects multiple sites for each document through a machine learning model. In this paper, we propose an approach to select a unique site for each document. We call this site the master site of the document. We formally define this problem in Section 3.1.

2.2 Query processor

Processing queries in a distributed search engine is a challenging task. The result quality is crucial to ensure user satisfaction. The results computed by the search engine should not be affected by the distribution of the index among several sites. The main technique investigated so far is query forwarding [1, 7]. A search site first computes results using its local index and then determines through heuristics if the other sites may have different documents that would be ranked higher. If that is the case, the query is forwarded in order to compute more accurate results. The heuristic may overestimate the scores of the other sites to achieve a result similar in quality to that of a centralized setup.

While forwarding a query can improve the quality of the results, this may increase the response time of the search engine as well as the computational load. It is therefore crucial to reduce the number of forwarded queries. This can be done both by improving the accuracy of the score estimation heuristics and by ensuring that documents relevant to the users of a site are present in its local index. In this paper, we assume the existence of a query forwarding algorithm with an associated heuristic [1, 7]. The content of the index of a site is the direct consequence of the master selection performed by the crawler. Hence, we evaluate the accuracy of the master selection process by computing the proportion of results served by a site that was present in its local index.

2.3 Indexer and replicator

An indexer extracts terms from documents and generates an inverted index in order to match documents to queries. Each site has its own indexer which receives documents from the crawler according to the master selection process. An indexer has a maximum capacity, due to storage, memory, or computational limits. Artificially limiting the size of an index can also be an efficient way of reducing the query response time, as smaller indexes are faster to process. Each document is assigned to a master which is responsible for keeping the document in its index. The forwarding mechanism implemented by the query processor ensures that a document matching a query is always taken into account in ranking, even when the document is indexed in another site.

The popularity of Web pages follows a power law, a few Web pages are extremely popular and constitute most of the search results. If these documents were indexed only by their master site, any query matching one of them and issued at another site would always have to be forwarded. This would degrade the performance of the search engine. As a consequence, the master selection process is used in conjunction with a replication algorithm. After indexing the documents that are assigned to itself, each site uses its remaining index capacity to index other documents that are assigned to other sites but are frequently accessed by its users. This process replicates popular documents at each site. Still, contrary to Baeza-Yates *et al.*'s approach [1], the set of replicated documents is not statically determined and common to all sites. Each site can locally decide which documents to replicate, and this decision takes into account the activities of the users of that site in particular. The replication decisions are local. As each document has a master that maintains it in its index, a replicated document can be deleted without synchronization with the other sites, it will not be evicted from the distributed search engine.

This paper focuses on the problem of selecting a master for each document. While the replication mechanism is crucial for the performance of the search engine, we leave this study as part of future work. Since the master of a document is in charge of maintaining it, it is important to accurately assign it to the site where users are most likely to access it.

3. DOCUMENT ASSIGNMENT

3.1 Problem definition

We consider the problem of selecting exactly one site for each document while crawling. This site is referred to as the *master* of the document, and it is responsible for keeping this document in its index. The existence of a master site guarantees the recall of the search engine and simplifies the index replication process.

$$master : \mathcal{D} \rightarrow \mathcal{S}$$

Without loss of generality, defining the choice of a master site is equivalent to providing the crawler with a function *mScore* such that:

$$mScore : \mathcal{D} \times \mathcal{S} \rightarrow \mathbb{R}$$
$$master(D_j) = \arg\max_{S_i \in \mathcal{S}} mScore(D_j, S_i)$$

The goal of the master selection process is to place documents in sites where they are likely to be requested by users. Therefore, $mScore(D_j, S_i)$ should produce higher scores when it predicts that the document D_j matches the interests of the users of site S_i.

3.2 Document language

The language of a document is a good indicator of which region could be interested in it. Regional documents are more likely to be requested from the countries whose language is the same. Brefeld *et al.* [4] use the languages as one of the features of a machine learning algorithm. They observe that the language of a document has a large impact in the precision of the document's placement. In our experiments, we use a commercial language classifier to assign a language to each document.

Using past search engine activity, we compute the following conditional probability: given that a document in a language L_j is returned as a result to a user, what is the probability that the user is from site S_i? The index partitioner computes the language of new documents and assigns each of them to the site with the highest probability. In this case, we approximate *mScore* with $p(S_i|L_j)$. In the evaluation, we refer to this solution as LANG.

3.3 Document assignment by likelihood

While the language of a document leverages, to some extent, the content of the document, the language is a coarse-grain information. It would be possible to achieve a better precision by taking into account all the terms in the document. Hence, we propose to compute *mScore* using a probability estimation. In general, the optimum placement for a document D_j at a master site S_i depends on the queries that will be issued in the future Q_i^f in which D_j appears among the top results. We make use of two sources of information: C_i is a random vector that represents the content of site S_i, and Q_i is a random vector representing the most recent recent query stream processed by S_i. Both these informations can be extracted from the cache of the search engines or its query logs. That is, we want to select the most probable site maximizing the following log-likelihood:

$$\log p(S_i|D_j) = \int \log p(S_i|Q_i^f, D_j) p(Q_i^f|D_j) dQ_i^f$$
$$= \int \log p(C_i, Q_i|D_j, Q_i^f) + \log p(Q_i^f|D_j) dQ_i^f.$$

In order to estimate Q_i^f, we make use of Q_i as an approximation of the future query stream, and we have

$$\log p(S_i|D_j) \approx \int \log p(C_i, Q_i|D_j, Q_i) + \log p(Q_i|D_j) dQ_i \quad (1)$$
$$\approx \log p(C_i|D_j) + \frac{1}{|Q_i|} \sum_{q_z \in Q_i} \log p(q_z|D_j) . \quad (2)$$

Here, we assume that the queries in the stream are conditionally independent given a document.

This formulation has two components: one that uses the contents of a given site and its relatedness to the document $p(C_i|D_j)$ and another one that uses the available query stream Q_i as a source of evidence. We relate the former probability with the *term distribution* of the site, and the latter as the fraction of queries that are *invalidated* by a given document, as explained next. We experiment how both probabilities perform for the problem of master assignment independently and we combine them later on.

3.3.1 Document as a query

Our first classification method stems directly from the estimation of $p(C_i|D_j)$ (Eq. (2)), which assigns a document D_j to a master site S_i based on the likelihood of observing the content C_i at the site S_i given the content of D_j. It is possible to compute the likelihood of the content to the document using a similarity function, in the same way standard language models for IR score documents with respect to their likelihood to a query. In this case, the whole contents of the site plays the role of the document and the document to be indexed as the query. We employ a bag of words representation for the document to be indexed where C_i is the concatenation of all content of S_i. The rationale is that if the contents of the documents returned by a site matches the queries it receives, we should assign a new document to the data center that has the closest term distribution.

To estimate $p(C_i|D_i)$, we employ the language-model-based KL divergence [16], which measures how similar a certain distribution is (query) with respect to a reference distribution (document). We smooth the unigram language model counts of both the document and site contents using Dirichlet priors smoothing [17]. This ranking function contains a tunable parameter μ that controls the amount of probability mass that is assigned to unseen terms:

$$mScore(D_j, S_i; \mu) = KL(D_j||C_i; \mu).$$

In our experiments, we consider two different ways to represent the content of a search site. For the first one, which we call KL-D, we use the content of the documents returned as results to the users of the site. The second approach, KL-Q, directly uses the term distribution of user queries to represent the content of the site, as an approximation of the most recent term distribution. It is important to notice that both of these approaches are directly driven by user activity and not influenced by the master selection process. An alternative approach could be to use the documents indexed by a site to represent its content. A drawback of this approach is that previous indexing decisions would influence the future ones and mis-classification error would affect future decisions degrading the performance over time. We therefore discarded this possibility in our experiments and focus on using the term distribution in the cache contents only.

3.3.2 Cache invalidation

The second classification method estimates the probability of $p(Q_i|D_j)$ (Eq. (1)). The likelihood of the query stream to the document has been studied in the past in the context of *cache invalidation*. Search engines cache the results served to the users in order to avoid computing multiple times the answer to a given query. While this increases the performance of the search engine, it also raises the problem of results staleness [?], especially in the case of incremental indexing. Cache entries need to be invalidated in order to reflect the changes in the index. Blanco *et al.* [3] experiment different cache invalidation policies to strike a good balance between the risk of serving stale results and the hit-rate of the cache. In practice, upon adding a document to the index, the search engine matches the terms in the document with queries present in the cache and if the document is expected to be in the top-k of a query, its cache entry is invalidated. Then, we define $p(Q_i|D_j)$ as the fraction of queries in the cache of S_i that would be invalidated by D_j, that is, D_j would be in the top-k results of those queries:

$$mScore(D_j, S_i) = \frac{1}{|Q_i|} \sum_{q_z:Q_i} I(q_z||D_j) ,$$

where $I(q_z||D_j)$ is 1 if D_j would be in the top-k results for q_z and 0 otherwise.

The query cache of a search site is a good indicator of the interests of the users in its region. Hence, we propose to use the number of cache invalidation caused by a document at a given site as an indicator of its relevance to this site. If the document would have had a high impact on the results of the past queries, it is likely to appear in the future results as well. The main advantage of this approach is that, contrary to the approach presented in Section 3.3.1, it does not concatenate all the queries into a bag of words. Since the co-occurrence of terms is preserved, we expect cache invalidation to have a slightly better performance. In the remainder of this paper, we refer to the assignment based on cache invalidation as CACHE.

4. EXPERIMENTAL SETUP

4.1 Search engine

4.1.1 Distributed search engine

We consider a distributed search engine, such as the one described in Section 2. We devise a configuration in which the search engine is deployed on five sites $\mathcal{S} = \{S_1 \ldots S_5\}$, distributed over different continents. While the sites are located in different countries, some countries have people speaking the same language, which complicates the assignment of documents. We assume that the query processor of the search engine implements a query forwarding scheme (Section 2). As a consequence, given a query and a document collection, the results computed by the distributed search engine are equal to the ones returned by a centralized one, and do not depend on the site that the query originates from. Thus, we perform our experiments using a centralized commercial search engine, but label each query with the site it originates from and label each document with the site that is selected as the document's master.

4.1.2 Ranking function

The ranking function of a search engine is a key component, as it directly impacts the quality of the results returned to the users. While the main focus or our work is not related to the relevance of the results of the search engine, it is important to consider a realistic ranking function because it impacts the distribution of the documents' popularity. We rely on the following ranking function to assign a score to a document d with respect to a query q:

$$score(d, q) = \lambda \times relevance(d, q) + (1 - \lambda) \times quality(d)$$

The ranking function assesses both the relevance of the document and its quality, and weights them using the λ parameter. We use BM25 to compute the relevance, while the quality of a document is evaluated through a link-based metric. We optimize its parameters using a separate training dataset that contains queries with relevance information and keep the best parameters for our own test evaluation. While BM25 and KL divergence are both effective ranking functions and therefore, exhibit correlations in their behavior, it is important to notice that we use a completely different setup to rank documents in the search engine and to assign documents to sites. Hence, our results are not specific to a ranking function and can be applied in more general cases.

4.2 Dataset

4.2.1 Documents

We use a random sample of 31,599,910 Web pages obtained from the Web crawl of a commercial search engine. We randomly split the documents into a training and a testing set, holding 75% and 25% of the documents, respectively.

4.2.2 Queries

We rely on query logs to simulate user activity. The log consists of consecutive queries issued in a single day to different frontends of a commercial search engine. We only consider queries of less than 20 terms where the users clicks a result on the first page of results. The queries are converted to lower case, and duplicate terms are removed. Each query is labeled with the country of the user who issued the query. We generate a collection of queries for each site of the search engine by keeping queries originating from the country of the site and, when this is not sufficient, from neighboring countries. We sample a total of 7,023,102 queries, which we equally split for training and testing for each region. As queries are sorted in arrival order, the first half of the queries constitute the training set, while the rest forms the test set.

4.2.3 Document popularity

In our experiments, we assume that the top-10 documents returned by the search engine to a query are all relevant. We evaluate the training queries on an index containing the training documents. The popularity of a document is the number of times it occurs in the results of a query. We display the distribution of the popularity of the documents in the training set in Fig. 2. As already observed in many search engine studies (e.g., by Brefeld *et al.* [4]), the distribution follows a power law: a few documents are very popular while many documents have a very low frequency in top search results. From all the documents in the training set, only 4,370,608 appear at least once in the results of the training queries. The documents in the test set exhibit a similar popularity pattern, where 2,729,205 of them appear in the results of the test queries. Given the large amount of diversity in document popularity, it seems that a reactive replication scheme may be more efficient than a static replication scheme, determined at the discovery time of the document. Precisely predicting the popularity of a new document is indeed a difficult problem. In the approach we propose, the search engine first selects a single master site for a

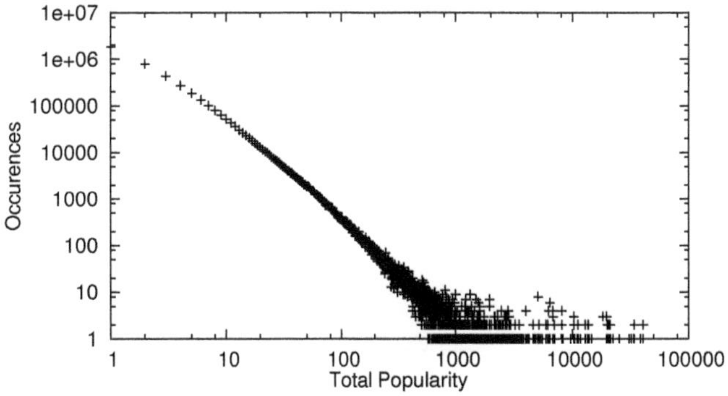

Figure 2: Document popularity distribution in the training set

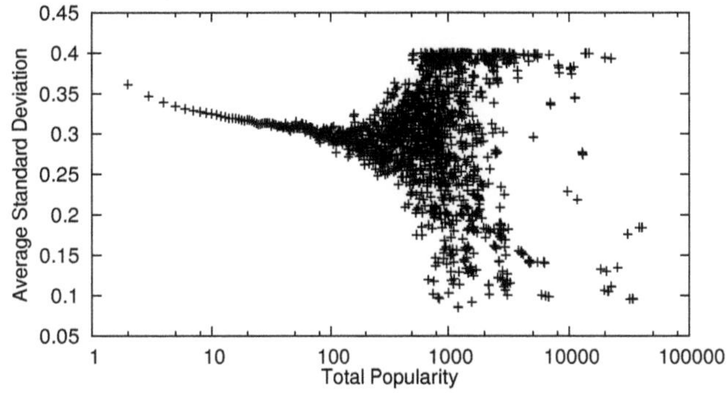

Figure 3: Divergence of document popularity distribution in the training set

document, and then replicates the documents depending on the observed popularity of the document.

As each query is labeled with the search engine site it originates from, it is also possible to study the popularity of documents with respect to the users of each site. In particular, we are interested in knowing if documents are equally popular among all the sites, or if they only of interest to users from a particular site. For each document, we compute the normalized standard deviation of its popularity among the five sites of the search engine. We average the divergence of the documents that exhibit the same total popularity and display the results in Fig. 3. Given the power law distribution of the document popularity, the right part of the graph contains a lot of noise, as the averages are computed from very few samples. Nevertheless, the results show a clear trend: popular documents present a lower deviation in their popularity among the different sites. This means that popular documents are more likely to be queried by users from different sites. Still, the average standard deviation remains high (above 0.2), even for very popular documents. This shows that, while some documents are accessed uniformly by users from all sites, many popular documents are accessed by users of a given site in particular. This observation confirms the validity of our approach, the access pattern of documents shows that they indeed have a natural master site. Furthermore, as some documents, while being very popular, remain local to one site, this also argues in favor of local replication decisions, as opposed to using global popularity statistics.

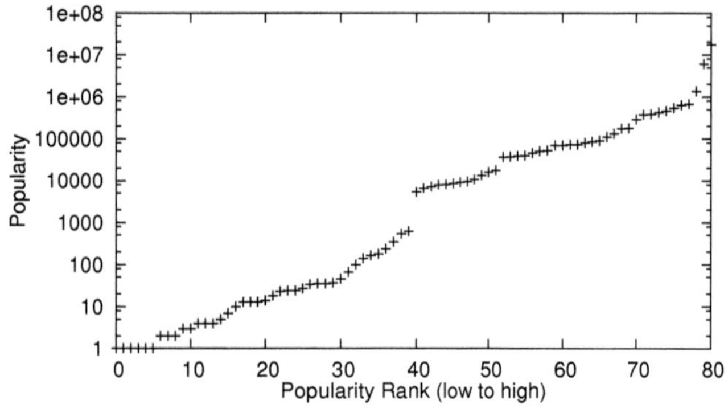

Figure 4: Popularity of the languages

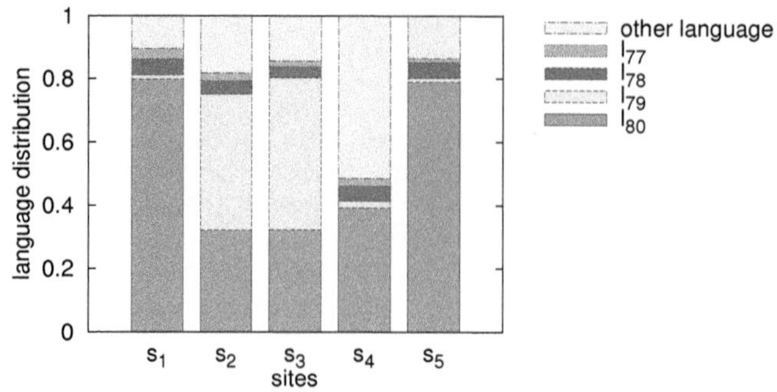

Figure 5: Distribution of the most popular languages at the different sites

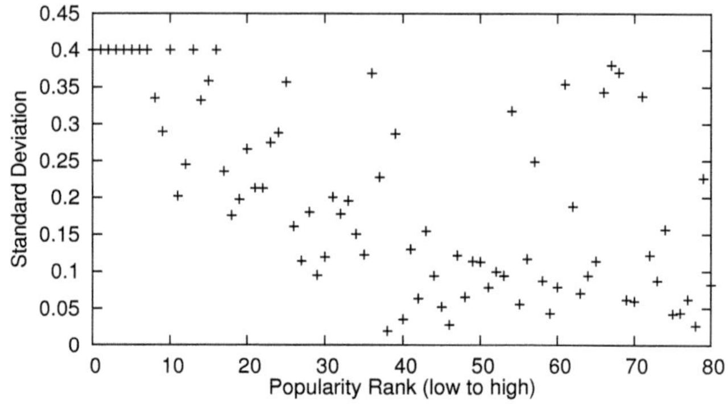

Figure 6: Divergence of the languages with respect to their popularity

5. EXPERIMENTS

5.1 Metrics and theoretical baselines

The main focus of our work is the selection of a master site for each document indexed by the search engine. We rely on existing query forwarding algorithms to process the queries (Section 2). Therefore, we do not evaluate the quality of the results returned by the search engine. As explained by Brefeld *et al.* [4], distributed search engines should achieve a good trade-off between the amount of data indexed by each site and the proportion of forwarded queries. In the approach we propose, a document is only indexed by its master site. Hence, the total size of the indexes is fixed. Our main evaluation criterion is the locality of the results delivered by a search site. The first metric we use to evaluate the quality of our results is the proportion of documents returned as results by a site that are part of its index:

$$locality(S_i) = \frac{1}{\sum_{Q_j \in \mathcal{Q}_i} |result(Q_j)|} \sum_{Q_j \in \mathcal{Q}_i} |results(Q_j) \cap \mathcal{D}_i|,$$

where $\mathcal{D}_i$ is the set of test documents assigned to S_i, $\mathcal{Q}_i$ is the set of test queries submitted to S_i, and $results(Q_j)$ is the set of documents that the search engine returns as a result to query Q_j.

This metric reflects the activity of the search engine, as each query is taken into account with the same weight. However, making an error in the assignment of a popular document has more impact, since it affects more queries. We define a second metric that takes into account each document with an equal weight. For each document, we sort the sites according to the popularity of the document at each one of them. A perfect master assignment would index the document at the first site of this list. We compute the rank of the site selected by the feature in this list and score it using NDCG [9]. We then average this value over the collection of documents.

From this information, we also compute theoretical baselines in order to facilitate the interpretation of our results: BEST always indexes a document at the site where it is most popular, WORST indexes at the site where the document is least popular, and RAND selects a site at random.

5.2 Language

We observe 81 different languages in our training data. In Fig. 4, we display the popularity of each language in the query results. The most popular language represents 58% of the results of the queries and the second one has a 20% share. This clearly demonstrates an imbalance in the popularity of the languages, i.e., some languages are dominant and widely used while others are very rare. The language classifier assigns the *unknown* label to 2.2% of the results.

We examine the distribution of languages in the results of each site in Fig. 5. The overall most popular language, l_{80}, represents a large fraction (over 30%) of the results returned by each site. However, the second most popular language, l_{79} is mostly used by the users of the sites s_2 and s_3. Over 50% of the results returned by s_4 are not in one of the most frequent languages. This suggests that users in these region tend to use multiple less common languages.

For each language, we compute the probability that the query originated from each site, as explained in Section 3.2. Fig. 6 displays the divergence of these probabilities for the five sites, while Fig. 7 compares the highest probability with the others. These results show that while some languages are clearly localized and match a particular site, many of the most popular languages have a more uniform usage. The lower the divergence of the popularity at each site, the more difficult it is to precisely assign documents to sites solely based on their language. This is problematic as popular languages are difficult to assign, and they represent most of the documents in the Internet.

5.3 Document as a query

We evaluate the performance of KL divergence in assigning documents to sites using different smoothing parameters μ. In Fig. 8, we display the performance of the assignment using the locality metric. It appears that computing KL divergence with respect to the terms in the result documents,

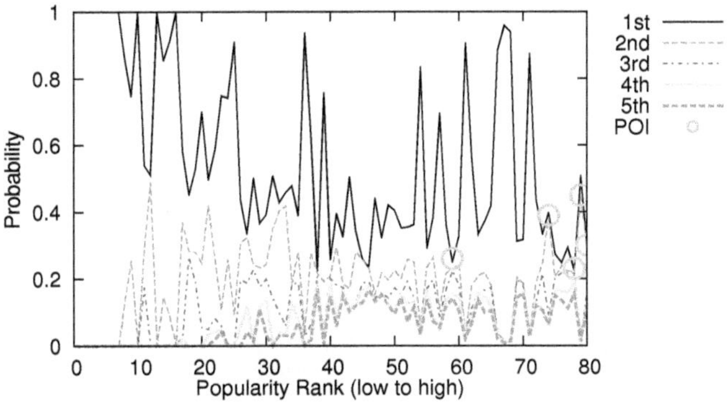

Figure 7: Probabilities of the languages with respect to their popularity

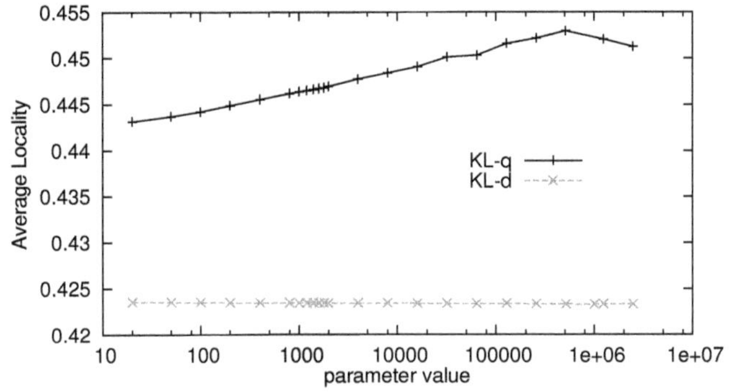

Figure 8: Influence of the μ parameter in KL divergence performance

KL-D, is not affected by the parameter value and maintains a constant performance. On the contrary, KL-Q, which takes into account the terms in the queries, exhibits the maximum performance for $\mu \approx 500{,}000$. We confirm these results by cross-validating on different subsets of the test collections. The performance measurements through NDCG lead to the same conclusions. Hence, we do not report them here. Note that when comparing the performance of KL divergence with other approaches, we only consider the best parameter.

5.4 Cache invalidation

We generate a cache of results at each site using the training queries and documents. For each query, this cache records the number of results as well as the ranking score obtained by the last result. We then simulate the addition of the test documents to the index of each site. Following the strategy of Blanco *et al.* [3], we count the number of cache entries invalidated at each location, weighted by the number of occurrences of the query. Fig. 9 depicts the distribution of the number of invalidations. These results are very similar to the distribution of document popularity and clearly indicate a power-law distribution. This result is not surprising, as the cache invalidation process is very close to the ranking process of the search engine.

We evaluate the divergence of the number of invalidations at each site and present the results in Fig. 10. Once again, this distribution resembles the divergence of the popularity of documents. The similarity between cache invalidation and query processing is encouraging: if the query distribution of the users does not vary too much, the distribution of

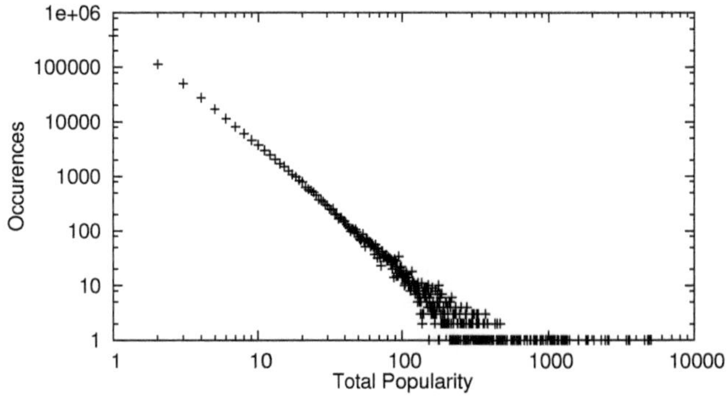

Figure 9: Distribution of the number of invalidations

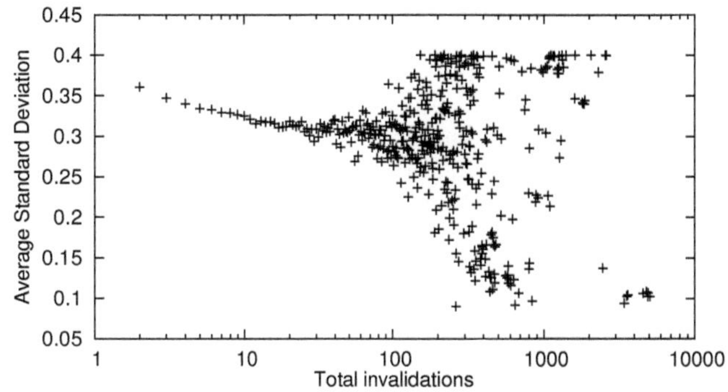

Figure 10: Divergence of cache invalidation distribution

cache invalidations should be a good indicator of the popularity of documents for future queries. However, cache invalidation suffers from the same problem as query processing: some documents have a very low popularity and are never returned in query results. Similarly, a large fraction of documents do not generate any cache invalidation. In our experiments, 648,184 documents cause cache invalidations in at least one site. This means that CACHE can be used to infer a prediction for 24% of the test documents. From these, we also need to remove the documents that do not match any query of the test set although they invalidate cache entries in the training set. This leaves us with 531,646 documents to measure the performance of CACHE.

5.5 Comparison

Table 1 (left) presents the performance of all the features on the full document test dataset. As CACHE cannot be applied on all documents, we perform a separate comparison. The first observation is that the best locality achievable is 72.9%. As the most popular documents are queried from different sites, it is not possible to obtain 100% locality without any replication. Still, this score, while impossible to achieve in practice, remains very high. A random assignment provides 20% locality, since the search engine is deployed on five sites. As few very popular documents are queried from all five sites of the search engine, the worst possible score is not 0%, but 1.2%. LANG, in spite of being a simple feature, achieves 38, 1%. KL-D and KL-Q achieve better performance, with 42, 3% and 45, 3% locality, respectively. While these three features all leverage the content of the document to compute a prediction, KL divergence is more reliable as it learns directly from the behavior of the users. In particular,

feature	All documents		Invalidation subset	
	locality	NDCG	locality	NDCG
BEST	72.9%	0.500	70.6%	0.500
WORST	1.2%	0.031	1.4%	0.031
RAND	20.0%	0.194	20.0%	0.194
LANG	38.1%	0.344	39.5%	0.342
KL-D	42.3%	0.355	46.2%	0.359
KL-Q	45.3%	0.362	48.7%	0.368
CACHE	NA	NA	52.0%	0.368

Table 1: Overall performance

as LANG mostly relies on a dictionary, it does not benefit from particular words such as names and locations. KL-Q outperforms KL-D, which indicates that mining the queries of the users is more reliable than mining the results. This may seem counterintuitive, as this metric is applied on the terms of a new document to index. Hence, it would seem more natural to compare it with terms in other documents. Nevertheless, the queries seem to contain less noise, which increases the precision of the assignment.

Table 1 (right) shows results computed on the set of documents that trigger at least one cache invalidation. These documents have higher quality and are more likely to be accessed in several sites. This explains why BEST scores are lower while all other features, except for RAND, obtain higher results. CACHE obtains the best locality score with 52%. This can be explained by the similarity of the cache invalidation process to the computation of search results.

In Figs. 11 and 12, we evaluate the locality achieved by the features with respect to the popularity of the document. In order to avoid noise, we group together different ranges of popularity. The more popular a document is, the lower BEST scores. Indeed, popular documents have a higher probability to be accessed from different locations. On the left part of the plot, we can see that while LANG has a constant behavior, KL-D, KL-Q and CACHE obtain better results on popular documents. One of the explanations could be that popular documents have a higher quality, which provides these last three features with more terms to leverage. Unpopular documents have more random access patterns and are less reliable due to the lack of samples of users accessing them. Interestingly, around a popularity of 1,000, CACHE achieves a performance very close (88%) to the optimal BEST. The right part of the plot, for very high popularity, exhibits a different behavior. All features but BEST obtain lower scores. On of the possible explanations to this phenomenon is that very popular documents are more universal and are accessed from all locations. Hence, this could be caused by a temporary event that would have reflected in the queries.

5.6 Combination

Our experiments show that CACHE generates the most accurate document placement. However, it cannot be applied on all documents, as some of them do not generate any query invalidation. One simple possibility to increase the precision of master selection overall is to rely on CACHE when this information is available, and otherwise use a more general method, such as KL-Q. This leads to a locality performance of 46.0%, which constitutes an improvement of 20.8% over the language baseline.

As explained in Section 3.3, KL-Q, KL-D and CACHE can be interpreted as probabilities and can therefore be combined with different coefficient. We evaluate this possibility over a wide range of coefficients. Nevertheless, as shown in Fig. 12, these three predictors exhibit a similar behavior and only little gain can be achieved by combining them. We obtain a maximum locality of 52.6% on the documents that generate cache invalidations by combining CACHE and KL-Q. This is unexpected, as both these metrics are based on terms in the queries. More interestingly, combining them has a higher impact on the NDCG performance. This means that combining predictors has a smoothing effect, as fewer false decisions are made.

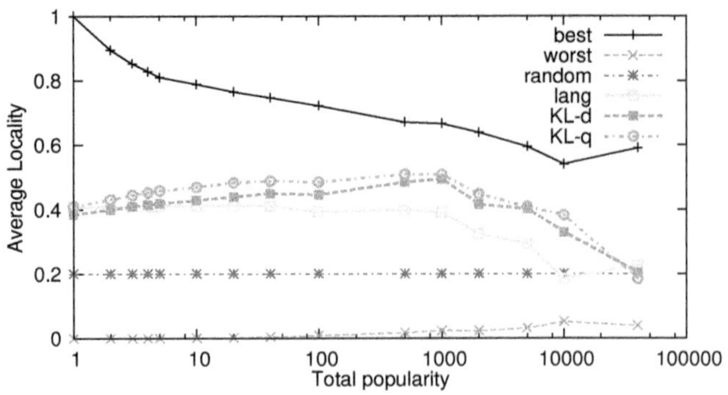

Figure 11: Performance with respect to document popularity (all documents)

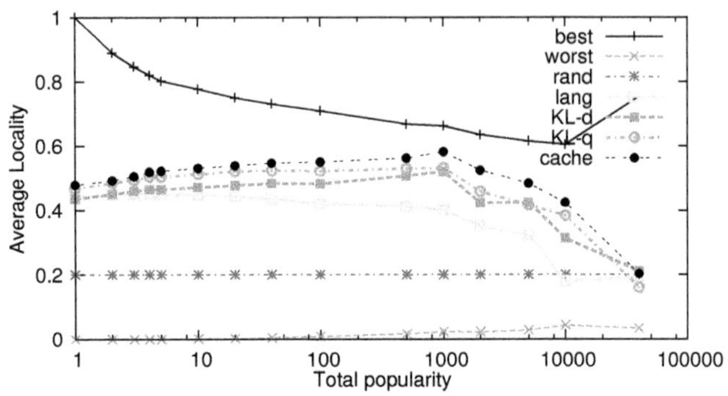

Figure 12: Performance with respect to document popularity (invalidation subset)

6. PRACTICAL CONSIDERATIONS

Throughout this paper, we consider different metrics to assign sites to new documents. We evaluate them on a large collection of data to assess their efficiency. In this section, we discuss the practical implementation aspects.

6.1 Language

The document placement policy is by far the easiest to implement. The only requirement is the presence of a classifier that assigns a document to a language depending on the terms it contains. Most of this information is static. It may be interesting to regularly enrich it with new popular terms, in particular if they differentiate users from different regions. Given its simplicity, this method achieves a reasonable precision. It can be used in contexts where there is little access to the information of the data centers, as reasonable approximations about the language statistics of regions can be obtained from demographic studies. However, if more information can be obtained from the search engine, it is more cost efficient to implement more complex measurements as mistakes in document placement cause query forwarding.

6.2 Document as a query

The computation of KL divergence requires statistics about the content of the different search sites. In this paper, we propose two sources of information: the queries of the users and the content of the results. Aggregating the terms of queries is simpler than extracting data from the documents. Indeed, the later would be a two steps process, in which the list of results is used to extract the documents and obtain their content. To reduce the cost of extracting this information, it is possible to leverage the text from the snippets computed by the search engine. This information does not contain the full document and could constitute an interesting trade-off between document information and query information. Furthermore, snippets of documents are usually cached by search engines, making their access faster.

Our experiments show that using queries to summarize the content of a search site is more efficient. In practice, each search site needs to transfer term statistics about its query log to the crawler. This data should be updated regularly to reflect changes of user interest. This is not problematic, as this data is small, typically in the order of hundreds of megabytes, and can be easily compressed.

6.3 Cache invalidation

Contrary to the other approaches, the number of cache invalidations caused by a document cannot be computed locally by a crawler. A search engine cache typically contains millions of entries, which makes its replication on the crawler impractical [3]. Consequently, the crawler has to transmit the document to each search site to determine how many invalidations this causes. Blanco *et al.* [3] propose an approach to summarize the content of a document and reduce the amount of data transmitted to the cache. Using term frequency statistics, they select the terms that have the highest impact in the ranking function of the search engine. At the cost of a few invalidations misses, this significantly reduces the size of the data representing a document. In this paper, we do not evaluate the impact of such techniques on the index partitioning. Nevertheless, this constitutes a potential optimization for the system, as it would reduce the size of the data transmitted to computed the invalidation scores.

While relying on the number of cache invalidations to estimate the relevance of a document may seem to generate more communications than the other approaches, it is important to notice that cache invalidation is a desirable mechanism in a search engine. This is particularly true if the index is updated incrementally. Therefore, if such a mechanism is already in place, it is possible to use invalidation statistics without generating any additional traffic.

Our experiments demonstrate that metrics based on cache invalidation provide the most accurate information to place documents among several search sites. The main goal of a placement strategy is to increase the locality of the computation of results. Hence, even a small improvement in locality can significantly reduce the traffic caused by query forwarding, as well as the additional processing it incurs. It is difficult to accurately evaluate these costs without implementing a real prototype. Depending on the amount of queries with respect to the number of new documents, the cache invalidation mechanism may compensate part of its bandwidth usage, or even save on network usage overall. Finally, forwarding queries also increases the latency observed by the users. Thus, any gain in document placement accuracy translates into an improvement in quality of service.

7. RELATED WORK

The inverted index partitioning problem is considered by many works in literature [10, 11, 13, 15]. The two commonly used techniques are to partition the index based on document ids or term ids. The main challenge addressed by these works is to distribute the index over a parallel computing system such that both the storage and query processing loads are evenly distributed. All these works assume that the index is distributed over a search cluster located within a single search site. Our work investigates the problem in a geographically distributed setting, where the main problem is to reduce the workload of the search system rather than establishing a load balance across search sites.

In practice, in a multi-site web search engine, partitioning of the index can be performed based on the language or the region of documents. So far, all research works investigated the very simple region-based index partitioning strategy [1, 7]. In these works, the index in each data center is built over the documents that are in the geographical neighborhood of the data center with partial replication of popular documents on all sites. Our technique goes one step beyond these works by taking into account the past query distributions observed in local search sites.

The closest work to ours is the work of Brefeld *et al.*, which proposes a machine learning model to replicate Web documents across data centers [4]. The main difference between this work and our approach is that we aim to achieve an effective one-to-one mapping between documents and sites, whereas the model in [4] replicates a document on many sites. Brefeld *et al.* rely mostly on the language and the region of a document to assign it to several sites. As shown in our experiments in Section 5.2, this can be problematic, as popular languages are used by many users in different regions. In our dataset, the most popular language constitutes over 30% of the results of each search site. An approach purely based on languages is likely to index all documents in this language in all different sites. As a consequence, a large proportion of the indexes will be used to reference low quality documents, solely on the basis of their language. We believe that it is preferable to rely on observed documents popularity before replicating it on many location. Hence, we propose a two phase approach, in which we first select a master, and then replicate the document using real popularity observations. Assigning a master site to each document ensures that it remains in the index, while giving the possibility to the other sites to replicate the document without synchronizing. Our experiments confirm that the language of a document is indeed quite accurate for assigning masters to documents. However, we go one step further by using the distribution of terms in the document to build a more accurate predictor. Finally, our work is more practical in that it does not rely on a learning model, but instead uses some simple statistical evidence about user interests.

In this paper, we rely on KL divergence [17] to evaluate the similarity between a document and the content of a site. In the early stages of our work, we also considered alternative approaches. Callan *et al.* use inference networks to select collections of documents relevant to a given query [5]. In the context of distributed search, this avoid forwarding a query to a site that does not contain any potential result. This algorithm could also be used to determine which site would be most likely to contain a document, and therefore would be a suitable master. We performed evaluations using inference networks. The performance is quite close to the one of KL divergence. Hence, we do not report on these numbers.

8. CONCLUSION

We evaluated two different document assignment techniques for multi-site distributed Web search engines. Compared to a naive baseline, which assigns documents to sites based on documents' language, our techniques achieved a large improvement (20.8%) in increasing the locality of documents. Using cache invalidation knowledge, we achieve up to 88% of the optimal performance when documents are sufficiently popular. This directly impacts the amount of query forwarding needed to compute results, thus improves the quality of service and reduces the cost of the search engine.

The next steps involve designing a dynamic index replication scheme. This work will be facilitated by the presence of a master for each document. This setup favors dynamic policies, in which documents can be easily added and removed from the index to reflect users' interests. Depending on the replication mechanism, it may also be possible to design a master migration procedure, to transfer the responsibility of a document from the master site to a site hosting a replica. We believe that this approach is quite promising as, by adaptively re-partitioning our index, we will be able to capture the temporal patterns of document accesses.

Acknowledgement

This work has been partially supported by the COAST project (ICT-248036), funded by the European Community.

9. REFERENCES

[1] R. Baeza-Yates, A. Gionis, F. Junqueira, V. Plachouras, and L. Telloli. On the feasibility of multi-site web search engines. In *Proceedings of the 18th ACM Conference on Information and Knowledge Management*, pages 425–434, 2009.

[2] L. A. Barroso, J. Dean, and U. Hölzle. Web search for a planet: the Google cluster architecture. *IEEE Micro*, 23(2):22–28, 2003.

[3] R. Blanco, E. Bortnikov, F. P. Junqueira, R. Lempel, L. Telloli, and H. Zaragoza. Caching search engine results over incremental indices. *Proceeding of the 33rd International ACM SIGIR Conference on Research and Development in Information Retrieval*, pages 82–89, 2010.

[4] U. Brefeld, B. B. Cambazoglu, and F. P. Junqueira. Document assignment in multi-site search engines. In *Proceedings of the Fourth ACM International Conference on Web Search and Data Mining*, pages 575–584, 2011.

[5] J. P. Callan, Z. Lu, and W. B. Croft. Searching distributed collections with inference networks. In *Proceedings of the 18th Annual International ACM SIGIR Conference on Research and Development in Information Retrieval*, pages 21–28, 1995.

[6] B. B. Cambazoglu, V. Plachouras, and R. Baeza-Yates. Quantifying performance and quality gains in distributed web search engines. In *Proceedings of the 32nd International ACM SIGIR Conference on Research and Development in Information Retrieval*, pages 411–418, 2009.

[7] B. B. Cambazoglu, E. Varol, E. Kayaaslan, C. Aykanat, and R. Baeza-Yates. Query forwarding in geographically distributed search engines. In *Proceedings of the 33rd International ACM SIGIR Conference on Research and Development in Information Retrieval*, pages 90–97, 2010.

[8] W. Gao, H. C. Lee, and Y. Miao. Geographically focused collaborative crawling. In *Proceedings of the 15th International Conference on World Wide Web*, pages 287–296, 2006.

[9] K. Järvelin and J. Kekäläinen. Cumulated gain-based evaluation of IR techniques. *ACM Trans. Inf. Syst.*, 20:422–446, 2002.

[10] C. Lucchese, S. Orlando, R. Perego, and F. Silvestri. Mining query logs to optimize index partitioning in parallel web search engines. In *Proceedings of the 2nd International Conference on Scalable Information Systems*, pages 1–9, 2007.

[11] A. MacFarlane, J. A. McCann, and S. E. Robertson. Parallel search using partitioned inverted files. In *Proceedings of the 7th International Symposium on String Processing Information Retrieval*, pages 209–220, 2000.

[12] B. Ribeiro-Neto, E. S. Moura, M. S. Neubert, and N. Ziviani. Efficient distributed algorithms to build inverted files. In *Proceedings of the 22nd Annual International ACM SIGIR Conference on Research and Development in Information Retrieval*, pages 105–112, 1999.

[13] B. A. Ribeiro-Neto and R. A. Barbosa. Query performance for tightly coupled distributed digital libraries. In *Proceedings of the 3rd ACM Conference on Digital Libraries*, pages 182–190, 1998.

[14] B. A. Ribeiro-Neto, J. P. Kitajima, G. Navarro, C. R. G. Sant'Ana, and N. Ziviani. Parallel generation of inverted files for distributed text collections. In *Proceedings of the 18th International Conference of the Chilean Computer Science Society*, pages 149–157, 1998.

[15] A. Tomasic and H. Garcia-Molina. Query processing and inverted indices in shared: nothing text document information retrieval systems. *The VLDB Journal*, 2(3):243–276, 1993.

[16] C. Zhai and J. Lafferty. Model-based feedback in the language modeling approach to information retrieval. In *Proceedings of the tenth international conference on Information and knowledge management*, CIKM '01, pages 403–410, New York, NY, USA, 2001. ACM.

[17] C. Zhai and J. Lafferty. A study of smoothing methods for language models applied to information retrieval. *ACM Trans. Inf. Syst.*, 22:179–214, April 2004.

Discovering URLs through User Feedback

Xiao Bai
Yahoo! Research
Barcelona, Spain
xbai@yahoo-inc.com

B. Barla Cambazoglu
Yahoo! Research
Barcelona, Spain
barla@yahoo-inc.com

Flavio P. Junqueira
Yahoo! Research
Barcelona, Spain
fpj@yahoo-inc.com

ABSTRACT

Search engines rely upon crawling to build their Web page collections. A Web crawler typically discovers new URLs by following the link structure induced by links on Web pages. As the number of documents on the Web is large, discovering newly created URLs may take arbitrarily long, and depending on how a given page is connected to others, such a crawler may miss the pages altogether. In this paper, we evaluate the benefits of integrating a passive URL discovery mechanism into a Web crawler. This mechanism is passive in the sense that it does not require the crawler to actively fetch documents from the Web to discover URLs. We focus here on a mechanism that uses toolbar data as a representative source for new URL discovery. We use the toolbar logs of Yahoo! to characterize the URLs that are accessed by users via their browsers, but not discovered by Yahoo! Web crawler. We show that a high fraction of URLs that appear in toolbar logs are not discovered by the crawler. We also reveal that a certain fraction of URLs are discovered by the crawler later than the time they are first accessed by users. One important conclusion of our work is that web search engines can highly benefit from user feedback in the form of toolbar logs for passive URL discovery.

Categories and Subject Descriptors

H.3.3 [**Information Storage Systems**]: Information Retrieval Systems

General Terms

Performance, Experimentation

Keywords

Search engines, Web crawling, URL discovery, toolbar

CIKM'11, October 24–28, 2011, Glasgow, Scotland, UK.

1. INTRODUCTION

Web crawling is an integral part of a search engine. A Web crawler continuously discovers new URLs and fetches their content to populate a large Web repository, mandatory to build an inverted index to serve user queries. Even though the basic mechanism of a crawler is simple, crawling efficiently and effectively is a difficult problem. The Web is very large and has a dynamic nature. To keep up with the rate of changes to Web pages, the crawler not only has to continuously enlarge its repository by expanding its frontier, but also needs to refresh previously fetched pages to incorporate in its index the changes on those pages.

In practice, crawlers prioritize the pages to be fetched, taking into account various constraints: available network bandwidth, peak processing capacity of the backend system, and politeness constraints of Web servers [24]. As a result of these constraints, the delay to discover a Web page can be quite long after its creation and some Web sites may be only partially crawled. Another important challenge is the discovery of hidden Web content, which crawlers cannot reach by following links on Web pages [4]. Hidden Web pages often contain dynamic content and are backed by a database. Fetching such pages requires different techniques [32], which a Web crawler does not typically implement. Pages that are disconnected or are part of small connected components are also unlikely to be discovered by a crawler. Consequently, the crawler misses the opportunity to incorporate such pages into its repository, and the search engine cannot serve them.

The main goal of our work is to understand whether user feedback can be beneficial to improve the URL discovery process in a Web crawler. Even though different forms of user feedback (*e.g.*, click-through history [31] and eye tracking [19]) have been considered to enhance the search result quality, to the best of our knowledge, our work is the first to evaluate the benefits of using the URLs collected from a Web browser toolbar as a form of user feedback to the crawling process. In this work, we quantify the effectiveness of this technique, which we refer to as toolbar-enhanced Web crawling, through extensive experimental analysis.

Contributions. Our work seeks answers to these questions:

- What fraction of URLs discovered through the toolbar logs are useful for increasing the coverage of a crawler?
- How do these URLs differ in terms of quality?
- How long does it take for the crawler to discover a URL that is first observed in the toolbar logs before it is discovered by the crawler?

- If the URLs discovered early via toolbar logs are displayed in search results before they are discovered by the crawler, what would be the impact on the search result quality?
- What would be the impact of the URLs only discovered in the toolbar logs on the search result quality, if they are incorporated to the search engine index?

To answer the above-raised questions, we conduct a large-scale experimental study on a snapshot of the entire Yahoo! Web crawl and the URL access logs obtained via the Yahoo! toolbar. Our study shows that there is a non-negligible fraction of Web pages, accounting for 80% of URLs in daily toolbar logs, which are not discovered by the crawler. If these pages are incorporated to the search engine index, 26.2% of the top-k query results are among them. We also observe that the crawler, on average, has a high delay of 121 days in discovering 2% of URLs that appear in daily toolbar logs. These URLs are shown to have higher link-based quality and content-based quality than those only discovered by the crawler, and serve up to 60 million queries before they are discovered by the crawler.

Roadmap. The paper is organized as follows. We introduce the active and passive URL discovery concepts in Section 2, together with the concept of toolbar-enhanced Web crawling. We discuss our experimental methodology in Section 3. We carry out a user study, in Section 4, to quantify usefulness of URLs. The impact of the proposed approach on the content and runtime systems of a search engine are discussed in Sections 5 and 6, respectively. Section 7 surveys the previous work. The paper is concluded in Section 8.

2. ACTIVE VS. PASSIVE DISCOVERY

2.1 Active URL Discovery

Most Web crawlers rely on the same basic mechanism to fetch the content on the Web. The crawler first fetches the pages pointed by a set of seed links. The downloaded pages are stored in a repository. The crawler then parses the content of these pages to discover links that are not seen before. The newly discovered links are stored in a download queue, referred to as the frontier of the crawler. The entire process, which involves fetching, storing, and parsing of pages, is iteratively repeated using the links in the frontier. In commercial Web crawling systems, additionally, previously downloaded pages are selectively refetched. This helps maintaining the freshness of the content in the repository.

Unfortunately, this form of crawling, where the Web is actively harvested by the crawler, has two important weaknesses. The first weakness is its limited coverage. In active Web crawling, the content discovery is limited to following links, and not all content on the Web can be accessed by following the link structure of Web pages [4]. For example, a high fraction of the content on the Web is accessible through Web forms. This type of dynamically generated content is hidden to a standard Web crawler as exposing such pages requires that the crawler knows how to fill out such forms.

The second weakness is the inaccuracy in estimating importance of the URLs in the frontier. In practice, it is not always trivial for the crawler to accurately estimate the importance of a Web page.[1] Traditional importance estimation techniques rely on the connectivity of a page to decide on its importance, *e.g.*, pages that are highly linked by other pages are predicted to be high-quality or important. Unfortunately, these techniques can only capture the importance attributed to a page in the past, but they fail to capture how important the page currently is or will be in the future. More specifically, a page that has accumulated many incoming links in the past, may not be relevant at the moment. In fact, a newly created page that has not yet accumulated enough links may be very important. More recent techniques use feedback from the popularity of the page in search results, *e.g.*, highly viewed or clicked pages are deemed to be important and are fetched earlier. Such techniques perform better in estimating the current, user-perceived importance of pages. However, although these techniques are useful for prioritizing the URLs in the refresh queue, they are not useful for the URLs in the frontier since, for these URLs, no popularity information can be obtained from search results.

2.2 Passive URL Discovery

Web pages can be discovered by means other than active URL discovery, which relies on link following. For example, users may push the URLs of their newly created Web pages or even their content to the search engine.[2] Other alternatives include obtaining URLs from emails, instant messages, and browser toolbars. In an extreme scenario, URLs can be discovered and pushed to the crawler by ISPs or even network routers while the content is being consumed by users.

All examples mentioned above are different forms of passive URL discovery, where URLs are discovered by means other than link following. Passive URL discovery has three advantages over the active URL discovery approach. First, it has the potential to improve the coverage of the crawler as certain URLs that are not accessible by the crawler are discoverable through such techniques. For example, a link to a hidden Web page can be extracted from the email logs. In fact, this is especially useful to improve the coverage of real-time generated content. For example, a link to a newly created streaming video of a soccer game can be extracted from instant messages. It may take hours or even days after the game has ended to discover such links via active URL discovery. Second, it improves the accuracy of the importance estimations by using the popularity (*i.e.*, the occurrence frequency) of passively obtained URLs, which is particularly useful for newly generated content that has not accumulated enough in-links but is worth fetching earlier. Third, performing the necessary processing for URL discovery in external agents or software components does not impose additional workload on the crawler.

2.3 Toolbar-Enhanced Web Crawling

Major commercial search engines provide a toolbar software that can be deployed on users' Web browsers. These toolbars provide additional functionality to users, such as quick search option, shortcuts to popular sites, and malware detection. However, from the perspective of the search engine companies, their main use is on branding and collecting marketing statistics. A typical toolbar tracks some of the actions that the user performs on the browser (*e.g.*, typing a URL, clicking on a link) and reports these actions to the search engine, where they are stored in a log file.

[1]Typically, the crawler prioritizes the URLs in the frontier in decreasing order of importance so that pages that are predicted to be more important are fetched earlier.

[2]`http://siteexplorer.search.yahoo.com/submit`

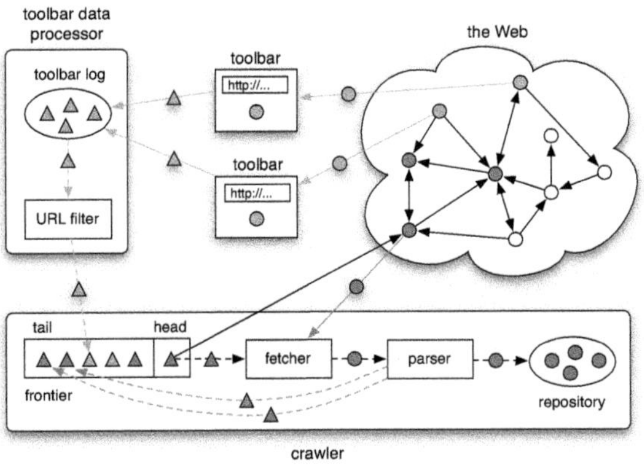

Figure 1: Toolbar-enhanced crawling architecture.

In this work, our goal is to use the feedback obtained from toolbar logs to improve effectiveness of Web crawling, *i.e.*, we specifically focus on a particular type of crawling enhanced with passive URL discovery: toolbar-enhanced Web crawling, where URLs are extracted from toolbar logs and pushed to the crawler's frontier. We note that our approach carries all potential benefits of passive URL discovery.

Fig. 1 illustrates the toolbar-enhanced crawling idea in more detail. As described in Section 2.1, the crawler continues to extend its frontier by fetching pages from the Web, extracting new links, and storing them in the download queue. In the mean time, users continue to access the content on the Web. As mentioned above, all page accesses that are performed through the browser are reported by the toolbar software to the search engine, *i.e.*, the URLs accessed via the browser are simply transferred to the search engine and are stored in a common log file.[3] A URL filtering daemon takes new URLs discovered through the toolbar and selectively adds them to the frontier of the crawler. We note that only the URLs that are not seen by the crawler are selected.[4] Further filtering is possible (*e.g.*, malformed URLs can be eliminated here). Since our focus herein is not on the design of the URL filter, we omit such details. In this work, we are more specifically interested in the impact of toolbar data on crawling and the degree of potential benefits in toolbar-enhanced Web crawling.

3. DATASET AND METHODOLOGY

In experiments, we use a snapshot of the full Yahoo! Web crawl. The snapshot contains all URLs "discovered" by the crawler before March 23, 2010. We note that the original snapshot does not contain any URLs obtained through passive URL discovery. For confidentiality reasons, we cannot disclose the size of the crawl, but we could safely claim that it is one of the biggest Web collections ever crawled to date and is of the order of hundreds of billions URLs.

We also use a very large log of URLs accessed by users through Yahoo! toolbar. Again, we cannot disclose the size of the toolbar log, but it is safe to state that it is one of the most popular toolbars currently used in Internet browsers. The toolbar log contains information about the access times of each URL.

[3]Alternatively, along with the URL, the links extracted from the page content can also be transferred.

[4]This can be performed through a standard URL seen test, available in crawlers running in active mode [20].

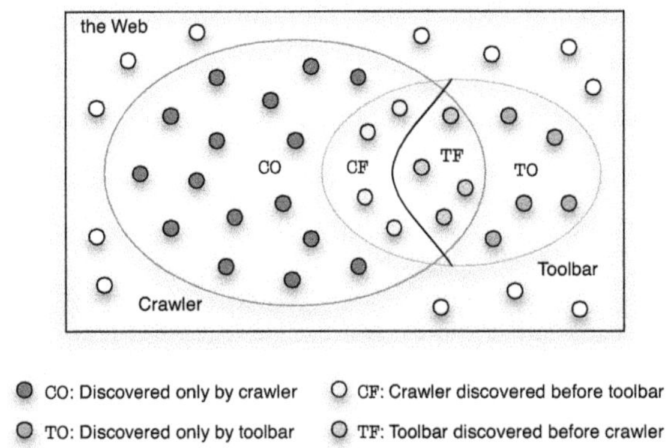

Figure 2: The four sets formed based on the discovery time of URLs by the crawler and the toolbar.

To assess the benefits that toolbar-enhanced crawling brings to the runtime system of a search engine, *i.e.*, the improvement in search result quality, we also use a large web query log obtained from the Yahoo! search engine. The query log on each day used in our experiments represents a fraction of the search engine's daily workload. For each query, the query log records the query terms along with the top-k matching results. All of our experiments are conducted on a very large Hadoop cluster. We do not provide details on our computing platform and the software we developed, as this potentially deserves a separate study on its own.

Our experimental methodology divides the URL space into different sets, based on URL's discovery time in toolbar logs and by the crawler. We then observe, at certain checkpoint dates, the distribution of URLs in these sets to obtain lower and upper bounds on the potential gains in using the toolbar data. Specifically, we form the following four sets (Fig. 2).

- `CO` (crawler only): URLs that are discovered by the crawler, but not in toolbar logs.
- `TO` (toolbar only): URLs that are discovered in toolbar logs, but not by the crawler.
- `CF` (crawler first): URLs that are first discovered by the crawler and then in toolbar logs.
- `TF` (toolbar first): URLs that are first discovered in toolbar logs and then by the crawler.

Since the toolbar logs do not affect the URLs in the `CO` set, we focus our study mostly on the URLs discovered through the toolbar (*i.e.*, the `TO`, `TF`, and `CF` sets). We note that only the URLs in the `TO` and `TF` sets have a potential for positive impact on the search engine.

Among the identified sets, the size of the `TO` set gives us an upper-bound on the portion of the Web discoverable through toolbar, but not through Web crawling. Moreover, the size of the `TF` set gives us a lower-bound on the fraction of URLs that can be discovered in toolbar logs before they are discovered by the crawler. These are only bounds because some portion of the URLs in the `TO` set may later be discovered by the crawler and move into the `TF` set.

In this section, as an initial experimental result, we report the sizes of the `TO`, `TF`, and `CF` sets, for our data. In this experiment, we select two sets of checkpoint days, sampled in different ways. The first set consists of the first seven days

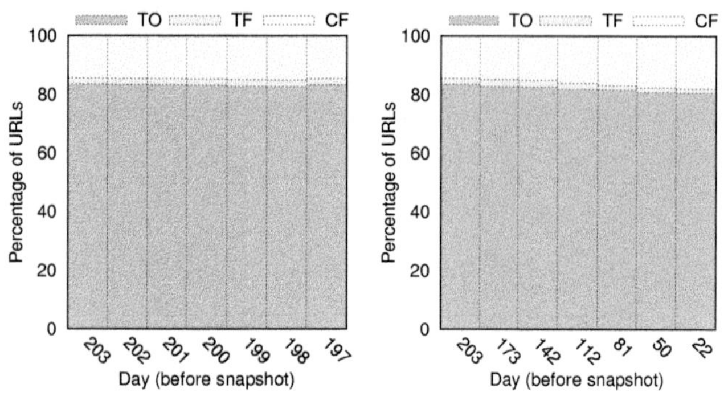

(a) Consecutive checkpoints. (b) Scattered checkpoints.

Figure 3: Sizes of different URL sets.

of September 2009 (starts from 203 days before the date of the crawl snapshot). The second set consists of the first day of each month from September 2009 to March 2010. For each checkpoint day, we identify all URLs crawled before the checkpoint day and the toolbar URLs obtained on that particular day. We then compute the URL distribution over the three sets at every checkpoint day.

Fig. 3 shows the fraction of URLs that fall in the three sets. We observe that more than 80% of the URLs accessed by users within a day are not discovered by the crawler (`TO`). This is a much higher number than what one may expect. However, in the next section, we will show through a user study that this is only a loose bound on the potential coverage of toolbar URLs. We also observe that about 2% of the URLs are first accessed through the toolbar (`TF`). If the checkpoint dates are consecutive (Fig. 3(a)), the fractions remain stable. However, when we use checkpoints with enough time distance (Fig. 3(b)), the increase in the size of the `CF` set is evident. This is simply because the crawler is given more time to discover URLs. Nevertheless, there is still a large fraction of toolbar URLs that are not discovered early enough or at all by the crawler. More concretely, the URLs in the `TO` and `TF` sets of each checkpoint day count for about 0.02% of the full Web crawl we use. Given the huge size of our crawl (in order of hundreds of billions), this percentage corresponds to a large number of Web pages that are worth exploiting.

4. STUDY ON TOOLBAR-ONLY URLS

We assess in this section the importance of URLs in the `TO` set. We quantify the fraction of URLs that are really useful for enhancing the crawler (Section 4.1) and analyze the reasons for which such URLs are not discovered by the crawler (Section 4.2). Since no information is available to the search engine about the content of the URLs in the `TO` set, the only option to evaluate the usefulness and discoverability of these URLs is to obtain their content and conduct a user study. To this end, we independently sample 10 sets of URLs from the `TO` set observed on September 1, 2009. Each sample set contains 1000 URLs selected uniformly at random.

4.1 Usefulness of URLs

As stated above, we first aim to understand through a user study whether the URLs that are only viewed by the users are useful for a crawler as a complementary source of information. Our user study comprises two steps. In the first step, for each sample URL, we send an HTTP get request to its server. We place the URLs in different bins according to the HTTP status codes returned by their servers. This automatic classification step gives us an idea about the reachability of the sample URLs. In this step, we filter out all URLs that are invalid or not accessible. In the second step, we download the remaining URLs and manually check their content to place them under different categories according to their usefulness.

Table 1: Distribution of status codes.

	HTTP status codes				Parse
	2**	3**	4**	5**	error
Avg. percentage	77.2	13.2	7.4	0.5	1.9
Std. deviation	0.026	0.022	0.008	0.002	0.005

Automated filtering. According to RFC 2616[5], the status codes in the form of `2**` indicate that the requests are successfully received, understood, and accepted; the codes in the form of `3**` mean that the requested resource resides under another URL and the current URL is redirected to that URL; the codes in the form of `4**` or `5**` correspond to the client-side or the server-side errors, respectively. If a request fails to get any response, it is due to the fact that the requested URL is invalid, *i.e.*, the URL cannot be correctly parsed using the URL syntax.[6] This happens mainly due to misspellings introduced by users when typing URLs.

In Table 1, we provide the distribution of HTTP status codes obtained for our 10 sets of sample URLs. We observe that about 90.4% of the sample URLs are valid URLs that receive a `2**` or `3**` code.[7] This indicates that if the URLs in the `TO` set are queued for crawling, there is a high potential to increase the coverage of the crawler. The URL with status codes `4**` and `5**` are clearly not useful for the crawler. We thus filter out these URLs as well as those that cannot be parsed and focus only on the remaining URLs for the manual classification step, conducted next.

Manual classification. We classify the URLs under the following classes, according to the usefulness of their content. In our classification, URLs can be uniquely assigned to classes, except for the `Adult` class. Hence, we assumed that the `Adult` class has higher precedence and a URL assigned to it would not be assigned to any other class.

Regular (`Regular`): These are pages that contain useful information. If there is any reasonable information in the page content, we place the page under this class.

Private with useful content (`Private-Useful`): These are the pages whose full content can be viewed after logging into a server, but a portion of the information on the page is publicly accessible. For instance, public user profiles in `www.tagged.com` are available only to registered users. However, some information about the users (*e.g.*, name, gender, photo) may still be displayed on the page. Hence, we consider such pages useful.

[5]Hypertext Transfer Protocol – HTTP/1.1, `http://www.rfc-archive.org/getrfc.php?rfc=2616`.
[6]Uniform Resource Locators (URL), `http://www.rfc-archive.org/getrfc.php?rfc=1738`.
[7]Although URLs with a `3**` code may be redirects to known URLs, we make an optimistic assumption and include them in our manual classification.

Table 2: Fraction of pages under different content classes in the TO and CO sets.

	Useful content classes					Useless content classes		
	Regular	Prv-Useful	Search-Web	Search-DB	Adult	Prv-Useless	Blank	Soft404
TO	23.1	2.3	12.7	6.2	2.8	48.4	1.1	3.4
CO	46.7	7.0	1.1	15.2	1.1	11.7	1.7	15.5

Table 3: Impact of robot exclusion protocol on discovery of useful content (+R: excluded, -R: not excluded).

	Regular		Prv-Useful		Search-Web		Search-DB		Adult	
	+R	-R	+R	-R	+R	-R	+R	-R	+R	-R
Fraction	2.3	20.8	0.1	2.2	11.0	1.7	1.4	4.8	0.3	2.5

Private without useful content (Private-Useless): These URLs are either redirects to a login page or contain a simple message telling the user to login to the server. Since no useful information is provided, we consider such pages useless.

Web search engine results (Search-Web): These pages contain the search results generated by a Web search engine for a given query. Following the links on such result pages provides a unique opportunity to find high-quality content discovered by other search engines but may have been omitted or not discovered by the Yahoo! Web crawler.

Database search results (Search-DB): In some online Web sites (*e.g.*, eBay and Amazon), users issue queries against an item databases to retrieve items of interest. If the result page URLs returned by such sites are included in the index of a search engine, items can be located by issuing queries directly to the Web search engine. Hence, we consider such URLs useful.

No content (Blank): These pages are simply those having an accessible URL with no useful information in its content. They are thus not likely to be useful.

Adult (Adult): These pages contain adult content. Although it is arguable, we consider adult pages useful as they are of interest to some people and appear frequently enough among the URLs accessed via toolbar.

Link not found (Soft404): Some websites display customized "404 not found" messages with a HTTP "200 OK" status code. Crawling such pages does not bring any useful information but only waste the crawling time and may harm the search result quality as well.

We manually classify the sampled 1000 URLs in the set whose status code distribution is the closest to the average distribution over the 10 sample URL sets. This sample contains 905 valid URLs after the automated filtering step. Table 2 shows the distribution of URLs in the usefulness classes we defined. The distribution of URLs from a CO sample is shown to give a general idea of the usefulness of URLs. Not surprisingly, compared to the crawler, the users are more likely to access private pages that require login. However, there is still half of the pages that contain useful information and might be useful to the search engine.

4.2 Discoverability of Useful URLs

We now analyze the characteristics of the useful URLs in order to understand why they are not discovered by the crawler. One obvious reason is the robot exclusion protocol, through which website owners can advisorily prevent crawling of certain pages in their sites. To understand the impact of the robot exclusion protocol, we retrieve the `robots.txt` files from the server of every URL that is identified as useful. Then, we check whether the URL is excluded by the protocol or not. Table 3 displays the fraction of the useful URLs that are excluded or not excluded. According to the table, about one-third of the useful URLs are excluded and hence cannot be crawled (+R). Interestingly, most of the excluded URLs are in the Search-Web category. This is because search engines use the robot exclusion protocol as a precaution to prevent their URLs from being scraped and stolen by the competitors.

Table 4: Fraction of static and dynamic URLs.

	TO		CO	
	Static	Dynamic	Static	Dynamic
Fraction	27.1	72.9	55.5	44.5

We continue our analysis with the remaining two-thirds of useful URLs that are not excluded by the robot exclusion protocol. A very large number of Web pages are in the hidden Web, which are only accessible by submitting queries to a database. As a result, regular crawlers are unable to find these dynamic pages if there is no link pointing to them. Table 4 compares the fraction of static and dynamic URLs[8] in the TO and CO sets. The high variation in distributions confirms our claim that the toolbar data can enhance a Web crawler's coverage by providing dynamic pages that are often not discoverable by the crawler.

Some commercial search engine crawlers are known to limit the number of query parameters in dynamic pages.[9] In Fig.4(a), we compare the number of query parameters in dynamic URLs for the TO and CO sets.[10] Not surprisingly, most URLs in the CO set (90%) have no more than three parameters. In contrast, the number of parameters are evenly distributed for the URLs in the TO set and 27% of such URLs have more than three parameters.

Crawlers typically limit the depth of the URLs they follow. To observe if this has an impact on coverage, we compute the depth distribution for static URLs in the TO and CO sets. Fig. 4(b) confirms that toolbar is more effective for discovering the static URLs with depth not smaller than 5.

5. IMPACT ON THE CONTENT SYSTEM

In this section, we assess the impact of toolbar data on the content quality of a search engine. We first evaluate the importance of the URLs in different sets. Next, we inves-

[8]Note that this number is a lower bound for the proportion of dynamic URLs since some dynamic URLs do not have a query parameter and may appear to be static.

[9]Dynamic versus static URLs, available at `http://googlewebmastercentral.blogspot.com/2008/09/dynamic-urls-vs-static-urls.html`

[10]URLs without a parameter are dynamic URLs rewritten in the form of a static URL.

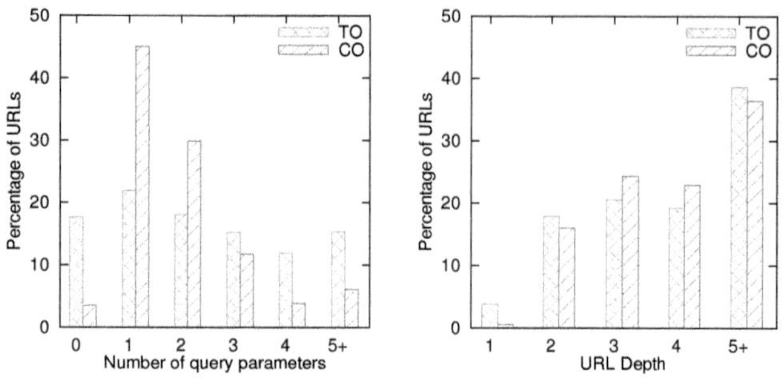

(a) (b)

Figure 4: Distribution of URL properties: (a) Distribution of dynamic URLs, according to the number of query parameters in the URL; (b) Distribution of static URLs, according to depth measured by the number of slashes in the URL.

tigate to which extent the URLs discovered in toolbar logs can affect the content discovery time.

5.1 Importance of URLs

We use two different proprietary metrics to assess the importance of pages. The first is a link analysis metric (`link metric`) that measures the importance of a page based on the number of links it receives from other pages. The second is a content quality metric (`content metric`) that uses the textual content of a page to decide on its importance. In both metrics, increasing values indicate higher importance.

Unfortunately, the metric values are available to us only for pages discovered by the crawler. Therefore, we focus on the URLs discovered only by the crawler (`CO`) and those discovered by both the toolbar and the crawler (`TF`). For these experiments, we sample about 15 million URLs, uniformly at random, from the `CO` set and use all URLs in the `TF` set obtained on September 1, 2009.

Fig. 5(a) shows the distribution of `link metric` values for the `TF` and `CO` sets. The average value of the `link metric` is 0.27 for the `TF` set, whereas it is 0.21 for the `CO` set. It is also seen that there are more URLs in the `TF` set with a larger `link metric` value. Fig. 5(b) shows the distribution of the `content metric`. We similarly observe that the URLs in the `TF` set have larger `content metric` values.[11] Knowing that a crawler always crawls important URLs first, the fact that more URLs in the `TF` set have positive `content metric` indirectly confirms our observation. These two experiments indicate that the URLs discovered by both toolbar and crawler are more important than the URLs discovered only by the crawler, *i.e.*, there is an opportunity to discover high-quality content via user feedback.

5.2 Discovery Time of URLs

We have seen that the URLs discovered both in toolbar logs and by the crawler are more important than those discovered only by the crawler. Yet, these URLs would be useful for improving the content system of a search engine only if they are discovered earlier in toolbar logs. We are thus interested in knowing how early a toolbar can discover such URLs (*i.e.*, those in the `TF` set).

Fig. 6 illustrates the fraction of URLs discovered first in

[11]The value of `content metric` is 0 if a URL has not yet been crawled. URLs with a value of 0 are omitted from Fig. 5(b).

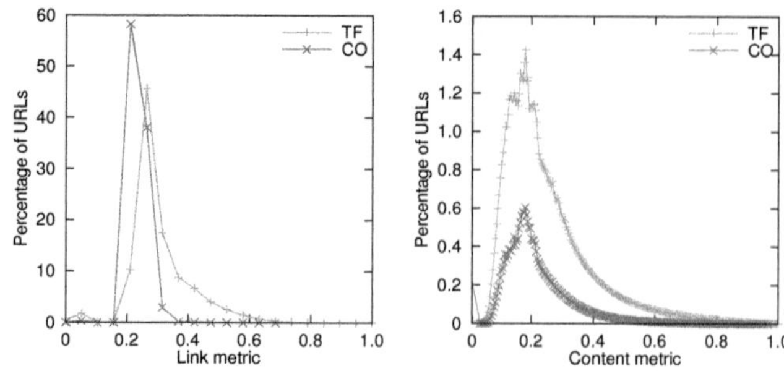

(a) Link metric (b) Content metric

Figure 5: Distribution of URL importance.

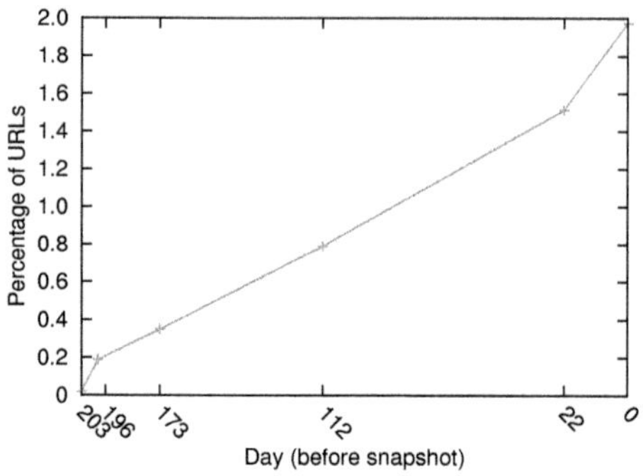

Figure 6: Fraction of URLs that were initially in the `TO` set (on September 1, 2009) and then moved into the `TF` set as they were discovered by the crawler.

toolbar logs on September 1, 2009 and then discovered by the crawler before the date indicated on the x-axis. We observe that the fraction of URLs that moved from the `TO` set to the `TF` set increases linearly over time. By the date of our crawl snapshot, 2% of the URLs have moved from the `TO` set to the `TF` set. These URLs are certainly useful for improving the content system.

Herein, we further evaluate how long it takes for the crawler to discover a URL already discovered in toolbar logs. Fig. 7(a) compares the distribution of delay for the URLs in the `TF` set that are discovered on each day of the first week of September 2009. As expected, the distributions are similar. It is important to note that more than 60% of the URLs in the `TF` set are discovered by the toolbar at least 90 days earlier than the crawler. This result illustrates the potential in using toolbar logs to improve search engine coverage and to compute more accurate page importance values for the known URLs. Fig. 7(b) further compares the distribution of the delay for the URLs in the `TF` set that are discovered on the first day of each month from September 1, 2009 to March 1, 2010. The difference in the maximum delay is due to the fact that fewer days are available to the crawler to discover the same URLs after they are discovered in toolbar logs. Yet, even though the crawler had only 23 days to discover the URLs first discovered in toolbar logs, 40% of the URLs in the `TF` set were discovered 7 days later.

6. IMPACT ON THE RUNTIME SYSTEM

Typically, after a URL is indexed, it starts to appear in the top-k result sets of queries to which the URL is considered to be relevant by the search engine. Obviously, a URL cannot be incorporated into any set of search results before it is

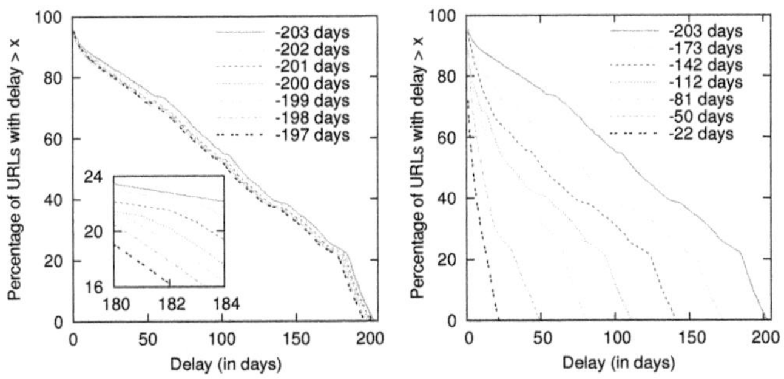

(a) Consecutive dates (b) Scattered dates

Figure 7: Distribution of the delay in discovery of TF URLs by the crawler.

discovered, crawled, and indexed. Consequently, some of the queries that could benefit from a URL cannot retrieve it until the URL is made available through the index. Herein, our goal is to estimate the impact of the discovery of TF and TO URLs on the result quality of a search engine, as well as to identify the type of queries for which the discovery of such URLs is important.

6.1 Impact of Toolbar-First URLs

We evaluate the impact of the early discovered URLs, *i.e.*, those in the TF set, on the search result quality by answering two questions: *(i)* given a set of queries, how many of them would retrieve a TF URL in their top-10 results, before these TF URLs are discovered by the crawler? We refer to such queries and TF URLs as *benefited queries* and *beneficial URLs* respectively; *(ii)* given a set of benefited queries, how frequently would they be issued before their beneficial URLs are discovered by the crawler?

In the experiments, as the toolbar URLs, we use the TF URLs discovered on September 1, 2009. We also use queries from the daily query logs of the Yahoo! search engine. We rely on the Yahoo! search engine's ranking mechanism to assess the relevance of a TF URL to a given query. Since a TF URL would not appear in the search results of any query before it is discovered by the Yahoo! Web crawler, we first identify a set of queries from the query logs which contain in their top-10 results at least one URL from the TF set, referred to as *relevant queries*, and then derive the benefited queries by comparing a given set of previously issued queries against them.

Fig. 8(a) displays the fraction of the relevant queries (observed on each day between April 1, 2010 and May 30, 2010) that contain in their top-10 results at least one URL from the TF set (obtained on September 1, 2009). The figure also provides the same information using unique relevant queries (*i.e.* ignoring repetition). On average, 0.03% of queries issued during a day have at least one URLs from the TF set in their top-10 results and are relevant to our experiment. The number goes to 0.14% when the relevant queries are unique, indicating that the URLs in the TF set are more likely to appear in the results of infrequent queries.

The first question we aim to answer is the fraction of benefited queries among a given set of queries. To this end, we focus on the queries issued on September 1, 2009 and count the occurrences of the unique relevant queries shown in Fig. 8(a) during that day. We observe from Fig. 8(b) that the number of benefited queries increases linearly with the

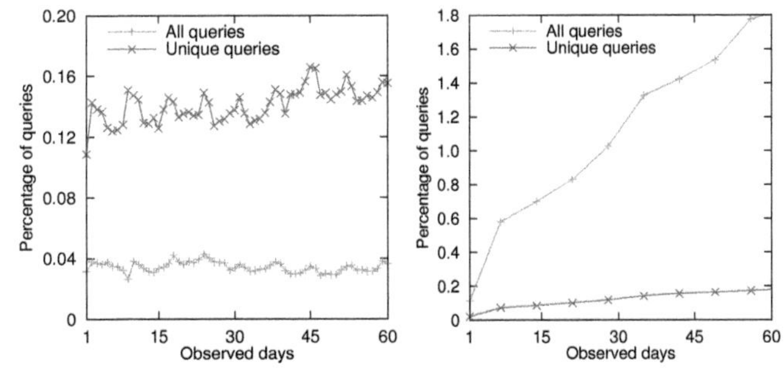

(a) Relevant queries (b) Benefited queries

Figure 8: Distribution of queries related to TF URLs

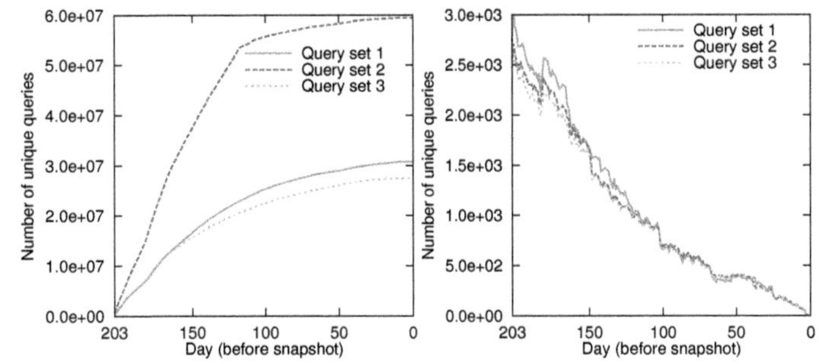

(a) All queries (b) Unique queries

Figure 9: Distribution of benefited queries w.r.t. different sets of relevant queries

length of observed period (*i.e.*, x-axis days). If the period of 60 days is considered, up to 1.8% of the queries on September 1, 2009 have a TF URL as a top-10 result, assuming those URLs are incorporated to the index once they are accessed via toolbar. In fact, this number is only a lower bound and more benefited queries should be expected if the relevant queries are obtained in a longer period. Note that this number is much larger than the fraction of the unique benefited queries. This is due to the fact that given a specific day the probability for an infrequent query (having a TF URL in its top-10 results) to be issued is low.

Now, we address the second issue by measuring the occurrences of the benefited queries issued on September 1, 2009, before all the corresponding beneficial URLs are discovered by the crawler, *i.e.*, during the period from September 1, 2009 to the date of our crawl snapshot. We consider three sets of relevant queries in this experiment. Each set consists of the unique relevant queries of a randomly selected observed day, as shown in Fig. 8(a).

Fig. 9(a) shows the total number of the benefited queries issued from September 1, 2009 to the x-axis day. We present absolute numbers instead of percentages to give an idea of the magnitude of the results. We observe that the number of benefited queries increases over time. Before all the TF URLs accessed via toolbar on September 1, 2009 are discovered by the crawler, the beneficial ones appear up to 60 million times in the top-10 results of the benefited queries. Fig. 9(b) shows the number of the unique benefited queries on the x-axis day. Issuing a query later reduces the probability that a TF URL appears in its top-10 results so that the number of unique benefited queries decreases with time.

Fig. 10 shows the distribution of benefited queries as a function of the crawler's delay. Only the queries related to

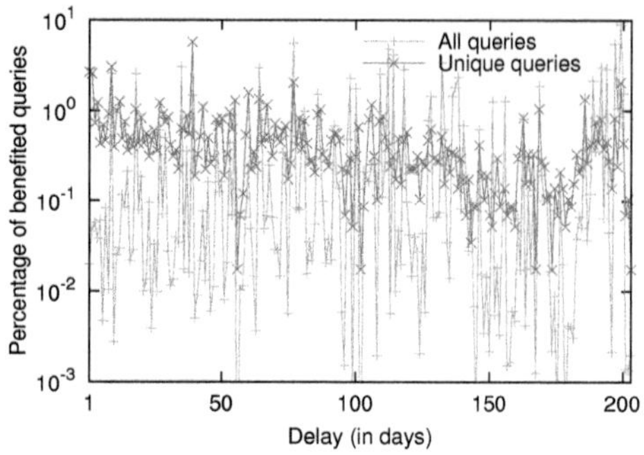

Figure 10: Query distribution for different delays.

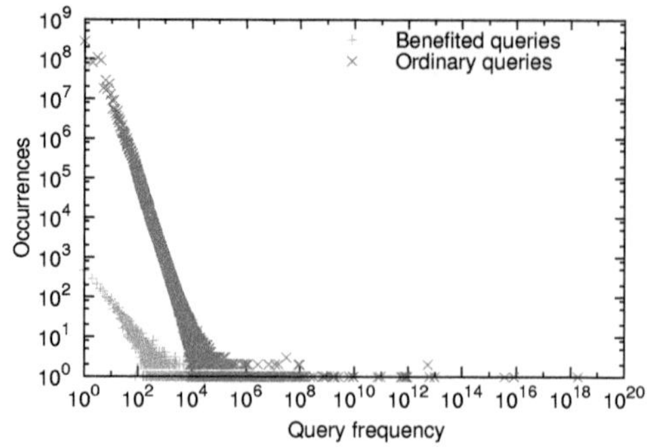

Figure 11: Frequency of queries (log-log).

Table 5: Content of queries.

Query type	Domain queries	Question queries
Benefited queries	22.09%	0.01%
Ordinary queries	6.16%	3.42%

Table 6: Length of queries.

Query type	Average length	Standard deviation
Benefited queries	1.52	1.08
Ordinary queries	2.01	0.08

the first set of relevant queries are shown. Interestingly, the number of queries in each delay interval is independent of the length of the delay. In other words, even a small delay may significantly impact the query results. This observation confirms that discovering URLs earlier via toolbar impacts a large number of queries.

6.2 Characterization of Benefited Queries

We have observed that the `TF` URLs help improving the search result quality of certain queries. We are now interested in the characteristics of the benefited queries to understand for which queries the `TF` URLs are crucial. To this end, we evaluate the content, the frequency and the length of the benefited queries, and compare them against those of ordinary queries. In this experiment, we use all the benefited queries issued during the period from September 1, 2009 to the date of our crawl snapshot with respect to the first set of relevant queries. All the queries issued during the same period are considered as ordinary queries.

We analyze the content of the queries by measuring the fraction of *domain queries* and *question queries*, which can be easily identified by matching the query terms with predefined keywords. Here, by *domain query* we mean a query that contains a domain name, such as ".com", ".edu", etc. A *question query* is a query starting with an interrogative word, such as "what", "why", etc. For each type of queries, we develop a complete list of relevant keywords and run an automatic classifier against it. Table 5 summarizes our observation that a significant fraction of benefited queries are domain queries while very few queries look for specific information. Fig. 11 depicts the distribution of query frequency, following a power-law distribution. We observe that none of the benefited queries occurs more than 10,000 times during the observed period, while 90% of them occur more than once. In contrast, some ordinary queries appear up to 10^{18} times during the same period. Table 6 shows the average length of queries. Not surprisingly, since there are much more domain queries among the benefited queries, they are shorter than the ordinary queries, on average. Generally, the URLs first discovered via toolbar are crucial for the domain queries with medium frequency to retrieve the recently created pages earlier.

6.3 Impact of Toolbar-Only URLs

As we have seen, a large fraction of URLs discovered through toolbar logs are not discovered by the crawler but contain useful information. To understand the contribution of such URLs, *i.e.*, those in the `TO` set, to the search results, we conduct the following experiments. We obtain the content of two million URLs, half of which are randomly sampled from the `TO` set on September 1, 2009 and the remaining half are randomly sampled from our crawl snapshot. We index these URLs using the open source information retrieval platform Terrier[12] and evaluate one million queries randomly selected from the query logs against this index. The relevance of a URL to a query is computed by summing the BM25 score of each query term. For each top-k result set retrieved for a query, we are interested in the number (fraction) of `TO` URLs in that set.

Fig. 12 displays the distribution of queries according to the number of `TO` URLs in their top-10 results. On average, 2.6 results out of 10 are from the `TO` set, confirming that incorporating the URLs discovered through toolbar logs into the search engine index positively impacts the search results. We infer from the different distribution of unique queries that `TO` URLs are more likely to appear in the top-10 results of infrequent queries, *i.e.*, queries looking for tail content. Finally, we repeat this experiment with different values of k and observe that the fraction of `TO` URLs in the top-k result sets remains stable, and 26.2% of the top-k results are from the `TO` set on average. This independence of k further confirms the impact of `TO` URLs on the runtime system of the search engine.

7. PREVIOUS WORK

Web crawling is a well-studied topic [29]. In the literature, there have been a significant number of design alternatives, including sequential [24], parallel [5, 8, 20, 33, 36], and geographically distributed [6, 14, 15] Web crawlers. The three main quality objectives, common to most crawling architectures, were achieving high collection quality through download scheduling [10, 26], maintaining page freshness [7, 9, 16, 30, 35], and obtaining high Web coverage [11, 23].

[12]`http://terrier.org/`.

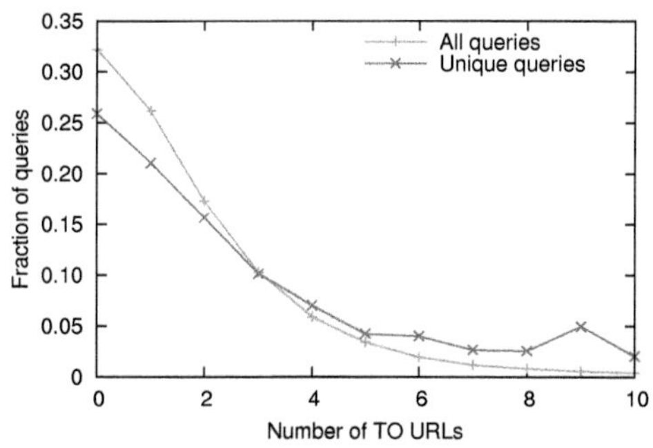

Figure 12: Distribution of queries w.r.t. number of TO URLs in the top-10 result set.

Quality. A notable technique to improve the download content quality is to fetch the links in the frontier in decreasing order of the predicted importance values [10, 26]. In former studies, the importance of a link mainly depends on the structure of the Web graph and is link-based [10, 13] (*e.g.*, pages are prioritized based on their PageRank values). A more recent work [30] took into account the impact of a page on search result quality. In this metric, newly created pages and tail pages that have not received enough in-links but are likely to appear in the search results are given more priority to improve the utility of crawled pages.

Freshness. Keeping the page repository fresh requires refetching already downloaded pages. A number of studies investigated the evolutionary properties of the Web [2, 17, 27] and proposed page refreshing policies for crawlers [7, 9, 16, 30, 35]. Some policies aimed to refresh more often the content that is more important [7] or more likely to change [9, 12]. Others tried to maximize the impact on search result quality [16, 30, 35].

Coverage. To achieve a high Web coverage, a crawler needs to continuously discover new pages. Although outdated, an analysis of the coverage of commercial search engines is available in [23]. The discoverability of newly created pages is intensively analyzed in [11]. Not surprisingly, this study showed that about a quarter of the new content is not easily discoverable by following the links in known pages.

Hidden Web. In practice, the size of the hidden Web [4, 32] is a limiting factor for the coverage of a Web crawler. The main challenge in hidden Web crawling is to discover entry points to hidden Web sites [3] and to sample them via automated form filling [18, 25, 28]. Moreover, the hidden Web crawler should try to discover useful information without putting too much burden on sites.

Passive URL discovery. As we discussed in Section 2.2, a promising technique is to incorporate other sources of information rather than solely relying on the crawler to discover new pages. The client-side applications, like Web browsers and toolbars, appear to be good candidates for gathering such information. To the best of our knowledge, the only previous work exploring this idea is a recent patent [34], which proposes using search toolbar data to locate and index multimedia resources that are not discoverable by Web crawlers. However, the patent is mostly about how multimedia resources can be identified and added to the search index, but does not give any evidence to which extent a search engine can benefit from passive URL discovery.

URL discovery through user feedback. A recent work [21] proposes using the URLs posted on social bookmarking sites (in this particular case, del.icio.us) to improve Web search. The study reports that approximately 25% of URLs posted by users are new, not indexed pages. Since the existence of URLs in the search engine is checked over the index, 25% forms an upper bound on the URLs not discovered by the crawler. The same work states that the fraction of unique URLs obtained via social bookmarking represents a tiny fraction of the URLs on the Web. In this respect, our toolbar-based URL discovery approach has a much larger coverage. Moreover, our approach focuses on tail content rather than the popular content in social bookmarking. Finally, we note that the work in [21] does not form an instance of passive URL discovery since the URLs in social bookmarking sites are accessible through link following.

Toolbar data. In [22], through an analyses of Yahoo! toolbar data, authors propose a new taxonomy for online browsing behavior of users. In [1], URL revisitation patterns of users is analyzed using URLs accessed by a toolbar. In [2], the change in Web content is studied by restricting the URLs to the toolbar data. All these studies use toolbar data for either characterization or filtering purposes, but do not give any clue about its potential use.

8. CONCLUSION

We conducted a large-scale study, using toolbar logs, a large Web crawl, and search query logs obtained from Yahoo!, to investigate the role toolbar data can play in improving the content and the runtime systems of a search engine. Through a user study, we showed that there exist a large portion of useful URLs that are not discovered by the crawler, but are accessed by the users via Web browsers. We then showed that, on average, URLs accessed by the users are more important than those found in the repository of a crawler. We found that the crawler has a significant delay in discovering URLs that are first accessed by the users. Finally, we have shown that URL discovery via toolbar have positive impact on search result quality, especially for queries seeking recently created content and tail content.

There are a few potential extensions to our work we envision. One extension is to repeat our study with other forms of passive URL discovery (*e.g.*, email messages, communication logs of Internet messengers). An interesting yet challenging example of passive URL discovery is to delegate the discovery process to the network itself (*e.g.*, agents on Internet routers or ISPs). This way URLs can be discovered at a much larger scale with almost no delay. Another extension is to perform passive crawling in a privacy-preserving fashion, since proper anonymization of URLs is important to prevent search results from leaking confidential user information.

Acknowledgement

This work has been partially supported by the COAST project (ICT-248036), funded by the European Community.

9. REFERENCES

[1] E. Adar, J. Teevan, and S. T. Dumais. Resonance on the Web: Web dynamics and revisitation patterns. In *Proc. 27th Int'l Conf. on Human Factors in Computing Systems*, pages 1381–1390, 2009.

[2] E. Adar, J. Teevan, S. T. Dumais, and J. L. Elsas. The web changes everything: Understanding the dynamics

of web content. In *Proc. 2nd ACM Int'l Conf. on Web Search and Data Mining*, pages 282–291, 2009.

[3] L. Barbosa and J. Freire. An adaptive crawler for locating hidden-web entry points. In *Proc. 16th Int'l Conf. on World Wide Web*, pages 441–450, 2007.

[4] M. K. Bergman. White paper: The deep web: Surfacing hidden value. *The Journal of Electronic Publishing*, 7(1):online, 2001.

[5] P. Boldi, B. Codenotti, M. Santini, and S. Vigna. UbiCrawler: A scalable fully distributed web crawler. *Softw. Pract. Exper.*, 34(8):711–726, 2004.

[6] B. B. Cambazoglu, V. Plachouras, F. Junqueira, and L. Telloli. On the feasibility of geographically distributed web crawling. In *Proc. 3rd Int'l Conf. on Scalable Information Systems*, pages 1–10, 2008.

[7] J. Cho and H. Garcia-Molina. The evolution of the Web and implications for an incremental crawler. In *Proc. 26th Int'l Conf. on Very Large Data Bases*, pages 200–209, 2000.

[8] J. Cho and H. Garcia-Molina. Parallel crawlers. In *Proc. 11th Int'l Conf. on World Wide Web*, pages 124–135, 2002.

[9] J. Cho and H. Garcia-Molina. Effective page refresh policies for web crawlers. *ACM Trans. Database Syst.*, 28(4):390–426, 2003.

[10] J. Cho, H. Garcia-Molina, and L. Page. Efficient crawling through URL ordering. *Comput. Netw. ISDN Syst.*, 30(1-7):161–172, 1998.

[11] A. Dasgupta, A. Ghosh, R. Kumar, C. Olston, S. Pandey, and A. Tomkins. The discoverability of the Web. In *Proc. 16th Int'l Conf. on World Wide Web*, pages 421–430, 2007.

[12] J. Edwards, K. McCurley, and J. Tomlin. An adaptive model for optimizing performance of an incremental web crawler. In *Proc. 10th Int'l Conf. on World Wide Web*, pages 106–113, 2001.

[13] N. Eiron, K. S. McCurley, and J. A. Tomlin. Ranking the web frontier. In *Proc. 13th Int'l Conf. on World Wide Web*, pages 309–318, 2004.

[14] J. Exposto, J. Macedo, A. Pina, A. Alves, and J. Rufino. Geographical partition for distributed web crawling. In *Proc. 2005 Workshop on Geographic Information Retrieval*, pages 55–60, 2005.

[15] J. Exposto, J. Macedo, A. Pina, A. Alves, and J. Rufino. Efficient partitioning strategies for distributed web crawling. In *Information Networking. Towards Ubiquitous Networking and Services*, volume 5200 of *Lect. Notes Comput. Sc.*, pages 544–553. 2008.

[16] D. Fetterly, N. Craswell, and V. Vinay. The impact of crawl policy on web search effectiveness. In *Proc. 32nd Int'l ACM SIGIR Conf. on Research and Development in Information Retrieval*, pages 580–587, 2009.

[17] D. Fetterly, M. Manasse, M. Najork, and J. L. Wiener. A large-scale study of the evolution of web pages. *Softw. Pract. Exper.*, 34(2):213–237, 2004.

[18] A. d. C. Fontes and F. S. Silva. SmartCrawl: A new strategy for the exploration of the hidden web. In *Proc. 6th Annual ACM Int'l Workshop on Web Information and Data Management*, pages 9–15, 2004.

[19] L. A. Granka, T. Joachims, and G. Gay. Eye-tracking analysis of user behavior in WWW search. In *Proc. of the 27th Int'l ACM SIGIR Conf. on Research and Development in Information Retrieval*, pages 478–479, 2004.

[20] A. Heydon and M. Najork. Mercator: A scalable, extensible web crawler. *Proc. 8th Int'l Conf. on World Wide Web*, 2(4):219–229, 1999.

[21] P. Heymann, G. Koutrika, and H. Garcia-Molina. Can social bookmarking improve web search? In *Proc. 1st Int'l Conf. on Web Search and Data Mining*, pages 195–206, 2008.

[22] R. Kumar and A. Tomkins. A characterization of online browsing behavior. In *Proc. 19th Int'l Conf. on World Wide Web*, pages 561–570, 2010.

[23] S. Lawrence and C. L. Giles. Accessibility of information on the Web. *Intelligence*, 11(1):32–39, 2000.

[24] H.-T. Lee, D. Leonard, X. Wang, and D. Loguinov. IRLbot: Scaling to 6 billion pages and beyond. In *Proc. 17th Int'l Conf. on World Wide Web*, pages 427–436, 2008.

[25] J. Madhavan, D. Ko, L. Kot, V. Ganapathy, A. Rasmussen, and A. Halevy. Google's deep web crawl. *Proc. VLDB Endowment*, 1(2):1241–1252, 2008.

[26] M. Najork and J. L. Wiener. Breadth-first crawling yields high-quality pages. In *Proc. 10th Int'l Conf. on World Wide Web*, pages 114–118, 2001.

[27] A. Ntoulas, J. Cho, and C. Olston. What's new on the web?: The evolution of the web from a search engine perspective. In *Proc. 13th Int'l Conf. on World Wide Web*, pages 1–12, 2004.

[28] A. Ntoulas, P. Zerfos, and J. Cho. Downloading textual hidden web content through keyword queries. In *Proc. 5th ACM/IEEE-CS Joint Conf. on Digital Libraries*, pages 100–109, 2005.

[29] C. Olston and M. Najork. Web crawling. *Found. Trends Inf. Retr.*, 4(3):175–246, 2010.

[30] S. Pandey and C. Olston. User-centric web crawling. In *Proc. 14th Int'l Conf. on World Wide Web*, pages 401–411, 2005.

[31] F. Radlinski and T. Joachims. Query chains: Learning to rank from implicit feedback. In *Proc. of the 11th Int'l Conf. on Knowledge Discovery in Data Mining*, pages 239–248, 2005.

[32] S. Raghavan and H. Garcia-Molina. Crawling the hidden web. In *Proc. 27th Int'l Conf. on Very Large Data Bases*, pages 129–138, 2001.

[33] V. Shkapenyuk and T. Suel. Design and implementation of a high-performance distributed web crawler. In *Proc. 18th Int'l Conf. on Data Engineering*, page 357, 2002.

[34] H. E. Williams. Discovering web-based multimedia using search toolbar data, 2007. US 2007/0136263 A1.

[35] J. L. Wolf, M. S. Squillante, P. S. Yu, J. Sethuraman, and L. Ozsen. Optimal crawling strategies for web search engines. In *Proc. 11th Int'l Conf. on World Wide Web*, pages 136–147, 2002.

[36] D. Zeinalipour-Yazti and M. D. Dikaiakos. Design and implementation of a distributed crawler and filtering processor. In *Proc. 5th Int'l Workshop on Next Generation Information Technologies and Systems*, 2002.

User Browsing Behavior-driven Web Crawling

Minghai Liu†‡*, Rui Cai†, Ming Zhang‡, and Lei Zhang†
†Microsoft Research Asia ‡School of EECS, Peking University
†{ruicai, leizhang}@microsoft.com ‡{lmh, mzhang}@net.pku.edu.cn

ABSTRACT

To optimize the performance of web crawlers, various measures of page importance have been studied to select and order URLs in crawling. Most sophisticated measures (*e.g.* *breadth-first* and *PageRank*) are based on link structure. In this paper, we treat the problem from another perspective and propose to directly measure page importance through mining user interest and behaviors from web browse logs. Unlike most existing approaches which work on single URL, in this paper, both the log mining and the crawl ordering are performed at the granularity of URL pattern. The proposed URL pattern-based crawl orderings are capable to properly predict the importance of newly created (unseen) URLs. Promising experimental results proved the feasibility of our approach.

Categories and Subject Descriptors

H.3.3 [**Information Storage and Retrieval**]: Information Search and Retrieval—*information filtering*

General Terms

Algorithms, Performance, Experimentation.

Keywords

web crawling, URL pattern discovery, web log mining

1. INTRODUCTION

A web crawler cannot download everything but should be selective. The strategy of a crawler to choose URLs from its crawling queue is called crawl ordering policy [14]. The essence of designing crawl ordering policy is to quantitatively measure the "importance" of a page.

In the past decade, a series of ordering policies have been proposed, based on various importance measures. Most popular measures are based on link structure. For example, the breadth-first policy [19] believes pages located within a few links to a website's portal are important. More sophisticated measures like in-degree [7], PageRank [15], and their derivatives [2, 3, 8, 9] take more complicated link structures into account to estimate page importance. Besides link structure, some new measures were proposed recently to leverage other information. For example, topical crawler [13, 18] (also called focused crawler [6]) was introduced to prioritize pages according to their content relevance to some pre-defined semantic topics. And in [16, 17], URLs with higher search impact (in terms of click-through rates) are prompted in crawling. Another noticeable trend is to design site-specific importance measures. For example, the structure-driven approach [21] is interested in selecting some certain kinds of target pages in a website; and for forum crawling, only pages containing user-generated content are considered to be important [5, 22]. In the literature, promising results have been reported using all these approaches. Some of them (*e.g.* PageRank) have been proven to work well in industry [4].

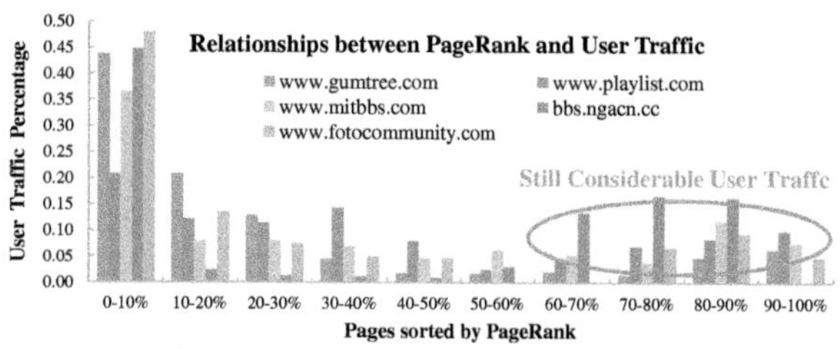

Figure 1: The relationships between PageRank and user traffic distribution on several example websites.

In nature, these importance measures adopt different hypotheses to predict how a page could be interesting to users [19]. All these hypotheses are reasonable but just characterize user interest indirectly and incompletely. Fig. 1 shows that even the most successful PageRank still lose considerable user traffic. This is because user interest is influenced by multifarious factors when the Web becomes more dynamic and complex. Therefore, we propose in this paper to directly measure page importance through mining user interest and behaviors from web browse logs.

Simply prioritizing a URL according to its frequency being recorded is impractical as the log data is very sparse in comparison with the Web. In addition, user behaviors on a single URL are usually noisy and unstable. We propose to summarize log data with URL patterns, and design crawl ordering policies at pattern-level. The motivation is that in a website, URLs generally follow some syntax schemes (patterns) pre-defined by the designers, and URLs belonging to the same pattern usually act similar roles [12]. Moreover, pattern-level statistics are more reliable and robust. In practice, our approach has two additional advantages:

*This work was performed at Microsoft Research Asia.

CIKM'11, October 24–28, 2011, Glasgow, Scotland, UK.

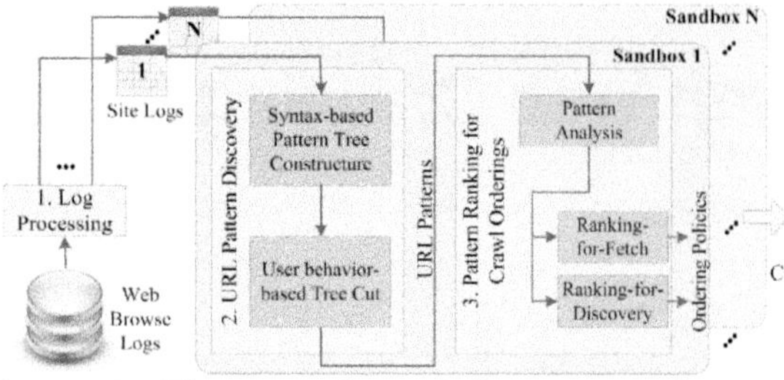

Figure 2: The overview of the proposed approach.

- First, our approach *is capable of predicting the importance of unseen URLs.* URL patterns of a website are steady in a relatively long period, and the user behaviors related to a certain pattern won't change too much.
- Second, our approach *integrates the merits of both general and site-level crawl ordering policies.* General policies like PageRank deal with a majority of websites but cannot optimize the efficiency of a particular one; while site-level policies [21, 22] are designed for specific websites but are hard to be scaled up to the whole Web. By contrast, our approach can go deep to optimize site-level crawl efficiency, as well as go wide to provide a general solution.

Two technical obstacles are solved to make the proposed approach work:

- *How to determine the granularities of URL patterns?* General patterns are apt to mix up URLs with different characteristics and cannot help crawling; while subtle patterns have the risk of over-fitting which leads to poor generalization ability on unseen data. We propose to organize URL patterns in a tree structure, and select appropriate patterns from the tree through investigating the corresponding user behaviors.
- *How to properly leverage URL patterns to design crawl ordering policies?* URLs from various patterns act different roles in a website. We propose a behavior graph-based solution to rank URL patterns for two common crawling scenarios–*comprehensive fetch a website* and *timely discover new pages.*

Elaborate experiments have been carried out and the results are quite promising. First, the discovered URL patterns can describe user behaviors very well. Furthermore, the patterns are temporally reliable and with good generalization ability to unseen data. Second, the crawling efficiencies are noticeably improved. Under the same download throughput, the proposed approach discovers and fetches more informative pages than several traditional methods.

2. DATA AND FRAMEWORK OVERVIEW

The framework overview of the proposed approach is shown in Fig. 2, which mainly consists of three components: (1) *log processing*, (2) *URL pattern discovery*, and (3) *pattern ranking for crawl ordering.*

We work on browse log collected from anonymous users who have agreed to contribute their surfing history. Records in the raw log data are in the form of a triple

$$(URL_t, URL_r, GUID)$$

where URL_t is the target being browsed and URL_r is the referrer the user comes from. $GUID$ is a hexadecimal string to identify anonymous users. Duplicate records (*i.e.* the same user transit from URL_r to URL_t for multiple times) are removed to avoid bias brought by individual users. Several measurements are statistically defined to characterize user browsing behaviors:

- $\mathcal{F}_{in}(u)$. The frequency of a URL u being a visit target. It is defined as the number of records whose URL_t is u.
- $\mathcal{F}_{out}(u)$. The frequency of a URL u being a referrer. It is defined as the number of records whose URL_r is u.
- $\mathcal{F}_{trans}(u, v)$. The frequency of transiting from a URL u to v. It is defined as the number of records whose URL_t is v and URL_r is u.

To discover appropriate URL patterns, as shown in Fig. 2, we first construct a pattern tree to organize URLs based on their syntax structures. The "parent-child" relationship between tree nodes characterizes the syntax similarity very well at various granularities. Then we tailor the tree through merging child nodes to their parent if they have consistent user behaviors.

Next, we analyze the statistical characteristics of user behaviors on each URL pattern. For example, how many URLs in a pattern act as referrer in browsing? And what is the frequency that users transiting from URLs in one pattern to URLs in another? From such statistics we can estimate how users browse a website, and analogically design crawl ordering policies. Currently two crawling scenarios – *comprehensive fetch* and *timely discovery* – are considered and their ordering policies are discussed in the modules *ranking-for-fetch* and *ranking-for-discovery* in Fig. 2.

At last, we would like to emphasize that the proposed approach can be run in parallel in multiple sandboxes, each of which handles one website, as shown in Fig. 2. The only input of a sandbox is the site-level logs. It is easy to deploy this approach on a cluster to deal with millions of websites.

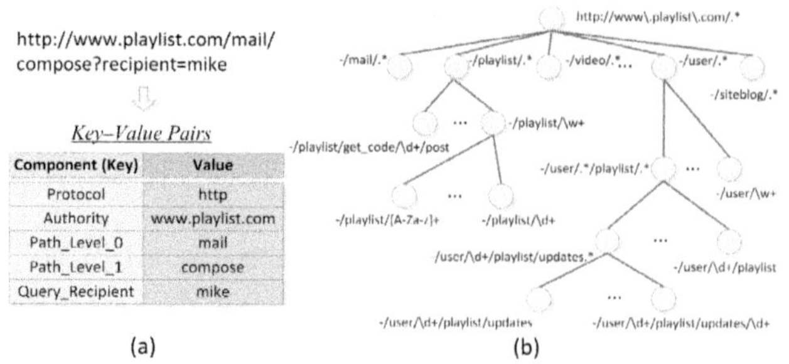

Figure 3: Illustrations of (a) URL decomposition and (b) the pattern tree (only shows a partial part for a clear view) for URLs from www.playlist.com.

3. DISCOVERING URL PATTERNS

In this section, we introduce how to discover appropriate URL patterns from web browse logs.

3.1 Syntax-based Pattern Tree Construction

A URL is not an ordinary string but complies with the syntax scheme strictly defined in [1]. Based on the syntax scheme, a URL can be decomposed into a series of "key–value" pairs, as shown in Fig. 3 (a). In addition, URLs in the same website usually follow some designing principles. Specifically, different keys usually have different functions and play different roles.

Following the recursive split process in [12], we construct a pattern tree in a top-down manner. That is, we start from the root (which contains all the input URLs), and iteratively divide URLs into subgroups according to their values under a particular key. The selected key in each iteration is the one

Table 1: Pattern-level statistics of user behaviors.

Statistics	Description
$\lVert\mathbb{P}\rVert$	$\lVert\{u, u \in \mathbb{P}\}\rVert$
$\mathcal{F}_{in}(\mathbb{P})$	$\mathcal{F}_{in}(\mathbb{P}) = \sum_{u \in \mathbb{P}} \mathcal{F}_{in}(u)$
$\mathcal{F}_{out}(\mathbb{P})$	$\mathcal{F}_{out}(\mathbb{P}) = \sum_{u \in \mathbb{P}} \mathcal{F}_{out}(u)$
$\mathcal{F}_{trans}(\mathbb{P}_a, \mathbb{P}_b)$	$\mathcal{F}_{trans}(\mathbb{P}_a, \mathbb{P}_b) = \sum_{u \in \mathbb{P}_a, v \in \mathbb{P}_b} \mathcal{F}_{trans}(u, v)$

who has the most concentrated distribution of values. For more details please refer to [12]. Fig. 3 (b) shows an example pattern tree constructed for the website `www.playlist.com`.

3.2 User Behavior-based Pattern Selection

Table 1 defines several pattern-level statistics, which are statistically significant than URL-level ones. Two browsing behaviors, *visit* and *transit*, are then considered in sequence to cut down the syntax-based tree, as shown in Fig. 4.

3.2.1 Visit-based Tree-Cut

Visit-based tree-cut is to remove sibling nodes having similar visit traffic (*e.g.* the nodes in the red dashed ellipse in Fig. 4 (b)). The process can be considered as using a model (a tree-cut plan) to characterize a dataset (URL-based user traffic). A model with lower complexity is preferred if it can describe the data well. In this paper, the well-known minimum description length (MDL) principle [20] is adopted to balance the model complexity and the fit to the data. Let $\mathbb{U}$ be the set of input URLs. A tree-cut plan is denoted by a set $\Gamma = \{\mathbb{P}_1, \cdots, \mathbb{P}_K\}$ in which each $\mathbb{P}_k (1 \le k \le K)$ is a leaf node survived after the cut. The best plan Γ_{best} is the one that minimizes the sum of *model description length* $L(\Gamma)$ and *data description length* $L(\mathbb{U}|\Gamma)$, as

$$\Gamma_{best} = \arg\min_{\Gamma} L(\Gamma) + L(\mathbb{U}|\Gamma). \quad (1)$$

According to [20], $L(\Gamma)$ can be estimated by

$$L(\Gamma) = \frac{K-1}{2} \log \mathcal{F}_{in}(\mathbb{P}_{root}), \quad (2)$$

where $\mathcal{F}_{in}(\mathbb{P}_{root}) = \sum_{u \in \mathbb{U}} \mathcal{F}_{in}(u)$ is the total traffic on all the URLs in $\mathbb{U}$, and K is the size of Γ. $L(\mathbb{U}|\Gamma)$ can be described by the negative log-likelihood of the data given the model [10],

$$L(\mathbb{U}|\Gamma) = -\log p(\mathbb{U}|\Gamma) = -\sum_{u \in \mathbb{U}} p(u|\Gamma), \quad (3)$$

where $p(u|\Gamma)$ is defined as

$$p(u|\Gamma) = \frac{1}{\lVert\mathbb{P}_k\rVert} \frac{\mathcal{F}_{in}(\mathbb{P}_k)}{\mathcal{F}_{in}(\mathbb{P}_{root})}. \quad (4)$$

In other words, the probability of a single URL being visited is smoothed by the corresponding pattern-level average.

3.2.2 Transit-based Tree-Cut

As user behaviors are easy to be disturbed by temporal interruptions, child nodes belonging to the same functional role are still possible to have different visit frequencies. In such a case, transit behavior can help remove redundant nodes. For example, it is reasonable to remove the two nodes in the blue rectangle in Fig. 4 (b) if they have identical in-links and out-links, as shown in Fig. 4 (c).

Given a pattern $\mathbb{P}_k$, it is straightforward to characterize its in-link distribution $\mathbf{p}_k^{in}$ and out-link distribution $\mathbf{p}_k^{out}$ as

$$\begin{array}{ll} \mathbf{p}_k^{in} = \{p_{i \to k}^{in}, 1 \le i \le K\}, & p_{i \to k}^{in} = \frac{\mathcal{F}_{trans}(\mathbb{P}_i, \mathbb{P}_k)}{\mathcal{F}_{in}(\mathbb{P}_k)} \\ \mathbf{p}_k^{out} = \{p_{k \to i}^{out}, 1 \le i \le K\}, & p_{k \to i}^{out} = \frac{\mathcal{F}_{trans}(\mathbb{P}_k, \mathbb{P}_i)}{\mathcal{F}_{out}(\mathbb{P}_k)} \end{array}. \quad (5)$$

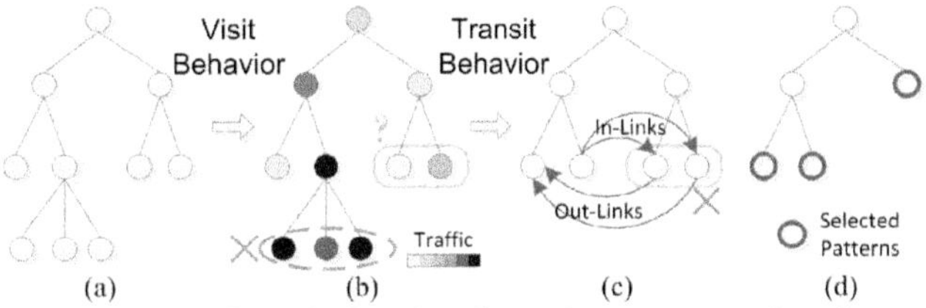

Figure 4: User behavior-based pattern selection.

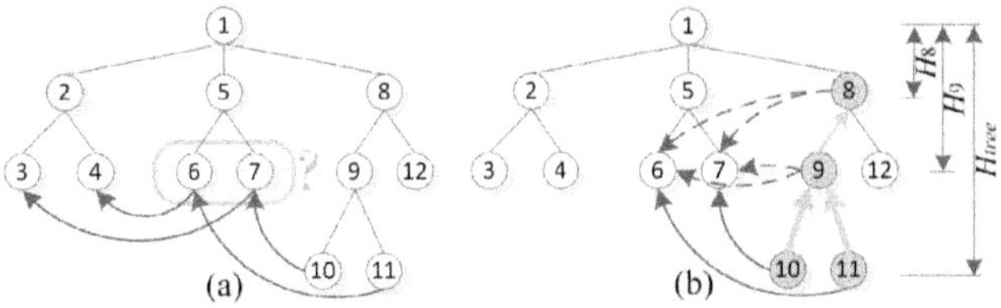

Figure 5: Illustrations of (a) a complex case to judge the transit similarity of node 6 and 7; and (b) propagate transit possibilities on the tree to smooth the in-link distributions of 6 and 7.

Such a definition can handle the simple case in Fig. 4 (c), while real cases are more complicated. As shown in Fig. 5 (a), the nodes 6 and 7 have different in-link and out-link nodes. However, it is noticed that their in-link nodes (10 and 11) and out-link nodes (3 and 4) are siblings of each other. The nodes 6 and 7 still have similar transit relationships if node 9 and 2 are respectively treated as their in-link and out-link nodes. To smooth the in-link and out-link distributions, the transits are propagated on the tree, as shown in Fig. 5 (b). The propagation is defined by a $K \times N$ matrix whose element$\mathbf{P}_{k,n}$is defined as

$$\mathbf{P}_{k,n} = \begin{cases} \prod_{h=H_n}^{H_k-1} \frac{h}{H_{tree}} & k \text{ is a leaf, } n \text{ is its ancestor} \\ 1 & k = n \\ 0 & \text{otherwise} \end{cases} \quad (6)$$

where H_k and H_n are the heights of k and n on the tree, H_{tree} is the total tree height, and N is the total number of tree nodes. Eq. (6) is defined following two criteria:

- The transit possibility of a leaf node can only be propagated to its direct ancestors.
- The transit possibility keeps weakening when the propagation goes farther. The decay factor is experimentally set as H_{father}/H_{tree} where H_{father} is the depth of the father node.

With the $\mathbf{P}$ matrix, the K-dimensional sparse vectors in Eq. (5) are converted to N-dimensional dense ones, as

$$\hat{\mathbf{p}}_i^{in} = \mathbf{p}_i^{in} \times \mathbf{P} \quad \text{and} \quad \hat{\mathbf{p}}_i^{out} = \mathbf{p}_i^{out} \times \mathbf{P}. \quad (7)$$

And the transit similarity $sim_{transit}(i, j)$ between $\mathbb{P}_i$ and $\mathbb{P}_j$ is defined as the average of their in-link and out-link cosine similarities on the smoothed distributions, as

$$sim_{transit}(i, j) = \frac{1}{2}[\cos(\hat{\mathbf{p}}_i^{in}, \hat{\mathbf{p}}_j^{in}) + \cos(\hat{\mathbf{p}}_i^{out}, \hat{\mathbf{p}}_j^{out})]. \quad (8)$$

Based on Eq. (8), the cutdown process is carried out in a bottom-up way, as shown in Algorithm 1.

4. PATTERN RANKING FOR CRAWLING

In this section, we introduce how to design crawl ordering policies based on the discovered URL patterns.

Algorithm 1 Transit-based Tree Cut. The input is a pattern tree and the output is a series of URL patterns.

```
Let 𝒬 be a priority queue in which tree nodes are sorted in
   descending order according to their depths on the tree.
Initializing 𝒬. For each node, add it to 𝒬 if the node itself is
   not a leaf but all its children are leaves.
while 𝒬 is not empty do
  Pop the first node q from 𝒬, 𝒞_q is the set of q's children.
  ξ_q = min{sim_transit(m, n), ∀m, n ∈ 𝒞_q & m ≠ n}
  if ξ_q > ξ_thresh-to-cut then
    Turn q into a leaf by cutting all the nodes in 𝒞_q.
    Update p_i^in, p_i^out and P following Eq. (5) and (6).
    if all the siblings of q are leaves then
      Add q's parent to 𝒬.
    end if
  end if
end while
return URL patterns of all the remaining leaf nodes.
```

4.1 Two Crawling Scenarios

Two common crawling scenarios–*batch* and *incremental* modes [14]–are exported to site-level here, as:

- *Comprehensive fetching a website* is similar to the *batch* mode, to periodically snapshot a website. The goal is to fetch as much as possible valuable information from the target website. Importance measurement in this situation should describe the value of a downloaded page itself.
- *Timely discovering new pages* partially realizes the function of the *incremental* mode, to discover newly created URLs via frequently checking a few "hub" pages. This is useful to monitor websites of social network or news. Importance measurement here should consider the total value of URLs linked from the downloaded page.

It is straightforward to design ordering strategies directly based on the pattern-level statistics of browsing behaviors.

Ranking-for-fetch strategies:

- *Rank-by-Volume.* URL patterns are sorted in descending order based on its volume $||\mathbb{P}||$. Large volume means that pattern is a dominant resource in a website, and should provide more information to users.
- *Rank-by-Overall-Visit.* Patterns attracting more overall user visit traffic, *i.e.* $\mathcal{F}_{in}(\mathbb{P})$, are with higher priorities.
- *Rank-by-Average-Visit.* Patterns are ordered according to the averaged visit frequency $\mathcal{F}_{in}(\mathbb{P})/||\mathbb{P}||$.

Ranking-for-discovery strategies:

- *Rank-by-Overall-Referral.* The importance of a pattern is evaluated based on the total amount of times that its URLs act as referrers in browse logs, *i.e.*, $\mathcal{F}_{out}(\mathbb{P})$.
- *Rank-by-Average-Referral.* Patterns are ranked based on the average frequency that their URLs play a referrer role in browsing, *i.e.*, $\mathcal{F}_{out}(\mathbb{P})/||\mathbb{P}||$.

All these strategies are partially reasonable from certain perspectives. However, they just locally consider the characteristics of an individual pattern, but neglect the relationships between patterns. To better combine both the behavior statistics and the relationships between URL patterns, we propose to use graph-based strategy to rank patterns.

4.2 Behavior Graph-based Pattern Ranking

The graph constructed in this paper is called behavior graph as it is different from the traditional link graph in several aspects. First, link graph in existing work is based on URLs, while nodes in the behavior graph are URL patterns. Therefore, the behavior graph is small and the related computation is cheap. Second, the behavior graph is initialized based on statistics at pattern-level, while link graphs are initialized almost randomly. Third, the transition probabilities (*i.e.* weights of graph edges) of the behavior graph are voted by users, while the edge weights of a link graph are based on hyper-links (*e.g.* in-degree and out-degree).

Of course, PageRank-like link analysis strategy is still feasible for the behavior graph. However, it measures the overall importance of a graph node and thus is only suitable for *comprehensive fetch.* In comparison, another popular link analysis method, the HITS algorithm [11], measures page importance from two aspects–*authority* and *hub.* For each node, the *authority* score depicts the value of its content and the *hub* score describes the value of its links. This perfectly matches the requirements of both *comprehensive fetch* and *timely discovery.* Following the instruction of the HITS algorithm, the two scores of a node $\mathbb{P}_i$ are initialized as

$$auth^0(\mathbb{P}_i) = \frac{\mathcal{F}_{in}(\mathbb{P}_i)}{\mathcal{F}_{in}(\mathbb{P}_{root})} \quad hub^0(\mathbb{P}_i) = \frac{\mathcal{F}_{out}(\mathbb{P}_i)}{\mathcal{F}_{out}(\mathbb{P}_{root})}. \quad (9)$$

The two scores are continually updated in a series of iterations. The updating formulas of the kth iteration are

$$\begin{array}{l} auth^k(\mathbb{P}_i) = \sum_j p_{j\to i}^{out} \times hub^{k-1}(\mathbb{P}_j) \\ hub^k(\mathbb{P}_i) = \sum_j p_{i\to j}^{in} \times auth^{k-1}(\mathbb{P}_j) \end{array}. \quad (10)$$

Both $auth^k(\mathbb{P}_i)$ and $hub^k(\mathbb{P}_i)$ are normalized to unit magnitude after the update. The converged *authority* and *hub* of each node can properly estimate the possibilities of URLs in that pattern to be targets or referrers. Consequently, for *comprehensive fetch*, URL patterns are ranked in descending order based on $0.5 \times [auth(\mathbb{P}_i) + hub(\mathbb{P}_i)]$; and for *timely discovery*, patterns are simply ordered by $hub(\mathbb{P}_i)$.

Table 2: The dataset scales (#URLs) in evaluation.

Website	Mirror	30-day Log	Search Result
www.mitbbs.com	9,903,107	265,464	27,757
www.gumtree.com	9,135,292	973,317	64,663
www.cooks.com	3,555,610	353,492	200,354
6.cn	6,996,186	234,936	53,962
bbs.ngacn.cc	2,901,950	490,818	49,980
www.fotocommunity.de	8,282,845	1,699,434	22,226
ku6.com	17,896,352	1,613,165	214,059
www.playlist.com	10,831,023	964,819	20,783
fantong.com	4,952,562	67,060	6,789
Total	**74,454,927**	**6,662,505**	**660,573**

5. EVALUATION AND DISCUSSION

Elaborate experiments have been carried out to demonstrate the feasibility of the proposed approach, for both URL pattern discovery and efficient site-level crawling.

5.1 Experiment Setup

The experiments were carried out on 9 websites, as shown in Table 2. These websites include forums, video websites, and several popular Web 2.0 portals. For each website there are three data resources: (1) the mirror cached at May 2010, using a brute-force crawler; (2) 6-month browse logs from Nov. 2009 to Apr. 2010, collected by web browsers; and (3) search results returned by Google, Bing, and Yahoo!, including URLs from that website and were clicked in web search. Browse logs and search results can be considered to describe user interest from two different perspectives. The scales of these data resources are listed in Table 2. In the experiments, the URL patterns were mined based on one-month log data (Nov. 2009), and the other five months' logs

Table 3: The statistics of pattern trees

Pattern Tree	#Leaf Node			Tree Height		
	Min	Max	Avg	Min	Max	Avg
$\mathbb{T}_{SYN}$	28	1076	283.7	7	17	11.3
$\mathbb{T}_{VISIT}$	20	106	60.9	6	12	8.4
$\mathbb{T}_{TRAN}$	16	100	51.1	6	11	7.8

Table 4: Several evaluations of pattern qualities

Quality	$\mathbb{T}_{SYN}$	$\mathbb{T}_{VISIT}$	$\mathbb{T}_{TRAN}$	Random
Mirror Coverage	91.2%	99.1%	99.9%	–
Layout Similarity	0.915	0.889	0.881	0.322
Traffic Approximation	0.165	0.166	0.166	–

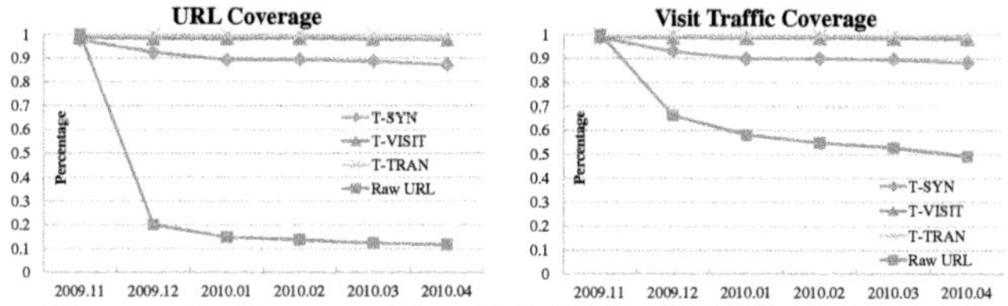

Figure 6: Temporal reliability of URL patterns.

were used for evaluation. All the crawling was simulated on the mirrors, which provide a consistent experimental environment. In the following evaluations, the average performances of all the 9 websites are reported.

5.2 Quality of URL Patterns

According to the steps in Section 3, the generated pattern trees are denoted as $\mathbb{T}_{SYN}$, $\mathbb{T}_{VISIT}$ and $\mathbb{T}_{TRAN}$. Some basic statistics of these pattern trees are listed in Table 3. Several evaluations were designed to measure the URL pattern qualities from four aspects.

Mirror coverage is to measure the *generalization ability* of URL patterns. Specifically, we measure how many URLs in the mirrors can be covered by the discovered patterns. From Table 4, it is noticed that around 10% URLs in the mirrors cannot be covered by the patterns from $\mathbb{T}_{SYN}$. In other words, these patterns somewhat overfit the training log data. In comparison, the patterns from $\mathbb{T}_{VISIT}$ and $\mathbb{T}_{TRAN}$ significantly improve the generalization ability and can cover almost all the URLs in the mirrors.

Page layout similarity is to measure the *distinguishability* of URL patterns. That is to say, a pattern should contain only one certain resource in a website. Here, the distinguishability is evaluated via checking the layout similarity between pages under the same pattern. This makes sense as most modern websites are built based on templates [5, 21]. We computed the pair-wise layout similarities between pages under the same patterns, as well as some random pages from different patterns for comparison. From Table 4, it is clear that pages grouped by URL patterns have better layout consistencies than randomly selected pages.

Visit traffic approximation is to measure the *summarization ability* of URL patterns. The pattern-level summarizations smooth the user browsing behaviors on individual URLs. However, such smoothing shouldn't distort the browsing behaviors too much. We calculated the Jensen-Shannon divergences between the visit traffic distribution on original URLs and the smoothed distributions on pattern-level. From Table 4, it is clear that the smoothing process (*e.g.* $\mathbb{T}_{SYN}$ *vs.* $\mathbb{T}_{TRAN}$) just slightly hurt the distribution of browsing behaviors.

Temporal reliability is to measure the period of validity of URL patterns. Both the URL coverage and the traffic

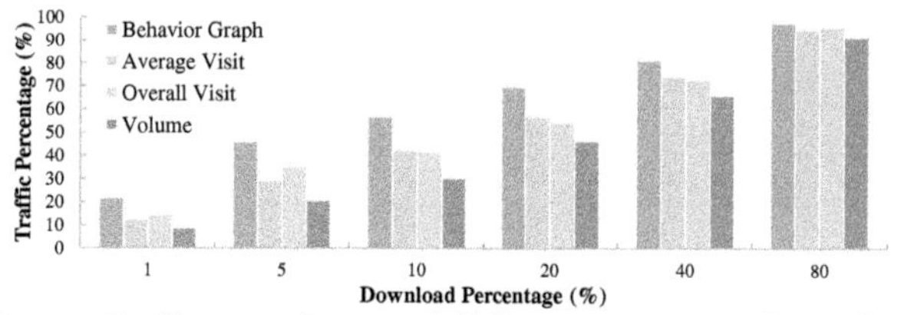

Figure 7: Comparisons of different pattern-based ordering strategies, for *comprehensive fetch.*

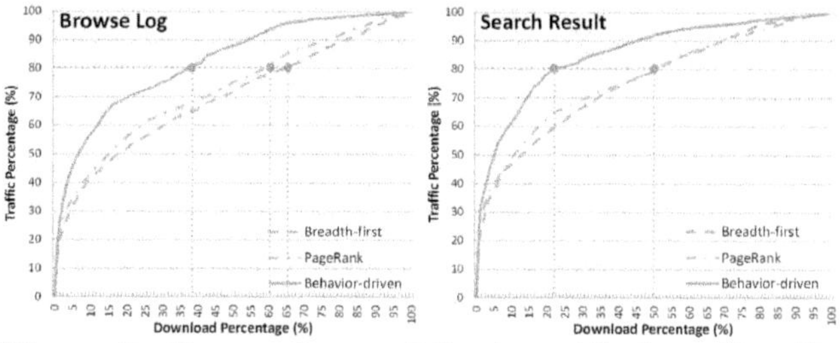

Figure 8: Comparisons of the breadth-first, PageRank, and the proposed behavior-driven approach, for *comprehensive fetch.*

coverage were evaluated along time. For comparison, we also measured the URL-level reliability, that is, the intersection percentage of URLs in logs of different periods. As shown in Fig. 6, the URL-level reliability drops very quickly, which perfectly echoes the statement in [14] that URLs retire rapidly. By contrast, URL patterns (especially those from the final tree-cut $\mathbb{T}_{TRAN}$) are quite reliable. This is a convincing justification to do pattern-level crawl ordering.

5.3 Crawling Efficiency

The evaluations of crawling performance were set up respectively for *comprehensive fetch* and *timely discovery.*

5.3.1 Comprehensive Fetch a Website

Two factors were monitored for the evaluation of the *comprehensive fetch* scenario. One is the throughput which indicates how many web pages have been downloaded; the other is the amount of downloaded information which is described by the sum of traffic[1] of the fetched URLs.

In Fig. 7, we compare the behavior graph-based ranking strategy with the three naïve ranking-for-fetch strategies in Section 4.1. Several different throughput conditions, from 1% to 80%, were investigated. Among the four strategies, rank-by-volume is always the worst. This indicates that the visit traffic is not in proportion to the resource scale (a URL pattern can be considered as a kind of resource in a website). Rank-by-overall-traffic and rank-by-average-traffic are more efficient but still not good enough. In comparison, the behavior graph-based strategy remarkably outperforms all those naïve strategies, especially when the throughput is small. This is a nice advantage as throughput is always the biggest bottleneck in crawling.

Fig. 8 compares the proposed approach with two popular ordering policies, *breadth-first* and *PageRank*, deployed in industry. The link-depth and PageRank scores were calculated based on the mirrored websites. Besides the browse logs, the information amount was also estimated based on the click numbers in the search results. It is noticeable that

[1]For a URL in browse log, the traffic is $\mathcal{F}_{in}(u)$; for a URL in search results, the traffic is its click number; otherwise the traffic is simply set as zero.

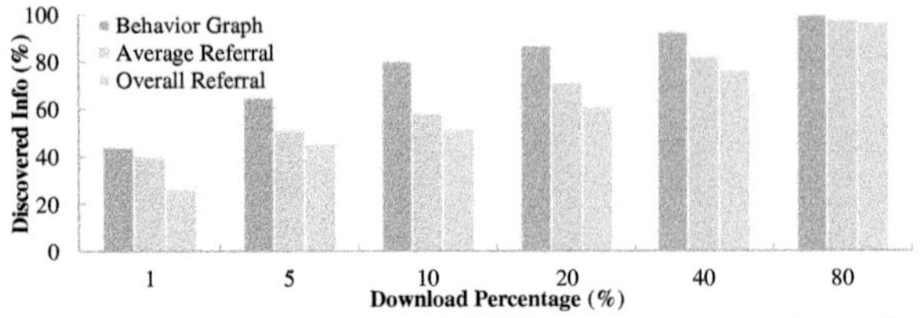

Figure 9: Comparisons of different pattern-based ordering strategies, for *timely discovery*.

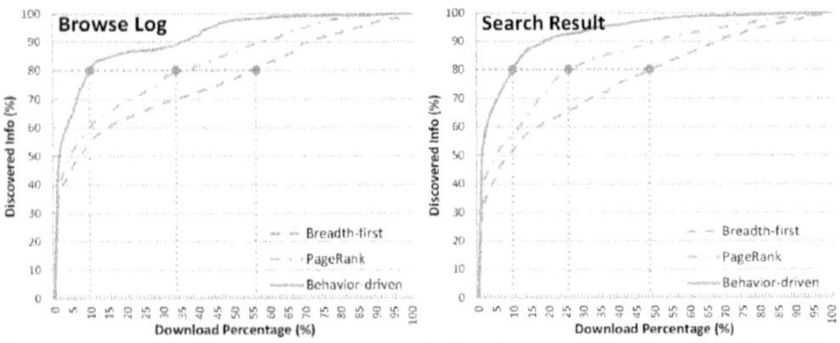

Figure 10: Comparisons of the breadth-first, PageRank, and the proposed behavior-driven approach, for *timely discovery*.

the proposed approach is much better than the breadth-first and PageRank methods. For example, to download 80% visit traffic, our approach needs to fetch less than 40% pages form a website; while the other two methods need to download more than 60% pages to achieve this goal. Under the measurement of click number in search results, the superiority is even more obvious, as shown in the right part of Fig. 8. This is a good news to search engines, as URLs frequently clicked in search results are quite important to search relevance.

5.3.2 Timely Discover New Pages

For evaluation of the *timely discovery* scenario, we replace the amount of downloaded information to the amount of discovered information. The discovered information is defined as the sum of traffic of all the seen URLs. A URL is called a seen URL once it was parsed from a fetched page and has been added to the crawling queue. The discovered information provides an expectation of the amount of information can be downloaded in the future.

In Fig. 9, we compare the behavior graph-based ranking strategy with the other two ranking-for-discovery strategies in Section 4.1. Among the three strategies, rank-by-average-referral is better than rank-by-overall-referral. This makes sense as dominant hub patterns in a website usually have only a few URLs which frequently act as referrers in browsing. Although the count of overall referral may be small, the average number of referrals on each page is large. Again, the behavior graph-based strategy is the best under all the throughputs. This suggests the quality of referrals is also important in ranking a referrer.

Finally, the efficiencies of the breadth-first, PageRank, and our approach are compared in Fig. 10. Our approach is still better than the breadth-first and PageRank methods. For instance, to discover 80% traffic, our approach needs to download around 10% pages; while PageRank needs to download about 35% pages and the breadth-first needs to fetch 55%. In other words, a crawler equipped with our approach can monitor 80% information of a website via only downloading and checking 10% URLs. This is especially useful for the crawling of Web 2.0 websites. In addition, our approach also held the superiority under the measurement of click number, as shown in the right part of Fig. 10.

6. CONCLUSIONS

In this paper we proposed a user behavior-driven method for efficient crawling. The contributions are four-fold:

- Propose to leverage web log data to help web crawling. This is more direct than existing technologies to predict user interest and optimize crawl ordering.
- Propose to summarize web logs with URL patterns. Come up with a pattern tree-based method to identify URL patterns in a proper granularity from log data.
- Propose several strategies to rank patterns for two crawling scenarios, comprehensive fetch and timely discovery.
- The proposed approach goes deep to optimize site-level crawl ordering policies, and is capable of going wide to deal with millions of websites in parallel mode.

7. REFERENCES

[1] Uniform resource identifier: Generic syntax. RFC 3986.
[2] S. Abiteboul, M. Preda, and G. Cobena. Adaptive on-line page importance computation. In *Proc. WWW*, pages 280–290, 2003.
[3] R. Baeza-Yates, C. Castillo, M. Marin, and A. Rodriguez. Crawling a country: better strategies than breadth-first for web page ordering. In *Proc. WWW*, pages 864–872, 2005.
[4] S. Brin and L. Page. The anatomy of a large-scale hypertextual web search engine. *Computer Networks*, 30(1–7):107–117, 1998.
[5] R. Cai, J.-M. Yang, W. Lai, Y. Wang, and L. Zhang. iRobot: an intelligent crawler for web forums. In *Proc. WWW*, pages 447–456, 2008.
[6] S. Chakrabarti, M. van den Berg, and B. Dom. Focused crawling: a new approach to topic-specific web resource discovery. *Computer Networks*, 31(11–16):1623–1640, 1999.
[7] J. Cho, H. Garcia-Molina, and L. Page. Efficient crawling through URL ordering. *Computer Networks*.
[8] J. Cho and U. Schonfeld. RankMass crawler: a crawler with high personalized PageRank coverage guarantee. In *Proc. VLDB*, pages 375–386, 2007.
[9] D. Fetterly, N. Craswell, and V. Vinay. The impact of crawl policy on web search effectiveness. In *Proc. SIGIR*, pages 580–587, 2009.
[10] P. Grünwald. *A tutorial introduction to the minimum description length principle.* Advances in Minimum Description Length: Theory and Applications. MIT Press, 2005.
[11] J. Kleinberg. Authoritative sources in a hyperlinked environment. *Journal of the ACM*, 46(5):604–632, 1999.
[12] T. Lei, R. Cai, J.-M. Yang, Y. Ke, X. Fan, and L. Zhang. A pattern tree-based approach to learning URL normalization rules. In *Proc. WWW*, pages 611–620, 2010.
[13] F. Menczer, G. Pant, and P. Srinivasan. Topical web crawlers: evaluating adaptive algorithms. *ACM Trans. Internet Techn.*, 4(4):378–419, 2004.
[14] C. Olston and M. Najork. Web crawling. *Foundations and Trends® in Information Retrieval*, 4(3):175–246, 2010.
[15] L. Page, S. Brin, R. Motwani, and T. Winograd. The PageRank citation ranking: bringing order to the Web. Technical report, Stanford University, 1999.
[16] S. Pandey and C. Olston. User-centric web crawling. In *Proc. WWW*, pages 401–411, 2005.
[17] S. Pandey and C. Olston. Crawl ordering by search impact. In *Proc. WSDM*, pages 3–14, 2008.
[18] G. Pant and P. Srinivasan. Learning to crawl: comparing classification schemes. *ACM Trans. Inf. Syst.*
[19] B. Pinkerton. Finding what people want: experiences with the web crawler. In *Proc. WWW*, pages 3–14, 1994.
[20] J. Rissanen. Stochastic complexity and modeling. *The Annals of Statistics*, 14(3):1080–1100, 1986.
[21] M. L. A. Vidal, A. S. da Silva, E. S. de Moura, and J. M. B. Caval-canti. Structure-driven crawler generation by example. In *Proc. SIGIR*, pages 292–299, 2006.
[22] Y. Wang, J.-M. Yang, W. Lai, R. Cai, L. Zhang, and W.-Y. Ma. Exploring traversal strategy for efficient web forum crawling. In *Proc. SIGIR*, pages 459–466, 2008.

Diversifying Search Results of Controversial Queries

Mouna Kacimi
Free University of Bozen-Bolzano
Italy
Mouna.Kacimi@unibz.it

Johann Gamper
Free University of Bozen-Bolzano
Italy
gamper@inf.unibz.it

ABSTRACT

Diversifying search results of queries seeking for different view points about controversial topics is key to improving satisfaction of users. The challenge for finding different opinions is how to maximize the number of discussed arguments without being biased against specific sentiments. This paper addresses the issue by first introducing a new model that represents the patterns occurring in documents about controversial topics. Second, proposing an opinion diversification model that uses (1) *relevance* of documents, (2) *semantic diversification* to capture different arguments and (3) *sentiment diversification* to identify positive, negative and neutral sentiments about the query topic. We have conducted our experiments using queries on various controversial topics and applied our diversification model on the set of documents returned by Google search engine. The results show that our model outperforms the native ranking of Web pages about controversial topics by a significant margin.

Categories and Subject Descriptors

H.3 [**Information Storage and Retrieval**]: Information Search and Retrieval]

General Terms

Algorithms, Experimentation

1. INTRODUCTION

In the last decade, Web search has become the predominant method to access information. Typically, queries are expressed using few keywords which are often ambiguous and have different interpretations [1, 12]. For example, the query "jaguar" may refer to the *car*, the *cat*, the *operating system*, or the *classic Fender guitar*. Since no additional information is always available to determine the real user intent, several result diversification techniques have been proposed to solve this problem [7, 1, 4, 13]. Their aim is to produce a set of results that cover different interpretations. While there is a considerable effort on diversifying search results of ambiguous queries, there is a little effort on covering different view points in the result set of controversial queries, meaning queries about debatable topics, such as "assisted suicide", "human evolution", "UFOs existence", and queries looking for different versions of the same breaking news. Users seeking for such type of knowledge are not necessarily interested in a specific way of looking at a given issue, but possibly learning about that topic and interested in finding all different view points. Thus, it is important to focus on how best to produce a set of diversified results that cover different arguments and sentiments.

Diversifying results of controversial queries involves mining opinions (also called sentiment analysis), a problem that have been widely studied in the past few years [20, 6, 21]. Most of these efforts have focused on product reviews, while few attempts [2, 5] have addressed the problem of mining controversial documents (i.e., documents about controversial topics). Typically, mining controversial documents has followed the same line of mining product reviews, where a pro/con classification is used to identify documents that have either positive or negative sentiment regarding a given topic. However, discussing a controversial topic involves much more than just positive, negative or neutral sentiments. It involves different ways of looking at the problem using different arguments. For example, two documents can be both negative about "human evolution" but for completely different reasons. One is negative because of the *high deleterious mutation rate in humans*, while the other is negative because it promotes *creationism*. These two documents are not diverse with respect to their sentiments, but they are diverse with respect to the arguments they provide. Thus, one need to use both sentiment analysis and novelty detection to diversify search results of controversial queries.

Addressing queries looking for both various arguments and sentiments face two main challenges. First, finding documents discussing similar arguments without being mislead by the difference they might exhibit in presenting them. Second, diversifying a set of documents by maximizing the number of discussed arguments without being biased against specific sentiments. This paper presents a solution towards solving the above problems by first introducing a new model that captures the main features of controversial documents, and second proposing an opinion diversification model that uses (1) *relevance* to select relevant documents for the query topic , (2) *semantic diversification* to avoid redundancy and cover a diverse set of documents presenting different argu-

CIKM'11, October 24–28, 2011, Glasgow, Scotland, UK.

ments, and (3) *sentiment diversification* to cover different types of sentiments that can be positive, negative, or neutral. The diversification model is presented with a new technique for computing similarity between documents based on the discussion arguments. We applied the proposed diversification model on the set of documents returned by Google search engine. The results show that our opinion diversification model always outperforms the native ranking of controversial Web pages by a significant margin.

2. RELATED WORK

Search result diversification has been investigated extensively following two different approaches.The first one is *taxonomy-independent* where no knowledge base is used to diversify search results [19, 12, 13, 7, 15]. Some of the works falling into this category include the work by Gollapudi et al. [7] that uses a diversification model combining both novelty and relevance of search results. Zhai et al. [18] propose a risk minimization framework that allows users to define an arbitrary loss function for a given set of results. Radilinski et al. [12] use query expansion to enrich search results generating more relevant documents for various interpretations. The second approach to result diversification is *taxonomy-based.* [1, 4, 3]. Representative works include the one by Agrawal et al. [1] which makes use of a taxonomy for classifying queries and documents and create a diverse set of results according to this taxonomy. Clarke et al. [4] focus on developing a framework of evaluation that takes into account both novelty and diversity. Carterette et al. [3] propose a probabilistic approach to maximize the coverage of the retrieved documents with respect to the aspects of a query.

In our work, we use a *taxonomy-independent* diversification model that exploits both relevance and novelty. The difference between our work and existing approaches is the integration of sentiments in the diversification model. The closest work to ours is by Demartini et al. [5]. They propose a diversification model for search results based on positive, negative, and neutral sentiments. The difference with our work is that we do not restrict the diversification to these three sentiments but we exploit also novelty to capture various arguments about controversial topics.

Another research problem that is directly related to our work is *opinion mining*, also called *sentiment analysis.* This problem has been studied in the past few years [14, 6, 16] exploiting two main directions: (1) finding product features that have been commented on by reviewers and (2) deciding whether the comments are positive or negative. The second direction is the one we are exploiting in our work. Two main categories of classifying sentiments have been explored: classification at the *document* level [11, 14] and a more fine-grained classification at the *sentence level* [16, 6]. As stated in [6], most *sentence level* and *document level* classification methods follow two approaches: (1) *corpus-based* approaches, and (2) *lexical-based* approaches. Corpus-based approaches find co-occurrence patterns of words to determine the sentiments of words or phrases, e.g., the work in [14]. Lexical-based approaches use synonyms and antonyms in WordNet to determine word sentiments based on a set of seed words. Such approaches are studied in [6].

Most of the techniques described above focus on product reviews. Few attempts [2, 5] have addressed the problem of mining documents about controversial topics. In our work, we take a more general approach to address the problem of classifying search results of controversial queries, depending on their sentiment orientations. To this end, we propose a model that can handle both sentence-level and document level classification. Depending on the granularity of classification, both corpus-based and lexical based approaches can be used.

3. MODELING CONTROVERSIAL DOCUMENTS

We define a controversial document as a document that discusses a debatable topic. A controversial document is represented as a set of *topic elements*, E=$\{e_1, e_2, ..., e_n\}$, which reflect the different points of the discussion. For instance, a document about "Abortion" discusses: the *pregnancy*, the *choice* of abortion, the *right* to abort, the *privacy* of the action, the *fetus*, the *ethics* of abortion, and the *family* role. Concretely, topic elements are assumed to be the nouns that occur in the text. Each topic element occurs within a set of sentences. These sentences give the context in which the topic element was discussed. We define the *context* C_i of a topic element e_i by the set of words composing the sentences to which it belongs. We call these words, *context words* and we write $C_i = \{cw_1, cw_2, ..., cw_m\}$ where cw_j is a context word of topic element e_i . We restrict context words only to nouns, adjectives, and adverbs. For example, we take the topic element "fetus" that occurs in the following sentence: "*If the fetus is a person, then abortion is murder and should be illegal*". In this case, the set of context words would be $\{person, abortion, murder, illegal\}$. Note that the topic element "fetus" is linked to topic elements *person*, *abortion*, and *murder*, which are basically the nouns. For each context word, we define its sentiment orientation, which will be used to predict the sentiment assigned to the corresponding topic element. Words that encode a desirable state (e.g., perfect, right) have a positive orientation, while words that represent undesirable states have a negative orientation (e.g., illegal, against). While sentiment orientations apply to many words, there are also those words that have no sentiment orientation (e.g., person, universe) that we call neutral. Combining topic elements, context words, and sentiment orientations, we define a document as a set of triples:

$$d = \{< e_i, cw_j, o_j >\}$$

where e_i is a topic element, cw_j is a context word associated with e_i, and o_j is the sentiment orientation of cw_j. Note here that we have used OpenNLP[10] to extract the different types of words from the text, while the extraction of sentiments is done through classification.

This model is used both to compute similarity between documents and classify their sentiments. It allows both *sentence-level* and *document-level* classification of sentiments. In *sentence-level* classification, sentiments are assigned to each topic element depending on its context. By contrast, *document-level* classification assigns one sentiment orientation to the whole document with respect to the query topic (e.g., Abortion). In this paper, we focus on *document-level* classification as a first step towards diversifying search results of controversial queries.

We consider a multi-class classification model where we have three classes $\{positive, negative, neutral\}$. Each document with features $\{f_1, ..., f_N\}$ is assigned to one class. The features, we use in our classification model, are the set of *context words* that have either *positive* or *negative* sentiment orientation. This can include nouns as well as adjectives and adverbs. To know the sentiment orientation of a context word, we use the opinion lexicon provided by [6]. In this paper, we have used both *NaiveBayes* classifier and *Logistic Regression* provided by [17]

4. OPINION DIVERSIFICATION

This section introduces an opinion diversification model and algorithm. Before describing our approach, we define an *opinion* about a controversial topic to be composed of a set of *arguments* and *sentiments*. Formally, we extend the framework proposed in [7] by adding sentiment diversification to diversify search results of controversial queries. We are given a set of documents $D = \{d_1, d_2, ..., d_n\}$ where $n \geq 2$, and a set of queries Q. Given a query $q \in Q$ and an integer k, our goal is to select a subset $L_k \subseteq D$ of documents that is diverse. We assume three main components that define the diversity of a set of documents about controversial topics: *relevance*, *semantic diversity*, and *sentiment diversity*. Naturally, before discussing whether a set is diverse or not, it should first contain relevant documents to the query. The *relevance* of each document is given by a function $r : D \times Q \rightarrow R^+$, where a higher value implies that the document is more relevant to the query. To diversify a set of documents, we need to give more preference to dissimilar documents. In the context of controversial queries, two documents are dissimilar if (1) they use different arguments to discuss the query topic, and/or (2) they exhibit different sentiments about the query topic, including positive, negative, and neutral sentiments. To satisfy these two requirements, we define two distance functions. The first one is a *semantic distance* function $d : D \times D \rightarrow R^+$ between documents, where smaller the distance, the more similar the two documents are. The second one is a *sentiment distance* function $s : D \times D \rightarrow R^+$ between documents, where smaller the distance, the closest in sentiments the two documents are.

We formalize a set selection function $f : 2^D \times Q \times r \times d \times o \rightarrow R^+$, where we assign scores to all possible subsets of D, given a query $q \in Q$, a relevance function $r(.)$, a semantic distance function $d(.,.)$, a sentiment distance function $s(.,.)$, and a given integer $k \in Z^+ (k \geq 2)$. The goal is to select a set $L_k \subseteq D$ of documents such as the value of f is maximized. In other words, the objective is to find:

$$L_k^* = Max_{L_k \subseteq D, |L_k| = k} f(L_k, q, r(.), d(.,.), s(.,.))$$

where all arguments other than L_k are fixed inputs to the function. Based on this objective function, we present an opinion diversification model that extends the Max-sum diversification model presented in [7]. The goal of this model is to maximize the sum of the relevance, the semantic dissimilarity, and the sentiment dissimilarity of the selected set. The function we aim at maximizing can be formalized as follows:

$$f(L) = \alpha(k-1) \sum_{a \in L} r(a) + 2\beta \sum_{a,b \in L} d(a,b) + 2\gamma \sum_{a,b \in L} s(a,b)$$

where $|L| = k$, and $\alpha, \beta, \gamma > 0$ are parameters specifying the trade-off between relevance, semantic diversity, and sentiment diversity. The model allows to put more emphasis on relevance, on semantic diversity, on sentiment diversity, or on any mixture of these measures. Note that we need to scale up the three terms of the function. The reason is that there are $\frac{k(k-1)}{2}$ numbers in the semantic similarity sum, and $\frac{k(k-1)}{2}$ in the sentiment sum as opposed to k numbers in the relevance sum.

In the context of controversial queries, we are particularly interested in detecting documents that use similar arguments to discuss a given topic. Thus, we do not use the whole vocabulary of a document to compute the semantic distance.We rather use only the topic elements to compute the distance between two documents. Formally, we define an opinion-based Jaccard similarity function $O\_Jaccard$ as follows:

$$O\_Jaccard(a,b) = \frac{|E(a) \cap E(b)|}{|E(a) \cup E(b)|}$$

where $E(a)$ and $E(b)$ are the set of topic elements of document a and document b respectively. We note that Jaccard similarity is known to be a metric. As for sentiment distance, we define it as follows:

$$s(a,b) = \begin{cases} 0, & \text{if } a \text{ and } b \text{ have the same sentiment;} \\ 1, & \text{otherwise.} \end{cases}$$

where the sentiment orientation includes *positive*, *negative*, and *neutral* sentiments.

Algorithm 1 Algorithm for MaxSumDispersion

Input: Documents D, k
Output: Set $L(|L| = k)$ that maximizes $f(L)$
Initialize the set $L = \emptyset$
for $i \leftarrow 1$ **to** $\frac{k}{2}$ **do**
  $Find(a,b) = Max_{x,y \in D} d(x,y)$
  Set $L = L \cup \{a,b\}$
  Delete all edges from E that are incident to a or b
end for
If k is odd, add an arbitrary document to L

The problem of diversifying search results is NP-hard [7, 1]. Therefore, we need to exploit existing approximation algorithms to solve it. Gollapudi et al., [7] show that their Max-sum diversification objective can be casted to a facility dispersion problem, known as the MaxSumDispersion problem [8, 9]. In our work, we follow the same principle and model our diversification problem as a MaxSumDispersion problem which aims at maximizing the sum of the pairwise distances between nodes in a metric space:

$$f'(L) = \sum_{a,b \in L} d'(a,b)$$

where d'(.,.) is a distance metric. We show in the following that f' is equivalent to our f function. To this end, we define the distance function $d'(a,b)$ as follows:

$$d'(a,b) = \begin{cases} 0, & \text{if } a = b; \\ \alpha(r(a) + r(b)) + 2\beta d(a,b) + 2\gamma s(a,b) & \text{otherwise.} \end{cases}$$

Considering the binary sentiment function, we claim that if d(.,.) is a metric then d'(.,.) is also a metric (proof skipped). We replace d'(.,.) by its definition in f'(L), disregarding pairwise distances between identical pairs, thus we obtain:

$$f'(L) = \alpha(k-1)\sum_{a\in L} r(a) + 2\beta \sum_{a,b\in L} d(a,b) + 2\gamma \sum_{a,b\in L} s(a,b)$$

we can easily see that each $r(a)$ is counted exactly $(k-1)$ times. Hence, the function f' is equivalent to our function f. Given this mapping, we can use a 2-approximation algorithm proposed in [8, 9] and illustrated by algorithm 1 to maximize our MaxSum objective f.

5. EXPERIMENTS

5.1 Setup

We evaluated our opinion diversification model using two different types of controversial queries: (1) *informative queries* and (2) *debatable* queries. *Informative queries* calls for different theories and information about a given topic rather than sentiments. For example, search results of queries like "Origin of the universe" or "Overpopulation" typically do not express positive or negative sentiments about the subject but rather present different theories and arguments. Note that search results of informative queries typically contain one predominant sentiment rather than a variety of sentiments. Examples include "Child abuse" and "Racism" where you can hardly find, in the search results, Web pages that are positive about these topics. By contrast, a *debatable* query is a query for which search results can express different sentiments including positive, negative, or neutral. For example, "Feminism", "Arranged Marriage" and "Assisted Suicide" are issues one can be for, against, or neutral about them.

To assess the effectiveness of our model, we used 50 queries: 25 *informative* queries and 25 *debatable* queries. We posed each query to Google search engine and we collected the *top*50 from the results list. Before applying any diversification, we showed the entire pool of results to human judges for assessment. The judges proceeded with the assessment of positive, negative, and neutral Web pages. The assessment was done as follows. First, Web pages giving definitions about the query topic or stating some facts (historical facts, events, or statistics) were considered *neutral* because they do not express any sentiment. Examples of these Web pages include Wikipedia pages, factual news, dictionary definitions, and historical articles. Additionally, pages describing both positive and negative sentiments about a topic were considered *neutral* due to their objectivity. Second, Web pages with clear positive statements were considered *positive*. For example, pages stating explicitly that "death penalty is the right punishment for killers because it reduces crime rates" are obviously positive. There are also some pages with a known and determined position, for instance, Church pages which are clearly positive about "God existence". Third, Web pages with clear negative statements were considered *negative*. For example, pages stating explicitly that "death penalty should be abolished". In this case, we can also find pages with a determined position such as Amnesty International pages that are clearly against "death penalty".

Recall that our goal, in diversifying search results of controversial queries, is to cover many different view points. Thus, a natural way to assess the effectiveness of our model is to measure the number of different topic elements and sentiments covered, as a function of the size of the selected set. We call this measure *Novelty* and note that it is the same *S-recall* measure proposed in [18] and $Novelty_q$ measure presented in [7]. More precisely, consider a topic T with N topic elements e_1 . . . , e_N and a set $p_1, ..., p_k$ of k Web pages. Let $elm(p_i)$ be the set of topic elements covered by p_i. We define the *Novelty* of a set of size k as follows:

$$Novelty_k = \frac{|\cup_{i=1}^{k} elm(p_i)|}{N}$$

This *Novelty* measure helps quantifying the success in covering different arguments. However, it does not capture the sentiment with which the argument was brought into discussion. To address this problem, we define an opinion-based novelty measure that we call *O_Novelty*. The idea is to consider, for each topic element, three different contexts: *Positive, Negative*, and *Neutral*. To do so, we define three sets of sub topic elements: (1) $elm^{pos}(p_i)$ the set of topic elements covered by p_i in a positive context about the query topic, (2) $elm^{neg}(p_i)$ the set of topic elements covered by p_i in a negative context about the query topic, and (3) $elm^{neu}(p_i)$ the set of topic elements covered by p_i in a neutral context about the query topic. Now, we define the *O_Novelty* of a set of size k as follows:

$$O\_Novelty_k = \frac{\sum_{op\in\{pos,neg,neu\}} |\cup_{i=1}^{k} elm^{op}(p_i)|}{3\times N}$$

Note here that we divide by $3\times N$ since a topic element might be counted three times if it is covered in the three different contexts.

To find the set of topic elements related to a given query, we make use of Wikipedia portals. A portal introduces the reader to key articles and categories that further describe a given topic. We submit each query of our test set to Wikipedia and get all its related portals. Then, we analyze the page of each portal and take its title and categories as the topic elements related to the query. Examples of topic elements extracted from the portals related to the query "Abortion Ethics" include *Embryology, Surgery, Medical-treatments, Religion-and-politics, Liberalism, Human-rights, Social-inequality, Humanists, Personal-life, Family, Women-rights, Feminist-movement, Ethical-theories*, etc.

5.2 Strategies Under Comparison

Relevance-based selection. The selection of the best set of Web pages for a given query is based solely on relevance. This is translated by setting the model parameters as follows: $\alpha \gg \beta$ and $\alpha \gg \gamma$. In our experiment $\alpha = 1$, $\beta = 1^{-8}$, and $\gamma = 1^{-8}$. To compute the relevance score, we inverse the Google rank of each Web page and normalized it in such a way that scores are ranging from 0 to 1, with 1 being the score of the top page. Note that using relevance selection, the best set of size k would always correspond to the *topk* results from Google. This method represents the baseline approach of our work.

Semantic-based selection. The selection of the best set of Web pages for a given query is based solely on semantic diversity. This is translated by setting the model parameters as follows: $\beta \gg \alpha$ and $\beta \gg \gamma$. In our experiment $\alpha = 1^{-8}$, $\beta = 1$, and $\gamma = 1^{-8}$. We have used both Jaccard similarity distance and *O_Jaccard*.

Sentiment-based selection. The selection of the best set of Web pages for a given query is based solely on sen-

Table 1: Evaluation of different diversification strategies using informative queries

	Relevance (Google)	Semantic		Relevance + Semantic	
		Jaccard	*O_Jaccard*	*Jaccard*	*O_Jaccard*
Novelty$_5$	0.332	0.334	**0.381**	0.330	0.367

Table 2: Examples of $Novelty_5$ values for individual informative queries

	Relevance (Google)	Semantic		Relevance + Semantic	
		Jaccard	*O_Jaccard*	*Jaccard*	*O_Jaccard*
Pacifism	0.357	0.285	0.500	0.428	0.500
Smoking	0.181	0.181	0.218	0.181	0.200
Slavery	0.189	0.168	0.210	0.189	0.189
Racism	0.175	0.175	0.228	0.175	0.192
Fundamentalism	0.461	0.461	0.615	0.461	0.538
Global Warming	0.163	0.122	0.183	0.122	0.183
Meaning of Life	0.500	0.583	0.583	0.583	0.583

timent diversity. This is translated by setting the model parameters as follows: $\gamma \gg \alpha$ and $\gamma \gg \beta$. In our experiment $\alpha = 1^{-8}$, $\beta = 1^{-8}$, and $\gamma = 1$.

Integrated selection. An integrated selection involves more than one measure to select the best set of Web pages. This requires setting the values of the parameters α, β, and γ accordingly. For informative queries we mainly use the relevance and semantic diversity measures while for debatable queries all the three measures can be used.

5.3 Results

Informative Queries. The results using informative queries are shown in Table 1 using a set size of 5. We can see that our model improves the novelty measure and outperforms the baseline approach. Compared to the original *top*5 results returned by Google, our diversification model increases the novelty value from 0.334 to 0.381 using semantic diversification. This means that 4.7% of new discussion elements were added compared to the original *top*5 results. The interesting observation that we can make here is that our *O_Jaccard* distance outperforms the standard *Jaccard* distance. We can see that the standard *Jaccard* almost does not improve the novelty measure and it even loses some information when combining it with the relevance. Having a closer look at the results of individual informative queries shown in Table 2, we can clearly see that in many cases, the standard *Jaccard* distance decreases the novelty measure when using semantic diversification. The reasons for this behavior are discussed further in section 5.4.

Debatable Queries. The results of *debatable queries* are shown in Table 3. We can see that for the relevance baseline, our model always improves the novelty measure. Compared to the original *top*5 results returned by Google, our diversification model increases the novelty value from 0.393 to 0.606. This means that we can include 21.3% of new topic elements and sentiments in the best 5 results compared to the original set. Looking at the different diversification methods, we observe that the novelty value increases by combining different measures for set selection. While semantic diversification is improving the baseline with 8.6%, a combination with sentiment diversification gives further improvement of 12.7%. It is also important to note that sentiment diversification is improving the novelty up to 0.549%. This is also due to the fact that the set selection process is ordered starting from the sets of highly ranked documents. In the integrated selection, combining all three measures, we observe that adding relevance seems to decrease slightly the novelty, however, we still improve considerably compared to the baseline. An interesting observation, in the results of individual queries presented in Table 4, is that in some cases the standard *Jaccard* distance performs better than our distance for the semantic diversification (e.g., Abortion Ethics). However a combined semantic and sentiment diversification always performs best with our *O_Jaccard* distance. The reasons for this behavior are discussed further in section 5.4.

5.4 Discussion

The experimental results show our model always outperforms the native ranking of controversial Web pages by a significant margin. We are performing particularly well in the case of *debatable queries*, for which the full set of search results contains various sentiments and discussion elements. This rich pool of results allows our model to effectively select Web pages having dissimilar contents and sentiments. Thus, overcoming the bias of the top results of the native ranking. By contrast, in the case of *informative queries*, search results are more monotonous in terms of sentiments, thus we only apply semantic diversification to learn about various arguments and view points about the topic. Although the gains for *informative queries* are smaller than *debatable queries*, we are always able to provide a richer set of results with novel information.

We observed through the experiments of individual queries that, in the context of controversial Web pages, a standard distance (e.g., *Jaccard*) does not perform well for semantic diversification. The main reason is that two pages can discuss the same aspect of a controversial topic but using different context words. Sometimes authors use different words and approaches to describe the same idea. Therefore, a standard distance is successful to measure how different the two pages are but not how different are the topic elements being discussed. By contrast, our opinion-based distance *O_Jaccard* shows better performance by taking into account only topic elements. Semantic diversification focuses on topic elements while sentiment diversification focuses on the sentiments derived from their context. In this way, the results are effectively merged giving a better performance.

Table 3: Evaluation of different diversification strategies using debatable queries

	Relevance (Google)	Semantic		Sentiment	Semantic+Sentiment		Relevance +Semantic +Sentiment
		Jaccard	*O_Jaccard*		*Jaccard*	*O_Jaccard*	
O_Novelty$_5$	0.393	0.425	0.479	0.549	0.555	**0.606**	0.566

Table 4: Examples of $O\_Novelty_5$ values for individual debatable queries

	Relevance (Google)	Semantic		Sentiment	Semantic+Sentiment		Relevance +Semantic +Sentiment
		Jaccard	*O_Jaccard*		*Jaccard*	*O_Jaccard*	
Abortion Ethics	0.215	0.505	0.408	0.537	0.419	0.612	0.548
Vegetarianism	0.250	0.416	0.458	0.458	0.375	0.525	0.458
God Existence	0.281	0.510	0.354	0.437	0.510	0.523	0.437
Censorship	0.382	0.390	0.404	0.553	0.574	0.581	0.560
Human Cloning	0.484	0.454	0.424	0.545	0.454	0.636	0.515
Homosexality	0.535	0.190	0.619	0.535	0.380	0.630	0.595
Illegal Immigration	0.378	0.196	0.606	0.606	0.590	0.621	0.606

6. CONCLUSIONS

Diversifying search results of controversial queries is a promising direction to satisfy users looking for different versions and information about the same topic. A challenging issue is the nature of opinions in controversial topics that goes beyond being *positive*, *negative*, or *neutral*. An opinion also includes different arguments and angles from which the problem can be addressed. In this paper, we proposed a new model for representing controversial documents as a set of *topic elements* and *contexts*. These two main components represent the basis for computing semantic and sentiment similarity between documents. Additionally, we proposed an opinion diversification model that combines *relevance*, *semantic*, and *sentiment* measures. The experiments showed that our model always outperforms the native ranking of opinionated Web pages by a significant margin. For pragmatic reasons, our choice of queries was heavily dependent on how well Wikipedia covers a given topic which calls for exploring additional data sources about controversial issues.

7. REFERENCES

[1] R. Agrawal, S. Gollapudi, A. Halverson, and S. Ieong. Diversifying search results. In *WSDM*, pages 5–14, 2009.

[2] R. Awadallah, M. Ramanath, and G. Weikum. Language-model-based pro/con classification of political text. In *SIGIR*, pages 747–748, 2010.

[3] B. Carterette and P. Chandar. Probabilistic models of ranking novel documents for faceted topic retrieval. In *CIKM*, pages 1287–1296, 2009.

[4] C. L. A. Clarke, M. Kolla, G. V. Cormack, O. Vechtomova, A. Ashkan, S. Büttcher, and I. MacKinnon. Novelty and diversity in information retrieval evaluation. In *SIGIR*, pages 659–666, 2008.

[5] G. Demartini. Ares: A retrieval engine based on sentiments - sentiment-based search result annotation and diversification. In *ECIR*, pages 772–775, 2011.

[6] X. Ding, B. Liu, and P. S. Yu. A holistic lexicon-based approach to opinion mining. In *WSDM*, pages 231–240, 2008.

[7] S. Gollapudi and A. Sharma. An axiomatic approach for result diversification. In *WWW*, pages 381–390, 2009.

[8] R. Hassin, S. Rubinstein, and A. Tamir. Approximation algorithms for maximum dispersion. *Operations Research Letters*, 21(3):133–137, 1997.

[9] B. Korte and D. Hausmann. An analysis of the greedy heuristic for independence systems. *Algorithmic Aspects of Combinatorics*, 2:65–74, 1978.

[10] openNLP. http://opennlp.sourceforge.net/.

[11] B. Pang, L. Lee, and S. Vaithyanathan. Thumbs up? sentiment classification using machine learning techniques. *CoRR*, cs.CL/0205070, 2002.

[12] F. Radlinski and S. T. Dumais. Improving personalized web search using result diversification. In *SIGIR*, pages 691–692, 2006.

[13] R. L. T. Santos, C. Macdonald, and I. Ounis. Selectively diversifying web search results. In *CIKM*, pages 1179–1188, 2010.

[14] P. D. Turney. Thumbs up or thumbs down? semantic orientation applied to unsupervised classification of reviews. In *ACL*, pages 417–424, 2002.

[15] J. Wang and J. Zhu. Portfolio theory of information retrieval. In *SIGIR*, pages 115–122, 2009.

[16] T. Wilson, J. Wiebe, and R. Hwa. Just how mad are you? finding strong and weak opinion clauses. In *AAAI*, pages 761–769, 2004.

[17] I. H. Witten and E. Frank. *Data Mining: Practical Machine Learning Tools and Techniques with Java Implementations*. Morgan Kaufmann, 1999.

[18] C. Zhai, W. W. Cohen, and J. D. Lafferty. Beyond independent relevance: methods and evaluation metrics for subtopic retrieval. In *SIGIR*, pages 10–17, 2003.

[19] C. Zhai and J. D. Lafferty. A risk minimization framework for information retrieval. *Inf. Process. Manage.*, 42(1):31–55, 2006.

[20] Z. Zhai, B. Liu, H. Xu, and P. Jia. Clustering product features for opinion mining. In *WSDM*, pages 347–354, 2011.

[21] L. Zhuang, F. Jing, and X. Zhu. Movie review mining and summarization. In *CIKM*, pages 43–50, 2006.

Relevance Weighting using Within-document Term Statistics

Kai Hui
Graduate University of Chinese Academy of Sciences
huikai10@mails.gucas.ac.cn

Ben He
Graduate University of Chinese Academy of Sciences
benhe@gucas.ac.cn

Tiejian Luo
Graduate University of Chinese Academy of Sciences
tjluo@gucas.ac.cn

Bin Wang
Institute of Computing Technology, Chinese Academy of Sciences
wangbin@ict.ac.cn

ABSTRACT

With the rapid development of the information technology, there exists the difficulty in deploying state-of-the-art retrieval models in environments such as peer-to-peer networks and pervasive computing, where it is expensive or even infeasible to maintain the global statistics. To this end, this paper presents an investigation in the validity of different statistical assumptions of term distributions. Based on the findings in this investigation, a variety of weighting models, called NG (standing for "no global statistics") models, are derived from the Divergence from Randomness framework, in which only the within-document statistics are used in the relevance weighting. Compared to the state-of-the-art weighting models in extensive experiments on various standard TREC test collections, our proposed NG models can provide acceptable retrieval performance in ad-hoc search, without the use of global statistics.

Categories and Subject Descriptors: H.3.3 [Information Storage and Retrieval]: Information Search and Retrieval

General Terms: Experimentation, Performance, Algorithms

Keywords

Probabilistic models, Term frequency distribution fitting, Within-document statistics

1. INTRODUCTION

The probabilistic models are among the most popular information retrieval models for their efficiency and effectiveness. The BM25 probabilistic weighting function [9], the PL2 Divergence from Randomness (DFR) model [1] and the KL-divergence language model (KLLM) [13], have been shown effective in TREC experimentation[1]. All of these three models consider the global term statistics, e.g. the document frequency and the collection-wide term frequency, for the relevance weighting. The use of global statistics in the weighting models can be beneficial to the retrieval effectiveness. However, in large-scale Web applications such as the distribution IR, peer-to-peer network and pervasive computing, it is difficult or even infeasible to maintain the global statistics [2, 11]. To this end, the aim of this paper is to explore the possibility of developing the fairly simple retrieval models that use only within-document statistics for the relevance weighting.

The main contribution of this paper is tri-fold. First, we study the term frequency distribution on various recent IR datasets, results show that other than the classical Poisson assumption proposed by Harter in 1975 [4], there are quite a few appropriate approximations of the actual term frequency distribution in recent datasets. Second, we propose a family of *NG* (No Global statistics) weighting models that use only the within-document statistics for the relevance weighting. Evaluation shows that the weighting models based on the Weibull approximation of the term frequency distribution demonstrates the best retrieval performance and robustness. Third, we develop a new weighting framework that is a simplified form of the DFR framework which can improve not only the retrieval performance, but also the robustness by reducing the parameter sensitivity.

The remainder of this paper is organized as follows. Section 2 introduces the related work. Section 3 applies a list of distribution functions to fit the actual term frequencies in standard TREC collections. A list of new NG weighting models using only the within-document statistics for relevance weighting are proposed in Section 4. Evaluation results of these new models are then presented in Section 5. Finally, Section 6 concludes the work and suggests possible future research directions.

2. RELATED WORK

A well-known empirical description of the term frequency distribution in text collection is the so-called Zipf's law, in which a given term's collection-wide frequency is inversely proportional to its rank in the frequency table [15]. Luhn's

[1]Although these three weighting models are based on different assumptions of relevance, they are usually considered to be within the category of probabilistic models [7].

work in 1957 is among the earliest research on the term frequency distribution and IR. His research gave an outline for building a system based on statistical method for literature searching by machine [5]. Later in 1975, Harter proposed the 2-Poisson assumption for keyword indexing, in which the informative terms in the documents, namely specialty words, follow Poisson distribution in both the entire document collection, and the elite set [4].

The 2-Poisson assumption has been widely recognized as the standard approximation of the term frequency distribution. The BM25 and PL2 DFR models, both derived based on the 2-Poisson assumption, are currently among the most popular and effective IR models. The formulas of these two models, as well as the KLLM model, are introduced below. These three popular probabilistic models are used as the baselines in our evaluation.

As one of the most established weighting models, BM25 computes the relevance score of a document d for a query Q by the following formula [9]:

$$score(d, Q) = \sum_{t \in Q} w^{(1)} \frac{(k_1 + 1)tf}{K + tf} \frac{(k_3 + 1)qtf}{k_3 + qtf} \quad (1)$$

where qtf is the query term frequency; $w^{(1)}$ is the *idf* factor, which is given by:

$$w^{(1)} = \log_2 \frac{N - N_t + 0.5}{N_t + 0.5}$$

N is the number of documents in the whole collection. N_t is the document frequency of term t. K is given by $k_1((1 - b) + b\frac{l}{avg\_l})$, where l and avg_l are the document length and the average document length in the collection, respectively. The document length refers to the number of tokens in a document. k_1, k_3 and b are parameters. The default setting is $k_1 = 1.2$, $k_3 = 1000$ and $b = 0.75$ [9]. qtf is the number of occurrences of a given term in the query; tf is the within document frequency of the given term.

Let $tfn = \frac{tf}{(1-b)+b\cdot\frac{l}{avg\_l}}$, where tfn denotes the normalized term frequency, we obtain:

$$score(d, Q) = \sum_{t \in Q} w^{(1)} \frac{k_1(k_1 + 1)tfn}{k_1 tfn + 1} \frac{(k_3 + 1)qtf}{k_3 + qtf}$$

Hence the term frequency normalization component of the BM25 formula can be seen as:

$$tfn = \frac{tf}{(1 - b) + b \cdot \frac{l}{avg\_l}} \quad (2)$$

The Kullback-Leibler divergence language model (KLLM) with Dirichlet smoothing assigns the relevance score as follows [13, 14]:

$$score(d, Q) = \sum_{t \in Q} p(t|\hat{\theta}_Q) log_2(1 + \frac{tf}{\mu P(t|\mathcal{C})}) + log_2 \frac{\mu}{\mu + l} \quad (3)$$

where $p(t|\hat{\theta}_Q)$ is the maximum likelihood of generating query term t from a query model. $p(t|\mathcal{C})$ is the generation probability from the collection model. In this paper, the free parameter μ is set by simulated annealing on training queries.

PL2 is one of the weighting models derived from the Divergence from Randomness (DFR) framework. The DFR framework assigns the relevance score of a document d for a query Q as follows [1]:

$$score(d, Q) = \sum_{t \in Q} qtf \cdot Inf_1 \cdot Inf_2 \quad (4)$$

where qtf is the query term frequency. The first measurement of the information amount Inf_1 is given by the information content $-log_2 P(t, tf|d)$. $P(t, tf|d)$ is the probability of having *tf* occurrences of query term t in document d. The second measurement of the information amount Inf_2 is given by Laplace succession $\frac{1}{tfn+1}$. The normalized term frequency tfn is given by Normalization 2:

$$tfn = tf \cdot \log_2(1 + c \cdot \frac{avg\_l}{l}), (c > 0) \quad (5)$$

where the recommended setting of free parameter c ranges from 1 to 7, depending on the search task.

Assuming the Poisson distribution of the term frequency in the collection leads to the PL2 model, where the relevance score of a document d for a query Q is given by [1]:

$$\begin{aligned} score(d, Q) \quad = \quad & \sum_{t \in Q} qtf \cdot \frac{1}{tfn + 1} (tfn \cdot \log_2 \frac{tfn}{\lambda} \\ & + (\lambda + \frac{1}{12 \cdot tfn} - tfn) \cdot \log_2 e + \\ & 0.5 \cdot \log_2(2\pi \cdot tfn)) \end{aligned} \quad (6)$$

where λ is the mean and variance of the assumed Poisson distribution. Estimation of λ requires the global statistics of the term's distribution in the whole document collection.

In this paper, we propose to eliminate the need for global statistics in the DFR models by treating the $P(t, tf|d)$ as a function of the within-document term frequency *tf*, and its parameters of the term frequency distribution function. Various distribution functions are tested in our study on the distribution fitting in the following sections. In addition, as explained in Section 4.2, the average document length avg_l is obtained by averaging the document length of random samples from the collection.

3. FITTING THE TERM FREQUENCY DISTRIBUTION

Harter's [4] study on the term frequency distribution was based on the analysis on a sample of the archives at the Graduate Library of University of Chicago. With the fast growth of the internet in both size and the amount of information in text documents or Web pages, an interesting research question arises: do the terms still follow the Poisson distribution in recent datasets?

In this section, we attempt to answer the above research question by using a list of statistical distribution functions (Section 3.1) to fit the term frequency distribution in standard TREC collections, as described in Section 3.2. Detailed analysis on the distribution fitting is provided in Section 3.3.

3.1 Distribution Functions

We study a variety of distribution functions as follows:

- Poisson distribution:

$$P(t, tf|d) = \frac{e^{-\lambda} \lambda^{tf}}{tf!} \; (tf = 0, 1, 2, \cdots) \quad (7)$$

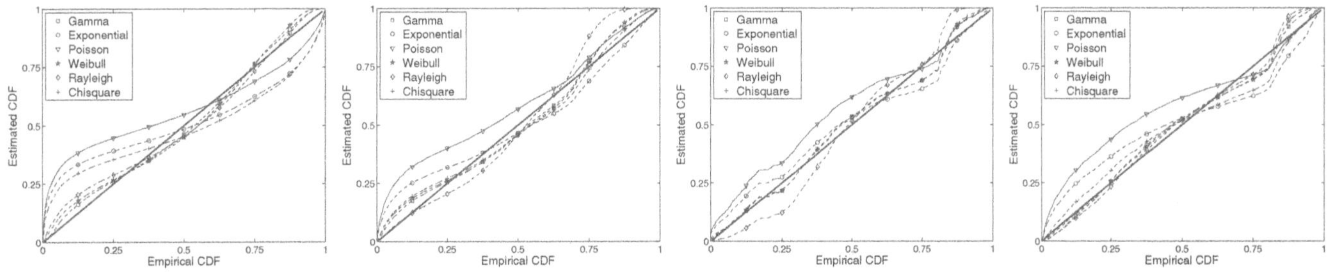

(a) disk1&2 (b) disk4&5 (c) WT10G (d) .GOV2

Figure 1: The empirical probabilities (X-axis) against the estimated probabilities (Y-axis) of the distribution fitting.

where λ is a positive real number, which is the expected number of occurrences.

- Gamma distribution:

$$P(t,tf|d) = \frac{\lambda^{\alpha}}{\Gamma(\alpha)} x^{\alpha-1} e^{-\lambda x} (tf \geq 0) \quad (8)$$

where $\alpha > 0$ is the shape parameter and $\lambda > 0$ is the scale parameter.

- Exponential distribution:

$$P(t,tf|d) = \lambda e^{-\lambda tf}, (tf \geq 0) \quad (9)$$

where $\lambda > 0$ is called the rate parameter of the distribution. The distribution is supported on the interval $[0, \infty)$.

- Weibull distribution:

$$P(t,tf|d) = \frac{k}{\lambda}\left(\frac{tf}{\lambda}\right)^{k-1} e^{-(\frac{tf}{\lambda})^k} (tf \geq 0) \quad (10)$$

where $k > 0$ is the shape parameter and $\lambda > 0$ is the scale parameter of the distribution.

- Rayleigh distribution:

$$P(t,tf|d) = \frac{tf}{\sigma^2} e^{-\frac{tf^2}{2\sigma^2}} (tf \geq 0) \quad (11)$$

where $\sigma > 0$ is the parameter of this distribution.

- χ^2 distribution:

$$P(t,tf|d) = \frac{(\frac{1}{2})^{\frac{n}{2}}}{\Gamma(\frac{n}{2})} tf^{\frac{n}{2}-1} e^{-\frac{tf}{2}} (tf \geq 0) \quad (12)$$

where $n = 1, 2, 3 \cdots$ is the degrees of freedom.

3.2 Datasets and the Fitting Method

We use four standard TREC test collections in our study: disk1&2, disk4&5, WT10G and .GOV2. For all four test collections used, each term is stemmed using Porter's English stemmer, and standard English stopwords are removed. Only the query terms in the title field are used.

Weighted Least Squares (WLS) regression is used to determine the optimal parameters in a given distribution function by fitting the target function, namely the empirical cumulative distribution function (ECDF). The use of the CDF function instead of the probability density function (PDF) as the target of the distribution fitting is a common practise because CDF can uniquely determine a distribution, while PDF may not, for example when the PDF of a given distribution cannot be derived, or simply does not exists. The mean sum of square error (SE) between the estimated distribution and the observed distribution of all query terms in the title field is used to indicate the goodness of the fitting.

Table 1: Information about the test collections used.

Coll.	TREC Task	Topics	# Docs
disk1&2	1, 2, 3 ad-hoc	51-200	741,856
disk4&5	Robust 2004	301-450, 601-700	528,155
WT10G	9, 10 Web	451-550	1,692,096
GOV2	2004-2006 Terabyte Ad-hoc	701-850	25,178,548

3.3 Results of the Distribution Fitting

In Harter's work, the distribution fitting is done on the raw term frequencies [4]. We base our investigation on the distribution of the normalized term frequency (*tfn*) instead. For space reason, we only report the results obtained using BM25's default setting $b = 0.75$.

Figure 1 plots the P-P figures between the fitted probabilities and the empirical probabilities on the four datasets used. The average linear correlation coefficients between ECDF and CDF of the Poisson, χ^2, Exponential, Gamma, Rayleigh, Weibull distribution are 0.9908, 0.9735, 0.9743, 0.9904, 0.9874, and 0.9832 respectively. It shows that all the six distributions can fit the term frequency distribution to some extent on the four test collections being used.

Finally, we conduct ANOVA to investigate the differences of the fitness among the distributions being used. In Figure 2), objects on the left have better fitting goodness than its right ones. Vertical dashed lines separating the objects shows the significant fitness differences in the group. According to Figure 2, Gamma and Weibull distributions demonstrate better fitness than the others.

4. PROPOSED NG MODELS

We describe our proposed NG models (no global statistics models) in Section 4.1, and estimate the average document length, which is a global variable, in Section 4.2.

4.1 Formulas

Our proposed NG models follow the DFR framework as introduced in Equation (4). Under the general probability platform of DFR framework, we can generate new NG

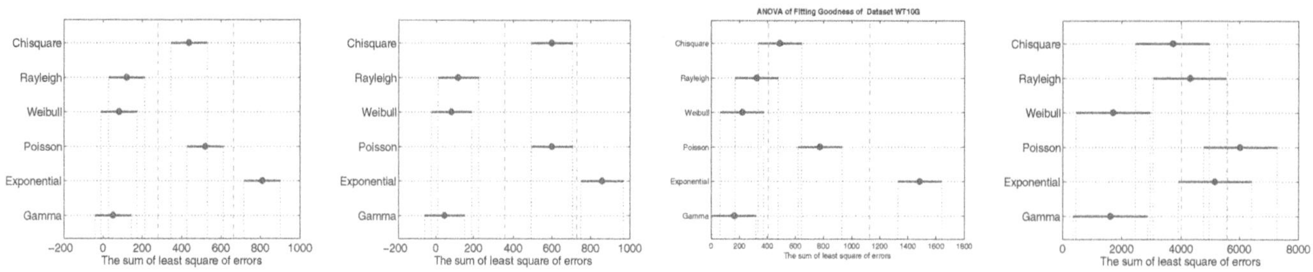

(a) disk1&2 (b) disk4&5 (c) WT10G (d) GOV2

Figure 2: The ANOVA test for the significance of difference in fitting goodness of different distribution functions on the four datasets used.

weighting models by replacing the probability $P(t, tf|d)$ with the proper function form which can fit the real normalized term frequency distribution well.

Table 7 explains how the proposed NG models are generated named. For example, the WL2d model assigns relevance score as follows:

$$\begin{aligned} score(d,Q) &= \sum_{t\in Q} qtf \cdot Inf_1 \cdot Inf_2 \quad (13) \\ &= \sum_{t\in Q} qtf \cdot (-log_2 P(t, tf|d)) \cdot Inf_2 \\ &= \sum_{t\in Q} qtf \cdot (-log_2 \frac{k}{\lambda}\left(\frac{tfn}{\lambda}\right)^{k-1} e^{-(\frac{tfn}{\lambda})^k}) \\ &\cdot \frac{1}{1+tfn} \end{aligned}$$

where the probability $P(tf, t|d)$ is estimated by Weibull (W) distribution in Equation (10), Inf_2 is given by Laplace succession (L) as explained in Table 7. The normalized term frequency *tfn* is given by Normalization 2 in Equation (5). A d at the end of the model name stands for within-document term statistics, indicating that the model is derived from the DFR framework in Equation (4). The distribution parameters λ and k are treated as free parameters that require tuning on training queries.

A notable difference between our proposed NG models and the state-of-the-art probabilistic models is that the former does not involve the use of the global statistics. However, we need to apply term frequency normalization, such as the normalization 2 in Equation (5) and BM25's normalization method in Equation (2), to cope with the bias towards long documents. Both of the above mentioned normalization methods use an expected document length, given by the average document length in the entire document collection, as a normalization factor. In this paper, we propose a method to get the average documents length by estimating through random sampling in the collection and our stimulating experiments have shown good estimating results.

4.2 Estimating the Expected Document Length

We use Systematic Sampling to estimate the average document length in the tf normalization part. A unique feature of Systematic Sampling is that it can give a stable estimate of the random variable, i.e. the average document length

Table 2: The estimated (*EstL*) and the actual average document length (*avg_l*) on the four test collections used, and the error in percentage.

Coll.	*EstL*	*avg_l*	Error (%)
disk1&2	266.10	261.30	1.84
disk4&5	301.22	297.10	1.39
WT10G	406.68	399.28	1.85
GOV2	673.76	648.42	3.91

Table 3: The average error rate (Avg.), maximum positive error rate (MaxPos), minimum negative error rate (MinNeg) of the 10,000 estimated average document length. Avg. is the mean of the absolute values of MaxPos and MinNeg.

Coll.	Avg. (%)	MaxPos (%)	MinNeg (%)	CV
disk1&2	3.15	3.55	-9.23	0.8348
disk4&5	2.72	2.98	-6.8	0.7021
WT10G	3.07	3.90	-8.38	0.8306
GOV2	3.89	0.53	-8.37	0.4470

(*avg_l*) in our case, with only few samples from the dataset, which is therefore very suitable for our study.

Our stimulated tests of the estimates of the average document length on four datasets show that most of the sampled average document length *EstL* fall around the actual average document length, showing the reliability of the sampling method. Some detailed statistics of the tests are shown in Table 3. The table shows that a descent approximation result is observed in the 10,000 times of systematic sampling experiments. When sampling 2.5% of the collection's document length, the average error rate is less than 4%, and the maximum error rate is less than 10%.

5. RETRIEVAL EVALUATION

Section 5.1 introduces the evaluation settings and Section 5.2 presents the experimental results.

5.1 Evaluation Settings

Our proposed NG models are evaluated against the KLLM, BM25, and PL2 weighting models, which are among the most effective weighting models as shown by the evaluation results in the literature such as the TREC experimentation [12]. The experiments are conducted using an in-house version of the Terrier toolkit [8].

We again use the same TREC collections and their associated title-only queries as in Section 3.2. On each collection,

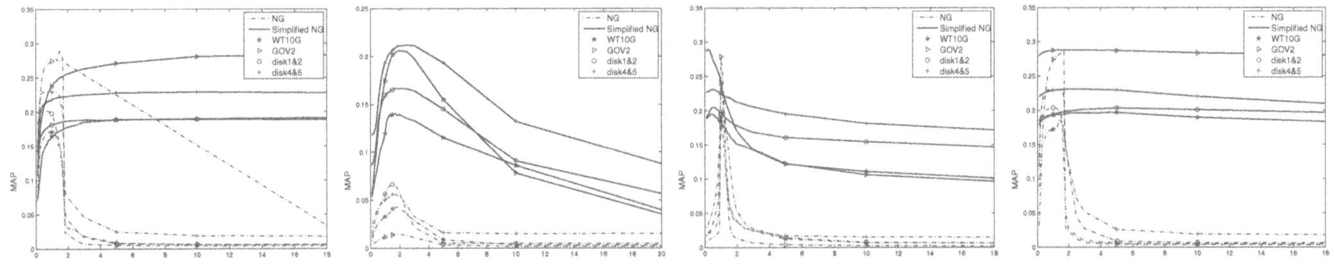

(a) Gamma distribution's parameter λ (see Eq. 8) (b) Rayleigh distribution's parameter σ (see Eq. 11) (c) Weibull distribution's parameter k (see Eq. 10) (d) Weibull distribution's parameter λ (see Eq. 10)

Figure 3: The parameter value of the distribution functions (X-axis) against the MAP obtained (Y-axis) using the NG models (dashed lines) and its simplified forms (solid lines).

we evaluate the NG models by a two-fold cross-validation. The test topics associated to each collection are split into two equal-size subsets by parity. We use one subset of topics for training, and use the remaining subset for testing. The overall retrieval performance is averaged over the two test subsets of topics. We use the TREC official evaluation measures in our experiments, namely the Mean Average Precision (MAP) [12]. All statistical tests are based on Wilcoxon matched-pairs signed-rank test at the 0.05 level.

Table 4: Experimental results of the baselines.

Coll.	KLLM	PL2	BM25
disk1&2	.2351	.2336	.2404
disk4&5	.2565	.2570	.2535
WT10G	.2153	.2126	.2080
GOV2	.3028	.3042	.2997

5.2 Evaluation Results

The evaluation results of the NG models are presented in this section. Tables 4 and 5 contain the evaluation results of the three state-of-the-art probabilistic models and our proposed NG models, respectively. According the results, we have the observations as follows:

First, the NG models based on Weibull and Poisson distributions provide the best retrieval performance, while those based on the Rayleigh and χ^2 distributions are not as good as expected. This indicates that the effectiveness of the models in the term frequency distribution fitting and the retrieval is not necessarily completely related.

Second, the use of two different normalization methods leads to in general comparable retrieval performance of our proposed models, which conforms to our previous finding in Section 3.3 that these two different normalization methods lead to similar fitting effectiveness.

Third, our proposed NG models based on Weibull and Poisson distribution can lead to comparable retrieval performance with the baseline models as the performance is sometimes not significant different between our models and the BM25 model 5. As a matter of fact, without using global statistics, we indeed have less information than the baseline models, for instance the collection information, e.g. the document frequency and the term frequency in the collection. So our models' performances mainly depend on what distribution function to use and how to use them to describe the real situation.

Finally, Figure 3 examines how the parameter setting affects the NG models' retrieval performance. From the experiments, we find that the retrieval performance of the NG models are highly sensitive to their parameters of their underlying distribution functions, which can potentially hurt the robustness of the models. In the next section, we improve the robustness by a simplified DFR framework.

5.3 Improving the Robustness

In this section, we propose to improve the robustness of the NG models. The underlying idea of our method is to fit the relevance scores produced by a given NG model using a function that is more simple than the information content components in the original DFR framework (i.e. $Inf_1 \cdot Inf_2$ in Equation (4)). In IR applications, it is a common practise to simplify the mathematical forms that are relatively complicated, in order to achieve an easier implementation or a better robustness. For example, Robertson & Walker simplified the 2-Poisson model by fitting the actual term frequency distribution, which eventually led to the proposal of the BM25 model [9, 10].

With an idea similar to [10], we propose a simple form of the DFR framework as given by the following function:

$$score(d, Q) \propto \sum_{t \in Q} qtf \cdot (1 - \beta \cdot P(tf, t|d))$$

Following the similar steps of the distribution function fitting in Section 3, we obtain $\beta = 1$. Thus, a simplified DFR framework is given as follows:

$$score(d, Q) \propto \sum_{t \in Q} qtf \cdot (1 - P(tf, t|d)) \qquad (14)$$

In Table 6, the retrieval performance of the simplified NG models is compared to the state-of-the-art models, and the NG models. The Poisson distribution is not suitable to the simplified DFR framework because of the difficulty caused by expanding the factorials using Stirling formula [1]. From Table 6, we can see that the simplified NG models achieve statistically significant improvement over the NG models on most cases, showing that the simplified DFR framework can indeed enhance the retrieval performance of the NG models.

Moreover, from Figure 3, we can see that the simplified NG models markedly reduce the parameter sensitivity. Overall, the simplified NG models based on the Weibull esti-

Table 5: Experimental results of the comparison between our proposed models and the baselines in Table 4. Statistically significant difference with KLLM, PL2, and BM25 are marked with $*$, $\dagger$, and $\ddagger$, respectively.

Coll.	PL2d	PLBd	CL2d	CLBd	EL2d	ELBd	GL2d	GLBd	RL2d	RLBd	WL2d	WLBd
disk1&2	.2044∗ † ‡	.2032∗ † ‡	.1630∗ † ‡	.1190∗ † ‡	.2004∗ † ‡	.2034∗ † ‡	.2004∗ † ‡	.1988∗ † ‡	.0664∗ † ‡	.0678∗ † ‡	.2024∗ † ‡	.2048∗ † ‡
disk4&5	.2301∗ † ‡	.2178∗ † ‡	.1936∗ † ‡	.1388∗ † ‡	.2294∗ † ‡	.2298∗ † ‡	.2289∗ † ‡	.2132∗ † ‡	.0541∗ † ‡	.0532∗ † ‡	.2300∗ † ‡	.2300∗ † ‡
WT10G	.1934∗†	.1808∗ † ‡	.1055∗ † ‡	.0739∗ † ‡	.1760∗ † ‡	.1926∗ † ‡	.1702∗ † ‡	.1286∗ † ‡	.0436∗ † ‡	.0486∗ † ‡	.1774∗ † ‡	.1878∗ † ‡
GOV2	.2855∗†	.2705∗ † ‡	.1538∗ † ‡	.0715∗ † ‡	.2778∗ † ‡	.2844∗ † ‡	.2635∗ † ‡	.2580∗ † ‡	.0305∗ † ‡	.0200∗ † ‡	.2890∗†	.2890∗†

Table 6: Experimental results using the *simplified* NG models, whose model names end with an *S* for *simplified*. Statistically significant difference with KLLM, PL2, and BM25 (see in Table 4) are marked with $*$, $\dagger$, and $\ddagger$, respectively. A $\star$ indicates a statistically significant improvement over the corresponding model in Table 5, e.g. on disk1&2, R2dS leads to a statistically significant difference over RL2d, which is marked by a $\star$.

Coll.	C2dS	CBdS	E2dS	EBdS	G2dS	GBdS	R2dS	RBdS	W2dS	WBdS
disk1&2	.1924∗ † ‡⋆	.1974∗ † ‡⋆	.1967∗ † ‡	.1966∗ † ‡	.1898∗ † ‡	.1918∗ † ‡⋆	.1664∗ † ‡⋆	.1656∗ † ‡⋆	.2029∗ † ‡	.2048∗ † ‡
disk4&5	.2245∗ † ‡⋆	.2284∗ † ‡⋆	.2258∗ † ‡	.2247∗ † ‡	.2283∗ † ‡	.2280∗ † ‡⋆	.2104∗ † ‡⋆	.1930∗ † ‡⋆	.2304∗ † ‡	.2284∗ † ‡
WT10G	.1857∗ † ‡⋆	.1946∗ † ⋆	.1844∗ † ‡⋆	.1871∗ † ‡⋆	.1904∗ † ‡⋆	.1934∗ † ⋆	.1365∗ † ‡⋆	.1276∗ † ‡⋆	.1934∗†	.1920∗†
GOV2	.2590∗ † ‡⋆	0.2586∗ † ‡⋆	.2664∗ † ‡	.2630∗ † ‡	.2804∗ † ‡⋆	.2866∗ † ⋆	.2012∗ † ‡⋆	.1938∗ † ‡⋆	.2884∗†	.2878∗†

mation of the term frequency distribution, especially W2dS, has demonstrated the best retrieval effectiveness and robustness out of all the NG models proposed. Therefore, it is recommended to apply the W2dS model in large-scale IR applications where it is difficult to maintain the global statistics.

6. CONCLUSIONS AND FUTURE WORK

We have conducted a thorough study of the term frequency distribution on recent TREC collections. Six different distribution functions are used to fit the actual frequency distribution of query terms from TREC collections. Our experimental results show that apart from Poisson distribution there are other probabilistic models of term occurrences are suitable for describing the term frequency distribution in document collections.

Based on the above finding, we have proposed a list of the NG models generated from the DFR framework. A unique feature of the NG models is the exclusion of global statistics. Extensive experiments on four TREC test collections show that our proposed NG models can provide acceptable retrieval performance for ad-hoc search. In addition, we have improved the robustness of the NG models by fitting relevance scoring fitting using simplified NG models. Finally, it is recommended to apply th W2dS model based on the Weibull distribution in large-scale IR applications, for its effectiveness and robustness.

While our proposed models' evaluation results are not good enough, and as to we have conducted a wide investigation about which distributions can be deployed, we plan to refine the form of the distributions appeared in the weighting formula in the future to improve the performance.Besides. Devising a method that automatically estimates the parameters on a per-term basis without the use of global statistics is also scheming. Another future research direction is to investigate the application of query expansion and the term proximity models [6] on top of the NG models. Finally, we plan to investigate the effectiveness of the proposed NG models in large-scale distributed IR applications such as in peer-to-peer networks or sensor networks in practise.

7. REFERENCES

[1] G. Amati and C. J. van Rijsbergen. Probabilistic models of information retrieval based on measuring the divergence from randomness. ACM Trans. Inf. Syst. 20(4): 357-389, 2002.

[2] M. Bender, S. Michel, P. Triantafillou, and G. Weikum. Global Document Frequency Estimation in Peer-to-Peer Web Search. In *Proc. WebDB*, 2006.

[3] Witschel, H. F. *Global term weights in distributed environments*. Inf. Process. Manage. 44(3): 1049-1061, 2008.

[4] S. Harter. A probabilistic approach to automatic keyword indexing (part I & II). *Journal of the American Society for Information Science*, 2(6): 197-206 (Part I), 280-289 (Part II), 1975.

[5] H. P. Luhn. A statistical approach to mechanized encoding and searching of literary information. *IBM Journal of Research and Development*, 1(4), 309-317, 1957.

[6] C. Macdonald and I. Ounis. Global Statistics in Proximity Weighting Models. In *Proc. Web N-gram Workshop of ACM SIGIR*, 2010.

[7] C. Manning, P. Raghavan, and H. Schutze. *Introduction to Information Retrieval*. Cambridge University Press, 2009.

[8] I. Ounis, G. Amati, V. Plachouras, B. He, C. Macdonald, and C. Lioma. Terrier: A High Performance and Scalable Information Retrieval Platform information retrieval. In *Proc. ACM OSIR*, 2006.

[9] S. E. Robertson, S. Walker, M. Hancock-Beaulieu, M. Gatford, and A. Payne. Okapi at TREC-4. In *Proc. TREC-4*, 1995.

[10] S. E. Robertson, and S. Walker. Some Simple Effective Approximations to the 2-Poisson Model for Probabilistic Weighted Retrieval. In Proc. ACM SIGIR: 232-241, 1994.

[11] C. Viles and J. French. Dissemination of collection wide information in distributed information retrieval systems, In *Proc. ACM SIGIR*, 12-20, 1995.

[12] E. Voorhees. *TREC: Experiment and Evaluation in Information Retrieval*. The MIT Press, 2005.

[13] C. Zhai. Statistical Language Models for Information Retrieval A Critical Review. *Foundations and Trends in Information Retrieval*, 2(3): 137-213, 2008.

[14] C. Zhai and J. Lafferty. A study of smoothing methods for language models applied to ad hoc information retrieval. In *Proc. ACM SIGIR*, 334-342, 2001.

[15] G. Zipf. *Human Behavior and the Principle of Least Effort*. Addison-Wesley. 1949.

Appendix: Table 7 explains the notations in naming the NG models.

Table 7: Naming of the proposed NG models.

Distribution function for $P(tf, t\|d)$			
P:	Poisson, Eq. 7	C:	χ^2, Eq. 12
E:	Exponential, Eq. 9	RL:	Rayleigh, Eq. 11
WB:	Weibull, Eq. 10	G:	Gamma, Eq. 8
Inf_2 in Eq. 4			
L:	Laplace succession, $\frac{1}{tf+1}$		
Term frequency normalization			
2:	Normalization 2, Eq. 5	B:	BM25's normalization, Eq. 2
Suffix of the model name			
d:	NG model derived from the original DFR framework in Eq. 4		
dS:	NG model derived from the simplified DFR framework in Eq. 14		

Acknowledgements: This work is supported in part by CAS e-Learning Fund (Y129017EA2) and the President Fund of GUCAS (Y15101FY00).

Suggestion Set Utility Maximization Using Session Logs

Umut Ozertem
Yahoo! Labs
701 First Ave.
Sunnyvale CA 94089
umut@yahoo-inc.com

Emre Velipasaoglu
Yahoo! Labs
701 First Ave.
Sunnyvale CA 94089
emrev@yahoo-inc.com

Larry Lai
Yahoo! Labs
701 First Ave.
Sunnyvale CA 94089
larrylai@yahoo-inc.com

ABSTRACT

Assistance technology is undoubtedly one of the important elements in the commercial search engines, and routing the user towards the right direction throughout the search sessions is of great importance for providing a good search experience. Most search assistance methods in the literature that involve query generation, query expansion and other techniques consider each suggestion candidate individually, which implies an independence assumption. We challenge this independence assumption and give a method to maximize the utility of a given set of suggestions. For this, we will define a measure of conditional utility for query pairs using query-URL bipartite graphs based on the session logs (clicked and viewed URLs). Afterwards, we remove the redundant queries from the suggestion set using a greedy algorithm to be able to replace them with more useful ones. Both offline (based on user studies and session log analysis) and online (based on millions of user interactions) evaluations show that modeling the conditional utility and maximizing the utility of the set of queries (by eliminating redundant ones) significantly increases the effectiveness of the search assistance both for the presubmit and postsubmit modes.

Categories and Subject Descriptors

H.3.3 [**Information Systems**]: Information Storage and Retrieval

General Terms

Experimentation, Algorithms

Keywords

Search Assistance, Diversification, User Browsing Models

1. INTRODUCTION

Search assistance modules are significant elements in commercial search engines. Two main flavors of the search assistance are the *presubmit* and the *postsubmit* modes, namely the assistance before and after the users submit their queries. Presubmit technology is based on target auto-completion, whereas in the postsubmit, suggestions might be specializations, generalizations or lateral moves. Specializations are suggestions that add terms to the original query such as "python tutorial","monthy python" for the query "python" and generalizations are queries that drop terms from the original query such as suggesting "sfo" for "sfo flight status". Lateral moves are suggestions to related entities or concepts that do not impose any lexical overlap in either direction, such as "canon 50d" to "nikon d90" or "walmart" to "target".

The dominant presubmit search assistance technology in the search industry is based on completing user's partially typed query (will be referred as the prefix hereafter) to help the users save time by not requiring them to manually type the whole query into the search box, and also help them phrase their query when they start typing but do not exactly know which query terms to use or how to spell them. The common solution to this problem is to suggest the most popular (hence, most frequent) queries that match the user's prefix. Presubmit search assistance is a very clear case where the intent of the user is not defined. Let alone the ambiguities in the search queries, in presubmit, the input from the user is not even a full query yet. In this application, the aim is to minimize the number of characters that the user types before she finds at least one useful suggestion. This understanding assumes that as long as the user does not find *at least one useful suggestion* in the suggestion set she will keep typing the query manually. Therefore, if the aim is to minimize the time/effort by the user before she finds a useful suggestion, one needs to maximize the utility of the suggestion set, by trading some popularity (analogous to the relevance in web search ranking) for some diversity.

In the postsubmit mode, after the user issues the query, the intent is much more clear. Therefore, postsubmit assistance technology includes more sophisticated techniques, but still the core techniques are some derivatives of the marginal query frequency that lexically matches the query and popular query reformulations -which handle each suggestion independently. Query reformulations use the probability distribution of possible next queries that the current query is formulated to; more formally $p(q_{next}|q_{current})$. Furthermore, to ensure that the next query is related to the current query, rather than having a high reformulation probability just because it has a high marginal probability, the pointwise mutual information $p(q_{next}, q_{current})/(p(q_{current}) \times p(q_{next}))$ can be used. Here $p(q_{next}, q_{current})$ denotes the probability that these two queries were issued by the same user within a short time frame. In addition to the above, there are also more sophisticated methods that use the geolocation and the search history of the user [18, 6] to provide a more contextualized and personally relevant information. Regardless of the underlying suggestion technology, if the approach is handling each suggestion candidate independently and sorting by some suggestion level score, there might be redundant suggestions in the suggestion sets in postsubmit.

Understanding the user intent is the key for designing an effective search assistance system and when such knowledge is lacking,

CIKM'11, October 24–28, 2011, Glasgow, Scotland, UK.

search engines need to diversify the query suggestions in order to improve the quality of search assistance. The need for diversifying the presented query suggestions to maximize the total utility of a given suggestion set finds a good analogy to the web search ranking problem. In web search ranking, since a particular query might have multiple intents, it is well-known that presenting the most relevant results on the top positions might be suboptimal, and one should trade-off some relevance in return for some diversity in the result set [7]. In this view, the goal is to maximize the probability that the user will find *at least one relevant document* in the result set, hence minimizing query abandonment. The need to do some trade-off between relevance and diversity can be regarded as finding a relevant but also diverse set of documents. It is not well-defined how to adjust the trade-off between these two somewhat conflicting criteria, and the ill-defined nature of the problem yields many different techniques and formulations [1, 8, 9, 26, 2, 20]. A good summary and comparison of the approaches and a unifying view is presented in [13]. Although not nearly as much in web ranking, diversity has also been studied in the context of query suggestions. There are two recent publications on this subject based on random walks over query-URL bipartite graph [17] and manifold ranking [27]. In the next section, we will describe these two recently published methods in more detail, and we will also provide experimental comparisons.

We give a model to maximize the utility of a given suggestion set based on a diversity definition that we derive from a intuitive user browsing model. Since both the hitting time method and the manifold ranking method require the input query, to our knowledge, our approach is the only query suggestion diversification method that is applicable to presubmit, where only the partially-typed query is available. We show that in postsubmit the proposed examination model based utility maximization works better than existing methods, especially for less frequent queries. Another contribution is a path-based evaluation metric for measuring the utility of postsubmit suggestions that we call path gain/loss (PGL). PGL aims to measure the quality of the postsubmit suggestions by the average time it takes the user to reach a destination URL.

This paper is structured as follows. In the next section, we present several related query expansion/generation/rewriting methods in the recent literature, and our suggestion utility model is given in Section 3. In Section 4, we provide the details of our experimental setup. We present results on both offline (based on user studies and analysis of past session logs) and online (based on user interactions in session logs of a major search engine) evaluations of the model in Section 5, and conclude the paper with a discussion and proposed future work in Section 6.

2. RELATED WORK

Our suggestion set utility model is based on defining the conditional utility between pairs of queries, which has similar characteristics to defining a query similarity. There are many methods in the literature that define similarities between queries, and also utilize these for various problems, such as query rewriting, query generation or query suggestions.

Cui et al. look at the co-occurrences of query terms and document terms of the clicked documents and some term clustering to find similar queries [11]. Jones et al. use independence hypothesis log-likelihood ratio to find popular reformulations and use these as candidate suggestions [16], and build a supervised model to build a scoring scheme for suggestions. Probably Baeza-Yates & Tiberi and Craswell & Szummer are the first to use a query-url biparite graph for finding semantic relations [4, 10]. In a more recent work, Mei et al. build a bipartite graph of query-URL pairs, and use the click frequencies as the edges [18]. Using this graph, they generate query suggestions by looking at the pairs of queries that lead to clicks on same set of URL's. They also suggest using the same conditioning on a particular user's -or a user group's- click data only to generate personalized query suggestions. Cao et. al. use the same query-URL clickthrough bipartite graph idea, but they compliment it with a concept-tree [6]. Sahami and Heilman take another approach by investigating the common terms in the top n retrieved documents, and they build a similarity function using tf-idf vectors of these terms [21]. A similar idea is presented by Baeza-Yates et al., where they do clustering based on the aggregation of the term-weight vectors of the clicked URL's [3].

Overall, similarity measures defined over a query-URL bipartite graph that has the clickthrough values on the edges, and cosine similarity or Jensen-Shannon (or Kullback-Leibler) divergence over a set of most common terms in the top retrieved URL's are the most commonly used methods to define query similarity. In our view, the utility of each query is conditioned on the results of the earlier (higher-ranked) suggestions -also the results of the original query in postsubmit mode. Note that all above work focuses on defining a similarity measure between queries and our work is different mostly because we do not model the similarity of two queries; our aim is to model the conditional utility of one query given the other one is already presented.

Recently, studying diversity in the context of query suggestions has also attained some interest [27, 17, 5]. In [5], although the authors do not specifically aim for diversifying the query suggestions, they define an intuitive measure -distinct URLs in the multiset- for measuring the diversity of the suggestion sets that produce. In [27], authors build a query nearest neighbor graph to obtain a query manifold, and use a manifold ranking approach to generate a diverse set of suggestions. Although this approach is theoretically appealing and works effectively for frequent queries, practical usefulness of this approach is rather limited since the relevance of the suggestions drop very significantly for infrequent queries, since the query manifold becomes very sparse. In [17], Ma et al. use random walks over query-URL bipartite graph and hitting time to get a diversified set of query suggestions, and this is similar to the hitting time based method presented earlier by Mei et al. [18].

To our knowledge, the manifold ranking idea by Zhu et al. [27] and the hitting time approach by Ma et al. [17] are the only papers in the literature that are aiming to introduce diversity into query suggestions. One common shortcoming of both these two methods is they define the objective as "*given a query, generate a diverse and relevant suggestion set*", hence neither one of them is -neither directly nor with trivial modifications- suitable for presubmit, where the query is yet to be defined. We define the problem as "*given a set of suggestions of size N, rerank the suggestions such that the overall utility in top K rank is maximized for all* $K \leq N$", which is suitable for presubmit as well as postsubmit.

3. SUGGESTION UTILITY MODEL

Our model is based on estimating the pairwise conditional utility on the returned and clicked URLs[1] for each query pair. We argue that a query suggestion should be presented only if it can lead the user to the URLs that are not reachable more easily via the already presented suggestions -as well as the URLs presented for the original query for the postsubmit mode. We define a measure of utility that a query suggestion provides, conditioned on the original query and higher ranked suggestions. Using this, we define a submodular objective function over the set of queries, and develop a greedy algorithm to maximize the utility of a given suggestion set.

[1] A presentation group of title-abstract-URL tuple is referred as the URL through-out.

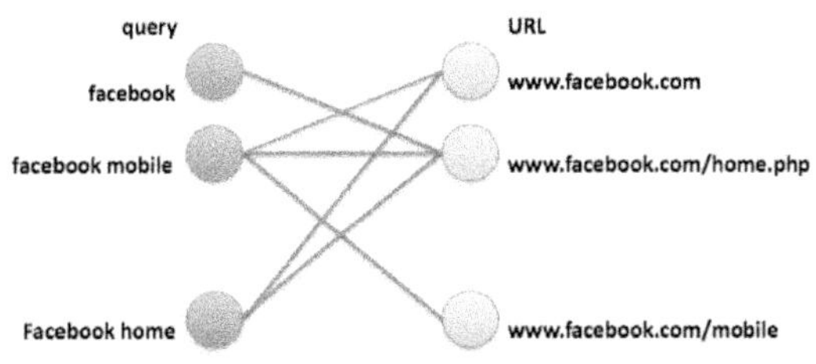

Figure 1: Query-URL bipartite graph

3.1 Query-URL Bipartite Graphs

We build the click bipartite graph of queries and clicked URLs, and the edges are the clickthrough values. Namely the weight on the edge that connects a particular URL u and a query q we have,

$$p(c(u) = 1|q) = N^u_{click}/N^u_{disp} \quad (1)$$

where $c(u)$ is a binary random variable, denoting whether the URL u is clicked or not, and N^u_{disp} and N^u_{click} are the number of times u is displayed and clicked for query q, respectively.

Similarly, we also build a view bipartite graph for queries and displayed URLs, where the edges are the average rank discount of the URL. In search, it is reasonable to assume that the importance of a document depends on its probability of being examined by the user. Therefore, Discounted Cumulative Gain (DCG) is among the most commonly used information retrieval metrics [14], which is given by

$$DCG_n = \sum_{r=1}^{N} \frac{rel_r}{\log_2(r+1)} \quad (2)$$

where r represents the rank of the results, and the typical values for N are 1,3,5. Note that the DCG formula can be considered as the inner product of two vectors, relevance vector $\mathbf{rel} = [rel_1, \ldots, rel_r]$ and discount vector $\mathbf{d} = [1, \ldots, 1/\log_2(r+1)]$, where the relevance vector represents the gain, and the discount vector represents the examination probabilities. In our view bipartite graph, the edges are discount values that DCG uses; however, since the results that the search engine change in time, if one looks into the query logs for a long period of time, one can see that a particular URL might have been returned at different ranks for a given query. Therefore here we use the average rank discount given by

$$E\{d(q,u)\} = \frac{1}{K} \sum_{i=1}^{K} \frac{1}{\log_2(r_i+1)} \quad (3)$$

where K is the number of times the URL u is returned for the query q in the session logs.

3.2 Pairwise Conditional Suggestion Utility

We assert that a query suggestion should be presented only if it leads to a sufficiently different result set as compared to those of the already presented suggestions and the original query. Therefore, we define $U(q_s|q_p)$, the utility of the suggestion q_s conditioned on q_p, a query that is already presented to the user. Simply, q_p is either the original query in the postsubmit mode or the partial query at the word boundaries in the presubmit mode or an already presented suggestion.

Intuitively, given two queries q_s and q_p, for each URL in the result set of q_s, we would like to check whether the same URL is in the result set of q_p; and if so, whether the URL is ranked as high as in q_s or not (so that the user is at least as likely to examine it). The simplest case is that the two queries q_s and q_p having exactly the same result sets. There are many such pairs of queries, mainly due to query rewriting widely used by search engines [24, 15, 22]. For example, for the prefix "bed", the two most frequent suggestions are "bed bath and beyond" and "bed bath & beyond", leading to *exactly* the same result set. If queries are sorted by popularity (for a given prefix), there are examples of such duplicate suggestions for even the simplest case of exactly same result sets.

Note that, in general using the query similarity of some type is not a good choice to model the utility of the suggestions, since it assumes $U(q_s|q_p) \doteq U(q_p|q_s)$ by definition, which is fundamentally incorrect. The relevant URLs in the result set of q_p might be a superset of those in q_s. A symmetric query similarity measure would not capture the required difference between a missing good result in the result set of q_s versus an additional good result in q_p, and the similarity drops in both cases.

Given q_s and q_p, let us define the result sets of these two queries as $URL_s = [u_{s1}, \ldots, u_{sN}]$ and $URL_p = [u_{p1}, \ldots, u_{pN}]$. For q_s, the click probabilities on the URL's are given as in (1). Here we don't consider any constraints in the rank of the URL's.

$$p(c(u_{si}) = 1|q_s) = N^{u_{si}}_{click}/N^{u_{si}}_{disp} \quad (4)$$

To make the model more stable for queries with very few clicks and pageviews, we introduce a prior on the click probabilities based on the average rank, which is available in the view bipartite graph.

$$p(c(u_{si}) = 1|q_s) = N^{u_{si}}_{click}/N^{u_{si}}_{disp} + \alpha\, E\{d(q_s, u_{si})\} \quad (5)$$

where α adjusts the strength of the prior distribution. Low values of α leads to a low precision model for queries with very few clicks, whereas a high α value leads to a too conservative model; hence a significant decrease in recall. We experimented with different values of α, and empirically found $\alpha = 1$ works best.

For each $u_{si} \in URL_s$, we define the examination probability that the user will examine the URL in the result page of q_p as follows,

$$p(e(u_{si}) = 1|q_p) = \begin{cases} 0 & : u_{si} \notin URL_p \\ 1 & : \begin{array}{c} u_{si} \in URL_p, \\ E\{d(q_p,u_{si})\} \geq E\{d(q_s,u_{si})\} \end{array} \\ \frac{E\{d(q_p,u_{si})\}}{E\{d(q_s,u_{si})\}} & : \begin{array}{c} u_{si} \in URL_p, \\ E\{d(q_p,u_{si})\} < E\{d(q_s,u_{si})\} \end{array} \end{cases} \quad (6)$$

where $e(u)$ is a binary random variable denoting whether u is examined or not. In words,

- u_{si} cannot be observed via q_p, if it is not in the result set of q_p, hence the examination probability is zero.
- If q_p returns u_{si} at least as high as q_s does, the examination probability is 1. The underlying assumption here is that a user that would examine the results of q_p at least as deep as she would go in the result set of q_s.
- If q_p returns u_{si} at a lower rank than q_s does, the examination probability of this URL is the ratio of the rank discounts of the two corresponding ranks. This ratio decreases when the rank difference increases, and for a given rank difference, it increases and gets close to 1 when both of the ranks are getting lower. With this, we want to capture two main effects presented in a comprehensive study on how people examine, recall, and reuse search results [23]:
  - The probability that people will recall a result decreases monotonically with the rank.
  - The probability that people will realize that a pair of documents were swapped increases with the difference in the rank, and decreases as the maximum of these two ranks are getting lower.

Combining (5) and (6), we define the conditional utility $U(q_s|q_p)$:

$$U(q_s|q_p) = 1 - \sum_{u \in URL_s} p(c(u) = 1|q_s)\, p(e(u) = 1|q_p) \quad (7)$$

where both terms in the summation can be obtained from the click and view bipartite graphs directly. Intuitively, the first term in the summation gives how important this particular URL is for the query q_s, and the second term gives how likely it is that the same user would examine this URL in q_p, with the assumption that the user would go as deep into the result set in q_p as well. Hence, $U(q_s|q_p)$ is, by definition 0 if the results of the two queries are exactly the same (since $p(e(u) = 1|q_p) = 1$ for all URLs, and $p(c(u) = 1|q_s)$ sums up to 1). Also, $U(q_s|q_p)$ would be close to 0 for queries that share many URLs and rank them similarly, and vice versa.

One missing piece in the utility definition is that it measures the amount of novelty that the suggestion may bring, however it does not model the relevance of the suggestion in any way. For example for two queries that are totally irrelevant, we have $U(q_s|q_p)$ values very close to 1. Same can be said about the diversity measures in web ranking; they are not useful by themselves, and have to be used along with some relevance criteria. Next section presents how we use this pairwise measure for a set of suggestions also taking their relevance into account.

3.3 Suggestion Set Utility Maximization

People with the same/similar intent do not phrase their queries in exactly the same way. Therefore, a search assistance system that is handling each suggestion candidate independently may perform poorly. For example, in the presubmit, the most popular queries that are matching the prefix "wal" include "wal mart", "wal mart stores", and "wal mart online", leading to almost identical result pages. Similarly, in the postsubmit, two most popular reformulations of the query "wal mart" includes "target" and "target stores". The missing piece is to model the additional utility of a suggestion, given the other ones that are already presented.

The pairwise conditional utility definition given in (7) can be regarded as the probability that q_s might satisfy the user given that she is not satisfied by q_p. We now state the problem of suggestion set utility maximization, as given an input (prefix or full query) maximizing the probability that an average user finds at least one useful suggestion within the suggestion set of size K.

Let sat be a binary random variable that denotes the probability that the user is satisfied, and S denote the suggestion set. For a particular user input q_{in}, given the satisfaction probabilities $p(sat = 1|s)$ for each suggestion $s \in S$, we would like to find the subset of suggestions $S' \subseteq S$ with $|S'| = K$ that maximizes the probability of satisfaction

$$p(sat = 1|S') = \sum_{s_i \in S'} p(sat = 1|s_i) \prod_{\substack{s_j \in S' \\ s_j \neq s_i}} U(s_i|s_j) \quad (8)$$

The satisfaction probability $p(sat = 1|s)$ depends on the application and might be popularity for presubmit, and reformulation probability for postsubmit. For brevity, we drop the conditioning on q_{in} since the formulation and all below derivation is given for a particular user input.

Intuitively, we would like to find a set of queries, with highest individual probability of satisfaction and all of which are sufficiently different from each other. One important observation is that the objective $p(sat = 1|S')$ is submodular, and a greedy algorithm that picks the query with highest marginal utility at each step can approximately solve the problem [19]. Submodularity is defined as follows,

Definition 1: Given a finite set N, a set function $f : 2^N \rightarrow \mathbb{R}$ is submodular iff for all sets S_1 and $S_2 \subseteq N$ such that $S_1 \subseteq S_2$, and $e \in N\ S_2$, $f(S_1{+}e) - f(S_1) \geq f(S_2{+}e) - f(S_2)$.

In words, a function is submodular if it satisfies *the principle of diminishing returns.* In our case the utility of adding a suggestion into a larger set is no more than the utility of adding the same suggestion into a smaller set, because a larger set of suggestions has higher probability that more of the users have already been satisfied, and the added value of the same additional suggestion gets smaller as the size of the set increases. More formally, let $T_1 = S_1 \cup e$, and $T_2 = S_2 \cup e$. Following the notation in Definition 1, one can write

$$\begin{aligned} p(sat = 1|T_1) = & \textstyle\sum_{s_i \in T_1} p(sat = 1|s_i) \prod_{\substack{s_j \in T_1 \\ s_j \neq s_i}} U(s_i|s_j) \\ = & \textstyle\sum_{s_i \in S_1} p(sat = 1|s_i) \prod_{\substack{s_j \in T_1 \\ s_j \neq s_i}} U(s_i|s_j) \\ & + p(sat = 1|e) \prod_{\substack{s_j \in T_1 \\ s_j \neq e}} U(e|s_j)) \end{aligned} \quad (9)$$

Then, the additional utility becomes

$$p(sat = 1|T_1) - p(sat = 1|S_1) = p(sat = 1|e) \prod_{\substack{s_j \in T_1 \\ s_j \neq e}} U(e|s_j)) \quad (10)$$

Very similarly, one can write the same for the other sets, S_2 and T_2

$$p(sat = 1|T_2) - p(sat = 1|S_2) = p(sat = 1|e) \prod_{\substack{s_j \in T_2 \\ s_j \neq e}} U(e|s_j)) \quad (11)$$

Since we have $0 \geq U(e|s_j) \geq 1$, and $T_1 \subseteq T_2$, we can conclude

$$p(sat = 1|T_1) - p(sat = 1|S_1) \geq p(sat = 1|T_2) - p(sat = 1|S_2) \quad (12)$$

Hence, the objective function given in (8) is submodular. For a submodular function, Nemhauser et al. show that the error of a greedy algorithm that selects the maximum marginal utility at each step is bounded [19], and the constructed set satisfies

$$f(S') \geq (1 - 1/e) f(S^*) \quad (13)$$

where S^* is the optimal set and S' is the set selected by the greedy algorithm. We will design a such greedy algorithm to select S', however one thing to consider is that this submodular objective function is defined over the set, hence it does not take the ordering into account. This is due to the assumption that the users will examine all K suggestions, which in practice is not true; users have higher probability of examining the suggestions that are ranked higher. Therefore, our algorithm is also designed to give an ordered list rather than a set, which is of the following form;

- Given the user input (either a prefix or full query), get the set of suggestions S, ordered with descending $p(sat = 1|s)$.
- Place the query that has the highest $p(sat = 1|s)$ into the output set S'.
- For all remaining queries in the input set S, get the query with highest $p(sat = 1|s) \prod_{\substack{s_j \in S' \\ s_j \neq s_i}} U(s|s_j)$.

One constraint we have here is that the algorithm should not increase the latency significantly, and the bottleneck here is the utility function has to be stored for all query pairs. To increase the time efficiency of the algorithm we binarize the conditional utility, and use $U(s|s_j) < \gamma$ at the last step. For the optimal γ value that we found with editorial tests (will be presented shortly), the utility function does fit into the memory, even for the web scale.

Another observation is that the above approach captures the utility optimization within the presented suggestions and rank them with optimal order, but one piece that is missing is to compare the suggestion candidates against the original query, to ensure that all presented suggestions satisfy $U(q_s|q_{in})$ as well. However, one thing that one should consider in the prefix phase is that we don't know q_{in} is a full query or not. For example, "faceb" is a very common misspelling of "facebook" and since the search engine corrects this misspelling, the result sets of these two queries are identical, therefore $U(\text{“}facebook''|\text{“}faceb'') = 0$. This suggests that "facebook" should not be displayed for the prefix "faceb", which is quite counter-intuitive. Therefore we examine the conditional utility with the user input (and remove the suggestion q_s, when $U(q_s|q_{in}) < \gamma$), only if the marginal query frequency of q_{in} is greater than q_s.

One final remark is, to preserve the optimal ordering of the output set S', one should account for the probability of satisfaction of the queries that are not included into the set. This is in fact one of the main differences of our greedy algorithm compared to the existing greedy algorithms proposed for result set diversification [1]. For a query, $p(sat = 1|s)$ should be its satisfaction probability plus the satisfaction probabilities of all of its near-duplicates (all suggestions that were not added to the output set S' since they failed to pass the conditional utility thresholding due to this particular query). For example, assume for the prefix "awk" the suggestions in the input set S are, "awkward", "awkward tv moments", "awk example", "awk examples" and "unix awk example", with decreasing $p(sat = 1|s)$. If "awk examples" and "unix awk example" are removed from the list since they are a duplicate of an earlier presented suggestion "awk example", then one should adjust $p(sat = 1|\text{“}awk\ example'')$ as $p(sat = 1|\text{“}awk\ example'') += p(sat = 1|\text{“}awk\ examples'') + p(sat = 1|\text{“}unix\ awk\ example'')$, so that after the duplicate removal the total satisfaction probability of this intent is properly represented, and this query has the chance to move upwards in the suggestion list.

Let us give a few definitions for formalizing the algorithm.

$f(q)$: The marginal query frequency

$S_{list}(q)$: A function which given an input query q, returns the set of query suggestions in descending probability of satisfaction.

$S_{dup}(q, \gamma)$: A function which given an input query and a threshold γ, returns the set of query suggestions with utility lower than the given threshold, $U(q_s|q_p) < \gamma$. We implement this as a look up table for a predetermined γ value, which yields a very fast computation time. Even for the web scale, the database required for this step fits into the memory for the optimal γ value.

S_{pre}: A function which given an input query q and the output set S', returns the set of queries within S', that q is a duplicate of. Simply, $S_{pre}(q)$ is the query (or queries) that caused q to be removed. In almost all cases this only returns one query, but in general, a new query might be a near-duplicate of more than one query in S'.

The pseudo-code of the set utility maximization algorithm is presented in Algorithm 1. After the initializations (lines 1-4), the first for-loop eliminates the duplicates of the user input (prefix or full query) by also considering the marginal frequency of the input (lines 5-9). Afterwards, the second for-loop does the greedy utility optimization within the suggestion set (lines 10-21). Every time a suggestion is decided to be added to the output set S', this query and all its duplicates are added to the set Dup, the set of queries that we remove the duplicates of which keeps growing as the for-loop proceeds (line 14). Every time a query is decided not to be added to the output set S', we move its satisfaction probability to the corresponding query (or queries) in the output set S' (lines 16-19), and once we reach the desired set size K, we sort results with decreasing probability of satisfaction to present them in the optimal order (line 22). At the end, all queries in S' are sufficiently different from each other (and sufficiently different from the user input q_{in} if q_{in} is a full query), and the queries in S' are sorted by descending satisfaction probability.

Algorithm 1 Greedy Suggestion Set Utility Maximization

1: $I = S_{list}(q_{in})$
2: $S' = \{\}$
3: $Dup = \{\}$
4: $Dup_q = S_{dup}(q_{in}, \gamma)$
5: **for** $q \in Dup_q$ **do**
6:   **if** $f(q) < f(q_{in})$ **then**
7:     $Dup += q$
8:   **end if**
9: **end for**
10: **for** $q \in I$ **do**
11:   **if** $q \notin Dup$ **then**
12:     $S' += q$
13:     $Dup_q = S_{dup}(q, \gamma)$
14:     $Dup += Dup_q$
15:   **else**
16:     $P = S_{pre}(q, S')$
17:     **for** $p \in P$ **do**
18:       $p(sat = 1|p) += p(sat = 1|q)/length(P)$
19:     **end for**
20:   **end if**
21: **end for**
22: Sort S' by descending $p(sat = 1|s)$

4. EXPERIMENTAL SETUP

Before going into the results that we obtained with our model, in this section we describe the session logs data that we used to build the bipartite graphs presented in Section 3.1, and the details of our offline and online test setup.

4.1 Model Training Data

We use 6-month of anonymized session logs of a major commercial search engine to build the view and click bipartite graphs. To make the data size tractable we ignored queries that appeared less than 3 times in this 6-month period, and bipartite graphs consist of roughly 119M unique queries and 658M unique URLs in total. The view graph is much denser than the click graph, since by definition the edges in the view graph are a superset of the edges in the click graph. After building the graphs we construct the non-symmetric conditional utility matrix, whose entries are $U(q_s|q_p)$, for all query pairs. Given a γ value, constructing the look-up table needed for S_{dup} is rather straightforward from this conditional utility matrix.

4.2 User Studies

In the user study, we provide a pair of queries to the judges and ask them to assess the utility of the second query suggestion, given that the first one is already presented. Note that small differences in queries that seem insignificant to people just by looking at the query strings can have very different intents and search results (for example, "office" vs "the office"). Therefore, in this task, we specifically ask the judges to examine the search results of each query before assessing the utility/redundancy. We also do a side-by-side test, where we present two sets of queries to the judges and ask them to assess which of the suggestion sets is better. All judges are professionals trained to evaluate search engines, and this test includes 12 individuals. The judges were asked to check the search result pages of each suggestion before making a decision according to the following guidelines in a 4-level grade scale.

3 - Useful: This suggestion introduces distinct, useful, unique information that is different from that of the presented suggestion.

2 - Somewhat useful: There is some content overlap with the presented suggestion, but there is enough of a difference that you do not consider the suggestions wholly redundant.

1 - Somewhat redundant: There is a minor difference in intent between the first suggestion and second, but they are mostly the same. Showing this suggestion might offer a somewhat different experience for the user, but the overlap between first and second suggestion is great and the second is not likely to be useful.

0 - Redundant: This suggestion definitely does not add any new information to presented suggestion. It would not be useful to show to any user because its intent/content is wholly redundant with the presented suggestion.

4.3 Session Log Analysis

In the session log analysis, we perform comparisons of suggestion relevance and diversity, with respect to the following evaluation metrics.

Relevance metric: In presubmit, the query is yet to be defined and relevance cannot be defined. Therefore, we use average query popularity -average marginal query frequency- instead of relevance. In postsubmit evaluation, we will use the reformulation probability $p(q_{next}|q_{current})$ estimated from the query logs and averaged over the suggestions in the set, as the relevance measurement. Reformulation probability is defined as follows, given the user issued $q_{current}$ the probability that the same user issues q_{next} within 10 minutes. Not to introduce a presentation bias, here we only consider manual reformulations (reformulations due to query suggestion clicks are not counted).

Diversity metric: To measure diversity, we adopt a similar measure as in [5], the total number of URLs in the multiset per query: the total number of unique URLs at top 5 ranks for all queries in the suggestion set, divided by the number of queries in the set.

The set of algorithms to be compared in the session log analysis are given below.

`REL`: Optimize for relevance; at any point add the query that maximizes the relevance metric into the suggestion set. Optimizing for relevance is in fact the dominant approach in the commercial search engines.

`DIV`: Optimize for diversity and use relevance to break ties; start with the most popular query, and at any point among the queries that maximize the diversity metric, add the query with maximum query frequency into the suggestion set.

`DQS`: The random walk hitting time based method in [17].

`UM`: Our suggestion utility maximization algorithm.

Note that we decided not to include manifold ranking method in [27] into the comparisons. Although this method is theoretically appealing, it seems applicable to only frequent queries, where there exist a sufficient number of related queries in the query neighborhood to construct the query manifold reliably. In their paper, the authors provide results over queries that have appeared at least 700 times in a month of query logs, which roughly corresponds to 0.002% of the overall unique query traffic. For infrequent queries, the query manifold becomes very unreliable and the relevance of the query suggestions drop very significantly, making this method impractical for real applications.

4.4 Online Test Setup

The online test is a classical A/B test setting, where the search traffic is split into two exclusive groups, the baseline (control) and the test buckets. In the A/B test the method and the baseline is presented to millions of users, and their interactions are recorded for the analysis. The user populations in the baseline and the test buckets are uniformly sampled, hence they are not biased towards heavy or light users. The query volume, and query distributions (for example the proportion of navigational and informational queries or other similar statistics etc.) are very similar in both buckets. The test bucket implements our suggestion set utility maximization algorithm, both in the presubmit and postsubmit. For both presubmit and postsubmit, we log when our algorithm modifies the suggestion set in order to be able to find the subset of queries which we will refer to as *affected queries*. In the following, we describe the configuration in the baseline bucket as well as the search assist modules within which the test and baseline configurations are applied. Except these search assist modules mentioned below, everything on the search result page is identical for both the test and baseline buckets, including the search results, sponsored search results, page layout and user interface. The test is kept alive for a sufficient period of time such that all metrics that we are interested can reach statistically significant values.

Baseline Configuration: The baseline configuration is a simple modification of `REL`. It disregards diversity and does not consider the conditional utility of each suggestion and it is optimized for relevance (popularity in presubmit), except that it implements two simple query string based deduping operations:

- If two query suggestions in the list are identical except for one word is plural (for example, "hp laptop" and "hp laptops"), remove the less frequent of these two from the suggestions, and add the popularity mass of the less popular suggestion to the more popular one.
- If one of the query suggestions is identified as a misspelling of one of the others, remove the misspelled query from the suggestions and add the popularity mass of the misspelled query to the correctly spelled one.

Test Configuration: `UM`, our suggestion utility maximization method.

Search Assistance Modules: There are three search assistance modules that we will apply the changes in this A/B test. *Suggest-as-you-type* (SAYT) is the presubmit search assistance module. Given a prefix, the top 5 queries with the highest score that match the prefix are presented under the query box like a dropdown menu. *North Also Try* (NAT) is the postsubmit search assistance module that is displayed above the search results. The user is likely to see these suggestions -probably even before examining the search results. *South Also Try* (SAT) is the postsubmit search assistance module that is displayed below the 10 search results, right above the next page button. For a given query, the suggestions presented in NAT and SAT modules are exactly the same (same suggestion set in the same order), and depending on the number of characters in each suggestions, up to 5 suggestions can be displayed.

5. EXPERIMENTAL RESULTS

Our experiments consist of three parts, (i) user studies that we did for selecting the γ value and to measure the accuracy at this operating point, (ii) session log analysis to compare our method (at this γ value) to relevance and diversity baselines as well as an earlier proposed method for both presubmit and postsubmit, (iii) a thorough analysis of the results from the A/B test, again independently for presubmit and postsubmit.

5.1 User Studies

We present two user studies. First one is a pairwise test for tuning the γ value presented in the greedy algorithm, which is basically the threshold of $U(q_s|q_p)$ that we will consider q_s redundant if q_p is already presented. The second test is a side-by-side test at the particular γ value selected.

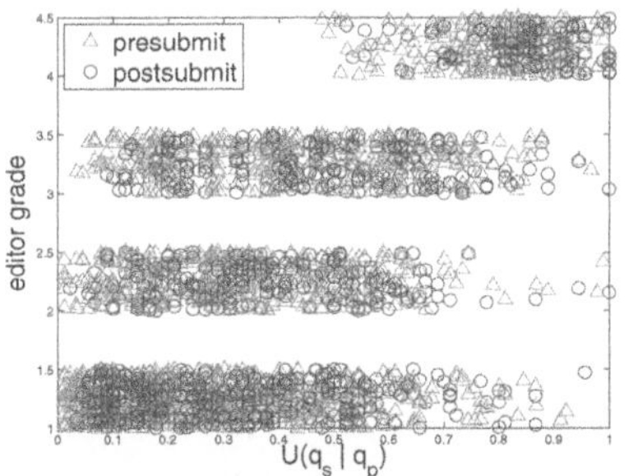

Figure 2: $U(q_s|q_p)$ vs. the editorial grades (3-useful, 2-somewhat useful, 1-somewhat redundant, 0-redundant) Query pairs sampled from presubmit (red) and postsubmit (blue) are presented.

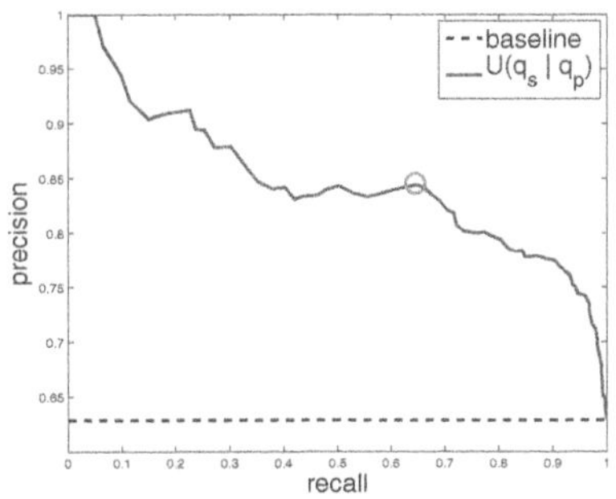

Figure 3: precision-recall curve of the $U(q_s|q_p)$ and the precision-recall curve of the majority classifier. The marker shows the selected operating point where $\gamma = 0.24$.

5.1.1 Pairwise Comparison

To find the optimal γ value to execute the greedy algorithm, we sampled 2400 unique (q_s, q_p) pairs. 1600 of these samples are coming from query pairs that were displayed together in Suggest-as-you-type. While collecting the supervised learning data for training/testing a query classifier or some retrieval model, it is a common practice to generate sample set weighted with the traffic, hence the frequent queries are respected more and added into the training set with greater likelihood. With the same motivation, we collect this sample in a way that the sampling probability of a particular query pair is directly proportional to the number of times that they are displayed together (so pairs like "facebook" and "facebook login" displayed millions of times in the suggest-as-you-type together for the same prefix have much higher likelihood of getting into this sample set). Similarly, we sampled 800 query pairs from the postsubmit suggestion pairs that are popular reformulations of the same query, where the sampling probability is directly proportional with the reformulation probability. Hence, we again sample more from more frequent query pairs.

The editorial test evaluates how useful the suggestion q_s is given that q_p is already presented to the user in a four grade scale (3-useful, 2-somewhat useful, 1-somewhat redundant, 0-redundant). Figure 2 shows the distribution of the data samples, $U(q_s|q_p)$ vs. the editorial grade. We binarize this 4-grade by mapping useful and somewhat useful to 1, and redundant and somewhat redundant to 0. We investigate the precision-recall curve of this dataset (shown in Figure 3) to select γ, and decided to use $\gamma = 0.24$. This corresponds to 0.85 precision and 0.65 recall on this dataset.

5.1.2 Side-by-side Evaluation

To measure the performance of UM at the particular γ value selected, we designed a side-by-side test. For a given prefix or full

Table 1: A side-by-side sample of REL (left) and UM (right)

netf	netf
netflix	**netf**lix
netflix rentals	**netf**irms
netflix movies	blockbuster vs **netf**lix
netflix queue	**netf**ile
netfirms	**netf**ront
wal m	wal m
wal mart	**wal m**art
wal mart stores	**wal m**art canada
wal mart supercenter	**wal m**art black friday 2008
wal mart online	**wal m**art benefits
wal mart canada	**wal m**art black friday 2009
faceb	faceb
facebook	**faceb**ook
facebook login	farmville **faceb**ook
facebook home	**faceb**ook farm town
facebooklogin	**faceb**ook layouts
facebook friends	**faceb**ook ipo
well	well
wells fargo	**well**s fargo
wellsbutrin	**well**sbutrin
wells fargo bank	tom **well**ing
wells fargo online	**well**point
tom **well**ing	dawn **well**s

query, we provide the judges the top 5 suggestions of the baseline configuration and the test configurations defined in Section 4.4 (REL with some tweaks and UM), and ask them which of the suggestion sets is better.

To construct the sample set first we get the 500 most frequent queries in our session logs. From these, for each query we grab 3 random prefixes between 2-6 characters, and we end up with 758 unique prefixes. For these 758 prefixes, the side-by-side test significantly favors the UM against REL. The judgments are 42 (5.5%) REL is better, 191 (25.2%) UM is better, and 525 (69.3%) no noticeable difference. Table 1 shows some samples from this side-by-side test.

To follow up with the cases that the editor thinks UM is worse, for these 42 cases we provided the editors the individual (q_s, q_p) pairs, and asked them to do a pairwise comparison (exactly as in the previous subsection), to identify the useful suggestions that we incorrectly removed. For 28 of these 42 cases, the editors did not report any useful suggestion that is removed, and mentioned that the problem is not the useful suggestions that are incorrectly removed, but the relevance of the suggestions that rank higher after removing these. For example, see the "wal m" example in Table 1 where the algorithm removes "wal mart stores", "wal mart supercenter", "wal mart online" as reduntant since "wal mart" is presented, and the editor agrees that these are all redundant suggestions. However, the editor notes that the relevance of the suggestions (originally ranked 7th, 8th and 9th) that bump up after removing the redundant ones are really low, and despite the redundancy, the original suggestion set *looks* better.

The small follow-up study over the negative side-by-side examples suggests that tuning γ in a query-dependent manner can further improve the accuracy, and will be the focus of our future work. Overall, the side-by-side test shows that the judges think that UM leads to better results as compared to the baseline REL more than 82% of the time, when it introduces noticeable changes.

5.2 Session Logs Analysis

Having set the γ value, before designing an online test we evaluate UM against the baseline algorithms (REL and DIV) as well as a recently proposed algorithm DQS by analyzing our past session

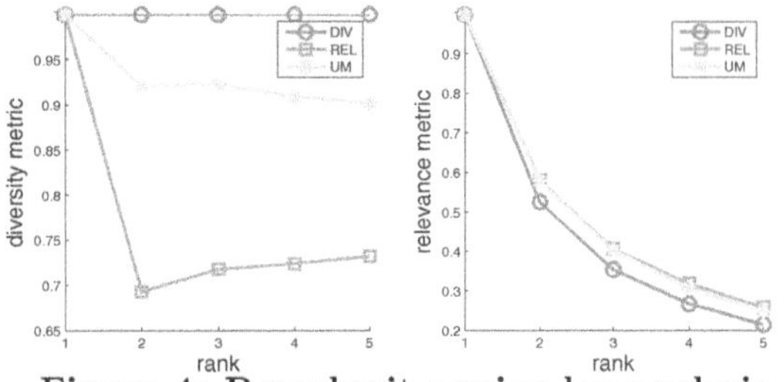

Figure 4: Presubmit session log analysis

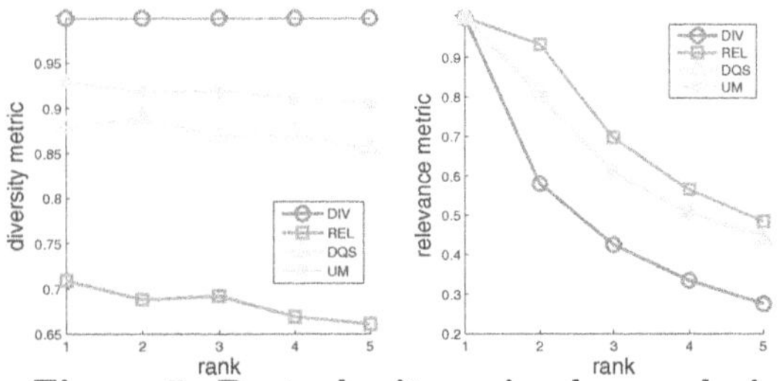

Figure 5: Postsubmit session log analysis

logs. We present two comparisons, one for presubmit and one for postsubmit using the metrics defined in Section 4.3.

For presubmit evaluation, we randomly sample 25K prefixes from query logs and evaluate the diversity and relevance metrics (relevance metric at prefix is marginal query frequency) at each rank up to 5. Note that `DQS` method is not included in the presubmit evaluation, since by definition it requires the input query, which is yet to be defined in presubmit. Figure 4 shows the presubmit evaluation from session logs, and we normalize the relevance and diversity metrics to [0,1]. Similarly for postsubmit evaluation, we randomly sample 25K queries and repeat the same experiment with `DQS` also included, results are shown in 5.

In both presubmit and postsubmit, the diversity baseline `DIV` seems that it is always -at least up to rank 5- able to find some query suggestion that keeps the diversity metric maximal at 1.0, however it has significantly worse relevance at all ranks. Also, the relevance baseline `REL` with the optimal relevance metric has the worst diversity metrics at all ranks for both presubmit and postsubmit. Note that unlike the diversity metric, the optimal relevance metric, hence average marginal query frequency (presubmit) and average reformulation probability (postsubmit) decreases with rank.

In presubmit, for the relevance baseline `REL`, the average diversity at rank 2 is significantly lower than the average over top 3, 4 or 5 ranks. This is presumably due to the fact that popular queries of generally navigational nature and their redundant variants appear together at top two ranks more frequently. Overall, in presubmit, `UM` improves the diversity metric over the relevance baseline `REL` significantly, without inducing any noticeable loss in relevance.

In postsubmit, relevance baseline `REL` again has the worst diversity metric, and diversity baseline `DIV` has the worst relevance metric. In terms of diversity, `UM` and `DQS` both improve significantly over the baseline with similar amount of compromise on the relevance metric. In terms of diversity, `UM` performs better than `DQS` and similar to the postsubmit, it brings roughly a 30% improvement in the diversity metric over the relevance baseline `REL`.

5.3 Online Evaluation

In this section we will provide the evaluation of the session logs obtained by the A/B test on a major search engine, and unless stated otherwise, all presented results are statistically significant. The key for evaluating the online tests effectively is to interpret the user interactions correctly. Therefore, throughout this section we will

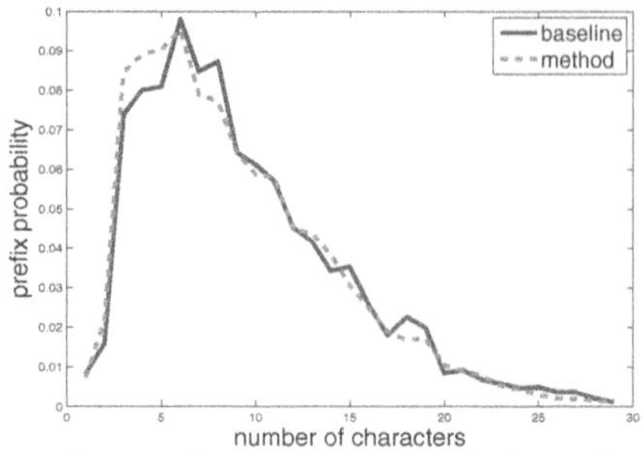

Figure 6: The probability of prefix length (as a function of number of characters), for queries that the algorithm modified the results before a query suggestion is clicked.

also briefly provide the reason why we think the metrics mentioned here are useful ones.

5.3.1 Presubmit

The overall aim of Suggest-as-you-type is to auto-complete the user's prefix, hence to minimize the time and effort it takes to the users while they enter their search queries. Therefore, a natural metric for comparing the test and baseline configurations in the presubmit phase is measuring the change in the time and effort.

Let us define the affected queries as follows: the algorithm affected the query if the Suggest-as-you-type suggestion set was modified by the algorithm *at anytime before the query is submitted.* We found that, for this definition, on the affected queries the utility maximization model decreases the average number of characters typed by the user before submitting the query by 1.2% (p-value<0.0001) against the baseline. Although in the right direction, this does not seem to be a big difference. The reason why becomes clearer after observing Figure 6, where we show the probability that the user stops (either clicks a suggestion, or finishes typing the whole query) at a given prefix length, as a function of number of characters typed. Both distributions show very similar characteristics except the 3 to 8 characters region, and that is presumably because this is not a good definition of affected queries. The reason is, for example, if what the user has in mind was "faucet handle opens wrong way" she probably did not care too much about that our algorithm modified results along the way, for example the fact that the "facebook" variants were removed for the prefix "fa".

Let us now define the affected queries as: Suggest-as-you-type suggestion set was modified by the algorithm *at the prefix that a query suggestion is clicked.* For this definition of affected queries, we see a much more significant difference as shown in Figure 7. The difference in average prefix length is -7.4% (p<0.0001), the probability that the user finished the search before 5 characters given that the query is longer than 5 characters increases by 31.3% (p=0.0004). Also, the time it takes the user to get to a long-dwell-time URL decreases by roughly one second on average (p=0.0021). One second might not sound that significant in the beginning, but considering the overall query volume, it adds up to a lot.

For these two definitions of affected queries, the overall suggest-as-you-type click through rate change is 1.14% increase, and 0.75% decrease against baseline, both not statistically significant. Hence, the overall clickthrough rate of the module is flat. Note that unlike the web search scenario, multiple clicks per query (here prefix) is not possible. One can either type the whole query manually (which can be regarded as abandonment of the suggestion module) or select a single suggestion, and a flat click through difference between the baseline and the bucket can be interpreted as `UM` does not remove many useful queries while introducing diversity into the sug-

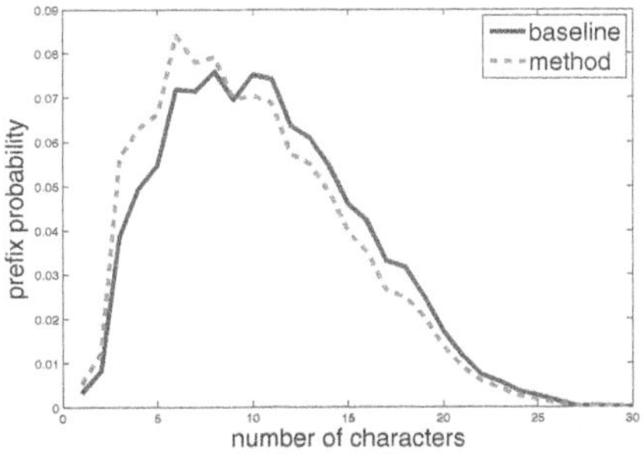

Figure 7: The probability of prefix length (as a function of number of characters), for queries that the algorithm modified the results at the prefix that a query suggestion is clicked.

gestion set, and the suggest-as-you-type does not get abandoned more. We don't directly aim to increase the number of clicks in this module, we just want the users to get what they want sooner.

5.3.2 *Postsubmit*

In the postsubmit, we tested both algorithms for two different suggestion placements, above the search results (NAT) and beneath the search results (SAT). For both the baseline and the bucket, the NAT and SAT suggestions are the same, hence we have four configurations to compare: 1) REL at NAT, 2) gUM at NAT, 3) REL at SAT, and 4) UM at SAT.

An argument similar to that in the prefix phase also applies here, we would like to present the suggestion set that minimizes the time it takes to the user to get to what they want. Note that suggestion click trough rate is not a good metric for this, since what the user want is not a suggestion anymore, it is a search result. In fact, there are many cases that decreasing the suggestion click through rate by removing low utility suggestions can save the user a lot of time. Suppose for the query "bank of america", the suggestion is "bank of america online". Clicking on this suggestion very rarely takes the user to a destination URL that was not already on the first search result page, and this suggestion just distracts and causes the user to lose time. We want the users to spend less time for reaching the destination URLs, and this is exactly the sort of suggestion click that we would like to get rid of. On the other hand, if a useful suggestion is removed that could take the user to a destination URL that is not on the original page, the user would have to reformulate the query manually, which would take longer time.

One thing that we have observed is when not distracted with low utility suggestions, users tend to click more on the search results. All result set click trough rate on the bucket is 1.296% (p=0.0007) higher than the baseline, where the biggest gains were in position 2 to 5 with 4.0%, 8.3%, 9.8% and 11.0% increase in clickthrough, respectively (all with $p<0.0001$). Also, while they show exactly the same suggestions and NAT click trough rate decreases very sharply -7.9% ($p<0.0001$) against the baseline, there is no statistically significant change in the SAT results -0.4% (p=0.11). Given that the same suggestions were displayed at NAT and SAT, the difference can be interpreted as UM is not removing suggestions that would be useful to the user after examining the first 10 results.

In addition to the click trough rates above, we also use a metric that based on user's search paths to evaluate the effectiveness of our utility maximization algorithm. A search path is the sequence of search events conducted by a search user that started from an initial query, possibly went through a few query reformulations and result clicks, finally reaching a destination page. Intuitively, if either the retrieval results and/or the suggestions are better, the average time of the search paths to final destination URL should get smaller.

Table 2: PGL results for four test configurations

Configuration	Total	Loss	Gain	PGL
REL, NAT	185,910	120,017	65,893	35%
UM, NAT	144,654	89,961	54,693	38%
REL, SAT	7,429	3,751	3,678	50%
UM, SAT	6,094	2,681	3,413	56%

We introduce a path-based metric which measures the performance of a suggestion algorithm in terms of additional gain/loss of suggestions observed by users. We call this metric as "path gain/loss" (PGL) metric. To calculate the PGL metric, we first mine the session logs of the A/B test and pulled out the competitive search paths that start from the same query and end at the same destination URL. There are several identification methods for destination URL in the literature [25, 12]. Without loss of generality, we used a simple destination URL classifier based on page dwell time. We consider a clicked page is a destination URL if its dwell time is greater than 100 seconds. Among those competitive search paths (i.e., paths having the same start and end points), we further divided them into two classes.

The first class of paths all involve some query suggestion clicks. We call this class of paths as *assisted paths*. For the other class of paths, they do not have any query suggestion click. This class of paths is called *algo paths*. Intuitively, if we see the time distribution for the assisted paths is shorter than that for algo paths, we can conclude the query suggestions are good at saving user's time.

To compare the time distribution between these two classes of paths, we sorted the algo paths by their path times and chose the path time at 20th percentile as the pivotal path time. We then compared the assisted path one by one against the pivotal path time. If the path time is shorter than the pivotal path time, we count it as a gain for the clicked query suggestion. If the path time is longer than the pivotal path time, we count it as a loss for the clicked query suggestion. (Note that the reason we chose 20th percentile point is our selected system requirement, and this selection is a design choice - we want our assisted paths to be significantly faster than algo paths on average.) In this process, we updated the gain/loss counters associated to each suggestion. We repeated the above gain/loss analysis for all combinations of starting query and destination page observed in the session logs. At the end, we aggregate the gain/loss counts across all clicked suggestions for the total gain/loss counts. The total gain/loss counts reflect the overall query suggestion performance observed by search users. We simply define PGL as the following equation:

$$PGL = \frac{gaincount}{gaincount + losscount} \qquad (14)$$

Note that PGL value is in the range of 0 to 1, and higher PGL value means the query suggestion algorithm that is being evaluated is on average reducing the time that it takes the user to reach a destination URL. Table 2 shows the PGL results for four test configurations. For both NAT and SAT, UM performs better than the baseline algorithm REL, with 8.5% and 12% relative improvements in PGL ratio, respectively.

Note that for both NAT and SAT, we see the utility maximization algorithm has fewer assisted paths than the baseline algorithm. This is expected since our goal is to remove useless suggestions that the user is likely end up at a destination URL that she could have found in the first result page anyway. Therefore, the algorithm tends to offer suggestions for the minor intents, saving time of the people that are interested in these minor intents to help them get where they want without typing the query manually, and saving time of the people that are interested in the major intent by not distracting them. On the affected queries, we found that the average search path in the test bucket is 0.87 seconds shorter than the baseline on

Table 3: PGL results and path time for example queries

Query	Config.	Total	Loss	Gain	PGL	Avg. Path Time	Suggestions
usps	REL	2212	116	34	22%	6.29s	usps tracking, usps rates, usps zip codes
usps	UM	2470	2	8	80%	5.96s	usps jobs, usps priority mail, usps liteblue
hulu	REL	4502	90	11	10%	6.67s	hulu tv, hulu movies, hulu saturday nitght live
hulu	UM	4977	9	9	50%	6.37s	hulu saturday night live, hulu family guy, hulu desktop
food network	REL	2266	43	6	12%	7.64s	food network recipes, tv food network, food network channel
food network	UM	2446	6	6	50%	7.19s	food network recipes, next food network star, food network canada
target	REL	6209	67	22	0.29	7.57s	target online stores, target stores, target department store
target	UM	7164	68	45	0.41	7.29s	target baby registry, target coupon, target jobs
wal mart	REL	2532	70	21	23%	10.77	wal mart stores, wal mart supercenter, wal mart online
wal mart	UM	2748	11	12	52%	10.35	wal mart canada, wal mart jobs, wal mart benefits

average. In Table 5.3.2, we show the NAT results of some example queries in our A/B test. The table columns shows the query itself, query suggestion algorithm, total number of queries received, total loss count for the query, total gain count, PGL value, and average path time, and the corresponding suggestions.

6. CONCLUSIONS

Most query expansion and query generation methods in the literature that are being used for search assistance handle the suggestion candidates individually, and diversity of the query suggestions is generally neglected. We present a utility maximization algorithm to introduce diversity into the suggestion sets by modeling the conditional utility for pairs of queries, and we use this pairwise measure to build an algorithm to maximize the utility of a suggestion set. Overall, the problem that we tackle and the method we provide is analogous to the result set diversification problem, while the formalization of added utility of a suggestion is novel, and the greedy algorithm we develop is customized for the search assistance.

Our problem formulation is different from existing suggestion diversification models in the literature that define the problem as "*given a query*, generate a diverse and relevant suggestion set" [27, 17]. Our approach is to frame the problem as "*given a set of suggestions of size N, rerank the suggestions such that the overall utility in top K rank is maximized for all* $K \leq N$", which not require the query to be given, hence the model is suitable for both presubmit and postsubmit suggestions. Our model is based on a user examination model, and its performance does not drop for infrequent queries -presumably thanks to the smoothing in (5) and the fact that the examination probabilities in (6), which are derived from the rank discount factors in DCG, can reliably be estimated even with a few observations. In the session logs analysis, our model performed better than the random walk based diversification approach presented earlier by Ma et al. [17]. In the online evaluations, we show that our a model gets the users to what they want -a query completion suggestion that they find useful in the presubmit mode, and a destination URL in the postsubmit mode- in shorter time.

7. REFERENCES

[1] R. Agrawal, S. Gollapudi, A. Halverson, and S. Ieong. Diversifying search results. In *WSDM '09*, pages 5–14, New York, NY, USA, 2009. ACM.

[2] A. Anagnostopoulos, A. Z. Broder, and D. Carmel. Sampling search-engine results. In *WWW '05*, pages 245–256, New York, NY, USA, 2005. ACM.

[3] R. A. Baeza-Yates, C. A. Hurtado, and M. Mendoza. Query recommendation using query logs in search engines. In *EDBT Workshops*, pages 588–596, 2004.

[4] R. A. Baeza-Yates and A. Tiberi. Extracting semantic relations from query logs. In *KDD*, pages 76–85, 2007.

[5] P. Boldi, F. Bonchi, C. Castillo, D. Donato, and S. Vigna. Query suggestions using query-flow graphs. In *Proceedings of the 2009 workshop on Web Search Click Data*, WSCD '09, pages 56–63, New York, NY, USA, 2009. ACM.

[6] H. Cao, D. Jiang, J. Pei, Q. He, Z. Liao, E. Chen, and H. Li. Context-aware query suggestion by mining click-through and session data. In *KDD '08*, pages 875–883, New York, NY, USA, 2008. ACM.

[7] J. Carbonell and J. Goldstein. The use of mmr, diversity-based reranking for reordering documents and producing summaries. In *SIGIR '98*, pages 335–336, New York, NY, USA, 1998. ACM.

[8] H. Chen and D. R. Karger. Less is more: probabilistic models for retrieving fewer relevant documents. In *SIGIR '06*, pages 429–436, New York, NY, USA, 2006. ACM.

[9] C. L. Clarke, M. Kolla, G. V. Cormack, O. Vechtomova, A. Ashkan, S. Büttcher, and I. MacKinnon. Novelty and diversity in information retrieval evaluation. In *SIGIR '08*, pages 659–666, New York, NY, USA, 2008. ACM.

[10] N. Craswell and M. Szummer. Random walks on the click graph. In *SIGIR*, pages 239–246, Amsterdam, The Netherlands, 2007.

[11] H. Cui, J.-R. Wen, J.-Y. Nie, and W.-Y. Ma. Probabilistic query expansion using query logs. In *WWW '02*, pages 325–332, 2002.

[12] D. Downey, S. Dumais, D. Liebling, and E. Horvitz. Understanding the relationship between searchers' queries and information goals. In *CIKM '08*, pages 449–458, New York, NY, USA, 2008. ACM.

[13] S. Gollapudi and A. Sharma. An axiomatic approach for result diversification. In *WWW '09*, pages 381–390, New York, NY, USA, 2009. ACM.

[14] K. Järvelin and J. Kekäläinen. Cumulated gain-based evaluation of IR techniques. *ACM Trans. Inf. Syst.*, 20(4):422–446, 2002.

[15] R. Jones and F. Peng. Web search query rewriting. In *Encyclopedia of Database Systems*, pages 3491–3493. 2009.

[16] R. Jones, B. Rey, O. Madani, and W. Greiner. Generating query substitutions. In *WWW '06*, pages 387–396, 2006.

[17] H. Ma, M. R. Lyu, and I. King. Diversifying query suggestion results. In *AAAI '10*, 2010.

[18] Q. Mei, D. Zhou, and K. Church. Query suggestion using hitting time. In *CIKM '08*, 2008.

[19] G. L. Nemhauser, L. A. Wolsey, and M. L. Fisher. An analysis of approximations for maximizing submodular set functions. *Math. Programming*, 14(3):265–294, 1978.

[20] F. Radlinski and S. Dumais. Improving personalized web search using result diversification. In *SIGIR '06*, pages 691–692, New York, NY, USA, 2006. ACM.

[21] M. Sahami and T. D. Heilman. A web-based kernel function for measuring the similarity of short text snippets. In *WWW '06*, pages 377–386, New York, NY, USA, 2006. ACM.

[22] B. Tan and F. Peng. Unsupervised query segmentation using generative language models and wikipedia. In *WWW '08*, pages 347–356, New York, NY, USA, 2008. ACM.

[23] J. Teevan. How people recall, recognize, and reuse search results. *ACM Trans. Inf. Syst.*, 26(4):1–27, 2008.

[24] X. Wei, F. Peng, H. Tseng, Y. Lu, and B. Dumoulin. Context sensitive synonym discovery for web search queries. In D. W.-L. Cheung, I.-Y. Song, W. W. Chu, X. Hu, and J. J. Lin, editors, *CIKM '09*, pages 1585–1588. ACM, 2009.

[25] R. W. White, M. Bilenko, and S. Cucerzan. Studying the use of popular destinations to enhance web search interaction. In *SIGIR '07*, pages 159–166, 2007.

[26] C. Zhai and J. Lafferty. A risk minimization framework for information retrieval. *Inf. Process. Manage.*, 42(1):31–55, 2006.

[27] X. Zhu, J. Guo, and X. Cheng. Recommending diverse and relevant queries with a manifold ranking based approach. In *SIGIR '10 Workshop on Query Representation and Understanding*, 2010.

Improving Context-Aware Query Classification via Adaptive Self-training

Minmin Chen[1]*, Jian-Tao Sun[2], Xiaochuan Ni[2], Yixin Chen[1]
[1]Department of Computer Science and Engineering
Washington University in Saint Louis, Saint Louis, MO, USA
[2]Microsoft Research Asia, Beijing, P.R. China
[1]{mc15, chen}@cse.wustl.edu, [2]{jtsun, xini}@microsoft.com

ABSTRACT

Topical classification of user queries is critical for general-purpose web search systems. It is also a challenging task, due to the sparsity of query terms and the lack of labeled queries. On the other hand, search contexts embedded in query sessions and unlabeled queries free on the web have not been fully utilized in most query classification systems. In this work, we leverage these information to improve query classification accuracy.

We first incorporate search contexts into our framework using a Conditional Random Field (CRF) model. Discriminative training of CRFs is favored over the traditional maximum likelihood training because of its robustness to noise. We then adapt self-training with our model to exploit the information in unlabeled queries. By investigating different confidence measurements and model selection strategies, we effectively avoid the error-reinforcing nature of self-training. In extensive experiments on real search logs, we have averaged around 20% improvement in classification accuracy over other state-of-the-art baselines.

Categories and Subject Descriptors

H.3.m [**Information Storage and Retrieval**]: Miscellaneous; I.5.2 [**Pattern Recognition**]: Design Methodology - Classifier design and evaluation

General Terms

Algorithms, Experimentation, Measurement, Performance

Keywords

Query classification, User search context, Unlabeled queries

*This work was done when Minmin Chen was an intern at Microsoft Research Asia.

CIKM'11, October 24–28, 2011, Glasgow, Scotland, UK.

1. INTRODUCTION

Recent years have witnessed the booming of web search and its related services. Commercial web search engines receive hundreds of millions of queries every day. Understanding user intents behind queries is essential in developing search engines. Query classification is a task studied for this purpose. In query classification, user queries are classified into one (or more) predefined target categories. Such category information later can be used for refining web page rankings, triggering the most appropriate vertical searches, and finding matched online advertisements, etc..

Challenges associated with query classification include sparsity of both query features and training data. First, user queries usually contain only several unique terms, thus it is difficult to derive a good feature representation. Previous works focused primarily on tackling this feature sparseness problem, e.g., by augmenting queries with external knowledge such as search engine results. Second, despite colossal volumes of unlabeled queries stored in search engine logs, manually labeled queries are very limited and expensive to obtain. Several works [1, 19] introduced semi-supervised learning methods to explore the information hidden in logs. However, most of the systems take a single query as a unit of search engine interaction, without considering search contexts.

It has been argued forcefully that exploiting search contexts can improve information retrieval systems [10, 13, 26]. Intuitively, introducing search contexts, such as the neighboring queries in the same query session, can help better understand users' search intents and thus improve classification accuracy. For instance, when a user issues a query "giant", it is unclear whether he or she is interested in the San Francisco National League baseball team, the bicycle manufacturer, or something else. However, if we knew that the query "MLB" (Major League Baseball) was issued in the same query session, we could have classified the query as "Sports" rather than "Products". Conversely, if the user issued queries related to other bicycle brands before the query "giant", it would have suggested the query was related to "Products".

In this paper, we utilize search contexts embedded in query sessions, together with the large number of unlabeled queries available free on the web, to improve query classification. To achieve this goal, we need to address the following questions: 1) How to model search contexts? 2) How to incorporate the information in unlabeled queries? 3) How

Table 1: **Two user query sessions with sequences of queries, clicked url titles and user dwell time in seconds ("-" indicates that there is no url clicks associated with the query).**

SID	observations				Category
	QID	Query	Url title	Time	
1	1	tires 75067	Lewisville tires | Find tires in Lewisville, TX	18	Compare products or services
	2	Traders Village Grand prairie	Traders Village / A Texas-Size Marketplace	4	Compare products or services
	3	craiger wheels	CRAIGER WHEELS	17	Compare products or services
	4	craiger wheels 75067	-	12	Find contact information
	5	Bing	Bing^{TM} Official Site	1	Find a specific miscellaneous fact
	6	wheels 75067	Listings for Wheels near Texas 75067	14	Find contact information
	7	Colleyville tx	Colleyville tx - Google Maps	53	Plan travel
2	1	discount tire lake jackson tx	-	446	
	2	michelin	-	43	
	2	michelin tires Angleton tx	-	20	

to integrate these two components? 4) How to scale our algorithm to handle web-scale data?

First, we model search contexts using a Conditional Random Field (CRF) model. Second, we explore the information in unlabeled query sessions by combining them with a few manually labeled ones using self-training (bootstrapping). Third, to integrate these two components, we investigate: 1) different training methods for CRFs; Discriminative training is favored as it is more robust to labeling noise introduced by self-training. 2) different confidence measurements and model selection strategies for self-training to help the CRF model converge faster. We refer to the resulting framework as *Adaptive Self-training with Conditional Random Field (ASCRF)*. Forth, we adopt a softmax approximation during the discriminative training of our CRF model, resulting in a formulation which can be efficiently computed and optimized by a slight variant of existing algorithms. As such, our solution can apply to web-scale data.

The rest of this paper is organized as follows. In Section 2, we introduce notations and problem settings. In Section 3, we briefly introduce the CRF model. We compare two commonly used CRF training methods, and apply an approximation to tailor the training algorithm to deal with web-scale data. In Section 4, we detail the ASCRF framework. A series of experiments are carried out to demonstrate the effectiveness of our proposed framework in Section 5. In Section 6, we review related works. Finally, we conclude our work in Section 7.

2. NOTATIONS AND SETTINGS

Search contexts are usually embodied as interactions between queries and related user behaviors within a query session. Various works [7, 24, 17, 14] proposed different methods for identifying the boundaries of query sessions. In this work, we follow a simple yet effective session segmentation rule; that is, two user queries are separated into different sessions if they were issued longer than 30 minutes apart [11, 6].

Table 1 shows two query sessions extracted from real log, one labeled and the other one not. They both consist of a sequence of queries and related user behaviors. Due to space limitations, the urls clicked are not listed. We can make two observations: 1) search contexts can help clarify ambiguous queries; The query "michelin" in Session 2 can either refer to the tire brand, or the Michelin guide book, or something else. However, considering the search context within the session can help correctly classify the query; 2) unlabeled query sessions can help relief the demand for a large number of labeled data. Intuitively, we can infer the category label of the first query in Session 2 based on its similarity to the queries in Session 1, and obtain the labels for the other queries based on context information. By doing so, we can expand the small labeled set with unlabeled queries to improve performance.

Motivated by these observations, we propose to build a semi-supervised context-aware query classification framework that takes advantage of both search contexts and unlabeled query sessions to improve query classification.

Let $\mathbf{x} = \langle \mathrm{x}_1, \mathrm{x}_2, \cdots, \mathrm{x}_T \rangle$ denote a query session, where each observation $\mathrm{x}_t, t = 1, \cdots, T$ includes a query q_t issued by the user, and sometimes related user behaviors, such as clicked urls, url titles and user dwell time. For any query $q_t (1 \leq t \leq T)$, the observations $\mathrm{x}_1, \cdots, \mathrm{x}_{t-1}$ are referred to as the search context of q_t [6].

Let $\mathcal{D} = \{(\mathbf{x}^{(n)}, \mathbf{y}^{(n)})\}_{n=1}^{N}$ be a set of labeled query sessions, where each $\mathbf{x}^{(n)}$ is a query session as defined, and $\mathbf{y}^{(n)}$ is its corresponding labeling sequence. Let $\mathcal{U} = \{\mathbf{x}^{(m)}\}_{m=1}^{M}$ be a set of unlabeled query sessions. We have, $N \ll M$. Our goal is to learn a classifier $h(\mathbf{x}; \mathbf{w})$ based on both the labeled and unlabeled query sessions, so that given a new query q_t, it can correctly classify q_t into one of the predefined categories, taking into account the search context of q_t.

3. MODELING SEARCH CONTEXT BY CRFS

Inspired by Cao's work [6], we model search contexts embedded in each query sessions with a linear-chain CRF model.

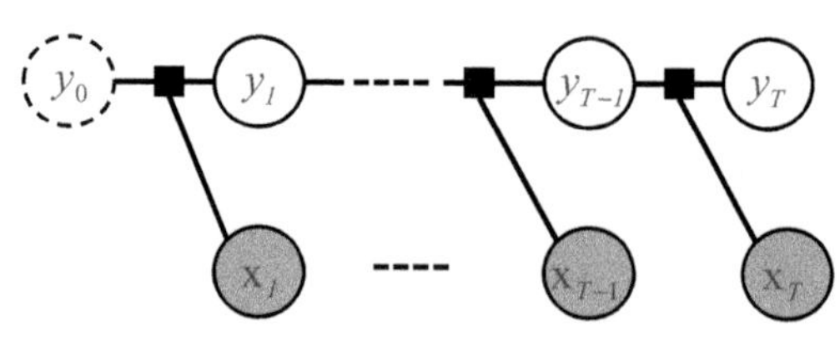

Figure 1: A linear-chain CRF modeling search context.

Let $\mathbf{x} = \langle \mathrm{x}_1, \mathrm{x}_2, \cdots, \mathrm{x}_T \rangle$ be a user query session, and $\mathbf{y} = \langle y_1, y_2, \cdots, y_T \rangle$ be its corresponding category labeling sequence. As shown in Figure 1, a CRF models the conditional distribution of the labeling sequence $\mathbf{y}$, given the observation sequence $\mathbf{x}$, as [18]

$$p(\mathbf{y}|\mathbf{x}) = \frac{1}{Z(\mathbf{x})} \exp\left(\sum_t \sum_k \omega_k f_k(y_{t-1}, y_t, \mathbf{x})\right) = \frac{e^{\mathbf{w}^\top \mathbf{f}_\mathbf{x}(\mathbf{y})}}{Z(\mathbf{x})},$$

where $\mathbf{f} = \{f_k\}$ is a set of predefined *feature* functions, and $Z(\mathbf{x}) = \sum_{\mathbf{y}'} e^{\mathbf{w}^\top \mathbf{f}_\mathbf{x}(\mathbf{y}')}$ is a normalization function.

Given a set of trained parameters $\mathbf{w}^*$, a new query session $\mathbf{x}$ is classified as

$$\hat{\mathbf{y}} = h(\mathbf{x}; \mathbf{w}^*) = \arg\max_{\mathbf{y}'} \mathbf{w}^{*\top} \mathbf{f}_\mathbf{x}(\mathbf{y}'). \tag{1}$$

3.1 Training CRFs

In this work, we investigate two commonly used training methods for CRF models, i.e., maximum likelihood training vs. margin maximization training.

3.1.1 Maximum Likelihood Training.

Given a set of i.i.d training data $\mathcal{D} = \{(\mathbf{x}^{(n)}, \mathbf{y}^{(n)})\}_{n=1}^N$, maximum likelihood training finds the parameters $\mathbf{w} = \{\omega_k\}$ such that the logarithm of the likelihood,

$$\ell(\mathcal{D}; \mathbf{w}) = \sum_{n=1}^N \log p(\mathbf{y}^{(n)}|\mathbf{x}^{(n)})$$

is maximized.

The method has been widely used for CRF training because both of its training and inference can be carried out efficiently using standard dynamic programming algorithms [25], making it scalable to large scale problems. However, as the approach explicitly considers only the probability of the exact training parses, it can easily overfit the training data without proper regularization [22, 9].

3.1.2 Margin Maximization Training.

Margin maximization training of CRF models is a popular alternative. Given a set of training data $\mathcal{D} = \{(\mathbf{x}^{(n)}, \mathbf{y}^{(n)})\}_{n=1}^N$, it finds a hyperplane that not only separates the training data, but also maximizes the score difference between the true label and the others, i.e. [27, 28],

$$\begin{aligned} \min_{\mathbf{w}} \quad & \frac{1}{2}\|\mathbf{w}\|^2 + C\sum \xi_n \\ \text{s.t.} \quad & -\mathbf{w}^\top \mathbf{f}_{\mathbf{x}^{(n)}}(\mathbf{y}^{(n)}) + \max_{\mathbf{y}} \left(\mathbf{w}^\top \mathbf{f}_{\mathbf{x}^{(n)}}(\mathbf{y}) + \Delta_{\mathbf{y}^{(n)}}(\mathbf{y})\right) \\ & \leq \xi_n, \forall n \end{aligned} \tag{2}$$

where $\Delta_{\mathbf{y}^{(n)}}(\mathbf{y}) = I(\mathbf{y}_t^{(n)} \neq \mathbf{y}_t)$ denotes the hamming distance between $\mathbf{y}^{(n)}$ and $\mathbf{y}$.

To simplify the optimization, we replace the "hard" max margin in (2) with a softmax $\log\sum\exp$ approximation as proposed in [23, 12]. Let

$$\rho_n(\mathbf{w}) = \max\left\{0, \begin{array}{l} -\mathbf{w}^\top \mathbf{f}_{\mathbf{x}^{(n)}}(\mathbf{y}^{(n)}) + \\ \log\left(\sum_{\mathbf{y}\neq\mathbf{y}^{(n)}} e^{\mathbf{w}^\top \mathbf{f}_{\mathbf{x}^{(n)}}(\mathbf{y}) + \Delta_{\mathbf{y}^{(n)}}(\mathbf{y})}\right) \end{array}\right\},$$

we can now eliminate the slack variables in (2) and rewrite our objective function as follows:

$$\textbf{SMMCRF:} \quad \min \ell(\mathcal{D}; \mathbf{w}, C) = \frac{1}{2}\|\mathbf{w}\|^2 + C\sum_n \rho_n(\mathbf{w}). \tag{3}$$

We refer to the resulting model as SoftMax Margin Conditional Random Field (SMMCRF). The objective is convex, and can be computed efficiently with a slight variation of the standard forward-backward algorithm used in maximum likelihood training [23]. We present an analysis of the generalization performance of SMMCRF as follows. The bound provides a natural way to bridge SMMCRF with semi-supervised learning to utilize unlabeled data to improve query classification.

3.1.3 Generalization Performance of SMMCRF.

Given a set of i.i.d. training data $\mathcal{D} = \{(\mathbf{x}, \mathbf{y})\}_N$, Vapnik [29] showed that with probability $1 - \eta$, the expected risk

$$R(\mathbf{w}) \leq R_{emp}(\mathbf{w}) + \Omega(N, d, \eta), \tag{4}$$

where $R_{emp}(\mathbf{w}) = \frac{1}{|\mathcal{D}|}\sum_{(\mathbf{x},\mathbf{y})\in\mathcal{D}} \Delta(\mathbf{y}, h_\mathbf{w}(\mathbf{x}))$ is the empirical risk on the training set, and the VC-confidence $\Omega(N, d, \eta)$ is a term depending on the number of training examples N and the VC-dimension d of the hypothesis class H.

PROPOSITION 1. *Let* $\mathbf{w}^*$ *be the optimal solution to (3). Then* $\frac{1}{|\mathcal{D}|}\sum_n \rho_n(\mathbf{w}^*)$ *upper bounds the empirical risk.*

The proof can be easily generalized from Tsochantaridis's proof for the generalization bound of structured SVM. We refer interested readers to [28].

It is known that the VC-dimension of margin-based classifiers grows inversely with the size of the margin [5]. In other words, the margin control factor C in (3) controls the tradeoff between the training error and the complexity of the classifiers. As $C \to \infty$, the empirical risk goes to zero, at the cost of increasing the complexity of the hypothesis class. Contrarily, as C decreases, the size of the margin increases, resulting in a hypothesis class of lower complexity. However, the empirical risk would be increased. In the next section, we will detail how we effectively control C to help avoid the error-reinforcing nature [32] of self-training.

4. INCLUDING UNLABELED QUERIES VIA ADAPTIVE SELF-TRAINING

Now we have a model that incorporates search contexts, in this section, we will be focusing on how to use semi-supervised learning to explore the information contained in unlabeled query sessions to further improve query classification.

4.1 Self-training

The general idea behind semi-supervised learning is to use a large amount of unlabeled data, together with a few labeled data, to build better classifiers. A variety of semi-supervised learning methods have been proposed [30, 4, 2, 16, 20, 15]. However, only a few of them work with graphical models, like CRFs. Self-training [30] is a very commonly used algorithm to wrap complex models for semi-supervised learning. It works as follows:

1. Train a base classifier using the small labeled set;
2. Infer the labels for the unlabeled data;
3. Add confident predictions to the training set;
4. Repeat the process.

Note that the classifier uses its own predictions to teach itself. The procedure is therefore also called self-teaching or bootstrapping.

The advantage of self-training lies in its simplicity and the ability to combine with complex models. On the other hand, the drawbacks of this approach are: 1) erroneous labels are introduced into the training set; and 2) errors are reinforced at each iteration. In other words, wrong predictions are strengthened during the self-teaching procedure, especially when combined with complex models. Nevertheless, the analysis of the generalization performance of the SMMCRF model in Section 3.1.3 provides heuristics on how to best integrate our model with self-training to avoid error-reinforcing.

4.2 Adaptive Self-training

In this section, we detail the adaptations we made to the self-training algorithm, based on the characteristics of the SMMCRF model.

4.2.1 Overall Framework

Algorithm 1 listed the details of the overall framework. We call our framework ASCRF, *Adaptive Self-training with Conditional Random Field.* We start a SMMCRF model trained on the small set of labeled data. A common practice to set the margin controlling factor C in (3) is through cross-validation. However, since manually labeled data is very limited in this case (in our experiments, only a few hundreds of the query sessions are labeled), it is not practical to do so. Structural risk minimization tells us that we get the smallest bound on the test error if we select a class of hypotheses H that minimizes the right hand side of (4). We start with a relatively large C, so that we can enforce zero empirical risk on the training set. As we gradually decrease C, the margin of our classifier is increased, so that the second term of the bound (4) is decreased. As proved in Proposition 1, $\sum \rho(\mathbf{w})$ upper bounds the empirical risk. We stop when the bound exceeds 0.

We then label query sessions in the unlabeled set $\mathcal{U}$ with the trained base classifier. That is, $\forall \mathbf{x} \in \mathcal{U}$, a prediction $\hat{\mathbf{y}} = h(\mathbf{x}, \mathbf{w})$ is assigned using the trained parameters $\mathbf{w}$. Then, num, the number of most confident predictions $(\mathbf{x}, \hat{\mathbf{y}})$ are picked out and added to the labeled set $\mathcal{D}'$. The model is then retrained with the augmented labeled data set $\mathcal{D} \cup \mathcal{D}'$. The process repeats until we can no longer find confident predictions to aid our learning. To further help our algorithm avoid stuck with wrong predictions in $\mathcal{D}'$, we remove predictions that our model deems unconfident during this process.

To complete our algorithm, we investigated 1) different confidence measurements for selecting unlabeled queries to expand the training set; 2) different model selection strategies (margin control schemes) to balance the capacity of the SMMCRF model to fit the training data, and the complexity of the models.

4.2.2 Confidence measurements

First, margin maximization training offers us a straightforward margin-based confidence measurement:

$$c_{\mathbf{w}}^{(1)}(\mathbf{x}, \hat{\mathbf{y}}) = \mathbf{w}^\top \mathbf{f}_{\mathbf{x}}(\hat{\mathbf{y}}) - \log \sum_{\mathbf{y}' \neq \hat{\mathbf{y}}} e^{\mathbf{w}^\top \mathbf{f}_{\mathbf{x}}(\mathbf{y}') + \Delta_{\hat{\mathbf{y}}}(\mathbf{y}')}.$$

It measures the gap between the prediction $\hat{\mathbf{y}}$ to any other sequence $\mathbf{y}'$ in the output space. The larger the gap, the more confident our model is about this prediction. We select the predictions with the maximum $c_{\mathbf{w}}^{(1)}$.

Second, as introduced in section 3, a CRF models the conditional distribution of a labeling sequence $\mathbf{y}$ given the observation $\mathbf{x}$. Given a trained model $\mathbf{w}$, we can also measure the confidence in a prediction by the conditional probability,

$$c_{\mathbf{w}}^{(2)}(\mathbf{x}, \hat{\mathbf{y}}) = p(\hat{\mathbf{y}}|\mathbf{x}) = \frac{e^{\mathbf{w}^\top \mathbf{f}_{\mathbf{x}}(\hat{\mathbf{y}})}}{\sum_{\mathbf{y}'} e^{\mathbf{w}^\top \mathbf{f}_{\mathbf{x}}(\mathbf{y}')}}.$$

Similarly, the larger the conditional probability, the more our model favors the prediction $\hat{\mathbf{y}}$. We select the prediction with the maximum $c_{\mathbf{w}}^{(2)}$

Third, the decision boundary of margin-based classifiers depends on the set of support vectors, i.e., the set of data points with

$$\mathbf{w}^\top \mathbf{f}_{\mathbf{x}}(\hat{\mathbf{y}}) - \log \sum_{\mathbf{y}' \neq \hat{\mathbf{y}}} e^{\mathbf{w}^\top \mathbf{f}_{\mathbf{x}}(\mathbf{y}') + \Delta_{\hat{\mathbf{y}}}(\mathbf{y}')} = 0.$$

Therefore, our third strategy is to select support vectors, i.e., the predictions that are closest to the decision boundary.

$$c_{\mathbf{w}}^{(3)}(\mathbf{x}, \hat{\mathbf{y}}) = -c_{\mathbf{w}}^{(1)}(\mathbf{x}, \hat{\mathbf{y}}) \cdot I\left(c_{\mathbf{w}}^{(1)}(\mathbf{x}, \hat{\mathbf{y}}) \geq 0\right)$$

Notice here, to avoid wrong predictions, only the predictions that are right on the margin or outside of the margin are considered. It is plausible to call $c_{\mathbf{w}}^{(3)}$ a confidence measurement since high $c_{\mathbf{w}}^{(3)}$ does not indicate that our model is confident about the correctness of the prediction. However, to be consistent with the rest of the notations, we still refer to it a confidence measurement.

By definition, the confidence measurement becomes less strict from $c^{(1)}$ to $c^{(3)}$. With a simple transformation, we can rewrite $c^{(1)}$ as

$$\exp\left(c_{\mathbf{w}}^{(1)}(\mathbf{x}, \hat{\mathbf{y}})\right) = \frac{e^{\mathbf{w}^\top \mathbf{f}_{\mathbf{x}}(\hat{\mathbf{y}})}}{\sum_{\mathbf{y}' \neq \hat{\mathbf{y}}} e^{\mathbf{w}^\top \mathbf{f}_{\mathbf{x}}(\mathbf{y}') + \Delta_{\hat{\mathbf{y}}}(\mathbf{y}')}}.$$

In other words, in order to obtain a high confidence $c^{(1)}$, a prediction $\hat{\mathbf{y}}$ has to maintain a dominant score even when the other parses $\mathbf{y}'$ is helped by $\Delta_{\hat{\mathbf{y}}}(y')$. In $c^{(2)}$, the hamming loss $\Delta_{\hat{\mathbf{y}}}(y'))$ is dropped,

$$c_{\mathbf{w}}^{(2)}(\mathbf{x}, \hat{\mathbf{y}}) = \frac{e^{\mathbf{w}^\top \mathbf{f}_{\mathbf{x}}(\hat{\mathbf{y}})}}{\sum_{\mathbf{y}'} e^{\mathbf{w}^\top \mathbf{f}_{\mathbf{x}}(\mathbf{y}')}},$$

resulting in a looser standard. $c^{(3)}$ further relax the requirement by only constraining the predictions to lie on or outside of the decision boundary. Therefore, we would expect that the predictions selected using confidence measurement $c^{(1)}$ contain the least noise, and the amount of noise increases when using $c^{(2)}$, and $c^{(3)}$ is the worst. However, in terms of the usefulness of the new predictions to the convergence of the self-training process, the order is reversed. In [31], Zhang et al. showed that knowing the label of an unlabeled data point, on which the current model has low confidence, has more potential in improving the classification. Intuitively, adding a prediction $(\mathbf{x}, \hat{\mathbf{y}})$ on which our model has already achieved a large margin over the other parses will not add any new constraints to our formulation in (2), since they are already satisfied by the current set of parameters $\mathbf{w}$. Thus, using confidence measurement $c^{(1)}$ leads to slow convergence. In contrast, the unlabeled points lying right on the decision boundary have great influence on the change of

Algorithm 1: Adaptive Self-training with Conditional Random Fields (ASCRF)

Input:

- Labeled query sessions $\mathcal{D} = \{(\mathbf{x}, \mathbf{y})\}^N$;
- Unlabeled query sessions $\mathcal{U} = \{\mathbf{x}\}^M$;
- $N \ll M$.

Parameters:

- β: constant for tuning the penalty factor C in (3);
- num: number of unlabeled query sessions to be labeled at each iteration;
- $c_{\mathbf{w}}(\mathbf{x}, \hat{\mathbf{y}})$: confidence measurement of the prediction $(\mathbf{x}, \hat{\mathbf{y}})$.

Output:

- $\mathbf{w}$ the set of optimal parameters

Initialize C to a relatively large number;
repeat
  $\mathbf{w} = \text{Train\_SMMCRF}(\mathcal{D}, C)$;
  $C \leftarrow C/\beta$;
until $\sum_n \rho_n(\mathbf{w}) > 0$;
repeat
  Label query sessions in $\mathcal{U}$ with the trained classifier: $\forall \mathbf{x} \in \mathcal{U} \longrightarrow \hat{\mathbf{y}} = h(\mathbf{x}; \mathbf{w})$;
  Extract num predictions $(\mathbf{x}, \hat{\mathbf{y}})$ of the highest confidence $c_{\mathbf{w}}(\mathbf{x}, \hat{\mathbf{y}})$ from $\mathcal{U}$ and add them to the labeled set $\mathcal{D}'$;
  Train a SoftMax Margin CRF with the data in $\mathcal{D} \cup \mathcal{D}'$: $\mathbf{w} = \text{Train\_SMMCRF}(\mathcal{D} \cup \mathcal{D}', C)$;
  Remove unconfident instances: $\forall (\mathbf{x}, \hat{\mathbf{y}}) \in \mathcal{D}'$, remove it from $\mathcal{D}'$ if $\mathbf{w}^\top \mathbf{f}_{\mathbf{x}}(\hat{\mathbf{y}}) < \max_{\mathbf{y}'} \mathbf{w}^\top \mathbf{f}_{\mathbf{x}}(\mathbf{y}') + \Delta_{\hat{\mathbf{y}}}(\mathbf{y}')$;
  Estimate the labeling noise ϵ newly introduced to $\mathcal{D}'$ by $\epsilon \approx \sum_{num}(1 - p(\hat{\mathbf{y}}|\mathbf{x}))/num$;
  Increase the margin of the classifier to take into consideration the noise by decreasing C: $C \leftarrow C/(1+\epsilon)$;
until *no more confident predictions can be found*;

$\mathbf{w}$. During our empirical study, we found that, as a tradeoff between $c^{(1)}$ and $c^{(3)}$, the confidence measurement $c^{(2)}$ performs the best. It introduces less noise than $c^{(3)}$, and it helps the classifier achieve faster convergence than $c^{(1)}$.

4.2.3 Model selection

At each iteration of the self-training procedure, we have to retrain our model based on the set of augmented training data $\mathcal{D} \cup \mathcal{D}'$. As self-training goes on, labeling noise would be introduced to the training set. In this case, instead of forcing the classifier to come up with a set of parameters $\mathbf{w}$ that perfectly classify the training data, we should increase the margin so that the mistakenly labeled training data can be ignored. As the margin increases, the second term of the generalization bound (4) can be reduced to ensure generalization performance. However, blindly enlarging the margin will result in a model with very high bias, increasing both the empirical and expected risk. The tradeoff here is balanced through the margin control factor C. Often the case, cross-validation is used to tune hyperparameters. However, it is prohibitive to do in this setting, due to the sparseness of training data, as well as the relatively long running time of the entire self-training process.

Instead, we came up with an updating rule for the penalty factor C that depends on an estimated error rate of the training data. With a set of trained parameter $\mathbf{w}$, we can estimate the error rate of the newly selected predictions by

$$\epsilon \approx \frac{\sum_{num}(1 - p_{\mathbf{w}}(\hat{\mathbf{y}}|\mathbf{x}))}{num};$$

where $p_{\mathbf{w}}(\hat{\mathbf{y}}|\mathbf{x})$ computes the conditional probability of the true parse being $\hat{\mathbf{y}}$ given the observation $\mathbf{x}$ under current model.

At each iteration, C is decreased by a factor proportional to the estimated error rate, that is,

$$C \leftarrow C/(1+\epsilon).$$

To further avoid error-reinforcement, we also drop the instances that were added into $\mathcal{D}'$ during the early stage of the self-training process, but later were found out to be unconfident ones. That is, a prediction $(\mathbf{x}, \hat{\mathbf{y}})$ is removed from the training set if

$$\tau_{\mathbf{w}}(\mathbf{x}, \hat{\mathbf{y}}) = \mathbf{w}^\top \mathbf{f}_{\mathbf{x}}(\hat{\mathbf{y}}) - \max_{\mathbf{y}'} \left(\mathbf{w}^\top \mathbf{f}_{\mathbf{x}}(\mathbf{y}') + \Delta_{\hat{\mathbf{y}}}(\mathbf{y}')\right) < 0.$$

This term can be efficiently computed with a slight variant of the standard Viterbi algorithm [21]. Note that our first confidence measurement $c^{(1)}$ upper bounds this term, that is, $\forall \mathbf{w}, (\mathbf{x}, \hat{\mathbf{y}}), c^{(1)}_{\mathbf{w}}(\mathbf{x}, \hat{\mathbf{y}}) > \tau_{\mathbf{w}}(\mathbf{x}, \hat{\mathbf{y}})$. The reason we did not use $c^{(1)}$ directly is that when it becomes less than zero, the prediction $(\mathbf{x}, \hat{\mathbf{y}})$ is not necessarily within the margin, which might cause correct predictions being removed.

5. EXPERIMENTAL RESULTS

In this section, we validate our proposed methods through systematic empirical comparisons with previous work on two real datasets.

5.1 Datasets

Both datasets were extracted from real search logs. Queries were segmented into different sessions according to the rule described in section 2.

5.1.1 *Dataset 1*

The first dataset is from previous work [6]. It contains 3,500 query sessions (8,988 queries) extracted from one day's search log of a commercial search engine. Three labelers were invited to label the queries of each session using the target taxonomy of ACM KDD Cup'05, which is a two-level taxonomy with seven level-1 categories and 67 level-2 categories.

5.1.2 *Dataset 2*

To make our story complete, we also apply our algorithm to a relatively larger second dataset. The set was extracted and labeled by a product team in 2010. It contains 1,727 query sessions (39,565 queries) in total. Instead of the ACM KDD Cup'05 taxonomy, the queries were labeled using a set of categories more closely related to users' search intents, such as, "Compare products, services, or activities for use", "Learn how to perform a task", and "Plan travel". There are 65 categories in total.

5.2 Evaluation Metric

In our experiments, we used only previous queries in the same session as the search contexts since related user behavior information was missing in Dataset 1. Different from classic sequential learning tasks in which the testing sequences come in batch, queries come in streaming. Hence, the testing phase for query classification was done differently. Given a sequence of queries $q_1, q_2, \ldots, q_t$, we take the query q_t as the test query, and the queries $q_1, q_2, \ldots, q_{t-1}$ as the context of q_t, and find the prediction of the session as in (1). Then the label of query q_t is set to $\hat{y}_t = \hat{\mathbf{y}}_t$. We do this for each time stamp t.

Given a set of queries q_t with true label y_t, and prediction $\hat{y}_t$, we report the accuracy of our trained classifier as

$$Acc = \frac{1}{|T|}\sum_t I(y_t = \hat{y}_t),$$

where $|T|$ is the total number of queries in the testing set.

5.3 Preliminary Experiments

We used the smaller set, Dataset 1, for preliminary study. We first compared different training methods for our CRF model. We then investigate different confidence measurements and model selection strategies for our adaptive self-training framework. Finally we validate our framework on Dataset 2.

5.3.1 *Robustness of SMMCRF*

In the first experiment, we compare the performance of softmax margin maximization training (denoted as SMMCRF) with maximum likelihood training (denoted as CRF), and maximum likelihood training with regularization $\|\mathbf{w}\|/2\sigma^2$ [22] (denoted as CRF-R) on Dataset 1.

Experiment Setup. We did 5-fold cross-validation. That is, the entire dataset was randomly split into five folds. Each time four of them were used as training, and the remaining one as testing. The average testing accuracy is reported. In this experiment, all of the training data are labeled, as opposed to the following experiments, in which only fraction of the training data are labeled. For this experiment, the margin control factor C in our loss function (3) and the Gaussian prior σ^2 of the regularized CRF [22] were both tuned on a validation set.

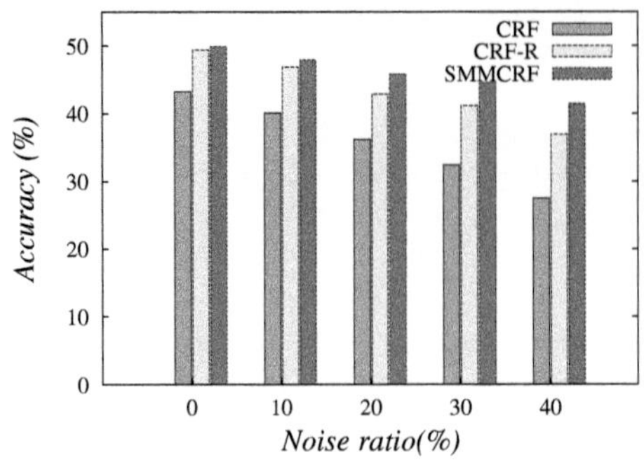

Figure 2: Comparison of softmax margin maximization and maximum likelihood training on dataset 1

In order to test the robustness of the trained models to noise, we added random labeling noise to our training data. The labeling noise goes from 10% to 40% of the data. To deal with the increasing noise, the margin control factor C of SMMCRF is decreased by a constant factor each time, same for the Gaussian prior σ^2 of CRF-R.

Discussion. As shown in Figure 2, the model obtained with maximum likelihood training without regularization is seriously overfitting the training data. At point 0, that is, when the data contains no noise, SMMCRF achieved over 20% improvement over CRF in term of generalization performance. CRF-R did relieve the overfitting problem. However, as more and more labeling noise is added into the dataset, we can clearly see the advantage of margin maximization training. While the performance of CRF and CRF-R deteriorates very quickly as more noise is added, SMMCRF turns out to be much more robust. We can see the performance gap between MMCRF and CRF-R/CRF becomes larger and larger as more noise is added to the training data from Figure 2.

5.3.2 *Adaptive Self-training with SMMCRF*

Now that we have a model shown to be robust to labeling noise both theoretically and empirically, in this part, we study the effects of different choices of confidence measurements and model selection strategies on the performance of our framework on Dataset 1.

Experiment Setup. As classical semi-supervised learning setting, we used 80% of the data as training, and the remaining 20% as testing. 10% of the training data are randomly selected to be labeled, and the others are used as unlabeled data. We did 10 runs of these experiments, each time with a different labeled set. Since the size of the training set is small, we used the level-1 categories of the ACM KDD Cup'05 taxonomy, which contains seven categories in total, as the output.

Confidence measurements. In this experiment, we study the effects of various confidence measurements on the performance of our framework. Figure 3(a) shows the progress of ASCRF framework with the three confidence measurements we introduced in Section 4.2.2. Figure 3(b) shows the percentage of noise introduced into our training set when unlabeled query sessions are extracted and added to the set $\mathcal{D}'$ using different confidence measurements.

The results are consistent with our discusion in Section 4.2.2. 1) In terms of noise rate (Figure 3(b)), $c_{\mathbf{w}}^{(1)}$ includes the least amount of noise into the training set, $c_w^{(2)}$ the second, and $c_w^{(3)}$ is the worst. Especially at the very beginning of the process, since our model is trained with a very small labeled set, it is seriously overfitting the training data, and does not generalize well to unseen data at that point. Therefore, the predictions close to the decision boundary under the current model are very likely to be wrong. 2) In terms of model convergence (Figure 3(a)), the few correct predictions selected by $c_w^{(3)}$ significantly drive up the performance, since they are the data points the original model not sure of. Knowing the labels for these query sessions have great potential in improving the performance. On the other hand, although the predictions selected by $c_w^{(1)}$ are of high accuracy, since they are the data points the current model is very confident about, adding these data points do not help much. 3) In the long run, as the self-training procedure goes on, the wrong predictions selected by $c_w^{(3)}$ start to hurt the learning process; while on the other hand, as the size of the margin increases, the highly accurate predictions selected by $c_w^{(1)}$ start to help the learning process. $c_w^{(2)}$, as a tradeoff between these two, leads our model to the best generalization performance. In the following experiments, we used $c_w^{(2)}$ as our confidence measurement.

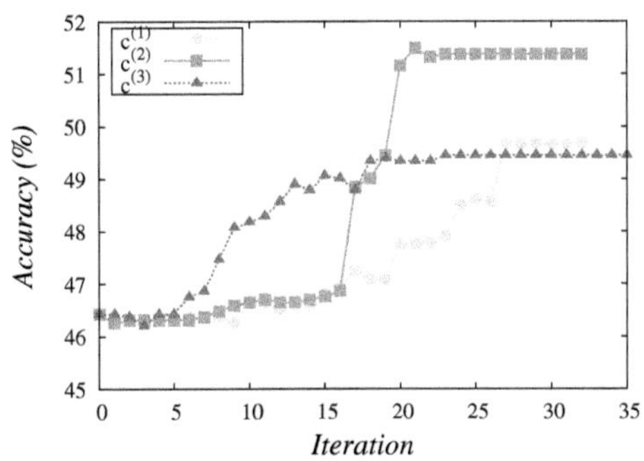

(a) Accuracy

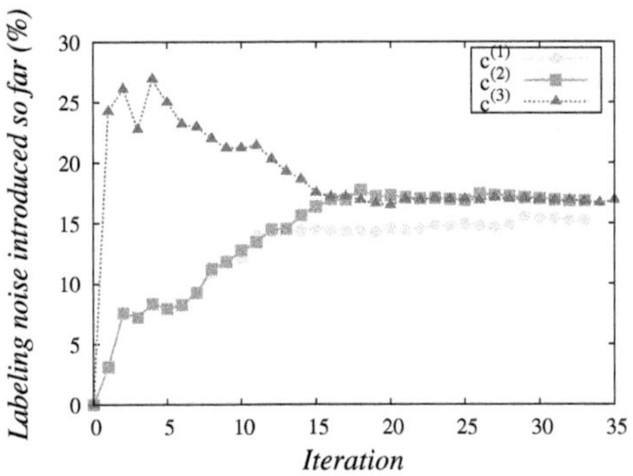

(b) Noise

Figure 3: Comparison of different confidence measurements: (a) Accuracy of Adaptive Self-training with different confidence measurements (b) Noise rate in $\mathcal{D}'$ with different confidence measurements.

Model selection. In this experiment, we test different model selection strategies introduced in Section 4.2.3. We proposed to update the margin control factor C in (3) with an estimate of the noise rate in set $\mathcal{D}'$. We compare this strategy with 1) a constant factor C; 2) a constant update,

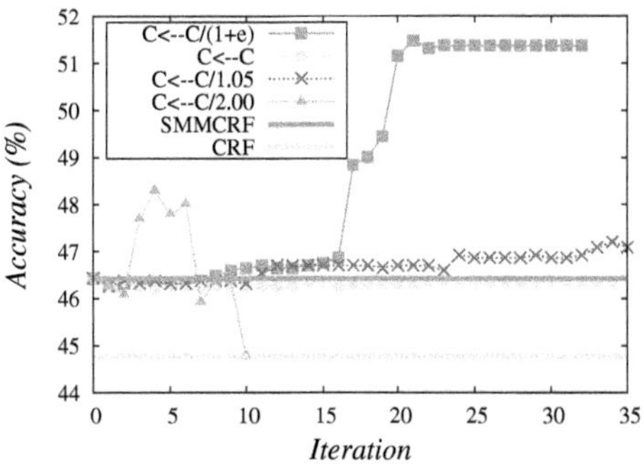

Figure 4: Comparison of different model selection strategies.

that is, $C \leftarrow C/\beta$ at each iteration of self-training. All experiments were carried out in the same setting, except with different updating rules for C. The confidence measurement $c_w^{(2)}$ is used.

For constant update, we tried $\beta = 1.05$ and $\beta = 2$. As shown in Figure 4, self-training with constant C is overwhelmed by the noise introduced, thus shows no progress. For constant update, a small β leads to slow convergence, while a large β results in a model of high bias. As shown in the magenta curve, when $\beta = 2$, the model can not find confident predictions within several iterations, and terminates very quickly. On the other hand, with the proposed updating rule, we achieved over 10% improvement compared to a SMMCRF model trained with only the labeled instances shown as red solid line, and around 20% improvement over a CRF model trained with maximum likelihood training, shown as green dotted line in Figure 4. To make comparison, we also trained a SMMCRF with all the training data labeled, it achieved 58.85% test accuracy (Notice here the number is higher than the one shown in Figure 2 because in this experiment we used only 7 level-1 categories as opposed to 67 level-2 categories in previous one), while our framework achieved 51.38% precesion with only 10% of the training data labeled.

5.4 Overall performance

In this experiment, we test our overall framework on Dataset 2. The experiment setting is same as previous, 80% of the data are used as training set, and the remaining 20% as testing. We only used 5% of the training data as labeled ones, and the remaining 95% are unlabeled. Same here, we did 10 runs of this experiments.

Figure 5 shows the progress of our framework on Dataset 2, with proposed model selection strategy and confidence measurement $c_w^{(2)}$. We compare our ASCRF framework to a baseline, which trains a SMMCRF with the labeled query sessions. As shown in the figure, in Run 1, we improved over the baseline for around 20% in accuracy; and in Run 2, we nearly doubled the performance.

Table 2 reports the overall experimental results. The results are consistent across the two datasets. We have averaged around 10% improvement on Dataset 1, and over 20% on Dataset 2. Our algorithm achieved more significant improvement and smaller deviation on Dataset 2. We believe this is due to the size of the unlabeled set is larger in Dataset 2 than Dataset 1.

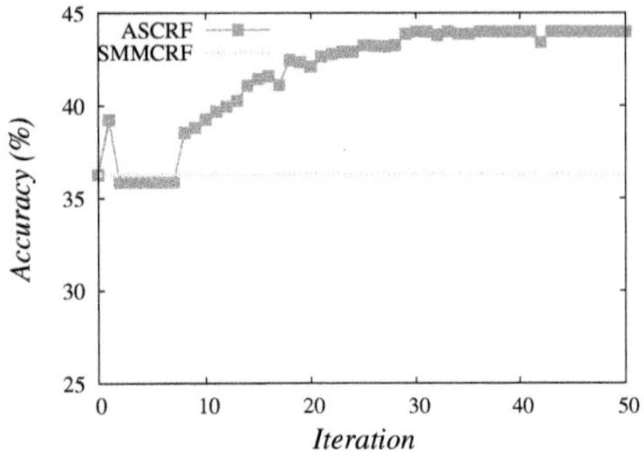

(a) Run 1

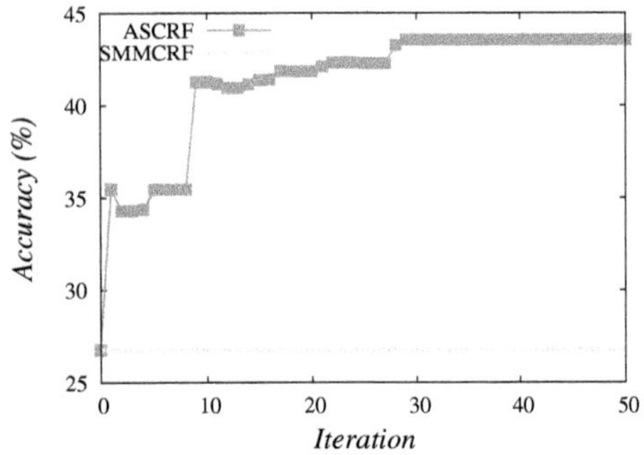

(b) Run 2

Figure 5: Two runs of ASCRF on Dataset 2: 5(a) Run 1; 5(b) Run 2.

Table 2: Overall performance comparison (Accuracy and Standard Deviation) of ASCRF vs. baseline on Dataset 1 and Dataset 2, with 10 runs each.

Accuracy(Std)	Baseline	ASCRF
Dataset 1	44.67%(1.48×10^{0})	49.94%(8.07×10^{-1})
Dataset 2	35.25%(4.95×10^{-2})	43.53%(4.44×10^{-3})

5.5 Efficiency

The main computational time of our algorithm comes from the training of SMMCRF. As stated in Section 3.1.2, using the softmax approximation, we can compute the objective and gradient for our formulation efficiently with a slight variant of the forward-backward algorithm used in the standard maximum likelihood training. Hence, the computational time is linear on the sequence length, and quadratic on the number of categories. Our algorithm was implemented on top of the Limited Memory Variable Metric (LMVM) solver in the Toolkit for Advanced Optimization (TAO) [3]. The experiments were run on a machine with Intel(R) Xeon(R) CPU 2.67GHz, and 4G memory. It takes us around 2 minutes to finish the entire adaptive self-training process for Dataset 1, with 7 level-1 categories, and 8,988 queries; and around 4 hours on Dataset 2, with 65 categories, and 39,565 queries. The time cost is acceptable for offline training. Also, the algorithm can run parallel to improve efficiency.

Web users often have very strict requirement on the response time of online applications. Fortunately, the testing phase of our algorithm can be done very efficiently using the standard Viterbi algorithm. During our experiment, it takes less than 1 second to finish the testing phase for Dataset 2, which contains around 7,000 test queries in total.

6. RELATED WORK

Cao et al.'s work [6] adopted CRF models to include context information in query classification. There are two major differences between our work and theirs: 1) The previous work was carried out under a supervised learning setting. In order to achieve satisfactory performance, a great number of labeling queries are required. In contrast, we propose to combine a small set of labeled instances with the abundant unlabeled queries free on the web to build a good query classifier, reducing human effort in labeling query sessions. 2) The previous work used the traditional maximum likelihood training for CRF models. However, during our study, we found that discriminative training of CRF models is much more robust to labeling noise. Empirical study also supports our claim, SMMCRFs consistently outperform CRFs trained with maximum likelihood training. It provides us not only with guaranteed generalization performance, but also a straightforward mechanism to adapt the popular semi-supervised learning method, self-training, to explore the information contained in unlabeled queries.

The second class of related work is semi-supervised learning [32, 8], which aims at utilizing the information in unlabeled data to improve supervised learning. This can be achieved in various ways [30, 4, 2, 16, 20, 15]. In 2005, Beitzel et al. [1] proposed a semi-supervised learning framework tailored specially for query classification. It uses labeled data to learn logical relationships between query terms and query categories, and unlabeled data to fully exploit the "syntactic" dependencies between query terms, so that more queries can be classified. Li et al. [19] used click graphs to increase the amount of training data. Specifically, class memberships of unlabeled queries are inferred from those of labeled ones according to their proximities in a click graph. However, both works ignored the context information contained in query sessions.

7. CONCLUSION AND FUTURE WORK

Accurate topical classification of user queries can benefit a variety of web applications. A great amount of works have been proposed to study the problem. However, the issue of lacking training data to obtain a high quality classifier has not been well addressed. Inspired by a previous work on context-aware query classification, we built a general framework that exploits the large number of unlabeled queries available free on the web, as well as search contexts embedded in query sessions to improve query classification. Extensive experiments on two datasets extracted from real search log demonstrated the efficacy of our framework.

In our experiments, we used only previous queries in the same session as search contexts. In future work, we plan to include related user behaviors, such as clicked urls, user dwell time, to enrich our feature set and investigate the impact of them. Li et al. [19] found that with a large amount of training data, classifiers using only query words/phrases as features can work remarkably well. It would be interesting to see if the statement still holds in our case.

8. REFERENCES

[1] S. Beitzel, E. Jensen, O. Frieder, D. Lewis, A. Chowdhury, and A. Kołcz. Improving automatic query classification via semi-supervised learning. In *Proc. ICDM*, pages 42–49, 2005.

[2] M. Belkin, I. Matveeva, and P. Niyogi. Regularization and semi-supervised learning on large graphs. *Learning theory*, pages 624–638, 2004.

[3] S. Benson, L. McInnes, J. Moré, and J. Sarich. TAO user manual (revision 1.9). *Mathematics and Computer Science Division, Argonne National Laboratory, Tech. Rep. ANL/MCS-TM-242*, 2005.

[4] A. Blum and T. Mitchell. Combining labeled and unlabeled data with co-training. In *Proc. COLT*, pages 92–100, 1998.

[5] C. Burges. A tutorial on support vector machines for pattern recognition. *Data mining and knowledge discovery*, 2(2):121–167, 1998.

[6] H. Cao, D. Hu, D. Shen, D. Jiang, J. Sun, E. Chen, and Q. Yang. Context-aware query classification. In *Proc. SIGIR*, pages 3–10, 2009.

[7] L. Catledge and J. Pitkow. Characterizing browsing strategies in the World-Wide Web. *Computer Networks and ISDN systems*, 27(6):1065–1073, 1995.

[8] O. Chapelle, B. Schölkopf, A. Zien, et al. *Semi-supervised learning.* MIT press Cambridge, MA, 2006.

[9] M. Chen, C. Y., M. Brent, and A. Tenney. Gradient-Based Feature Selection for Conditional Random Fields and Its Applications in Computational Genetics. In *Proc. ICTAI*, pages 750–757, 2009.

[10] B. Croft et al. The role of context and adaptation in user interfaces. *Journal of Man-Machine Studies*, 21(4):283–292, 1984.

[11] H. Cui, J. Wen, J. Nie, and W. Ma. Probabilistic query expansion using query logs. In *Proc. WWW*, pages 325–332, 2002.

[12] K. Gimpel and N. Smith. Softmax-margin crfs: Training log-linear models with cost functions. In *Proc. ACL*, pages 733–736, 2010.

[13] A. Goker. Context learning in Okapi. *Journal of Documentation*, 53(1):80–83, 1997.

[14] B. Jansen, A. Spink, C. Blakely, and S. Koshman. Defining a session on web search engines. *Journal of the American Society for Information Science and Technology*, 58(6):862–871, 2007.

[15] F. Jiao, S. Wang, C. Lee, R. Greiner, and D. Schuurmans. Semi-supervised conditional random fields for improved sequence segmentation and labeling. In *Proc. ACL*, pages 209–216, 2006.

[16] T. Joachims. Learning to classify text using support vector machines: Methods, theory, and algorithms. *Computational Linguistics*, 29(4):656–664, 2002.

[17] R. Jones and K. Klinkner. Beyond the session timeout: automatic hierarchical segmentation of search topics in query logs. In *Proc. CIKM*, pages 699–708, 2008.

[18] J. Lafferty, A. McCallum, and F. Pereira. Conditional random fields: Probabilistic models for segmenting and labeling sequence data. In *Proc. ICML*, pages 282–289, 2001.

[19] X. Li, Y. Wang, and A. Acero. Learning query intent from regularized click graphs. In *Proc. SIGIR*, pages 339–346, 2008.

[20] G. Mann and A. McCallum. Simple, robust, scalable semi-supervised learning via expectation regularization. In *Proc. ICML*, pages 593–600. ACM, 2007.

[21] N. Seshadri and C. Sundberg. List Viterbi decoding algorithms with applications. *Communications, IEEE Transactions on*, 42(234):313–323, 2002.

[22] F. Sha and F. Pereira. Shallow parsing with conditional random fields. In *Proc. Human Language Technology - NAACL*, pages 134–141, 2003.

[23] F. Sha and L. Saul. Large margin hidden Markov models for automatic speech recognition. In *Proc. NIPS*, pages 1249–1256, 2007.

[24] C. Silverstein, H. Marais, M. Henzinger, and M. Moricz. Analysis of a very large web search engine query log. In *ACM SIGIR Forum*, volume 33, pages 6–12, 1999.

[25] C. Sutton and A. McCallum. An Introduction to Conditional Random Fields for Relational Learning. *Introduction to statistical relational learning*, page 93, 2007.

[26] S. Talja, H. Keso, and T. Pietiläinen. The production of 'context' in information seeking research: a metatheoretical view. *Information Processing and Management*, 35(6):751–763, 1999.

[27] B. Taskar, C. Guestrin, and D. Koller. Max-margin Markov networks. In *Proc. NIPS*, 2003.

[28] I. Tsochantaridis, T. Hofmann, T. Joachims, and Y. Altun. Support vector machine learning for interdependent and structured output spaces. In *Proc. ICML*, page 104, 2004.

[29] V. Vapnik and V. Vapnik. *Statistical learning theory.* Wiley New York, 1998.

[30] D. Yarowsky. Unsupervised word sense disambiguation rivaling supervised methods. In *Proc. ACL*, pages 189–196, 1995.

[31] T. Zhang and F. Oles. A probability analysis on the value of unlabeled data for classification problems. In *Proc. ICML*, pages 1191–1198, 2000.

[32] X. Zhu. Semi-supervised learning literature survey. *Computer Science, University of Wisconsin-Madison*, 2006.

A Task Level Metric for Measuring Web Search Satisfaction and its Application on Improving Relevance Estimation

Ahmed Hassan
Microsoft Research
Redmond, WA
hassanam@microsoft.com

Yang Song
Microsoft Research
Redmond, WA
yangsong@microsoft.com

Li-wei He
Microsoft
Redmond, WA
lhe@microsoft.com

ABSTRACT

Understanding the behavior of satisfied and unsatisfied Web search users is very important for improving users search experience. Collecting labeled data that characterizes search behavior is a very challenging problem. Most of the previous work used a limited amount of data collected in lab studies or annotated by judges lacking information about the actual intent. In this work, we performed a large scale user study where we collected explicit judgments of user satisfaction with the entire search task. Results were analyzed using sequence models that incorporate user behavior to predict whether the user ended up being satisfied with a search or not. We test our metric on millions of queries collected from real Web search traffic and show empirically that user behavior models trained using explicit judgments of user satisfaction outperform several other search quality metrics. The proposed model can also be used to optimize different search engine components. We propose a method that uses task level success prediction to provide a better interpretation of clickthrough data. Clickthough data has been widely used to improve relevance estimation. We use our user satisfaction model to distinguish between clicks that lead to satisfaction and clicks that do not. We show that adding new features derived from this metric allowed us to improve the estimation of document relevance.

Categories and Subject Descriptors

H.3.3 [**Information Search and Retrieval**]: search process

General Terms

Algorithms, Experimentation, Measurement

Keywords

search engine evaluation, user behavior models, web search success, clickthrough data

CIKM'11, October 24–28, 2011, Glasgow, Scotland, UK.

1. INTRODUCTION

Web search systems are traditionally evaluated using classical methodologies that use query sets and relevance judgments. Search quality is then measured for individual queries using measures like mean average precision (MAP), and normalized discounted cumulative gain (NDCG). A single score for an information retrieval system is then computed by averaging across many queries. However, user information needs are usually complex and the search process may involve query reformulations. Hence, individual queries may only represent a part of the underlying information need. This gave rise to research efforts that try to evaluate the entire search task rather than individual queries.

To better understand this problem, we developed a Web browser add-in to monitor user search activity across search engines and collect explicit judgments of user satisfaction with the entire search goal. In addition to explicit satisfaction ratings, the add-in also collected several pieces of information describing user behavior throughout the search process. This resulted in a dataset of search goals and the corresponding satisfaction labels. The labels are very reliable because they were directly collected from users performing the search rather than guessed by judges. Results were analyzed using sequence models that incorporate user behavior to predict whether the user ended up being satisfied with her search or not. The trained model can be used as a search quality metric to compare search engines, compare different versions of the same engine, or optimize document relevance estimation.

Web search engines logs have been widely used for optimizing search engine performance. Clickthrough data can be perceived as a strong signal from users telling us which documents they find relevant. However, interpreting clickthrough data for use in optimizing search engines faces several challenges. For example, several methods that exploit clcikthrough data assume that the user examined all the documents in the ranked list and clicked on the relevant ones [14, 20]. Others assume that perceived relevance (i.e. attractiveness) is the same as actual relevance [6, 9], or assume that all clicks result in some information gain for the user [5].

In this work, we propose a new model for estimating document relevance using the search logs of a web search engine. Current relevance models, that use clickthrough data, make the simplistic assumption that the mere fact that a URL has been clicked is a strong indicator of its relevance to the query. Even though, clickthrough data is correlated with relevance, not all clicks result in an information gain for the user. Given a model to predict user satisfaction with search results, we can provide a more accurate interpretation of clicks and hence better estimation of document relevance. We show empirically that user behavior models trained using explicit judgments of user satisfaction outperform several other search quality metrics. We also show that the resulting metric can be used to compute features that better interpret clickthrough data. These features are used to improve a machine learning algorithm that learns to rank documents. Comparing the ranking function with and without the new features, we observe improvement in the ranking quality.

The reminder of this paper is organized as follows. In Section 2, we discuss related work in the areas of measuring search quality and improving query-URL relevance estimation using search log data. A summary of our contributions is presented in Section 3. We then describe a user study where we collected explicit satisfaction ratings from users in Section 4. Our user satisfaction model is described in Section 5, followed by a description of the model that we use to improve relevance estimation in Section 6. Finally we present experiments in Section 7, and conclude in Section 8.

2. RELATED WORK

In this section, we describe previous work on evaluating the quality of search results. We review methods that try to measure search quality on both query level and goal level basis. We also describe work on improving query URL relevance estimation using search logs.

2.1 Evaluating Search Results Quality

Ad hoc information retrieval evaluation had focused on mean average precision (MAP). MAP is optimized to cover both recall and precision aspects. It also takes the entire search result ranking into consideration. Studies of Web search results evaluation have shown that users are only interested in the first few results and hence high early precision is desirable [11]. State of the art measurements of query result relevance use discounted cumulative gain (DCG) [13]. DCG metrics lend themselves to a user model of scanning a ranked list of results to some depth. DCG can be calculated using manual query URL relevance judgments, or estimated query URL relevance [2, 17]. The problem with this approach is that it misses the complete picture by looking only at individual queries. User information needs may result in more than one query, and same queries may have different underlying information needs. Hence, individual query URL relevance may not always mean user satisfaction.

Fox et al. [7] found that a strong correlation between search log features and user satisfaction. They used Bayesian modeling and decision trees to model explicit satisfaction ratings using several kinds of features. They used clickthrough rate features, as well dwell time features, and features describing how users end their search sessions.

Huffman and Hochster [12] study the correlation between user satisfaction and simple relevance metrics. They report a relatively strong correlation between user satisfaction and linear models encompassing the query URL relevance of the first three results for the first query in the search task. Hassan et al. [10] showed that modeling action sequences representing user behavior is better than models based on the query URL relevance of the first three results for the first query. The main reasons are that different information needs sometimes underlie the same query, and that the first query does not tell the complete picture in terms of the entire search task.

Radlinski et al. [22] show that interleaving the results of two ranking functions and presenting the interleaved results to users is a good way for predicting relative search engine performance. They also look at using metrics including abandonment rate, reformulation rate, and time to first click to predict relative performance. They found out that those metrics do not perform as well as interleaving results. Using aggregated features extracted from user behavior is certainly correlated with satisfaction. However, it has been shown that modeling the transitions between actions performed by users during search is a stronger predictor of satisfaction [10].

The most relevant work to this study is that of Hassan et al. [10]. They use two Markov models characterizing the behavior of users in both successful and unsuccessful searches. Our study improves upon this model in several ways. We will describe this model in detail, and discuss how it relates to this study in Section 3.

2.2 Improving Relevance Estimation

One of the earliest studies that use search logs to improve search results ranking was presented in [14]. In this work, clickthrough data based features were used to train a support vector machine (SVM) ranking function.

Radlinski and Joachims [20] extended this work to account for the concept of query chains. They observed that users searching the web often perform a sequence, or a chain, of queries with similar information needs. They extract those chains and generate preference judgments from search logs taking the chains into consideration.

In [21], the authors approach the problem of learning ranking functions from clickthrough data in an active exploration setting. They develop a Bayesian approach for selecting rankings to present to users such that their interactions result in more informative training data. They test their hypothesis on the TREC Web corpus, and on synthetic data. Their experiments demonstrate that their strategy leads to improving the learned ranking function.

Unlike previous work that has focused mainly on clickthough data, Agichtein et al. [2] incorporated user behavior information to improve ranking. They used implicit features aggregated over a large number of users. They included traditional implicit feedback features such as clickthrough rate, and aggregate features such as deviation of the observed clickthrough number for a given query-URL pair from the expected number of clicks. They show that incorporating implicit feedback improves the performance of the ranking algorithm. A similar study that aims at predicting user preferences has been presented in [1].

All the methods we discussed so far assume that the user examined all the documents in the ranking list and clicked on the relevant ones. Hence, the relevance of any document may be estimated simply by counting the number of times it was clicked. However, users do not browse the whole list [6]. For example, documents that appear highly in the ranking have higher probability of being clicked regardless of their relevance [8]. This suggests that taking the probability of examining a result into consideration would improve the ranking. Dupret and Piwowarski [6] addressed this problem by estimating the probability of examination of a document given the rank of the document and the last clicked document. The model assumes that the user goes through the list of results sequentially in the order in which they are presented. The user clicks on a URL only if it is both *examined* and found *attractive*. The probability that a document is examined depends on its rank and the rank of the last examined document. The probability that a document is attractive depends on the title, snippet, etc. A similar model is described in [9], where the authors present two different models to interpret multiple clicks: the independent click model, and the dependent click model which takes into consideration dependencies between multiple clicks.

The work we just described tries to model the relation between multiple clicks and study how this affects relevance estimation. However, it assumes that the attractiveness of a particular URL equals its relevance. Obviously, this may not always be the case. This problem has been addressed in [5]. In this work, the authors present a model for estimating intrinsic relevance as opposed to perceived relevance. They estimate intrinsic relevance by examining the documents that have been clicked after the current document. They assume that if a user clicks on document B after clicking on document A, then the amount of utility the user gained from A was not enough to satisfy her information need. They proposed a model to predict whether, given a certain amount of utility, the user will stop or continue her search and use that to generate a utility feature that is later used to improve ranking. This model has several advantages over previous models that try to interpret clickthrough data and was shown to be useful. However, it makes the simplistic assumption that all goals with clicks are successful. Obviously this assumption is not verified in reality as we will show later. Our model goes one step beyond this model by differentiating between successful and unsuccessful search tasks. We introduce the notion of a user failing to fulfill her information need and abandoning the search out of despair. Given a user satisfaction model, we can assign *utility* values to clicks in satisfied search goals, and *despair* values to clicks in unsatisfied search goals, hence providing a better interpretation of clicks with respect to the entire search task.

3. CONTRIBUTIONS

Our contributions include (1) we perform a large scale user study where thousands of explicit satisfaction ratings were collected from users, (2) we use and improve the user satisfaction model based on user behavior that was presented in [10], (3) we perform a large scale evaluation of the model using real search traffic, and (4) we present an application of the user satisfaction model on Improving relevance estimation.

Our user study allowed us to collect reliable satisfaction ratings from users regarding their search experience. The collected data encompasses several search engines, and several search verticals. The data was manually checked to verify the integrity of all labels.

Our user satisfaction model is based on modeling user behavior [10]. Our model has several advantages compared to previous related work. The quality of the search metrics depends on both the method and the training data. In this work, we train the model using a more reliable training data collected directly from users right after performing search. This is clearly better than asking judges to predict whether a user has been satisfied with her search or not, because judges, at best, are only guessing on the user's information intent; especially because several queries may have different underlying information need. Unlike query based metrics, we predict search goal success by analyzing user behavior. This allows us to capture the whole picture and predict satisfaction with respect to the entire information need rather than individual queries. Hassan et al. [10] used server side logging to collect behavioral signals. We used, and compared, both client side logging and server side logging for modeling user behavior. Client side logging gives us access to more information and hence a better characterization of user behavior during search. Our dataset contained data from several search engines and several verticals. This ensures that our metric generalizes well for all search engines and hence can be used to compare their performance. Finally, we performed a large scale evaluation using millions of search goals from actual user traffic to a major commercial search engine to evaluate how powerful the proposed metric is.

The model we propose for improving relevance estimation is different from all previous work on using clickthough data for optimizing ranking algorithms. Most of previous work makes the simplistic assumption that a click on a URL is always associated with information gain for the user. We show that this is not always the case and introduce the notions of *utility*, which users gain when their information need is satisfied, and *despair*, which users develop when their information need is not met. The closest work to our model is that presented in [5]. However, it does not distinguish between satisfied and unsatisfied search goals.

4. DATA

Collecting the data required for this research was particularly challenging. Asking human judges to predict whether a user ended up being satisfied with her search or not is very tricky. No matter how hard judges try to re-enact the user's experience, they end up to be only guessing on the actual user intent. As a result, we decided to directly collect explicit ratings of user satisfaction from the actual users performing search. For that, we developed an add-in for a widely distributed browser within a client server architecture. The add-in consists of a browser helper object that monitors the user's search experience, and a toolbar that interacts with the user. The browser helper object detects when a user submits a query to any of the three major search engines (Google, Bing, and Yahoo). Users are instructed to submit an explicit satisfaction rating at the end of their search goal, where a search goal is defined as follows:

Definition A search goal is a single information need that may result in one or more queries.

In the rest of this paper, we will use the terms "goal" and "task" interchangeably to refer to an atomic information need that may result in any number of queries.

4.1 User Study

The objective of this user study is to collect explicit satisfaction ratings from users with respect to their search experience. Participants were instructed to vote only after their information need is met. We are collecting goal-level labels rather than query-level labels. A search goal is different from a physical session. The later usually uses the idea of a "timeout" cutoff between queries. A timeout is the time between two successive activities, and it is used as a session boundary when it exceeds a certain threshold. The later definition of a physical session means that it may include several information needs.

A typical search goal would begin with a user issuing a query to a search engine (Bing, Google, or Yahoo) in order to fulfill an information need. The user can read the search results page, read the pages linked by the result page (up to many levels of depth), reformulate the queries, or click on search features such as spelling correction, ads, or other search verticals (such as Images, News, etc.). The user's information need is either satisfied (SAT) or the effort is abandoned (UNSAT).

Participants were encouraged to use the add-in both at home and at work. That helped us collect a more diverse set of information goals. They were also encouraged to use the search engine that best suits their needs. That allowed us to collect data from all major web search engines.

Depending on the query and information need, users had to choose one of the following three outcomes for each information need:

1. Satisfied: user found what she wants
2. Unsatisfied: no matter what user tried, she could not find what she needs, and hence gave up.
3. No Opinion: user was not able to tell whether she is satisfied or not, or did not want this goal logged.

In addition to explicit satisfaction ratings, we collected several other pieces of information that characterize the behavior of users during search. Our log entries included a unique identifier for the user, a timestamp for each page view, a unique browser window and tab identifiers, and the URL of the visited web pages. Secure (https) URLs have not been collected. Any personally identifiable information was removed from the data prior to analysis. We further processed the collected URLs to identify queries, search result clicks, sponsored search clicks, related search clicks, spelling suggestion clicks, and browsing clicks that originated from a search result click. For each query, we identified the corresponding search engine and vertical. In addition, we collected the timestamp of every action. The start of a search goal was automatically detected by the add-in whenever the user submits a query to any major web search engine. The end of every goal is the time when the user submitted her satisfaction rating.

An example of an unsatisfied goal is shown in Table 1. The user started with the query "steven colbert painting". After two clicks with short dwell time, she decided to switch to the "Images" tab. Apparently, she still could not find what she was looking for so she decided to reformulate her query to "steven colbert recursive painting". That still did not help her fulfill her information need. Hence, she gave up and ended her search. An example of a satisfied goal with a related information need is shown in Table 2. Here, the user started with the query "van gogh self portrait", and quickly decided to click on an image results. She spent some time examining the result then she successfully ended her search.

Table 1: An Example of an Unsatisfied Goal

	Action	Dwell Time
Query	steven colbert painting	12
CLICK	url1	4
BACK	steven colbert painting	11
CLICK	url2	8
TAB SWITCH	IMAGES	8
Query	steven colbert recursive painting	8
END		-

Table 2: An Example of a Satisfied Goal

	Action	Dwell Time
Query	van gogh self portrait	7
IMG CLICK	url1	37
END		-

4.2 Participants

We collected data from 115 regular employees and college interns in a large company who volunteered for the experiments. We initially invited 1200 users to participate in the study. The group of invited users included both technical and administrative employees. 115 user opted in to participate in the study resulting in a 9.5% response rate. 75% of the opt in users were males, while the rest were females. Participants were instructed to use the add-in both on the internal corporate network and outside. We also encouraged participants to use the add-in both at home and at work. That helped us collect a more diverse set of information goals. Our user base included different genders, different age groups (i.e. regular employees vs. college interns), and different educational backgrounds (i.e. technical vs administrative employees). This helped reduce any bias in the collected data.

4.3 Data Characteristics

We collected data from 115 users over a span of 6 weeks. During this period, we collected more than 12,000 search goals and more than 33,000 page visits. The average number of queries per search goals was 2.1 queries. This is somewhat smaller than the values of 2.4 and 2.5 reported in Fox et al. [7], and Spink et al. [23] respectively. The average query length was 2.84 words which is similar the values of 2.99 and 2.35 reported in Fox et al. [7], and Spink et al. [23] respectively.

We collected data from all major web search engines. We also collected data from all search verticals. Expectedly, most of the goals had the first query submitted to the web vertical, however some of those goals switched to a different vertical later in the search process. Our data contains search goals involving almost all available search verticals. For example, we have data from the following verticals: images, video, news, shopping, academic,...etc.

We excluded users who submitted very small (less than 10) or very large (more than 200) number of queries. Most of the users (approximately 88%) submitted 10 to 200 votes.

5. MODELING USER SATISFACTION

5.1 Goals as Search Trails

The user satisfaction model is based on user behavior while interacting with the search engine. We use search trails to represent this behavior by recording all user Web search activities. Every search goal is represented by a trail. A search trail originates with the submission of a query to a search engine and contains all queries and all post-query navigation trails (i.e., pages viewed on the click stream following the query being issued) [27]. It terminates when user stops their information seeking activity. This happens either when the information need is met, or when the user gives up and decides not to pursue his information need anymore. The trails contain any reformulation of queries, and all page visits. A page visit could be a visit to the search engine homepage, a search results page, or by following a link from a result page.

A user search trail is represented by an ordered sequence of user actions along with the time between those actions. We included several types of actions in our search trail representation like a query submission, an algorithmic search click, a sponsored search click, a related search click, a spelling suggestion click, an answer click, a tab switch, a click on a link on a search result page, or navigating back to SERP (i.e. the search engine results page).

Consider the following example: A user enters the query "steven colbert painting", then 12 seconds later she clicks on one of the search results. She spends only 4 seconds on this page and then goes back the SERP which she examines for 12 seconds then clicks on another search result. She spends 5 seconds examining the new result page, then switches to the "images" tab where she reformulates her query to "steven colbert recursive painting" then ends her information seeking activity. This user goal can be represented by the following trail:

Q 12s SR 4s SERP 11s SR 8s IMG 8s Q 8s END

Here, Q represents a query, SR is a search result click, SERP represents going back to the search engine results page, IMG is a switch to the "images" tab, and finally END denotes the end of the user information seeking activity. We notice that we have a single state "Q" that represents both the first query and any further query rewrites. The reason is that we model transitions rather than states, and hence the transition to the first query will be always "START Q", and that will be different from transitions to further query rewrites.

5.2 Learning Model Parameters

If we examine the example of the user searching for "steven colbert painting" from Table 1, we will find out that her information need was not met and hence she was not satisfied with her search experience. This goal is represented by this trail: Q 12s SR 4s SERP 11s SR 8s IMG 8s Q 8s END. Now let us contrast this example with the example in Table 2. This goal is represented by the following trail: Q 7s SR 37 END. The later user fulfilled her information need and ended up being satisfied with her search experience. If we examine the trails, we notice that the behavior that leads to satisfaction is different from the behavior that leads to dissatisfaction. Hence, if we are able to build a model to characterizes the behavior of users in the case of satisfaction, and another model that characterizes the behavior of users in the case of dissatisfaction, we can use those models to predict whether any new unseen goal is satisfied or not as in [10].

Given a set of trails representing a set of search goals, we can build a graph $G = V, E, w$ where V is the set of all possible tokens (i.e. actions) that may appear in the trails. $E = V \times V$ is the set of possible transitions between any two tokens. $w : E \rightarrow [0..1]$ is a weighting function that assigns to every pair of states (i, j) a weight $w(i, j)$ representing the probability that we have a transition from state i to state j.

This graph corresponds to a Markovian model. The set of states are the vocabulary, and the transition probabilities between states are estimated using Maximum Likelihood estimation as follows:

$$P_{ij} = \frac{N_{ij}}{N_i}$$

where N_{ij} is the number of times we saw a transition from i to state j, and N_i is the total number of times we saw state i in the training data. We used smoothing to account for any data scarcity.

We build two such models. The first model is built using all trails that appeared in the training dataset and was labeled as satisfied, and the second model is built using all trails in the training dataset that are not satisfied.

To model time, we assume that there is a distinctive distribution that governs the amount of time the user spends at each transition. We assume that transition times follow a gamma distribution. We again split our training data into two splits; the first containing all satisfied goals and the second containing all unsatisfied goals. We then estimate the gamma distribution parameters for every transition once in each model as in [10].

5.3 Classifying New Goals

We split our training data into two splits; the first containing all trails of satisfied goals and the second containing all trails of unsatisfied goals. Given the methodology described in the previous section, we build a pair of Markov models: One using all satisfied goals and the other using all unsatisfied goals. The first model characterized the behavior of satisfied users and the second model characterizes the behavior of unsatisfied users. We also estimate the time distribution parameters for every transition in both models. Given any new goal, we extract the corresponding trail and estimate the log likelihood that this sequence of actions was generated from every model. If a certain goal ended with user satisfaction, we expect that the likelihood of the corresponding behavior being generated from the SAT model will be higher and vice versa.

Given a model M, and sequence of actions (i.e. search trail) $T = (T_1, T_2, \ldots TS_n)$, the probability of this trail being generated from M is:

$$P_M(T) = \prod_{i=2}^{n} P(T_i|T_1, \ldots, T_{i-1}) = \prod_{i=2}^{n} W(T_{i-1}, T_i)$$

where n is the number of actions in the trail, and W is the probability transition function.

The log likelihood is then defined as:

$$LL_M(T) = \sum_{i=2}^{n} \log W(T_{i-1}, T_i)$$

Then we use the log likelihoods ratio to predict whether the search goal was satisfied or not :

$$f = \frac{LL_{M_{sat}}(T)}{LL_{M_{unsat}}(T)}$$

where T is the search trail, $LL_{M_{att}}(T)$ is the log likelihood of the trail given the satisfaction model, and $LL_{M_{unsat}}(T)$ is the log likelihood of the trail given the non-satisfaction model. If f is greater than a particular threshold, we classify the goal as SAT, otherwise we classify it as UNSAT. The threshold is estimated empirically using a development set.

6. IMPROVING RELEVANCE ESTIMATION

We propose a new model for estimating document relevance using the search logs of a Web search engine. The model is based on analyzing the overall activity of users during search goals. In particular, we propose a better interpretation of clickthrough data by putting the click in its context. Current relevance models, that use clickthrough data, make the simplistic assumption that the mere fact that a URL has been clicked is a strong indicator of its relevance to the query. Even though clickthrough data is correlated with relevance, there are several problems that arise when using it as an explicit relevance measure. When a user decides to click on a particular URL, he is usually affected by the results presentation. That includes the snippet, the position of different URLs, other displayed results, etc. Hence when a user decides to click on a URL, she is only guessing that this URL is relevant to her information need, which may or may not be correct. On the other hand, if we know whether the information need of the user has been met or not, we would be able to provide a much better estimation of the relevance of a particular document given the clickthrough data.

The proposed model makes use of the user satisfaction model we described earlier. It assumes that users, who end up being satisfied with their search, keep clicking on search results till they collect enough "utility" to satisfy their information need. On the other hand, users who end up being dissatisfied with their search develop "despair" as they click on more and more irrelevant results. They give up when they develop a certain amount of despair. We collect a large number of search goals from the search logs and use our overall goal success metric to predict whether users ended up being satisfied or not. We then estimate the average utility, and despair for every query document pair. These will be used as features to train a machine learning ranking function. We compare this ranking function to a baseline using both content features and features extracted from clickthrough data.

Let us reconsider the example from Section 5.1 where a user was searching for "steven colbert painting". In this example, the user clicked on two different URLs, yet this did not fulfill her information need. Systems that use clickthrough rate (CTR) as a predictor of actual relevance will incorrectly assume that the two URLs are relevant to the query "steven colbert painting". The model we propose will not only avoid this, but will also reduce the predicted relevance of those URLs causing other, possibly more relevant, results to move up in the ranking.

6.1 Utility Despair Model

Assume our unit of analysis is a search goal as described earlier in Section 5. Assume a user U_1 starts a search to satisfy a certain information need. During her search she clicked on three URLs U_1, U_2, and U_3. Also assume that our satisfaction model predicted that this user was satisfied with her search. The basic intuition behind the model we propose is that the user kept clicking on results until she collected enough utility. after which her information need was met and she concluded her search activity. Every result she clicked contributed a certain amount of utility toward satisfying her need.

We tried two different methods to assign a particular amount of utility to every result. The first assumes that utility is distributed uniformly between all clicked results and hence:

$$Util(u_i) = \frac{1}{n} \tag{1}$$

where n is the number of clicked results.

The second method assumes that the more time a user spends on a search result, the more utility she gains from it. Hence the utility gain from a particular click is proportional to its dwell time. Hence utility is defined as:

$$Util(u_i) = \frac{T_i}{\sum_{j=1}^{n} T_j} \tag{2}$$

where T_i is dwell time of the click with order i and n is the number of clicked results.

Now assume the same user starts another search where she clicks on some results . But in this case, our satisfaction model predicted that this user was not satisfied with her search. This user kept trying to fulfill her information need till she finally gave up. we assume that unsatisfied users keep trying to fulfill their information need till they develop a certain amount of "despair", after which they give up. Every click the user makes contributes to that despair. In cases, where a user does not click on any results, we assume that she at least spent an equal amounts of time examining the titles and snippets of the first two results, and did not find them relevant. Hence, we treat them as if they were clicked. The choice of the first two results in case of no clicks is justified by the eye tracking studies [8] that show that the mean time users fixate on a presented result is almost equal for links ranked 1 and 2, and that it drops off sharply after the second link. Despair is distributed among URLs in the same way we described for utility (i.e. either uniformly or using dwell time). When using dwell time, it is assumed that the less time the user spends on the result, the more despair she develops.

7. EXPERIMENTS

7.1 User Satisfaction Model

7.1.1 *Evaluation using Labeled Data*

Our experiments use the search goals collected during the user study described in Section 4. Our search goals come from several search engines and several verticals. Labels were directly collected from users in the form of explicit satisfaction ratings. We evaluate our results in terms of *Precision*, *Recall*, *F-measure*, and *Accuracy*. We used ten fold cross validation for all experiments and evaluated statistical significance using a 1-tailed paired t-test. All results are statistically significant unless otherwise stated.

We compare our results to two different baselines. The first is based on the time to first click which is the difference between the timestamp from serving up the page, and the timestamp of the first user click on the page. It has been previously shown that this number is highly correlated with satisfaction. The second baseline is based on the number of successful clicks in the search goal. A successful click is defined to be either a click on a result link (answer, ad, or web result) that has a dwell time of 30 second or the last click in a user's goal was on an answer, ad, or a web result.

We compare our method to the baselines using 10-fold cross validation on the labeled data. We also perform a large scale evaluation using real user traffic. In the later scenario, we use two ranking functions; one of which is hypothesized to be better by the ranking function developers. Results from the two functions were shown to a small fraction of a commercial search engine system and millions of queries and clicks are observed. We use the proposed method and the baselines to compare the two ranking functions and examine which methods succeed and which methods fail in finding the difference between the two ranking functions.

More than 83% of our data was for goals where users ended up being satisfied with their search experiment. Hence the class distribution was not balanced. Imbalance in the class distribution often causes machine learning algorithms to perform poorly on the minority class [25]. In our case, we are more interested in the minority (DSAT) class. Hence, the cost of misclassifying the minority class is usually higher than the cost of misclassifying the majority class. Several researchers have experimentally evaluated the benefit of using sampling to artificially balance imbalanced data [4, 18, 26]. A common way of addressing class imbalance is to artificially rebalance the training data. To do this we down-sample the majority class (SAT goals) by holding the M DSAT goals constant, randomly selecting without replacement M SAT goals, and training our model on the 50/50 split. This was repeated several times until all SAT goals have been used which resulted in 5 different models. Finally decisions are made by taking the majority vote among all models.

Figure 1 compares the precision-recall curves for the two baselines described earlier and the proposed model for the SAT case. Figure 2 compares the precision-recall curves for the same systems for the DSAT case. If we examine the curves for the SAT class, we notice that the baseline based on the number of successful clicks does pretty well for very low recall regions (i.e. recall less than or equal to 0.2). The proposed model significantly outperforms the baseline based on the number of successful clicks for all operating points where recall is greater than 0.2. The proposed model significantly outperforms the baseline based on time to first click for all operating points. The superior performance of the baseline based on the number of successful clicks at low recall is not surprising. The reason is that the few number of goals with so many successful clicks are almost always satisfied. If we examine the precision-recall curves for the DSAT class, we notice that the proposed model significantly outperforms the baselines at all operating points. The model also subsumes the information in the baselines. This became clear, when we trained a classifier using features from the baselines along with the log likelihood ratio calculated by the proposed model. The difference in performance before and after adding features from the baselines was not statistically significant. The Markov model based on search trails representing user behavior has several advantages compared to the baseline. The most important advantage is that it provides a more accurate picture of the user behavior, while the baselines only use aggregated feature to create a rough approximation of behavior.

We now measure the performance of the proposed method when the system is allowed to abstain from classifying goals for which it have low confidence. We regard the log likelihood ratio as a confidence measure and evaluate the top goals with the highest confidence level at different values of threshold. Figure 3 shows the accuracy and the DSAT precision at different thresholds. We notice that both metrics improve by abstaining from classifying the difficult goals. This is particularly important for the DSAT precision, because one of the possible applications for our metric is to mine dissatisfaction cases. These are cases where a search engine fails and hence need improvement. We notice from the figure that if we abstain from classifying the 30% of the goals where we have the least confidence, we can achieve precision as high as 93%.

Finally we compared the performance of the model when restricted to using information available on the server side logs only to that using the richer information available at the client side. We found out that when using server side logs , accuracy drops by approximately 1%. This shows that the model is useful for use with both kinds of logs, yet it is capable of using the richer information available in the client side logs.

7.1.2 Large Scale Evaluation using User Traffic

The second part of our evaluation uses real user traffic. We used two ranking functions developed by a large commercial search engine. One of the ranking functions is intentionally degraded by the ranker developers. The two ranking functions were shown to a small fraction of a commercial search engine system users and millions of queries and clicks were observed. We extracted 1,000,000 search goals for each ranking function. We ran the proposed system on all search goals corresponding to the two ranking functions. The p-values for the time to first click baseline, the number of successful clicks baseline, and the proposed system were 0.5694, 0.0048, and 2.2×10^{-8} respectively. This shows that the proposed metric was able to tell the two ranking functions apart with a significantly smaller p-value than the baselines. We also used another pair of ranking functions for testing. All previously mentioned metrics failed to find any statistically significant difference between their performance. The only two metrics that were able to report any statistically significant difference are our metric, and a metric based on an interleaved evaluation [19]. According to recent studies, interleaving experiments can identify large differences in retrieval effectiveness with high reliability. The advantage of our metric is that it eliminates the need for creating and collecting traffic for a third ranking function that interleaves the results of the two functions we need to compare [19].

We also studied how many search goals are needed for our metric to reliably compare two systems. We studied the effect of the amount of user traffic collected on the outcome of the comparison between the first pair of ranking functions. We sample n goals from the user traffic data without replacement for the two ranking functions. We measure the performance of every ranking function and determine which one wins. We repeat the sampling 1,000 times for every n and report the percentage of trials where the better ranking function wins. Figure 4 shows the fraction of samples where the better ranker gets a better score using the proposed user satisfaction model versus the size of the dataset used for evaluation in terms of the number of goals. For small numbers of goals, each ranker gets a better score for almost 50% of the time. As the number of goals increase, a constant preference for the better ranker to win is observed. More sensitive metrics are more desirable because they can work with less amounts of data. The figure shows that with

100,000 goals, the better function wins more than 90% of the time. This figures tells us how much data do we need to collect to get meaningful results from the metric.

Figure 1: Precision Recall Graph for the SAT Class.

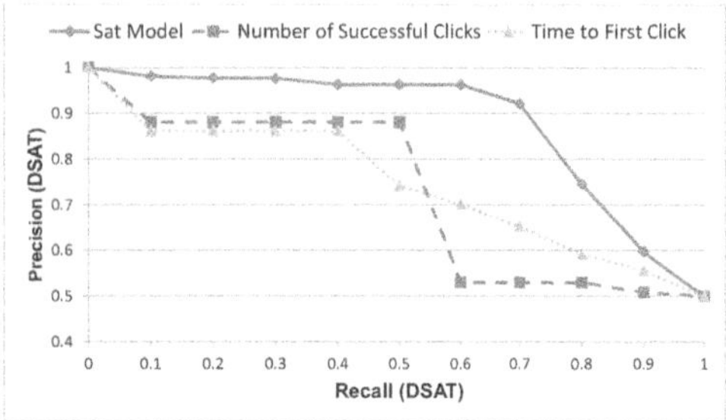

Figure 2: Precision Recall Graph for the DSAT Class.

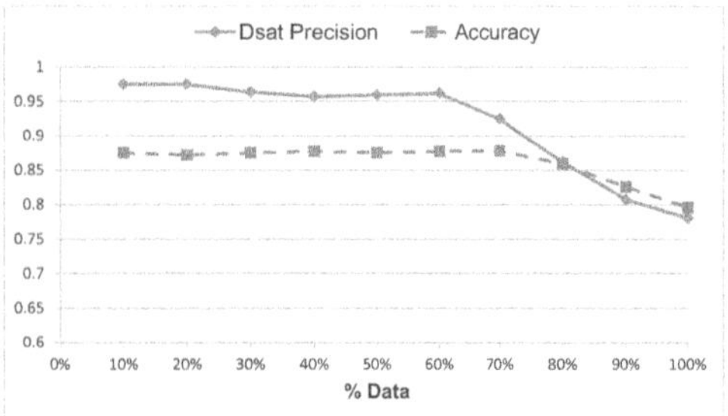

Figure 3: Confidence in Prediction vs. Performance.

7.2 Relevance Estimation Evaluation

We explained in previous sections how to use the user satisfaction model and a large amount of user traffic to assign utility and despair values to query URL pairs. We evaluate those values by using them as features to train a learning to rank algorithm.

We compare the results of two ranking functions. The first uses content based features (i.e. BM25F [24], word overlap,..etc.), and link based features. We then added the utility and despair values as features and create a new ranking function.

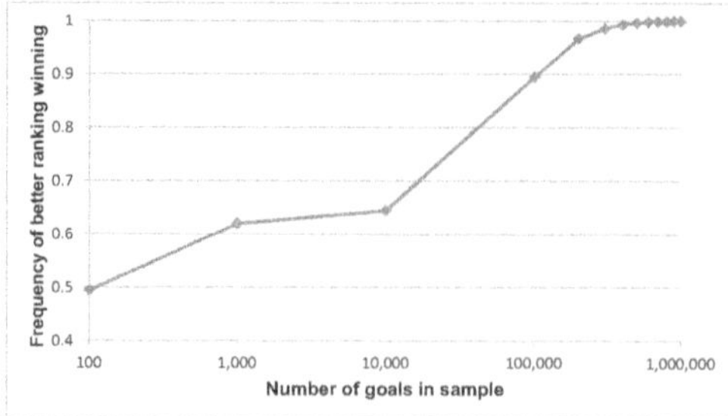

Figure 4: Number of Goals in Test Data vs. Frequency of Better Ranking Winning.

We use Normalized Discounted Cumulative Gain (NDCG) [13] for evaluation. It is defined as:

$$NDCG@K = \frac{1}{Z@K} \sum_{i=1}^{k} \frac{2^{g(i)} - 1}{\log(i+1)} \quad (3)$$

where K is the cut-off threshold, and $g(i)$ is the relevance of the ith document. $g(i)$ can take any integer value between 1, and 5 which corresponds to the "Perfect", "Excellent", "Good", "Fair", and "Bad" relevance grades. $Z@K$ is a normalization factor that represents the DCG of the ideal ranking.

Our test data consists of 750 queries for which we have human relevance judgments. For every query result pair, a human annotator was asked to examine the pair and decide whether the result is relevant to the query or not. Annotators used a five point scale, where every pair is judged as either "Perfect", "Excellent", "Good", "Fair", or "Bad". We also collected a large amount of user traffic over the span of a two weeks period from users using a commercial search engine. We segmented the search log data into search goals using a simple linear classifier that uses the time between queries, word level edit distance and character level edit distance as features. The parameters of the classifier were set using grid search. We can also use more sophisticated techniques for boundary identification following the method proposed in Jones and Klinkner [16] which reports accuracy of around 92%. After identifying search goal boundaries, we keep only goals that has one or more of the queries for which we have human relevance judgments. Then, we apply our user satisfaction model to every goal and calculate a utility and/or despair values for every query URL pairs as discussed in Section 6. We use those feature to train a learning to rank algorithm. We use SVMRank [15] for all ranking experiments. All experiments use 10-fold cross validation. All experiments distribute utility/despair based on dwell time unless otherwise stated.

Figure 5 shows the NDCG@K for different values of K for the baseline ranking function with and without the utility and despair features. We notice from the figure that adding the features improves the performance of the baseline for all values of K. Next, we tried to add click-through rate features to the baseline to test whether adding the utility and despair features will still improve performance. The result of this experiment is shown in Figure 6. The figure shows an improvement in NDCG@K for all values of K even after

Table 3: Example of an Unsatisfied Goal

NDCG @k	Uniform	Dwell Time
1	0.116	0.129
2	0.239	0.251
3	0.326	0.338
4	0.372	0.385
5	0.402	0.414

we add the CTR features to the baseline. All improvements are statistically significant at the 0.05 level.

We compare the NDCG gain for informational versus navigational queries [3] in Figure 7. We notice that the improvement in case of informational queries is larger than the improvement in case of navigational queries. This is a desirable property because informational queries are usually more challenging.

Finally we compare the two utility distribution methods in Table 3. The table shows the NDCG@K values for the uniform distribution method, and the one based on dwell time. We notice that the dwell time yields the better results. However, the results are only numerically better but not statistically significant. This supports the hypothesis that the more time a user spends on a result page, the more utility she gains from it.

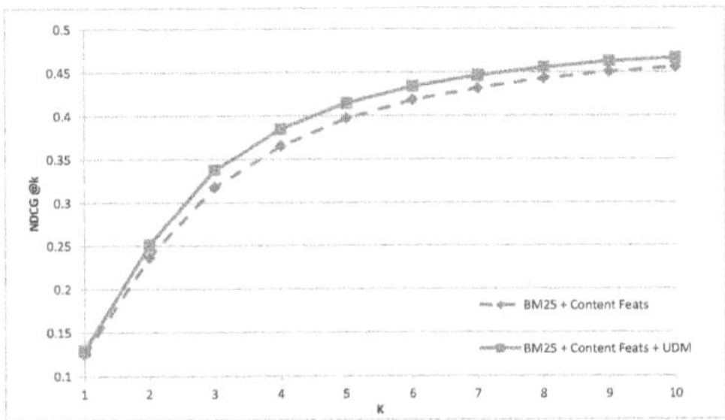

Figure 5: NDCG@n Improvement when Adding Utility and Despair Features.

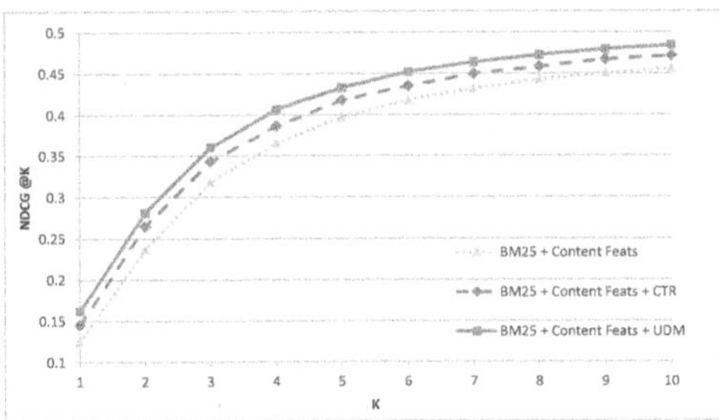

Figure 6: NDCG@n Improvement when Adding CTR vs. Improvement when Adding Utility and Despair Features.

8. DISCUSSION AND CONCLUSIONS

We performed a user study to collect explicit satisfaction ratings from users across search engines. We developed a browser add-in for a well distributed web browser to collect satisfaction ratings from participants, as well as monitor their behavior during search. We managed to collect approximately 12,000 search goals and 33,000 page visits from 115 users over a span of 6 weeks. The dataset we collected contains a reliable satisfaction ratings for a diverse set of search goals from several search engines.

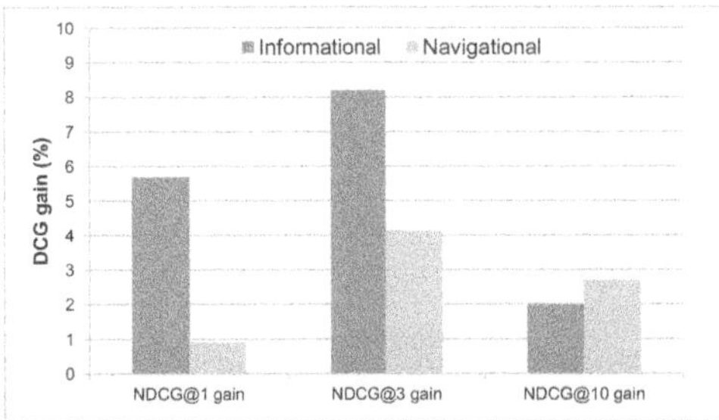

Figure 7: NDCG Gain for Informational vs. Navigational Queries.

We have shown that training a supervised model that learns user behavior in satisfied and unsatisfied scenarios results in an accurate satisfaction/dissatisfaction prediction. We extensively evaluated our model using cross validation on the labeled data. We also evaluated it by comparing two ranking functions using millions of goals from real user traffic on a commercial search engine. The results show that our model is accurate and robust.

We also showed preliminary results for an application of how our user satisfaction model can be used to improve relevance estimation. We presented a new model for interpreting clickthrough data that distinguished between clicks in satisfied, and unsatisfied goals. We introduced the notions of utility and despair, where users gain utility when clicking on results in satisfied goals, and develop despair when clicking or examining results in unsatisfied goals. We described how utility and despair values can be calculated for query-URL pairs and used as features for a learning to rank algorithm. We showed that adding those features improves the performance of a strong ranking function used as a baseline.

One direction of future work is improve the user satisfaction model by adding the notion of effort as a component of predicting over all satisfaction. Another direction is to extend the model to the semi-supervised setting where we learn from both labeled and unlabeled. We also intend to explore how the satisfaction model can be used in real time settings where the search engine predicts that a user will end up being unsatisfied and interfere to prevent that. Another direction of future work is to improve the relevance estimation model by using different ways, that are more sensitive to user behavior, to distribute utility or despair among clicks.

9. REFERENCES

[1] E. Agichtein, E. Brill, S. Dumais, and R. Ragno. User interaction models for predicting web search result preferences. In *Proceedings of the 29th annual international ACM SIGIR conference on Research and development in information retrieval*, pages 3–10, 2006.

[2] E. Agichtein, E. Brill, and S. T. Dumais. Improving web search ranking by incorporating user behavior information. In *SIGIR 2006: Proceedings of the 29th annual international ACM SIGIR conference on Research and development in information retrieval*, pages 19–26, New York, NY, USA, 2006. ACM.

[3] A. Broder. A taxonomy of web search. *SIGIR Forum*, 36(2):3–10, 2002.

[4] C. Drummond and R. C. Holte. C4.5, class imbalance, and cost sensitivity: Why under-sampling beats over-sampling. In *ICML'2003 Workshop on Learning from Imbalanced Datasets II*, pages 1–8, 2003.

[5] G. Dupret and C. Liao. A model to estimate intrinsic document relevance from the clickthrough logs of a web search engine. In *Proceedings of the third ACM international conference on Web search and data mining*, pages 181–190, New York, NY, USA, 2010. ACM.

[6] G. E. Dupret and B. Piwowarski. A user browsing model to predict search engine click data from past observations. In *SIGIR '08: Proceedings of the 31st annual international ACM SIGIR conference on Research and development in information retrieval*, pages 331–338, New York, NY, USA, 2008. ACM.

[7] S. Fox, K. Karnawat, M. Mydland, S. Dumais, and T. White. Evaluating implicit measures to improve web search. *ACM Transactions on Information Systems*, 23, 2005.

[8] L. A. Granka, T. Joachims, and G. Gay. Eye-tracking analysis of user behavior in www-search. In *Proceedings of the 27th annual international conferenceon Research and development in information retrieval*, pages 478–479, 2004.

[9] F. Guo, C. Liu, and Y. M. Wang. Efficient multiple-click models in web search. In *Proceedings of the Second ACM International Conference on Web Search and Data Mining*, pages 124–131, 2009.

[10] A. Hassan, R. Jones, and K. L. Klinkner. Beyond dcg: user behavior as a predictor of a successful search. In *WSDM '10: Proceedings of the third ACM international conference on Web search and data mining*, pages 221–230, New York, NY, USA, 2010. ACM.

[11] D. Hawking, N. Craswell, P. Thistlewaite, and D. Harman. Results and challenges in web search evaluation. In *WWW '99: Proceedings of the eighth international conference on World Wide Web*, pages 1321–1330, New York, NY, USA, 1999. Elsevier North-Holland, Inc.

[12] S. B. Huffman and M. Hochster. How well does result relevance predict session satisfaction? In *Proceedings of the 30th annual international ACM SIGIR conference on Research and development in information retrieval*, pages 567–574, 2007.

[13] K. Järvelin and J. Kekäläinen. Cumulated gain-based evaluation of ir techniques. *ACM Trans. Inf. Syst.*, 20(4):422–446, 2002.

[14] T. Joachims. Optimizing search engines using clickthrough data. In *KDD '02: Proceedings of the eighth ACM SIGKDD international conference on Knowledge discovery and data mining*, pages 133–142, New York, NY, USA, 2002. ACM.

[15] T. Joachims, T. Finley, and C.-N. Yu. Cutting-plane training of structural svms. *Machine Learning*, 77(1):27–59–59, October 2009.

[16] R. Jones and K. Klinkner. Beyond the session timeout: Automatic hierarchical segmentation of search topics in query logs. In *Proceedings of ACM 17th Conference on Information and Knowledge Management (CIKM 2008)*, 2008.

[17] S. Jung, J. L. Herlocker, and J. Webster. Click data as implicit relevance feedback in web search. *Information Processing and Management (IPM)*, 43(3):791–807, 2007.

[18] X.-Y. Liu, J. Wu, and Z.-H. Zhou. Exploratory undersampling for class-imbalance learning. *Trans. Sys. Man Cyber. Part B*, 39(2):539–550, 2009.

[19] F. Radlinski and N. Craswell. Comparing the sensitivity of information retrieval metrics. In *Proceeding of the 33rd international ACM SIGIR conference on Research and development in information retrieval*, SIGIR '10, pages 667–674, 2010.

[20] F. Radlinski and T. Joachims. Query chains: learning to rank from implicit feedback. In *KDD '05: Proceedings of the eleventh ACM SIGKDD international conference on Knowledge discovery in data mining*, pages 239–248, New York, NY, USA, 2005. ACM.

[21] F. Radlinski and T. Joachims. Active exploration for learning rankings from clickthrough data. In *KDD '07: Proceedings of the 13th ACM SIGKDD international conference on Knowledge discovery and data mining*, pages 570–579, New York, NY, USA, 2007. ACM.

[22] F. Radlinski, M. Kurup, and T. Joachims. How does clickthrough data reflect retrieval quality? In J. G. Shanahan, S. Amer-Yahia, I. Manolescu, Y. Zhang, D. A. Evans, A. Kolcz, K.-S. Choi, and A. Chowdhury, editors, *CIKM*, pages 43–52. ACM, 2008.

[23] A. Spink, D. Wolfram, B. Jansen, B. J. Jansen, and T. Saracevic. Searching the web: The public and their queries. 2001.

[24] S. J. M. H.-B. Stephen E. Robertson, Steve Walker and M. Gatford. Okapi at trec-3. In *Proceedings of the Third Text REtrieval Conference (TREC 1994)*, 1994.

[25] J. Van Hulse, T. M. Khoshgoftaar, and A. Napolitano. Experimental perspectives on learning from imbalanced data. In *Proceedings of the 24th international conference on Machine learning*, pages 935–942, 2007.

[26] G. M. Weiss and F. Provost. Learning when training data are costly: The effect of class distribution on tree induction. *Journal of Artificial Intelligence Research*, 19:315–354, 2003.

[27] R. W. White and S. M. Drucker. Investigating behavioral variability in web search. In *Proceedings of the 16th international conference on World Wide Web*, 2007.

Multi-view Random Walk Framework for Search Task Discovery from Click-through Log

Jianwei Cui[1], Hongyan Liu[2], Jun Yan[3], Lei Ji[3], Ruoming Jin[4],
Jun He[1†], Yingqin Gu[1], Zheng Chen[3], Xiaoyong Du[1]

[1]Key Labs of Data Engineering and Knowledge Engineering, Ministry of Education, China.
School of Information, Renmin University of China, {cjwruc, guyingqin, hejun, duyong}@ruc.edu.cn
[2]Department of Management Science and Engineering, Tsinghua University, hyliu@tsinghua.edu.cn
[3]Microsoft Research Asia, Beijing, China, {leiji, junyan, zhengc}@microsoft.com
[4]Computer Science Department, Kent State University, jin@cs.kent.edu

ABSTRACT

Search engine users often have clear search tasks hidden behind their queries. Inspired by this, the modern search engines are providing an increasing number of services to help users simplify their key tasks. However, the problem of *what are the major user search tasks with high traffic for which search engines should design special services* is still underexplored. In this paper, we propose a novel Multi-view Random Walk (*MRW*) algorithm to measure the search task oriented similarity between queries, and then group search queries with similar tasks so that the major search tasks of users can be identified from search engine click-through log. The proposed *MRW*, which is a general framework to combine knowledge from different views in a random walk process, allows the random surfer to walk across different views to integrate information for search task discovery. Experimental results on click-through log of a commonly used commercial search engine show that our proposed *MRW* algorithm can effectively discover user search tasks.

Categories and Subject Descriptors

H.3.3 **[Programming Languages]: Information Search and Retrieval**

General Terms

Algorithm, Experimentation

Keywords

Search task, Query clustering, Multi-view random walk

1. INTRODUCTION

During search process, users often have different search intentions and tasks, which are hidden behind search queries. For example, if a user issues a query "Seattle weather", the search task is to check the weather of a city. Recently, many commercial search engines are providing various services to simplify users' search tasks. For example, after one issues the query "Seattle weather" to some commercial search engines, several of them will directly provide the weather information on top of the search results as shown in Figure 1, which requires no user effort to browse the long list of search results. This emerging trend requires that the search engine has to "smart and intelligent" to be able to accurately capture users' search tasks and then route the queries to their corresponding online services.

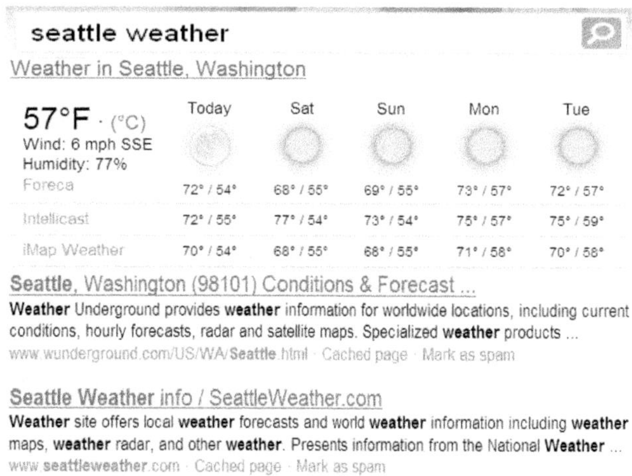

Figure 1. Search result of "Seattle Weather"

Though there are some existing work [1, 5, 9, 10] trying to address the identification of user search tasks, these studies either target different stage of the search process or explore only single aspect of the query, such as word similarity. To address this problem, we aim to discover the high traffic user search tasks from real users' search behaviors, which are logged in the search engine click-through log. To achieve this goal, in this paper, we aim to measure the task oriented similarity between queries, and then cluster queries according to their possible search tasks. Thus, the clusters with high traffic in search engine click-through log are recognized as the query clusters to reflect the major user search tasks. However, it is a challenging problem to group queries according to their tasks since the tasks are generally hidden behind short search queries. For some queries, such as "dell inspiration price" and "dell laptop price", the fact that they share

†Corresponding author.

CIKM'11, October 24–28, 2011, Glasgow, Scotland, UK.

the same search task can be observed from the query contents. However, for many other queries, whether they have the same task cannot be directly observed. For example, queries "computer price" and "laptop amazon" share the same task since they usually share the same group of clicked Web pages but they have no term level overlap. Indeed, different information sources, such as query content, query document click-through and search session information all can provide some knowledge of the underlying search task. However, how to integrate and combine them to better estimate the search task oriented similarity between queries is still an open problem.

In this paper, we propose a novel Multi-view Random Walk (*MRW*) algorithm, which measures similarity between queries according to their search tasks by integrating information from different views. Here, each information source is represented as a single view. Theoretically, *MRW* offers a powerful framework to combine multiple heterogeneous information sources, which generalizes the existing classical linear combination methods [2]. Meanwhile, this framework enables us to better combine different information sources by assigning cross-view transition probabilities properly for different queries with respect to view characteristics and mining tasks.

The rest of this paper is organized as follows. In Section 2, we formally introduce multi-view random walk algorithm. In Section 3, we implement *MRW* model. After that in Section 4, we study the experimental results. Then, we summarize the related works and draw conclusion in Section 5 and Section 6 respectively.

2. MULTI-VIEW RANDOM WALK

2.1 Problem Statement

In this paper, we aim to grouping queries according to their search tasks so that identifying the high traffic user search tasks from the search engine click-through log. To do this, the key challenge we are facing is how to measure the similarities between queries such that they can reflect users' hidden intention and search tasks. Specifically, in this work, we consider heterogeneous information sources such as query content, query document click-through, search session information, etc. as different views, i.e. different spaces, and integrate them to better measure the search task oriented similarity between queries. Mathematically, we use Q and V to represent the set of queries and the set of different views (information sources) respectively. Then the query search task discovery problem we aim to solve is formulated as follows.

Problem Formulation. Given Q and V, we measure the task oriented similarity $\mathrm{sim}(q_a, q_b)$ between queries q_a and q_b from the multiple views V. Then we group queries in Q into query clusters based on $\mathrm{sim}(q_a, q_b)$, in which the high traffic query clusters are served as major search tasks of users.

2.2 Building the MRW Model

The intuition of our multi-view random walk (*MRW*) model contains two aspects. First, if we model each view v as a graph G_v in which queries are represented by nodes and the relationships between queries from view v are represented by edges with weights, G_v has a natural interpretation as Markov model, with the edges describing the transitions between queries. Here, G_v is denoted as query transition graph for view v and the overall graph which contains all query transition graphs for each view is denoted as multi-view graph. Given this, the random walk can be used to measure the similarity between queries even when they are not directly linked. Secondly, by allowing the transitions across views, relationships from multiple views can also be integrated in the random walk process; consequently, by assigning cross-view transitions appropriately for different queries, we can get a similarity metric which better reflects whether two queries share the similar search task.

Based on the above intuition, the multi-view random walk can be illustrated in the multi-view graph (three views) in Figure 2. Imagining there is a random surfer who transits from q_b to q_a in Figure 2. The walk consists of two parts. First, the random surfer will transit across views. For example, the random surfer may transit from v_2 to v_1 with certain probability which is called cross-view probability and denoted as $p(v_1|q_b, v_2)$. Next, after the across-view transition, the random surfer exploits the relationships between queries in the corresponding views to walk to q_a. Here, the transition between queries in the same view is called intra-view probability and can be calculated by Equation (1), in which $r^v(q_a, q_b)$ is the edge weight between queries q_a and q_b in view v. The edge weights correspond to the strength of relationships between queries in each individual view. We will detail their calculation in the next section. To sum, the multi-view random walk is combined by applying these two types of transition in an alternating fashion.

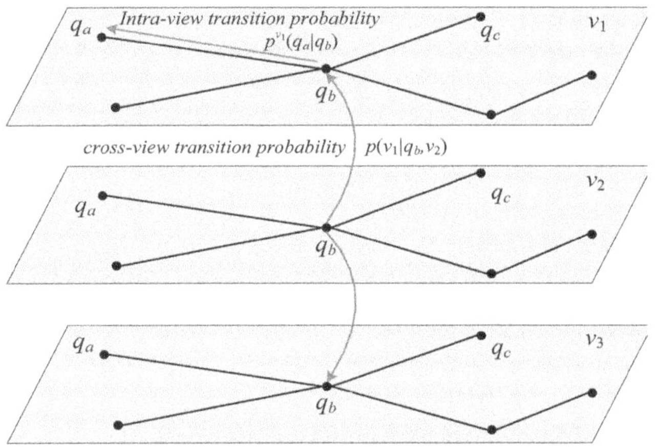

Figure 2. Illustration of multi-view transition

$$p^v(q_a|q_b) = r^v(q_a, q_b) / \sum_{q \in Q} r^v(q_b, q) \quad (1)$$

Transition Probabilities Computation for *MRW*: We now present the method to compute the transition probability between queries for *MRW*. Key notations are given in Table 1.

Table 1. Notations used in this paper.

Symbol	Meaning
$\boldsymbol{M}, \boldsymbol{P}, \boldsymbol{T}^n, \boldsymbol{A}$	four $\lvert Q\rvert \times \lvert Q\rvert$ matrixes
$\vec{p}$	row vector
$\vec{p}[i]$	the ith element of row vector $\vec{p}$
$\vec{\times}$	product operation for two n dimensional row vectors $\vec{p}_a$ and $\vec{p}_b$, the result is also a n dimensional row vector $\vec{p}$ which satisfies $\vec{p}[i] = \vec{p}_a[i] \cdot \vec{p}_b[i]$.
$\vec{p}'$	column vector, transpose of $\vec{p}$
$\boldsymbol{M}[i,j], \boldsymbol{P}[i,j], \boldsymbol{T}^n[i,j], \boldsymbol{A}[i,j]$	the element at the ith row and the jth column of matrix $\boldsymbol{M}, \boldsymbol{P}, \boldsymbol{T}^n$ *and* $\boldsymbol{A}$ respectively.
$p(v_j\|q, v_i)$	across-view transition probability from v_i to v_j when a random surfer starts from q
$p^v(q_a\|q_b)$	intra-view transition probability from q_b to q_a when a random surfer in view v

The first part of *MRW* is that the random surfer transits across views. To represent such transition, we use a $|V| \times |V|$ matrix $\boldsymbol{M}_k$ to store the cross-view transition probabilities for query q_k, in which $\boldsymbol{M}_k[i,j]$ is $p(v_j|q_k, v_i)$. Then the cross-view transition probabilities for all queries can be stored in a $|Q| \times |Q|$ diagonal transition matrix $\boldsymbol{M}$ in which the *k*th diagonal element $\boldsymbol{M}[k,k] = \boldsymbol{M}_k$ as shown in Figure 3(a).

The second part is that the random surfer performs random walk inside the individual view after each across-view transition. Here, we use a $|V|$ dimension row vector $\vec{p}^V(q_a|q_b)$ to denote the intra-view transition probabilities in all the views from q_b to q_a, in which the *i*th element $\vec{p}^V(q_a|q_b)[i]$ is $p^{v_i}(q_a|q_b)$ defined by Equation (1). Then, the intra-view transition probabilities for all queries can be stored in a $|Q| \times |Q|$ matrix $\boldsymbol{P}$ with $\boldsymbol{P}[b,a] = \vec{p}^V(q_a|q_b)$ as shown in Figure 3(b).

Combining the two parts, the transition matrix $\boldsymbol{T}^{t+1}$, which records the transition probabilities for all query pairs after $t+1$ ($t \geq 0$) step random walks in multi-view graph, is computed by Equation (2), in which $\boldsymbol{T}^{t+1}[i,j]$ is a $|V|$ dimension row vector calculated by Equation (3) that records the transition probability from q_j to q_i after $t+1$ step random walk. In equation (3), $\boldsymbol{T}^t[i,k] \cdot \boldsymbol{M}_k$ represents the cross-view transition for q_k if the random surfer has transited to q_k from q_i after t step random walk; meanwhile, the $\vec{\times}\, \vec{p}^V(q_j|q_k)$ operator corresponds to the transition in the same views after cross-view transitions. Here, the operator $\vec{\times}$ defined in Table 1 is the product of two row vectors.

$$\boldsymbol{M} = \begin{pmatrix} \boldsymbol{M}_1 & \cdots & 0 \\ \cdots & \cdots & \cdots \\ 0 & \cdots & \boldsymbol{M}_{|Q|} \end{pmatrix} \qquad \boldsymbol{P} = \begin{pmatrix} \vec{p}^V(q_1|q_1) & \cdots & \vec{p}^V(q_{|Q|}|q_1) \\ \cdots & \cdots & \cdots \\ \vec{p}^V(q_1|q_{|Q|}) & \cdots & \vec{p}^V(q_{|Q|}|q_{|Q|}) \end{pmatrix}$$

(a) (b)

Figure 3. (a) cross-views transition matrix. (b). Intra-views transition matrix.

$$\boldsymbol{T}^{t+1} = (\boldsymbol{T}^t \cdot \boldsymbol{M}) \cdot \boldsymbol{P} \tag{2}$$

$$\boldsymbol{T}^{t+1}[i,j] = \sum_{k=1}^{|Q|} (\boldsymbol{T}^t[i,k] \cdot \boldsymbol{M}_k)\, \vec{\times}\, \vec{p}^V(q_j|q_k) \tag{3}$$

$$\boldsymbol{A}_n = (\boldsymbol{T}^n) \cdot \boldsymbol{1} = \boldsymbol{T}^0 \cdot (\boldsymbol{M} \cdot \boldsymbol{P})^n \cdot \boldsymbol{1} \tag{4}$$

As a starting point in Equation (2), we set $\boldsymbol{T}^0$ as a diagonal matrix with each element being a uniform $|V|$ dimensional row vector in which each element is $1/|V|$. Therefore, $\boldsymbol{T}^{t+1}[i,j]$ is also a $|V|$ dimensional row vector which records how the random surfer walks from q_i to q_j from different views after $t+1$ step walks. Therefore, to measure the transition probability after random walk across all the views, we need to sum up the transition from q_i to q_j in each view by Equation (4). In Equation (4), $\boldsymbol{1}$ is a $|Q| \times |Q|$ diagonal matrix with each diagonal element is a $|V|$ dimensional column vector in which every element is equal to 1. Then, all the transitions between queries after n step multi-view random walks will be stored in a $|Q| \times |Q|$ matrix $\boldsymbol{A}_n$.

2.3 Discussion

In this subsection, we discuss the relation between *MRW* with three existing models ***SVRW***, ***VIRW*** and ***LCV***; and then show they are all special cases of *MRW*.

SVRW stands ***Single View Random Walk*** model, in which there is only on information source; so it is clearly that *SVRW* is the special case when $|V| = 1$ for *MRW*.

For *VIRW*, it denotes ***View Independent Random Walk***, which means first applies random walks in each view independently and then combines the random walk results linearly. Mathematically, we can prove that the *VIRW* is a special case of *MRW* when the cross-view transition probability for any query is zero.

Lastly, for *LCV*, which presents ***Liner Combination of Views***, it first linearly combines the transition between views by Equation (5) with the constraint $\sum_{v \in V} w_v = 1$, and then applies random walk based on a transition matrix $\widehat{\boldsymbol{P}}$ in which each element $\widehat{\boldsymbol{P}}[i,j]$ is defined by Equation (5). In this situation, we can prove the *LCV* is also a special case when $p(v_i|q, v_j)$ is proportional to w_i for any query q transits from any view $v_j (j \neq i)$ to v_i.

$$p^{\vec{w}}(q_a|q_b) = \sum_{v \in V} w_v \cdot p^v(q_a|q_b) \tag{5}$$

2.4 Query Similarity Measurement

In this subsection, we formally define the search task oriented similarity between queries based on *MRW* model by Equation (6) which is the weighted sum of transition probabilities in different steps in multi-view random walk. In Equation (6), $\boldsymbol{A}_t$ is the *t*-step transition matrix calculated by Equation (4) and β is a decay factor in the range (0, 1).

$$t(q_j|q_i) = \sum_{t=1}^{\infty} \beta^t \cdot \boldsymbol{A}_t[i,j] \tag{6}$$

$$Sim(q_i, q_j) = \frac{(t(q_j|q_i) + t(q_i|q_j))}{2} \tag{7}$$

Equation (6) is motivated by the work of [15] in which the transition probabilities at different steps will be weighted by β^t to accumulate up to $t(q_j|q_i)$, making the longer step transitions have less contribution to $t(q_j|q_i)$. Then, we define the similarity between queries by Equation (7), which is an average value of the transition probability from q_i to q_j and from q_j to q_i.

Theorem 1. The similarity defined by Equation (7) will converge.

Proof. The correctness of Theorem 1 could be observed as follows. Firstly, it is easy to see that $Sim(q_i, q_j) = \sum_{t=1}^{\infty} \beta^t \cdot$ ***A****ti,j+****A****t[j,i]2* and ***A****ti,j+****A****t[j,i]2≤1*, so that *Simqi,qj* is upper bounded by $\frac{\beta}{1-\beta}$; Secondly, we can see $\beta^t \cdot \frac{\boldsymbol{A}_t[i,j] + \boldsymbol{A}_t[j,i]}{2} \geq 0$ for any *t*. Therefore, based on the monotone convergence theorem [27], $Sim(q_i, q_j)$ will converge when $t \to \infty$.

3. MODEL IMPLEMENTATION

3.1 Building View Graphs

We consider the following three views for search task discovery.

Query Term View: This view corresponds to the fact that the search tasks of many queries can be observed from their terms. To evaluate the relationship of the two queries in this view, each query q will be represented by a term vector $\vec{t}(q)$ in the term space of all queries, in which each element $\vec{t}(q)[i]$ is the $tf \cdot idf$ value of the *i*th term in query q. Then, the weight associated with edge (q_i, q_j) between two queries in this view is measured by cosine similarity of their term vectors: $\cos\left(\vec{t}(q_i), \vec{t}(q_j)\right)$.

Document Click View: This view corresponds to the fact that queries are likely to share the same search task if users tend to click the same Web documents after they issued these queries. More specifically, assume the Web document set is D; then the query can be represented by a vector $\vec{d}(q)$ in which the *i*th element is the number of times users clicked the Web document $d_i \in D$ after q was issued. Therefore, similar to the query term view, the weight for edge (q_i, q_j) between queries in this view is calculated by $\cos\left(\vec{d}(q_i), \vec{d}(q_j)\right)$.

Search Session View: The intuition behind this view is that queries are likely to share the same search task if they tend to appear in same search sessions. The relationship of the two queries in this view can be measured straightforwardly by the probability that they co-occur in the same search sessions: $|S(q_i) \cap S(q_j)|/|S(q_i) \cup S(q_j)|$ in which $S(q_i)$ is the set of search sessions which contain the query q_i.

After measuring the relationship between queries, we can build G_v and compute intra-view transition probabilities by Equation (1).

3.2 Cross-view Transitions

The key of applying *MRW* model is to properly assign cross-view transitions for each individual query. To tackle this problem, we develop a method to evaluate the ability that the view captures the search task of a given query; so that the more possible a view indicates the search task of a query, the higher probability the cross-view transitions should be.

We evaluate the ability that a view v represents the search task of query through analyzing the characteristic of G_v. In detail, we collect 1.08 million queries about computer (collecting method will be given in Section 6) and use 3 month query log to build G_v for each view. Figure 4 shows the node degree distribution for document click view in log-log scale. The x-axis represents the node degree ordered by ascending order and the y-axis represents the number of query nodes which have corresponding degree. The distribution can be modeled well by power law distribution [3]. The transition graphs for other two views also exhibit similar degree distribution as the document click view.

In Figure 4, the head ($1 \le degree \le 5$) of the power law distribution corresponds to queries with few neighbors in the view. In other words, the relationships in the view for these queries are too sparse to find queries with similar search task. On the other hand, the relationships for queries with very big degree ($1000 \le degree \le 10000$) are too general and consequently not distinctive enough to measure the similarity with other queries, make many queries with different search tasks become similar when measuring similarity for these queries in this view.

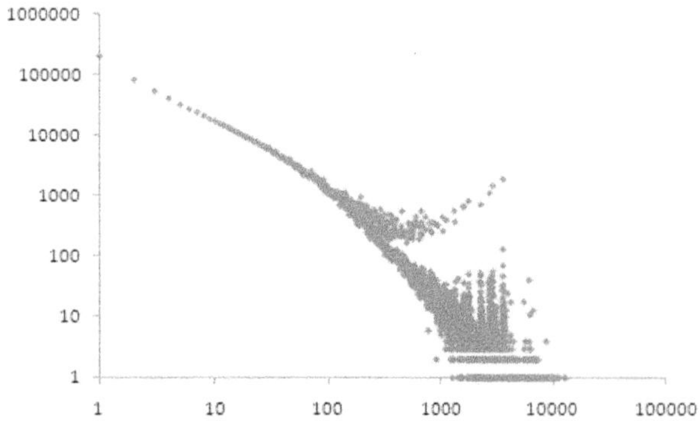

Figure 4. Degree distribution of document click view

Based on the observation, we can see the relationship which is too sparse or too general lacks the ability to identify the search task behind query. Therefore, we define the quality of view v for a query by Equation (8), where $degree^v(q)$ is the degree of query q in G_v and $d_s = max_{q \in Q}(degree^v(q))/2$ serve as a moderate node degree in v. Therefore, only queries with neither too small nor too big degree can get a high quality score by Equation (8).

$$Qual^v(q) = \frac{d_s}{d_s + |d_s - \log(degree^v(q))|} \quad (8)$$

Based on the view quality defined by Equation (8), we expect the view of higher quality contributes more towards identifying the query search task. Therefore, we define the cross-view transition for query q by Equation (9) in which $p(v_j|q, v_i)$ is proportional to $Qual^{v_j}(q)$. On the other hand, the surfer has an extra probability α $(0 \le \alpha \le 1)$ to transit to the same view v_i. Therefore, the parameter α controls the degree that the random surfer is more likely to retain in the same view or transit across views.

$$p(v_j|q, v_i) = \begin{cases} \frac{(1-\alpha) \cdot Qual^{v_j}(q)}{\sum_{v_k \in V} Qual^{v_k}(q)} & for\ i \ne j \\ \frac{(1-\alpha) \cdot Qual^{v_j}(q)}{\sum_{v_k \in V} Qual^{v_k}(q)} + \alpha & for\ i = j \end{cases} \quad (9)$$

4. EXPEREIMENT

4.1 Data Collection

In this section, we evaluate the effectiveness of *MRW* by mining the search tasks for eight types of queries

Table 2 lists the query types in which the domain column gives the query types. Each domain is identified by a group of instances known as name entities (entity for short). For example, for computer domain, example name entities may be "hp", "ibm thinkpad". Such entities could be easily discovered using proposed methods from web resources. The number of entities we collect for each domain is given in column 2. Then, the domain of a query can be judged easily based on the entity it contains. For example, for query such as "dell laptop price", it will be classified into computer domain. Although this method is very simple, it is yet effective because more than 70% queries contain entities [4]. We then use a one-week log of Bing search from 2010-02-01 to 2010-02-07. For query which appears at least 20 times in the query log, we judge whether it belongs to any of the 8 domains and the number of queries of each domain is also given in Table 2.

Table 2. Eight types of queries for evaluation

Domain	Entity #	Entity Examples	Query #
Computer	6340	dell, ibm thinkpad	14054
City	11388	seattle, new york city	20330
Car	7381	ford, toyota	20310
Cellphone	11476	iphone, nokia	15857
Music Player	11190	ipod, zune, apple nano	21728
Game	12804	world of warcaft	17896
Disease	9370	cough, fever	23335
Restaurant	17444	pizza hut, starbucks	16184

4.2 MRW Effectiveness

We implement *MRW* for each domain to measure the search task oriented similarity between queries. As we introduced above, we build query transition graphs for three views. For document click view, the relationship between queries can be predicted directly from query log because the query log also records the clicked documents after a user issued a query. For search session view, the search session is defined as a logical unit of time-ordered user search behaviors [5]. Then, the relationship between queries of this view can be computed. Lastly, for query term view, we first remove stop words from query. In this paper, the entity names also serve as stop words because we aim to mine the specific search tasks under the domain. Then, each query term is stemmed before measuring the relationship between queries in this view.

After building query transition graphs for each view, we get the search task based similarity between queries by implementing *MRW* in which we set $\alpha = 0.4$ in Equation (9). Then, we cluster queries for each domain based on their similarities. In this paper, we choose agglomerate hierarchy based clustering (*HAC*) [16] to group queries. We use *Avg-Link* [16] to measure the distance between two clusters and choose the clustering result which has the biggest Silhouette Coefficient as the final clustering result. For details, please refer to work [7]. Therefore, the number of clusters will be determined automatically.

Table 3. Some High Traffic Search Tasks for some domains

City		
Tasks	TR	Query examples
Search Lottery Result	4.7	florida lottery, ny lottery org, ny lottery win number, ny pawer ball, Colorado lottery result
Find Education Information	2.3	university of utah, florida colledge and university, Washington county school
Find Local News	1.8	san dieago newspaper, alaska news, boston channel 5 news, channel 7 detroit
Find Local Job Information	1.6	florida job search, ontario labor law, florida employment, texas unemployment payment
Check Weather	1.3	washington dc weather, weather forecast ny, orlando 15 day weather, maryland snow storm
Computer		
Tasks	TR	Query examples
Maintain Driver	19.2	Sony vaio driver download, driver for dell inspiron 6000, hp pavilion sound
Review Computer	11.3	macbook pro review, hp pavilion rate, sony vaio series, dell zino review
Maintain Memory	2.6	dell dimension memory, dell dimension memory upgrade, install ram on dell dimension
Buy Computer	1.4	Lenovo g550 coupon uk, sony vaio ecoupon, dell xps deal sale coupon, discount mini laptops
View Accessory	1.1	Apple macbook accessory, macbook hard cover, mini laptop case, skin for dell inspiron

Table 3 illustrates some high traffic clusters (tasks) for each domain (Due to limited space, we only show the results of two domains). The traffic of a cluster is the sum of traffic of queries in this cluster, and the query traffic is the number of times the query appears in the query log. "*TR*" means traffic rate, the percentage of the cluster traffic in the total traffic of the domain. From Table 3, we can see after clustering queries based on similarities computed by *MRW*, many interesting search tasks are captured for these domains. The names of search tasks in Table 3 are the most frequent query terms of corresponding clusters. We can see that for city domain, the top high traffic clusters correspond to check the "Lottery", "Education", "News", "Job" and "Weather" of a city, which all have traffic more than 1%. These clusters describe the main information need when users issue queries about city. For computer domain, we can see that there are two search tasks "Driver maintain" and "Review computer" which account for a very high traffic rate. This reveals two major search tasks of computer domain are "Review computer" before buying a computer and "Driver maintain" after owning a computer. Some other interesting search tasks of computer domain are "Memory maintain", "Buy computer" and "Computer Accessory".

Parameter Turning

As we mentioned in the above section, *MRW* depends on a parameter $\alpha \in [0,1]$, which is the extra possibility a random surfer retains in the same view when transiting between views. We select α to achieve best performance by manually studying search tasks of some domains. Specifically, we manually study the high traffic search tasks for three domains as shown in Table 4, in which the column represents the domain name, search task names and number of queries annotated for these search tasks.

Table 4. Labeling data for three domains.

Domain	Search Tasks	# of queries
City	Map, News, Real estate, Rental, Tax, Law, Weather…	1304
Computer	Driver, review, Battery, Memory, Motherboard, Buy…	1084
Car	Part, Car Recall, Sale, Payment service, Dealer, Forum…	1959

Then, we evaluate the effectiveness of *MRW* by the average $SimQuality$ coefficient for all annotated search tasks in three domains, in which $SimQuality$ is defined by Equation (10). In Equation (10), $IntraSim(st_i)$and $InterSim(st_i)$ are the average similarity between queries into the same cluster and across clusters respectively. For detail, please see [17].

$$SimQuality(st_i) = IntraSim(st_i)/InterSim(st_i) \qquad (10)$$

Based on $SimQuality$, in Figure 5, we plot the *SimQuality* of *MRW* for different values of α with *SimQuality* being normalized into [0, 1). From Figure 5, we can see when $\alpha \in [0,0.8]$, the *SimQuality* doesn't change too much. *SimQuality* achieves the highest when $\alpha = 0.4$, which corresponds to that the random surfer has about equal possibility to retain in the same view or transit between views. Meanwhile, we can see the best situation is 3% higher than the situation when $\alpha = 0$. This result demonstrates that although involving extra possibility to retain in the same view when transiting across views, the improvement is not so significant. On the other hand, we can see when $\alpha \geq 0.8$, the *SimQuality* decreases sharply. This phenomenon demonstrates that *MRW* tends to get high quality similarity when using big transitions across views, which just proves that the view quality is reasonable measure to guide the walking process.

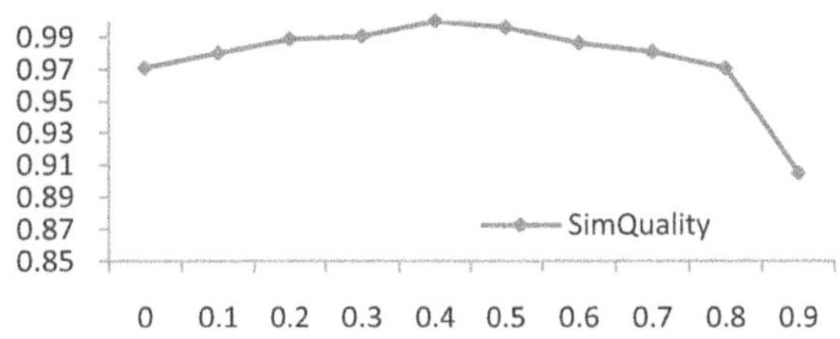

Figure 5. *SimQuality* for *MRW* with different α

Comparison

In Section 2.3 we have prove the *SVRW*, *VIRW* and *LCV* are all special cases of *MRW*. We compare *MRW* with these models via *SimQuality* coefficient. The result is given in Table 5.

Table 5. *SimQuality* Comparison between algorithms.

MRW	*QTV*	*DCV*	*SSV*	*VIRW*	*LCV*
1	0.078	0.352	0.047	0.537	0.848

In Table 5, *QTV*, *DCV* and *SSV* are all *SVRW* models which only use query term view, document click view and search session view respectively. The *SimQuality* of other models are normalized by the *SimQuality* of *MRW*. For *LCV*, we enumerate the parameters to get the best performance. From Table 5, we can see that the *MRW* gets the highest *SimQuality* comparing with the other five algorithms. Table 5 also indicates that the combination of information from different views greatly helps improve the performance for search task discovery. For example, the best situation for single-view random walk is *DCV*, but *DCV* is about 19% percent lower than the situation of *VIRW*, the worst one among algorithms combining the three views. On the other hand, *MRW* has about 15% improvement over *LCV*, which demonstrates that compared with combining the relationship globally for different queries; *MRW* which assigns different cross-view transitions for different queries can actually improve the results.

5. RELATED WORK

The work of this paper focuses on discovering query search task, which has been studied by several previous works. Early efforts of query search task discovery classified the user search goal into given categories [6][8][9][10] which was also known as query classification. Recent query classification works [11][12] tend to leverage the external knowledge of *WordNet* or *Wikipedia* respectively to classify queries. Compared with these works, in this work, we develop a data-driven way to mine search tasks from query log in which the search tasks are not needed to be defined manually as previous works do.

Recently, there are more works focusing on understanding the specific information need behind query by analyzing the query log, such as [1][5][13]. Different from these works which focus on understanding the search task of a single query or simply combine relationships from different views, in this paper, we develop a general framework *MRW* to measure the relationships between queries from multi-sources, in which different information aspects, such as query content, query document click-through and search session, etc, can easily be integrated under *MRW* framework to better identify the query search task. From this aspect, our work is also related to multi-source learning such as [14], in which multi-view spectral clustering is proposed to extend classic single-view normalized cut. Different from [14], our focus in this paper is clustering queries according to their search tasks, in which the size of query clusters need not be normalized. Further correlations between our work and other multi-source learning researches is our ongoing study issues, in which more detailed comparisons and learnings will be conducted in future works.

6. CONCLUSION AND FUTURE WORK

In this paper, we address the problem of discovering the high traffic search tasks from web search queries. Because the query search task may be reflected from different views. We develop a random walk algorithm *MRW*, which combines the relationships between queries from different views in a random walk process. The experiment results demonstrate that *MRW* is effective to discover query search tasks.

The *MRW* algorithm provides us a general way to combine information from different sources. Therefore, the future works could focus on developing better ways to assigning the inter-view transitions for different queries. For example, if we can collect a large number of training data, such inter-view transitions could be learnt appropriately as [2] do.

7. ACKNOWLEDGEMENT

The work was supported in part by the National Nature Science Foundation of China under Grant No. 70871068 and 70890083 and HGJ project 2010ZX01042-002-002-03.

8. REFERENCES

[1] Sadikov, E., Madhavan, J., Wang, L., and Halevy, A. 2010. Clustering query refinements by user intent. In WWW '10.

[2] Sandler, T., Ungar, L. and Crammer K. Resolving Identity Uncertainty with Learned Random Walks. ICDM 2009.

[3] Reed, W-J. The Pareto, Zipf and other power laws. Economics Letters, 74(1):15-19, December 2001.

[4] Xu, G., Yang, S., and Li, H. 2009. Named entity mining from click-through data using weakly supervised latent dirichlet allocation. In SIGKDD 2009. 1365-1374

[5] Cheng, Z., Gao, B., and Liu, T. 2010. Actively predicting diverse search intent from user browsing behaviors. In WWW '10. 221-230.

[6] White, R. W., Bilenko, M., and Cucerzan, S. 2007. Studying the use of popular destinations to enhance web search interaction. In SIGIR '07. 159-166.

[7] Cui, J., Liu, H., He, J., Li, P., Du, X-Y and Wang, P. TagClus: a random walk-based method for tag clustering. In Knowledge and Information Systems Journal. 13 June, 2010.

[8] A. Broder : A taxonomy of web search. SIGIR Forum 2002.

[9] Lee, U., Liu, Z., and Cho, J. 2005. Automatic identification of user goals in Web search. In WWW 2005.

[10] Rose, D. E. and Levinson, D. 2004. Understanding user goals in web search. In WWW 2004. 13-19.

[11] Shen, D., Sun, J., Yang, Q., and Chen, Z. 2006. Building bridges for web query classification. In SIGIR 2006.131-138.

[12] Hu, J., Wang, G., Lochovsky, F., Sun, J., and Chen, Z. 2009. Understanding user's query intent with wikipedia. In WWW 2009. 471-480.

[13] Yin, X. and Shah, S. 2010. Building taxonomy of web search intents for name entity queries. In WWW 2010. 1001-1010.

[14] Zhou. D., Burges, CJ. C. 2007. Spectral clustering and transductive learning with multiple views. ICML 2007

[15] Minkov, E. and Cohen, W. W. 2008. Learning graph walk based similarity measures for parsed text. ACL 2008

[16] Chuang, S-L., Chien, L-F. 2002. Towards automatic generation of query taxonomy: a hierarchical query clustering approach. In ICDM 2002. 75-82.

[17] Ilaria Bordino, Carlos Castillo, Debora Donato, and Aristides Gionis. 2010. Query similarity by projecting the query-flow graph. In SIGIR 2010. 515-522.

Query Sampling for Learning Data Fusion

Ting-Chu Lin and Pu-Jen Cheng
Department of Computer Science and Information Engineering
National Taiwan University, Taiwan
tingchu134@gmail.com and pjcheng@csie.ntu.edu.tw

ABSTRACT

Data fusion is to merge the results of multiple independent retrieval models into a single ranked list. Several earlier studies have shown that the combination of different models can improve the retrieval performance better than using any of the individual models. Although many promising results have been given by supervised fusion methods, training data sampling has attracted little attention in previous work of data fusion. By observing some evaluations on TREC and NTCIR datasets, we found that the performance of one model varied largely from one training example to another, so that not all training examples were equivalently effective. In this paper, we propose two novel approaches: greedy and boosting approaches, which select effective training data by query sampling to improve the performance of supervised data fusion algorithms such as *BayesFuse*, *probFuse* and *MAPFuse*. Extensive experiments were conducted on five data sets including TREC-3,4,5 and NTCIR-3,4. The results show that our sampling approaches can significantly improve the retrieval performance of those data fusion methods.

Categories and Subject Descriptors

H.3.3 [**Information Storage and Retrieval**]: Information Search and Retrieval

General Terms

Algorithms, Experimentation

Keywords

Data fusion, query sampling, *AdaFuse*

1. INTRODUCTION

In the data fusion task [7], the document collections searched by different models should be the same. It is quite different from so-called collection fusion [21], where the search results come from distinct document collections. Data fusion is important in order to exploit multiple models to achieve better performance than any of the individual models. Several earlier studies have shown significant improvement using data fusion such as on the datasets of TREC-2 [5] and Encyclopedia Britannica [4]. Data fusion can also benefit many information retrieval applications such as meta-search [3] and multimodal search [11].

A general solution to the data fusion problem is to develop a score function, which calculates a ranking score for each document in the merged search results; this score determines the final rank of the document. In the previous works, the learning of the function could be unsupervised or supervised. Unsupervised fusion methods such as *BordaFuse* [3], *Condorect Fusion* [17] and *CombMNZ* [7] heuristically determine such a score based merely on the evidences provided by the search results like similarity, rank, and the number of the models retrieving the document. Supervised methods, for example, *SegFuse* [20], *SlideFuse* [14], *PosFuse* [13] and *PLQA* [23], get a better approximation of the score based on the given training data, which shows information about how well the models performed for some given queries before. With such training data, supervised methods can further estimate the quality of the evidences such as the accuracy of a rank position for a specific model [13] and the weight of a model [15], and then adjust the ranking score accordingly.

Supervised methods generally perform better than unsupervised ones [7]. Previous work on supervised methods mostly used all of the training data to learn their fusion models [3, 13, 15]. They assumed ineffective training data was tolerable and could be remedied via data fusion in the process of document retrieval. However, by observing some evaluations on several datasets, we found that the performance of one model varied largely from one training data to another, showing that not all training data should be considered in learning.

Take the *probFuse* algorithm [13] as an example, which is a supervised method. In probFuse, each search-result ranked list is divided into (ranked) segments. The ranking score S_d for document d is defined by:

$$S_d = \sum_{m=1}^{M} \frac{P(d_{k^*}|m)}{k^*} \quad \text{and} \quad P(d_k|m) = \frac{\sum_{q=1}^{Q} \frac{|R_{k,q}|}{|k|}}{Q} \qquad (1)$$

where M is the number of retrieval models, and k^* is the segment that d returned by model m appears in. $P(d_k|m)$ is the probability that document d returned in segment k by model m, where Q is the number of training queries, $R_{k,q}$ is the number of documents in segment k which is relevant to

CIKM'11, October 24–28, 2011, Glasgow, Scotland, UK.

Table 1: Terminology and Explanations

Notations	Explanations
$X = \{(R(q_n), J(q_n))\}_{n=1}^{\|Q\|}$	Training data set
$R(q_n) = \{f_m(D, q_n)\}_{m \in M}$	Ranked lists of q_n
$J(q_n) = \{(d_i, r_i)\}_{i=1}^{\|D\|}, r_i \in \{0, 1\}$	Relevance judgement of query q_n (1:relevant, 0:irrelevant)
$f_m(D, q_n) = [f_m(d_1, q_n), \quad f_m(d_2, q_n), \cdots, f_m(d_{\|D\|}, q_n)]$	Relevance scores of D to q_i
$f_m(d, q_n)$	Relevance score of d to q_n by m
Q	Query set, $q_n \in Q$
D	Document collection, $d \in D$
M	Model set, $m \in M$

query q, and $|k|$ is the total number of documents in segment k. In our experiments, we observed that the variance of segment relevance ($\frac{|R_{k,q}|}{|k|}$) among different training queries was large. When a retrieval model had a higher density of relevant documents at the top for some training queries, the average of the ratios dropped significantly at small k. In this case, sampling all queries for constructing training data could not estimate well for all $P(d_k|m)$. This observation is supported by [13], where probFuse was examined on different size of training sets. The results (in [13]'s Table 4) show that the largest training set didn't achieve the best performance but the size of 20% did. In this paper, we are interested in figuring out how to sample effective queries as training data.

The goal of this paper is to sample a set of queries from given training data, which is used to learn a given data fusion method. Three supervised methods are considered, including *BayesFuse* [3], *probFuse* [13], and *MAPFuse* [15]. We propose two novel query sampling approaches: greedy and boosting. Extensive experiments have been conducted on five data sets including TREC-3,4,5 and NTCIR-3,4. The experimental results show that our sampling approaches can significantly improve the retrieval performance of those data fusion methods.

In the rest of this paper, we first make a brief review on related work in section 2, and describe the proposed greedy and boosting approaches in Section 3. The experiments and discussions are presented in Sections 4. Finally, in Section 5, we present our conclusions and future work.

2. RELATED WORK

It has been shown that the data instances are not equally informative in information retrieval task [10]. The selections of documents and topics (queries) have been studied to affect the efficiency and effectiveness of retrieval evaluation in information retrieval community. With large scale corpora and limited resource, the selection of the best subset of topics which is sufficient for evaluation purpose are discussed in some papers [18, 9], and the collection of documents which balances reducing the corpora size and effectiveness of learning are also studied [2]. However, the purpose of our query sampling is quite different to those works. Our sampling algorithms is for data fusion, in which the input format is several outputs of learning-to-rank or retrieval model. Besides, our goal is to increase the fusion performance by selecting informative training queries from a clean and well-defined data set.

Training data selection has been well studied in machine learning community [6], but relatively little research has been conducted on data fusion in such issue. It has been proposed that learning can be more efficient by actively selecting particular salient training data [16]. In addition, Selection methods for particular learning algorithms such as Support Vector Machine are also discussed [22]. However, there is difficulty in applying above conventional selection methods to the problem of data fusion. The data format of traditional machine learning problem is (feature vector, label) pair, which is different to that of data fusion problem. For performance evaluation, the predictions in machine learning are considered as correctness, but in data fusion, the criteria is the improvement by fusion, i.e., the performance increasing after fusing results. Those gaps are still not sufficiently investigated.

3. QUERY SAMPLING

3.1 Problem Specification

Given a supervised data fusion method and its training data, the goal of this paper is to select a set of effective training data from original one by query sampling for maximizing the retrieval performance of the fusion method. Note that our method should be independent to the adopted fusion method. The process consists of two phases: sampling phase and fusion phase. In the sampling phase, based on the fusion method, our problem is how to sample a set of queries to construct effective training data. Suppose the given training data is denoted as X and the given fusion method is $Fuse$. We want to find

$$X^* = \underset{X' \subseteq X}{\text{argmax}}\ \Omega(Fuse_{\ X'}(X)) \quad (2)$$

where $Fuse_{\ X'}(X)$ stands for the fusion of X using X' as training data, and Ω is the measure of evaluating a fusion model, such as MAP, NDCG and p@k, in this work, MAP (Mean Average Precision) is used. The selected training data $X^* \subseteq X$ should be able to maximize $\Omega(Fuse_{\ X^*}(X))$. In the fusion phase, fusion model $Fuse_{\ X^*}$ is built by applying the given fusion method on sampled training data X^*. The fusion model $Fuse_{\ X^*}$ is then used to merge a set of search results from the retrieval models for a new query. The formal terminology of training data X is listed in Table 1. In this section, two approaches to query sampling for learning data fusion are presented: greedy and boosting.

3.2 Greedy Approaches

To select the most effective training data for improving query performance, one can evaluate the effectiveness of each training instance by sampling a single query. To achieve this, one can exhaustively select each training instance and decide whether a selected data instance improves the query success rate. One can apply either incremental (take-one-in) or decremental (leave-one-out) strategies for the training

Algorithm 1 Independent Greedy Approaches

Top-k take-one-in Indep. Algorithm

1. Given $X = \{T(q_n)\}_{n=1}^{|Q|}$, $T(q_n) = (R(q_n), J(q_n))$
2. For each training example $T(q_n) \in X$:
   - score$(T(q_n)) = \Omega(Fuse_{\{T(q_n)\}}(X))$
3. Sorting: $score(T(q_{\pi(1)})) \geq score(T(q_{\pi(2)})) \geq \cdots score(T(q_{\pi(|Q|)}))$.
   Return top k examples.

Top-k leave-one-out Indep. Algorithm

1. Given $X = \{T(q_n)\}_{n=1}^{|Q|}$, $T(q_n) = (R(q_n), J(q_n))$
2. For each training example $T(q_n) \in X$:
   - $score(T(q_n)) = \Omega(Fuse_{X-\{T(q_n)\}}(X))$
3. Sorting: $score(T(q_{\pi(1)})) \leq score(T(q_{\pi(2)})) \leq \cdots score(T(q_{\pi(|Q|)}))$.
   Return top k examples.

data selection process. Algorithm 1 illustrates the take-one-in procedure, which samples a query data instance at each iteration and determines whether that instance improves the performance. Similar to *Take-one-in*, we also consider *Leave-one-out* for comparison, which iteratively removes the most ineffective training example.

We note that this strategy might not be preferred in traditional machine learning tasks such as classification, since using only few data instances in the first few iterations is typically insufficient to describe the associated learning model, but such method is reasonable in data fusion because that a training example is not just a (feature vector, label) pair. For data fusion purposes, the take-one-in procedure actually utilizes a set of ranked lists and relevant judgments, i.e $(R(q_n), J(q_n))$. Besides, most of the time top-ranked documents from most of the retrieval models have more chances to be relevant to a query. It's adequate to sample a single query for estimating such probabilities.

The dependent greedy approach, as shown in Algorithm 2, always considers those have been collected in the training data when sampling new query. Generally, the independent greedy approach tends to sample queries with high individual co-relations. The dependent one is helpful in sampling those queries that are individually uncorrelated but jointly more correlated for learning data fusion. The parameter k is the specified preferable size of sampled subset, i.e. the k most effective queries.

3.3 Boosting Approaches

The greedy approaches only sample a set of queries as training data. In this section, we extend the *AdaBoost* algorithm [8] to sample a set of weighted queries; the given fusion method is treated as a base learner. We name our boosting approach as *AdaFuse*, which repeatedly constructs base learners on the basis of re-weighted training examples and finally linearly combines them for fusion. Multiple subsets from training data are selected in the process of boosting; each subset improves fusion performance based on partial (weighted) training data.

Algorithm 2 Top-k Take-one-in Dependent Algorithm

1. Given $X = \{T(q_n)\}_{n=1}^{|Q|}$, $X^S = \{\}$, $X^{US} = X$
2. Repeat k times:
   - For each training example $T(q_n) \in X$:
     - $score(T(q_n)) = \Omega(probFuse_{X-\{T(q_n)\}}(X))$
     - Sorting: $score(T(q_{\pi(1)})) \geq score(T(q_{\pi(2)})) \geq \cdots score(T(q_{\pi(|Q|)}))$
     - $X^S = X^S \cup \{T(q_{\pi(1)})\}$,
       $X^{US} = X^{US} - \{T(q_{\pi(1)})\}$
3. Return X^S

3.3.1 Hypothesis Set for Base Learners

Similar to the greedy approaches, AdaFuse is flexible for data fusion since any supervised fusion method can serve as a base learner. The hypothesis set is a set of possible base learners, i.e., fusion models. In this paper, we focus on sampling effective training data; therefore the base learners are constructed by the given fusion method learning with different subset of training data. We define the hypothesis set H in the form of

$$H : R(q) \longrightarrow f(D, q) = \{Fuse_{X'}((R(q))\}_{X' \subseteq X}.$$

We start to achieve H by $\{Fuse_{\{q_n\}}((R(q))\}_{q_n \in Q}$ as the idea of *decision stump* [1]. We construct a base learner for each training query q_n, and repeatedly select the most effective one. This simple hypothesis set improves the fusion performance efficiently. Moreover, considering those queries that are not effective individually but jointly more informative for learning, we enlarge the $\{q_n\}$ to a very small subset with particular size κ, so the H is $\{Fuse_{X'}(R(q))\}_{X' \subseteq X(\kappa)}$, where set $X(\kappa)$ includes $C_\kappa^{|Q|}$ κ-elements-subsets, i.e., the κ-combinations from training query set. The κ is the degree of dependency, which controls the impact of query co-occurrence.

3.3.2 Differences from AdaBoost

The *AdaBoost* algorithm is designed for prediction, namely, the binary classification. Besides that the format of training examples of data fusion differs from that of classification, the main difference between the two tasks is how to evaluate the performance. In classification, a prediction to an example by a hypothesis is evaluated in terms of correctness, i.e., error or correct, but in data fusion, an example fused by a hypothesis is measured by a real value which presents the quality of the merged ranked list, namely, the improvement in performance measure, such as MAP, NDCG and P@k.

It has been proposed that the effectiveness of learned hypothesis can be evaluated based on the concept of *prediction margin* [12, 19]. Given hypothesis h is a function in the form of $h : x_i \rightarrow \Re$; the output $\{+1, -1\}$ is the sign of $h(x_i)$, and the magnitude $|h(x_i)|$ is interpreted as the confidence in this prediction [19]. For a prediction $h(x_i)$, its *prediction margin* is defined as $y_i h(x_i)$, and thus the correct predictions with high confidence may have large prediction margin. The prediction margin represents the "effectiveness of prediction", that is to say, how effective this prediction is.

We interpret the "effectiveness of fusion" as the performance improvement after fusion. Therefore, we propose an new concept of the *improvement margin* ϕ as

$$\phi(J(q_n), f(D, q_n), \overline{\{f_m(D, q_n)\}_{m \in M}}),$$

where ϕ is a function, and $\overline{\{f_m(D, q_n)\}_{m \in M}}$ is the average performance of basis models; we simplify it as $\phi(J(q_n), f(D, q_n))$. The larger the improvement margin is, the better the performance comparing to the basis retrieval models is. This conversion of margin: $y_n h_t(x_n) \Longrightarrow \phi(J(q_n), f(D, q_n))$ helps us to extend the AdaBoost to a variation of boosting algorithm for data fusion. We give a definition of *margin* ϕ which is transformed to $[-1, +1]$ by tan^{-1}.

$$\begin{aligned} &\phi(f(D, g_n), J(q_n), \overline{\{f_m(D, q_i)\}_{m \in M}}) \\ &= tan^{-1}\left(\frac{\Omega(f(D, q_n)) - Mean(\{\Omega(f_m(D, q_n))\}_{m \in M}}{Mean(\{\Omega(f_m(D, q_n))\}_{m \in M}}\right) \end{aligned} \quad (3)$$

Besides, any definition in the range $[-1, +1]$ can be used.

3.3.3 A Variation of Boosting for Data Fusion

By extending the Adaboost with our improvement margin, we propose AdaFuse as the boosting algorithm for data fusion, which learns a simple rule to maximize the weighted sum of improvement margin from weighted training examples; the confidence of each hypothesis is evaluated in terms of such rule. The details are shown in Algorithm 3.

Algorithm 3 AdaFuse: Boosting for Data Fusion

1. Given the training data: $\{(R(q_n), J(q_n))\}_{n=1}^{N}$
2. Initialize: $P_1(n) = 1/N$ for all n
3. For $t = 1, 2, 3, ..., T$:
   - Define margin of prediction: $\phi(J(q_i), h_t(D, q_i)) \rightarrow [-1, +1]$
   - Define hypothesis set: H
   - Base learner's goal now is to maximize $|r_t|$

   $$\begin{aligned} h_t &= argmax_{h \in H}\, r_t \\ r_t &= E_{n \sim P_t}[\phi(J(q_n), h_t(D, q_n))] \\ &= \sum_{n=1}^{N} P_t(n)\phi(J(q_n), h_t(D, q_n)) \end{aligned}$$

   - Confidence $\alpha_t = \frac{1}{2} ln(\frac{1+r_t}{1-r_t})$
   - Update weight $P_{t+1}(n) = \frac{P_t(n)}{Z_t} exp(-\alpha_t \cdot \phi(J(q_n), h_t(D, q_n)))$ where Z_t is a normalization factor (chosen so that P_{t+1} will be a distribution)
4. Output the final hypothesis:

   $$f(D, q) = \sum_{t=1}^{T} \alpha_t h_t(D, q)$$

   $$h_t(D, q) = Fuse_{X_t^*}(q)$$

   - X_t^* : best subset chosen by iteration t

4. EXPERIMENTS

Two data sets were used in the experiments. One was from the TREC-3, TREC-4 and TREC-5 (CategoryA only) ad-hoc IR tasks. The other was from NTCIR-3 and NTCIR-4 ad-hoc IR tasks, and the relax judgment was used rather than the rigid one. We used the Lemur toolkit[1] to support the construction of the 7 retrieval models in our experiments.

Two experimental settings were considered. The first setting is evaluated by the output of the 5-folds cross validation (CV) with all models used. We followed [13, 15] to perform five random runs (RR) as the second setting. Each run had 6 models without repetitiveness. 50% of queries were treated as training data and the rest as testing data. Each algorithm in our experiments was compared in the same division of training data, testing data and retrieval models.

We tested our query sampling approaches on 3 fusion methods, including *BayesFuse* [3], *MAPFuse* [15] and *probFuse* [13], which have been shown to superior than the papular unsupervised fusion method CombMNZ [7]. These methods without training data selection were viewed as the baselines.

The *BayesFuse* algorithm is based on Bayesian inference [3] and ranks documents by

$$rel(d) = \sum_{m=1}^{M} log \frac{Pr[r_m(d)|rel]}{Pr[r_m(d)|irr]} \quad (4)$$

where $Pr[r_m(d)|rel]$ is the probability that a relevant document would be ranked at level r by retrieval m, and $Pr[r_m(d)|irr]$ is the probability of an irrelevant document.

MAPFuse approximates the probability of a document returned at rank position x by model m is relevant by $\frac{MAP_m}{x}$. MAP_m is the MAP score of training query set by retrieval model m. The final ranking score R_d for document d is

$$\sum_{m \in M} \frac{MAP_m}{p_m(d)} \quad (5)$$

where M is the set of retrieval models and $p_m(d)$ is the ranking position that retrieval model m ranks document d. The training process only needs the MAPs of training queries.

We compared the MAPs of applying Top-k Take-One-In indep., Leave-One-Out indep., and Top-k Take-One-In dep. with the k most effective queries. Figures 2 lists the performance evaluated by CV and RR. In general, the MAP scores for CV are higher than those for RR because all models were used in CV where only some models were used in RR. Most of the MAP curves share an interesting tendency: the curves keep going up in the first few interactions. After the peak is reached, the curves go down. Notice that the peaks were achieved for $k < 10$ in BayesFuse cases, $k < 5$ for probFuse cases and even less for MAPFuse, meaning only a few training examples were critical to constructing a high-performance fusion model. Take-One-In dep. performed better than Take-One-In indep., but some cases they both failed in improvement because unsuitable queries were selected in early stages. Although there was significant performance improvement in TREC data sets, greedy approaches were only observed limited gain in NTCIR.

To observe the boosting behavior of each iteration, we examined the five CV folds of boosting process. Figure 1

[1]http://www.lemurproject.org/, Build-in retrieval models: (1)TFIDF (2)Okapi (3)Simple KL (4)INQUERY (5)CORI CS (6)Cosine Similarity and (7)INDRI.

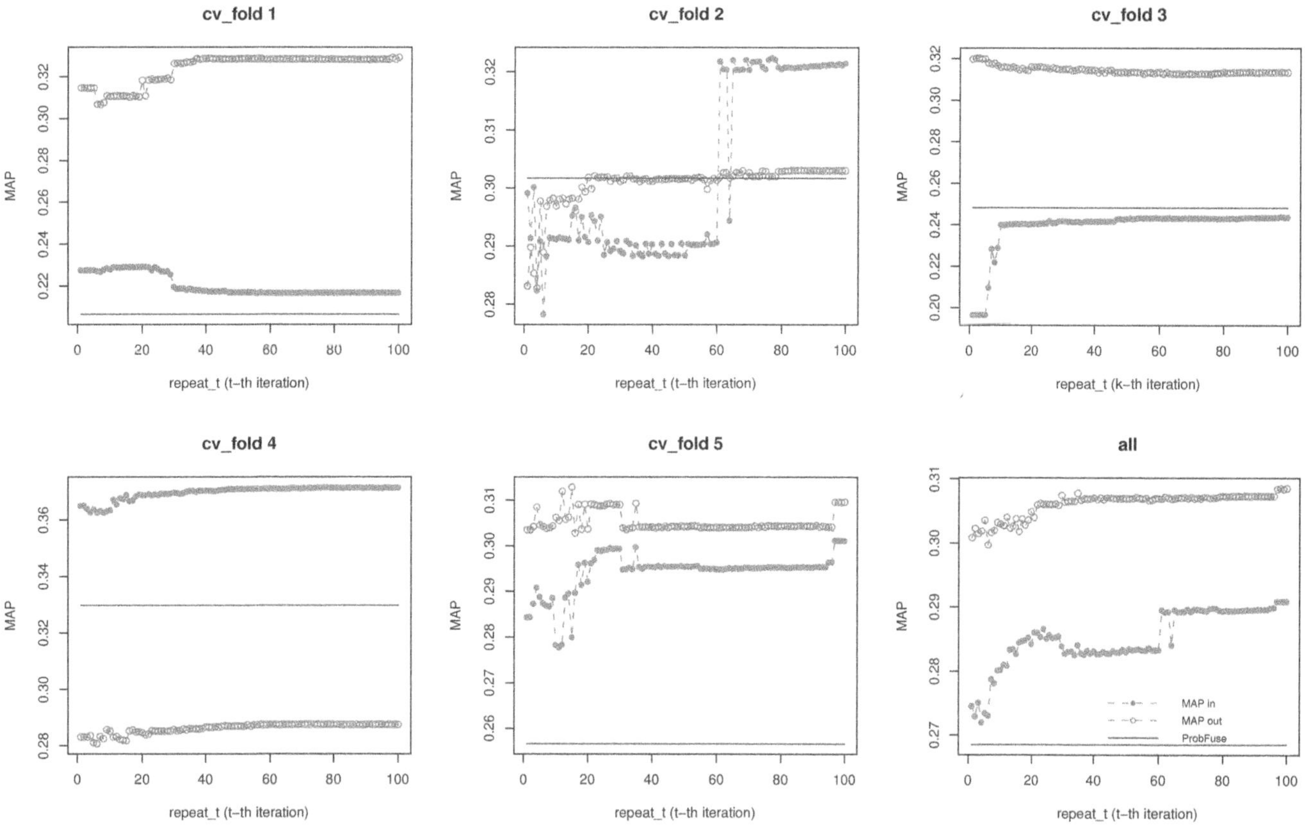

Figure 1: MAP scores of greedy approaches

demonstrates the analysis of individual fold in NTCIR-3 with AdaFuse. The MAP-in was MAP score obtained by fusion only training queries, and the MAP-out is that from testing set. We marked the two curves in order to observe the tendency of learning; note that the MAP-in increased with each training iteration and the MAP-out followed the same tendency except in the fold 1, which maybe slightly over-fitting. The baseline was compared with only MAP-out, since the MAP-in and MAP-out are fused from different queries and could not be compared.

The greedy approaches selected only 5-6 queries to achieve promising results, so we tried the degree of dependency $\kappa = 1, 2, 3, 4$ and reported the best MAP of the four results. The union of each multiple subset selection by each iterator was larger than 5-6 queries, but in our experiments with 100 iterators, none of our approaches sampled more than half of original training queries, which still supports our assumption that not every query is effective.

We summarized the experiments in Table 2. In most of the cases, the two-tailed P-value of t-test less being than 0.01 showed that the difference is statistically significant comparing with the baseline: probFuse, MAPfuse and BayesFuse. The boosting approaches performed much higher than the greedy approaches, but the time complexity of the boosting approach is much larger than the greedy approach, and both fusion processes take the same time. Note that the NTCIR data set, on which greedy approaches did not performed well, got a large improvement by boosting approaches; improving even more than the TREC dataset. In general, the boosting process needs more training time, but the performance is more stable than greedy approaches because if some biased queries are chosen at an early stage, greedy approaches fail to compensate, but boosting processes have a chance to emphasize other effective queries by iteratively updating weight.

5. CONCLUSIONS AND FUTURE WORK

By means of query sampling, the retrieval performance can be improved significantly for conventional supervised data fusion methods. In this paper, we proposed two useful approaches for query sampling. Extensive experiments have been conducted on five data sets, including TREC-3,4,5 and NTCIR-3,4. The results show the feasibility of the proposed approaches. Our AdaFuse is a framework for any fusion algorithm and possible hypothesis set, not limited in queries sampling purpose. Future work will include the adoption of more complicated and powerful base learners and use new definition of margin in our boosting framework.

6. REFERENCES

[1] W. I. Ai and P. Langley. Induction of one-level decision trees. In *ICML*. Morgan Kaufmann, 1992.

[2] J. A. Aslam, E. Kanoulas, V. Pavlu, S. Savev, and E. Yilmaz. Document selection methodologies for efficient and effective learning-to-rank. In *SIGIR*. ACM, 2009.

[3] J. A. Aslam and M. Montague. Models for metasearch. In *SIGIR*. ACM, 2001.

[4] B. T. Bartell, G. W. Cottrell, and R. K. Belew. Automatic combination of multiple ranked retrieval systems. In *SIGIR*, 1994.

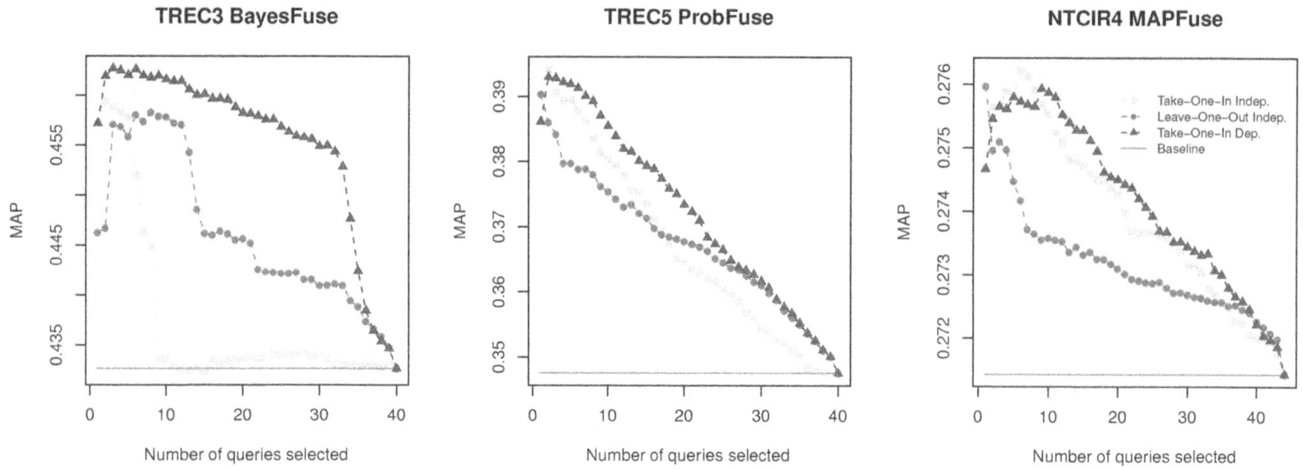

Figure 2: MAP scores of greedy approaches

Table 2: Summery of all the query sampling approaches. * p-value < 0.01

	Cross Validation					Random Runs		
	TREC3	TREC4	TREC5	NTCIR3	NTCIR4	TREC3	TREC4	TREC5
probFuse	0.41866	0.38924	0.34756	0.26778	0.26942	0.33496	0.32843	0.32331
take-1-in	0.43994*	0.40836*	0.39422*	0.27049*	0.27074*	0.35148*	0.33668*	0.33396*
leave-1-out	0.43485*	0.40880*	0.39037*	0.26972*	0.27072*	0.34910*	0.33201*	0.33203*
take-1-in.Dep	0.44068*	0.41241*	0.39301*	0.26860	0.27133*	0.35234*	0.33956*	0.33445*
AdaFuse	0.45887*	0.41268*	0.40156*	0.29241**	0.29476*	0.37195*	0.35260*	0.35949*
BayesFuse	0.43266	0.38339	0.33256	0.27224	0.27270	0.36107	0.27090	0.29515
take-1-in	0.45945*	0.38842*	0.37017*	0.27903*	0.27438	0.36234*	0.34247*	0.31755*
leave-1-out	0.45831*	0.38495*	0.36915*	0.27224	0.27438	0.36925*	0.31705*	0.32704*
take-1-in.Dep	0.46268*	0.41277*	0.37712*	0.27511*	0.27438	0.37005*	0.34688*	0.32643*
AdaFuse	0.45126*	0.40298*	0.39295*	0.30508*	0.29477*	0.35779*	0.34439*	0.35561*
MAPFuse	0.39799	0.36232	0.33691	0.29008	0.27143	0.31662	0.31292	0.33452
take-1-in	0.44303*	0.39458*	0.39035*	0.29227*	0.27622*	0.33387*	0.33257*	0.35254*
leave-1-out	0.44252*	0.38844*	0.36658*	0.28980	0.27579*	0.33399*	0.32934*	0.35088*
take-1-in.Dep	0.44303*	0.39420*	0.38879*	0.29059	0.27593	0.33387*	0.33257*	0.35370*
AdaFuse	0.45179*	0.41583*	0.40147*	0.30472*	0.29026*	0.36212*	0.35179*	0.35318*

[5] N. J. Belkin, P. Kantor, E. A. Fox, and J. A. Shaw. Combining the evidence of multiple query representations for information retrieval. *IP&M*, 1995.

[6] A. L. Blum and P. Langley. Selection of relevant features and examples in machine learning. *Artificial Intelligence*, 1997.

[7] J. A. S. Edward A. Fox. Combination of multiple searches. In *TREC-2*. NIST, 1994.

[8] Y. Freund and R. E. Schapire. A decision-theoretic generalization of on-line learning and an application to boosting. In *EuroCOLT*. Springer, 1995.

[9] J. Guiver, S. Mizzaro, and S. Robertson. A few good topics: Experiments in topic set reduction for retrieval evaluation. *TOIS*, 2009.

[10] C. Hauff, D. Hiemstra, F. de Jong, and L. Azzopardi. Relying on topic subsets for system ranking estimation. In *CIKM*. ACM, 2009.

[11] L. S. Kennedy, A. P. Natsev, and S.-F. Chang. Automatic discovery of query-class-dependent models for multimodal search. In *MULTIMEDIA*. ACM, 2005.

[12] L. Li, A. Pratap, H. tien Lin, and Y. S. Abu-mostafa. Improving generalization by data categorization. In *PKDD 2005*. Springer, 2005.

[13] D. Lillis, F. Toolan, R. Collier, and J. Dunnion. Probfuse: a probabilistic approach to data fusion. In *SIGIR*. ACM, 2006.

[14] D. Lillis, F. Toolan, R. Collier, and J. Dunnion. Extending probabilistic data fusion using sliding windows. In *ECIR*. Springer, 2008.

[15] D. Lillis, L. Zhang, F. Toolan, R. W. Collier, D. Leonard, and J. Dunnion. Estimating probabilities for effective data fusion. In *SIGIR*. ACM, 2010.

[16] D. J. C. MacKay. Information-based objective functions for active data selection. *Neural Computation*, 1992.

[17] M. Montague and J. A. Aslam. Condorcet fusion for improved retrieval. In *CIKM*. ACM, 2002.

[18] S. Robertson. On the contributions of topics to system evaluation. In *ECIR*. Springer, 2011.

[19] R. E. Schapire and Y. Singer. Improved boosting algorithms using confidence-rated predictions. *Machine Learning*, 1999.

[20] M. Shokouhi. Segmentation of search engine results for effective data-fusion. In *ECIR*. Springer, 2007.

[21] E. M. Voorhees, N. K. Gupta, and B. Johnson-laird. The collection fusion problem. In *TREC-3*. NIST.

[22] J. Wang, P. Neskovic, and L. N. Cooper. Training data selection for support vector machines. In *ICNC. LNCS*. Springer, 2005.

[23] R. Yan and A. G. Hauptmann. Probabilistic latent query analysis for combining multiple retrieval sources. In *SIGIR*. ACM, 2006.

Query Session Detection as a Cascade*

Matthias Hagen Benno Stein Tino Rüb

Bauhaus-Universität Weimar
99421 Weimar, Germany
<first name>.<last name>@uni-weimar.de

ABSTRACT

We propose a cascading method for query session detection, the problem of identifying series of consecutive queries a user submits with the same information need. While the existing session detection research mostly deals with effectiveness, our focus also is on efficiency, and we investigate questions related to the analysis trade-off: How expensive (in terms of runtime) is a certain improvement in F-Measure? In this regard, we distinguish two major scenarios where query session knowledge is important: (1) In an online setting, the search engine tries to incorporate knowledge of the preceding queries for an improved retrieval performance. Obviously, the efficiency of the session detection method is a crucial issue as the overall retrieval time should not be influenced too much. (2) In an offline post-retrieval setting, search engine logs are divided into sessions in order to examine what causes users to fail or to identify typical reformulation patterns etc. Here, efficiency might not be as important as in the online scenario but the accuracy of the detected sessions is essential.

Our cascading method provides a sensible treatment for both scenarios. It involves different steps that form a cascade in the sense that computationally costly and hence time-consuming features are applied only after cheap features "failed." This is different to previous session detection methods, most of which involve many features simultaneously. Experiments on a standard test corpus show the cascading method to save runtime compared to the state of the art while the detected sessions' accuracy is even superior.

Categories and Subject Descriptors: H.3.3 [Information Storage and Retrieval]: Query formulation, Search process
General Terms: Algorithms, Experimentation
Keywords: Web Search, Session Detection, Cascading Method

1. INTRODUCTION

We tackle the problem of query session detection, which aims at identifying consecutive queries a user submits for the same information need. Detecting such search sessions is of major interest as they offer the possibility to analyze potential techniques for supporting users stuck in longer sessions, to learn from the users' query reformulation patterns, or to obtain knowledge on how users behave when their initial queries were not satisfactory.

*Extended version of a paper presented at the ECIR 2011 Workshop on Information Retrieval over Query Sessions (SIR 11) [7].

CIKM'11, October 24–28, 2011, Glasgow, Scotland, UK.

Usually, the queries of a user form a stream ordered by submission time and are recorded in a query log by the search engines. Session detection for a single user then can be modeled as the task of deciding for each pair of chronologically consecutive queries whether the two queries were submitted for the same information need or not. This applies for an online scenario where the search engine is observing the user while searching, but also for an offline scenario where a recorded query log should be divided into the contained query sessions for further examination.

In an online scenario, session detection aims at supporting the user in satisfying her information need. Incorporating the knowledge of the queries that belong together may help the engine to present better results (e.g., the task of the TREC Sessions track) or to suggest queries that other users used in similar situations. Since online session detection is most useful when applied pre-retrieval, the efficiency of the detection method plays a crucial role. The overall retrieval time should not be increased too much in order not to cause a worse search experience at user site.

In an offline post-retrieval scenario, the goal of session detection is to identify typical reformulation patterns or to examine how search processes that finished satisfactory are different from such that are not. The efficiency of the session detection method is not as crucial as in the online scenario although faster methods are still favorable. However, the accuracy of the detected sessions is even more important than in the online scenario as conclusions drawn from examining large logs become more reasonable when the underlying data in form of detected query sessions is more reliable.

Our new approach for session detection—the cascading method—addresses both scenarios, online and offline detection. Unlike former approaches to the problem the cascading method does not require the simultaneous evaluation of all features. Instead, it processes the features in different steps one after the other by increasing computational costs and thus by increasing runtime requirements. Whenever a computationally cheap feature allows for a reliable decision, features with higher cost and runtime are not considered. If, however, the cheaper features do not provide a reliable decision basis, additional features are involved. For example, if a query contains the preceding query (e.g., `istanbul` and `istanbul archeology`), it is reasonable to assume that both queries belong to the same session. No other feature besides a simple query subset test is needed for that decision. For more complex situations like `istanbul archeology` and `constantinople`, the simple subset test fails but computationally more costly features that are able to identify semantic similarities can support the desired decision of also assigning these two queries to the same session (as Constantinople is the ancient name of Istanbul).

Query sessions are an interesting field of research with many published detection methods and also many studies that examine search behavior in sessions, query reformulation patterns, or improved retrieval techniques for known query sessions. In such studies, session detection is applied in a pre-processing step to obtain experimental data in form of sessions from a stored log. However, there is a huge gap between the state-of-the-art session detection methods and the ones that are practically used in the pre-processing of such studies. Most often the studies apply a simple time threshold: two queries belong to the same session iff the time gap between the queries is smaller than a given threshold (e.g., 5 or 10 minutes). The time threshold criterion is a very fast method but with a bad accuracy compared to more sophisticated methods. Is it the runtime alone that "bribes" so many studies to use time thresholds, although the bad accuracy is well known? In our opinion, there is an additional third critical issue that influences success of session detection methods besides the already mentioned efficiency and effectiveness: the simplicity of the method or, more precisely, the ease of re-implementation. In fact, time threshold methods are both very easy to be operationalized and extremely fast—two arguments that might give a reasonable trade-off for accepting inferior accuracy. In order to have a practical impact and to be applied by researchers, we argue that new detection methods should be equally fast and simple as time thresholds (and by far more accurate).

Our cascading method aims at bridging the described gap between developed and practically used methods. It is more easy to be implemented than many sophisticated state-of-the-art detection methods which often require intricate and not documented parameter tuning or training on data not available to the public. Furthermore, the cascading method is only about 4–5 times slower than a simple time threshold, making it faster than the current state of the art. These features come with an even superior accuracy of the detected sessions on a standard test corpus.

2. RELATED WORK

The earliest methods for session detection were mostly time based: two consecutive queries belong to the same session whenever the time elapsed is smaller than some threshold. Different time gaps have been tried and documented in the literature: 5 minutes [4], 10–15 minutes [8], 30 minutes [16], 60 minutes [2], or even 120 minutes [2]. The time thresholds were usually not intended to detect queries with the same information need but rather to study search behavior on bunches of queries. Nevertheless, time thresholds are an often used method to gather sessions in the "modern" notion of queries with the same information need (although the achievable accuracy is at most 70% [12]). As elaborated earlier, one reason for using time thresholds might be the very attractive simplicity compared to other existing session detection methods.

To overcome the bad accuracy of time thresholds, other methods also incorporate lexical features. For instance, queries that do not share any term often indicate a new session [10]. Other applied lexical features are the Levenshtein distance (how many operations are needed to transform one query into the other) [12] or the Jaccard coefficient (how large is the overlap) [13]. Some methods judge typical patterns like repeated query, specialization, or generalization as session continuations [11] or try to identify reformulations based on rules for changed words, deleted word suffixes, etc. [9].

However, all these lexical features are not able to determine semantic relatedness like in our introducing `istanbul archeology` vs. `constantinople` example. These two queries share no term and have very few overlapping character n-grams. For such cases several semantic features have been examined. An interesting idea is to enrich the short query strings in order to get a longer representation of the underlying information need. One possibility is to use the actual search results and researchers have tried the first 10 results [16], 50 results [18], 100 results [3], or even 500 results [14]. The methods then check the overlap of the set of URLs, the standard cosine similarity of the page titles and snippets, or even the cosine similarity of the result documents themselves [17]. In a very recent method the well-known ESA framework is applied for semantic similarity checks [13]. The ESA framework evaluates semantic similarity by comparing representations of the queries in a background collection (like Wikipedia documents) [5].

Table 1: Example query log. First the user had a Turkish history intent and then turned to a CIKM venue sports intent.

ID	Query	Click domain + rank		Time
42	`istanbul`	en.wikipedia.org	1	2011-05-22 20:34:17
42	`istanbul archeology`			2011-05-23 12:02:54
42	`istanbul archeology`	www.turizm.tr	6	2011-05-23 12:03:15
42	`istanbul archeology`	www.arkeoloji.tr	13	2011-05-23 18:24:07
42	`constantinople`			2011-05-23 19:12:40
42	`constantinople`	en.wikipedia.org	4	2011-05-23 19:13:02
42	`soccr glasgo`			2011-05-23 19:16:01
42	`soccer glasgow`			2011-05-23 19:16:11
42	`soccer glasgow`	www.soccer.uk	3	2011-05-23 19:16:15
42	`celtics vs rangers`			2011-05-23 20:33:04
42	`celtics vs rangers`	en.wikipedia.org	5	2011-05-23 20:33:12
42	`old firm`			2011-05-23 22:42:48

Most of the aforementioned features are not used alone (time thresholds being the main exception) but applied in different combinations. However, different features come with different computation costs and thus influence efficiency. For a query repetition it is obviously not necessary to check the search results in order to assign both queries to the same session. But none of the published session detection methods explicitly examines the efficiency aspect. Different to that line of research, we carefully design our new cascading method with respect to efficiency aspects. We also combine several features but involve time-consuming features only when cheaper features do not allow for a reliable decision.

We compare our method to the state-of-the-art geometric method by Gayo-Avello [6]. In his survey, Gayo-Avello compares most of the existing session detection approaches on a gold standard of human annotated queries and shows the geometric method's superiority in terms of detection accuracy. The geometric method is a very simple and fast method; it involves only the two basic features time threshold and lexical similarity. However, as a stand-alone approach, the geometric method is not able to detect semantic similarities. Hence, our cascading method builds upon the geometric method but equips it with simple additional steps. Our objective is threefold: a runtime performance comparable to the geometric method, a similar ease of implementation, and a further improved accuracy. In our cascading method we use an adapted version of the geometric method as the second of our four steps. In a first pre-processing step, simple patterns (repetitions, specializations, or generalizations) are identified and in two post-processing steps semantically related queries are detected. The pre-processing step ensures to save runtime compared to the original geometric method while the post-processing further improves accuracy.

3. PRELIMINARIES

A query q consists of a set of keywords. The search engine log additionally contains a user ID and a time stamp. If the user clicked on a result, the clicked result's rank and URL are also logged. We explain our cascading framework for the queries submitted by one user ordered by submission time. The problem of session detection is modeled as the problem of deciding for each consecutive pair q, q' of queries whether the session s that contains q continues with q' or whether q' starts a new session.

An example of a typical query log is given in Table 1 (the log

Table 2: Detected sessions after processing Step 1.

ID	Query	Click domain + rank		Time
42	istanbul	en.wikipedia.org	1	2011-05-22 20:34:17
42	istanbul archeology			2011-05-23 12:02:54
42	istanbul archeology	www.turizm.tr	6	2011-05-23 12:03:15
42	istanbul archeology	www.arkeoloji.tr	13	2011-05-23 18:24:07
42	constantinople			2011-05-23 19:12:40
42	constantinople	en.wikipedia.org	4	2011-05-23 19:13:02
42	soccr glasgo			2011-05-23 19:16:01
42	soccer glasgow			2011-05-23 19:16:11
42	soccer glasgow	www.soccer.uk	3	2011-05-23 19:16:15
42	celtics vs rangers			2011-05-23 20:33:04
42	celtics vs rangers	en.wikipedia.org	5	2011-05-23 20:33:12
42	old firm			2011-05-23 22:42:48

even contains a misspelled query right after the indicated intent boundary). Note that time is not a good indicator of session boundaries in the example as the user sometimes stopped working for longer time periods and then continued a pending session. For instance, in the last two queries, `old firm` is the name of the Glasgow `celtics vs rangers` soccer derby and both queries obviously have the same search intent. Regardless of the time passed, we assume that in such cases the user just continued the session. Another interesting observation is that at the highlighted search intent switch the passed time is quite short.

4. THE CASCADE: STEP BY STEP

Our cascading session detection method consists of four steps. From step to step the required features get more expensive in the sense of needed runtime but later steps are invoked only if the previous steps were not able to come to a reliable decision.

Step 1: Simple Query String Comparison

The most simple patterns that two consecutive queries q and q' may form can be detected by a simple comparison of the keywords: repetition ($q = q'$), generalization ($q' \subset q$), and specialization ($q \subset q'$). Whenever two consecutive queries represent one of these three cases, the cascading method assigns the queries to the same session regardless of the time that has passed between their submission. The rationale is that in case of a longer time gap, we assume the user to have continued a pending session. The effect of Step 1 in the example scenario is shown in Table 2. Note that Step 1 reliably detects generalizations and specializations, and captures all the interactions for the same queries. No other features have to be involved "inside" of the sessions that Step 1 detected. However, all the session boundaries cannot be trusted. Hence, for these cases, our cascading method invokes the geometric method [6] in Step 2 as a more sophisticated comparison of the query strings.

Step 2: Geometric Method

The geometric method [6] relaxes Step 1's query overlap condition with respect to the elapsed time between the queries. Let t and t' be the submission times of a pair q and q' of consecutive queries. Using the offset $t' - t$, the geometric method computes the time feature $f_{\text{time}} = \max\{0, 1 - \frac{t'-t}{24h}\}$. Thus, chronologically very close queries achieve scores near to 1 whereas longer time periods between query submissions decrease the score until it gets 0 for queries with a gap of 24 hours or larger. The lexical similarity f_{lex} for q' is computed as the cosine similarity of the character 3- to 5-grams of the query q' and the session s whose current last query is q. The geometric method votes for a session continuation

Table 3: Detected sessions after processing Step 2.

ID	Query	Click domain + rank		Time
42	istanbul	en.wikipedia.org	1	2011-05-22 20:34:17
42	istanbul archeology			2011-05-23 12:02:54
42	istanbul archeology	www.turizm.tr	6	2011-05-23 12:03:15
42	istanbul archeology	www.arkeoloji.tr	13	2011-05-23 18:24:07
42	constantinople			2011-05-23 19:12:40
42	constantinople	en.wikipedia.org	4	2011-05-23 19:13:02
42	soccr glasgo			2011-05-23 19:16:01
42	soccer glasgow			2011-05-23 19:16:11
42	soccer glasgow	www.soccer.uk	3	2011-05-23 19:16:15
42	celtics vs rangers			2011-05-23 20:33:04
42	celtics vs rangers	en.wikipedia.org	5	2011-05-23 20:33:12
42	old firm			2011-05-23 22:42:48

iff $\sqrt{(f_{\text{time}})^2 + (f_{\text{lex}})^2} \geq 1$. This inequality can be geometrically interpreted as plotting the point $(f_{\text{time}}, f_{\text{lex}})$ in the $\mathbb{R}^2$ and checking whether it lies inside or outside the unit circle (cf. Figure 1 (a)).

The effect in our example scenario is shown in Table 3 (remember that Step 2 is invoked only when Step 1 decided for new session). The geometric method correctly decides to remove the intent switch between the queries `soccr glasgo` and `soccer glasgow` as the elapsed time is rather short and many character n-grams overlap. This way, the geometric method is able to catch many typos and their corrections as often the corrected queries are lexically very similar and submitted within a small time gap.

Nevertheless, there are problematic cases where the geometric method cannot be trusted. There are three such session boundaries in Table 3 where this happens. One example is the pair `istanbul archeology` and `constantinople`. The only overlapping 3- to 5-grams of `constantinople` with the previous session are `sta`, `stan`, and `tan` such that the geometric method decides for a new intent. However, knowing that the ancient name of Istanbul was Constantinople, one would expect both queries to belong to the same session as semantically they are very similar. The other pairs in our example scenario are `soccer glasgow` and `celtics vs rangers`, and `celtics vs rangers` and `old firm`. As the Celtics and the Rangers are soccer teams from Glasgow and their derby is named "Old Firm," there should be no intent breaks.

Common to all three cases in the example scenario is that for the query pairs f_{time} is large (i.e., queries are chronologically close) but the lexical similarity reflected by f_{lex} is rather low. We conducted a pilot experiment to further examine where the geometric method fails. Therefore, we took a 10% sample of consecutive query pairs from the standard session detection corpus by Gayo-Avello [6] and analyzed the accuracy of the geometric method. Note that the remaining 90% of the corpus form our test set also used for evaluation in Session 5. Especially for pairs with $f_{\text{lex}} < 0.4$ and $f_{\text{time}} > 0.8$ the sample contained many wrong decisions (feature values tested in steps of 0.2).

To show that the derived bounds $f_{\text{lex}} < 0.4$ and $f_{\text{time}} > 0.8$ are also reasonable for the test set, Figures 1 (b) and (c) show the points in the $\mathbb{R}^2$ that the geometric method derives on the test set. Obviously, most pairs within a session are close to the right vertical border of the diagram, while pairs with a session break are close to the lower border. Cases where the geometric method decides wrongly are all the black dots in Figure 1 (b) that lie inside the unit circle and all the red dots in Figure 1 (c) that lie outside the unit circle. Figure 1 (d) gives the frequencies of the geometric method's errors. In the lower right corner ($f_{\text{lex}} < 0.4$ and $f_{\text{time}} > 0.8$) there are $583 + 14$ query pairs wrongly assigned to different sessions

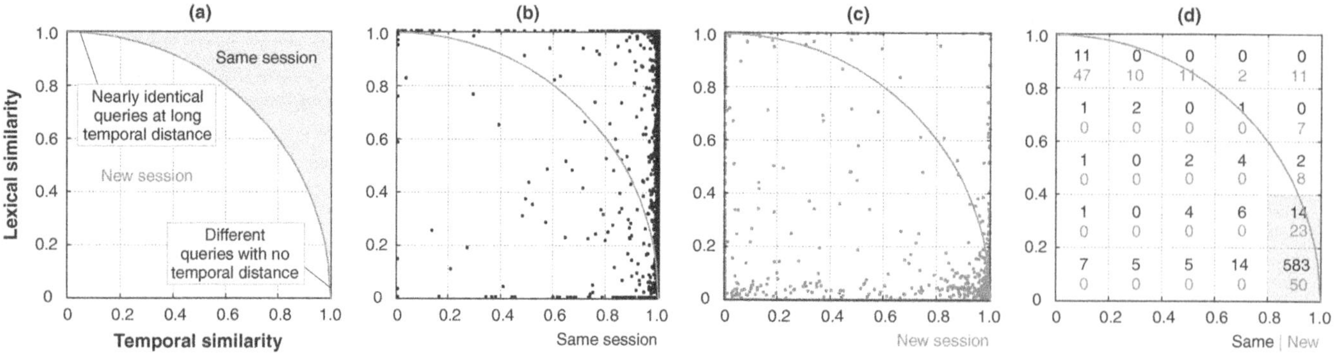

Figure 1: (a) Geometric interpretation of the geometric method. (b) Feature values of the geometric method for query pairs with "same session" annotation in the test corpus. (c) Feature values of the geometric method for query pairs with "new session" annotation in the test corpus. (d) Error frequency distribution of the geometric method's decisions. Black frequencies are query pairs wrongly assigned to different sessions. Red frequencies are pairs wrongly assigned to the same session.

although semantically related and $23 + 50$ query pairs wrongly assigned to the same session although semantically different.

Hence, for query pairs that are chronologically very close and lexically very different, the decisions of the geometric method are not reliable. Some of the respective pairs will not be related and correspond to real intent switches but some will have high semantic similarity and thus correspond to session continuations with different wordings. To detect these semantic relatedness or difference of queries, our cascading method drops the geometric method's decision for pairs that fall in the lower right corner and invokes Step 3 to further analyze semantic similarity.

Step 3: Explicit Semantic Analysis

An elegant way to compare semantic similarity of two short texts is the explicit semantic analysis (ESA) introduced by Gabrilovich and Markovitch [5]. The idea is to not compare the given two texts directly but to use an indexed background collection against which similarities are calculated. Since the index collection (e.g., the Wikipedia articles) can be pre-processed and stored, invoking ESA is not too expensive compared to the basic session detection features such as n-gram overlap or query submission time.

The ESA principle works as follows. During a pre-processing step, a $tf \cdot idf$-weighted term-document-matrix of the Wikipedia articles is stored as the ESA matrix. During runtime, the two to-be-compared texts represented as vectors are multiplied with the ESA matrix and the cosine similarity of the resulting vectors yields the ESA similarity feature f_{esa}. In our setting, the two texts that should be ESA-compared are the keywords of q' and all the keywords of the queries in the session s to which the previous query q belongs. As Anderka and Stein [1] showed that the ESA performance varies only very little with the size of the index collection, we conducted a pilot experiment on the 10% subsample of Gayo-Avello's corpus also used in the analysis of Step 2. We randomly sampled English Wikipedia articles (10 000, 100 000, 1 million, all) and could verify Anderka and Stein's observation that the size of the index collection did not really matter for the accuracy of the session decisions except that 10 000 articles performed a little worse than the larger sizes. Hence, the cascading method's Step 3 implementation uses a random sample of 100 000 Wikipedia articles as the ESA index collection. Our pilot experiment also reveals that for $f_{\text{esa}} \geq 0.35$ (we tested in steps of 0.05) a quite reliable decision can be made that the two examined queries belong to the same session.

Table 4 shows the effect of Step 3 in our example scenario. The intent switches between the queries `istanbul archeology` and `constantinople` and between `soccer glasgow` and `celtics vs rangers` are correctly removed. However, the session break

Table 4: Detected sessions after processing Step 3.

ID	Query	Click domain + rank	Time
42	`istanbul`	en.wikipedia.org 1	2011-05-22 20:34:17
42	`istanbul archeology`		2011-05-23 12:02:54
42	`istanbul archeology`	www.turizm.tr 6	2011-05-23 12:03:15
42	`istanbul archeology`	www.arkeoloji.tr 13	2011-05-23 18:24:07
42	`constantinople`		2011-05-23 19:12:40
42	`constantinople`	en.wikipedia.org 4	2011-05-23 19:13:02
42	`soccr glasgo`		2011-05-23 19:16:01
42	`soccer glasgow`		2011-05-23 19:16:11
42	`soccer glasgow`	www.soccer.uk 3	2011-05-23 19:16:15
42	`celtics vs rangers`		2011-05-23 20:33:04
42	`celtics vs rangers`	en.wikipedia.org 5	2011-05-23 20:33:12
42	`old firm`		2011-05-23 22:42:48

between `celtics vs rangers` and `old firm` still remains as the corresponding ESA similarity is to low. Hence, for $f_{\text{esa}} < 0.35$ the decision is still questionable (remember that `old firm` is just another name for the `celtics vs rangers` soccer match). Accordingly, the cascading method does not immediately view q' as the start of a new session in this case but invokes Step 4 that aims at further enlarging the representation of the queries.

Step 4: Search Result Comparison

Step 4 compares the search results of the queries. As retrieving such results requires time-consuming index accesses at search engine site or even the submission of two web queries from an external client, the web results are applied only when all previous steps failed to provide a reliable decision. Using web search results to detect semantically similar queries is applied in different variants in the literature (cf. the discussion in Section 2). We evaluated different settings in a pilot study on the 10% sample of Gayo-Avello's test corpus also used in the analyses of Steps 2 and 3. As a result, we chose to compare the sets of URLs of the top-10 retrieved documents via the Jaccard coefficient. Whenever q' returns at least one of the top-10 results of q, we view this as an argument for a session continuation. Otherwise, q' starts a new session.

In our running example scenario, Step 4 correctly removes the intent switch between the queries `celtics vs rangers` and `old firm` as both return the "Old Firm" Wikipedia article in their top-10 Google results. Hence, the decisions after processing all four steps of the cascading method match the desired outcome depicted in Table 1. But note that a "new session" decision after Step 4 still cannot be guaranteed to be correct as semantically related queries may exist with low f_{esa}-value and no shared top-10 search results.

The Complete Cascade

Putting all the pieces together, the cascading method's pseudo code is given as Algorithm 1.

Algorithm 1 Cascading method for one query pair q and q'

```
if q ⊆ q' or q ⊃ q' then "same session"                          ▷ Step 1
else if f_lex ≥ 0.4 or f_time ≤ 0.8 then
    if √((f_time)² + (f_lex)²) ≥ 1 then "same session"            ▷ Step 2
    else "new session"
else if f_esa ≥ 0.35 then "same session"                         ▷ Step 3
else if shared top-10 result then "same session"                 ▷ Step 4
else not sure, but probably "new session"
```

5. EXPERIMENTAL EVALUATION

We conduct a two-part experimentation to examine the performance of our new cascading method. In a first experiment, we compare against the state-of-the-art geometric method on a standard session detection test corpus. In a second experiment, we show the scalability of our method on a large query log.

Comparison with the State of the Art

To ensure comparability, we evaluate our cascading method on the annotated gold standard query corpus that Gayo-Avello used in his experiments showing the geometric method to be superior to other approaches for session detection [6]. Note that using the same corpus, we have to compare our cascading method only with the best performing method of Gayo-Avello's comprehensive study to ensure comparability with all other approaches as well. The corpus contains 11 484 queries of 223 users sampled from the 2006 AOL query log [15]. The queries are manually subdivided into 4 254 sessions with an average of 2.70 queries per session. As we have sampled 10% of the corpus for parameter tuning of Steps 2–4, the experimental evaluation is done on the remaining 90% of the corpus. For evaluation purposes we use the F-Measure $F_\beta = \frac{(1+\beta^2)\cdot prec\cdot rec}{\beta^2\cdot prec+rec}$, where precision and recall of the detected sessions are measured against the human gold standard. We follow Gayo-Avello and set $\beta = 1.5$, which emphasizes wrong session continuations as the bigger problem compared to wrong breaks.

The results of this experiment can be found in Table 5. First of all, we could verify Gayo-Avello's reported good performance of his geometric method achieving an F-Measure of 0.9181. Note however, that the cascading method improves upon this value and achieves an F-Measure of 0.9327 (the difference is statistically significant according to a paired t-test with confidence level $p = 0.05$). The better accuracy is due to an improved session recall that more than compensates for a slightly worse precision.

We further analyze the impact step by step. The results are given in Table 6 and should be read as follows. After Step 1 (the subset test) about 40% of the test set's query pairs are reliably judged (column "reliable") and the F-Measure is 0.8303 if one would stop the processing after Step 1. Note that the runtime for invoking Step 1 on a pair of queries is about 0.08 ms on average (experimentation done on a standard quad-core desktop PC with 8 GB RAM). After Step 2 another 35% of all queries are judged reliably (altogether about 75%) with an F-Measure of 0.9292. Hence, applying the pre-processing Step 1 improves the accuracy of the geometric method.

Table 5: Accuracy values on the Gayo-Avello corpus.

	Precision	Recall	F-Measure
Geometric method	**0.8667**	0.9430	0.9181
Cascading method	0.8622	**0.9679**	**0.9327**

Table 6: Step by step performance on the Gayo-Avello corpus.

	reliable	F-Measure	time	factor
Step 1	40.49%	0.8303	0.08 ms	1.0
Step 2	35.15%	0.9292	0.20 ms	2.5
Step 3	2.05%	0.9316	0.27 ms	3.4
Step 4	0.85%	0.9327	9.85 ms	123.1

That the pre-processing also significantly speeds up the whole process can be seen as Step 2 requires about 0.20 ms per query pair (2.5 times more than Step 1 (column "factor")).

Step 3 is invoked on about 25% of all queries and runs with a pre-computed ESA matrix in main memory. Nevertheless, Step 3 is a little slower than Step 2 with an average time of about 0.27 ms per query pair. Step 3 reliably assigns "same session" for another 2.05% of all queries raising the F-Measure to 0.9316 if one would stop the cascading method after Step 3. Note that after Step 3 the cascading method is still faster than the original geometric method: 2.5 times faster on about 40% of the queries and 1.35 times slower on about 25% (0.27 ms vs. 0.20 ms).

The only crucial issue for runtime is Step 4 which is invoked on about 22% of all query pairs. For our experimental setting we modeled Step 4 as follows. All the queries on which Step 4 would be invoked were submitted to the Bing-API and the top-10 result URLs stored. On runtime of the cascading method, these result lists were held in memory to simulate a very fast index lookup at search engine site. Nevertheless, even in this artificial setting, Step 4 on average needs about 9.35 ms per query pair. This yields a factor of more than 100 compared to the time for Step 1. Applying Step 4 against the API's of commercial search engines would be even inferior as then a typical query needs at least 200 ms. Furthermore, note that Step 4 only assigns a "same session" decision to about 0.85% of all queries (column "reliable") and only slightly increases the resulting F-Measure by 0.011. That the improvement is so small is due to the fact that the ESA step already catches many of the semantically related query pairs that can be detected automatically. Hence, when efficiency is an issue, Step 4 is the obvious bottleneck even in the simulated environment of having the results in memory.

Improved Cascading Method: Drop Last Step

As Step 4 is the clear efficiency "problem" within the cascading method, we also suggest a very fast three-step variant of the cascade by removing Step 4. As described above, the resulting method is about 15% faster than the original geometric method while the accuracy of the detected sessions is even improved from 0.9181 to 0.9316 (again found to be a statistically significant difference).

Furthermore, consider the scenario in which session detection is applied offline and not at search engine site with access to a web index etc. Consider for instance some academic non-industry researcher whose use case is not to break a complete search engine log into all contained sessions but just to sample sessions with very high detection accuracy for further experiments. This might for instance be the case in the pre-processing step of studies that want to evaluate new retrieval ideas for improved handling of query sessions etc. In this scenario, Step 4 of the original cascade would have to be implemented against the public API of some commercial search engine with time requirement of at least 200 ms per query. For larger logs this is prohibitive and for such cases we suggest an additional tweak to the three-step cascading method. This second variant of the three-step cascading method assigns a "not sure, maybe new session" decision when Step 3 votes for a new session (about 22% of all query pairs in the Gayo-Avello test corpus). In a post-processing, all sessions starting with such a "not sure" decision can be deleted. In case of the Gayo-Avello test corpus this removes about 30% of the sessions but the remaining ones then achieve an almost perfect F-Measure of 0.9755. Hence, this version of the three-step cascading method with post-processing can be used as a very fast and very accurate session detection method that extracts very high quality sessions for further experimentation.

Scalability on a Large Log

We tested the suggested three-step variants of the cascading method on the 2006 AOL query log [15]. To this end, we cleaned the original log of about 36.4 million interactions collected in 3 months from about 650 000 users in order to remove users that probably are bots or that are not relevant for session detection. We had three simple rules for the cleaning: (1) we removed all users that only had one interaction (session detection would be senseless on these), (2) we removed all users that on average had less than 10 seconds between two consecutive interactions (probably bots), and (3) we removed all users whose median query length is more than 100 characters (probably bots). All in all, the cleaning removed about 1 million interactions and 130 000 users. Hence, the remaining log contains about 35.4 million interactions. With the figures from the experiments on Gayo-Avello's corpus one would expect about 8 million queries (22% of 35.4 million) to have to be submitted to a search engine when applying the full four-step cascade. Further assuming an average time of about 300 ms per web query against a typical API of some commercial search engine would yield 1 month of processing time. Of course, some queries could be parallelized etc.; but nevertheless the time consumption remains in the order of days compared to several minutes for the other three steps. Hence, these figures emphasize the fact that for larger analyses the three-step cascading method should be applied.

The three-step cascade on the cleaned AOL log takes about 27 minutes on a standard quad-core desktop PC with 8 GB RAM (compare this to several days for the full four step variant). We also tested the effect of removing all the sessions starting with a "not sure" decision after Step 3: as in the Gayo-Avello test corpus this affects about 30% of the sessions.

Altogether, our experiments show that for analyses of smaller logs the full four-step cascade can be applied although the accuracy is only slightly better than for the three-step cascade. If, however, the focus is on larger logs or the online scenario, the efficiency issue comes into play and the three-step cascading method should be chosen. It is about 15% faster than the original geometric method and comes with an even improved accuracy. Furthermore, for the task of sampling a few sessions with very high detection accuracy, an adapted version of the three-step cascade can remove the about 30% of sessions on which it is not sure. The remaining sessions then have a very good quality compared to human judgments.

6. CONCLUSION AND OUTLOOK

We have presented the cascading method for query session detection, which is based on the combined use of the geometric method and the well-known ESA model. The cascading method achieves a very high detection accuracy against a human gold standard and is superior to the current state-of-the-art geometric method. In contrast to other published methods, the cascading method sensibly invokes time-consuming features only if cheaper features fail to provide a reliable session detection. In its three-step variant our method is more accurate than the geometric method while saving 15% of the runtime. If equipped with a post-processing step that drops sessions with "not sure" decisions, the achieved accuracy is almost perfect on Gayo-Avello's gold standard. Hence, the cascading method is an ideal pre-processor for many evaluations that need to extract high quality sessions from query logs as experimental data. Another salient characteristic of the cascading method is its simplicity, which renders costly training data or an intricate hyperparameter tuning superfluously: the three-step cascade just involves a basic pre-processing, the simple geometric method, and the standard ESA framework.

An interesting aspect for future research is the integration of a post-processing that accounts for multitasking at user site, or for hierarchies of different search goals and missions [12, 13, 19, 20]. The idea of multitasking is that users may shortly interrupt longer search sessions for some completely different intent, and, after the short interruption, continue the original session. The idea of search goals and missions is that larger user search missions like planning the next vacation comprise of smaller goals like booking a flight, searching a nice hotel, etc. In future work, we plan to enhance the cascading method to also find search hierarchies or goals/missions. A potential way to achieve this would be to run the current cascade and then carefully merge the detected sessions into an appropriate hierarchy also respecting multi-tasking issues.

7. REFERENCES

[1] M. Anderka and B. Stein. The ESA retrieval model revisited. In *SIGIR 2009*, pp. 670–671.

[2] N. Buzikashvili and B. J. Jansen. Limits of the web log analysis artifacts. In *WWW 2006 Workshop on Logging Web Activity*.

[3] S.-L. Chuang and L.-F. Chien. A practical web-based approach to generating topic hierarchy for text segments. In *CIKM 2004*, pp. 127–136.

[4] D. Downey, S. T. Dumais, and E. Horvitz. Models of searching and browsing: languages, studies, and application. In *IJCAI 2007*, pp. 2740–2747.

[5] E. Gabrilovich and S. Markovitch. Computing semantic relatedness using Wikipedia-based explicit semantic analysis. In *IJCAI 2007*, pp. 1606–1611.

[6] D. Gayo-Avello. A survey on session detection methods in query logs and a proposal for future evaluation. *Information Sciences*, 179 (12):1822–1843, 2009.

[7] M. Hagen, B. Stein, and T. Rüb. Query Session Detection as a Cascade. In *ECIR 2011 Workshop on IR over Query Sessions*.

[8] D. He and A. Göker. Detecting session boundaries from web user logs. In *BCS-IRSG Colloquium 2000*, pp. 57–66.

[9] J. Huang and E. N. Efthimiadis. Analyzing and evaluating query reformulation strategies in web search logs. In *CIKM 2009*, pp. 77–86.

[10] B. J. Jansen, A. Spink, C. Blakely, and S. Koshman. Defining a session on web search engines. *JASIST*, 58(6):862–871, 2007.

[11] B. J. Jansen, A. Spink, and B. Narayan. Query modifications patterns during web searching. In *ITNG 2007*, pp. 439–444.

[12] R. Jones and K. L. Klinkner. Beyond the session timeout: automatic hierarchical segmentation of search topics in query logs. In *CIKM 2008*, pp. 699–708.

[13] C. Lucchese, S. Orlando, R. Perego, F. Silvestri, and G. Tolomei. Identifying task-based sessions in search engine query logs. In *WSDM 2011*, pp. 277–286.

[14] D. Metzler, S. T. Dumais, and C. Meek. Similarity measures for short segments of text. In *ECIR 2007*, pp. 16–27.

[15] G. Pass, A. Chowdhury, and C. Torgeson. A picture of search. In *Infoscale 2006*, paper 1.

[16] F. Radlinski and T. Joachims. Query chains: learning to rank from implicit feedback. In *KDD 2005*, pp. 239–248.

[17] M. Sahami and T. D. Heilman. A web-based kernel function for measuring the similarity of short text snippets. In *WWW 2006*, pp. 377–386.

[18] X. Shen, B. Tan, and C. Zhai. Implicit user modeling for personalized search. In *CIKM 2005*, pp. 824–831.

[19] A. Spink, H. C. Özmutlu, and S. Özmutlu. Multitasking information seeking and searching processes. *JASIST*, 53(8):639–652, 2002.

[20] A. Spink, M. Park, B. J. Jansen, and J. O. Pedersen. Multitasking during web search sessions. *Inf. Process. Manage.*, 42(1):264–275, 2006.

Discovering Missing Click-through Query Language Information for Web Search

Xing Yi and James Allan
Center for Intelligent Information Retrieval
Computer Science Department
University of Massachusetts, Amherst, MA, USA
{yixing,allan}@cs.umass.edu

ABSTRACT

The click-through information in web query logs has been widely used for web search tasks. However, it usually suffers from the data sparseness problem, known as the missing/incomplete click problems, where large volume of pages receive few or no clicks. In this paper, we adapt two language modeling based approaches to address this issue in the context of using web query logs for web search. The first approach discovers missing click-through query language features for web pages with no or few clicks from their similar pages' click-associated queries in the query logs, to help search. We further propose combining this content based approach with the random walk approach on the click graph to further reduce click-through sparseness for search. The second approach follows the query expansion method and utilizes the queries and their clicked web pages in the query logs to reconstruct a structured variant of the relevance based language models for each user-input query for search. We design experiments with a publicly available query log excerpt and two TREC web search tasks on the GOV2 and ClueWeb09 corpora to evaluate the search performance of different approaches. Our results show that using discovered semantic click-through query language features can statistically significantly improve search performance, compared with the baselines that do not use the discovered information. The combination approach that uses discovered click-through features from both random walk and the content based approach can further improve search performance.

Categories and Subject Descriptors: H.3.3 [**Information Storage and Retrieval**]: Information Search and Retrieval–*Search process,Retrieval models*;H.3.5 [**Information Storage and Retrieval**]:Online Information Services–*Web-based services*

General Terms: Algorithms, Experimentation

1. INTRODUCTION

Click-through data provide important user preference information (both individual and collective) over the returned web search results and play important roles in designing and improving web search engines. For example, click-through information can be used to derive labeled training data for optimizing web ranking functions used by web search engines [14, 26]; user clicks can be directly used as relevance judgments of the clicked URLs to generate evaluation data for comparing different retrieval approaches[28, 3]; and collective click-through features can be extracted to enhance the ranking models of search engines[30, 1].

Unfortunately, click-through data usually suffer from a data sparseness problem where large volume of queries have few or no associated clicks [9, 11]. This problem may be caused by two related user click behaviors. One is that users may only click a very limited number of pages for a query so that the clicks are not complete; the other one is that users may just browse the returned snippets to fetch some useful information while not clicking any results even they are relevant. Gao et al. [11] referred to these two situations as the *incomplete click* problem and the *missing click* problem, respectively. These problems greatly limit the possibility and reliability of using click-through features for web search. For example, click-through features cannot be extracted for pages with no clicks. To overcome the click-through sparseness, Craswell and Szummer [9] built a query-URL bipartite click graph from a web query log and then proposed a *random walk* algorithm on the graph to discover missing clicks between query nodes and URL nodes. The intuition behind this approach is to use the transitions of the semantic relation between queries and their clicked URLs on the click graph to find plausible missing clicks.

However, the random walk approach can only partially alleviate the click-through sparseness because it requires specific link structures in the click graph to discover missing clicks. For example, URLs (web pages) that have not yet received any clicks in the search history can never be associated with any previously issued queries in the query logs. To address this issue, Gao et al. [11] considered an alternative approach to compute click-through features from sparse click-through data. They introduced a Good-Turing estimator [12] based discounting method to smooth click-through features of web pages, so that pages with no clicks can have very small *non-zero* click-through features computed by discounting the average of the click-through features of all pages that receive exactly *one* click. Intuitively, their approach follows the smoothing approach of computing out-of-vocabulary (OOV) words' probabilities in statistical language models to compute missing click-through features for web pages with no clicks.

CIKM'11, October 24–28, 2011, Glasgow, Scotland, UK.

Notice that although OOV words and missing clicks of web pages can be both viewed as events unseen in training data and thus handled in a similar way, there is an important difference between the two types of unseen events: we usually have little semantic information about OOV words while we normally have indexed the content of the web pages that have not received clicks yet. Gao et al.'s smoothing approach does not use any semantic information in the web page content, thus *pages that have completely different content but no clicks will obtain the same smoothed click-through features*. This is counter-intuitive and makes some smoothed features ineffective for ranking. Indeed, in the experiments they found that using the smoothed click-through features extracted from the content of a web page's *click-associated* query strings (called *query-dependent* features by them) helped little for retrieval [11].

To overcome the weaknesses of the random walk approach [9] and the Good-Turing smoothing approach [11], we propose to utilize the content similarity between web pages to address the click-through sparseness problem. Our content based approach is able to discover click-through query language model features that can properly convey semantic information in the content of pages with no clicks to help retrieval.

Specifically, we hypothesize that *web pages that are similar in content may be clicked by web searchers issuing similar queries*. Under this assumption, we introduce a language modeling based technique for discovering a target web page's plausible missing click-associated queries, using the queries that led to the clicks on the target page's *similar* pages. We then use the discovered query language features for search. We further present a way of combining the advantages of both the random walk approach and the content based approach for helping search. In addition, we adapt an alternative approach, based on the relevance-based language models (RM)[18] to address the click-through sparseness issue for search. This approach, Structured Relevance Models, has been used to handle missing fields when searching semi-structured documents[19].

We evaluate the retrieval performance of different approaches using the Microsoft Live Search 2006 search query log excerpt (MS-QLOG), which has been used in some query log studies [28, 3], and two different sets of *ad hoc* web search tasks: (1) the ones in the TREC 2004-2005 Terabyte Tracks [8, 7] and (2) the ones in the TREC 2009-2010 Web Tracks [6, 15][1]. Our work has four major contributions: 1) To the best of our knowledge, we are the first to utilize web content similarity to discover missing click-through query language features for improving web search, although content similarity has been used in many other applications. 2) We adapt two language modeling based approaches to address click-through sparseness in the context of using query logs for web search; we also propose combining the content based approach and the random walk approach [9] for computing effective ranking features from query logs that have the click-through sparseness issue. 3) We empirically show that using our approaches can statistically significantly improve web search performance. 4) We empirically compare different approaches of discovering missing click-through query language features for web search and do in-depth analysis on their advantages and weaknesses.

[1]http://plg.uwaterloo.ca/~trecweb/2010.html

We begin by reviewing some related work. In §3, we describe three approaches for discovering missing click-through query language features. In §4 we present how we use different discovered information for search, then compare and analyze retrieval performance of different approaches using the TREC *ad hoc* web search tasks. Then we conclude in §5.

2. RELATED WORK

Previous research has encountered the data sparseness problem in click-through data, including the incomplete click problem and the missing click problem, when leveraging web query logs for helping different web search tasks [9, 1, 26]. However, there is relatively little of work directly handling the click-through sparseness. Craswell and Szummer [9] proposed a random walk approach on the query-URL click graph to discover plausible missing clicks. Gao et al. [11] have recently proposed a discounting method inspired by the Good-Turing estimator [12] to smooth click-through features for web pages that have received no clicks. Different from previous work, we propose using web content similarity to address the click-through sparseness. Recently, Seo et al. [27] proposed applying spectral graph analysis on the web content similarity graph to smooth click counts in the query logs for search. Our approach is similar to their approach in terms of using web content similarity to address click-through sparseness; however, we specifically focus on discovering click-through query language features for search.

Our approach is closely related to other similarity-based techniques, such as clustering similar documents for smoothing document language models[16, 21], smoothing documents based on document-content similarity graph [22], and using web content similarity for missing anchor text discovery [31]; however, we focus on enriching web pages' semantic click-through features for web search by using their similar pages' click-associated queries. We further consider combining web content similarity and click graph information to improve discovered missing semantic click-through features for web search. We notice that Li et al. [20] considered combining query language features and click graph information for mitigating the click-through sparseness in a different task of classifying the search intents of web queries in query logs. Different from them, we further consider using web content similarity for reducing the click-through sparseness and use the discovered query language features for retrieval.

There is significant research on using click-through data in the query log for enhancing web search performance: using query-page click-through pairs to derive labeled training pairs for learning web page ranking functions [14, 26], extracting click-through features and incorporating them into ranking models for web search [30, 1, 11]. The incomplete/missing click problems present major challenges for both approaches of using click-through data for web search. Our research on discovering missing click-through features can benefit the latter research direction in particular.

3. DISCOVERING MISSING CLICK INFORMATION FOR WEB PAGES

We first describe two different approaches for discovering plausible missing click-through query language information for web pages with few or no clicks. Next, we present one way to combine the advantages of the two approaches. We emphasize that in our research we are particularly interested

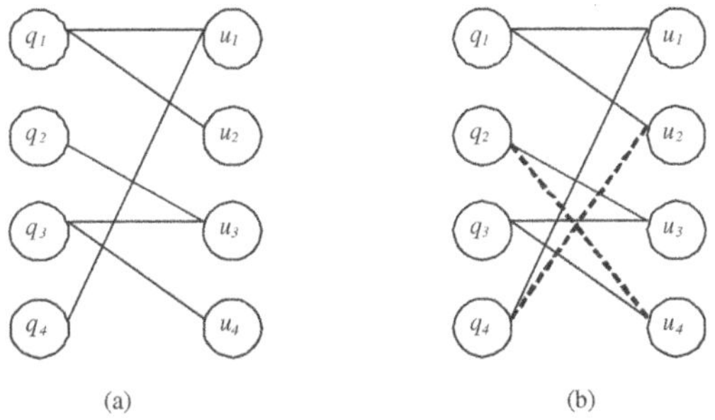

Figure 1: An illustration example of using random walk approach to discover plausible missing clicks (denoted by dashed lines): (a) the original click graph; (b) the link-enriched click graph after applying rank walk algorithm.

in *obtaining click-through query language features, which can convey some semantic information of the target web page*, for search.

3.1 Finding More Click-associated Queries by Random Walk on Click Graph

We start by reviewing the random walk approach that uses co-clicks in the click-through data to discover plausible missing clicks for web pages [9, 11]. We follow Gao et al. [11] and use the forward random walk [9] instead of the backward one for our task. This approach first builds a query-URL *bipartite* click graph from a web query log, by assigning the same query strings/URLs to the same query/URL nodes and linking them according to the click pairs in the query log; then it uses a random walk algorithm to discover plausible missing click edges. Intuitively, this approach assumes there exists close semantic relation among neighbor nodes in the click graph, and uses the transitions of the semantic relation on the graph for missing click edge discovery. For example, in Figure 1, q_1 and q_4 both lead to the clicks on u_1, thus q_1 and q_4 may be semantically related; therefore q_4 may also lead to the click on u_2, which is q_1's clicked URL. Similarly, due to the co-clicks on u_3 by q_2 and q_3, q_2 may also lead to the click on q_3's clicked URL u_4.

Formally, assume a bipartite click graph $G =< Q, U, E >$ is constructed from a set of query nodes $Q = \{q_1 \ldots q_m\}$, a set of web page URL nodes $U = \{u_1 \ldots u_n\}$ and the edges E between the query nodes and the URL nodes. $(q_i, u_j) \in E$ is an edge in G when q_i leads to at least one click on u_j, and $w(q_i, u_j)$ represents the click count associated with the edge (q_i, u_j). We can normalize the $w(q_i, u_j)$ to obtain the transition probability $p(u_j|q_i)$ on the click graph between a query q_i and each of its clicked web page u_j by:

$$p(u_j|q_i) = \frac{w(q_i, u_j)}{\sum\limits_{k\in\{1\ldots n\},(q_i,u_k)\in E} w(q_i, u_k)}, \tag{1}$$

and also the transition probability $p(q_i|u_j)$ between a page u_j and each of its click-associated queries q_i by:

$$p(q_i|u_j) = \frac{w(q_i, u_j)}{\sum\limits_{k\in\{1\ldots m\},(q_k,u_j)\in E} w(q_k, u_j)}. \tag{2}$$

# click pairs	#unique queries (query nodes)	#unique URLs (URL nodes)
12,251,067	3,545,174	4,971,990

	# click edges in the graph
original counts	6,853,498
random walk($t = 1$)	
$\alpha = 0$ (no noise filtering)	42,999,932
$\alpha = 0.001$	32,240,647
$\alpha = 0.005$	24,365,787
$\alpha = 0.01$	20,265,365

Table 1: Some summary statistics of the click graph built from the MS-QLOG dataset and different enriched graphs by the random walk approach with different noise filtering parameters.

We can use the above transition probabilities $p(u_j|q_i), p(q_i|u_j)$, $i \in \{1 \ldots m\}, j \in \{1 \ldots n\}$ to compute the probability $p^{(2t)}(q_j|q_i)$ of one query q_i transiting to another one q_j on the click graph in $2t$ steps by the following iterative equations:

$$\begin{aligned}
p^{(2t)}(q_j|q_i) &= \sum_{k\in\{1\ldots n\},(q_j,u_k)\in E} [p(q_j|u_k)p^{(2t-1)}(u_k|q_i)], t \geq 1; \\
p^{(2t-1)}(u_j|q_i) &= \sum_{k\in\{1\ldots m\},(q_k,u_j)\in E} [p(u_j|q_k)p^{(2t-2)}(q_k|q_i)], t > 1; \\
p^{(1)}(u_j|q_i) &= p(u_j|q_i), i \in \{1 \ldots m\}, j \in \{1 \ldots n\}.
\end{aligned} \tag{3}$$

We can see that longer transition steps can discover transitions to additional queries for a target query q_i while the discovered semantic relation between them becomes weaker and noisier. Thus for effectiveness and efficiency, we follow Gao et al.[11] to set $t = 1$ in our experiments. In order to further filter some plausible noise, we follow their approach and require that the discovered transitions for the target query q_i should satisfy $p^{(2)}(q_j|q_i) > \alpha$, where α is a controlling parameter and tuned empirically on training data for different tasks.

After discovering similar queries for each query using the random walk approach, Gao et al.[11] expanded each web page's click-associated queries with discovered similar queries. In this way, web pages are linked with more semantically related queries so that the incomplete click problem is partially mitigated. Then they used the enriched representation of the click-associated queries for each web page to extract click-through features to improve web search performance.

Table 1 shows some summary statistics of the original click graph and the enriched click graphs by the random walk approach when we use the click pairs in MS-QLOG to build the graph. The first four rows in Table 1 show some summary statistics of the original click graph, indicating the click-through information is very sparse even for the pages that received some clicks – on average, each page only received 2.5 clicks and has about 1.4 unique click-associated queries. The last four rows show the number of click edges in each enriched graph by the random walk approach using different noise filtering parameters, indicating that incomplete click problem can be partially mitigated – on average, the number of the unique click-associated queries of each web page has been raised to 6.5 when $\alpha = 0.001$.

3.2 Discovering Missing Click-associated Queries through Finding Similar Pages

Notice that the random walk approach needs specific click graph structures to discover plausible missing clicks, meaning it cannot handle web pages with no clicks. Therefore, we propose to adapt a content based approach, which was originally proposed by Yi and Allan for addressing the missing anchor text issue in web search [31]. Intuitively, our approach assumes that web pages that are similar in content may receive clicks from web searchers issuing similar queries. Under this assumption, we aim to discover a query language model for each page, in order to obtain effective missing semantic click-through features to help search.

We adapt Yi and Allan's contextual translation approach of discovering missing anchor text [31] for our task. Briefly speaking, their approach first views the content of web pages as their anchor text's descriptive context and utilizes the contextual translation approach [28] to measure the semantic relation between the anchor text associated with different pages. Given any page P_i and a target page P_0, the semantic relation between their associated anchor text A_i and A_0 is measured by the contextual translation probability $t(A_i|A_0)$, computed from the Kullback-Leibler divergence (KL-div) between the document language models of P_i and P_0. Then they use $t(A_i|A_0)$ to compute a relevant anchor text language model $p(w|A_0)$ for a target page P_0 to discover P_0's plausible missing anchor terms by:

$$p(w|A_0) = \sum_{A_i \in \mathcal{A}} p(w|A_i) \times t(A_i|A_0), \quad (4)$$

where $\mathcal{A}$ denotes the complete anchor text space of all pages and $p(w|A_i)$ is a multinomial distribution of anchor terms (w) over the vocabulary $\mathcal{V}_{\mathcal{A}}$.

Similarly, we first view each page P_i's content as the descriptive context of the page's click-associated queries Q_i and use P_i's document language model, $p_i = \{p(w|P_i)\}$, as Q_i's *contextual* language model, which is computed by applying Dirichlet smoothing [17] on the original un-smoothed document language model:

$$p(w|P_i) = \frac{N_{P_i}}{N_{P_i} + \mu} p_{ML}(w|P_i) + \frac{\mu}{N_{P_i} + \mu} p(w|\mathcal{C}), \quad (5)$$

where $p_{ML}(w|P_i)$ is the maximum likelihood (ML) estimate of observing a word w in the page, $p(w|\mathcal{C})$ is w's probability in the collection $\mathcal{C}$, N_{P_i} is the length of P_i's content and μ is the Dirichlet smoothing parameter.

Then given any page P_i and a target page P_0, we measure the semantic relation between their click associated queries Q_i and Q_0 by their contextual translation probability $t(Q_i|Q_0)$, computed from the KL-div $Div(\cdot||\cdot)$ between their contextual models p_0 and p_i:

$$t(Q_i|Q_0) = \frac{\exp(-Div(p_0||p_i))}{\sum_i \exp(-Div(p_0||p_i))} \propto \prod_w p(w|P_i)^{p(w|P_0)}. \quad (6)$$

The end of Equation 6 is the likelihood of generating Q_0's context P_0 from the smoothed language model of Q_i's context P_i, being normalized by Q_0's context length.

After that, for each given target page P_0, we calculate a relevant (click-associated) query language model (**RQLM**) $p(w|Q_0)$ to discover P_0's plausible click-associated query terms by:

$$p(w|Q_0) = \sum_{Q_i \in \mathcal{Q}} p(w|Q_i) \times t(Q_i|Q_0), \quad (7)$$

where Q_i denotes all the queries that may lead to the clicks on P_i but may be *incomplete* or *missing*, $\mathcal{Q}$ denotes the complete textual space of the click-associated queries of all pages, $p(w|Q_i)$ is a multinomial distribution of query terms (w) over the click-associated query language vocabulary $\mathcal{V}_{\mathcal{Q}}$.

To compute the RQLM $p(w|Q_0)$ in Equation 7, we use each page P_i's click-associated queries originally *observed* in the query log to estimate a query language model $p_{obs}(w|Q_i)$ to approximate $p(w|Q_i)$, which should be estimated ideally from some unknown *complete* set of P_i's all plausible click-associated queries in the query log[2]. In practice, for effectiveness and efficiency we compute the RQLM of the target page P_0 using the click-associated queries of P_0's top-k most similar pages in the query log. This choice is due to two reasons: (1) $t(Q_i|Q_0)$ is very small for other pages thus has less impact on the RQLM; (2) increasing k can increase the number of query samples for better estimating RQLM but also may introduce more noise to degrade the quality of the estimated RQLM. We tune k's value on the training data for each different retrieval task.

3.3 Combining Random Walk Approach and Finding Similar Approach

We can take advantages of both the random walk approach in §3.1 and our content based approach to further reduce the click-through sparseness and calculate better semantic click-through features for search. Here we present one language modeling based way to combine the advantages of two approaches.

We first employ the random walk approach to enrich the original bipartite click graph and discover more click-associated queries for each web page. Then we estimate a query language model $p(w|Q_{aug})$ for each web page from the new added click-associated queries, which we call *augmented* queries, of the page. We also estimate a query language model $p(w|Q_{orig})$ for each page from its click-associated queries originally observed in the query log that has not been enriched by the random walk approach. Next, we employ the mixture model approach [23, 24] to combine two query language models $p(w|Q_{orig})$ and $p(w|Q_{aug})$, and compute a better smoothed query language model $\tilde{p}(w|Q)$ by:

$$\tilde{p}(w|Q) = \gamma p(w|Q_{orig}) + (1-\gamma) p(w|Q_{aug}), \quad (8)$$

where γ is a meta-parameter to control the mixture weight (or prior probability) of each component and can be tuned on training data for different tasks. Then we use the updated query language model $\tilde{p}(w|Q)$ of each page to better approximate the $p(w|Q_i)$ in Equation 7 so that we can better estimate the RQLM $p(w|Q_0)$ of each page to help retrieval.

Next, we describe how we utilize missing click-through query language information discovered by these different approaches to help improve search performance.

4. USING DISCOVERED CLICK-THROUGH INFORMATION FOR WEB SEARCH

We have described several ways to infer click-through information when in situations where a page or query has few clicks. In this section we consider how to use the inferred information and measure its utility. We first present how we utilize discovered missing click-through query language information for retrieval in §4.1, following the language modeling based retrieval framework[25]. Then in §4.2 we consider an approach that expands the query with additional

[2]We will use this fact in §3.3 to combine the random walk approach and the content based approach for discovering missing click-through features.

terms, also inferred from the click-through log. For the convenience of discussing different retrieval models and baselines, we start by briefly describing the data and methodology we used for evaluating different approaches.

Mainly due to privacy and security concerns, there are very limited *publicly available* query log data for research. Here we use the MS-QLOG dataset which contains about 12m click-through events and also information of about 15m additional user-issued web queries that received no clicks, sampled from the query log of Microsoft's web search engine during 05/01/2006 to 05/31/2006. We only use the click-through records in this dataset for our experiments.

We use the queries and the relevance judgments in two different sets of the TREC web search tasks to design retrieval experiments. The first set consists of the *ad hoc* web search tasks in the TREC 2004-2005 Terabyte Tracks [8, 7], where the GOV2 collection (a TREC web collection crawled from government web sites during early 2004) was used for search; the second set consists of the *ad hoc* web search tasks in the TREC 2009 Web Track [6, 15] and the TREC 2010 Web Track[3], where the search was originally performed on the ClueWeb-09 Dataset[4](a larger TREC web collection recently crawled during 01/06/2009 to 02/27/2009 from all domains of the Web).

Because our approach depends on web page content similarity, we crawl the web pages of all the *clicked* URLs in MS-QLOG and use the crawled pages and their click-associated queries in MS-QLOG as the training data for extracting semantic click-through features. The GOV2 collection and the TREC category B subset of the ClueWeb09 web collection (or ClueWeb09-T09B dataset), are used as the searched targets in our experiments. Each ClueWeb09 or GOV2 web page can be viewed as a page whose click information is completely missing[5], thus we need to handle the click-through sparseness problem in both the training pages and the searched collections.

More details about the data and methodology used for evaluating the retrieval performance of different approaches will be described in §4.3.1. Then we will discuss the experimental results in §4.3.2 and §4.3.3.

4.1 Document Smoothing Approach

The first baseline is a query likelihood baseline following the typical language modeling based retrieval approach[25]. This baseline does not use any click-through features and ranks each web page P for a query Q by the likelihood of the page P's document language model $p(w|P)$ generating the query Q:

$$p(Q|P) = \prod_{w \in Q} p(w|P). \tag{9}$$

We use Dirichlet smoothing [17] to compute the document language model $p(w|P)$ used in the above equation and denote this query likelihood baseline **QL** here. We tune the Dirichlet parameter μ for QL to achieve the best retrieval performance for different tasks. Note that μ is fixed to 2500 when using Equation 5 to compute the document models of the crawled clicked pages for estimating RQLMs (relevant click-associated query language models described in §3.2).

[3]`http://plg.uwaterloo.ca/~trecweb/2010.html`

[4]`http://boston.lti.cs.cmu.edu/Data/clueweb09/`

[5]Some research showed that there is very small overlap between the clicked URLs in MS-QLOG and the GOV2 collection[3].

We follow the mixture model approach [23, 24] to use the discovered click-through query language model features to help search. After we estimate the RQLM $p(w|Q_0)$ for each page, we mix a web page P's document language model $p(w|P)$ with the RQLM to obtain a better document language model $\tilde{p}(w|P)$ by:

$$\tilde{p}(w|P) = \beta p(w|P) + (1-\beta)p(w|Q_0), \tag{10}$$

where $p(w|P)$ is the original smoothed document model in the QL baseline and β is the meta-parameter controlling the mixture weights of the component distributions. Then we can use the updated document language model $\tilde{p}(w|P)$ and Equation 9 for retrieval.

We have described three different approaches of discovering semantic missing click-through features in §3. We point out *because the searched items here are ClueWeb09 or GOV2 web pages with no click information, only using the random walk approach cannot discover any click-associated queries for them.* Therefore, we do not use the sparse click count (which is *zero* for almost all pages and not helpful for retrieval) in our experiments, but use our content based approach and the combination approach for improving search performance. In the combination approach, we first discover plausible missing links in the click graph (built from MS-QLOG) by the random walk approach and then use the enriched click graph to estimate better RQLMs for the ClueWeb09 or GOV2 pages as described in §3.3. We denote the retrieval baseline that employs our content based approach to update document models for search as **RQLM**, and the baseline that uses combination approach for search as **RW+RQLM** in later discussions.

4.2 Query Expansion Approach

Besides document smoothing approaches, we are also interested in exploring some *query-side* alternative approaches of handling missing click-through information for search. Here we adapt a structured variant of the relevance based language models [18], which was proposed by Lavrenko et al.[19] and called Structured Relevance Models (SRM), for discovering useful click-through query information to reconstruct queries. The SRM technique was originally developed to search *semi-structured* documents with incomplete/missing fields; thus, here we introduce field structure for the queries and pages, represent click-through information using this structure and then utilize the SRM approach for search.

Formally, we view each web page as a semi-structured document containing two fields: (1) the *PageContent* field (denoted by $\mathbf{w}_p$) which contains the original page content and (2) the *QueryContent* field (denoted by $\mathbf{w}_q$) which contains all the click-associated queries of the page in the web query log. Then for each unstructured query q, we generate a semi-structured query $\mathbf{q} = \{\mathbf{w}_p, \mathbf{w}_q\}$ that has the same semi-structure as the web page document by duplicating the query string in both fields, i.e. $\mathbf{w}_p = \mathbf{w}_q = q$: intuitively, *the query is searching for pages that match the query in content and/or their click-associated queries.* We assume that both fields are incomplete and then use the SRM approach to estimate plausible missing field values in $\mathbf{q}$ based on the observed $\{\mathbf{w}_p, \mathbf{w}_q\}$.

We use our crawled pages of the clicked URLs in MS-QLOG and their click-associated queries in MS-QLOG to form the *training* semi-structured document collection $\mathcal{W}$. We then use the training collection to calculate the SRM

$\{R_p(\cdot), R_q(\cdot)\}$ for $\mathbf{q}$, where each relevance model $R_i(w)$ specifies how plausible it is the word w would occur in the field i ($i \in \{p, q\}$) of $\mathbf{q}$ given the observed $\mathbf{q} = \{\mathbf{w}_p, \mathbf{w}_q\}$, i.e.

$$R_i(w) = P(w \circ \mathbf{w}_i | \mathbf{q}) = P(w \circ \mathbf{w}_i | \mathbf{w}_p, \mathbf{w}_q), i \in \{p, q\}, w \in \mathcal{V}_i, \quad (11)$$

where $w \circ \mathbf{w}_i$ denotes appending word w to the string $\mathbf{w}_i$ and $\mathcal{V}_i$ denotes the vocabulary of the field i. Using the training web page documents $\mathbf{w}' \in \mathcal{W}$ and Equation 11, $R_i(w)$ can be further calculated by:

$$R_i(w) = \sum_{\mathbf{w}' \in \mathcal{W}} p(w|\mathbf{w}'_i) \times P(\mathbf{w}'|\mathbf{q}), i \in \{p, q\}, w \in \mathcal{V}_i. \quad (12)$$

To calculate the posterior probability $P(\mathbf{w}'|\mathbf{q})$,we use the following equations:

$$\begin{aligned} P(\mathbf{w}'|\mathbf{q}) &\propto P(\mathbf{q}|\mathbf{w}') * P(\mathbf{w}'), \\ P(\mathbf{q}|\mathbf{w}') &= P(\mathbf{w}_p|\mathbf{w}'_p)^{\beta_p} * P(\mathbf{w}_q|\mathbf{w}'_q)^{\beta_q}, \end{aligned} \quad (13)$$

where $P(\mathbf{w}')$ is assumed to be a uniform distribution, the meta-parameters β_p, β_q are used to control the impact of each field on the posterior probability and tuned with the training queries. When computing $P(\mathbf{w}_i|\mathbf{w}'_i), i \in \{p, q\}$ in Equation 13, we fix the Dirichlet smoothing parameter $\mu_p = 50, \mu_q = 1$ for the *PageContent* and *QueryContent* fields, respectively.[6]

For efficiency and effectiveness we use $\mathbf{q}$'s top-k most similar documents instead of all $\mathbf{w}' \in \mathcal{W}$ to calculate $R_i(w)$. k is tuned with the training queries. Because the click information is completely missing in our two searched target collections $\mathcal{W}''$ (ClueWeb09-T09B and GOV2), the *QueryContent* field is missing there. Therefore, we only use the relevance model $R_p(w)$ of the estimated SRM in the *PageContent* field to search each target collection. We interpolate it with the original query language model to obtain a better relevance model for retrieval:

$$R'_p(w) = \lambda * (p(w|\mathbf{w}_p)) + (1 - \lambda) * R_p(w), \quad (14)$$

which is similar as in the Relevance Model 3 [10]. We use the parameter λ to control the impact of the original query language model on the updated relevance model and tune it with the training queries. Then the searched documents $\mathbf{w}'' \in \mathcal{W}''$ are ranked by their weighted cross-entropy [17] based similarity to $R'_p(w)$:

$$H(R'_p; \mathbf{w}''_p) = \sum_{w \in \mathcal{V}_p} R'_p(w) \log p(w|\mathbf{w}''_p) \quad (15)$$

We denote this query expansion retrieval baseline as **SRM** in our experiments.

For comparison, we also provide the typical highly effective language modeling based query expansion baseline – Relevance Model [18] – in our experiments. We use the version of Relevance Model 3 [10] and denote it as **RM**. Note that different from SRM, here RM *does not use any click-through information* for search: it builds a relevance model from the top results of the QL baseline, which is obtained by running the original query directly against the search target (ClueWeb09-T09B or GOV2); then it mixes the built relevance model with the original query language model (similar as in Equation 14) and ranks the searched pages again using the updated model.

In addition, we consider an approach that combines the advantages of both the RM approach and the combination approach (RW+RQLM in §4.1) for further improving search performance. This approach first uses discovered click-through query information from RW+RQLM to get a better query-likelihood ranked list of pages for a given query, and then uses the top ranked pages to compute a plausibly better relevance model for query expansion and re-retrieval. This approach is similar in spirit to previous research that combines document expansion techniques and RM for further improving search [29]. We denote this approach as **RW+RQLM +RM** in the experiments.

4.3 IR Experiments

4.3.1 Data and Methodology

As described at the beginning of §4, we consider two set of retrieval tasks. The first one is performed on GOV2 which contains about 25m U.S. government web pages; the second one is performed on ClueWeb09-T09B which contains about 50m English web pages. We use the Indri Search Engine[7] to index each collection by removing a standard list of 418 INQUERY [4] stopwords and applying Krovetz stemmer.

For the first retrieval task, we use 50 *ad hoc* queries (topic id:701-750,title-only) in the TREC 2004 Terabyte Track [7] for train and 50 *ad hoc* queries (topic id:751-800,title-only) in the TREC 2005 Terabyte Tracks[8] for test. For the second retrieval task, we use 50 *ad hoc* queries (title-only) in the TREC 2009 Web Track [6, 15] for train and 50 queries (title-only) in the TREC 2010 Web Track for test. Moreover, instead of using the whole ClueWeb09 collection as the search target as in the TREC 2010 Web Track, we only use the ClueWeb09-T09B subset here; thus only relevant pages in this subset collection are used for evaluation.

We crawled the web pages of the clicked URLs in the MS-QLOG during June 2010 and use the HTML pages downloadable during that time period and their click-associated queries in the MS-QLOG as the training collection for our experiments. Originally there are about 5m unique clicked URLs in this query log, as shown in Table 1; we successfully crawled about 3m HTML pages of the clicked URLs and indexed them using the Indri Search Engine. We remove 418 INQUERY stopwords and apply Krovetz stemmer during the indexing and call the indexed collection as MS-QLOG-Web, which contains about 21.5 million unique words and 4.1 billion word postings. These training pages are then used to discover click-through query language features for the GOV2 or ClueWeb09 pages. We also preprocess the queries in the MS-QLOG using the same stopwords removing and stemming procedure.

To evaluate the retrieval performance, we calculate typical IR evaluation measurements including Mean Average Precision (MAP), Precision at position k (P@k), Normalized Discounted Cumulative Gain (NDCG) [13]. For the TREC 2009 Web Track queries, we report two additional measurements: *statMAP* and *MPC(30)*, which were used by the TREC community for that track [6] and computed

[6]When using some sampled queries in MS-QLOG to search their clicked URLs in our crawled web collection, we found that these smoothing parameters can perform the best, if the user click is directly used as the relevance indicator of a web page. Note that only very sparse, biased and incomplete relevance judgments may be obtained in this way.

[7]http://www.lemurproject.org/indri/

by the TREC evaluation tool *statAP_MQ_eval_v3.pl* [8]; thus, we can compare our results with other researchers' published results on the same query set. Intuitively, both statMAP and MPC(30) measurements are used for addressing the incomplete judgment issue [2]: the former one is a statistical version of the MAP measurement and the latter one is a statistical version of the measurement P@30.

In each retrieval task, we first tune the Dirichlet smoothing parameter μ in Equation 5 to obtain the best QL baseline that can achieve the highest MAP with training queries on each searched target collection (GOV2 or ClueWeb09-T09B). Then for both the RQLM baseline (using our content based approach) and the RW+RQLM baseline (using the combination approach), we follow the *reranking* scheme, where we use the updated document language model by each approach to recompute the query likelihood scores of the top-1000 web pages returned by the QL baseline for each query and then rerank the pages. For the RQLM baseline, we tune these two parameters: the number (k) of the similar pages whose click-associated queries are used to compute the RQLM and the mixture weight β in Equation 10. For the RW+RQLM baseline, we tune two additional parameters: the transition probability threshold α (discussed in §3.1) and the query language model updating weight γ in Equation 8. For the SRM baseline, as described in §4.2, we tune the number of the similar pages (k) used to build SRM, the number of terms (N) in each field of the built SRM, the meta-parameters λ in Equation 14 and β_p, β_q in Equation 13. For the RM baseline, we tune the number of top ranked pages (k), the number of terms (N) used to build a relevance model and the mixture weight λ' between the relevance model and the original query model. For the RW+RQLM+RM baseline, we first use the tuned RW+RQLM baseline to obtain a best query likelihood ranked list of pages, then we use this best ranked list to build a relevance model and tune the number of top ranked pages (k'), the number of terms (N) and the mixture weight λ' similarly as in the RM baseline.

In each retrieval task, we tune the parameters of each approach with the training queries, and then test their performance on the test queries.

4.3.2 Results

Table 2 and 3 show the retrieval performance of different approaches with the training and testing queries, respectively, in the first retrieval task (TREC 2005 queries are widely known to perform well, explaining why they outperform the training queries.) Table 4 and 5 show the retrieval performance of different approaches with the training and testing queries, respectively, in the second retrieval task. The ‡ and † in these tables indicate *statistically* significant improvement over of the QL baseline based on one-sided t-test with $p < 0.05$ and $p < 0.1$,respectively. The * indicates *statistically significant improvement over of the highly effective RM baseline* based on one-sided t-test with $p < 0.05$. Table 2 and 4 also show the corresponding tuned parameters of each approach in the first and second retrieval task, respectively. These tables show using discovered click-through query information can help for improving web search performance. We have the following main observations:

1. Using click-through query language features from MS-QLOG benefit more for the web search tasks on the ClueWeb09 data than the ones on the GOV2 data. This is not surprising because the TREC *ad hoc* search tasks on the ClueWeb09 data are, in nature, more similar to real-world web search scenarios as those recorded in MS-QLOG: (1) the ClueWeb09 dataset were crawled from the general web while the GOV2 data was crawled only from government web sites; (2) the TREC Web Tracks queries were created to closely simulate the real-world web search scenarios, while the TREC Terabyte Track queries targeted government web pages in order to have some relevant pages in the GOV2 data.

2. On the test query sets in both retrieval tasks, (a) both RQLM and RW+RQLM performed statistically significantly better than QL in terms of MAP,P@10 and NDCG; (b) RW+RQLM+RM performed *statistically significantly better than RM* in terms of MAP and NDCG. This result demonstrates that using click-through query language model features discovered by our content based approach can help to improve the web search performance significantly, even compared with a highly effective typical query expansion baseline. This also indicates that our content based approach can effectively alleviate the click-through sparseness problem. In addition, RW+RQLM performed slightly better than RQLM on the training query sets in both retrieval tasks and the test query set in the ClueWeb09 retrieval task, indicating that the combination of our content based approach and the click-graph based random walk approach can further reduce the click-through sparseness and refine the discovered missing click-through features for search.

3. The structured query expansion approach (SRM) achieved very good performance (3rd on GOV2 and 2nd on ClueWeb data) on the training query sets in both retrieval tasks. This shows when the model parameters are carefully tuned, SRM can use click-through information to discover miss-

[8]It is downloadable at: `http://trec.nist.gov/data/web09.html`

	MAP	P@10	P@30	NDCG
QL	0.2617	0.5102	0.4694	0.4829
SRM	$0.2777^{\ddagger}$	$0.5551^{\ddagger}$	$0.5020^{\ddagger}$	0.4945
RQLM	0.2688	$0.5388^{\ddagger}$	0.4796	$0.4927^{\ddagger}$
RW+RQLM	$0.2691^{\dagger}$	$0.5347^{\ddagger}$	$0.4823^{\dagger}$	$0.4933^{\ddagger}$
RM	$0.2824^{\ddagger}$	$0.5449^{\ddagger}$	$0.4966^{\ddagger}$	0.4928
RW+RQLM+RM	$0.2875^{\ddagger}$	$0.5612^{\ddagger}$	$0.5061^{\ddagger}$	$0.4974^{\ddagger}$
	Optimal Parameters:			
QL	$\mu = 1000$			
SRM	$k = 10, N = 50, \lambda = 0.3, \beta_p = 0.99, \beta_q = 0.01$			
RQLM	$k = 100, \beta = 0.95$			
RW+RQLM	$k = 100, \beta = 0.95, \alpha = 0.01, \gamma = 0.6$			
RM	$k = 50, N = 50, \lambda' = 0.2$			
RW+RQLM+RM	$k' = 50, N = 50, \lambda' = 0.2$			

Table 2: Retrieval performance and tuned parameters on the TREC 2004 Terabyte Track queries (train).

	MAP	P@10	P@30	NDCG
QL	0.3043	0.5560	0.4980	0.5475
SRM	0.3110	0.5700	0.5060	0.5502
RQLM	$0.3161^{\ddagger}$	$0.5960^{\ddagger}$	0.5120	$0.5601^{\ddagger}$
RW+RQLM	$0.3132^{\dagger}$	$0.5840^{\ddagger}$	0.5067	$0.5579^{\ddagger}$
RM	$0.3540^{\ddagger}$	$0.5800^{\ddagger}$	$0.5440^{\ddagger}$	$0.5797^{\ddagger}$
RW+RQLM+RM	$0.3617^{\ddagger *}$	$0.6080^{\ddagger *}$	$0.5580^{\ddagger}$	$0.5866^{\ddagger *}$

Table 3: Retrieval performance on the TREC 2005 Terabyte Track queries (test).

	MAP	P@10	P@30	statMAP	MPC(30)
QL	0.1951	0.3408	0.3354	0.1732	0.3636
SRM	0.2258‡	0.4388‡	0.3959‡	0.2069	0.4661
RQLM	0.2107‡	0.3714†	0.3694‡	0.1916	0.4215
RW+RQLM	0.2123‡	0.3796‡	0.3728‡	0.1908	0.4359
RM	0.2113†	0.3939‡	0.3646‡	0.1993	0.3970
RW+RQLM +RM	0.2284‡*	0.4408‡*	0.3891‡*	0.2213	0.4299
	Optimal Parameters:				
QL	$\mu = 1000$				
SRM	$k = 5, N = 100, \lambda = 0.4, \beta_p = 0.01, \beta_q = 0.99$				
RQLM	$k = 25, \beta = 0.9$				
RW+RQLM	$k = 25, \beta = 0.9, \alpha = 0.01, \gamma = 0.5$				
RM	$k = 50, N = 200, \lambda' = 0.3$				
RW+RQLM +RM	$k' = 50, N = 200, \lambda' = 0.3$				

Table 4: Retrieval performance and tuned parameters on the TREC 2009 Web Track queries (train).

	MAP	P@10	P@30	NDCG
QL	0.1761	0.2292	0.2451	0.3347
SRM	0.1808	0.2354	0.2556	0.3264
RQLM	0.1925‡	0.2646†	0.2708†	0.3509‡
RW+RQLM	0.1995‡	0.2688‡	0.2715†	0.3526‡
RM	0.1751	0.2729‡	0.2535	0.3233
RW+RQLM+RM	0.1979‡*	0.3125‡	0.2958‡*	0.3401*

Table 5: Retrieval performance on the TREC 2010 Web Track queries (test).

ing query language information to improve the search effectiveness. $\beta_p = 0.99, \beta_q = 0.01$ in the first retrieval task implies that the reconstructed query field content mainly comes from the content of the MS-QLOG-Web pages that have the highest likelihoods of generating the original query. In contrast, $\beta_p = 0.01, \beta_q = 0.99$ in the second retrieval task implies that the reconstructed query field content mainly determined by each query's similar queries' clicked pages, thus the query log information is more helpful for the search task on the ClueWeb09 data. However, we observe that on the test queries SRM achieved little improvement over the QL baseline. We will do more analysis on this issue in §4.3.3 to investigate some plausible causes, such as the sensitivity of the performance of SRM is to the change of its model parameters and irrelevant noise in the training data across different query sets.

4. The typical query expansion approach (RM) failed (i.e. performed worse than QL) on the TREC 2010 Web Track web search task (in Table 5), but leveraging the click-through query information discovered from random walk and our content based approach can make RM more resistent to irrelevant noise in the searched collection and effectively reduce the risk of *topic-drifting*. Indeed, on both training and test queries across different searched collections and retrieval tasks, RW+RQLM+RM approach performed robustly and very well: it achieved the best MAP on 3 of 4 query sets and the second best MAP on the remained query set.

It is worthwhile to compare our results with some very recently published results on the TREC Web Track *ad hoc* web search tasks on the ClueWeb09-T09B collection (our second retrieval task). Table 6 shows some results on the TREC 2009 Web Track *ad hoc* search task from some participants [15]. The 2nd-4th rows of the table show Koolen and Kamps' results[15] on the same retrieval task when they

	statMAP	MPC(30)
QL	0.1442	0.3079
Anchor	0.0567	0.5558
Mix	0.1643	0.4812
UDWAxQEWeb	0.1999	0.5010
uogTrdphCEwP	0.2072	0.4966
ICTNETADRun4	0.1746	0.4368

Table 6: Retrieval performance of some published results on the TREC 2009 Web Track *ad hoc* queries.

examined the potential of using existing anchor text in large scale web corpora for helping search. One major difference between their QL baseline and ours is that they used linear smoothing approach while we used Dirichlet smoothing. The 5th-7th rows of Table 6 show the top3 best official TREC submissions for the same retrieval task from other participants. Comparing Table 6 with our results in Table 4, our retrieval approaches that use discovered click-through query language information from sparse click-through data achieved similar or better performance, compared to these top-performing TREC submissions.

To summarize, our content based approach can effectively discover missing click-through query language information to help improving retrieval performance. The content based approach can be combined with the random walk approach to further improve the quality of the discovered language model information from click-through data. The query-side approach of handling click-through sparseness performs very well on some query sets but not on other query sets. The discovered click-through query information can be combined with the typical relevance model to further improve web search performance.

4.3.3 *Impact of Change of Model Parameters*

We are concerned about how sensitive different approaches' performance is to the change of their retrieval model parameters. Specifically, for the content based approach (RQLM), we are interested in the number of similar pages needed to build RQLMs for each page to be able to perform reasonably well and how the change of this number will affect the retrieval performance; for the combination approach (RW+RQLM), we are further interested in the impact of the augmented queries discovered by the random walk approach on the performance. For the SRM based approach, we are concerned about the impact of different number of feedback pages used to build SRM and the mixture weight between the original query language and the built SRM on the retrieval performance. As discussed in the previous section, our second retrieval task on the ClueWeb09-T09B collection better simulates the real-world web search scenarios; therefore, here we use this task for our investigation.

Figure 2(a) and (b) depict the model parameters' impact for RW+RQLM with training/testing queries in this retrieval task, respectively, where we fix $\alpha = 0.01, \beta = 0.9$ while varying γ and k. Figure 3(a) and (b) depict the model parameters' impact for SRM with training/testing queries, respectively, where we fix $\beta_p = 0.01, \beta_q = 0.99, N = 100$ while varying λ and k.

From Figure 2, we have the following major observations: **1.** Using click-associated queries from about 25 $\sim$ 35 most similar pages to build RQLM for each page can achieve near optimal retrieval performance on both training/test query sets. Increasing k beyond 35 brings little additional benefit to (or even hurt) the retrieval performance, and only changes the performance very slowly. This property means that in real-world use, for efficiency we need only index click-through information from a small number of similar pages of each page, without sacrificing the retrieval effectiveness. **2.** Using augmented queries discovered by the random walk approach from the click graph can slightly help the retrieval effectiveness. The mixture weight γ's value can be selected between $0.4 \sim 0.6$ across different query sets and the change of this value among this range has little impact on the retrieval performance. This also indicates that the augmented queries discovered by the random walk approach are at least as useful as the click-through query information discovered from the content based approach for search.

Figure 3 shows that the performance of SRM mainly depends on whether the training web pages (the MS-QLOG-Web collection here) contains useful content for helping to search the target web collection (the ClueWeb09-T09B here). For example, on the training queries, using only top-5 feedback pages for re-constructing the *PageContent* query field can achieve very good performance; in contrast, on the test queries, the improvement is very little. Furthermore, the mixture weight λ also affects SRM's retrieval performance significantly.

Figure 2 and 3 also reveal that for different query sets the optimal model parameters are very similar for RW+RQLM while different for SRM; therefore, if we exchange TREC 2009/2010 queries for training/test, RW+RQLM's parameters will be nearly the same and so will achieve near optimal retrieval performance while SRM's performance will significantly degrade.

5. CONCLUSIONS

In this paper, we adapt two language modeling based approaches to address the click-through sparseness problem in the context of using web query logs for helping web search.

Our first approach stems from the contextual translation approaches [28, 31] and uses web content similarity for discovering missing click-through query language model information for web pages with no or few clicks, in order to help search. This approach computes a relevant (click-associated) query language model, called RQLM, for each web page from the click-associated queries of its similar pages in the web query log, and then uses the RQLM to smooth the original document language model of each page for achieving better retrieval performance. Compared with the random walk approach [9], this content based approach does not need to use specific click graph structure to discover missing clicks thus can further mitigate the click-through sparseness. Furthermore, we present a combination approach that takes advantage of both random walk and the content based approach to further improve search.

Our second approach follows the query expansion approach and utilizes the semantic relation between the queries and the content of their clicked URLs in the web query log to reconstruct a structured variant of the relevance based language models, called Structured Relevance Models (SRM)[18, 19], for each user-input query, to help search.

We then demonstrated the effectiveness and compared the performance of different approaches of handling the click-through sparseness problem for web search with two recent sets of TREC *ad hoc* web search tasks. The results showed that discovering missing click-through query language information from click-through data can statistically significantly improve search performance, compared with two retrieval baselines (QL and RM) that did not use the discovered information. The document smoothing approaches (RQLM and RW+RQLM), performed well across different query sets while the query expansion approach (SRM) of using sparse click-through information was more sensitive to model parameter selection and irrelevant noise in the click-through data. The random walk approach complemented the content approach for addressing the click-through sparseness problem: the combination approach performed slightly better than the content-only approach in three of the four query sets in our experiments. In addition, the most complex approach (RW+RQLM+RM) that combines to use the typical query expansion approach (RM) and the discovered click-through query language information from RW+RQLM can **statistically significantly improve the highly effective RM baseline.**

There are several interesting directions of future work. It is worthwhile to explore using the discovered missing click-through query language features beyond the language modeling based retrieval framework, for example, using the discovered features in the learning-to-rank retrieval approach [5], so that we can combine different approaches described here with the Good-Turing based smoothing approach [11] to see whether the retrieval performance can be further improved. Moreover, here we have only explored using the contextual translation probability $p(P_i|P_0)$ between web pages to discover useful missing click-through query language features; theoretically, we may also use this probability to compute an expected feature $E(f_{P_0}) = \sum_{f_{P_i} \in \mathcal{F}} f_{P_i} \times p(P_i|P_0)$ for a page P_0 for any selected click-through feature from the same click-through features f_{P_i} of the page's similar pages P_i. Intuitively, this approach aims to smooth the click-through features for web pages with no clicks as in Gao et al.'s approach, but leverages the web content similarity during the smoothing. We would like to explore the utility of these smoothed click-through features for web search.

6. ACKNOWLEDGMENTS

This work was supported in part by the Center for Intelligent Information Retrieval, in part by NSF CLUE IIS-0844226, and in part by NSF grant #IIS-0910884. Any opinions, findings and conclusions or recommendations expressed in this material are the authors' and do not necessarily reflect those of the sponsors.

7. REFERENCES

[1] E. Agichtein, E. Brill, and S. Dumais. Improving web search ranking by incorporating user behavior information. In *SIGIR*, pages 19–26, 2006.

[2] J. A. Aslam and V. Pavlu. A practical sampling strategy for efficient retrieval evaluation. Technical report, Northeastern University, 2007.

[3] M. Bendersky and W. B. Croft. Analysis of long queries in a large scale search log. In *Workshop on Web Search Click Data*, pages 8–14, 2009.

[4] J. Broglio, J. P. Callan, and W. B. Croft. An overview of the INQUERY system as used for the TIPSTER project. Technical report, University of Massachusetts, Amherst, 1993.

[5] C. Burges, T. Shaked, E. Renshaw, A. Lazier, M. Deeds, N. Hamilton, and G. Hullender. Learning to rank using gradient descent. In *Proceedings of ICML*, pages 89–96, 2005.

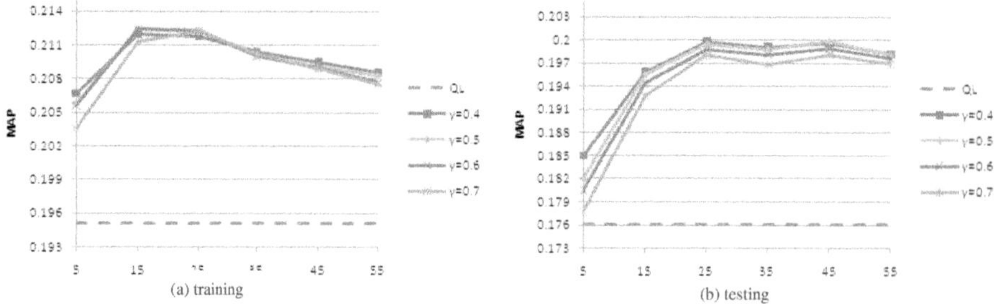

Figure 2: The impact of choosing different number (k) of most similar pages (represented by X-axis) and mixture weight γ (between the original click-associated query language model and the language model from the augmented queries discovered by the random walk approach) on RW+RQLM 's retrieval effectiveness. (a) with the training queries; (b) with the test queries.

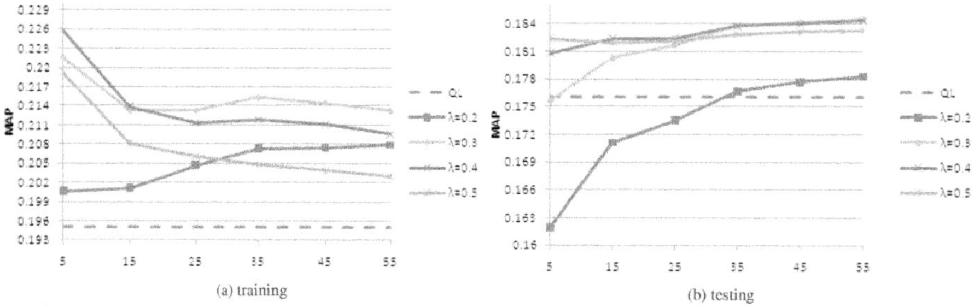

Figure 3: The impact of choosing different number (k) of retrieved pages (represented by X-axis) to build SRM and mixture weight λ (between the built SRM and the original query language model) on SRM's retrieval effectiveness. (a) with the training queries; (b) with the test queries.

[6] C. A. Clarke, N. Craswell, and I. Soboroff. Overview of the TREC 2009 Web Track. In *TREC*, 2009.

[7] C. L. A. Clarke, N. Craswell, and I. Soboroff. Overview of the TREC 2004 Terabyte Track. In *TREC*, 2004.

[8] C. L. A. Clarke, F. Scholer, and I. Soboroff. The TREC 2005 Terabyte Track. In *TREC*, 2005.

[9] N. Craswell and M. Szummer. Random walks on the click graph. In *SIGIR*, pages 239–246, 2007.

[10] F. Diaz and D. Metzler. Improving the estimation of relevance models using large external corpora. In *SIGIR*, pages 154–161, 2006.

[11] J. Gao, W. Yuan, X. Li, K. Deng, and J.-Y. Nie. Smoothing clickthrough data for web search ranking. In *SIGIR*, pages 355–362, 2009.

[12] I. Good. The population frequencies of species and the estimation of population parameters. *Biomerika*, 40(3):237–264, 1953.

[13] K. Järvelin and J. Kekäläinen. Cumulated gain-based evaluation of IR techniques. *ACM Transactions on Information Systems*, 20(4):422–446, 2002.

[14] T. Joachims. Optimizing search engines using clickthrough data. In *SIGKDD*, pages 133–142, 2002.

[15] M. Koolen and J. Kamps. The importance of anchor text for ad hoc search revisited. In *SIGIR*, pages 122–129, 2010.

[16] O. Kurland and L. Lee. Respect my authority!: Hits without hyperlinks, utilizing cluster-based language models. In *SIGIR*, pages 83–90, 2006.

[17] J. Lafferty and C. Zhai. Document language models, query models, and risk minimization for information retrieval. In *SIGIR*, pages 111–119, 2001.

[18] V. Lavrenko and W. B. Croft. Relevance based language models. In *SIGIR*, pages 120–127, 2001.

[19] V. Lavrenko, X. Yi, and J. Allan. Information retrieval on empty fields. In *NAACL-HLT*, pages 89–96, 2007.

[20] X. Li, Y. Wang, and A. Acero. Learning query intent from regularized click graphs. In *SIGIR*, pages 339–346, 2008.

[21] X. Liu and W. B. Croft. Cluster-based retrieval using language models. In *SIGIR*, pages 186–193, 2004.

[22] Q. Mei, D. Zhang, and C. Zhai. A general optimization framework for smoothing language models on graph structures. In *SIGIR*, pages 611–618, 2008.

[23] R. Nallapati, W. B. Croft, and J. Allan. Relevant query feedback in statistical language modeling. In *CIKM*, pages 560–563, 2003.

[24] P. Ogilvie and J. Callan. Combining document representations for known-item search. In *SIGIR*, pages 143–150, 2003.

[25] J. M. Ponte and W. B. Croft. A language modeling approach to information retrieval. In *SIGIR*, pages 275–281, 1998.

[26] F. Radlinski and T. Joachims. Active exploration for learning rankings from clickthrough data. In *SIGKDD*, pages 570–579, 2007.

[27] J. Seo, W. B. Croft, K. Kim, and J. Lee. Smoothing click counts for aggregated vertical search. In *Proceedings of ECIR*, pages 387–398, 2011.

[28] X. Wang and C. Zhai. Mining term association patterns from search logs for effective query reformulation. In *CIKM*, pages 479–488, 2008.

[29] X. Wei and W. B. Croft. LDA based document models for ad hoc retrieval. In *SIGIR*, pages 178–185, 2006.

[30] G.-R. Xue, H.-J. Zeng, Z. Chen, Y. Yu, W.-Y. Ma, W. Xi, and W. Fan. Optimizing web search using web click-through data. In *CIKM*, pages 118–126, 2004.

[31] X. Yi and J. Allan. A content based approach for discovering missing anchor text for web search. In *SIGIR*, pages 427–434, 2010.

Interactive Sense Feedback for Difficult Queries

Alexander Kotov
akotov2@illinois.edu

ChengXiang Zhai
czhai@illinois.edu

Department of Computer Science
University of Illinois at Urbana-Champaign
Urbana, IL, 61801, USA

ABSTRACT

Ambiguity of query terms is a common cause of inaccurate retrieval results. Existing work has mostly focused on studying how to improve retrieval accuracy by automatically resolving word sense ambiguity. However, fully automatic sense identification and disambiguation is a very challenging task. In this work, we propose to involve a user in the process of disambiguation through interactive sense feedback and study the potential effectiveness of this novel feedback strategy. We propose several general methods to automatically identify the major senses of query terms based on global analysis of document collection and generate concise representations of the discovered senses to the users. This feedback strategy does not rely on initial retrieval results, and thus can be especially useful for improving the results of difficult queries. We evaluated the effectiveness of the proposed methods for sense identification and presentation through simulation experiments and user studies, which both indicate that sense feedback strategy is a promising alternative to the existing interactive feedback techniques such as relevance feedback and term feedback.

Categories and Subject Descriptors

H.3.3 [**Information Storage and Retrieval**]: Information Search and Retrieval—*search process, query formulation, relevance feedback*

General Terms

Algorithms, Experimentation

Keywords

Query Analysis, Query Reformulation, Interactive Feedback, Sense Disambiguation

1. INTRODUCTION

Ambiguity is a fundamental property of natural language, which negatively affects the quality of retrieval results by decreasing precision. Generally, an ambiguous query can be defined as any query which contains one or several polysemous terms. The difficulty of lexical ambiguity resolution (or sense disambiguation) varies greatly depending on several factors. When a query is sufficiently long, other terms in the query may serve as effective disambiguation clues due to the collocation effects [12]. In such cases, a search system may attempt to resolve ambiguity in an unsupervised way or by leveraging external resources, such as on-line dictionaries [13] or thesauri (e.g., WordNet [34] [30] [15]). Automatic disambiguation, however, proved to be very challenging, particularly because queries are usually very short and even humans cannot perform it with perfect accuracy.

The problem of ambiguity is exacerbated when a user's information need corresponds to a minority (non-popular) sense of an ambiguous query term in the collection. In such a case, the initial retrieval results would most likely be dominated by a large number of non-relevant documents covering the popular, but distracting senses of an ambiguous query term, while the relevant documents covering the non-popular sense that the user is interested in may be ranked so far down in the ranked list that even diversification of search results would not be very helpful. Clearly, for such difficult queries, any feedback techniques that rely on the assumption that there is some relevant information in the top ranked results (e.g., pseudo feedback, document-level relevance feedback, top results-based term feedback) would not work well either. Consequently, designing an effective feedback method for such difficult queries is a theoretically and practically important problem, particularly in those domains, where short and ambiguous queries prevail, such as Web search.

In this work, we propose *interactive sense feedback* (ISF), a new method for interactive query disambiguation and reformulation, which, unlike the previously proposed methods for interactive relevance feedback [21], such as explicit [9] and term feedback [10] [31], does not rely on the assumption that the initial retrieval results contain relevant documents. Because of its independence of the initial retrieval results, ISF can leverage user interaction both during the early stages of the search process or after it is complete.

At the high level, the proposed ISF is similar to query spelling correction, a popular and widely used feature of all major search engines. When a user submits a misspelled query, she may not be aware (at least immediately) of the reason the search results are of poor quality. A search system, however, can detect the problem, step in and try to improve the results by asking a user if she accidentally mis-

CIKM'11, October 24–28, 2011, Glasgow, Scotland, UK.

spelled the query. Similarly, when users submit ambiguous queries, they are likely to spend some time and effort perusing search results, not realizing that the sense of a polysemous term that they had in mind is not the most common sense in the collection being searched. Similar to spelling correction, along with presenting the initial search results, a search system can provide sense suggestions to narrow down the scope of the query. Ideally, sense suggestions can be presented as clarification questions (e.g., *"Did you mean <ambiguous query term> as <sense label>?"*), where the *sense label* can be either a single term or multiple terms.

Our approach is aiming to *only signal and reveal the ambiguity* of one or several query terms, leaving the final decision whether to disambiguate the query or not to the user. In some sense, our approach takes the best of both worlds: search systems can leverage the vastness of the data and their processing capabilities to infer the *collection-specific senses* of query terms and signal potential problems early on, while the users can leverage their intelligence and world knowledge to interpret the signals from the system and make the final decision. If the users are satisfied with search results, they may simply disregard sense suggestions. However, if the quality of search results is poor and a user can easily identify the desired sense of an ambiguous query term, she may indicate that sense and rely on the search system to update the results, according to the provided feedback.

We illustrate the idea of interactive sense feedback with the following example scenario. Suppose a user submits an ambiguous short query like "piracy" and is looking for documents about instances of copyright law violations as opposed to armed ship hijackings. In a collection of recent news documents, the intended sense of "piracy" corresponds to a minority sense, and one would expect the top-ranked retrieved documents to be non-relevant. Instead of having a user go through the search results and locate the relevant documents, a search system can instead find all the contexts, in which the query term occurred in the collection, indicate that the query term likely has two distinct collection-specific senses and ask the user *"Did you mean piracy as copyright infringement?"* or *"Did you mean piracy as ship hijacking?"*.

From the above discussion, it follows that interactive sense feedback needs to address the following two major problems. The first problem is designing an efficient algorithm for automatic off-line identification of discriminative senses of query terms through the *global* analysis of document collection. We emphasize the global analysis because a local analysis method such as pseudo-feedback cannot discover minority senses when the initial search results are poor, a scenario which we focus on in this work. The second problem is how to generate a representation of the discovered senses in such a way that each sense is easily interpretable and the best sense (i.e. the sense that results in the best retrieval performance) is easily identifiable by the users.

To solve the first problem, we propose and study several different algorithms for discovering the query term senses based on the global analysis of the collection. We compare these algorithms based on their upper bound retrieval performance and select the best performing one.

To solve the second problem, we propose several alternative methods for concise representation of the discovered senses and conducted a user study to evaluate the effectiveness of each method with the actual retrieval performance of user sense selections.

The rest of the paper is organized as follows. In the next section, we review the related work. In Section 3, we introduce the general idea and formally define the concept of interactive sense feedback. In Sections 4 and 5, we provide a detailed description of the methods used for sense detection and representation, respectively. In Section 6, we experimentally determine the potential and actual retrieval effectiveness of sense feedback and report the results of our user study. Finally, section 7 concludes the work and provides directions for future research.

2. RELATED WORK

Methods to improve the quality of retrieval results by reducing the negative impact of lexical ambiguity have been studied for many years and this research direction proved to be very challenging. Below we briefly overview three major lines of related previous work.

The first line is aimed at understanding the nature of lexical ambiguity in IR. This direction has been started by the work of Krovetz and Croft [12], who conducted a series of experiments in order to examine the quantitative aspects of lexical ambiguity in IR test collections and determined its influence on retrieval performance. They concluded that achieving benefits from disambiguation methods is dependent on how successful a sense-aware IR system is in discriminatingly applying them, however an effective and robust automatic disambiguation method is still an open problem in IR. Their results were later enhanced by a series of works by Sanderson [26, 23, 24, 22]. In [22], Sanderson concluded that improvements in IR effectiveness from using automatic disambiguation methods can be observed only if those methods can provide the accuracy close to that of humans and wrong disambiguation decisions can dramatically hurt the retrieval performance.

The second line aims at performing automatic sense disambiguation during retrieval by using external resources (such as machine-readable dictionaries [13], thesauri (e.g., WordNet) or supervised methods. Voorhees [34] conducted the first large scale study of a retrieval system which featured automatic word sense disambiguation based on WordNet and concluded that automatic sense disambiguation did not improve the performance. Mandala et al. [17] proposed a method to combine three different thesaurus types for query expansion: manually constructed (WordNet), automatically constructed based on document co-occurrence relations and automatically constructed based on head-modifier relations and found out that improvements in retrieval performance can be achieved by combining all three types of resources. Liu et al. [15] proposed several heuristics for disambiguating the query terms that used adjacent query terms and WordNet. Kim [11] proposed an approach for coarse-grained disambiguation of nouns by mapping them into 25 unique terms associated with the root synsets of each of the noun hierarchies in WordNet. Gonzalo et al. [8] showed that the performance of vector space retrieval model can be improved if WordNet synsets are chosen as the indexing space. In general, approaches relying on external resources share the common problems of coverage (a query term may have a specialized sense in a particular domain, which may not be covered by a generic lexical resource) and domain mismatch (some of the dictionary senses may not occur in the collection being searched). Automatic disambiguation has also been addressed in the context of vector space retrieval methods. Schütze et al. [27] proposed a method to learn the senses from a vector space representation of the term contexts during training and classify the senses during testing. They achieved the best experimental results by allowing a word to be tagged with up to three senses and combining term and sense ranking. Stokoe et al. [29] used state-of-the-art disambiguation algorithm based on supervised machine learning that was trained on an external corpus to perform retrieval experiments on the TREC WT10G data set and concluded that sense based vector space retrieval consistently outperformed traditional vector space models even if the accuracy of the disambiguation algorithm is below 90%. The query expansion method proposed by Qiu and Frei [20] for generalized vector-space retrieval models used global term co-occurrence data to select the best expansion terms by ranking them according to the vector-space based similarity score of a term to the entire query. Fonseca et al. [7] represented the query concepts as a set of related past queries from the search logs and proposed an interactive query expansion technique for web queries.

The third line aims at addressing the problem of ambiguity indirectly by improving the initial retrieval results through various types of relevance feedback. In the context of pseudo-relevance feedback (PRF), the problems of minority sense and query drift have been addressed through clustering [32] [14] [33]. In particular, Liu and Croft [16] proposed to cluster the initially retrieved documents and used the discovered clusters to smooth the document language model. Pu and He [19] went one step further and proposed to use independent component analysis as a dimensionality reduction technique and cluster the top retrieved documents in the latent semantic space. Xu et al. [36] used a combination of query-specific clustering and external resource (Wikipedia) for query expansion. However, both the traditional and clustering-based PRF can be effective only when there are some relevant documents in the top results, which is generally not the case for difficult queries. In the context of interactive term feedback, an alternative to the document-based relevance feedback, Anick and Tipireni [3] proposed a method for creating lexical hierarchies of expansion terms, based on the linguistically-aware processing of the document collection. A similar method, but based on using simple co-occurrence statistics has been proposed by Sanderson and Croft [25]. Carmel et al. [5] proposed to use lexical affinities to automatically select the expansion terms in such a way that the information gain of the retrieved document set is maximized. Tan et al. [31] proposed a method for interactive term feedback based on clustering the initial retrieval results. They reported that users were having difficulties in selecting the good expansion terms, primarily because term clustering generally lacks semantic coherence. We believe that term feedback has two major limitations. First, similar to PRF, it uses the initially retrieved documents for generating feedback terms, which makes it ineffective for difficult queries. Second, since term feedback does not take into account the relationships between individual terms, it cannot capture the semantics of the feedback terms well. Wang et al. [35] proposed the concept of negative feedback, when only negative signals are used for improving difficult queries, however, to the best of our knowledge, there has been no prior work on improving difficult queries through interactive relevance feedback. Therefore, the primary motivation behind interactive sense feedback is to overcome the limitations of existing relevance feedback methods for difficult queries, when poor search results are caused by query ambiguity.

3. INTERACTIVE SENSE FEEDBACK

3.1 General idea

Despite years of research, there is still no consensus within the AI and IR research communities about what kind of information is the most useful for sense disambiguation. Depending on the definition of a word sense, there are two major ways to approach word sense disambiguation. Within the first view, the sense of a word is defined as its intrinsic property, which corresponds to the high-level concepts denoted by the word lexeme. This view assumes that the correct and comprehensive specification of the word sense requires complete knowledge about the world and can only be provided in the form of a manually created knowledge base. The second view assumes that the sense of a word, rather than being its predefined property, is determined by various contextual clues, such as its syntactic role and the nearby context.

This work adopts the latter view and is based on the assumption that *the senses of a query term can be differentiated by grouping and analyzing all the contexts, in which it appears in the collection.* Consequently, a sense-aware retrieval model should consider not only individual terms, but also all the contexts, in which those terms appear in the collection. It uses two types of contexts: the *local context*, which corresponds to an individual co-occurrence of a term with other terms within a certain unit of text (such as a text window or the entire document) and the *global context*, which aggregates all the local contexts associated with a word. Such aggregation allows to eliminate noise and identify strong, collection-wide contextual co-occurrence relations of a given term with other terms in the vocabulary of a collection. The global context for a particular term can then be analyzed to identify the subsets of terms, which consistently appear in the global contexts of each other. We consider such subsets of terms as the *collection-specific senses* of a query term.

Algorithm-wise, sense feedback works as follows:

1. First, a document collection is preprocessed to construct a contextual similarity matrix, which includes all the terms in the vocabulary of a collection using one of the methods in Section 4.1; the *contextual similarity matrix* is a sparse matrix, in which the rows corresponds to the global contexts of each term in the vocabulary of a collection.

2. Given a query, the retrieval system first constructs a *query term similarity graph* for each query term, which includes all the terms appearing in the global context of the given query term and the contextual co-occurrence relations between them. Next the system identifies clusters of terms in the query term similarity graph. Each of those clusters is then converted into a language model, which takes into account the strength of relations between the terms in the contextual similarity matrix and represents the *collection-specific sense* of a query term.

3. For each of the identified senses, the system generates a concise representation using the method described in Section 5, which can be presented to a user. If a user recognizes the intended sense among those presented by the system, the language model of the original query is updated with the language model of the selected sense. The updated query language model can then be used to retrieve a new set of documents reflecting user feedback and focused on the specific sense of the initially ambiguous query term.

The interactive sense feedback approach has several advantages over the existing feedback methods. Firstly, sense feedback does not rely on the initial retrieval results and can be used either on-line or off-line. Secondly, only those senses that actually occur in the collection would be presented to the users. Finally, sense feedback does not rely on any external resources, and hence is completely general.

3.2 Formal definition

We study interactive sense feedback with the language modeling approach to IR, specifically the KL-divergence retrieval model [37], according to which the retrieval task involves estimating a query language model, Θ_q for a given term-based query q and document language models Θ_{D_i} for each document D_i in the document collection $C = \{D_1, \ldots, D_m\}$. The documents in the collection are scored and ranked according to the Kullback-Leibler divergence:

$$\mathrm{KL}(\Theta_q || \Theta_D) = \sum_{w \in V} p(w|\Theta_q) \log \frac{p(w|\Theta_q)}{p(w|\Theta_D)}$$

Within the KL-divergence retrieval model, relevance feedback is considered as the process of updating the query language model Θ_q, given the feedback obtained after the initial retrieval results are presented to the users. Such feedback may be explicitly provided by the user or implicitly derived from the retrieved results. According to this view, sense feedback can be treated as the process of updating Θ_q with the sense of an ambiguous query term identified by the user as relevant to her information need.

By following the language modeling approach, given a term-based query $q = \{q_1, \ldots, q_n\}$, a particular sense s of the query term q_i is represented as a *sense language model* $\hat{\Theta}^s_{q_i}$.

Definition 1. Sense Language Model $\hat{\Theta}^s_t$ *for a particular sense s of term $t \in V$ is a probability distribution $p(w|\hat{\Theta}^s_t)$ over a subset of words $S \subseteq V$, where V is a vocabulary of a particular document collection C.*

Given that a user selects a particular sense s for the query term q_i, the language model $\hat{\Theta}^s_{q_i}$ associated with the selected sense can be naturally used for updating the original query language model Θ_q through linear interpolation:

$$p(w|\tilde{\Theta}_q) = \alpha p(w|\Theta_q) + (1-\alpha) p(w|\hat{\Theta}^s_{q_i})$$

where α is the interpolation coefficient between the sense language model and the original query model.

Definition 2. Contextual Term Similarity Matrix *is a sparse matrix $\mathbf{S}$ of size $n \times n$ where $n = |V|$. Each row $\mathbf{S}_i$ corresponds to a word $w_i \in V$ and represents a probability distribution over all other words w in the vocabulary V, such that the probability mass would be concentrated on the terms, which are strongly semantically related to w_i. Each element $\mathbf{S}_{ij}$ of the matrix corresponds to a probability $p(w_j|w_i)$, which indicates the strength of semantic relatedness of the words w_i and w_j in a document collection C.*

Definition 3. Term Similarity Graph $G_{w_i} = (V_{w_i}, E_{w_i})$ *for a term w_i is a graph, in which $\forall j \in V_{w_i}, \mathbf{S}_{ij} \neq 0$ and $\forall u, v$, such that $(u, v) \in E_{w_i}$, $\mathbf{S}_{uv} \neq 0$.*

Having formally defined the concept of a sense, in the following sections we discuss the proposed approaches to sense detection and presentation in more detail.

4. SENSE DETECTION

Our sense detection method has two components: constructing the contextual similarity matrix and clustering the query term similarity graph. We discuss each below.

4.1 Contextual term similarity matrix construction

Constructing the contextual similarity matrix for a document collection requires a method to calculate the strength of relations between the terms in the vocabulary. In this work, we experiment with two such methods: mutual information (MI) and HAL scores.

4.1.1 Mutual Information

Given two words w and v, the mutual information between them is calculated by comparing the probability of observing w and v together with the probabilities of observing them independently, according to the following formula:

$$MI(w,v) = \sum_{X_w=0,1} \sum_{X_v=0,1} p(X_w, X_v) \log \frac{p(X_w, X_v)}{p(X_w)p(X_v)}$$

where X_w and X_v are binary variables indicating whether w or v are present or absent in a document. The probabilities are estimated as follows:

$$\begin{aligned}
p(X_w = 1) &= \frac{c(X_w = 1)}{N} \\
p(X_w = 0) &= 1 - p(X_w = 1) \\
p(X_v = 1) &= \frac{c(X_v = 1)}{N} \\
p(X_v = 0) &= 1 - p(X_v = 1) \\
p(X_w = 1, X_v = 1) &= \frac{c(X_w = 1, X_u = 1)}{N} \\
p(X_w = 1, X_v = 0) &= \frac{c(X_w = 1) - c(X_w = 1, X_v = 1)}{N} \\
p(X_w = 0, X_v = 1) &= \frac{c(X_v = 1) - c(X_w = 1, X_v = 1)}{N} \\
p(X_w = 0, X_v = 0) &= 1 - p(X_w = 1, X_v = 0) - \\
&\quad p(X_w = 0, X_v = 1) - p(X_w = 1, X_v = 1)
\end{aligned}$$

where $c(X_w = 1)$ and $c(X_v = 1)$ are the numbers of documents containing the words w and v, respectively, and $c(X_w = 1, X_v = 1)$ is the number of documents that contain both w and v. Mutual information measures the strength of association between the two words and can be considered as a measure of their semantic relatedness. The higher the mutual information between the two words, the more often they tend to occur in the same document, and hence, the more semantically related they are. For each term in the vocabulary of the collection, we identify the top k terms that have the highest mutual information scores with the given term and use them as a global similarity context of a term in the contextual similarity matrix of the collection.

4.1.2 Hyperspace Analog to Language

Hyperspace Analogue to Language (or HAL) [4] is a representational model for high dimensional concept spaces. It was created based on the studies of human cognition. Previous work [28] has demonstrated that HAL can be effectively applied to IR. Constructing the HAL space for an n-term

	the	eff	of	poll	on	pop
the	1	2	3	4	5	
eff	5					
of	4	5				
poll	4	5				
on	2	3	4	5		
pop	5	1	2	3	4	

Table 1: HAL space matrix for the sentence "the effects of pollution on the population"

vocabulary involves traversing a sliding window of width w over each word in the corpus, ignoring punctuation, sentence and paragraph boundaries. All words within a sliding window are considered as the local context of the term, over which the sliding window is centered. Each word in the local context receives a score according to its distance from the center of the sliding window (words that are closer to the center receive higher score). After traversing the entire corpus, an $n \times n$ HAL space matrix $\mathbf{H}$, which aggregates the local contexts for all the terms in the vocabulary is produced. In this matrix, the row vectors encode the preceding word order and the column vectors encode the posterior word order. An example HAL space matrix for the sentence "the effects of pollution on the population" constructed using the sliding window of size 10 (5 words before and after the center word) is shown in Table 1.

In the HAL-based approach, the global co-occurrence matrix is first produced by merging the row and column corresponding to each term in the HAL space matrix. Each term t corresponds to a row in the global co-occurrence matrix $\mathbf{H}_t = \{(t_1, c_1), \ldots, (t_m, c_m)\}$, representing the number of co-occurrences of the term t with all other terms in the vocabulary. After the merge, each row $\mathbf{H}_t$ in the global co-occurrence matrix is normalized to obtain the contextual term similarity matrix for the collection:

$$\mathbf{S}_{ti} = \frac{c_i}{\sum_{j=1}^{m} c_j}$$

Unlike mutual information, HAL uses the contextual windows of sizes smaller than the entire document to create the local contexts, which presumably would produce less noisy sets of semantically related terms.

4.2 Sense detection algorithm

Algorithm 1 is a high-level representation of a method to detect the senses of a given query term q_i.

Algorithm 1 Sense detection for a query term q_i

1. **forall** $j : \mathbf{S}_{ij} \neq 0$
   $V_{q_i} \leftarrow V_{q_i} \cup j$
2. **forall** $(u, v) : (u, v) \in V_{q_i} \times V_{q_i}$
   if $\mathbf{S}_{uv} \neq 0$
   $E_{q_i} \leftarrow E_{q_i} \cup ((u, v); \mathbf{S}_{uv})$
   $G_{q_i} \leftarrow G(V_{q_i}, E_{q_i})$
3. $C \leftarrow cluster(G_{q_i})$
   for $k = 1$ to $|C|$
   forall $t : t \in V_{C_k}$
4. $p(t|\hat{\Theta}^k_{q_i}) = \frac{\sum_{v:(t,v) \in E_{C_k}} \mathbf{S}_{tv}}{\sum_{w \in V_{C_k}} \sum_{u:(w,u) \in E_{C_k}} \mathbf{S}_{wu}}$

The algorithm works as follows:

1. Given a query term q_i, a set of terms related to q_i from the contextual similarity matrix $\mathbf{S}$ forms a set of vertices of the term similarity graph G_{q_i};
2. For each pair of vertices in G_{q_i}, check if there exists a relation in $\mathbf{S}$ with non-zero weight between the terms corresponding to those vertices. If so, the strength of relation becomes the weight of the edge between those terms in G_q;
3. The dynamically constructed query term similarity graph G_q is clustered into a set of subgraphs using one of the graph clustering algorithms;
4. Each cluster (subgraph) C_k is converted into a sense language model $\hat{\Theta}^k_{q_i}$, by normalizing the sum of the weights of all edges adjacent to each term node in the cluster with the sum of the weights of all edges in the cluster.

The hypothesis that the query term similarity graphs contain inherent clustering structure is based on the observation that they are likely to be small world graphs. Small world graphs correspond to a subset of graphs, in which most pairs of nodes are connected with very short paths. Small world graphs are known to contain inherent community or cluster structure. In this work, we experiment with two methods for finding this structure: Clauset-Newman-Moore community clustering algorithm [6] and clustering by committee [18].

5. SENSE PRESENTATION

In the proposed sense feedback approach, a sense is represented as a sense language model. Although such a representation is effective for retrieval, it may not be suitable for presenting the senses to the users, since interpreting it may place a significant cognitive burden on them. Therefore, we need to generate a concise representation of a sense that can be easily interpreted. We explore two sense presentation methods: using the top k terms with the highest probability in the sense language model and selecting a small number of the most representative terms from the sense language model as a sense label. The latter approach uses a subgraph of the query term similarity graph, from which the sense language model was created to find a subset of terms that cover the subgraph in such a way that the sum of the weights of the vertices in the cover is maximized. This is known as the Dominating Set Problem, which is NP-complete.

Algorithm 2 Generate a set of labels L for a sense language model $\hat{\Theta}^s_q$

$L \leftarrow \varnothing$
$C \leftarrow \varnothing$
$W \leftarrow \varnothing$
forall $t : t \in \hat{\Theta}^s_q$
1. $W_t \leftarrow W_t \cup \sum_{v:(t,v) \in E_{C_s}} \mathbf{S}_{tv}$
   $W \leftarrow sort(W)$
2. **forall** $t : t \in W_t$
   if $t \notin C$
3. $L \leftarrow L \cup t$
   forall $v : (t, v) \in E_{C_s}$
   $C \leftarrow C \cup v$

Therefore, we employ a greedy Algorithm 2, which works as follows:

1. Sort the vertices according to their weights;
2. Traverse the sorted set of vertices W_t, each time selecting the remaining *uncovered* vertex with the highest weight and add this vertex to the set of sense labels L;

3. Add the selected vertex and all the vertices adjacent to it in the cluster subgraph to the set of covered vertices and select the next label, until all the vertices of the subgraph, which corresponds to the labeled sense, are covered.

6. EXPERIMENTS

In this section, we present the results for experimental evaluation of sense feedback. We first describe our experimental setup and two experimental settings used to study the upper-bound and actual retrieval effectiveness of sense feedback. In the first setting, in order to determine the upper bound for potential retrieval effectiveness of sense feedback on several standard TREC datasets, we simulated the optimal user behavior by measuring the retrieval performance of all the senses discovered by each sense detection method and saving only the results of the optimal (best performing) sense. We also determined the optimal parameter settings for each sense detection method through simulation experiments and compared the upper-bound effectiveness of each method with the baselines. In the second setting, in order to find out whether the users can recognize the query term senses discovered by the best sense detection method and effectively use them to improve the quality of retrieval results, we conducted a user study by asking the users to pick one sense for each query based on different sense presentation methods. We then determined the best method for sense presentation and the actual performance of sense feedback, using different sense presentation methods.

6.1 Datasets and experimental setup

All experiments were conducted on three standard TREC collections: AP (Associated Press), which was used for various Ad Hoc tracks; ROBUST04, which was used for the 2004 Robust track [1] and AQUAINT, which was used for the 2005 HARD [2] and Robust tracks. Various statistics for the experimental datasets are summarized in Table 2.

Corpus	#Docs	Size(Mb)	#Topics	Avg. top.
AP88-89	164,597	507	100	3.5
ROBUST04	528,155	1910	250	2.65
AQUAINT	1,033,461	3042	50	2.56

Table 2: Statistics of the experimental datasets

The TREC topics 51-150 for the AP88-89 collection are long, sentence-like queries, including on average more than 3 query terms. The TREC topics 301-450 and 601-700 for the ROBUST04 collection are mostly 2-3 term queries with a small number of highly ambiguous one term queries (e.g, metabolism, robotics, tourism, creativity). The AQUAINT topics include 50 topics, known to be hard (i.e. resulting in very low retrieval performance) from the previous Robust tacks. All documents and queries have been preprocessed by stemming with the Porter stemmer and removing the stop words. For each of the test collections, we precomputed the contextual term matrices using both the mutual information and HAL scores as measures of similarity. We did not include very rare terms (the ones that occur less than 5 times in the entire collection) or very popular ones (the ones that occur in more than 10% of documents) in the contextual term similarity matrices. A maximum of 100 most contextually similar terms according to the particular similarity measure have been stored for each term in the contextual term similarity matrix. For the construction of the query term similarity graphs, we selected only those terms with a similarity value greater than 0.001.

6.2 Upper-bound performance

We experimentally determine the upper bound for retrieval performance of sense feedback and compare it with the baseline feedback method on all three test collections. As a baseline, we use the model-based feedback method proposed in [38] with the suggested parameter settings: mixture noise was set to 0.95 and feedback coefficient to 0.9. Note that since the proposed sense feedback method is meant to be a complementary, rather than a competing method to pseudo feedback (any pseudo feedback method can be easily combined with sense feedback), we only include pseudo feedback as a reference baseline and are not interested in comparing with the best performing pseudo feedback methods.

The upper bound for the retrieval performance of sense feedback is determined through simulation of a user who is always able to select the optimal sense for each query. Specifically, we first determine all possible senses for each query term and use each sense to update the initial query model, perform retrieval, and estimate its effectiveness using the relevance judgments. The sense that maximizes the average precision of the retrieved results is then chosen as the best sense for a given query. For model-based pseudo-relevance feedback we used the top 10 retrieved documents. For initial retrieval, we used the KL divergence retrieval method with a Dirichlet smoothing prior set to 2000. Before comparing different sense detection methods to the baseline in the following section we determine the optimal configuration for each of them. We use the AP88-89 dataset for parameter tuning.

6.2.1 *Parameter setting*

First, we set the interpolation coefficient α to 0.9 and empirically determined the optimal size of the sliding window, used for construction of the HAL-based contextual similarity matrix. Figure 1 shows the performance of Community Clustering (CC) and Clustering By Committee (CBC) with respect to MAP on the HAL-based contextual similarity matrix by varying the size of the sliding window used for its construction.

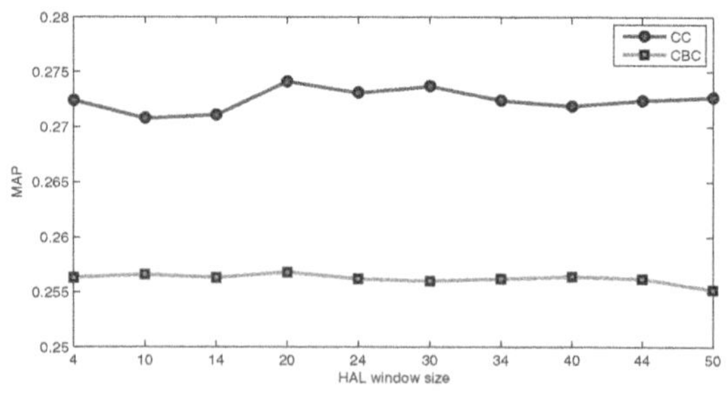

Figure 1: Performance of sense detection methods by varying the size of the HAL sliding window

Two important conclusions can be made based on the analysis of Figure 1. First, community clustering consistently outperforms clustering by committee for all sizes of the HAL window. Second, the optimal size of the HAL window for both sense detection methods is 20 (10 words to the left and 10 words to the right from the target word).

Next, we determine the optimal value of the interpolation coefficient α for different combinations of methods for construction of the contextual term similarity matrix and sense detection. In these experiments, we set the size of the HAL window to its optimal value of 20.

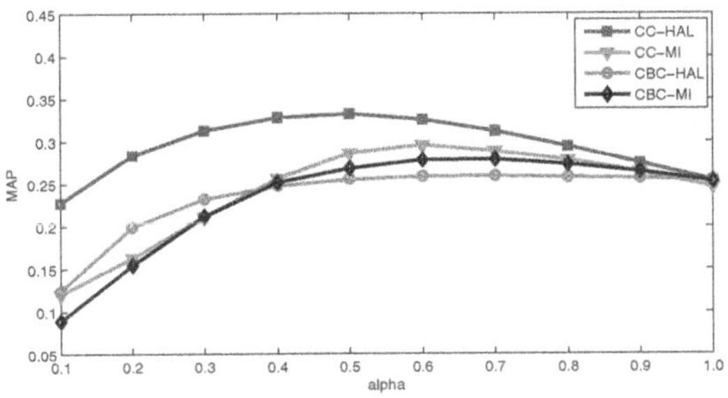

Figure 2: Performance of sense detection methods by varying the interpolation parameter α (the name of the sense detection method is before the hyphen and the similarity measure is after the hyphen).

From Figure 2, it follows that the combination of community clustering and HAL-based similarity matrix outperforms all other sense detection methods. The best configuration for each sense detection method is as follows: $w = 20$ and $\alpha = 0.5$ for CC-HAL; $w = 20$ and $\alpha = 0.7$ for CBC-HAL; $\alpha = 0.6$ for CC-MI and $\alpha = 0.7$ for CBC-MI. Having determined the optimal parameter setting for each sense detection method, in the next section we determine the best sense feedback method with respect to the upper-bound retrieval performance and compare it to the baselines.

6.2.2 *Upper-bound comparison of sense feedback*

The upper-bound performance of different combinations of methods for construction of contextual similarity matrix and sense detection on all three experimental datasets is summarized and compared with the baselines in Table 3. For these experiments, we used the best configuration for each sense detection method empirically determined in the previous section. All feedback methods are evaluated based on their ranking of the top 1000 documents with respect to the mean average (non-interpolated) precision (MAP), precision at top 5 and 20 documents (Pr@5 and Pr@20) and the total number of relevant documents retrieved (RR). We also report the retrieval performance of the initial KL-divergence based retrieval (KL), which is used for model-based pseudo-feedback (KL-PF). As explained earlier, we include pseudo feedback only as a reference baseline since sense feedback is meant to be complementary with pseudo feedback, and they can be easily combined.

From the analysis of Table 3, we can make the following conclusions:

1. The combination of community clustering and HAL-based construction of contextual similarity matrix outperforms all other methods and the baselines both in terms of MAP and Pr@N, indicating the potential of using the identify senses of the query terms to improve retrieval;

2. Community clustering generally outperforms clustering by committee both in combination with mutual information-based similarity matrix construction and HAL-based similarity matrix construction;

3. Sense feedback is effective for both short AQUAINT and ROBUST04 queries and longer AP queries.

Next, we compared the upper-bound effectiveness of sense feedback to the baselines in case of difficult queries (i.e., queries whose initial retrieval results have a MAP value less than 0.1). The results are presented in Table 4. As follows from Table 4, sense feedback effectively improves performance of difficult queries and outperforms both baselines, particularly improving the ranking of the top results, as indicated by significant improvement in Pr@5 and Pr@10, whereas for the AQUAINT dataset, pseudo-feedback decreased the retrieval performance.

		KL	KL-PF	SF
AP88-89	MAP	0.0346	0.0744	0.0876*
	Pr@5	0.1118	0.1529	0.25
	Pr@10	0.0824	0.1412	0.2031
ROBUST04	MAP	0.04	0.067	0.073*†
	Pr@5	0.1567	0.1675	0.3054
	Pr@10	0.1527	0.1554	0.2608
AQUAINT	MAP	0.0473	0.0371	0.0888*†
	Pr@5	0.125	0.075	0.2875
	Pr@10	0.1188	0.0813	0.2375

Table 4: Comparison of the upper-bound performance of sense feedback with KL-divergence retrieval model (KL) and model-based pseudo-relevance feedback (KL-PF) on difficult topics. * indicates statistically significant difference relative to KL (95% confidence level), according to the Wilcoxon signed-rank test. † indicates statistically significant difference relative to KL-PF (95% confidence level), according to the Wilcoxon signed-rank test.

The absolute numbers of difficult and normal topics improved by pseudo-feedback and sense feedback on different datasets are shown in Table 5.

	T	D	N	KL-PF		SF	
				D+	N+	D+	N+
AP	99	34	65	19	44	31	37
ROBUST04	249	74	175	37	89	68	153
AQUAINT	50	16	34	4	26	12	29

Table 5: Number of difficult (D) and normal (N) topics improved by pseudo-feedback (KL-PF) and sense feedback (SF) in different datasets.

As follows from Table 5, sense feedback improved the retrieval performance of a significantly larger number of both difficult and normal queries than pseudo-feedback in each dataset.

6.3 User study

Although it is clear from the simulation experiments that automatically identified senses have the potential to improve the quality of retrieval, the next important question is whether the users can recognize and select the optimal sense from retrieval perspective. In order to answer this question, we conducted a user study. For the user study we selected the AQUAINT topics, since those topics were used in 2005 TREC HARD track, which was created to explore

		KL	KL-PF	CC-MI	CC-HAL	CBC-MI	CBC-HAL
AP88-89	MAP	0.2492	0.3066	0.2955	0.3323	0.2786	0.2588
	RR	6833	7767	7058	7588	7141	6794
	Pr@5	0.4121	0.4444	0.5089	0.5771	0.4708	0.4371
	Pr@20	0.3652	0.4096	0.4417	0.4818	0.4042	0.3820
ROBUST04	MAP	0.2462	0.2569	0.2538	0.3002	0.2477	0.2571
	RR	10227	11386	9401	10842	9993	10387
	Pr@5	0.4659	0.4426	0.5159	0.5871	0.4840	0.4851
	Pr@20	0.3490	0.3454	0.3737	0.4116	0.3634	0.3657
AQUAINT	MAP	0.1942	0.2189	0.2237	0.2286	0.2060	0.2004
	RR	4107	4142	4166	4166	4153	4155
	Pr@5	0.496	0.488	0.5833	0.6120	0.5224	0.5
	Pr@20	0.394	0.427	0.4573	0.456	0.3959	0.389

Table 3: Comparison of the upper-bound performance of sense feedback methods with the baselines on all topics and all collections.

the methods for improving the accuracy of retrieval systems through "highly focused, short-duration interaction with the searcher". In the study, we asked the six participants to assume that they are typing a provided TREC query into the search engine box and the search engine asks to clarify the meaning of a query by first selecting a query term and one of its senses that best fits the description of the query and makes the entire query less ambiguous.

We used the best performing combination of community clustering and HAL scores to generate the candidate senses of the query terms for the user study and presented the discovered senses using one-term labels, two-term labels, three-term labels, top-three terms from the sense language model and the top 10 words from the sense language model. We then compared query term and sense selections made by the users with the query term and sense selections resulting in the best upper-bound retrieval performance determined through simulation. Table 6 shows the accuracy of sense selection by the users as the fraction (in percentages) of the users, who select *both* the optimal term and the optimal sense for feedback (in boldface) and the optimal term only (in parenthesis), regardless of whether the selected sense of the term is optimal.

	LAB1	LAB2	LAB3	SLM3	SLM10
User 1	**18**(56)%	**18**(60)%	**20**(64)%	**36**(62)%	**30**(60)%
User 2	**24**(54)%	**18**(50)%	**12**(46)%	**20**(42)%	**24**(54)%
User 3	**28**(58)%	**20**(50)%	**22**(46)%	**26**(48)%	**22**(50)%
User 4	**18**(48)%	**18**(50)%	**18**(52)%	**20**(48)%	**28**(54)%
User 5	**26**(64)%	**22**(60)%	**24**(58)%	**24**(56)%	**16**(50)%
User 6	**22**(62)%	**26**(64)%	**26**(60)%	**28**(64)%	**30**(62)%

Table 6: Percentage of users selecting the optimal sense of the optimal term for sense feedback (in boldface) and the optimal term, but suboptimal sense (in parenthesis).

As follows from Table 6, on average for most labeling methods the users were able to select the best term for sense feedback at least for half of the queries in the study, which indicates that users are able to identify the potentially ambiguous query terms that can benefit most from sense feedback. The percentages of times that the users can select *both* the best term for sense feedback *and* the best sense of that term are less, achieving the maximum of 36%. The following interesting conclusions can also be made from the analysis of Table 6:

1. Users do not tend to select the best sense more often when they observe more terms both in the label and the sense language model. One-term label is often sufficient to recognize the best sense and adding more terms can potentially mislead and confuse the user. The best result of 36% correctly identified best sense selections for one of the users is achieved when the top-3 terms in the sense language model are presented as a sense label.

2. 3-term labeling and choosing the top 3 terms from the sense language model perform comparably, which suggests that terms with the highest probability are generally the most representative for a sense, and vertices corresponding to them cover most of the sense subgraph.

In order to determine the practical utility of interactive sense feedback, we generated and evaluated the retrieval results based on the actual user sense selections. First we tuned α, the parameter for interpolating the sense language model into the original language model. Using sense selections of users for the best sense representation method (we used top 10 terms with the highest weights in the sense language model for parameter tuning and evaluation, since it is the best sense representation method, according to Table 6), we varied the value of the interpolation coefficient α and plotted the resulting performance on all AQUAINT queries with respect to MAP in Figure 3.

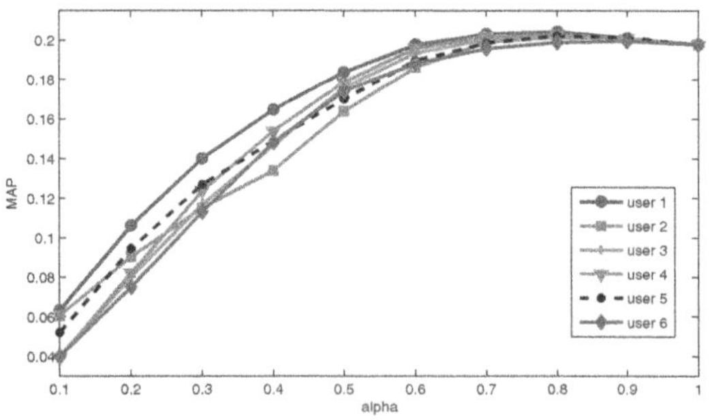

Figure 3: Retrieval performance of user sense selections for all queries in terms of MAP, depending on the value of interpolation parameter α.

From Figure 3 it follows that when $\alpha = 0.8$ sense feedback is consistently most effective in terms of MAP for all the users. Setting α to its optimal value, we determined the retrieval performance of user sense selections on difficult topics, according to different sense presentation methods. The results are presented in Table 7.

KL MAP=0.0473					
KL-PF MAP=0.0371					
	LAB1	LAB2	LAB3	SLM3	SLM10
User 1	0.0543	0.0518	0.0520	0.0564	0.0548
User 2	0.0516	0.0509	0.0515	0.0544	0.0536
User 3	0.0533	0.0547	0.0545	0.0550	0.0562
User 4	0.0506	0.0506	0.0507	0.0507	0.0516
User 5	0.0519	0.0529	0.0517	0.0522	0.0518
User 6	0.0526	0.0518	0.0524	0.056	0.0534

Table 7: Retrieval performance of user sense selections on difficult topics with respect to MAP, depending on the sense presentation method. Performance of the baselines is shown in the first two rows of the table.

As follows from Table 7, although the user sense selections do not achieve the upper bound performance, we can conclude that interactive sense feedback can effectively improve the retrieval performance of difficult queries.

6.4 Examples of discovered senses

To gain some insight at what the senses presented to the user look like, in Tables 8 and 9, we show some sample senses discovered by using the community clustering algorithm in combination with the HAL scores for the query term "stealth" of the AP topic #132 "stealth aircraft" and for the query term "cancer" of the AQUAINT topic # 310 "radio waves and brain cancer". Inferring the meaning behind each sense from the top representative terms is not hard, but sometimes requires certain background knowledge. For example Sense 2 of the query term "stealth" clearly corresponds to aircrafts with low radar visibility.

In case of the term "cancer", senses are less distinguishable, but nevertheless correspond to semantically coherent aspects of the query topic. For example, sense 1 most likely corresponds to cancer research, sense 2 is about different types of cancer, sense 3 is about cancer treatment and sense 4 is likely to correspond to cancer statistics in the US.

6.5 Error analysis

It is important to note that most TREC queries consist of at least 2-3 terms and are generally not highly ambiguous. Therefore, several collection-based senses of a query term may have comparable retrieval performance to the best sense and users often select these senses instead of the best performing sense. For example, for the query #625 "arrests bombing WTC" the best sense is the sense labeled as "police" for the query term "bombing". However, all the users who participated in the study selected the sense labeled as "arrest" for the query term "WTC". Similarly, for the query #639 "consumer on-line shopping" most users selected the sense labeled as "web" for the query term "consumer", whereas the best sense is the sense labeled "online" for the query term "shopping".

7. DISCUSSION AND FUTURE WORK

In this work, we presented a novel idea of interactive sense feedback. Sense feedback can automatically discover collection specific senses of query terms, present those senses to the users and update the queries based on user sense selections. Because the senses are discovered from the entire collection, this feedback strategy is not biased to focus on the popular senses covered in the top-ranked results, and thus is especially useful for improving performance for difficult queries.

We experimentally determined the upper bound for the retrieval performance of all possible combinations of several different methods for automatic sense discovery and measuring the strength of semantic relatedness between the terms. Experimental results show that the combination of Community Clustering and Hyperspace Analog to Language (HAL) results in the best overall retrieval performance and can also significantly improve the retrieval accuracy for difficult queries. We also proposed different presentation methods for the discovered senses and evaluated the effectiveness of user sense selections when senses are concisely represented. The results show that users are able to select the best senses in most cases, leading to improvement of average retrieval accuracy for difficult queries. Therefore, sense feedback has all the potential to be used as an alternative or supplemental technique to the existing interactive feedback methods, such as term, relevance and pseudo-feedback, particularly for difficult queries.

Our work can be extended in several ways. First, we can explore other methods for automatic sense detection and compare them with the ones proposed in this work. Second, we can investigate alternative ways of effectively presenting senses to the users. Finally, it would be very interesting to experiment with sense feedback on real ambiguous Web-style queries and incorporate sense feedback into search engine infrastructure as a complimentary strategy to search results diversification. We envision that sense feedback will show its full real potential in this case.

8. ACKNOWLEDGMENTS

This material is based upon work supported by the National Science Foundation under Grant Numbers IIS-0713581, CNS-0834709, and CNS 1028381, by a Sloan Research Fellowship, and by a Microsoft gift grant.

9. REFERENCES

[1] J. Allan. Overview of the trec 2004 robust retrieval track. In *Proceedings of TREC 13*, 2004.

[2] J. Allan. Hard track overview in trec 2005 - high accuracy retrieval from documents. In *Proceedings of TREC 14*, 2005.

[3] P. G. Anick and S. Tipirneni. The paraphrase search assistant: Terminological feedback for iterative information seeking. In *Proceedings of ACM SIGIR'99*, pages 153–161, 1999.

[4] C. Burgess, K. Livesay, and K. Lund. Explorations in context space: Words, sentences and discourse. *Discourse Processes*, 25:211–257, 1998.

[5] D. Carmel, E. Farchi, Y. Petruschka, and A. Soffer. Automatic query refinement using lexical affinities with maximal information gain. In *Proceedings of ACM SIGIR'02*, pages 283–290, 2002.

[6] A. Clauset, M. E. J. Newman, and C. Moore. Finding community structure in very large networks. *Physical Review E*, 70(6):066111, 2004.

[7] B. M. Fonseca, P. Golgher, B. Pôssas, B. Ribero-Neto, and N. Ziviani. Concept-based interactive query expansion. In *Proceedings of CIKM'05*, pages 696–703, 2005.

[8] J. Gonzalo, F. Verdejo, I. Chugur, and J. Cigarran. Indexing with wordnet synsets can improve text retrieval. In *Proceedings of ACL/COLING Workshop*

Sense 1		Sense 2		Sense 3		Sense 4	
w	$p(w\|s)$	w	$p(w\|s)$	w	$p(w\|s)$	w	$p(w\|s)$
budget	0.05	117a	0.068	missil	0.33	technolog	0.187
senat	0.05	us	0.05	midgetman	0.22	research	0.15625
fiscal	0.045	plane	0.047	mx	0.17	advanc	0.15625
cut	0.0421	fighter	0.0463	trident	0.14	new	0.06
chenei	0.0391	f	0.0461	nuclear	0.12	make	0.06

Table 8: Examples of senses discovered for the term "stealth" in the query "stealth aircraft"

Sense 1		Sense 2		Sense 3		Sense 4	
w	$p(w\|s)$	w	$p(w\|s)$	w	$p(w\|s)$	w	$p(w\|s)$
research	0.065	diseas	0.076	treatment	0.062	us	0.1847
new	0.057	caus	0.058	chemotherapi	0.06	women	0.1086
studi	0.050	liver	0.051	doctor	0.06	men	0.086
scientist	0.048	lung	0.049	tumor	0.052	breast	0.0976
dr	0.0448	drug	0.049	patient	0.05	ovarian	0.068

Table 9: Examples of senses discovered for the term "cancer" in the query "radio waves and brain cancer"

on Usage of WordNet for Natural Language Processing, 1998.

[9] M. Iwayama. Relevance feedback with a small number of relevance judgments: Incremental relevance feedback vs. document clustering. In *Proceedings of ACM SIGIR'00*, pages 10–16, 2000.

[10] D. Kelly and X. Fu. Elicitation of term relevance feedback: An investigation of term source and context. In *Proceedings of ACM SIGIR'06*, pages 453–460, 2006.

[11] S.-B. Kim, H.-C. Seo, and H.-C. Rim. Information retrieval using word senses: Root sense tagging approach. In *Proceedings of ACM SIGIR'04*, pages 258–265, 2004.

[12] R. Krovetz and W. B. Croft. Lexical ambiguity and information retrieval. *ACM Transactions on Information Systems*, 10(2):115–141, 1992.

[13] M. Lesk. Automatic sense disambiguation using machine readable dictionaries: How to tell a pine cone from an ice cream cone. In *Proceedings of SIGDOC'86*, pages 24–26, 1986.

[14] A. Leuski. Evaluating document clustering for interactive information retrieval. In *Proceedings of CIKM'01*, pages 33–40, 2001.

[15] S. Liu, F. Liu, C. Yu, and W. Meng. An effective approach to document retrieval via utilizing wordnet and recognizing phrases. In *Proceedings of ACM SIGIR'04*, pages 266–272, 2004.

[16] X. Liu and W. B. Croft. Cluster-based retrieval using language models. In *Proceedings of ACM SIGIR'04*, pages 186–193, 2004.

[17] R. Mandala, T. Tokunaga, and H. Tanaka. Combining multiple evidence from different types of thesaurus for query expansion. In *Proceedings of ACM SIGIR'99*, pages 191–197, 1999.

[18] P. Pantel and D. Lin. Discovering word senses from text. In *Proceedings of KDD'02*, pages 613–619, 2002.

[19] Q. Pu and D. He. Pseudo relevance feedback using semantic clustering in relevance language model. In *Proceedings of ACM CIKM'09*, pages 1931–1934, 2009.

[20] Y. Qiu and H.-P. Frei. Concept based query expansion. In *Proceedings of ACM SIGIR'93*, pages 160–169, 1993.

[21] I. Ruthven and M. Lalmas. A survey on the use of relevance feedback for information access systems. *Knowledge Engineering Review*, 18(2):95–145, 2003.

[22] M. Sanderson. Word sense disambiguation and information retrieval. In *Proceedings of ACM SIGIR'94*, pages 49–57, 1994.

[23] M. Sanderson. Retrieving with good sense. *Information Retrieval*, 2(1):49–69, 2000.

[24] M. Sanderson. Ambiguous queries: Test collections need more sense. In *Proceedings of ACM SIGIR'08*, pages 499–506, 2008.

[25] M. Sanderson and W. B. Croft. Deriving concept hierarchies from text. In *Proceedings of ACM SIGIR'99*, pages 206–213, 1999.

[26] M. Sanderson and C. van Rijsbergen. The impact on retrieval effectiveness of skewed frequency distributions. *ACM Transactions on Information Systems*, 17(4):440–465, 1999.

[27] H. Schütze and J. O. Pedersen. Information retrieval based on word senses. In *Proceedings of the 4th Annual Symposium on Document Analysis and Information Retrieval*, pages 161–175, 1995.

[28] D. Song and P. Bruza. Towards context sensitive information inference. *JASIST*, 54(4):321–334, 2003.

[29] C. Stokoe, M. P. Oakes, and J. Tait. Word sense disambiguation in information retrieval revisited. In *Proceedings of ACM SIGIR'03*, pages 159–166, 2003.

[30] M. Sussna. Word sense disambiguation for free-text indexing using a massive semantic network. In *Proceedings of CIKM'93*, pages 67–74, 1993.

[31] B. Tan, A. Velivelli, H. Fang, and C. Zhai. Term feedback for information retrieval with language models. In *Proceedings of ACM SIGIR'07*, pages 263–270, 2007.

[32] A. Tombros, R. Villa, and C. J. van Rijsbergen. The effectiveness of query-specific hierarchic clustering in information retrieval. *Information Processing and Management*, 38(4):559–582, 2002.

[33] R. Udupa, A. Bhole, and P. Bhattacharyya. ä term is known by the company it keeps: On selecting a good expansion set in pseudo-relevance feedback. In *Proceedings of ICTIR'09*, pages 104–115, 2009.

[34] E. M. Voorhees. Using wordnet to disambiguate word senses for text retrieval. In *Proceedings of ACM SIGIR'93*, pages 171–180, 1993.

[35] X. Wang, H. Fang, and C. Zhai. A study of methods for negative relevance feedback. In *Proceedings of ACM SIGIR'08*, pages 219–226, 2008.

[36] Y. Xu, G. J. Jones, and B. Wang. Query dependent pseudo-relevance feedback based on wikipedia. In *Proceedings of ACM SIGIR'09*, pages 59–66, 2009.

[37] C. Zhai and J. Lafferty. Document language models, query models, and risk minimization for information retrieval. In *Proceedings of SIGIR'01*, pages 111–119, 2001.

[38] C. Zhai and J. Lafferty. Model-based feedback in the language modeling approach to information retrieval. In *Proceedings of CIKM'01*, pages 403–410, 2001.

Reranking Search Results for Sparse Queries

Elif Aktolga and James Allan
Center for Intelligent Information Retrieval
Department of Computer Science
University of Massachusetts Amherst
Amherst, Massachusetts
{elif, allan}@cs.umass.edu

ABSTRACT

It is well known that clickthrough data can be used to improve the effectiveness of search results: broadly speaking, a query's past clicks are a predictor of future clicks on documents. However, when a new or unusual query appears, or when a system is not as widely used as a mainstream web search system, there may be little to no click data available to improve the results. Existing methods to boost query performance for sparse queries extend the query-document click relationship to more documents or queries, but require substantial clickthrough data from other queries.

In this work we describe a way to boost rarely-clicked queries in a system where limited clickthrough data is available for all queries. We describe a probabilistic approach for carrying out that estimation and use it to rerank retrieved documents. We utilize information from co-click queries, subset queries, and synonym queries to estimate the clickthrough for a sparse query. Our experiments on a query log from a medical informatics company demonstrate that when overall clickthrough data is sparse, reranking search results using clickthrough information from related queries significantly outperforms reranking that employs clickthrough information from the query alone.

Categories and Subject Descriptors: H.3.3 [**Information Search and Retrieval**]: Search process

General Terms: Experimentation, Algorithms

Keywords: Sparse Queries, Reranking, Query Log Mining, Sparse Clickthrough Data, Query Selection

1. INTRODUCTION

Clickthrough data from query logs is widely used to improve document ranking [1, 8, 9, 10, 14, 15, 25]. But how does it work for new or unusual queries in a search system? Such (sparse) queries are problematic because little or no clickthrough information is available for them in query logs. This situation can be attributed to three causes: (1) either the query is unpopular or new and therefore very few searches have been issued with this query; (2) the query is not unpopular but the displayed ranking of the search results does not fulfill users' information needs to the extent that results are rarely clicked; or (3) the query is not unpopular but the retrieved list of documents is of poor quality so that reranking with the same set would not improve the results. Mostly, such queries can be boosted with their own sparse clickthrough data if available [23], or information from other more popular queries such as co-click queries may be used to enrich the results [8, 25]. Existing approaches however require substantial clickthrough data from *somewhere* for solid improvements due to noise that is introduced in gathering the additional data [10, 23]. In this context, our work aims at answering the following question: how can we rerank search results for rare or sparse queries in a system for which *limited clickthrough data* is available?

Our aim is in particular to achieve a better ranking of documents for underrepresented or sparse queries of types (1) and (2) described above. We do not deal with case (3) since this situation must be approached with a better retrieval algorithm and not with reranking.

We deal with issues (1) and (2) indirectly by estimating how likely a document is to be clicked given a query by using a language modeling framework [19]. Our hypothesis is that using clickthrough data from *related* queries for sparse queries aids in achieving a better ranking than solely using the query's own sparse clickthrough data. The difficulty of the task arises from the fact that little or no clickthrough data is available not only for the query in question, but also for *all other queries* in the query log. In this situation, we cannot afford to use an approach that introduces too much noise.

For our task, we employ queries related to the query whose results are to be reranked. They come from one of the following three sources: 1. *Similar queries:* these share at least one co-click with the original query, which is a well-known feature from previous work [8, 10, 13, 23]; 2. *Subset queries:* these are contained in the original query as an n-gram sequence; 3. *Synonym queries:* these are lexically, semantically, or syntactically related to the original query. We use the clickthrough data of these related queries in our models.

We test our models on queries from a medical query log that was obtained from a medical informatics company, UpToDate. We also use their Lucene-based search system that yields the initially ranked search results for a query. The users of this system are doctors and nurses in practices and hospitals – i.e., specialists in their domain. Therefore, the medical queries are very specific to the domain. In such a

CIKM'11, October 24–28, 2011, Glasgow, Scotland, UK.

system, sparsity of clickthrough data is experienced more strongly than in general search engines that quickly acquire vast amounts of queries per day.

Our results show that all reranking models outperform the baseline for which clickthrough-boosting is employed with information from the original query only. Further, we observe some interesting trends among the reranking models when reducing clicks in the dataset. Reranking with subset queries and a merged version that uses all related queries perform best, which is expected.

Our results are specific to a particular medium-scale search system, though we believe they are general enough to apply to any similar setting. We hypothesize that the same ideas will extend to general search engines with much greater levels of activity, but do not have access to the resources needed to test that belief.

This paper is organized as follows: the next Section 2 reviews relevant related work in the area. In Section 3 we detail the empirical setting that motivated us for this research and that constrains our possible solutions. Then, we describe the baselines and reranking models that use clickthrough data from related queries in Section 4. This is followed by the experiments and the results in Section 5. Finally, we conclude our work in Section 6.

2. RELATED WORK

It is well known that by means of clickthrough data search results can be reranked to significantly improve the results [1, 8, 9, 10, 14, 15, 25]. However, clickthrough data sparsity poses a problem [6, 8, 10, 13], since many queries often have a small number of clicks, which makes them incomplete. Indeed, queries often have no clicks at all. Gao et al. [10] apply two smoothing methods to overcome the data sparsity problem, one of which is based on Good Turing smoothing. This is achieved by smoothing the features of 0-click queries with features of 1-click queries. The other 'smoothing' method is based on query clustering on the clickthrough graph [8]. Here, the query-document click graph is extended with more queries and documents by following links between them. However, in their experiments on a dataset with less clickthrough data available, Gao et al. [10] show that the query clustering approach on the clickthrough graph does not help. This method only works well when substantial clickthrough data is available, since the introduction of additional documents in the click graph is likely to be noisy for queries originally not having a click with such documents.

One similarity between our work and Craswell and Szummer's random walk on the click graph [8] is that we use information from co-click queries to estimate parts of the reranking models – this is equivalent to following a link between a document and a co-click query. However, one major difference is that we do not include new documents in the document list to be reranked, since this is prone to be noisy when clickthrough data is sparse. This means that we do not go beyond the scope of 1-hop co-click queries. Another major difference is that in Craswell et al.'s work the query content is not considered in the reranking process, whereas we also attempt to use information from other related queries for which the subqueries and synonyms of a query have to be analyzed.

There has been a lot of previous research that uses information from co-click queries for reranking [8, 10, 13, 23]. These queries are what we refer to as 'similar queries', and they are one possible source of related queries in our reranking models. Zhao et al. [25] use clickthrough frequencies of subqueries in their reranking approach while calculating the likelihood of a document being retrieved, given a query. Synonym queries on the other hand have been explored in the literature in the form of query reformulation, query expansion and query rewriting [11, 17, 22].

There are several learning to rank approaches that incorporate clickthrough data [1, 9, 20]. Although we employ a simple regression approach to estimate the similarity of some queries (Section 4.3.2), we do not otherwise use learning approaches. For reasons explained in the following section, our empirical evaluation is constrained to use a black-box retrieval system, for which we are combining very few features. A straightforward parameter sweep is as powerful as any learning method in this case.

To the best of our knowledge, although previous approaches have tested their retrieval and reranking algorithms on sparse queries, they have not employed them on sparse queries in a sparse system where the overall clickthrough data available is limited *for all queries*. In our work, we aim at addressing this aspect in particular. We note that such a setting seems unusual, but is common in the early days of any new search system. Indeed, major search engines have the same problem – i.e., they have queries which have rarely been seen before. Further, their total count of such queries is almost certainly vastly greater. However, since these queries are a more noticeable part of the search experience for smaller search engines like that of UpToDate, this work is more valuable in such a setting. Our results will show that 'sparse' means up until queries have close to 500 clicks.

3. EMPIRICAL SETTING

The motivation for this research arose during discussions with the medical informatics company UpToDate. UpToDate hosts medical information that is searched on a daily basis by a large number of physicians. Although it receives a substantial number of queries each day, the volume is minuscule compared to major search engines: our collection contains around 10 million queries per month compared to an estimated more than 10 billion queries handled by Google this past March [7].

The search engine used by UpToDate is based on version 1.4 of the open source Apache Lucene system[1]. It has been extensively tuned over several years, using parameter sweeps, evaluations on subsets of users, careful editing of the hosted information, and human intuition. A user's query is converted into a complex weighted combination of the original query words, synonyms from a controlled vocabulary, and field references. In this work, we incorporate clickthrough information in the Lucene-based ranking, improving retrieval effectiveness to the point that it is exceptionally good. As we show in Section 5.2, the system is extremely accurate, achieving NDCG closing in on 90% on average.

Not surprisingly, there are a number of queries that perform much worse, the 'sparse queries' in particular. The empirical parts of this study are carried out in this environment. Whereas the baseline search system is a carefully crafted Lucene implementation that incorporates clickthrough information for all queries with enough click history, our ex-

[1]http://lucene.apache.org/java/docs/index.html

periments investigate methods for applying clickthrough information for sparse queries in addition.

The goal of our empirical work is to explore the impact of several approaches for using sparse information to improve the ranking of the UpToDate-based system. That means we are constrained to combining a carefully crafted Lucene score with other information – here, clickthrough information from the query and its related queries. We leave for future work approaches that expose the inner workings of the Lucene black-box system and integrate clickthrough information more elaborately.

4. RERANKING METHODS

In this section we first detail two baseline methods before describing the reranking models that incorporate clickthrough data from related queries.

4.1 Baseline System (Luc)

As mentioned before, the query log and search system we have for this work are based on the Apache Lucene system used by UpToDate. Lucene by default employs a combination of the vector space model and the boolean model for retrieval. The system has further been extended and tuned for this work as described in Section 3. We convert this retrieval system's raw output score, $\text{score}_{\text{Luc}}(Q, D)$, to probabilities for our reranking models (Section 4.3) as follows:

$$P_{\text{Luc}}(D|Q) = \frac{\text{score}_{\text{Luc}}(Q, D)}{\sum_i \text{score}_{\text{Luc}}(Q, D_i)} \quad (1)$$

where the denominator of this equation sums over all documents D_i retrieved for the query Q.

4.2 Clickthrough-Boosted Baseline (BoosLuc)

The Clickthrough-Boosted Baseline (BoosLuc) is an extension of the Lucene system in that every query is boosted with its own clickthrough information from the training data. A Lucene retrieved document D for query Q is reranked as follows:

$$P_{\text{BoosLuc}}(D|Q) = \gamma \cdot \frac{c_{\text{CT}}(Q, D)}{c_{\text{CT}}(Q)} + (1 - \gamma) \cdot P_{Luc}(D|Q) \quad (2)$$

where $c_{\text{CT}}(Q, D)$ is the clickthrough count for query Q with document D, $c_{\text{CT}}(Q)$ is the total clickthrough count for Q used for normalization, and $P_{Luc}(D|Q)$ is from Equation 1. γ is defined as follows:

$$\gamma = \frac{c_{\text{CT}}(Q)}{c_{\text{CT}}(Q) + \rho} \quad (3)$$

which is Dirichlet-like smoothing, ensuring heavier weight on the clickthrough part in Equation 2 when more clickthrough data is available for Q, and less otherwise. With less clickthrough data, $P_{Luc}(D|Q)$, which estimates how likely D is to be relevant by content, has a larger impact. We determine ρ with a parameter sweep on the training data.

4.3 Reranking Models

In this section we describe the reranking models for sparse queries that use clickthrough data from related queries. All reranking models have the same base model, but they differ in their source of related queries from which the information is drawn. The base model estimates the relevance of a document D given a query Q as follows:

$$P_{\text{RelQ}}(D|Q) = \alpha \cdot P_{\text{CT}}(D|Q) + (\alpha - 1) \cdot P_{\text{Luc}}(D|Q) \quad (4)$$

where α is Jelinek-Mercer smoothing tuned on training data. The first component $P_{\text{CT}}(D|Q)$ indicates how likely D is to be clicked based on the clickthrough information obtained from related queries:

$$P_{\text{CT}}(D|Q) = \beta \cdot \sum_{Q' \in \mathcal{Q}} P(D|Q') \cdot P(Q'|Q) + (1 - \beta) \cdot \frac{c_{\text{CT}}(Q, D)}{c_{\text{CT}}(Q)} \quad (5)$$

where $\mathcal{Q}$ is a set of related queries that varies depending on the particular model used. β is again determined by means of Dirichlet-like smoothing as in Equation 3, with the parameter ρ replaced with κ. $P(D|Q')$ indicates the likelihood of D to be retrieved by the related query Q':

$$P(D|Q') = \frac{c_{\text{CT}}(Q', D)}{c_{\text{CT}}(Q')} \quad (6)$$

which is a normalized probability based on Q's clickthrough data so that $\sum_D P(D|Q') = 1$.

$P(Q'|Q)$ in Equation 5 stands for the quality of the relation between Q' and Q. Intuitively, Q and Q' are most related if Q' can predict the way Q's Lucene ranked documents are going to be clicked. In other words, given the Lucene ranked list Q_{Luc} of Q and the clickthrough ranked list Q'_{CT} of Q', the two queries are most related if Q_{Luc} ranks documents in the order they are clicked in Q'_{CT}. The list Q'_{CT} is sorted in decreasing order of frequencies $c_{\text{CT}}(Q', D)$ for Q'. This means that ideally exactly those documents in Q_{Luc} should be ranked lowest that were not clicked for Q' and are thus missing in Q'_{CT}. Hence, we compare Q_{Luc} and Q'_{CT} as follows:

$$P(Q'|Q) = NDCG(Q_{\text{Luc}}) \quad (7)$$

where the relevance judgments for NDCG come from the ranking of Q'_{CT}. That is, we map the clicks given by Q'_{CT} to relevance grades, with which Q_{Luc} is evaluated (see Section 5.1.) In particular, here we use NDCG@n, where $n \leq 10$ – the NDCG value at the highest rank available, not exceeding 10. The NDCG values are normalized to probabilities so that $\sum_{Q' \in \mathcal{Q}} P(Q'|Q) = 1$.

Note that with this approach, documents in Q_{Luc} that are ranked lowest and which were not clicked for Q' (absent in Q'_{CT}) will get a relevance grade of 0 in Q_{Luc}. If those documents are perfectly ranked at the bottom of the list, this will not result in a lower NDCG score.

To summarize, Equation 5 has the following consequences in extreme cases:

1. if there is no clickthrough data available *at all* for Q or any $Q' \in \mathcal{Q}$, then the reranking model will not alter the original ranking as given by the Lucene baseline;
2. if there is no clickthrough data available for *any* of the related queries, or no related queries could be found, but there is information for Q, then the reranking model will utilize the clickthrough likelihood of Q and rank exactly like BoosLuc (Equation 2).

In the usual case where some sparse clickthrough data is available for both Q and related queries, the model is a combination of all these components. Each related query contributes to the likelihood of D being relevant for Q. If there is no evidence for $c_{\mathrm{CT}}(Q', D)$ given a particular Q', then this results in D not being boosted by Q'. Neither do we apply a special form of smoothing here, nor do we use clicks with related queries on other documents to boost D, which would introduce noise into the estimation. The idea is that by means of different ways of locating related queries, we can find enough evidence to boost the right documents.

4.3.1 Similar Query Reranking (Sim)

In this model a related query is a similar query Q' that shares at least one co-click on a document with the original query Q. The domain of similar queries therefore consists of all the training queries in the entire 'clickthrough corpus' that have at least one click in common with Q's ranked list. We constrain the clickthrough corpus here to have a limited and meaningful set of similar queries that excludes junk queries. We locate similar queries efficiently via the reverted indexing approach [18]:

Build Reverted Index.

This is a preparation step for which we obtain the clicked document ids for every training query Q from the clickthrough data from which the index is built. The entries look as follows:

$$docid(D) = \{\text{queries that retrieve } D \text{ having } c_{\mathrm{CT}}(Q, D)\}$$

This way we accumulate the queries that were clicked with every *docid* for all the training queries. The clickthrough counts are normalized so that $\sum_i c_{\mathrm{CT}_{\mathrm{norm}}}(Q, D_i) = 1$, where each D_i has at least one click with Q.

Retrieve Similar Queries.

This is how similar query lookup is achieved. Given an initial query Q, we retrieve similar queries $Q' \in \mathcal{Q}$ by querying the reverted index with each of the clicked *docids* for Q. This yields a combined list of similar queries with their normalized clickthrough counts. We conflate multiple entries of a similar query Q' in this list to obtain the set $\mathcal{Q}$ by averaging the normalized clickthrough count for each Q'. This is then used to estimate $P(D|Q')$ (Equation 6).

Rank Similar Queries.

The similar queries are ranked in decreasing order of $P(Q'|Q)$ as described in Section 4.3 (Equation 7). By construction, every similar query has a non-zero $P(Q'|Q)$.

4.3.2 Subset Query Reranking (Sub)

Under this model a related query Q' is defined as a subquery of Q. The domain of related queries is therefore the power set of all non-empty n-gram subqueries of Q. Considering subqueries is useful when the original query is too specific, such as in *pediatric migraine headache*, since subqueries such as *migraine headache* or *headache* often capture more general content. We analyzed in our training data how frequently subqueries of sparse queries are clicked. For this, we took all training queries with fewer than 100 clicks, of which there are about 1 million queries, and obtained their subqueries. Table 1 contrasts the number of these training subqueries having clicks in a certain range versus the total number of training queries having click counts in the same range. The numbers show that subqueries of sparse queries are not as sparse as their corresponding super queries (bold entries in 2nd column), with 10,368 of them having at least 100 clicks. But the subqueries are not more popular either, since the numbers in the higher click count bins are comparable (bold entries in 2nd versus 3rd columns).

Table 1: Number of training subqueries having clicks in a certain range whose super queries have less than 100 clicks, versus the number of all training queries having clicks in that range.

clicks	*#Subqueries of sparse queries*	*#All queries*
1-9	108,807	960,423
10-49	28,421	42,915
50-99	6435	7234
100-499	**7291**	**7489**
500-999	**1426**	**1430**
1000-2499	**1077**	**1078**
2500-4999	**369**	**370**
>5000	**205**	**208**

In the subset query ranking model (Sub), we estimate $P(D|Q')$ as described in Equation 6, but for $P(Q'|Q)$, we train a linear regression function with several features on a portion of the training data, since this form of estimation yields better performance with subset queries. As the truth label during training we use $NDCG(Q_{\mathrm{CT}})$ (with relevance judgments from Q'_{CT}) from a different training split. The features are the following:

overlap(Q, Q') number of overlapping terms between the query and subquery

kcc(Q), *kcc*(Q') Key Concept Classifier (KCC) score [4]

sim(Q, Q') weighted overlapping terms, where weight $w(t)$ for a term t is either the Google n-gram count [5] or KCC(t):

$$sim_{\mathrm{google/kcc}}(Q, Q') = \frac{\sum_{t \in Q'} w(t)}{\sum_{t \in Q} w(t)} \tag{8}$$

$\mathrm{score_{Luc}}(Q)$, $\mathrm{score_{Luc}}(Q')$ total Lucene retrieval score for query and subquery

popweight(Q, Q') popularity weight of Q' with Q:

$$\mathrm{popweight}(Q, Q') = \frac{c_{\mathrm{CT}}(Q)}{\sum_{Q^* \supset Q'} c_{\mathrm{CT}}(Q^*)} \tag{9}$$

where $Q^* \supset Q'$ represents queries Q^* that contain Q'. The popularity weight thus contrasts how popular Q' is as a subquery of Q versus being a subquery of other queries, estimated by means of clickthrough counts.

popscore(Q, Q') popularity score of Q' with Q:

$$\mathrm{popscore}(Q, Q') = \frac{\mathrm{popweight}(Q, Q')}{\sum_{Q'' \in 2^Q} \mathrm{popweight}(Q'', Q)} \tag{10}$$

where Q'' iterates over all subqueries in Q. The popularity score indicates how popular the subquery Q' is as opposed to other subqueries Q'' in Q.

We ensure all features are between 0 and 1 through normalization. For the subset queries model, $P(Q'|Q)$ is then a linear combination of these features with the trained weights. Note that most of these features just described are applicable to subset queries only. We tried training a function for the other reranking models, too, by including $NDCG(Q_{\text{Luc}})$ as an additional feature. This feature proved to be the strongest one for them, which is what we use to estimate $P(Q'|Q)$ for those approaches.

4.3.3 Synonym Query Reranking (Syn)

In Synonym Query Reranking (Syn), a synonym query is syntactically, semantically, or lexically related to the original query. So variations of a query such as singular/plural or paraphrases such as in *hypernatremia* and *high plasma sodium level* are valid synonym queries. As a synonym resource we use a carefully constructed medical vocabulary by deputy editors from UpToDate. It has 24,415 canonical keyword entries with 150,383 synonym entries in total.

Given a query, we construct the set of synonym queries $\mathcal{Q}$ as follows: first, if a canonical keyword entry exists for the query, we use the synonym entries associated with it. If there is no canonical entry for a query (which often happens with very general medical terms), we take the n-gram subset queries of the query and again look for canonical keyword entries for those subset queries. If still no synonym queries could be found after this step, we try to match the original query and its subqueries in the synonym entries, to then include the associated canonical entry and the remaining synonym entries for that query. The found set of synonyms is filtered to exclude 0-click queries. We use at most 10 synonyms from this set.

$P(Q'|Q)$ and $P(D|Q')$ of these synonym queries are then estimated by means of the training clickthrough data as described in Equations 6 and 7, Section 4.3.

4.3.4 Merged Reranking (Merged)

For this model, we merge the different kinds of related queries to one set, i.e.,

$\mathcal{Q}$ = similar queries $\cup$ subqueries $\cup$ synonyms

For each type of related query we estimate $P(Q'|Q)$ and $P(D|Q')$ the way it was described for the query in Section 4.3 and its subsections. We do not reduce the number of related queries in this process. Therefore, the effect on Equation 5 is that the sum is performed over a larger set of related queries.

The reason for having this merged reranking model is to compensate for a bad choice of related queries for any one of the methods – such as poor synonyms, no similar queries (for 0-click queries), or no subset queries (for original unigram queries).

5. EXPERIMENTS

5.1 Data and Evaluation

Our query log is from UpToDate. The query log has 4 months of data. Tables 2 and 3 contain some statistics about the entire data set. We split the query log into three folds: two training folds for parameter tuning and one test fold on which the results are reported in Section 5.2. The folds are roughly equal in size.

For the experiments, we use 1407 queries together with the training portion of the query log and 972 queries with the test set. To avoid biasing parameters toward certain queries, the training queries used in parameter tuning are *distinct* from the test queries for which the results in this paper are reported. All training and test queries are popular (i.e., each query has at least 500 clicks). We perform the experiments both on these popular queries and we also simulate them as sparse queries by reducing the amount of training click data available to the models. This is done to understand the performance of sparse queries in a *sparse environment.*

Table 2: Some statistics about the query log.

Feature	Quantity
Total # queries	39,248,767
Unique queries	4,896,827
Queries/day	256,528
Unique queries/day	32,005
Queries/month	7,849,753
Unique queries/month	979,365

Table 3: Distribution of clicks for all queries in the training and test data sets.

Click Range	Train	Test
1-9	960423	634761
10-49	42915	28569
50-99	7234	4838
100-499	7489	5221
500-999	1430	956
1000-2499	1078	660
2500-4999	370	170
> 5000	208	74

Each query comes with clicks in the training folds as well as clicks in the test fold. For some of our experiments we use all of the clicks available. In others we reduce the number of clicks available to the algorithms in order to simulate a sparse situation. The reduction of clicks for sparsity is achieved as follows: to have K clicks for a query, we evenly reduce the click count for each document so that the sum of all the clicks for the query roughly equals K (with some small error, due to multiplication with a small fraction). If the total click count for a query is less than K, the clicks are not altered. Therefore, this reduction of clicks preserves the distribution of the click counts. We choose this form of click reduction to preserve the trend in the data, i.e., the most frequently clicked document will still be the same after reduction. Note that clicks can be reduced within a single fold, but can also be reduced across two or three.

Our aim in reranking the Lucene results is to better approximate the ranking as given by the click frequencies from users, similar to Zhao et al's work [25]. Hence we use the clicks in the test fold as a representation of "truth." For the experiments reported in this paper, clickthrough truth comes from the test fold and model estimation is done with the training folds. Note that while the training clicks are reduced in some of the experiments, the clickthrough truth data from the test split is never reduced.

Given a query Q, in order to evaluate its ranked list of n documents R, we use two different measures. One of them uses relevance judgments from clickthrough truth, whereas the other compares the rank correlation to the clickthrough truth list. For the former measure, we use the truth clicks for Q from the test fold as relevance judgments. We do this by mapping the clicks to relevance grades for the well-known NDCG measure (Normalized Discounted Cumulative Gain) [12]:

$$\text{NDCG(Q, R)} = \frac{1}{Z_Q} \sum_{i=1}^{n} \frac{2^{rel_i} - 1}{\log_2(1+i)} \quad (11)$$

where i is the ith document in R and rel_i is the relevance grade of document i. This measure is normalized with Z_Q so that NDCG=1.0 when ranking is perfect. We would like to be able to uniformly map the clicks to a reasonable range of relevance grades to be used with NDCG for *any given query*. We experimented with various schemes of mapping the clicks for all the queries in the training query log portion to find the most suitable approach. We discovered that we can achieve a reasonable range of real-valued relevance grades roughly between 1 and 4 if we use $\log_{10}(clicks)$ for the mapping.

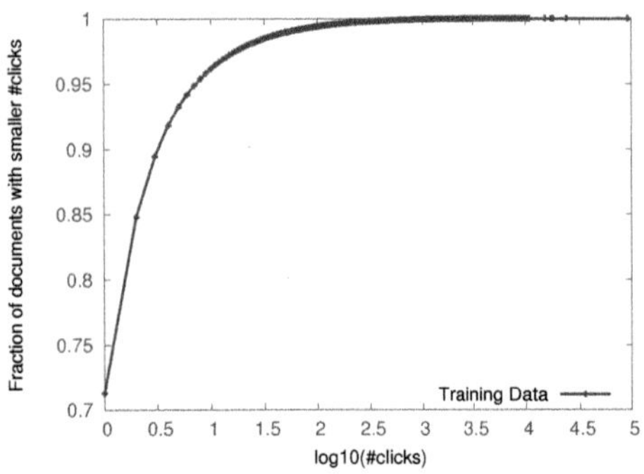

Figure 1: Mapping clickthrough data to NDCG relevance grades for all queries in the training query log.

Table 4: Relevance judgments from the entire test set rounded to discrete values.

Rel. Grade	Test total
1	7121
2	2772
3	1115
4	30

Figure 1 shows the effect of choosing $\log_{10}(clicks)$ with a cumulative distribution function of the clicks on the documents of all the queries in the training data. Note that by this construction relevance grades are real-valued rather than discrete.

Table 4 shows the corresponding relevance judgments for the entire test set. For this, we rounded the real-valued relevance grades to discrete values. The numbers indicate that across the dataset, there are only 30 'perfect' documents, 1115 'excellent' documents, 2772 'fair' documents, and 7121 'bad' documents, which should not be ranked highly.

Therefore, given a query Q and a ranked list R obtained through a reranking method as detailed in Section 4, we evaluate the ranking of each $D \in R$ by means of the *truth clicks* of (Q, D) from the *test fold* mapped to NDCG relevance grades as follows: $\log_{10}(c_{\text{CT}}(Q, D))$. Similarly, in Equation 7 where we estimate the quality of the relation $P(Q'|Q)$ by means of NDCG, the frequencies $c_{\text{CT}}(Q', D)$ in Q'_{CT} are also mapped to NDCG relevance grades in the same manner.

Since NDCG has been criticized in past research for not correlating well with user satisfaction [2, 21, 24], we also use a measure that directly evaluates the rank correlation between two lists. Unlike NDCG, this measure does not require relevance judgments; the ranking of the lists are compared directly. We still show our results with NDCG, since it is a well-known measure widely used in the information retrieval community. As the rank correlation metric, we use the M Measure [3] which penalizes differences in rankings depending on the rank position, similarly to the weighted generalized version of Kendall's Tau and Spearman's footrule presented in recent work by Kumar and Vassilvitskii [16]. The M Measure is defined as follows:

$$M(t,r)@k = 1 - \frac{M'(t,r)@k}{norm} \quad (12)$$

where t and r are two ranked lists for which M yields 1 if t and r are identical at rank k, and 0 if they are completely disjoint at rank k. M' is defined as follows:

$$\begin{aligned} M'(t,r)@k = &\sum_Z \left| \frac{1}{\text{rank}_t(i)} - \frac{1}{\text{rank}_r(i)} \right| \quad (13) \\ &+ \sum_S \left(\frac{1}{\text{rank}_t(j)} - \frac{1}{k+1} \right) \\ &+ \sum_T \left(\frac{1}{\text{rank}_r(l)} - \frac{1}{k+1} \right) \end{aligned}$$

where $i \in Z$ is the set of overlapping documents between t and r, $j \in S$ is the set of documents occurring in t but not in r, and $l \in T$ is the set of documents occurring in r but not in t. Note that a document being 'absent' in a list is assumed to have rank $k+1$, which is denoted by the penalizing denominator $k+1$ in S and T. The notation $\text{rank}_x(y)$ denotes the rank of document y in list x. The M Measure gives a higher weight to documents whose rankings are closer in high ranks of r and t, whereas the weight is lower with greater disagreements and lower rankings in the lists. The normalization constant in Equation 12 depends on k, referring to the case when Z is empty and all documents in r and t fall into the sets S and T.

In our evaluation, we observe $M(t,r)@k$ for t being the *truth list* – the clickthrough ranked list in decreasing order of click frequencies – and for r – the reranked list by one of the reranking methods.

5.2 Results

We first conduct the experiments on the unreduced 972 test queries to measure the performance of the baselines and all reranking models. For all models, the parameters α and κ (for the reranking models) and ρ (for BoosLuc) are set using the training data. For estimating the components in these runs, the models have full access to the training clickthrough data. Table 5 shows the results for the popular queries.

We can see that the baseline system Luc is already very good with NDCG@1 = 0.894 and M@1 = 0.682, increasing at lower ranks up until 0.925 for NDCG@20 and 0.705 for M@20. However, we can significantly improve on this by just boosting with clickthrough data, which is what the second baseline BoosLuc represents. We observe NDCG@1 = 1.0, and at the other ranks we have almost perfect ranking, which is also reflected in the M Measure rank correlation. As for the reranking models Sim, Sub, Syn and Merged – they also perform very similarly to BoosLuc with Syn (the synonym queries reranking model) showing the largest gain. Syn beats all other methods significantly with p-value < 0.04

Table 5: **Comparing the reranking methods on 972 popular test queries. All bold numbers are statistically significant over all non-bold ones at same ranks with p-value < 0.04 using the paired two-sided t-test.**

Average NDCG@rank	Luc	BoosLuc	Sim	Sub	Syn	Merged
1	0.894	**1.0**	**1.0**	0.999	**1.0**	0.999
2	0.89	0.997	0.996	0.996	**0.998**	0.995
5	0.907	0.992	0.988	0.99	**0.994**	0.987
10	0.914	0.99	0.984	0.987	**0.991**	0.984
20	0.925	0.989	0.984	0.986	**0.991**	0.984
Average M@rank	Luc	BoosLuc	Sim	Sub	Syn	Merged
1	0.682	0.983	0.978	0.972	**0.989**	0.971
2	0.678	0.971	0.964	0.962	**0.978**	0.957
5	0.699	0.948	0.933	0.938	**0.957**	0.93
10	0.707	0.928	0.908	0.916	**0.935**	0.906
20	0.705	0.90	0.878	0.888	**0.907**	0.876
Fixed Parameters	–	$\rho = 1000$	$\alpha = 0.5$ $\kappa = 20000$	$\alpha = 0.6$ $\kappa = 20000$	$\alpha = 0.6$ $\kappa = 20000$	$\alpha = 0.5$ $\kappa = 20000$

using the paired two-sided t-test for both measures. This experiment shows that with popular queries in a popular system when a substantial amount of clickthrough data is available, we can successfully boost a well-performing baseline such as the Lucene system with clickthrough data from the query only. For even better performance, the synonym queries reranking model can be used.

We now consider what happens if far fewer clicks are available on documents. We vary the number of clicks available for *all queries*, N, between 0 and 20,000 to simulate a sparse system that gradually progresses to a system with larger amounts of clickthrough data. Tables 6 and 7 and Figure 2 with the graphs show the simulated sparse query runs in a sparse system with little clickthrough data available *for all queries.* With higher N, the performance eventually becomes identical to what is reported in Table 5, since this corresponds to running the models with maximum N.

In Tables 6 and 7 we present all the reranking models in comparison to BoosLuc with only at most 1-50 clicks available for every query in the system. We notice a big, significant difference between BoosLuc and the reranking models at all ranks for these clicks, with BoosLuc catching up as the number of clicks increases. At NDCG@1 and M@1, all reranking models are almost perfect, whereas at lower ranks Sub and Merged perform best. This is also the case for 10 clicks, although Merged is not statistically significant over all methods at NDCG@5, but it is significantly better according to the M Measure. Sub clearly dominates for both 1 and 10 clicks for both measures. At 20 clicks, Sub is not the strongest method any more. The merged reranking model shows the best performance together with Sim at ranks 1 and 2. At 50 clicks we can also see that Merged dominates the results. This is not surprising, since Merged contains related queries from all models and it therefore has an advantage over the other methods in extreme cases, such as when no subset queries are available, or no co-click queries or synonyms could be found. It is surprising that Merged does not perform best in Table 5, where more clickthrough data is available. One reason might be that the scores of many documents are heavily boosted due to the large number of related queries – and that unfortunately many of those documents are non-relevant.

The parameters were fixed on training data individually for every different click setting for each of the methods. Note that the fixed parameter α is consistently higher in Tables 6 and 7 ($\alpha = 0.8, 0.9$) for most reranking models than it was in Table 5 (0.5, 0.6), which is the weight on the related queries reranking part in Equation 4. This is required for making up for the sparsity of clicks, whereas for more popular queries such a high emphasis on the information from the related queries is not required. κ is very sensitive for different reranking models and depends on the number of clicks available in a sparse system, although lower values are preferred. In the runs with the popular queries in Table 5 it is more stable with $\kappa = 20000$.

Figure 2 shows all the runs for the reranking models and BoosLuc (always the solid line) with NDCG and M Measure performance at the measured ranks 1, 10, and 20 for varying click counts. Each graph shows the results at a fixed NDCG or M Measure rank on the y axis with varying clicks on the x axis for the methods. In all the graphs, the BoosLuc curve starts off low and improves the more clicks (on the query itself for this baseline) are available. However, after 500 clicks the effectiveness has plateaued and no further gains occur. In fact, there is only modest value to clicks after the first 300. Therefore, the presented click range is between 0 and 800 or at most 2,000 for the graphs; the numbers do not change much afterwards and gradually progress into the results in Table 5.

As for the first two graphs with NDCG@1 and M@1 on the y axis, there is little noticeable difference between the reranking methods, except for the fact that they all outperform BoosLuc. A slight dominance of Sub is visible in the M@1 graph. At NDCG@10 and M@10, this becomes much clearer: the lines for Syn and Sim are noticeably below the lines for Sub and Merged. This fact becomes even more evident at NDCG@20 and M@20, with the gap between the lines growing larger. Another point is that between 0 and 100 clicks, in all the graphs the performance between the related query reranking models is very similar. With more than 100 clicks, the changes become noticeable.

Figure 2: Comparing different reranking methods and BoosLuc on 972 simulated sparse queries. The x axis shows the maximum number of clicks available, whereas the y axis is NDCG or M Measure @ different ranks.

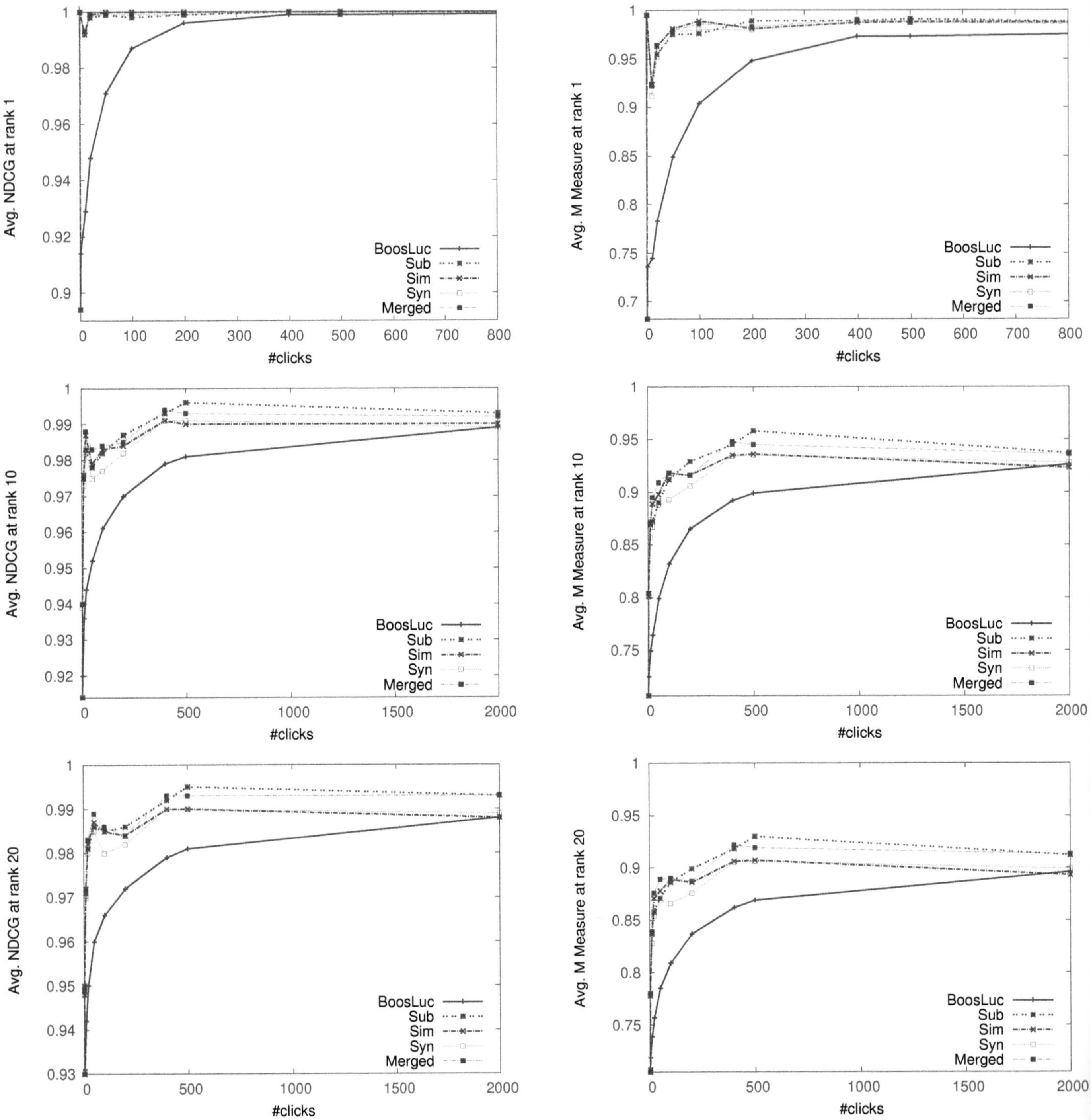

Table 6: NDCG results on comparing the reranking methods to BoosLuc on 972 simulated sparse queries when clickthrough data is sparse. The same results for ranks 1, 10, and 20 are shown in full in Figure 2. All bold numbers are statistically significant over all non-bold ones at same ranks and clicks with p-value < 0.004 using the paired two-sided t-test.

clicks			$N = 1$					$N = 10$		
Average NDCG@ rank	BoosLuc	Sub	Merged	Sim	Syn	BoosLuc	Sub	Merged	Sim	Syn
1	0.914	**1.0**	**1.0**	**1.0**	**1.0**	0.929	**0.993**	**0.993**	0.992	0.992
2	0.903	**0.952**	**0.952**	0.949	0.949	0.919	**0.985**	**0.984**	0.982	0.977
5	0.915	**0.94**	**0.94**	0.939	0.939	0.932	**0.983**	0.982	0.981	0.979
10	0.92	**0.94**	**0.94**	0.939	0.939	0.936	**0.976**	**0.975**	0.975	0.973
20	0.931	**0.949**	**0.949**	0.948	0.948	0.942	**0.972**	**0.971**	0.971	0.97
Fixed Parameters	$\rho = 1000$	$\alpha = 0.8$ $\kappa = 1000$	$\alpha = 0.8$ $\kappa = 1000$	$\alpha = 0.9$ $\kappa = 5000$	$\alpha = 0.9$ $\kappa = 5000$	$\rho = 1000$	$\alpha = 0.9$ $\kappa = 10000$	$\alpha = 0.9$ $\kappa = 20000$	$\alpha = 0.9$ $\kappa = 5000$	$\alpha = 0.9$ $\kappa = 5000$
clicks			$N = 20$					$N = 50$		
Average NDCG@ rank	BoosLuc	Sub	Merged	Sim	Syn	BoosLuc	Sub	Merged	Sim	Syn
1	0.948	**0.998**	**0.999**	**0.999**	0.998	0.971	**0.999**	**0.999**	**1.0**	**1.0**
2	0.937	0.992	**0.995**	0.993	0.99	0.964	0.995	**0.997**	**0.997**	**0.997**
5	0.937	0.974	**0.983**	0.98	0.971	0.952	0.982	**0.987**	0.984	0.981
10	0.944	0.983	**0.988**	0.987	0.982	0.952	0.978	**0.983**	0.979	0.975
20	0.95	0.981	**0.983**	0.982	0.98	0.96	0.986	**0.989**	0.987	0.985
Fixed Parameters	$\rho = 1000$	$\alpha = 0.8$ $\kappa = 20000$	$\alpha = 0.8$ $\kappa = 1500$	$\alpha = 0.9$ $\kappa = 1000$	$\alpha = 0.9$ $\kappa = 15000$	$\rho = 1000$	$\alpha = 0.5$ $\kappa = 1000$	$\alpha = 0.9$ $\kappa = 1000$	$\alpha = 0.9$ $\kappa = 5000$	$\alpha = 0.8$ $\kappa = 1500$

Table 7: M Measure results on comparing the reranking methods to BoosLuc on 972 simulated sparse queries when clickthrough data is sparse. The same results for ranks 1, 10, and 20 are shown in full in Figure 2. All bold numbers are statistically significant over all non-bold ones at same ranks and clicks with p-value < 0.02 using the paired two-sided t-test.

clicks			$N = 1$					$N = 10$		
Average M@ rank	BoosLuc	Sub	Merged	Sim	Syn	BoosLuc	Sub	Merged	Sim	Syn
1	0.736	**0.995**	**0.995**	**0.995**	**0.995**	0.745	**0.923**	**0.922**	**0.924**	0.912
2	0.715	**0.895**	**0.895**	0.891	0.891	0.73	**0.90**	**0.90**	0.899	0.878
5	0.724	**0.832**	**0.832**	0.828	0.828	0.742	**0.878**	**0.877**	0.876	0.86
10	0.725	**0.804**	**0.804**	0.801	0.801	0.749	**0.871**	**0.87**	0.869	0.857
20	0.719	**0.78**	**0.78**	0.778	0.778	0.739	**0.839**	**0.838**	0.837	0.828
Fixed Parameters	$\rho = 1000$	$\alpha = 0.8$ $\kappa = 1000$	$\alpha = 0.8$ $\kappa = 1000$	$\alpha = 0.9$ $\kappa = 5000$	$\alpha = 0.9$ $\kappa = 5000$	$\rho = 1000$	$\alpha = 0.9$ $\kappa = 10000$	$\alpha = 0.9$ $\kappa = 20000$	$\alpha = 0.9$ $\kappa = 5000$	$\alpha = 0.9$ $\kappa = 5000$
clicks			$N = 20$					$N = 50$		
Average M@ rank	BoosLuc	Sub	Merged	Sim	Syn	BoosLuc	Sub	Merged	Sim	Syn
1	0.783	0.955	**0.964**	**0.963**	0.952	0.849	**0.975**	**0.979**	**0.981**	**0.978**
2	0.769	0.933	**0.948**	**0.944**	0.926	0.836	0.957	**0.97**	**0.969**	**0.963**
5	0.764	0.886	**0.91**	0.902	0.88	0.814	0.92	**0.938**	0.929	0.921
10	0.764	0.872	**0.895**	0.889	0.867	0.799	0.89	**0.909**	0.898	0.888
20	0.757	0.858	**0.876**	0.871	0.854	0.785	0.871	**0.889**	0.878	0.869
Fixed Parameters	$\rho = 1000$	$\alpha = 0.8$ $\kappa = 20000$	$\alpha = 0.8$ $\kappa = 1500$	$\alpha = 0.9$ $\kappa = 1000$	$\alpha = 0.9$ $\kappa = 15000$	$\rho = 1000$	$\alpha = 0.5$ $\kappa = 1000$	$\alpha = 0.9$ $\kappa = 1000$	$\alpha = 0.9$ $\kappa = 5000$	$\alpha = 0.8$ $\kappa = 1500$

The results show very interesting trends: subset queries seem to be a more reliable clickthrough source for reranking than synonyms or co-click queries at lower clicks, which is an interesting observation. For best performance over a wider range of low clicks, the merged model together with the subset query model are most helpful, as we learned from Tables 6 and 7. When substantial clickthrough data is available, however, Syn outperforms all other methods as we saw in Table 5. Further, the results at rank 1 are near perfect for almost all the reranking models, whereas maintaining perfect reranking quality at lower ranks until 20 seems slightly more difficult for some of the methods. These results show the sensitivity of the methods to the number of clicks available and high-rank versus low-rank performance. What is evident in all the results however is that in a sparse system with sparse queries – even queries with up to 400 clicks – clickthrough boosting solely with the information from the original query is a poor choice, as is done with BoosLuc. Furthermore, using synonym queries can be helpful even when a system has large numbers of clicks available.

Finally, it is evident in Tables 6 and 7 and in Figure 2 that the two measures NDCG and M Measure mostly agree with one another with small exceptions, although the absolute improvement between BoosLuc and the reranking methods is greater with the M Measure.

6. CONCLUSIONS

In this paper, we tackled improving search results for sparse queries when the overall availability of clickthrough data is sparse. The aim was to approximate the ranking as defined by users' clicks. For this, we presented several reranking models that use clickthrough counts from related queries to better estimate the relevance of a document, given a query. The general reranking model estimates the relevance of a document by considering the quality of the related query and the likelihood that the related query will retrieve the given document. The models differ in their source of related queries, which may be similar queries sharing at least one co-click with the original query, subqueries, or synonym queries. Finally, a merged model combines the various sources of related queries into one as evidence for reranking documents.

The experimental results showed that with popular queries the synonym queries reranking model significantly outperforms basic clickthrough boosting of the original query, although all methods were able to greatly improve over the basic Lucene baseline often achieving nearly perfect results. For sparse queries in a simulated sparse system we observed that the related query reranking models are able to maintain the strong performance and significantly improve over the clickthrough boosted baseline with large gains. In a very sparse system with only 1-50 clicks available for every query, the subset query and merged reranking models performed best.

As future work, it would be interesting to conduct further experiments on other sparse web data sets or on other domain-specific query logs from small- or medium-sized systems to understand the generalizability and limitations of our models.

7. ACKNOWLEDGMENTS

This work was supported in part by the Center for Intelligent Information Retrieval, in part by NSF grant #IIS-0910884, and in part by UpToDate. We wish to thank UpToDate for access to its query log and retrieval system. We are particularly grateful to Jerry Greene's help in the time-consuming process of tagging data for our experiments. Any opinions, findings and conclusions or recommendations expressed in this material are the authors' and do not necessarily reflect those of the sponsors.

8. REFERENCES

[1] E. Agichtein, E. Brill, and S. Dumais. Improving web search ranking by incorporating user behavior information. In *Proceedings*, SIGIR '06, pages 19–26, New York, NY, USA, 2006. ACM.

[2] A. Al-Maskari, M. Sanderson, and P. Clough. The relationship between ir effectiveness measures and user satisfaction. In *Proceedings*, SIGIR '07, pages 773–774, New York, NY, USA, 2007. ACM.

[3] J. Bar-Ilan, M. Mat-Hassan, and M. Levene. Methods for comparing rankings of search engine results. *Comput. Netw.*, 50:1448–1463, July 2006.

[4] M. Bendersky and W. B. Croft. Discovering key concepts in verbose queries. In *Proceedings*, SIGIR '08, pages 491–498, New York, NY, USA, 2008. ACM.

[5] T. Brants and A. Franz. Google n-grams, Web 1T 5-gram Version 1, 2006.

[6] A. Broder, P. Ciccolo, E. Gabrilovich, V. Josifovski, D. Metzler, L. Riedel, and J. Yuan. Online expansion of rare queries for sponsored search. In *Proceedings*, WWW '09, pages 511–520, New York, NY, USA, 2009. ACM.

[7] comScore. comScore Releases March 2011 U.S. Search Engine Rankings. `http://www.comscore.com`.

[8] N. Craswell and M. Szummer. Random walks on the click graph. In *Proceedings*, SIGIR '07, pages 239–246, New York, NY, USA, 2007. ACM.

[9] Z. Dou, R. Song, X. Yuan, and J.-R. Wen. Are click-through data adequate for learning web search rankings? In *Proceedings*, CIKM '08, pages 73–82, New York, NY, USA, 2008. ACM.

[10] J. Gao, W. Yuan, X. Li, K. Deng, and J.-Y. Nie. Smoothing clickthrough data for web search ranking. In *Proceedings*, SIGIR '09, pages 355–362, New York, NY, USA, 2009. ACM.

[11] J. Huang and E. N. Efthimiadis. Analyzing and evaluating query reformulation strategies in web search logs. In *Proceedings*, CIKM '09, pages 77–86, New York, NY, USA, 2009. ACM.

[12] K. Järvelin and J. Kekäläinen. Cumulated Gain-based Evaluation of IR Techniques. *ACM Trans. Inf. Syst.*, 20:422–446, October 2002.

[13] X.-M. Jiang, W.-G. Song, and H.-J. Zeng. Applying associative relationship on the clickthrough data to improve web search. In *Advances in Information Retrieval*, volume 3408 of *Lecture Notes in Computer Science*, pages 475–486. Springer Berlin / Heidelberg, 2005.

[14] T. Joachims, L. Granka, B. Pan, H. Hembrooke, and G. Gay. Accurately interpreting clickthrough data as implicit feedback. In *Proceedings*, SIGIR '05, pages 154–161, New York, NY, USA, 2005. ACM.

[15] T. Joachims, L. Granka, B. Pan, H. Hembrooke, F. Radlinski, and G. Gay. Evaluating the accuracy of implicit feedback from clicks and query reformulations in web search. *ACM Trans. Inf. Syst.*, 25, April 2007.

[16] R. Kumar and S. Vassilvitskii. Generalized distances between rankings. In *Proceedings*, WWW '10, pages 571–580, New York, NY, USA, 2010. ACM.

[17] A. Mastora, M. Monopoli, and S. Kapidakis. Exploring query formulation and reformulation: A preliminary study to map usersÕ search behaviour. In *Research and Advanced Technology for Digital Libraries*, volume 5173 of *Lecture Notes in Computer Science*, pages 427–430. Springer Berlin / Heidelberg, 2008.

[18] J. Pickens, M. Cooper, and G. Golovchinsky. Reverted indexing for feedback and expansion. In *Proceedings*, CIKM '10, pages 1049–1058, New York, NY, USA, 2010. ACM.

[19] J. M. Ponte and W. B. Croft. A language modeling approach to information retrieval. In *Proceedings*, SIGIR '98, pages 275–281, New York, NY, USA, 1998. ACM.

[20] F. Radlinski and T. Joachims. Query chains: learning to rank from implicit feedback. In *Proceedings*, KDD '05, pages 239–248, New York, NY, USA, 2005. ACM.

[21] S. E. Robertson, E. Kanoulas, and E. Yilmaz. Extending Average Precision to Graded Relevance Judgments. In *Proceedings*, SIGIR '10, pages 603–610, New York, NY, USA, 2010. ACM.

[22] X. Wei, F. Peng, H. Tseng, Y. Lu, and B. Dumoulin. Context sensitive synonym discovery for web search queries. In *Proceedings*, CIKM '09, pages 1585–1588, New York, NY, USA, 2009. ACM.

[23] G.-R. Xue, H.-J. Zeng, Z. Chen, Y. Yu, W.-Y. Ma, W. Xi, and W. Fan. Optimizing web search using web click-through data. In *Proceedings*, CIKM '04, pages 118–126, New York, NY, USA, 2004. ACM.

[24] H. Zaragoza, B. B. Cambazoglu, and R. Baeza-Yates. Web search solved?: all result rankings the same? In *Proceedings*, CIKM '10, pages 529–538, New York, NY, USA, 2010. ACM.

[25] M. Zhao, H. Li, A. Ratnaparkhi, H.-W. Hon, and J. Wang. Adapting document ranking to users' preferences using click-through data. In *Information Retrieval Technology*, volume 4182 of *Lecture Notes in Computer Science*, pages 26–42. Springer Berlin / Heidelberg, 2006.

Searching Microblogs: Coping with Sparsity and Document Quality

Nasir Naveed Thomas Gottron Jérôme Kunegis Arifah Che Alhadi
WeST – Institute for Web Science and Technologies
University of Koblenz-Landau, 56070 Koblenz, Germany
{naveed, gottron, kunegis, alhadi}@uni-koblenz.de

ABSTRACT

Two of the main challenges in retrieval on microblogs are the inherent sparsity of the documents and difficulties in assessing their quality. The feature sparsity is immanent to the restriction of the medium to short texts. Quality assessment is necessary as the microblog documents range from spam over trivia and personal chatter to news broadcasts, information dissemination and reports of current hot topics. In this paper we analyze how these challenges can influence standard retrieval models and propose methods to overcome the problems they pose. We consider the sparsity's effect on document length normalization and introduce *interestingness* as static quality measure. Our results show that deliberately ignoring length normalization yields better retrieval results in general and that interestingness improves retrieval for underspecified queries.

Categories and Subject Descriptors

H.3 [**Information Storage and Retrieval**]: Content Analysis and Indexing; H.3.3 [**Information Search and Retrieval**]: *Information filtering, Relevance feedback, Retrieval models*

General Terms

Algorithms, Experimentation, Performance

Keywords

Microblog, Twitter, Retweet, Interestingness

1. INTRODUCTION

Microblogging documents are – by definition – very short. In the most renown microblogging service Twitter, the length of messages is restricted to 140 characters. While the conciseness of messages has been cited as a major reason for Twitter's success, it is at the same time problematic for text retrieval: Term frequencies, for instance, are typically used as a parameter in the estimation of term importance within a given document. In short texts, however, this essential feature does not discriminate much between different documents, as it is nearly a binary value. In fact, our analysis across several large datasets shows that about 85% of all Twitter messages contain each term at most once (see Figure 1). In consequence, most retrieval models are effectively reduced to using global term weights, that measure the discriminativeness of terms.

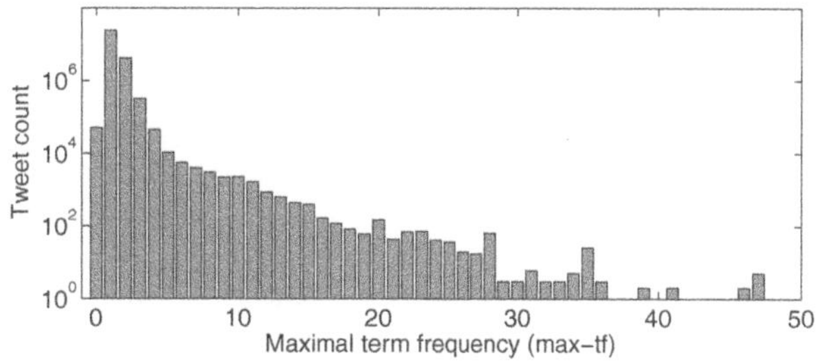

Figure 1: Distribution of maximal term frequencies (*max-tf*) in Twitter messages of the *choudhury-ext* dataset after removing stop words.

A second challenge for retrieval on microblogs is the nature of the medium. With regard to the purpose Twitter documents are different from documents in the classical sense. Classical documents address a wider, open audience, as in principle everyone has access to the document. Microblog messages, instead, typically have a more restricted and better defined audience provided by the social network of a user. Thus, while the primary purpose of a tweet can be to communicate information (e.g. news, sharing resources, broadcast an alert) it might, alternatively, also serve other primary purposes, such as social interaction, promotion, requesting feedback or expressing emotions [5]. In a general retrieval scenario, the rather private and personal messages in a social interaction context are typically of less interest for a user with a concrete information need. This implies that a retrieval criterion for microblog messages should relate to the *interestingness* of a tweet.

Information retrieval on microblogs needs to address these two challenges that are immanent to the technical and social context of the medium. Classical retrieval models do not consider these aspects; they are directed to longer texts and assume the intention of a document to primarily be the transmission of information. Also, recent approaches transferring the concepts of authority in reference networks, such as citations or hyperlinks, to the social network of Twitter do not take into consideration that the semantic of the social network is not equivalent to a content motivated reference network.

In this paper we make two contributions:

- We analyze term and length features of microblog messages and provide theoretical and empirical evidence that length normalization introduces an unjustified bias for Twitter.
- We introduce a static quality measure of *interestingness* and show that it improves retrieval results in particular on short, underspecified queries.

2. RELATED WORK

People seek information within microblogs in two ways: by asking questions to their followers or by querying microblogs in order to discover information that has already been posted. Looking at the user's side, people mainly search microblogs to find in particular timely information (e.g. news, trending topics, events), social information (information related to other users) and topical information (e.g. topic of interest) [15]. Another observed and important difference between search on microblogs and on the Web is the length of queries. While Web queries are on average 3.08 words long, queries on mircoblogs are far shorter: on average 1.64 words.

Massoudi et al. [8] incorporate quality indicators such as emoticons, post length, shouting, capitalization, hyperlinks, reposts, followers, and recency into a retrieval model for searching microblog posts for a given topic of interest. Previous studies have also measured the influence of users on tweet quality. Cha et al. [4] discovered that a very large number of followers do not necessarily have an impact on a user being retweeted more often.

However, some researchers [7, 10] found that the context of a tweet (number of followers/followees, timestamp) strongly correlates with retweetability along with content features such as the presence of URLs and hashtags. Kwak et al. [10] found that rankings based on the number of followers and PageRank are very similar, while rankings based on the number of retweeted messages differ, concluding that interest does not necessarily correlate with social status. In analogy with PageRank, Weng et al. [16] define the TwitterRank measure to rate users. Nagmoti et al. [11] state that social graph network features (number of followers and followees) can be used as a ranking measure of microblog search.

Hong et al. [7] use retweets as a measure of popularity and apply machine learning techniques to predict how often new messages will be retweeted. The authors analyze the content of messages, temporal information, metadata of messages and users, and the user's social graph as the features in predicting the messages to be retweeted.

In summary, these recent studies listed here indicate that the likelihood of a tweet to be retweeted is based on context and content of the tweet. Our work focuses on the applicability of a content-based probability of retweet as a static quality measure. Therefore, we put a much stronger emphasis on the content and analyze a wider set of low-level content-based features as well as derived, high-level content-based features (topic and sentiment of a tweet).

3. RETRIEVAL ON MICROBLOGS

In this section we consider the two challenges for retrieval on microblogs we mentioned in the introduction: sparsity and quality. We look at the impact of sparsity on length normalization in retrieval models and motivate to ignore document length in a microblog scenario. Further we introduce a way to measure quality in tweets, which helps to overcome underspecified queries and allows for adding a static quality measure that can compensate for the lack of meaningful term frequencies in microblog messages.

3.1 Term Sparsity and Length Normalization

We already mentioned that microblog messages contain few terms in general and very rarely contain a term more than once (see Figure 1). Intuition dictates that this term sparsity will have an impact in a retrieval setting. The most obvious impact is that a potentially relevant tweet will not be retrieved at all if among its few terms it does not contain one of the query terms. This risk is much higher than with classical documents, as the length restrictions prevent an author from using synonyms or elaborating concepts with additional words. But, a second and more subtle impact lies in the length restriction itself, as we will see in a moment.

Length normalization is an essential ingredient to modern retrieval models. The motivation for length normalization is to counterbalance the potential advantages of longer documents [14] that are commonly explained based on the *verbosity hypothesis* and the *scope hypothesis*.

Verbosity Hypothesis A long document elaborates the same topic longer and repeatedly. Therefore it also contains the same terms repeatedly while not adding further information to the document. This leads to a higher term frequency and in consequence to higher weights for the repeated terms.

Scope Hypothesis A long document addresses several topics. Therefore, it contains more different terms and might seem relevant to wider range of different queries. The general line of thought here is that a user would prefer a short and focused document over a long document relating to several topics.

Given the restriction of microblog messages to contain very few terms, intuition tells us that neither the verbosity nor the scope hypothesis can serve to explain the document length in Twitter messages. To verify our intuition, we analyze a large collection of Twitter messages with respect to two questions: (a) can we observe a tendency of longer tweets to be verbose, i.e. contain terms repeatedly and (b) can we observe a tendency of longer tweets to have a larger scope, i.e. to cover several topics.

To discover verbosity we look at redundancy in a tweet and how it correlates with document length. As measure for document length we employ once the number of characters and once the total number of terms. Given the non-normal distribution of document length (c.f. Figure 2 for the distribution of messages w.r.t. character length) we calculated Spearman's rank correlation on the two observed values for document length and the amount of redundant words. Between the character length of a tweet and redundancy we observed a correlation of $\rho = 0.381$. This indicates no or at most a very weak correlation. Also for the total number of words and the number of redundant word we found a quite

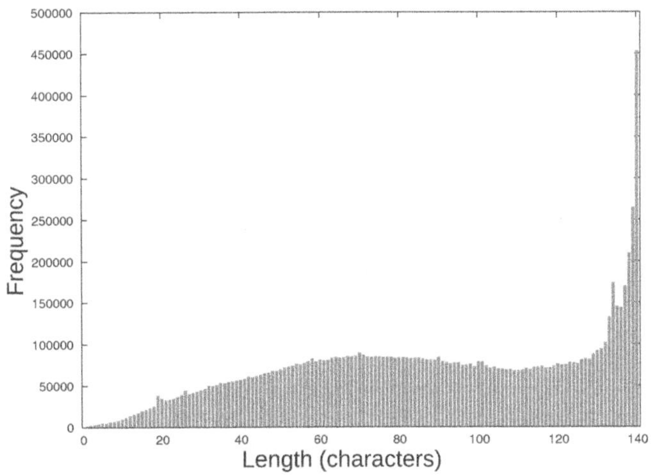

Figure 2: Distribution of document length (in characters) in the *choudhury* dataset.

low value of $\rho = 0.377$, allowing us to conclude that in a microblogging environment document length does not seem to be caused by verbosity.

A larger scope within a document is more difficult to detect. In order to get an idea of how many topics a tweet might cover, we applied latent Dirichlet allocation (LDA) to our dataset. LDA discovers latent topics in text documents and represents them as a distribution over terms. At the same time, documents are seen as a random mixture of topics, i.e. each document is a distribution over topics. The latter allows us to obtain insights on the number of topics a tweet is associated with.

We used LDA to obtain 100 topics and the likelihood of each tweet to belong to this topic. Given this model, we found around 8.5% of the tweets not being strongly related to any topic[1]. Among the remaining tweets, we analyzed the tweets for the number of topics that contribute to more than half of the probability of associated topics. To do so we analyzed how many topics we have to consider for each tweet to cover more than 50% of the probability in the topic mixture. We observed that in 77.1% of the tweets this point is already reached with one topic, meaning that the most prominent topic dominates the overall topic of the tweet. And for 99.6% the two top ranking topics contribute half the probability in the topic mixture. Our scope observations are also in line with the work of Zhao et al. [17] that observed that a single tweet usually covers a single topic. As a result, we can say that microblog messages in general are very focused – typically one LDA topic explains very well the composition of the entire tweet.

As neither the verbosity nor the scope hypothesis seem to apply to Twitter, we conjecture that length normalization for Twitter messages is not necessary. On the contrary, it might be counterproductive, as it introduces a bias favoring short over long messages without a justification.

3.2 Interestingness as Static Quality Measure

Microblog documents have different aspects of quality. Obviously, there is the distinction of spam, the trustworthiness or the purpose of a message. Quality is a static measure for a document that is independent from an actual query. Such a static quality measure is of particular interest when documents are likely to obtain homogeneous relevance values in a retrieval model. This is the case for Twitter, given that term frequency is nearly a binary value on microblogs and queries are typically composed of very few or even single terms.

The motivation of introducing interestingness into a general retrieval setting is, that when searching for messages a user would want to leave his closer social sphere and get results also from other areas in the social graph. We base our notion of interestingness on the *retweet* function. As a retweet is relayed to all the followers of a user, the message being retweeted can therefore be considered of general interest. This notion of a tweet being potentially interesting to other users is then a suitable way to capture the static content quality we have in mind.

Studies of tweets and retweets have revealed that the context of a tweet influences its actual chance to be retweeted. Most prominent context features are the social graph and the time of the original tweet. As our focus is on the message itself, we will deliberately ignore such context information, and rely only on features extracted from the message itself[2]. We use logistic regression on content features to predict the probability of an unseen message to be retweeted and use this probability as a static quality measure for tweets.

We follow our approach from [12] to determine interestingness via the probability of a tweet being retweeted. There, only the following features based on the tweets themselves were considered and a tweet's author and timestamp was ignored. All features except term odds, sentiment and topic scores are binary.

URLs, usernames and hashtags. Without further differentiation we consider the presence of particular items typical for tweets. These are the presence of a URL, the mention of a username or a hashtag. These constitute three binary features.

Exclamation and question marks. We use the presence of exclamation marks "!" and question marks "?" at the end of tweets as two binary features.

Positive and Negative Terms. We look for positive and negative words from a short predefined list. Positive terms comprise exclamations of happiness, such as *excellent* or *great*, while negative exclamations contain swear words or expressions of disgust (e.g. *eww* or *fail*).

Emoticons. Emoticons or smileys are short character sequences representing emotions. We parse the tweets to find positive emoticons such as `:-)` and negative emoticons such as `:-(`, giving two binary features.

Sentiments. Many tweets are personal and express sentiments. To detect the sentiments expressed by a tweet, we follow previous Twitter research and select a simple dictionary-based approach [9]. We use the Affective Norms of English Words dictionary [3], which provides numerical values for 1,030 English words to capture valence (pleasure vs. displeasure), arousal (excitement vs. calmness) and dominance (weakness vs. strength).

Terms. The most obvious content features in text are the contained terms. We extract terms and normalize them

[1] No topic had an association of more than 1%

[2] Our aim is to capture a relevant and interesting tweet even if it was written by a new user with no followers and at an unsuitable time in the middle of the night.

using case folding and the Porter Stemmer. For each message M we compute the odds of it being a retweet. Modeling a retweet as event RT, assuming independence between the occurrences of terms and employing Bayes' theorem the odds value can be brought into a form that is easier to handle:

$$O(\mathrm{RT} \mid M) = O(\mathrm{RT}) \cdot \prod_{t \in M} \frac{P(t \mid \mathrm{RT})}{P(t \mid \overline{\mathrm{RT}})}$$

where $O(\mathrm{RT})$ are the a priori odds of a retweet, and the product ranges over the ratios of the probabilities of each contained term to occur in a retweeted or a non-retweeted message. To estimate these probabilities we use maximum likelihood estimation and Laplace smoothing to handle unseen terms.

Topics. The topic of a tweet is a latent feature and can be inferred by analyzing a tweet's content. Modeling Twitter content requires methods that are suitable for short texts with heterogeneous vocabulary. Recent work shows that one such method is LDA and its extensions [2, 16]. We use LDA to find latent topics that characterize the corpus. In topic modeling the standard model used to describe a topic is as a distribution over terms and documents, generated as a mixture of latent topics.

Based on these features we trained a logistic regression model to be able to obtain for an individual tweet a probability of retweet. We interpret this probability to be the quality of a microblog message. If the probability of retweet is high, the message is seen as interesting for a wider audience and, therefore, of better quality in a general retrieval scenario.

4. EVALUATION

We empirically evaluate our approach in two different ways. We use a relevance-based evaluation following the classical Cranfield paradigm and a subjective evaluation asking users which result sets they prefer for a given query.

To analyze empirically the impact of length normalization and message quality in the sense of interestingness on the retrieval performance we set up three systems making use of two Lucene-based indices over a collection of 10 million tweets. As baseline we use an index-based on an out-of-the-box implementation of Lucene, i.e. a vector space retrieval model (VSM) including length normalization. The second Lucene index was modified not to perform length normalization, but otherwise use the Lucene retrieval function.

In order to incorporate interestingness as static quality measure, we use an approach based on reranking relevant results. For this purpose we take the top-100 entries in a relevance-based result set and rerank them according to descending probability of retweet. This means rank 1 is the tweet that has the highest value for interestingness among the tweets with 100 highest relevance values.

4.1 Methodology

To the best of our knowledge, there is currently no established dataset for evaluating retrieval in a microblog setting. Therefore, we had to develop an own configuration of microblog corpus, topics and relevance decisions. As corpus we employed an existing dataset [6] covering 118,506 users.

Table 1: Twitter datasets used in our experiments.

Dataset	Users	Tweets	Retweets
CHOUDHURY [6]	118,506	9,998,756	7.89%
CHOUDHURY-EXT [6]	277,666	29,000,000	8.64%
PETROVIĆ [13]	4,050,944	21,477,484	8.46%

The ratio of actual retweets in the dataset was 7.89%. The full list of datasets we used is given in Table 1.

To formulate information needs on Twitter data we selected the most prominent terms from 20 distinct LDA topics. To cover different query lengths, we created five queries each of length one to four terms. In this way we could simulate a range of quite general and quite specific information needs, for which the data set should also provide relevant documents.

To assess the objective performance of retrieval on microblogs in a classical Cranfield setting, we needed objective relevance judgements. We applied pooling on the top 5 retrieved tweets for each method and evaluated the messages in the pool for relevance. As relevance is typically judged as *aboutness*, i.e. to which degree a document covers the topic of an information need, we additionally had the judges determine if a tweet was actually interesting. The purpose of this extension is to distinguish between technically relevant (i.e. about the topic, containing the query terms) and actually informative tweets (i.e. about the topic and providing general information on the topic). As we will see later quite often retrieval results on microblog messages are technically relevant, because they contain the query terms, but are practically not informative because they contain no other terms. Other tweets are rather personal messages, that do not satisfy a general information need.

To further measure user satisfaction, we set up a second experiment in which we confronted the judges with two top-10 result lists for a given query, originating from two different retrieval setups anonymized as System A and System B. The users were asked if they preferred the results of System A, of System B, or were indifferent. The intention of this evaluation setup was to capture a subjective preference of a particular system over another one in direct comparison.

For both evaluation tasks we used crowdsourcing to obtain relevance judgements and system preferences respectively. To assert the quality of our crowdsourcing approach we introduced artificial non-relevant results to identify and eliminate spammer results. Further, we collected for each evaluation task the feedback from seven different judgements and derived the final judgement based on the recommendations provided in [1].

4.2 Results

We measured the objective performance using average P@5 and MAP. Figure 3 gives the achieved values on a all queries and a break down for the different query lengths. The plots list the Lucene system in its out-of-the-box configuration (i.e. a VSM with length normalization) as a baseline, the modified Lucene setup which does not perform any length normalization, and the setup using the retweet odds for reranking the top-100 results.

With respect to both evaluation metrics, we observe a global and local trend. Globally we can confirm our theory, that length normalization on microblog messages is counterproductive. The standard Lucene approach is outperformed on all levels and independent of query length. Looking at the tweets retrieved, length normalization favors shorter messages. In particular for short queries, the tweets quite often consist only of the query terms, thus, not satisfying any information need. Turning off the length normalization bias leads to better results. The gap is narrower for longer queries, but on average, the approach without length normalization still leads to better results.

The second trend is depending on the query length. For short and underspecified queries a simple relevance-based ranking provides relatively poor results. Deactivating length normalization does improve the results, but not to a level that can be observed for longer queries. Here, incorporating interestingness as static quality measure leads to a big improvement. This is of particular interest, as queries on Twitter are typically short: 1.64 words on average [15].

Tables 2 and 3 demonstrate the positive effect of reranking based on interestingness with a very clear and illustrative example of the query beer. The top ranking results in Table 2 contain only the query term, repeated many times. Technically these results are relevant as they contain the query term, but they do not convey much information. The results employing reranking based on interestingness in Table 3, instead, are technically relevant and informative.

In general, with an average P@5 value of 1.00 and a MAP value of 0.78, retweet odds reranking on one term queries achieves the overall best results we observed in our evaluation. Looking again at the data we saw two explanations: (a) the top-100 results coming out of the relevance ranking were all more or less related to the topic, thus, reranking did not bring irrelevant documents to the top of the list and (b) the top relevance ranking results consisted mainly of tweets formed by the query term, as already noted above. The longer and more specific the queries are, the less the top relevance ranked documents consists of query terms alone and the more irrelevant tweets come into the top-100 documents used for reranking. Therefore, the advantage of interestingness as static quality measure wears off and might actually put highly interesting, but only marginally relevant tweets to the top of the result lists.

Table 2: Top 5 tweets for the query beer using the Lucene-noLen setting.

	Tweet
1	Beer beer beer beer beer beer beer beer beer beer beer beer beer. Er, guess what I'm looking forward to?
2	BEER^5. RT @dewbelle: BEER BEER BEER BEER. RT @kulturbrille: BEER BEER BEER. RT @Bluebarrow: BEER BEER. RT @WalterMitty007: BEER
3	http://ping.fm/p/Bnra7 - In!!! BEER, BEER, BEER, BEER, BEER, BEER, BEER, BEER, BEER, BEER,
4	Lompoc. beer beer beer beer beer beer beer beer beer beer. http://twitpic.com/168ld
5	Beer, beer beer, beer, beer beer, beer and a little bit more beer.

Our second evaluation looked at subjective performance. Also here we observed the same trends as above. Table 4 shows how many times a system was preferred over an opposed system. Figure 4 further summarizes these results and shows for each query length how many times the result set of an individual system was preferred. We observe the same

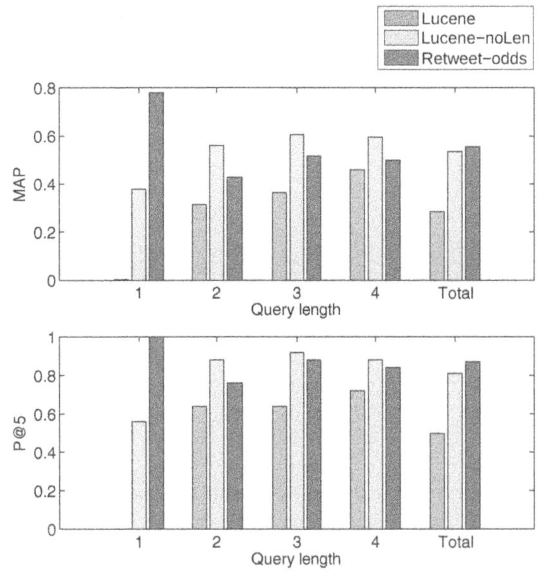

Figure 3: MAP and P@5 performance: in total and resolved by query length.

Table 3: Top 5 tweets for query beer using the Retweet-Odds setting.

	Tweet
1	UK beer mag declares "the end of beer writing." @StanHieronymus says not so in the US. http://bit.ly/424HRQ #beer
2	beer summit @bspward @jhinderaker no one had billy beer? heehee #narm - beer summit @bspward @jhinde http://tinyurl.com/n29oxj
3	Go green and turn those empty beer bottles into recycled beer glasses! | http://bit.ly/2src7F #beer #recycle (via: @td333)
4	Great Divide beer dinner @ Porter Beer Bar on 8/19 - $45 for 3 courses + beer pairings. http://trunc.it/172wt
5	Interesting Concept-Beer Petitions.com launches&hopes 2help craft beer drinkers enjoy beer they want @their fave pubs. http://bit.ly/11gJQN

tendency, that the classical Lucene implementation is rarely preferred over another setup. Further we note strong preference towards the Retweet-odds based reranking on shorter and underspecified queries, while on longer queries the users prefer the relevance based ranking over the Retweet-odds reranking approach. This corresponds to the observations made for the objective evaluation setting.

5. CONCLUSIONS AND SUMMARY

In this paper we looked into the particularities of information retrieval on microblogs: sparsity and document quality. Sparsity is inherent to microblog documents, as it reflects the technical constraints on the message length. The quality of a document with respect to its ability to satisfy an information need originates from the different purposes and environments in which microblog messages are generated. We motivated from a theoretical and data analytical point of view, that document length normalization introduces an unmotivated bias towards short documents in microblog retrieval. Further, we introduced interestingness as a static quality measure for microblog messages. We empirically showed, that both approaches improve retrieval performance

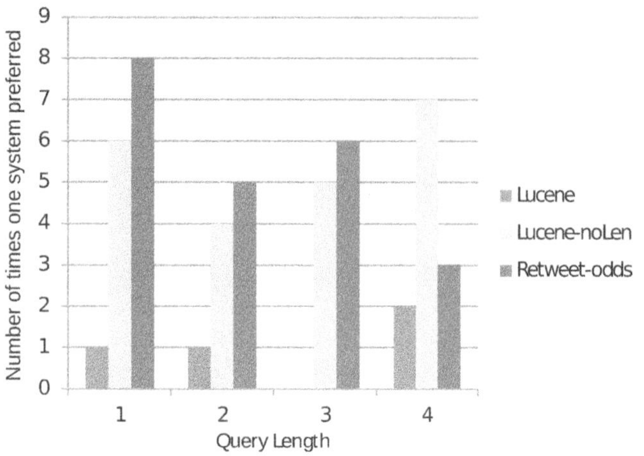

Figure 4: Number of times each system is preferred over the others for different query lengths.

Table 4: User preference of systems.

Opposed	Preferred system		
Q1	Lucene	Lucene-noLen	Retweet-odds
Lucene	–	4	5
Lucene-noLen	1	–	3
Retweet-odds	0	2	–
Q2	Lucene	Lucene-noLen	Retweet-odds
Lucene	–	3	2
Lucene-noLen	0	–	3
Retweet-odds	1	1	–
Q3	Lucene	Lucene-noLen	Retweet-odds
Lucene	–	2	4
Lucene-noLen	0	–	2
Retweet-odds	0	3	–
Q4	Lucene	Lucene-noLen	Retweet-odds
Lucene	–	3	2
Lucene-noLen	0	–	1
Retweet-odds	2	4	–

in the sense of providing more relevant and generally interesting messages in the search results.

As a next step, we plan to incorporate further static quality measures in the process. These will include the social context of a user, the global network structure and the freshness of results.

Acknowledgments

The research leading to these results has received funding from the European Community's Seventh Framework Programme (FP7/2007-2013) under grant agreement no. 257859, ROBUST and grant agreement no. 248512, WeGov. This work was supported in part by HEC, Govt. of Pakistan in collaboration with DAAD, Germany. This work was also partly funded by the German Research Foundation (DFG) under the Multipla project (grant 38457858).

6. REFERENCES

[1] O. Alonso and R. A. Baeza-Yates. Design and implementation of relevance assessments using crowdsourcing. In *Proc. European Conf. on Information Retrieval*, pages 153–164, 2011.

[2] D. M. Blei, A. Y. Ng, and M. I. Jordan. Latent Dirichlet allocation. *J. of Machine Learning Research*, 3:993–1022, 2003.

[3] M. M. Bradley and P. J. Lang. Affective norms for English words (ANEW): Instruction manual and affective ratings. Technical report, The Center for Research in Psychophysiology, University of Florida, 1999.

[4] M. Cha, H. Haddadi, F. Benevenuto, and K. P. Gummadi. Measuring user influence in Twitter: the million follower fallacy. In *Proc. Int. Conf. on Weblogs and Social Media*, pages 10–17, 2010.

[5] A. Che Alhadi, S. Staab, and T. Gottron. Exploring user purpose writing single tweets. In *Proc. Web Science Conf.*, 2011.

[6] M. D. Choudhury, Y.-R. Lin, H. Sundaram, K. S. Candan, L. Xie, and A. Kelliher. How does the data sampling strategy impact the discovery of information diffusion in social media? In *Proc. Conf. on Weblogs and Social Media*, pages 34–41, 2010.

[7] L. Hong, O. Dan, and B. D. Davison. Predicting popular messages in Twitter. In *Proc. Int. World Wide Web Conf.*, pages 57–58, 2011.

[8] M. Karam, T. Manos, d. R. Marten, and W. Wouter. Incorporating query expansion and quality indicators in searching microblog posts. In *Proc. European Conf. on Information Retrieval*, 2011.

[9] E. Kim, S. Gilbert, M. J. Edwards, and E. Graeff. Detecting sadness in 140 characters: Sentiment analysis and mourning Michael Jackson on Twitter. Technical report, Web Ecology Project, Aug 2009.

[10] H. Kwak, C. Lee, H. Park, and S. Moon. What is Twitter, a social network or a news media? In *Proc. Int. World Wide Web Conf.*, pages 591–600, 2010.

[11] R. Nagmoti, A. Teredesai, and M. De Cock. Ranking approaches for microblog search. In *Proc. Int. Conf. on Web Intelligence and Intelligent Agent Technology*, pages 153–157, 2010.

[12] N. Naveed, T. Gottron, J. Kunegis, and A. Che Alhadi. Bad news travel fast: A content-based analysis of interestingness on twitter. In *Proc. Web Science Conf.*, 2011.

[13] S. Petrović, M. Osborne, and V. Lavrenko. The Edinburgh Twitter corpus. In *Proc. Workshop on Computational Linguistics in a World of Social Media*, pages 25–26, 2010.

[14] A. Singhal, C. Buckley, and M. Mitra. Pivoted document length normalization. In *Proc. Int. Conf. on Research and Development in Information Retrieval*, pages 21–29, 1996.

[15] J. Teevan, D. Ramage, and M. R. Morris. #twittersearch: a comparison of microblog search and Web search. In *Proc. Int. Conf. on Web Search and Data Mining*, pages 35–44, 2011.

[16] J. Weng, E.-P. Lim, J. Jiang, and Q. He. TwitterRank: Finding topic-sensitive influential twitterers. In *Proc. Int. Conf. on Web Search and Data Mining*, pages 261–270, 2010.

[17] W. X. Zhao, J. Jiang, J. Weng, J. He, E.-P. Lim, H. Yan, and X. Li. Comparing twitter and traditional media using topic models. In *Proc. European Conf. on Information Retrieval*, pages 338–349, 2011.

Finding Images of Difficult Entities in the Long Tail

Bilyana Taneva
Max-Planck Institute for Informatics
Saarbrücken, Germany
btaneva@mpi-inf.mpg.de

Mouna Kacimi
Free University of Bozen-Bolzano
Italy
Mouna.Kacimi@unibz.it

Gerhard Weikum
Max-Planck Institute for Informatics
Saarbrücken, Germany
weikum@mpi-inf.mpg.de

ABSTRACT

While images of famous people and places are abundant on the Internet, they are much harder to retrieve for less popular entities such as notable computer scientists or regionally interesting churches. Querying the entity names in image search engines yields large candidate lists, but they often have low precision and unsatisfactory recall. In this paper, we propose a principled model for finding images of rare or ambiguous named entities. We propose a set of efficient, light-weight algorithms for identifying entity-specific keyphrases from a given textual description of the entity, which we then use to score candidate images based on the matches of keyphrases in the underlying Web pages. Our experiments show the high precision-recall quality of our approach.

Categories and Subject Descriptors

H.3 [**Information Storage and Retrieval**]: Information Search and Retrieval

General Terms

Algorithms, Experimentation

1. INTRODUCTION

1.1 Motivation

The digital information world is getting more and more organized. Knowledge bases such as DBpedia [1] or Freebase (`freebase.com`) systematically organize millions of entities and billions of facts into a formal representation based on the RDF data model. However, despite these advances in moving from raw data to value-added knowledge, there are still major shortcomings in organizing multimedia information such as images of named entities. For example, out of the 735 articles in the Wikipedia category *2010 FIFA World Cup players*, many articles do not have an image of the football (soccer) player. The same problems hold for scientists, artists, and politicians in the long tail of entities. Even if Wikipedia contains a picture, users may be interested in obtaining a wide variety of pictures at different occasions or different ages. Likewise, for geographic or cultural landmarks (mountains, temples, etc.), users may want to see different perspectives, weather/light conditions, etc.

It is often a tedious task to find good images using search engines. Even when the top-20 results contain some true matches, the user may have to look at the actual Web pages to figure out which image shows which entity (unless the user was already familiar with the requested person, waterfall, cathedral, etc.). Ideally, we would like to have a knowledge base, perhaps as an extension of Wikipedia or DBpedia, that contains a wide variety of different pictures for all named entities. This collection should be automatically constructed and maintained as new images appear on the Web. This paper addresses this very topic. While projects like `image-net.org` are collecting large amounts of images for general concepts (e.g., sunsets, cats, kiwis), there is no counterpart for individual entities (e.g., the Bridge of Sighs in Venice, as opposed to any kind of bridge).

The outlined endeavor is challenging for the following reasons. Names can be highly ambiguous, and search engines do not always favor the interpretation that the user is interested in. For example, assume you want to find pictures of the economist David Gale. Searching with "David Gale" yields results that are dominated by the actor Kevin Spacey who acted in the movie "The Life of David Gale" (totally unrelated to the economist). Entities in the long tail may be rare on the Web, despite being well worthy of inclusion in a universal knowledge base. For example, the top-100 search results for Carsten Lund, who has received the Goedel prize (the most prestigious award for theoretical computer science), contain only few correct images at low ranks. Unfortunately, the names themselves do not give any cues if an entity is a difficult case in terms of rarity or ambiguity.

A practically viable solution should be able to operate with minimum human supervision. The main prior work on this problem [16] highly depends on explicitly labeled training samples for each class of entities, and performs computationally expensive query expansions and aggregation steps.

Our goal is not just finding one image on the first result page (ideally rank 1), but to find as many (ideally different) images of the entity on high ranks. Thus we aim at a high value of the area under the precision-recall curve.

1.2 Contribution

Our approach of finding images for ambiguous or rare named entities is illustrated in Figure 1. It consists of the

CIKM'11, October 24–28, 2011, Glasgow, Scotland, UK.

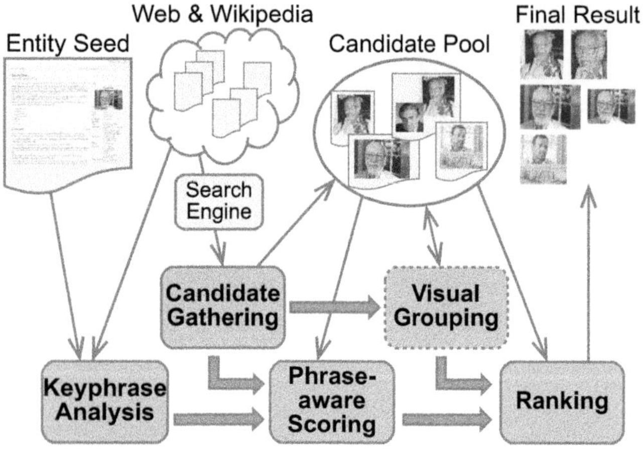

Figure 1: System Architecture. Rectangles are system components. *Visual grouping* is optional.

following steps. For a given entity of interest, we start from a salient *seed page* (or ask the user for it, find it in a knowledge base, etc.). This could be the Wikipedia article for the entity, but we can handle arbitrary seed pages on the Web such as people's home pages or short descriptions. The only requirement is that the user herself can uniquely identify the entity from solely seeing the seed page. If there is no other information about the entity but its name, the task becomes ill-defined for the machine and the only possible output can be a mixture of results for different entities with the same name. The *keyphrase analysis* component then automatically extracts from the seed page a ranked list of *keyphrases* that are characteristic for the entity. The *candidate gathering* component sends a keyword query using only the entity name to image search engines and obtains a pool of candidate images fetched with their underlying Web pages. Then the *phrase-aware scoring* component uses a new model for *re-ranking* the results in the candidate pool, based on the entity-characteristic keyphrases found earlier. For each image in the pool it identifies *full or partial matches* of keyphrases in the Web page containing the image, and computes a new form of relevance score used for re-ranking. Optionally, the *visual grouping* component groups visually similar images aiming at a diversified final list of results.

The paper makes the following novel contributions: 1) a principled model for re-ranking of images for rare or ambiguous named entities in the long tail; 2) a phrase-aware scoring model for image candidates based on partial keyphrase matches in an image's underlying Web page; 3) a robustness test for entity difficulty that allows us to selectively apply our ranking model only when it is likely to improve the result list; 4) a comprehensive experimental evaluation with a variety of entity categories, demonstrating the high precision-recall quality of our approach, and the improvements over various baseline methods including the original image-search result list and a language-model-based ranking method that directly uses the seed page of an entity.

2. RELATED WORK

A number of recent projects have aimed at enhancing the *semantic organization of image collections.* Prominent examples are TinyImage [19] and LabelMe [15]. TinyImage is a dataset of low resolution images collected from the Internet by sending all nouns in WordNet [4] as queries to several image search engines. It uses the hypernymy relation of WordNet in conjunction with nearest-neighbor methods to automatically classify the retrieved images. LabelMe is a large collection of images with ground truth labels to be used for object detection and recognition research. It aims at object class recognition (e.g., bridge) as opposed to instance recognition (e.g., Golden Gate Bridge).

A few projects tackle the more specific problem of *integrating images into knowledge bases* [3, 16]. ImageNet [3] builds a large-scale labeled image collection based on the taxonomic hierarchy of WordNet. To this end, it exploits the hypernymy relation between entity classes and nearest-neighbor-based classification with visual features. While ImageNet focuses on finding images of semantic classes such as towers, churches, etc., our work addresses photos of *individual entities* like the Blue Mosque in Istanbul. Closest to our paper is the work of [16], which aims to populate a knowledge base of individual entities with their images. The latter harnesses relational facts about entities for generating expanded queries posed to image search engines. The approach retrieves all result lists from the generated expanded queries, merges the lists, and ranks the individual images by weighted voting procedure. Weights are dependent on the type of entity (e.g., scientist vs. politician) and computed from training entities for each type. This approach achieved very good experimental results but had significant limitations: dependence on ontological facts which are not always available, the need for training samples for each entity type which is a bottleneck, and the high overhead caused by query expansions resulting in a large number of search-engine requests. In our work, we propose a very different, more lightweight technique that overcomes these limitations.

Keyphrase extraction is one of the components in our system. There are both supervised [5, 8] and unsupervised [7, 11] approaches. Supervised methods crucially depend on the availability of manually labeled training data, while unsupervised methods do not need labeled samples and are domain-independent. They typically use IR measures like tf-idf, consider linguistic features, and harness document structure such as XML tags. We adopt an unsupervised approach for keyphrase extraction to avoid training bottlenecks and for domain-independence. We use noun phrases ranked by Mutual Information, as described in Section 3.

3. KEYPHRASE MINING & WEIGHTING

Finding good images of entities is not always straightforward, especially when the user is not familiar with the (look of the) requested entity. Given a list of image results, the user sometimes has to look at the Web pages that contain the image results to figure out which image shows which entity. To automate this challenging task, we exploit characteristic phrases of entities to select good matches of images from the result pool that we obtain from querying image search engines with entity names.

For a given entity, we start from a salient *seed page.* We assume that the page has enough information so that a human user can uniquely identify the entity and there is no confusion about other entities with the same name. We then automatically extract from the seed page a *ranked list of keyphrases* that are characteristic for the entity. These keyphrases are later used to re-rank images.

Keyphrase extraction. On first thought, a good method for extracting keyphrases would be to identify all noun phrases in the seed page. We use the OpenNLP tool [12] for this purpose. For example, from the seed page of the economist David Gale (`en.wikipedia.org/wiki/David_Gale`), we gather phrases like "economist", "Professor Emeritus", "partner Sandra Gilbert", "poet", "daughters", etc. Some of them are characteristic for the entity, but others dilute the focus by being either too broad or misleading (e.g., the phrase "poet" actually refers to Gale's partner). To overcome these issues while keeping the approach computationally efficient (e.g., avoiding deep natural-language parsing), we introduce a notion of *focused keyphrases* that are truly characteristic for an entity. For David Gale, we prefer phrases like "University of California, Berkeley", "economist", "game theory", etc.

Depending on whether the entity seed page is a Wikipedia article or an arbitrary Web page, we use two different strategies to select focused keyphrases. Given a Wikipedia seed page, we extract from the article's text part all outgoing links that point to other Wikipedia articles. Then, we select the anchor text of these links as focused keyphrases. We use the WikiPrep tool [6] for this purpose. For an arbitrary Web page, we select all noun phrases that are titles of Wikipedia articles, including redirects. This way, we restrict the vocabulary of keyphrases to named entities and informative nouns.

Keyphrase weigthing. For each selected keyphrase of a given entity, we also compute and assign a weight, which measures how well the keyphrase characterizes the entity. We use the standard *Mutual Information* measure (*MI*) for this purpose, but other measures can be applied as well. The *MI* of a given keyphrase and an entity indicates how much information the keyphrase contains about the entity. The higher the *MI* is, the more dependent they are. More formally, for each entity we have two possible classes of pages: one for pages about the entity (c), and one for other pages ($\bar{c}$). The *MI* of a keyphrase and an entity is then given by:

$$MI(X;Y) = \sum_{x_k \in \{1,0\}} \sum_{y_c \in \{1,0\}} P_{XY}(x_k, y_c) \log_2 \frac{P_{XY}(x_k, y_c)}{P_X(x_k) P_Y(y_c)}$$

where X is a random variable that takes values 1 if the page contains the keyphrase and 0 otherwise, and Y is a random variable that takes values 1 if the page is in class c and 0 if the page is in class $\bar{c}$. In our implementation we typically have one seed page per entity. Thus, the class c contains only this page, and all other pages in the corpus (e.g., all other Wikipedia articles) belong to class $\bar{c}$.

Note that keyphrases often consist of multiple words. We compute the *MI* weight for the entire keyphrase and also for each of its constituent words. The usage of the weights of individual words is described in Section 4.

Our model can also be specialized to use individual words only, for example, all words that constitute the keyphrases of an entity. In this special case, referred to as the *words-aware model* (as opposed to *phrase-aware model*), words lose their phrase context but can still be good cues for an entity, especially with our weighting method. For example, David Gale would be characterized by single words like "economist", "university", "Berkeley", "game", etc.

4. PHRASE-AWARE SCORING

Assume that for an entity of interest e we are given its candidate pool of images with their underlying Web pages, and its set of characteristic keyphrases ranked by *MI* as described in Section 3. We denote the keyphrases of e by $k_1(e), \ldots, k_m(e)$, or $k_1, \ldots, k_m$ if the entity is given by the context. Then for each image/page p in the candidate pool we compute a *phrase-aware score* $s(p)$, which is later used to rank the images in the pool:

$$s(p) = \sum_{i=1}^{m} w(k_i)\; \mathcal{S}(k_i, p)$$

Here $w(k_i)$ is the *MI* weight of keyphrase k_i and by $\mathcal{S}(k_i, p)$ we denote a *keyphrase score* for phrase k_i and image/page p. The keyphrase score $\mathcal{S}(k_i, p)$ is estimated by identifying matches or partial matches of a phrase k_i in a page p. Note that in the special case of the words-aware model, $\mathcal{S}(k_i, p)$ is either 0 or 1, as a single word is either in the page or not.

The best image pages for a given entity would ideally match exactly the entity's keyphrases. However, partial matches of keyphrases can still be good cues for the entity. For example, if "University of California, Berkeley" is a keyphrase, we are still interested in pages that contain pieces and variants such as "Berkeley University" or "UC Berkeley". In such cases, a good image page should contain as many of the keyphrase words as possible within close distance.

We compute keyphrase scores using a *Minimum Cover model*. We also explored two further alternative models, Büttcher's and Spans scoring models, but they achieved slightly inferior results to the minimum-cover-based model (see [17] for more details). All these models are extensions of prior work on proximity-aware scoring. The original models aimed at enhancing the scoring for standard keyword search by considering the proximity of the query keywords in a result candidate. In contrast, we apply and adapt these kinds of models to entity-specific keyphrases, not queries.

Scoring based on Minimum Cover. The Minimum Cover [18, 2] of a set of words in a text sequence is defined as the length of the shortest subsequence that contains all words at least once. We introduce an extension of this model to compute the keyphrase score for given entity keyphrase k and image page p:

$$\mathcal{S}(k,p) = \frac{|k \cap p|}{mincover(k \cap p, p)} \left(\frac{\sum_{t \in k \cap p} w(t)}{\sum_{t \in k} w(t)} \right)^{\lambda}$$

Here $k \cap p$ denotes the set of words from a keyphrase k that are matched in page p, and $mincover(k \cap p, p)$ returns the length of the shortest text segment of p where all words in $k \cap p$ appear at least once. We use the reciprocal of $mincover(k \cap p, p)$ to obtain high scores for short text segments and low scores for long segments. To capture how many keyphrase words are reflected by the *mincover* score, we multiply the reciprocal of the *mincover* by the number of matched keyphrase words $|k \cap p|$. In this way, we distinguish pages with comparable *mincover* scores but with different number of matched keyphrase words. The first factor in the formula ranges from 0 to 1. It is equal to 1 if there is an exact match of the words in $k \cap p$ in p, and to 0 if $|k \cap p| = 0$.

The original Minimum Cover model of [18, 2] for improved result ranking of standard text queries would consider only the first factor in the formula (with adaptation to its respective setting). However, this would still favor pages with fewer matched keyphrase words. For example, consider a keyphrase k with 5 words, and two pages p and q. Assume, $|k \cap p| = 2$ and $mincover(k \cap p, p) = 2$, and $|k \cap q| = 4$ and $mincover(k \cap q, q) = 4$. In this case, both p and q would have score 1 for the first factor in the formula, even though they match different number of keyphrase words. To solve this inconsistency, we introduce the second factor of the formula. It captures how many keyphrase words are missing from the page and how characteristic they are for the keyphrase. This is expressed by the weighted fraction of keyphrase words that appear in the page, where words are weighted by *MI* (see Section 3). This factor ranges from 0 to 1. It is equal to 1 if $|k \cap p| = |k|$, and to 0 if $|k \cap p| = 0$.

We adjust the influence of the two factors in the formula using a parameter λ. To favor pages containing more phrase words with relatively low *mincover*, we set $\lambda > 1$ (e.g., 2).

5. ENTITY DIFFICULTY

For some entities the image search engines perform already very good, with perfect precision for the first result page. In such cases we want to keep the original ranking of images and should not apply our re-ranking model. For deciding whether to re-rank the search engine's results or not, we perform a *robustness test* for *entity difficulty*.

The robustness test uses the top-15 results retrieved from image search engines by querying with the entity name only. We cluster the set of Web pages that contain the image results using a simple density-based method, which produces a variable number of clusters depending on a threshold for intra-cluster similarity. If an entity's results produce many clusters (e.g., ≥ 4), we conclude that the entity is difficult (i.e., ambiguous, rare, or both). Only then we apply our re-ranking; otherwise the entity is considered easy and we keep the original ranking.

The clustering method processes the pages in their original ranking order. For each page we find its first sufficiently similar neighbor from the already processed pages. If such a page exists, we assign the current page to the cluster of that previous page; otherwise we create a new cluster. As a similarity measure between two pages, we use the cosine similarity of their *tf-idf* vector representations. The *tf* value of a given word is based on the frequency of the word in the page, and the *idf* value – on the full Wikipedia corpus.

6. VISUAL GROUPING OF IMAGES

In addition to exploring the text of the pages containing the candidate images for the entity-specific keyphrases, we can optionally consider the visual content of the images. Our approach groups visually similar images and assigns to each group a representative image. Having already assigned to each candidate image in the pool its phrase-aware score (see Section 4), every representative image of a visual group is given a *group score* by summing over all phrase-aware scores of the images in its visual group. Finally, in the result list of images only the representatives are included, ranked by their group scores. This way we obtain visually diverse images.

To consider the visual content of the images we use visual features like *SIFT* feature descriptors [9] and *MPEG-7* features [10]. For testing pairwise similarity between images we applied similar techniques as in [16].

	Keyphrases
Entity: Peter Naur Category: Turing Award laureates	1) Backus-Naur form 2) ALGOL 60 3) ACM A.M. Turing Award 4) Niels Bohr Institute 5) Regnecentralen
Entity: Wapta Falls Category: Waterfalls of British Columbia	1) BC Geographical Names Information System 2) Yoho National Park 3) Kicking Horse River 4) waterfall 5) British Columbia

Table 1: Keyphrases from Wikipedia seed pages.

7. EXPERIMENTS

7.1 Setup

Methodology. We evaluated our method using entity collections such as waterfalls or Turing award winners. We focused on difficult entities in the long tail, and did not consider prominent entities such as "Niagara Falls". To decide whether an entity is difficult or not, we used our robustness test for entity difficulty presented in Section 5. We also disregarded extreme cases like "Basalt Falls" (located in BC, Canada), for which we could not find a single good result in the top-50 results returned by image search engines.

For each entity we used its seed page to extract (focused) keyphrases, for which we computed *MI* measures, as described in Section 3. Table 1 shows two entities and their best focused keyphrases ranked by *MI*. To collect a candidate pool of images for each test entity, we posed a query with the entity name to `images.google.com` and retrieved the top-50 image results and their underlying Web pages.

We manually assessed the candidate pictures for each test entity by assigning one of three possible labels: relevant, not relevant, undefined. The last label was assigned to pictures, for which we could not decide whether they are relevant or not (e.g., if a person was possibly shown in a group, but the photo quality was too poor to truly tell). The undefined results were not considered in our experiments.

We performed two types of experiments: one based on Wikipedia seed pages and one based on seed pages which were not Wikipedia articles, but simple Web pages varying in text length and quality of entity description.

Test data. Our test data is based on Wikipedia categories of named entities. We used 2 Wikipedia categories with specific themes, which we perceived as typical for the long tail of entities: "Turing Award laureates" with 56 entities, out of which 34 are difficult, as concluded by the test for entity difficulty, and "Waterfalls of British Columbia" with 20 entities, 14 of which are difficult. We also used 2 entity lists with broader but heterogeneous themes: "Economists" with 589 entities and "Ruins" with 788 entities. We completely assessed the image results for all entities in the first two categories. For the other two categories we randomly sampled 25 entities from each, excluding extremely prominent entities with perfect precision for the first result page. We applied the entity difficulty test on the two samples of 25 entities: there were 23 difficult entities from the "Economists" category and 17 from the "Ruins" category.

Methods under comparison. We compared five methods: 1) our new ranking method based on the minimum-cover matching of (focused) keyphrases (**Phr**); 2) the words-aware model as a special case of our method (**Word**); 3) the original search engine, as a main baseline (**G**); 4) the original search engine with query expansion, by including the highest-MI keyphrase in the entity query (**GQE**); 5) a language-model-based ranking, using the Kullback-Leibler divergence $KL(LM(e)|LM(p))$ between a result page p and the entity seed page e (in the role of a query), with Dirichlet smoothing for p using the entire Wikipedia as a background corpus. This baseline represents state-of-the-art IR methods for document retrieval [13, 20] (**KL**).

Quality measures. We used four quality measures: Mean Average Precision (MAP), Normalized Discounted Cumulative Gain (NDCG), Precision at k (P@k), and Mean Reciprocal Rank (MRR). Our main measures of interest are MAP and NDCG, as we are interested in the entire precision-recall curve. We include P@k and MRR for completeness. We compute MAP and NDCG similarly to [14] and refer to [17] for more details.

7.2 Results

Ranking based on Wikipedia seed pages. The results for the ranking models using Wikipedia seed pages are shown in Table 2. The phrase-aware model almost always improves all measures in comparison to the original search engine and the search engine with query expansion. The original search engine is better than the phrase-aware model only in terms of our secondary measures P@k and MRR for "Turing Award winners" and "Waterfalls of BC" respectfully. The gains of the phrase-based model depend on the category with highest gains on the "Ruins" category.

The words-aware model and the KL-divergence-based model perform amazingly well. They perform worse than the search engine baseline for the waterfalls category, but outperform the baseline on all other categories. The phrase-aware model almost always outperforms the words-aware and the KL-divergence-based models. The exception is the "Economists" category, for which the KL-divergence model is slightly better than the phrase-based model in terms of NDCG and MRR.

Another observation is that the search engine with query expansion performs worse than the original search engine. The reason is that the highest-MI keyphrase used for query expansion is often too long or too specific and hence dilutes the results of the expanded query.

The results in Table 2 are obtained by using only focused keyphrases for our phrase-aware model. We also compared the use of focused keyphrases versus using all noun phrases. The results show that the first are essential for the good performance of our model [17].

Ranking with visual grouping of images. Table 3 compares the re-ranking models when we group visually similar images, using the technique of Section 6. For consistency, we apply visual grouping to Google's ranking as well: starting from the top ranks of Google's list, whenever we meet a result that is visually similar to a result higher in the ranking, we remove the lower-ranked one. As a consequence of the visual grouping, the search engine's results are slightly better than the same results without grouping.

The phrase-aware model always improves MAP and NDCG compared to the search engine baseline. The words-aware and the KL-divergence-based models are also better than the baseline. They perform very well in this setting, but still lose against the phrase-aware model in most cases.

		Phr	Word	KL	G	GQE
T	MAP@50	0.599	0.591	0.591	0.587	0.344
	NDCG@50	0.931	0.924	0.926	0.885	0.893
	P@10	0.759	0.759	0.756	0.770	0.638
	MRR	0.956	0.941	0.944	0.897	0.910
W	MAP@50	0.618	0.593	0.589	0.588	0.210
	NDCG@50	0.894	0.882	0.876	0.883	0.682
	P@10	0.714	0.714	0.671	0.700	0.378
	MRR	0.886	0.889	0.848	0.964	0.611
E	MAP@50	0.628	0.621	0.625	0.572	0.163
	NDCG@50	0.895	0.887	0.897	0.855	0.664
	P@10	0.678	0.674	0.656	0.569	0.291
	MRR	0.935	0.917	0.946	0.935	0.625
R	MAP@50	0.594	0.578	0.552	0.499	0.259
	NDCG@50	0.934	0.924	0.909	0.823	0.742
	P@10	0.765	0.747	0.723	0.635	0.447
	MRR	0.970	1.000	0.970	0.779	0.778

Table 2: Evaluation for Turing Award winners (T), Waterfalls of BC (W), Economists (E), and Ruins (R), with Wikipedia seed pages.

Ranking based on non-Wikipedia seed pages. For all 4 entity categories, we also performed experiments using non-Wikipedia seed pages, obtained from the "wild Web". For each category we chose the five entities that performed worst in terms of MAP and NDCG of the Wikipedia-based experiment. This experiment was meant as a stress-test, geared towards the most difficult entities. Seed pages for the waterfalls or some of the ruins were typically very sparse, containing only a short paragraph. Seed pages for economists or Turing award winners were almost the opposite: very detailed but fairly verbose and thus very noisy.

As keyphrases, we extracted from the non-Wikipedia seed pages all noun phrases that are titles of Wikipedia articles, but did not use phrases with MI below some noise threshold. The results are shown in Table 4. For these very difficult entities, we observe that the phrase-aware model outperforms the search engine baseline and the KL-divergence-based model by a large margin. The words-aware model performs comparably to the phrase-based model, as, in these cases, many keyphrases were merely one-word phrases.

7.3 Discussion

Comparing the three main competitors – phrase-based model, words-aware model, and KL-divergence-based model – to the search engine baseline, we observe the following major trends. All three methods perform better than the search engine. The phrase-based method is almost never outperformed by the search engine, whereas the other two models are sometimes inferior to the baseline. The words-aware and KL-divergence-based models sometimes slightly outperform the phrase-based model, but the gains are statistically insignificant. Conversely, the gains of the phrase-based model over the KL-divergence-based one are statistically significant; they are most pronounced for the entities with Wikipedia seed pages from the "Ruins" and "Waterfalls" categories (see Table 2) and the most difficult entities

		Phr	Word	KL	G	GQE
T	MAP@50	0.643	0.639	0.615	0.604	0.422
	NDCG@50	0.928	0.926	0.902	0.873	0.891
W	MAP@50	0.647	0.643	0.610	0.625	0.208
	NDCG@50	0.889	0.888	0.857	0.878	0.675
E	MAP@50	0.632	0.649	0.636	0.612	0.197
	NDCG@50	0.874	0.884	0.887	0.859	0.668
R	MAP@50	0.592	0.584	0.564	0.512	0.251
	NDCG@50	0.915	0.908	0.904	0.814	0.726

Table 3: Evaluation with Wikipedia seed pages and visual grouping of images.

		Phr	Word	KL	G	GQE
T	MAP@50	0.476	0.484	0.405	0.308	0.375
	NDCG@50	0.906	0.911	0.853	0.686	0.863
W	MAP@50	0.644	0.646	0.557	0.518	0.178
	NDCG@50	0.915	0.913	0.856	0.823	0.562
E	MAP@50	0.542	0.498	0.489	0.344	0.272
	NDCG@50	0.909	0.854	0.876	0.725	0.786
R	MAP@50	0.558	0.546	0.459	0.331	0.297
	NDCG@50	0.920	0.920	0.884	0.686	0.706

Table 4: Evaluation with non-Wikipedia seed pages.

from all four categories for which we used noisy and sparse non-Wikipedia seed pages (see Table 4).

The phrase-based method performs particularly well for ambiguous names. For such entities, the search engine returns a mixture of relevant and irrelevant results, while our method successfully disambiguates the correct entity. An example is the "Sans-Souci Palace" from the "Ruins" category (Figure 2). There exist (at least) two palaces with the same name, one in Potsdam and one in Haiti.

In addition to entities with ambiguous names, our method performs very well also for rare entities in the Internet image space. For example, searching for images of the computer scientist "Robert Floyd" yields only 2 correct results in the top-50 result list, on ranks 3 and 15, while the phrase-based method ranks these matches on the first two ranks.

Figure 2: Top-5 results (no vis. grouping) for David Gale (economist) and Sans-Souci Palace (Haiti).

8. CONCLUSIONS

We have shown that our phrase-based approach can substantially enhance the ranking quality of image search for difficult entities in the long tail. Some of our techniques may resemble internal ranking techniques of commercial search engines, but these are not publicly documented at all. Moreover, Google and Bing operate solely at the level of query keywords and their proximity to images, whereas our approach is specifically designed for target entities of interest and uses automatically computed keyphrases for scoring. Our experiments have demonstrated that this entity-oriented re-ranking of Google image results leads to major improvements.

9. REFERENCES

[1] S. Auer et al. DBpedia: A nucleus for a web of open data. In *ISWC/ASWC*, 2007.

[2] R. Cummins and C. O'Riordan. Learning in a pairwise term-term proximity framework for information retrieval. In *SIGIR*, pages 251–258, 2009.

[3] J. Deng et al. ImageNet: A Large-Scale Hierarchical Image Database. In *CVPR*, 2009.

[4] C. Fellbaum. *WordNet: An Electronical Lexical Database*. The MIT Press, Cambridge, MA, 1998.

[5] E. Frank et al. Domain-specific keyphrase extraction. In *IJCAI*, pages 668–673, 1999.

[6] E. Gabrilovich and S. Markovitch. Computing semantic relatedness using wikipedia-based explicit semantic analysis. In *IJCAI*, 2007.

[7] K. Hofmann et al. The impact of document structure on keyphrase extraction. In *CIKM*, 2009.

[8] X. Jiang, Y. Hu, and H. Li. A ranking approach to keyphrase extraction. In *SIGIR*, pages 756–757, 2009.

[9] D. G. Lowe. Distinctive image features from scale-invariant keypoints. *IJCV*, 60:91–110, 2004.

[10] P. S. Member and J. R. Smith. Mpeg-7 multimedia description schemes. *IEEE TCSVT*, 11:748–759, 2001.

[11] R. Mihalcea and P. Tarau. TextRank: Bringing order into texts. In *EMNLP*, 2004.

[12] OpenNLP. http://opennlp.sourceforge.net/.

[13] J. M. Ponte and W. B. Croft. A language modeling approach to information retrieval. In *SIGIR*, 1998.

[14] F. Radlinski and N. Craswell. Comparing the sensitivity of information retrieval metrics. In *SIGIR*, pages 667–674, 2010.

[15] B. C. Russell et al. LabelMe: A database and web-based tool for image annotation. *IJCV*, 77(1-3):157–173, 2008.

[16] B. Taneva, M. Kacimi, and G. Weikum. Gathering and ranking photos of named entities with high precision, high recall, and diversity. In *WSDM*, 2010.

[17] B. Taneva, M. Kacimi, and G. Weikum. Finding images of rare and ambiguous entities. Research Report MPI-I-2011-5-002, MPII, 2011.

[18] T. Tao and C. Zhai. An exploration of proximity measures in information retrieval. In *SIGIR*, 2007.

[19] A. Torralba, R. Fergus, and W. T. Freeman. 80 million tiny images: A large data set for nonparametric object and scene recognition. *IEEE TPAMI*, 30(11):1958–1970, 2008.

[20] C. Zhai and J. Lafferty. A study of smoothing methods for language models applied to information retrieval. *ACM TOIS*, 22:179–214, 2004.

Learning to Rank User Intent

Giorgos Giannopoulos*
NTU Athens -
IMIS, "Athena" R.C.
Greece
giann@dblab.ece.ntua.gr

Ulf Brefeld
Yahoo! Research
Barcelona, Spain
brefeld@yahoo-inc.com

Theodore Dalamagas
IMIS, "Athena" R.C.
Greece
dalamag@imis.athena-innovation.gr

Timos Sellis
NTU Athens -
IMIS, "Athena" R.C.
Greece
timos@imis.athena-innovation.gr

ABSTRACT

Personalized retrieval models aim at capturing user interests to provide personalized results that are tailored to the respective information needs. User interests are however widely spread, subject to change, and cannot always be captured well, thus rendering the deployment of personalized models challenging. We take a different approach and study ranking models for user intent. We exploit user feedback in terms of click data to cluster ranking models for historic queries according to user behavior and intent. Each cluster is finally represented by a single ranking model that captures the contained search interests expressed by users. Once new queries are issued, these are mapped to the clustering and the retrieval process diversifies possible intents by combining relevant ranking functions. Empirical evidence shows that our approach significantly outperforms baseline approaches on a large corporate query log.

Categories and Subject Descriptors

H.3.3 [**Information Search and Retrieval**]: Information Search and Retrieval – Relevance feedback, Search process, Clustering

General Terms

Algorithms, Experimentation, Measurement

Keywords

Search engine, ranking, training, clickthrough data, relevance judgement, clustering, search behavior

*This research has been co-financed by the European Union (European Social Fund - ESF) and Greek national funds through the Operational Program "Education and Lifelong Learning" of the National Strategic Reference Framework (NSRF) - Research Funding Program: Heracleitus II. Investing in knowledge society through the European Social Fund.

1. INTRODUCTION

Modern data collections and recordings of historic user interaction pave the way for personalized information retrieval which exploits user profiles and historic usage data to re-rank and filter retrieved documents to serve individual information needs.

Personalized retrieval aims at computing a ranking model for every user or groups of similar users. Different approaches including the impact of short- and long-term search histories [21, 22], context [14, 21], query categories [8, 24], and search behavior and feedback [1, 9, 12, 16] have been studied. Additionally, collaborative filtering techniques for personalized search [22] and learning to rank-based approaches [1, 6, 12, 17, 19, 26] also proved effective in many scenarios. Many of the above techniques are also applicable to registered users of search engines, however, to have all users benefit from the re-ranking they need to be perfectly disambiguated. This is, particularly on shared computers, an issue and renders personalized web search difficult in practice.

In this paper, we study an orthogonal approach to re-ranking for web search which does not share these limitations, so that all users benefit equally from re-ranking the results. Our approach is based on the observation that existing approaches mainly focus on the retrieved content and on users search histories, thus leaving an important aspect unaddressed: The analysis of user search behavior. The user behavior is directly observable by user feedback in form of clicks on the result page and allows to reason about the intent of the users. The intent therefore acts like an unobserved, latent variable and is (partially) captured by user behavior.

Consider a user who issues a query for a new mobile phone. Her search history so far contains only unrelated queries. A personalized model would have to resort to the average user model for processing the query and possibly return text documents about phones. By contrast, our approach does not rely on user-specific models but aims at capturing the user intent by grouping queries entailing similar behavior. The results proposed to the user thus consist of different media types (e.g. reviews, videos, etc) that have been associated with mobile phones in the past. In other words, our system re-ranks the retrieved results, so that they represent the broad spectrum of user behavior for a given query.

To build models for user intent, we propose to cluster queries with respect to the user intent and learn a ranking function for every cluster. Optimally, the clustering and the ranking models are optimized jointly to capture interdependencies between the tasks. The corresponding optimization problem however turns out to be a mixed-integer problem with cubic constraints in the number of queries and and renders large-scale deployment infeasible. We therefore present an approximation that consists of three stages: Firstly, a ranking function is learned for every query to capture the user behavior by adaptation to user feedback given by click data. Secondly, the ranking models are grouped so that the resulting clusters correspond to similar user intents. Thirdly, a ranking function is learned for each cluster to represent the contained intent. At deployment time, queries are mapped to the clustering to compute scores expressing how likely the intent of the query is captured by the respective cluster. The final ranking is then induced by a weighted linear combination of ranking functions that are likely to cover the intent of the user, given the query. Combining the ranking functions of several clusters diversifies the results in terms of the captured intents.

Empirically, we observe our approach to capture user intent better than baseline methods on a large sample from the Yahoo! query log. Our method achieves higher precision values on top-ranks compared to content-based baselines. Additionally, the underlying clustering is observed to effectively group queries with similar intents together while content-based baselines do not exhibit interpretable clusterings.

The remainder is organized as follows. Section 2 reviews related work. We present our main contribution, the joint optimization problem and its approximation, in Section 3. Section 4 reports on the empirical evaluation and Section 5 concludes.

2. RELATED WORK

In [10] the author proposes a topic-based refinement of the PageRank algorithm that allows the offline computation of a fixed number of PageRank vectors corresponding to certain topic categories. The final result is a weighted combination of these vectors, where weights are proportional to the similarity of the query and the respective topic. In [20] the authors utilize concept hierarchies, like ODP[1], to categorize queries and to generate user profiles. Query results are re-ranked based on those profiles using collaborative filtering techniques. By contrast, our method does not rely on user profiles and is independent of static topic hierarchies.

Another prominent strand of research is based on exploiting historic user feedback. The impact of short-term versus long-term histories has been studied by [22, 23] while [5, 21] aim at capturing the context of the users, for instance by taking documents on the virtual desktop into account. The resulting models are essentially user profiles that are used to expand future queries and to refine the retrieved results. Compared to our method, these approaches focus on content similarity and do not exploit collaborative user data.

Many approaches incorporate state-of-the-art machine learning techniques to improve ranking results. [4] study modifications of ranking support vector machines to reduce the error on top-ranks and to increase the importance of queries with only a few relevant documents in the training sample. In [17], the authors propose to learn multiple ranking functions for different ranks which are aggregated to induce the final ranking. By contrast, we propose to learn different ranking functions for different behavior and intents. Furthermore, the above approaches do not take the inherent relations between queries and their clickthrough data into account.

The closest work to ours is [3] who propose to learn multiple ranking models by clustering queries based on the topical information extracted by their results. They represent queries by aggregating feature vectors which are then clustered to obtain specific ranking models. The final ranking for new queries is being made by combining the models. Their work differs in several aspects, the two main differences being as follows: Firstly, the method in [3] relies on pseudo feedback to extract the top results of each query and does not distinguish between positive and negative judgements. Secondly, the proposed approach computes the mean feature representation of the results for a given query and uses these averages to group queries. By contrast, we propose to cluster the ranking functions themselves.

Finally, clustering methods are studied in combination with learning to rank strategies. [15] propose to cluster results to discard probably redundant examples from a large training sample to render the resulting optimization feasible, while [7] cluster personalized ranking functions to group users for recommendation purposes.

[1] http://www.dmoz.org/

3. RANKING MODELS FOR USER INTENT

In this section we present our main contribution, ranking models for user intent. The following section introduces the problem setting and notation. Section 3.2 presents a joint optimization problem that directly solves the problem in theory but is infeasible in practice. In Section 3.3 we devise an efficient approximation that can be solved on large scales. Section 3.4 details the application of the model for new queries at execution time.

3.1 Preliminaries

We are given n historic queries $q_1, \ldots, q_n$ and their top-m retrieved documents $(x_1^{(q)}, y_1^{(q)}), \ldots, (x_m^{(q)}, y_m^{(q)})$ where $y_j^{(q)} = 1$ if $x_j^{(q)}$ was clicked and 0 otherwise. The click feedback induces a partial ranking on the documents such that

$$x_i^{(q)} \text{ is preferred over } x_j^{(q)} \;\Leftrightarrow\; y_i^{(q)} > y_j^{(q)}$$

holds. We collect the preference relations for query q in the index set $\mathcal{P}_q = \{(i,j) : y_i^{(q)} > y_j^{(q)}\}$, see also [12, 18]. A ranking function $f : (q,x) \mapsto \mathbb{R}$ can now be adapted to the pairwise preferences $\mathcal{P} = \bigcup_q \mathcal{P}_q$. In this paper we focus on linear models of the form $f(q,x) = \langle \vec{w}, \phi(q,x) \rangle$, where $\phi(q,x)$ denotes a joint embedding of query and document in some feature space. To avoid overloading the notation, we'll use $\phi(q,x) = x$ in the remainder and note that generalizations are straight forward, see for instance Table 2 for the features we used in the experiments. Following a large-margin approach leads to the optimization problem [13]

$$\min_{\vec{w},\xi_{ij}\geq 0} \quad \langle \vec{w}, \vec{w} \rangle + \lambda \sum_{ij} \xi_{ij}$$
$$\text{s.t.} \quad \forall (i,j) \in \mathcal{P} : \langle \vec{w}, x_i \rangle \geq \langle \vec{w}, x_j \rangle + 1 - \xi_{ij},$$

where $\lambda > 0$ determines the trade-off between margin maximization and error minimization. The latter is the sum of individual losses ξ_{ij} and constitutes an upper bound on the 0/1-loss of mistaken preference relations. The constraints enforce $\langle \vec{w}, x_i \rangle > \langle \vec{w}, x_j \rangle$ whenever possible and penalize violations thereof. Once optimal parameters $\vec{w}^*$ have been

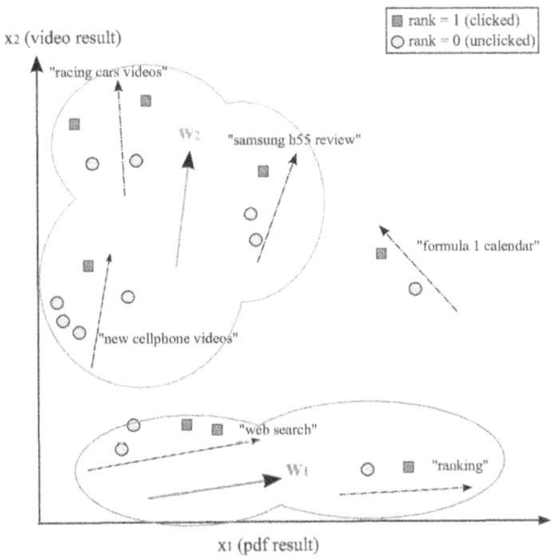

Figure 1: Visualization of the problem setting.

found, these are used as plug-in estimates to induce rankings of the documents for new queries.

3.2 Joint Optimization

In a nutshell, we aim at learning ranking functions for *similar* queries, where similar refers to the latent user intent. Figure 1 shows a simple two-dimensional visualization of the problem setting, focusing on pdf (dimension x_1) and video (dimension x_2) results. Different queries (e.g., *racing cars videos*, *web search*) are visualized by relevant clicked (red squares) and not clicked results (green circles) documents. The task is to group the queries so that similar intents are close with respect to some distance measure in the feature space so that they are clustered together.

Since there is no ground-truth for the intrinsic clustering, the respective error of the ranking functions serves as a makeshift for the missing performance measure at the clustering stage. That is, if the error-rate of a ranking function is high, the queries in the respective cluster are too diverse to allow for a good fit; the goal is therefore to find a grouping of the queries such that the ranking models are well adapted. Thus, a natural approach is to jointly optimize the clustering *and* the ranking models.

Let K be the number of desired clusters. We intend to find (i) K ranking models $\vec{w}_1, \ldots, \vec{w}_K$, one for each cluster, and (ii) find a clustering $\vec{c}_1, \ldots, \vec{c}_K$ with $c_{kj} = 1$ if query q_j belongs to cluster k and $c_{kj} = 0$ otherwise, that gives rise to an optimal fit of the ranking models. The following optimization problem realizes this task straight forwardly,

$$\begin{aligned} \min_{\vec{w}_k, \vec{c}_k, \xi_{ij}} \quad & \sum_{k=1}^{K} \left[\|\vec{w}_k\|^2 + \lambda_k \sum_{\ell=1}^{n} c_{k\ell} \sum_{(i,j) \in \mathcal{P}_{q_\ell}} \xi_{ij}^k \right] \\ \text{s.t.} \quad & \forall k, \forall (i,j) \in \mathcal{P}(k) : \langle \vec{w}_k, x_i \rangle \geq \langle \vec{w}_k, x_j \rangle + 1 - \xi_{ij}^k \\ & \forall k, \forall (i,j) \in \mathcal{P}(k) : \xi_{ij}^k \geq 0 \\ & \forall i, j, \ell : \; c_{ki} c_{kj} + c_{ki} c_{k\ell} \leq c_{kj} c_{k\ell} + 1 \qquad (1) \\ & \forall k, \forall j : \; c_{kj} \in \{0, 1\} \end{aligned}$$

where we defined $\mathcal{P}(k) = \bigcup_{j:c_{kj}=1} \mathcal{P}_{q_j}$ as the union of all members of cluster k, and trade-off parameters $\lambda_k > 0$.

The above optimization problem suffers from major drawbacks. Firstly, the optimization interweaves real and integer variables; that is, directly solving the mixed-integer program is expensive and one usually resorts to relaxing the binary variables to the interval $[0, 1]$ to obtain an approximate solution. Secondly and more severely, the number of triangle inequalities guaranteeing a proper clustering in Eq. (1) is cubic in the number of queries and renders the optimization infeasible at larger scales. We present an efficient approximation and propose a pipelined approach in the next section.

Table 1: Ranking Models for User Intent

Require: n queries q_j with preference relations $\mathcal{P}_{q_j}$

---

for $1 \leq j \leq n$ **do**
  learn ranking function $\vec{w}_j$ for q_j using $\mathcal{P}_{q_j}$
end for
cluster $w_1, \ldots, w_n$
for $1 \leq k \leq K$ **do**
  learn ranking function $\vec{w}_k$ using $\bigcup_{j:c_j=k} \mathcal{P}_{q_j}$
end for

Ensure: ranking models $\vec{w}_1, \ldots, \vec{w}_K$

3.3 Learning to Rank User Intent

We now present a sequential model that approximates the infeasible optimization problem and that can be solved efficiently on large scales. The novel approach consists of three stages and generates the desired ranking models for each cluster of queries: Firstly, we learn a ranking function for every query. Secondly, these ranking functions are clustered, and thirdly, we learn a ranking function for each cluster using the original queries and documents. The algorithm in pseudo-code is depicted in Table 1.

3.3.1 *Ranking Models for Queries*

The initial step of the approximation consists in learning a ranking model for every query. To this end we solve the standard ranking SVM for every query and the respective preference relations assembled from the click data. Analogously to Section 3.1, the ℓ-th optimization problem can either be solved by quadratic programming or online gradient-based approaches [12, 18, 13] and is given by

$$\begin{aligned} \min_{\vec{w}_\ell, \xi_{\ell ij} \geq 0} \quad & \langle \vec{w}_\ell, \vec{w}_\ell \rangle + \lambda \sum_{ij} \xi_{\ell ij} \\ \text{s.t.} \quad & \forall (i,j) \in \mathcal{P}_{q_\ell} : \langle \vec{w}_\ell, x_i \rangle \geq \langle \vec{w}_\ell, x_j \rangle + 1 - \xi_{\ell ij}. \end{aligned}$$

In general, the trade-off parameter λ needs to be set appropriately to obtain optimally adapted models. In our large-scale experiments, tuning the parameters manually or deploying model selection techniques like cross-validation is not feasible due to the large amount of data. Anecdotal evidence however shows that for binary representations and features in the interval $[0, 1]$, values around $\lambda \approx 1$ are often a reasonable choice. We thus use $\lambda = 1$ for the initial ranking SVM models and note that there is potentially room for improvement. The result of this step is n ranking functions $\vec{w}_1, \ldots, \vec{w}_n$, one for each query.

3.3.2 *Clustering Ranking Functions*

The goal of the second step of our approach is to group similar ranking models together as they capture similar intents. As the absolute locations of the $\vec{w}_i$ are negligible and only the direction of the vectors is of interest, the ranking functions are ℓ_2-normalized by $\vec{w} \leftarrow \vec{w}/\|\vec{w}\|$ so that they lie on the unit hyperball. The similarity of two ranking

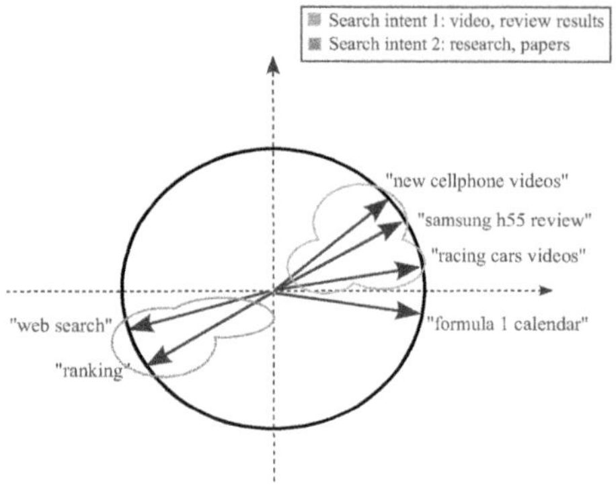

Figure 2: Query-specific models on the unit sphere.

functions $\vec{w}$ and $\vec{w}'$ can now be measured by their cosine which reduces to the inner product for normalized vectors, $\cos(\vec{w}, \vec{w}') = \langle \vec{w}, \vec{w}' \rangle$. Unit vectors are usually modeled by a von Mises-Fisher distribution [2], given by $p(\vec{x}|\vec{\mu}, \kappa) = Z_d(\kappa) \exp\{\kappa \langle \vec{\mu}, \vec{x} \rangle\}$ where $\|\vec{\mu} = 1\|$ and $\kappa \geq 0$ and $d \geq 2$ and partition function $Z_d(\kappa) = \kappa^{d/2-1}/(2\pi)^{d/2} I_{d/2-1}(\kappa)$ where $I_r(\cdot)$ denotes the modified Bessel function of the first kind and order r. Applied to the n ranking functions $\vec{w}_1, \ldots, \vec{w}_n$, a mixture model of von Mises-Fisher distributions with K components (clusters) has the density

$$f(\vec{w}_i|\vec{\mu}_1, \ldots, \vec{\mu}_K, \vec{\kappa}) = \sum_{i=1}^{n} \alpha_{c_i} p(\vec{w}_i|\vec{\mu}_{c_i}, \kappa_{c_i})$$

with mixing parameters α_i with $0 \leq \alpha_i \leq 1$ and $\sum \alpha_i = 1$. The latent variables $c_i \in \{1, \ldots, K\}$ indicate the generating components for the $\vec{w}_i$; that is, $c_i = k$ indicates that the ranking function $\vec{w}_i$ is sampled (generated) from the k-th component $p(\cdot|\vec{\mu}_k, \kappa_k)$.[2] If the latent variables were known, finding maximum likelihood estimates for the parameters $\vec{\mu}_1, \ldots, \vec{\mu}_k$ and $\kappa_1, \ldots, \kappa_k$ would be trivial. Since this is not the case, we resort to a constrained Expectation Maximization approach to jointly optimize the log-likelihood.

3.3.3 Ranking Models for Clusters

Given the clustering induced by the latent variables c_i of the previous section, we now learn a ranking function for each cluster. The approach is similar to learning the initial ranking models for the queries, however, this time, all queries in the cluster have to be taken into account. The optimization for the k-th cluster can again be solved with the ranking SVM and is given by

$$\min_{\vec{w}_k, \xi_{ij} \geq 0} \quad \langle \vec{w}_k, \vec{w}_k \rangle + \lambda \sum_{ij} \xi_{ij}$$

$$\text{s.t.} \quad \forall (i,j) \in \bigcup_{\ell : c_\ell = k} \mathcal{P}_{q_\ell} : \langle \vec{w}_k, x_i \rangle \geq \langle \vec{w}_k, x_j \rangle + 1 - \xi_{ij}.$$

3.4 Application

Once the ranking functions are adapted to the clusters, our method can be deployed to re-rank retrieved documents for new queries. Our approach aims at diversifying possible

[2]Note that the variables $\vec{c}_k$ in Section 3.2 are analogous binary encodings of the latent variables c_i. That is, if the j-th query is in the k-th cluster, we have $c_{kj} = 1$ and $c_j = k$, respectively. We overloaded the notation to indicate that both represent the actual clustering.

Table 2: Feature categories

<table>
<tr><td></td><td>Textual similarity features</td></tr>
<tr><td>4</td><td>Sum of TFs of query terms in result title|URL|text|all</td></tr>
<tr><td>4</td><td>Lucene score between query and result title|URL|text|all</td></tr>
<tr><td></td><td>Result characteristics features</td></tr>
<tr><td>1</td><td>Result initial rank</td></tr>
<tr><td>4</td><td>Number of words in result title|url|text|all</td></tr>
<tr><td>1</td><td>Result URL length in characters</td></tr>
<tr><td>72</td><td>Result URL domain (boolean values)</td></tr>
<tr><td>83</td><td>Popular sites the result might belong to (boolean)</td></tr>
<tr><td>200</td><td>Top most frequent urls in the dataset</td></tr>
<tr><td></td><td>Result special words features</td></tr>
<tr><td>10</td><td>Special words in result URL ("forum", "pdf", etc.)</td></tr>
<tr><td>10</td><td>Result site category (news, search, blog etc)</td></tr>
<tr><td>200</td><td>Top most frequent words in the dataset</td></tr>
</table>

intents as the same query might end up in more than just one cluster, for instance if users clicked on different media types (e.g., videos, pdfs, etc.). Thus, the goal is to map a new query to the clustering and combine the respective ranking functions of the top matching clusters.

To this end, we represent historic queries together with their positively judged results as pseudo documents which are indexed and made searchable by a search engine. In our implementation we used the Lucene[3] IR engine, however, other choices are straight forward. Given a new query q, the Lucene scoring function is used to obtain historic queries which are similar to q.

We select the top-u most similar historic queries and the clusters they belong to. By doing so, we compute a weighted mapping of the new query to the clustering as follows. Let v_j, $1 \leq j \leq u$, be the scores for the top-u historic queries q_j, these are ℓ_1-normalized and translated into cluster-scores s_k, $1 \leq k \leq K$, such that $s_{qk} = \sum_{j:c_j=k} v_j / \sum_{i=1}^{u} v_i$, where the c_j are the latent cluster memberships. That is, if a cluster occurs more than once, the respective scores are aggregated. Due to the normalization, the scores s_{qk} act like probabilities, quantifying the likelihood that cluster k contains the intent expressed by query q.

Finally, the ranking of the documents for the query q is assembled from the clustering by weighting the contribution of each cluster k by its score s_{qk}. Let r_{kj} denote the ranking of the j-th document by the ranking function of cluster k, the final ranking score is given by linearly weighting the cluster rankings r_{kj} with the cluster importance s_{qk} for query q,

$$score(q, j) = \sum_{k=1}^{K} s_{qk} r_{qkj}.$$

4. EMPIRICAL EVALUATION

For the experimental evaluation, we sample queries from the Yahoo! query log. From the sample, we discard queries with less than 5 results, queries without clicks, and queries from users with less than 100 searches. This leaves us with 76,037 queries posed by 453 distinct users. We split the obtained data, that is query and top-10 results, chronologically into 30,053 (40%) queries for training and 45,984 (60%) queries for test set.

Ground-truth is given by user clicks in terms of relevance judgments [12, 18] as follows: If a document x_i has been clicked, the relevance judgment equals $y_i = 1$. Unclicked documents that are higher ranked than clicked results receive a relevance judgment of $y_j = 0$ which is also used for unclicked results occuring right after a clicked result. This

[3]http://lucene.apache.org/

Table 3: Mean average precision.

Method	MAP	Increase
Single	0.709	-
User	0.806	13.7%
Content-1	0.748	5.5%
Content-2	0.734	3.5%
Intent	0.754	6.3%

process results in a total of 96,030 relevance judgments for the training dataset and 144,021 for the test set. This gives an average of about 3.2 relevance judgments per query on the data. The query-result pairs are represented by feature vectors. The respective features are depicted in Table 2.

4.1 Baselines

We compare our method, denoted as *Intent* with four alternative approaches for re-ranking search results: Firstly, we deploy a single ranking SVM (*Single*) for all users which is trained on all available training data and used to rank the documents for the test queries. Secondly, we train an SVM for every user (*User*) to capture state-of-the-art personalization approaches. According to [22], short- and long-term search histories are well captured by personalized, user-specific models and we thus expect the *User* baseline to perform best while the *Single* baseline is expected to be too simple to capture the diverse behavior in the data.

Furthermore, we apply *Content-1* which clusters queries in the training set based on their content similarity and learns a ranking SVM for each cluster which are finally combined to re-rank documents for the test queries. Note that – except for the clustering – the processing pipeline is exactly the same as in our method; at the clustering stage, queries are grouped based on their textual similarity including text from their positive results (the clicked documents). Finally, we apply a variant of topical RankSVMs [3] (*Content-2*). The document representation is extended by incorporating means and variances as dimensions for each feature; the new representation is computed by using the top-5 results of each query. Note however that this baseline is not identical to [3] in the sense that we use the standard ranking SVM for solving the optimization problems.

4.2 Ranking Performance

The first experiment aims at measuring the performance of the algorithms in a static environment. We use the complete training set for the learning processes and all available test queries for evaluation. We report on MAP, Precision@n, and NDCG@n.

Results for MAP are shown in Table 3. Unsurprisingly, learning user specific models performs best, achieving about 14% precision increase compared to the a single model that serves everyone. The setting resembles an ideal scenario and the baselines *Single* and *User* constitute the expected lower and upper bound on the performance, respectively. Note that a real-world deployment of the personalized user model would require perfect disambiguation of users which is still an open problem.

By contrast, *Content-1*, *Content-2*, and *Intent* are user independent and form groups of similar content or intent, respectively. In that sense, they constitute realizable approaches. However, they differ significantly in terms of predictive performance. Among these three, *Content-2* is the weakest method although it still increases the performance over the *Single* baseline by 3.5%. *Content-1* allows for improvements about 5.5% and *Intent* even by 6.3%.

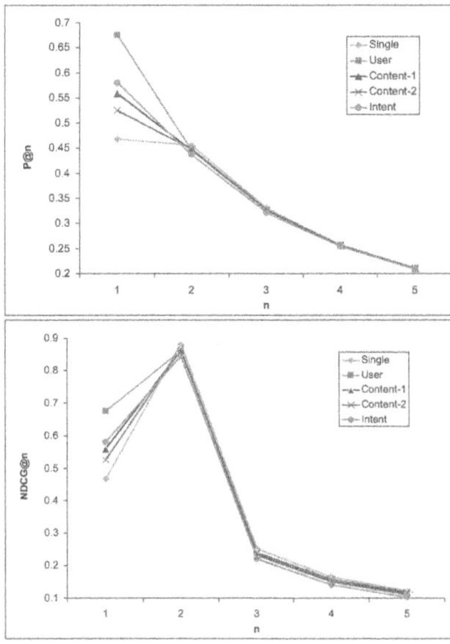

Figure 3: Precision@k and NDCG@k.

A similar picture is drawn by the precision at n scores that are displayed in Figure 3 (top). The methods are indifferent for $n > 1$ due to the relatively small number of relevance judgments (on average 3.2 per query). More specifically, for the 45,984 test queries, there are 51,089 positive relevance judgements (user clicks) which translate to about 1.1 clicks per query on average. At P@1, however, we observe significant differences in performance that confirm the previous findings. *Single* and *User* establish lower and upper bounds and *Intent* performs better than *Content-1/2*. Figure 3 (bottom) corroborates the observations for NDCG@n.

4.3 Cluster Analysis

To shed light on the nature of intent- and content-based methods, we analyze and compare respective clusterings for *Intent*, *Content-1*, and *Content-2* in Table 4. We picked clusters with queries for which the respective methods perform well.

The qualitative results are as follows. Firstly the approaches differ significantly in the amount of clusters, where the optimal number of clusters is determined by model selection for each method. While the content-based methods generate between 20 (*Content-1*) and 32 (*Content-2*) clusters, the solution of *Intent* consists of 75 distinct clusters. Though clusterings of this size are generally difficult to interpret, the numbers already indicate that the solution found by *Intent* is more specialized than the content-based ones due to the, on average, smaller clusters. In fact, it turns out that the *Intent* performs well in many specific information needs as Table 4 (left) shows. The first set of queries corresponds to a cluster that contains information needs in textual form, perhaps enriched with pictures while the second group contains specific questions which are probably best answered by appropriate text documents, too.

By contrast, Table 4 (center and right) show exemplary clusters for the two content-based methods. The former shows two clusters for *Content-1*. While the top cluster

Table 4: Exemplary results of the clustering.

Intent	Content-1	Content-2
1968 yamaha trailmaster 100 yl2 value	austro diesel gmbh schwechat	mila kunis photo
spendor s3 5 system	skeleton reference of human muscle	marie osmond classical beauty doll margot
sonic video game 2011	double din dash facia for pt cruiser	mickey mouse pictures
85 mustang ignition module harness	keilwerth tenor ex90	batman action ↓gure power pack
owner of gold 39 s gym in wichita	seiko ladies watch bracelet elegant	lego star wars 2
72 chevy fuel tank swap	conn 37m tenor sax	↓ghter jets
artist lessons mountain painting	new jersey animal shelters	dental o¡ce for sale in california
who makes jet skis	best food to sell for pro↓t	barrio indios puerto rico house rentals
why does spray paint come o↑	fbi national academy 2010 boston	tv shows solar power
where can i buy centrum materna in us	passport renewal	logo design
why is the order of operations for algebra	oprah wearing philip stein watches	hotel dei mellini rome
shooting a wedding without a 'ash	top scottish baby names	gem kitchens and bath dublin

is similar to corresponding one of the *Intent*, the bottom is more or less a random collection of queries expressing a diverse set of information needs. Finally, the right column of Table 4 shows examples for well performing clusters for *Content-2*. The baseline exhibits typical content-based clusters formed by common tokens. The noisy membership can be explained by keywords which are central for the cluster and only occur on the result documents and not in the query.

4.4 Discussion

At first sight our method seems to be outperformed by a personalized solution. However, the latter is not always applicable. Consider, for instance, scenarios such as web search where only a fraction of all users are registered and can be disambiguated only after the login. Including the personalized user model thus mirrors an ideal but unrealistic scenario. As an alternative for scenarios that do not allow personalized methods, we propose to deploy ranking models for user intent. Our method significantly increases MAP and also outperforms traditional content-based baselines for P@n and NDCG@n.

In our setting, the increase in P@n and NDCG@n performance is achieved by a significant increase in P@1, that is, *Intent* performs well in ranking relevant result on top. This observation is explained by the model itself: by grouping queries into clusters with similar intent, multiple ranking models are established, each one based on queries with similar user clicks in terms of the resulting types of documents. Results for new queries are re-ranked using the clustering; the final ranking score is computed by a linear mixture of relevant ranking functions. In case the textual matching is inaccurate, for instance because textual similarity does not necessarily imply similar search intentions, the final score diversifies the most likely intents and counterbalances possible errors at earlier stages.

5. CONCLUSION

In this paper, we presented a methodology for improving the quality of ranking functions for web search by capturing and exploiting latent search behavior. The underlying idea grounds on the observation that search behavior is not necessarily content-dependent and we show that it can be used to train more effective ranking models.

Our method clusters ranking models trained on search queries and their results. The produced clusters represent implicit search behavior and are used to train ranking models for user intent. The experimental evaluation demonstrates the effectiveness of our method compared to traditional content-based baselines, leading to significant increases in MAP, P@1 and NDCG@1. An analysis of the resulting clusterings revealed that the novel method groups similar queries together while the content-based baselines suffer from noise that is incorporated by additional content from the documents. Although our approach cannot compete with personalized methods, we note that it is generally deployable and does not rely on user disambiguation. It thus proved a valid alternative for scenarios in which personalized models cannot be applied such as web search.

Acknowledgments

The authors wish to thank B. Barla Cambazoglu for helping us with data extraction and experimental evaluation.

6. REFERENCES

[1] E. Agichtein, E. Brill, and S. Dumais. Improving web search ranking by incorporating user behavior information. In *Proc. of the ACM SIGIR Conference*, 2006.

[2] A. Banerjee, I. Dhillon, j. Ghosh and S. Sra. Clustering on the Unit Hypersphere using von Mises-Fisher Distributions. *Journal of Machine Learning*, 38(6):1345–1382, 2005.

[3] J. Bian, X. Li, F.-Li. Liu, Z. Zheng, and H. Zha. Ranking Specialization for Web Search: A Divide-and-Conquer Approach by Using Topical RankSVM. In *Proc. of the ACM WWW Conference*, 2010.

[4] Y. Cao, J. Xu, T.-Y. Liu, H. Li, Y. Huang, and H.-W. Hon. Adapting ranking svm to document retrieval. In *Proc. of the ACM SIGIR Conference*, 2006.

[5] P.-A. Chirita, C.-S. Firan, and W. Nejdl. Summarizing local context to personalize global web search. In *Proceedings of the ACM CIKM Conference*, 2006.

[6] W. Chu, and S.-S. Keerthi. Support Vector Ordinal Regression. *Neural Computation*, 19:792–815, 2007.

[7] J. Diez, J. J. del Coz, O. Luaces, and A. Bahamonde. Clustering people according to their preference criteria. *Expert Systems with Applications: An International Journal*, 34:1274–1284, 2008.

[8] Z. Dou, R. Song, J.-R. Wen, and X. Yuan. Evaluating the E↑ectiveness of Personalized Web Search. *IEEE TKDE*, 21:1178–1190, 2008.

[9] S. Fox, K. Karnawat, M. Mydland, S. Dumais and T. White. Evaluating implicit measures to improve web search. *ACM TOIS*, 23(2):147–168, 2005.

[10] T.-H. Haveliwala. Topic-sensitive PageRank. In *Proceedings of the ACM WWW Conference*, 2002.

[11] R. Herbrich, T. Graepel and K. Obermayer. Large margin rank boundaries for ordinal regression. *Advances in Large Margin Classifiers, MIT Press*, 2000.

[12] T. Joachims. Optimizing search engines using clickthrough data. In *Proc. of the ACM SIGKDD Conference*, 2002.

[13] T. Joachims. Training Linear SVMs in Linear Time. In *Proceedings of ACM SIGKDD Conference*, 2006.

[14] J.-W. Kim, and K.-S. Candan. Skip-and-prune: cosine-based top-k query processing for e¡cient context-sensitive document retrieval. In *Proceedings of the ACM SIGMOD Conference*, 2009.

[15] X. Li, N. Wang, and S.-Y. Li. A fast training algorithm for svm via clustering technique and gabriel graph. In *Proceedings of the International Conference on Intelligent Computing*, 2007.

[16] S. Pandey, S. Roy, C. O. J. Cho, and S. Chakrabarti. Shu¿ing a stacked deck: the case for partially randomized ranking of search engine results. In *Proceedings of the VLDB Conference*, 2005.

[17] T. Qin, X.-D. Zhang, D.-S. Wang, T.-Y. Liu, W. Lai, and H. Li. Ranking with multiple hyperplanes. In *Proceedings of the ACM SIGIR Conference*, 2007.

[18] F. Radlinski and T. Joachims. Query chains: Learning to rank from implicit feedback. In *Proceedings of the ACM SIGKDD Conference*, 2005.

[19] F. Radlinski and T. Joachims. Active exploration for learning rankings from clickthrough data. In *Proc. of the ACM SIGKDD Conference*, 2007.

[20] U. Rohini and V. Ambati. Improving Re-ranking of Search Results Using Collaborative Filtering. *Information Retrieval Technology, AIRS*, 2006.

[21] X. Shen, B. Tan, and C. Zhai. Context-sensitive information retrieval using implicit feedback. In *Proceedings of the ACM SIGIR Conference*, 2005.

[22] K. Sugiyama, K. Hatano, and M. Yoshikawa. Adaptive web search based on user pro↓le constructed without any e↑ort from users. In *Proceedings of the ACM WWW Conference*, 2004.

[23] B. Tan, X. Shen, and C. Zhai. Mining long-term search history to improve search accuracy. In *Proceedings of the ACM SIGKDD Conference*, 2006.

[24] J. Teevan, S.-T. Dumais, and D.-J. Liebling. To Personalize or Not to Personalize: Modeling Queries with Variation in User Intent. In *Proceedings of the ACM SIGIR Conference*, 2008.

[25] G.-R. Xue, H.-J. Zeng, Z. Chen, Y. Yu, W.-Y. Ma, W. Xi, and W. Fan. Optimizing web search using web click-through data. In *Proceedings of the ACM CIKM Conference*, 2004.

[26] Z. Zheng, K. Chen, G. Sun, and H. Zha. A regression framework for learning ranking functions using relative relevance judgments. In *Proceedings of the ACM SIGIR Conference*, 2007.

Learning to Aggregate Vertical Results into Web Search Results

Jaime Arguello[*]
School of Information and Library Science
University of North Carolina
Chapel Hill, NC, USA
jarguello@unc.edu

Fernando Diaz
Yahoo! Labs New York
New York, NY, USA
diazf@yahoo-inc.com

Jamie Callan
Language Technologies Institute
Carnegie Mellon University
Pittsburgh, PA, USA
callan@cs.cmu.edu

ABSTRACT

Aggregated search is the task of integrating results from potentially multiple specialized search services, or *verticals*, into the Web search results. The task requires predicting not only which verticals to present (the focus of most prior research), but also predicting where in the Web results to present them (i.e., above or below the Web results, or somewhere in between). Learning models to aggregate results from multiple verticals is associated with two major challenges. First, because verticals retrieve different types of results and address different search tasks, results from different verticals are associated with different types of predictive evidence (or features). Second, even when a feature is common across verticals, its predictiveness may be vertical-specific. Therefore, approaches to aggregating vertical results require handling an inconsistent feature representation across verticals, and, potentially, a vertical-specific relationship between features and relevance. We present 3 general approaches that address these challenges in different ways and compare their results across a set of 13 verticals and 1070 queries. We show that the best approaches are those that allow the learning algorithm to learn a vertical-specific relationship between features and relevance.

Categories and Subject Descriptors

H.3 [**Information Storage and Retrieval**]: Information Storage and Retrieval

General Terms

Algorithms

General Terms

aggregated search, federated search, query intent, learning to rank

[*]Work done at Carnegie Mellon University.

CIKM'11, October 24–28, 2011, Glasgow, Scotland, UK.

1. INTRODUCTION

In addition to providing Web search, commercial search engines provide access to specialized search services (referred to as *verticals*) that focus on a specific information-seeking task (e.g., search for news, images, video, local businesses, items for sale, weather forecasts, etc.). Aggregated search refers to the detection and integration of relevant vertical content into the Web search results page. The problem is typically decomposed into two sub-tasks. It is impractical, if not impossible, to issue the query to every vertical. Thus, the first sub-task (*vertical selection*) is to predict *which* verticals, if any, are relevant [2, 3, 6]. Typically, this is done without issuing the query to the vertical [2, 3]. The second sub-task (*vertical results presentation*) is to predict *where* in the web results to display those verticals selected [16, 1]. This work focuses on the vertical results presentation task.

If we assume that vertical results must be presented in specific positions relative to the Web search results (i.e., above, below, or in between certain Web results), then the vertical results presentation task can be cast as *block-ranking*. A *block* is defined as a short sequence of Web or same-vertical results which must be presented grouped together—vertically (e.g., *news*) or horizontally (e.g, *images*)—in the final search results page. A Web block corresponds to a set of Web results which cannot be partitioned in the final presentation (e.g., Web results 1-3, 4-6, and 7-10). A vertical block corresponds to the top results from a particular vertical. The goal of block-ranking is to predict a ranking of blocks that approximates, based on some metric, a gold standard ranking. We propose and evaluate three supervised machine learning approaches to block-ranking.

Casting block-ranking as a supervised machine learning problem is associated with two main challenges. First, because verticals retrieve different types of results (e.g., news articles, images, videos, local business information, weather forecasts), blocks from different verticals are associated with different types of predictive evidence or features. For example, *news* results are associated with a publication date, *local* results are associated with a geographical location, and *community Q&A* results are associated with a number of suggested answers. Thus, block-ranking requires approaches that can handle an inconsistent feature representation across verticals. Secondly, even if a feature is common to multiple verticals, it may not be equally predictive. For example, the number of results retrieved by the vertical will likely be more predictive for *news* than *weather*, which retrieves at most a *single* result. Alternatively, a feature may be predictive for different verticals, but in the *opposite* direction. For example, the query-term "pics" may be positive evidence for *images*, but negative evidence for *shopping*. Thus, block-ranking may require approaches that can exploit a vertical-*specific* predictive relationship between features and relevance. We propose methods that address both challenges in different ways.

We evaluate approaches that rank blocks as a function of a set of features. We partition features into two general classes: *pre-retrieval* and *post-retrieval* features. During vertical results presentation, we assume that the system has already issued the query to each vertical, or at least those predicted relevant during vertical selection. Thus, post-retrieval features can be derived directly from the vertical results. We investigate the cost-benefit of post-retrieval features. Are they useful for predicting *where* a vertical should be presented? Can they *also* be used to re-evaluate vertical selection decisions in light of the vertical results? Answering these questions affects, for example, whether the end-to-end system should attempt to issue the query to as many verticals as possible (to derive these features), or whether it should cache post-retrieval features for future impressions of the query.

2. RELATED WORK

Research in aggregated search can be described along several dimensions: number of verticals considered, number of positions in which vertical content can be integrated, and sources of training data. The earliest work in aggregated search integrated the content from a single vertical above the first Web result [6, 10, 12]. Unfortunately, evaluating the performance of a single vertical in isolation ignores possible contention with other verticals. As a result, more realistic models were developed which considered several verticals simultaneously [2, 3, 7]. Limiting integration to the top position is rather crude when considering the nuanced nature of user intent. For example, if a query's dominant intent is navigational, there may be a secondary, less popular, news intent which should be surfaced lower in the ranked list. In order to address this, more recent work has focused on integrating at arbitrary positions in the ranked list [1, 16]. Finally, all of the prior work in aggregated search uses machine learning methods and, as a result, sources of training data become important. Training data has included editorial judgments [2, 1, 12], click information [6, 10, 16], and indirect labels from other verticals [3].

We focus our experiments on methods of learning orderings of generic Web and vertical content using pairwise labels [14]. This is quite different from prior work which focuses on minimizing misclassification of vertical relevance [2, 3, 7, 12] or regressing against a click-based target [6, 10, 16]. In the language of 'learning to rank', these previous approaches are based on pointwise sources of relevance while our approach focuses on pairwise sources.

3. PROBLEM DEFINITION

At query time, the aggregated search system issues the query to the Web search engine and to those verticals selected, which we refer to as the *candidate* verticals. The aggregation task is subject to a set of layout constraints. We assume the following constraints. First, we assume that results from the same vertical must be presented together. Second, vertical results can only be embedded in specific positions relative to the Web results. We assume four slotting positions: above the first Web result, between Web results 3 and 4, between results 6 and 7, and below the tenth Web result. Third, Web results are always presented and maintain their original order. Fourth, each candidate vertical is associated with a set of top results, which are given. That is, the system does not predict which results from a particular vertical to present. Finally, we assume that users prefer to not see non-relevant vertical results even below the last Web result. The system is free to suppress a candidate vertical, for example, based on its results.

Combined, these layout constraints form a set of blocks. Each candidate vertical forms its own vertical block and our four slotting positions divide the top 10 Web results into three Web blocks: Web results 1-3 (w_1), 4-6 (w_2), and 7-10 (w_3). We define the block-ranking task as follows. Let $\mathcal{B}_q$ denote the set of Web and vertical blocks associated with query q and let σ_q^* denote the optimal ordering of $\mathcal{B}_q$ for query q, referred to as the *reference* ranking. The objective of block ranking is to predict a ranking of blocks σ_q that approximates σ_q^*. The quality of the approximation can be measured using a rank-based distance metric, such as Kendall's τ. We discuss this in Section 6.5.

In addition to deciding where to present vertical results, the task is also to filter non-relevant candidate verticals. Suppressed verticals are modeled using an imaginary "end of search results" block, denoted as *eos*. The *eos* block is included in $\mathcal{B}_q$, and, therefore, appears in both σ_q and σ_q^*. Let $\sigma_q(i)$ denote the rank of block i in σ_q. Blocks ranked above *eos* are considered to be displayed to the user and those ranked below it are suppressed. Because the sub-ranking of blocks below rank $\sigma_q(eos)$ is not observed by the user, for the purpose of comparing σ_q with σ_q^*, all blocks ranked below *eos* in σ_q are considered tied at rank $\sigma_q(eos) + 1$.

4. FEATURES

We propose machine learning approaches to rank blocks as a function of a set of features. We use various types of features which we believe are predictive of a particular block's relevance to a query. These can be divided into two general classes. *Pre-retrieval features* can be generated without issuing the query to the Web or vertical search engine. These include, for example, the topic of the query or whether the query contains a particular named-entity type (e.g., the name of a person, product, or location). *Post-retrieval features* must be generated *after* the query is issued to the Web or vertical search engine. These include, for example, the total number of results retrieved by the block's search engine or the average text-similarity between the query and the results presented in the block. We investigate the contribution of post-retrieval features to performance.

4.1 Pre-retrieval Features

Pre-retrieval features can be generated before the query is issued to the Web or vertical search engine.

Named-Entity Type Features.

These binary features correspond to named-entity types possibly appearing in the query. Queries were automatically annotated using the BBN IdentiFinder named-entity tagger [4]. Named-entity features include *location* (possibly predictive for *local*, *maps*, and *weather*), *product* (possibly predictive for *shopping*), *person* (possibly predictive *news* and *images*), and *organization* (possibly predictive for *finance*). In total, we focused on 24 named-entity types. Each binary feature equals 1 if the named-entity type appears at least once in the query and 0 otherwise.

Category Features.

Some verticals may be topically focused. Thus, knowing the general topic of the query may help in block ranking. We focused on 30 topical categories, derived as follows. First, we selected 150 categories from the Open Directory Project (ODP) hierarchy and crawled Web documents associated with these ODP nodes. Then, in order to reduce the number of category features, these 150 categories were clustered into 30 clusters. Clustering was done using complete-link agglomerative clustering [15]. The distance between ODP categories was computed using the symmetric Kullback-Leibler divergence [8] between category language models. We used unigram language models with add-one smoothing to avoid zero probabilities. Let θ_i denote the language model associated with cluster/category i. We set the ith category feature for query q according to, $\frac{1}{\mathcal{Z}} \prod_{w \in q} P(w|\theta_i)$ where $\mathcal{Z}$ normalizes across clusters/categories.

Click-through Features.

User clicks are often viewed as surrogates for relevance. The queries associated with clicks on a particular document convey the types of information needs the document satisfies. Likewise, the queries associated with clicks on vertical results convey the types of information needs the vertical satisfies. Our click-through features harness this type of evidence by considering the similarity between the query and those associated with clicks on vertical content (or content very similar to the vertical's).

Click-through data was derived from the AOL query-log. We derived one click-through feature per vertical as follows. First, for each vertical, we manually selected a set of Web domains which we believe have content closely related to the vertical. For *local*, we selected www.local.yahoo.com, www.citysearch.com, and www.yellowpages.com. Then, we constructed vertical-specific (unigram) language models using all queries (allowing duplicates) associated with click-events on the vertical's corresponding domains. Finally, given a query, we generate one feature per vertical based on the query generation probability given the vertical's query-based language model. Given query q, we set the click-through feature for vertical i according to, $\frac{1}{\mathcal{Z}} \prod_{w \in q} P(w|\theta_i)$ where $\mathcal{Z}$ normalizes across verticals.

Vertical-Intent Features.

Users often express vertical-intent *explicitly* using keywords such as "news" (for the *news* vertical), "pics" (for the *images* vertical) or "buy" (for the *shopping* vertical). The goal of our explicit vertical-intent features is to determine vertical relevance based on how often the query co-occurs with keywords used in explicit requests for the vertical. For example, given the query "britney spears", we may predict that *images* is relevant because users often issue the query "britney spears pics". Co-occurrence statistics were derived from the AOL query-log.

Vertical-intent features were generated as follows. First, we manually associated each vertical with a small set of keywords which we believe are often used in explicit requests for the vertical. For example, the *images* vertical was associated with "picture(s)", "photo(s)", "pic(s)", and "image(s)".[1] Then, to measure the affinity between the query and a particular vertical, we use the chi-squared statistic to measure the lack of independence between two events: the occurrence of the query in the AOL query-log and the occurrence of any of the vertical's vertical-intent keywords. To reduce sparsity (particularly for long queries), we compute the chi-squared statistic for each query-term individually and use the geometric average. The geometric average (rather than the arithmetic average) was used to favor queries with terms that *consistently* co-occur with keywords used in explicit requests for the vertical.

4.2 Post-retrieval Features

Post-retrieval features must be generated after the query is issued to the Web or vertical search engine.

Hit Count Features.

This feature considers the number of results retrieved from the Web or vertical search engine. For some verticals, an abundance of query-related content in the index may be predictive of its relevance. This may be true, for example, for *news*, where the rate of content production may correlate with the rate of content demand. However, we do not expect this feature to be useful for every vertical. For example, the number of retrieved results contributes no useful information for verticals that retrieve at most a *single* result (*finance*, *maps*, and *weather*).

Temporal Features.

Some verticals may be time sensitive. Prior work shows that recency is important in news search [6]. Temporal information was available for four verticals: *news*, *blogs*, *community Q&A*, and *twitter*. Our assumption is that, for these verticals, users care primarily about recent results. If this is true, then the average age of results presented in the block should affect its relevance. Temporal features are generated as follows. For each individual vertical result, we measure the elapsed time (in hours) between the current and created date/time. We included four features for each time-sensitive vertical: the minimum, maximum, mean, and standard deviation of the elapsed time across results within the block.

Text-Similarity Features.

The goal of these features is to characterize the text-similarity between the query and the results presented in the block. The challenge in deriving text-similarity features is that results from different sources (i.e., results from the Web search engine and from different verticals) are associated with *different* sets of textual representations. For example, each Web result is associated with three representations: a title, URL, and summary snippet. Each *community Q&A* result is associated with two representations: a question and an optional "best answer". Each *weather* result is associated with a single representation: the location, which we define as the concatenation of the city, state, and country of the weather forecast.

[1]The full vertical-to-keyword and vertical-to-domain mappings are available at `http://www.ils.unc.edu/~jarguell/cikm11/`.

Text-similarity features are generated for a query-block pair in two steps. In the first step, for each result within the block, we measure the text similarity between the query and each representation associated with the result. We use four different text-similarity measures: (1) the cosine similarity between the query and the representation, (2) the maximum number of query-terms appearing consecutively in the representation, (3) the percentage of query-terms appearing in the representation, and (4) the percentage of the representation corresponding to a query-term. Similar text-similarity features were used in prior learning-to-rank research (for document ranking) [14, 9].

The second step depends on whether the block-type is associated with a single result per block (e.g., *weather*, *finance*, and *maps*) or multiple results per block (e.g., *news*, *local*, and *shopping*). For block-types with a single result, we simply include our four similarity measures for each of its text representations. For block-types with multiple results, for each query-representation similarity measure, we use the minimum, maximum, mean, and standard deviation across results within the block.

4.3 Summary of Features

Pre-retrieval features are independent of the block. Thus, every block-type is associated with the same set of 80 pre-retrieval features: 24 named-entity type features, 30 category features, 13 click-through features, and 13 vertical intent features. Notice that we included all 13 click-through features (one per vertical) and all 13 vertical intent features (one per vertical) in every block's feature representation, irrespective of its type. Post-retrieval features, as opposed to pre-retrieval features, are derived directly the block (e.g., the average text-similarity between the query and the title of results within the block) or from the search engine's response to the query (e.g., its hit count). Different block-types were associated with a different set of post-retrieval features. Hit count features were omitted for verticals that retrieve at most a *single* result (i.e., *finance*, *maps*, and *weather*). Temporal features were only available for *news*, *blogs*, *community Q&A*, and *twitter*. Text-similarity features are inconsistent because different block-types are associated with different representations and a different number of results—block-types with multiple results per block require aggregating evidence by taking the minimum, maximum, mean, and standard deviation of query-representation similarities across results.

5. BLOCK-RANKING APPROACHES

As previously mentioned, casting block-ranking as a supervised machine learning problem is associated with two main challenges. First, different types of blocks are associated with different features. Second, even when a feature is common to multiple block-types, it may have a type-*specific* relationship with relevance. We propose three general approaches which address both challenges in different ways.

5.1 Classification Approach

Our classification framework takes the form of n independent binary classifiers (one per vertical). We choose to use logistic regression due to its prediction accuracy and training speed on large-scale classification tasks [13].

Each binary classifier is trained to predict whether a particular vertical should be presented (ranked above *eos*) or suppressed (ranked below *eos*). While training the classifier for vertical v, a query is considered a positive instance if v is ranked above *eos* in the reference ranking σ_q^* and a negative instance otherwise. To compensate for class imbalance (verticals are more often suppressed), each positive training instance is weighted according to the number of negative instances in the training set and vice-versa [5].

The classification approach produces a block-ranking by assigning vertical blocks to slots. Consistent with our layout constraints, we assume four vertical slotting positions relative to the Web results: slot s_1 (above w_1), slot s_2 (between w_1 and w_2), slot s_3 (between w_2 and w_3), and slot s_4 (between w_3 and *eos*). In the output ranking, a slot may contain zero or more vertical blocks.

The classification approach combines all n vertical-specific binary classifiers as follows. First, the query, represented as a vector of features, is submitted to each candidate vertical's classifier. Each classifier outputs a prediction probability that its vertical should be presented (i.e., ranked above *eos* in the predicted ranking σ_q). Let $P(\sigma_q(v) < \sigma_q(eos))$ denote the prediction probability that v should be presented. Then, each candidate vertical is assigned to a slot (or is suppressed) using four threshold parameters τ_{1-4}. Vertical v is assigned to slot x if $P(\sigma_q(v) < \sigma_q(eos)) \geq \tau_y \; \forall \; x \leq y$. In other words, vertical v is assigned to the highest slot for which v's prediction probability is greater than or equal to all thresholds below it. At this point, vertical blocks assigned to the same slot are tied. Finally, ties are broken by ordering vertical blocks within the same slot by descending order of prediction probability.

The classification approach addresses the two challenges mentioned above by training a different binary classifier per vertical. Each classifier adopts its own feature representation, which is unique to the vertical, and learns a vertical-specific relationship between features and block relevance.

5.2 Voting Approach

In the classification approach, each independent binary classifier is trained to predict whether a particular vertical should be presented or suppressed. Our voting approach also combines independent binary classifiers. However, these are trained to make more fine-grained predictions. Independent binary classifiers are trained to predict the relative ordering between pairs of blocks of a particular type. Each classifier is trained to predict whether block i (of a particular type) should be ranked above or below block j (of another particular type) for a given query. The voting approach uses one binary classifier per block-type pair.

The training phase proceeds as follows. Recall that $\mathcal{B}_q$ denotes the set of block associated with query q and includes one block per candidate vertical, all three Web blocks (w_{1-3}), and the *eos* block. While training a classifier specific to a block-type pair, the query is considered a positive or negative instance depending on the pair's relative rank. Certain block-type pairs occur more frequently in one order versus the other. To correct for class imbalance, each positive training instance is weighted according to the number of negative instances in the training set and vice-versa [5].

To predict a block-ranking for query q, first, every block-pair $i, j \in \mathcal{B}_q$ is submitted to the appropriate classifier, depending on the type of i and the type of j. Let $P(\sigma_q(i) < \sigma_q(j))$ denote the prediction probability that i should be ranked above j. This probability can be treated as a preference score between i and j. The voting approach produces the output block-ranking σ_q by combining these preference scores as input to the Schulze voting method [17].

As in the classification approach, each binary classifier is associated with a unique feature representation. More specifically, each classifier is associated with three sets of features: one set of pre-retrieval features, which are independent of the block-types under consideration, and two separate sets of post-retrieval features (one set specific to each type in the block-type-pair).

The voting approach addresses both challenges mentioned above (block-type-specific features and a potentially different predictive relationship across types) by training a different binary classifier per block-type pair. Each classifier adopts its own feature representation and learns a predictive relationship that is specific to the block-type-pair.

Given n verticals and m non-vertical block-types, the total number of binary classifiers used by the voting approach is given by $\binom{n+m}{2} - \binom{m}{2}$. The second term accounts for the fact that Web results are always presented and always ranked in their original order (i.e., $\sigma_q(w_1) < \sigma_q(w_2) < \sigma_q(w_3) < \sigma_q(eos)$). Thus, it is not required to learn a classifier to determine the relative ordering between pairs of non-vertical blocks. In our case, $n = 13$ and $m = 4$, which results in 130 independent binary classifiers. The large number of binary classifiers used by this method may be viewed as a disadvantage. An alternative to learning one model per block-type pair is to learn one model per vertical/non-vertical block-type pair. This results in four models per vertical: three which predict the vertical's relevance compared to each Web block (w_{1-3}) and one which predicts its relevance compared to *eos* (i.e., it predicts whether to display/suppress the vertical). As before, given a query, every block-pair $i, j \in \mathcal{B}_q$, where one is a vertical- and the other a non-vertical block, is submitted to the appropriate classifier. Then, the output prediction probabilities are combined as the input to the Schulze voting method in order to derive σ_q.

5.3 Learning to Rank Approaches

The block-ranking task can also be cast as a learning to rank (LTR) problem. Many different learning to rank methods have been proposed. In this work, we adopt a *pairwise* learning to rank approach. Pairwise approaches optimize over the set of pairwise preferences implicit in the training data. More specifically, we adopt a method that solves the classic RankSVM optimization problem, first proposed by Joachims [9]. RankSVM learns a linear model $f_{\mathbf{w}}$ parameterized by feature weight vector $\mathbf{w}$.

Casting block-ranking as an LTR problem requires training a *single* model $f_{\mathbf{w}}$ to predict a block's rank irrespective of its type. In our situation, this is problematic because different block-types are associated with different features (i.e., some features may be specific to a handful of types and some may be unique to a particular one). In addition, it is problematic because those features that are common to *multiple* types (e.g., whether the query contains a city name) may be predictive for some types more than others, or even predictive for different types in the opposite direction. Next, we propose three LTR variants which address these challenges in different ways. Each variant makes a different assumption about how features may be correlated with block relevance across block-types.

Equally Correlated Features.

One alternative is to assume that each feature is equally predictive of block relevance (in the same direction) independent of the block-type. The feature representation is as follows. Pre-retrieval features are independent of the block. This model uses a *single* copy of each pre-retrieval feature. Post-retrieval features are block-specific (i.e., they are generated directly from the block or the block's search engine results). Similar to pre-retrieval features, this approach *also* uses a *single* copy of each post-retrieval feature. If a block is not associated with a particular post-retrieval feature, then the feature is zeroed-out in that instance. Consider, for example, our post-retrieval features which determine the text-similarity between the query and the summary snippets presented in the block. These features are only associated with *news* and Web blocks w_{1-3}. Therefore, if the block is not one of these types, all these features are zeroed-out.

This approach assumes that features are equally correlated with relevance irrespective of the block-type. Once trained, model $f_{\mathbf{w}}$ will apply the *same* weight to a feature independent of the instance's block-type. We denote this LTR variant as `LTR-G` because it assumes a vertical-*general* relationship between features and relevance.

Uniquely Correlated Features.

This approach makes the opposite assumption as the previous one. It assumes that every feature—whether it is a pre- or post-retrieval feature—is uniquely correlated with relevance across different block-types. The feature representation is as follows. We make a separate, block-type-specific copy of each feature. So, for example, given 17 block-types (13 verticals + 3 Web blocks and the *eos* block), we make 17 copies of each pre-retrieval feature (one per block-type). Given an instance, all copies are zeroed-out except for those corresponding to the instance's block-type. For post-retrieval features, we make one copy per block-type for which the feature is available. Consider, for example, our temporal features, which are available for blocks from *blogs*, *community Q&A*, *news*, and *twitter*. We make 4 copies of each temporal feature.

This approach assumes that features are correlated differently with relevance depending on the block-type. Once trained, model $f_{\mathbf{w}}$ can apply a *different* weight to a feature, depending on the instance's block-type. While this added flexibility may be advantageous, the increased number of features may introduce predictive noise and result in overfitting. Thus, this LTR variant may require more training data than `LTR-G`. We denote this LTR variant as `LTR-S` because it assumes a vertical-*specific* relationship between features and relevance.

Equally and Uniquely Correlated Features.

The previous two approaches make opposite assumptions: features are either equally correlated or uniquely correlated with relevance for different block-types. A third alternative is to make neither assumption *a priori*, but to give the algorithm the freedom to exploit both types of relationships using training data.

For this approach, we maintain a single copy of each pre- and post-retrieval feature which is shared across all block-types. As before, if an instance's block-type is not associated with a shared feature, the feature is zeroed-out for that instance. In addition to these shared features, we make one block-type-specific copy of each pre- and post-retrieval feature. Given an instance, all copies corresponding to types other than the instance's block-type are zeroed-out. The canonical feature representation for this approach is the union of features used by the previous two approaches.

This approach makes no assumption about how a feature is correlated with relevance across block-types. If a feature is equally correlated across block-types, then the algorithm can assign a large (positive or negative) weight to the copy of the feature which is shared across types. Alternatively, if a feature is correlated differently for different block-types, then the algorithm can assign a large positive weight to some copies of the feature and a large negative weight with to others. We denote this LTR variant as `LTR-GS` because it has the flexibility of learning a vertical-specific and vertical-general relationship for each feature. Of all three LTR variants, `LTR-GS` has the largest number of features and may therefore need the most training data to avoid overfitting.

6. METHODS AND MATERIALS

We evaluate performance using a set of 13 verticals and 1070 queries. Our evaluation methodology is based on that proposed in Arguello *et al.* [1]. For each query, a reference block-ranking σ_q^* is derived from human preference judgements on block-pairs $i, j \in \mathcal{B}_q$. These 1070 reference presentations are used for training and evaluation. That is, during training, algorithms are tuned to predict a block-ranking σ_q that approximates the reference block-ranking σ_q^*. During testing, we evaluate algorithms based on the quality of their approximation on unseen queries. Following Arguello *et al.* [1], we evaluate the predicted block-ranking σ_q based on its *generalized* Kendall's τ distance to σ_q^*, denoted by $K^*(\sigma_q^*, \sigma_q)$ [11]. Arguello *et al.* [1] presented a user study which shows that when assessors strongly prefer one block-ranking over another, the preferred block-ranking is scored as being superior by this metric. That is, on average, the preferred presentation is the one closest to σ_q^* based on K^*.

Approaches are compared based on average performance across queries using 10-fold cross-validation. Unless otherwise stated, statistical significance is tested using a one-tailed paired t-test (at the $p < 0.05$ level) by comparing performance across test queries (i.e., the concatenation of all 10 test-folds). Next, we describe the methodology for deriving σ_q^*, the human relevance assessment process, the evaluation metric $K^*(\sigma_q^*, \sigma_q)$, our set of verticals and queries, and some algorithm implementation details.

6.1 Deriving the Reference Block-Ranking

We provide a general overview of how σ_q^* is derived from human relevance assessments and refer the reader to Arguello *et al.* [1] for more details.

Given query q, the reference presentation σ_q^* is derived from *redundant* pairwise preference judgements collected for *all* block-pairs $i, j \in \mathcal{B}_q$. That is, every candidate block-pair for the query is shown to multiple assessors, who are asked to state a preference or to state that both blocks i and j should be suppressed. Let π_q denote the full set of block-pair judgements collected for query q and let $\pi_q(i, j)$ denote the strength with which block i is preferred over j given q. We collected 3 redundant judgements per triplet (q, i, j) and set $\pi_q(i, j)$ equal to the number of assessors who prefer i over j given q. $\pi_q(eos, i)$ was set equal to the number of assessors who stated that i should be suppressed in conjunction with another block j. Finally, to derive σ_q^*, block-pair judgements π_q are input to the Schulze voting method [17], which converts these block-pair preferences into a ranking of blocks. A detailed explanation of the Schulze voting method is given in Schulze [17] and a description of how it is used to infer σ_q^* from π_q is given in Arguello *et al.* [1].

6.2 Human Relevance Assessment

Block-pair assessments for 1070 queries were collected using Amazon's Mechanical Turk (AMT). Assessors were compensated US$ 0.01 per block-pair assessment. For a given triplet (i, j, q), assessors were presented with the query q and blocks i and j presented side-by-side in random order. The only difference between our assessments and those collected in Arguello *et al.* [1] is that assessors were not given a topic description for the query. Instead, they were instructed to judge blocks based on their best guess of the hypothetical user's intent. To do quality control, 10% of all block-pair assessments were traps. In a trap assessment, the assessor is given a triplet (q, i, j), but either block i or j is taken from a query other than q. If the assessor selects the extraneous block as the preferred block, we consider it a *failed* trap. Assessors with more than 2 failed traps had all their judgements removed and re-submited to AMT.

6.3 Verticals and Queries

We focused on 13 verticals constructed using free APIs from eBay (*shopping*), Google (*blogs, books, weather*), Recipe Puppy (*recipes*), Yahoo! (*community Q&A, finance, images, local, maps, news*), Twitter (*twitter*), and YouTube (*video*). For the *local, maps,* and *weather* verticals, queries were mapped to a geographical location using Yahoo!'s GeoPlanet API. For queries with no target location explicitly mentioned (e.g., "home depot"), we assumed a particular location and instructed assessors to interpret such queries as a resident of that location. Blocks were constructed using the vertical's top results, assuming a maximum number of results (e.g., 5) per vertical block.

A set of 1,070 queries for model learning and evaluation was collected using sampling. We are interested not only in performance across queries, but also across verticals. Therefore, our sampling approach is biased towards coverage across our set of 13 verticals. For space reasons, we omit the details of our sampling approach.[2]

6.4 Modeling Bias Towards Vertical Results

In some cases, one may prefer a system that is biased towards vertical results. The aggregated web search provider may want to tune the system so that it more frequently presents vertical results and/or presents them higher in the output presentation. This may occur, for example, in order to gather user-interaction data or to satisfy contractual obligations with vertical providers or advertisers.

Vertical bias can be modeled in our evaluation framework using vertical *pseudo-votes*, a parameter p in the range $[0, \infty)$. As previously noted, $\pi_q(i, j)$ corresponds to the number of assessors who prefer i over j given q. A vertical bias can be introduced by incrementing this value by some number of pseudo-votes p, but only if i corresponds to a vertical block. If i and j correspond to blocks from different verticals, this method increments both $\pi_q(i, j)$ and $\pi_q(j, i)$ by

[2] A description of our sampling approach is available at `http://www.ils.unc.edu/~jarguell/cikm11`.

an equal number of pseudo-votes. This has the effect that, after producing σ_q^* using the Schulze voting method, vertical results are ranked higher in σ_q^*. However, the ranking of verticals relative to each other is unchanged. Modeling vertical bias using vertical pseudo-votes changes σ_q^* and, therefore, changes model learning and evaluation. Rather than select a single pseudo-vote parameter p, we learn and evaluate models across several values of p (i.e., $p = \{0, 1, 2, 3, 4, 5\}$). Across values of p, the verticals ranked higher in σ_q^* were *video*, *local*, *news*, *blogs*, and *community Q&A*.

6.5 Evaluation Metric

The primary evaluation metric is the *generalized* Kendall's τ distance between the predicted block-ranking σ_q and the reference block-ranking σ_q^*, denoted as $K^*(\sigma_q^*, \sigma_q)$ [11]. Generalized Kendall's τ is related to Kendall's τ, which measures the number of discordant pairs between two rankings of the same set of elements. For our purpose, however, Kendall's τ has a major limitation: it considers *all* discordant pairs equally important. In aggregated search, users typically scan results from top to bottom. Thus, discordant pairs at the top of the ranking should be more influential. As suggested in Kumar and Vassilvitskii [11], discordances at the top of the ranking can be made more influential by using a DCG-like cost function. See Arguello *et al.* [1] for details.

6.6 Implementation Details

The classification framework described in Section 5.1 requires tuning threshold parameters τ_{1-4}, which are used to slot verticals based on each classifier's prediction confidence value. In addition to these parameters, logistic regression requires tuning cost factor C, which determines the cost of misclassifying a training set instance. These 5 parameters were tuned using 10-fold cross-validation. More specifically, they were tuned for each train/test pair individually by doing a second level of 10-fold cross-validation on each primary fold's training set. An exhaustive search was used to find the parameter values with the best average performance across secondary train/test pairs. The voting approach described in Section 5.2 also uses logistic regression models: one per block-type-pair. The C parameter was tuned as described above. In both approaches, models were trained using the `LibLinear` toolkit.[3]

The prior probability that a particular vertical is ranked high is fairly low. This is a problem if during training the LTR model learns that the best alternative is to present w_{1-3} and suppress all verticals. In the classification and voting approach, we balanced the training data using instance weighting (i.e., assigning more weight to the minority class). Casting block-ranking as a learning-to-rank approach may also require some form of instance weighting.

Our approach to instance weighting is as follows. Let σ_q^w denote a block-ranking which presents Web blocks w_{1-3} in their original order and suppresses all verticals. Given a training query q, $-K^*(\sigma_q^*, \sigma_q^w)$, which is in the range $[-1, 1]$, measures the distance between σ_q^* and σ_q^w. If $-K^*(\sigma_q^*, \sigma_q^w)$ is close to $+1$, it means that σ_q^* has verticals presented in the top ranks. If $-K^*(\sigma_q^*, \sigma_q^w)$ is close to -1, it means that σ_q^* has Web blocks w_{1-3} presented in the top ranks and verticals presented in the low ranks or suppressed. Our approach to instance weighting is to replicate queries in the training set proportional to this distance. This has the effect that queries which deviate from σ_q^w are oversampled. The amount of replication is controlled using parameter α. First, we scale $-K^*(\sigma_q^*, \sigma_q^w)$ to zero min and unit max (using queries from the training set). Then, we multiply this value by α. Given training query q, the number of *additional* copies of q in the training set is given by $-\alpha K^*_{\text{min-max}}(\sigma_q^*, \sigma_q^w)$. Note that when $\alpha = 0$, no additional copies of q are added to the training set. We evaluate the effect of parameter α in Section 8.1.

In addition to parameter α, RankSVM has a regularization parameter λ. Both parameters were tuned using two levels of 10-fold cross-validation. An exhaustive search was used to find the parameter values with the best average performance across secondary train/test pairs. We trained LTR models using the `sofia-ml` toolkit.[4]

7. EVALUATION RESULTS

We evaluate three general approaches to block-ranking: the classification approach, the voting approach, and the LTR approach. One limitation of the voting approach is that it requires a large number of independent binary classifiers. Thus, we evaluate a second version of the voting approach that trains a binary classifier only for block-type-pairs where one type corresponds to a vertical block-type and the other corresponds to a non-vertical block-type. Both are included in this evaluation. We also include all three variants of the LTR approach, with parameter α tuned using cross-validation.

Results in terms of average $K^*(\sigma_q^*, \sigma_q)$ are presented in Table 1. As previously mentioned, pseudo-vote parameter p controls for vertical bias. The higher its value, the greater the bias towards verticals ranked high. Rather than choose a single parameter p, results are presented for $p = \{0, 1, 2, 3, 4, 5\}$. When $p = 0$, the σ_q^*'s used for training and evaluation have no vertical bias. The second row in Table 1 (`WEB`) corresponds to a degenerate baseline that suppresses all vertical results and simply presents w_{1-3} above *eos* in their original order.

Table 1 shows several meaningful trends. Performance for all methods decreases with greater values of p (this was expected for `WEB`). One possible reason is the following. As p increases, the number of queries with top-ranked verticals increases. This means that the room for error also increases. When p is low, ranking w_{1-3} above all verticals is a reliable and effective strategy.

When $p = 0$, `WEB` performs well. In fact, the only two approaches that significantly outperform `WEB` when $p = 0$ are `LTR-S` and `LTR-GS`. Significance with respect to `WEB` is not shown in Table 1. For values of $p \geq 3$, *all* block-ranking approaches significantly outperform `WEB`. Thus, given a vertical bias, any of the three general block-ranking approaches is better than presenting only Web results.

Both voting approaches perform similar to each other. This is interesting because the second version (which learns one binary classifier per vertical/non-vertical block-type) uses many fewer binary classifiers than the first (which learns one classifier per block-type). The performance for both voting approaches, however, deteriorates for $p \geq 2$.

The classification approach does surprisingly well considering that it uses a just one binary classifier per vertical. Its

[3]`http://www.csie.ntu.edu.tw/cjlin/liblinear/`

[4]`http://code.google.com/p/sofia-ml/`

Table 1: **Block-ranking results in terms of average $K^*(\sigma_q^*, \sigma_q)$. A $\triangle(\triangledown)$, $\blacktriangle(\blacktriangledown)$, and $\wedge(\vee)$ denotes significantly better(worse) performance compared to the classification, voting (all pairs), and `LTR-G` approaches, respectively.**

	$p=0$	$p=1$	$p=2$
`WEB`	$0.982^{\triangle}$	$0.959^{\triangle\vee}$	$0.896^{\triangledown\vee}$
classification$^{\triangle\triangledown}$	$0.950^{\blacktriangledown\vee}$	$0.943^{\blacktriangledown\vee}$	$0.924^{\blacktriangle}$
voting (all pairs)$^{\blacktriangle\blacktriangledown}$	$0.984^{\triangle}$	$0.960^{\triangle\vee}$	$0.898^{\triangledown\vee}$
voting (only v-w pairs)	$0.980^{\triangle\blacktriangledown}$	$0.956^{\triangle\blacktriangledown\vee}$	$0.898^{\triangledown\vee}$
`LTR-G` $^{\wedge\vee}$	$0.980^{\triangle}$	$0.967^{\triangle\blacktriangle}$	$0.932^{\blacktriangle}$
`LTR-S`	$0.986^{\triangle\wedge}$	$0.970^{\triangle\blacktriangle}$	$0.937^{\triangle\blacktriangle}$
`LTR-GS`	$0.986^{\triangle\wedge}$	$0.973^{\triangle\blacktriangle\wedge}$	$0.936^{\triangle\blacktriangle}$

	$p=3$	$p=4$	$p=5$
`WEB`	$0.773^{\triangledown\blacktriangledown\triangledown}$	$0.656^{\triangledown\blacktriangledown\triangledown}$	$0.520^{\triangledown\blacktriangledown\triangledown}$
classification$^{\triangle\triangledown}$	$0.878^{\blacktriangle}$	$0.824^{\blacktriangle\wedge}$	$0.775^{\blacktriangle\wedge}$
voting (all pairs)$^{\blacktriangle\blacktriangledown}$	$0.830^{\triangledown\vee}$	$0.744^{\triangledown\vee}$	$0.734^{\triangledown\vee}$
voting (only v-w pairs)	$0.822^{\triangledown\vee}$	$0.760^{\triangledown\blacktriangle\vee}$	$0.734^{\triangledown}$
`LTR-G` $^{\wedge\vee}$	$0.871^{\blacktriangle}$	$0.798^{\triangledown\blacktriangle}$	$0.754^{\triangledown\blacktriangle}$
`LTR-S`	$0.883^{\blacktriangle\wedge}$	$0.838^{\triangle\blacktriangle\wedge}$	$0.792^{\triangle\blacktriangle\wedge}$
`LTR-GS`	$0.882^{\blacktriangle\wedge}$	$0.843^{\triangle\blacktriangle\wedge}$	$0.795^{\triangle\blacktriangle\wedge}$

performance is competitive across all values of p, showing that it can be effectively trained to fit different degrees of vertical bias.

Comparing among the three LTR variants, performance is significantly worse for `LTR-G`. It never performs better and often performs significantly worse than `LTR-S` and `LTR-GS`, particularly for values of $p \geq 3$. For values of $p \geq 4$, `LTR-G` performs significantly worse than the classification approach. The improvement of `LTR-S` and `LTR-GS` over `LTR-G` reveals the importance of exploiting vertical-specific evidence. Imposing the constraint that features must be similarly correlated with relevance across different block-types degrades performance. `LTR-G` and `LTR-S` perform better by allowing the learning algorithm to exploit a block-type-specific relationship between features and block relevance.

Compared to the classification approach, `LTR-S` and `LTR-GS` both perform better. The improvement is significant for all values of p, except $p = 3$, where all three perform at the same level. We view this as a positive result in favor of casting block-ranking as a learning-to-rank task. In contrast with the classification approach, both of these LTR variants perform better and require training only a single model (rather than one per vertical). Relative to each other, `LTR-S` and `LTR-GS` are statistically indistinguishable across all values of p (statistical significance not shown in Table 1). We provide an explanation for this in Section 8.3.

8. DISCUSSION

8.1 Effect of Parameter α on LTR variants

The goal of parameter α is to focus LTR training on those queries that have verticals ranked high. Given enough evidence in favor of a particular vertical, we want to the LTR model to overcome the prior probability that the vertical is ranked low. Our method for instance weighting is to replicate queries in the training set proportional to the K^* distance between the reference block-ranking σ_q^* and a one that presents w_{1-3} and suppresses all verticals. Parameter α controls the amount of replication.

We were interested in the effect of parameter α on performance. Each LTR variant is evaluated under two conditions. In the first condition, $\alpha = 0$, which corresponds to *no replication*—each training query q appears just once in the training set. In the second condition, α is tuned by sweeping across $\alpha = \{0, 10, 25, 50\}$. Notice that $\alpha = 0$ (no replication) is a parameter choice. These results are identical to those in Table 1. Table 2 presents results (in terms of average $K(\sigma_q^*, \sigma_q)$) for all three LTR variants under these two conditions. As a second point of reference, we also present results for the classification approach. To conserve space, we limit results to $p = \{0, 2, 4, 5\}$.

Table 2: **Block-ranking results in terms of $K(\sigma_q^*, \sigma_q)$. A $\triangle(\triangledown)$ denotes significantly better(worse) performance compared to the classification approach. A $\blacktriangle(\blacktriangledown)$ denotes a significant improvement(drop) in performance for an LTR variant (with α tuned) compared to its counterpart for which $\alpha = 0$.**

	$p=0$	$p=2$	$p=4$	$p=5$
classification	0.950	0.924	0.824	0.775
`LTR-G`,α=0	$0.983^{\triangle}$	0.923	$0.775^{\triangledown}$	$0.701^{\triangledown}$
`LTR-S`,α=0	$0.986^{\triangle}$	0.928	$0.798^{\triangledown}$	$0.723^{\triangledown}$
`LTR-GS`,α=0	$0.986^{\triangle}$	$0.940^{\triangle}$	0.812	$0.743^{\triangledown}$
`LTR-G`	$0.980^{\triangle\blacktriangledown}$	$0.932^{\blacktriangle}$	$0.798^{\triangledown\blacktriangle}$	$0.754^{\triangledown\blacktriangle}$
`LTR-S`	$0.986^{\triangle}$	$0.937^{\triangle\blacktriangle}$	$0.838^{\triangle\blacktriangle}$	$0.792^{\triangle\blacktriangle}$
`LTR-GS`	$0.986^{\triangle}$	$0.936^{\triangle}$	$0.843^{\triangle\blacktriangle}$	$0.795^{\triangle\blacktriangle}$

The relative performance between LTR variants when $\alpha = 0$ (rows 3-5) is consistent with their relative performance when α is tuned (rows 6-8). That is, `LTR-S` and `LTR-GS` outperform `LTR-G`. Thus, we focus the discussion on `LTR-S` and `LTR-GS`. For both approaches, tuning α (vs. setting it to zero) has either no effect or significantly improves performance. For $p \geq 4$, setting $\alpha = 0$ degrades performance even compared to the classification approach. Thus, casting block-ranking as a learning-to-rank task benefits not only from allowing the algorithm to learn a block-type-specific relationship between features and relevance, it also benefits re-weighting training-phase instances in order to overcome the prior probability that verticals are ranked low.

8.2 Feature Contribution to Performance

A feature ablation study was conducted to test each feature group's contribution to overall performance, measured in terms of average $K(\sigma_q^*, \sigma_q)$. The analysis is conducted for both the classification approach and the `LTR-S` approach because they performed the best in Section 7. Each feature group was individually omitted and this model was compared to a model with access to all features. Because features may be correlated, a non-significant drop in performance does not necessarily mean that the feature group contributes no useful information.

Results are presented in Table 3 for the classification approach and the `LTR-S` approach. The top four feature groups are pre-retrieval features. The next four features are post-retrieval features. The last row corresponds to a model that ignores *all* post-retrieval features.

Table 3 shows several interesting results. The `LTR-S` approach appears to be slightly more robust to missing features. One possible reason is the following. The classification approach trains one independent binary classifier per vertical. The `LTR-S` approach, on the other hand, trains a single model. It may be that training a single model allows the `LTR-S` approach to better shift its focus towards block-types for which it is more confident.

Table 3: Feature ablation results for the classification and LTR-S approaches. A ▲(▼) denotes a significant improvement(drop) in performance compared to the model with access to all features.

classification approach

	$p = 0$	$p = 2$	$p = 4$	$p = 5$
all	0.950	0.924	0.824	0.775
no ne-type	0.003	-0.005	0.001	0.005
no cat	0.004	-0.83%▼	0.003	0.000
no click	-0.004	-1.71%▼	-1.97%▼	-2.05%▼
no vert-intent	-0.001	-1.15%▼	0.000	-0.009
no hit	0.003	-0.005	0.002	0.013
no loc	-0.001	-0.003	0.002	0.001
no temp	-0.002	0.000	-0.002	0.000
no text-sim	-0.003	-0.94%▼	-2.34%▼	-3.97%▼
no post-ret	-0.001	-0.86%▼	-2.29%▼	-3.44%▼

LTR-S

	$p = 0$	$p = 2$	$p = 4$	$p = 5$
all	0.986	0.937	0.838	0.792
no ne-type	-0.02%	0.19%	-0.42%	1.28%
no cat	-0.10%	0.31%	-0.35%	0.21%
no click	-0.04%	0.26%	-0.20%	-0.13%
no vert-intent	-0.03%	0.12%	0.16%	0.60%
no hit	-0.15%	-0.26%	-0.45%	-0.23%
no loc	-0.01%	0.12%	-0.65%	1.61%▲
no temp	0.01%	0.05%	-0.10%	0.65%
no text-sim	-0.09%	-0.41%	-2.60%▼	-3.44%▼
no post-ret	-0.02%	0.08%	-2.95%▼	-3.79%▼

The features with the greatest drop in performance (at least for $p \geq 4$) are text-similarity features, which are a type of post-retrieval feature. This shows the importance of deriving evidence directly from those results presented in the block. Also, it suggests the importance of issuing the query to as many vertical search engines as possible (in order to derive this type of evidence) or caching these post-retrieval features for future impressions of the query. Text-similarity features may have contributed the most to performance because many of the block-types often ranked high in σ_q^* were associated with text-rich information. These included Web blocks w_{1-3}, *news*, *blogs*, and *community Q&A*.

Finally, omitting most feature groups did not result in a significant drop in performance. There are two reasons for this. First, features may be correlated. Second, most verticals are rarely ranked high in σ_q^*. Some of our features may be essential to minority verticals, but this may not have a noticeable effect on the average $K^*(\sigma_q^*, \sigma_q)$. We explore this further in the next section.

8.3 Feature Contribution to Per-Vertical Performance

We also investigated each feature group's contribution to per-vertical ranking performance. Evaluating a feature's contribution to a particular vertical is not trivial. Suppose, for example, that we omit temporal features and want to evaluate the effect on the *news* vertical. One possibility might be to compare the *news* vertical's predicted rank and its ideal rank across a set of queries. However, omitting temporal features may affect *other* verticals as well. And, if so, then ranking mistakes for those verticals would displace *news* from its ideal rank. For this reason, we focus our analysis on the classification approach, which trains one binary classifier per vertical. Each vertical-specific classifier is

Table 4: Feature contribution to per-vertical performance, based on AP. Statistical significance is tested using a one-tailed paired t-test, comparing across cross-validation test-folds. A ▲(▼) denotes a significant improvement(drop) in performance compared to the model with access to all features.

	q & a	blogs	book	finance	image
all features	0.284	0.431	0.088	0.638	0.323
no ne-type	10.15%▲	2.65%▲	34.41%▲	-18.69%▼	9.19%▲
no cat	15.49%▲	-6.61%▼	7.77%	21.95%▲	6.61%▲
no click	2.32%▲	0.32%	-1.29%	-14.35%▼	-9.23%▼
no vert-intent	7.80%▲	2.60%▲	1.97%	0.00%	-19.34%▼
no hit	5.53%▲	-0.61%▼	3.65%▲	2.44%▲	0.81%
no loc	0.00%	0.00%	0.00%	0.00%	0.00%
no temp	0.12%	-0.43%▼	0.00%	0.00%	0.00%
no text-sim	-8.44%▼	-12.35%▼	-31.16%▼	-3.38%▼	2.47%
no post-ret	-6.03%▼	-14.20%▼	-31.07%▼	-3.71%▼	2.20%
	local	**map**	**news**	**recipe**	**shopping**
all features	0.546	0.419	0.594	0.48	0.377
no ne-type	-3.97%▼	-1.99%	13.04%▲	6.97%▲	1.35%
no cat	-8.67%▼	-0.36%	21.92%▲	18.10%▲	-32.93%▼
no click	-10.44%▼	-16.86%▼	3.27%▲	-0.01%	-8.88%▼
no vert-intent	7.37%▲	-74.42%▼	2.73%	-3.63%▼	-0.65%
no hit	-2.89%▼	-1.94%▼	-4.21%▼	3.78%▲	0.21%
no loc	-8.84%▼	13.12%▲	0.00%	0.00%	0.00%
no temp	0.00%	0.00%	0.51%	0.00%	0.00%
no text-sim	-16.93%▼	0.00%	-48.88%▼	0.00%	-8.02%▼
no post-ret	-18.04%▼	13.15%▲	-45.26%▼	3.78%▲	-10.96%▼
	twitter	**video**	**weather**		
all features	0.053	0.571	0.938		
no ne-type	-14.19%▼	2.14%▲	4.55%▲		
no cat	-0.91%	3.35%▲	-17.31%▼		
no click	1.99%	-4.48%▼	-50.11%▼		
no vert-intent	0.31%	4.41%▲	-1.11%▼		
no hit	-5.90%▼	-0.75%▼	-0.45%		
no loc	0.00%	0.00%	-17.68%▼		
no temp	-5.71%▼	0.00%	0.00%		
no text-sim	-26.78%▼	-12.11%▼	0.00%		
no post-ret	-27.64%▼	-12.46%▼	-17.81%▼		

trained to predict whether the vertical should be displayed (ranked above *eos*) or suppressed (ranked below *eos*) in σ_q.

Performance for a particular vertical is evaluated by considering the quality of confidence values produced by the vertical's corresponding classifier. Let $\mathcal{Q}_v$ denote the queries for which v is a candidate vertical. We evaluate the quality of confidence values output from v's classifier by computing the average precision (AP) metric on a ranking of $\mathcal{Q}_v$ (ranked in descending order of confidence value that v should be presented). In computing AP, a ranked query q is considered "relevant" if $\sigma_q^*(v) < \sigma_q^*(eos)$ and "non-relevant" otherwise. Results in terms of AP are presented in Table 4. We limit our discussion to the case where $p = 5$ because it is associated with verticals ranked higher in σ_q^*.

Table 4 shows several noteworthy trends. First, performance across verticals varied widely (see row "all features"). The best-performing verticals were *weather* (AP=0.938), *finance* (AP=0.638), and *news* (AP=0.594). Interestingly, both *weather* and *finance* were minority verticals. Both were presented (i.e., ranked above *eos* in σ_q^*) for only 14 and 21 queries, respectively. In spite of having few positive instances for training, performance for both these verticals was good. As it turns out, *weather* was easy because *every* query for which it was presented had the query term "weather" (e.g., "weather louisville ky"). This explains why the most predictive feature for *weather* was the click-through feature (i.e., the query's similarity to queries with clicks on weather-related content, many of which contain the term "weather"). Similarly, *finance* was easy because 10/21 queries for which it was presented had the query term "stock(s)" (e.g., "boeing stock"). In other words, performance was high for *weather* and *finance* because their queries often had explicit vertical intent, which is easy to detect.

It is interesting that *news* was among the best performing verticals. This is inconsistent with previous results on vertical selection [2]. The most useful features for *news* were text-similarity features, which are a type of post-retrieval feature. Thus, while it is difficult to detect that a query is newsworthy using only pre-retrieval evidence (as in Arguello *et al.* [2]), useful evidence can be harnessed by issuing the query to the *news* vertical.

The worst performing verticals were *twitter* (AP=0.053), *books* (AP=0.088), and *community Q&A* (AP=0.284). Both *twitter* and *books* were minority verticals, while *community Q&A* was fairly common. Predicting *twitter* may require predicting that the query is about a trending topic, which we did not explicitly address. Predicting *books* and *community Q&A* seems difficult. Queries for which these verticals were relevant had no clear pattern. For *books*, for example, some queries had the keyword "book" (e.g., "books on giraffes"), some corresponded to a book title (e.g., "lolita"), some corresponded to an author name (e.g., "dr. phil"), and, finally, others corresponded to encyclopedic information needs (e.g., "wedding cake ideas", "why don't babies sleep at night", "perennials"). *Community Q&A* queries showed a similar pattern. This may explain why text-similarity features were the only ones to significantly improve performance for both. In the absence of a clearly predictive query-pattern, it seems useful to derive evidence directly from the block.

Features contributed to performance differently for different verticals. Vertical intent features, which exploit vertical-related keywords, were predictive for *maps* and *images*. Many queries for which *maps* was relevant had the keyword "map(s)". Similarly, many queries for which *images* was relevant had the keywords "photo(s)", "pic(s)", and "picture(s)". Category features were predictive for *shopping* because one of our category clusters was related to the shopping ODP node. Different features also hurt performance for different verticals. Named-entity type features hurt performance for *books* and *news*. Category features hurt performance for *community Q&A*, *finance*, *news*, and *recipe*. Click-through features hurt performance for *communtiy Q&A* and *news*.

The only features that did not significantly hurt performance for *any* vertical were text-similarity features. In the previous section, text-similarity features had the greatest contribution to overall performance. In this analysis, text-similarity features were the most consistently predictive for different verticals.

9. CONCLUSION

We proposed and evaluated three general machine learning approaches to block-ranking—ordering blocks of Web and vertical results in response to a query. The best overall performance was obtained by casting this as a learning-to-rank problem. We showed, however, that to be successful, the LTR model must be able to learn a vertical-*specific* relationship between features and block relevance. Our solution to this problem is through feature replication (i.e. by making a block-type-specific copy of each feature). This allows the model to weight a feature as positive evidence for some verticals and negative evidence for others.

Consistent with most prior work in aggregated search, evidence integration is key to block-ranking. Different features were predictive for different verticals. The features that contributed the most to overall performance, and those that were *consistently* predictive for different verticals, were text-similarity features, which are a type of post-retrieval feature. Their contribution to performance suggests the importance of issuing the query to a vertical when possible or of caching this type of evidence for future impressions of the query (or queries similar to it).

10. ACKNOWLEDGMENTS

This work was supported in part by the NSF grant IIS-0916553 and a gift from Yahoo! through its Key Scientific Challenges program. Any opinions, findings, conclusions, and recommendations expressed in this paper are the authors' and do not necessarily reflect those of the sponsors.

11. REFERENCES

[1] J. Arguello, F. Diaz, J. Callan, and B. Carterette. A methodology for evaluating aggregated search results. In *ECIR 2011*, pages 141–152. Springer Berlin / Heidelberg, 2011.

[2] J. Arguello, F. Diaz, J. Callan, and J.-F. Crespo. Sources of evidence for vertical selection. In *SIGIR 2009*, pages 315–322. ACM, 2009.

[3] J. Arguello, F. Diaz, and J.-F. Paiement. Vertical selection in the presence of unlabeled verticals. In *SIGIR 2010*, pages 691–698. ACM, 2010.

[4] D. M. Bikel, R. Schwartz, and R. M. Weischedel. An algorithm that learns what is in a name. *Machine Learning*, 34:211–231, 1999.

[5] L. Breiman, J. Friedman, C. J. Stone, and R. A. Olshen. *Classification and Regression Trees.* Chapman and Hall/CRC, 1984.

[6] F. Diaz. Integration of news content into web results. In *WSDM 2009*, pages 182–191. ACM, 2009.

[7] F. Diaz and J. Arguello. Adaptation of offline vertical selection predictions in the presence of user feedback. In *SIGIR 2009*, pages 323–330. ACM, 2009.

[8] H. Jeffreys. An invariant form for the prior probability in estimation problems. *Proceedings of the Royal Society of London. Series A, Mathematical and Physical Sciences*, 186(1007):453–461, 1946.

[9] T. Joachims. Optimizing search engines using clickthrough data. In *KDD 2002*, pages 133–142. ACM, 2002.

[10] A. C. König, M. Gamon, and Q. Wu. Click-through prediction for news queries. In *SIGIR 2009*, pages 347–354. ACM, 2009.

[11] R. Kumar and S. Vassilvitskii. Generalized distances between rankings. In *WWW 2010*, pages 571–580. ACM, 2010.

[12] X. Li, Y.-Y. Wang, and A. Acero. Learning query intent from regularized click graphs. In *SIGIR 2008*, pages 339–346. ACM, 2008.

[13] C.-J. Lin, R. C. Weng, and S. S. Keerthi. Trust region newton methods for large-scale logistic regression. In *ICML 2007*, pages 561–568. ACM, 2007.

[14] T.-Y. Liu. Learning to rank for information retrieval. *Foundations and Trends in Informaton Retrieval*, 3:225–331, 2009.

[15] C. D. Manning, P. Raghavan, and H. Schtze. *Introduction to Information Retrieval.* Cambridge University Press, New York, NY, USA, 2008.

[16] A. K. Ponnuswami, K. Pattabiraman, Q. Wu, R. Gilad-Bachrach, and T. Kanungo. On composition of a federated web search result page: Using online users to provide pairwise preference for heterogeneous verticals. In *WSDM 2011*, pages 715–724. ACM, 2011.

[17] M. Schulze. A new monotonic, clone-independent, reversal symmetric, and condorcet-consistent single-winner election method. *Social Choice and Welfare*, 36:267–303, 2011.

Coreference Aware Web Object Retrieval

Jeffrey Dalton*
Center for Intelligent Information Retrieval
Department of Computer Science
University of Massachusetts Amherst
Amherst, Massachusetts
jdalton@cs.umass.edu

Peter Mika and Roi Blanco
Yahoo Research
Barcelona, Spain
{pmika, roi}@yahoo-inc.com

ABSTRACT

As user demands become increasingly sophisticated, search engines today are competing in more than just returning document results from the Web. One area of competition is providing web object results from structured data extracted from a multitude of information sources. We address the problem of performing keyword retrieval over a collection of objects containing a large degree of duplication as different Web-based information sources provide descriptions of the same object. We develop a method for coreference aware retrieval that performs topic-specific coreference resolution on retrieved objects in order to improve object search results. Our results demonstrate that coreference has a significant impact on the effectiveness of retrieval in the domain of local search. Our results show that a coreference aware system outperforms naive object retrieval by more than 20% in P5 and P10.

Categories and Subject Descriptors: H.3.3 [Information Search and Retrieval]: Selection Process

General Terms: Algorithms, Experimentation

Keywords: Semantic Search, Vertical Search, Structured Data, Object Retrieval, Coreference

1. INTRODUCTION

Web search engines compete today by looking for ways to provide specific results to their users beyond the familiar list of "ten blue links." One approach pursued in the past is to integrate object search results from vertical search databases maintained by the provider of the Web search engine. An example is Yahoo! Local, a vertical for business listings, which searches over a curated collection of structured data sourced from multiple trusted providers. Though costly, careful aggregation of the underlying data feeds also ensures that there are no duplicate business listings in the data set. Results from Yahoo! Local are integrated into the main search engine through an information box that appears on top of the search results, and shows a small number of related results from vertical search.

A significant problem with this approach is that vertical search engines built in this manner suffer from a lack of coverage compared to Web search and rely on expensive data feeds sourced from commercial providers. In this context, the emerging Web of Data provides an opportunity for search providers to significantly extend the coverage of their vertical search results, and also to create more compelling search result presentations [13]. Based on the success of the Semantic Web and particular efforts such as microformats[1] and Linked Data[2], the Web of Data has grown considerably in size in the past years [14]. In addition, improved methods of Information Extraction allow web-scale extraction of information with increasing accuracy [6].

In this work, we address a crucial challenge of this approach: the presence of multiple descriptions of the same object from multiple sources. The problem is demonstrated on the case of Yahoo!, where the search for business listings extracted from the Web of Data is offered as an option on the left bar of the search engine, shown in Figure 1. The retrieval base of this search is significantly larger than that of the curated Yahoo! Local database. It searches over structured business objects extracted from the web. A typical query such as *pizza Amherst, MA* returns 926 results in Yahoo! Local, while Yahoo!'s web object search returns 6,420 local business objects. However, as Figure 1 also shows, greater recall comes at the price of *coreferent* results, i.e. object results that describe the same real-world entity. Figure 1 shows that four of the top results are for Antonio's pizza and that Athena's Pizza occurs twice. There are only six unique objects on the first page of search results. This search experience could be significantly improved by performing coreference resolution on the objects in the search collection, either globally or in response to the query.

To address these shortcomings, we introduce the concept of *coreference aware object retrieval*. The context of our work is Ad-hoc Object Retrieval (AOR), which is different from text retrieval in a number of crucial aspects. First, the objects consist mainly of structured attributes and links to other entities, with only a few short pieces of text. Crucially, the coreference of two objects is determined not only by textual features but also by key structural differences. The nature of the search tasks over these objects is also different because the objects contain structured and actionable values: location, phone number, rating, and price informa-

*Work performed while intern at Yahoo! Research.

[1]http://microformats.org
[2]http://linkeddata.org

CIKM'11, October 24–28, 2011, Glasgow, Scotland, UK.

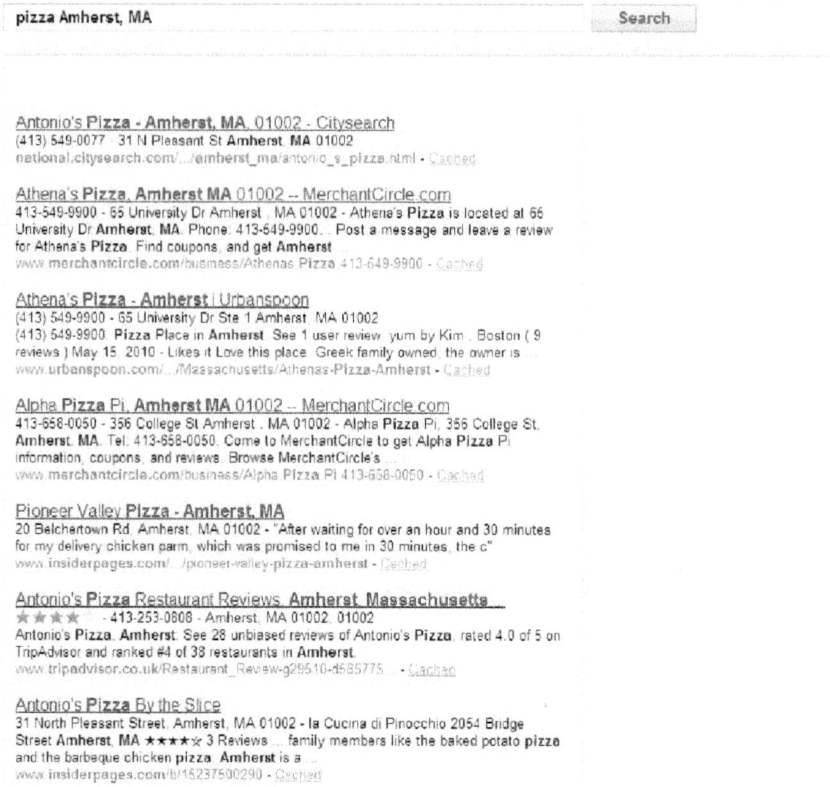

Figure 1: Local business listing objects for *pizza Amherst MA*.

tion. We explain these differences in more detail in Section 2 where we discuss AOR.

The key contribution of our work is to establish coreference aware information retrieval and show the following:

- A substantial amount of redundancy exists in existing object data that can be retrieved from the Web of Data, indicating a large potential impact on applications using the data.
- Demonstrating that coreference aware evaluation has a significant impact on retrieval effectiveness. In particular, systems that do not handle coreference, dramatically overestimate their effectiveness when coreference is considered.
- Coreference aware retrieval approaches outperform naive IR systems by increasing the unique objects returned in the search results. The results also show that errors made by state-of-the-art coreference systems have a significant effect on retrieval and motivates further work considering the tasks jointly.

The area of our study is local search, i.e. search queries where the user is explicitly looking for local businesses and services. However, our conclusions apply to all web search engines that exploit structured data from the Web in any domain of retrieval.

2. PRELIMINARIES

2.1 Ad-hoc Object Retrieval

Pound *et al.* [19] are the first to provide a formal treatment of object retrieval from an information retrieval perspective. They formalize the problem as the Ad-hoc Object Retrieval (AOR) task in Web of Data collections. They define the AOR task as follows:

- INPUT: a user query (a keyword query, without structure) q which has query type t and query intent z, and a data graph G.
- OUTPUT: a ranked list of object identifiers $o = (o_1; o_2; ...o_k)$ such that each o_i occurs in G.
- EVALUATION: each object o_i is labeled with a score (independently of the rest) by a judge with access to all the information contained in or linked to by o_i, with respect to the query q, query type t, and the query intent z.

Based on an analysis of query logs, they suggest a typology of web queries and note that the two most prevalent types of queries are **Entity** and **Type** queries. In an Entity query, the intention of the user is to find references to a particular real-world entity. In a Type query, the intention is to find entities of a particular type or class. The process of evaluating an object retrieval system is similar to web search evaluation. The objects are rated on a four point scale for relevance to the query (Perfect, Good, Fair, Not Relevant).

Field	tok1	tok2	tok3	tok4
vcard:fn	Antonio's	Pizza		
vcard:street-address	31	N	Pleasant	St
vcard:locality	Amherst			
vcard:region	MA			
vcard:postal-code	1002			
vcard:tel	413	253	808	

Table 1: Example of tokenized hCard data mapped to indexable fields

2.2 Ranking models for AOR

In order to test the impact of coreference on retrieval we use well-known retrieval models proven to be effective. Specifically, models based on the Markov Random Field retrieval model (MRF-IR) [12] using unigram and sequential dependence models. We also use the probabilistic BM25 model. In the recent SemSearch 2010 Workshop these methods were the basis for the most effective object retrieval systems for the Entity Search track [10].

The AOR task models typical search workloads performed by semantic search engines, which provide the ability to retrieve resources based on words that appear in the values of properties. The data collection used in retrieval is represented using the Resource Description Framework (RDF) to model it as a series of triples (resource, property, value), also known as (subject, predicate, object). The values may contain textual content or refer to the URI of other resources. To construct objects, triples are grouped by resource. Each property (also referred to as a predicate) is mapped onto fields which can then be tokenized where appropriate to support keyword matching. An example of an object derived from hCard microformat data is presented in Table 1.

We now describe the retrieval models utilized to rank a structured object O, contained in a collection C of $|N|$ objects, with respect to a keyword query Q formed of $q_1, \dots q_n$ query terms. The models we use do not leverage the RDF property structure for field matching or weighting. The selected models can be applied across all Web of Data objects and represent typical baseline retrieval systems. The effectiveness of more advanced models is inconsistent across collections and is very sensitive to parameter tuning.

2.2.1 BM25

BM25 is a probabilistic retrieval model that is an effective approximation of the two-poisson model of term frequency distributions. For an object O the score with respect to a query Q is defined as:

$$s(Q,O) = \sum_{i=1}^{|Q|} \log \frac{N - tf(q_i,C) + 0.5}{tf(q_i,C) + 0.5} \cdot \quad (1)$$

$$\cdot \frac{(k_1+1)\cdot tf(q_i,O)}{k_1 \cdot (1 - b + b \cdot \frac{N}{dl(O)}) + tf(q_i,O)}, \quad (2)$$

where $dl(O)$ is the length of the object in tokens, $tf(q_i, O)$ the number of times q_i occurs in O, $tf(q_i, C)$ the number of times q_i occurs in C and b and k_1 are parameters. We set k_1 to its default value of 1.2 as it has little effect in retrieval performance.

2.2.2 MRF-IR

Two standard retrieval models in the MFR-IR framework are the unigram and sequential dependence models. The unigram model treats the document as a bag-of-words with the underlying assumption of term independence. The probability with Dirichlet smoothing is rank-equivalent to the following score:

$$\log p(Q|O) = \sum_{i=1}^{|Q|} \log \frac{tf(q_i,O) + \mu\frac{c_{q,i}}{|C|}}{|O| + \mu} \quad (3)$$

where $c_{q,i}$ is the number of times a word occurs in a collection of documents, $|C|$ is the number of words in the collection, and μ is the smoothing parameter that is set empirically.

The sequential dependence model relaxes the term independence assumption allowing for adjacent term dependencies. It uses the following formulation:

$$s(Q|O) = \lambda_T \textstyle\sum_{i=1}^{|Q|} f_T(q_i, O) + \quad (4)$$

$$+\lambda_{OW} \textstyle\sum_{q_i,q_{i+1}\in Q} f_{OW}(q_i, q_{i+1}, O) + \quad (5)$$

$$+\lambda_{UW} \textstyle\sum_{q_i,q_{i+1}\in Q} f_U(q_i, q_{i+1}, O)\ , \quad (6)$$

where

$$f_T(q_i,O) = \log \left[\frac{tf(q_i,O) + \mu \cdot \frac{tf(q_i,C)}{N}}{dl(O) + \mu} \right] \quad (7)$$

and f_{OW} and f_{UW} are computed like f_T but replacing the $tf(q_i, \cdot)$ function with the count $tf(q_i, q_{i+1}, \cdot)$ where q_i and q_{i+1} appear ordered and unordered windows in the text respectively. λ_T, λ_{OW}, λ_{UW} are weighting parameters as suggested by Metzler *et al.* [12].

3. RELATED WORK

We now consider work related to keyword search over structured objects. We also discuss the relationship to previous work on redundancy and diversity in information retrieval. To our knowledge, ours is the first work to address the impact of coreference in object retrieval.

3.1 Keyword search over structured data

The area of keyword search over structured objects is well studied. At a recent SIGMOD conference, Chen [7] provides an overview of recent work in the database community. Agrawal *et al* [2] and Paprizos *et al* [16] both address the problem of returning structured objects in response to web keyword queries. These works assume a clean database where coreference, if necessary, has been performed and therefore do not address coreference.

3.2 Diversity in retrieval

There is significant recent focus on the problems of diversity and redundancy in document retrieval. The work in this area deals primarily with unstructured and semi-structured documents without clearly defined structured relationships. Our work differs from previous studies because we focus on objects in the Web of Data where the relationships between objects is well-defined. The subject of diversity received attention at a recent SIGIR workshop [20] on the topic. The workshop identified two classes of diversity, *extrinsic diversity* and *intrinsic diversity*. Extrinsic diversity models uncertainty about the information need due to query ambiguity (e.g. pumps). Intrinsic diversity focuses on avoiding redundancy by presenting novel and useful results to a well defined need. The problem of coreferent objects is specific form of intrinsic diversity for structured object retrieval.

Recently developed are "diversity aware" retrieval models that combine relevance scores with inter-document similarity for retrieval over unstructured documents. An important early work is that of Carbonell and Goldstein [5] who define Maximal Marginal Relevance (MMR). MMR combines relevance and novelty by ranking documents according to both their similarity to the query and their dissimilarity to other documents. They performed a small scale evaluation on 42 queries and used content based features to define similarity. We apply a similar approach to retrieval over structured objects and explicitly model the object coreference relationship. Clarke *et al.* [8] study diversification of results for Question Answering. They develop α-nDCG which models documents containing information nuggets and relevance as a function of those nuggets. The issue of coreference does not conceptually fit well with the 'nugget' based approach for unstructured documents.

Bernstein and Zobel measure the impact of syntactically redundant documents on the TREC GOV1 and GOV2 collections [3]. As our results show, although some coreferent documents are duplicates, there is a significant amount of non-trivial object redundancy in Web of Data collections. For web search, a number of approaches have recently been developed to address minimizing risk by diversifying search results [26] [24] [21]. These studies focus on exploiting topical and host-based correlation between documents. In our work we instead focus on the structured coreference relationships between documents.

There have also been attempts to develop evaluation methods for queries requiring extrinsic diversity. These include 'Intent Aware' versions of normalized discounted cumulative gain (NDCG), mean reciprocal rank (MRR), and mean average precision (MAP) [1]. In our study most queries are well defined and do not require extrinsic diversification. We therefore utilize the standard non-diversity aware evaluation measures.

Vee *et al.* [23] demonstrate methods for efficiently computing diverse query results when querying structured data in the context of online shopping. However, they do not evaluate the relevance of the returned objects.

3.3 Object Coreference

Coreference is a common thread across many communities and is referred to as: entity matching, entity disambiguation, cross-document coreference, duplicate record detection, and record linkage. These terms all describe the process for determining whether two records model unique entities. For a survey of various approaches to the problem we refer the interested reader to the recent survey on duplicate detection by Elmagarmid *et al.*[9].

In the database community Benjelloun *et al.* develop a generic framework for merging entities. They demonstrate their algorithm on a collection of 3000 iPod related objects from Yahoo! Shopping and 15,000 hotel records. For efficiency, they perform blocking to limit the number of pairwise comparisons. Nie *et al.* [15] perform entity disambiguation on author objects extracted from the web. In the Semantic Web community Hogan, Harth, and Decker [11] address the problem of object consolidation to merge identifiers of objects across data sources. They perform global object consolidation across a large collection of RDF data where consolidation is performed mostly on Person instances from the FOAF (Friend-of-a-Friend) ontology. There was little overall redundancy. In contrast, for the local business objects extracted from the web we find that there is a significant level of redundancy in returned object results. In addition, all of these works perform global coreference. Our work performs coreference resolution on the scope of retrieved object results in response to a query.

Bhattacharya and Getoor [4] perform query time entity resolution over 'unclean' databases. They describe an 'expand and resolve' strategy for collective resolution. Similarly, we perform object coreference over results returned in response to a ranked keyword query. However, they use structured queries without relevance ranking. Our work differs because we study the impact of coreference on the relevance of returned objects and the interaction between these aspects.

4. COREFERENCE AWARE RETRIEVAL

The problems of object coreference and object retrieval are usually modeled as independent tasks. By considering these tasks together, our goal is to improve the experience for users of object retrieval systems. We now provide an overview of this process.

First, retrieval is first performed over the underlying unclean object collection. Next, coreference classification is performed on the objects retrieved, creating clusters of coreferent objects. Optionally, at this point the clusters may be reranked. Finally, a representative object from each cluster is selected or created by merging objects.

We now examine some of the underlying issues that this process presents. We first discuss underlying indepedence assumptions between objects during retrieval. Next, we explore the impact of coreference error on effectiveness. Finally, we outline additional steps that are necessary beyond the traditional evaluation processes needed to perform coreference aware evaluation for object retrieval.

4.1 Text Retrieval

In conventional text retrieval, a fundamental assumption is that document relevance is independent from other retrieved documents. The probability ranking principle (PRP) states that:

If an IR system's response to each query is a ranking of documents in order of decreasing probability of relevance, the overall effectiveness of the system to its user will be maximized. [22]

However, this is problematic when performing retrieval over *unclean* object data-sets that contain many objects that represent the same real world entity. The effectiveness of a system depends on both the relevance of retrieved objects as well as the number of unique entities presented.

4.2 Object Retrieval

Because of the well-defined coreference relationship between objects, we can model the novelty of a retrieved object in a ranked list. For an object O_k retrieved at position k in a result set we define novelty with respect to the previous retrieved results as follows:

$$novelty(O_k) = \begin{cases} 1 & O_k \text{ is not coref. w/ } O_1, \ldots, O_{k-1} \\ 0 & \text{Otherwise} \end{cases}$$

In other words, only the first retrieved object of a coreference cluster has utility for the user. Subsequent occurrences of coreferent objects do not provide additional information. We must then define a measure that captures this property of an object result set.

We borrow from the data integration community and define the *conciseness* for a retrieved object result set, R. We define the conciseness of R as:

$$conciseness(R) = \frac{NumUniqueObjects \in R}{|R|} \quad (8)$$

An object retrieval system should rank documents in decreasing probability of relevance, $p(Rel|D)$, combined with decreasing probability that the object is coreferent with a previously retrieved document, $p(O_k = unique|O_1, \ldots, O_{k-1})$.

4.3 Coreference Errors

In this section, we examine the impact of coreference error on retrieval effectiveness when the top ranked object is selected as the cluster representative (the other coreferent objects are removed from the final results R).

4.3.1 False Negatives

For a false negative coreference error, an object is classified as non-coreferent when in truth the objects are coreferent. The result of the error is that a redundant object is included in R, lowering the conciseness of the returned results. In this case, whether or not the result was relevant does not matter because coreferent objects of previously retrieved results are redundant and provide no additional benefit.

4.3.2 False Positives

For the false positive case, the object is incorrectly identified as coreferent. The impact on retrieval depends on whether or not the result is relevant. If the object is relevant, then retrieval effectiveness decreases because the relevant object is incorrectly removed from the final result set. In contrast, if the object is non-relevant then removing it does not decrease the retrieval effectiveness. In fact, there is potential for effectiveness to improve because removing a non-relevant object could allow lower-ranked relevant results to be moved higher in the ranked list. Counterintuitively, this means that queries with coreference errors can outperform queries with perfect coreference! The exact impact on effectiveness depends on the number and position of relevant and non-relevant objects incorrectly clustered.

4.4 Utilizing Coreference

Coreference information can also be leveraged during retrieval in other ways. In this section we discuss two possibilities: data fusion and popularity priors.

Data Fusion. In the above formulation all coreferent objects are assumed to be equally reliable and contain identical information. In practice, the objects have different values for their properties and come from sources of varying reliability. In fusion, coreference objects O_c are combined into a single new result in R, O_n. Various data fusion methods have been studied in other previous work [9]. The resulting object can be used to rerank results and possibly display to the users.

Popularity priors. The coreference information can also be used as a feature to indicate object popularity. The correct approach to leveraging coreference depends on the nature of the objects being retrieved, the confidence in coreference information, and the retrieval domain.

For the experiments in Section 5 we do not perform reranking and use the top ranked object as the cluster representative. Exploring the above options is an area for future work.

4.5 Evaluation

To perform coreference aware retrieval evaluation, an additional level of judgments beyond relevance is necessary to determine whether retrieved objects are coreferent with one another. The result is that coreference aware evaluation is significantly more expensive and time consuming than evaluating only topical relevance. In addition to relevance judgments, this evaluation also requires a coreference judgment be made for each result to all previously retrieved objects in R.

In traditional IR evaluation the runs from different systems are pooled and individual result order is ignored. For coreference, the lack of ordering after pooling means that all combinations of documents need to be evaluated. Because the coreference relationship is symmetric, the number of comparisons is defined as the number of unordered pairs of documents: $N \cdot (N-1)/2$. For example, given a query with where $|R| = 10$ the result is 45 coreference judgments are needed.

To reduce the number of judgments needed we utilize several properties. The first is based on transitivity of coreference. If $coref(A,B) = true$ and $coref(B,C) = true$ then this implies $coref(A,C) = true$. We can use this in an online method to reduce the number of positive pairs judged by 1/3. No reduction can be made when the objects are not all coreferent.

A follow-up to this would build on the work of Carterette *et al.* and only compare pairs of objects that could significantly impact the retrieval results enough to change comparative effectiveness of the retrieval algorithms being evaluated.

5. EXPERIMENTS

In this section we describe the results of performing keyword search over a collection of local business objects crawled from the web. We first describe the experimental setup including the query selection process and details on the web object collection. Next, we discuss the evaluation process including relevance assessment and coreference judgments.

We evaluate the object retrieval systems using the Adhoc Object Retrieval (AOR) methodology [19]. Next, we contrast the AOR effectiveness results with an evaluation that is coreference aware. Finally, we show the impact of coreference aware retrieval on these systems.

5.1 Local Object Queries

To evaluate the effectiveness of retrieval we identified a sample of object queries with local intent from the Yahoo! Search query log. Each query was first manually classified as to whether it had local intent. We define queries with local intent as follows:

A query where the goal appears to be an interaction or transaction in a specific geographical location.

Query	Class
morristown west high school	entity
Troy Sports Center	entity
swallows inn	entity
syracuse SPCA	entity
the addison park aberdeen nj	entity
oakland flea market	type
traverse city mi hotel	type
co pug rescue	type
san diego recording studio	type
things to do in toledo ohio	other
map of springfield	other
brewton alabama zip code	attribute

Table 2: Examples of local object queries

AOR class	Count
Entity	659
Type	104
Attribute	2
Relationship	0
Other	11

Table 3: Local queries by AOR class

This definition includes queries which explicitly or implicitly refer to local entities such as business, schools, hospitals, etc. The queries were manually classified by looking at the query keywords and the results returned by a web search engine. We judged results from the *Yahoo! Search Query Log Tiny Sample v1.0* dataset provided as part of the Yahoo! WebScope[3] program. This query set contains 4497 queries sampled randomly from queries submitted at least three times to the Yahoo! US search engine in January, 2009. The log contained 538 queries with implicit and explicit local intent. Because this query set contained fewer local queries than desired, the classification procedure was repeated for another random sample query set containing 7303 queries from Yahoo! Search US query logs from Q3 of 2009. From this set we included 198 queries with explicit local intent.

The local queries were then manually categorized according to the AOR taxonomy described in Section 2.1. The AOR query class breakdown for these queries is shown in Table 3. One finding is that our sample contains a smaller fraction of *Other* and *Relationship* queries than reported from a study of general web query logs [19]. We attribute this to the fact that the local domain is narrower than general web search and more likely to contain references to entities.

From the manually classified local queries we selected a subset to use for testing. Six queries relate to local job intent were filtered out. Random sampling was performed to produce 55 queries from the entity and type query classes for a total of 110 queries. The Type class was oversampled because coreference is particularly important for these queries where users are seeking multiple objects. These are likely to be affected by redundancy in the object collection.

We now describe how the keyword queries were transformed for retrieval. The queries were lowercased and punctuation removed. The queries were spell corrected using the Yahoo! search spelling corrector. A small domain-specific list of stop-words were removed: locator, location, locations, and stores. A gazetteer of state abbreviation names was used to replace full state names to their abbreviations. This is important because local business objects typically contain mailing addresses that utilize the abbreviated form. The queries were not stemmed, but plural terms were depluralized based on the query context [17].

[3]http://webscope.sandbox.yahoo.com/

	Count
Resources (Objects)	106,192,950
Unique Terms	110,564,059
Total terms	1,533,269,855

Table 4: vCard Object Collection Statistics

	Relevant
All	1930
De-duplicated	865
Unique	546

Table 5: Number of relevant objects before and after clustering based on coreference.

5.2 Documents: Local Business Objects

For our experiments, we used local business objects extracted from web pages by Yahoo!'s web search indexing pipeline. The majority of this data is extracted from webpages that use the hCard[4] microformat, an encoding of vCard address book data in HTML pages. A smaller part of the data comes RDFa such as Google's Rich Snippets[5] markup or extracted using proprietary Information Extraction techniques.

The collection was indexed using the Indri[6] search engine. Indri natively supports indexing and retrieval over fielded documents using extents. The data objects were converted to fielded documents and indexed using the procedure described in Section 2.2. No stop-words were removed and stemming was not applied.

As shown in Table 4, the collection contains a sizable 106 million local business objects. The virtual business cards are concise with an average length of 14.4 tokens per object.

5.3 Evaluation Process

The normalized queries were executed using the three retrieval methods described in Section 2.2. The top 20 resources for each query were pooled. This resulted in 4964 unique returned resources to evaluate for relevance. The complete RDF representation of each query-object pair was shown to a human judge and evaluated for relevance. Relevance judgments were made on the four point scale described in Section 2.2. These were converted to binary relevance values where a value of 2 or 3 is considered to be relevant. Six queries were skipped by the human annotator because their intent is unclear. The final query set consists of 104 queries; 54 entity queries and 50 type queries. After relevance assessment, the results were then evaluated for coreference.

To measure coreference, the evaluation procedure described

[4]http://microformats.org/wiki/hcard
[5]http://www.google.com/support/webmasters/bin/answer.py?answer=99170
[6]http://www.lemurproject.org/indri/

	Relevant	MAP	nDCG@15	MRR	P5	P10	P20
BM25	1300	42.55	49.50	59.74	41.73	35.38	29.28
QL	1494	51.19†	55.39†	63.72†	44.81	39.71†	33.37†
SD	1495	54.80†	60.40†	69.83†	50.96†	43.85†	35.38†

Table 7: Object retrieval on all 104 queries. †indicates significance over BM25 at p < .05

True Positive	683
True Negative	8381
False Positive	159
False Negative	155
Accuracy	96.65%

Table 6: SVM coreference evaluation

in Section 4.5 was followed. Fully evaluating coreference on the set of pooled objects proved infeasible in practice. There are on average 47.7 unique objects per query and evaluating all pairs would result in over one hundred thousand pairs to annotate. In order to evaluate the difference between coreference aware and traditional evaluation, we fully evaluated all pairs of relevant documents for a query. The presence of redundant non-relevant results is less critical to retrieval effectiveness. Therefore, to reduce annotator effort we did not judge coreference on non-relevant documents.

To evaluate the coreference of the retrieved objects, we performed coreference judgments on the complete relevant set for each query. Across all queries there are 915 unique relevant results, creating 9378 pairs of objects to evaluate. Each pair of objects with their full RDF representation was shown to an annotator who manually evaluated whether or not they were coreferent.

There are 838 pairs of coreferent objects, 8.94% of the total number of pairs. The pairs are used to induce a clustering of coreferent results. The impact of this on the number of relevant objects is shown in Table 5. The number of relevant objects is reduced by 71.7% from all objects and 36.9% from the de-duplicated relevant results. This indicates that there is a significant degree of non-trivial object coreference that could significantly impact the diversity of retrieved results. We now explore the impact of this redundancy on the retrieval process.

5.4 Coreference Classification

In order to identify coreferent objects at retrieval time we trained a support vector machine (SVM) classifier using LIBSVM[7]. The classifier takes as an input a vector that represents the similarity between two objects using a set of individual features, and produces a binary class label that indicates whether the two objects are coreferent or not. Each one of the features in the input vector corresponds to the output of a similarity function over pairs of attributes corresponding to the same property, this is, their *field* similarity. We compute three similarity functions for the attributes in each pair: Levenshtein distance, Jaccard distance over 3-grams and the exact match of numerical fields (such as telephone numbers or zip codes). The final feature vector contains three similarity values for each matching pair of properties. We note that these similarity distances are used in a plethora of applications from database de-duplication and record linkage but also on spell checking and classification. The combination of these metrics with the classifier sufficed to identify coreferent objects.

We mapped the input data $\mathbf{x_i}$ into a higher dimensional space using a radial basis kernel of the form $K(\mathbf{x}, \mathbf{x_i}) = exp(-\gamma||\mathbf{x} - \mathbf{x_i}||^2)$, where γ is a parameter. This kernel is able to handle the case when the relation between class labels and attributes is not linear. SVMs also contain a tunable penalty parameter $C > 0$ that introduces the tolerance of the model upon misclassified instances. Given that both γ and C affect the performance of the SVMs, we learn them from the training data using 10-fold cross validation. Our classification set consists of 9378 pairs of objects which have been manually classified as coreferent or distinct.

The overall results are shown in Table 6, where the accuracy averaged over the 10 folds is higher than 95%. The classifier is able to distinguish coreferent objects using with very high precision and recall. However, in our experiments we will show that the false positive errors are particularly problematic when we remove coreferent objects. Before examining coreference aware retrieval, we first evaluate retrieval using traditional non-coreference aware evaluation.

5.5 Coreference Based Diversification

In this section we measure the object retrieval effectiveness of three widely used object retrieval models: BM25, Query Likelihood (QL), and the Sequential Dependency model (SD) over all objects. The results returned include coreferent pairs of objects. For each method, the top 100 results are retrieved for each of the 104 object queries. We use cross-validation to tune the BM25 b parameter and the μ Dirichlet priors smoothing parameter for QL and SD. We set the SD parameters using the settings in [12], which were shown to be robust to tuning. The b and μ parameters control the influence of document length normalization in the final scores. It is worth noting that the objects we are dealing with are short the parameters have a considerable influence in the final performance of all three methods. Regarding parameter stability, both QL and SD tuned parameters using the folds are close to the over-fitted optimum using the 104 queries ($\mu = 100$). The tuned b for the BM25 runs vary between the folds, although their final performance is less affected by a particular choice of b.

The 2-fold cross-validated results are shown in Table 7. Significance testing is done using the sign test and we report significance at $p < 0.05$. The results show that keyword document retrieval methods perform very well on vCard objects. In particular, the SD model strongly outperforms both the BM25 and QL models, which is consistent with previous findings [12] for document retrieval. The results are promising; however, they do not provide a full and accurate representation of utility for users. The evaluation so far does not consider the impact of redundancy in the search results due to coreferent objects.

[7]http://www.csie.ntu.edu.tw/~cjlin/libsvm/

	RelRet	MAP	nDCG@15	P5	P10	ΔRelRet	ΔMAP	ΔnDCG@15	ΔP5	ΔP10
BM25	1300	42.55	49.50	41.73	35.38					
BM25-util	340	15.84	28.14	22.69	14.33	-73.85%	-62.77%	-43.15%	-45.63%	-59.50%
QL	1494	51.19	55.39	44.81	39.71					
QL-util	393	18.22	30.61	24.04	15.96	-73.69%	-64.41%	-44.74%	-46.35%	-59.81%
SD	1495	54.80	60.40	50.96	43.85					
SD-util	416	20.57	33.44	26.15	17.50	-72.17%	-62.46%	-44.64%	-48.69%	-60.09%

Table 8: Coreference Aware Evaluation

	MAP	P5	P10	Δmap	ΔP5	ΔP10
BM25	33.82	37.78	33.52			
BM25-util	9.98	22.59	15.37	-70.49%	-40.21%	-54.15%
QL	38.33	38.52	36.85			
QL-util	9.37	23.33	16.67	-75.55%	-39.43%	-54.76%
SD	42.80	47.78	44.44			
SD-util	12.68	26.30	19.63	-70.37%	-44.96%	-55.83%

Table 9: Coreference aware evaluation restricted to the 50 type queries

5.6 Baseline Object Retrieval

We now address the problem of redundancy in object results and demonstrate that it is of critical consideration when evaluating retrieval effectiveness. As discussed in Section 4.2, for this evaluation we assume that coreferent objects provide no additional value over previous objects in the ranked list. Consequently, for coreference aware evaluation only the first occurrence of a unique object is counted as relevant, all subsequent retrieved occurrences are counted as non-relevant. Given that we are measuring the number of *useful* relevant objects, we denote this approach as *util*. The results for this handling of coreferent documents is shown in Table 8, we omit MRR from the figures because the first relevant document is unchanged. The table shows that the number of relevant results retrieved is reduced by more than 70% across all methods. There is a similar effect on all retrieval models independent of their effectiveness. Although the ordering of the systems is unchanged, the differences between the retrieval models is greatly reduced.

Next, we examine the impact of coreference on Type queries specifically (those in which the goal is to find objects of a particular type). The results for only Type queries are shown in Table 9. The baseline retrieval results for the Type queries is lower than the effectiveness of all queries. This indicates that they are more difficult queries. We also observe that the change in MAP is greater than for all queries. The Type queries have on average almost twice the number of relevant objects than for Entity. There is therefore greater opportunity to identify and replace coreferent documents in these queries. The reduction in precision scores is comparable to the overall query set, indicating that the coreferent documents being removed are below result ten.

Overall, the results of coreference aware evaluation show that the impact of coreferent documents on the retrieval effectiveness score is very significant. The effectiveness of the retrieval models id reduced by more than half for the number of returned relevant documents, MAP, and P10. This indicates that there is significant possibility for improvement improvements using coreference aware retrieval.

5.7 Coreference Aware Evaluation

In this section we study the effect of using coreference information to diversify the object results. We first retrieve 100 results per query. To introduce diversity, we test several methods to identify and remove coreferent objects from the results. For diversification we utilize the SVM coreference classifier described in Section 5.4. We also utilize the gold standard annotations of relevant objects.

The result of removing coreferent documents is shown in Table 10. The *ret* column shows the percentage of objects removed by coreference. It shows that between 27% and 33% of the overall number of objects are removed. This represents a substantial reduction in the redundancy of the results. The greater diversity is reflected in improved retrieval effectiveness. We observe that there is a trend for better retrieval models to see greater improvement over the non-diversified results. These models are more likely to replace a coreferent object with one that is relevant. The greatest improvements are the precision scores, P5 and P10. For a web search engine these results are compelling because they represent the first page of objects a user is shown.

Table 10 shows that approximating coreference improves retrieval over the baseline, but is significantly outperformed by using the gold standard judgments on only the relevant documents. In particular, the *relret* column indicates that the SVM is making false positive errors on relevant documents, causing them to be incorrectly removed from the results. The number of incorrectly removed relevant documents is consistent across all retrieval methods. For BM25, 29 objects are removed, for QL 30 objects, and 34 for Sequential Dependency. For a search engine, these mistakes are very costly. However, despite removing some relevant documents, more non-relevant coreferent documents are removed, resulting in improved retrieval effectiveness by moving relevant documents higher in the results.

We now discuss the impact of SVM classifier errors on retrieval in more detail and improve the effectiveness by leveraging the posterior probability estimates. As previously shown, despite the 96.55% accuracy of the SVM coreference classifier, the errors hurt retrieval. In particular, the 159 false positive mistakes result in the incorrect removal of approximately 8% of the relevant results. Therefore, a classifier

	Ret	RelRet	MAP	nDCG@15	P5	P10	ΔRet	ΔRelRet	ΔMAP	ΔnDCG@15	ΔP5	ΔP10
BM25	10400	340	15.84	28.14	22.69	14.33						
BM25-SVM	7562	311	16.72	30.43	26.15	17.69	-27.29%	-8.53%	5.56%	8.14%	15.25%	23.45%
BM25-gt	7591	340	17.48	31.74	27.31	19.23	-27.01%	0.00%	10.35%	12.79%	20.36%	34.19%
QL	10400	393	18.22	30.61	24.04	15.96						
QL-SVM	7386	363	19.38	33.49	29.62	19.81	-28.98%	-7.63%	6.37%	9.41%	23.21%	24.12%
QL-gt	7417	393	20.25	34.66	30.58	21.25	-28.68%	0.00%	11.14%	13.23%	27.20%	33.15%
SD	10400	416	20.57	33.44	26.15	17.50						
SD-SVM	6982	382	22.18	37.39	34.04	22.69	-32.87%	-8.17%	7.83%	11.81%	30.17%	29.66%
SD-gt	7017	416	22.99	38.54	35.00	23.94	-32.53%	0.00%	11.76%	15.25%	33.84%	36.80%

Table 10: Impact of diversifying object results by removing redundant objects. The baselines are coreference aware evaluation without removal. The SVM variants approximates coreference on relevant objects and removes them, the gt removes coreferent objects using the gold standard judgments.

	Ret	Rel Ret	MAP	nDCG@15	P5	P10
BM25-SVM	7562	311	16.72	26.90	26.15	17.69
BM25-SVMpp	7220	364	17.54†	28.06†	26.73	19.23
QL-SVM	7386	363	19.38	30.11	29.62	19.81
QL-SVMpp	6999	431	20.14†	31.13†	30.38	21.92
SD-SVM	6982	382	22.18	32.89	34.04	22.69
SD-SVMpp	6627	448	22.90†	33.93†	35.19	24.33

Table 11: Diversifying object results using an SVM leveraging posterior probability estimates. The SVM variants approximates coreference on relevant objects and removes them, the SVMpp modifies the SVM output using the posterior probability estimates. †indicates significance over SVM at $p < .05$

with fewer false positives could potentially be more effective. We utilize Platt's [18] sigmoid probabilistic outputs as an estimate of posterior probability of the SVM classifier. The errors analysis showed that a significant number of false positive cases were near the SVM threshold. We lowered the classification threshold from .75 to .53. The threshold value of 0.53 was selected based on the distribution of data points to reduce the number of false positive labels. The number of data points below the .53 threshold value increases significantly and a lower value would result in a high number of documents not being labeled correctly as coreferent.

The results comparing the baseline SVM coreference with one leveraging the posterior probabilities is shown in Table 11. The number of false positives is reduced and the number of false negatives is increased. The net effect on retrieval is a small effectiveness improvement across all retrieval methods. The MAP and NDCG improvements are statistically significant.

Performing coreference as a separate step with the SVM creates problems when used in retrieval. The loss function of the SVM does not model the impact of coreference. For example, it does not model position of the objects being considered or the cost of a mistake on retrieval score. Returning a redundant result early in the list is much more costly than returning one later in the list. Considering these two tasks separately is problematic and this study motivates the need to model them jointly. This is analogous to the joint modeling of coreference with other NLP tasks, which has recently shown significant gains [25].

Overall, these experiments demonstrate significant improvement in retrieval effectiveness using coreference to diversify results. The improvements are particularly notable in the precision of the top 5 and top 10 results, which are of particular compelling for keyword retrieval in web search. We show that false positive errors are particularly costly and can be reduced by using the classifier posterior probabilities.

6. CONCLUSIONS

Large Web of Data collections hold the promise to offer significant recall improvements over vertical search engines that leverage only a narrow amount of clean data. In this paper, we considered the problem of performing keyword retrieval over a collection of objects extracted from the Web of Data. We are the first to address the problem of coreference in this setting and to consider the impact in the context of object retrieval. We performed large-scale experiments on a collection of over 100 million real web business objects and local queries from a Web search engine. Our results on a representative sample of state-of-the-art retrieval models show that naive object retrieval systems overestimate their effectiveness by more than 50% when they do not handle coreference. In our experiments, we show retrieval effectiveness improves significantly when redundant objects are removed. The retrieval results improve by 20-40% for precision at 5 and 10. This change reflects a significant improvement in the search experience for users of object retrieval systems.

Coreference aware retrieval approaches significantly outperform traditional IR systems by increasing the diversity of search results. The errors made by state-of-the-art coreference systems have a significant effect on retrieval and motivates further work considering the tasks jointly. In future work, we hope to generalize and verify that these models work across a variety of heterogenous object domains, i.e. that the problem can be addressed in a horizontal fashion. In our experiments we focus on removing redundant coreferent objects. However, other ways of handling coreference, including reranking and data fusion should be considered in the future. Furthermore, relationships other than coreference could be incorporated into our models, and handled in retrieval such as subsumption of one object result by another. For example, a hotel and related spa and restaurant are distinct but closely related entities.

In document retrieval on the Web, the removal of syntactically identical and very similar webpages is vital. For object retrieval, the same challenge remains for identifying coreference, but with multiple ways of improving the experience for search users.

7. ACKNOWLEDGMENTS

This work is partially supported by the EU Large Scale Integrated Project LivingKnowledge (contract no. 231126).

8. REFERENCES

[1] R. Agrawal, S. Gollapudi, A. Halverson, and S. Ieong. Diversifying search results. In *WSDM '09*, pages 5–14, New York, NY, USA, 2009. ACM.

[2] S. Agrawal, K. Chakrabarti, S. Chaudhuri, V. Ganti, A. C. Konig, and D. Xin. Exploiting web search engines to search structured databases. In *WWW '09*, pages 501–510, New York, NY, USA, 2009. ACM.

[3] Y. Bernstein and J. Zobel. Redundant documents and search effectiveness. In *CIKM '05*, pages 736–743, New York, NY, USA, 2005. ACM.

[4] I. Bhattacharya and L. Getoor. Query-time entity resolution. In *SIGKDD '06*, 2006.

[5] J. Carbonell and J. Goldstein. The use of mmr, diversity-based reranking for reordering documents and producing summaries. In *SIGIR '98*, pages 335–336, New York, NY, USA, 1998. ACM.

[6] A. Carlson, J. Betteridge, R. C. Wang, E. R. Hruschka, Jr., and T. M. Mitchell. Coupled semi-supervised learning for information extraction. In *WSDM '10*, pages 101–110, New York, NY, USA, 2010. ACM.

[7] Y. Chen, W. Wang, Z. Liu, and X. Lin. Keyword search on structured and semi-structured data. In *SIGMOD '09*, pages 1005–1010, New York, NY, USA, 2009. ACM.

[8] C. L. A. Clarke, M. Kolla, G. V. Cormack, O. Vechtomova, A. Ashkan, S. Büttcher, and I. MacKinnon. Novelty and diversity in information retrieval evaluation. In *SIGIR '08*, pages 659–666, New York, NY, USA, 2008. ACM.

[9] A. K. Elmagarmid, P. G. Ipeirotis, Vassilios, S. Verykios, A. K. Elmagarmid, P. G. Ipeirotis, V. S. Verykios, D. Ahmed, K. Elmagarmid, P. G. Ipeirotis, Vassilios, and S. Verykios. Duplicate record detection: A survey. *Transactions on Knowledge and Data Engineering*.

[10] H. Halpin, D. M. Herzig, P. Mika, R. Blanco, J. Pound, H. S. Thompson, and D. T. Tran. Evaluating Ad-Hoc Object Retrieval. In *Int. Workshop on Evaluation of Semantic Technologies (IWEST 2010), ISWC*, 2010.

[11] A. Hogan. Performing object consolidation on the semantic web data graph. In *In Proceedings of 1st I3: Identity, Identifiers, Identification Workshop*, 2007.

[12] D. Metzler and W. B. Croft. A markov random field model for term dependencies. In *SIGIR '05*, pages 472–479, New York, NY, USA, 2005. ACM.

[13] P. Mika. Anatomy of a searchmonkey. *Nodalities Magazine*, 2008.

[14] P. Mika, E. Meij, and H. Zaragoza. Investigating the semantic gap through query log analysis. In *ISWC '09*, pages 441–455, Berlin, Heidelberg, 2009. Springer-Verlag.

[15] Z. Nie, J.-R. Wen, and W.-Y. Ma. Object-level vertical search. In *CIDR*, pages 235–246, 2007.

[16] S. Paparizos, A. Ntoulas, J. Shafer, and R. Agrawal. Answering web queries using structured data sources. In *SIGMOD '09*, pages 1127–1130, New York, NY, USA, 2009. ACM.

[17] F. Peng, N. Ahmed, X. Li, and Y. Lu. Context sensitive stemming for web search. In *SIGIR '07*, pages 639–646, New York, NY, USA, 2007. ACM.

[18] J. C. Platt. Probabilistic outputs for support vector machines and comparisons to regularized likelihood methods. In *ADVANCES IN LARGE MARGIN CLASSIFIERS*, pages 61–74. MIT Press, 1999.

[19] J. Pound, P. Mika, and H. Zaragoza. Ad-hoc object retrieval in the web of data. In *WWW '10*, pages 771–780, New York, NY, USA, 2010. ACM.

[20] F. Radlinski, P. N. Bennett, B. Carterette, and T. Joachims. Redundancy, diversity and interdependent document relevance. *SIGIR Forum*, 43(2):46–52, 2009.

[21] D. Rafiei, K. Bharat, and A. Shukla. Diversifying web search results. In *WWW '10*, pages 781–790, New York, NY, USA, 2010. ACM.

[22] Robertson, S. E. The Probability Ranking Principle in IR. *Journal of Documentation*, 33(4):294–304, 1977.

[23] E. Vee, U. Srivastava, J. Shanmugasundaram, P. Bhat, and S. A. Yahia. Efficient computation of diverse query results. In *ICDE '08*, pages 228–236, Washington, DC, USA, 2008. IEEE Computer Society.

[24] J. Wang and J. Zhu. Portfolio theory of information retrieval. In *SIGIR '09*, pages 115–122, New York, NY, USA, 2009. ACM.

[25] M. L. Wick, K. Rohanimanesh, K. Schultz, and A. McCallum. A unified approach for schema matching, coreference and canonicalization. In *Proceeding of the 14th ACM SIGKDD international conference on Knowledge discovery and data mining*, KDD '08, pages 722–730, New York, NY, USA, 2008. ACM.

[26] J. Zhu, J. Wang, I. J. Cox, and M. J. Taylor. Risky business: modeling and exploiting uncertainty in information retrieval. In *SIGIR '09*, pages 99–106, New York, NY, USA, 2009. ACM.

Tag Clouds Revisited

Dimitrios Skoutas
L3S Research Center
Hanover, Germany
skoutas@L3S.de

Mohammad Alrifai
L3S Research Center
Hanover, Germany
alrifai@L3S.de

ABSTRACT

Tagging has become a very common feature in Web 2.0 applications, providing a simple and effective way for users to freely annotate resources to facilitate their discovery and management. Subsequently, tag clouds have become popular as a summarized representation of a collection of tagged resources. A tag cloud is typically a visualization of the top-k most frequent tags in the underlying collection. In this paper, we revisit tag clouds, to examine whether frequency is the most suitable criterion for tag ranking. We propose alternative tag ranking strategies, based on methods for random walk on graphs, diversification, and rank aggregation. To enable the comparison of different tag selection and ranking methods, we propose a set of evaluation metrics that consider the use of tag clouds for search, navigation and recommendations. We apply these tag ranking methods and evaluation metrics to empirically compare alternative tag clouds in a dataset obtained from Flickr, comprising 488,112 tagged photos organized in 451 groups, and 112,514 distinct tags.

Categories and Subject Descriptors

H.3 [**Information Storage and Retrieval**]: Information Search and Retrieval; H.5.1 [**Information Interfaces and Presentation**]: Multimedia Information Systems

General Terms

Algorithms, Measurement

Keywords

Web 2.0, Tagging, Web Resources

1. INTRODUCTION

With the abundance of content on the Web, especially with the rapidly increasing amount of user generated content in Web 2.0, retrieving and managing information remains a significant and challenging problem. Although content-based retrieval usually performs sufficiently well for text, such as documents or Web pages, the same does not hold for other types of content. For example, for multimedia resources or bookmarks, it has become clear that exploiting metadata is often crucial for achieving good performance. However, although the Semantic Web aims at annotating Web resources to facilitate their search and management, attempts in this direction are hindered by the significant effort required to create and maintain formal annotations, as well as the ontologies on which they rely upon. In contrast, *tagging* has emerged as a very simple, easy and effective solution for annotations. Most Web 2.0 applications allow users to tag resources created by themselves or others, and exploit these tags to improve search, navigation and recommendations [21].

The fact that tagging is such an easy and fast process that any user can perform has been the main driving factor for its widespread adoption by most Social Web applications, such as Flickr, Delicious, Technorati, Facebook or Last.fm. However, this also makes the results of the tagging process very noisy. To address this problem, several approaches have proposed methods for extracting semantics from tags or computing the relevance of a tag to a resource in order to improve or recommend the assignment of tags to resources (e.g. [14, 12, 18, 23, 13, 7]). These approaches focus on (re-)ranking or suggesting tags for an *individual* resource, based on its content (e.g., visual features of an image), as well as the content and tags of other similar resources.

In this paper, we consider instead the problem of selecting and ranking tags to describe *groups* of tagged resources. For example, in Flickr or Facebook, users can create albums to organize their photos; similarly, in Last.fm, they can create playlists containing tracks from similar artists or for specific occasions. Such item collections can become arbitrarily large over time. Relying on a title or a short text to describe the group contents is not sufficient and may easily become outdated or reflect only the owner's perspective. On the other hand, listing all the contents is impractical for large collections, while selecting only a few representatives to display may not be straightforward. When dealing with collections of tagged resources, tag clouds have become a common way for describing the group contents and allowing navigation.

The goal of a *tag cloud* is to display the most relevant and important tags for the items in a group. In practice, tag clouds typically display the most frequently occurring tags, since this is both intuitive and easy to compute. Figure 1

CIKM'11, October 24–28, 2011, Glasgow, Scotland, UK.

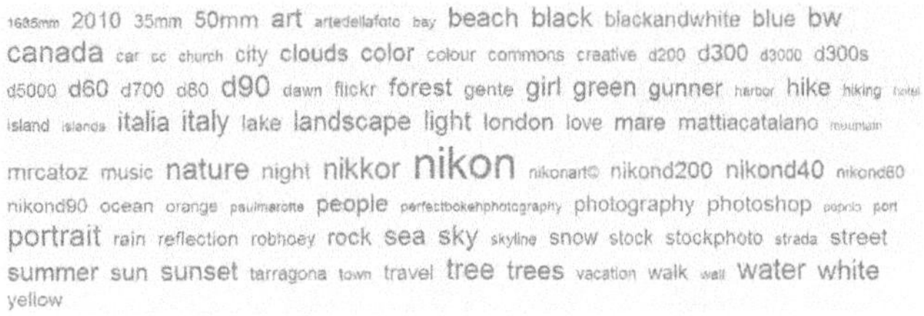

Figure 1: Example of a tag cloud from Flickr.

shows an example of a tag cloud displayed by Flickr for a group of photos with title "This is nikon art".

In this paper, we deal with the problem of *selecting and ranking tags for tag clouds*, addressing two main questions: (a) how effective is the strategy of ranking tags in item collections based on their frequency, and (b) are there any better strategies for this task? To address these questions, we propose and examine alternative methods to select and rank tags in groups of tagged objects, and we compare these methods on a large real-world dataset containing groups of tagged photos obtained from Flickr. To compare the different methods, we measure their effectiveness in terms of a set of proposed metrics that characterize the usefulness of a tag cloud for search and navigation. Moreover, we measure their accuracy for the task of recommending groups for a tagged item, when groups are represented by different tag clouds. The results of our evaluation show that although ranking tags based on their frequency performs well in most cases, even more effective rankings can be obtained using other methods. Specifically, our contributions can be summarized as follows:

- We formalize the problem of ranking tags to represent groups of tagged objects, and we propose different ranking strategies that go beyond the simple frequency-based method.
- We propose a set of metrics to objectively and automatically evaluate the effectiveness of alternative tag clouds for a given group of objects.
- We empirically evaluate the presented tag selection and ranking methods in terms of the described evaluation methodology, using a large real-world dataset from Flickr, comprising 451 groups, 488,112 tagged photos, and 112,514 distinct tags.

The rest of the paper is organized as follows. The next section discusses related work. Section 3 introduces the basic framework and notation. In Section 4, we present different strategies for selecting and ranking tags for tag clouds. Section 5 proposes a set of evaluation metrics that allow to objectively compare different tag clouds for the tasks of search, navigation and recommendations.Section 6 presents the results of our experimental evaluation on a large collection of tagged photos and groups obtained from Flickr. Finally,Section 7 concludes the paper.

2. RELATED WORK

Due to the popularity and wide adoption of manual tagging of resources in content sharing Web sites, this area has attracted a lot of research interest. In the following, we review some of the main related research efforts, including also some related work on faceted browsing.

2.1 Tag Ranking

The most relevant work to the one presented in this paper is a recent effort described in [22], which addresses the problem of selecting tags to summarize query results. It combines frequency and diversity to increase the coverage of the query results. However, it does not consider other methods such as tag co-occurrence or rank aggregation or different variations for diversification as in this paper. In addition, it proposes a set of metrics for evaluating different tag clouds. Although some of these metrics are common to our work, such as coverage and overlap, it focuses on measures for relevance, balance and cohessiveness of results, while we are more interested in characteristics such as selectivity, navigation cost and accuracy for recommendations.

Some recent efforts have dealt with the problem of (re-) ranking the set of tags assigned to an object. [14] focuses specifically on images and computes a relevance score between an image and each tag assigned to it by performing a random walk on a graph representing tag similarities. Apart from tag co-occurrences, these similarities take into consideration the content of the photos using low-level visual features. In the same direction, [12] estimates the relevance of a tag to an image based on its occurrence or not in visually similar images. Furthermore, extracting event and place semantics from tags of photos has been investigated in [18].

In contrast, our goal is to select and rank tags for groups of objects rather than each single object. However, it is interesting to examine how the methods and metrics presented in our work can be adapted for individual resources or extended to exploit semantics and content-based similarity.

2.2 Tag Recommendations

To reduce the noise and the effort in tagging, several approaches have focused on recommending tags to users for a given resource. In [23], tag recommendation for images is formulated as a learning problem, proposing a multimodality recommendation based on both tag and visual correlation. [13] proposes a re-tagging scheme for images that maintains consistency of visual and semantic similarity between tags and images. In [2], tags are propagated along edges in a graph connecting similar documents. A graph-based ranking algorithm is proposed in [7] for personalized tag recommendation. When a user issues a tagging request, both the resource and the user are treated as queries, accounting for relevance and personalization, respectively. Then, the top ranked tags are recommended to the user.

Again, these approaches focus on recommending tags for individual objects and they rely on content-based (visual) similarity for relevance.

2.3 Visualization of Tag Clouds

In a different line of research, the impact of the visualization aspects of tag clouds on the user experience has been studied. A comparative study of several tag cloud layouts (e.g. sequential, circular and clustered layouts) has shown that they clearly affect task performance, and thus should be carefully designed [15]. Another experimental evaluation indicated that semantically clustered tag clouds can provide improvements over random layouts in specific search tasks, increasing also the attention towards tags in small fonts [20]. A method for displaying large-scale tag clouds using a topographical image has been proposed in [5].

Visualization and layout aspects are not considered in our

work. However, it is interesting to examine how the proposed tag selection and ranking algorithms can be combined with different tag cloud layouts. For example, a clustered layout might be more suitable for a tag diversification algorithm, while a sequential layout for a rank aggregation method.

2.4 Faceted Browsing

Finally, our work has many commonalities with methods for automatically selecting facets and facet-value pairs in faceted browsing interfaces, which are also used in many applications to help users navigate through large collections of resources [8]. Facets are attributes describing resources in a collection. For example, typical facets for scientific publications are *author*, *title*, *conference*, *year*, etc. Each facet may have a very large list of possible values; however, only a few facets and facet-value pairs can be displayed in a user interface. Thus, several works have focused on the problem of ranking facets and facet-value pairs, going beyond the standard frequency-based approach.

Facetedpedia [11] automatically selects and ranks facets in wikipedia, based on a user navigation model to define the cost of different facets. This is extended with a definition of similarity between facets to allow the ranking of combinations of facets. To make the navigation model manageable, some simplifying assumptions are made; for example, deselecting a previously selected facet is not allowed. A set of metrics for determining which facets constitute good "navigators" in RDF datasets is proposed in [17]. These include *predicate balance*, which compares the sizes of the result sets of different facet-value pairs, *object cardinality*, which is the number of possible values for a facet, and *predicate frequency*, which is the number of objects that have a non-null value for a given facet. To select facets that minimize the navigation cost in a database, [19] finds the minimum cost decision tree that distinguishes each tuple from other tuples based on its attributes values. This is similar, to some extent, with our metric for selectivity. Finally, personalized and interactive faceted search is studied in [9], focusing on a methodology to evaluate alternative selections of facets. A user simulation model is used to define a utility score for alternative faceted search interfaces.

Summarizing, since tag clouds and faceted browsing interfaces serve similar purposes, there are some similar ideas underlying methods, models and metrics in both categories. However, due to the different nature of facets, which are structured and have the form of attribute-value pairs, those approaches are usually not suitable or directly applicable for tag selection and ranking.

3. TAG SELECTION FRAMEWORK

Assume a set of objects $\mathcal{U}$, a set of (possibly overlapping) groups $\mathcal{G}$, and a set of tags $\mathcal{T}$. Objects are assigned to groups according to a mapping function $m_g : \mathcal{U} \times \mathcal{G} \rightarrow \{0, 1\}$. Similarly, tags are assigned to objects according to a mapping function $m_t : \mathcal{U} \times \mathcal{T} \rightarrow \{0, 1\}$.

Let $T(u)$ denote the set of tags assigned to an object u. Similarly, $U(t)$ denotes the set of objects tagged with t. Typically, the latter refers to the objects within a particular group G under consideration, but to simplify notation we omit G since it is clear from the context.

Given a group G, the set $T(G)$ of all the tags related to it is the union of the sets of tags assigned to its objects, i.e.,

$$T(G) = \bigcup_{u \in G} T(u) \quad (1)$$

This set can be arbitrarily large, depending on the size of the group and the number and variety of tags assigned to its objects. Applications need to select and visualize a few of these tags to represent a summary of the group contents. Thus, the goal is to select a subset $T_G \subseteq T(G)$ of size k (for a given, relatively small, integer k) to describe the group. In addition, the tags in T_G should be ranked, since this ranking is typically taken into consideration when visualizing a tag cloud. Therefore, we consider T_G as an ordered list of tags $\{t_1, t_2, \ldots, t_k\}$. We denote the rank of a tag t in the tag cloud T_G by $r(t)$ (with the first tag having $r(t) = 0$).

Let $f(t)$ be a scoring function that assigns to each tag t of a tag cloud T_G a utility value in the interval $[0, 1]$. We define the overall utility value of T_G as

$$F(T_G) = \frac{\sum_{t \in T_G} \alpha(r(t)) \cdot f(t)}{|T_G|} \quad (2)$$

where $\alpha()$ is a discount function that adjusts the utility of each tag according to its position in the cloud, e.g.:

$$\alpha(i) = \frac{1}{\beta \cdot i + 1} \quad (3)$$

where the parameter β determines the rate of reduction.

Given a group G and an integer k, the optimal tag cloud for G is the set T_G that is a subset of $T(G)$ with size k and maximizes the utility function F:

$$T_G = \underset{T \in 2^{T(G)} \& |T|=k}{\arg\max} \; F(T) \quad (4)$$

Therefore, the main question is how to specify the utility function f, and subsequently, to maximize it. In the following section, we propose different tag selection methods based on different approaches for defining the utility function f for the members of the tag cloud.

4. TAG SELECTION STRATEGIES

We consider different strategies for ranking tags to describe sets of tagged objects. In particular, we first start with the standard frequency-based ranking, and we examine two possible extensions. Then, we present two methods based on diversification algorithms, and finally we present a method based on an algorithm for rank aggregation.

4.1 Based on Frequency

4.1.1 *Frequency scoring*

The simplest, most straightforward and most widely used approach for selecting the contents of a tag cloud for a set of objects is to rank tags based on their frequency, i.e., the number of objects to which a tag is assigned. This is based on the assumption that, if a large number of objects in the group has been tagged with a tag t, then t has high utility for describing the contents of the group. Therefore, the utility function of a tag $t \in T(G)$ is defined in this case as

$$f(t) = \frac{|U(t)|}{|G|} labeleq : frequency \quad (5)$$

Then, the tag cloud is simply formed by selecting the top k most frequent tags. In practice, it is possible that some objects are more important or relevant for the group than others. Equation **??** can be easily extended to include a weight parameter for each object. For example, these weights could be determined based on the number of views for each item. For simplicity, we assume in this paper that all objects have equal weights.

In the following, we examine two other approaches for defining the utility function f, which can be seen as extensions of the frequency based approach. Since the frequency of a tag, as defined in Equation **??**, is used as basis for these and also for subsequent definitions of the utility function, we denote it as $fr(t, G)$ for later reference.

4.1.2 TF.IDF scoring

The first extension is to rank tags based on the same idea as *tf.idf* scoring for document retrieval. This is based on the assumption that a tag has lower utility in describing the contents of a group if it also occurs frequently in several other groups. In other words, the computation of the utility score of a tag t with respect to a group G relies not only on the contents of this particular group but also on the contents of the other groups in the collection. In particular, we can define the utility function as

$$f(t) = fr(t, G) \cdot idf(t) \tag{6}$$

where the *idf* of a tag in the collection is computed by

$$idf(t) = \log \frac{|\mathcal{G}|}{|\{G \in \mathcal{G} : t \in T(G)\}|} \tag{7}$$

The tag cloud comprises the top k tags in terms of $f(t)$.

4.1.3 Graph-based scoring

The second extension is based on the assumption that co-occurrence of tags is important. Typically, tags assigned to objects are keywords freely chosen by the users without restricting them to the use of an ontology or controlled vocabulary. This significantly facilitates the process of tagging and has contributed to its popularity and widespread adoption, but as a consequence tags may often be ambiguous or used in different ways by different users. For this reason, considering combinations of tags that occur together rather than individual tags may be more informative, since it provides context information.

To take this into consideration when constructing the tag cloud of a group G, we create a graph of the tags in $T(G)$, where an edge between two tags t_i and t_j denotes that there is an object in G tagged with both t_i and t_j. Then, the utility score of a tag is derived by performing a random walk on this graph [16]. Note that this is similar to the method applied in [14] for ranking the tags of individual objects.

Initially, the score of each tag t is set to its frequency, i.e., $f_0(t) = fr(t, G)$. The transition probability from a tag t_i to a tag t_j is computed as

$$p(t_i, t_j) = \frac{sim(t_i, t_j)}{\sum_{t \in T(G)} sim(t_i, t)} \tag{8}$$

The similarity $sim(t_i, t_j)$ between two tags can be computed using the Google similarity distance [3], which takes into account the number of objects tagged with each tag, the number of objects tagged with both tags, and the total number of objects in the group:

$$sim(t_i, t_j) = \exp[-\frac{\max(n_i, n_j) - n_{ij}}{\log |G| - \min(n_i, n_j)}] \tag{9}$$

where $n_i = \log |U(t_i)|$, $n_j = \log |U(t_j)|$ and $n_{ij} = \log |U(t_i) \cap U(t_j)|$. After each iteration q, the utility score of each tag is updated according to:

$$f_q(t_i) = z \cdot \sum_{t_j \in T(G)} f_{q-1}(t_j) \cdot p(t_j, t_i) + (1 - z) \cdot f_0(t_i) \tag{10}$$

with z being a weight parameter. The process is repeated until the utility score of each tag t converges to a value $f(t)$. Then, the top k tags with respect to $f(t)$ are selected to construct the tag cloud for the group.

4.2 Based on Diversity

A limitation of the approaches examined above is that the utility score of each tag is computed independently, without taking into consideration the rest of the tags in the cloud. This may result in cases where certain objects of the group are over-represented in the tag cloud, i.e., they have many of their tags appearing in the cloud, while other objects are under-represented, having very few or no tags in the cloud. Especially the latter case constitutes a very negative scenario, since it implies that these objects are not reachable via the tag cloud. This problem can be addressed by following a strategy that aims at increasing the *diversity* or *novelty* of the members of the tag cloud [6, 4]. In the following, we describe two approaches that can be used for this purpose.

4.2.1 Diversity

The goal in this case is to select tags that are as dissimilar as possible from each other, in the sense that appear in different sets of objects. Specifically, a tag has high utility, if there are no other tags already in the cloud that have a high similarity to it, i.e., that appear approximately in the same set of objects. This can be quantified by computing the minimum distance between the considered tag t and the currently selected tags in the cloud T_G. Since we do not wish to completely discard the criterion of frequency, we include it as an additional factor in computing the utility score of a tag. Specifically, the utility score of a tag t is defined as

$$f(t) = \lambda \cdot fr(t, G) + (1 - \lambda) \cdot (1 - \max_{t_i \in T_G} sim(t, t_i)) \tag{11}$$

where the parameter λ is used to weight the importance of frequency with respect to the factor of diversity. For example, assume that $\lambda = 0$. If a tag t appears in exactly the same set of objects as another tag t_i already selected in the cloud, then $sim(t, t_i) = 1$, and therefore $f(t) = 0$. On the contrary, if there is no tag in the cloud that appears in any of the objects tagged with t, then the maximum similarity of t with the current members of T_G is 0, and therefore the utility of t becomes equal to 1.

As can be seen by Equation 11, the selection of a tag now can not be done independently, but depends instead on the selection of other tags in the cloud. However, examining all possible combinations is clearly impractical due to the high computational cost. For this reason, a greedy approximation algorithm can be used, as is typically done in search results diversification. The algorithm is simple and proceeds as follows. First, the tag cloud is initialized with the tag that has the highest frequency. Then, the remaining $k - 1$ tags are selected by adding to the cloud, at each iteration, the tag that maximizes the utility value in Equation 11, with respect to the contents of the cloud up to that step.

4.2.2 Novelty

Another approach to diversify the members of a tag cloud is to emphasize on the novelty of newly selected tags, while the cloud is constructed. In document retrieval, this is formalized using the notion of *information nuggets*. An information nugget v is a piece of information contained in a document. Each document may contain one or more information nuggets, and the same information nugget may appear in more than one documents. When documents are retrieved, a document is selected if it contains as many previously unseen information nuggets as possible.

In our case, we consider each object to constitute one information nugget[1]. Selecting a tag t, provides a set of information nuggets $V(t)$ corresponding to the objects that this tag is assigned to. Under the above assumption for the definition of an information nugget, we have $V(t) = U(t)$. Let n_{v,T_G} be the number of times that a nugget v has already appeared in the tags currently contained in the cloud, i.e., $n_{v,T_G} = |\{t_i \in T_G : v \in V(t_i)\}|$. Also, let N_V be the total number of information nuggets in the group; in our case, $N_V = |G|$. Given a tag t and the current contents of the tag cloud T_G, the utility score of t is defined as

$$f(t) = \frac{\sum_{v \in V(t)} \gamma(n_{v,T_G})}{N_V} \quad (12)$$

The function $\gamma()$ is a discount function that reduces the contribution of each information nugget of the tag t based on the number of times it has already been seen by previously selected tags. To maximize the emphasis on novelty, this function can be defined to return 1 if $n_{v,T_G} = 0$, and 0 otherwise. In that case, if, for example, a tag t appears only in a single object u, and there is already another tag of u in the cloud, then the utility score of t is 0.

As with Equation 11, in this definition of the utility function f the score of a tag depends also on the other tags existing in the cloud. Therefore, tags may again be selected using a similar greedy algorithm to the one described in the previous section. Specifically, the algorithm starts by selecting first the tag that provides the highest number of information nuggets. According to our definition of nuggets, where there is a one-to-one mapping between objects and information nuggets, this is the tag having the highest frequency. At each subsequent iteration, the tag providing the highest number of new nuggets is identified and added to the cloud, until a total number of k tags have been selected.

4.3 Based on Rank Aggregation

The tag ranking strategies presented so far take into consideration the criteria of frequency and novelty. However, there is another source of information that can be taken into account, when constructing the tag cloud of a group of objects: the order in which the tags appear in these objects. Although in typical applications there are no explicit semantics or criteria determining the order in which users assign tags to an object, it is reasonable to assume that there exists some (even small) correlation between this order and the relevance or importance of the tags for the target object. Alternatively, it is also possible to determine and use a different ranking for the tags of each object, according to a specified criterion, as in [14].

To take the order of tags into account, we define a utility function based on the Borda Count method. This is a voting algorithm that has been shown to be optimal with respect to desired symmetry properties of typical election systems, and has also been used for metasearch in IR [1]. The Borda Count method works as follows. Each voter ranks a fixed set of c candidates in order of preference. For each voter, the top ranked candidate receives c points, the second ranked candidate receives $c - 1$ points, and so on. At the end, the candidates are ranked in order of their total points. The candidate with the most points wins the election.

In our case, voters correspond to objects and candidates correspond to tags. To take the ranking of tags into account, we discount the "vote" given by an object to a tag based on the position of this tag in the object's tag list, using a discount function as discussed for Equation 2. Thus, we define the utility score of each tag as follows:

$$f(t) = \frac{\sum_{u \in U(t)} \alpha(r_u(t))}{|G|} \quad (13)$$

where $r_u(t)$ is the position (starting from zero) of the tag t in the list of tags assigned to object u. For example, if the tag t appears in the first position of the tag list of all the objects in the group, then $f(t) = 1$. The tag cloud comprises the top k tags ranked in decreasing order of their utility score.

#	Method					
	Freq.	TF.IDF	R.W.	Div.	Nov.	Rank Aggr.
1	nikon	panoramio	nikon	nikon	nikon	nikon
2	people	wiki	d5000	people	people	wiki
3	d5000	ulisse	people	italy	love	wikipedia
4	italia	gps	italy	music	hotel	people
5	italy	wikipedia	italia	canada	ottawa	d5000
6	portrait	aci	flickr	portrait	macro	cc
7	flickr	basalt	creative	love	sky	gente
8	creative	faraglioni	portrait	d90	rome	panoramio
9	cc	cc	cc	2010	barcelona	portrait
10	common	fishermen	common	london	d300	sicilia

Table 1: Top 10 tags selected by the different algorithms for the Flickr group "This is nikon art".

5. EVALUATION METHODOLOGY

In the previous section, we have presented different approaches for selecting and ranking tags for a group of objects. Table 1 shows the top 10 tags selected by these methods for the Flickr group "This is nikon art". One can notice, for example, that frequency-based ranking selects tags like *flickr* or both *italy* and *italia*, which in other methods are replaced by other more intresting tags, such as *fishermen*, *music*, *hotel*, *rome*, *sicilia*, etc.

The question that arises is which of these tag clouds is better and why. In the following, we propose an evaluation methodology for comparing different tag clouds. The typical purpose of a tag cloud is to serve as a summarized representation of a group in order to allow users to search and navigate through its items, to drill down to specific items of

[1] A more fine grained definition for information nuggets is possible if the content of the objects is analyzed and taken into consideration; however, this is orthogonal to our work.

interest, and to receive recommendations for groups when adding a new item (e.g., [10, 14]). The methodology and metrics presented in this section aim at providing an objective and automatic way to compare the characteristics and effectiveness of different tag clouds with respect to these properties and tasks.

5.1 Metrics for Search and Navigation

In the following, we consider characteristics of a tag cloud that make it useful for search and navigation. Notice that similar metrics have been also proposed for evaluating faceted search interfaces (see Section 2 for more details).

5.1.1 *Coverage*

Since a tag cloud aims at providing an entry point for searching and navigating through the objects of a group, ideally every object should be reachable through the tag cloud. That is, for every object, at least one of its tags should appear in the tag cloud. Otherwise, any tag that the user may select would lead to a subset of results that does not contain this particular object. To measure this property, we define the *coverage* of a tag cloud T_G with respect to the group of objects G it represents as the portion of the objects in the group that have at least one tag appearing in the cloud, i.e.,

$$coverage(T_G) = \frac{|\{u \in G : T(u) \cap T_G \neq \emptyset\}|}{|G|} \quad (14)$$

The higher the coverage, the more effective the tag cloud is.

5.1.2 *Overlap*

Another aspect is that a tag cloud, similar to a (multi-) document summary, should avoid redundancy. This means that we would like to avoid cases where different tags in the cloud, when selected, lead to the same or very similar subsets of objects. To quantify this aspect, we measure the overlap between two tags t_i and t_j by computing the portion of objects tagged with t_j that are also tagged with t_i, i.e., $|U(t_i) \cap U(t_j)| \;/\; |U(t_j)|$. Assume, for example, that a user selects first t_i, browses the results, then goes back, and selects t_j. If the overlap between t_i and t_j is high, the second step will return little or no new results. Thus, we define the *overlap* of the tag cloud as the average overlap between each pair of tags:

$$overlap(T_G) = \frac{\sum_{t_i, t_j \in T_G} \frac{|U(t_i) \cap U(t_j)|}{|U(t_j)|}}{|T_G| \cdot (|T_G| - 1)} \quad (15)$$

The lower the overlap, the more effective the tag cloud is.

5.1.3 *Selectivity*

As already mentioned, a tag cloud should facilitate users to drill down to specific objects of interest. Selecting all the common tags between an object and the cloud provides the best "zoom in" that can be achieved for this object. The question then is how many other objects remain after this selection is made. Assume that a user is insterested in the object u, and that all the tags of u appearing in the tag cloud, i.e., $T(u) \cap T_G$, have been selected. The result list will then contain u, as well as all other objects that also have (at least) those tags. That is, the result list will comprise every object $u_i \in G$ such that $T(u) \cap T_G \subseteq T(u_i)$, while the rest of the objects will have been filtered out. The number of filtered out objects should be as high as possible. We call this number, normalized to the total number of objects, the selectivity of u with respect to the tag cloud T_G. Thus, we measure the *selectivity* of the tag cloud by computing the average selectivity of the objects in the group:

$$selectivity(T_G) = \frac{\sum_{u \in G} \frac{|\{u_i \in G : (T(u) \cap T_G) \nsubseteq T(u_i)\}|}{|G|}}{|G|} \quad (16)$$

The higher the selectivity, the more effective the tag cloud.

5.2 User Navigation Model

The metrics described so far allow to quantify different properties of a tag cloud with respect to search and navigation. However, they are "static", in the sense that they do not consider the (order and cost of) actions taken by a user when using the tag cloud to find items of interest. Next, we describe a user navigation model that can be used to evaluate different tag clouds in this respect.

The reasons for preferring a simulation model to an actual user study are the following. On the one hand, if the same user evaluates alternative tag clouds for a group, the results can not be easily compared, because, when using one tag cloud for navigating and searching for items, the acquired knowledge about which tags were more or less useful will affect the choices made when using the other tag clouds. On the other hand, if different users evaluate the alternative tag clouds for a group, again the results can not be easily compared, due to cognitive differences among the users or differences regarding what each user perceives as interesting or relevant. A possible solution would be to use non-overlapping, sufficiently large sets of users for evaluating alternative tag clouds, and then comparing the average results among those sets. However, this makes the user study even more expensive to conduct and to reproduce. Instead, the proposed simulation model provides an easy and objective way for comparison. Notice that such a methodology has also been followed in [9] to evaluate user interfaces for personalized and interactive faceted search instead of relying on actual user studies forsimilar reasons. To simulate user navigation, we assume that the user is trying to find items of interest in a group that are described by a set of tags T_{nav}. To find an item, the user can perform two types of actions: she can scan the list of results or she can select a tag in the cloud to reduce the size of the result set. Each of these actions is associated with a cost. The goal is to measure the total cost for finding an item.

Initially, the list of items presented to the user contains all the objects of the group, typically organized in pages of fixed size (e.g., 10 objects per page). Let c_p be the cost of scanning one page of objects. We also assume that the user is willing to scan up to a relatively small number of pages, say n_p; otherwise, if the list comprises more than n_p pages, she would prefer instead to select a tag to narrow down the list of results. To capture this, we set the cost c_t of selecting a tag to be equal to scanning n_p pages, i.e., $c_t = n_p \cdot c_p$.

The process works as follows:

1. The result list is initialized with all the objects in the group.

2. If the current result list contains at most n_p pages or

if there are no more tags left to use, the user scans the results and the session ends.

3. Otherwise, the user selects one tag from $T_{nav} \cap T_G$ and the result list is updated. The process repeats from step 2.

At the end of the session, the navigation cost is the sum of the costs of all the actions performed by the user (i.e., tag selections and page scans). This cost is divided by the cost needed to scan all the initial list of objects without using the tag cloud, to obtain a normalized value in $[0, 1]$. Therefore, if the user performed n_1 tag selections and n_2 page scans, then the navigation cost is:

$$nav\_cost = \frac{n_1 \cdot c_t + n_2 \cdot c_p}{n_0 \cdot c_p} \quad (17)$$

where $n_0 = \lceil (|G| / (page\_size) \rceil$.

There are two questions still to be answered to fully specify the simulation process. First, which are the tags T_{nav} that are used for the navigation. Second, when a user selects one tag from $T_{nav} \cap T_G$, which tag is selected.

Regarding the first question, for the purpose of the simulation, we assume that for each object u in the group there exists one user that wants to navigate the collection using the tags of this object, i.e., $T_{nav} = T(u)$, and we compute the average navigation cost among all users. Of course, in practice, more users may be interested in certain objects rather than others. In that case, it is possible to generalize the process using different weights for the users, as discussed also in Section 4.1.1.

For the second issue, we adopt the approach used in [9] for selecting facet-value pairs when simulating user behavior in a faceted browsing interface. Specifically, three types of users are considered. *First-match users* select the tag in $T_{nav} \cap T_G$ that has the highest rank in T_G. The intuition for this lies in the fact that tags in a cloud are visualized according to their ranking, with top tags being presented more prominently than others (typically, in terms of font size). Thus, users are more likely to spot and select highly ranked tags first. In contrast, *last-match users* select the tag having the lowest rank. The reason for this behavior is that those tags are less frequent, and therefore more selective, leading to a smaller subset of results. Finally, *random-match users* select a tag randomly.

5.3 Group Recommendation Accuracy

So far, we have considered the task of using the tag cloud to find items of interest within a group. Another important and common task is to recommend groups for new items. In this case, we assume that we are given an object u tagged with a set of tags $T(u)$, and the system needs to recommend groups for u from the set of groups $\mathcal{G}$ existing in the collection. A straightforward approach is to compare u with each object in each available group and recommend the group that contains the most similar objects to u. However, this is clearly very expensive, especially when this operation needs to be done online. Instead, we want to use the tag cloud of each group for this purpose.

To assign an object to a group, we compute a similarity score based on the common tags between the object and the tag cloud of the group, taking also into consideration the importance (i.e., the ranking) of these tags in the tag cloud. Specifically, we define this similarity as follows:

$$sim(u, G) = \frac{\sum_{t \in T(u) \cap T_G} \alpha(r(t))}{|T(u)|} \quad (18)$$

where $a(r(t))$ is a discount function applied on the rank $r(t)$ of the tag t in T_G, as in Equation 2.

Given an object u, groups are then recommended in decreasing order of similarity. Using different tag clouds, results in different lists of retrieved groups. In addition, if we assume that we know the relevant groups for the given object, i.e., the correct assignments, then it is possible to evaluate different tag clouds using standard IR metrics.

6. EXPERIMENTAL EVALUATION

We have conducted an empirical evaluation of the tag ranking algorithms presented in Section 4, using a large, real-world dataset obtained from Flickr containing groups of tagged images. First, we describe the characteristics of this dataset, and then we present the results of the evaluation with respect to the metrics presented in Section 5.

6.1 Dataset

To evaluate the tag ranking methods, we collected a dataset comprising groups of tagged photos from Flickr. We chose Flickr among a set of several popular Web 2.0 applications that provide tagging functionality and use tag clouds, such as Delicious, Technorati, Facebook or Last.fm, for mainly two reasons. First, there exists a very large number of groups of photos in Flickr, with groups often containing hundreds or thousands of photos, having several tags assigned to each of them. This allowed us to obtain a very large dataset in order to make the evaluation more interesting and challenging. Second, obtaining the data was significantly facilitated by the API[2] provided by Flickr for such purposes.

The Flickr API was used to collect data about groups of photos over a period of two weeks. Flickr does not provide a direct way to browse all available groups; instead, one needs to search for groups based on keywords. Thus, to obtain groups of photos we used a total of 10 keywords, in particular: *autumn*, *animals*, *architecture*, *city*, *beach*, *food*, *film*, *christmas*, *art*, and *car*. These were selected from the list of "all time most popular tags" in Flickr[3].

For each one of these keywords, we retrieved the top 60 groups returned by the API. Specifically, for each group, we retrieved up to 2000 photos, storing for each photo its ID, its owner, the date posted, the group(s) it belongs to, and the list of assigned tags (with the order they appear in Flickr). Note that in some cases, some groups or photos could not be retrieved, either because of being set as private or due to some connection error. Thus, there exist variations in the number of groups that were finally collected per keyword, as well as the number of photos per group, which however corresponds to a realistic scenario. Moreover, some pre-processing was done on the collected data to reduce noise, including stopword removal and stemming. After this process, we also removed: tags that had been used by less than 2 users; photos that had less than 4 tags; and groups that contained less than 50 photos.

[2]`http://www.flickr.com/services/api/`

[3]`http://www.flickr.com/photos/tags/`

Keyword	# of groups	# of photos per group			# of distinct tags per group			# of tags per photo		
		avg	max	min	avg	max	min	avg	max	min
animals	56	1248	1758	843	3068	5106	1114	10	142	4
architecture	59	1416	1748	510	2865	5245	579	12	71	4
art	55	1164	1650	418	3098	5820	1232	12	73	4
autumn	29	1220	1620	519	2655	5361	134	11	69	4
beach	38	1216	1548	426	2175	4581	616	13	72	4
car	48	1391	1719	973	2625	5262	1027	13	92	4
christmas	15	844	1438	417	1644	3438	605	10	68	4
city	49	1278	1865	415	2586	4331	581	11	72	4
film	53	1367	1862	460	2758	4407	1034	12	72	4
food	49	1212	1741	559	2578	4387	1070	10	70	4
TOTAL	451	1270	1865	415	2707	5820	134	11	142	4

Table 2: Dataset statistics.

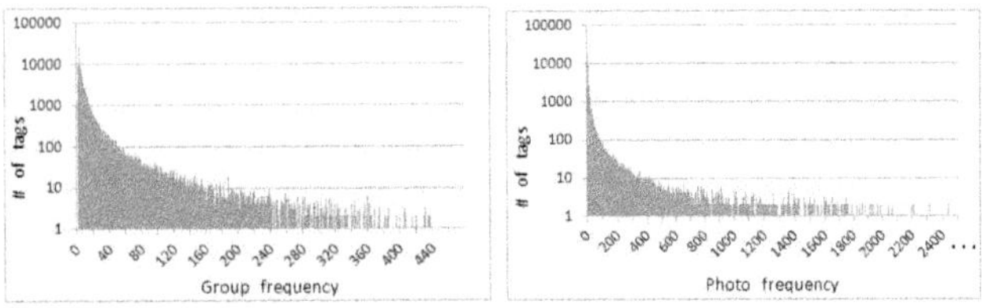

(a) (b)

Figure 2: Distribution of (a) group frequency and (b) photo frequency of tags.

The final dataset contained 451 groups, 488,112 photos, and 112,514 tags, with each group having on average 1270 photos and 2707 distinct tags. Table 2 provides detailed statistics about the dataset. Moreover, Figure 2 plots the distribution of tag frequencies, in terms of number of groups and number of photos they appear in. For example, one can see that the majority of the tags has a relatively low group frequency, e.g., less than 30 groups, while there are only a few tags that appear in more than half of the groups. The distribution is similar for the photo frequency, with most tags appearing in not more than 100 different photos. Of course, there are also some tags like names of colors, cities or countries, or tags such as *sky*, *sea*, *street*, that appear in the majority of the groups and in more than 10,000 photos.

6.2 Results

We now present the results of our experiments on the Flickr dataset described above. We have implemented the algorithms described in Section 4, and we compare them applying the evaluation methodology presented in Section 5.

In the implementation and experiments, we used the following configuration. For the random walk algorithm (Equation 10) and for the diversification algorithm (Equation 11), we used $z = 0.5$ and $\lambda = 0.5$, respectively. As discount function in Equation 2 we used the one in Equation 3 with $\beta = 0.1$. In Equation 12, we set $\gamma(n) = 1$ for $n = 0$, or 0 otherwise, to emphasize novelty. Finally, in the user navigation model, we used $n_p = 2$ and we assumed that each page of results displays (at most) 10 objects.

In the following discussion and in the plots, we refer to the methods presented in Section 4 using the abbreviations FRQ, TFIDF, RW, DIV, NOV, and RA, respectively. The presented results refer to average values over all the 451 groups in the dataset.

6.2.1 *Coverage, Overlap and Selectivity*

Figure 3 displays the results for the different tag ranking algorithms with respect to the metrics for search and navigation presented in Section 5, and for different values of the number of tags k in the cloud.

As shown, FRQ performs reasonably well, mainly for the metrics of coverage and selectivity and less for overlap. For example, it provides a coverage starting from 87% for top-k = 20, reaching 95%, for top-k = 100. RW and RA exhibit a similar performance to FRQ, with the latter outperforming the other two regarding overlap. In contrast, the performance of TFIDF is very low both for coverage and selectivity, but it outperforms all three previous approaches in overlap. Finally, DIV and NOV perform better than all other approaches. Especially for coverage, NOV achieves excellent results, starting from 93% for top-k = 20 and reaching 99% for top-k = 100. It also has good results for overlap for all values of k, although for $k > 60$ DIV becomes equally good or even better.

As expected, increasing the size of the tag cloud improves the performance of all methods in all metrics.

6.2.2 *Navigation Cost*

Figure 4 displays the navigation cost for the tag clouds created with the different ranking algorithms, considering the three types of users described in Section 5.2, and for different tag cloud sizes.

A first observation is that TFIDF has a much higher navigation cost than all other methods. This is a direct consequence of its low coverage, since photos that are not covered by the tag cloud can not benefit from it during navigation. For the rest of the methods, the observations are similar to the results presented above. This has to do with the fact that the navigation cost is affected by coverage and selectivity. Thus, for example, since NOV performed better than all other methods in both those metrics, this also contributed to having the lowest navigation cost. As expected, the navigation cost decreases for all methods as the tag cloud size increases; also, it is higher for first-match users and lower for last-match users.

6.2.3 *Recommendation Accuracy*

Here we consider the task of group recommendation. Given a tagged photo and a set of groups, the goal is to recommend groups for this photo based on their tag clouds. For each of the 451 group, we selected as test photos the 10 most recent ones added to it by different users. Then, for each test

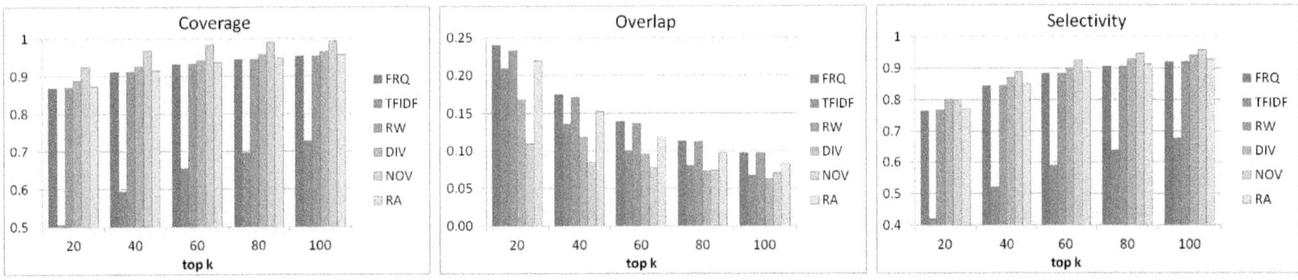

(a) coverage (b) overlap (c) selectivity

Figure 3: Evaluation results for the metrics (a) coverage (b) overlap and (c) selectivity.

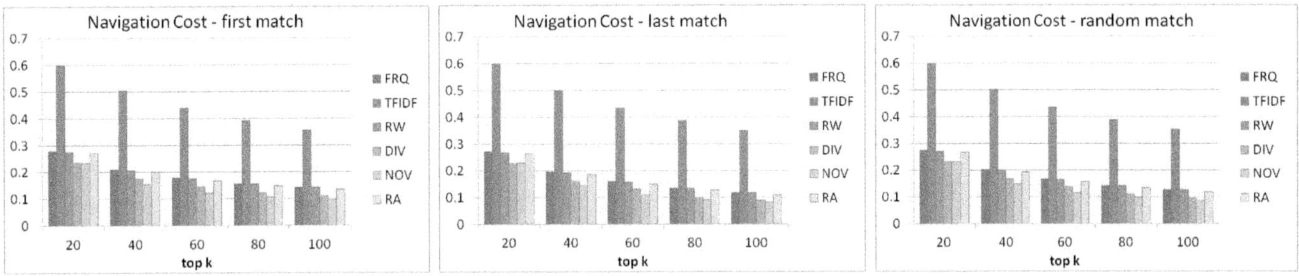

(a) first-match (b) last-match (c) random-match

Figure 4: Navigation cost for (a) first-match (b) last-match and (c) random-match users.

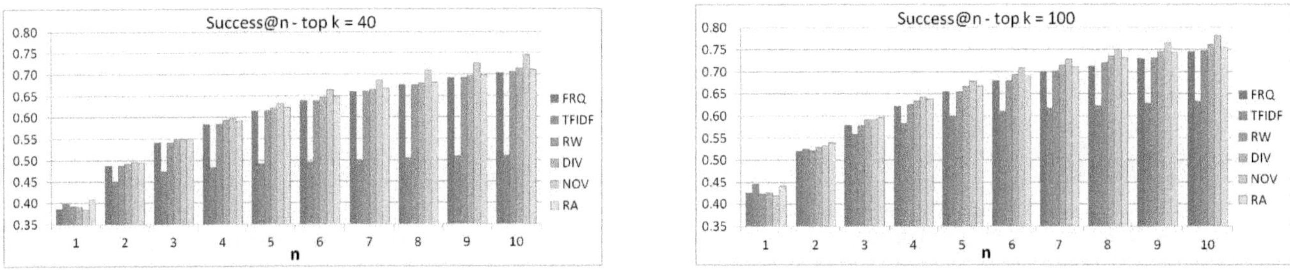

(a) top-k = 40 (b) top-k = 100

Figure 5: Success@n for group recommendation with (a) top-k = 40 and (b) top-k = 100.

photo, we computed a ranked list of recommended groups, using the different tag clouds provided by the ranking algorithms. The similarity between a photo and the tag cloud of a group was computed according to Equation 18.

The performance of each tag cloud is determined by how high the relevant group(s) of a photo appear in the list of recommendations. As relevant, we considered the group from which the photo was selected, as well as any other groups it might also belong to. Since very few photos appear in more than one group, we used the common IR metric *success@n*, which takes the values 1 or 0, depending on whether a relevant result is found among the top n recommendations.

Figure 5 displays the average values of *success@n* over all the test photos, for different values of n and for tag clouds of size 40 and 100 tags. Interestingly, when only the first recommendation is considered, TFIDF and RA achieve the highest accuracy. However, the performance of TFIDF remains approximately at the same levels as n increases. This is attributed to the fact that TFIDF discards many frequent tags. This helps to make a more accurate recommendation for photos that are covered by the tag cloud, but it misses for all the rest. Instead, RA and DIV continue to be better for $n = 2$ or 3. For higher values of n, NOV achieves the best performance.

6.2.4 *Execution Time*

Finally, we also measured the execution time for the different ranking algorithms. The following table shows the average time (in sec) per group, for top-k = 100:

FRQ	TFIDF	RW	DIV	NOV	RA
0.002	0.003	87.813	9.552	0.296	0.008

FRQ, TFIDF and RA are simple, one-pass algorithms, therefore their execution time was very low. The diversification algorithms are more expensive, since they need to perform k passes. At each pass, each of the remaining tags is compared either with each tag already in the cloud (DIV) or with the set of information nuggets in the cloud (NOV). Thus, DIV requires even more computations than NOV. Indeed, the execution time of NOV was below half second, while DIV required a few seconds. Finally, RW exceeded 1 min, which makes it not suitable for online computation.

6.2.5 Summary of Results

Summarizing the results, we can make the following main observations:

- As a baseline, FRQ achieved reasonably good results, which verifies that it is a good criterion for selecting tags. Nevertheless, it was outperformed by other methods in all metrics.
- TFIDF showed a very poor performance for all metrics except overlap. This is because it penalizes frequent tags that occur also in many groups. Although this lowers the overlap also within each group, excluding those tags results in many photos not having any common tags with the cloud.
- RW failed to show a noticeable improvement over FRQ. This means that, in our setting, propagating the scores in the tag graph did not improve the ranking. Even worse, it significantly increased the computational cost. Still, it would be worth investigating whether enriching the tag graph with content-based similarity of tags and photos provides a more positive effect.
- The diversification methods, DIV and NOV, achieved the best performance in all metrics. NOV clearly outperformed all methods, especially for coverage, as well as for recommendations. This is due to the fact that it selects tags that cover as many not previously seen items as possible. In some cases, the performance of DIV was equally or slightly better than NOV; however, NOV has also a lower computational cost.
- Finally, RA performed overall a little better than FRQ but not as well as DIV and NOV. Also, its execution time was similar to frequency.

7. CONCLUSIONS

In this paper, we have presented a set of methods and metrics for constructing and evaluating tag clouds to describe groups of tagged resources. The presented algorithms include frequency or *tf.idf* based ranking, random walk on tag graphs, diversification of tags, and rank aggregation. The proposed metrics cover several aspects of tag clouds for search, navigation and recommendations. The results of our large-scale evaluation on groups of Flickr photos have shown that methods employing diversification or rank aggregation can improve the performance of tag clouds with respect to these metrics, compared to the traditional frequency-based ranking, while still having a similar or comparable computation time and without relying on content-based analysis. There exist several interesting directions for future work, as already pointed out while discussing related efforts. These include extracting semantics of tags and exploiting content-based similarity of objects.

8. REFERENCES

[1] J. A. Aslam and M. H. Montague. Models for metasearch. In *SIGIR*, pages 275–284, 2001.

[2] A. Budura, S. Michel, P. Cudré-Mauroux, and K. Aberer. To tag or not to tag - harvesting adjacent metadata in large-scale tagging systems. In *SIGIR*, pages 733–734, 2008.

[3] R. Cilibrasi and P. M. B. Vitányi. The Google similarity distance. *IEEE Trans. Knowl. Data Eng.*, 19(3):370–383, 2007.

[4] M. Drosou and E. Pitoura. Search result diversification. *SIGMOD Record*, 39(1):41–47, 2010.

[5] K. Fujimura, S. Fujimura, T. Matsubayashi, T. Yamada, and H. Okuda. Topigraphy: visualization for large-scale tag clouds. In *WWW*, pages 1087–1088, 2008.

[6] S. Gollapudi and A. Sharma. An axiomatic approach for result diversification. In *WWW*, pages 381–390, 2009.

[7] Z. Guan, J. Bu, Q. Mei, C. Chen, and C. Wang. Personalized tag recommendation using graph-based ranking on multi-type interrelated objects. In *SIGIR*, pages 540–547, 2009.

[8] M. A. Hearst. Clustering versus faceted categories for information exploration. *Comm. ACM*, 49(4):59–61, 2006.

[9] J. Koren, Y. Zhang, and X. Liu. Personalized interactive faceted search. In *WWW*, pages 477–486, 2008.

[10] B. Y.-L. Kuo, T. Hentrich, B. M. Good, and M. D. Wilkinson. Tag clouds for summarizing web search results. In *WWW*, pages 1203–1204, 2007.

[11] C. Li, N. Yan, S. B. Roy, L. Lisham, and G. Das. Facetedpedia: dynamic generation of query-dependent faceted interfaces for wikipedia. In *WWW*, pages 651–660, 2010.

[12] X. Li, C. G. M. Snoek, and M. Worring. Learning social tag relevance by neighbor voting. *IEEE Trans. on Multimedia*, 11:1310–1322, Nov. 2009.

[13] D. Liu, X.-S. Hua, M. Wang, and H.-J. Zhang. Retagging social images based on visual and semantic consistency. In *WWW*, pages 1149–1150, 2010.

[14] D. Liu, X.-S. Hua, L. Yang, M. Wang, and H.-J. Zhang. Tag ranking. In *WWW*, pages 351–360, 2009.

[15] S. Lohmann, J. Ziegler, and L. Tetzlaff. Comparison of tag cloud layouts: Task-related performance and visual exploration. In *INTERACT (1)*, pages 392–404, 2009.

[16] L. Lovász. Random walks on graphs: A survey. *Combinatorics Paul Erdos is Eighty*, 2(1):1–46, 1993.

[17] E. Oren, R. Delbru, and S. Decker. Extending faceted navigation for RDF data. In *ISWC*, pages 559–572, 2006.

[18] T. Rattenbury, N. Good, and M. Naaman. Towards automatic extraction of event and place semantics from Flickr tags. In *SIGIR*, pages 103–110, 2007.

[19] S. B. Roy, H. Wang, G. Das, U. Nambiar, and M. K. Mohania. Minimum-effort driven dynamic faceted search in structured databases. In *CIKM*, pages 13–22, 2008.

[20] J. Schrammel, M. Leitner, and M. Tscheligi. Semantically structured tag clouds: an empirical evaluation of clustered presentation approaches. In *CHI*, pages 2037–2040, 2009.

[21] G. Smith. *Tagging: People-powered Metadata for the Social Web.* New Riders Publishing, Thousand Oaks, CA, USA, 2008.

[22] P. Venetis, G. Koutrika, and H. Garcia-Molina. On the selection of tags for tag clouds. In *WSDM*, pages 835–844, 2011.

[23] L. Wu, L. Yang, N. Yu, and X.-S. Hua. Learning to tag. In *WWW*, pages 361–370, 2009.

Ranking-based Processing of SQL Queries

Hany Azzam, Thomas Roelleke, and Sirvan Yahyaei
Queen Mary, University of London, UK. E1 4NS
{hany,thor,sirvan}@eecs.qmul.ac.uk

ABSTRACT

A growing number of applications are built on top of search engines and issue complex structured queries. This paper contributes a customisable ranking-based processing of such queries, specifically SQL. Similar to how term-based statistics are exploited by term-based retrieval models, ranking-aware processing of SQL queries exploits tuple-based statistics that are derived from sources or, more precisely, derived from the relations specified in the SQL query. To implement this ranking-based processing, we leverage PSQL, a probabilistic variant of SQL, to facilitate probability estimation and the generalisation of document retrieval models to be used for tuple retrieval. The result is a general-purpose framework that can interpret any SQL query and then assign a probabilistic retrieval model to rank the results of that query. The evaluation on the IMDB and Monster benchmarks proves that the PSQL-based approach is applicable to (semi-)structured and unstructured data and structured queries.

Categories and Subject Descriptors

H.3.3 [**Information Storage and Retrieval**]: Information Search and Retrieval; H.2.3 [**Database Management**]: Languages; H.3.4 [**Information Storage and Retrieval**]: Systems and Software—Performance evaluation (efficiency and effectiveness)

General Terms

Algorithms, Languages, Performance

Keywords

PSQL (Probabilistic SQL), retrieval models, integrated DB+IR

1. INTRODUCTION

Applications built on top of search engines such as question answering and data mining are gradually leveraging rich language resources such as microformats (e.g."geo" and "hAtom") and RDF/RDFa markup which can be integrated with content-based resources [14]. Using these resources effectively requires complex structural representations of information needs [2]. Additionally, there may be retrieval environments where users are expert searchers willing to use structured query languages. Librarians, application developers, patent searchers and users of legal information systems often form complex queries.

Both search applications and expert searchers rely on information retrieval (IR) approaches that can support constraint-checking and ranking with respect to document structure and annotations as well as keywords. Such approaches enable direct expression of higher-level constraints on answer structures which can be checked at retrieval time. One approach is to use SQL, which is still the most widely used standard for formulating structured and semantic-expressive queries, and extend it with similarity predicates to perform the ranking, e.g. [3]. However, most of these approaches use physical SQL math and aggregation operators (e.g. log, sum) to express the ranking function. In other words, they specify the information need *and* the ranking function in the same query. From an abstraction point of view, this mix is *physical*, since bare SQL is used to implement the ranking. Other approaches, such as [4] implement the ranking function directly on top of a physical document representation. Such engineering approaches can also be problematic because they result in implementations that are difficult to maintain and re-use [9, 6, 10].

A general-purpose framework for ranking structured queries can address these issues by providing transparent and effective ranking. We propose such a framework that interprets *any* SQL query and then assigns a probabilistic retrieval model to rank the results of that query. The interpretation is part of a processing strategy that focuses on satisfying the information need while concurrently adding the model as part of the processing. To implement these models we use Probabilistic SQL (PSQL, [20]), which helps to express them in an abstract and logical way. The abstraction takes control of tuple (the results from the structured query) probability estimation and aggregation, which replaces the physical approaches that use SQL aggregation operators. The resulting implementation is easy to understand, debug and customise.

1.1 Contributions & Outline

To achieve the ranking-based processing of SQL, retrieval models (due to space constraints, we mainly focus on the TF-IDF and language modelling) which are designed primarily for document retrieval are generalised for tuple-based retrieval. The main contribution of this paper are the SQL-to-PSQL algorithms which transform the SQL queries to PSQL programs. These programs deliver an IR-model-based ranking of tuples retrieved for the genuine SQL query and are evaluated using several benchmarks.

The remainder of the paper is organised as follows: Section 2 provides the essential background on probabilistic DB technology, retrieval models and PSQL. Sections 3 and 4 cover the core contributions of this paper: the generalisation from document retrieval to tuple retrieval, and the evaluation. Section 5 summarises the paper and concludes the discussion.

CIKM'11, October 24–28, 2011, Glasgow, Scotland, UK.

2. BACKGROUND & PRELIMINARIES

2.1 Probabilistic Databases

The research in this paper draws upon advances in probabilistic data models. Early work that discusses the notion of quality and its estimation in databases using a probabilistic approach can be found in [15]; the relational model was extended and a quality specification was associated with each relation instance. [13] introduced RankSQL, which integrates ranking support into SQL. Another significant approach is the framework for probabilistic ranking of tuples based on a variant of the BIR retrieval model [4]. This framework, which measures the correlation between the specified and unspecified attributes to produce the ranking, differs from the framework proposed here. We support any probabilistic retrieval model and its variations, and the probability estimation need not be modelled outside the probabilistic framework. Efficient query evaluation in probabilistic databases is discussed by [7], which proposes a system that efficiently ranks the top-k answers to an SQL query on a probabilistic database. This system provides an optimisation technique referred to as "safe-plan" that facilitates the efficient computation of probabilistic results for queries. This technique also ensures that the correctness of the probabilistic semantics is maintained. Another approach for improving query processing times, proposed by [17], is based on materialising probabilistic views in probabilistic databases. Other approaches concerned with the efficient ranking of tuples, but geared towards specific types of data such as semi-structured, have been initiated. [21] compute approximate top-k results using probabilistic score estimators. As a result, retrieval efficiency improves without a major loss in effectiveness.

The probabilistic relational modelling concepts employed herein build upon the aforementioned research and the theoretical foundations by [8], [7] and [17]. The contribution of this paper is to leverage such concepts for the probabilistic ranking of tuples.

2.2 The Core Retrieval Models

This section reviews the core retrieval models used in this paper. To define this models, let $N_D(c)$ denote the number of *Documents* in collection "c", and let $n_D(t,c)$ denote the number of *Documents* with term "t" in collection "c", where $\mathrm{df}_t := n_D(t,c)$ is the *document frequency*. Similarly, let $N_L(c)$ denote the number of *Locations* in collection "c", and let $n_L(t,c)$ denote the number of *Locations* with term "t". $N_L(d)$ and $n_L(t,d)$ are the *Location-based* counts for document "d", where $\mathrm{tf}_d := n_L(t,d)$ is the within-document *term-frequency*. The dual notation helps to achieve the unifying definitions of TF-IDF and LM shown next.

DEFINITION 1. *TF-IDF RSV:*

$$\mathrm{TF}(t,d) := \begin{cases} \frac{n_L(t,d)}{n_L(t,d)+K_d} & \textit{BM25-like TF norm.} \\ \frac{n_L(t,d)}{N_L(d)} & \textit{max-likelihood estimate} \end{cases} \tag{1}$$

$$\mathrm{IDF}(t,c) := \begin{cases} -\log_2 \frac{n_D(t,c)}{N_D(c)} \\ -\log_{N_D(c)} \frac{n_D(t,c)}{N_D(c)} \end{cases} \tag{2}$$

The TF-IDF term weight is a combination of TF and IDF values.

$$w_{\textit{TF-IDF}}(t,d,q,c) := \mathrm{TF}(t,d) \cdot \mathrm{TF}(t,q) \cdot \mathrm{IDF}(t,c) \tag{3}$$

The RSV is the sum over the TF-IDF weights.

$$\textit{RSV}_{\textit{TF-IDF}}(d,q,c) := \sum_{t \in d \cap q} w_{\textit{TF-IDF}}(t,d,q,c) \tag{4}$$

The definition captures traditional TF-IDF and some of the probabilistic and information-theoretic interpretations proposed in [5, 18]. $\mathrm{TF}(t,d)$ is the within-document term frequency component. $\mathrm{TF}(t,d)$ can be set to one of the following: the BM25-motivated quantification $\mathrm{tf}_d/(\mathrm{tf}_d + K_d)$, K_d is a normalisation factor reflecting the document length and is usually proportional to the pivoted document length ($\mathrm{pivdl} := \mathrm{dl} / \mathrm{avgdl}$); and the maximum-likelihood estimate $P_L(t|d) := n_L(t,d)/N_L(d)$, which estimates the within-document term probability ($\mathrm{dl} := N_L(d)$ is the document length, i.e. the number of locations in document d).

$\mathrm{IDF}(t,c)$ is the inverse document frequency component. This can be the negative logarithm of the term probability $P_D(t|c) := n_D(t,c)/N_D(c)$. $\mathrm{IDF}(t,c)$ can also be normalised, for example, $\mathrm{idf}(t,c)/\mathrm{maxidf}$. This corresponds to the logarithm to base $N_D(c)$, since the maximum idf value is $\mathrm{maxidf} := -\log 1/N_D(c)$ [20].

The setting of the $\mathrm{TF}(t,d)$ to the BM25-motivated quantification and the $\mathrm{IDF}(t,c)$ to the normalised (probabilistic) one are the settings used for the experiments in Section 4.

DEFINITION 2. *LM RSV: Language modelling (LM) [16] consists of two term probabilities: the within-document term probability $P(t|d)$ (foreground model) and the collection-wide term probability $P(t|c)$ (background model).*

$$P(t|d) := P_L(t|d) := \frac{n_L(t,d)}{N_L(d)} \left(= \frac{\mathit{tf}(t,d)}{\sum_{t'} \mathit{tf}(t',d)} \right) \tag{5}$$

$$P(t|c) := P_L(t|c) := \frac{n_L(t,c)}{N_L(c)} \left(= \frac{\mathit{tf}(t,c)}{\sum_{t'} \mathit{tf}(t',c)} \right) \tag{6}$$

The LM term weight is defined as follows:

$$w_{\mathit{LM}}(t,d,c) := \log \left(1 + \frac{\lambda}{1-\lambda} \cdot \frac{P(t|d)}{P(t|c)} \right) \tag{7}$$

$$\mathit{RSV}_{\mathit{LM}}(d,q,c) := \sum_{t \in d \cap q} \mathrm{TF}(t,q) \cdot w_{\mathit{LM}}(t,d,c) \tag{8}$$

The RSV is derived from the conditional probability $P(q|d)$, which is based on $P(q|d)/(P(q) \cdot \prod_{t \in q}(1-\lambda)^{\mathrm{TF}(t,q)})$, i.e. a query-based but document-independent normalisation of the query probability $P(q|d)$.The $0 < \lambda < 1$ is the mixture parameter. The query probabilities are decomposed as follows: $P(q|d,c) = \prod_{t \in q} P(t|d,c)^{\mathrm{TF}(t,q)}$ and $P(q|c) = \prod_{t \in q} P(t|c)^{\mathrm{TF}(t,q)}$, where $P(t|d,c)$ is the mixed term probability.

2.3 Probabilistic SQL (PSQL)

The syntax of PSQL is like SQL apart from a few additional syntactic elements. For example, in the PSQL SELECT statement, one can specify an *aggregation assumption* in front of the target list, an *estimation assumption* per source, and an *estimation assumption* for the SELECT statement. One feature of PSQL is, hence, the estimation assumption, which locates probability estimation within the probabilistic relational paradigm. This differs from probabilistic relational algebra [8] and approaches such as [1] where probability estimation is modelled outside the relational paradigm, a feature perceived as disadvantageous by both developers and designers.

Below we illustrate the most commonly used syntactic elements particular to PSQL and their definitions. Their theoretical underpinnings are described in [20], and to improve readability, a summarised version of the syntax of PSQL is illustrated in Figure 1.

DEFINITION 3. ***Aggregation assumption:*** *DISJOINT, INDEPENDENT and SUBSUMED are the main aggregation assumptions. For DISJOINT, the aggregation corresponds to the sum of probabilities. For INDEPENDENT, the aggregation is based on the usual set overlap: $P(A \vee B) = P(A) + P(B) - P(A) \cdot P(B)$. For SUBSUMED, the aggregation yields the maximal probability.*

```
view ::= 'CREATE' 'VIEW' relName 'AS' query ';'
query ::= 'SELECT' [assumption] targetList
  'FROM' sourceList
  'WHERE' condition
  [ 'EVIDENCE' 'KEY' '(' key ')' ]
  [ 'ASSUMPTION' assumption ]
source ::= tradSrc | condSrc
tradSrc ::= relName | relName varName
condSrc ::= tradSrc '|' [assumption] '(' key ')'
key ::= | attrName | attrName ',' key
assumption ::= ... % see Definition 5
```

Figure 1: PSQL Syntax (extract)

DEFINITION 4. ***Evidence key:*** *An evidence key is a set of attributes. The notion "evidence" is borrowed from the conditional probability $P(h|e)$ where h is the hypothesis and e is the evidence.*

In the relational world, $P(\text{Term}|\text{Doc})$ is a probability that can be defined for a relation with attributes "Term" and "Doc". The set {Doc} is the evidence key. Evidence keys can be specified for the targets (SELECT targets) or for the sources (FROM source1, source2, ...) of an SQL query.

DEFINITION 5. ***Estimation assumption:*** *The estimation assumption is related to the evidence key and describes the way $P(h|e)$ is estimated. The main assumptions are: Disjoint, Independent, Subsumed and the so-called complex assumptions (e.g. VALUE_FREQ (VF), INVERSE_VALUE_FREQ (IVF), MAX_IVF, and similar for TUPLE_FREQ (TF)).*

One important feature of the estimation is whether the assumption is based on *value frequency*, or *tuple frequency*. Value frequency corresponds to the number of distinct relations in which a term occurs. For document-based retrieval (and IR in general), the *value* in a (Key, Value) pair corresponds to a *document*, i.e. (Term, Doc). Value-frequency-based estimation, for instance, is fundamental for estimating the IDF. An example of an assumption that facilitates such an estimation is the MAX_IVF assumption, which computes a probability according to the maximal inverse value frequency. For IR, this is the maximal IDF, i.e. MAX_IDF.

Tuple frequency, on the other hand, corresponds to the number of tuples (locations) in which a term occurs. For example, tuple-based probability corresponds to the so-called within-document term frequency (TF) of a term. This probability can be estimated using the TUPLE_FREQ (TF) assumption.

3. TUPLE RETRIEVAL

In [20] the application of PSQL to document retrieval was demonstrated. This lays the groundwork for this section where the generalisation from document retrieval to tuple retrieval is presented. For the demonstration, assume a term-based representation of queries and documents. The schema consists of two extensional relations, "qIdx(Term, QueryId)" and "docIdx(Term, DocId)". Given such a schema, document retrieval is:

```
-- Document retrieval in SQL
SELECT DISTINCT DocId, QueryId
 FROM qIdx Q, docIdx D   WHERE Q.Term = D.Term;
```

A typical SQL query, as the one shown above, can be decomposed into two parts: an indexing part and a retrieval part. This decomposition, which facilitates the discussion about the ranking of tuples, is illustrated using the following SQL query on table "properties(Type, Area, Price)": *find the areas with flats or studios in the price range 200-250k.*

```
SELECT Area FROM properties
 WHERE (Price BETWEEN 200 AND 250)
 AND (Type='Flat' OR Type='Studio');
```

Step 1: Create a view to index the source "properties".

```
CREATE VIEW areaIndex AS
 SELECT Type, Area   FROM properties
 WHERE Price BETWEEN 200 AND 250;
```

The view illustrates how an index ("areaIndex(Type, Area)") can be obtained for one attribute (here, the property type) and then used to retrieve areas with flats or studios in the price range 200-250k.

Step 2: Retrieve in document-retrieval fashion.

```
SELECT DISTINCT Area FROM areaIndex D
 WHERE D.Type = 'Flat' OR D.Type = 'Studio';
```

Figure 2 illustrates that this general decomposition helps to transform any SQL query into a form aligned with that of document retrieval. The significance of this alignment is that the ranking functions for document retrieval, such as the ones illustrated in [20], become applicable to tuple retrieval.

```
SELECT DISTINCT Doc
 FROM docIdx D
 WHERE D.Term = 'sailing'
 OR D.Term = 'east';
```

```
SELECT DISTINCT Area
 FROM areaIndex D
 WHERE D.Type = 'Flat'
 OR D.Type = 'Studio';
```

Figure 2: Alignment of Document and Tuple Retrieval

Having attained this aligned, or in other words, generalised SQL structure, a translation process takes place through which a well defined ranking is attached to this SQL query. This translation process is the transformation of the generalised SQL structure into PSQL programs that implement ranking functions, such as TF-IDF or LM. Note that the original information need ("Find from table properties the areas ...") is intact; yet, instead of a set-based processing of the SQL query, a rank-based processing takes place.

The following illustrates the SQL-to-PSQL (SQL2PSQL) translation process. To define the algorithms that automate the SQL2PSQL translation, we use the following notation. Each SQL query has a set of *conditioned attributes* (referred to as X), a set of *target attributes* (referred to as Y) and a *source relation(s)* (referred to as Z). For example, in document retrieval $X = \{\text{Term}\}$, $Y = \{\text{DocId}\}$ and $Z = \text{docIdx}$. Figure 3 presents the generalised structure of an SQL query.

```
SELECT DISTINCT Y                                  -- Y: {target attributes }
 FROM Z                                            -- Z: {sources}
 WHERE Z.X1='value1' OR Z.X1='value2' ...;          -- X: {conditioned attr.}
```

Figure 3: Generalised Structure of an SQL Query

The first algorithm decomposes the SQL expression and generates probabilistic views (spaces) that are later combined according to the ranking rationales of retrieval models, such as TF-IDF and LM. With respect to the generalisation of document retrieval to tuple retrieval, the location frequency corresponds to the tuple frequency, and the document frequency corresponds to the value frequency.

ALGORITHM 1. *SQL2PSQL: Basic Views*

For each conditioned attribute in X in SQL query "SELECT DISTINCT Y FROM Z WHERE X" create the following views:

1. *Tuple-based (Location-based) probabilities: p_Z_X. Probability $P_Z(X)$ is the tuple-based probability of X. View naming example: p_docIdx_Term.*

```
-- Tuple retrieval                 -- Document retrieval
CREATE VIEW p_Z_X AS               -- p_docIdx_Term
  SELECT SUM X                     -- X=Term
  FROM Z | ();                     -- Z=docIdx
-- Prob semantics: P_Z(X)          -- P_docIdx(Term)
```

2. *Value-based (Document-based) probabilities: p_Y_Z_X. Probability $P_{Z[Y]}(X)$ is the value-based probability of X. View naming example: p_DocId_docIdx_Term.*

```
-- Tuple retrieval                 -- Document retrieval
CREATE VIEW p_Y_Z_X AS             -- p_DocId_docIdx_Term
  SELECT X                         -- X={Term}
  FROM Z                           -- Z=docIdx
  ASSUMPTION VALUE_FREQ            -- DocId_Freq
  EVIDENCE KEY ();
  -- Prob semantics: P_Z[Y](X)     -- P_docIdx[DocId](Term)
```

3. *Conditional probabilities in sources: p_Z_X_Y. Probability $P_Z(X|Y)$ is the conditional probability of X. View naming example: p_docIdx_Term_DocId.*

```
-- Tuple retrieval                 -- Document retrieval
CREATE VIEW p_Z_X_Y AS             -- p_docIdx_Term_DocId
  SELECT SUM X, Y                  -- X={Term} Y={DocId}
  FROM Z | (Y);                    -- Z=docIdx
  -- Prob semantics: P_Z(X|Y)      -- P_docIdx_Term_DocId
```

4. *Information-based probabilities: p_inv_Y_Z_X. Probability P_Z(X informs) is the probability of X is informative. View naming example: p_inv_DocId_docIdx_Term.*

```
-- Tuple retrieval                 -- Document retrieval
CREATE VIEW p_inv_Y_Z_X AS         -- p_inv_DocId_docIdx_Term
  SELECT X FROM Z                  -- X={Term} Y={DocId} Z=docIdx
  ASSUMPTION MAX_IDF               -- idf(t)/max_idf
  EVIDENCE KEY ();
```

The SQL2PSQL algorithm generates probabilistic views independent of a particular retrieval model. The algorithms illustrated in the following sections show how and which of these views are used to construct retrieval models such as TF-IDF and LM.

3.1 TF-IDF-based Processing of SQL Queries

Algorithm 2 shows how a TF-IDF PSQL program is automatically generated for the genuine SQL query in Figure 3.

ALGORITHM 2. *SQL2PSQL(TF-IDF)*

Step 1: Create for each conditioned attribute X in SQL query "SELECT DISTINCT Y FROM Z WHERE cond(X)" one view to reflect tf and another one to reflect idf.

```
-- PSQL views generated for TF-IDF-based Retrieval

-- Tuple retrieval                     -- Document retrieval
CREATE VIEW Z_X_Y_tf                   -- docIdx_Term_DocId_tf
  SELECT X, Y FROM p_Z_X_Y;            -- p_docIdx_Term_DocId

CREATE VIEW pidf_Z_X                   -- pidf_docIdx_Term
  SELECT X FROM p_inv_Y_Z_X;           -- p_inv_DocId_docIdx_Term
```

Step 2: In the genuine query, replace each source (Z) by the tf (variable D) and idf (variable Q) relations of the specified attributes. Replace each ordinary *condition Z.X='value' by Q.X='value' AND Q.X=D.X. Replace each* join *condition Z1.X=Z2.X by D1.X=D2.X AND Q1.X=D1.X AND Q2.X=D2.X.*

For a genuine query SELECT Y FROM Z WHERE Z.X='value1' OR Z.X='value2', the output is:

```
SELECT SUM D.Y                               -- Y={DocId}
 FROM pidf_Z_X Q, Z_X_Y_tf D                 -- Z=docIdx, X={Term}
 WHERE Q.X='value1' AND Q.X=D.X
 OR    Q.X='value2' AND Q.X=D.X;
```

To improve readability, we omit the output for the join conditions. The algorithm generates a PSQL program for TF-IDF retrieval.

THEOREM 1. *Algorithm SQL2PSQL(TF-IDF) is correct.*

PROOF. The view Z_X_Y_tf (for document retrieval, p_docIdx_Term_DocId, i.e. the "TF" component) has the probabilistic semantics $P_Z(X|Y)$ ($P_{\text{docIdx}}(\text{Term}|\text{DocId})$). The view pidf_Z_X (for document retrieval, pidf_docIdx_Term) has the semantics $P(\text{X is informative}) = \text{idf}(X)/\text{maxidf}(c)$. The probabilities in the SQL query "SELECT SUM D.Y" correspond to $\sum_{t \in d \cap q} \text{TF}(t,d) \cdot \text{IDF}(t,c)/\text{maxidf}(c)$. □

3.2 LM-based Processing of SQL Queries

Algorithm 3 shows how an LM PSQL program is automatically generated for the genuine SQL query in Figure 3.

ALGORITHM 3. *SQL2PSQL(LM)*

Step 1: Create for each conditioned attribute X in query "SELECT DISTINCT Y FROM Z WHERE cond(X)" one view for the foreground *and one view for the* background *model. These correspond to the document and the collection model, respectively. The models are weighted with the respective mixture parameters. Next, the foreground is united with the background model. This yields the LM mixture in view "Z_X_mix".*

```
-- PSQL views generated for LM-based Retrieval

-- Tuple retrieval                    -- Document retrieval
-- foreground (fg) model              -- document model: P(t|d)
CREATE VIEW Z_X_Y_fg AS               -- docIdx_Term_DocId_fg
  SELECT X, Y                         -- X={Term}, Y={DocId}
  FROM p_Z_X_Y;                       -- p_docIdx_Term_DocId

-- background (bg) model              -- collection model: P(t|c)
CREATE VIEW Z_X_bg AS                 -- docIdx_Term_bg
  SELECT X                            -- X={Term}
  FROM p_Z_X;                         -- p_docIdx_Term

-- To conserve space, the automatic generation of weighted
-- foreground model and background model is omitted

CREATE VIEW Z_X_mix AS                -- docIdx_Term_mix
  lambda_Z_X_fg UNION DISJOINT        -- lambda_docIdx_Term_fg
  lambda_Z_X_bg;                      -- lambda_docIdx_Term_bg
```

Step 2: In the genuine SQL query, replace each source (Z) by Z_X_mix. For a genuine query SELECT Y FROM Z WHERE Z.X='value1' OR Z.X='value2', the output is:

```
SELECT PROD D.Y
 FROM Z_X_mix D
 WHERE D.X = 'value1' OR D.X = 'value2' ...
```

THEOREM 2. *Algorithm SQL2PSQL(LM) is correct.*

PROOF. The probabilistic views Z_X_Y_fg ($P(t|d)$) and Z_X_bg ($P(t|c)$) correspond to the docModel and collModel views in the reference implementation. The view Z_X_mix has the semantics $P(t|d,c) = \lambda \cdot P(t|d) + (1-\lambda) \cdot P(t|c)$. The probabilities in the SQL query "SELECT PROD D.Y" correspond to $P(q|d,c) = \prod_{t \in q} P(t|d,c)$. □

This concludes the ranking-based processing of SQL queries. The SQL2PSQL translation has been given for a simple SQL query (one source relation, one specified attribute, one target attribute). The translation, however, applies to multiple sources, ordinary and joined conditions and several attributes in the target list, all of which have been demonstrated in the algorithms and proofs.

4. EVALUATION

The purpose of the evaluation is twofold. Firstly, it demonstrates the feasibility of the proposed technology, namely the PSQL framework and the SQL2PSQL functionality. Secondly, using the TREC benchmark [20] demonstrated how the PSQL framework is capable of solving traditional IR tasks (e.g. TREC experiments). The evaluation is now extended to more structured/semantic benchmarks.

4.1 Set-up

The evaluation employs the *IMDB* and *Monster* benchmarks. The former consists of 437,281 documents with 40 topics, and the latter consists of 1,040,000 documents with 60 topics. The experiments were run on a single CPU using a DB+IR prototype [20] that supports the retrieval of text, structured and semi-structured data. The prototype provides customisable concepts to represent the data and supports PSQL to implement the ranking models.

To demonstrate how the modelling framework performs, we evaluate the generated retrieval models, TF-IDF and LM (settings in Section 2.2), with respect to a restricted evidence size. In standard IR this corresponds to processing the most selective terms first and choosing the top-k document Ids from the posting list. The aim is to investigate how much quality can be achieved by the implemented retrieval models and at what *cost*. This cost-based evaluation is with respect to the retrieval model itself and how favourably or poorly it utilises the underlying evidence. One achievement is to support nested expressions whereby the required efficiency can be achieved via top-k and evidence-based processing. Nowadays, relational approaches to IR often rely on materialisation and are based on stepwise processing pipelines. The views used to implement the models, however, have *not* been materialised, and, hence, the cost includes the time to generate and process them.

We report the retrieval quality of the generated programs and the average retrieval time (total retrieval time divided by the total number of queries) of the generated programs against the number of evidence tuples. The number of considered evidence tuples ranges from 10,000 to 200,000. We use Mean Average Precision (MAP) and Reciprocal Rank (RecipRank) as the evaluation metrics.

The *baselines* are based on the document-oriented TF-IDF and LM retrieval models with no top-k processing. In other words, the structure of the data is not taken into consideration by the retrieval model and a bag-of-words representation is utilised. In the case of tuple retrieval, however, the document structure (see Section 4.2 for the list of element types) is considered when constructing the SQL queries. Note that the purpose of the evaluation is primarily to present the *feasibility* of the modelling framework and translation algorithms. Other task-specific retrieval models can be generated.

To *formulate the SQL queries*, the keyword queries and the *ideal* mapped attribute for each query term are used. This ideal attribute is extracted from the set of relevant documents for each query term.

The intuition behind the mapping is that if a term occurs frequently within a certain element type then it is more likely to be "characterised" by that type [12]. This method offers an easy way to automatically transfer a keyword-based query to a structured one. The correctness of the extracted attribute is verified manually. After the SQL query is formulated it is automatically augmented with the desired ranking strategy which results in a relevance-based processing of that query. Below is an SQL-based formulation of IMDB query number 28 "*gladiator action maximus scott*".

```
SELECT Movie
 FROM movies WHERE Title = 'gladiator' AND Genre = 'action'
 AND Plot = 'maximus' AND Director = ' scott ' ;
```

As noted above, when creating the SQL queries, only the top-mapped attribute for each query term is considered. For example, the top-mapped attribute for query term "gladiator" is "Title". This is particularly important when evaluating a larger and noisier dataset such as Monster because the significant term overlap among the different elements makes estimating the correct attributes a challenge. However, the focus of our experimental study is not on the mapping process, and the SQL2PSQL facility is flexible enough to process queries with multiple attributes in the target list and any other customisations.

4.2 IMDB

The IMDB dataset is formatted in XML and was constructed from text data (http://www.imdb.com/interfaces#plain). Each document corresponds to a movie.

	MAP	RecipRank	Time (s)
SQL2PSQL(TF-IDF:10k)	44.01	45.42	00.24
SQL2PSQL(TF-IDF:20k)	46.09	47.42	00.59
SQL2PSQL(TF-IDF:50k)	48.80	48.58	00.70
SQL2PSQL(TF-IDF:100k)	49.96	49.27	00.87
SQL2PSQL(TF-IDF:200k)	**54.37**† (+13.06)	**55.64**† (+13.92)	01.28
Baseline: TF-IDF:All	48.09	48.84	
SQL2PSQL(LM:10k)	27.75	29.19	00.19
SQL2PSQL(LM:20k)	31.30	32.19	00.50
SQL2PSQL(LM:50k)	42.70	43.89	00.75
SQL2PSQL(LM:100k)	*43.90*† (+09.37)	*44.43*† (+08.63)	01.05
SQL2PSQL(LM:200k)	41.85	42.47	01.27
Baseline: LM:All	40.13	40.90	

Table 1: Quality w.r.t number of evidence tuples considered; the best overall result is in bold, and the best result out of the baseline and its tuple-based variant is italicised; results that are statistically significant ($p < 0.05$) above the baseline are denoted by †, as determined by a signed t-test.

There are several processing steps that present the data in the form that is best situated for achieving effective retrieval. For example, we have opted to propagate the keywords occurring within elements such as "actor" and "director" upwards to their corresponding part. Having a coarser schema helps to improve the accuracy of the derived attributes for each query term. Another example is that the terms that occur in a specific context have also been propagated upwards to the root element. This propagation helps to model document-based retrieval as opposed to element-based one.

[12] provided the test-bed which included 40 queries. These queries were created assuming a situation in which a user wants to find a movie using partial information spanning over many elements. Relevant documents were found manually.

As discussed in Section 3, the SQL queries are decomposed into two parts: an indexing part and a retrieval part. In the retrieval part, for each query the SQL2PSQL algorithm (Algorithm 1) generates a set of probabilistic views independently of a particular retrieval model. These views are then used to construct the desired retrieval model. For the evaluation, the generated relevance-based ranking of the SQL queries is based on SQL2PSQL(TF-IDF) and SQL2PSQL(LM) algorithms (Algorithm 2 and Algorithm 3).

In Table 1 the values in parenthesis represent the relative (percentage) difference in performance from the baseline results. If evidence beyond the 200,000 tuples for the generated TF-IDF program is considered, retrieval quality continues to monotonically increase. However, considering further evidence tuples for the generated LM program (optimal performance $\lambda \approx 0.7$) does not significantly increase the quality; in fact, after a certain amount of evidence is considered, it starts to decrease. This degradation is due to the top-k operators, which are optimised for the TF-IDF-based models.

4.3 Monster

The benchmark contains longer documents with more complex structure and full text content than the IMDB. Moreover, the queries, job requests created by users of the Monster service, are longer and more complex. An example of a keyword-based query is "*aircraft airplane mechanic technician tech fort riley kansas*". This query seeks an Aircraft Structural Mechanic to determine the methods to repair malfunctioning or damaged components of aircrafts in Fort Riley, Kansas. Similar to the IMDB we have adopted a coarse schema to improve the accuracy of the derived SQL queries.

	MAP	RecipRank	Time (s)
SQL2PSQL(TF-IDF:10k)	22.00	39.17	00.41
SQL2PSQL(TF-IDF:20k)	23.89	42.51	00.98
SQL2PSQL(TF-IDF:50k)	24.79	46.94	01.13
SQL2PSQL(TF-IDF:100k)	27.04	51.84	01.32
SQL2PSQL(TF-IDF:200k)	**29.22**† (+11.34)	**54.45**† (+13.39)	01.85
Baseline: TF-IDF:All	26.23	48.02	
SQL2PSQL(LM:10k)	17.10	22.25	00.42
SQL2PSQL(LM:20k)	18.04	26.51	00.78
SQL2PSQL(LM:50k)	20.91	30.94	00.91
SQL2PSQL(LM:100k)	*22.84*† (+08.09)	*32.84*† (+08.24)	01.31
SQL2PSQL(LM:200k)	21.02	31.45	01.78
Baseline: LM:All	21.13	30.34	

Table 2: Quality w.r.t Number of Evidence Tuples Considered

Table 2 illustrates the quality results of the TF-IDF and LM generated programs. As previously observed, considering evidence tuples beyond 200,000 does not significantly increase retrieval quality. The average retrieval times demonstrate the processing cost for the ranking-based processing of the SQL queries. The retrieval quality is reasonable at the one second ceiling, but further precision requires longer retrieval times. Although the retrieval times appear to be scalable, the processing costs can present a further challenge if lager text-based or semi-structured datasets are used. One solution is [11], which demonstrates how the probabilistic descriptive approach employed herein can be parallelised.

5. SUMMARY & CONCLUSION

This paper advances the feasibility of using IR models for processing SQL queries and develops the application of PSQL for tuple retrieval. The SQL2PSQL translation algorithms were shown to generate PSQL programs that assign an IR-model-based, probabilistic ranking to the tuples retrieved for an SQL query.

The evaluation showed that the PSQL framework and the SQL2PSQL facility deliver good retrieval performance. This outcome is a direct consequence of the IR models. The main contributions are customisable rankings and the expressiveness to model tuple retrieval while incorporating keyword-based document retrieval models. A quality-oriented evaluation is required. Ideally, however, this evaluation should measure how DB+IR technology improves *productivity*, and specifically, how it adapts to customer-tailored and changing relevance criteria. Developing such an evaluation measure is part of future research.

The ranking-aware processing of SQL queries is particularly relevant at a time when SQL queries, and more generally, structured queries, are increasingly being generated by applications built on top of search engines. The SQL2PSQL facility is also applicable to other structured query languages such as SPARQL. For example, a SPARQL2SQL translation, which acts as a query processing front-end, or a more direct one, such as SPARQL2PSQL, can be implemented. This re-use of the proposed SQL2PSQL technology can lead to general-purpose DB+IR solutions.

The automatic generation of PSQL from SQL has a twofold impact. The generation of "seamless" DB+IR technology becomes more accessible since applications/users are not required to learn PSQL to achieve customisable and re-usable retrieval strategies. Moreover, well-defined rankings are available as modules ready to be tailored to specific search tasks and to other structured query languages. In summary, the presented DB+IR approach supports the use of SQL and extends the well-defined IR models for the effective ranking of documents *and* tuples.

6. ACKNOWLEDGMENTS

We are grateful for the support of Yahoo! Labs Barcelona. We would also like to thank Prof. Bruce Croft for providing us with the two benchmarks, and the reviewers for their excellent suggestions.

7. REFERENCES

[1] D. Barbara, H. Garcia-Molina, and D. Porter. A probabilistic relational data model. In *Proc. of EDBT*, 1990.

[2] J. Callan. Search engine support for software applications. In *Proc. of CIKM*, 2010.

[3] A. Chandel, O. Hassanzadeh, N. Koudas, M. Sadoghi, and D. Srivastava. Benchmarking declarative approximate selection predicates. In *Proc. of SIGMOD*, 2007.

[4] S. Chaudhuri, G. Das, V. Hristidis, and G. Weikum. Probabilistic IR approach for ranking of DBs query results. *ACM TODS*, 31(3):1134–1168, 2006.

[5] K. Church and W. Gale. Inverse document frequency (IDF): A measure of deviation from Poisson. In *Proc. of the Workshop on Very Large Corpora*, 1995.

[6] R. Cornacchia and A. de Vries. A Parameterised Search System. In *Proc. of ECIR*, 2007.

[7] N. Dalvi and D. Suciu. Efficient query evaluation on probabilistic DBs. In *Proc. of VLDB*, 2004.

[8] N. Fuhr and T. Roelleke. A probabilistic relational algebra for the integration of IR and DB systems. *ACM TOIS*, 14(1):32–66, 1997.

[9] D. Hawking. Challenges in enterprise search. In *Proc. of ADC*, 2004.

[10] D. Hiemstra and V. Mihajlovic. A DB approach to IR: The remarkable relationship between language models and region models. Technical Report, 2010.

[11] I. Klampanos, H. Azzam, T. Roelleke: A case for probabilistic logic for scalable patent retrieval. In *Proc. of the Workshop on Patent Information Retrieval*, 2009.

[12] J. Kim, X. Xue, and W. Croft. A probabilistic retrieval model for semistructured data. In *Proc. of ECIR*, 2009.

[13] C. Li, K. Chen-Chuan Chang, I. Ilyas, and S. Song. RankSQL: Query algebra and optimization for relational Top-k queries. In *Proc. SIGMOD*, 2005.

[14] P. Mika, E. Meij, and H. Zaragoza. Investigating the semantic gap through query log analysis. In *Proc. of ISWC*, 2009.

[15] A. Motro. Vague: A user interface to relational DBs that permits vague queries. *ACM Trans. on Office Information Systems*, 6(3):187–214, 1988.

[16] J. Ponte and W. Croft. A language modeling approach to IR. In *Proc. of SIGIR*, 1998.

[17] C. Ré and D. Suciu. Materialized views in probabilistic DBs: for information exchange and query optimization. In *Proc. of VLDB*, 2007.

[18] S. Robertson. Understanding inverse document frequency: On theoretical arguments for IDF. *Journal of Documentation*, 60:503–520, 2004.

[19] S. Robertson, S. Walker, and M. Hancock-Beaulieu. Large test collection experiments on an operational interactive system: Okapi at TREC. *IP&M*, 31:345–360, 1995.

[20] T. Roelleke, H. Wu, J. Wang, and H. Azzam. Modelling retrieval models in a probabilistic relational algebra with a new operator: The relational Bayes. *VLDB Journal*, 17(1):5–37, January 2008.

[21] M. Theobald, R. Schenkel, and G. Weikum. An efficient and versatile query engine for TopX search. In *Proc. of VLDB*, 2005.

Keyword Search over RDF Graphs

Shady Elbassuoni *†
Max-Planck Institute for Informatics
Saarbrücken, Germany
elbass@mpii.de

Roi Blanco
Yahoo! Labs
Barcelona, Spain
roi@yahoo-inc.com

ABSTRACT

Large knowledge bases consisting of entities and relationships between them have become vital sources of information for many applications. Most of these knowledge bases adopt the Semantic-Web data model RDF as a representation model. Querying these knowledge bases is typically done using structured queries utilizing graph-pattern languages such as SPARQL. However, such structured queries require some expertise from users which limits the accessibility to such data sources. To overcome this, keyword search must be supported. In this paper, we propose a retrieval model for keyword queries over RDF graphs. Our model retrieves a set of subgraphs that match the query keywords, and ranks them based on statistical language models. We show that our retrieval model outperforms the-state-of-the-art IR and DB models for keyword search over structured data using experiments over two real-world datasets.

Categories and Subject Descriptors

H.3.3 [**Information Storage and Retrieval**]: Information Search and Retrieval—*retrieval models, search process*

General Terms

Algorithms, Design, Experimentation

1. INTRODUCTION

The continuous growth of knowledge-sharing communities like Wikipedia and the advances in automated information-extraction from Web pages [5, 23] have made it possible to build large-scale knowledge bases. Examples of such knowledge bases include YAGO [26], DBpedia [1] and Freebase [7]. These repositories contain entities such as people, movies, books, etc. and the relationships between them such as `bornIn` , `actedIn` , `isAuthorOf` and so on. Such data is typically represented in the form of subject-predicate-object triples of the Semantic-Web data model RDF [22], where subjects and objects are entities and predicates are relationships between pairs of entities. An RDF collection conceptually forms a large graph, which we refer to as an RDF graph, with nodes corresponding to subjects and objects and edges denoting predicates. Table 1 shows a set of RDF triples from a movie knowledge base.

*Work performed while intern at Yahoo! Research.
†This work is partially supported by the EU Large Scale Integrated Project LivingKnowledge (contract no. 231126).

CIKM'11, October 24–28, 2011, Glasgow, Scotland, UK.

Subject (S)	Property (P)	Object (O)
Traffic	hasWonPrize	Academy_Award
Innerspace	hasWonPrize	Academy_Award
Innerspace	hasGenre	Comedy
Joe_Dante	directed	Innerspace
Toy_Story	hasWonPrize	Academy_Award
Road_Trip	hasGenre	Comedy
Toy_Story	hasGenre	Comedy
Tom_Hanks	actedIn	Toy_Story
Diner	hasWonPrize	Academy_Award
Diner	type	Comedy_films
Steve_Guttenberg	actedIn	Diner
The_Pink_Panther	type	Criminal_comedy_films
The_Pink_Panther	hasWonPrize	Academy_Award
Police_Academy	type	Comedy_films
Steve_Guttenberg	actedIn	Police_Academy
The_Darwin_Awards	type	Comedy_films

Table 1: A set of RDF triples from a movie knowledge base

RDF data can be queried using a conjunction of *triple patterns*, where a triple pattern is a triple with variables and the same variable in different patterns denotes a join condition. For example, the information need of finding comedies that have won the Academy Award can be expressed using the following 2 triple-patterns: `<?x hasGenre Comedy; ?x hasWonPrize Academy_Award>`.

Structured queries like the one above are very expressive, yet very restrictive. They require the users to be familiar with the underlying data and a structured-query language like SPARQL. Empowering users to search RDF graphs using keywords only can increase the usability of such data sources. In addition, it enables adapting the-state-of-the-art IR searching and ranking techniques.

In this paper, we develop a retrieval model that enables users to search RDF graphs using *keywords*. Our model takes as an input a keyword query and returns a ranked list of *RDF subgraphs*. By retrieving subgraphs instead of just entities, we treat triples in a holistic manner and we explicitly take into account the relationships between the entities. This can be particularly beneficial for both result retrieval and result representation. As an example, consider running the query "comedy academy award" against the RDF collection in Table 1. One possible result to such a query retrieved by our model is the 2-triple subgraph `<Innerspace hasGenre Comedy; Innerspace hasWonPrize Academy_Award>`.

To be able to process keyword queries over RDF graphs, we associate each triple with a set of keywords derived from the subject and object of the triple, as well as representative keywords for the predicate. We explain how we do this in Section 3. To retrieve all subgraphs that match a given keyword query, we utilize a backtracking algorithm over graphs, which is described in Section 4.

Once candidate subgraphs have been retrieved, we need to rank them. We try to identify the *structured-information need* intended by the keyword query. For instance, consider the query "comedy academy award". It is likely that the user is looking for movies of genre comedy that have won the Academy Award. Thus, we need to rank the subgraphs that match this information need higher. Our ranking model is based on statistical language-models and it utilizes the distribution of terms in the whole knowledge base as a means of inferring the structured-information need of a user keyword query. For instance, given that the term 'comedy' appears often in the object of triples with predicate `hasGenre` and the terms 'academy' and 'award' appear often in the object of triples with predicate `hasWonPrize`, we can infer that the most likely structured triple-pattern query intended by the keyword query "comedy academy award" is `<?x hasGenre Comedy; ?x hasWonPrize Academy_Award>`. We thus rank subgraphs that match this implicit structured-query higher. We explain our ranking model in Section 5.

To show the effectiveness of our retrieval model, we create a benchmark for keyword queries over two real-world RDF datasets and use it to compare our ranking model to well-known IR and DB techniques for keyword search over structured data. Our evaluation results are highlighted in Section 6.

2. RELATED WORK

The work on keyword search over structured data can be classified into two classes. The first class aims at mapping the keyword query into one or more structured query. For instance, the authors in [27] assume that the user keyword-query is an implicit representation of a structured triple-pattern query. They try to infer such structured query using the RDF graph and retrieve the top-k most relevant structured queries. They then provide the user with the retrieved queries and let her choose the most appropriate structured query to be evaluated. Their approach involves user interaction, and in addition suffers from a loss-of-information phenomenon since typically k is set to a small number.

The work on query inference from a user's natural language question in [18] is also closely related. It utilizes natural-language processing tools and try to parse a user's question in order to infer the most-likely structured query. Their technique however relies heavily on the quality of the parsing process and it also suffers from the information-loss problem highlighted above.

The second class of work on keyword search over structured data overcomes the aforementioned issues by directly retrieving results of the keyword query. The work on keyword search over XML data for instance falls into this category. XKSearch [29] returns a set of nodes that contain the query keywords either in their labels or in the labels of their descendant nodes and have no descendant node that also contains all keywords. Similarly, XRank [9] returns the set of elements that contain at least one occurrence of all of the query keywords, after excluding the occurrences of the keywords in subelements that already contain all of the query keywords. However, all these techniques assume a tree-structure and thus can not be directly applied to graph-structured data such as RDF graphs.

Also, closely related to our work is the language-modeling approach for keyword search over XML data proposed in [14]. The authors assume that a keyword query has an implicit mapping of each keyword into XML element(s). Their ranking is based on the hierarchal language-models proposed in [20] and they utilize the distribution of terms in the elements of the XML collection to weight the different component of the LMs. However, the setting of XML data is quite different from that of RDF since in XML the retrieval unit is an XML document (or a subtree). In an RDF setting, we are interested in ranking subgraphs that match the user's query. These subgraphs are not known in advance and are computed on the fly during retrieval time, and thus most of the prior work on XML IR would not apply.

Keyword search on graphs which returns a ranked list of Steiner trees [2, 12, 10, 8] (the exception is [17] which returns graphs) deals with the latter problem of having a predefined retrieval unit. However, the result ranking in each of the above is based on the structure of the results [2, 13] (usually based on aggregating the number or weights of nodes and edges), or on a combination of these properties with content-based measures such as tf-idf [4, 10, 17] or language models [19].

A closely related work that combines structure and content for ranking is the LM-based ranking model in [19] for ranking objects (entities in an RDF setting). This model however assumes that the retrieval unit is entities only, while our ranking model goes beyond this to treat triples in a holistic manner by taking into account the relationships between the entities. In addition, it assumes the presence of a document associated with each Web Object or entity, something that we lack in the case of RDF data in general.

The Semantic Search Challenge provided a benchmark for keyword queries over RDF data, however the judgments were made over entities built by assembling all the triples that shared the same subject. The best performing approach [3] ranked the entities using a combination of BM25F and additional hand-crafted information about some predicates, properties and sites. In contrast, we retrieve the set of subgraphs that match the query keywords and rank them. We believe that the graph representation provides more concise answers to the user information need than a set of entities.

3. SYSTEM OVERVIEW

Our knowledge base consists of a set of SPO-triples such as the one shown in Table 1. To be able to process keyword queries, we construct a virtual document for each triple t_i which we refer to as D_i. D_i contains a set of keywords that are extracted from the subject and object of the triple, and representative keywords for the predicates (these can be generated from extraction patterns for instance [25]). For example, the triple `<Innerspace hasWonPrize Academy_Award>` would be associated with the following document: {*innerspace, won, prize, academy, award*}. In case there are any textual information associated with the triple t_i such as the contextual text from which the triple was extracted [6], we can also extract all the keywords there and add them to D_i. We stem the terms in document D_i using any standard stemmer and store them in an inverted index. In addition, we also store the term frequency of term w in D_i, which we refer to as $c(w, D_i)$.

Given a keyword query, we utilize our inverted index to retrieve, for each query keyword, a list of matching triples. We then join the triples from different lists based on their subjects and objects to retrieve subgraphs with one or more triples. However, we only construct subgraphs that contain triples from *different* lists, corresponding to matches to different (sets of) keywords. The intuition behind this is that we assume that the user has a precise information need in mind that can be precisely represented using a set of triple patterns. However, since the user cannot express her information need using triple patterns, she represents each triple pattern using a set of keywords. Without any knowledge about which keywords map to which triple pattern, we need to consider all extremes: from all keywords representing a single triple pattern up to each single keyword representing an individual triple pattern. Thus, the results

Subgraphs	Keywords
Traffic hasWonPrize Academy_Award	academy, award
Innerspace hasGenre Comedy Innerspace hasWonPrize Academy_Award	comedy academy, award
Toy_Story hasGenre Comedy Toy_Story hasWonPrize Academy_Award	comedy academy, award
Road_Trip hasGenre Comedy	comedy
Diner type Comedy_films Diner hasWonPrize Academy_Award	comedy academy, award
The_Pink_Panther type Criminal_comedy_films The_Pink_Panther hasWonPrize Academy_Award	comedy academy, award
Police_Academy type Comedy_films The_Darwin_Awards type Comedy_films	academy, comedy award, comedy

Table 2: All subgraphs retrieved for the query "comedy academy award"

to the user information need would be subgraphs with one or more triples up to the number of keywords in the user query. Our algorithm for retrieving subgraphs is described in Section 4.

For example, consider the information need of finding comedies that have won the Academy Award. Furthermore assume that the user expressed this information need using the keyword query "comedy academy award". The results for such a query would then be single triples matching one or more query keywords, subgraphs with 2 triples matching at least 2 query keywords and so on. Table 2 shows all subgraphs retrieved given the query from our example RDF collection in Table 1. The second column shows the set of matched keywords by each triple in the corresponding subgraph.

Since keyword queries introduce additional ambiguity that is not present in the case of structured triple-pattern queries, result ranking becomes very crucial. For instance, the subgraphs in Table 2 differ in their size (i.e., how many triples they contain) as well as how many keywords they match. In addition, they also differ in their semantics. For instance, consider the last subgraph in Table 2. It states the fact that the movies `Police_Academy` and `The_Darwin_Awards` are both comedy movies. The rest of the subgraphs in Table 2 describe movies that have genre comedy and have won the Academy Award. Recall our earlier observation that the user keyword query is a representation of an implicit structured triple-pattern query. Thus, in order to provide an effective ranking, the system must infer what is the most likely structured query the user has in mind, and rank the subgraphs based on how well they match this implicit structured query. Our ranking model, described in Section 5, does this by combining the structure and the contents of the triples in the ranking function.

4. SUBGRAPH RETRIEVAL

As mentioned in the previous section, the first step is to retrieve the set of subgraphs that match the user keyword query. In order to avoid retrieving subgraphs that are arbitrarily long, we restrict the subgraphs retrieved to have the following two properties:

1. The subgraphs should be unique and maximal. That is, each subgraph retrieved should not be a subset of any other subgraph retrieved.
2. The subgraphs should contain triples matching different sets of keywords. That is, no triples in the same subgraph would match the exact same set of keywords. If two triples match the same set of keywords, they are parts of two different possible results to the user query, and should be considered as parts of two separate subgraphs.

Our subgraph-retrieval algorithm starts by retrieving the lists of all triples matching the query keywords. That is, given a query

Algorithm 1 RETRIEVESUBGRAPHS(E)

for each edge $t \in E$ **do**
  $X \leftarrow \{t \in A(t)\}$
  EXTENDSUBGRAPH($\{t\}$, X)
end for

Algorithm 2 EXTENDSUBGRAPH(G, X)

1: **while** $X \neq \phi$ **do**
2:   Remove an arbitrary chosen edge t from X
3:   **if** $L(\{t\}) \not\subseteq L(G)$ and $L(G) \not\subseteq L(\{t\})$ **then**
4:     $X' \leftarrow X \cup \{t' \in NEIGHBORS(t, G)\}$
5:     EXTENDSUBGRAPH($G \cup \{t\}$, X')
6:   **end if**
7: **end while**
8: **if** MAXIMAL(G) $\neq true$ **then**
9:   **print** G
10:   **return**
11: **end if**

$q = \{q_1, q_2, ..., q_m\}$ where q_i is a single keyword, we utilize our inverted index to retrieve lists $\{L_1, L_2, ..., L_m\}$ where L_i is the list of all triples that match the keyword q_i (see Table **??**). Let the set of all unique triples in all the lists be E. This set E can be viewed as a disconnected graph which we refer to as the *query graph* . Recall that each triple can be viewed as an edge where its subject and object are nodes.

We adapt the backtracking algorithm for network-motif detection in [28] to retrieve the subgraphs from the query graph. The modified algorithm utilizes adjacency lists for edges. Given an edge t_i from list L_i, its adjacency list $A(t_i)$ would contain all neighbor edges t_j from all other lists L_j. Two edges are considered neighbors if they share a common node. That is, given an edge $t_i = \langle s_i\ p_i\ o_i \rangle$, an edge $t_j = \langle s_j\ p_j\ o_j \rangle$ would be a neighbor of t_i if $s_i = s_j$, $s_i = o_j$, $o_i = s_j$ or $o_i = o_j$. In order to retrieve only unique subgraphs, we associate with each edge t_i an id and we only add a neighbor to the adjacency list of t_i if its id is greater than that of t_i. Also, to ensure that we do not consider joining triples that match the same set of keywords, we only add a neighbor t_j to the adjacency list $A(t_i)$ of triple t_i if and only if $t_i \notin L_j$ and $t_j \notin L_i$. Finally, we loop over all edges and generate all unique subgraphs using the following two algorithms.

Algorithm 1 loops over all the edges and for each edge t extracts its neighbors from its adjacency list $A(t)$. Algorithm 2 takes as an input a subgraph and a list of neighbors and recursively tries to add edges to this subgraph. The condition in line 3 of Algorithm 2 ensures that only edges that belong to at least one different list other than the lists the edges of the current subgraph G belong to are considered. This ensures that we construct only subgraphs whose edges match different sets of keywords. The function $L(G)$ returns the set of lists the edges of a subgraph G belong to. Once an edge is added to the current subgraph, we also add its neighbors that are not neighbors of edges in G to the current list of neighbors and continue. The function $NEIGHBORS(t, G)$ retrieves all neighbors of an edge t that are not neighbors to edges in G. Finally, the function $MAXIMAL(G)$ ensures that the retrieved subgraph is unique and maximal.

5. RANKING MODEL

In the previous section, we presented a graph-searching algorithm that retrieves a set of subgraphs matching a given keyword query. We now explain how we rank these subgraphs. Our ranking model is based on statistical language-models (LMs) [21] and works as follows. Given a query $Q = \{q_1, q_2, ..., q_m\}$ where q_i is a single term and a subgraph $G = \{t_1, t_2, ..., t_n\}$ where t_j is a triple, we rank the subgraph G based on the *query likelihood* or the probability of generating the query Q given the subgraph G's LM. Assuming independence between the query terms, the query likelihood $P(Q|G)$ is computed as follows:

$$P(Q|G) = \prod_{i=1}^{m} P(q_i|G) \tag{1}$$

where $P(q_i|G)$ is the probability of the term q_i in the LM of G. The LM of subgraph G is computed as a mixture model of the LMs of its constituent triples as follows:

$$P(q_i|G) = \sum_{j=1}^{n} \frac{1}{n} P(q_i|t_j) \tag{2}$$

That is, the probability of a term q_i in the subgraph LM is the average of its probability in the triples LMs. Note that more than one triple in subgraph G can match the same keyword q_i and thus averaging over all the triples is a natural choice. The LM of a triple t_j can then be directly computed using the document of the triple . Recall from Section 3 that each triple t_j is associated with a virtual document D_j which is composed of all the terms associated with the triple. However, this approach completely ignores the structure of the triples and treats every triple as a bag-of-words. For instance, consider the query "comedy academy award" to find comedies that have won the Academy award. Now, consider the 2 subgraphs G_1 = `<Innerspace hasGenre Comedy; Innerspace hasWonPrize Academy_Award>` and G_2 = `<The_Darwin_Awards type Comedy_films; Police_Academy type Comedy_films>` matching the query. Given the intended information need of the query, we should rank the subgraph G_1 higher.

In our ranking model, we try to take into consideration the structure of the triples as an additional evidence of how well they match the structured-information need intended by the keyword query. This is motivated by our earlier remark that we built our retrieval model on: a user keyword query is a representation of an implicit structured triple-pattern query. Considering our example query "comedy academy award", the term 'comedy' most likely refer to the triple pattern `<?x hasGenre Comedy>` given the fact that the term 'comedy' appears more often in the documents of triples of the form `<s hasGenre Comedy>`. Similarly, the terms 'academy' and 'award' would likely refer to the pattern `<?x hasWonPrize Academy_Award>` . Thus, it would be desirable to assign higher probability mass to triples that match these patterns (i.e., triples with predicate `hasGenre` for the keyword 'comedy' and `hasWonPrize` for the keywords 'academy' and 'award').

To this end, we set the probability of a term q_i in the triple t_j's LM or $P(q_i|t_j)$ in equation 2 to $P(q_i|D_j, r_j)$. That is, the probability of a term in a triple LM does not only depend on the document of the triple t_j, but also on its predicate which we denote by r_j. Applying Bayes' rule, we have:

$$P(q_i|D_j, r_j) = \frac{P(q_i|D_j)P(r_j|q_i, D_j)}{P(r_j|D_j)} \tag{3}$$

Furthermore, we set $P(r_j|q_i, D_j)$ as a linear combination of the following two components [24, 16, 15]:

$$P(r_j|q_i, D_j) = \beta P(r_j|q_i) + (1-\beta)P(r_j|D_j) \tag{4}$$

The first component in equation 4 is the probability that the predicate r_j is relevant to the term q_i whereas the second component is the probability that the predicate of triple t_j is r_j. The latter can be set to the extraction accuracy of triple t_j for instance. Since this value is not generally present in RDF knowledge bases, we assume that we are always fully confident in the extraction quality of any triple, and set $P(r_j|D_j)$ to 1. The parameter β is a weighting parameter that controls the effect of each component on the ranking and can be set using training queries.

Substituting equation 4 in equation 3 and simplifying, we have:

$$P(q_i|D_j, r_j) = \beta P(q_i|D_j)P(r_j|q_i) + (1-\beta)P(q_i|D_j) \tag{5}$$

where $P(q_i|D_j)$ is the probability of generating the term q_i from the triple document D_j which can be estimated using a maximum likelihood estimator after smoothing with the collection probability as follows:

$$P(q_i|D_j) = \alpha \frac{c(q_i, D_j)}{|D_j|} + (1-\alpha)\frac{c(q_i, Col)}{|Col|} \tag{6}$$

where $c(w, D_j)$ is the term frequency of term w in document D_j, $|D_j|$ is the length of document D_j (i.e., the sum of the term frequencies of all terms in D_j), Col is the whole collection constructed by concatenating all the documents of all the triples in the knowledge base and $|Col|$ is the length of the whole collection. Finally, the parameter α is a smoothing parameter and is set according to Dirichlet prior smoothing [30].

The only remaining component to estimate in equation 5 is the probability of relevance of the predicate r_j to the query term q_i. In order to estimate this probability, we first construct a document R_j for each predicate r_j in the knowledge base concatenating the documents of all the triples with such predicate. For instance, given the predicate `hasGenre` , we construct a document which is a concatenation of all the documents of all triples of the form `<s hasGenre o>` . Once we have constructed a document R_j for each predicate r_j, we set the probability of relevance of r_j to a term q_i or $P(r_j|q_i)$ in equation 5 to the $P(R_j|q_i)$ (i.e., the probability of relevance of the document R_j to the term q_i). Applying Bayes' rule, the probability $P(R_j|q_i)$ can be estimated as follows:

$$P(R_j|q_i) = \frac{P(q_i|R_j)P(R_j)}{P(q_i)} = \frac{P(q_i|R_j)P(R_j)}{\sum_k P(q_i|R_k)P(R_k)} \tag{7}$$

where $P(w|R_j)$ is the probability of generating the term w given the document R_j which is estimated using a maximum-likelihood estimator as in equation 6 and $P(R_j)$ is the prior probability of the document R_j being relevant to any term, which we set uniformly. For example, using the above technique, the probability $P(hasGenre|comedy)$ would be higher than $P(actedIn|comedy)$ given the fact that the keyword 'comedy' appears much more often in the documents of triples that have predicate `hasGenre` than those that have predicate `actedIn` .

6. EXPERIMENTAL EVALUATION

6.1 Setup

We evaluated our retrieval model using a comprehensive user-study over two RDF datasets. The first dataset was derived from the LibaryThing community, which is an online catalog about books. The second dataset was derived from the Internet Movie Database (IMDB). The data from both sources was automatically parsed and converted into RDF triples.

Recall that our retrieval model assumes that each triple t_i is associated with a document D_i. The triples documents were constructed by using keywords derived from the triple entities, and representative words for the relations. For example, the relation `isMarriedTo` was represented using the terms *{marry, wife, husband, spouse, etc}*. This was done manually since we did not

#entities	Example entity types	#triples	Example relations	#unique terms
		LibraryThing Dataset		
48,000	book, author user, tag	700,000	wrote, hasFriend, hasTag, type	21,821
		IMDB Dataset		
59,000	movie, actor director, producer, country, language	600,000	actedIn, directed, won, marriedTo, produced, hasGenre	80,584

Table 3: Overview of the datasets

have that many relations in our datasets, but for bigger datasets, the representations of relations can be generated automatically using a dictionary, or by utilizing the textual extraction-patterns in case the triples were extracted using some IE technique from free-text[25]. Once each triple was associated with a set of keywords, we stemmed all the keywords using the Stanford stemmer, removed stop words and created an inverted index over the triples. Table 3 gives an overview of the datasets.

Due to the lack of an appropriate query benchmark for *keyword search* over RDF data, we had to create a benchmark and gather relevance assessments ourselves. The queries we used for evaluation were a subset of the query benchmark in [6]. The benchmark there contains a set of structured queries, possibly augmented with keywords, along with their descriptions. We extracted *30* queries from there, 15 for each dataset and represented each query using a set of keywords. We opted for 30 queries only since we pooled 50 results per each query, and gathered relevance assessment for each result using at least 4 different human judges. Overall, we had about *15,000* unique relevance assessments for the 30 queries. All evaluation queries, results and relevance assessments are available at `http://www.mpii.de/~elbass/demo/rdftext.txt`.

We compared our ranking model, which we refer to as the *Structured LM* approach, to 3 competitors: 1) a baseline language-modeling approach (Baseline LM), 2) the Web Object Retrieval Model (WOR) [19] and 3) the BANKS system [2]. We chose these 3 competitors since they represent the family of approaches applicable to our setting, namely: keyword search over structured data. The rest of the approaches sketched in Section 2 do not directly apply to our setting and thus were omitted from our preliminary evaluation.

6.2 Relevance Assessments

For each evaluation query, we retrieved the top-50 results retrieved using each one of the 4 models described above. We then pooled all the results together and presented the set of all unique results from the pool to 13 human judges in no particular order, along with the query description. The judges were all computer-scientists in two different research institutes. For the case of results retrieved using WOR, we presented the entity name as a result and provided the judges with a link to the Wikipedia article for that entity (in case there was one) in order to help them decide whether a result is relevant or not. For the rest of the results, we just presented the subgraphs for judgment.

We asked the judges to assess the results on a 4-levels scale: 3 corresponding to results that completely match the information need as given by the query description, 2 corresponding to results that do not completely match the information need but are still highly related to it, 1 corresponding to results that do not really match the information need of the query, but the results still make sense and add valuable information to the user and finally 0 corresponding to trivial, or nonsense results. Each result was evaluated by 4 different judges. The levels of agreement between the judges as measured by the Kappa coefficient were *0.449* for the LibraryThing dataset and *0.542* for the IMDB dataset. We also computed

Model	NDCG @20	NDCG @10	NDCG @5
Structured	**0.764**	**0.817**	**0.840**
BANKS	0.637	0.647	0.639
WOR	0.576	0.596	0.621
Baseline	0.397	0.368	0.351

Table 4: Average NDCG values for both datasets

Model	NDCG @20	NDCG @10	NDCG @5
	Librarything		
Structured	**0.861**	**0.880**	**0.889**
BANKS	0.762	0.734	0.710
WOR	0.621	0.624	0.623
Baseline	0.395	0.361	0.333
	IMDB		
Structured	**0.667**	**0.754**	**0.791**
BANKS	0.513	0.560	0.569
WOR	0.530	0.567	0.618
Baseline	0.399	0.376	0.370

Table 5: Average NDCG values with parameter learning

the agreement for relevant and irrelevant results only (i.e., assuming that levels 3,2,1 are relevant and 0 is irrelevant). We obtained a Kappa coefficient of *0.397* for LibraryThing and *0.671* for IMDB which are in line with the numbers reported for standard TREC evaluation campaigns. For instance, the TREC legal track for 2006 reports a Kappa value of 0.49 on 40 queries, the opinion detection task in 2009 reports a Kappa value of 0.34, and the TREC 2004 Novelty track reports a value of 0.54 for sentence relevance.

6.3 Evaluation Results

We conducted 3 experiments: an overall evaluation using all evaluation queries, a training experiment to set the parameters of the models that involve ones, and a cross-validation to predict how well our parameter-learning approach would generalize.

Overall Evaluation. In the first experiment, we report the average NDCG values (Normalized Discounted Cumulative Gain [11]) over all *30* evaluation queries at levels 20, 10 and 5 using all 4 different models in Table 4. The values for the Structured LM approach and the BANKS system reported in the table are the ones achieved when the models parameters were set to their optimum values (i.e., $\beta = 0.9$ for the Structured LM approach and $\lambda = 1$ for BANKS).

As can be seen from Table 4, the Structured LM approach significantly outperforms ($p - value < 0.05$ with a one-tailed t-test) all other methods in terms of NDCG values at all levels. In the next experiment, we explain how to set the models parameters using training queries.

Training Results. In the second experiment, we used one dataset for training and the other for testing. That is, the 15 queries for the IMDB dataset were used as a training set to learn the optimal parameter setting for the Structured LM approach and BANKS. The 15 queries for LibraryThing were then used to test the performance of the different methods. We did the same thing using the LibraryThing queries for training and the IMDB queries for testing. The learning procedure was as follows. For the Structured LM approach, we computed the average NDCG at level *50* over the 15 training queries, setting the parameter β to a value between 0 and 1. We achieved the highest average $NDCG@50$ for both datasets when β was set to 0.9. For BANKS, we did the same thing using the same set of training queries and setting the parameter λ to a value between 0 and 1, and we achieved the highest average NDCG at level 50 when λ was set to 1. Table 5 shows the average NDCG values over the test queries at levels 20, 10 and 5.

Similar to the first experiment, the Structured LM approach significantly outperforms ($p - value < 0.05$ with a one-tailed t-test) all other methods in terms of NDCG values at all levels for both datasets. In order to test how well our training strategy generalizes, we performed a cross-validation experiment which we report next.

Cross-Validation Results. The third experiment was a cross-validation experiment to show how well the parameter learning procedure we described above generalizes over unseen datasets. We performed a leave-one-out cross validation, where 14 out of the 15 queries for each dataset were used as a training set to determine the the value of the parameter β, and then the left-out query was used for testing. We repeated the same process such that each evaluation query is used for validation once, and we averaged the NDCGs over all the validation queries. For BANKS, we also performed a cross-validation to validate the learning of its parameter λ, and again averaged the NDCGs over all the queries. For the IMDB dataset, the results were identical to those reported in Table 5 for all approaches, and for the LibraryThing dataset, the results were also the same as in the training experiment, except for a slight change in the case of the Structured LM approach (with NDCG values of *0.814*, *0.833* and *0.841* at levels 20,10 and 5, respectively). That is, similar to the results of the first two experiments, the Structured LM approach outperforms all other methods for both datasets.

7. CONCLUSION

We proposed a retrieval model for keyword queries over RDF graphs. Our retrieval model adopts backtracking algorithms to retrieve subgraphs matching the query keywords. Our model provides a result ranking based on a novel structure-aware language-modeling approach. We have shown through a preliminary, yet comprehensive user-study that our retrieval model outperforms well-known techniques for keyword search over structured data.

8. REFERENCES

[1] S. Auer, C. Bizer, G. Kobilarov, J. Lehmann, R. Cyganiak, and Z. Ives. Dbpedia: A nucleus for a web of open data. In *ISWC/ASWC*, 2007.

[2] G. Bhalotia, A. Hulgeri, C. Nakhe, S. Chakrabarti, and S. Sudarshan. Keyword searching and browsing in databases using banks. In *ICDE*, 2002.

[3] R. Blanco, P. Mika, and H. Zaragoza. Entity search track submission by yahoo! research barcelona. SemSearch, 2010.

[4] T. Cheng, X. Yan, and K. Chen-Chuan Chang. Entityrank: Searching entities directly and holistically. In *VLDB*, 2007.

[5] A. Doan, L. Gravano, R. Ramakrishnan, and S. Vaithyanathan (Editors). Special issue on managing information extraction. *ACM SIGMOD Record*, 37(4), 2008.

[6] S. Elbassuoni, M. Ramanath, R. Schenkel, M. Sydow, and G. Weikum. Language-model-based ranking for queries on RDF-graphs. In *CIKM*, 2009.

[7] Freebase: A social database about things you know and love. http://www.freebase.com.

[8] K. Golenberg, B. Kimelfeld, and Y. Sagiv. Keyword proximity search in complex data graphs. In *SIGMOD*, 2008.

[9] L. Guo, F. Shao, C. Botev, and J. Shanmugasundaram. Xrank: ranked keyword search over xml documents. In *SIGMOD*, 2003.

[10] V. Hristidis, H. Hwang, and Y. Papakonstantinou. Authority-based keyword search in databases. *TODS*, 33(1), 2008.

[11] K. Järvelin and J. Kekäläinen. Ir evaluation methods for retrieving highly relevant documents. In *SIGIR*, 2000.

[12] Varun Kacholia, Shashank Pandit, Soumen Chakrabarti, S. Sudarshan, Rushi Desai, and Hrishikesh Karambelkar. Bidirectional expansion for keyword search on graph databases. In *VLDB*, 2005.

[13] G. Kasneci, M. Ramanath, M. Sozio, F. M. Suchanek, and G. Weikum. Star: Steiner tree approximation in relationship-graphs. In *ICDE*, 2009.

[14] J. Kim, X. Xue, and W. B. Croft. A probabilistic retrieval model for semistructured data. In *ECIR*, 2009.

[15] O. Kurland. The opposite of smoothing: a language model approach to ranking query-specific document clusters. In *SIGIR*, 2008.

[16] O. Kurland and L. Lee. Corpus structure, language models, and ad hoc information retrieval. In *SIGIR*, 2004.

[17] G. Li, B.C. Ooi, J. Feng, J. Wang, and L. Zhou. Ease: an effective 3-in-1 keyword search method for unstructured, semistructured and structured data. In *SIGMOD*, 2008.

[18] V. Lopez, V. Uren, E. Motta, and M. Pasin. Aqualog: An ontology-driven question answering system for organizational semantic intranets. *Web Semant.*, 5(2):72–105, 2007.

[19] Z. Nie, Y. Ma, S. Shi, J. Wen, and W. Ma. Web object retrieval. In *WWW*, 2007.

[20] P. Ogilvie and J. Callan. Hierarchical language models for xml component retrieval. *Advances in XML Information Retrieval*, 2005.

[21] J. Ponte and W. B. Croft. A language modeling approach to information retrieval. In *SIGIR*, 1998.

[22] W3c: Resource description framework (rdf). www.w3.org/RDF/.

[23] S. Sarawagi. Information extraction. *Foundations and Trends in Databases*, 2(1), 2008.

[24] L. Si, R. Jin, J. Callan, and P. Ogilvie. A language modeling framework for resource selection and results merging. In *CIKM*, 2002.

[25] F. Suchanek, M. Sozio, and G. Weikum. SOFIE: A self-organizing framework for information extraction. In *WWW*, 2009.

[26] F. M. Suchanek, G. Kasneci, and G. Weikum. Yago: A large ontology from wikipedia and wordnet. *J. Web Sem.*, 6(3), 2008.

[27] T. Tran, H. Wang, S. Rudolph, and P. Cimiano. Top-k exploration of query candidates for efficient keyword search on graph-shaped (rdf) data. In *ICDE*, 2009.

[28] S. Wernicke. A faster algorithm for detecting network motifs. In *WABI*, 2005.

[29] Y. Xu and Y. Papakonstantinou. Efficient keyword search for smallest lcas in xml databases. In *SIGMOD*, 2005.

[30] C. Zhai and J. Lafferty. A study of smoothing methods for language models applied to ad hoc information retrieval. In *SIGIR*, 2001.

Frequency-aware Similarity Measures

Why Arnold Schwarzenegger is Always a Duplicate

Dustin Lange Felix Naumann
Hasso Plattner Institute, Potsdam, Germany
firstname.lastname@hpi.uni-potsdam.de

ABSTRACT

Measuring the similarity of two records is a challenging problem, but necessary for fundamental tasks, such as duplicate detection and similarity search. By exploiting frequencies of attribute values, many similarity measures can be improved: In a person table with U.S. citizens, Arnold Schwarzenegger is a very rare name. If we find several Arnold Schwarzeneggers in it, it is very likely that these are duplicates. We are then less strict when comparing other attribute values, such as birth date or address.

We put this intuition to use by partitioning compared record pairs according to frequencies of attribute values. For example, we could create three partitions from our data: Partition 1 contains all pairs with rare names, Partition 2 all pairs with medium frequent names, and Partition 3 all pairs with frequent names. For each partition, we learn a different similarity measure: we apply machine learning techniques to combine a set of base similarity measures into an overall measure. To determine a good partitioning, we compare different partitioning strategies. We achieved best results with a novel algorithm inspired by genetic programming.

We evaluate our approach on real-world data sets from a large credit rating agency and from a bibliography database. We show that our learning approach works well for logistic regression, SVM, and decision trees with significant improvements over (i) learning models that ignore frequencies and (ii) frequency-enriched models without partitioning.

Categories and Subject Descriptors

I.5 [**Pattern Recognition**]: Clustering—*Similarity Measures*

General Terms

Algorithms

Keywords

similarity measures, duplicate detection, similarity search

1. COMPARING RECORDS

The problem of determining the similarity (or distance) of two records in a database is a well-known, but challenging problem. Suitable similarity measures help to find duplicates and thus cleanse a data set, or they can help finding nearest neighbors to answer search queries. The problem comprises two main difficulties: First, the representations of same real-world objects might differ due to typos, outdated values, and sloppy data or query entries. Second, the amount of data might be very large, thus prohibiting exhaustive comparisons. The first problem is overcome by devising sophisticated similarity measures (the focus of this paper); the second problem is alleviated by efficient algorithms and indexes that avoid comparing each entry or query with all other entries.

Our original motivation stems from a cooperation with Schufa, a credit rating agency that stores data of about 66 million citizens, which are in turn reported by banks, insurance agencies, etc. To ensure the quality of the data, it is necessary to detect and fuse duplicates therein [14]. Also, queries about the rating of an individual must be responded to as precisely as possible.

We propose a novel comparison method that partitions the data using value frequency information and then automatically determines similarity measures for each individual partition. We show that this method indeed finds a different configuration for each partition and that we achieve an overall better precision. Note that while we motivate our ideas using a person data use case, our approach is general and can be used with any composed similarity measure. We report on experiments with the person data set, but also with a bibliographic data set from DBLP.

Example: Two Arnold Schwarzeneggers. Assume a table in which each row represents a person. We know a person's name, birth date, and address. We need to decide whether two different records represent the same person. Usually, we use some similarity measure to answer this question. A common approach is to use the same, carefully crafted similarity measure across all records. We argue that it makes sense to use different similarity measures for different groups of records.

We explain the intuition of our idea by means of Arnold Schwarzenegger. In a person table containing US citizens, we cannot find many Arnold Schwarzeneggers. In fact, it is highly unlikely that there are two Arnold Schwarzeneggers stored in our table. Arnold Schwarzenegger is our representative for a rare name. From this rarity, we conclude that another record with this same name is already quite likely to be a duplicate of the earlier. We are less rigorous about the similarity of birth date and address: For two rows with rare names, we argue that address and date-of-birth similarity are less important than for rows with frequent names. □

With this paper, we make the following contributions:
Exploiting frequencies: We propose two approaches to exploit frequencies in learnable similarity measures: The first directly incorporates frequencies in machine learning models. The second partitions the data according to value frequencies and learns a composite similarity measure for each partition.
Partitioning strategies: We propose different partitioning strategies: a greedy partitioning algorithm, equi-depth partitioning, random partitioning, as well as a novel partitioning algorithm inspired by genetic programming.
Evaluation on two real-world data sets: The first is a person data set from Schufa, a large credit rating agency. The data set contains ca. 66m person records and 2m search queries, from which we evaluate 10,000 of the most difficult ones. The second data set is from the DBLP bibliography, from which we created a data set that contains 10,000 paper reference pairs (available from our website, see Sec. 5).

2. RELATED WORK

In the last decades, many researchers have worked on duplicate detection. For a general overview on duplicate detection, we refer the reader to excellent surveys [4, 15].

Bilenko et al. use machine learning techniques to learn similarity measures [3]. They learn base similarity measures using SVMs and apply another SVM to combine the base similarity measures. Sarawagi and Bhamidipaty use active learning for interactive duplication detection [11]. They also employ machine learning techniques (decision trees, Naive Bayes, and SVMs) to combine base learners. We adapt and greatly extend this approach by creating a set of learners for different partitions of the data. Shen et al. [12] propose to create a set of different matchers for different portions of the data. They focus on the task of integrating a set of data sources and create different similarity measures for comparing entities from the different sources. In contrast to their work, we partition data according to frequencies and not based on different sources of the data. Moreover, we employ a set of similar matchers, i.e., we learn one similarity function for each of the partitions – but all of them with the same machine learning technique. Another idea is to use actual attribute values for partitioning (e.g., using a Country attribute, we learn one measure for US citizens and one measure for Austrian citizens). While this idea depends on the availability of attributes values that are suitable for partitioning, our approach is more generally applicable as it only exploits meta-information of the values (frequencies).

There are also approaches to duplicate detection/entity resolution that exploit knowledge about frequencies. Bhattacharya and Getoor apply collective entity resolution; by incorporating knowledge about references between entities, entity resolution can be improved [2]. Their approach starts by resolving entities with least frequent names, since "two references with the name 'A. Ansari' are more likely to be the same, because 'Ansari' is an uncommon name." Torvik and Smalheiser propose a probabilistic approach to author name disambiguation [13]. In their model, they include the frequency of names to predict the probability that two names match. They also recognize that "if the name is very unusual (e.g., D. Gajdusek), the chances are better that any two randomly chosen articles with that name are written by the same individual than if the name is very common (e.g., J. Smith)." We also exploit this insight, but with an entirely different approach.

3. COMPOSING SIMILARITY

In this section we describe the similarity model used throughout the paper. We follow the common and proven notion of defining individual similarity measures for different attributes and attribute types; for instance, dates are compared differently than names or addresses. These individual similarities are subsequently combined to define some global similarity of two records.

Base Similarity Measures.

We first split the problem of measuring the similarity of two records into smaller subproblems. We define a set of **base similarity measures** $sim_p(r_1, r_2)$, each responsible for calculating the similarity of a specific attribute p of the compared records r_1 and r_2 from a set R of records. In our use case, we have three functions sim_{Name}, $sim_{\mathsf{BirthDate}}$, and sim_{Address}. All base similarity measures can be chosen independently. For example, we could use Jaro-Winkler distance for sim_{Name} [15], the relative distance between dates for $sim_{\mathsf{BirthDate}}$, and Euclidean distance for sim_{Address}. The base similarity measures can also test for equality (e.g., for email addresses) or boolean values (e.g., for gender).

Each base similarity measure is a function

$$sim_p : (R \times R) \to [0, 1] \subset \mathbb{R} \tag{1}$$

In the following, we assume the domain of the similarity measures to be between 0 and 1, with 1 representing identity and 0 dissimilarity of the compared record parts.

Composition of Base Similarity Measures.

To calculate the overall similarity of two records, we integrate the base similarity measures into an overall judgement. We consider the task of judging whether two records are similar a classification task: the classes are *isSimilar* and *isDissimilar*; the features are the results of the base similarity measures. To derive a general model, we employ machine learning techniques. We have enough training data for supervised learning methods. In case of lacking training data, active learning methods could be chosen [11].

Due to their popularity and strong performance in different classification tasks, we selected the following three classification methods for further analysis: logistic regression, decision trees, and support vector machines.

4. EXPLOITING FREQUENCIES

In our use case, we have data about a large set of persons. We need to define a similarity measure for comparing persons, but our findings are equally applicable to other use cases, such as products, bills, etc. We want to answer the question: Can information about data distribution improve our similarity measurement?

In this section, we propose two approaches to exploit frequencies in learning similarity measures. A requirement for both approaches is a frequency function that is introduced in

Sec. 4.1. In Sec. 4.2, we describe how to adapt the machine learning techniques to exploit frequencies. As an alternative approach, a partitioning idea is discussed in detail in Sec. 4.3.

4.1 Frequency Function

First of all, we need to select attributes for frequency evaluation (in our use case, we select the attributes FirstName and LastName). For two compared records, we then determine the value frequencies of the selected attributes. We define a frequency function f that takes as arguments two records and determines a frequency:

$$f : R \times R \to \mathbb{N} \tag{2}$$

Modeling the frequency function is a domain-specific task. In the following, we describe how we modeled this function in the Schufa use case. Our goal is to partition the data according to the name frequencies. We have two name attributes in our data model (FirstName and LastName) and need to handle several data quality problems: swapping of first and last name, typos, and combining two attributes (so that one frequency value is calculated). First and last name may be switched (e. g., FirstName=`Arnold`, LastName=`Schwarzenegger`; FirstName=`Schwarzenegger`, LastName=`Arnold`). We take this possible switch into account by calculating the attribute similarities for both attribute value combinations (switched and non-switched) and proceeding with the combination that results in a larger similarity value. Next, typos may occur in attribute values (e. g., `Arnold; Arnnold`). We assume that at least one of the spellings is correct and that a typo leads to a less frequent name. Although this is not always true, this heuristic works in most cases. Thus, we take the larger frequency value of both spellings. Lastly, we combine the frequency values of first and last name. We argue that the less frequent name is more distinguishing and helpful (e. g., `Schwarzenegger` is more distinguishing than `Arnold`). Thus, we take the smaller frequency of the different attribute values as the result of our frequency function. Experiments with alternatives, namely using the maximum or the average instead of the minimum, showed that minimum is in fact the best accumulation function in our use case.

This description reflects the characteristics of our person data use case; for other data sets, the individual frequency function must be adjusted accordingly. For the DBLP data set, our frequency function works similar to the Schufa function explained above, except that there is no check for switched first and last names, since the name parts are not split in this data set.

4.2 Frequency-enriched Models

A first idea to exploit frequency distributions is to alter the models that we learned with the machine learning techniques explained in Sec. 3. One could manually add rules to the models, e.g., for logistic regression, we could say "if the frequency of the name value is below 10, then increase the weight of the name similarity by 10% and appropriately decrease the weights of the other similarity functions". Manually defining such rules is cumbersome and error-prone.

Another idea is to integrate the frequencies directly into the machine learning models. We add the frequencies of the compared entities' attribute values as an additional attribute to the discussed models. Some machine learning techniques can only handle normalized feature values (e. g., logistic regression and SVMs). Since all similarity values are required to lie in the range $[0,1]$, we need to scale the frequency values accordingly. We apply the following scaling function:

$$scaled\_f(r_1, r_2) = \frac{f(r_1, r_2)}{M}, \tag{3}$$

where M is the maximum frequency in the data set.

Adding attributes to the learned model means adding complexity and mixing information. The models become "polluted" with frequency information. The comprehensibility of the created models is lower, since each model contains mixed decisions based on similarity values and frequencies. As our experiments in Sec. 5 show, this idea is outperformed by the partitioning approach that we describe in the following.

4.3 Partitioning

We propose to partition compared record pairs based on frequencies and create different models for the different partitions. These models are equal to the ones learned in Sec. 3, we just create several of them. The models still decide only on the basis of similarities. Since the models do not contain any additional information about the frequencies, they are still as easy to interpret and adjust as before.

We now partition compared record pairs into n partitions using the determined frequencies. The number of partitions is an important factor for partitioning. A too large number of partitions results in small partitions that can cause overfitting. A too small number of partitions leads to partitions too large for discovering frequency-specific differences. To determine a good number of partitions as well as a good partitioning, we need a partitioning strategy. We introduce several strategies in Sec. 4.4.

In the following, we formally define partitions. The entire frequency space is divided into non-overlapping, continuous partitions by a set of thresholds:

$$\Theta = \{\theta_i \mid i \in \{0, \dots, n\} \wedge \theta_0 < \dots < \theta_n\} \tag{4}$$

with $\theta_0 = 0$ and $\theta_n = M + 1$, where M is the maximum frequency in the data set. The partitions are then defined as frequency ranges I_i:

$$I_i = [\theta_i, \theta_{i+1}) \tag{5}$$

A partitioning I is then a set of partitions that covers the entire frequency space:

$$I = \{I_j \mid j \in \{0, \dots, n-1\}\} \tag{6}$$

A partition covers a set of record pairs. A record pair (r_1, r_2) falls into a partition $[\theta_i, \theta_{i+1})$ iff the frequency function value for this pair lies in the partition's range:

$$\theta_i \leq f(r_1, r_2) < \theta_{i+1} \tag{7}$$

For each partition, we learn a composite similarity measure using the learning techniques presented in Sec. 3. It is now the task of the learning method to derive an appropriate model for each partition. In other words, we shift the problem of appropriately handling rare or frequent values to the learning method. If the learning method cannot exploit frequencies, then we expect the method to generate the same model for each partition (assuming each partition is large enough for creating appropriate models).

With the set of composite similarity measures for all partitions at hand, we can judge new record pairs. For a record pair, we first determine the partition that the pair belongs to with Formula (7). We then apply only the composite similarity measure that has been learned for this partition. By retaining frequency lists for all frequency-relevant attributes, the frequency lookup is quite fast. Thus, our approach hardly affects the query time. This is quite important for our use case as each query needs to be answered in less than a second.

4.4 Partitioning Strategies

An important problem in partitioning our data is to determine the number of partitions as well as the thresholds that separate the partitions. Since the number of partitions is determined by the number of thresholds, we only need to determine a set of thresholds.

A complete search on the threshold space is too expensive. For a maximum frequency M, we could define up to $M-1$ thresholds, resulting in a separate partition for each possible frequency. Overall, there are 2^{M-1} possibilities to choose threshold sets, since each distinct frequency $f \in \{0, \ldots, M\}$ can be either contained or not contained in a threshold set. For a reasonable maximum frequency of $M = 1,000,000$, there are obviously too many threshold combinations to consider. Even if we consider only the number of distinct frequencies that actually occur as possible thresholds in the data set, the computation costs are too high. In our use case data set, the frequency of the most frequent last name is 616,381. The number of distinct frequencies is 4629, which results in 2^{4628} theoretically possible different partitionings.

To efficiently determine a good partitioning, we suggest the following partitioning strategies, which we empirically compare in Sec. 5.1 and Sec. 5.2:

Random partitioning: To create a random partitioning, we randomly pick several thresholds $\theta_i \in \{0, \ldots, M+1\}$ from the set of actually occurring frequencies of the considered attribute values. The number of thresholds in each partitioning is also randomly chosen. The maximum number of partitions in one partitioning as well as the total number of generated initial partitionings are fixed. For our use case, we define a maximum of 20 partitions in one partitioning.

Equi-depth partitioning: We divide the frequency space into e partitions. Each partition contains the same number of tuples from the original data set R. For our use case, we create partitionings for $e \in \{2, \ldots, 20\}$.

Greedy partitioning: We define a list of threshold candidates $C = \{\theta_0, \ldots, \theta_n\}$ by dividing the frequency space into segments with the same number of tuples (similar to equi-depth partitioning, but with fixed, large e, in our case $e = 50$). We then begin learning a partition for the first candidate thresholds $[\theta_0, \theta_1)$. Then we learn a second partition that extends the current partition by moving its upper threshold to the next threshold candidate: $[\theta_0, \theta_2)$. We compare both partitions using F-measure. If the extended partition achieves better performance, the process is repeated for the next threshold slot. If not, the smaller partition is kept and a new partitioning is started at its upper threshold; another iteration starts with this new partition. This process is repeated until all threshold candidates have been processed.

This greedy partitioning algorithm stops after encountering a worse F-measure. A worse F-measure is an indicator for a more difficult set of tuples in the analyzed partition; thus, it makes sense to create a new partition for this set.

Genetic partitioning: Another partitioning approach is inspired by genetic algorithms. Since we have achieved overall best results with this approach in our experiments, we dedicate the following section to genetic partitioning.

4.5 Genetic Partitioning

To determine a good partitioning, but keep the number of generated and evaluated partitions low, we apply ideas inspired by genetic algorithms [1, 8]. Genetic algorithms in turn are inspired by biological evolution. From an initial population, the fittest individuals are selected. These individuals "breed" offspring that are assumed to be fitter than their parents. Random genetic mutation and crossover produce even fitter offspring.

Indeed, genetic algorithms are a good fit to our problem. A specific partitioning contains several thresholds, some of which are a good choice, while others should be moved by a small portion and again others should be replaced or removed completely. Deciding whether a threshold is a good choice is difficult, as we can only evaluate performance of partitions, and these are defined by *two* thresholds. In addition, we do not know the optimal number of partitions in advance. Due to their intelligent selection algorithms and random events, genetic algorithms can efficiently handle these choices and are a promising choice for partitioning (as we also empirically show in Sec. 5.1 and 5.2).

Genetic Partitioning Algorithm. The detailed steps of the genetic partitioning algorithm are the following:

Initialization: We first create an initial population consisting of several random partitionings. These partitionings are created as described above with the random partitioning approach.

Growth: Each individual is grown. We learn one composite similarity function for each partition in the current set of partitionings using the techniques presented in Sec. 3.

Selection: We then select some individuals from our population for creating new individuals. A fitness function determines which partitionings to select. In our case, we choose F-measure as fitness function using our training data. For each partition, we determine the maximum F-measure that can be achieved by choosing an appropriate threshold for the similarity function. We weight the partitions' F-measure values according to the compared record pairs in each to calculate an overall F-measure value for the entire partitioning. We then select the partitionings with highest weighted F-measure. For our use case, we select the top five partitionings. Note that we use a test set for evaluation that is different from the training set used for learning the composite similarity measure for each partition.

Reproduction: We build pairs of the selected best individuals (during all iterations) and combine them to create new individuals. Two techniques are applied to each new partitioning. *Recombination:* We first create the union of the thresholds of both partitionings. For each threshold, we randomly decide whether to keep it in the result partition or not. Both decisions have equal chances. *Mutation:* We randomly decide whether to add another new (also randomly picked) threshold *and* whether to delete a (randomly picked) threshold from the current threshold list. All possibilities have equal chances. If a partition is too small, then we have too little training and test data available. To avoid too small partitions (and thus overfitting), we define a minimum partition size (we set this value to 20 record pairs in our use case). Randomly created partitionings with too small partitions are discarded. In our use case, we create two new partitionings for each partitioning pair processed in the reproduction phase.

Termination: The resulting partitions are evaluated and added to the set of evaluated partitions. The selection/reproduction phases are repeated until a certain number of iterations is reached or until no significant improvement can be measured. In our use case, we require a minimum F-measure improvement of 0.001 after 5 iterations. The algorithm returns the partitioning that has been evaluated best during all iterations.

5. EVALUATION

In this section, we provide a detailed evaluation of our approach. We describe the Schufa data set in Sec. 5.1. We compare different partitioning strategies and show improvements achieved by our approach. In Sec. 5.2, we show results of experiments on a data set extracted from DBLP.

We performed all tests on a workstation PC. Our test machine runs Windows XP with an Intel Core2 Quad 2.5 GHz CPU and 8 GB RAM. We used Weka [6] as implementation of the machine learning techniques.

5.1 Evaluation on Schufa Data Set

We evaluated our approach on real-world data from Schufa, a large credit agency. The Schufa database contains information about the credit history of about 66m people.

Preparation. Our data set consists of two parts: a person data set and a query data set. The person data set contains about 66 million records. The most relevant fields for our search problem are name, date and place of birth, and address data (street, city, zip). The query data set consists of 2 million queries to this database. For each query, we know the exact search parameters (most record fields are mandatory), and the result obtained by Schufa's current system. This result contains up to five candidate records.

The Schufa system automatically evaluates its performance. A confidence value is assigned to each result. If only one result could be found and if its confidence is above a pre-determined high threshold, then the result is automatically accepted. Results with a confidence below a predetermined low threshold are automatically discarded. For all other results, Schufa is particularly careful: An expert needs to determine whether one of the results can be accepted or not.

Thus, there are many manually evaluated queries (the least confident cases) that we can use for evaluating our approach. We randomly selected 10,000 of these most difficult queries for evaluating our system: we built record pairs of the form *(query, correct result)* or *(query, incorrect result)*, depending on how the result has been evaluated by the expert. We can compare with the results of Schufa's current system and we can show whether our system would allow Schufa to save some of the (expensive) manual decisions without losing precision.

The automatically evaluated cases are not interesting for us: by comparing with Schufa's current system, we could only determine whether our system would act in the same way, without knowing whether these decisions are correct.

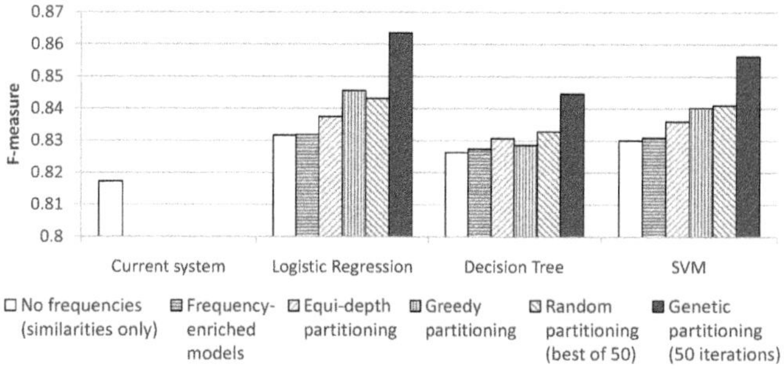

Figure 1: Comparison of frequency approaches and partitioning strategies for Schufa data set

Results. In this experiment, we compare the results of the learned similarity measures when applying all partitioning strategies described in Sec. 4.4. All results are determined using 10-fold CV on the 10k query data set containing difficult queries. We show the results in Fig. 1.

We observe improvements with partitioning for all learning methods and almost any partitioning strategy. The partitioning approaches also achieve better results than the frequency-enriched models.

For equi-depth partitioning, greedy partitioning, and random partitioning, we can see no clear leader across all learning methods. The achieved results are specific to each method. For all learning methods, genetic partitioning achieves the overall best results.

When comparing learning methods for genetic partitioning, logistic regression achieves better results than SVM, while decision trees are relatively far behind. Logistic regression can gain the largest profit from genetic partitioning. Thus, this method can even exceed SVM results. Decision trees profit less from genetic partitioning than SVMs or logistic regression.

We further show the result of Schufa's manually developed current system. In total, we can improve this system's F-measure by approx. 6%. This improvement translates to 600 of the 10,000 evaluated most difficult queries (with least confident results) and is a significant and valuable improvement for this use case.

5.2 Evaluation on DBLP Data Set

To investigate whether our approach also works for other data sets, we prepared another data set from DBLP [9], a bibliographic database for computer sciences. The main problem in DBLP is the assignment of papers to author entities. As described by Ley, DBLP is not perfect and needs to handle joins and splits: Author entries that falsely summarize publications from several authors need to be split into distinct author entries; author entries that represent the same entity, but have different names, need to be joined [9]. In contrast to other work that focuses on artificially injected errors [10] or specific groups of names [5, 7], we want to handle the actual DBLP problems on a larger scale. We constructed our data set from cleaned parts of DBLP, where different aliases for a person are known or ambiguous names have been resolved. In DBLP, cleaning is done manually (due to author requests) and automatically (using fine-tuned heuristics) [9].

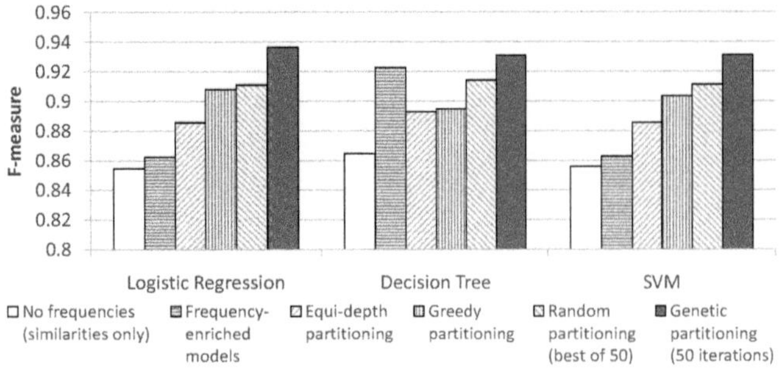

Figure 2: Comparison of frequency approaches and partitioning strategies for DBLP data set

Preparation. We created a new data set consisting of paper reference pairs that can be assigned to the following categories: (1) Two papers from the same author, (2) Two papers from the same author with different name aliases (e. g., with/without middle initial), (3) Two papers from different authors with the same name, (4) Two papers from different authors with different names.

For each paper pair, the matching task is to decide whether the two papers were written by the same author. The data set contains 2,500 paper pairs per category (10k in total). This does not represent the original distribution of ambiguous or alias names in DBLP (where about 99.2 % of the author names are non-ambiguous), but makes the matching task more difficult and interesting. We provide this data set on our website[1].

Results. Similar to the previous experiment on the Schufa data set, we applied 10-fold cross validation to compare the partitioning strategies from Sec. 4.4. The results in Fig. 2 look similar to the results of the Schufa data set. Without partitioning, all three machine learning techniques achieve similar F-measure results of about 0.86.

Incorporating only frequencies into these models (without partitioning) improves performance only by a small amount. An exception are decision trees, for which we can measure a significant improvement. For this data set, the decision tree algorithm could determine that the frequency attribute is relevant for the classification task.

From the partitioning strategies, genetic partitioning clearly outperforms all other strategies with overall F-measure results of about 0.93. The results show that random partitioning is not enough to achieve best results. The equi-depth and greedy partitioning strategies perform worse than the other partitioning strategies, but still better than the no-partitioning approach without frequencies. For this data set, too, partitioning always improves the results.

Overall, we can measure a significant improvement by genetic partitioning of about 9 %, which is larger than the improvement on the Schufa data set. Our experiments show that our approach works on different data sets, but that the actual amount of improvement depends on the data set.

6. CONCLUSION

With this paper, we introduced a novel approach for improving composite similarity measures. We divide a data set consisting of record pairs into partitions according to frequencies of selected attributes. We learn optimal similarity measures for each partition. Experiments on different real-world data sets showed that partitioning the data can improve learning results and that genetic partitioning performs better than several other partitioning strategies.

[1]`http://www.hpi-web.de/naumann/data`

Acknowledgments

We thank Schufa Holding AG for supporting this work. We especially thank Stephan Springob, Boris Zerban, and Michael Stolz for their valuable input. In addition, we are grateful to Tobias Vogel for fruitful discussions and Arvid Heise for his help on preparing the DBLP data set.

7. REFERENCES

[1] W. Banzhaf, P. Nordin, R. E. Keller, and F. D. Francone. *Genetic Programming – An Introduction; On the Automatic Evolution of Computer Programs and its Applications.* Morgan Kaufmann, San Francisco, CA, USA, Jan. 1998.

[2] I. Bhattacharya and L. Getoor. Collective entity resolution in relational data. *ACM Transactions on Knowledge Discovery from Data (TKDD)*, 1, March 2007.

[3] M. Bilenko and R. J. Mooney. Adaptive duplicate detection using learnable string similarity measures. In *Proc. of the ACM Intl. Conf. on Knowledge Discovery and Data Mining (SIGKDD)*, pages 39–48, Washington, DC, USA, 2003.

[4] A. K. Elmagarmid, P. G. Ipeirotis, and V. S. Verykios. Duplicate record detection: A survey. *IEEE Transactions on Knowledge and Data Engineering (TKDE)*, 19(1):1–16, 2007.

[5] A. A. Ferreira, A. Veloso, M. A. Gonçalves, and A. H. Laender. Effective self-training author name disambiguation in scholarly digital libraries. In *Proc. of the Joint Conference on Digital Libraries (JCDL)*, pages 39–48, Gold Coast, Australia, 2010.

[6] M. Hall, E. Frank, G. Holmes, B. Pfahringer, P. Reutemann, and I. H. Witten. The WEKA data mining software: An update. *SIGKDD Explorations*, 11, 2009.

[7] H. Han, L. Giles, H. Zha, C. Li, and K. Tsioutsiouliklis. Two supervised learning approaches for name disambiguation in author citations. In *Proc. of the Joint Conference on Digital Libraries (JCDL)*, pages 296–305, Tuscon, AZ, USA, 2004.

[8] J. R. Koza. *Genetic Programming: On the Programming of Computers by Means of Natural Selection.* MIT Press, Cambridge, MA, USA, 1992.

[9] M. Ley. DBLP – some lessons learned. *Proc. of the VLDB Endowment*, 2(2):1493–1500, 2009.

[10] V. Rastogi, N. N. Dalvi, and M. N. Garofalakis. Large-scale collective entity matching. *Proc. of the VLDB Endowment*, 4(4):208–218, 2011.

[11] S. Sarawagi and A. Bhamidipaty. Interactive deduplication using active learning. In *Proc. of the ACM Intl. Conf. on Knowledge Discovery and Data Mining (SIGKDD)*, pages 269–278, Edmonton, Alberta, Canada, 2002.

[12] W. Shen, P. DeRose, L. Vu, A. Doan, and R. Ramakrishnan. Source-aware entity matching: A compositional approach. In *Proc. of the Intl. Conf. on Data Engineering (ICDE)*, pages 196–205, Istanbul, Turkey, 2007.

[13] V. I. Torvik and N. R. Smalheiser. Author name disambiguation in MEDLINE. *ACM Transactions on Knowledge Discovery from Data (TKDD)*, 3:11:1–11:29, July 2009.

[14] M. Weis, F. Naumann, U. Jehle, J. Lufter, and H. Schuster. Industry-scale duplicate detection. *Proc. of the VLDB Endowment*, 1(2):1253–1264, 2008.

[15] W. E. Winkler. The state of record linkage and current research problems. Technical report, Statistical Research Division, U.S. Census Bureau, 1999.

A Probabilistic Method for Inferring Preferences from Clicks

Katja Hofmann, Shimon Whiteson and Maarten de Rijke
ISLA, University of Amsterdam
{K.Hofmann, S.A.Whiteson, deRijke}@uva.nl

ABSTRACT

Evaluating rankers using implicit feedback, such as clicks on documents in a result list, is an increasingly popular alternative to traditional evaluation methods based on explicit relevance judgments. Previous work has shown that so-called *interleaved comparison methods* can utilize click data to detect small differences between rankers and can be applied to learn ranking functions online.

In this paper, we analyze three existing interleaved comparison methods and find that they are all either biased or insensitive to some differences between rankers. To address these problems, we present a new method based on a probabilistic interleaving process. We derive an unbiased estimator of comparison outcomes and show how marginalizing over possible comparison outcomes given the observed click data can make this estimator even more effective.

We validate our approach using a recently developed simulation framework based on a learning to rank dataset and a model of click behavior. Our experiments confirm the results of our analysis and show that our method is both more accurate and more robust to noise than existing methods.

Categories and Subject Descriptors

H.3 [**Information Storage and Retrieval**]: H.3.3 Information Search and Retrieval

General Terms

Algorithms, Experimentation

Keywords

Evaluation, Implicit feedback, Interleaved comparison

1. INTRODUCTION

In information retrieval (IR), most techniques for evaluating rankers require *explicit feedback*, in which assessors manually judge the relevance of documents for given queries. Unfortunately, obtaining such explicit judgments is expensive and error-prone. Since annotators usually judge documents for queries they did not formulate, the judgments may be biased towards their interpretation of the underlying information needs [2]. Consequently, evaluating rankers using *implicit feedback* such as click data is a promising alternative. Since click data is a by-product of the normal interactions between the user and the retrieval system, it can be collected unobtrusively and at minimal cost. In addition, since it is based on the behavior of real users, it more accurately reflects how well their actual information needs are met [23].

Previous work demonstrated that two rankers can be successfully compared using click data. In the *balanced interleave* method [15], an *interleaved list* is generated for each query based on the two rankers. The user's clicks on the interleaved list are attributed to each ranker based on how they ranked the clicked documents, and the ranker that obtains more clicks is deemed superior. These comparisons are repeated for a large number of queries, to obtain a reliable estimate of the relative performance of the two rankers.

Unfortunately, the balanced interleave approach suffers from a bias that can make it prefer the wrong ranker [23]. The alternative *team draft* method avoids this form of bias by assigning each document to the ranker that contributed it to the interleaved list and only crediting clicks to the ranker to which the clicked document is assigned. In contrast to the balanced interleave and team draft methods, the *document constraint* method takes relations between documents into account [10].

In this paper, we analyze existing interleaved comparison methods and find that the document constraint method suffers from a bias similar to that of the balanced interleave method. We also find that the team draft method, though unbiased, is insensitive to some differences between rankers. We illustrate these problems using examples, and show how they can affect comparison outcomes.

Furthermore, we propose a new approach for comparing rankers that utilizes a probabilistic model of the interleave process and is based on the team draft method. The main idea is to replace the original rankers with softmax functions that define probability distributions over documents. Contributing a document to an interleaved list is formulated as sampling without replacement from a probability distribution. To infer comparison outcomes, we derive an unbiased estimator. Because this estimator is based on our probabilistic model, it smooths over click assignments, making the method both unbiased and sensitive to small differences between rankers. Finally, we show how comparisons can make more effective use of observed data by marginalizing over all possible comparison outcomes for each observed sample.

We present experiments using a large set of explicitly labeled data and a recently developed user click model that simulates the resulting implicit feedback. These experiments confirm the results of our analysis, and show that our method can identify the correct ranker more reliably than existing methods. Furthermore, our method improves over previous methods in terms of efficiency and robustness to noise.

CIKM'11, October 24–28, 2011, Glasgow, Scotland, UK.

In the next section we give an overview of related work (§2). We then formulate requirements for interleaved comparison methods and analyze existing methods (§3). Our probabilistic method is described in §4 and experiments are detailed in §5. We present and discuss experimental outcomes in §6 and conclude in §7.

2. RELATED WORK

Implicit feedback has long been used in a variety of settings, e.g., to infer users' interest in specific web pages. Many forms have been considered, such as the time spent on a page, scrolling, and clicks [5, 17]. In IR, implicit feedback has been used for relevance feedback, to refine search results throughout a search session [27].

Unfortunately, implicit feedback tends to be noisy. For example, a long-term study of "time spent reading" found no clear relation between this form of implicit feedback and a document's perceived usefulness, and that the time spent on the page varies considerably across users and tasks [18].

Clicks, the most easily collected form of feedback, are difficult to use for evaluation because they do not correspond well to absolute relevance. Jung et al. [16] found that click data does contain useful information, but that variance is high. They propose aggregating clicks over search sessions and show that focusing on clicks towards the end of sessions can improve relevance predictions. Similarly, Scholer et al. [24] found that click behavior varies substantially across users and topics, and that click data is too noisy to serve as a measure of absolute relevance. Fox et al. [7] found that combining several implicit indicators can improve accuracy, though it remains well below that of explicit feedback.

Nonetheless, in some applications, click data has proven reliable. In searches of expert users who are familiar with the search system and document collection, clicks can be as reliable as purchase decisions [11]. Methods for optimizing the click-through rates in ad placement [19] and web search [22] have also learned effectively from click data.

Methods that use implicit feedback to infer the relevance of specific document-query pairs have also proven effective. Shen et al. [25] show that integrating click-through information for query-document pairs into a content-based retrieval system can improve retrieval performance substantially. Agichtein et al. [1] demonstrate dramatic performance improvements by re-ranking search results based on a combination of implicit feedback sources, including click-based and link-based features. Chapelle and Zhang [4] learn a Bayesian model that accurately predicts the relevance of documents to specific queries from click data.

These applications learn the value of specific documents for specific queries, for which implicit feedback appears to be accurate. However, since implicit feedback varies so much across queries, it is difficult to use it to learn models that generalize across queries. To address this problem, several methods have been developed that use implicit feedback, not to infer absolute judgments, but to compare two rankers by observing clicks on an interleaved result list. In the remainder of this section, we overview these methods.

The *balanced interleave* method [15] takes as input two result lists l_1 and l_2 for a given query q, and produces an outcome $o \in \{-1, 0, 1\}$ that indicates whether the quality of l_1 is judged to be lower, equal to, or higher than that of l_2, respectively. The method first generates an interleaved list l (see Figure 1, part 1). One of $\{l_1, l_2\}$ is selected at random as the starting list and its first document is placed at the top of the interleaved list. Then, the non-starting list contributes its highest-ranked document if it is not already part of the list. These steps repeat until the interleaved list has the desired length. The clicks c that are observed when the interleaved list is presented to the user are attributed to each list as

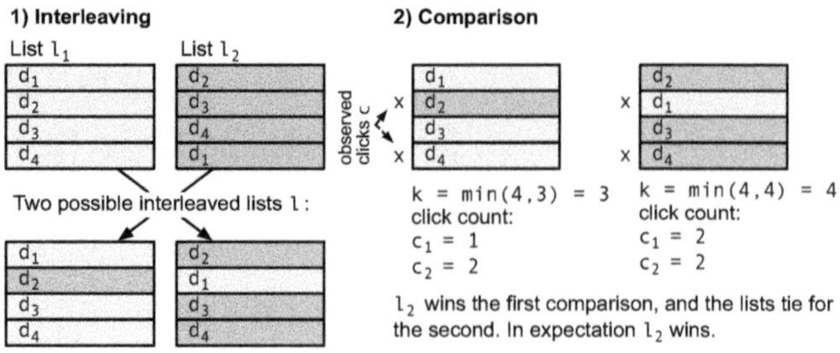

Figure 1: Interleaved comparisons using *balanced interleave*.

follows (Figure 1, part 2). For each list, the lowest-ranked document that received a click is determined, and the minimum of their ranks is denoted k. Then, the clicked documents ranked at or above k are counted for each list. The list with more clicks in its top k is deemed superior (they tie if they obtain the same number of clicks).

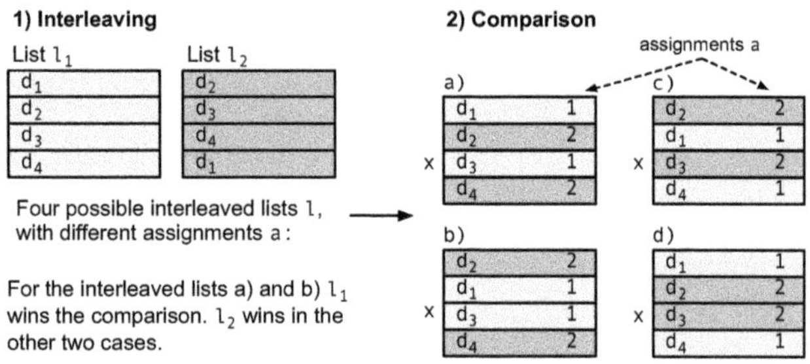

Figure 2: Interleaved comparisons using *team draft*.

The alternative *team draft* method [23] creates an interleaved list following the model of "team captains" selecting their team from a set of players (see Figure 2). For each pair of documents to be placed on the interleaved list, a coin flip determines which list gets to select a document first. It then contributes its highest-ranked document that is not yet part of the interleaved list. The method also records which list contributed which document in an *assignment* a. To compare the lists, only clicks on documents that were contributed by each list are counted towards that list. This method of assignments ensures that each list has an equal chance of obtaining clicks. Recent work demonstrates that the team draft method can reliably identify the better of two rankers in practice [21].

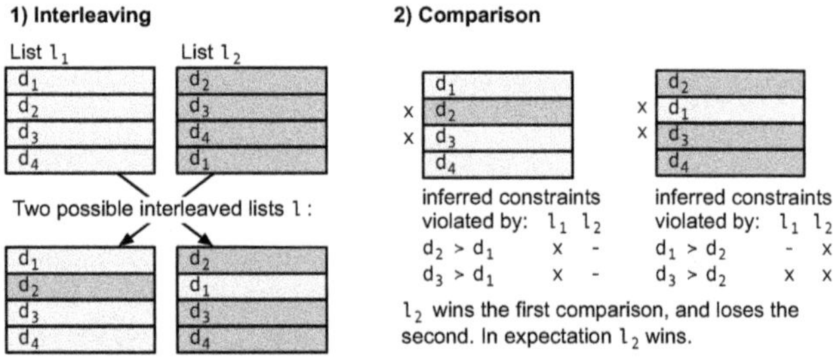

Figure 3: Interleaved comparisons using *document constraints*.

Neither the balanced interleave nor the team draft method takes relations between documents explicitly into account. To address this, He et al. [10] propose an approach that we call the *document-constraint* method (see Figure 3). Result lists are interleaved and clicks observed as for the balanced interleave method. Then, following [14], the method infers constraints on pairs of individual documents, based on their clicks and ranks. For each pair of a clicked document and a higher-ranked non-clicked document, a constraint is inferred that requires the former to be ranked higher than the latter.[1] For example, in the first interleaved list shown in Figure 3, d_2 is ranked lower than d_1. If d_2 is clicked while d_1 is not, the constraint $d_2 \succ d_1$ is inferred. The method then compares these constraints to the original result lists and counts how many constraints are violated by each. The list that violates fewer constraints is deemed superior. Though more computationally expensive, this method proved more reliable than either balanced interleave or team draft on a synthetic data set [10].

3. ANALYSIS

To analyze interleaved comparison methods, we need a set of criteria against which such methods can be evaluated. We propose two criteria. First, an interleaved comparison method should not suffer from *bias*, i.e., it should not prefer either ranker when clicks are random. Second, it should possess *sensitivity*, i.e., it should be able to detect differences in the quality of document rankings. In this section, we detail both criteria and analyze to what degree they are met by existing methods.

3.1 Bias

Our first criterion for interleaved comparison methods is that they not suffer from *bias*. We define an interleaved comparison method to be biased if, under a random distribution of clicks, it prefers one ranker over the other in expectation. Bias is problematic because it means that noise in click feedback can affect the expected outcome of comparisons, making the comparison method unreliable.

For the balanced interleave method, Radlinski [23] demonstrated bias in cases where l_1 and l_2 are very similar. This problem is illustrated in Figure 1. The interleave process can result in interleaved lists that are identical, or very similar, to one of the original lists. In the example, the first interleaved list is equal to l_1, and the second is similar to it, with only the first two documents switched. Consequently, clicks towards the top of the interleaved list are more likely to be attributed to l_1, while clicks on lower-ranked documents tend to benefit l_2. This is problematic for two reasons. First, the biases for either list do not necessarily cancel each other out, so that even randomly distributed clicks can yield a preference for one of the lists. For example, in Figure 1, l_2 wins in expectation, i.e., the outcome converges to l_2 in the limit; this can easily be verified using truth tables. Second, documents displayed at the top of a result list are typically more likely to be clicked, due to position bias [6]. In the example, strong position bias would favor l_1.

For the document constraint method, we identify a similar bias. Since interleaving is done as in the balanced interleave method, the interleaved lists can again be very similar to one of the original lists. Here, the list that is more similar to a presented interleaved list has a disadvantage because it is more likely to attract clicks. These clicks translate into constraints that are more likely to be violated by the more similar list. For example, in the first interleaved list constructed in Figure 3, clicks on the second and third rank of the interleaved list result in two violated constraints for the similar l_1 and no violated constraints for l_2. For randomly distributed clicks, l_2 wins in expectation.

The team draft method addresses the issue of bias by ensuring that each click can only be attributed to one list (the one assigned to that document). Because the interleaving process also ensures that in expectation each list contributes the same number of documents to each rank, the method is unbiased, both under random clicks and in the face of position bias.

[1]In the original description in [10], additional constraints are inferred between the lowest-clicked document and its successor. To simplify analysis, we consider only the first type of constraints. The additional requirements do not qualitatively affect our analytical or experimental results.

Table 1: Notation used throughout this paper. Uppercase letters indicate random variables and lowercase letters indicate the values they take on.

Symbol	*Description*
q	query
d	document
l	interleaved list
r	rank of a document in a document list
a	assignment, a vector of length $\|l\|$ where each element $a[r] \in \{1, 2\}$ indicates whether the document at rank r of an interleaved list l, $l[r]$ was contributed by l_1 or l_2 (or by softmax functions s_1 or s_2, respectively)
c	a vector of clicks observed on an interleaved list l
s_x	softmax function, cf., §4.1, Equation 1
$o(c, a)$	outcome of a comparison computed from clicks c and assignments a

3.2 Sensitivity

Our second criterion for assessing interleaved comparison methods is *sensitivity*. We define sensitivity as the ability of an interleaved comparison method to detect differences in the quality of rankings. As in standard evaluation measures like Normalized Discounted Cumulative Gain (NDCG) [13], we assume that the quality of a ranking depends on how highly it ranks relevant documents.

Clearly, all interleaved comparison methods will fail to be sensitive if user clicks are not correlated with relevance. However, in some cases, the team draft method can suffer from insensitivity even when such correlations exist. Figure 2 illustrates this phenomenon. Assume that d_3 is the only relevant document, and is therefore more likely to be clicked than other documents. Because l_2 ranks this document higher than l_1 it should win the comparison. To compare l_1 and l_2 using the team draft method, four possible interleaved lists can be generated, all of which place document d_3 at the same rank. In two interleaved lists, d_3 is contributed by l_1, and in two it is contributed by l_2. Thus, in expectation, both lists obtain the same number of clicks for this document, yielding a tie. Therefore, the method fails to detect the preference for l_2.

Hence, since the team draft method is insensitive to some ranking differences, it can fail to detect a difference between rankers or infer a preference for the wrong ranker. In contrast, the balanced interleave and document constraint methods can detect these differences in ranking, but because of the bias discussed above, small differences between rankers can result in erratic behavior.

4. METHOD

As discussed above, existing interleaved comparison methods are either biased or insensitive to certain differences between rankings. In this section we develop a probabilistic method that fulfills both criteria. We do so by devising a probabilistic model in §4.1, which is based on the team draft method. Instead of interleaving documents deterministically, we model the interleaving process as random sampling from *softmax* functions that define probability distributions over documents. This model allows us to derive an estimator in §4.2 that is both unbiased and sensitive to even small ranking changes. Finally, in §4.3, we derive a second estimator that marginalizes over all possible assignments to make estimates more reliable. Table 1 shows notation used throughout this section.

4.1 Probabilistic interleaving

We propose a probabilistic form of interleaving in which the interleaved document list l is constructed, not from fixed lists l_1 and l_2, but from *softmax* functions s_1 and s_2 that depend on the query q. The use of softmax functions is key to our approach, as it ensures that every document has a non-zero probability of being selected by each ranker. As a result, the distribution of credit accumulated for clicks is smoothed, based on the relative rank of the document in the original result lists. If both rankers place a given document at the same rank, then the corresponding softmax functions have the same probability of selecting it and thus they accumulate the same number of clicks in expectation.

More importantly, rankers that put a given document at similar ranks receive similar credit in expectation. Furthermore, the difference in expected value reflects the magnitude of the difference between the two rankings. In this way, the method becomes sensitive to even small differences between rankings and can accurately estimate the magnitude of such differences.

Starting with the ranked lists l_1 and l_2 that two rankers generated for a given query q, we construct corresponding softmax functions s_1 and s_2. Each s_x is a probability distribution over documents in which documents with a higher rank according to l_x have a higher probability. Many softmax functions are possible [20, 26]. We use a function in which the probability of selecting a document is inversely proportional to a power of the rank $r_x(d)$ of a document d in list l_x:

$$P_{s_x}(d) = \frac{\frac{1}{r_x(d)^\tau}}{\sum_{d' \in D} \frac{1}{r_x(d')^\tau}}, \quad (1)$$

where D is the set of all ranked documents, including d. The denominator applies a normalization to make probabilities sum to 1. Because it has a steep decay at top ranks, this softmax function is suitable for an IR setting in which correctly ranking the top documents is the most important. It also has a slow decay at lower ranks, preventing underflow in calculations. The parameter τ controls how quickly selection probabilities decay as rank decreases, similar to the Boltzmann temperature in the normalized exponential function [26]. In our experiments, $\tau = 3$, though preliminary experiments with higher τ yielded qualitatively similar results.

After constructing s_1 and s_2, l is generated similarly to the team draft method. However, instead of randomizing the ranker to contribute the next document per pair, one of the softmax functions is randomly selected at each rank. Doing so is mathematically convenient, as the only component that changes at each rank is the distribution over documents. The system records which softmax function was selected to contribute the next document in assignment a. Then, a document is randomly sampled without replacement from the selected softmax function and added to the interleaved list. The document is also removed from the non-sampled softmax function and both are renormalized. This process repeats until l has the desired length.

This approach has several properties that ensure no bias is introduced. First, in expectation, each ranker contributes the same number of documents to the interleaved list. Second, the softmax functions constructed for each ranker have the same shape, i.e., the probability allocated to each document depends only on its rank. Third, the use of assignments guarantees that each click is attributed to only one list, as in the team draft method.

Figure 4 depicts a probabilistic model of this process. It has four random variables: the user's query q, the interleaved list l generated in response to q, the assignments a that specify which softmax function contributed which document to l, and the user's clicks c. Samples of all four random variables can be observed. In addition,

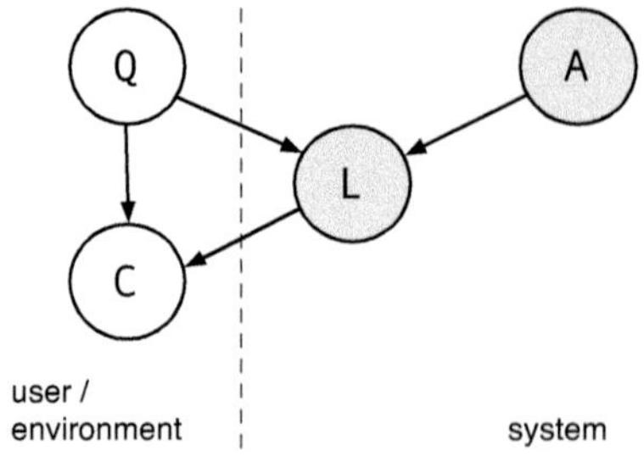

Figure 4: Probabilistic model for comparing rankers. Conditional probability tables are known only for variables in gray.

the distributions L and A are completely specified given a query q. In the next section we show how observed samples (q, l, a, c) can be used to estimate comparison outcomes.

4.2 Unbiased comparison

If we define a deterministic outcome function $o(c, a) \in \{-1, 0, 1\}$ that compares the number of clicks obtained by each ranker, as in the team draft method, then the relative quality of the two rankers is given by the expected outcome, defined as follows:

$$E[o(C, A)] = \sum_{c \in C} \sum_{a \in A} o(c, a) P(c, a). \quad (2)$$

While this cannot be computed directly, it can be estimated from a given set of n samples of the form (c, a):

$$E[o(C, A)] \approx \frac{1}{n} \sum_{i=1}^{n} o(c_i, a_i), \quad (3)$$

where c_i and a_i are vectors containing the observed clicks and assignments for the i-th sample.

Eq. 3 is an unbiased estimator of the expected outcome. If this estimator was used with deterministic ranking functions, it would reduce to the team draft method. However, because of the smooth credit assignment enabled by the softmax functions, it is more sensitive to differences in ranking quality than the team draft method, while still avoiding bias.

4.3 Marginalized comparison

In this section, we derive a second unbiased estimator that achieves better reliability by marginalizing over all possible assignments for an observed interleaved list, instead of using noisy samples from the true distribution.

In Eq. 3, the expected outcome is estimated directly from the observed clicks and assignments. However, in the probabilistic model shown in Figure 4, the distributions for A and L are known given an observed query q. As a result, we need not consider only the observed assignments. Instead, we can consider all possible assignments that could have co-occurred with each observed interleaved list. i.e., we can marginalize over all possible values of A for each observed interleaved list l_i and query q_i. Marginalizing over A leads to the following alternative estimator:

$$E[o(C, A)] \approx \frac{1}{n} \sum_{i=1}^{n} \sum_{a \in A} o(c_i, a) P(a | l_i, q_i), \quad (4)$$

To estimate $P(A|L, Q)$ we can follow Bayes' rule:

$$P(A|L, Q) = \frac{P(L|A, Q) P(A|Q)}{\sum_{a \in A} P(L|a, Q)}. \quad (5)$$

Since A and Q are independent, $P(A|Q) = P(A)$. $P(L|A, Q)$ is the product of the probabilities of selecting the documents at each

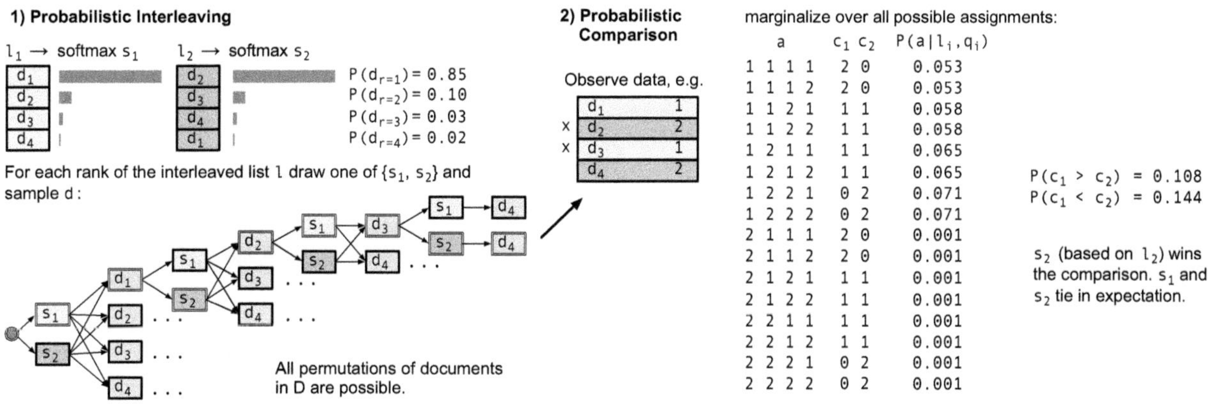

Figure 5: Example of an interleaved comparison using our *probabilistic marginalization* method with softmax functions.

rank:

$$P(L|A, Q) = \prod_{r=1}^{|L|} P(L[r] \mid A[r], L[1, r-1], Q), \qquad (6)$$

where $A[r] \in \{1, 2\}$ specifies which softmax function contributed $L[r]$, the document at rank r, and $L[1, r-1]$ is the list of all documents between ranks 1 and $r-1$.

Figure 5 illustrates the resulting probabilistic method for comparing rankers based on implicit feedback. For an incoming query, the system generates an interleaved document list, as described in §4.1. After observing clicks, the system computes the probability of each possible outcome. All possible assignments are generated, and the probability of each is computed using Eq. 5. The example shows that, while the softmax functions tie in expectation (because our method is unbiased), s_2 has a higher probability of winning, because it has a higher probability of generating the clicked documents than s_1 (because the method is sensitive to such differences in rankings).

Generating all possible assignments and computing their probabilities for a given list is computationally expensive. However, assignments and probabilities need to be calculated only up to the lowest observed click. In the worst case, the lowest click is at the lowest rank of the interleaved list, which is a small constant, e.g., 10.[2] In practice, we perform computations using logs and sums instead of probabilities and products to avoid buffer underflow.

5. EXPERIMENTS

We present three sets of experiments, designed to answer the question: *To what extent do the analytical differences between the comparison methods translate into performance differences?*

In our first set of experiments, we address this question on a large scale. We compare a large number of ranker pairs to examine how the analytical differences between comparison methods affect the accuracy of ranker comparisons. In the second experiment, we use these first results to select a small subset of ranker pairs with which to study convergence characteristics in more detail. In the third, we use the same subset of rankers to examine the effect of noise in click data.

All experiments employ the same experimental setup that simulates user interactions. This setup is described in the next section (§5.1). After this, we specify our data (§5.2) and runs (§5.3).

[2]To further reduce computation, probabilities for documents below a certain rank can be set to a small constant, trading a small loss in sensitivity for gains in speed.

5.1 Experimental setup

Our experiments are based on a recently developed experimental setup that simulates user interactions based on datasets with explicit relevance judgments and user click models [12]. This simulator fulfills the assumption made by all comparison methods that more relevant documents are more likely to be clicked. Simulating user interactions makes it possible to study the comparison methods at different levels of noise in user clicks. In addition, the experiments can be repeated for many comparisons.

The simulation takes as input a dataset with queries and explicit relevance judgments and simulates user interactions as follows. It simulates a user submitting a query by randomly sampling from the set of available queries (with replacement).[3] On the system side, the interleaved comparison method observes the sampled query and produces an interleaved result list that is presented to the user (sent back to the simulator). User clicks are then simulated using a click model and the relevance judgments provided with the dataset.

The click model simulates user interactions according to the Dependent Click Model (DCM) [8, 9], an extension of the cascade model [6]. According to this model, users traverse result lists from top to bottom. For each document they encounter, they decide whether the document representation is promising enough to warrant a click (e.g., based on the title and document snippets). If, after clicking on a document, the users' information need is satisfied (likely if the document was relevant), then they stop browsing the result list. Otherwise, they continue examining the result list (likely if the document was not relevant).

We implement the click model following [12], with the difference that we define click and stop probabilities based on graded relevance assessments instead of binary ones. Simulated users examine the result list starting at the top. For each document they encounter, they decide whether to click or not, with probability $P(c|R(d))$, i.e., the probability of a click given the relevance level of the examined document $R(d)$. While the relevance level is not known to the user before clicking, we assume that its presentation in the result list is informative enough to make relevant documents more likely to be clicked. The probability that a user is satisfied with the obtained results and stops after clicking a document with relevance level $R(d)$ is modeled by $P(s|R(d))$.

We instantiate the click model in two ways (for 5 relevance lev-

[3]In the absence of information about the original distribution of the queries in the data set, we sample uniformly. An advantage of doing so is that frequent queries cannot dominate performance. Different query distributions may affect convergence speed, but not the qualitative differences between the comparison methods we evaluate.

Table 2: Instantiations of the click model used in our experiments.

perfect model					
$R(d)$	0	1	2	3	4
$P(c\|R(d))$	0.00	0.20	0.40	0.80	1.00
$P(s\|R(d))$	0.00	0.00	0.00	0.00	0.00
realistic model					
$R(d)$	0	1	2	3	4
$P(c\|R(d))$	0.05	0.10	0.20	0.40	0.80
$P(s\|R(d))$	0.00	0.20	0.40	0.60	0.80

els) to study the behavior of comparison methods under *perfect* and *realistic* conditions. The perfect click model is used to examine the behavior of comparison methods in an ideal setting. The stop probabilities are 0 for all relevance levels, i.e., the user continues to examine documents regardless of the relevance of previously encountered documents. Therefore, all documents in the top 10 of each result list are examined. The click probabilities are defined such that highly relevant documents ($R(d) = 4$) are always clicked, and that non-relevant documents ($R(d) = 0$) are never clicked. Click probabilities for relevance levels between these extremes decrease monotonically. The realistic click model was designed to approximate noisier click behavior. Here, highly relevant documents are most likely to be clicked ($P(c|R(d) = 4) = 0.8$), and click probabilities decrease for lower relevance levels. Similarly, stop probabilities for this model are highest after seeing a highly relevant document and decrease for lower probabilities. Besides the different levels of noise, the two models differ in the overall expected number of clicks, which is lower for the realistic click model because the click probabilities are consistently lower and the stop probabilities are higher. Table 2 lists the probabilities defined for the two models.

The click models instantiated here are appropriate for our evaluation of comparison methods, as they satisfy the assumptions made by all these methods. In preliminary experiments, we found that the level of noise introduced by the realistic click model is of the same order of magnitude as observed in previous work [21]. In addition, we observed qualitatively similar results for all other instantiations we tested. Finer details, such as click behavior that takes relations between documents into account are not captured. Therefore, extending our evaluation to include real-life experiments is important future work.

5.2 Data

All experiments make use of the MSLR-WEB30k Microsoft learning to rank (MSLR) data set.[4] This data set consists of approximately $30,000$ queries with 136 precomputed document features and relevance judgments. Relevance judgments are provided on a 5-point scale. Unless stated otherwise, our experiments use the training set of fold 1. This set contains $18,919$ queries, with an average of 9.6 judged documents per query.

To generate rankers to compare in our experiments, we make use of the features provided for the documents of the data set. Specifically, we take each feature to be a ranker, and formulate the task of the comparison method as identifying the ranking features that are expected to give the best performance. In our first set of experiments, we exhaustively compare all distinct ranker pairs that can be generated in this way. For the second and third sets, we select a small subset that appears most suitable for more detailed analysis.

[4]Downloaded from `http://research.microsoft.com/en-us/projects/mslr/default.aspx`.

The experiments are designed to evaluate the comparison methods' ability to identify the better of two rankers based on (simulated) user clicks. To set the ground truth for which ranker is better, we use NDCG based on the explicit relevance judgments provided with the data set, following previous work [21]. We use the complete set of documents provided with the data set to determine NDCG for the ground truth, i.e., no cut-off is used. Note that comparisons between rankers using implicit feedback depend not only on the true difference in NDCG between two rankers but also on the magnitude of the difference per query and the number of affected queries.

5.3 Runs

All our experiments evaluate the same four interleaved comparison methods. As baselines, we use three existing methods (cf., §2):

- **balanced interleave**, as described in [23].
- **team draft**, as introduced in [23]; as in the original, clicks on top results are ignored when the documents are placed in identical order by both rankers.
- **document constraint**, introduced in [10], as described in §2.

In addition, we evaluate the experimental condition:

- **marginalized probabilities**: our model using the probabilistic interleave process (cf. §4.1) and the probabilistic comparisons defined in Eq. 4 (cf. §4.3).

Below we describe the three sets of experiments designed to assess interleaved comparison methods in terms of accuracy, convergence behavior, and robustness to noise.

Accuracy. The first experiment assesses the accuracy of interleaved comparison methods when evaluated on a large set of ranker pairs. We construct a ranker for each of the 136 individual features provided with the MSLR data set. We then evaluate the interleaved comparison methods on all $9,180$ possible distinct pairs that can be obtained from these rankers. We evaluate the methods on this large set of ranker pairs using the perfect click model and a fixed subset of the data consisting of $1,000$ queries. We then compare the outcome predicted by the interleaved comparison methods to the true NDCG of the rankers, computed on the same set of queries. We report on *accuracy* after $1,000$ queries: the percentage of pairs for which a comparison method correctly identified the better ranker.

Convergence. Based on the findings of the first experiment, we select a small subset of ranker pairs with which to investigate the methods' behavior in more detail. These experiments were designed to follow the setup used in [21] as closely as possible, with the difference that we use simulated interactions with the perfect click model instead of real-life search engine traffic, as discussed in §5.1. For each pair of rankers, each comparison method was run on randomly sampled query sets of size 1 to $10,000$; queries for which an interleaved list did not obtain any clicks were ignored. Each experiment was repeated $1,000$ times. We evaluate each method by computing, for each sampled query set size, the fraction of these $1,000$ repetitions for which it detected a preference for the correct ranker. We compute binomial confidence intervals on this fraction using Wilson score intervals at the 95% level [3].

Noise. The third set of experiments assesses the robustness of interleaved comparison methods to noise in click feedback. The setup is identical to the previous one except that the *realistic* click model is used instead.

6. RESULTS AND DISCUSSION

In this section we present and discuss the results of our experiments. Results from the exhaustive experiment, designed to assess the accuracy of interleaved comparison methods are presented first (§6.1). Based on the results of that experiment we select a subset of rankers to further investigate the convergence of these methods (§6.2), and their robustness to noise in click feedback (§6.3).

6.1 Accuracy

Table 3 gives an overview of the accuracy achieved by the four interleaved comparison methods in our first set of experiments. The highest accuracy is achieved by our probabilistic marginalization method. It correctly identifies the better ranker for 91.4% of the pairs. This constitutes a 1.7% increase (or 143 additional pairs) in accuracy over the second-best run, team draft. The team draft method achieves an accuracy of 89.8%, followed by balanced interleave at 88.1%. The accuracy achieved by the document constraint method is substantially lower (85.7%).

Table 3: Accuracy for the comparison methods on ranker pairs constructed from individual features (after 1,000 queries).

run	*accuracy*
balanced interleave	0.881
team draft	0.898
document constraint	0.857
marginalized probabilities	**0.914**

To gain further insight into the performance characteristics of each method, we analyzed what type of ranker pairs each method judged correctly or incorrectly. The balanced interleave, team draft, and marginalized probabilities methods correctly identify the better ranker in all pairs with an NDCG difference of at least 0.05. This is in line with [21], which found that the team draft method can be used to reliably compare ranker pairs with a difference in NDCG of 0.05 within approximately 1,000 queries. The document constraint method made mistakes on much more distant ranker pairs, with an NDCG difference of up to 0.12.

We further find that the document constraint method makes a number of systematic errors, meaning that an unexpectedly large number of pairs involving a particular ranker are judged incorrectly. For example, a large number of comparisons involving the ranker constructed from one of the best features, query-click count (feature id 134 in the MSLR data set), are incorrect. The ranked lists that are generated in these cases differ substantially, so that there is little overlap. The documents ranked highly by the better ranker contain many more relevant documents, so more constraints involving these documents are inferred from clicks. As most of these documents are not included in the top ranks of the worse ranker, the inferred constraints are not counted as being violated by this ranker, while they do count against the better ranker.

For the balanced interleave method, we also observe systematic errors, but to a much lesser degree. These errors typically involve pairs of rankers that are very similar, or that are likely related, such as the minimum term frequency and the minimum tf-idf (feature id 27 and 77, respectively). For the team draft and marginalized probabilities methods, we found no such systematic bias. Errors appear to be randomly distributed over ranker pairs.

The results of our first set of experiments indicate that the marginalized probabilities method is more accurate than other methods. On a large set of rankers it was able to infer the correct relation between rankers the most often. This method, as well as balanced interleave and team draft, are able to reliably compare rankers with a difference in NDCG of at least 0.05 after 1,000 queries. For the document constraint method, we found systematic errors even when the difference in NDCG between two rankers was very large.

Table 4: Ranker pairs used for the second set of experiments.

pair	*ranking features (feature id)*	*NDCG*
	"easy" ranker pairs	
1	term frequency of the document url, normalized by mean stream length (64)	0.301
	mean stream length of the document url (14)	0.201
2	bm25 score on the document title (108)	0.306
	maximum tf-idf on the url (84)	0.256
	"problem" ranker pairs	
3	click-count for a query-url pair of a search engine over a given period (134)	0.341
	boolean retrieval score on the document body (96)	0.219
4	boolean retrieval score on anchor text (97)	0.303
	bm25 score on the document body (106)	0.253
5	minimum tf-idf on anchor text (77)	0.262
	number of covered query terms (1)	0.231

6.2 Convergence

Based on the outcomes of the first set of experiments, we selected a small set of ranker pairs for more in-depth analysis. We used these rankers to run a second set of experiments with a large number of randomly sampled queries and many repetitions, to distinguish performance characteristics due to chance from more systematic issues.

The ranker pairs used for this second set of experiments are shown in Table 4. For each pair, the table includes a description of the two ranking features, the corresponding feature id in the MSLR data set, and the NDCG that is obtained on the whole data set if the feature is used for ranking documents for each query.

The pairs of rankers were selected as follows. First, we selected two pairs of rankers for which all methods had correctly identified the better ranker. These "easy" pairs have an NDCG difference of 0.1 (pair 1) and 0.05 (pair 2) percentage points, respectively. The second pair is on the threshold at which three of the methods achieved perfect accuracy within 1,000 queries, and corresponds to the "major" experiments in [21].

Second, we selected a set of "problem" pairs, on which one or more of the comparison methods had made mistakes. For each method, we selected the incorrectly judged pair of rankers with the highest difference in NDCG. Because pairs with a large difference in NDCG are typically easier to distinguish, these pairs are most useful for diagnosis. If the method again comes to the wrong conclusion after evaluation with a much larger set of queries and repetitions, then we can conclude that the mistake is systematic and that similar errors will likely occur for more difficult ranker pairs with smaller differences in NDCG.

The problematic pair selected for the document constraint method is pair 3. This method made many mistakes involving the click-count feature (134), and we select the pair with the highest NDCG difference (0.12). Pair 4 is the pair that was judged incorrectly by the team draft and marginalized probabilities methods with the highest difference in NDCG (0.05). As these runs did not appear to have systematic difficulties, we assumed that a pair that had been judged wrong by both methods would be most likely to point to a systematic problem. The balanced interleave method made systematic mistakes on pairs with relatively small differences, of which the selected pair 5 is the one with the biggest difference in NDCG (0.03).

Figures 6 to 9 show the results of our second set of experiments, using the perfect click model. The figures show the fraction of repetitions in which the hypothesized better ranker won the comparison (on the y-axis) vs. the number of sampled queries (on the x-axis). A comparison method that performs well will converge to 1 quickly, meaning that it detects a preference for the correct ranker after observing a relatively small number of samples.

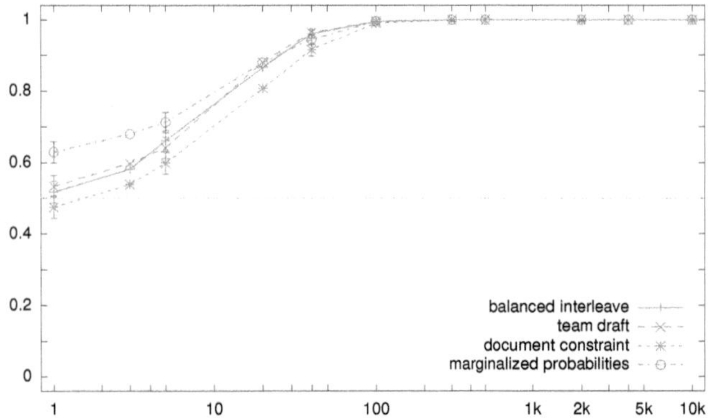

Figure 6: Results, pair 1, perfect click model (see text for results for pair 2).

Figure 6 shows the results obtained when comparing pair 1 using (simulated) user clicks. We observe that for "easy" pairs, all methods converge to the correct decision quickly, in this case after approximately 100 observed queries. Results for pair 2 are qualitatively similar to those obtained for pair 1, so we only include one of the figures due to space limitations. Convergence on pair 2 is slower, as expected. All methods converge within $1,000$ observed queries, a result that is in line with [21].

To further investigate what constitutes "easy" ranker pairs, we analyzed how NDCG differences are distributed over queries. For pair 1 and 2 we found that these differences are distributed over a large portion of queries. Thus, a consistent NDCG difference on a large number of queries appears to make the detection of such differences using interleaving techniques easiest.

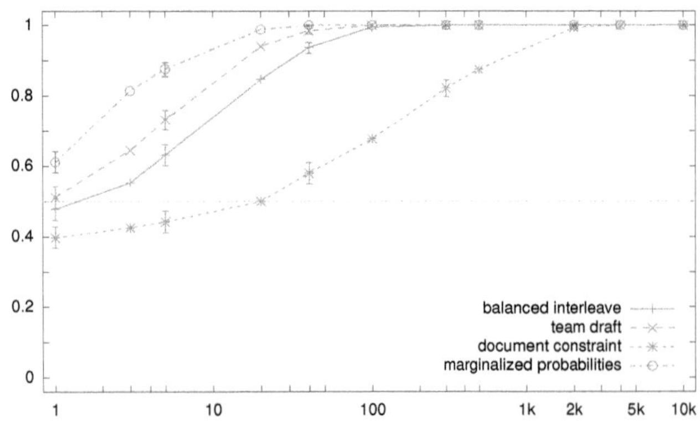

Figure 7: Results, pair 3, perfect click model.

Figure 7 shows the results obtained for pair 3, which was selected as a problematic pair for the document constraint method. Indeed, this method is slowest to converge. However, it does identify the hypothesized better ranker correctly, and converges within approximately $2,000$ observed samples (half as fast as other methods). Marginalized probabilities converges significantly faster than all other methods, after only 50 observed samples.

To analyze this performance difference, we again examine the NDCG differences between rankers and how they are distributed over queries. We find that the relatively large difference in NDCG is distributed over a relatively small number of queries. Thus, there is a relatively small set of queries for which the first ranker performs dramatically better than the second and a large set of queries for which the difference is negligible, or where the second ranker is preferred. In such situations, the magnitude of the differences between rankers can play a critical role. Our method's use of softmax functions and marginalization enables it to more accurately assess these magnitudes, leading to better, faster comparisons.

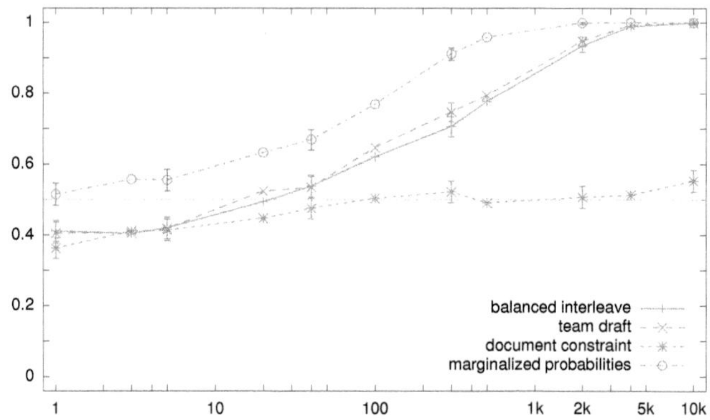

Figure 8: Results, pair 4, perfect click model.

Results for pair 4 are presented in Figure 8. This pair of rankers was selected as problematic for the team draft and marginalized probabilities methods. However, it appears that the selected pair is simply more difficult than previous ones and that this difficulty is not specific to these two methods. Though convergence on this pair is much slower than on those discussed previously, the marginalized probabilities method still converges much faster than other methods ($\approx 2,000$ impressions, vs. $4,000$ for the second-fastest team draft method). Note that the document constraint method has still not converged to a decision after $10,000$ impressions.

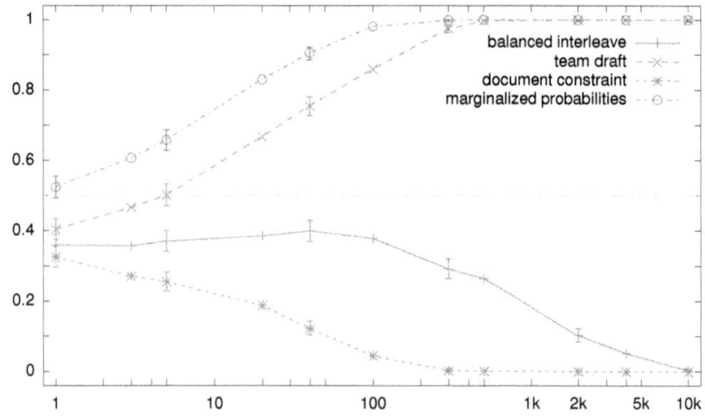

Figure 9: Results, pair 5, perfect click model.

Results for the last pair of rankers we examine, pair 5, are shown in Figure 9. This pair was selected as problematic for the balanced interleave method. The NDCG difference of this pair is smallest (0.03), as is the number of affected queries. The team draft and marginalized probabilities methods quickly identify the correct ranker, with the marginalized probabilities method converging much faster than the team draft method. The other two methods are unable to identify the better ranker for this pair. For this pair, the interleaved lists tend to be very similar to the worse ranker, creating bias towards that ranker. As a result, the balanced interleave and document constraint methods converge to the wrong decision.

Overall, results for all the pairs considered in this section show a similar pattern. The marginalized probabilities method performs best overall, identifying the better rankers correctly for all pairs, and converging to the correct solution quickly, often substantially and significantly faster than all other methods. The team draft method performs second best, identifying the better ranker correctly in all cases and typically converging faster than the balanced interleave and document constraint methods, which select the wrong ranker in one case. Of course, there may exist pairs of rankers for which the document constraint and balanced interleave methods converge faster than team draft and probabilistic marginalization due to bias towards the ranker that is in fact better. However, there is in general no guarantee that these methods will select the better ranker, no matter how large the number of observed queries.

6.3 Noise

In the previous section, we studied the performance of interleaved comparison methods under simulated perfect conditions, in which the simulated user examined all top 10 documents, clicked on all highly relevant and no non-relevant documents (with click probabilities decreasing for in-between relevance levels; cf. §5.1). Here, we use a more realistic user model to study the influence of noise on the performance of the comparison methods. Our *realistic* click model defines click probabilities such that there is a 0.8 probability of highly relevant documents being clicked, with click probabilities cut in half for each subsequently lower relevance level. Stop probabilities increase with the relevance level of previously seen documents. Hence, the chance that clicks prefer a less relevant document is higher than with the perfect model and documents ranked towards the top of the result list are more likely to be clicked. Ideally, noise should slow the convergence of interleaved comparison methods but not alter the final outcome.

For the third set of experiments, we omit graphs for pairs 1, 2, and 5, as the results are very similar to those presented in the previous section. For pairs 1 and 2, all methods identify the better ranker correctly but converge more slowly than under perfect conditions. For pair 1, the correct ranker is identified after between 300 impressions (marginalized probabilities) and 500 impressions (document constraint), respectively; for pair 2 this occurs after approximately 2,000 impressions. For pair 2, only the marginalized probabilities and team draft methods identify the correct rankers (after approximately 2,000 impressions).

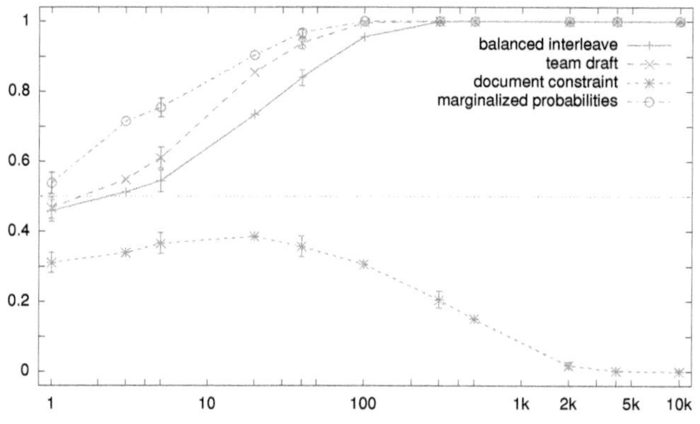

Figure 10: Results, pair 3, realistic click model.

Interesting performance differences can be seen for pairs 3 and 4. For pair 3 (Figure 10), noise affects the outcome for the document constraint method to such an extent that the method is unable to identify the better ranker. The reason for this change in outcome is that the realistic user model results in noisier clicks that are more concentrated towards the top of the result list. Documents contributed by the better ranker are generally more relevant and clicked more often in expectation. Clicks on documents other than the top-ranked one will result in constraints that are more often violated by the better ranker, while fewer clicks on documents contributed by the worse ranker result in fewer violated constraints for that ranker. This result suggests that the document constraint method is not appropriate for use with noisy click feedback, especially when the true quality difference between rankers is very large.

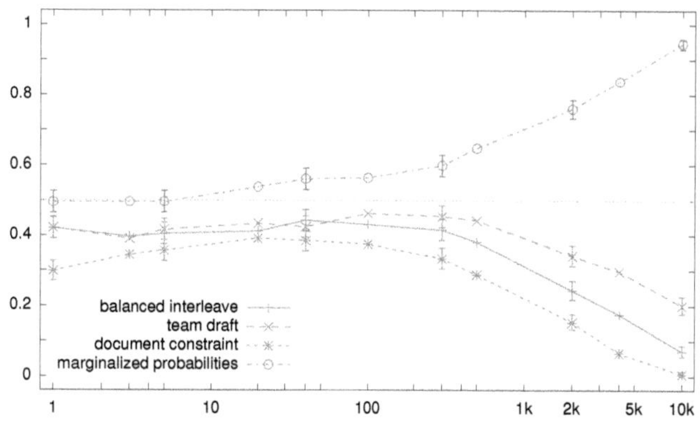

Figure 11: Results, pair 4, realistic click model.

Figure 11 shows the noisy results obtained with pair 4. Only the marginalized probabilities method correctly identifies the better ranker and it converges more slowly than under perfect conditions. None of the baseline methods identifies the correct ranker. For the team draft method, which preferred the predicted better ranker in the perfect setting, the influence of more realistic stop probabilities plays a role. Previously, the simulated user examined all results in the top 10 interleaved list, so relevant documents at similar ranks had the same chance of being clicked. Now, the simulated user may stop browsing the result list after clicking on the link to a document, creating a disadvantage for one of the rankers, especially in cases where rankers place relevant documents at similar ranks (which is particularly likely in cases where the rankers produce similar result lists). Here, this phenomenon creates a systematic disadvantage for the true better ranker. This demonstrates that an insensitivity to some changes in rankings can result in the team-draft method inferring a preference for the wrong ranker.

Our evaluation of interleaved comparison methods with noisy and less exhaustive user clicks shows that our marginalized probabilities method is robust to such changes in click behavior. In all cases, the method was able to correctly identify the better ranker. As predicted, noise slowed convergence. For all the baseline methods, the addition of noise caused them to infer a preference for the wrong ranker more often than under perfect conditions.

7. CONCLUSION

Methods for evaluating rankers using implicit feedback are promising because implicit feedback can be collected directly while users interact with a search engine, which reduces cost and allows tuning to the true preferences of users. Previous work introduced the *balanced interleave*, *document constraint*, and *team draft* methods for comparing rankers using click feedback based on interleaving lists. The *team draft* method has previously been shown to reliably detect small differences between rankers in practice.

The first contribution of our paper is an analysis of interleaved comparison methods. We formulated criteria in terms of bias and sensitivity and analyzed how well existing methods fulfill them. In addition to the previously known bias of the balanced interleave method, we identified a similar bias affecting the document constraint method, and a lack of sensitivity to specific differences in ranking for the team draft method.

Our second contribution is a new, probabilistic interleaved comparison method that is both unbiased and sensitive to differences between rankings. Central to the method is the use of softmax functions, which assign to each document a non-zero probability of being placed in the interleaved result list. As a result, click assignment to rankers is smoothed, yielding credit assignment that accurately reflects the magnitude of differences between rankers. Furthermore, we showed how the method can be made more efficient by marginalizing over all possible assignments for an observed interleaved list.

We validated the results of our analysis and our proposed method using experiments based on a recently developed simulation framework. The probabilistic method for comparing rankers using click data is more accurate than any of the previous methods. In particular, on pairs of rankers that are difficult for other methods to compare, e.g., because the rankers perform very differently on only a few queries, our method can correctly identify the better ranker, with substantially and significantly fewer observed queries. In addition, the method is more robust to noise than previous methods.

Our simulation setup allowed us to undertake many comparisons under different conditions (e.g., varying noise). However, as with any simulation, these experiments cannot replace experiments with real users. Therefore, in the future we aim to evaluate our method in a real-life setting. In addition, with more reliable and faster convergence, our approach can pave the way for online learning to rank methods that require many comparisons. Applying the method in such settings is another interesting direction for future research.

Acknowledgements

This research was partially supported by the European Union's ICT Policy Support Programme as part of the Competitiveness and Innovation Framework Programme, CIP ICT-PSP under grant agreement nr 250430, the PROMISE Network of Excellence co-funded by the 7th Framework Programme of the European Commission, grant agreement no. 258191, the Netherlands Organisation for Scientific Research (NWO) under project nrs 612.061.814, 612.061.-815, 640.004.802, 380-70-011, the Center for Creation, Content and Technology (CCCT), the Hyperlocal Service Platform project funded by the Service Innovation & ICT program, the WAHSP project funded by the CLARIN-nl program, and under COMMIT project Infiniti.

8. REFERENCES

[1] E. Agichtein, E. Brill, and S. Dumais. Improving web search ranking by incorporating user behavior information. In *SIGIR '06*, pages 19–26, 2006.

[2] P. Bailey, N. Craswell, I. Soboroff, P. Thomas, A. P. de Vries, and E. Yilmaz. Relevance assessment: are judges exchangeable and does it matter. In *SIGIR '08*, pages 667–674, 2008.

[3] L. D. Brown, T. T. Cai, and A. DasGupta. Interval estimation for a binomial proportion. *Statistical Science*, 16(2):pp. 101–117, 2001.

[4] O. Chapelle and Y. Zhang. A dynamic bayesian network click model for web search ranking. In *SIGIR '09*, pages 1–10, 2009.

[5] M. Claypool, P. Le, M. Wased, and D. Brown. Implicit interest indicators. In *IUI'01*, IUI '01, pages 33–40, 2001.

[6] N. Craswell, O. Zoeter, M. Taylor, and B. Ramsey. An experimental comparison of click position-bias models. In *WSDM '08*, pages 87–94, 2008.

[7] S. Fox, K. Karnawat, M. Mydland, S. Dumais, and T. White. Evaluating implicit measures to improve web search. *ACM TOIS*, 23(2):147–168, 2005.

[8] F. Guo, L. Li, and C. Faloutsos. Tailoring click models to user goals. In *WSCD '09*, pages 88–92, 2009.

[9] F. Guo, C. Liu, and Y. M. Wang. Efficient multiple-click models in web search. In *WSDM '09*, pages 124–131, 2009.

[10] J. He, C. Zhai, and X. Li. Evaluation of methods for relative comparison of retrieval systems based on clickthroughs. In *CIKM '09*, pages 2029–2032, 2009.

[11] K. Hofmann, B. Huurnink, M. Bron, and M. de Rijke. Comparing click-through data to purchase decisions for retrieval evaluation. In *SIGIR '10*, pages 761–762, 2010.

[12] K. Hofmann, S. Whiteson, and M. de Rijke. Balancing exploration and exploitation in learning to rank online. In *ECIR'11*, pages 251–263, 2011.

[13] K. Järvelin and J. Kekäläinen. Cumulated gain-based evaluation of IR techniques. *ACM Trans. Inf. Syst.*, 20(4): 422–446, 2002.

[14] T. Joachims. Optimizing search engines using clickthrough data. In *KDD '02*, pages 133–142, 2002.

[15] T. Joachims. Evaluating retrieval performance using clickthrough data. In J. Franke, G. Nakhaeizadeh, and I. Renz, editors, *Text Mining*, pages 79–96. Springer Verlag, 2003.

[16] S. Jung, J. L. Herlocker, and J. Webster. Click data as implicit relevance feedback in web search. *IPM*, 43(3): 791 – 807, 2007. Special Issue on Heterogeneous and Distributed IR.

[17] D. Kelly. Implicit feedback: Using behavior to infer relevance. In *New directions in cognitive information retrieval*, pages 169–186. Springer, 2005.

[18] D. Kelly and N. Belkin. Display time as implicit feedback: understanding task effects. In *SIGIR '04*, pages 377–384, 2004.

[19] J. Langford, A. Strehl, and J. Wortman. Exploration scavenging. In *ICML '08*, pages 528–535, 2008.

[20] R. Lippmann. Pattern classification using neural networks. *Communications Magazine, IEEE*, 27(11): 47–50, 2002.

[21] F. Radlinski and N. Craswell. Comparing the sensitivity of information retrieval metrics. In *SIGIR '10*, pages 667–674, 2010.

[22] F. Radlinski, R. Kleinberg, and T. Joachims. Learning diverse rankings with multi-armed bandits. In *ICML '08*, pages 784–791, 2008.

[23] F. Radlinski, M. Kurup, and T. Joachims. How does clickthrough data reflect retrieval quality? In *CIKM '08*, pages 43–52, 2008.

[24] F. Scholer, M. Shokouhi, B. Billerbeck, and A. Turpin. Using clicks as implicit judgments: expectations versus observations. In *ECIR'08*, pages 28–39, 2008.

[25] X. Shen, B. Tan, and C. Zhai. Context-sensitive information retrieval using implicit feedback. In *SIGIR '05*, pages 43–50, 2005.

[26] R. S. Sutton and A. G. Barto. *Introduction to Reinforcement Learning*. MIT Press, Cambridge, MA, USA, 1998.

[27] R. White, I. Ruthven, J. Jose, and C. Rijsbergen. Evaluating implicit feedback models using searcher simulations. *ACM TOIS*, 23(3):325–361, 2005.

Intent-Aware Query Similarity

Jiafeng Guo[†], Xueqi Cheng[†], Gu Xu[‡], Xiaofei Zhu[†]

[†]Institute of Computing Technology, CAS
Beijing, P. R. China
guojiafeng@software.ict.ac.cn,cxq@ict.ac.cn,
zhuxiaofei@software.ict.ac.cn

[‡]Microsoft Research Asia
Beijing, P. R. China
guxu@microsoft.com

ABSTRACT

Query similarity calculation is an important problem and has a wide range of applications in IR, including query recommendation, query expansion, and even advertisement matching. Existing work on query similarity aims to provide a single similarity measure without considering the fact that queries are ambiguous and usually have multiple search intents. In this paper, we argue that query similarity should be defined upon search intents, so-called *intent-aware query similarity*. By introducing search intents into the calculation of query similarity, we can obtain more accurate and also informative similarity measures on queries and thus help a variety of applications, especially those related to diversification. Specifically, we first identify the potential search intents of queries, and then measure query similarity under different intents using intent-aware representations. A regularized topic model is employed to automatically learn the potential intents of queries by using both the words from search result snippets and the regularization from query co-clicks. Experimental results confirm the effectiveness of intent-aware query similarity on ambiguous queries which can provide significantly better similarity scores over the traditional approaches. We also experimentally verified the utility of intent-aware similarity in the application of query recommendation, which can suggest diverse queries in a structured way to search users.

Categories and Subject Descriptors

H.3.3 [**Information Storage and Retrieval**]: Information Search and Retrieval—*Query formulation*

General Terms

Algorithms, Experimentation, Performance, Theory

Keywords

Query Similarity, Search Intent, Regularized Topic Model, Pair-wise Measure, Graph-based Measure

CIKM'11, October 24–28, 2011, Glasgow, Scotland, UK.

1. INTRODUCTION

Calculating similarities between queries is a key element of various IR applications. For example, query recommendation [2, 34] manages to provide similar queries to users and help them to reformulate their queries regarding their information needs. In query expansion [14, 17], similar terms (words) are added to improve the recall of search, and the expanded query can also be considered as a similar query to the original query. Besides, query similarity can also be helpful to advertisement matching [29]. However, due to the high ambiguity of queries, how to properly define the similarity between queries is not a trivial problem. For example, given query "apple", it is similar to "apple tree" if the searcher is looking for apple fruits, while it is also similar to "apple store" if the search intent is to find products of the apple company. The similarity is actually not comparable across different search intents, which means that we cannot say "apple tree" is more similar to "apple" than "apple store" and vice versa. In this paper, we argue that the similarity between queries should be defined upon search intents, so-called *intent-aware query similarity*. Note that search intent here refers to the goal or need of a user during a search. In this manner, we can provide more precise and also informative similarity information without being biased by popular intents or wrongly making queries from different intents similar. Evidently intent-aware query similarity will be especially helpful for various diversity problems.

To the best of our knowledge, none of existing work formally addressed the problem of similarity calculation with the awareness of search intents and thus it is the unique position of this paper. Also it is important to notice that traditional similarity measures may encounter some problems when dealing with ambiguous queries, namely the queries with multiple search intents. Various data sources, including search results [30], user clicks [2, 26, 13] and search sessions [34, 9], have been employed to enrich the representation of search queries. While similarity measures defined on these representations can be divided into two major categories:

Pair-wise Measures. The similarity is independently measured on each query pair, using similarity functions like cosine similarity [2, 33], Jaccard coefficient [3], kernel functions [30], etc. For ambiguous queries, the information from multiple search intents are actually mixed together and thus pair-wise measures without the awareness of search intents will be easily biased by dominant search intents and ignore unpopular ones, for example query "apple" is only similar to "apple store" but not related to "apple tree".

Graph-based Measures. The similarity between queries is

defined on a query graph, or query relation graph [13, 9]. It means that the similarity is not pair-wise independent and the similarity of adjacent queries is considered. In some sense, graph-based measures can be considered as propagating the similarity on top of the query graph. However, if the queries are ambiguous, the propagation should not cross the boundary of different search intents. Without the awareness of search intents, the queries with different search intents will be wrongly connected, for example "apple store" becomes similar to "apple tree".

In this paper, as the first attempt, we cast some light on the problem of "intent-aware query similarity". Specifically, we propose first identifying the potential search intents of queries, and then measuring query similarity under different search intents using intent-aware representations. Note that the identification of potential search intents of queries are largely different from classifying the queries into a set of predefined categories [23, 12], since the search intents of queries are usually fine-grained and substantial. In our work, a regularized topic model is employed to automatically learn the potential intents of queries by using both the words from search result snippets and the regularization from query co-clicks. Based on the learned intents of queries, we then extract the query representation under each intent, and thus different measures can be applied to measure query similarity with respect to different search intents. Both pair-wise measures (e.g., cosine similarity measure) and graph-based measures (e.g., spectral embedding [4]) can be easily applied.

While there are many applications requiring a similarity measure between queries, one direct application in the context of search is query recommendation. In this paper, we adopt query recommendation as an example to demonstrate the usefulness of introducing search intent into the calculation of query similarity. With our approach, we can identify similar queries to the user's initial query with respect to different search intents, and then a structured query recommendation [19] can be easily built by grouping diverse recommendations based on the search intents.

We conducted experiments based on a large collection of query logs and search results from a commercial search engine, and demonstrated the effectiveness of our intent-aware query similarity by comparing with other baseline methods. Experimental results show that by identifying search intents of queries, we can measure query similarity significantly better than traditional approaches. We also demonstrate that by grouping query recommendations based on search intents and presenting them in structured way, we can largely enhance users' click behaviors on recommendations.

The rest of the paper is organized as follows. Section 2 introduces related work. Section 3 describes our solution to intent-aware query similarity. Section 4 discusses applying our application to query recommendations. Experimental results are presented in Section 4. Conclusions are made in the last section.

2. RELATED WORK

Measuring similarity between queries is an interesting and difficult problem. A reliable query similarity measure can be very useful for a variety of applications such as query recommendation [2, 34, 26], query reformulation [32, 1, 22], query expansion [14, 17], and advertising [29]. However, since queries are usually very short and ambiguous, it is difficult to calculate their similarity only based on query terms. Many existing approaches resolve the information inadequate problem in query by leveraging auxiliary information, including search results [30], clickthrough [2, 26, 13] or search sessions [34, 9], to enrich query representation for better similarity measurement.

Based on the augmented representation of queries, two major approaches are then applied to measure similarity between queries:

Pair-wise Measures. The similarity is independently measured on each query pair using pair-wise metrics. For example, Beeferman et al. [3] leveraged Jaccard similarity coefficient over the clickthrough vector of queries as the similarity measure. Baeza-Yates et al. [2] calculated query similarity using cosine similarity based on the aggregation of the term-weight vectors of the URLs clicked after the query. Wen et al. [33] applied various similarity metrics over both query term vectors and clickthrough vectors to measure query similarity, including term overlap, cosine similarity, edit distance, and Jaccard coefficient. Typical approaches using the hybrid similarity measurements over queries can also be found in [34, 22]. In [16], Deng et al. introduced two new schemes for representing queries based on clickthrough and applied both cosine similarity and Jaccard coefficient for measuring query similarity. In [30], Sahami et al. proposed a Kernel Function for measuring the query similarity based on the Tf-Idf weighted vectors of search result snippets. However, for ambiguous queries, the information from multiple search intents are actually mixed together and thus pair-wise measures without the awareness of search intents will be easily biased by dominant search intents and ignore unpopular ones.

Graph-based Measures. The similarity between queries is defined on a query graph, or query relation graph [13, 9]. Therefore, the similarity is not pair-wise independent and the similarity of adjacent queries is considered. In some sense, graph-based measures can be considered as propagating the similarity on top of the query graph. For example, Craswell et al. [13] applied two types of random walk process to propagate the query similarity along the query-URL bipartite graph and obtain better similarity scores between queries. Mei et al. [26] described a random walk on the one-mode query graph and employed the hitting time as the similarity measure. In [1], Antonellis et al. used the bipartite SimRank on the query-URL graph to measure query similarity. In [24], matrix factorization was employed to calculate query similarity based on the user-query-URL tripartite graph. Recently, Bordino et al. [9] introduced the query-flow graph based on the session data and employed graph projection to measure query similarity. Work on such a graph to compute query similarity can also be found in [7, 8]. However, if the queries are ambiguous, the graph-based measures without the awareness of search intents will wrongly connect the queries with different search intents.

Related work also includes topic modeling. Topic modeling has been popularly used for data analysis in various domains including topic discovery, document classification, citation analysis, and social network analysis. Topic models, such as Probabilistic Latent Semantic Indexing (PLSI) [21] and Latent Dirichlet Allocation (LDA) [6] have shown impressive empirical success in revealing the hidden structures of documents and in related applications like document classification and collaborative filtering. Based on the above models, a set of variants and extensions [18, 5, 31] have been further proposed to address document modeling problems in different scenarios. Our work exploits topic modeling in a new application (i.e., query similarity measure), and we employed a regularized topic model to fully leverage both search result snippets and co-clicks to help learn the search intents of queries. There have been several regularized topic models proposed to incorporate auxiliary knowledge as a constraint into topic model learning process and show the resulting benefits. For example, Cai et al. proposed two topic models, Laplacian pLSI (LapPLSI) [10] and Locally-consistent Topic Modeling (LTM) [11], which incorporate manifold structure information as a constraint into the PLSI model to smooth the probability density functions. Similarly, Mei et al. [25] regularized the statistical topic model PLSI with a harmonic regularizer based on a graph structure in the data. In [20], Guo et al. introduced a weakly supervised topic model, i.e. WS-LDA, by incorporating human labels as a soft constraints into the LDA model to supervise the topic alignment.

3. OUR APPROACH

In our work, we propose to measure query similarity with the awareness of search intents. The key idea is that we first identify the potential search intents of queries, and then measure the query similarity under different search intents using their intent-aware representations. As aforementioned, there are a large amount fined-grained potential search intents behind different queries (e.g. the fruit or product intent for query "apple"), and it is usually difficult to define an appropriate prior taxonomy for search intents. Therefore, we propose to leverage the large amount of hidden topics in topic model to help capture the potential search intents of queries.

Specifically, a regularized topic model is employed to automatically learn the potential intents of queries by using both the words from search result snippets and the regularization from query co-clicks. Based on the learned intents of queries, we then extract the query representation under each intent, and thus different measures can be applied to measure query similarity with respect to different search intents. Both pair-wise measures (e.g., cosine similarity measure) and graph-based measures (e.g., spectral embedding) can be easily applied.

In this section, we will first introduce the auxiliary data we leveraged for identifying the search intents of queries. We then describe the regularized topic model for the key learning problem. Finally, we show how to extract the query representation under each intent, and apply different similarity metrics to measure query similarity with respect to search intent.

3.1 Data for Identifying Search Intents of Queries

In order to identify the potential search intents of queries, we need to leverage some auxiliary data to provide a rich representation for short queries. Different types of auxiliary data, including search results [30], clickthrough [2, 26, 13] or search sessions [34, 9], have been leveraged to enrich query representation for similarity measurement in many existing approaches. For ambiguous queries, such auxiliary data is a mixture of information from multiple search intents. However, traditional approaches usually directly leverage such kind of mixed-intent representations of queries for similarity measure. In our work, we leverage both search result snippets and clickthrough of queries to help learn the potential search intents of queries. This is largely different from the traditional work.

Although both the two types of data can provide rich information for identifying potential search intents of queries, they have some natural different characteristics. The search result snippets provide a great context for the query. We can thus construct a virtual document by the words from the snippets of the top search results to well "describe" the given query. Thanks to the advance of modern search engines, such a description often show a high recall of potential search intents of the given query. Take the query "office" for example, a typical search results from the commercial search engines (e.g. Google, Bing or Yahoo!) may contain the content about the microsoft office software, the office tv series, and even some office furniture or supplies. However, search results may also have some irrelevant, spam or advertisement information, and words itself may have ambiguity. All these factors may hurt the quality or precision of the search result snippets on resolving search intents of queries.

Meanwhile, the large amount of clickthough data from search logs also provide us useful information for identifying search intents of queries. Unlike the search result snippets, clickthrough information is a resource with higher precision but lower recall. As we can see, although one query may convey multiple search intents, it is often determined when a specific URL is clicked. Therefore, if two queries share a set of same clicked URLs, they will convey similar search intent [2, 3]. The "wisdom of the crowds" property thus makes clickthrough, especially the query co-clicks, a more precise resource for identifying similar search intent of queries. However, query co-click information is relative sparse (i.e. lower recall) in describing search intents compared with the search result snippets, since usually there are limited clicks for each query.

Based on the above analysis of the different characteristics in search result snippets and clickthrough, we propose to simultaneously leverage the two types of auxiliary data in our work so that they can supplement each other in resolving search intents of queries.

3.2 Learning Potential Search Intents with a Regularized Topic Model

From previous section we can see, the search result snippets provide rich context information for a given query. We can thus construct a virtual document by the words from the search result snippets to describe the given query and capture its major search intents. Since queries may convey multiple search intents, it is natural to apply a mixture model (e.g. topic model) over the virtual document of the query to help learn the potential search intents. Meanwhile, the clickthrough information, especially the query co-clicks, provides us clear evidence about which queries convey the similar search intent. Such evidence can be used as a powerful constraint over the intent distribution of queries to help us reveal the search intents of queries more accurately. Therefore, we propose to employ a regularized topic model to fully leverage the two types of auxiliary data to help learn the potential search intents of queries.

3.2.1 The Regularized Topic Model

Suppose there is a collection of N queries $\mathcal{Q} = \{q_1, \ldots, q_N\}$ sharing the same set of K potential search intents $\mathcal{S} =$

$\{s_1, \ldots, s_K\}$, and each query is represented by a set of words $w \in \mathcal{W} = \{w_1, \ldots, w_M\}$, which are collected from its top search result snippets. By viewing queries as virtual "documents", words from top search result snippets as "words", and potential search intents as "topics", we can apply the Probabilistic Latent Semantic Indexing (PLSI) [21] to model the generation of each query and its words from top search result snippets by the following scheme:

1. select a query q_i with probability $P(q_i)$,
2. pick a potential search intent s_k with probability $P(s_k|q_i)$,
3. generate a word w_j with probability $P(w_j|s_k)$.

By summing out the latent variable s, the joint probability of an observed pair (q_i, w_j) can be computed as

$$\begin{aligned} P(q_i, w_j) &= P(q_i)P(w_j|q_i) \\ &= P(q_i)\sum_{k=1}^{K} P(w_j|s_k)P(s_k|q_i) \end{aligned} \quad (1)$$

Based on this joint probability, we can calculate the log-likelihood as

$$\tilde{\mathcal{L}} = \sum_{i=1}^{N}\sum_{j=1}^{M} n(q_i, w_j) \log\Big(P(q_i)\sum_{k=1}^{K} P(w_j|s_k)P(s_k|q_i)\Big) \quad (2)$$

where $n(q_i, w_j)$ denotes the number of times word w_j occurred in the top search result snippets of query q_i. Following the maximum likelihood principle, one can determine the model parameters $\{P(w_j|s_k), P(s_k|q_i)\}$ by maximizing the relevant part of Equation (2).

Recall that the query co-clicks provide us clear evidence about similar search intent between queries. That is, if two queries share many same clicked URLs, they convey similar search intent. Therefore, we can use the co-click information as a constraint over the search intents of queries to help us reveal the intents more accurately. More formally, we need to minimize the proximity of the probability distribution $P(s|q)$ of co-clicked query pairs, expressed by

$$\mathcal{R} = \sum_{i,j=1}^{N}\sum_{k=1}^{K} C_{ij}(P(s_k|q_i) - P(s_k|q_j))^2 \quad (3)$$

where matrix C contains the co-click relationship between queries with C_{ij} set as unique co-clicked URL number of the query pair (q_i, q_j). Note that other definitions for the co-click matrix C and proximity measure can also be used.

Now we give out the regularized topic model for identifying potential search intents of queries. The model adopts the generative scheme of PLSI. It aims to maximize the *regularized* log-likelihood as follows:

$$\begin{aligned} \mathfrak{L} &= \mathcal{L} - \lambda\mathcal{R} \\ &= \sum_{i=1}^{N}\sum_{j=1}^{M} n(q_i, w_j) \log\Big(P(q_i)\sum_{k=1}^{K} P(w_j|s_k)P(s_k|q_i)\Big) \\ &\quad -\lambda \sum_{i,j=1}^{N}\sum_{k=1}^{K} C_{ij}(P(s_k|q_i) - P(s_k|q_j))^2 \end{aligned} \quad (4)$$

where λ is the regularization parameter. Note that the regularized topic model essentially have the same form of the LapPLSI model proposed by Cai et al. [10]. However, in their case, they adopted the manifold structure information from document dataset to help modeling latent topics in the same document collections. While in our problem, we adopt the regularized topic model to effectively combine the two different types of data (i.e. search result snippets and query co-clicks) in the learning task for identifying the potential search intents of queries.

3.2.2 Model Fitting

The standard procedure for maximum likelihood estimation in latent variable model is the Expectation Maximization (EM) algorithm [15]. Here we use the Generalized EM algorithm [27] for parameter estimation in our regularized topic model as [10]. The major difference between Generalized EM and traditional EM is that in the M-step, Generalized EM only finds parameters that "improve" the expected value of the *complete* data log-likelihood function rather than "maximizing" it.

In our model, we have $NK + MK$ parameters $\{P(w_j|s_k), P(s_k|q_i)\}$ to be estimated, which is the same as PLSA. For simplicity, we define $\Phi = \{P(w_j|s_k)\}$ and $\Theta = \{P(s_k|q_i)\}$.

E-step: The E-step of the regularized topic model is exactly the same as that of PLSI. By applying Bayes' formula, we compute posterior probabilities.

$$P(s_k|q_i, w_j) = \frac{P(w_j|s_k)P(s_k|q_i)}{\sum_{k'=1}^{K} P(w_j|s_{k'})P(s_{k'}|q_i)} \quad (5)$$

M-step: In M-step, we maximize the expected complete data log-likelihood which is

$$\begin{aligned} Q(\Phi, \Theta) &= Q_1(\Phi, \Theta) - \lambda Q_2(\Theta) \\ &= \sum_{i=1}^{N}\sum_{j=1}^{M} n(q_i, w_j)\sum_{k=1}^{K} P(s_k|q_i, w_j) \log[P(w_j|s_k)P(s_k|q_i)] \\ &\quad -\lambda \sum_{i,j=1}^{N}\sum_{k=1}^{K} C_{ij}(P(s_k|q_i) - P(s_k|q_j))^2 \end{aligned} \quad (6)$$

The M-step re-estimation equation for Φ is exactly the same as PLSI since the regularization term does not include $P(w_j|z_k)$.

$$P(w_j|z_k) = \frac{\sum_{i=1}^{N} n(q_i, w_j)P(s_k|q_i, w_j)}{\sum_{j'=1}^{M}\sum_{i=1}^{N} n(q_i, w_{j'})P(s_k|q_i, w_{j'})} \quad (7)$$

However, we do not have a closed form re-estimation equation for Θ. Based on the concepts of Generalized EM, we re-estimate Θ by increasing $Q(\Theta)$ rather than maximizing it. Specifically, let $\{\Phi_n, \Theta_n\}$ denote the parameter values of the previous iteration and $\{\Phi_{n+1}, \Theta_{n+1}\}$ denote the parameter values of the current iteration. We first find $\{\Phi_{n+1}, \Theta_{n+1}^{(1)}\}$ which maximizes $Q_1(\Phi, \Theta)$ instead of the whole $Q(\Phi, \Theta)$ using the re-estimation Eqn. (7) and (8) for Φ and Θ respectively.

$$P(z_k|q_i) = \frac{\sum_{j=1}^{M} n(q_i, w_j)P(s_k|q_i, w_j)}{\sum_{j=1}^{M} n(q_i, w_j)} \quad (8)$$

We then try to start from $\Theta_{n+1}^{(1)}$ and decrease $Q_2(\Theta)$, by using the Newton-Raphson method [28]. Therefore, we can obtain the closed form solution for updating Θ_{n+1}

$$P(s_k|q_i)_{n+1}^{(t+1)} = (1-\gamma)P(s_k|q_i)_{n+1}^{(t)} + \gamma\frac{\sum_{j=1}^{N} C_{ij}P(s_k|q_j)_{n+1}^{(t)}}{\sum_{j=1}^{N} C_{ij}} \quad (9)$$

Algorithm 1 Generalized EM for Regularized Topic Model

Input: N: # of queries, M: size of vocabulary, K: # of topics, C: co-click matrix, λ: regularization parameter, γ: Newton step parameter, δ: Termination condition.

Output: $\Phi = \{P(w_j|s_k)\}$, $\Theta = \{P(s_k|q_i)\}$

Randomly initialize Φ_0 and Θ_0.
$n \leftarrow 0$
while (**true**) **do**
  E-step:
  Compute $P(s_k|q_i, w_j)$ using Φ_n and Θ_n as in Eqn. (5)
  M-step:
  Re-estimate Φ_{n+1} as in Eqn. (7)
  Re-estimate Θ_{n+1} as in Eqn. (8)
  $\Theta^{(1)}_{n+1} \leftarrow \Theta_{n+1}$
  Compute $\Theta^{(2)}_{n+1}$ from $\Theta^{(1)}_{n+1}$ as in Eqn. (9)
  while $(Q(\Phi_{n+1}, \Theta^{(2)}_{n+1}) \geq Q(\Phi_{n+1}, \Theta^{(1)}_{n+1}))$ **do**
    $\Theta^{(1)}_{n+1} \leftarrow \Theta^{(2)}_{n+1}$
    Compute $\Theta^{(2)}$ from $\Theta^{(1)}$ as in Eqn. (9)
  end while
  if $(Q(\Phi_{n+1}, \Theta^{(1)}_{n+1}) \geq Q(\Phi_n, \Theta_n))$ **then**
    $\Theta_{n+t} \leftarrow \Theta^{(1)}_{n+t}$
  else
    $\Phi_{n+1} \leftarrow \Phi_n$
    $\Theta_{n+1} \leftarrow \Theta_n$
  end if
  if $(Q(\Phi_{n+1}, \Theta_{n+1}) - Q(\Phi_n, \Theta_n)) \leq \delta)$ **then**
    break
  end if
  $n \leftarrow n + 1$
end while
return Φ_{n+1}, Θ_{n+1}

where $0 \leq \gamma \leq 1$ is the step parameter. It can be easily verified that $\sum_{k=1}^{K} P(s_k|q_i)^{(t+1)}_{n+1} = 1$ and $P(s_k|q_i)^{(t+1)}_{n+1} \geq 0$ hold in Eqn. (9) as long as $\sum_{k=1}^{K} P(s_k|q_i)^{(t)}_{n+1} = 1$ and $P(s_k|q_i)^{(t)}_{n+1} \geq 0$. Note here Φ_{n+1} will be fixed since $Q_2(\Theta)$ does not include Φ.

The iteration of Eqn. (9) is repeated until $Q(\Phi_{n+1}, \Theta^{(t+1)}_{n+1}) \leq Q(\Phi_{n+1}, \Theta^{(t)}_{n+1})$. We then test whether $Q(\Phi_{n+1}, \Theta^{(t+1)}_{n+1}) \geq Q(\Phi_n, \Theta_n)$. If it is not true, we reject the proposal of $\{\Phi_{n+1}, \Theta^{(t+1)}_{n+1}\}$ and return $\{\Phi_n, \Theta_n\}$ as the result of the M-step, and continue with the next E-step. The specific model fitting algorithm for the regularized topic model is summarized in Algorithm 1.

Finally, we obtain the probability $P(s_k|q_i)$ for each query q_i, which denotes the distribution of potential search intents of the query, and the probability $P(w_j|s_k)$ for each intent s_k, which denotes the distribution of words under each search intent. Here we further cut off the search intent with the proportion under a pre-defined threshold (e.g. 0.1 in our case) for each query to only preserve its major intents and avoid potential noises.

3.3 Intent-Aware Similarity Measure

Based on the learned intents of queries, here we show how to extract the query representation under each intent, and apply different metrics to measure query similarity with respect to different search intents. Both pair-wise measures (e.g. cosine similarity) and graph-based measures (e.g. spectral embedding) are adopted in our work as examples.

Pair-wise Measures: For pair-wise measures, the similarity of each query pair is independently measured by pair-wise metrics over the corresponding representations of queries. A typical representation for query q_i is the word vector from its search result snippets, where the l-th element of query q_i's vector is denoted as

$$\vec{q_i}[l] = n(q_i, w_l)$$

Such a word vector is a mixed-intent representation since words describing different intents of the query are merged together. In order to apply pair-wised measures to estimate query similarity with respect to search intents, we need to extract the word vector representation of the query under different search intents. This can be easily obtained with the topic model learned above.

As we can see, with our learned model, we can infer the probability $P(s_k|q_i, w_l)$ using the Eqn. (5), which denotes the expected search intent distribution for each word occurrence w_l given query q_i. In other words, we have the specific topic assignment for each word w_l from the top search result snippets of query q_i. Therefore, it is straightforward to represent query q_i under the k-th search intent using the word vector with the l-th element defined as

$$\vec{q}_{ik}[l] = n(q_i, w_l) P(s_k|q_i, w_l)$$

With the query representation under different search intents in hand, we can directly apply pair-wise measures to calculate the similarity between queries with respect to search intents. Here we take the traditional *cosine similarity* for example. Given query q_i and q_j, the similarity between the two queries under the k-th search intent can be calculated as follows

$$Sim_k(q_i, q_j) = \frac{\vec{q}_{ik} \cdot \vec{q}_{jk}}{\| \vec{q}_{ik} \| \| \vec{q}_{jk} \|} \qquad (10)$$

Graph-based Measures: For Graph-based measures, the similarity between queries is defined on a query graph, or a query relation graph [13, 9]. A typical query graph is the query similarity graph, which is an undirected graph $G = (V, E, A)$, where V is the set of unique queries $\mathcal{Q} = \{q_1, \ldots, q_N\}$, $E \subseteq V \times V$ is the set of edges, and $A = [W_{ij}]_{i,j=1,\ldots,N}$ is the adjacency matrix with W_{ij} defined as the similarity between the i-th and j-th queries. Here we simply define W_{ij} as the Jaccard coefficient on clicked URLs between the i-th and j-th queries for demonstration. Obviously, such a query graph is a mixed-intent representation of queries, since queries from different search intents are connected together. To leverage graph-based measures to estimate query similarity with respect to search intent, the key problem is to extract the query graph representation under different search intents.

In our topic model, we obtain the probability $P(s_k|q_i)$ for each query q_i, which denotes the probability that query q_i conveys the search intent s_k. Here, we define the probability that an edge will generated between query q_i with search intent s_k and query q_j with search intent $s_{k'}$ is $P(s_k|q_i)P(s_{k'}|q_j)$. This probability obviously satisfies the normalization condition $\sum_{k,k'} P(s_k|q_i)P(s_{k'}|q_j) = 1$. In this way, we can obtain the query graph representation under the k-th search intent by re-define the edge weight between query q_i and q_j as

$$W^k_{ij} = W_{ij} P(s_k|q_i) P(s_k|q_j)$$

With the query similarity graph representation under different search intents in hand, we can then apply graph-based measures to calculate the similarity between queries with respect to search intents. Here we take the graph projection method, referred as spectral embedding [4], as an example.

The basic idea of spectral embedding is to project the original graph into a low-dimensional Euclidean space and then measure distances between graph nodes by considering the distances of the corresponding projected points. The spectral embedding has the property of preserving the distances in the projected space. The process of applying spectral embedding on the query graph representation under k-th search intent is described briefly below:

1. Given the adjacency matrix $A_k = [W_{ij}^k]_{i,j=1,\ldots,N}$ of the graph G under the k-th search intent, we compute the eigenvalues and eigenvectors for the generalized eigenvector problem:
$$L_k\mathbf{y} = \lambda D_k\mathbf{y} \qquad (11)$$
where D_k is diagonal matrix whose entries are column sums of A_k. $L_k = D_k - A_k$ is the Laplacian matrix.

2. Let $\mathbf{y}_0, \ldots, \mathbf{y}_{l-1}$ be the solution of Eqn. (11), ordered according to their eigenvalues with $\mathbf{y}_0$ having the smallest eigenvalue. We then obtain, for the k-th search intent, the query q_i under the embedding into the lower dimensional space $\mathbb{R}^m$ is given by $\vec{q}_{ik}= (\mathbf{y}_1(i), \ldots, \mathbf{y}_m(i))$

On the projected space under each search intent, we can take cosine similarity as the metric to measure the similarity between queries. The similarity between query q_i and q_j under the k-th search intent is obtained by

$$Sim_k(q_i, q_j) = \frac{1 + cos(\vec{q}_{ik}, \vec{q}_{jk})}{2} \qquad (12)$$

Note here we follow the way in [9] to rescale the cosine to ensure a measure in $[0, 1]$.

4. APPLICATION TO QUERY RECOMMENDATION

After describing our approach for measuring query similarity with respect to search intents, we turn our attention to the task of developing a simple application based on our approach. While there are many applications requiring a similarity measure between queries, one particularly useful application in the context of search is query recommendation. Query recommendation is to suggest a set of potentially related queries to search users to help them refine their original query. Here we use query recommendation as one example to show the potential utility of our approach and also demonstrate its effectiveness.

Traditionally, query recommendation provide search users a list of related queries. Since queries are often ambiguous in search intent, the recommendation list is thus a mixture of related queries from different search intents, or even worse, dominated by related queries from one popular search intent. As proposed in [19], a structured approach is effective in providing users with diverse query recommendations and thus enhance users' click behavior on recommendations. With our approach to intent-aware similarity, we can identify similar queries to the user's initial query with respect to different search intents, and thus a structured query recommendation can be easily built by grouping diverse recommendations based on the search intents.

More specifically, the structured query recommendation based on our approach can be divided into two stages, i.e. the offline learning stage and the online testing stage. In the offline learning stage, we applied the regularized topic model described in previous section to learn the potential search intents of queries and extract the query representations under each search intent. We can then index all the result representations for fast retrieval later. In the online testing stage, for a given user query q^*, we find its major search intents and corresponding representations under those intents. For each of its major search intent, we retrieve all the existing queries in the repository that potentially match q^* (i.e., a query q's vector representation matches q^*'s in at least one dimension), calculate the similarity between them using certain metrics, and sort the queries under that search intent. Finally, we provide users the structured recommendation results, where similar queries under the same search intent are grouped together and the groups are further ordered according to the proportion of the search intents of the initial query.

5. EXPERIMENTS

We have conducted experiments to verify the effectiveness our similarity measure approach. In this section, we first compare the performance of query similarity calculation of our approach with two baseline methods. We then compare the performance on identifying search intents of queries between our approach and traditional PLSI model. Finally, we apply our approach to query recommendation and evaluate its effectiveness by users' click behavior.

5.1 Experiment Setting

In our experiments, we obtained a query clickthrough data set by randomly sampling from a commercial search engine's search logs during a time period of one month. This sampled clickthrough data set contains about 15 million records. The queries were processed via the following normalization steps (i) trimming of each query, (ii) converting letters into lower case, and (iii) space sequence reduction to one space character. Queries and corresponding clickthrough data containing adult content were filtered out. For each query, we then collected its top N (i.e. $N = 10$ in our case) search results from the same search engine. A virtual document was constructed for each query by aggregating all the words from its top search result snippets with the stop words removed. Finally, we obtained 11,524 unique queries, 87,415 unique URLs, and 45,882 unique words.

Two types of similarity measures (i.e., pair-wise measures and graph-based measures) were adopted as baselines in our evaluation. For pair-wise measures, we used cosine similarity based on Tf-Idf weighted word vector from top search results as a baseline measure, referred as **Cos-Word**. For graph-based measures, we used the spectral embedding over the query similarity graph based on clickthrough (described in section 3.3) as another baseline measure, referred as **Embed-Click**. Note that a similar approach has been used in [9] for measuring query similarity. In our experiments, we empirically set the embedding dimension to 10 since we found that increasing the number of dimensions does not determine a considerable gain in terms of quality.

For our approach, we identified potential search intents of queries with our regularized topic model, and adopted pair-wise measure (i.e. cosine similarity) and graph-based measure (i.e. spectral embedding) based on the intent-aware representations of queries for similarity measure. We denote our two approaches as **Cos-Intent** and **Embed-Intent**, respectively. In our experiments, we empirically set the value

Table 1: Example Queries Pairs with Similarity Scores Calculated by Different Methods

Method	Intent†	apple					
		apple store	apple company	apple ipod	apple fruit	apple tree	apple juice
Cos-Word	N/A	0.86	0.78	0.65	0.17	0.15	0.11
Cos-Intent	fruit	0	0	0	0.44	0.41	0.39
	company	0.92	0.83	0.77	0	0	0
Embed-Click	N/A	0.89	0.81	0.87	0.46	0.37	0.41
Embed-Intent	fruit	0	0	0	0.83	0.77	0.79
	company	1	0.96	0.99	0	0	0

Method	Intent†	taylor					
		taylor swift	taylor swift new songs	taylor ice cream	taylor soft serve machine	taylor acoustic	taylor guitars
Cos-Word	N/A	0.55	0.51	0.49	0.58	0.62	0.59
Cos-Intent	singer	0.76	0.68	0	0	0	0
	instrument	0	0	0	0	0.87	0.85
	company	0	0	0.52	0.61	0	0
Embed-Click	N/A	0.48	0.47	0.47	0.46	0.44	0.51
Embed-Intent	singer	1	1	0	0	0	0
	instrument	0	0	0	0	0.60	0.63
	company	0	0	0.87	0.72	0	0

†the search intents are manually labeled for illustration

Table 2: Examples of Similar and Dissimilar Query Pairs

Type	Query Pair	Traditional Method		Intent-Aware Method†	
		Cos-Word	**Embed-Click**	**Cos-Intent**	**Embed-Intent**
Similar Pairs	(apple, apple store)	0.86	0.89	0|0.92	0|1
	(apple, apple fruit)	0.17	0.46	0.44|0	0.83|0
Dissimilar Pairs	(apple store, apple fruit)	0.09	0.37	0|0	0|0
	(apple ipod, apple tree)	0.08	0.34	0|0	0|0
Similar Pairs	(taylor, taylor swift)	0.55	0.48	0.76|0|0	1|0|0
	(taylor, taylor soft serve machine)	0.58	0.46	0|0|0.61	0|0|0.72
Dissimilar Pairs	(taylor swift, taylor soft serve machine)	0.28	0.36	0|0|0	0|0|0
	(taylor ice cream, taylor acoustic)	0.24	0.38	0|0|0	0|0|0

†similarity scores under different intents are separated by vertical bars for clarity

of Newton step parameter γ to 0.1, the value of the regularization parameter λ to 10, and the number of potential search intent to 500. We found that when the number of potential search intents is reasonable large (i.e. ≥ 500), the performance would be relatively stable.

5.2 Evaluation of Similarity Measurement

5.2.1 Qualitative Evaluation

To get a cursory evaluation for how well our approach performs, we show some example query pairs with the similarity scores calculated by different methods in Table 1. In this table, we take the two multi-intent queries "apple" and "taylor" as the central queries and show the similarity scores between the central query and their similar queries from different search intents.

From Table 1 we can see, both the Cos-Word and Embed-Click measures, which do not take search intent into account, assign a single similarity score for each pair of queries. Take the Cos-Word measure for example, the similarity score between "taylor" and "taylor swift" is 0.55, while the similarity score between "taylor" and "taylor soft serve machine" is 0.58. Since they are calculated under the same measure, it seems that we can derive a strange conclusion that "taylor soft serve machine" is more similar to "taylor" than "taylor swift". In fact, "taylor soft serve machine" and "taylor swift" are from different search intents of the query "taylor", one about a company and the other about a famous singer. The similarity is actually not comparable across different search intents in such case. The similar problem can also be found in the query "apple" which is also shown in Table 1 and many other multi-intent queries.

On the other hand, by identifying potential search intents of queries, both the Cos-Intent and Embed-Intent measures show a more proper similarity measure for the same set of queries. For example, we can see that queries like "taylor swift" and "taylor swift new songs" both obtain high similarity scores under the search intent about the singer, while low similarity scores (i.e. zero) under other search intents. Note here the names of the search intents are manually labeled for illustration. Clearly, under the search intent about the singer, "taylor swift" is much more similar to "taylor" than "taylor soft serve machine", while under the search intent about the company, it is the opposite. Similar results can also be found for the query "apple".

To have a deeper understanding of the problems in similarity measures without the awareness of search intents, we further extract some pairs of similar and dissimilar queries for comparison as shown in Table 2. From the results we can see, the pair-wise measure Cos-Word gives the query pair ("apple", "apple store") a much higher similarity score (i.e. 0.86) than the query pair ("apple", "apple tree"). The major reason is that, for the ambiguous query "apple", the representation (i.e. words from top search result snippets) used by Cos-Word for similarity measure is actually a mixture of its multiple search intents but dominated by the intent about the apple company. Therefore, without the awareness of

Table 3: Examples of Manually Built Test Set

Query	Major Intents
24 hours	1. tv show 24, 24 on fox, 24 the series
	2. 24 fitness, 24hr fitness, 24 hour gym
sigma	1. sigma aldrich, sigma chemicals, sigma biology
	2. greek alphabet sigma, sigma symbol, sigma maths
	3. sigma camera, sigma photo, sigma lenses
svm	1. svm cards, svm gift card, svm gas cards
	2. svm kernel, svm tutorial, support vector machine

search intents, the similarity measure Cos-Word is easily biased by dominant search intents and ignore unpopular ones. On the contrary, the intent-aware pair-wise measure Cos-Intent calculates the similarity for each pair under different search intents using intent-aware representations. Such intent-aware representations convey precise information of each query under each intent. Therefore, our approach can produce more reasonable similarity scores without the bias on only popular intents. For example, "apple tree" receives a much higher similarity score (i.e. 0.44) to "apple" than "apple store" (i.e. 0) under the fruit intent.

Moreover, we observe that the dissimilar query pairs also obtain reasonably large similarity scores under the traditional graph-based measure Embed-Click. For example, the query pair ("apple store", "apple fruit") receives a similarity score of 0.37 and the query pair ("taylor swift", "taylor soft serve machine") receives a similarity score of 0.36 under the Embed-Click measure. As we know, the Embed-Click measure leverages the spectral embedding technique, which in some sense propagates the similarity on top of the query graph during embedding. Therefore, since query "apple store" and "apple fruit" are both close to "apple" in the original graph, without the awareness of search intents, the similarity will be propagated cross the boundary of different search intents and thus query "apple store" and "apple fruit" will become similar after embedding. On the contrary, the intent-aware graph-based measure Embed-Intent extracts the intent-aware graph representation under each search intent, where queries not conveying that intent will not be connected (or connected with a very large distance). In this way, we can see that the similarity is properly propagated among queries, and dissimilar queries like "apple store" and "apple fruit" will not be wrongly connected any more.

5.2.2 *Quantitative Evaluation*

We further conducted quantitative comparison between our approaches and baseline approaches. For evaluation, we first constructed a test set based on our query logs. We collected a set of single-term queries that are likely to have more than one search intent. From these candidate queries, we asked three human judges to figure out the queries which have multiple search intents. Specifically, for each candidate query, queries that share co-clicks with it were collected as its potential similar queries. The human judges then exam each candidate query whether there are at least two distinct clusters in its potential similar queries. Finally, we collected 200 seed queries that have multiple search intents which are agreed by at least two human judges. For each seed query, we then created a test set of similar queries by extracting 3 representative similar queries under each major intent. In this way, we obtained a test set with total $1,581$ queries labeled. Such a test set represents the ground truth for our evaluation. Table 3 show examples of the test set.

We then apply different similarity measures over the queries in the test set, and evaluate their agreement with human labeled search intents. Specifically, given a seed query, let $\mathcal{Q}$ be the set of its similar queries which can be categorized into K search intents $S = \{S_1, \ldots, S_K\}$. Obviously, we have $\mathcal{Q} = \cup_i S_i$. For a similarity measure $Sim(q, q')$, we introduce two scores similarly as [9]:

Expected Intra-intent Similarity:

$$IntraSim(S) = \frac{1}{K}\sum_{k=1}^{K}\left[\sum_{q_i,q_j \in S_k, i\neq j}\frac{2Sim(q_i,q_j)}{|S_k||S_k-1|}\right]$$

Expected Inter-intent Similarity:

$$InterSim(S)=\frac{1}{K(K-1)}\sum_{S_k,S_{k'}\in S,k\neq k'}\left[\sum_{q_i\in S_k}\sum_{q_j\in S_{k'}}\frac{Sim(q_i,q_j)}{|S_k||S_{k'}|}\right]$$

The intuition is that a similarity measure agrees with human labeled search intent if the expected inter-intent similarity score is small compared to the expected intra-intent similarity score. Therefore, we calculate the following expected ratio to evaluate the quality of a similarity measure

$$\mathcal{H}_{\hat{S}}(Sim) = E\left[\frac{InterSim(S)}{IntraSim(S)}\right]_{S\in\hat{S}} \quad (13)$$

Given two different similarity measures, the best one is the one that minimize the measure $\mathcal{H}_{\hat{S}}(Sim)$.

The results are reported in Table 4. From the results we can see, for the traditional measures which do not take search intent into account, the pair-wise measure Cos-Word performs better than the graph-based measure Embed-Click. The major reason is that the Embed-Click measure would generate a higher inter-intent similarity, since the similarity propagation often wrongly connects the dissimilar queries and assign them a large similarity score. By considering search intent of queries, both Cos-Intent and Embed-Intent can significantly outperform the baseline measures (p-value$<$ 0.01). With some further analysis, we find that our approach generates a much smaller inter-intent similarity as well as a larger intra-intent similarity as compared with the traditional measures. It shows that, by measuring query similarity with respect to search intent, we can generate more precise similarity scores for both similar and dissimilar queries.

Table 4: $\mathcal{H}_{\hat{S}}(Sim)$ for Different Similarity Measures

Method	$\mathcal{H}_{\hat{S}}(Sim)$	Significant differences[†]
Cos-Word	0.47±0.06	>Embed-Click***
Cos-Intent	0.08±0.03	>Cos-Word*** >Embed-Click***
Embed-Click	0.54±0.02	
Embed-Intent	0.09±0.03	>Cos-Word*** >Embed-Click***

[†]the significant levels are denoted as 0.1* 0.05 ** 0.01 ***

5.3 Evaluation of Topic Models

In our approach, we employ the regularized topic model to learn the potential search intents of queries by using both words from search results and regularization from query co-clicks. A natural question is how about learning the search intents only based on words from search results, e.g., to just apply the traditional PLSI model over the virtual document of queries. In other words, does the regularization from query co-clicks really helps for the learning problem?

To answer this question, we compared our regularized topic model with traditional PLSI model on the performance of identifying potential search intents. We applied PLSI over

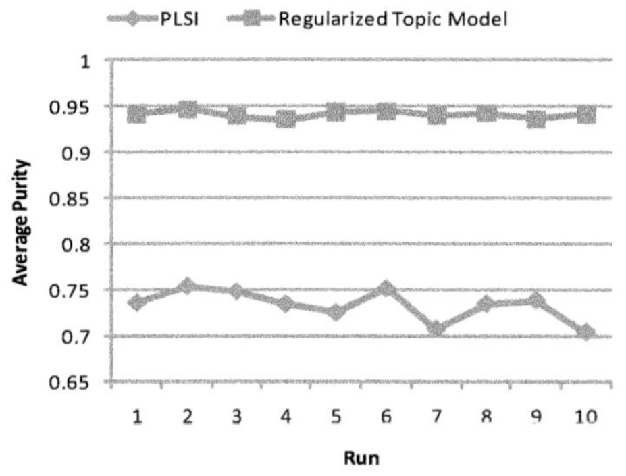

Figure 1: Comparison between PLSI and Regularized Topic Model on Average Purity Score

the search result snippets of queries to learn the search intents. To make the comparison fair, we use the same intent number for PLSI and our regularized topic model. For evaluation, we use the same test set described above. With the topic model learned in hand, we assign each query in the test set to an intent group according to its largest intent. The intuition is that the topic model learns better if the predicted intent groups are more like the human labeled results. For each seed query, let $S = \{s_1, \ldots, s_J\}$ denote the intent groups predicted by the topic model, and $\hat{S} = \{\hat{s}_1, \ldots, \hat{s}_K\}$ denote its manually labeled intent groups. We then borrow the *purity* metric [35] from traditional clustering problem to evaluate the quality of predicted intent groups, which is defined as

$$Purity(S, \hat{S}) = \frac{1}{N} \sum_j \max_K |s_j \cap \hat{s}_k| \quad (14)$$

where N is the total number of similar queries in the test set for a seed query. A higher purity score means a better prediction on intent groups.

The average purity scores for both PLSI and our regularized topic model over different runs are depicted in Fig. 1. The results show that our regularized topic model can consistently outperform PLSI. The average purity score obtained by our regularized topic model is about 0.94, while the average purity score obtained by PLSI is about 0.73. The results indicate that the query co-clicks can largely help resolve the ambiguity in search intents of queries. By leveraging the regularization from query co-clicks, we can learn the potential search intents of queries significantly better than using the search results alone. Moreover, we can also observe that the performance of our regularized topic model is more stable than PLSI. It shows that the regularization from query co-clicks can help our model produce high accuracy in prediction constantly.

5.4 Evaluation on Query Recommendation

In this section, we applied our approach to query recommendation. As described in Section 4, we can easily generate a structured query recommendation for a given query to suggesting diverse related queries from different search intents. We also implemented a traditional *list-based* recommendation system for comparison, where similar queries are ranked according to their similarity scores under a traditional measure and the top ones are returned in a list. For demonstration, here we employ the Cos-Word and Cos-Intent measures for the list approach and structured approach, respectively. We used the previous selected 200 multi-intent queries plus 200 randomly sampled queries for evaluation. For each query, top 10 recommendations are used for performance comparison.

Table 5: Comparisons between List Approach and Our Approach on Click Performance

	List Approach	Our Approach
Ave. CRN	4.10	4.63 (+12.9%)
Ave. CRS	0.43	0.47 (+9.3%)
Ave. TRS	0.15	0.17 (+13.3%)

We follow the way proposed in [19] to compare the performances of different recommendation methods by users' click behavior. The manual labeling process is almost the same, where human judges are required to label for each recommendation how likely he would like to click it with a 6-point scale (0, 0.2, 0.4, 0.6, 0.8, and 1) as the willingness measure. We asked 5 judges with or without computer science background to label the recommendations.

We also adopted the *Clicked Recommendation Number (CRN)*, *Clicked Recommendation Score (CRS)*, and *Total Recommendation Score (TRS)* as evaluation measures [19]. Given a query q, let $R = \{r_1, \ldots, r_k\}$ denote the k recommendations generated by a certain approach, and $L = \{l_1, \ldots, l_k\}$ denote the corresponding label scores on these recommendations. The three measures for a query q are then defined as follows

$$CRN_q = |\{r_i | l_i > 0, i \in [1, k]\}|,$$

$$CRS_q = \frac{\sum_{i=1}^{k} l_i}{CRN_q},$$

$$TRS_q = \frac{\sum_{i=1}^{k} l_i}{k},$$

where $| * |$ denotes the size of a set.

Table 5 shows the evaluation results of the two approaches. The numbers in the parentheses are the relative improvements of our approach compared with list approach. The results show that by recommending structured queries based on our intent-aware approach, we can largely improve both the click number and click willingness on recommendations. When compared with list approach, the relative improvements obtained by our approach are about 12.9%, 9.3% and 13.3% in terms of average CRN, average CRS and average TRS, respectively. This simple experiment demonstrates the utility and effectiveness of our intent-aware approach in real applications.

6. CONCLUSIONS

In this paper, we propose to measure query similarity with the awareness of potential search intents. A regularized topic model is employed to effectively identify search intents of queries using words from search result snippets and regularization from query co-clicks. We then extract the query representation under different intents, and apply two types of similarity measures to estimate query similarity with respect to search intent. Experimental results verify the effectiveness of our approach to intent-aware query similarity. We also demonstrate the utility of intent-aware similarity in the application of query recommendation, which can suggest diverse queries in a structured way to search users.

For the future work, we will consider using more context information of queries, e.g. search sessions, for identifying search intents better. It is also interesting to apply our intent-aware query similarity in other real applications in the search context.

7. ACKNOWLEDGMENTS

This research work was funded by the National High-tech R&D Program of China under grant No. 2010*AA*012500, and the National Natural Science Foundation of China under Grant No. 61003166 and Grant No. 60933005.

8. REFERENCES

[1] I. Antonellis, H. G. Molina, and C. C. Chang. Simrank++: query rewriting through link analysis of the click graph. *Proc. VLDB Endow.*, 1:408–421, August 2008.

[2] R. A. Baeza-Yates, C. A. Hurtado, and M. Mendoza. Query recommendation using query logs in search engines. In W. Lindner, M. Mesiti, C. Tíźrker, Y. Tzitzikas, and A. Vakali, editors, *EDBT Workshops*, volume 3268 of *Lecture Notes in Computer Science*, pages 588–596. Springer, 2004.

[3] D. Beeferman and A. Berger. Agglomerative clustering of a search engine query log. In *Proceedings of the sixth ACM SIGKDD international conference on Knowledge discovery and data mining*, KDD '00, pages 407–416, New York, NY, USA, 2000. ACM.

[4] M. Belkin and P. Niyogi. Laplacian eigenmaps and spectral techniques for embedding and clustering. *Advances in Neural Information Processing Systems*, 14:585–591, 2001.

[5] D. M. Blei and J. D. Lafferty. Dynamic topic models. In *Proceedings of the 23rd international conference on Machine learning*, ICML '06, pages 113–120, New York, NY, USA, 2006. ACM.

[6] D. M. Blei, A. Y. Ng, and M. I. Jordan. Latent dirichlet allocation. *J. Mach. Learn. Res.*, 3:993–1022, March 2003.

[7] P. Boldi, F. Bonchi, C. Castillo, D. Donato, A. Gionis, and S. Vigna. The query-flow graph: model and applications. In *Proceeding of the 17th ACM conference on Information and knowledge management*, CIKM '08, pages 609–618, New York, NY, USA, 2008. ACM.

[8] P. Boldi, F. Bonchi, C. Castillo, D. Donato, and S. Vigna. Query suggestions using query-flow graphs. In *Proceedings of the 2009 workshop on Web Search Click Data*, WSCD '09, pages 56–63, New York, NY, USA, 2009. ACM.

[9] I. Bordino, C. Castillo, D. Donato, and A. Gionis. Query similarity by projecting the query-flow graph. In *Proceeding of the 33rd international ACM SIGIR conference on Research and development in information retrieval*, SIGIR '10, pages 515–522, New York, NY, USA, 2010. ACM.

[10] D. Cai, Q. Mei, J. Han, and C. Zhai. Modeling hidden topics on document manifold. In *Proceeding of the 17th ACM conference on Information and knowledge management*, CIKM '08, pages 911–920, New York, NY, USA, 2008. ACM.

[11] D. Cai, X. Wang, and X. He. Probabilistic dyadic data analysis with local and global consistency. In *Proceedings of the 26th Annual International Conference on Machine Learning*, ICML '09, pages 105–112, New York, NY, USA, 2009. ACM.

[12] B. Cao, J.-T. Sun, E. W. Xiang, D. H. Hu, Q. Yang, and Z. Chen. Pqc: personalized query classification. In *Proceeding of the 18th ACM conference on Information and knowledge management*, CIKM '09, pages 1217–1226, New York, NY, USA, 2009. ACM.

[13] N. Craswell and M. Szummer. Random walks on the click graph. In *Proceedings of the 30th annual international ACM SIGIR conference on Research and development in information retrieval*, SIGIR '07, pages 239–246, New York, NY, USA, 2007. ACM.

[14] H. Cui, J.-R. Wen, J.-Y. Nie, and W.-Y. Ma. Query expansion by mining user logs. *IEEE Trans. on Knowl. and Data Eng.*, 15:829–839, July 2003.

[15] A. P. Dempster, N. M. Laird, and D. B. Rubin. Maximum likelihood from incomplete data via the EM algorithm. *Journal of the Royal Statistical Society*, B(39):1–38, 1977.

[16] H. Deng, I. King, and M. R. Lyu. Entropy-biased models for query representation on the click graph. In *Proceedings of the 32nd international ACM SIGIR conference on Research and development in information retrieval*, SIGIR '09, pages 339–346, New York, NY, USA, 2009. ACM.

[17] L. Fitzpatrick and M. Dent. Automatic feedback using past queries: social searching? In *Proceedings of the 20th annual international ACM SIGIR conference on Research and development in information retrieval*, SIGIR '97, pages 306–313, New York, NY, USA, 1997. ACM.

[18] T. L. Griffiths, M. Steyvers, D. M. Blei, and J. B. Tenenbaum. Integrating topics and syntax. In *In Advances in Neural Information Processing Systems 17*, pages 537–544. MIT Press, 2005.

[19] J. Guo, X. Cheng, G. Xu, and H. Shen. A structured approach to query recommendation with social annotation data. In *Proceedings of the 19th ACM international conference on Information and knowledge management*, CIKM '10, pages 619–628, New York, NY, USA, 2010. ACM.

[20] J. Guo, G. Xu, X. Cheng, and H. Li. Named entity recognition in query. In *Proceedings of the 32nd international ACM SIGIR conference on Research and development in information retrieval*, SIGIR '09, pages 267–274, New York, NY, USA, 2009. ACM.

[21] T. Hofmann. Probabilistic latent semantic indexing. In *Proceedings of the 22nd annual international ACM SIGIR conference on Research and development in information retrieval*, SIGIR '99, pages 50–57, New York, NY, USA, 1999. ACM.

[22] R. Jones, B. Rey, O. Madani, and W. Greiner. Generating query substitutions. In *Proceedings of the 15th international conference on World Wide Web*, WWW '06, pages 387–396, New York, NY, USA, 2006. ACM.

[23] Y. Li, Z. Zheng, and H. K. Dai. Kdd cup-2005 report: facing a great challenge. *SIGKDD Explor. Newsl.*, 7:91–99, December 2005.

[24] H. Ma, H. Yang, I. King, and M. R. Lyu. Learning latent semantic relations from clickthrough data for query suggestion. In *Proceeding of the 17th ACM conference on Information and knowledge management*, CIKM '08, pages 709–718, New York, NY, USA, 2008. ACM.

[25] Q. Mei, D. Cai, D. Zhang, and C. Zhai. Topic modeling with network regularization. In *Proceeding of the 17th international conference on World Wide Web*, WWW '08, pages 101–110, New York, NY, USA, 2008. ACM.

[26] Q. Mei, D. Zhou, and K. Church. Query suggestion using hitting time. In *Proceeding of the 17th ACM conference on Information and knowledge management*, CIKM '08, pages 469–478, New York, NY, USA, 2008. ACM.

[27] R. M. Neal and G. E. Hinton. *A view of the EM algorithm that justifies incremental, sparse, and other variants*, pages 355–368. MIT Press, Cambridge, MA, USA, 1999.

[28] W. H. Press, S. A. Teukolsky, W. T. Vetterling, and B. P. Flannery. *Numerical recipes in C: the art of scientific computing*. Cambridge University Press, New York, NY, USA, 1992.

[29] F. Radlinski, A. Broder, P. Ciccolo, E. Gabrilovich, V. Josifovski, and L. Riedel. Optimizing relevance and revenue in ad search: a query substitution approach. In *Proceedings of the 31st annual international ACM SIGIR conference on Research and development in information retrieval*, SIGIR '08, pages 403–410, New York, NY, USA, 2008. ACM.

[30] M. Sahami and T. D. Heilman. A web-based kernel function for measuring the similarity of short text snippets. In *Proceedings of the 15th international conference on World Wide Web*, WWW '06, pages 377–386, New York, NY, USA, 2006. ACM.

[31] M. Steyvers, P. Smyth, M. Rosen-Zvi, and T. Griffiths. Probabilistic author-topic models for information discovery. In *The Tenth ACM SIGKDD International Conference on Knowledge Discovery and Data Mining*, 2004.

[32] E. Terra and C. L. Clarke. Scoring missing terms in information retrieval tasks. In *Proceedings of the thirteenth ACM international conference on Information and knowledge management*, CIKM '04, pages 50–58, New York, NY, USA, 2004. ACM.

[33] J.-R. Wen, J.-Y. Nie, and H. Zhang. Query clustering using user logs. *ACM Trans. Inf. Syst.*, 20(1):59–81, 2002.

[34] Z. Zhang and O. Nasraoui. Mining search engine query logs for query recommendation. In *Proceedings of the 15th international conference on World Wide Web*, WWW '06, pages 1039–1040, New York, NY, USA, 2006. ACM.

[35] Y. Zhao and G. Karypis. Criterion functions for document clustering: Experiments and analysis. Technical report, 2002.

Semi-supervised Learning to Rank with Preference Regularization

Martin Szummer
Microsoft Research
Cambridge, UK
szummer@microsoft.com

Emine Yilmaz
Microsoft
Cambridge, UK
eminey@microsoft.com

ABSTRACT

We propose a semi-supervised learning to rank algorithm. It learns from both labeled data (pairwise preferences or absolute labels) and unlabeled data. The data can consist of multiple groups of items (such as queries), some of which may contain only unlabeled items. We introduce a preference regularizer favoring that similar items are similar in preference to each other. The regularizer captures manifold structure in the data, and we also propose a rank-sensitive version designed for top-heavy retrieval metrics including NDCG and mean average precision.

The regularizer is employed in SSLambdaRank, a semi-supervised version of LambdaRank. This algorithm directly optimizes popular retrieval metrics and improves retrieval accuracy over LambdaRank, a state-of-the-art ranker that was used as part of the winner of the Yahoo! Learning to Rank challenge 2010. The algorithm runs in linear time in the number of queries, and can work with huge datasets.

Categories and Subject Descriptors

H.3.3 [**Information Search and Retrieval**]: Retrieval models; I.2.6 [**Learning**]: Parameter learning

General Terms

Algorithms

Keywords

Learning to rank, semi-supervised, partially labeled data, regularization, LambdaRank

1. INTRODUCTION

A ranking function, or ranker, is a function that orders items in a set based on their features. For example, a search engine orders the documents in a corpus based on features of document content and the search query, such as how many query words the document contains. The ranking function strives to maximize some ranking objective, e.g. to order documents by descending relevance to the query. Modern ranking systems can combine many features to build complex ranking functions. Learning to rank algorithms aim to learn ranking functions that achieve good ranking objectives on test data. Such learning methods require labeled data for training. In the case of search engines, the training data consist of queries, documents and the labels are human relevance judgments of documents with respect to queries. To learn a complex ranking function, a significant amount of labeled data may be required.

CIKM'11, October 24–28, 2011, Glasgow, Scotland, UK.

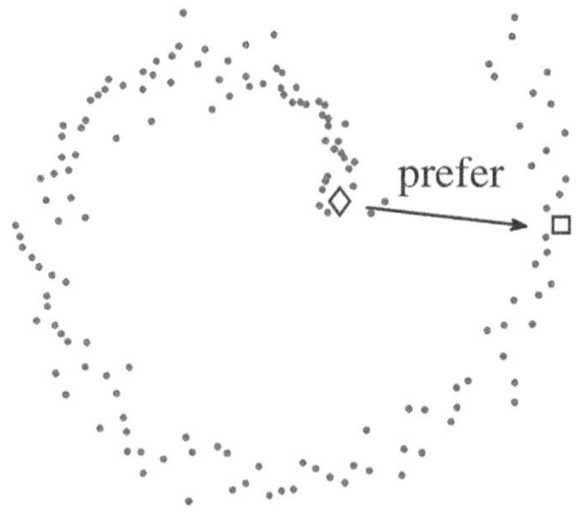

Figure 1: A semi-supervised ranking instance: labeled items, in the form of a preference pair (rhomb and square), and unlabeled items (dots).

In many cases, it is difficult to acquire labeled data, but easy to collect unlabeled training data. For example, unlabeled queries and documents can be obtained mechanically from query logs and web crawls, but the labeling requires paid human assessors. When building systems for small markets, such as for minority languages, specialized domains, or narrow query segments, it can be cost-ineffective to acquire sufficient label data. It can also be impractical to keep large label sets up to date; by the time judges have completed their assessments, some label information may no longer be fresh. As another example, when building personalized rankers for individuals or enterprises, we can only expect individuals to provide relatively few labeled examples.

A well-established retrieval scenario is *relevance feedback*, in which a user issues a query, and labels a few of the resulting documents from a (typically) hand-tailored ranker (BM25 or language modeling), but leaves most documents unlabeled.

The ranker then incorporates the partially labeled results to produce refined results.

In this paper, we propose semi-supervised learning to rank methods. Such methods learn both from labeled as well as unlabeled data, so called partially labeled data. Commonly, there is a small amount of labeled data and a large amount of unlabeled data. By leveraging both types of data, the need for labeled examples can be reduced. In web search, the labeled data consists of labeled (judged) query-document features (or preference relationships between items), whereas the unlabeled data are simply query-document feature vectors without any labels (or preference information).

There is a wealth of work in semi-supervised classification [27, 28] and regression. These tasks involve predicting class labels or function values of individual items. The labels are assigned to individual items and are absolute. In contrast, there is comparatively little prior work in semi-supervised ranking. Ranking has the different goal of learning a function that orders multiple items correctly. In this setting, labeled data can be provided as relative preferences among items. Absolute labels are not required, but can still be used by inducing pairwise preferences.

The key to semi-supervised learning is a principle connecting the structure of the unlabeled data with the function to be learned. In classification, a commonly used principle is the cluster assumption [24], which states that data points in each high-density region (cluster) should have the same labels. Essentially, the unlabeled data define the extent of the clusters, whereas the labeled data determine the class of the clusters. In this paper, we formulate such a principle for ranking: we favor that similar documents are similar in preference to each other with respect to a query. We embody this principle in a preference regularizer that exploits unlabeled data. The regularizer tries to capture manifold structure in the data. The regularizer is general and can be applied to any paired comparison ranking model.

For many problems, we desire ranking functions that correctly order the top of the ranking in particular. For this purpose, we develop a rank-sensitive preference regularizer that emphasizes the influence of unlabeled data at the top of the ranking.

We apply this rank-sensitive regularizer to obtain a semi-supervised version of LambdaRank [7], a state-of-the-art learning to rank algorithm. LambdaRank can optimize NDCG, mean average precision, and many other popular ranking metrics. It has proven to be one of the most effective and practical algorithms and the winner of the Yahoo! Learning to Rank challenge 2010 [9] used an used an ensemble of Lambda-Gradient models.

Data and resources for this paper are available at `http://purl.org/net/semisupervised-ranking-cikm11.html`.

2. BACKGROUND

The semi-supervised ranking problem consists of a set of ranking instances. Each ranking instance is a set $X = \{\boldsymbol{x}_i \in \mathbb{R}^n\}$ of items with feature vectors, to which we would like to assign a ranking $\boldsymbol{r}$, a permutation of the numbers $1, \ldots, |X|$. Here r_i refers to the rank of item i and the top (preferred) rank is 1.

Figure 1 illustrates the semi-supervised ranking task. It depicts two labeled items, which by themselves offer very limited information for learning a ranking function. The distribution of unlabeled items suggests that there is additional structure in the data; for example, it would make sense for the ranking function to be smooth along the spiral shape.

In ranking, label information can take several forms, such as absolute labels (e.g. relevance grades), preference relations, complete orderings or partial orderings. We convert these by inducing pairwise preference relations of form "item i is preferred to j", and denoted by $i \succ j$. Then, let L be a set of pairs with given preferences, and U a set of items that will be used in an unsupervised way (and whose preferences may be unknown). We will typically include all available items in U and induce all possible pairs within a rank instance.

Our task is to learn a function $f(\boldsymbol{x}; \boldsymbol{w})$ with parameters $\boldsymbol{w}$ that ranks the items of a ranking instance X. We will consider rankers that assign a score $s_i = f(\boldsymbol{x}_i; \boldsymbol{w})$ to each item, where high scores indicate preference. A ranking can be produced simply by sorting the scores[1]. We will consider probabilistic models that assign a probability of preference $P(i \succ j)$, based on score differences. Such models are referred to as "paired comparison" models.

We will mostly employ the Bradley-Terry model [22], a long-standing model that has been successfully applied in learning to rank [6]. It associates a parameter s_i with each item, which can be thought of as a score. Then it defines the probability $P(i \succ j)$ that item i is preferred to j to be the logistic function of their score difference

$$P(i \succ j) = 1/(1 + \mathrm{e}^{-(s_i - s_j)}). \tag{1}$$

For example, if $s_i > s_j$, then $P(i \succ j) > 0.5$. By construction, pairwise preferences from the model are transitive, so that $P(i \succ j) > 0.5$ and $P(j \succ k) > 0.5$ implies $P(i \succ k) > 0.5$; in fact, $P(i \succ j)$ and $P(j \succ k)$ uniquely determine $P(i \succ k)$ [6].

Let L be a set of observed preferences, $L = \{i_1 \succ j_1, j_1 \prec i_1, i_2 \succ j_2, \ldots\}$ (where pairs (i,j) are included both ways (i,j) and (j,i)). We can estimate item scores s (or parameters $\boldsymbol{w}$) by maximizing the likelihood

$$C = \sum_{(i,j) \in L} \mathbb{I}_{i \succ j} \log P(i \succ j). \tag{2}$$

Here the indicator $\mathbb{I}_{i \succ j}$ denotes the observed pairwise preferences, and $\mathbb{I}_{i \succ j} = 1$ when $i \succ j$, and 0 otherwise.

For notational convenience, we have displayed just a single ranking instance (consisting of a single set of items, and a single rank ordering); in practice, we will have training data consisting of multiple item sets (queries) with associated orderings, $\{X^{(q)}, \boldsymbol{r}^{(q)}\}$, from which we learn a single ranking function f. We note that some of the ranking instances may be completely unsupervised. For example, in information retrieval, the training set consists of multiple queries each with an associated partial ranking of documents (where the partial ranking may be empty). For a new test query, the goal is to rank all the documents in the collection.

2.1 Related Work

Related semi-supervised work falls in three broad classes: self-training, feature extraction approaches, and graph-based regularization.

The self-training approach, termed *pseudo relevance feedback*, is very popular in retrieval. It assumes that the top k retrieved results from the ranker are relevant, and uses them to retrain the ranker. A variation of this is to take the results below rank k to be negative (non-relevant); this

[1] We resolve ties randomly.

is a fairly safe assumption, as the vast majority of items are non-relevant, and including such items improves ranker training in practice.

Other self-training approaches [2, 33] and co-training [21] first train a standard supervised ranker (RankBoost and RankNet&BM25 respectively) on the labeled items. They then apply a nearest neighbor classifier to assign labels to k unlabeled items that are the most similar to the labeled ones. Finally they retrain the supervised ranker including the newly labeled points, and repeat the process. It is important to control k to reduce the propagation of errors as noisily classified points accumulate in the training set.

The feature extraction approach [14] also employs an existing supervised ranker (RankBoost), but apply it not to the given features, but instead to the output of an unsupervised feature extractor (kernel PCA) trained separately on unlabeled data. The method thus involves two stages, and the structure extracted from unlabeled data is not guided by labeled data.

Graph-based regularization is another way to combine labeled and unlabeled data, via a manifold regularizer (the second term below) [5, 34, 12]. This is usually done in the context of regression, where we have

$$\min_f \sum_{i \in L} \|f(\boldsymbol{x}_i) - y_i\|^2 + \beta \sum_{i,j \in U} W_{ij} \|f(\boldsymbol{x}_i) - f(\boldsymbol{x}_j)\|^2. \quad (3)$$

This formulation fits the function f to target labels y_i while also making sure that function values of similar items $\boldsymbol{x}_i$ and $\boldsymbol{x}_j$ are close, according to a similarity measure W_{ij}, commonly defined in terms of graph Laplacians.

This is typically formulated as a transductive approach, meaning that unlabeled test data can (and must) be included at learning time, something difficult to do when the goal is to learn a model for ranking novel (unseen) queries. The approach can be extended to transductive ranking by handling input given as pairwise preference relations [26], and the function f can be a Gaussian process [11]. These approaches are currently defined only for a single ranking instance, corresponding to a single graph, and have high computational cost $O(|U|^3)$.

Rank-aggregation [10, 25] involves combining multiple ranked lists to produce a better overall ranking, and has been performed in a semi-supervised way by combining large-margin preference constraints with a manifold regularizer.

A preliminary version of the present work was presented in [30]. See also [29] for a broad overview that positions semi-supervised ranking in the context of cost-sensitive machine learning for information retrieval.

2.2 Motivations for Our Work

Our work is related to the graph-based regularization approaches, but formulates the regularizer specifically for paired comparison ranking models, rather than for regression models. It is also the first algorithm to satisfy all of the following properties:

Preference learning: labeled data is given as (or interpreted as) pairwise item preferences; it neither requires [ordinal] labels, nor assigns any [ordinal] labels. The output is simply a ranked list.

End-to-end optimization of ranking metrics: it directly optimizes most established ranking metrics (e.g. mean average precision, NDCG), including their emphasis of top rank positions.

Single-stage learning: The learning is done jointly on labeled and unlabeled data in a single stage. Information in the labeled data can guide the extraction of structure extracted from unlabeled data.

Multiple and completely unlabeled rank instances: in information retrieval, the training data usually comes grouped into queries, some of which have labeled and unlabeled documents, but some of which have exclusively unlabeled ones. Our method can utilize information from queries for which no labeled items are available.

Scalability: linear time in the number of queries, and approximately linear in the number of unlabeled items (section 5.1).

Performance: it extends one of the most effective learning to rank algorithms, LambdaRank, to the semi-supervised setting.

Generality: the regularization principle can be applied to many learning to rank algorithms and settings, beyond semi-supervised learning, such as cases with fully-labeled data in order to reduce overfitting, adaptation, etc.

In the following sections, we first introduce a preference regularizer for learning to rank. This main idea is generally applicable to most paired learning to rank algorithms. As LambdaRank is one of the strongest learning to rank algorithms, we illustrate how to apply the regularizer to it.

3. PREFERENCE REGULARIZATION

The key to semi-supervised learning is a principle connecting the structure of the unlabeled data with the function to be learned. In classification, a commonly used principle is the cluster assumption [24], which states that data points in each high-density region (cluster) should have the same labels. In regression, a principle is to assume that the function value changes slowly in high-density regions (as formalized by Eq. 3). In retrieval, it has been observed that closely related documents tend to be relevant to the same query [16, 32], which is termed the "cluster hypothesis".

We adapt the cluster hypothesis to a ranking context, and require that similar documents be similar in preference to each other, with respect to a query. Specifically, neither document should be much preferred to the other; ideally, they should tie in preference — an indifference of preference.

This preference similarity assumption is weaker than the classification one, as it only constrains relative item order, and not absolute score or class. For a pair of similar documents, it does not assume which document is preferred.

The two spaces we need to connect are: i) the feature space of the unlabeled data, and ii) the preference space of the ranking function. In the feature space, the type of structure we hope to exploit is manifold structure of the unlabeled data. To do this, we quantify the similarity between documents i and j as the probability of transitioning between them under a noise model. We base the transition probability on the exponentiated distance $d_{ij}^2 = \|\boldsymbol{x}_i - \boldsymbol{x}_j\|^2/\sigma_i^2$ between the (suitably normalized) document feature vectors, where σ_i is a length scale. However, we only allow transitions to K-nearest neighbors $N_K(i)$, as we want to follow the local manifold relying only on local distances. The probability of an i to j transition is

$$\hat{q}_{j|i} = \begin{cases} \mathrm{e}^{-d_{ij}^2/\sigma_i^2} / \sum_{k \in N_K(i)} \mathrm{e}^{-d_{ik}^2/\sigma_i^2} & \text{if } j \in N_K(i), \\ 0 & \text{otherwise.} \end{cases} \quad (4)$$

The probability of going there and back is then $\hat{q}_{ij} = \hat{q}_{i|j}\hat{q}_{j|i}/Z$, where Z normalizes $\hat{q}_{ij}$ to sum to one over all pairs.

In the preference space, we hope to constrain the preference structure of the ranking function. To do so, we quantify the probability that neither document is preferred to the other. This is given by $P(i \not\succ j)P(j \not\succ i)$, where $P(i \not\succ j) = 1 - P(i \succ j) = P(j \succ i)$. The lowest possible preference is a tie, when $P(i \succ j) = P(j \succ i) = 0.5$. These probabilities can be produced by the Bradley-Terry model, or any paired comparison ranking model. Via this model, the probabilities will depend on the ranking function with parameters $\boldsymbol{w}$.

To form the regularizer, we must link the feature space similarity to the preference similarity. Recall the manifold regularizer for regression (Eq. 3) that penalized the output difference between a pair of items (i, j) according to their input similarity. In the ranking case, for every pair (i, j) we have a probabilistic preference similarity, and a probabilistic input similarity. We shall penalize the difference between these two distributions according to their KL divergence. This penalty is the same as the stochastic neighbor embedding (SNE) objective [31], which ensures that probabilistic neighborhood relations in a high-dimensional space are preserved when the points are embedded in a low-dimensional space. One can think of this regularizer as penalizing bad embeddings from the input space to the low-dimensional preference space.

Definition. The *preference regularizer* is

$$\sum_{(i,j) \in U} \hat{q}_{ij} \log P(i \not\succ j)P(j \not\succ i). \quad (5)$$

It strongly penalizes models for which similar documents (high $\hat{q}_{ij}$) have dissimilar preference (probabilities close to 0 and 1, yielding a low product $P(i \not\succ j)P(j \not\succ i)$). However, it only weakly penalizes the converse: dissimilar documents can be similar in preference. This behavior springs from the asymmetry of the KL-divergence. It is desirable, as we can assume more about preferences between similar documents than about dissimilar ones.

4. SEMI-SUPERVISED BRADLEY-TERRY MODEL

To obtain a semi-supervised ranking model, we add the preference regularizer to a paired comparison likelihood, obtaining

$$C = \sum_{(i,j) \in L} \mathbb{I}_{i \succ j} \log P(i \succ j) + \beta \sum_{i,j \in U} \hat{q}_{ij} \log P(i \not\succ j)P(j \not\succ i). \quad (6)$$

The parameter β weights the preference regularizer against the likelihood. The combination of these two terms mirrors manifold regularization (Eq. 3).

The above is general and applies to any probabilistic ranking model that can be expressed in terms of paired comparison probabilities. For example, we can apply it to the Bradley-Terry model by substituting Eq. 1 to get

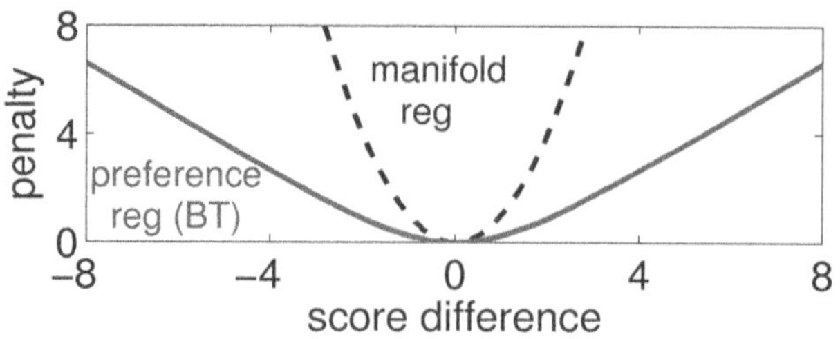

Figure 2: Comparison between the preference regularizer applied to the Bradley-Terry model and the manifold regularizer. We have subtracted a constant from the preference regularizer to align it with the manifold regularizer at the origin (constant offsets have no effect on training).

$$C = \sum_{(i,j) \in L} \mathbb{I}_{i \succ j} \log \frac{1}{1 + \mathrm{e}^{-(s_i - s_j)}} \quad (7)$$

$$+ \beta \sum_{i,j \in U} \hat{q}_{ij} \log \frac{0.5}{1 + \cosh(s_i - s_j)}. \quad (8)$$

In the context of the Bradley Terry model, we see that the regularizer operates on score differences $(s_i - s_j)$, which it tries to reduce proportionally to $\hat{q}_{ij}$. We can directly compare it with the manifold regularizer, since that also operates on score differences. The manifold regularizer imposes a quadratic penalty, whereas the preference regularizer grows linearly for large score differences (Figure 2). The latter is milder. Importantly, our regularizer is matched to the ranking task and the chosen Bradley-Terry model, so it should nicely balance the likelihood; a score-difference for labeled data will be treated consistently with a score-difference in unlabeled data, which would not be the case if one added a manifold regularizer to a ranking likelihood.

Learning to Rank Algorithm. At this point, we can already design a simple semi-supervised learning to rank algorithm. Given scores, the Bradley-Terry model defines pairwise preference probabilities, but our task is to go from item features to a ranking. So, we could for example choose a neural network to assign the scores s_i for the Bradley-Terry model. To obtain a semi-supervised ranker, we then simply include the preference regularizer during training. We learn it by maximizing regularized likelihood (Eq. 7 and 8) via gradient descent with respect to $\boldsymbol{w}$.

Experiment on Spiral Data. Here we train a ranker on the spiral dataset from Figure 1. We choose the ranking function to be a 1-hidden layer neural network, with x and y coordinates as inputs, and 8 hidden units. First, we train the ranker using only labeled data. As shown in the contour plot in Figure 3 (left), we obtain a ranking function $f(\cdot)$ that decreases uniformly from left to right. This function correctly ranks the given labeled preference, but it ignores the structure in the unlabeled points.

Next, we add the preference regularizer, employing $K = 6$ nearest neighbors, and with length scale $\sigma_i = 0.2$ for all i (the input data ranges from -1 to 1 along both axes). Semi-supervised training then yields a ranking function that de-

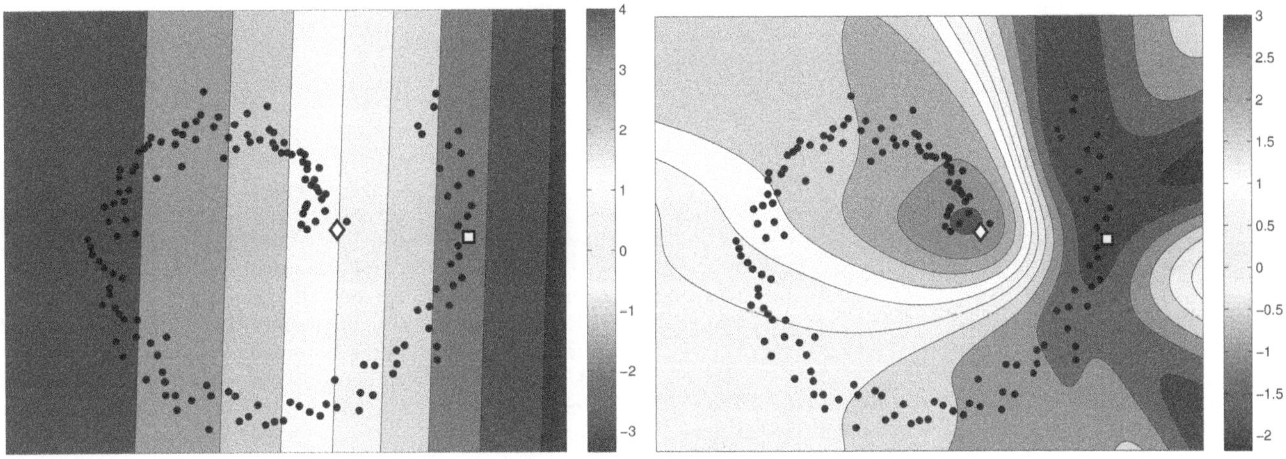

Figure 3: Left: Ranking function trained in a supervised way on a single preference pair (the rhomb is preferred to the square), ignoring unlabeled data. Right: ranking function trained in a semi-supervised way on a single preference pair plus unlabeled data.

creases smoothly along the spiral shape, while still satisfying the labeled preference (Figure 3, right).

This approach is adequate for generic ranking scenarios. However, we now move on to a more sophisticated approach, suitable to retrieval problems.

5. SEMI-SUPERVISED RANK-SENSITIVE BRADLEY-TERRY MODEL

In this section we extend the semi-supervised ranking framework to fit rank-sensitive objectives used in information retrieval, such as normalized discounted cumulative gain (NDCG) [17]. These objectives are rank-sensitive in that they take rank position of the documents into account. We focus on NDCG here, but note that it is straightforward to derive semi-supervised objectives for other popular objectives, such as mean average precision (MAP) and reciprocal rank (RR) metrics, using results from [13]. Ranking objectives give superior performance compared to classification or regression objectives in retrieval applications [23].

NDCG. The NDCG ranking metric captures two common requirements. Firstly, it focuses on the top of the ranking by weighting rank positions according to a decreasing discount function $R(r_i)$. Secondly, it caters for multi-grade relevance information given in terms of ordinal labels l_i for items i, by assigning a utility value $L(l_i)$ for each label. The relevance label l_i of a document can be 0, 1, 2, etc. depending on whether the document is nonrelevant, relevant, highly relevant, etc. for a query, respectively. Then, the NDCG objective is defined as

$$\mathrm{NDCG} = \frac{1}{\mathrm{DCG}_{\max}} \sum_i L(l_i) R(r_i), \tag{9}$$

where $\mathrm{DCG}_{\max}$ is the maximum value of the sum achieved by an ideal ranking. $L(l_i)$ is usually referred to as a gain function which measures the utility ("gain") a user obtains by observing a document that has label (relevance) l_i. We use $L(l_i) = 2^{l_i} - 1$ as it is the most commonly used gain function in the literature [7].

A useful quantity is the change in the metric value if items i and j were to be swapped in the ranking. We denote this *swap cost* by $|\Delta_{ij}|$, and it is given by

$$|\Delta_{ij}| = |L(l_i)R(r_i) + L(l_j)R(r_j) - L(l_i)R(r_j) - L(l_j)R(r_i)|. \tag{10}$$

For notational convenience we will also absorb the $\mathrm{DCG}_{\max}$ normalization into $|\Delta_{ij}|$. For unlabeled data, we introduce an unlabeled swap cost that depends only on the discount difference between items in the ranking (as there are no labels):

$$|\Delta^U_{ij}| = |R(r_i) - R(r_j)|. \tag{11}$$

Rank-sensitive Bradley-Terry. We incorporate the rank-sensitivity of retrieval metrics into the Bradley-Terry model by weighting item pairs in the likelihood by swap cost $|\Delta_{ij}|$, to produce the objective

$$C = \sum_{(i,j)\in L} |\Delta_{ij}| \mathbb{I}_{i\succ j} \log P(i \succ j). \tag{12}$$

The gradients of this objective coincide with the gradients that were manually crafted for the LambdaRank algorithm [7]. We note that LambdaRank successfully reaches optima of NDCG and MAP [13] using those gradients. This fact supports the design of the proposed rank-sensitive Bradley-Terry objective.

Rank-sensitive Preference Regularization. We would like the preference regularizer to be rank-sensitive in a similar way to the ranking objective above. Hence, we analogously weight item pairs in the preference regularizer by their unlabeled swap cost:

Definition. The *rank-sensitive preference regularizer* is given by

$$\sum_{i,j\in U} |\Delta^U_{ij}| \, \hat{q}_{ij} \log P(i \not\succ j) P(j \not\succ i). \tag{13}$$

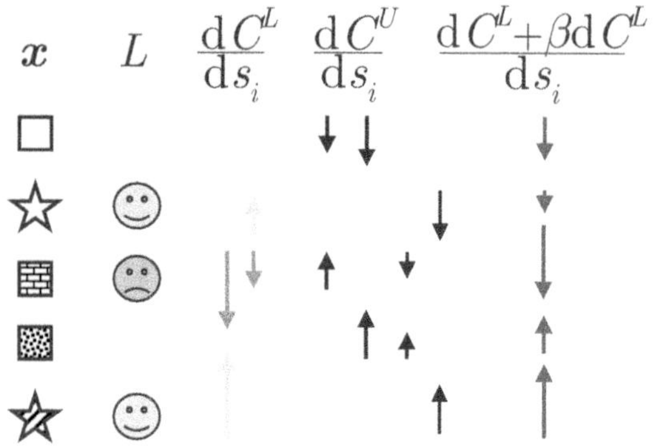

Figure 4: Example gradients during a run of SS-LambdaRank. $\mathrm{d}C^L/\mathrm{d}s_i$ and $\mathrm{d}C^U/\mathrm{d}s_i$ refer to the gradients computed using labels and document similarities (unlabeled), respectively.

Semi-supervised Rank-sensitive Bradley-Terry Model. To obtain a semi-supervised ranking model, we add the rank-sensitive Bradley-Terry objective to the rank-sensitive regularizer:

$$C = \sum_{(i,j)\in L} |\Delta_{ij}| \mathbb{I}_{i\succ j} \log P(i \succ j) \quad (14)$$

$$+ \beta \sum_{i,j\in U} |\Delta^U_{ij}| \hat{q}_{ij} \log P(i \not\succ j) P(j \not\succ i), \quad (15)$$

with gradients

$$\mathrm{d}C/\mathrm{d}s_i = \sum_{\{j|(i,j)\in L\}} |\Delta_{ij}| (\mathbb{I}_{i\succ j} - P(i \succ j)) \quad (16)$$

$$+ \beta \sum_{j\in U} |\Delta^U_{ij}| \hat{q}_{ij} (0.5 - P(i \succ j)), \quad \forall i. \quad (17)$$

Comparing the labeled and unlabeled terms (Eq. 14 and 15), one sees that the document similarity probability $\hat{q}_{ij}$ serves a role similar to preferences $\mathbb{I}_{i\succ j}$ in the labeled data. One difference between the labeled and unlabeled gradients, is that the unlabeled gradient (Eq. 17) always tries to reduce the difference in ranks between i and j; the gradient sign is controlled by $0.5 - P(i \succ j)$ which is positive if $i \prec j$, or 0 if equal, or negative otherwise. In contrast, the labeled gradients (Eq. 16) can either increase or decrease the rank difference depending on the labels, as $\mathbb{I}_{i\succ j} - P(i \succ j)$ is positive when $i \succ j$ or negative when $j \succ i$ (or 0).

The gradients can be intuitively visualized as "forces" acting on each pair of documents (Figure 4), pushing the more relevant document up in the ranking, and the other one down. The resultant force on document i is a sum over forces from other documents j (as shown in Eq. 16 and 17). The forces depend on the current ranks and scores, as well as the labels of the documents. In the figure, the column marked $\boldsymbol{x}$ shows items in the training data, where items with similar shapes are assumed similar to each other (squares and stars). The L column shows the labels of the items in the training data (positive and negative), and $\mathrm{d}C^L/\mathrm{d}s_i$ shows the magnitude and direction of the labeled gradients. For each pair of items, positive items are pushed up and negative items are pulled down in the ranking. The force magnitude is dictated by the difference in rank between the two items. Similarly, $\mathrm{d}C^U/\mathrm{d}s_i$ shows the unlabeled gradients for the data. Similar items are pulled towards each other. The last column in the figure shows the total semi-supervised gradient.

Learning to Rank Algorithm: SSLambdaRank. We now proceed to implement the semi-supervised rank-sensitive model above in a learning algorithm, which we will call SSLambdaRank. We choose the ranking function $s_i = f(\boldsymbol{x}_i; \boldsymbol{w})$ to be a 1-hidden layer neural network, although any differentiable function will do. We aim to calculate $\mathrm{d}C/\mathrm{d}\boldsymbol{w} = \sum_i (\mathrm{d}C/\mathrm{d}s_i)(\mathrm{d}s_i/\mathrm{d}\boldsymbol{w})$ for gradient descent training.

The challenge in learning the ranking function $f(\boldsymbol{x}; \boldsymbol{w})$ is that the ranks are discontinuous in the parameters $\boldsymbol{w}$; in particular, the ranking is determined by sorting the scores $\{s_i\}$. The swap costs $|\Delta_{ij}|$ and $|\Delta^U_{ij}|$ both depend on ranks, which implies that the gradients are discontinuous in the parameters $\boldsymbol{w}$.

LambdaRank [7] is an algorithm that successfully applies stochastic gradient descent in this discontinuous setting. Given a parameter state $\boldsymbol{w}$, it calculates item scores, sorts the scores to determine item ranks, calculates swap costs $|\Delta_{ij}|$, computes stochastic gradients, and takes a gradient step to update the parameters. The updated parameters may yield a discontinuous change in $|\Delta_{ij}|$, but the algorithm works well empirically. In fact, LambdaRank is state of the art in ranking: the winning entry in the Yahoo! Learning to Rank Challenge [9] used an ensemble of Lambda-Gradient models, including LambdaRank. SSLambdaRank is applied in the same way, but to the semi-supervised gradients.

5.1 A (Near) Linear Time Algorithm

In semi-supervised learning, we often want to use very large unlabeled datasets, thus computational efficiency is required. The proposed learning algorithms scale linearly in the number of queries. In our settings, the scalability is dominated by the number of queries, as the number of items per query is bounded by 1000 (the max number of documents the search engine returns per query), so overall we observe linear scaling behavior.

However, in other settings, scalability may be dominated by the number of items per query (both labeled and unlabeled). A naive implementation that considered all item pairs would scale quadratically in the number of items. Fortunately, our formulation regularizes only with respect to the K nearest neighbors of each item in the feature space, which reduces to linear scaling behavior. This also has the benefit of trusting the feature space dissimilarity d_X only in local neighborhoods, giving it a local manifold behavior.

We also require a preprocessing step to find the K nearest neighbors of every item. Here we can apply approximation techniques such as locality sensitive hashing, which can bucket items in near linear time, or use fast exact K-nearest neighbor techniques [4].

Finally, the learning algorithm requires sorting item scores to form the ranked list for each query. This step can be done in linear time via radix sort, given that the scores have finite precision.

6. EXPERIMENTAL RESULTS

6.1 Datasets

In order to demonstrate the quality of the SSLambdaRank algorithm, we use two different datasets: TREC 6, 7, 8 adhoc

	Features
1.	BM25
2.	LogBM25
3.	LM_ABS
4.	LM_DIR
5.	LM_JM
6.	LogNormalizedTF
7.	SumLogTF
8.	TF
9.	TF_IDF
10.	LogTF_IDF_V2
11.	NormalizedTF

Table 1: Feature Set

tracks, and the semi-supervised Million Query 2008 (MQ 2008) dataset [1] from LETOR 4.0 [23].

6.1.1 The TREC Ad-hoc Dataset

The first dataset we use consists of queries and documents from the TREC 6, 7 and 8 adhoc tracks, as set up by Aslam et al. [3]. The dataset has depth-100 pools from the TREC tracks, along with the associated relevance judgments. In total, there are 150 queries in the dataset, and approximately 1000 labeled documents per query.

The features used are those of LETOR 3.0, excluding web features that require link information, which is not available for this corpus. The features (Table 1) are computed over the document text with and without the title, resulting in 22 features in total. Detailed feature descriptions can be found in [23].

In order to avoid judging the entire document collection, the most commonly used technique is depth-m pooling, where in the case of depth-100 pooling, for example, only the top 100 documents retrieved by the systems are judged and the rest of the documents are assumed nonrelevant. We will simulate the effect of varying the number of labeled documents per query, in a similar spirit to depth pooling. For this, we include judgments for m of the labeled documents with the highest BM25 [20] score for each query, varying $m \in \{2, 3, 5, 10, 15\}$ and treating the rest of the documents as unlabeled. In this way, we include labels for likely relevant documents that appear towards the top of the ranking, as commonly done in the literature [23].

The distance between documents, $d_X()$ was computed using two different approaches: one content-based, the other feature-based. In the content-based approach, we first identified the top 50 words in the labeled documents with highest tf-idf score, and represented each document only using these terms, to compute Euclidean distance between such tf-idf document vectors. In the feature-based approach, we used the Euclidean distance between the ranking features (BM25, LogBM25, LM_ABS, etc.) for the documents. The goal of this was to examine whether semi-supervised learning could help even when exactly the same features were used for regularization as for ranking.

6.1.2 The Million Query 2008 Dataset

The second dataset we use is the semi-supervised Million Query 2008 (MQ 2008) query set [1] from LETOR 4.0 [23].

The MQ 2008 dataset uses the Gov2 web page collection (containing approximately 25M pages). It consists of 800 queries, with approximately 15000 labeled documents and 88000 unlabeled documents in total. The LETOR 4.0 data also provides cosine-similarities between tf-idf document vectors, which we directly used as our distances $d_X()$.

6.2 Experimental Setup

Both datasets were split in five parts: three for training, one for validation, and one for testing. The splits were done five ways for 5-fold cross validation. The documents in the training and validation sets are samples of the complete collection, as described above. The test set consists of the complete set of documents. We report averages across the 5 folds.

The neural network architecture was tuned for the supervised case where we only use the labeled documents (*L only*) by varying the number of hidden units; 3 hidden units performed best on the validation set. Even though the optimal number of hidden units for our semi-supervised algorithm may be larger, we used the same model size as the supervised LambdaRank algorithm to ensure the same learning capacity in both cases.

We also validated other important model parameters: β, the weight of labeled and unlabeled data, was varied between 0.1 and 5 in 0.1 increments, and the best value on the validation set was chosen. Likewise, the epoch for early stopping was validated. Other parameters were fixed to reasonable defaults: the learning parameters K=5, σ_i=∞ for all i, yielding $\hat{q}_{ij}$=0.2 for K neighbors or 0 otherwise. The effect of number of number of neighbors, K, will be analyzed in section 6.3.3.

RankBoost [15] and Ranking SVM [19] are two commonly used learning to rank algorithms. Semi-supervised RankBoost [2] and Transductive SVM (TSVM) [18] are semi-supervised variations of these algorithms. TSVM is really a classification algorithm, but is applicable since the collections have absolute judgments. We use these algorithms as baselines. For semi-supervised RankBoost, the weight of unlabeled documents needs to be specified (similar to our β parameter). To set this value for RankBoost, we used the same validation approach as we used for specifying the β parameter for our algorithm.

6.3 Results

We use two different retrieval tasks to compare the performance of different learning to rank algorithms: ranking novel queries, and a relevance feedback task. When ranking novel queries, training and test sets are separate. In the relevance feedback task, a user issues a query and labels a few of the resulting documents from a traditional ranker (e.g. BM25). Then the system trains a query-specific ranker incorporating the user feedback, and re-ranks the collection.

6.3.1 Ranking Novel Queries Task

The left plot in Figure 5 shows the quality of our algorithm on the TREC test set (averaged across all five folds). All LambdaRank variants are trained to optimize NDCG and the accuracy is measured using the NDCG metric at rank cutoff 10. Our semi-supervised algorithm is trained on varying numbers of labeled preference pairs from 90 training queries, and all documents associated with those queries (nearly 90,000) are used as unlabeled data. All LambdaRank methods work on preference pairs; a very large number of pairs are induced from the labels: about 3500 labeled pairs and over 40 million unlabeled pairs. This experiment thereby demonstrates the scalability of our algorithms.

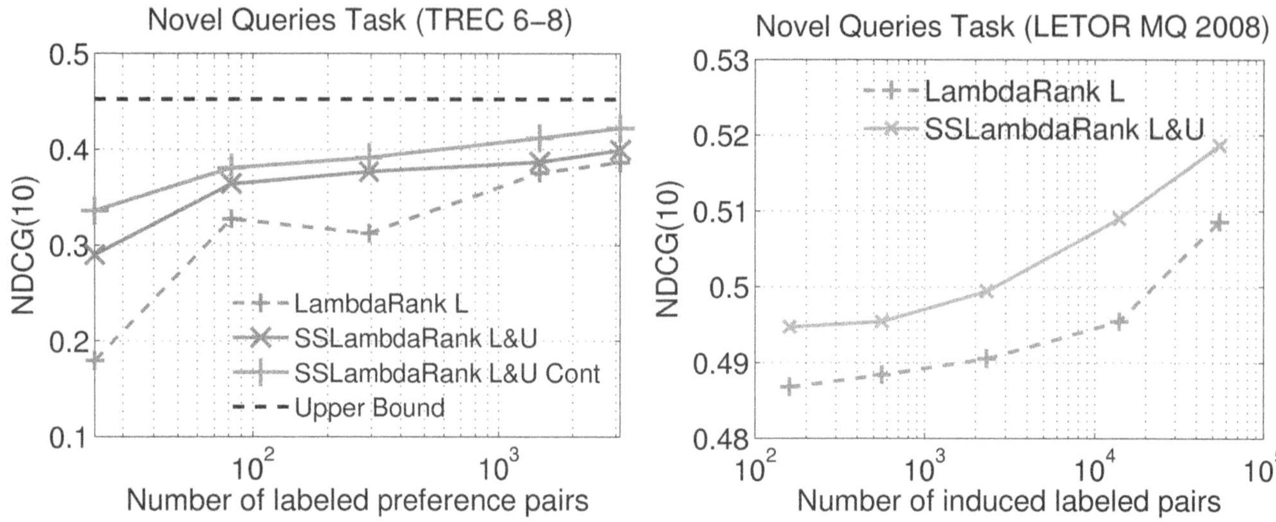

Figure 5: NDCG accuracy at rank cutoff 10 for the test set averaged over 5 folds for the (left) TREC and (right) Million Query 2008 datasets. We show supervised methods (dashed lines, suffix L) and semi-supervised methods (solid lines, suffix L & U). Feature-based SSLambdaRank has suffix (L & U), content-based SSLambdaRank has suffix (L & U Cont).

The *Upper bound*, is attained by taking all ~150,000 docs and using them in supervised LambdaRank providing labels, which is "cheating" compared to semi-supervised methods which treat most of these documents as unlabeled. This corresponds to an ideal case in which the true labels of the unlabeled data became available.

The figures show that SSLambdaRank using either distance metric outperforms LambdaRank (*LambdaRank L*). Since the LambdaRank algorithms use preference pairs in training, the x axis in this plot displays the number of preference pairs (on a log scale) as opposed to the number of labeled documents per query. Except for the last data point (with the most labeled pairs), the differences between SSLambdaRank and LambdaRank are statistically significant in all cases according to the Wilcoxon sign-rank test at $p = 0.05$ significance level. We note that the semi-supervised ranker still benefits from unlabeled data despite the large number of labeled preferences.

The right plot of Figure 5 shows the quality of our algorithm on the LETOR MQ2008 dataset. In this experiment, we only use the document similarity values that were provided by the LETOR collection. To analyze the effect of varying the number of labeled examples, we form different training sets by sampling l% of the documents from each query ($l \in 5, 10, 20, 50, 100$), assuming the sampled documents are labeled and the rest of the documents are unlabeled. The x axis in the plot shows the number of induced pairs (on a log scale) when l% of documents are used from the complete set. SSLambdaRank beats LambdaRank consistently. All the improvements are statistically significant according to the Wilcoxon sign-rank test at $p = 0.05$ significance level. Since the LETOR MQ2008 dataset does not contain the labels for all documents (the collection itself is partially judged), no *Upper bound* information is available for this dataset.

The two semi-supervised baselines, semi-supervised RankBoost and Transductive SVM could not be used in this setting. The semi-supervised RankBoost code [2] does not apply to the problem of ranking unseen queries as it only works for a single rank instance (i.e., train on a single query, test on the same query). For both datasets, Transductive SVM was trained for more than two days without terminating. Our proposed algorithm can be trained in an hour even for a large dataset as the MQ 2008 collection.

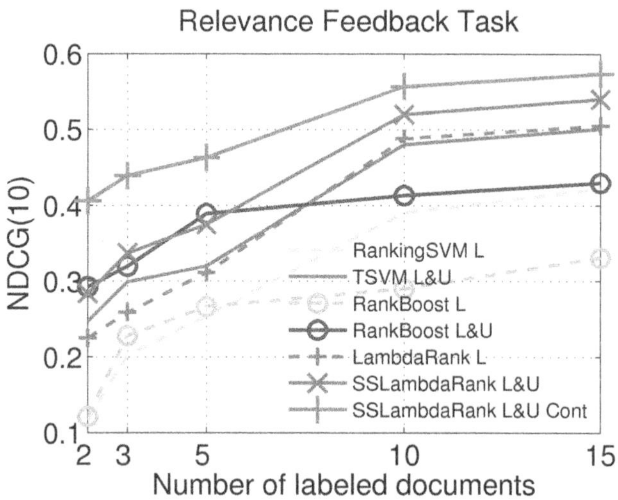

Figure 6: NDCG accuracy at rank 10 for the relevance feedback task. We show supervised methods (dashed lines, suffix L) and semi-supervised methods (solid lines, suffix L & U).

6.3.2 *Relevance Feedback Task*

Next, we focus on the relevance feedback task as this task is approachable by the other semi-supervised algorithms. Here, we can compare the quality of our semi-supervised algorithm with that of our two baselines (semi-supervised RankBoost

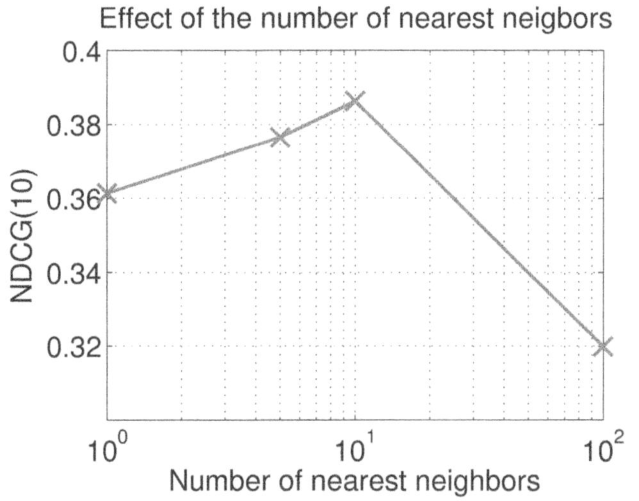

Figure 7: Effect of K, the number of nearest neighbors, on SSLambdaRank (L & U cont), for the novel queries task.

and Transductive SVM). In the relevance feedback task, a user issues a query and labels a few of the resulting documents from a traditional ranker (BM25). The system then trains a query-specific ranker incorporating the user feedback, and re-ranks the collection (test on the query the algorithm is trained on, similar to the assumption the semi-supervised RankBoost algorithm is based on). This is a transductive setting, as both labeled and unlabeled documents for the test query are available at training time. Since the training is done per query, the training data is much smaller. Hence, Transductive SVM can be run in a reasonable amount of time. For this task, we only report results from the TREC dataset.

Figure 6 shows retrieval accuracy for varying numbers of labeled training documents for the relevance feedback task. Since the relevance feedback experiment involves training on a single query and testing on the same query (excluding the training documents), we plot the mean NDCG across all queries. The figure shows that the SSLambdaRank using either distance metric outperforms LambdaRank. The differences between SSLambdaRank and LambdaRank are statistically significant in all cases according to the Wilcoxon sign-rank test at $p = 0.05$ significance level. Furthermore, our proposed algorithm consistently and significantly ($p = 0.05$) outperforms the other two semi-supervised algorithms.

6.3.3 *Effect of the Number of Nearest Neighbors (K)*

One important parameter in SSLambdaRank algorithm is the number of nearest neighbors K. Figure 7 explores the effect of K for the novel queries task using 300 labeled preference pairs per query for the TREC collection. $K = 10$ nearest neighbors results in the best performance.

Note that in all experiments we used $K = 5$ number of nearest neighbors. The performance of SSLambdaRank could be further improved had we used $K = 10$ neighbors.

7. DISCUSSION AND CONCLUSIONS

We proposed a preference regularizer for semi-supervised ranking; and showed how it could be used to extend LambdaRank to a semi-supervised setup. Experiments show that the proposed algorithm outperforms both the supervised version of itself as well as other available semi-supervised baselines.

Even though our semi-supervised algorithm can work with absolute labels, our guiding principle in this paper has been to design an algorithm for relative as well as absolute labels. We learn from neighborhood relations in the feature space, and preference relations in the preference space. Preferences are the essence of ranking, distinguishing it from classification and ordinal regression. Importantly, studies show that humans produce more consistent rankings and do so quicker when giving preferences rather than absolute labels [8]. Preference relations arise naturally as user choices from lists (e.g. clicks on search results). Thus, there are strong justifications for algorithms in this category.

We could have been more purist by optimizing a preference metric (e.g. ppref) rather than NDCG that employs absolute labels. The algorithm is designed for this setting, but preference metrics are not well-established yet.

The regularizer exploits structure in the unlabeled data. We have chosen to focus on manifold structure. However, the question remains what part of the manifold should be included; equivalently, what pairs of data points should be used in the regularizer? We included unlabeled data retrieved at the top of the ranking; since common ranking objectives emphasize top ranks, unlabeled data in that region regularizes the ranking function where it matters the most. Random items would generally be non-relevant and spread out thinly in the space, having little in common with each other. With the rank-sensitive regularizer, one could include all unlabeled data, as data at the bottom would be discounted anyway.

Future work could explore the effectiveness of different label information: *depth* (many preferences for few rank instances (queries)) vs. *breadth* (few preferences for many rank instances (queries)), as well as preferences within top vs. across top-bottom for a ranking instance. It may also be interesting to apply the regularizer with differentiable hypothesis classes other than neural networks, in particular random forests.

Acknowledgements

We thank Massih Reza Amini for making the semi-supervised RankBoost [2] implementation available, and Tom Minka and Vishwa Vinay for helpful discussions.

8. REFERENCES

[1] J. Allan, B. Carterette, J. A. Aslam, V. Pavlu, and E. Kanoulas. Million query track 2008 overview. In *The Sixteenth Text REtrieval Conference Proceedings (TREC 2008)*. National Institute of Standards and Technology, 2009.

[2] M. R. Amini, T. V. Truong, and C. Goutte. A boosting algorithm for learning bipartite ranking functions with partially labeled data. In *SIGIR Conf. Research and Development in Information Retrieval*, 2008.

[3] J. A. Aslam, E. Kanoulas, V. Pavlu, and E. Yilmaz. Document selection methodologies for efficient and effective learning-to-rank. In *SIGIR Conf. Research and Development in Information Retrieval*, 2009.

[4] R. J. Bayardo, Y. Ma, and R. Srikant. Scaling up all pairs similarity search. In *Proc. Intl. conf. World Wide Web (WWW)*, pages 131–140, 2007.

[5] M. Belkin, P. Niyogi, and V. Sindhwani. Manifold regularization: a geometric framework for learning from labeled and unlabeled examples. *Journal of Machine Learning Research*, 2006.

[6] C. Burges, T. Shaked, E. Renshaw, A. Lazier, M. Deeds, N. Hamilton, and G. Hullender. Learning to rank using gradient descent. In *Intl. Conf. on Machine Learning (ICML)*, 2005.

[7] C. J. Burges, R. Ragno, and Q. V. Le. Learning to rank with nonsmooth cost functions. In *Advances in Neural Information Processing Systems (NIPS)*, 2006.

[8] B. Carterette, P. Bennett, D. Chickering, and S. Dumais. Here or there: Preference judgments for relevance. In *European Conf. Information Retrieval (ECIR)*, 2008.

[9] O. Chapelle and Y. Chang. Yahoo! learning to rank challenge overview. In *Proc. Yahoo! Learning to Rank Challenge 2010*, 2011.

[10] S. Chen, F. Wang, Y. Song, and C. Zhang. Semi-supervised ranking aggregation. *Information Processing & Management*, 47:415–425, May 2011.

[11] W. Chu and Z. Ghahramani. Extensions of gaussian processes for ranking: Semi-supervised and active learning. In *NIPS workshop on Learning to Rank*, 2005.

[12] F. Diaz. Regularizing query-based retrieval scores. *Information Retrieval*, 10(6):531–562, 2007.

[13] P. Donmez, K. M. Svore, and C. J. Burges. On the local optimality of Lambdarank. In *SIGIR Conf. Research and Development in Information Retrieval*, 2009.

[14] K. Duh and K. Kirchhoff. Learning to rank with partially-labeled data. In *SIGIR Conf. Research and Development in Information Retrieval*, 2008.

[15] Y. Freund, R. Iyer, R. Schapire, and Y. Singer. An efficient boosting algorithm for combining preferences. *Journal of Machine Learning Research*, 4:933–969, 2003.

[16] N. Jardine and C. J. van Rijsbergen. The use of hierarchic clustering in information retrieval. *Information Storage and Retrieval*, 7:217–240, 1971.

[17] K. Järvelin and J. Kekäläinen. IR evaluation methods for retrieving highly relevant documents. In *SIGIR Conf. Research and Development in Information Retrieval*, 2000.

[18] T. Joachims. Transductive inference for text classification using support vector machines. In *Intl. Conf. on Machine Learning (ICML)*, pages 200–209, 1999.

[19] T. Joachims. Optimizing search engines using clickthrough data. In *Intl. conf. Knowledge discovery and data mining (KDD)*, pages 133–142, 2002.

[20] K. S. Jones, S. Walker, and S. E. Robertson. A probabilistic model of information retrieval: development and comparative experiments. In *Information Processing & Management*, pages 779–840, 2000.

[21] M. Li, H. Li, and Z.-H. Zhou. Semi-supervised document retrieval. *Information Processing & Management*, 45(3):341–355, 2009.

[22] J. Marden. *Analyzing and Modeling Rank Data.* Chapman & Hall, 1995.

[23] T. Qin, T.-Y. Liu, J. Xu, and H. Li. LETOR: A benchmark collection for research on learning to rank for information retrieval. *Information Retrieval Journal*, 2010.

[24] M. Seeger. Learning with labeled and unlabeled data. Technical Report, Dec. 2002.

[25] D. Sheldon, M. Shokouhi, M. Szummer, and N. Craswell. LambdaMerge: Merging the results of query reformulations. In *Conf. Web search and data mining (WSDM)*, pages 795–804, 2011.

[26] A. Shivani. Ranking on graph data. In *Intl. Conf. on Machine Learning (ICML)*, 2006.

[27] M. Szummer and T. Jaakkola. Kernel expansions with unlabeled examples. In *Advances in Neural Information Processing Systems (NIPS)*, volume 13, pages 626–632. MIT Press, 2001.

[28] M. Szummer and T. Jaakkola. Partially labeled classification with markov random walks. In *Advances in Neural Information Processing Systems (NIPS)*, volume 14, pages 945–952. MIT Press, 2002.

[29] M. Szummer and F. Radlinski. Cost-sensitive machine learning for information retrieval. In Krishnapuram, Yu, and Rao, editors, *Cost-sensitive Machine Learning.* Chapman and Hall/CRC, 2011.

[30] M. Szummer and E. Yilmaz. Semi-supervised ranking via ranking regularization. In *Advances in Ranking, workshop at NIPS*, 2009.

[31] L. van der Maaten and G. Hinton. Visualizing data using t-SNE. *Journal of Machine Learning Research*, 9:2579–2605, 2008.

[32] C. J. van Rijsbergen. *Information Retrieval.* Butterworths, London, 2nd ed edition, 1979.

[33] J.-N. Vittaut and P. Gallinari. Supervised and semi-supervised machine learning ranking. In *Comparative Evaluation of XML Information Retrieval Systems*, volume 4518 of *Lecture Notes in Computer Science*, pages 213–222. Springer, 2007.

[34] C. Wang, E. Yilmaz, and M. Szummer. Relevance feedback exploiting query-specific document manifolds. In *Conf. Information and Knowledge Management (CIKM)*, 2011.

Simultaneous Clustering of Multi-Type Relational Data via Symmetric Nonnegative Matrix Tri-Factorization

Hua Wang
Department of Computer Science and Engineering
University of Texas at Arlington, TX 76019, USA
huawangcs@gmail.com

Heng Huang
Department of Computer Science and Engineering
University of Texas at Arlington, TX 76019, USA
heng@uta.edu

Chris Ding
Department of Computer Science and Engineering
University of Texas at Arlington, TX 76019, USA
chqding@uta.edu

ABSTRACT

The rapid growth of Internet and modern technologies has brought data involving objects of multiple types that are related to each other, called as *multi-type relational data*. Traditional clustering methods for single-type data rarely work well on them, which calls for more advanced clustering techniques to deal with multiple types of data simultaneously to utilize their interrelatedness. A major challenge in developing simultaneous clustering methods is how to effectively use all available information contained in a multi-type relational data set including *inter-type* and *intra-type* relationships. In this paper, we propose a Symmetric Nonnegative Matrix Tri-Factorization (S-NMTF) framework to cluster multi-type relational data at the same time. The proposed S-NMTF approach employs NMTF to simultaneously cluster different types of data using their inter-type relationships, and incorporate the intra-type information through manifold regularization. In order to deal with the symmetric usage of the factor matrix in S-NMTF, we present a new generic matrix inequality to derive the solution algorithm, which involves a fourth-order matrix polynomial, in a principled way. Promising experimental results have validated the proposed approach.

Categories and Subject Descriptors

H.3.3 [**Information Storage And Retrieval**]: Information Search and Retrieval—*Clustering*; I.2.6 [**Artificial Intelligence**]: Learning

General Terms

Algorithms, Experimentation, Performance

Keywords

Clustering, Multi-Type Relational Data, Web, Nonnegative Matrix Tri-Factorization

1. INTRODUCTION

Clustering aims to partition a set of objects into groups or clusters such that objects in a same cluster are similar while those in different clusters are dissimilar. Most traditional clustering algorithms concentrate on dealing with *homogeneous* data, in which all the objects are of one single type. Recently, the rapid progress of Internet and computational technologies have brought data much richer in structure, involving objects of multiple types that are related to each other. For example, in a Web search system in Figure 1, we have four different types of data objects including words, Web pages, search queries and Web users. Each of the four types of entities have their own attributes. Meanwhile different types of data are also interrelated to each other by various means, *e.g.*, Web pages and words are related via co-occurrences. Due to their high heterogeneity and close interrelationships, these data are called as *multi-type relational data* [10]. The information contained in a multi-type relational data set typically appears in two forms as follows:

- **Inter-type relationships** characterize the relations between data objects from different types, such as the co-occurrences between data objects from different types, as illustrated by the green solid lines in Figure 1.
- **Intra-type relationships** characterize the native relations between objects within one data type, *e.g.*, as illustrated by the blue dashed lines in Figure 1, the internet hyperlinks among Web pages, the pairwise affinities among users that are induced from user attributes, *etc.*

Inter-type relationships appear exclusively in multi-type relational data, while intra-type information, due to its homogeneity, appears in both multi-type relational data and traditional single-type data.

The rich structures of multi-type relational data provide a potential opportunity to improve the clustering accuracy, which, however, also present a new challenge on how to take advantage of all available information. In this paper, we tackle this new, yet important, problem to simultaneously cluster multiple types of relational data. Our goal is to make full use of the both forms of information of a multi-type relational data set.

1.1 Difficulties of Traditional Clustering Methods on Multi-Type Relational Data

Because each type of a multi-type relational data set can be viewed as homogeneous data, one may argue that clustering heterogeneous data can be solved using traditional methods to cluster each type of objects independently. However, this may not work well.

First, various data types in a multi-type relational data set are interrelated to each other. Clustering each data type independently will lose these interaction information, such as that conveyed by internet hyper-links or co-occurrences, which are essential to gain a full understanding of the Web data.

Second, in practice the clustering of a data type may not be the one based on the intra-type relationships (*i.e.*, the similarity of fea-

CIKM'11, October 24–28, 2011, Glasgow, Scotland, UK.

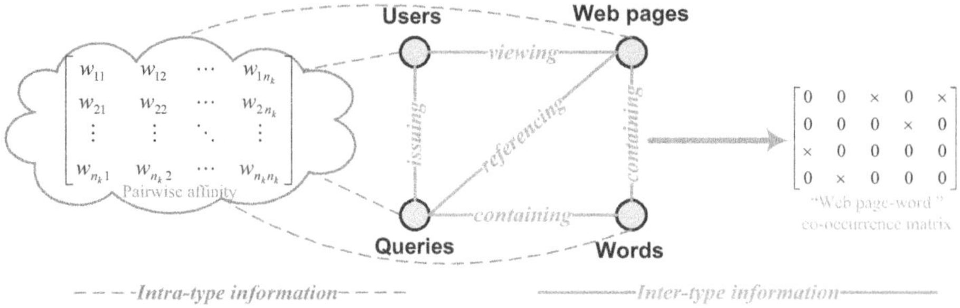

Figure 1: A Web search system is an example of multi-type relational data, involving (1) *Inter-type relationships* (green solid lines): the relations between objects in different data types. (2) *Intra-type relationships* (blue dashed lines): the relations between different objects in a same data type.

tures) but the one based on the inter-type relationships between this data type and others. For example, in the Web search system in Figure 1, instead of the similarity between Web pages themselves, people are often interested in the relationships between user groups and Web page styles.

Last, but not least, heterogeneous data contain different types of objects. Processing and interpreting them in one single way may not be appropriate and presents a major challenge. Ad hoc integration or normalization (*e.g.*, concatenating different features into a vector of fixed length) rarely works.

As a result, recent research has advanced swiftly from simple clustering of one type of data to simultaneous clustering of multiple types of data, for both two data types (pairwise co-clustering) [3, 6, 7, 16] and multiple (more than two) data types (high-order co-clustering) [10, 12, 15]. Through simultaneous clustering, one can discover the hidden global structures in the heterogeneous data, which seamlessly integrates multiple data types to provide a better picture of the underlying data distribution.

1.2 Our Contributions

Given the inter-type relationships and the intra-type information, we present a Symmetric Nonnegative Matrix Tri-Factorization (S-NMTF) framework for simultaneous clustering of multi-type relational data. In our new approach, we use NMTF to simultaneously cluster different types of data upon their inter-type relationship matrices. Meanwhile, users are allowed to provide optional intra-type information for different types of data in form of pairwise affinity, which is incorporated as manifold regularization to NMTF. Promising empirical results in extensive experiments validate the proposed method. We summarize our contributions as following.

1. We present a simple, yet effective, framework to tackle the complicated problem of simultaneous clustering of multi-type relational data, which aims to fully exploit all available information.

2. Existing NMF algorithms usually deal with asymmetric (rectangle data-feature) matrix factorization [4, 6, 12–14] and optimize one factor matrix at a time, which only involve second-order matrix polynomials. When dealing with symmetric matrix factorization, a fourth-order matrix polynomial is involved, which is much harder to be dealt with and heuristics are usually used in existing works. In this paper, as an important theoretical contribution, we present a new generic matrix inequality (in Lemma 4), such that the difficulty is tackled in a principled way.

2. SIMULTANEOUSLY CLUSTER MULTI-TYPE RELATIONAL DATA BY S-NMTF

In this section, we first briefly review NMTF based co-clustering of two-type relational data, from which we gradually develop the proposed S-NMTF approach for simultaneous clustering of multi-type relational data. Our approach employs both inter-type relationships as well as intra-type information.

2.1 Problem Formalization

We first formalize the problem of simultaneous clustering of multi-type relational data.

We denote a K-type relational data set as $\mathcal{X} = \{\mathcal{X}_1, \mathcal{X}_2, \ldots, \mathcal{X}_K\}$, where $\mathcal{X}_k = \{\mathbf{x}_1^k, \mathbf{x}_2^k, \ldots, \mathbf{x}_{n_k}^k\}$ represents the data objects of the k-th type. Suppose that we are given a set of relationship matrices $\{R_{kl} \in \Re^{n_k \times n_l}\}_{(1 \le k \le K, 1 \le l \le K)}$ between different types of data objects, and we have $R_{kl} = R_{lk}^T$. Our goal is to simultaneously partition the data objects in $\mathcal{X}_1, \mathcal{X}_2, \ldots, \mathcal{X}_K$ into $c_1, c_2, \ldots, c_K$ disjoint clusters respectively.

Most existing simultaneous clustering algorithms only rely on inter-type relationships, *i.e.*, R_{ij}. However, in practice we may also have intra-type information for each type of data. For the k-th type of data, for example, we usually have pairwise affinities $W_k \in \Re^{n_k \times n_k}$ between the objects of the type. In this study, we aim to make full use of both inter-type relationships R_{kl} (in Section 2.3) and intra-type information W_k (in Section 2.4).

Throughout this paper, we denote $A_{(ij)}$ as the entry at the i-th row and j-th column of a matrix A.

2.2 A Brief Review of Co-Clustering of Two-Type Relational Data Using NMTF

The close connection between Nonnegative Matrix Factorization (NMF) and clustering [4] provides the potential theory to develop co-clustering methods. Ding *et al.* proposed to use NMTF [6] to simultaneously cluster the rows and columns of an input nonnegative relationship matrix R_{12} by decomposing it into three nonnegative factor matrices, which minimizes the following objective:

$$J_1 = \|R_{12} - G_1 S_{12} G_2^T\|^2, \; s.t. \; G_1 \ge 0, G_2 \ge 0, S_{12} \ge 0, \quad (1)$$

where $\|\cdot\|$ denotes the Frobenius norm of a matrix, $G_1 \in \Re_+^{n_1 \times c_1}$ and $G_2 \in \Re_+^{n_2 \times c_2}$ are the cluster indicator matrices for $\mathcal{X}_1$ and $\mathcal{X}_2$ respectively, and $S_{12} \in \Re_+^{c_1 \times c_2}$ absorbs the different scales of R_{12}, G_1 and G_2. Note that, the original NMF problem [9] requires R_{12} to be nonnegative. In co-clustering scenarios, this constraint (thereby the nonnegativity constraint on S_{12}), however, can be relaxed [5], which leads to the semi-NMTF problem to minimize:

$$J_2 = \|R_{12} - G_1 S_{12} G_2^T\|^2, \quad s.t. \quad G_1 \ge 0, G_2 \ge 0 \; . \quad (2)$$

Simultaneous clustering on $\mathcal{X}_1$ and $\mathcal{X}_2$ is then achieved by solving Eq. (2). Because the rows of the resulted G_k ($k \in \{1, 2\}$) (with normalization) can be interpreted as the posterior probability for clustering on $\mathcal{X}_k$ [4, 6], the cluster label of $\mathbf{x}_i^k$ is obtained by

$$l\left(\mathbf{x}_i^k\right) = \arg\max_j G_{k(ij)} \; . \quad (3)$$

2.3 Simultaneous Clustering of Multi-Type Relational Data Using Inter-Type Relationships

A natural generalization of the co-clustering objective in Eq. (2) to simultaneous clustering of multi-type relational data is to solve the following optimization problem [10, 12]:

$$\min\ J_3 = \sum_{1\le k<l\le K} \|R_{kl} - G_k S_{kl} G_l^T\|^2, \quad s.t.\quad G_k \ge 0,\ \forall\, 1 \le k \le K\ . \tag{4}$$

However, it is not straightforward to solve Eq. (4) by generalizing existing iterative multiplicative NMTF solution algorithms. Motivated by [3] that deals with bipartite graphs, we propose to solve the optimization problem in Eq. (4) by solving an equivalent Symmetric NMTF problem.

We first introduce the following useful lemma.

LEMMA 1. *The optimization problem in Eq.* (2) *can be equivalently solved by the following S-NMTF problem:*

$$\min\ J_4 = \|R - GSG^T\|^2, \quad s.t.\quad G \ge 0, \tag{5}$$

in which

$$R = \begin{bmatrix} 0^{n_1\times n_1} & R_{12}^{n_1\times n_2} \\ R_{21}^{n_2\times n_1} & 0^{n_2\times n_2} \end{bmatrix},$$
$$G = \begin{bmatrix} G_1^{n_1\times c_1} & 0^{n_1\times c_2} \\ 0^{n_2\times c_1} & G_2^{n_2\times c_2} \end{bmatrix},\quad S = \begin{bmatrix} 0^{c_1\times c_1} & S_{12}^{c_1\times c_2} \\ S_{21}^{c_2\times c_1} & 0^{c_2\times c_2} \end{bmatrix}, \tag{6}$$

where the superscripts denote the matrix sizes, and $R_{21} = R_{12}^T$, $S_{21} = S_{12}^T$. $0^{n_1\times n_1}$ *is a matrix with all zero entries of size* $n_1 \times n_1$.

PROOF. Following the definitions of R, G and S, we can derive

$$\|R - GSG^T\|^2 = \left\| \begin{bmatrix} 0 & R_{12} \\ R_{12}^T & 0 \end{bmatrix} - \begin{bmatrix} 0 & G_1 S_{12} G_2^T \\ G_2 S_{12}^T G_1^T & 0 \end{bmatrix} \right\|^2 = 2\|R_{12} - G_1 S_{12} G_2^T\|,$$

which proves the lemma. □

Based upon Lemma 1, we have the following theorem.

THEOREM 1. *It is equivalent to solve Eq.* (4) *and to solve*

$$\min\ J_5 = \|R - GSG^T\|, \quad s.t.\quad G \ge 0, \tag{7}$$

in which

$$R = \begin{bmatrix} 0^{n_1\times n_1} & R_{12}^{n_1\times n_2} & \cdots & R_{1K}^{n_1\times n_K} \\ R_{21}^{n_2\times n_1} & 0^{n_2\times n_2} & \cdots & R_{2K}^{n_2\times n_K} \\ \vdots & \vdots & \ddots & \vdots \\ R_{K1}^{n_K\times n_1} & R_{K2}^{n_K\times n_2} & \cdots & 0^{n_K\times n_K} \end{bmatrix},$$
$$G = \begin{bmatrix} G_1^{n_1\times c_1} & 0^{n_1\times c_2} & \cdots & 0^{n_1\times c_K} \\ 0^{n_2\times c_1} & G_2^{n_2\times c_2} & \cdots & 0^{n_2\times c_K} \\ \vdots & \vdots & \ddots & \vdots \\ 0^{n_K\times c_1} & 0^{n_K\times c_2} & \cdots & G_K^{n_K\times c_K} \end{bmatrix}, \tag{8}$$
$$S = \begin{bmatrix} 0^{c_1\times c_1} & S_{12}^{c_1\times c_2} & \cdots & S_{1K}^{c_1\times c_K} \\ S_{21}^{c_2\times c_1} & 0^{c_2\times c_2} & \cdots & S_{2K}^{c_2\times c_K} \\ \vdots & \vdots & \ddots & \vdots \\ S_{K1}^{c_K\times c_1} & S_{K2}^{c_K\times c_2} & \cdots & 0^{c_K\times c_K} \end{bmatrix},$$

where $R_{ji} = R_{ij}^T$ *and* $S_{ij} = S_{ji}^T$.

The proof of Theorem 1 can be easily obtained by generalizing the proof of Lemma 1 to multi-type relational data.

Theorem 1 presents a general framework via S-NMTF to simultaneously cluster multi-type relational data using the mutual relationship matrices. However, the symmetric usage of the factor matrix G in NMTF leads to a fourth-order matrix polynomial when deriving the iterative algorithm, which is harder to be dealt with compared to the second-order matrix polynomials involved in standard (asymmetric) NMTF. In Section 3, we will introduce a new matrix inequality in Lemma 4 to solve this problem.

2.4 Incorporating Intra-Type Information via Graph Regularization

The optimization objectives in Eq. (2) and Eq. (7) only involve the inter-type relationships of a multi-type relational data set, whereas the intra-type information, though often available, are not used. We incorporate them through Laplacian regularization [2, 7].

For a two-type relational data set, given the intra-type information in form of the pairwise affinity matrices W_1 and W_2 for $\mathcal{X}_1$ and $\mathcal{X}_2$ respectively, we can incorporate them into Eq. (2) as following:

$$J_6 = \|R_{12} - G_1 S_{12} G_2^T\|^2 + 2\lambda \left[\mathbf{tr}\left(G_1^T L_1 G_1\right) + \mathbf{tr}\left(G_2^T L_2 G_2\right)\right], \quad s.t.\quad G_1 \ge 0,\ G_2 \ge 0, \tag{9}$$

where D_k is the diagonal degree matrix with $D_{k(ii)} = \sum_j W_{k(ij)}$, and $L_k = D_k - W_k$ is the corresponding graph Laplacian. Because L_k is the discrete approximation of the Laplace-Beltrami operator on the underlying data manifold [1], the last two terms reflects the label smoothness of the two types of data points. The smoother the data labels are with respect to the underlying data manifolds, the smaller their values will be.

Using R, S and G defined in Eq. (8), and denote

$$W = \begin{bmatrix} W_1^{n_1\times n_1} & 0^{n_1\times n_2} & \cdots & 0^{n_1\times n_K} \\ 0^{n_2\times n_1} & W_2^{n_2\times n_2} & \cdots & 0^{n_2\times n_K} \\ \vdots & \vdots & \ddots & \vdots \\ 0^{n_K\times n_1} & 0^{n_K\times n_2} & \cdots & W_K^{n_K\times n_K} \end{bmatrix}, \tag{10}$$

we approach simultaneous clustering on multi-type relational data by solving the following optimization problem:

$$\min\ J_{\text{S-NMTF}} = \|R - GSG^T\|^2 + 2\lambda\, \mathbf{tr}\left[G^T (D - W) G\right], \quad s.t.\quad G \ge 0, \tag{11}$$

where D is the diagonal degree matrix with $D_{(ii)} = \sum_j W_{(ij)}$. We call Eq. (11) as our proposed S-NMTF approach. As can be seen, the complicated problem of simultaneous clustering of multi-type relational data is finally modeled by a very simple mathematical formulation, which is the first contribution of this work.

3. ALGORITHM FOR S-NMTF

The computational algorithm for the proposed S-NMTF approach is listed in Algorithm 1. Upon solution, the final cluster labels are obtained from the resulted G_k using Eq. (3).

The main challenge to derive Algorithm 1 is the fourth-order matrix polynomial incurred by the symmetric usage of G in Eq. (11). Existing works [4, 6, 12] tackle this difficulty in an intuitive way: solve the problem as a standard NMF problem with two different factor matrices and set them as same in the solution. In this work, as a theoretical contribution, we present a new matrix inequality in Lemma 4 to tackle this difficulty in a principled way.

Algorithm 1: Algorithm to solve S-NMTF in Eq. (11)

Data: Relationship matrices: $\{R_{ij}\}_{1\leq i<j\leq K}$
Unsupervised pairwise affinity matrices: $\{W_k\}_{1\leq k\leq K}$
Result: Factor matrices: $\{G_k\}_{1\leq k\leq K}$
1. Construct R, G, S as in Eq. (8), and W as in Eq. (10).
2. Initialize G as in [6].
repeat
  3. Compute $S=\left(G^TG\right)^{-1}G^TRG\left(G^TG\right)^{-1}$.
  4. Update $G_{ij}\leftarrow G_{ij}\left[\frac{(RGS+\lambda WG)_{ij}}{\left(GSG^TGS+\lambda DG\right)_{ij}}\right]^{\frac{1}{4}}$.
until *Converges*

3.1 Correctness of the Algorithm

The following theorem guarantees the correctness of Algorithm 1.

THEOREM 2. *If the updating rules of G and S in Algorithm 1 converges, the final solution satisfies the KKT optimal condition.*

PROOF. For the objective in Eq. (11), following the standard theory of constrained optimization, we introduce the Lagrangian multipliers 4Λ and minimize the Lagrangian function as follows:

$$L(G,S)=J_{\text{S-NMTF}}+\textbf{tr}\left(4\Lambda G^T\right), \tag{12}$$

which gives

$$\frac{\partial L}{\partial G}=-4RGS+4GSG^TGS-4\lambda WG+4DG+4\Lambda, \tag{13}$$

$$\frac{\partial L}{\partial S}=-2G^TRG+2G^TGSG^TG. \tag{14}$$

Fixing G, letting $\partial L/\partial S=0$, from Eq. (14) we obtain

$$S=\left(G^TG\right)^{-1}G^TRG\left(G^TG\right)^{-1}. \tag{15}$$

The KKT complementary condition for the nonnegativity of G_{ij} gives $G_{ij}\Lambda_{ij}=0$. Setting $\partial L/\partial G=0$, from Eq. (13) we have:

$$\left(-4RGS+4GSG^TGS-4\lambda WG+4DG\right)_{ij}G_{ij}=0\ . \tag{16}$$

This is the fixed point relationships that the solution must satisfy. At convergence, $G^{(\infty)}=G^{(t+1)}=G^{(t)}$, thus we can derive

$$\left(-4RGS+4GSG^TGS-4\lambda WG+4DG\right)_{ij}G_{ij}^4=0,$$

which is identical to Eq. (16) and proves Theorem 2. □

3.2 Convergence of the Algorithm

Now, we analyze the convergence of Algorithm 1 using the auxiliary function approach [9].

LEMMA 2. *[9] $Z(h,h')$ is an auxiliary function of $F(h)$ if the conditions $Z(h,h')\geq F(h)$ and $Z(h,h')=F(h)$ are satisfied. [9] If Z is an auxiliary function for F, then F is non-increasing under the update $h^{(t+1)}=\arg\min_h Z(h,h')$.*

LEMMA 3. *[6] For any matrices $A\in\Re_+^{n\times n}$, $B\in\Re_+^{k\times k}$, $S\in\Re_+^{n\times k}$ and $S'\in\Re_+^{n\times k}$, and A and B are symmetric, the following inequality holds:*

$$\sum_{ip}\frac{(AS'B)_{ip}S_{ip}^2}{S'_{ip}}\geq\textbf{tr}\left(S^TASB\right). \tag{17}$$

As one of our contribution, we prove the following generic matrix inequality to analyze objective functions involving 4-th order matrix polynomials, such as that our S-NMTF objective in Eq. (11).

LEMMA 4. *For any nonnegative symmetric matrices $A\in\Re_+^{k\times k}$ and $B\in\Re_+^{k\times k}$, for $H\in\Re_+^{n\times k}$ the following inequality holds:*

$$\textbf{tr}\left(HAH^THBH^T\right)\leq\sum_{ik}\left(\frac{H'AH'^TH'B+H'BH'^TH'A}{2}\right)_{ik}\frac{H_{ik}^4}{H_{ik}'^3}. \tag{18}$$

PROOF. Let $H_{ik}=H'_{ik}u_{ik}$. The 1st term in RHS of Eq. (18) is

$$\sum_{ik}(H'AH'^TH'B)_{ik}\frac{H_{ik}^4}{H_{ik}'^3}=\sum_{ijkrpq}H'_{jr}A_{rk}H'_{ik}H'_{ip}B_{pq}H'_{jq}u_{jq}^4$$

Now, switching indexes: $i\Leftrightarrow j, p\Leftrightarrow q, r\Leftrightarrow k$, we obtain

$$\sum_{ik}(H'AH'^TH'B)_{ik}\frac{H_{ik}^4}{H_{ik}'^3}=\sum_{ijkrpq}H'_{ik}A_{kr}H'_{jr}H'_{jq}B_{qp}H'_{ip}u_{ip}^4$$

The 2nd term in RHS of Eq. (18) is

$$\sum_{ik}(H'BH'^TH'A)_{ik}\frac{H_{ik}^4}{H_{ik}'^3}=\sum_{ijkrpq}H'_{ip}B_{pq}H'_{jq}H'_{jr}A_{rk}H'_{ik}u_{ik}^4\ .$$

Now, switching indexes: $i\Leftrightarrow j, p\Leftrightarrow q, r\Leftrightarrow k$, we obtain

$$\sum_{ik}(H'BH'^TH'A)_{ik}\frac{H_{ik}^4}{H_{ik}'^3}=\sum_{ijkrpq}H'_{jq}B_{qp}H'_{ip}H'_{ik}A_{kr}H'_{jr}u_{jr}^4$$

A careful examination of the RHS of the above four equations shows that they are identical except u^4 terms. Thus, the RHS of Eq. (18) is

$$\sum_{ijkrpq}H'_{ip}B_{pq}H'_{jq}H'_{jr}A_{rk}H'_{ik}\frac{u_{ik}^4+u_{jr}^4+u_{jq}^4+u_{ip}^4}{4}. \tag{19}$$

The LHS of Eq. (18) is $\sum_{ijkrpq}H'_{ip}B_{pq}H'_{jq}H'_{jr}A_{rk}H'_{ik}u_{ik}u_{jr}u_{jq}u_{ip}$. For any $a,b,c,d>0$, we have $a^4+b^4+c^4+d^4\geq 2(a^2b^2+c^2d^2)\geq 4(ab)(cd)$, thus $u_{ik}u_{jr}u_{jq}u_{ip}\leq\left(u_{ik}^4+u_{jr}^4+u_{jq}^4+u_{ip}^4\right)/4$, which proves Lemma 4. □

Based upon the above lemmas, we prove the following theorem.

THEOREM 3. *Let*

$$J_{\text{S-NMTF}}(G)=\textbf{tr}\left(-2RGSG^T+GSG^TGSG^T+2\Lambda G^TDG-2\lambda G^TWG\right), \tag{20}$$

then the following function

$$Z(G,G')=-2\sum_{ijkl}G'_{ji}S_{jk}G'_{kl}R_{li}\left(1+\log\frac{G_{ji}G_{kl}}{G'_{ij}G'_{kl}}\right)+\sum_{ij}\left(G'SG'^TG'S\right)_{ij}\frac{G_{ij}^4}{G_{ij}'^3}+\sum_{ij}(DG'\Lambda)_{ij}\frac{G_{ij}^4+G_{ij}'^4}{G_{ij}'^3}-2\lambda\sum_{ijk}G'_{ji}W_{jk}G'_{ki}\left(1+\log\frac{G_{ji}G_{ki}}{G'_{ji}G'_{ki}}\right)$$

is an auxiliary function of $J_{\text{S-NMTF}}(G)$. Furthermore, it is a convex function in G and its global minimum is

$$G_{ik}=G_{ik}\left[\frac{(RGS+\lambda WG)_{ik}}{(GSG^TGS+DG\Lambda)_{ik}}\right]^{\frac{1}{4}}. \tag{21}$$

PROOF. By applying Lemma 4, we have

$$\mathbf{tr}\left(GSG^TGSG^T\right) \le \sum_{ij}\left(G'SG'^TG'S\right)_{ij}\frac{G_{ij}^4}{G_{ij}'^3}.$$

Because of Lemma 3 and the inequality of $2ab < a^2 + b^2$, we have

$$\mathbf{tr}\left(\Lambda G^TDG\right) \le \sum_{ij}\left(DG'\Lambda\right)_{ij}\frac{G_{ij}^2}{G_{ij}'} \le \sum_{ij}\left(DG'\Lambda\right)_{ij}\frac{G_{ij}^4 + G_{ij}'^4}{G_{ij}'^3}.$$

Because $z \le 1 + \log z, \forall\, z > 0$, we have

$$\mathbf{tr}\left(RGSG^T\right) \ge \sum_{ijkl}G'_{ji}S_{jk}G'_{kl}R_{li}\left(1 + \log\frac{G_{ji}G_{kl}}{G'_{ij}G'_{kl}}\right).$$

$$\mathbf{tr}\left(G^TWG\right) \ge \sum_{ijk}G'_{ji}W_{jk}G'_{ki}\left(1 + \log\frac{G_{ji}G_{ki}}{G'_{ji}G'_{ki}}\right).$$

Summing over all these bounds, we get $Z(G, G')$, which clearly satisfies (1) $Z(G, G') \ge J_{\text{S-NMTF}}(G)$ and (2) $Z(G, G) = J_{\text{S-NMTF}}(G)$. Therefore, $Z(G, G')$ is an auxiliary function of $J_{\text{S-NMTF}}(G)$.

Following the same derivations as in [5–7, 12, 13], it can be verified that the Hessian matrix of $Z(G, G')$ is a positive definite diagonal matrix (we skip the derivations due to space limit). Thus $Z(G, G')$ is a convex function of G. We can obtain the global minimum of $Z(G, G')$ by setting $\partial Z(G, G')/\partial G_{ij} = 0$ and solving for G, from which we can get Eq. (21). This completes the proof of Theorem 3. □

THEOREM 4. *Updating G using the rule in Algorithm 1 monotonically decreases $J_{\text{S-NMTF}}(G)$ in Eq.* (20).

PROOF. According to Lemma 2 and Theorem 3, we can get that $J_{\text{S-NMTF}}(G^0) = Z(G^0, G^0) \ge Z(G^1, G^0) \ge J_{\text{S-NMTF}}(G^1) \ldots$. Thus $J_{\text{S-NMTF}}(G)$ is monotonically decreasing. □

Because of Eqs. (14–15), in each iteration step of Algorithm 1 $S^{(t+1)} = \arg\min_{S^{(t)}} J_{\text{S-NMTF}}\left(S^{(t)}, G^{(t)}\right)$, which, together with Theorem 3 and 4, guarantees the convergence of Algorithm 1, because $J(G)$ in Eq. (11) is obviously lower bounded by 0.

4. EMPIRICAL STUDIES

In this section, we experimentally evaluate the proposed S-NMTF approach. Our new method has only one parameter λ in Eq. (11). Empirically, we set it as $\lambda = 0.01$.

4.1 Co-Clustering of Two-Type Relational Data

We first evaluate the proposed method on two-type relational data, the simplest multi-type relational data. We use the following three data sets: Newsgroup4 data set, WebKB4 data set, WebACE data set, whose details can be found in [7].

4.1.1 *Experimental Settings*

For co-clustering of two-type relational data, we need two inputs from a data set: the relationship matrix between the two types of data, and the pairwise affinity matrices for each type of data. We obtain the relationship matrices directly from the testing data sets. We construct neighborhood graphs from the both sides of the relationship matrix following [7] to obtain the pairwise affinity matrices for the both types of the entities, where, following [7], the neighborhood size is set as 10.

We compare the proposed S-NMTF approach against two related clustering methods that combine NMF and Laplacian regularization: graph regularized NMF (GNMF) [2] method and dual regularized co-clustering (DRCC) [7] method. These two methods are largely same, except that the former uses two-factor factorization and imposes Laplacian regularization on one side factor, while the latter uses the three-factor factorization and imposes Laplacian regularizations on the both side factors. Following [7], two graphs are built on both feature side and data point side for DRCC method, and its parameters are set as $\lambda = \mu$ which is same as in [7].

Table 1: Clustering accuracy in co-clustering tasks.

Methods	Newsgroup4	WebKB4	WebACE
GNMF	0.889	0.731	0.513
DRCC	0.931	0.738	0.568
PMF	0.923	0.727	0.566
CKMeans	0.643	0.594	0.477
S-NMTF	**0.937**	**0.783**	**0.613**

Table 2: Normalized mutual information in co-clustering tasks.

Methods	Newsgroup4	WebKB4	WebACE
GNMF	0.716	0.462	0.618
DRCC	0.782	0.491	0.629
PMF	0.758	0.488	0.602
CKMeans	0.612	0.375	0.491
S-NMTF	**0.795**	**0.554**	**0.643**

In addition, we also compare our approach against the following two methods: penalized matrix factorization (PMF) [12] method and constrained K-means (CKmeans) [11] method.

To evaluate the clustering results, we adopt two standard measures widely used for clustering [2]: clustering accuracy and normalized mutual information (NMI).

4.1.2 *Experimental Results*

The clustering performance measured by clustering accuracy and normalized mutual information of the compared methods on the three data sets are listed in Table 1 and Table 2. The results show that the proposed S-NMTF approach consistently outperforms the other methods, sometimes very significantly, which demonstrate the effectiveness of the proposed S-NMTF approach in co-clustering of two-type relational data.

4.2 Simultaneous Clustering of Multi-Type Relational Web Data

Finally we evaluate the proposed S-NMTF approach for simultaneous clustering on multi-type relational data by using both inter-type relationships and intra-type information, which is the ultimate goal of this work.

4.2.1 *Data Set*

For the data set and experimental settings in this subsection, we largely follow those in [12] (We acknowledge the author of [12] for sharing the data).

We use a data set sampled from the Bulletin Board Systems (BBS) in [8]. In a BBS system, the users first register IDs. Using their IDs, the users can read others' published messages and leave their own messages. The whole system consists of many discussion fields, each of which contains many boards with similar themes. The boards are named to reflect the contents of the articles in them [8]. Once an ID posts a new article (initial article) on one board, the others can show their opinions by replying the initial article using reply articles. The initial article and reply articles

Table 3: A subset of data sampled from a BBS data set [8].

Field name	Board name
Computer Science	C++ Builder
Computer Science	Delphi
Computer Science	Database
Sports	Basketball
Sports	Volleyball
Sports	Badminton

Table 4: The F1 measure of the four compared algorithms.

	MLSA	SRC	PMF	S-NMTF
$d = 3$	0.712	0.731	0.795	**0.832**
$d = 5$	0.756	0.634	0.815	**0.839**
$d = 7$	0.711	0.621	0.780	**0.811**
$d = 9$	0.699	0.482	0.734	**0.759**

constitute a topic. Each board contains many topics. Each topic connects with several IDs through articles.

We use a subset of the BBS data in [8], in which several boards are sampled from several discussion fields. In each board, 80 topics are sampled randomly. The names of the fields and boards that we use are listed in Table 3. The user IDs related to these topics and boards are found out. Then the tensor is constructed by the co-occurrence of these three data types.

4.2.2 Experimental Settings

In the experiments, there exist three data types: topics ($\mathcal{X}_1$), user IDs ($\mathcal{X}_2$) and boards ($\mathcal{X}_3$). The topic-user matrix (R_{12}) is constructed with the number of articles each user posted in each topics with TF-IDF normalization. The topic-board matrix (R_{13}) is constructed such that if a topic belongs to a board, then the corresponding entry of R_{13} is 1. R_{23} is constructed such that if the user had posted any articles on that board, then the corresponding element of R_{23} is set to 1. Finally the elements of R_{23} are also normalized using TF-IDF scheme.

We only use the pairwise affinity matrices W_1 and W_2 for $\mathcal{X}_1$ and $\mathcal{X}_2$, which are constructed using R_{12} in a same way as in Section 4.1. We set $W_3 = I$ to simulate the case in real applications when the intra-type information for $\mathcal{X}_3$ is not available.

Besides our approach, the results of applying the Spectral Relational Clustering (SRC) [10] method and Multiple Latent Semantic Analysis (MLSA) [15] method, and PMF method are also included for comparison. All these three methods are for simultaneous clustering on multi-type relational data.

The evaluation metric is the F1 score computed using the clustering results on topics, the ground truth of which is set to be the classes corresponding to the field names they belong to.

4.2.3 Experimental Results

The experimental results are shown in Table 4, in which the value of d represent different number of clusters. From the table we can clearly see the superiority of the proposed S-NMTF approach. Besides, we also see that PMF method is always better than the other two methods. By examining the implementation details, we can see that these results are consistent with the information used by these methods: MLSA and SRC methods only use the inter-type relationships, while our S-NMTF approach additionally utilizes the intra-type information.

5. CONCLUSIONS

In this paper, we presented a general Symmetric Nonnegative Matrix Tri-Factorization (S-NMTF) framework to simultaneously cluster multi-type relational data. Our approach clusters different types of data at the same time using inter-type relationships by transforming the original problem into a symmetric NMF problem, into which we can optionally incorporate the intra-type information. In order to deal with the symmetric usage of the factor matrix in S-NMTF, we presented a new generic matrix inequality to derive the solution algorithm, which involves a fourth-order matrix polynomial, in a principled way. Extensive empirical studies in evaluating various aspects of our approach have demonstrated encouraging results, which validate the usefulness of the proposed S-NMTF approach.

Acknowledgment.

This research was supported by NSF-IIS 1117965, NSFCCF-0830780, NSF-DMS-0915228, NSF-CCF-0917274.

6. REFERENCES

[1] M. Belkin, P. Niyogi, and V. Sindhwani. On manifold regularization. In *AISTAT*, 2005.

[2] D. Cai, X. He, J. Han, and T. S. Huang. Graph regularized non-negative matrix factorization for data representation. *IEEE TPAMI*, 99, 2010.

[3] I. Dhillon. Co-clustering documents and words using bipartite spectral graph partitioning. In *SIGKDD*, 2001.

[4] C. Ding, X. He, and H. Simon. On the equivalence of nonnegative matrix factorization and spectral clustering. In *SDM*, 2005.

[5] C. Ding, T. Li, and M. Jordan. Convex and semi-nonnegative matrix factorizations. *IEEE TPAMI*, 32(1):45–55, 2010.

[6] C. Ding, T. Li, W. Peng, and H. Park. Orthogonal nonnegative matrix t-factorizations for clustering. In *SIGKDD*, 2006.

[7] Q. Gu and J. Zhou. Co-clustering on manifolds. In *SIGKDD*, 2009.

[8] Z. Kou and C. Zhang. Reply networks on a bulletin board system. *Physical Review E*, 67(3):36117, 2003.

[9] D. Lee and H. Seung. Algorithms for non-negative matrix factorization. In *NIPS*, 2001.

[10] B. Long, Z. Zhang, X. Wu, and Y. P. Spectral clustering for multi-type relational data. In *ICML*, 2006.

[11] K. Wagstaff, C. Cardie, S. Rogers, and S. Schrödl. Constrained k-means clustering with background knowledge. In *ICML*, 2001.

[12] F. Wang, T. Li, and C. Zhang. Semi-supervised clustering via matrix factorization. In *SDM*, 2008.

[13] H. Wang, H. Huang, F. Nie, and C. Ding. Cross-language web page classification via dual knowledge transfer using nonnegative matrix tri-factorization. In *SIGIR*, 2011.

[14] H. Wang, F. Nie, H. Huang, and C. Ding. Dyadic transfer learning for cross-domain image classification. In *ICCV*, 2011.

[15] X. Wang, J. Sun, Z. Chen, and C. Zhai. Latent semantic analysis for multiple-type interrelated data objects. In *SIGIR*, 2006.

[16] H. Zha, X. He, C. Ding, H. Simon, and M. Gu. Bipartite graph partitioning and data clustering. In *CIKM*, 2001.

Collaborative Online Learning of User Generated Content

Guangxia Li Kuiyu Chang Steven C.H. Hoi Wenting Liu
School of Computer Engineering
Nanyang Technological University
Singapore 639798
{ligu0005,askychang,chhoi,wliu7}@ntu.edu.sg

Ramesh Jain
School of Information and
Computer Sciences
University of California
Irvine, CA 92697
jain@ics.uci.edu

ABSTRACT

We study the problem of online classification of user generated content, with the goal of efficiently learning to categorize content generated by individual user. This problem is challenging due to several reasons. First, the huge amount of user generated content demands a highly efficient and scalable classification solution. Second, the categories are typically highly imbalanced, i.e., the number of samples from a particular useful class could be far and few between compared to some others (majority class). In some applications like spam detection, identification of the minority class often has significantly greater value than that of the majority class. Last but not least, when learning a classification model from a group of users, there is a dilemma: A single classification model trained on the entire corpus may fail to capture personalized characteristics such as language and writing styles unique to each user. On the other hand, a personalized model dedicated to each user may be inaccurate due to the scarcity of training data, especially at the very beginning; when users have written just a few articles. To overcome these challenges, we propose learning a global model over all users' data, which is then leveraged to continuously refine the individual models through a collaborative online learning approach. The class imbalance problem is addressed via a cost-sensitive learning approach. Experimental results show that our method is effective and scalable for timely classification of user generated content.

Categories and Subject Descriptors

H.3.3 [**Information Search and Retrieval**]: Information Filtering; I.2 [**Artificial Intelligence**]: Machine Learning

General Terms

Experimentation

Keywords

online learning, classification, imbalanced class distribution

CIKM'11, October 24–28, 2011, Glasgow, Scotland, UK.

1. INTRODUCTION

The popularity of Web 2.0, along with the increasing use of blogs, wikis, and social networks has catalyzed the quantity and frequency of user generated content (UGC, also known as consumer generated media) for public consumption. With the proliferation of UGC comes the demand for discovering useful information from it. Consider Facebook, one of the world's largest online social networks, as an example. Facebook users generate 60 million status updates per day as of February 2010[1]. Status updates are short postings, and can be analyzed by a computer to reveal personal characteristics such as emotional state (happy or sad), sentiments towards things or issues, etc.

A machine learning model can be trained to classify UGC. However, applied to a group of users, classical approaches always face a dilemma: A single global classification model trained on a collection of users' data may fail to capture the peculiarity of different users and thus works poorly. On the other hand, a personalized model for each user may be inaccurate due to the scarcity of training data. As an example, consider the problem of personalized music recommendation. The recommendation should rely on the user's own data, e.g., user profile, history of music enjoyed in the past, etc. Yet it is also reasonable to take other similar users' preferences into consideration. The issue of how group characteristics and individual traits can be combined to achieve a result that is greater than the sum of its parts warrants further study.

In this paper, we present a highly efficient and scalable online classification method that is designed to classify UGC generated by a group of users by combining group and individual characteristics. We opt for the online learning framework, which incrementally learns a classification model from a stream of samples, for its high efficiency and scalability. The basic idea of the proposed collaborative online learning is to first build a generic *global* model from large amounts of UGC of various users, and then subsequently leveraging the global model to build the *personalized* online classification model for individual user in a *collaborative* learning manner. Moreover, UGC are typically highly imbalanced in class distribution. We use a cost penalty in the objective function to address this problem. We evaluate the performance of our algorithm on two real-life problems — spam email filtering and micro-blog sentiment classification. We show that learning multiple related tasks collaboratively outperforms learning each task independently by comparing our algorithm with state-of-the-art online learners. We also match

[1]http://blog.facebook.com/blog.php?post=466369142130

our algorithm against batch learning methods that are updated periodically, to show that ours are not only orders of magnitude faster, but also equally effective for the UGC classification task.

The rest of this paper is organized as follows. Section 2 introduces related work. Section 3 presents the proposed algorithm. Section 4 gives experimental results and discussions. Section 5 concludes this paper.

2. RELATED WORK

Unlike typical machine learning methods, which assume all training examples are available before the learning task begins, online learning is more appropriate for some real-world problems where training data arrives sequentially. It has been extensively studied in the machine learning community [14, 12, 13, 9, 8]. Moreover, the vast majority of existing work in online learning only studies the prediction mistake rates or accuracies, without regard to class distributions or actual classification accuracies. Notably, methods that perform seemingly well on balanced datasets may not perform well on real-world imbalanced datasets [1, 7]. As a result, such performance evaluations are not always appropriate for real world applications, where datasets are often imbalanced. To address class-imbalance problem, a multi-class cost-sensitive extension to the original online passive aggressive algorithm has been proposed by Crammer et al. [8], along with theoretical loss bounds. Our work extends Crammer's approach by adding the collaborative learning element.

Our work is also related to learning multiple related tasks in parallel. Multi-task learning solves multiple related learning problems simultaneously instead of independently. Empirical evidence shows that multi-task learning can improve classifier's performance [3, 4, 5]. Ando et al. [2] considered learning predictive structures on hypothesis spaces from multiple learning tasks. Evgeniou et al. [10] extended the single-task kernel learning methods to multi-task learning by defining a family of multi-task kernel functions. Instead of defining specific kernel functions, we use a generic model shared by many parallel learners to leverage the information embedded in individual tasks. Our approach not only enjoys an improvement on classification performance, but also retains the hallmark low computational cost of online learning algorithms.

3. METHODOLOGY

Figure 1 illustrates the idea of collaborative online learning. Our method operates in a sequential manner. At each learning round, it collects the current global set of data; one from each of the engaged users, which are employed to update the global classification model. At the same time, a collaborative personalized model is maintained for each user. The individual collaborative classification model is subsequently updated using the latest individual data and the global model's parameters.

For simplicity, we assume that the training data from all users can be represented in a global feature space and the sequence of training data is ordered chronologically. Denote by $(\mathbf{x}_t, y_t)$ a training instance at round t, where $\mathbf{x}_t \in \mathbb{R}^d$ is a d-dimensional vector representing the example and $y_t \in \{1, \ldots, m\}, m \geq 3$ refers to its class label. Further, denote by $\mathcal{D}_i = \{(\mathbf{x}_t, y_t) : t = 1, \ldots, T_i\}$ a collection of training

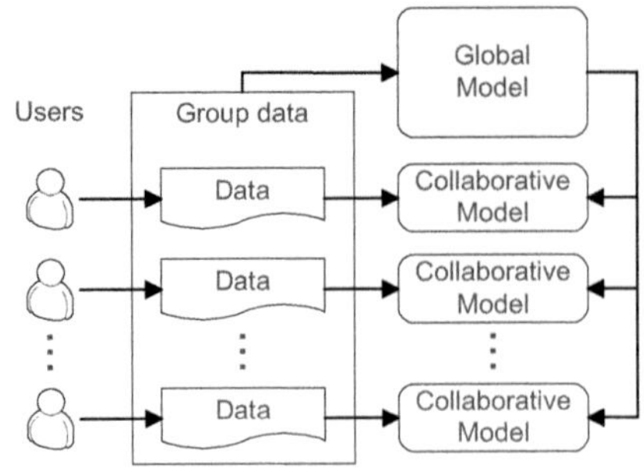

Figure 1: Collaborative online learning.

data for the i-th user, and $\mathcal{D} = \{(\mathbf{x}_t, y_t) : t = 1, \ldots, T\}$ the whole collection of training data from a group of K users, where $T = \sum_i T_i$ denotes the total number of data over all users. The goal is to learn a set of K classification models, i.e., $f^{(i)}(\cdot) : \mathbb{R}^d \mapsto \mathbb{R}^m, i = 1, \ldots, K$, where each element in the m-dimensional output vector corresponds to a score assigned to the respective class label. The output of the algorithm is simply set to the label with the highest score.

We adopt the online passive aggressive (PA) framework [8] to build a global classification model using data collected from *all* users at round t, that is

$$f_t(\bar{\mathbf{x}}) = \mathbf{u}_t \cdot \bar{\mathbf{x}}$$

where $\mathbf{u}_t \in \mathbb{R}^{dm}$ is the weight vector of the updated model learned at round t, and $\bar{\mathbf{x}} \in \mathbb{R}^{dm}$ is formed by concatenating m replications of $\mathbf{x} \in \mathbb{R}^d$ together.

At round t, the algorithm uses the latest training instance $(\mathbf{x}_t, y_t)$ to update the classification model as follows

$$\mathbf{u}_{t+1} = \underset{\mathbf{u} \in \mathbb{R}^{dm}}{\text{argmin}} \quad \frac{1}{2}\|\mathbf{u} - \mathbf{u}_t\|^2 + C\xi \tag{1a}$$

$$\text{s.t.} \quad \ell(\mathbf{u}; (\mathbf{x}_t, y_t)) \leq \xi \tag{1b}$$

$$\xi \geq 0 \tag{1c}$$

where C is a positive parameter that controls the influence of the slack term ξ on the objective function, and ℓ is a loss function defined as follows

$$\ell(\mathbf{u}; (\mathbf{x}_t, y_t)) = \max(0, 1 - \mathbf{u}^{\mathrm{T}}\mathbf{I}_r\mathbf{x}_t + \mathbf{u}^{\mathrm{T}}\mathbf{I}_s\mathbf{x}_t) \tag{2}$$

where the superscript T denotes the transpose of a matrix. $\mathbf{I}_r$ and $\mathbf{I}_s$ are $dm \times d$ matrices whose r-th and s-th blocks are identity matrices with other elements zero, respectively. Subscripts r and s are chosen from {1,…,m}. Specifically, r is the index of relevant label y_t, and s is the index of the highest ranked irrelevant class, given by

$$s = \text{argmax}_{s \notin y_t} \mathbf{u}^{\mathrm{T}}\mathbf{I}_s\mathbf{x}_t \tag{3}$$

As an example, consider a three-class classification problem and training instance $\mathbf{x}_t$ with label $y_t = 1$. Here, $r = 1$, and s is chosen from $\{2, 3\}$ by applying equation (3). The loss function (2) defines the margin as the score difference between the relevant label and the highest ranked irrelevant label (see [8] for details). For binary class classification problems, one can replace (2) with the hinge loss function.

The solution to the optimization problem (1) is

$$\mathbf{u}_{t+1} = \mathbf{u}_t + \tau(\mathbf{I}_r - \mathbf{I}_s)\mathbf{x}_t \tag{4}$$

where τ is given by $\tau = \min\{C, \frac{\ell}{2\|\mathbf{x}_t\|^2}\}$.

A critical step of our algorithm is to apply the existing global model to collaboratively learn the individual model for each of the K users. Using the same PA formulation, the goal is to learn a classification model for the i-th user as

$$f_t^{(i)}(\bar{\mathbf{x}}) = \mathbf{w}_t^{(i)} \cdot \bar{\mathbf{x}}$$

where $\mathbf{w}_t^{(i)} \in \mathbb{R}^{dm}$ is the weight vector of the i-th user's model learned at round t. To ease the discussion, we shall use $\mathbf{w}_t$ to denote $\mathbf{w}_t^{(i)}$ henceforth.

We formulate learning the collaborative model as a convex optimization problem that minimizes the deviation of the new weight from the prior collaborative weight and the global weight, as follows

$$\mathbf{w}_{t+1} = \underset{\mathbf{w}\in\mathbb{R}^{dm}}{\operatorname{argmin}} \frac{\eta_1}{2}\|\mathbf{w}-\mathbf{w}_t\|^2 + \frac{\eta_2}{2}\|\mathbf{w}-\mathbf{u}_t\|^2 + C\xi \quad (5a)$$

$$\text{s.t.} \quad \ell(\mathbf{w};(\mathbf{x}_t, y_t)) \le \xi \quad (5b)$$

$$\xi \ge 0 \quad (5c)$$

where η_1 and η_2 are regularization parameters that balance the tradeoff between the global model $\mathbf{u}_t$ and the collaborative model $\mathbf{w}_t$, and parameter $C \ge 0$ controls the influence of the slack variable ξ on the objective function.

The above formulation aims to achieve a balance between the global and individual models, i.e., in spite of its uniqueness, each individual also shares some commonness with other members in the group. It coherently combines the collaborative model with the global one. In particular, if we set $\eta_2 = 0$, the optimization reduces to the approach of learning an individual classification model without engaging the global model; if we set $\eta_1 = 0$, it reduces to the global model. Accordingly, we can fine tune the contribution of each model by setting appropriate parameters.

Applying the Lagrangian multiplier technique, the update rule for optimization problem (5) can be derived as

$$\mathbf{w}_{t+1} = \frac{\eta_1 \mathbf{w}_t + \eta_2 \mathbf{u}_t + \tau(\mathbf{I}_r - \mathbf{I}_s)\mathbf{x}_t}{\eta_1 + \eta_2} \quad (6)$$

where τ is given by

$$\tau = \min\left\{C, \frac{\eta_1 + \eta_2 - (\eta_1 \mathbf{w}_t^{\mathrm{T}} + \eta_2 \mathbf{u}_t^{\mathrm{T}})(\mathbf{I}_r - \mathbf{I}_s)\mathbf{x}_t}{2\|\mathbf{x}_t\|^2}\right\}$$

To alleviate the class imbalance problem, we define a new loss function that assigns a penalty for rare class higher than that for majority class, as follows

$$\ell^*(\mathbf{u};(\mathbf{x}_t, y_t);\rho_i) = \max(0, \rho_i - \mathbf{u}^{\mathrm{T}}\mathbf{I}_r\mathbf{x}_t + \mathbf{u}^{\mathrm{T}}\mathbf{I}_s\mathbf{x}_t)$$

where $\rho_i \ge 1, i = 1 \ldots m$ are biased penalties setting in inverse ratio to the amount of the i-th class.

By replacing the loss function in (5) with this, we obtain the cost-sensitive collaborative online learning optimization problem. The update rule has the same form as equation (6), and τ is given by

$$\tau = \min\left\{C, \frac{\rho_i(\eta_1 + \eta_2) - (\eta_1 \mathbf{w}_t^{\mathrm{T}} + \eta_2 \mathbf{u}_t^{\mathrm{T}})(\mathbf{I}_r - \mathbf{I}_s)\mathbf{x}_t}{2\|\mathbf{x}_t\|^2}\right\}$$

Finally, Algorithm 1 summarizes our approach. It is clear that the algorithm has linear time complexity with respect to the number of instances and dimensions, which is not different from typical online learners. In terms of space complexity, for a group of K users, in addition to a set of K collaborative models, it only needs to keep an extra global model. Therefore, our algorithm is both efficient and scalable for large-scale online learning task.

Algorithm 1: Cost-sensitive collaborative online learning

Input: training data of K users $(\mathbf{x}^k, y^k)$, $k = 1, \ldots, K$, parameters $\eta_1 \ge 0$, $\eta_2 \ge 0$, $C \ge 0$, $\rho_i \ge 1$
Initialize $\mathbf{w}_0^k \leftarrow \mathbf{0}$, $\mathbf{u}_0 \leftarrow \mathbf{0}$;
for $t \leftarrow 1$ **to** T **do**
  `// Update the collaborative models`
  for $k \leftarrow 1$ **to** K **do**
    receive weight vector of the global model $\mathbf{u}_t$;
    receive training instance $(\mathbf{x}_t^k, y_t^k)$;
    set $r \in y_t^k$ and $s = \operatorname{argmax}_{s \notin y_t^k} \mathbf{w}^{\mathrm{T}}\mathbf{I}_s\mathbf{x}_t^k$;
    set ρ_i according to y_t^k;
    set loss $\ell^*(\mathbf{w}^k;(\mathbf{x}_t^k, y_t^k);\rho_i) = \max(0, \rho_i - \mathbf{w}^{\mathrm{T}}\mathbf{I}_r\mathbf{x}_t^k + \mathbf{w}^{\mathrm{T}}\mathbf{I}_s\mathbf{x}_t^k)$;
    if $\ell^*(\mathbf{w}^k;(\mathbf{x}_t^k, y_t^k);\rho_i) = 0$ **then**
      $\tau = 0$
    else
      $\tau = \min\{C, \frac{\rho_i(\eta_1+\eta_2) - (\eta_1\mathbf{w}_t^{\mathrm{T}} + \eta_2\mathbf{u}_t^{\mathrm{T}})(\mathbf{I}_r - \mathbf{I}_s)\mathbf{x}_t^k}{2\|\mathbf{x}_t^k\|^2}\}$
    end
    update $\mathbf{w}_{t+1}^k = \frac{\eta_1\mathbf{w}_t^k + \eta_2\mathbf{u}_t + \tau(\mathbf{I}_r - \mathbf{I}_s)\mathbf{x}_t^k}{\eta_1+\eta_2}$;
  end
  `// Update the global model`
  for $k \leftarrow 1$ **to** K **do**
    receive training instance $(\mathbf{x}_t^k, y_t^k)$;
    set $r \in y_t^k$ and $s = \operatorname{argmax}_{s \notin y_t^k} \mathbf{u}^{\mathrm{T}}\mathbf{I}_s\mathbf{x}_t^k$;
    set loss $\ell(\mathbf{u};(\mathbf{x}_t^k, y_t^k)) = \max(0, 1 - \mathbf{u}^{\mathrm{T}}\mathbf{I}_r\mathbf{x}_t^k + \mathbf{u}^{\mathrm{T}}\mathbf{I}_s\mathbf{x}_t^k)$;
    if $\ell(\mathbf{u};(\mathbf{x}_t^k, y_t^k)) > 0$ **then**
      $\sigma = \min\{C, \frac{1 - \mathbf{u}^{\mathrm{T}}\mathbf{I}_r\mathbf{x}_t^k + \mathbf{u}^{\mathrm{T}}\mathbf{I}_s\mathbf{x}_t^k}{2\|\mathbf{x}_t^k\|^2}\}$;
      update $\mathbf{u}_{t+1} = \mathbf{u}_t + \sigma(\mathbf{I}_r - \mathbf{I}_s)\mathbf{x}_t^k$;
    end
  end
end

---

4. EXPERIMENTAL RESULTS

4.1 Benchmark Setup

We compare our COL algorithm with two batch learning methods (LIBSVM [6] with linear kernel and LIBLINEAR [11]) and two online learning algorithms (ROMMA [13] and PA [8]). Apart from testing various values of the penalty parameter C for the two batch learning methods, all other parameters were set to default values. Batch learning methods were modified to handle online data by periodically retraining them with the most recent 50 samples after every new sample arrives. To further examine the effectiveness of learning multiple related tasks in together, we compare our method with a few variations of the PA algorithm [8] as described below.

- **PA-Global** It learns a single classification model from *all* users' data by applying the PA algorithm. At each learning round, the algorithm receives a training in-

Table 1: **Cumulative error rate and F1-measure (%) on the spam email dataset**

	pu1			pu2			pu3			pua		
	Error	Legit F1	Spam F1	Error	Legit F1	Spam F1	Error	Legit F1	Spam F1	Error	Legit F1	Spam F1
SVM	8.99	92.05	89.66	7.32	95.58	78.69	8.99	92.31	89.20	9.75	89.97	90.52
LINEAR	6.79	93.99	92.19	7.46	95.53	77.25	5.04	95.51	94.26	6.67	93.21	93.44
ROMMA	11.83	89.20	86.85	14.08	90.22	70.89	7.65	93.05	91.46	14.14	85.69	86.04
PA-Global	7.16	93.65	91.81	8.45	94.81	77.27	4.07	96.38	95.36	9.39	90.75	90.64
PA-Personal	5.50	95.13	93.67	10.85	93.30	71.59	3.73	96.69	95.73	8.43	91.59	91.55
PA-Simple	5.60	95.04	93.59	8.73	94.66	75.97	3.83	96.60	95.63	8.87	91.15	91.12
COL	**4.13**	**96.33**	**95.28**	**6.62**	**95.96**	**81.71**	**2.98**	**97.36**	**96.59**	**5.88**	**94.14**	**94.10**

stance from each user, and uses that instance to update its weight vector.

- **PA-Personal** It employs the PA algorithm to train a personal classification model for *each* user only using his/her own data. In other words, every user is associated with a personalized classification model.

- **PA-Simple** It simply switches between the PA-Global and PA-Personal models according to their cumulative error counts in previous rounds. In particular, at each learning round, it always sets the weight vector to that of the best model (PA-Global or PA-Personal), i.e., one with the least cumulative errors to-date. Benchmarking against this method is important as it will show whether the proposed COL algorithm is more effective than a naive combination.

We adopt the *cumulative error rate*, i.e., the ratio of the number of mistakes made by the online learning algorithm over total number of examples received up-to-date as a metric for comparing different algorithms. Despite its extensive usage in online learning studies, the cumulative error rate is not suitable for evaluating performances on class-imbalanced datasets. Because for a highly imbalanced dataset, it is possible to deploy a trivial classifier (i.e., blanket prediction of the majority class) that has low error rates but actually is of little use. We thus report the F1-measure in addition to cumulative error rate. It is typically harder for a classifier to achieve a good F1-measure compared to error rate on an imbalanced dataset. For simplicity, we fix the parameter C to 1 for all PA variations and our algorithm. We also fix η_2 to 1 and only choose η_1 from a small range of values.

4.2 Spam Email Filtering

We apply online collaborative learning to construct effective personalized spam email filters. The task is to classify each new incoming email message into two categories: *legitimate* or *spam*. We use a dataset hosted by the Internet Content Filtering Group[2]. The dataset contains emails collected from the mailboxes of four users (denoted by *pu1*, *pu2*, *pu3*, and *pua*). Strictly speaking, the set of all emails received by a user is not generated per se by that specific user. However, the characteristic of each user's email can be said to match his or her interest, whatever that may be. Each email entry is converted to a word document vector using the TF-IDF (term frequency-inverse document frequency) representation. Table 2 summarizes the characteristics of this dataset.

Since the email dataset has no time stamp, each user's email was shuffled into a random sequence. The cumulative

[2]http://labs-repos.iit.demokritos.gr/skel/i-config/

Table 2: Details of spam email dataset

User ID	# Instance	# Legit	# Spam
pu1	1090	610	480
pu2	710	570	140
pu3	4129	2310	1819
pua	1139	570	569
Total	7068	4060	3008

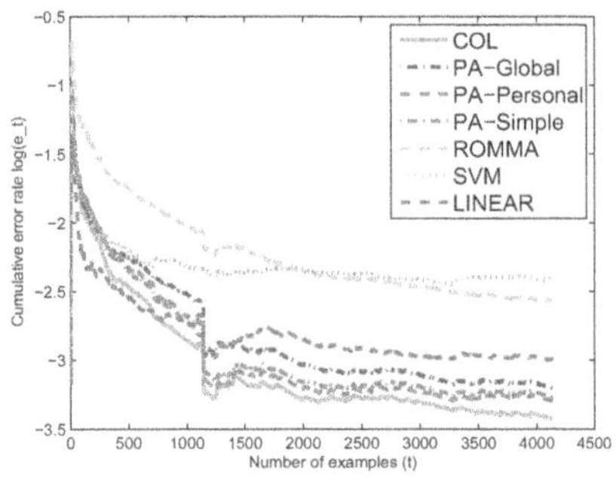

Figure 2: Average cumulative error rate (log scale) of four users on the spam email dataset.

error rate and F1-measure results are listed in Table 1. We exclude CS-COL result from the table since its performance is similar to COL. The cost sensitive approach doesn't help much here because the data is not that imbalanced, with a 4:3 ratio of legit to spam email ratio as seen from Table 2. The average cumulative error rate of the four users is plotted in Figure 2. We also report each algorithm's run-time, i.e., the time consumed by both training and test phase during the complete online learning process in Table 3.

We can see that the proposed COL model consistently beats the other competitors in terms of error rate and F1-measure. It should be noted that compared with online learners who update models based only on the current sample, batch learning methods enjoy the advantage of keeping a substantial amount of recent training samples, at the cost of storage space and higher complexity. In fact, the proposed COL algorithm is more efficient than batch incremental methods, e.g., it is 100 times faster than batch SVM as shown in Table 3. COL does not store recent training samples. It only uses the current training sample and a simple rule to update the model. In contrast, batch learning algorithms need to keep a certain number of recent training samples in memory, leading to extra burden on storage and complexity. What's more, both SVM and LINEAR algorithm need to solve an optimization problem in an iterative way. SVM has to additionally compute the kernel matrix. For practical applications involving hundreds of millions of users and features, the batch learning algorithms are no longer feasible, while online learners are still highly efficient.

Lastly, Table 3 shows that COL is slightly slower than the original PA algorithm. This is expected since COL has to update one global model. However, for a group of users, only one group model is needed. The extra computational cost is trivial compared to the combined cost to update every user model. Therefore, the proposed COL algorithm is efficient and applicable for solving large-scale problems.

Table 3: Run-time (in seconds) for each algorithm

	COL	PA-G	PA-P	ROMMA	SVM	LINEAR
Spam	1.02	0.67	0.70	0.53	109.33	7.84
Twitter	9.76	6.75	7.10	10.24	44.69	9.73

4.3 Micro-blog Sentiment Analysis

With the growing popularity of micro-blogs like *Twitter*[3] comes the demand to understand their users. We present an interesting problem, namely the micro-blog sentiment analysis, which aims to automatically classify each micro-blog post into three categories: *positive emotion*, *negative emotion*, and *non-emotional*. This problem is challenging because a micro-blog post is often very short and each person may have his/her unique way of expressing sentiments. Moreover, the proportion of emotional posts is typically very small, and varies across individuals. Ideally, a personalized classifier should be created for each micro-blogger. However, there is a dearth of training data for each user, making the personalized sentiment model vastly inaccurate unless the model has been trained over hundreds of micro-blogs.

A post on *Twitter* is called a tweet. We crawled 7131 tweets written by six influential users according to *wefollow.com*[4]. The latest tweet in our dataset was published in May, 2010, and the oldest one was in February, 2008. Each tweet was converted to a word vector using the TF-IDF representation. A human annotator was employed to label tweets as one of three categories: positive emotion (class 1), negative emotion (class 2), and non-emotional (class 3). Table 4 summarizes the labeling result. We can see that on average, 20-30% of a user tweets are sentimental (belonging to positive or negative emotion). This result matches our conjecture that emotional tweets are generally a minority for *Twitter* users.

Table 4: Details of *Twitter* sentiment dataset

User Name	# Instance	# Pos	# Neg	% Emotion
JamesKysonLee	1187	152	48	16.85
JimGaffigan	1161	98	280	32.56
1capplegate	1185	134	196	27.85
elizadushku	1420	242	129	26.13
jessetyler	1040	131	168	28.75
peterfacinelli	1138	233	106	29.79
Total / Average	7131	990	927	26.88

The experimental results are reported in Table 5. For fairness, cost-sensitive learning is also applied to SVM and LIBLINEAR via setting a larger penalty parameter C for the minority classes. To make a clear comparison between collaborative online learning and PA algorithm, we show the variation of their cumulative error rates along the entire online learning process in Figure 3. The biased penalty parameters for CS-COL are set to $\rho_1 = 25$, $\rho_2 = 50$, and $\rho_3 = 1$ for class 1, 2, and 3, respectively.

[3]http://twitter.com

[4]http://wefollow.com

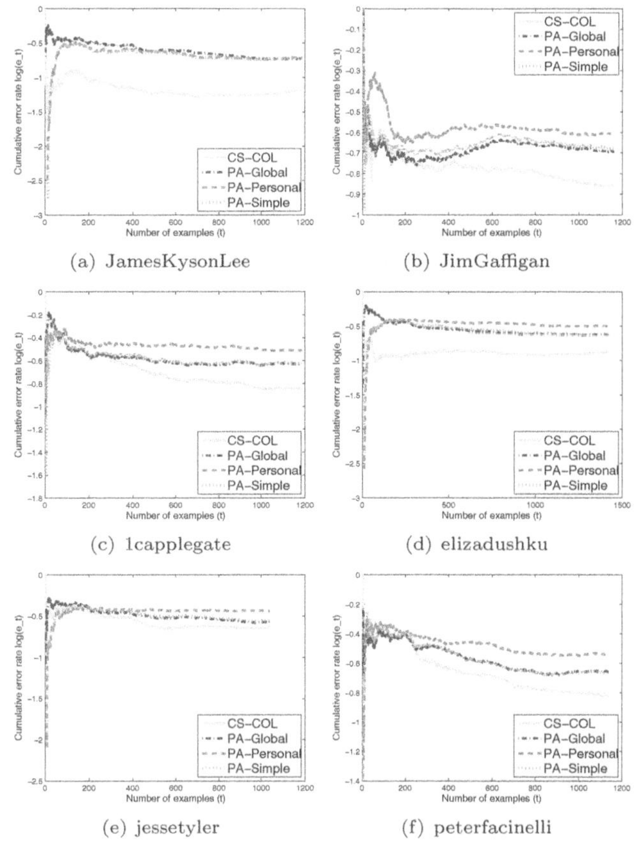

(a) JamesKysonLee (b) JimGaffigan (c) 1capplegate (d) elizadushku (e) jessetyler (f) peterfacinelli

Figure 3: Cumulative error rate (log scale) on the *Twitter* dataset.

It can be seen that two of the models trained with PA — PA-Global and PA-Personal, match each other in strength, but loose to the collaborative models. This result validates our previous concern that simply learning a single global model from all users' data is insufficient for solving the micro-blog sentiment classification task, since each user expresses emotions differently. The simple combination of global model and personal model — PA-Simple is able to approach the best model between PA-Global and PA-Personal, but fails to outperform the best one. This is because the "simple" scheme selects between the global and personal models by comparing their *historical* cumulative error counts. It is possible for a model with few mistakes in the earlier learning rounds to misclassify an incoming sample. Similarly, a model with large historical cumulative errors may score a lucky hit on that sample. This makes sticking to the first model an unwise choice.

Table 5 shows that CS-COL achieves better F1-measure on the minority classes (positive or negative emotion tweet) than the other competitors. It indicates that the proposed CS-COL is effective for online sentiment classification of imbalanced data. On the other hand, by examining the majority class (non-emotional tweet), we find that the F1-measure performance of CS-COL is not better than the other competitors. This is reasonable as the CS-COL was tuned to focus on the minority class, at the slight expense of the majority class. Nonetheless, if we ignore the cost-sensitive concern, we find that the F1-measure performance of the COL method without biased penalty is still better than the other

Table 5: Cumulative error rate and F1-measure (%) on the *Twitter* sentiment dataset

(a) Cumulative error rate (%)

	Jam.	Jim.	1ca.	eli.	jes.	pet.	Avg.
SVM	30.33	61.76	58.57	64.79	64.81	61.07	56.89
LINEAR	28.64	46.25	44.64	40.63	47.12	42.36	41.61
ROMMA	36.23	46.60	48.19	46.27	51.83	47.19	46.05
PA-G	48.44	50.04	53.16	53.73	56.44	51.85	52.28
PA-P	49.12	54.69	60.08	60.63	64.33	58.44	57.88
PA-S	48.44	50.90	53.50	54.01	57.21	51.67	52.62
COL	**22.91**	**34.28**	**31.98**	**31.20**	**35.67**	**31.11**	**31.19**
CS-COL	38.75	44.44	45.49	48.24	49.71	43.94	45.10

(b) Class 1 (positive emotion) F1-measure (%)

	Jam.	Jim.	1ca.	eli.	jes.	pet.	Avg.
SVM	**30.50**	5.53	9.40	25.45	13.81	**35.23**	19.99
LINEAR	28.27	10.65	11.69	24.38	15.52	33.43	20.65
ROMMA	18.25	9.98	11.20	21.32	14.31	26.94	17.00
PA-G	26.30	13.60	17.78	25.82	20.59	29.56	22.27
PA-P	26.89	13.39	11.19	**27.98**	16.48	30.71	21.11
PA-S	25.68	13.85	16.74	27.92	16.67	30.60	21.91
COL	27.27	14.22	17.07	25.30	19.87	31.13	22.48
CS-COL	26.28	**15.96**	**19.19**	24.97	**21.31**	31.13	**23.14**

(c) Class 2 (negative emotion) F1-measure (%)

	Jam.	Jim.	1ca.	eli.	jes.	pet.	Avg.
SVM	0.00	40.20	23.40	5.15	21.81	3.87	15.74
LINEAR	2.86	36.60	20.69	7.38	15.52	9.74	15.46
ROMMA	6.52	31.61	20.36	9.63	14.04	13.53	15.95
PA-G	3.88	30.55	21.58	12.80	15.63	17.90	17.05
PA-P	5.91	34.70	21.07	6.71	14.19	9.98	15.43
PA-S	5.98	27.44	20.08	5.99	12.44	11.85	13.96
COL	4.23	36.22	21.21	11.93	14.71	16.51	17.47
CS-COL	**9.80**	**44.64**	**32.88**	**16.77**	**25.18**	**21.14**	**25.07**

(d) Class 3 (non-emotional) F1-measure (%)

	Jam.	Jim.	1ca.	eli.	jes.	pet.	Avg.
SVM	80.60	33.67	50.14	40.87	39.28	40.85	47.57
LINEAR	82.01	61.94	67.61	71.59	65.25	67.87	69.38
ROMMA	76.35	63.22	63.88	66.05	60.45	63.14	65.52
PA-G	84.84	73.53	76.91	77.57	75.36	77.72	78.09
PA-P	89.15	74.51	78.15	81.31	76.10	79.46	77.53
PA-S	**89.34**	74.69	77.79	**81.85**	75.80	**79.58**	77.99
COL	86.32	**75.61**	**79.07**	79.74	**76.11**	79.32	**79.08**
CS-COL	72.94	60.06	62.54	61.71	58.61	64.69	63.43

competitors for most cases, again verifying the effectiveness of the proposed technique for online micro-blog sentiment classification.

5. CONCLUSION

In this paper, we proposed a collaborative online learning algorithm that is able to take advantage of individual and global models to achieve an overall improvement in classification performance for processing UGC of a group of users. We showed that it is possible to outperform both the global and personal models by coherently integrating them in a unified collaborative learning framework. The experimental results show that our algorithm is both effective and efficient for online spam email filtering. For the micro-blog sentiment classification task, the cost-sensitive mechanism of CS-COL produced improvements to the classification of both positive and negative emotional tweets, however, at the slight expense of the majority class (F1-measure reduced from 79.08% to 63.43%). From a theoretical standpoint, this is a serious trade-off. In practice, users will be happy if the system can accurately predict positive and negative emotions, even if it performed poorly on the non-emotional tweets. Moreover, despite the significant improvements, the overall F1-measure of both the positive and negative class tweets still have a long way to go, as both are extremely low at around 25%. In conclusion, our collaborative online learning is a significant first step towards a more effective online user-based classification method.

6. ACKNOWLEDGMENTS

This research was supported in part by Singapore Ministry of Education's Academic Research Fund Tier 1 grant RG30/09.

7. REFERENCES

[1] R. Akbani, S. Kwek, and N. Japkowicz. Applying support vector machines to imbalanced datasets. In *ECML*, pages 39–50, 2004.

[2] R. K. Ando and T. Zhang. A framework for learning predictive structures from multiple tasks and unlabeled data. *J. Mach. Learn. Res.*, 6:1817–1853, 2005.

[3] A. Argyriou, T. Evgeniou, and M. Pontil. Multi-task feature learning. In *NIPS*, pages 41–48, 2006.

[4] B. Bakker and T. Heskes. Task clustering and gating for bayesian multitask learning. *J. Mach. Learn. Res.*, 4:83–99, 2003.

[5] S. Ben-David and R. Schuller. Exploiting task relatedness for mulitple task learning. In *COLT*, pages 567–580, 2003.

[6] C.-C. Chang and C.-J. Lin. *LIBSVM: a library for support vector machines*, 2001. Software available at http://www.csie.ntu.edu.tw/ cjlin/libsvm.

[7] N. V. Chawla, N. Japkowicz, and A. Kotcz. Editorial: special issue on learning from imbalanced data sets. *SIGKDD Explorations*, 6(1):1–6, 2004.

[8] K. Crammer, O. Dekel, J. Keshet, S. Shalev-Shwartz, and Y. Singer. Online passive-aggressive algorithms. *J. Mach. Learn. Res.*, 7:551–585, 2006.

[9] K. Crammer and Y. Singer. Ultraconservative online algorithms for multiclass problems. *J. Mach. Learn. Res.*, 3:2003, 2001.

[10] T. Evgeniou, C. A. Micchelli, and M. Pontil. Learning multiple tasks with kernel methods. *J. Mach. Learn. Res.*, 6:615–637, 2005.

[11] R.-E. Fan, K.-W. Chang, C.-J. Hsieh, X.-R. Wang, and C.-J. Lin. LIBLINEAR: A library for large linear classification. *J. Mach. Learn. Res.*, 9:1871–1874, 2008.

[12] Y. Freund and R. E. Schapire. Large margin classification using the perceptron algorithm. *Machine Learning*, 37(3):277–296, 1999.

[13] Y. Li and P. M. Long. The relaxed online maximum margin algorithm. In *NIPS*, pages 498–504, 1999.

[14] F. Rosenblatt. The perceptron: A probabilistic model for information storage and organization in the brain. *Psychological Review*, 65(6):386–408, 1958.

Structured Learning of Two-Level Dynamic Rankings

Karthik Raman
Dept. of Computer Science
Cornell University
Ithaca NY 14850 USA
karthik@cs.cornell.edu

Thorsten Joachims
Dept. of Computer Science
Cornell University
Ithaca NY 14850 USA
tj@cs.cornell.edu

Pannaga Shivaswamy
Dept. of Computer Science
Cornell University
Ithaca NY 14850 USA
pannaga@cs.cornell.edu

ABSTRACT

For ambiguous queries, conventional retrieval systems are bound by two conflicting goals. On the one hand, they should diversify and strive to present results for as many query intents as possible. On the other hand, they should provide depth for each intent by displaying more than a single result. Since both diversity and depth cannot be achieved simultaneously in the conventional *static* retrieval model, we propose a new *dynamic* ranking approach. In particular, our proposed *two-level* dynamic ranking model allows users to adapt the ranking through interaction, thus overcoming the constraints of presenting a one-size-fits-all static ranking. In this model, a user's interactions with the first-level ranking are used to infer this user's intent, so that second-level rankings can be inserted to provide more results relevant to this intent. Unlike previous dynamic ranking models, we provide an algorithm to efficiently compute dynamic rankings with provable approximation guarantees. We also propose the first principled algorithm for learning dynamic ranking functions from training data. In addition to the theoretical results, we provide empirical evidence demonstrating the gains in retrieval quality over conventional approaches.

Categories and Subject Descriptors

H.3.3 [**Information Search and Retrieval**]: Retrieval Models

General Terms

Algorithms, Experimentation, Theory

Keywords

Diversified Retrieval, Structured Learning, Submodular Optimization, Web Search, Ranked Retrieval

1. INTRODUCTION

Search engine users often express different information needs using the same query. For such *ambiguous queries*, a single query can represent multiple intents – ranging from coarse (*e.g.*, queries such as *apple*, *jaguar* and *SVM*) to fine-grained ambiguity (*e.g.*, the query *apple ipod* with the intent of either buying the device or reading reviews).

Conventional retrieval methods do not explicitly model query ambiguity, but simply rank documents by their probability of relevance independently for each result [8]. A major limitation of this approach is that it favors results for the most prevalent intent. In the extreme, the retrieval system focuses entirely on the prevalent intent, but produces no relevant results for the less popular intents. Diversification-based methods (e.g. [3, 12, 4, 11, 9]) try to alleviate this problem by including at least one relevant result for as many intents as possible. However, this necessarily leads to fewer relevant results for each intent. Clearly, there is an inherent trade-off between *depth* (number of results provided for an intent) and *diversity* (number of intents served) in the conventional ranked-retrieval setting, since increasing one invariably leads to a decrease of the other. How can we avoid this trade-off and obtain diversity while not compromising on depth?

We argue that a key to solving the conflict between depth and diversity lies in the move to *dynamic* retrieval models [2] that can take advantage of user interactions. Instead of presenting a single one-size-fits-all ranking, dynamic retrieval models allow users to adapt the ranking dynamically through interaction. Brandt et al. [2] have already given theoretical and empirical evidence that even limited interactivity can greatly improve retrieval effectiveness. However, Brandt et al. [2] did not provide an efficient algorithm for computing dynamic rankings with provable approximation guarantees, nor did they provide a principled algorithm for learning dynamic ranking functions. In this paper, we resolve these two open questions.

In particular, we propose a new *two-level dynamic ranking model*. Intuitively, the first level provides a diversified ranking of results on which the system can sense the user's interactions. Conditioned on this feedback, the system then interactively provides a second-level rankings. A possible layout is given in Figure 1. The left-hand panel shows the first-level ranking initially presented to the user. The user then chooses to expand the second document (*e.g.* by clicking) and a second-level ranking is inserted as shown in the right panel. Conceptually, the retrieval system maintains two levels of rankings, where each second-level ranking is conditioned on the head document in the first-level ranking.

To operationalize the construction and learning of two-level rankings in a rigorous way, we define a new family of submodular performance measure for diversified retrieval. Many existing retrieval measures (e.g., Precision@k, DCG, Intent Coverage) are special cases of this family. We then

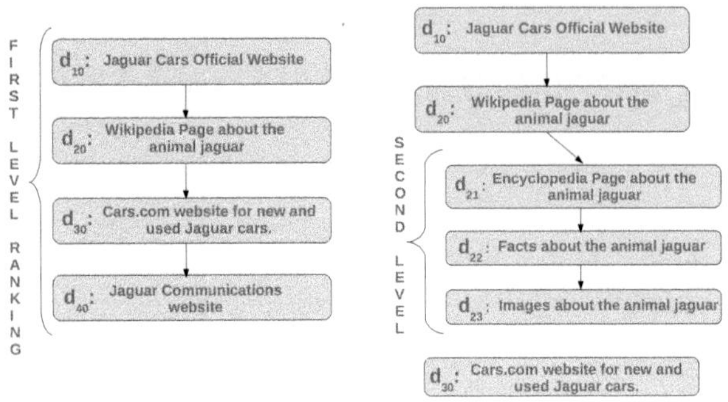

Figure 1: A user interested in the animal "jaguar" interacts with the first-level ranking (left) and obtains second-level results (right).

operationalize the problem of computing an optimal two-level ranking as maximizing the given performance measure. While this optimization problem is NP-hard, we provide an algorithm that has an $1-e^{-(1-\frac{1}{e})}$ approximation guarantee.

Finally, we also propose a new method for learning the (mutually dependent) relevance scores needed for two-level rankings. Following a structural SVM approach, we learn a discriminant model that resembles the desired performance measure in structure, but learns to approximate unknown intents based on query and document features. This method generalizes the learning method from [11] to two-level rankings and a large class of loss functions.

2. TWO-LEVEL DYNAMIC RANKINGS

Current methods for diversified retrieval are *static* in nature, *i.e.,* they stay unchanged through a user session. On the other hand, a *dynamic* model can adapt the ranking based on interactions with the user. The primary motivation for using a dynamic model is addressing the inherent trade-off between depth and diversity in static models.

Consider the example with four (equally likely) user intents $\{t_1, ..., t_4\}$ and documents $\{d_1, ..., d_9\}$ with relevance judgments $U(d_j|t_i)$ as given in Table 1. On the one hand, a non-diversified static ranking method could present $d_7 \rightarrow d_8 \rightarrow d_9$ as its top three documents, providing two relevant documents for intents t_3 and t_4 but none for intents t_1 and t_2. On the other hand, a diversified static ranking $d_7 \rightarrow d_1 \rightarrow d_4$ covers all intents, but this ranking lacks depth since no user gets more than one relevant document.

As an alternative, consider the following two-level dynamic ranking. The user is presented with $d_7 \rightarrow d_1 \rightarrow d_4$ as the first-level ranking. Users can now expand any of the first-level results to view a second-level ranking. Users interested in d_7 (and thus having intent t_3 or t_4) can *expand* that result and receive a second-level ranking consisting of d_8 and d_9. Similarly, users interested in d_1 will get d_2 and d_3; and users interested in d_4 will get d_5 and d_6.

For this dynamic ranking, every user gets at least one relevant result after scanning at most three documents (i.e. the first-level ranking). Furthermore, users with intents t_3 and t_4 receive two relevant results in the top three positions of their dynamically constructed rankin $d_7 \rightarrow d_8 \rightarrow d_9 \rightarrow d_1 \rightarrow d_4$. Similarly, users with intent t_1 also receive two relevant results in the top three positions while those with intent t_2 still receive one relevant result. This illustrates how a dynamic two-level ranking can simultaneously provide diversity and increased depth.

$U(d_j\|t_i)$	d_1	d_2	d_3	d_4	d_5	d_6	d_7	d_8	d_9
t_1	1	1	1	0	0	0	0	0	0
t_2	0	0	0	1	1	1	0	0	0
t_3	0	0	0	0	0	0	1	1	0
t_4	0	0	0	0	0	0	1	0	1

Table 1: Utility $U(d_j|t_i)$ of document d_j for intent t_i.

In the above example, interactive feedback from the user was the key to achieving both depth and diversity. More generally, we assume the following **model of user behavior**, which we denote as policy π_d. Users expand a first-level document if and only if that document is relevant to their intent. When users skip a document, they continue with the next first-level result. When users expand a first-level result, they go through the second-level rankings before continuing from where they left off in the first-level ranking. It is thus possible for a user to see multiple second-level rankings. Hence we do not allow documents to appear more than once across all two-level rankings.

Note that this user model differs from the one proposed in [2] in several ways. First, it assumes feedback only for the first-level ranking, while the model in [2] requires that users give feedback many levels deep. Second, unlike in [2], we model that users return to the top-level ranking. We conjecture that these differences make the two-level model more natural and appropriate for practical use.

We now define some notation used in this paper. The documents shown in a first-level ranking of **length** L are called the **head** documents. The documents shown in a second-level ranking are called the **tail** documents. The number of tail documents is referred to as the **width** W. A **row** denotes a **head** document and all its **tail** documents. Static rankings are denoted as θ while two-level rankings are denoted as $\Theta = (\Theta_1, \Theta_2, ...\Theta_i, ..)$. Here $\Theta_i = (d_{i0}, d_{i1}, ..., d_{ij}, ...)$ refers to the ith row of a two-level ranking, with d_{i0} representing the head document of the row and d_{ij} denoting the jth tail document of the second-level ranking. We denote the candidate set of documents to rank for a query q by $\mathcal{D}(q)$, the set of possible intents by $\mathcal{T}(q)$ and the distribution over an intent $t \in \mathcal{T}(q)$, given a query q, by $\mathbf{P}[t|q]$. Unless otherwise mentioned, dynamic ranking refers to a two-level dynamic ranking in the following.

3. PERFORMANCE MEASURES FOR DIVERSIFIED RETRIEVAL

To define what constitutes a good two-level dynamic ranking, we first define the measure of retrieval performance we would like to optimize. We then design our retrieval algorithms and learning methods to maximize this measure. In the following, we start with evaluation measures for one-level rankings, and then generalize them to the two-level case.

3.1 Measures for Static Rankings

Existing performance measures range from those that do not explicitly consider multiple intents (e.g. NDCG, Avg Prec), to measures that reward diversity. Measures that reward diversity give lower marginal utility to a document, if the intents the document is relevant to are already well represented in the ranking. We call this the *diminishing returns* property. The extreme case is the "intent coverage" measure (e.g. [9, 11]), which attributes utility only to the first document relevant for an intent.

We now define a family of measures that includes a whole range of diminishing returns models, and that includes most existing retrieval measures. Let $g : \mathbb{R} \to \mathbb{R}$ with $g(0) = 0$ be a concave, non-negative, and non-decreasing function that models the diminishing returns, then we define the utility of the ranking $\theta = (d_1, d_2, ..., d_k)$ for intent t as

$$U_g(\theta|t) = g\Big(\sum_{i=1}^{|\theta|} \gamma_i U(d_i|t)\Big). \quad (1)$$

The $\gamma_1 \geq ... \geq \gamma_k \geq 0$ are discount factors and $U(d|t)$ is the relevance rating of document d for intent t. For a distribution of user intents $\mathbf{P}[t|q]$ for query q, the overall utility of a static ranking θ is the expectation

$$U_g(\theta|q) = \sum_{t \in \mathcal{T}(q)} \mathbf{P}[t|q]\, U_g(\theta|t). \quad (2)$$

Note that many existing retrieval measures are special cases of this definition. For example, if one chose g to be the identity function, one recovers the intent-aware measures proposed in [1] and the modular measures defined in [2]. Further restricting $\mathbf{P}[t|q]$ to put all probability mass on a single intent leads to conventional measures like DCG for appropriately chosen γ_i. At the other extreme, chosing $g(x) = \min(x, 1)$ leads to the intent coverage measure [9, 11]. Since g can be chosen from a large class of functions, this family of performance measures covers a wide range of diminishing returns models.

3.2 Measures for Dynamic Rankings

We now extend our family of performance measures to dynamic rankings. The key change for dynamic rankings is that users interactively adapt which results they view.

How users expand first-level results was defined in Section 2 as π_d. Under π_d, it is natural to define the utility of a dynamic ranking Θ analogous to Equation (1).

$$U_g(\Theta|t) = g\Big(\sum_{i=1}^{|\Theta|}\Big(\gamma_i U(d_{i0}|t) + \sum_{j=1}^{|\Theta_i|} \gamma_{ij} U(d_{i0}|t) U(d_{ij}|t)\Big)\Big). \quad (3)$$

Like for static rankings, $\gamma_1 \geq \gamma_2 \geq ...$ and $\gamma_{i1} \geq \gamma_{i2} \geq ...$ are position-dependent discount factors. Furthermore, we again take the expectation over multiple user intents as in Equation (2) to obtain $U_g(\Theta|q)$.

Note that the utility of a second-level ranking for a given intent is zero unless the head document in the first-level ranking has non-zero relevance for that intent. This encourages second-level rankings to only contain documents relevant to the same intents as the head document, thus providing depth. The first-level ranking, on the other hand, provides diversity as controlled through the choice of function g. The "steeper" g diminishes returns of additional relevant documents, the more diverse the first-level ranking gets.

4. COMPUTING DYNAMIC RANKINGS

In this section, we provide an efficient algorithm for computing dynamic rankings that maximize the performance measures defined in the previous section. In the proposed greedy Algorithm 1, the operator $\oplus$ denotes either adding a document to a row, or adding a row to an existing ranking. In each iteration, Algorithm 1 considers every document in the remaining collection as the head document of a candidate row. For each candidate row, W documents are greedily added to maximize the utility $U_g(\Theta|q)$ of the resulting partial dynamic ranking Θ. Once rows of length W are constructed, the row which maximizes the utility is added to the ranking. The above steps are repeated until the ranking has L rows. Algorithm 1 is efficient, requiring $O(|\mathcal{T}|)$ space and $O(|\mathcal{T}||\mathcal{D}|^2)$ time.

Algorithm 1 for computing a two-level dynamic ranking.

```
Input: (q, D(q), T(q), P[t|q] : t ∈ T(q)), g(·), L, W.
Output: A dynamic ranking Θ.
Θ ← new_two_level()
while |Θ| ≤ L do
  bestU ← −∞
  for all d ∈ D(q) s.t. d ∉ Θ do
    row ← new_row();   row.head ← d
    for j = 1 to W do
      bestDoc ← argmax_{d' ∉ Θ∪row} U_g(Θ ⊕ (row ⊕ d')|q)
      row ← row ⊕ bestDoc
    if U_g(Θ ⊕ row|q) > bestU then
      bestU ← U_g(Θ ⊕ row|q);   bestRow ← row
  Θ ← Θ ⊕ bestRow
```

Our greedy algorithm is closely related to submodular function maximization. Maximizing monotonic submodular functions is a hard problem, but a greedily constructed set gives an $(1-1/e)$ approximation [6] to the optimal. Since the definition of our utility in (2) involves a concave function, it is not hard to show that selecting a ranking of rows is a submodular maximization problem. Moreover, given the head document, finding the best row is also a submodular maximization problem. Thus, finding a dynamic ranking to maximize our utility is a *nested* submodular maximization problem, and we can show the following approximation guarantee for Algorithm 1.

LEMMA 1. *Algorithm 1 is* $(1 - e^{-(1-\frac{1}{e})})$ *approximate.*

The proof can be found in [7]. It follows [5], but generalizes the result from max coverage to our more general setting.

5. LEARNING DYNAMIC RANKINGS

In the previous section, we showed that a dynamic ranking can be efficiently computed when all the intents and relevance judgments for a given query are known. In this section, we propose a supervised learning algorithm that can predict dynamic rankings on previously unseen queries.

Our goal here is to learn a mapping from a query q to a dynamic ranking Θ. We pose this as the problem of learning a weight vector $\mathbf{w} \in \mathbb{R}^N$ from which we can make a prediction as follows:

$$h_{\mathbf{w}}(q) = \underset{\Theta}{\operatorname{argmax}}\ \mathbf{w}^\top \Psi(q, \Theta). \quad (4)$$

As further explained below, $\Psi(q, \Theta) \in \mathbb{R}^N$ is a joint feature-map between query q and dynamic ranking Θ.

Given a set of training examples $(q^i, \Theta^i)_{i=1}^n$, the structural SVM framework [10] can be use to learn a discriminant function by minimizing the empirical risk $\frac{1}{n}\sum_{i=1}^n \Delta(\Theta^i, h_{\mathbf{w}}(q^i))$, where Δ is a loss function. Unfortunately, however, the Θ^i are typically not given directly as part of the training data. Instead, we assuming that we are given training data of the form $(q^i, \mathcal{D}(q^i), \mathcal{T}(q^i), \mathbf{P}[t|q] : t \in \mathcal{T}(q^i))_{i=1}^n$, and we then compute the dynamic rankings Θ^i by maximizing the utility U_g (approximately) using Algorithm 1. These Θ^i's will be used as the training labels henceforth.

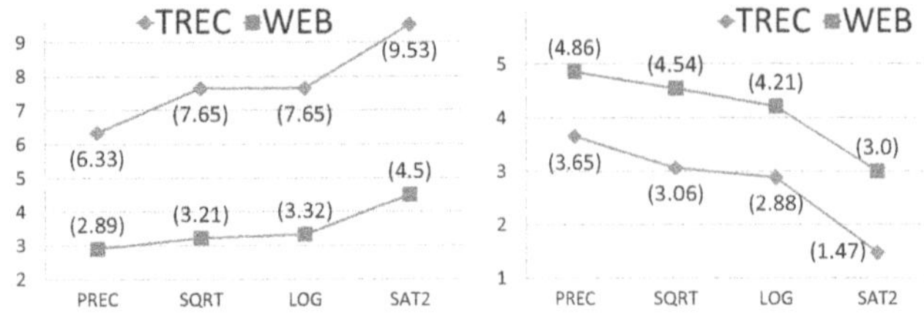

Figure 2: Average number of intents covered (left) and average number of documents for prevalent intent (right) in the first-level ranking.

A key aspect of structural SVMs is to appropriately define the joint-feature map $\Psi(q, \Theta)$. For our problem, we propose

$$\mathbf{w}^\top \Psi(q,\Theta) := \sum_{v \in V_{\mathcal{D}(q)}} \mathbf{w}_v^\top \phi_v U_g(\Theta|v) + \sum_{s \in V_{\mathcal{D}(q)\times\mathcal{D}(q)}} \mathbf{w}_s^\top \phi_s(\Theta), \quad (5)$$

where $V_{\mathcal{D}(q)}$ denotes an index set over the words in the candidate set $\mathcal{D}(q)$. The vector ϕ_v denotes word-level features (for example, how often a word occurs in a document) for the word corresponding to index v. The utility $U_g(\Theta|v)$ is analogous to (3) but is now over the words in the vocabulary (rather than over intents). The word-level features are reminiscent of the features used in diverse subset prediction [11]. The key assumption is that the words in a document are correlated with the intent since documents relevant to the same intent are likely to share more words than documents that are relevant to different intents.

The second term in Eq. 5 captures the similarity between head and tail documents. In this case, $V_{\mathcal{D}(q)\times\mathcal{D}(q)}$ denotes an index set over all document pairs in $\mathcal{D}(q)$. Consider an index s that corresponds to documents d_1 and d_2 in $\mathcal{D}(q)$. $\phi_s(\Theta)$ is a feature vector describing the similarity between d_1 and d_2 in Θ when d_1 is a head document in Θ and d_2 occurs in the same row as d_1 ($\phi_s(\Theta)$ is simply a vector of zeros otherwise). An example of a feature in $\phi_s(\Theta)$ that captures the similarity between two documents is their TFIDF cosine.

Using these features, $\mathbf{w}^\top\Psi(q,\Theta)$ models the utility of a given dynamic ranking Θ. During learning, $\mathbf{w}$ should be selected so that better rankings receive higher utility than worse rankings. This is achieved by solving the following structural SVM optimization problem for $\mathbf{w}$:

$$\min_{\mathbf{w},\xi\geq 0} \frac{1}{2}||\mathbf{w}||^2 + \frac{C}{n}\sum_{i=1}^{n}\xi_i \quad (6)$$

$$\text{s.t.} \forall i, \forall\Theta: \mathbf{w}^\top\Psi(q^i,\Theta^i) - \mathbf{w}^\top\Psi(q^i,\Theta) \geq \Delta(\Theta^i,\Theta|q^i) - \xi_i$$

The constraints in the above formulation ensure that the predicted utility for the target ranking Θ^i is higher than the predicted utility for any other Θ. The objective function in (6) minimizes the empirical risk while trading it off (via the parameter $C > 0$) with the margin. The loss between Θ^i and Θ is given by $\Delta(\Theta^i, \Theta|q^i) := 1 - \frac{U_g(\Theta|q^i)}{U_g(\Theta^i|q^i)}$ which ensures that the loss is zero when $\Theta = \Theta^i$. It is easy to see that a dynamic ranking Θ has a large loss when its utility is low compared to the utility of Θ^i.

Even though the Eq. (6) has an exponential number of constraints, the quadratic program in Eq. 6 can be solved in polynomial time using a cutting-plane algorithm [10]. In each iteration of the cutting-plane algorithm, the most violated constraints in (6) are added to a working set and the resulting quadratic program is solved. Given a current $\mathbf{w}$, the most violated constraints are obtained by solving:

$$\underset{\Theta}{\text{argmax}}\ \mathbf{w}^\top\Psi(q^i,\Theta) + \Delta(\Theta^i,\Theta|q^i). \quad (7)$$

Algorithm 1 can be used to solve the above problem, even though the formal approximation guarantee does not hold in this case. Once a weight vector $\mathbf{w}$ is obtained, the dynamic ranking for a test query can be obtained from Eq. (4).

6. EXPERIMENTS

Experiments were conducted on the TREC 6-8 Interactive Track (TREC) and the Diversity Track of TREC 18 using the ClueWeb collection (WEB). The 17 queries in TREC contain between 7 to 56 different manually judged intents. In the case of WEB, we used 28 queries with 4 or more intents. We consider the probability $\mathbf{P}[t]$ of an intent proportional to the number of documents relevant to that intent. A key difference between the two datasets is that the most prevalent intent covers 73.4% of all relevant documents for the WEB dataset, but only 37.6% for TREC.

The number of documents in the first-level ranking was set to 5. The width of the second-level rankings was set to 2. For simplicity, we chose all factors γ_i and γ_{ij} in Equations (1) and (3) to be 1. Further, we chose $U(d|t) = 1$ if document d was relevant to intent t and set $U(d|t) = 0$ otherwise.

More details about the experiments and additional results can also be found in [7].

6.1 Controlling Diversity and Depth

The key design choice of our family of utility measures is the concave function g. As Algorithm 1 directly optimizes utility, we explore how the choice of g affects various properties of the two-level rankings produced by our method.

We experiment with four different concave functions g, each providing a different diminishing-returns model. At one extreme, we have the identity function $g(x) = x$ which corresponds to modular returns. Using this function in Eq. (1) leads to the intent-aware Precision measure proposed in [1], and it is the only function considered in [2]. We therefore refer to this function as PREC. It is not hard to show that Algorithm 1 actually computes the optimal two-level ranking for this choice of g. On the other end of the spectrum, we study $g(x) = \min(x, 2)$. By remaining constant after two, this function discourages presenting more than two relevant documents for any intent. This measure will be referred to as SAT2 (short for "satisfied after two"). In between these two extremes, we study the square root function (SQRT) $g(x) = \sqrt{x}$ and the log function (LOG) $g(x) = \log(1 + x)$.

To explore how dynamic rankings can differ, we used Algorithm 1 to compute the two-level rankings (approximately) maximizing the respective measure. Figure 2 shows how g influences diversity. The left-hand plot shows how many different intents are represented in the top 5 results of the first-level ranking on average. The graph shows that the stronger the diminishing-returns model, the more different intents are covered in the first-level ranking. In particular, the number of intents almost doubles on both datasets when moving from PREC to SAT2. In contrast, the number of documents on the most prevalent intent in the first-level ranking decreases, as shown in the right-hand plot. This illustrates how the choice of g can be used to control the desired amount of diversity in the first-level ranking.

Table 2 provides further insight into the impact of g, now also including the contributions of the second-level rankings.

Eval. \ Optim.	PREC	SQRT	LOG	SAT2
PREC	**0.315**	0.302	0.294	0.164
SQRT	1.612	**1.664**	1.659	1.333
LOG	1.216	1.267	**1.27**	1.046
SAT2	1.18	1.335	1.349	**1.487**

Table 2: Performance when optimizing and evaluating using different performance measures for TREC.

The rows correspond to different choices for g when evaluating expected utility according to Eq. (3), while the columns show which g the two-level ranking was optimized for. Not surprisingly, the diagonal entries of Tables 2 show that the best performance for each measure is obtained when optimizing for it. The off-diagonal entries show that different g used during optimization lead to substantially different rankings. This is particularly apparent when optimizing the two extreme performance measures PREC and SAT2; optimizing one invariably leads to rankings that have a low value of the other. In contrast, optimizing LOG or SQRT results in much smoother behavior across all measures, and both seem to provide a good compromise between depths (for the prevalent intent) and diversity. The results for WEB are qualitatively similar and are omitted for space reasons.

6.2 Static vs. Dynamic Ranking

The ability to simultaneously provide depth and diversity was a key motivation for our dynamic ranking approach. We now evaluate whether this goal is indeed achieved. We compare the two-level rankings produced by Algorithm 1 (denoted *Dyn*) with several static baselines. These static baselines are also computed by Algorithm 1, but with the width of the second-level rankings to 0.

First, we compare against a diversity-only static ranking that maximizes intent coverage as proposed in [11] (denoted *Stat-Div*). Second, we compare against a depth-only static ranking by chosing g to be the identity function (denoted *Stat-Depth*). And, third, we produce static rankings that optimize SQRT, LOG, and SAT2 (denoted *Stat-Util*). Note that both Dyn and Stat-Util optimize the same measure that is used for evaluation.

To make a fair comparison between static and dynamic rankings, we measure performance in the following way. For static rankings, we compute performance using the expectation of Eq. (1) at a depth cutoff of 5. In particular, we measure PREC@5, SQRT@5, LOG@5 and SAT2@5. For two-level rankings, the number of results viewed by a user depends on how many results he or she expands. So, we truncate any user's path through the two-level ranking after visiting 5 results and compute PREC@5, SQRT@5, LOG@5 and SAT2@5 for the truncated path.

Results of these comparisons are shown in Figure 3. First, we see that both Dyn and Stat-Util outperform Stat-Div, illustrating that optimizing rankings for the desired evaluation measure leads to much better performance than using a proxy measure as in Stat-Div. Note that Stat-Div never tries to present more than one result for each intent, which explains the extremely low "depth" performance in terms of PREC@5. But Stat-Div is not competitive even for SAT2, since it never tries to provide a second result.

Second, at first glance it may be surprising that Dyn outperforms Stat-Depth even on PREC@5, despite the fact that Stat-Depth explicitly (and globally optimally) optimizes depth.

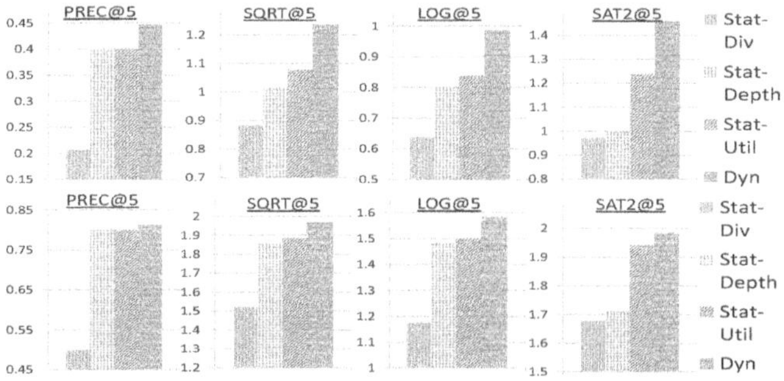

Figure 3: Comparing the retrieval quality of Static vs. Dynamic Rankings for TREC and WEB.

To understand consider the following situation where A is the prevalent intent, and there are three documents relevant to A and B and three relevant to A and C. Putting those sets of three documents into the first two rows of the dynamic ranking provides better PREC@5 than sequentially listing them in the optimal static ranking.

Overall we find the dynamic ranking method outperforming all static ranking schemes on all the metrics – in many cases with a substantial margin. This gain is more pronounced for TREC than for WEB. This can be explained by the fact that WEB queries are less ambiguous, since the single most prevalent intent accounts for more than 70% of all queries on average.

6.3 Learning Two-level Ranking Functions

So far we have evaluated how far Algorithm 1 can construct effective two-level rankings if the relevance ratings are known. We now explore how far our learning algorithm can predict two-level rankings for previously unseen queries. For all experiments in this section, we learn and predict using SQRT as the choice for g, since it provides a good trade-off between diversity and depth as shown above.

We performed standard preprocessing such as tokenization, stopword removal and Porter stemming. Since the focus of our work is on diversity and not on relevance, we rank only those documents that are relevant to at least one intent of a query. This simulates a candidate set that may have been provided by a conventional retrieval method. This setup is similar to that used by Yue and Joachims [11].

Many of our features in ϕ_v follow those used in [11]. These features provide information about the importance of a word in terms of two different aspects. A first type of feature describes the overall importance of a word. A second type of feature captures the importance of a word in a document. An example of this type of feature is whether a word appears with frequency at least y% in the document? Finally, we also use features ϕ_s that model the relationship between the documents in the second-level ranking and the corresponding head document of that row. Examples of this type of feature are binned features representing TFIDF similarity of document pairs and the number of common words that appear in both documents with a frequency at least x%.

Dynamic vs. Static: In the first set of experiments, we compare our learning method (*Dyn-SVM*) for two-level rankings with two static baselines. The first static baseline is the learning method from [11] which optimizes diversity (referred to as *Stat-Div*). It is one of the very few learning methods for learning diversified retrieval functions, and was shown to outperform non-learning methods like Essen-

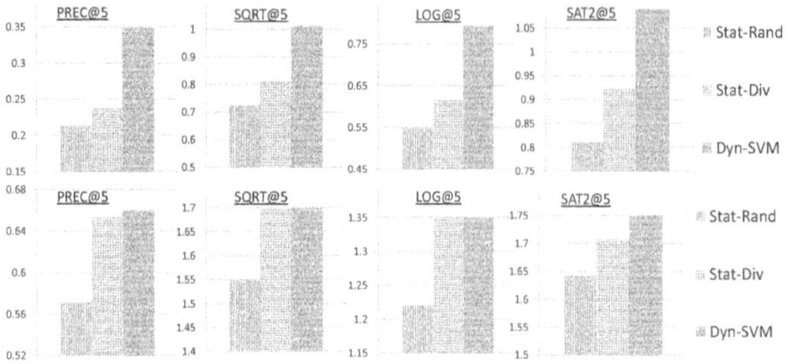

Figure 4: Performance of learned functions, comparing static & dynamic rankings for TREC and WEB.

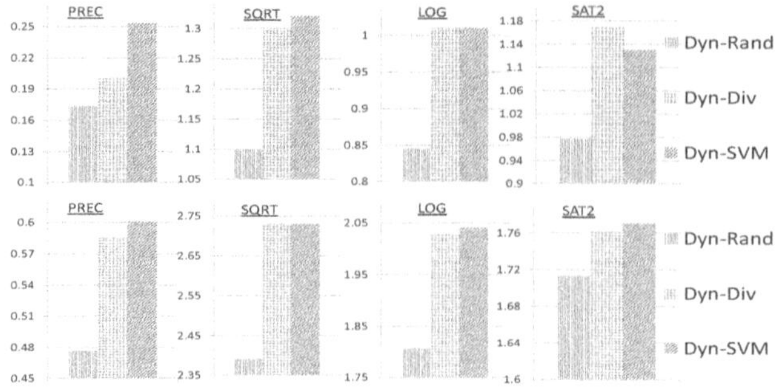

Figure 5: Comparing learned dynamic rankings with heuristic baselines for TREC and WEB.

tial Pages [9]. We also consider a *random* static baseline (referred to as *Stat-Rand*), which randomly orders the candidate documents. This is a competent baseline, since all our candidate documents are relevant to at least one intent.

Figure 4 shows the comparison between static and dynamic rankings. For TREC, *Dyn-SVM* substantially outperforms both static baselines across all performance metrics, mirroring the results we obtained in Section 6.2 where the relevance judgments were known. This shows that our learning method can effectively generalize the multi-intent relevance judgments to new queries. On the less ambiguous WEB dataset the differences between static and dynamic rankings are smaller. While *Dyn-SVM* substantially outperforms *Stat-Rand*, *Stat-Div* is quite competitive on WEB.

Learning vs. Heuristic Baselines: We also compare against alternative methods for constructing two-level rankings. We extend the static baselines *Stat-Rand* and *Stat-Div* using the following heuristic. For each result in the static ranking, we add a second-level ranking using the documents with the highest TFIDF similarity from the candidate set. This results in two dynamic baselines, which we call *Dyn-Rand* and *Dyn-Div*. The results are shown in Figure 5.

Since we compare two-level rankings of equal size, we measure performance in terms of expected utility. On both datasets *Dyn-SVM* performs substantially better than *Dyn-Rand*. This implies that our method can effectively learn which documents to place at the top of the first-level ranking. Surprisingly, simply extending the diversified ranking of *Dyn-Div* using the TFIDF heuristic produces dynamic rankings are are competitive with *Dyn-SVM*. In retrospect, this is not too surprising for two reasons. First, our experiments with *Dyn-SVM* use rather simple features to describe the relationship between the head document and documents in the second-level ranking – most of which are derived from their TFIDF similarity. Stronger features exploiting document ontologies or browsing patterns could easily be incorporated into the feature vector. Second, the learning method of *Dyn-Div* is actually a special case of *Dyn-SVM* when using the SAT1 loss (i.e. satisfied after a single relevant document) and second-level rankings of width 0. However, we argue that it is still highly preferable to directly optimize the desired loss function and two-level ranking using *Dyn-SVM*, since the reliance on heuristics may fail on other datasets.

7. CONCLUSIONS

We proposed a two-level dynamic ranking approach that provides both diversity and depth for ambiguous queries by exploiting user interactivity. In particular, we showed that the approach has the following desirable properties. First, it covers a large family of performance measures, making it easy to select a diminishing returns model for the application setting at hand. Second, we presented an efficient algorithm for constructing two-level rankings that maximizes the given performance measure with provable approximation guarantees. Finally, we provided a structural SVM algorithm for learning two-level ranking functions, showing that it can effectively generalize to new queries.

This work was funded in part under NSF Awards IIS-0905467, IIS-0713483, and IIS-0812091.

8. REFERENCES

[1] R. Agrawal, S. Gollapudi, A. Halverson, and S. Ieong. Diversifying search results. In *WSDM*, 2009.

[2] C. Brandt, T. Joachims, Y. Yue, and J. Bank. Dynamic ranked retrieval. In *WSDM*, 2011.

[3] J. Carbonell and J. Goldstein. The use of MMR, diversity-based reranking for reordering documents and producing summaries. In *SIGIR*, 1998.

[4] H. Chen and D. R. Karger. Less is more: probabilistic models for retrieving fewer relevant documents. In *SIGIR*, 2006.

[5] D. S. Hochbaum and A. Pathria. Analysis of the greedy approach in problems of maximum k-coverage. *Naval Research Logistics (NRL)*, 45:615–627, 1998.

[6] G. L. Nemhauser, L. A. Wolsey, and M. L. Fisher. An analysis of approximations for maximizing submodular set functions. *Math Programming*, 14:265–294, 1978.

[7] K. Raman, P. Shivaswamy, and T. Joachims. Structured learning of two-level dynamic rankings. Arxiv 0298967, August 2011.

[8] S. Robertson. The probability ranking principle in ir. *Journal of Documentation*, 33(4):294–304, 1977.

[9] A. Swamintahan, C. Metthew, and D. Kirovski. Essential pages. In *Technical Report, MSR-TR-2008-15*, Microsoft Research, 2008.

[10] I. Tsochantaridis, T. Joachims, T. Hofmann, and Y. Altun. Large-margin methods for structured and interdependent output variables. *Journal of Machine Learning Research*, 6:1453–1484, 2005.

[11] Y. Yue and T. Joachims. Predicting diverse subsets using structural SVMs. In *ICML*, 2008.

[12] C. X. Zhai, W. W. Cohen, and J. Lafferty. Beyond independent relevance: methods and evaluation metrics for subtopic retrieval. In *SIGIR*, 2003.

Efficiency Optimizations for Interpolating Subqueries

Marc-Allen Cartright
CIIR
Dept. of Computer Science
Univ. of Massachusetts
Amherst, MA 01003
irmarc@cs.umass.edu

James Allan
CIIR
Dept. of Computer Science
Univ. of Massachusetts
Amherst, MA 01003
allan@cs.umass.edu

ABSTRACT

A large class of queries can be viewed as linear combinations of smaller subqueries. Additionally, many situations arise when part or all of one subquery has been preprocessed or has cached information, while another subquery requires full processing. This type of query is common, for example, in relevance feedback settings where the original query has been run to produce a set of expansion terms, but the expansion terms still need to be processed. We investigate mechanisms to reduce the time needed to process queries of this nature.

We use RM3, a variant of the Relevance Model scoring algorithm, as our instantiation of this arrangement. We examine the different scenarios that can arise when we have access to the internal structure of each subquery. Given this additional information, we investigate methods to utilize this information, reducing processing costs substantially. Depending on the amount of accessibility we have into the subqueries, we can reduce processing costs over 80% without affecting the score of the final results.

Categories and Subject Descriptors: H.3.3 Information Search and Retrieval: Relevance Feedback, Retrieval Models

General Terms: Algorithms, Performance

Keywords: query optimization, pseudo-relevance feedback, query modeling

1. INTRODUCTION

Recent research in information retrieval has recognized the utility of structure in queries [14, 12, 7, 8, 3, 9], further justifying complex query languages in some search engines (i.e. InQuery, Indri). In addition, various evaluation conferences have led efforts towards researching the use of structure in queries, such as INEX[1] and TREC's Entity Track[2]. Assuming that queries have some structure has become the expectation in retrieval; unfortunately large complex queries are likely to be slow to process, indicating a clear need for optimization if such queries have any hope of being called interactievly. Towards this end, we look to improve query processing on a recurring pattern in information retrieval models: linear combinations.

Linear combinations of scores lie at the heart of many well-known models in information retrieval. The class of probabilistic models contains, or easily translates to, linear combinations of unigrams or n-grams. The Language Model [13] is technically a ranking based on joint probability of the query terms $q_1 q_2 \dots q_k = Q$ occurring in document D; however in order to avoid underflow the scores produced are the sum of the log-probabilities: $Score(Q, D) = \sum_{q \in Q} \log P(q|D)$. A term-order aware extension to the Language Model, the Sequential Dependence Model, uses the weighted geometric mean to combine the unigram, ordered, and unordered components of a given query [12]. When we take the logarithm of these quantities, the entire equation again reduces to a series of sums over log-probabilities. The Relevance Model [10], after generating the estimates for the likelihood of a term w coming from relevance model R, denoted $P(w|R)$, is a linear combination of log-probabilities as well: $\sum_{w \in V} P(w|R) \log P(w|D)$. Likewise, the binary independence models, most famously the BM25 model [15], are also linear combinations of term weights.

If we look to vector space models, we can observe a similar phenomenon. The standard cosine similarity scoring function takes the inner product of D and Q — which in turn is a sum of products between the two vectors [17]. The Rocchio algorithm for relevance feedback [16] creates an interpolation between the components of each query term:

$$q'_j = \alpha \cdot q_j + \beta \cdot \frac{1}{\|R\|} \sum_{D_i \in R} d_{ij} - \gamma \cdot \frac{1}{\|\bar{R}\|} \sum_{D_i \in \bar{R}} d_{ij}$$

These new weights are then used to provide a "more complete" vector representation of the information need. In implementation, the score consists of calculating the dot product, as before. There are numerous other examples of established models that operate as linear combinations of various components, and linear combination is often one of the first methods tried when adding new information into existing models.

The major contribution of this work is to provide optimization mechanisms to interpolating subquery components, depending on what we can assume about the subqueries. Given the increasing use of structure in retrieval, optimization algorithms should operate on queries as structured objects. We focus our efforts on linear combinations

[1]http://www.inex.otago.ac.nz/
[2]http://ilps.science.uva.nl/trec-entity/

CIKM '11, October 24–28, 2011, Glasgow, Scotland, UK

as they are a basic structure used throughout the field.

2. RELATED WORK

Query processing optimization has been a constant activity in information retrieval since the field's inception. Many strategies have been developed for various models, providing different guarantees. While we cannot cover the entire history of optimization in IR, some prior work has more directly influenced the work here.

The use of an inference network as a retrieval model was introduced by Turtle and Croft in the early 1990s [22, 23]. Their analyses showed that a significant number of existing retrieval models at the time could be efficiently represented in the inference network framework, a form of directed graphical model, making it capable of representing a wide range of retrieval models. This framework is the inspiration for the graphic representation of queries used here, which affords us an efficient way to manipulate the query structure.

Turtle and Flood developed the MAXSCORE optimization for early-termination in both document-at-a-time (daat) and score-at-a-time (saat) query evaluation strategies. Following on this work, Strohman et al. combined the "topdocs" caching method of Brown [6] with Turtle and Flood's MAXSCORE algorithm, producing a hybrid algorithm that outperformed both prior techniques [21]. We make use of this version of the algorithm several times here.

In work focusing on saat index organization, Anh and Moffat extended the work of pruned query evaluation to impact-sorted indexes [2]. The document scores are first binned and truncated to integers, allowing for better compression and faster query evaluation. They then use an algorithm to limit the size of the accumulator table during scoring. They maintain a top candidate list in addition to the accumulator table, and use score bounds to determine when they can stop adding candidates, as well as stop tallying scores. Their paper also provides an excellent overview of index models and optimization strategies to date. Our approach here is not directly comparable to their work, as we study a different index organization; however several of our algorithms would work in conjunction with optimizations designed for saat-organized indexes.

Research in the area of efficient query expansion includes Billerbeck and Zobel, who conduct several rounds of experiments examining the use of auxiliary data structures for improving the efficiency of query expansion [5, 4]. They discovered that using short summaries of documents significantly reduced the time needed to analyze the documents used for feedback, which they considered to be the largest bottleneck during automatic expansion. In contrast, our concern is not with generating the expansion query - the techniques shown here are applied after such generation. The methods described by Billerbeck and Zobel should smoothly integrate with the merging techniques shown here, although experiments to prove this hypothesis are beyond the scope of this work.

Cartright et al. first look into the problem of specifically optimizing the Relevance Model [11]. They considered a document-document similarity matrix to serve as the offline store for supplemental data. They then tried to reduce the size of this matrix in order to improve its scalability to larger scale collections. Their results indicate that both static (i.e., index time) and dynamic (i.e., query time) pruning techniques have potential to dramatically reduce the size of the matrix with minor negative impact on the effectiveness of the original Relevance Model. Their approach attempted to directly optimize retrieval scores via document-document similarity rather than manipulating the structure of the query components, as we do here.

Collection	# docs (10^6's)	terms (10^6's)	unique terms (10^3's)
AQUAINT	1.0	484	892
GOV2	25.2	2,552	62,433
ClueWeb-B	50.2	39,834	468,380

Table 1: Statistics on the collections used in experiments.

3. APPROACH

In this section we describe the different algorithms we test in our experiments. We begin with data, software, and evaluation in order to provide context necessary for the remaining discussion in this section.

3.1 Data and Software

We conduct our experiments on three collections, as shown in Table 1. The AQUAINT collection refers to the dataset and 50 queries from the TREC 2005 Robust Track. GOV2 uses the dataset and 150 automatic run queries from the Adhoc task of the TREC 2006 Terabyte Track. Clue-B refers to the ClueWeb Category B sub-collection and 50 queries used in the Adhoc task of the TREC 2009 Web Track.

We conduct all retrieval experiments using the Galago 3.0 search engine[3]. We generate all on-disk data structures, such as the indexes and the topdocs lists [21] described in later sections, using the TupleFlow distributed processing framework [19].

3.2 Evaluation

Our primary concern is improving query processing time. We perform two separate kinds of evaluation to measure the effect on processing time. First, we record the number of times we call SCORE on a term scoring node, which is the only construct in our model that directly iterates over data stored on the disk. Since the optimizations described here focus on reducing this factor, we get an upper bound of how effective these algorithms can be in reducing processing load. Second, we record the actual elapsed time of each query to determine the improvement in processing time in a live system. We use the first evaluation as the focus of our initial analysis of the algorithms, and we discuss the second type of evaluation in Section 4.4.2.

Some techniques presented here guarantee that if a document appears in R, the final ranked list, the score is the same as the unoptimized version. We call an algorithm with this property *score-accurate to rank k*. Prior work has referred to a similar property, *rank-safe up to k*, meaning the ranks of documents up to rank k are unchanged from the original ranking function [24]. As defined, these two properties are unrelated: an algorithm may exhibit the *score-accurate* property, but not the *rank-safe* property, and vice-versa. This occurs, for example, when an algorithm only

[3]http://galagosearch.org

fully scores a subset of the entire candidate list. A document in the original R may not be scored by the algorithm, therefore is not in the new R, however all documents appearing in the new R have been scored correctly. The REWIND algorithm, described in Section 3.4.2, behaves in this fashion. For the remainder of this work, we assume r is the number of documents requested, so we abbreviate *score-accurate to rank r* to *score-accurate*, and *rank-safe up to r* to *rank-safe*.

In the cases where an optimization is score-accurate and rank-safe, we do not report the effect on retrieval effectiveness. Otherwise, we report Mean Average Precision (MAP) as implemented by the `trec_eval` program[4]. In calculating the statistical significance between score count samples, we use a paired randomization test, as described by Smucker et al. [18]. When determining statistical significance of the real time measurements, we use a standard randomization test to maintain tractability. In both cases we set our sample size to 10^6.

3.3 Representation

We choose to focus on the RM3 scoring function [1] as our exemplar scoring model for this work, for several reasons: 1) previous research has shown it to be effective in practice [1]; 2) it interpolates only two subquery components, making it a canonical case for our study; and 3) the internals of both subqueries also have simple structure, affording easy manipulation.

RM3 is a variant of the Relevance Model that interpolates the Language Model [13] and Relevance Model [10] scores for a given query Q and document D:

$$Score_{RM3}(Q,D) = \lambda Score_{LM}(Q,D) + (1-\lambda) Score_{RM}(Q,D)$$

Typical implementations of RM3, such as the implementation in Indri [20], construct an interpolated query after an initial round of retrieval and submit the entire revised query for scoring. That is, the LM scores are used to build the query that generate the RM scores. The algorithms described here are applied after the expansion terms have been selected. Clearly if $\lambda \in \{0,1\}$, then we can simply drop the zero-weighted subquery, and only evaluate the remaining subquery. However in cases where $0 < \lambda < 1$, both subqueries matter, and we must evaluate both. This is the situation we address here. Instead of re-submitting the revised query, including the initial query as a subquery, we intervene to leverage structure in this expanded two-part query in order to improve performance.

Given the point of intervention, we slightly recast the formula above to specify the components involved. The original query we label P, which is the processed subquery at this point. The expansion terms we label U, the unprocessed part of the query. Therefore we reformulate the RM3 scoring function to reflect this:

$$Score_{RM3}(Q,D) = \lambda Score_{LM}(P,D) + (1-\lambda) Score_{RM}(U,D)$$

Note that in order to create U, the system must have generated an initial ranked list based solely on P; we call that list R_P. We allow the system to access this initial ranked list during processing.

In order to organize the remaining discussion, we represent the query structure as a network of interconnected nodes, similar to an Inference Network [22]. As an example, suppose P is the query *hydrogen energy*, and we construct U using 3 expansion terms, *science*, *nuclear*, and *research*. Assume that each term comes with an associated weight. We label the associated weights as follows: the ith term in subquery P has associated weight p_i, likewise the jth term in subquery U has associated weight u_j. Let $\pi(t,D)$ and $v(t,D)$ represent the scoring functions of a single term given a document D and term t for subqueries P and U, respectively. Mathematically, the score of a document D for this query is:

$$\begin{aligned} Score(Q,D) &= \lambda Score_{LM}(P,D) + (1-\lambda) Score_{RM}(U,D) \\ &= \lambda(p_1\pi(\text{hydrogen},D) + p_2\pi(\text{energy},D)) \\ &\quad + (1-\lambda)(u_1 v(\text{science},D) + u_2 v(\text{nuclear},D) \\ &\quad + u_3 v(\text{research},D)) \end{aligned} \tag{1}$$

In choosing RM3 as our scoring function, π and v are in fact the same term scoring function: the log of the smoothed term likelihood of t in D.

The graphical representation of this query is shown in Figure 1. The construction provides us with a clean way of expressing the query visually. The nodes at the bottom of the tree are *term scoring nodes* - they represent the scoring functions π and v in Equation 1. The nodes up the tree are all *combining nodes* - they combine the incoming scores according to the weights along the incoming edges. In our case, all combining nodes represent a weighted sum over the contributed scores. Assuming N is a combining node, let $\hat{N}$ denote the subtree rooted at node N, excluding N itself. In implementation, the term scoring nodes act as iterators over the posting list of the given term, and the combining nodes act as meta-iterators that ensure the scoring over documents proceeds correctly.

The processing model uses document-at-a-time processing, meaning each document is scored in its entirety before another document is scored. Under this model, we construct the network once, and iterate over all documents, having each term scoring node score each document (a term scoring must produce a score for any document), combine the scores, then move to the next document. We assume all iterators are capable of the following functions: 1) *score* a given document, 2) *tell* the document id that the iterator is currently on in the posting list, 3) *reset* to the beginning of its posting list, and 4) *move* to/past a particular document id in its posting list[5]. Combining nodes simply pass the command forward to all nodes under them. For example, the statement 'We reset P ...' means that the term scoring iterators under P are all reset to the beginning of their respective posting lists.

During description and analysis of the algorithms, we will also consider the set of documents that appear in the posting list of a given term. We denote this as $\Delta(N)$, where N is a node in the network. If N is a combining node, then $\Delta(N) = \bigcup_{M \in \hat{N}} \Delta(M)$.

3.3.1 *Visibility*

Given the graphical representation of a query, we now assume that we have varying amounts of information about

[4]http://trec.nist.gov

[5]All posting lists are sorted in increasing document id order, so any id can be found in log time using binary search over a sample of positions from the list.

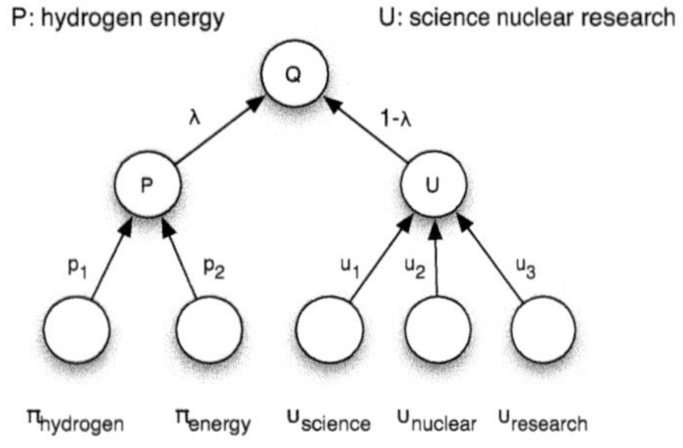

Figure 1: Graphical representation of an example query.

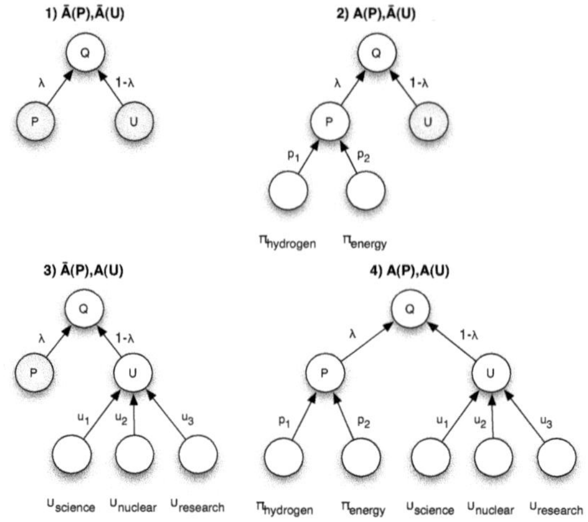

Figure 2: 4 cases under investigation, with varying amounts of accessibility. Shaded nodes are inaccessible.

each combining node that we can leverage. We define an additional property over the combining nodes, known as its *visibility*, which has two values: *accessible* and *inaccessible*. We say a combining node N is accessible if we have the capability to examine and modify the weights and nodes in the subtree of N. We denote this as $A(N)$. If N is inaccessible, denoted $\bar{A}(N)$, we cannot examine or modify the internals of N. Note that even if a node is inaccessible, we may still perform the previously mentioned operations on it; therefore an inaccessible node may still be scored, as is the case in federated search or when using a third-party system.

We examine 4 distinct cases, shown in Figure 2. In the first case, we have $\bar{A}(P)$ and $\bar{A}(U)$, meaning we cannot directly observe or modify the structure of either subquery. Treating a node as inaccessible guarantees that the semantics of the subquery are not inadvertently changed, which is desirable in some cases. This situation may occur in federated search or distributed search, where a query comes from an external source, and the ability of the system to restructure the query is restricted. This may also occur when both P and U represent scoring nodes that the system cannot modify, for example if both subqueries are phrases. In the second case, we have $A(P)$ and $\bar{A}(U)$ and in the third case $\bar{A}(P)$ and $A(U)$. Since we assume that P has undergone some amount of processing whereas U has not, we do not assume the optimizations available between cases 2 and 3 will be the same. These cases occur whenever we encounter a subquery the system may understand (e.g., a subquery that is also a linear combination, such as a Language Model query), but the other subquery cannot be understood or is implemented externally, for example if the node represents a function that calculates a score for D based on geolocation data. We can still use the node to score documents, but we have no way of reorganizing the implementation of the node. Finally, we have $A(P)$ and $A(U)$ which is the fourth case. This represents the fortunate case where the system can manipulate both subqueries. As shown earlier, this case occurs frequently across various text-based retrieval models. We do not consider the case when $\bar{A}(Q)$, as that leaves us with no information about the query structure, therefore the methods described here do not apply.

3.3.2 Maxscore

In addition to the standard linear combining nodes in our network, we also implement the MAXSCORE algorithm described by Turtle and Flood [24] as a combining node. Fundamentally a MAXSCORE node is a combining node that performs extra bookkeeping to determine if it can stop combining scores early. If it stops early, then the candidate document would not have passed the threshold score (the lowest score in the list of top r documents so far) and it returns the incomplete score early. Otherwise the node completes scoring and returns the correct score. We denote a MAXSCORE combining node N as N^M. We define a function, MAKE-MAXSCORE, which accepts a regular combining node and produces the MAXSCORE-enabled version of that node. Mathematically, the two node types will return the exact same documents and scores for the number of documents requested (r). While we may replace any combining node in the network with its MAXSCORE equivalent, we consider the direct interaction of multiple MAXSCORE nodes outside the scope of this work.

We also augment MAXSCORE similar to Strohman et al. by including *topdocs lists* for the term scoring nodes [21]. The topdocs implementation in Galago operates similar to the implementation in Indri. Every posting list over length l has its best b scoring documents stored in a short list, known as its topdocs list. When MAXSCORE accesses these lists, it partially scores the union of all available topdocs lists, allowing the algorithm to immediately lower its threshold to filter candidates, as well as lowering the potential on each term scoring node with a topdocs list. Both l and b are set to 1000 for our experiments.

In Galago, the topdocs are kept as a separate posting list file in the index, and are only accessed when requested by the retrieval model. While this organization may not be as real-time efficient as Indri, we believe this creates a better interface for future experimentation with such data structures where supplemental information can be made available on demand. We implemented the MAXSCORE node to check for topdocs lists. Therefore if a term scoring node has a topdocs list available, the MAXSCORE node will utilize that extra information.

We now describe the experimental algorithms we test in each scenario. For the following discussion, we assume R is the final ranked list returned by the algorithm.

3.4 $\bar{A}$(P) and $\bar{A}$(U)

We begin with the first case, where both P and U are inaccessible.

3.4.1 *Fusion*

FUSION is the first, and simplest, of the algorithms we present. The intuition behind this algorithm is simple: RM3 scores using both P and U. Instead, FUSION only makes use of whatever R_P provides, and ignores P. The pseudocode for FUSION is shown below. We assume R_P and R_U act as maps from the documents returned to their scores, for notational convenience. The algorithm begins by evaluating U, producing ranked list R_U (lines 1-4). To guarantee that every document receives some kind of score, we establish lower bounds for each list (lines 5 and 6). These bounds acts as the default score for any document not explicitly in the corresponding list. We then take the linear interpolation of R_P and R_U using parameter λ (lines 7-14). Finally, we return the highest-scoring r items from this merge (lines 15-19).

FUSION(R_P, U, λ, r)

1 $R_U \leftarrow$NEW-MAP
2 **foreach** $d \in \Delta(U)$
3   INSERT($R_U, \langle d,$ SCORE$(U,d)\rangle$)
4 TRIM(R_U, r)
5 $min_P \leftarrow \min_{d \in R_P} R_P[d]$
6 $min_U \leftarrow \min_{d \in R_U} R_U[d]$
7 $A \leftarrow$ NEW-MAP()
8 **foreach** $d \in R_P$
9     $A[d] \leftarrow \lambda R_P[d] + (1-\lambda) min_U$
10 **foreach** $d \in R_U$
11   **if** $d \in A$
12         $A[d] \leftarrow A[d] + (1-\lambda)(R_U[d] - min_U)$
13   **else**
14         $A[d] \leftarrow \lambda min_P + (1-\lambda) R_U[d]$
15 $R \leftarrow$ NEW-QUEUE()
16 **foreach** $d \in A$
17   INSERT($R, \langle d, A[d]\rangle$)
18 TRIM(R, r)
19 **return** R

The FUSION algorithm is simple, requires no further disk-accesses after evaluation, and two linear passes through R_P and R_U, which are typically much smaller than the number of documents evaluated to produce the corresponding lists. Note that the only time we call the SCORE function is at the beginning, when we populate R_U (line 3). We do not score any document against P, whereas the standard RM3 algorithm would. This is where we receive the gain in efficiency over RM3. This method also has the advantage that it can be applied across virtually all scoring and processing strategies, as long as the final scores can be combined independently of each other (i.e. the final score of a document does not rely on any other score in the same list).

FUSION is neither score-accurate nor rank-safe: a document that does not appear in R_P will not receive the correct score - instead it will receive the lowest available score in R_P. This in turn can cause a change in the ordering of documents in R. Consequently all documents not in R_P are overestimated if they appear in R_U. The converse is true as well. Also, the ability of this method to reduce the number of accesses is limited – as the number of expansion terms grows, the percent of processing that FUSION will save relative to processing the whole query will decrease.

3.4.2 *Rewind*

In an effort to improve correctness among the final scores, we present another algorithm, which caches R_P and makes use of the scores in it when possible; otherwise we use P to score the document. We call this algorithm REWIND, since we rewind P, and use it to score documents as requested by U. The pseudocode for REWIND is shown below.

REWIND(P, R_P, U, λ, r)

1 RESET(P)
2 R $\leftarrow$ NEWQUEUE()
3 **foreach** $d \in \Delta(U)$
4   **if** $d \in R_P$
5         $score \leftarrow \lambda R_P[d] + (1-\lambda)$SCORE$(U,d)$
6   INSERT($R, \langle d, score\rangle$)
7   **else**
8   MOVETO(P, d)
9         $score \leftarrow \lambda$SCORE$(P,d) + (1-\lambda)$SCORE(U,d)
10   INSERT(R, $\langle d, score\rangle$)
11 TRIM(R, r)
12 **return** R

The REWIND algorithm is not as efficient as FUSION; in addition to calling SCORE with node U, it also will frequently call SCORE using node P (line 9). However iteration is directed by U (line 3), so REWIND still makes less SCORE calls than the original RM3 algorithm.

REWIND is a score-accurate algorithm but it is not rank-safe. Consider the set $\Delta(P) - \Delta(U)$. These are documents in the posting list(s) of P that are not in U. They will never be considered as candidates, therefore they will never receive a score, and have no chance of making it into R, the final ranked list. Therefore, all of the scores returned in R are correct, however some documents that should be in R may be omitted.

3.5 A(P) and $\bar{A}$(U)

We now assume that P is accessible, therefore we have access to its internal structure. The first modification we make is to replace P with P^M, its MAXSCORE equivalent, to improve evaluation over P's subtree. However we can go even further, and incorporate U directly into P^M's subtree. We do not need access to U to do this; we only need to take care to properly adjust the weight of U when we add it. We call this algorithm MAX-PLUS.

3.5.1 *Max-Plus*

Our plan is to add U to the subtree of P^M. However we must take care to properly adjust the weights when adding P. Fortunately, we have access to the weights associated with $\hat{P}^M$ as well as λ, our interpolation weight between the two components. Using these we can derive the appropriate weight for U. Let W_U be the desired weighting for U, $W_{PM} = \sum_{i=|P^M|} p_i$, $W = W_{PM} + W_U$ and by definition $\lambda + (1-\lambda) = 1$. We know the ratios of $\lambda : 1$ and $W_{PM} : W$

are equivalent:

$$\frac{\lambda}{1} = \frac{W_{PM}}{W} \rightarrow \lambda = \frac{W_{PM}}{W}, \quad \text{implying that}$$
$$\lambda W = W_{PM} \rightarrow W = \frac{W_{PM}}{\lambda}$$

Substituting into the ratio for W_U:

$$\frac{1-\lambda}{1} = \frac{W_U}{W} \rightarrow 1-\lambda = W_U \frac{\lambda}{W_{PM}}, \quad \text{we see that}$$
$$W_U = (1-\lambda)\frac{W_{PM}}{\lambda}$$

meaning we can represent the required weight for U in terms of the weights of $\hat{P}^M$ and λ. The conversion of the query example is shown graphically in Figure 3.

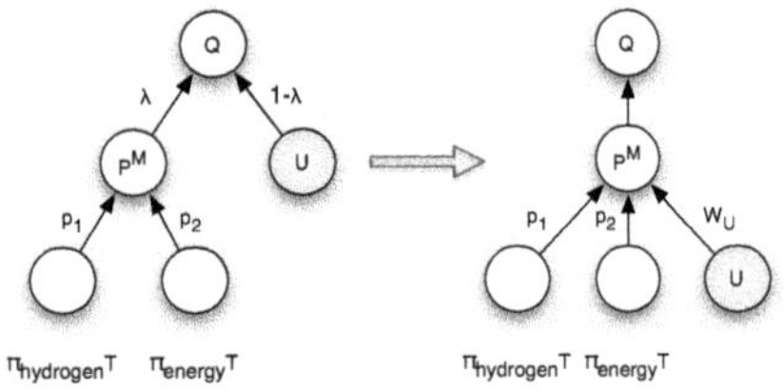

Figure 3: Converting the standard maxscore expansion to maxscore-plus.

3.6 $\bar{A}$(P) and A(U)

We now assume that U is accessible but P is not. As before, we replace U with U^M, to prune as much as we can over U's subtree. We can use the MAX-PLUS modification to incorporate P directly into the subtree of U^M. The calculation for W_P proceeds in the same fashion as for W_U earlier, therefore $W_P = \lambda(1-\lambda)^{-1}W_{U^M}$. To differentiate this version of the algorithm from MAX-PLUS, we use the label MAX-PLUS-U in the results section.

3.6.1 Warmup

Unlike the case of $A(P)$ and $\bar{A}(U)$, we can now make use of R_P to modify the operation of U. We would like to avoid adding P into the subtree of U^M, to save the cost of iterating over the posting lists in P again. Instead, we only use R_P to populate the internal candidate list of U^M; in other words we "warm up" the cache in U^M. From this point forward, we use the FUSION algorithm to produce final results. We define the SETBOUNDS function, which populates the candidate list of U^M with R_P. The pseudocode for WARMUP is shown below.

WARMUP(R_P, U, λ, r)
$U^M \leftarrow$ MAKE-MAXSCORE(U)
SETBOUNDS(U^M, R_P, λ, r)
return FUSION(R_P, U^M, λ, r)

3.7 A(P) and A(U)

We come to the situation where we can observe the internal structure of both P and U.

3.7.1 Max-Flat

We continue in the vein of MAX-PLUS and rewrite the query in order to flatten it into a single layer. Figure 4 shows the flattening of our query example from earlier. As before, we replace Q with Q^M to use pruning where possible. We remove nodes P and U entirely, and report scores directly to Q^M. Note that P and U themselves do not contribute to the scoring tally for our measurements. Therefore their removal does not affect the number of nodes being tallied; any change in the count will come from pruning.

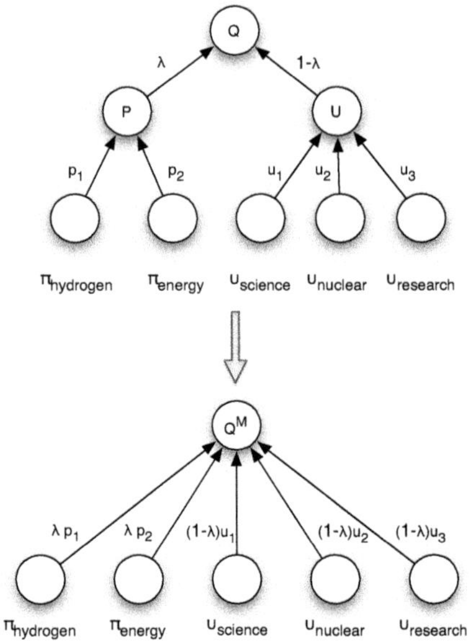

Figure 4: Flattening the query tree.

This assumption, that our components P and U may be expressed as linear combinations themselves, holds true for many of the popular retrieval models studied today. Therefore while it is a strong assumption, it also applies to a large portion of models studied to date.

4. EXPERIMENTS AND RESULTS

We vary three parameters when performing experiments:

Interpolation Weight The weight λ determines the importance of each subquery. We investigate three distinct values of λ: 0.2, 0.5, and 0.8 to examine how changing the importance of the subqueries affects each of the algorithms.

Number of Expansion Terms The ratio of terms between P and U will most likely impact the effectiveness of the algorithms. Let $\tau = |\hat{U}|$, the number of terms in the expansion. We use values of 10 and 100 for τ to examine minor and major imbalance.

Number of Items Requested We vary r, the number of documents requested in R, to determine how the algorithms are affected by needing to maintain larger candidate lists. This should affect the non score-accurate algorithms the most. We use values of 100 and 1000 to observe this effect.

AQUAINT	RM3	RM3+	Rewind	Fusion	Warmup	Max-Plus-U	Max-Plus	Max-Flat
Default	8515351	-4.4†	-5.1	-23.6	-50.6	-68.3	-7.1†	-85.3
$r = 1000$	8515351	-4.4†	-5.2	-23.6	-26.6	-64.6	-7.1†	-79.1
$\tau = 100$	104815675	-1.6†	-0.04	-2.5	-5.4	-46.8	-1.5†	-61.9
$\lambda = 0.2$	8515351	-3.0†	-5.1	-23.6	-66.5	-73.1	-2.7†	-80.0
$\lambda = 0.8$	8515351	-86.5	-5.1	-23.6	-32.0	-69.4	-92.3	-87.6
GOV2	RM3	RM3+	Rewind	Fusion	Warmup	Max-Plus-U	Max-Plus	Max-Flat
Default	193233121	-7.2	-7.0	-29.1	-63.3	-56.5	-9.0	-88.2
$r = 1000$	193233121	-0.6†	-7.0	-29.1	-40.2	-53.4	-9.0	-82.1
$\tau = 100$	2351713435	-2.8	-0.022	-3.3	-15.7	-50.8	-2.9	-75.2
$\lambda = 0.2$	193233121	-2.4	-7.0	-29.1	-76.4	-74.7	-1.5	-78.0
$\lambda = 0.8$	193233121	-86.7	-7.0	-29.1	-41.1	-54.5	-94.2	-87.6
CLUE-B	RM3	RM3+	Rewind	Fusion	Warmup	Max-Plus-U	Max-Plus	Max-Flat
Default	400366062	-23.7	-10.4	-26.5	-63.2	-58.0	-27.1	-90.7
$r = 1000$	400366062	-23.7	-10.5	-26.5	-42.1	-57.0	-27.1	-90.7
$\tau = 100$	4428706966	-11.6	-2.5	-2.5	-14.7	-58.3	-14.8	-81.2
$\lambda = 0.2$	400366062	-13.3	-10.5	-26.5	-73.9	-81.2	-8.5	-87.6
$\lambda = 0.8$	400366062	-68.9	-10.5	-26.5	-44.7	-58.1	-90.6	-93.6

Table 2: Results over AQUAINT, GOV2, and ClueWeb-B, using 36, 150, and 50 queries, respectively. The † indicates a change that is *not* statistically significant. The number in the RM3 column is the number of score requests under the unmodified algorithm. The numbers in the remaining columns are the percent change relative to the the unmodified RM3 model. We calculate this as $-(A - B)/A$, where A is RM3 and B is the algorithm in question.

We present the main efficiency results in Table 2. Each row provides the results for a particular parameter setting in a given collection, and a column is the performance of a method over the different parameter settings. For each parameter setting, we provide the average number of times the SCORE function was called, and the percent change from the average for the RM3 method. In all cases, the *default* setting indicates the following parameter values: $r = 100$, $\lambda = 0.5$, and $\tau = 10$. We include an RM3 run that makes use of MAXSCORE (RM3+), for comparison. In the graphical representation, we accomplish this by replacing node Q with Q^M, therefore we use the MAXSCORE algorithm directly on nodes P and U.

The results from the three datasets look largely equivalent, suggesting that the methods described here will retain their ability to improve over the baseline as the collection size increases. Both RM3+ and MaxPlus seem to generally perform better on the Clueweb-B dataset; analysis of this phenomenon reveals that the proportion of queries actively optimized (i.e. pruned) is much higher in Clueweb-B ($> 45\%$ in both cases) than in the other two collections ($< 23\%$). This in turn produces a larger impact on the average SCORE count.

Method	Default	$\tau = 100$	$r = 1000$	$\lambda = 0.2$	$\lambda = 0.8$
Baseline	0.0827	0.0827	0.1565	0.0827	0.0827
RM3	0.1153	0.1177	0.1984	0.1000	0.0991
Fusion	0.0978	0.1096	0.1888	0.0911	0.0912
Rewind	0.1153	0.1177	0.1945	0.1000	0.0993
Warmup	0.0824	0.0958	0.1678	0.0777	0.0793

Table 3: MAP results over the AQUAINT collection. Only methods that are non-safe are shown. The baseline method is the query-likelihood model, shown for comparison.

4.1 $\bar{A}$(P) and $\bar{A}$(U)

The behavior between the REWIND and FUSION algorithms is consistent between the collections; FUSION provides a significant decrease in the number of scores requested, while REWIND only reduces the evaluation cost by less than 10%. However we must also consider MAP scores for these algorithms. Table 3 shows the MAP scores produced by the non-safe[6] algorithms across the different parameter settings. Generally, the FUSION algorithm only provides a relatively small increase in performance over the baseline method (Language Model), and only in the case of $r = 1000$ does the performance of FUSION approach that of RM3.

Conversely, REWIND seems to stay true to the original scoring model, except in two cases. When $r = 1000$, the score is slightly lower than RM3. Analysis of the mean precision at different ranks shows identical precision scores until past rank 200. When $\lambda = 0.8$, the score is slightly higher than RM3, most likely due to the increased weight on U. Hence, more relevant documents would come from U, which are all correctly scored using REWIND.

4.1.1 *Fusing Larger Lists*

Given the results above, we wonder if increasing the number of results from just U would improve results. We have no control over R_P, however we can instruct U to return a larger list of documents that we could use in merging. We run a few experiments to observe this behavior (Table 4). We do not show the average number of scores requested, as they are the same across all runs. We express the increase as a percentage of the original list, i.e. a value of 10 indicates that we request $1.1r$ (10% more) documents to be scored, where r is the original list size.

The results suggest that increasing the size of the list returned from U can provide some minor benefits, but only

[6]Non-safe indicates an algorithm lacks either the rank-safe or the score-accurate property.

% More	0	10	25	50	100
MAP	0.0978	0.0977	0.0984	0.0986	0.0983

Table 4: Changes in MAP when varying the number of results requested from U.

up to a point. The decrease when we double the size of the list indicates that around that point we stop adding useful documents to the merging procedure, and that the overestimated score from P for those documents introduces noise in R.

4.1.2 *Maxscore Under the Hood*

While we have no control over the internals of either subquery in this configuration, we examine how FUSION and REWIND may interact with MAXSCORE. To test this effect, we replace P and U with their MAXSCORE version where appropriate. In FUSION, we apply it to U, and in REWIND, we apply it over the cached P and U. The results over the default parameter set are shown in Table 5. We can immediately see a large improvement in efficiency over the baseline methods. This indicates that FUSION and REWIND can combine with MAXSCORE to improve other using either technique alone. We leave further analysis as future work.

Method	# Scores	% Chg.	Orig
RM3	8143117.5	0.0	-4.4
Fusion	1791606.1	-78.0	-72.4
Rewind	2352511.6	-71.1	-77.8

Table 5: Results over the AQUAINT collection, now using the MAXSCORE optimization. The rightmost column indicates the change over the same method without the optimization.

4.2 A(P) and $\bar{A}$(U)

The MAX-PLUS algorithm is the only algorithm tested for this scenario. Under the default and $r = 1000$ parameter settings, MAX-PLUS provides a consistent minor improvement over the original algorithm. The differences are not statistically significant in the AQUAINT collection, however they are for GOV2. If the number of feedback terms is increased, the effectiveness of the algorithm decreases, which we expect — we have no control over U, therefore if its organization changes, it will have an effect on MAX-PLUS.

The most interesting result comes when $\lambda = 0.8$. Both RM3+ and MAX-PLUS perform exceptionally well. Further inspection reveals that in both cases, the bias towards P allowed for massive pruning during query processing. The only documents that have a chance to enter the candidate list are documents that contain components from P; specifically, the entire subquery. Therefore the only documents that are even considered are in $\Delta(P)$. The main difference between these algorithms is that MAX-PLUS directly integrates U into its early-termination algorithm, whereas RM3-Maxscore can only interact with the nodes opaquely. We believe this allows the MAX-PLUS algorithm to converge to a stable threshold more rapidly, resulting in the increase in performance over RM3-Maxscore.

4.3 $\bar{A}$(P) and A(U)

We now look to the performance of WARMUP and MAX-PLUS-U. Both algorithms provide substantial improvements over the original RM3 algorithm. As anticipated, WARMUP consistently outperforms the FUSION algorithm in efficiency, where we do not pre-set the candidate list for the U node. However if we consider effectiveness (Table 3), we see that in fact WARMUP performs worse than FUSION in all cases, and in some cases performs worse than the baseline method.

In contrast, the MAX-PLUS-U method appears to consistently provide substantial gains in efficiency, while maintaining score correctness. The only noticeable drop in performance for the MAX-PLUS-U algorithm comes from increasing the number of feedback terms ($\tau = 100$), which is consistent with the behavior of the other algorithms. However unlike several of the other algorithms, MAX-PLUS-U appears to be more robust to the parameter change.

4.4 A(P) and A(U)

Clearly, having access to both sub-nodes allows the most effective optimization of the entire set. The MAX-FLAT procedure consistently shaves off over 80% of the scoring requests, except when we increase the number of feedback terms by a factor of 10. Even under such conditions, MAX-FLAT still cuts over half of the scoring requests. Deeper analysis of this model shows that like MAX-PLUS and MAX-PLUS-U, having all of the term nodes managed by one MAXSCORE node allows for the fastest stabilization of the threshold scores. The only case where this is not true is when $\lambda = 0.8$, where P has so much weight that it largely overwhelms the contributions of U, allowing MAX-PLUS and RM3+ to perform on par with MAX-FLAT.

4.4.1 *Modifying the Scoring Order*

In the original MAXSCORE algorithm, the term scoring nodes are ordered according to the estimated lengths of their posting lists, the intuition being that if pruning occurs by the nodes processed first during a scoring pass, then moving the shortest posting lists to the front should minimize the number of documents considered. However our model has scoring nodes scaled by weights. Not only must we consider weights now, but as we rescale the weights of the nodes managed by the algorithm, as we do in the MAX-* algorithms, we often have the situation that some subset of the nodes have weights orders of magnitude larger than the others.

Considering these new factors, we explore the possibility of ordering by weight to increase pruning further. We reason as follows: If the pruning decision is contingent on the heavily weighted nodes, then if we order by length of the posting lists, this weight imbalance is ignored. Hence we tend to prune wherever we hit these heavily weighted nodes, no matter where they fall in the scoring order. Ordering by weight pushes these nodes to the front of the scoring list, removing the wasted effort of scoring nodes that do not trigger pruning. We test this hypothesis on the MAX-FLAT algorithm, and call it MAX-FLAT-W. Results are shown in Table 6 for different values of λ, and for $\tau = 100$.

Surprisingly, ordering by weight is only effective when $\lambda = 0.8$ or when $\tau = 100$. This indicates that the weight imbalance between the subquery components must be quite high for it to be effective. Worse performance of MAX-FLAT-W when $\lambda = 0.2$ supports this hypothesis. This weight brings the individual component weights closer to unifor-

Method	Max-Flat	Max-Flat-W	% Chg
$\lambda = 0.2$	1876666.2	3430090.9	+82.3
$\lambda = 0.5$	1248424.9	1795394.2	+43.8
$\lambda = 0.8$	1053798.0	615244.3	-41.6
$\tau = 100$	39932114.8	37111540.1	-7.1

Table 6: Comparing list length and weight ordering for the MAX-FLAT algorithm.

mity, reducing the importance of ordering the scoring list by weight.

4.4.2 *Effect on Wall-Clock Time*

We now examine changes in performance based on system time measurements. We perform 5 runs of the GOV2 collection, with the queries permuted randomly in each run to lessen any dependence on query order. We record the time to execute each query for each method, making a total of 750 samples for each algorithm. The system used is a non-dedicated cluster of 32 nodes, each node having 2 Xeon 3.2 GHz cores with 4Gb of RAM and having access to a shared disk-server, where the index resides. Therefore a single run executes on a single core in this cluster. To compute statistical significance between algorithms, we use a randomization test of 1 million samples with the sample mean as the sufficient statistic. We also determine what percentage of the queries shows some "positive effect" relative to unmodified RM3. Let $\mathcal{A}$ be the algorithm in question. If the value for $\mathcal{A}$ is less than 90% of the value for RM3 for a particular measure (either SCORE count or real time), we consider that to be a positive effect. For example, a value of 10 in the table indicates that 10% of the queries (75 of 750) had that measure reduced by at least 10% compared to RM3. Table 7 shows the mean runtimes of the samples, the percent change from RM3, and percentage of queries affected when measuring via SCORE count and real time.

Based on the results from Table 7, the algorithms seem to fall into 3 distinct groups. The strongest of these is MAX-FLAT, and to a slightly lesser degree, MAX-PLUS-U, which seem to consistently reduce both the SCORE count and the system time by a significant amount. Their average impact is high, and they cover a high percentage of the queries. The next group includes the WARMUP and FUSION algorithms. They also have a consistent impact, but their average impact is less pronounced. The final group, consisting of RM3+, REWIND, and MAX-PLUS, have average runtimes are greater than the unmodified RM3, but they still register at least a 10% measurement improvement for some number of the queries tested. Further analysis of this last group shows that when the algorithms work, they have a significant impact on both measurements, often resulting in reductions over 40%. However, as the table shows, these algorithms do not "trigger" very often, and the added logic used to continually check for a pruning opportunity results in a notable increase in execution time.

5. DISCUSSION AND CONCLUSION

We have shown that it is possible to greatly improve the efficiency of queries represented by a linear combination of subqueries, a common mechanism for integrating partial scores in information retrieval. Our results show that when the two subqueries are inaccessible, our options for safe optimization are limited, but there are several courses of action we can take that typically have little negative effect on the accuracy of results. When we have access to the internal structures, we can manipulate the query structure further, providing greater efficiency gains while making stronger correctness guarantees. Under the correct conditions, we can reduce the scoring cost by over 50%, and in many cases by over 80%, while not affecting the ranking results at all.

Method	Mean Time	Pct Chg	Pct. Affected	
			Score	Time
RM3	134.8	0	Score	Time
Max-Flat	19.4	-85.6✦	100.0	100.0
Max-Plus-U	68.6	-49.1✦	87.3	86.1
Fusion	129.3	-4.1✦	98.7	41.9
Warmup	119.4	-11.4✦	100.0	60.4
RM3+	245.9	+82.4	12.0	7.1
Rewind	139.9	+3.7	20.0	44.9
Max-Plus	230.7	+71.1	22.0	13.7

Table 7: Statistics over 750 queries run over GOV2. Mean times are in seconds. The ✦ indicates statistical significance at $p \leq 0.02$. The Score and Time columns report the percentage of queries that experienced at least a 10% drop in the given measurement.

Several phenomena here require further study to fully explain. All of the algorithms presented here appear to be sensitive to τ, therefore, determining the underlying cause of this sensitivity will give us even further insight into the interaction between the subquery components. Given the emergent behaviors shown by the algorithms, understanding what properties of the algorithms cause such behavior would help to predict the interactions between optimizations, queries, and collections.

Although several described algorithms provide substantial gains in efficiency, our experiments also raise new interesting questions to pursue. The results suggest that for different values of λ, different algorithms afford the greatest reduction in cost. Query analysis may enable us to choose which algorithm to use based on the value of λ, thereby leveraging the best possible optimization available. Also, the real-time analysis here shows that if we can cheaply predict whether a certain optimization will activate on a given query, we may be able to avoid unnecessary overhead by not trying to optimize the query in the first place.

The above results show how we can reduce the processing cost of the RM3 algorithm, implying a similar impact on other retrieval models as well. RM3 serves as an archetype of interpolated subqueries: many other retrieval models share structure similar RM3, therefore the algorithms developed here should easily transfer to those instances. Furthermore, we can look to apply these algorithms to even more diverse query types. Consider, for example, an n-gram index, where these mechanisms could significantly impact the processing time of scanning the term-level posting lists by making use of the stored n-grams. Recent research has made use of n-gram posting lists [8, 7], therefore we can consider the pre-calculated n-gram posting list as the subquery containing information, and the rest of the query (the unigrams) as not. We may encounter subqueries that must be evaluated against different indexes, such as in desktop search as described by Kim and Croft [9] or graph-based data, such as citation analysis information. One subquery may apply to the graph data, whereas the other applies to textual information. Other applications include temporal information, precalculated statistics for document or collection-level data, and geolocation information.

In the context of web search, the optimizations discussed here would most likely not impact the head queries that are heavily cached and optimized for performance. However tail queries could benefit greatly, as the use of psuedo-relevance feedback can still improve retrieval performance for such queries. The results here indicate that we can apply pseudo-relevance feedback, among other expansion techniques, to improve ranked results without suffering from high overhead.

In the past it was sufficient to investigate optimizations for queries that were simply bags of words - therefore one could assume that each component in the query represented a single iterator over a posting list. However with the advent of structured queries that are now being applied over increasingly larger and larger sets of data, the need to respect this additional structure while designing optimizations for query processing has become evident. We believe this research moves towards addressing this need, and we intend to continue this line of research to provide even greater improvements for structured query processing.

6. ACKNOWLEDGEMENTS

This work was supported in part by the Center for Intelligent Information Retrieval and in part by NSF grant #IIS-0910884. Any opinions, findings and conclusions or recommendations expressed in this material are the authors and do not necessarily reflect those of the sponsors. We would like to thank all reviewers for their helpful comments during the development of this work.

7. REFERENCES

[1] N. Abdul-jaleel, J. Allan, W. B. Croft, O. Diaz, L. Larkey, X. Li, D. Metzler, M. D. Smucker, T. Strohman, H. Turtle, and C. Wade. UMass at TREC 2004: Notebook. In *TREC 2004*, pages 657–670, 2004.

[2] V. N. Anh and A. Moffat. Pruned query evaluation using pre-computed impacts. In *Proceedings of the 29th annual international ACM SIGIR conference on Research and development in information retrieval (SIGIR)*, pages 372–379, New York, NY, USA, 2006. ACM.

[3] M. Bendersky and W. B. Croft. Discovering key concepts in verbose queries. In *Proceedings of the 31st SIGIR*, pages 491–498, New York, NY, USA, 2008. ACM.

[4] B. Billerbeck and J. Zobel. Techniques for efficient query expansion. In A. Apostolico and M. Melucci, editors, *Proceedings of the 14th International Symposium on String Processing and Information Retrieval (SPIRE)*, volume 3246 of *Lecture Notes in Computer Science*, pages 99–134. Springer Berlin / Heidelberg, 2004.

[5] B. Billerbeck and J. Zobel. Efficient query expansion with auxiliary data structures. *Information Systems*, 31:573–584, November 2006.

[6] E. W. Brown. Fast evaluation of structured queries for information retrieval. In *Proceedings of the 18th SIGIR*, pages 30–38, New York, NY, USA, 1995. ACM.

[7] Hao Yan, Shuming Shi, Fan Zhang, Torsten Suel, and Ji-Rong Wen. Efficient term proximity search with term-pair indexes. In *Proceedings of the Nineteenth International Conference on Information and Knowledge Management (CIKM)*, pages 39–45, Toronto, Ontario, Canada, October 2010. ACM, ACM.

[8] S. Huston, A. Moffat, and W. B. Croft. Efficient Indexing of Repeated n-Grams. In *Fourth ACM International Conference on Web Search and Data Mining*, 2011.

[9] J. Kim and W. B. Croft. Retrieval experiments using pseudo-desktop collections. In *Proceedings of the 18th CIKM*, pages 1297–1306, New York, NY, USA, 2009. ACM.

[10] V. Lavrenko and W. B. Croft. Relevance based language models. In *Proceedings of the 24th SIGIR*, pages 120–127, New York, NY, USA, 2001. ACM.

[11] Marc-Allen Cartright, James Allan, Victor Lavrenko, and Andrew McGregor. Fast query expansion using approximations of relevance models. In *Proceedings of the 19th CIKM*, pages 1573–1576, Toronto, Ontario, Canada, October 2010. ACM, ACM.

[12] D. Metzler and W. B. Croft. A markov random field model for term dependencies. In *Proceedings of the 28th SIGIR*, pages 472–479, New York, NY, USA, 2005. ACM.

[13] J. M. Ponte and W. B. Croft. A language modeling approach to information retrieval. In *Proceedings of the 21st SIGIR*, pages 275–281, New York, NY, USA, 1998. ACM.

[14] S. Robertson, H. Zaragoza, and M. Taylor. Simple BM25 extension to multiple weighted fields. In *Proceedings of the 13th CIKM*, pages 42–49, New York, NY, USA, 2004. ACM.

[15] S. E. Robertson and S. Walker. Some simple effective approximations to the 2-Poisson model for probabilistic weighted retrieval. In *Proceedings of the 17th SIGIR*, pages 232–241, New York, NY, USA, 1994. Springer-Verlag New York, Inc.

[16] J. Rocchio. Relevance feedback in information retrieval. In G. Salton, editor, *The SMART retrieval system: Experiments in automatic document processing*, pages 313–323. Prentice-Hall, Englewood Cliffs, NJ, 1971.

[17] G. Salton, A. Wong, and C. S. Yang. A vector space model for automatic indexing. *Communications of the ACM*, 18:613–620, November 1975.

[18] M. D. Smucker, J. Allan, and B. Carterette. A comparison of statistical significance tests for information retrieval evaluation. In *Proceedings of the 16th CIKM*, pages 623–632, New York, NY, USA, 2007. ACM.

[19] T. Strohman. *Efficient Processing of Complex Features for Information Retrieval*. Ph.D. dissertation, University of Massachusetts Amherst, December 2007.

[20] T. Strohman, D. Metzler, H. Turtle, and W. B. Croft. Indri: a language-model based search engine for complex queries. Technical report, in Proceedings of the International Conference on Intelligent Analysis, 2005.

[21] T. Strohman, H. Turtle, and W. B. Croft. Optimization strategies for complex queries. In *Proceedings of the 28th SIGIR*, pages 219–225, New York, NY, USA, 2005. ACM.

[22] H. Turtle and W. B. Croft. Inference networks for document retrieval. In *Proceedings of the 13th SIGIR*, pages 1–24, New York, NY, USA, 1990. ACM.

[23] H. Turtle and W. B. Croft. Evaluation of an inference network-based retrieval model. *ACM Transactions on Information Systems*, 9:187–222, July 1991.

[24] H. Turtle and J. Flood. Query evaluation: strategies and optimizations. *Information Processing & Management*, 31:831–850, November 1995.

Efficiently Encoding Term Co-occurrences in Inverted Indexes

Marcus Fontoura*
Google Inc.
Mountain View, CA, USA
marcusf@google.com

Maxim Gurevich
Yahoo! Research
Santa Clara, CA, USA
maximg@yahoo-inc.com

Vanja Josifovski
Yahoo! Research
Santa Clara, CA, USA
vanjaj@yahoo-inc.com

Sergei Vassilvitskii
Yahoo! Research
New York, NY, USA
sergei@yahoo-inc.com

ABSTRACT

Precomputation of common term co-occurrences has been successfully applied to improve query performance in large scale search engines based on inverted indexes. The results of such precomputations are traditionally stored as additional posting lists in the index. During query evaluation, these precomputed lists are used to reduce the number of query terms, as the results for multiple terms can be accessed through a single precomputed list. In this paper, we expand this paradigm by considering an alternative method for storing term co-occurrences in inverted indexes. For a selected set of terms in the index, we store *bitmaps* that encode term co-occurrences. A bitmap of size k for term t augments each posting to store the co-occurrences of t with k other terms, across every document in the index. At query evaluation, size k bitmaps can be used to answer queries that involve any of the 2^k combinations of the additional terms. In contrast, a precomputed list, although typically shorter, can only be used to evaluate queries containing all of its terms. We evaluate the bitmaps technique we propose, and the baseline of adding precomputed posting lists and show that they are complementary, as they capture different aspects of the query evaluation cost. We perform an experimental evaluation on the TREC WT10g corpus and show that a hybrid strategy combining both methods significantly lowers the cost of query evaluation compared to each method separately.

Categories and Subject Descriptors

H.3.3 [**Information Search and Retrieval**]: Selection process

*The work was done while the author was at Yahoo! Research

CIKM'11, October 24–28, 2011, Glasgow, Scotland, UK.

General Terms

Algorithms, Measurement

Keywords

Inverted index, term co-occurrence, precomputation, bitmaps

1. INTRODUCTION

Inverted indexes have been successfully deployed to solve scalable retrieval problems where documents are represented as bags of terms. Each term t is associated with a *posting list*, which encodes the documents that contain t. The cost of query evaluation depends both on the number of query terms and the length of their posting lists. To reduce this cost, previous approaches [16, 18] have used precomputation of common subqueries.

This precomputation is performed in advance, during index construction, and it is then used during query evaluation where multiple query terms are replaced with one composite term. The precomputed combinations are determined based on their frequencies in logs of past usage of the system. Precomputed lists are stored in the index as regular posting lists, and thus their number is limited by the available memory. For example, terms *New* and *York* can be substituted with the precomputed list for *New York*. While this approach has been shown to be successful in reducing the query evaluation time, it is limited by the fact that each additional posting list can only be used for queries containing *all* of the pre-joined terms. Moreover, given additional available memory, only a limited number of term combinations can be precomputed. We use this precomputation technique as a baseline.

In this paper we introduce a more flexible way to encode term co-occurrence using *bitmaps*. A bitmap is associated with each posting and encodes co-occurrence of the posting term with a fixed set of other terms, chosen offline at index construction time. Given k bits we can encode the co-occurrence of k different terms with the posting list term in a list with bitmaps. This allows us to use the posting list of a single term to resolve queries involving that term and any of the 2^k combinations of the chosen terms. Had we chosen to represent each of these combinations by a separate posting list, the memory cost, as well as the complexity of picking the right combinations during query evaluation, would have become prohibitive. As they represent many

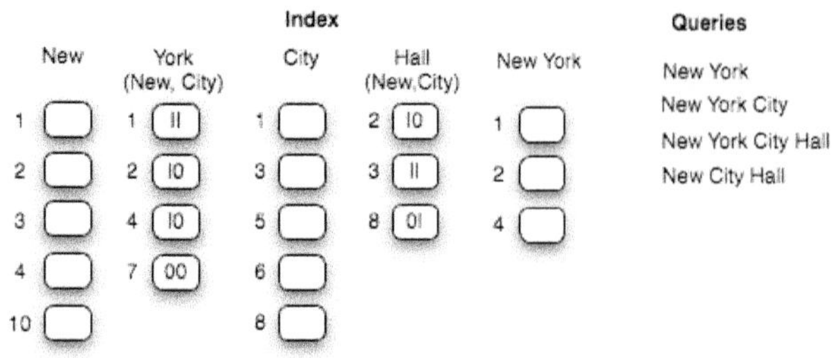

Figure 1: An example index with bitmaps for terms York and Hall and a precomputed list for New York (left) and example query workload (right).

term combinations, bitmaps are triggered more frequently during query evaluation, although this benefit is somewhat offset by the fact that postings lists with bitmaps are typically longer than precomputed lists.

In Figure 1 we present an example to illustrate the intuition behind the use of bitmaps. On the left of the figure we have an index with five posting lists corresponding to the terms *New, York, City, Hall* and the precomputed list for *New York*. Each posting list has document identifiers *(docids)* in sorted order. Besides *docids*, we represent bitmaps inside the oval. In this example each bitmap is 2 bits long. The terms corresponding to each bit in the bitmap are identified inside the parenthesis. An empty oval denotes no bitmaps for that term. There are two lists with bitmaps in this figure: York and Hall. The postings for term York contain bits for its co-occurrence with terms New and City. If we examine the bitmap for the posting of York in *docid* 2 we can see that it indicates that document 2 also contains term New but it does not contain term City. This is also apparent by the presence of *docid* 2 in New's posting list and by its absence in City's posting list.

On the right side of Figure 1 we show a sample query workload using the terms in the index. The index bitmaps have been optimized for this workload. We now provide some intuition on how to chose the terms to be represented in the bitmaps. Examining the workload we notice that the terms New and York co-occur in many of the queries. Thus, it would be beneficial to place a bit for New in York's list or vice versa. Since the posting list of York is shorter, we chose to place a bit for New in York's list. As terms City and Hall are both present in queries involving terms New and York, we can also add a bit for these two. In this example we are limited to bitmaps of size 2, we chose to add a bit for City in York's list. Now the first two queries can be evaluated by accessing only York's posting list. Similar reasoning is used to store the bits for New and City into Hall's posting list.

To contrast bitmaps with precomputed lists, consider again the query New York. This query can be answered either with the precomputed posting list New York or with York's list, which contains a bitmap that encodes co-occurrences of term New. In both cases only one list is accessed. The precomputed list has the advantage of being shorter, as it only contains the documents in the intersection of the lists for New and York. Therefore, using the precomputed list is more efficient as it contains only the *docids* that belong to the query results. On the other hand, bitmaps are more space efficient and more flexible – York's posting list can be used to answer queries York, New York, York City and New York City, while the precomputed posting list for New York can only be used in two of these cases. In this paper, we show that the bitmaps and precomputed posting lists capture *different* aspects of the query evaluation cost. These complementary properties lead to improved performance when using both techniques simultaneously.

1.1 Contributions

To determine which terms should be listed in the bitmaps of each posting list, we develop a model of the query evaluation cost as a function of the number of query terms and the lengths of the posting lists corresponding to these query terms. This cost model allows us to formulate the problem of selecting bitmap terms for each posting list as an optimization problem. Given a query workload (e.g., from a historical query log) and a memory budget, the goal is to select the optimal set of bitmap terms for all posting lists in the index, so as to minimize the evaluation cost of the workload. The optimization problem is NP-hard, but we show that the cost function is submodular, allowing for efficient approximation [15].

In this study we focus on the analysis of Boolean evaluation algorithm for conjunctive (AND) queries, which are prevalent in display advertising scenarios [24]. Boolean AND queries are also common in the first phase selection for web search queries, where the first phase results are reranked by machine learning scoring methods. We experimentally evaluate precomputed lists, bitmaps and their combination on the TREC WT10g corpus and a query workload derived from the AOL query log [20]. We show that the two techniques are complementary, as their combination achieves higher latency reduction than each technique individually. Latency reduction ranges from 25% for 3% growth in index size, to 71% for 4-fold index size increase. We also show that both precomputation techniques benefit not only past queries, contained in the workload used for building the index, but also new, previously unseen "long tail" queries.

In summary, the main contributions of this paper are the following.

- We introduce the concept of posting bitmaps as a flexible way to index term co-occurrences.
- We formally define the problem of selecting terms to precompute given a query workload and a memory budget, and propose an efficient solution for it.
- We show that bitmaps and precomputed lists complement each other, and that the combination significantly outperforms each technique individually.
- We present experimental results over the TREC WT10g corpus demonstrating the benefits of the approach in practice.

The rest of the paper is organized as follows. Section 2 contains background on indexing and query evaluation. In Section 3 we model the cost function of query evaluation and discuss the trade off between index size and evaluation time. Section 4 describes the index construction algorithms for bitmaps and precomputed lists, while Section 5 presents the corresponding query evaluation algorithms. Section 6 describes our experimental results. Section 7 reviews the related work. Finally, Section 8 presents our conclusions and future research directions.

2. PRELIMINARIES

2.1 Inverted indexes

Most search engines and information retrieval systems use inverted indexes as their main data structure for full-text indexing [28]. We remark that many modern applications are geared for high-throughput and low-latency scenarios (see, for example, [9, 24]), and consequently, the index data structures reside in main memory and are not swapped in from disk. There is a considerable body of literature on efficient index construction (e.g. [3, 6, 12, 14, 19, 26, 28]) and query evaluation (e.g. [7, 17, 26, 28]) algorithms.

In inverted indexes, the occurrence of a term t within a document d is called a *posting*. A posting has the form $\langle$*docid, payload*$\rangle$, where *docid* is the document identifier of d and where the payload is used to store arbitrary information about each occurrence of t within d. In this paper, we use part of the payload to store the co-occurrence bitmaps. The set of postings associated with a term t is stored in a *posting list.*

Each posting list is sorted in increasing order of *docid.* Often, B-trees [13] or skip lists are used to index the posting lists [12, 19]. This facilitates searching for a particular *docid* within a posting list, or for the smallest *docid* in the list greater than a given *docid.* In this work we use the following basic operations on posting lists:

1. *first():* returns the list's first posting;
2. *next():* returns the next posting or signals the end of list;
3. *search(d):* returns the first posting with *docid* $\geq d$, or end of list if no such posting exists. This operation is typically implemented efficiently using the posting lists indexes.

2.2 Query evaluation strategies

Although both precomputed lists and bitmaps can be used with different query evaluation algorithms, in this paper, we assume conjunctive Boolean queries and the document-at-a-time query evaluation model (DAAT) [23], commonly used in Web search engines. With Boolean queries no extra information, such as term weights, is required in the bitmaps and precomputed lists. In DAAT, the documents that satisfy the query are usually obtained via a join of the posting lists of the query terms. Given a conjunctive query $q = t_1t_2 \ldots t_n$, a search algorithm returns R – the set of *docids* of all documents that match all terms $t_1t_2 \ldots t_n$.

Let $L_1, L_2, \ldots, L_n$ be the posting lists of terms $t_1, t_2, \ldots, t_n$ respectively. A naive algorithm would scan $L_1, L_2, \ldots, L_n$ and return the set of documents that appear in all the lists. Clearly, the naive algorithm accesses $\sum_{i=1}^{n} |L_i|$ postings, where $|L_i|$ is the number of postings in L_i.

A more efficient algorithm is Max Successor [8], shown in Algorithm 1. It sorts terms in ascending order of their list lengths and traverses them in parallel. In each iteration, the algorithm checks whether the current candidate document from the shortest list appears in other lists. Instead of scanning over possibly numerous postings in longer lists, this step is implemented by skipping to the first position containing *docid* greater than or equal to the current candidate. If all lists contain the current candidate, it is added to the result set and the position in the shortest list is advanced by 1. Otherwise, the algorithms advances the shortest list to the following potentially matching document. The algorithm iterates until it reaches the end of one of the lists. The advantage of this algorithm that the number of list accesses is proportional to the length of the shortest list. We use this algorithm as the basis for our analysis and evaluation.

Algorithm 1 Max Successor: *search*(q)

1: Assume that $|L_1| \leq |L_2| \leq \ldots \leq |L_n|$
2: $R \leftarrow \emptyset$
3: $d_1 \leftarrow L_1.first()$
4: **while** d_1 is defined **do**
5:   **for** $i \leftarrow 2$ to n **do**
6:     $d_i \leftarrow L_i.search(d_1)$
7:     **if** $d_1 \neq d_i$ **then**
8:       $d_1 \leftarrow max(d_i, L_1.next())$
9:       break
10:     **else if** $i = n$ **then**
11:       $R \leftarrow R \bigcup d_1$
12:       $d_1 \leftarrow L_1.next()$
13: **return** R

3. EVALUATION TIME VS. INDEX SIZE

Our work trades off the size of the index with the query evaluation speed. Generally, query latency is directly correlated with the number of postings that are accessed during the evaluation of the query. We begin by analyzing the cost of query evaluation as a function of the lengths of the postings lists that are accessed and define an analytic cost function. We then discuss the trade off between the size of the index and query evaluation performance and show that bitmaps and precomputed lists capture different aspects of this trade off.

3.1 The cost function

The latency of the Max Successor query evaluation algorithm [8] increases both when the algorithm has to access more lists, and when the lists accessed are themselves longer. Understanding the exact interplay between these two parameters is integral to making principled decisions as to which precomputed lists and bitmaps should be added to the index.

In each iteration of the algorithm the cursor in the shortest list advances by at least 1, and therefore the main loop of the algorithm (line 4) is executed at most $|L_1|$ times. For the remaining lists, in each iteration the algorithm advances the cursors to the next relevant *docid*, skipping other postings along the way (line 6). These skips are significant, as the total number of accesses to a secondary list is *sublinear* in the length of the list.

With this in mind, we considered the family of functions expressed as:

$$F(q) = |L_1| \sum_{i=2}^{n} G(|L_i|),$$

where G is the sublinear function quantifying the number of accesses to the secondary lists. We validated this cost function experimentally using the TREC WT10g corpus and the AOL query log [20], measuring the lengths of the accessed postings lists and the evaluation time for each query. Typical implementation of skipping by B-trees or binary search suggests that the function G is logarithmic in shape. To test this hypothesis we considered $G(x)$ to be coming from the parametric family:

$$G(x) = C_1 + C_2 \log(x).$$

The best fit to the data was achieved by setting $C_1 = 12$ and $C_2 = 1$, which yielded an R^2 (R squared correlation coefficient) value of 0.65. Thus, this simple function explains almost 2/3 of the variation that occurs in the data. For the remainder of the paper, we then fix the cost function for evaluating query q to be:

$$F(q) = |L_1| \sum_{i=2}^{n} (12 + \log |L_i|) .$$

3.2 Optimizing the cost function

We now describe how precomputed lists and bitmaps minimize the two components of the above cost function (1) the shortest list length $|L_1|$ and (2) the random access cost $12 + \log |L_i|$. Suppose terms t_1 and t_2 frequently occur as a subquery and assume $|L_1| \leq |L_2|$.

Using precomputed lists we would store the co-occurrences of $t_1 t_2$ as a new term t_{12}. The size of t_{12}'s list is exactly $|L_1 \cap L_2|$ as it contains only the documents in the intersection of these lists. Therefore, precomputed lists reduce not only the number of posting lists accessed during query evaluation, but also the size of these lists, potentially impacting the length of the shortest list in the query. This technique decreases both components of the cost function while increasing the index by $|L_1 \cap L_2|$ postings.

In the case of bitmaps, we add a bit to the payload of each posting in L_1, where the value of the bit is 1 for postings whose document contains t_2 and 0 otherwise. This allows the query evaluation algorithm to avoid accessing L_2, cutting the second component of the cost function, $12 + \log |L_2|$. The extra space is a bit for each posting in L_1.

To demonstrate the complementary nature of the two precomputation techniques we analyze their applicability to different queries in our evaluation dataset (described in Section 6). For each query of at least two terms we computed the *minimum relative intersection size* (MRIS) — the relative size of the shortest list resulting from an intersection of two query terms to the shortest list of a single term: $\frac{\min_{i,j} |L_i \cap L_j|}{|L_1|}$. MRIS captures the potential benefit of adding the optimal precomputed list of two terms for this particular query: the lower the MRIS, the lower evaluation cost can be achieved; and, moreover, the lower is the storage cost of that precomputed list. Figure 2 shows the cumulative distribution function of queries as a function of their MRIS. While the majority of the queries have low MRIS and thus can benefit from precomputed lists, a non-negligible fraction of queries have relatively high MRIS, where precomputed lists are less beneficial. Indeed, in our experimental results we show that the potential benefit of precomputed lists declines sharply with increasing MRIS, while the benefit of bitmaps rises moderately (see Figure 5).

We note here that adding bitmaps to postings does not prevent delta compression of the *docids*. Traditionally, for disk based indexes *docids* are compressed in compact array that is separated from the payload to pack as many *docids* as feasible in the available memory. Accessing the payload is done only when needed and requires additional I/Os. For in-memory indexing, the access penalty is a lot smaller and

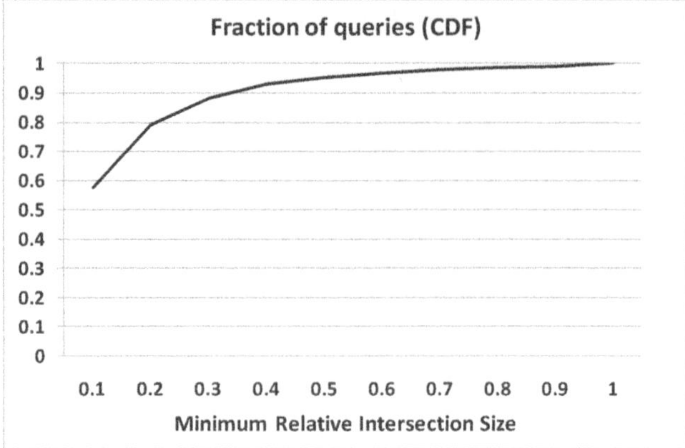

Figure 2: CDF of fraction of queries as a function of their minimum relative intersection size.

both options are applicable: storing the bitmap with the compressed *docids*, as well as using a separate payload array to store the bitmap. In either option the added cost of accessing the payload is captured by the C_1 and C_2 constants.

Given a typical query workload and additional memory budget, our goal is to find the optimal set of bitmaps and precomputed lists that minimizes the query evaluation cost function based on the given workload.

4. INDEX CONSTRUCTION

At index construction time, the central question is which bitmaps and precomputed lists should be added to the index to reduce the expected latency under the given query load. In both of these approaches we face a tension between the improvement in latency caused by using precomputed objects (whether bitmaps or precomputed lists) and the extra space required for precomputed results. Moreover, the problem does not decompose nicely, the contribution of a particular precomputation (whether bitmap or precomputed list) depends on the set of bitmaps and precomputed lists already added to the index. We first consider the problems of selecting bitmaps and precomputed lists separately, and then propose a hybrid algorithm for selecting them simultaneously.

4.1 Bitmaps

In the case of bitmaps the extra space required for adding a bitmap for term t_j to term t_i's list is exactly $|L_i|$ since every posting in L_i grows by one bit. The benefit of the extra bitmap varies. Suppose, for example, that we have terms New, York, and City, with list lengths $|L_{\text{New}}| \geq |L_{\text{City}}| \geq |L_{\text{York}}|$, and the queries are New York, City York, and New York City. Consider the benefit of adding a bitmap for term New to City's posting list. In the case that no previous bitmaps exist, this bitmap improves the evaluation of query New York City from $|L_{\text{York}}|(G(|L_{\text{New}}|) + G(|L_{\text{City}}|))$ to $|L_{\text{York}}|G(|L_{\text{City}}|)$. However, if the list York already has bits for terms New and City, the extra bitmap provides no additional benefit. In this case the total latency would be $|L_{\text{York}}|$ regardless of whether a bit for term New was added to City's list.

This leads us to formulate the bitmap selection problem as follows. Let B be the association matrix where $b_{ij} = 1$ if there is a bit for term t_j in list L_i's bitmap, and 0 otherwise. For example, we set $b_{\text{City New}} = 1$ in the example above. Given a set of bitmaps B and a query q, $F(B,q)$ is the latency of evaluating q with the bitmaps indicated by B. Here we assume q is evaluated using the optimal set of lists and bitmaps minimizing the evaluation cost. Finally, let S denote the total space available for storing extra information and $Q = \{q_1, q_2, \ldots\}$ the query workload. The problem is then:

$$\begin{aligned} \text{minimize:} \quad & \sum_{q \in Q} F(B,q) \\ \text{subject to:} \quad & \sum_i b_{ij}|L_i| \le S \\ & b_{ij} \in \{0,1\} \end{aligned}$$

Although the problem looks daunting, the cost function F has extra structure which allows us to find a near optimal solution. Consider the benefit of an extra bitmap, b_{ij}, when a previous set B has already been selected. This is exactly $F(B \cup \{b_{ij}\}, q) - F(B,q)$. Contrast this with the extra benefit when a larger set, $\hat{B} \supseteq B$ has already been selected, $F(\hat{B} \cup \{b_{ij}\}, q) - F(\hat{B}, q)$. The cost function defined in Section 3.1 exhibits diminishing returns, that is, the extra benefit of b_{ij} can only decrease as other bitmaps are added. More formally, the function is submodular.

LEMMA 1. *Let F be the cost function as above, and $B \subseteq \hat{B}$ be two sets of bitmaps already selected. Then for any b_{ij}, $F(\hat{B} \cup \{b_{ij}\}, q) - F(\hat{B}, q) \le F(B \cup \{b_{ij}\}, q) - F(B,q)$.*

Since the sum of submodular functions is itself submodular, we know that the objective in the mathematical problem defined above is also submodular. We now appeal to the theory of submodular function maximization subject to a budget constraint. As [15] shows, the simple greedy algorithm achieves a constant factor approximation to the optimum. At every iteration, for every potential bitmap b_{ij}, the algorithm computes the ratio of the benefit to the increase in index size:

$$\lambda_{ij} = \frac{\sum_{q \in Q} F(B \cup \{b_{ij}\}, q) - F(B,q)}{|L_i|}. \tag{1}$$

Then b_{ij} with the maximum λ_{ij} is selected as the next bitmap to be added, and the benefit ratios λ_{ij} are recomputed.

LEMMA 2 ([15]). *The greedy algorithm finds a set B that forms a $1/2(1 - 1/e) - \epsilon$ approximation to the optimal value of $\sum_{q \in Q} F(B,q)$.*

4.2 Precomputed lists

The problem and the algorithm for selecting precomputed posting lists is similar in spirit to the one for bitmaps. Given a set of precomputed lists $P = \{p\}_{ij}$, where p_{ij} is the indicator variable representing whether the results of query $t_i t_j$ were precomputed, we denote by $F(P,q)$ the cost of evaluating query q given P. We assume q is evaluated using the optimal set of posting lists minimizing the evaluation cost. Adding an extra precomputed list p to P can obviously only reduce F, but at the cost of storing a new list of size $|L_i \cap L_j|$.

Note that although precomputed lists can encode conjunctions of more than two terms, the utility of precomputed lists drops sharply with each new term, as the list requires that *all* of the terms be present in the query. We found that in the AOL query log (described in Section 6) the 100 most frequent three-term conjunctions appear in only one quarter of the 100 most frequent two-term conjunctions. Moreover, since the number of possible multi-term conjunctions grows exponentially with the number of terms in a query, considering them during index construction and during query evaluation becomes computationally expensive. We thus consider only precomputed lists of two terms that capture most of the benefit of such lists.

We can again describe the optimization problem as follows:

$$\begin{aligned} \text{minimize} \quad & \sum_{q \in Q} F(P,q) \\ \text{subject to} \quad & \sum_{ij} p_{ij}|L_i \cap L_j| \le S \\ & p_{ij} \in \{0,1\} \end{aligned}$$

An argument similar to the one in the last section shows that the objective function remains submodular and thus the same submodular function optimization technique described in [15] can be applied to quickly obtain a constant approximation to the optimum solution. Given a set of already selected precomputed lists P, we sort the potential precomputed lists by:

$$\lambda'_{ij} = \frac{\sum_{q \in Q} F(P \cup \{p_{ij}\}, q) - F(P,q)}{|L_i \cap L_j|}, \tag{2}$$

and select the precomputed list p_{ij} that maximizes λ'_{ij}.

LEMMA 3 ([15]). *The greedy algorithm finds a set P that forms a $1/2(1 - 1/e) - \epsilon$ approximation to the optimal value of $\sum_{q \in Q} F(P,q)$.*

4.3 Hybrid

Unfortunately, we cannot solve the optimization problem for selecting both bitmaps and precomputed list as above. The difficulty arises from the fact that while precomputed lists can carry bitmaps, we can only add bitmaps to the precomputed lists that are already selected. That is, the benefit of adding a bitmap to a precomputed list *increases* (becomes positive) after adding that precomputed list, violating submodularity requirement of the greedy algorithm [15]. Since we are not aware of an alternative optimization technique for achieving constant approximation to the optimum solution for such a problem, we resort to a heuristic approach.

One strategy could be to partition the budget between the two methods, and use each of the above two algorithms to first select precomputed lists and then bitmaps (some of which are added to the precomputed lists). However, deciding upon the budget fraction allocated to precomputed lists and to bitmaps may be hard, as the fraction depends on the distribution of the posting list lengths as well as on the query workload.

We thus use a hybrid algorithm that in each step selects a precomputed list *or* a bitmap that maximizes marginal benefit relative to the precomputed lists and bitmaps selected so far. That is, at each step we select either b_{ij} or p_{ij} that has the maximum marginal benefit given by Equations 1 and 2. To make the marginal benefit functions λ_{ij} and λ'_{ij} directly comparable, they have to be normalized according on the number of bits used for each bitmap and posting in precomputed lists. Let the number of bits per posting used for a bitmap be β_1 (naturally, $\beta_1 = 1$), and the number of bits per posting in a precomputed list be β_2 (β_2 is the size of the ⟨*docid, payload* ⟩ tuple, in our experiments $\beta_2 = 32$ bits). Then, we divide λ_{ij} by β_1 and λ'_{ij} by β_2.

5. QUERY EVALUATION

Given a query q and its matching posting lists our goal is to select a subset $\mathcal{L}$ of the lists to use for query evaluation. When there are no precomputed lists or bitmaps present, this algorithm has no choice but to use one list per query term. However, when additional information in the form of bitmaps or precomputed lists is available some lists may not be necessary.

5.1 Bitmaps

In the case of bitmaps, we can formally state the problem facing the algorithm as follows. We are given a set of query terms $t_1, t_2, \ldots, t_n$ and a set of postings lists associated with each term $L_1, L_2, \ldots, L_n$. In addition, the algorithm has access to the association matrix B where $b_{ij} = 1$ if there is a bit for term t_j in list L_i's bitmap. Our goal is to find a subset of the lists that minimizes the query cost, yet covers all of the terms. Formally, let $\mathcal{L} \subseteq \{L_1, L_2, \ldots, L_n\}$ be the set of lists that we will be using for query evaluation. $\mathcal{L}$ covers the query q if and only if:

$$\forall t_i \in q, \exists j \text{ such that } L_j \in \mathcal{L} \wedge (b_{ji} = 1 \vee j = i)$$

Then the goal is to find $\mathcal{L}$ that covers q and minimizes $F(B, q)$. Finding the optimum subset of lists is an NP-complete problem, which follows via a simple reduction from the set cover problem. We therefore use a greedy algorithm to select the best subset of the lists (Algorithm 2).

Algorithm 2 Query rewrite algorithm using bitmaps

```
Assume that |L_1| ≤ |L_2| ≤ ... ≤ |L_n|
Unmark terms t_1, t_2, ..., t_n
𝓛 ← ∅
for i ← 1 to n do
    if t_i is unmarked then
        𝓛 ← 𝓛 ∪ {L_i}
        Mark t_i
        for j ← i + 1 to n do
            if b_ij = 1 then
                Mark t_j
return 𝓛
```

The algorithm begins with all of the query terms unmarked. It proceeds by examining lists in increasing order of their lengths, since our cost function (Section 3.1) has a monotone dependence on the length of the lists – processing longer lists takes more time. If a given list L is unmarked, it is marked and added to $\mathcal{L}$. The algorithm then checks to see if any of the longer unmarked lists are present in the bitmap of L (and can hence be evaluated using only the information in L). It marks all of the lists that satisfy this condition and continues with the next shortest unmarked list. Although this greedy heuristic carries no formal optimization guarantees, it performed well in practice (see Table 1).

5.2 Precomputed lists

In the case of precomputed lists, the approach is nearly identical to the one described in the previous section. Our goal is to find the set of lists that minimize the cost function and jointly cover all of the query terms. Algorithm 3 begins with all of the query terms unmarked and examines the posting lists in increasing order of their lengths. If a given list for term t_i is unmarked, the algorithm marks it and looks for a precomputed list of term t_i and another unmarked term t_j. If found, the precomputed list L_{ij} is added to $\mathcal{L}$, otherwise L_i is added.

Algorithm 3 Query rewrite algorithm using precomputed lists

```
Assume that |L_1| ≤ |L_2| ≤ ... ≤ |L_n|
Unmark terms t_1, t_2, ..., t_n
𝓛 ← ∅
for i ← 1 to n do
    if t_i is unmarked then
        L ← L_i
        Mark t_i
        for j ← i + 1 to n do
            if p_ij = 1 ∧ t_j is unmarked then
                L ← L_ij
                Mark t_j
                break
        𝓛 ← 𝓛 ∪ {L}
return 𝓛
```

5.3 Hybrid

When both bitmaps and precomputed lists are available, we use a hybrid algorithm that first invokes Algorithm 3 to identify precomputed lists and then invokes Algorithm 2 for removing some of these lists that are covered by bitmaps in shorter lists. The rationale for first looking for precomputed lists is the higher potential benefit of identifying a precomputed list that becomes the shortest list for the query, therefore minimizing $|L_1|$ (the first component of our cost function defined in Section 3.1).

6. EXPERIMENTAL RESULTS

We conducted series of experiments to evaluate our algorithms. All experiments were performed on a Linux-based 8-core 1.8GHz server with 16GB memory. Our index construction and retrieval algorithms were implemented as single-threaded Java applications. We report *in memory* list access latencies measured after query rewrite and after preloading all posting lists into memory, averaged over several runs. We focus on the evaluation of in memory indexes since the strict requirements of high-throughput and low-latency, combined with the fact that today's commodity server machines have main memory that can exceed the disk capacities of a decade ago, makes disk-based indexes rarer for the large scale applications such as web search [9] or online advertising platforms that are the focus of our work. Although typical indexes are much larger than the memory capacity of a single machine, the indexes are typically divided into many partitions (shard) so that each partition fits into memory. The intent of our experiments is to highlight the benefits of precomputation in a single index partition.

We indexed the TREC WT10g corpus consisting of 1.68

million web pages. We extracted the textual content of the documents and discarded HTML tags. We built an inverted index where each posting contains a *docid* of four bytes and variable size payload containing bitmaps. Bitmap sizes vary from 0 to 32 bits, rounded up to the next byte boundary. The size for the basic index (with no precomputed lists or bitmaps) was 1.5GB. In our experiments we allowed for precomputation budget of up to three times the index size, which means that our largest index of 6GB (4.5GB occupied by precomputed results) still fits in memory.

The average query latency we measure directly translates to hardware costs of serving a query stream. The average latency of a query over the original index was 2.5 milliseconds. This latency corresponds to 1 on the y-axis in the figures showing query latency.

For query workload, we used the AOL query log [20]. We sorted all queries according to their timestamps and discarded queries containing non-alphanumeric characters, as well as all additional information contained in the log beyond query strings. The resulting 23.6M queries were split into training and testing sets. The training set consists of the first 21M queries from the AOL log, spanning 2.5 months. The testing set is a sample of 50K queries from the remaining 2.6M queries, spanning the following two weeks. The training set was used for creating indexes while the testing set was used for query evaluation.

Using the (properly anonymized) AOL query log has become very common in the research community, despite the controversy surrounding its release and subsequent withdrawal, as it is the largest and the most recent of the publicly available query logs. To make our results reproducible, we have chosen to use the AOL log, and not a proprietary query log.

6.1 Bitmaps and precomputed lists

We first examine the effects of each of the two precomputation techniques alone and then study their combination. We allowed for a memory budget equal to the size of 25% of the original index, for precomputed results. We then evaluated the benefit of allocating this budget for (1) bitmaps only, (2) precomputed lists (the baseline), and (3) both bitmaps and precomputed lists using the hybrid algorithm (Section 4.3). The ratio between the average query latency when using the index with precomputed results and the average latency using the original index is depicted in Figure 3. The figure shows that precomputed lists alone reduce the average query latency by 32% while the bitmaps alone by 41%. A combination of the two techniques achieves an even higher latency reduction of 53%.

We note that the above is not a completely fair comparison, as our algorithm only allows for pairwise intersection lists, while a bitmap may contain information about multiple terms. In order to demonstrate that this is not a limitation, we observe that going from pairwise intersections to triples does *not* reduce the size of the most frequently accessed lists significantly. The total number of postings in the lists for the top 1000 most frequent bigrams is 173.9 million, whereas the total number of postings in the top 1000 trigram lists is 169.9 million, a reduction of only 2.4%. At the same time, the top 1000 trigram lists cover less than one third of the queries covered by the top 1000 bigram lists. Thus, not allowing for larger intersection lists is not a major limitation. Furthermore, this data suggests that the top trigrams have a significant overlap with each other, and, we find this to be the case. Of the top 1000 trigrams 92.5% share a bigram with at least one other trigram in the list. This is exactly the situation where the bitmap approach is superior to simple intersection lists.

We next evaluate two strategies of allocating the shared memory budget for bitmaps and precomputed lists: (1) allocating a fixed fraction of the memory budget for bitmaps and precomputed lists, first selecting precomputed lists and then bitmaps using algorithms described in sections 4.1 and 4.2; and (2) bitmaps and precomputed lists simultaneously using the hybrid algorithm (Section 4.3). The ratio between the average query latency when using the index with precomputed results and the average latency using the original index is depicted in Figure 4. It is evident that the hybrid index construction algorithm successfully finds the optimal allocation without the need to decide on how to partition the memory budget between bitmaps and precomputed lists.

Finally, we use the index constructed using the hybrid algorithm and compare the fraction of queries that benefit from at least one precomputed list or at least one bitmap as a function of query MRIS (defined in Section 3.2). Figure 5 shows that while queries with low MRIS are effectively optimized using precomputed lists, as MRIS increases their effectiveness drops to almost zero. The effectiveness of bitmaps, on the other hand, is independent of the MRIS, thus their marginal benefit (captured by the hybrid algorithm) rises with MRIS.

6.2 Memory budget

We next evaluate the marginal benefit of allocating memory for precomputed results using the hybrid algorithm. Figure 6 shows the average query latency as a function of the precomputation budget, from 0% (the original index without precomputation) to 300% (precomputed results occupy 3/4 of the index). The figure shows that allocating as little as 3% of additional memory for precomputed results decreases average query latency by 25%. As the index grows to twice the original size, the latency decreases by almost 2/3. The benefit of further increasing precomputation budget is relatively low.

Note that although we experimented with encoding term co-occurrences with single bits ($\beta_1 = 1$), the results suggest that using multiple-bit encodings (e.g., to indicate terms proximity or term weights) would yield lower but still favorable index size vs. latency tradeoff. For example, for $\beta_1 = 4$ (i.e., 4 bits instead of 1), the index size cost of achieving 25% latency decrease would grow by the factor of 4, that is, the index would increase by 12% only.

6.3 Coverage of new queries

Many query streams, such as user queries to search engines, follow a "heavy tail" distribution – queries that have never been seen before comprise as much as half of all arriving queries [2]. It is thus important to not overfit the training data. To evaluate the effect of precomputation on long tail queries, we identify all queries in the test set that did not appear in the training set. These queries comprise 46% of our test set. Figure 7 shows the latency of all queries and compares it to that of the long tail queries, with and without precomputation. Note that without precomputation the average latency of long tail queries is lower by 22% than the average latency of all queries, since the posting lists

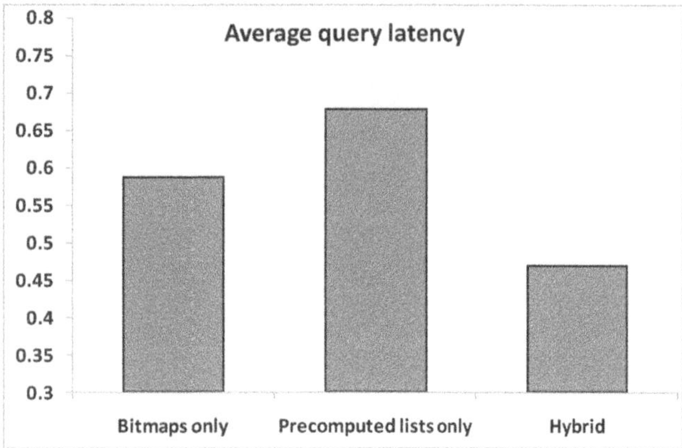

Figure 3: Query latency reduction with different precomputation techniques. Precomputation budget is 25% the size of the original index size.

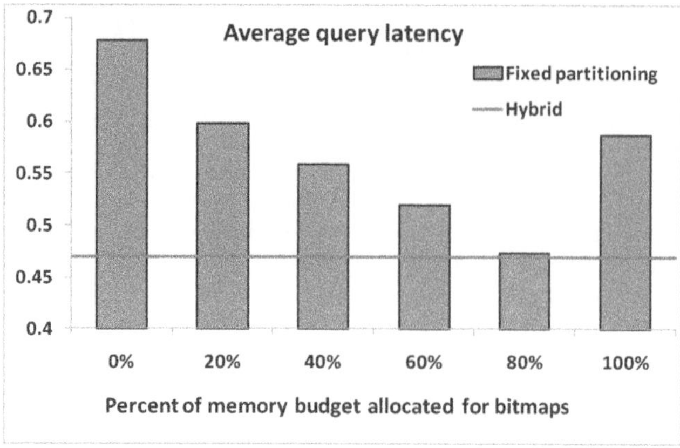

Figure 4: Query latency reduction as a function of memory sharing between bitmaps and precomputed lists. Total precomputation budget is 25% the size of the original index size.

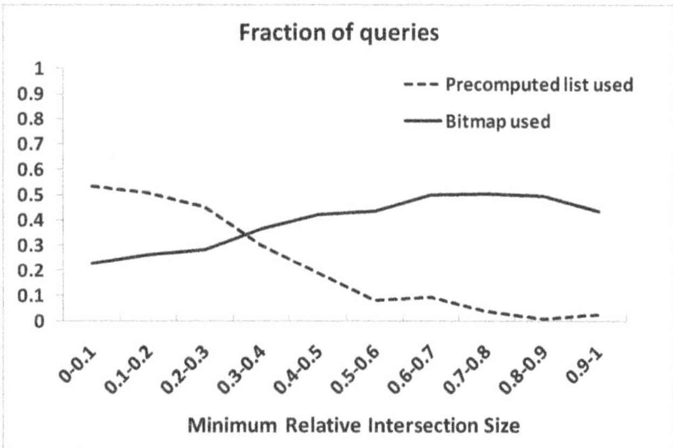

Figure 5: Fraction of queries optimized by at least one precomputed list or one bitmap, by query MRIS.

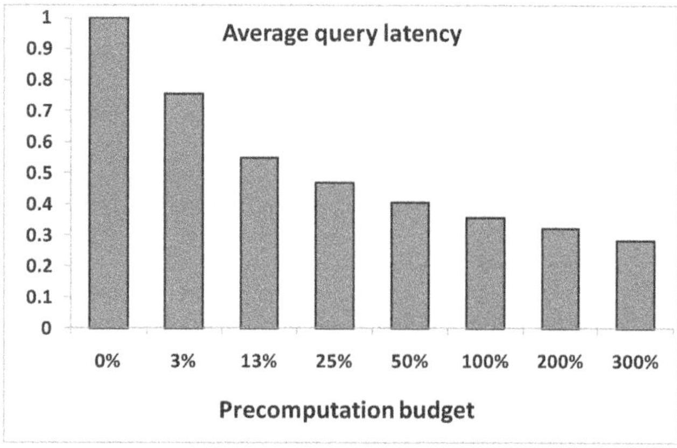

Figure 6: Query latency reduction with increasing precomputation budget (in percents of the original index size).

of terms in long tail queries tend to be shorter than average. This could possibly happen due to higher fraction of rare terms (e.g., names, foreign words, misspellings) in these queries. Yet, although the potential benefit from precomputation is lower for the long tail queries, and despite these exact queries did not appear in the training set, precomputation reduces their average latency by 33%.

To further demonstrate that precomputed results do not overfit the training we fix index and examine the average query latency of AOL queries spanning two weeks. Figure 8 shows that the average latency does not change, indicating that in this timeframe, while the query mix might have changed, the common subqueries remain the same and thus there is no degradation in performance. We conclude that for web search query logs, precomputation successfully captures common subqueries submitted in the future.

6.4 Query rewrite performance

We next evaluate how well the greedy query rewrite algorithm performs compared to the optimal algorithm. We identify the optimal query rewrite by evaluating our cost function on all possible rewrites given the index and selecting the one with the lowest cost. Table 1 summarizes the results for different precomputation budgets ("Avg. lists" stands for the average number of posting lists used to compute query results). Expectedly, as the precomputation budget increases, the quality of our heuristic approximation goes down, albeit only slightly. Even when half of the index contains precomputed results, the evaluation cost due to heuristic approximation is only two percent higher than with the optimal rewrite.

Metric \ Budget	3%	25%	100%
Avg. lists before rewrite	2.83	2.83	2.83
Avg. lists after heuristic rewrite	2.49	2.13	1.92
Avg. lists after optimal rewrite	2.48	2.12	1.90
Fraction of rewritten queries	28%	50%	60%
Heuristic rewrite is optimal	97%	91%	87%
Heuristic cost over optimal	0.2%	0.8%	1.7%

Table 1: Query rewrite performance for precomputation budget of 3%, 25%, and 100% of the original index size.

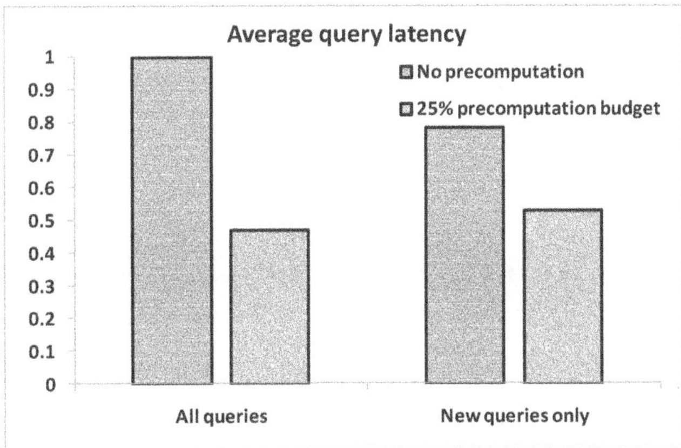

Figure 7: Query latency reduction of long tail queries compared to all queries. Precomputation budget is 25% of the original index size.

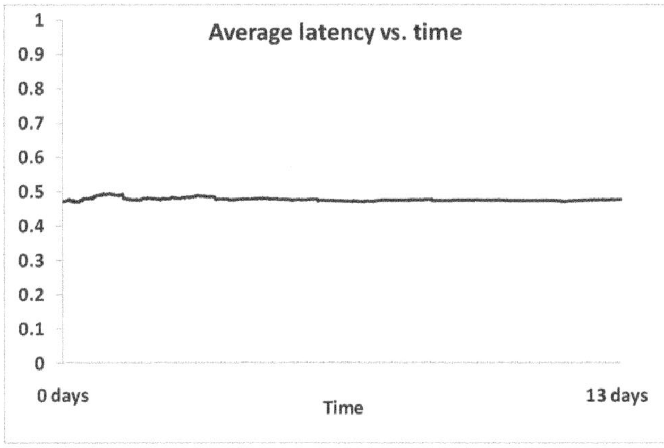

Figure 8: Query latency reduction as a function of time after the last query appearing in the training set. Precomputation budget is 25% of the original index size.

6.5 Index construction overhead

While in this work we focus on query evaluation costs, and not on efficient index construction, we report index construction overhead using straightforward batch implementation of the algorithms we describe. We used a single-threaded code that used up to 16G of memory.

Recall that the TREC WT10g corpus we index consists of 1.68 million documents of average length 217 (after discarding non-textual content), corresponding to 365 million postings. Index inversion takes about 50 minutes. For selecting bitmaps, precomputed lists, and the hybrid approach we used the same code that could be configured to implement either approach. For precomputation budget of 25%, the analysis of the query log (21M training queries) and the greedy submodular optimization take about 160 minutes, while adding the selected precomputation lists and bitmaps to the index takes additional 13 minutes. Thus, the total overhead of adding precomputed results to the index is of the same order as the time it takes to construct the standard inverted index. Obviously, for a partitioned index, index construction can be parallelized across partitions.

7. RELATED WORK

To the best of our knowledge, this is the first work that uses the posting list payloads to encode term co-occurrence. Several other works explored using payloads for different kinds of precomputation. In [25] the authors propose to index phrase queries using a combination of a nextword and a phrase index, achieving significant reduction in the query evaluation latency at the expense of small increase of the index size. In [11] the authors explore the use of the posting payloads to improve processing of phrase queries by using algebraic signatures of the content preceding the current posting. In [27] the authors propose to precompute and store in the index term proximity information, and then use it to speed-up retrieval.

There is an extensive line of works on list intersection techniques, [4, 5, 8, 10] to name a few. These works mainly focus on the worst-case complexity of computing intersections of arbitrary lists. Conversely, in this paper our goal is optimizing query performance for the *given* index and query workload, exploiting the fact that some lists are more likely to be intersected than the others.

One of the first works that explored the use of precomputed posting lists was done by Long and Suel [18]. They proposed a three-level caching strategy, where the second level consisted of precomputed posting lists of frequently occurring pairs of terms. A similar strategy was also proposed in the context of P2P search [22]. In [16], the authors show how to use precomputed posting lists together with early termination in order to improve the query performance of information retrieval systems. The contribution of that work is combining these two techniques using rigorous theoretical analysis. In addition, the authors performed empirical tests on the TREC GOV2 data set and on real web queries showing the performance gains of their early termination method.

Several authors have focused on improving top-k query performance through optimized DAAT and TAAT query evaluation algorithms (e.g. [7, 23]). These algorithms focus on vector space model queries and use upper bounds on term weights to *skip* posting entries that are guaranteed to not influence query results. Turtle and Flood [23] propose both TAAT and DAAT versions of the *max score* algorithm. Broder et. al [7] propose the WAND (Weighted AND) DAAT algorithm, which uses upper bounds to reduce the number of full score computations. In [1] weight quantization is used to reduce the evaluation cost at the expense of slight decrease in accuracy.

Another related line of work is the use of *fancy lists* to improve query performance [17, 21]. Fancy lists are small posting lists that contain the documents with the highest score for each term in the dictionary. In [21], for instance, a new DAAT algorithm that improves upon the DAAT *max score* [23] is proposed. This algorithm uses fancy lists to set a better initial threshold for DAAT *max score*.

8. CONCLUSIONS

In this paper we introduced the concept of bitmaps for optimizing query evaluation over inverted indexes. Bitmaps allow for a flexible way of storing information about term co-occurrences and complement the traditional approach of precomputed lists. We proposed a greedy procedure for the problem of selecting bitmaps and precomputed lists that is a constant approximation to the optimal algorithm. The analysis of bitmaps and precomputed lists over the TREC WT10g corpus shows that the hybrid approach achieves 25% query performance improvement for 3% growth in index size and 71% for 4-fold index size increase. An interesting future work is exploring the application of bitmaps to non-Boolean top-k retrieval. In this case one needs to store extra information in the bitmaps, such as weights in the case of vector space queries and term positions in the case of phrase queries.

9. REFERENCES

[1] V. N. Anh, O. de Kretser, and A. Moffat. Vector-space ranking with effective early termination. In *SIGIR*, pages 35–42, 2001.

[2] R. Baeza-Yates, A. Gionis, F. Junqueira, V. Murdock, V. Plachouras, and F. Silvestri. The impact of caching on search engines. In *Proc. 30th SIGIR*, pages 183–190, 2007.

[3] R. Baeza-Yates and B. Ribeiro-Neto. *Modern Information Retrieval.* Addison Wesley, 1999.

[4] R. A. Baeza-Yates. A fast set intersection algorithm for sorted sequences. In *CPM*, pages 400–408, 2004.

[5] J. Barbay, A. L?pez-Ortiz, and T. Lu. Faster adaptive set intersections for text searching. In *Experimental Algorithms*, volume 4007 of *Lecture Notes in Computer Science*, pages 146–157. Springer Berlin / Heidelberg, 2006.

[6] S. Brin and L. Page. The anatomy of a large-scale hypertextual Web search engine. In *WWW*, 1998.

[7] A. Z. Broder, D. Carmel, M. Herscovici, A. Soffer, and J. Zien. Efficient query evaluation using a two-level retrieval process. In *CIKM*, 2003.

[8] J. S. Culpepper and A. Moffat. Compact set representation for information retrieval. In *SPIRE*, pages 137–148, 2007.

[9] J. Dean. Challenges in building large-scale information retrieval systems: invited talk. In *WSDM*, page 1, 2009.

[10] B. Ding and A. C. König. Fast set intersection in memory. *Proc. VLDB Endow.*, 4:255–266, January 2011.

[11] C. du Mouza, W. Litwin, P. Rigaux, and T. Schwarz. As-index: a structure for string search using n-grams and algebraic signatures. In *CIKM 2009*, pages 295–304, New York, NY, USA, 2009. ACM.

[12] M. Fontoura, E. J. Shekita, J. Y. Zien, S. Rajagopalan, and A. Neumann. High performance index build algorithms for intranet search engines. In *VLDB*, 2004.

[13] H. Garcia-Molina, J. Ullman, and J. Widom. *Database System Implementation.* Prentice Hall, 2000.

[14] S. Heinz and J. Zobel. Efficient single-pass index construction for text databases. *JASIST*, 54(8), 2003.

[15] A. Krause and C. Guestrin. A note on the budgeted maximization of submodular functions. Technical Report CMU-CALD-05-103, Carnegie Mellon University, 2005.

[16] R. Kumar, K. Punera, T. Suel, and S. Vassilvitskii. Top-k aggregation using intersections of ranked inputs. In *WSDM 2009*, pages 222–231, New York, NY, USA, 2009. ACM.

[17] X. Long and T. Suel. Optimized query execution in large search engines with global page ordering. In *VLDB*, 2003.

[18] X. Long and T. Suel. Three-level caching for efficient query processing in large web search engines. In *WWW 2005*, pages 257–266, New York, NY, USA, 2005. ACM.

[19] S. Melnik, S. Raghavan, B. Yang, and H. Garcia-Molina. Building a distributed full-text index for the web. In *WWW*, 2001.

[20] G. Pass, A. Chowdhury, and C. Torgeson. A picture of search. In *Proc. 1st InfoScale*, 2006.

[21] T. Strohman, H. R. Turtle, and W. B. Croft. Optimization strategies for complex queries. In *SIGIR*, pages 219–225, 2005.

[22] B. B. Sudarshan, S. Chawathe, V. Gopalakrishnan, P. Keleher, and B. Silaghi. Efficient peer-to-peer searches using result-caching. In *In Proc. of the 2nd Int. Workshop on Peer-to-Peer Systems*, 2003.

[23] H. Turtle and J. Flood. Query evaluation: strategies and optimizations. *Inf. Process. Manage.*, 31(6), 1995.

[24] S. Whang, C. Brower, J. Shanmugasundaram, S. Vassilvitskii, E. Vee, R. Yerneni, and H. Garcia-Molina. Indexing boolean expressions. *PVLDB*, 2(1):37–48, 2009.

[25] H. E. Williams, J. Zobel, and D. Bahle. Fast phrase querying with combined indexes. *ACM Trans. Inf. Syst.*, 22(4):573–594, 2004.

[26] I. Witten, A. Moffat, and T. Bell. *Managing Gigabytes.* Morgan Kaufmann, 1999.

[27] H. Yan, S. Shi, F. Zhang, T. Suel, and J.-R. Wen. Efficient term proximity search with term-pair indexes. In *Proc. 19th CIKM*, pages 1229–1238, 2010.

[28] J. Zobel and A. Moffat. Inverted files for text search engines. *ACM Computing Surveys*, 38(2), 2006.

SIMD-Based Decoding of Posting Lists

Alexander A. Stepanov, Anil R. Gangolli, Daniel E. Rose
Ryan J. Ernst, Paramjit S. Oberoi

A9.com
130 Lytton Ave.
Palo Alto, CA 94303
{stepanov,gangolli,danrose,rjernst,paramjit}@a9.com

ABSTRACT

Powerful SIMD instructions in modern processors offer an opportunity for greater search performance. In this paper, we apply these instructions to decoding search engine posting lists. We start by exploring variable-length integer encoding formats used to represent postings. We define two properties, *byte-oriented* and *byte-preserving*, that characterize many formats of interest. Based on their common structure, we define a taxonomy that classifies encodings along three dimensions, representing the way in which data bits are stored and additional bits are used to describe the data. Using this taxonomy, we discover new encoding formats, some of which are particularly amenable to SIMD-based decoding. We present generic SIMD algorithms for decoding these formats. We also extend these algorithms to the most common traditional encoding format. Our experiments demonstrate that SIMD-based decoding algorithms are up to 3 times faster than non-SIMD algorithms.

Categories and Subject Descriptors

E.4 [**Coding and Information Theory**]: Data Compaction and Compression; H.3.1 [**Information Storage and Retrieval**]: Content Analysis and Indexing—*indexing methods*; C.1.2 [**Processor Architectures**]: [Single-instruction-stream, multiple-data-stream processors (SIMD)]

General Terms

Algorithms, Performance, Measurement, Experimentation

Keywords

variable-length integer encoding, SIMD

1. INTRODUCTION

The central data structure in search engines is the *inverted index*, a mapping from index terms to the documents that contain them. The set of documents containing a given word is known as a *posting list*. Documents in posting lists are typically represented by unique nonnegative integer identifiers. Posting lists are generally kept in sorted order to enable fast set operations which are required for query processing.

Because posting lists typically account for a large fraction of storage used by the search engine, it is desirable to compress the lists. Smaller lists mean less memory usage, and in the case of disk-based indices, smaller lists reduce I/O and therefore provide faster access. A common way to compress posting lists is to replace document IDs in the list with differences between successive document IDs, known as Δ-*gaps* (sometimes just *gaps* or *d-gaps*). Since Δ-gaps are on average necessarily smaller than raw document IDs, we can use a variable-length unsigned integer encoding method in which smaller values occupy less space. In a sorted list the Δ-gaps are always non-negative, so we are only concerned with encoding nonnegative integers; for the remainder of the paper "integer" means unsigned integer.

The integer encoding for a posting list is performed infrequently, at indexing time. The decoding, however, must be performed for every uncached query. For this reason, efficient integer decoding algorithms are essential, as are encoding formats that support such efficient decoding.

We started by exploring several commonly-used variable-length integer encodings and their associated decoding algorithms. Based on their common structure, we defined a taxonomy that encompassed these existing encodings and suggested some novel ones. Our investigation was motivated by the desire to incorporate fine-grained parallelism to speed up integer decoding. We were able to develop decoding methods that use SIMD instructions available on many general-purpose processors, in particular current Intel and forthcoming AMD processors. In this paper, we present these methods and evaluate them against traditional techniques. Our results indicate significant performance benefit from applying SIMD to these new formats.

The remainder of the paper is organized as follows. We review some related work on encoding formats and decoding algorithms in Section 2. Section 3 presents our taxonomy of byte-oriented encodings. Section 4 describes three particular encoding formats which are well suited to SIMD parallelism in more detail. Section 5 gives an overview of our use of SIMD on Intel-compatible processors. In Section 6 we provide SIMD algorithms for decoding the formats introduced in Section 4. Section 7 contains an evaluation of the results, followed by our conclusions in Section 8.

CIKM'11, October 24–28, 2011, Glasgow, Scotland, UK.

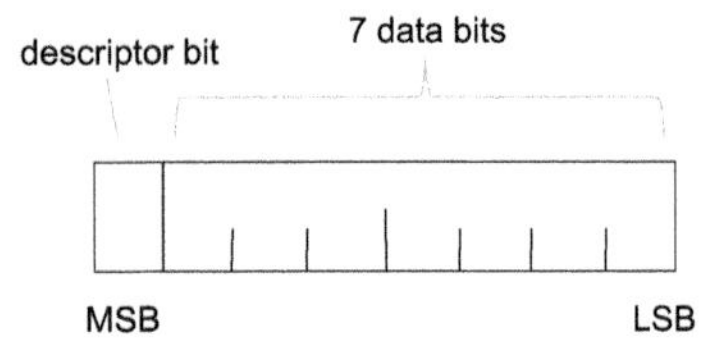

Figure 1: Format known in the literature as "vbyte", "vint", etc. Called *varint-SU* in the taxonomy of Section 3.

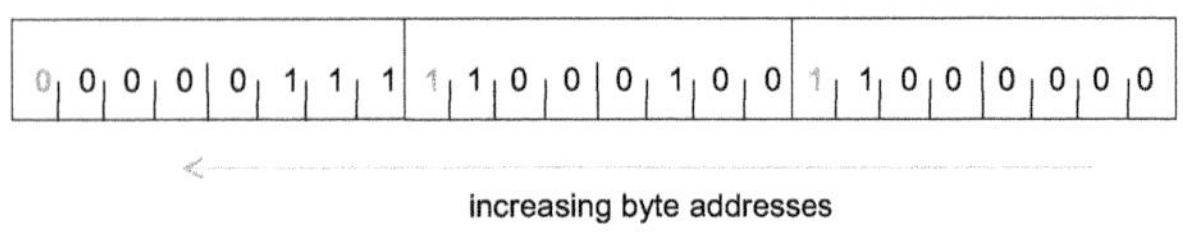

Figure 2: Storing the integer 123456 in varint-SU format.

2. RELATED WORK

The problem of integer encoding has been studied for several decades. General compression techniques such as Huffman coding often utilize analysis of the data to choose optimal representations for each codeword. Many applications, however, use techniques that do not depend on data distribution. These are called *nonparametric* codes [4].

Encoded representations of data may also be classified as byte- or bit-aligned, depending on whether codewords are required to end on byte boundaries. In addition, Anh [1, 2] introduced an interesting class of *word-aligned* encodings (e.g. Simple-9). These encodings occupy an intermediate place between bit-aligned and byte-aligned encodings by allowing codewords to end at an arbitrary bit position as long as they do not cross the machine word boundary.

While there are multiple choices for encoding posting lists in information retrieval applications, in this paper we concentrate exclusively on non-parametric, byte-oriented encodings.

The most common such encoding format uses 7 bits of each byte to represent data, and one bit to represent whether the encoded representation of the integer continues into the next byte (see Figure 1). This format has a long history, dating back at least to the MIDI specification in the early 1980s [14], and foreshadowed by earlier work on byte-based vocabulary compression by H.S. Heaps [11]. As early as 1990, Cutting and Pedersen [7] used this format to encode Δ-gaps in an inverted index. The information retrieval literature refers to the format by many different names, including vbyte, vint, and VB. Different authors give slightly different versions that vary on endianness, location of the continuation bit (most significant vs. least significant), and whether 0 or 1 indicates continuation. Figure 2 illustrates this encoding for the integer 123456 with little-endian, most significant bit and 1 for continuation.

Another format *BA*, introduced by Grossman in 1995 [10] uses 2 bits of the first byte to indicate the length of the encoded integer in binary. In his 2009 WSDM keynote, Dean [8] described a format he calls *group varint* that extends the BA format (which he calls *varint-30*) and reported significant performance gains obtained at Google by adopting it. A similar but more general format was described by Westmann et al. [19] in the database context. Schlegel et al. [17] applied SIMD-based decompression algorithms to a specialized version of Westmann's format that coincides exactly with group varint, but under the name *k-wise null suppression*. While they do not precisely describe the decoding and table generation, we believe that their algorithms are special cases of the generalized algorithms we describe in Section 6. All of these encodings fall into the taxonomy defined in this paper.

Büttcher et al. [4] have compared performance of several encoding techniques using posting lists from the GOV2 corpus on a particular query sample. They originally reported vbyte being the fastest at decoding, with Simple-9 being second. They recently updated their analysis [5] to include the group varint format, reporting that it outperforms both vbyte and Simple-9. Our experiments (presented in Section 7) show that the SIMD techniques described in this paper significantly outperform all of these in decoding speed.

3. BYTE-ORIENTED ENCODINGS

Encoding formats are generally distinguished by the granularity of their representation. We focus on encodings satisfying the following definition.

DEFINITION 1. *We call an encoding* byte-oriented *if it satisfies the following conditions:*

1. *All significant bits of the natural binary representation are preserved.*
2. *Each byte contains bits from only one integer.*
3. *Data bits within a single byte of the encoding preserve the ordering they had in the original integer.*
4. *All bits from a single integer precede all bits from the next integer.*

A byte-oriented encoding is fixed-length *if every integer is encoded using the same number of bytes. Otherwise it is* variable-length.

Since variable-length byte-oriented formats must encode the length of the encoded data, they vary along the following three dimensions:

- The length can be expressed in binary or unary.
- The bits representing the length can be stored adjacent to the data bits of the corresponding integer so that some data bytes contain both data and length information; alternatively, lengths of several integers can be grouped together into one or more bytes distinct from the bytes containing data bits.
- If the length is represented in unary, the bits of the unary representation may be packed contiguously, or split across the bytes of the encoded integer.

It is evident that for byte-oriented formats, the natural unit of length is a byte. We call the set of bits used to represent the length the *descriptor*, since it describes how the data bits are organized.

Table 1: Nomenclature of Byte-Oriented Integer Encoding Formats

Descriptor Arrangement	Descriptor Length Encoding	Abbreviation	Names in the Literature
split	unary	varint-SU	v-byte [6], vbyte [4], varint [8], VInt [3], VB [13] (earlier references [14], [7] do not name the format)
packed	unary	varint-PU	none (format introduced in this paper)
group	unary	varint-GU	none (format introduced in this paper)
split	binary	varint-SB	none
packed	binary	varint-PB	BA [10], varint30 [8]
group	binary	varint-GB	group varint [8], k-wise (k=4) null suppression [17]

We assume that each encoded integer requires at least one byte, so both binary and unary descriptors can represent the length n by recording the value $n-1$. This reduces the number of bits required to represent a given length.[1]

The dimensions listed above provide the basis of a taxonomy of byte-oriented encoding formats for integers that can be encoded in four bytes or less. Selecting one of the possible options for each dimension determines a position in the taxonomy. This taxonomy, shown in Table 1, provides a unifying nomenclature for the encoding formats, several of which have been described previously under various names.

For example, Grossman's BA format becomes *varint-PB* in our taxonomy, since it is a *variable*-length encoding of *integers* with descriptor bits *packed* together and representing the length in *binary*.

For the unary formats, we follow the natural convention where the quantity is represented by the number of consecutive 1 bits, followed by a terminating 0. We start from the least significant bit. Thus 0111 represents the number 3.

Accordingly, the vbyte encoding may be viewed as representing the length $-$ 1 of the encoded representation in the sequence of continuation bits. For example, a three-byte integer encoding would look like this:

```
1xxxxxxx
1xxxxxxx
0xxxxxxx
```

Notice that the leading bits form the unary number 2, representing the length 3. Thus we call this representation *varint-SU*, since it is a *variable*-length representation of *integers* with length information *split* across several bytes and represented in *unary*. While unary length representation has been widely used in bit-oriented encodings, for byte-oriented encodings the concept of continuation bits obscured their interpretation as unary lengths.

If binary length descriptors are used, the descriptor length must be fixed in advance, or additional metadata would be required to store the length of the descriptor itself. For this reason, all binary formats in the taxonomy use fixed-length descriptors of 2 bits per integer. Furthermore, since splitting a fixed-length k-bit binary descriptor (one bit per byte) results in a byte-oriented integer encoding that requires at least k bytes, the split binary encoding format does not offer a competitive compression rate and we do not consider it further.

[1]Storing length as n would allow the length zero to represent an arbitrary constant with zero data bytes. Such an encoding, however, does not in general satisfy the first property of Definition 1.

There are also additional variations of some of these formats. Bytes of the encoded data may be stored in little-endian or big-endian order; descriptor bits may be stored in the least significant or most significant bits. While these choices are sometimes described as arbitrary conventions, in practice there are efficiency considerations that make certain variants attractive for certain machine architectures. For example, in varint-SU, representing termination as 0 in the most significant bit allows the common case of a one-byte integer to be decoded without any shifts or masks. While traditional decoding algorithms run more efficiently when the representation preserves native byte ordering, the performance of the SIMD algorithms presented in Section 6 does not depend on the ordering. Without loss of generality, for the remainder of the paper we restrict our attention to little-endian encodings.

The byte-oriented encoding taxonomy suggests two encodings, *varint-PU* and *varint-GU*, that, to our knowledge, have not been previously described.

Varint-PU is similar to varint-SU, but with the descriptor bits packed together in the low-order bits of the first byte rather than being split across all bytes. (The choice of low-order bits to hold the descriptor is appropriate for little-endian encodings on little-endian architectures so that all data bits for one integer are contiguous. For the same reason, on big-endian architectures placing the descriptor in the high-order bits and using big-endian encoding is more efficient to decode.) The compression rate of varint-PU is the same as that of varint-SU, since the bits in each encoded integer are identical but rearranged. The decoding performance of varint-PU using unaligned reads, masks, and shifts in a table-driven algorithm similar to that for varint-PB is faster than traditional varint-SU, but significantly slower than the group formats such as varint-GU, described in detail in the next section.

4. THE GROUP ENCODING FORMATS

Within our taxonomy, encoding formats that group several integers together provide opportunities for exploiting SIMD parallelism. These encodings satisfy the following important property.

DEFINITION 2. *We call a byte-oriented encoding* **byte-preserving** *if each byte containing significant bits in the original (unencoded) integer appears without modification in the encoded form.*

Neither split nor packed formats satisfy this property, since the descriptor bits are intermingled with data bits in some bytes. The separation of descriptor bytes from data

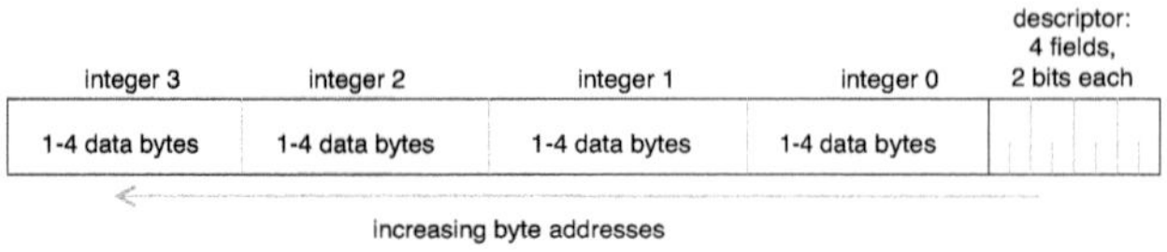

Figure 3: The varint-GB format.

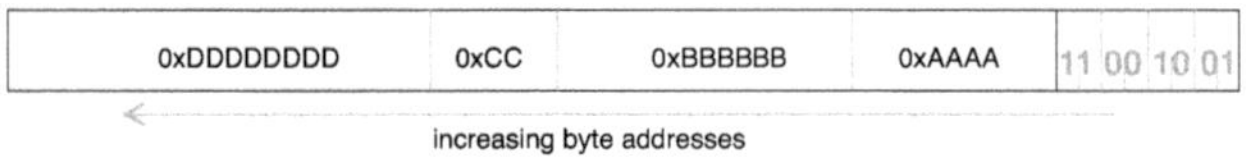

Figure 4: Storing the four integers 0xAAAA, 0xBBBBBB, 0xCC, 0xDDDDDDDD in varint-GB format. The value of each pair of bits in the descriptor is one less than the length of the corresponding integer. Byte addresses increase from right to left, matching the order of increasing bit significance. The order of pairs of bits in the descriptor matches the order of the integers.

bytes in group formats allows for more efficient decoding. It facilitates the use of tables to simplify the decoding process and avoids bitwise manipulations that are required to eliminate interspersed descriptor bits. In particular, we shall see in Section 6 that byte-preserving encodings are especially amenable to decoding with the SIMD techniques described in this paper.[2]

There are two classes of group formats, group binary (varint-GB) and group unary (varint-GU).

In the *varint-GB* format (called group varint in [8] and k-wise null supression (with $k = 4$) in [17]) a group of four integers is preceded by a descriptor byte containing four 2-bit binary numbers representing the lengths of the corresponding integers. Figure 3 illustrates this format for one such group. The actual number of bytes in a group may vary from 4 to 16. Figure 4 shows how the four hexadecimal numbers 0xAAAA, 0xBBBBBB, 0xCC, 0xDDDDDDDD would be represented. The four integers require, correspondingly, 2 bytes, 3 bytes, 1 byte, and 4 bytes. For each integer, its length n is represented in the descriptor by the 2-bit binary value $n - 1$. Therefore, the descriptor byte contains the values 01, 10, 00, and 11 respectively. To maintain a consistent order between descriptor bits and data bytes, we store the first binary length in the least significant bits, and so on. Thus the descriptor byte for these four integers is 11001001.

Varint-GB operates on a fixed number of integers occupying a variable number of bytes, storing their lengths in binary. In contrast, the varint-GU format operates on a fixed number of bytes encoding a variable number of integers, storing their lengths in unary.

Varint-GU groups 8 data bytes together along with one descriptor byte containing the unary representations of the lengths of each encoded integer. The 8 data bytes may encode as few as 2 and as many as 8 integers, depending on their size. The number of zeros in the descriptor indicates the number of integers encoded. This format is shown in

[2]Note that what Anh [1] calls *word-aligned* is neither byte-oriented nor byte-preserving as defined in this paper.

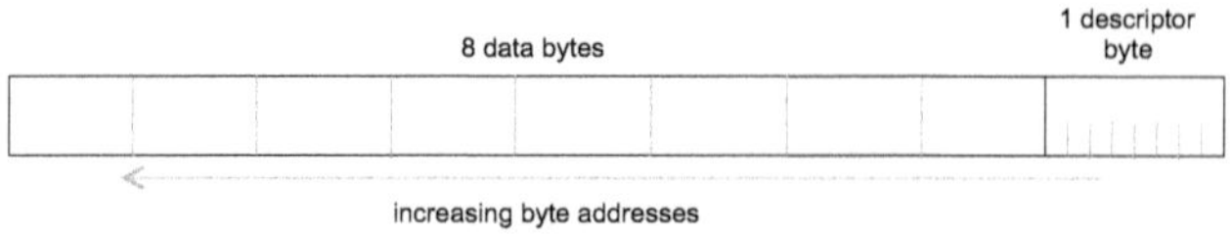

Figure 5: The varint-GU format.

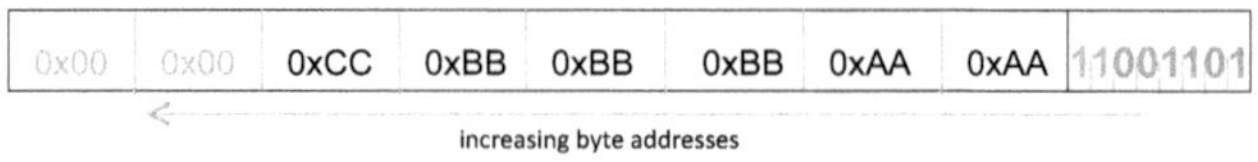

Figure 6: Storing the three integers (0xAAAA, 0xBBBBBB, 0xCC) in varint-G8IU format. The descriptor bits express the unary lengths of the integers. Since the next integer 0xDDDDDDDD in our example does not fit in the data block, the block is left incomplete and padded with 0s, while the descriptor is padded with 1s.

Figure 5. The block size of 8 is the minimal size that can use every bit of the descriptor byte; larger multiples of 8 are possible, but did not improve performance in our experiments.

Since not every group of encoded integers fits evenly into an 8-byte block, we have two variations of the encoding: incomplete and complete.

In the *incomplete* block variation, which we call *varint-G8IU*, we store only as many integers as fit in 8 bytes, leaving the data block incomplete if necessary.[3] The remaining space is padded with zeros, but is ignored on decoding.[4] When there is no additional integer to decode, the final (most significant) bits of the descriptor will be an unterminated sequence of 1 bits.

An example is shown in Figure 6. We use the same four integers 0xAAAA, 0xBBBBBB, 0xCC and 0xDDDDDDDD to illustrate. Encoding these values requires 10 bytes, but we have only 8 bytes in the block. The first three integers fit into the block using 6 bytes, leaving 2 bytes of padding. The final integer 0xDDDDDDDD is left for the next block (not shown). The descriptor contains the three unary values 01, 011, and 0, and two padding bits 11. These are arranged in the same order as the integers, giving the descriptor a binary value of 11001101.

In the *complete* block variation, which we call *varint-G8CU*, we always fill all eight bytes in a data block.[5] As before, the number of zero bits in the descriptor indicates the number of complete integers encoded. In situations where an integer exceeds the remaining space in the current block, as much of that integer as fits is placed in the current block. The remaining bytes of that integer are carried over into the

[3]In our notations for the encoding, the number 8 represents the size of the data block.

[4]There is also a variation of this encoding format that uses variable size data blocks and avoids padding. Its performance characteristics are between those of varint-G8IU and varint-G8CU described later.

[5]As before, the number 8 represents the size of the data block.

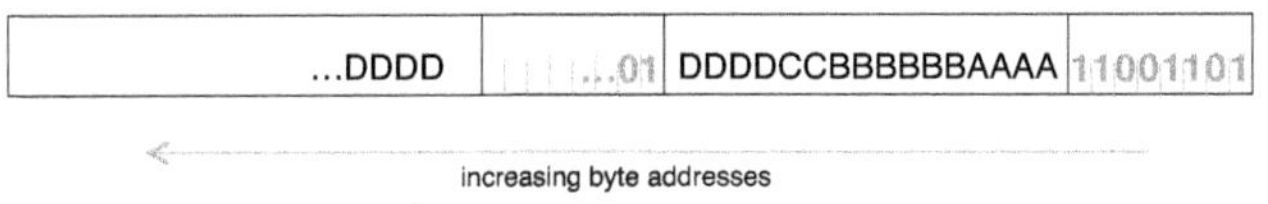

Figure 7: Storing four integers (0xAAAA, 0xBBBBBB, 0xCC and 0xDDDDDDDD) in varint-G8CU format. The last two bytes of the fourth integer carry over to the subsequent data block, and its descriptor bits carry over to the subsequent descriptor byte.

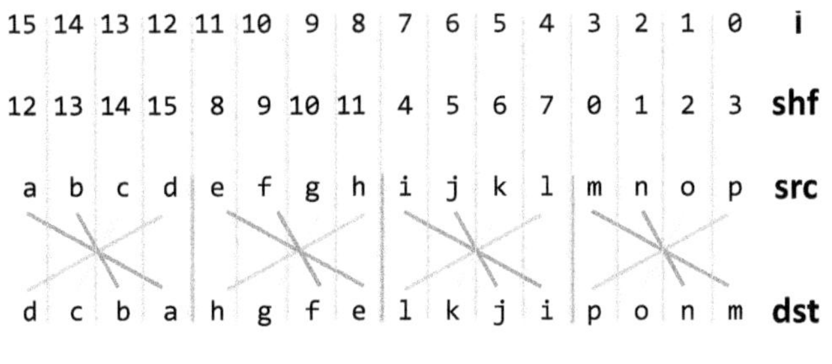

Figure 8: Using the PSHUFB instruction to reverse the byte order of four integers in parallel. The shf vector determines the shuffle sequence used to transform src to dst.

next data block. Similarly, the corresponding descriptor bits are carried over to the next block's descriptor byte.

An example is shown in Figure 7. Again we use the same four integers 0xAAAA, 0xBBBBBB, 0xCC and 0xDDDDDDDD. The first three integers and the corresponding descriptor bits are stored exactly as in varint-G8IU. However, varint-G8CU handles the fourth integer differently. Its first two bytes are placed in the first data block, filling it entirely, and the remaining two bytes go into the following block. The two descriptor bits corresponding to these last two bytes go into the next block's descriptor byte. Although spread across two descriptor bytes, the unary value of the descriptor bits for this fourth integer still equals $n-1$, where n is the length of the encoded integer.

5. SIMD ON INTEL/AMD

Facilities for fine-grained parallelism in the SIMD (Single Instruction, Multiple Data) paradigm are widely available on modern processors. They were originally introduced into general-purpose processors to provide vector processing capability for multimedia and graphics applications. Although SIMD instructions are available on multiple platforms, we restricted our focus to Intel-compatible architectures [12] implemented in current Intel processors in extensive use in many data centers, as well as forthcoming AMD processors.

In these architectures, a series of SIMD enhancements have been added over time. Among the current SIMD capabilities are 16-byte vector registers and parallel instructions for operating on them.

The PSHUFB instruction, introduced with SSSE3 in 2006, is particularly useful.[6] It performs a permutation ("shuffle") of bytes in a vector register, allowing the insertion of zeros in specified positions. PSHUFB has two operands, a location containing the data and a register containing a shuffle sequence. If we preserve the original value of the data operand, we can view PSHUFB as transforming a source sequence of bytes *src* to a destination sequence *dst* according to the shuffle sequence *shf*, implementing the following algorithm:

for $0 \leq i < 16$ **parallel do**
  if $shf[i] \geq 0$ **then**
    $dst[i] \leftarrow src[shf[i] \bmod 16]$
  else
    $dst[i] \leftarrow 0$
end

In other words, the ith value in the shuffle sequence indicates which source byte to place in the ith destination byte. If the ith value in the shuffle sequence is negative, a zero is placed in the corresponding destination byte.

The example illustrated in Figure 8 shows how PSHUFB can be used to reverse the byte order of four 32-bit integers at once.

6. SIMD DECODING

Since byte-preserving formats remove leading zero bytes while retaining the significant bytes intact, the essence of decoding is reinserting the zero bytes in the right places. Our discovery is that we can make PSHUFB do virtually all of the work for many formats. We construct a shuffle sequence by inserting -1s in a sequence $\{0, 1, 2, 3, ...\}$. With this sequence, the PSHUFB instruction will copy the significant data bytes while inserting the missing zeros.

An example of using PSHUFB to decode varint-G8IU is shown in Figure 9. This is the same data represented in Figure 6.

For a given format, we can precompute what the correct shuffle sequence is for a particular data block and its corresponding descriptor byte. For all possible values of the descriptor (and sometimes additional state) we build a table of any shuffle sequence that might be needed at decode time.

The table entries also contain a precomputed offset. For the varint-GB format, the offset indicates how many bytes were consumed to decode 4 integers; it always outputs 16 bytes. For the varint-GU formats, the offset indicates how many integers were decoded; it always consumes 8 bytes.

Table construction occurs only once, while table lookup occurs every time a group is decoded.

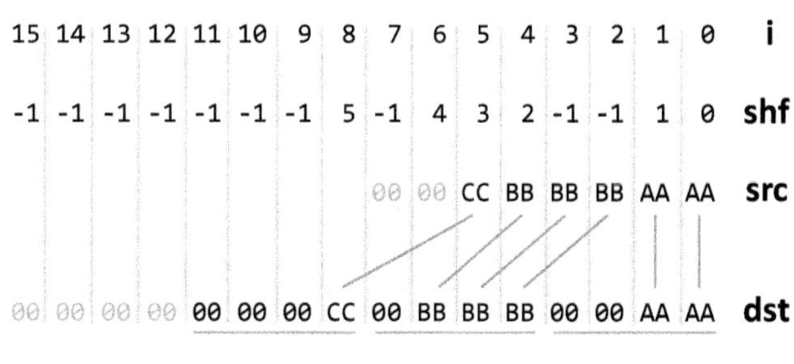

Figure 9: Using the PSHUFB instruction to decode the varint-G8IU format.

[6] A similar instruction, vperm, is part of the AltiVec/VMX instruction set for the PowerPC processor family.

Given the availability of these tables, the general strategy of all the decodings is:

1. read a chunk of data and its corresponding descriptor;
2. look up the appropriate shuffle sequence and offset from the table;
3. perform the shuffle;
4. write the result;
5. advance the input and output pointers.

This approach allows us to decode several integers simultaneously with very few instructions. It requires no conditionals, and thus avoids performance penalties due to branch misprediction. Two techniques make this possible. First, the logical complexity has been shifted from the code to the table. Second, the algorithm always reads and writes a fixed amount and then relies on the table to determine how much input data or output data it has actually processed.[7]

Data blocks are not aligned on any fixed boundary. We depend on the ability of the CPU to perform unaligned reads and writes efficiently, and we have observed this to be true on modern Intel processors.

6.1 Details of the Decoding Algorithm

All of the group formats can be decoded using the generalized algorithm shown in Algorithm 1.

Algorithm 1: decodeBlock

Decodes a block of data using SIMD shuffle.
input : *src*, *dst*, *state*
output: *src*, *dst*, *state*

begin
  $data \leftarrow \text{read}(src + 1, 16)$
  $entry \leftarrow table_{format}[desc, state]$
  $shf \leftarrow \text{shuffleSequence}(entry)$
  $\text{shuffleAndWrite}(data, shf, dst)$
  $src \leftarrow src + \text{inputOffset}(entry)$
  $dst \leftarrow dst + \text{outputOffset}(entry)$
  return $src, dst, \text{nextState}(entry)$
end

Because this algorithm constitutes the inner loop of the decoding process, it is essential to inline the implementation to avoid function call overhead. The algorithm takes three inputs:

- *src* – a pointer to the input byte stream of encoded values
- *dst* – a pointer to the output stream of integers in case of varint-GB, and varint-G8IU; in the case of varint-G8CU, *dst* is a pointer to an output stream of bytes, since decoding a block of varint-G8CU may result in writing a portion of a decoded integer.
- *state* – auxiliary state. This is required only for varint-G8CU, where it is an integer i, with $0 \leq i < 4$ indicating the number of bytes modulo 4 of the last integer written.

[7]This requires that the input and output buffers always have at least this amount available to read or write.

The algorithm reads encoded values from the input stream, outputs decoded integers to the output stream and returns as its result the new positions of *src*, *dst*, and the updated *state*.

We always read 16 bytes, the size of the vector register used by the **PSHUFB** operation. The number of bytes corresponding to a single byte descriptor is 8 for the unary formats and at most 16 for the binary format. While it is possible to read only 8 bytes for the unary formats, in our evaluation we found that doing so did not improve performance, and in fact made the implementation slightly slower.

A different table is used for each format. There is a table entry corresponding to each possible descriptor value and state value. The table has 256 entries for the varint-GB and varint-G8IU formats. For varint-G8CU format, the table has $4 \times 256 = 1024$ entries, because we have an entry for each descriptor and state pair, and the state is an integer i, with $0 \leq i < 4$.

Each table entry logically contains four things:

- a shuffle sequence
- an input offset
- an output offset
- the state value to use for the subsequent block

The shuffleSequence, inputOffset, outputOffset, and nextState functions are accessors for these fields. For some of the formats, some of these values are constant over all entries in the table, and are not stored explicitly; the accessors simply return constant values.

The shuffleAndWrite operation uses the **PSHUFB** operation with the provided shuffle sequence to expand the 16 bytes of data, inserting zeros into the correct positions. It then writes its result to the destination.

In the varint-GB case, the shuffle sequence is a 16-byte sequence describing a single **PSHUFB** operation. A single **PSHUFB** is sufficient because the group always contains four encoded integers, and thus the output never exceeds 16 bytes.

For decoding the varint-GU formats, the shuffle sequence is a 32-byte sequence specifying two **PSHUFB** operations. The second **PSHUFB** is required for the unary formats because an 8-byte data block may encode up to 8 integers, which can expand to 32 bytes. The output of the first **PSHUFB** is written to locations beginning at *dst*, and the output of the second **PSHUFB** to locations beginning at $dst + 16$. To avoid conditionals, the second shuffle is always performed, even when the output does not exceed 16 bytes. Since **PSHUFB** rearranges the register in place, the corresponding register needs to be reloaded with the original data before the second **PSHUFB**.

For unary formats, the input offset, by which we increment the *src*, is always 8 bytes. For varint-G8IU, the output offset measured in units of decoded integers varies between 2 and 8, except for the last block of a sequence, which may contain only 1 integer. For varint-G8CU, decoding one block may result in writing a portion of a decoded integer, so the output is a byte stream and the offset is measured in byte units. It varies between 8 and 32 bytes, except for the last block of the sequence which may output only 1 byte.

In the case of varint-GB, the output offset is always a

constant 4 integers.[8] The input offset varies between 4 and 16 bytes.

For all of the encodings, the input offset needs to account for the additional one byte of the descriptor as well. All variable offsets are precomputed and stored in the format table.

For the varint-G8CU format, the table also contains the new state information indicating the number of bytes in the last integer to be used to decode the subsequent block.

6.2 Building the Tables

For each of the group formats, the decoding table used by Algorithm 1 is constructed in advance. The construction process takes as input a descriptor byte value and a state value. It builds the shuffle sequence for the entry and computes the input offset, output offset, and next state (unless they are constant for the format).

We assume we deal only with valid descriptor values, those which could actually arise from encoding. For varint-GB, all possible byte values are valid. For the group unary formats, a descriptor is valid if and only if the distance between consecutive zero bits does not exceed 4.

The algorithms for constructing shuffle sequences, offset values, and the next state value depend on the following abstract functions:

- $\text{num}(desc)$ gives the number of integers whose encoding is completed in the group described by the descriptor value *desc*. For varint-GB this is always 4. For the group unary formats, this value is the number of 0 (termination) bits in *desc*.

- $\text{len}(desc, i)$ gives the length of the ith integer in the group, for each i, $0 \leq i < \text{num}(desc)$. This is the length determined by the ith individual bit pair in *desc* for varint-GB, or the ith unary value in *desc* for the unary formats.

- $\text{rem}(desc)$ gives the number of bytes modulo 4 in the last encoded integer in the group. This is needed only for varint-G8CU, where it is equal to the number of leading 1s in the descriptor *desc*. For the other formats it is always zero.

Again, the basic idea in constructing a shuffle sequence is to insert -1s in a sequence $\{0, 1, 2, 3, ...\}$ representing the byte positions in one block of the source data being decoded. The resulting shuffle sequence is used by the `PSHUFB` instruction to copy the significant data bytes while inserting the missing leading zeros. The details of the construction are shown in Algorithm 2. The algorithm takes two inputs:

- *desc* the descriptor value

- *state* the number of bytes modulo 4 written from the last integer in the prior group.[9]

[8]The varint-GB format requires auxiliary information to deal with sequences of length not divisible by 4. This may be done using length information stored separately or the convention that zero values do not appear in the sequence, so terminal zeros can be ignored.

[9]For varint-GB and varint-G8IU, the value of state is always zero, since only complete integers are written in a given data block in these formats.

The algorithm produces one output, *shf*, the shuffle sequence to be used for the given descriptor and state. The first loop iterates over every completed integer in the group corresponding to the given descriptor. For each completed integer in the group, the inner loop sets the shuffle sequence to move the encoded bytes from the source of the shuffle operation, inserting -1s to produce the leading zeros necessary to complete the decoded integer. Here the variable j advances over the source data positions in the data block, while the variable k advances over the positions in the shuffle sequence, which correspond to destination positions of the shuffle operation.

The concluding loop only executes for varint-G8CU. It sets the remainder of the shuffle sequence to transfer encoded bytes from the source for the last incomplete integer in the group.

Algorithm 2: constructShuffleSequence

```
input  : desc, state
output: shf
begin
    j, k ← 0
    s ← 4 − state
    for 0 ≤ i < num(desc) do
        for 0 ≤ n < s do
            if n < len(desc, i) then
                shf[k] ← j
                j ← j + 1
            else
                shf[k] ← −1
            end
            k ← k + 1
        end
        s ← 4
    end
    for 0 ≤ n < rem(desc) do
        shf[k] ← j
        j ← j + 1
        k ← k + 1
    end
    return shf
end
```

Computing input offsets is easy. For the unary formats the input offset is always 9; we always consume a block of 8 bytes of data and 1 descriptor byte. For the group binary format varint-GB, the input offset for a given descriptor *desc* is

$$1 + \sum_{i=0}^{3} \text{len}(desc, i)$$

which is the sum of the lengths of the integers in the group plus 1 for the descriptor byte.

The output offset for varint-GB and varint-G8IU is equal to $\text{num}(desc)$ integers (which is always 4 for varint-GB). The output offset is

$$4 \cdot \text{num}(desc) - state + \text{rem}(desc)$$

for the varint-G8CU format.

The state value for the subsequent block is always 0 for varint-GB and varint-G8IU (and the state can be ignored for these formats). For varint-G8CU it is $\text{rem}(desc)$.

Table 2: **Decoding rates in millions of integers per second; larger is better**

encoding	algorithm	Wikipedia	Reuters	GOV2
varint-SU	traditional	424	516	491
varint-SU	SIMD	547	640	477
varint-GB	mask table	766	831	763
varint-GB	SIMD	1159	1276	1024
varint-G8IU	SIMD	**1321**	**1518**	**1059**
varint-G8CU	SIMD	1231	1398	1033

Table 3: Compression ratios; smaller is better

encoding	Wikipedia	Reuters	GOV2
varint-SU	0.34	0.30	0.32
varint-GB	0.38	0.35	0.37
varint-G8IU	0.37	0.33	0.35
varint-G8CU	0.36	0.33	0.34

6.3 Applying SIMD to varint-SU

Although varint-SU is not a byte-preserving encoding, Algorithm 1 can be applied as a component for decoding it. By efficiently gathering the descriptor bits from each byte into a single value for a table lookup, we can treat a sequence of 8 consecutive varint-SU-encoded bytes almost as if they were a varint-GU-encoded block. The Intel instruction `PMOVMSKB`, which gathers the most-significant bits from 8 bytes into a single byte, provides the needed functionality. After applying a shuffle as in Algorithm 1, the descriptor bits must be "squeezed out" to finish the decoding; this removal of the interspersed descriptor bits requires masks and shifts. Despite this additional step, the SIMD implementation still outperforms the traditional method in most cases as shown in Section 7.

7. EVALUATION

We used three corpora in our evaluation: Wikipedia [20] (6M documents[10], 27 GB), Reuters RCV1 [16] (0.8M documents, 2.5 GB), and GOV2 [15] (25M documents, 426 GB). To satisfy the resource constraints of our test environment, we randomly sampled 50% of the Wikipedia documents and 15% of GOV2. We removed all XML/HTML markup and five common stopwords (`a, an, and, of, the`) and applied stemming to conflate singular and plural nouns.

The C++ implementation was compiled using gcc 4.5.1.[11] Measurements were done using a single-threaded process on an Intel Xeon X5680 processor (3.3GHz, 6 cores, 12 MB Intel Smart Cache shared across all cores), with 24 GB DDR3 1333 MHz RAM. Measurements are done with all of the input and output data in main memory.

Decoding speed results are shown in Table 2. For each corpus, this table shows the decoding speed measured in millions of integers per second; the fastest result is shown in boldface. In every case, a SIMD algorithm strongly outperformed a conventional algorithm; in all cases, the implementation of our varint-G8IU format was fastest. The "traditional" implementation of varint-SU shown in the table is our best implementation for this encoding using traditional techniques. The "mask table" implementation of varint-GB is our implementation of the technique described in Dean [8].

Compression ratios are shown in Table 3. Here the compression ratio indicates the ratio between the bytes required for the integers encoded in the format and their original size of 4 bytes each. Compression ratios depend only on the encoding and not on the implementation.

7.1 Comparison with Other Evaluations

There seems to be no standard benchmark for measuring integer decoding implementations in the information retrieval field. Even with conventional test corpora, there are many variations possible in producing the posting lists. Evaluation methods are also not standardized. Some research on compression only reports compression rate but not speed. Speed is reported using different metrics and data.

Büttcher et al. [4] start with the GOV2 corpus and the 10000 queries from the efficiency task of the TREC Terabyte Track 2006. They indicate they used components of the Wumpus search engine to index the GOV2 corpus, and then decoded the posting lists for non-stopword terms contained in the query set. They do in-memory measurements, but also compute a "cumulative overhead" for decoding and disk I/O by estimating the I/O time based on compression rate.

Schlegel et al. [17] use 32MB synthetic data sets constructed by sampling positive 32-bit integers from the Zipf distribution with different parameter values. They measure the amount of uncompressed data that can be processed per second.

Dean [8] uses millions of integers decoded per second as a performance metric (as we do), but he does not provide details on the data or evaluation method used in his measurements.

We measured performance on standard corpora decoding every posting list once, repeating the test to achieve stable timing. While it is easy to reproduce, this method does not account for different term distributions in queries. To account for different frequencies of terms in real queries, one needs a representative query mix. Since GOV2 and Reuters

[10]This counts all documents from the English Wikipedia dump except empty documents and redirect pages.

[11]It uses the GCC intrinsics `__builtin_ia32_pshufb128`, `__builtin_ia32_loaddqu`, and `__builtin_ia32_storedqu` to invoke the `PSHUFB` and unaligned load and store instructions.

RCV1 are not used in real world search tasks, such a mix is not available.

Creation of a standard benchmark containing several sequences of integers with distinct but representative statistical characteristics would allow meaningful comparisons of different implementations.

8. CONCLUSIONS AND FUTURE WORK

We discovered a taxonomy for variable-length integer encoding formats. This led us to identify some new encodings that offer advantages over previously known formats. We identified the *byte-preserving* property of encoding formats which makes them particularly amenable to parallel decoding with SIMD instructions. The SIMD-based algorithms that we developed outperformed the traditional methods by 300%, and the best previously published methods by over 50%. Furthermore the new group unary formats offer better compression than the group binary format on all of the corpora tested.

Schlegel et al. [17] also reported success applying SIMD to Elias γ [9], which is not aligned on byte boundaries at all. Further investigations are needed to see whether SIMD techniques can be similarly applied to other encodings which are not aligned on byte boundaries, such as Simple-9 [2], PForDelta [21] and VSEncoding [18].

We restricted our investigation to integers that can be encoded in four bytes or less. We believe, however, that some of the encodings that we introduced could be easily extended to larger values.

SIMD instructions, a powerful but under-utilized resource, offer the opportunity for significant performance improvements in modern search engines.

Acknowledgments

We thank Thomas London for suggestions on a draft of this paper and Bill Stasior for supporting this research.

References

[1] V. N. Anh. *Impact-Based Document Retrieval.* PhD thesis, University of Melbourne, April 2004.

[2] V. N. Anh and A. Moffat. Inverted index compression using word-aligned binary codes. *Information Retrieval*, 8(1):151–166, 2005.

[3] Apache Software Foundation. Lucene 1.4.3 documentation. `http://lucene.apache.org/java/1_4_3/fileformats.html`, 2004.

[4] S. Büttcher, C. L. A. Clarke, and G. V. Cormack. *Information Retrieval: Implementing and Evaluating Search Engines.* MIT Press, Cambridge, MA, 2010.

[5] S. Büttcher, C. L. A. Clarke, and G. V. Cormack. Information retrieval: Implementing and evaluating search engines, addenda for chapter 6: Index compression. `http://www.ir.uwaterloo.ca/book/addenda-06-index-compression.html`, 2010.

[6] W. B. Croft, D. Metzler, and T. Strohman. *Search Engines: Information Retrieval in Practice.* Pearson Education, Boston, 2010.

[7] D. Cutting and J. Pedersen. Optimizations for dynamic inverted index maintenance. In *Proceedings of the 13th Annual International ACM SIGIR Conference on Research and Development in Information Retrieval*, SIGIR '90, pages 405–411, New York, NY, USA, 1990. ACM.

[8] J. Dean. Challenges in building large-scale information retrieval systems. Keynote, WSDM 2009, `http://research.google.com/people/jeff/WSDM09-keynote.pdf`, February 2009.

[9] P. Elias. Universal codeword sets and representations of the integers. *IEEE Transactions on Information Theory*, 21(2):194–203, 1975.

[10] D. A. Grossman. *Integrating Structured Data and Text: A Relational Approach.* PhD thesis, George Mason University, 1995.

[11] H. S. Heaps. Storage analysis of a compression coding for a document database. *INFOR*, 10(1):47–61, February 1972.

[12] Intel Corporation. *Intel 64 and IA-32 Architectures Software Developers Manual.* Intel Corporation, Santa Clara, California, USA, September 2010. Version 37.

[13] C. D. Manning, P. Raghavan, and H. Schütze. *Introduction to Information Retrieval.* Cambridge University Press, 2008.

[14] MIDI Manufacturers Association. *MIDI 1.0 Specification*, 1982-2001.

[15] NIST. GOV2 collection. `http://ir.dcs.gla.ac.uk/test_collections/`, 2010.

[16] Reuters. Reuters RCV1 Corpus. `http://trec.nist.gov/data/reuters/reuters.html`, 2010.

[17] B. Schlegel, R. Gemulla, and W. Lehner. Fast integer compression using SIMD instructions. In *Proceedings of the Sixth International Workshop on Data Management on New Hardware (DaMoN 2010)*, Indianapolis, Indiana, June 7 2010.

[18] F. Silvestri and R. Venturini. VSEncoding: efficient coding and fast decoding of integer lists via dynamic programming. In *Proceedings of the 19th ACM international conference on Information and knowledge management*, CIKM '10, pages 1219–1228, New York, NY, USA, 2010. ACM.

[19] T. Westmann, D. Kossmann, S. Helmer, and G. Moerkotte. The implementation and performance of compressed databases. *SIGMOD Rec.*, 29:55–67, September 2000.

[20] Wikimedia Foundation. Wikipedia database download (english). `http://en.wikipedia.org/wiki/Wikipedia:Database_download`, September 2010.

[21] M. Zukowski, S. Héman, N. Nes, and P. A. Boncz. Super-scalar RAM-CPU cache compression. In *Proceedings of the 22nd International Conference on Data Engineering*, ICDE '06, pages 59–, Washington, DC, USA, 2006. IEEE Computer Society.

Factorization-based Lossless Compression of Inverted Indices

George Beskales
University of Waterloo
Waterloo, ON, Canada
gbeskale@cs.uwaterloo.ca

Marcus Fontoura
Google Inc.
Mountain View, CA, USA
marcusf@google.com

Maxim Gurevich
Yahoo! Labs
Santa Clara, CA, USA
maximg@yahoo-inc.com

Sergei Vassilvitskii
Yahoo! Labs
New York, NY, USA
sergei@yahoo-inc.com

Vanja Josifovski
Yahoo! Labs
Santa Clara, CA, USA
vanjaj@yahoo-inc.com

ABSTRACT

Many large-scale Web applications that require ranked top-k retrieval are implemented using inverted indices. An inverted index represents a sparse term-document matrix, where non-zero elements indicate the strength of term-document associations. In this work, we present an approach for lossless compression of inverted indices. Our approach maps terms in a document corpus to a new term space in order to reduce the number of non-zero elements in the term-document matrix, resulting in a more compact inverted index. We formulate the problem of selecting a new term space as a matrix factorization problem, and prove that finding the optimal solution is an NP-hard problem. We develop a greedy algorithm for finding an approximate solution.

A side effect of our approach is increasing the number of terms in the index, which may negatively affect query evaluation performance. To eliminate such effect, we develop a methodology for modifying query evaluation algorithms by exploiting specific properties of our compression approach.

Categories and Subject Descriptors

H.3.1 [**Information Storage And Retrieval**]: Indexing methods

General Terms

Algorithms, Experimentation, Performance

1. INTRODUCTION

Web search engines and other large-scale information retrieval systems typically have to process query workloads of thousands of requests per second over large collections of documents. Usually, the result of the retrieval is a ranked list of the top few (k) results.

Top-k retrieval is defined as follows. Given a query Q and a document corpus $Docs$, find the k documents $\{D_1, D_2, \ldots, D_k\} \subset Docs$ that have the highest score, according to some scoring function $Score(D, Q)$. Both the query and the documents are sets of *terms* from the same high-dimension space. Scoring is usually performed based on the overlapping terms between the query and the document. The document corpus $Docs$ can be represented as a two dimensional matrix, denoted as V, with m terms (rows) and n documents (columns). The values of elements in V reflect how strongly terms are associated with documents (e.g., tf-idf).

Inverted indices are the prevailing implementation of scalable top-k retrieval. In an inverted index, each term T appearing in the corpus $Docs$ is associated with a *posting list*, which enumerates the documents that contain T. Each posting list consists of a sequence of document identifiers, each of which associated with an optional payload (e.g., term frequency). An inverted index can also be viewed as a sparse representation of the matrix V that stores only non-zero matrix elements.

In several applications, top-k queries are processed while the user is waiting for the results, which imposes very strict bounds on query latency. Due to such requirements, memory-resident indices are becoming more popular. To reduce the amount of required memory, and hence the system cost, compression techniques (e.g., [6, 18, 21]) are heavily used to reduce the size of the inverted indices. Compression techniques are divided into two categories: lossy compression, where quality of the results might be affected by compression, and lossless compression, where the quality is not affected. In this work, we focus on lossless compression.

In this paper, we propose a novel lossless compression technique that holistically compresses multiple posting lists by taking advantage of similarities between them. This in contrast to the many existing lossless compression approaches that compress each posting list individually [16, 21]. The compression approach we propose can be applied before the standard per-posting-list compression in order to combine the benefits of both methods. In spirit, the technique presented in this paper is related to matrix factorization methods such as Non-negative Matrix Factorization [10, 13], Latent Dirichlet Allocation [4], Singular Value Decomposition [19], and Principal Component Analysis [11]. All of these techniques map the documents from the space of the original terms into a lower dimensional space. However, unlike previous factorization methods, we aim at providing an *exact* factorization of the input matrix in order to avoid any information loss, while reducing the number of non-zero elements in the resulting factors. Furthermore, we do not restrict the dimensionality of the factor matrices.

For example, the top term-document matrix in Figure 1 is factored into two matrices W and H such that: (1) the product of the factors is equal to the input matrix, and (2) the factor matrices contain fewer non-zeros than the input matrix. Note that the rank of

CIKM'11, October 24–28, 2011, Glasgow, Scotland, UK.

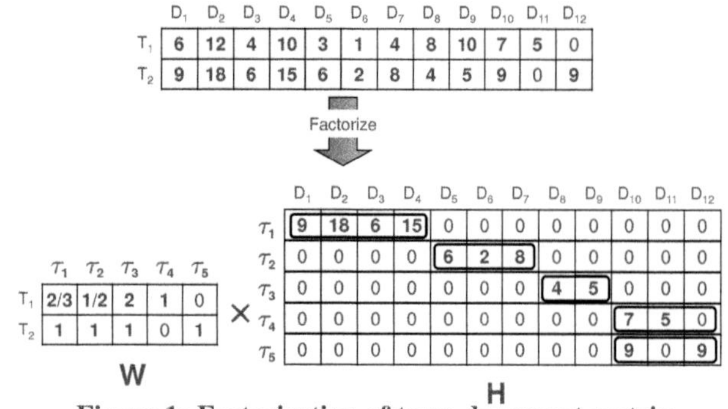

Figure 1: Factorization of term-document matrix

the second factor H (five), is higher than the rank of the input matrix (two). To answer queries, we use the first factor to map (i.e., rewrite) query terms from the original term space to a new space of meta-terms (e.g., T_1 is mapped to $\tau_1, \tau_2, \tau_3, \tau_4$ in Figure 1). The rewritten query is used for searching the index built from the second factor using any top-k search algorithms. In this paper, we prove that finding the optimal (i.e., the sparsest) factorization is NP-hard, and we develop a greedy algorithm that efficiently finds an approximate solution.

Although lossless compression helps reducing the amount of memory required for storing a given index, it usually incurs a computational overhead due to the need of decompressing the index data [18, 21]. Such overhead should be minimized in order to keep query latency small. The computational overhead in our approach is due to rewriting a query using a number of meta-terms that is greater than the number of the original terms. For example, the number of meta-terms in Figure 1 is five, while the original number of terms is two. We show how to eliminate such negative effect by exploiting some unique characteristics of our compression technique. More specifically, we show that standard query processing approaches such as No-Random-Access (NRA) algorithm [8] can be modified to search the compressed index as fast as the original algorithm searches the uncompressed index.

2. PRELIMINARIES

In this paper, we use the vector-space representation of documents and queries. That is, documents and queries are represented as vectors in a multidimensional space, where each term is a dimension. Let $\Omega = \{T_1, T_2, \ldots, T_m\}$ be a set of terms. A document D_j is a vector $(d_j^1, d_j^2, \ldots, d_j^m)$. When a term T_i occurs in a document D_j, the element d_j^i is non-zero, and its value is typically related to the number of times T_i occurs in D_j. Similarly, a query Q is represented by a vector $(w_1, w_2, \ldots, w_m)$, where non-zero elements correspond to terms appearing in the query, and their values are term weights in the query.

Given a corpus of n documents $Docs = \{D_1, \ldots, D_n\}$, and a query Q, a common task in many information retrieval systems is to retrieve the k documents with the highest score according to some scoring function $Score(D, Q)$. In this work, we assume the scoring function is defined as the inner product of document and query vectors: $Score(D_j, Q) = \sum_{i=1}^{m} d_j^i \cdot w_i$.

Many information retrieval systems use inverted indices as their main data structure for top-k retrieval. An inverted index is a collection of *posting lists* $L_1, L_2, \ldots, L_m$: a list for each term in Ω. List L_i is a vector containing weights of term T_i in all documents (i.e., $L_i = (d_1^i, d_2^i, \ldots, d_n^i)$). Usually, sparse representation of posting lists is used, where zero entries are omitted.

A naïve top-k algorithm would examine all entries in the posting lists relevant to the query, compute the scores of found documents, and return the top-k documents. However, the total number of documents in the relevant posting lists is typically much larger than k, especially when Q contains frequent terms. Many top-k search algorithms (e.g., [5, 8]) aim at retrieving the top-k documents while examining only a fraction of entries in the relevant posting lists.

3. INDEX COMPRESSION USING MATRIX FACTORIZATION

We represent an index by an $m \times n$ term-document matrix V (Figure 1). We denote by $V[T, D]$ the value of the element in V corresponding to a row T and a column D. We use $\|V\|_0$ to denote the number of non-zero elements in V. Top-k retrieval is defined as computing scores of all documents, represented by a size-n vector S, and picking the top-k documents with highest scores. The transpose of vector S is equal to $Q^T V$, where the superscript T denotes the transpose operator.

Typical document collections, such as Web corpora, contain redundant elements in their term-document matrices due to duplicate or near-duplicate contents. For example, news articles are usually shared across multiple Web sites. In this case, two documents D_x and D_y that refer to the same article would contain several identical sentences consisting of terms $T_a, T_b, \ldots, T_p$. Consequently, the term-document matrix would contain two identical sets of values: $V[T_a, D_x], \ldots, V[T_p, D_x]$, and $V[T_a, D_y], \ldots, V[T_p, D_y]$. Another example that leads to redundancy in term-document matrix is co-occurrence of subsets of terms in multiple documents. For example, terms "Britney" and "Spears" usually co-occur in documents related to music.

A known technique for reducing redundancy in a matrix is matrix factorization. The simplest form of factorization is decomposing V into two matrices: an $m \times r$ matrix W and an $r \times n$ matrix H, such that $V = WH$. Note that since our goal is lossless index compression, we consider the exact formulation and not the approximate one ($V \approx WH$). Our objective is to minimize the total number of non-zero elements in W and H (i.e., $\|W\|_0 + \|H\|_0$).

Intuitively, factoring V into WH transforms the set of terms Ω into another space, denoted Θ, consisting of r *meta-terms* $\{\tau_1, \tau_2, \ldots, \tau_r\}$. Matrix W linearly maps terms in Ω to meta-terms in Θ (and vice-versa), while matrix H represents an inverted index of *Docs* in space Θ. Figure 1 is an illustration of such a factorization, where terms $\{T_1, T_2\}$ are linearly mapped into meta-terms $\{\tau_1, \ldots, \tau_5\}$ using matrix W, and documents are represented as combinations of these meta-terms in matrix H. Note that although $r > m$ (i.e., the number of rows in H is greater than the number of rows in V), the total number of non-zeros in W and H is less than the number of non-zeros in V.

Evaluation of query Q is performed on the inverted index represented by H, after rewriting Q according to W. Specifically, we rewrite the query vector Q into vector Q' such that $Q'^T = Q^T W$. In other words, each term T in Q is replaced by a set of meta-terms $\{\tau : W[T, \tau] \neq 0\}$, and the weight of each term τ in Q' is $w \cdot W[T, \tau]$, where w is the weight of T in Q. Any standard search algorithm can be used to retrieve the top-k documents from the compressed index H using query Q'. The following theorem proves that searching the original inverted index using Q is equivalent to searching the index represented by H using Q'.

THEOREM 1. *Let W and H be the result of factoring V (i.e., $WH = V$). Let $\mathcal{A}(V, Q, k)$ be the top-k documents for query Q using inverted index V and the scoring function in Section 2 (ties are broken by some predefined criteria). Let the rewritten query be Q' such that $Q'^T = Q^T W$. Then, $\mathcal{A}(V, Q, k) = \mathcal{A}(H, Q', k)$.*

The proof is described in [3]. An immediate consequence is that standard top-k algorithms can still be used for searching the compressed indices without any loss in quality.

REMARK It is possible to interpret the intermediate space Θ as a space of *meta-documents*, rather than *meta-terms*. In this case, the matrix W represents an inverted index of meta-documents in the original term space Ω, and H is a mapping from meta-documents to documents in $Docs$. However, existing top-k retrieval algorithms that employ early termination cannot be used on W, since top-k meta-documents do not necessarily contain the top-k documents.

4. SPARSE MATRIX FACTORIZATION

In this section, we consider the following exact sparse matrix factorization problem. Given a matrix V, obtain W and H that

$$\begin{array}{ll} \text{minimize} & \|W\|_0 + \|H\|_0 \\ \text{subject to} & WH = V. \end{array}$$

The following theorem states that the problem of obtaining the sparsest exact factorization is NP-hard.

THEOREM 2. *Given a matrix V, the problem of obtaining two matrices W and H, subject to the constraint $WH = V$, such that $\|W\|_0 + \|H\|_0$ is minimum is NP-hard.*

Proof of Theorem 2 is provided in [3]. Hardness of the problem is proved by a reduction from an NP-complete problem, namely the SPARSESTVECTOR problem [9].

Since obtaining the optimal factorization is computationally infeasible, we propose an iterative greedy algorithm for getting an exact factorization that might not have the minimal number of non-zeros. The key idea is to start with a trivial factorization $W_0 = I_m$ (I_m is the identity matrix of rank m) and $H_0 = V$, and iteratively improve the current solution (W_t, H_t) by a sequence of local transformations on W_t and H_t, obtaining W_{t+1} and H_{t+1}. At each step, we ensure that $\|W_{t+1}\|_0 + \|H_{t+1}\|_0 < \|W_t\|_0 + \|H_t\|_0$, and $W_{t+1}H_{t+1} = V$.

The transformation performed at each step is described as follows. At step t, given matrices W_t and H_t, the algorithm looks for a submatrix H_t^s of H_t defined by a subset R of H_t's rows, and a subset C of H_t's columns, such that the rank of H_t^s is one (i.e., rows are multiples of each others):

$$\forall(\tau_i, \tau_j) \in R \times R,\ \forall(D_p, D_q) \in C \times C \quad \Big(\frac{V[\tau_i, D_p]}{V[\tau_j, D_p]} = \frac{V[\tau_i, D_q]}{V[\tau_j, D_q]}\Big). \tag{1}$$

Clearly, keeping only one representative row from H_t^s, and encoding other rows in H_t^s as multiples of the representative row, would reduce the number of non-zero values in H_t. Unfortunately, identifying the largest rank-1 submatrix H_t^s is equivalent to the problem of finding the largest bi-cluster [15], which is an NP-hard problem. Thus, our algorithms considers only submatrices consisting of exactly two rows (i.e., $|R| = 2$) at each step.

For efficiency, in each iteration, our algorithm identifies z rank-1 submatrices that are composed of two rows $R = \{\tau_i, \tau_j\}$ and z sets of columns $C_1, \ldots, C_z$ (i.e., Equation 1 holds for submatrices (R, C_1) through (R, C_z)). Rows τ_i and τ_j can then be rewritten as linear combinations of a set of z new common subvectors, denoted $\tau_{r+1}, \ldots, \tau_{r+z}$, and two new remainder vectors τ_{r+z+1} and τ_{r+z+2} that retain values of columns that are not in $C_1 \cup \cdots \cup C_z$.

$$\tau_i = \alpha_1 \cdot \tau_{r+1} + \alpha_2 \cdot \tau_{r+2} + \cdots + \alpha_z \cdot \tau_{r+z} + \tau_{r+z+1} \tag{2}$$

$$\tau_j = \beta_1 \cdot \tau_{r+1} + \beta_2 \cdot \tau_{r+2} + \cdots + \beta_z \cdot \tau_{r+z} + \tau_{r+z+2} \tag{3}$$

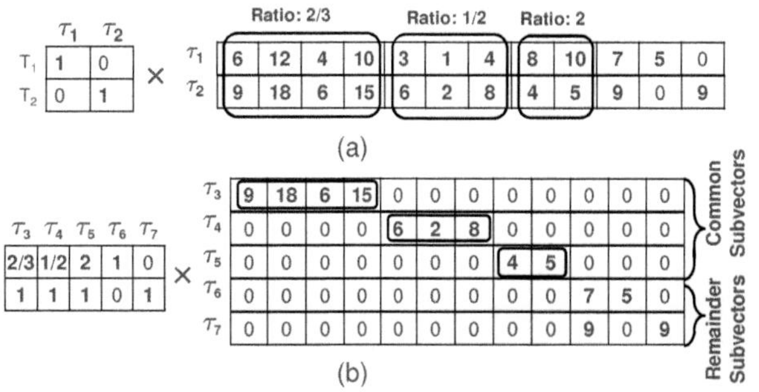

Figure 2: Combining term vectors (a) matrices W_t and H_t (b) matrices W_{t+1} and H_{t+1} after combining τ_1 and τ_2

The new vectors $\tau_{r+1}, \ldots, \tau_{r+z+2}$ are appended to matrix H_t, and vectors τ_i and τ_j are removed from H_t, resulting in matrix H_{t+1}. Matrix W_t is modified by mapping the original terms τ_i, τ_j to $\tau_{r+1}, \ldots, \tau_{r+z+2}$, obtaining W_{t+1}. Algorithm 1 describes the procedure in more details. Function $GetCorrelatedSubmatrices(H_t)$, which we describe in Section 4.1, is responsible for extracting the sets R and $C_1, \ldots, C_z$ that maximize space saving.

Figure 2 shows an example of combining two meta-terms τ_1 and τ_2 into common subvectors τ_3, τ_4, τ_5, and remainder vectors τ_6, τ_7. Without loss of generality, we assume hereafter that $\beta_1 = \cdots = \beta_z = 1$.

Algorithm 1 `ComputeFactorization(V)`

$W_0 \leftarrow I_m$; $H_0 \leftarrow V$
$r \leftarrow m$
$t \leftarrow 0$
repeat
  $H_{t+1} \leftarrow H_t$
  $(R, C_1, \ldots, C_z) \leftarrow GetCorrelatedSubmatrices(H_t)$
  if failed to find correlated submatrix **then**
    break
  remove rows $R = \{\tau_i, \tau_j\}$ from H_{t+1}, and add the new rows $\tau_{r+1}, \ldots, \tau_{r+z+2}$ to H_{t+1}
  construct an $r \times (r+z+2)$ transformation matrix W_M that linearly maps τ_i and τ_j to $\tau_{r+1}, \ldots, \tau_{r+z+2}$ using Equations 2 and 3, and trivially maps all other meta-terms in W_t to themselves.
  $W_{t+1} \leftarrow W_t W_M$.
  $r \leftarrow r + z + 2$
  $t \leftarrow t + 1$
until $\|W_t\|_0 + \|H_t\|_0$ converges
return W_t, H_t

4.1 Identifying Correlated Submatrices

The goal of function $GetCorrelatedSubmatrices(H_t)$ is to return correlated submatrices, defined by $R = \{\tau_i, \tau_j\}$ and $C_1, \ldots, C_z$. Our algorithm heuristically finds the submatrices that would result in the highest reduction of space. In the following, we first describe how to find the sets $C_1, \ldots, C_z$ given R, then formulate the potential saving from combining two meta-terms, and finally how to find R.

Denote by $X[p]$ the value of the element at index p in vector X. For two rows τ_i and τ_j in H_t, we compute vector γ of length n such that for $q \in \{1, \ldots, n\}$, $\gamma[q] = \frac{\tau_i[q]}{\tau_j[q]}$ if $\tau_j[q] \neq 0$, and equals 0 otherwise. Each set C_p is a maximal subset of columns (documents) in H_t that have the same *non-zero* value in γ (which is eventually the value of the corresponding coefficient α_p in Equation 2). For example, in Figure 2, the first four cells have the same value in γ, namely $2/3$, and thus constitute a common subvector (τ_3). If is clear that $C_1, \ldots, C_z$ are pairwise disjoint because each set C_p corresponds to a unique non-zero ratio in γ. We rely on this property to improve query evaluation performance (Section 5).

The space saving resulting from combining τ_i and τ_j is computed as follows. Combining τ_i and τ_j in Algorithm 1 reduces the number of non-zero elements in H_t by $\sum_{p=1}^{z} |C_p|$ because each subvector corresponding to C_p is stored twice in H_t and only once in H_{t+1}. All the terms that were mapped to either τ_i or τ_j in W_t are now mapped to additional z meta-terms $\tau_{r+1}, \ldots, \tau_{r+z}$ in W_{t+1}. For example, in Figure 2, T_1 is originally mapped to τ_1. After combining τ_1 and τ_2, T_1 is mapped to extra 3 meta-terms, namely τ_3, τ_4, τ_5, (besides the remainder meta-term τ_6), which results in three additional elements in W. Formally, the overall space saving when combining τ_i and τ_j is:

$$saving(\tau_i, \tau_j, C_1, \ldots, C_z, W_t) = \sum_{p=1}^{z} |C_p| - z \cdot |\{T \in \Omega : W_t[T, \tau_i] \neq 0 \vee W_t[T, \tau_j] \neq 0\}|. \quad (4)$$

In the following, we describe how to efficiently identify a pair of rows in H_t, with the highest potential savings. A straightforward approach is to compute the potential space saving, based on Equation 4, for all pairs of rows and return the pair with the highest savings. However, the complexity of such approach is quadratic in the number of rows in H_t, which is prohibitively expensive. To reduce the number of pair-wise comparisons, we use a *blocking* technique to heuristically prune a large number of pairs that have low potential space saving. Specifically, we partition the rows in H_t into several disjoint blocks, based on the number of non-zeros in each row, and we only compute the potential saving for pairs of rows within the same block. The main hypothesis here is that rows that have significantly different number of non-zero elements are uncorrelated, and they are unlikely to have overlapping elements.

4.2 Other Issues

Limiting the Number of Subvectors. Our compression approach iteratively reduces the index size at the cost of increasing the number of meta-terms. That is, there is a trade-off between the space savings and the increase in the number of meta-terms. In particular, it may not be beneficial to introduce new meta-terms whose space savings are below some threshold. The length of a new meta-term τ_{r+p} represents its maximum potential saving, according to Equation 4. Therefore, we modify algorithm $GetCorrelatedSubmatrices(H_t)$ such that it generates a new meta-term only if its length is greater than or equal to a threshold μ. Consider the example depicted in Figure 2. Assuming that $\mu = 3$, only the first two meta-terms τ_3, τ_4 would be generated, while the third meta-term τ_5 would not be generated (i.e., it becomes part of the remainder meta-terms τ_6, τ_7).

MapReduce Implementation. To scale the algorithm to large matrices, we parallelize it according to the MapReduce model [12]. We notice that combining two rows of matrix H_t is done independently of other rows on H_t. Therefore, it is possible to combine multiple pairs of rows of H_t in parallel, as long as pairs are mutually disjoint. Such observations allow the following parallelization scheme: (1) map each row in H_t to a specific block, based on the number of non-zeros in each row, (2) compute the potential space saving for each pair of rows in the same block in parallel, (3) for each block, identify a set of disjoint pairs of rows that maximize the overall saving, (4) for each block, combine all pairs and output the (disjoint) parts of H_{t+1} and W_M, and (5) collect all the parts and construct H_{t+1}, and $W_{t+1} = W_t W_M$.

Updating the Compressed Index. Due to the dynamic nature of documents copra that are found in the Web, we must be able to update inverted indices with minimal computational cost, without the need of reconstructing the entire index from scratch. In the following, we show how to append a new document to the index, and how to remove an existing document (updating a document can be decomposed into removing the old version of the document, and inserting the new version). We notice that at least one meta-term is a remainder meta-term, denoted $Rem(T_i)$, that is uniquely mapped to the original term T_i (i.e, $W[T_i, Rem(T_i)] = 1$, and $\forall j \neq i(W[T_j, Rem(T_i)] = 0)$). In order to add a new document D that mention term T_i, it is sufficient to add a new posting to the posting list of $Rem(T_i)$. To remove a document D from the index, we remove all elements in the column in H that corresponds to D. Note that the index should be reconstructed periodically (e.g., at idle times) to compress the newly inserted documents.

5. OPTIMIZING QUERY PROCESSING

A side-effect of our approach is having a number of meta-terms in the rewritten query that is larger than the number of terms in the original query, which can lead to longer query response times. In this section, we show how to mitigate this undesirable effect by exploiting unique characteristics of our compression scheme. As a case study, we show how to modify the Non-Random-Access algorithm (NRA) [8]. Note that there exist a plethora of search algorithm that might be more efficient than NRA, especially for memory-resident indices. However, we chose the NRA algorithm because of its simplicity.

We denote by $L_1, \ldots, L_h$ the posting lists corresponding to the terms with non-zero weight in query Q, where $h = \|Q\|_0$, and let $w_1, \ldots, w_h$ be the weights associated with $L_1, \ldots, L_h$ in Q. The score of a document D can be rewritten as $Score(D, Q) = \sum_{i=1}^{h} w_i \cdot L_i(D)$, where $L_i(D)$ denotes the weight of document D in list L_i. The NRA algorithm requires posting lists to be sorted in descending order of term frequencies.

The NRA algorithm retrieves documents from lists $L_1, \ldots, L_h$ in a round robin order. Having the lists sorted enables computing upper and lower bounds on document scores in each list. Every time a document is retrieved, the lower and upper bounds of retrieved documents, as well as unseen documents, are updated. Once k documents are found whose lower bounds are greater than or equal to the upper bounds of all other documents (including the unseen ones), the algorithm terminates.

Score bounds are computed as follows. Let $\overline{x}_i$ denote the weight of the last document retrieved from list L_i, if L_i is not completely read by the algorithm, or 0 otherwise. During execution of the algorithm, the score upper bound of each retrieved document D, denoted $\overline{Score}(D, Q)$, is computed as follows:

$$\overline{Score}(D, Q) = \sum_{i=1}^{h} w_i \cdot \overline{L_i}(D). \quad (5)$$

where $\overline{L_i}(D)$ is the weight of D in list L_i if D has appeared in L_i, and $\overline{x}_i$ otherwise. The upper bound for unseen documents is $\sum_{i=1}^{h} w_i \cdot \overline{x}_i$. Similarly, the lower bound of each retrieved document D, denoted $\underline{Score}(D, Q)$, is

$$\underline{Score}(D, Q) = \sum_{i=1}^{h} w_i \cdot \underline{L_i}(D). \quad (6)$$

where $\underline{L_i}(D)$ is the weight of D in list L_i, if D has appeared in L_i, and 0 otherwise.

In the following, we describe our modifications to the NRA algorithm. The score upper bound of each retrieved document D is computed by assuming that each undiscovered weight $L_i(D)$ is equal to $\overline{x}_i$ (Equation 5). Recall that all meta-term lists corresponding to the same original term are disjoint (Section 4.1). Thus, it is possible to compute a tighter score upper bound by setting undiscovered weight $L_i(D)$ to zero, instead of $\overline{x}_i$, if D has appeared in some list L_j such that L_i and L_j are disjoint.

Therefore, instead of considering lists of meta-terms independently, we create a two-level document retrieval scheme as follows. We create a *virtual list* for each original query term T_i. Each virtual list is traversed by probing the *disjoint* lists of the corresponding meta-terms. We use a priority queue PQ_i to implement retrieval from the virtual list of T_i. Let $M(T_i) \triangleq \{\tau : W[T_i, \tau] \neq 0\}$ be the set of meta-terms that term T_i is rewritten into. Initialization of a priority queue PQ_i is performed by inserting a pair (τ, D) for each meta-term τ in $M(T_i)$, where D is the document with the highest score in τ. The score of each pair (τ, D) in the queue is equal to the score of D in list τ multiplied by the weight $W[T_i, \tau]$. Retrieving next document from the virtual list of T_i is equivalent to retrieving the document D in the pair (τ, D) at the head of the priority queue. After each retrieval from PQ_i, we insert a new pair (τ, D') in PQ_i, where D' is the next document to be retrieved from the list of τ.

We modify the NRA algorithm to use virtual lists as follows. The algorithm initializes priority queues $PQ_1, \ldots, PQ_h$ for the original query terms $T_1, \ldots, T_h$. Retrievals from each list L_i are replaced by retrievals from the corresponding virtual list. The following theorem states the correctness of the modifications, and gives an upper bound on the runtime overhead.

THEOREM 3. *Query results obtained by the NRA algorithm when processing query Q using the uncompressed index V are equal to the results obtained by the modified NRA algorithm when processing the same query Q using a compressed index H and a term rewriting matrix W such that $V = WH$. Furthermore, the modified NRA algorithm performs at most $\sum_{T_i \in Q} |M(T_i)|$ more probes than the unmodified NRA algorithm.*

The proof is provided in [3]. Some meta-terms in the rewritten query might be shared across multiple terms in the original query (i.e., $M(T_i) \cap M(T_j) \neq \phi$ for $T_i, T_j \in Q$ and $i \neq j$). We further reduce the number of probes by keeping each meta-term τ in exactly one priority queue PQ_i of a term T_i such that $\tau \in M(T_i)$, and removing occurrences of τ in other priority queues.

6. EXPERIMENTAL EVALUATION

In this section, we evaluate the effectiveness of our compression technique and its impact on query execution time. We show that our technique is orthogonal to the compression techniques that compress posting lists individually (e.g., var-byte encoding [16]), and thus can be integrated with such techniques as we demonstrate in this section. We perform our evaluation on memory-resident indices since this is the dominant approach in modern search engines due to the growing memory capacities of modern machines, as well as index partitioning techniques.

6.1 Setup

Our index factorization algorithm ran on a Hadoop cluster. Query evaluation latency was measured by a single-threaded Java process running on an Intel Xeon 2.00GHz 8-core machine with 32GB RAM. Both compressed and uncompressed indices were preloaded into RAM prior to query evaluation. We used TREC WT10g document corpus [1], which contains 1.7M documents. We indexed only the textual content of the documents and discarded HTML tags. We removed rare terms that appear in less than three documents, thus reducing the number of unique terms from 5.4M to 1.6M. These rare terms account for less than 1% of the index size. Each posting contains 4-byte integer for *docID* and 4-byte integer

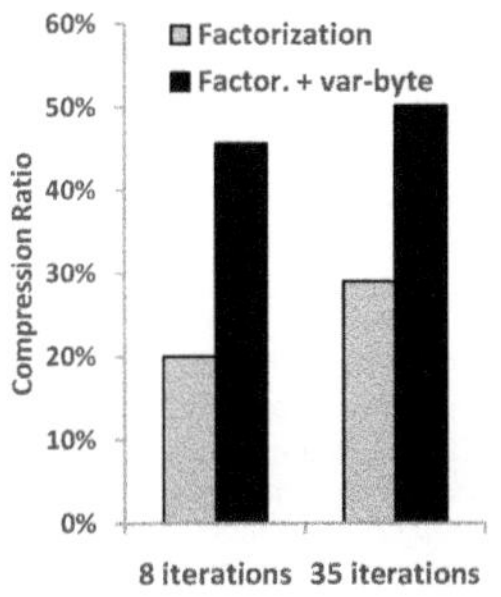

Figure 3: Compression ratio

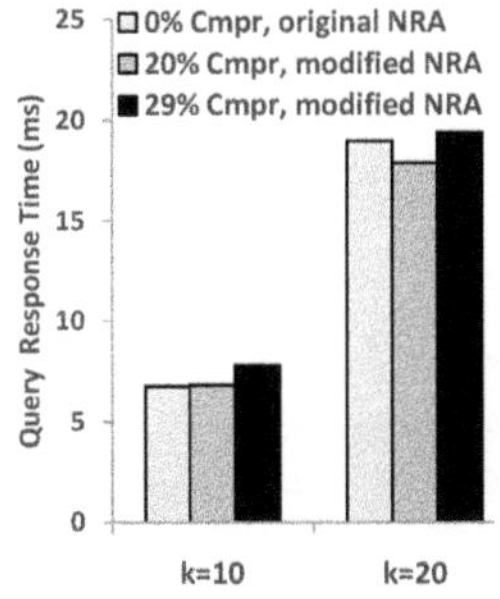

Figure 4: Average query response time

for term frequency. For query workload, we used 50,000 queries that are randomly selected from the AOL query log [17]. Unless specified otherwise, the minimum savings threshold μ is set to 100.

To measure the compression ratio, we use the relative reduction in the size of the inverted index: (Uncompressed Index Size - Compressed Index Size) / (Uncompressed Index Size). We consider both matrices W and H when computing the size of a compressed index. Note that for factorization-based compression only, the compression ratio is equal to $\frac{\|V\|_0-(\|W\|_0+\|H\|_0)}{\|V\|_0}$.

6.2 Results

Compression Performance. We selected two compressed indices obtained after 8 and 35 iterations of our algorithm. Figure 3 shows the compression ratio for the two indices. We observe that after 8 iterations, our algorithm compresses the index by 20%. When we additionally compress each posting list in the compressed index using the gap-based var-byte encoding [16], the overall compression reaches 46%. At iteration 35, the compression ratios further increase to 29% and 50%, respectively. The size of matrix W, which maps the original terms to the meta-terms, is less than 1% of the compressed index size in all iterations.

By lowering the saving threshold μ to 0, our approach archives a compression ratio of 35% after 30 iterations (Figure 7(b)).

When limiting the number of mappers/reducers to 100 per each job, each iteration took 22 minutes in average. The runtime of the first few iterations is slightly above average (e.g., the first iteration took 27 minutes, while the second iteration took 23 minutes).

Query Evaluation Latency. Figure 4 shows the average query latency for different numbers of retrieved documents (k) using the compressed indices at iterations 8 and 35. We do not show the latency of the unmodified NRA algorithm on the compressed indices as it is orders-of-magnitude higher and would distort the plot. In some cases, searching a compressed index outperforms searching the uncompressed index (e.g., for $k = 20$, the latency at compression ration of 20% is 6% lower than the latency when using the uncompressed index).

Size of the Factor Matrices. Figure 5 depicts the relative number of non-zero elements in W and H compared to the number of non-zeros in V at various iterations of the compression algorithm. Observe the monotonicity of the curve due to the property of our algorithm that never increases the number of non-zero elements in the factors. Matrix W, which is used for query rewriting, is much smaller than H (e.g., $\|W\|_0$ is less than 1% of $\|V\|_0$).

Integration with Var-byte Encoding. In this experiment, we show the behavior of var-byte encoding [16] when applied to our compressed index. Figure 6 shows the effectiveness of the var-byte encoding at various compression ratios of our factorization algorithm. The relative stability of effectiveness of var-byte encoding

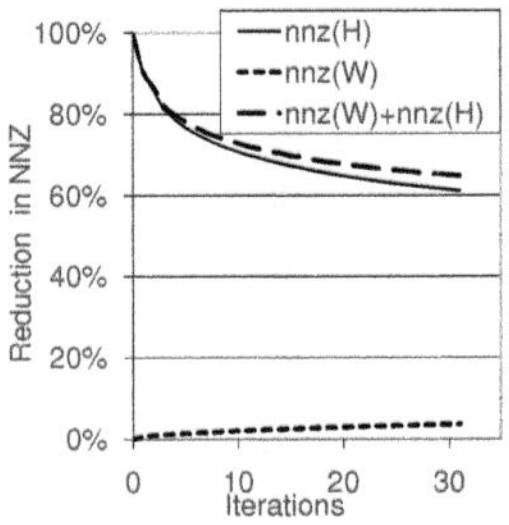

Figure 5: Relative reduction in non-zeros

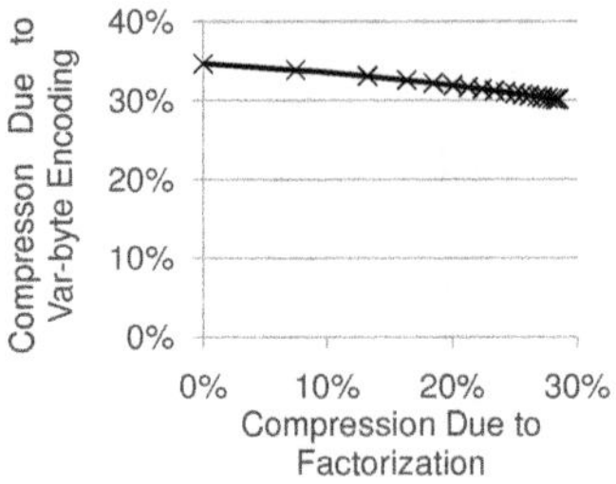

Figure 6: Effectiveness of var-byte encoding

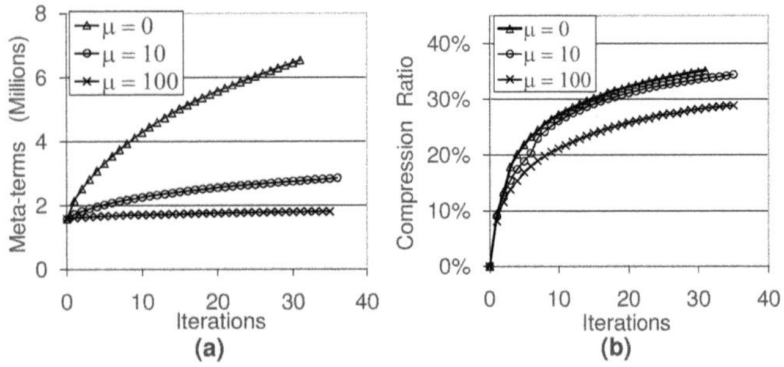

Figure 7: The effect of μ on (a) the number of meta-terms, and (b) the compression ratio

suggests that it is orthogonal to our compression technique, and thus both techniques can be used together to achieve higher compression ratios. For example, combining the two techniques enables compression ratio of 50% at iteration 35 (Figure 3), which is higher than using our compression technique alone (29%), or using var-byte encoding alone (34%).

The Saving Threshold μ. In this experiment, we analyze the effect of μ on the total number of meta-terms in the compressed index (Figures 7(a)), and on the compression ratio (Figures 7(b)). Changing μ from 0 to 100 reduces the total number of meta-terms in the compressed index at iteration 30 from 6.5M to 1.8M. At the same time, the compression ratio is reduced by only 6%.

7. RELATED WORK

Lossless compression of inverted indices has been an active topic for the past few years. Most of the developed techniques (e.g., variable-byte encoding, gamma-coding and delta-coding [16, 18]) aim at generating an efficient encoding of the entries in a posting list, and thus can be integrated with our approach (cf. Section 6). We also envision integrating our approach with lossy compression techniques, such as static pruning [6].

Several matrix factorization approaches have been proposed such as Non-negative Matrix Factorization [10, 13, 14], Principal Component Analysis [11], Latent Semantic Analysis [7], and Singular Value Decomposition [19]. Their goal is to factor a given matrix into two (or three) factor matrices that (optionally) exhibit some level of sparseness. Such techniques provide a *close approximation* of the input matrix, while our approach provides an *exact* factorization of the input matrix. Modifying such algorithms to be lossless is not straightforward. For example, one naïve approach is to compute the remainder matrix $R = V - WH$ so that V can be compactly represented using W, H, and R (i.e., $V = WH + R$). Unfortunately, there is no guarantee that sparseness of W and H would lead to sparseness of R. In fact, the size of R can be larger than the size of V because elements in V with values equal to zero may have non-zero values in the product WH. Another related work in the context of signal and image processing considers the problem of representing a *signal* (i.e., a vector) using a linear combination of a small number of basis vectors from a *dictionary* (e.g., [2, 20]). The problem of selecting the optimal dictionary is similar to the problem we consider, with two main differences: (1) the dimensions of the factor matrices are selected in advance, and (2) the sparseness is required only for the encoding vectors (matrix W) and not for the basis vectors (matrix H).

8. CONCLUSION

We presented a novel approach for lossless compression of inverted indices based on exact matrix factorization. We proved that obtaining the optimal factorization is NP-hard, and developed an efficient greedy factorization algorithm. We described how to modify a typical top-k search algorithm to eliminate the query time overhead. Our experiments show that our technique achieves compression ratio of 35% while incurring negligible increase in the query evaluation time. Variable-byte encoding can be integrated with our approach to achieve overall compression ratios up to 50%.

9. REFERENCES

[1] TREC WT10g Dataset, http://ir.dcs.gla.ac.uk/test_collections/wt10g.html.

[2] On the uniqueness of overcomplete dictionaries, and a practical way to retrieve them. *Linear Algebra and its Applications*, 2006.

[3] G. Beskales, M. Fontoura, M. Gurevich, S. Vassilvitskii, and V. Josifovski. Factorization-based lossless compression of inverted indices. Technical report, 2011. http://arxiv.org/abs/1108.1956.

[4] D. M. Blei, A. Y. Ng, and M. I. Jordan. Latent dirichlet allocation. *Journal of Machine Learning Research*, 3:993–1022, 2003.

[5] A. Z. Broder, D. Carmel, M. Herscovici, A. Soffer, and J. Zien. Efficient query evaluation using a two-level retrieval process. In *CIKM*, 2003.

[6] D. Carmel, D. Cohen, R. Fagin, E. Farchi, M. Herscovici, Y. S. Maarek, and A. Soffer. Static index pruning for information retrieval systems. In *SIGIR*, 2001.

[7] S. Deerwester, S. T. Dumais, G. W. Furnas, T. K. Landauer, and R. Harshman. Indexing by latent semantic analysis. *Journal of The American Society for Information Science*, 41(6):391–407, 1990.

[8] R. Fagin, A. Lotem, and M. Naor. Optimal aggregation algorithms for middleware. *J. Comput. Syst. Sci.*, 66(4):614–656, 2003.

[9] S. Foucart and M.-J. Lai. Sparsest solutions of underdetermined linear systems via l_q-minimization for $0 < q \leq 1$. *Applied and Computational Harmonic Analysis*, 26(3):395 – 407, 2009.

[10] P. O. Hoyer. Non-negative matrix factorization with sparseness constraints. *J. Mach. Learn. Res.*, 5:1457–1469, 2004.

[11] I. Jolliffe. *Principal Component Analysis*. Springer Verlag, 1986.

[12] R. Lämmel. Google's mapreduce programming model — revisited. *Sci. Comput. Program.*, 68(3):208–237, 2007.

[13] D. D. Lee and H. S. Seung. Algorithms for non-negative matrix factorization. In *In NIPS*, pages 556–562. MIT Press, 2001.

[14] C. Liu, H.-c. Yang, J. Fan, L.-W. He, and Y.-M. Wang. Distributed nonnegative matrix factorization for web-scale dyadic data analysis on mapreduce. In *WWW*, 2010.

[15] S. C. Madeira and A. L. Oliveira. Biclustering algorithms for biological data analysis: A survey. *IEEE/ACM Trans. Comput. Biol. Bioinformatics*, 1(1):24–45, 2004.

[16] C. D. Manning, P. Raghavan, and H. Schütze. *Introduction to Information Retrieval*. Cambridge University Press, 1 edition, 2008.

[17] G. Pass, A. Chowdhury, and C. Torgeson. A picture of search. In *Proc. 1st InfoScale*, 2006.

[18] F. Scholer, H. E. Williams, J. Yiannis, and J. Zobel. Compression of inverted indexes for fast query evaluation. In *SIGIR*, 2002.

[19] L. N. Trefethen and D. Bau. *Numerical Linear Algebra*. SIAM: Society for Industrial and Applied Mathematics, 1997.

[20] J. A. Tropp. Greed is good: algorithmic results for sparse approximation. *IEEE Trans. on Info. Theory*, 2004.

[21] H. Yan, S. Ding, and T. Suel. Inverted index compression and query processing with optimized document ordering. In *WWW*, 2009.

TOPSIG: Topology Preserving Document Signatures

Shlomo Geva
Faculty of Science and Technology
Queensland University of Technology
Brisbane, Australia
s.geva@qut.edu.au

Christopher M. De Vries
Faculty of Science and Technology
Queensland University of Technology
Brisbane, Australia
chris@de-vries.id.au

ABSTRACT

Comparisons between file signatures and inverted files for text retrieval have shown the shortcomings of traditional file signatures. It has been widely accepted that traditional file signatures are inferior alternatives to inverted files. This paper describes TopSig, a new approach to the construction of file signatures that extends recent advances in semantic hashing and dimensionality reduction. These were not so far linked to general purpose, signature file based, search engines. We demonstrate significant improvements in the performance of signature file based indexing and retrieval. Performance is comparable to the state of the art inverted file based systems, including language models and BM25. These findings suggest that file signatures offer a viable alternative to inverted files in suitable settings and positions the file signatures model in the class of Vector Space retrieval models.

Categories and Subject Descriptors

H.3.3 [**Information Storage and Retrieval**]: Information Search and Retrieval—*Retrieval Models, Relevance Feedback, Search Process, Clustering*

General Terms

Algorithms, Experimentation, Performance, Theory

Keywords

Signature Files, Random Indexing, Topology, Quantisation, Vector Space IR, Search Engines, Document Clustering, Document Signatures

1. INTRODUCTION

Document signatures have been largely absent from mainstream IR publications about *general purpose* search engines and ranking models for several years. The decline in the attention paid to this approach started with the publication of the paper "Inverted Files Versus Signature Files for Text Indexing" by Zobel et al [19]. This paper offers an extensive comparison between signature files and inverted files for text indexing. The authors concluded that inverted files are distinctly superior to signature files. Signature files are found to be slower, offer less functionality and require larger indexes. They conclude that the bit sliced signature files under-perform on almost all counts and offer very little if any advantages over inverted files. A similar picture emerges during the discussion of signature files by Witten et al [15]. The presumed advantages of efficient bit-wise processing and the potential for index compression are not generally achievable in practice. For a detailed explanation of signature files consult the work of Faloutsos and Christodoulakis [4].

Recent approaches to similarity search [17] have explored similar ideas to TopSig for mapping documents to N bit strings for comparison using Hamming distance. The approach taken by Zhang et al [17] and prior publications focus on similarity comparisons between documents. Their models have not been applied to general purpose ad-hoc retrieval. More importantly, Zhang et al [17] use a complicated approach to the static, off-line derivation of signatures, which involves supervised and unsupervised learning to generate document signatures. This in effect prevents the application of the approach to ad-hoc retrieval where a query signature has to be derived at run-time. It is not practical in a very large collection due to the excessive computational load of supervised and unsupervised learning.

Unlike earlier attempts, we approach the design of TopSig document signatures from basic principles. TopSig is radically different in the construction of file signatures and in the manner in which the search is performed. We present results of extensive experiments, performed with large standard IR collections, where we compare TopSig with standard retrieval models such as BM25 and various language models. We also describe document clustering experiments that demonstrate the effectiveness of the approach relative to standard document representation for clustering.

The remainder of this paper is organised as follows. Section 2 introduces the TopSig approach in detail. Sections 3, 4 and 5 define and evaluate the use of this approach for ad-hoc retrieval and clustering. The paper is concluded with a discussion in Section 6.

2. TOPSIG

TopSig represents a radically different approach to the construction of signature files. Unlike the traditional ad-hoc approach [4], TopSig is principled and signature files emerge naturally from a highly effective compression of the well understood and commonly used Vector Space representation of documents.

CIKM'11, October 24–28, 2011, Glasgow, Scotland, UK.

We approach the design of document signatures from the perspective of dimensionality reduction. TopSig starts from a straight forward application of a vector space representation of the collection - the term-document weight matrix. We then derive the signatures through extreme and lossy compression, in two steps, to produce topology preserving binary document signatures. While the actual mechanism that is proposed is highly efficient in signature construction and in searching, we first focus the discussion on the conceptual approach, its justification and theoretical grounding, while leaving the implementation and performance analysis details for later in the paper.

In this section we describe the concepts that underpin TopSig. These concepts are not new - Random Indexing and Numeric Quantisation - but when put together to form file signatures, the results are remarkable.

2.1 Random Indexing vs LSA

Latent Semantic Analysis [3] is a popular technique that is used with word space models. LSA creates context vectors from a document term occurrence matrix by performing Singular Value Decomposition (SVD). SVD is computationally expensive and this limits its application in large collections.

Random Indexing (RI) [11] is an efficient, scalable and incremental approach to dimensionality reduction. At the foundation of RI is the Johnson-Lindenstrauss lemma [5]. It states that if points in a high-dimensional space are projected into a randomly chosen subspace, of sufficiently high-dimensionality, then the distances between the points are approximately preserved.

Word space models often use RI as an alternative to LSA. Both LSA and RI start from the term-document frequency matrix. RI has linear complexity in the number of terms in a document and also in the collection size. This is a significant advantage over LSA whose time complexity is prohibitive in large collections. As stated by Manning et al [9] in 2008, in relation to LSA - *"The computational cost of the SVD is significant; at the time of this writing, we know of no successful experiment with over one million documents"*. RI can be performed incrementally and online as data arrives. Any document can be indexed independently from all other documents in the collection. This eliminates the need to build and store the entire document-by-term matrix. Additionally, newly encountered terms are naturally accommodated without having to recalculate any of the projections of previously encoded documents.

2.2 TopSig Signatures

Document signatures are fixed length bit patterns. In order to transform the real-valued projected term-document matrix into a signatures matrix, we proceeded to reduce numerical precision. TopSig takes the reduction in numerical precision to its ultimate conclusion by and reducing the precision all the way to a single bit. Binary signatures are obtained by taking only the *sign-bits* of the projected document vectors (!!). This is a key step in TopSig signature calculation; it may appear to be highly excessive precision reduction, but it is in fact surprisingly effective, as we shall demonstrate with search and clustering experiments in the following sections. Both clustering and ranking applications are concerned not with the actual similarity values, but rather with their rank order. As long as rank order is preserved the distortion due to reduced numerical precision is not problematic.

To complete the generation of a document signature we need to pack the ± 1 representation of signatures, onto binary strings. This is done by representing positive signs as 1s, and negative signs as 0s. The final result is thus a binary digital signature, but it still conceptually represents ± 1 signatures.

To measure the impact of aggressive dimensionality reduction we measure the root mean squared differences (RMSE) between the normalised mutual distance matrices of 1000 document vectors and their compressed counterparts. Figure 1 depicts the results of our experiment. On the y-axis is the topological distortion, measured by RMSE. On the x-axis is the number of dimensions in the projection. Each of the curves on the plot corresponds to a different numerical precision. The bottom curve corresponds to double precision, and then the plots above correspond to 8-bit quantisation, through 7-bit quantisation, and so on all the way down to 1-bit quantisation.

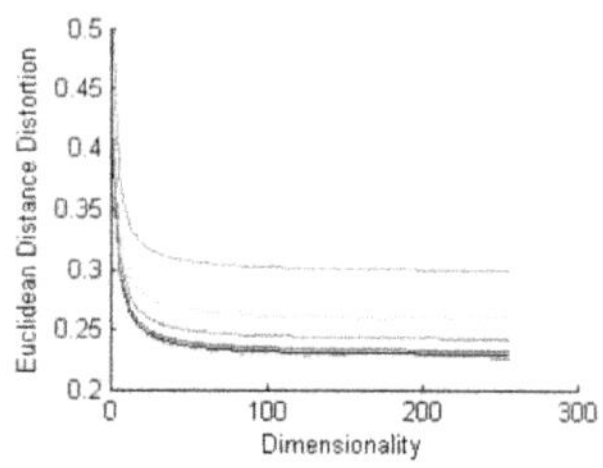

Figure 1: RMSE Drop Precision

As the dimensionality of the projected subspace is increased the distortion becomes smaller and is true regardless of numerical precision. Most of the gain is achieved quite early with relatively small dimensionality and is the expected behaviour of both RI and LSA. Unexpectedly, as we reduce the numerical precision the deterioration is very small. The lowest curve in Figure 1 corresponds to double precision. It is only when precision is dropped to 3-bits and below that the difference in RMSE becomes noticeable. Even with 1-bit precision we are still able to significantly preserve topology quite early with very small dimensionality.

3. AD-HOC RETRIEVAL

We provide a concrete description of TopSig components used for ad-hoc retrieval and describe the evaluation of document retrieval using the INEX Wikipedia collection and the TREC Wall Street Journal (WSJ) collection.

3.1 Document Signatures

We have not addressed the weighting of terms. The most effective weighting function we have found is described by $P(t|D) = \frac{tdf}{|D|}$, $P(t|C) = \frac{tcf}{|C|}$ and $W(t, D) = log\left(\frac{P(t|D)}{P(t|C)}\right)$. $W(t, D)$ is the weight for term t in document D, tdf is the term frequency for term t in document D, $|D|$ is the total number of term occurrences in document D, tcf is the collection frequency for term t, and $|C|$ is the total number of term occurrences in the collection. $P(t|D)$ is an estimate of the probability of finding the term t given a document D, and $P(t|C)$ is an estimate of the probability of finding term t given the collection C.

The weighting function $W(t, D)$ produces a larger value if the frequency of a term in a document is higher than expected, and smaller if the frequency is lower than expected. The logarithm of the ratio of these expected values is taken, so as to dampen the effect of an inordinately large frequency of a term in a document. Negative weight values are set to zero.

3.2 Query Signatures

In order to search the collection with a given query, we need to generate a query signature. Query document vectors are generated using standard TF-IDF weighting. This real valued query vector is then converted to a signature using exactly the same process as used with document signatures. It is necessary to use exactly the same process and parameters in generating the query signature as when generating document signatures.

Document signatures are represented in binary form, where 1-bits correspond to +1, and 0-bits correspond to -1. Query signatures, before taking the sign bits, may contain a mix of 3 classes of values: positive, negative, or zero. This depends on the signs of term signatures, and a value of zero is obtained when none of the query terms occupy some bit positions. As a matter of fact, with short queries and sparse term signatures this is almost invariably the case. These zero valued bit positions are those for which the query does not specify any preference. To account for this, a query mask is also generated to accompany the query signature. This mask has 1-bits in all positions other than those that are not covered by any term in the query. The 1-bits in the mask identify the subspace in signature space which the query terms cover. When comparing the query signature against document signatures, the similarity measure must not take account of differences in those bit positions. Conceptually, those are neither $+1$ nor -1.

3.3 Ranking

Ranking with TopSig is performed with the Hamming distance, calculating the similarity score for each document. The Hamming distance is rank equivalent to the Euclidean distance since all signatures have the same vector length - we note that the signatures correspond to $+1$ and -1 values, not 1 and 0 values, and hence the length of each signature of N bits is $\sqrt{N}$. Since the mask is almost invariably different for each query, the Hamming distance for each query will generally be calculated in a different subspace. The distance metric is therefore a *masked* Hamming distance.

If the document and query are identical in the query subspace then the Hamming distance will be zero. The Hamming distance between two signatures of N bits is restricted to the range $[0, 1, 2, ..N]$. For a signature file with 1024 bits per document there are at most 1025 possible distances between the query and a document, and many less if the query is short. This means that in a collection such as the Wikipedia, with millions of documents, if we rank all the documents by the Hamming distance from the query, we are bound to get numerous ties.

Although document signatures are not completely random - they are biased by the document contents, and similar documents have similar signatures - we still expect the vast majority of the documents to be centred at about a Hamming distance of $N/2$ from the query signature. Indeed this is always observed. The distribution of distances always resembles a binomial distribution, which we expect if the distribution of signatures was indeed random. It is not quite that, but we still observe strong resemblance to truly random distribution.

We are interested in early precision and so TopSig can still achieve granularity in ranking of documents. This is so because a large number of documents falls much closer than $N/2$ to the query signature, and the number of ties diminishes rapidly as the distance becomes smaller. Some ties still remain nevertheless and these may be broken arbitrarily or by using simple heuristics or document features. For instance, page-rank can be used, or any one of hundreds of document features that are reportedly used in commercial search engines.

3.4 Relevance Feedback

Psuedo relevance feedback is known to improve the performance of a retrieval system. TopSig can implement pseudo relevance in the usual manner, through query expansion. This however is a generic approach and can be be used with any search engine. There is however an additional opportunity to apply pseudo relevance feedback, an opportunity that is unique and specific to TopSig.

An initial TopSig search is performed in the subspace of the query signature by using the masked Hamming distance to rank all the documents in the collection. TopSig can expand the query signature by completing information from the *top-k* ranked documents and populating bits *not* in the original query subspace. The mean of the *top-k* ranked documents populates query bits *not* in the original query. This signature is now spans the full signature space and takes into account information from highly ranked results, including in bit positions that were not informed directly by the query terms. The new query is constructed by inserting only the missing bits into the original signature.

The ranking of documents in relation to the new query is then repeated by re-ranking a very small fraction of the nearest signatures - usually those that were retained in a shortened result list following the initial search. The feedback leads to statistically significant improvement in performance.

4. EVALUATION AND RESULTS

We have evaluated TopSig using the INEX Wikipedia 2009 collection, and the TREC Wall Street Journal (WSJ) Collection. INEX Wikipedia collection contains 2,666,192 documents with a vocabulary of 2,132,352 terms. The mean document length in the Wikipedia has 360 terms, the shortest has 1 term and the longest has 38,740 terms. We used all 68 queries from INEX 2009 for which there are relevance judgements. The Wall Street Journal Collection consists of 173,252 documents and a vocabulary of 113,288 terms. The mean WSJ document length is 475 terms, the shortest has 3 terms, and the longest has 12,811 terms. We used TREC WSJ queries 51-100.

To compare TopSig with state-of-the-art approaches, we have used the ATIRE search engine (formerly k [12]. ATIRE is a highly efficient state-of-the-art system which implements several ranking functions, over an inverted file system. The ATIRE search engine has been thoroughly tested at INEX against other search engines, including several well known systems such as Zettair, Lucene, and Indri, and has been shown to produce accurate and reliable results.

The references given herein to the ranking functions that were compared with TopSig, are to the actual papers that were followed in implementing the methods, as documented in the ATIRE search engine manual. These are Jelineck-

Mercer (LMJM) [16], DLH13 [8], Divergence from Randomness [1], and Bose-Einstein [1]. The ranking functions were evaluated with relevance judgements from TREC and INEX, and the *trec_eval* program.

4.1 Recall-Precision

Figure 2 depicts the precision-recall curves for INEX 2009 topics, against a tuned BM25 system, using $k = 1.1$ and $b = 3$, and with Rocchio pseudo relevance feedback. This BM25 baseline curve is optimistic - it is tuned with the actual queries, and performs better than any official run at INEX 2009. This provides a very conservative yardstick by which to measure the performance. The figure shows several TopSig indexes, encoding the signature with 64, 128, 256, 512, 768, 1024, 2048, 3072, and 4096 bits per signature. We have tested signatures of no more than 4096 bits because that signature file size is just below the size of the most efficient Inverted File index that we have been able to produce with ATIRE. ATIRE produces a significantly smaller index than Lucene, Indri and Zettair without sacrificing performance. Only one in 12 vector elements were set in the random term signatures, to either $+1$ or to -1, with the rest of the elements set to 0. As the number of bits in the signature increases, so does the recall. The performance of the file signatures is quite respectable once we allow for about 512 bits per signature - particularly at early precision. All the other language model based ranking functions produce a recall-precision curve that falls below BM25, and just above the best TopSig curve, but are not shown on the plot so as to reduce the clutter.

4.2 Early recall

While Figure 2 may at first suggest that file signatures produce inferior performance, we must focus our attention on the early precision, and this requires some justification before we do that.

Moffat and Zobel [10] found that P@N correlates with user satisfaction. A user who is given 7 relevant documents in the top 10 is better off than one who is only given 2. They argue that recall does not have a similar use case that reflects user satisfaction. Even for a recall oriented task, a user is unlikely to look past the top 30 results. For most tasks, the first page or top 10 results are most useful to the user. Users achieve recall not through searching the entire ranked list but by reformulating queries. Recent work by Zobel and Moffat [18] suggests recall is not important except for a few recall oriented tasks such as retrieval in medical and legal domains. If a system provides 100% recall, it implies that the user can create a perfect query. Even in recall based tasks, users tend to re-probe the collection with multiple queries to minimise the risk they have missed important documents.

The same argument is applied to discount the importance that is attributed the commonly used measure of Mean Average Precision (MAP) as it too depends on higher recall and a long tail of relevant results. Again, it is not clear what user satisfaction is correlated with MAP. Turpin and Scholer [13] performed retrieval experiments where users completed search tasks using search results with MAP scores between 55% and 95%. They were unable to find a correlation between MAP scores and a precision based task requiring the first relevant document to be found. For recall based tasks, they only found a weak link between MAP and the number of relevant documents found in a given time period.

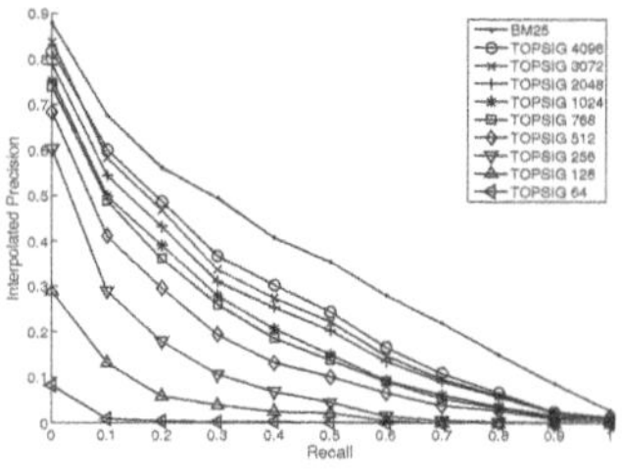

Figure 2: INEX 2009 Precision vs Recall

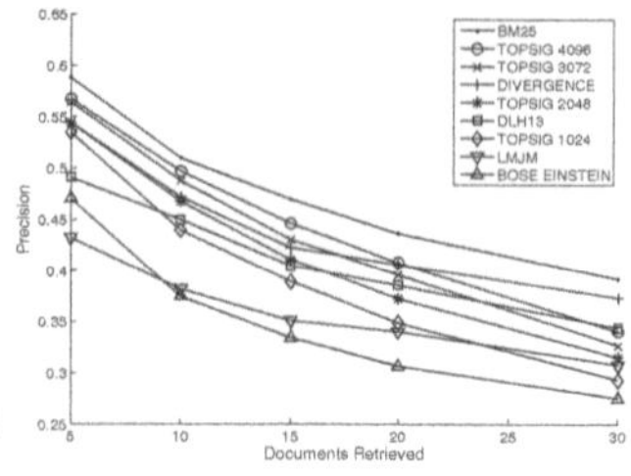

Figure 3: INEX 2009 P@n

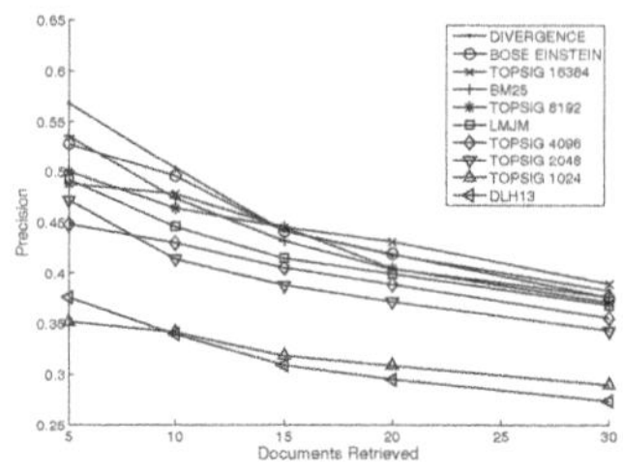

Figure 4: Wall Street Journal P@n

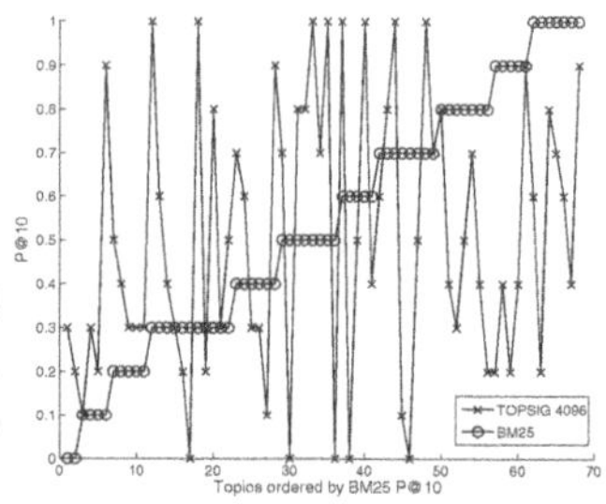

Figure 5: P@10 by Topic

They conclude that MAP does not correlate with user performance on simple information finding web search tasks.

Recall is not likely to be important to users except in some specific domains. Therefore, we focus our attention on comparison of P@N results between TopSig and state of the art inverted file approaches. The results immediately make it obvious that TopSig is a viable option for common information finding tasks

To assess TopSig at early precision we look at early precision in the P@N plots on Figures 3 and 4, for the 68 INEX 2009 ad-hoc queries and the TREC Wall Street Journal queries 51-100. It is immediately clear that TopSig performs similarly.

In order to look more carefully at the differences, we focused on the P@10 performance differences on the Wikipedia collection, between the best performing ranking function - BM25, and TopSig with 4096 bit signatures. The average P@10 for BM25 is 0.54, and for TopSig it is 0.51. We look at all 68 queries and performed two-tailed paired t-test. There is no statistically significant difference with $p = 0.41$. Figure 5 depicts the P@10 values for all 68 queries. The topics on the X axis are ordered by increasing P@10 values for BM25. The TopSig P@10 values are plotted in the same order. It is obvious that the two approaches produce very different results on a per-topic comparison. The two systems do not agree on which topics are difficult and which are not, and both sometime fail (on different topics) to produce any relevant result in the top-10. It is a common and well understood phenomena that this should occur and it is true for all the ranking functions that we tested. However, there is a much stronger correlation between all the language models, and BM25, as to which topics are hard and which are easy. No such correlation is observed for TopSig which seems to behave quite differently despite producing similar overall precision. This leads us to conjecture that combining TopSig with BM25 (or any of the other models tested) may lead to better results than emerge from combining any other pair of more correlated ranking functions. Testing this conjecture is outside the scope of this paper.

4.3 Storage and Processing overheads

TopSig is efficient and compares well with the inverted file approach. On a standard PC, a 1024 bit signature index can be searched by brute force in about 175 milliseconds, with a collection of 2.7 million signatures of the English Wikipedia documents. The signatures file size for this collection is only 325 MB, less than 0.65% of the collection size, and so it easily fits in memory. By contrast, the highly compressed inverted file of ATIRE (formerly known as ANT) that underlies all the other models, occupies 1.5GB, or about 3% of the uncompressed text collection size. ATIRE itself is highly efficient and for comparison, the Indri index for the same collection occupies about 11% of the space.

Searching with TopSig is also efficient. We have not implemented a parallel multicore search which offers linear speedup in the number of cores. Even so, all 68 queries for INEX collection were completed in 12 seconds for the Wikipedia collection and all 50 WSJ topics were completed in 4 seconds, on a basic Laptop. This is comparable to the performance that is obtained with the inverted file system.

5. CLUSTERING EVALUATION

The goal of clustering is to place documents into topical groups. The space and time efficiency of the TopSig representation allows it to outperform current approaches. It is also competitive in terms of document cluster quality. We have modified the k-means algorithm to work with signatures. This approach is compared to the implementation of k-means in the CLUTO clustering toolkit [6] that is popular in the IR community. CLUTO uses full precision sparse vectors to represent documents.

The k-means [7] algorithm was modified to work with the bit string representation of TopSig. Cluster centroids and documents are N bit strings. Each bit in a centroid is the median for all documents it represents. If more than half the documents contain a bit set to 1 then the centroid contains this value in the corresponding position. As the 1 and 0 values represent +1 and -1 this is equivalent to adding all the vectors and taking the sign of each position. The standard Hamming distance measure is used to compare all vectors. The algorithm is initialized by selecting k random documents as centroids. This modified version of k-means always converged when the maximum number of iterations was not limited. Whether this modified version has the same convergence guarantees as the original algorithm is unknown.

5.1 Clustering Results

We have evaluated document clustering using a 144,265 Wikpedia document subset - the INEX 2010 XML Mining collection [2]. The standard approach of comparing clusters to a "ground truth" set of categories is measured via Micro Purity. On this collection, Purity produces approximately the same relationships between different clustering approaches as F1, Normalized Mutual Information and Entropy. There are 36 categories for documents that are extracted from the Wikipedia category graph.

An alternative evaluation is performed that has a specific application in information retrieval. Ad-hoc retrieval relevance judgements are used to measure the spread of relevant documents over clusters. This is motivated by the cluster hypothesis [14], stating that documents relevant to the same information need tend to cluster together. If this hypothesis holds then most of the results will be in a small number of

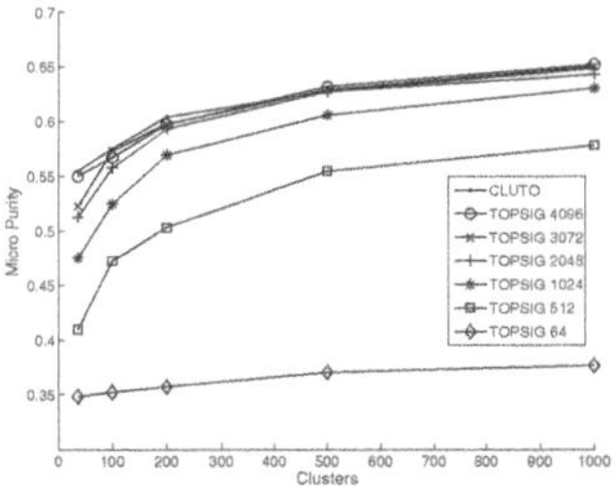

Figure 6: INEX 2010 Micro Purity

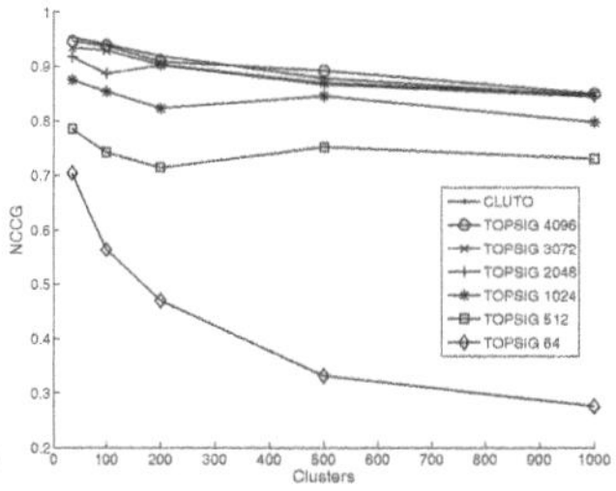

Figure 7: INEX 2010 NCCG

clusters. The Normalized Cumulative Cluster Gain measure represents how relevant documents are spread over clusters. It falls in the range $[0, 1]$ where a score of 1 indicates all relevant documents were contained in 1 cluster and a score of 0 indicates all relevant documents were evenly spread across all clusters. Complete details of the evaluation are available in a track overview paper from INEX 2010 [2].

The sparse document vectors used to create the TopSig document signatures are used as input to the k-means implementation in CLUTO. Therefore, we are comparing the same algorithm on the same data except for the fact the TopSig representation is extremely compressed and has a different centroid representation and distance measure. Both implementations of k-means are initialized randomly and are allowed to run for a maximum of 10 iterations. 36, 100, 200, 500 and 1000 clusters were produced by each approach where 36 was chosen to match the number of categories. This allows the trend of the measures to be visualised as the number of clusters are varied.

5.2 Analysis of Clustering Results

Figures 6 and 7 represent the quality of the clustering approaches using the Micro Purity and NCCG measures respectively. The TopSig representation nears the quality of CLUTO at 1024 bits and matches it at 4096 bits according to both measures. The best NCCG scores are all greater than 0.84 for all numbers of clusters, strongly supporting the cluster hypothesis, even when splitting the collection into 1,000 clusters.

Figure 8 shows how many times faster the TopSig clustering is than the traditional sparse vector approach in CLUTO. For example, using 4096 bit signatures to create 500 clusters is completed 20 times faster than CLUTO and 80 times faster at 1024 bits. This is one to two orders of magnitude increase in efficiency while still achieving the same quality as traditional approaches.

Figures 6, 7 and 8 can not be significance tested as they are a single run of the algorithms. However, the graphs allow the general trends to be visualised. CLUTO k-means takes approximately 5 hours to produce 1,000 clusters on this relatively small collection. Therefore, the CLUTO and TopSig k-means algorithms were repeatedly run to produce 36 clusters given different starting conditions. Given each random initialisation, k-means converges to a different local minima. The k-means implementations were run 20 times to measure this variability. Table 9 contains the results of this experiment where TopSig approaches that are equivalent to the CLUTO approach are highlighted in boldface. Equivalence was tested using the t-test with $p > 0.05$ indicating no statistically significant difference.

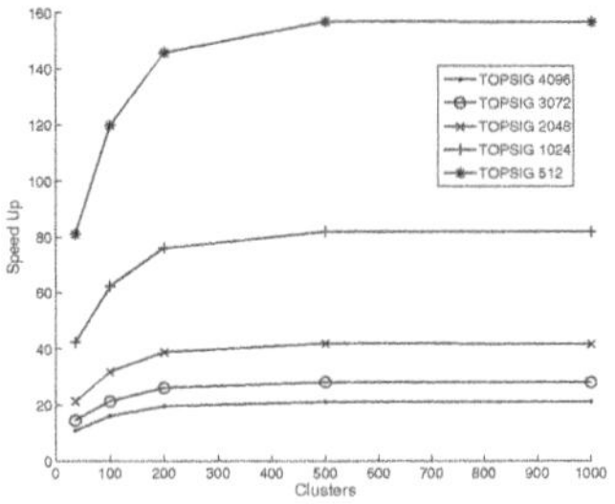

Figure 8: INEX 2010 Clustering Speed Up

Method	Micro Purity	NCCG
CLUTO	0.543 ± 0.008	0.955 ± 0.003
TOPSIG 4096	$\mathbf{0.540 \pm 0.008}$	$\mathbf{0.951 \pm 0.007}$
TOPSIG 3072	0.528 ± 0.009	0.939 ± 0.005
TOPSIG 2048	0.520 ± 0.007	0.926 ± 0.007
TOPSIG 1024	0.480 ± 0.007	0.867 ± 0.012

Figure 9: Detailed Evaluation of 36 clusters

6. DISCUSSION

We have described TopSig, an approach to the construction of file signatures that emerges from aggressive compression of the conventional term-document weight matrix that underlies the most common and most successful inverted file approaches. When focusing on early precision, TopSig is shown to be as effective as even the best models available, while requiring equal or less amounts of space for storing signatures. Significant reductions in signature index size can be achieved with TopSig as a trade-off. Testing with standard clustering benchmark tasks demonstrates TopSig to be equally effective and as accurate as a state-of-the-art clustering solution such as CLUTO, with processing speedup of one to two orders of magnitude.

TopSig had been applied to documents of greatly varying lengths. Both the WSJ and the Wikipedia collections have very short to very long documents, varying in size by up to five orders of magnitude. It had been suggested that file signatures are susceptible to this situation because of the increased probability of collisions on terms, but TopSig still performs well on these collections. In particular, we have tested TopSig with WSJ - the same collection that was used by Zobel et al to demonstrate the superiority of conventional inverted files. TopSig clearly outperforms conventional file signatures that were previously discredited. In this paper we compare TopSig directly with inverted file approaches to demonstrate similar performance levels.

There are certain differences between TopSig and inverted file based retrieval which may offer advantages in some application settings. TopSig performs the search in constant time and independently of query length. Comparing full documents to the collection (filtering task), or processing long queries, take exactly the same time as comparing a single term query. This may be useful in applications where predictability and quality of service guarantees are critical. The index size can be reduced by shortening the signature length, with smooth degradation in retrieval performance. Signatures may offer significant advantages where storage space is at a premium and a robust trade off is sought.

Distributed search is an attractive setting for TopSig - distributed indexing and retrieval have to resolve the problems of collection splitting and result fusion. With TopSig these operations are trivial to implement since the Hamming distance between signatures can be used as a universal metric across the system. If each text object in an enterprise carries its own signature then crawling and indexing the enterprise collection is a simple as collecting the signatures. Alternatively, TopSig can support the implementation of massively parallel search simply by distributing the query signature to every participating sub-system that maintains its own set of signatures. It is also trivial to implement distributed filtering with TopSig by maintaining a "watch list" of signatures that can be compared with incoming text objects at run time.

TopSig represents a principled approach to the construction of file signatures, placing it in the same conceptual framework as other models. It offers a view of file signatures as a highly compressed vector space representation of the collection, or alternatively, it offers a geometric representation of documents as points on the vertices of a collection hypercube. This is very different from the bitwise-efficiency motivated conventional ad-hoc formulation of file signatures.

7. REFERENCES

[1] G. Amati and C.J. van Rijsbergen. Probabilistic models of information retrieval based on measuring the divergence from randomness. *ACM Trans. Inf. Syst.*, 20:357–389, October 2002.

[2] C.M. De Vries, R. Nayak, S. Kutty, S. Geva, and A. Tagarelli. Overview of the INEX 2010 XML mining track. *INEX 2010, LNCS*, 2011.

[3] S. Deerwester, S.T. Dumais, G.W. Furnas, T.K. Landauer, and R. Harshman. Indexing by latent semantic analysis. *Journal of the American Society for Information Science*, 41(6):391–407, 1990.

[4] C. Faloutsos and S. Christodoulakis. Signature files: an access method for documents and its analytical performance evaluation. *ACM Trans. Inf. Syst.*, 2:267–288, October 1984.

[5] W.B. Johnson and J. Lindenstrauss. Extensions of Lipschitz mappings into a Hilbert space. *Contemporary mathematics*, 26(189-206):1–1, 1984.

[6] G. Karypis. CLUTO-A Clustering Toolkit. 2002.

[7] S. Lloyd. Least squares quantization in pcm. *IEEE Transactions on Information Theory*, 28(2):129–137, March 1982.

[8] C. Macdonald and I. Ounis. Voting for candidates: adapting data fusion techniques for an expert search task. In *CIKM 2006*, pages 387–396. ACM, 2006.

[9] C.D. Manning, P. Raghavan, and H. Schütze. *An introduction to information retrieval.* Cambridge University Press Cambridge, UK, 2008.

[10] A. Moffat and J. Zobel. Rank-biased precision for measurement of retrieval effectiveness. *ACM Trans. Inf. Syst.*, 27:2:1–2:27, December 2008.

[11] M. Sahlgren. An introduction to random indexing. In *TKE 2005*, 2005.

[12] A. Trotman, X. Jia, and S. Geva. Fast and effective focused retrieval. In *Focused Retrieval and Evaluation*, LNCS, pages 229–241. 2010.

[13] A. Turpin and F. Scholer. User performance versus precision measures for simple search tasks. In *SIGIR 2006*, pages 11–18. ACM, 2006.

[14] C. J. van Rijsbergen. *Information Retrieval.* Butterworths, 1979.

[15] I.H. Witten, A. Moffat, and T.C. Bell. *Managing gigabytes: compressing and indexing documents and images.* Morgan Kaufmann, 1999.

[16] C. Zhai and J. Lafferty. A study of smoothing methods for language models applied to information retrieval. *ACM Trans. Inf. Syst.*, 22:179–214, April 2004.

[17] D. Zhang, J. Wang, D. Cai, and J. Lu. Self-taught hashing for fast similarity search. In *SIGIR 2010*, pages 18–25. ACM, 2010.

[18] J. Zobel, A. Moffat, and L.A.F. Park. Against recall: is it persistence, cardinality, density, coverage, or totality? *SIGIR Forum*, 43:3–8, June 2009.

[19] J. Zobel, A. Moffat, and K. Ramamohanarao. Inverted files versus signature files for text indexing. *ACM Trans. Database Syst.*, 23:453–490, December 1998.

Implementation Techniques for Large-Scale Latent Semantic Indexing Applications

R. B. Bradford
Agilex Technologies Inc.
5155 Parkstone Drive
Chantilly, VA 20151
1-703-889-3916
r.bradford@agilex.com

ABSTRACT

The technique of latent semantic indexing (LSI) has wide applicability in information retrieval and data mining tasks. To date, however, most applications of LSI have addressed relatively small collections of data. This has been due partly to hardware and software limitations and partly to overly pessimistic estimates of the processing requirements of the singular value decomposition (SVD) process. In recent years, advances in hardware capabilities and software implementations have enabled much larger LSI applications. Moreover, experience with large LSI indexes has shown that the SVD is not the limitation on scalability that it was long thought to be. This paper describes techniques applicable to creating large-scale (multi-million document) LSI indexes. Detailed data regarding the LSI index creation process is presented for collections of up to 100 million documents. Four key factors are shown to contribute to the scalability of LSI. First, in most situations, the time required for calculation of the singular value decomposition (SVD) of the term-document matrix is not the dominant factor determining the overall time required to build an LSI index. Second, the time required to calculate the SVD in LSI is linear in the number of objects indexed. Third, incremental index creation greatly facilitates use of LSI in dynamic environments. Fourth, distributed query processing can be employed to support large numbers of users. It is shown that LSI is well-suited for implementation in modern distributed computing environments. This paper provides the first measurements of the execution time for large-scale LSI build processes in a cloud environment.

Categories and Subject Descriptors

H.3.4 **[Information Storage and Retrieval]**: Systems and Software – *performance evaluation.*

General Terms

Algorithms, Performance, Experimentation.

Keywords

Latent Semantic Indexing, LSI, SVD, scaling, large-scale applications, cloud computing.

1. INTRODUCTION

Latent semantic indexing (LSI) is a powerful analytic technique that has proven to be useful in a wide variety of applications [8]. Based on a technique from linear algebra, LSI provides an elegant solution to the key problem of dimensionality reduction. Considering the impressive performance of LSI in multiple applications [2], it has not achieved as wide usage as might be expected. One of the principal reasons for this has been a significant underestimate of the scalability of the technique.

This paper provides an overview of the technical considerations involved in applying LSI to large document collections. Section 2 provides a brief synopsis of the LSI technique. Section 3 presents an historical perspective on the LSI scalability issue. Section 4 describes the software, data, and parameter choices employed in the experiments and applications reported here. Section 5 presents details on the infrastructure and techniques applicable to deployment of large-scale LSI applications. Section 6 provides concluding remarks.

2. LATENT SEMANTIC INDEXING

Latent semantic indexing (LSI) is a machine learning technique that (classically) takes as input a collection of documents and produces as output a vector space representation of the documents and terms of the collection.[1] The central feature of LSI is the use of singular value decomposition (SVD) to achieve a large-scale dimensionality reduction for the problem addressed.

2.1 The Indexing Process

The technique of latent semantic indexing (as applied to text) consists of the following primary steps [5]:

1) A matrix is formed, wherein each row corresponds to a term that appears in the documents of interest, and each column corresponds to a document. Each element (m,n) in the matrix corresponds to the number of times that the term m occurs in document n.

[1] LSI actually can be used for a wide variety of data types. The discussion here focuses on text, the traditional domain of LSI. However, all of the results presented here are immediately applicable to large-scale LSI analysis of other data types.

2) Local and global term weighting is applied to the entries in the term-document matrix.

3) Singular value decomposition (SVD) [9] is used to reduce this matrix to a product of three matrices, one of which has non-zero values (the singular values) only on the diagonal.

4) Dimensionality is reduced by deleting all but the k largest values on this diagonal, together with the corresponding columns in the other two matrices. This truncation process is used to generate a k-dimensional vector space.

5) Both terms and documents are represented by k-dimensional vectors in this vector space.

2.2 Folding in

In many applications, it is desirable to represent in the LSI space documents that were not present in the original collection indexed. The technique of folding-in allows rapid creation of vectors that represent new documents in the space. To fold in a document, it is parsed, and a vector created that is a weighted average of the vectors for all of the constituent terms of the document [5].

3. HISTORICAL PERSPECTIVE

The idea of latent semantic indexing was first introduced in 1988 [5]. The SVD technique that lies at the heart of LSI is computationally intensive. In 1988, this was a significant drawback for LSI.

Throughout the 1990s and early 2000s, most published papers on LSI dealt with data collections of no more than a few tens of thousands of documents. Many authors made negative statements about the scalability of the technique. In general, these comments were based on two factors: a belief that the SVD calculation was the most time-consuming step in the LSI algorithm and an overestimate of the time required for that calculation.

Even quite recent publications have shown significant hesitancy regarding the scalability of LSI. For example, in a major textbook on information retrieval, published in 2008, the authors noted that they were not aware of any successful experiment using LSI on a collection of over one million documents [12].

The authors of a 2009 paper expressed the commonly-held feeling that large-scale LSI applications require supercomputers or even special-purpose hardware [10].

A 2010 paper described a collection of 131,321 documents as a very large dataset for LSI indexing [15].

4. TESTING AND APPLICATIONS

This paper presents details of the creation of LSI representation spaces built from collections of from 1 to 100 million documents. Roughly half of the data presented comes from testing activities. The rest comes from instrumentation of deployed LSI-based data mining and knowledge discovery applications. All data presented here is for LSI indexing of textual data. All results shown here encompass calculation of the (rank reduced) SVD for all documents and all selected terms (see section 4.2 for term selection criteria) for each respective document collection.

4.1 Data

Data used in the reported *test* activities consisted primarily of news articles comparable to those used in TREC testing. Some of the largest tests employed data from the Gov2 collection. Data from *applications* included news articles, resumes, technical articles, biomedical reports, and government documents. Such material includes large numbers of abbreviations, acronyms, technical terms, and proper names. Accordingly, the number of terms in these collections grows far beyond the number of dictionary words present in the material.

In most of the examples presented here, the documents have been processed using entity extraction software prior to creating the LSI indexes. For example, when a name such as *John Smith* has been identified by the entity extraction software, it has been treated as a single term in the creation of the term-document matrix. Depending on the specific documents, the entity types chosen, and the entity extractor employed, this process increases the number of terms in these collections by a factor of two to three. Thus, most of the LSI index creation (build) times shown here are significantly larger than would be the case for classical LSI indexes of the same documents, where entity extraction is not employed.

4.2 LSI Parameter Choices

Except for the dimensionality testing described in section 5.6, all LSI spaces discussed here were created with the number of dimensions set equal to 300. Stopword lists of $\approx$ 600 terms were used. There was no stemming of terms. Terms generally were indexed only if they occurred at least twice and in at least two different documents. This is a frequently employed occurrence threshold, which eliminates many noise terms but few desirable terms (particularly in very large collections).

4.3 LSI Software

In all cases presented here, the LSI software employed was the Content Analyst LSI engine from Content Analyst Company in Reston, Virginia.[2] Multiple versions were employed, with the most recent data obtained using version 3.7. This software implements the classical LSI algorithm as described in [5], with extensions allowing multi-process / multi-host parallel execution of a Lanczos technique for computing the largest singular values of the SVD [16].

5. LARGE-SCALE LSI PERFORMANCE

The following sections provide details of the creation of LSI indexes for large document collections.

5.1 LSI Process Steps

The key computational tasks to be carried out in creating an LSI space are:

- Creation of the term versus document matrix.
- Calculation of the rank-reduced SVD of that matrix.

[2] This software was chosen as it is the only known LSI engine that provides a full parallel implementation of both build and query functions.

- Expression of all terms and documents as vectors based on the calculated singular values.

In addition to computational demands, the initial step requires large volumes of I/O activity in order to ingest all of the documents of interest.

Figure 1 presents the times required for each of the fundamental elements of LSI index creation for collections ranging from 1 to 100 million documents.[3] The x-axis corresponds to the total number of objects indexed, both terms and documents. Two aspects of this figure are of particular interest:

- Total index creation (build) time (the sum of the three steps) is roughly linear in the number of documents.
- Total build time is not dominated by the time required for SVD calculation.

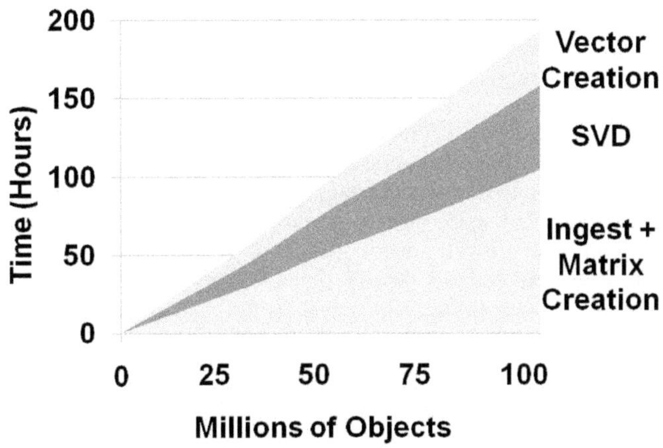

Figure 1. Timing of steps in the creation of an LSI space.

Figure 2 shows the number of terms versus number of documents for a range of representative LSI applications.

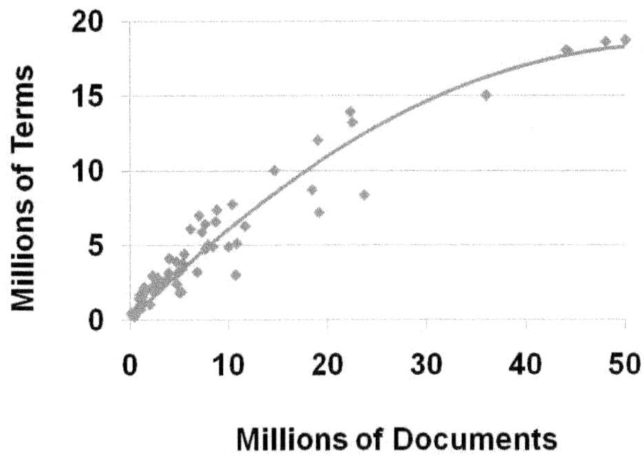

Figure 2. Term growth with increasing collection size.

[3] LSI indexing using 8 processors on HP DL 580 servers.

The high term counts reflect the large number of acronyms, abbreviations, proper names, technical terms, equipment designators, etc. that occur in real-world text collections. In addition, of the text collections described here, nearly all have been pre-processed using entity extraction software, which typically expands the number of terms by a factor of two to three.

The time required for LSI index creation results from a complex interaction among multiple factors:

- Inherent aspects of the LSI technique itself.
- The hardware employed (CPU and I/O capabilities).
- The operating system employed.
- The LSI software implementation architecture.
- The LSI indexing parameters chosen.
- Characteristics of the data (e.g., term distribution).

The following sections address these factors, with emphasis on the infrastructure and techniques required to enable large-scale applications using LSI.

5.2 Hardware Advances

Over the past few years, the time required to build large LSI spaces using modest hardware (mid-range servers) has decreased dramatically, as shown in Figure 3.

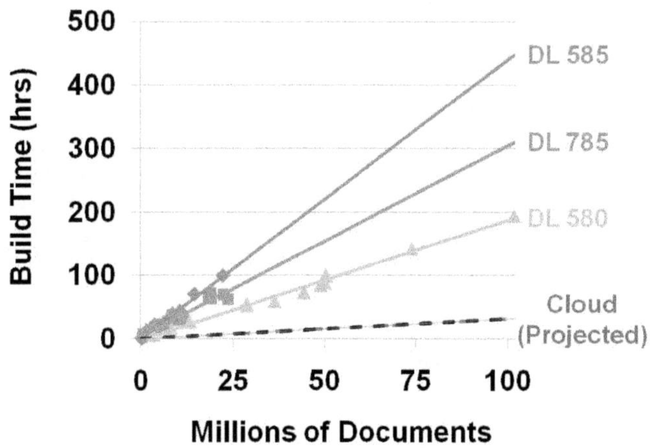

Figure 3. Reduction of build times with improving technology.

The advances shown in Figure 3 are due primarily to the confluence of four technology developments:

- Modern multi-processor / multi-core server architectures are well-suited to support both the build and query phases of LSI operations.
- High-speed backplanes available on modern servers facilitate the interprocess communication required to exploit distributed LSI processing.
- Solid-state disks (SSDs) reduce I/O delays in comparison to magnetic disks.
- Large amounts of RAM can be configured in modern server architectures for modest cost.

The top three trend lines presented in Figure 3 represent (from top to bottom) older, intermediate, and current mid-range server technology[4], as summarized in Table 1. Most of the data presented in this paper is from testing and applications employing DL 580 servers.

Table 1. Server characteristics

Server	Processor	Cores Per Processor	Clock Rate (GHz)	Bus Speed (GHz)	Cache			RAM (GB)	Disk Type
					L1 (KB)	L2 (MB)	L3 (MB)		
DL 585	4 X AMD Opteron 8220	2	2.8	1	256	2	0	128	Mag
DL 785	8 X AMD Opteron 8356	4	2.3	1	256	.5	2	256	SSD
DL 580	4 X Intel Xeon X7550	8	2.0	3.2	384	2	18	512	SSD

The line labeled cloud (projected) in Figure 3 is based on initial tests using a cloud computing architecture for implementation of the key steps in the LSI algorithm. Key constituent processes required for creation of an LSI space: ingestion, parsing, matrix population, and vector creation; are all well-suited to the map-reduce paradigm.

5.3 Data Ingestion

For all of the collections represented in Figure 1 above, the time required to ingest the documents, parse them, and create the term-versus document matrix was significantly greater than the time required for (truncated) SVD processing of the resulting matrix. High-speed magnetic disks, efficient RAID arrays, and solid state disks are all applicable approaches for minimizing ingest time.

5.4 Matrix Creation

One key requirement for creating large LSI indexes is that all of the intermediary processes must be carried out in RAM. If insufficient RAM is available, and the hardware begins to page, build times will be dramatically increased. (All build times presented here are from servers where sufficient RAM is available to prevent paging). Having a sufficient amount of RAM is a key scalability enabler for large-scale LSI applications. The matrix generation stage of LSI index creation is the most memory-intensive, as shown in Figure 4. One key reason for this is that pruning based on term occurrence[5] occurs in this phase.

[4] When purchased new, these servers originally cost in the range of \$50K-\$100K apiece. These HP servers are similar to those from several vendors that are used for large database applications and in virtualization environments.

[5] As noted in section 4.2, a term occurrence threshold requiring at least two occurrences of a term in at least two different documents was applied in the spaces reported here.

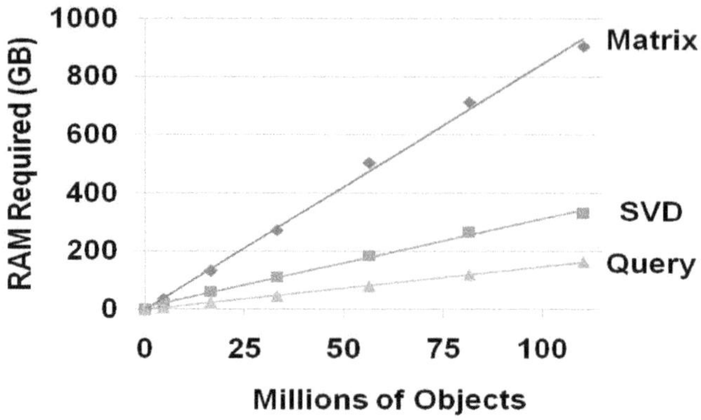

Figure 4. RAM requirements for LSI processing stages.

Requirements for high-speed memory also apply to LSI query operations. In order to obtain acceptable query times, the vectors for objects of interest (terms and documents) must all be kept in RAM. In Figure 4, note that the amount of RAM required for query operations is less than a fifth of what must be available during the creation of the LSI space. This characteristic is of great practical importance for applications. It allows approaches wherein a single server with large memory is used to build an LSI space, with that space then being distributed to a smaller server (or multiple servers) for query operations. Replication of the term and document vectors across multiple servers is a standard approach for supporting large numbers of users.

5.5 SVD Calculation

Historically, discussions of the scalability of LSI have focused on the time required for SVD computation. As shown in Table 2, a variety of estimates for the time complexity of the truncated SVD have been produced. In general, there has been a tendency for the estimated complexity to decrease over the years as researchers have become more familiar with LSI.

Table 2. Estimates of SVD computation time

Year	Author	Estimate	Ref
1990	Deerwester et al	$O([M+N]^2 \cdot k^3)$	[6]
1996	Dumais	$O(4 \cdot Z + 3.5 \cdot k)$	[7]
1997	Carbonell et al	$O(\max\{M,N\} \cdot k)$	[3]
2001	Chen et al	$O(M \cdot N \cdot k^2)$	[4]
2003	Xu & Umemura	$O(k \cdot Z^2)$	[14]
2004	Skillicorn	$O(Z \cdot k)$	[13]
2008	Landauer & Dumais	$O(Z+k)$	[11]

Where:
M = # of Terms
N = # of Documents
Z = # of nonzero Entries in Term- Document Matrix
k = # of Dimensions

Figure 5 shows actual times for the truncated SVD calculation for several large LSI indexes. The measured SVD calculation time is plotted as a function of the total number of objects (terms plus documents) being indexed. The growth in required time is linear over the entire range of applications, through 100 million documents. This behavior is due, in great part, to the fact that the term-document matrices being operated on are extremely sparse –

typically ≈ .003% populated. The calculations are carried out using sparse matrix techniques.

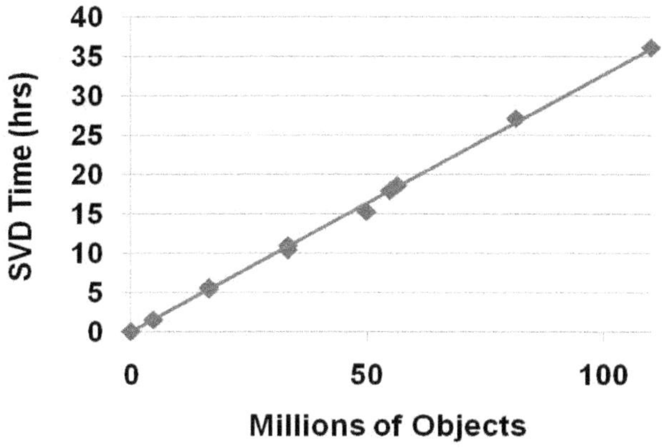

Figure 5. SVD calculation times.

5.6 Dimensionality

In general, there is reason to believe that, the larger the document collection, the more dimensions will be required in order to appropriately represent the range of concepts in that collection. One study has suggested that the number of dimensions should scale according to the log of the size of the collection [1]. Increasing the number of dimensions increases the total truncated SVD calculation time, as additional singular values must be computed. In addition, the vector creation time is increased, as more components have to be calculated. The combined increase is essentially linear in the number of dimensions, as shown in Figure 6.[6] As the number of dimensions increases, the amount of RAM required for the build process increases. Also, as noted in section 5.4, all vectors for objects of interest must be held in RAM for query operations to be efficient. Thus, as the number of dimensions is increased, the RAM requirements for the query server also increase.

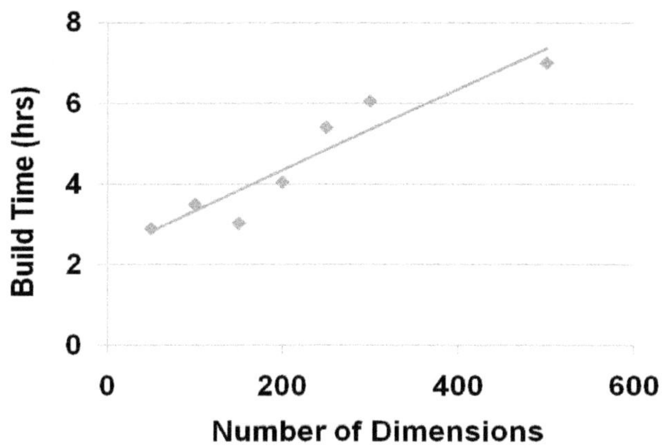

Figure 6. Build time versus number of dimensions.

[6] Collection of 1.6 million documents, 2 million terms, built on a DL 585 using hard disk storage.

5.7 Disk Storage Requirements

Once an LSI build process is complete, there are several files which constitute the repository for that space. The most important files are those containing the documents themselves (if they are stored locally), metadata about the documents, the term and document vectors, ancillary data used to speed query processing, and intermediate results. The storage requirements for the repositories grow roughly linearly with the number of objects indexed, as shown in Figure 7.

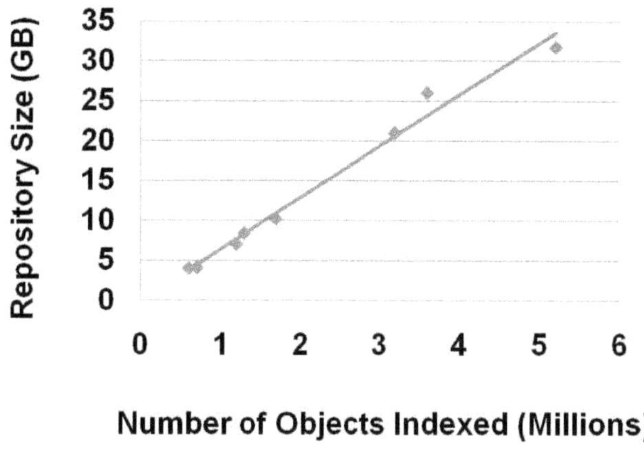

Figure 7. Linear Growth of repository size.

The repository size also grows linearly with the number of dimensions chosen, as shown in Figure 8.

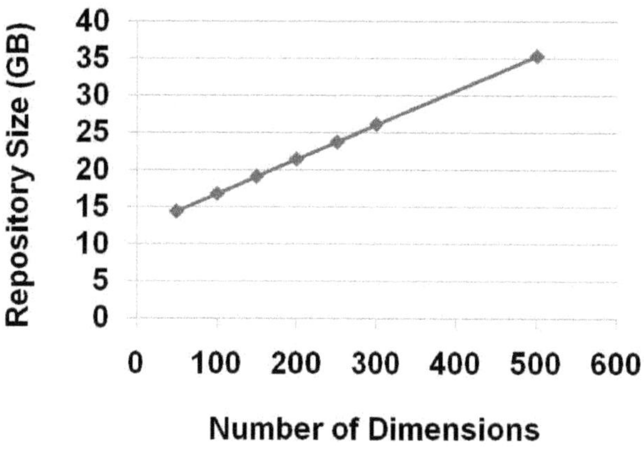

Figure 8. Repository size vs. dimensions.

5.8 Saving Intermediate Results

In many LSI applications there is a requirement to accommodate ongoing acquisition of new documents. On a short-term basis, this typically is done through use of the folding-in process described in section 2.2. On a longer-term basis, periodic re-indexing of the data typically is carried out. As noted above, the time required to ingest documents and create the term-document matrix currently is the dominant factor in determining the total time required to produce an LSI index. Accordingly, in large LSI applications with updating, there is much to be gained from saving intermediate results. Storing the term-document matrix (sans global weighting) typically can yield a savings of ≈50% in the time required for creating an updated index. As noted in section 5.5, the term-document matrix is very sparse and is represented using sparse matrix techniques. Thus, the size of the intermediate result file that must be stored is manageable.

6. CONCLUSION

To date, the technique of latent semantic indexing typically has been applied to relatively small collections of data. Systematic analysis of the technique, however, shows that this need not be the case. All of the constituent processes making up the overall LSI algorithm can be executed in time that is linear in the number of objects being indexed. Moreover, all of these processes are amenable to a high degree of parallel execution.

Historically, it has been felt that the time required for calculation of the singular value decomposition of the LSI matrix was the primary impediment to large-scale LSI applications. However, this turns out not to be the case. With today's hardware architectures, calculation of the SVD typically is not the most resource-intensive component of the basic LSI indexing processes. Moreover, the time required for (truncated) SVD calculation is linear in the number of objects being indexed. Thus, this process does not fundamentally constrain the ability to apply LSI to large problems.

With today's multi-core, multi-processor architectures, the time required to ingest the data being indexed typically is the most resource-intensive element of LSI index creation. Use of high-performance disk arrays and solid state disks can significantly reduce the time required for this data ingestion. In dynamic LSI applications, saving intermediate results (e.g., the term-document matrix in a text application) obviates the need to re-ingest and re-parse earlier data. This can result in dramatic time savings when re-building LSI indexes to accommodate new data.

The requirements for storage and for processing differ significantly for the individual steps in LSI indexing. Most of the key steps are well-suited to the map-reduce paradigm. Accordingly, modern cloud computing architectures are ideal for large-scale LSI applications. Such architectures will enable much larger LSI applications in the near future.

The ability to address large data collections also will make LSI an increasingly attractive approach for applications involving non-textual data, including audio, video, and sensor data.

7. ACKNOWLEDGMENTS

I would like to thank the Semantic Engineering Team at Agilex Technologies for their pioneering work in creating the large-scale LSI implementations represented here.

8. REFERENCES

[1] Bradford, R. 2008. An empirical study of required dimensionality for large-scale Latent Semantic Indexing applications. In *Proceedings, ACM 17th Conference on Information and Knowledge Management* (Napa, California, 26-30 October 2008).

[2] Bradford, R. 2009. Comparability of LSI and human judgment in text analysis tasks. In *Proceedings, Applied Computing Conference* (Athens, Greece, 28-30 September 2009).

[3] Carbonell, J., et al. 1997. Translingual information retrieval: a comparative evaluation. In *Proceedings of the Fifteenth International Joint Conference on Artificial Intelligence* (Nagoya, Japan, August 23-29, 1997), 708-714.

[4] Chen, C., et al. 2001. Telcordia LSI engine: implementation and scalability issues. In *Proceedings of the 11th International Workshop on Research Issues in Data Engineering* (Heidelberg, Germany, Apr. 1-2, 2001).

[5] Deerwester, S., et al. 1988. Improving information retrieval with Latent Semantic Indexing. In *Proceedings of the 51st Annual Meeting of the American Society for Information Science* (1988), 36-40.

[6] Deerwester, S., et al. 1990. Indexing by Latent Semantic Analysis. *Journal of the American Society for Information Science*, 41, 1990, 391-407.

[7] Dumais, S. 1996. Information retrieval: finding needles in massive haystacks. In *Proceedings of the National Academy of Sciences Workshop on Massive Data Sets* (1996), 23-31.

[8] Dumais, S. 2004. Latent Semantic Analysis. *Annual Review of Information Science and Technology*, Vol. 38. Information Today Inc., (2004), 189-230.

[9] Kalman, D. 1996. A singularly valuable decomposition: the SVD of a matrix. *College Math Journal*, 27 (1996), 2-23.

[10] Kettani, H., and Newby, G. 2009. On the ranking of text documents from large corpuses. In *Proceedings of the 2009 International Conference on Data Mining (DMIN'09)* (Las Vegas, Nevada, July 13-16, 2009).

[11] Landauer, T., and Dumais, S. 2008. Latent semantic analysis. Scholarpedia, 3(11):4356. Available from: http://www.scholarpedia.org/article/Latent_semantic_analysis.

[12] Manning, C., Raghavan, P., and Schutze, H. 2008. *Introduction to Information Retrieval*, Cambridge University Press, New York, N.Y. p. 382.

[13] Skillicorn, D. 2004. *Applying Matrix Decompositions to Counterterrorism.* Technical report. Queen's University, Kingston, Ontario, Canada, May 2004.

[14] Xu, Y., and and Umemura, K. 2003. Very low-dimensional latent semantic indexing for local query regions. In *Proceedings of the Sixth International Workshop on Information Retrieval with Asian Language* (Sappro, Japan, July 7, 2003), 84-91.

[15] Zaman, A., and Brown, C. 2010. Latent semantic indexing and large dataset: study of term-weighting schemes. In *Proceedings of the Fifth IEEE International Conference on Digital Information Management, ICDIM 2010* (Thunder Bay, Canada, July 5-8, 2010), 1-4.

[16] Berry, M., et al. 1993. *SVDPACKC User's Guide.* Technical Report Number CS-93-194, Department of Computer Science, University of Tennessee, May, 1993.

Statistical Source Expansion for Question Answering

Nico Schlaefer
School of Computer Science
Carnegie Mellon University
nico@cs.cmu.edu

Jennifer Chu-Carroll
IBM T.J. Watson
Research Center
jencc@us.ibm.com

Eric Nyberg
School of Computer Science
Carnegie Mellon University
ehn@cs.cmu.edu

James Fan
IBM T.J. Watson
Research Center
fanj@us.ibm.com

Wlodek Zadrozny
IBM T.J. Watson
Research Center
wlodz@us.ibm.com

David Ferrucci
IBM T.J. Watson
Research Center
ferrucci@us.ibm.com

ABSTRACT

A source expansion algorithm automatically extends a given text corpus with related content from large external sources such as the Web. The expanded corpus is not intended for human consumption but can be used in question answering (QA) and other information retrieval or extraction tasks to find more relevant information and supporting evidence. We propose an algorithm that extends a corpus of seed documents with web content, using a statistical model to select text passages that are both relevant to the topics of the seeds and complement existing information.

In an evaluation on 1,500 hand-labeled web pages, our algorithm ranked text passages by relevance with 81% MAP, compared to 43% when relying on web search engine ranks alone and 75% when using a multi-document summarization algorithm. Applied to QA, the proposed method yields consistent and significant performance gains. We evaluated the impact of source expansion on over 6,000 questions from the Jeopardy! quiz show and TREC evaluations using Watson, a state-of-the-art QA system. Accuracy increased from 66% to 71% on Jeopardy! questions and from 59% to 64% on TREC questions.

Categories and Subject Descriptors

H.3 [**Information Storage and Retrieval**]: Information Search and Retrieval

General Terms

Algorithms, Experimentation, Performance

1. INTRODUCTION

In question answering (QA), it is common to locally store and index document collections that provide good coverage of the information required for a given question domain. For instance, encyclopedias and dictionaries are useful sources for answering trivia questions, and newswire corpora provide relevant information about politics and the economy. However, these resources may not contain the answers to all questions, and answers may be hard to find if there is little redundancy in the sources. To improve the coverage of local sources and to facilitate the extraction and validation of answers, the sources can be expanded automatically with related information from large external text corpora such as the Web. In this paper, we present a fully implemented statistical approach to source expansion and compare it to several baselines for selecting relevant source content. We further demonstrate that source expansion consistently and significantly improves QA performance on large datasets drawn from the Jeopardy! quiz show and TREC evaluations.

We decompose the source expansion (SE) task into a four-stage process. Given a corpus of seed documents, our approach (1) retrieves, for each seed, related documents from the Web or other external sources, (2) extracts paragraph- or sentence-length text nuggets from the retrieved documents, (3) estimates the relevance of the nuggets with regard to the seed document using a statistical model, and (4) compiles a new pseudo-document from the most relevant text. The pseudo-documents can be indexed along with the seeds, yielding a larger corpus with increased coverage and reformulations of existing information. Note that this expansion is performed only once in a preprocessing step and does not require specific knowledge of the questions that will be asked at QA runtime.

SE is an effective method for improving QA performance because it addresses the most common types of failures in state-of-the-art systems:

1. *Source failures*, i.e. the knowledge sources do not contain the information sought by a question. SE helps by adding more relevant content.

2. *Search and candidate extraction failures*, i.e. the system cannot retrieve or extract a correct answer, often because of insufficient keyword overlap with the question. SE helps by adding paraphrases of existing information.

3. *Answer selection failures*, i.e. the answer is outscored by a wrong answer, often because of insufficient supporting evidence in the sources or because the relevant search results ranked too low. SE again helps by adding reformulations and increasing redundancy.

CIKM'11, October 24–28, 2011, Glasgow, Scotland, UK.

In contrast, by performing query expansion or using pseudo-relevance feedback (PRF) in the search phase of the QA system, one can (at most) address failures of types 2 and 3. In practice, these approaches may introduce noise and hurt performance [28]. Often, they are only applied as a fallback solution if an initial query yields low recall [19, 3].

Source expansion performed as a preprocessing step can also be preferable over live web searches at QA runtime. While web search engines must be used as black boxes, local sources can be indexed with open-source IR systems such as Indri[1] or Lucene[2], which allow full control over the retrieval model. Local sources can also be preprocessed and annotated with syntactic and semantic information, which can be leveraged to formulate queries that better describe the information need expressed in a question [30, 6]. Furthermore, in applications where speed and availability matter, where the knowledge sources contain confidential data or restricted-domain knowledge, or where a self-contained system is required, a live web search may be infeasible. Local sources also guarantee reproducible results, whereas the Web and search engines change constantly. Finally, local sources can be consolidated e.g. by merging related content into a single document and removing noise.

Source expansion has many potential applications beyond QA. For instance, the pseudo-documents generated through SE could be added to the document representations of the seeds to improve retrieval accuracy of a traditional document retrieval system. The expanded documents could also be used by a relation extraction algorithm to validate instances of relations found in the seeds and to find additional instances. This paper, however, focuses on QA as one example of a task where SE helps consistently. We show that SE significantly improves the performance of Watson [17], one of the most effective QA systems to date, yielding gains of 4.2%–8.6% in search recall and 7.6%–12.9% in QA accuracy on large datasets of Jeopardy! and TREC questions.

2. RELATED WORK

Source expansion is related to a number of NLP tasks, including content-based information filtering, topic tracking, multi-document summarization and definitional QA. The problem of extracting text nuggets from documents that relate to a given topic is perhaps most similar to multi-document summarization (e.g. [18, 27]) but differs in important ways: (1) the extraction is guided by the content of a seed document which is used to model topicality, (2) while we avoid lexical redundancy, semantically redundant text that phrases the same information differently is desirable, and (3) the generated summaries need not be coherent as they are not intended for human consumption.

Recent research on definitional QA has led to various algorithms for compiling relevant texts on topics such as people, organizations or events (e.g. [7, 32]). However, these algorithms generate answers to individual questions from existing sources at QA runtime, whereas the proposed method compiles new source material that can be used by a QA system to answer a wide range of questions with little computational overhead.

QA systems often use the Web as a large, redundant knowledge source [14, 16], but it has been noted that there are situations where a local search is preferable [13, 22]. Clarke et al. [13] evaluated the performance impact of locally indexed web crawls on TREC QA data. They found that large crawls of over 50 GB were required to outperform the 3 GB reference corpus used in TREC, and that performance degraded if the crawl exceeded about 500 GB. Our approach improves on earlier work by using statistical models to reduce the size of the retrieved web data by two orders of magnitude and to filter out noise that may hurt QA performance.

Balasubramanian and Cucerzan [4] propose an algorithm for generating documents about given topics from web content. The usefulness of sentences extracted from web pages is determined with aspect models built from web search logs. These aspect models consist of terms that frequently co-occur with a given topic or related topics in the query logs. In contrast, our SE method leverages the content of existing seed corpora to model topicality. While query logs may be hard to come by, particularly when starting out in a new domain (e.g. medical or legal search), suitable seed corpora are often readily available (e.g. medical encyclopedias, legal dictionaries).

A variety of techniques have been proposed for expanding text documents to facilitate their retrieval if the queries do not exactly match the terminology used in those documents. For example, documents can be augmented with terms extracted from related documents retrieved from the same collection or an auxiliary corpus. It has been shown that document expansion improves retrieval performance on various tasks, including spoken document retrieval [29], cross-lingual IR [24] and topic tracking [23]. When indexing a collection of web pages, the anchor texts associated with hyperlinks provide high-level descriptions of the linked documents and can be added to their index representations [15]. Similarly, in a scientific corpus, terms that appear in the vicinity of citations can be associated with the referenced articles [8]. Conversely, the content of linked or cited documents can be propagated to the documents that contain the references [25].

Similarly to query expansion and PRF, these document expansion techniques are unlikely to help if the information sought by an IR system is missing in the corpus (failure type 1 in the introduction). In contrast, the proposed SE method augments a seed corpus with additional information that can be used by applications such as QA, increasing the amount of useful content several-fold. SE can also help if the expanded sources are used directly by an information extraction system (e.g. for relation extraction) without performing a search.

3. APPROACH

The input of the source expansion (SE) algorithm is a collection of documents in which each document contains information about a distinct topic. We refer to each of the documents as a *seed document* or simply *seed*, and to the entire collection as the *seed corpus*. Examples of pre-existing seed corpora that are suitable for SE are encyclopedias (such as Wikipedia) and dictionaries (such as Wiktionary). For each seed, a new pseudo-document is generated that contains related information retrieved from large external resources. By expanding the seed documents, we gather additional relevant content about their topics, as well as paraphrases of information that was already covered. A question answering

[1]http://www.lemurproject.org/indri/

[2]http://lucene.apache.org/

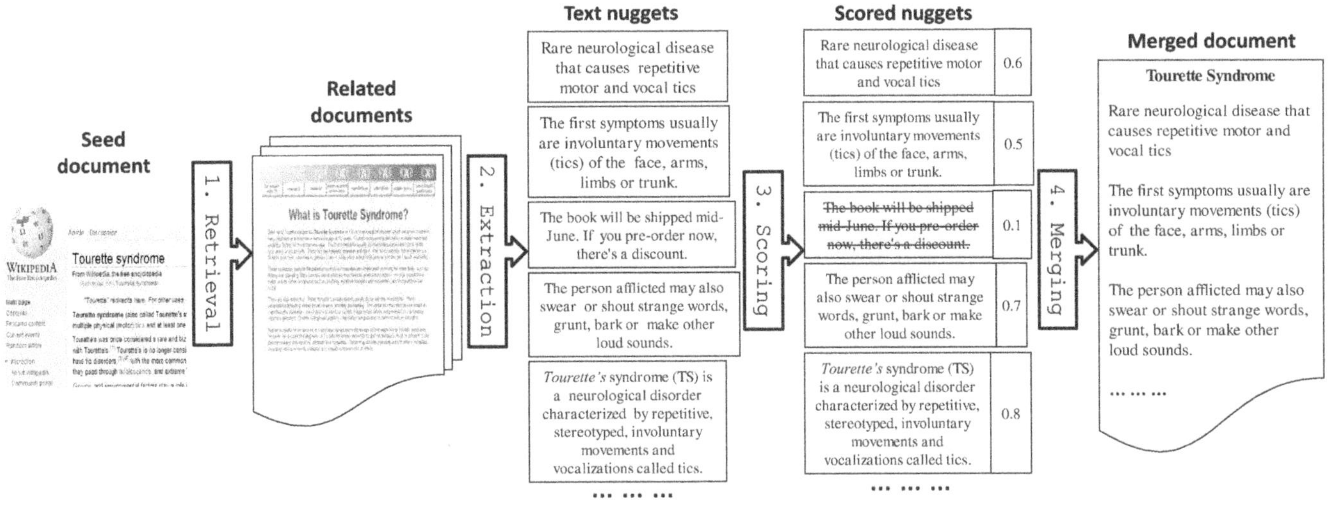

Figure 1: Four-stage source expansion pipeline processing the Wikipedia seed about *Tourette Syndrome*.

system can benefit both from the increased coverage and the added semantic redundancy.

Seed documents are expanded in a four-stage pipeline, illustrated in Figure 1 using the Wikipedia article about *Tourette Syndrome* as an example. For each seed, the SE system retrieves related documents from an external source (*retrieval* stage in Figure 1). We used the Web as a large source of related content for all experiments reported in this paper. The retrieved documents are divided into paragraph- or sentence-length text nuggets (*extraction* stage), and their relevance to the topic of the seed is estimated using a statistical model (*scoring* stage). Finally, a pseudo-document is compiled from the most relevant nuggets (*merging* stage). Note that this expansion is performed as a separate preprocessing step, and the expanded sources can then be used in conjunction with the seed corpora by a QA system and other information retrieval or extraction applications.

3.1 Retrieval

For each seed, the retrieval component generates a query, performs a Yahoo! search for related content, and fetches up to 100 web pages linked from the highest ranking search results. In experiments with Wikipedia and Wiktionary, we used the document titles as queries since they already provide fully disambiguated descriptions of the topics. However, queries can also be generated from documents that do not have descriptive titles by extracting topical terms from their bodies based on markup information or using statistical techniques.

3.2 Extraction

The extraction component splits the retrieved web documents into paragraph-length text nuggets. For HTML documents, structural markup can be used to determine boundaries. Typical text nuggets are HTML paragraphs, list items or table cells. They range in length from short fragments (e.g. *born: 1968*) to narratives of multiple sentences. Since in the merging stage individual nuggets are selected and added to the pseudo-document, the text nuggets should ideally be self-contained (i.e. meaningful on their own) and either entirely relevant or irrelevant. Nuggets that are delimited by structural markup are mostly self-contained, but are often only partially relevant. Thus we further split the nuggets into sentences and experimented with both markup-based nuggets and sentence-level nuggets. In Section 4.2 we present evaluation results for both granularities.

3.3 Scoring

The core component of our SE approach is a statistical model that scores the extracted text nuggets based on their relevance to the topic of the seed document. A large dataset of manually labeled nuggets described in Section 4.1 was used to fit the relevance model. We experimented with various features that estimate the topicality or textual quality of nuggets and are thus predictive of their relevance. In Table 1 we briefly describe and motivate each feature, and specify its type (*topicality*, *search* or *surface* feature), its range and whether it is generated at the level of *documents* or individual *nuggets*. The most predictive topicality features (*TopicLRSeed*, *TFIDFSeed* and *MMR*) utilize the body of the seed document, which provides useful information about the topicality of text nuggets that is not available in definitional QA or summarization tasks. For the features that are based on language models (*TopicLRSeed* and *TopicLRNuggets*), we used simple unigrams with Good-Turing discounting since often not much data is available to fit the topic models.

We first fitted a logistic regression (LR) model [1] using these features to estimate the relevance of each text nugget independently. However, we found that text nuggets should not be evaluated independently since they are more likely to be relevant if the surrounding text is relevant. Thus we relaxed the independence assumption by adding features of adjacent nuggets to the LR model. More precisely, in addition to the original relevance features, we added the nugget-level features (i.e. all features except *DocRank*) of the previous nugget and the next nugget, and fitted a model using this larger feature set. In Section 4.2 we show that this simple extension improves nugget ranking performance.

3.4 Merging

The merging component ranks the text nuggets by their relevance scores in descending order. A filter reduces lexical redundancy by removing nuggets whose keywords are sub-

Table 1: **Features for estimating the relevance of text nuggets to the topic of a seed document.**

Feature (Type)	Description (Range, Level)	Motivation
TopicLRSeed *(Topicality)*	Likelihood ratio of the nugget estimated with topic and background language models. The topic model is estimated from the seed document, the background model from a large sample of Wikipedia articles. *(continuous, per nugget)*	Nuggets with large likelihood ratios are often thematically related to the seed.
TopicLRNuggets *(Topicality)*	Similar to *TopicLRSeed*, but the topic model is estimated from the nuggets that were retrieved for the given topic, and the background model from a large sample of nuggets retrieved for different topics. *(continuous, per nugget)*	More stable than *TopicLRSeed* for short seed documents.
TFIDFSeed *(Topicality)*	Average *tf.idf* score of the tokens in the nugget. The *tf* scores are estimated from the seed document, the *idf* scores from a large sample of Wikipedia articles. *(continuous, per nugget)*	Tokens with high *tf.idf* scores are often central to the topic.
TFIDFNuggets *(Topicality)*	Similar to *TFIDFSeed*, but the *tf* scores are estimated from the nuggets that were retrieved for the given topic, and the *idf* scores from a large sample of nuggets retrieved for different topics. *(continuous, per nugget)*	More stable than *TFIDFSeed* for short seed documents.
MMR *(Topicality)*	Relevance score from the maximal marginal relevance (MMR) summarization algorithm with $\lambda = 1$ [10, 18]. Originally used as a baseline, then adopted as an additional feature. See Section 4.2 for details. *(continuous, per nugget)*	Nuggets with large MMR scores have a similar word distribution as the seed and are thus likely to be topical.
QueryTerms *(Topicality)*	Fraction of the terms in the query used in the retrieval stage that occur in the text nugget. Terms are weighted with *idf* scores that are normalized to sum to 1. *(continuous, per nugget)*	Nuggets that contain rare query terms are more likely to be topical.
3PPronoun *(Topicality)*	Whether the nugget contains a third person pronoun. *(binary, per nugget)*	Third person pronouns often refer to the topic.
DocRank *(Search)*	Yahoo! search rank of the web page the nugget was extracted from. *(discrete, per document)*	Documents with high ranks usually contain more relevant text.
AbstractCoverage *(Search)*	Fraction of the tokens in the Yahoo! search abstract covered by the nugget. *(continuous, per nugget)*	The abstract is the search engine's view of the most relevant text.
Known3Grams *(Surface)*	Fraction of token 3-grams found in a dictionary of known 3-grams. *(continuous, per nugget)*	High-quality English text should contain many known 3-grams.
NuggetLength *(Surface)*	Length of the nugget measured in tokens. *(discrete, per nugget)*	Very short nuggets are usually not relevant.
NuggetOffset *(Surface)*	Offset of the nugget in the document measured in nuggets. *(discrete, per nugget)*	Text at the beginning of a document is often more relevant.
TypeTokenRatio *(Surface)*	Ratio of the number of distinct tokens over the total number of tokens in the nugget. *(continuous, per nugget)*	Penalizes nuggets that repeat topical terms over and over.
SpecialCharRatio *(Surface)*	Ratio of the number of special characters over the total number of characters in the nugget. *(continuous, per nugget)*	Penalizes nuggets that are not well-formed English text.

sumed by higher ranking nuggets or the seed. Nuggets are also dropped if their relevance scores are below an absolute threshold, or if the total character length of all nuggets exceeds a threshold that is relative to the length of the seed. In Section 5.2 we describe how thresholds were chosen in our experiments. The remaining nuggets are compiled into a pseudo-document that can be indexed and searched along with the seed.

3.5 Examples

To better understand how source expansion improves QA performance, consider the TREC question *What is the name of the rare neurological disease with symptoms such as: involuntary movements (tics), swearing, and incoherent vocalizations (grunts, shouts, etc.)?* The expanded version of the Wikipedia article about *Tourette syndrome* in Figure 1 contains the following nuggets, which originated from different web pages and jointly almost perfectly cover the question terms (underlined):

- *<u>Rare neurological disease</u> that causes repetitive motor and vocal <u>tics</u>*
- *The first <u>symptoms</u> usually are <u>involuntary movements (tics)</u> of the face, arms, limbs or trunk.*
- *Tourette's syndrome is a <u>neurological</u> disorder characterized by repetitive, stereotyped, <u>involuntary movements</u> and <u>vocalizations</u> called <u>tics</u>.*
- *The person afflicted may also <u>swear</u> or <u>shout</u> strange words, <u>grunt</u>, bark or make other loud sounds.*

This example supports the claim in Section 1 that SE helps consolidate sources by merging related content into a single document. The expanded document is retrieved by Watson, enabling it to correctly answer the question. Note that this article was expanded along with many other Wikipedia articles in a preprocessing step, without knowing yet which articles will be relevant for answering questions.

Now consider the TREC question *When were the first postage stamps issued in the United States?* The article on *Postage stamp* in our copy of Wikipedia only mentions the year (*1847*) and the relevant passage does not match the question well enough to be retrieved by Watson. However, the expanded version of the article contains the snippet *on*

```
<DOC>
<TITLE>Postage stamp</TITLE>
<TEXT>
<NUGGET SCORE="0.9942" URL="http://www.answers.com/topic/postage-stamp">Postage stamp, government stamp affixed to mail to indicate payment of postage. The term includes stamps printed or embossed on postcards and envelopes as well as the adhesive labels. The use of adhesive postage stamps was advocated by Sir Rowland Hill; it was adopted in Great Britain in 1839. Zuerich (Switzerland) and Brazil issued stamps in 1843, and by 1850 the custom had spread throughout the world. Although the postmasters of several cities had previously issued provisional stamps, the first U.S. official issue was in 1847. [...]</NUGGET>
<NUGGET SCORE="0.9718" URL="http://www.answers.com/topic/postage-stamp">The postage stamp is a relatively modern invention, first proposed in 1837 when Sir Rowland Hill, an English teacher and tax reformer, published a seminal pamphlet entitled Post Office Reform: Its Importance and Practicability. Among other reforms, Hill's treatise advocated that the English cease basing postal rates on the distance a letter traveled and collecting fees upon delivery. Instead, he argued, they should assess fees based on weight and require prepayment in the form of stamps. [...]</NUGGET>
<NUGGET SCORE="0.9512" URL="http://www.edinformatics.com/inventions_inventors/postage_stamp.htm">The adhesive postage stamp and the uniform postage rate were devised in Great Britain by James Chalmers around 1834. The same ideas were brought forward by Lovrenc Kosir, a Slovenian postal clerk at the Viennese court in 1835, but did not meet a favorable response. [...]</NUGGET>
[...]
<NUGGET SCORE="0.3312" URL="http://www.postalmuseum.si.edu/resources/6a2p_1847s.html">This summer the National Postal Museum celebrates the anniversary of a watershed event in America's postal history. One hundred and fifty years ago, on July 1, 1847, the first federal United States postage stamps were issued in New York City. [...]</NUGGET>
[...]
</TEXT>
</DOC>
```

Figure 2: Pseudo-document for the Wikipedia seed article about *Postage stamp* (abbreviated).

July 1, 1847, the first federal United States postage stamps were issued, which perfectly matches the question and enables Watson to retrieve the complete answer. An abbreviated version of the pseudo-document that includes the snippet is shown in Figure 2. This example illustrates how SE adds new information to a corpus, addressing source failures (type 1 in Section 1), and how reformulations facilitate the retrieval of relevant text, mitigating search failures (type 2).

4. INTRINSIC EVALUATION

4.1 Dataset

A large dataset of manually annotated web pages was created to evaluate different relevance estimation strategies. For a sample of 15 Wikipedia articles about people, things and events, we retrieved 100 web pages each and presented them to human annotators with instructions to select relevant substrings. The annotators were given guidelines in the form of a checklist for making consistent decisions. A nugget was considered relevant if any of its tokens were selected by an annotator. Table 2 lists the topics along with the total number of extracted markup-based nuggets and the number of nuggets labeled as relevant. The agreement between annotators was high, with κ scores of 0.9085 to 0.9379.

Table 2: Summary of relevance estimation dataset.

Topic	# Nuggets	# Relevant
Amy Van Dyken	8,502	969 (11.4%)
Anne Frank	11,360	830 (7.3%)
Berlin Wall	10,280	1,300 (12.6%)
Fort Boise	8,756	73 (0.8%)
Harry Blackmun	9,750	641 (6.6%)
Iran-Iraq War	15,193	1,929 (12.7%)
Jenny Toomey	10,789	145 (1.3%)
John Rolfe	10,490	283 (2.7%)
José de San Martín	11,984	206 (1.7%)
Karriem Riggins	10,120	105 (1.0%)
Lincoln assassination	11,632	542 (4.7%)
Mother Teresa	11,507	1,383 (12.0%)
Ross Powless	13,410	97 (0.7%)
Vasco Núñez de Balboa	7,939	508 (6.4%)
XYZ Affair	12,726	210 (1.7%)
All	**164,438**	**9,221 (5.6%)**

4.2 Experiments

Using this dataset, we evaluated different relevance models through 15-fold cross-validation (one fold for each topic). The nuggets were ranked by relevance estimates in descending order, and performance was measured in terms of mean average precision (*MAP*) and micro-averaged precision-recall curves. Precision and recall were computed at the level of tokens rather than text nuggets so that results are comparable across different nugget granularities. For instance, precision is the percentage of tokens up to a given cutoff point in the ranking that were annotated as relevant. We present evaluation results on sentence-level nuggets (*Sentence*) and markup-based nuggets (*Markup*) for the independent logistic regression model (*LR Independent*), the model with features of adjacent instances (*LR Adjacent*) and these baselines:

- *Random.* Nuggets are ranked randomly. We report the expected performance if each token is treated as an independent nugget.
- *Round Robin.* Selects the first nugget from all documents, followed by the second nugget, and so forth, assuming that relevant text is more concentrated at the top of documents.

Table 3: MAP of baselines and statistical models.

Model	MAP	
	Sentence	Markup
Random	28.48%	28.48%
Round Robin	32.59%	35.78%
Search Rank	42.67%	42.67%
MMR	61.46%	74.75%
LR Independent	71.95%	79.69%
LR Adjacent	**77.19%**	**80.59%**

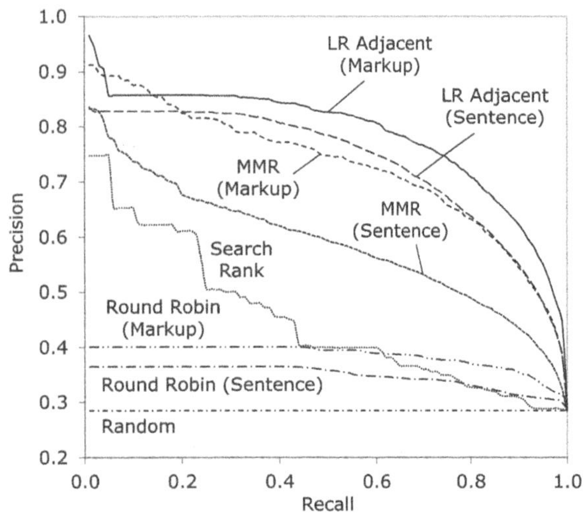

Figure 3: Precision-recall curves for baselines and statistical models.

- *Search Rank.* Preserves the ranking of the documents by the search engine and the order of the text nuggets within the documents.
- *MMR.* The maximal marginal relevance (MMR) algorithm [10, 18] is used to rank the text nuggets. MMR is one of the most effective algorithms for multi-document summarization. It iteratively selects text passages with high "marginal relevance", i.e. passages that are relevant to a query and add novel information. We used the full seed documents as queries and set the parameter $\lambda = 1$, i.e. the algorithm selects the most relevant nuggets regardless of their novelty. This setup worked best in a preliminary study.

Table 3 shows MAP scores for all ranking strategies and Figure 3 illustrates their performance in terms of precision-recall curves. Note that *Random* breaks down nuggets into tokens and *Search Rank* preserves the original order of the nuggets, and thus these strategies do not depend on the size of the nuggets. Among the baselines, MMR is clearly most effective, followed with some distance by the search engine rankings. The LR models outperform the baselines, with the only exception that MMR-based rankings have higher precision on markup-based nuggets at very low recall levels (too low to generate expanded documents of reasonable length). The independent nugget scoring model performs worse than the model with features of adjacent instances and has been omitted in the precision-recall plot for ease of presentation. The results also indicate that it is more effective to rank the longer markup-based text nuggets, even though they are often only partially relevant. This is because some features, such as the likelihood ratios and average *tf.idf* scores, are less reliable for short nuggets.

When adopting the source expansion approach, one could initially use the *MMR* baseline to rank text nuggets since it is easy to implement and does not require training data. Its performance (74.75% MAP on markup-based nuggets) comes relatively close to the best statistical model (80.59%), but the baseline solely relies on the seed content and is only effective if the seeds are long and of high quality. Other features that are predictive on their own include *TopicLRSeed* (69.40%) and *AbstractCoverage* (50.93%).

Table 4: Summary of QA datasets.

Regular Jeopardy!	Final Jeopardy!	TREC 8–12 Factoid
3,508 questions (66 episodes)	788 questions (1 per episode)	2,137 questions (no *NIL* questions)

5. APPLICATION TO QA

5.1 Datasets

The source expansion approach was evaluated on large datasets of Jeopardy! and TREC questions. A summary of the datasets is given in Table 4.

Jeopardy! questions and their answers were retrieved from J! Archive[3]. Most of these questions ask for factoid answers that can be extracted from text corpora, but there are also puzzles, word plays and puns that require additional processing and specialized inference. In each Jeopardy! episode, human contestants compete in answering up to 60 regular questions (sometimes not all questions are revealed) and one Final Jeopardy! question. Most questions in Jeopardy! only have a single correct answer. In the following experiments we use both regular Jeopardy! and Final Jeopardy! datasets. Final Jeopardy! questions are usually harder, both for human players and Watson, which will be reflected in the results. Questions with audio or visual clues were excluded.

For experiments with TREC datasets, we used independent factoid questions from the TREC 8–12 evaluations [31]. The questions and corresponding answer keys were obtained from the NIST website[4]. *NIL* questions without known answers were removed. TREC questions often have more than one acceptable answer, and the answer keys only cover answers that were found in the reference corpora used in the evaluations. When we evaluated end-to-end QA results, assessors who were not involved in the development of the approach judged the top answers returned by Watson and extended the answer keys with additional correct answers. However, when measuring search performance, we did not further extend the answer keys because it was impractical to judge all search results manually.

5.2 Sources

We expanded two sources that are both useful for Jeopardy! and TREC question answering: Wikipedia and the online dictionary Wiktionary[5]. Wikipedia, in particular, has

[3]http://www.j-archive.com/

[4]http://trec.nist.gov/data/qamain.html

[5]http://www.wiktionary.org/

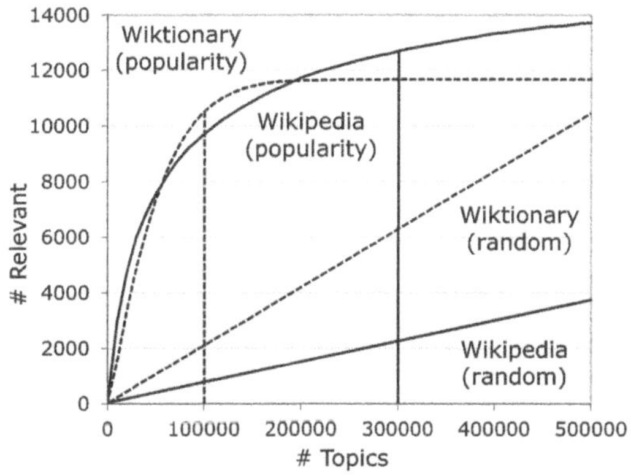

Figure 4: Relevance of Wikipedia and Wiktionary seeds for Jeopardy! when ranked by popularity or randomly.

proven to be a valuable resource for a variety of natural language processing tasks [9, 26] and has been used successfully in QA [2, 21]. The sources differ in two significant ways that affect SE: (1) Wiktionary entries are on average much shorter than Wikipedia articles (780 vs. 3,600 characters), and (2) Wiktionary entries are often about common terms. The shorter Wiktionary seeds render some topicality features less effective. Web queries for common terms yield more noise, which we alleviated by adding the keyword "define" to all queries and dropping search results that did not contain the topic in their title or URL.

Our cleansed copies of Wikipedia and Wiktionary contain about 2.1 million and 600,000 documents, respectively. To reduce computational costs and to avoid adding noise, we focused on expanding seeds that we deemed most relevant for Jeopardy! and TREC. Questions in both QA tasks are often about topics of common interest, such as famous people or well-known events, and thus SE should be prioritized to cover the most *popular* seeds first. For Wikipedia, in which rich hyperlink information is available, we defined the popularity of an article as the number of references from other articles in Wikipedia. Since Wiktionary contains only sparse hyperlink information, we estimated the popularity of a Wiktionary entry based on its frequency in a large collection of English documents across a variety of topics and genre. We sorted the seeds by popularity in descending order and plotted the number of seeds versus the number of those seeds that are *relevant* for the Jeopardy! task. A seed was considered relevant if its title was the answer to one of 32,000 Jeopardy! questions selected randomly from episodes that are not part of our test sets. This is an approximation of relevance based on the potential impact of a seed if only document titles are retrieved. The relevance curves for both sources, shown in Figure 4, have decreasing slopes, indicating that popularity-based rankings outperform random rankings of the seeds, which are illustrated by straight lines. We also performed this analysis for all factoid questions in TREC 8–15 and obtained very similar curves.

Based on these relevance curves, we chose to expand the top 300,000 Wikipedia articles and the top 100,000 Wiktionary entries. The size of the expanded pseudo-documents was restricted to at most 10 times the length of the seeds, and nuggets with relevance scores below 0.1 were dropped. We analyzed a sample of the pseudo-documents and chose

Table 5: Sizes of seed and expanded corpora.

Source	# Docs	Size
Wikipedia	2,114,707	7.0 GB
Expanded Wikipedia	100,000	4.8 GB
	200,000	7.6 GB
	300,000	9.8 GB
Wiktionary	565,335	420 MB
Expanded Wiktionary	100,000	590 MB

parameter values that resulted in reasonable cutoff points. That is, with these cutoff values the final pseudo-documents contained a large number of relevant nuggets but little noise. Later we also performed QA experiments using different parameter settings and found that the precise thresholds have very little impact on QA performance. In general, more lenient thresholds yield slightly better results at the expense of larger expanded sources and thus longer QA runtime.

The text nuggets were scored using the model with features of adjacent instances, trained on all 15 topics. Overall, we processed about 40 million web pages, totaling about 2 TB of web data and 4 billion text nuggets. The expansion of each seed took around 15–45s and was dominated by the retrieval of web pages from different hosts. These numbers illustrate the necessity of a highly efficient and robust implementation. The sizes of the seed corpora and expanded sources are given in Table 5. The SE algorithm condensed the web data by two orders of magnitude, yielding a corpus that can be indexed and searched on a single node.

5.3 QA Search Experiments

We evaluated the impact of SE on search performance using Watson [17], a state-of-the-art QA system. As baselines, we used (1) Wikipedia, (2) Wiktionary and (3) a large collection of existing sources that we manually identified to be relevant for Jeopardy! and TREC based on an iterative error analysis. The collection (subsequently referred to as *All Sources*) comprises 23 GB of text, including encyclopedias such as Wikipedia and World Book, dictionaries such as Wiktionary, thesauri, newswire sources such as the AQUAINT corpus and a New York Times archive, literature and other sources of trivia knowledge [12]. We compare the Wikipedia and Wiktionary baselines to configurations that include the corresponding expanded sources. The collection of all sources is compared to a corpus to which only expanded versions of Wikipedia and Wiktionary were added.

The sources were indexed and searched with both Indri and Lucene, and the results were pooled. Queries were generated with Watson's retrieval component [11]. Two search strategies were evaluated: (1) we fetched a total of 20 *passages* and aligned them with sentence boundaries, and (2) we retrieved 50 documents in total and used their *titles* as results. The title searches target questions asking for an entity that matches a given description, such as the Jeopardy! question *From the Latin for "evening", it's a service of Evening Worship*[6] (answer: *vesper*) or the TREC question *What is the fear of lightning called?* (answer: *astraphobia*). Here source expansion helps by generating more complete descriptions of such terms that are more likely to match the question. Search results were judged as relevant if any token sequence matched the answer key. Performance was

[6]Jeopardy! questions are given in the form of statements.

Table 6: Search recall on Wikipedia, Wiktionary and all sources for Jeopardy! and TREC. For each setup, we show the percentage gain and the number of questions gained/lost. All improvements are significant with $p < .001$ based on a one-sided sign test.

Sources	Regular Jeopardy!			Final Jeopardy!			TREC 8–12		
	Passages	Titles	Total	Passages	Titles	Total	Passages	Titles	Total
Wikipedia	74.54%	65.19%	81.33%	52.54%	44.92%	63.32%	72.30%	49.42%	76.74%
Expansion	80.05%	71.86%	86.23%	59.39%	55.84%	72.21%	79.50%	52.32%	82.17%
% Gain	*+7.4%*	*+10.2%*	*+6.0%*	*+13.0%*	*+24.3%*	*+14.0%*	*+10.0%*	*+5.9%*	*+7.1%*
# Gain/Loss	*+280/-87*	*+293/-59*	*+211/-39*	*+77/-23*	*+104/-18*	*+88/-18*	*+203/-49*	*+150/-88*	*+157/-41*
Wiktionary	21.84%	18.93%	30.39%	8.12%	8.12%	13.32%	23.12%	15.96%	29.15%
Expansion	42.47%	32.47%	51.20%	19.67%	18.27%	27.79%	47.92%	26.02%	52.46%
% Gain	*+94.5%*	*+71.5%*	*68.5%*	*+142.2%*	*+125.0%*	*+108.6%*	*+107.3%*	*+63.0%*	*+80.0%*
# Gain/Loss	*+856/-132*	*+558/-83*	*+852/-122*	*+110/-19*	*+93/-13*	*+138/-24*	*+596/-66*	*+269/-54*	*+556/-58*
All Sources	78.48%	71.07%	**85.55%**	57.11%	52.54%	**69.54%**	75.76%	51.90%	**79.64%**
Expansion	82.38%	76.54%	**89.17%**	62.94%	61.42%	**75.51%**	80.30%	54.33%	**83.29%**
% Gain	*+5.0%*	*+7.7%*	***+4.2%***	*+10.2%*	*+16.9%*	***+8.6%***	*+6.0%*	*+4.7%*	***+4.6%***
# Gain/Loss	*+255/-118*	*+248/-56*	***+171/-44***	*+82/-36*	*+85/-15*	***+73/-26***	*+158/-61*	*+128/-76*	***+119/-41***

measured in search recall, the percentage of questions with relevant results. Search recall is an important metric in QA as it constitutes an upper bound on end-to-end accuracy.

Table 6 shows the impact of source expansion on search recall when retrieving only titles or passages and when combining these search results. We also indicate for each setup the number of questions gained and lost and the percentage gain. The performance on regular Jeopardy! is higher than on Final Jeopardy! since the regular questions are generally easier to process and ask about less obscure facts. The TREC performance numbers are lower than the regular Jeopardy! results because the answer keys were incomplete and because most of our development effort focused on Jeopardy! questions. On all datasets, SE yields consistent and significant ($p < .001$) improvements over the baselines, independently of the search strategy used. Even if a seed corpus with reasonable coverage for a QA task exists, such as Wikipedia for Jeopardy! and TREC, SE improves performance substantially. If a corpus with lower coverage is expanded, such as Wiktionary, very large gains can be realized. Compared to the strongest baseline, SE improves total search recall by 4.2% on regular Jeopardy! questions, 8.6% on Final Jeopardy! and 4.6% on TREC questions. The improvements are significant, even though of all the sources used in the baseline only Wikipedia and Wiktionary (one third of the collection) were expanded. It can also be seen that relatively few questions are hurt (e.g. 171 regular Jeopardy! questions are gained but only 44 out of 3,508 are lost). This distinguishes source expansion from most query expansion techniques: SE adds noise to the sources in addition to relevant content, but that is less likely to cause a search to fail than irrelevant keywords added to the query.

The recall curves in Figure 5 illustrate that SE improves search recall independently of the hit list length on both Jeopardy! and TREC questions. For these experiments we used only Indri and performed only one title search and one passage search to have a single hit list for each strategy. The gains in passage search recall are larger on Jeopardy! than on TREC questions because there is more headroom in Jeopardy! search performance. Passage recall on the TREC dataset approaches 90% even though the answer keys are often incomplete. Title searches are less effective for TREC since the questions targeted by this strategy are relatively infrequent in this dataset. The results also show that when adding the expanded sources, fewer titles or passages yield the same search recall as longer hit lists without source expansion. Decreasing the hit list lengths can be worthwhile since this reduces the number of candidate answers and improves the efficiency and effectiveness of answer selection.

Table 7: Search recall when expanding increasing numbers of Wikipedia seed articles for Jeopardy! and TREC.

	Regular J!	Final J!	TREC 8–12
Wikipedia	81.33%	63.32%	76.74%
Top 100,000	85.46%	71.32%	**80.91%**
Top 200,000	86.03%	72.08%	**80.91%**
Top 300,000	**86.09%**	**72.21%**	80.67%

Table 7 shows the impact of SE when expanding varying numbers of Wikipedia seeds. The top 100,000 seeds are responsible for most of the performance gain, which confirms that popularity-based seed selection is effective. On TREC, performance even degrades (though not significantly) if more than 200,000 seeds are expanded.

5.4 End-to-End QA Experiments

The Watson system was also used to evaluate the impact of source expansion on end-to-end QA accuracy, the percentage of questions answered correctly. Watson extracts candidate answers from the passage and title search results and scores them using a statistical model. During this answer scoring phase, additional supporting passages are retrieved for each of the top candidate answers, using a query comprising key terms from the question and the candidate itself. The supporting passages come from the same collection used in the initial searches, including the expanded sources. They are used to assess whether a candidate matches the information need expressed in the question and play a crucial role in answer scoring [17]. Thus Watson not only uses the expanded sources in the initial searches for candidate answers but also leverages them to score the candidates.

We again use the collection of manually acquired sources as a baseline and compare it to a configuration including expanded versions of Wikipedia and Wiktionary only. Watson

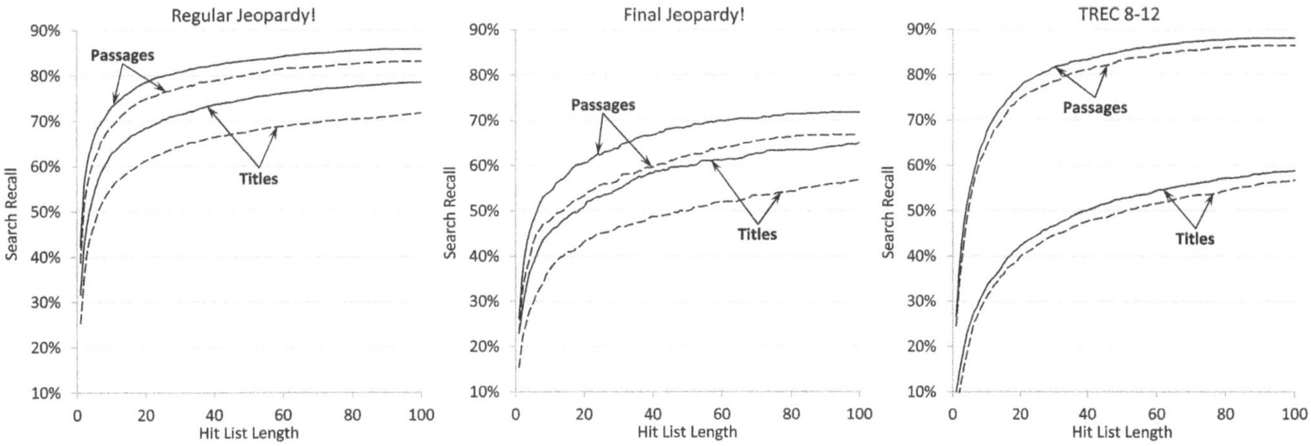

Figure 5: Search recall as a function of the hit list length for Jeopardy! and TREC. Dashed lines: all sources without expansion; solid lines: all sources with expansion of Wikipedia and Wiktionary.

Table 8: QA accuracies for Jeopardy! and TREC. For each dataset, we show the percentage gain and the number of questions gained/lost. All improvements are significant with $p < .01$ based on a one-sided sign test.

	Regular J!	Final J!	TREC 11
All Sources	66.08%	45.43%	59.46%
Expansion	71.12%	51.27%	63.96%
% Gain	*+7.6%*	*+12.9%*	*+7.6%*
# Gain/Loss	*+286/-109*	*+82/-36*	*+44/-24*

scores and ranks candidate answers using supervised models trained on question-answer pairs with relevance judgments. For the Jeopardy! task, we trained these models on separate datasets and used the same test sets as in previous experiments. For TREC, we had to reserve most data for training, leaving TREC 11 (444 questions with known answers) as an independent test set.

Table 8 shows that source expansion improves QA accuracy by 7.6% on regular Jeopardy! questions, 12.9% on Final Jeopardy! and 7.6% on TREC 11. The improvements in QA performance are significant with $p < .01$, even though only a fraction of the sources in the baseline were expanded. It is also worth noting that the baseline includes the AQUAINT corpus, which was used as the reference source in TREC 11 and thus contains the answers to all TREC questions. The improvements in accuracy exceed the gains in search recall on all datasets, which supports our claim that SE also improves answer selection (failure type 3 in Section 1).

6. CONCLUSIONS AND FUTURE WORK

We proposed a statistical approach for source expansion and evaluated its impact on large datasets of Jeopardy! and TREC questions, using different seed corpora and applying different search strategies. The proposed method yields significant gains in search performance on all datasets, improving search recall by 4.2–8.6%. These improvements were achieved *without* retrieving more text at QA runtime. Recall can always be increased through additional or longer search results, but this often comes at the expense of adding noise and hurting answer scoring efficiency and effectiveness. SE also significantly improves the overall performance of Watson, one of the most effective QA systems to date, increasing accuracy by 7.6–12.9% on Jeopardy! and TREC datasets.

It may seem that search performance always improves if more source content is added, but we found that this is not the case. For instance, just adding large web crawls is ineffective since the vast majority of web pages do not contain useful information [13]. We have shown that it is important to select relevant seed content for source expansion (Figure 4) and that performance can degrade if too many seeds are expanded (Table 7). Even if the most relevant seeds are chosen, an effective model is needed to accurately estimate the relevance of related text and avoid adding noise.

It is usually possible to make large improvements early in the development of a QA system, but as the system becomes more effective at its task the gains invariably get smaller. Often the impact of new algorithms depends on the order in which they are added because different approaches address similar issues. Yet we found that the impact of SE did not diminish as Watson was improved over time because advances in other components also helped better utilize the additional source content. For instance, more correct answers could be found in the expanded sources because of improved question analysis, search and answer extraction, and advances in answer scoring helped cope with the added noise. Because the gains from SE are largely orthogonal to other improvements, it is likely that this method will also help other QA systems and will be useful for other applications beyond QA. Since the approach is fully automated, it can be applied to new tasks with low effort.

We have begun working on sequential models for relevance estimation that predict transitions between relevant and irrelevant text using lexical coherence features derived from text segmentation algorithms [20, 5]. Preliminary results indicate that these models can outperform the logistic regression models discussed in this paper. We are also extending SE to seed corpora in which there is no one-to-one correspondence between documents and topics, such as newswire sources or web pages, by automatically detecting relevant topics and building pseudo-documents about them. Finally, SE can be applied to QA in different languages, and to other information retrieval and extraction tasks, such as document retrieval and relation extraction.

7. ACKNOWLEDGMENTS

The authors would like to thank Jamie Callan and Jaime Carbonell for helpful discussions on document expansion and multi-document summarization.

8. REFERENCES

[1] A. Agresti. *Categorical Data Analysis*. Wiley, 2002.

[2] D. Ahn, V. Jijkoun, G. Mishne, K. Müller, M. de Rijke, and S. Schlobach. Using Wikipedia at the TREC QA track. In *Proceedings of the Thirteenth Text REtrieval Conference*, 2004.

[3] G. Attardi, A. Cisternino, F. Formica, M. Simi, and A. Tommasi. PiQASso: Pisa question answering system. In *Proceedings of the Tenth Text REtrieval Conference*, 2001.

[4] N. Balasubramanian and S. Cucerzan. Automatic generation of topic pages using query-based aspect models. In *Proceedings of CIKM*, 2009.

[5] D. Beeferman, A. Berger, and J. Lafferty. Statistical models for text segmentation. *Machine Learning*, pages 177–210, 1999.

[6] M. Bilotti, P. Ogilvie, J. Callan, and E. Nyberg. Structured retrieval for question answering. In *Proceedings of SIGIR*, 2007.

[7] S. Blair-Goldensohn, K. McKeown, and A. Schlaikjer. Answering definitional questions: A hybrid approach. *New Directions In Question Answering*, 2004.

[8] S. Bradshaw. Reference directed indexing: Redeeming relevance for subject search in citation indexes. In *Proceedings of the 7th European Conference on Research and Advanced Technology for Digital Libraries*, 2003.

[9] R. Bunescu, E. Gabrilovich, and R. Mihalcea. Wikipedia and artificial intelligence: An evolving synergy. *Papers from the 2008 AAAI Workshop*, 2008.

[10] J. Carbonell and J. Goldstein. The use of MMR, diversity-based reranking for reordering documents and producing summaries. In *Proceedings of SIGIR*, 1998.

[11] J. Chu-Carroll and J. Fan. Leveraging Wikipedia characteristics for search and candidate generation in question answering. *AAAI Conference on Artificial Intelligence*, 2011.

[12] J. Chu-Carroll, J. Fan, N. Schlaefer, and W. Zadrozny. Textual resource acquisition and engineering. *Submitted to IBM Journal of Research and Development*, 2011.

[13] C. Clarke, G. Cormack, M. Laszlo, T. Lynam, and E. Terra. The impact of corpus size on question answering performance. In *Proceedings of SIGIR*, 2002.

[14] C. Clarke, G. Cormack, and T. Lynam. Exploiting redundancy in question answering. In *Proceedings of SIGIR*, 2001.

[15] N. Craswell, D. Hawking, and S. Robertson. Effective site finding using link anchor information. In *Proceedings of SIGIR*, 2001.

[16] S. Dumais, M. Banko, E. Brill, J. Lin, and A. Ng. Web question answering: Is more always better? In *Proceedings of SIGIR*, 2002.

[17] D. Ferrucci, E. Brown, J. Chu-Carroll, J. Fan, D. Gondek, A. A. Kalyanpur, A. Lally, J. W. Murdock, E. Nyberg, J. Prager, N. Schlaefer, and C. Welty. Building Watson: An overview of the DeepQA project. *AI Magazine*, 31(3):59–79, 2010.

[18] J. Goldstein, V. Mittal, J. Carbonell, and M. Kantrowitz. Multi-document summarization by sentence extraction. In *Proceedings of the ANLP/NAACL Workshop on Automatic Summarization*, 2000.

[19] S. Harabagiu, D. Moldovan, M. Paşca, R. Mihalcea, M. Surdeanu, R. Bunescu, R. Gîrju, V. Rus, and P. Morărescu. The role of lexico-semantic feedback in open-domain textual question-answering. In *Proceedings of the 39th ACL Conference*, 2001.

[20] M. Hearst. TextTiling: Segmenting text into multi-paragraph subtopic passages. *Computational Linguistics*, 23(1):33–64, 1997.

[21] M. Kaisser. The QuALiM question answering demo: Supplementing answers with paragraphs drawn from Wikipedia. In *Proceedings of the ACL-08 HLT Demo Session*, 2008.

[22] B. Katz, J. Lin, D. Loreto, W. Hildebrandt, M. Bilotti, S. Felshin, A. Fernandes, G. Marton, and F. Mora. Integrating web-based and corpus-based techniques for question answering. In *Proceedings of the Twelfth Text REtrieval Conference*, 2003.

[23] G.-A. Levow and D. W. Oard. Signal boosting for translingual topic tracking: Document expansion and n-best translation. In *Topic Detection and Tracking: Event-based Information Organization, Chapter 9*, pages 175–195. Kluwer Academic Publishers, 2002.

[24] Y.-C. Li and H. M. Meng. Document expansion using a side collection for monolingual and cross-language spoken document retrieval. In *ISCA Workshop on Multilingual Spoken Document Retrieval*, 2003.

[25] M. Marchiori. The quest for correct information on the Web: Hyper search engines. *Computer Networks and ISDN Systems*, 29(8-13):1225–1235, 1997.

[26] O. Medelyan, C. Legg, D. Milne, and I. Witten. Mining meaning from Wikipedia. *International Journal of Human-Computer Studies*, 67(9):716–754, 2009.

[27] A. Nenkova, L. Vanderwende, and K. McKeown. A compositional context sensitive multi-document summarizer: Exploring the factors that influence summarization. In *Proceedings of SIGIR*, 2006.

[28] L. Pizzato, D. Mollá, and C. Paris. Pseudo relevance feedback using named entities for question answering. In *Proceedings of the Australasian Language Technology Workshop (ALTW)*, 2006.

[29] A. Singhal and F. Pereira. Document expansion for speech retrieval. In *Proceedings of SIGIR*, 1999.

[30] J. Tiedemann. Integrating linguistic knowledge in passage retrieval for question answering. In *Proceedings of HLT/EMNLP*, 2005.

[31] E. Voorhees. Overview of the TREC 2003 question answering track. In *Proceedings of the Twelfth Text REtrieval Conference*, 2003.

[32] R. Weischedel, J. Xu, and A. Licuanan. A hybrid approach to answering biographical questions. *New Directions In Question Answering*, 2004.

Passage Retrieval for Incorporating Global Evidence in Sequence Labeling

Jeffrey Dalton, James Allan, and David A. Smith
Center for Intelligent Information Retrieval
Department of Computer Science
University of Massachusetts Amherst
Amherst, Massachusetts
{jdalton, allan, dasmith}@cs.umass.edu

ABSTRACT

Many forms of linguistic analysis, such as part of speech tagging, named entity recognition, and other sequence labeling tasks are performed on short spans of text and assume statistical dependence within a window of only a few tokens. We propose using passage retrieval to induce non-local dependencies in structured classification that generalizes earlier work in context aggregation for named-entity recognition. We introduce a new method for feature expansion inspired by psuedo-relevance feedback (PRF). Our results on the CoNLL 2003 task show that features from cross-document feature expansion improves NER effectiveness over previous aggregation models. Utilizing all the tokens in a sentence for query context consistently perform best on both intrinsic and extrinsic evaluations. Tagging models incorporating feature expansion outperform the leading NER system when evaluated on out of domain data, a collection of publicly available scanned books on the topic of historic Deerfield, MA. Finally, the results show that retrieval based feature expansion using an external collection of unlabeled text can result in further effectiveness improvements.

Categories and Subject Descriptors: H.3.3 [Information Search and Retrieval]: Selection Process

General Terms: Algorithms, Experimentation

Keywords: Named Entity Recognition, Passage Retrieval, Pseudo-Relevance Feedback, Information Extraction

1. INTRODUCTION

Despite the increased application of Natural Language Processing (NLP) on queries and documents to improve retrieval, there is little work exploring the use of retrieval to improve NLP tasks. In this work, we use passage retrieval to improve the effectiveness of Named Entity Recognition (NER). NER is one of many commonly performed sequence labeling tasks including part of speech tagging, syntactic chunking, and other types of information extraction. In these problems, we are given an input sequence of observed variables, $\mathbf{x}$, which consists of a sequence of words. For each observed variable, $x_i \in \mathbf{x}$ the goal is to infer a corresponding output label.

CIKM'11, October 24–28, 2011, Glasgow, Scotland, UK.

In most statistical sequence models the decision about the output label of a given token depends only on a small local window of adjacent text. These local features sometimes do not provide enough evidence to accurately infer the output label. This problem is exacerbated by tables, lists, and other structures containing non-grammatical text with little or no contextual clues. To improve NER effectiveness for these tokens, we need methods that utilize non-local dependencies within and across documents.

Specifically, we use a technique inspired by Pseudo-Relevance Feedback (PRF) to aggregate observed features from retrieved passages to more accurately estimate a feature distribution used to label a token. PRF consistently improves retrieval effectiveness by providing a better estimate of the query model [12, 3].

In PRF, the top retrieved documents are assumed to be relevant, and terms are selected from these documents to add to the original query. When labeling in NER, for each x_i in $\mathbf{x}$ meeting specified criteria, we perform passage retrieval using the context of $\mathbf{x}$ to construct a query. We assume that the top retrieved passages containing x_i have the same label as the source word sequence. Given this assumption, we extract features from the retrieved passages and aggregate them to provide a better estimate of the observation sequence. This feature expansion method addresses the problems of feature sparsity and labeling consistency.

PRF based feature expansion has several important properties that make it attractive for handling non-local dependencies in NLP tasks. First, the context of the token is used to rank passages. As we show in our retrieval evaluation, using passage context is highly effective at selecting passages with matching labels in the top ranks, even for ambiguous tokens. Second, the number of dependencies created by the model can be controlled by varying the number of feedback documents. Third, the features extracted from the retrieved passages are weighted by the retrieval model's estimate of their similarity to the source passage. Finally, the number of expansion features can be restricted to those with the highest probability in the retrieved set, reducing the number of features added to the model.

The idea of tying labels and features across tokens has been explored in previous work modeling non-local dependencies, such the skip-chain CRF model [20]. However, efforts to model non-local dependencies directly in the graph structure result in complex graphical models with loopy graphs that require approximate inference methods, such as Loopy BP and Gibbs sampling. The use of approximate inference for NER results in significant slower performance [7]. Consequently, these models are not used often in practice.

Another approach to handling non-local dependencies is based on copying and aggregating observed features [23, 19]. Copying features allows the use of simple linear models where efficient exact inference techniques for training and decoding, such as the Viterbi algorithm, can be used. However, results using this approach in the past have been mixed. The recent results of Villain et al. [23] show that feature copying improves the results on the CoNLL 2003 shared task, but not as much as they expect. One cause of error that they highlight is ambiguous tokens that refer to the same entity but take on different labels depending on the context. For example, consider the word *China* which in: "China beat out Finland in the match..." is an ORG and "The Beijing Olympics took place in China." where it is a LOC. Previous models treat all occurrences of a token within a document identically without consideration of the context. Our method addresses this problem by generating a query from the passage context and weighting passage features based on retrieval similarity.

A problem with existing models [20] is that they do not improve effectiveness on tokens that occur infrequently within a document. Our method utilizes features from external documents to aggregate features across documents. We also show that PRF feature expansion can leverage volumes of unlabeled text to improve effectiveness.

One of the stated design goals of NER systems is that they should be robust to unseen text. However, state-of-the-art systems such as the Stanford NER system and the LBJ NER tagger perform poorly when evaluated on out of domain data. Liu et. al. [14] recently demonstrated that the effectiveness of the Stanford NER tagger trained on CoNLL data drops to 45.8% F1 when tagging entities from Twitter microblog documents. In our experiments, we find similar degradation in performance to 51% when tested on the Deerfield collection of historical books. We observe that across multiple out of domain data sets the F1 score of models trained on newswire decreases by approximately 40%. Our experiments show that models incorporating feature based expansion are more robust than previous systems when evaluated on out of domain data. We note that the LBJ tagger also utilizes a greedy form of non-local dependency handling and does better than the other systems tested, but not as well as models using the principled aggregation methods proposed in this paper.

Our main contributions are:

- proposing a new method for incorporating non-local dependencies using passage retrieval;
- demonstrating that retrieval based feature expansion outperforms previous models of feature aggregation and consistently improves effectiveness;
- evaluating the effectiveness of various retrieval models to rank passages based on the likelihood that shared tokens have the same entity label;
- showing that feature expansion using external unlabeled data results in more significant improvement than using only labeled data; and
- demonstrating that models that utilize retrieval features are more robust when evaluated on out of domain data, outperforming the current leading sequence tagging system.

The remainder of the paper is structured as follows. In Section 2 we provide an overview of related work utilizing non-local dependencies in sequence labeling. In Section 3 we outline our approach for NER. Section 4 describes passage retrieval for sequence labeling and pseudo-relevance feedback for feature expansion. In Section 5 we evaluate our methods for passage retrieval and compare the effectiveness of feature expansion approaches to improve NER.

2. RELATED WORK

Named entity recognition, due to its wide array of practical applications, has received substantial attention from researchers for the past twenty years. Nadeau and Sekine [17] survey much of this literature. Here we focus on attempts to augment NER systems with information beyond a candidate token's local neighborhood to improve model consistency and address feature sparsity.

2.1 Label Consistency

Recent efforts have focused on adding dependencies, mostly within a document that penalizes inconsistent labeling and enforce some degree of consistency constraints. Finkel et. al. [7] show that predictions for the same entity are inconsistent within the same document and across the corpus. Sutton and McCallum [20] use a skip-chain CRF with loopy BP inference to enforce consistent decoding among string-identical tokens. Finkel [7] penalizes inconsistent labeling and performs inference using Gibbs sampling. Bunescu and Mooney [4] use a Relational Markov Network (RMN) to explicitly model long-distance dependencies and use loopy BP for inference. Instead of modifying the graph to explicitly encode dependencies our approach aggregates feature information and allows the use of efficient exact inference methods for decoding.

2.2 Two-Pass Systems

A simpler, but still effective, approach to global inference is taken by two-pass or stacked architectures. A token which appears in an unindicative context in one sentence may appear in a very obvious context in another sentence. In a two pass model the predictions of a first-pass system are used as features in a second-pass model that "fixes up" the labeling [10]. The simplest version of this approach enforces consistency in certain labelings by majority vote or other heuristics [16]. Other versions use nearest neighbor classification to incorporate predictions in other parts of the document or corpus [14].

Two pass models fix mistakes on frequent entities with little or no ambiguity. However, the limitations of these models were recently examined by Villain et al.[23]. They fail when the first pass labels the instance incorrectly more often than correctly. Furthermore, for rare tokens the prediction information remains sparse and there may only be weak evidence in each passage considered in isolation. Aggregating feature level information across occurrences can be more effective than coordinating output decisions.

Bendersky at al.[1] tag sparse and ungrammatical web search queries by utilizing labels from top retrieved documents where instances are weighted using pseudo relevance feedback. Instead of aggregating labels, which can be noisy, our method utilizes the underlying features.

2.3 Context Aggregation

Our work on feature expansion is mostly closely related to work on context aggregation, which copies features across token instances. Ratinov and Roth [19] aggregate features for string-identical tokens within a fixed window size of 200, even across document boundaries. The idea of our work is related to that of Villain et. al.[23], who copy "displaced features" across related tokens within the same document. Their method uses information to copy only the most predictive features for related tokens. It requires a preprocessing step over the entire corpus to identify these features over the corpus before training or decoding. The model suffers from ambiguous token contexts, introducing noise. In contrast, our uses all features weighted based on the retrieved passage's similarity to the source sequence.

Feature
words = W_{i-2}, ... W_{i+2}
POS tags = o_{i-1}, o_i, o_{i+1}
W_i capitalization patterns
Char Prefixes = W_{i-1}, W_i, W_{i+1}
Char Suffixes = W_{i-1}, W_i, W_{i+1}

Table 1: Baseline NER features

2.4 Feature Sparsity

A fundamental cause of inconsistent tagging is that local contexts in isolation may be noisy and contain sparse or contradictory features. Lower-dimensional representations are useful, however, not only as a way of transferring information across domains but for mitigating sparsity within the source domain [22]. Many state-of-the-art systems exploit flat or hierarchical distributional similarity clustering to induce better feature representations [8, 19]. As Turian et al. [22] detail, these models are expensive to train and can take days or weeks on modest sized RCV1 news collection.

3. NER APPROACH

The methods we propose can be incorporated into a variety of models used to infer output values in sequence labeling. For this work we incorporate our feature expansion technique with a state sequence model based on Conditional Random Fields (CRFs) [11]. CRFs are a type of discriminatively trained undirected graphical model trained to maximize the conditional probability of output labels given an input observation sequence. Given an observed sequence of words $\mathbf{x}$, the goal is to predict the values of the unobserved random variables $\mathbf{y}$, which are the corresponding output labels. In this work, we utilize a linear-chain CRF with a first order Markov assumption made on hidden variables in the graph where only adjacent vertices are connected by edges. Just as with first-order HMMs, our model admits efficient inference using the forward-backward and Viterbi algorithms for training and decoding.

CRFs are the state-of-the-art in many sequence modeling tasks [18, 11], and their effectiveness on NER tagging is competitive with the best reported by the LBJ NER tagger [10, 23, 19]. The CRF framework allows flexibility to integrate retrieval based features. Unlike generative models like HMMs, CRFs do not attempt to model the joint distribution $p(\mathbf{x}, \mathbf{y})$. Instead, they estimate $p(\mathbf{y} \mid \mathbf{x})$. We train the CRF model using stochastic gradient descent (SGD). Our system is based on a popular open-source implementation, LingPipe,[1]. This model corresponds roughly to the local Viterbi model described in by Finkel et al[7]. This class of models are widely used because of their efficiency and reliability.

The features used in the model include words within a window size of 4, adjacent word character prefixes and suffixes, part of speech tags, and capitalization patterns. The baseline feature set is summarized in Table 1. For each of these features there is a binary feature function $f_k(x_i, \mathbf{x})$ that indicates the presence of the feature in the observed variables. We also evaluate stronger models that include the Wikipedia gazetteers and hierarchical Brown word clusters [2] used by Ratinov et al [19]. In Section 5 we test the combination of these models with our method for incorporating non-local dependencies using various feature expansion techniques.

[1]`http://www.alias-i.com/lingpipe`

4. PASSAGE RETRIEVAL FOR NER

This section formalizes the use of passage retrieval in the context of a sequence labeling task. We first explore various definitions of the retrieval collection and relate this to previous work. Second, we present methods for generating the query, Q, to retrieval similar passages from the observation sequence. Third, we provide an overview of passage retrieval models. Finally, we present a new method for feature expansion based on pseudo-relevance feedback.

For the purposes of discussion, we define the observation sequence of tokens $\mathbf{x}$ to consist of a single sentence. Likewise, the passages indexed in the collection C are also sentences.

4.1 Corpus Definition

C is a set of passages over which retrieval is performed. The set of passages used is an important factor in the effectiveness of retrieval based feature aggregation. It determines the scope of the non-local dependencies. We now examine several corpus definitions and relate them to previous work.

Within Document.

The within document restriction defines the collection of passages to be the sentences that occur in the same document as $\mathbf{x}$. In previous work this is the most commonly used model [20, 7, 23]. It is simple to implement because an entire document is typically available during labeling. Since documents that mention the same entity multiple times are likely referring to the same entity, there is strong evidence that the entity shares the same label. However, this definition does not consider dependencies between occurrences across documents. This hurts recall and is problematic for short documents and rare entities.

Fixed Token Window.

The fixed window definition restricts the retrieved passages to ones that occur within a specified range of tokens in relation to the observed token, x_i. This is the cross-document context aggregation model utilized by the LBJ NER tagger [19]. The LBJ tagger uses a token window size of 200. The fixed window definition is an ad-hoc model developed based on the observation that documents close together in a newswire stream tend to be topically related. The LBJ results demonstrate that utilizing cross-document feature information improves effectiveness, but the heuristic is highly specific to the CoNLL data format. We include it in our experiments for completeness.

Global.

The global corpus utilizes all passages. The size and scope of the collection can vary significantly. Incorporating global dependencies provides the largest amount of information. This can be useful when labeling very rare entities.

4.2 Query Generation

In this section, we describe methods for generating a query, Q, from an observed input sequence of tokens, $\mathbf{x}$. The process of query generation for sequence labeling has two separate components: query triggering and query context generation.

4.2.1 *Query Triggering*

Query triggering is the process of determining the variables for which feature expansion should be performed. In the simplest case for each observed variable x_i in $\mathbf{x}$ we generate a query, Q, to retrieve passages and perform expansion. This results in |C| queries, one for each token in the collection, which is infeasible.

Feature	Description
notStop	Negative feature indicating presence of x_i in Lemur 418 stopword list
notBos	Negative feature indicating presence x_i at the beginning of a sentence
isFirstCap	Is the first character of x_i capitalized
isCapOnly	Does x_i match the Aa capitalization pattern

Table 2: Query trigger features

We define a binary decision function, g that determines whether to generate a query, Q for each x_i in $\mathbf{x}$.

$$g(x_i) = \begin{cases} 1 & \text{if } x_i \text{ creates a non-empty query, Q} \\ 0 & \text{if no query is generated} \end{cases}$$

The optimal decision function should minimize overall retrieval time while maximizing the improvement in NER effectiveness. The correct balance of these factors depends on the efficiency vs. effectiveness trade-offs of the application and we do not explore them in detail.

For our experiments we utilize several boolean combinations of the features in Table 2. For the data sets in these experiments the capitalization heuristics work well and have been successfully used in previous work [20, 7]. Beyond capitalization, very common stopword tokens represent a large number of terms and queries generated from them can be slow to execute. Tokens that are short or all capitalized are likely abbreviations and are often ambiguous; not performing expansion for these tokens can avoid errors. The capitalization features at the beginning sentences are also uncertain. Given labeled training data, it is possible to learn feature combination weights using a machine learning technique. Instead, we created several hand-crafted combinations of these features which are evaluated in Section 5. A more thorough investigation of triggering is an area for future work. In practice, the rules are effective for our evaluation data sets.

4.2.2 *Query Context*

In this section we outline several methods for generating a query, Q, from the input sentence, $\mathbf{x}$. The goal is to generate a query likely to retrieve passages where the target variable x_i shares the same output label. We only utilize the token text, which generalizes across sequence labeling tasks and feature sets.

No context.

In this method, the query consists of only the current observed token, x_i. In previous work cite[19] [20] [7] on modeling non-local dependencies, this is the only method utilized.

Adjacent tokens.

This method makes a first order markov assumption and utilizes only adjacent tokens (x_{i-1}, x_i, x_{i+1}). This is an important feature used in NER classification.

All tokens.

All of the observed tokens in $\mathbf{x}$ are utilized in the query. This utilizes the largest amount of context information. It is also the most expensive to execute because these queries can become quite large for long sequences.

Capitalized Tokens.

Tokens that match the capitalization pattern Aa+ are utilized in the query. These tokens that are likely to be other related named entities.

For retrieving similar passages in NER, an important consideration is how the tokens are normalized. This includes case folding, stemming or lemmatization, and stopword removal. As we show in our experiments, in Section 5, features such as case sensitivity significantly impact the effectiveness of retrieval.

4.3 Passage Retrieval Models

Given a query, Q, generated from our source sentence, we now describe how we rank passages, r, in the collection, C. This defines the similarity function between the query, Q, and other sentences in the collection. For comparison with previous work the basic model is a simple set based retrieval model that performs exact string matching. The remaining models are based on the Markov Random Field retrieval model (MRF-IR) [15] using unigram and sequential dependence models.

4.3.1 *Exact match*

The simplest model we test is an exact match between a query, Q, consisting of the single token x_i in the source sequence.

$$p(r|Q) = \begin{cases} 1 & \text{if } x_i \text{ is in r} \\ 0 & \text{if } x_i \text{ is not in r} \end{cases}$$

This model performs exact string matching where all passages containing the matching token are returned. All retrieved passages have the same score. This is the method used in previous feature aggregation models [20, 23]. For cross-document dependencies on larger collections the number of passages retrieved can be prohibitively large.

4.3.2 *Unigram*

The unigram model is equivalent to the Query Likelihood model that ranks documents according to the probability of relevance using a bag of words assumption of term independence. Using Dirichlet smoothing this is defined as:

$$logp(Q|r) = \sum_{i=1}^{|Q|} \log \frac{f(q_i, r) + \mu \frac{c_{q,i}}{|C|}}{|D| + \mu} \quad (1)$$

where $f(q_i, r)$ is the frequency of the query term in the passage, $c_{q,i}$ is the number of times a word occurs in a collection of documents, $|C|$ is the number of words in the collection, and μ is the smoothing parameter that is set empirically.

4.3.3 *Sequential Dependence*

To model dependencies between terms in the source query we utilize the sequential dependence variant of the Markov Random Field IR model. The model goes beyond individual query terms and utilizes phrases and word proximity for adjacent terms in the query.

This model can specified using the Indri [2] query language as,

[2] http://www.lemurproject.org/indri

```
#weight( 0.8 #combine(United Arab Emirates)
0.15 #combine( #owl(United Arab)
#owl(Arab Emirates) )
0.05 #combine( #uw8(United Arab)
#uw8(Arab Emirates)) )
```

The weighting parameters are set according to those suggested by Metzler and Croft, which were shown to be stable across collections [15].

4.4 PRF Feature Expansion

We now describe our approach to using non-local information. At inference time, we use **weighted feature copying** to provide a better estimate of $p(\mathbf{y} \mid \mathbf{x})$. Specifically, when an input token x_i triggers a query, we generate a query and retrieve r passages. We append NER classifier features from these passages onto the vector of features $\mathbf{f}(x_i, \mathbf{x})$ that fires for x_i. The weights for the appended features are those features' weights learned during CRF training, down-weighted by the passage's score under the retrieval model, as we now describe.

We utilize a pseudo feedback method based on Relevance Models (RM) [12]. RM provides a framework for better estimating a query language model. Given an initial short query, Q, the relevance model result is a distribution $P(w|\theta_Q)$.

$$p(w|\theta_Q) = \sum_{r \in C} P(w|\theta_r)P(\theta_r|Q) \quad (2)$$

Given the set of all passages, r in the collection, the model is an aggregation of term probabilities in the collection weighted by the passage's similarity to the query. We can utilize a similar formulation for generating an expanded feature distribution for our target input passage we are labeling. Given the query, Q_{x_i} generated from $\mathbf{x}$ given the formulation:

$$p(f_k|Q_{x_i}) = \sum_{r \in C} p(f_k|r)P(\theta_r|Q_{x_i}) \quad (3)$$

As discussed in Section 3, each f_k is a binary feature function used to define the features in the CRF. The $p(f_k|r)$ is estimated as a binary indicator function, 1 if the feature occurs in r and 0 otherwise. The result of the model is a distribution over feature values. It is an aggregation of the feature counts in the collection weighted by the similarity of the passage to the source query.

Since for most documents the conditional probability of $p(Q_{x_i}|\theta_r)$ is very small, we can closely approximate the above distribution by using the set of R top retrieved documents in response to the query, giving us:

$$p(f_k|Q_{x_i}) \approx \sum_{r \in R} p(f_k|r)P(\theta_r|Q_{x_i}) \quad (4)$$

We utilize this new feature distribution in place of the distribution extracted from the original observed variable x_i and use the local inference methods for linear chain CRFs.

Note that for exact match retrieval the $P(Q_{x_i}|\theta_r)$ values are all one, so it is simply an average of the feature values across the collection without context based weighting.

A variant of the relevance model that has been shown to be effective when constructing an expanded query is RM3, where the original query is linearly interpolated with the expanded relevance model query [9] using a parameter, λ. We perform a similar form of interpolation by adding the feature values estimated from the relevance model as distinct features in our CRF separate from the feature space of the original passage. This allows the CRF to learn separate weights for expanded features from retrieval. In place of a fixed λ value, each feature has its own weight which is learned by the CRF.

Adding features from the relevance model as separate features significantly expands the number of features used in the model. Over large collections the number of features can become prohibitively expansive. The relevance modeling framework provides parameters to control this: varying the size of R and only using a top-k subset of the highest weighted features instead of the entire distribution.

	Count
Tokens	10,050
Person	273
Miscellaneous	98
Location	241
Organization	49

Table 3: Historic Deerfield NER collection statistics

5. EXPERIMENTS

In this section, we report experimental results utilizing retrieval based feature expansion. First, we evaluate the quality of passage retrieval for various retrieval models. Second, we measure the effectiveness of passage based expansion on NER labeling in the CoNLL03 shared task. Third, we test NER models that utilize external corpora as a source for expansion features. Finally, we assess the robustness of the models by labeling an out of domain a collection of scanned historical texts.

5.1 Datasets

We perform our experiments on two data sets. Our primary data set is the standard CoNLL NER collection. As a secondary data set, we constructed an NER collection using publicly available scanned OCRed books on the history of Deerfield, Massachusetts.

5.1.1 CoNLL 2003

We first use the standard CoNLL 2003 English data set, which was created for the shared task of the Seventh Conference on CoNLL, which focused on entity recognition. The data consists of Reuters newswire documents from 1996. The training set consists of 945 documents from August 1996 containing 14987 sentences and approximately 200,000 tokens. The test (b) set consists of 231 documents from December 1996 with 3584 sentences and approximately 46,000 tokens. The data set is annotated with four entity types: Person (PER), Location, (LOC), Organization (ORG), and Miscellaneous (MISC).

5.1.2 Deerfield Book Collection

Recent book digitization efforts by the Internet Archive [3] and Google Books are making large volumes of public domain books widely available. To simulate the task of a historical researcher, we created a focused topic collection of material relevant to the history of the town of Deerfield, Massachusetts. The books were scanned and processed with OCR software, which introduces noise due to OCR errors and page structure recognition issues.

The Historic Deerfield collection has ten books containing 3,311 pages with 98,444 sentences, 2.1 million tokens, and over 60 thousand distinct words. It contains diverse historical resources: biographies, encyclopedias, and historical catalogues of artifacts. To

[3] http://www.archive.org/details/texts

Trigger	Num Queries	TP	FN	FP	TN	Precision	Recall
isFirstCap	44906	33359	684	11547	158028	74.29	97.99
isFirstCap & notStop	41344	33273	768	8071	161504	80.48	97.74
isFirstCap & notStop & notBos	32552	27413	6628	5139	164438	84.21	80.53
CapOnly & notStop	33429	27912	6132	5517	164060	83.50	81.99
CapOnly & notStop & notBos	27240	24004	10040	3236	166341	88.12	70.51

Table 4: Query Trigger evaluation on the CoNLL training data. It compares boolean combinations of the features from Table 2.

Retrieval	ZeroResults	MAP	Mean Prec.	Relevant Passages	Returned Passages
Case Folding	2491	87.30	84.56	1497893	1844301
Case Sensitive	3112	90.57	88.35	1161370	1297002

Table 5: Evaluation of case normalization in retrieval using the Query Likelihood ranking and no context for the 33429 queries.

Retrieval	MAP
CaseFold QL NoContext	87.30
CaseFold QL Adjacent	90.10
CaseFold QL All	91.14
CaseFold SD Capitalized	91.43
CaseFold SD All	91.70
CaseSens QL NoContext	90.57
CaseSens QL Adjacent	92.63
CaseSens QL All	93.50
CaseSens SD Capitalized	93.55
CaseSens SD All	**93.92**

Table 6: Evaluation of passage retrieval ranking using Mean Average Precision (in %). Various combinations of case sensitivity, retrieval model, and query generation method are evaluated. QL indicates Query Likelihood retrieval, SD indicates Sequential Dependence. The last word indicates the query generation method from Section 4.2.2.

create a evaluation set for NER, we randomly sampled two pages from each book in the collection. The resulting test set contains 20 pages with 481 sentences and approximately 10 thousand tokens. The pages were manually annotated with entities consistent with the CoNLL task [4]. The dataset contains 661 entity mentions. The distribution is shown in Table 3.

5.2 Passage Retrieval Evaluation

We now evaluate the retrieval effectiveness of the retrieval models described in Section 4.3 on the CoNLL data set. All results utilize the entire training corpus. Unlike traditional adhoc retrieval evaluation, the goal is not simply to return passage relevant to a topic. For NER expansion, the aim is to identify passages whose features are useful in the predicting the correct y_i of the observed x_i in the source sequence $\mathbf{x}$.

5.2.1 Query Trigger Evaluation

In the section we test the effectiveness of several combinations of query trigger features described in Section 4.2.1. Query triggering determines which variables are expanded. It should occur when expansion will improve labeling effectiveness; however, this is difficult to estimate directly. For a straightforward evaluation method, feature expansion should be performed only if the token is part of a named entity. This definition ensures that non-local entity information is considered in classification. The triggering evaluation results are shown in Table 4.

From the results, we observe that the heuristic utilizing capitalized letters has high recall. It captures all but 2% of entity tokens, which are mostly stopwords that are part of a longer entity string (e.g. of, the), but has a significant number of false positives. The precision improves by removing stopwords, which are expensive queries to execute and are ambiguous tokens. The *CapOnly* heuristic excludes mixed and all-caps tokens which improves precision over *isFirstCap*. Although recall is reduced significantly, manual inspection shows that many of the missed tokens are abbreviations such as US, UN, and EU. *CapOnly* combined with excluding stopwords reduces the number of queries by 19%, reducing the number of false positives in half compared with the baseline *isFirstCap*. This is a significant savings in the number of queries executed. Most of the remaining false positives are temporal expressions such as month and days which are not labeled as named entities.

The addition of the restriction to exclude tokens at the beginning of sentences, *notBos*, where virtually all tokens are capitalized improved precision but resulted in a significant reduction in recall. Furthermore, capitalized tokens at the beginning of sentences are often ambiguous and expansion can improve effectiveness by providing more features to disambiguate them. We found tagging effectiveness improved by expanding these tokens.

We utilize the *CapOnly & notStop* combination for the remaining experiments. It is simple and provides a satisfactory trade-off between efficiency and recall.

5.2.2 Passage Retrieval Effectiveness

For retrieval based feature expansion the effectiveness of the first pass retrieval is an important factor in expansion quality because the features are weighted by the model probabilities. We therefore

Approach	F1	% Err. Red.
Local (baseline)	82.16	
FixedWindow	**84.55***	13.4%
Global	83.86*	9.5%
Local (Brown + Wiki)	86.08	
FixedWindow	**86.44***	2.6%
Global	86.11	0.2%

Table 8: F1 scores on CoNLL for feature expansion using exact string matching for varying corpus scopes described in Section 4.2.2. The top is the baseline model with features from Table 1. The bottom results are for a stronger model with Brown clusters and Wikipedia features. Statistically significant over local models where indicated with a * with p $\leq$ .05.

[4]We make the judgments file available at `http://ciir.cs.umass.edu/~jdalton/deerfield`. It contains the publicly available book ids and annotations

Approach	LOC	MISC	ORG	PER	ALL
Baseline	87.02	73.19	78.37	84.53	82.16
Stanford	86.11	77.78	78.50	85.39	82.62
Baseline + Brown	88.79	74.23	79.15	89.73	84.53
Stanford DistSim	89.64	77.35	81.08	90.63	85.88
Baseline + Brown + Wiki	89.59	74.48	81.49	91.91	86.08

Table 7: Phrase level F1 scores for base NER models described in Section 3 compared with the Stanford NER tagger on the CoNLL 2003 Named Entity Recognition test (b) set.

Approach	F1	% Err Red
Local (Brown + Wiki)	86.08	
QL Capitalized	86.36*	2.0%
QL All	86.47*	2.8%
SD Capitalized	86.28	1.4%
SD All	**86.60***	3.7%

Table 9: CoNLL F1 scores for feature expansion using ranked passage retrieval with the Global retrieval scope. (QL) indicates Query Likelihood and (SD) indicates Sequential Dependence retrieval models. The query context was varied, Capitalized includes only capitalized tokens, All has all tokens excluding stopwords. Significant differences over the local model with p $\leq$ .05 are indicated with by *.

evaluate various retrieval methods to determine which is the most effective. For evaluation purposes a retrieved passage r is defined to be relevant with respect to a source query Q_{x_i} for variable x_i as follows:

$$Rel(r) = \begin{cases} 1 & \text{if } x_i = x_j \text{ and } y_i = y_j \\ 0 & \text{Otherwise} \end{cases}$$

where x_j and y_j are the corresponding variables contained in in r. The above definition states that a passage is relevant only if it contains a string-identical observed variable where the output labels have the same entity class.

The CoNLL newswire documents are indexed using the open-source Galago [5] retrieval system. The documents are split into sentences using the boundaries provided and indexed to create a passage level index. We perform stopping using the Lemur 418 stopword list and stemming using the Porter stemmer. Default Dirichlet smoothing was used with μ=2500. For evaluation, the set of 33429 queries resulting from the query triggering method selected in Section 5.2.1 is used. The search index is loaded into memory for fast retrieval during tagging.

We first examine the impact of case folding on effectiveness. As previously discussed, capitalization is an important feature that strongly indicates a token is an entity. To utilize this we test case-folded and case sensitive retrieval. The results are shown in Table 5. Case sensitive matching improves precision but decreases recall, the number of relevant passages decreases by approximately 20%. The number of queries with no results increases by 25%, no expansion can be performed for these queries. It is notable that both models have very high MAP scores. The high MAP score indicates that most tokens in the CoNLL dataset are not ambiguous.

Next, varying combinations of retrieval models described in Section 4.3 and context query generation in Section 4.2.2 are tested. The results of the evaluation on Mean Average Precision (MAP) are shown in in Table 6. The table shows that case sensitive retrieval results in consistent effectiveness improvements across all models. Using the entire sentence as context to generate the query performs the best. Generating the query only using the capitalized words in the sentence performs only slightly worse than using all of the words in the sentence. This is significant because these queries are significantly more efficient to run because they contain fewer terms that occur less frequently in the collection.

The best performing model is the Sequential Dependence model using all words in the source sentence to generate the query. As shown later in Section 5.3.3, this model also performs the best for NER feature expansion. This indicates that our relevance evaluation correlates with real NER improvements in the final combined system.

5.3 CoNLL NER Evaluation

In this section we measure the impact of adding non-local feature information from retrieved passages to our baseline CRF model. We begin by evaluating the local baseline CRF models. For comparison with previous work we also evaluate unweighted exact match boolean retrieval. Finally, we evaluate effectiveness of ranked feature expansion models.

5.3.1 Local NER Models

We now evaluate the baseline local tagging models systems. Table 7 shows various local NER systems and feature combinations on the CoNLL named entity recognition task. We compare the effectiveness of the our baseline tagger with the the Stanford NER system [6]. The base CRF model performance is comparable to the out-of-the-box Stanford system. Although these models are widely used for their efficiency, they are not state-of-the-art.

To the baseline system we add features from external knowledge sources. In particular, they are augmented with gazetteers from Wikipedia and Brown word cluster information. These resources are bundled with the freely available Illinois LBJ Named Entity tagger [7]. Consistent with the findings of Ratinov et. al. [19], the external features provide significant improvement over the baseline model. These local NER models are the baselines we use to assess the impact of feature expansion from retrieval.

5.3.2 Exact Match Feature Expansion

Next, we present the results of cross-document feature expansion using passages with string-identical tokens. Table 8 shows that expansion provides consistent improvements over the local models. The FixedWindow expansion corresponds to the context aggregation method used by the LBJ tagger [19].

For the baseline retrieval system, the FixedWindow expansion method provides a 13.4% reduction in F1 error on the CoNLL dataset. The global expansion model using all passages in the collection provides a smaller 9.5% reduction. FixedWindow outperforms unweighted global feature expansion. FixedWindow restricts

[5] http://www.galagosearch.org/

[6] http://nlp.stanford.edu/software/CRF-NER.shtml

[7] http://cogcomp.cs.illinois.edu/page/software_view/4

Approach	LOC	MISC	ORG	PER	ALL	% Error Red
ExactMatch	53.43	57.29	18.90	55.97	51.97	
LBJ (Win 200)	62.10	57.31	11.84	67.12	58.05	12.7%
QL All	64.62	53.47	23.64	63.79	59.31	15.3%
SD All	64.40	58.42	21.71	65.89	**60.15***	17.0%

Table 11: F1 scores for CoNLL models evaluated on the Deerfield collection. The table compares global ranked feature expansion compared with baseline exact string matching. We compare against the state-of-the-art LBJ NER model that uses Fixed Window feature aggregation. All differences are statistically significant over the baseline ExactMatch model with a with p $\leq$ .05, a * indicates significance over LBJ.

Approach	F1	% Err Red
Local (Baseline)	49.86	
Win200	51.41	3.1%
Global	**55.36***	11.0%
Local (Brown+Wiki)	51.58	
Win200	51.06	-1.1%
Global	51.97	0.8%

Table 10: F1 scores of the NER model trained on CoNLL and evaluated on the Deerfield collection. The results show local systems and unweighted feature expansion with varying collection scopes. The top is a tagger model with baseline features. The bottom is a stronger baseline model with word clustering and Wikipedia features. The differences are statistically significant with local models where indicated with a * with p $\leq$ .05.

the passages to match those near the source sentence in the news stream. It exploits locality in the CoNLL dataset. It does not perform well on collections that do not have this property, as we show later in the Deerfield evaluation. Neither aggregation method applied to the baseline model outperforms a stronger local model that uses Brown word clustering and Wikipedia gazetteers.

The results of adding exact match expansion to a stronger model incorporating Brown and Wikipedia is shown in the bottom of Table 8 there is a small, but significant improvement using the FixedWindow model. The expansion with the global retrieval over all passages provides no significant benefit. The unweighted global aggregation has less topical cohesion and the unweighted expansion contains more noise. The exact match model acts as a type of global prior for a token. This can be problematic for ambiguous tokens. We now explore the use of ranked expansion models that utilize sentence context to address the problem of ambiguity.

5.3.3 Ranked Feature Expansion

The results for feature expansion from ranked retrieval are shown in Table 9. Because the retrieval corpus is small all passages are used for expansion. Unlike the exact match based expansion, the results show that use all expansion models result in significant improvement over the strongest local NER model. The SD AllTok combination provides a 3.7% reduction in error over the best performing local model.

The models with the AllTok context outperform models using only capitalized tokens. The Sequential Dependence model provides a small improvement over Query Likelihood. The models using AllTokens outperform the exact match expansion limited to the 200 token fixed window described in the previous section.

5.4 Deerfield Evaluation

In this section we evaluate the robustness of the models trained on newswire by testing them on the collection of scanned books described in Section 5.1.2. For the Global retrieval scope all the sentences in the 20 books are indexed. Sentence splitting is performed using the OpenNLP MaxEnt classifier.

The results for the evaluation on the Deerfield dataset are shown in Table 10. The results show that the F1 score of the tagger drops by approximately 40% compared with the CoNLL results. We investigated the errors and found that many of errors are due to sparsity in the target domain. A significant number of the entities in the book collection are not present in the newswire training collection. Our error analysis finds that often LOC chunks are confused for PER. The cause of this is that for unseen capitalized tokens the tagger relies heavily on the class prior, which is strongly biased towards PER tags in the newswire data. We now show the impact of feature expansion on addressing these problems.

5.4.1 Exact Match Expansion

Table 10 shows that expansion using Fixed Window of 200 tokens does not improve effectiveness significantly. The Global scope outperforms the Fixed Window method when applied to the baseline model.

It is curious that global retrieval aggregation does not significantly improve the stronger local model that incorporates Wikipedia based gazetteers. In fact, the model performs worse than expansion applied to a weaker model. We believe this is due to the phenomena of model undertraining [21] where the strong Wikipedia features in the newswire domain result in the model underweighting token and context features.

5.4.2 Ranked Feature Expansion

The results for ranked feature expansion are shown in Table 11. The weighted expansion models result in very substantial improvements in NER effectiveness. The Sequential Dependence model using a query generated from the entire sentence results in a 17% reduction in error. It outperforms the LBJ Layer 1 model which is currently the top performing NER tagger on newswire data. The results indicate that non-local dependencies created from retrieval feature expansion create a model that is more robust across domains.

The improvement in model effectiveness from expansion does not address OCR errors. We only copy features for identical observed tokens. Relaxing this constraint to copy features for similar strings could potentially improve accuracy further for these tokens, but we do not focus on this problem.

5.5 Expansion using External Collections

Retrieval based feature expansion can also be used to improve NER effectiveness by using unlabeled data from external collections. The previous experiments utilized small collections. The labeled CoNLL data contains less than 20 thousand sentences. We can create a more general model by incorporating external features from larger collections.

Approach	F1	% Err Red.
CoNLL SD AllTokens	86.60	
CoNLL QL AllTokens + Ext100	86.66	0.4%
CoNLL SD AllTokens + Ext50	**87.01***	3.1%
Deerfield SD AllTokens	60.15	
Deerfield QL AllTokens + Extl100	60.07	-0.2%
Deerfield SD AllTokens + Ext50	**61.22***	2.7%

Table 12: F1 scores for external feature expansion including a 50k document subset of the RCV1 reuters news collection. Ext100 indicates 100 feedback passages, Ext50 indicates 50 passages. A * indicates significance over non-external model with p $\leq$ .05.

Approach	F1 Score	% Err. Red.
CoNLL Best Local	86.08	
CoNLL Expansion	86.60	3.7%
CoNLL Expansion + External	**87.01**	**6.7%**
Deerfield Best Local	51.58	
Deerfield Expansion	60.15	17.7%
Deerfield Expansion + External	**61.22**	**19.9%**

Table 13: Summary Table comparing the F1 score of the strongest models in each category, a purely local model incorporating word clustering and gazetteers, a model using ranked feature expansion, and feature expansion including an external corpus. All results are statistically significant with p $\leq$ .05.

5.5.1 Reuters RCV1 subset

As an external source for PRF feature expansion we use a subset of the Reuters RCV1 collection [13]. RCV1 consists of Reuters newswire data collected in 1996 and 1997. It contains documents from the same source and time period as the CoNLL data set. We use the first 50,000 documents of the collection. The RCV1 subset contains 931,822 sentences and 20.5 million words.

5.5.2 Evaluation

In previous experiments all of the passages in the collection without a cutoff were used because of their limited size. For these experiments, feature expansion only uses top ranked passages. We experimented with the number of retrieved passages and report results using the top 50 and 100 passages.

The results on both the CoNLL and Deerfield collections are shown in Table 12. The results compare against the top performing feature expansion models that does not utilize external data. The Sequential Dependence model with 50 feedback documents results in significant improvement in both the CoNLL and Deerfield evaluations. It provides a 3.1% error reduction in CoNLL and a 2.7% error reduction in Deerfield.

The model using 100 feedback documents and QL retrieval does not significantly improve effectiveness and slightly hurts effectiveness on the Deerfield data. We are unsure why this model does not perform as well, especially on the CoNLL data. More error analysis is needed to fully understand the causes. However, we note that the QL retrieval model is less effective than the Sequential Dependence model. Also, the larger number of feedback documents may introduce noisy features from off-topic passages. For the Deerfield data, the additional newswire data may not contain the topics in the dataset and therefore may not be as useful for expansion.

Despite some mixed results, the external feature expansion models result in the overall best performing system.

6. FUTURE WORK

The most significant area of future work is a better method for determining which tokens in the observation sequence require feature expansion. Using our current heuristics there are over 8000 queries needed on the CoNLL test set. While we used in memory indices for fast retrieval performance, the retrieval time could be significantly reduced with little loss in effectiveness. For sequences with strong evidence feature expansion is unnecessary. Furthermore, a more advanced triggering model could also leverage the training data to identify where expansion hurts effectiveness due to poor retrieval effectiveness.

Another area that could be improved is a more principled approach to selecting the passage collection to use for feature expansion. We would like to utilize strong local evidence within the document and back off to models of similar documents, and finally the entire collection. This could be done using a technique similar to the Mixture of Relevance Models (MoRM) [6]. Diaz and Metzler also investigate the utility of different external corpora for query expansion [6]. They introduce a theory of "concept density" that measures the utility of a collection for expansion.

7. CONCLUSIONS

Many state-of-the-art named entity recognition systems pool information about the context of different entity tokens. This aggregation may be at the level of features or by enforcing consistency in decoding. Context aggregation in documents often exploits discourse constraints [5]; aggregation across adjacent documents in a news feed exploits the local salience of particular stories [19].

We presented a framework that embraces these and other context aggregation methods as forms of passage retrieval. In particular, we can retrieve, and use features from, topically similar passages. A summary of the results is presented in Table 13. In addition to showing that passage retrieval can achieve significant improvements on in-domain accuracy, we showed it surpasses other context aggregation methods when evaluating NER models in new domains.

8. ACKNOWLEDGMENTS

This work was supported in part by the Center for Intelligent Information Retrieval, in part by NSF CLUE IIS-0844226 and in part by NSF grant #IIS-0910884. Any opinions, findings and conclusions or recommendations expressed in this material are those of the authors and do not necessarily reflect those of the sponsors.

9. REFERENCES

[1] M. Bendersky, W. B. Croft, and D. A. Smith. Structural annotation of search queries using pseudo-relevance feedback. In *Proceedings of the 19th ACM international conference on Information and knowledge management*, CIKM '10, pages 1537–1540, New York, NY, USA, 2010. ACM.

[2] P. F. Brown, P. V. deSouza, R. L. Mercer, V. J. D. Pietra, and J. C. Lai. Class-based n-gram models of natural language. *Comput. Linguist.*, 18:467–479, December 1992.

[3] C. Buckley. Automatic query expansion using smart : Trec 3. In *In Proceedings of The third Text REtrieval Conference (TREC-3*, pages 69–80.

[4] R. Bunescu and R. J. Mooney. Collective information extraction with relational markov networks. In *Proceedings of the 42nd Annual Meeting on Association for Computational Linguistics*, ACL '04, Stroudsburg, PA, USA, 2004. Association for Computational Linguistics.

[5] H. L. Chieu and H. T. Ng. Named entity recognition: a maximum entropy approach using global information. In *COLING*, pages 1–7, 2002.

[6] F. Diaz and D. Metzler. Improving the estimation of relevance models using large external corpora. In *Proceedings of the 29th annual international ACM SIGIR conference on Research and development in information retrieval*, SIGIR '06, pages 154–161, New York, NY, USA, 2006. ACM.

[7] J. R. Finkel, T. Grenager, and C. Manning. Incorporating non-local information into information extraction systems by gibbs sampling. In *ACL*, pages 363–370, 2005.

[8] F. Huang and A. Yates. Distributional representations for handling sparsity in supervised sequence-labeling. In *ACL-IJCNLP*, pages 495–503, 2009.

[9] N. A. Jaleel, J. Allan, W. B. Croft, F. Diaz, L. Larkey, X. Li, M. Smucker, and C. Wade. Umass at trec 2004: Novelty and hard. 2005. Proc. TREC 2004, http://trec.nist.gov/.

[10] V. Krishnan and C. D. Manning. An effective two-stage model for exploiting non-local dependencies in named entity recognition. In *ACL*, pages 1121–1128, 2006.

[11] J. Lafferty, A. McCallum, and F. Pereira. Conditional random fields: Probabilistic models for segmenting and labeling sequence data. In *ICML*, pages 282–289, 2001.

[12] V. Lavrenko and W. B. Croft. Relevance-based language models. In *Proceedings of the ACM SIGIR 01 conference*, pages 120–127, 2001.

[13] D. D. Lewis, Y. Yang, T. G. Rose, and F. Li. Rcv1: A new benchmark collection for text categorization research. *J. Mach. Learn. Res.*, 5:361–397, December 2004.

[14] X. Liu, S. Zhang, F. Wei, and M. Zhou. Recognizing named entities in tweets. In *ACL*, 2011.

[15] D. Metzler and W. B. Croft. A markov random field model for term dependencies. In *Proceedings of the 28th annual international ACM SIGIR conference on Research and development in information retrieval*, SIGIR '05, pages 472–479, New York, NY, USA, 2005. ACM.

[16] A. Mikheev. A knowledge-free method for capitalized word disambiguation. In *ACL*, pages 159–166, 1999.

[17] D. Nadeau and S. Sekine. A survey of named entity recognition and classification. *Lingvisticæ Investigationes*, 30(1):3–26, 2007.

[18] D. Pinto, A. McCallum, X. Wei, and W. B. Croft. Table extraction using conditional random fields. In *Proceedings of the 26th annual international ACM SIGIR conference on Research and development in informaion retrieval*, SIGIR '03, pages 235–242, New York, NY, USA, 2003. ACM.

[19] L. Ratinov and D. Roth. Design challenges and misconceptions in named entity recognition. In *CoNLL*, pages 147–155, 2009.

[20] C. Sutton and A. McCallum. Collective segmentation and labeling of distant entities in information extraction. In *ICML Workshop on Statistical Relational Learning and its Connections to Other Fields*, 2004.

[21] C. Sutton, M. Sindelar, and A. McCallum. Reducing weight undertraining in structured discriminative learning. In *HLT-NAACL*, pages 89–95, 2006.

[22] J. Turian, L. Ratinov, and Y. Bengio. Word representations: a simple and general method for semi-supervised learning. In *ACL*, pages 384–394, 2010.

[23] M. Vilain, J. Huggins, and B. Wellner. A simple feature-copying approach for long-distance dependencies. In *Proceedings of the Thirteenth Conference on Computational Natural Language Learning*, CoNLL '09, pages 192–200, Stroudsburg, PA, USA, 2009. Association for Computational Linguistics.

Effective and Efficient Polarity Estimation in Blogs based on Sentence-Level Evidence

Jose M. Chenlo
Centro de Investigación en Tecnoloxías da Información (CITIUS)
Universidade de Santiago de Compostela, Spain
josemanuel.gonzalez@usc.es

David E. Losada
Centro de Investigación en Tecnoloxías da Información (CITIUS)
Universidade de Santiago de Compostela, Spain
david.losada@usc.es

ABSTRACT

One of the core tasks in Opinion Mining consists of estimating the polarity of the opinionated documents found. In some scenarios (e.g. blogs), this estimation is severely affected by sentences that are off-topic or that simply do not express any opinion. In fact, the key sentiments in a blog post often appear in specific locations of the text. In this paper we propose several effective and robust polarity detection methods based on different sentence features. We show that we can successfully determine the polarity of documents guided by a sentence-level analysis that takes into account topicality and the location in the blog post of the subjective sentences. Our experimental results show that some of our proposed variants are both highly effective and computationally-lightweight.

Categories and Subject Descriptors

H.3 [**Information Storage and Retrieval**]: Information Search and Retrieval

General Terms

Theory, Experimentation

Keywords

Opinion mining, blog retrieval, sentence retrieval, polarity estimation, efficiency

1. INTRODUCTION

The rise of social networks and blogs has led to new opportunities and challenges regarding how to effectively deal with the opinionated nature of these resources. Our research is focused on one of the most important web sentiment-oriented resources, the blogosphere. People frequently read blogs to determine the viewpoints of others. In order to build an effective information retrieval (IR) system that helps users to find out what other people think, we need to have an understanding regarding whether or not an opinion is present in a text and, if so, whether that opinion is positive or negative [14].

In recent years, several studies have been conducted to determine opinions in blog posts. Most of these address this challenge as a two-stage process that involves a topic retrieval stage (i.e. retrieve on-topic documents given a user query), and a re-ranking stage that takes into account opinion-based features [12]. In blogs, this second Opinion Mining (OM) stage usually involves two further subtasks: an opinion-finding task, where the main aim is to find opinionated posts related to the query, and a subsequent polarity task to identify the orientation of a blog post with respect to the topic (e.g. positive, negative or neutral).

We are concerned here with polarity estimation, a challenging area that is much more demanding than topicality estimation [14]. One problem in polarity estimation is that there may be conflicting opinions in a blog post. For example, a blog writer may summarise pros and cons of a particular argument before settling on an overall recommendation. This mixed set of opinions severely affects the quality of automatic methods designed to estimate the overall orientation of the post. This issue is illustrated particularly well in the following example (taken from a popular film reviews' blog[1]). Despite the start of the post being predominantly negative, with several negative comments being made, the overall recommendation is positive:

> *Gran Torino also includes a few easy outs built into the story ... And even without those easy outs, the storytelling's fairly obvious ... Gran Torino is a curdled mess, politically ... but considering that Gran Torino's heading towards the sunset of Eastwood's acting career, that's a good enough reason to watch it go by.*

Observe that the location of the subjective sentences may offer important clues when attempting to establish the polarity of the blog post. In the example above the last sentence is the one that expresses the overall view. Nevertheless, existing literature on blog polarity estimation has disregarded this valuable information. For instance, the most effective polarity systems participating in the TREC blog tracks [12, 7] do not incorporate any feature based on this flow of sentiments, but rather focus on a document-level estimation

[1] `http://blog.moviefone.com`

CIKM'11, October 24–28, 2011, Glasgow, Scotland, UK.

of polarity that combines relevance to the topic with some sort of global orientation of the sentiments in the document (e.g. counting positive/negative terms). We argue that this is a rather strong simplification and claim that more effective polarity estimation methods can be designed using a sentence-level approach.

In more restricted scenarios, such as corpus of movie or product reviews, some authors have found that the location of the sentiments could be valuable [13, 15, 1]. However, in blogs, the presence of noise (off-topic information or on-topic information that is non-opinionated) makes it difficult to locate the key polar sentences. In this respect, our thorough study of polarity gives useful insights on how sentiments are expressed in blog posts.

In the literature, it has been shown that the noise introduced by off-topic content in documents is a major issue that needs to be addressed to facilitate progress in OM [3, 19]. Therefore, we propose a refined analysis of the documents that takes into account not only the location of the sentiments, but also their relevance to the query. More specifically, we propose effective algorithms that consider two main factors when determining the key sentences for polarity estimation: the relatedness of the sentence and the query topic, and the location of a sentence in the post. We argue that this information, combined with evidence of polarity (i.e. positive/negative terms in the sentence), is extremely valuable when attempting to detect the overall orientation of a post.

The contributions of this paper are:

- We show that sentence-level methods are able to yield state-of-the-art performance in polarity estimation.
- We demonstrate that small subsets of subjective sentences obtained from certain locations of the post are good indicators of the overall polarity.
- We show that estimating polarity from these narrower parts of the document leads to substantial gains in terms of efficiency.

The rest of the paper is organized as follows. In section 2 we explain the blog subjectivity and polarity estimation methods, and the methodology followed to combine sentence-level information with document scores. Sections 3 and 4 report the experiments and analyze their outcomes. Section 5 presents related work. The paper ends with Section 6, where we present the conclusions and outline our ideas for future work.

2. METHOD

As we argued above, the noise introduced by off-topic content in documents may severely harm OM performance because documents might have query terms in a wrong context. Moreover, finding robust OM techniques that can be applied effectively across different underlying topic retrieval baselines is a real challenge. In the past TREC Blog tracks most polarity approaches did not give any added value over the topic retrieval baseline (meaning that the baseline, with no polarity-oriented capabilities, is not beaten by these approaches) [12]. Actually, it is interesting to note that only one participant in TREC 2008 had on average improved the polarity performance of the five topic retrieval baselines provided by the task. This illustrates how difficult it is to design effective polarity estimation methods.

To deal with this challenging problem, we define a general OM polarity approach that involves searching for on-topic polar sentences and location-aware estimation of the document polarity. Given an initial topic retrieval baseline, we work at sentence level to find positive and negative sentences related to the query. Next, our method builds a ranking of positive posts and a ranking of negative posts by aggregating relevance scores and sentence-level polarity information. Within this process we study different location-aware strategies to represent the overall view of the post. An alternative approach with no polarity capabilities is also studied. This final method, which is explained in subsection 2.4, simply promotes subjective documents (regardless of their polarity) and serves as a reference comparison.

The resources utilized in this research to estimate the opinions expressed in texts, and the methods to compute polarity and subjectivity scores based on these resources are explained below.

2.1 OpinionFinder

To estimate subjectivity and polarity we use OpinionFinder (OF) [22][2]. OF is a state of the art subjectivity classifier that works as follows. First, the text is processed using part-of-speech tagging, name entity recognition, tokenization, stemming, and sentence splitting. Next, a parsing module builds dependency parse trees where subjective expressions are identified using a dictionary-based method. This is powered by Naive Bayes classifiers that are trained using subjective and objective sentences. These sentences are automatically generated from a large corpus of unannotated data by two high-precision, rule-based classifiers.

Sentences are classified by OF as subjective or objective (or unknown if it cannot determine the nature of the sentence). Two classifiers are implemented: accuracy classifier and precision classifier. The first one yields the highest overall accuracy. It tags each sentence as either subjective or objective. The second classifier optimizes precision at the expense of recall. It classifies a sentence as subjective or objective only if it can do so with confidence. Furthermore, OpinionFinder marks various aspects of the subjectivity in the sentences, including the words that are estimated to express positive or negative sentiments or the confidence of the decisions made for the accuracy classifier (*diff*).

2.2 Finding On-Topic Polar Sentences

In order to have a precise representation of the mixed set of opinions in a blog post, we compute polarity at sentence level.

With the polar terms tagged by OF [23] we can naturally define the positive or negative polarity score of a sentence. To promote polar sentences that are on-topic, we run a sentence retrieval process to determine the relatedness between the query and each polar sentence. More specifically, we use the Lemur [20] implementation of tf-idf, with BM25-like weights[3].

The combination of relevance and polarity is done through

[2] `www.cs.pitt.edu/mpqa/opinionfinderrelease`

[3] We build a sentence-level index and apply the well-known BM25 suggested configuration ($k1 = 1.2, b = 0.75$), which has proved to be very robust in many retrieval experiments [18].

linear interpolation:

$$pol(S,Q) = \beta \cdot rel_{norm}(S,Q) + (1-\beta) \cdot pol(S) \quad (1)$$

where $rel_{norm}(S,Q)$ is the Lemur's tf-idf score after a query-based normalization into [0,1] and $pol(S)$ represents the number of positive (resp. negative) terms tagged in the sentence S divided by the total number of terms in S[4]. $\beta \in [0,1]$ is a free parameter.

2.3 Document Polarity Score

Our objective in this paper is to apply sentence-level features combined with location information to improve blog polarity estimation. To this end we score sentences using eq. 1, but only take into account those subjective sentences that have at least one term tagged as positive/negative (i.e. sentences with $pol(S)$ equal to 0 are discarded). We refer to the these sentences as *polar* sentences. To aggregate the individual sentence polarity scores in a document-level polarity measure we work with the following alternatives to define a document polarity score ($pol_S(D,Q)$):

- *PolMeanAll:* The mean of *pol* scores computed across all polar sentences in the document. This measure is a natural choice to estimate the overall polarity of a document.
- *PolMeanBestN:* The mean of *pol* scores from the n sentences with the highest *pol* scores (sentences with the highest aggregated score of topicality and polarity). Focusing on the on-topic sentences with high polarity (e.g. the most controversial contents of the post) we expect to detect properly the polarity of a document.
- *PolMeanFirstN* and *PolMeanLastN:* The mean of *pol* scores from the first/last n polar sentences in the document. As argued above, the position of the sentence in the post may be an important clue when attempting to understand the polarity of the document. Therefore, we study whether the subsets consisting of the first/last polar sentences are good indicators of the overall view in a post. Observe that these strategies are more sophisticated than simply splitting the document into parts. In fact, the polar sentences selected by *PolMeanFirstN* and *PolMeanLastN* depend on the flow of sentiments of the documents, which is specific to each post. For instance, a post whose last part is objective might have its last polar sentence in the middle of the post.

Finally, we combine relevance and polarity evidence as follows:

$$pol(D,Q) = \gamma \cdot rel_{norm}(D,Q) + (1-\gamma) \cdot pol_S(D,Q) \quad (2)$$

where rel_{norm} is the document's relevance score (obtained from the initial topic retrieval baseline) after a query-based normalization in [0,1], $pol_S(D,Q)$ is one of the aggregation alternatives sketched above and $\gamma \in [0,1]$ is a free parameter. Note that some aggregation techniques have an extra parameter: the number of sentences (n). By studying the behavior of this parameter we might discover valuable patterns about the way in which bloggers express their views.

[4]For positive document retrieval $pol(S)$ is the percentage of positive terms in the sentence, and for negative document retrieval $pol(S)$ is the ratio of negative terms in the sentence.

2.4 Document-Level Subjectivity Estimation

As an alternative approach focused only on subjectivity, we use the proportion of subjective sentences in each retrieved post and the accumulated confidence about their subjectivity (OF's confidence [17, 21]) as subjectivity indicators. This approach has been adopted successfully in other studies [5]:

$$subj(D) = sumdiff \cdot \frac{\#subj}{\#sent} \quad (3)$$

where $\#subj$ and $\#sent$ are the number of subjective sentences and the number of sentences in a document, respectively. *sumdiff* is the sum of the confidence values of the subjective sentences in the document.

Next, we combine the relevance and subjectivity scores to promote subjective documents that are on-topic. The function used to combine the topic and subjective score of a document is simply:

$$subj(D,Q) = \alpha \cdot rel_{norm}(D,Q) + (1-\alpha) \cdot subj_{norm}(D,Q) \quad (4)$$

where rel_{norm} is the normalized relevance score (obtained from the initial topic retrieval baseline) and $subj_{norm}$ is a query-based normalization of eq. 3. $\alpha \in [0,1]$ is a free parameter. This method, with no polarity capabilities, serves as a reference comparison for polarity-oriented approaches.

3. EXPERIMENTAL DESIGN

In our evaluation we aim at answering the following research questions:

1. Are sentence-level methods effective for polarity estimation?
2. Is sentence location valuable in blog polarity estimation?
3. How does performance change as we focus the estimation of polarity on narrower parts of the documents? What are the implications in terms of efficiency?

To answer the first question, we apply the sentence-level methods defined in subsection 2.3 to a set of different baselines provided by TREC. This helps to assess the impact of our polarity techniques across a range of different topic-relevance baselines. We also compare the performance of our strategies against the best polarity methods participating in TREC and against the subjectivity method sketched in subsection 2.4. We address the second question by analyzing whether we can achieve competitive performance taking only a few sentences from each post (the initial/last polar sentences). We answer the third question by studying the relationship between the number of sentences used and the performance achieved by our location-aware methods. This study takes into account both effectiveness and efficiency.

The remainder of this section describes the experimental setup used to support these investigations.

3.1 Collection and Topics

Our experiments are based on the BLOGS06 collection [8], which is one of the most renowned blog test collections with relevance, subjectivity and polarity assessments. Some statistics of the collection are reported in Table 1.

Number of Unique Blogs	100,649
RSS	62%
Atom	38%
First Feed Crawl	06/12/2005
Last Feed Crawl	21/02/2006
Number of Feeds Fetches	753,681
Number of Permalinks	3,215,171
Number of Homepages	324,880
Total Compressed Size	25GB
Total Uncompressed Size	148GB
Feeds (Uncompressed)	38.6GB
Permalinks (Uncompressed)	88.8GB
Homepages (Uncompressed)	20.8GB

Table 1: The main statistics of the BLOGS06 collection. This collection was utilized in the TREC 2006, TREC 2007 and TREC 2008 blog tracks

We worked with the TREC 2006, TREC 2007 and TREC 2008 blog track's benchmarks. All of them utilize the BLOGS06 document collection as the reference collection for the retrieval experiments. Every year a new set of topics was provided and new judgments were made according to the documents retrieved by the participants. Details about these topics are reported in Table 2.

Blog Track	Topics(#)
2006	851-900 (50)
2007	901-950 (50)
2008	1001-1050 (50)

Table 2: Topics provided in the TREC Blog tracks

Each TREC topic contains three different fields (i.e. title, description and narrative) but we only utilized the title field, which is short and the best representation of real user web queries, as reflected in the official TREC Blog track literature [11, 9, 12]. Documents and topics were preprocessed with Krovetz stemmer and 733 English stopwords were removed.

For the assessment, the content of a blog post was defined as the content of the post itself and the contents of all comments to the post (i.e. permalink document). Documents were judged in two different levels by TREC assessors:

- relevance level: A post can be relevant, not relevant or not judged.
- opinion level: If the post or its comments are not only on target, but also contain an explicit expression of opinion or sentiment about the target, showing some personal attitude of the writer(s), then the document is tagged as positive, negative or mixed (if the opinion expressed is ambiguous, mixed, or unclear). Note that a post tagged as positive (negative) can still contain some negative (positive) opinions provided that the overall document expresses clearly a positive (negative) view with respect to the topic. For instance, the BLOGS06 document below was assessed as positive for the topic *'MacBook Pro'*. Observe that in spite of the presence of conflicting opinions the document was not tagged as mixed because the overall sentiment seems to be positive.

> *[...]the MacBook Pro doesn't come with a modem [...] If you're a business traveller then you WILL be in a situation where the only way to phone home is on an actual phone. You can always add a modem to the MacBook Pro, but that's another expense and another thing to carry. And that's fine, really. Since most people won't need the modem, take it out and gain back the space.*

Blog web pages have noisy information within their internal structure (e.g. links and advertisements). To remove such noise we built a preprocessing unit which can identify the main permalink components (i.e. title, post and comments) and discard the rest of the documents' content. This unit uses a common HTML parser [6] to process the structure of permalinked documents and a set of heuristics to find the core components. The main idea is to detect pieces of text in different HTML blocks and then classify them according to their positional information and size. This type of heuristic has been used successfully in other contexts [16]. We only used the information from title and post, because the comments could be misleading. Deciding how to use comments to effectively guide the estimation of polarity of the document is an interesting challenge that is out of the scope of this paper.

3.2 Retrieval Baselines

In TREC 2008, to allow the study of the performance of a specific opinion-finding technique across a range of different topic-relevance baseline systems, a set of five topic-relevance baselines was provided. These standard baselines use a variety of different retrieval approaches, and have varying retrieval effectiveness[5]. Participants were encouraged to apply their opinion-finding techniques on as many standard baselines as possible. This aims at drawing a better understanding of the most effective and stable opinion-finding techniques, by observing their performance on common standard topic-relevance baselines. Here we adopt this evaluation methodology and apply our methods on these five topic-relevance baselines to assess the robustness of our techniques.

3.3 Polarity Task

The polarity task was introduced in TREC 2007 as a natural extension to the opinion-finding task. This task was initially defined as a classification problem where the systems had to identify the real polarity of a blog post (i.e. positive, negative or mixed). To draw a better simulation of a real user search scenario the task was redefined in TREC 2008 as a typical adhoc retrieval task where the systems had to return a ranking of positive opinionated documents and a ranking of negative opinionated documents. We follow this

[5]The baselines were selected by TREC from the runs submitted to the initial ad-hoc retrieval task in the TREC blog track. These baselines were introduced in 2008 but runs were provided not only for the TREC 2008 topics but also for earlier topics.

Label	Training	Testing
TREC 2007	2006	2007
TREC 2008	2006, 2007	2008

Table 3: Training and testing configurations.

	Int.	Step	Desc.	Form.
α	[0..1]	0.1	Doc. Subjectivity (Comb.)	eq. 4
β	[0..1]	0.1	Sentence Polarity (Comb.)	eq. 1
γ	[0..1]	0.1	Doc. Polarity (Comb.)	eq. 2
n	[1..10]	1	Number of Sentences	eq. 2

Table 4: Parameters to train: the interval, the step used to train, a description and the formula affected by the parameters.

definition of the polarity task. The measures applied to evaluate performance are mean average precision (MAP), and precision at 10 documents (P@10).

3.4 Training and Testing

We built two realistic and chronologically organized query datasets with the topics provided by TREC. Details about these configurations are shown in Table 3. The training topics were used to set all the parameters of our methods. In Table 4 we report some details about the parameters and their characteristics.

Two different training-testing processes focused on maximizing MAP were ran: one for positive polarity retrieval and another for negative polarity retrieval.

4. EXPERIMENTAL RESULTS

In this section, we analyze the results obtained with the datasets described above and address our three research questions. Subsection 4.1, which is related to our first question, reports the results of our polarity estimation methods. Subsection 4.2 addresses the second question, by investigating how location-aware methods work in comparison with other approaches that do not take into account location-based information. Finally, in subsection 4.3 we cover the third research question by studying the impact of the number of sentences used by our polarity approaches and the performance obtained.

4.1 Polarity Task

Tables 5 and 6 show the results of the polarity retrieval approaches. Each run is evaluated in terms of its ability to rank positive (resp. negative) opinionated permalinks higher up in the ranking. In order to have an overall performance for each method, we compute the mean of the positive and negative MAPs and P10s of each run (denoted Mix MAP and Mix P10 respectively)[6]. The best value in each column for each baseline is underlined. Statistical significance was estimated using the paired t-test at the 95% level. The symbols $\triangle$ and $\triangledown$ indicate a significant improvement or decrease over the corresponding baseline. To specifically measure the benefits of our polarity methods we also compare their performance against the results obtained from the subjectivity method (eq. 4, results reported in the rows labeled as Subj). The symbols ▲ and ▼ indicate a significant improvement or decrease over the subjectivity method.

Sentence-level polarity methods. The technique that shows the best performance across all different baselines is *PolMeanBestN*. In TREC 2007, *PolMeanBestN* is the best method in 17 out of 30 cases, showing usually significant improvements in performance with respect to the baseline and with respect to the subjectivity method. *PolMeanAllN* performs the best in 6 cases and *PolMeanLastN* is the best approach in 4 cases. Although *PolMeanFirstN* was never the best option, their results are close to the best ones in most scenarios. We will go back to this issue in subsection 4.2. Observe also that, on average (mix column), some methods yield to a statistically significant decrease in performance for one of the baselines in TREC 2007 (baseline5) but *PolMeanBestN* does not. In TREC 2008, the relative merits of the methods remain the same.

Subjectivity Method. Not surprisingly, subjectivity information alone is not useful in polarity scenarios (the subjectivity method hardly shows any significant improvement in performance with respect to the baseline).

Positive vs Negative rankings. Another observation is that the performance of negative document rankings is quite poor. It is interesting to note that TREC systems (see Table 8) show similar trends. We argue that this is due to the difficulty to retrieve negative posts. As a matter of fact, these collections have many more positive documents than negative ones. The difference is greatest in TREC 2007, where the number of positive documents is 2960 and the number of negative documents is 1844. In TREC 2008, the difference between the number of positive and negative documents is not so marked (3338 against 2789).

Comparison against TREC Systems. To put things in perspective, we report in Table 8 how our methods compare with those proposed by teams participating in TREC [12]. Here, we show the mean of the relative improvements over the five standard baselines. Observe that this polarity task is quite challenging: most TREC polarity systems failed to retrieve more positive or negative documents than the baselines[7]. The methods proposed in this paper perform as well as the best TREC polarity approach (KLE, Pohang University of Science and Technology) [7], showing better performance for some configurations. Observe that our methods and these TREC systems were evaluated under the same testing conditions. Going back to our first research question, these results show that sentence-level methods are an effective strategy for polarity estimation, performing comparably to state-of-the-art TREC systems.

Parameters Trained. Table 7 reports the parameter values trained for each method. Observe that, although the methods proposed have up to three parameters, their optimal values are quite stable across collections.

The subjectivity approach gets a high value of α (0.9). This parameter controls the relative weight of relevance over subjectivity in eq. 3. The value of this parameter indicates

[6]Do not confuse with mixed polarity documents, which refer to documents with mixed opinions.

[7]We can only report the 2008 results because the polarity task was not defined as a ranking process until TREC 2008. Therefore, there are not official results for systems with earlier topics.

	Negative MAP	Negative P@10	Positive MAP	Positive P@10	Mix MAP	Mix P@10
baseline1	.0569	.0620	.1779	.2640	.1174	.1630
+Subj	.0603	.0920△	.1599	.2540	.1101	.1730
+PolMeanAll	.0737	.0980△	.1673	.2680	.1205	.1830
+PolMeanBestN	.0818▲	.1240△ ▲	.1819▲	.2880	.1318▲	.2060△ ▲
+PolMeanFirstN	.0742	.0960△	.1668	.2660	.1205	.1810
+PolMeanLastN	.0731	.0980△	.1718	.2640	.1224▲	.1810
baseline2	.0657	.0640	.1590	.2260	.1124	.1520
+Subj	.0656	.0800	.1582	.2260	.1119	.1530
+PolMeanAll	.0719△ ▲	.0740	.1673△ ▲	.2420	.1196△ ▲	.1580
+PolMeanBestN	.0723	.0960	.1624△ ▲	.2320	.1174▲	.1640
+PolMeanFirstN	.0715△ ▲	.0840	.1624△ ▲	.2300	.1170△ ▲	.1570
+PolMeanLastN	.0715△ ▲	.0760	.1655△ ▲	.2360	.1185△ ▲	.1560
baseline3	.0787	.0940	.1919	.2660	.1353	.1800
+Subj	.0792	.0940	.1927△	.2640	.1360△	.1790
+PolMeanAll	.0842△ ▲	.1000	.1956△ ▲	.2780	.1399△ ▲	.1890
+PolMeanBestN	.0843	.1080	.1933△	.2720	.1388	.1900▲
+PolMeanFirstN	.0837△ ▲	.1020	.1933△	.2720▼	.1385△ ▲	.1870
+PolMeanLastN	.0839△ ▲	.1000	.1948△ ▲	.2740△	.1394△ ▲	.1870
baseline4	.0872	.0780	.2176	.2760	.1524	.1770
+Subj	.0878	.0760	.2171	.2740	.1524	.1750
+PolMeanAll	.0912	.0860	.2235△ ▲	.2780	.1574	.1820
+PolMeanBestN	.0899	.1120△ ▲	.2208△ ▲	.2820	.1554	.1970△ ▲
+PolMeanFirstN	.0896	.0860	.2212△ ▲	.2760	.1554	.1810
+PolMeanLastN	.0915	.0840	.2235△ ▲	.2900▲	.1575	.1870
baseline5	.0931	.0960	.2239	.2860	.1585	.1910
+Subj	.0926	.1120△	.2093▽	.2600	.1510▽	.1860
+PolMeanAll	.0843	.1080	.1922▽▼	.2600	.1382▽▼	.1840
+PolMeanBestN	.0785▼	.1100	.2273▲	.2880	.1529	.1990
+PolMeanFirstN	.0818▽▼	.1080	.2181▲	.2820	.1500▽	.1950
+PolMeanLastN	.0834	.1100	.2032▽▼	.2700	.1433▽▼	.1900

Table 5: Polarity Retrieval Results in TREC 2007.

	Negative MAP	Negative P@10	Positive MAP	Positive P@10	Mix MAP	Mix P@10
baseline1	.1175	.1700	.1364	.1860	.1270	.1780
+Subj	.1148	.1580	.1379	.1760	.1264	.1670
+PolMeanAll	.1223	.1860	.1477	.2300△ ▲	.1350	.2080▲
+PolMeanBestN	.1280	.1920	.1498	.2200▲	.1389	.2060▲
+PolMeanFirstN	.1315	.2100▲	.1489△ ▲	.2360△ ▲	.1402▲	.2230△ ▲
+PolMeanLastN	.1212	.1920	.1453△	.2200▲	.1332	.2060▲
baseline2	.0865	.1420	.0952	.1400	.0908	.1410
+Subj	.0865	.1380	.0934▽	.1360	.0900▽	.1370
+PolMeanAll	.1026△ ▲	.1480	.1000△ ▲	.1440	.1013△ ▲	.1460
+PolMeanBestN	.0981△ ▲	.1700	.1019△ ▲	.1520	.1005△ ▲	.1610▲
+PolMeanFirstN	.1049△ ▲	.1500	.0975△ ▲	.1420	.1012△ ▲	.1460
+PolMeanLastN	.1000△ ▲	.1460	.0980△ ▲	.1400	.0990△ ▲	.1430
baseline3	.1266	.1520	.1376	.1680	.1321	.1600
+Subj	.1275△	.1540	.1378	.1680	.1326△	.1610
+PolMeanAll	.1333△ ▲	.1700△	.1398△ ▲	.1660	.1366△ ▲	.1680
+PolMeanBestN	.1358△	.1900△ ▲	.1410△ ▲	.1760	.1384△ ▲	.1830△ ▲
+PolMeanFirstN	.1325△ ▲	.1640	.1386△ ▲	.1680	.1356△ ▲	.1660
+PolMeanLastN	.1317△ ▲	.1660	.1386△	.1680	.1352△ ▲	.1670
baseline4	.1288	.1600	.1532	.1980	.1410	.1790
+Subj	.1294	.1640	.1529	.1880▽	.1412	.1760
+PolMeanAll	.1388	.1660	.1576	.2060	.1482△ ▲	.1860
+PolMeanBestN	.1333	.1820	.1559	.1940	.1446	.1880
+PolMeanFirstN	.1423△ ▲	.1900△	.1555△ ▲	.1980	.1489△ ▲	.1940▲
+PolMeanLastN	.1380	.1820	.1552	.2020▲	.1466△ ▲	.1920▲
baseline5	.1085	.1680	.1229	.1780	.1157	.1730
+Subj	.1087	.1620	.1232	.1800	.1160	.1710
+PolMeanAll	.0971	.1640	.1301	.1860	.1136	.1750
+PolMeanBestN	.0988	.1760	.1204	.1980	.1096	.1870
+PolMeanFirstN	.1051	.1780	.1270	.1940	.1160	.1860
+PolMeanLastN	.0991	.1740	.1357	.2000	.1174	.1870

Table 6: Polarity Retrieval Results in TREC 2008.

	TREC 2007		TREC 2008	
	Negative	Positive	Negative	Positive
Subj	$\alpha = 0.9$	$\alpha = 0.9$	$\alpha = 0.9$	$\alpha = 0.9$
PolMeanAll	$\beta = 0.6, \gamma = 0.8$	$\beta = 0.4, \gamma = 0.9$	$\beta = 0.6, \gamma = 0.8$	$\beta = 0.3, \gamma = 0.7$
PolMeanBestN	$\beta = 0.5, \gamma = 0.6, n = 1$	$\beta = 0.1, \gamma = 0.8, n = 1$	$\beta = 0.6, \gamma = 0.6, n = 3$	$\beta = 0.2, \gamma = 0.5, n = 1$
PolMeanFirstN	$\beta = 0.6, \gamma = 0.8, n = 6$	$\beta = 0.2, \gamma = 0.9, n = 5$	$\beta = 0.5, \gamma = 0.8, n = 3$	$\beta = 0.2, \gamma = 0.9, n = 9$
PolMeanLastN	$\beta = 0.6, \gamma = 0.8, n = 10$	$\beta = 0.3, \gamma = 0.9, n = 1$	$\beta = 0.5, \gamma = 0.8, n = 3$	$\beta = 0.2, \gamma = 0.8, n = 1$

Table 7: Parameters trained.

that the relevance component is much more important than the subjectivity component. This seems to indicate that the subjectivity approach is extremely sensitive to off-topic material.

Regarding β, we observe different trends in positive and negative polarity rankings. Positive rankings have lower values of β (the value of this parameter is around 0.2 for positive document retrieval and around 0.5 for negative document retrieval). The β parameter controls the trade-off between relevance and polarity at sentence level (see eq. 1). This means that in positive rankings the polarity evidence is more important than content-match evidence. This might be due to a more reliable estimation of polarity for positive sentences (i.e. OF might be more reliable for positive polarity estimation) or it might be due to the presence of more noisy text (off-topic sentiments) in negative documents. This will be subject to further research in our future work.

Another important trend found affects the number of sentences used by *PolMeanFirstN* and *PolMeanLastN* (i.e. the parameter n). In general, *PolMeanFirstN* takes more sentences to estimate polarity than *PolMeanLastN*. This fact seems to indicate that bloggers briefly summarise their views in the last part of the post. In contrast, if we want to have a reliable summary of the overall opinion obtained from the initial part of the post we need to take a longer subset of sentences. From Table 7 it is also interesting to observe that the number of sentences used by *PolMeanBestN* was 1 in most of the cases. This indicates that we can use the highest *pol*-sentence as the best guidance to understand the overall sentiment of a blog. This finding can be also useful, for example, to build polarity-biased snippets in a blog retrieval scenario.

4.2 Number of Polar sentences needed to achieve state-of-the-art performance

The results reported above suggest that the best way to estimate the overall polarity of a post is to take the highest-*pol* sentences as a representation of the sentiments of the author. However, the methods based on sentences taken from specific document locations work often quite well. Figure 1 depicts the evolution of performance of *PolMeanFirstN* and *PolMeanLastN* against the number of polar sentences taken. For each point in the plot, a ▼ indicates a significant decrease in performance over *PolMeanBestN*, while a • indicates a non-significant difference in performance with respect to *PolMeanBestN*. With few polar sentences the performance is not statistically different to the performance achieved by the best method. Interestingly, the number of sentences needed to achieve similar performance with respect to the best method differs between *PolMeanFirstN* and *PolMeanLastN*. With *PolMeanLastN*, the last two polar sentences are enough to have a level of effectiveness that is not statistically different to *PolMeanBestN* (for both MAP and P@10). With *PolMeanFirstN*, the initial four polar sentences seem to be a good choice to estimate polarity (with fewer sentences we obtain statistically significant decreases for some measure in some of the collections).

We have therefore successfully addressed our second research question: the use of location information is valuable in blog post polarity estimation, because the first four or last two polar sentences of a blog are good indicators of the overall sentiment.

4.3 Effectiveness vs Efficiency

In the previous section we have compared the performance of the best blog polarity estimation method (*PolMeanBestN*) against the location-aware methods. The reader might wonder why we should bother with these location-based methods if we can achieve state-of-the-art performance with *PolMeanBestN*. In this respect, we argue that there are important implications in terms of efficiency. *PolMeanBestN*, *PolMeanAllN* and *Subj* need to classify all sentences in the post to compute the polarity score of a document. In contrast, the location-based methods just need to classify a small set of sentences.

In the literature, many authors have expressed their concerns about efficiency when using tools such as OF for opinion-finding [5, 4]. We argue that by reducing the amount of data we can substantially decrease the computational cost associated to polarity estimation. To further explore this issue, we took a random sample of 100 documents from the BLOGS06 text collection that had a mean of 6.5 polar sentences according to OF[8]. For each document we created new files based on the first four or the last two polar sentences (appropriate configurations for the *PolMeanFirstN* and *PolMeanLastN* methods, respectively, as discussed in subsection 4.2). For example, for the first four polar sentences of a document, we built a new file that contains the text of all sentences until the fourth polar sentence is found. Finally, we applied OF on each file and on the original document and recorded the average time needed to process each file (preprocessing, tagging and classification). In Table 9 we report the results of this experiment. The use of location-aware methods to estimate the polarity of a blog has a very positive impact in terms of efficiency. *PolMeanLastN* and *PolMeanFirstN* reduce substantially the computation time

[8]The mean of polar sentences per document in the collection is 6.45. The standard deviation is 27.03. This high deviation is likely because of the presence of smap documents, which tends to be large.

	Negative		Positive		Mix	
	MAP	△ MAP	MAP	△ MAP	MAP	△ MAP
KLE	**.1180**	**3.51%**	**.1370**	**6.08%**	**.1274**	**4.86%**
UoGtr	.1103	-2.76%	.1226	-4.62%	.1165	-3.77%
UWaterlooEng	.0987	-12.33%	.1252	-1.69%	.1119	-6.70%
UIC_IR_Group	.0568	-49.60%	**.1313**	**2.12%**	.0941	-22.10%
UTD_SLP_Lab	.0799	-29.23%	.1068	-17.51%	.0934	-22.96%
fub	.0569	-50.18%	.0521	-59.81%	.0545	-55.26%
tno	.0260	-77.02%	.0312	-75.93%	.0286	-76.42%
UniNE	.0584	-48.49%	.0775	-39.41%	.0680	-43.68%
PolMeanAll	**.1189**	**4.80%**	**.1350**	**4.75%**	**.1269**	**4.92%**
PolMeanBestN	**.1190**	**4.89%**	**.1338**	**3.86%**	**.1264**	**4.37%**
PolMeanFirstN	**.1234**	**9.18%**	**.1335**	**3.45%**	**.1284**	**6.07%**
PolMeanLastN	**.1180**	**4.08%**	**.1346**	**4.39%**	**.1263**	**4.36%**

Table 8: Comparison against TREC systems using all 5 of the standard baselines and TREC 2008 topics. TREC results are reported in the first set of rows (top 8 rows). The performance of the polarity methods proposed in this paper is reported in the second set of rows (bottom 4 rows). Positive improvements with respect to baselines are bolded.

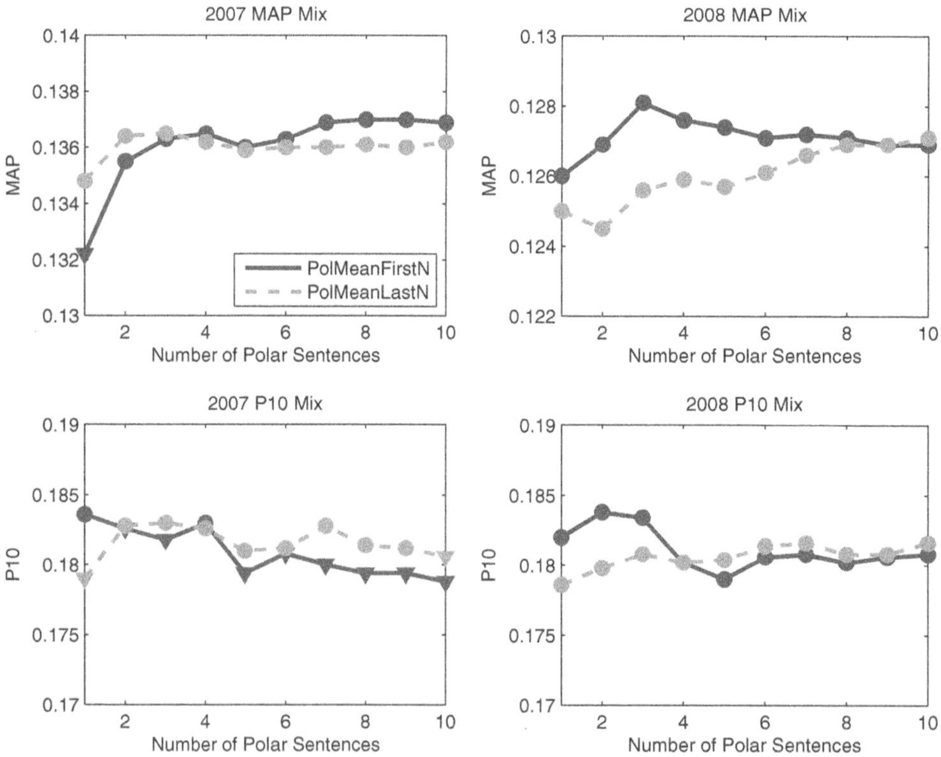

Figure 1: Performance of polarity methods against the number of sentences utilized. A ▼ indicates a significant decrease in performance over the PolMeanBestN method, while a • indicates a non significant difference in performance with respect to the PolMeanBestN method.

	Avg. Time(s)	Δ %
Complete Document	2.6	
Last Two Polar Sentences	1.26	−51.5%
First Four Polar Sentences	1.81	−30.4%

Table 9: Average time taken to classify complete documents vs the time taken to classify narrower subsets containing the first/last polar sentences.

with respect to the full document approach (time required is reduced by 51.5% and 30.4%, respectively).

Observe that this classification, which is required to compute $pol(S)$, can be done offline (at indexing time) but, still, there are also benefits on-line. With *PolMeanBestN* it is necessary to process all sentences at query time (to compute $pol_S(D, Q)$ in eq. 2) while *PolMeanFirstN* and *PolMeanLastN* only need to score a small set of sentences. Observe also that the best TREC polarity system (KLE) also treats the full document to find opinionated terms [7]. We argue that location-aware methods are more convenient because they get to similar levels of effectiveness with little computational effort. Furthermore, our findings are potentially applicable not only to learning approaches such as those based on OF but also to other methods that currently process whole documents.

This study answers our third research question: we can substantially improve the efficiency of the OM processes by focusing on small sets of sentences (initial/last polar sentences), and this reduction in the representation of the post does not affect the effectiveness of the polarity estimations.

5. RELATED WORK

Many opinion detection approaches have been proposed in the literature. Among the most successful studies in this subject are those focused on finding document contents that are both opinionated and on-topic [19, 3]. To meet this aim, some papers consider term positional information to find opinionated information related to the query. Santos et al. [19] applied a novel OM approach that takes into account the proximity of query terms to subjective sentences in a document. Gerani et al. [3] proposed a proximity-based opinion propagation method to calculate the opinion density at the position of each query term in a document. These two studies led to improvements over state of the art baselines for blog opinion retrieval. Although we focus on polarity estimation (rather than opinion finding), we also need to filter out off-topic material. In this respect, we worked here with simple sentence retrieval methods and showed that they are consistent to estimate which polar sentences are on-topic.

Pang and Lee [13] considered the impact of the location of the opinionated sentences on the accuracy of two state-of-the art polarity classifiers of film reviews. They built polarity classifiers based on sentences from different parts of a document (e.g. first sentences, last sentences), however these classifiers were not able to overcome local-unigram state-of-the-art systems. Nevertheless, the results obtained showed that the last sentences of a document might be a good indicator of the overall polarity of the review.

Pang et al. [15] considered the impact of term positions in polarity classifiers and argued that the position of a word in the text might make a difference (e.g. movie reviews normally conclude by summarising the author's overall view). Each word was tagged according to whether it appeared in the first quarter, last quarter, or middle half of the document and this information was incorporated in a state-of-the-art unigram classifier. The results did not differ greatly from those obtained using unigrams alone, but the authors argue that the study of more refined notions of positions could be useful in polarity retrieval scenarios.

Beineke et al. [1] proposed several sentiment summarisation approaches based on the analysis of data from a popular film reviews website[9]. This study revealed that the first and the last sentences of the reviews are more important for summarising opinions. To show the importance of the sentence locations, an automatic classifier was built based on two kind of sentence-location features: location within paragraph (i.e. opening, ending, interior or complete paragraph) and location within document (as the fraction of the document that has been completed until the sentence appears). These features were utilized in film reviews to predict whether a particular span of text should be chosen as a summary sentence. The authors found that the use of location-based features alone were insufficient to create proper summaries, being the best results achieved by a classifier that incorporated both term frequencies in the sentences and positional information of the sentences.

In [10], Mao and Lebanon predict the global sentiment of a document by analyzing the sentiment flow at sentence-level. The results indicate that the classification performance is better than a bag of words approach.

In our paper we revisited these issues and studied whether this location information is also a good guidance in blogs (where, typically, we have much more noise than in movie reviews). The techniques proposed here are more sophisticated than the methods applied in film or product reviews, which simply take into account the first or the last part of a document. We analyzed here the first/last sentences *that are subjective with respect to the query*. This allowed us to successfully incorporate location-based information into a large-scale multi-topic scenario, such as the blogosphere. Furthermore, we conducted experiments to understand the implications of location-aware methods in efficiency.

6. CONCLUSIONS AND FUTURE WORK

In this paper we have investigated the impact of sentence-level information in a challenging problem: polarity estimation in blogs. In particular, we have deeply studied different ways to aggregate sentence-level evidence into a document polarity measure. We have also assessed the impact of sentence locations in polarity estimation and evaluated the performance of these techniques in terms of effectiveness and efficiency.

From the results obtained, we found that location-aware polarity methods yield state-of-the-art performance, which is robust across different topic-relevance baselines. We were also able to detect some patterns related to the way in which people write in blogs. More specifically, the overall polarity of posts relies on a few specific sentences (taken from the beginning, from the end, or from the set of high polarity sentences related to the query). This result could be also valuable for creating polarity-biased snippets. We have also

[9] `www.rottentomatoes.com`

demonstrated that we can improve efficiency with no impact on effectiveness.

Most of the methods proposed in this paper are based on simple combinations of polarity and topicality. We are aware that there might be better and more formal ways to approach this combination of evidence (e.g. subjectivity and relevance might be combined using formal methods to learn query-independent weights [2]). This will be explored in the near future. Another problem relates to the number of free parameters to train. Although the optimal parameter values seem to be stable across collections, we plan to study alternative ways to introduce location information in our models. Related to this, we are also interested in studying more refined ways of representation of the sentiment flow of the documents. We also expect to explore the benefits of the use of sentence location for creating opinion-biased summaries.

Acknowledgments

The authors thank the financial support given by Ministerio de Ciencia e Innovación through research project ref. TIN2010-18552-C03-03. We would also like to thank David Elsweiler, Álvaro Barreiro and Leif Azzopardi for their useful comments and suggestions.

7. REFERENCES

[1] P. Beineke, T. Hastie, C. Manning, and S. Vaithyanathan. Exploring sentiment summarization. In *Proceedings of the AAAI Spring Symposium on Exploring Attitude and Affect in Text Theories and Applications*, pages 12–15, 2004.

[2] N. Craswell, S. E. Robertson, H. Zaragoza, and M. J. Taylor. Relevance weighting for query independent evidence. In *SIGIR*, pages 416–423, 2005.

[3] S. Gerani, M. J. Carman, and F. Crestani. Proximity-based opinion retrieval. In *Proc. 33rd Annual International ACM SIGIR Conference*, pages 403–410, 2010.

[4] B. He, C. Macdonald, J. He, and I. Ounis. An effective statistical approach to blog post opinion retrieval. In *CIKM*, pages 1063–1072, 2008.

[5] B. He, C. Macdonald, and I. Ounis. Ranking opinionated blog posts using opinionfinder. In *SIGIR*, pages 727–728, 2008.

[6] M. Jericho. Jericho HTML parser. `http://jericho.htmlparser.net/docs/index.html`, 2009.

[7] Y. Lee, S.-H. Na, J. Kim, S.-H. Nam, H.-Y. Jung, and J.-H. Lee. KLE at TREC 2008 blog track: Blog post and feed retrieval. In *Proc. TREC 2008, the 17th Text Retrieval Conference*, Gaithersburg, United States, 2008.

[8] C. Macdonald and I. Ounis. The TREC Blogs 2006 collection: Creating and analysing a blog test collection. Technical Report TR-2006-224, Department of Computing Science, University of Glasgow, 2006.

[9] C. Macdonald, I. Ounis, and I. Soboroff. Overview of the TREC 2007 blog track. In *Proc. TREC 2007, the 16th Text Retrieval Conference*, Gaithersburg, United States, 2007.

[10] Y. Mao and G. Lebanon. Sequential models for sentiment prediction. In *ICML Workshop on Learning in Structured Output Spaces*, 2006.

[11] I. Ounis, C. Macdonald, M. de Rijke, G. Mishne, and I. Soboroff. Overview of the TREC 2006 blog track. In *Proc. TREC 2006, the 15th Text Retrieval Conference*, 2006.

[12] I. Ounis, C. Macdonald, and I. Soboroff. Overview of the TREC 2008 blog track. In *Proc. TREC 2008, the 17th Text Retrieval Conference*, Gaithersburg, United States, 2008.

[13] B. Pang and L. Lee. A sentimental education: Sentiment analysis using subjectivity summarization based on minimum cuts. In *Pr. of the Association for Computational Linguistics*, pages 271–278, 2004.

[14] B. Pang and L. Lee. Opinion mining and sentiment analysis. *Foundations and Trends in Information Retrieval*, 2(1-2):1–135, 2007.

[15] B. Pang, L. Lee, and S. Vaithyanathan. Thumbs up? sentiment classification using machine learning techniques. In *Pr. of the Conference on Empirical Methods in Natural Language Processing*, 2002.

[16] J. Parapar and A. Barreiro. An effective and efficient web news extraction technique for an operational newsir system. In *XIII Conferencia de la Asociación Española para la Inteligencia Artificial CAEPIA - TTIA 2007*, pages 319–328, Salamanca, Spain, November 2007. Actas Vol II.

[17] E. Riloff and J. Wiebe. Learning extraction patterns for subjective expressions. In *Proc. of Conference of Empirical Methods in Natural Language Processing*, pages Pages 105–112, 2003.

[18] S. Robertson. How okapi came to TREC. *E.M. Voorhees and D.K. Harman (eds.), TREC: Experiments and Evaluation in Information Retrieval*, pages 287–299, 2005.

[19] R. L. T. Santos, B. He, C. Macdonald, and I. Ounis. Integrating proximity to subjective sentences for blog opinion retrieval. In *Proc. 31st European Conference on Information Retrieval , ECIR 2009*, pages 325–336, 2009.

[20] The Lemur Project. `http://www.lemurproject.org/`, 2009.

[21] J. Wiebe and E. Riloff. Creating subjective and objective sentence classifiers from unannotated texts. In *Proc. of 6th International Conference on Intelligent Text Processing and Computational Linguistics*, 2005.

[22] T. Wilson, P. Hoffmann, S. Somasundaran, J. Kessler, J. Wiebe, Y. Choi, C. Cardie, E. Riloff, and S. Patwardhan. Opinionfinder: A system for subjectivity analysis. In *HLT/EMNLP*, 2005.

[23] T. Wilson, J. Wiebe, and P. Hoffmann. Recognizing contextual polarity in phrase-level sentiment analysis. In *Proc.of Human Language Technologies Conference/Conference on Empirical Methods in Natural Language Processing (HLT/EMNLP 2005)*, 2005.

Sentiment Classification Based on Supervised Latent n-gram Analysis

Dmitriy Bespalov
NEC Labs America
CS Dept, Drexel University
db59@drexel.edu

Bing Bai
NEC Labs America
Princeton, NJ, USA
bbai@nec-labs.com

Yanjun Qi
NEC Labs America
Princeton, NJ, USA
yanjun@nec-labs.com

Ali Shokoufandeh
Computer Science Dept.
Drexel University
Philadelphia, PA, USA
as79@drexel.edu

ABSTRACT

In this paper, we propose an efficient embedding for modeling higher-order (n-gram) phrases that projects the n-grams to low-dimensional latent semantic space, where a classification function can be defined. We utilize a deep neural network to build a unified discriminative framework that allows for estimating the parameters of the latent space as well as the classification function with a bias for the target classification task at hand. We apply the framework to large-scale sentimental classification task. We present comparative evaluation of the proposed method on two (large) benchmark data sets for online product reviews. The proposed method achieves superior performance in comparison to the state of the art.

Categories and Subject Descriptors

H.3.3 [**Information Storage and Retrieval**]: Information Search and Retrieval—*Information filtering*; I.2.7 [**Artificial Intelligence**]: Natural Language Processing—*Text analysis*

General Terms

Algorithms, Experimentation

Keywords

sentiment analysis, supervised embedding, deep learning

1. INTRODUCTION

Sentiment analysis (SA) or polarity mining refers to identifying and extracting subjective information from natural language text. The problem of automatic sentiment analysis has received significant attention in recent years, largely due to the explosion of online social-oriented content (e.g., user reviews, blogs, etc). As one of its main applications, sentiment classification targets to rate the polarity of a given text accurately towards a label or a score, predicting whether the expressed opinion in the text is positive, negative, or neutral.

In this paper, we will explore the use of high order n-grams for classifying the sentiment orientation of a given text at article level. The motivation is that longer phrases tend to be less ambiguous in terms of their polarity. The authors in [10] pointed out that a discriminating classifier combined with high order n-grams as features can achieve comparable, or better SA performance than state of the art on large-scale data sets. Indeed, e.g., while term "good" is likely a positive sentiment, "not good" or "not very good" are less likely to appear in positive comments. Needless to say, models such as bag-of-unigrams or bag-of-bigrams will possibly fail to deal with "not good" and "not very good", respectively. The other facet of SA is the degree of positivity or negativity of long phrases. As one such example, consider the compounding effect of the phrase "... terrible terrible terrible ..." in contrast to three dispersed "terrible" in a text. The use of n-gram features can provide a remedy for such scenarios [10]. Unfortunately, this comes at a very high computational cost associated with modeling n-grams for $n \geq 3$. This is due to the extremely large parameter space associated to n-grams. For instance, assuming English word dictionary $\mathcal{D}$ of size $|\mathcal{D}|$, then bigram representation of text relates to $|\mathcal{D}|^2$ free parameters, while trigram relates to $|\mathcal{D}|^3$ free parameters. This will become intimidating even for a dictionary of moderate size. When the number of training samples is limited, it can easily lead to overfitting. If unigram dictionary has the size $|\mathcal{D}| = 10,000$, we have $|\mathcal{D}|^2 = 10^8$ free parameters or $|\mathcal{D}|^3 = 10^{12}$ that need to be estimated, which is far too many for a small corpora. As more and more web-scale sentimental data sets become available, large corpora with sentimental labels could easily be accessible for researchers. The availability of large datasets also encourages us to explore n-grams. To the best of our knowledge, there are only a few experimental evaluations involving large-scale data sets [12, 8].

This paper partly motivated our idea and we believe that potentially, using higher order n-grams is beneficial in capturing sentiments in the text. For example, term *good* commonly appears in positive reviews, but "not good" or "not very good" are less likely to happen in positive comments. If using bag-of-unigram, "not" is separated from "good", which does not have the ability to describe the "not good" combination. Similarly using just bag-of-bigrams,

CIKM'11, October 24–28, 2011, Glasgow, Scotland, UK.

the model can not represent the short pattern "not very good" either. Another example is: if a product review uses the phrase "Terrible Terrible Terrible", it contains more negative opinion than three "Terrible" separately occur in the text. Building n-gram features is a method to remedy this issue [10], but it is computationally very difficult to model n-grams (for $n >= 3$) raw features directly.

We utilize a multi-level embedding strategy to project n-grams into a low-dimensional latent semantic space where the projection parameters are trained in a supervised fashion together with the sentiment classification task.

In this paper, we present a novel approach for using high-order n-grams for sentimental classification problem. We will also devise a new embedding mechanism of n-grams, called "latent n-grams", that will enable us to deal with the curse of dimensionality. Next, the proposed embedding of n-grams to low-dimensional latent semantic space will be tied to a classifier, trained for sentiment analysis tasks. Using a deep neural network allows one to learn the parameters for the latent space and the classifier jointly in one unified discriminative framework. It is worth noting that performing dimensionality reduction in the original feature space is a common practice for various classification methods. However, as we discuss in Section 3, methods that bias parameters of the embedding towards specific classification task has not received much attention until recently. The proposed multi-layer embedding and classification model provides two major advantages. First, the latent model greatly reduces the dimensionality and computational efficiency in comparison to raw n-gram features. Moreover, the parameters of latent space are learned using supervised signals arising from the sentiment classification. Two clear advantages to use the proposed method involves that (1), the system utilizes an embedding space to greatly reduce the dimensionality of n-gram, and is thus much easier to model than n-grams raw features. (2), The n-gram embeddings are learned using supervised signals with the main sentiment classification task which means they are optimized for the task and require little human labors in feature engineering.

We evaluate the performance of the proposed method along with several state of art baselines using two typical tasks relevant for SA: (1) binary classification, predicting binary (positive or negative) sentiment of the text; and (2) multi-score sentiment classification, predicting a range of scores on Likert-scale (e.g. 1-5 stars) that reflect both polarity and strength of the sentiment in the text. The presented empirical evidence demonstrate the superior performance of the proposed system on two major publically available benchmark datasets: Amazon[1] and TripAdvisor[2].

The rest of this paper is organized as follows. Section 2 describe our method in details. Section 3 provides an overview of related work. In Section 4 we present the experimental results, and conclude the paper in Section 5.

2. METHOD

Sentiment classification can be stated as the general task of classifying an input text-sequence into certain types or as rating the input text with a certain score. Feature extraction and feature-based representation are critical to the effectiveness of sequence analysis, since text sequences cannot be readily described as feature vectors. Traditional text categorization methods use feature vectors indexed by all possible words (e.g., the so-called "bag-of-words") of a given dictionary to represent text documents. The bag-of-words strategy treats articles as an unordered set of features (words), for which the critical word ordering information is not preserved.

[1] http://times.cs.uiuc.edu/~wang296/Data/TripAdvisor.tar.gz

[2] http://www.cs.jhu.edu/~mdredze/datasets/sentiment/unprocessed.tar.gz

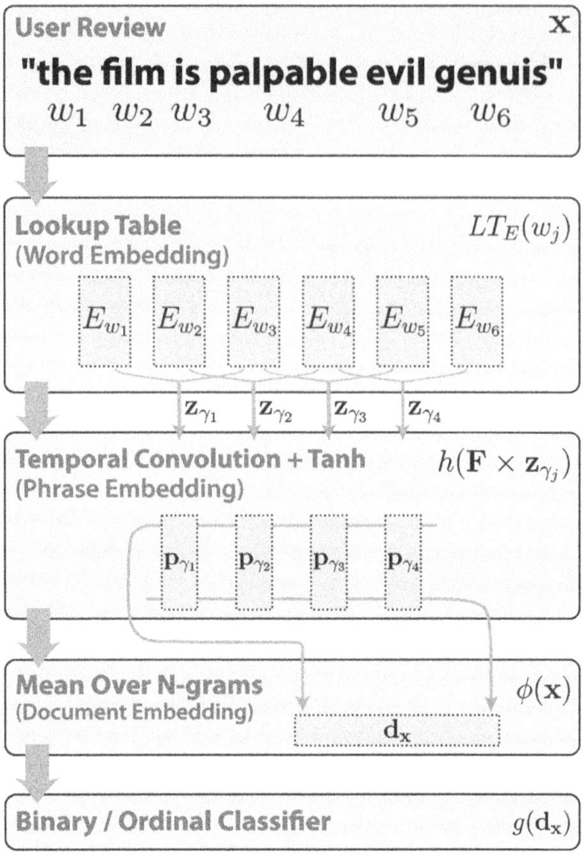

Figure 1: The overall structure of the proposed system.

To take word ordering into account, text articles can be considered as bags of short sequences of words with feature vectors corresponding to all possible word n-grams (n adjacent words from vocabulary $\mathcal{D}$). In the sequel, we will refer to this as "bag-of-ngram" (BON). [20, 10] showed that introducing 2-grams into the bag representation significantly improves the performance of sentiment classification. However, adding higher order n-grams, for $n \geq 3$, into BON model can be prohibitively expensive, since the dimensionality of a BON vector grows exponentially as a function of n.

There are two possible approaches to remedy the curse of dimensionality associated with n-gram representation. First is the feature selection approach. To this ends, pre-selected n-gram patterns or short phrases (e.g. with certain semantic meaning) will be utilized for modeling the sequences. Another possible approach is the use of the dimensionality reduction to approximate the original space – e.g., latent semantic indexing (LSI), an embedding based on term-document matrix.

In this paper, we will use a supervised embedding strategy. We represent a document using its n-gram embedding, which in turn is built upon its word embedding. The step utilizes the supervised signal and acts as feature learning for sentiment classification. Next, the document representation is fed into a perceptron classifier to learn a function mapping toward sentiment labels. The embedding feature learning and the sentiment classification are trained jointly in an end-to-end fashion, which can be illustrated using a multi-layer perceptron (MLP) network structure, as illustrated in Figure 1.

2.1 Embedding of n-Grams

Formally, the basic bag-of-word representation for text applies a mapping $\phi(\cdot)$ to strings of variable length into a feature space of fixed dimension. It is in this space that a standard classifier such as linear perceptron or support vector machine can be applied. Let $\mathcal{D}$ denote the underlying dictionary and $\mathcal{S}$ denote the set of all finite length sequences of words from $\mathcal{D}$. We use $|.|$ to denote the cardinality of a set. We will also assume the aforementioned mapping $\phi : \mathcal{S} \rightarrow \mathbf{R}^M$ maps words sequences in $\mathcal{S}$ to finite dimension feature space. The sentiment labels will form a set $\mathcal{Y} = \{1, ..., K\}$, e.g., $K = 2$ denotes sentiment classes such as "positive" or "negative". We will also denote a labeled training-set with training labels from $\mathcal{Y}$ as $\{\{(\mathbf{x}_i, y_i)\}_{i=1,...,L} | x_i \in \mathcal{S}, y_i \in \mathcal{Y}\}$. An input text sequence of length N will be denoted as $\mathbf{x} = (w_1, \ldots, w_N)$, where $w_j \in \mathcal{D}$. Let Γ denote the vocabulary of n-grams in the corpus, and $\gamma_j = (w_j, w_{j+1}, \ldots, w_{j+n-1})$, where j indicates the j-th position in $\mathbf{x}$. Given the bag-of-unigram representation, $\phi(\mathbf{x})$ maps the input $\mathbf{x}$ in a natural way as a (sparse) vector of dimensionality $M = |\mathcal{D}|$. Similarly, In a bags-of-ngrams $\phi(\mathbf{x})$ maps $\mathbf{x}$ to a $M = |\Gamma|$-dimensional representation, with $|\Gamma| = O(|\mathcal{D}|^n)$.

Motivated by the fact that individual words carry significant semantic information, we learn a mapping of each word into a real-valued vector space, referred to as an "embedding". Specifically, each word $w_j \in \mathcal{D}$ is embedded into an m-dimensional feature space using a *lookup table* $LT_E(\cdot)$ defined as

$$\begin{aligned} LT_E(w_j) &= E \times (0, \ldots, 0, \underset{\text{at index } w_j}{1}, \ldots, 0)^\top \\ &= E_{w_j} = [E_{1,w_j}, E_{2,w_j}, \ldots, E_{m,w_j}]^\top \end{aligned}$$

where $E \in \mathbf{R}^{m \times |\mathcal{D}|}$ is a matrix with word embedding parameters to be learn. Here, $E_{w_j} \in \mathbf{R}^m$ is the embedding of the word w_j in the dictionary $\mathcal{D}$ and m denotes the target word embedding dimensionality. It is important to note that the parameters of E are automatically *trained* during the learning process using backpropagation.

In our framework, formation of n-grams will be carried through a sliding window of length n. As illustrated in Figure 1, setting $n = 3$, the first n-gram is (w_1, w_2, w_3), second n-gram will be (w_2, w_3, w_4), etc. Given an n-gram of adjacent words, we represent its embedding based on the embedding of individual words it contains. Specifically, given $\gamma_j = (w_j, w_{j+1}, \ldots, w_{j+n-1})$, define $\mathbf{z}_{\gamma_j} = [E_{w_j}^\top, E_{w_{j+1}}^\top, \ldots, E_{w_{j+n-1}}^\top]^\top$ as an operator concatenating embeddings of words in the n-gram γ_j, resulting in an nm-dimensional vector $\mathbf{z}_{\gamma_j}$. The embedding of the γ_j can then be defined as

$$\mathbf{p}_{\gamma_j} = h(\mathbf{F} \times \mathbf{z}_{\gamma_j}),$$

where projection matrix $\mathbf{F} \in \mathbb{R}^{M \times nm}$ maps the vector $\mathbf{z}_{\gamma_j}$ into a M-dimensional latent space, and $h(\cdot) = \tanh(\cdot)$[3].

Finally, we use the n-gram embeddings to form a vector representation for each input text document. Formally, the document representation will be defined as

$$\phi(\mathbf{x}) \equiv \mathbf{d}_\mathbf{x} = \frac{1}{N} \sum_{j=1}^{N} \mathbf{p}_{\gamma_j} \tag{1}$$

where $\mathbf{d}_\mathbf{x} \in \mathbb{R}^M$ and $\mathbf{x} = (w_1, \ldots, w_N)$. In other words, $\mathbf{d}_\mathbf{x}$ is the centroid of the vector associated with n-grams of the document $\mathbf{x}$. Intuitively, the sentiment of a document is related to the aggregated polarity of all its n-grams; that is, the more positive n-grams that exist in the document, it is more likely for it to express a positive opinion. While there are many possibilities for aggregation function, mean value provides a good summarization of the document's sentiment in this latent space. As suggested by [9], one can also use the $\mathbf{max}$ function that selects the maximum value along each latent dimension. Our empirical evidence indicate that the $\mathbf{mean}$ function is a more appropriate choice for the SA task.

Another fundamental reason for this formulation is that the number of phrases in the sentence is variable depending on the sentence length n. Thus, we need a function to compress the information from these phrases into a fixed length document embedding vector.

2.2 Sentiment Classification

We will consider two types of sentiment classification in this paper. First, similar to most prior approaches, we will consider binary classification setting that classifies a document either as a positive or negative. Next, we try to predict the text polarity toward its star-scale score directly using ordinal regression. It is our believe that this setting will become more prominent in the future since most of the online evaluation system are utilizing Likert-scale (e.g. 1-5 stars).

Given the document representation $\mathbf{d}_\mathbf{x}$ defined as above, the binary sentiment classification learns a function by optimizing the following loss measure:

$$\mathcal{L} = \sum_{\mathbf{x} \in S} (\text{sgn}(g(\mathbf{d}_\mathbf{x})) - y_\mathbf{x}), \tag{2}$$

where $\text{sgn}(g(\cdot)) \in \{1, -1\}$ are the prediction obtained from the classifier, and $y_\mathbf{x} \in \{1, -1\}$ is the label of the document $\mathbf{x}$. We chose a linear function for g, where

$$g(\mathbf{d}_\mathbf{x}) = \mathbf{a} \cdot \mathbf{d}_\mathbf{x} + b,$$

Linear classifiers have proven record of achieving the state of the art performance in previous sentiment classification results [19].

The Likert-scale classification problem belongs to the more general class known as "Ordinal Classification" [1], where the class labels have orderings. Utilizing this ordinal information in the classification will achieve better performance than treating each class separately without the order. There exist different methods to tackle ordinal classification or regression. Here, we present a simple marginal ordinal loss based strategy. We aim to learn a function g that optimizes the following loss:

$$\begin{aligned} \mathcal{L} = \sum_{\mathbf{x} \in S} \{ \quad & \textstyle\sum_{1 \le l \le y_\mathbf{x}} \max(0, 1 - g(\mathbf{d}_\mathbf{x}) + \beta_l) \\ + \quad & \textstyle\sum_{y_\mathbf{x} < l \le L} \max(0, 1 - \beta_l + g(\mathbf{d}_\mathbf{x}))\}. \end{aligned} \tag{3}$$

In this case, we are handling a L-likert-scale system. We have a set of boundaries β_l for each class $l \in [1, L]$. These boundaries are in ascending order, i.e $\beta_i < \beta_j, \forall i < j$. The function $g(\cdot)$ outputs a score for a document vector $\mathbf{d}_\mathbf{x}$. The discriminative training estimates the parameters of function $g(\cdot)$ and class boundaries $\beta_i, i \in [1, L]$ by minimizing the loss function $\mathcal{L}$.[4] The final classifier $g(\mathbf{d}_\mathbf{x})$ is defined as:

$$\underset{l \in [1,L]}{\arg\min} (\beta_{l-1} < g(\mathbf{d}_\mathbf{x}) < \beta_l).$$

The ordinal classification can be related to Rank Loss used in information retrieval society. Given a set of objects $x_i \in X, i \in$

[3]the non-linear function $\tanh(\cdot)$ converts unbounded range of the input into $[-1, 1]$

[4]For simplicity, we define $\beta_0 = -\infty$, for the first class that does not need a lower boundary for $g(\cdot)$

$[1, |\mathcal{S}|]$, their corresponding labels $y_i \in Y, i \in [1, |\mathcal{S}|]$, and a scoring function, the rank loss can be defined as:

$$\mathcal{L} = \sum_{i,j \text{ s.t. } y_i > y_j} \max(0, 1 - g(\mathbf{d}_{\mathbf{x}_i}) + g(\mathbf{d}_{\mathbf{x}_j})).$$

The objective is to learn function $g(\cdot)$ while minimizing the loss function $\mathcal{L}(\cdot)$. Clearly the score $g(\cdot)$ will try to put the objects in the order just like their labels. This order is consistent with the ordinal classification objective.

2.3 Embedding and Sentiment Classification within a Unified Model

We use the multi-layer perceptron network to implement the above modules in a unified framework. As illustrated in Table 1, the overall system can be represented in a 6-layer network architecture ($T = 6$):

level	layer	params
f_1	lookup table (word embedding)	$\mathbf{E}$
f_2	temporal convolution (n-gram embedding)	$\mathbf{F}$
f_3	transfer layer tanh (n-gram embedding)	-
f_4	mean function (document representation)	-
f_5	binary/ordinal classifier	$\mathbf{a}, b, \boldsymbol{\beta}$
f_6	loss function	-

Table 1: Parameters learned at each level.

We take advantages of the simple and efficient backpropagation process to train this layered network. The stacked layers in our network can be written in a more general form of multi-level functions:

$$l_{\mathbf{x}} = \mathbf{f}_T(\mathbf{f}_{T-1}(...(\mathbf{f}_1(\mathbf{x}))...)),$$

where $l_{\mathbf{x}}$ denotes the loss on a single example $\mathbf{x}$, and the exact loss function f_T is defined in Equation 2 and Equation 3. For a layer $\mathbf{f}_i, i \in [1, T]$, the derivative for updating its parameter set $\boldsymbol{\theta}_i$ is using the delta rule:

$$\frac{\partial l}{\partial \boldsymbol{\theta}_i} = \frac{\partial \mathbf{f}_T}{\partial \mathbf{f}_i} \times \frac{\partial \mathbf{f}_i}{\partial \boldsymbol{\theta}_i},$$

and the first factor on the right can be recursively calculated:

$$\frac{\partial \mathbf{f}_T}{\partial \mathbf{f}_i} = \frac{\partial \mathbf{f}_T}{\partial \mathbf{f}_{i+1}} \times \frac{\partial \mathbf{f}_{i+1}}{\partial \mathbf{f}_i}.$$

Note that $\mathbf{f}$ and θ are usually vectors (the scalar loss $l = \mathbf{f}_T$ can be treated as an all 1's vector), so $\frac{\partial \mathbf{f}_T}{\partial \mathbf{f}_{i+1}}$ and $\frac{\partial \mathbf{f}_i}{\partial \boldsymbol{\theta}_i}$ are Jacobian matrices, and "$\times$" is matrix multiplication.

We can use stochastic gradient descent (SGD) method to to perform training of parameters [7]. For a set of training samples, instead of calculating true gradient of the objective on all training samples, SGD calculates gradient and updates accordingly on each training sample. SGD is proved to be scalable and more efficient than batch-mode gradient descent methods, especially when dealing with large-scale datasets. The training procedure is presented in Algorithm 2.3. The 3rd column in Table 1 specify the parameters that will be learned during this end-to-end learning process in each layer.

Algorithm 1 End-to-End Training procedure for the proposed system

```
for j = 1 to MaxIter do
  if converge then
    break
  end if
  x, y ← random sampled data point and label
  calculate loss l(x; y)
  cumulative ← 1
  for i = 6 to 1 do
    ∂l/∂θ_i ← cumulative * ∂f_i/∂θ_i
    θ_i ← θ_i − λ ∂l/∂θ_i
    cumulative ← cumulative * ∂f_{i+1}/∂f_i
  end for
end for
```

We also want to point out that when using "deep learning" network, unsupervised pre-training of lower-layers is a common practice [3] and shows to improve the results. We adopt a similar strategy and use the projection matrix learned via LSI (using the term-doc matrix on a large unlabeled text set) to initialize the word embedding - E matrix, i.e. unsupervised pre-training, in our experiment.

3. RELATED WORK

Our proposed framework is closely related to the following areas and research topics.

3.1 Sentiment Analysis

An in-depth survey of the earlier methods for sentiment analysis has been presented in [20]. We will primarily focus on related works on polarity classification with similar objective tasks. The main approaches classify the polarity of a given text at either the word, sentence or paragraph, or document levels. In the most intuitive model, the polarity of an article can be related to the sentiment orientation of its words [13]. Latent semantic analysis has been used in [23] to to calculate the semantic orientation of the extracted words according to their co-occurrences with the seed words, such as "excellent" and "poor". The polarity of the article is then determined through averaging the sentimental orientation of its corresponding words. Instead of limiting the sentiment analysis at the word level, the mainstream research community performs sentiment classification at the article level. Various methods based on this principle have been proposed. These methods can be contrasted in terms of features they use: utilizing either unigram features [20] and/or filtered bigrams [6]. It is claimed that unigram and bigram features beat other features in the evaluation of several small-scale benchmark data sets [10]. It should also be noted that [19] investigated the use of several inverse document frequency (IDF) weighting schemes as features. They observed that such features improve the accuracy of sentiment classification. The third noteworthy trend is based on capturing existing substructures and their ordering in the text. In a recent paper, [22] used an HMM-based model to describe the dependency between local substructures to improve sentiment prediction. Similarly, [8] proposed a learning method for local content modeling (aspect-sentiment sense) using large-scale unsupervised data sets.

3.2 Latent Topic/Concept Models

There exists a number of word-level embedding methods that are able to capture semantic similarity between word pairs. One of the earliest but widely used approaches is Latent Semantic Indexing (LSI) [11]. LSI applies SVD to term-document co-occurrence matrix, producing a low-dimensional representation for both documents (including unseen ones) and words, and enables efficient computation of semantic similarity between them. LSI is considered the pioneering work that inspired methods such as probabilistic LSI (pLSI) [14] and Latent Dirichlet Allocation (LDA) using a generative probabilistic framework [5].

There are also supervised variants that try to compute embedding by fitting to the labeled data. Such approaches have been applied to a variety of information retrieval tasks such as link prediction, cross-lingual retrieval, and image annotations [2, 25]. Another variant of supervised embedding method was recently introduced by [21] that learns (128 bit) hash-coding for term-frequency vectors of documents in the corpus, enabling semantic similarity-based hashing.

3.3 String Classification Using String Kernel

Broadly speaking, the proposed method is applicable to the general string classification problem. A variety of methods have been proposed to tackle the string classification problem, including generative (e.g., HMMs) or discriminative approaches, such as string kernel-based machine learning methods [15, 26]. The key idea of basic string kernels is to map text strings of variable length into a vectorial feature space of fixed length. In this space a standard classifier such as a support vector machine (SVM) can then be applied. As SVMs require only inner products between examples in the feature space, rather than the feature vectors themselves, one can define a *string kernel* which *implicitly* computes an inner product in the feature space. String kernels are designed so that the high similarity value between two text documents indicates that they have numerous n-grams in common.

We note that our proposed method implements a variation of inexact matching between n-grams which is also a critical component in the string kernel research, usually tackled by using different families of mismatch in the string kernel [16].

3.4 Deep Learning for Natural Language Processing

Lately, "deep learning" research grows to bring in attentions. As pointed out by [3], recent results have suggested that in order to learn the kind of complicated functions that can represent high-level abstractions (e.g. in natural language, or vision), one would need deep architectures. Each layer in the architecture represents features at a different level of abstraction, defined as a composition of lower-level features. Statistical language modeling is a key topic in natural language processing (NLP), where the difficulty is the curse of dimensionality, especially when modeling joint distribution between many discrete random variables. [4, 18] proposed a language model based on the multi-layered neural networks, which tries to model a distributed representation for each word and the probability function for word sequences, simultaneously. Later, [9] utilized a single multi-layered convolutional neural network architecture to handle multiple classic NLP tasks at the same time. The proposed unified framework provides an end-to-end system that, given a sentence, outputs a host of language processing predictions.

Our proposed method is motivated by the above approach and uses a multi-layer "deep" neural network to combine the n-gram embedding and sentiment classification in a single framework. It is our belief that the word embedding and n-gram embedding are feature learning in some sense.

4. EXPERIMENTS

4.1 Datasets

We have evaluated the performance of the proposed method on two sentiment dataset, Amazon and TripAdvisor that were introduced by [6] and [24], respectively. The Amazon dataset contains customer reviews of 25 various categories including apparel, automotive, baby, DVDs, electronics, magazines, tools and hardware, etc. The TripAdvisor data set contains customer reviews for various hotels across the globe. In addition to the overall reviewer's sentiment rating, this corpus contains scores for various aspects such as rooms, location, cleanliness, etc. However, sentiment scores for the specific aspects are absent from a significant number of the reviews in the TripAdvisor data set, so In our experiments we only consider overall ratings for this data set. These are considered some of the largest SA data sets currently available. We note that, our approach requires training for a large number of parameters in comparison to a simple shallow BOW model. Consequently, the advantage of our model becomes more obvious on larger datasets (we will show the effect in section 4.3.3).

Both datasets contain user-generated reviews where an overall sentiment for each review is quantified with an integer 1 through 5 (a.k.a the 5 stars scale). A sentiment score of 1 star corresponds to the lowest (negative) sentiment, while the score of 5 stars corresponds to the highest (positive) sentiment. For each dataset, we create a *balanced* version of the data that contains equal number of positive (4 and 5 stars) and negative (1 and 2 stars) reviews. TripAdvisor data also contains neutral reviews (3 stars) that do not exceed the number of positive nor negative reviews, so we add the neutral reviews to the balanced version of the data as well. In addition, we drop very small number of reviews from TripAdvisor with overall sentiment scores of zero stars, since the meaning of this sentiment rating is ambiguous. Statistics of both datasets can be found in Table 2.

We split balanced datasets with 70%/30% ratio into training and testing sets, respectively. We sample positive, negative, and (optionally) neutral reviews separately. This results in equal number of positive and negative reviews in both training and testing sets. Furthermore, in the case of Amazon dataset, each of the 25 categories is handled separately, resulting in balanced version of the data and splitting it into training/testing sets. This is done to obtain equally split sets in terms of polarity for each category, as the number of reviews varies significantly across the categories (e.g., from couple of hundreds to tens of thousands). Finally, once training and testing sets are constructed, we sample the training sets to obtain subsets required for validation. We use 20,000 and 3,000 reviews for validation from the Amazon and TripAdvisor datasets, respectively. The datasets used in our experiments are made available online. [5]

4.2 Evaluation Methodology

We have evaluated the performance of sentiment prediction using binary and ordinal classifications described in Section 2. We also present comparative results between our method and linear classifiers on bag-of-word features (1-gram and 2-gram). The latter approaches are considered to achieve the state of the art performance on sentiment prediction [19].

First, we outline the baseline procedure producing 1-gram and 2-gram features. We follow the method used by [6] to limit vocabulary size to 10,000 terms with highest mutual information (MI), shared with the binary labels (positive or negative). As was men-

[5] http://mst.cs.drexel.edu/datasets/CIKM2011

	Amazon	TripAdvisor
⋆	103,953	15,152
⋆⋆	80,278	20,040
⋆⋆⋆	0	25,968
⋆⋆⋆⋆	48,086	15,141
⋆⋆⋆⋆⋆	136,145	20,051
Train	237,900	64,445
Test	110,562	28,907
Validate	20,000	3,000
Total	368,462	96,352
$\|\mathcal{D}\|$	448,146	158,997
$\|\Gamma_1\|$	54,334	54,000
$\|\Gamma_2\|$	127,337	127,000

Table 2: Selected statistics for Amazon and TripAdvisor data sets. The table lists the number of reviews for each star rating, as well as for training, testing and validation sets separately. In addition, total number of reviews in each data set is provided. Original dictionary size ($|\mathcal{D}|$) for each data set is listed along with 1-gram (Γ_1) and 2-gram (Γ_2) vocabulary sizes. All of the numbers listed are obtained from the *balanced* versions of the datasets, containing equal number of positive and negative reviews.

tioned earlier, Amazon dataset contains reviews for 25 categories of consumer products. As a result, the MI-based procedure for building 1- and 2-gram vocabularies for the Amazon is performed on each category separately. In the interest of fairness, the MI-based procedure is performed only on the training data. Then $10,000$ terms for each of the 25 categories are concatenated together to form the final vocabulary that contains $54,334$ unique terms. This vocabulary is then used to filter all three sets of data; training, testing, and validation, for both Supervised Latent n-gram Analysis (SLNA) input and BOW input.

In addition to selecting single terms with highest mutual information to form 1-gram vocabulary Γ_1, we perform the same procedure on both unigrams and bigrams to form 2-gram vocabulary Γ_2, yielding $127,337$ features. For the TripAdvisor corpus, we also use MI-based procedure to build 1-gram and 2-gram vocabularies. However, since there is only one category for this corpus, we simply limit the vocabulary size to match the size of the corresponding vocabulary obtained from the Amazon training set. Table 2 lists 1- and 2-gram vocabulary sizes for both sentiment datasets.

We train the SVM classifier with linear kernel using LibLinear SVM tool[6]. Note that the size of the training data, as well as its dimensionality makes it impractical to use any non-linear kernel for the SVM classifier. This was previously pointed out by [19]. The SVM classifier is obtained using the entire training data, and its performance is evaluated on whole testing set. For each term, we used two weighting schemes, regular TF-IDF and Δ-IDF (we have implemented $a\Delta(t')n$ variant). According to [19], Δ-IDF achieves state of art performance on a small subset of the Amazon dataset. The optimal value for the cost constant C was chosen using validation set with simple parameter grid search on $C = \{2^{-7}, 2^{-6}, \ldots, 2^{6}, 2^{7}\}$. We found that for both datasets, setting $C = 32$ and $C = \frac{1}{32}$ for TF-IDF and Δ-IDF weighting schemes, respectively, yield the best validation performance.

The training of the perceptron classifiers is different under two representations: BOW linear or SLNA. Specifically, we perform training and validation of the perceptrons simultaneously in batches, where each batch consists of training for $100,000$ iterations followed by the validation testing on the entire set. Each iteration consists of one positive and one negative reviews selected at random from the appropriate set. We stop the training either after 250 batches were performed ($25,000,000$ training iterations), or when the running average validation error over the last 50 batches increased for the three consecutive batches. Following the training procedure, the classification error rate (reported in all of our experiments) is computed on the entire testing set using trained neural network. In our experiments, we set the dimensionality of the word embedding (Level 1 in Table 1) to $m = 50$, dimensionality of the n-gram embedding to $M = 30$ (Level 2 in Table 1), and size of the window to $n = 5$ words (reducing the window size increased error rate). Dimensionality of the word embedding ($m = 50$) was selected to match dimensionality of the LSI-based embedding, and is a common choice for the latter. Furthermore, reducing the dimensionality of the n-gram embedding to $M = 30$ slightly improved classification accuracy in our preliminary evaluations. Thus, we chose to fix this parameter throughout all experiments presented in Section 4.3.

[6] http://www.csie.ntu.edu.tw/~cjlin/liblinear/

4.3 Empirical Results

4.3.1 Binary Classification

The first experiment that we performed was to evaluate the performance of the proposed Latent n-gram Analysis method for a binary classification task – predicting polarity of the review (positive or negative). Binary classification setup was chosen, since it is the most common measure of performance for the sentiment prediction task. The binary classification error rates for Amazon and TripAdvisor datasets can be found in Table 3.

Method	Amazon	TripAdvisor
BOW Prc 1g	10.96	8.27
BOW SVM 1g	11.10	8.89
BOW Prc 2g	7.59	**7.37**
BOW SVM 2g	7.45	7.47
BOW SVM Δ-IDF 1g	10.91	8.74
BOW SVM Δ-IDF 2g	7.39	7.96
BOW LSI SVM 1g	21.40	24.18
SLNA	9.84	8.92
SLNA LSI	**7.12**	8.33
SLNA LT-FIX	15.4	-

Table 3: Average error rate under binary classification.

The results indicate that for Amazon dataset, SLNA initialized with LSI embedding achieved better performance in comparison to both 1-gram and 2-gram, including the SVM classifier using Δ-IDF. However, on TripAdvisor data, SLNA does not outperform the BOW methods. Our hypothesis is that this is due to the size limitation of the training data (60k) for the model. This will be further confirmed in Section 4.3.3. As a comparison of SLNA to an unsupervised embedding method, we also include results of a linear SVM trained on BOW LSI embeddings (BOW LSI SVM), and also a SLNA with fixed lookup table: i.e., classifier and n-gram embeddings are trained, but word embeddings are fixed to LSI embeddings (SLNA LT-FIX). Note that for BOW LSI SVM method, LSI-based document embedding was obtained in transductive setting (i.e., using entire balanced dataset), and the best error rate for 5-fold cross validation on each set is reported (cost parameters used: $C = \{2^{-7}, 2^{-6}, \ldots, 2^{6}, 2^{7}\}$). It is clear from Table 3

1g	vocabulary with unigrams
2g	vocabulary with unigrams and bigrams
BOW	bag-of-words text representation
Prc	perceptron classifier
SVM	support vector machine classifier
SLNA	Supervised Latent n-gram Embedding
LSI	lookup table is initialized with LSI-based latent vocabulary
BOW LSI	50-dimensional LSI document embedding for BOW
LT-FIX	SLNA structure initialized by LSI, except that we don't update word embedding in training
RL	The neural network for ordinal classification is initialized with the network pre-trained for margin ranking loss

Table 4: Acronym legend.

that neither of these two methods reaches the level of SLNA. For a description of acronyms, please refer to Table 4.

4.3.2 Rank Loss and Ordinal Classification

Table 5 shows the results on rank loss.

Method	Amazon	TripAdvisor
BOW Prc 2g	12.5	16.0
SLNA LSI	**10.2**	**13.7**

Table 5: Average error when using margin ranking loss. For TripAdvisor dataset, the experiments were performed on the data containing neutral reviews.

Clearly, SLNA outperforms BOW approaches on both Amazon and TripAdvisor datasets. This is different from the results we observed for binary classifications. We believe this behavior can be attributed to the fact that pair-wise training examples generates more training data than simple binary classification. Furthermore, the rank loss is consistent with the ordinal classification results presented in Table 6, where SLNA yields the best performance in all scenarios. We are not aware of any prior art reporting results for ordinal classification on these two datasets, so direct comparisons is not possible. For the sake completeness, we calculated mean squared error (MSE) based on predictions with ordinal classification. We obtained MSE $= 1.03$ on Amazon dataset using SLNA LSI RL model, which is considerably better than previously reported MSE ≈ 1.5 on a small subset of Amazon dataset [17].

Method	Amazon	TripAdvisor
BOW Prc 2g	37.8	44.9 (52.1)
BOW Prc 2g RL	35.8	41.5 (51.6)
SLNA LSI	30.7	42.7 (51.4)
SLNA LSI RL	**28.2**	**39.6 (49.2)**

Table 6: Ordinal classification average error rate. The error rate for 5 star classification (i.e., including neutral reviews) are provided in parentheses.

4.3.3 Effect of the training set size

In table 2, we train Amazon data on the binary classification task, while varying the size of the training data. We can see that as we increase the size of the training set, the gap between SLNA and BOW diminishes and eventually SLNA out-performs 2-gram BOW.

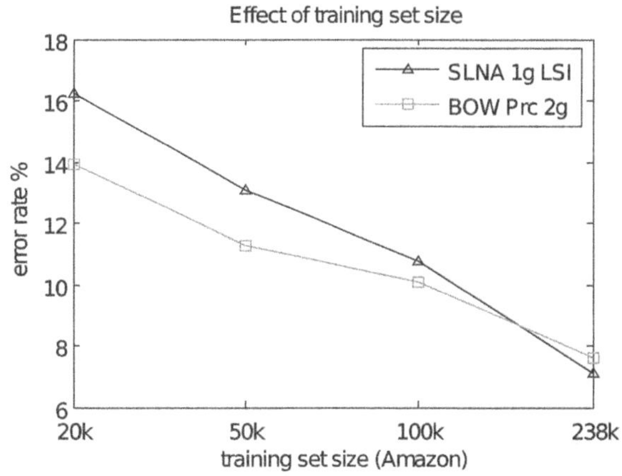

Figure 2: Testing error on Amazon with different training set size.

5. CONCLUSIONS

It is our belief that an n-gram model, combined with latent representation, will produce an more suitable embedding for document-level classification tasks, such as sentiment polarity prediction. Our proposed embedding combines n-gram representation with a latent model to produce a simple and efficient embedding for short segments of text. Our experimental evaluation indicates that for binary classification and regression tasks, our method with 1-gram (i.e., single words) dictionary of size $|\mathcal{D}|$ achieves accuracy of BOW representation with a 1- and 2-gram dictionary of size $|\mathcal{D}|^2$. Furthermore, we show that in a multi-class experimental setting (i.e., predicting star values for reviews) our embedding outperforms the baseline methods based on BOW with 2-gram dictionary.

One potential limitation associated with the proposed method is its need of large enough training set for model training. However, due the increasing availability of large scale SA datasets become available, this is not considered a major shortcoming. Moreover, our study indicates the model trained on mixed categories has excellent performance on both mixed and separated categories. These are all indications of great potential of proposed method in sentiment analysis. This model is not restricted to the task of sentiment classification and can potentially be applied for other document classification applications.

6. ACKNOWLEDGMENTS

Ali Shokoufandeh and Dmitriy Bespalov gratefully acknowledges the support from the National Science Foundation Grant #0803670 under the IIS Division and Office of Naval Research Grant ONR-N000140410363.

7. REFERENCES

[1] A. Agresti. *Analysis of Ordinal Categorical Data*. John Wiley and Sons Inc., 2010.

[2] B. Bai, J. Weston, R. Collobert, D. Grangier, K. Sadamasa, Y. Qi, O. Chapelle, and K. Weinberger. Supervised semantic indexing. In *Proceeding of the 18th ACM Conference on Information and Knowledge Management*, pages 187–196. ACM, 2009.

[3] Y. Bengio. *Learning Deep Architectures for AI*. Now Publishers Inc., Hanover, MA, USA, 2009.

[4] Y. Bengio, R. Ducharme, P. Vincent, and D. D. E. R.

Operationnelle. A neural probabilistic language model. *Journal of Machine Learning Research*, 3:1137–1155, 2000.

[5] D. Blei, A. Ng, and M. Jordan. Latent dirichlet allocation. *The Journal of Machine Learning Research*, 3:993–1022, 2003.

[6] J. Blitzer, M. Dredze, and F. Pereira. Biographies, bollywood, boomboxes and blenders: Domain adaptation for sentiment classification. In *In ACL*, pages 187–205, 2007.

[7] L. Bottou. Stochastic learning. In O. Bousquet and U. von Luxburg, editors, *Advanced Lectures on Machine Learning*, Lecture Notes in Artificial Intelligence, LNAI 3176, pages 146–168. Springer Verlag, Berlin, 2004.

[8] S. Brody and N. Elhadad. An unsupervised aspect-sentiment model for online reviews. In *Human Language Technologies: The 2010 Annual Conference of the North American Chapter of the Association for Computational Linguistics*, HLT '10, pages 804–812, Stroudsburg, PA, USA, 2010. Association for Computational Linguistics.

[9] R. Collobert and J. Weston. A unified architecture for natural language processing: Deep neural networks with multitask learning. In *International Conference on Machine Learning, ICML*, 2008.

[10] H. Cui, V. Mittal, and M. Datar. Comparative experiments on sentiment classification for online product reviews. In *proceedings of the 21st national conference on Artificial intelligence - Volume 2*, pages 1265–1270. AAAI Press, 2006.

[11] S. Deerwester, S. T. Dumais, G. W. Furnas, T. K. Landauer, and R. Harshman. Indexing by latent semantic analysis. *Journal of The American Society for Information Science*, 41(6):391–407, 1990.

[12] G. Ganu, N. Elhadad, and A. Marian. *Beyond the stars: improving rating predictions using review text content*. 2009.

[13] V. Hatzivassiloglou and K. R. McKeown. Predicting the semantic orientation of adjectives. In *Proceedings of the 35th Annual Meeting of the Association for Computational Linguistics and Eighth Conference of the European Chapter of the Association for Computational Linguistics*, ACL '98, pages 174–181, Stroudsburg, PA, USA, 1997. Association for Computational Linguistics.

[14] T. Hofmann. Probabilistic latent semantic indexing. In *Proceedings of the 22nd annual international ACM SIGIR conference on Research and development in information retrieval*, pages 50–57. ACM Press New York, NY, USA, 1999.

[15] P. Kuksa, P.-H. Huang, and V. Pavlovic. Scalable algorithms for string kernels with inexact matching. In *NIPS*, 2008. Spotlight Presentation. Acceptance rate: 123/1022 (12

[16] C. S. Leslie, E. Eskin, J. Weston, and W. S. Noble. Mismatch string kernels for SVM protein classification. In *NIPS*, pages 1417–1424, 2002.

[17] Y. Mansour, M. Mohri, and A. Rostamizadeh. Domain adaptation with multiple sources. In *NIPS'08*, pages 1041–1048, 2008.

[18] F. Morin. Hierarchical probabilistic neural network language model. aistatsâĂŹ05. In *In AISTATS*, pages 246–252, 2005.

[19] G. Paltoglou and M. Thelwall. A study of information retrieval weighting schemes for sentiment analysis. In *Proceedings of the 48th Annual Meeting of the Association for Computational Linguistics*, ACL '10, pages 1386–1395, Stroudsburg, PA, USA, 2010. Association for Computational Linguistics.

[20] B. Pang and L. Lee. Opinion mining and sentiment analysis. *Foundations and Trends in Information Retrieval*, 2(1-2):1–135, 2008.

[21] R. Salakhutdinov and G. Hinton. Semantic hashing. *Int. J. Approx. Reasoning*, 50:969–978, July 2009.

[22] C. Sauper, A. Haghighi, and R. Barzilay. Incorporating content structure into text analysis applications. In *EMNLP'10*, pages 377–387, 2010.

[23] P. Turney and M. Littman. Measuring praise and criticism: Inference of semantic orientation from association. *ACM Transactions on Information Systems*, 21:315–346, 2003.

[24] H. Wang, Y. Lu, and C. Zhai. Latent aspect rating analysis on review text data: a rating regression approach. In *Proceedings of the 16th ACM SIGKDD international conference on Knowledge discovery and data mining*, KDD '10, pages 783–792, New York, NY, USA, 2010. ACM.

[25] J. Weston, S. Bengio, and N. Usunier. Large scale image annotation: Learning to rank with joint word-image embeddings. *Machine learning*, 81(1):21–35, 2010.

[26] J. Weston, C. Leslie, E. Ie, D. Zhou, A. Elisseeff, and W. S. Noble. Semi-supervised protein classification using cluster kernels. *Bioinformatics*, 21(15):3241–3247, 2005.

Legal Document Clustering with Built-in Topic Segmentation

Qiang Lu, William Keenan
Thomson Reuters
Research & Development
50 Broad Street
Rochester, New York 14694 USA
{qiang.lu, william.keenan}@thomsonreuters.com

Jack G. Conrad, Khalid Al-Kofahi
Thomson Reuters
Research & Development
610 Opperman Drive
St. Paul, Minnesota 55123 USA
{jack.g.conrad, khalid.al-kofahi}@thomsonreuters.com

ABSTRACT

Clustering is a useful tool for helping users navigate, summarize, and organize large quantities of textual documents available on the Internet, in news sources, and in digital libraries. A variety of clustering methods have also been applied to the legal domain, with various degrees of success. Some unique characteristics of legal content as well as the nature of the legal domain present a number of challenges. For example, legal documents are often multi-topical, contain carefully crafted, professional, domain-specific language, and possess a broad and unevenly distributed coverage of legal issues. Moreover, unlike widely accessible documents on the Internet, where search and categorization services are generally free, the legal profession is still largely a fee-for-service field that makes the quality (e.g., in terms of both recall and precision) a key differentiator of provided services.

This paper introduces a classification-based recursive soft clustering algorithm with built-in topic segmentation. The algorithm leverages existing legal document metadata such as topical classifications, document citations, and click stream data from user behavior databases, into a comprehensive clustering framework. Techniques associated with the algorithm have been applied successfully to very large databases of legal documents, which include judicial opinions, statutes, regulations, administrative materials and analytical documents. Extensive evaluations were conducted to determine the efficiency and effectiveness of the proposed algorithm. Subsequent evaluations conducted by legal domain experts have demonstrated that the quality of the resulting clusters based upon this algorithm is similar to those created by domain experts.

Categories and Subject Descriptors

H.3.3 [**Information Storage and Retrieval**]: Information Search and Retrieval—*Clustering*; H.3.5 [**Information Storage and Retrieval**]: Online Information Services—*Commercial Services*

General Terms

Algorithms, Experimentation, Evaluation

CIKM'11, October 24–28, 2011, Glasgow, Scotland, UK

Keywords

clustering, unsupervised learning, topic segmentation

1. INTRODUCTION

Search is but one tool of a comprehensive information retrieval system. Other tools include recommendation, navigation, clustering, query suggestion, and personalization, among others. Such tools are often featured more prominently in a vertical domain than they are in the open Web. This is primarily because the underlying use cases are more clearly defined; more information about the users is also available; and in the case of fee-based models, information providers often deploy editorial resources in addition to algorithmic means to organize and index content to further support specific information needs.

Topical taxonomies and encyclopedias are two examples of editorial tools that are designed to help legal researchers discover critical information via navigation. West's Key Number System is one noteworthy example of such a taxonomy. It segments the American system of law into common research and practice areas (e.g., Civil Rights, Negligence, and Pretrial Procedure). Other legal information providers, such as Lexis provide similar tools, but the Key Number System,[1] which contains about 100,000 nodes and existed since the 1870s, is considered by many to be the gold standard. The Key Number System still has its limitations as stated in [ ]. We have found that document clustering can be very beneficial to supplement the traditional, often manual analysis and interpretation of the legal text corpora.

Most clustering algorithms view documents as single atomic units in that they do not segment them further into topics. This is also true of some soft clustering algorithms, where soft clustering refers to the fact that a document may be assigned to multiple clusters. While this may work well for short single-topic news stories, we claim it to be ineffective for complex legal documents. For example, a judicial opinion may deal with a driver's complaint about the liability of an automobile insurer, where the driver caused personal injury, was denied insurance coverage, and where compensation was subsequently awarded by summary judgment.

Given the complexity and multi-topical nature of the majority of legal documents, we developed a recursive soft clustering framework with a built-in topic segmentation algorithm. We have successfully applied it to millions of legal documents and generated high quality legal topical clusters.

[1] http://west.thomson.com/westlaw/advantage/keynumbers/

Evaluations of these machine-generated clusters by trained legal professionals were overwhelmingly positive, as the quality was determined to be close to that of human-generated clusters.

Given a document, e.g., in a search result, a user is presented with more documents, in a manner similar to the "more-like-this" feature found on the open Web. However, we group the recommended documents by issues (or clusters), thus it can be viewed as issue-based more-like-this.

Logically, our work can be described as follows: (1) identify the universe of legal issues, (2) for every legal issue, identify the set of most important documents for that issue, and (3) associate every document in our collections with one or more of these issues. The distinction between documents that are most important to a legal issue (i.e., members of a cluster), and those that are merely related to one (i.e., are associated with a cluster) is important because it allows us to distinguish between documents that are an authority on a subject and those that are merely relevant to it. Note that under such an organization, a document can be a *member* of some clusters and *associated* with others at the same time.

Collectively, these two clustering relationships produce a powerful, coherent, utility-based approach to supplementing search results with additional relevant documents, ones that share the same common issue if not the same common query terms. Such a conceptual tool permits users to explore a topic at greater depth rather than simply surveying the topic through trial and error querying.

Figure 1 illustrates the overall workflow of the clustering processes and applications of the underlying algorithm. At the highest level, the primary tasks (described above) generate the two key types of document-to-cluster relationships, (1) membership, and (2) associations (shown in the two blue boxes delineated by dotted lines). As the sub-components indicate, both the clustering membership and associations processes rely on the topic segmentation results that precede them. Other significant components of the workflow include (a) merging, since the algorithm can be invoked recursively, and (b) labeling, which is an important piece of any outward facing rendering of the clusters. Each of these components will be discussed in the remainder of the paper to the extent necessary to explicate them.

The paper is organized as follows. Section 2 briefly discusses related work. Section 3 gives a short description of the metadata available in the legal domain. Section 4 introduces definitions and notation used throughout this paper. Section 5 presents the overall clustering framework, which includes the topic segmentation algorithm, and the recursive clustering algorithm. Some potential applications using the generated clusters are discussed in Section 6. We describe our evaluation of cluster quality and system performance in Section 7. Finally, Section 8 concludes the work while discussing future research directions.

2. RELATED WORK

The ability to identify and partition a document into segments is important for many Natural Language Processing (NLP) tasks, including information retrieval, summarization, and text understanding. One of the most important applications of topic segmentation is the Topic Detection and Tracking (TDT) task, as described in [ ]. Much research has been done on topic segmentation. Many unsupervised, domain independent approaches [, ,] exploit lexical cohesion information. The fact that related or similar words and phrases tend to be repeated in topically coherent segments and segment boundaries often correspond to a change in the vocabulary [ ]. Other approaches rely on complementary semantic knowledge extracted from dictionaries and thesauruses, or from collocations collected in large corpora, which use additional domain knowledge such as the use of hyponyms or synonyms [, , ,].

Clustering is an active area of research and a variety of algorithms have been developed in recent years. Clustering algorithms can be categorized into agglomerative schemes or partitioning schemes (depending on how the final clusters are generated), or hard/soft clustering (depending on the nature of the membership function, i.e., whether single vs. multiple assignments are permitted). A comprehensive survey on clustering algorithms is presented in [ ]. The legal community has also benefited from this technology [,].

Soft clustering is often used when algorithm designers want to capture the multi-topical nature of documents. The fuzzy C-means algorithm is one of the most widely used of these algorithms; it allows one document to be assigned to more than one cluster by using a fuzzy membership function. It has been applied to text document collections with some success [ ]. However, the well-known limitation of fuzzy C-means and algorithms of this type–its dependency on its initialization–limits their application to very large document collections. Other soft clustering solutions also exist, such as probabilistic clustering frameworks built upon Expectation-Maximization (EM) algorithms [,], Fuzzy Adaptive Resonance Theory (Fuzzy-ART) neural network [ ] and the Suffix Tree Clustering (STC) algorithm [ ], to cite a few examples.

Tagarelli and Karypis [ ] incorporate document topic segmentation into their clustering framework by first breaking documents into paragraph-based segments and then grouping these segments into clusters using the spherical K-means algorithm. These segment-clusters, based on all the documents in the collections, are then further grouped into high level clusters (segment-sets) using a "fuzzy" version of the spherical K-means algorithm. In their framework, an induction process is introduced to map the segment-sets clustering solution to document-level clusters in order to provide the user with a more useful organization of the input texts. In the case addressed by the authors, the text/topic segmentation algorithm assumes that documents are multi-topical. It further assumes that document paragraphs represent coherent topics and topics shift on or around paragraph boundaries.[2] Issues of scale are the prime differences between this work and our own. The segments with which we start are four magnitudes greater than those used in this study.

3. LEGAL DOMAIN CHARACTERISTICS

Documents in the legal domain have some unique characteristics. These characteristics include being intrinsically multi-topical, relying on well-crafted, domain-specific language, and possessing a broad and unevenly distributed coverage of legal issues.

[2]The extent to which a framework will actually lead to effective solutions depends in part on the validity of its assumptions. In the legal domain, there is no guarantee that paragraphs will possess a single topic only. This work is performed on document sets of 2.5K-6.5K using 15-25 underlying classes and where the number of clusters is tied to the number of known classes, a rather unrealistic scenario.

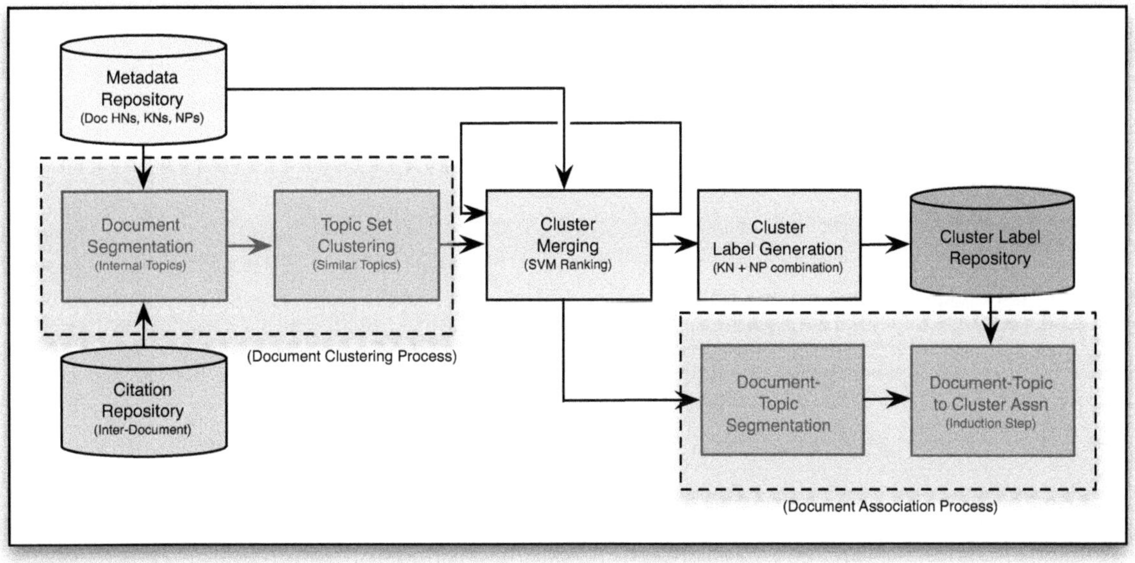

Figure 1: Workflow of topic clustering process and subsequent document-to-cluster associations application.

3.1 Data and Metadata Resources

Legal documents in the U.S. are complex in nature because they are the product of a highly analytical and adversarial process that involves determining relevant law, interpreting such law and applying it to the dispute to which it pertains. In doing so, courts must be careful not to diverge from established precedents or risk being overturned on appeal or criticized by future courts. This is because each case law document not only attempts to resolve a particular legal dispute, but also serves to help resolve similar disputes in the future. Legal publishers not only collect and publish the judicial opinions from the courts, but also summarize and classify them into topical taxonomies – such as the Key Number System (described in 3.1.3).

We mention some features of Thomson Reuters' products below to illustrate a point about the kinds of resources legal publishers harness in order to offer researchers multiple entry points and search indexes into the content. Other legal publishers have their own analogous means of accessing their content.

3.1.1 Judicial Opinions making Case Law Corpus

A judicial opinion (or a case law document) contains a court's analysis of the issues relevant to a legal dispute, citations to relevant law and historical cases to support such analysis and the court's decision. In other words, a judicial opinion expounds the law as applied to the case, and details the reasons upon which the judgment is based. By contrast, caselaw or legal cases refer to the *collection* of reported cases that forms a body of jurisprudence (i.e., the law on a particular subject formed by the decided cases), and is distinct from statutes and other sources of law. Generally considered among the most important legal documents, judicial opinions represent the bedrock of our clustering environment. A judicial opinion typically consists of several conventional components. These include the parties involved in the case, the jurisdiction, the court and judge(s) hearing the case, the background and facts of the case, the case history (if this is an appellate court document), the holdings made by the court, and the mandate or binding legal decision. In addition, Thomson Reuters' Westlaw System adds several annotations to these documents to summarize the points of law within and make them more accurate using a consistent language for the purposes of legal research. These include a synopsis of the case, a series of summaries of the points of law addressed in the case (3.1.2), classification of these points to a legal taxonomy (3.1.3), and an historical analysis of the case to determine whether its holdings and mandate remain intact or whether they have been overruled in part or in whole (3.1.4). Westlaw currently has just over 7 million annotated caselaw documents in the system and an additional 5 million unannotated caselaw documents available to legal researchers.[3]

3.1.2 Caselaw Annotated Points of Law

Thomson Reuters' Westlaw System creates "headnotes" for case law documents, which are short summaries of the points of law made in the cases. A typical case law document produces approximately 7 headnotes, but cases with over one hundred headnotes are not rare. On average, about 500,000 new headnotes are created each year, and the total repository now contains over 22 million headnotes corresponding to over 7 million annotated cases. West has been writing headnotes for over 120 years and the 7 headnotes per case average is more reflective of the last 10-15 years.

3.1.3 Headnote Classification, Key Number System

Headnotes are further classified to a legal taxonomy known as the West Key Number System, an hierarchical classification of the headnotes across more than 100,000 distinct legal categories. Each category is given a unique alpha-numeric code, known as a Key Number, as its identifier along with

[3] Unannotated cases on Westlaw tend to be cases from lower level courts such as county courts or very short cases such as certain summary judgments or other cases with few if any citations.

313A Products Liability
313AII Elements and Concepts
313Ak132 Warnings or Instructions
313Ak134 k. Obvious Danger. Most Cited Cases
(Formerly 313Ak54)

313A Products Liability KeyCite Citing References for this Headnote
313AIII Particular Products
313Ak256 k. Ladders and Scaffolds. Most Cited Cases
(Formerly 313Ak54)

Danger or potential danger of electrocution posed by use of aluminum ladder near high-voltage overhead power lines was danger which was generally known and recognized such that manufacturer of ladder had no duty to warn users to stay clear of power line, and thus manufacturer of aluminum ladder was not liable in products liability action based on theory of strict liability brought by personal representative of roofer who was killed by electrocution when conveyor ladder came into contact with power lines. (Per Goolsby, J., with one Judge concurring and Chief Judge dissenting.)

Figure 2: A example of a headnote with its assigned key number.

a descriptive name.[4] An example of a headnote with its assigned key number is shown in Figure 2.

3.1.4 Citation System

Equivalent to the links among Web pages, legal documents contain rich citation information just as documents from other domains do, such as scientific publications and patents. A case law document tends to cite previous related cases to argue for or against its legal claims; therefore, it is not unusual to have landmark cases decided by the U.S. Supreme Court with hundreds of thousands of cites to them.

KeyCite, a citation system created and maintained by West, is an example of such a citation network that keeps track of these rich relations between legal documents. Two types of citations are maintained in the system, *citing* (out-links to other legal documents) and *cited* (in-links to the instant document). KeyCite's key functionality includes: indicating whether a document represents good (valid) law (i.e., has a decision been overruled or weakened in a subsequent opinion?), the depth of treatment a citation may receive in the citing document, and whether the citing document directly quotes the cited document.[5]

These rich metadata provide useful information not only to legal researchers but also to data mining algorithms for better understanding of complicated legal issues.

4. DEFINITIONS AND NOTATION

Let $D = \{d_1, \ldots, d_N\}$ denote the set of documents. Each document $d_i \in D$ is seen as being comprised of a set of topics which contains text and other metadata information. A set of topics, T, is called a topic-set. We denote with T_j a topic-set from a document d_i, and further with T_{ij} being the j_{th} topic in the document d_i. Also we use $TS = \cup_{i=1 \ldots N} \cup_{d_i \in D, j=1 \ldots k} T_{ij}$ for k topics in d_i to represent the set of topic-sets from all the documents in the collection.

For clustering purposes, we use $C = \{c_1, \ldots, c_M\}$ to denote the distinct cluster set that exists in the document collection D, of which c_k is one cluster consisting of similar topics from different documents.

In general, the vector-space model is used to represent the documents to be clustered. A vector not only contains items from textual space, such as terms, but also contains items from other metadata, such as legal classification assignments, citator information based on inter-document citing and cited relationships, and click stream data from user behavior databases. For textual data, unless otherwise specified, text term relevance is weighted by using the standard *tf.idf*, which computes the weight of any term w as $tf.idf(w) = tf(w) \times log(N/N(w))$, where $tf(w)$ is the number of occurrences of w in a document (term frequency), N is the total number of documents in the collection D, and $N(w)$ is the portion of text documents in N that contains term w. Weights for the metadata representations are defined in the next section. The length of each vector is normalized so that it is of a unit length.

The cosine similarity is applied to compute the similarity between two vectors x_1 and x_2 in the vector-space model, which is defined to be $cos(x_1, x_2) = (x_1 \cdot x_2)/(||x_1|| \times ||x_2||)$, and $||x||$ to be the length of a vector.

5. LEGAL DOCUMENT CLUSTERING VIA TOPIC SEGMENTATION

At a high level, our clustering approach consists of two steps. First, each document in the document set D is processed to identify its topic-set and the collection of topic-sets from all documents in D is aggregated to generate the topic-sets, TS. In the second step, similar topics in the topic-sets TS are grouped together to form final clusters using a soft clustering algorithm. See Figure 3, where the topic sets, $TS = \{ts_1, ts_2, ts_3, \ldots ts_N\}$, populate clusters $C = \{c_1, \ldots, c_M\}$. The rest of this section describes how these two steps are performed.

5.1 Topic Segmentation in Legal Documents (Document Segmentation by Topics)

The topic segmentation algorithm leverages available metadata such as headnotes, key numbers, and citations. We found this approach to provide better results (in terms of coverage and quality of topics) over traditional topic segmentation algorithms that rely upon lexical cohesion and utilize only document text. For the purposes of emphasizing the segmentation task, we will subsequently focus only on legal documents possessing headnotes, i.e., case law documents. As stated in 3.1.2, headnotes are short summaries of points of law in case law documents, there-

[4] http://west.thomson.com/westlaw/advantage/keynumbers/
http://west.thomson.com/documentation/westlaw/wlawdoc/wlres/keynmb06.pdf
[5] http://west.thomson.com/documentation/westlaw/wlawdoc/web/kcwlcqr4.pdf

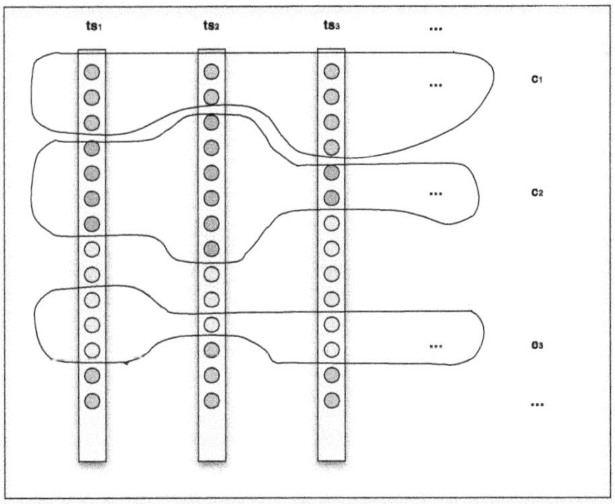

Figure 3: Topic sets populating final soft clusters.

fore have a near-complete coverage of the main legal issues in them. By grouping headnotes based on their "similarities" within a case law document, it is possible to identify the main legal topics within a document.

We use the vector-space model to represent headnotes in a case law document. A headnote is represented in terms of four types of features: text, key numbers, KeyCite citations, and noun phrases.[6] Thus, a headnote feature vector, h, is composed of four separate feature components, one per feature type. The similarity between a pair of headnotes, $sim(h_i, h_j)$, is defined as the weighted sum of the similarities between the corresponding component vectors. The weights are determined using heuristics.[7]

The similarity functions for the component vectors are defined as follows. For text-related features (i.e., headnote text and noun phrases) we use cosine similarity with a *tf.idf* weighting scheme. An analogous similarity function is also used for the key number features, where each key number is treated as if it was a word. For the KeyCite component vector we define similarity in terms of co-citations:

$$cite\_sim(h_i, h_j) = \frac{cite(h_i \cap h_j)}{cite(h_i \cup h_j)} \tag{5.1}$$

in which $cite(h_i \cap h_j)$ represents the number of documents that cite both headnotes h_i and h_j, and $cite(h_i \cup h_j)$ the number of documents that cite either headnote h_i or h_j.

An agglomerative clustering algorithm groups similar headnotes to generate the topic-set for a document. The algorithm merges two headnotes together while maximizing the following equations,

$$F = maximize \frac{\tau}{\epsilon} \tag{5.2}$$

where,

$$\tau = maximize \sum_{r=1}^{k} \sum_{h_i \in T_r} sim(h_i, \overline{T_r}) \tag{5.3}$$

[6]An in-house study found that noun phrases, e.g., from headnotes, closely approximated the associated key legal concepts, e.g., "product liability."

[7]We determined empirically that the key number feature was the most discriminating. Given that it is assigned by humans, is independent of any particular terms or phrases, and is highly granular (having O(100K) leaf nodes), the finding is not surprising.

and

$$\epsilon = minimize \sum_{r=1}^{k} n_r sim(\overline{T_r}, \overline{T}) \tag{5.4}$$

$$\overline{T_r} = \frac{\sum_{hinT_r} h}{n_r} \tag{5.5}$$

$$\overline{T} = \frac{\sum_{rinT} \overline{T_r}}{k} \tag{5.6}$$

where τ is the intra-cluster similarity and ϵ is the inter-cluster similarity, k denotes the total number of topics in a document, T denotes the topic-set for a document, T_r denotes an individual topic, and n_r is the number of headnotes in the topic T_r. Also, $\overline{T_r}$ and $\overline{T}$ represents the center of a single topic and all topics, respectively.

Notice that the algorithm does not require the number of topics as an input parameter; rather, it depends on an intra-topic similarity threshold to control the granularity of the topics in a document. The threshold is determined empirically by analyzing the histogram of intra-cluster similarities. We use a set of documents with known topic-segmentations to guide our threshold selection process.

5.2 Topic Set Clustering

The above document segmentation process resulted in a large number of topics, over 10 million in total. Clearly, many of these topics are duplicative and thus called for further merging or clustering. This section describes the clustering process.

First, we needed to reduce computational complexity of the underlying problem. We do this in two ways: we reduced the dimensionality of the topics themselves, and we reduced the computational complexity of the clustering algorithm.

We performed aggressive feature selection to reduce the dimensionality of the topics from hundreds of words, noun phrases, and key numbers to a much smaller set. We use a ranker support vector machine (SVM) [illegible] to rank noun phrases in a cluster, and select the top n most descriptive and discriminative ones (n was set empirically to 5).

We then used a technique similar to that described in [illegible] to reduce the computational complexity of the algorithm. In [illegible], McCallum, et al. describe a "canopy" based clustering technique for large and high-dimensional data sets. The main idea is to use a cheap, approximate distance measure to efficiently divide the data into overlapping subsets, or "canopies" and then apply (traditional) clustering algorithms by measuring exact distances only between points that occur in a common canopy. This reduces the overall computational complexity of clustering dramatically.

Our methods are similar in that we first index the set of 10 million+ topics and for each topic we retrieve the top n most similar topics using several simple features. To merge topics, we use measurements in more extensive feature sets, but only against the set of most similar topics, thus producing dramatic improvements in processing speed without negatively affecting quality.

A topic can be a member of as many clusters as appropriate, a general property of soft clustering algorithms. A seed topic is a topic that can start its own cluster. However, a topic that is already a member of another cluster cannot be used as a seed for a new cluster. This means that the resulting clusters are order dependent. To increase the likelihood that popular topics are represented in their own clusters we order topics according to their popularity (in terms of number of citations to the headnotes in a cluster), and start with most popular topics first.

We used a document classification engine, CaRE [ ], to retrieve similar topics (clusters). CaRE allows the utilization of an ensemble of classifiers and comes equipped with a number of meta-classifiers to be used to combine the results of individual classifiers. For each topic (e.g., cluster), we have three classifiers – one per feature type – headnote texts, key numbers, and citation patterns. Other indexing engines (e.g., Lucene[8]) could have been used.

Given a seed topic, we use CaRE to retrieve a pool of candidate topics. We then use a ranker SVM to determine which of the topics in the candidate pool can be merged with the seed topic. To do this, we represent each seed-candidate pair in terms of a feature vector. The features include CaRE scores, as well as the four similarity functions described in section 5.1. In addition, the feature vector includes a coclick similarity feature. The basic idea is that documents that are frequently viewed (clicked on) in the same session, by different users, tend to share common topics. This feature is computed as follows:

$$coclick\_sim(d_i, d_j) = \frac{coclick(d_i \cap d_j)}{coclick(d_i \cup d_j)} \quad (5.7)$$

in which $coclick(d_i \cap d_j)$ represents the number of times that both documents d_i and d_j have been clicked in the same session, and $coclick(d_i \cup d_j)$ is the number of times that either document d_i or d_j has been clicked in all sessions.

The above similarity features are then used to train a ranker SVM to rank clusters in the retrieved pool and top ranked clusters are then merged into the seed cluster.

The algorithm is designed as a recursive process such that multiple rounds can be performed if needed. The initial input of the algorithm is the set of 10 million+ topics, and the output of each round is the input to subsequent rounds. The process stops when the inter-cluster similarities between any two clusters are lower than a predefined threshold if a subsequent merge took place. In all, we performed 3 rounds. After the first round, we ended up with 1.4 million clusters, and these were further reduced to approximately 360,000 clusters after the third and final round.

5.3 Additional Notes about the Clusters

We relied upon two Linux servers, each with 32 GB RAM, and two quad core 2.66 MHz CPUs. One of them was used for the central clustering and merging tasks and the other for CaRE similarity services. These servers reduced processing time from days to tens of hours. Table 1 contains a sample of clusters as well as their metadata. Notice that the majority of the 360,000 clusters are jurisdiction neutral. The clusters represent the universe of legal issues, some of which are state specific, others are federal and others are a mix of both. However, not all legal issues are represented in all jurisdictions. In fact, the resulting clusters only contain descriptions of legal issues. The process of "populating" these clusters with legal documents is evaluated in section 7.

No clustering algorithm is complete without a discussion about labeling. As one can see in Table 1, cluster labels are hierarchical (separated by '/') and coherent. The algorithm for generating these labels is quite complex and will be the subject of another paper.

[8] http://lucene.apache.org

6. ASSOCIATING DOCUMENTS WITH CLUSTERS

By design, clusters are meant to contain the most important case law documents on a legal topic. Hence, not every case law document is a member of a cluster. Yet although clusters are case-centric, they are also populated with other types of legal documents such as statutes, regulations, administrative decisions. The utility of clusters as a means to organize legal content around issues or topics is as much a function of the quality of the clusters themselves as it is a function of their coverage. Without this universal coverage, one could not envision an issue-based "more like this," where legal researchers can discover topics related to a document they are examining or dig deeper into a topic of interest. In other words, it is critical that most if not all legal documents (regardless of their type) be linked to these clusters. To address this challenge, we designed a process by which documents are associated with (or linked to) existing clusters. In other words, clustering defines the space of legal topics as well as the most important case law documents which are cluster members under that topic, while association indexes all types of legal content relative to the discovered topics.

As such, *association* is not part of the algorithm for cluster *membership*, but we mention it here because it significantly improves the utility of the resulting clusters. Very briefly, the document association algorithm consists of two steps: (1) segment documents into topics and (2) associate topics with clusters. The document segmentation step is tailored to the various content types but is analogous to the process described in Section 4. The association step is based on the similarity between topics and clusters. In summary, we have established a two-tier relationship between documents and clusters. The strongest relationship, for the most *authoritative* documents under a given topic, is one of membership. By contrast, the second relationship for documents that remain *relevant* to a given topic, is that of association.

7. EVALUATION AND PERFORMANCE

To assess the performance of our clustering approach, we clustered the set of headnoted case law documents on Westlaw. This consists of about 7 million U.S. case law documents, and collectively contains more than 22 million headnotes classified to about 100,000 key numbers.

7.1 Evaluation Design

We designed three different experiments as follows:

7.1.1 Evaluation I: Cluster Quality – Coherence and Utility

Coherence was defined as the extent to which the documents in a given cluster address the same specific legal issue. Utility was defined as the usefulness of the documents in the given cluster to a legal researcher. The rationale behind why utility was assessed in addition to coherence was because it would be possible to have a cluster with a high coherence score, but not be very useful to a legal researcher, for example, if the documents contained within were clustered based upon a common dimension such as "all litigation involving a company." So a cluster is considered to be useful to a legal

Cluster ID	Label	Noun Phrases	Key Numbers
12799254	Eminent Domain/ Compensation/ Nature of Property and Neighborhood and Estimated Replacement Value	"fair cash" "right way" "landowner right access" "diversion traffic" "access controlled highway"	148k221 148k141(1) 148k107
12436744	Opinion Evidence/ Challenged Portion of Expert Witness Opinion	"admissible expert testimony" "qualify expert witness" "product liable action" "direct examination manufacturer expert' "subject matter testimony"	157k536 157k546 157k539
12957372	Automobiles/ Arrest, Stop, or Inquiry; Bail or Deposit/ Stop and Arrest by Police Officers	"police officer" "valid traffic stop" "defendant drive license" "reason suspicion criminal activity" "law enforcement officer"	48Ak349(4) 35k63.5(6) 48Ak349(2.1)
13080456	Mines and Minerals/ Titles, Conveyances, and Contracts/ Prior Conveyance of Rights of the Oil Gas and Mineral Royalty Estate	"half mineral interest" "severance mineral estate" "gas mineral" "surface land" "possession surface"	260k55(4) 260k55(2) 260k55(5)
12879050	Child Custody/ Removal from Jurisdiction/ Best Interests and Welfare of Children and Rights of Other Parent	"admissible expert testimony" "modify child custody" "noncustodial parent child" "child father" "child quality life"	76Dk261 76Dk76 76Dk921(1)

Table 1: A sample set of clusters and their metadata

researcher not simply because it groups documents containing a similar "topic" together, but it also presents a useful legal concept with respect to the topic. In Evaluation I the top ranked 25 case law documents were evaluated for 128 clusters. These documents were ranked by relevance to the cluster definition. For both metrics, the reviewers used a five-point Likert scale ranging from 1 (low coherence with the current cluster's central topic or low utility to a legal researcher) to 5 (high coherence with the current cluster's central topic or high utility to a legal researcher).

7.1.2 Evaluation II: Cluster-to-Document Association Quality

In Evaluation II, the quality was evaluated indirectly through a document association process briefly described in Section 6. The quality of the associated clusters to documents of different types was graded by expert researchers using a five-point scale from A (high quality of associated clusters) to F (low quality of associated clusters).

7.1.3 Evaluation III: Legal Issue Detection Quality, Legal Issue Clustering Quality

In Evaluation III, a group of legal professionals were involved in creating 10 research reports from a cross-section of U.S. jurisdictions and covering different topical areas. Each of the reports included 7 or fewer of *the most authoritative documents*, including both primary sources, such as case law and statutes, and secondary sources such as analytical materials. Legal topics were identified manually for each of the documents by these experts. Further, they found that each of the 10 reports in this study has a common 'thread' (i.e., a common legal issue) running through it. However, the common thread did not always appear in each document in each of the reports.

Our algorithm was applied to the same set of reports to detect clusters in the documents. The objective of the assessment in this evaluation was two-fold: (1) is the clustering algorithm able to discover all the legal clusters in these documents, and (2) is the clustering algorithm able to find the common legal issue in each of the reports.

We used precision P and recall R to measure the performance for the first objective, in which:

- **P** is defined by the number of correctly identified clusters of a document (compare to the manually identified clusters) divided by the total number of clusters, and

- **R** is defined by the number of correctly identified clusters of a document divided by the total number of manually identified clusters of a document (as ground truth).

For the second objective, we used precision P for evaluation, which is defined by the number of common legal issues identified among documents in all reports divided by the number of common legal issues manually identified among documents in all reports by experts.

7.2 Performance

7.2.1 Evaluation I

Table 2 shows the quality assessment by legal experts of 128 randomly selected clusters. Each cluster was given three scores, for coherence, utility, and an overall score (an additional score to assess the overall cluster quality, using a simpler 3-point scale, A-C-F, representing high-medium-low).

The result clearly demonstrates the effectiveness of the clustering framework even when applied to such a large scale data set. The results are significantly higher than the ones reported in the authors' earlier work in [ ].

The slight discrepancy between the coherence score and utility score suggests a unique advantage of this human assessment. A cluster can contain highly coherent topics from different documents, but that in itself does not guarantee they will be equally useful, thus a slightly lower score for utility is possible. For example, a "summary judgment" cluster is a less interesting and less useful topic to a legal researcher due to its commonality in the legal litigation process; therefore one would expect it to receive a lower utility grade, even though it may contain highly related documents. This type of quality characteristic can only be revealed though human expert assessments. Traditional machine-generated cluster quality measurements, such as entropy and purity, as used in [ ], are not suitable for this purpose.

Grade	Expert Assessment		
	Coherence	Utility	Overall Cluster Grade
5	41	37	65
4	71	54	0
3	15	29	60
2	1	7	0
1	0	1	3
Average	4.11	3.93	3.97

Table 2: Quality of Randomly Selected Clusters

7.2.2 Evaluation II

In Evaluation II, more than a thousand documents from different content types were run through our association algorithm to associate clusters to each of the documents. Besides cases, documents from nine other types were tested by the system. These include U.S. statutes, U.S. government regulations, U.S. secondary law materials (a.k.a. analytical materials), and others indicated in Figure 4. Figure 4 shows the quality of the associated clusters of tested documents from all ten types.

When legal experts were evaluating the quality of the associated clusters, they reached a consensus on the clusters with grade A being "excellent", B being "good", C being "acceptable", D being "marginal", and F being "poor". In addition, the experts defined the "precision rate" as the ratio of A+B graded clusters, and the "success rate" as the ratio of A+B+C grade clusters, to the total associated clusters, respectively. The algorithm shows a consistently high success rate and good precision rate in documents across different content types.

One reason why two of the content types have poorer performance when compared to others, e.g. Analytical Materials and Expert Witness Reports, is that the language used in these types is quite different. For example, a typical expert witness report is recorded in a "Question and Answer" format with less specific legal terminologies such as those corresponding to common layman's terms. By contrast, Analytical Materials may address more conventional legal topics. However, Analytical content is difficult as it does not follow standards in terms of style, breadth or depth of material; so without tuning the segmentation algorithm to such stylistic variations, performance is bound to suffer. As an illustration, *American Law Reports (ALR)* is very different from *American Jurisprudence (AmJur)* in terms of document and section lengths, while both are dramatically different from the format of law reviews.

7.2.3 Evaluation III

Regarding the first objective, the precision and recall of the system on 10 reports across different document types is shown in the Figure 5. Overall, we achieved reasonably high precision, but the recall was quite low especially for case law documents. The main reason for this is the aggressive filtering, by adopting much higher thresholds, in the post processing of the system to achieve high precision.

For the second objective, Table 3 shows the performance of the system in each individual report, as well as overall.

In this analysis, each of the 10 reports has a common legal issue running through it. However, the common 'thread' did not appear in each document in each of the reports.

In summary, the experts manually created clusters by identifying a common thread through all documents in 7 of the 10 reports; our system identified a common thread through all documents in 6 of the 10 reports. In one of the reports, our system missed a common thread in one of the documents in that report, and is thus considered as a failure. Across the entire set, experts manually created clusters and identified the common thread in 52 of the 58 documents (89.7%). Our system created clusters and identified the "common thread" in 51 of the 58 documents (87.9%).

As demonstrated in three different evaluations, the assessment of our proposed clustering system for legal documents consistently achieved significantly reliable results overall.

8. CONCLUSIONS AND FUTURE WORK

This paper describes a large scale soft clustering algorithm that relies on topic-segmentation. The performance of the algorithms is encouraging, especially given its validation by human legal experts through different test assessments.

Clustering large document collections remains a challenging problem, especially in the legal domain where documents with multiple topics are very common. Traditional clustering algorithms have shown limited success in this area. In the research we have conducted, we have shown that our topic segmentation-based soft clustering framework not only successfully incorporates metadata information into the topic segmentation process for a given document, but also develops a practical soft clustering system which is highly scalable.

In this paper, we have attempted to demonstrate the utility of highly refined issue-based clusters created through two important kinds of document-cluster relationships. The first, *membership*, identifies and populates these document clusters by defining a comprehensive set of legal issues. The second, *association* associates these clusters with the documents retrieved by users who seek "more-like-this" functionality, whether or not these documents have any terms in common with the original query. As such, this paper makes three contributions to the field. First, it implements a highly practical means for defining and populating clusters along issue-based dimensions. Second, it demonstrates how one can expand the set of original relevant legal documents using "more like this" functionality, one that does not require the intersection between original user query terms and those in the candidate documents. And third, by focusing on high precision clusters, we show how users can expand both the breadth and depth of their legal research, rather than conducting research that only surveys the documents returned by a given query. This approach has been

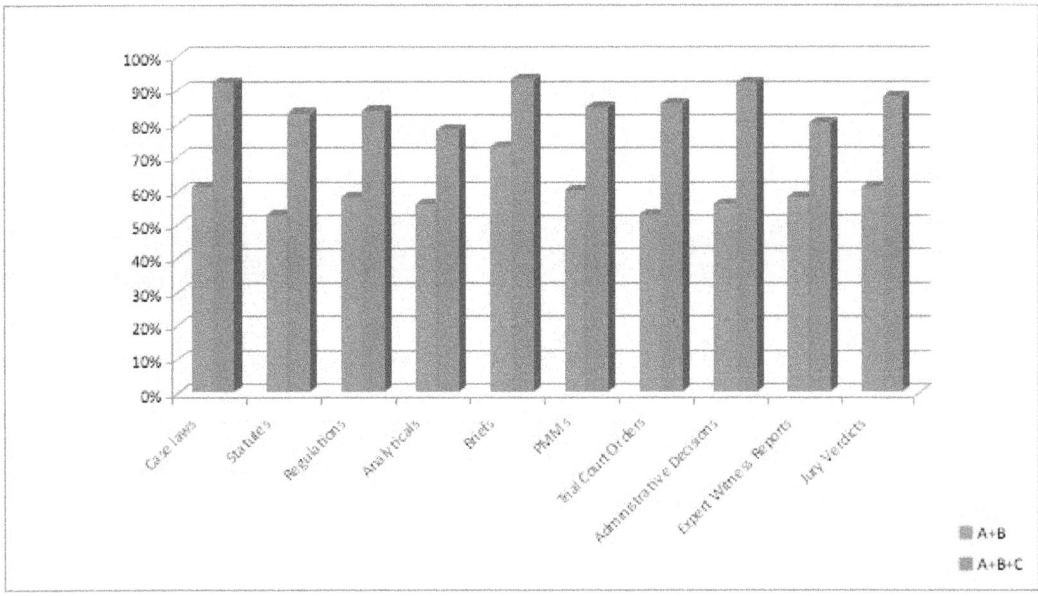

Figure 4: Quality Assessment of Associated Clusters for Different Content Types

Report IDs	Total No. of Documents	Documents with Common Theme Editorially Created Associations	Documents with Common Theme Algorithmically Created Associations
AE_2	6	6	6
AE_20	6	6	6
AE_22	4	4	4
AE_24	5	3	3
AE_31	6	6	6
AE_32	7	5	5
AE_35	6	6	5
AE_36	6	6	6
AE_37	5	3	3
AE_39	7	7	7
Total	58	52	51
Precision		89.7%	87.9%

Table 3: Precision of common legal issues of Evaluation III

scaled initially to address O(10M) clusters, which is another strength of the underlying techniques. Users, especially legal researchers, often prefer to have ability to drill down and focus on key concepts within a document set as opposed to getting a high-level overview of a document collection. Attention to fine-grained legal issues, robustness and resulting heterogeneous document clusters, and scalability are the characteristics that transform this cluster-based application into a highly resourceful research tool.

Topic segmentation for documents with little metadata information will be one focus of our future research work. Topic modeling algorithms, such as latent semantic indexing (LSI) [ ] or probabilistic LSI [ ], and Latent Dirichlet Allocation (LDA) [ ], have been shown to be capable of modeling topics beyond lexical coherence from text documents into some conceptual aspects of basic linguistic notations, such as synonymy and polysemy. They have yet to be applied to complex documents—as far as we know, such as those in the legal domain—and produce promising outcomes.

The MapReduce framework introduced by Google [ ] to support distributed computing on very large data sets of clusters across commodity or dedicated computers has ignited much excitement given its ability to tackle very large scale document processing problems [ ]. The development of the Apache Lucene Mahout [ ] machine learning algorithm libraries implemented on top of the Apache Hadoop MapReduce paradigm [ ] also holds promise to resolve critical problems, including those of very large scale document clustering and classification. We are looking into these subjects as another future research direction.

9. ACKNOWLEDGEMENTS

We thank John Duprey, Helen Hsu, Debanjan Ghosh and Dave Seaman for their help in developing software for this work, and we are also grateful for the assistance of Julie Gleason and her team of legal experts for their detailed quality assessments and invaluable feedback.

10. REFERENCES

[1] K. Al-Kofahi, et al. Combining multiple classifiers for text categorization. In *Proceedings of the 10th International*

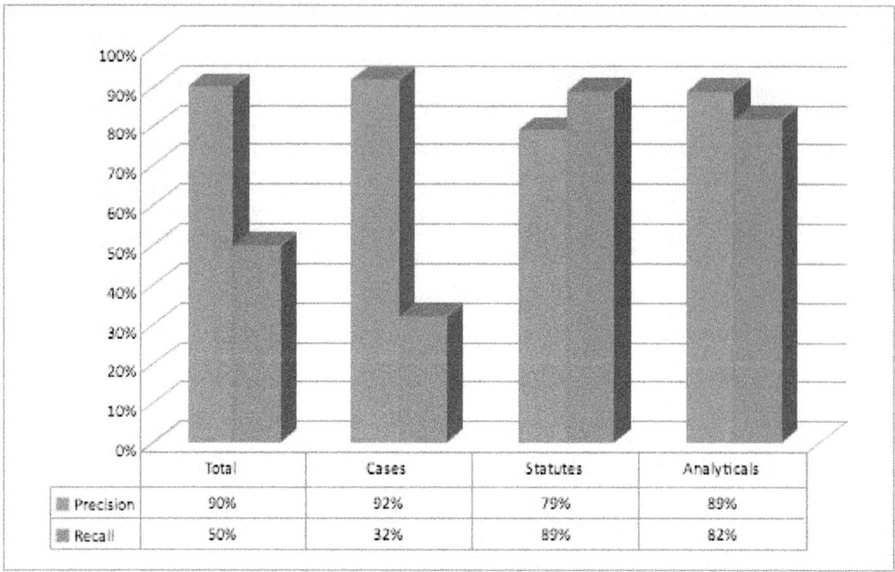

Figure 5: Precision and Recall of Evaluation III

Conference on Information and Knowledge Management (CIKM01), pages 97–104, 2001.

[2] J. Allen, et al. Topic detection and tracking pilot study – final report. In *Proceedings of the DARPA Broadcast News Transcription and understanding Workshop*, 1998.

[3] D. Beeferman, A. Berger, and J. Lafferty. A model of lexical attraction and repulsion. In *Proceedings of the ACL*, pages 373–380, 1997.

[4] P. Berkhin. A survey of clustering data mining techniques. *Grouping Multidimensional Data*, pages 25–71, 2006.

[5] D. Blei, A. Ng, and M. Jordan. Latent dirichlet allocation. *Journal of Machine Learning Research*, 3:993–1022, 2002.

[6] P. Bradley, C. Reina, and U. Fayyad. Clustering very large databases using em mixture models. In *Proceedings of ICPR*, volume 2, pages 2076–2080, 2000.

[7] F. Choi. Advances in domain independent linear text segmentation. In *Proceedings of the Association for Computational Linguistics*, pages 26–33, 2000.

[8] F. Choi, P. Wiemer-Hastings, and J. Moore. Latent semantic analysis for text segmentation. In *Proceedings of EMNLP*, pages 109–117, 2001.

[9] J. Conrad, K. Al-Kofahi, Y. Zhao, and G. Karypis. Effective document clustering for large heterogeneous law firm collections. In *Proceedings of the 10th International Conference on Artificial Intelligence and Law (ICAIL05)*, pages 177–187, 2005.

[10] J. Dean and S. Ghemawat. Mapreduce: Simplified data processing on large clusters. In *Proceedings of the Sixth Symposium on Operating System Design and Implementation (OSDI04)*, 2004.

[11] S. Deerwester, et al. Indexing by latent semantic analysis. *Journal of the American Society of Information Science*, 41(6):391–407, 1990.

[12] Apache hadoop. `http://hadoop.apache.org/`, 2010.

[13] Marti Hearst. Texttiling: Segmenting text into multi-paragraph subtopic passages. *Computational Linguistics*, 23:33–64, 1997.

[14] T. Hofmann. Probabilistic latent semantic indexing. In *Proceedings of 22rd Annual International SIGIR Conference*, 1999.

[15] M.C. Hung and D.L. Yang. An efficient fuzzy c-means clustering algorithm. In *Proceedings of the IEEE International Conference on Data Mining*, pages 225–232, 2001.

[16] R. Kondadadi and R. Kozma. A modified fuzzy art for soft document clustering. In *Proc. of International Joint Conference on Neural Networks IJCNN*, pages 2545–2549, 2002.

[17] H. Kozima. Text segmentation based on similarity between words full text. In *Proc. of the ACL*, pages 286–288, 1993.

[18] H. Kozima and T. Furugori. Similarity between words computed by spreading activation on an english dictionary. In *Proceedings of the ACL*, pages 232–239, 1993.

[19] J. Lin and C. Dyer. Data-intensive text processing with mapreduce. *Synthesis Lectures on Human Language Technologies*, 2010.

[20] Apache mahout overview. `http://lucene.apache.org/mahout/`, 2010.

[21] A. McCallum, K. Nigam, and L. Ungar. Efficient clustering of high-dimensional data sets with application to reference matching. In *Proceedings of the Sixth ACM SIGKDD International Conference on Knowledge Discovery and Data Mining (KDD00)*, pages 169–178, 2000.

[22] D. Merkl and E. Schweighofer. En route to data mining in legal text corpora: Clustering, neural computation, and international treaties. In *Proceedings of the 8th International Workshop on Database and Expert Systems Applications (DEXA '97)*, 1997.

[23] C. Ordonez and E. Omiecinski. Frem: Fast and robust em clustering for large data sets. In *Proceedings of CIKM*, pages 590–599, 2002.

[24] M. Shafiei and E. Milios. A statistical model for topic segmentation and clustering. *Lecture Notes in Computer Science*, 5032, 2008.

[25] Svm light. `http://svmlight.joachims.org/`, 2010.

[26] A. Tagarelli and G. Karypis. A segment-based approach to clustering multi-topic documents. In *Proceedings of the Text Mining Workshop, SIAM Data Mining Conference*, 2008.

[27] M. Utiyama and H. Isahara. A statistical model for domain-independent text segmentation. In *Proceedings of the ACL*, pages 499–506, 2001.

[28] N. Vaughn and D. Boley. Automated clustering and extraction of distinctive words in legal documents. Dept. of computer science and engineering report, University of Minnesota, 2001.

[29] O. Zamir and O. Etzioni. Web document clustering: A feasibility demonstration. In *Proceedings of the 21st Int'l ACM SIGIR Conference on Research and Development in Information Retrieval*, pages 46–54, 1998.

What and How Children Search on the Web

Sergio Duarte Torres
University of Twente
Drienerlolaan 5
Enschede, The Netherlands
duartes@cs.utwente.nl

Ingmar Weber
Yahoo! Research Barcelona
Avda. Diagonal 177
E-08018 Barcelona, Spain
ingmar@yahoo-inc.com

ABSTRACT

The Internet has become an important part of the daily life of children as a source of information and leisure activities. Nonetheless, given that most of the content available on the web is aimed at the general public, children are constantly exposed to inappropriate content, either because the language goes beyond their reading skills, their attention span differs from grown-ups or simple because the content is not targeted at children as is the case of ads and adult content. In this work we employed a large query log sample from a commercial web search engine to identify the struggles and search behavior of children of the age of 6 to young adults of the age of 18. Concretely we hypothesized that the large and complex volume of information to which children are exposed leads to ill-defined searches and to disorientation during the search process. For this purpose, we quantified their search difficulties based on query metrics (e.g. fraction of queries posed in natural language), session metrics (e.g. fraction of abandoned sessions) and click activity (e.g. fraction of ad clicks). We also used the search logs to retrace stages of child development. Concretely we looked for changes in the user interests (e.g. distribution of topics searched), language development (e.g. readability of the content accessed) and cognitive development (e.g. sentiment expressed in the queries) among children and adults. We observed that these metrics clearly demonstrate an increased level of confusion and unsuccessful search sessions among children. We also found a clear relation between the reading level of the clicked pages and the demographics characteristics of the users such as age and average educational attainment of the zone in which the user is located.

Categories and Subject Descriptors

H.3.3 [**Information Search and Retrieval**]: Query formulation, Search process; H.1.2 [**User/Machine Systems**]: Human Factors

General Terms

Experimentation, Human Factors, Measurement

Keywords

children, query logs, session analysis, topic classification, web search

CIKM'11, October 24–28, 2011, Glasgow, Scotland, UK.

1. INTRODUCTION

Both the fraction of children using the web and the amount of time they spend online has increased significantly in the past years. For instance, in the U.K. 63%, 76% and 83% percent of users 5 to 7, 8 to 11 and 12 to 15 years old respectively have access and use the Internet at home.[1] In the U.S. 32.4 million of children under the age of 18 years old were active users of the Internet in 2008, accounting for up to 19% of the online population.[2] Similar trends have been reported in other developed countries.

Given the small amount of content carefully designed for this audience and the lack of specialized search engines dedicated to help children find appropriate content on the web, there is an increasing need for research aimed at understanding the current difficulties these users experience searching for information on the Web.

To exemplify the difficulties that children encounter during the search process, consider the following two search session derived from the query log sample studied.

(1) A 10 years old girl submits the query *what is love*, the search engine triggers advertisements related to dating and casual encounters. Thinking that this ad is a result to the query, the girl clicks on it, after spending few seconds trying to understand what it is happening she goes back and then clicks on the first web result, which explains the chemical processes involved when people feel love. The content of this website goes beyond her reading skills and she quits the search session, most likely frustrated.

(2) When a 9 years old boy submits the query *hun*, the search engine suggests queries such as *hun school* (Princeton college), *hun sen* (primer minister of Cambodia) and *hun empire* (former empire ruled by Attila). Although this user is targeting the last topic suggested by the search engine, he does not seem to notice any of the query suggestions and simply continues with his initial query. Then he clicks on the first web result which happens to be a web directory of

[1] `http://stakeholders.ofcom.org.uk/binaries/research/media-literacy/ukchildrensml1.pdf`
[2] `http://www.iab.net/insights_research/530422/1675/600835`

links with adult content. Hun is also a popular term used to refer to a specific type of adult content. The user who is probably confused by the content he found decides to go back and then he clicks on the second web result which is the Wikipedia article of the Hun empire. As it was the case with our previous example, the article is dense and its language is too advanced for the reading capabilities of this user who after few seconds aborts the search session.

In these two examples, we observed that young users have a tendency to click on higher ranked results, spend short time on each url and in general have shorter sessions than those observed in older users. Although we observed that children do use the query suggestions provided by the search engine, these are less frequently used when they are displayed while the user is typing. In the first part of this paper, we quantify the struggle children experience while using a search engine using both established and novel query log metrics. Concretely, we present detailed information about queries, clicks and sessions. Details include aspects of query structure, click duration and session duration, among other features. All results are aggregated on a per-user basis and macro-averaged over age ranges that reflect human development stages. We explore how search suggestions can influence the success in their search process. We also investigated the likelihood of children to click on ads and to click on adult content by accident.

In the second part of the paper, we employ the query log as a mean to retrace the stages of child development. We point out differences in the topic distribution of what users search at different ages and gender. We show that the reading level of the pages clicked also varies according to the age and demographics such as the average income of the user's location.

The paper is organized as follows: in Section 2 we present the most relevant related work of previous studies on query logs and children search behavior. In Section 3.1 the data set used by us is described and the methodology followed to estimate the measures that we report is explained. In Section 4 we present the results and discussion of children's search difficulty. Section 5 discusses our findings on retracing child development stages using query logs. Both Section 4 and 5 are subdivided according to concrete research questions. We conclude in Section 6 with a discussion of our main findings and how they could be applied.

2. RELATED WORK

The most relevant literature on children search behavior on the web and query log analysis are described in the following paragraphs.

2.1 Information seeking on the web by children

Bilal [3, 4] investigated the behavior of children using the web directory Yahooligans![3] to solve open and well-defined informational tasks. The author reported that children are more successful in finding information when they used a navigational approach instead of keyword search. The author also reported that children are often ineffective at finding information as a consequence of frequent looped searches, hyperlink backtracking and poor query formulation. Druin et al. [7] characterized the search roles that children adopt during the search process and studied how these roles depend on the children's environment and their motivation. Our work differs from theirs in that we quantify the search characteristics and search difficulty of children based on aggregated results of thousands of users across a broad age range, which makes our observations more representative on a web-scale. Additionally we report topic interest trends over a population with diverse demographic characteristics.

[3]Today known as Yahoo! kids: http://kids.yahoo.com/

2.2 Related query log analysis

Duarte et al. [9, 8] compared users accessing general purpose information with users accessing information aimed at children. They reported significant differences between these type of users and show that some of their results are in line with previous case studies on children search behavior. Nonetheless, the authors argued that is not possible to assure that the users studied were children.

In [23] query logs are employed to study how search differs on users with different demographics. They used demographic information derived from the US-census and user profile information to describe search patterns and behaviors for population segments with different demographic characteristics. In this work, we employed an analogous methodology to show that the reading level of the urls clicked by children also varies across demographic features.

In [24] the authors tried to explain how the "who searches", the "what he searches", and the "how he searches" interact. Related to our work, they also gave details about topical distributions as function of a user's age. Though we apply similar methodological techniques, such as analyzing session characteristics, the main difference is one of breadth vs. depth. With our focus on a particular demographic group, namely children, we can go into far more details and paint a fine-grained picture of children's struggles and search behavior online.

3. DATA SET AND METHODOLOGY

3.1 Data set

The data set employed in this study was extracted from a large sample of the Yahoo! search logs of May to August of 2010. The following restrictions were employed to filter out search log data:

- Log entries of users without a valid Yahoo! account
- Log entries of users with unspecified birth year, gender and zip code in the Yahoo! profiles. Ill defined fields were also excluded (e.g. invalid zip codes)
- Queries containing personally identifiable information, such as credit card numbers or full street addresses
- Queries that were issued by only a single user
- Queries containing only a single token consisting exclusively of non-alphanumerical characters

For users below 10 years old we collected search volume in the order of hundreds of thousands of queries from tens of thousands of users. For users aged 10 or more years old we employed search volumes in the order of millions of queries from hundreds of thousands of users. As certain aspects of this data set are considered business sensitive, for various metrics we report *relative* differences between age groups, as opposed to *absolute* differences including, say, actual click-through-rates on ads.

The motivation of this study is to characterize the search activity of young web searchers and identify crucial differences between the search behavior across children of different ages and adults. For this purpose, we aggregated entries from the log data according to the user's birth year. Concretely, we estimate the age of the users by setting the date of birth as the 31 of December of the birth year provided in the user profiles and considering that the search was carried out in 2010. The following age ranges were created

- early elementary: 6-7 years old
- readers: 8-9 years old
- old children: 10-12 years old
- teenagers: 13-15 years old
- old teenagers: 16-18 years old
- adults: Above 18 years old

Children from 5 to 6 years old refine their motor skills and start to be involve in social games. Children from 6 to 8 years old start to expand their vision of the world beyond their immediate surroundings. Children from 8 to 12 years old acquire the ability to represent the entities of the world in terms of concepts and abstract representations. Teenagers on the other hand become more interested in social interactions [16]

Our selection of the age groups follows the development changes present in these stages of life. As we will show in this work, theses stages also have an impact on what children search on the web and on the way they interact with the search engine.

It can be argued that it is unreliable to trust the user information provided in the Yahoo! profiles since people can lie about their age, gender or geographical location. Nonetheless, since at last as early as 2007 Yahoo! has required the consent of a parent or legal responsible for users under 13 years old to create an account [4]. Currently Yahoo! charges a symbolic amount of $.50 to confirm that a guardian is responsible for the child creating the account. Apart from the (small) financial cost, the corresponding time and effort increases the chances of having veridical information for these age groups. Note that even if a small fraction of supposed child users lied about their true age, this is less problematic for general *trends* to be present or not, though the actual *absolute* numbers will be affected. It is also interesting to notice that in social networks, children tend to lie to make themselves appear older and this practice is often backed by parents [19].

As mentioned, we only used search and click events of users for whom we could obtain (self-provided) age, gender and US ZIP code. We then used the ZIP code in combination with US census information[5] to further annotate users with demographic estimates about their education level (the fraction of the population in a certain age range holding a bachelor's degree or higher). This techniques has been previously used in the context of query log analysis in [23, 24].

3.2 Methodology

In all of our work, we take a user-centric approach as we want to provide insights into how children search online. This means that *all* of our statistics are macro-averages, where things are averaged with each user contributing equally, as opposed to micro-averages, where things are averaged over all query instances and heavy users will have a bigger importance.

For various parts of our analysis, we also make use of the notion of a *search session*. To break sequences of queries and clicks into sessions, we used a very simple approach that splits sequences of query and click events into sessions using a sliding window of 30 minutes. A similar approach has been used in several query log studies [14, 22].

For the queries and clicked documents (if any) we computed various metrics which will be explained in the sections where they are analyzed. However, the distinction between navigational and non-navigational queries [5] is used in several sections and so we describe here how this distinction was computed. We used two different approaches in parallel. First, we used the *click entropy* [24] to get estimates about how diverse the clicked results in response to a particular query were. Queries that had a sufficient support, a minimum of 2 occurrences, were judged as navigational if the click entropy was no larger 1.0. This approach works well for head queries and, e.g. detects the query "utube" as a navigational query. Additionally, we used a simple heuristics on given (query, click) pairs. Note that this heuristics does not label the query as such as navigational, but rather individual (query, click) pairs. So *facebook* could be non-navigational if the user clicks `http://en.wikipedia.org/wiki/Facebook`. Our heuristics works as follows: First query and url are tokenized (by white-spaces and dot characters respectively), then tokens are sorted and plurals are stemmed. We label the pair as navigational if the query contains a domain extension (i.e. www, .com, .org), the domain of the URL is contained in the query (or vice versa), or the edit distance between the query and the domain of the url is smaller that an threshold value (in the results reported we used 2 as threshold for queries containing more than 4 characters). For instance, this method is able to detect the navigational intent of the pair (kids abercrombi, `www.abercrombiekids.com/`).

In our arguments, comparisons between (macro-)averages computed for different groups, say session lengths of children between 6 and 7 and adults between 40 and 70, are core elements in our arguments. Hence, we were careful to test the various differences we report for statistical significance, using a two-tailed t-test for the equality of means with unequal variance and sample size.[6] We consider a difference to be statistically significant if the probability of the null hypothesis, i.e. the two means being equal, is smaller than 5%. Recall that the averages for each group are *macro*-averages across the users in the corresponding group.

4. SEARCH DIFFICULTY

Query, click and session characteristics were collected to identify differences in the search process between users of different ages and gender. In the following paragraph we analyze each one of these types of metrics. Our focus here is on finding metrics that give insight into the *search difficulty*

[4] `http://info.yahoo.com/privacy/us/yahoo/family/details.html`

[5] `http://factfinder.census.gov/`

[6] `http://en.wikipedia.org/wiki/Student\%27s_t-test#Unequal_sample_sizes.2C_unequal_variance`

Table 1: Query length averages by query intent

Age	Global		Non-Nav.		Nav.	
	T. length	C. length	T. length	C. length	T. length	C. length
6 to 7	2.55	16.49	2.80	17.40	2.14	15.16
8 to 9	2.56	16.59	2.77	17.27	2.24	15.91
10 to 12	2.56	16.62	2.81	17.54	2.17	15.49
13 to 15	2.60	16.82	2.84	17.67	2.18	15.67
16 to 18	2.64	17.08	2.86	17.92	2.19	15.68
19 to 25	2.71	17.34	3.03	18.72	2.22	15.16
26 to 30	2.68	17.34	3.02	18.83	2.25	15.32
31 to 40	2.65	17.43	3.00	18.88	2.26	15.76
> 40	2.80	19.05	3.12	20.09	2.43	17.73

that children face. In particular, we are interested in metrics related to *confusion*.

4.1 Do children pose longer queries?

The formulation of a well-defined query is an crucial part of the search process in IR systems [6]. The correlation between query length and IR effectiveness has widely been explored before [2, 13]. On TREC ad-hoc settings it has been found that longer queries lead to better search performance and user satisfaction [2]. Nonetheless, recent studies show that this result does not always hold on the Web-scale [6]. Query length has also been associated to the specificity of the user's query intent, longer queries representing more specific and less ambiguous information needs [17]. In this work, the obvious two query length metrics were considered: token length and character length. Token length is measured as the number of tokens separated by white-spaces and character length is simply the number of characters (including white-spaces) in the query.

Table 1 summarizes the results obtained by age range and query intent. A clear increasing trend of length was observed from younger to older ages. This result suggests that younger users tend to formulate simpler information's goals. Given that the difference margin is larger for non-navigational queries, this result may also indicate that younger users have difficulties finding the right keywords to formulate more elaborated information needs.

4.2 Do children pose queries using natural language?

Children have been observed to pose queries in natural language given their lack of familiarity with the keyword approach of search engines. Moreover, at younger stages children typically have a greater sense of curiosity which we hypothesized is reflected in the searches they performed. The following query types were created to quantify these phenomena.

1. Question queries: Queries for which the first token is a question word (how, where, what, ...), or the last character of the query is a question mark (e.g. what is the only immortal animal?)

2. Modal queries: Queries containing auxiliary verbs as will, won't, don't or modal verbs as shall, should, can, etc. (e.g., I don't want to go school)

3. Knowledge questions: Queries containing the words *describe, about, explain, define* or *interesting*

Table 2: Fraction of query types

Age	quest.	modal	knowl. quest.	superl.	for kids
6 to 7	2.07%	0.41%	0.16%	0.91%	2.36%
8 to 9	2.56%	0.29%	0.08%	1.48%	1.74%
10 to 12	3.53%	0.58%	0.11%	1.46%	0.97%
13 to 15	3.84%	0.71%	0.16%	1.33%	0.43%
16 to 18	3.33%	0.69%	0.20%	1.15%	0.34%
19 to 25	2.80%	0.49%	0.20%	1.23%	0.32%
25 to 30	2.54%	0.44%	0.16%	1.16%	0.54%
31 to 40	2.19%	0.33%	0.14%	1.09%	0.68%
>40	1.69%	0.24%	0.11%	1.07%	0.31%

4. Superlatives: Queries containing superlative adjectives (e.g, the fastest dog)

5. Kids targeted queries: Queries with the terms *for kids* or *for children*

Knowledge queries attempt to measure the fraction of queries intended to fetch a specific explanation about an issue or topic. Superlative queries are commonly employed to satisfy the curiosity about certain topic such as in "fastest animal". These queries were detected by looking at tokens with the suffix *est* and filtering out those matched tokens that are not listed as adjectives in Wordnet[7] or that have a locational meaning (e.g., west). Kids targeted queries are employed to focus the search on content oriented for children. Table 2 summarizes the results obtained by age for the set of non-navigational queries. Although the age range 10 to 18 has the highest fraction of question queries, the 6 to 9 years group does not have a noticeably higher fraction than, say, the 31 to 40 years age range. Similarly, *lacks* of clear trends over the age groups can be observed for the other features. Only the "for kids" query type came close to behaving as expected. The fraction of superlative queries peaks for children in the 8 to 12 years age range.

4.3 Do children have a position click bias?

We collect the macro-averaged distribution of the result ranks clicked by the users. The macro rank distribution is computed by estimating the probability of each user to click at each rank position, only taking into account query instances with click, and then averaging the distributions across users belonging to the same age range. Figure 1 presents the distribution of clicks for the first five results

[7]`http://wordnet.princeton.edu/`

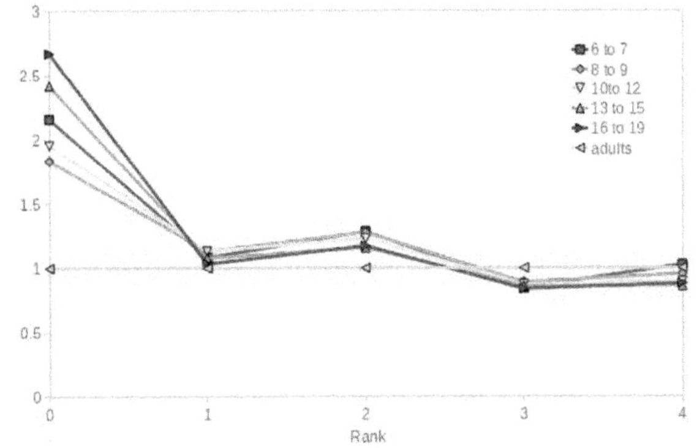

Figure 1: Relative rank frequency distribution across age ranges

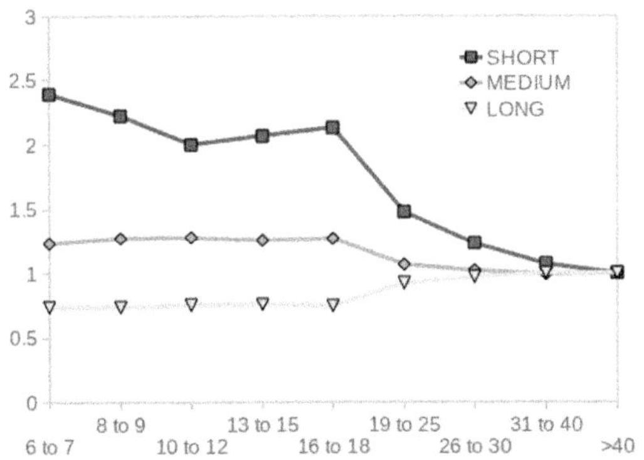

Figure 2: Distribution of click length across the age groups

where all click-through-rates are relative to those of adults. A rank of "0" refers to any kind of "special result" which includes links to current news, shopping results or any other high quality content which is typically only shown for high volume queries. Not surprisingly we found that younger users tend to click on higher ranked results, clicking twice as often as adults on the special rank 0 results. Similarly, for positions 1 and 2 were a factor between 1.1 and 1.3 as likely as adults to click. For lower positions this behavior is reversed.

4.4 Do children have more "long" clicks?

Previous work showed that one signal use to detect search success occurs in the form of *long clicks*. Here a long click is a click on a result such that after the click the user does not issue a new query or click on another result for at least 100 seconds. However, before the session times out (time limit of 30 minutes) he does submit another event so that the click duration can be estimated. Clicks at the end of a session have unknown click duration. We broke down non-final clicks into the three classes short (0-10 seconds), medium (11-99 seconds) and long ($\geq$ 100 second) [12]

Fig 2 shows that the fraction of long clicks is comparatively low for children of all ages, before it suddenly jumps to a higher level for users in the 19 to 25 years age range. This result indicates search frustration in younger users since they tend to abort the clicked pages sooner than adults.

Table 3: Relative ad click through rates

Age	Click ratio
6 to 7	1.28
8 to 9	1.14
10 to 12	1.04
13 to 15	0.89
16 to 18	0.9
19 to 25	0.84
25 to 30	0.8
30 to 40	0.86
$>$ 40	1.20

4.5 Are children more or less likely than adults to click on ads?

We employed the macro-fraction of ad-clicks to quantify how likely it is for an user of a given age range to click on an ad. Since not all the queries trigger advertisements, the estimation was performed only for clicks on results that were generated by queries that had triggered at least one click on an ad. Table 3 reports the fraction ratios of ad-clicks in respect to the group of adults users between 30 and 40 years old. Values greater than *1* means that users are more likely to click on ads than this age range of adults. Surprisingly, we observed higher ratios of ad-clicks for users at very young ages (6 to 12) which suggests disorientation during the search process for these users since ads are most of the time not targeted at this demographic segment. This observation is in line with previous research that showed that in the context of online games children are also more likely to click on ads as they fail to recognize them as such [1, 18]. It also reconfirms the findings concerning the position click bias from Section 4.3.

4.6 Are they relying more on search suggestions?

Druin et al. [7] reported in a detailed case study with 12 participants that children aged 7 to 12 often ignore the auto-completion and query suggestion facilities provided by search engines. This behavior occurs as a consequence of their longer attention on the typing instead of on the screen which make children ignore the queries suggested by the search engine. Figure 3 shows the fraction of queries that were submitted to the search engine as a product of a query suggestion or query correction. Query suggestions are triggered by the search engine when the user is typing the query (i.e. query auto-completion) or as the form of related searches right after the user has submitted the query. The automatic query correction functionality is triggered by spelling mistakes and are commonly displayed by the search engine by informing the user *We have included "britney spears" results - Show only "brittnay spears"*.

Figure 3 shows that, somewhat surprisingly, children are *not* more likely to make use of query suggestions or query corrections. However, we did observe the trend that the younger a user is, the more likely is he to *undo* a query suggestion, i.e. to insist on the (incorrect) spelling by clicking on the option like "Show only 'brittnay spears'". The fraction for users aged 6 to 7 to click such an in-correction was a factor of 1.62 higher than for a user in the age range 26 to 30.

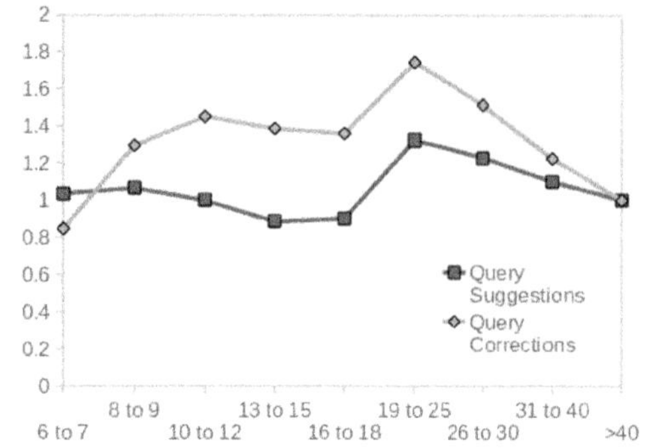

Figure 3: Query suggestions and correction usage

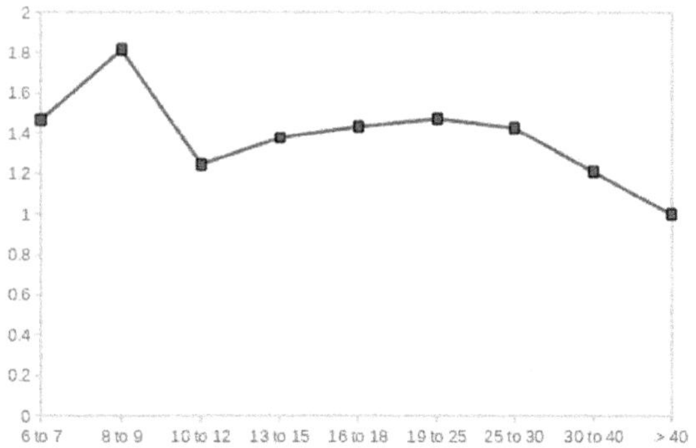

Figure 4: Relative likelihoods of accidental clicks on adult content websites.

4.7 Are children more likely to accidentally click on adult content, only to immediately correct their choice?

Children are potentially exposed to adult and explicit material on the Web given its large volume and the lack of parental supervision. Although, we observed lower volume of queries accessing adult explicit content for users below 13 years old (as it will be depicted in Section 5.1.1) it is important to quantify how often this content is accessed accidentally.

We hypothesized that users clicking by accident on a website with adult content would immediately go back and click on a different web result. Thus, we estimate the likelihood of having a click on a website without adult content after a short clicked on a website with adult content was registered during the same user session. Note that this process may occur more that once during the same user session. The last event of the sessions were ignored in the calculations since their click duration are unknown.

Figure 4 shows the relative frequencies for the event of an accidental short and immediately reverted click on adult content. Note that even though children in the 6 to 9 years age range have a comparatively high probability of immediately reverting to a different result after a (supposedly accidental) click on adult content, their *absolute* probability of clicking on this type of result or of issuing a related query is very low. The fact that the probability of these accidents-with-immediate correction is higher for children aged 6 to 7 than for children aged 8 to 9 can potentially be explained by the fact that the youngest children might take too long to read an entry page explaining that the site contains adult material and that the visitor needs to be of legal age (typically 18) to view the content.

Table 4: Session characteristics

Age	S.duration	S. length	Query ref.	Click ref.
6 to 7	3.79	3.76	0.24	0.17
8 to 9	3.51	3.71	0.24	0.15
10 to 12	3.63	3.71	0.23	0.14
13 to 15	3.91	3.76	0.26	0.14
16 to 18	4.04	3.82	0.26	0.13
adults <25	8.20	5.45	0.32	0.22
adults <30	8.45	5.43	0.30	0.20
adults <40	8.39	5.28	0.29	0.20
adults <70	8.42	5.25	0.34	0.24

4.8 Are children's search sessions ill defined?

One indication for a user struggling with a query is the fact that a user goes back to a question issued earlier in the same session after temporarily exploring different queries. As our sessions were quite short, with an average of 3.51 minutes for ages between 8 and 9 years old, it is unlikely that the second occurrence of a query is indicative of a renewal of the earlier information need. More likely, it indicates that the user has not yet fulfilled the earlier information need. We call such queries that repeated with a session "query refindings and their fraction is computed as follows. For each user we estimate the fraction of refinding queries inside a session (in respect to the total number of queries inside the session). Then, we averaged this fractions for all the sessions of the same user to generate a per users estimate of query refinding usage. As with all the other metrics reported in this work, we report the macro-averages across users. Similarly, if a user clicks the same URL repeatedly (which can be interspersed with other events) this can be seen as an indication that he is struggling and trying to make up his mind about the most relevant result.

Apart from the fraction of refinding queries and clicks, Table 4 also shows two simple measures for the average session length, one for the length measured in minutes and one counting the number of events (queries, clicks and next result page) in a session. It is important to clarify that these estimations exclude sessions containing only one entry (i.e. sessions in which a query was submitted and no clicks were registered)

Table 4 shows that search sessions of children are considerably shorter that for adults. Surprisingly, this statement includes the 16 to 19 age range and the jump to "adulthood" occurs suddenly in the group 20 to 25.

The fraction of query refinding and, in particular, click refinding sessions is *lower* for children. However, rather than to be taken as an indication for a lower level of confusion it is more likely to be a result of the fact that children have (considerably) shorter sessions and so there is simply less opportunity to issue the same query or click the same URL again.

5. TRACING CHILDREN DEVELOPMENT STAGES

Previous work showed that, given enough search history of a user, attributes such as gender, age and location can

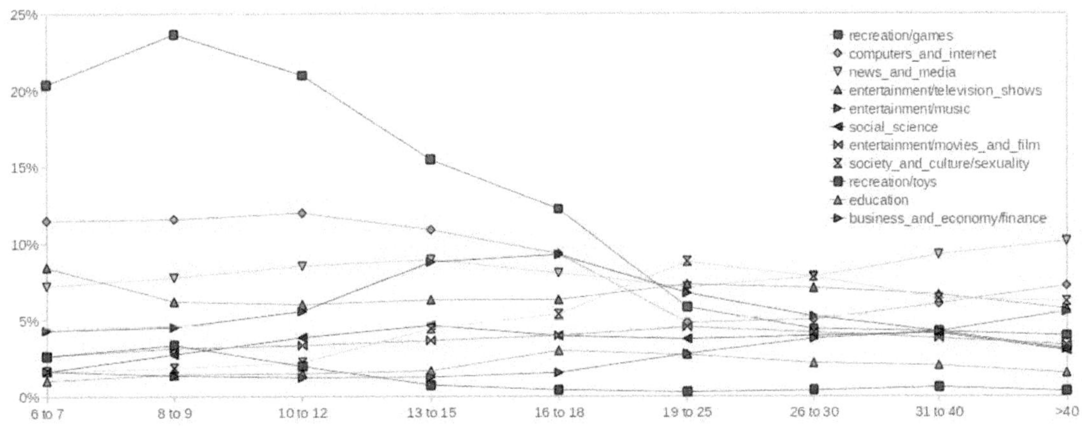

Figure 5: Topic progression through the ages

Table 5: Examples of queries and their mapped entities

Query	entity
facebook, facebook login	`en.wikipedia.org/wiki/Facebook`
disney cars games, 2011 cars, cars 2 2011	`en.wikipedia.org/wiki/Cars_2`
what to do with hummus, ideal protein, hummus recipe	`en.wikipedia.org/wiki/Hummus`
download b.o.b. airplanes, bob airplanes lyrics, airplanes part 2	`en.wikipedia.org/wiki/Airplanes_(song)`
youtuyoutube, youtui, youtuyoutube	`en.wikipedia.org/wiki/Youtube`
back to school clothes, london school uniforms, dress code for christian school	`en.wikipedia.org/wiki/School_uniform`

be estimated [15]. In this work, we looked at a related but different problem: can we find hints in the query logs that give indications about a child's development stage? In particular, can we confirm existing hypothesis and knowledge about child psychology?

5.1 What do children search for?

We investigated what children search for and how this evolves along two dimensions. First, which high level topics do they search for. Second, which concrete entities do they search for and which are typical characteristics of these entities. In both cases we tried to link our findings back to existing knowledge about child psychology, such as the development of gender differences or the orientation of children in certain age groups towards idols/heroes.

5.1.1 Which topics are children interested in?

We used a proprietary classifier to map web pages to entries in the Yahoo! Directory[8]. To obtain a classifier for *queries*, not pages, we then used a weighted majority voting scheme on the top 10 organic results returned by the Yahoo! search engine. See [24] for details. In total, there were 95 different topics. Figure 5 presents the average topic fractions for the 11 most frequent topics searched by users below 18 years old.

The behavior of Figure 5 is intuitive. Kids have a much higher fraction of queries falling into recreation/games than adults and the same holds, though at a lower level, for recreation/toys. The interest in music is most expressed in the teenage age range (13 to 18). The fraction of business/finance increases steadily as users grow older.

[8]`http://dir.yahoo.com/`

While we are most interested in understanding age-related differences, there are also important gender-related differences, even in children [10, 11]. We were interested in how gender differences evolve as children grow up. Are gender differences more pronounced in, say, teenagers than in adults? To answer this question we quantified gender differences by looking at the topical distribution for particular age groups. Each such topical distribution corresponds to a probability distribution, summing to 100%. We used the 1-norm to quantify the differences between the probability distributions belonging to boys and, respectively, girls for a given age group.

The blue line in Figure 6 shows that the gender differences for children are a lot smaller than for adults. However, a lot of these gender differences are due to a gender bias in the topic for adult content. The red line shows the gender differences when this topic has been removed and the remaining topics renormalized. As can be seen in the plot, this modification removes a large part of the age-related increase in gender differences.

The largest differences between genders were observed in the categories business and economy, computers and Internet and society and culture/sexuality. Nonetheless, this differences were significantly higher for users male and females above 16 years old, which is the trend that is observed in Figure 6.

5.1.2 Which entities are children interested in?

As the topics we used were fairly broad, such as "music" or "finance & investment", we were also interested in obtaining more fine-grained information by looking at the (main) *Wikipedia entity* a query refers to. To map queries to Wikipedia articles we used the following simple, yet effec-

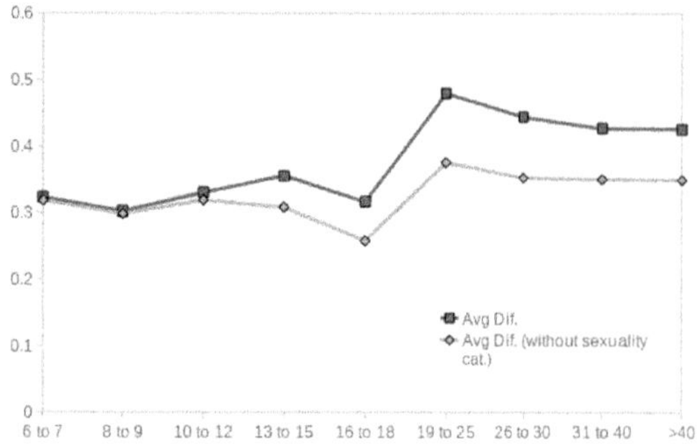

Figure 6: Average topic difference between genders through the ages as measured by the ||1||-norm

Table 6: Entity fractions for Child related content and Living People according to the Wikipedia categories

Age	Children and Kids	Living people
6 to 7	5.81%	8.11%
8 to 9	5.49%	6.97%
10 to 12	3.38%	7.59%
13 to 15	1.46%	9.47%
16 to 18	0.95%	10.86%
19 to 25	0.62%	11.96%
26 to 30	0.63%	11.54%
31 to 40	0.89%	11.09%
>40	0.62%	10.88%

tive approach: we ran each of the millions of distinct queries on the Yahoo! search engine and limited the results to results from `http://en.wikipedia.org/wiki/`. The first result was then used as the entity representation for the query. Note that these queries against Wikipedia were only run fairly recently, though the original queries were submitted about one year earlier. This ensured that even for recent events almost always a Wikipedia page could be found. Table 5 shows some examples of this mapping.

An overview of the entities searched by young and adults users is presented by the tag clouds in Figure 7 and 8 respectively. These entities correspond only to the non-navigational queries found in our data set. Entities related to adult content were also manually removed.

One of the advantages of mapping queries to Wikipedia pages is that Wikipedia pages come with a categorical classification and that this classification is both more fine-grained and in a certain sense orthogonal to our own topic classification (see Section 5.1.1). For example, pages about current celebrities almost always belong to the "Living People" category. Similarly, there are many child-related categories such as "Early childhood education". We used a simple pattern match for the prefixes "child" and "kid" to identify these pages. In Table 6 we present the fraction of entities associated to children content in Wikipedia and the fraction of famous people found in the queries for the age groups.

We expected young children or at least teenagers to have a large fraction of celebrity related fraction. However, that did not turn out to be the case and the highest fraction of such queries was observed for people of college age. The trend for child-related categories was much more intuitive and, as expected, this fraction is the more pronounced the younger the user is.

Table 7: Mean query sentiment values scores

Age	Positive	Negative	Diff
6 to 7	1.233	-1.211	0.0216
8 to 9	1.253	-1.237	0.0161
10 to 12	1.257	-1.248	0.009
13 to 15	1.284	-1.274	0.0101
16 to 18	1.274	-1.258	0.0165
19 to 25	1.300	-1.283	0.023
26 to 30	1.302	-1.275	0.026
31 to 40	1.322	-1.297	0.0248
>40	1.400	-1.376	0.0279

5.2 Do children express stronger sentiments in their queries?

To find out if children or adults are "more rational" in formulating a query we looked at the presence or absence of *sentiments* in queries. This was motivated by the fact that children in the age range of 9 to 12 tend to experience extreme changes of mood [20], which we hypothesized could be reflected in the formulation of queries.

To assign numerical scores to sentiments being present in queries, we used the SentiStrength[9] tool developed by Thelwall et al. [21]. This tool simultaneously assigns both a positive and a negative score to bits of English text, the idea being that users can express both types of sentiments at the same time such as in "I love you but I also hate you". Positive sentiment strength scores range from $+1$ (not positive) to $+5$ (extremely positive). Similarly, negative sentiment strength scores range from -1 to -5. The tool works by assigning scores to tokens in a dictionary which includes common emoticons. For example, "love" is mapped to $+3/-1$ and "stink" is mapped to $+1/-3$. Modifier words or symbols can boost the score such that "really love" is mapped to $+4/-1$ (the same for "love!!" or "looove"). The final positive sentiment strength for a bit of text is then computed by taking the maximum score among all individual positive scores. The negative sentiment strength is similarly calculated.

As can be seen in Table 7, sentiment analysis applied to individual queries did *not* reveal the expected trend. It did however reveal that the tendency to use both more positive and negative words in a question *increases* as users get older. This phenomenon is at least partly explained by the fact that they issue longer queries (see Table 1) and hence the probability of positive/negative sentiment words appearing is higher.

5.3 Does the reading level of the clicked results vary across ages and education levels?

One of the most noticeable factors in child development and its relation to web search behavior is an improvement in reading skills. As children improve their reading proficiency they will be able to (i) make sense of a wider range of web results, and (ii) potentially understand better the various elements of a web search engine, such as query suggestions or advertisements.

[9]`http://sentistrength.wlv.ac.uk/`

Figure 7: Entity tag cloud: 10 to 12 years old

Figure 8: Entity tag cloud: above 40 years old

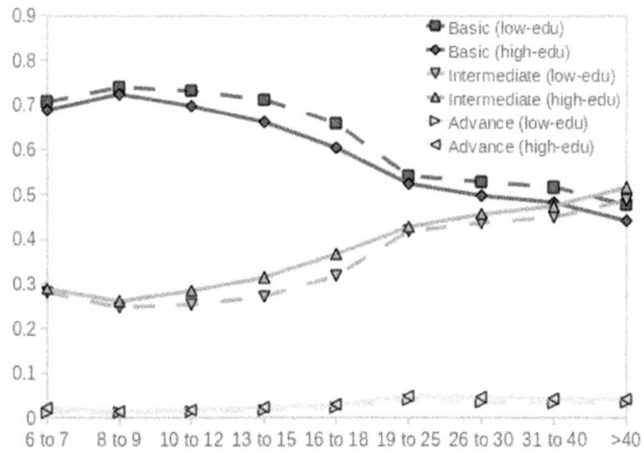

Figure 9: Reading level across age and average educational level

To retrace and quantify the improvement in reading level in our data set, we mapped clicked result pages to a 3-scale reading level using Google's "annotate results with reading levels" option.[10] Here, we simply issued the URL of the page of interest as a query to Google. In cases where the full URL did not return any results, or at least no results with an annotated reading level, we used backtracking by iteratively chopping of parts from the end of the URL, hopefully finding a shorter URL for which information could be obtained.

Table 8 gives a few examples for each of the three reading levels. Note that a single host such as `http://en.wikipedia.org` can host pages of all three reading levels. Averaged across all web pages, irrespective of the corresponding query volume, 51.6% of our URLs were classified as "basic", 35.8% as "intermediate" and 2.9% as advanced. For 10.2% we could not obtain a reading level with the current approach.

We observed a general and strong trend for the fraction of clicks on "basic" reading level pages to decline for older users. At the same time we observed a weak increase for the "advanced" level and a strong increase for the "intermediate" level.

To understand which other factors, apart from age, influence the preferred reading level of users, we also broke down users according to the education level in their self-report ZIP code. Here we used the census feature "percentage of population of the age of 25 or higher holding a bachelor degree or higher". We sorted users according to this features and investigated the lowest 20%-tile, and the highest 20%-tile. Figure 9 shows that, for the fraction of basic reading level pages, children from well-educated areas have about 3 years of advantage over children from poorly-educated areas. For example, a child from the age range 16 to 18 has a fraction of basic result clicks of 65%. This is slightly lower than the fraction for children in the age range 13 to 15 from well-educated areas, which is 66%, and much higher than the fraction of 60% for other children in the 16 to 18 age range also coming from well-educated areas.

6. CONCLUSIONS AND FUTURE WORK

In several aspects of our analysis, we observed a notable difference between children and adults but often, and this came as a surprise to us, the differences between the different age groups were quite small and children between 16 and 18 behaved more like children between 8 to 9 than young adults in the 19 to 25 range. This "sudden jump to adulthood", albeit not for all features, could potentially be explained by children leaving home and starting college or a job.

As far as useful lessons learned are concerned, the position click bias for children is worth pointing out. This bias also leads to a higher fraction of ad clicks and to a higher fraction of cases where (useful and correct) spelling corrections are *undone* by the user as he clicks on, say, "Show only 'brittnay spears'". Both of these indicate that very young users have a tendency to "click whatever is presented at a prominent position" which has implications for the design of an appropriate search interface.

In the future, we plan to continue the line of thought that "child development can be observed through search logs". Concretely, we would like to investigate (i) how the differences between concrete and abstract entities depends on the

[10]`http://www.google.com/support/websearch/bin/answer.py?hl=en&answer=1095407`

Table 8: Examples of websites for each of the three reading levels

reading level	example urls
basic	www.cookingtips-recipes.com, www.funbrain.com, en.wikipedia.org/wiki/Toy_Story, www.pbteen.com
intermediate	en.wikipedia.org/wiki/John_Wooden, horoscopes.astrology.com, www.sprint.com/, www.foxnews.com
advanced	www.answers.com/topic/mathematics, www.medicinenet.com/tinnitus/article.htm, www.merriam-webster.c

age, (ii) if FSK levels of movies or suggested age limits for games match the age of the user, and (iii) if "how to" or "how can I" queries and their topics can be used to describe what type of problems children are facing at different development stages.

Our hope is that a deeper understanding of children's search behavior and their struggles will lead to a reduction of the prevalent "one size fits all" search interface. In particular, our work suggests that due to the strong position click bias a linear, ranked list might not be the best way of presenting search results and alternatives should be explored.

7. ACKNOWLEDGMENTS

We would like to thank Alejandro Jaimes for helpful discussions at an early stage of this work. The pointers to the New York Times articles [18, 19] inspired parts of this work. We are also thankful to Mounia Lalmas and Djoerd Hiemstra for their encouraging and valuable comments.

This research was partially funded by the European Community's Seventh Framework Programme FP7/2007-2013 under grant agreement no. 231507

8. REFERENCES

[1] S. An and S. Stern. Mitigating the effects of advergames on children; do advertising breaks work? *Journal of Advertising*, 40(1):43 – 56, 2011.

[2] N. J. Belkin, C. Cool, D. Kelly, G. Kim, J. y. Kim, H. j. Lee, G. Muresan, M. c. Tang, and X. j. Yuan. Query length in interactive information retrieval. In *In Proceedings of the 26th Annual ACM International Conference on Research and Development in Information Retrieval (SIGIR '03)*, pages 205–212, 2003.

[3] D. Bilal. Children's use of the yahooligans! web search engine: II cognitive and physical behaviors on research tasks. *Journal of the American Society for Information Science and Technology*, 52:118–136, January 2001.

[4] D. Bilal. Children's use of the yahooligans! web search engine: III cognitive and physical behaviors on fully self-generated search tasks. *Journal of the American Society for Information Science and Technology*, 53:1170–1183, November 2002.

[5] A. Broder. A taxonomy of web search. *SIGIR Forum*, 36:3–10, September 2002.

[6] D. Downey, S. Dumais, D. Liebling, and E. Horvitz. Understanding the relationship between searchers' queries and information goals. In *Proceeding of the 17th ACM conference on Information and knowledge management*, CIKM '08, pages 449–458, 2008.

[7] A. Druin, E. Foss, L. Hatley, E. Golub, M. L. Guha, J. Fails, and H. Hutchinson. How children search the internet with keyword interfaces. In *Proceedings of the 8th International Conference on Interaction Design and Children*, IDC '09, pages 89–96, 2009.

[8] S. Duarte Torres, D. Hiemstra, and P. Serdyukov. An analysis of queries intended to search information for children. In *Proceeding of the third symposium on Information interaction in context*, IIiX '10, pages 235–244, 2010.

[9] S. Duarte Torres, D. Hiemstra, and P. Serdyukov. Query log analysis in the context of information retrieval for children. In *Proceeding of the 33rd international ACM SIGIR conference on Research and development in information retrieval*, SIGIR '10, pages 847–848, 2010.

[10] J. Eccles, A. Wigfield, R. D. Harold, and P. Blumenfeld. Age and gender differences in children's self- and task perceptions during elementary school. *Child Development*, 64(3):830–847, 1993.

[11] J. S. Eccles, J. E. Jacobs, and R. D. Harold. Gender role stereotypes, expectancy effects, and parents' socialization of gender differences. *Journal of Social Issues*, 46(2):183–201, 1990.

[12] A. Hassan, R. Jones, and K. L. Klinkner. Beyond DCG: user behavior as a predictor of a successful search. In *Proceedings of the third ACM international conference on Web search and data mining*, WSDM '10, pages 221–230, 2010.

[13] B. Jansen, M. Bernard, J. Jansen, A. Spink, and T. Saracevic. Real life, real users, and real needs: A study and analysis of user queries on the web. *Information Processing & Management*, 36:207–227, March 2000.

[14] R. Jones and K. L. Klinkner. Beyond the session timeout: automatic hierarchical segmentation of search topics in query logs. In *Proceeding of the 17th ACM conference on Information and knowledge management*, CIKM '08, pages 699–708, New York, NY, USA, 2008. ACM.

[15] R. Jones, R. Kumar, B. Pang, and A. Tomkins. "i know what you did last summer": query logs and user privacy. In *Proceedings of the sixteenth ACM conference on Conference on information and knowledge management*, CIKM '07, pages 909–914, 2007.

[16] R. Kail. Children and their development. Pearson Education, 2009.

[17] N. Phan, P. Bailey, and R. Wilkinson. Understanding the relationship of information need specificity to search query length. In *Proceedings of the 30th annual international ACM SIGIR conference on Research and development in information retrieval*, SIGIR '07, pages 709–710, 2007.

[18] M. Richtel. Children fail to recognize online ads, study says, April 2011. http://bits.blogs.nytimes.com/2011/04/21/children-fail-to-recognize-online-ads-study-says/?hpw.

[19] M. Richtel and M. Helft. Facebook users who are under age raise concerns. *New York Times*, page B1, March 2011. http://www.nytimes.com/2011/03/12/technology/internet/12underage.html?pagewanted=1&_r=1.

[20] P. Smith, H. Cowie, and M. Blades. Understanding children's developments. BlackWell, 2003.

[21] M. Thelwall, K. Buckley, G. Paltoglou, D. Cai, and A. Kappas. Sentiment in short strength detection informal text. *Journal of the American Society for Information Science and Technology*, 61:2544–2558, 2010.

[22] S. K. Tyler and J. Teevan. Large scale query log analysis of re-finding. In *Proceedings of the third ACM international conference on Web search and data mining*, WSDM '10, pages 191–200, 2010.

[23] I. Weber and C. Castillo. The demographics of web search. In *Proceeding of the 33rd international ACM SIGIR conference on Research and development in information retrieval*, SIGIR '10, pages 523–530, 2010.

[24] I. Weber and A. Jaimes. Who uses web search for what: and how. In *Proceedings of the fourth ACM international conference on Web search and data mining*, WSDM '11, pages 15–24, 2011.

Personalizing Web Search Results by Reading Level

Kevyn Collins-Thompson
Paul N. Bennett
Ryen W. White
Microsoft Research
One Microsoft Way
Redmond, WA 98052
{kevynct, pauben, ryenw}
@microsoft.com

Sebastian de la Chica
Microsoft Bing
One Microsoft Way
Redmond, WA 98052
sedelach@microsoft.com

David Sontag
Microsoft Research
New England
One Memorial Drive
Cambridge, MA 02142
dsontag@csail.mit.edu

ABSTRACT

Traditionally, search engines have ignored the reading difficulty of documents and the reading proficiency of users in computing a document ranking. This is one reason why Web search engines do a poor job of serving an important segment of the population: children. While there are many important problems in interface design, content filtering, and results presentation related to addressing children's search needs, perhaps the most fundamental challenge is simply that of providing relevant results at the right level of reading difficulty. At the opposite end of the proficiency spectrum, it may also be valuable for technical users to find more advanced material or to filter out material at lower levels of difficulty, such as tutorials and introductory texts.

We show how reading level can provide a valuable new relevance signal for both general and personalized Web search. We describe models and algorithms to address the three key problems in improving relevance for search using reading difficulty: estimating user proficiency, estimating result difficulty, and re-ranking based on the difference between user and result reading level profiles. We evaluate our methods on a large volume of Web query traffic and provide a large-scale log analysis that highlights the importance of finding results at an appropriate reading level for the user.

Categories and Subject Descriptors: H.3.3 [**Information Retrieval**]: Retrieval Models; **General Terms:** Algorithms, Experimentation; **Keywords:** Reading difficulty, re-ranking, personalization.

1. INTRODUCTION

Our goal is to show how modeling reading proficiency of users and the reading difficulty of documents can be used to improve the relevance of Web search results. This goal is motivated by the fact that content on the Web is written at a wide range of different reading levels: from easy introductory texts and material written specifically for children, to difficult, highly-technical material for experts that requires advanced vocabulary knowledge to comprehend. Web users differ widely in their reading proficiency and ability to understand vocabulary, depending on factors such as age, educational background, and topic interest or expertise. Web search engines, however, typically use algorithms optimized for the 'average' user, not specific individuals. These facts currently impair the ability of users to carry out successful searches by finding material at an appropriate level of reading difficulty for them.

As an example of the need, and potential, for personalization by reading level, consider the query [*insect diet*], whose actual top-ranked results from a major search engine are shown in Table 1. While a younger child may be more likely to have chosen query terms like [*bug diet*] or [*what do bugs eat?*], the choice of [*insect diet*] could have been made by a child doing a class project, or an elementary school teacher searching for low-difficulty material; parents or middle-school science students may require intermediate material, and more advanced high school and college users may require sites describing entomology research, as the top results do here. Only one result (`www.tutorvista.com`), at rank position eight, is at a low level of difficulty (American school grade level of 5.0). There are several results, however, including the top two, that contain highly technical research-oriented content most appropriate for specialists only. Clearly there is a need for improvement in ranking search results at an appropriate level of reading difficulty.

To address this problem, we describe a tripartite approach based on user profiles, document difficulty, and re-ranking. First, we discuss how snippets and Web pages can be labeled with reading level and combined with Open Directory Project (ODP, `www.dmoz.org`) category predictions. Second, we describe how a user's reading proficiency profile may be estimated automatically from their current and past search behavior. Third, we use this profile to train a re-ranking algorithm that combines both relevance and difficulty in a principled way, and which generalizes easily to broader tasks such as expertise-based re-ranking. In this view, the overall relevance of a document is a combination of two factors: a general relevance factor, provided by an existing ranking algorithm, and a user-specific reading difficulty model, based on the gap between a user's proficiency level and a document's difficulty level. While users may self-identify their desired level of result difficulty, such information may not always be provided. We therefore investigate methods for estimating a reading proficiency profile for users based on their online search interaction patterns.

We structure our study as follows. In Section 2 we review related work in reading difficulty prediction, modeling user expertise, and search systems for children. We then describe three key problems that must be addressed in using reading level to improve Web search relevance: estimating

CIKM'11, October 24–28, 2011, Glasgow, Scotland, UK.

Rank	URL Domain	Title	Category	Reading Level (Grade level)
1	`insectdiets.com`	Insect Diet & Rearing Research	Technical/Research	High (10.0)
2	`imfc.cfl.rncan.gc.ca`	Insect Diet	Technical/Research	High (10.0)
3	`www.sugar-glider-store.com`	Insect-Eater Diet	Commercial	Medium (7.0)
4	`insectdiets.com`	Insect Rearing Research	Technical/Research	High (10.0)
5	`insectrearing.com`	Bio-Serv Entomology Division	Commercial, Technical	Medium (8.0)
6	`www.ehow.com`	Aquatic Insects & Diet	Educational	Medium (7.0)
7	`www.exoticnutrition.com`	Insect-eater Diet...	Commercial	Medium (6.0)
8	`www.tutorvista.com`	Insect diet: Questions & Answers	Educational	Low (5.0)
9	`www.encarta.msn.com`	Dictionary	Not relevant (empty)	N/A
10	`deltafarmpress.com`	Producers may put fish on insect diet	Technical/News	High (10.0)

Table 1: Top ten results, in rank order, for the query [*insect diet*] from a commercial search engine, showing the wide variation in reading level that can occur for material retrieved on the same query. Reading level here is estimated using the statistical model described in Section 3.1 and shown in brackets. (Query issued on January 20, 2011.)

a profile of the user's reading proficiency, estimating a document's reading difficulty, and re-ranking algorithms that can effectively combine relevance and difficulty signals to improve search quality. Section 3 then develops the theoretical models and algorithms we use to address each of these three areas. In Section 4 we contrast the search behavior of two groups: users looking for 'kids'-related material and general users, by performing a large-scale log analysis of query, session, and result properties. This analysis helps provide insights into features that may be useful for improving re-ranking by reading-level. Section 5 evaluates the effectiveness of those algorithms according to implicit relevance judgments obtained from actual Web search logs comprising queries, search result clicks, and post-click navigation events. Finally, in Sections 6 and 7 we discuss areas for future research and summarize our findings.

2. RELATED WORK

Personalizing search using reading level touches on several research areas with relevant prior work: search systems for children and students; modeling user expertise and topic familiarity; algorithms for predicting reading difficulty; and personalization or re-ranking methods based on additional user-specific relevance signals.

Effective search systems for children and students have been the focus of increased interest in recent years. Progress in improved user interfaces, crawling and indexing strategies, and models of child-centered relevance are all important in creating a better search experience for children. The PuppyIR project [15] has begun to examine these types of important questions around the design of search engines, especially user interfaces and finding appropriate Web sites for children [7]. To date, however, there has been little, if any, published work on user modeling and re-ranking algorithms based on reading level and their deployment and evaluation in a commercial-scale search engine. Gyllstrom and Moens [10] proposed a binary labeling of Web documents: material for children versus adults, where the label is inferred using a PageRank-inspired graph walk algorithm called AgeRank. For queries, recent work has explored query expansion methods for queries formulated by children [18]. Our approach operates at a lower level and assumes that common operations such as spelling correction have already been performed by the retrieval system to obtain the top-ranked documents, although such additional processing may well be improved using the methods and features that we develop in this paper. Torres *et al.* [17] performed an analysis of the AOL query log to characterize so-called 'Kids' queries. A query was labeled as a Kids query if and only if it had a corresponding clicked document whose domain was listed as an ODP entry in the 'Kids&Teens' ODP top-level category. Our study includes analysis based on the same definition, but we also explore the important dimension of reading level.

An emerging community of human-factors researchers has been focusing on children's experiences in searching for information online. Hirsh [11] carried out a detailed study of the relevance criteria that children employ when searching for information online. The study offers important findings on what criteria matter to children as they search the Web (e.g., topicality was viewed as much more important than authority). Bilal [2] investigated children's cognitive, affective, and physical behaviors as they use the Yahooligans! search engine to find information on a specific search task. Bilal found that childrens' search processes were ineffective and inefficient, as well as of low quality, suggesting that children need to be better trained in how to search – or search engines need to adapt, as we are advocating for in this paper. More recently, Druin *et al.* [6] studied how children use keyword-based Web search and found that children exhibit a number of different roles (e.g., content searcher, distracted searcher) that have implications for the design of new search interfaces tailored toward children's information needs and search behaviors.

Search engines have attempted to adapt to children's use in other ways. For example, many search engines provide a degree of parental control filtering, which blocks inappropriate material. Other sites provide a corpus of high-quality but highly controlled 'white-listed' sites that is curated by human editors, but limited in scope and recency compared to the standard Web. Since these other areas are either existing technologies or outside the scope of our research, we focus on the core problem of improving search result relevance for users, given an estimate of their reading proficiency.

Estimating reading difficulty has been studied for decades, but traditional formulae such as Flesch-Kincaid provide only a crude combination of vocabulary and syntactic difficulty estimates [5]. Recent progress has been made in applying statistical modeling and machine learning to improve reading difficulty estimation for non-traditional documents [5][12] such as Web pages or short snippets. An earlier study on predicting query readability level [14] attempted automatic recognition of reading levels from user queries by using Support Vector Machines with syntactic and vocabulary-based features. A study by Clarke *et al.* [4] showed that the features of snippets provided by search engines have the potential for significant influence on clickthrough behavior. Their study included an ad-hoc readability measure for each snippet: the percentage of words that occur in a list of the 100 most frequent English words. They did not experimentally validate this measure, but it is related to the Dale readability feature we include (Section 3.1.2).

Reading difficulty is related to, but separate from, the *topic familiarity* of a document to a user. Kumaran *et al.* [13] examined re-ranking Web search results with respect to topic familiarity. Their study results suggested that traditional reading difficulty features and formulas such as Flesch-Kincaid alone could not predict whether a document was an introductory or advanced text for a given topic. However, our study retains a focus on general language proficiency, where it is somewhat easier to distinguish between levels. We also do not rely exclusively on traditional difficulty measures as these have been shown to perform poorly for Web texts [5]. Instead, we apply a robust statistical modeling approach that is able to capture detailed, per-word distinctions in usage across grades.

White *et al.* [22] examined how domain expertise influences Web search behavior, and their analysis of numerous query and session features inspired our own choice of features for result re-ranking. Earlier work by Teevan *et al.* [16] examined general personalization based on a variety of user behavior and content-based features, and re-ranked using a simple interpolation formula. A number of studies have investigated combining a base relevance score with auxiliary user- or group-associated features to perform personalized re-ranking. This includes subtopic coverage and novelty [24], which gives a multiplicative re-ranking update but also assumes a particular retrieval model. We emphasize that this paper is about solving multiple problems to provide an end-to-end solution that assumes little about the base ranking score or underlying retrieval model and thus can be applied in a wide variety of systems.

With this research we extend previous work in a number of ways. First, we introduce a document labeling methodology that assigns reading level and ODP category predictions to both documents and the corresponding query-biased snippet that searchers use when making search engine result page (SERP) clickthrough decisions. These labels play an important role in re-ranking and the evaluation of re-ranking. Second, we describe how a user's reading proficiency profile may be estimated automatically from their current and past search behavior. Finally, we train and evaluate at Web scale a re-ranking algorithm that combines both relevance and difficulty in a principled way, and allows proficiency profile features to be used to re-rank Web search results.

3. PROBLEM FORMULATION

There are three key problems to solve in order to incorporate reading level as a relevance signal for Web search: (i) estimating reading level of documents and snippets, (ii) estimating reading proficiency of users, and (iii) ranking documents based on reading level of users and documents. We now treat each of these in turn.

3.1 Estimating reading difficulty of documents and snippets

We represent the reading difficulty of a document or text as a random variable R_d taking values in the range $[1, 12]$. In this study, these values correspond to American school grade levels, although they could easily be modified for finer or coarser distinctions in level, or for different tasks or populations. We computed reading level predictions for two different representations of a page: the combined title and summary text, which we call a 'snippet', that appears for that page in the search engine results page; and the full body text extracted from the HTML of the underlying page. The snippet text and full-page text are complementary sources of information. While the snippet provides a relatively short sample of content for the underlying page, it is query-specific, and is what users see in choosing whether or not the corresponding page may be relevant and thus whether to click the result. The full-page text, in contrast, is not affected by a query, and is what users see *after* clicking on a result hyperlink on the search result page. We were interested in the interaction of snippet and page level estimates as well as their individual effectiveness. Indeed, we discovered a strong interaction of snippet-page difficulty difference with page dwell time (see Section 4.4 for more details).

3.1.1 Prediction using language models

The reading difficulty prediction method that we use for this study, summarized in this section, has been shown to be effective for both short, noisy texts, and full-page Web texts. Unlike traditional measures that compute a single numeric score, methods based on statistical language modeling provide extra information about score reliability by computing the likely *distribution* over levels, which can be used to compute confidence estimates. Moreover, language models are vocabulary-centric and can capture fine-grained patterns in individual word behavior across levels. Thus, they are ideal for the noisy, short, fragmented text that occurs on the Web in queries, titles, result snippets, image or table captions. Because of this short, noisy nature of Web snippets we applied a robust, vocabulary-oriented reading difficulty prediction methods that is a hybrid of the original smoothed unigram approach [5] and a more recent model based on estimated age of word acquisition [12].

Following [12], we say that a document D has an (r, s)-reading level t if at least s percent of the words in D are familiar to at least r percent of the general population[1]. We say that a word has r-acquisition level $\mu_w(r)$ if r percent of the population have acquired the word by grade μ_w. For a fixed (but large) vocabulary V of distinct words, we define an approximate age-of-acquisition for all words $w \in V$ using a truncated normal distribution with parameters (μ_w, σ_w). We estimated (μ_w, σ_w) from a corpus of labeled Web content from [5]. With these word parameters, we can then apply the above definition of (r, s)-readability. To compute the readability distribution of a text passage, we accumulate individual word predictions into a stepwise cumulative density function (CDF). Each word contributes in proportion to its frequency in the passage. The reading level of the text is then the grade level corresponding to the s-th percentile of the text's word acquisition CDF. Details are given in Kidwell *et al.* [12].

3.1.2 Prediction using traditional semantic variables

We also compute a traditional measure of vocabulary-based difficulty: the fraction of unknown words in a query or snippet (which we call the 'Dale readability measure') relative to the Dale 3000 word list, which is the semantic component of the Dale-Chall reading difficulty measure [3].

3.1.3 Category prediction

We used automatic classification techniques to assign a category label to each page. A logistic regression classifier using an L2 regularizer was trained over each of the ODP topics identified: for the experiments reported in this study we had available the 219 topical categories from the top two levels of the ODP hierarchy, although we focus primarily on the Kids&Teens category in this study. Our classi-

[1]In that study, the authors found that setting $r = 0.80$ and $s = 0.65$ provided the greatest reduction in training error, and so we use the same settings for r and s here.

fier assigned one or more labels using a similar approach to that described in [1]. We chose to use the Open Directory Project (ODP) for classification because of its broad, general purpose topic coverage; the availability of reasonably high-quality training data; and of special interest is the Kids&Teens category, which was created in Nov. 2000 with its own set of editorial guidelines with the goal of providing kids-safe content for the under-18 age group.

3.2 Estimating reading proficiency of users

One approach is to have users self-identify their level of reading proficiency. For example, this is the approach that Google has recently used as part of their advanced search tools: users may choose to filter the results to show only 'basic', 'intermediate', or 'advanced' reading level. This approach has as its advantages both simplicity of user interaction and transparency of search behavior. One disadvantage of such an approach is that it may be difficult for users to properly calibrate their reading level. Also, reading proficiency may change over time, and it may be dependent on the actual query issued. Thus, we can consider ways to construct a reading proficiency profile automatically from search behavior. This may include the previous queries and click-throughs in either the session, or the user's long-term history. We discuss one such approach now.

To match the difficulty distribution $p(R_d)$ of a document given in Sec. 3.1.1, we define a proficiency profile for user u to be a distribution $p(R_u)$ over levels, allowing us to compute the probability that a user understands a document. As with the document, R_u can take values in the range $[1, 12]$. Here, we give a generative model for a user's search sessions that we will use in estimating $p(R_u)$ from a user's search behavior. Although the prior distribution $p(R_u)$ is assumed to be the same for all of a user's search sessions, the posterior $p(R_u \mid \text{query})$ depends on the query and may differ between sessions. Let Q denote the set of queries that the user has issued in this session, and let D_q denote the documents that the user clicks on in response to the query. We make the assumption that a user clicks and *dwells* on a document only if they can understand it - or more generally, if they like the page because the reading level is appropriate to their intent[2]. A session is generated as follows:

1. $r_d \sim p(R_d)$ (given in Sec. 3.1.1)
2. $r_u \sim p(R_u)$ (to estimate)
3. For all $q \in Q$:
   (a) $q \sim p(\text{query} \mid r_u)$
   (b) For all $d \in D_q$:
   SAT-click $= 1 \sim p(u \text{ likes reading level of } d \mid r_u, r_d)$

Typically, users will like reading documents whose difficulty is at or below their average proficiency level, and dislike documents more and more as their difficulty increases above this average level. To reflect this, we may choose a definition such as

$$p(u \text{ likes level of } d \mid r_u, r_d) = \exp(-\max(0, r_d - r_u)). \quad (1)$$

However, the appropriate form of Eq. 1 may vary depending on the user and their intent. For example, some expert users looking for high-difficulty technical material may actually want to penalize easier documents, to avoid introductory material. Other users, such as students, may also want material that is neither too difficult nor too easy relative to their level. Thus, we can instead define

$$p(u \text{ likes level of } d \mid r_u, r_d) = \exp(-(r_d - r_u)^2).$$

In this study we use Eq. 1 but exploring other forms or learning this from data is a topic for future work.

The distribution $p(\text{query} \mid R_u)$ would ideally be a language model that is directly estimated using query logs. An alternative is to use the language model that we developed for document classification. However, query readability may be very different from document readability. The distinction is that the words a user *recognizes* may be different from the words that they choose to use in queries. A much simpler approach is to simply model the length of the query, ignoring the actual words. As we show in Figure 1, the query length can be informative about a user's reading proficiency.

We use the above ideas to compute a session-based query difficulty feature based on the average reading level of the satisfied clicks that a user enacts in previous queries within the session.

If we also have access to the set of web sites that a user frequently visits, we could use these to help predict the reading proficiency of a user. For example, Club Penguin and Funbrain are two sites often visited by children, but less frequently visited by adults. This is a topic for future work.

3.3 Re-ranking based on reading difficulty

To learn effective re-rankings and to explore the importance of features related to reading level, we use the LambdaMART [23] algorithm, a state-of-the-art ranking algorithm based on boosted regression trees. Compared with other ranking approaches LambdaMART is typically more robust to sets of features with widely varying ranges of values, such as categorical features. Since LambdaMART produces a tree-based model, it can be used as a feature selection algorithm or to rank features by their importance (Section 5.1.2). Based on the results of our analysis in Section 4, along with evidence on the effectiveness of specific features gathered by other authors in previous studies of expertise [22], we chose the following set of features for study.

Query features. These features rely only on the query string and include query length in characters and query length in space-delimited words.

Query/session features. If previous queries were present in a session, we estimate a dynamic reading level for a user by taking the average reading level of the clicked snippets from previous queries in the same user search session. Because of the sparse nature of clicks we also compute a confidence value for this query level that increases with the sample size of clicked snippets. We also include a measure of the length of a session, in terms of the number of previous queries.

Snippet features. We compute the estimated reading difficulty of a page's snippet using the algorithm described in Section 3.1.1, and the Dale-Chall semantic variable from Section 3.1.2. We also include the relative difficulty of the snippet compared to the levels of the other top-ranked result snippets: snippets are sorted by descending reading level, and then the reciprocal rank of the snippet is computed with respect to that ranking.

Page features. Using the same reading level prediction algorithm used for snippets, we compute reading difficulty for the body text of the Web page corresponding to a snippet. We also include a confidence feature for this prediction.

Snippet-page features. We compute the (signed) difference between the full page reading level and the snippet reading level.

Query-page features. These features capture the strength of a query-document match: the main signals here are the

[2]A widely-used dwell time satisfaction threshold in Web search is 30 seconds, termed a 'satisfied' click or SAT-click. In reality, dwell time may vary with a number of factors, such as the age or reading proficiency of the user.

Source	Feature Name	Description
Query	query_char_len	Query length (in characters)
	query_word_len	Query length (in words)
Query (Session)	session_user_level	Session-based user reading level estimate
	session_user_level_confidence	Confidence estimate for user reading level
	prev_queries_in_session	Number of previous queries in current search session
Snippet	snippet_difficulty	Reading level of snippet
	relative_snippet_difficulty	Relative snippet difficulty in top 10 results
	dale_snippet_difficulty	Dale difficulty level
Page	full_page_difficulty	Reading level of page body text
	full_page_difficulty_confidence	Confidence level for full-page reading level
Snippet-Page	snippet_page_level_difference	Difference between reading levels of snippet and full page
	snippet_page_difference_confidence	Confidence level for snippet-page level difference
Query-Page	norm_production_score	Normalized ranker score for a page
	reciprocal_rank_score	Reciprocal rank of page
Query-Snippet	snippet_query_diff	Signed difference in reading level between query and snippet
	snippet_query_diff_abs	Absolute difference in reading level between query and snippet

Table 2: The features used by LambdaMART reranking. Features that potentially make use of previous queries in a session are denoted (Session).

normalized ranker score from the search engine, and the reciprocal rank of a page in the top ten results.
Query-snippet features. We compute the absolute and signed differences between the estimated user reading level and the estimated snippet reading level.

Table 2 summarizes the set of features used for ranking.

4. LARGE-SCALE QUERY LOG ANALYSIS

In this section we perform a summary analysis of search log data in order to contrast the properties of Kids and non-Kids users and data sources. We conjectured that Kids sessions and queries would exhibit differences, especially with respect to the reading level of preferred result snippets. Our analysis also estimates coverage for Kids queries to assess the likely impact of personalization in this area, and shows that having both snippet- and page-level reading level predictions is valuable.

4.1 Data set and evaluation methodology

The primary source of data for this study was a proprietary data set containing the anonymized logs of URLs visited by users who consented to provide interaction data through a widely-distributed browser plug-in. The data set contained browser-based logs with both searching and browsing episodes from which we extract search-related data. These data provide us with examples of real-world searching behavior that may be useful in understanding and modeling kids-related search. Log entries include a browser identifier, a timestamp for each page view, and the URL of the Web page visited. To remove variability caused by geographic and linguistic variation in search behavior, we only include log entries generated in the English-speaking United States locale. The results described in this paper are based on URL visits during the first week of October 2010 representing millions of Web page visits from hundreds of thousands of unique users. From these data we extracted search sessions from a major commercial Web search engine, using a session extraction methodology similar to [20]. Search sessions begin with a query, occur within the same browser and tab instance (to lessen the effect of any multi-tasking that users may perform), and terminate following 30 minutes of user inactivity.

From these search sessions we extracted search queries and for each query, we obtained the top ten search results retrieved by the Web search engine and the titles and the snippets for each result that were displayed on the search engine's result page at query time. We then estimated the grade level distribution for each of those results using the snippet text and the full text of the corresponding Web page, per the method described in Section 3.1.1.

In addition, we also obtained binary relevance judgments for each result in the top 10 using a methodology similar to that in [9]. We define a satisfied (SAT) click in a similar way to previous work [19] (i.e., with either a dwell time post-click of 30 seconds or the last SERP click in the session). Advantages of these log-based judgments are that many judgments can be easily gathered, and that they are personalized to the user and the query, which is important in the evaluation of personalized search algorithms. With these judgments, we define two evaluation scenarios: 'Last-SAT', which assigns a positive judgment to one of the top 10 URLs if it is the *last* satisfied SERP click in the session (by click time); and 'All-SAT', which assigns a positive judgment to *any* satisfied click in a session. (In both cases, the remaining top-ranked URLs receive a negative judgment.) While Last-SAT has been shown to be highly indicative of a user's goal [9], we also examine All-SAT since informational queries, which are more likely to have multiple relevant results, may exhibit different performance qualities.

For the Last-SAT case, the Mean Reciprocal Rank (MRR) of the positive judgment is used to evaluate retrieval performance before and after re-ranking. For All-SAT, we evaluate average precision on the top 10 results.

Queries for which we cannot assign a positive judgment to any top-10 URL are excluded from the feature set. We also excluded queries corresponding to twelve very high frequency navigational queries[3]. Although there are benefits to including these queries, such as detecting engine switching behavior [21], their highly predictable nature across users makes them less interesting for a personalization study, and removing them also greatly reduces data processing demands.

After this filtering, 759,671 queries remained. Of these, 555,048 queries (73%) had no previous queries in the same session and 205,623 had at least one previous query, leaving 27% of queries potentially amenable to session-based improvements. The 27% is low, since previous work has found

[3]facebook, google, myspace, gmail, bing, yahoo, yahoomail, craigslist, youtube, ebay, aol, hotmail.

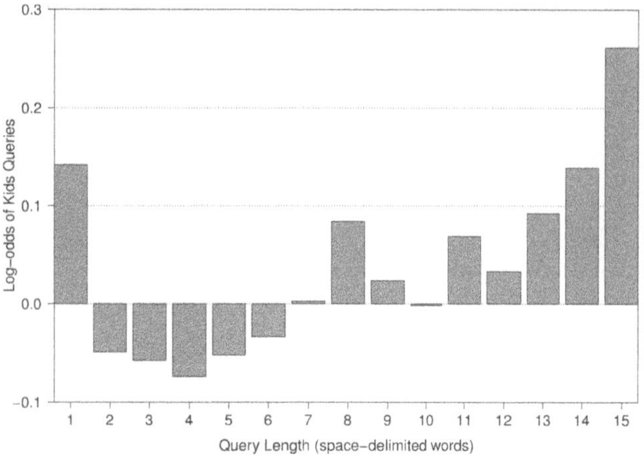

Figure 1: Log-odds of query length (in words) for Kids vs. All queries, showing that single-word queries and queries with eight words or more are more likely for Kids queries than general queries.

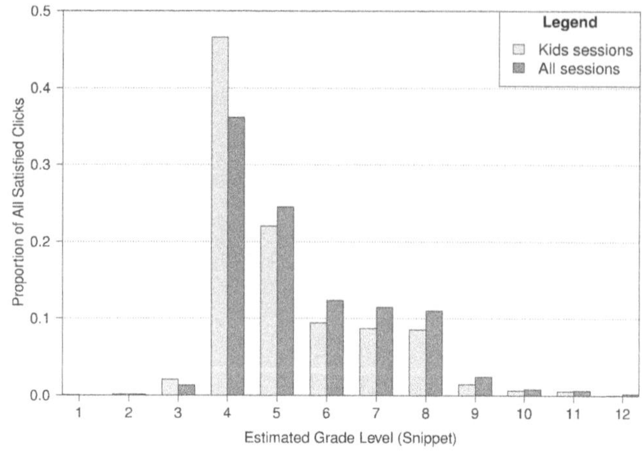

Figure 2: The estimated reading difficulty of snippets for pages with satisfied clicks, for Kids sessions and all sessions.

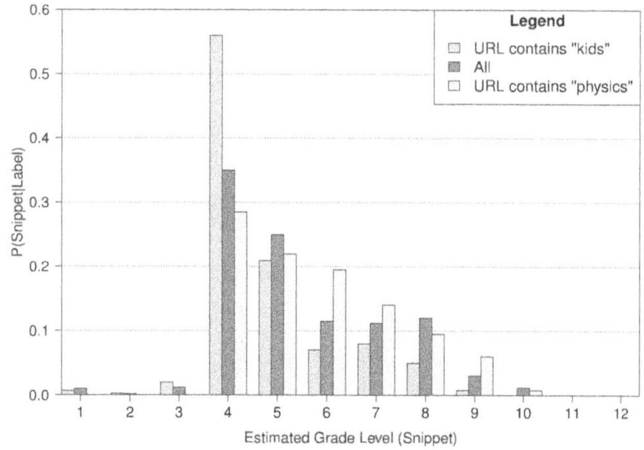

Figure 3: The estimated reading difficulty of snippets of pages with different substrings in their URL: 'kids' and 'physics' have sharply different difficulty distributions, with the All distribution lying in between.

that 60% of search sessions contained multiple queries [20]. This may be explained in part by differences in the search behavior of users issuing Kids queries and perhaps even the removal of the small set of high-frequency navigational queries.

4.2 Query properties

We used our development set (Section 5.1) to extract 29,498 total queries and 19,601 unique queries having at least one click on a SERP result labeled with the Kids&Teens ODP category. We compared this to the properties of the full development set, with no filtering, which we call the All queries set.

Many of the most frequent queries found in a recent AOL query log analysis by Torres *et al.* [17] also appeared highly ranked in our list in various forms, such as [*nick jr*], [*starfall.com*], [*coloring pages*] and [*dora*]. We found that the distribution of query lengths for Kids sessions was also similar to Torres *et al.* , with longer queries being more likely on average, as shown in Figure 1, possibly due to a greater frequency of natural language queries. Query lengths above the line (positive log-odds) are more likely for Kids queries, and those below the line are more likely for All queries. Our data also showed that single-word queries were more likely, as the result of a larger proportion of navigational queries.

4.3 Reading level distribution of snippets

Of all SERP clicks, 3.6% were satisfied clicks in our Kids sessions sample. The distribution of snippet reading levels for all SAT clicks for Kids and All queries is shown in Figure 2. The figure shows that the estimated reading difficulty of snippets associated with satisfied clicks is skewed toward lower grade levels for queries coming from Kids sessions, compared to all queries.

As an example of the connection between simple syntactic features within a page's URL string and the estimated reading level of its snippet, we extracted URLs containing the substring 'kids' and another set containing the substring 'physics'. Figure 3 shows that the two reading level distributions are very different: the 'physics' distribution is shifted toward a much higher level of difficulty. The All distribution lies in an intermediate area between the two. Our comparison here makes the assumption that documents about physics are of higher difficulty whereas the vast majority of kids documents are of lower difficulty. Indeed, we can see this reflected in the actual distributions in Figure 3.

Note that Figure 2 is computed from user clicks while Figure 3 is computed from properties of URL strings, which are user-agnostic. Thus, Figure 2 shows whether users take reading difficulty into consideration in deciding whether they like a page. For example, it could be that for the query [*physics*] all users click on documents with reading level 10 – this would be captured in the type of histogram shown in Figure 2 but not in Figure 3.

4.4 Snippet-page difficulty gap predicts average dwell time

To assess the importance of using both snippet and page representations of reading level, we examined the correlation between the *difference* in the predicted reading levels of a SERP snippet vs. the full text of the corresponding Web page, and the average user dwell time (in seconds) for that Web page. We found a strong relationship between these quantities: for example, the more difficult the underlying page is, compared to the clicked snippet for that page, the

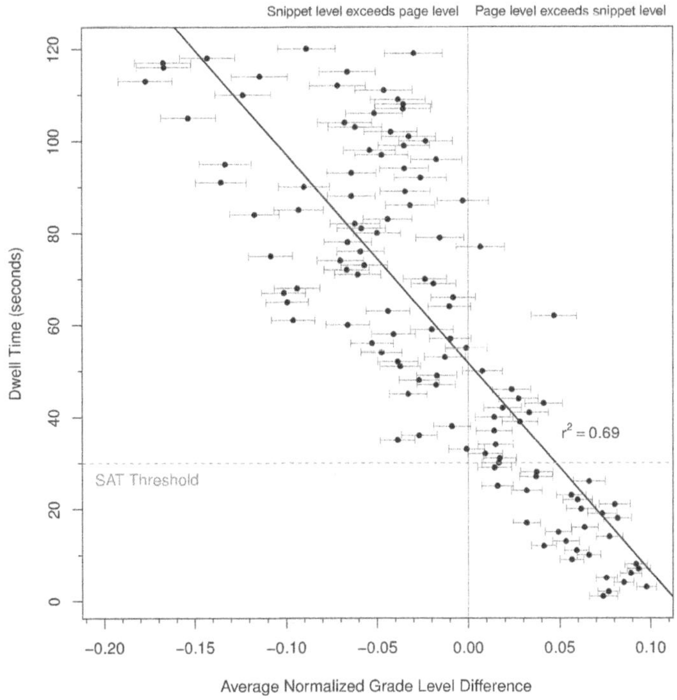

Figure 4: Average user dwell time is strongly predicted by the difference between the query-specific snippet reading difficulty and the underlying page reading difficulty. As actual page difficulty increases relative to the displayed snippet, user will be more likely to abandon that page quickly. Error bars denote 95% confidence intervals.

more likely it became that the user would be unsatisfied and leave that page quickly (e.g., spend less than 30 seconds reading it). This is summarized in Figure 4. The means and confidence intervals for each dwell time, conditioned on snippet-page reading level difference, are shown in Figure 4 and were computed by the bootstrap method [8], using 100 iterations over the search log data. Each iteration sampled $N = 630,000$ click instances with replacement. The Pearson correlation coefficient over all dwell times of 120 seconds or less was $r^2 = 0.69$: a strong signal about the behavior of a user population. This is an important finding with a number of implications. First, it provides clear evidence that modeling *both* snippet and page level provides a valuable generic relevance signal. As we show later in Section 5.1.2, the difference between snippet and page level does have high relative weight among effective ranking features. Second, it suggests that snippet quality could be improved by constraining a snippet's expected reading level to closely match the underlying page reading level.

4.5 Coverage for Kids-related queries

To understand what percentage of queries may be related to children's information needs and thus might be candidates for reading level-based personalization, we extracted all URLs from the Kids&Teens categories in the ODP and considered them to be children-friendly URLs given the ODP editing guidelines for these categories.

We used a query-click bipartite graph from anonymous search data containing a node for each query and each clicked URL for one month of 2010 query traffic in the English-speaking United States locale from a large commercial search engine. Query nodes are connected via edges to the URLs

ODP Kids&Teens URLs	45,879
Unique Queries (with clicks on these URLs)	1,360,341
Impressions from these queries	286,174,932
Coverage	13.62%

Table 3: Kids&Teens-related traffic statistics (one month).

users actually clicked on for those queries during a search session. We looked up the ODP children-friendly URLs in this graph and extracted the queries leading to clicks on these URLs. While it is impossible to know if these queries were issued by users in the age range targeted by ODP with the Kids&Teens categories, we used this method to characterize such queries as having some degree of Kids&Teens intent. Using this technique, we estimated the coverage of Kids&Teens queries to be 13.62% of non-bot traffic. Summary statistics are shown in Table 3.

The dataset used to identify queries with Kids&Teens intent includes impressions collected from multiple revisions of the underlying Web search results ranking algorithm, meaning that there was significant variance Web search results returned for the same queries. As a result, we consider the 13.62% coverage presented here as a ceiling of opportunity for personalization of the search experience for children. In addition, our earlier analysis (from Section 4.1) shows that at least 27% of those Kids&Teens queries might be amenable to additional session-based improvements.

5. EVALUATION

Our evaluation section consists of three parts: re-ranking results, an analysis of relative feature importance, and robustness evaluation.

5.1 Re-ranking performance

In this section we confirm the effectiveness of re-ranking Web search results using reading level features. We examine not only basic retrieval performance in Section 5.1.1 but also the relative importance of different features (Section 5.1.2), and the robustness in rank gains and losses (Section 5.1.3).

We partitioned our log data as described in Section 4 randomly into two sets: 25% was used as a development set for LambdaMART parameter optimization, and the remaining 75% was used for training/test splits using 10-fold cross-validation. To avoid bias toward longer sessions, these sets were further subsampled to one random query per session.

5.1.1 Basic retrieval performance

In order to account for the possibility of query sets with relevant documents biased lower in the ranking (such as difficult queries), we trained a learned rank-only baseline reranking model using two features: the commercial search engine ranker score, and the rank position of a document. This model always performs at least as well as the original commercial ranker score. As described in Section 4, our main evaluation measures are the change in Mean Reciprocal Rank (MRR) of the last satisfied click ('Last-SAT'), and Mean Average Precision (MAP) using all satisfied clicks ('All-SAT'). In practice, because the vast majority of queries have only one click, there turns out to be almost no difference in performance between Last-SAT and All-SAT on this dataset, but we report both numbers for the full query set experiment for completeness. Because of the proprietary nature of our search engine system we do not report absolute MRR, but instead report relative change in MRR on a point scale from 0 to 100: $(MRR_{MODEL} - MRR_{BASE}) \cdot 100$, where MRR_{BASE} is the learned rank-only baseline MRR for

Experiment	Last-SAT (MRR Change)	All-SAT (MAP Change)
Rank-only Baseline	0.0	0.0
Query+Session	$+0.7^{\star}$	$+0.6^{\star}$
Query+Session+Page	$+0.8^{\star}$	$+0.8^{\star}$
Query+Session+Snippet	$+1.0^{\star}$	$+0.9^{\star}$
All Features	$+1.2^{\star}$	$+1.1^{\star}$

Table 4: Summary of the relative performance for different feature sets on full query set, in terms of change points in MRR (Last-SAT) and MAP (All-SAT). The Rank-only Baseline is used as the baseline for comparison and thus set to 0.0. Superscripts $\star$ and $+$ denote significance of change at $p < 0.01$ and $p < 0.10$ respectively using a paired t-test.

Query subset	Num. queries	% Total	Baseline Rel. MRR	Model Rel. MRR	Gain
Kids	15,796	4.4%	−4.1	−3.1	$+1.0^{\star}$
Science	23,059	6.8%	−9.0	−4.7	$+4.3^{\star}$
Sports	41,139	11.6%	+7.2	+8.2	$+1.0^{\star}$
Health	21,581	6.1%	−7.3	−7.3	0.0
All	545,255	100%	0.0	+1.2	$+1.2^{\star}$

Table 5: Summary of gains in MRR for Last-SAT click from re-ranking with reading-level features. To show the relative difficulty of different query sets, the Baseline Relative MRR Change is computed relative to the Rank-only Baseline for all queries in the test set, so that relative MRR for the 'All' query set is zero. Similarly, the Model Relative MRR Change is also computed relative to the Rank-only Baseline for all queries. Gain is the difference between the Model and Baseline. Superscripts $\star$ and $+$ denote significance of change at $p < 0.01$ and $p < 0.10$ respectively using a paired t-test.

all queries. We note that the baseline ranking, representing a highly-tuned commercial search engine, is very competitive, and even a 1-point change in MRR, when statistically significant, is considered a notable gain.

Table 4 compares the performance of the learned rank-only baseline to our model, for different features of the system. Across the full query set, there was a statistically significant +1.2 point MRR gain for Last-SAT clicks, and +1.1 point MAP gain for All-SAT clicks. Starting with the Rank-only baseline, we added a basic set of Query+Session features that made no use of snippet or page-level reading difficulty predictions, which gave an MRR gain of +0.7. To compare the relative utility of page vs. snippet features, we then added either all snippet-based features, or all page-based features, to the basic Query+Session set. The snippet-based features gave a slightly larger gain (+1.0) compared to adding full-page features (+0.8). Finally, we achieved the best overall performance when both snippet and page features were used together with the other features.

To investigate the effect of re-ranking using reading difficulty features on queries of different topics, we chose the ODP Kids&Teens, Science, Sports, and Health categories. For each of these categories, we extracted individual queries having at least one click on a URL belonging to that ODP category[4]. Table 5 shows gains and losses achieved by re-ranking for Kids, Science, Sports, and Health subsets of queries[5]. An increasingly negative (resp. positive) value for Base Relative MRR indicates a harder (resp. easier) retrieval task compared to the All Queries scenario.

Across several useful subclasses of queries, re-ranking with reading level features gave consistent, statistically significant gains in MRR compared to the learned rank-only baseline. The most challenging query set in terms of low baseline (Science) had a rank-only relative baseline of -9.0 compared to the rank-only baseline of the full query set, while the 'easiest' subclass was Sports, whose rank-only baseline change was +7.2 over the full query set. After adding reading level features, our ranking model achieved net MRR point gains of +1.0 for Kids queries, +4.3 for Science queries, and +1.0 for Sports queries. Somewhat surprisingly, Health queries showed no gain - the reasons for this require further study.

It is encouraging to find a class of queries like Science queries that obtain a particularly large benefit from reading level features. The Science category contains a higher proportion of more technical material than most other ODP categories[6] and thus search results for those queries might be expected to have higher reading difficulty entropy, leading to greater potential for personalization. Kids&Teens pages, in contrast, are typically already tailored for children and thus have less variation in reading level, which may explain the reduced effect of reading level features on those queries.

5.1.2 *Relative effectiveness of ranking features*

To understand the relative contribution of our query, session, snippet, and page-based reading difficulty features to re-ranking effectiveness, we used LambdaMART to obtain scores representing relative feature importance. These scores are computed as the average reduction in residual squared error when applying the given feature, averaged over all trees and over all splits. The scores are then normalized relative to the most informative feature, which has a score of 1.000. Table 6 lists the top-scoring features resulting from our main experiment using all features over all queries, averaged over 10 cross-validation splits.

Examining the top five features in this list, the highest-weighted feature - perhaps not surprisingly - was the reciprocal rank score of a page, reflecting the extreme bias toward top-ranked clicks that is typical of Web search results. Rela-

[4]For classifying queries in this way, the click did not have to be a satisfied click.

[5]Note that according to our definition, a query can belong to potentially multiple ODP categories depending on the user's clicked pages, so the query counts in Table 5 do not sum to the total number of all queries. Also, total queries reported here are about 70% of the total queries reported in Section 4, due to combined effects of query subsampling to reduce session length bias, and 10-fold cross-validation split.

[6]For example, the average reading difficulty level estimated for snippets for Kids&Teens pages was 4.53, for Sports was 4.79 and for Science was 5.34.

Feature	Rel. Weight
Reciprocal rank score	1.000
Relative snippet difficulty	0.295
Query length in characters	0.237
Session-based user reading level	0.216
Snippet-page reading level difference	0.207
Dale snippet difficulty level	0.186
Normalized ranker score	0.183
Query-snippet reading level difference	0.142
Query length in words	0.116
Snippet-page level difference confidence	0.081
Snippet reading level	0.076
Page reading level	0.048
Number of previous queries in session	0.030
Session-based user reading level confidence	0.019

Table 6: The relative importance of features computed by LambdaMART reranking for all queries. Feature importance in the right column is the average reduction in residual squared error over all trees and over all splits, relative to the most informative feature.

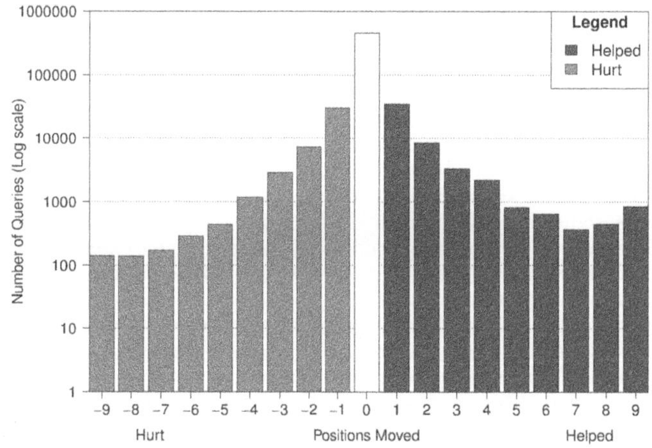

Figure 5: Histogram showing the variance of losses (left tail) and gains (right tail) using re-ranking by reading level features on All queries. The loss or gain in rank position of the last satified click is given on the x-axis. The y-axis denotes the number of queries (note the log scale).

tive snippet difficulty was the second-most important feature (0.295), which matches what we have observed informally: that when picking from a list of otherwise similar results, users tend to pick the snippet with lowest reading difficulty. Query length in characters was more influential (0.237) than query length in words (0.116), although both contributed to the prediction performance. The predictive power of query length is in accordance with the log-odds length distribution shown in Figure 1. Estimating the user's reading proficiency from their previous session queries proved to be another highly-ranked feature (0.216), showing the importance of user-specific personalization. As predicted by our analysis in Section 4.4, the reading level difference between a snippet and its corresponding Web page also carries valuable information, and this is reflected in its position as one of the top 5 features (0.207).

Among the remaining features, the Dale difficulty feature of the snippet, with a relative weight of 0.186, proved moderately effective as a complementary level prediction. Several base features, such as snippet-page level difference, have corresponding confidence features: one of these (for snippet-page level difference) did appear in the top 10 (0.081) while the others had much weaker feature scores.

5.1.3 *Robustness of re-ranking*

While improving a retrieval metric's average gain across queries is important, in the case of re-ranking an existing set of results, the *variance* of relative gains and losses compared to the initial ranking is also critical to measure. An algorithm may improve average performance, but also increase the number of queries dramatically hurt by re-ranking.

Figure 5 shows the distribution of gains and losses across all queries for the re-ranking model used in Section 3.3, as measured by the change in rank position of the last satisfied click. A robust algorithm is one that is able to achieve good on-average results, while having a minimal failure profile – as measured by a statistic like the number of queries hurt by re-ranking (the left half of histogram in Figure 5). Out of a total of 545,245 queries, 450,921 queries (82.7%) had no change; 51,759 (9.4%) were helped (rank of the last SAT click increased at least one position); and 42,565 (7.8%) were hurt (rank of the last SAT click decreased by at least one rank position). While more work is needed on methods to reduce the loss side of the histogram, the multi-position gains we obtain are encouraging. In particular, for changes of 6 or more rank positions, we achieve a ratio of queries helped to hurt of greater than 2 to 1.

6. DISCUSSION

Personalization by reading level can be considered somewhat orthogonal, but complementary, to other dimensions of personalization such as location, domain expertise, or topical interest. Our study is, to our knowledge, the first of its kind to study and evaluate personalization by reading level as an aspect of large-scale Web search. From our work it is clear that some problems, such as automatically estimating a reliable user profile of reading proficiency, and finding more accurate or effective features for re-ranking, are non-trivial and require further research. Furthermore, while our study included some features defined over a single user session, we believe learning and applying a longer-term user history could also be quite valuable.

Many improvements and interesting directions remain to help users find and understand material appropriate to their needs and reading level. For example, while personalization seeks to adapt the content to the user, we can also consider the reverse goal: adapting the *user* to the content. By this we mean applying models of reading level and vocabulary difficulty to identify *learning opportunities* that would help reduce the gap between the user's reading proficiency and document reading level. For example, a search engine might identify critical 'words to learn' on a topic, such as *bronchitis* for coughs in a home medical care page. A similar idea could be used to help non-native language learners.

The role of reading level features in improving query and document representations is also a rich area for further study. As our findings on dwell time in Section 4.4 suggest, identifying differences in vocabulary or reading level distribution between the different representation streams of a Web page, such as anchor text and captions, and those of the underlying page could help identify problems with snippet or document quality, or even distinctions in usage between different user groups. Also, the variation of dwell times across different ages or reading proficiency levels may also be interesting to investigate further. When processing a likely Kids query, the search engine could provide more child-appropriate snippets or query suggestions for that query. Since the reading level distribution of a page can be pre-computed and stored in the index, improvements in reranking that require reading level could be applied quickly and reliably. We also believe that the interaction of reading level with topic is important and intend to explore this combination in future work.

In general, reading difficulty level can serve as a valuable contextual signal to improve the ranking of documents presented to individual users during a search session. Document relevance may be improved using the language models in this paper because they can characterize user intent based on vocabulary usage during and across search sessions. Search engines could further leverage these models to personalize all aspects of the user experience, including captions, ads, images, videos, or even pure presentation features such as font size, site previews, and page composition. While the actual impact of such personalization efforts on overall user satisfaction remains a point for further investigation, reading level modeling may provide a powerful tool to bridge the vocabulary gap between search engines and their users.

7. CONCLUSION

We have shown how incorporating reading level features for users and documents can provide a valuable new signal for relevance in Web search. We explored three key problems in improving relevance for search using reading difficulty: estimating models of user reading proficiency, estimating models of result difficulty, and combining relevance and difficulty signals to re-rank based on the difference between user and result reading level. We also provided a large-scale analysis of log data to characterize certain aspects of user behavior and classes of features and queries that were likely to be effective in personalization using reading difficulty predictions. Our results show that statistically significant gains may be obtained with a commercial search engine, even for general queries, by incorporating reading difficulty features. Furthermore, we found specific sub-classes of queries, such as science-oriented queries, that are particularly amenable to improvement. Our work could easily be generalized to model domain expertise in specific subject areas, such as those defined in the Open Directory Project. For example, Web search results could be ranked with the introductory material first, followed by increasingly technical material. Other advances such as level-appropriate query suggestions, result snippets, and site recommendations are also possible.

Acknowledgements

We thank Dan Liebling and Misha Bilenko for technical assistance, and Sue Dumais, Jaime Teevan, and the anonymous reviewers for their valuable suggestions.

8. REFERENCES

[1] P. N. Bennett, K. Svore, and S. T. Dumais. Classification-enhanced ranking. In *Proc. of WWW 2010*, 111–120.

[2] D. Bilal. Children's use of the yahooligans! web search engine: Cognitive, physical, and affective behaviors on fact-based search tasks. *J. Am. Soc. Inf. Sci.*, 51(7):646–665, 2000.

[3] J. Chall, E. Dale. *Readability Revisited: The New Dale Chall Readability Formula.* Brookline Books, 1995.

[4] C. L. Clarke, E. Agichtein, S. Dumais, and R. W. White. The influence of caption features on clickthrough patterns in web search. In *Proc. of SIGIR 2007*, 135–142.

[5] K. Collins-Thompson and J. P. Callan. A language modeling approach to predicting reading difficulty. In *HLT-NAACL*, 193–200.

[6] A. Druin, E. Foss, H. Hutchinson, E. Golub, and L. Hatley. Children's roles using keyword search interfaces at home. In *Proc. of CHI 2010*, 413–422.

[7] C. Eickhoff, P. Serdyukov, and A. de Vries. A combined topical/non-topical approach to identifying web sites for children. In *Proc. of WSDM 2011*, 505–514.

[8] B. Efron, R. J. Tibshirani. *An Introduction to the Bootstrap.* Chapman & Hall/CRC, New York, 1994.

[9] J. Gao, W. Yuan, X. Li, K. Deng, and J.-Y. Nie. Smoothing clickthrough data for web search ranking. In *Proc. of SIGIR 2009.*

[10] K. Gyllstrom and M.-F. Moens. Wisdom of the ages: toward delivering the children's web with the link-based agerank algorithm. In *Proc. of CIKM 2008*, 159–168.

[11] S. Hirsh. Children's relevance criteria and information seeking on electronic resources. *JASIST*, 50(14):1265–1283.

[12] P. Kidwell, G. Lebanon, and K. Collins-Thompson. Statistical estimation of word acquisition with application to readability prediction. In *Proc. of EMNLP 2009.*

[13] G. Kumaran, R. Jones, and O. Madani. Biasing web search results for topic familiarity. In *Proc. of CIKM 2005*, 271–272.

[14] X. Liu, W. B. Croft, P. Oh, and D. Hart. Automatic recognition of reading levels from user queries. In *Proc. of SIGIR 2004*, 548–549.

[15] PuppyIR. PuppyIR: An open source environment to construct information services for children. 2011. http://www.puppyir.eu/.

[16] J. Teevan, S. T. Dumais, and E. Horvitz. Personalizing search via automated analysis of interests and activities. In *Proc. of SIGIR 2005*, 449–456.

[17] S. D. Torres, D. Hiemstra, and P. Serdyukov. An analysis of queries intended to search information for children. In *IIiX 2010*, 235–244.

[18] M. van Kalsbeek, J. de Wit, D. Trieschnigg, P. van der Vet, T. Huibers, and D. Hiemstra. Automatic reformulation of children's search queries. Technical Report TR-CTIT-10-23, June 2010.

[19] K. Wang, T. Walker, and Z. Zheng. Estimating relevance ranking quality from web search clickthrough data. In *Proc. of SIGKDD 2009*, 1355–1364.

[20] R. W. White, P. N. Bennett, and S. T. Dumais. Predicting short-term interests using activity-based search context. In *Proc. of CIKM 2010*, 1009–1018.

[21] R. W. White and S. T. Dumais. Characterizing and predicting search engine switching behavior. In *Proc. of CIKM 2009*, 87–96.

[22] R. W. White, S. T. Dumais, and J. Teevan. Characterizing the influence of domain expertise on web search behavior. In *Proc. of WSDM 2009*, 132–141.

[23] Q. Wu, C. J. C. Burges, K. M. Svore, and J. Gao. Adapting boosting for information retrieval measures. *Information Retrieval*, 3(13):254–270, 2010.

[24] C. X. Zhai, W. W. Cohen, and J. Lafferty. Beyond independent relevance: methods and evaluation metrics for subtopic retrieval. In *Proc. of SIGIR 2003*, 10–17.

Location-aware Click Prediction in Mobile Local Search

Dimitrios Lymberopoulos[‡], Peixiang Zhao[†], Christian König[‡], Klaus Berberich[§], Jie Liu[‡]
[†] UIUC, Urbana-Champaign, IL, USA
[‡] Microsoft Research, Redmond, WA, USA
[§] MPI, Saarbrücken, Germany
pzhao4@illinois.edu, {dlymper,chrisko,liuj}@microsoft.com, kberberi@mpi-inf.mpg.de

ABSTRACT

Users increasingly rely on their mobile devices to search, locate and discover places and activities around them while on the go. Their decision process is driven by the information displayed on their devices and their current context (e.g. traffic, driving or walking etc.). Even though recent research efforts have already examined and demonstrated how different context parameters such as weather, time and personal preferences affect the way mobile users click on local businesses, little has been done to study how the location of the user affects the click behavior. In this paper we follow a data-driven methodology where we analyze approximately 2 million local search queries submitted by users across the US, to visualize and quantify how differently mobile users click across locations. Based on the data analysis, we propose new location-aware features for improving local search click prediction and quantify their performance on real user query traces. Motivated by the results, we implement and evaluate a data-driven technique where local search models at different levels of location granularity (e.g. city, state, and country levels) are combined together at run-time to further improve click prediction accuracy. By applying the location-aware features and the multiple models at different levels of location granularity on real user query streams from a major, commercially available search engine, we achieve anywhere from 5% to 47% higher Precision than a single click prediction model across the US can achieve.

Categories and Subject Descriptors

H.4 [**Information Systems Applications**]: Miscellaneous

General Terms

Measurement, Human Factors

Keywords

mobile local search, search log analysis, feature extraction

1. INTRODUCTION

The wide availability of internet access on mobile devices, such as phones and personal media players, has allowed users to search, locate and access web information while on the go. Currently, there are 54.5 million mobile internet users and market analysis shows that this number will increase to 95 millions by 2013 [16]. This rapid growth indicates that it is only a matter of time when mobile devices will overtake desktop as the web/search access point of choice.

A significant part of mobile query volume is represented by local search queries, where users search for nearby businesses, parks, attractions and activities. Even though mobile local search is similar to desktop local search, there are two fundamental differences. First, mobile devices provide significantly more accurate location information (e.g. GPS, cell tower and/or wifi triangulation) compared to desktop devices (e.g. reverse IP localization techniques). Accurate location estimation is critical in mobile search since the users are on the go and their range of reach might be limited.

Second, when compared to desktop search, mobile search is more "actionable" in the sense that mobile users usually take an action immediately after a local search session (e.g. visit a restaurant, a grocery store etc.). Because of mobile search's actionable nature, the role of the user's *current* context is particularly important in successfully answering a query. For instance, knowing that a mobile user searching for restaurants is walking in downtown Manhattan during rush hour on a Friday evening, can provide invaluable information such as how much distance this user is willing to travel to visit a business or what type of businesses he might be interested in given the day and time of his search. On the other hand, the context of a desktop user that searches for restaurants from the comfort of his house right before he goes to sleep on a Monday night, might be irrelevant given that the search session might be triggered by a totally different context (i.e. plan a night out with friends for next Saturday).

The context of a mobile query can be defined by a collection of different features such as time of day, day of week, weather, traffic, user preferences and more. Several research efforts have already looked at the importance of context in local search or have attempted to analyze how mobile users click on local businesses [14, 1, 6]. The ultimate goal of these approaches is to learn a ranking function that properly balances the importance of all these different features to provide accurate business rankings. However, the way these features should be balanced might be different across locations. Users at different locations can have different decision processes either due to geographic properties of their regions or demographics of the area they live in. For instance, a mobile user in Manhattan on a Friday evening around 5pm, most probably is willing to travel a short distance to visit a business because of the

Category	Query Volume (%)
Food & Dining	35.36
Shopping	9.31
Arts & Entertainment	7.87
Health & Beauty	7.34
Home & Family	6.64
Automotive & Vehicles	5.61
Travel	5.39
Government & Comm.	4.46
Real Estate & Construction	4.12
Sports & Recreation	3.97
Computers & Technology	3.56
Legal & Finance	2.64
Professional & Services	2.36
Education	1.37

Table 1: Profile of the analyzed mobile search log dataset.

heavy traffic and the difficulty to access the highway. On the other hand, a mobile user in Texas might be willing to use his car and drive a longer distance because of the ease of acess to the highway. Consequently, the relative importance of the different context features might vary across locations. A mobile local search engine can capture these variations by (i) properly leveraging location-aware features to implicitly condition the ranking function on location, (ii) training multiple ranking functions across locations or (iii) by simultaneously combining both approaches.

Properly defining the location granularity at which local search models should be trained to effectively capture location context is quite challenging. While training models at the country level (i.e. US) might mask the importance of local context, training models at low levels of location granularity (i.e. zip code level) can also be inefficient due to data sparsity and data over-fitting issues. In addition, an optimal location resolution at which local search models should be trained might not exist. For instance, even though a high query volume area, such as Manhattan, may provide enough data to accurately train a local model, other nearby locations to Manhattan, such as Bedford, NY, might not. Hence, a more general model obtained at the state or even country level could be used to answer queries that originate from Bedford. In general, the number of local search models to be trained, the location resolution at which these models should be trained and how these models are combined at run-time to answer queries needs to be determined.

2. CONTRIBUTIONS

In this paper we study the impact of location context in mobile local search and make the following contributions. First, we quantify how differently mobile users click across locations by analyzing 2 million local search queries submitted in the United States.

Second, we implement and evaluate two approaches to encode location context in current state-of-the-art models: *implicit* and *explicit* location-aware training. In both approaches we augment the feature space with a set of new location-aware features and allow the model at the training phase to automatically decide the importance of these features. By picking up those features, the trained model implicitly takes location context into account. In the case of *implicit* training a single model is trained across the US, while in the case of *explicit* training, multiple models at different levels of location granularity (e.g. city, state, and country levels) are trained by segmenting the training dataset based on geographical and volume characteristics. At run time, the model at the lowest level of location granularity that is available for the location where the query originated from, is used to rank nearby businesses. By

Figure 1: US coverage of the analyzed dataset. Each query is represented as a point at the location where it was submitted.

applying these techniques on real user query streams, we show that Precision can be improved by up to 47% when compared to to the Precision achieved by a single click prediction model for the whole US.

Third, we demonstrate that mobile search logs can be used to extract a model mapping at the zip code level that can guide the application of multiple models at different levels of location granularity at run time to improve click prediction accuracy. In the offline phase, we leverage the search logs to train models at the city, state, and country levels. By applying these models on search log traces and comparing their accuracies at the zip code level, we automatically learn a mapping between zip codes and models for each state in the US. At run-time, we lookup the appropriate model (city, state or country level) to use for each query based on the zip code where the query originates from and the learnt mapping. Through a 10-fold cross validation on real user query streams from a commercially available search engine, we show that we can achieve up to 4% higher Precision compared to the Precision that a single click prediction model at the state level with the location-aware features can achieve.

3. DATASET AND TOOLS

In this section we give an overview of the analyzed mobile search log dataset and describe the learning tools we use to train local search click prediction models.

3.1 Data Profile

The dataset used in this paper consists of approximately 2 million local search queries submitted to a major search engine across the United States over a period of 3 months. All the queries were submitted from mobile users that opted to download and install the search engine's mobile application on iPhone and Android devices. The information recorded and analyzed for every query included the GPS location where the query was submitted, the actual query string, the unique ID of the business that was clicked by the user, the unique IDs of the businesses shown to the user, and a timestamp. To protect the privacy of the users, no other information about the user or the query was recorded.

The original information recorded in the search logs was augmented with publicly available demographic data from recent CENSUS reports [17]. Using the GPS location available in every search log entry, we retrieved the zip code from where each query was submitted. Based on this information, we were able to associate zip code level demographic data (i.e. population density, average household size etc.) to every search log entry from the 2000 CENSUS report.

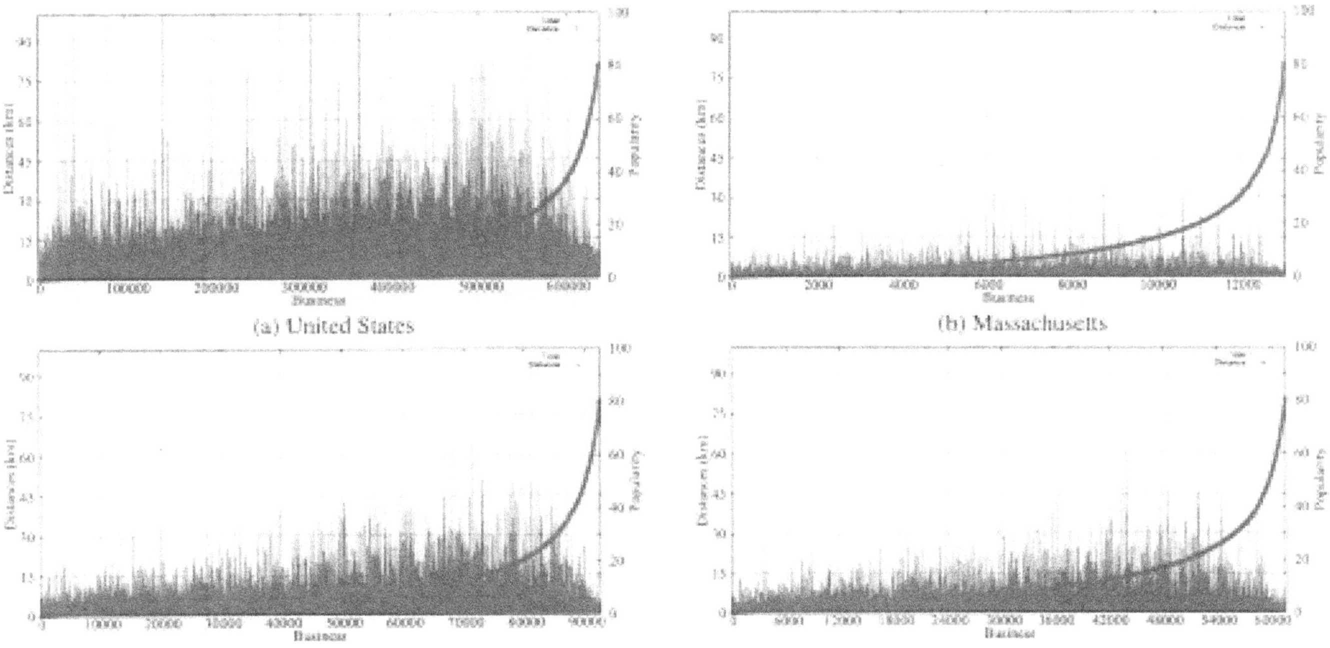

(a) United States (b) Massachusetts

(c) California (d) Texas

Figure 2: Distance-popularity relationship across the US and 3 representative states. For every business ID (x-axis) in the search logs, the average distance in km between the location of the query that resulted into a click for that business and the location of the business is shown (y-axis on the left). The business' normalized popularity based on the number of clicks it received in the logs (histogram, y-axis on the right) is also shown. Businesses are sorted based on average distance.

In addition, the unique ID of every business was used to retrieve more detailed information such as business' location and zip code.

Table 1 shows the breakdown of the analyzed query volume based on the type of businesses clicked. More than half of the query volume targeted businesses in the dining, entertainment and shopping categories. Another 20% of the volume targeted businesses around personal, home and automotive care. The remaining 30% of the query volume was distributed over travel and sports related businesses as well as over various public and private services.

Figure 1 shows the geographical coverage of the 2 million search queries analyzed in this paper. The query volume is distributed across the United States with the states of CA, WA, MA, AZ, NY, and TX being among the highest query volume producing states.

3.2 Training Tools

To provide a common training framework on top of which we can compare the performance of different modeling techniques and features, we adopt MART [20], a learning tool based on *M*ultiple *A*dditive *R*egression *T*rees. MART is based on the stochastic gradient boosting approach described in [4, 5, 7]. We formulate the mobile local search problem as a *click prediction* problem[1] and leverage MART to solve it. Each entry in the training and validation data contains a set of n features, $\mathcal{F}_q = \{f_{q1}, f_{q2}, \ldots, f_{qn}\}$, that might be related to a query q (e.g. query zip code), a business object b (e.g. popularity), or both (e.g. distance between query and business) in conjunction with a click label which records the user's response c (1 for click and 0 otherwise). The training data is fed into MART to build a classification model, $\mathcal{M}$, which we use to estimate the probability of clicks $p_{\mathcal{M}}(c|q, b)$ in the test data. In our experiments we use the log-likelihood as the loss function (optimization criterion), steepest-descent (gradient-descent) as the optimization technique, and binary decision trees as the fitting function.

In addition to the trained model $\mathcal{M}$, MART reports a relative ordering of all the features $\mathcal{F}_q$. This ordering indicates the *"relative importance"* of the features during click prediction and provides insight on how the model is built. The most important feature has a relative importance of 1, while the rest of the features have a relative importance between 0 and 1.

For each experiment, we report the relative feature importance, and the Precision achieved by the different models for different Recall values.

The baseline set of features used for training MART models consisted of 5 representative features that were selected based on previous research studies [14, 1, 6]. For every business click and non-click, we record: *(i)* the position in the search results where the business appeared, *(ii)* the distance between the query and the business locations, *(iii)* the popularity of the business as defined by the number of clicks in the search logs, *(iv)* the time frame within a day (one out of four 6-hour time frames) that the query was submitted, and *(v)* a binary feature that represents if the query was submitted on a workday or over the weekend. For every training experiment, the input dataset is split to training, verification and test data with the data volume ratio being 70% : 20% : 10% respectively.

4. MOBILE SEARCH LOG ANALYSIS

In this section we visualize and quantify how differently mobile users click across locations. In particular, we compare click behavior at the country, state and zip code levels.

In this analysis, we characterize click behavior using different forms of two features that recent research studies [14, 6] as well as our current experience with 2 million queries has shown to be among the most important features: *traveling distance* (or simply distance) and *business popularity*. The former corresponds to the distance that a mobile user is willing to travel to visit a business

[1] Click prediction is a proxy for ranking quality. Given the close relationship between clicks on a search result and its relevance, it is very likely that features that help improve click prediction will be useful in ranking as well.

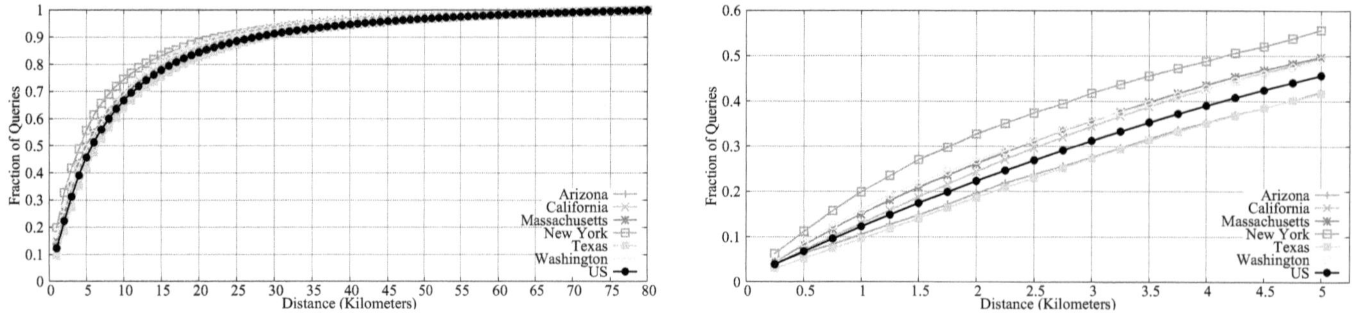

(a) (b)

Figure 3: CDF of the distance between the location of the query and the location of the clicked business for 6 representative states and the US.

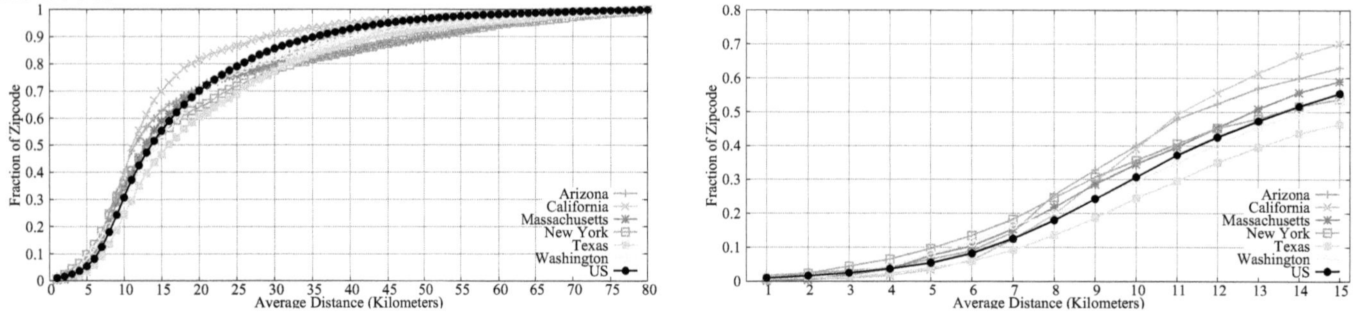

(a) (b)

Figure 4: CDF of the average distance between the location of the query and the location of the clicked business across zip codes for 6 representative states and the US.

and is calculated as the distance between the location of the query and the location of the clicked business. The latter corresponds to the popularity of a business and is calculated based on the number of clicks each business receives in the search logs.

Due to space constraints, we only present the results for a representative subset of locations, features and demographic data studied.

4.1 Country and State Level Statistics

First, we look at the tradeoff between distance and business popularity. In general, mobile users wish to travel short distances, but at the same time they are willing to visit popular businesses around them. The way users tradeoff these two features is vital during ranking.

Figure 2 shows the tradeoff between distance and business popularity when examining the queries across the whole US, and the states of MA, CA and TX independently. Current techniques use data across the whole US to capture the distance/popularity tradeoff in a single model (Figure 2(a)). According to Figure 2(a), the mostly clicked businesses can be roughly classified into two categories based on the distance the mobile user is willing to travel. About 30% of the popular businesses are clicked within a 2-km radius of the mobile user's location. However, mobile users are willing to travel anywhere between 5km and 15km to reach about 70% of the most clicked businesses.

Aside from the fact that mobile users in the US are willing to travel a surprisingly large distance to visit a business, interesting observations can be made by comparing the statistics across the whole US with that of individual states. The states of CA and TX seem to share the same trends with the US as the most clicked businesses tend to be located between 5-15km from the user's location. However, the number of clicked businesses within a 2-km radius from user's location, is lower for the state of CA and significantly lower for the state of TX. Even more astounding is the comparison between Figures 2(a) and 2(b), that shows that mobile users in the state of MA tradeoff distance and business popularity in a different way than people across the US.

4.2 Variation Across States

Figure 3 provides deeper insight on how much distance mobile users are willing to travel and how this distance varies across different states. Surprisingly, only 12.5% of the mobile queries across the US result into clicking a business that is within a 1-km radius of the user's location. Looking at individual states, only 10% of the queries in the state of TX result into clicking a business within 1km of user's location. However, this percentage doubles (20%) when considering the sate of NY. The gap across states increases as the distance increases. For instance, the percentage of queries that results in a business click within 5km of user's location is 56% in NY; approximately 32% higher than TX (42.5%). In other words, mobile users in the state of NY are willing to travel shorter distances when compared with users in the state of TX. These differences could be caused, among others, by the geographical differences between Manhattan and TX. Given the heavy traffic conditions in Manhattan and the excellent subway network, mobile users in Manhattan are more likely to want to travel a short distance. On the other hand, mobile users in TX that have easy access to a well built highway networks might be more willing to travel longer distances to visit a business. A click prediction model that can effectively capture this information can have the flexibility to provide more location-aware, and thus more accurate, click predictions.

4.3 Variation Across Zip Codes

To quantify the variation across zip codes, we grouped the queries for every state based on the zip code that they originated

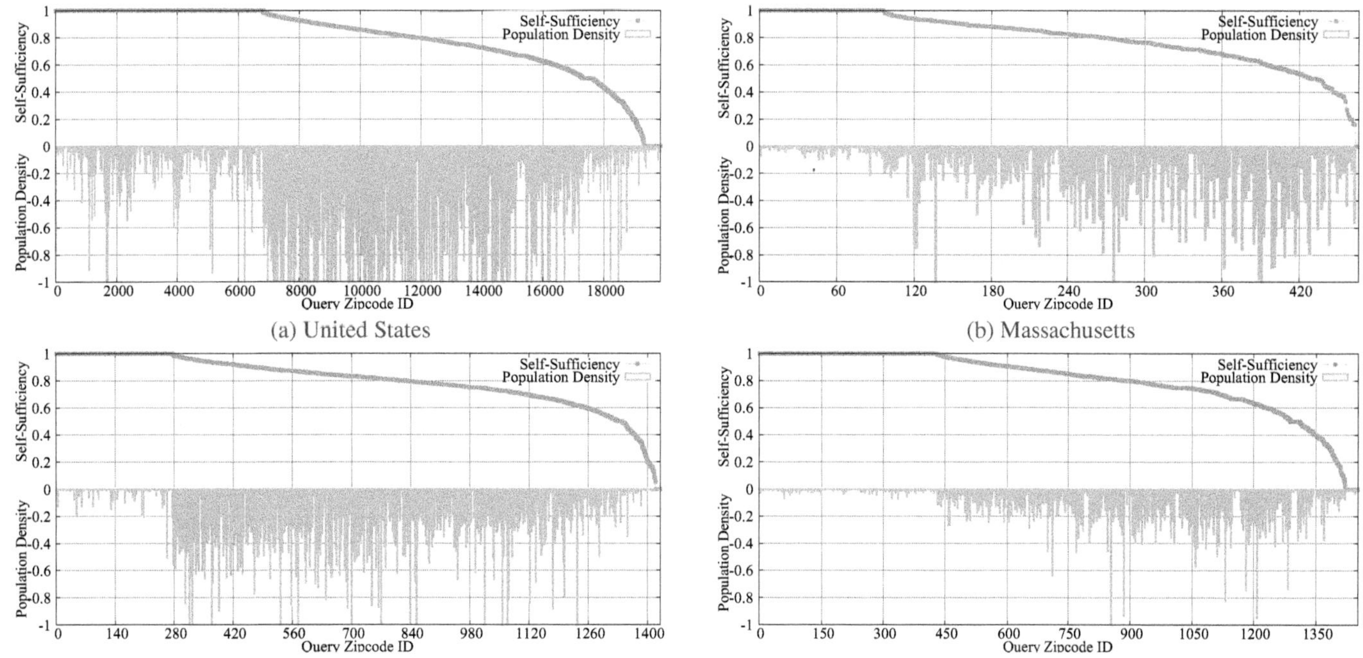

(a) United States

(b) Massachusetts

(c) California

(d) Texas

Figure 5: The fraction of queries where the zip codes of the query and the clicked business match. A value of 1 means that all the queries from the given zip code resulted into clicking businesses in a different zip code. The histogram at the bottom part of the figure shows the normalized population density for the given zip code across all zip codes.

from and computed the average traveling distance for every zip code. Figure 4 shows the CDF of the average traveling distance across zip codes for 6 representative states and the US. At a high level, users click on businesses within 5km from their location from only 5% of the zip codes. Conversely, for 30% of the zip codes, mobile users tend to click on businesses that are more than 20km away from their current location. The average traveling distance for the remaining 65% of the zip codes varies significantly across states. For instance, the percentage of zip codes in the state of TX where the average distance is less than 20km is 60%, as opposed to 82% for the state of CA. This difference represents a gap of approximately 37% across states (60% vs. 82%), indicating that even at the zip code level granularity mobile users exhibit different click behaviors.

Figure 5 sheds more light on the variation across zip codes. For every zip code we compute the *self-sufficiency* value, that is the fraction of queries where the query and clicked business zip codes are different. A value of 0 on the y-axis means that all the queries from the given zip code resulted into clicking businesses in the same zip code, and therefore we call that zip code *self-sufficient*. A value of 1 means that all the queries from that zip code resulted into clicking businesses in a different zip code and therefore we call that zip code *self-insufficient*. Figure 5 shows a clear segmentation of zip codes. Approximately 35% of the zip codes across the US are self-insufficient, while only 5% of the zip codes are self-sufficient. The rest 60% of the zip codes have a *self-sufficient* value between 0 and 1, with the majority having a value above 0.7. In other words, mobile users are willing to move away from their immediate vicinity in about 70% of the zip codes across the US.

In addition, the distribution of zip codes in terms of their *self-sufficient* value varies across states. For instance, in the state of TX, 40% of the zip codes are *self-insufficient*, while in California less than 20% of the zip codes are *self-insufficient*. Figure 5 also shows the normalized population density for each zip code. From the individual states figures, it is apparent that zip codes with low population density are usually *self-sufficient* or *self-insufficient*. However, Figure 5(a) suggests that about 25% of the *self-insufficient* zip codes across the US exhibit medium to high population densities.

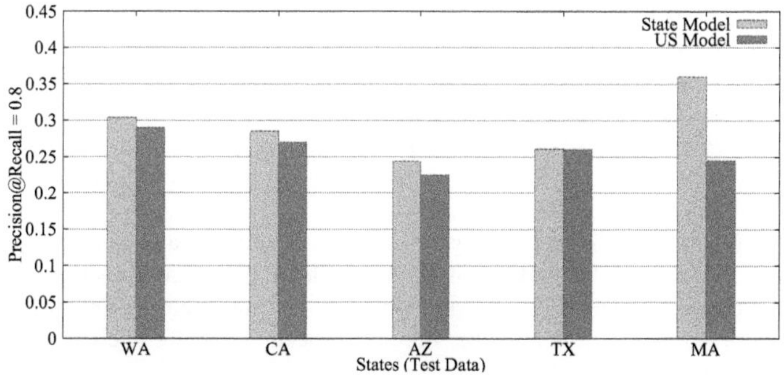

Figure 6: Precision achieved for Recall value of 0.8 when the state and US models are applied on each state's test dataset for 5 representative states.

Figures 4 and 5 show clearly that mobile click behavior varies at the zip code level across states as well as within a state. Thus, knowing the zip code from where a query originated from, can provide significant insight on how to answer the query.

4.4 The Effect of Location on Click Prediction Accuracy

To quantify the impact of our findings on the local search click prediction accuracy, we leveraged the MART training tool, described in Section 3.2, to train, validate and test different click prediction models on the recorded search log data.

Using the query volume from 5 representative states, a local search click prediction model was trained for every state. In a similar way, a US click prediction model was trained using the search log data across the whole US. To quantify how differently these

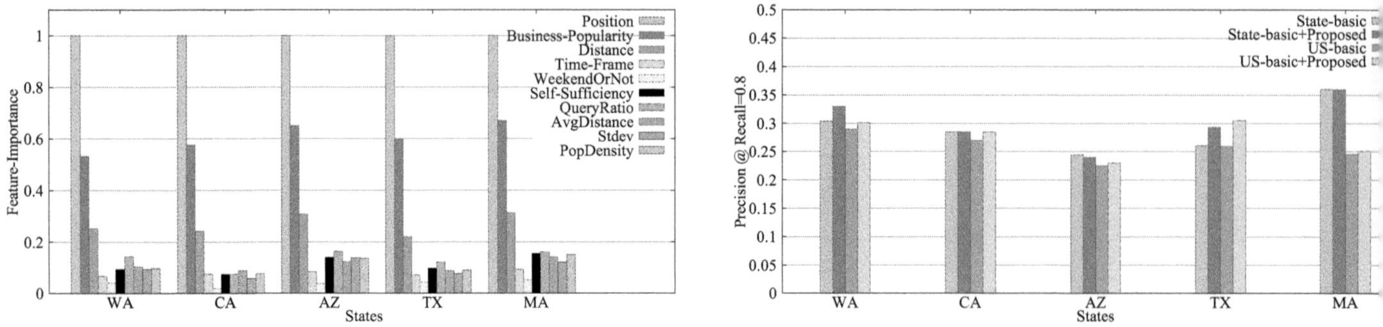

(a) Feature Importance (b) Precision @ Recall= 0.8

Figure 7: (a) Feature importance and (b) Precision performance for the US and 5 representative state models with and without the proposed location-aware features. All models were evaluated against the test dataset of each state (x-axis).

models perform across locations, we applied both the US and state models on each state's test dataset.

The results are shown in Figure 6. The state models consistently achieve higher Precision compared to the US model indicating the importance of location context. The increase in Precision by the use of state models varies anywhere from 0.4% to 47% depending on the individual state. In general, the state models for the states for which click behavior is similar to the click behavior across the whole US (*i.e.*, TX and CA states as shown in Figure 2) achieve minor or modest Precision improvements (0.4% and 4.8% respectively). On the other hand, states for which click behavior is significantly different than that across the US (*i.e.*, MA state as shown in Figure 2), the increase in Precision can be as high as 47%.

Table 2 provides more insight on the performance of models at different levels of location granularity by comparing the achieved Precision for different Recall values. *Columns 2 and 4 in Table 2 show that the state model achieves on average 3%, 6%, 11%, and 13% higher Precision than the US model for a Recall value of 0.5, 0.6, 0.7, and 0.8 respectively.* Only in the case of CA and TX states (that according to Figure 2 share the same click behavior as the whole US) and for high Recall values, the US and state models achieve identical Precision. Overall, simply training models at the state level, can provide significant improvement in Precision performance indicating the impact of location content in click prediction.

	Model(Features) (B): Basic Features, (P): Proposed Features			
Recall Value	WA(B)	WA(B+P)	US(B)	US(B+P)
50%	0.509	**0.52**	**0.485**	0.5
60%	0.434	**0.462**	**0.42**	0.44
70%	0.35	**0.401**	**0.326**	0.375
80%	0.304	**0.33**	**0.29**	0.301
	MA(B)	MA(B+P)	US(B)	US(B+P)
50%	0.47	**0.47**	**0.436**	0.437
60%	0.434	**0.432**	**0.355**	0.36
70%	0.389	**0.387**	**0.276**	0.29
80%	0.36	**0.36**	**0.245**	0.251
	AZ(B)	AZ(B+P)	US(B)	US(B+P)
50%	0.37	**0.371**	**0.369**	0.378
60%	0.325	**0.328**	**0.317**	0.32
70%	0.272	**0.273**	**0.26**	0.267
80%	0.244	**0.245**	**0.225**	0.23
	CA(B)	CA(B+P)	US(B)	US(B+P)
50%	0.43	**0.43**	**0.427**	0.43
60%	0.349	**0.369**	**0.349**	0.36
70%	0.294	**0.297**	**0.294**	0.3
80%	0.285	**0.285**	**0.272**	0.285
	TX(B)	TX(B+P)	US(B)	US(B+P)
50%	0.423	**0.423**	**0.415**	0.42
60%	0.346	**0.37**	**0.335**	0.36
70%	0.28	**0.322**	**0.28**	0.33
80%	0.261	**0.293**	**0.26**	0.305

Table 2: Precision for different Recall values for the state and US models with and without the proposed location-aware features in the case of 5 representative states in the US.

5. LOCATION-AWARE CLICK PREDICTION

To effectively capture the variance of mobile click behavior across locations, we propose and evaluate two different approaches: *implicit* and *explicit* location-aware modeling. In the case of *implicit* location-aware modeling, we train a single click prediction model for the whole US but we augment the feature set described in Section 3.2 with new location-aware features. In the case of *explicit* location-aware modeling, we still expand the feature space with the same location-dependent features, but this time a different click prediction model is built for every state or even city (given that it generates a high-enough search log volume (e.g. Manhattan, NY)).

Based on the analysis presented in the previous sections we introduce 5 new location-aware features:

1. *Self-sufficiency* value of the zip code the query originated from.

2. Average traveling distance within the zip code where the query originated from.

3. Standard deviation of the distance within the zip code where the query originated from.

4. Population density of the zip code where the query originated from.

5. Fraction of the state's query volume generated from the zip code the query originated from.

Note that all the features introduced encode information about the zip code where the query originated from. Providing these features can guide the training process to identify local properties at the zip code level and properly capture variance across zip codes in the trained model. Also, by training individual state models, we explicitly take into account the variance across states.

Figure 7 shows the results for both implicit and explicit location-aware modeling. Figure 7(a) shows the relative feature impor-

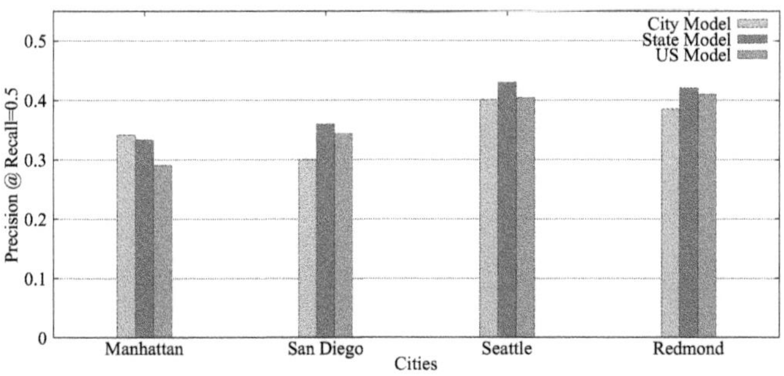

Figure 8: Precision achieved (for Recall=0.5) by models at the city, state and country levels for 4 representative high query volume cities. All models were evaluated against the test dataset of each city.

tance reported by the MART tool for every input feature across all state models and the US model. All the proposed location-dependent features are leveraged in the training process across all models. As expected, features such as the traveling distance still remain the most important features in terms of click prediction. However, location-dependent features are shown to be more important than temporal features such as the time window, or the weekday/weekend feature that have been previously shown to have a significant impact on mobile click prediction [14, 1, 6]. Furthermore, even though the feature importance trends are similar across all models, the importance of each location-dependent feature varies across different state models demonstrating the variance in mobile click behavior across locations.

Figure 7(b) shows the Precision achieved by the state and US models on the state's test dataset for all 5 states. To facilitate the discussion, we also show the Precision achieved by the state and the US models when none of the proposed location-dependent features is used. When examining the US model's performance across states, the use of location-dependent features leads to a Precision improvement that lies anywhere between 2.2% (AZ test dataset) and 17% (TX test dataset) depending on the state considered. When examining the performance of individual state models, the Precision improvement varies between 0% (CA and MA test datasets) and 12% (TX test dataset) when the proposed location-dependent features are used. *Comparatively, the Precision performance of state click prediction models is anywhere between 6.5% (AZ state) and 43.4% (MA state) better when compared to the US model, and when both basic and proposed features are leveraged.* The only exception are the CA and TX states, for which similar Precision is achieved for both the state and US models when all the features are leveraged. This is expected given the similarity of click behavior in these states and across the US (Figure 2).

Most importantly, the Precision achieved by the state model when both basic and proposed features are used is significantly higher compared to the US model that leverages only the basic features and represents the current state-of-the-art approach. *In particular, the improvement in Precision performance is anywhere between 4.8% (CA state) and 46.7% (MA state).*

Note that the introduced location-dependent features have greater impact on the US model (implicit location-aware training) when compared to individual state models (explicit location-aware training). This trend is expected since the latter modeling methodology already leverages the location context by explicitly training different models for every state.

Table 2 quantifies in more detail the effect of the proposed location-dependent features on the Precision/Recall performance of the state and US models for the 5 representative states in Figure 7(b). Columns 3 and 5 in Table 2 show that both the state and US models achieve consistently higher Precision for a given Recall value when leveraging the proposed location-dependent features. *Specifically, in the case of WA state's dataset, state model's Precision increases anywhere between 2.2% and 14.6%, while US model's Precision increases anywhere between 3% and 15%, demonstrating the importance of the proposed features.* In addition, columns 3 and 4 show the improvement of leveraging models at the state level and incorporating the proposed location-aware features. Depending on the state and Recall value, an improvement of anywhere between 0.5% and 46.7% in Precision is achieved when compared to the Precision achieved by the US model when only the set of basic features is leveraged.

	Model		
Recall Value	Manhattan	NY	US
50%	0.342	0.334	0.291
60%	0.33	0.284	0.281
70%	0.32	0.262	0.282
80%	0.295	0.262	0.263
	Model		
	Seattle	WA	US
50%	0.401	0.43	0.404
60%	0.35	0.365	0.355
70%	0.32	0.281	0.302
80%	0.281	0.252	0.26
	Model		
	Redmond	WA	US
50%	0.385	0.42	0.41
60%	0.335	0.34	0.354
70%	0.278	0.245	0.263
80%	0.21	0.135	0.15
	Model		
	San Diego	CA	US
50%	0.3	0.36	0.344
60%	0.258	0.329	0.265
70%	0.233	0.267	0.201
80%	0.214	0.238	0.211

Table 3: Precision for different Recall values for the city, state, and US models in the case of 4 representative high query volume cities. Each model was applied on the test dataset of the individual city.

5.1 City-level Modeling

Training click prediction models at lower levels of location granularity can be extremely challenging due to data sparsity and data over-fitting problems. Even though the search log data provide a good indication of high volume areas within a state that one can successfully train click predictions models, the performance of these models might not be the best possible. For instance, Figure 8 shows the Precision performance of models at the city, state, and country levels for 4 of the cities that were among the highest query volume producing cities in the dataset. Surprisingly, city-level models don't always achieve the best Precision. Similar trends can also be seen in Table 3 where the Precision/Recall performance of the city, state and US models are shown on the test dataset of a representative set of cities. Different models achieve the highest Precision across different Recall values.

This observation can be explained by the fact that location-independent features, such as the position of a business in the search results list, are among the most important features during click prediction (Figure 7(a)). When we train models at lower lev-

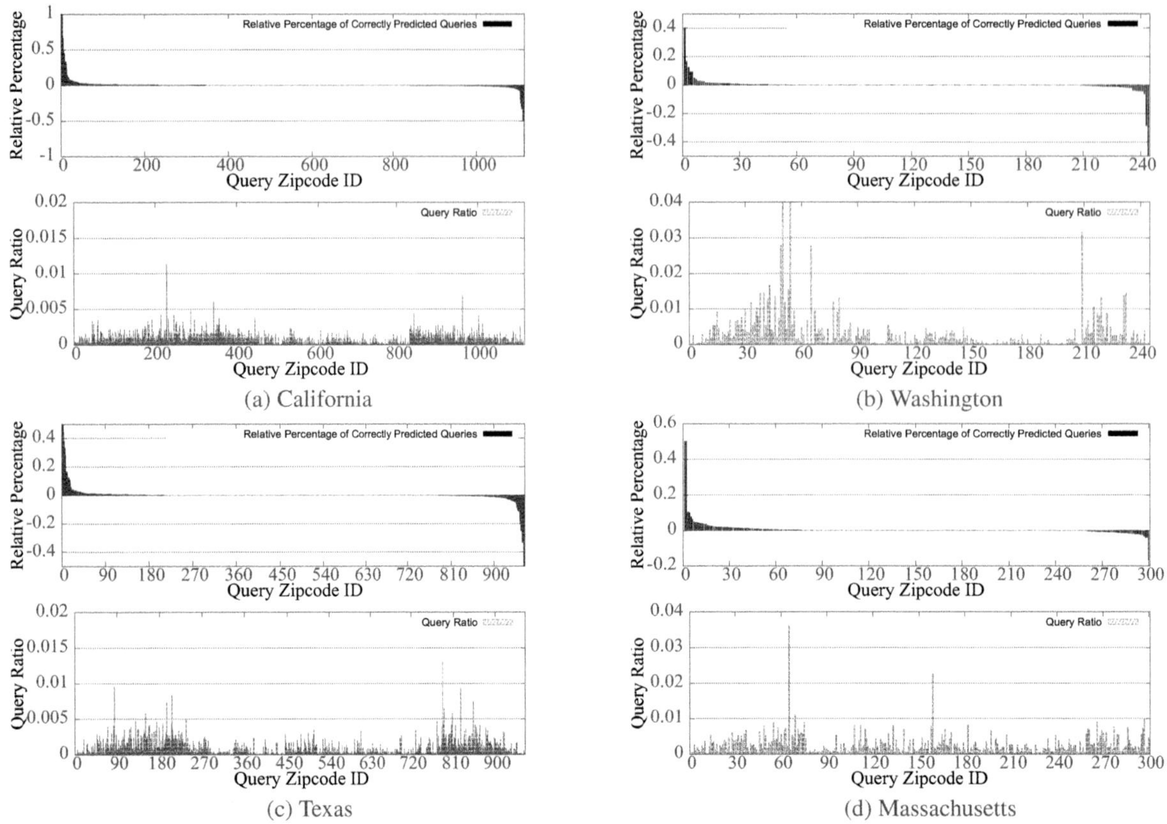

Figure 9: Relative percentage of correctly predicted queries per zip code. A positive value, say 0.5, indicates that the state model is able to successfully predict 50% *more* clicks at the given zip code when compared to the US model. Conversely, a negative value, say −0.5, indicates that the state model is able to successfully predict 50% *fewer* clicks at the given zip code when compared to the state model. The histogram at the bottom part of the figure shows the normalized query volume for the given zip code across all zip codes.

els of location granularity (*e.g.*, city level), we enable better modeling of the location-aware features. However, because the volume of data available for training is naturally lower at lower levels of granularity (e.g. city-level vs. state level), the modeling of location-independent features might not be as accurate as when data a coarser level of location granularity is used. Given that location-independent features are significantly more important than location-dependent features (Figure 7), it is possible that models at the city level can achieve worse click prediction.

Even though Figure 8 suggests that city-level click prediction models are ineffective, this is not the case. As we show in the next sections, city-level models are valuable when applied intelligently on the test dataset.

5.2 Leveraging Multiple Models at Run-time

Our data analysis so far has shown that training models at the state level and leveraging the proposed location-dependent features, allows for singificantly more accurate click prediction in mobile local search.

However, a more careful comparison of Precision performance results in Figure 7, and in Table 3 indicates an interesting inconsistency. According to Figure 7 the click prediction of state-level models is consistently better than the click prediction of the US model. However, Table 3 suggests that this is not true when examining subsets of a state's test dataset. For instance, even though the WA state model achieves the best Precision on the state's test dataset, in the case of Redmond, the US model is able to achieve lower Precision compared to the WA state model. This inconsistency indicates that the relative performance of the models might be different across locations even within a state.

Motivated by the observed variance across zip codes in Section 4 and to further investigate this inconsistency, we study the click prediction performance for every model at the zip code level. In particular, for every state and for both the state and US models [2], we compute the percentage of correctly predicted clicks for every zip code that appears in the test dataset. Figure 9 shows the relative percentage of correctly predicted clicks at the zip code level for 4 representative state datasets. A positive value, say 0.5, indicates that the state model is able to successfully predict *50% more* clicks at the given zip code when compared to the US model. Conversely, a negative value, say −0.5, indicates that the state model is able to successfully predict *50% fewer* clicks at the given zip code when compared to the state model. Surprisingly, for the queries that originate from approximately 80% of the zip codes the state and US models exhibit very similar performance. However, for approximately 10% of the zip codes, the state model can successfully predict up to 60% more clicks, while for another 10% of the zip codes, the US model can successfully predict up to 40% more clicks.

As a result, in order to achieve the highest number of successful click predictions (and thus the highest Precision) over a state's dataset, we would like to apply the state model only on these zip codes for which it can successfully predict more clicks than the US model (these are the zip codes with *positive* relative percentage val-

[2]The exact same trends apply when considering other combinations of models such as city and state models, or city and country models. The results are not shown due to space constraints.

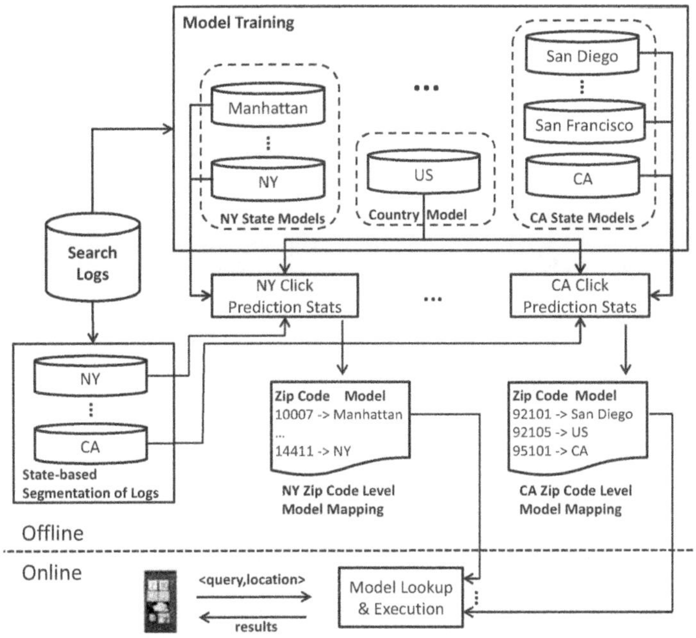

Figure 10: A mapping between zip codes and click prediction models at different levels of location granularity is automatically learned from the search logs.

	Model		
	WA	US	Combo
50%	0.455	0.41	0.457
60%	0.4	0.351	0.405
70%	0.347	0.292	0.348
80%	0.29	0.253	0.29
	MA	US	Combo
50%	0.444	0.351	0.445
60%	0.418	0.29	0.418
70%	0.392	0.257	0.391
80%	0.365	0.245	0.364
	AZ	US	Combo
50%	0.372	0.339	0.38
60%	0.33	0.295	0.34
70%	0.29	0.255	0.293
80%	0.272	0.223	0.272
	CA	US	Combo
50%	0.367	0.365	0.37
60%	0.315	0.298	0.32
70%	0.266	0.256	0.27
80%	0.235	0.234	0.235
	TX	US	Combo
50%	0.365	0.365	0.375
60%	0.311	0.31	0.32
70%	0.274	0.272	0.281
80%	0.25	0.25	0.26

Table 4: Precision for different Recall values for the state, US, and combination of city, state and country models (Combo) on the test datasets of 5 representative states.

ues in Figure 9). Similarly, the US model should only be applied on these zip codes for which it can successfully predict more clicks than the state model (these are the zip codes with *negative* relative percentage values in Figure 9). As Figure 9 suggests such a mapping between zip codes and click prediction models exists, and can be automatically learned from the mobile search logs.

Based on this observation, we implement a data-driven technique for leveraging multiple models at different levels of location granularity. The proposed scheme is described in Figure 10. Initially, the search logs are geographically segmented to different datasets; one for each state. At the same time the search log data across the US, individual states, and high query volume cities are used to train click prediction models at the country, state and city levels. The click prediction models available for a given state (country, state and available city models) are evaluated against the dataset of the state. *By computing and comparing the click prediction accuracy for each model at the zip code level (similarly to Figure 9), we create a mapping between zip codes and models so that each zip code is associated to the model that achieves the highest click prediction accuracy on this zip code's query trace.* When a query is submitted at run time, we leverage the learnt mapping to choose the appropriate model to use based on the zip code that the input query originates from.

5.3 Evaluation

The performance of the approach described in Figure 10 depends heavily on the ability to accurately learn the mapping between zip codes and click prediction models. To evaluate the effectiveness and stability of the approach, we perform a 10-fold cross validation on the mobile search log dataset.

Each dataset is split to 10 different collections of training, validation and test datasets with the data volume ratio being 70%:20%:10% respectively. For each collection of training, validation and test data, we leverage the training data to automatically learn the mapping between models and zip codes as described in the previous section (Figure 10). Then, we leverage the learnt mapping to properly apply the trained models on the actual test dataset.

The click prediction models were generated once and independently of the 10-fold cross validation experiments. We trained models at the country, state and city levels using the corresponding segments of the search log data and splitting them into 70% training, 20% validation and 10% test data. All models leverage both the basic set of 5 features described in Section 3.2 as well as the location-dependent features introduced in Section 5. For each experiment, we report the Precision/Recall performance for every model and test dataset combination.

Table 4 shows the achieved Precision for different Recall values that the state, US and the combination of state, US and city models achieve for 5 representative states' test datasets. Consistently across all Recall values and test datasets, the US model achieves the lowest Precision. When compared to the US model, the Precision achieved by the combo model is anywhere between 0.5% (CA @ Recall=0.8) and 52% (MA @ Recall=0.7) higher. On average, across all states and recall values, the combo model achieves 16% higher Precision compared to the US model.

When compared to the state model, the Precision improvement that the combo model achieves is more modest. On average, across all states and Recall values, the combo model achieves 1.2% higher Precision compared to the state model. Note that this improvement is additional to the one introduced by the location-dependent features that was quantified in Table 2. For individual states, such as AZ and TX, the Precision improvement is on average 2.5%, while for other states, such as MA, the combination of models at run time seems to have a negligible effect. This is expected given that the performance of the US model in the MA state's test dataset has been drastically lower compared to the state model's performance (Table 2). In this case, the performance of the state model dominates the performance of the other models, causing the combo model to become very similar to the state model.

6. RELATED WORK

Search logs have been studied extensively in the past for web search query profiling [3, 10, 11, 21, 2, 12, 13], topic or result clustering [18] and query intent detection [9, 15, 19].

The analysis closest to our work is the one on web search query profiling [3, 10, 11, 21, 2, 12, 13]. These efforts have analyzed search query volumes that vary from hundreds of thousands to several tenths of millions of queries across the US, Canada, Europe, and Asia. However, these efforts mainly focus on analyzing mobile web search trends such as repeatability of queries across users, length of queries and types of queries submitted. Few of these search log analysis efforts [10, 21] have provided insight about mobile local search, but only in terms of reporting the breakdown of business types that mobile users typically click on. Our work is among the first to analyze millions of mobile local search queries to understand how mobile users click on local businesses and how their click behavior varies across locations. In addition, our work goes beyond reporting general statistics. We propose new location-aware features to capture the variance of mobile click behavior across locations and quantify their impact in click prediction by leveraging state-of-the-art learning techniques.

In [19], Weber and Castillo show how demographic information can be leveraged to improve web search relevance and query suggestions. Conversely to [19], our work focuses on mobile local search, and most importantly, it goes beyond incorporating demographics into the ranking process and studies the variability of mobile local click behavior across locations.

Close, but complimentary to our work, is the work presented in [14]. Lane et al. analyzed approximately 80,000 queries in the state of WA to understand how the context of a mobile query (i.e. traveling distance, business popularity, time, weather etc.) affects the quality of business ranking. They propose a set of context-aware features (several of these features were included in the basic set of features used in our experiments) and demonstrate their effectiveness by training click prediction models and evaluating them against real user query traces. Our work differs in two ways. First, we analyze mobile local search logs across the whole US and not within a specific state, and report on how mobile click behavior varies across locations. Second, we propose and evaluate new features that can efficiently capture the variance of mobile click behavior across locations in the click prediction models. This is something that the work in [14] does not focus on.

Researchers in the area of mobile context-aware systems have also performed user studies to highlight the importance of context in mobile local search. Amin et al. [1] and Froehlich et al. [6] highlight the importance of temporal context as well as the strong correlation between traveling distance and business popularity in mobile local search through long term user studies. In addition, Issaacman et al. [8] analyze call logs to understand specific aspects of mobile behavior across locations. In particular, they demonstrate that mobile users' behavior varies across locations by comparing the traveling distance of AT&T cellular customers in Manhattan and Los Angeles. However, none of these efforts has explicitly studied and quantified how mobile click behavior changes across locations, let alone evaluate its impact on click prediction models.

7. CONCLUSIONS

We have presented an in-depth analysis of mobile local search click behavior across the US. Our contributions were threefold. First, we analyzed 2 million local search queries to better understand mobile local search click behavior and to quantify how this behavior varies across locations. Second, based on our analysis we proposed a set of location-aware features to efficiently capture the variance of mobile click behavior across locations in the click prediction model. By leveraging these features and training models at different levels of location granularity, we showed, using real query traces, that Precision can be improved anywhere from 5% up to 47% across states. Third, we demonstrated that mobile search logs can be used to extract a model mapping at the zip code level that can guide, at run time, the application of multiple models at different levels of location granularity. By applying this approach on real query traces, we showed that Precision can be *additionally* improved by up to 4%.

8. REFERENCES

[1] A. Amin, S. Townsend, J. Ossenbruggen, and L. Hardman. Fancy a drink in canary wharf?: A user study on location-based mobile search. In *Proceedings INTERACT*, 2009.

[2] K. Church, B. Smyth, K. Bradley, and P. Cotter. A large scale study of european mobile search behaviour. In *Proceedings of MobileHCI*, 2008.

[3] K. Church, B. Smyth, P. Cotter, and K. Bradley. Mobile information access: A study of emerging search behavior on the mobile internet. *ACM Trans. Web*, 1(1):4, 2007.

[4] J. H. Friedman. Greedy function approximation: A gradient boosting machine. *Annals of Statistics*, 29:1189–1232, 1999.

[5] J. H. Friedman. Stochastic gradient boosting. *Comput. Stat. Data Anal.*, 38(4):367–378, 2002.

[6] J. Froehlich, M. Y. Chen, I. E. Smith, and F. Potter. Voting with your feet: An investigative study of the relationship between place visit behavior and preference. In *Proceedings of Ubicomp*, 2006.

[7] J. Gao, Q. Wu, C. Burges, K. Svore, Y. Su, N. Khan, S. Shah, and H. Zhou. Model adaptation via model interpolation and boosting for web search ranking. In *Proceedings of EMNLP*, 2009.

[8] S. Isaacman, R. Becker, R. Cáceres, S. Kobourov, J. Rowland, and A. Varshavsky. A tale of two cities. In *Proceedings of HotMobile'10*.

[9] B. J. Jansen, D. L. Booth, and A. Spink. Determining the user intent of web search engine queries. In *Proceedings of WWW*, 2007.

[10] M. Kamvar and S. Baluja. A large scale study of wireless search behavior: Google mobile search. In *Proceedings of CHI*, 2006.

[11] M. Kamvar and S. Baluja. Deciphering trends in mobile search. *Computer*, 40(8):58–62, 2007.

[12] M. Kamvar, M. Kellar, R. Patel, and Y. Xu. Computers and iphones and mobile phones, oh my!: a logs-based comparison of search users on different devices. In *Proceedings of WWW*, 2009.

[13] E. Koukoumidis, D. Lymberopoulos, K. Straus, J. Liu, and D. Burger. Pocket cloudlets. In *Proceedings of ASPLOS (to appear)*, 2011.

[14] N. D. Lane, D. Lymberopoulos, F. Zhao, and A. T. Campbell. Hapori: context-based local search for mobile phones using community behavioral modeling and similarity. In *Proceedings of Ubicomp'10*.

[15] Y. Lu, F. Peng, X. Wei, and B. Dumoulin. Personalize web search results with user's location. In *Proceedings of SIGIR*, 2010.

[16] Mobile Search Trends Report, `http://www.marketingcharts.com/`.

[17] U.S. Census Bureau, `http://www.census.gov/`.

[18] X. Wang and C. Zhai. Learn from web search logs to organize search results. In *Proceedings of SIGIR*, 2007.

[19] I. Weber and C. Castillo. The demographics of web search. In *Proceedings of SIGIR*, 2010.

[20] Q. Wu, C. J. C. Burges, K. M. Svore, and J. Gao. Ranking, boosting, and model adaptation. Technical Report MMSR-TR-2008-109, Microsoft Research, 2008.

[21] J. Yi, F. Maghoul, and J. Pedersen. Deciphering mobile search patterns: a study of yahoo! mobile search queries. In *Proceeding of WWW*, 2008.

Text vs. Space: Efficient Geo-Search Query Processing

Maria Christoforaki
Computer Science & Eng.
Polytechnic Institute of NYU
christom@cis.poly.edu

Jinru He
Computer Science & Eng.
Polytechnic Institute of NYU
jhe@cis.poly.edu

Constantinos Dimopoulos
Computer Science & Eng.
Polytechnic Institute of NYU
constantinos@cis.poly.edu

Alexander Markowetz
Computer Science
University of Bonn, Germany
alex@iai.uni-bonn.de

Torsten Suel
Computer Science & Eng.
Polytechnic Institute of NYU
suel@poly.edu

ABSTRACT

Many web search services allow users to constrain text queries to a geographic location (e.g., yoga classes near Santa Monica). Important examples include local search engines such as Google Local and location-based search services for smart phones. Several research groups have studied the efficient execution of queries mixing text and geography; their approaches usually combine inverted lists with a spatial access method such as an R-tree or space-filling curve. In this paper, we take a fresh look at this problem. We feel that previous work has often focused on the spatial aspect at the expense of performance considerations in text processing, such as inverted index access, compression, and caching. We describe new and existing approaches and discuss their different perspectives. We then compare their performance in extensive experiments on large document collections. Our results indicate that a query processor that combines state-of-the-art text processing techniques with a simple coarse-grained spatial structure can outperform existing approaches by up to two orders of magnitude. In fact, even a naïve approach that first uses a simple inverted index and then filters out any documents outside the query range outperforms many previous methods.

Categories and Subject Descriptors

H.3.3 [**INFORMATION STORAGE AND RETRIEVAL**]: Information Search and Retrieval; H.3.4 [**INFORMATION STORAGE AND RETRIEVAL**]: Systems and Software

General Terms

Algorithms, Experimentation, Performance

Keywords

Efficient query processing, Geographic web search engines

CIKM'11, October 24–28, 2011, Glasgow, Scotland, UK.

1. INTRODUCTION

In just a few years, *geographic web search* has emerged from a niche service to one of the most popular applications. It allows users to focus queries to a particular geographic region; e.g., "yoga lessons near Los Angeles" to yoga schools in the LA area, or "pizza" to pizza stores near the user's current location (as reported by her smartphone). The underlying data collections usually either originate from business directories (yellow pages), or consist of *geo-coded* web documents. In the latter case, the search provider found a *geographic reference* (e.g., a city name, or an address) in a document, and was able to map this to a location. As data on the web grows in size, more and more detailed local information becomes available, making geographic web search more useful. In addition to the increase in geo-coded documents, the increasing use of GPS-enabled smartphones further boosts the number of geographic queries.

This massive amount of geographic queries necessitates efficient query processing. Commercial search providers maintain vast server farms to process this workload, and even a small increase in efficiency results in significant savings. However, geographic queries differ significantly from traditional text queries. Standard inverted indexes hence do not directly extend to geographic search, nor do the existing techniques for query optimization. The main challenge lies in the combination of textual and spatial constraints, i.e., finding pages that contain query terms *and* are close to the intended location. Both textual and spatial queries have been extensively studied within their respective communities, but much less work has been spent on combining them.

On the one hand, research in *Information Retrieval* (IR) has resulted in extremely fast algorithms for textual search using inverted indexes. In particular, major web search engines employ a range of performance optimizations including caching, index compression, and early termination. For typical setups, these techniques are able to execute most (or all) queries directly from main memory, running in just a few milliseconds. The rare cache misses only lead to sequential disk access, still significantly cheaper than random I/O. On the other hand, research in spatial databases has proposed numerous specialized index structures such as quad-trees or R*-trees. These however commonly result in a fair amount of random I/O, once the data exceeds main memory. This behavior is partially due to (geo-)database systems having different objectives than web search systems. However, it raises the question of how to best integrate spatial structures in geographic web search.

Over the past years, several studies have explored techniques for efficient processing of geographic queries over document collections. While there are a number of different algorithms, most of them rely on a single R-tree, into which the textual index entries are then inserted. The resulting index structure contains a tremendous number of small textual index structures at the leaves of the R-tree. Significant amounts of CPU are hence spent navigating the spatial structure, even after employing various pruning heuristics. Moreover, when the data does not fit in main memory, this approach necessitates multiple random I/Os per query, rendering it too expensive for web search applications.

We observe that in any typical geo web search scenario, textual clearly dominates spatial data. In particular, the average web page contains several hundred distinct terms, but only one or few geographic references. Even yellow page entries commonly contain at least tens of terms, but only a single location (the address of the business). Any efficient method for processing geographic web queries thus has to primarily address text indexing. Namely, it has to encorporate the various performance optimizations employed in current web search engines. Conversely, a solution that focuses on organizing documents into a fine-grained spatial structure results in significantly decreased performance.

In this paper, we substantiate this claim by experimentally comparing three basic approaches: First, a *Naïve R*-Tree* maintains an inverted index at each leaf, indexing all documents within the leaf's MBR. Second, a *Clairvoyant R*-Tree* assumes an oracle that can prune unproductive subtrees, and thus supersedes many of the optimizations in the literature. Third, a brute-force *Text-First* baseline first determines all textually relevant documents using a state-of-the-art inverted index implementation. Only thereafter, it discards documents outside the query area. Our experimental results show that *Text-First* beats both R*-tree methods, and substantially outperforms the numbers reported in previous papers.

Of course, we should expect a geographic search query to run faster than the Text-First approach, since it actually only needs to be evaluated on a subset of "local" documents. We thus further optimize our approach, by integrating fairly coarse-grained, and thus light-weight, spatial structures into the inverted index without adversely impacting its performance. This leads us to algorithms based on kd-trees and space-filling curves that outperform the CPU cost of our baseline by up to two orders of magnitude.

In our experimental evaluation, we try to create setups that closely resemble scenarios encountered by commercial geographic search services. Thus, we use documents and queries extracted from real data sets that preserve the natural correlation between text and geographic location. In addition, we consider cases where (i) data is completely in main memory, (ii) data is on disk but partially cached in main memory, and (iii) data is on disk with no caching. The latter case is in fact not realistic in current engines, which all have at least a substantial cache of index data in main memory. In fact, cache hit rates commonly range at 90% or higher, due to the natural skew in query term frequencies. We also evaluate the algorithms on additional synthetic data sets, in order to observe the impact of various parameters. Overall, our contributions can be summarized as follows:

- We show that a brute-force inverted index-based method without any spatial index structure outperforms the previous techniques from the literature.
- We describe, implement, and evaluate several optimizations, integrating a coarse-grained spatial structure into the inverted index. The proposed approaches achieve significant speed-ups over the baseline method, and thus over previous work.
- We evaluate the various methods through extensive experiments on real and synthetic data.

The remainder of the paper is structured as follows. First, Section 2 provides background and discusses previous work on text indexing, spatial data structures, and geographic IR. Next, Section 3 outlines the basic application scenario and describes the data setup. Section 4 presents the baseline approaches and performs a brief experimental comparison of these methods. Then, Section 5 discusses how to further optimize performance using coarse kd-trees and space-filling curves. Section 6 evaluates the various approaches and optimizations through a large set of experiments. Finally, Section 7 concludes the paper.

2. BACKGROUND AND RELATED WORK

Geographical search engine technology builds on contributions from several research communities, in particular (i) text indexing and query processing, (ii) spatial index structures, and (iii) geographical information retrieval. In the following, we give a short overview of relevant techniques in these areas and subsequently discuss previous work on query processing in geographic search queries.

2.1 Indexing and Querying in Search Engines

There are a number of textual index structures in the literature including inverted indexes [28], signature files [9], and suffix arrays [18, 1]. However, almost all current web search engines and text information retrieval systems are based on inverted indexes, and substantial efforts have been invested in optimizing the construction, size, and access speed of these structures; see, e.g., [28, 26].

An *inverted index* contains one *inverted list* for each distinct term (word) in the document collection. Each list consists of postings describing occurrences of the term in the collection. We assume that a posting contains the ID of the document where the term occurs (docID), and the number of times it occurs (frequency). Postings may contain additional data such as the precise positions of the terms in the document. However, docIDs and frequencies already suffice to compute simple common ranking functions such as BM25 or Cosine measures. The postings in each list are usually sorted by docID, and an additional dictionary structure stores for each distinct term a pointer to the start of the corresponding list. Query processing basically involves intersecting (conjunctive queries) or merging (disjunctive queries) the inverted lists of the query terms and then computing the ranking function on top. The main performance challenge is the length of the inverted lists for common query terms, which increases with collection size.

While inverted indexes and basic query mechanisms seem almost trivial, there are a number of non-trivial optimizations such as index compression, caching, index pruning and reorganization, early termination, and parallel query processing. These can increase query throughput drastically [28]. As a result, state-of-the-art search tools achieve impressive query processing, typically in the range of a few milliseconds per query, on machines indexing millions of pages. We refer to [26, 22] for recent numbers on the widely used GOV2 collection of 25 million pages. As we demonstrate in this paper, such state-of-the-art techniques for text query processing are crucial for building high-performance geographic search engines.

2.2 Spatial Indexing

There exists a tremendous body of work in spatial databases and geographic information systems on index structures for spatial data. The main approaches can be classified into: (i) tree-based methods [8], (ii) grid structures [20], and (iii) space-filling curves [12, 3, 21]. Most relevant to our work here are tree-based methods and space-filling curves.

Tree-based indexing structures can be divided into (i) space- and (ii) data-partitioning. The former divides space into disjoint tiles, while the latter divides the spatial objects into disjoint subsets. Important examples of space-partitioning techniques are quad-trees [11] and kd-trees [2]. Their major drawback is that objects that span across a border between tiles are stored twice. This problem occurs for relatively large objects, but not when objects are fairly small or just points. The most widely used data-partitioning approach is the R-tree family of index structures [13]. These store each object only once, but use overlapping subareas that may result in a search operation having to visit multiple subtrees. An optimized version, the R*-tree, employs an improved partitioning heuristic, and is widely used in many applications. We refer to [8] for a more detailed discussion of tree-based spatial index structures.

Space-filling curves (SFCs) are continuous curves that cover the entire space. The basic goal of a SFC is that most points that are close to each other in space should also be reasonably close to each other on the curve. There are a number of different SFCs in the literature, with the Z curve and Hilbert curve being the most widely used. For an overview of space-filling curves, we refer to [12, 3, 21]. In this paper, we use index structures for geo search based on R*-trees, kd-trees, and space-filling curves.

2.3 GIR and Geo Query Processing

Geographic information retrieval (GIR) deals with items (documents) containing both spatial data and unstructured data, most commonly text. We refer to [16] for early work, and to [15] for a recent overview. This area commonly requires techniques from both textual information retrieval and spatial data processing.

We focus on efficient query processing over web documents and yellow page collections under both textual and spatial constraints, as motivated by the local and mobile search services provided by all the major search engines. Thus, we have a set of documents, each containing textual content and one or more locations (points or rectangles). Given a query consisting of terms and a rectangle, the goal is to find (and possibly rank) all documents that contain the query terms and have a location in the query rectangle.[1]

[1]There are several variations of this problem, but for now this basic version suffices.

A number of researchers have studied this and related problems over the last few years, starting with the early work in [23], where three techniques based on a grid scheme for spatial indexing along with inverted indexes are proposed. In the first approach, an inverted index is built for each grid cell and each query is performed by first applying spatial filtering and then textual. In their second technique, the postings are spatially clustered based on the grid cells their footprints belong to. The third approach separately applies spatial and textual filtering and merges the results. This work is the most closely related to our work. The main drawback of the second proposed approach, which is similar to our work, is that the documents in lists do not preserve a sorted order which in turn does not permit performing effective skipping while processing the inverted lists.

Some follow-up work was done in [27, 6]. In particular, Zhou et al. in [27] studies three approaches combining inverted indexes and R*-trees: (i) keeping separate indexes, (ii) an inverted file on top of an R*-tree (the overall best), and (iii) an R*-tree on top of an inverted file.

The work by Chen et al. in [6] combines inverted indexes with space-filling curves. More precisely, efficient query processing is achieved by laying out the inverted lists along a space-filling curve. This work is also different from [27] as it focuses on disk performance and assumes that larger spatial payloads (not just points or rectangles) may be attached to the documents, and that a document may relate to several locations. However, the CPU performance in [6] suffers from bottlenecks in the inverted index implementation.

Several more recent papers have proposed additional query processing algorithms based on combining inverted indexes with R*-trees [14, 10, 7, 17]. These papers all use R*-trees as the main structure, and basically insert the document data into the R*-tree. Basic query processing involves traversing the R*-tree to visit leaf nodes satisfying the spatial constraint, and then traversing the (fairly small) textual indexes in the leaves. Additional improvements are obtained by pushing some textual information up in the tree, allowing pruning of subtrees that do not contain the query terms or cannot contain high-scoring results.

In particular, in the KR*-tree algorithm [14], dictionary information is propagated from leaves to internal nodes. In the IR^2-tree algorithm in [10], R*-trees are combined with signature files [10]. Thus, every node in the IR^2-tree maintains a signature of the textual content in its subtree. Cong et al. [7] look at a slight variation of the problem where only the top-k results need to be returned, based on textual relevance and spatial proximity (but without an a-priori cut-off distance as implied by a query rectangle). They build an optimized R*-tree structure for this problem that also stores suitable summary information in the internal nodes. Follow-up work in [4] studies a modified ranking function based on textual relevance, proximity, and a new prestige measure derived from query logs. Finally, the work in [17] presents a structure called IR-Tree that stores impact and location information for selected high-scoring terms in intermediate nodes of the R*-tree, enabling additional pruning during top-k query processing.

In this paper, we revisit the problem of efficient geo query processing, with emphasis on both CPU time and disk performance. Our goal is to design techniques that integrate state-of-the-art techniques from IR query processing, and that achieve significant improvements over existing approaches.

In our experiments we will show that a fairly general class of approaches based on R*-trees cannot come close to our best techniques in the most commonly studied scenarios.

3. PROBLEM AND EXPERIMENT SETUP

We assume conditions similar to those encountered by commercial geo search engines such as Google Local. Specifically, we envision a scenario where entities have a precise location; e.g., a web page about a cafe that is assigned the business' street address. Thus, each document in our collection is associated with a single point location. (Though, we could extend this to multiple locations or small areas with negligible modifications in the code.) In the remainder of the paper, we refer to these markers as the *geographic footprint* of a document. Each query consists of several keywords, and a rectangular geographic search area. The latter is usually small, at least compared to the continental U.S., the region under investigation. We refer to this set of rectangles as *query footprints*.

We pursue a realistic geographic web search scenario, similar to that encountered by a large local (geographic) search engine. For a realistic setting, it is of utmost importance to use data sets that reflect the natural relationship between (i) terms and positions and (ii) keywords and documents. For example, a page about opera tickets is more likely to relate to a large city; the query "cattle feed" most likely originates from a rural location.

To maintain this natural relationship between terms and locations, we geo-coded real web documents and search queries. To this end, we scanned each document for geographic markers, such as zip codes or names of counties, cities, and towns. Next, we assigned a geographic position to the document, using the "Census 2000 U.S. Gazetteer" [5]. This data collection maps 95,000 geographical entities (zip codes and location names) to geographic coordinates. In cases where we found more than one location in a document, we chose the one with the larger population. For example, if a document contained a reference to New York City as well as Smalltown, we assumed it belonged to the former. Similarly, we geo-coded web queries. Namely, we first parsed real web queries for geographic terms, subsequently translated into a geographic position. Finally, we associated each query with a search rectangle, corresponding to the square miles of the geographical location found.

We conduct our experiments on two sets of documents. First, we use 6.1 million pages from a broad web crawl performed by our group (referred to as $R6.1$). These documents were assigned locations by means of geo-coding, as described above. They were part of a larger collection, from which we removed all web pages that did not refer to a U.S. location. Second, we use the 25 million documents of the $GOV2$ data set (referred to as $F25$). Here we assign random locations, however according to the distribution observed in $R6.1$. The characteristics of the $R6.1$ web data collection summarize as follows. There are a total of 6.1 million geo documents, containing $29,872,888$ distinct terms. The size of the uncompressed inverted index is 17.9 GB, whereas its compressed version is only 3.36 GB. Our collection contains $14,134$ distinct geographic footprints. The $F25$ data set consists of $25,205,179$ documents, $36,759,149$ distinct words and $6,797$ M postings. We also obtained much larger data sets of size 50, 75 and 100 million documents by suitably replicating the $F25$ data set.

A set of geographic web queries was obtained by geocoding entries of the 2006 AOL search log. In particular, we selected queries containing the name of a town, county, or a zip code. The query was then assigned a search rectangle centered around this location.Consequently, the term indicating the geographic position (e.g., the name of a town) was removed from the query string. The resulting query trace contains $49,978$ geo queries, $5,841$ distinct locations and an average of 2.8 textual terms per query.

We do not assume any particular search scenario, as could arise from a person on foot vs. a person travelling by car (larger area of interest). To model different scenarios, we partition our geo queries into four subsets, called *small, medium, large*, and *mixed*, based on the sizes of their footprints. In particular, the small set corresponds to areas of less than 0.5 sq. miles, the medium set to areas between 0.5 and 450 sq. miles and the large set to areas larger than 450 sq. miles. For every experiment we used $1,000$ queries from each set.

We compute the precise relevance scores for all documents, but allow the choice of any k in top-k pruning approaches. We focus on conjunctive queries and retrieve all the documents that satisfy the textual and geographical constraints of the query. To be more specific, we consider every document that (i) has a non-zero term-based score, and (ii) whose spatial focus lies strictly within the query rectangle. For the purpose of this paper, we use a simple scoring function. In particular, we employ a linear combination of a term-based measure (BM25) and a geographic score, the distance between the center of the query footprint and the geographic footprint of the document. However, our approach also applies to many other ranking functions.

4. BASELINES AND PRELIMINARIES

In this section, we first describe several basic solutions, and then show experimentally that a simple *Text-First* index already outperforms previous approaches. Finally, we discuss these observations, providing valuable insights for the subsequent optimizations.

4.1 The Naïve R*-Tree Algorithm

As described in Section 2, a number of previous approaches have used R(*)-trees. We describe the *Naïve R*-Tree*, the most basic such approach. This method inserts documents into an R*-Tree according to their geographic locations. At each leaf node, there is a small inverted index over all documents residing therein. Given a query, we first traverse the R*-tree to find all leaf nodes intersecting the query footprint. Subsequently, we access the inverted indexes stored at each of these leaves. The approach thus first filters by space, and only thereafter by text. We implemented the Naïve R*-Tree by adding inverted indexes to the leaf nodes of the canonical R*-tree implementation of [19].

4.2 The Clairvoyant R*-Tree Algorithm

While the Naïve R*-Tree does not perform any textual filtering before reaching the leaf level, several authors have proposed textual pruning at intermediate nodes. We hence conceptualize a *Clairvoyant R*-Tree*, employing perfect textual pruning inside the R*-Tree, at zero cost. This hypothetical data structure would thus outperform any of the approaches using R*-trees, as presented in the literature.

The Clairvoyant R*-Tree structurally resembles a Naïve R*-Tree, but employs an oracle that indicates if a path leads to a leaf containing results. Recall that while traversing the Naïve R*-Tree we may visit leaves that do not contain a single result. For example, consider the query "cat, dog", on the index structure of Figure 1. Assume that the query rectangle intersects spatially with all depicted leaf nodes. The intermediate nodes of the Naïve R*-Tree only store spatial information. One would thus visit all leaves, and traverse the inverted lists for "cat" and "dog" in nodes n_3 and n_4. However, only n_4 actually returns a result, and exploring n_3 wastes considerable resources, due to R*-tree traversal, dictionary lookup, and inverted index access. In contrast, the Clairvoyant R*-Tree features an oracle at each intermediate node of the R*-tree. For a given query, it directs us exclusively to leaves in the subtree that contain at least one result. The oracle thus allows us to avoid any nodes in the tree that are not on a path between the root and leaves containing results. In our example, it would spare us from visiting n_3 as well as exploring this leaf's inverted index, while still finding the results at n_4.

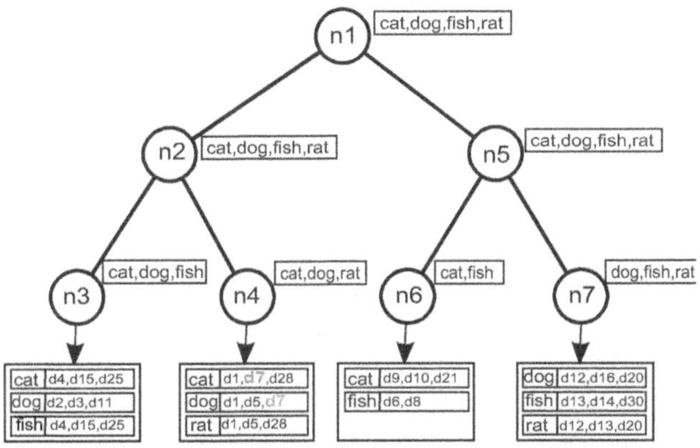

Figure 1: A hybrid R-Tree based structure.

Obviously, this data structure is entirely hypothetical. Yet, it makes an excellent contestant for our experiments, as it subsumes all optimizations storing textual hints at intermediate nodes. In fact, it subsumes many optimizations not in the literature. We simulated its implementation by executing every query twice. First, we issue an exploratory query, recording all inner nodes that actually lead to a result. Subsequently, we execute the actual query, only visiting these productive nodes.

The main limitation of the Clairvoyant R*-Tree is that the algorithm must visit and score every document that satisfies the textual and spatial filters. Some top-k early termination techniques such as in [7, 17] however do not score every document passing the filters. The performance of these data structures is not bounded by the Clairvoyant R*-Tree. We further elaborate on this topic below.

4.3 Text-First Baseline

We now describe a trivial algorithm that relies on an inverted index, and uses no spatial index structure at all. While this algorithm is trivial, we are not aware of any previous work that compares an optimized implementation of it to the various R-Tree based methods. More precisely, we use an inverted index structure, and a simple array storing the geo locations of the documents. This array, almost two orders of magnitude smaller than the inverted index, fits into main memory. This *Text-First* algorithm then executes a query as follows:

1. Issue a query against the inverted index, retrieving the docID of any document containing all query terms.
2. For each docID returned, perform a lookup in the array to check if the document's location is in the query interval.
3. For any docID passing this spatial check, fetch the frequency values of the postings and compute the BM25 score.

In our implementation, we used an inverted index that compresses docIDs and frequencies in blocks of 128 elements using the OPT-PFD algorithm [25]. We executed queries on our own *document-at-a-time* (DAAT) query processor, optimized through block-wise compression and forward skips in the inverted lists. DocIDs were assigned to documents at random; thus we did not try to obtain additional benefits due to sorted assignment as described in [25]. Overall, this implementation contains many of the techniques used in state-of-the-art IR query processors. To illustrate its performance, we later also report experimental results on this text index alone (*Text-Only*), without applying any geographic filtering at all.

4.4 Preliminary Experimental Evaluation

We implemented the baseline methods and conducted experiments using the *R*6.1 data set and the mixed query set. Table 1 shows the CPU costs of the above methods in milliseconds when both spatial and textual indexes reside in memory. Observe that the trivial Text-First method clearly outperforms both R*-tree methods. The Clairvoyant R*-Tree is much faster than the Naïve R*-Tree, but still significantly slower than Text-First. This illustrates the importance of comparing newly proposed spatial optimizations to simple baselines employing state-of-the-art IR query processing techniques. Comparing Text-First and Text-Only, the former performs additional table lookups and intersections with the query rectangle. This spatial check however results in fewer frequency values being fetched and BM25 scores computed. The performance of both algorithms is thus very similar. Note that to guarantee fairness during this preliminary evaluation, both spatial and textual index structures are memory-resident.

Method	time/query
Naïve R*-Tree	33.0ms
Clairvoyant R*-Tree	12.0ms
Text-Only	7.2ms
Text-First	6.9ms

Table 1: CPU costs of baseline approaches (R6.1)

We now compare the CPUs costs to those reported in previous papers. The best published results appear to be those in [7], where queries on 2.5 million web pages take about 20 ms of CPU time on a similar processor, while our results are for 6.1 million pages. Thus, even though our Clairvoyant R*-Tree does not provide a bound for the top-k methods in [7], as discussed earlier, all our numbers compare well to their reported CPU numbers. In fact, [7] also provides numbers for larger data sets up to 10 million pages, but performance degrades in this case. We note that results reported in other previous papers are limited to even smaller data sets, and achieve much slower performance relative to data size.

In conclusion, it is important to integrate state-of-the-art IR query processing into geographic search. Moreover, for several million pages, R-tree based methods do not appear to perform as well as a carefully implemented trivial baseline. Note that these findings are not restricted to R(*)-trees in particular; any other deep spatial data structure (e.g., kd-trees) would have shown similar performance. All these indexes spend significant amounts of time navigating the fine-grained spatial structure and performing the multiple dictionary lookups to find the inverted lists in the leaf nodes. The Text-First baseline algorithm does not have these overheads.

Of course, when further increasing data size to tens and hundreds of millions of pages, the trivial baseline will eventually fail. In the next section, we thus add coarse-grained spatial optimizations that achieve significant improvements. We evaluate these algorithms on data sets up to 100 million pages, assuming data to be entirely in memory, entirely on disk, and cached in memory. This scenario thus exceeds any experimental setup in literature.

5. IMPROVED ALGORITHMS

As seen in the previous section, even the simple Text-First approach outperforms the best results in the literature in terms of CPU performance. In this section, we present various improved algorithms with optimizations, which as we will see through the experimental results in Section 6 perform significantly better than the baseline solutions. In fact, we outline and compare two approaches and their variations: (i) a coarse-space partitioning (CSP) and (ii) a spatial indexing based on a space-filling curve (SFC).

5.1 Coarse Space Partitioning

The first improved algorithm uses a fairly coarse-grained partitioning of the geographic space into a limited number of regions. Subsequently, it runs Text-First on any region intersecting the query (typically just one, as regions are larger than most query rectangles). We would thus like to divide space into a small number of k regions such that each contains approximately the same number of documents. One could think of various optimizations that try to avoid, e.g., cutting through major metropolitan areas, but we decided to partition space using a simple kd-tree. We hence recursively divide space along vertical and horizontal axes, until the desired number of regions has been obtained. The optimal choice of k naturally depends on the size of the collection and the sizes of the query footprints, a trade-off explored thereafter. Choosing a relatively small value of k allows us to fit the dictionary structures of all regions into main memory, avoiding random I/O at query time. (Caching is also known to perform extremely well on disk-based dictionaries, due to the extreme skew in query term frequencies). We obtain the following simple query processing algorithm:

1. Determine all regions that intersect the query rectangle, using either a scan over an array or a traversal of the (small) kd-tree structure.
2. Run Text-First in each intersecting region, fetching list data from disk if needed.

We implemented two versions of this method, using different layouts of inverted lists. In the first approach, called *CSP-SEQ*, the k inverted lists for each term are stored sequentially. They are thus organized as a single inverted list with the k dictionaries pointing to the starts of the k sublists. In the second approach, *CSP-SUB*, each region builds its own index substructure independently. As seen later, the choice of layout does not significantly affects CPU time. However, when data resides on disk, CSP-SEQ tends to outperform CSP-SUB. Its sequential layout commonly consumes only a single disk seek, even when several regions intersect with the query rectangle. Only in rare cases do lists get so long that it would be preferable to utilize two or three separate seeks. In our memory-resident experiments we present only the results of the CSP-SEQ algorithm for simplicity, since the choice of layout doesn't affect CPU time of the coarse-space partitioning methods.

5.2 Space-Filling Curves

This approach uses space-filling curves [12] to lay out index structures in geo search engines. In fact, as recently disclosed in [24], all the major search engines currently use index structures based on space-filling curves in their local search services. Thus, our results can be seen as providing experimental support that such methods indeed outperform methods based on other, more involved, spatial data structures. Its core idea was proposed by [6], albeit under a very different setup. The authors of [6] assumed that each location may have an associated *document footprint record* of up to several hundred bytes. These may contain polygon data or textual annotations that needs to be fetched at query runtime. Space-filling curves were thus utilized to organize these footprints on disk. Also, the work in [6] did not employ a state-of-the-art IR query processor, and thus reports higher CPU costs.

We use a so-called Z curve [21], which is a fairly simple but still effective SFC. (The approach extends directly to other types of space-filling curves, such as Hilbert.) We first assign to each document a docID that corresponds to the position of its location on the SFC, and then build a standard block-compressed inverted index. The idea is that all documents in the query rectangle are likely close to each other on the SFC, and thus close to each other in the inverted list. This allows skipping large parts of the list. To achieve this skipping effect, we explore two approaches described in the following.

SFC-QUAD: The first approach uses a quad-tree structure to enable skipping. We built a fairly shallow and thus small quad-tree over the document space, roughly consuming 0.5 MB. We then first traverse the quad-tree to determine up to m docID *ranges* that contain all documents intersecting the query footprint. The query processor, adapted again from the Text-First approach, hence only accesses (decompresses) these m docID ranges and can skip the rest of the inverted lists. Moreover, when data resides on secondary storage, the query processor only retrieves the relevant ranges of the inverted lists from disk.

We evaluated different values of m, and found that in main memory, values in the order of several hundred perform best. When fetching inverted list from disk, such a fine-grained approach fails, since for any given list, one should spend only a few (often just one, and rarely more than three) random seeks. We thus merge the m ranges into a smaller number of k disk *sweeps*. In fact, we can choose the number of sweeps optimally, based on the lists lengths and layouts as well as disk model. Overall, we obtain the following algorithm:

1. Traverse the quad-tree and obtain m docID ranges covering all documents in the query rectangle.
2. For each term t whose inverted list is not in main memory, determine $k = 1, 2,$ or 3 docID ranges. These should cover the above m docID ranges and minimize total I/O cost.
3. For each such term perform k seeks on disk to fetch the needed parts of the inverted list.
4. Run Text-First on the m docID ranges.

SFC-SKIP: We also explored an alternative, yet natural, way to skip parts of the docID space. Remember that our inverted lists are compressed in blocks of 128 postings. Suppose that for each such block we store a *minimum bounding rectangle* (MBR), encompassing all of the locations of documents represented in the block. During query processing, we can skip any block whose MBR does not intersect with the query rectangle. This skipping fits naturally into any typical IR query processor, which already performs skips over compressed blocks of postings. In fact, we can store additional MBRs for groups of, say, 2, 4, 8, etc. blocks. The resulting structure thus allows hierarchical skipping. This structure differs from the others approaches presented in this paper, because it is defined on a per-list basis. Thus, we have more detailed skipping information for longer lists, and no such information at all for lists with fewer than 128 postings.

We explored different settings and found that storing MBRs and shortcut pointers on 3 levels, for 4, 16, and 64 compressed blocks, provided excellent performance. The MBRs and shortcuts are stored separately from the lists and are usually kept in main memory. Using this information, we can again determine optimized sweeps for fetching index data from disk, as in the SFC-QUAD method. In our disk-resident experiments we found that the performance of the two versions of the SFC approach is similar. Thus, in our experiments when data reside on disk, we only present the performance of SFC-QUAD for simplicity.

6. EXPERIMENTS

In this section we present the results of an extensive performance evaluation of our proposed algorithms.

6.1 Experimental Evaluation

In Section 4, preliminary experiments showed that the Text-First *baseline* outperforms the commonly considered R-Tree based approaches in terms of CPU. In this section, we investigate the benefits achieved by the various optimizations from Section 5. In particular, we evaluate three approaches: (i) *Coarse Space Partitioning* (CSP), (ii) *Space Filling Curve Quad Tree* (SFC-QUAD), and (iii) *Space Filling Curve Skip pointers* (SFC-SKIP). The parameters under investigation are: (a) the size of the query rectangle, (b) the number k of sweeps, (c) the amount of memory available for caching index data, and (d) the size of the data set. By default, we used query rectangles of mixed size, and a choice of up to three sweeps. In every set of experiments, we modify one parameter, while the others remain at their default. All experiments were conducted on a single core of an Intel Xeon server with 2.27*Ghz*.

We first conduct experiments in main memory. Subsequently, we evaluate setups where data resides on secondary storage. In particular, we use a standard disk model to estimate the time spent retrieving data from disk. We assume $8ms$ access time for each random access, and $50MB/s$ sequential transfer rate, settings typical for current SATA disks. In the remainder of the paper, we refer to the total disk cost including both seek and transfer time as I/O cost. For CPU results all structures are kept in main memory, while for disk and disk-cached results, only the spatial structures plus the stated amount of cached inverted lists are in memory while the rest of the inverted list is on disk.

Index size: Table 2 reports the space required to store the inverted index with docIDs and term frequencies. We index (and compress) gaps between docIDs, so smaller gaps among docIDs achieve better compression. We observe that CSP has larger index size than other methods, because docIDs are scattered into separate indexes (partitions). The relative gap between docIDs of the same partition hence increases, resulting in a larger docID index. On the other hand, the baseline and SFC approach achieve smaller index size due to their smarter docID assignment scheme. Of course, the increased index size for CSP also has an adverse effect on disk access costs (both with and without caching).

in *GB*	docID	freq	total
Baseline	2.49	0.87	3.36
CSP	4.55	1.12	5.67
SFC	2.50	0.87	3.37

Table 2: Compressed index size (R6.1)

Spatial structure size: Table 3 presents the size of the spatial structures in memory. We observe that the R*-Tree is significantly larger than the CSP and SFC methods. For each document we assign footprints of 8 bytes and thus need roughly 48 MB of memory for maintaining this information for the R6.1 data set. The size of these footprints is not included in any of the spatial structure sizes reported, and is thus listed separately. Moreover, we assume that the document footprints always reside in memory.

	size in MB
R*-tree	680.935
CSP-SEQ	0.004
SFC-QUAD	0.513
SFC-SKIP	17.502
Doc footprints	48.8

Table 3: Size of spatial structures (R6.1)

Query footprint size: First, we vary the size of the query rectangles. Table 4 illustrates the effects of this parameter on CPU consumption, using the R6.1 data set. We observe that all methods significantly improve over the Text-First baseline. These results confirm our expectation that coarse spatial partitioning outperforms any fine grained partitioning. Overall, light-weight spatial indexing techniques such as SFC achieve best performance. The spatial ordering of documents in the inverted lists according to SFC answers even queries with large footprint in less than one millisecond. For this setting, we also evaluated different index layout for the CSP method. Results however indicated that the choice of layout in main memory does not noticeably affect performance. Next, we evaluate the proposed methods on disk-resident data. In Table 5 we show experimental results, assuming that the inverted index resides entirely on disk and

in ms	mixed	small	medium	large
Baseline	6.95	6.81	6.97	7.10
CSP-SEQ	0.50	0.14	0.28	1.27
SFC-QUAD	0.14	0.07	0.08	0.40
SFC-SKIP	0.17	0.08	0.09	0.48

Table 4: Query footprint size vs. CPU (R6.1)

using the R6.1 data set. Note that the CSP-SEQ and SFC approaches achieve significantly better performance than the baseline method. The SFC-QUAD method clearly dominates all other approaches. The experimental results allow the following observations. First, we observe the same ordering of the algorithms for I/O cost as for CPU cost. Second, the layout of inverted lists on disk significantly affects efficiency. In particular, the CSP-SEQ method with sequential layout outperforms its rival CSP-SUB using smaller independent inverted indexes. It is thus beneficial to write all inverted lists for the same term sequentially on disk. Queries located close to a partition border can thus be answered with a single seek operation per term.

in ms	mixed	small	medium	large
Baseline	79.1	79.1	79.1	79.1
CSP-SEQ	29.1	24.8	27.3	44.2
CSP-SUB	41.2	34.5	40.2	62.9
SFC-QUAD	25.1	23.6	24.9	34.1

Table 5: Query footprint size vs. I/O (R6.1)

For this parameter, we also investigate seek and transfer time individually. Table 6 presents the transfer time for various query footprint sizes. In contrast, seek time remains stable between $22ms$ to $28ms$ for all methods and settings. This is not surprising, if we recall that queries on average contain 2.8 terms. For each term, we need to perform at least one seek (of about $10ms$), and thus expect a total seek time of $28ms$. Only in the case of large footprints and the CSP-SUB method, seek time increases to $43.2ms$. This is expected, since large footprints are more likely to cross partition borders, thus necessitating multiple random seeks for the same term.

For the Text-First baseline, transfer cost strongly dominates seek time, since the method ignores spatial filtering, and thus frequently retrieves redundant blocks. Note that the baseline's transfer time remains the same for different footprint sizes, since inverted lists are always retrieved in full length; the same holds for the seek time. All proposed optimizations achieve notably lower transfer cost than the baseline, because the spatial filtering enables them to retrieve fewer blocks. Also, note that the layout of inverted lists on disk affects transfer cost. In particular, sequential layout shows smaller transfer cost for small query footprints. As footprints become larger, both layouts start to achieve similar transfer cost.

in ms	mixed	small	medium	large
Baseline	56.7	56.7	56.7	56.7
CSP-SEQ	5.9	3.1	4.7	17.8
CSP-SUB	13.2	10.5	12.2	19.7
SFC-QUAD	2.3	1.2	2.1	10.1

Table 6: Query footprint vs. disk transfer (R6.1)

Number of sweeps: Next, we evaluate the degree to which the number of sweeps affects performance. Table 7 depicts I/O cost as the number of sweeps increases. Since SFC-QUAD and SFC-SKIP perform exactly the same I/O, we only report the numbers of the former. In the *normal* setting, the algorithm performs exactly k sweeps. Using the *hybrid k-sweeps* technique, the optimum of up to k sweeps is chosen. In particular, it is beneficial to choose a large k for long inverted lists. As these become longer, multiple sweeps improve performance by skipping redundant blocks. In both data sets we observe that, as the number of sweeps increases, performance drops significantly. On the R6.1 data set, hybrid methods exhibit stable performance, very close to 1-sweep. On the F25 data set, the option of using larger k in the hybrid approach yields more substantial benefits. This effect can largely be explained by F25 having longer inverted lists than R6.1.

	*R*6.1		*F*25	
in ms	normal	hybrid	normal	hybrid
1 sweep	26.5	26.5	41.4	41.4
2 sweeps	58.1	25.6	68.6	36.8
3 sweeps	79.6	25.1	93.4	35.2

Table 7: Effects of the number of sweeps in SFC

Cache size: So far, we have assumed that the index structure is either completely in main memory, or only on disk. However, the latter case is not realistic. In real large-scale local search engines the index is either entirely in memory or a significant fraction of the index is cached. To determine the impact of caching, we apply a simple scheme that maintains a static subset of lists in memory. Inverted lists are cached according to (i) their frequency in a large query trace, and (ii) their length. Caching small lists is slightly more preferable, due to the high cost of random accesses on disk. As shown in Figure 2, the I/O cost decreases significantly as cache size grows. Allowing $512MB$ of cache, the total disk cost for SFC-QUAD decreases to less than 10% of the cost without caching. Also, we observe that the relative performance gap between SFC-QUAD versus coarse-grained methods increases with cache size.

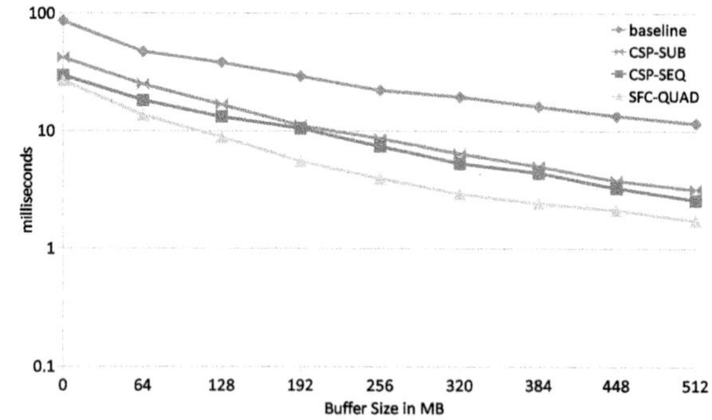

Figure 2: Effects of cache size (R6.1)

Data set size: Table 8 shows the CPU costs (SFC-Quad and SFC-Skip) and I/O-costs (Hybrid k-sweeps) when evaluating the SFC methods for document collections of various sizes. Namely, we use 50, 75 and 100 million documents. The total cost is the sum of the CPU and I/O costs. We observe that all optimizations scale extremely well to larger data. Also, note that the quad-tree approach consistently outperforms skip pointers.

Partition size: Next, we explore the optimal number of partitions under the CSP approach. Again, we experiment in main memory as well as on disk. Coarse partitioning is

in *ms*	6.1	25	50	75	100
SFC-QUAD	0.14	0.23	0.55	0.75	0.89
SFC-SKIP	0.17	0.24	0.57	0.81	0.93
Hybrid k-sweeps	25.1	29.7	31.2	32.8	34.4

Table 8: Number of documents vs. performance

tested by scaling the number of partitions (of the continental US) from 8 to 1024. As expected, the optimal partition granularity differs between main memory and disk. In Figure 3, we observe the effect of partition granularity in main memory for different query footprint sizes. Initially, as the number of partitions increases, performance also improves. Note that with 256 partitions, performance for different query footprint sizes converges to optimal. Increasing the number of partitions does not further reduces the cost of query processing.

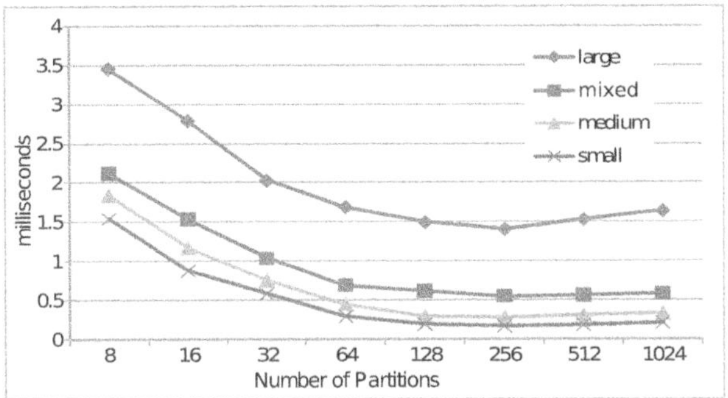

Figure 3: Partition granularity vs. CPU (R6.1)

Figure 4 depicts the impact of the number of partitions on I/O cost. Overall, we observe that as the number of partitions increases, performance degrades. This is reasonable, since more partitions intersect with each query on average, resulting to an increase in the number of disk seeks for fetching all inverted lists. When partition size is set to 64, we observe that all algorithms achieve optimal performance. Further fine grained partitioning leads to additional disk overhead. This experiment supports our claim that fine grained partitioning does not further improve performance. In terms of I/O efficiency, this setting encounters a trade-off between transferring large inverted lists and performing multiple seeks. The best choice for the number of partitions naturally depends on the size of the collection and the sizes of the query footprints.

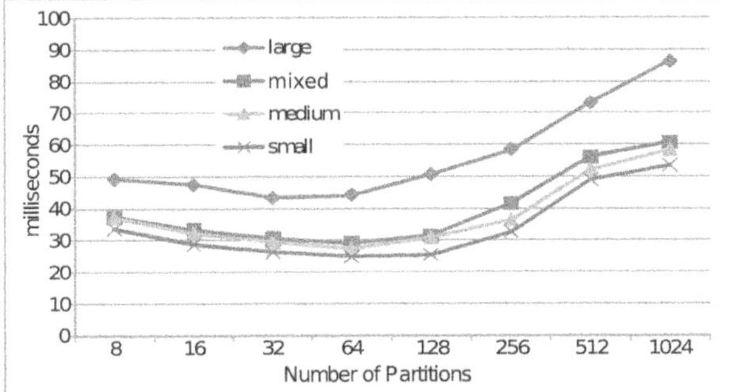

Figure 4: Partition granularity vs. I/O (R6.1)

Query terms: We also tested the effect of the number of query terms on the performance in main memory, using the R6.1 data set. According to Table 9, the CSP-SEQ and SFC methods show significant improvements over the baseline. The SFC approaches outperform CSP-SEQ, while SFC-QUAD performs slightly better than SFC-SKIP. The performance of all algorithms decreases as the number of the query terms increases, due to more lists being accessed.

in *ms*	1	2	3	4 or 5	≥ 6	mean
Baseline	4.01	6.71	6.92	8.21	8.43	6.95
CSP-SEQ	0.43	1.23	1.53	1.91	2.43	1.51
SFC-QUAD	0.07	0.12	0.16	0.21	0.27	0.14
SFC-SKIP	0.07	0.13	0.16	0.23	0.31	0.17

Table 9: Query length vs. CPU (R6.1)

Document size: Next, we study how CPU performance changes depending on the average number of distinct terms in each document. Table 10 shows the impact on the query time for our methods, as we utilize 100, 50 and 30% of the text, meaning the percentage of random distinct terms per document taken into account. More text naturally results in longer inverted lists. Therefore, more blocks must be retrieved which leads to additional performance overhead. CSP-SEQ and SFC methods achieve much better response time than our baseline. SFC approaches achieve remarkably smaller time than other proposed methods. The relative order between the different algorithms is not changed by varying the document size.

in *ms*	100%	50%	30%
Baseline	6.95	3.21	2.01
CSP-SEQ	0.51	0.33	0.21
SFC-QUAD	0.14	0.07	0.05
SFC-SKIP	0.17	0.10	0.07

Table 10: Document size vs. CPU (R6.1)

Query footprint size ($F25$): We also evaluate the impact of the size of the query footprint. In particular, we compare the performance of our proposed methods when tested on the $F25$ data set. Furthermore, we evaluate query performance when data resides (i) in memory as well as (ii) on disk. The SFC approaches once again perform best, across all query footprint sizes. As seen in Table 11, they outperform their competitors in terms of CPU cost, even on large document collections. Also, the CPU cost increases with the size of query footprints, since more inverted list data needs to be retrieved.

in *ms*	mixed	small	medium	large
Baseline	9.78	9.53	9.61	9.98
CSP-SEQ	1.05	0.35	0.63	3.97
SFC-QUAD	0.23	0.13	0.15	0.60
SFC-SKIP	0.24	0.14	0.17	0.65

Table 11: Query footprint size vs. CPU (F25)

According to Table 12, our proposed methods also outperform the baseline on disk. Query footprints naturally affect performance, since larger query rectangles intersect with more documents.

7. DISCUSSION AND CONCLUSIONS

This paper studied the query processing problem that arises in geographic search services such as local search and search on mobile devices. We described several new and existing algorithms, and experimentally evaluated their performance on real and synthetic data sets. Our best methods achieve very substantial improvements over all previous results.

in *ms*	mixed	small	medium	large
Baseline	122.72	122.72	122.72	122.72
CSP-SEQ	37.13	34.59	36.14	56.78
CSP-SUB	46.32	41.33	47.78	74.61
SFC-QUAD	29.7	28.4	31.5	39.7

Table 12: Query footprint size vs. I/O (F25)

The main lessons to be taken away from our results are as follows:

1. State-of-the-art query processing techniques for text data are quite efficient. For related problems such as geographic web search, it is thus important to consider approaches that preserve and exploit these techniques.

2. As there is significantly more textual than spatial data in current geo search engines, it is important to focus on the textual aspect of the problem.

3. Approaches based on fine-grained spatial structures may result in significant CPU and I/O overheads compared to more coarse-grained structures.

4. Efficient algorithms must avoid random I/O, since a single random I/O is significantly more expensive than the entire CPU cost of a query on millions of pages.

5. The best approaches use a careful layout of the inverted lists (and corresponding assignment of docIDs) according to spatial structure.

6. Since current search engines cache a substantial amount (or all) of the index data in memory, focusing on the disk-only case is not sufficient.

There are of course still many open problems in geographic search. Additional optimizations and other methods are an obvious research direction. It would also be interesting to look at parallel query processing in geo search engines, where data is distributed over many nodes. Also, in this paper we focused on simple ranking functions such as BM25, while current engines use several ranking phases that apply increasingly sophisticated ranking functions. Finally, there are many open problems on aspects of geographic search other than efficiency.

Acknowledgments

This research was supported by NSF Grant IIS-0803605, "Efficient and Effective Search Services over Archival Webs".

8. REFERENCES

[1] R. Baeza-Yates and B. Ribeiro-Neto. *Modern Information Retrieval.* Addision Wesley, 1999.
[2] J. L. Bentley. Multidimensional binary search trees used for associative searching. *Commun. ACM*, 18(9):509–517, 1975.
[3] C. Böhm, G. Klump, and H.-P. Kriegel. XZ-Ordering: A Space-Filling Curve for Objects with Spatial Extension. In *SSD*, pages 75–90, 1999.
[4] X. Cao, G. Cong, and C. S. Jensen. Retrieving top-k prestige-based relevant spatial web objects. *PVLDB*, 3(1):373–384, 2010.
[5] Census 2000 U.S. Gazetteer. `http://www.census.gov/geo/www/gazetteer/places2k.html`.
[6] Y.-Y. Chen, T. Suel, and A. Markowetz. Efficient query processing in geographic web search engines. In *SIGMOD Conference*, pages 277–288, 2006.
[7] G. Cong, C. S. Jensen, and D. Wu. Efficient retrieval of the top-k most relevant spatial web objects. *PVLDB*, 2(1):337–348, 2009.
[8] M. de Berg, M. van Krefeld, M. Overmars, and O. Schwarzkopf. *Computational Geometry: Algorithms and Applications.* Springer, 2000.
[9] C. Faloutsos and S. Christodoulakis. Signature files: An access method for documents and its analytical performance evaluation. *ACM Trans. Inf. Syst.*, 2(4):267–288, 1984.
[10] I. D. Felipe, V. Hristidis, and N. Rishe. Keyword search on spatial databases. In *ICDE*, pages 656–665, 2008.
[11] R. A. Finkel and J. L. Bentley. Quad trees: A data structure for retrieval on composite keys. *Acta Inf.*, 4:1–9, 1974.
[12] V. Gaede and O. Günther. Multidimensional access methods. *ACM Comput. Surv.*, 30(2):170–231, 1998.
[13] A. Guttman. R-trees: A dynamic index structure for spatial searching. In *SIGMOD Conference*, pages 47–57, 1984.
[14] R. Hariharan, B. Hore, C. Li, and S. Mehrotra. Processing spatial-keyword (SK) queries in geographic information retrieval (GIR) systems. In *SSDBM*, page 16, 2007.
[15] C. B. Jones and R. S. Purves. Geographical information retrieval. *International Journal of Geographical Information Science*, 22(3):219–228, 2008.
[16] R. Larson. Geographic information retrieval and spatial browsing. In *GIS and Libraries: Patrons, Maps and Spatial Information*, pages 81–124, 1996.
[17] Z. Li, K. C. K. Lee, B. Zheng, W.-C. Lee, D. L. Lee, and X. Wang. IR-Tree: An Efficient Index for Geographic Document Search. *IEEE Trans. Knowl. Data Eng.*, 23(4):585–599, 2011.
[18] U. Manber and E. W. Myers. Suffix arrays: A new method for on-line string searches. *SIAM J. Comput.*, 22(5):935–948, 1993.
[19] Marios Hadjieleftheriou. Spatial Index Library. `http://www2.research.att.com/~marioh/spatialindex/`.
[20] J. Nievergelt, H. Hinterberger, and K. C. Sevcik. The grid file: An adaptable, symmetric multikey file structure. *ACM Trans. Database Syst.*, 9(1):38–71, 1984.
[21] H. Samet. *Foundations of Multidimensional and Metric Data Structures.* Morgan Kaufmann, 2006.
[22] T. Strohman and W. B. Croft. Efficient document retrieval in main memory. In *SIGIR*, pages 175–182, 2007.
[23] S. Vaid, C. B. Jones, H. Joho, and M. Sanderson. Spatio-textual indexing for geographical search on the web. In *SSTD*, pages 218–235, 2005.
[24] P. Venetis, H. Gonzalez, C. S. Jensen, and A. Y. Halevy. Hyper-local, directions-based ranking of places. *PVLDB*, 4(5):290–301, 2011.
[25] H. Yan, S. Ding, and T. Suel. Inverted index compression and query processing with optimized document ordering. In *WWW*, pages 401–410, 2009.
[26] J. Zhang, X. Long, and T. Suel. Performance of compressed inverted list caching in search engines. In *WWW*, pages 387–396, 2008.
[27] Y. Zhou, X. Xie, C. Wang, Y. Gong, and W.-Y. Ma. Hybrid index structures for location-based web search. In *CIKM*, pages 155–162, 2005.
[28] J. Zobel and A. Moffat. Inverted files for text search engines. *ACM Comput. Surv.*, 38(2), 2006.

One is Enough: Distributed Filtering for Duplicate Elimination

Georgia Koloniari
Computer Science Dept.
University of Ioannina, Greece
kgeorgia@cs.uoi.gr

Nikos Ntarmos
Computer Science Dept.
University of Ioannina, Greece
ntarmos@cs.uoi.gr

Evaggelia Pitoura
Computer Science Dept.
University of Ioannina, Greece
pitoura@cs.uoi.gr

Dimitris Souravlias
Computer Science Dept.
University of Ioannina, Greece
dsouravl@cs.uoi.gr

ABSTRACT

The growth of online services has created the need for duplicate elimination in high-volume streams of events. The sheer volume of data in applications such as pay-per-click clickstream processing, RSS feed syndication and notification services in social sites such Twitter and Facebook makes traditional centralized solutions hard to scale. In this paper, we propose an approach based on distributed filtering. To this end, we introduce a suite of distributed Bloom filters that exploit different ways of partitioning the event space. To address the continuous nature of event delivery, the filters are extended to support sliding window semantics. Moreover, we examine locality-related tradeoffs and propose a tree-based architecture to allow for duplicate elimination across geographic locations. We cast the design space and present experimental results that demonstrate the pros and cons of our various solutions in different settings.

Categories and Subject Descriptors

H.3.3 [**Information Storage and Retrieval**]: Information Search and Retrieval—*Information Filtering*

General Terms

Algorithms, Design, Experimentation, Performance

Keywords

Distributed Bloom Filters, Duplicate Elimination

1. INTRODUCTION

The growth of the Internet and the advent of large-scale computing infrastructures, have given ample ground to researchers and developers to create applications and systems that gather and process huge amounts of data from all over the world, usually in a streaming fashion. In turn, the problem of eliminating duplicates from such streams of events has become very important in a number of different settings. When it comes to large amount of data, duplicate-free event delivery is important from two perspectives (a) from the perspective of the event recipients, since it avoids overwhelming them with large amounts of similar data and (b) from a system perspective, since it eliminates the cost of processing and communicating duplicate data.

A recent example is that of click-fraud avoidance in pay-per-click online ad services. In this scenario, malicious parties generate fraudulent accesses to online ads, leading to an arbitrary inflation of related charges. Relevant large-scale systems (such as, Google AdWords/AdSense and Yahoo! Search Marketing) usually filter-out successive identical accesses as a first (and usually most important) step in fighting back[1]. Another example is the re-syndication of events that occurs in applications such as Twitter and Facebook, where events are re-posted (re-tweeted) by a number of different sources besides their original source resulting in multiple appearances of the same event in users feeds. Related research usually relies on variations of Bloom filters [2] to identify and drop duplicates [14, 13]. A common theme in these works is that the naive solution of using a single large Bloom filter for everything does not scale well, due to problems such as excessive memory footprint, lock contention or reduced parallelism. The authors advocate breaking up the filter into smaller units, while incoming events are "rehashed" and assigned to a number of these filter partitions. With this work, we extend such solutions to function in the widely distributed settings of modern data management infrastructures. Such architectures range for partitioning the Bloom filter among threads on a single host to spreading (groups of) such partitions and the related filtering load across multiple hosts and data centers.

The contribution of our work lies in casting the design space regarding the distribution of Bloom filters and their use for duplicate-free event dissemination. In particular, we propose two fundamental ways of partitioning the filters: a *horizontal* and a *vertical* one. We study the two partitioning methods both theoretically and experimentally in terms of accuracy, efficiency, load balance and fault tolerance. Vertical partitioning achieves in practice better load balance and fault tolerance but induces higher communication costs. We further present timer-based filters to support sliding window semantics. In this case, an event is considered a duplicate, only if it was previously delivered in the same time window. A nice property of our extension is that it allows us to improve accuracy through a heuristic we call "equal timers".

[1] `http://adwords.blogspot.com/2007/02/invalid-clicks-googles-overall-numbers.html`

CIKM'11, October 24–28, 2011, Glasgow, Scotland, UK.

Our structures are dynamic, in the sense that they automatically adjust their size thus being capable of handling bursts of events.

To exploit the geographical or network locality of sources, we propose multiple levels of filtering through Bloom trees. We introduce two variations of Bloom trees, namely the sparse and dense Bloom tree. The *sparse Bloom tree* is built based on a simple "first test for duplicates and then set" principle that results in each event being stored only once in the structure. On the other hand, the *dense Bloom tree* is built based on a simple "test and set" principle that results in each event being maintained many times in the structure. Both structures have the same accuracy but differ in efficiency.

The rest of this paper is structured as follows. Section 2 briefly presents our system model. In Section 3, we introduce our distributed filters. Filters are extended to support sliding windows in Section 4 and bursts of events in Section 5. In Section 6, we introduce the Bloom tree. Section 7 presents our experimental results, while Section 8 includes a comparison with related work. Section 9 offers conclusions.

2. MODEL AND PROBLEM DEFINITION

We consider a system where users are interested in events generated by a number of distributed data sources. The data sources that generate the events are called *producers*, while the users that are interested in the events are called *consumers*. The generated events are delivered (pushed) to the consumers by some notification service or mechanism.

We are interested in delivering distinct events to the consumers. To this end, we add a filtering component. All events generated by the producers are first passed through this component that filters out/discards duplicate events, i.e., events that have reached the system before. The straightforward solution for implementing such a filtering component would be to centrally collect and store all produced events. Any new event is compared against these events and is delivered to the consumers only if found to be distinct. The problem with this approach is that it induces large space, communication and processing overheads. To address these issues, we propose using Bloom filters to summarize the set of events.

A Bloom filter [2] is a compact data structure for representing a set of elements. The idea is to allocate an array *bf* of m bits, initially all set to 0, and then choose k independent hash functions, h_i, $1 \leq i \leq k$, each with range 0 to *m-1*. For each element $a \in A$, the bits at positions $h_i(a)$ in *bf* are set to 1. Given a query for c, the bits at positions $h_i(c)$ are checked. If any of them is 0, then certainly $c \notin A$. Otherwise, we conjecture that c is in the set, although there is a certain probability that we are wrong, called *false positive*. For a Bloom filter with n distinct elements, the false positive probability, i.e., the probability that a distinct event is characterized as a duplicate, is:

$$P_{fp}(m,k,n) = (1-(1-\frac{1}{m})^{k \cdot n})^k \quad (1)$$

For large m, Eq. (1) is closely (i.e., within $O(1/m)$) approximated by:

$$P_{fp}(m,k,n) \approx (1-e^{-k \cdot n/m})^k \quad (2)$$

Using Eq. (2), one can set the parameters of a Bloom filter (i.e., number of hash functions k and size m) so as to minimize the false positive probability. In particular, P_{fp} is minimized for $k = \ln 2 \cdot m/n$, in which case $P_{fp} = 0.6185^{m/n}$.

Filtering works as follows. For each incoming event, the corresponding bits in the filter are checked and if they are set, the event is considered a duplicate; otherwise it is considered distinct. If the event is determined as a duplicate, no further action is required. Otherwise, the event is inserted in the filter by setting the above bits. We call this the *first-test-then-set* primitive. We also define a *test-and-set* primitive, where a non-set bit is set when tested.

Instead of forwarding the actual event to the filtering component, the producers can just send the bit positions corresponding to the event. This way, the communication overhead between the producers and the notification service is reduced. In particular, only $k \cdot \log_2(m)$ bits are required. Note that in this case, the communication cost depends on the number of hash functions and their range. The producer of the event needs to forward the actual event to the notification service, only if the event is found to be distinct.

3. SLICING THE BLOOM FILTER

Using Bloom filters reduces the space and processing overheads for detecting duplicates. However, the Bloom filter constitutes a single point of failure and a potential bottleneck for the notification service. To address these issues, we propose distributing the filter by slicing it.

3.1 Horizontal and Vertical Slicing

The Bloom filter is partitioned into disjoint parts, called *slices*, each being placed at a different system site. Clearly, the number of slices determines the degree of distribution. We propose two different approaches for slicing the Bloom filter: horizontally and vertically.

Definition 1. A horizontal Bloom filter is a basic Bloom filter of size m split into S slices, s_i ($1 \leq i \leq S$), each of which is a basic Bloom filter of size m/S. Each event u is inserted in one of the S slices chosen uniformly at random by an additional hash function H_S with range $[1, S]$.

To test whether an event u belongs to the horizontal Bloom filter, the slice $s_i = H_S(u)$ is selected, and u is looked up against it by applying the k hash functions with range $[0,(m/S)-1]$. If the event is determined as distinct the corresponding bit positions in s_i are set. The processing cost is $O(k)$, and if the message regarding the event corresponds to bits positions in the respective slice, the communication cost is $k \cdot \log_2(m/S)$ bits.

A *vertical Bloom filter* splits the filter vertically into slices corresponding to a subset of the range of the original filter.

Definition 2. A vertical Bloom filter is a Bloom filter of size m split into S slices, s_i, $1 \leq i \leq S$, such that each slice s_i is assigned bits $((i-1) \cdot m/S)$ to $(i \cdot m/S - 1)$ of the original Bloom filter.

For an incoming event u, the appropriate filter slices that contain the corresponding bits are located by applying the k hash functions to u. In the worst case, all k bits for the event are contained in k different filter slices and a message has to be sent to each of them to set the bits in their filters.

Note that each producer needs to know the location of the slices to communicate with the corresponding sites. This information can be distributed among the sites holding the filter slices, so that each producer knows the location of just one of the sites. This can be achieved by building an overlay network among the sites that maintain the slices. The sites can use this overlay for forwarding the event (or hash functions) to the site(s) holding the appropriate slices.

3.2 Properties

False Positive Probability. Assume that we slice a Bloom filter of size m with k hash functions into S slices. In the case of vertical Bloom filters, all elements are inserted into the same size m filter, thus as in Eq. (1), the false positive probability is equal to:

$$VP_{fp}(m,k,S,n) = (1-(1-\frac{1}{m})^{k \cdot n})^k \quad (3)$$

In the case of horizontal Bloom filters, each slice has size m/S. Assuming that H_S distributes the n elements uni-

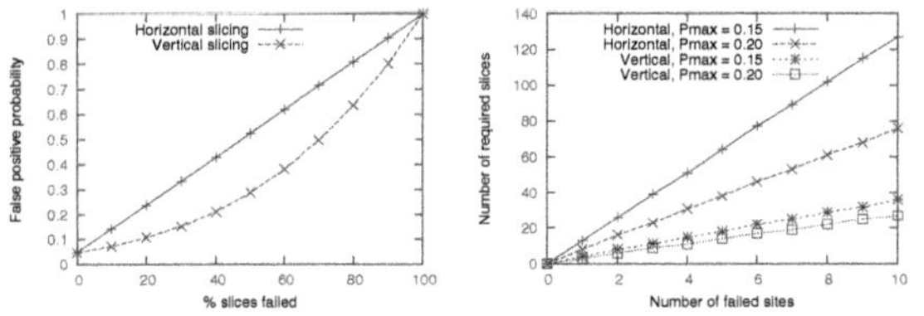

(a) (b)

Figure 1: Fault tolerance.

formly at random at the S slices, each one of the slices receives approximately n/S elements. Thus, the false positive probability is equal to:

$$HP_{fp}(m,k,S,n) = (1-(1-\frac{S}{m})^{k\cdot n/S})^k. \quad (4)$$

From Eq. (3) and (4), $HP_{fp}(m,k,S,n) > VP_{fp}(m,k,S,n)$, for $S > 1$. For small $\frac{S}{m}$, $HP_{fp}(m,k,S,n)$ is closely (within a factor of $O(S/m)$) approximated by $(1-e^{-k\cdot n/m})^k$, which in conjunction with Eq. (2) leads to the following conclusion:

Proposition 1. The false positive probability for both horizontal and vertical Bloom filters is asymptotically the same and equal to that of the non-sliced filter.

Load. Assume an incoming stream of N events taking values in a domain N_D, according to some distribution. For this input, N lookups/filter tests are required in a single Bloom filter. By slicing the filter, this load is distributed among the S slices.

With horizontally sliced filters, each of the N events is inserted/looked-up at only one slice, as $H_S(u)$ partitions N_D uniformly into parts of N_D/S size each (on average), each assigned to a different slice. Thus, the input load is also distributed uniformly across the S slices. Therefore, for a uniform input distribution, the load is balanced among the S slices, with each slice receiving approximately N/S test requests. Whereas, for a skewed distribution, the load at each slice follows this distribution.

Vertical slicing, on the other hand, results in each input event being inserted at k (possibly) different sites, as dictated by the k hash functions. In this case the total load for N events is increased by a factor of k. This added communication overhead comes at the benefit of load distribution; as each of the k functions also spreads its input domain uniformly over its output domain, the final load distribution is the sum of k permutations of the input distribution and thus more balanced than with horizontal slicing. We study this issue in more detail experimentally.

To conclude, while both horizontal and vertical filters distribute uniform input distributions evenly among the slices, vertical filters also manage to balance skewed distributions more evenly in the cost of increasing the total load.

Parallelism & Pipelining. With vertical Bloom filters, k sites need to be contacted. Both the first-test-then-set and the test-and-set primitives can be implemented either in parallel or using pipelining. In the first case, the k sites are contacted in parallel and each site independently tests, sets, or tests-and-sets the corresponding bits. To determine whether the event is distinct, the sites need to inform the producer of the event with their decision. With pipelining, the k sites test, set and test-and-set their bits in turn. In this case, only one site communicates the final outcome; this site is either the first site having a slice with an unset bit, or the last site in the pipeline, if the bits are set in all sites. In addition, the procedure for test stops, once the first unset bit is encountered, thus the response time is improved.

Fault Tolerance. Let us now compute the false positive probability in the case of failures. We assume that all sites have an equal probability to fail.

In the case of horizontal Bloom filters, each event is inserted in just one of the S filters. This filter constitutes a single point of failure for the event. If we treat events that hash to a failed site as duplicates, the false positive probability in the case of f failures is given by:

$$\frac{f}{S} + (1-\frac{f}{S}) \cdot (1-e^{-k\cdot n/m})^k \quad (5)$$

Vertical Bloom filters exhibit better fault tolerance, since information for each event is available in more than one site. For each incoming event u, if there is at least one site that has not failed and at this site the corresponding bit is not set, we can safely characterize u as distinct. Thus, additional false positives are introduced only in the case in which, for an event u, the corresponding bits in all the non-failed sites are set.

We assume that the bits that the events set are distributed uniformly among the S slices. Thus, for f failed slices, the probability that a bit is not available is $\frac{f}{S}$. The false positive probability in this case is:

$$(\frac{f}{S} + (1-\frac{f}{S}) \cdot (1-e^{-k\cdot n/m}))^k \quad (6)$$

Fig. 1(a) shows the false positive probability of horizontal and vertical filters with increasing percentage of failed sites.

Since the increase in the false positive probability depends on the number of slices S of the filter, we can tune S, so that for a given number of failed sites (filters) f, the false positive probability is not increased above a desired threshold P_{fp}^{max}.

Definition 3. Given a Bloom filter bf with size m and k hash functions with n inserted elements, we define its fault tolerance parameter S_f, as the number of slices we need to split bf into so as to achieve a false positive probability that does not exceed P_{fp}^{max} when f out of the S_f sites fail.

For horizontal Bloom filters, by solving Eq. (5) for S_f we get: $S_f \geq \frac{f\cdot(1-P_{fp})}{P_{fp}^{max}-P_{fp}}$. Similarly using Eq. (6), we get for vertical filters: $S_f \geq \frac{f\cdot(1-\sqrt[k]{P_{fp}})}{\sqrt[k]{P_{fp}^{max}}-\sqrt[k]{P_{fp}}}$. Fig. 1(b) illustrates how the fault tolerance parameter S_f varies for different number of failed sites and maximum false positive thresholds. Vertical filters show better fault tolerance than horizontal ones. For instance, for the same maximum false positive probability of 0.15 and f=4 failed sites, vertical filters require less than 20 slices, while horizontal filters require more than 30.

A symmetric approach is also possible, where instead of treating events that hash at failed sites as duplicates, we treat them as distinct. By doing so, we do not increase false positives, but instead introduce false negatives. This approach leads to an alternative definition of S_f such that the false negative probability does not exceed a given P_{fn}^{max} threshold and to the following hybrid approach:

VERTICAL FAULT TOLERANCE HEURISTIC. An event is considered to be a duplicate, if there are at least x bits in non-failed sites with their bits set, and distinct, otherwise.

To have a false negative, it means that one or more of the bits corresponding to the failed sites would have not been set. The probability of a false negative for horizontal Bloom filters is $\frac{f}{S}$, as any event corresponding to a failed site will be considered as distinct. In this case, the false positive probability is reduced to $(1-\frac{f}{S}) \cdot (1-e^{-k\cdot n/m})^k$.
For vertical filters, the false negative probability is:

$$\sum_{i=1}^{k} \left(\frac{f}{S}\right)^i \cdot \left(1-\frac{f}{S}\right)^{k-i}$$

while the false positive one becomes: $((1-\frac{f}{S})\cdot(1-e^{-k\cdot n/m}))^k$.

Now consider the hybrid approach for vertical Bloom filters, where an event is considered to be a duplicate, if there are at least x bits in non-failed sites with their bits set, and distinct, otherwise. Using this heuristic, we get:

$$VP_{fp} = ((1-\frac{f}{S}) \cdot (1-e^{-k\cdot n/m}))^x$$

and

$$VP_{fn} = \sum_{i=k-x+1}^{k} \left(\frac{f}{S}\right)^i \cdot \left(1-\frac{f}{S}\right)^{k-i}.$$

3.3 Other Types of Slicing

Let us first examine whether there is a better way to slice a Bloom filter in terms of improving the false positive probability. The most general way to split a Bloom filter into S slices is by using two sets of hash functions. For inserting an event into the filter, one set of k_1 hash functions is used to select k_1 of the S slices. Then, for each of the selected slices, a second set of k_2 hash functions is used to set the corresponding k_2 bits. Note that for horizontal Bloom filters, $k_1 = 1$ and $k_2 = k$, whereas for vertical Bloom filters, $k_1 = k$ and $k_2 = 1$. It can be shown that:

Proposition 2. The false positive probability cannot be improved regardless of how we choose k_1 and k_2, given that we maintain the total size and number of hash functions fixed.

Proof. We split a Bloom filter into S slices using two sets of hash functions. For inserting an event into the filter, the first set of hash functions (k_1 hash functions) is used to select k_1 of the S slices. Then, for each of the selected slices a second set of k_2 hash functions is used to set to 1 the corresponding k_2 bits. Therefore, to insert each event we apply $k_1 * k_2$ hash functions. To maintain the same number of hash functions as for the single Bloom filter, we set $k_1 \cdot k_2 = k$. Let us assume n inserted events into the filter and slices of the same size m/S. Then each slice has $n \cdot k_1/S$ elements on average, making the per slice s_i false positive probability:

$$(1-(1-S/m)^{k_2 \cdot k_1 \cdot n/S})^{k_2} \approx (1-e^{k_1 \cdot k_2 \cdot n/m})^{k_2}$$

Since for each event we check all k_1 slices indicated by the first set of hash functions, the total probability for a false positive to occur is: $(1-e^{k_1 \cdot k_2 \cdot n/m})^{k_2 \cdot k_1}$. Since $k_1 \cdot k_2 = k$, we conclude that the false positive probability cannot be improved regardless of how we choose to slice a Bloom filter, given that we want to maintain the total size and number of hash functions fixed.

Let us now consider combinations of vertical and horizontal Bloom filters, called *diced Bloom filters*. There are two possible combinations: *h-v diced* Bloom filters are horizontal Bloom filters with k hash functions and S slices of size m/S, with each slice being a vertical Bloom filter of S' slices of size $m/(S \cdot S')$; *v-h diced* Bloom filters are vertical Bloom filters with k hash functions and S slices of size m/S, each being a horizontal Bloom filter of S' slices of size $m/(S \cdot S')$.

Assuming all mappings and hash functions are known, the communication and processing cost for both diced Bloom filters is O(k). For the h-v diced Bloom filter, we first consider the horizontal Bloom filter consisting of S slices and ignore the vertical partitioning. The false positive probability is:

$$\left(1-(1-\tfrac{S}{m})^{\frac{k \cdot n}{S}}\right)^k$$

The vertical partitioning does not influence the false positive probability, and thus, the false positve for the h-v diced Bloom filter is equal to the false positive probability of a horizontal Bloom filter with S slices and k hash functions. For the v-h diced Bloom filter, the vertical partitioning again does not influence the false positive probability. Thus, the total false positive probability is influenced by the horizontal partitioning and given by:

$$\left(1-(1-\tfrac{S \cdot S'}{m})^{\frac{k \cdot n}{S \cdot S'}}\right)^k$$

Again, for small $\frac{S \cdot S'}{m}$, we conclude that slicing the Bloom filter does not influence its false positive probability.

With respect to load balance, both communication and processing cost is split equally among the $S \cdot S'$ sites that maintain the corresponding filter slices. As for fault tolerance, the diced Bloom filter inherits the fault tolerance properties of the vertical Bloom filters as information about each event is distributed among multiple sites. In particular, the diced Bloom filter behave similarly to a vertical Bloom filter but with $S \cdot S'$ slices. For instance, the false positive probability if we consider that any bit corresponding to a failed site is set, is given by:

$$\left(\frac{f}{S \cdot S'} + (1-\frac{f}{S}) \cdot (1-e^{-k \cdot n/m})\right)^k \quad (7)$$

The false positives in case of failures are the same for both diced Bloom filters if we also consider that both their initial false positive probability is $(1-e^{-k \cdot n/m})^k$ by using the e approximation. If instead we use the accurate formulas then the measure differs for the two structures as we need to replace in Eq. (7) the corresponding false positive for each variation as we have evaluated them above.

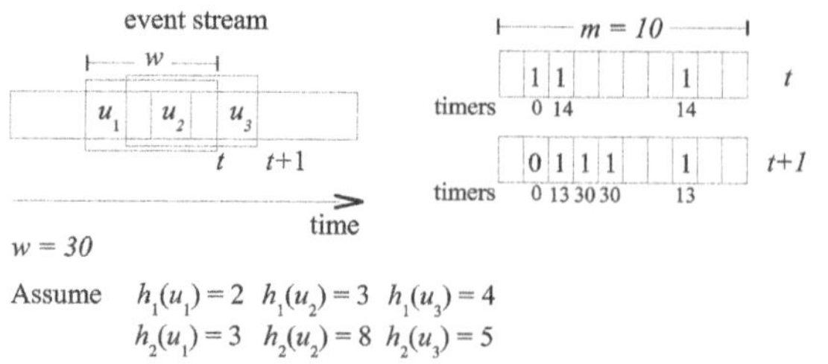

Figure 2: Event stream and the corresponding sliding Bloom filter at time t and $t+1$.

4. SLIDING WINDOWS

In many applications where duplicate-free delivery is desired, events are only considered during specific time frames (windows). For instance, in a pay-per-click online ad service, an access made one day should not forbid the payment for an access made the next day, i.e., the second access should not be considered a duplicate.

Definition 4. An event u is considered distinct in a *sliding window* of size w, if it has not been delivered during the previous w time units.

So far, our Bloom filters are append-only: events are inserted in the filters but never deleted. However, to support sliding-window semantics, an event must be deleted from the filter, once it exits the current window. To allow deletions, we extend each Bloom filter array bf to an array bf^T of the same size whose elements are integers called *timers* initially set to zero. To insert an event u, instead of setting the bits $h_j(u)$ of bf to one, we set the timers at the same positions of bf^T equal to w. At each time unit, all non-zero timers are decremented by one. Consequently, a non-zero value t of the timer in position j in bf^T indicates that the last event that has set the corresponding timer j in bf^T was delivered $w-t$ time units ago. A position is considered to be zero, when the corresponding timer becomes equal to zero, since this means that the last event that has set the corresponding timer was delivered w time units ago, thus no longer belongs to the current window. Consequently, the above technique ensures that Definition 4 holds. An example is shown in Fig. 2. The maximum value that any timer can take is w, thus timers need to be $\lceil log_2(w) \rceil$ bits long.

The above approach assumes that all k positions associated with an event are set at the same time. This may not be possible when these positions belong to slices stored at different sites, as it may be the case with vertical Bloom filters. To address possible network delays, the producer may assign to each event u a timestamp t_u equal to the time instant of its delivery to the filtering service. Let t_i be the current time at a slice. When u is inserted, we set the timers at the corresponding positions at this slice to $w-(t_i-t_u)$.

The timers are set only if an event is distinct and not for duplicate events. Thus, using the test-and-set primitive is not possible, since, we cannot determine whether to reset any given timer without testing all associated positions first. Instead, with first-test-then-set, we can safely reset the timers that belong to events already tested as distinct.

Note that our sliding windows are time-based. Alternatively, an event-based sliding window would require that the same event is not among the last w events previously delivered. Our approach can be extended to this case as well, but such semantics are hard to achieve in a distributing setting, since some form of counting of the events is required.

Equal Timers Heuristic. The timers of the sliding Bloom filters can be used to improve the false positive probability. The intuition is that, if during the lookup for an event all k timers are non-zero, and in addition all the corresponding k timers are equal, then the timers have been most probably set by the same event. Thus, the event is a true duplicate with high probability.

We can evaluate the probability for a false positive if all the k corresponding timers are equal as follows. For a false positive, that is for an element that is not maintained in the filter to correspond to k equal timers, and if we assume that two events cannot be inserted in the same time unit, a different element that has been previously inserted in the filter needs to have set the exact same k timers. That is, the k hash functions must have identical outputs for two different elements. The false positive probability in this case may be evaluated as the false positive probability for a lookup when a single element is inserted in a Bloom filter, that is: $(1 - e^{-k/m})^k$. Generalizing the above idea, the more the equal timers among the k ones, the smaller the probability for a false positive. Based on this observation, we introduce the following heuristic:

EQUAL TIMERS HEURISTIC: A sliding Bloom filter with equal timers indicates an event as a duplicate, iff all the corresponding k timers are non-zero and at least k' of the k corresponding timers are equal; else, the event is considered distinct.

Exploiting the timers induces an overhead of k comparisons for each look-up.

5. DYNAMIC SIZE

Given an estimate of the number of events to be inserted in each Bloom filter, we can pre-allocate a maximum size per filter so that the false positive probability is kept below a certain threshold. However, this may either result in unnecessarily large filters if the actual event arrival rate is smaller than the assumed value, or in a higher false positive rate if the event arrival rate is larger. Instead, we can further enhance the flexibility of our Bloom filters, by letting the size of their slices grow dynamically as more events are inserted, so that the false positive probability is kept below a certain threshold.

Specifically, for a given filter configuration (i.e., size m and k hash functions), solving Eq. (1) for n, we get: $n = -\frac{m}{k} \cdot \ln\left(1 - \sqrt[k]{P_{fp}}\right)$. Now, substituting for a target P_{fp} we can derive a *cardinality-based* threshold. If the number n is not known, we can instead use for controlling the false positive probability the *density* of the filter, defined as the ratio z/m where z is the number of bits set to 1 in the filter. It holds: $P_{fp} = (\frac{z}{m})^k$. By solving for z, we get $z = m \cdot \sqrt[k]{P_{fp}}$ and substituting for the target P_{fp} we can derive a *density-based* threshold.

Let m_0 be the filter size initially assigned to each slice. When the density or cardinality of a slice exceeds the specified threshold, a new empty filter of the same characteristics (size and hash functions) is created. From this point on, events are checked against both filters. For an event to be delivered, both filters must indicate the event as distinct. New events are inserted only in the newly created filter. This process is repeatedly applied every time the newest filter reaches the threshold. Clearly, there is a trade-off involved in starting with small versus large initial filters. Small initial filters offer good space utilization; however, they result in many small filters and thus incur additional look-ups and a slightly worse total false positive rate.

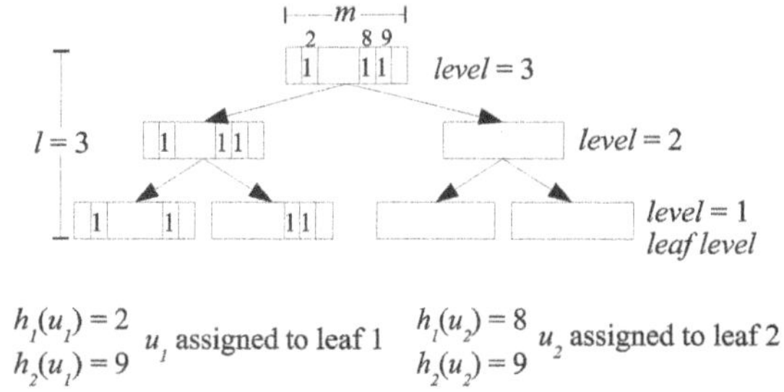

Figure 3: A Bloom tree with filters of size 10 and 2 hash functions, after the insertion of two events.

In the sliding window case, as the window slides ahead, the timers of older filters will eventually be reset to 0. Any empty filter is then discarded. When cardinality is used, n (i.e., the number of items) is incremented, each time an item is inserted in the filter. Since it is not possible to accurately detect when an item exits the window, we cannot decrement n; the old "full" filter is left to live, until it becomes empty. The density-based approach uses the actual load of the filter. Thus, the last (or only) filter may live past w time units, as window sliding gradually resets some of its timers to 0; if the event arrival rate is smaller than the rate by which the filter slides, the last filter will never need to grow. However, when growing based on cardinality, the filter will fluctuate between one and two filters if the arrival rate of events is less than the window sliding rate.

The growing and shrinking of filters is applied per slice, i.e., each slice may grow depending on the number of events it receives, independently of the other slices. This allows better space utilization when dealing with non-uniform inputs. Further, the number of alive filters depends on the rate of the arriving events versus the size of the filter, the target probability of false positive, and the sliding rate of the window. Thus, besides addressing the problem of pre-allocating an appropriate size, using dynamic sizes allows filters to efficiently handle bursts of events, by dynamically growing and shrinking their size over time.

6. MULTI-LEVEL FILTERING

In this section, we focus on multi-level filtering to explore locality so that the communication cost is reduced. The simplest form of multi-level filtering is achieved by assigning a *local Bloom filter* at each producer, in addition to the main Bloom filter. Each producer first tests for the events it produces in its local filter. If the local filter indicates a match, the event is a duplicate of an event that the producer has generated before. Otherwise, the producer forwards the event to the main filtering component.

Locality can be exploited further by multi-level filtering through a tree of Bloom filters (i.e., a *Bloom tree*) that places filters in the proximity of the producers. Events are assigned to the same tree node based on the geographical or network proximity of their producers. Thus, events are first tested against filters nearby in the physical network and are forwarded to remote parts of the network only in case of misses. Besides location criteria, other criteria such as the similarity of events that are usually looked up together or generated together may also be used to build the Bloom tree.

Algorithm 1 Test-and-Set Algorithm

Input: An incoming event u, a Bloom tree T
Output: Whether u is duplicate or not.

```
i = the leaf node associated with the producer of u
duplicate = false;
while i NOT NULL do
  if u ∈ bf_i then
    duplicate = true;
    return duplicate;
  else
    set u in bf_i
    i = parent node of i in T
  end if
end while
return duplicate;
```

Algorithm 2 First-Test-Then-Set Algorithm

Input: An incoming event u, a Bloom tree T
Output: Whether u is duplicate or not.

```
i = the leaf node associated with the producer of u
duplicate = false;
S = NULL {stack storing the path from i to the root of T}
while i NOT NULL do
  if u ∈ bf_i then
    duplicate = true;
    return duplicate;
  else
    push i into stack S
    i = parent node of i in T
  end if
end while
i = pop(S)
while i NOT NULL do
  set u in bf_i
  i = pop(S)
end while
return duplicate;
```

Definition 5. A Bloom tree for a set of events is a tree where each node is a Bloom filter such that:

- each internal node maintains the union of the events that are maintained by its children,
- each leaf node maintains a subset of the total events inserted in the tree, and
- each event is inserted in at least one leaf.

An example Bloom tree is shown in Fig. 3.

To exploit locality, we try to filter each event as close to its producer as possible, through a bottom-up traversal. An event is first tested against the filter of the leaf associated with its producer and if not found there, the process forwards the request to nodes higher in the tree. Definition 5 ensures that if the same event has appeared, reaching the root ensures that this is detected. Moreover, sites located nearby the producer are examined first and remote parts of the network are contacted later if necessary.

We study two types of trees. A *sparse Bloom tree* is a Bloom tree, where the leaf nodes maintain disjoint subsets of the total events inserted into the Bloom tree, while in a *dense Bloom tree* the sets of events maintained by its leaf nodes may overlap. With a dense Bloom tree, we aim at moving the events closer to the producers that generate them so that more requests can be resolved locally. To implement the dense Bloom trees, the test-and-set primitive is used, whereas for the sparse Bloom trees, we use the first-test-then-set primitive.

TEST-AND-SET FOR DENSE BLOOM TREES. Consider an event u generated at leaf i of a dense Bloom tree T. The event is first tested against the filter bf_i of node i. If bf_i indicates a hit, u is considered a duplicate and the process stops. Otherwise, the bits corresponding to u are set in bf_i. This miss does not ensure that u is not a duplicate, since it may have been inserted previously at some other leaf of T. Thus, the process continues up the tree by forwarding a test-and-set request for u to the parent node of i. The process continues until either the event is found, or the root is reached, in which case we determine that u is distinct (Alg. 1).

FIRST-TEST-THEN-SET FOR SPARSE BLOOM TREES. The first-test-then-set primitive starts similarly to the test-and-set one by testing for event u in bf_i. Again, if u is found in bf_i, the event is considered a duplicate and the process stops. The difference lies in the case that bf_i indicates a miss. Then, a test request for u is again forwarded to the parent node of i, but without setting any bits in bf_i. The process continues, until either we have a hit or we reach the root. If the root is reached and u is determined as distinct, the testing stops, and setting is initiated. The same path the event has followed to the root is traversed now backwards and the bits corresponding to the event are set at each node in the path (Alg. 2).

Using a bottom-up traversal for testing and setting events in the Bloom tree alleviates some of the load at the upper levels in the case of duplicates. However, the nodes in the upper levels still receive a considerable amount of load. We can address this problem by slicing the root Bloom filter or the filter of any other overloaded node in the tree.

Bloom trees can also be enhanced with timers to support sliding windows. However, as with vertical Bloom filters, the test-and-set primitive cannot be used. Instead, the first-test-then-set primitive can be used both for sparse Bloom trees and for implementing the dense Bloom trees.

Top-down testing. Since filters in higher levels maintain more events, in general, the higher in the tree we locate a match for an event, the higher the probability of a false positive. In this case, for both dense and sparse Bloom trees, we may improve the false positive probability for the testing process by using the following heuristic.

TOP-DOWN TESTING HEURISTIC. Let us assume that a match for u has occurred at a node i at level j. If we consider level j as a level with high false positive probability, instead of terminating the process, we continue by exploring the subtree rooted at i. In particular, given a threshold level d, testing proceeds as follows:

- If $j < d$, a test request is forwarded to all children of i except the one i received the initial test request for u from.
- If all the children indicate a miss, then u is considered distinct, the match at i is determined as a false positive and the process stops.
- For all children of i that indicate a match for u, the test request is forwarded similarly to the children of these nodes.
- This process continues until we reach level d.

Note that even in dense Bloom trees, the top-down process consists of tests only, i.e., no bits are set.

False Positives. Let us assume a Bloom tree with a single filter configuration of size m and k hash functions used by all of its nodes. To evaluate the false positive probability we follow a bottom up approach. Assume n distinct inserted elements in the Bloom tree filter in total. We denote as $bf_{(j,i)}$, a filter bf maintained by the i-th node at the j-th level of the tree. Thus, for each leaf filter i with n_i inserted elements, the false positive probability is given by:

$$P_{fp_{(l,i)}} = (1 - e^{-k \cdot n_i / m})^k,$$

where the sum of the n_is of all the leaves in the tree are equal to n for sparse Bloom trees, and greater or equal to n for the dense ones.

Let us consider now a filter corresponding to the i-th internal node at the j-th level of the hierarchy. Its filter $bf_{(i,j)}$ maintains the union of the events maintained by its children. Let us denote as $\mathcal{C}_r$ the set of distinct events inserted in the r-th child of i which has d children in total. Then, the false positive probability of this filter is 1 if any of its children has indicated a match, and given that none of its children has indicated a match it is:

$$P_{fp_{(i,j)}} = (1 - e^{-k\cdot|\mathcal{C}_1 \bigcup\cdots\bigcup \mathcal{C}_d|/m})^k,$$

where $|\mathcal{C}_1 \bigcup\cdots\bigcup \mathcal{C}_d|$ denotes the cardinality of the union of all events inserted in any of the d children of i. For sparse Bloom trees, this is equal to the sum of events inserted in all the d children as there are no double insertions, while for dense ones it may be smaller since one event may be inserted in more than one child.

Proposition 3. For the same input data and tree configuration, the false positive probability of the sparse and the dense Bloom trees is the same.

Proof. To determine whether an event is distinct in the worst case the bottom-up testing will reach the root in both trees. However, the root nodes of the two trees are identical for the same input data. Even if the distinct events inserted may not be the same, the set bits are. The only difference may be caused by a false positive occurring in the dense Bloom filter that may prevent the insertion of an event, but that means that the corresponding bits are already set.

Proposition 4. If an event is determined as distinct by a single Bloom filter, then it is also determined as distinct by any Bloom tree in which all nodes use the same filter configuration with the single Bloom filter.

Proof. If an event is determined as distinct by the single Bloom filter, it is also determined as distinct by the tree.

We can equivalently show that, if an event is determined as a duplicate by the Bloom tree, then it is determined as a duplicate by the Bloom filter. Thus, if the Bloom tree indicates a false positive for an event, then this event would cause a false positive in the single Bloom filter.

Each node filter maintains a subset of the events inserted in the single Bloom filter, and since the same hash functions are used, the bits set in each node are also a subset of the bits set in the single Bloom filter. Therefore, if a false positive appears at a node filter for an event, a false positive will appear for the same event in the single Bloom filter.

Note that if a node filter indicates a false positive for an event that has not been generated in its rooted subtree but has been inserted by some other path in the tree, then this event is not an actual false positive, since if it would reach the single Bloom filter it would be correctly identified as a duplicate. Thus, even in this case Prop. 4 still holds. However, Prop. 4 does not hold for horizontal Bloom filters. If we configure the node filters similar to the slice of a horizontal Bloom filter, with size m/S and k hash functions, the events in one filter in this case are in general directed to more than one slices in the horizontal Bloom filter. Thus, the slices are not supersets of the node filters. If we configure the node filters for horizontal Bloom filters similarly to the case of vertical Bloom filters, i.e., as a single Bloom filter with size m and k hash functions, while we do not increase the false positive probability as with vertical Bloom filters, still Prop. 4 does not hold.

Let us consider now the case where the main filtering component compared to our tree is a sliced Bloom filter. That is, let us consider that the root of our tree is now a sliced Bloom filter.

Lemma 1. With vertical Bloom filters, Prop. 4 holds if the tree filters are configured as the basic Bloom filter that was split vertically, i.e., with size m and k hash functions.

Concurrency. Inserting and testing for items in the Bloom filter involves accessing a number of bits. We can view the first-test-then-set primitive as a sequence of read(b) followed by write(b) operations, and test-and-set as a sequence of readwrite(b) operations, b being a Bloom filter bit. With concurrent accesses, an interleaving of these operations may lead to false negatives. For instance, assume two producers of the same event u, and that $h_1(u) = i$ and $h_2(u) = j$ for two of the hash functions. Further, assume that both bits i and j are equal to 0. If one producer tests i and then j and the other one j and then i, they both decide that u is distinct. One way to handle this is to implement both primitives as atomic operations or transactions. Implementing concurrency at the bit level is too fine grained; implementing concurrency at the slice level is more reasonable. In the case of vertical filtering, more than one site needs to be contacted for testing/setting the corresponding bits thus some coordination is needed. Note that slicing actually improves concurrency, since we lock smaller units. For trees, it suffices to lock the root, as all first-test-then-set requests will pass through the root node before setting any bits in the tree.

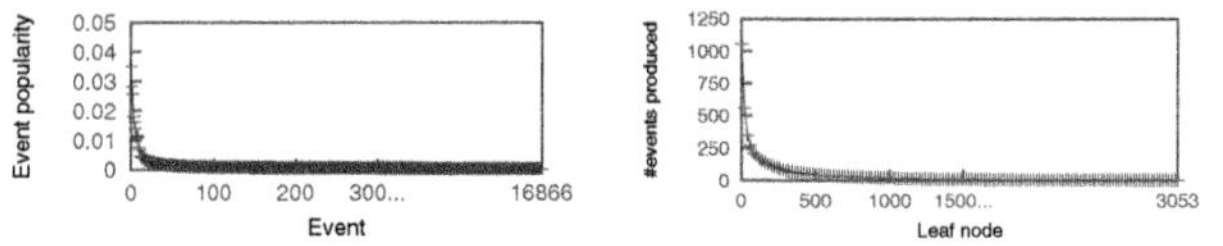

(a) Event popularity (b) Source distribution

Figure 4: Web log data distribution.

7. EXPERIMENTAL EVALUATION

In this section, we present experimental results regarding the performance of the proposed distributed Bloom filters. We used two real-world datasets - namely, a log of entries of the web server of our department and a network flow log from Yahoo - as well as a set of synthetic datasets. Unless stated otherwise, the presented figures refer to the web log dataset.

For the web log, the initial log file consisted of approximately 4.5 million entries, each including (among others) the IP address of the requesting client, the accessed URL, and a timestamp. We initially pruned all entries with IPs belonging to subnets of our institution, so as to include only remote accesses and avoid biasing the dataset. This pruning step brought the total log entry count down to 2.5 million entries. We then randomly sampled 100000 of these entries to create our input dataset. In this dataset, the client IP is used as the source (i.e., producer) identifier and the URL as the event data. The popularity of accessed URLs (i.e., the percentage of times each URL appears in the input stream) follows a highly skewed Zipf-like distribution as shown in Fig. 4(a). The Yahoo network flow log dataset contains 100000 communication patterns between end-users and Yahoo servers collected from three border routers in October 11 2007. In this dataset, the client IP is treated as the event data to be filtered. Figure 6 illustrates the popularity of each distinct item in this dataset, which also follows a highly skewed Zipf-like distribution. Lastly, for the synthetic datasets, we used both a uniform and a Zipf distribution with parameter α=1.0 for generating the events and further control the number of duplicates by drawing the events from domains having different sizes.

The accuracy of Bloom filters depends on the filter configuration, that is, the filter size and the number of hash functions. Typically, the filter size is set so that, given the number of distinct events, a maximum probability of false positive (P_{fp}) is achieved. Unless stated otherwise, the size of the filter is preset at the optimal size given an estimation of the input size. In particular, we use as default k=4 hash functions, and for example, for the web log dataset that includes $\approx$ 4300 distinct URLs, for P_{fp} = 0.02, 0.05, and 0.08, the filter consists of $m\approx$14300, 105000, and 89000 elements (bits/timers) respectively.

Bloom Slicing. The goal of this set of experiments is to examine the performance of Bloom filter slicing and pitch it against the theoretic formulae, using an append-only setting

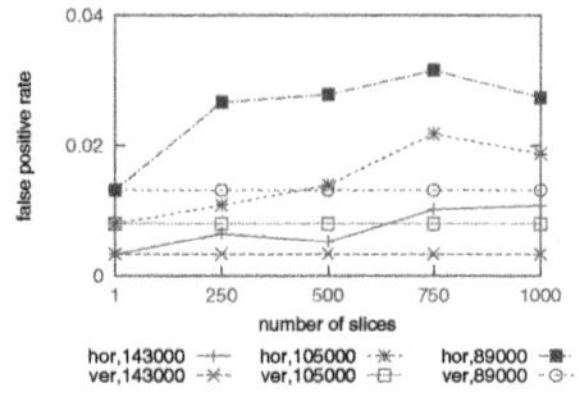

(a) False positive

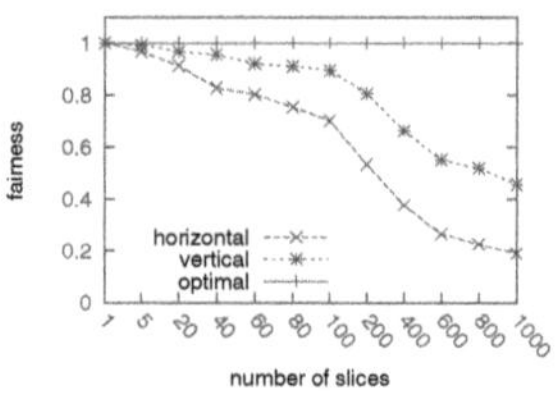

(b) Fairness

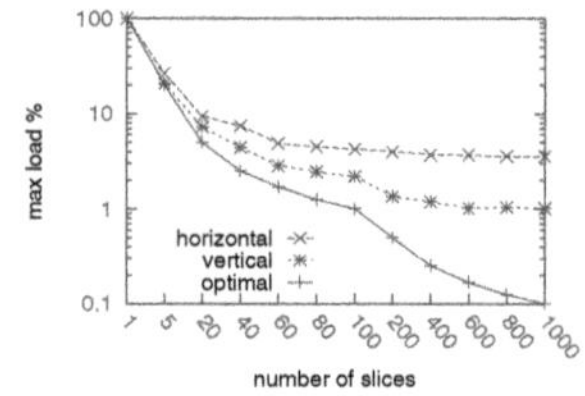

(c) Load

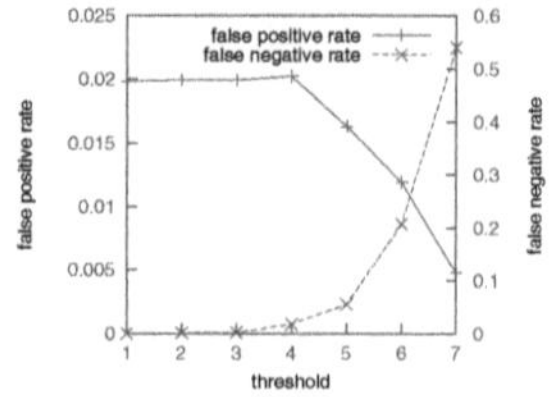

(d) Fault tolerance heuristic

Figure 5: Results for vertical and horizontal Bloom filters for varying number of slices (web log).

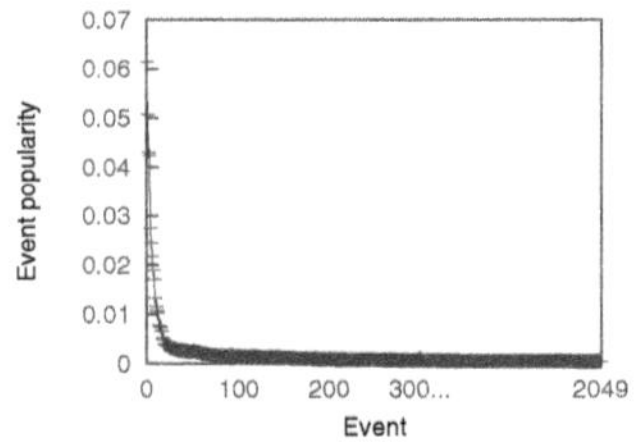

Figure 6: Yahoo dataset event popularity.

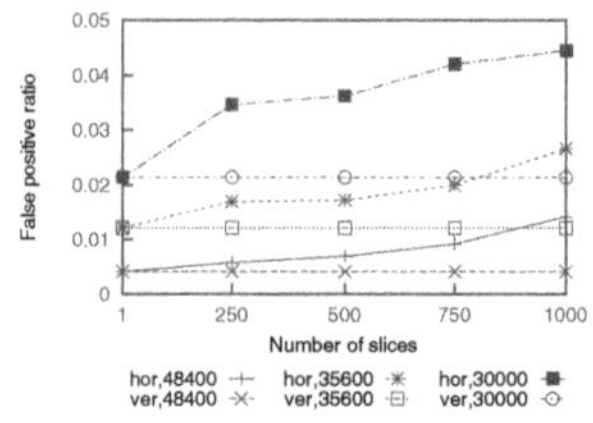

(a) False positive (synthetic)

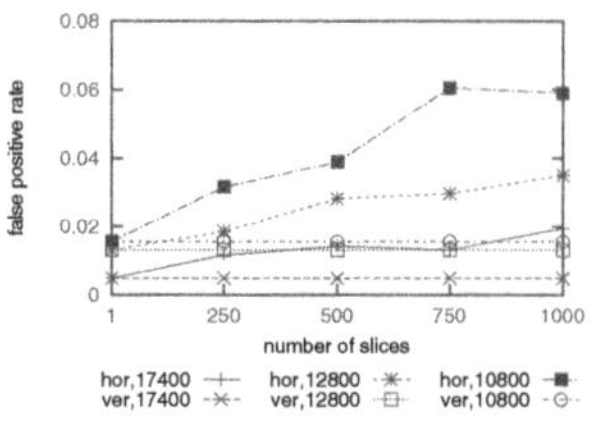

(b) False positive (Yahoo)

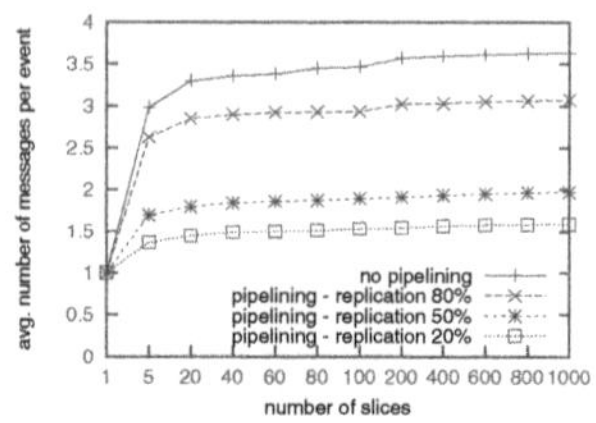

(c) Pipelining

Figure 7: False positives for (a) the synthetic and (b) Yahoo datasets, and (c) pipelining for synthetic data.

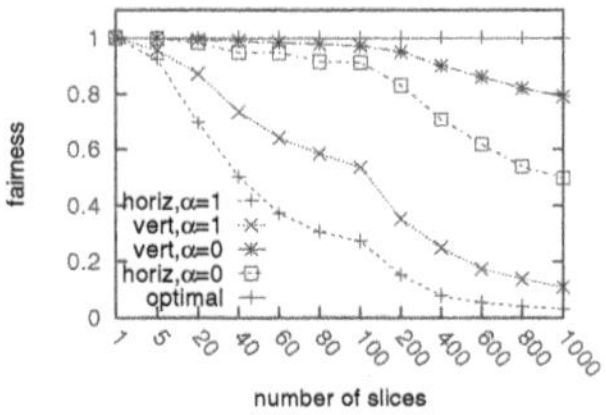

(a) Fairness (synthetic)

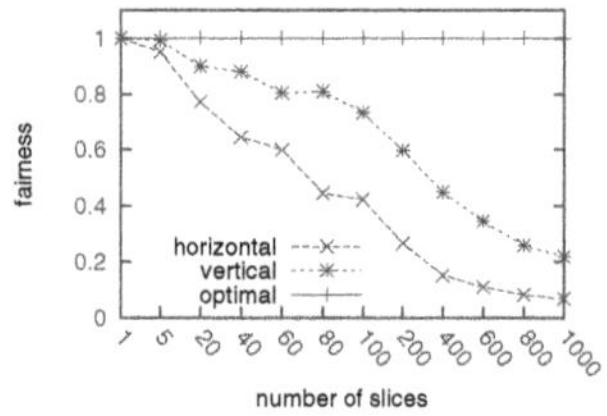

(b) Fairness (Yahoo)

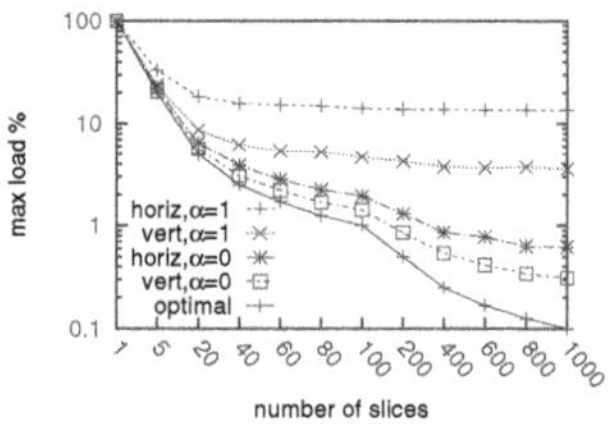

(c) Load (synthetic)

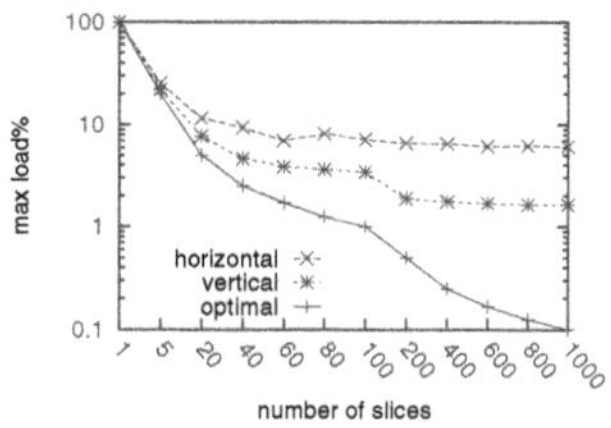

(d) Load (Yahoo)

Figure 8: (a,b) Fairness and (c,d) load for the synthetic and Yahoo datasets respectively.

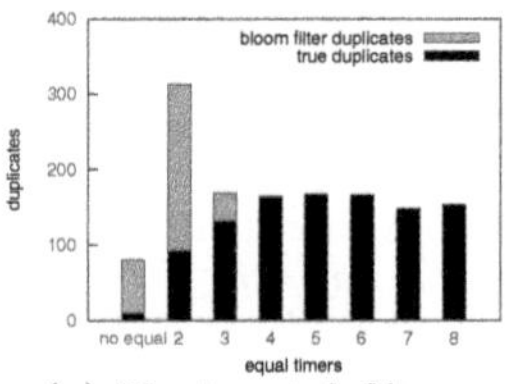

(a) Horizontal filters

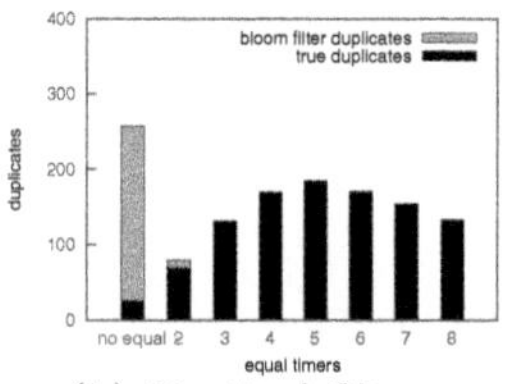

(b) Vertical filters

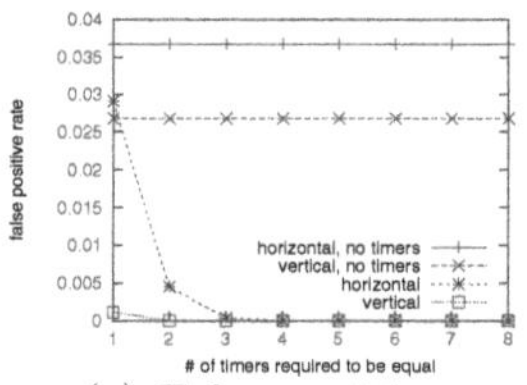

(c) False positive

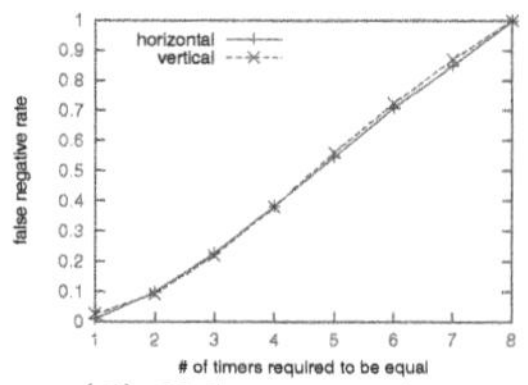

(d) False negative

Figure 9: Equal timers (web log).

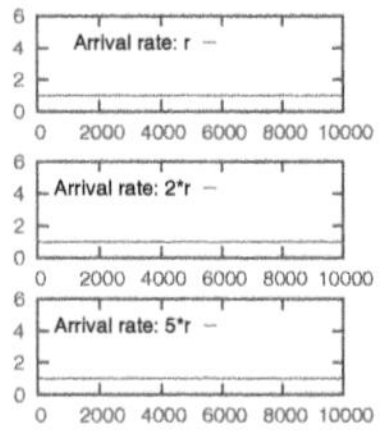

(a) w=100

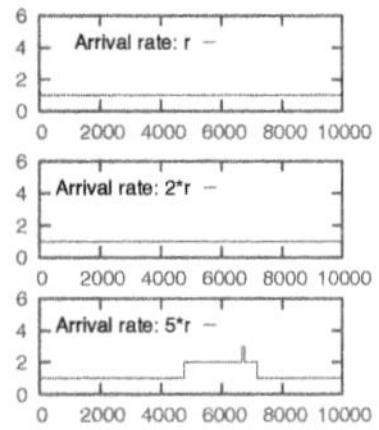

(b) w=500

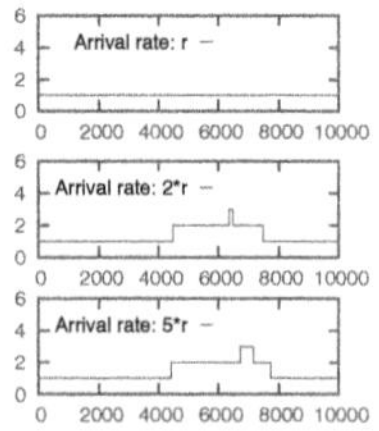

(c) w=1000

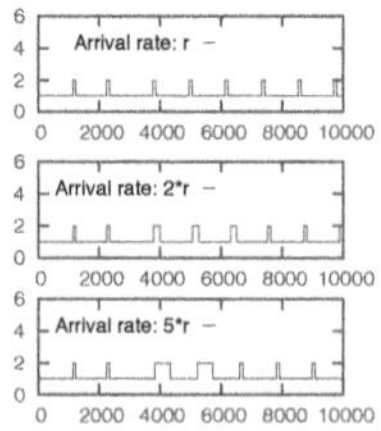

(d) w=100

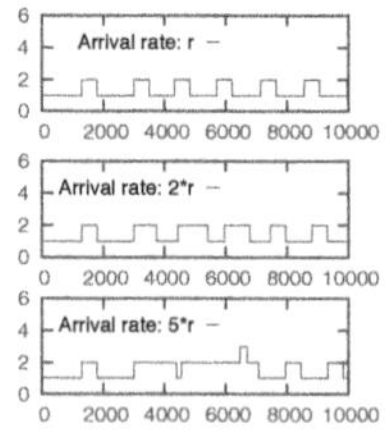

(e) w=500

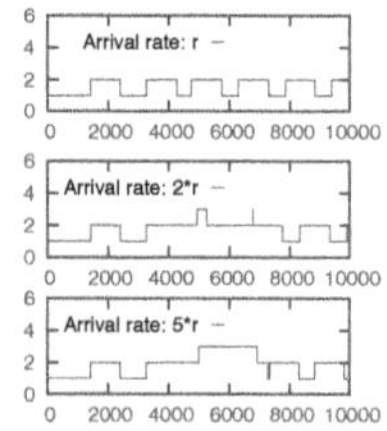

(f) w=1000

Figure 10: Dynamic size – (a,b,c): density-based, (d,e,f): cardinality-based (web log).

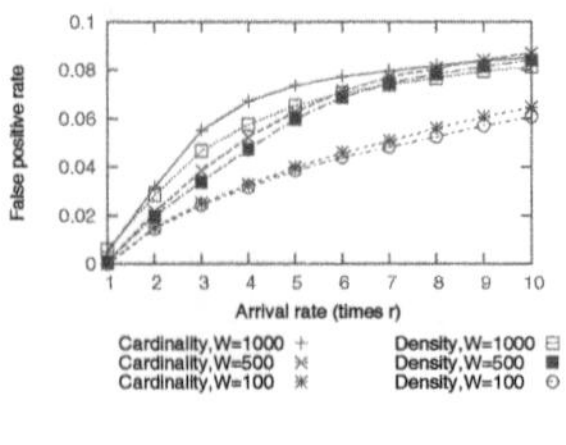

Figure 11: Dynamic size – false positive (web log).

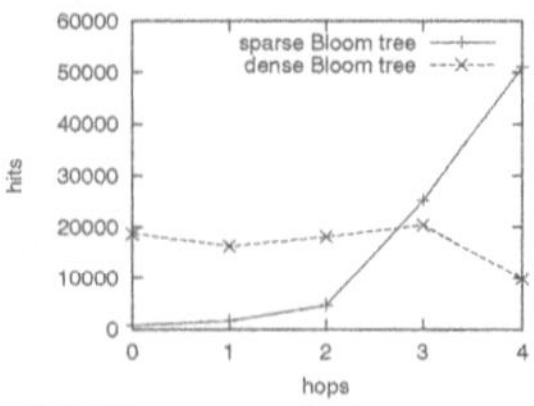

(a) Hops until detection

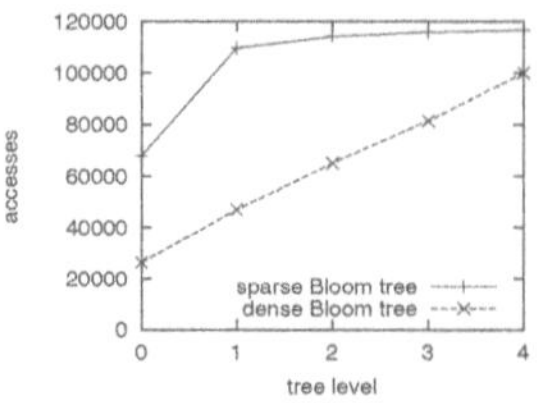

(b) Accesses per level

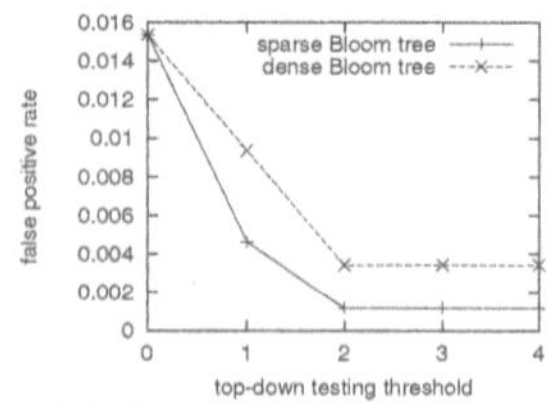

(c) Top-down heuristic

Figure 12: Bloom trees (web log).

in which events are gradually inserted in an initially empty filter. Figure 5(a) plots the false positive rate – that is, the ratio $\frac{FP}{FP+TN}$, where FP and TN are the numbers of false positives and true negatives for the whole input stream respectively – for an increasing number of slices. Although theoretically the false positive rate is not (asymptotically) affected by slicing (see Section 3), this only holds for vertical filters; for horizontal filters the more the slices, the more the false positive rate deviates from the theoretic value. This is caused primarily by imbalances in the way items are spread across horizontal partitions and by the range of the k hash functions becoming very small as the size of individual slices decreases.

This load imbalance is also evident in Fig. 5(b) that depicts the fairness [11] of the load distribution – defined as $(\sum_{i=1}^{S} x_i)^2/(S \cdot \sum_{i=1}^{S}(x_i)^2)$, where S is the number of slices and x_i the percentage of load received by the i-th slice, with the optimal fairness value being 1 – with the number of slices. In addition, Fig. 5(c) reports the maximum percentage of the load received by any of the slices, the optimal being $1/S$. Both figures verify the intuition in Section 3, showing vertical filters outperforming horizontal ones for skewed distributions. Note that since the load distribution characteristics are not affected by the filter parameters (m, k), only a single curve is plotted for each case.

The false positives (Fig. 7(a), 7(b)) and load characteristics (Fig. 8) for the synthetic and Yahoo data sets are similar. Note that, since the number of distinct items in these datasets are different from the web log, the filters are configured differently. Specifically, for the synthetic datasets (≈5700 distinct items) and for the same target P_{fp}s of 0.02, 0.05, and 0.08, the filters consist of approximately 48400, 35600, and 30000 elements respectively; whereas, for the Yahoo dataset (≈2049 distinct items), the corresponding sizes are approximately 17400, 12800, and 10800 elements.

We also evaluated our fault-tolerance heuristic (Fig. 5(d)). Here, we use 8 hash functions, to depict how the heuristic works more clearly. In this case, in order to characterize an event as duplicate, we need at least x ($x \in [1, 7]$) of the corresponding bits to be alive and set, else we characterize it as distinct, potentially introducing false negatives. We consider a 20% failure rate (i.e., 8 out of 40 slices failing). As shown in Fig. 5(d), a threshold value of 3 or 4 is the best, since it almost minimizes both the false positive and false negative rate.

Finally, we study how pipelining improves the communication cost for vertical Bloom filters. We use three synthetic datasets that exhibit different degrees of replication. In particular, we consider a scarcely, a medium, and a highly replicated dataset, where the distinct events correspond respectively to about 80%, 50%, and 20% of the input data. Pipelining reduces the average number of messages, i.e., the slices accessed per lookup (Fig. 7(c)) for vertical partitioning. Note that with horizontal partitioning, only one slice is accessed per lookup. The savings are more evident when there are few duplicates, since seeing the first bit equal to 0 suffices to characterize an event as distinct. Note that some hash functions may lead to the same slice, thus the average number of slices accessed without pipelining is at most equal to the number of functions.

In summary, vertical Bloom filters achieve slightly better false positive rates, fault tolerance and load distribution, but induce higher communication costs that can be somewhat reduced using pipelining.

Sliding Bloom Filters and Dynamic Size. In this set of experiments, events are continuously inserted in a timer-based filter, with the timers decaying over time as described in Section 4. We first evaluate the equal timers heuristic in terms of accuracy gains. Again, we use 8 hash functions for better clarity. Figures 9(a) and 9(b) show the distribution of true duplicates over all duplicates when x ($x \in [1, 8]$) out of the 8 timers are equal, for both horizontal and vertical partitioning. Characterizing an event as distinct when all timers are unequal for vertical and at most 2 timers are equal for horizontal seems to strike a good balance between false positives (Fig. 9(c)) and false negatives (Fig. 9(d)).

We also experimented with the dynamic adjustment of the size of the sliding Bloom filters for handling bursts in the arrival rate of events. We show the growth of the filter size when a burst in the rate of events appears after 1/3 of the stream has passed, lasts for 1/3 and then events continue to arrive with the initial rate. We consider two such bursts, one with events appearing at twice the initial arrival rate and one with events appearing at five times the arrival rate. We further experiment with various window sizes, ranging from 100 to 500 and 1000 time slots. We show the number of Bloom filters that are created with (i) a density-based method (Fig. 10(a), 10(b), and 10(c)) and (ii) a cardinality-based method (Fig. 10(d), 10(e), and 10(f)) and the corresponding false positive rate (Fig. 11). In both cases, additional filters are temporarily created to handle the peaks. As expected, the cardinality-based method exhibits larger fluctuations in the number of additional created filters than the density-based method, as the former has no easy way of estimating the actual number of items in the filter at any time, while the latter knows exactly how many bits are set. We can also see that, the larger the window size, the more extra filters are created during the burst period and the longer they live, as older events are phased out more slowly. We also repeated the sliding window experiments with the Yahoo flow and synthetic datasets with similar results, thus omitted for space conservation reasons.

Table 1: Local filters.

	Hits		Accesses	
	dense	sparse	dense	sparse
L0	34K	77K	50K	111K
L1	49K	5K	100K	116K

Multi-level Filtering. Since locality is clearly application-dependent, to evaluate the benefits of multi-level filters, we used the client IPs from the web log to create the tree hierarchy. Figure 4(b) plots the distribution of events across the leaf level of our tree. Table 1 shows the locality achieved with local filters, that is with 2 levels, where level 0 corresponds to the root and level 1 to the leaves. The number of hits indicates the number of events detected as duplicates at each level. Clearly, for dense trees most duplicates are detected by using only the local filters, whereas for sparse trees, the vast majority of events are detected as duplicates at the root. Thus, dense trees are better in terms of locality, since they avoid contacting the root filter. The number of accesses refers to the number of filters accessed per level. Again, dense filters exploit locality better as expected. They also reduce the number of accesses, since for sparse trees, in the case of non-duplicates, each filter is accessed twice, once during testing and once during setting.

We also built a Bloom tree with 5 levels for the same dataset. Figure 12(a) shows the number of levels each event goes up the tree before detected as a duplicate or not, and Fig. 12(b) the distribution of accesses per level. Again, the dense tree resolves most requests locally (i.e., at lower levels). Figure 12(c) shows the reduction of false positives achieved with the top-down heuristic for various levels. A threshold value of 2 seems the best choice for both trees, since continuing at lower levels practically does not improve the false positive rate any further. Similar results were obtained for the second real and the synthetic datasets as well. In summary, both sparse and dense trees exploited the locality in the dataset. Dense trees are more efficient and should be used, unless sliding-window semantics must be supported.

8. RELATED WORK

In this paper, we have proposed distributed filtering for duplicate-free event delivery. Our solution is based on distributed Bloom filters. The contribution of our work lies in casting the design space regarding the distribution of Bloom filters and their use for duplicate-free event dissemination. Horizontal vs vertical partitioning, sparse and dense trees and their analysis are novel in this paper.

Bloom filters have been used in a variety of applications (see [3] for a survey). For example, Bloom filters are deployed for cache sharing among web proxies; each proxy contains Bloom filters that summarize the cache content of all other participating proxies to quickly determine which of them contains an item of interest [9]. Bloom filters have also been used for computing the union of non-distinct sets residing at distributed sites by providing compact summaries of the content of each site [6]. In addition, Bloom filters have been deployed for query routing in distributed overlays, summarizing the content of a single node or sets of nodes in its neighborhood. In the latter case, multi-level Bloom filters have been proposed, most notably attenuated Bloom filters [16] and filters for hierarchical overlays [12]. An attenuated Bloom filter of depth d is an array of d Bloom filters. Each node in the overlay maintains an attenuated Bloom filter for each of its links such that the i-th filter, $1 \leq i \leq d$, provides a summary of the content of all nodes reachable through that link within at most i-hops. In [12], Bloom filters are placed on the nodes of a hierarchical overlay of nodes sharing XML data, where the filter at each node summarizes the XML content of all descendants in the overlay. In contrary to our approach, these works use Bloom filters to summarize the content of nodes, focusing on using the filters for routing and on lazy filter update methods for changing content.

There has been some previous work regarding streaming and dynamic-size filters. To handle unbounded streams of items, in stable Bloom filters, some randomly chosen bits are reset to 0, as new items are inserted, such that old items that have become stale are deleted from the filter [7], with applications in click-fraud detection [13]. Sliding windows with counters are used in [14] and [18] for a single stream and in [17] for distributed streams but using a centralized filter. The equal-timers heuristic and the distributed system aspects are new in this paper. Dynamic [10] and Scalable [1] Bloom filters start with a small filter and add filters when the current ones get full. Block partitioned Bloom filters [15] use blocks of Bloom filters where each block can grow dynamically. The combination of dynamic size with sliding windows for handling bursts and the distributed issues considerations are novel in this paper.

Finally, counting Bloom filters have been used for frequency estimation [5], finding most frequent items [8] and long duration network flows [4]. Spectral Bloom filters use counters to estimate the multiplicities of items [5], while multistage Bloom filters use multiple filters to reduce false positives for identifying large network flows [8, 4]. In such applications, sampling could also be applied for duplicate elimination. However, sampling suffers from false negatives while inducing much larger space, communication, and computation overheads than Bloom filters.

9. SUMMARY

In this paper, we address the problem of large-scale duplicate-free delivery of events produced by distributed sources. To this end, we have proposed a distributed filtering mechanism based on Bloom filters. We have presented a suite of distributed Bloom filters that exploit different ways of slicing the filter. To address the dynamic nature of event dissemination, we have proposed extensions that provide sliding windows semantics and dynamically adjustable sizes. To exploit locality, sparse and dense Bloom filters have been introduced that support multi-level filtering. We have studied both theoretically and experimentally the properties of the various proposed structures.

10. REFERENCES

[1] P. S. Almeidaa, C. Baqueroa, N. Preguiça, and D. Hutchison. Scalable bloom filters. *Information Processing Letters*, 101(6):255–261, 2007.

[2] B. H. Bloom. Space/time trade-offs in hash coding with allowable errors. *Communications of the ACM*, 13(7):422–426, 1970.

[3] A. Broder and M. Mitzenmacher. Network applications of bloom filters: A survey. *Internet Mathematics*, 1(4):485–509, 2002.

[4] A. Chen, Y. Jin, J. Cao, and L. E. Li. Tracking long duration flows in network traffic. In *INFOCOM*, 2010.

[5] S. Cohen and Y. Matias. Spectral bloom filters. In *SIGMOD Conference*, 2003.

[6] I. Dar, T. Milo, and E. Verbin. Optimized union of non-disjoint distributed data sets. In *EDBT*, 2009.

[7] F. Deng and D. Rafiei. Approximately detecting duplicates for streaming data using stable bloom filters. In *SIGMOD Conference*, 2006.

[8] C. Estan and G. Varghese. New directions in traffic measurement and accounting: Focusing on the elephants, ignoring the mice. *ACM Trans. Comput. Syst.*, 21(3):270–313, 2003.

[9] L. Fan, P. Cao, J. M. Almeida, and A. Z. Broder. Summary cache: a scalable wide-area web cache sharing protocol. *IEEE/ACM Trans. Netw.*, 8(3):281–293, 2000.

[10] D. Guo, J. Wu, H. Chen, Y. Yuan, and X. Luo. The dynamic bloom filters. *IEEE TKDE*, 22(1):120–133, 2010.

[11] R. Jain, D. Chiu, and W. Hawe. A quantitative measure of fairness and discrimination for resource allocation in shared computer systems. *DEC Research Report TR-301*, 1984.

[12] G. Koloniari and E. Pitoura. Content-based routing of path queries in peer-to-peer systems. In *EDBT*, 2004.

[13] S. Majumdar, D. Kulkarni, and C. Ravishankar. Addressing click fraud in content delivery systems. In *Proc. INFOCOM*, 2007.

[14] A. Metwally, D. Agrawal, and A. E. Abbadi. Duplicate detection in click streams. In *WWW*, 2005.

[15] O. Papapetrou, W. Siberski, and W. Nejdl. Cardinality estimation and dynamic length adaptation for bloom filters. *Distributed and Parallel Databases*, 28(2,3):119–156, 2010.

[16] S. C. Rhea and J. Kubiatowicz. Probabilistic location and routing. In *Proc. INFOCOM*, 2002.

[17] X. Wang, Q. Zhang, and Y. Jia. Efficiently filtering duplicates over distributed data streams. In *Proc. CSSE*, 2008.

[18] T. Xia, C. Jin, X. Zhou, and A. Zhou. Filtering duplicate items over distributed data streams. In *WAIM*, 2005.

Duplicate Detection Through Structure Optimization

Luís Leitão
IST/INESC-ID
Av. Professor Cavaco Silva
2744-016 Porto Salvo, Portugal
luis.leitao@ist.utl.pt

Pável Calado
IST/INESC-ID
Av. Professor Cavaco Silva
2744-016 Porto Salvo, Portugal
pavel.calado@ist.utl.pt

ABSTRACT

Detecting and eliminating duplicates in databases is a task of critical importance in many applications. Although solutions for traditional models, such as relational data, have been widely studied, recently there has been some focus on solutions for more complex hierarchical structures as, for instance, XML data. Such data presents many different challenges, among which is the issue of how to exploit the schema structure to determine if two objects are duplicates. In this paper, we argue that structure can indeed have a significant impact on the process of duplicate detection. We propose a novel method that automatically restructures database objects in order to take full advantage of the relations between its attributes. This new structure reflects the relative importance of the attributes in the database and avoids the need to perform a manual selection. To test our approach we applied it to an existing duplicate detection system. Experiments performed on several datasets show that, using the new learned structure, we consistently outperform both the results obtained with the original database structure and those obtained by letting a knowledgeable user manually choose the attributes to compare.

Categories and Subject Descriptors

H.2.5 [**Database Management**]: Heterogeneous Databases

General Terms

Standardization, Algorithms, Experimentation

Keywords

data quality, duplicate detection, hierarchical data, object structure, support vector machine, simulated annealing

1. INTRODUCTION

Fuzzy duplicates, or duplicates for short, are multiple representations of a same real-world object in a given data source, such as a relational database or an XML document. Their presence can cause analysis applications to generate wrong results, based on the assumption that each representation describes a different object. Detecting and eliminating duplicates is, therefore, a task of critical practical relevance in many applications, including data cleaning [27], data integration [10], and personal information management [13].

The challenge in duplicate detection lies in the fact that duplicate object representations usually cannot be identified using a universal identifier (e.g., the ISBN of a book) and are not exactly equal, due to errors or inconsistencies. Typical errors are typos, misspellings, the lack of a standard representation, and missing, outdated, or contradictory data. As a consequence, in order to detect duplicates, more sophisticated methods than the comparison of object representations based on equality have to be devised.

Duplicate detection has been studied extensively for relational data stored in a single table [21, 28, 5, 12, 3, 7, 8, 13, 31]. Algorithms performing duplicate detection in a single table generally compare tuples, each of which represents an object, based on attribute values. However, data usually comes in more complex structures. For instance, data stored in a relational table relates to data in other tables through foreign keys. Recently, duplicate detection algorithms for data stored in such complex structures have been proposed [1, 18].

Among these, several works focus on the special case of detecting duplicates in hierarchical and semi-structured data, most notably, on XML data [34, 20, 17, 22]. Methods devised for duplicate detection in a single relation do not directly apply to XML data, due to the differences between the two data models [34]. In particular, the hierarchical relationships in XML provide useful additional information that can help improve the quality of duplicate detection. Nevertheless, such solutions do not typically consider the relative importance of attributes, individually. They rely on human knowledge to determine which attributes are significant to use. This carries two different problems: (i) the user may not always have knowledge about data and (ii) some attributes, though considered less significant, may provide a useful contribution to the process.

In this paper, we confirm that data structure is indeed a factor to be considered when searching for duplicates in hierarchical data. More specifically, we show that by carefully choosing the relationships between object attributes, we can effectively improve the duplicate detection process. We present a novel method to automatically discover such

CIKM'11, October 24–28, 2011, Glasgow, Scotland, UK.

relationships and apply it in a duplicate detection framework called XMLDup [20].

Using Machine Learning techniques, we are able to determine a new structure for the objects being compared that can optimize duplicate detection. Determining a new structure means automatically changing the nesting characteristics of its hierarchical data tree, i.e., its depth, breadth and node positions. In fact, although the XMLDup framework was initially designed for duplicate detection in XML data, here we show that it can be equally applied to flat data records. Our approach is therefore independent of the initial object structure and can also be applied to relational data.

To achieve this, we combine an optimization method, based on Simulated Annealing [19], with a Support Vector Machine [32] classifier. Although this is a supervised technique, and therefore requires a known set of duplicate objects, we show that the classification model can be learned on completely different databases. Thus, no previous knowledge of the database being processed is required and user intervention is reduced to a minimum.

Through experiments, performed on a set of 8 distinct databases, we were able to achieve R-precision gains of up to 35%, when compared to the original objects structure. Furthermore, our optimization managed to outperform the results obtained when using only the attributes selected by a user with deep knowledge of the datasets.

The contributions of this work are, therefore, twofold. First, we show that object structure can effectively be used to improve duplicate detection. Second, we present a novel method for object restructuring that not only enhances the duplicate detection results, but also performs the task automatically, avoiding the need for a knowledgeable user to perform attribute selection.

The remainder of this paper is organized as follows. In Section 2, we present previous related work. In Section 3, we describe the XMLDup framework and discuss how object structure can influence the outcome of the duplicate detection process. In Section 4, we present our structure optimization approach. In Section 5, we present our experiments and the achieved results. Finally, in Section 6, we conclude the paper and suggest future research directions.

2. RELATED WORK

Duplicate detection, originally defined by Newcombe et al. [24] and formalized by Fellegi and Sunter [14], has been extensively studied, particularly for relational databases [15, 4, 35, 11]. Only more recently, solutions directed to more structured data models have emerged.

The work developed in [1] presents an algorithm for eliminating duplicates in a data warehouse. The authors explore the hierarchies between dimensional tables to relate co-occurrences in the database. With this strategy, Ananthakrishna et al. show that the quality of duplicate detection can be effectively improved for entities stored across multiple tables, connected by a foreign key.

In [6], the authors propose a solution to the problem of integrating tree-structured data extracted from the Web. Two object representations, e.g. two hierarchical representations of person elements, are compared by transforming each into a vector of terms and using a variation of the cosine measure to evaluate their similarity [2]. The hierarchical structure of object representations is mostly ignored, and a linear combination of weighted similarities is used to account for the relative importance of the different fields within the vectors. The authors show that this simple strategy manages to achieve high precision values in a collection of scientific publications. Nevertheless, and because of its more general nature, their approach does not take advantage of the useful features existing in Web data, such as the element structure or tag semantics.

Solutions that directly address the problem of detecting duplicates in XML data have more recently been proposed. Works like [17, 33, 34, 20, 22, 26], explore the native characteristics of the XML data model. Therefore, aspects like the object structure along with element contents and semantics are considered in the process.

In [17, 33] the authors provide strategies to match XML documents. To determine the degree of similarity, the content and structure of the documents is taken into consideration, by combining node paths with text contents similarity. In order to improve the similarity results, element names are relabeled according to their semantic similarity.

The work proposed in [34] aims at both efficiency and effectiveness in duplicate detection. Their framework consists of three main steps: candidate definition, duplicate definition, and duplicate detection. Whereas the first two provide the data necessary for duplicate detection (i.e., the set of object representations to compare and the duplicate classifier to use), the third component includes the actual algorithm, an extension to XML data of the work of Ananthakrishna et al. [1].

The XMLDup system [20] uses a Bayesian Network model for XML duplicate detection. The model is used to capture not only the textual information contained by data objects but also the information provided by their structure. Its approach is further described in Sec. 3.1 and serves as basis to our structure optimization solution.

Milano et al. propose a distance measure between two XML object representations that is defined based on the concept of overlays [22]. An overlay between two XML trees U and V is a mapping between their nodes, such that a node $u \in U$, is mapped to a single node $v \in V$ if, and only if, they have the same path from the root. This measure is then used to perform a pairwise comparison between all candidates. If the distance measure determines that two XML candidates are closer than a given threshold, the pair is classified as a duplicate.

Finally, SXNM (Sorted XML Neighborhood Method) [26] is a duplicate detection method that adapts the relational sorted neighborhood approach (SNM) [15] to XML data. Like the original SNM, the idea is to avoid performing useless comparisons between objects by grouping together those that are more likely to be similar

It is worth noting that all the proposals described above use the object structure in its original form. This means that they assume the original database schema already provides sufficient information on how to compare two object representations. Here, we follow a different approach, trying to discover an object structure that best reflects the properties of data.

3. USING OBJECT STRUCTURE AND THE XMLDUP SYSTEM

The process of detecting if two objects are duplicates relies in confronting the information they both contain. This information is typically found as values of the objects attributes. Nevertheless, we know that some attributes are more useful than others to differentiate the objects. Thus, we can assume that they should be given more relevance in the duplicate detection process. In this section we present the XMLDup system, which uses the hierarchical structure of the database to determine the impact that each attribute should have when comparing objects. We then argue that the original object structure may not produce the best results and that there may be an optimal structure, which maximizes duplicate detection effectiveness.

3.1 The XMLDup System

XMLDup is a duplicate detection system, originally proposed for XML data. Its approach for duplicate detection is centered around one basic assumption: *The fact that two XML nodes are duplicates depends only on the fact that their values are duplicates and that their children nodes are duplicates.* Thus, we say that two XML trees are *duplicates* if their root nodes are duplicates. Note that we assume a schema mapping step has preceded duplicate detection, so that all XML documents comply to the same schema.

To illustrate this idea, consider the goal of detecting that both people represented in Figure 1 are duplicates. This means that the two *person* objects, represented by nodes tagged *prs*, are duplicates depending on whether or not their children nodes, tagged *pob* (place of birth) and *cnt* (contact), and their values for attributes *name* and *dob* (date of birth) are duplicates. Furthermore, the nodes tagged *pob* are duplicates depending on whether or not their values are duplicates, and the nodes tagged *cnt* are duplicates depending on whether or not their children nodes, tagged *eml* (email) and *add* (address) are duplicates. This process goes on recursively until the leaf nodes are reached.

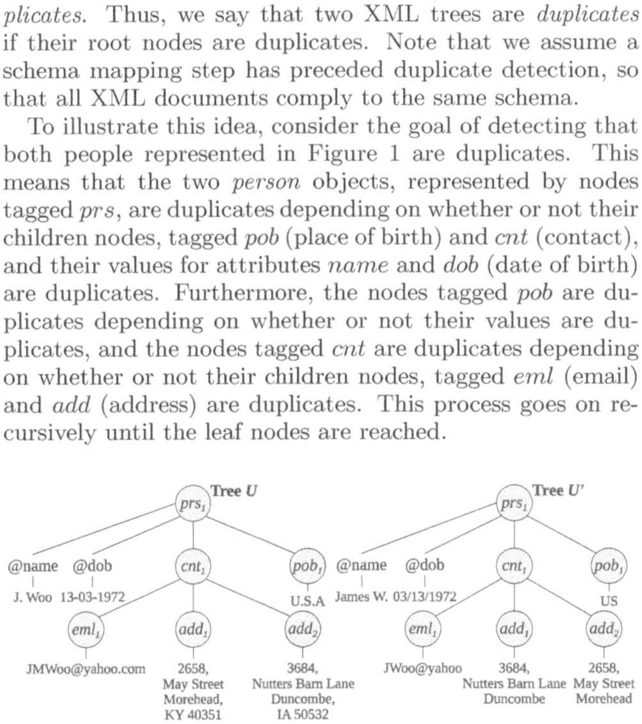

Figure 1: Two XML objects that represent the same person. Nodes are labeled by their XML tag name and an index for future reference.

In XMLDup, this process is represented by the Bayesian Network illustrated in Figure 2. In this network, the node labeled prs_{11} represents the possibility of node prs_1 in tree U being a duplicate of node prs_1 in tree U'. This node has two parent nodes: $V_{prs_{11}}$, which represents the possibility of the values in the *prs* nodes being duplicates, and node $C_{prs_{11}}$, which represents the possibility of the children of the *mv* nodes being duplicates. Following the same reasoning, node $V_{prs_{11}}$ has two parent nodes, shown as rectangles in Fig. 2, which represent the possibility of the *name* values in the *prs* nodes being duplicates and of the *dob* values in the *prs* nodes being duplicates. This can be repeated recursively until all node comparisons are represented.

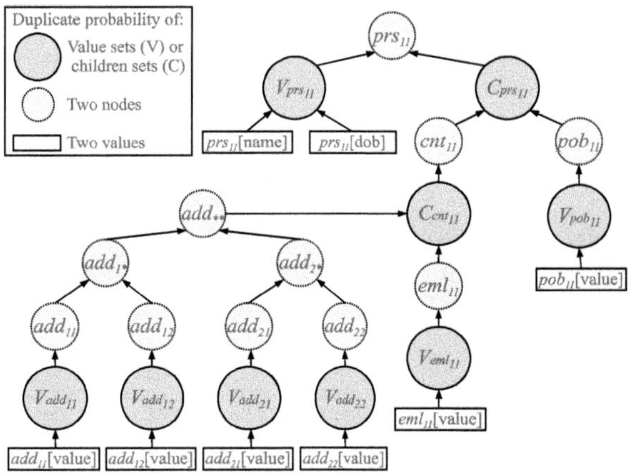

Figure 2: BN to compute the similarity of the trees in Figure 1.

All nodes are assigned binary random variables, taking the value 1 to represent the fact that the corresponding data in trees U and U' are duplicates, and taking the value 0 to represent the opposite. Thus, to decide if two objects are duplicates the algorithm has to compute the probability of the root nodes being duplicates, $P(prs_{11} = 1)$, which can be interpreted as a similarity value between the two XML elements. To obtain this probability, the algorithm propagates the prior probabilities associated to the network leaf nodes, which will set the intermediate nodes probabilities, until the root probability is found. This yields the formula:

$$P(prs_{11}) = \Big(w_{name}P(prs_{11}[name]) + w_{dob}P(prs_{11}[dob])\Big) \times \Big(P(pob_{11}[value]) + \big(1 - \prod_{i=1}^{2}(1 - P(add_{1i}[value])) + 1 - \prod_{i=1}^{2}(1 - P(add_{2i}[value])) + 2P(elm_{11}[value])\big) \times \frac{1}{4}\Big) \times \frac{1}{2} \quad (1)$$

To compute the probability $P(prs_{11})$, the prior probabilities in Eq. (1) need to be given a value. This can be accomplished using a any chosen similarity measure between the values in the corresponding XML nodes, normalized to fit between 0 and 1 (0 meaning that the values are totally dissimilar and 1 meaning that they are exactly equal). A normalized version of Levenshtein's string edit distance is a common choice.

For further details of this process, we refer the reader to [20]. Detailed information on Bayesian Networks and their applications can be found in [25].

3.2 Impact of Object Structure

If we examine Eq. (1), we can see that, implicitly, XMLDup assigns more importance to the values that are closer to the root of the XML trees. In our example, the similarity between person names ($P(prs_{11}[name])$) and between dates of birth ($P(prs_{11}[dob])$) carries as much weight as all the remaining attributes together. XMLDup relies, therefore, on the assumption that, when creating database schemas, we tend to group together and emphasize attributes that we believe to be more distinctive.

However, this may not always be the case. Either by design or, for instance, if we are dealing with a flat structure, such as a relational table, structure may not reflect the actual importance of the attributes. In fact, many other characteristics of the attribute values, unrelated to structure, can have a critical impact on the outcome of the duplicate detection process. For instance, although the name of a person is expected to be a reliable source of information, it may happen that, in our particular instance of the database, the values for *name* contain many typographical errors, thus rendering it useless.

To take advantage of the capabilities of XMLDup using structure to give the appropriate weight to the attributes being compared, we could redesign the objects structure, placing the most important elements closer to the root, and those that carry less information in lower levels. For example, the objects in Fig. 1 could be restructured so that elements *dob* and *pob* are grouped together under a new element called *brt* (birth), as shown in Fig. 3. In this case, the equation for determining the probability of tree U and tree U' being duplicates would be:

$$P(prs_{11}) = \Big(P(prs_{11}[name])\times \Big((P(pob_{11}[value]) \times P(brt_{11}[dob]))+ (1-\prod_{i=1}^{2}(1-P(add_{1i}[value]))+ 1-\prod_{i=1}^{2}(1-P(add_{2i}[value]))+2P(elm_{11}[value])\Big)\times\frac{1}{4}\Big)\times\frac{1}{2} \tag{2}$$

As an implication, the similarity of nodes *name* has now gained in importance, actually acting as a scale on the remaining similarity values.

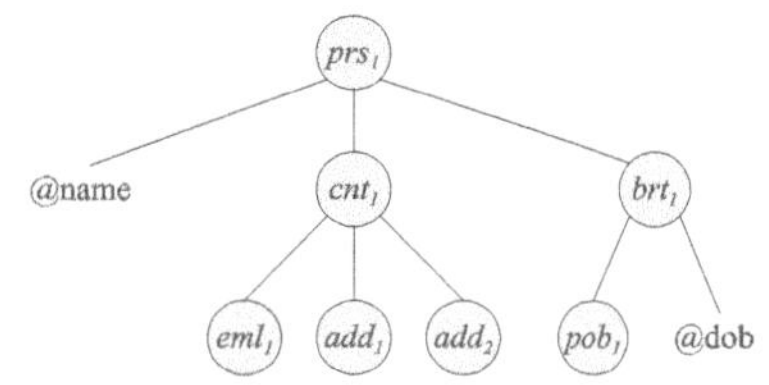

Figure 3: XML object that represents a person, restructured so that the most important elements are placed closer to the root.

Of course, there is no guarantee that this structure would yield better results than the one shown in Fig. 1. It might happen that combining the name with date of birth is better to distinguish people than just using the name alone. In fact, to find an optimal new structure, the user interested in the duplicate detection process would need a thorough knowledge of the database contents and of the relationships between the attributes. Unfortunately, such knowledge is often unavailable.

In the following section, we show that a quasi-optimal structure can be found automatically by analyzing some statistical properties of the objects attributes. This is achieved without user intervention and does not require any previous knowledge of the data.

4. OPTIMIZING OBJECT STRUCTURE

As argued in the previous section, object structure can influence the outcome of the duplicate detection process. In this section we propose a strategy to solve this problem, by automatically restructuring the database objects in order to maximize the impact of highly informative attributes, while minimizing the impact of attributes that carry less information.

4.1 Building the New Structure

Our object restructuring proposal consists in the following. Let D be an instance of a database, i.e., a set of objects where we intend to discover duplicates. Let $\mathcal{A}$ be the set of attributes in the schema of D, where by *attribute* we mean any element that can carry a value. Each attribute $a_i \in \mathcal{A}$ is represented as vector of features $f_i = (f_{i1}, f_{i2}, \ldots, f_{iN})$, where each feature corresponds to a statistical property of the attribute.

The idea is to find a mapping function $\mathcal{M} : \mathcal{A} \to L$, where $L = \{1, 2, \cdots\}$ is the set of possible levels in the new hierarchic object schema (level 1 is immediately below the root, level 2 is below level 1, and so on). This function will allow us to build a new object structure, by placing each attribute $a_i \in \mathcal{A}$ at level $\mathcal{M}(a_i)$ in the new schema.

To discover the mapping function $\mathcal{M}$, we use a Support Vector Machine classifier [32]. The classifier is trained by taking as input a set of example attribute feature vectors and their corresponding level on an *ideal object structure*. Thus, let $\mathcal{T} = \{T_1, T_2, \ldots, T_N\}$ be a set of database instances. Each T_i does not need to have any intersection with D, nor does it need to be on the same domain. This means that, for instance, D might contain objects representing movies, while T_1 might contain objects representing people or bank accounts, or any other thing.

Assume, for now, that, for each T_i, we know its ideal structure, i.e., the schema that maximizes the effectiveness of the duplicate detection process. We can use $\mathcal{T}$ to provide the example *(attribute,level)* pairs to train our classifier. For example, if we knew that the best duplicate detection results could be achieved using the structure in Fig. 1, our classifier would receive as examples the pairs $(f_{prs}, 1)$, $(f_{name}, 1)$, $(f_{dob}, 1)$, $(f_{pob}, 1)$, $(f_{eml}, 2)$, and $(f_{add}, 2)$. Once trained, we can use the classifier to map each attribute to its corresponding level. This is achieved by Algorithm 1.

Algorithm 1 Algorithm for building a new object structure.

Require: A mapping function $\mathcal{M} : \mathcal{A} \to L$
Ensure: A new schema for the objects

$n \leftarrow$ new root node R
$l \leftarrow 1$ {current level}
$l' \leftarrow \max_{a \in \mathcal{A}} \mathcal{M}(a)$ {maximum level returned by $\mathcal{M}$}
for $i \leftarrow 1, \ldots, l'$ **do**
  $A' \leftarrow \{a \in \mathcal{A} \mid \mathcal{M}(a) = i\}$
  Place all nodes in A' (if any) under node n
  if $i \neq l'$ **then**
    $n' \leftarrow$ a new node, placed under node n
    $l \leftarrow l + 1$
    $n \leftarrow n'$
  end if
end for
return the new schema, represented by the tree rooted at R

It is important to note that, by using a function that simply maps attributes to hierarchic levels, we are not exploring every possible alternative object structure. Nevertheless, our experiments show that this simplification is still capable of achieving high quality results, while reducing the complexity of the problem to a manageable level.

Fig. 4 summarizes our restructuring procedure. Two issues, thus, remain. First, how do we discover such an ideal structure? Second, what statistical features are appropriate to represent the object attributes? We propose an answer to both questions in the following sections.

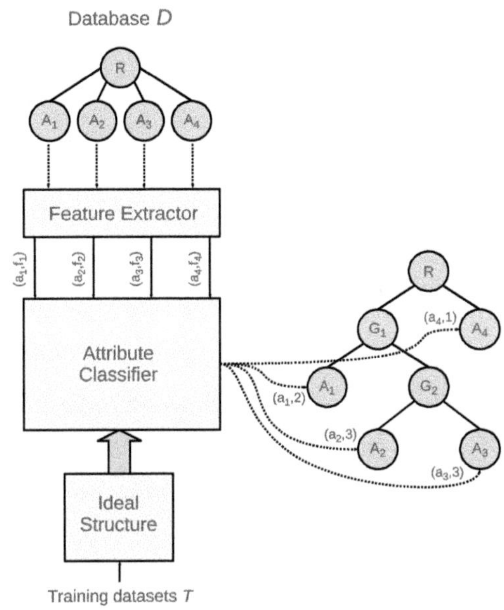

Figure 4: Training and structure classification process.

4.2 Discovering the Ideal Structure

To discover the ideal structure in a database $T_i \in \mathcal{T}$, we require that, in each T_i, some of the duplicate objects are known. A brute force solution to this problem would be to simply take all possible structure configurations, apply them in a duplicate detection process using XMLDup, and choose that which yielded the best results, i.e., that which would maximize some criteria for result quality.

This approach is, of course, unfeasible. Thus, we take an approximate approach, using the well-known search algorithm of Simulated Annealing (SA) [19] to find an optimal or sub-optimal solution. We chose SA because of its simplicity, allowing a straightforward adaptation to our problem domain.

SA is an algorithm intended to determine the maximum (or minimum) value of a function with several independent variables, under a fraction of the time needed to find an absolute maximum (or minimum) in a large search space. This function is called the *objective function* and its results depend on the possible variable configurations, or *states*. SA consists in shifting among candidate states in order to approximate the *objective function* to a global optimum, using an *acceptance function* to decide if the new state should be accepted.

Our duplicate detection problem is modeled in SA as follows. Each state corresponds to a specific object structure. In Fig. 5, we illustrate with four possible states, on a database were the objects contain four attributes (A_1, A_2, A_3, and A_4). For an objective function, we choose the measure of *R-precision* [2]. R-precision is the percentage of correctly determined duplicates among the first R items in the list, where R is the total number of known duplicate objects. In this case, our goal is to maximize R-precision.

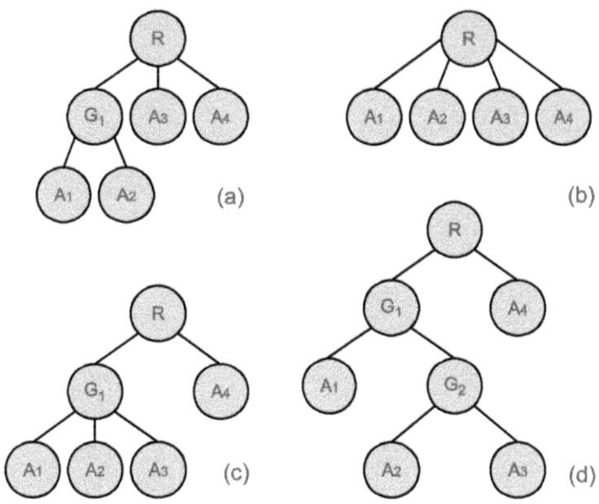

Figure 5: Structure topologies generated from the attributes A_1, A_2, A_3 and A_4.

Thus, given a state s, we execute our duplicate detection system on the database, building the Bayesian Network according to the corresponding structure. As a result, we obtain a list of object pairs, ordered according to the probability of being duplicates. Using this list, we compute our objective function. It should be noted that, although, in the worst case, building the network for each state can be quadratic in the number of attributes, in practice this process is linear [20]. Furthermore, this is only performed during the structure learning phase, and thus can be done offline.

To determine if the algorithm should change state, we use the acceptance function defined in Eq. (3):

$$P(p_s, p_n, t) = \begin{cases} 1 & \textit{if } p_n > p_s \\ e^{\left(\frac{p_n - p_s}{t}\right)} & \text{otherwise} \end{cases} \qquad (3)$$

where p_s is the objective function value for the current state, p_n is the objective function value for the new state, and t is the fraction of iterations the algorithm still needs to execute. Eq. (3) is a commonly used function in SA implementations and returns the probability of accepting the new state.

To select the candidate new states, the algorithm chooses those that represent close neighbors of the current state, i.e., states that differ from the current by one edit operation in the structure. An edit operation can be swapping two nodes, moving an attribute to a different level, or the insertion/deletion of a node. Since the search space is still too large to provide viable results, we impose an additional restriction: any non-leaf node can only have one child node that is not itself a leaf node. This means that we will not have several attributes grouped under different nodes at the same level of the tree.

We believe that, despite this restriction, it is still possible to find a near-optimal structure, which is confirmed by our experiments. In fact, convergence is achieved relatively fast, with an average of about 53 iterations for the datasets with the highest number of attributes.

4.3 Attribute Features

As stated above, each attribute a_i in a database is represented as a vector of features $f_i = (f_{i1}, f_{i2}, \ldots, f_{iN})$. These features represent particular statistical characteristics of the attribute, computed by examining the different values it contains in the database D. We now explain each feature used and the rationale for choosing it. Since some features are similar in the type of information they provide about attributes, we have grouped them accordingly.

In the remaining of this section, we use the following notation:

O	total number of objects in the database
N	number of objects that contain attribute a
t	total number of values of attributes a
d	set of distinct values in attribute a
ds	set of distinct string lengths of the values in attribute a

Group 1: Uniqueness features

Uniqueness features try to capture the diversity with which attribute values occur in the dataset. Intuitively, attributes with more distinct values should be better at distinguishing objects.

- **Distinctiveness:** Provides a ratio between distinct attributes versus the total amount of objects that contain the attribute.

$$D = log(\frac{N}{|d|}) \tag{4}$$

- **Distinctiveness entropy:** This feature is obtained by measuring the entropy of the attribute values [29].

$$DE = -\sum_{i=1}^{|d|} p(d_i) \log p(d_i), \tag{5}$$

where $p(d_i)$ is the probability mass function of the i-th element of set d. To provide a more accurate measure, we consider that strings within a certain edit distance are the same. For instance, attributes with values "Brasil" and "Brazil" are considered to have the same content.

- **Value harmonic mean:** The harmonic mean between the number of times each distinct value occurs. This measure should capture if all values are similarly distributed in the database.

$$HM = \frac{|d|}{\sum_{i=1}^{|d|} \frac{1}{|d_i|}} \tag{6}$$

where $|d_i|$ is the number of times value d_i occurs in the database.

- **Value standard deviation:** Shows how disperse attribute contents are within a dataset, in relation to the average.

$$SD = \sqrt{\frac{1}{|d|}\sum_{i=1}^{|d|}(|d_i| - \mu)^2} \tag{7}$$

where $\mu = \sum_{i=1}^{|d|} |d_i|/|d|$

- **Diversity index:** Measures the diversity of the values, as defined in [30].

$$DI = \frac{\sum_{i=1}^{|d|} |d_i|(|d_i| - 1)}{t(t-1)} \tag{8}$$

Group 2: Format features

Format features provide information about the type of contents present in the attribute values. The intuition is that values composed of alphabetical characters may be better to distinguish objects than those based on numbers, or vice-versa.

- **Non-Numeric content rate:** (NNR) Measures the percentage of values that are composed only by alphabetical characters.
- **Numeric content rate:** (NR) Measures the percentage of values that are composed only by numeric characters.
- **Mixed content rate:** (MCR) Measures the percentage of values that are composed both by alphabetical and numeric characters.

Group 3: Content length features

Since in XMLDup, as in most other duplicate detection frameworks, values are compared using a string edit distance, the string length of the attribute values can influence the results. For instance, attributes with a smaller length are more affected by typographical errors than attributes with a greater length.

- **Average string size:** Indicates the average of the string lengths for the attribute.

$$AS = \frac{\sum_{i=1}^{|ds|} ds_i}{|ds|} \tag{9}$$

where ds_i is the i-th element of set ds.

- **String size entropy:** Measures the variation of string lengths along the dataset.

$$SE = -\sum_{i=1}^{|ds|} p(ds_i) \log p(ds_i), \tag{10}$$

Group 4: Absence features

Missing data is the characteristic that affects most negatively the duplicate detection results [20]. With this feature we intend to measure the absence of data in the attributes.

- **Emptiness:** Emptiness measures the proportion between the number of objects that do not contain the attribute, over the complete set of objects.

$$EMP = \frac{O - N}{O} \tag{11}$$

Group 5: Occurrence features

Several elements with the same label can occur within an object (e.g., element *add* in Fig. 1). This can increase the probability of finding contradictory information when comparing objects. This feature tries to infer if the number of occurrences can influence the quality of the outcome.

- **Attributes per object:** Indicates if there are more values of a given attribute than there are objects containing that attribute.

$$APO = \frac{t}{N} \quad (12)$$

Using this set of features and the process described above, we have performed several experiments, to validate our approach. We describe the experimental setup and the results achieved in the following section.

5. EXPERIMENTAL EVALUATION

In this section we present an evaluation of our structure optimization strategy. We start by evaluating the impact that the choice of features has in the optimization results and then test our approach in four real world datasets, using the best set of features obtained.

5.1 Datasets

Our tests were performed using eight different datasets, representing six different data domains. The first four datasets, *Country*, *CD*, *IMDB* and *Person*, consist of a set of XML objects taken from a real database and artificially polluted by inserting duplicate data and different types of errors, such as typographical errors, missing data, and duplicate erroneous data. Contrarily to the other datasets, where data was originally in XML format, the *Person* dataset was stored in a plain text file, presenting one record per line. Thus, we converted it to the XML format respecting its original flat form, that is, every field from the person record was converted to a node placed immediately below the root node.

The remaining four datasets, *Cora*, *IMDB+FilmDienst*, another dataset containing CD records (which we are going to refer to as *CD 2*), and *Restaurant*, are composed exclusively of real world data, containing naturally occurring duplicates. The characteristics of the *Restaurant* dataset are similar to those of the *Person* dataset.

The *Cora*, *Country*, *IMDB*, *IMDB+FilmDienst* and both *CD* datasets are available at the Hasso Plattner Institute website[1]. The *Restaurant* and *Person* datasets were obtained from the University of Texas Machine Learning Research Group website[2] and from the FEBRL record linkage tool package [9], respectively.

5.2 Experimental Setup

To assess the effectiveness of our method, we applied the commonly used *precision* and *recall* and *r-precision* measures [2]. Precision measures the percentage of correctly identified duplicates, over the total set of objects determined as duplicates by the system. Recall measures the percentage of duplicates correctly identified by the system, over the total set of duplicate objects. R-precision measures the precision at cut-off R, where R is the number of duplicates in the dataset. We used the SVMLight implementation for our classifier [16], with a linear function kernel.

[1] `http://www.hpi.uni-potsdam.de/naumann/projekte/repeatability/datasets.html`

[2] `http://www.cs.utexas.edu/users/ml/riddle/data.html`

5.3 Results

We performed two sets of experiments. The first set aimed at discovering the best features to build the attribute classification model. The second set aimed at evaluating the performance of our method on real-world datasets. We now present the achieved results.

In all experiments, the classifier was trained using all the datasets, except the one being tested. Again, we note that the datasets used for training do not need to have any objects nor attributes in common with the tested dataset and, therefore, no knowledge of the testing dataset is needed.

5.3.1 Selecting the best features

With this set of experiments we intended to discover which of the features described in Sec. 4.3 are more reliable to perform the structure classification. We started by verifying the impact of each group of features in the duplicate detection results. To this effect, we tested each group in isolation and also the removal of each group from the full set of features. Tab. 1 shows the R-precision values obtained.

Group	Single group	Group excluded
G1	80	68
G2	57	80
G3	71	81
G4	67	82
G5	70	82

Table 1: Average R-precision for all datasets, using only one feature group (Single group) or all features excluding one group (Group excluded).

As we can see, G1 presents the more distinctive features, showing a significant higher R-precision than the remaining groups. This is reinforced by the score obtained when G1 is excluded, which is clearly the lowest from all tests. Aside from G1, none of the other groups show a similar behavior. However, we can observe that G3 exhibits the second highest individual score and that, when it is excluded, the score is at an intermediate value. This suggests that G3 may contain features that, although not as important as those in G1, provide useful complementary information.

To further explore the interaction between groups of features, we experimented several combinations. Due to space constraints, we show only the results obtained by combining the best individual groups with the remaining. Results are shown in Tab. 2. As a baseline we used the results obtained with the original object structure (All attributes) and with the original object structure, manually choosing only the attributes more appropriate to compare the objects (Best attributes).

Results show that most combinations are able to perform effectively. In particular, sets (G1, G3, G5) and (G1, G3, G4) present better results than the original structure for all datasets. In fact, (G1, G3, G4) managed to present better or equal results than the those obtained with manually selected attributes. This reveals the importance accounting for missing data and confirms our intuition about the importance of the length of strings to the duplicate detection. In fact, the size of the strings being compared seems to be more decisive to the process than the actual contents, since the combination (G1, G2, G3) shows worse results.

The high scores from (G1, G3, G5) also stress the impor-

Original Structures	Country	CD	IMDB	Person	Cora	IMDB+FD	CD 2	Restaurant
All attributes	48	82	46	92	73	90	45	70
Best attributes	63	82	78	92	82	93	75	80
Features	-	-	-	-	-	-	-	-
All features	**76**	**90**	**81**	**95**	**83**	90	18	**88**
G1,G2,G3	58	**88**	**81**	55	74	91	72	**88**
G1,G3,G5	**76**	**88**	**81**	**96**	**83**	**93**	72	**84**
G1,G3,G4	**68**	**88**	**81**	**96**	**83**	**94**	**75**	**84**
G1,G3,G4,G5	**68**	**90**	**81**	**96**	68	**96**	70	70
G1,G3	58	79	**81**	85	68	**93**	72	**88**
G1	**76**	**88**	**82**	**96**	50	**93**	72	**84**
DE,DI,APO,D,SD	**68**	**88**	**81**	**96**	**83**	**93**	**75**	77
DE,DI,APO,D,SD,HM,EMP,MCR	**68**	**88**	**82**	**94**	**83**	90	72	**84**

Table 2: R-precision scores obtained by combining feature groups. Text in bold indicates that the scores are equal or higher than *Best attributes*.

tance of considering the replication of attributes of the same type in a single object. Interestingly, when combining (G1, G3, G4, G5) results show a decrease in three databases. This indicates that some features in G4 and G5 might be causing cause mutual interference and, although absence and occurrence features are both useful, they should not be used together.

Results are also inferior when using one or two groups of features, showing that the additional complementary information is needed by the classifier in order to obtain a ground-base to evenly provide effective structures for different domains.

To evaluate the impact of single features, we sorted the full set of features according to the measure of information gain for each feature [23]. We then tested all combinations of the features with the highest information gain. In Tab. 2, we show the two combination that yielded the best results. We note that, only when combining 5 or more features, the results became comparable to those achieved by the baselines. Also, most features are from group 1 and group 5, which confirms their importance.

5.3.2 *Structure optimization in real world data*

We now present precision-recall results for four real world datasets from distinct domains. By showing these plots we intend to provide a more detailed analysis on how restructuring the objects influences the duplicate detection outcome.

Fig. 6 shows results of performing duplicate detection on three different structures: the original structure, the original structure with only the most significant attributes manually selected, and the structure learned by our structure optimization strategy, using the sets of features G1, G3 and G4.

Similarly to what was observed in previous experiments, the duplicate detection results obtained using the optimized structure are, in general, similar or better than those using both versions of the original structure. In the *Restaurant* dataset, our learned structure presents a generalized gain over both versions of the original structure, showing a significant increase in precision for recall values above 80%.

For the *Cora* dataset, the optimized structure presents a similar curve to that showed by the best attributes. However, after 90% of recall, the learned structure shows a less abrupt decrease in the quality of the duplicates detected. This is symptomatic of the importance of building an accurate object structure. For duplicate pairs where the objects contain attributes with very distinct or very similar values, the final score is not much affected. However, when the attribute values get more similar, it becomes important to have all attributes contributing to the score, although weighted by their relative importance, which explains the higher precision at later recall values.

In the *IMDB+FD* and *CD 2* datasets the results gathered from the two best structures are very similar. For the *CD 2* dataset the learned structure presented an initial decrease in the early ranking places, caused by the occurrence of two false positives, though it recovered quickly to higher precision scores. The *IMDB+FD* dataset presents very similar results. However, given that the best version of the original structure already produces a near optimal result, it becomes difficult to improve the outcome. Nevertheless, our optimization manages to present a slightly smoother decrease at later recall values.

5.4 Discussion

As the experimental evaluation revealed, the placement of attributes inside the object structure has a significant impact in duplicate detection. Results showed that our method was able to learn a structure that, in the best case, caused R-precision improvements of 13% over the original structure, with the best attributes manually selected, and 35% over the original structure considering all attributes. The superior results achieved by the learned structure in real world data, confirm our intuition that attributes with less distinctive power should, although in a less emphasized way, contribute to duplicate detection.

Moreover, the dataset object structures were learned from a model which was trained with datasets from different contexts. This shows that our strategy does not require the classifier to be trained with specific domain data. This fact also stresses that data should be looked at according to its statistical characteristics and not necessary according to its semantic domain. Our method also has the advantage that, once the classifying model is created from the training data, it can be used to restructure any object from any dataset where one needs to find duplicates.

Finally, since this approach is independent of the data structure because it only considers the individual attributes to build the hierarchy, it can virtually be applied to any dataset where information can be segmented in the form of attributes as, for example, in the case of the traditional

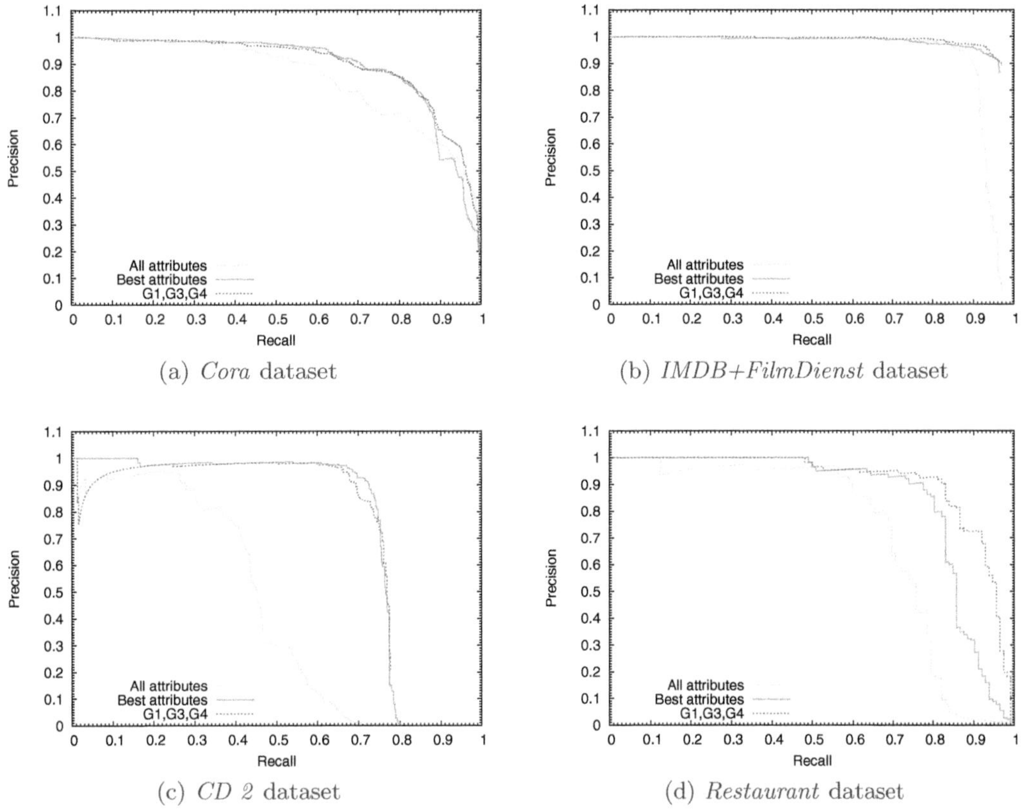

(a) *Cora* dataset

(b) *IMDB+FilmDienst* dataset

(c) *CD 2* dataset

(d) *Restaurant* dataset

Figure 6: Restructuring results for the *Cora* dataset (a), the *IMDB+FilmDienst* dataset (b), the *CD 2* dataset (c), and the *Restaurant* dataset (d).

relational databases. Besides the improvements it delivers, the process is performed in a fully automatic way, therefore relieving the user from the need to have prior knowledge of data.

6. CONCLUSION

In this paper we presented a novel method to automatically restructure data objects in order to improve duplicate detection effectiveness. Our approach places the objects attributes in a hierarchical structure, according to a set of statistical characteristics extracted from the data, and does not require user intervention.

This method relies on the premise that data attributes should be placed in the structure according to their overall importance in distinguishing between two objects and that, to this end, objects should be looked at by their intrinsic characteristics rather than by the domain they belong. Our approach maps attributes from an original object structure into a new structure level according to their relevance to the duplicate detection process. To achieve this we used a Simulated Annealing algorithm combined with a Support Vector Machine classifier.

Experiments performed on eight different datasets showed that the learned structure consistently produced better results than the original object structure and than a selection of attributes performed by a knowledgeable user. Additionally, the method obtained effective results, even when using trained data from completely different domains.

The success demonstrated in our experimental results leaves motivation for future work. Despite the good results obtained by looking at attributes individually and mapping their relative importance into a single level, the correlation between attributes at the same or different levels may provide additional information that can be useful to further optimize the process. Therefore, the classification of more complex features, such as the co-occurrences of attributes with certain characteristics is an issue we should address. A more complex classification strategy may benefit from withdrawing the topology restriction that avoids the appearance of two grouping nodes with the same parent. This requires the search space reduction strategy to be adapted to a larger domain, a problem we also intend to consider in future work.

Acknowledgements

This work was partially supported by FCT, through project SMARTIS (ref. PTDC/EIA-EIA/115346/2009) and PhD grant SFRH/BD/41450/2007 (Luís Leitão).

7. REFERENCES

[1] R. Ananthakrishna, S. Chaudhuri, and V. Ganti. Eliminating fuzzy duplicates in data warehouses. In *Conference on Very Large Databases (VLDB)*, pages 586–597, Hong Kong, China, 2002.

[2] R. A. Baeza-Yates and B. Ribeiro-Neto. *Modern Information Retrieval*. Addison-Wesley Longman Publishing Co., Inc., Boston, MA, USA, 1999.

[3] I. Bhattacharya and L. Getoor. Relational clustering

for multi-type entity resolution. *Workshop on Multi-Relational Data Mining (MRDM)*, 2005.

[4] I. Bhattacharya and L. Getoor. Collective entity resolution in relational data. *ACM Transactions on Knowledge Discovery from Data*, 1(1), 2007.

[5] M. Bilenko and R. J. Mooney. Adaptive duplicate detection using learnable string similarity measures. In *Conference on Knowledge Discovery and Data Mining (KDD)*, pages 39–48, Washington, DC, 2003.

[6] J. C. P. Carvalho and A. S. da Silva. Finding similar identities among objects from multiple web sources. In *CIKM Workshop on Web Information and Data Management (WIDM)*, pages 90–93, New Orleans, Louisiana, USA, 2003.

[7] S. Chaudhuri, V. Ganti, and R. Motwani. Robust identification of fuzzy duplicates. In *International Conference on Data Engineering (ICDE)*, pages 865–876, Tokyo, Japan, 2005.

[8] Z. Chen, D. V. Kalashnikov, and S. Mehrotra. Exploiting relationships for object consolidation. In *SIGMOD Workshop on Information Quality in Information Systems (IQIS)*, Baltimore, MD, 2005.

[9] P. Christen and A. Pudjijono. Accurate synthetic generation of realistic personal information. In *Pacific-Asia Conference on Advances in Knowledge Discovery and Data Mining (PAKDD)*, pages 507–514, Berlin, Heidelberg, 2009. Springer-Verlag.

[10] W. W. Cohen and J. Richman. Learning to match and cluster large high-dimensional data sets for data integration. In *Conference on Knowledge Discovery and Data Mining (KDD)*, pages 475–480, Edmonton, Alberta, Canada, 2002.

[11] D. Dey, V. Mookerjee, and D. Liu. Efficient techniques for online record linkage. *IEEE Trans. on Knowl. and Data Eng.*, 23:373–387, March 2011.

[12] A. Doan, Y. Lu, Y. Lee, and J. Han. Profile-based object matching for information integration. *IEEE Intelligent Systems*, 18(5):54–59, 2003.

[13] X. Dong, A. Halevy, and J. Madhavan. Reference reconciliation in complex information spaces. In *Conference on the Management of Data (SIGMOD)*, pages 85–96, Baltimore, MD, 2005.

[14] I. P. Fellegi and A. B. Sunter. A theory for record linkage. *Journal of the American Statistical Association*, 1969.

[15] M. A. Hernández and S. J. Stolfo. The merge/purge problem for large databases. In *Conference on the Management of Data (SIGMOD)*, pages 127–138, San Jose, CA, 1995.

[16] T. Joachims. *Making large-scale support vector machine learning practical*, pages 169–184. MIT Press, Cambridge, MA, USA, 1999.

[17] A. M. Kade and C. A. Heuser. Matching XML documents in highly dynamic applications. In *ACM Symposium on Document Engineering (DocEng)*, pages 191–198, New York, NY, USA, 2008. ACM.

[18] D. V. Kalashnikov and S. Mehrotra. Domain-independent data cleaning via analysis of entity-relationship graph. *ACM Transactions on Database Systems (TODS)*, 31(2):716–767, 2006.

[19] S. Kirkpatrick, C. D. Gelatt, Jr., and M. P. Vecchi. Optimization by simulated annealing. *Science*, 220:671–680, 1983.

[20] L. Leitão, P. Calado, and M. Weis. Structure-based inference of XML similarity for fuzzy duplicate detection. In *Conference on Information and Knowledge Management (CIKM)*, pages 293–302, 2007.

[21] E.-P. Lim, J. Srivastava, S. Prabhakar, and J. Richardson. Entity identification in database integration. In *International Conference on Data Engineering (ICDE)*, pages 294–301, Vienna, Austria, April 1993.

[22] D. Milano, M. Scannapieco, and T. Catarci. Structure aware XML object identification. In *VLDB Workshop on Clean Databases (CleanDB)*, Seoul, Korea, 2006.

[23] T. Mitchell. *Machine Learning*. Mc-Graw-Hill, 1997.

[24] H. Newcombe, J. Kennedy, S. Axford, and A. James. Automatic linkage of vital records. *Science 130*, (3381):954–959, 1959.

[25] J. Pearl. *Probabilistic Reasoning in Intelligent Systems: Networks of plausible inference*. Morgan Kaufmann Publishers, 2nd edition, 1988.

[26] S. Puhlmann, M. Weis, and F. Naumann. XML duplicate detection using sorted neigborhoods. In *Conference on Extending Database Technology (EDBT)*, pages 773–791, Munich, Germany, 2006.

[27] E. Rahm and H. H. Do. Data cleaning: Problems and current approaches. *IEEE Data Engineering Bulletin*, 23:3–13, 2000.

[28] S. Sarawagi and A. Bhamidipaty. Interactive deduplication using active learning. In *Conference on Knowledge Discovery and Data Mining (KDD)*, pages 269–278, Edmonton, Alberta, 2002.

[29] C. E. Shannon. A mathematical theory of communication. *Bell System Technical Journal*, vol. 27:pages 379–423 and 623–656, 1948.

[30] E. H. Simpson. Measurement of diversity. *Nature*, 163:688, 1949.

[31] P. Singla and P. Domingos. Object identification with attribute-mediated dependences. In *Conference on Principals and Practice of Knowledge Discovery in Databases (PKDD)*, pages 297–308, Porto, Portugal, 2005.

[32] V. N. Vapnik. *The nature of statistical learning theory*. Springer-Verlag New York, Inc., New York, NY, USA, 1995.

[33] W. Viyanon and S. K. Madria. A system for detecting xml similarity in content and structure using relational database. In *Proceeding of the 18th ACM conference on Information and knowledge management*, CIKM '09, pages 1197–1206, New York, NY, USA, 2009. ACM.

[34] M. Weis and F. Naumann. Dogmatix tracks down duplicates in XML. In *Conference on the Management of Data (SIGMOD)*, pages 431–442, Baltimore, MD, 2005.

[35] S. E. Whang, D. Menestrina, G. Koutrika, M. tin Theobald, and H. Garcia-Molina. Entity resolution with iterative blocking. In *Conference on the Management of Data (SIGMOD)*, Providence, Rhode Island, USA, 2009.

SISP:A New Framework for Searching the Informative Subgraph Based on PSO

Chen Chen Guoren Wang Huilin Liu Junchang Xin Ye Yuan
Key Laboratory of Medical Image Computing (Northeastern University), Ministry of Education, China
College of Information Science and Engineering, Northeastern University, China
neuchenchen@163.com, {wanggr, liuhuilin, xinjunchang, yuanye}@ise.neu.edu.cn

ABSTRACT

A significant number of applications on graph require the key relations among a group of query nodes. Given a relational graph such as social network or biochemical interaction, an informative subgraph is urgent, which can best explain the relationships among a group of given query nodes. Based on Particle Swarm Optimization (PSO), a new framework of SISP (Searching the Informative Subgraph based on PSO) is proposed. SISP contains three key stages. In the initialization stage, a random spreading method is proposed, which can effectively guarantee the connectivity of the nodes in each particle; In the calculating stage of fitness, a fitness function is designed by incorporating a sign function with the goodness score; In the update stage, the intersection-based particle extension method and rule-based particle compression method are proposed. To evaluate the qualities of returned subgraphs, the appropriate calculating of goodness score is studied. Considering the importance and relevance of a node together, we present the PNR method, which makes the definition of informativeness more reliable and the returned subgraph more satisfying. At last, we present experiments on a real dataset and a synthetic dataset separately. The experimental results confirm that the proposed methods achieve increased accuracy and are efficient for any query set.

Categories and Subject Descriptors

H.3.3 [**INFORMATION SEARCH AND RETRIEVAL**]: Search process

General Terms

Algorithms, Experimentation, Performance

Keywords

Relational graph, informative subgraph, SISP, Preference NodeRank

CIKM'11, October 24–28, 2011, Glasgow, Scotland, UK.

1. INTRODUCTION

Due to the rapid development of information science, many real problems are expressed as relational graph models for the reason of further processing. In a graph, one node always stands for a special object and the edges depict some kinds of relationships between these objects, such as the interaction in protein networks, the bandwidth or delay time in computer networks and the acquaintance in friend networks. The problem that the paper is trying to solve focuses on a new application. For a given query set, we try to find a subgraph which can best explain the relationships among the n query nodes.

Generally speaking, the graphs mentioned above have a large scale. Though the large-scale graph can cover vast information, it is quite difficult to be used under some specific conditions. As a concrete example of entity relational graph, Figure 1 exhibits a co-authorship network of scientists. The challenge is how to meet the query requirement about the relations between "HOLME,P", "SNEPPEN K" and "JEONG H". Although all the three scientists are included in the initial large graph, we still cannot get a clear answer depicting the key relationships among them because of the disturbance of many remote or uncorrelated nodes. In such a condition, a small and compact subgraph composed of a few key paths will be more satisfying than the whole graph.

Suppose the expected scale of the answer is predefined, using the proposed method, we can clearly know what are the most informative paths connecting the three persons from Figure 2, such as the close co-authorship with "ROSVALL,M", "TRUSINA,A", "KIM,B", "YOON,C", and "MINNHAGEN, P".

Formally, the problem of interest is as follows:

Given: an undirected graph G; a query $Q = \{q_i\}(i = 1,\dots n)$,$n = |Q|$; and an integer budget b.

Find: a suitably connected subgraph H that (1)contains all the n query nodes; (2)contains at most b other vertices; and (3)maximizes a goodness function $g(H)$;

In the problem above, b expresses the largest scale that H can have; and the g function determines the quality of specific H. For different applications, $g(H)$ can be defined as multiple different forms. For example, Faloutsos and McCurley [1] use the current delivered by H to find an optimal subgraph with two query nodes; Hanghang Tong and Faloutsos [2] define $g(H)$ as the sum of relevance score for each node of H to find the Center-Piece subgraphs.

By Theorem 1 given in the following, we can see that the proposed problem is NP-complete. So the heuristic method

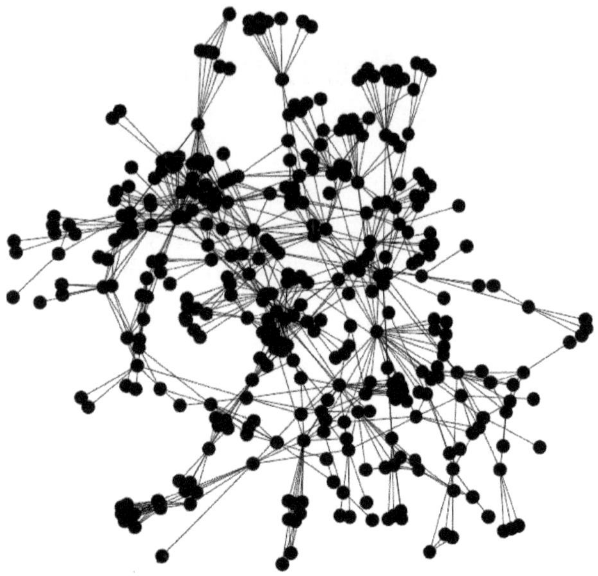

Figure 1: Part of netscience

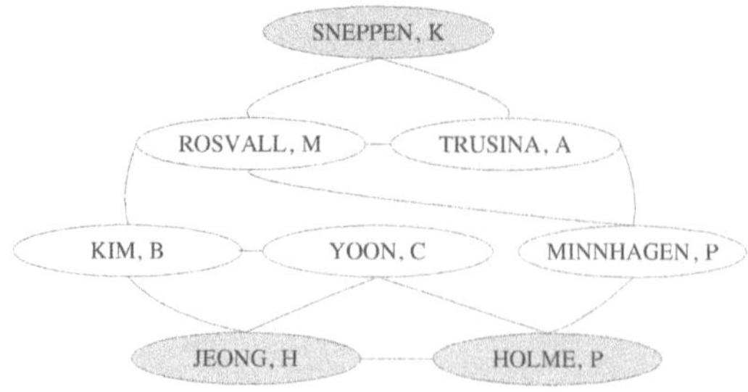

Figure 2: An example of subgraph mining

and approximate method are adopted separately to find the target H.

THEOREM 1. *It is NP-complete to find the target informative subgraph H.*

PROOF. Specially, we set n to 2 and b to the number of nodes in G. Then it is obvious that our problem is reduced to computing the maximum weight path between two query vertices. It is well-known that it is NP-complete to determine maximum weight path between two vertices in a graph [24], and thus our problem is NP-complete. □

In any case, according to the problem definition, to get a subgraph like Figure 2, two important issues should be considered. One is how to quickly find the target H and the other is how to design the goodness function to let H make sense.

For the first issue, the paper gives two solutions: sampling method and PSO-based SISP. The former, a simple way, can quickly return an approximate subgraph. The latter is a new framework which contains three key stages: particle initialization, fitness calculation and particle update. For each stage, some appropriate algorithms are proposed. First, we use a random spreading method that can effectively guarantee the connectivity of each particle; Second, by a sign function, we design an appropriate fitness function which can well compute the fitness score of a particle with specific size; Third, based on the precondition of connectivity, we propose the intersection-based particle update strategy which makes each particle move towards a better fitness. Additionally, some effective rules are made to quickly compress the large particles.

For the second issue, considering the importance and relevance of a node together, this paper proposes the Preference NodeRank(PNR) method to evaluate the goodness of each node in the large graph and then gives an appropriate description of $g(H)$. The experimental results show that the returned subgraph is satisfying.

The contributions of this work are as follows.

1. Based on the key idea of PSO, we propose a new framework of SISP. For each stage of the framework, some appropriate algorithms are proposed to fit the practical needs.The experimental results prove the efficiency of the proposed methods;

2. We use the sampling method to quickly find the target H. When the number of samples is large enough, the returned subgraph has high accuracy.

3. By combining the importance and relevance together, we propose the PNR based method to depict the goodness score of H;

4. We do experiments on two different datasets. The experimental results confirm that the proposed methods achieve high accuracy and are efficient for any different query set.

The rest of the paper is organized as follows: in Section 2, we review some related works; Section 3 introduces the overall framework of SISP and then gives the detail discussions for each stage of SISP. In Section 4, the sampling method is proposed. In Section 5, we give the detail description of the goodness measurement. We present several important experimental results in Section 6 and conclude the paper in Section 7.

2. RELATED WORKS

Along with the frequent application of complex networks, there are increasing search interests in large graph mining such as the frequent substructure discovery [4], graph summary [5], and dense graph mining [6] and so on. The community detection [7] is a similar problem. It aims to find groups of nodes within which connections are dense, but between which connections are sparser. However, as pointed out in[2] , we cannot directly apply community detection to find the target informative subgraph especially when the source queries are remotely related or lie in different communities.

As far as we know, there are few works devoted to the research. [1] is an early research for the problem. It exploits a current-flow algorithm to extract an important subgraph for two query nodes. The authors interpret the graph as an electric network and make the subgraph which delivers maximum current between the query nodes as the answer. In [14], the authors extend the current-flow method to multi-relational graphs. However, the number of query nodes in both their papers is restricted to two.

In [2], the authors propose the CEPS method, which can handle more than two query nodes. The method first chooses the central-piece nodes closely connected with most of the query nodes. Then based on the center pieces, key paths are added into the subgraph until the terminal condition is satisfied. To deal with different types of query scenarios, the paper introduces and handles the $KsoftAND$ queries, which include AND and OR queries as special cases. In [15], a steiner tree which connects all the query nodes is viewed as a part of the target subgraph. Then by a product of the two-step random walk probabilities, some extra good nodes are gradually added until the subgraph reaches the expected scale. Both the methods do some hypothesizes that some nodes are forced to become the members of target subgraph, such as the node of central-piece in [2] and the nodes in steiner tree in [15]. Although these hypothesizes simplify the proposed problem, the searching space of solutions is also shrunken, which will decrease the precision of the final returned subgraph.

Considering the shortcomings of methods above, we propose the sampling method and the PSO-based SISP framework for searching the informative subgraph. PSO [19] is a computational method that optimizes a problem by iteratively trying to improve a candidate solution with regard to a given measure of quality. PSO has an adequate biology background [20], with easy understanding and realization. Due to the excellent global search capability on the nonlinear and multi-modal problems, PSO is widely used in scientific research and engineering practice [21, 22]. As far as we know, PSO has not been used in the area of subgraph searching.

The problem of finding important nodes and entity ranking [8, 9] in a large graph are also related with our work. In [10], the authors propose a simple way to measure the graph entropy and a systematic way to find important nodes based on their effect on graph entropy. The approach of [11] views an undirected graph as a Euclidean space and depicts the connection of two nodes using commute time distance. Besides the works above, there are still many methods which calculate the importance of each node based on the connection structures. Typically, PageRank [3] , Sim-Rank [12], and HITs [13] are popular choices. By combining the importance and relevance of a node together, we further propose the Preference NodeRank method which makes the returned subgraph more meaningful.

3. THE SISP METHOD FOR SEARCHING INFORMATIVE SUBGRAPH

3.1 Framework

According to the definition of target subgraph, we can reconsider the problem as finding a optimal solution of H which maximizes $g(H)$ and meets the two constraints: (1)H is connected; and (2)H contains all query nodes and at most b other nodes.

Based on the basic idea of PSO, the new framework of SISP is proposed in this section. SISP contains three key stages and the particles are the basic operating units. In the background of graph, each particle is viewed as a subset of G and each dimension of the particle stands for a specific node. We will discuss how to select the best nodes in detail in Section 3.2.

SISP starts from initializing m particles, X_1,X_2,...,X_m. Then, by a specific fitness function, we can find the best particle X_{gbest} which has the maximum fitness score. At last, we iteratively update the m particles. Each loop contains two operations. First, every particle is updated by the guidance of X_{gbest}. And second the fitness of each new particle is re-computed. When the loop is over, the final X_{gbest} will be the optimal solution. The overview of SISP is shown as algorithm 1.

Algorithm 1 The SISP framework for searching informative subgraph

Input: the initial graph G, the query Q, the budget b and particle number m
Output: the target subgraph H
Initialize m particles X_1,X_2,...,X_m, and each particle stands for a subset of G;
for each X_i **do**
  Compute $f(X_i)$; \\ $f(X_i)$ is the fitness value of X_i
end for
X_{gbest} = argmax$f(X_i)$;.
while (!(terminal conditions)) **do**
  for each X_i **do**
    $X_i = Update(X_i, X_{gbest})$;
    Compute $f(X_i)$;
  end for
  X_{gbest} = argmax$f(X_i)$;
end while
return X_{gbest};

Generally speaking, the loop can be terminated either when the number of loop exceeds certain given threshold or when X_{gbest} has changed little within multiple loops. In practice, the two conditions are used simultaneously to better control the loop.

PSO is a kind of evolutionary algorithm, so the returned subgraph may not be the optimal one. In fact, a sub-prime solution is also acceptable to users. For example, if the minimum amount of nodes connected with all the query nodes is still bigger than b, according to the problem definition the optimal solution does not exist.

The following sections will give detail discussions for initialization, fitness calculation and update strategy separately.

3.2 Initialization of Particles

In SISP, the first step is to initialize a group of particles. Essentially the initialization is a process of finding some random solutions of the proposed problem. For different problems, the particles can be initialized by different rules. In the paper, each particle is viewed as a subset of G. Following the constraints of connectivity and scale, the most direct way is to initialize each particle as a group of nodes which are connected with Q and its size is not more than b. By this way, the generated particles meet with all the constraints. However, this initialization costs a lot of time. And the greater disadvantage is that the activity space of each particle is confined to a limit small range, which may make the searching process stay locally optimum.

Therefore, we loosen the constraints and make each particle fit only one condition. The simple way is to select randomly b nodes from G as a particle. This kind of initialization is fast. However, many isolated nodes will be generated, to make difficult construction of fitness function

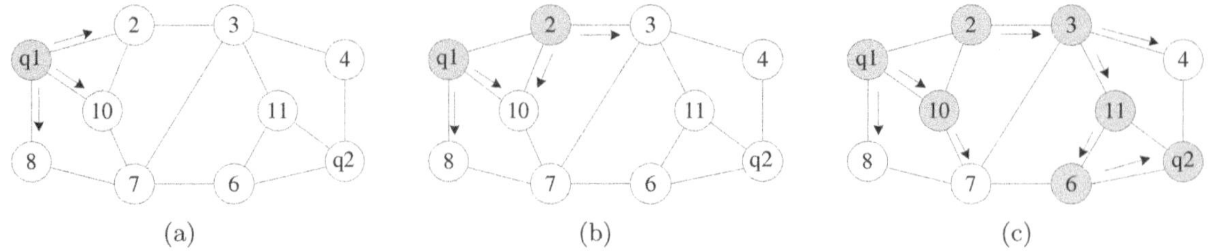

Figure 3: The initialization of particle

and update of particles. So taking no account of the dimension, we initialize each particle as a group of connected nodes. For an arbitrary particle X_i, we first add a random query node of Q into X_i, and continue to add the neighbors of X_i into X_i until all the nodes in X_i have been connected with all the query nodes. Figure 3 shows a sample initialization. Starting from a random query node, such as q_1 (Figure 3(a)), the algorithm finds all the neighbor nodes of q_1 and adds a random node into X_i, such as $X_i = \{q_1, 2\}$ in Figure 3(b); Based on the current X_i, we repeat the finding and adding until X_i is connected with all the n query nodes. In Figure 3(c), the final form of X_i is $Xi = \{q_1, 2, 3, 10, 11, 6, q_2\}$.

The only drawback of random spreading is that the scale of each initial particle is not controlled. Namely a particle can be initialized with any dimension. Actually, this drawback will not cause tremendous effects. For the particles beyond the scale, their dimensions can be adjusted gradually in the update stage, which will be discussed in detail in Section 3.4.

In the paper, the vector is used to restore each particle. The pseudo code of initialization is shown as algorithm 2.

Algorithm 2 Initialization of particles

Input: the initial graph G, the query vector Q and particle number m

Output: $X = \{X_1, X_2, \ldots, X_m\}$

```
for int i=1 to i=m do
    Initialize two vectors as X_i = null, neighbor_i = null;
    Add a random node of Q into X_i;
    while (!(X_i contains all the query nodes in Q)) do
        neighbor_i = getNeighbor(X_i); //get the neighbor nodes of X_i.
        Node tempn = getRandomNode(neighbor_i );
        if (! (X_i contains tempn)) then
            Add tempn into X_i;
        end if
    end while
end for
return X_1,X_2,..., X_m
```

Given all that, the initial particles have the following character.

CHARACTER 1. *Every initial particle is a connected subgraph and contains all the n query nodes.*

To speed up algorithm 2, a boolean array is created for each particle. In the array, the subscript is used as the identifier of each node. Each element of the array is initialized as false, and when a node is added into the particle, the corresponding position of the array is set to true. By doing this, it is directly judged whether a node has been used or not, and thus the scanning count of X_i decreases.

3.3 Calculation of Fitness

To get X_{gbext} in every loop, a proper fitness function is needed. According to the definition of target informative subgraph, the fitness of a particle X_i should be considered from the connectivity with Q, the dimension and the goodness of X_i together.

Throughout the whole framework of SISP, there are two places where the constituent of a particle is changed, the initialization and the update. According to Character 1, we have known that the nodes in initial particles are connected with Q. And faithfully speaking, the update strategy described in Section 3.4 can still keep the connectivity. So in the whole searching process we are always concentrating on the particles which are actually connected subgraphs. Given all that, the factor of connectivity can be ignored when calculating the fitness for each particle.

For a given query vector Q, suppose the normalized goodness score of $g(j, Q)$ for each $j \in H$ has been pre-calculated, we use formula 1 to calculate the fitness of each particle.

$$f(X_i) = \frac{1}{2} + sign(X_i) \times \frac{g(X_i)}{2} \tag{1}$$

where $g(X_i)$ is the goodness of X_i, which is calculated as formula 2; $sign(X_i)$ is a sign function, which is calculated as formula 3.

$$g(X_i) = \sum_{j \in X_i} g(j, Q) \tag{2}$$

$$sign(X_i) = \begin{cases} 1 & \text{if } (d(x_i) \text{ - } (b+n)) \leqslant 0, \\ -1 & \text{if } (d(x_i) \text{ - } (b+n)) > 0 \end{cases} \tag{3}$$

where $d(X_i)$ is the dimension of X_i.

The random spreading-based initialization makes all the query nodes members of each particle. So the difference between the $d(X_i)$ and $(b+n)$ will determine whether a particle meets the expected scale or not. The fitness function of formula 1 will generate different ranges for the two kinds of particles. For example, Figure 4 shows a statistical curve distribution for $b = 9$ and $n = 3$.

By Figure 4, the designed fitness function has the following characters.

CHARACTER 2. *$0.5 < f(X_i) \leq 1$, for each $d(X_i) \leq (b+n)$; $0 \leq f(X_j) < 0.5$, for each $d(X_j) > (b+n)$; and always $f(X_i) > f(X_j)$.*

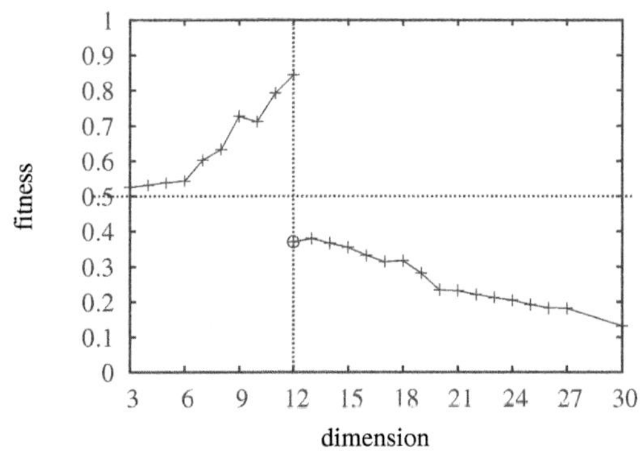

Figure 4: Overall fitness distribution related with particle dimension

PROOF. $0<g(X_i)\leq 1$, $0<g(X_i)/2\leq 0.5$. If $d(X_j)\leq(b+n)$, then $0<sign()g(X_i)/2\leq 0.5$, $0.5<f(X_i)\leq 1$; if $d(X_j)>(b+n)$, then $-0.5\leq sign()g(X_i)/2<0$, $0\leq f(X_i)<0.5$.

So, the $f(X_i)>f(X_j)$ for all $d(X_i)\leq(b+n)$ and $d(X_j)>(b+n)$. □

Character 2 ensures that the X_{gbest} will be generated from the particles whose dimensions are close to $b+n$.

3.4 Update of Particles

In each loop, according to the formula 1, we can get a specific X_{gbest}. This section proposes an effective update strategy to make each particle move towards X_{gbest} in next loop.

Different from the basic PSO, the nodes in a particle are co-dependent in our problem. Namely the value of each dimension is greatly related with other dimensions. So we cannot update the value of each dimension one by one. A better update strategy is to consider each particle as an ensemble unit.

On the whole, the update should follow the following two principles. First, every X_i should be move towards X_{gbest} to improve the similarity of contents between them; Second, the scale of X_i is extended or compressed to fit the dimension of X_{gbest}.

Given a specific X_{gbest}, for a random particle X_i, the intersection-based extension way is adopted to guarantee the content similarity which is related with the number of common nodes between them. Figure 5 shows the extension process of a particle with 9 dimensions. For the given X_i(Figure 5(a)) and X_{gbest} (Figure 5(b)), we first get the intersection set $Iset$=$\{q_1$, 4, 10, $q_2\}$(Figure 5(c)). Then we find the neighbor set of $Iset$ from G, and add a random node into X_i, such as the node labeled as 22 in Figure 5(d). In each update, the number of nodes which can be added into X_i can be freely set. Generally speaking, the users will not expect a large returned subgraph, so a slow expansion is effective. In the paper, we add only one node into X_i for each update. The extension makes X_i more similar to X_{best} to some degree.

Meanwhile, the dimension of X_i is expected to approximate to X_{gbest} as possible. For the scale constraint, there are two situations. If the dimension of X_i is smaller than $b+n$, X_i can be extended as Figure 5, and if bigger some nodes in X_i should be removed to reduce the scale.

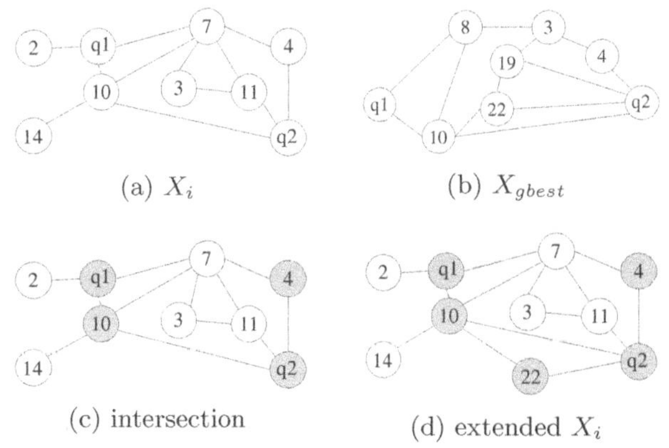

Figure 5: Particle extension based on intersection

The principle of removal is that the rest nodes in X_i are still connected. It is necessary to judge whether the connectivity of X_i is broken when its node is removed. However, when the given X_i is relatively large, the calculating of connectivity is time-consuming. So some simple rules are set to control the removing.

For a random node j in particle X_i, it can be removed if (1)the degree of j is 1, or (2)the degree of j is 2 and the two adjacent nodes of j also have an edge.

Take the particle of Figure 5(d) as an example, the nodes 2 and 14 can be removed by the first rule; the node of 3 can be removed by the second rule. Because the rules are only aimed at the nodes whose degrees are 1 and part of nodes whose degrees are 2, we cannot identify all the nodes which can be removed. However, the compression is a cycling program. When some nodes are removed, some other satisfying the rules will appear. So in practical, these simple rules can achieve good performance. Noticeability the compression of particle begin with the node with the lowest goodness score, which can effectively guarantee the quality of the compressed particles.

Combined with extension and compression, the pseudo code of update is shown as algorithm 3. The $compress()$ is a compression function whose pseudo code is shown as algorithm 4.

Algorithm 3 The update for particle X_i

Input: X_{gbest}, X_i
Output: X_i

Compute the intersection set between X_i and X_{gbest} as $Iset$;
$Nv = getNeighbor(Iset)$;
$extendnode = getRadomNode(Nv)$;
$X_i = X_i.\text{add}(extendnode)$;
if $(d(X_i)>(b+n))$ **then**
  $X_i = compress(X_i)$
end if
return X_i

According to the initialization, all the query nodes are put into the particles. So the intersection set $Iset$ in algorithm 3 always is non-empty (In the worst case, the intersection set still contains all the n query nodes.). Importantly, the

Algorithm 4 Algorithm for *compression*()

Input: X_i
Output: X_i

```
for int i=1 to i=(d(X_i) − (b + n)) do
    Select the node with minimum goodness as currentnode;
    \\ judge whether the currentnode can be removed or not
    if (judgeDelByRules(currentnode)) then
        X_i.remove(currentnode)
    end if
end for
return X_i
```

non-empty character ensures the possibility of extension of X_i towards X_{gbest}

Through the analysis above we get the third character.

CHARACTER 3. *For any given X_i, the nodes in X_i are still connected even when X_i is updated.*

Character 3 guarantees the constraint of connectivity, which makes the definition of fitness function shown as formula 1 sense.

4. THE SAMPLING METHOD FOR SEARCHING INFORMATIVE SUBGRAPH

The most direct way of finding H is to traverse all the G's possible subsets (the query nodes are not included) whose sizes are not more than b. For each such subset, by judging the connectivity with Q and calculating the goodness score of $g(H)$, we can find the final target subgraph. Undoubtedly, this searching way can fully guarantee the precision of returned H. However, when the graph is large, the searching space is so huge that we cannot suffer it. So as an approximation, the sampling method is used. Each time, we sample a random subgraph H_i of G which meets the following two constrains: (1)the nodes in H_i are connected with Q; and (2)the size of H_i is not bigger than b. For the N sampled subgraphs, the one with maximal goodness will be finally returned. The pseudo code is shown as algorithm 5.

Algorithm 5 The sampling method for searching informative subgraph

Input: the initial graph G, the query Q, the budget b and sampling times N
Output: the target subgraph H

```
Initialize H = null, maxscore = 0 ;
for i = 1 to i = N do
    H_i = getRandomH(G, Q); \\ get a random H which meets the connectivity with Q
    if (the node number of H_i is not bigger than b) then
        if g(H_i) > maxscore then
            maxscore = g(H);
            H = H_i;
        end if
    end if
end for
return H;
```

When the sampling times N is big enough, [23] gives the accuracy assurance of the the returned subgraph.

THEOREM 2. *For arbitrary $\delta(0 < \delta < 1)$ and $\tau(\tau>0)$, if $N \geq (3ln\frac{2}{\delta})$, then, $Pr|(maxscore\text{-}E(\varphi(H))) < \tau E(\varphi(H))| \geq 1\text{-}\delta$.*

In Theorem 2, $E(\varphi(H))$ stands for the expected value of maximum goodness score.

In application, we can adjust the parameter of δ and τ to balance the quality and time cost.

5. PNR BASED CALCULATION OF G(H)

A natural way to measure the goodness of H is to measure the goodness of the nodes it contains. Similar to [2], the goodness of H is defined as formula 4.

$$g(H) = \sum_{j \in H} g(j, Q) \tag{4}$$

where $g(j, Q)$ is the goodness score of a given node j with regard to the query set Q.

According to formula 4, the most informative subgraph, which maximizes $g(H)$, is chosen by formula 5.

$$H^* = \arg\max_{H} g(H) \tag{5}$$

So the key problem of getting H^* is how to calculate $g(j, Q)$. Let $g(j, q_i)$ be the goodness score of a given node j with regard to q_i, then the paper calculates $g(j, Q)$ as the sum of $g(j, q_i)$ for each $q_i \in Q$. Now, the problem is how to calculate $g(j, q_i)$. In this section, the effective Preference NodeRank(PNR) is proposed to calculate such goodness for each (j, q_i) pair. PNR considers $g(j, q_i)$ from two factors. First, the importance of each node in a large graph is different and the importance of j can greatly affect $g(j, q_i)$; Second, $g(j, q_i)$ can also be affected by the relevance between j and q_i.

The link structures are useful resources in evaluating the importance of each node in a large graph. So utilizing the links in the given graph G, we adopt the PageRank [3] to calculate the importance of each node. The concrete is shown as formula 6.

$$NR(j) = (1 - \beta) + \beta \times \sum_{u \in B(j)} NR(u)/|N(u)| \tag{6}$$

where $NR(j)$ is the importance of node j, $B(j)$ is node set of the outlinks of j, $N(u)$ is the set of nodes which node u links to, and β is a damping factor set between 0 and 1. In the undirected graph, the outlinks are equal to inlinks. The importance by formula 6 is query-independent, which cannot well reflect the goodness of j with regard to specific q_i. So PNR further incorporates the relevance between j and q_i into $NR(j)$.

The path information is used to evaluate the relevance of a node. We assume that sufficient short paths between j and q_i can express a good relevance of j with regard to q_i. Formally, the relevance is calculated as formula 7.

$$r(j, q_i) = \sum_{p \in P(j, q_i)} |p|^{-\lambda} \tag{7}$$

where $P(j, q_i)$ is the set of paths connecting j and q_i; and λ is a damping parameter for adjusting the influence of each path on $r(j, q_i)$. In fact, a long path contributes little to $r(j, q_i)$.

Therefore, to reduce the computation cost we abandon the paths whose lengths are bigger than k. According to the real scale of graph, k can be assigned to different values. In the paper, we set k as 4. Incorporating $r(j, q_i)$ into $NR(j)$, we get the final calculation of $g(j, q_i)$ as formula 8.

$$g(j, q_i) = NR(j)_q = (1-\beta)P(j)_q + \beta \sum_{u \in B(j)} NR(u)_q P(j|u) \tag{8}$$

where $P(j)_q$ and $P(j|u)$ are similar to [26] and defined as formula 9 and formula 10.

$$P(j)_q = \frac{r(j, q_i)}{\sum_{u \in G} r(u, q_i)} \tag{9}$$

$$P(j|u) = \frac{r(j, q_i)}{\sum_{k \in N(u)} r(k, q_i)} \tag{10}$$

Now we explain how the two formulas of 9 and 10 affect the node ranking. Actually, formula 6 can be considered as a random walk [16, 17]. Starting from a specific node j, the surfer can walk along a path or jump to a new node. $P(j)_q$ is the probability that the surfer jumps to j. So by formula 9, the surfer tends to jump to the nodes which are relevant to q_i. Similar, $P(j|u)$ is the probability that the surfer transits to node j given that it is on node u. So by formula 10, the surfer tends to follow the nodes relevant to q_i.

PNR is an iterative algorithm. Suppose the initial rank value of each node is $1/|G|$. We can get the final goodness score for each node by enough iterations. To reduce the online response time, we store the ranking lists for as many nodes as possible. Then when a new query is coming, we can get the score of $g(j, Q)$ by directly adding each $g(j, q_i)$. Additionally, all the scores are normalized for operation convenience.

6. EXPERIMENTS

In this section, we demonstrate some experimental results. The experiments are designed to answer the following questions.

(1) Does the proposed goodness criterion based on PNR make sense?

(2) Do the methods of SISP and sampling capture the optimal target subgraph?

(3) How do the parameters balance the quality and response time?

6.1 Data Sets and Settings

(1)Datasets. We use two datasets to evaluate the proposed method. Firstly, we use the netscience dataset to test the quality of the returned subgraph. The network is compiled from the bibliographics of several review articles. Here each author is denoted as a node in G and the edge is added when at least one co-authored paper exists between the corresponding two authors. On the whole, the network has 1,589 nodes and 2,742 edges.

Besides the netscience dataset, we also use a synthetic data set to test the scalability. To make the synthetic data more realistic, we generate a scale-free graph by the BA[25] model. Totally, the synthetic dataset contains 10k nodes and 35k edges.

(2)Source Queries. To test the proposed algorithm, we select several persons from different communities to compose the source-query repository. From the real dataset, we select 50 famous persons who come from different areas such as network, physics, intelligence and informatics. The query size is restricted to 2 to 10. Namely a query can be composed of 2 to 10 arbitrary persons from the query repository.

(3) Baseline method. This paper compares the experimental results with the MING proposed by Gjergji Kasneci[15] in CIKM 2009. The authors first construct a steiner-tree that closely interconnects all nodes in Q and label the nodes in steiner tree as '+'. Then for each node in the candidate graph, the authors classify it as '+' or '-' by a product of the two-step random walk probabilities. At last, within a limited size, the subgraph with maximal probability of '+' is returned.

(4) Software architecture. Our system was implemented in the Java programming language, and it runs on a Pentium class machine with a 2.0GHz processor. User can submit a group of queries, and then the system will initialize a specified number of particles. By multiple update of particles, the system will finally return a connected subgraph to user. The Java library of GraphStream[18] is used to deal with all the basic operations about the graph.

6.2 Evaluation of The Goodness g(H): Case Study

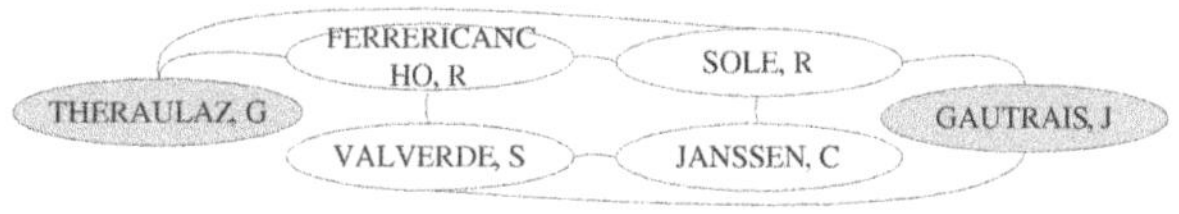

(a) H returned by MING

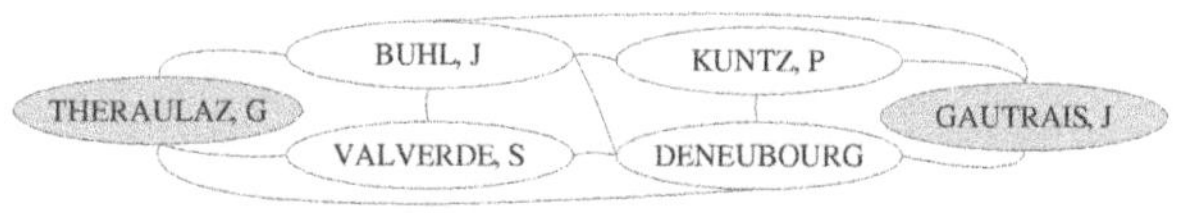

(b) H returned by SISP

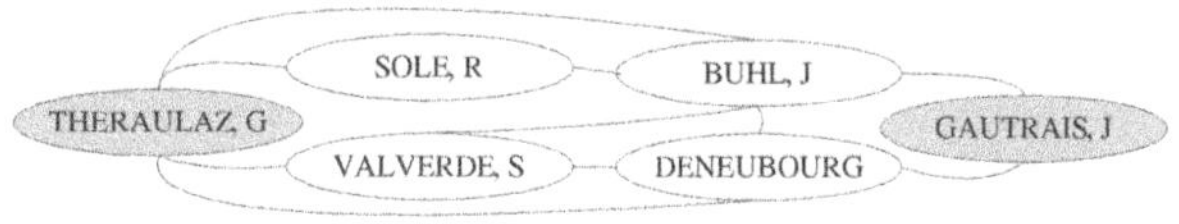

(c) H returned by Sampling

Figure 6: The informative subgraph for Q = {"THERAULAZ,G", "GAUTRAIS,J"}.

Using the real dataset, we exhibit some running cases to prove the effectiveness of the proposed method. By three methods, Figure 6 shows the different connection subgraphs with budget 4 for the query nodes "THERAULAZ,G" and "GAUTRAIS,J". Both the two persons are working in the fields of swarm intelligence in natural and artificial systems and self-organization in biological systems.

We can see that the returned subgraphs are composed of different persons. Figure 6(a) shows close connections among 6 persons by MING. However, the connections presented by Figure 6(b) and 6(c) are obviously stronger than

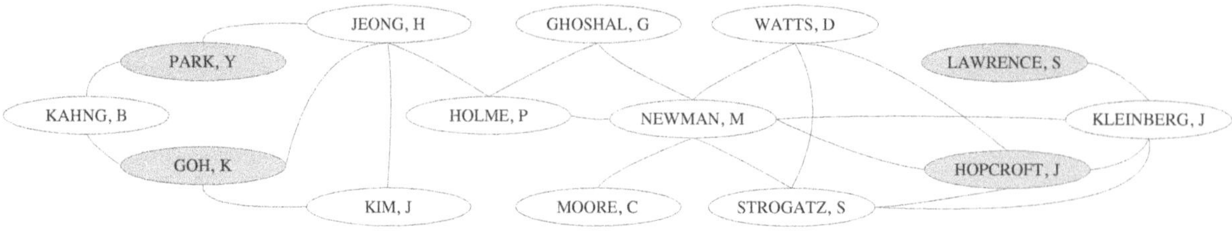

(a) H returned by MING

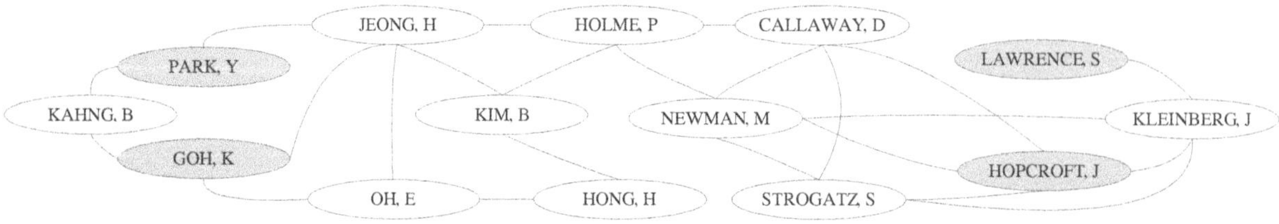

(b) H returned by SISP

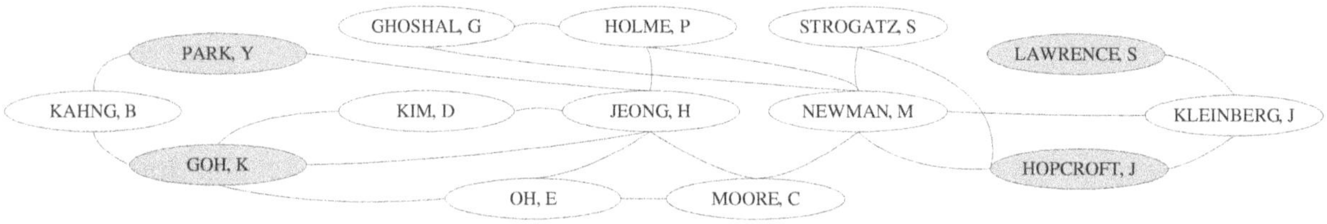

(c) H returned by Sampling

Figure 7: The informative subgraph for Q={"PARK,Y", "GOH,K", "LAWRENCE,S" and "HOPCROFT,J"}

Figure 6(a). In fact, all the five persons "BUHL,J", "SOLE,R", "KUNTZ,P", "VALVERDE,S" and " DENEUBOURG,J" in Figure 6(b) and 6(c), contribute to investigation in relative industry with self-organization and there are much cooperation in paper among them. So as we expected, the returned subgraphs by proposed methods are satisfactory.

Now consider a more complicated query requirement. We want to know the key relationships between the 4 different persons, "PARK,Y", "GOH,K", "LAWRENCE,S" and "HOPCROFT,J". By resumes, we can see that the 4 persons come from largely disjoint communities. And without the returned subgraph, it would be difficult to find the key paths between them.

Running the three algorithms MING, sampling and SISP, we get the results shown as Figure 7(a), Figure 7(b) and Figure 7(c) separately. Compared with Figure 7(a), the subgraphs by Sampling and SISP are more compact. For example, In Figure 7(b) and 7(c) the person "OH,E" has close relations with "GOH,K", they cooperate in many papers about structure and evolution of online social relationships; in Figure 7(c), the person "CALLAWAY,D" has close relations with "HOPCROFT,J" and "NEWMAN,M", they have cooperated in many fields such as the network evolution, data mining and so on.

6.3 Evaluation of SISP and Sampling

To further test the performance of the two proposed methods, we use the evaluation criterion of $NRatio$ [2] to exhibit the quality of the retrieved subgraph. $NRation$ expresses how many important/good nodes are captured by $g(H)$ and it is calculated by formula 11.

$$NRatio = \frac{\sum_{j\in H} g(Q,j)}{\sum_{j\in G} g(Q,j)} \tag{11}$$

To speed up the response time, we do all the following experiments on a candidate subgraph C of G. C contains many key connections among the query nodes. Expanding the query nodes by heuristics, we adopt the similar method of [1] to realize the candidate generation. Then the extracted candidate subgraph is treated as the full graph for the algorithms of sampling, SISP and MING.

For different b and n, we compare $NRatio$ with the baseline method. The default values of τ, δ and particle number m are to 0.1, 0.1 and 60. Utilizing the netscience dataset, we show the the mean $NRatio$ vs. b as Figure 8(a) and the mean $NRatio$ vs. n as Figure 8(b).

In both cases, the proposed methods capture most of important nodes by any number of budget b or n. For example, when b is 40, SISP captures 95% important nodes on average; when n is 4, SISP captures 85% important nodes on average. From Figure 8(a) we can see that the subgraph captures higher $NRatio$ when the budget b increases. That is because a bigger b makes more nodes with high goodness scores be added into H. So the ratio of good nodes in H is also increasing; From Figure 8(b) we can see that the subgraph with more source queries captures higher $NRatio$ than those with less ones. The explanation is that the goodness score of each node becomes more skewed by increasing the number of source queries. So the extracted subgraph contains more important nodes with high goodness scores.

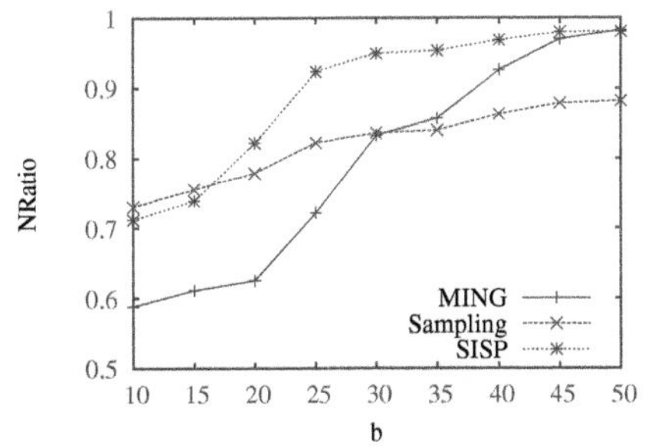

(a) *RNatio* vs. *b*

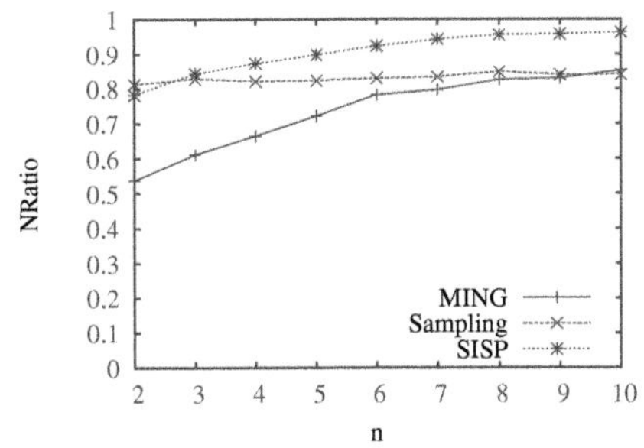

(b) *RNatio* vs. *n*

Figure 8: *RNatio* for different methods

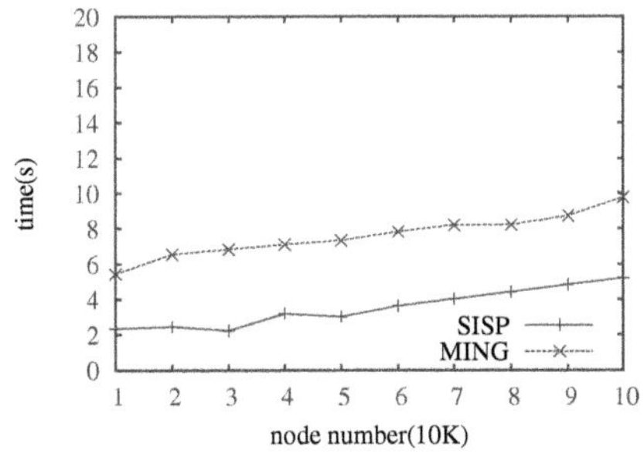

(a) time vs. graph scale

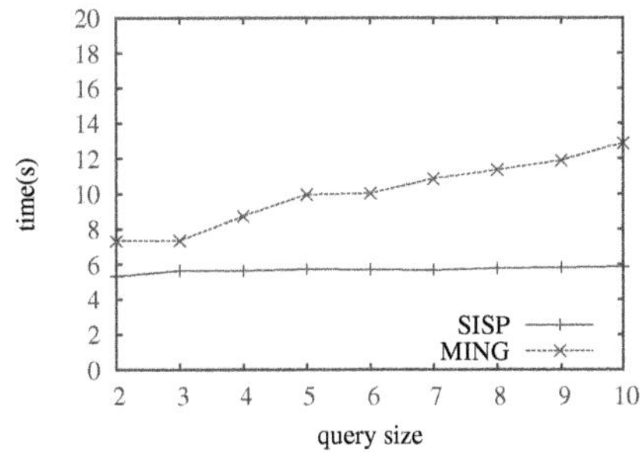

(b) time vs. *n*

Figure 9: Response time for different methods

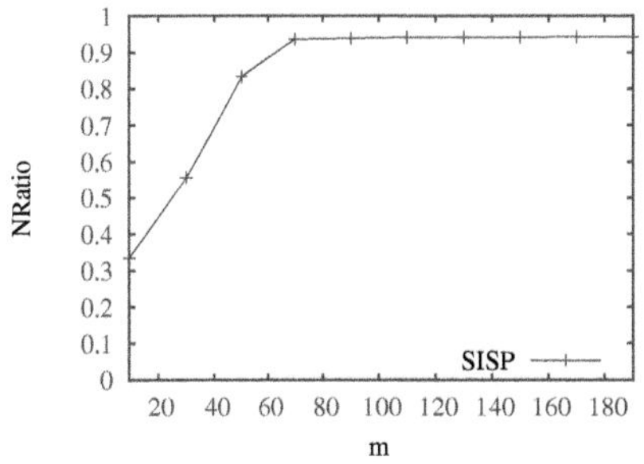

(a) *NRatio* vs. *m*

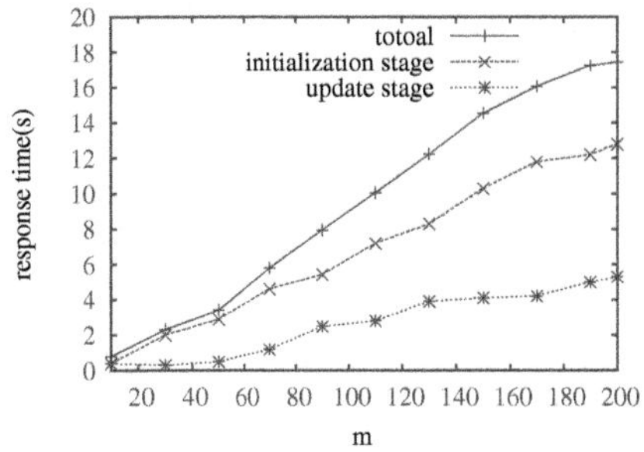

(b) time vs. *m*

Figure 10: The impact of particle number

Besides *NRatio*, we also report the response time of MING and SISP on the dataset with different scales. We do this experiment on the synthetic dataset. For 5 different scales, the average response time of SISP and MING are reported as Figure 9(a). When b is 30, we also record the response time for the queries with different sizes. The experimental results are shown as Figure 9(b). From the both figures, we can see that the proposed SISP has obviously lower response time. Additionally, in SISP, the size of a query has not a great effect on the response time, which is better than MING.

For SISP, we study the impact of m on *NRatio* and response time in the synthetic data. From Figure 10(a) we can see that *NRatio* grows rapidly when m increases from 20 to 60 and converges for bigger m. It is because that more particles can greatly extend the searching space of the optimal solution. So the number of captured good nodes is increasing. When the solution space has been covered by multiple particles, the continuous growth of m cannot make more good nodes involved. So the curve is convergent when m is greater than 60.

To find out the time cost of each step for different m, we report the response time by 3 curves shown as Figure 10(b). The amount of time spent on each stage is increasing along with the increase of m. We can see that the main time consumption is in the stage of initialization. Given all that, for a large graph with 10k nodes, the informative subgraph can be returned in 5 seconds when m is less than 60.

In the sampling method, the quality of returned subgraph depends on the sampling times. According to Theorem 2, the smaller δ is, the better quality is, but the longer response time becomes. The balance between quality and sampling times for different node scales is shown as Figure 11(a). We

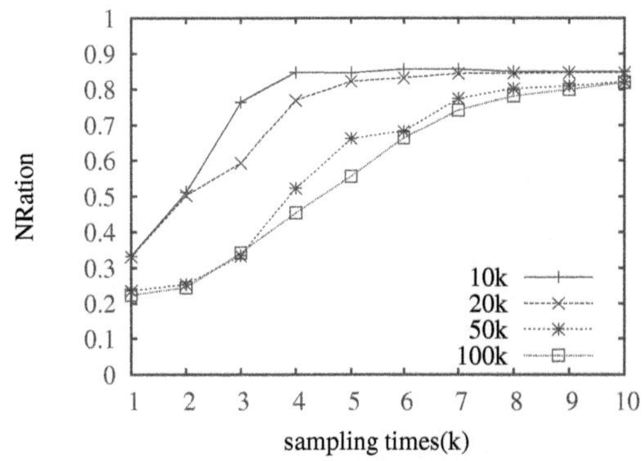

(a) *NRatio* vs. N for different graph scale

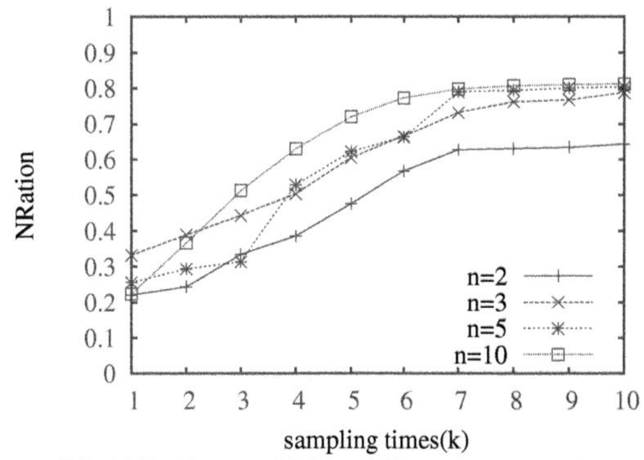

(b) *NRatio* vs. N for different query size

Figure 11: the balance between sampling times and quality

can see that *NRation* grows along with the increase of sampling times for each dataset. The bigger the dataset, the more the sampling times are needed to get a high *NRation*.

When b is 30, the balance between quality and sampling times for different query size is shown as Figure 11(b). We can see that H captures higher *NRatio* when the query size n is increasing. This can be explained similar to figure 8(b). Bigger query size makes H involve more important nodes, so the corresponding convergence velocity is faster than that of smaller one.

7. CONCLUSIONS

We have proposed the sampling and SISP for solving the problem of searching the informative subgraph. Every key stage in SISP is discussed and some efficient algorithms are proposed. In initialization, we use a random spreading method, which can effectively guarantee the connectivity of each particle; In fitness calculation, the designed fitness function, the goodness and dimension considered, can well reflect the quality of each particle.; In update stage, we propose the intersection-based particle extension and rule-based particle compression method. To make the returned subgraph satisfactory, we further present the PNR method which considers the importance and relevance of a node together

The experimental results prove that the proposed methods achieve increased accuracy and are efficient for any query set.

For the future work, we will continue our research by optimizing the initialization to decrease time cost.We will also use the SISP framework to solve other problems related with graph searching such as community detection, frequent subgraph discovery and so on.

8. ACKNOWLEDGMENTS

This research is supported by the National Basic Research Program of China (2011CB302206), National Natural Science Foundation of China (61025007, 60933001, 61073063) and Fundamental Research Funds for the Central Universities (Grant No. N090304007).

9. REFERENCES

[1] C. Faloutsos, K. S. McCurley, and A. Tomkins. Fast discovery of connection subgraphs. In *KDD*, pages:77-99, 2004.

[2] H. Tong, C. Faloutsos. Center-piece subgraphs: problem definition and fast solutions. In *KDD*, pages: 404-413, 2006.

[3] L. Page, S. Brin, R. Motwani, T. Winograd. The PageRank citation ranking:Bringing order to the web. Technical report, Stanford University, 1998.

[4] D. J. Cook, L. B. Holder. Substructure discovery using minimum description length and background knowledge. *Journal of Artificial Intelligence Research*, pages:231-255, 1994.

[5] S. Navlakha, R. Rastogi, N. Shrivastava. Graph summarization with bounded error. In *proc. of SIGMOD* , pages: 419-432, 2008.

[6] X. L. Li, S. H. Tan, C. S. Foo, S. K. Ng. Interaction graph mining for protein complexes using local clique merging. *Genome Inform Ser* , 16(2):260-269, 2008.

[7] N. Du, B. Wu, X. Pei, B. Wang, L.Xu. Community detection in large-scale social networks. In *proc. of KDD*, pages:16-25, 2007.

[8] A. M. Vercoustre, J. A. Thom, J. Pehcevski. Entity ranking in WikiPekia. *In porc. of ACM on Applied computing*, pages:1101-1106, 2008.

[9] J. P. Jiang, W. Lu, X.Q. Rong, Y. Y. Gao. Adapting language modeling methods for expert search to rank wikipedia entities. *Lecture Notes in Computer Science*, pages:264-272, 2009.

[10] J. Shetty, J. Adibi. Discovering important nodes through graph entropy the case of Enron email database. *In proc. of LinkKDD*, pages:74-81, 2004.

[11] S. Vast ,P. Dupont ,Y. Deville, P. S. Barbe. Automatic extraction of relevant nodes in biochemical networks. *Atelier Apprentissage et Bioinformatique*, pages:21- 31, 2005.

[12] G. Jeh, J. Widom. Simrank: A measure of structural context similarity. *In proc. of KDD*, pages:538-543, 2002.

[13] J. M. Kleinberg. Authoritative sources in a hyperlinked environment. *In proc. of ACM*, pages:668-677, 1998.

[14] C. Ramakrishnan, W. Milnor, M. Perry, and A. Sheth. Discovering informative connection subgraphs in multi-relational graphs. *ACM SIGKDD Explorations Newsletter*, pages: 56-63, 2005.

[15] G. Kasneci, S. Elbassuoni, G. Weikum. MING:Ming informative entity relationship subgraphs. *In CIKM*, pages:1653-1656, 2009.

[16] H. Tong, C. Faloutsos, J. Pan. Fast Random Walk with Restart and Its Applications. *In proc. of ICDM*, pages: 613-622, 2006.

[17] A. Agarwal, S. Chakrabarti. Learning random walks to rank nodes in graphs. *In proc. of ICML*, pages:9-16, 2007.

[18] http://graphstream.sourceforge.net/

[19] J. Kennedy, R. Eberhart. Particle swarm optimization. *In proc. of the 4th IEEE International Conference on Neural Networks*, pages:1942-1948, 1995.

[20] S. Garnier, J. Gautrais, G. Theraulaz. The biological principles of swarm intelligence. *Swarm Intelligence*, 2007.

[21] R. Eberhart, Y. Shi. Particle swarm optimization: developments, applications and resources. *In proc. of IEEE Congr.Evol.Comput*, 2001.

[22] K. Parsopoulos, M. Vrahatis. Recent approaches to golbal optimization problems through particle swarm optimization. *Natural Computing*, 2002.

[23] D. Angluin ,L.G. Valiznt. Fast probabilistic algorithms for hamiltonian circuits and matchings. *In proc. of STOC*, 1977.

[24] M. R. Garey, D. S. Johnson. Computers and intractability: a guide to the theory of NP-completeness. New York, NY, USA, 1990.

[25] A. Barablcsi, R.Albert. Statistical mechanics of complex. *Revieews of Modern Physics*, 2002.

[26] M. Richardson, P. Domingos. The intelligent surfer:probabilistic combination of link and content information in PageRank. *In proc. of NIPS*, 2001.

Indexes for Highly Repetitive Document Collections

Francisco Claude
School of Computer Science,
University of Waterloo
Waterloo, Canada
fclaude@cs.uwaterloo.ca

Antonio Fariña
Database Lab.,
University of A Coruña,
A Coruña, Spain.
fari@udc.es

Miguel A. Martínez-Prieto
Dept. of Computer Science,
University of Valladolid,
Valladolid, Spain.
Dept. of Computer Science,
University of Chile,
Santiago, Chile,
migumar2@infor.uva.es

Gonzalo Navarro
Dept. of Computer Science,
University of Chile,
Santiago, Chile.
gnavarro@dcc.uchile.cl

ABSTRACT

We introduce new compressed inverted indexes for highly repetitive document collections. They are based on run-length, Lempel-Ziv, or grammar-based compression of the differential inverted lists, instead of gap-encoding them as is the usual practice. We show that our compression methods significantly reduce the space achieved by classical compression, at the price of moderate slowdowns. Moreover, many of our methods are universal, that is, they do not need to know the versioning structure of the collection.

We also introduce compressed self-indexes in the comparison. We show that techniques can compress much further, using a small fraction of the space required by our new inverted indexes, yet they are orders of magnitude slower.

Categories and Subject Descriptors

E.1 [**Data Structures**]; E.4 [**Coding and Information Theory**]; H.3.3 [**Information Storage and Retrieval**]: Information Search and Retrieval

General Terms

Algorithms

1. INTRODUCTION

Large versioned document collections, such as *Wikipedia* (`www.wikipedia.org`) and the *Wayback Machine* from the *Internet Archive* (`www.archive.org/web/web.php`), are examples of the emergence of highly repetitive document collections, where most documents are near-duplicates. Apart from versioned document collections, other cases where this problem arises are software repositories (where the tree of versions is maintained), biological databases (where many DNA or protein sequences of the same or related species are maintained), periodic technical publications (where the same data, with small updates, are republished), and so on.

These collections may be very large, but at the same time highly compressible. While Lempel-Ziv compressors [24] are successful in capturing their repetitiveness, such compression is suitable only for archival purposes. The applications we have enumerated require, instead, fast searching and direct access capabilities. Thus, we need to compress not only the data, but also the indexes.

There is a burst of recent activity in exploiting this repetitiveness at the indexing structures in order to provide fast searches into the collection within little space. Both inverted indexes for word and phrase queries over natural language texts [2, 5, 11, 12], and other indexes for general string collections [16, 6, 14, 7], have been pursued.

The focus of this paper is on natural language text collections, which can be decomposed into words, and queried for words or phrases. The classical data structure to index such collections is the inverted index, where a list of the occurrences of each distinct word is maintained. The variant where the lists are sorted by increasing document identifier has gained relevance, since such ordering is most useful for list intersections. Intersections of inverted lists arise as a fundamental task under the Google-like default policy of treating bag-of-word queries as ranked AND-queries. Therefore, intersections conform the heaviest part of the search process, and relevance ranking is done as a postprocessing step [9]. Intersections are also used for phrase queries.

In this context, there are two different types of indexes. *Non-positional* indexes find, given a word or bag-of-words query, the documents containing all the words. They store, for each word, the increasing list of documents containing it. *Positional* indexes retrieve the precise positions in each document where a word or phrase query appears. They store, in addition to the document identifiers, the word offset of the occurrences within each document.

Traditional techniques to compress inverted indexes [25] represent the differences between consecutive document or position values. Many of those differences tend to be small, and thus they are encoded in a way that favors small numbers. While very effective for traditional collections, this compression technique fails to capture the repetitiveness that arises in versioned collections.

He et al. [11, 12] have presented alternative compression

CIKM'11, October 24–28, 2011, Glasgow, Scotland, UK.

methods specifically targeted at highly repetitive collections. Their approach merges all versions of each document for creating the inverted lists and then keeps a secondary index that allows one to list the versions of a document that contain a given term. They obtained spectacular compression results for non-positional inverted indexes.

In this paper we introduce techniques for compressing inverted indexes on highly repetitive collections. Some of those are *universal* in the sense that they do not need to identify which document is a version of which. The techniques of He et al. [11, 12] work under a model where there exists a set of independent documents, each of which has a number of versions, and this versioning information must be available to the index. Our techniques can also work on cases where the versions form a tree structure (as in collaborative document creation, software repositories, or phylogenetic trees), or where it is unknown or unclear which documents are versions of which (as in DNA sequence databases).

Instead of using the classical encoding of differences, we adapt and apply run-length, grammar [15] or Lempel-Ziv [24] compression on the lists of differences. Our techniques largely outperform classical inverted index compression in this scenario. For example, our Lempel-Ziv-based index is 15 times smaller than a Rice-encoded index (the best choice for classical text collections), and at most 70% slower on word and conjunctive queries. Our grammar-based compressed index is up to 18 times smaller and up to 3 times slower. Our experiments also show that other classical encodings, such as Simple9 [1] and PforDelta [26], perform surprisingly well on repetitive collections, yet they still require 5 times more space than ours. Our techniques still do not match the performance of He et al.'s methods [12] when their assumptions hold, but these methods are not universal.

Some of our methods work well also for positional indexes, where the work of He et al. does not apply but other techniques are possible. Our Lempel-Ziv based index is 3.6 times smaller, yet up to 8 times slower, than classical inverted indexes. For this case we also consider self-indexes, which are compressed indexes (not based on inverted indexes) that encompass the text and the index. We use and adapt existing self-indexes designed for highly repetitive collections (mostly for computational biology scenarios) [16, 6, 14]. They compress up to 16 times more than our Lempel-Ziv-based index, yet their query times are 10 to 500 times higher.

2. RELATED WORK

2.1 Data structures for inverted lists

The compression of inverted lists usually represents each list $\langle p_1, p_2, p_3, \ldots, p_\ell \rangle$ as a sequence of d-gaps $\langle p_1, p_2 - p_1, p_3 - p_2, \ldots, p_\ell - p_{\ell-1} \rangle$, and uses a variable-length encoding for these differences, such as Rice codes [25]. Those methods assign shorter codes to smaller values, taking advantage of the fact that, on longer lists, the d-gaps are shorter.

If the lists reside on disk, reducing their space (and then the I/O cost to fetch them) is the most important criterion. If they reside in RAM, we must also consider the time to traverse them. We pay attention to both in this paper.

Gap encoding techniques that allow very fast in-memory traversals are `Vbyte` [23], `Simple9` [1] and `PforDelta` [26].

Intersections can be carried out by traversing the lists sequentially. When one list is much shorter than the other, it is advantageous to provide direct access so that the longer list can be searched for the elements of the shorter one. It was shown experimentally [3] that in practice the best is to sort the lists by length, taking the shortest as the "candidate" list, and iteratively intersect the candidate list with longer and longer lists, making it shorter and shorter. A technique to provide random access [8] samples regularly the compressed list and stores separately the array of samples, which is searched with exponential search. Very long lists are replaced by a bitmap. Given a parameter k, a list of length ℓ is sampled every $k \log_2 \ell$ positions. Another good method [22] regularly samples the universe of positions, so that the exponential search is avoided. Given a parameter B, it samples the universe of size u at intervals $2^{\lceil \log_2(uB/\ell) \rceil}$.

In the particular case of highly repetitive collections, the best figures so far have been presented by He et al. [12] in the non-positional case. They model versioned document collections using so-called *two-level indexes*. The first level of the inverted list of a term stores all the documents where the term appears in, at least, one of its versions. The second level is a bit vector that marks all document versions where the term appears. Experiments on Wikipedia and Internet Archive subsets report improvements in space and query times with respect to the original one-level techniques.

2.2 Re-Pair compression algorithm

Re-Pair [15] is a linear-time compressor that repeatedly finds the most frequent pair of symbols in a sequence of integers and replaces it with a new symbol, until no more replacements are useful. Over a sequence L, Re-Pair: (1) Identifies the most frequent pair ab in L; (2) Adds the rule $s \rightarrow ab$ to a dictionary R, where s is a new symbol not appearing in L; (3) Replaces every occurrence of ab in L by s; (4) Iterates until every pair in L appears once.

We call C the sequence resulting from L after compression. Every symbol in C represents a *phrase* (a substring of L), which is of length 1 if it is an original symbol (called a *terminal*) or longer if it is an introduced one (a *non-terminal*). Any phrase can be recursively expanded in optimal time (i.e., proportional to its length), even if C is stored on secondary memory (as long as the rules R fit in RAM).

We represent R using a method [10] that allows accessing any rule without decompressing the whole set of rules. It represents the DAG of rules as a set of trees. Each tree is represented as a sequence of leaf values (collected into a sequence R_S) and a bitmap that defines the tree shapes in preorder (collected into a bitmap R_B). Nonterminals are represented by the starting position of their tree (or subtree) in R_B. In R_B, internal nodes are represented by 1s and leaves by 0s, so that the value of the leaf at position i in R_B is found at $R_S[rank_0(R_B, i)]$. Operation $rank_0$ counts the number of 0s in $R_B[1, i]$ and can be implemented in constant time, after a linear-time preprocessing that stores only $o(|R_B|)$ bits of space [18] on top of the bitmap. To expand a nonterminal, we traverse R_B and extract the leaf values, until we have seen more 0s than 1s. Leaf values corresponding to nonterminals must be recursively expanded.

2.3 Lempel-Ziv compression

The Lempel-Ziv 1977 (*LZ77*) compression algorithm [24] works by decomposing the text from left to right into maximal phrases, so that each phrase is a substring of the previous text. The main drawback of LZ77 is that it does not support random access to the compressed text.

An alternative parsing called *LZ-End* [13] limits the substrings to end at a previous phrase, and uses this limitation to offer reasonable access time. This approach was shown [13] to compete very closely in space with LZ77.

2.4 Compressed self-indexes

Compressed self-indexes are data structures that enable efficient searches over an arbitrary string collection (called the text), and also replace the text by supporting extraction of arbitrary snippets or documents. The supported searches obtain all the positions of a substring in the collection, which makes them candidates to compete in the positional setting.

Self-indexes have undergone much progress in the last decade [19]. Recently they have been adapted to index highly repetitive sequences [16, 6, 14]. While general self-indexes have been successful by targeting at statistical compression, they have been proved insufficient on highly repetitive collections [16]. The indexes aimed at repetitive collections seek instead to capture repetitions in the text.

The first self-index successfully capturing high repetitiveness was the `RLCSA` [16]. This index adapts the well-known `CSA` of Sadakane [21] to better cope with the regularities that arise when indexing highly repetitive sequences. A variant aimed at indexing natural language, `WCSA` [4], regards the text as a sequence of words and separators instead of characters, but it is not so oriented to much repetitiveness. Another index aimed at repetitive collections is the `SLP` [7, 6], which exploits the regularities of highly repetitive sequences because its structure is determined by a grammar-based compressor (Re-Pair). We adapt the `SLP` to words (`WSLP`) in this paper. Finally, other strong indexes for repetitive sequences are `LZ77-index` and `LZend-index` [14], which are based on the LZ77 or LZ-End compression algorithms, respectively. The LZ77 parsing is, at least, as powerful as any grammar representation [20], and thus, it is also a good candidate for highly repetitive sequences.

3. NEW LIST REPRESENTATIONS

Our basic idea, for both non-positional and positional indexes, is to differentially encode the inverted lists, transforming a sequence $\langle p_1, p_2, p_3, \ldots, p_\ell \rangle$ into the d-gap sequence $\langle p_1, p_2 - p_1, p_3 - p_2, \ldots, p_\ell - p_{\ell-1} \rangle$, and then apply a general compression algorithm to the sequence formed by the concatenation of all the lists. Each vocabulary word will store a pointer to the beginning of its list in the compressed data.

3.1 Using run-length compression

A typical regularity in highly repetitive collections arises when the versions of a document happen to receive consecutive identifiers. As most of the words in such documents will appear in all versions, a consecutive sequence of numbers will appear in each inverted list of non-positional indexes. Consider the word w_t appearing in documents $d_i, \ldots, d_{i+k}$: the d-gapped list for w_t will contain $k-1$ consecutive ones.

In this representation we use any variable-length encoding for the differences. However, when this difference is 1, the next encoded number is the number of 1s in that run (k, in the previous paragraph). This encoding allows us skipping whole runs in a single operation, when processing intersections. It also allows combining with sampling techniques that support intersection methods other than the sequential one [8, 22]. In this paper we combine run-length compression with Rice coding, giving rise to method `Rice-Runs`.

Note that this technique works well only under the assumption that the documents can be linearized so that close documents receive consecutive numbers. While such kinds of assumptions are used in previous work [11, 12], we aim to handle more general cases in this paper. Moreover, this technique can be efficient only for non-positional indexes.

3.2 Using LZMA

This representation (already used for compressing q-gram indexes on DNA [6]) compresses each d-gap list with `Vbyte` and then with the *LZMA* variant of LZ77 (`www.7-zip.org`). LZMA is applied only on the lists where it reduces space. A bitmap marks which words were compressed with LZMA.

This representation, called `Vbyte-LZMA`, only supports extracting a list from the beginning, that is, we cannot jump to a random position on the list, and thus the only intersection algorithm supported is the sequential one. Moreover, unlike run-length compression, it cannot skip a compressed subsequence without fully processing it.

In this paper we apply LZMA to non-positional indexes as well, and evaluate it at intersections. LZMA handles more complex regularities than run-length compression. In particular, it works well on positional indexes: Consider r repetitions of a long substring S in the collection, for example in any r similar documents across the collection. For each word w_t in S, with occurrences at relative positions $i_1, i_2, \ldots, i_k$ in S, the sublist $i_2 - i_1, \ldots, i_k - i_{k-1}$ appears r times in the list of word w_t. Hence, LZMA will capture this repetition and represent $r-1$ of those sublists with just one reference. Note that this will occur independently of whether the versions are consecutive, and even without any need to know which documents are close versions of which.

4. RE-PAIR COMPRESSED LISTS

LZMA is limited to spotting intra-list regularities. A grammar-based compressor aimed at globally compressing the lists of d-gaps could spot inter-list similarities as well. In the same example of Section 3.2, consider that we have a phrase $w_{t_1} w_{t_2} \ldots w_{t_s}$ occurring k times in S. Then the sequence $i_2 - i_1, \ldots, i_k - i_{k-1}$ will appear r times inside each of the s lists, and a grammar compressor could be able to replace $rs - 1$ of the occurrences by a single reference. LZMA would have replaced only $rs - s$.

We use Re-Pair as our grammar compressor. We operate over the integer values and not over their `Vbyte` encodings.

We prevent phrases from spanning multiple lists, which can be easily enforced at compression time. Thus we can store pointers from the vocabulary to the points in the compressed sequence C where the lists begin, and any list can be expanded in optimal time. We also store the Re-Pair dictionary, in the compact format described in Section 2.2.

The terminal symbols are directly the corresponding differential values (e.g. value *3* is represented by the terminal integer 3). This saves table accesses at decompression time.

4.1 Skipping

An attractive feature of our Re-Pair method is that we can add extra information to nonterminals that enables fast skipping over the compressed list data without decompressing. This yields much faster sequential list intersections.

The key idea is that *nonterminals also represent differential values*, namely the sum of the differences they expand into. We call this the *phrase sum* of the nonterminal.

Phrase sums will be stored in sequence R_S, aligned with the 1 bits of sequence R_B. Thus *rank* is not anymore necessary to move from one sequence to the other. The 0s in R_B are aligned in R_S to the leaf data, and the 1s to the phrase sums of the corresponding nonterminals.

In order to find whether a given document d is in the compressed list, we first scan the entries in C, adding up in a sum s the value $C[i]$ if it is a terminal, or $R_S[C[i]]$ if it is a nonterminal. If at some point we get $s = d$, then d is in the list. If instead $s > d$ at some point, we consider whether the last $C[i]$ processed is a terminal or not. If it is a terminal, then d is not in the list. If it is a nonterminal, we restart the process from $s - C[i]$ and process the R_S values corresponding to the 0s in $R_B[C[i], \ldots]$, recursing as necessary until we get $s = d$ or $s > d$ after reading a terminal.

4.2 Intersection algorithm

To intersect several lists, we sort them in increasing order of their *uncompressed* length (which we store separately). Then we proceed iteratively, searching in step i the list $i+1$ for the elements of the candidate list (recall Section 2.1).

At each intersection, the candidate list is sequentially traversed. Let x be its current element. We skip phrases of list $i+1$, accumulating gaps until exceeding x, and then consider the previous and current cumulative gaps, $x_1 \leq x < x_2$. Then the last phrase represents the range $[x_1, x_2)$. If $x_1 = x$ we report x and shift to the next element in the candidate list. In either case, we advance in the candidate list until finding the largest $x' < x_2$. Then, we process all the interval $[x, x']$ within the phrase representing $[x_1, x_2)$ in R_S in a recursive fashion, until one of the two lists gets empty.

This procedure can be speeded up by adding samples, but we do not consider them in this paper. We will only consider a variant that stores skipping information on nonterminals (`RePair-Skip`), and one that does not (`RePair`).

5. SELF-INDEXES

Self-indexes support positional indexing. We will apply them on the concatenated text collection, $\mathcal{D}$. The self-index will find all the occurrences of the pattern, yet usually not in order, so a sorting post-processing is necessary.

Some self-indexes compared in this paper (see Section 2.4), are character-oriented: `LZ77-index`, `LZend-index`, `RLCSA`, and `SLP` (this one including several improvements upon its previous version [6]). They regard the text as a sequence of characters and report any substring matching the pattern.

Two self-indexes, instead, are word-oriented: `WCSA` and `WSLP` (this one created for this paper). Words and *separators* (maximal spaces between words) are mapped to integers, and the indexes represent the integer sequence. We use the spaceless words model [17], where the single whitespace separator is omitted and assumed by default.

6. EXPERIMENTAL RESULTS

We tested the non-positional and positional scenarios. We used the 108.5 GB Wikipedia collection described by He et al. [12], which is a 10% of the complete English Wikipedia. This collection is formed by 240,179 articles, each of which has a number of versions. There are 8,467,927 versions, of average size 13,757 bytes. We chose a random subset of the articles, and collected all their versions. Each version is considered as a document in our collection. For the non-positional setting our subset contained 24.77 GB, whereas for positional indexes we chose 1.94 GB of random articles.

We consider four query sets, with 1000 queries per set. Two sets are one-word searches, chosen at random from the vocabulary of the indexed subcollection. In the first we take words with up to 1000 occurrences in the subcollection. In the second we take words with more than 1000 occurrences. The other two query sets correspond to phrases of 2 and 5 words chosen at random from the text of the subcollection. For non-positional indexes this is taken as an AND query, whereas for the positional ones it is taken as a phrase query.

6.1 Non-positional indexes

The machine used in this scenario has an Intel(R) Xeon(R) E5520 CPU running at 2.27 GHz, 8 MB cache, 72 GB of RAM memory, 4 cores. The operating system installed is an Ubuntu GNU/Linux version 9.10 running kernel 2.6.31-19-server (64 bits) and `g++` compiler version 4.4.1. Our code was compiled with the `-O9` directive. We measure user times.

We use in these indexes exactly the same parsing of words of He et al. [12], which involves case folding, removing 20 very common stopwords, and no stemming. This reduces the original 108.5 GB to about 85.55 GB, and the 24.79 GB of text we index to about 19.54 GB. Yet we report the space results with respect to the original text size.

We compared a number of variants. The first are representatives of the best classical techniques we are aware of, see Section 2. These include various encodings of the d-gaps with no sampling (`Rice`, `Simple9`, `PforDelta`, and `Vbyte`), and a Vbyte encoding of the d-gaps with samplings in the type of Culpepper and Moffat [8] with $k = 32$ (`Vbyte-CM`), or Sanders and Transier [22] with $B = 128$ (`Vbyte-ST`).

The second group is formed by methods proposed in this paper to handle repetitive sequences. None uses sampling, so intersections are sequential: `Rice-Runs` (Section 3.1), `Vbyte-LZMA` (Section 3.2), `RePair` and `RePair-Skip` (Section 4).

Figure 1 shows the space/time tradeoffs for all the non-positional indexes. The space is given as a percentage of that used by the text in plain form (we are not considering in this experiment the compressed representation of the text itself). The time is shown in microseconds per occurrence.

We can see that, among classical compression methods, the newer methods `Simple9` and `PforDelta` are much better in space than older techniques like `Rice` (one third the space) and `Vbyte` (one fifth the space). In typical collections `Rice` achieves the best space, but these newer methods take advantage of the many runs of 1s. They are also several times faster than `Rice`, and roughly as fast as `Vbyte` on word queries. On conjunctive queries, however, `Vbyte` is faster. In those queries adding samples [8, 22] is advantageous: `Vbyte-CM` and `Vbyte-ST` are significantly faster than `Vbyte` (more than 3 times faster on 5-word queries). The little impact (and even reduction) in size owes to the fact that values stored in the samples are removed from the differential sequence. All the other methods (except `Vbyte-LZMA`) can be combined with such samplings to speed up long queries. Yet, the most important conclusion with regard to classical encoding methods is that they are unsuitable for highly repetitive collections. Our new techniques take one order of magnitude less space, yet they are also significantly slower than the fastest classical variants.

Our first simple method to take advantage of repetitiveness, `Rice-Runs`, makes an important leap in space, from 1%

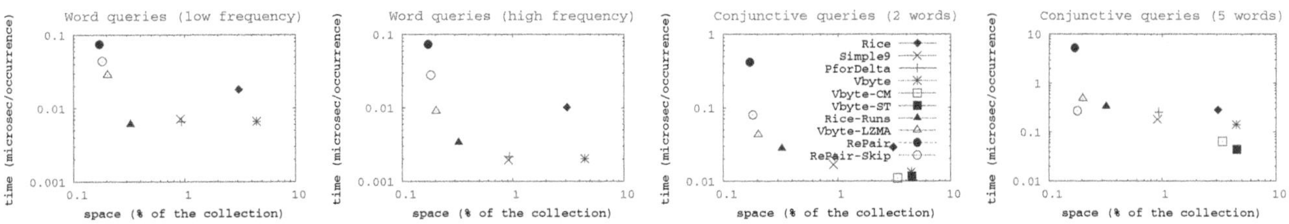

Figure 1: Space/time tradeoffs for non-positional indexes. Logscale.

taken by `Simple9` and `PforDelta` to around 0.3%. It takes one tenth the space of plain `Rice` and is at the same time faster, as it needs much less decompression work. It does not, however, get close to the space of stronger methods like `Vbyte-LZMA`, which achieves around 0.2% by exploiting other types of redundancy, but it is significantly faster than `Vbyte-LZMA` (up to 3 times). We recall that runs can only be exploited if we can arrange the versions consecutively.

`Vbyte-LZMA` is close to the smallest space that we can achieve. It is significantly faster than `RePair` (up to 10 times) and than `RePair-Skip` (up to 3 times) at word queries, as it decompresses faster the inverted list. However, on conjunctive queries, where many of the decoded values have to be discarded, the ability of `RePair-Skip` to skip nonterminals without decompressing them finally makes it almost twice as fast as `Vbyte-LZMA`, and even faster than `Rice-Runs`.

Note that `RePair` obtains lower space (85%) than `Vbyte-LZMA`, despite the fact that LZ77 compression is more powerful than Re-Pair. This is a consequence of LZMA exploiting only intra-list regularities, and shows that significant further repetitions are captured when considering the inter-list redundancies. The skipping information added to Re-Pair adds very little space (6%), but significantly improves time performance (almost 20 times faster on long phrases). This improvement occurs even on one-word queries (up to 2.6 times faster), since `RePair-Skip` does not need to carry out *rank* operations on R_B (recall Section 2.2).

Comparison with previous work. As described in Section 2.1, the best previous work for repetitive collections is by He et al. [12]. Our experiments show that they still obtain roughly half the space and time than `RePair-Skip`. The advantage of `RePair-Skip` is that it works for more general scenarios their techniques are not designed for.

6.2 Positional indexes

For this scenario we used an Intel(R) Xeon(R) E5335 CPU running at 2.00 GHz, 4 MB cache, 16 GB of RAM memory, 8 cores. The operating system installed is an Ubuntu GNU/Linux version 8.04.4 LTS running kernel 2.6.24-29-server (64 bits) and `g++` compiler version 4.2.4. Our code was compiled with the `-O9` directive. We measure user times.

Since self-indexes must reproduce the precise text, we cannot apply case folding nor any kind of filtering in this scenario. We index the original text as is. As explained, word-based self-indexes will regard (and index) the text as a sequence of words and separators. For fairness, the positional inverted indexes will index separators as valid words as well, and phrase queries will choose sequences of tokens, be they words or separators. Still, we note that character-based self-indexes will return more occurrences than word-based self-indexes (or than inverted indexes), as they report all the non-word-aligned ones too. Times per occurrence still seem comparable, yet they slightly favor character-based self-indexes since the time per occurrence drops as more occurrences are reported (there is a fixed time cost per query).

We consider the same techniques of the non-positional setting, now operating on position lists. We used sampling $k = 32$ for `Vbyte-CM` and $B = 64$ for `Vbyte-ST`. We had to adapt `Simple9` because it is unable to represent gaps longer than 2^{28}. While such gaps do not arise on document lists, they occur in position lists. We use the gap $2^{28} - 1$ as an escape code and then the next 32 bits represent the real gap. We exclude `PforDelta` because it has the same limitation, fixing it is more cumbersome, and its performance is not very different from that of `Simple9`. We also exclude `Rice-Runs`, as runs do not arise in the positional setting.

In order to compare fairly with self-indexes, we compress the text with Re-Pair without any sampling and add the space to that of the inverted indexes. This adds just 1.21% of the text size. Adding sampling would slightly increase this space and provide progressively faster extraction time.

We compare the self-indexes described in Section 5: `RLCSA` and `WCSA` (the curves come from using different sampling steps for internal data structures), `SLP` and `WSLP`, and `LZ77-index` and `LZend-index` (the latter using their minimum-space variant [14]). Figure 2 shows the space/time tradeoffs achieved for the four types of queries.

All classical inverted indexes achieve similar space, slightly over 35% ratio. `Simple9` is slightly faster than `Vbyte` for decompressing (i.e., one-word queries), yet `Vbyte` becomes much faster on phrases. Adding sampling, particularly `Vbyte-ST`, improves phrase query times significantly while almost not affecting the space. `Rice` is not competitive.

`RePair` and `RePair-Skip` achieve almost the same space, slightly below 30%, and the latter is always faster for the same reasons as on non-positional indexes. While for words `RePair-Skip` is slower than the classical methods, their times become similar on phrases.

The best space of inverted indexes is achieved by `Vbyte-LZMA`, which reaches a compression ratio near 10%. This represents a significant improvement upon the state of the art. Moreover, for single-word queries its times are only slightly worse than those of `RePair-Skip`, yet on phrase queries its need to fully decompress the list makes it clearly slower, and closer to the times of `Rice`.

Self-indexes are able to use much less space. `WSLP` is only slightly better than `SLP`. This shows that grammar-based compressors do not gain much from handling words instead of characters. They achieve 2%–3% compression ratio. This important reduction in space is paid with a sharp increase in search times. On words they are up to 500 times slower than `Vbyte-LZMA`. This gap, however, reduces to 50 times on 2-word queries and to 5 on 5-word queries. Self-indexes are usually mostly insensitive to the number of words in the

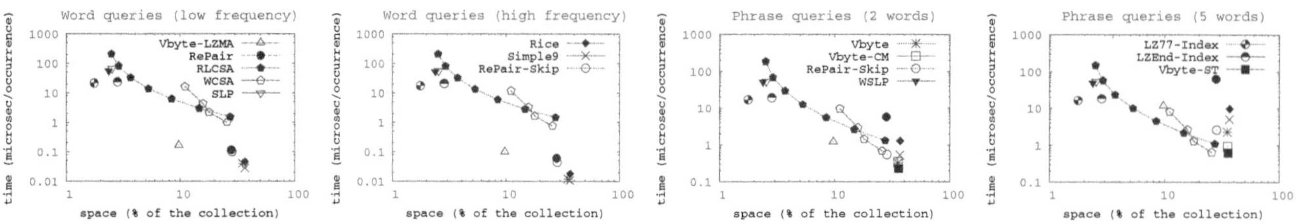

Figure 2: Space/time tradeoffs for positional indexes. Logscale.

query, whereas inverted indexes become much slower when looking for longer phrases.

The RLCSA offers a space/time tradeoff that goes from the space of SLP (where the latter is faster) to that of classical inverted indexes. These are faster for word searches, but slower as the search phrase becomes longer. The WCSA can be regarded as a word-based variant of the RLCSA, yet it is not so well optimized for highly repetitive sequences. It is indeed faster than RLCSA when using sufficient space. For that space, other indexes are much faster on word queries, but the WCSA retains a niche on phrase queries.

Finally, the LZ77-index achieves the least space, overcoming its variant LZend-index and grammar-based compressors both in time and space. The LZ77-index takes less than 2% space and answers queries in less than 20 microseconds per occurrence. Other indexes need at least twice its space to achieve faster query processing.

Acknowledgments

We thank J. He, J. Zeng, and T. Suel, for providing their input collection and help to use it.

This work was funded in part by NSERC of Canada and a David R. Cheriton Scholarship (FC); by Fondecyt Grant 1-110066, Chile (GN); by the Millennium Institute of Cell Dynamics and Biotechnology (ICDB), Grant ICM P05-001-F, Mideplan, Chile (GN and MMP); by Ministerio de Ciencia e Innovación, Grants TIN2009-14009-C02-02 (MMP), TIN2009-14560-C03-02 (AF), and CDTI CEN-20091048 (AF); and by Xunta de Galicia, Grant 2010/17 (AF).

7. REFERENCES

[1] V. Anh and A. Moffat. Inverted index compression using word-aligned binary codes. *Inf. Retr.*, 8:151–166, 2005.

[2] P. Anick and R. Flynn. Versioning a full-text information retrieval system. In *SIGIR*, pages 98–111, 1992.

[3] J. Barbay, A. López-Ortiz, and T. Lu. Faster adaptive set intersections for text searching. In *WEA*, pages 146–157, 2006.

[4] N. Brisaboa, A. Fariña, G. Navarro, A. Places, and E. Rodríguez. Self-indexing natural language. In *SPIRE*, pages 121–132, 2008.

[5] A. Broder, N. Eiron, M. Fontoura, M. Herscovici, R. Lempel, J. McPherson, R. Qi, and E. Shekita. Indexing shared content in information retrieval systems. In *EDBT*, pages 313–330, 2006.

[6] F. Claude, A. Fariña, M. Martínez-Prieto, and G. Navarro. Compressed q-gram indexing for highly repetitive biological sequences. In *BIBE*, pages 86–91, 2010.

[7] F. Claude and G. Navarro. Self-indexed text compression using straight-line programs. In *MFCS*, pages 235–246, 2009.

[8] J. Culpepper and A. Moffat. Compact set representation for information retrieval. In *SPIRE*, pages 137–148, 2007.

[9] S. Ding, J. Attenberg, and T. Suel. Scalable techniques for document identifier assignment in inverted indexes. In *WWW*, pages 311–320, 2010.

[10] R. González and G. Navarro. Compressed text indexes with fast locate. In *CPM*, pages 216–227, 2007.

[11] J. He, H. Yan, and T. Suel. Compact full-text indexing of versioned document collections. In *CIKM*, pages 415–424, 2009.

[12] J. He, J. Zeng, and T. Suel. Improved index compression techniques for versioned document collections. In *CIKM*, pages 1239–1248, 2010.

[13] S. Kreft and G. Navarro. LZ77-like compression with fast random access. In *DCC*, pages 239–248, 2010.

[14] S. Kreft and G. Navarro. Self-indexing based on LZ77. In *CPM*, pages 41–54, 2011.

[15] J. Larsson and A. Moffat. Off-line dictionary-based compression. *Proc. IEEE*, 88(11):1722–1732, 2000.

[16] V. Mäkinen, G. Navarro, J. Sirén, and N. Välimäki. Storage and retrieval of highly repetitive sequence collections. *J. Comp. Biol.*, 17(3):281–308, 2010.

[17] E. Moura, G. Navarro, N. Ziviani, and R. Baeza-Yates. Fast and flexible word searching on compressed text. *ACM Trans. Inf. Sys.*, 18(2):113–139, 2000.

[18] I. Munro. Tables. In *FSTTCS*, pages 37–42, 1996.

[19] G. Navarro and V. Mäkinen. Compressed full-text indexes. *ACM Comp. Surv.*, 39(1):article 2, 2007.

[20] W. Rytter. Application of Lempel-Ziv factorization to the approximation of grammar-based compression. In *CPM*, pages 20–31, 2002.

[21] K. Sadakane. New text indexing functionalities of the compressed suffix arrays. *J. Alg.*, 48(2):294–313, 2003.

[22] P. Sanders and F. Transier. Intersection in integer inverted indices. In *ALENEX*, 2007.

[23] H. Williams and J. Zobel. Compressing integers for fast file access. *The Comp. J.*, 42:193–201, 1999.

[24] J. Ziv and A. Lempel. A universal algorithm for sequential data compression. *IEEE Trans. Inf. Theory*, 23(3):337–343, 1977.

[25] J. Zobel and A. Moffat. Inverted files for text search engines. *ACM Comp. Surv.*, 38(2):article 6, 2006.

[26] M. Zukowski, S. Heman, N. Nes, and P. Boncz. Super-scalar RAM-CPU cache compression. In *ICDE*, page 59, 2006.

Partial Duplicate Detection for Large Book Collections

Ismet Zeki Yalniz
Dept. of Computer Science
University of Massachusetts
Amherst, MA, 01003
zeki@cs.umass.edu

Ethem F. Can
Dept. of Computer Science
University of Massachusetts
Amherst, MA, 01003
efcan@cs.umass.edu

R. Manmatha
Dept. of Computer Science
University of Massachusetts
Amherst, MA, 01003
manmatha@cs.umass.edu

ABSTRACT

A framework is presented for discovering partial duplicates in large collections of scanned books with optical character recognition (OCR) errors. Each book in the collection is represented by the sequence of words (in the order they appear in the text) which appear only once in the book. These words are referred to as "unique words" and they constitute a small percentage of all the words in a typical book. Along with the order information the set of unique words provides a compact representation which is highly descriptive of the content and the flow of ideas in the book. By aligning the sequence of unique words from two books using the longest common subsequence (LCS) one can discover whether two books are duplicates. Experiments on several datasets show that DUPNIQ is more accurate than traditional methods for duplicate detection such as shingling and is fast. On a collection of 100K scanned English books DUPNIQ detects partial duplicates in 30 min using 350 cores and has precision 0.996 and recall 0.833 compared to shingling with precision 0.992 and recall 0.720. The technique works on other languages as well and is demonstrated for a French dataset.

Categories and Subject Descriptors

H.3.3 [**Information Storage and Retrieval**]: Information Search and Retrieval; H.3.7 [**Digital Libraries**]: Collection, Systems Issues

General Terms

Algorithms, Experimentation

Keywords

partial duplicate detection, sequence matching, unique words

1. INTRODUCTION

This paper describes an approach to finding partial duplicates of documents. The focus here is on long noisy documents. By long it is meant book length rather than short messages, records, or short documents of the type seen on the web. The particular application here is to scanned and recognized books from collections such as the Internet Archive or Google Books but it also applies to government, company and legal documents. Partial duplicates help us to explore the relationships between books - for example which ones are multiple editions or versions of a given book.

Books are different from traditional web documents or the kinds of documents used in TREC. Different editions or versions of books are often not straight copies or near duplicates but may show a lot of variation. Such variations include new prefaces or introductions, additional footers and headers and formatting changes. Two editions of Shakespeare's Othello may differ substantially. For example, one may contain only the main text while a second variorum edition may contain only 30% of the main text on the page with the rest being footnotes. In addition there may be spelling changes and OCR errors. To simplify matters we will refer to this process of finding editions and versions as one of finding partial duplicates. Note that a near duplicate or an exact duplicate is a special case of a partial duplicate. It is not common to find near duplicates in books - both because of OCR errors and the addition of new material.

Books must preserve the linear progression of ideas for them to be valid duplicates. Re-ordering the chapters of a book such as Twain's Huckleberry Finn would either not make it meaningful or make it a different book. This structure is preserved even if material is inserted in the form of footnotes or a preface is inserted. One approach, therefore, to finding a duplicate is to consider each book as a sequence of words and do a full alignment. This has been suggested for various tasks such as finding plagiarized portions of documents [8, 11]. However, methods to fully align two texts are expensive even for papers (let alone books) and do not scale well to large collections. Most plagiarism detection techniques instead use a prefiltering stage which involves chunk overlap to detect possible duplicates before running a full alignment to detect which portions are duplicated [11].

We propose an alternative representations for finding partial duplicates efficiently for books which works for documents in the same language. We exploit the characteristics of language - specifically Zipf's law - to come up with a representation. The crux of the idea is to represent each document using the *sequence of unique words* in the document (not in the collection). By unique words we mean words which occur only once in the document. A sequence is created from the unique words by following their natural

CIKM'11, October 24–28, 2011, Glasgow, Scotland, UK.

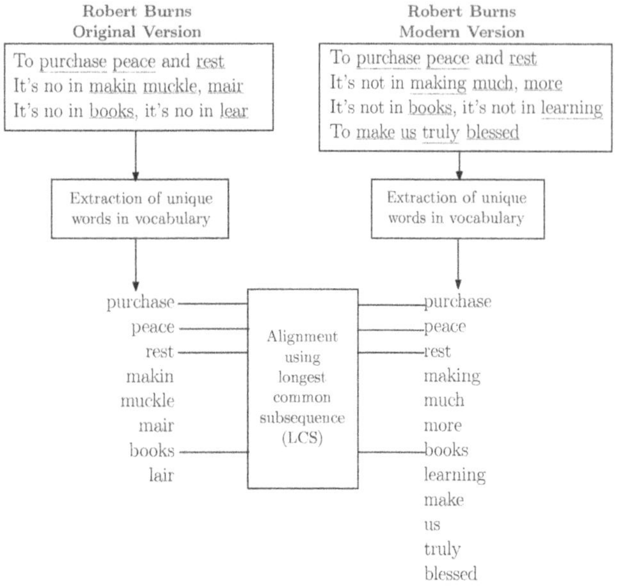

Figure 1: Illustration of partial duplicate detection. Two versions of Robert Burns' poem. Unique words are underlined in the text. The two sequences of unique words are aligned using LCS.

order in the document. Two documents are similar if their sequences are similar [1]. Figure 1 shows two versions of a portion of Robert Burns' poem. For each document, the sequence of unique words is shown from top to bottom.

This representation is compact since unique words are a small percent of all the words in the document. A typical 100K word English book has around 2-3K unique words. Two books are compared by finding the longest common subsequence (LCS) between the two unique word sequences. Since the LCS is done over the sequence of unique words and not over the sequence of all words, the alignment time is drastically reduced. There are additional characteristics of this representation which make the alignment even more efficient and it will be discussed later. For a 100K dataset of books (over 5 billion book pairs), DUPNIQ has a precision of 0.996 and a recall of 0.833. It is more accurate than a 0 mod p shingling technique with p = 50 and 4-grams which has a precision of 0.992 and a recall of 0.720. Our technique is also fast and comparable to shingling in terms of speed. Total processing time for the 100K dataset is 30 min on a 350 core cluster. Experiments over several data sets are also reported including a collection of French books.

There are many uses of such duplicate detection work. The humanities and library communities have a great interest in aggregating works and finding all versions of say Shakespeare's Othello. IFLA's Functional Requirements for Bibliographic Records (FRBR) proposes that the new generation of cataloging systems will include works aggregation [21]. Search engines such as those at the Internet Archive could collapse duplicate books or show the most appropriate work in a set of duplicates - for example an ordinary reader may prefer an uncommented version while a scholar might want a commented version.

[1]Unlike web documents, books don't have the problem of dealing with spammers who might create documents containing only unique words.

In the next section, we characterize the problem of duplicate detection. This is followed by a review of the literature. Section 4 discusses how to find duplicates explaining the unique word representation, the sequence alignment and the scoring used. Datasets and experiments are described next. Finally, we conclude and point to future research directions.

2. PROBLEM CHARACTERIZATION

Our aim here is to find segments of texts which are partial duplicates - for example, this may include an entire book, the main text of a Shakespeare play, a story from a selection of short stories or long excerpts. We exclude quotations or short passages the reason being that a quotation may be used almost anywhere (see [23] on finding quotations). Documents on the same topic (e.g. optics) are not necessarily duplicates so our problem is different from topic detection.

Figure 2 illustrates the variety of duplicates. These images are a selection of duplicates found by the 100K dataset. A full alignment was done on each pair of duplicates. The lengths show the relative lengths of the two book pairs. The books are binned and if the alignment density of a bin is greater than 50% the bin is green, otherwise it is red. Note that the actual play is only a third of the (bottom) Tempest book in Figures 2(b) and 2(c). The figures show that even small portions of duplicates in books can be found even when the metadata gives little hint that the books are duplicates.

Sometimes one may have two collections of short stories with some overlapping stories. However, the overlapping stories may not have the same order in both books. Note that we just need one short story to do the duplicate detection. Identifying which portion of each book aligns (the full alignment task) is more complicated but that is not the focus of this paper. Certain books like dictionaries, word lists and encyclopedias have an unusually large number of unique words which follow an alphabetical order. This leads to many false matches. Our focus is not on such books.

Note that metadata is not a good solution to finding duplicates since it is often erroneous. Even when correct it is not easy to tell two books are duplicates. Table 1 shows three versions of Shakespeare's Othello. It is not easy to find an automatic algorithm (which works for all books) which will tell from the metadata alone that all contain Shakespeare's Othello. Exact title matches may not also always indicate duplicates. For example, there are two books titled "1914" - one a book of fiction while another is a non-fiction book.

3. RELATED WORK

Several approaches have been previously studied for finding duplicates in different contexts. One well-known application, the Unix program "diff" [17] first creates chunks from each line and then computes the LCS between two sequences of chunks. It works well for comparing different versions of source codes but fails for finding duplicates in scanned book collections because of noise (OCR errors) and variations in line formatting which cause chunks not to be consistent across books.

Most of the work in near duplicate detection involves using either fingerprinting algorithms or using relative frequency techniques (based on using words with similar frequencies) [3]. The fingerprint techniques [3, 5] assume that each document can be broken up into "distinctive" chunks or shingles and two documents which have a large number of chunks

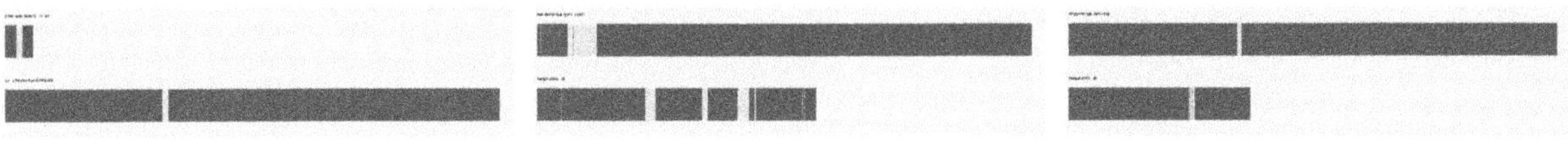

(a) (b) (c)

Figure 2: Examples of duplication. Green bars show matching portions of text with 50% or above word overlap. (a) The book Points of Humour (top) contains a selection of verses from the Complete Works of Robert Burns (bottom). (b) Tales from Shakespeare (top) contains selections from Shakespeare's plays including the Tempest (bottom). (c) Clegg's Elocutionist (top) contains a wide selection of texts including a passage from the Tempest (bottom).

#	Creator	Title
1	No Author	Shakespeare's Tragedy of Othello
2	William Shakespeare and H. H. Furness	A New Variorum Edition of Shakespeare
3	Wiliam Shakespeare, Tommaso Salvini and James Henry Mapleson	Othello: A Tragedy in Five Acts

Table 1: Internet Archive catalogue records for *Othello*

in common are likely to be similar to each other compared to documents which only have a small number in common. Chunks are created by n-grams of words or characters. Note that this is more likely to make the chunks unique since an n-gram is less common than the original word. Hash-keys are generated by hashing the chunks and then indexed using an inverted file (sometimes the chunks are also indexed). Since a document can contain a large number of chunks, most algorithms subsample this set of chunks and differences in sampling strategy distinguish the various approaches [16]. Several sampling techniques have been tried such as full sampling, random sampling, picking every k^{th} chunk [14]. Another approach windows the chunks [22] by picking the chunk with the lowest hash-key as a window is moved over the document. [3] use the fact that every sub-chunk of a duplicated chunk must be non-unique to reduce the number of chunks in multiple passes. Other chunking algorithms include those by [4, 20, 25]. The sub-sampling required in practice means that many of these algorithms do not work as well [3] when the documents are only partial duplicates or noisy OCR output is considered. I-Match [7] extracts words with certain statistical characteristics and hashes their aggregation. These hash values are compared to determine duplication. Talent [9] similarly finds certain kinds of content words and hashes them. Note that both I-Match and Talent use collection statistics rather than individual document statistics as done here. Charikar [6] applied a random projection based method - essentially locality sensitive hashing on the terms of a document - to find near duplicates and Henzinger [15] applied this to the web domain. Hajishirzi et al. [13] also worked on near duplicates by representing each document as a sparse ngram vector and learning the weights depending on the similarity measure being optimized.

Relative frequency techniques assume that two documents with similar words and frequencies must be similar or duplicated [16, 24] and claim to be more accurate than chunking based methods. Local text reuse is a related problem where the duplicates may not be exact. [23] used a Discrete Cosine Transform (DCT) fingerprinting algorithm for this problem.

In plagiarism detection full alignment has been used to find plagiarized passages [8] but is impractical for long documents and large collections. For example, eTBLAST was used to align Medline abstracts [11] but is too computationally expensive for whole documents and instead an essentially chunking based approach was used.

The idea of using sequences of unique words to find duplicates is an extension of Feng and Manmatha's work [12]. Given the OCR output and the ground truth text, Feng and Manmatha find OCR errors with a HMM based alignment approach using unique words as anchors. This approach was later used by Stewart et al. [26] for OCR error correction.

4. FRAMEWORK

The duplicate detection framework DUPNIQ consists of two stages. In the first stage unique words in the document along with their relative positions are extracted from the documents. For efficiency this is done once for every book in the entire collection and thus the process is linear in the number of documents. For a collection consisting of 100K books, it takes about 3.5 min on a cluster of 350 cores to extract and record lists of unique words sorted by their original order in documents. In the second stage the sequences of unique words from two books is compared using an alignment algorithm. If the duplication score is greater than a threshold, the pair is classified as a duplicate. Although there are $d(d-1)/2$ book pairs in a collection of size d, pair-wise comparisons can be done rapidly.

4.1 Extraction of Unique Words

Each book in the collection is represented by the sequence of words (in the order they appear in the text) which appear only once in the context of the book. These words are referred to as "unique words" and they constitute a small percent of all the words in a typical book. The representation is tolerant to OCR errors. While an OCR error may map a non-unique word to a unique word, it is unlikely that two books will have the same corrupted word let alone in the same position in the sequence. Punctuation and numeric characters are removed since the recognition accuracy and consistency is low for them. This also eliminates page numbers which may not be consistent across books but can form a sequence of their own. In addition, the unique words are fairly frequent further reducing the effect of OCR errors and other noise. In a book of 100K words, every second sentence of the document contains a unique word.

4.2 Sequence Matching

Each pair of books in the collection is compared using the sequence of their unique words. The aim is to find the longest subsequence (LCS) of unique words which preserves

Table 2: DUPNIQ-cs and DUPNIQ-its scores for three pairs of books. X and Y refer to the sequences of unique words for Book X and Book Y respectively. GT is the ground truth.

Book X	Book Y	|X|	|Y|	$\|X \cap Y\|$	|LCS|	DUPNIQ-cs	DUPNIQ-its	GT
Shakespeare's Law; S. G. Greenwood	Shakespeare's Law; S. G. Greenwood	1482	1563	1406	1404	0.922	0.979	Yes
Departmental ditties and other verses; R. Kipling	Departmental ditties ballads barrackroom ballads & other verses; R. Kipling	1787	4512	955	739	0.260	0.765	Yes
Metrical Translations; J. Muir	Ausonius	7526	12695	689	53	0.005	0.400	No

the same order in both books. The problem turns out to be a search for the longest common subsequence between the sequences. The length of the LCS is a good indication of duplication between two books (see Figure 1).

There are a number of LCS algorithms in the literature. The standard dynamic programming algorithm has $O(mn)$ time and space requirements, where m and n are the lengths of the two input sequences. There are also algorithms requiring $O(mn)$ time and linear space for computing the LCS. There is also a $O(nloglogn)$ time algorithm with the restriction that no word appears more than once within either input string [18]. This algorithm is actually suitable for the duplication detection case since input sequences are composed of only unique words. For a more detailed discussion on longest common subsequences, please refer to [10].

It is not necessary to compute the LCS length for each book pair in the collection. Given the duplication threshold, it is possible to solve for a lower bound for the LCS length L which makes the book pair a duplicate. If the total number of common unique words between the two sequences is less than L, then the pair is guaranteed to have a duplication score which is below the threshold and therefore the pair can be skipped without any alignment. It is observed that less than 1% of book pairs in the collection pass this test. This test, therefore, provides a considerable speed-up. It is also not necessary to compute the LCS over the entire sequences of unique words. The reason is that a word must appear in both sequences to be in the LCS. Therefore, LCS is run over the sequence of unique words which appear in both sequences [10]. Table 2 shows that the number of common words $X \cap Y$ is much smaller than the unique words in either sequence.

4.3 Scoring Function

The LCS length is used to detect duplicates. However, the LCS length is a function of book length and needs to be normalized. Below two normalization schemes are proposed. Other approaches involving normalizing the LCS length by the minimum or average of the lengths of the two sequences did not work well and therefore, are not reported.

4.3.1 Correlation Score (CS)

The CS score for two (unique word) sequences X and Y is defined by analogy with correlation as:

$$cs(X,Y) = \frac{|LCS(X,Y)|}{\sqrt{(|X||Y|)}} \tag{1}$$

where $|LCS(X,Y)|$ is the LCS length of the two sequences. $|X|$ and $|Y|$ denote the length of X and Y respectively. The range of values is [0,1] and the highest score is obtained when the two sequences are identical.

4.3.2 Information Theoretic Score (ITS)

From an information theoretic point of view, the similarity between two objects X and Y maybe defined as [19]:

$$similarity(X,Y) = \frac{\log \Pr(common(X,Y))}{\log \Pr(description(X,Y))} \tag{2}$$

where X and Y are any objects generated by a probabilistic model. According to the formula, two objects are more similar if they share more features. The similarity value is maximized when the two objects are identical.

In our case, X and Y are sequences of unique words. The overlapping content between X and Y is defined by the longest common subsequence:

$$common(X,Y) = LCS(X,Y) \tag{3}$$

and the total information content (description) of X and Y is defined by the alignment of X and Y. Assuming that the probability of any word sequence is inversely proportional to its length, then Eq.2 simplifies as:

$$its(X,Y) = \frac{\log |LCS(X,Y)|}{\log (|X| + |Y| - |LCS(X,Y)|)} \tag{4}$$

The score has a range [0,1] and the maximum value is obtained when the sequences are identical. If $|X|$ and $|Y|$ have no common words, then the score is assumed to be zero.

Table 2 shows two duplicates (first two rows) and a non-duplicate. Duplicates have higher LCS scores and higher DUPNIQ-cs and DUPNIQ-its scores. The thresholds are 0.12 and 0.72 for DUPNIQ-cs and DUPNIQ-its respectively.

5. SYNTHETIC EXPERIMENTS

Synthetic documents are generated for investigating the effect of OCR errors and the amount of overlapping text between two books. A pair of texts is created as follows: A clean (without OCR errors) book from the Project Gutenberg website [2] is used as a reference text. The second text is created by replacing a random portion of the reference text with a sample from another book from the Gutenberg website while ensuring that its length remains the same. A specified amount of character level document noise is added to the second text to simulate OCR errors creating a synthetic document [12]. DUPNIQ-cs and DUPNIQ-its scores are computed between the synthetic and reference book. Experiments are performed 20 times and the scores are averaged. Two different scenarios are experimented: In the first scenario two different books on different topics by different authors are used to generate the reference and the synthetic documents. In the second scenario, the same process is applied using two different novels from the same writer (Joseph A. Altsheler) on the same subject (Civil War). Figure 3

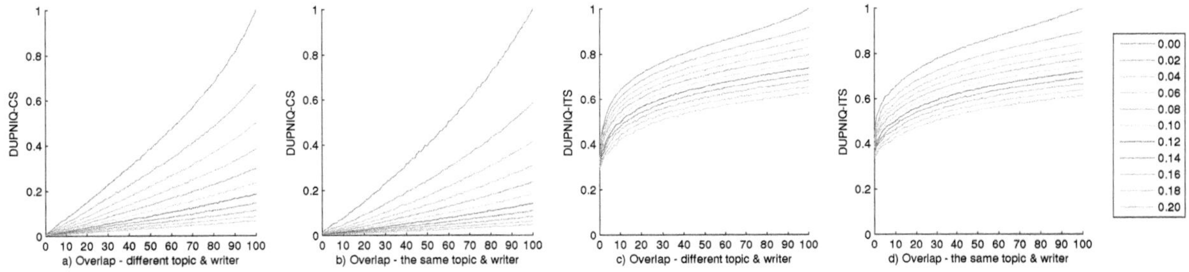

Figure 3: DUPNIQ-its and DUPNIQ-cs versus percentage of overlap and character level document noise. Each line in the plot represents results for the given amount of noise. Note that word error rate is around 75% for 20% character level noise.

shows the duplication scores as the amount of noise and the percentage of text overlap are varied for both scenarios. It is seen that the duplication score does not significantly depend on which scenario is used. DUPNIQ-cs is more sensitive to OCR errors as the amount of noise increases.

6. DUPLICATION EXPERIMENTS

Books from the Internet Archive (IA) [1] were used to construct datasets of various sizes in English and French. The datasets are diverse and include religious books, literary works, technical reports, engineering books, and novels. Language identification was run on all datasets to ensure that the dominant language of each book is as desired. Some of these datasets will be made publicly available at http://ciir.cs.umass.edu/downloads/

The **Training Set** consists of 151 English books containing 67 duplicate pairs labeled manually. This set is used to learn duplicate detection thresholds. The **1K Set** consists of 1,092 English books containing 258 duplicate pairs. The **3K Set** consists of 2,884 French books containing 483 duplicate pairs. The ground truth for 1K and 3K sets are created using a manual technique. The **100K Set** is a large dataset consisting 103,455 English books containing 45,485 duplicate pairs. A major challenge is to estimate the ground truth for this dataset. Metadata alone is not sufficient to create the ground truth since it may be missing, incorrect or incomplete. We made a best effort approach to finding the groundtruth duplicates in this dataset by pooling the outputs of the three different techniques (i.e. DUPNIQ-cs, DUPNIQ-its, and Shingling). Pooling is the strategy used by TREC to judge relevant documents. For pooling we use a lower threshold than the one we estimated on the training set to identify candidate duplicate pairs. Then we do a full alignment on those candidate pairs which is guaranteed to align all duplicate parts. By analyzing the results of the full alignment experiments, we created a subset from the candidate pairs and used the subset as ground truth. In the future we expect to improve the groundtruth on this set. The **Partial Set** has 458 books and tests how well the techniques work on partial duplicates. There are 460 partial duplicate pairs (e.g. ranging from 15% to 80% of a book).

6.1 Evaluation

The threshold is taken to be the value which maximizes the F-measure (the harmonic mean of recall and precision) on the training set. This threshold is used for all datasets including the French dataset.

We considered four baselines - the overlap of unique words (UWO), the overlap of vocabulary words (VO), a 0 mod p Shingling algorithm [3, 20] and I-match. Jaccard similarity is used for the first three. For shingling we tried ngrams with n=2, 4 and 8 and p = 10, 25 and 50. The best shingling results over all datasets were obtained for n=4, p=50 and are reported below. I-match performed poorly. This is understandable given that books are very rarely near duplicates and contain a lot of OCR and other errors. We note that VO - the overlap of vocabulary words - does much better than I-match (see below) indicating that the problem is the global hash function in I-match is sensitive to even small numbers of vocabulary words being wrong (in other words noisy words are found at a variety of IDF values and can't easily be filtered out). We do not discuss I-match further. For the other baselines thresholds are estimated by maximizing the F-measure over the training set as for DUPNIQ.

We provide precision and recall scores for different methods on the datasets in Table 3. For the smaller datasets, DUPNIQ-its did best in terms of F-measure while DUPNIQ-cs did slightly better for the 100K dataset. While shingling did reasonably well on the smaller datasets it did not perform well on the 100K dataset. It is interesting to note that a threshold trained on English books does fine on a French dataset. On the 100K set DUPNIQ-cs and DUPNIQ-its did much better than any other technique in terms of F-measure (DUPNIQ-cs - 0.918, DUPNIQ-its - 0.907, UWO - 0.724, VO - 0.552, Shingling - 0.834). We can understand the performance of the top 3 techniques better by looking at their performance on the Partial dataset. As the results show, both DUPNIQ techniques work better than shingling. DUPNIQ-its, in particular, is a lot better than shingling on partial duplicates. DUPNIQ-its has better performance over DUPNIQ-cs and it is consistent with the synthetic experiments. Between UWO and VO, UWO is the best on most counts. Besides, UWO is much faster since it has many fewer words to deal with.

Results on the 100K set show that some duplicates are missed by DUPNIQ-its and DUPNIQ-cs because their score is slightly lower than the threshold even though they have a high LCS length. This indicates that there is scope for further improvement in length normalization. It may also help to use a larger training set to compute the threshold. 14% of the false negatives are due to dictionaries and encyclopedias. As mentioned before the technique is not meant to work on such books because of their alphabetical ordering. 16% of the false matches are religious book pairs (e.g. gospels, hymns, and prayer books), 12% are literary books, and 6% of them are technical book pairs. The flavor of re-

Table 3: Precision (P) and Recall (R) scores for Training, 1K, 3K, 100K and Partial sets.

Dataset	Training Set		1K Set		3K Set		100k Set		Partial Set	
	P	R	P	R	P	R	P	R	P	R
DUPNIQ-cs	0.971	0.985	**1.000**	0.945	0.940	0.940	0.903	**0.933**	0.989	0.808
DUPNIQ-its	**1.000**	0.985	**1.000**	**0.957**	**0.991**	**0.944**	**0.996**	0.833	**0.995**	**0.919**
UWO	0.956	0.970	0.979	0.937	0.833	0.915	0.593	0.929	-	-
VO	0.970	0.940	0.987	0.887	0.958	0.722	0.440	0.741	-	-
Shingling	0.971	**1.000**	0.983	0.941	0.932	0.892	0.992	0.720	0.963	0.799

sults obtained is similar to that shown in Figure 2. There are also some unusual duplicates. For example, two technical reports published by Johns Hopkins University matched because they contained very similar mailing distribution lists at the end.

7. CONCLUSIONS

The sequence of unique words in a document is proposed as a representation for long documents. In this context, a long document is considered to be one which has at least a few pages of text. The effectiveness of our approach is shown for finding partial duplicates on different datasets in different languages at different scales. Experiments also show that the proposed approach is quite scalable. Although it checks every pair of documents in the collection, partial duplicates can be found in a 100K dataset of books in 30 min on a 350 core cluster with high precision and recall figures. Future work includes further speed-ups, extensions to multiple languages and mapping duplicated portions to each other.

8. ACKNOWLEDGMENTS

We thank James Allan, Bruce Croft and David Smith for discussions and Marek Blat and Logan Giorda for helping with annotations. This work was supported in part by the Center for Intelligent Information Retrieval and in part by NSF grant #IIS-0910884. Any opinions, findings and conclusions or recommendations expressed in this material are the authors' and do not necessarily reflect those of the sponsor.

9. REFERENCES

[1] Internet Archive. http://www.archive.org, 2010.
[2] Project Gutenberg. http://www.gutenberg.org, 2010.
[3] Y. Bernstein and J. Zobel. A scalable system for identifying co-derivative documents. In *SPIRE*, pages 55–67, 2004.
[4] S. Brin, J. Davis, and H. Garcia-Molina. Copy detection mechanisms for digital documents. In *ACM SIGMOD*, pages 398–409, 1995.
[5] A. Z. Broder, S. C. Glassman, M. S. Manasse, and G. Zweig. Syntactic clustering of the web. *Computer Networks*, 29(8-13):1157–1166, 1997.
[6] M. S. Charikar. Similarity estimation techniques from rounding algorithms. In *34th Ann. ACM Symp. on Theory of computing*, pages 380–388, 2002.
[7] A. Chowdhury, O. Frieder, D. A. Grossman, and M. C. McCabe. Collection statistics for fast duplicate document detection. *ACM Trans. Inf. Syst.*, 20(2):171–191, 2002.
[8] P. Clough. Old and new challenges in automatic plagiarism detection. National UK Plagiarism Advisory Service, http://www.ir.shef.ac.uk/cloughie/papers/pas_plagiarism.pdf, 2003.
[9] J. Cooper, A. Coden, and E. Brown. Detecting similar documents using salient terms. In *CIKM*, pages 245–251, 2002.
[10] S. Deorowicz. Solving longest common subsequence and related problems on graphical processing units. *Softw. Pract. Exper.*, 40:673–700, July 2010.
[11] M. Errami, Z. Sun, A. C. George, T. C. Long, M. A. Skinner, J. D. Wren, and H. R. Garner. Identifying duplicate content using statistically improbable phrases. *Bioinformatics*, 26(11):1453–1457, 2010.
[12] S. Feng and R. Manmatha. A hierarchical, HMM-based automatic evaluation of OCR accuracy for a digital library of books. In *JCDL*, pages 109–118, 2006.
[13] H. Hajishirzi, W. tau Yih, and A. Kolcz. Adaptive near-duplicate detection via similarity learning. In *SIGIR'10*, pages 419–426, 2010.
[14] N. Heintze. Scalable document fingerprinting. In *USENIX Workshop on Electronic Commerce*, 1996.
[15] M. Henzinger. Finding near-duplicate web pages: a large-scale evaluation of algorithms. In *ACM SIGIR*, pages 284–291, 2006.
[16] T. C. Hoad and J. Zobel. Methods for identifying versioned and plagiarized documents. *JASIST*, 54(3):203–215, 2003.
[17] J. W. Hunt and M. D. McIlroy. An algorithm for differential file comparison. Technical Report CSTR 41, Bell Laboratories, Murray Hill, NJ, 1976.
[18] J. W. Hunt and T. G. Szymanski. A fast algorithm for computing longest common subsequences. *Commun. ACM*, 20:350–353, May 1977.
[19] D. Lin. An information-theoretic definition of similarity. In *ICML '98*, pages 296–304, 1998.
[20] U. Manber. Finding similar files in a large file system. In *USENIX Winter 1994 Tech. Conf*, pages 1–10, 1994.
[21] D. Mimno, G. Crane, and A. Jones. Hierarchical catalog records: Implementing a FRBR catalog. In *D-Lib Magazine, http://www.dlib.org/dlib/october05/crane/10crane.html*, volume 11, Oct 2005.
[22] S. Schleimer, D. Wilkerson, and A. Aiken. Winnowing: local algorithms for document fingerprinting. In *ACM SIGMOD conference*, pages 76–85, 2003.
[23] J. Seo and W. B. Croft. Local text reuse detection. In *ACM SIGIR*, pages 571–578, 2008.
[24] N. Shivakumar and H. Garcia-Molina. Scam: A copy detection mechanism for digital documents. In *Ann. Conf. on the Theory and Practice of Digital Libraries*, 1995.
[25] N. Shivakumar and H. Garcia-Molina. Finding near-replicas of documents on the web. In *Intl. Workshop on the World Wide Web and Databases*, 1999.
[26] G. Stewart, G. Crane, and A. Babeu. A new generation of textual corpora: mining corpora from very large collections. In *JCDL*, pages 356–365, 2007.

This Image Smells Good: Effects of Image Information Scent in Search Engine Results Pages

Faidon Loumakis
Fluent Interaction Ltd.
17g Clerkenwell Road
London EC1M 5RD
faidon@fluent-interaction.co.uk

Simone Stumpf
Centre for HCI Design
City University London
London EC1V 0HB
Simone.Stumpf.1@city.ac.uk

David Grayson
Fluent Interaction Ltd.
17g Clerkenwell Road
London EC1M 5RD
dave@fluent-interaction.co.uk

ABSTRACT

Users are confronted with an overwhelming amount of web pages when they look for information on the Internet. Current search engines already aid the user in their information seeking tasks by providing textual results but adding images to results pages could further help the user in judging the relevance of a result. We investigated this problem from an Information Foraging perspective and we report on two empirical studies that focused on the information scent of images. Our results show that images have their own distinct "smell" which is not as strong as that of text. We also found that combining images and text cues leads to a stronger overall scent. Surprisingly, when images were added to search engine results pages, this did not lead our participants to behave significantly differently in terms of effectiveness or efficiency. Even when we added images that could confuse the participants' scent, this had no significantly detrimental impact on their behaviour. However, participants expressed a preference for results pages which included images. We discuss potential challenges and point to future research to ensure the success of adding images to textual results in search engine results pages.

Categories and Subject Descriptors

H.3.5 [**Information Storage and Retrieval**]: On-line Information Services – *Web-based services*, H.5.2 [**Information Interfaces and Presentation**]: User Interfaces – *screen design, H.1.2 User/Machine Systems – Human Information Processing.*

General Terms

Human Factors, Theory, Design.

Keywords

Information foraging, information scent, search engine results pages, images, visual search, usability.

1. INTRODUCTION

There are currently billions of web pages, presenting the user with an overwhelming amount of information to be sifted through during their information seeking tasks. To aid users in finding the information that they are looking for, modern search engines retrieve results based on keyword queries and present them in a ranked list which usually gives details of the page title, URL and a short text snippet. In order to further help the user judge the results' relevance in search engine results pages (SERPs), some search engines now also add a visual representation of the target page, for example, a page preview (Figure 1) gives a thumbnail visual representation of the result page. In addition to page thumbnails, there are also other approaches that aim to visually summarise the content of the target page by providing representative images [11].

Text results and visual representations in SERPs can be viewed as components within Information Foraging Theory [15, 16, 19]. Information Foraging posits that users will seek out information patches with the strongest scent, where the strength of scent is determined by textual and visual cues from the environment, reflecting the cue's relevance to the search task. In SERPs, scent can come from text cues – the text in the title, the URL and the text snippets – and also visual cues, such as styling of text or associated images. While textual cues have been explored extensively from an Information Foraging perspective, visual cues on the other hand, especially the role of images in providing scent, have received scant attention.

This paper describes two empirical studies which investigated scent of images and the effects of adding visual cues in the form of images to SERPs on user behaviour. Our first study aimed to *determine information scent for images* and *investigate the relationship between the presence of text and images in information scent.* Our second study built on these findings to further investigate adding images to SERPs. This second study explored *the effect of adding images to SERPs in terms of user effectiveness, efficiency and satisfaction.*

Previous work has attended to retrieved objects' relevance for a topical area within a work task and users' assessment of intellectual topicality [2]. Our approach has a different focus. We explore the usefulness of images as a visual representation of the results page when added to textual results. In our search tasks we assume the user is looking for textual information, not searching for images specifically.

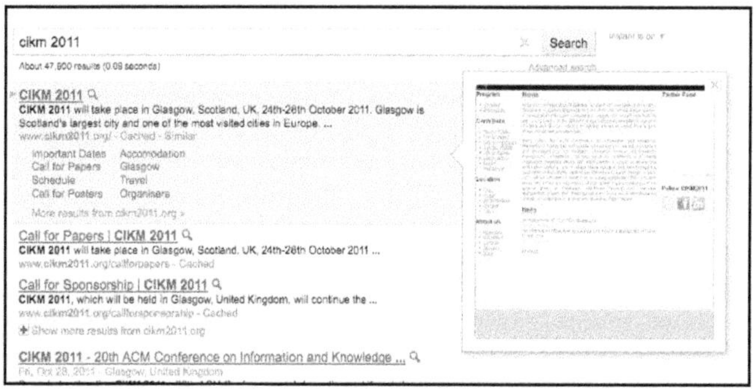

Figure 1. Search results in Google. This interface makes use of a number of scent cues: Textual cues (e.g. text snippets, URL, etc.) and visual cues (e.g. text styling, page preview image).

CIKM'11, October 24–28, 2011, Glasgow, Scotland, UK.

In the remainder of this paper, we will explore previous research relevant to Information Foraging and the presentation of SERPs. We then present the set-up and results of our first study, followed by the methods and findings for our second study. We end with an overall discussion of the combined findings from both studies and directions for future work.

2. RELATED WORK

2.1 Information Foraging

Information Foraging Theory [15, 16, 19] aims to explain how information seekers navigate information environments such as the web, drawing on an analogy of how animals forage for food. According to this theory, users forage for information by seeking out information patches, e.g. web pages, drawn by the patch's "scent". The strength of scent is determined by textual and visual cues, and it is argued that if scent decreases or is not strong enough, users will move on to the next information patch.

Models built on this theory have been used to predict user behaviour during the information seeking process [5, 10, 13, 18] and also to predict the information scent for specific interfaces and web pages [1, 6, 7]. However, in these models involving information scent, visual cues are mostly ignored. Although information scent has been recognised as an important concept in interface design [24], no studies have been carried out that leverage Information Foraging for making design decisions involving SERPs with images.

2.2 Search Engine Results Pages

Current SERPs usually present textual cues in the form of words in the page title, URL, text snippet, etc., combined with some visual cues such as text styling and visual treatment. More recently, other visual cues such as page previews have been added. Research into the presentation of SERPs has shown the importance of the length of text snippets on a user's click behaviour [9], however, what matters to a user in the presentation of results is strongly tied to the user's task [9, 20]. Search tasks can be categorised into informational, navigational, and transactional types [3]. In this paper, we focus on informational tasks, i.e. how to find pages that contain relevant information, and will not further discuss navigational tasks, e.g. how to re-find pages using SERPs.

Visual cues are often combined with text such as colour styling on sponsored ads, text size, and so on, to draw attention to them. Styling needs to be carefully used because, whilst it can increase users' efficiency, it may also interfere if it draws attention to the wrong item [21]. However, some research has also suggested that styling does not override textual cues in users' information seeking behaviour [4].

Visual cues can also come from images associated with search results. Again, there are problems with using this type of cue in SERPs. Woodruf et al. [25, 26] compared textually enhanced thumbnails of target pages, plain thumbnails and text as elements of a SERP. Results showed that enhanced thumbnails proved to be more consistently successful than plain thumbnails. When presenting users with visual summaries in addition to text results, users have been shown to be less effective in finding relevant information [14].

Our studies in contrast focus on the scent of images, and compare them to textual cues. In addition, we were interested in the behaviour of users when the scent of images is manipulated in SERPs. Our studies therefore contribute to deepening the understanding of image scent, the impact of images on users' information foraging behaviour and the design of SERPs extended with images.

3. STUDY 1: INFORMATION SCENT OF IMAGES

How can we determine the scent of an image, and how does it compare to the scent of text? In this first study, we aimed to measure information scent for images and investigate the relationship between cues from text and images in information scent.

3.1 Methodology

There are two main approaches to measuring information scent. The most common way is to use independent human judges to rate scent on a scale [16, 19]. The second is to use algorithms which automatically assign scent based on keywords found in the text using a model-driven approach [12, 17]. There is currently no automatic way to determine the information scent of an image, thus our study used human judges to rate the images.

Previous studies involving human judges of scent used between four and ten judges [19]. Since images can be more ambiguous than text, we decided to use a much higher number of judges by distributing a scent rating elicitation tool (SRET) over the Internet. Invitations to take part were distributed via email, Facebook and Twitter. Participants who completed all the tasks in the SRET were offered the chance to enter a competition to win a £30 voucher from Amazon.co.uk. In total, we had 81 participants.

We presented a series of questions to participants, stimulating an information need and mimicking a search task. Topic familiarity has previously been shown to influence the rating of relevance criteria [22], thus we chose questions so that that they covered a wide breadth of topics and so that it would be unlikely that the participants would know the answers. In total we asked eight questions:

1. *What is the problem with the antenna of the iPhone 4 and how can it be fixed?*
2. *What is the length of a Japanese bullet train?*
3. *Where does the blobfish live?*
4. *How many stairs does the Eiffel tower have?*
5. *What is the maximum speed a cheetah can reach?*
6. *When (day, month, year) did Martin Luther King deliver the famous "I have a dream" speech?*
7. *Who invented the pen Bic and how did they come up with the idea?*
8. *What is the address of the Google offices in London?*

For each question, we provided a number of "search results" i.e. cues that may lead to a target page on which to find the right answer. These cues were presented in three cue treatments:

- *Text-only* cues, where the cue showed a link with the title of the result, a text snippet, and a URL,
- *Image-only* cues, where the cue was a visual representation of the results page information,

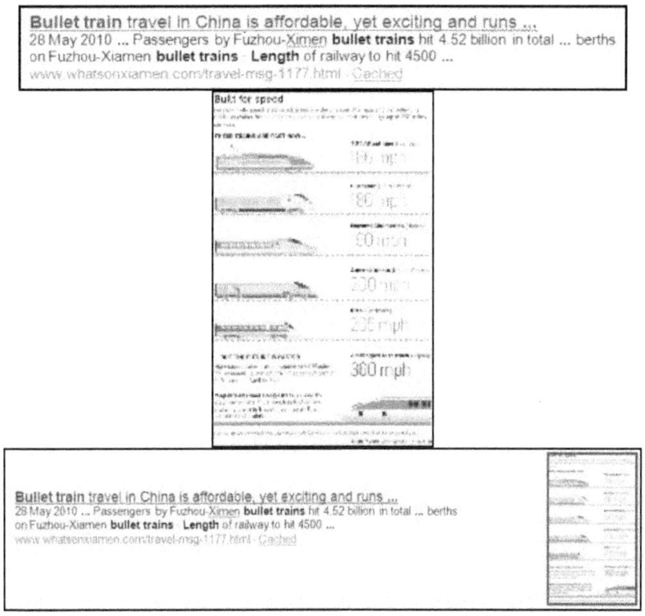

Figure 2. Cue treatments: Text-only cue (top), Image-only cue (middle), Text+Image cue (bottom) for *Bullet train* question.

Table 1 – Query keywords used to retrieve cues for questions.

Question	Query keywords
What is the problem with the antenna of the iPhone 4 and how can it be fixed?	iPhone 4 antenna problem
What is the length of a Japanese bullet train?	Bullet train length
Where does the blobfish live?	Blobfish
How many stairs does the Eiffel tower have?	Eiffel tower stairs
What is the maximum speed a cheetah can reach?	Cheetah
When (day, month, year) did Martin Luther King deliver the famous "I have a dream" speech?	Martin Luther King I have a dream
Who invented the pen Bic and how did they come up with the idea?	Bic pen
What is the address of the Google offices in London?	Google London

Text Cue	Image cue
Let's work together. - UK jobs - Google Our UK offices are based in **London** and other locations around the UK. ... Please do not forward CVs to our jobs alias, **Google** employees or any other company ... www.**google**.co.uk/intl/en/jobs/index.html - Cached	
London - Student Jobs - Google Human resources, finance, legal, facilities, marketing, communications, business development and corporate development staff also work at **Google London**. ... www.**google**.com/jobs/students/emea/spotlight**london**/ - Cached - Similar	
Google Maps of London street gangs: Do the Mozart Bloods prowl ... 30 Mar 2010 ... Is your neighbourhood blighted by the Ghetto Diplomats or the Manor Park Goons? Do the Mozart Bloods walk your West **London** street? blogs.telegraph.co.uk/.../**google**-maps-of-**london**-street-gangs-do-the-mozart-bloods-prowl-your-neighbourhood/ - Cached	
Revealed: the environmental impact of Google searches - Times Online 11 Jan 2009 ... Alex Wissner-Gross decribes his research in detail | **Google's** response to th ... 894646 Registered office: 1 Virginia Street, **London**, E98 1XY. technology.timesonline.co.uk/tol/news/tech.../article5489134.ece - Similar	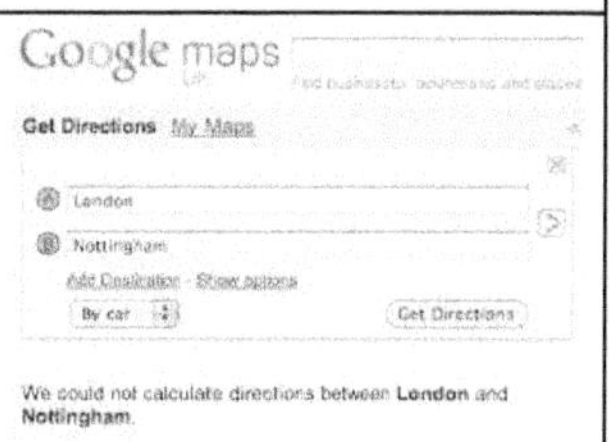

Table 2. Example of Text cues and Image cues for *Google London* question.

- *Text+Image* cues, where a cue showed both text and an image.

The three cue treatments are displayed in Figure 2. In order to counter-balance practice effects in this study, we randomised the order in which cue treatments appeared to participants.

For each question, we selected four text cues and four image cues as a basis for investigating scent. Image and text cues were found through Google Search and Google Images using keywords associated with the questions that a researcher generated (Table 1). For each cue, we tried to choose a range of items that would span the spectrum of scent, i.e. some potentially high-scent and low-scent cues. Table 2 shows the four text cues and four image

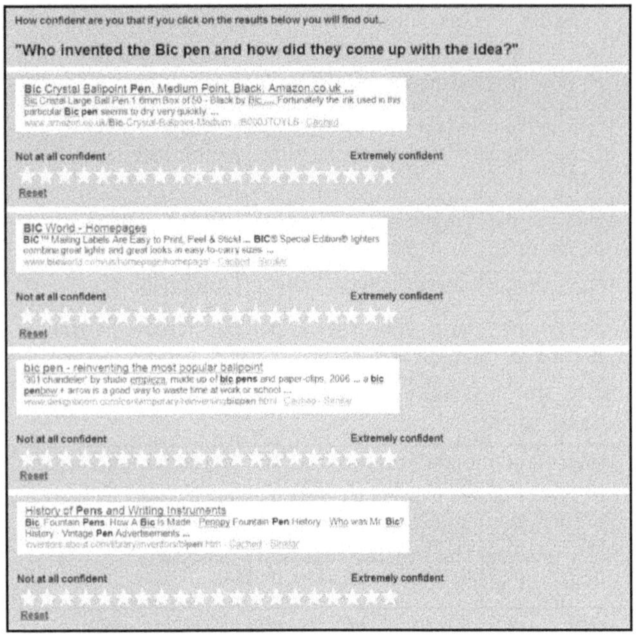

Figure 3. *Bic pen* question in Text-only cue treatment.

cues used for the *Google London* question. For the Text+Image treatment we randomly paired text cues and image cues.

For their main task, we asked participants to rate how confident they were that this cue would lead them to the answer to the question i.e. how strong was the cue's information scent? The participants were able to rate the scent of cues on a 20-point Likert scale from "Not at all confident" (1) to "Extremely confident" (20). We chose a large scale instead of the more traditional five- or seven-point scale, because we believed this scale would give the users the freedom to intuitively select one point without spending much time thinking and trying to assign ratings into few categories. Figure 3 shows the presentation of question, cues and rating scale for the *Blobfish* question in the Text-only treatment.

Of the 81 people who took part in this study, 63 completed all rating tasks. Overall, we managed to obtain 6776 scent ratings across 96 individual cues (96 cues are derived from the 8 questions * (4 Text-only cues + 4 Image-only cues + 4 Text+Image cues)).

3.2 Study 1 Results

3.2.1 Do you think I smell?

We wondered first of all if scent is a reliable measure that could be utilised in SERPs. To investigate this, we calculated simple descriptive statistics for each cue.

Overall, we observed some divergence on scent ratings between users. Across all cues, there was a 25% spread of ratings, with an average standard deviation of 5.38. This was true for the majority of cues: 22.9% of cues received ratings from the whole 20-point spectrum of the scent scale, while 87.5% received ratings from a not much narrower 17-point spectrum. For example, Figure 4 shows the distribution of ratings for the "map" image for the *Blobfish* question. It can be seen that the majority of the participants rated the scent of this image very high; 58% rated it at 15 or above. However, there are 13 participants who rated the image as not very high, with a scent rating of less than 10. Thus, for the same cue, there was disagreement about whether it had a high scent or a low scent – participants' opinions diverged

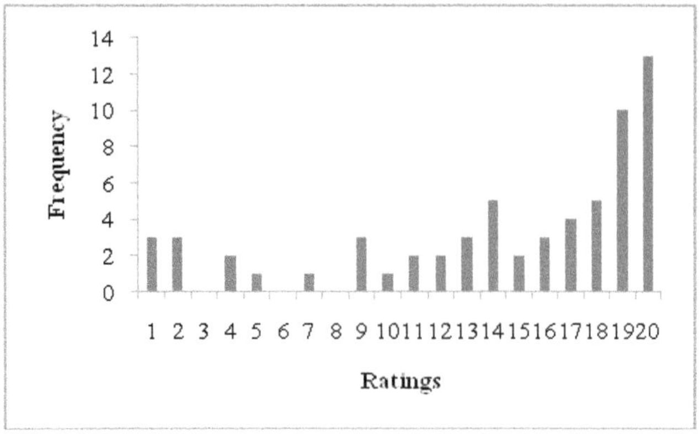

Figure 4. Frequency of scent ratings for the "map" image in the Blobfish question (mean = 14.4 , median = 17).

sometimes widely. This range pattern remained consistent across different cues and opinions diverged just as much for Text-only cues as for Image-only or Text+Image cues (Table 3).

Intuitively, it may be assumed that the more relevant the image is, the less disagreement there should be. However, standard deviation was *not* related to the median scent ratings of the images. This means that participants disagreed with each other consistently, even on images that were generally judged to be more relevant. From these results it appears that there is an individualistic component to ratings, in which one user's nose for information scent may be working differently to another user's.

However, fairly reliable scent ratings for cues can be obtained. In the best case (*Bic pen* question: "History of pens and writing instruments" text + "BIC think" image, SD=3.59), the spread of ratings was less than 20%. Although some images may be affected by outlier scent ratings, median values of scent rating can still reflect the most prevalent scent for an image.

However, reliable scent ratings may not be enough to justify adding images to SERPs; if image cues do not have a strong scent by themselves there may be no value in adding them to SERPs in the first place. In order to find out what scent dominates, we looked at the scent ratings of Text-only cues and Image-only cues across the questions in more detail (Table 4). In five of the eight questions, participants gave higher scent ratings to Text-only cues than Image-only cues. In fact, a t-test showed that Text-only scent was rated significantly higher than Image-only scent overall ($t(4483) = 2.85$, $p = 0.004$). Text-only cues therefore have a significant advantage in terms of scent compared to images. However, there are exceptions: For some image sets and questions (e.g. *Blobfish* and *Eiffel tower*), Image-only scent ratings were higher than Text-only ratings.

These results are important for the design of SERPs in terms of choice of images. It shows that however relevant the image may

Table 3. Lowest and highest median scent ratings for individual cues observed and mean standard deviation by cue treatment

Cue Treatment	Lowest median cue rating	Highest median cue rating	Mean SD
Text	1	17	6.14
Image	2	17	6.14
Text+Image	2	18	6.21

Table 4. Mean scent ratings and standard deviation for Text-only and Image-only cues per question. Shaded cells indicate where Image-only scent is higher rated than Text-only scent.

Question	Mean scent rating		Standard Deviation	
	Text-only	Image-only	Text-only	Image-only
iPhone	12.00	11.25	2.16	2.63
Bullet train	10.50	10.50	3.79	5.20
Blobfish	8.25	11.75	4.19	4.11
Eiffel tower	8.33	10.25	6.66	4.65
Cheetah	10.50	6.75	2.12	4.11
MLK	12.25	8.50	1.89	3.11
Bic pen	7.25	5.67	6.08	2.52
Google London	11.75	9.00	4.79	6.48
Mean	**10.10**	**9.21**	**3.96**	**4.10**

seem to the designer (or an algorithm that extracts relevant images), it may not align with the scent that the user smells. However, cues from images appear to have a scent of their own and therefore adding images to text cues may be a viable option to explore.

3.2.2 Does text with an image smell even better?

We were interested in what happens to scent if images are added to text. How do text scent and image scent combine? By looking at the ratings of all three types of treatments, a pattern that emerged was that, in most cases, the Text+Image cues were rated higher by participants than both the Text-only cue or the Image-only cue. A t-test comparing the scent ratings of text with the scent ratings of Text+Image showed that the Text+Image were rated significantly higher than the text ($t(4028) = -6.68$, $p = 2.65e-11$). Moreover, a multiple regression test showed that the rating of the Text+Image result was predicted by both the text and the image ratings (multiple regression, $R^2=0.3426$, $p = 3.952E-184$). The text is the most influential element in the scent rating, with the image contributing a little scent by itself, shown by the regression function:

*Text+Image scent = 0.53 *Text scent + 0.19 * Image scent + 4.05*

It follows from this function that a very good image scent could overpower the scent of text. In other words, could a relevant image overcome irrelevant text? Table 5 shows the instances in our study when this happened. In all cases the Image scent ratings were significantly higher than the Text-only rating. Our findings show that participants rated some Text+Image ratings higher when high-scent images were paired with low-scent text.

Conversely, consistent with the scent regression function, when a high-scent text was combined with a low-scent image, participants usually ignored the low-scent image and rated the combined result highly. This shows that images played a mediating role when added to text and in some cases counteracted textual cues.

Our findings have implications for the design of novel SERP interfaces. Adding images to textual search results will affect what the user smells, however the scent of text will dominate – the role of the image in SERPs is generally of minor importance. In some cases however, adding an image can raise the relevance of results

Table 5 - The six results in which the high-scent image caused a significant increase in the Text+ Image results' score

Text+Image combination	Scent ratings		
	Text-only	Image-only	Text + Image
"Reinventing the most popular pen"+"BIC inventor"	6	13.5	10
"London street gangs"+ "Google Map"	1	16	4
"Bullet train of Shinkansen"+"Blueprint"	8	15	11
"Blobfish" + "map"	11	17	15
"sometimes we all feel like the blobfish" + "WWF"	2	13	4
"Cheetah"+"Cheetah running"	10	14	14.5

and can lead it to smelling better overall. In other words: adding images, even if they are bad, probably will not matter that much. If images are good, they could make even a bad result appear more relevant.

4. STUDY 2: EFFECTS OF SCENT ON USER BEHAVIOUR IN SERPS

With the ratings gathered in Study 1, we designed a second experiment to investigate the effect of adding images to SERPs on user behaviour in terms of effectiveness, efficiency and satisfaction:

- We wanted to explore whether adding images to SERPs can lead users to choose results more accurately and whether users would be confused by placing images next to text cues where their scents conflict (Effectiveness).
- We also wanted to investigate whether adding images helps the user to choose more quickly or whether they are delayed by conflicting scents of images and text cues (Efficiency).
- We were interested in whether users liked having image cues added to SERPs (Satisfaction).

4.1 Methodology

We decided to include only the questions from Study 1 where there were distinctive scent ratings for images and text, i.e. not all cues were rated to have roughly equal scent. Hence, we only gathered data about the following four questions (original numbers from Study 1 in brackets):

1. What is the problem with the antenna of the iPhone 4 and how can it be fixed? (1)

2. What is the length of a Japanese bullet train? (2)

3. What is the maximum speed a cheetah can reach? (5)

4. What is the address of the Google offices in London? (8)

To investigate user behaviour upon adding images, we developed four SERP versions to explore variations in combinations of scent in images and text:

V1 Baseline (Text-only): A SERP showing no images but giving textual cues and visual cues only in terms of styling. This is the traditional SERP presentation.

V2 (Text+Image scent-matched): A SERP which gives both textual cues and image cues and where the high-scent text is shown with the high-scent image.

V3 (low-scent Text+high-scent Image): A SERP which gives both textual cues and image cues but where a low-scent text is shown with the high-scent image. This will allow us to investigate whether an image that smells very good can outweigh "bad-smelling" text.

V4 (high-scent Text+low-scent Image): A SERP which gives both textual cues and image cues but where a high-scent text is shown with the low-scent image. Again, this allowed us to investigate if image scent would confuse users.

For each question, no matter the SERP version, the best result was shown in the same rank position. However, that position was not the same for all questions as we wanted to avoid a "training effect" that would help the user choose a result realising that the "best" result is always in the same position.

Each SERP showed seven results since we wanted to mimic a realistic SERP task, in which a user is confronted with a number of results that have an impact on effectiveness and efficiency. In addition to our four results from Study 1 for which we had scent ratings, we therefore had to insert additional "filler" search results to make up the seven results. For these "filler" results, we chose three generic or unrelated text results and images, being careful not to introduce a new high-scent item.

We adopted a within-subject experiment design, in which each participant was faced with all four questions and all four SERP versions. We developed four alternative experiment treatments where we counterbalanced the SERP versions against questions using a Latin square design to remove ordering confounds (e.g. Participant 1 saw V1 with Question 1 whereas Participant 2 saw V1 with Question 2, and so on).

The SERPs were implemented using a static visual prototyping tool to resemble Google search result pages, using the same fonts and colours in order to feel familiar to the users (e.g. the title of the text result was coloured blue and underlined using an Arial 12pt font). The images were resized not to exceed 180pt in height and 200pt in width and an outer blue stroke was added to them to resemble Google linked images. All other features of the Google search results page (search box, number of pages, left bar faceting tools etc.) were removed so as not to distract the participants from their task. A search results page, as was displayed to the participants for V2, can be seen in Figure 5.

A total of 64 participants completed this experiment. Participants were recruited at a university in a main pass-through area, used by

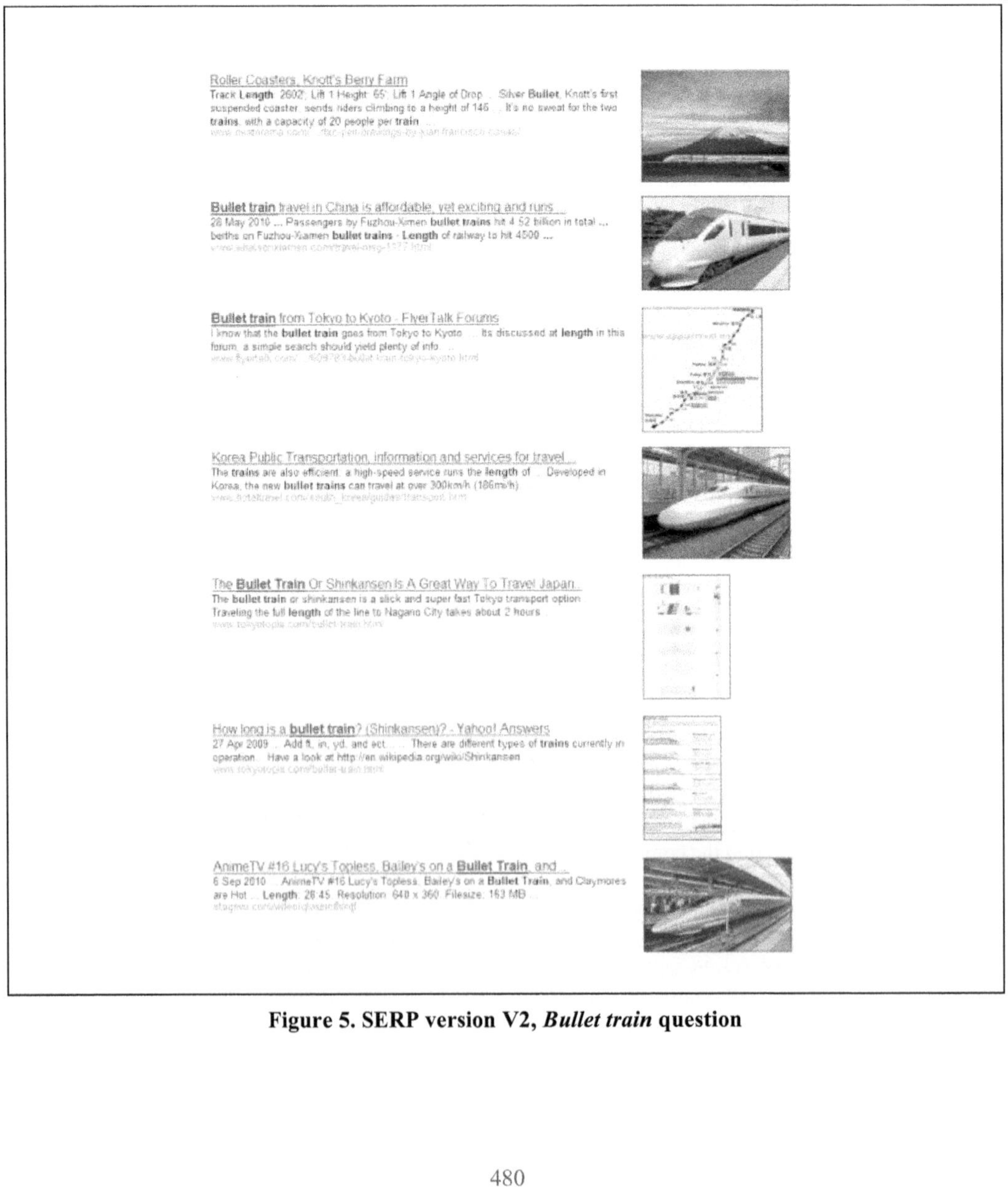

Figure 5. SERP version V2, *Bullet train* question

staff and students from different disciplines. The experiment lasted approximately 2 minutes. All participants were asked not to talk during the experiment and to use the mouse in order to keep the experiment conditions as consistent as possible. The experiments were conducted on a SONY VAIO laptop with an Intel® Core™ 2 Duo CPU P8400 at 2.26GHz, using a wireless Logitech mouse and the participants' screen was captured using CamStudio 2.0. All pages that were shown to participants were locally stored in the computer so there was virtually no delay between pages.

After a brief description of the experiment by the researchers, the participants were presented with a screen with instructions for the experiment. This was done in order to ensure that all participants would receive exactly the same information. This was followed by an example task. This example task's only purpose was to familiarise the participants with the procedure. The data from the example task was not included in the analysis.

Each question consisted of three screens. The first screen featured the question and a button which, upon being clicked, lead to the results page. The second screen was the SERP version. When a participant clicked on any link on the SERP (title of result or image) they would leave the SERP and continue on to a "thank you" page, asking them if they were ready to proceed to the next question. They would then click on a "next question" button which led to the next question, then the SERP, and so on. Once all questions and versions were completed by the participant, they were presented with a page asking them to rate their preference of SERP presentation.

For this study we captured three measures: effectiveness, efficiency and satisfaction. For effectiveness, we measured how many participants selected the "correct" highest-scent rated item out of the seven results shown. To measure efficiency, we took the time that participants spent between starting the task and selecting a result. The start of the task is defined by the moment a participant clicked on the "see the results" button on the question page. We analysed the selection of results and timing of the selections from the screen capture. Satisfaction ratings were obtained from participants at the end of the experiment using a 5-point scale, indicating their preference on a spectrum between 1 (Strongly prefer Text-only version) to 5 (Strongly prefer Text+Image version). Screenshots of the two versions were also shown on this page that acted as a reminder to participants.

4.2 Study 2 Results

4.2.1 How effective is image scent added to SERPs?

In order to test the effectiveness of adding images to SERPs, we set up two hypotheses:

(H1) Adding images to text cues will result in more correct selections – V2 (Text+Image scent-matched) will result in more correct selections than V1 Baseline (Text-only) version.

(H2) Placing image cues where their scent conflicts with the scent of text cues will cause more incorrect selections – there will be more incorrect selections with either V3 (low-scent Text + high-scent Image) or V4 (high-scent Text + low-scent Image) than with V2 (Text+Image scent-matched).

Figure 6 shows the breakdown of correctly and incorrectly selected results for all versions. As can be seen, participants in our study only chose marginally more correctly in V2 where images were added than compared to V1, the Text-only baseline version; this improvement is not statistically significant. This means that

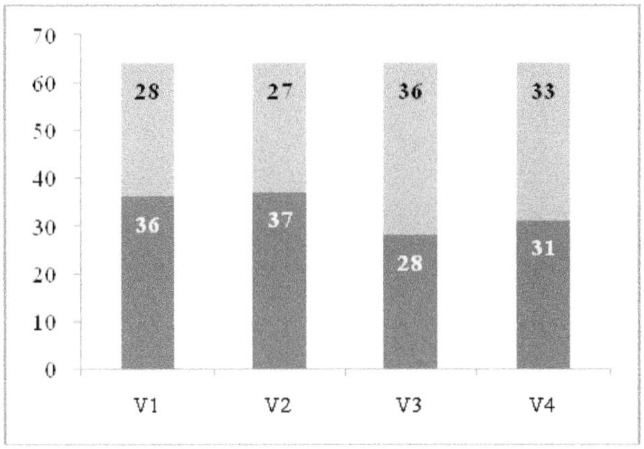

Figure 6. Number of correct (dark grey) and non-correct (light grey) selections by SERP versions indicating Effectiveness.

the high-scent image did not help users choose more accurately and therefore H1 is rejected.

Did confusing scent have any negative impact on participants' effectiveness? It would seem that there is a tendency towards more incorrect selections in both V3 and V4, where scents by text and image cues clashed, than in V2, where scent of text and images matched. However, the difference between V2 and V3 is not statistically significant ($\chi^2(3, N=64) = 1.63$, $p = 0.65$). Since V4 has a higher number of correct selections than V3, by implication there will be no significant difference between V4 and V2. Therefore, hypothesis H2 is also rejected.

For the design of SERPs integrating images, this means that adding an image to a SERP result will not significantly help users in identifying correct results but neither will it significantly hinder them if an image is placed with text cues where the scents may conflict.

4.2.2 Does image scent make SERP choices quicker?

We also investigated the effects of adding images to SERPs on users' efficiency. We surmised that

(H3) Adding images to text cues will result in selections being made in less time – Results in V2 (Text+Image scent-matched) will be selected faster than in V1 Baseline (Text-only).

(H4) Adding image cues to text where their scents conflict will confuse users and lead to longer selection times – Results in V3 (low-scent Text + high-scent Image) and V4 (high-scent Text + low-scent Image) will be selected slower than in V2 (Text+Image scent-matched).

The average timings of the four versions are displayed in Figure 7. According to H1, we expected that images would help with efficiency compared to the Text-only version. In our study, we found that, on average, participants tended to select results *slightly slower* in V2 where images were added than in V1 without images but this difference was not statistically significant ($t(123) = -0.45$, $p = .65$).

What about efficiency when scent confusion was added to the mix? We found that participant's selected a result *slightly quicker* in V3 (low-scent Text + high-scent Image) compared to V2 (without scent confusion) and *slightly slower* in V4 (high-scent Text + low-scent Image) than in V2. Again, this partially went against our initial expectations as we expected scent conflicts to have a detrimental effect on selection times. However, the time

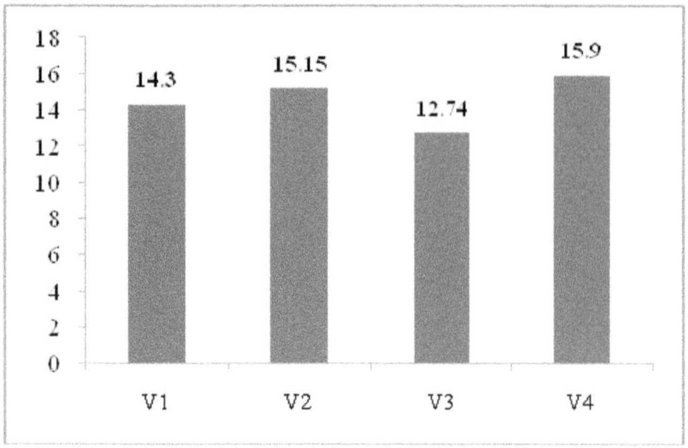

Figure 7. Average time (seconds) to select a result in the four SERP versions indicating Efficiency

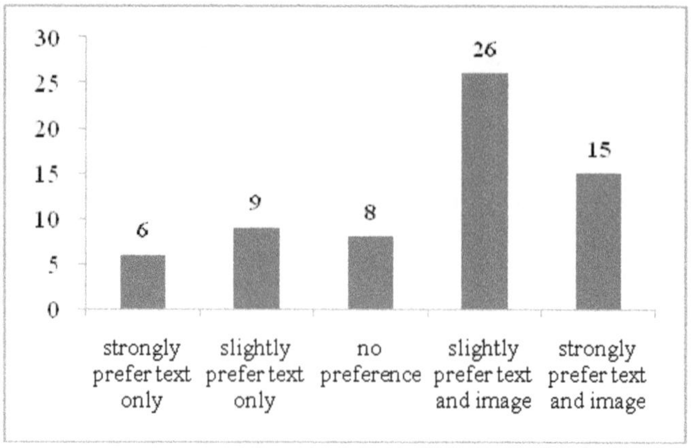

Figure 8. Frequency of participants' preference ratings for Text versus Text+Image

that participants took is not statistically significantly different from V2 which is the best case where scents matched (Table 6).

Therefore, our hypotheses H3 and H4 are both rejected. This means that overall, adding images to SERPs will not lead to a substantial difference in user efficiency. Moreover, adding the "wrong" kinds of images to texts result also did not lead to significantly detrimental effects on participants in terms of efficiency.

4.2.3 Is added image scent appreciated in SERPs?

We also wondered if images had any effect on user satisfaction. In our post-study questionnaire, we asked participants to rate their preference for the Text-only version and versions with images added. The preference ratings were collated for the 64 participants who took part in the experiment and are presented in Figure 8.

Our findings show that there were a clear majority of participants who preferred Image versions over the Text-only version: 41 participants preferred images combined with text compared to 15 who preferred Text-only versions. A test confirmed this trend: there is a significant difference between ratings ($\chi^2(4, N=64) = 20.53$, $p = .0003$). This means that in terms of user satisfaction adding images to SERPs has a clear advantage – participants liked the added scent from image cues.

5. DISCUSSION AND FUTURE WORK

The results from our two studies on image information scent have important implications for the presentation of SERPs, and in addition, could also be of interest to the area of image retrieval in general.

Firstly, it appears that adding images to SERPs is, in general, a good idea. Combined scent from images and text cues resulted in higher scent ratings by participants in the first study, and participants in our second study preferred when images were added to SERPs.

However, our work also shows that some caution is advised in the choice of images. One immediate problem is that individual users may interpret the scent of an image differently to each other, to a designer or to an algorithm that extracts suitable images from web pages automatically. This means that there will never be a "perfect" image to accompany a textual search result but neither is it understood what aspects contribute to the scent of an image. Some work on users' needs, when they are specifically searching for images, has started to shed light on this area [8, 23] but more research is required to determine what aspects affect the scent of an image in order to develop a suitable model of image information scent.

Table 6. t-test result of timings

Comparison	t-test results
V2 - V3	$t(122) = 1.39$, $p = .16$
V2 - V4	$t(119) = -0.37$, $p = .72$

Secondly, our work shows that scent from images smells less than scent from text but we did not investigate the role that visual styling of text may contribute to scent. Previous research [4] has suggested that text styling does not override text cues but it is not clear how the scent from visual styling compares to the scent of images.

Thirdly, the regression function we developed and the scent rating results we obtained from our participants show that image scent in some instances may outweigh the scent of text. Although we did not find any evidence that these confounding images significantly affected user behaviour in SERPs in our study, previous research has found that text styling can increase users' efficiency but may also trick users into selecting the wrong result [21]. A careful investigation into the factors that could confuse users' sense of smell is warranted.

Finally, our results on user behaviour in SERPs in terms of effectiveness, efficiency and user satisfaction also yielded interesting insights. We found that our participants were not significantly better or quicker in completing search tasks when images were added than with traditional textual results pages, which contradicts previous research [14, 25, 26]. However, we also observed some very counter-intuitive trends when we added confusing scent cues: placing high-scent images with low-scent text made participants tend to select results slightly quicker. Future research employing larger field studies may want to shed more light on user effectiveness and efficiency in SERPs by investigating subtle interactions between scent strength and cue type, especially as users interactively refine their search needs.

6. CONCLUSION

This paper has investigated adding images to SERPs from an Information Foraging perspective. We conducted two empirical studies to explore the information scent of images and the effects of adding images to SERPs on user behaviour. In our first study, we found that:

- Image information scent has user-dependent aspects and that users' scent ratings of the same image may differ.
- Overall, the combined scent of text and images is stronger than each on its own.
- Text has a stronger scent than images, however in some cases, the scent of images can outweigh the scent of text.

In addition, our second study showed that

- Adding images to SERPs may not have very much effect on changing user behaviour in terms of either effectiveness or efficiency, even when confounding images are presented.
- Overall, users appear to appreciate the addition of images to SERPs.

Our results have important implications for the design of SERP interfaces. We found that it will be extremely problematic to choose the "perfect" image to accompany textual results. In addition, although users may mainly rely on text cues to find search results, some images may throw users off the scent. Furthermore, it appears that there may not be a directly quantifiable benefit or detriment to users when adding images to SERPs – our participants did not select the correct results significantly better/worse, or slower/quicker. Further research into the basis of how users determine image information scent and the contribution of image scent to user behaviour in SERPs is therefore warranted. Our studies provide a valuable first step into image information scent and innovative SERP interfaces that take into account whether an image smells good.

7. ACKNOWLEDGMENTS

We thank the participants of our study. We thank Hannah Locke for her help in preparing this paper.

8. REFERENCES

[1] Blackmon, M.H., Polson, P.G., Kitajima, M., and Lewis, C. 2002. Cognitive walkthrough for the web. *Proceedings of CHI 2002.*

[2] Borlund P. 2003. The concept of relevance in IR. *Journal of the American Society for information Science and Technology.* 54(10):913-925.

[3] Broder, A. 2002. A taxonomy of Web search. *SIGIR Forum*, 36(2).

[4] Buscher, G., Dumais, S.T., and Cutrell, E. 2010. The good, the bad, and the random: An Eye-Tracking study of Ad Quality in Web Search. *Proceedings of SIGIR 2010.*

[5] Chi, E., Pirolli, P., Chen, K., and Pitkow, J. 2001. Using information scent to model user information needs and actions on the web, *Proceedings of CHI 2001.*

[6] Chi, E., Rosien, A., Supattanasiri, G., Williams, A., Royer, C., Chow, C., Robles, E., Dalal, B., Chen, J. and Cousins, S. 2003. The Bloodhound Project: Automating discovery of web usability issues using the InfoScent Simulator. *Proceedings of CHI 2003.*

[7] Chi, E.H., Pirolli, P., and Pitkow, J. 2000. The scent of a site: A system for analyzing and predicting information scent, usage, and usability of a web site. *Proceedings of CHI 2000.*

[8] Cunningham SJ, Masoodian M. 2006. Looking for a picture: an analysis of everyday image information searching. *Proceedings of the 6th ACM/IEEE-CS joint conference on Digital libraries*. Chapel Hill, NC, USA: ACM 2006. p. 198–199.

[9] Cutrell, E. and Guan, Z. 2007. What are you looking for? An eye-tracking study of information usage in web search. *Proceedings of CHI 2007.*

[10] Fu, W-T. and Pirolli, P. 2007. SNIF-ACT: A cognitive model of user navigation on the World Wide Web. *Proceedings of HCI 2007.*

[11] Jiao, B., Yang, L., Xu, J., and Wu, F. 2010. Visual Summarizations of web pages. *Proceedings of SIGIR 2010.*

[12] Katz, M. A., and Byrne, M. D. 2003. Effects of scent and breadth on use of site specific search on e-commerce web sites. *ACM Transactions on Computer-Human Interaction*, 10(3).

[13] Kitajima, M., Blackmon, M. H., and Polson, P. 2005. Cognitive architecture for website design and usability evaluation: Comprehension of information scent in performing by exploration. *Proceedings of HCI International 2005.*

[14] Al Maqbali, H., Scholer, F., Thom, J.A., and Wu, M. 2010. Evaluating the effectiveness of visual summaries for web search. *Proceedings of the Australasian Document Computing Symposium.*

[15] Pirolli, P. and Card, S. 1995. Information Foraging in information access environments. *Proceedings of CHI 1995.*

[16] Pirolli, P. and Card, S. 1999. Information Foraging. *Psychological Review,* 106(4).

[17] Pirolli, P., Card, S., and Van Der Wege, M. 2001. Visual information foraging in a focus + context visualization. *Proceedings of CHI 2001.*

[18] Pirolli, P. and Fu, W-T. 2003. SNIF-ACT: A model of information foraging on the World Wide Web. *Proceedings of User Modeling 2003.*

[19] Pirolli, P. 2007. *Information Foraging Theory: Adaptive Interaction with Information,* Oxford University Press, New York.

[20] Rele, R.S. and Duchowski, A.T. 2005. Using eye tracking to evaluate alternate search results interfaces. *Proceedings of HFES.*

[21] Tamborello II, F. P. and Byrne, M. D. 2005. Information Search: The intersection of visual and semantic space. *Proceedings of CHI 2005.*

[22] Wen L, Ruthven I, Borlund P.2006. The effects on topic familiarity on online search behaviour and use of relevance criteria. *Advances in Information Retrieval 2006* 456-459.

[23] Westman, S. 2009. Image Users' Needs and Searching Behaviour. *Information Retrieval: Searching in the 21st Century*, Goker and Davies (eds.), Wiley.

[24] Withrow, J. 2002. Do your links stink? Techniques for good web information scent. *American Society for Information Science and Technology Bulletin, 28(5).*

[25] Woodruf, A., Rosenholtz, R., Morrison, J.B., Faulring, A., and Pirolli, P. 2001. A comparison of the use of text summaries, plain thumbnails, and enhanced thumbnails for Web search tasks. *Journal of the American Society for Information Science and Technology*, 53(20).

[26] Woodruf, A., Faulring, A., Rosenholtz, R., Morrison, J.B., and Pirolli, P. 2001. Using thumbnails to search the web. *Proceedings of CHI 2001*

Retrieving and Ranking Unannotated Images through Collaboratively Mining Online Search Results

Songhua Xu
Oak Ridge National Laboratory
Oak Ridge, Tennessee 37831, USA

Hao Jiang
Dept. of Computer Science
The University of Hong Kong
Hong Kong S.A.R., P.R. China

Francis C.M. Lau
Dept. of Computer Science
The University of Hong Kong
Hong Kong S.A.R., P.R. China

ABSTRACT

We present a new image search and ranking algorithm for retrieving unannotated images by collaboratively mining online search results which consist of online image and text search results. The online image search results are leveraged as reference examples to perform content-based image search over unannotated images. The online text search results are utilized to estimate the reference images' relevance to the search query. The key feature of our method is its capability to deal with unreliable online image search results through jointly mining visual and textual aspects of online search results. Through such collaborative mining, our algorithm infers the relevance of an online search result image to a text query. Once we obtain the estimate of query relevance score for each online image search result, we can selectively use query specific online search result images as reference examples for retrieving and ranking unannotated images. We tested our algorithm both on the standard public image datasets and several modestly sized personal photo collections. We also compared our method with two well-known peer methods. The results indicate that our algorithm is superior to existing content-based image search algorithms for retrieving and ranking unannotated images.

Categories and Subject Descriptors

H.5.1 [**Information Interfaces and Presentation**]: Multimedia Information Systems; I.4.9 [**Image Processing and Computer Vision**]: Applications; H.3.3 [**Information Storage and Retrieval**]: Information Search and Retrieval—*Query Formulation, Retrieval Models, Search Process*

• Corresponding author: S. Xu; contact him at xus1 "*at*" ornl "*dot*" gov.

• This manuscript has been authored by UT-Battelle, LLC, under Contract No. DE-AC05-00OR22725 with the U.S. Department of Energy. The United States Government retains and the publisher, by accepting the article for publication, acknowledges that the United States Government retains a non-exclusive, paid-up, irrevocable, world-wide license to publish or reproduce the published form of this manuscript, or allow others to do so, for United States Government purposes.

CIKM'11, October 24–28, 2011, Glasgow, Scotland, UK.

General Terms

Algorithms, Experimentation, Performance

Keywords

Multimedia information retrieval, web information retrieval, online reference image collection, query processing, retrieving unannotated images, web search mining

1. INTRODUCTION

Today, many people need to manage their photos, which by no means is an easy task especially when the photo collection becomes very large. One of the frequent management tasks is to search for a photo. Using the mainstream image search tools, which mostly rely on traditional text based retrieval methods, can be cumbersome and frustrating because ordinary photos are rarely annotated. If there are annotations, they tend to be terse, subjective, and biased.

To enable searching and ranking unannotated images, we introduce a new content-based image retrieval algorithm by leveraging online image search results—using them as reference examples to inform and guide the unannotated image search and ranking process. A key feature of our algorithm is its capability of automatically inferring the relevance of an online image search result to its corresponding textual query through collaboratively mining both visual contents of and text clues associated with the online image search result. After having derived the estimate of image-to-query relevance for each reference image obtained from the online image search step, we can further compute the relevance of an arbitrary unannotated image to a textual query according to the unannotated image's collective visual similarity with the entire reference image set. We calculate the collective visual similarity between an unannotated image and the reference image set by accumulating the individual pairwise image visual similarities between the unannotated image and each example image in the reference image set. During this accumulation process, we also take into account the query relevance score of each reference image example. All in all, an unannotated image that has higher visual similarities with more query relevant example images tends to obtain a higher collective visual similarity score. Finally, based on the derived collective visual similarity score for each candidate unannotated image with respect to the reference image set, we can search and rank all the unannotated images accordingly.

2. RELATED WORK

2.1 Content-Based Image Retrieval

Fergus et al. [9] proposed a method that dynamically derives a visual object model through learning from Google image search results. Their method however does not leverage the annotation or description text of an online image. Popescu et al. [1] proposed a content-based image retrieval method using an ontology driven approach for improving image retrieval precision. Kidambi and Narayanan [17] introduced a human computer integrated approach for content-based image retrieval, taking advantage of user feedbacks. Hsiao et al. [12] represented an image as a visual bag-of-words followed by a relevance feedback scheme for ranking images. Jing and Baluja [15] adapted Google's PageRank algorithm for product image search. Their approach is based on image similarities estimated from low-level visual features proposed in [23]. Compared with our algorithm, their method does not look into the text clues associated with an image. Liu et al. [22] gave a high-level overview of content-based image retrieval research from the perspective of semantics understanding. For more comprehensive reviews on recent progress in content-based image retrieval and web image search, readers are referred to [27, 16, 5, 22, 28, 24]. These are also many surveys on domain specific content-based image retrieval methods and systems, e.g. Muller et al.'s survey [25] on content-based image retrieval for medical applications.

2.2 Image Search and Re-Ranking through Mining Text Clues

Lin et al. contributed a probabilistic model based algorithm [19] for re-ranking image search results according to images' surrounding texts. In comparison, our algorithm does more—it also explores the visual content of an image. Cai et al. [3] proposed a hierarchic image clustering method through jointly analyzing visual, textual, and link information of an image. However, their algorithm is proposed for clustering images, which cannot be directly applied to retrieving or re-ranking images. Zhou and Huang's image retrieval algorithm [31] jointly uses the keywords and the visual content of an image for image retrieval. But their method uses reference images in isolation during the image retrieval process whereas our algorithm considers the collective image similarity between a given candidate unannotated image and an entire reference image set. Jia et al. [14] proposed a personal album annotation algorithm. Their algorithm and Feng et al.'s [7] algorithm, similar to ours, use clues from the visual content and HTML text of an image for image content understanding. Jia et al.'s method is a supervised learning approach, which needs a set of pre-labelled images as training samples, whereas our method does not need any human labels. Feng et al.'s method independently trains two separate classifiers, one using text features and the other using visual features of an image. In contrast, our method collaboratively analyzes the visual and text aspects of online image search results in one unified procedure. Through our integral analysis based on image and text data fusion, our method can adaptively prioritize relevant online reference images. As a result, our algorithm can deal with noisy reference image samples more superbly than Feng et al.'s algorithm, which will be proved through our experiments. Recently, Liu et al. [20] [21] developed a textual query based personal photo retrieval system, which also uses web image search results to facilitate querying unannotated personal photos. However, their method focuses on leveraging the relevance feedback strategy to deal with the noisy unreliable online image search results. In contrast, our method collaboratively mines the visual contents and text clues accompanying each online image search result to discriminate reliable online image search results from irrelevant ones. Compared with their relevance feedback based strategy, which requires end user participation, our method can autonomously apply online image search results in a selected manner to guide the unannotated image search and ranking process. The hybrid mining feature of our algorithm allows our method to automatically cope with the noisy and unreliable nature of web image search results. It is possible to further strengthen the image search capability of our algorithm by adopting the relevance feedback strategy proposed in Liu et al.'s work, which is a meaningful topic for future exploration. Fergus et al. [8] proposed an algorithm that learns object categories from Google's image search results. The key part of their algorithm is a model that considers spatial and scalar information of images for learning the potential categories and tags of Google search result images. They also incorporatd an incremental learning algorithm [18] in their method to support relevance feedback by end users. People have also explored the idea of mining web text search results for establishing tagged image databases. For example, Schroff et al. [26] proposed to build image databases by collecting images within webpages of web text search results. In their method, they utilize the textual contents of web search results for image tag identification and selection.

3. OUR METHOD

3.1 Finding Reference Images for an Image Query through Online Image Search

Given a textual query Q, we first use a third party commercial image search engine (Google Image Search in our current implementation) to perform an online image search. The purpose is to acquire a set of reference images to perform content-based image search over the candidate unannotated image set. Assume there are $\zeta(Q)$ reference images obtained for the input image query Q, which are organized as a reference image set $\mathbf{G}(Q) \triangleq \{G_1(Q), G_2(Q), \cdots, G_{\zeta(Q)}(Q)\}$, where each $G_i(Q)$ is an online search result image.

It is common knowledge that not all the online image search results are closely related to the query; some are completely irrelevant. Treating these noisy online search result images indiscriminately will introduce great noise and instability to our content based image search process. To overcome this problem, in our method, we estimate each reference image's relevance to the image search query. The resultant image-to-query relevance scores can help our algorithm differentiate between good reference images and noisy or irrelevant ones, which improves the overall accuracy and reliability of our method. In Sec. 3.2–Sec. 3.4 below, we will explain how we estimate reference images' query relevance through collaboratively mining online search results, in both the text and image domains.

3.2 Estimating Initial Image-to-Query Relevance for Reference Images

To estimate each reference image's relevance to a text query Q, we first compare the similarity between the text context associated with the reference image and the text context of Q. Our assumption is: the more aligned the two contexts is, the more likely the reference image reflects the image search intent as expressed by the text query Q. In the following, we explain in detail our text analysis based initial image-to-query relevance estimation procedure.

3.2.1 Characterizing word frequency distribution in online text search result

Given a text query Q, we first submit the query to Google (text) search and retrieve the top N text search results. In our experiments, the typical value assignment for N falls in $[100, 500]$, which shall never exceed the total number of search result documents returned by Google for the query. Let the j-th text search result document be D_j ($j \in [1, N]$). All these search result documents form an online text search result set for Q, denoted as

$\mathbf{D}(Q) \triangleq \{D_1, D_2, \cdots, D_N\}$. Next, we derive non-stop words' frequency distribution in $\mathbf{D}(Q)$ to characterize these words' respective importance. To balance between text search result documents with different lengths, we work with *relative word frequency* rather than absolute word frequency. The derivation process for a word's relative frequency is as follows: assume a non-stop word wd_i occurs $y_{i,j}$ times in the document D_j and the total number of occurrence of all the non-stop words in D_j is m_j. We then calculate the relative word frequency of wd_i in D_j as $\frac{y_{i,j}}{m_j}$. We accumulate wd_i's relative word frequencies for all the documents in $\mathbf{D}(Q)$ and treat the sum as wd_i's *accumulated relative word frequency*, $t_i(Q)$, i.e. $t_i(Q) \triangleq \sum_{j=1}^{N} \frac{y_{i,j}}{m_j}$. In addition, we introduce an inverse word frequency term for each non-stop word in $\mathbf{D}(Q)$. Assume n_i is the total number of documents containing the word wd_i in $\mathbf{D}(Q)$. Then, the word wd_i's inverse word frequency term with respect to $\mathbf{D}(Q)$ is formulated as $\ln(1 + \frac{N}{n_i})$. Given wd_i's accumulated relative word frequency $t_i(Q)$ and its inverse word frequency $\ln(1+\frac{N}{n_i})$, we follow the TF-IDF rule and use the product of the two terms, $t_i(Q)\ln(1 + \frac{N}{n_i})$, to indicate the importance of wd_i. Finally, we organize the TF-IDF terms of all the non-stop words occurring in $\mathbf{D}(Q)$ as a vector $\mathbf{\Omega}_{\text{text}}(Q)$, i.e.

$$\begin{aligned}\mathbf{\Omega}_{\text{text}}(Q) \triangleq \; & \left(t_1(Q)\ln(1 + \tfrac{N}{n_1}), t_2(Q)\ln(1 + \tfrac{N}{n_2}),\right. \\ & \left.\cdots, t_{V(Q)}(Q)\ln(1 + \tfrac{N}{n_{V(Q)}})\right),\end{aligned} \tag{1}$$

where $V(Q)$ is the number of distinct non-stop words in $\mathbf{D}(Q)$.

3.2.2 Characterizing word frequency distribution associated with online image search results

It should be noted that each reference image in our method is obtained through an online image search process. A property of images obtained in this way is that every image is linked back to its source webpage where we can obtain surrounding text for the image. Denote a reference image $G_j(Q)$'s source webpage as $P_j(Q)$. The source documents of all the webpages associated with the online image search results $\mathbf{G}(Q)$ form a document set $D'(Q) \triangleq \{P_1(Q), \cdots, P_{\zeta(Q)}(Q)\}$. For each non-stop word wd_i that occurs in the source document of the webpage $P_j(Q)$, we also calculate its relative word frequency among all the non-stop words occurring in the source document and denote the result as $f_{i,j}(Q)$. In a similar procedure as described in Sec. 3.2.1, we also derive a non-stop word wd_i's inverse word frequency with respect to the webpage source document set $D'(Q)$ as $\ln(1 + \frac{\zeta(Q)}{n'_i})$ where n'_i is the total number of webpage source documents containing the non-stop word wd_i. We organize the product of the above calculated relative word frequencies and inverse word frequencies for all the non-stop words occurring in $P_j(Q)$ as a $V'_j(Q)$ dimensional vector $\mathbf{\Omega}_{\text{img}}(Q)$, assuming there are $V'_j(Q)$ distinct non-stop words appearing in $P_j(Q)$. That is,

$$\begin{aligned}\mathbf{\Omega}_{\text{img},j}(Q) \triangleq \; & \left(f_{1,j}(Q)\ln(1 + \tfrac{\zeta(Q)}{n'_1}), f_{2,j}(Q)\ln(1 + \tfrac{\zeta(Q)}{n'_2}),\right. \\ & \left.\cdots, f_{V'_j(Q),j}(Q)\ln(1 + \tfrac{\zeta(Q)}{n'_{V'_j(Q)}})\right).\end{aligned} \tag{2}$$

3.2.3 Measuring the semantic alignment between two types of text context

Previously in Sec. 3.2.1 and Sec. 3.2.2 we derived two types of text contexts, one from the online text search results and the other from the webpage source document associated with an online image search result. We have also looked at how to characterize the two types of text contexts via their respective word frequency distribution vectors $\mathbf{\Omega}_{\text{text}}(Q)$ and $\mathbf{\Omega}_{\text{img},j}(Q)$. Next, we derive an online reference image $G_i(Q)$'s relevance to its query Q, which is denoted as $r_i(Q)$, by measuring the semantic alignment between the two types of text contexts through computing the inner product of their respective word frequency distribution vectors. That is,

$$r_i(Q) \triangleq \mathbf{\Omega}_{\text{text}}(Q)\mathbf{\Theta}_i\mathbf{\Omega}^{\text{T}}_{\text{img},i}(Q), \tag{3}$$

where $\mathbf{\Theta}_i$ is a $V(Q) \times V'_i(Q)$ dimensional matrix whose element on the u-th row and v-th column is the semantic relatedness between the u-th non-stop word in the online text search results and the v-th non-stop word in $P_i(Q)$, measured by the algorithm proposed in [10]. We then treat the resulting $r_i(Q)$ as our initially estimated image-to-query relevance for the online reference image $G_i(Q)$. We organize all the estimated initial reference image to query relevance as a $\zeta(Q)$ dimensional vector, i.e. $\mathbf{R}^{\text{init}}(Q) \triangleq (r_1(Q), r_2(Q), \cdots, r_{\zeta(Q)}(Q))$. The reason why we call this the initial relevance estimation is because not all the reference images acquired through online image search are accompanied by quality annotation texts. Such unreliability in the surrounding text of online reference images will surely affect the quality of our text analysis based image to query relevance estimation, a problem commonly suffered by nearly all annotation text based image search methods. Hence we call the above estimation on online reference images' relevance to the textual query *the initial estimation*. In the following, we will discuss how to refine this initial estimation.

3.3 Measuring Pairwise Reference Image Similarity

Given the initial image-to-query relevance estimation for all the reference images, we then refine the estimated image-to-query relevance through conducting an image content similarity based propagation procedure, which will be presented in Sec. 3.4. A key step of the procedure is to measure the pairwise image similarity between reference images. In our method, we introduce a visual patch set based pairwise image similarity estimation method, which collaboratively mines the online text and image search results.

In our method, we calculate pairwise reference image similarity through analyzing image content similarity at the granularity of visual patch sets rather than at the whole image level. Such finer granularity offers us a more elaborate analysis capability, which we will make clear shortly. To extract visual patch sets from the reference image set, we first apply the feature extraction algorithm proposed in [2] to obtain a collection of visual patches for every reference image in the reference image set $\mathbf{G}(Q)$. These visual patches are defined as Speeded-Up Robust Features (SURF), each of which includes a circular effective feature region and a feature descriptor. More concretely, we represent a visual patch v as $v = (C, Des)$, where C represents v's circular effective feature region, and Des is v's feature description vector. We further define the distance between two visual patches as the L_2 distance between the description vectors of the two visual patches. Two visual patches are considered identical if their L_2 distance is below 0.01.

Based on the concept of visual patches just introduced, we can define a visual patch set which is a set of visual patches detected from an image whose circular regions are overlapping. Formally, a visual patch set of size l is defined as:

$$\phi \triangleq (v_1, v_2, \cdots, v_l), \tag{4}$$

where $v_i = (C_i, Des_i)$ and $\forall i, j = 1, 2, \cdots, l$, v_i connects with

v_j. Here the relationship connects with is defined as follows:

$$v_i \text{ connects with } v_j \iff \begin{array}{c} C_i \cap C_j \neq \emptyset \\ \text{or} \\ \exists v_k \in \phi,\ s.t.\ C_i \cap C_k \neq \emptyset, C_j \cap C_k \neq \emptyset \end{array} \quad (5)$$

In the above, $\emptyset$ represents an empty set. In the following, we use the notation $|\phi|$ to denote the size of the visual patch set ϕ.

Finding all the visual patch sets contained in a reference image set incurs an exponential amount of computational overhead. Fortunately, we only need to derive some most frequently occurring visual patch sets in our method as they provide the most essential evidence for estimating pairwise image similarity. Calculating frequently occurring visual patch set is a much more affordable computational task. In our method, we extracted visual patch sets from all the reference images in $\mathbf{G}(Q)$ whose occurrence numbers exceed a certain threshold using the method proposed in [30]. A typical threshold value used in our experiments is 5. Two visual patch sets are identical if they contain the same set of constituent visual patches. Let $\phi_i(Q)$ denote a frequent visual patch set detected from the reference image set $\mathbf{G}(Q)$. All the frequently occurring visual patch sets detected from the reference image set $\mathbf{G}(Q)$ are organized as a collection, which is denoted as $\mathbf{\Phi}(Q) \triangleq \{\phi_1(Q), \phi_2(Q), \cdots, \phi_{z(Q)}(Q)\}$, assuming there are $z(Q)$ frequent visual patch sets contained in the reference image set $\mathbf{G}(Q)$.

It is noted that in [30], the authors also proposed to use visual patch sets to estimate pairwise image similarity. Unlike our method, their algorithm only detects visual patch sets containing no more than two patches; our algorithm explores visual patch sets of all sizes. The reason why their algorithm tightly limits the size of visual patch sets considered is because their algorithm relies on extracting visual patch sets from a large number of sample images to perform content-based image search, an image collection that aims to work universally for all the queries. Such an algorithm design feature translates to a high degree of computational overhead in visual patch set extraction. In contrast, our algorithm is designed to use a much smaller set of sample images acquired from online image searches in a query specific manner. The query-specific nature of our algorithm's reference image acquisition process allows us to work with a very limited number of sample images each time for performing content-based image retrieval. Such careful control of reference image set size successfully restricts the time spent on extracting visual patch sets from the reference image set. This algorithm feature enables us to explore visual patch sets of larger sizes in our method, leading to a richer set of image features for image content understanding.

Once we have detected the visual patch sets from all the reference images, we can then analyze those patch sets commonly occurring in a pair of reference images for estimating pairwise image similarity. This practice is inspired by the classic $TF \times IDF$ based document similarity measurement method [29]. Borrowing their idea for document similarity estimation in the text domain, in our method, we attempt to estimate pairwise image similarity through counting the common visual patch sets existing among two images and in a weighted way, prioritizing co-occurrence of salient visual patch sets. The assumption is, the larger the number of salient visual patch sets commonly existing among two reference images is, the more similar the two images would be.

3.4 Refining Image-to-Query Relevance Estimation for Reference Images

Based on the pairwise reference image similarity estimation method introduced in the previous subsection, we now introduce a multi-step propagation procedure to refine the initial image-to-query relevance estimation for reference images. We call the resultant estimation the *refined image-to-query relevance.* Our work is inspired by the recent work on product image ranking by Jing and Baluja, who modified the traditional Pagerank algorithm for ranking images through an iterative process [15].

First, we construct a pairwise image similarity matrix $\mathbf{S}_{\zeta(Q)\times\zeta(Q)}$, where the element on the i-th row and the j-th column of $\mathbf{S}_{\zeta(Q)\times\zeta(Q)}$ is the image similarity between the i-th and the j-th reference images, $G_i(Q)$ and $G_j(Q)$. The pairwise image similarity is estimated using the method introduced in Sec. 3.3. Noticing that the more steps we take in propagating a belief, the less reliable the propagated belief tends to be, we penalize the results obtained with more steps of propagation using an attenuation factor β. To formally define this multi-step propagation process, we employ the matrix exponent notation [11], as follows:

$$\begin{aligned} \mathbf{R}^{\text{refined}} &\triangleq e^{\beta\mathbf{S}}\mathbf{R}^{\text{init}} \\ &= (\mathbf{I}_{\zeta(Q)\times\zeta(Q)} + \beta\mathbf{S} + \tfrac{\beta^2\mathbf{S}^2}{2!} + \tfrac{\beta^3\mathbf{S}^3}{3!} + \cdots)\mathbf{R}^{\text{init}}, \end{aligned} \quad (6)$$

where $\mathbf{S}_{\zeta(Q)\times\zeta(Q)}$ is the pairwise image content similarity matrix; $\mathbf{R}^{\text{init}}$ and $\mathbf{R}^{\text{refined}}$ are respectively the initial and refined estimated image-to-query relevance for all the reference images; β is the propagation attenuation constant. A typical value assignment for β, as used in all our experiments reported in this paper, is 0.3.

The propagation procedure described in (6) can be concisely represented as $\mathbf{R}^{\text{refined}} \triangleq e^{\beta\mathbf{S}}\mathbf{R}^{\text{init}}$, where the matrix exponent can be efficiently computed by observing the fact that $\mathbf{S}$ is symmetric. Therefore, we can decompose $\mathbf{S}$ as $\mathbf{S} \triangleq \mathbf{QDQ}^{-1}$, where $\mathbf{Q}$ is an orthogonal $\zeta(Q)\times\zeta(Q)$ matrix containing the eigenvectors of $\mathbf{S}$, and $\mathbf{D}$ is an $\zeta(Q)\times\zeta(Q)$ diagonal matrix containing the eigenvalues of $\mathbf{S}$. We can then rewrite $e^{\beta\mathbf{S}}$ as follows:

$$\begin{aligned} e^{\beta\mathbf{S}} &= \mathbf{I} + \beta\mathbf{QDQ}^{-1} + \tfrac{\beta^2(\mathbf{QDQ}^{-1})^2}{2!} + \tfrac{\beta^3(\mathbf{QDQ}^{-1})^3}{3!} + \ldots \\ &= \mathbf{I} + \beta\mathbf{QDQ}^{-1} + \tfrac{\beta^2\mathbf{QD}^2\mathbf{Q}^{-1}}{2!} + \tfrac{\beta^3\mathbf{QD}^3\mathbf{Q}^{-1}}{3!} + \ldots \\ &\approx \mathbf{I} + \beta\mathbf{QDQ}^{-1} + \tfrac{\beta^2\mathbf{QD}^2\mathbf{Q}^{-1}}{2!} + \tfrac{\beta^3\mathbf{QD}^3\mathbf{Q}^{-1}}{3!} \\ &\quad + \tfrac{\beta^4\mathbf{QD}^4\mathbf{Q}^{-1}}{4!} + \tfrac{\beta^5\mathbf{QD}^5\mathbf{Q}^{-1}}{5!}. \end{aligned} \quad (7)$$

The truncation decision of stopping at the fifth term is emprically made in our experimentation. We plan to explore more systematically the optimal assignment of this truncation threshold in our future work. According to this new representation, the matrix exponentiation can be efficiently computed by an eigenvalue decomposition process followed by a few matrix multiplication and addition operations. As mentioned earlier, the constant β is the propagation attenuation parameter that penalizes the results obtained through multiple steps of propagation.

Combining (6) and (7), we have:

$$\mathbf{R}^{\text{refined}} = e^{\beta\mathbf{S}}\mathbf{R}^{\text{init}} \approx (\mathbf{I} + \sum_{i=1}^{5} \frac{\beta^i\mathbf{QD}^i\mathbf{Q}^{-1}}{i!})\mathbf{R}^{\text{init}}. \quad (8)$$

Each time when a query Q is submitted, the initial image-to-query relevance score $\mathbf{R}^{\text{init}}$ is first estimated and then the corresponding $\mathbf{R}^{\text{refined}}$ can be derived through matrix multiplications and additions according to (8). The i-th component of $\mathbf{R}^{\text{refined}}$ is denoted as $r_j^{\text{refined}}(Q)$, which represents the j-th reference image $G_j(Q)$'s relevance to the query Q.

3.5 Retrieving and Re-Ranking Unannotated Images

Given an arbitrary unannotated image I_x, to estimate I_x's relevance to the textual query Q, we refer to a set of reference images highly similar to I_x and use these reference images' query relevance for estimating I_x's relevance to the query. Our idea is to leverage the "intelligence of the crowd," i.e., if multiple reference images that are highly relevant to the query exhibit a high visual similarity with I_x, I_x is then more likely to be closely related to the query.

More concretely, given a textual query Q, we perform an online image search to obtain a collection of reference images $\mathbf{G}(Q) = \{G_1(Q), G_2(Q), \cdots, G_{\zeta(Q)}(Q)\}$ (Sec. 3.1). In Sec. 3.2–Sec. 3.4, we have explained our method for estimating an arbitrary reference image $G_j(Q)$'s relatedness to the query Q, which is denoted as $r_j^{\text{refined}}(Q)$. We have also explained our method to extract frequent visual patch sets from $\mathbf{G}(Q)$, which are denoted as $\mathbf{\Phi}(Q) = \{\phi_k\}$, where each ϕ_k is an extracted frequent visual patch set (see Sec. 3.3).

For each visual patch set ϕ_k, we first estimate its relevance to the query Q. Since we have estimated each reference image G_i's relevance to the query Q, our method estimates each visual patch set's relevance to the query by distributing the image to query relevance to the individual visual patch sets' relevance to the query. To realize the above idea, we first estimate the salience of each visual patch set contained in a reference image G_i. Again, we borrow the traditional TF-IDF scheme in the text processing domain for characterizing a visual patch set's salience. Let $m_j(\phi_k)$ be the number of times the visual patch set ϕ_k occurs in the j-th reference image $G_j(Q)$. Then we can mimic the TF term for the visual patch set ϕ_k as $(1+\ln m_j(\phi_k))$. Let $m(\phi_k)$ be the number of images in the reference image collection $\mathbf{G}(Q)$ that contain the visual patch set ϕ_k. Then we can emulate the IDF term for ϕ_k as $\ln(1+\frac{\zeta(Q)}{m(\phi_k)})$. Recall that $\zeta(Q)$ is the total number of images in the reference image collection. Overall, we define the TF-IDF term for the visual patch set ϕ_k as $(1+\ln m_j(\phi_k))\ln(1+\frac{\zeta(Q)}{m(\phi_k)})$. We can then calculate the relative salience of the visual patch set ϕ_k among all the visual patch set contained in the reference image G_i as follows:

$$\rho(\phi_k) = \frac{(1+\ln m_j(\phi_k))\ln(1+\frac{\zeta(Q)}{m(\phi_k)})}{\sum_{\phi_t \in G_i}(1+\ln m_j(\phi_t))\ln(1+\frac{\zeta(Q)}{m(\phi_t)})}. \quad (9)$$

According to the relative salience of each visual patch set contained in G_i, we then proportionally attribute G_i's relevance score to the query Q to individual visual patch sets present in the image. That is, the fraction of query relevance score allocated for the visual patch set Φ_k is $r_j^{\text{refined}}(Q)\rho(\phi_k)$. Recall that $r_j^{\text{refined}}(Q)$ is the j-th reference image $G_j(Q)$'s refined estimated relevance score to the query Q. Finally, we derive ϕ_k's overall relevance score to the query, denoted as $\theta(\phi_k, Q)$, by summing up the fractional relevance scores ϕ_k acquired from all the reference images, i.e.:

$$\theta(\phi_k, Q) = \sum_{j=1}^{\zeta(Q)} r_j^{\text{refined}}(Q)\rho(\phi_k). \quad (10)$$

With every visual patch set's query relevance estimated through (10), we can now estimate an unannotated image I_x's image-to-query relevance, denoted as $\widehat{\theta}(I_x, Q)$, based on the query relevance of all the visual patch sets carried in I_x, as follows:

$$\widehat{\theta}(I_x, Q) = \sum_{\phi_k \in I_x} \theta(\phi_k, Q), \quad (11)$$

Overall, via (11), we can estimate an unannotated image's relativeness to a textual query through weighted sum of the query relevance of all the visual patch sets present in the image.

Finally, given an input query Q, each search candidate image I_x will be assigned a query relevance score $\widehat{\theta}(I_x, Q)$ via (11). Those candidate images whose estimated query relevance scores are above a certain threshold will be returned as image search results for the query. All the search result images are also ranked in a descendent order according to each image's estimated query relevance score.

4. EXPERIMENTAL RESULTS

We invited eight volunteers to participate in our experiments conducted on two standard image datasets: the Caltech101 image collection [6] and the MIRFLICKR collection [13]. We compared the measured performance of our algorithm with that of two peer content-based image retrieval algorithms. All our experiments were performed on a desktop computer with 2.66GHz Intel Core 2 Duo CPU and 2GB main memory, running Windows XP.

4.1 Evaluation Metric

We evaluate the quality of an image search and ranking result by adopting the normalized discounted cumulative gain (NDCG) metric. The participating users would assign a numerical label to each of the top N_{top} search result images to indicate their opinions on these images' relevance to the corresponding queries. The numeric label, in the range of $[0, 1]$, represents the image's relevance with the query (1: "fully relevant"; 0: "fully irrelevant"). For those image search experiments performed on the standard image collections, since all the images in the collection have been carefully classified and labeled, we automatically assign a binary value of either 0 or 1 to indicate whether a search result image is relevant to the query or not. In all the experiments reported in this paper, we restrict N_{top} to be no more than 50.

4.2 Execution Efficiency

Much of the execution time of our algorithm is spent on downloading online reference images through Google image search. For a typical query performed in our experiments for the Caltech101 data set, we use the top 50 images retrieved from Google image search as the reference image collection, i.e. $\zeta(Q) = 50$. Table 1 shows the run-time breakdown statistics for each part of our algorithm. The exact duration of downloading time needed varies from query to query, which also heavily depends on the quality of a particular user's Internet connection. For real world deployment, our algorithm can run on the server side in order to avoid the reference image downloading time. Therefore, in our analysis, we exclude the online reference image downloading step.

4.3 Image Retrieval on Standardized Image Sets

The Caltech101 image collection contains 8677 images, pre-labelled with 101 textual tags, which has been widely used as a benchmark for image retrieval and object recognition. We use each textual tag as the image query keyword and take all the 8677 images in the entire Caltech101 image collection as the candidate image search result set. Therefore, all together, we would perform 101 sessions of image retrieval experiments over the collection. At the end of each image querying experiment, we evaluate the performance of our algorithm by calculating its NDCG score for the image querying session. If the search result image comes from the then chosen image class, it is considered a correct image retrieval result; otherwise, it is a false retrieval result. We also perform the same image query sessions on the MIRFLICKR collection, which consists of

Algorithm Step		Execution Time
Step 1:	Download reference images	ISP-dependent
Step 2:	Estimate initial image-to-query relevance for reference images	20 $\sim$ 30 sec.
Step 3:	Detecting visual patch sets	10 $\sim$ 40 sec.
Step 4:	Refine image-to-query relevance for reference images	< 1 sec.
Step 5:	Retrieve and rank unannotated images	< 1 sec.

Table 1: Run-time breakdown of different components of our algorithm for performing a typical image search query in our experiments. We report the time consumed by every step of our algorithm individually.

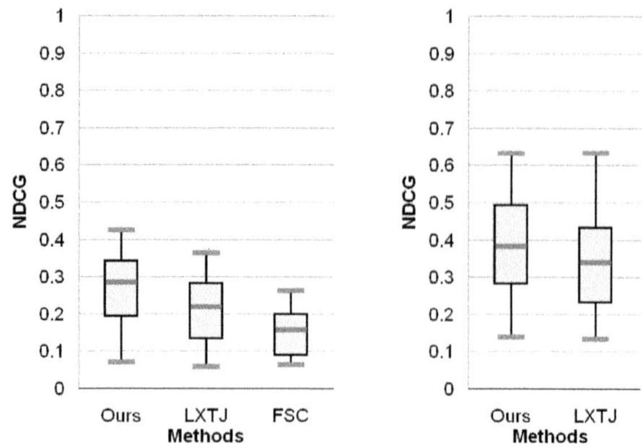

(a) without relevance feedback (b) with relevance feedback

Figure 1: NDCG scores of image search experiments conducted over the MIRFLICKR image set using "LXTJ," "FSC," and our algorithm respectively. We illustrate the key statistics of all the NDCG scores using boxplots.

25000 pre-tagged images that were used in recent years for ImageCLEF cross language image retrieval tasks [4].

For comparison purposes, we also implemented two recent image retrieval algorithms respectively proposed in [21] and [7], which we abbreviate as "LXTJ" and "FSC" in our following discussions. We chose these two algorithms to compare with because they share the same idea of mining online information for image search as our method; the two peer algorithms also achieve today's leading performance among all existing methods for image search. During our comparison, we apply the three algorithms respectively over the Caltech101 and MIRFLICKR collections for image retrieval experiments. Note that the "FSC" algorithm requires a labelled training set. We employed the 10-fold cross validation as our evaluation strategy.

4.4 Comparing Algorithm Performance without Relevance Feedback

In Figure 1(a) and Figure 2(a), we report the NDCG scores obtained by three algorithms respectively over the image querying sessions. All these results are generated fully automatically, i.e. no user feedback is provided for the algorithms. From these results, we can clearly see that our algorithm consistently outperforms the other two algorithms.

4.5 Comparing Algorithm Performance with Relevance Feedback

In practice, a frequent strategy for improving the performance of an image retrieval system is to incorporate relevance feedback. For example, "LXTJ" proposed a relevance feedback based approach to enhance their image classifiers' performance interactively via cross-domain learning. To explore our algorithm's image search capability and potential more thoroughly, we also conduct experiments with relevance feedback. In our comparative study, we perform three rounds of relevance feedback when executing each query. In each feedback round, a user randomly selected from our participation group is asked to mark one relevant image and one irrelevant image among the top N_{top} (usually 50) images in the query result. For the algorithm of "LXTJ," their method is designed with a relevance feedback module and hence can directly use the provided relevance feedback data to improve its image search result. Our algorithm however is not equipped with a relevance module because we focus on providing a fully automatic mechanism for image search, aiming at the most convenient user experience. For a fair comparison, when comparing search results of our algorithm with those of LXTJ under the relevance feedback setting, we introduce a trivial relevance feedback step for our algorithm—if a user indicates a negative search result item, i.e. the item is not related to the query, we simply remove the item from the returned search image list. If a user indicates a positive search result item, our algorithm simply ignores the user input. Figure 1(b) and Figure 2(b) report the respective NDCG scores of image search experiments performed over two public image datasets by our algorithm and LXTJ with a three-round user feedback. The results show that our algorithm still outperforms the LXTJ algorithm with three rounds of user feedback.

4.6 Comparing Algorithm Performance with Query Keywords Extended

We aim to more realistically emulate users' image search behaviors and scenarios in reality. This time, when doing an image retrieval, instead of using the original query keyword, we use a synonym of the keyword as the query text. For example, for the query keyword of "lotus," we use "lily" or "lily lotus" or "lotus flower" or "water-lily" as the query text in our image retrieval experiments. For this new set of experiments, we randomly select 10 image tags from the Caltech101 collection as our retrieval target objects to perform ten image retrieval experiments, one experiment for each tag. In each experiment, we invited five volunteers. We asked each volunteer to give a few words that could best describe the common content of a few randomly selected images from the same image tag in the Caltech101 collection. In this process, we hide the original image tag to these volunteers; and the answer given by each volunteer is kept hidden from other volunteers. Therefore, each volunteer needs to come up with a name for the image tag independently. For each image tag, if there is a word that appears in at least three volunteers' description texts, we will accept the word as a commonly agreed *user nominated search query* for the image query. If there are more than one word commonly named by more than three volunteers during our image querying experiments, we will randomly choose one word as the keyword to compose the image query. We designed this set of experiments to emulate image search scenarios in reality when the query text submitted by the end user does not use exactly the same word as the labels of an online image. For the "FSC" algorithm, again half of images in each class of Caltech101 were used as the training set and the other half were used as the testing set. Figure 3 shows key statistics on the results of our image search experiments achieved by all three algorithms.

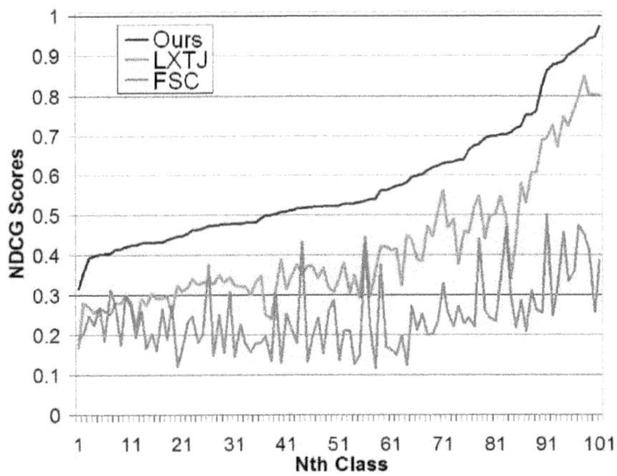

(a) Experiments without relevance feedback on Caltech101

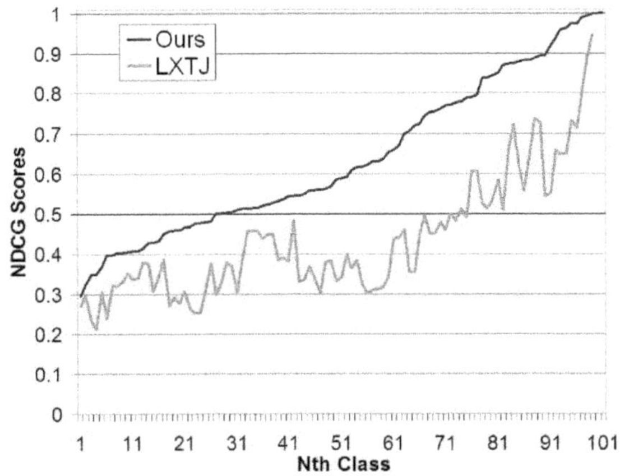

(b) Experiments with relevance feedback on Caltech101

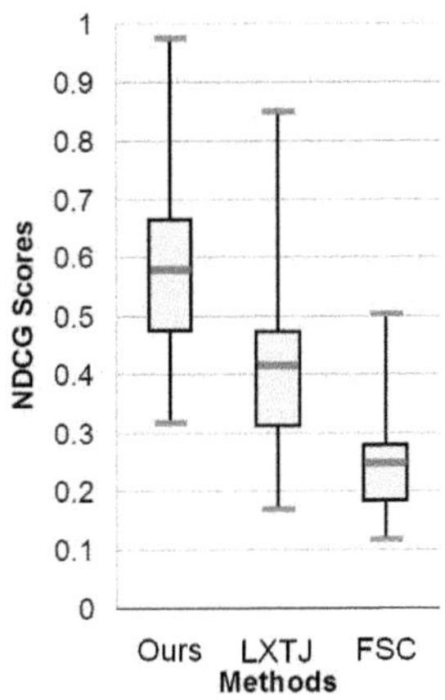

(c) Box-plots of (a)

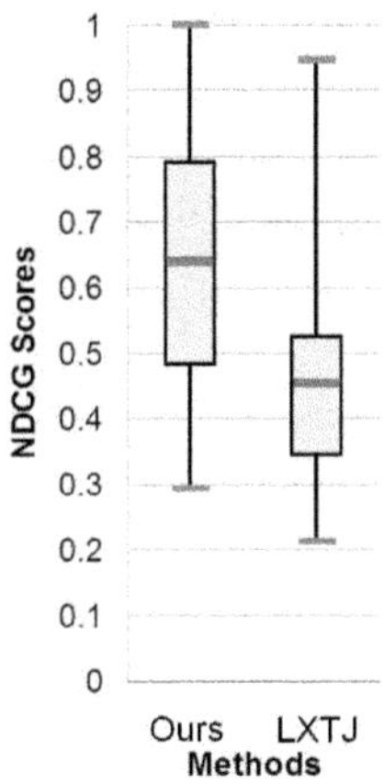

(d) Box-plots of (b)

Figure 2: NDCG scores of 101 image search experiments conducted over the Caltech101 image set using "LXTJ," "FSC," and our algorithm respectively. We report the NDCG scores for all 101 image search sessions (a), (b) and also illustrate their key statistics using boxplots (c), (d). For easy reading, all the NDCG scores are sorted in the ascending order according to the NDCG score of our method. In (a) & (c) we compare our algorithm's performance with that of LXTJ and FSC, all without using any relevance feedback measurement; in (b) & (d) we compare the performance of our algorithm and that of LXTJ, both using three rounds of relevance feedback.

Image Tag	User Nominated Query Keywords	
brain	neuron	nervous
cannon	gun	weapon
dollar bill	dollar	money
ferry	ship	boat
laptop	notebook	computer
menorah	candle	candelabrum
motorbike	motorcycle	pedal bicycle
pyramid	Egypt	triangle
stop sign	sign	car sign
sunflower	flower	flora

(a)

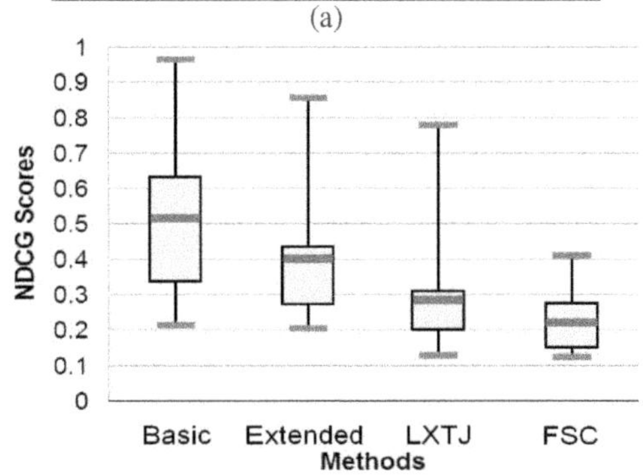

(b)

Figure 3: Statistics of the NDCG scores attained by "LXTJ," "FSC," and our method respectively, in our experiments simulating real-world user search scenarios. (a) lists user nominated query keywords. In (b), we illustrate NDCG scores using boxplot diagrams, where the box-plots "Basic" and "Extended" respectively indicate search scores achieved by our method when we use the exact image class names (basic) and the user nominated keywords (extended) as image search queries to perform image searches. We also provide search scores achieved by "LXTJ" and "FSC" for image searches using user nominated search keywords for comparison.

These results again demonstrate the superiority of our algorithm to the other two peer methods.

4.7 Image Retrieval on Personal Photo Collections

Eight volunteers were invited to use the prototype image search system that implements our algorithm to retrieve images from their respective personal photo albums. The number of photos in a volunteer's personal photo album is between 500 and 4000. The number of photos in the eight volunteers' personal photo albums are 1172, 729, 2305, 671, 1380, 2768, 3884, 3374 respectively.

We ask every volunteer in our study to perform 30 image searches. For each volunteer, his or her 30 image search queries are formulated by the volunteer himself or herself by freely choosing 30 search keywords. We then rank all the image search query words suggested by the eight volunteers according to the frequency that a query word was commonly suggested by multiple users. Once all the query words are ranked, we select the top 20 most frequently suggested query keywords. Figure 4(a) lists these twenty image query keywords used in our experiments. Figure 5 shows some example image search results by our algoirthm in our personal photo retrieval experiments. Image searches are performed using these query words over each user's personal photo collection. After that, we evaluate the NDCG score for each query performed over a user's personal photo collection, following the procedure introduced earlier in Sec. 4.1. For each user, we perform twenty image search sessions, where each time we use one of the twenty image search keywords as the image search query and performed the search session over the user's personal photo collection. Hence for each user, we obtain twenty NDCG scores, one for each image query session performed. Figure 4(b) reports the key statistics on the distributions of these twenty NDCG scores attained by our method for personal photo search experiments performed for every user respectively.

For comparison, we also report the NDCG scores of personal image retrieval experiments, performed using "LXTJ" and "FSC" respectively, under the same experiment setup. Concerning the "FSC" algorithm, we notice that the algorithm cannot be run in a straight-forward manner on a personal photo album because it needs a labelled training set. To enable the "FSC" algorithm to run in our comparison, we first retrieve the top 500 images for each query keyword using Google image search as its training set. In Figure 4, we use yellow, red, and blue boxplots to respectively illustrate the statistic distributions of search scores obtained using "LXTJ," "FSC," and our algorithm when performing twenty personal image retrieval sessions for every user in our study. According to results shown in the figure, for all the subjects in our user study, the image search scores obtained using our algorithm are noticeably higher than the image search scores of the other two peer methods, which demonstrates the general superiority of our algorithm to the two existing methods for retrieving unannotated personal photos.

5. CONCLUSION

We have introduced a new content-based image search and ranking algorithm for unannotated images. Our algorithm infers the relevance of an unannotated image to a text query through a set of reference images from online image search. To deal with noisy reference image samples, we introduced an elaborate joint text analysis and image visual content analysis procedure to set apart the good and the bad (i.e., irrelevant) reference images. Then through a weighted visual phrase based scheme, we transfer the image-to-query relevance information on the reference images to an arbitrary unannotated image. The transferred relevance is then used to retrieve and rank unannotated images. The experimental results convincingly show the effectiveness and advantages of our new algorithm for searching unannotated images given an input textual query.

In the future, we plan to explore advanced machine learning algorithms that can more reliably and comprehensively understand the semantics of an unannotated images for content-based image search. We also plan to design an intelligent and friendly user interface that can leverage user feedback or utilizes social tags to improve the retrieval quality through online learning. We may consider extending our algorithm to automatically and efficiently annotate unlabelled images on the Internet. This problem is related to the task tackled by our algorithm in this paper, which is to find relevant images for a given text query, but in the automatic image labeling task, the goal is to look for text term(s) that can maximize their relevance to a given image. We expect many steps of our current algorithm can be readily used to address that new problem.

Acknowledgement

Songhua Xu and Hao Jiang contribute equally to this paper. Songhua Xu has performed this research as a Eugene P. Wigner Fellow and staff member at the Oak Ridge National Laboratory, managed by UT-Battelle, LLC, for the U.S. Department of Energy under Contract DE-AC05-00OR22725. This research is also partially sponsored by Centers for Medicare & Medicaid Services of United States Department of Health and Human Services.

6. REFERENCES

[1] P. Adrian, M. Christophe, and M. Pierre-Alain. Ontology driven content based image retrieval. In *CIVR '07: Proceedings of the 6th ACM International Conference on Image and Video Retrieval*, pages 387–394, New York, NY, USA, 2007. ACM.

[2] H. Bay, A. Ess, T. Tuytelaars, and L. V. Gool. Speeded-up robust features (surf). *Computer Vision and Image Understanding*, 110(3):346–359, 2008.

[3] D. Cai, X. He, Z. Li, W.-Y. Ma, and J.-R. Wen. Hierarchical clustering of www image search results using visual, textual and link information. In *MULTIMEDIA '04: Proceedings of the 12th Annual ACM International Conference on Multimedia*, pages 952–959, New York, NY, USA, 2004. ACM.

[4] P. Clough, M. S, and H. MÍźller. H.: A proposal for the clef cross language image retrieval track (imageclef) 2004. In *CIVR '04: The Challenge of Image and Video Retrieval*, page 3115. Springer LNCS, 2004.

[5] R. Datta, J. Li, and J. Z. Wang. Content-based image retrieval: approaches and trends of the new age. In *MIR '05: Proceedings of the 7th ACM SIGMM International Workshop on Multimedia Information Retrieval*, pages 253–262, New York, NY, USA, 2005. ACM.

[6] L. Fei-Fei, R. Fergus, and P. Perona. Learning generative visual models from few training examples: An incremental bayesian approach tested on 101 object categories. In *CVPRW '04: Proceedings of the 2004 Conference on Computer Vision and Pattern Recognition Workshop (CVPRW'04) Volume 12*, page 178, Washington, DC, USA, 2004. IEEE Computer Society.

[7] H. Feng, R. Shi, and T.-S. Chua. A bootstrapping framework for annotating and retrieving www images. In *MULTIMEDIA '04: Proceedings of the 12th Annual ACM International Conference on Multimedia*, pages 960–967, New York, NY, USA, 2004. ACM.

[8] R. Fergus, L. Fei-Fei, P. Perona, and A. Zisserman. Learning object categories from google's image search. In *Tenth IEEE International Conference on Computer Vision*, ICCV '05, pages 1816–1823. IEEE, 2005.

[9] R. Fergus, P. Perona, and A. Zisserman. A visual category filter for google images. In *ECCV '04: 8th Proceedings of the European Conference on Computer Vision*, pages 242–256, London, UK, 2004. Springer-Verlag.

[10] E. Gabrilovich and S. Markovitch. Computing semantic relatedness using wikipedia-based explicit semantic analysis. In *Proceedings of the 20th International Joint Conference on Artifical Intelligence*, pages 1606–1611, San Francisco, CA, USA, 2007. Morgan Kaufmann Publishers Inc.

[11] R. A. Horn and C. R. Johnson. *Topics in Matrix Analysis*. Cambridge University Press, 1991.

[12] J.-H. Hsiao, C.-S. Chen, and M.-S. Chen. A novel language-model-based approach for image object mining and re-ranking. In *ICDM '08: Proceedings of the Eighth IEEE International Conference on Data Mining*, pages 243–252, Washington, DC, USA, 2008. IEEE Computer Society.

apple	baby
beach	chair
cloud	desert
everest	flower
girl	green trees
house	jokul
lotus	mountain
park	people
pyramid	railway
river	rocket

(a)

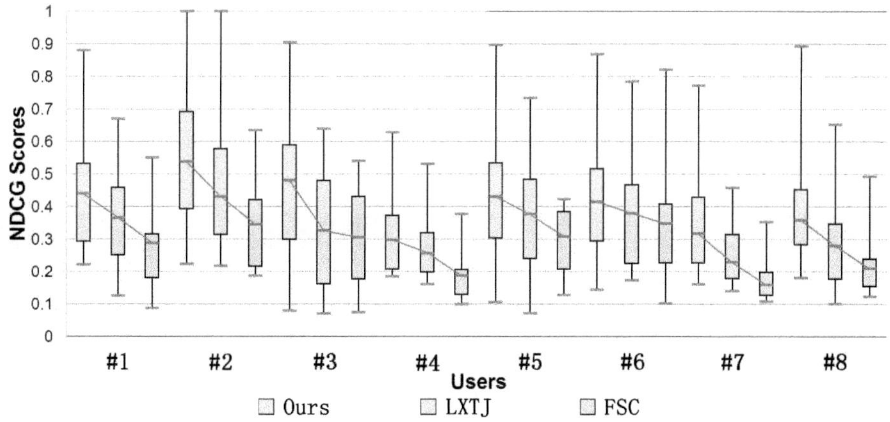

(b)

Figure 4: (a) Twenty image queries performed over each user's personal photo collection in our experiments. (b) Distributions of NDCG scores of three algorithms for searching unannotated images over eight users' personal photo collections in box-plots. Twenty image queries were performed over each user's personal photo collection using "LXTJ" (without relevance feedback), "FSC," and our algorithm respectively.

[13] M. J. Huiskes and M. S. Lew. The mir flickr retrieval evaluation. In *Proceeding of the 1st ACM International Conference on Multimedia Information Retrieval*, MIR '08, pages 39–43, New York, NY, USA, 2008. ACM.

[14] J. Jia, N. Yu, and X.-S. Hua. Annotating personal albums via web mining. In *Proceeding of the 16th ACM International Conference on Multimedia*, MM '08, pages 459–468, New York, NY, USA, 2008. ACM.

[15] Y. Jing and S. Baluja. Pagerank for product image search. In *WWW '08: Proceedings of the 17th International Conference on World Wide Web*, pages 307–316, New York, NY, USA, 2008. ACM.

[16] M. L. Kherfi, D. Ziou, and A. Bernardi. Image retrieval from the world wide web: Issues, techniques, and systems. *ACM Computing Survey*, 36(1):35–67, 2004.

[17] P. Kidambi and S. Narayanan. A human computer integrated approach for content based image retrieval. In *ICCOMP'08: Proceedings of the 12th WSEAS International Conference on Computers*, pages 691–696, Stevens Point, Wisconsin, USA, 2008. World Scientific and Engineering Academy and Society (WSEAS).

[18] L.-J. Li and L. Fei-Fei. Optimol: Automatic online picture collection via incremental model learning. *International Journal of Computer Vision*, 88:147–168, 2010.

[19] W.-H. Lin, R. Jin, and A. Hauptmann. Web image retrieval re-ranking with relevance model. *Proceedings of IEEE/WIC International Conference on Web Intelligence*, pages 242–248, 2003.

[20] Y. Liu, D. Xu, I. W. Tsang, and J. Luo. Using large-scale web data to facilitate textual query based retrieval of consumer photos. In *Proceedings of the 17th ACM International Conference on Multimedia*, MM '09, pages 55–64, New York, NY, USA, 2009. ACM.

[21] Y. Liu, D. Xu, I. W. Tsang, and J. Luo. Textual query of personal photos facilitated by large-scale web data. *IEEE Transactions on Pattern Analysis and Machine Intelligence*, 33:1022–1036, May 2011.

[22] Y. Liu, D. Zhang, G. Lu, and W.-Y. Ma. A survey of content-based image retrieval with high-level semantics. *Pattern Recognition*, 40(1):262–282, 2007.

[23] D. G. Lowe. Distinctive image features from scale-invariant keypoints. *International Journal of Computer Vision*, 60(2):91–110, 2004.

[24] R. Marée, P. Denis, L. Wehenkel, and P. Geurts. Incremental indexing and distributed image search using shared randomized vocabularies. In *Proceedings of the International Conference on Multimedia Information Retrieval*, MIR '10, pages 91–100, New York, NY, USA, 2010. ACM.

[25] H. Muller, N. Michoux, D. Bandon, and A. Geissbuhler. A review of content-based image retrieval systems in medical applications–clinical benefits and future directions. *International Journal of Medical Informatics*, 73(1):1–23, 2004.

[26] F. Schroff, A. Criminisi, and A. Zisserman. Harvesting image databases from the web. *IEEE Transactions on Pattern Analysis and Machine Intelligence*, 33:754–766, April 2011.

[27] A. W. M. Smeulders, M. Worring, S. Santini, A. Gupta, and R. Jain. Content-based image retrieval at the end of the early years. *IEEE Transactions on Pattern Analysis and Machine Intelligence*, 22(12):1349–1380, 2000.

[28] L. Torresani, M. Szummer, and A. Fitzgibbon. Learning query-dependent prefilters for scalable image retrieval. In *CVPR '09: IEEE Conference on Computer Vision and Pattern Recognition*, pages 2615–2622, Washington, DC, USA, 2009. IEEE Computer Society.

[29] I. H. Witten, A. Moffat, and T. C. Bell. *Managing gigabytes: compressing and indexing documents and images*. Morgan Kaufmann, 1999.

[30] Q.-F. Zheng and W. Gao. Constructing visual phrases for effective and efficient object-based image retrieval. *ACM Transactions on Multimedia Computing, Communications and Applications*, 5(1):1–19, 2008.

[31] X. S. Zhou and T. Huang. Unifying keywords and visual contents in image retrieval. *IEEE Multimedia*, 9(2):23–33, 2002.

(a) Top 20 image search results for "cloud"

(b) Top 20 image search results for "beach"

(c) Top 20 image search results for "jokul"

Figure 5: Three personal photo album search experiments using the keywords "cloud," "beach," and "jokul" respectively. For each experiment, we show its top 20 search result images, along with each image's relevance to the query (beneath the image).

Adaptive Parallel Approximate Similarity Search for Responsive Multimedia Retrieval

George Teodoro
Dept. of Computer Science
University of Maryland
College Park, MD
teodoro@cs.umd.edu

Eduardo Valle
FEEC
State University of Campinas
Campinas, Brazil
dovalle@dca.fee.unicamp.br

Nathan Mariano
Dept. of Computer Science
Federal U. of Minas Gerais
Belo Horizonte, MG
nathanr@dcc.ufmg.br

Ricardo da Silva Torres
Institute of Computing
State University of Campinas
Campinas, Brazil
rtorres@ic.unicamp.br

Wagner Meira Jr.
Dept. of Computer Science
Federal U. of Minas Gerais
Belo Horizonte, MG
meira@dcc.ufmg.br

ABSTRACT

This paper introduces Hypercurves, a flexible framework for providing similarity search indexing to high throughput multimedia services. Hypercurves efficiently and effectively answers k-nearest neighbor searches on multigigabyte high-dimensional databases. It supports massively parallel processing and adapts at runtime its parallelization regimens to keep answer times optimal for either low and high demands. In order to achieve its goals, Hypercurves introduces new techniques for selecting parallelism configurations and allocating threads to computation cores, including hyperthreaded cores. Its efficiency gains are throughly validated on a large database of multimedia descriptors, where it presented near linear speedups and superlinear scaleups. The adaptation reduces query response times in 43% and 74% for both platforms tested, when compared to the best static parallelism regimens.

Categories and Subject Descriptors

H.2.2 [**Database management**]: Physical design — access methods; H.2.4 [**Database management**]: Systems — multimedia databases; H.3.1 [**Information storage and retrieval**]: Content analysis and indexing — indexing methods

General Terms

Algorithms, Measurement, Performance, Design, Experimentation.

Keywords

Descriptor indexing, Local descriptors, Information retrieval.

1. INTRODUCTION

In the past decades, content-based multimedia retrieval has been proposed by the scientific community as a sophisticated alternative to the often impractical keyword-based retrieval of multimedia documents. Though the concretization of those goals in the marketplace has been much more elusive, in the past few years, a quick sequence of successful applications has brought content-based retrieval from the pages of scholarly articles to the reality of consumer service business. Those services include the obvious web image retrieval search engines, but also the less obvious image recognition for handheld devices, real-time song identification, and a myriad of assorted applications.

The alluring diversity of those services is somewhat deceptive, for behind the multitude of media formats, query modalities and database genera, content-based multimedia retrieval and classification is backed by the unifying principle of the descriptor. The descriptors give the multimedia documents a perceptually meaningful geometry, which bridges the so called "semantic gap", i.e., the meaninglessness of their low-level coding (the pixels in the image, the samples in the audio, etc.) and the complexity of the high-level task at hand. In that geometry, the documents may be seen as vectors in a space, which can be closer or further apart, according to their perceptual properties.

In terms of database systems, the pivotal operation is similarity search on the descriptors. From that point of view, looking for similar multimedia documents is equivalent to look for documents whose descriptors are similar. The complete multimedia query processing may actually be more complex than that, and consist of several phases. Nevertheless, similarity search on the descriptors will often be the first step and, surprisingly, one of the most expensive.

In this paper we are concerned with that core operation of similarity search. We introduce a flexible architecture, which we call Hypercurves, for providing similarity search to online multimedia services.

Hypercurves is built upon the synergy of two ideas: the sequential multidimensional index Multicurves [35] and the concurrent execution environment Anthill [31]. It addresses many challenges, presenting several novel contributions:

1. In order to address large scale databases and heavy request loads, Hypercurves employs several dimensions of parallelism: task, data, pipeline, and intra-filter; allowing data partition in the distributed environments without the need of any replication.
2. Hypercurves is intended for online services, with variable, user-dependent demands. On those environments, any static

CIKM'11, October 24–28, 2011, Glasgow, Scotland, UK.

choice for the parallelism configuration will become sub-optimal as operational conditions fluctuate. We have developed efficient (low overhead) and effective algorithms for dynamically selecting parallelism configurations (Section 4.3) and allocating tasks to computational cores, including hyper-threaded cores (Section 4.4);

3. Hypercurves performance (almost linear speedup and super-linear scaleup) rests upon the fact Multicurves design fit extremely well into the execution model of Anthill. Nevertheless the transition from sequential to parallel indexing remains very challenging, and depends crucially on the fact each partition of the data can be accessed independently. We demonstrate that this can be done efficiently, while keeping the algorithms equivalent with almost certain probability (Section 4 and Section 5).

It is opportune to highlight that the extensions proposed to Anthill, though tailored to Hypercurves, are useful to a large class of online services. The equivalence proof can also be applied in other contexts, since it is general to the problem of searching on distributed sorted lists.

All contributions are tested throughly in several experimental scenarios.

1.1 Image retrieval and similarity search

Classification and retrieval of multimedia documents is almost always mediated by descriptors, which embed multimedia documents into a space, thus bridging the gap between the amorphous low level coding and the complex semantic relationships.

In what concerns visual documents (images and videos), the last decade witnessed the ascent of descriptors inspired by Computer Vision, especially the so-called local descriptors [21, 33], with the remarkable success of the SIFT local descriptors [18]. Meanwhile, the idea of using compact representations based on codebooks of those descriptors became popular and one of the main tools in the literature [4].

But regardless of the representation employed, a key operation in all systems is retrieving similar descriptors. This operation can be used either directly (many early CBIR systems were little more than a similarity search engine attached to a descriptor space [29]), either indirectly (the search may be part of a kNN classifier, it can retrieve a preliminary set of candidates to be refined by a more computationally intensive classifier, etc.). Nevertheless, it remains a critical component, if the system is to be used in real world, large-scale databases [17].

Efficient query-processing for multidimensional data has been pursued for at least four decades. Its applications are many, and go far beyond the matching of multimedia descriptors, including satisfying multicriteria searches and spatial and spatio-temporal constraints [24, 19, 12, 9, 23]. An exhaustive review is daunting, and beyond the scope of this text: for a comprehensive introduction and state of the art on the subject the reader is referred to [26, 27].

In multimedia we are almost always interested in approximate techniques. That is not only a result of the technical challenge of treating high dimensionalities; the information coded by the descriptors is always intrinsically approximate, so insisting on exact retrieval makes no sense. What is expected is a good trade-off between precision and speed. But if perfect accuracy can be excused, the efficiency requirements remain very challenging: the method should perform well for high-dimensional data (hundreds of dimensions) in very large databases (at least millions of records); it must adapt well to secondary-memory storage, which in practice means that few random accesses should be performed; it should be dynamic, i.e., allow data insertion and deletion without performance degradation.

Despite the huge assortment of methods available, those of practical interest in the context of content-based multimedia services are surprisingly few. Many methods assume that the implementation uses shared main memory (with cheap random access), other methods have prohibitively high index building times (with a forced rebuilding if the index changes too much), and so on.

MEDRANK is an interesting method, which projects the data into several random straight lines. The one-dimensional position on the line is used to index the data [11]. The method has an interesting theoretical analysis, establishing that under certain hypotheses, rank aggregation on straight line projections offers some (lax) bounds on approximation error. The techniques employed by the algorithm were extremely well succeeded in moderately-dimensional multicriteria databases, for which it is still feasible to search for exact solutions. In those cases many of its choices are provably optimal [12].

For high-dimensional multimedia information, however, the technique fails, mainly due to the lack of correlation between the distance in the straight lines and the distance in the high-dimensional space [34]. This phenomenon is known as "curse of dimensionality" and expresses the difficulty in partitioning the data or the space in efficient ways when dimensionality is high [3, 37]. Image descriptors with 30 dimensions are commonplace, and those at around 100 are not unusual. Dimensionalities of 400 and above are not unheard of. For spaces like those, kNN search is extremely challenging.

An interesting family of solutions employs the fractal space-filling curves. Like MEDRANK, those methods reduce multidimensional indexing to one-dimensional indexing, but using more sophisticated projections [16, 28]. The method upon which we build our work, Multicurves, is one of those methods and it is explained in detail in the next section.

1.2 Paper organization

The remainder of the text is organized as follows. In Section 2 we describe Multicurves in detail. In Section 3, the Anthill execution model is discussed. Section 4 is devoted to Hypercurves and its scheme of parallelization. In Section 5 we present an important result: the proof of the probabilitistic equivalence of the proposed parallel algorithm to the original sequential version. In Section 6 we present an experimental evaluation of the proposed scheme in many stress scenarios. With Section 7, we conclude the article.

2. MULTICURVES

Multicurves [35, 36] is an index for data immersed in Hilbert spaces, whose properties make it especially adapted for large-scale multimedia descriptor databases. Multicurves is based on space-filling curves that are fractal curves introduced by Peano and Hilbert [25], which provide a continuous mapping from the unit interval $[0;\ 1]$ to any unit hypercube $[0;\ 1]^d$. Most space-filling curves are constructed by recursive procedures, where, in the limit, the curve fills the entire space. Though these curves are fascinating by themselves, here we are interested in their ability to induce a "vicinity-sensitive" total order to the data: the curve produces a total order that, locally and with high-probability, preserves the neighborhood relations (putting near in the curve points also near in the space). The biggest problem when using those curves is the existence of boundary regions where locality-preserving properties are violated, and points close in space are placed far appart in the curve. This issue worsens significantly as dimensionality grows [16, 28].

Algorithm 1 Multicurves index construction

input:

$points$: *input data elements*

$curves$: *number of curves (and, thus, of sub-indexes)*

$dims[i]$: *dimensionality of the ith curve*

a: *correspondence between input data and subindexes — $a[i,j]$ is the dimension in the ith subindex to which the jth dimension of the input data should be attributed (see line 6 below)*

output: *an array of 'curves' sorted lists, which composes the index*

1: $subindexes[] \leftarrow$ *new array with* $curves$ *empty sorted lists*
2: **for all** $p \in points$ **do**
3:   **for** $c \leftarrow 1$ to $curves$ **do**
4:     $proj[] \leftarrow$ *new array with* $dims[c]$ *empty elements*
5:     **for** $d \leftarrow 1$ to $dims[c]$ **do**
6:       $proj[d] \leftarrow p[a[c,d]]$
7:     $key \leftarrow ExtendedKey(dims[c], proj)$
8:     *Insert* $< key, p >$ *into* $subindex[curve]$;
9: **return** $subindexes[]$

Multicurves proposes to alleviate this issue by making each curve responsible for only a subset of the dimensions. Because of the exponential nature of the "curse", it is more efficient to process several low dimensional queries than a single high-dimensional one. As we will see in Section 4.2, this structure also opens the opportunity for parallelism, since querying the sub-indexes is mostly independent.

Multicurves index construction is simple: the data elements are divided among a certain number of space-filling curves. Each curve projects the data on a corresponding subspace and then computes their extended-keys (the one-dimensional position in the curve). The pairs <extended-key, data element> are placed in lists sorted by extended-key, one list per curve. Each list is a subindex (Algorithm 1). For ease of understanding, it is described as a "batch" algorithm, but nothing prevents the index from being built incrementally, if the structure used to implement the sorted list allows so.

Algorithm 2 Multicurves search phase

input : *(in addition to $curves$, $a[]$ and $dims[]$, defined as above)*

k: *the number of desired nearest neighbors*

$depth$: *the* probe-depth *i.e., the number of elements to examine per subindex*

$query$: *the data element to be queried*

$subindexes[]$: *array of sorted lists composing the index, generated as above*

output : *a list with the k approximate nearest neighbors*

$best \leftarrow \emptyset$
for $c \leftarrow 1$ to $curves$ **do**
  $proj[] \leftarrow$ *new array with* $dims[c]$ *empty elements*
  for $d \leftarrow 1$ to $dims[c]$ **do**
    $proj[d] \leftarrow query[a[c,d]]$
  $key \leftarrow ExtendedKey(dims[c], proj)$
  $candidates \leftarrow$ *set of* $probe - depth$ *points whose keys are nearest to* key *in* $subindex[c]$
  $kLocal \leftarrow$ *the* k *points nearest to* $query\ from\ candidates$
  $best \leftarrow best \cup kLocal$
$knn \leftarrow$ *the* k *points from best nearest to* $query$
return knn

The search is conceptually similar: the query is decomposed into projections (whose subspaces must be the same used during the index construction) and each projection has its extended-key computed. Then, from each subindex, we obtain a certain number of candidate elements (**probe-depth**), whose extended-keys are the nearest to the extended-key of the corresponding projection of the query. At the end, we compute the actual distance from those elements to the query and keep the k nearest (Algorithm 2).

The extended-key computation depends on the space-filling curve employed. For the Hilbert curve, the most efficient algorithm is [6]. The extended-key on a Z-order curve, which we employ in Hypercurves, is simpler to compute: it suffices to intercalate the bits of the dimensions.

3. ANTHILL

Anthill [31, 32] is a flexible runtime system based on the dataflow model. As such, applications are decomposed into processing stages, called *filters*, which communicate with each other using unidirectional *streams*. The application is, therefore, described as a multi-graph representing the logical interconnections of the filters. At runtime, Anthill spawns on nodes of the cluster instances of each filter, called transparent copies. Anthill automatically handles runtime communication and state partitioning among those copies. A typical Filter-Stream application is shown in Figure 1, where we emphasize the copy mechanism and the possibility of creating loops among filters.

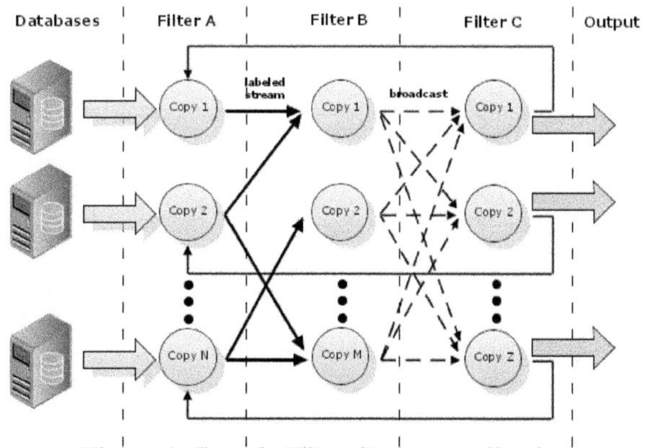

Figure 1: Sample Filter-Stream application.

The filter programming abstraction provided by Anthill is event-oriented, and derives heavily from the message-oriented programming model [22, 38]. The programmer provides functions that match input buffers from the multiple streams to a set of dependencies, creating event queues. Anthill will then take charge of the needed non-blocking I/O streaming.

The programmer also provides handling functions for each of the events on a filter that are automatically invoked by the runtime. Those events, in the dataflow model, amount to asynchronous and independent tasks. Since the filters are multithreaded, multiple tasks can be spawned provided there are pending events and computational resources. This feature not only is essential to fully exploit the capability of current multicore architectures, but also, in heterogeneous platforms, is used to spawn tasks on multiple devices. To accomplish that, Anthill allows the user to provide multiple handlers for the same event, with hints indicating which should be employed on each specific device.

The assignment of events to processors is demand-driven. Thus, when events are queued, they are not immediately assigned to a processor. Rather, this occurs on-demand as devices become available. In the current implementation, the demand-driven, first-come, first-served (DDFCFS) task assignment policy is used as default strategy of the event scheduler.

4. HYPERCURVES

The Hypercurves parallel execution strategy partitions the database among nodes of the distributed environment, while the search is performed locally in the subindexes managed by each node, and a reduction stage merges the results of those local searches. The cost of the algorithm is dominated by the local searches, which are further dependent on the probe-depth used (the number of candidates to retrieve from each subindex). When using the same probe-depth of the sequential algorithm for each local index of the distributed environment, the answer of Hypercurves is guaranteed at least as good as the sequential algorithm. However, this is an extremely pessimistic and costly choice for the local indexes probe-depth: it can be shown that the quality of Hypercurves is equivalent to that of Multicurves with very high probability by using a probe-depth a slightly higher than taking the original probe-depth and dividing it by the number of nodes (See Section 5).

Therefore, the parallelization we propose exploits this property to partition that subindexes among the nodes in a distributed environment, avoiding data replication and consequently improving the scalability of the solution. The user can further modify the probe-depth of the parallel algorithm accordingly using Equation 4 (Section 5) to guarantee that the quality of Hypercurves is equivalent to that of Multicurves with desired probability.

4.1 Filter-Stream based parallelization

Hypercurves consists of four filters, organized in two parallel computation pipelines, as shown in Figure 2. The first pipeline is conceptually an index builder/updater. Its first filter, "Input Reader" (IRR), reads the points from the input database and partitions them among the copies of the second filter, "Index Holder/Local Searcher" (IHLS). The default partition function divides the points equally among IHLS copies, by using a round-robin policy. (It is opportune to highlight, though, that other partition policies may be performed, for providing fault-tolerance or for balancing the load when computing nodes are heterogeneous. We expect to evaluate those scenarios in future works.) The IHLS filter adds the points received from IRR to its local index, according to Algorithm 1. Index building and database reading are performed concurrently, as ensured by Anthill's execution model. After the input is exhausted, IRR interacts with IHLS in case of updates to the database.

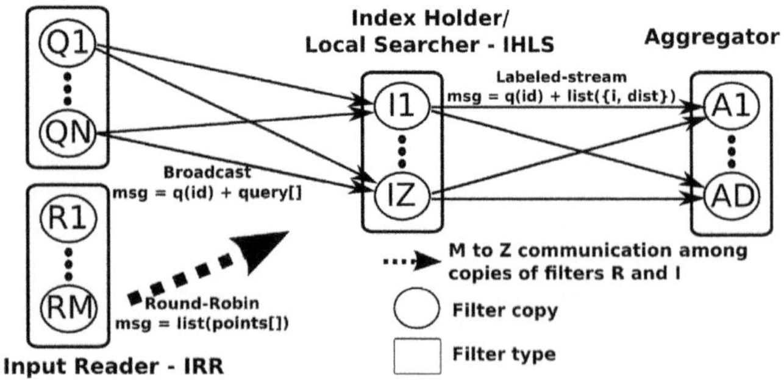

Figure 2: Hypercurves design overview.

The second computation pipeline, which corresponds conceptually to the search phase, contains three filters: (i) Query receiver (QR); (ii) IHLS (shared with the first pipeline); and (iii) Aggregator. QR is the entry point to the search server, receiving the queries and broadcasting them to all IHLS copies, since queries must be processed by all index partitions. That broadcast strategy has little impact on performance, because the search itself dominates the execution time. Thus the communication latency is offset by the speedups on computation.

For each query, IHLS instances independently perform the search on their local index partition, retrieving k nearest *local* data points, according to sequential Multicurves (Algorithm 2).

The final answer to the query is obtained by reducing the k points local to each IHLS copy into k *global* nearest points. This operation is performed by the Aggregator filter. We allow for multiple concurrent copies of this filter, performing reductions from different queries. It is, therefore, crucial that all messages related to some query be sent to the same copy of the Aggregator filter. That is guaranteed by making full use of Anthill Labeled-Stream communication policy, which provides an affordable way to map specific message tags to the same copy of the receiver filter in a stream. The Aggregator filter, itself, receives k nearest points from each IHLS instance, calculates the k global nearest values and emits the query final response. The operation performed between IHLS and Aggregator is very similar to a generalized parallel data reduction [40], except that it outputs a list of values for each output, and that an arbitrary number of reductions are executed in parallel.

Hypercurves scheme exploits all the four dimensions of parallelism: task, data, pipeline, and intra-filter. Task parallelism occurs as filters of different pipelines are executed in parallel, e.g., QR and IRR, which concurrently perform index updates and searches. Data parallelism is achieved as the input database is partitioned among copies of IHLS filters. Pipeline parallelism is a result of Anthill's ability to execute in parallel the filters which compose a single computational pipeline, e.g., IRR and IHLS for updating the index. The fourth dimension of parallelism (next section), refers to a single filter instance being able to process events in parallel. That provides the ability of efficiently exploiting multiple computing devices available in modern multicore computers.

4.2 Intra-filter parallelism

Inter-filter parallelism basically instantiates multiple copies of a sequential event handler. As a strategy, it is very convenient for the programmer, and very effective for many batch applications. However, as the number of independent events falls below the number of computing cores, that "embarrassingly parallel" approach fails to fully utilize the resources. In on-line applications like Hypercurves, there is the additional constraint of the demand being based on users requests, and thus varying during execution.

To fully exploit symmetric multiprocessing (SMP) machines when the number of ready events is lower than the available CC (computing cores), we propose in this work the concept of *parallel event handlers — PEH*. Those event handlers consists of parallel processing functions, capable, thus, of using multiple processing cores for computing a single event. Parallel event handlers introduce the opportunity of employing all available computing cores (even if the number of ready events is low), but at the cost of additional intrinsic overhead brought by the finer grained parallelism. Therefore, their use must be judicious in order to extract the maximum overall performance.

4.2.1 *Extending intra-filter parallelism*

With the addition of parallel handlers, two intra-filter degrees of parallelism exist: (i) the event level degree of parallelism, EP, which refers to the number of events that a filter instance executes in parallel; and, (ii) the degree of internal parallelism, HP, which is the number of cores or threads used by a handler when executing a single event. A parallelism strategy adopted by a filter copy (e.g. one of the instances of IHLS) is described by a set of pairs (EP, HP), each pair defining the number of events EP using a particular amount of threads HP in their PEH. For instance, a IHLS copy could be executing 3 events concurrently: two of them using 1 thread each, and the third using 6 threads at once; that strategy would correspond to the set $\{(2,1),(1,6)\}$.

The crucial point we want to emphasize again is that the parallelism of PEH is achieved at the cost of higher overheads, and thus, likely to be less scalable than the strategy using only event-level parallelism $(EP, 1)$. Therefore, the PEH should be employed judiciously in order to maximize application performance. To increase the challenge, the number of events ready to execute varies during the execution, and thus, the optimal intra-filter parallelism strategy changes dynamically. That problem is detailed and addressed in Sections 4.2.2 and 4.3.

Although crucial to fully exploit SMP machines, the parallelism of PEH requires extra effort from the programmers. Facilitating the development of SMP-based parallel codes is beyond the scope of this paper. However, it is a highly investigated subject, and much progress has been made on automatic parallelizing compilers [39], and other tools for parallel programming [8, 14, 15].

4.2.2 Hypercurves parallel event handler

We have implemented HyperCurves' own parallel event handler using OpenMP [8]. IHLS is Hypercurves' most computational intensive filter, and, thus, an ideal candidate for having a parallel event handler. Though the filter contains two handlers, we have parallelized the search phase that refers to retrieve the k nearest local points for each query, since it is the only handler in IHLS affected by users' behavior.

For this handler, the most expensive operations are examining each subindex/curve in order to retrieve the candidate points, and to reduce these candidates into k nearest points in that curve. This phase is parallelized in our approach, as the subindices are concurrently examined by multiple $threads$. This parallel section represents the lines 2 to 9 of the search phase shown in Algorithm 2. A small sequential section is still necessary in order to pre-aggregate the candidates from each $thread$ to produce the k local points, that are then forwarded to the Aggregator filter (Line 10 from Algorithm 2). However, the cost associated with those local sequential operations is usually very low.

4.3 Auto-tuning intra-filter parallelism

As mentioned before, Hypercurves poses a very interesting challenge with respect to intra-filter parallelism: the number of events ready to execute within a filter varies during the execution, according to the user request demand. Therefore, any intra-filter parallelism configuration chosen *prior* to execution may result in suboptimal response times (See Figure 4). The relation between load/demand (given by *query rate*) and optimal parallelism strategy is affected by complex factors, including hardware architecture and application parameters. Optimizing response times under variable workloads is, therefore, beyond the capabilities of static tuning.

The problem of selecting the adequate values for each parallelism level corresponds to defining a set Z of pairs (EP_i, HP_i), that minimizes the average response time for events created in a filter. To further constraint the optimization, we assume an 1:1 correspondence between the HP parallelism employed in Z and the available CC (computing cores). That corresponds to the following constraint:

$$\sum\nolimits_{(EP_i,HP_i)\in Z} EP_i \times HP_i = CC \qquad (1)$$

When this constraint is too restrictive, omitting sets Z with better performance (e.g., unscalable PEH) the programmer can handcraft another value to be used in the place of CC in the equation above. We believe, however, that the 1:1 assumption to be reasonable when targeting SMP machines.

More importantly, the formulation assumes different optimal solutions throughout the execution as the load varies. The algorithm proposed, called *Dynamic Selection of Parallelism Degrees — DSPD*, is independently executed by each filter instance at runtime. Its rationale is to minimize *query response time* = *event queued time* + *event processing time*. Therefore, our choice is to execute the highest possible number of events in parallel, increasing EP and reducing HP — this also tends to minimize the queued time of events and improve throughput. However, when the number of ready events is not enough to use all available CC, HP is increased to use multiple devices for a single event. In that scenario, event processing time is reduced, and an even better response time is delivered. In all cases, the scheduler works to minimize queuing time and response time (Algorithm 3). It runs during the execution every time that an I/O operation is performed (in background to the events processing), and the computed Z is used thereafter by that filter instance.

Algorithm 3 Dynamic selection of parallelism degrees — DSPD

1: $EP \leftarrow CC, HP \leftarrow 1$
2: **while** not $EndOfWork$ **do**
3:   **if** $EP < CC$ and $GetNumberReadyEvents() > 0$ **then**
4:     $EP \leftarrow Min(CC, GetNumberReadyEvents())$
5:   **else if** $GetNumberIdleThreads() > 0$ **then**
6:     $EP \leftarrow Max(1, EP - GetNumberIdleThreads())$
7:   $HP \leftarrow \lfloor CC \div EP \rfloor$
8:   **if** $EP \times HP = CC$ **then**
9:     $Z \leftarrow \{(EP, HP)\}$
10:   **else**
11:     $idleCores \leftarrow CC - EP \times HP$
12:     $Z \leftarrow \{(idleCores, HP + 1)\}$
13:     $Z \leftarrow Z \cup \{(EP - idleCores, HP)\}$

First step, DSPD checks whether there are events ready to execute. The outer, event parallelism EP is then kept as large as possible, in the limit of the number of waiting events and computing cores, in order to empty the queue as fast as possible (lines 3–5). If there are no events queued and available resources, a higher HP is employed to exploit them (lines 5–7). Finally, the parallelism strategy is set as one pair (if the product $EP \times HP$ fully occupies all cores) or two pairs (if a single "recipe" would leave idle cores) of parallelism strategies. Thus, all CC are employed and a minimum number of threads is used within each PEH.

Defining the right parallelism granularity is a complex problem, which has been studied for a long time, and has many applications, for instance, in the context of parallel nested loops [7]. Most works on this area, however, focus on applying loop transformations according to the available resources in order to adjust the parallelism granularity, aiming at gaining parallelism with reasonable synchronization overhead. However, the best parallelism configuration may be beyond any static tuning, as discussed. That has motived several recent works, which focus on runtime transformations [1, 2, 10]. Those interesting works aim at parallelism tuning for a lower level and are complementary to the strategy we propose.

Though they do not address the needs of adjusting application-level parallelism in changing working loads, they could be applied internally to a parallel event handler.

4.4 Architecture aware thread placement

The advances in multicore systems have turned traditional SMP machines into hierarchical computing environments. As a result, current processors are built using several levels of cache, with different interconnections among cores (*Non Uniform Memory Access — NUMA*), and *Symmetric Multithreaded Processors* (branded *HyperThreading* by Intel), are also available. To exploit those architectures, a deep analysis is required when scheduling computations ($threads$).

In Filter-Stream, thread assignment refers to the problem of choosing the computation cores employed when executing a parallel event handler, i.e., the assignment of each pair $(EP_i, HP_i) \in Z$ to the available computing cores. The challenge is heightened as DSPD changes dynamically the value of Z, requiring the placement to be recomputed.

Events ready to execute are independent tasks in the programming model and, as such, can be dispatched for execution in any order, without assumptions about co-scheduling. There is no communication between events, but only among groups of threads HP processing the same event. Thus, the placement of those threads should minimize their communication cost. However, threads of the same group are likely to execute similar operations (e.g., I/O followed by processing, etc.) in the same sequence, and thus are expected to request the same resources concurrently. That makes them bad candidates to employ virtual cores mapped to the same physical core (i.e., *HyperThreaded* cores), which achieve maximum performance for processes with different requirements [30]. In summary, the proposed solution is based on the following aspects to optimize: (i) distance among cores used by a PEH, according to memory hierarchy (cache and NUMA interconnections); and, (ii) load imbalance among cores, and better use of SMP.

Algorithm 4 Architecture-aware thread placement — TP

for all $(EP_i, HP_i) \in Z$ — *sorted by* HP **do**
  { For all handlers using HP_i threads}
  for $x \leftarrow 1$ to $|EP_i|$ **do**
    $coresSet_x \leftarrow$FindClosestCores(HP_i)

As mentioned above, this optimization is time critical, since it is performed at run time and repeated after every modification in Z. Therefore, we use a lightweight greedy algorithm presented in Figure 4. It first sorts the pairs (EP_i, HP_i) in descending order of HP_i. It then places the sets in this descending order: the goal is to benefit handlers with higher number of threads and communication/synchronization costs. The choice of the adequate cores for each HP_i is further executed by the $FindClosestCores$, which first creates a tree based representation of the computing cores, according to the memory level shared among them, using hwloc [5]. Thereafter, the mapping is made by navigating through the tree in a preorder basis, and assigning the closest set of cores according to the memory hierarchy for each call. The cores are then marked as used, preventing the algorithm from revisiting this tree branch during the next search. Moreover, when *HyperThreading* is available, we avoid employing the same physical core for an HP thread group, unless no other placement is available. By placing threads of different groups on the same physical core we intend to exploit temporal variability on resource demands among those threads. Our strategy differs from traditional approaches where processes that use different resources are executed in the same physical cores [30]. Instead, we exploit the temporal aspect to co-schedule similar computations with time varying demands. In the PEH used by IHLS the demand varies as it has an I/O intensive stage followed by a compute intensive phase. The first phase consists of consulting the subindexes, while the second refers to computing the distance of the candidates returned from the subindexes to the query.

5. PROBABILISTIC CORRECTNESS

Hypercurves was created by adapting the original sequential Multicurves algorithm to the Filter-Stream programming model implemented by Anthill. As seen in the previous sections, that task is far from trivial and required (i) identifying, as filter candidates, sections of the code at once computational intensive, logically concise; (ii) refining the filters boundaries by trading off parallelism and communication costs; (iii) further trade-offs between parallelism opportunities and degree of precision. The first two steps are general to most dataflow languages and runtime systems [13]. The latter step is particular to the approximate nature of the problem in hand.

Multicurves is based upon the ability of space-filling curves giving a total order to data. This is exploited on each subindex (Algorithm 2), where a number of candidates is retrieved from each sorted list. Those candidates are, then, measured against the query and the k nearest are kept. In Hypercurves, the index is further fragmented, and each IHLS filter instance has available only a subset of the database: a single filter cannot warrant the equivalent approximate k nearest neighbors. That is exactly the role of the Aggregator filter: collecting multiple local best neighbors and returning a refined answer set. Note that in terms of equivalence between Multi- and Hypercurves it matters little how the candidates are distributed among the IHLS instances (i.e., whether the "right" candidates end up in a single filter copy or whether they are dispersed). Because both the local aggregation at the end of IHLS and the final Aggregator filter consider all the candidates retrieved so far, they cannot result in a loss of precision.

The only way for both Multi- and Hypercurves to miss a correct answer in the kNN set is failing to retrieve it from the subindexes. In that sense Hypercurves can be made guaranteedly equivalent to Multicurves by employing on each filter copy a probe-depth equivalent to the one used in the sequential Multicurves. That way, no candidates are ever missed, but this is an extremely pessimistic choice.

Consider the same dataset, either in a Multicurves' subindex with probe-depth $= 2 \times \Phi$, or partitioned among ℓ Hypercurves' IHLS filter copies, each with probe-depth $= 2 \times \varphi$ (even probe-depths make the analyses more symmetric, but the argument is essentially the same for odd values). Both on Multi- and Hypercurves each subindex is conceptually a sorted list. For any query, the candidates that would be in a single sorted list in Multicurves are now distributed among ℓ sorted lists in Hypercurves.

The problem can be restated, in more general terms, as follows. We start with a single sorted list and retrieve the $2 \times \Phi$ elements closest to a query point. If we distribute randomly that single sorted list into ℓ sorted lists, how many elements must we retrieve from each of those new lists (i.e. which value for $2 \times \varphi$ must we employ) to ensure that none of the originally retrieved elements is missed.

Note that: (i) due to the sorted nature of the list, the elements before the query cannot exchange positions with the elements after the query; (ii) no element of the original list can be lost as long as all those $2 \times \ell$ "half-lists" are shorter than φ.

Due to (i), we can analyze each half of the list independently. The distribution of the elements among the ℓ lists, is given by an Multinomial distribution with Φ trials and all probabilities equal to ℓ^{-1}. The exact probability of no list being longer than φ involves computing a truncated part of the distribution, but the exact formulas are exceedingly complex and little elucidative. We can, however, bound it from below [20] with:

$$P\left(List_{max} \leq \varphi\right) \geq 1 - \left(\Phi \times P\left(List_i > \varphi\right)\right) \qquad (2)$$

Where $List_i$ is an arbitrary single component of the equiprobable Multinomial, which, by construction has a Binomial distribution for Φ trials and success rate of ℓ^{-1}. Thus, the probability of any miss on any of the $2 \times \ell$ half-lists is bounded from above by:

$$1 - Max\left[0; 1 - \Phi \times \sum_{k=\varphi+1}^{\Phi} \binom{\Phi}{k} \left(\frac{1}{\ell}\right)^k \left(1 - \frac{1}{\ell}\right)^{\Phi-k}\right]^2 = \qquad (3)$$

$$1 - Max\left[0; 1 - \Phi \times \left(1 - I_{1-\ell^{-1}}\left(\Phi - \varphi, \varphi + 1\right)\right)\right]^2 \qquad (4)$$

Where $I()$ is the regularized incomplete Beta function. This probability tends to zero for very reasonable values of φ, still much lower than Φ. This is more easily seen if we make $\varphi = (1 + \varsigma)\lceil\Phi/\ell\rceil$, i.e., if we "distribute" the probe-depth among the filters, adding a "slack factor" of ς. For all reasonable scenarios, the probability tends to zero very fast, even for small ς (Figure 3).

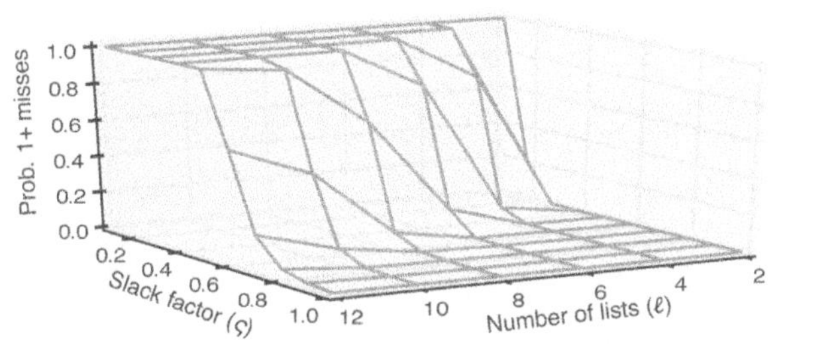

Figure 3: Equivalence between sequential Multicurves with a probe-depth of $2 \times \Phi = 256$ and parallel Hypercurves with distributed probe-depth of $2 \times \varphi$, with $\varphi = (1 + \varsigma)\lceil\Phi/\ell\rceil$ and ℓ = the number of filter copies. The probability of missing any of the candidate points drop sharply to zero for very low values of ς. For the large initial probe-depths actually employed in our experiments ($2 \times \Phi = 6000$), the convergence to zero is even faster.

6. EXPERIMENTAL RESULTS

The experiments were performed using two setups of machines. The first setup was composed of 2 PCs connected with Gigabit Ethernet, each with two quad-core AMD Opteron 2.0 GHz processors and 16 GB of main memory. The second setup was an 8-node cluster connected through Gigabit Ethernet, each node being a PC with two quad-core hyperthreaded Intel Xeon processors E5620 and 12 GB of main memory. All machines run Linux.

The main dataset used to evaluate our algorithm contained 233,852 "background" images from Web, and 225 "foreground" images from our personal collections — the foreground images were used to compute sets of descriptors that must be matched, while the background images were used to compute descriptors added to confound the method. The descriptors were computed using SIFT [18], summing up to 130,463,526 local descriptors with 128 dimensions. Due to the number of evaluations performed, we have also employed smaller partitions of that main database, in order to achieve feasible experimentation run times. The experiments were executed at least three times with standard deviation smaller than 3%.

The experiments concentrate on issues of efficiency, since, as demonstrated in Section 5, Hypercurves, with very high probability, returns the same results of Multicurves. Thus, by construction, it inherits the good trade-off between precision and speed of Multicurves [36].

6.1 Intra-filter scalability analysis

In this section, we evaluate the intra-filter parallelism scalability, as a function of the number of threads. For both node setups, we compare the $(1, HP)$ strategy (only one event at once, with an increasing number of threads employed internally by the parallel event handler) and the $(EP, 1)$ strategy (only one thread per event, with an increasing number of parallel events). The evaluation employed a small subsample of 150,000 descriptors randomly selected from the main database and 1,000 queries. The small dataset is appropriate for this evaluation, since it provides shorter execution times, and, thus, highlights existing overheads. For those experiments, all queries are sent to the filter QR in the beginning of the execution, and only one copy of the filter IHLS is running in a dedicated machine, while the other filters employ a second node.

Parallelism configuration	Number of cores / threads				
	1	2	4	6	8
(1,HP)	153	79.3	41.2	30.2	24.4
(EP,1)	153	76.5	37.6	25.5	19

(a) First setup (2-node AMD)

Parallelism configuration	Number of cores / threads					
	1	2	4	8	12	16
(1,HP)	60.6	31.7	16.3	9.8	8.7	8.5
(EP,1)	60.6	31.3	16.1	9.5	8	7.3

(b) Second setup (8-node Intel)

Table 1: Execution times of two extreme parallelism regimens: only internal parallelism (1,HP) and only event parallelism (EP,1). Note that the latter scales better.

Table 1 shows Hypercurves execution times as the number of threads increases. Both configurations achieve performance gains as the number of threads grows, but, as expected, the configuration with only event-level parallelism $(EP, 1)$ scales better, primarily due to the absence of thread communication / synchronization costs inside the event handler.

The experiments in Table 1 (b) also evaluate the impact of Intel Hyperthreading (which is present from 8 cores/threads and onwards) on both configurations. The configuration $(EP, 1)$ performed consistently better than $(1, HP)$, as expected, but the difference becomes more visible for the hyperthreading scenario: $(EP, 1)$ is 14% faster than $(1, HP)$ when using 16 hyperthreaded cores, and it has an speedup of $1.3\times$ when compared to the configuration with 8 non-hyperthreaded cores. The causes of the better gains of event-only parallelism in the hyperthreading scenario are (i) the lesser imbalance among threads; and, (ii) the independence of threads mapped to the same physical core (since they are processing different events). The fact the threads are likely to be in different phases of the computation, and thus employing distinct resources in time, is crucial to exploit hyperthreading.

6.2 Intra-filter degree of parallelism vs. load

Here, we have evaluated query response times according to the query rate submitted. We have used the same database and queries of the last section. The configurations of parallelism employed are those where all CC are used on a single (EP, HP) pair (i.e. there is a single configuration pair, with $EP \times HP = CC$). The query rate is varied in the interval of 10-120% of the maximum query rate that Hypercurves is able to answer. The maximum rate was calculated in previous executions, considering the configuration $(EP, 1)$, and all queries sent to execution at the beginning (those values are 45 and 138, respectively, for the 1st and 2nd setups).

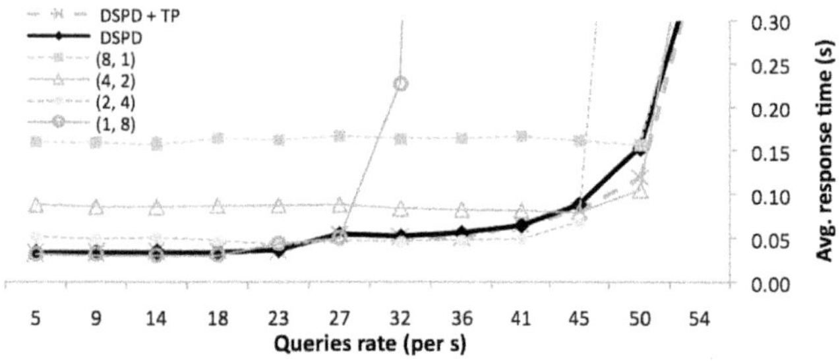

(a) First Setup (2-node AMD)

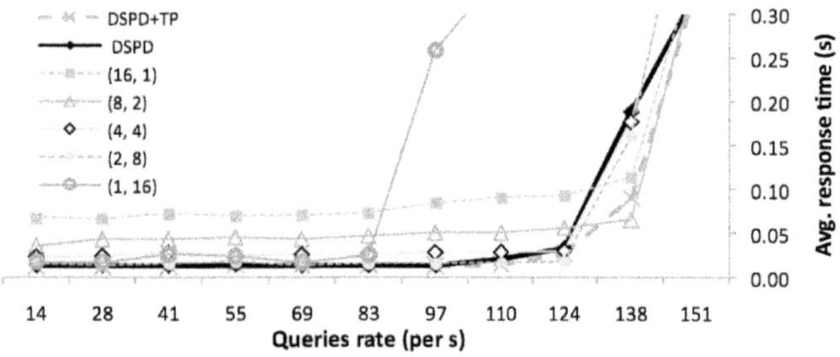

(b) Second Setup (8-node Intel)

Figure 4: Average query response times as a function of load (query rates) for different intra-filter parallelism configurations, on both machine setups. No static configuration is consistently optimal throughout the load variation.

In Figure 4, we present the average query response times for Hypercurves in both setups. The performance of the DSPD algorithm is depicted in this figure, for comparison purposes, but we will discuss it on the next section. The results for the 1st setup, Figure 4(a), show that none of the static configuration delivers the minimum query response times as the query rate varies: for instance, the $(8, 1)$ configuration, which provides the best throughput with a heavy load — query rate, is about 5× slower than the configuration $(1, 8)$, when the load is light. It is interesting to note that each static configuration has the best response times for at least one load. The same set of experiments, executed on the 2nd setup, is shown on Figure 4(b). Again, the best intra-filter parallelism configuration varies according to the query rate. Moreover, for those experiments, the configuration that maximizes throughput $(16, 1)$ has response times up to 7× worse than $(2, 8)$, for query rates lower than 90% of the maximum.

The experiments on both setups show that there is no obvious tradeoff to define the best configuration value. In addition, the choice should depend not only on the query rate (as shown), but also on the input data characteristics and application parameters. Thus, any static tuning is likely to achieve suboptimal performance if those factors change. These aspects motivated the auto-tuning algorithm, as proposed in Section 4.3

6.3 Auto-tuning intra-filter parallelism

This section evaluates the auto-tuning algorithm — DSPD. The first set of experiments, shown in Figure 4, present DSPD performance for static loads (each experimental point has a fixed query rate throughout execution). The initial DSPD configuration in all experiments is $(EP, 1)$, where EP is the number of cores used.

Parallelism configuration	Poisson avg.			
	0.4	0.6	0.8	1.0
Static (1,8)	0.053	0.09	0.256	1.427
Static (2,4)	0.046	0.043	0.048	0.149
Static (4,2)	0.088	0.086	0.084	0.085
Static (8,1)	0.159	0.158	0.161	0.169
DSPD	0.035	0.035	0.048	0.093
DSPD + TP	0.035	0.034	0.047	0.07

(a) First setup (2-node AMD)

Parallelism configuration	Poisson avg.			
	0.4	0.6	0.8	1.0
Static (1,16)	0.391	8.128	5.47	16.595
Static (2,8)	0.014	0.014	0.016	0.519
Static (4,4)	0.026	0.026	0.027	0.181
Static (8,2)	0.04	0.045	0.048	0.171
Static (16,1)	0.069	0.076	0.085	0.206
DSPD	0.014	0.013	0.015	0.241
DSPD + TP	0.012	0.012	0.01	0.17

(b) Second setup (8-node Intel)

Table 2: Average query response times (in s) for static and auto-tuned parallelism configuration under stochastic loads.

DSPD was able to adapt the parallelism, keeping the average response near to the best static configurations in nearly all cases. Moreover, it is able to surpass, on average, the best static configurations for all query rates (78% and 12% improvement, respectively, for 1st and 2nd setups).

We also contrast DSPD to the static parallelism configurations on runs whose query rate varies stochastically during the execution. In those experiments, the load follows a Poisson distribution. These results are presented in Table 2. Again, DSPD performed very well, delivering an equivalent or best performance on almost all cases. For both setups, a static configuration achieved better results when a high load is employed (Poisson average equals to maximum query rate), but the difference is only significant for the second setup. That phenomenon is mainly due to the flatter speedup curves of the intra-filter parallelism, caused by the non-linear speedup achieved by employing virtual cores available with the $Hyperthreading$ mechanism, making the $(8, 2)$ configuration a good choice up to very heavy loads. DSPD, however, starts migrating to intermediary configurations from $(8, 2)$ to $(1, 16)$, before the last becomes the best parallelism configuration.

6.4 Thread placement evaluation

The thread placement algorithm is proposed as an extension to DSPD (DSPD + TP). We start comparing DSPD and DSPD+TP under fixed query rates (Figure 4). On those experiments, DSPD+TP performs very similarly or superpasses DSPD, for both machine setups. The average gains in query response times over DSPD were: 6.45% on the first setup, and 19.3% on the 2nd setup.

The improvements on the 1st setup (2-node AMD) are purely due to faster communication among threads placed with the DSPD+TP. The benefits observed on the 2nd setup (8-node Intel), however, are even more exciting. In this case, most of the gains are due to Hyperthreading-aware placement. When the same evaluation is performed without considering the existence of this mechanism the gains are reduced to about 7%.

For stochastic, time-varying loads, the results are shown on Table 2. Here, DSPD+TP achieves even better results, being equal or better than any other configuration for all runs, with average improvement of 43% and 74%, respectively, for the 1st and 2nd setups when compared to the best static parallelism regimens.

6.5 Assessing distributed memory scalability

The distributed memory analysis in this section has focused in evaluating Hypercurves speedup and scaleup. We consider the compromises between parallelism performance and quality preservation, as data is partitioned among the computing nodes. The query rate delivered by the algorithm considers two parameterization scenarios named *Optimist* and *Pessimist* (Table 3), which differ in their guarantees of equivalence (in terms of precision of the kNN search) to the sequential Multicurves algorithm.

The Optimist parameterization divides the probe-depth equally among the nodes, without any slack — it will only be equivalent to Multicurves in the unlikely case that all candidates of that query are equally distributed among the nodes. The Pessimist parameterization uses a slack such to guarantee that a point encountered in probe-depth of the sequential algorithm may not be in the probe-depth of the distributed version with probability smaller than 1% (the proof details are on Section 5). Note that this choice is still extremely conservative, because, in order to effectively affect the answer, the missed points from the candidate set have to be among the actual *top k* set, and k is much smaller than the probe-depth.

For those experiments, 1/8 of the database is used, such that it occupies 96% of the main memory in each machine. As presented in Table 3, the speedup of the Optimist case is nearly linear in the number of nodes employed. A maximum of 38,932 queries per minute are answered when the entire cluster of the *2nd setup* is employed. The Pessimist case also achieves a near to linear speedup in the number of nodes, but with a smaller factor as it performs extra computation due to the slack added to guarantee the quality.

The Optimist and Pessimist cases are interesting, since they may be considered extreme choices, and taken together, they reflect well the upper and lower bounds on speedup. They enclose a number of reasonable configurations, where the trade-off between performance and quality of the answer can be examined to define the appropriated "slack" in the choice of probe-depth.

We also investigate how the use of more machines allows Hypercurves to process larger datasets. In Table 4, we present the number of queries answered per minute by Hypercurves during that scaleup evaluation. For this experiment we also added a slack to the probe-depth such that we guarantee that with a probability smaller than 1% a point in the probe-depth of the sequential execution will not be in probe-depth of the distributed execution. Those experiments started with 1 computing node, using the 16 virtual cores available, and 1/8 of the main database. The number of machines and the database fraction were increased proportionally up to the configuration with 8 nodes and the entire input database (130,463,526 descriptors). The performance of the Hypercurves in this scenario is even more exciting as it achieved *superlinear scaleup*. The performance of the algorithm is impressive in scaleup experiments because it is only affected by the number of points in the dataset when it is retrieving the probe-depth points from the curves or subindexes, and the cost of this phase grows logarithmic with the size of the database. The most costly phase refers to computing the distance of the query to the probe-depth points. However, the probabilistic correctness (Section 5) allows the distance computation costs to be efficiently distributed among the nodes, as the probe-depth of the sequential executions is divided by the number of nodes and increased by a small slack.

7. CONCLUSIONS AND FUTURE WORK

This work evaluated the similarity search problem on very large databases, focusing on the aspects that arise when it is employed in the context of online search. We have proposed a parallel self-adaptable approximate search algorithm — Hypercurves, which was implemented utilizing the Filter-Stream programming model and is based on space-filling curves concepts. Hypercurves has been designed in order to fully exploit massively parallel machines under variable load. Thus, it can self-adapt the types of parallelism employed within its computation stages, in response to variations on query request rate submitted, to minimize response times.

Also, as a future work, we intend to examine the performance of Hypercurves in heterogeneous clusters and grid environments. An important extension to this algorithm would be the use of accelerators (e.g. GPUs), in order to further improve its performance. The use of GPUs is very challenging with respect to the online demands of Hypercurves, as this type of processor is normally used for throughput oriented computations.

8. ACKNOWLEDGMENTS

The authors would like to express their gratitude to the reviewers of our paper for their valuable comments. This work is partially supported by CNPq, Capes, Fapemig, InWeb - Brazilian INCT for the Web, and FAPESP (project 2009/05951-8).

9. REFERENCES

[1] F. Aleen, M. Sharif, and S. Pande. Input-driven dynamic execution prediction of streaming applications. In *Proc. of the 15th ACM SIGPLAN symposium on Principles and practice of parallel programming*, PPoPP '10. ACM, 2010.

[2] F. Blagojevic, D. S. Nikolopoulos, A. Stamatakis, C. D. Antonopoulos, and M. Curtis-Maury. Runtime scheduling of dynamic parallelism on accelerator-based multi-core systems. *Parallel Comput.*, 33:700–719, November 2007.

[3] C. Böhm, S. Berchtold, and D. A. Keim. Searching in high-dimensional spaces: Index structures for improving the performance of multimedia databases. *ACM Comput. Surv.*, 33:322–373, September 2001.

[4] Y.-L. Boureau, F. Bach, Y. LeCun, and J. Ponce. Learning mid-level features for recognition. *Computer Vision and Pattern Recognition, IEEE Computer Society Conference on*, 0:2559–2566, 2010.

[5] F. Broquedis, J. Clet-Ortega, S. Moreaud, N. Furmento, B. Goglin, G. Mercier, S. Thibault, and R. Namyst. hwloc: a Generic Framework for Managing Hardware Affinities in HPC Applications. In *Proc. of the 18th Euromicro Int. Conf. on Parallel, Distributed and Network-Based Processing (PDP2010)*, pages 180–186, 2010.

[6] A. R. Butz. Alternative algorithm for hilbert's space-filling curve. *IEEE Trans. on Computers*, C-20, 1971.

[7] D.-K. Chen, H.-M. Su, and P.-C. Yew. The impact of synchronization and granularity on parallel systems. *SIGARCH Comput. Archit. News*, 18:239–248, May 1990.

Number of nodes	1	2	3	4	5	6	7	8
# of cores/threads	16	32	48	64	70	86	102	118
Optimist — queries per min	4910	10316	15252	20583	26015	31672	36902	38932
Pessimist — queries per min	4910	9957	14484	19272	24087	29003	33486	35010

Table 3: Speedup evaluation: query rate as number of nodes increase, according to the depth probe used.

Number of nodes	1	2	3	4	5	6	7	8
# of cores/threads	16	32	48	64	70	86	102	118
Pessimist — queries per min	4910	9946	14412	19235	24004	29002	33289	34813

Table 4: Scaleup evaluation: query rate as database and number of nodes increase proportionally.

[8] L. Dagum and R. Menon. Openmp: an industry standard api for shared-memory programming. *Computational Science and Engineering, IEEE*, 5(1):46–55, Jan-Mar 1998.

[9] C. Doulkeridis, A. Vlachou, K. Nørvåg, Y. Kotidis, and M. Vazirgiannis. On the selectivity of multidimensional routing indices. In *Proceedings of the 19th ACM international conference on Information and knowledge management*, CIKM '10, pages 109–118. ACM, 2010.

[10] A. Duran, R. Silvera, J. Corbalán, and J. Labarta. Runtime adjustment of parallel nested loops. In B. M. Chapman, editor, *Shared Memory Parallel Programming with Open MP*, volume 3349 of *Lecture Notes in Computer Science*. Springer Berlin / Heidelberg, 2005.

[11] R. Fagin, R. Kumar, and D. Sivakumar. Efficient similarity search and classification via rank aggregation. In *Proceedings of the 2003 ACM SIGMOD international conference on Management of data*, SIGMOD '03, pages 301–312, New York, NY, USA, 2003. ACM.

[12] R. Fagin, A. Lotem, and M. Naor. Optimal aggregation algorithms for middleware. In *Proc. of the 20th ACM SIGMOD-SIGACT-SIGART Symp. on Principles of database systems*, PODS '01, pages 102–113. ACM, 2001.

[13] M. I. Gordon, W. Thies, and S. Amarasinghe. Exploiting coarse-grained task, data, and pipeline parallelism in stream programs. *SIGOPS Oper. Syst. Rev.*, 40, October 2006.

[14] IEEE. Threads extension for portable operating systems (draft 6), february 1992. p1003.4a/d6., 1992.

[15] Intel. Intel threading building blocks 2.0 for open source. http://threadingbuildingblocks.org/, 2003.

[16] S. Liao, M. A. Lopez, and S. T. Leutenegger. High dimensional similarity search with space filling curves. In *Proc. of the 17th Int. Conf. on Data Engineering*, pages 615–622, 2001.

[17] Y. Liu, D. Zhang, G. Lu, and W.-Y. Ma. A survey of content-based image retrieval with high-level semantics. *Pattern Recognition*, 40(1):262 - 282, 2007.

[18] D. G. Lowe. Distinctive image features from scale-invariant keypoints. *Int. J. Comput. Vision*, 60:91–110, November 2004.

[19] Y.-E. Lu, P. Lió, and S. Hand. On low dimensional random projections and similarity search. In *Proceeding of the 17th ACM conference on Information and knowledge management*, CIKM '08, pages 749–758. ACM, 2008.

[20] C. L. Mallows. An inequality involving multinomial probabilities. *Biometrika*, 55(2):pp. 422–424, 1968.

[21] K. Mikolajczyk and C. Schmid. A performance evaluation of local descriptors. *IEEE Transactions on Pattern Analysis and Machine Intelligence*, 27:1615–1630, 2005.

[22] S. W. O'Malley and L. L. Peterson. A dynamic network architecture. *ACM Trans. Comput. Syst.*, 10(2), 1992.

[23] H. Pang, X. Ding, and B. Zheng. Efficient processing of exact top-k queries over disk-resident sorted lists. *The VLDB Journal*, 19:437–456, June 2010.

[24] H. L. Razente, M. C. N. Barioni, A. J. M. Traina, C. Faloutsos, and C. Traina, Jr. A novel optimization approach to efficiently process aggregate similarity queries in metric access methods. In *Proceeding of the 17th ACM conference on Information and knowledge management*, CIKM '08, pages 193–202. ACM, 2008.

[25] H. Sagan. *Space-Filling Curves*. Springer-Verlag, New York, NY, USA, 1994.

[26] H. Samet. *Foundations of Multidimensional and Metric Data Structures (The Morgan Kaufmann Series in Computer Graphics and Geometric Modeling)*. Morgan Kaufmann Publishers Inc., San Francisco, CA, USA, 2005.

[27] G. Shakhnarovich, T. Darrell, and P. Indyk. *Nearest-Neighbor Methods in Learning and Vision: Theory and Practice (Neural Information Processing)*. The MIT Press, 2006.

[28] J. Shepherd, X. Zhu, and N. Megiddo. A fast indexing method for multidimensional nearest neighbor search. In *SPIE Conference on Storage and Retrieval for Im-age and Video Databases VII*, pages 350–355, 1999.

[29] A. Smeulders, M. Worring, S. Santini, A. Gupta, and R. Jain. Content-based image retrieval at the end of the early years. *Pattern Analysis and Machine Intelligence, IEEE Trans. on*, 22(12):1349 –1380, dec 2000.

[30] A. Snavely and D. M. Tullsen. Symbiotic jobscheduling for a simultaneous multithreaded processor. In *Proceedings of the ninth international conference on Architectural support for programming languages and operating systems*, ASPLOS-IX, pages 234–244. ACM, 2000.

[31] G. Teodoro, D. Fireman, D. Guedes, W. M. Jr., and R. Ferreira. Achieving multi-level parallelism in filter-labeled stream programming model. In *The 37th International Conference on Parallel Processing (ICPP)*, 2008.

[32] G. Teodoro, T. D. R. Hartley, U. Catalyurek, and R. Ferreira. Run-time optimizations for replicated dataflows on heterogeneous environments. In *Proc. of the 19th ACM International Symposium on High Performance Distributed Computing (HPDC)*, 2010.

[33] T. Tuytelaars and K. Mikolajczyk. Local invariant feature detectors: a survey. *Found. Trends. Comput. Graph. Vis.*, 3:177–280, July 2008.

[34] E. Valle, M. Cord, and S. Philipp-Foliguet. Fast identification of visual documents using local descriptors. In *Proceeding of the eighth ACM symposium on Document engineering*, DocEng '08, pages 173–176. ACM, 2008.

[35] E. Valle, M. Cord, and S. Philipp-Foliguet. High-dimensional descriptor indexing for large multimedia databases. In *Proceeding of the 17th ACM conference on Information and knowledge management*, CIKM '08, pages 739–748, New York, NY, USA, 2008. ACM.

[36] E. Valle, M. Cord, S. Phillip-Folliguet, and D. Gorisse. Indexing personal image collections: A flexible, scalable solution. *IEEE Trans. Consumer Elect.*, August 2010.

[37] R. Weber, H.-J. Schek, and S. Blott. A quantitative analysis and performance study for similarity-search methods in high-dimensional spaces. In *Proc. of the 24rd Int. Conf. on Very Large Data Bases*, VLDB '98, pages 194–205, San Francisco, CA, USA, 1998.

[38] M. Welsh, D. Culler, and E. Brewer. Seda: an architecture for well-conditioned, scalable internet services. *SIGOPS Oper. Syst. Rev.*, 35(5):230–243, 2001.

[39] M. J. Wolfe. *High Performance Compilers for Parallel Computing*. Addison-Wesley Longman Publishing Co., Boston, MA, USA, 1995.

[40] H. Yu and L. Rauchwerger. Adaptive reduction parallelization techniques. In *Proc. of the 14th Int. Conf. on Supercomputing*, ICS '00, pages 66–77. ACM, 2000.

A Linear-Time Approximation of the Earth Mover's Distance

Min-Hee Jang
Dept. of Electronics and Computer Engineering
Hanyang University, Korea
zzmini@hanyang.ac.kr

Sang-Wook Kim
Dept. of Electronics and Computer Engineering
Hanyang University, Korea
wook@hanyang.ac.kr

Christos Faloutsos
Dept. of Computer Science
Carnegie Mellon University, USA
christos@cs.cmu.edu

Sunju Park
School of Business
Yonsei University, Korea
boxenju@yonsei.ac.kr

ABSTRACT

Color descriptors are one of the important features used in content-based image retrieval. The dominant color descriptor (DCD) represents a few perceptually dominant colors in an image through color quantization. For image retrieval based on DCD, the earth mover's distance and the optimal color composition distance are proposed to measure the dissimilarity between two images. Although providing good retrieval results, both methods are too time-consuming to be used in a large image database. To solve the problem, we propose a new distance function that calculates an approximate earth mover's distance in linear time. To calculate the dissimilarity in linear time, the proposed approach employs the space-filling curve for multidimensional color space. To improve the accuracy, the proposed approach uses multiple curves and adjusts the color positions. As a result, our approach achieves order-of-magnitude time improvement but incurs small errors. We have performed extensive experiments to show the effectiveness and efficiency of the proposed approach. The results reveal that our approach achieves almost the same results with the EMD in linear time.

Categories and Subject Descriptors

H.3 [**Information Storage and Retrieval**]: Information Search and Retrieval

General Terms

Measurement, Performance

Keywords

Image retrieval, Distance function, Earth mover's distance

1. INTRODUCTION

As the interest in applications using multimedia contents grows fast, the importance of image retrieval has also increased. Many studies have worked on various techniques for accurately retrieving the image(s) the human user wants [13][28][21]. Content-Based Image Retrieval (CBIR) is the technique of searching for images in large databases [13][5]. The human user defines a query image as an example, and the CBIR finds images similar to the query image based on the color distribution, shapes, and textures of the image. This paper deals with the color-based image retrieval problem in CBIR.

How to represent the distribution of colors in an image has a significant implication in color-based image retrieval[15]. The method traditionally used is the color histogram that stores the information about the number of pixels for each color within a fixed set of color ranges. Although being able to represent the entire range of colors (by counting the number of pixels for each possible color), the color histogram may not be a suitable representation for image retrieval for two reasons [25][20]. First, representing and using all possible colors may slow down the search. Second, since only a fraction of the color ranges in a histogram may be useful, using the entire range of colors in an image does not necessarily improve the accuracy of search.

Since it is humans who evaluate the accuracy of the searched images, we need a color description that is tailored to human perception[9]. Humans, when looking at an image, analyze it based on dominant colors [17][7]. An image with blue sky and desert, for example, would be analyzed by humans as an image composed of two main colors: blue (the sky) and yellow (the sand). That is, humans perceive the shades of yellow as a single color. To represent the color in the way human interpret them, the dominant color descriptor (DCD) is proposed for describing color features [21]. By color quantization, the DCD represents an image using a small number of dominant colors, their weights in the image, and several optional parameters. The image retrieval based on the DCD has shown a better performance than that based on the color histogram [20].

To measure the dissimilarity between a given image and images in databases, one needs a distance function. The distance function should be able to measure the following: (1) the dissimilarity between the dominant colors in two images, and (2) the dissimilarity between the weights of dominant colors in two images [17]. As a distance function that satisfies the above criteria, one may use the minimum work, the minimum amount of work needed to transform the color and weight distribution of one image to the distribution of another.

The Earth Mover's Distance (EMD) computes the *optimal* minimum work needed to transform one distribution into the other [20]. The work is defined as the multiplication of the weight of a color transferred and the distance between the transfers. Since a dominant color in one distribution can be transformed into a color in the other distribution in many different ways, finding the minimum work requires a large amount of processing time [20].

Several efforts have been suggested to reduce the computational cost. The EMD finds the minimum work by solving the transportation problem [20]. The complexity of the EMD is $O(n^3 logn)$ where n is the number of the dominant colors. Optimal color composition distance (OCCD) is an approximate method that reduces the computational cost of finding the minimum work [17]. The OCCD quantized the dominant colors into a set of m color unit, each with the same weight, and finds an approximate minimum work by solving the minimum-cost graph-matching problem. The time complexity of the OCCD is $O(m^3)$.

Color-based image retrieval in large databases requires a large number of image comparisons. Both the EMD and the OCCD are not suitable for large databases, because each image comparison requires high computational cost. Although a multidimensional index such as M-tree [3] can reduce the number of image comparisons, a significant number of image comparisons would still be required. For example, 500 to 700 comparisons are required for the database with 100,000 images when the M-tree is used [3].

For large databases, we need a distance function that calculates the minimum work between two images in reasonable time. In previous works, the EMD-L_1 and the wavelet EMD were proposed. The EMD-L_1 reduces the time complexity of the original EMD to $O(n^2)$[12]. However it requires the L_1-distance instead of the usual Euclidean distance. The wavelet EMD was proposed as a linear-time approximate EMD computation [23]. The wavelet EMD, however, is applied to the histogram descriptor and not to the DCD. The wavelet EMD requires the dual function of the EMD, which cannot be created in the DCD. Details of the EMD-L_1 and the wavelet EMD are found in [12] and [23].

We propose a distance function that computes an approximate EMD in linear time of the number of dominant colors. The proposed method works as follows. First, the proposed method creates a linear order of the dominant colors in each distribution. Second, the method calculates the work between the first colors in order in each distribution. The second step is repeated until all dominant colors are considered. The result is the minimum work between two distributions, computed in linear time.

To linearize the distribution of dominant colors in the multidimensional space, we use a space-filling curve. The space-filling curve linearizes multidimensional space [18][11]. Among the various space-filling curves, we use the Hilbert curve, one of the most widely used linearization methods [8][18]. After the linearization using the Hilbert curve, we repeat to select two colors nearest to the starting point of each distribution and compute the work between them. While the selection of two colors compared is based on the Hilbert order, the distance used in computing the work is the actual distance between them in the multidimensional space. The minimum work between two images is computed in $O(n)$, because the dominant colors are scanned sequentially only once.

However, there are two potential problems in the proposed method. First, the distance of two dominant colors close to each other in the multidimensional space may be measured distant in the Hilbert curve. As a result, the order of the dominant colors may not correctly represent the actual distance between them, and the minimum work may be calculated inaccurately. To solve the problem, we create multiple Hilbert curves by changing the starting point and the direction of the Hilbert curve. We calculate the minimum work for each of multiple Hilbert orders and select the minimum value as the minimum work between two images.

Second, even when multiple Hilbert curves are used, there is a chance that the linearized order of dominant colors may not reflect the actual distance in multidimensional space. In particular, if two colors are on the opposite side from the center of the multidimensional space, the distance between them is measured distant in the Hilbert curve.

To solve this problem, we adjust the position of dominant colors to one of the corners of the multidimensional space. The position adjustment may decrease the discrepancy between the actual distance of the colors in multidimensional space and the distance in the Hilbert curve. Since, the distance between the colors is preserved with the position adjustment, no additional error is introduced. After the position adjustment, we create multiple Hilbert curves, compute the minimum work for each Hilbert order and select the minimum value as the minimum work between two images.

When adjusting the positions of dominant colors, we preserve the distance between the colors, and thus no additional error is introduced by the position adjustment. The proposed distance function calculates in linear time the minimum work that is almost the same as the EMD. To demonstrate the advantages of our method, we conduct an extensive set of experiments. The experimental results show that our method provides significant performance improvement over the EMD with small errors. It is also observed that the color-based image retrieval results of our method are comparable with the EMD.

This paper is organized as follows. Section 2 defines the problem and reviews two existing methods. Section 3 describes our method in detail. Section 4 evaluates the performance of our method. Finally, Section 5 concludes this paper.

2. COMPUTATION OF MINIMUM WORK

2.1 Problem Definition

Let $P = (p_1, w_{p_1}), \ldots\ldots ,(p_m, w_{p_m})$ be the color-weight distribution of an image with m dominant colors, where p_i is the dominant color and w_{p_i} is the weight of p_i. Let $Q = (q_1, w_{q_1}), \ldots ,(q_n, w_{q_n})$ be the distribution of another

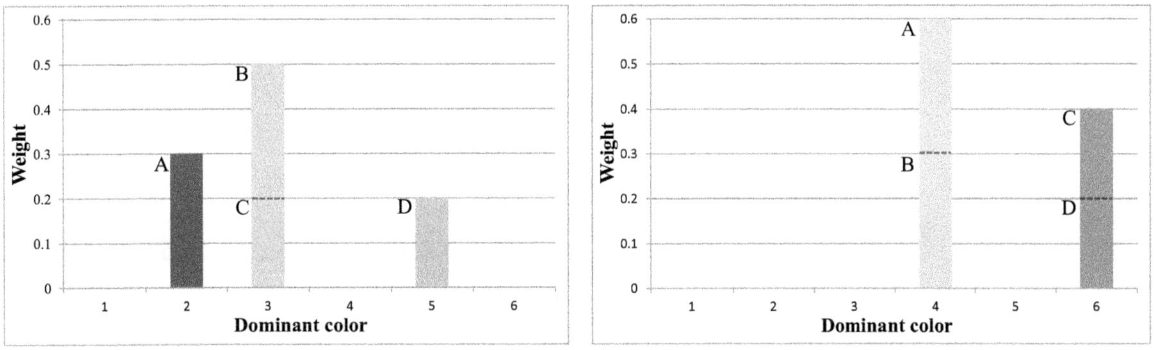

(a) color-weight distribution, *P*.   (b) color-weight distribution, *Q*.

Figure 1: Computation of the minimum work between two distributions.

image with n dominant colors. We assume the total weights of P and Q are the same. Let $D = [d_{ij}]$ be the ground distance matrix, where d_{ij} is the distance between p_i and q_j. The ground distance measures the dissimilarity between the dominant colors of two images and can be defined by any standard method, such as Euclidean distance or L_1 distance [20]. Let $F = [f_{ij}]$ be the transferred weight, where f_{ij} is the amount of weight transferred from p_i to q_j. The work between two colors, p_i and q_j, is defined as the multiplication of transferred weight f_{ij} and ground distance d_{ij}. The work between distributions P and Q is defined as:

$$WORK(P, Q, F) = \sum_{i=1}^{m} \sum_{j=1}^{n} d_{ij} f_{ij}$$

The minimum work between P and Q is defined as the minimum amount of work required to transform distribution P into distribution Q. That is, we want to find the flow, $F = [f_{ij}]$, that minimizes the amount of work required to transform P into Q [20].

We use Figure 1 as an example to describe the computation of the minimum work between P and Q. In Figure 1, P represents the distribution of an image composed of three dominant colors, and Q represents the distribution of an image with two dominant colors. When transforming P into Q, the dominant colors in P can be transferred into the positions in Q in many different ways, but the amount of work would be minimal when each dominant color of P is transferred into the position denoted by the same alphabet in Q. That is, the minimum work is 0.3×2 (for moving A) + 0.3×1 (for B) + 0.2×3 (for C) + 0.2×1 (for D).

The Earth Mover's Distance (EMD) computes the *optimal* minimum work, but requires a significant amount of processing time [20]. The processing time is as important as the accuracy in dissimilarity measures, especially for large databases. In this paper, we propose a new distance function that calculates an approximate minimum work in linear time.

2.2 Existing Methods

2.2.1 *Optimal color composition distance*

The optimal color composition distance (OCCD) is an approximate method that reduces the computational cost of the minimum work. To compute the OCCD, dominant colors are quantized into a set of m color units, each with the same weight, w, where $m\times w = 100$. By solving the minimum-cost graph-matching problem on the undirected graph with m nodes (that represents m color units), the OCCD finds an approximate minimum work.

When an undirected graph is given, the minimum-cost matching problem finds the set of disjoint edges with the minimum cost [10]. The time complexity of the OCCD is $O(m^3)$. The accuracy and the time complexity of the OCCD are influenced by the weight of the color unit. The weight of the color unit has a fixed size, while the weight of each dominant color varies. When dominant colors are quantized into a set of color units, therefore, color loss occurs due to the discrepancy between the weight of dominant color and the color unit. With larger weights, the computation takes less time but the accuracy suffers. When the weight of the color unit is divided into the minimum unit, no color loss occurs, and the OCCD is able to calculate the *optimal* minimum work, while the complexity would be higher. It is recommended to use $m = 20$, $w = 5$ [17].

2.2.2 *Earth Mover's Distance*

In the EMD, the minimum work is computed based on the solution to the transportation problem. Suppose that suppliers need to provide goods to several consumers. Each supplier has a given amount of goods, each consumer has a given demand, and the cost of transporting a single unit of goods is given for each supplier-consumer pair. The transportation problem is then to find the least expensive flow of goods from suppliers to consumers that satisfies consumers' demands [19].

The EMD defines that the dominant colors of one image as suppliers and those of the other image as consumers. The cost of a supplier-consumer pair is defined as the ground distance between the dominant colors. The minimum work can be calculated by solving the transportation problem. The complexity of the EMD is $O(n^3 logn)$. Due to the high computational complexity, both the EMD and the OCCD require a long retrieval time in content-based information retrieval.

3. THE PROPOSED METHOD

3.1 Basic Strategy

In this section, we propose a new distance function that calculates an approximate EMD in linear time. In the fol-

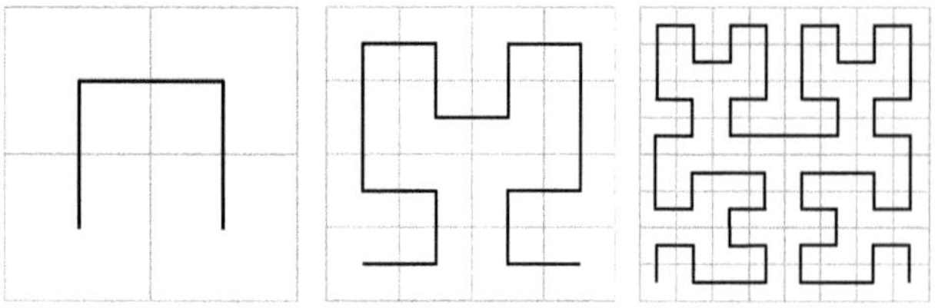

(a) level 1. (b) level 2. (c) level 3.

Figure 2: Examples of the Hilbert curve.

lowing, we assume that dominant colors are ordered in one-dimensional color space. The actual algorithm works in multidimensional space. First, the proposed method selects the color nearest to the starting point of the one-dimensional space from each distribution and computes the work between two colors by multiplying the ground distance between two colors and the maximum common weight (MCW). The MCW is defined as the smaller of the weights of the two colors compared. Second, the proposed method removes the amount of MCW from the two colors. By doing so, the weights used to compute the work are removed from the distributions. Third, the above two steps until all dominant colors of two images are used to compute the work. Finally, adding all the works, the proposed method calculates the minimum work between two images.

We use Figure 1 in Section 2 as an example. Figure 1 shows color-weight distributions of two images in the one-dimensional color space. The weight of the first dominant color in P is 0.3, and the weight of the first dominant color in Q is 0.6. The MCW between these two colors is 0.3. After computing the work (0.3×2), the MCW of the compared colors are removed. That is, the first dominant color at position 2 in P is removed, and the half of the weight of the first dominant color at position 4 in Q is removed. At the next step, the colors nearest to the starting point (and their weights) are at position 3 in P (with the weight of 0.5) and at position 4 in Q (with the weight of 0.3). The MCW between these two colors is 0.3. The work is 0.3×1. When repeating these processes in Figure 1, the minimum work is computed. In the one-dimensional space, our method can compute the optimal minimum work between two images in $O(n)$, where n is the number of dominant colors.

To apply this approach to the image retrieval, we need to establish the order of dominant colors by linearizing the three-dimensional color space. In this paper, we use Hilbert curve, one of the most widely-used space-filling curves [18][29]. Figure 2 shows several examples of the Hilbert curve in two-dimensional space. As shown in the figure, Hilbert curve fills two-dimensional space with a continuous curve. The Hilbert order of the dominant colors is created by this curve. With smaller granularity, multidimensional space is filled with a more complicated curve.

Because the color space, such as RGB and HSV, is three-dimensional space, we use three-dimensional Hilbert curve [18]. After the linearization, we compute the minimum work by above mentioned approach. Note that the work is computed based on the Hilbert order of dominant colors, but the actual ground distance between the dominant colors in three-dimensional space is used when computing the work.

3.2 Improvements

Note that in multidimensional space our method may not calculate the optimal minimum work, because the Hilbert order may not reflect the true proximity of the dominant colors. The distance of two neighboring dominant colors in multidimensional space might be measured distant by the Hilbert curve.

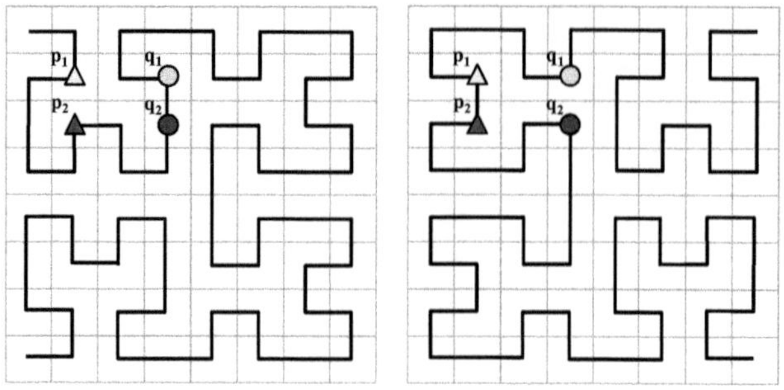

(a) Hilbert curve from the upper-left corner. (b) Hilbert curve from the upper-right corner.

Figure 3: Hilbert curves in two-dimensional space.

Figure 3 shows as an example of the Hilbert curve in two-dimensional space. Suppose P and Q are composed of two colors each, (p_1, p_2) and (q_1, q_2), respectively, and the weights of all colors are the same. The *optimal* minimum work between P and Q should be calculated by the sum of the work between p_1 and q_1 and the work between p_2 and q_2. The Hilbert order of dominant colors in Figure 3 (a), however, is $<p_1, p_2, q_2, q_1>$ such that, the distance between p_1 and q_1 is measured longer than the distance between p_1 and q_2. As a result, the minimum work would be calculated by the sum of the work between p_1 and q_2 and the work between p_2 and q_1.

This happens when the Hilbert order fails to reflect the proximity of dominant colors in multidimensional space. The order of $<p_1, p_2, q_2, q_1>$ in Figure 3 (a) does not reflect the proximity of (p_1, q_1) and (p_2, q_2). If we change the starting point and the direction to create another Hilbert curve as in Figure 3 (b), $<q_1, p_1, p_2, q_2>$ is created. In this order, the optimal minimum work between P and Q is calculated by the sum of the work between p_1 and q_1 and the work between p_2 and q_2. With the Hilbert curve in Figure 3 (b), we are able to extract the order that reflects the proximity of multidimensional space. Depending on the position of dominant colors in multidimensional space, the Hilbert order that may or may not reflect the proximity between them. Therefore, we propose to use multiple Hilbert curves. In k-dimensional space, $(2^k \cdot k!)/2$ Hilbert curves can be created. In three-dimensional color space, 24 Hilbert curves can be created. We compute 24 minimum works based on the 24 orders and select the minimum value among them as the minimum work between two images.

Even when multiple Hilbert curves are used, however, the orders of dominant colors might still be misarranged. Figure 4 shows an example where the proximity is not correctly reflected in the multiple Hilbert orders. In Figure 4, two-dimensional space is divided into quadrants, and the dominant colors of P and Q are on the opposite side of the boundary of quadrants I and II.

In Figure 4 (a), the work is calculated between p_1 and q_2 and p_2 and q_1, which results in inaccurate minimum work. This is because in most cases the distance of two colors that are on the opposite side of the boundary of the quadrant is

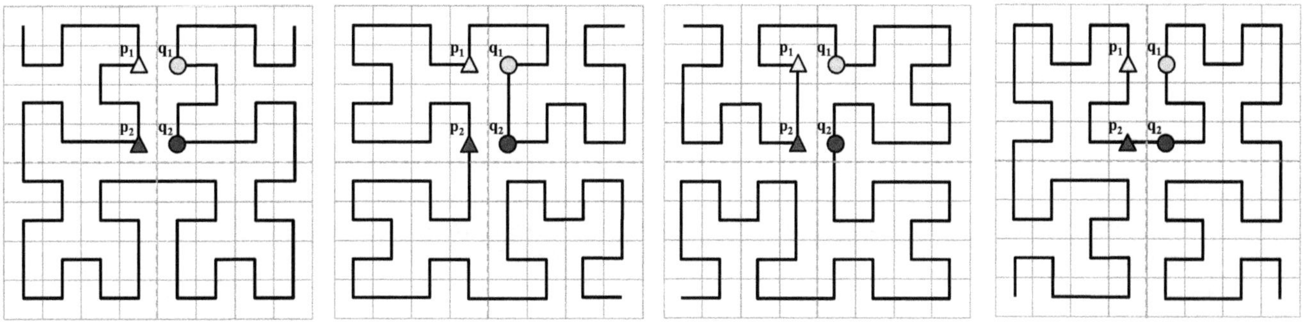

(a) Heading south from the upper-left corner. (a) Heading west from the upper-left corner. (a) Heading east from the bottom-left corner. (a) Heading north from the bottom-right corner.

Figure 4: An example where multiple Hilbert curves fail to reflect the proximity of dominant colors.

measured distant by the Hilbert curve. In Figure 4, (a), (b), (c), and (d), all Hilbert curves calculate inaccurate minimum work. That is, even if multiple Hilbert curves are used, the distance between the colors near the boundary in the Hilbert order may not reflect the true proximity.

To solve the problem, we adjust the position of dominant colors in multidimensional space. When calculating the minimum work between two images, what we need is the distance between dominant colors, not the precise position of them. As long as we preserve the distance between the colors, the minimum work between two images will not be affected even when we adjust the position of them. In this paper, we propose to adjust the position of dominant colors using the minimum bounding box (MBB) shift method. The MBB is defined as the smallest hyper-rectangle that contains all dominant colors in k-dimensional space[2].

The position adjustment method finds the MBB and shifts it to one of the corners in multidimensional space. In Figure 5 (a), the Hilbert order, $<q_2, q_1, p_1, p_2>$, does not reflect the proximity of the dominant colors. Figure 5 (b) shows the position adjustment. As shown in the figure, the MBB shift puts the dominant colors into one quadrant (and makes them avoid the boundary of the quadrant). After the MBB shift, the Hilbert curve is able to find the correct order of $<q_1, p_1, q_2, p_2>$ that reflects the proximity of multidimensional space.

Note that the difference between the distance in multidimensional space and the distance in the Hilbert curve increases with the increase in the granularity of the Hilbert curve. In Figure 2 (a) in Section 3.1, for example, the distance of the Hilbert curve between upper-left cell and upper-right cell is same as the distance of multidimensional space. In Figures 2 (b) and 2 (c), on the other hand, the difference between two distances grows with finer granularity. Also note that the Hilbert curve in the quadrant of a particular level is the same as the Hilbert curve of the previous level, as shown in Figure 2 in Section 3.1. These two facts indicate that if the MBB fits into a single quadrant (i.e., the entire dominant colors can be represented in the single quadrant), the level of the Hilbert curve decreases and the difference between two distances may decrease, which results in the proximity to be reflected correctly in the Hilbert curve in many cases.

Even when the MBB is bigger than the quadrant, we can adjust the position of the MBB and get different Hilbert

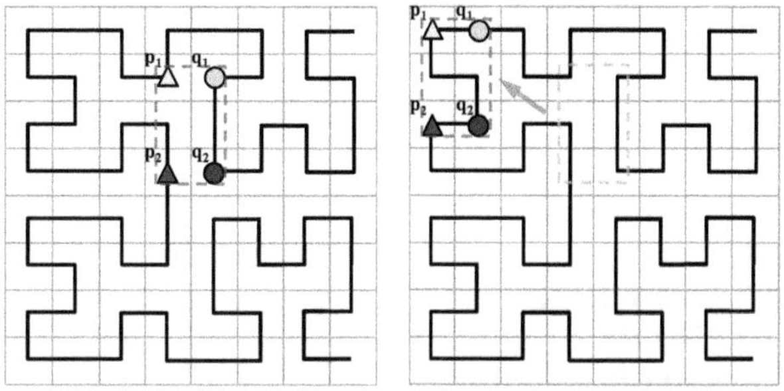

(a) original color distribution. (b) color distribution after the MBB shift

Figure 5: An example of MBB shift.

orders, which make it possible to reflect the proximity of colors. In this paper, we shift the MBB to the origin (ex: RGB(0,0,0)). The Hilbert order may be different depending on which corner the MBB is shifted to, and thus the approximate EMDs computed with different origins may be different. Since multiple Hilbert orders are created after the MBB shift, however, the experimental results (not reported in this paper) show that the impact of different origins is negligible.

After the position adjustment, we create $(2^k \cdot k!)/2$ Hilbert orders. Consequently, $2^k \cdot k!$ orders (48 orders in three-dimensional space) are created including the orders created using the original position of the dominant colors. We compute the approximate EMD of each order, and select the minimum value as the minimum work. Because generating $2^k \cdot k!$ orders requires a considerable time, we use *mappingTable(originCoord[h][i][j], HilberPosition)* for creating multiple Hilbert curves. The *mappingTable* receives as an input the position of the dominant colors in k-dimensional space as array ($originCoord[h][i][j]$), and maps its position in the Hilbert curve. Using the mapping table, the orders of the dominant colors are created with short memory access time. Also, if we use a parallel processing, the overhead of generating $2^k \cdot k!$ orders is only a little[6].

Figure 6 shows the algorithm of the proposed method. Suppose that $2^k \cdot k!$ orders have already been created by the *mappingTable*. The algorithm *CalculateAEMD* calculates the approximate EMD of each order. The dominant color nearest to the starting point from each distribution is selected (line 1), and the maximum common weight (MCW) between two colors is computed (line 3). If w_{q_j} is the MCW,

Algorithm *CalculateAEMD* (*P*, *Q*, *AEMD*)
Input:
- *P*: distribution $P = \{(p_1, w_{p1}, o_{p1}), \ldots, (p_n, w_{pn}, o_{pn})\}$
- *Q*: distribution $Q = \{(q_1, w_{q1}, o_{q1}), \ldots, (qm, w_{qm}, o_{qm})\}$
  /* p_i and q_i are dominant colors, w_i is the weight of the dominant color, o_i is the order in the Hilbert curve */

Output:
- *AEMD*: the approximate EMD between *P* and *Q*

1: **IF** $o_{pi} = o_{pfirst}$ **and** $o_{qj} = o_{qfirst}$; $i = 1$
2:   **WHILE**($i < n+m$)
3:     **IF** $w_{pi} > w_{qj}$
4:       $AEMD += \overline{p_i q_j} \cdot w_{q_j}$
5:       $w_{pi} = w_{pi} - w_{qj}$
6:       $w_{qj} = 0$
7:       q_j++
8:     **ELSE**
9:       $AEMD += \overline{p_i q_j} \cdot w_{p_i}$
10:       $w_{qj} = w_{qj} - w_{pi}$
11:       $w_{pi} = 0$
12:       p_i++
13:     **END IF**
14:   i++
15: **END WHILE**
16: **END IF**
17: **RETURN** *AEMD*
END *CalculateAEMD*

Figure 6: The *CalculatedAEMD* algorithm.

the work is computed by multiplying the distance between two colors and w_{q_j} (line 4). The weights used to compute the work are removed from two distributions (lines 5 and 6). The algorithm selects the next dominant color q_{j+1} because the $w_{q_j} = 0$ (line 7). If w_{q_j} is the MCW in line 3, the algorithm proceeds through line 9 to line 13. The algorithm repeats the above process until all dominant colors of two distributions are visited. Adding all the work, the algorithm calculates the approximate EMD between P and Q.

Figure 7 shows the algorithm *PositionAdjustment*. This algorithm shifts the position of the dominant colors to the origin *top_left*. In line 1 to 3, the algorithm searches for top_left_x, top_left_y, and top_left_z, the x, y, z coordinates of the dominant color nearest to the origin of the x, y, and $z$axises, respectively. In line 4 to 6, the dominant colors are shifted to the origin by subtracting top_left_x, top_left_y, and top_left_z from the x, y, z coordinate of each dominant color. In line 7, the Hilbert order is created. In line 9, the algorithm calculates approximate EMD by calling the algorithm *CalculateAEMD*.

4. PERFORMANCE EVALUATION

4.1 Experimental Setup

We performed our color-based image retrieval on the SIMPLIcity [24]. The SIMPLIcity is composed of 1,000 color images in 10 categories. Each category has 100 images. The data size of 1,000 images is reasonable, since our experiments are designed to test the time complexity of the EMD for each image comparison (and not necessarily the scalability). As mentioned in Section 1, 500 to 700 comparisons are needed for 100,000 image when the M-tree is used. Therefore, even if a larger dataset is used for scalability, we would have a similar number of image comparisons and would have drawn the conclusion similar to the following experimental results.

Algorithm *PositionAdjustment* (*P*, *Q*, *AEMD*)
Input:
- *P*: distribution $P = \{(p_1, w_{p1}), \ldots, (p_n, w_{pn})\}$
- *Q*: distribution $Q = \{(q_1, w_{q1}), \ldots, (qm, w_{qm}\}$

Output:
- *AEMD*: the approximate EMD between *P* and *Q*

1: **FOR** each dominant color in *P* and *Q*
2:   search (top_left_x, top_left_y, top_left_z)
3: **END FOR**
4: **FOR** each dominant color in *P* and *Q*
5:   $p_i = (p_{ix} - top\_left_x, p_{iy} - top\_left_y, p_{iz} - top\_left_z)$
6:   $q_j = (q_{jy} - top\_left_x, q_{jy} - top\_left_y, q_{iz} - top\_left_z)$
7:   map p_i and q_j to positions o_{pi} and o_{qj} in Hilbert curve
8: **END FOR**
9: **CALL** *CalculateAEMD*()
10: **RETURN** *AEMD*
END *PositionAdjustment*

Figure 7: The *PositionAdjustment* algorithm.

To extract the dominant colors of the SIMPLIcity, we applied the MPEG7 dominant color descriptor that extracts maximum 8 dominant colors of an image [16][4]. For the SIMPLIcity, the MPEG7 dominant color descriptor extracted the dominant colors in the 32×32×32 RGB space.

We performed extensive experiments on the SIMPLIcity to compare the processing time and the accuracy of the proposed method with the EMD, OCCD(20), and OCCD(100). The number in parentheses indicates the number of color units in OCCD. The 20 color units in OCCD(20) is the recommended number of the color unit in [17]. When the number of color unit is fixed at 20, the accuracy of the OCCD may suffer with the increase in the number of dominant colors. To measure the accuracy of the OCCD method fairly, we use both OCCD(20) and OCCD(100) in our experiments.

$$MAPE = \frac{1}{n}\sum_{i=1}^{n}|\frac{a_i - f_i}{a_i}|$$

As an accuracy measure, we used the mean absolute percentage error(MAPE) [22]. In the MAPE, a_i is the EMD value, and f_i is the approximate value computed by the proposed or the OCCD methods. The MAPE represents the accuracy as a percentage. As a processing time measure, we used the time elapsed during query processing, while excluding the time for file access. For accurate experimental results, we used the average of 100 queries, where each query calculates the dissimilarity of a query image to 1,000 images. The experiments were performed on a 2.80GHZ PC equipped with a Window7 OS and 2GH of main memory.

4.2 Experimental Results

In the first set of experiments, we evaluated the preprocessing time of the proposed method. The preprocessing time in Table 1 shows the time to create the mapping table.

Figure 8: Examples of SIMPLIcity images.

Table 1: Preprocessing time of the proposed method

	32x32x32	64x64x64	128x128x128	256x256x256
Time (sec.)	0.097	0.923	8.944	76.346

Table 2: Performances of the proposed method while varying the number of orders used

	MHC(8)	MHC(16)	MHC(24)	MHC(shift)
MAPE(%)	8.7	5.6	5.2	4.2
Time (sec.)	0.004	0.008	0.012	0.023

The preprocessing time increases as the granularity of the multidimensional space becomes finer. This is because the size of the mapping table increases with the finer granularity of the multidimensional space. Note that the mapping table can be used without additional overheads once created, since preprocessing can be done offline. Also, the mapping table maps the dominant colors to the order of the Hilbert curve directly, working as a hash table. Therefore, the performance of the proposed method does not degrade with finer granularity.

In the second set of experiments, we measured the processing time and the accuracy of the proposed method while varying the number of the orders used. We used the SIMPLIcity imagess. Table 2 shows the experiment results. In three-dimensional color space, 24 Hilbert curves can be created at maximum by creating 3 Hilbert curves from each corner of the space. In Table 2, MHC(8) used 8 orders by creating a Hilbert curve from each corner. Likewise, MHC(16) and MHC(24) used 16 and 24 orders by creating 2 and 3 Hilbert curves from each corner, respectively. After creating 24 orders from the original position of the dominant colors, MHC(shift) shifted the position of dominant colors to the origin and used the additional 24 orders created by position adjustment. As shown in Table 2, the accuracy improves with the increase in the number of orders used. This is because the order that reflects the true proximity of

Table 3: Performance comparison

	MHC(shift)	EMD	OCCD(20)	OCCD(100)
MAPE (%)	4.2	-	4.3	1.2
Time (sec.)	0.023	0.789	0.684	59.846

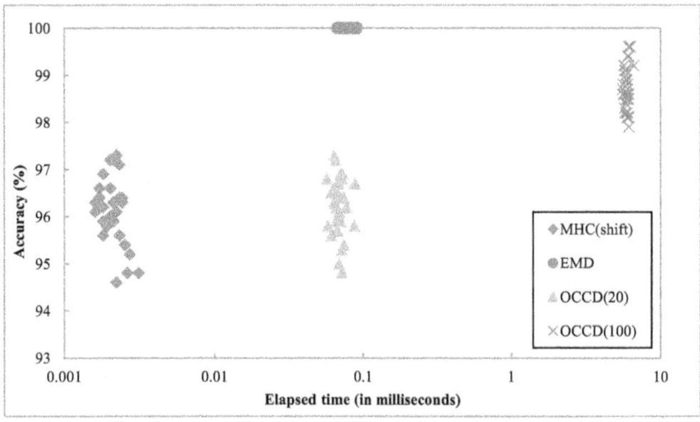

Figure 9: Time vs. accuracy.

Table 4: Precision and recall

(a) precision

Number of Retrieved images	MHC(shift)	EMD	OCCD(20)	OCCD(100)
10	88.2%	86.8%	85.4%	87.3%
20	75.0%	74.5%	75.5%	75.5%
30	66.1%	65.8%	65.4%	65.8%
50	54.5%	55.4%	53.6%	54.7%
100	37.8%	39.2%	38.5%	38.4%

(b) recall

Number of Retrieved images	MHC(shift)	EMD	OCCD(20)	OCCD(100)
10	8.8%	8.7%	8.5%	8.7%
20	15.0%	14.9%	15.1%	15.1%
30	20.0%	19.9%	19.7%	19.9%
50	27.25%	27.7%	26.8%	27.4%
100	37.8%	39.2%	38.5%	38.4%

the multidimensional space depends on the position of the dominant colors. The accuracy does not improve much from MHC(16) to MHC(24) for two reasons. First the problem near the boundary of the quadrant is more prominent with finer granularity. Second, most of 24 orders have similar sequences since they are created from the same position of the dominant colors. These problems can be solved by the position adjustment. The accuracy of the MHC(shift) is better

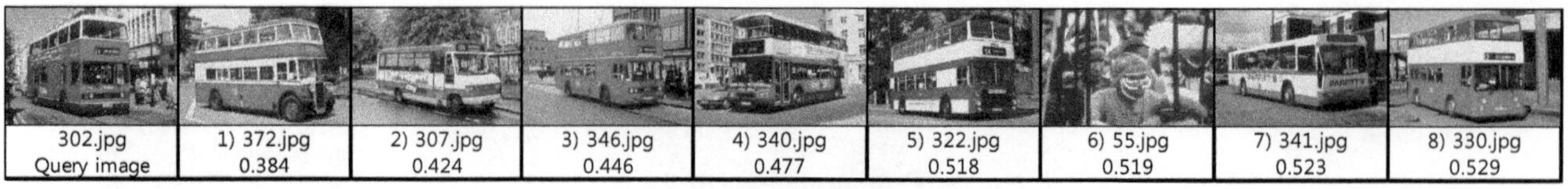

(a) MHC(shift)

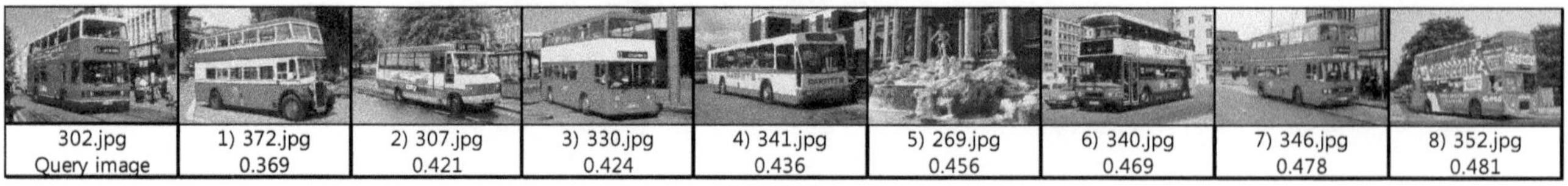

(b) EMD

(c) OCCD(20)

(d) OCCD(100)

Figure 10: Eight images closest to the query image 302.jpg.

than MHC(24). The elapsed time of the proposed method, although it increases linearly according to the number of the orders, is very short. The image retrieval can be done in a short time even when MHC(shift) is used. In the following, we used the MHC(shift).

In the third set of experiments, we compared the processing time and the accuracy of the proposed method with the EMD, OCCD(20), and OCCD(100). As shown in Table 3, the proposed method showed significantly better performance with small errors. The proposed method exhibits 4.2% MAPE, while shortens the image-retrieval time 34 times over the EMD. The proposed method calculates the approximate minimum work with an acceptable error bound in a very short time. OCCD(20) has 4.3% MAPE, similar to the MHC(shift), but the processing time of OCCD(20) is similar to that of EMD. Because the weight of the color unit is different from the weight of the dominant color, the error occurs in the OCCD. Also, the OCCD requires a considerable processing time to find the optimal color unit pairs that satisfies the approximate minimum work. As the weight of the color unit gets smaller, the accuracy increases, but the performance suffers. OCCD(100), although the MAPE is only 1.2%, exhibits the elapsed time of 59.846 seconds, too long to be used in any practical image-retrieval or search applications.

Figure 9 shows the correlation between the processing time and the accuracy. We calculated the dissimilarities of the 30 randomly-generated query images to 100 SIMPLIcity images. Each point in Figure 9 is the result of each query. The x-axis is the elapsed time to calculate the dissimilarity with 100 images, and the y-axis is the average of the 100 accuracy results.

As shown in Figure 9, the accuracy of the EMD is 100% in all points and the elapsed time of the EMD is between 67 and 91 milliseconds (ms). The accuracy of OCCD(20) is similar to that of MHC(shift), but the elapsed time is similar to that of the EMD. OCCD(100) shows the high accuracy between 98.1% and 99.6%, but the elapsed time is 5564 to 6611 ms. In comparison, MHC(shift) shows both good performance and high accuracy. The accuracy of MHC(shift) is 95.8% to 98.3%, and the elapsed time is between 1.7 and 3.1 ms.

In the next set of experiments, we examined the precision and the recall of the search to measure the impact of errors in real-world image retrieval. We used the average of 100 queries, where each query retrieved 10, 20, 30, 50, and 100 images, and calculated the precision and the recall. As shown in Table 4, all methods exhibit similar results. This is because errors are rare in approximate methods. Both the proposed method and the OCCD show almost the same results with the EMD.

Figure 10 shows an example of search results of each method. Each figure displays eight images closest to the query image 302.jpg, retrieved from the SIMPLIcity. The number below the image name represents the minimum work computed by each method. The images are ordered in terms of similarity. All methods retrieved bus images similar to the query image. MHC(shift) retrieved 55.jpg that is different from the query. The EMD retrieved 269.jpg that is the different from the query image. OCCD(20) retrieved 269.jpg incorrectly, and OCCD(100) retrieved 269.jpg and 55.jpg incorrectly. This is because the compositions of dominant colors in 269.jpg and

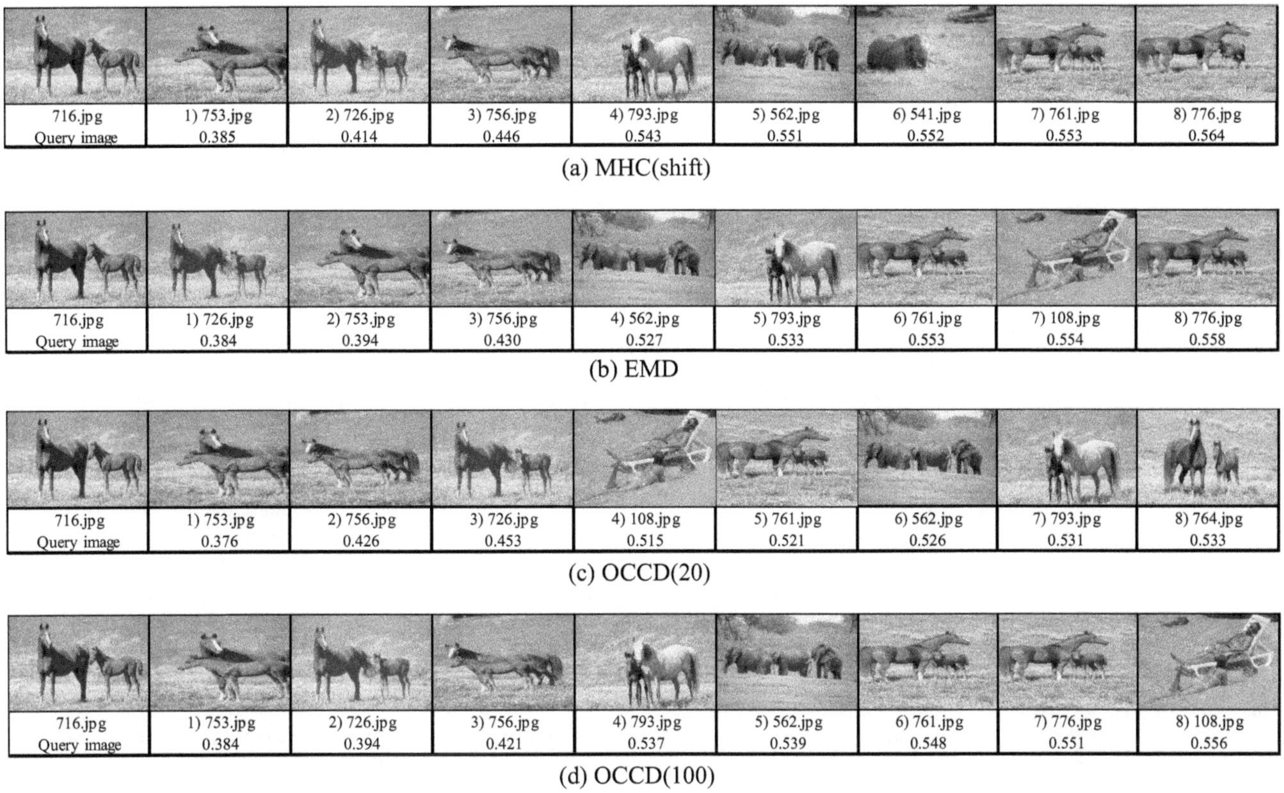

Figure 11: Eight images closest to the query image 716.jpg.

55.jpg are similar to the query image. The overall tendency of the retrieved images is similar in all methods. Figure 11 shows another example of search results, which indicates the tendency similar to that in Figure 10.

5. CONCLUSIONS AND FUTURE WORK

In this paper, we proposed a new distance function that calculates the approximate EMD in linear time. For the image retrieval based on the dominant color descriptor, the earth mover's distance and the optimal color composition distance have been used as the dissimilarity measure. They provide high-quality results in image retrieval but require high computational cost.

Our distance function linearizes the multidimensional color space using the Hilbert curve, thereby calculates the approximate minimum work in linear time. To improve the accuracy, the distance function adopts two improvements: the use of multiple Hilbert orders and the position adjustment. The extensive experiments reveal that our approach achieves the order-of-magnitude improvement on processing time and that the rate of error growth decreases as the number of the dominant color increases. The retrieval results of the proposed method in real-world images are almost the same as that of the EMD, which indicates the error of the proposed methods does not influence the quality of image-retrieval results. Given the $O(n)$ processing time and small errors, our distance function can be used effectively in image retrieval for large databases.

As a future work, we would like to extend our work to indexing in a high dimensional space. Recently, several works have been proposed to reduce the number of EMD comparisons in a high dimensional space [1][26][27][14]. Since the post-processing in these research needs a considerable number of EMD comparisons, they require high retrieval time. To solve the problem, we are in the process of developing an indexing scheme based on our approximate EMD in a high dimensional space.

6. ACKNOWLEDGEMENTS

This research was supported by the MKE(The Ministry of Knowledge Economy), Korea, under the Convergence-ITRC(Convergence Information Technology Research Center) support program (NIPA-2011-C6150-1101-0001) supervised by the NIPA(National IT Industry Promotion Agency) and was supported by the National Research Foundation of Korea(NRF) grant funded by the Korea government(MEST) (No. 2008-0061006)

7. REFERENCES

[1] I. Assent, A. Wenning, and T. Seidl. Approximation techniques for indexing the earth mover's distance in multimedia databases. In *Proc. IEEE Int'l. Conf. on Data Engineering, ICDE*, pages 1–12, 2006.

[2] B. Barequet and S. Peled. Analysis of the clustering properties of the hilbert space-filling curve. *Journal of Algorithms*, 38(1):91–109, 2001.

[3] P. Ciaccia, M.Patella, and P. Zezula. M-tree: An efficient access method for similarity search in metric spaces. In *Proc. Int'l. Conf. on Very Large Data Bases, VLDB*, 1997.

[4] M. Coimbra and J. Cunha. Mpeg-7 visual descriptors - contributions for automated feature extraction in capsule endoscopy. *IEEE Transaction on Circuits and Systems for Video Technology*, 16(5):628–637, 2006.

[5] R. Datta, J. Li, and J. Wang. Content-based image retrieval: Approaches and trends of the new age. In *Proc. of the 7th ACM SIGMM international workshop on Multimedia information retrieval*, 2005.

[6] J. Dean and S. Ghemawat. Mapreduce: Simplified data processing on large clusters. *Communications of the ACM*, 51(1):107–113, 2008.

[7] Y. Deng, B. Manjunath, C. Kenney, and M. M. ans H. Shin. An efficient color representation for image retrieval. *IEEE Transactions on Image Processing*, 10(1):140–147, 2001.

[8] H. Jagadish. Analysis of the hilbert curve for representing two-dimensional space. *Information Processing Letters*, 62(1):17–22, 1997.

[9] S. Landy and N. Graham. *Visual Perception of Texture*. MIT Press, 2004.

[10] E. Lawler. *Combinatorial Optimization: Networks and Matroids*. New York: Holt, Rinehart, and Winston, 1976.

[11] K. Lee, B. Zheng, H. Li, and W. Lee. Approaching the skyline in z order. In *Proc. Int'l. Conf. on Very Large Data Bases, VLDB*, pages 279–290, 2007.

[12] H. Ling and K. Okada. An efficient earth mover's distance algorithm for robust histogram comparison. *IEEE Transactions on PAMI*, 29(5):840–853, 2006.

[13] Y. Liu, D. Zhang, G. Lu, and W. Ma. A survey of content-based image retrieval with high-level semantics. *Pattern Recognition*, 40(1):262–282, 2007.

[14] V. Ljosa and A. S. A. Bhattacharya. Indexing spatially sensitive distance measures using multi-resolution lower bounds. In *Proc. Int'l. Conf. Extending Database Technology, EDBT*, pages 865–883, 2006.

[15] B. Manjunath, J. Ohm, V. Vasudevan, and A. Yamada. Color and texture descriptors. *IEEE Transactions on Circuits and Systems for Video Technology*, 11(6):703–715, 2001.

[16] J. Martnez. *MPEG-7 overview*. http://mpeg.chiariglione.org/standards/mpeg-7/mpeg-7.htm.

[17] A. Mojsilovic, J. Hu, and E. Soljanin. Extraction of perceptually important colors and similarity measurement for image matching, retrieval, and analysis. *IEEE Transactions on Image Processing*, 11(11):1238–1248, 2002.

[18] B. Moon, H. Jagadish, C. Faloutsos, and J. Saltz. Analysis of the clustering properties of the hilbert space-filling curve. *IEEE Transactions on Knowledge and Data Engineering*, 13(1):124–141, 2001.

[19] S. Rachev. The monge-kantorovich mass transference problem and its stochastic applications. *Theory of Probability and its Applications*, 29(4):647–676, 1984.

[20] Y. Rubner, C. Tomasi, and J. Guibas. The earth mover's distance as a metric for image retrieval. *International Journal of Computer Vision*, 40(2):99–121, 2000.

[21] W. Schwartz, A. Kembhavi, D. Harwood, and L. Davis. Human detection using partial least squares analysis. In *Proc. IEEE Int'l. Conf. on Computer Vision*, pages 24–31, 2009.

[22] J. Shepperd and C. Schofield. Estimating software project effort using analogies. *IEEE Transactions on Software Engineering*, 23(11):736–743, 1997.

[23] S. Shirdhonkar and D. Jacobs. Approximate earth mover's distance in linear time. In *Proc. IEEE Int'l Conf. on Computer Vision and Pattern Recognition, CVPR*, pages 334–348, 2009.

[24] J. Wang, J. Li, and G.Wiederhold. Simplicity: Semantics-sensitive integrated matching for picture libraries. *IEEE Transactions on Pattern Analysis and Machine Intelligence*, 23(9):947–963, 2001.

[25] J. Weijer and C. Schmid. Coloring local feature extraction. In *Proc. European Conference on Computer Vision, ECCV*, pages 334–348, 2006.

[26] M. Wichterich, I. Assent, P. Kranen, and T. Seidl. Efficient emd-based similarity search in multimedia databases via flexible dimensionality reduction. In *Proc. ACM SIGMOD Int'l. Conf. on Management of Data*, pages 199–211, 2008.

[27] J. Xu, Z. Zhang, A. Tung, and G. Yu. Efficient and effective similarity search over probabilistic data based on earth mover's distance. In *Proc. Int'l. Conf. on Very Large Data Bases, VLDB*, pages 758–769, 2010.

[28] R. Yan and W. Hsu. Recent developments in content-based and concept-based image/video retrieval. In *Proc. ACM Int'l Conf. on Multimedia*, pages 1155–1156, 2008.

[29] M. Yiu, Y. Tao, and N. Mamoulis. The b^{dual}-tree: indexing moving objects by space filling curves in the dual space. *The VLDB Journal*, 17(3):379–400, 2008.

Towards a Framework for Attribute Retrieval

Arlind Kopliku
IRIT
Paul Sabatier University
Toulouse, France
Arlind.Kopliku@irit.fr

Mohand Boughanem
IRIT
Paul Sabatier University
Toulouse, France
Mohand.Boughanem@irit.fr

Karen Pinel-Sauvagnat
IRIT
Paul Sabatier University
Toulouse, France
Karen.Sauvagnat@irit.fr

ABSTRACT

In this paper, we propose an attribute retrieval approach which extracts and ranks attributes from HTML tables. We distinguish between class attribute retrieval and instance attribute retrieval. On one hand, given an instance (e.g. University of Strathclyde) we retrieve from the Web its attributes (e.g. principal, location, number of students). On the other hand, given a class (e.g. universities) represented by a set of instances, we retrieve common attributes of its instances. Furthermore, we show we can reinforce instance attribute retrieval if similar instances are available.

Our approach uses HTML tables which are probably the largest source for attribute retrieval. Three recall oriented filters are applied over tables to check the following three properties: *(i)* is the table relational, *(ii)* has the table a header, and *(iii)* the conformity of its attributes and values. Candidate attributes are extracted from tables and ranked with a combination of relevance features. Our approach is shown to have a high recall and a reasonable precision. Moreover, it outperforms state of the art techniques.

Categories and Subject Descriptors

H.3.3 [**Information Systems**]: Information Search and Retrieval

General Terms

Measurement, Experimentation, Algorithms

Keywords

information retrieval, attribute retrieval

1. INTRODUCTION

Most information retrieval systems answer user queries with a list of documents, but there are many information needs that can be answered with one or more extracts of information coming from one or more documents. For instance, the query "features of Mac Book" is not asking for all pages speaking of Mac Books rather than for a list of features.

Inspired by the work in [6], we distinguish three types of information needs that can be answered differently:

- *query by attribute* ("GDP of UK", "address of Hotel Bellagio")
- *query by instance* ("Samsung Galaxy S", "Scotland", "Oscar Wilde")
- *query by class* ("Toshiba notebooks", "British writers")

When the query is specifically asking for an attribute, we can return its value right away. When the query is an instance, we can propose a summary of salient attributes (properties). When the query is a class of instances, the result can be a comparative table of the class instances with their attributes. Figure 1 shows what these results might look like. A direct application can be Google Squared[1], a commercial tool that produces similar results. We will call search based on attributes, instances and classes *relational search*.

Relational search is not the only application where attributes play a crucial role. They can also be used for query suggestion [4], faceted search [5] and aggregated search [15]. For instance, given the query "Indonesia" and using attributes of "Indonesia" we can produce suggestions such as "Indonesia climate", "Indonesia capital" and "Indonesia hotels", while in a faceted search context we can navigate returned results on the query "modern architecture" by attributes such as "country", "architecture style" and so on. Attributes can also be used to summarize content about instances/classes.

In this paper, we deal with attribute retrieval which falls in the above defined framework. More precisely, we deal with three attribute retrieval problems. First, we retrieve relevant attributes for one given instance (e.g. "University of Strathclyde"). Second, we retrieve attributes for a given class (e.g. "universities") represented as a set of instances. Third, we retrieve attributes for one instance when some other similar instances are given (from the same class).

Attributes are extracted from HTML tables in the Web. There are some main reasons behind this choice. First, tables are widespread across the Web. Second, many tables contain relational data (i.e. data in a relational form) [8]. Third, tables have already been used sucessfully for attribute extraction [10, 9].

[1]http://www.google.com/squared

CIKM'11, October 24–28, 2011, Glasgow, Scotland, UK.
Copyright 2011 ACM 978-1-4503-0717-8/11/10 ...$10.00.

Query: *president of France*
Result: Nicolas Sarkozy

Query: *Tower of Pisa*
Result:

Location	Italy
Width	Tuscany
Height	55.8m
Steps	296
...	

Query: *Macintosh notebooks*
Result:

	Mac Book	Mac Book Pro
Height	1.08 inches	0.11-0.68 inches
Width	13.00 inches	11.8 inches
Depth	9.12 inches	7.56 inches
Weight	4.7 pounds	2.3 pounds
...		

Figure 1: Examples of relational search results

However, the task is not easy. Many of the HTML tables are used for layout design and navigation. In [8], authors estimate that only about 1% of the Web tables contain relational data. Furthermore, some relational tables have no headers (schema of attributes) and it is not easy to retrieve all relevant tables for a given instance.

We propose an attribute retrieval approach at Web scale which takes into account the above issues. For every given instance, we issue the instance as a query to a search engine. The retrieved documents are used to extract tables from. Successively, we apply 3 filters to candidate tables to check the following properties: *(i)* is the table relational, *(ii)* has the table a header, *(iii)* the conformity of its attributes and values. Then, depending on the considered problem, we rank candidate attributes with a combination of relevance features.

Our approach integrates the work of Cafarella et al. [8]. Their work is at our knowledge the largest mining of Web tables for search purposes. They show we can filter out many tables that are not relational and that do not have a header. In addition to their work, we filter out many table columns (or rows) that do not contain attributes (name and values).

We also integrate our previous work [16, 17], which shows that we can rank attributes using a linear combination of relevance features such as table match, document relevance and external evidence from Web search, DBPedia and Wikipedia. In our previous work, we have focused on instance attribute retrieval, while in this paper we deal with instance and class attribute retrieval with an extended experimental setup. To the best of our knowledge, this is the first work that put together attribute retrieval at instance and class level through the use Web tables. We also introduce a technique to reinforce attribute retrieval and we show some initial work on attribute value retrieval (which is not the main goal of this paper). The combination of these techniques contributes to build a framework for attribute retrieval at Web-scale.

The paper is structured as follows. The next section is about related work. In section 3, we describe our approach including filtering and ranking of attributes. Then we describe the experimental setup (section 4) and results (section 5) following with conclusions.

2. RELATED WORK

Attributes can find different uses. They can be used for the summarization (representation) of content [29, 18], to assist search such as for query suggestion [4] and faceted search [5], or for question answering [13]. Attribute acquisition methods can be domain-independent or domain-dependent. Among domain-dependent approaches, we can mention approaches that focus on products. In this domain, attributes have been used to improve product search and recommendation [18, 22], but also to enable data mining [27].

Attribute retrieval provides another granularity in Web search. This can interest communities that propose a more focused access to information or communities that envision aggregating pieces of information such as aggregated search [19, 15].

To acquire attributes from the Web, it is common to use decoration markup [30, 27, 11] and text [4, 24, 20]. HTML tags (for tables, lists and emphasis) have also been shown to help for attribute acquisition [30, 27]. Wong et al. [27] combine tags and textual features in a Conditional Random Fields model to learn attribute extraction rules, but they need a seed of relevant documents manually fed.

Another common technique to acquire attributes is through the use of lexico-syntactic rules. For example, Pasca et al. [1, 21] use rules such as "A of I" and "I's A" to acquire attributes from query logs. Authors represent the class as a set of instances and multiple class instances are used to improve extraction. In [2], authors use more precise lexico-syntactic rules such as "the A of I is", but recall of these rules is lower. In [22], Popescu et al. use lexico-syntactic rules to extract product attributes from reviews.

At last, tables are known to be a mine for relational data and attributes. Cafarella et al. [8, 7] show we can identify billions of relational tables in the Web. In [10], Chen et al. identify attributes using column (or row) similarities. Another common technique to extract attribute from tables is through wrapper induction [9, 11, 26]. Given a training set or a set of similar documents, wrapper induction learns extraction rules. Many wrappers extract at record level, but they do not distinguish between attribute name and attribute value. Furthermore, wrappers are precision oriented and they work well only for some sites.

To summarize, current attribute acquisition techniques can obtain a high precision. Although many of these techniques produce a considerable number of attributes, they cannot cover the needs that can be answered with the Web. Most of them are conceived to work offline and they cannot extract instance attributes whatever the instance.

Our work is inspired by the work in [1] and [7, 8]. It differs from [1], in that we do not use lexico-syntactic rules but Web tables to identify attributes. It differs from the work in [7, 8], in that we do not use tables for relation search. We make use of learnings in [7, 8], but we introduce another filter at line level and we introduce relevance features. The combination of filters and relevance ranking allows us to enable attribute retrieval which was not investigated in [7, 8].

We retrieve attributes for instances and classes. A clear distinction among class attributes and instance attributes can be found in [1]. They represent the class as a set of instances and they extract class attributes using class instances. We use the same setup to retrieve attributes for classes.

Class instances can also be acquired automatically. Here,

we can mention the work done in named entity recognition [12, 23]. Class instances can be also acquired from hierarchies such as the ones that derive from quality sources such as Wikipedia or DBPedia. Hearst [14] shows that we can extract class instances using the pattern "*C* such as *LI*" (e.g. cities such as London, Paris and Rome). However, class acquisition methods need to be improved to have high recall and reasonable precision at Web scale.We prefer separating the class acquisition issues from class attribute retrieval. In this paper, we thus consider that class instances are given.

3. ATTRIBUTE RETRIEVAL

We consider three different attribute retrieval problems detailed below.

Problem 1: We consider an information retrieval situation where the query is an instance and the results is a list of attributes. Concretely, **given an instance i, attribute retrieval should extract and rank attributes with respect to their relevance to i.**

Retrieving attributes for whatever instance can be quite complex. There is no knowledge base with a list of attributes for the instance, but the Web with its size can help us retrieve many of them. We need methods that can work for most instances and are domain-independent. In this paper, we aim retrieving attributes at Web scale using HTML tables which are known to be a huge source for relational data.

Due to the complexity of the problem, we deal in this paper with attribute names only. To illustrate, given the instance "France", we want to retrieve its attributes such as "capital", "president", "area", "population", "GDP", "GDP per capita", etc. We do not focus on attribute values (e.g. "Paris" is the value of the attribute "capital" for the instance "France"). Although attribute names and values are usually met in the same line in tables (row or column), selecting the correct attribute value is not easy. We will discuss later shortly some of our experiments regarding attribute values, leaving for a future publication the entire study on attribute value retrieval.

We extract attributes from the lines (rows or columns) of HTML tables from the Web. To do so, we use the following procedure. Initially, we issue the instance i as a query to a search engine and we retrieve tables from the retrieved documents. These tables are potentially relevant for the instance and are used to extract attributes from. However, the problem is far away from being solved. Tables in the Web are quite heterogeneous and many of the retrieved tables are partially or not relevant.

Before ranking attributes, we apply three filters on tables and attributes namely *relational filter*, *header filter*, and *attribute line filter*. The first two are the same as in [8]. They are recall-oriented classifiers that can filter out many tables that are not relational and that do not have headers. Still, after applying these filters there remain many tables which are not relational. As well there are many tables which are almost relational such as table 2 in figure 2. Instead of filtering out this kind of tables, we introduce another filter at column (or row) level which we call *attribute line filter*. Each line is checked for its conformity for being an attribute line i.e. an attribute name followed with attribute values of similar format and length.

After applying the three filters, we rank the remaining attribute with respect to their relevance (depending on the retrieval problem). The task is not easy. If we consider only tables that match the instance, we would lose many relevant tables (e.g. table 2 in figure 2 is relevant for "France", but does not match it). To increase recall, we use all tables from all retrieved documents. Extracted attributes are ranked with a relevance score $\phi(a,i)$ which is applied over an instance i and an attribute a. $\phi(a,i)$ is a simple linear combination of relevance features which was shown to work well to rank attributes in previous work [16]. It will be described in details in section 3.3.

Problem 2: We consider that the query is a set of instances I that represents a class. For example the class "'countries"' can be represented by the set: "'France"', "'Italy"', "'UK"', etc. The goal is to retrieve common relevant attributes for the class. The relevant attributes should not be specific to one instance only, but to all the class.

For every instance $i \in I$, we repeat the same procedure as in problem 1 to retrieve candidate attributes. Then, we rank the set of all candidate attributes for all instances. The relevance score for the class (set of instances I) is :

$$\phi(a,I) = \frac{\sum_{i \in I} \phi(a,i)}{|I|} \quad (1)$$

In other terms, a relevant attribute for the class is likely to be present in many instances of the class. Though, we average the relevance score across all instances.

Problem 3: We reconsider retrieving attributes for an instance i, but we consider that a set of instances I_+ of the same class are given. The hypothesis is that having more instances can improve attribute retrieval due to the simple fact that similar instances share common attributes. However, even if most relevant attributes are shared among instances of the same class, many exceptions can occur. For example, "queen" is relevant for the instance "UK", but it is irrelevant for the instance "USA". To overcome this problem, when it comes to ranking, we privilege attributes retrieved for the instance i using only the instances in I_+ to reinforce ranking.

In practical terms, for every given instance (i, or $i_+ \in I_+$), we repeat the same procedure as in problem 1 to retrieve candidate attributes. The relevance score for the instance i is then computed as follows:

$$\phi'(a,i) = \begin{cases} 0 & \text{if } \phi(a,i) = 0 \\ \phi(a,i) + \phi(a,I_+) & \text{otherwise} \end{cases} \quad (2)$$

In the next sections, we will explain how our filters (*relational*, *header* and *attribute line*) work and which are relevance features used to compute $\phi(a,i)$.

3.1 Relational tables and headers

We build the relational filter and the header filter using the same features as done by Cafarella et al. in [8]. Features on the left of table 1 are used to learn a rule-based classifier for the relational filter and features on the right are used to learn a rule-based classifier for the header filter. Learning is done with a training set of human-classified tables described later in the experimental setup.

Features include the dimensions of the table (f_1, f_2), the fraction of lines with mostly nulls (empty cells) (f_3), the lines with non-string data (numbers, dates) (f_4), statistics on the character length of cells and their variation (f_5, f_6,

	Population	Median age
France	64,768,389	39.7 years
Italy	58,090,681	43.7 years

Table 1

Facts	
Capital	Paris
Demonym	French
Population	
Population	64,768,389
Median age	39.7 years

Table 2

1	Loud	Rihanna
2	The king of limbs	Radiohead
3	Femme fatale	Britney Spears

Table 3

Figure 2: Examples of interesting tables

	Relational Filter		Header Filter
f_1:	♯ rows	f_1:	♯ rows
f_2:	♯ cols	f_2:	♯ cols
f_3:	%rows w/mostly NULLS	f_8:	%head row cells with lower-case
f_4:	♯ cols w/non-string data	f_9:	% head row cells with punctuation
f_5:	cell strlen avg μ	f_{10}:	% head row cells with non string data
f_6:	cell strlen stddev σ	f_{11}:	% cols w/non-string data in *body*
f_7:	$\frac{\sigma}{\mu}$	f_{12}:	% cols w/$\lvert len(row\_1) - \mu \rvert > 2\sigma$
		f_{13} :	% cols w/$\lvert \sigma < len(row\_1) - \mu \rvert \leq 2\sigma$
		f_{14} :	% cols w/$\lvert \sigma > len(row\_1) - \mu \rvert$

Table 1: Features for the relational and header filter

f_7, f_{12}, f_{13}, f_{14}) and conformity of the header cells (lower-case, punctuation, non-string data) (f_8-f_{11}).

The main difference with the work of Cafarella et al. is that they consider that relational tables are all oriented vertically, i.e. the table header (if present) is on top of the table and the attribute lines are vertical (the columns). For example, tables 1 and 3 in figure 2 are oriented vertically and table 2 is oriented horizontally. We extend their approach to work for both horizontally and vertically oriented tables. This is not difficult. We consider the origin table t and another table $\bar{t}$ which is obtained from t considering its rows as columns and its columns as rows.

If t passes both the relational and header filter, table columns are considered as candidate attribute lines to extract attributes from. Similarly, if $\bar{t}$ passes both the relational and header filter, the table rows are considered as candidate attribute lines. It can happen that both columns and rows are considered as candidate attribute lines. The latter are then passed to the attribute line filter.

3.2 Attribute line filter

Let a be the first cell of the line (row or column) and V be the rest of the cells of the line. We consider that a conform attribute line should contain an attribute name in the first cell and attribute values in the rest of the cells. Attribute values can correspond to one instance or multiple instances.

Typically, attribute names do not have much punctuation except of the colon and parenthesis. They rarely contain numbers. On the other hand, attribute values are usually in the same format (number, string, date) and their length is similar. Based on the above observations, we define the following features for the attribute line filter:

- presence of punctuation (except colons, brackets) in a
- presence of numbers in a
- a is an English stop word
- length (char) of a; length (words) of a
- average and standard deviation of the length (char) of values: μ, σ
- ♯values $v \in V$ with $\lvert len(v) - \mu \rvert > 2\sigma$
- ♯values $v \in V$ with $\lvert \sigma < len(v) - \mu \rvert \leq 2\sigma$
- ♯values $v \in V$ with $\lvert \sigma > len(v) - \mu \rvert$
- data conformity : $\frac{max_{T \in int, string, date}(\sharp values\_of\_type(T))}{\lvert V \rvert}$

These features are then used to learn a rule-based classifier from a training set of human classified attribute lines described later in the experimental setup. Once candidate attributes are filtered, we rank the remaining set as explained in the following section.

3.3 Relevance

It is not easy to tell whether an attribute is relevant for a given instance. There are many tables relevant to the instance where the instance is not even present in its cells. We propose combining different features to estimate a relevance score $\phi(a, i)$ for a candidate attribute a and an instance i. These features include a score on the match of the instance on the table, document relevance and external evidence from DBPedia, Wikipedia and Web search. $\phi(a, i)$ is a simple linear combination of these features[2]. Relevance features are described below.

Table match: Tables from which attributes are extracted should be relevant for the instance. A necessary condition but not sufficient for a table to be relevant is to be present in a relevant document for the instance. In some tables, the instance appears explicitly. Such tables might be better candidates for extraction. In fact, we analyzed samples of Web tables and we observed a higher concentration of relevant attributes within tables that match the instance. The table match feature will measure at which extent the table matches the instance.

[2]This combination has been shown to be the most effective way to combine features in previous experiments.

Let a be an attribute extracted from a table T for an instance i. The match of an instance within a table cell $T_{x,y}$ is measured with the cosine distance among the terms of the instance and the terms of the table cell. Let i and c be the vector representation of the instance and the table cell content. We have $i = (w_{1,i}, w_{2,i}, ..., w_{n,i})$ and $c = (w_{1,c}, w_{2,c}, ..., w_{n,c})$. Each dimension corresponds to a separate term. If a term occurs in the instance, its value is 1 in i. If it occurs in the table cell content, its value is 1 in c. The match is computed with the cosine similarity among the vectors.
The table match score is computed as the maximal match within table cells:

$$match(i,T) = \max_{T_{x,y} \in T} cos(i, T_{x,y}) \quad (3)$$

However an attribute name is unlikely to be present in the same line (row or column) with the instance name, while the relevant attribute value is likely to appear in the same line with the instance. The latter can be also observed in table (1) in figure 2. We will define the shadow area of a cell O as the set of cells in the same row and same column with O. There are some exceptions to this rule. We call headline cells, the ones that have are spanned ($colspan > 1$)[3] that cover the entire table width such as the ones in table 2 in figure 2. Headline cells usually act as titles that introduce parts of the table. We consider that the headline cells are not part of the shadow of another cell (see figure 3).

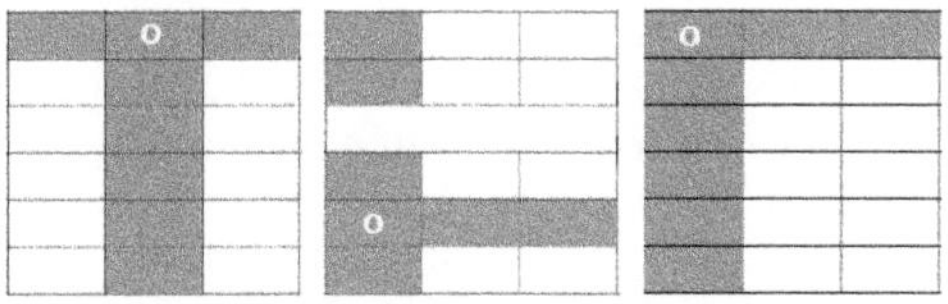

Figure 3: The shadow for a cell O, 3 cases

We define the match score of an attribute as the difference between the table match score and the shadow match score.

$$match(a,i,T) = match(i,T) - match(i, shadow(a)) \quad (4)$$

where

$$match(i, shadow(a)) = \max_{T_{x,y} \in shadow(a)} cos(i, T_{x,y})$$

Document relevance : If a document is relevant for the instance, the tables within the document are likely to be relevant for the instance. We should though take into account the document relevance. More precisely, let $\sharp results$ be the number of retrieved results for an instance i and $rank$ be the rank of a document d within this list. We compute:

$$drel(d,i) = \frac{\sharp results - rank}{\sharp results} \quad (5)$$

Search hits: Search hits is a feature that has already been used for attribute extraction [30, 22]. It corresponds to the number of search results returned by a Web search engine to a query "attribute of instance" within double quotes (successive ordering of terms is obligatory, e.g. "capital of France"). As done in literature, we use the logarithm (base 10) of the search hits count. To normalize, we used the following observation. Few attributes score higher than 6 i.e $log_{10}(search\_hits\_count(a\ of\ i)) > 6$. All the attributes that score higher than 6 were given a score of 1, the other scores were normalized by 6. Doing so, we have all scores in the interval $[0, 1]$.

DBPedia feature: DBPedia represents a large ontology of information which partly relies on information extracted from Wikipedia [3]. Given an instance i and an attribute a, the DBPedia feature $DBPedia(a,i)$ is equal to 1 if a is found as an attribute of i in DBPedia.

Wikipedia feature: Although information in DBPedia is much more uniform, there exist many attributes in Wikipedia *infobox* tables which are not present in DBPedia. *Infobox* tables are available for many Wikipedia pages. They contain lists of attributes for the page. Given an instance i and a candidate attribute a, we set the Wikipedia feature $Wikipedia(a,i)$ to 1 if a can be found in the infobox of a page for i in Wikipedia.

Other features: It is difficult to find features which help rank attributes that are domain-independent and apply at large-scale. We excluded from the relevance features the *frequency feature.* This feature is meant to measure how often an attribute appears within tables of relevant documents. Intuitively, we can think that a relevant attribute will repeat more frequently than non-attributes or irrelevant attributes. We observed that candidate attributes that repeat the most are the ones that are used in ads or forms. Thus, candidate attributes such as "login", "search", "previous", etc. were the ones that were favored by this feature. To tackle this issue, we developed a stop-word list for attributes, but even with this list, previous experiments did not show the interest of the frequency feature. This may be due to the fact that our list is still incomplete and need to be built using the whole web. Another alternative is to divide frequency by the frequency of the candidate attribute in the entire collection of documents being considered (analogous to *tf-idf*). In other terms, an attribute has to be more frequent in relevant documents than in a random sample of documents. Once again, preliminary experiments did not demonstrate the validity of the feature. We thus leave for future work a correct integration of this feature in the evaluation of $\phi(a,i)$.

Combination of features At last, $\phi(a,i)$ is evaluated according to the following formula:

$$\begin{aligned}\phi(a,i) &= match(a,i,T) + drel(d,i) \\ &+ log_{10}(search\_hits\_count(a\ of\ i)) \\ &+ DBPedia(a,i) + Wikipedia(a,i) \quad (6)\end{aligned}$$

with T the table from which a was extracted and d the document containing T.

4. EXPERIMENTAL SETUP

Data set: To evaluate our approaches, we built a dataset of classes and instances. First we chose a set of classes and then 10 instances per class. To choose instances and classes, we used sampling to avoid biases. 5 participants had to write down 10 classes each. Classes could be broad (e.g. *Countries*) or specific (*French speaking countries*). We sampled 20 classes out of the 50. This is a reasonable amount as in state of the art approaches [24, 30, 4, 28, 20], the number of assessed classes varies from 2-25 classes.

[3]The colspan is an HTML attribute that defines the number of columns a cell should span.

Horizontal			Vertical			Cafarella		
	prec.	recall		prec.	recall		prec.	recall
yes	0.50	0.82	yes	0.38	0.81	yes	0.41	0.81
no	0.98	0.94	no	0.98	0.95	no	0.98	0.87

Table 2: Precision and recall for the relational filter

Horizontal			Vertical			Cafarella		
	prec.	recall		prec.	recall		prec.	recall
yes	0.96	0.95	yes	0.76	0.89	yes	0.79	0.84
no	0.63	0.70	no	0.87	0.73	no	0.65	0.57

Table 3: Precision and recall for the header filter in relational tables

Similarly for each selected class, we asked the 5 participants to write down 10 instances. Sampling and removing duplicates we obtained 10 instances per class.

This is the list of classes: *rock bands, laptops, american universities, hotels, software, british army generals, chancellors of German, American films, IR papers, SLR cameras, 2000 novels, Nirvana songs, Nissan vehicles, programmable calculators, countries, drugs, companies, cities, painters, mobile phones.* The entire dataset can be found in: http://www.irit.fr/~Arlind.Kopliku/FORCEdataset.txt .

General setup: For each instance of the dataset (200 instances), we retrieved top 50 search results using the Yahoo! BOSS API. These pages are used as a seed to extract tables and attributes. For each table, we apply the three filters.

For the problem 1, candidate attributes are ranked using $\phi(a, i)$. For the second problem, attributes are ranked using $\phi(a, I)$ For the third problem attributes are ranked using $\phi(a, i)$ reinforced with $\phi(a, I_+)$ as described before.

Learning filters: The three filters correspond to rule-based classifiers. They were trained using the previously mentioned features using the WEKA package [25]. From the extracted tables, we randomly selected a sample of 3000 tables (with more than 1 row and more than 1 column) which were judged by 3 assessors. For each table assessors had to tell, if the table is relational. If "yes" they had to tell if the table is oriented vertically or horizontally and whether the table has a header.

Similarly, we choose a sample of 3000 random attribute lines from our dataset of tables. They are as well assessed from our assessors. For each attribute line, the assessor has to tell if it is a conform attribute line i.e. it contains an attribute name and attribute values.

Similarly to [8], we cross-validated the trained classifiers by splitting the human-judged dataset into five parts. Each time four parts are used training and the fifth for testing. We trained five different classifiers, rotating the testing set each time. Performance numbers are averaged from the resulting five tests.

Ranking: Candidate attributes are ranked based on the relevance features and depending on the problem being treated. 5 human participants evaluated this task assessing each a disjoint set of attributes. To measure the performance of ranking we had to measure top attributes retrieved for the three problems. To assess the performance over the first and third problem, assessors judged the 30 top ranked attributes for each instance being the target. To assess the performance for the problem 2, top 30 attributes were assessed for all classes of our dataset.

Assessments were binary. An attribute is assigned 1 if it is *relevant* for the instance/class it was retrieved for[4]. It were assigned 0 otherwise. During evaluation, assessors could access the source page of the attribute or other sources (Web search, dictionary) to make their decision. Attributes were shown in alphabetical order to avoid any bias.

5. EVALUATION RESULTS

This section is about experimental results. First, we present the performance of the three filters. We then analyze the performance of attribute retrieval.

5.1 Filtering

First, we analyzed all retrieved tables for all instances in our dataset. We found that only 16.9% of the tables had more than one row and more than one column. Within the 3000 tables that were assessed only 23% were considered relational. We can thus estimate a concentration of 3.9% relational tables within the entire set of tables in the retrieved Web pages. Now, we will analyze the effect of the filters. It is important to point out that our goal is not to compare with the results of Cafarella et al. [8], but to integrate their work and show its effect on attribute retrieval.

Relational filter: As we mentioned earlier, we learn separately a classifier for relational tables that are oriented horizontally and another classifier for relational tables that are oriented vertically. Results are shown in table 2 aside with the results obtained by Cafarella et al. [8].

We tuned classification for high recall over positives. The performance of our classifiers is similar to Cafarella et al. The classifier of relational tables oriented horizontally retains 82% of the true positives and it filters out 94% of the true negatives. Similarly, the classifier of relational tables oriented vertically retains 81% of the true positives and it filters out 95% of the true negatives. After this filtering step, we will have about 45% of relational tables within our corpus out of an initial estimated concentration of about 3.9%.

Header filter: In table 3, we show results for the header filter. Results are better than those obtained by Cafarella et al. This can be explained with the fact that we use top search resuts which are presumably of better quality than random Web pages. In particular, we found that most of the horizontally oriented relational tables have headers. They usually have two to three columns and are easier to classify.

The header classifier for relational tables oriented horizontally retains 95% of the true positives with a precision

[4]We recall that only attribute names were assessed.

of 96%. Although the header classifier of relational tables oriented vertically is less performant, it retains 89% of the true positives with a precision of 76%. After this filtering step, about 87.5% of the relational tables will have headers.

Attribute line filter: As well as the other filters, the attribute line filter is tuned for recall over positives. Results are shown in table 4. This filter retains 95% of the correct attribute lines, while it filters out about 55% of the incorrect attribute lines. It clearly helps in filtering out useless attribute lines at the cost of 5% of correct attribute lines.

	prec.	recall
yes	0.56	0.95
no	0.69	0.55

Table 4: Precision and recall for the attribute line filter in relational tables

In the next section, we will discuss on the effectiveness of the filters for the attribute retrieval task.

5.2 Instance attribute retrieval

For the first problem considered (instance attribute retrieval), attributes are ranked with $\phi(a,i)$. In figure 4, we show precision at rank averaged over all instances. We can say that results are promising. At rank 10, we have a precision of about 83%. At rank 20 we have a precision of about 72%. This means that if we apply this ranking for query suggestion, we will have that about 8.3 correct suggestions within top 10 suggestions and about 14.4 correct suggestions among the top 20.

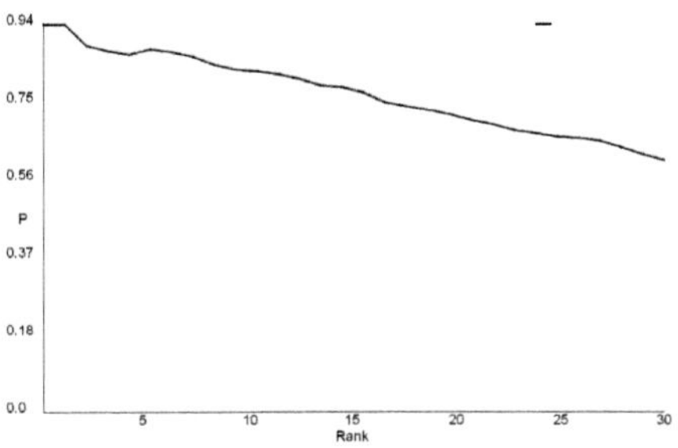

Figure 4: Precision at rank for instance attribute retrieval

Table 5 allows us to analyze the impact of each filter for attribute retrieval. Symbol * after the results of the first row indicates statistical significance using a paired t-test at $p < 0.05$ (all filters against no filters). We can see that the attribute line filter has a significant impact in the ranking as well as the relational and header filter. Combining all three filters provides the best performance. This is probably because the filters remove useless tables and table lines, making it easier to rank attributes.

Attribute values: The above results concern only attribute names. We will introduce here some of our work on attribute values. Given a set of candidate attribute lines, we can rank attribute values in different ways. An easy way to rank is the following. First, we rank attribute lines with $\phi(a,i)$. Then, if the attribute line has two rows (or columns), we use the second cell as attribute value. If the instance name appears ortogonally with some cell (except

Approach	p@1	p@10	p@20	p@30
All filters	0.94*	0.83*	0.72*	0.61*
Attribute line filter	0.90	0.82	0.70	0.61
Header and relat. filter	0.89	0.83	0.70	0.59
No filters	0.84	0.81	0.68	0.59

Table 5: The impact of filters

the first) in the attribute line, we select this cell as the attribute value for the attribute. Otherwise, we consider that the attribute value is the union of all cells (except the first). We call this attribute as multi-value. This simple method was shown to acquire correctly attribute values for 66% of relevant attributes in our dataset. These promising results will be completed by a complete analysis of attribute values retrieval in future work.

5.3 Class attribute retrieval

Figure 5 shows precision at rank for class attribute retrieval (problem 2) when we represent the class as a set of 10 instances. We retrieve attributes for each of the 10 instances of the class and we rank with the function $\phi(a,I)$ defined in section 3 for the second problem. As expected, results are better than for instance attribute retrieval. We have precision of 0.95 at rank 10, a precision of 0.84 at rank 20 and a precision of 0.77 at rank 30. For the same problem, if we use 5 instances per class, we obtain precision 0.89 at rank 10, precision 0.76 at rank 20 and precision 0.66 at rank 30. In general, we noticed that class attribute retrieval performance improves with the increase of available instances.

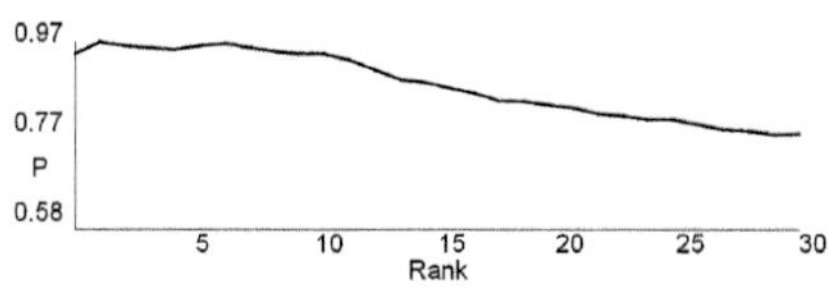

Figure 5: Precision at rank for class attribute retrieval

In figure 6, we show how results look like in one Web application we built. Here, we rank attributes names and values with $\phi(a,I)$ and then we select attribute values as described in section 5.2. Then we add some photos using image search, that can be seen as some decoration in our application. The example in figure 6 concerns a query composed of three instances from the class "mobile phones".

We also analyzed results class by class. Figure 7 shows precision at rank 30 by class. We can see that attribute retrieval can vary across classes. For some classes in our dataset, performance is lower such as for "drugs" and "programmable calculators", while for others precision remains high such as for "british army generals", "chancelors", "countries". The quality of attribute retrieval by class depends on the quality of attribute retrieval for every instance of the class. Results are relatively heterogeneous. Some instances are ambiguous. For some others, returned search results are slightly relevant. For some instances or class of instances, there is more tabular data than for other within search re-

	Nokia e72	Samsung Galaxy	iPhone
connectivity:	wlan wi-fi 802.11 b,g, integrated & assisted gps ...	usb 2.0, bluetooth 2.1, wi-fi b/g, gps ...	wi-fi (802.11 b/g/n) (2.4 ghz only)bluetooth 2.1 + ...
cpu:	600 mhz arm 11 processor ...	arm11 528 mhz + dsp 256 mhz ...	apple a4 (arm cortex-a8)[4] ...
dimensions:	114 x 59.5 x 10.1 mm ...	115 x 56 x 11.9 mm ...	115.2 mm (4.54 in) (h) 58.66 mm (2.309 in) (w) 9.3 ...
display:	320×240 px (0.1 megapixels), 2.36 in, up to 16.7 m ...	320 x 480 px , 3.2 in, amoled , touchscreen ...	3.5-inch (89 mm) diagonal 1.5:1 aspect ratio wides ...
form factor:	bar ...	candybar ...	slate bar ...
memory:	250 mb internal user storage rom: 512 mb sdram: 12 ...	128 mb ram ...	512 mb edram[5] ...
operating system:	s60 3rd edition feature pack 2 ui on symbian os ...	android v1.6 (donut)originally android 1.5upgrada ...	ios 4.3.2 (build 8h7) (gsm) released april 14, 2 ...
rear camera:	5 megapixel (2592 x 1944 pixels) with autofocus a ...	5 megapixel with auto focus; 720p hd video(12mbps ...	5 mp back-side illuminated sensorhd video (720p ...
weight:	128 g ...	114g ...	137 g (4.8 oz) ...
manufacturer:	nokia ...	samsung ...	foxconn (umts/gsm model)pegatron (cdma model)[1] ...
predecessor:	nokia e71 ...	samsung galaxy i-7500 ...	iphone 3gs ...
compatible networks:	gsm 800 / 900 / 1800 / 1900 mhz tri band utms / hs ...	dual band cdma2000 /ev-do rev. a 800 and 1,900 m ...	quad band gsm/gprs/edge (850, 900, 1800, 1900 mhz) ...

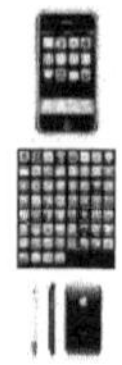

Figure 6: Attribute retrieval results for 3 mobile phone instances

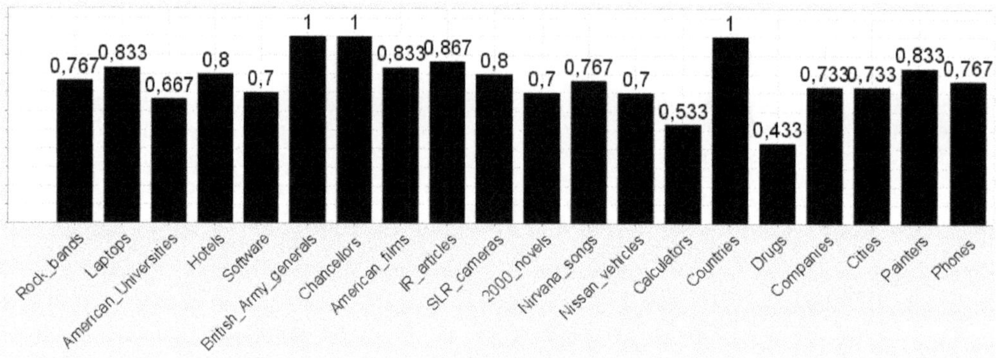

Figure 7: Precision at rank 30 by class

sults. Furthermore, for some classes there exist more relevant attributes than for others.

5.4 Reinforced attribute retrieval

To reinforce instance attribute retrieval (problem 3), for each target instance we use the 9 other instances of the same class. Attributes are ranked combining both $\phi(a, i)$ and $\phi(a, I_+)$ as described earlier. The intuition is that the other instances can provide additional evidence of relevance for attributes.

In figure 8, we can see the impact of reinforcement on instance attribute retrieval. The lower curve corresponds to instance attribute retrieval without reinforcement, while the upper curve corresponds to the reinforced attribute retrieval. We can see that reinforcement improves significantly results[6].

We can conclude that having multiple instances of the same class helps attribute retrieval for instance queries. We can explain this phenomena due to the fact that similar

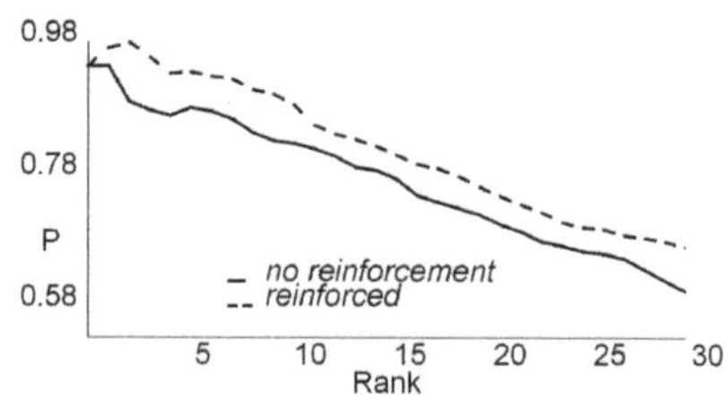

Figure 8: The impact of reinforcement

instances have similar attributes. Promoting common attributes has a positive impact on retrieval.

5.5 Estimating recall

To estimate in a reasonable time the recall of our method, we used 4 classes randomly selected from our dataset namely "SLR cameras", "countries", "companies", "Nissan vehicles". For all instances of the class, our assessors evaluated all candidate attributes (the ones that are not filtered out).

We found an average of 918 distinct candidate attributes per class (SLR cameras 689, countries 1253, companies 804,

[6]The significance of the improvement was validated using a paired t-test with $p<0.05$ for P@10, P@20, P@30.

vehicles 925). Among them, there are on average 256 relevant attributes per class (cameras 303, countries 213, companies 160, vehicles 347). This is a considerable amount of relevant attributes and it shows the potential of our method. We can say that tables are a good source for attributes and that our filters keep a high concentration of relevant attributes.

It is difficult to estimate how many relevant attributes there are for a given class or instance as it is difficult to write down all of them. We used Wikipedia and DBPedia to estimate their coverage in terms of attributes and then compare it to our method. We used 10 instances for each of the 4 classes mentioned above which have Wikipedia pages and are present in DBPedia. We then extracted attributes which are either present in DBPedia or in infoboxes from Wikipedia. We found an average of 25 distinct relevant attributes per class (cameras 8, countries 38, companies 37, vehicles 18). Although Wikipedia and DBPedia are quality and huge sources of information, they have a much lower recall than our method.

5.6 Comparison with state of the art

We also compared our approach to the ones based on lexico-syntactic rules [4, 30, 24, 21] Lexico-syntactic rules are common for attribute extraction . We tested the lexico-syntactic extraction rules in our retrieval framework with our dataset. Concretely, we use the patterns "*A* of *I*" and "*I*'s *A*" as done in [21, 24]. We collect candidate attributes for 10 instances of all classes.

To compare we used the class attribute retrieval approach (problem 2). We use top 50 search results for all instances of our dataset as extraction seed for both techniques. The attributes extracted by the lexico-syntactic extraction method are ranked with the same scoring (excluding table match score which does not apply to lexico-syntactic rules).
Results are shown in table 6. Our method performs significantly better with 61% of of relevant attributes at rank 30 against 33% for the lexico-syntactic rules. We recall that symbol * after the results indicates statistical improvement using a paired t-test ($p<0.05$).

Approach	p@1	p@10	p@20	p@30
Our approach	0.94*	0.83*	0.72*	0.61*
Lexico-syntactic rules	0.46	0.48	0.43	0.33

Table 6: Comparison with lexico-syntactic scores

We also compared both approach in term of recall, by considering only the 4 classes used to estimate recall. Lexico-syntactic rules have a lower recall, too. For each class, lexico-syntactic rules identify 55 candidate attributes on average. Among these there are about 24 relevant attributes per class (against 256 for our approach).

We can conclude that lexico-syntactic rules work well for certain applications such as queries, but they do not work well for long documents, especially in terms of precision.

6. CONCLUSIONS

In this paper, we propose 3 approaches for attribute retrieval using HTML tables from the Web. Our approaches combine 3 filters and they rank attributes using relevance features. Results are promising both in terms of precision and recall.

We combine three filters. Two of them are already known in literature. They apply to HTML tables to filter out non relational tables and tables without header. In our experimental setup they prove their effectiveness. In addition, we propose a third filter which is specific to attributes. Similarly to the other two, this filter is shown to have a high recall over positives and to filter out a reasonable amount of useless data.

We treat 3 different problems for attribute retrieval. First, we retrieve attributes for a given instance. Then, we retrieve attributes at class level. Retrieval is shown to have a high recall and a reasonable precision for both problems. Then we propose a reinforced approach for instance attribute retrieval. Using similar instances of the same class to reinforce attribute retrieval is shown to improve significantly results.

Our approaches have different advantages which were shown in this paper. First, they can be applied to whatever instances. They work at Web scale and they have a high recall. Furthermore, they outperform state of the art techniques for the same purpose.

We envision for future work the completition of the attribute retrieval framework with other recall-oriented or precision-oriented techniques. We believe that relations between classes, instances and attributes can be further explored for a better attribute retrieval. We will also explore more deeply the issue of attribute value retrieval.

7. REFERENCES

[1] E. Alfonseca, M. Pasca, and E. Robledo-Arnuncio. Acquisition of instance attributes via labeled and related instances. In *SIGIR '10*, pages 58–65, New York, NY, USA, 2010. ACM.

[2] A. Almuhareb and M. Poesio. Attribute-based and value-based clustering: An evaluation. In *EMNLP*. ACL, 2004.

[3] S. Auer, C. Bizer, G. Kobilarov, J. Lehmann, R. Cyganiak, and Z. G. Ives. Dbpedia: A nucleus for a web of open data. In *ISWC/ASWC*, pages 722–735, 2007.

[4] K. Bellare, P. P. Talukdar, G. Kumaran, O. Pereira, M. Liberman, A. Mccallum, and M. Dredze. Lightlysupervised attribute extraction for web search. In *Proceedings of Machine Learning for Web Search Workshop, NIPS 2007*, 2007.

[5] O. Ben-Yitzhak, N. Golbandi, N. Har'El, R. Lempel, A. Neumann, S. Ofek-Koifman, D. Sheinwald, E. Shekita, B. Sznajder, and S. Yogev. Beyond basic faceted search. In *WSDM '08*, pages 33–44, New York, NY, USA, 2008. ACM.

[6] M. J. Cafarella, M. Banko, and O. Etzioni. Relational Web Search. Technical report, University of Washington, 2006.

[7] M. J. Cafarella, A. Halevy, D. Z. Wang, E. Wu, and Y. Zhang. Webtables: exploring the power of tables on the web. *Proc. VLDB Endow.*, 1(1):538–549, 2008.

[8] M. J. Cafarella, A. Y. Halevy, Y. Zhang, D. Z. Wang, and E. Wu. Uncovering the Relational Web. In *WebDB*, 2008.

[9] C.-H. Chang, M. Kayed, M. R. Girgis, and K. F. Shaalan. A survey of web information extraction systems. *IEEE Trans. on Knowl. and Data Eng.*, 18:1411–1428, October 2006.

[10] H.-H. Chen, S.-C. Tsai, and J.-H. Tsai. Mining tables from large scale html texts. In *Proceedings of the 18th conference on Computational linguistics - Volume 1*, COLING '00, pages 166–172, Stroudsburg, PA, USA, 2000. ACL.

[11] V. Crescenzi, G. Mecca, and P. Merialdo. Roadrunner: Towards automatic data extraction from large web sites. In *VLDB '01*, pages 109–118, San Francisco, USA, 2001. Morgan Kaufmann.

[12] O. Etzioni, M. Cafarella, D. Downey, A.-M. Popescu, T. Shaked, S. Soderland, D. S. Weld, and A. Yates. Unsupervised named-entity extraction from the Web: an experimental study. *Artif. Intell.*, 165(1):91–134, 2005.

[13] M. Fleischman, E. Hovy, and A. Echihabi. Offline strategies for online question answering: answering questions before they are asked. In *ACL '03: Proceedings of the 41st Annual Meeting on Association for Computational Linguistics*, pages 1–7, 2003.

[14] M. A. Hearst. Automatic acquisition of hyponyms from large text corpora. In *Proceedings of the 14th conference on Computational linguistics*, pages 539–545, Morristown, NJ, USA, 1992. Association for Computational Linguistics.

[15] A. Kopliku. Aggregated search: From information nuggets to aggregated documents. In *CORIA 09 RJCRI Rencontre Jeunes Chercheurs en Recherche d'Information, Toulon, France*, 2009.

[16] A. Kopliku, K. Pinel-Sauvagnat, and M. Boughanem. Attribute retrieval from relational web tables. In *Symposium on String Processing and Information Retrieval, SPIRE*, page to appear, 2011.

[17] A. Kopliku, K. Pinel-Sauvagnat, and M. Boughanem. Retrieving attributes using web tables. In *Joint Conference on Digital Libraries JCDL*, pages 397–398, 2011.

[18] Z. Nie, Y. Ma, S. Shi, J.-R. Wen, and W.-Y. Ma. Web object retrieval. In *WWW '07: Proceedings of the 16th international conference on World Wide Web*, pages 81–90, New York, NY, USA, 2007. ACM.

[19] C. Paris, S. Wan, and P. Thomas. Focused and aggregated search: a perspective from natural language generation. *Information Retrieval Journal*, 44(3), 2010.

[20] M. Pasca and B. V. Durme. What you seek is what you get: Extraction of class attributes from query logs. In *IJCAI*, pages 2832–2837, 2007.

[21] M. Pasca and B. V. Durme. Weakly-supervised acquisition of open-domain classes and class attributes from web documents and query logs. In *ACL*, pages 19–27, 2008.

[22] A.-M. Popescu and O. Etzioni. Extracting product features and opinions from reviews. In *HLT '05*, pages 339–346, Stroudsburg, USA, 2005. ACL.

[23] F. M. Suchanek, G. Kasneci, and G. Weikum. Yago: a core of semantic knowledge. In *WWW '07: Proceedings of the 16th international conference on World Wide Web*, pages 697–706, New York, NY, USA, 2007. ACM.

[24] K. Tokunaga and K. Torisawa. Automatic discovery of attribute words from web documents. In *IJCNLP 05', Jeju Island, Korea*, pages 106–118, 2005.

[25] I. H. Witten and E. Frank. Data mining: practical machine learning tools and techniques with java implementations. *SIGMOD Rec.*, 31:76–77, March 2002.

[26] T.-L. Wong and W. Lam. A probabilistic approach for adapting information extraction wrappers and discovering new attributes. In *ICDM '04*, pages 257–264, Washington, DC, USA, 2004. IEEE Computer Society.

[27] T.-L. Wong and W. Lam. An unsupervised method for joint information extraction and feature mining across different web sites. *Data Knowl. Eng.*, 68:107–125, January 2009.

[28] F. Wu, R. Hoffmann, and D. S. Weld. Information extraction from wikipedia: moving down the long tail. In *KDD '08*, pages 731–739, New York, USA, 2008. ACM.

[29] M. Yoshida and K. Torisawa. A method to integrate tables of the world wide web. In *In Proceedings of the International Workshop on Web Document Analysis (WDA 2001*, pages 31–34, 2001.

[30] N. Yoshinaga and K. Torisawa. Open-domain attribute-value acquisition from semi-structured texts. In *Proceedings of the workshop on Ontolex*, pages 55–66, 2007.

Building Directories for Social Tagging Systems

Denis Helic
Knowledge Management Institute
Graz University of Technology
Graz, Austria
dhelic@tugraz.at

Markus Strohmaier
Knowledge Management Institute and
Know-Center
Graz University of Technology
Graz, Austria
markus.strohmaier@tugraz.at

ABSTRACT

Today, a number of algorithms exist for constructing tag hierarchies from social tagging data. While these algorithms were designed with ontological goals in mind, we know very little about their properties from an *information retrieval* perspective, such as whether these tag hierarchies support efficient *navigation* in social tagging systems. The aim of this paper is to investigate the usefulness of such tag hierarchies (sometimes also called folksonomies - from folk-generated taxonomy) as directories that aid navigation in social tagging systems. To this end, we simulate navigation of directories as decentralized search on a network of tags using Kleinberg's model. In this model, a tag hierarchy can be applied as background knowledge for decentralized search. By constraining the visibility of nodes in the directories we aim to mimic typical constraints imposed by a practical user interface (UI), such as limiting the number of displayed subcategories or related categories. Our experiments on five different social tagging datasets show that existing tag hierarchy algorithms can support navigation in theory, but our results also demonstrate that they face tremendous challenges when user interface (UI) restrictions are taken into account. Based on this observation, we introduce a new algorithm that constructs efficiently navigable directories on our datasets. The results are relevant for engineers and scientists aiming to improve navigability of social tagging systems.

Categories and Subject Descriptors

H.5.4 [**Information Interfaces and Presentation**]: Hypertext/ Hypermedia—*Navigation*; H.3.4 [**Information Storage and Retrieval**]: Systems and Software—*Information networks*; H.5.3 [**Information Interfaces and Presentation**]: Group and Organization Interfaces—*Collaborative computing*

General Terms

Experimentation, Measurement, Algorithms

Keywords

Navigation, Simulation, Social Tagging, Folksonomy

1. INTRODUCTION

Social tagging systems allow users to organize information in an unconstrained manner by freely choosing so-called *tags* to annotate a set of potentially diverse resources, such as photos in Flickr, Web pages in Delicious or scientific articles in CiteULike [11]. In addition to using tagging systems for personal organization of information, users can *share* annotations with each other.

In past research, our research community has aimed to capture emergent semantic structures from the vocabulary originating in such systems, for example in the form of tag hierarchies [3, 4, 8, 12, 13] or so-called "folksonomies[1]" – from folk-generated taxonomies. However, this line of research has mainly pursued an ontological goal, and did not focus on the usefulness of folksonomies for *navigation*. For example [3, 12, 23] propose algorithms for constructing semantically sound tag hierarchies from social tagging data. A detailed analysis of approaches to semantic relatedness of tags in social tagging systems can be found in e.g. [7]. In our own previous work [19, 20], we investigated the extent to which tag semantics are influenced by user motivation and usage practices.

While there are a number of studies on the usefulness of tags for general information retrieval purposes, we know very little about the usefulness of tag hierarchies as *directories*, i.e. to support activities such as *browsing* or *navigation*. Recent theoretical work in this area for example has shown that the ability of tags to efficiently encode resources for later retrieval decreases over time [9]. In our own previous work [10], we evaluated the suitability of different tag hierarchies to support navigation in social tagging systems on a theoretical level - not taking user interface constraints into account. The practicability and usefulness of integrating tag hierarchies into user interfaces of social tagging systems thus remains unclear, and - to the best of our knowledge - has not been investigated so far.

This paper sets out to address this gap. We aim to assess the usefulness of tag hierarchies for supporting navigation processes in user interfaces of social tagging systems by adopting simulation as our method of choice. We start by hypothetically inserting excerpts of tag hierarchies into user interfaces of tagging systems similar to the way concept hierarchies are used in other systems, such as the Google Directory, to guide users to resources (see Figure 1 for an example). We then model a user navigating this hypothetical user interface: The user starts at an arbitrary tag and navigates to another tag in the system using the directory. Adopting Kleinberg's decentralized search algorithm, we simulate this by using tag hierarchies as background knowledge that guides a navigator towards the destination tag. In addition, we model typical user interface restrictions through a series of adjustable parameters such as limiting the number of subcategories presented to a user or constraining the number of related categories (please see Figure 1). By doing simulations,

[1] http://www.vanderwal.net/folksonomy.html

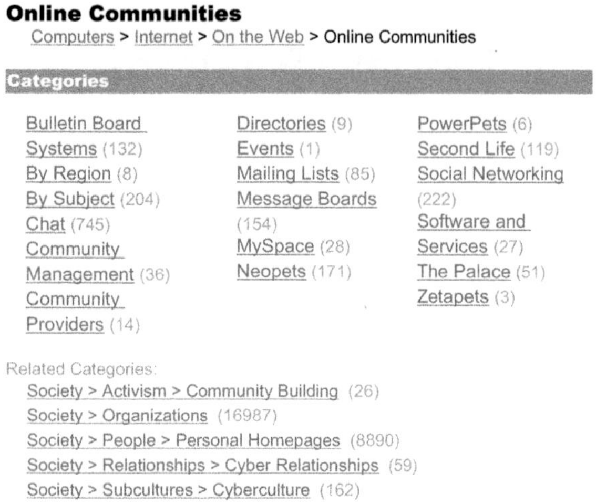

Figure 1: Google Directory user interface with typical directory elements including breadcrumbs, subcategories, and related categories.

we are able to conduct a thorough analysis of the effects of a variety of user interface restrictions on the usefulness of tag hierarchies for navigating 5 different real-world tagging datasets. This allows us to obtain novel insights and draw general conclusions about the drawbacks and promises of applying tag hierarchies as directories for navigating social tagging systems. We will show that tag hierarchies can support efficient navigation in social tagging systems in theory, but common user interface restrictions impair their practical suitability as a navigational aid significantly. Based on these results, we devise a novel directory algorithm capable of operating efficiently under typical user interface constraints.

In summary, this paper makes the following contributions:

- First, we introduce a framework for simulating navigation using different tag hierarchies in a social tagging system.
- Second, we show that although tag hierarchies can support efficient navigation in theory, under typical user interface restrictions (such as limiting the display of sub-categories) their ability to guide navigation is significantly impaired.
- Finally, we present a novel adaption of an existing algorithm [3] that restores efficient navigation under typical user interface restrictions.

The rest of this paper is organized as follows. In Section 2 we present a model for directory-based navigation using Kleinberg's algorithm for decentralized search in networks. In Subsection 2.3, we introduce the parameters for modeling user interface restrictions. In Section 3, we present our experimental setup and in Section 4 we discuss our experiment results. In Section 5 we introduce a new adaptation of an existing tag hierarchy algorithm and demonstrate how it can operate successfully under typical user interface constraints. Finally, we conclude the paper and provide some directions for future work.

2. MODELING DIRECTORY-BASED NAVIGATION

To investigate the implications of adopting tag hierarchies as a navigational aid in tagging systems, we model and simulate such navigation. Instead of observing real user behavior, we choose simulation mainly because current tagging systems do not offer directory support yet and simulation provides us with better experimental control and thus makes it possible to analyze different user interface issues across multiple datasets. In the following, we shortly introduce our simulation model and its theoretical background.

2.1 Greedy Search and Network Navigability

One of the research questions attracting a lot of interest in the field of networks is the relation between network structure and function, such as the relation between the structure and routing function of a network. Ever since the "small world" experiment [26] conducted by Stanley Milgram, researchers have been intrigued by the *routing efficiency* or *navigability* question in social networks – how people are able to find unknown people who are, potentially, geographically and socially distant to themselves. The key aspect of this question is the *absence of the global knowledge of the network* – people know only their friends and therefore *posses only the local knowledge of the network* but are still able to find unknown people. Similar navigability has been observed in other real networks such as metabolic or neural networks, or has been an important design goal for engineers of communication networks such as the Internet or different peer-to-peer networks (see e.g. [2]). Researchers identified the concept of *similarity between nodes* [22, 24, 32] or more generally the concept of *distance between nodes* [1, 15, 17, 18, 32] as an important aspect of establishing networking navigability. Combining the notion of distance between nodes with the algorithmic term of *greedy routing* [17], Kleinberg theoretically introduced network navigability [15, 18] in the following way: nodes use distance to select the next node in a routing session and the greedy algorithm selects the adjacent node closest (with the smallest distance) to the current destination node. The algorithm and its applications have been studied in the recent literature, see e.g. [16].

In [30] the authors abstract the notion of distance as introduced by Kleinberg to a *hidden distance* between nodes. Hidden distances define a *hidden metric spaces* which governs not only routing in the network but also the network formation and emergence of network structural properties such as power-law degree distributions and high node clustering. The authors connect observable emergent structural properties of a network with its navigability by defining a region of navigable networks in two dimensional space with clustering-coefficient [33] and power-law exponent as dimensions. On the other hand, a hidden metric space is also a geometric entity in which nodes are identified by their co-ordinates in it – distance between nodes is their geometric distance in that particular metric space. An interesting research question is the structure of such hidden metric spaces that underlie observable networks. In [5], the authors introduce a model with the circle as a hidden metric space and show its effects on routing in the global airport network. In [21] the authors discuss hyperbolic geometry as a hidden metric space whereas in [6] the authors apply hyperbolic geometry as a model of the hidden metric space of the Internet and design a novel greedy Internet routing algorithm.

The relation between Kleinberg's node distance and the recent work on hidden metric spaces can easily be established. In Kleinberg's model, the nodes are organized into a hierarchy according to their similarity – the distance between two nodes corresponds then to the height of their least common ancestor in that hierarchy [18] (Adamic [1] and Watts [32] introduce similar distance definitions). Hyperbolic geometry, as well as a hierarchy, distributes distances exponentially – it is, therefore, possible to approximate a hyperbolic metric space by a tree [21].

2.2 Simulating Navigation

We adopt a a tripartite hypernetwork model for social tagging systems where $V = R \cup U \cup T$, and R is the resource set, U is the user set, and T is the tag set [8, 27, 29]. An annotation of a particular resource with a particular tag produced by a particular user is a hyperedge (r, t, u), connecting three nodes from these three disjoint sets. Such a tripartite hypernetwork can be mapped onto three different bipartite networks connecting users and resources, users and tags, and tags and resources, or onto e.g. tag-to-tag networks. For different purposes it is often more practical to analyze one or more of these networks. For example, in the context of ontology learning, the bipartite networks of users and tags has been shown to be an effective projection [25]. In this paper, we focus on tag-to-tag networks (based on a tag-to-resource network) to mimic a tag-based user navigation task.

In a next step, we use a given tag hierarchy as a particular incarnation of a hidden metric space. We simulate greedy navigation through the observable tag-to-tag network querying the tag hierarchy for node distances – the idea is that the tag hierarchy is *useful* for supporting navigation *if* the greedy navigation using that hierarchy as the hidden metric space is successful.

The simulation algorithm starts its search at a randomly selected *start node* and tries to reach a randomly selected *destination node*. Search is carried out by moving along the links in the network in a number of intermediate steps. At each step, the link leading to the node that is closest (the node that is at the smallest hierarchy distance) to the destination node is selected. The basic idea behind such a greedy strategy is that there is a high probability to find a link to the destination node in the neighborhood of related nodes. The distance between two nodes v and w is calculated via a linear transformation of the height $h(v, w)$, which is the height of the least common ancestor of v and w in the tag hierarchy. More specifically, the parent node, the children nodes and the sibling nodes are considered to be at distance $d = 1$. From there on, the distance is recursively assigned, e.g., the parent's siblings and the grandchildren nodes are at distance $d = 2$, the children of the parent's siblings are at distance $d = 3$, the grandchildren of the parent's siblings are at distance $d = 4$ and so on. More details and an illustrative example of this particular simulation algorithm can be found in [10]. The algorithm is a variant of the simulation algorithm presented in [1].

For evaluation, we use the *length of the shortest path*. This reflects a typical scenario of navigation in tagging systems – the user will explore the tagging system by navigating to find relevant topics *as quickly as possible*, i.e., with as few clicks as possible. To model users behavior during navigation we apply the following strategy: if the agent arrives at a certain node for the second time, the search stops and is counted as a failure (no backtracking) – this mimics the situation where a user arrives at a tag that she has already visited, and then decides to, e.g., switch to the search field or to leave the system. In addition, if possible we try to avoid coming to a given node for the second time to model user exploration of alternative paths in the network. Thus, if the agent has two or more available paths with nodes at the same distances from the destination than a node that has not been already visited is preferred by the agent.

We simulate navigation in a large number of routing sessions (e.g. 1,000,000 sessions, see Section 3.3 for details on the experimental setup). Then, we quantify the quality of navigational support provided by a given tag hierarchy by measuring the success rate s of the greedy algorithm (the number of successfully reached destination nodes divided by the total number of routing sessions), and by the stretch τ [21], which is the ratio of the average greedy hops $\overline{h}$ to average shortest paths $\overline{l}$ (this measure tells us how longer are greedy paths as compared to global shortest paths). Those lengths are calculated over the e.g. 1,000,000 selected sessions. The measures are similar to those introduced in [6]. In addition to the global values calculated in [6], we calculate the measures for each observable shortest path in the networks.

In a final step, we analyze the structure of the greedy paths. This analysis provides insight into the importance of tag hierarchies and network nodes for the navigation process - in this way we can identify potential bottlenecks in folksonomies.

	BibSon.	CiteULike	Delicious	Flickr	LastFm
Tags	56,424	347,835	380,979	395,329	281,818
Links	2,003,986	27,536,381	39,808,439	17,524,927	84,787,780

Table 1: Dataset statistics.

2.3 UI Elements and Restrictions

Today, none of the popular tagging systems provide directory-based navigational aids. We therefore synthesize a model of a hypothetical user interface using user interface ideas from existing information systems with hierarchical organization of resources, such as Google Directory[2]. Such systems typically display the following user interface elements for any given node in a concept hierarchy (see Figure 1 for a screenshot or e.g. Google Directory[3]):

- **Breadcrumbs** provide the complete path to the root category.
- **Subcategories** provide links to more fine-grained categories. This list is typically limited in length. The user interface restricts how many subcategories are visible. We model this restriction by a parameter n.
- **Related categories** provide links to related categories. The user interface restricts how many related categories are visible. We model this second restriction by a parameter m.[4].

3. EXPERIMENTAL SETUP

We perform our experiments on five different tagging datasets. Directories are produced by a standard tag similarity network algorithm (see Section 3.2). General statistics about our datasets are depicted in Table 1, more details are presented next.

3.1 Datasets

Data from the following social tagging systems was used as an empirical basis:

- **Dataset BibSonomy**: This dataset[5] contains 916,495 annotations and 235,340 unique resources (scientific articles) from a dump of BibSonomy [14] until 2009-01-01. The tag-tag network comprises 56,424 nodes and 2,003,986 links.
- **Dataset CiteULike**: This dataset contains 6,328,021 annotations and 1,697,365 unique resources (scientific articles) and is available online[6]. The tag-tag network consists of 347,835 tags and 27,536,381 links.

[2] formerly DMOZ

[3] http://www.google.com/dirhp?hl=en

[4] In our model siblings of a particular node are considered to be related to that node

[5] http://www.kde.cs.uni-kassel.de/ws/dc09/

[6] http://www.citeulike.org/faq/data.adp

- **Dataset Delicious**: This dataset is an excerpt from the PINTS experimental dataset[7] containing a systematic crawl of Delicious and Flickr in 2006 and 2007. We extracted all data from November 2006. The resources in this dataset are Web addresses. The tag-tag network consists of 380,979 tags and 39,808,439 links.

- **Dataset Flickr**: This dataset is also an excerpt from the PINTS Flickr crawls. It contains the data from December 2005. The resources in Flickr are user-generated photos. The tag-tag network consists of 395,329 tags and 17,524,927 links.

- **Dataset LastFm** This dataset is from [28]. It contains annotations that were crawled from the last.fm website in the first half of 2009. The resources in this dataset are songs, artists and albums. The tag-tag network consists of 281,818 tags and 84,787,780 links.

3.2 Tag Hierarchy Algorithms

In previous work we have evaluated a series of existing tag hierarchy algorithms on a theoretical level, without taking user interface constraints into account [10]. As we have found that centrality-based algorithms outperform hierarchical clustering algorithms by a large margin (see [10, 31] for more details) we select one of these algorithms to conduct further investigations of their usefulness under typical user interface constraints. It is reasonable to assume that other centrality-based tag hierarchy algorithms will behave similarly under our constraints.

In this work we select an algorithm based on [12], where the authors propose to use so-called *tag similarity networks* and the centrality of tags for the construction of tag hierarchies. In their work, tag similarity networks are unweighted networks where each tag is a node in the network, and two nodes are linked to each other if their similarity is above a predefined similarity threshold. In the simplest case, the threshold is defined by tag overlap – if the tags do not overlap in at least one resource then they are not linked to each other in the tag similarity network. To construct tag hierarchies, the algorithm requires the ranking of nodes in a descending order according to how central the tags are in the tag similarity network. In particular, this ranking produces a centrality order where the most general tags from a dataset are in the top positions. The algorithm starts by a single node tree with the most general tag as the root node. The algorithm then proceeds by iterating through the centrality list and adding each tag to the tree – the algorithm calculates the similarities between the current tag and each tag currently present in the tree and adds the current tag as a child to its most similar tag. The authors define their algorithm in an extensible manner by supporting different similarity as well as different centrality measures. The presented algorithm uses cosine similarity and closeness centrality.

The work by [3] extends [12] by using tag co-occurrence as the similarity measure and the degree centrality as the centrality measure. In particular, the algorithm executes an extensive preprocessing of the dataset e.g. to remove synonym tags or to resolve ambiguous tags. For our work, we study this variation of the algorithm as both alternatives produce semantically and pragmatically comparable tag hierarchies. For reasons of simplicity, we skip the preprocessing of the dataset in this work and apply the alternative similarity and centrality measures only.

[7] https://www.uni-koblenz.de/FB4/Institutes/IFI/AGStaab/Research/DataSets/PINTSExperimentsDataSets/

3.3 Simulation Setup

With greedy navigation, we model and then simulate navigation in tagging systems. We select 1,000,000 distinct tag pairs that we call *search pairs* containing tags with degrees smaller or equal to 5 from the connected component of tag-to-tag tagging network. We adopt this low-degree selection strategy to make the simulated navigation task more "difficult" as finding e.g. the most central tag in a power law tag network is a trivial task. The first tag from the tag pair represents a *starting node* for navigation, modeling an arbitrary user entry page into the system (e.g. a landing page from a search engine, the latest tag from a news feed, or similar). We assume that users who come to the tagging system would *explore* the system to find one or more related topics or resources of current interest - we model this by means of the second tag (and the corresponding resource set) from the tag pair. We define this second tag as the *destination node* for the greedy navigation. The goal of the agent is to find a short path from the starting node to the destination node from the search pair.

To quantify the performance of the greedy navigator, we compare its path to the global shortest path (the shortest paths between two pairs assuming global knowledge of the network topology) between two selected nodes. We calculate the global shortest path between nodes from each search pair using breadth first search.

4. RESULTS

4.1 Navigational Efficiency of Tag Hierarchies

In this section we present the simulation results of adopting tag hierarchies as a navigational aid without any user interface restrictions, i.e. the entire tag hierarchy is accessible to a greedy navigator. It is important to note that this is a hypothetical setting, where a navigator has the entire directory at her disposal. In current directory-based systems (such as Google Directory), this is not the case. Therefore, these results are only of a theoretical value - they shed light on the nature of the greedy navigation process and help to identify potential pitfalls and bottlenecks, as well as ideas for solutions to those problems. Please note that these results are consistent with our previous results on theoretical suitability of tag hierarchies as a navigational support [10] – where here, we extend this investigation by discussing the structure of paths of the greedy navigator.

Consistently over all datasets, the greedy navigator performs very well with success rates close to 100%. Moreover, the navigator is very efficient in finding a short paths - in most cases it requires the same number of steps as the global shortest path - the global stretch is very close to 1 (see the far-left column of Figure 2).

As observed by [5], the path structure of the greedy navigator follows the zoom-out/zoom-in phase pattern. In the zoom-out phase, the navigator starts at a low degree node in the network periphery; it then exits the periphery and enters the network core visiting one of the high degree nodes there. In the zoom-in phase, the navigator leaves the core for its low-degree destination node in the periphery. Over all datasets, the top nodes are the most visited nodes - these are the nodes from the network core where the phase transition in the navigation process occurs (see the far-left column of Figure 3).

Table 2 shows the importance of the top degree nodes for greedy navigation – a huge fraction of all greedy paths go through the top 10% tags. This can be characterized as the main pitfall of tag hierarchies as a navigational tool. The top level categories in tag hierarchies have a huge number (hundreds, even thousands) of subcategories and related categories (see e.g. [10] or Figure 4a). The greedy navigator has no problems in finding the optimal path towards the network periphery from such a high-degree node – all

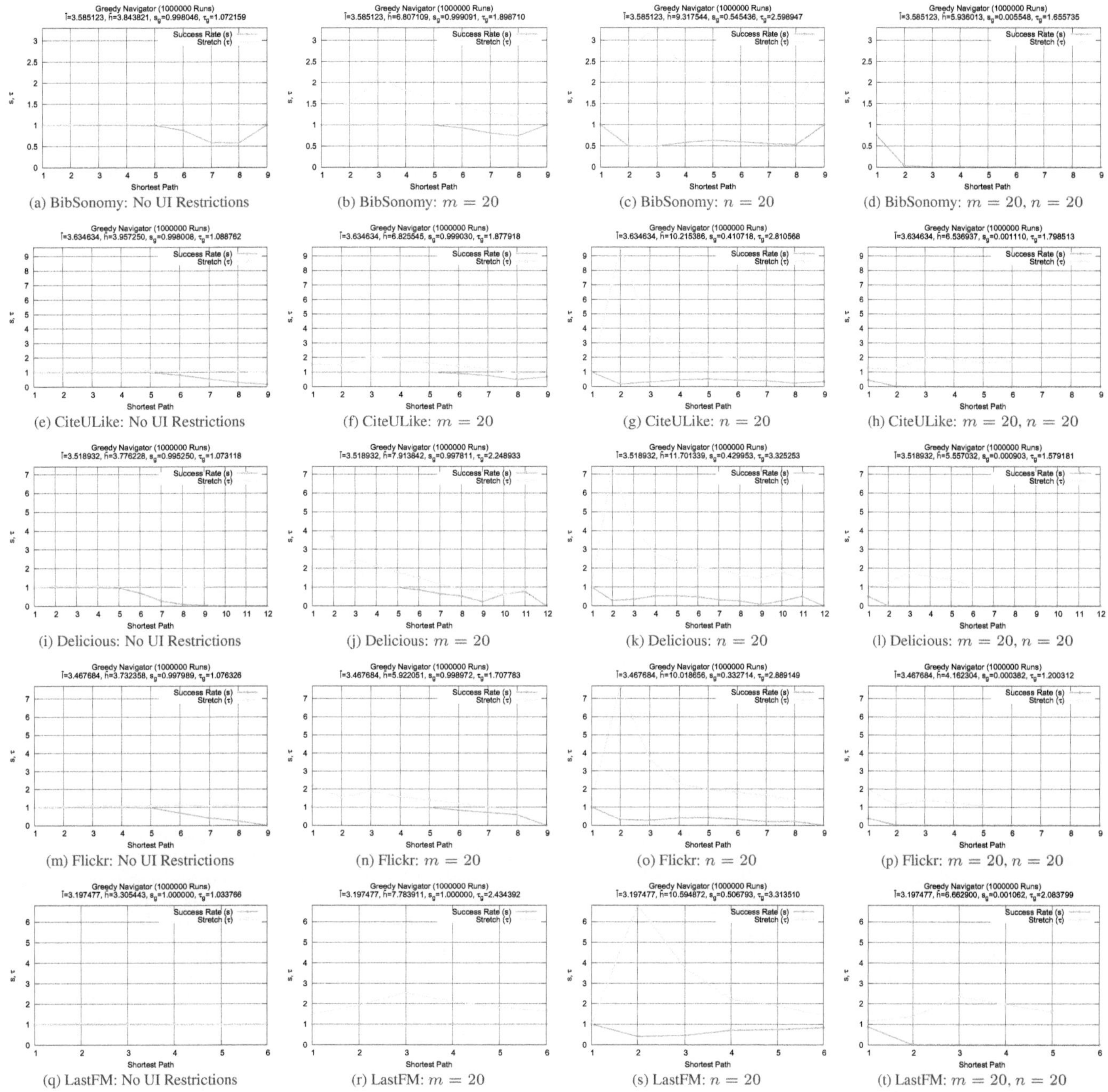

(a) BibSonomy: No UI Restrictions (b) BibSonomy: $m = 20$ (c) BibSonomy: $n = 20$ (d) BibSonomy: $m = 20, n = 20$

(e) CiteULike: No UI Restrictions (f) CiteULike: $m = 20$ (g) CiteULike: $n = 20$ (h) CiteULike: $m = 20, n = 20$

(i) Delicious: No UI Restrictions (j) Delicious: $m = 20$ (k) Delicious: $n = 20$ (l) Delicious: $m = 20, n = 20$

(m) Flickr: No UI Restrictions (n) Flickr: $m = 20$ (o) Flickr: $n = 20$ (p) Flickr: $m = 20, n = 20$

(q) LastFM: No UI Restrictions (r) LastFM: $m = 20$ (s) LastFM: $n = 20$ (t) LastFM: $m = 20, n = 20$

Figure 2: Greedy Navigator Success Rate (s) and Stretch (τ) - overall values and distributions per observable shortest path. *Far-Left:* (No UI restrictions) Theoretical evaluation of folksonomies as a navigational aid gives excellent results – both success rate and stretch are almost ideal. Slightly worst success rates for longer shortest paths (e.g. $l \geq 6$) are caused by poor connectivity and low degrees of the destination nodes and nodes leading to them. *Center-Left:* (Limited display of related categories with $m = 20$) Instead of taking a shortcut between related nodes the navigator needs to take a longer path over the parent node. Since less shortcuts between related nodes are being taken the number of navigator hops increases resulting in increased stretch values. On the other hand, the success rate remains almost untouched. *Center-Right:* (limited display of subcategories with $n = 20$) Under this restriction the navigator in many cases can not find the proper way towards the destination node in the periphery. The appropriate preceding nodes are very often not visible from a given high-degree node and this results in a failure. When successful the navigator bounces between the related and parent nodes, or between siblings until it finds the right path, see e.g. high stretch values for the shortest path of 2 (in a typical case we have here two low-degree siblings related via a high degree parent). *Far-Right:* ($m = 20$ and $n = 20$). Considering practical user interface restriction folksonomies are useless for supporting navigation. The success rate drops below 1%.

TopN(%)	Visits(%)
Root	4.94
1%	14.69
5%	33.99
10%	44.11

(a) BibSonomy

TopN(%)	Visits(%)
Root	4.18
1%	17.73
5%	30.01
10%	36.67

(b) CiteULike

TopN(%)	Visits(%)
Root	0.48
1%	19.83
5%	37.92
10%	45.38

(c) Delicious

TopN(%)	Visits(%)
Root	6.37
1%	20.09
5%	38.30
10%	46.27

(d) Flickr

TopN(%)	Visits(%)
Root	4.66
1%	35.80
5%	56.63
10%	62.74

(e) LastFM

Table 2: Percentage of greedy visits to the network core, i.e. visits to the (percentage of) the top degree nodes. Large proportion (36%-62%) of all greedy paths visit some of the top 10% nodes. This characterizes the two phase greedy navigation process - in the first "zoom-out" phase the greedy navigator exits the periphery and enters the network core whereas in the second "zoom-in" phase the greedy navigator leaves the core for its final destination in the network periphery.

paths at any given node are always *visible* to the greedy navigator. On the other hand, a typical user interface restricts visibility of subcategories to only a few, e.g. 10 or 20 categories which are sorted by a ranking algorithm. Typically, all other subcategories are only visible after clicking through e.g. a paginated category list.

In the next section we model such UI restrictions and investigate the *practical* usefulness of tag hierarchies to support navigation processes in user interfaces of social tagging systems.

4.2 Effects of UI Elements and Restrictions

In our simulations, we model the limited ability of user interfaces to display a directory in its entirety. This enables us to study the limitations of tag hierarchies where the number of subcategories is very high (in some cases, existing tag hierarchy algorithms produce nodes with thousands of children nodes). To model the constraints of a typical user interface, we set $n = 20$ and $m = 20$ and select randomly n tags as subcategories and respectively m tags as related categories. While similar constraints can be found in typical directory-based information systems such as Google Directory, our framework can easily evaluate and accommodate other values. For all practical purposes though, the results presented in this paper are based on the above parameter values.

Breadcrumbs. In all our experiments that model UI constraints, we introduce breadcrumb-aided navigation to our hypothetical user interfaces. In our simulations, breadcrumbs can speed up the zoom-out phase - in most cases the navigator jumps over low-degree nodes directly to the top nodes (see the center-left, center-right, and far-right columns in Figure 3). This is an intuitive behavior that can be expected from a greedy navigator.

In many cases, the effects of breadcrumbs on the greedy navigator is a decrease in the number of hops - often the navigator takes a direct, otherwise non-present, breadcrumb path to e.g. the root node. In some rare cases breadcrumbs can cause the stretch to even sink below 1 (see e.g. stretch values for $l \geq 8$ in 2j).

Subcategories. Constraining the display of subcategories to $n = 20$ impairs the success rate of the navigator tremendously. Destination nodes have small degrees - finding a path to those nodes requires the navigator to select appropriate preceding nodes from a given high-degree node. However, because of the particular user interface restriction, the appropriate nodes are very often not visible from a given high-degree node and this often leads to a failure. High stretch values indicate that the navigator bounces between the related and parent nodes until it finds its way down towards the destination node (see the center-right column of Figure 2).

Since the number of visible children is limited to a small value the zoom-in phase is disrupted - only few paths headed towards their final destination in the periphery find their way promptly. Instead, the navigator "bounces" between parent and sibling nodes to find its way down to the destination node (see the center-right column in Figure 3).

Related categories. The effect of limiting the number of related nodes (siblings) visible from the current node to $m = 20$ is that far less shortcuts between related nodes are being taken. Instead of taking a shortcut, the navigator often visits one of the parent nodes and only then one of the siblings or grand-siblings - this increases the number of necessary hops. Although breadcrumbs reduce the total number of hops the first effect is, by far, more significant - the total hops number and consequently the stretch increases (see the center-left column of Figure 2). On the other hand, the success rate remains almost uneffected. In certain cases it even increases (see e.g. 2b) - the navigator does not take the path over a non-visible sibling but takes an alternative (more successful) path via breadcrumbs or a visible sibling at the same distance to the destination node.

Concerning the path structure the following effects can be observed. While in the core, the majory of paths go up to the parent or root node. As the number of visible siblings is limited shortcuts are taken rarely (see the center-left column in Figure 3).

Related and subcategories restriction. When both user interface restrictions are applied at the same time (which again is typical in hierarchically organized information systems), the success rate drops drastically (see the far-right column in Figure 2). Even some of the nodes at $l = 1$ can not be found by the navigator - because of the user interface restrictions they are not visible anymore from the start node. On the one hand, the navigator can not find its way down towards the destination node. On the other, the "bouncing" between the related nodes is now also "forbidden" and this leads to disappointing success rates. Now - since both of the problems apply - the zoom-in phase is disrupted and the navigator does not "bounce" between siblings anymore. Most of the paths lead to the root node and then finish there without finding their way out of the core (see the far-right column in Figure 3).

In summary, these results suggest that existing algorithms for constructing tag hierarchies produce hierarchical structures that are not useful for aiding navigation under practical user interface constraints.

5. ALGORITHM

The main pitfall of the tag hierarchies that we simulated so far is their breadth – top level categories have too many subcategories, typically hundreds or thousands. Figure 4a depicts out-degree distributions of the tag hierarchies in our datasets. These distributions are essentially power-low distributions with a small number of high-degree tags (these are the top hierarchy nodes) and a large number of low-degree tags (these are the nodes from the lower hierarchy levels). As our previous analysis have shown the top level

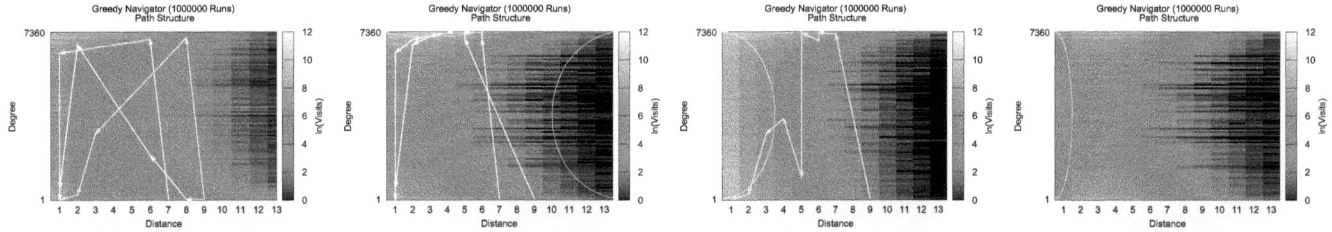

(a) BibSonomy:No UI Restrictions (b) BibSonomy: $m = 20$ (c) BibSonomy: $n = 20$ (d) BibSonomy: $m = 20, n = 20$

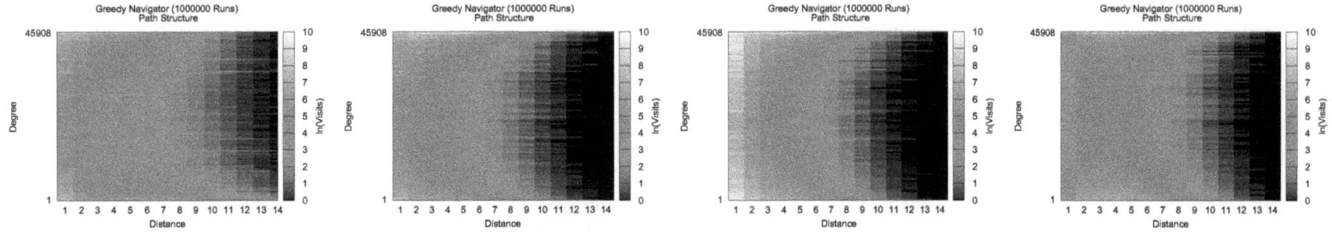

(e) CiteULike: No UI Restrictions (f) CiteULike: $m = 20$ (g) CiteULike: $n = 20$ (h) CiteULike: $m = 20, n = 20$

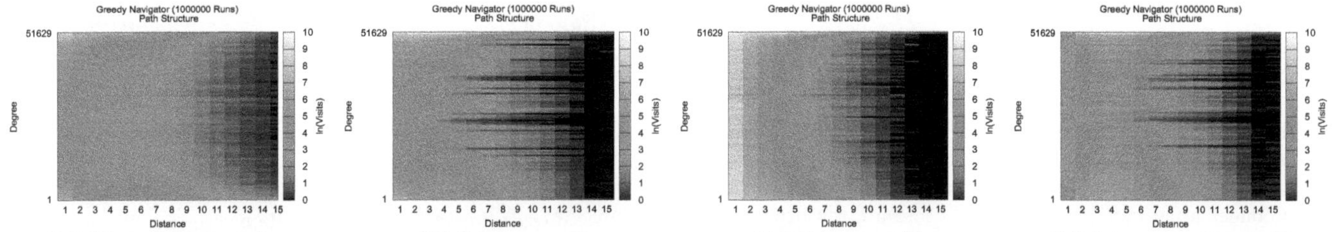

(i) Delicious: No UI Restrictions (j) Delicious: $m = 20$ (k) Delicious: $n = 20$ (l) Delicious: $m = 20, n = 20$

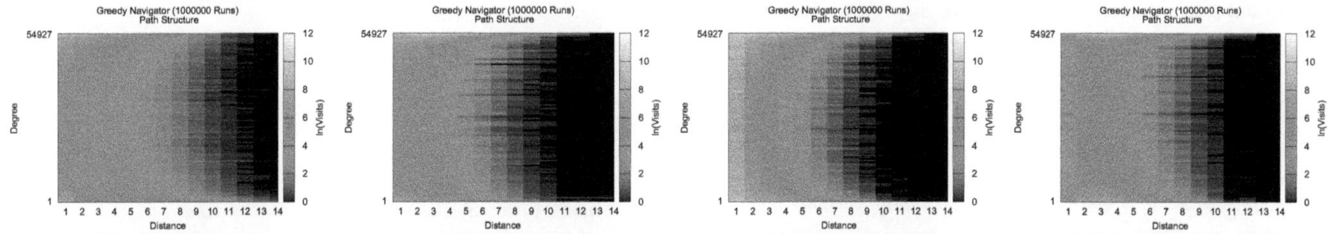

(m) Flickr: No UI Restrictions (n) Flickr: $m = 20$ (o) Flickr: $n = 20$ (p) Flickr: $m = 20, n = 20$

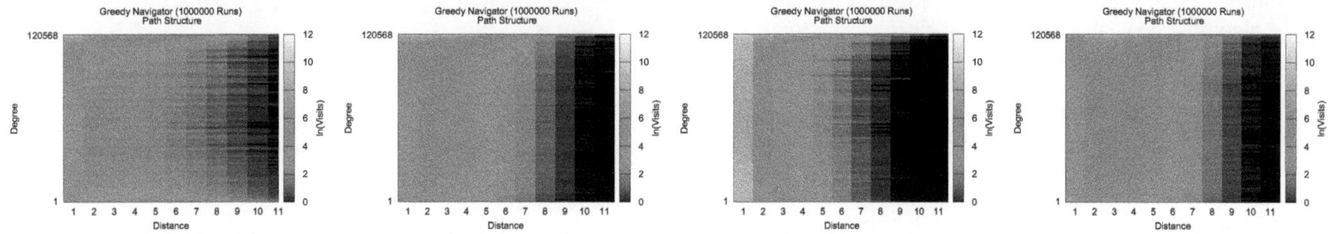

(q) LastFM: No UI Restrictions (r) LastFM: $m = 20$ (s) LastFM: $n = 20$ (t) LastFM: $m = 20, n = 20$

Figure 3: Greedy Navigator Path Structure. The density maps visualize visit frequency to nodes of a given degree at a given distance - the color is logarithm of the visit frequency (black indicating less visits; yellow indicating more visits). The zoom-out/zoom-in phase pattern can be observed across all experiments. *Far-Left:* (No UI restrictions) In 3a three typical paths are depicted with arrows. All paths start at low-degree nodes and long distances (the bottom-right side) proceeding to a core node in the zoom-out phase (the top-center position) and finishing again at a destination low-degree node (the bottom-left side). Many paths in the core proceed to the root node but many of those paths take also shortcuts between related high-degree siblings (see e.g. the yellow path in 3a). *Center-Left:* ($m = 20$) Because of breadcrumbs, the navigator skips low-degree nodes (cf. the white lines in 3a and 3b) and leaves the periphery immediately (more black/less violet in the white marked region in 3b). Same phenomenon can be observed in center-right and far-right diagrams. The majority of paths in the core go up to the root node. As the number of visible siblings is limited, shortcuts are taken rarely (greater numbers of yellow/orange pixels in the green marked region in 3b) increasing the total number of hops (cf. the yellow lines in 3a and 3b). *Center-Right:* ($n = 20$) The navigator "bounces" between parent and sibling nodes on its way down to the destination node (cf. the green lines in 3a and 3c). The number of mid-degree nodes visited at mid and small distances increases (more orange/yellow in the white marked region in 3c). *Far-Right:* ($m = 20$ and $n = 20$) The navigator is stuck at the root node without finding its way out of the core (more violet/less orange in the white marked region in 3d).

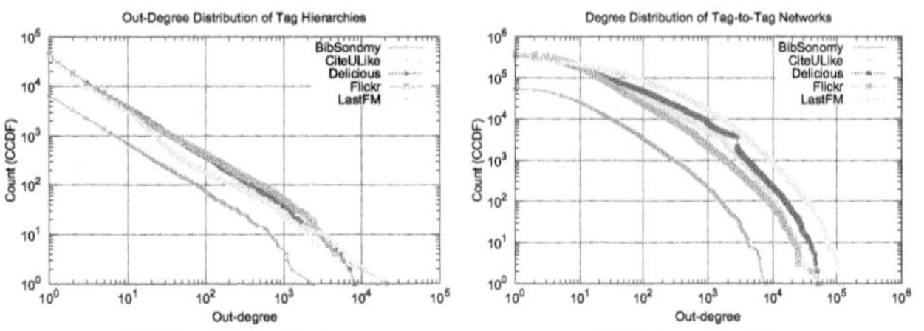

(a) Tag hierarchies (b) Tag networks

Figure 4: *Left:* Cumulative out-degree distribution of tag hierarchies produces by the algorithm described in [3]. Top level tags have hundreds, even thousands of subcategories – this makes those hierarchies useless for navigation as a typical user interface displays only a limited number of subcategories. *Right:* Cumulative degree distributions of tag-to-tag networks show existence of a large number of low-degree nodes that are typically connected to a single network hub.

nodes are crucial for the navigation. However, the UI limitations restrict the number of displayed subcategories to only a few and thus limit the usefulness of tag hierarchies as a navigational aid.

This requires a new tag hierarchy algorithm that is able to take into account display limitations of a typical user interface. In other words, the algorithm takes as an input parameter the display size and produces a tag hierarchy that can fit into a given user interface. Thus, the input parameter defines maximal number of subcategories and related categories that can be displayed. Technically, this input parameter defines branching factor b of the tag hierarchy.

In the following, we present a novel adaptation of the previously applied tag hierarchy algorithm that significantly recovers navigational support under typical user interface constraints by introducing a branching factor b as an input parameter. Moreover, we will demonstrate that *our algorithm produces tag hierarchies that efficiently support users in navigating social tagging systems.*

The new algorithm is a two-pass procedure. In the first pass the algorithm works similarly as proposed in [3] with the difference that the algorithm populates not only a single tree but a forest with multiple trees. The algorithm attaches maximally $b - 1$ subcategories to any given category in the forest. Before the second pass the algorithm sorts the produced trees in descending order of their size (the number of categories that they contain). We will call the largest tree in the forest the main tree.

In the second pass the algorithm attaches other trees to the main tree by linking the root node of a given tree to its most similar node from the main tree. If the most similar node has only one free subcategory spot left then a special misc category is first inserted in that free spot and then the given tree is attached to that misc category. The nesting of misc categories is necessary and it can be arbitrarily deep, e.g. if a misc category has only a single free subcategory spot left then another sub-misc category is first inserted in that spot and then a given tree is attached to that sub-misc category.

The goal of this approach is to connect as much trees as possible (and thus as much tags as possible) to the main tree without creating deep misc/sub-misc subtrees. However, such nested misc category constructs can not be avoided completely as the structure of the tag-to-tag network dictates their existence. Figure 4b shows the out-degree distributions of tag-to-tag networks in our analyzed datasets. The distributions show that there is a huge number of tags with a very small degrees – this means that these tags also have low centrality values. Further, these tags are typically connected only to high-degree tags. Because of their small centrality low-degree

Input: b **branching factor**
Output: $F =< V, E >$
add $C[0]$ to V
/* *Start of the first pass* */
for $i = 1 \ldots |C|$ **do**
  $t \leftarrow C[i]$
  add t to V
  $attached \leftarrow false$
  $j \leftarrow 0$
  repeat
    $candidate \leftarrow S_t[j]$
    if $(getOutDegree(V, candidate) < (b - 1))$ **then**
      add $(candidate, t)$ to E
      $attached \leftarrow true$
    end if
    $j \leftarrow j + 1$
  until $(j < |S_t|)$ && $(attached == false)$
end for
/* *End of the first pass* */
$WCCS \leftarrow getWccs(V)$
/* *Start of the second pass, WCSS[0] is the main tree* */
for $i = 1 \ldots |WCCS|$ **do**
  $t \leftarrow getRoot(WCCS[i])$
  $attached \leftarrow false$
  $j \leftarrow 0$
  repeat
    $candidate \leftarrow S_t[j]$
    if $(candidate \in WCCS[0])$ **then**
      if $(getOutDegree(V, candidate) < b)$ **then**
        add $(candidate, t)$ to E
        $attached \leftarrow true$
      else
        addToMiscCategory(candidate, t)
      end if
    end if
    $j \leftarrow j + 1$
  until $(j < |S_t|)$ && $(attached == false)$
  if $(attached == false)$ **then**
    addToMiscCategory(getRoot(WCCS[0], t)
  end if
end for
/* *End of the second pass* */

Figure 5: Tag Hierarchy Algorithm

tags are therefore added to the final tag hierarchy in the later stages of the process – typically when all of the free spots of high-degree tags are already taken.

For example, we want to discuss the following situation. Suppose there is a high-degree node in the network. Because of its degree the node possesses high centrality and resides therefore in one of the top hierarchy levels. In a typical power-law network, such node is connected to a small number of other high or mid-degree nodes with higher centrality values and to a significantly larger number of low-degree nodes with small centrality values (the latter representing the long tail). Thus, the algorithm first attaches adjacent high and mid-degree nodes as subcategories of the given node and uses all free subcategory spots. With high probability, the low-degree neighbors have links only to the given node (or similar high-degree nodes with no free subcategory spots) and need to be attached to that node via its misc subcategory. As the number of

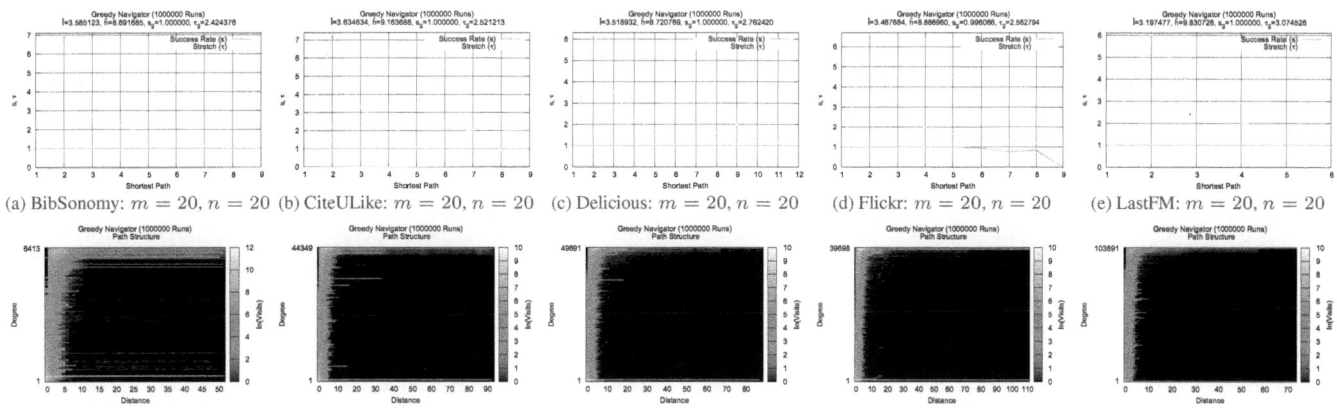

(a) BibSonomy: $m = 20, n = 20$ (b) CiteULike: $m = 20, n = 20$ (c) Delicious: $m = 20, n = 20$ (d) Flickr: $m = 20, n = 20$ (e) LastFM: $m = 20, n = 20$

(f) BibSonomy: $m = 20, n = 20$ (g) CiteULike: $m = 20, n = 20$ (h) Delicious: $m = 20, n = 20$ (i) Flickr: $m = 20, n = 20$ (j) LastFM: $m = 20, n = 20$

Figure 6: Top row: success rate and stretch of the improved algorithm. The new hierarchy is able to completely recover the success rate, however with increased stretch values. Bottom row: The density maps reveal a very clean zoom-out/zoom-in phase with zoom-out phase typically shortened by jumping over low degree nodes to the top level nodes via breadcrumbs. The long tail navigation is visible across all datasets as the orange/yellow line near the bottom of the diagrams.

such neighbors is larger than a typical branching factor nesting of misc categories is necessity.

Please note that the misc subtrees do not break semantics of the tag-to-tag networks, as no tags are attached to unrelated tags. Rather, the tags are pushed farther away from their most related tags into its nested misc categories.

The proposed algorithm (see Figure 5) requires:

- C is a array of tags sorted in descending order of their centrality in the tag-to-tag network.
- S is a array of arrays S_t. Each array S_t is sorted in descending order of similarity of tag t to other tags in the network.
- Function $getOutDegree(V, t)$ returns out-degree of node t in graph V.
- Function $getWccs(V)$ returns an array of weakly connected components of V sorted in descending order of components sizes. Function $getRoot(V)$ returns the root node of graph V.
- Function $addToMiscCategory(candidate, t)$ first creates a misc category for the $candidate$ tag and adds the tag t to that misc category. If the misc category is already full it will create a sub-misc category one level below in the hierarchy. The process is repeated recursively until a misc category with a free spot is found. In addition, the function *engineers* the tag-to-tag network linking each misc category to its parent, siblings, and children categories.

Our experiments with the hierarchies produced by the new algorithm show significant improvements in success rate across all datasets. Essentially, we were able to completely recover the success rate (see Figure 6). However, stretch increases and ranges between 2 and 3. This is caused by navigating the long tail of low degree tags – as those tags are situated within nested misc categories the number of hops before reaching the destination node increases with the number of hierarchy levels containing long tail tags. This phenomena is mostly visible for global shortest paths of 2 as two long tail tags are very often both linked to one and the same high-degree node.

6. CONCLUSION

While algorithms for constructing tag hierarchies have received much attention from a semantic research perspective, their usefulness for supporting *navigation* in social tagging systems under typical user interface constraints was generally unknown. The simulations and experimental results conducted in this work demonstrate that using existing tag hierarchies produced by existing algorithms as directories in user interfaces of social tagging systems yields sub-optimal results. Based on these insights, we presented and evaluated a novel adaptation of an existing algorithm that (i) significantly outperforms existing approaches, and (i) almost matches the results of the same algorithms in a hypothetical (i.e. unconstrained user interface) setting. The results of this work illuminate a way towards integrating tag hierarchies into user interfaces in an efficient way, i.e. in a way that enables users to navigate directories efficiently. Our work is relevant for engineers interested in integrating directory-based navigation support into user interfaces of social tagging systems and for scientists interested in the design and analysis of social tagging systems.

7. REFERENCES

[1] L. Adamic and E. Adar. How to search a social network. *Social Networks*, 27(3):187 – 203, 2005.

[2] L. A. Adamic, R. M. Lukose, A. R. Puniyani, and B. A. Huberman. Search in power-law networks. *Physical Review E*, 64(4):046135 1–8, Sep 2001.

[3] D. Benz, A. Hotho, and G. Stumme. Semantics made by you and me: Self-emerging ontologies can capture the diversity of shared knowledge. In *Proc. of the 2nd Web Science Conference (WebSci10)*, Raleigh, NC, USA, 2010. Web Science Trust.

[4] D. Benz, C. Körner, A. Hotho, G. Stumme, and M. Strohmaier. One tag to bind them all : Measuring term abstractness in social metadata. In G. Antoniou, M. Grobelnik, E. Simperl, B. Parsia, D. Plexousakis, J. Pan, and P. D. Leenheer, editors, *Proceedings of the 8th Extended Semantic Web Conference (ESWC 2011)*, Heraklion, Crete, May 2011.

[5] M. Boguñá, D. Krioukov, and K. C. Claffy. Navigability of complex networks. *Nature Physics*, 5:74–80, Jan. 2009.

[6] M. Boguñá, F. Papadopoulos, and D. Krioukov. Sustaining the Internet with hyperbolic mapping. *Nature Communications*, 1:62, Sept. 2010.

[7] C. Cattuto, D. Benz, A. Hotho, and G. Stumme. Semantic grounding of tag relatedness in social bookmarking systems. In A. P. Sheth, S. Staab, M. Dean, M. Paolucci, D. Maynard, T. W. Finin, and K. Thirunarayan, editors, *The Semantic Web - ISWC 2008, Proc. of International Semantic Web Conference 2008*, volume 5318 of *LNAI*, pages 615–631, Heidelberg, 2008. Springer.

[8] C. Cattuto, C. Schmitz, A. Baldassarri, V. D. P. Servedio, V. Loreto, A. Hotho, M. Grahl, and G. Stumme. Network properties of folksonomies. *AI Commun.*, 20(4):245–262, 2007.

[9] E. H. Chi and T. Mytkowicz. Understanding the efficiency of social tagging systems using information theory. In *Proc. of the nineteenth ACM conference on Hypertext and hypermedia, HT '08*, pages 81–88, New York, NY, USA, 2008. ACM.

[10] D. Helic, M. Strohmaier, C. Trattner, M. Muhr, and K. Lerman. Pragmatic evaluation of folksonomies. In *Proceedings of the 20th international conference on World wide web*, WWW '11, pages 417–426, New York, NY, USA, 2011. ACM.

[11] D. Helic, C. Trattner, M. Strohmaier, and K. Andrews. On the navigability of social tagging systems. In *Proc. of 2010 IEEE International Conference on Social Computing*, pages 161–168, Los Alamitos, CA, USA, 2010. IEEE Computer Society.

[12] P. Heymann and H. Garcia-Molina. Collaborative creation of communal hierarchical taxonomies in social tagging systems. Technical Report 2006-10, Stanford InfoLab, April 2006.

[13] A. Hotho, R. Jaeschke, C. Schmitz, and G. Stumme. Folkrank: A ranking algorithm for folksonomies. In *Proc. FGIR 2006*, pages 111–114, Bonn, Germany, 2006. Gesellschaft Für Informatik.

[14] A. Hotho, R. Jäschke, C. Schmitz, and G. Stumme. Bibsonomy: A social bookmark and publication sharing system. In A. de Moor, S. Polovina, and H. Delugach, editors, *Proceedings of the Conceptual Structures Tool Interoperability Workshop at the 14th International Conference on Conceptual Structures*, pages 87–102, Aalborg, Denmark, July 2006. Aalborg University Press.

[15] J. Kleinberg. The small-world phenomenon: an algorithm perspective. In *Proceedings of the thirty-second annual ACM symposium on Theory of computing*, STOC '00, pages 163–170, New York, NY, USA, 2000. ACM.

[16] J. Kleinberg. Complex networks and decentralized search algorithms. In *International Congress of Mathematicians (ICM)*, pages 1019–1044, Zürich, Switzerland, 2006. European Mathematical Society Publishing House.

[17] J. M. Kleinberg. Navigation in a small world. *Nature*, 406(6798):845, August 2000.

[18] J. M. Kleinberg. Small-world phenomena and the dynamics of information. In *Advances in Neural Information Processing Systems (NIPS) 14*, page 2001, Cambridge, MA, USA, 2001. MIT Press.

[19] C. Koerner, D. Benz, M. Strohmaier, A. Hotho, and G. Stumme. Stop thinking, start tagging - tag semantics emerge from collaborative verbosity. In *Proc. of the 19th International World Wide Web Conference (WWW 2010)*, Raleigh, NC, USA, Apr. 2010. ACM.

[20] C. Koerner, R. Kern, H. P. Grahsl, and M. Strohmaier. Of categorizers and describers: An evaluation of quantitative measures for tagging motivation. In *21st ACM SIGWEB Conference on Hypertext and Hypermedia (HT 2010), Toronto, Canada, ACM*, Toronto, Canada, June 2010.

[21] D. Krioukov, F. Papadopoulos, M. Kitsak, A. Vahdat, and M. Boguñá. Hyperbolic geometry of complex networks. *Phys. Rev. E*, 82(3):036106, Sep 2010.

[22] E. A. Leicht, P. Holme, and M. E. J. Newman. Vertex similarity in networks. *Phys. Rev. E*, 73(2):026120, Feb 2006.

[23] R. Li, S. Bao, Y. Yu, B. Fei, and Z. Su. Towards effective browsing of large scale social annotations. In *Proc. of the 16th international conference on World Wide Web, WWW '07*, page 952, New York, NY, USA, 2007. ACM.

[24] F. Menczer. Growing and navigating the small world web by local content. *Proc. Natl. Acad. Sci. USA*, 99(22):14014–14019, 2002.

[25] P. Mika. Ontologies are us: A unified model of social networks and semantics. *Web Semantics: Science, Services and Agents on the World Wide Web*, 5(1):5–15, 2007.

[26] S. Milgram. The small world problem. *Psychology Today*, 1:60–67, 1967.

[27] M. Ramezani, J. Sandvig, T. Schimoler, J. Gemmell, B. Mobasher, and R. Burke. Evaluating the impact of attacks in collaborative tagging environments. In *Computational Science and Engineering, 2009. CSE '09. International Conference on*, volume 4, pages 136 –143, Los Alamitos, CA, USA, aug. 2009. IEEE Computer Society.

[28] R. Schifanella, A. Barrat, C. Cattuto, B. Markines, and F. Menczer. Folks in folksonomies: social link prediction from shared metadata. In *Proc. of the third ACM international conference on Web search and data mining, WSDM '10*, pages 271–280, New York, NY, USA, 2010. ACM.

[29] C. Schmitz, A. Hotho, R. Jöschke, and G. Stumme. Mining association rules in folksonomies. In *Data Science and Classification: Proc. of the 10th IFCS Conf., Studies in Classification, Data Analysis, and Knowledge Organization*, pages 261–270, Berlin, Heidelberg, 2006. Springer.

[30] M. A. Serrano, D. Krioukov, and M. Boguñá. Self-similarity of complex networks and hidden metric spaces. *Phys. Rev. Lett.*, 100(7):078701, Feb 2008.

[31] M. Strohmaier, D. Helic, D. Benz, C. Körner, and R. Kern. Evaluation of folksonomy induction algorithms. under review.

[32] D. J. Watts, P. S. Dodds, and M. E. J. Newman. Identity and search in social networks. *Science*, 296:1302–1305, 2002.

[33] D. J. Watts and S. H. Strogatz. Collective dynamics of small-world networks. *Nature*, 393(6684):440–442, June 1998.

Workload-Aware Indexing for Keyword Search in Social Networks

Truls A. Bjørklund
Norwegian University of Science and Technology
trulsamu@idi.ntnu.no

Michaela Götz and Johannes Gehrke
Cornell University
{goetz,johannes}@cs.cornell.edu

Nils Grimsmo
Norwegian University of Science and Technology
nilsgri@idi.ntnu.no

ABSTRACT

More and more data is accumulated inside social networks. Keyword search provides a simple interface for exploring this content. However, a lot of the content is private, and a search system must enforce the privacy settings of the social network. In this paper, we present a workload-aware keyword search system with access control based on a social network. We make two technical contributions: (1) HeapUnion, a novel union operator that improves processing of search queries with access control by up to a factor of two compared to the best previous solution; and (2) highly accurate cost models that vary in sophistication and accuracy; these cost models provide input to an optimization algorithm that selects the most efficient organization of access control meta-data for a given workload. Our experimental results with real and synthetic data show that our approach outperforms previous work by up to a factor of three.

Categories and Subject Descriptors

H.3 [**Information Storage and Retrieval**]: Information Search and Retrieval—*Search Process*

General Terms

Performance, Security

1. INTRODUCTION

More and more data is accumulated inside social networks where users tweet, update their status, chat, post photos, comment on each other's lives, get updates through news feeds, and search for information. Examples of such social interaction platforms include Facebook, Twitter, LinkedIn, YouTube and Flickr. From a user's perspective, some of her content may be private and should only be accessible to a selected set of users in the network. To limit arbitrary information flow, social networks enable users to adjust their privacy settings at a fine granularity; e.g., to ensure that only friends can see the content they have posted. Thus any component that enables access to data in the social network *must* adhere to the privacy settings in place.

Search over collections of documents is a well-studied problem [37]. However, when supporting search over content in a social network, new opportunities and challenges arise. A document in a social network may be considered as consisting of two types of properties: *document-centric properties* and *network-centric properties*. The document-centric properties consist of the document and its metadata, for example the time when it was posted, the terms in the document, or properties of the user who posted the document. The network-centric properties consist of additional information added by other users, such as comments, tags, or ratings. The ranking of a document for a given search query could thus be based on both the document-centric and the network-centric part, where properties such as the relationship between the user who tagged a document and the user who submitted the query can be taken into account [1, 29].

When searching in social networks we need to enforce the access restrictions determined by the network structure, and we focus on the case where a user only has access to her friends' documents. This is a hard problem since as a result nearly every user has access to a unique subset of the documents and the resulting solution needs to scale not only with the number of documents but also the number of users.

In this paper, we propose to materialize special-purpose metadata called *author lists*, which are lists of identifiers for all documents authored by a set of users. When a user asks a search query, we use the author lists to filter the results of the query. This approach brings about two challenges. First, there is a large space of possible author lists, and we need to select which author lists to materialize to process a workload efficiently. Accurate cost models are required to identify a good set of lists. However, accurate cost models for query costs have received very limited attention in the literature as compared, for example, to cost models in database systems, probably because the space of possible query plans for a keyword search query is usually small compared to the space of possible query plans for an SQL query. To the best of our knowledge, this is the first paper that introduces highly accurate cost models for the operators in a search system. The second challenge is that a query may now need to access a very large number of author lists in order to determine the set of documents that a user has access to. Efficiently processing search queries with many author lists is essential for an efficient solution.

We focus on ranking functions based on simple document-centric properties in this paper, such as the time when the

CIKM'11, October 24–28, 2011, Glasgow, Scotland, UK.

document was posted or the user who posted the document. This provides an important step towards full support for search in social networks with access control for two reasons: First, there are situations where it is natural to rank documents only on simple properties and thus the techniques proposed in this paper solve the whole problem. An example is the search for tweets on Twitter where recency is a well-understood and reasonable ranking function. Second, the technical contributions of this paper can be used as building blocks in a solution that uses more general ranking functions. All solutions need to enforce access control, and query processing operators and data structures that efficiently enforce access control are therefore important building blocks.

We make the following technical contributions:

- We introduce a new operator called HeapUnion which efficiently allows us to process a large number of author lists while skipping over irrelevant documents. Compared to previous approaches, HeapUnion improves query processing time of queries with access control by up to a factor of two. (Section 3)
- We provide highly accurate cost models of the query operators in a keyword search system. We also describe how our cost models interact with the solution space of the problem of selecting a good author list design for a particular workload. (Section 4)
- In a thorough experimental analysis, we evaluate the efficiency of our novel HeapUnion operator, validate the accuracy of our cost models, and test the optimized access designs. (Section 5)

We discuss related work in Section 6 and conclude in Section 7. We now continue with a more formal description of the problem we address in Section 2.

2. PROBLEM DEFINITION

In this section, we will introduce some notation which is used to define the problem addressed in this paper.

2.1 Data and Query Model

We view a social network as a directed graph $\langle V, E\rangle$, where each node $u \in V$ represents a user. There is an edge $\langle u, v\rangle \in E$ if user v is a friend of user u, denoted $v \in F_u$, or alternatively that u is one of v's followers, denoted $u \in O_v$. We always have $u \in F_u$ and $u \in O_u$.

We consider workloads that consist of two different operations: posting new documents and issuing queries. A new document, which we also refer to as an *update*, consists of a set of terms. We will call the user who posted document d the *author* of d, and we will also say that the user *authored* d. The new document gets assigned a unique document ID; more recently posted documents have higher IDs. Let n_u denote the number of documents authored by user u, and let $N = \sum_u n_u$ denote the total number of documents.

A query submitted by a user u consists of a set of keywords. As mentioned in the previous section, we assume that only documents authored by users in F_u are accessible to u. For the remainder of this paper, we will also assume that the ranking is based on recency, with newer documents ranked higher than older documents. Thus the results of a keyword query are the k documents that (1) contain the query keywords, (2) are authored by a user in F_u, and (3) have the k highest document IDs among the documents that satisfy (1) and (2). Facebook currently supports these queries (with an artificial limit to posts of the last 30 days).[1] However, the technical details are proprietary.

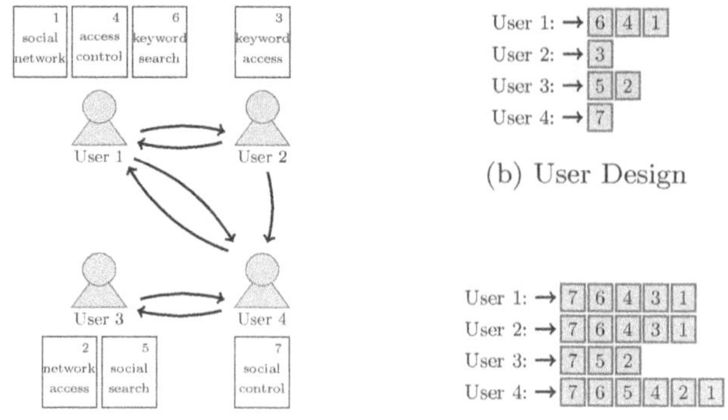

(a) Example social network with posted documents

(b) User Design

(c) Friends Design

Figure 1: Social Network and Basic Designs

Figure 1(a) shows an example of a social network with four users. User 4 is friends with Users 1 and 3, and User 2 is friends with Users 1 and 4. The users' posted documents are shown as well with their ID in the top right corner. User 3 has posted Documents 2 and 5, and in our model she can search through Documents 2, 5, and 7.

2.2 User and Friends Designs

In previous work we developed a conceptual framework of solutions to this problem based on two axes; the index axis and the access axis [12]. The *index axis* captures the idea that instead of creating one single inverted index over all the content in the social network, it is possible to create several inverted indexes, each containing a subset of the content. A set of inverted indexes and their content is called an *index design*. The *access axis* mirrors the index axis and describes the meta-data used to filter out inaccessible results; the meta-data is organized into *author lists*. As described in the introduction, an author list contains the IDs of all documents authored by a set of users. An *access design* describes a set of author lists.

Our experiments with some basic points in the solution space showed that two of the most promising solutions both use an index design with a single index containing all users' documents, while the access design in the two approaches differ. The first approach is called *user design* and has one author list per user that contains the document IDs posted by that particular user. The second approach is called *friends design*; it also has one author list per user, but this author list contains the documents posted by the user and all of her friends. The author lists for the user and friends designs for our example from Figure 1(a) are shown in Figures 1(b) and 1(c), respectively. In both of these designs, a keyword query from a user is processed in the single inverted index. To enforce access control, the results from the index are intersected with a set of author lists containing all friends of the user. In the friends design, all friends of the user are represented in the author list for the user, whereas in the user design, we need to calculate the union of the author lists for all friends.

Note that in the user design, updates are efficient because

[1] `http://blog.facebook.com/blog.php?post=115469877130`

only u's author list is updated when u posts a document; queries, however, need to access the author lists of all users in F_u. In the friends design, queries are more efficient because only the author list of u is accessed. Updates, however, need to change the author lists of all users in O_u.

2.3 Beyond User and Friends Designs

The relative merits of the user and friends designs motivate the work in this paper. In our new hybrid approach, we start out with the user design. In addition, we add one additional author list l_u for each user u; l_u contains the IDs of all documents authored by a selected set of users $L_u \subseteq F_u$. When user u submits a query, there is no need to access specific author lists for users in L_u, and queries therefore become more efficient as more users are represented in L_u. On the other hand, representing more users in L_u also leads to higher update costs. We therefore determine the contents of L_u (and thus l_u) based on the workload characteristics.

2.4 System Model

A system implementing the strategy we propose in this paper contains both posting lists and author lists. Both of these types of lists are lists of document IDs, and the resulting index is thus a standard inverted index including author lists that are identical to posting lists in structure.

An updatable keyword search system is usually implemented with a hierarchy of indexes [24, 14, 21, 26]. New data is accumulated in a small updatable structure that also supports concurrent queries, while the main part of the hierarchy consists of a set of read-only indexes. The read-only indexes are formed by merging a set of smaller read-only indexes. During a merge, queries are still processed in the old indexes, and an atomic switch to the new indexes is performed once the merge is finished. Then, after all searches in the old indexes are finished, the old indexes can be deleted. Thus documents will be merged into larger and larger indexes over time, and the largest read-only indexes will contain the least recent documents. Such an index hierarchy is well suited for search in social networks, especially when used in combination with an access design that adapts to the workload. The time at which indexes are merged represents an opportunity to modify the access design and adapt it to the current workload, so that different indexes in the hierarchy potentially have different access designs. When ranking documents based on recency as we do in this paper, the largest indexes in the hierarchy (with the oldest documents) will probably be accessed less frequently than smaller indexes, and using different access designs among the indexes in a hierarchy might be beneficial in such settings.

All individual indexes in the hierarchy except the small updatable part process *stratified* workloads because the index is constructed before it is used to answer queries. Because the stratified workloads therefore dominate in the index system, we focus on such workloads in this paper. We have implemented a system that constructs an index for a set of documents, and then processes search queries with the index. Our system is main-memory based and accumulates an index for a batch of documents at a time in a structure where the lists are compressed using VByte [30]. The batches are combined in the end to form the complete index, where the lists are compressed using PForDelta [38, 36]. Next, we describe how queries are processed.

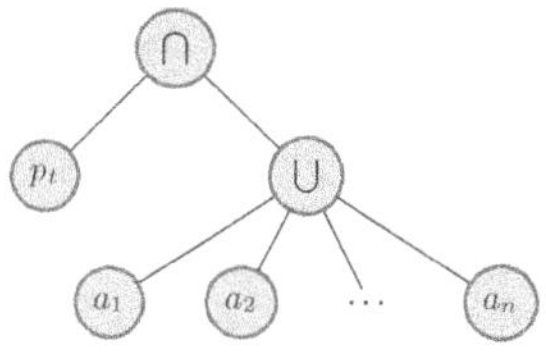

Figure 2: Query Template

3. THE HEAPUNION OPERATOR

In this section, we describe how our solution supports efficient query processing that scales to a large number of author lists. Without loss of generality, our explanation assumes single-term queries to simplify the presentation; extensions to multi-term queries are straightforward and our implementation supports the general case.

3.1 Query Processing

Our search system answers queries by computing the intersection of a posting list p_t for a term t with a union of author lists $a_1 \cup \cdots \cup a_m$.[2] A template for the query plan is shown in Figure 2. It uses three operators (intersection, union, and list iterator) that all support the following interface:

- *Init*(): Initialize the operator;
- *Current*(): Retrieve the current result;
- *Next*(): Forward to the next result and retrieve it;
- *SkipTo*(*val*): Forward to the next result $\leq$ *val*.

All results are returned in sorted order based on descending document IDs to facilitate efficient ranking on recency, and the query plan follows a document-at-a-time processing strategy [34]. The top-k ranked results are therefore found by calling *Next*() on the intersection operator k times. We use a standard intersection operator that alternates between the inputs and skips forward to find a value that occurs in both [20]. With this solution, the *SkipTo*(*val*) operation in the union operator will be called repeatedly, and thus its implementation is essential to the overall processing efficiency. We will therefore focus on the union operator in the remainder of this section. We use standard techniques to implement the other operators [19, 38, 9, 20].

There exist two basic algorithms for the union operator, Eager Merge and No Merge [28]. Eager Merge merges all inputs to the union first, and then supports skipping in the intermediate merged list. The initial merge is the dominating cost when using Eager Merge. Assuming a standard multi-way merge strategy and R entries in total in all m input lists, the worst-case total merge cost of Eager Merge is $\Theta(R \log m)$. No Merge, on the other hand, processes a skip operation on the union by performing a *SkipTo*(*val*) in each input and returning the maximum result. Eager Merge and No Merge are thus preferable in different situations: If there are many skip operations compared to the total number of entries in the inputs, Eager Merge is preferable. On the other hand, No Merge is preferable when the number of skip operations is small compared to the input sizes.

Raman et al. have introduced a union operator called Lazy Merge, which is based on the idea that if the number of skip operations in the union is large compared to the length of an input, it would have been ideal to pre-merge this input into

[2]Similar types of queries occur in several scenarios, e.g., in star joins in data warehouses [28].

a set of intermediate results. Lazy Merge adaptively merges an input into the intermediate results when the number of skip operations exceeds the length of the input times a constant α. Raman et al. show that Lazy Merge never uses more than twice the processing time of a solution that pre-merges the optimal set of inputs [28]. However, the approach has three drawbacks. First, although the analysis by Raman et al. argues that Lazy Merge adapts gracefully to all kinds of inputs, the analysis is, as the authors note, based on a simplifying approximation of the cost of merges. This approximation becomes increasingly inaccurate as the number of inputs and their sizes grow, and consequently, Lazy Merge does not scale well in practice. Second, the value of α has significant impact on performance, but it is non-obvious how to select the "right" value for this parameter. Third, we process top-k queries and therefore only need the first k results from the intersection during query processing. Thus any method that pre-merges complete inputs, such as Lazy Merge, will have poor performance in our setting.

3.2 The HeapUnion Operator

HeapUnion, our novel union operator, is designed (1) to scale gracefully to a very large number of inputs regardless of the characteristics of the skip operations; (2) not to have any parameters whose values may be difficult to determine, and (3) to be efficient regardless of whether all or only a fraction of the results are actually needed. HeapUnion is based on a binary heap which contains one entry for each input operator and is ordered based on the value obtained from calling *Current*() on each input operator (referred to as the current value for the input operator), just as in a standard multi-way merge strategy.

We support the standard operator interface by always having the input with the highest current value at the top of the heap, so that this value is also the current value for HeapUnion. The heap is initialized the first time *Next*() or *SkipTo*(*val*) is called. When the first call is a *Next*() (*SkipTo*(*val*) resp.), HeapUnion calls *Next*() (*SkipTo*(*val*)) on all inputs, and the heap is constructed using Floyd's Algorithm [18]. Floyd's Algorithm calls a recursive subprocedure called *heapify*() which constructs a legal heap from an entry with two legal sub-heaps as children. The *heapify*() operation has logarithmic worst-case complexity in the size of the heap, and Floyd's Algorithm runs in linear time [18]. We will also use *heapify*() for heap maintenance.

After initialization, HeapUnion works as shown in the pseudo code in Algorithm 1. The *Current*() operation either returns the current value from the input operator at the top of the heap, or it indicates that there are no more results if the heap is empty. The *Next*() operation forwards the input with the current value, and calls *heapify*() to ensure that the input with the new highest current value is at the top of the heap. The worst-case complexity of this operation is thus logarithmic in the number of input operators.

The most novel aspect of HeapUnion, however, is the very efficient *SkipTo*(*val*) operation that is based on a breadth-first search (BFS) in the heap. When forwarding to a value *val*, only the inputs with a current value $>$ *val* actually need to be forwarded. Because the heap is organized according to the current value for all inputs, we know that if a given input has a current value $\leq$ *val*, the same is true for all of its descendants. If we determine that no skip is necessary in a given input, we thus also know that no skip is required in any

Algorithm 1 HeapUnion Operator

```
function Init():
    Allocate heap

function Next():
    heap[0].Next()
    heapify(0)
    return Current()

function SkipTo(int val):
    Perform a breadth-first search in the heap from the root
    while BFS queue is not empty:
        if Current iterator is forwarded in SkipTo(val):
            Add to LIFO-list of entries for heap reorganization
            Add children to BFS queue
    Call heapify() for forwarded inputs in LIFO-list
    return Current()

function Current():
    if size(heap) == 0:
        return EOF
    else:
        return heap[0].Current()
```

of its children in the heap, and there is no need to process the children in the BFS. Furthermore, if an input is not forwarded, we know that its position in the heap relative to its children will not change. We also take advantage of this observation by calling *heapify*() only for the inputs where an actual skip occurred, and use a complete run of Floyd's algorithm only in the worst-case.

To illustrate how skipping in HeapUnion performs compared to both Lazy Merge and the basic union implementations described above, we will now present an example where HeapUnion outperforms all of them. Throughout the example, we assume that when merging a set of inputs, a standard multi-way merge is used. Furthermore, both the inputs and the pre-merged values are assumed to be represented as lists that support skipping forward with a cost logarithmic in the number of skipped entries. These assumptions agree with the implementations used in Section 5.

EXAMPLE 1. *Consider a union operator with* $k+1$ *inputs. The highest value in any input list is* $(k+\alpha)\cdot l$*, where* α *denotes the same constant that is used in Lazy Merge and* l *is a chosen constant. The first input contains the first* $\alpha \cdot l$ *values starting from the highest value. The rest of the values are partitioned equally among the rest of the inputs such that input* i *has the values* $\{i-1+k\cdot j | 0 \leq j < l\}$.

We will now evaluate the cost of a set of skip operations that can be partitioned into two phases: In the first phase, we skip to each of the αl *highest values in descending order. All these values are found in the first input. In the next phase, we perform a single skip to the value* 1*. We will evaluate the cost of both phases for both Eager Merge, No Merge, Lazy Merge and HeapUnion.*

Eager Merge: *For Eager Merge, we will analyze the cost of the merges for the two phases separately. The merge of Phase* 1 *will only involve accessing one input list, and thus have a constant cost per entry. In Phase* 2*, each input will move to a leaf in the heap once a value has been extracted in the merge, and the cost is therefore* $\Theta(k\cdot l\cdot \log(k))$*. The costs of the actual skip operations in this example are* $\Theta(\alpha \cdot l)$ *for the* $\alpha \cdot l$ *skips of length* 1 *in Phase* 1*, and* $\Theta(\log(k\cdot l))$ *for the single skip in Phase* 2*.*

No Merge: *In Phase* 1*, each skip operation with No Merge will result in a skip of length* 1 *in input* 1*, and an attempt* *at skipping in all other input lists, with total cost $\Theta(k\alpha l)$. Phase 2 has cost in $\Theta(k \log l)$ due to k skips of length l.*

***Lazy Merge**: Because the α in the example is the one used to configure Lazy Merge, this method will behave as No Merge in Phase 1. The remaining k inputs are merged before Phase 2, resulting in the same cost as Eager Merge in this phase.*

***HeapUnion**: HeapUnion will behave like a standard multi-way merge in Phase 1, and thus have the same cost as Eager Merge. In Phase 2 on the other hand, its costs are similar to with No Merge because the same skips are performed in each list, and the heap maintenance costs are in $O(k)$.*

In this example, Eager Merge is clearly preferable in Phase 1 as compared to No Merge with a speed-up factor of k. In Phase 2 on the other hand, No Merge is clearly preferable with a speed-up factor $\frac{l \log(k)}{\log(l)}$ compared to Eager Merge. Lazy Merge actually achieves the worst of both worlds in the two phases. HeapUnion, however, outperforms Lazy and No Merge by a factor k in Phase 1, and it outperforms Lazy and Eaper Merge by a factor $\frac{l \log(k)}{\log(l)}$ in Phase 2. HeapUnion thus scales much better than the other methods with increasing l and k.

We will now compare the worst-case performance of HeapUnion with the worst-case of Eager Merge and No Merge. First, we provide a bound on the combined complexity of all skip operations in one HeapUnion:

LEMMA 1. *Assuming that the cost of skipping forward s entries in an input is in $O(s)$ and that each skip operation on HeapUnion forwards at least one input, the total cost of all skip operations for a HeapUnion is in $O(R \log m)$.*

We omit the proof due to space constrains. As a consequence of Lemma 1, the worst-case cost for all skip operations in HeapUnion is no worse than the worst-case cost of all skips in Eager Merge because the initial merge in Eager Merge has worst-case complexity $\Theta(R \log m)$.

Furthermore, the following lemma follows immediately from the fact that the heap maintenance reduces to Floyd's algorithm in the worst-case and that Floyd's algorithm is $O(m)$ for m heap entries.

LEMMA 2. *The heap maintenance cost in one skip operation in HeapUnion is $O(m)$.*

As a consequence of Lemma 2, the cost of a specific skip operation with HeapUnion is comparable to the cost of the same skip operation with No Merge: In both methods, the same skips will occur on the inputs, and No Merge may potentially try to skip on more inputs that are not forwarded compared to HeapUnion (due to the BFS). Furthermore, the cost of finding the largest return value with No Merge is $\Theta(m)$, and the cost of heap maintenance in HeapUnion is $O(m)$. The worst-case cost of one skip operation in HeapUnion is therefore not worse than with No Merge.

HeapUnion will thus achieve the best of both worlds: When there are only a few skip operations compared to the lengths of the inputs, it is an advantage that its worst-case performance for each operation is as good as with No Merge. And, when there are many skip operations, it is an advantage that its worst-case performance is as good as with Eager Merge. In addition, HeapUnion does not pre-merge any inputs, and retrieving only a fraction of the results is therefore supported efficiently. Compared to Lazy Merge it also has the advantage that no configuration parameters are required. An experimental validation of the efficiency of HeapUnion is presented in Section 5.2.

	Update Cost ($\|l_u\| = n$)
Monotonic	$c_{update} n$
Non-monotonic	$\begin{cases} c_{1b} * n & \text{if } \frac{N}{n} < b_1 \\ c_{2b} * n & \text{if } b_1 \leq \frac{N}{n} < b_2 \\ c_{3b} * n & \text{otherwise} \end{cases}$

Figure 3: Overview of Update Cost Estimates

4. COST MODELS AND OPTIMIZATION

The efficiency of our system for a particular workload depends on the contents of the additional author lists, and selecting a good set of lists is therefore essential. For each user u, any subset of F_u can be included in L_u, which leads to $2^{\sum_{u \in V} |F_u|} = 2^{|E|}$ possible designs. We use cost models to explore this large space. In information retrieval, cost models have traditionally been used to explain and compare the relative merits of different algorithms [35, 34, 14, 16]. In this paper, however, the cost models are used in optimization algorithms to select between different access designs for a stratified workload of updates and queries.

It turns out that accurate cost models are required in order to find close-to-optimal access designs, and as we will show in Section 5, adaptations of cost models used in related work are not accurate enough for our purposes. However, accuracy is not the only factor when choosing a cost model, because an advantage of simpler models is that they can allow analytically reducing the number of potentially optimal solutions, i.e., the search space of an optimization algorithm.

In the following subsections, we will introduce two accurate cost models. With the first model, *Monotonic*, we try to achieve the best possible accuracy while ensuring that the search space of the optimization algorithm is limited. *Non-monotonic* increases the accuracy further at the expense of an increase in the size of the search space. Both *Monotonic* and *Non-monotonic* model the processing time of the individual query operators, and they can therefore be employed in other applications that attempt to estimate the processing time of different query plans.

4.1 Monotonic

Monotonic is designed to be an accurate yet tractable cost model, where only a small number of access designs must be checked in the optimization algorithm to find a globally optimal solution. The model for updates in Monotonic simply assumes that the cost of constructing a list is linear in the number of document IDs in the list. For modelling query costs, Monotonic has one cost model for each operator and the total query costs are estimated by combining the models for all operators in the query. The cost model for an operator describes the cost of each method supported by the operator. For operators that have other operators as inputs, like HeapUnion and Intersection, the cost is calculated by combining the cost of operations within the operator with the cost of method calls on the inputs. To find the cost of the queries we use in this paper, we combine the operators according to the template in Figure 2, and calculate the cost of k *Next*() calls for the Intersection to retrieve the top-k results (assuming there are at least k).

Monotonic is described in Figures 3 and 4. *Skip*(s) is a model for *SkipTo*(val). If *SkipTo*(val) forwards the current value of an operator with Δv document IDs, we model the cost of the operation by *Skip*($\frac{r\Delta v}{N}$), where r is the num-

	Init()	*Next()*	*Skip(s)*
List Iterator	$\begin{cases} c_{einit} & \text{empty list} \\ c_{init} & \text{otherwise} \end{cases}$	c_{next}	$\begin{cases} c_c + \frac{s}{b}c_d + scan(s)c_{sc} & \text{if } s \leq b \\ Skip(b) + c_g \log\left(\frac{s}{b}\right) & \text{otherwise} \end{cases}$
Intersection	$k_1.Init() + k_2.Init()$	$k_1.Next() + (t-1)k_1.Skip(1 + \frac{r_1}{r_2})$ $+ t \cdot k_2.Skip(\frac{t-1}{t}(1 + \frac{r_2}{r_1}) + \frac{r_2}{r_1 t})$	not used
Monotonic HeapUnion	$\sum_{i=1}^{m} k_i.Init()$	$\begin{cases} \sum_{i=1}^{m} k_i.Next() + (\gamma + \frac{1}{2}) \cdot m \cdot c_h & \text{first call} \\ \sum_{i=1}^{m} \frac{r_i}{R} k_i.Next() + (\gamma + 1) \cdot c_h & \text{otherwise} \end{cases}$	$\begin{cases} \sum_{i=1}^{m} k_i.Skip(\frac{r_i s}{R}) + (\gamma + \frac{1}{2}) \cdot m \cdot c_h & \text{first call} \\ \sum_{i=1}^{m} \min(1, \frac{r_i s}{R}) k_i.Skip(\max(1, \frac{r_i s}{R})) \\ \quad +(\gamma + 1) \cdot m_s \cdot c_h & \text{otherwise} \end{cases}$
Non-monotonic HeapUnion	$\sum_{i=1}^{m} k_i.Init()$	$\begin{cases} \sum_{i=1}^{m} k_i.Next() + (\gamma + \frac{1}{2}) \cdot m \cdot c_h & \text{first call} \\ \sum_{i=1}^{m} \frac{r_i}{R}(k_i.Next() + \log(1 + p_i) \cdot c_h) & \text{otherwise} \end{cases}$	$\begin{cases} \sum_{i=1}^{m} k_i.Skip(\frac{r_i s}{R}) + (\gamma + \frac{1}{2}) \cdot m \cdot c_h & \text{first call} \\ \sum_{i=1}^{m} \min(1, \frac{r_i s}{R}) k_i.Skip(\max(1, \frac{r_i s}{R})) \\ \quad + \max(m_s\gamma + \min(m_s, \frac{m}{2}), \\ \quad m_s(\sum_{j=1}^{m} \frac{r_j}{R} \log(1 + p_j)) - h(\lfloor m_s \rfloor)) \cdot c_h & \text{otherwise} \end{cases}$

Figure 4: Overview of Query Cost Estimates

ber of results of the operator. The number of results for an operator is the number of times we can call *Next*() and retrieve a new result. Monotonic and Non-monotonic use the same models for List Iterator and Intersection, but they have different models for HeapUnion. We will now explain Monotonic's model for HeapUnion; models for the other operators are explained in the full version of this paper along with the microbenchmarks used to determine the constants in the model [11].

HeapUnion. Let us assume that HeapUnion has m inputs $k_1, \ldots, k_m$. We use r_i to denote the number of results from input i, and define $R = \sum_{i=1}^{m} r_i$. We assume that the cost of initialization within the HeapUnion operator itself is negligible, and therefore model the cost of initialization as the sum of the initialization costs for all inputs.

Recall from Section 3.2 that the first call to either *Next*() or *SkipTo*(*val*) will involve construction of the heap; we therefore have two different cases in the model for *Next*() and *SkipTo*(*val*), depending on whether it is the first or a subsequent call. The cost of the first call to *Next*() includes the cost of calling *Next*() on all m inputs, and the cost of the heap construction using Floyd's Algorithm. For heap construction, we model the cost of each call to *heapify*() as being constant, c_h. With Floyd's algorithm, *heapify*() is called for half the heap entries, and then recursively every time there is a reorganization. The average case complexity of Floyd's algorithm is well known, and the number of relocations in the heap is approximately $\gamma m = 0.744m$ [33]. Thus we model the cost of heap construction as $(\gamma + \frac{1}{2}) \cdot m \cdot c_h$.

A first call to *SkipTo*(*val*) involves skipping in all inputs, in addition to heap construction. Given that s results are skipped in this operation, we simply assume that the number of entries skipped in input i is proportional to its length, i.e. it is $\frac{r_i s}{R}$, resulting in a cost of $\sum_{i=1}^{m} k_i.Skip(\frac{r_i s}{R})$. The cost of heap construction is modeled as explained for *Next*() above.

Subsequent calls to *Next*() involve a call to *Next*() for the input at the top of the heap and heap reorganization. We estimate the cost of the call to *Next*() for the input at the top as a weighted average over the inputs. The model for the cost of heap maintenance is simple. We assume that there will be γ relocations when a single operator is forwarded, leading to $\gamma + 1$ calls to *heapify*().

Subsequent calls to *SkipTo*(*val*) will potentially forward all inputs, and then reorganize the heap according to the new current values of the inputs. On average, each input will be forwarded past $\frac{r_i s}{R}$ entries. However, HeapUnion will ensure not to call *SkipTo*(*val*) for inputs that will not be forwarded. Therefore, when the average skip length for an input is less than 1, we model the cost as $\frac{r_i s}{R}$ calls that skip 1 entry. To find the cost of heap maintenance we estimate the number of forwarded inputs as: $m_s = \sum_{i=1}^{m} \min(\frac{s r_i}{R}, 1)$. Assuming that there will be as many relocations in the heap as when constructing a heap with m_s entries, the cost of heap maintenance is modeled as $(\gamma + 1) \cdot m_s \cdot c_h$.

Optimization Algorithm. We will now show in two steps that an optimization algorithm that uses Monotonic as the cost model only has to test $|E|$ different access designs in order to find the optimal solution. First, we show in the following lemma that we can find a globally optimal solution by choosing the contents of the additional author list for each user individually; it follows directly from the definitions in Figures 3 and 4.

LEMMA 3. *When using Monotonic as a cost model, the cost of including a user v_1 in L_{u_1} is independent of the cost of including a user v_2 in L_{u_2} for $u_1 \neq u_2$.*

Lemma 3 reduces the number of access designs to test in the optimization algorithm from $2^{\sum_{u \in V} |F_u|}$ to $\sum_{u \in V} 2^{|F_u|}$. The following theorem shows that we can reduce the size of the search space further under certain conditions.

THEOREM 4. *If Monotonic estimates that for a user u and a given workload, the performance is improved if $v \in F_u$ is included in L_u, then Monotonic will predict that it leads to a performance improvement to also include user w in L_u if $w \in F_u$, $0 < n_w < n_v$, and $c_d - \frac{c_{sc}}{2b} \geq \frac{c_g}{\ln 2}$.*

The proof of Theorem 4 is found in the full version of this paper [11]. We notice that in our case, $c_d - \frac{c_{sc}}{2b} \geq \frac{c_g}{\ln 2}$ translates to $0.331 \geq 0.114$, which holds with a significant margin. Theorem 4 implies that if we sort all friends of u based on the number of documents they post, the optimal contents of L_u is a prefix of this sorted list. We thus need to check only $|E|$ designs in total in order to find the optimal solution. Furthermore, notice that there is no cost associated with including users who do not post documents in the additional author lists, and it is therefore always beneficial to do so.

4.2 Non-monotonic

Non-monotonic is designed to be more accurate than Monotonic; however, it sacrifices the nice property that only a small number of designs must be checked to find the globally optimal access design. To achieve better accuracy, we improve the model for heap maintenance costs, and we use a slightly more advanced update model. The formal description of Non-monotonic is found in Figures 3 and 4.

The update model from Monotonic is extended by taking list compression into account. During accumulation, the lists are compressed using VByte, which implies that lists with few entries result in long deltas that use more space. The model assumes that the cost of updating a list depends on the number of bytes used by VByte to represent the average delta length.

The models for heap maintenance in subsequent calls to *Next*() and *SkipTo*(*val*) reflect that the cost of heap maintenance often depends on the total number of inputs as well as on the number of forwarded inputs. Given that input i is at the top of the heap when *Next*() is called, let p_i denote the number of inputs that will have *Current*() values larger than input i after the call to *Next*(). We estimate p_i as $\sum_{k=1}^{m} \min(\frac{r_k}{r_i}, 1)$. [3] We replace the rough heap maintenance cost estimate of $(\gamma + 1)c_h$ with $\log(1 + p_i)c_h$ when input i is at the top of the heap. By calculating a weighted average over all inputs, we end up with an average cost of heap maintenance for a *Next*() as shown in Figure 4.

The model for heap maintenance in *SkipTo*(*val*) is slightly more complex, and the maximum of two different estimates is used: (1) The first alternative is similar to the estimate in Monotonic, but incorporates that Floyd's algorithm will never call *heapify*() for more than half the inputs, which yields the following estimate: $(\gamma m_s + \min(m_s, \frac{m}{2}))c_h$. (2) The other alternative reflects that the cost can be logarithmic in the number of inputs when the number of forwarded inputs is low. We have already estimated the average number of calls to *heapify*() when only one input is forwarded in the model for *Next*(), denoted h_{next} in the following. We now assume that all forwarded inputs will lead to h_{next} *heapify*() operations, but compensate for the fact that many of the inputs are not at the top of the heap when *heapify*() is called. The compensation is achieved with the function $h(m_s)$ in Figure 4, which returns the minimum possible total distance from the root to m_s entries in the heap.

Optimization Algorithm. Lemma 3 also holds for Non-monotonic. However, the proof of Theorem 4 does not hold due to the extensions in Non-monotonic. As a result, an optimization algorithm that uses Non-monotonic must test $\sum_{u \in V} 2^{|F_u|}$ access designs to find the optimal approach. In social networks, users have hundreds of friends, and it is therefore not feasible to test such a large space of access designs. We thus choose to limit the space to the same space that the optimization algorithm explores for Monotonic. If Non-monotonic is actually more accurate than Monotonic, the resulting design should be at least as efficient.

5. EXPERIMENTS

We will now present experiments evaluating the efficiency of our novel HeapUnion operator, validate the accuracy of our cost models, and test the optimized access designs.

5.1 Experimental Setup

Workloads. In our experiments we are using a set of workloads that are based on a crawl of a subset of Twitter from February 2010. The first workload is based on the actual crawled Twitter network and is denoted Workload Real. The workload consists of 417,156 users with 74,326,889 unique friendships, and their 2,500,000 most recently posted documents. Due to a restriction in the Twitter API, none of the users have more than 200 posted documents in this workload. We have also generated two workloads with synthetic networks, Workload 1 and Workload 2, to enable to test our solutions with varying social network characteristics. Workload 1 has 10,000 users and Workload 2 has 100,000. In both networks, users have 100 friends each and the friendships are generated with the widely used preferential attachment model [6]. Documents in both workloads were obtained from the Twitter crawl. In both workloads, each user is assigned a posting frequency from a Twitter user, and the documents are assigned to users according to the resulting distribution. In Workload 1, we pick the posting frequency for a user dependent on the user's number of followers, which creates a strong correlation between the number of followers and the number of posted documents. We assign 1,500,000 documents accordingly. In Workload 2 we pick a frequency for a user independent of the number of followers and assign 2,500,000 documents accordingly.

The workloads also involve search queries. As we do not have access to actual search logs for the crawled data, we generated the search queries based on the actual document collection. The query terms were selected by removing all the stop words in the collection, and then choose a random remaining term. We thus select query terms based on term frequency except for stop words. We use two different strategies for selecting the user who submits the search query. We either use a uniform distribution such that each user is selected with equal probability, or a Zipfian distribution with exponent 1.5 such that a few users are selected much more frequently than others. In our plots, the workloads using the Zipfian distribution have "Z" as a suffix. Different complete workloads are generated by combining the 3 basic workloads above with 100,000 subsequent queries (with the exception of the last experiment). We return the top-100 results for all queries unless explicitly stated otherwise.

Hardware. All experiments were run on a computer with an Intel Xeon 3.2 GHz CPU with 6 MB cache and 16 GB main memory running RedHat Enterprise 5.3; our system is implemented in Java, and we ran Java 1.6.

5.2 Performance of HeapUnion Operator

We compare the relative efficiency of HeapUnion and Lazy Merge [28] by exchanging the HeapUnion operator in our query template with Lazy Merge. Our implementation of Lazy Merge stores the intermediate results in an uncompressed list where skips are implemented with a galloping search [9]. The parameter α describes how eager Lazy Merge is at merging inputs into the intermediate results. When setting α to 0, Lazy Merge behaves as Eager Merge, and with $\alpha = \infty$, Lazy Merge behaves as No Merge.

In the experiments with HeapUnion, we limit the access design to the user design because it provides a real test of any solutions' ability to process queries with many author lists efficiently. We report the query processing time for each of the workloads, and vary α between 0 and ∞. We have argued that one of the reasons why Lazy Merge is not ideal for our workloads is that we typically process top-k queries. To isolate this effect, we experiment both with only returning the top-100 results and with returning all results.

[3] $\frac{r_k}{r_i}$ is the average number of *Next*() calls in input k for each *Next*() call in input i. If both inputs each had values at equal distances this estimation would be exact.

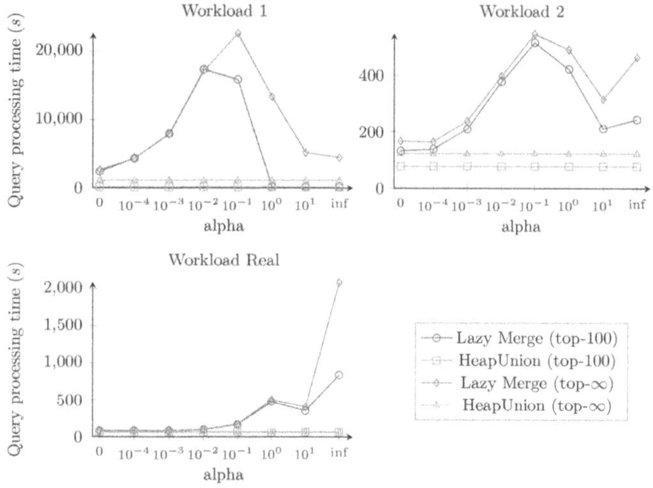

Figure 5: HeapUnion vs. Lazy Merge varying α.

The results from the experiments are shown in Figure 5. Notice that HeapUnion does not depend on α, and its cost is therefore constant. When using Lazy Merge, the difference between the cost of top-100 queries and retrieving all results increases with the size of α. This reflects the inadequacy of approaches that pre-merge when processing top-k queries. The processing time of HeapUnion is clearly dependent on the number of retrieved results, and HeapUnion is therefore an attractive solution for top-k queries as expected.

We observe that Workload 1 incurs the slowest performances across workloads. In Workload 1 users have access to more posts on average. This is particularly challenging to LazyMerge as it merges some of these longer lists. Lazy Merge performs best with α set to extreme values. Poor performance otherwise is often caused by the large number of merges resulting from many inputs with different lengths. In what end of the scale the best α value is found for a particular workload depends on the average length of the author lists compared to the posting list. HeapUnion outperforms the best configurations of Lazy Merge in all workloads with a speed-up between 1.12 and 2.36, reflecting that HeapUnion is efficient regardless of workload characteristics.

5.3 Validation of Cost Models

To test the accuracy of our cost models, we compare their predictions to the actual running times in our system for Workloads 1 and 2. We also need to define a set of access designs to test so that the results will be indicative of to which extent using the different cost models in an optimization algorithm will lead to efficient access designs. Here we make the observation that the optimization algorithms associated with all our cost models will select a limit for each user, u, such that all friends of u who post fewer documents than this limit will be included in L_u. For testing purposes, we choose a single *limit* per access design, such that all users will include a friend v in their L_u if the number of documents n_v posted by user v satisfies $n_v < limit$. By choosing a set of different values for *limit*, we obtain a set of designs ranging from empty L_us to L_us that include all friends.

As a basis for comparison in our experiments, we use a straight-forward cost model based on the one introduced by Silberstein et al. for the problem of finding the most recent posts to compose user event feeds in social networks [31]. We refer to this model as *Simple*; it assumes that the cost of processing a query is linear in the number of accessed author lists, and that the cost of constructing a list is linear in the number of document IDs in the list.

Figure 6 compares the actual running times of our system to predictions from both Monotonic and Non-monotonic as well as for Simple. As we can see, the query cost estimates with Monotonic are much more accurate than the estimates with Simple, but there is still room for improvement when *limit* is close to 0 in Workload 2. Inaccurate modeling of the cost of heap maintenance is one factor that contributes to this error, and the accuracy of Non-monotonic is therefore higher. The extended update model in Non-monotonic also leads to a slight improvement in terms of accuracy.

5.4 Workload-Aware Designs

We have tested the accuracy of the different cost models above, but the key success factor for a cost model is whether using it in an optimization algorithm leads to efficient designs. We therefore conducted a set of experiments to compare the access designs suggested by the different cost models and associated optimization algorithms. To do so, we use the basic workloads in Section 5.1, and combine them with different numbers of queries to vary the ratio of queries to updates in the workload. We compare the performance of the designs based on Simple, Monotonic and Non-Monotonic to the user design and the friends design.

The results of our experiments are shown in Figure 7, where the first three columns in the first line show the results for workloads where the queries are uniformly distributed among the users. To get a better view of the relative differences between the methods, the second line shows the performance of the approaches relative to the best of the user design and the friends design.

For the workloads with uniformly distributed queries, Simple often leads to designs that are slower than choosing the best of the user design and the friends design due to the prediction inaccuracies. Compared to Monotonic and Non-monotonic, the designs from Simple are up to 67% slower, a difference that occurs in Workload Real. Monotonic and Non-monotonic generally lead to reasonable designs that are comparable to or faster than the basic approaches. However, for Workload 2, both approaches lead to sub-optimal designs when queries are frequent relative to updates. This reflects the inaccuracies in the estimates for low limits for Workload 2 in Figure 6. However, Non-monotonic clearly results in better designs than Monotonic in this case; the designs from Monotonic are up to 12% slower, so the additional complexity pays off.

The results from Workload 2 with Zipfian queries are shown in the last column in Figure 7, denoted Workload 2Z. We have omitted the results for other workloads with Zipfian queries because the same patterns are observed. The results show that our overall solution performs much better compared to the basic designs when there is skew, with a speed-up of up to 3.4. With skew, the optimization problem is simple because a few users submit almost all queries, and all cost models are able to reflect that these users should have additional author lists with nearly all their friends represented. Non-monotonic is still slightly better than the others, but the difference is small.

In summary, these experiments confirm the benefits of

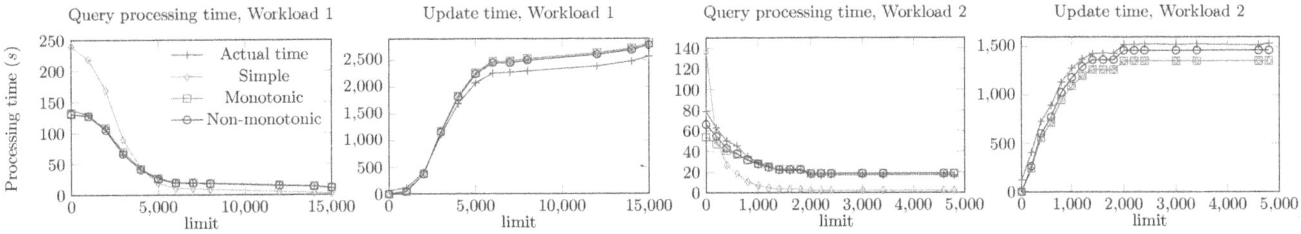

Figure 6: Accuracy of cost models for queries and updates in Workload 1 and Workload 2

using our more accurate cost models and associated optimization algorithms; we are able to find access designs that result in significantly better performance than the basic approaches from previous work.

6. RELATED WORK

Due to its clear commercial value there has recently been significant interest in search in social networks, and Bing for example supports real-time search over public Twitter posts. Unlike Google+, Facebook allows users to search their friends' posts. However, the details of these commercial solutions have not been published.

Several recent papers also address search in social networks [29, 2, 12, 22, 5, 1]. Some of these papers address the design and evaluation of new ranking functions that incorporate different network-centric properties of social networks (see for example [22, 5]). Others are concerned with efficient processing techniques for top-k queries with a focus on social tagging sites [2, 29]. However, none of these methods enforce access control because they may return any document tagged by users connected to the user who submitted the query, and this may include inaccessible documents.

Another related problem studied by Silberstein et al. [31] is that of computing event feeds containing the most recent posts of friends in a social network. Our work and the work of [31, 2] took a workload-aware approach to find a design in a large design space. Despite the fact that each work seeks to compute a different function (event feeds, vs. query results based on tags by friends vs. query results based on post content and access rights) there is a nice parallel between our design space and that of Silberstein et al. However, as we saw in the experimental section, adapting the cost model of Silberstein et al. produces poor results in our setting and we therefore developed our own cost models that perform much better.

The problem we address is related to access control in both information retrieval [13, 32] and for structured data [10].

Cost models have been used to estimate the efficiency of processing strategies in both information retrieval and databases [35, 14, 16, 25]. There exist advanced cost models to evaluate different index construction and update strategies [14, 35]. For search queries, however, simple models are most commonly used, sometimes without verification on an actual system [16]. Unlike previous models that estimate an abstract notion of cost (such as memory accesses [25]), we developed models to estimate the exact running time of a workload. This is more challenging and advanced models are required to predict query processing costs accurately as shown in our experimental evaluation.

The problems of calculating unions and particularly intersections of lists have attracted a lot of attention, both through the introduction of new algorithms with theoretical analyses [23, 20, 3, 7], and experimental investigations [8, 4]. The algorithms for single operators are also combined into full query plans [28, 17]. Our implementation computes intersections and unions over compressed lists with synchronization points for skipping following [19, 27]. Our intersection operator is based on the ideas from Demaine et al. [20]. For the union operators we also could have employed the practical implementations of Raman et al. [28], but we instead developed HeapUnion and demonstrated its superiority experimentally. Other implementations seem less suitable because [20] does not support skipping and would thus be inefficient in our setting, and [17] has a theoretical focus. HeapUnion saves work in the heap maintenance compared to a multi-way merge by carefully analyzing what parts of the heap need to be examined and rebuilt. The idea of optimized heap maintenance has been used in the context of tf-idf-based ranking [15]. Our techniques are different and can be used to improve previous work in case many documents contain only a subset of the queried terms.

7. CONCLUSIONS

In this paper we have presented an efficient system for keyword search in social networks with access control. Through the introduction of accurate cost models and associated workload-aware optimization algorithms, we are able to find designs of access control meta-data that speed up performance by a factor of up to 3.4 over previous work. We also introduced HeapUnion, a novel query processing operator that efficiently supports skipping over unions of sorted inputs. HeapUnion improves query processing efficiency with a factor between 1.12 and 2.36 in our system.

With this foundation in place, we have the basis for extensions to more advanced ranking functions such as ranking based on network-centric properties in social networks [29, 2] while enforcing access control. We may also be able to apply the techniques in this paper in other areas, such as in star joins in data warehouses [28], where HeapUnion might be an interesting query processing operator.

8. REFERENCES

[1] S. Amer-Yahia, M. Benedikt, and P. Bohannon. Challenges in searching online communities. *IEEE Data Eng. Bull.*, 30(2):23–31, 2007.

[2] S. Amer-Yahia, M. Benedikt, L. V. S. Lakshmanan, and J. Stoyanovich. Efficient network aware search in collaborative tagging sites. *Proc. VLDB Endow.*, 1(1):710–721, 2008.

[3] R. Baeza-Yates. A fast set intersection algorithm for sorted sequences. In *Proc. CPM*, 2004.

[4] R. Baeza-Yates and A. Salinger. Fast intersection

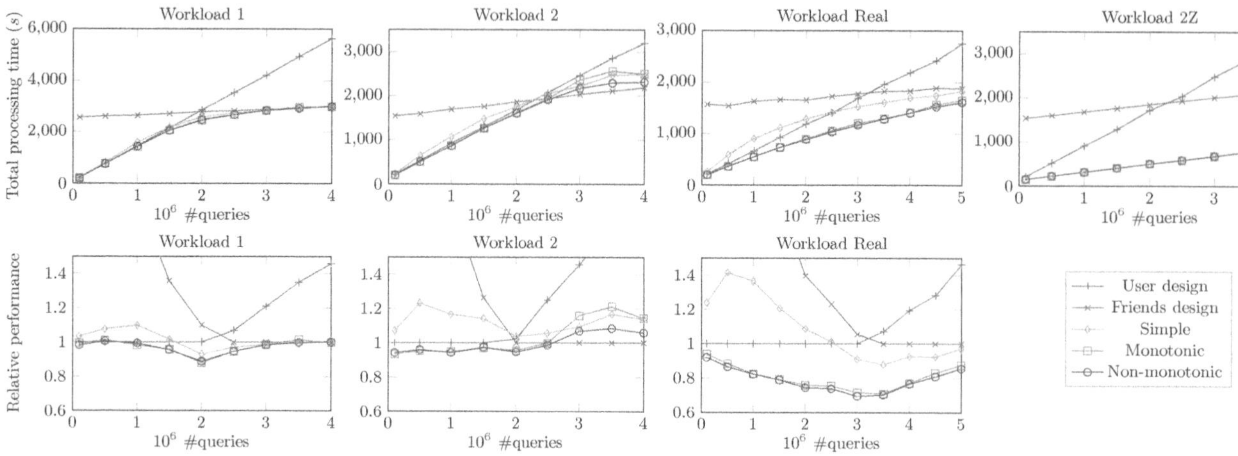

Figure 7: Performance for workloads with different fractions of documents vs. queries

algorithms for sorted sequences. *Algorithms and Applications*, 2010.

[5] S. Bao, G. Xue, X. Wu, Y. Yu, B. Fei, and Z. Su. Optimizing web search using social annotations. In *Proc. WWW*, 2007.

[6] A. L. Barabasi and R. Albert. Emergence of scaling in random networks. *Science*, 286(5439):509–512, 1999.

[7] J. Barbay and C. Kenyon. Alternation and redundancy analysis of the intersection problem. *ACM Trans. Algorithms*, 4(1), 2008.

[8] J. Barbay, A. López-Ortiz, T. Lu, and A. Salinger. An experimental investigation of set intersection algorithms for text searching. *J. Exp. Algorithmics*, 14, 2009.

[9] J. L. Bentley and A. C.-C. Yao. An almost optimal algorithm for unbounded searching. *Information Processing Letters*, 5(3), 1976.

[10] E. Bertino, S. Jajodia, and P. Samarati. Database security: research and practice. *Inf. Syst.*, 20(7), 1995.

[11] T. A. Bjørklund. *Column Stores versus Search Engines and Applications to Search in Social Networks*. PhD thesis, NTNU, 2011.

[12] T. A. Bjørklund, M. Götz, and J. Gehrke. Search in social networks with access control. In *Proc. KEYS*, 2010.

[13] S. Büttcher and C. L. A. Clarke. A security model for full-text file system search in multi-user environments. In *FAST*, 2005.

[14] S. Büttcher, C. L. A. Clarke, and B. Lushman. Hybrid index maintenance for growing text collections. In *Proc. SIGIR*, 2006.

[15] B. B. Cambazoglu and C. Aykanat. Performance of query processing implementations in ranking-based text retrieval systems using inverted indices. *Inf. Process. Manage.*, 42, 2006.

[16] B. B. Cambazoglu, V. Plachouras, and R. Baeza-Yates. Quantifying performance and quality gains in distributed web search engines. In *Proc. SIGIR*, 2009.

[17] E. Chiniforooshan, A. Farzan, and M. Mirzazadeh. Worst case optimal union-intersection expression evaluation. In *ICALP*, 2005.

[18] T. H. Cormen, C. E. Leiserson, R. L. Rivest, and C. Stein. *Introduction to Algorithms, Second Edition*. The MIT Press, 2001.

[19] J. S. Culpepper and A. Moffat. Compact set representation for information retrieval. In *Proc. SPIRE*, 2007.

[20] E. D. Demaine, A. López-Ortiz, and J. I. Munro. Adaptive set intersections, unions, and differences. In *Proc. SODA*, 2000.

[21] S. Gurajada and S. K. P. On-line index maintenance using horizontal partitioning. In *Proc. CIKM*, 2009.

[22] A. Hotho, R. Jäschke, C. Schmitz, and G. Stumme. Information retrieval in folksonomies: Search and ranking. In *The Semantic Web: Research and Applications*, 2006.

[23] F. K. Hwang and S. Lin. Optimal merging of 2 elements with n elements. *Acta Informatica*, 1(2), 1971.

[24] N. Lester, A. Moffat, and J. Zobel. Efficient online index construction for text databases. *ACM Trans. Database Syst.*, 33(3), 2008.

[25] S. Manegold, P. Boncz, and M. L. Kersten. Generic database cost models for hierarchical memory systems. In *Proc. VLDB*, 2002.

[26] G. Margaritis and S. V. Anastasiadis. Low-cost management of inverted files for online full-text search. In *Proc. CIKM*, 2009.

[27] A. Moffat and J. Zobel. Self-indexing inverted files for fast text retrieval. *ACM Trans. Inf. Syst.*, 14(4), 1996.

[28] V. Raman, L. Qiao, W. Han, I. Narang, Y.-L. Chen, K.-H. Yang, and F.-L. Ling. Lazy, adaptive rid-list intersection, and its application to index anding. In *Proc. SIGMOD*, 2007.

[29] R. Schenkel, T. Crecelius, M. Kacimi, S. Michel, T. Neumann, J. X. Parreira, and G. Weikum. Efficient top-k querying over social-tagging networks. In *Proc. SIGIR*, 2008.

[30] F. Scholer, H. E. Williams, J. Yiannis, and J. Zobel. Compression of inverted indexes for fast query evaluation. In *Proc. SIGIR*, 2002.

[31] A. Silberstein, J. Terrace, B. F. Cooper, and R. Ramakrishnan. Feeding frenzy: Selectively materializing users. event feeds. In *Proc. SIGMOD*, 2010.

[32] A. Singh, M. Srivatsa, and L. Liu. Efficient and secure search of enterprise file systems. In *Proc. ICWS*, 2007.

[33] R. Sprugnoli. Recurrence relations on heaps. *Algorithmica*, 15(5), 1996.

[34] H. Turtle and J. Flood. Query evaluation: strategies and optimizations. *Inf. Process. Manage.*, 31(6), 1995.

[35] I. Witten, A. Moffat, and T. C. Bell. *Managing Gigabytes*. Academic Press, 1999.

[36] J. Zhang, X. Long, and T. Suel. Performance of compressed inverted list caching in search engines. In *Proc. WWW*, 2008.

[37] J. Zobel and A. Moffat. Inverted files for text search engines. *ACM Comput. Surv.*, 2006.

[38] M. Zukowski, S. Heman, N. Nes, and P. Boncz. Super-scalar ram-cpu cache compression. In *Proc. ICDE*, 2006.

Effective Retrieval of Resources in Folksonomies Using a New Tag Similarity Measure

Giovanni Quattrone and Licia Capra
Dept. of Computer Science
University College London, UK
{g.quattrone,l.capra}@cs.ucl.ac.uk

Pasquale De Meo and Emilio Ferrara
Dept. of Physics, Dept. of Mathematics
University of Messina, Italy
{pdemeo,eferrara}@unime.it

Domenico Ursino
DIMET
Università Mediterranea di Reggio Calabria, Italy
ursino@unirc.it

ABSTRACT

Social (or folksonomic) tagging has become a very popular way to describe content within Web 2.0 websites. However, as tags are informally defined, continually changing, and ungoverned, it has often been criticised for lowering, rather than increasing, the efficiency of searching. To address this issue, a variety of approaches have been proposed that recommend users what tags to use, both when labeling and when looking for resources. These techniques work well in dense folksonomies, but they fail to do so when tag usage exhibits a power law distribution, as it often happens in real-life folksonomies. To tackle this issue, we propose an approach that *induces* the creation of a dense folksonomy, in a fully automatic and transparent way: when users *label* resources, an innovative tag similarity metric is deployed, so to enrich the chosen tag set with related tags already present in the folksonomy. The proposed metric, which represents the core of our approach, is based on the mutual reinforcement principle. Our experimental evaluation proves that the accuracy and coverage of searches guaranteed by our metric are higher than those achieved by applying classical metrics.

Categories and Subject Descriptors

I.5.3 [**Pattern Recognition**]: Clustering—*similarity measures*

General Terms

Algorithms, Experimentation, Performance, Measurement

Keywords

Folksonomy, tag similarity, tag recommendations

CIKM'11, October 24–28, 2011, Glasgow, Scotland, UK.

1. INTRODUCTION

Social media applications, such as blogs, multimedia sharing sites, question and answering systems, wikis and online forums, are growing at an unprecedented rate and are estimated to generate a significant amount of the content currently available on the Web. This has exponentially increased the amount of information that is available to users, from videos on sites like YouTube and MySpace, to pictures on Flickr, music on Last.fm, blogs on Blogger, and so on. This content is no longer categorised according to pre-defined taxonomies (or ontologies). Rather, a new trend called *social* (or *folksonomic*) *tagging* has emerged, and quickly become the most popular way to describe content within Web 2.0 websites. Unlike taxonomies, which overimpose a hierarchical categorisation of content, folksonomies empower end users by enabling them to freely create and choose the tags that best describe a piece of information (a picture, a document, a blog entry, a video clip, etc.). However, this freedom comes at a cost: since tags are informally defined, continually changing, and ungoverned, finding content of interest has become a main challenge because of the number of synonyms, homonyms and polysemies, as well as the inevitable heterogeneity of users and the noise they introduce.

In order to assist users finding content of their own interest within this information abundance, new approaches, inspired by traditional recommender systems, have been developed [3, 14, 13]. These often exploit an underlying tag similarity measure; whenever a user labels a resource or searches for it by adopting a set of tags, they suggest new tags to be added to the resource label or to the user query, on the basis of their *similarity* to the original tags expressed by the user herself. They do so to increase the chances of finding content of relevance in these extremely sparse settings.

Various classic metrics have been used to compute tag similarity, including, for instance, cosine similarity, Jaccard coefficient, and Pearson Correlation. Some of the approaches exploiting these metrics [9, 4] have proved to achieve excellent results; however, they do so *only if* the underlying folksonomy is *already dense*, and they operate by making it even denser. Nevertheless, we observe that this assumption does not hold true; rather, most real life folksonomies exhibit a *power law* distribution of tag usage [1, 2], with few tags labeling most resources, and most tags labeling just a few resources instead. This means that, in practical cases, if we were select any two tags, the probability that the resources jointly labeled by them is non-zero is extremely low. As a result, computing tag similarity on real folksonomies, using traditional metrics like cosine similarity, would almost always yield close-to-zero values, thus failing to support users in retrieving resources relevant to their queries.

In this paper, we propose an approach that transparently *induces* the creation of a *dense folksonomy*, thus supporting the effective retrieval of resources *by construction*. At the core of our approach lies an innovative tag similarity metric, used to recommend tags both when labeling resources and when querying the folksonomy. This metric is based on the *mutual reinforcement* principle, and thus computed following an iterative algorithm: two tags are deemed similar if they label similar resources, and vice-versa, two resources are similar if they have been labeled by similar tags. When a user labels a new resource, or when she is submitting a query to retrieve some resources, the above metric is used to automatically expand the user-selected tag set with those tags, already present within the folksonomy, that are: *(i)* most similar to those she initially submitted, and *(ii)* among those most widely used in the folksonomy.

We have conducted an extensive experimental evaluation on two large-scale datasets, namely BibSonomy and CiteULike. The obtained results demonstrate that our similarity metric operates effectively even in very sparse settings, where traditional metrics (including cosine similarity, SimRank [10] and Latent Semantic Indexing (LSI) [11]) fail.

2. DESCRIPTION OF OUR APPROACH

In this section we provide a detailed description of our approach to support effective resource retrieval in large-scale folksonomies. Before illustrating it, we formalize the concept of a folksonomy as done in [7].

DEFINITION 2.1. *Let* $US = \{u_1, \ldots, u_{n_u}\}$ *be a set of users,* $RS = \{r_1, \ldots, r_{n_r}\}$ *a set of resource URIs, and* $TS = \{t_1, \ldots, t_{n_t}\}$ *a set of tags. A* folksonomy F *is a tuple* $F = \langle US, RS, TS, AS \rangle$, *where* $AS \subseteq US \times RS \times TS$ *is a ternary relationship called* tag assignment set. □

In the above definition we do not make any assumption about the nature of resources; they could be a URL associated with a Web page (like in Delicious), photos (as in Flickr), music files (as in Last.fm), documents (as in CiteULike), and so on.

According to Definition 2.1, a folksonomy F is a "three-dimensional" data structure whose "dimensions" are represented by users, tags and resources. In particular, an element $a \in AS$ is a triple $\langle u, r, t \rangle$, indicating that user u labeled resource r with tag t. To simplify folksonomy modelling and management, the inherent tripartite graph structure is often mapped into three matrices, whereby each matrix models one relationship at a time [12].

In this paper, we adopt the same matrix-based representation. Specifically, the association between tags and resources can be modelled by a $n_t \times n_r$ matrix **TR**, called *Tag-Resource* matrix, being n_t and n_r the number of tags and resources, respectively. The generic entry of such a matrix $\mathbf{TR}_{ij}$ is the number of times the ith tag labels the jth resource. In an analogous fashion we can introduce the *Tag-User* and the *Resource-User* matrices, **TU** and **RU**.

Our approach consists of two phases: the former, executed offline, computes pairwise tag similarities, by means of an innovative tag similarity metric. The second phase, executed in real-time (online), follows a well-established process: when a user is labeling a new resource, or is querying the system to retrieve some resources, the tag set she has chosen is automatically expanded using the tags that are deemed most related to the user-elected ones, based on the similarities previously computed. We now illustrate each phase in more detail; we then conclude this section with a discussion on how our approach can be efficiently realised in practice.

2.1 Phase 1: Tag Similarity Computation

As previously pointed out, this phase aims at computing pairwise similarity of all tags in use within the folksonomy. A variety of metrics have been proposed in the literature, mostly based on tag co-occurrence (such as cosine similarity); however, we claim these approaches fail to work in the sparse settings we target. To see why, let us consider cosine similarity. Given an arbitrary pair of tags t_i and t_j, their cosine similarity $s(t_i, t_j)$ would be computed as

$$s(t_i, t_j) = \frac{\langle \mathbf{t}_r(i), \mathbf{t}_r(j) \rangle}{\sqrt{\langle \mathbf{t}_r(i), \mathbf{t}_r(i) \rangle} \cdot \sqrt{\langle \mathbf{t}_r(j), \mathbf{t}_r(j) \rangle}} \quad (1)$$

where $\mathbf{t}_r(i)$ and $\mathbf{t}_r(j)$ denote the ith and the jth row of **TR**.

Equation 1 states that the similarity score of a pair of tags is high if they *jointly co-occur* in labeling the same subset of resources. One important underlying assumption must hold for cosine similarity to work well: matrix **TR** must be densely populated. Unfortunately, this assumption does not hold in real folksonomies.

As an example, let us consider a real-world folksonomy like BibSonomy. BibSonomy [6, 8] is a social bookmarking service in which users are allowed to tag both URLs and scientific papers. A *power law* distribution of tags on scientific references emerges. In particular, roughly 81% of resources were described by no more than 5 different tags (and roughly 58% by less than 3). Furthermore, there is a small portion of frequently adopted tags, and a long tail of tags (roughly 81%) being used less than 5 times overall. Matrix **TR** is thus rather sparse: if we were to select any pair of tags t_i and t_j, most of the components of the corresponding vectors $\mathbf{t}_r(i)$ and $\mathbf{t}_r(j)$ would be 0, and so would be their inner product. In other words, the cosine similarity between *any* two folksonomy tags would be very close to 0, regardless of what the selected tags are; recommending tags (in Phase 2) based on such metric would thus be unfruitful.

Although classical similarity measures based on co-occurrences are inadequate in scenarios characterized by power law distributions, other metrics have been proposed and successfully used in Information Retrieval which could potentially be applied in our domain. We considered, in particular, one of the state-of-the-art techniques, namely *Latent Semantic Indexing* (LSI) [11]. LSI approximates the matrix **TR** by computing its *top* k eigenvalues. This is equivalent to mapping **TR** onto a low-dimensional vectorial space, with k dimensions (called *Latent Space*). Similarities between tags (respectively, resources) are computed in the Latent Space by applying the cosine similarity. Unfortunately, the application of this technique raised several concerns, because: *(i)* the computation of LSI on large matrices is very costly (and could indeed be practically unfeasible in real folksonomies); *(ii)* the tuning of parameter k is complex and time-expensive, and the quality of the produced results is very sensitive to such value.

More suitable to the folksonomy domain are techniques that rely on the *mutual reinforcement principle.* One of the most popular techniques based on it is *SimRank* [10]. SimRank uses an *iterative approach* to compute similarities whereby, in each iteration, the similarity between any two objects (be them tags or resources) is computed, based on the similarities already computed in the previous iteration.

If we were to adopt SimRank, the equations used at the kth iteration would be

$$st^k(t_a, t_b) = \frac{C_1}{|r(t_a)| \cdot |r(t_b)|} \sum_{r_i \in r(t_a)} \sum_{r_j \in r(t_b)} sr^{k-1}(r_i, r_j) \quad (2)$$

$$sr^k(r_a, r_b) = \frac{C_2}{|t(r_a)| \cdot |t(r_b)|} \sum_{t_i \in t(r_a)} \sum_{t_j \in t(r_b)} st^{k-1}(t_i, t_j) \quad (3)$$

where: *(i)* $st^k(t_a, t_b)$ (resp, $sr^k(r_a, r_b)$) denotes the similarity between t_a and t_b (resp, r_a and r_b) at the kth iteration; *(ii)* the set $r(t_a)$ (resp., $t(r_a)$) is the set of resources (resp, tags) associated with t_a (resp., r_a); *(iii)* C_1 and C_2 are two *normalization constants* belonging to the real interval [0, 1].

Equations 2–3 suffer from some main drawbacks that limit their applicability in our setting:

- SimRank does not take into account the number of times a tag intervenes in labeling a resource, thus discarding valuable information available within the folksonomy.
- SimRank does not distinguish between tags that have labeled exactly the same resource, and tags that (by means of one or more iterative steps) have been labeling related, but different, resources.

Although we share with SimRank the idea of computing tag/resource similarity by means of an application of the mutual reinforcement principle, we advocate for some main changes, in line with the discussion above. To begin with, the frequency with which a tag intervenes in labeling a resource is a very important piece of information that should be leveraged in the similarity computation process. Furthermore, a new factor (which we will call *mutual reinforcement factor*) should be introduced, to give more relevance to tags that labeled the very *same* resources, with respect to those that labeled related (but not the very same) resources.

We have thus derived a novel similarity metric, specifically conceived for the folksonomy setting. In detail, the similarity computation is performed recursively. For the base case, given a pair of tags $\langle t_a, t_b \rangle$ and a pair of resources $\langle r_a, r_b \rangle$, the *tag similarity* $st^0(t_a, t_b)$ and the *resource similarity* $sr^0(r_a, r_b)$ is defined as follows

$$st^0(t_a, t_b) = \delta_{ab} \qquad sr^0(r_a, r_b) = \delta_{ab} \quad (4)$$

Equation 4 states that, in the initial step, each tag (resp., resource) is similar only to itself and it is dissimilar to all other tags (resp., resources).

At the kth step, let $st^{k-1}(t_a, t_b)$ (resp., $sr^{k-1}(r_a, r_b)$) be the tag (resp., resource) similarity between t_a and t_b (resp., r_a and r_b). The following rules can be applied to compute $st^k(t_a, t_b)$ (resp., $sr^k(r_a, r_b)$)

$$st^k(t_a, t_b) = \frac{ST^k(t_a, t_b)}{\sqrt{ST^k(t_a, t_a)} \cdot \sqrt{ST^k(t_b, t_b)}} \quad (5)$$

$$sr^k(r_a, r_b) = \frac{SR^k(r_a, r_b)}{\sqrt{SR^k(r_a, r_a)} \cdot \sqrt{SR^k(r_b, r_b)}} \quad (6)$$

where

$$ST^k(t_a, t_b) = \sum_{i,j=1}^{n_r} \mathbf{TR}_{ai} \cdot \Psi_{ij} \cdot sr^{k-1}(r_i, r_j) \cdot \mathbf{TR}_{bj} \quad (7)$$

$$SR^k(r_a, r_b) = \sum_{i,j=1}^{n_t} \mathbf{TR}_{ia} \cdot \Psi_{ij} \cdot st^{k-1}(t_i, t_j) \cdot \mathbf{TR}_{jb} \quad (8)$$

Here Ψ_{ij} is equal to 1 if $i = j$, while it is equal to ψ if $i \neq j$. ψ is what we call *mutual reinforcement factor*, and is a value belonging to the real interval [0, 1].

Equations 5–6 rely on the following intuitions. Given a pair of tags $\langle t_a, t_b \rangle$, at the k iteration, we consider *all pairs of resources* $\langle r_i, r_j \rangle$ in the folksonomy and we take their similarity $sr^{k-1}(r_i, r_j)$ into account to compute $st^k(t_a, t_b)$. In particular, we compute a *weighted sum* of all the similarity values $sr^{k-1}(r_i, r_j)$, where the weights reflect the *strength of the association* between the tag t_a and the resource r_i, and the tag t_b and the resource r_j. As a consequence, the higher the similarity between r_i and r_j, the higher the contribution of the association between t_a and r_i, as well as t_b and r_j. Finally, the mutual reinforcement factor ψ is instrumental to give higher relevance to tags that labeled the very *same* resources, (resp., to resources labeled by the very same tags): indeed, the higher ψ, the higher the relevance assigned to similar resources (resp., tags) in the tag (resp., resource) similarity computation.

We argue that Equations 5–6 are able to effectively address the power law challenge we outlined above. In fact, when computing tag (resp., resource) similarity, our measure leverages the similarity of all pairs of resources (resp., tags) in the folksonomy. While cosine similarity restricts its attention to those resources jointly labeled by two tags (resp., those tags jointly labeling two resources), which are usually very few, our metric *iteratively propagates* similarity scores by considering all the pairs of similar resources jointly labeled by the two tags (resp., all the pairs of similar tags jointly labeling two resources). In this way, our measure can be applied in settings characterized by power law distributions of tag usage.

Similarly to state-of-the-practice recommender systems, we expect the above tag similarity computation to be performed offline, at regular intervals of time (e.g., daily, weekly), depending on the growth of the system and the available computational resources. With these similarities pre-computed, we now proceed to discuss how tag recommendation and expansion is performed, both when labeling new resources and when querying the folksonomy.

2.2 Phase 2: Tag Expansion

Key to our approach is the use of the previously computed tag similarities to automatically expand the tag set chosen by the user, both when labeling a new resource and/or when querying the folksonomy. Note that, by performing tag expansion upon *adding* a new resource in the system, we implicitly *induce the creation of a denser folksonomy*; furthermore, by performing tag expansion upon *querying* the system using the very same approach, we implicitly *induce the community to use a common vocabulary.* Taken together, these tag expansions have the effect of providing more accurate answers to users' searches within large-scale folksonomy.

The approach can be summarised as follow. Let $tSet = \{t_1, \ldots, t_n\}$ be the set of user-selected tags, either to label a resource or to submit a query in the folksonomy. Let t_j

be a tag in $tSet$ and t_i a tag not in $tSet$. We assign a score $sc(t_i, t_j)$ to t_i with respect to t_j based on: *(i)* $st(t_i, t_j)$ - the similarity between t_i and t_j as previously computed; *(ii)* $count(t_i)$ - the number of times t_i appears in the folksonomy; *(iii)* $IRF(t_i)$ - the inverse resource frequency of t_i (similar to IDF in Information Retrieval). This is a measure of the general importance of t_i within the whole folksonomy, and it is obtained by dividing the total number of resources in the folksonomy by the number of resources labeled by t_i, and then taking the logarithm of the quotient.

More precisely, $sc(t_i, t_j)$ is computed as follows

$$sc(t_i, t_j) = st(t_i, t_j) \cdot \log count(t_i) \cdot IRF(t_i) \quad (9)$$

Equation 9 assigns high scores to those tags that are both similar to $t_j \in tSet$ (as per our similarity metric) *and*, crucially, which are both *largely used* ($count(t_i)$) and *important* ($IRF(t_i)$) in the overall folksonomy. Intuitively, our approach expands user-selected tags with related tags that are part of the emerging common vocabulary of widely used tags. Note that we compute the logarithm of $count(t_i)$ to give equal weight to frequently used tags and to important ones (as computed by $IRF(t_i)$, which, by definition, already computes the logarithm).

Finally, the total score SC of t_i with respect to $tSet$ is obtained by summing the scores of t_i with respect to all the tags of $tSet$

$$SC(t_i, tSet) = \sum_{t_j \in tSet} sc(t_i, t_j) \quad (10)$$

Although in this paper we will be evaluating a fully automatic approach, whereby the user-selected set of tags $tSet$ is transparently expanded with the k highest scoring tags according to Equation 10, a more interactive approach could be adopted, whereby users are suggested up to k expansion tags, and they can decide which ones, if any, to use. Such an approach may lead to even more accurate results than those we will report in Section 3, and it is thus worth exploring in the future, by means of controlled user studies.

2.3 Taming Computational Complexity

The practical usability of our approach is strictly linked to the computational complexity of Equations 5–6. In particular:

- From a theoretical standpoint, the computation of each pairwise tag similarity may require an infinite number of iterations. As a consequence, a stopping criterium is required so that the execution of Equations 5–6 terminates after a finite (and hopefully low) number of iterations.
- Equation 5 (resp., Equation 6) requires the computation of n_r^2 resource-resource (resp,. n_t^2 tag-tag) similarities, at each kth step. This could make our similarity measure inapplicable in practical cases, because each iteration would require exactly $n_r^2 \times n_t^2$ computations.

However, we can prove that these theoretical limits do not apply in practice, and that, in fact, our new tag similarity metric requires a computational complexity comparable to that of cosine similarity. First of all, convergence of Equations 5–6 has been demonstrated.

THEOREM 1. *Let $st^k(t_a, t_b)$ and $sr^k(r_a, r_b)$ be defined as in Equations 5–6. Given any pair of tags t_a and t_b and any pair of resources r_a and r_b, the sequences $st^k(t_a, t_b)$ and $sr^k(r_a, r_b)$ converge.* □

The proof of the above theorem is available in full at `http://tinyurl.com/proof-cikm2011` and is based on the demonstration that the sequences $st^k(t_a, t_b)$ and $sr^k(r_a, r_b)$ are both bounded and not-decreasing. To complement this theoretical result, our experiments on two real folksonomies (Section 3.3) will provide evidence of very fast convergence indeed.

The second important result is that Equations 5–6 can be defined, without any loss of generality, as simple matrix products (such as in cosine similarity). Specifically, let $\mathbf{st}^k$ and $\mathbf{sr}^k$ be the tag-tag and resource-resource similarity matrices, respectively, with $\mathbf{st}^0 = \mathbf{I}_t$ and $\mathbf{sr}^0 = \mathbf{I}_r$, where $\mathbf{I}_t$ (resp., $\mathbf{I}_r$) is the $n_t \times n_t$ (resp., $n_r \times n_r$) *identity matrix*. We use symbol "∘" to refer to the Hadamard matrix product [5]. At the kth step the $\mathbf{st}^k$ and $\mathbf{sr}^k$ matrices are computed as

$$\mathbf{st}^k = \mathbf{ST}^k \circ \mathbf{DT}^k \quad \text{and} \quad \mathbf{sr}^k = \mathbf{SR}^k \circ \mathbf{DR}^k \quad (11)$$

where

$$\mathbf{ST}^k = \mathbf{TR} \times \left(\mathbf{\Psi_r} \circ \mathbf{sr}^{k-1}\right) \times \mathbf{TR}^t \quad (12)$$

$$\mathbf{SR}^k = \mathbf{TR}^t \times \left(\mathbf{\Psi_t} \circ \mathbf{st}^{k-1}\right) \times \mathbf{TR} \quad (13)$$

$$\mathbf{DT}^k_{ab} = \frac{1}{\sqrt{\mathbf{ST}^k_{aa}} \cdot \sqrt{\mathbf{ST}^k_{bb}}} \quad \mathbf{DR}^k_{ab} = \frac{1}{\sqrt{\mathbf{SR}^k_{aa}} \cdot \sqrt{\mathbf{SR}^k_{bb}}} \quad (14)$$

In the above equations, $\mathbf{\Psi}_r$ (resp., $\mathbf{\Psi}_t$) refers to a square matrix $n_r \times n_r$ (resp., $n_t \times n_t$) where all the elements are set equal to the mutual reinforcement factor ψ, with the exception of the diagonal, where the elements are set to 1; the symbol $\mathbf{TR}^t$ represents the transpose of $\mathbf{TR}$. Each step of the tag similarity computation can thus be performed by means of a simple matrix product. This result, coupled with the empirical observation that only a few iterative steps are required to reach convergence (Section 3.3), makes our similarity metric suitable in practical contexts. This conclusion is even more valid if we consider that, in our approach, tag similarity computations are performed offline.

3. EVALUATION

In order to evaluate the performance of our approach, we built a prototype in Java and MySQL and we performed experiments using two well known social tagging websites, i.e., Bibsonomy and CiteULike. The experiments we carried out aimed at answering the following questions: *(i)* Is our approach able to increase the accuracy of searches? And, if so, to what extent does the improvement depend on the underlying similarity metric in use? *(ii)* Does our approach scale to large folksonomies?

After presenting the two datasets used for experimentation, we will address each of the above questions in turn.

3.1 Datasets

We performed experiments on the following two datasets extracted from real large-scale folksonomies.

- *Bibsonomy* (`http://www.bibsonomy.org/`) is a social bookmarking website promoting the sharing of both scientific references and general URLs. We downloaded a snapshot of this Web site in June 2009, containing

648,924 bookmarks[1] and 4,696 users who had tagged 578,587 scientific references overall, using 147,076 distinct tags.

- *CiteULike* (`http://www.citeulike.org/`) is a social bookmarking website that aims at promoting and developing the sharing of scientific references amongst researchers. We downloaded a snapshot dataset with 57,053 users, 1,928,302 papers, 401,620 different tags, and 2,281,609 bookmarks.

3.2 Accuracy of User Searches

3.2.1 Simulation Setup

The first experiment we conducted aimed at determining the ability of our approach to retrieve resources of relevance to the user querying the folksonomy. This experiment was enacted as follow: we split each dataset into two different ones, called *train set* and *test set*; the split was performed multiple times at random, with the former containing 90% of bookmarks, and the latter containing the remaining 10%. After this split, we considered two different versions of the involved datasets, which we will refer to as *original* (unmodified) ones and *enriched* ones. The enriched version f^+ of each dataset f was obtained as follows. We computed similarities between all pairs of tags in the train set. After this, we examined all bookmarks in the original f; each bookmark $\langle u, r, tSet \rangle$ was then enriched by adding to $tSet$ the k tags that our approach would recommend, as per Equation 10. In this experiment, k was set equal to $\lceil 0.5 \cdot tSet \rceil$ if $tSet > 6$, equal to 3 otherwise.

In so doing, we simulate the automatic expansion of user-selected tags, as it would happen when labeling resources. The folksonomy f would thus be induced to grow to the enriched f^+, an emerging folksonomy containing a more common and widely accepted vocabulary.

Having performed this preparatory step, we considered f and, for each bookmark $\langle u, r, tSet \rangle$ in the test set, we used $tSet$ to query the train set and retrieve the q resources most relevant to the query. Note that, according to our approach, the query tag set $tSet$ was first expanded with the k most related tags, k set as above. To determine the relevance of a resource to a query $tSet$, we computed the *TF-IDF* coefficient assigned to such resource for each query tag $t_j \in tSet$, then summed up these values. The q most relevant resources were then offered to the user as answer to her query. We have experimented with $q \in \{5, 10, 20\}$, and measured the percentage of times the searched resource r appeared in the top q retrieved resources. We call this measure *retrieved ratio*. We repeated the same procedure for the folksonomy f^+ to see if the corresponding retrieved ratio increased (or decreased) with respect to the one of f.

The above process follows the intuition that, if a user *labeled* a specific resource r with the set of tags $tSet$, then $tSet$ would very likely be the set of tags such user would employ to *query* the folksonomy when willing to retrieve r. However, due to the number of synonyms, homonyms and polysemies, as well as the heterogeneity of users, r could have been described by users with different tags. This implies that $tSet$ could be unsuitable to retrieve r per se, and thus tag expansion, performed both when labeling and when querying the

[1]In this context, a bookmark is defined as a triplet $\langle u, r, tSet \rangle$, where $tSet$ is the set of tags originally assigned by the user u to label the resource r.

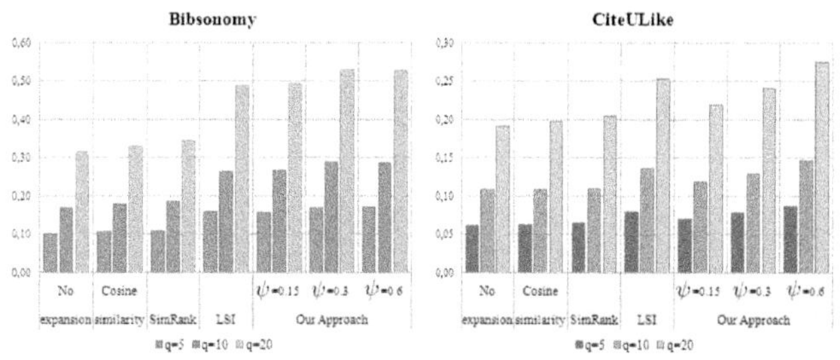

Figure 1: Retrieved Ratio on Bibsonomy and CiteULike

system (i.e., f^+), should yield better results (i.e., increased retrieved ratio).

We repeated the described process 10 times over different train and test random splits of the datasets. The results we describe next represent the average values of these runs.

3.2.2 Results

Figure 1 shows how the retrieved ratio of our approach varies across the two datasets, for different values of ψ, with respect to the case where no enrichment was performed. The same figure also illustrates a comparison of our approach with respect to cases where cosine similarity, Latent Semantic Indexing, and SimRank were used as the underlying tag similarity metric. The following two main observations can be drawn:

- The lowest retrieved ratio is the one obtained when no enrichment is performed. In particular, the retrieved ratio is up to 70% better when using an enriched folksonomy than when used an unmodified one. This means that, by transparently enriching the folksonomy when labeling resources, we successfully induce the construction of a denser and more meaningful folksonomy, over which resource retrieval performs better overall. This result underlines the importance of supporting users in their tagging and querying activity.

- Within the enriched folksonomy, the approach based on our novel tag similarity metric outperformed all others, followed by LSI, while SimRank and cosine lag behind. More precisely, results obtained by applying our similarity metric are up to 50% better than those obtained by applying cosine similarity or SimRank, and up to 8% better than those obtained by applying LSI.

3.3 Scalability

3.3.1 Simulation Setup

As previously pointed out, the highest cost caused by our approach lies in the computation of pairwise tag similarities. In Section 2.1, we have shown that our metric is recursive and that each step is no more expensive than the computation of classical similarity measures, such as cosine similarity. We have also proved that our formulation is convergent (Theorem 1). However, it is necessary to investigate how many steps are necessary to reach convergence in practice.

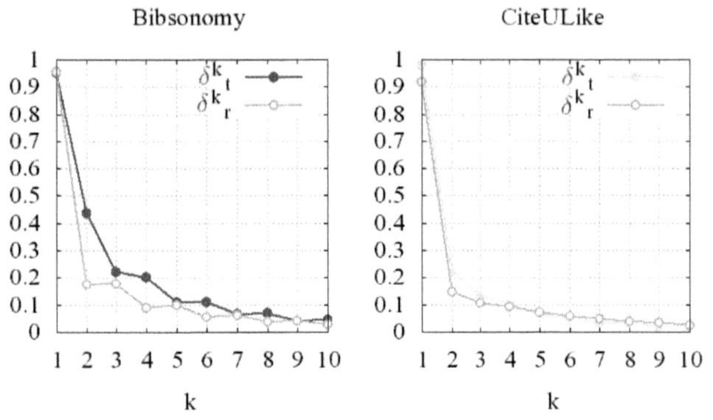

Figure 2: Scalability of our Approach on Bibsonomy and CiteULike

To experimentally perform this computation, we have defined the following parameters

$$\delta_t^k = \frac{||\mathbf{st}^k - \mathbf{st}^{k-1}||_1}{||\mathbf{st}^k||_1} \quad \text{and} \quad \delta_r^k = \frac{||\mathbf{sr}^k - \mathbf{sr}^{k-1}||_1}{||\mathbf{sr}^k||_1} \tag{15}$$

Here, $\mathbf{st}^k$ (resp., $\mathbf{sr}^k$) are the tag-tag (resp., resource-resource) similarity matrices at the kth step (see Equation 11), whereas symbol $||\cdot||_1$ indicates the 1-norm of a matrix.

3.3.2 Results

Figure 2 plots the variation of δ_t^k and δ_r^k as k increases, for each of our datasets. As shown, in the practical settings we have experimented with, the computation of our similarity metric exhibits very fast convergence. As an example, across all considered datasets, δ_t^k and δ_r^k are less than 0.1 after just six iterations. In other words, in the datasets we used, by accepting a negligible error in the similarity computation, we can stop our iterative procedure in less than six iterations. Using a server equipped with a quad-core processor and 32GB of RAM (which is much smaller than any server deployed in practice by actual businesses), we computed all similarity measures across all two datasets in less than 48 hours. As the computation of pairwise tag similarity is performed periodically (e.g., weekly) offline, this result confirms that our similarity measure is scalable and well suited to be applied even when operating in large folksonomies.

4. CONCLUSIONS

In this paper, we have proposed an approach that enables the effective retrieval of resources within folksonomies. The approach relies on an innovative tag similarity metric that is based on the mutual reinforcement principle. This metric is used both when users label resources, so to automatically enrich the user-selected tag set with highly-related tags already present in the folksonomy, and when users query the folksonomy. Our experimental evaluation has demonstrated that the accuracy of searches entailed by our metric are neatly higher than those achieved by applying classical metrics, thus confirming its suitability in scenarios characterized by power-law distributions of tags (as is the case in many real world folksonomies). Finally, the computational cost of our iterative approach is limited, as convergence is guaranteed, and in practice reached after a handful of iterations.

5. REFERENCES

[1] C. Cattuto, C. Schmitz, A. Baldassarri, V.D.P. Servedio, V. Loreto, A. Hotho, M. Grahl, and G. Stumme. Network properties of folksonomies. *AI Communications*, 20(4):245–262, 2007.

[2] P. De Meo, G. Quattrone, and D. Ursino. Exploitation of semantic relationships and hierarchical data structures to support a user in his annotation and browsing activities in folksonomies. *Information Systems*, 34(6):511–535, 2009.

[3] C.S. Firan, W. Nejdl, and R. Paiu. The benefit of using tag-based profiles. In *Proc. of the Latin American Web Congress*, pages 32–41. IEEE, 2007.

[4] J. Gemmell, T. Schimoler, M. Ramezani, and B. Mobasher. Adapting K-Nearest Neighbor for Tag Recommendation in Folksonomies. *CEUR Workshop Proceedings*, Vol. 528, 2009.

[5] G.H. Golub and C.F. Van Loan. *Matrix Computations, third edition.* Johns Hopkins University Press, 1996.

[6] A. Hotho, R. Jäschke, C. Schmitz, and G. Stumme. BibSonomy: A social bookmark and publication sharing system. In *Proc. of the 1st Conceptual Structures Tool Interoperability Workshop*, pages 87–102, 2006.

[7] A. Hotho, R. Jäschke, C. Schmitz, and G. Stumme. Information retrieval in folksonomies: Search and ranking. *The Semantic Web: Research and Applications*, pages 411–426, 2006.

[8] R. Jäschke, A. Hotho, C. Schmitz, and G. Stumme. Analysis of the publication sharing behaviour in BibSonomy. *Conceptual Structures: Knowledge Architectures for Smart Applications*, pages 283–295, 2007.

[9] R. Jäschke, L. Marinho, A. Hotho, L. Schmidt-Thieme, and G. Stumme. Tag Recommendations in Folksonomies. In *Proc. of the 11th European conference on Principles and Practice of Knowledge Discovery in Databases*, pages 506–514. Springer-Verlag, 2007.

[10] G. Jeh and J. Widom. SimRank: a measure of structural-context similarity. In *Proc. of the ACM SIGKDD International Conference on Knowledge Discovery and Data Mining*, pages 538–543, 2002.

[11] C.D. Manning, P. Raghavan, and H. Schutze. *Introduction to Information Retrieval.* Cambridge University Press, 2008.

[12] P. Mika. Ontologies are us: A unified model of social networks and semantics. *Web Semantics: Science, Services and Agents on the World Wide Web*, 5(1):5–15, 2007.

[13] K.H.L. Tso-Sutter, L.B. Marinho, and L. Schmidt-Thieme. Tag-aware recommender systems by fusion of collaborative filtering algorithms. In *Proc. of the ACM Symposium on Applied Computing*, 2008.

[14] V. Zanardi and L. Capra. Social Ranking: Uncovering Relevant Content Using Tag-based Recommender Systems. In *Proc. of the International Conference on Recommender Systems*, pages 51–58. ACM, 2008.

Content-Driven Detection of Campaigns in Social Media

Kyumin Lee, James Caverlee, Zhiyuan Cheng
Department of Computer Science and Engineering
Texas A&M University
College Station, TX 77843
{kyumin, caverlee, zcheng}@cse.tamu.edu

Daniel Z. Sui
Department of Geography
Ohio State University
Columbus, OH 43210
sui.10@osu.edu

ABSTRACT

We study the problem of detecting coordinated free text campaigns in large-scale social media. These campaigns – ranging from coordinated spam messages to promotional and advertising campaigns to political astro-turfing – are growing in significance and reach with the commensurate rise of massive-scale social systems. Often linked by common "talking points", there has been little research in detecting these campaigns. Hence, we propose and evaluate a content-driven framework for effectively linking free text posts with common "talking points" and extracting campaigns from large-scale social media. One of the salient aspects of the framework is an investigation of graph mining techniques for isolating coherent campaigns from large message-based graphs. Through an experimental study over millions of Twitter messages we identify five major types of campaigns – Spam, Promotion, Template, News, and Celebrity campaigns – and we show how these campaigns may be extracted with high precision and recall.

Categories and Subject Descriptors: H.3.5 [Online Information Services]: Web-based services; J.4 [Computer Applications]: Social and behavioral sciences

General Terms: Algorithms, Design, Experimentation

Keywords: social media, campaign detection

1. INTRODUCTION

Social media is inherently a persuasive technology, supporting the rapid insertion of new memes, near instantaneous global reach, and unprecedented leveraging of massive-scale interpersonal connections. On the one hand, many users of social media organically engage with social media to share opinions and interact with friends; on the other, social media is a prime target for strategic influence.

For example, there is widespread anecdotal evidence of "astroturfing" campaigns [3], in which political operatives insert memes into sites like Twitter and Facebook in an effort to influence discourse about particular political candidates and topics. In addition, there are large campaigns of coordinated spam messages in social media [4], templated messages (e.g., auto-posted messages to social media sites from third-party applications announcing a user action, like joining a game or viewing a video), high-volume time-synchronized messages (e.g., many users may repost news headlines to social media sites in a flurry after the news has been initially reported), and so on. In the case of spam and promotion campaigns, the relative openness of many social media sites (typically requiring only a valid email address to register) suggests coordinated campaigns could be a low-cost approach for strategically influencing participants.

User-driven campaigns – often linked by common "talking points" – appear to be growing in significance and reach with the commensurate rise of massive-scale social systems. However, there has been little research in detecting these campaigns. While there has been some progress in detecting isolated instances of long-form fake reviews (e.g., to promote books on Amazon), of URL-based spam in social media, and in manipulating recommender systems [4, 5, 6, 7], there is a significant need for new methods to support web-scale detection of campaigns in social media.

Hence, we focus in this paper on detecting one particular kind of coordinated campaign – those that rely on "free text" posts, like those found on blogs, comments, forum postings, and short status updates (like on Twitter and Facebook). For our purposes, a campaign is a collection of users and their posts bound together by some common objective, e.g., promoting a product, criticizing a politician, or inserting disinformation into an online discussion. Our goal is to link messages with common "talking points" and then extract multi-message campaigns from large-scale social media. Detecting these campaigns is especially challenging considering the size of popular social media sites like Facebook and Twitter with 100s of millions of unique users and the inherent lack of context in short posts.

We explore in this paper several content-based approaches for identifying campaigns from the massive scale of real-time social systems. Concretely, we propose and evaluate a content-driven framework for effectively linking free text posts with common "talking points" and extracting campaigns from large-scale social media. We find that over millions of Twitter messages, the proposed framework can identify 100s of coordinated campaigns, ranging in size up to several hundred messages per campaign.

2. OVERALL APPROACH

In this section, we describe the problem of campaign de-

CIKM'11, October 24–28, 2011, Glasgow, Scotland, UK.

tection in social media, introduce the data, and outline the metrics for measuring effective campaign detection.

2.1 Problem Statement

We consider a collection of n participants across social media sites $U = \{u_1, u_2, \ldots, u_n\}$, where each participant u_i may post a time-ordered list of k messages $M_{u_i} = \{m_{i1}, m_{i2}, \ldots, m_{ik}\}$. Our hypothesis is that among these messages, there may exist *coordinated campaigns.*

Given the set of users U, a *campaign* M_c can be defined as a collection of messages and the users who posted the messages: $M_c = \{m_{ij}, u_i | u_i \in U \cap m_{ij} \in M_{u_i} \cap theme(m_{ij}) \in t_k\}$ such that the campaign messages belong to a coherent theme t_k. Themes are human-defined logical assignments to messages and application dependent. For example, in the context of spam detection, a campaign may be defined as a collection of messages with a common target product (e.g., Viagra). In the context of astroturf, a campaign may be defined as a collection of messages promoting a particular viewpoint (e.g., the veracity of climate change). Additionally, depending on the context, a message may belong to one or multiple themes. For the purposes of this paper and to focus our scope of inquiry, we consider as a theme all messages sharing similar "talking points" as determined by a set of human judges.

2.2 Data

To evaluate the quality of a campaign detection approach, we would ideally have access to a large-scale "gold set" of known campaigns in social media. While researchers have published benchmarks for spam webpages, ad-hoc text retrieval, and other types of applications, we are not aware of any standard social media campaign dataset. Hence, we take in this paper a twofold approach: (i) a small-scale validation over hand-labeled data; and (ii) a large-scale validation over 1.5 million Twitter messages for which ground truth is not known.

CD$_{\textbf{Small}}$: First, we sample a small collection of messages (1,912) posted to Twitter in October 2010. Over this small *campaign dataset* (CD_{Small}), two judges labeled all pairs of the 1,912 tweets as sharing similar "talking points" or not, finding 298 pairs of messages sharing similar "talking points". Based on these initial labels, the judges considered all combinations of messages that may form campaigns consisting of four messages or more, and found 11 campaigns ranging in size from four messages to eight messages. While small in size, this hand-labeled dataset allows us to evaluate the precision and recall of several campaign detection methods.

CD$_{\textbf{Large}}$: Second, we supplement the small dataset with a large collection of messages (~1.5 million) posted to Twitter between October 1 and October 7, 2010. We sampled these messages using Twitter's Streaming API, resulting in a representative random sample of Twitter messages. Over this large *campaign dataset* (CD_{Large}), we can test the precision of the campaign detection methods and investigate the types of campaigns that are prevalent in-the-wild. Since we do not have ground truth knowledge of all campaigns in this dataset, our analysis will focus on the campaigns detected for which we can hand-label as actual campaigns or not.

2.3 Metrics

To measure the effectiveness of a campaign detection method, we use variations of average precision, average recall, and the average F_1 measure. The average precision (AP) for a campaign detection method is defined as:

$$AP = \frac{1}{n} \sum_{i=1}^{n} \frac{\max CommonMessages(PC_i, TCs)}{|PC_i|}$$

where n is the total number of predicted campaigns by the campaign detection method, PC is a predicted campaign, and TC is an actual (true) campaign. $MaxCommonMessage$ function returns the maximum of the number of common messages in both the predicted campaign i (PC_i) and each of the actual (true) campaigns (TCs). For example, suppose a campaign detection method identifies a three-message campaign: $\{m_1, m_{10}, m_{30}\}$. Suppose there are two actual campaigns with at least one message in common: $\{m_{30}, m_{38}, m_{40}\}$ and $\{m_1, m_{10}, m_{35}, m_{50}, m_{61}\}$. Then the Precision is $max(2, 1)/3 = 2/3$. In the aggregate, this individual precision will be averaged with all n predicted campaigns.

Similarly, we can define the average recall (AR) as:

$$AR = \frac{1}{n} \sum_{i=1}^{n} \frac{\max CommonMessages(PC_i, TCs)}{|TC_j|}$$

where n is the number of the predicted campaigns, and TC_j is a true campaign which has the largest common messages with the predicted campaign i (PC_i). Continuing the example from above, the Recall would be $max(2, 1)/5 = 2/5$.

Finally, we can combine precision and recall as the average F_1 measure (AF):

$$AF_1 = \frac{2 * AP * AR}{AP + AR}$$

An effective campaign detection approach should identify predicted campaigns that are composed primarily of a single actual campaign (i.e., have high precision) and that contain most of the messages that actually belong to the campaign (i.e., have high recall). A method that has high precision but low recall will result in only partial coverage of all campaigns available (which could be especially disastrous in the case of spam or promotional campaigns that should be filtered). A method that has low precision but high recall may identify nearly all messages that belong to campaigns but at the risk of mislabeling non-campaign messages (resulting in false positives, which could correspond to mis-labeled legitimate messages as belonging to spam campaigns).

3. CONTENT-DRIVEN CAMPAIGN DETECTION

To detect coordinated campaigns, we explore in this paper several content-based approaches for identifying campaigns. Our goal is to identify methods that can balance both precision and recall for effective campaign detection. We primarily consider a graph-based framework, where we model messages in social media as a *message graph.* Each node in the message graph corresponds to a message; edges correspond to some reasonable notion of content-based correlation between messages, corresponding to pairs of messages with similar "talking points." Formally, we have:

DEFINITION 1 (MESSAGE GRAPH). *A message graph is a graph $G = (V, E)$ where every message in M corresponds*

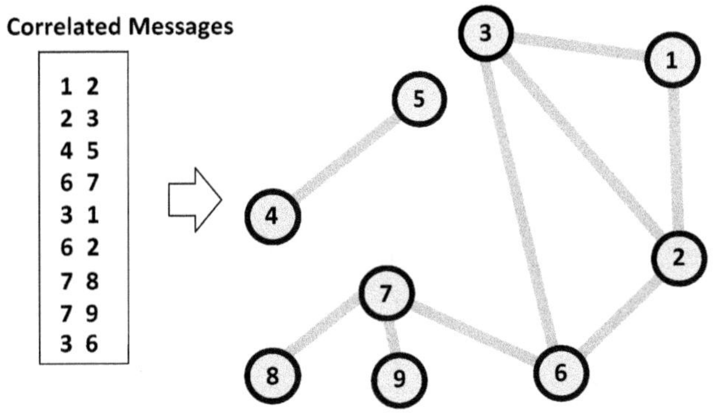

Figure 1: The campaign message graph

to a vertex m_{ix} in the vertex set V. An edge $(m_{ix}, m_{jy}) \in E$ exists for every pair of messages (m_{ix}, m_{jy}) where $corr(m_{ix}, m_{jy}) > \tau$, for a measure of correlation and some parameter τ.

A message graph which links unrelated messages will necessarily result in poor campaign detection (by introducing spurious links). Traditional information retrieval approaches for document similarity (e.g., cosine similarity, KL-divergence) as well as efficient near-duplicate detection methods (e.g., Shingling [1], I-Match [2] and SpotSigs [8]) have typically not been optimized for the kind of short posts of highly-variable quality common in many social media sites (including Facebook and Twitter). Hence, we shall investigate experimentally several possible approaches for determining pairwise message correlation which guides the formation of the message graph.

Given a message graph, we propose to explore three graph-based approaches for extracting campaigns:(i) loose extraction; (ii) strict extraction; and (iii) cohesive extraction. Experimentally, we compare these graph-based approaches versus a traditional k-means clustering approach and reach poor results for clustering as compared to the graph methods. For now, we focus our attention on extracting content-driven campaigns via graph mining.

3.1 Loose Campaign Extraction

The first approach for content-driven campaign detection is what we refer to as *loose campaign extraction.* The main idea is to identify as a logical campaign all chains of messages that share common "talking points". In this way, the set of all loose campaigns is the set of all maximally connected components in the message graph:

DEFINITION 2 (LOOSE CAMPAIGN). *A loose campaign is a subgraph $s = (V', E')$, such that s is a maximally connected component of G, in which s is connected, and for all vertices m_{ix} such that $m_{ix} \in V$ and $m_{ix} \notin V'$ there is no vertex $m_{jy} \in V'$ for which $(m_{ix}, m_{jy}) \in E$.*

As an example, Figure 1 illustrates a collection of 10 messages, edges corresponding to messages that are highly correlated, and the two maximal components (corresponding to loose campaigns): $\{1, 2, 3, 6, 7, 8, 9\}$ and $\{4, 5\}$. Such an approach to campaign detection faces a critical challenge, however: not all maximally connected components are necessarily campaigns themselves (due to long chains of tangentially-related messages). For example, a chain of similar messages A–B–C–...–Z, while displaying local similarity properties (e.g., between A and B and between Y and Z) will necessarily have low similarity across the chain (e.g., A and Z will be dissimilar since there is no edge between the pair, as in the case of messages 9 and 1 in Figure 1). In practice, such maximally connected components could contain disparate "talking points" and not strong campaign coherence.

3.2 Strict Campaign Extraction

A natural alternative is to constrain campaigns to be maximal cliques, what we call *strict campaigns*:

DEFINITION 3 (STRICT CAMPAIGN). *A strict campaign $s' = (V'', E'')$ in a message graph $G = (V, E)$, in which $V'' \subseteq V$ and $E'' \subseteq E$, such that for every two vertices m_{ix} and m_{jy} in V'', there exists an edge $(m_{ix}, m_{jy}) \in E''$ and the clique cannot be enlarged by including one more adjacent vertex (corresponding to a message in M).*

To identify these strict campaigns, we can first identify all loose campaigns – by identifying all maximally connected components over the message graph, we can prune from consideration all singleton messages and are left with a set of candidate campaigns. Over these candidates, we can identify the strict campaigns through maximal clique mining. However, discovering all maximal cliques from a graph is an NP-hard problem (i.e., the time complexity is exponential). Finding all maximal cliques takes $O(3^{n/3})$ in the worst case where n is the number of vertices [9]. Over large graphs, even with parallelized implementation over MapReduce-style compute clusters, the running time is still $O(3^{n/3}/m)$ in the worst case, where n is the number of vertices and m is the number of reducers [11].

And there is still the problem that even with a greedy approximation, strict campaign detection may overconstrain the set of campaigns, especially in the case of loosely-connected campaigns. Returning to the example in Figure 1, the maximal cliques $\{1, 2, 3\}$ and $\{2, 3, 6\}$ would be identified as strict campaigns, but perhaps $\{1, 2, 3, 6, 7\}$ form a coherent campaign even though the subgraph is not fully-connected. In this case the strict approach will identify multiple overlapping campaigns and will miss the larger and (possibly) more coherent campaign. In terms of our metrics, the expectation is that strict campaign detection will favor precision at the expense of recall.

3.3 Cohesive Campaign Extraction

Hence, we also consider a third approach which seeks to balance loose and strict campaign detection by focusing on what we refer to as *cohesive campaigns*, which relaxes the conditions of maximal cliques:

DEFINITION 4 (COHESIVE CAMPAIGN). *Given a message graph G = (V,E), a subgraph G' is called a* ***cohesive campaign*** *if the number of edges of G' is close to the maximal number of edges with the same number of vertices of G'.*

The intuition is that a cohesive campaign will be a dense but not fully connected subgraph, allowing for some variation in the "talking points" that connect subcomponents of the overall campaign. There are a number of approaches mining dense subgraphs and the exact solution is again NP-hard in computation complexity, so we adopt a greedy approximation approach following the intuition in [10]. The approach to extract cohesive campaigns requires a notion of maximum co-clique $CC(m_{ix}, m_{jy})$ for all neighbors:

DEFINITION 5 (MAXIMUM CO-CLIQUE: $CC(m_{ix}, m_{jy})$). *Given a message graph $G = (V,E)$, the maximum co-clique $CC(m_{ix}, m_{jy})$ is the (estimated) size of the largest clique containing both vertices m_{ix} and m_{jy}, where $m_{jy} \in V$ and m_{jy} is a neighbor vertex of m_{ix} (i.e., they are connected).*

Considering all of a vertex's neighbors, we define the largest of the maximum co-cliques as $C(m_{ix})$:

DEFINITION 6 ($C(m_{ix})$). *Then, $C(m_{ix})$ is the largest value between m_{ix} and any neighbor m_{jy}, formally defined as $C(m_{ix}) = max\{CC(m_{ix}, m_{jy}), \forall m_{jy} \in Neighbor(m_{ix})\}$.*

With these definitions in mind, our approach to extract cohesive campaign is as follows:

1. Estimate each vertex's $C(m_{ix})$: In the first step, our goal is to estimate the C values for every vertex in a candidate campaign which indicates the upper bound of the maximum clique size the vertex belongs to. Starting at a random vertex m_{ix} in s, we compute the maximum co-clique size $CC(m_{ix}, m_{jy})$, where $m_{jy} \in V'$ and m_{jy} is a neighbor vertex of m_{ix}. Then, we compute $C(m_{ix})$. We insert m_{jy} into a priority queue and sort all m_{jy} by $CC(m_{ix}, m_{jy})$. Next, we greedily advance to the m_{jy}, which has the largest $CC(m_{ix}, m_{jy})$ among all m_{jy}, and remove it from the queue. Finally, we compute $C(m_{jy})$. We repeat this procedure for every vertex in the candidate campaign. At the conclusion of this procedure, we have an estimated $C(m_{ix})$ for every vertex.

2. Cohesive campaign extraction: Given the estimated $C(m_{ix})$ for every vertex in a candidate campaign, by considering the order in which the greedy algorithm in Step 1 encounters each vertex, we can consider consecutive neighbors as potential members of the same coherent campaign. Intuitively, the $C(m_{ix})$ values should be high for vertices in dense subgraphs but should drop as the algorithm encounters nodes on the border of the dense subgraph, then rise again as the algorithm encounters vertices belonging to a new dense subgraph. We identify the first vertex with an increasing $C(m_{ix})$ over its neighbor as the initial boundary of a cohesive campaign. We next include all vertices between this first boundary up to and including the vertex with a $C(m_{ix})$ value larger than or equal to some threshold (= the local peak value * λ). By tuning λ to 1, the extracted cohesive campaigns will be nearly clique-like; lower values of λ will result in more relaxed campaigns (i.e., with less density). We repeat this procedure until we extract all cohesive subgraphs in the candidate campaign.

The output of the cohesive campaign extraction approach is a list of cohesive campaigns, each of which contains a list of vertices forming a cohesive subgraph.

4. EXPERIMENTAL STUDY

In this section, we explore campaign discovery over social media through an application of the framework to messages sampled from Twitter. We begin by examining how to accurately and efficiently construct the campaign message graph, which is the critical first step necessary for campaign detection. We find that a short-text modified Shingling-based approach results in the most accurate message graph construction. Based on this finding, we next explore campaign detection methods over the small hand-labeled Twitter dataset, before turning our sights to analysis of campaigns discovered over the large (1.5 million messages) Twitter dataset.

4.1 Message Graph Construction

Recall that each node in the message graph corresponds to a message; edges correspond to some reasonable notion of "relatedness" between messages corresponding to human-labeled similar "talking points". Our first goal is to answer the question: can we effectively determine if two messages are correlated (i.e., algorithmically determine if they share similar "talking points") across hundreds of millions of short messages for constructing the message graph in the first place? This step is critical for accurate message graph formation for discovering campaigns.

Using the small *campaign dataset* (CD_{Small}), we consider the 298 pairs of messages sharing similar "talking points" (as determined by human judges) as the ground truth for whether an edge should appear in the message graph between the two messages. We can measure the effectiveness of a message correlation method by precision, recall, and F_1.

We investigate the identification of correlated messages through a comparative study of five distinct techniques: unigram-based overlap between messages, edit distance, and three representative near-duplicate detection algorithms (Shingling [1], I-Match [2], SpotSigs [8]). Near-duplicate detection approaches have shown great promise and effectiveness by web search engines to efficiently identify duplicate web content, but their application to inherently short messages lacking context is unclear.

In our experiment, we see that the Shingling approach performs the best, with an $F_1 = 0.81$. To improve the performance of the Shingling approach with Jaccard coefficient, we propose as a measure of correlation the overlap coefficient ($corr_{overlap}(A, B) = \frac{|A \cap B|}{min(|A|,|B|)}$). With the overlap coefficient, we get $F_1 = 0.88$. In the further experiments, we use the Shingling approach with overlap coefficient.

4.2 Campaign Detection over Small Data

In the previous experiment, we evaluated several approaches to measuring message correlation. Now we turn our attention to evaluating campaign detection methods. We begin in this section with the small data set (which recall allows us to measure precision and recall against ground truth) before considering the large data set.

Over the hand-labeled campaigns in CD_{Small}, we apply the three graph-based campaign extraction methods: (i) loose; (ii) strict; and (iii) cohesive, over the message graph generated via the best performing message correlation method identified in the previous section. We also compare campaign extraction using a fourth approach based on text clustering. For this non-graph-based approach, we consider k-means clustering, where each message is treated as vector with 10K bag-of-words features, weighted using TF-IDF, with Euclidian distance as a distance function. We vary the choice of k value, and report the best result.

Table 1 presents the experimental results of the four cam-

Table 1: Effectiveness Comparison of Campaign Detection Approaches

Approach	NumC	F_1	Precision	Recall
Loose	12	0.962	0.986	0.940
Strict	12	0.906	0.907	0.904
Cohesive	11	**0.963**	0.977	0.950
k-means	5	0.89	1	0.805

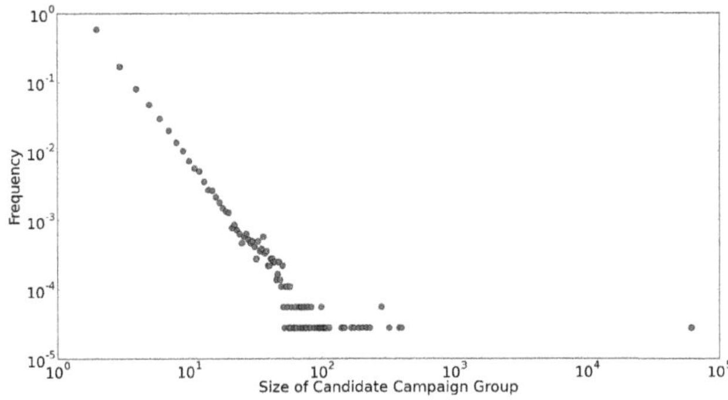

Figure 2: Size of Candidate Campaigns

paign detection approaches. The cohesive campaign detection approach found 11 campaigns ($NumC$) like the ground truth, but missed a message in two campaigns. The strict approach found 12 campaigns, missed one message in a true campaign, and divided a true campaign to two predicted campaigns because the approach due to the strict campaign rule (all nodes in a campaign should be completely connected). The loose approach found 12 campaigns, one of which is not an actual campaign (false positive) and some predicted campaigns contain dissimilar messages due to long chains. The k-means clustering algorithm found only 5 campaigns. Overall, the cohesive and strict approaches outperformed the loose and cluster-based approaches. In practice, the ideal approach should return the same number of campaigns of the ground truth in order to reduce post-labeling time and to further analysis. In this perspective, the cohesive approach may be preferred over the strict approach.

4.3 Campaign Detection over Large Data

We next examine campaign extraction from the large Twitter data set, CD_{Large}. Can we detect coordinated campaigns in a large message graph with 1.5 million messages? What kind of campaigns can we find? Which graph technique is the most effective to find campaigns?

Message Graph Setup: Based on the best message graph construction approach identified in the previous section, we generated a message graph consisting of 1.5 million vertices (one vertex per message). Of these, 1.3 million vertices are singletons, representing messages without any correlated messages in the sample (and hence, not part of any campaign). Based on this sample, we find 199,057 vertices have at least one edge; in total, there are 1,027,015 edges in the message graph.

Identifying Loose Campaigns: Based on the message graph, we identify as *loose campaigns* all of the maximally connected components, which takes about 1 minute on a single machine (relying on a breadth-first search with time complexity $O(|E| + |V|)$. Figure 2 shows the distribution of the size of the candidate campaigns on a log-log scale. We

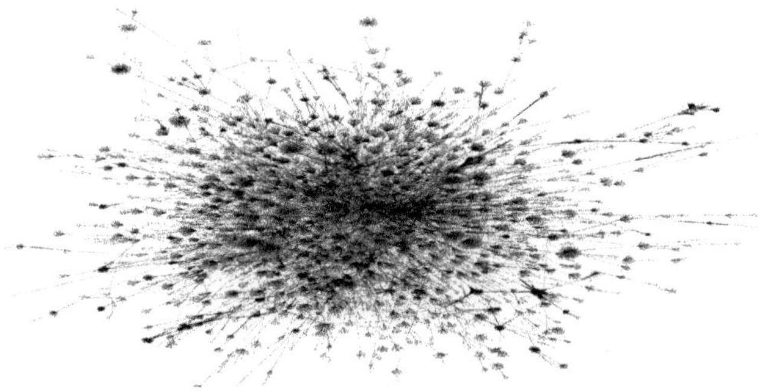

Figure 3: Candidate with 61,691 Vertices

see that the candidate campaign sizes approximately follows a power law, with most candidates consisting of 10 or fewer messages. A few candidates have more than 100 messages, and the largest candidate consists of 61,691 messages. On closer inspection, the largest candidate (as illustrated in Figure 3) is clearly composed of many locally dense subgraphs and long chains. Examining the messages in this large candidate, we find many disparate topics (e.g., spam messages, Justin Bieber retweets, quotes, Facebook photo template) and no strong candidate-wide theme, as we would expect in a coherent campaign.

Identifying Strict Campaigns: To refine these candidates, one approach suggested in Section 3 is *strict campaign detection*, in which we consider only maximal cliques as campaigns (in which all message nodes in a subgraph are connected to each other). While maximal clique detection may require exponential time and not be generalizable to all social message datasets, in this case we illustrate the maximal cliques found even though it required ~7 days of computation time (which may be unacceptable for campaign detection in deployed systems). Considering the top-10 strict campaigns discovered in order of size: [559, 400, 400, 228, 228, 227, 227, 217, 217, 214], we find high overlap in the campaigns discovered. For example, the 2nd and 3rd strict campaigns (each of size 400) have 399 nodes in common. Similarly, the 4th, 5th, 6th, 7th, and 10th strict campaigns have over 200 nodes in common, suggesting that these five different strict campaigns in essence belong to a single coherent campaign (see Figure 4). This identification of multiple overlapping strict campaigns – due to noise, slight changes in message "talking points", or other artifacts of short messages – as well as the high cost of maximal clique detection suggests the cohesive campaign detection approach may be preferable.

Identifying Cohesive Campaigns: We next applied the *cohesive campaign extraction* approach to the set of candidate campaigns corresponding to maximal connected components. We assign λ to 0.95 and use the CSV tool [10] for an efficient implementation of computing each vertex m_{ix}'s $C(m_{ix})$ by mapping edges and vertices to a multidimensional space. Although computing $C(m_{ix})$ of all vertices takes $O(|V|^2 \log |V| 2^d)$ where d is a mapping dimension, the performance for real datasets is typically sub-quadratic. Like the candidate campaign sizes, the distribution of the size of the cohesive campaigns follow a power law. Since the cohesive campaign extraction approach can isolate dense subgraphs, we see that the large 61,691 message candidate has been broken into 609 sub-components. Compared to

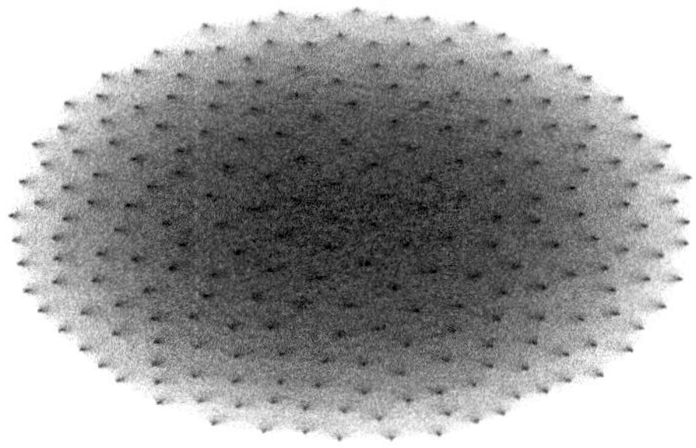

Figure 4: An Example Dense Subgraph Campaign: Strict Campaign Detection Identifies 5 Different Maximal Cliques; Cohesive Campaign Detection Identifies a Single Coherent Campaign

Table 2: Top-10 Largest Campaigns

Msgs	Users	Talking Points
560	34	Iron Man 2 spam
401	390	Facebook photo template
231	231	Support Breast Cancer Research (short link)
218	218	Formspring template
203	197	Chat template (w/ link)
166	166	Support Breast Cancer Research (full link)
165	154	Quote "send to anyone u don't regret meeting"
153	153	Justin Bieber Retweets
145	31	Twilight Movie spam
111	111	Quote "This October has 5 Fridays ..."

strict campaign detection, the cohesive campaign extraction approach required only 1/7 the computing time on single workstation.

Examining the top-10 campaigns (shown in Table 2) we see that the cohesive campaign detection approach overcomes the limitations of strict campaign detection by combining multiple related cliques into a single campaign (recall Figure 4). The biggest campaign contains 560 vertices and is a spam campaign. The "talking point" of this campaign is an Iron Man 2 promotion of the form: "#Monthly Iron Man 2 (Three-Disc Blu-ray/DVD Combo + Digital Copy) ... http://bit.ly/9L0aZU", though individual messages vary the exact wording and inserted link.

Based on a manual inspection of the identified campaigns, we categorize the campaigns into five categories:

- *Spam campaigns*: These campaigns typically post duplicate spam messages (changing @username with the same payload), or embed trending keywords; often with a URL linking to a malware website, phishing site or a product website. Example: "Want FREE VIP, 100 new followers instantly and 1,000 new followers next week? GO TO `http://alturl.com/bpby`".
- *Promotion Campaigns*: Users in these campaigns promote a website or product. Their intention is to expose it to other people. Example: "FREE SignUp!!! earn $450 Per Month Do NOTHING But Getting FREE Offers In The Mail!! `http://budurl.com/PPLSTNG`".
- *Template Campaigns*: These are automatically-generated messages typically posted by a third-party service. Example: "I'm having fun with @formspring. Create an account and follow me at `http://formspring.me/xnadjeaaa`".
- *News Campaigns*: Participants post recent headlines along with a URL. Example: "BBC News UK: Rwanda admitted to Commonwealth: Rwanda becomes the 54th member of the Commonwealth g.. `http://ad.vu/nujv`".
- *Celebrity Campaigns*: Users in these campaigns send messages to a celebrity or retweet a celebrity's tweet. Example: "@justinbieber please follow me i love youuu<3".

Some of these campaigns are organic and the natural outgrowth of social behavior, e.g., a group of Justin Bieber fans retweeting a message, or a group posting news articles of interest. On closer inspection, we observe that many of the less organic campaigns (e.g., spam and promotion campaigns) are driven by a higher ratio of messages to participants. For example in Table 2, the Iron Man 2 spam campaign consists of 560 messages posted by only 34 different participants. In contrast, the Justin Bieber retweet campaign consists of 153 messages posted by 153 different participants.

5. CONCLUSION AND FUTURE WORK

In this paper, we have investigated the problem of campaign detection in social media. We have proposed and evaluated an efficient content-driven graph-based framework for identifying and extracting campaigns from the massive scale of real-time social systems. Based on the success of the system we are extending this work to incorporate adaptive statistical machine learning approaches for isolating artificial campaigns from organic campaigns. Do we find that strategically organized campaigns engage in particular behaviors that make them clearly identifiable? Our results suggest that campaigns are not necessarily "invisible" to automated detection methods. We are also interested in exploring if campaigns are centralized around common types of users or are they embedded in diverse groups. How early in a campaign's lifecycle can a strategic campaign be detected with high confidence? Do we find a change in campaign membership and detection effectiveness after it reaches a critical mass? These challenges motivate our continuing research.

6. REFERENCES

[1] A. Z. Broder, S. C. Glassman, M. S. Manasse, and G. Zweig. Syntactic clustering of the web. *Comput. Netw. ISDN Syst.*, 29(8-13):1157–1166, 1997.

[2] A. Chowdhury, O. Frieder, D. Grossman, and M. C. McCabe. Collection statistics for fast duplicate document detection. *ACM Trans. Inf. Syst.*, 20(2):171–191, 2002.

[3] L. Films. (astro)turf wars. `www.astroturfwars.com`, 2011.

[4] H. Gao, J. Hu, C. Wilson, Z. Li, Y. Chen, and B. Y. Zhao. Detecting and characterizing social spam campaigns. In *Proceedings of the 10th annual conference on Internet measurement (IMC)*, 2010.

[5] N. J. Hurley, M. P. O'Mahony, and G. C. M. Silvestre. Attacking Recommender Systems: A Cost-Benefit Analysis. *Intelligent Systems, IEEE*, 22(3):64–68, 2007.

[6] S. K. Lam and J. Riedl. Shilling recommender systems for fun and profit. In *WWW*, 2004.

[7] E. P. Lim, V. A. Nguyen, N. Jindal, B. Liu, and H. W. Lauw. Detecting product review spammers using rating behaviors. In *CIKM*, 2010.

[8] M. Theobald, J. Siddharth, and A. Paepcke. Spotsigs: robust and efficient near duplicate detection in large web collections. In *SIGIR*, 2008.

[9] E. Tomita, A. Tanaka, and H. Takahashi. The worst-case time complexity for generating all maximal cliques and computational experiments. *Theor. Comput. Sci.*, 363:28–42, 2006.

[10] N. Wang, S. Parthasarathy, K.-L. Tan, and A. K. H. Tung. Csv: visualizing and mining cohesive subgraphs. In *SIGMOD*, 2008.

[11] B. Wu, S. Yang, H. Zhao, and B. Wang. A distributed algorithm to enumerate all maximal cliques in mapreduce. In *Proceedings of the Fourth International Conference on Frontier of Computer Science and Technology*, 2009.

Exploring Categorization Property of Social Annotations for Information Retrieval

Peng Li
Inst. of Computing Technology
Chinese Academy of Sciences
Beijing, China
lipeng01@ict.ac.cn

Bin Wang
Inst. of Computing Technology
Chinese Academy of Sciences
Beijing, China
wangbin@ict.ac.cn

Wei Jin
Dept. of Computer Science
North Dakota State University
Fargo, USA
wei.jin@ndsu.edu

Jian-Yun Nie
Dept. of Computer Science
University of Montreal
Montreal, Canada
nie@iro.umontreal.ca

Zhiwei Shi
Inst. of Computing Technology
Chinese Academy of Sciences
Beijing, China
shizhiwei@ict.ac.cn

Ben He
Graduate University of
Chinese Academy of Sciences
Beijing, China
benhe@gucas.ac.cn

ABSTRACT

User generated social annotations provide extra information for describing document contents. In this paper, we propose an effective method to model the categorization property of social annotations and explore the potential of combining it with classical language models for improving retrieval performance. Specifically, a novel TR-LDA model is presented to take annotations as an additional source for generating document contents apart from the document itself. We provide strategies for representing and weighting the categorization property and develop an efficient inference algorithm, where space saving is taken into account. Experiments are carried out on synthetic datasets, where documents and queries come from the standard evaluation conference TREC and annotations come from the website Delicious.com. Our results demonstrate the effectiveness of the proposed method on the ad-hoc retrieval task, which significantly outperforms state-of-art baselines.

Categories and Subject Descriptors

H.3.3 [**Information Storage and Retrieval**]: Information Search and Retrieval

General Terms

Algorithms, Design, Experimentation

Keywords

Social Annotations, Categorization, Topic Models, Language Models

CIKM'11, October 24–28, 2011, Glasgow, Scotland, UK.

1. INTRODUCTION

Social bookmarking has become one of the most important and popular activities for online users to manage and share resources. Typical systems like Delicious[1] and Bibsonomy[2] allow people to annotate documents with freely chosen terms, called tags. The tagging process for a document can be seen as somewhat a classification of the document into categories represented by the annotations and this is also referred to as categorization property of annotations[22].

A lot of studies have been conducted to analyze social annotations, e.g., their motivations, types, quantities and statistical characteristics[11, 3, 5, 10], and all these works serve for almost the same purpose, that is to apply this resource in real web search applications. However, there are limited approaches proposed in direct use of annotations[25, 22, 2, 13] and most existing works model tags as additional keywords[19, 25]. How to utilize the categorization property to improve search effectiveness is an interesting research question that remains unexplored.

Modeling annotations as categories are prominent in the following aspects which previous methods cannot handle well: (1) Many tags are composed of multiple terms, such as "Carpal-tunnel-syndrome" or "Computer_storage". Taking them as additional words would reduce their descriptive power for documents regardless of tokenization. (2) Many tags are from personal vocabulary but are meaningful on describing topic connections of documents. Taking them as words would not generate such an effect. (3) The tags on the Web are often multilingual and it is easy to treat synonyms from tags and words as multiple terms. The weights of these tags on topic estimation would be further reduced if they are used as words.

To leverage the categorization property, the following issues need to be addressed: category representation, category weighting and search-oriented category utilization. In this paper, we take all the above three aspects into consideration. First we propose a new topic model called TR-LDA based on the categorization property which combines the advantages of global text analysis and local categorization knowledge inferred from annotations. The learned topic model can then

[1]http://www.delicious.com

[2]http://www.bibsonomy.org

be used to smooth the classical language model to improve IR performance. In our proposed TR-LDA model, category representation is an independent component and category weights can be specified according to their relative accuracies on describing the document. We explore two methods for the representation according to whether users are considered as one element in category representation and their performances are further compared. We conclude that annotations working as categories provide stronger constraints for the learned topic model than working as keywords for which lots of tags are needed.

Our contributions in this paper lie in the following points. (1) We bring up a new method for modeling documents based on the categorization property of annotations and explore the impact of incorporating this factor on retrieval performance. (2)We compare several strategies to represent and weight annotation categories. (3)We develop an effective evaluation scheme as well as construct several evaluation datasets for the general social tag based retrieval task.

The rest of the paper is organized as follows: Section 2 reviews the existing work related to this paper. Section 3 presents our proposed TR-LDA model and its implementation issues. Section 4 discusses the TR-LDA based retrieval method in more detail. Section 5 introduces the evaluation process and presents experimental results. Finally, Section 6 concludes and discusses possible directions for future work.

2. RELATED WORK

Social annotations have been utilized for estimating web page importance[13, 2] as well as estimating document models[19, 25]. These two aspects are the major concerns of web search and we target the document modeling aspect in this paper. On modeling annotations, most existing works emphasize the keyword property, where tags are taken as observations at the same level as words. Specifically, [25] used one common topic specific distribution for words and tags while [19] demonstrated that independent modeling of word and tag distributions is desired, but both methods need a comparative number of tags to guarantee their performances.

Besides, methods on extracting one kind of data given its alternative counterpart have also been proposed, such as extracting content-related annotations[14] and annotation-related contents[18]. However, the common strategy used in the above works is that the topic distribution of extracted data is limited within the scope of the given data. This may not be suitable for the general IR task, because in this context, the goal is to find the best topic model to describe the document collection without any prior knowledge about which data source is more desirable; trusting one source only may be biased without fully exploring the information contained in the other.

Another related work concerns language models[17], for which smoothing is critical and has been well studied[24, 15, 21, 12]. Recent researches show that sophisticated topic models may provide no additional gains over the basic LDA model for smoothing[23]. We believe this is because using only the statistical information from document collections may not be sufficient and additional domain knowledge is needed to train a more accurate model.

Wikipedia categories have also been explored for ad hoc retrieval[14], where they are taken as references to align queries and documents. However, it is difficult to apply the same method to annotation categories because their quality is much lower than Wikipedia categories.

3. MODELING ANNOTATION CATEGORIES

This section starts with the introduction of proposed method for modeling documents by leveraging categorization property of annotations. Then we describe an inference framework for learning the model parameters. Finally, we discuss the implementation issues involving parameter settings and parameter updates.

3.1 The Proposed TR-LDA Generative Model

Since tags are mostly accurate topic descriptors, it is natural to consider tags as potential categories. Under this interpretation, a document with certain tags is assumed to be consistent with the topic(s) embodied by the tag term(s), and naturally tags should lie in a higher level compared to the traditional use of taking them at the word level. But note that the same tag term from different users may have different topic granularities and thus categories may be better represented by raw annotations, which are defined as <user,tag> tuples. The two kinds of category representations with or without user involvement are discussed in Section 3.3 and hereafter, we simply use *annotation categories* to refer to them.

Formally, we use D to represent the document collection. For each document $d \in D$, suppose C_d is the annotation categories of the document d, then the union of C_d forms the global category set C of document collection D. Note that a proportion of categories in C would appear in multiple documents as used for the purpose of organization. We use D_c to represent the set of documents associated with a certain annotation category c.

To reflect the constraint effect of categories, we take a certain proportion of word observations as generated from the annotation source. Specifically, suppose this proportion is $1 - \lambda(\lambda \leq 1)$ and if document d has N_d words, then $(1 - \lambda)N_d$ words are generated by its annotation categories, and the remaining λN_d are generated from the document itself. In this process, each word variable is in fact replaced with two random variables representing its generative patterns from the document source and annotation source respectively. The two variables having their appearances of λ and $1 - \lambda$ are independent though they share the same word form. Similarly, we can further model the generation from the annotation source using $|C_d|$ category specific random variables and define the appearance proportion of each as μ_{dc}. Note that the observation unit is now continuous rather than discrete as adopted in traditional LDAs and the generated random variables are assumed to be exchangeable as in the "bag-of-words" assumption[1]. This generative process is further illustrated in Figure 1 and Table 1.

As we can see, the proposed TR-LDA model maintains a global category component, which makes the documents with the same annotations have partial topic consistence since they may share the same θ_c.

In the TR-LDA model, λ and μ are parameters to be specified beforehand. These two parameters control how much we trust the social annotation source and its different annotation categories. The details of setting up them are discussed in Section 3.3. All other parameters can be inferred from the document collection. You may also easily observe

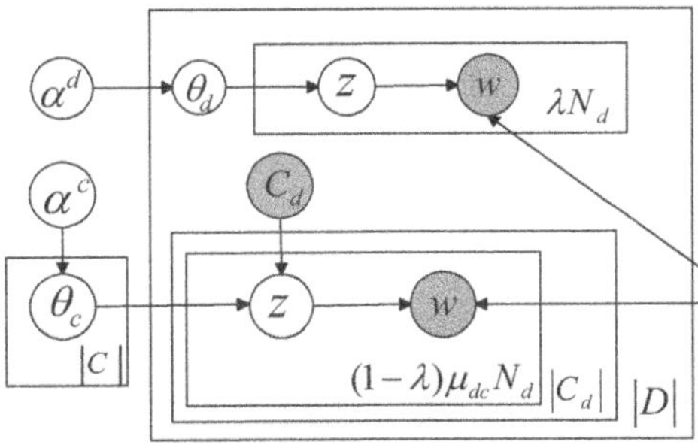

Figure 1: Graphic representation of TR-LDA Model

For each annotation category $c \in C$:
  Generate $\theta_c \sim \text{Dirichlet}(\cdot|\alpha^c)$
For each document $d \in D$
  Generate $\theta_d \sim \text{Dirichlet}(\cdot|\alpha^d)$
  For each word index $n \in 1, \ldots, N_d$:
    Generate λ times from document source:
      $z_{dn} \sim \text{Multinomial}(\cdot|\theta_d)$
      $w_{dn} \sim \text{Multinomial}(\cdot|\beta_{z_{dn}})$
    For each annotation category $c \in C_d$:
      Generate $(1-\lambda)\mu_{dc}$ times from category c
      $z_{dn} \sim \text{Multinomial}(\cdot|\theta_c)$
      $w_{dn} \sim \text{Multinomial}(\cdot|\beta_{z_{dn}})$

Table 1: The Generative process of TR-LDA

that LDA can be seen as a special case of TR-LDA, where $\lambda = 1$.

3.2 The Inference Framework for TR-LDA

Given the parameters $\Theta = \{\alpha^c, \alpha^d, \mu_d, \lambda, \beta\}$, the likelihood of a word w appearing in a document d is then the product of two source related word likelihoods,

$$P(w) = P(w|d)^\lambda P(w|C_d)^{1-\lambda} = P(w|d)^\lambda \Big(\prod_{c\in C_d} P(w|c)^{\mu_{dc}}\Big)^{1-\lambda}$$

where $\sum_{c\in C_d} \mu_{dc} = 1$. The corpus likelihood is defined as follows:

$$P(D|\Theta) = \int_{\theta_d,\theta_c: d\in D, c\in C} \prod_{d\in D} P(\theta_d|\alpha^d) \prod_{c\in C} P(\theta_c|\alpha^c) \times$$

$$\prod_{d=1}^{|D|} \Big(\prod_{n=1}^{N_d} (P(w_n|\theta_d,\beta)^\lambda \prod_{c\in C_d} P(w_n|\theta_c,\beta)^{\mu_{dc}(1-\lambda)}) \Big) d_{\theta_d,\theta_c}$$

where

$$P(w_n|\theta_d,\beta) = \sum_{z_n} P(z_n|\theta_d)P(w_n|z_n,\beta)$$

$$P(w_n|\theta_c,\beta) = \sum_{z_n} P(z_n|\theta_c)P(w_n|z_n,\beta)$$

As for TR-LDA, we would like to know the posterior distribution of $P(\theta_d, \theta_c, z|C, D, \Theta)$ and the parameter β. The former is used to estimate the document topic(s), while the latter is to estimate the topic-specific word distribution.

A variety of algorithms have been proposed to estimate the parameters in topic models. The two most common methods are Gibbs sampling [9] and variational inference [4]. Here we develop a variational inference method to approximate the posterior distribution of latent variables. The approximate distribution used in our algorithm is given as follows:

$$q(\theta_d, \theta_c, z|\Lambda) = \prod_{c=1}^{|C|} q(\theta_c|\gamma_c) \prod_{d=1}^{|D|} \Big(q(\theta_d|\gamma_d) \prod_{n=1}^{N_d} q(z_n|\phi_{dn}) \Big)$$

where $\Lambda = \{\gamma_c, \gamma_d, \phi_{dn} | c \in C, d \in D, dn \in 1, \ldots, N_d\}$ are variational parameters. Specifically, γ_d and γ_c are Dirichlet parameters and ϕ_{dn} are multinomial parameters. Using the variational EM algorithm, we get the following parameter updates

E-step

$$\phi_{dni} \propto \beta_{ij} \exp \Big(\lambda[\Psi(\gamma_{di}) - \Psi(\sum_{j=1}^{K} \gamma_{dj})] + (1-\lambda) \sum_{c:c\in C_d} \mu_{dc}[\Psi(\gamma_{ci}) - \Psi(\sum_{j=1}^{K} \gamma_{cj})] \Big) \quad (1)$$

$$\gamma_{di} = \alpha_i^d + \lambda \sum_{n=1}^{N_d} \phi_{dni} \quad (2)$$

$$\gamma_{ci} = \alpha_i^c + \frac{1-\lambda}{|D_c|} \sum_{d\in D_c} \mu_{dc} \sum_{n=1}^{N_d} \phi_{dni} \quad (3)$$

M-step

$$\beta_{ij} \propto \sum_{d} \sum_{n=1}^{N_d} \phi_{dni} \delta_j(w_n) \quad (4)$$

In this paper, we use fixed values for α^c and α^d for simplicity, though they can also be estimated by Newton-Raphson algorithm.

3.3 Implementation Issues

3.3.1 λ and μ_d

λ is a parameter which controls how likely the observed word is sampled from the document source. A smaller λ(which means bigger $1-\lambda$), indicates that we have more trust on the annotation source and the learned topic representation would be prone to reflect the underlying annotation categories. In our experimental setting, λ is closer to 1 rather than to 0 with the assumption that the statistical information contained in document is more important.

μ_d controls the proportion of words sampling from annotation categories for document d. We assume μ_{dc}, the proportion sampling from a certain category c, is consistent with its importance to the document d.

According to previous analysis, the categories can be represented by **only tags** after aggregating users out or by **raw annotations**. For the first representation, two heuristic methods are developed to compute μ_d according to different assumptions. Specifically, we first compute the weights for each tag and then use L1 norm to generate its corresponding proportion. The tag weights can be calculated using (1) the TF method. By aggregating annotations with the same tag term, we can calculate the term frequency of each tag assigned to the document. (2) the TF-IDF method. This method punishes the common tag terms appearing in multiple documents and emphasizes rare tag term(s) for a document. For the second representation(i.e. with user information), no prior knowledge on the relative importance of raw annotations is assumed, therefore uniform distribution is employed for μ_d. It is found that using tags as categories and TF based weighting scheme is the most effective through our experiments.

3.3.2 Parameter updates

In the above inference algorithm, at E-step, the estimation for variational parameters is done through cycling over all the parameters and replacing each in turn with an updated estimate by using the current estimates of other related parameters. Obviously, the associated parameters have to be kept in memory so as to update each other. In TR-LDA, each document update needs the parameters of its annotation categories and each category update needs all its associated document parameters(shown in Eq.(2) and Eq.(3) respectively). In fact, annotations and documents constitute a bipartite graph. The maximum memory needed depends on the size of the maximum subgraph. Suppose the maximum subgraph contains D_s documents and C_s annotation categories, the space required for inference is at least $K\sum_{d\in D_s} N_d + K|D_s| + K|C_s|$. In real annotation networks, the maximum subgraph could often consist of tens of thousands of nodes, therefore space saving is an immediate issue which needs to be addressed.

A basic idea to control the memory consumption is to remove unnecessary edges from the graph. Here, we adopt a principled graph cut approach to solve this problem. Graph cut is a method which can find the best graph partition with the least cut cost based on the graph structure[16, 8]. We use it here to split document-annotation subgraphs into smaller and balanced pieces according to the memory constraint. One can see that the edges removed would not participate in estimating related document and category topics, but we believe the negative impact is limited. Specifically, each edge is assigned the same weight, and we use the technique of normalized cut[20] to split the graph.

Besides, for those documents without annotations, we set $\lambda = 1$ to update ϕ_{dni} in Eq.(1).

4. DOCUMENT RETRIEVAL BASED ON TR-LDA

The basic language model(LM) uses query likelihood to score documents. Formally, for a query Q, the score of a document d is given as follows:

$$P(Q|d) = \prod_{q\in Q} P(q|d) \tag{5}$$

where q is a query term in Q and $P(q|d)$ is the estimated document model from the document observation. Obviously, the estimation of document model is the key element for LM based retrieval and it is demonstrated that some sort of smoothing is a must[21]. LDA based smoothing methods use the Eq.(6) to estimate $P(w|d)$.

$$P(w|d) = \tau\left(\frac{N_d}{N_d+\delta}P_{ml}(w|d) + (1-\frac{N_d}{N_d+\delta})P(w|coll)\right) + (1-\tau)P_{tp}(w|d) \tag{6}$$

$$P_{tp}(w|d) = E_{P(\theta_d,z|D)}[P(w|z)P(z|\theta_d)P(\theta_d|d)] \tag{7}$$

$P_{ml}(w|d)$ and $P(w|coll)$ are the maximum likelihood estimates of word w in the document and in the entire collection respectively. δ is the Dirichlet prior while τ controls the preference for exact term matching and inexact semantic matching. $P_{tp}(w|d)$ is the component estimated from topic models such as LDA and PLSI, etc.

In our proposed method, we use TR-LDA to calculate the $P_{tp}(w|d)$ component and the corresponding formula is shown in Eq.(8). Specifically, posterior distributions for θ_d and z are estimated based on the TR-LDA model. The rest of the retrieval process is the same as described before. The semantic matching provided by TR-LDA is assumed to be better because human categorization knowledge is incorporated in addition to the unsupervised analysis purely based on statistical information such as LDA.

$$P_{tp}(w|d) = E_{P(\theta_d,z|D,C)}[P(w|z)P(z|\theta_d)P(\theta_d|d)] = \sum_i^K P(w|\beta_i)\frac{\gamma_{di}}{\sum_{i=1}^K \gamma_{di}} \tag{8}$$

5. EXPERIMENTS

5.1 Data Set Construction

To evaluate the performance of tag based retrieval methods, the dataset should consist of two components: a document collection and its related annotations, and a query set and its relevance judgements. Here we resort to the standard evaluation conference TREC[3] and try to build test collections based on its tasks. We select the ad-hoc retrieval tasks of Web Track 2009[7] and Web Track 2010[6] as bases to construct our datasets. It is mainly because TREC datasets are carefully constructed and the used document collection ClueWeb09 dataset[4] was crawled from January to February in 2009, whose documents could be found in current bookmarking systems such as Delicious. Particularly, the ClueWeb09 dataset contains two types, the complete "Category A" dataset and the smaller "Category B" dataset.

Our construction process is composed of the following sequential steps:

1. The documents appearing in the relevance judgements of "Category B" dataset were taken as seeds to crawl related annotations. Specifically, the seeds can be divided into two portions: the relevant document set $D(rel)$ and the non-relevant document set $D(nonrel)$. Their corresponding annotation sets crawled are $A(rel)$ and $A(nonrel)$. Each annotation is in the form of a <user,tag> tuple.

2. The annotations in $A(rel)$ and $A(nonrel)$ were further submitted to the Delicious website to fetch web pages, which form two expanded document collections $DE(rel)$ and $DE(nonrel)$. New annotations of $DE(rel) + DE(nonrel)$ were added to $A(rel) + A(nonrel)$.

3. By intersecting $DE(rel)$ and $DE(nonrel)$ with the document set of "Category B", we got two new document sets $DC(rel)$ and $DC(nonrel)$. The annotations of those documents not in $DC(rel) + DC(nonrel)$ were deleted from $A(rel) + A(nonrel)$.

Now we define the dataset type R as follows:

$$R = \{D(rel) + DC(nonrel) + D(nonrel), A(rel) + A(nonrel)\}$$

Note that the documents in $DC(rel)$ are likely to be relevant due to the fact that they share the same annotations with $D(rel)$. Since no human judgements are available for $DC(rel)$, we removed this portion from R. $DC(nonrel)$ may

[3]http://trec.nist.gov/

[4]http://boston.lti.cs.cmu.edu/Data/clueweb09/

Web Track	no. topics	no. judged	no. rels
09 adhoc	50	13,118	4,002
10 adhoc	48	15,845	3,090

Table 2: Statistics about Web Track adhoc tasks.

name	no. docs	no. posts	no. users	no. tags
09R	37,108	122,016	12,074	7,472
10R	39,029	83,180	17,828	11,037

Table 3: Statistics about the datasets

also contain relevant documents, but the possibility would be much lower and therefore we assume that all its documents are not relevant.

Specifically, two evaluation datasets are constructed and used in the experiments which are derived from Web Track 2009 and Web Track 2010. The statistics about Web Tracks and the constructed datasets are shown in Table 2 and Table 3 respectively. For the relevance judgements provided by Web Track 2010, only those with documents appearing in "Category B" dataset were included, resulting in 48 queries for evaluation.

5.2 Retrieval Experiments

In this section, we examine the performance of TR-LDA based retrieval method(TBDM) to answer the following two questions: (1) Can annotations improve search effectiveness? (2) Does the TR-LDA model have advantage over other tag based models for IR?

For answering the first question, we implemented the following baselines: (1) Language model with Dirichlet prior(LM); (2) Language model using LDA smoothing (LBDM) [21]. In fact, LBDM is a strong baseline which is currently the best document smoothing method based on our knowledge[23, 21]. For answering the second question, we implemented three baselines. One is the language model using LDA smoothing (LBDM-T), where each document is represented by the set of its words and associated tags at inference. The other two baselines are WT-LDA and WT-QDAU+ from[25] which is also the most related work to ours.

$09R$ is our training collection to estimate parameters and $10R$ is used for testing whether the optimized parameters are consistent in other collections. The queries and relevance judgements in ad-hoc retrieval tasks are used and documents not appearing in the relevance judgements are taken as non-relevant at evaluation. The performance of each run is evaluated based on its top 100 documents instead of traditional 1000 documents. All the experiments were done with lemur toolkit[5]. Documents are indexed as trecweb type and stemmed using Porter stemmer. Queries are taken from the "query" field of the initial topic release. The performance is measured using mean average precision(MAP). In fact, for comparison, the whole experiment part follows the paradigm of [21], including the selection of parameters and the usage of training set and testing set.

5.2.1 Topic Model Estimation

For the retrieval methods mentioned above, each has a topic component which needs to be estimated before combining with the language model. We primarily examine the performances of LBDM and TBDM to study the impact of topic model estimation on IR. Other methods show similar properties as LBDM .

We use tags as categories and the TF based strategy for μ_d according to previous conclusions. This leads to a new document-tag bipartite graph. Considering the memory limitation, we select 20 for $09R$ and 50 for $10R$ as the Ncut partition number respectively. This makes around 7,000 documents have to be kept in memory at inference and the proportion of documents with tags is 68%for $09R$ and 63% for $10R$ after the partition. To estimate topic models, we use the most frequent 100,000 word terms in the collection and hyper parameters α^d,α^c and β prior are set to 1.

There are mainly four factors that determine the actual performance of the proposed TR-LDA method for retrieval:

(1) The iteration number. Generally, more iterations mean that the learned model tends to have stable predictive ability, however, for the retrieval task, better topic representation may be generated in the process of iterations, not in the final converged model. We found that the retrieval performance based on 5 iterations is generally good enough and the later iterations may even harm the performance.

(2) The local maximum problem. We ran 10 times for a given topic number with various random initializations for TR-LDA and LDA respectively. The average MAP across 10 runs was used as the performance measure for later comparison.

(3) The number of topics. The number of topics determines the granularity of the learned topics. To find an optimal topic number K, we vary it from 10 to 80 with 10 as the step. Both TBDM and LBDM reach their optimal performances at $K = 20$.

(4) The λ parameter. λ controls the preference of information source for generating document words. We set it from 0.6 to 1.0 with 0.05 as step. The optimal performance is achieved at $\lambda = 0.85$.

5.2.2 Comparison of Retrieval Performance

Parameters δ and τ are selected through exhaustive search on $09R$. $\tau = 0.9$ is the best value for both TBDM and LBDM. The optimal δ is a little bit different, that is $\delta = 1750$ for TBDM and $\delta = 1500$ for LBDM. The retrieval results on $09R$ are presented in Table 4. Statistically significant improvements are found for TBDM over LBDM and QL at multiple recall levels. With the trained parameter setting from $09R$, we examined the performances of these methods on $10R$. As shown from Table 5, TBDM still outperforms LBDM and QL significantly. This demonstrates that social annotations could bring benefits for web search.

To further compare with other tag based retrieval methods, we implemented LBDM-T, WT-LDA and WT-QDAU+, where the topic estimations were done in a similar way as LBDM. Their parameters were also tuned at $09R$. Table 6 shows that TBDM outperforms WT-LDA and WT-QDAU+ significantly, which demonstrates the benefit of modeling annotations as categories.

6. CONCLUSIONS AND FUTURE WORK

In this paper, we explore the use of the categorization property of social annotations for modeling document contents. We have proposed a new topic model TR-LDA, where annotations and documents determine the latent topic dis-

[5]http://www.lemurproject.org

Table 4: Comparison of QL, LBDM and TBDM in the 09R dataset. $*$ indicates a statistically significant improvement with a one-tailed Wilcoxon signed-rank test($p < 0.05$).

	QL	LBDM	TBDM	%chg over QL	%chg over LBDM
Rel.	4002	4002	4002		
Rel. Retr.	1844	1844	1877.9	+1.79	+1.79
0.00	0.5800	0.6371	0.6380	+10.00*	+0.15
0.10	0.4631	0.4972	0.5125	+10.67*	+3.09*
0.20	0.4406	0.4630	0.4803	+9.00*	+3.72*
0.30	0.4156	0.4206	0.4401	+5.90	+4.64*
0.40	0.3447	0.3406	0.3558	+3.23	+4.47*
0.50	0.1888	0.2224	0.2243	+18.80*	+0.82
0.60	0.1050	0.1384	0.1577	+50.10*	+13.91*
0.70	0.0788	0.0715	0.0760	-3.51	+6.29
0.80	0.0370	0.0343	0.0387	+4.78	+12.98
0.90	0.0138	0.0178	0.0198	+42.80*	+10.88
1.00	0.0115	0.0120	0.0119	+3.36	-0.83
Avg	0.2134	0.2312	0.2414	+13.12*	+4.41*

tribution together. The proposed model is demonstrated effective in the ad hoc retrieval task.

Future directions include the exploration of other alternative approximation methods to identify a better annotation-document partition. We are also interested in the performance of applying the proposed TR-LDA to document collections with much fewer annotations.

7. ACKNOWLEDGMENTS

This work is supported by the Major State Basic Research Project of China under Grant No. 2007CB311103 and the National Science Foundation of China under Grant No. 61070111 and 60873166.

8. REFERENCES

[1] D. Aldous. Exchangeability and related topics. In *Ecole d'Ete de Probabilities de Saint-Flour XIII 1983*, pages 1–198. Springer, 1985.

[2] S. Bao, G. Xue, X. Wu, Y. Yu, B. Fei, and Z. Su. Optimizing web search using social annotations. In *WWW*, pages 501–510. ACM, 2007.

[3] K. Bischoff, C. S. Firan, W. Nejdl, and R. Paiu. Can all tags be used for search? In *ACM CIKM*, pages 193–202. ACM, 2008.

[4] D. M. Blei, A. Y. Ng, and M. I. Jordan. Latent dirichlet allocation. *J. Mach. Learn. Res.*, 3, 2003.

[5] M. J. Carman, M. Baillie, R. Gwadera, and F. Crestani. A statistical comparison of tag and query logs. In *ACM SIGIR*, pages 123–130. ACM, 2009.

[6] I. S. G. V. C. Charles L. A. Clarke, Nick Craswell. Overview of the trec 2010 web track. 2010.

[7] C. L. Clarke, N. Craswell, and I. Soboroff. Overview of the trec 2009 web track. 2009.

[8] I. S. Dhillon. Co-clustering documents and words using bipartite spectral graph partitioning. In *ACM SIGKDD*, pages 269–274. ACM, 2001.

[9] T. L. Griffiths and M. Steyvers. Finding scientific topics. *Proceedings of the National Academy of Sciences of the United States of America*, 101(Suppl 1):5228–5235, April 2004.

[10] H. Halpin, V. Robu, and H. Shepherd. The complex dynamics of collaborative tagging. In *WWW*, pages 211–220. ACM, 2007.

[11] P. Heymann, G. Koutrika, and H. Garcia-Molina. Can social bookmarking improve web search? In *ACM WSDM*, pages 195–206. ACM, 2008.

Table 5: Comparison of QL, LBDM and TBDM in the 10R dataset. $*$ indicates a statistically significant improvement with a one-tailed Wilcoxon signed-rank test($p < 0.05$).

	QL	LBDM	TBDM	%chg over QL	%chg over LBDM
Rel.	3090	3090	3090		
Rel. Retr.	1308	1303.6	1333.4	+1.94	+2.29
0.00	0.4357	0.4627	0.4751	+9.04	+2.68
0.10	0.3720	0.3677	0.3884	+4.04	+5.63*
0.20	0.3316	0.3149	0.3284	-0.96	+4.29*
0.30	0.2927	0.2839	0.2890	-1.26	+1.80
0.40	0.2287	0.2393	0.2452	+7.21*	+2.47
0.50	0.1625	0.1763	0.1843	+13.41*	+4.54
0.60	0.1434	0.1307	0.1412	+1.53	+8.03
0.70	0.0695	0.0657	0.0708	+1.87	+7.76
0.80	0.0237	0.0250	0.0289	+21.94*	+15.6*
0.90	0.0000	0.0009	0.0027	–	–
1.00	0.0000	0.0002	0.0000	–	–
Avg	0.1623	0.1626	0.1716	+5.73*	+5.53*

Table 6: Comparison of LBDM, LBDM-T, WT-LDA, WT-QDAU+ and TBDM.

	LBDM	LBDM-T	WT-LDA	WT-QDAU+	TBDM
09R	0.2312	0.2332	0.2092	0.2079	0.2414
10R	0.1626	0.1621	0.1538	0.1578	0.1716

[12] T. Hofmann. Probabilistic latent semantic indexing. In *ACM SIGIR*, pages 50–57. ACM, 1999.

[13] A. Hotho, R. Jäschke, C. Schmitz, and G. Stumme. Information retrieval in folksonomies: Search and ranking. In *The Semantic Web: Research and Applications*, volume 4011 of *LNCS*, pages 411–426. Springer, 2006.

[14] R. Kaptein, M. Koolen, and J. Kamps. Using wikipedia categories for ad hoc search. In *ACM SIGIR*, pages 824–825. ACM, 2009.

[15] X. Liu and W. B. Croft. Cluster-based retrieval using language models. In *ACM SIGIR*, pages 186–193. ACM, 2004.

[16] U. Luxburg. A tutorial on spectral clustering. *Statistics and Computing*, 17:395–416, December 2007.

[17] J. M. Ponte and W. B. Croft. A language modeling approach to information retrieval. In *ACM SIGIR*, pages 275–281. ACM, 1998.

[18] D. Ramage, D. Hall, R. Nallapati, and C. D. Manning. Labeled lda: a supervised topic model for credit attribution in multi-labeled corpora. In *EMNLP*, pages 248–256. ACL, 2009.

[19] D. Ramage, P. Heymann, C. D. Manning, and H. Garcia-Molina. Clustering the tagged web. In *ACM WSDM*, pages 54–63. ACM, 2009.

[20] J. Shi and J. Malik. Normalized cuts and image segmentation. *IEEE Trans. Pattern Anal. Mach. Intell.*, 22:888–905, August 2000.

[21] X. Wei and W. B. Croft. Lda-based document models for ad-hoc retrieval. In *ACM SIGIR*, pages 178–185. ACM, 2006.

[22] S. Xu, S. Bao, B. Fei, Z. Su, and Y. Yu. Exploring folksonomy for personalized search. In *ACM SIGIR*, pages 155–162. ACM, 2008.

[23] X. Yi and J. Allan. Evaluating topic models for information retrieval. In *ACM CIKM*, pages 1431–1432. ACM, 2008.

[24] C. Zhai and J. Lafferty. A study of smoothing methods for language models applied to information retrieval. *ACM Trans. Inf. Syst.*, 22:179–214, April 2004.

[25] D. Zhou, J. Bian, S. Zheng, H. Zha, and C. L. Giles. Exploring social annotations for information retrieval. In *WWW*, pages 715–724. ACM, 2008.

Context-Aware Search Personalization with Concept Preference

Di Jiang, Kenneth Wai-Ting Leung, Wilfred Ng
Department of Computer Science and Engineering
The Hong Kong University of Science and Technology
Clear Water Bay, Kowloon, Hong Kong
{dijiang, kwtleung, wilfred}@cse.ust.hk

ABSTRACT

As the size of the web is growing rapidly, a well-recognized challenge for developing web search engines is to optimize the search result towards each user's preference. In this paper, we propose and develop a new personalization framework that captures the user's preference in the form of concepts obtained by mining web search contexts. The search context consists of both the user's clickthroughs and query reformulations that satisfy some specific information need, which is able to provide more information than each individual query in a search session. We also propose a method that discovers search contexts by one-pass of raw search query log. Using the information of the search context, we develop eight strategies that derive conceptual preference judgment. A learning-to-rank approach is employed to combine the derived preference judgments and then a *Context-Aware User Profile* (CAUP) is created. We further employ CAUP to adapt a personalized ranking function. Experimental results demonstrate that our approach captures accurate and comprehensive user's preference and, in terms of Top-N results quality, outperforms those existing concept-based personalization approaches without using search contexts.

Categories and Subject Descriptors

H.3.3 [**Information Search and Retrieval**]: Search Process

General Terms

Algorithms, Experimentation

Keywords

Search Personalization, Clickthrough, Query Reformulation

1. INTRODUCTION

With the exponential growth of information available on the Web, search engines have become an indispensable tool of people's daily activities [7]. However, as search queries are typically short and ambiguous, search engines have limited clues to infer a user's true search intents and thus can only return roughly the same result for the same query. This *one size fits all* strategy makes search engines perform only suboptimally for many users [5]. To alleviate this problem, search personalization has been studied in order to adapt search results to individual's explicit or implicit feedback. Since users are largely reluctant to provided explicit feedback due to the extra efforts involved, implicit feedback is commonly used as the major resource for search personalization [4, 8].

The most widely used implicit feedback is the user's clickthrough information [4]. Several personalization approaches have been proposed to personalize search results based on each individual query's clickthrough information [4, 8]. However, as the user usually submits a sequence of queries to satisfy the same information need [11], the search context that is composed of previous queries, previous clickthroughs as well as the semantic relations between queries become a potential resource to infer the user's preference with higher accuracy and broader information coverage.

We propose a framework that utilizes search context to personalize search results. Figure 1 shows the general process of the proposed framework, which consists of two fundamental activities: (1) Profile Updating and (2) Re-ranking.

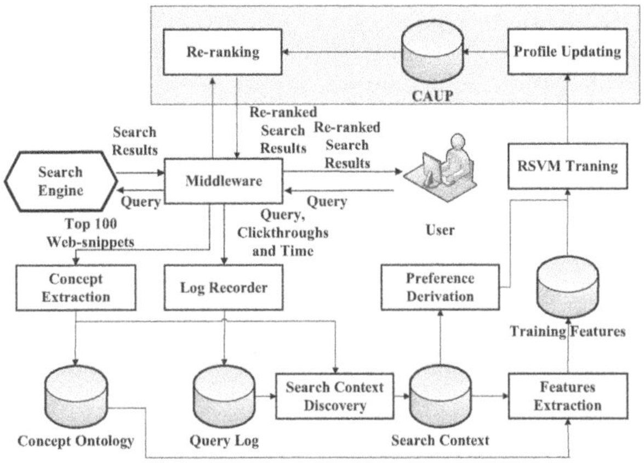

Figure 1: Main Processes in Personalization Framework

- **Profile Updating**: When the search results are returned from the backend search engine, the concepts (i.e. important terms and phrases) and their rela-

CIKM'11, October 24–28, 2011, Glasgow, Scotland, UK.

tions are mined from the search results and stored in *Concept Ontology*. Queries, submitting times and clickthrough behaviors are also recorded in *Query Log*. Then search contexts are extracted from the stored information and eight strategies are employed to derive conceptual preference. The conceptual preference is used in RSVM [4] training to update CAUP.

- **Re-ranking**: When a user submits a query, the search results are obtained from the backend search engines (Google) and then re-ranked according to CAUP.

In order to realize the proposed personalization approach, we need to overcome some challenging issues. First, we need to develop a method that automatically discovers search context from raw search query log. Although many existing methods assume that the context is already known, obtaining search context for personalization usage is non-trivial. As providing irrelevant results for the user is frustrating, a high coherency is required to avoid involving irrelevant information and meanwhile the integrity should also be kept to avoid breaking a context into several separated ones. Thus, we propose a method that utilizes a range of techniques concerning temporal cutoff, query relevance and *Search Engine Result Pages* (SERPs) similarity in order to discover search context by one-pass of the query log.

Second, search context contains different types of information. Based on the diverse nature of the observed evidence in search context, we need to design different strategies to infer the user's preference. Additionally, preference derived from different sources should be seamlessly combined to update CAUP for the user. To meet these requirements, our framework uses three strategies to derive preference judgment from the user's clickthrough behaviors and five strategies to derive preference judgment from the user's query reformulation behaviors. Then a learning-to-rank method is used to combine the derived preference judgment and update CAUP, which is further used to personalize search results.

The main contributions of this paper can be summarized as follows:

- Our search personalization is based on search context related to a specific information need rather than individual queries. We propose a new method that discovers search contexts from query log with high coherency and integrity.

- Eight preference derivation strategies are proposed to infer the user's conceptual preference through mining search context. We study in detail the characteristics and effectiveness of each proposed preference derivation strategy.

- A learning-to-rank approach is proposed to seamlessly combine preference judgment from different preference derivation strategies and utilize them to update CAUP, based on which the search results are re-ranked.

- We implement a working prototype to verify the proposed ideas. It consists of a middleware for capturing user interaction information, performing personalization, and interfacing with backend search engine. Empirical results show that our approach successfully captures the user's real search preference and outperform methods without considering contextual information.

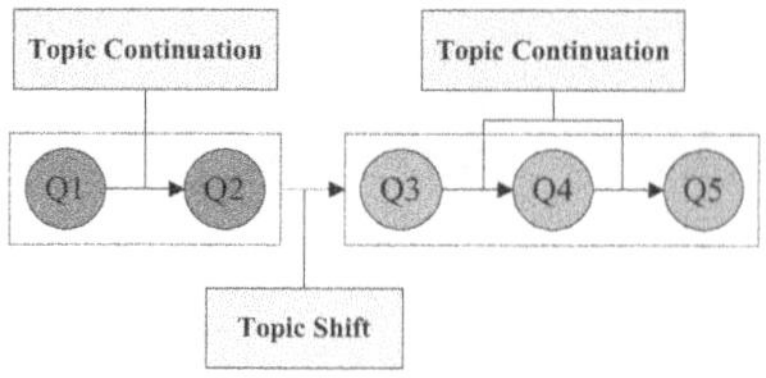

Figure 2: Relations Between Queries

The rest of the paper is organized as follows. Section 2 reviews the related work. Section 3 presents the method of concept extraction. Section 4 details our search context discovery technique. Section 5 explains the strategies of deriving conceptual preferences from search context. Personalized ranking function is described in Section 6 and experimental results are given in Section 7. Finally, we conclude the paper in Section 8.

2. RELATED WORK

The proposed framework utilizes interaction evidence in search context to support search personalization. In this section, we review two related fundamental topics: *session segmentation* and *search personalization*.

2.1 Session Segmentation

In the field of session segmentation, the relations between queries are categorized as *Topic Continuation* and *Topic Shift*, which are illustrated in Figure 2. Assume that query Q1 and Q2 are semantically related, thus they are grouped in the same session and the relation between them is *Topic Continuation*. Similarly, Q3, Q4 and Q5 are also from the same session and the relations between them are *Topic Continuation*. On the contrary, Q2 and Q3 have no semantic relation and the relation between them is *Topic Shift*, which generates a session boundary.

In previous studies, a fixed temporal cutoff is widely used as the indicator of *Topic Shift*. Radlinski *et al.* [11] used a half-an-hour cutoff on the log of a library search engine and discovered that this helps achieve a good precision in finding search sessions. However, Jones *et al.* [6] reported that only using timeout cutoff is not good enough for logs from general search engines. Gayo-Avello [1] provided a good survey about several session segmentation methods, which primarily based on temporal cutoff and lexical similarity between queries. More recently, in order to have a better understanding of the relation between search queries, Huang *et al.* [3] built a rich taxonomy of query refinement strategies and developed a high precision rule-based classifier to detect related queries. *Topic Continuation* is further characterized as different types of query reformulation.

Our work on search context discovery is different from previous studies in two ways. First, as high accuracy is required for personalization, keeping the coherency of search context is prioritized by our search context discovery method and meanwhile it also keeps the context integrity to avoid breaking a search context into several separated ones. Second, the search context discovered by our approach is not simply a group of semantically related queries. Through one-pass of the query log, our method also captures the query reformulation type between consecutive queries, which contains valuable information for inferring the user's preference.

2.2 Search Personalization

Search personalization aims to return the most relevant search results according to the user's interests and preferences. In order to achieve this goal, clickthrough is widely used in previous works to infer the user's preferences. Based on the research of search engine users' browsing behaviors, Joachims [5] first developed a framework that utilized clickthrough data to infer users' preferences on documents and then learned to adapt the ranking function. Radlinski *et al.* [11] extended Joachims' method to infer the user's document preference based on the clickthrough raised by different queries. As Radlinski's method can deduce new types of preference judgment, the learned ranking function outperformed the methods that only used information of individual query. Shen *et al.* [12] proposed a method which incorporates previous queries and clickthroughs to build language models. Luxenburger *et al.* [10] proposed a personalization framework that match users' information need with their searching history. Xiang *et al.* [15] proposed four strategies to re-rank search results by the relation between queries, and their method showed performance improvement compared with those without context information. Leung *et al.* [8] developed several profiling methods to capture the user's positive and negative preferences by concepts. By analyzing each search query individually, the profiling methods in [8] captures the user's preference with fine granularity and demonstrates better performance than those based on document preference. However, with the importance of context and the advantage of concept-based preference representation, few works has been done to study concept-based search personalization in a context-aware approach.

The differences between our work and the previous counterparts are: First, our framework utilizes search context rather than individual queries to derive preference and thus obtains more comprehensive information coverage, which improves the accuracy of generated preference judgment. Second, the user's preference is represented by concepts in current search results as well as the related concepts from the concept ontology. In this way, our framework captures the user's preference on more concepts and thus improves personalization accuracy. Third, we propose a learning-to-rank method that seamlessly combines different conceptual preference judgment and use the combined preferences to update the *Context-Aware User Profile*.

3. CONCEPT EXTRACTION

Informally, if a term/phrase c appears frequently in the web-snippets [1] arising from a query q, then c represents an important concept related to q, as it co-exists in close proximity with the query in the top documents. Our concept extraction method first extracts all the terms and phrases from the web-snippets arising from q and denote a term or a phrase as c_i. After obtaining a set of term/phrase, we use the following formula to clean the concept set and delete those concepts that are not related to the query or the user's interests.

$$\theta < support(c_i) = \frac{sf(c_i)}{n} \cdot |c_i|$$

where $sf(c_i)$ is the snippet frequency of the term/phrase c_i (i.e. the number of web-snippets containing c_i), n is the number of web-snippet returned and $|c_i|$ is the number of term in the term/phrase c_i. θ is the frequency threshold we use to distinguish concepts from other terms. θ is set to 0.03 in the experiments. We choose a relative small threshold in order to obtain good information coverage.

[1] A "web-snippet" denotes the title, summary and URL of a Web page returned by search engines.

ID	Reformulation Type	Example
1	Repeat	Apple -> Apple
2	Add Whitespace/Punctuation	Apple Pie -> Apple, Pie
3	Remove Whitespace/Punctuation	Apple Pie -> ApplePie
4	Add URL	apple -> www.apple.com
5	Strip URL	www.apple.com -> apple
6	Word Reorder	Apple Pie -> Pie Apple
7	Expand Acronym	UN -> United Nations
8	Form Acronym	United Nations -> UN
9	Expand Abbreviation	Soft App -> Software Application
10	Form Abbreviation	Software Application -> Soft App
11	Word Substitution	Apple -> Fruit
12	Stemming	Running -> Run
13	Singular/Plural Conversion	Woman -> Women
14	Substring	Music Record -> Music Rec
15	Superstring	Music Rec -> Music Record
16	Add Words	Apple -> Apple Pie
17	Remove Words	Apple Pie -> Apple
18	Spelling Correction	Appple -> Apple
19	Multiple Reformulation	Running hound -> Dog

Figure 3: Query Reformulation Taxonomy

4. SEARCH CONTEXT DISCOVERY

Search context consists of queries sharing the same topic, clickthrough raised by these queries and various reformulation types between queries. In this section, we present our search context discovery method, which captures this information through one-pass of raw search query log.

4.1 Temporal Cutoff

Temporal cutoff is widely used as the indicator of topic shift. Temporal cutoffs ranging from 5 minutes to 30 minutes are frequently used to identify session boundaries. In order to evaluate the effectiveness of these cutoffs, we utilize different temporal cutoffs within 90 minutes to evaluate their performance of search context discovery. We observe that a 30-minute cutoff achieves fairly good performance and the results are presented in Section 7.

4.2 Query Relevance

We utilize query reformulation taxonomy to evaluate the relevance between query strings. The reasons of using query reformulation taxonomy are twofold: First, the taxonomy-based approach demonstrates the state-of-the-art precision of detecting *Topic Continuation*, i.e., the approach has a high precision in detecting query relatedness. Second, reformulation taxonomy captures the reformulation type between consecutive queries and we will show later that various reformulation types contain valuable information that helps infer the user's preference.

The taxonomy is presented in Figure 3. Reformulation types except the last one belong to *Single Reformulation*, which is used to detect a certain type of change between two queries. The *Single Reformulation* we use is an enriched version of that in [3] and readers may refer to it for more detailed information. As Huang *et al.* [3] reported that only using *Single Reformulation* tends to damage the integrity of search context. To resolve this problem, we use *Multiple Reformulation* to handle the scenario that a user

Table 1: Weight of Term Similarity Features

Features	Weight
Same	≃1.99
Singular/Plural Conversion	≃1.99
Stemming	≃1.99
Spelling Correction	<0.01
Superstring	<0.01
Substring	<0.01
AddURL	<0.01
StripURL	<0.01

reformulates his/her queries by combining more than one reformulation types. For example, *horses race* → *horse* is a reformulation that combines *SingularAndPlural* and *RemoveWords*. Although these two queries are semantically related, reformulation types in *Single Reformulation* are too strict to capture them. As exhaustively enumerating each combination of reformulation types is infeasible, we propose to evaluate the relevance between two queries by the similarity of each pair of their terms. We first tokenize each query into terms by whitespace and then use six term similarity features to train an SVM model. The weight of each feature is listed in Table 1, from which we observe that the features *Same*, *Singular/Plural Conversion* and *Stemming* play the dominant roles.

4.3 SERPs Similarity

The limitation of taxonomy-based method is that it cannot capture reformulations beyond the predefined taxonomy. As search results returned from search engine usually contain abundant information about the query, *Search Engine Result Pages* (SERPs) are potentially helpful to detect the similarity between queries. For each query q, we extract concepts from the top 100 snippets returned by the search engine and then the query is represented as a concept vector $\vec{C_q}$. For simplicity, we utilize cosine similarity to evaluate the similarity between two SERPs. It is defined as follows:

$$SERPs(q_1, q_2) = cos(\vec{C_{q1}}, \vec{C_{q2}}) = \frac{\vec{C_{q1}} \cdot \vec{C_{q2}}}{\|\vec{C_{q1}}\|\|\vec{C_{q2}}\|}$$

Based on the three metrics proposed in Section 4.1, 4.2 and 4.3, we present our search context discovery method in Algorithm 1. Technically, separating queries from different users is straightforward, since each query is associated with user identifiers in search query log. Thus, we focus on how to discover search context for queries submitted by the same user.

Algorithm 1 Search Context Discovery

Input: Temporal Cutoff T; Query Reformulation Taxonomy Tax; SERPs Similarity Threshold θ_{SERPs};
Output: Search contexts segmented by *Topic Shift*;

for all q_i in log **do**
  if Time(q_{i+1})-Time(q_i)>T **then**
    Relation(q_i, q_{i+1}) ← *Topic Shift*
  else
    if (Reformulation(q_i,q_{i+1})∈ Tax)=FALSE **then**
      if $SERPs(q_i, q_{i+1}) < \theta_{SERPs}$ **then**
        Relation(q_i, q_{i+1}) ← *Topic Shift*
      else
        Relation(q_i, q_{i+1}) ←Unknown Reformulation
      end if
    else
      Relation(q_i, q_{i+1}) ←Reformulation(q_i,q_{i+1})
    end if
  end if
end for

5. CONCEPT PREFERENCE DERIVATION

In this section, we discuss the strategies of deriving the user's conceptual preference from the search context. We propose three strategies to derive preference from clickthrough behavior and five strategies to derive preference from query reformulation behavior.

5.1 Preference Derivation by Clickthrough

Joachims *et al.* [5] made an in-depth study about a user's browsing behaviors in the process of web searching and proposed three assumptions:

- Users scan the results in order from top to bottom.
- Users at least read the top two result snippets and the first one is much more likely to be clicked on.
- Users read one snippet below any they click on.

Based the aforementioned assumptions, we define a user's examination range of the search results as follows:

- If a snippet ranked i is the last snippet that a user clicked on the result, the examination range of the result is $1 \rightarrow (i + 1)$.
- If no snippet is clicked on the result, the examination range of the result is $1 \rightarrow 2$.

The following three strategies focus on snippets within the examination range and ignore those beyond it.

1. Click $>_q$ Skip Above: *Assume* $(s_1, s_2, ...)$ *is the ranking of snippets arising from query* q*, the corresponding concept set for each snippet is denoted as* $(C_1, C_2, ...)$*. If* s_i *is clicked while* s_j *is not clicked and* $i > j$*, derive a concept preference judgement* $c_a >_q c_b$ *for concept* c_a *from* C_i *and concept* c_b *from* C_j*.*

The intuition behind this strategy is that a user scans the search results from top to bottom. If he/she skipped a snippet s_i before clicking on snippet s_j, he/she must have scanned s_i and decided not to click on it. Based on this observation, we infer that concepts in s_j are more likely to be preferred than concepts in s_j and pairwise preference judgment is generated for each concept pair between s_i and s_j.

2. Click $>_q$ No-Click Next: *Assume* $(s_1, s_2, ...)$ *is the ranking of snippets arising from query* q*, the corresponding concept set for each snippet is denoted as* $(C_1, C_2, ...)$*. If* s_i *is clicked while* s_j *is not clicked and* $j = i + 1$*, derive a concept preference judgment* $c_a >_q c_b$ *for concept* c_a *from* C_i *and concept* c_b *from* C_j*.*

The intuition behind this strategy is that a user would not scan much below a clicked snippet s_i, and he/she usually view the immediately following snippet s_j. Therefore concepts in s_i are more likely to be preferred than concepts in s_j and pairwise preference judgment is generated for each concept pair between s_i and s_j. Note that the preference generated by this strategy confirms the original ranking.

3. Click $>_{q'}$ No-Click Earlier: *Assume q' is an earlier query of q within the search context. $(s'_1, s'_2, ...)$ is the ranking of snippets arising from q' and the corresponding concept set for each snippet are denoted as $(C'_1, C'_2, ...)$. Similarly, $(s_1, s_2, ...)$ is the ranking of snippets arising from q and the corresponding concept set for each snippet are denoted as $(C_1, C_2, ...)$. If s_i is clicked while s'_j is skipped by the user, derive a concept preference judgment $c_a >_{q'} c'_b$ for concept c_a from C_i and concept c'_b from C'_j.*

The intuition behind this strategy is that concepts in clicked snippets are more likely to be preferred than concepts in skipped snippets arising from earlier query. This strategy can generate preference judgment over concepts arising from different queries. By applying this strategy, we are able to compare concepts from different queries and thus capture more information to infer the user's preference.

5.2 Preference Derivation by Query Reformulation

Query reformulation reflects the semantic relation between two consecutive queries. We first evaluate the distribution of query reformulation types from a 10K search query log. We invite human judges to manually label the reformulation type between queries. The result is shown in Table 2.

Table 2: Distribution of Reformulation Types

Type	Percentage	Design Strategy
Repeat	42.0%	Yes
SpellingCorrection	8.9%	Yes
AddWords	6.6%	Yes
RemoveWords	2.5%	Yes
StripURL	2.2%	Yes
Multiple Reformulation	18.1%	No
Unknown Reformulation	15.6%	No
Others	4.1%	No

We design reformulation-based strategies for the first five types in Table 2. These query reformulation types cover 62.2% of the overall reformulations. As *Multiple Reformulation* is the hybrid of different reformulation types, we design no strategy for it. *Unknown Reformulation* is the reformulation types that cannot be captured by the reformulation taxonomy. From our empirical evaluation, we observe that most of *Unknown Reformulation* need external information such as SERPs to infer the relevance. Thus, no query reformulation-based preference derivation strategy is designed for *Unknown Reformulation*. As query reformulation types in *Others* only take up a small proportion, no strategy is designed for it either. However, in practice the effort of capturing *Multiple Reformulation*, *Unknown Reformulation* and *Others* by the context discovery algorithm would not be wasted. Capturing the three reformulation types is still helpful to glue semantically related queries in the same search context, from which we can derive preference judgment by *Click $>_{q'}$ No-Click Earlier*, otherwise related queries would be separated into different search contexts.

Table 3: Click/Skip Pattern of Reformulation Types

Type	S-S	C-S	S-C	C-C(S)	C-C(D)
Repeat	51%	13%	15%	8%	13%
SpellingCorrection	45%	5%	47%	1%	2%
AddWords	29%	14%	33%	2%	22%
RemoveWords	41%	10%	28%	2%	19%
StripURL	40%	6%	42%	6%	6%

In order to better understand the nature of the five query reformulation types, we also conduct an empirical study on the user's Click/Skip behavior before and after query reformulation. A query is labeled as Click(C) if it results in clickthrough, otherwise, it is labeled as Skip(S). Five Click/Skip patterns and their proportions for each reformulation type are listed in Table 3. In the table, the C-C pattern is further categorized as C-C(S/D) if the clicked URL is the same/different for the two queries. We notice that for each reformulation type, S-S and C-S patterns take a large proportion of the observed behavior patterns, indicating that query reformulation usually fails to bring satisfactory results. As there is no guarantee that a reformulated query would bring better result, we consider a reformulated query closer to the user's information need only if it results in some clickthrough.

4. Repeat Strategy: *Assume q' is an earlier query of q within the search context and q is the repeated query of q'. $(s'_1, s'_2, ...)$ is the ranking of snippets arising from q' and $(s_1, s_2, ...)$ is the ranking of snippets arising from q. The combined snippet ranking is denoted as $(s^c_1, s^c_2, ...)$ and s^c_i is labeled as clicked if s_i or s'_i is clicked. Derive preference using **Click $>_q$ Skip Above** and **Click $>_q$ No-Click Next** from the combined ranking list instead of original ones.*

After Repeat reformulation, the second query brings the same result as the previous one. For S-C pattern and C-C(D) pattern, applying the three clickthrough-based strategies would generate conflicting preference judgment as well as redundant preference judgment. For C-C(S) pattern, applying the three clickthrough-based strategies would generate redundant preference judgment. In order to alleviate this problem, we propose *Repeat Strategy* to avoid the undesirable effects arising from "judgment conflict" and "judgment inflation".

5. SpellingCorrection Strategy: *Assume q' is an earlier query of q within a search context. If q results in clickthrough while q' results in no clickthrough, only derive preference judgment for q by **Click $>_q$ Skip Above** and **Click $>_q$ No-Click Next**.*

S-C pattern takes a large proportion for SpellingCorrection. We infer that the user usually corrects the spelling mistake and does the search again. Such behavior pattern results from clicking the query suggested by the search engine. As there may be no real "preference judgment" made by the user, we constrain that for S-C pattern of SpellingCorrection, preference judgment is only derived from the search result of the second query.

6. AddWords Strategy: *Assume q' is an earlier query of q within a search context. Terms belong to q/q' are denoted by the set S. If q results in clickthrough, concepts containing terms in S is preferred over those skipped concepts for query q.*

Through AddWords reformulation, the second query q contains some terms that do not exist in the first query q'. We denote these terms as q/q', which form a set S. If the second query results in clickthrough, we infer that these terms successfully represent the user's information need and thus concepts containing these terms should be preferred to concepts in skipped snippets. From the Click/Skip pattern, we observe that S-C and C-C(D) take a relative large proportion. For these two patterns, the clickthrough indicates that the added terms bring results that are closer to the user's information need.

7. RemoveWords Strategy: *Assume q' is an earlier query of q within a search context. Terms belong to q'/q are denoted by the set S. If q results in clickthrough, clicked concepts is preferred over those containing terms in S for query q.*

Through RemoveWords reformulation, some terms in query q' are removed from q. We denote these terms as q'/q, which form a set S. If the second query results in clickthrough, we infer that the user is looking for more general information than that obtained from q'. Query terms in earlier queries that make the search result too specific would not be preferred by the user and clicked concepts are preferred to concepts containing these obsolete terms. From the Click/Skip pattern, we also observe that S-C and C-C(D) take a large proportion for RemoveWords. For these two patterns, the clickthrough indicates that removing these terms successfully brings relevant results to the user.

8. StripURL Strategy: *Assume q' is an earlier query of q within a search context. If q is obtained by stripping URL from q', snippets whose URLs sharing terms with q are preferred by the user.*

StripURL implies that the user has navigational search intent, i.e., the user is looking for a specific Web page rather than some informational contents. In our data set, through StripURL reformulation, 80.64% of the clicked URLs share terms with the reformulated query. In contrast to other query reformulation-based strategies, we capture the user's preference with respect to URLs rather than concepts. Thus, we design this strategy to promote results whose URLs share terms with the reformulated query.

6. PERSONALIZED RANKING FUNCTION

Based on the preference judgment obtained from the previous section, we evaluate each concept's attractiveness and generate a ranking function that utilizes weighted concepts to personalize search results.

Suppose we have input preference judgment over concepts c_i and c_j for a given query q in the following form: $c_i >_q c_j$. We write the above preference as a constraint as follows:

$$\vec{w} \cdot \Phi(q, c_i) > \vec{w} \cdot \Phi(q, c_j),$$

where Φ is a function that maps a query to a concept vector. RSVM [4] is employed to find $\vec{w}$ by which the maximal pairwise preference judgment can be satisfied.

The mapping Φ determines which kind of function RSVM to learn. We first build a *concept space*, which contains concepts in the preference judgment as well concepts have semantic relation with them in the concept ontology. Then, for each c_i arising from q, we create a feature vector $\phi(q, c_i) = (f_1, f_2, \ldots, f_n)$ based on all concepts in the *concept space*. The value of each feature is given by:

$$f_k = \begin{cases} 1 & if \quad k = i \\ sim(c_i, c_k) & if \quad sim(c_i, c_k) > 0 \\ 0 & otherwise. \end{cases}$$

The benefit of building *concept space* from concept ontology is to capture the semantic relation between concepts. For example, a user submitted the query "sun" and clicked on a snippet containing concept "star". From the concept ontology, we observe that "star", "planet" and "solar system" have relative strong relation, thus we infer that these concepts would be favored by the user and results interpreting "sun" as a company or a newspaper would not be relevant to the user's information need.

The semantic relation between two concepts, $sim(c_i, c_k)$, is measured by *Pointwise Mutual Information* (PMI). Let $p(c_i)$ and $p(c_j)$ denote the probability of c_i and c_j. Let $p(c_i, c_j)$ be the joint probability of c_i and c_j. The formula used to calculate PMI is given by:

$$PMI(c_i, c_j) = \log\left(\frac{p(c_i, c_j)}{p(c_i)p(c_j)}\right),$$

$$p(c_i) = N_{c_i}/N; p(c_j) = N_{c_j}/N; p(c_i, c_j) = N_{c_i,c_j}/N,$$

where N_{c_i} is the number of snippets containing c_i, N_{c_j} and is the number of snippets containing c_j and N_{c_i,c_j} is the number of snippets containing both c_i and c_j. N is the total number of snippets. The value of N_{c_i}, N_{c_j}, N_{c_i,c_j} and N are obtained from statistics stored in the concept ontology. PMI may yield negative values; in this case we replace it by zero. In this work, $sim(q, c_i, c_k)$ is replaced by normalized PMI which is denoted by $PMI_N(c_i, c_j)$. We adapt the formula of normalized PMI used in [2] as follows:

$$PMI_N(c_i, c_j) = PMI(c_i, c_j)/(-\log P(c_i, c_j))$$

Suppose the original ranking of search results arising from q is denoted by $R(s_1, s_2, ..., s_n)$, where s_i denotes the snippet ranked at position i. Let C_i be the set of concepts extracted from snippet s_i. The preference score for s_i is obtained by summing up the attractiveness of each concept in C_i weighted by $\vec{w}$.

$$P(s_i) = \sum_{\forall c \in C_i} \vec{w} \cdot \phi(q, c)$$

Based on the preference score of each snippet, we obtain a new ranking and present it to the user. Note that the aforementioned re-ranking method will not be apply to StripURL, which relies on URLs rather than concepts. For StripURL, we simply apply *StripURL Strategy*.

7. EXPERIMENTS

In this Section, we present a comprehensive evaluation of the proposed personalization framework. In Section 7.1, we detail the experimental setup. In Section 7.2, we compare the performance of our search context discovery algorithm with several baseline methods. In Sections 7.3 and 7.4, we evaluate the clickthrough-based strategies and query reformulation-based strategies. In Section 7.5, we evaluate the effectiveness of combining preference derivation strategies and provide an example of the obtained CAUPs.

7.1 Experimental Setup

For the evaluation of search context discovery, we prepare the experimental data from AOL search query log. Each record contains the attributes of user ID, query, timestamp and the URLs that the user clicked. The 8,852 search records are manually segmented into 4,598 search contexts, which are used as the ground truth when evaluating our context discovery algorithm. Table 4 shows the statistics of our experimental data. We compare our context discovery method with several baseline methods such as fixed temporal cutoff and the taxonomy-based method proposed in [3].

Table 4: Statistics of the Experimental Data

Number of users	215
Number of queries	8,852
Average number of queries per user	41.2
Average number of clicks per user	31.3
Number of search contexts	4,254

For the evaluation of personalization strategies, we compare our approach with two methods proposed in [8], which shows state-of-art of performance to capture the user's conceptual preference. In the evaluation of traditional information retrieval systems [14], expert judges are employed to judge the relevance of a set of documents (e.g., TREC) based on a description of the information need. However, the same evaluation method cannot be applied to personalize Web search, because the same query issued by two different users may have different goals behind it. Thus, instead of having expert judges to evaluate the results with optimized information goals, we invite the users to examine the results and judge what they would consider as relevant for precision computation. A similar evaluation approach has also been used in [13]. We collect the experimental data from the prototype shown in Figure 1. The users were asked to perform relevance judgment on the top 100 results for each query by filling in a score for each search result to reflect the relevance of the search result to the query. We define three level of relevancy (Good, Fair and Poor) on documents. Documents rated as "Good" are considered relevant while those rated as "Poor" are considered irrelevant to the user's information need. Documents rated as "Fair" are treated as unlabeled. In our experiments, documents rated as "Good" are used to compute the Top-N precisions for different methods.

7.2 Evaluation of Search Context Discovery

We evaluate the performance of our search context discovery approach in terms of coherency (Precision), integrity (Recall) and overall performance (F-measure). Precision is defined as the fraction of true topic continuation in all the detected topic continuations. Recall is the fraction of true topic continuation that has been detected by the method. F-measure is a metric involving both precision and recall and it is defined as $(2 \times Precision \times Recall)/(Precision + Recall)$.

We first evaluate the effectiveness of fixed temporal cutoffs and the result is shown in Figure 4(a). The result demonstrates that a cutoff between 25 minutes to 30 minutes is a fairly good cutoff for balancing precision and recall because it achieves the highest F-measure. Thus, we choose 30 minutes cutoff to be the default value for context discovery methods involving temporal cutoff. The evaluation result of SERPs similarity threshold is presented in Figure 4(b). We observe that SERPs similarity thresholds between 0.5 and 0.9 demonstrate very high precision and low recall. In order to strike a balance between precision and recall,

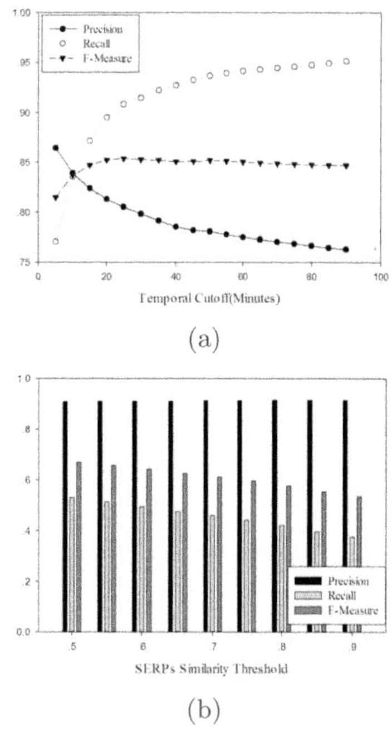

Figure 4: Temporal Cutoff and SERPs Threshold

we choose threshold 0.75 to be the default value for context discovery methods involving SERPs similarity.

The performance comparison of different context discovery methods is presented in Table 5. We observe that the temporal cutoff method tends to group both relevant and irrelevant queries together, and thus results in a high recall (92.73%), but low precision (78.48%). The low precision results from the risky assumption that queries within a period should be submitted to satisfy the same information need. The Single Reformulation method is solely based on the taxonomy proposed in [3] and demonstrates a high precision (93.13%). The high precision shows that, by utilizing strict reformulation rules, Single Reformulation can effectively detect query relatedness. However, a major drawback of Single Reformulation is that reformulation rules are too strict, and thus it cannot effectively discover similar queries (e.g., semantically rephrased queries) that are not covered by the reformulation rules, resulting low recall (66.33%). Low recall indicates that Single Reformulation tends to split a search context into several separated ones and therefore context integrity is damaged.

New Reformulation is the method based on the reformulation taxonomy in Figure 3. It yields fairly good precision (86.20%) and recall (84.40%). We observe that, by incorporating multiple reformulation, it boosts the recall by 18.07% while sacrifices 11.00% precision. The *Multiple Reformulation* type contributes a lot to the recall improvement. The method only using SERPs similarity is denoted by SERPs, which yields a precision of 91.23% and a recall of 44.14%. The result is consistent with the argument in [9], which reported that methods based on document overlap suffer from data sparseness problem, meaning that the chance for two queries to have common documents is very low. The method incorporating new reformulation taxonomy and SERPs similarity boosts the precision to 99.40%. However, it still suf-

Table 5: Comparison of Search Context Discovery Methods

Search Context Discovery Methods	Precision	Recall	F-measure	Capture Query Reformulation
Temporal Cutoff	78.48%	92.73%	0.8501	No
Single Reformulation	93.13%	66.33%	0.7748	Yes
New Reformulation	86.15%	84.38%	0.8525	Yes
SERPs	91.23%	44.15%	0.5950	No
SERPs and New Reformulation	86.15%	84.75%	0.8544	Yes
Temporal Cutoff and New Reformulation	96.89%	78.01%	0.8643	Yes
Temporal Cutoff and SERPs	99.41%	40.28%	0.5733	No
Temporal Cutoff, New Reformulation and SERPs	96.89%	78.36%	0.8664	Yes

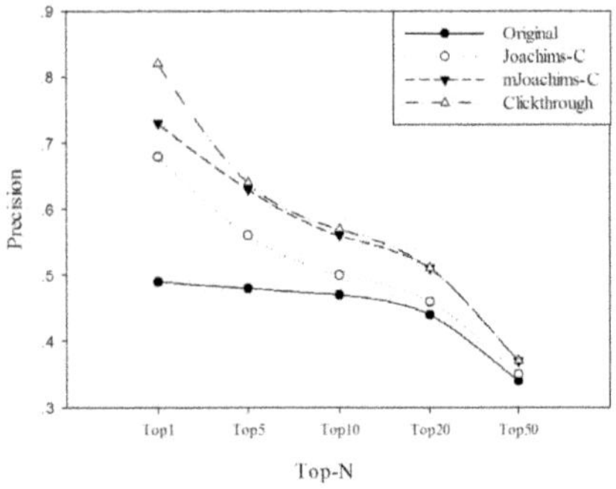

Figure 5: Effectiveness of Clickthrough-based Strategies

fers from the data sparseness problem, and thus yielding low recall (40.30%).

The method combining New Reformulation and temporal cutoff achieves good performance, yielding a precision of 96.89% and a recall of 78.01%. Compared with New reformulation, this approach improves the precision by 10.74% while sacrifices the recall by 6.37%. The result indicates that temporal cutoff is a good complementary factor for improving precision. The method based SERPs similarity and temporal cutoff shown the highest precision (99.41%), however, due to the data sparseness inherent from SERPs similarity, the method also has the lowest recall (40.28%).

Finally, by integrally using temporal cutoff, New Reformulation and SERPs similarity, the context discovery method proposed in Algorithm 1 yields a high precision (96.89%) while keeps a good recall (78.36%). It also achieves the highest F-measure. We use this method in our prototype and experiments.

7.3 Personalization with Clickthrough Strategies

Following the definitions in [8], the method embodying *Click* $>_q$ *Skip Above* is denoted as *Joachims-C* and the method embodying both *Click* $>_q$ *Skip Above* and *Click* $>_q$ *No-Click Next* is denoted as *mJoachims-C*. As the two methods have been proved useful in [8], we compare them with a new method taking into all the three clickthrough-based strategies. The new method is denoted by *Clickthrough*.

Figure 5 shows the Top-N precisions of the three methods. The Top-N precisions of all the three personalization methods have an obvious increase compared to the original ranking, meaning that all the obtained user profiles can correctly capture the users' preferences. Comparing to the original ranking, *Joachims-C* and *mJoachims-C* have a significant improvement in Top1 (19% and 24%), Top5 (18% and 25%) and Top10 precisions (3% and 9%). However, the improvement for Top20 (2% and 5%) and Top50 (1% and 3%) are not so obvious. We also observe that the extra preferences inferred by *mJoachims-C* help improve the personalization effectiveness. For example, if only the first search result is clicked, *Joachims-C* does not generate any preference judgment, while *mJoachims-C* can still deduce some preference judgments with *Click* $>_q$ *No-Click Next* to personalize the search results.

By introducing contextual clickthrough information, the *Clickthrough* method demonstrates significant improvement comparing to *Joachims-C* and *mJoachims-C* in term of Top1 precision(increased by 14% and 9%). We observe that if a user does not click on any search result for a particular query, *Joachims-C* and *mJoachims-C* then obtain no preference judgment, and thus no personalization can be done for the query. On the other hand, the *Clickthrough* method can still deduce preference judgment by utilizing *Click* $>_{q'}$ *No-Click Earlier*. There are two reasons for the performance improvement of incorporating *Click* $>_{q'}$ *No-Click Earlier*: (1) This strategy is robust to queries that result in no clickthrough; (2) It enables concepts raised from different queries comparable and therefore results in better information coverage. Utilization of the two information sources helps yield higher precision comparing to *Joachims-C* and *mJoachims-C*.

7.4 Personalization with Reformulation Strategies

We now study the effectiveness of each query reformulation-based strategy. In case the evaluation is biased by other factors, for each reformulation type, we sample 50 search contexts only containing the corresponding reformulation type.

We evaluate each strategy by comparing with the original ranking from search engine (denoted as Original) and the personalized ranking by integrally applied the three clickthrough based strategies (denoted as Clickthrough). The method of applying all three clickthrough-based strategies as well as the reformulation strategy under evaluation is denoted by (Clickthrough+ *corresponding* Strategy). The experiment results are shown in Figure 6. A special case is the *StripURL Strategy*, which is applied without any clickthrough-based strategies.

We observe that *Repeat Strategy* is effective in boosting the overall precisions. By applying *Repeat Strategy* reformulation, the precision is improved by 8.4% comparing to that without applying it for Top5 precision, 7.8% for Top10 precision, 5.5% for Top20 precision, and 4.5% for Top50 precision. The result validates that, by removing judgment inflation and judgment conflict, this strategy avoids distorting

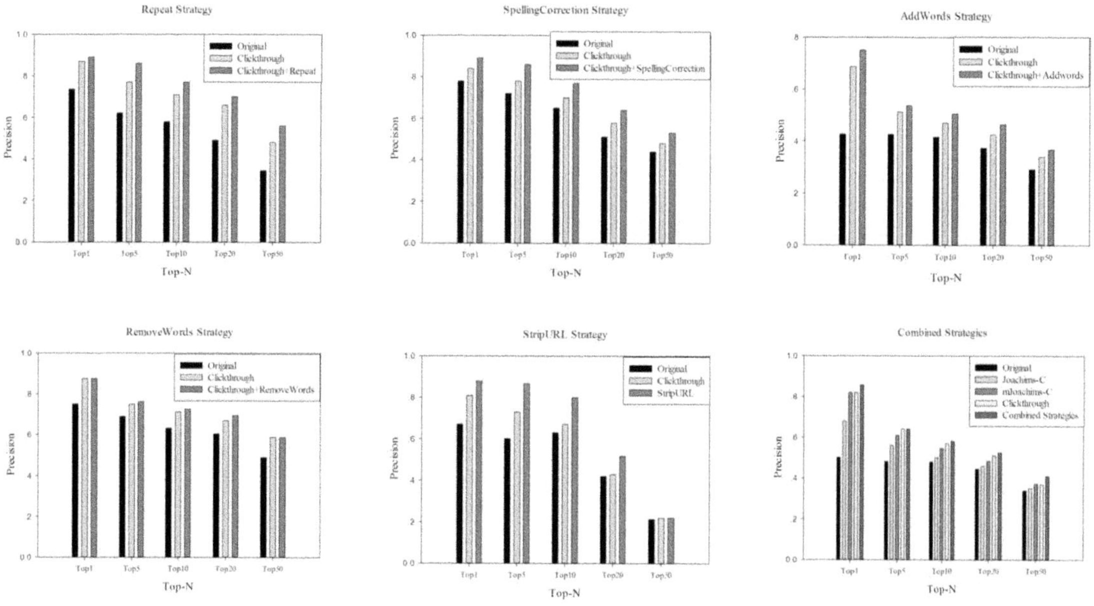

Figure 6: Effectiveness of Query Reformulation-based Strategies and Combined Strategy

the user's real search preference and thus boosts the overall personalization effectiveness, especially for Top1, Top5 and Top10 precision.

By combining *SpellingCorrection Strategy*, the Top1 and Top5 precisions have been improved by roughly 5% compared with that without applying this strategy. We also observe that the *Clickthrough* method is plagued by *Click* $>_{q'}$ *No-Click Earlier* for two reasons. First, for some queries with spelling mistakes, the backend search engine can successfully correct them and brings relevant results, in this case, the top two results of the first query may be relevant to the user's information need, even though no clickthrough is raised by the user. Second, if the spelling mistake cannot be corrected by the backend search engine, *Click* $>_{q'}$ *No-Click Earlier* generates preference judgment with some information raised from an irrelevant query and these judgment are not helpful to improve the result quality of current query. By applying this strategy, we avoid making such corrupted preference judgment and thus the personalization performance is improved accordingly.

AddWords Strategy is very helpful to boost the Top-N precision. By applying this strategy, the precision is improved by 6.25% comparing to that without it for Top1 precision, 2.5% for Top5 precision, 3.4% for Top10 precision, 4.1% for Top20 precision, and 2.8% for Top50 precision. It can significantly improve the Top1 precision, showing that when a user reformulates his/her query by adding some terms, these terms bear valuable information for inferring his/her preference. Thus, if a user clicks on the search results of a reformulated query, it is very likely that the reformulated query with the added terms successfully represents the user's actual information need and thus brings satisfactory search results.

RemoveWords Strategy is not as effective as the aforementioned strategies. The performance improvement obtained by applying this strategy is not obvious. For Top1 precision and Top5 precision, the improvement obtained by applying this strategy is less than 2%. The reason is that this strategy's effectiveness highly relies on the amount of concepts which are raised by the reformulated query and also contain the discarded terms. We observe that very few concepts raised from the new query contains the obsolete terms, and thus only a few additional preference judgments can be deduced for the personalization. The sparseness of preference judgment limits the effectiveness of this strategy.

Table 6: Example Queries and the Clickthroughs

Query	Clicked URL
q_1 =sun	oracle.com/sun
q_2 =sun microsystems	wikipedia.org/sun_micro..
q_3 =sun microsystems history	thocp.net/sun_micro..

StripURL Strategy is effective for improving the quality of Top1, Top5 and Top10 results. We observe that by applying this strategy, the personalized result outperforms the original ranking as well as that obtained by applying *Clickthrough* method. In the experiments, we also find that the extent of improvement relies on the popularity of the query. If the query itself is a popular navigational query, such as "www.apple.com", the original result obtained from the backend search engine is already very good and therefore the improvement is limited. However, if the query is not so popular, this strategy can effectively boost results with preferred URLs and thus brings a better personalization performance.

7.5 Personalization with Combined Strategies

In this section, we demonstrate the effectiveness of integrally applying the eight proposed strategies on fifty search contexts. We denote the combined strategies as *Combined Strategies* and compare it with the original ranking, *Joachims-C*, *mJoachims-C* and *Clickthrough*. The result is shown in Figure 6. We observe that the *Combined Strategies* can effectively improve the quality of the top-ranked search results and achieves the best performance in terms of Top-N precision.

Table 7: Example CAUPs for q_3="sun microsystems history"

Concept	Joachims-C	mJoachims-C	Clickthrough	Combined Strategies
company	0.4136	1.1500	1.1704	1.0272
oracle and sun	-0.2898	-0.4053	-0.4931	0.3205
solar system	-0.0318	-0.2293	-0.2754	-0.2220
technology	0.4873	0.4327	0.3713	0.2880
history	-0.1761	-0.5672	-0.4366	0.4118
sport	-0.3423	-0.2293	-0.4478	-0.4644

In order to gain a better insight for the profiles obtained from different approaches, we provide an example of the CAUPs obtained by different preference derivation methods. Table 6 shows the queries and the clickthroughs for a user who is searching for the history of "Sun Microsystems". Table 7 shows the user profile obtained from the four preference derivation methods running on the data in Table 6. We observe that the *Joachims-C*, *mJoachims-C*, and *Clickthrough* methods predicted the wrong preferences on the concepts "oracle and sun' and "history" due to the limited information coverage. The *Combined Strategies* can fix up the wrong preferences the concepts "oracle and sun' and "history". It predicts the correct preferences (i.e., positive preferences on "company", "oracle and sun", "technology", and "history", while negative preferences on "solar system" and "sport") from the input training data as shown in Table 6. Comparing to the existing *Joachims-C* and *mJoachims-C* methods, the extra cost of CAUP profiling is minimal. The extra cost comes from the additional preferences derived from the simple strategies (i.e. the third clickthrough-based strategy and query reformulation-based strategies), and it is minimal comparing to the overall cost spent in the training and ranking, which is roughly the same for all the strategies.

8. CONCLUSIONS

In this paper, we study the problem of using search contexts to facilitate concept-based search personalization. We introduce a new method that discovers search contexts from raw search query log. This method captures comprehensive information through one-pass of the query log and has good performance in keeping context coherency and integrity. Eight strategies are then developed to infer the user's conceptual preference from the search context. Through mining clickthroughs and query reformulations, the proposed strategies is able to capture the user's preference with higher accuracy than existing approaches that only consider individual query. We further adopt a learning-to-rank approach to seamlessly combine preference judgment derived from different strategies and update the *Context-Aware User Profile*, which is used to personalize the search results returned from the backend search engine. Empirical studies show that our proposed personalization framework yields higher Top-N precision compared to those without considering contextual information. Importantly, the extra cost of incorporating CAUP into personalized web searching is minimal, since we only incorporates a few more simple rules that manipulate the concept weight in the re-ranking process.

9. ACKNOWLEDGEMENTS

This work is partially supported by RGC GRF under grant number HKUST 618509.

10. REFERENCES

[1] Daniel Gayo-Avello, *A survey on session detection methods in query logs and a proposal for future evaluation*, Information Sciences **179** (2009).

[2] A. Herdagdelen and et al., *Generalized syntactic and semantic models of query reformulation*, Proc. of the SIGIR Conference, 2010.

[3] J. Huang and E. N. Efthimiadis, *Analyzing and evaluating query reformulation strategies in web search logs*, Proc. of the CIKM Conference, 2009.

[4] T. Joachims, *Optimizing search engines using clickthrough data*, Proc. of the SIGKDD Conference, 2002.

[5] T. Joachims and et al., *Evaluating the accuracy of implicit feedback from clicks and query reformulations in web search*, ACM TOIS **25** (2007).

[6] R. Jones and K. L. Klinkner, *Beyond the session timeout: automatic hierarchical segmentation of search topics in query logs*, Proc. of the CIKM Conference, 2008.

[7] Y. Ke, L. Deng, W. Ng, and D. L. Lee, *Web dynamics and their ramifications for the development of web search engines*, Computer Networks **50** (2006), no. 10.

[8] K. W. T Leung and D. L. Lee, *Deriving concept-based user profiles from search engine logs*, IEEE TKDE **22** (2010).

[9] K. W. T. Leung, W. Ng, and D. L. Lee, *Personalized concept-based clustering of search engine queries*, IEEE TKDE **20** (2008).

[10] J. Luxenburger, S. Elbassuoni, and G. Weikum, *Matching task profiles and user needs in personalized web search*, Proc. of the CIKM Conference, 2008.

[11] F. Radlinski and T. Joachims, *Query chains: learning to rank from implicit feedback*, Proc. of the SIGKDD Conference, 2005.

[12] X. Shen, B. Tan, and C. X. Zhai, *Context-sensitive information retrieval using implicit feedback*, Proc. of the SIGIR Conference, 2005.

[13] Jaime Teevan, Meredith Ringel Morris, and Steve Bush, *Discovering and using groups to improve personalized search*, Proc. of the ACM WSDM Conference, 2009.

[14] E. Voorhees and D. Harman, *Trec experiment and evaluation in information retrieval*, MIT Press, Cambridge, MA, 2005.

[15] B. Xiang, D. Jiang, J. Pei, X. Sun, E. Chen, and H. Li, *Context-aware ranking in web search*, Proc. of the SIGIR Conference, 2010.

A Framework for Personalized and Collaborative Clustering of Search Results

David C. Anastasiu
Texas State University-San Marcos
San Marcos, TX, USA
da1143@txstate.edu

Byron J. Gao
Texas State University-San Marcos
San Marcos, TX, USA
bgao@txstate.edu

David Buttler
Lawrence Livermore National Laboratory
Livermore, CA, USA
buttler1@llnl.gov

ABSTRACT

How to organize and present search results plays a critical role in the utility of search engines. Due to the unprecedented scale of the Web and diversity of search results, the common strategy of ranked lists has become increasingly inadequate, and clustering has been considered as a promising alternative. Clustering divides a long list of disparate search results into a few topic-coherent clusters, allowing the user to quickly locate relevant results by topic navigation. While many clustering algorithms have been proposed that innovate on the automatic clustering procedure, we introduce `ClusteringWiki`, the first prototype and framework for personalized clustering that allows direct user editing of the clustering results. Through a Wiki interface, the user can edit and annotate the membership, structure and labels of clusters for a personalized presentation. In addition, the edits and annotations can be shared among users as a mass-collaborative way of improving search result organization and search engine utility.

Categories and Subject Descriptors: H.3.3 [Information Storage and Retrieval]: Information Search and Retrieval – *Clustering*

General Terms: Algorithms, Design, Human Factors

Keywords: Personalized clustering, Search result clustering, Search result organization, Document clustering, Wiki, Mass collaboration, Social tagging, Information retrieval

1. INTRODUCTION

The way search results are organized and presented has a direct and significant impact on the utility of search engines. The common strategy has been using a flat ranked list, which works fine for homogeneous search results.

However, queries are inherently ambiguous and search results are often diverse with multiple senses. With a list presentation, the results on different sub-topics of a query will be mixed together. The user has to sift through many irrelevant results to locate those relevant ones.

With the rapid growth in the scale of the Web, queries have become more ambiguous than ever. For example, there are more than 20 entries in Wikipedia for different renown individuals under the name of Jim Gray and 74 entries for Michael Smith as of today. Consequently, the diversity of search results has increased to the point that we must consider alternative presentations, providing additional structure to flat lists so as to effectively minimize browsing effort and alleviate information overload [12, 25, 34, 5]. Over the years clustering has been accepted as the most promising alternative.

Clustering is the process of organizing objects into groups or clusters that exhibit internal cohesion and external isolation. Based on the common observation that it is much easier to scan a few topic-coherent groups than many individual documents, clustering can be used to categorize a long list of disparate search results into a few clusters such that each cluster represents a homogeneous sub-topic of the query. Meaningfully labeled, these clusters form a topic-wise non-predefined, faceted search interface, allowing the user to quickly locate relevant and interesting results. There is good evidence that clustering improves user experience and search result quality [23].

Given the significant potential benefits, search result clustering has received increasing attention in recent years from the communities of information retrieval, Web search and data mining. Many clustering algorithms have been proposed [12, 25, 34, 35, 36, 20, 32, 21]. In the industry, well-known cluster-based commercial search engines include Clusty (www.clusty.com), iBoogie (www.iboogie.com) and CarrotSearch (carrotsearch.com).

Despite the high promise of the approach and a decade of endeavor, cluster-based search engines have not gained prominent popularity, evident by Clusty's Alexa rank [13]. This is because clustering is known to be a hard problem, and search result clustering is particularly hard due to its high dimensionality, complex semantics and unique additional requirements beyond traditional clustering.

As emphasized in [32] and [5], the primary focus of search result clustering is NOT to produce optimal clusters, an objective that has been pursued for decades for traditional clustering with many successful automatic algorithms. Search result clustering is a highly user-centric task with *two unique additional requirements*. First, clusters must form interesting sub-topics or facets from the user's perspective. Second, clusters must be assigned informative, expressive, meaningful and concise labels. Automatic algorithms often fail to fulfill the human factors in the objectives of search result clustering, generating meaningless, awkward or nonsense cluster labels [5].

In this paper, we explore a completely different direc-

CIKM'11, October 24–28, 2011, Glasgow, Scotland, UK.

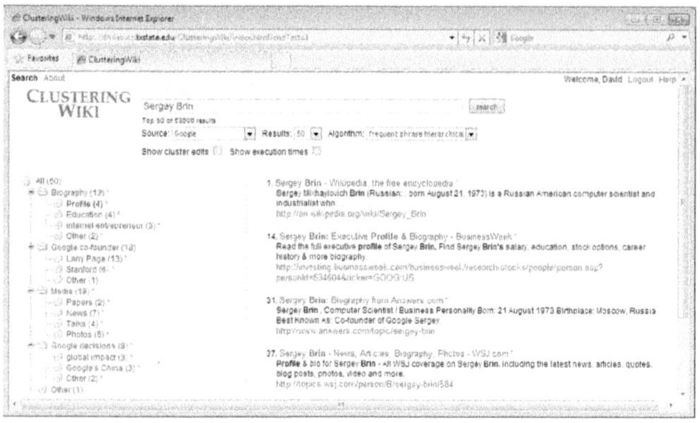

Figure 1: Snapshot of `ClusteringWiki`.

tion in tackling the problem of clustering search results, utilizing the power of direct user intervention and mass-collaboration. We introduce `ClusteringWiki`, the first prototype and framework for personalized clustering that allows direct *user* editing of the *clustering results*. This is in sharp contrast with existing approaches that innovate on the *automatic* algorithmic *clustering procedure*.

In `ClusteringWiki`, the user can edit and annotate the membership, structure and labels of clusters through a Wiki interface to personalize her search result presentation. Edits and annotations can be implicitly shared among users as a mass-collaborative way of improving search result organization and search engine utility. This approach is in the same spirit of the current trends in the Web, like Web 2.0, semantic web, personalization, social tagging and mass collaboration.

Clustering algorithms fall into two categories: partitioning and hierarchical. Regarding clustering results, however, a hierarchical presentation generalizes a flat partition. Based on this observation, `ClusteringWiki` handles both clustering methods smoothly by providing editing facilities for cluster hierarchies and treating partitions as a special case. In practice, hierarchical methods are advantageous in clustering search results because they construct a topic hierarchy that allows the user to easily navigate search results at different levels of granularity.

Figure 1 shows a snapshot of `ClusteringWiki`[1]. The left-hand *label panel* presents a hierarchy of cluster labels. The right-hand *result panel* presents search results for a chosen cluster label. A logged-in user can edit the current clusters by creating, deleting, modifying, moving or copying nodes in the cluster tree. Each edit will be validated against a set of predefined consistency constraints before being stored.

Designing and implementing `ClusteringWiki` pose non-trivial technical challenges. User edits represent user preferences or constraints that should be respected and enforced next time the same query is issued. Query processing is time-critical, thus efficiency must be given high priority in maintaining and enforcing user preferences. Moreover, complications also come from the dynamic nature of search results that constantly change over time.

Cluster editing takes user effort. It is essential that such user effort can be properly reused. `ClusteringWiki` considers two kinds of reuse scenarios, *preference transfer* and *preference sharing*. The former transfers user preferences from one query to similar ones, e.g., from "David J. Dewitt" to "David Dewitt". The latter aggregates and shares clustering preferences among users. Proper aggregation allows users to collaborate at a mass scale and "vote" for the best search result clustering presentation.

In social tagging, or collaborative tagging, users annotate Web objects, and such personal annotations can be used to collectively classify and find information. `ClusteringWiki` extends conventional tagging by allowing tagging of structured objects, which are clusters of search results organized in a hierarchy.

Contributions.

- We introduce `ClusteringWiki`, the first framework for personalized clustering in the context of search result organization. Unlike existing methods that innovate on the automatic clustering procedure, it allows direct user editing of the clustering results through a Wiki interface.
- In `ClusteringWiki`, user preferences are reused among similar queries. They are also aggregated and shared among users as a mass-collaborative way of improving search result organization and search engine utility.
- We implement a prototype for `ClusteringWiki`, perform experimental evaluation and a user study, and maintain the prototype as a public Web service.

Outline. The rest of the paper is organized as follows. Section 2 reviews the related work. Section 3 overviews the `ClusteringWiki` framework. Section 4 introduces the framework in detail. Section 5 presents experiments and user study. Section 6 concludes the paper.

2. RELATED WORK

Clustering. Clustering is the process of organizing objects into groups or clusters so that objects in the same cluster are as similar as possible, and objects in different clusters are as dissimilar as possible. Clustering algorithms fall into two main categories, partitioning and hierarchical. Partitioning algorithms, such as k-means [22], produce a flat partition of objects without any explicit structure that relate clusters to each other. Hierarchical algorithms, on the other hand, produce a more informative hierarchy of clusters called a dendrogram. Hierarchical algorithms are either agglomerative (bottom-up) such as AGNES [18], or divisive (top-down) such as DIANA [18].

Clustering in IR. As a common data analysis technique, clustering has a wide array of applications in machine learning, data mining, pattern recognition, information retrieval, image analysis and bioinformatics [14, 8]. In information retrieval and Web search, document clustering was initially proposed to improve search performance by validating the *cluster hypothesis*, which states that documents in the same cluster behave similarly with respect to relevance to information needs [26].

In recent years, clustering has been used to organize search results, creating a cluster-based search interface as an alternative presentation to the ranked list interface. The list interface works fine for most navigational queries, but is less effective for informational queries, which account for the majority of Web queries [4, 27]. In addition, the growing scale of

[1] dmlab.cs.txstate.edu/ClusteringWiki/index.html.

the Web and diversity of search results have rendered the list interface increasingly inadequate. Research has shown that the cluster interface improves user experience and search result quality [12, 35, 30, 16].

Search result clustering. One way of creating a cluster interface is to construct a static, off-line, pre-retrieval clustering of the entire document collection. However, this approach is ineffective because it is based on features that are frequent in the entire collection but irrelevant to the particular query [10, 28, 5]. It has been shown that query-specific, on-line, post-retrieval clustering, i.e., clustering search results, produces much superior results [12].

Scatter/Gather [12, 25] was an early cluster-based document browsing method that performs post-retrieval clustering on top-ranked documents returned from a traditional information retrieval system. The Grouper system [34, 35] (retired in 2000) introduced the well-known Suffix Tree Clustering (STC) algorithm that groups Web search results into clusters labeled by phrases extracted from snippets. It was also shown that using snippets is as effective as using whole documents. Carrot2 (www.carrot2.org) is an open source search result clustering engine that embeds STC as well as Lingo [24], a clustering algorithm based on singular value decomposition.

Other related work from the Web, IR and data mining communities exists. [36] explored supervised learning for extracting meaningful phrases from snippets, which are then used to group search results. [20] proposed a monothetic algorithm, where a single feature is used to assign documents to clusters and generate cluster labels. [32] investigated using past query history in order to better organize search results for future queries. [21] studied search result clustering for object-level search engines that automatically extract and integrate information on Web objects. [5] surveyed Web clustering engines and algorithms.

While all these methods focus on improvement in the automatic algorithmic procedure of clustering, `ClusteringWiki` employs a Wiki interface that allows direct user editing of the clustering results.

Clustering with user intervention. In machine learning, clustering is referred to as unsupervised learning. However, similar to `ClusteringWiki`, there are a few clustering frameworks that involve an active user role, in particular, semi-supervised clustering [2, 6] and interactive clustering [31, 15, 3] These frameworks are also motivated by the fact that clustering is too complex, and it is necessary to open the "black box" of the clustering procedure for easy understanding, steering and focusing. However, they differ from `ClusteringWiki` in that their focus is still on the clustering procedure, where they adopt a constraint clustering approach by transforming user feedback and domain knowledge into constraints (e.g., must-links and cannot-links) that are incorporated into the clustering procedure.

Search result annotation. Prototypes that allow user editing and annotation of search results exist. For example, U Rank by Microsoft (research.microsoft.com/en-us/projects/urank) and Searchwiki by Google (googleblog.blogspot.com/2008/11/searchwiki-make-search-your-own.html). Rants [9] implemented a prototype with additional interesting features including the incorporation of both absolute and relative user preferences. Similar to `ClusteringWiki`, these works pursue personalization as well as a mass-collaborative way of improving search engine utility. The difference is that they use the traditional flat list, instead of cluster-based, search interface.

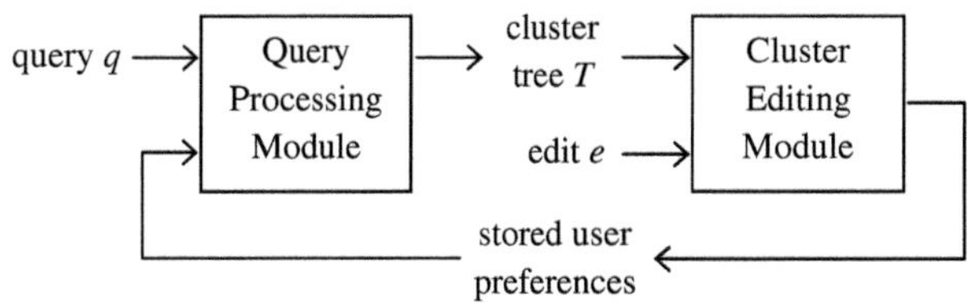

Figure 2: Main architecture of `ClusteringWiki`.

Tagging and social search. Social tagging, or collaborative tagging, allows users to create and associate objects with tags as a means of annotating and categorizing content. While users are primarily interested in tagging for their personal use, tags in a community collection tend to stabilize into power law distributions [11]. Collaborative tagging systems leverage this property to derive folksonomies and improve search [33]. In `ClusteringWiki` users tag clusters to organize search results, and the tags can be shared and utilized in the same way as in collaborative tagging. Since clusters are organized in a hierarchy, `ClusteringWiki` extends conventional tagging by allowing tagging of structured objects. Similar to tag suggestion in social tagging, the base clustering algorithm in `ClusteringWiki` provides suggested phrases for tagging clusters.

Social search is a mass-collaborative way of improving search performance. In contrast to established algorithmic or machine-based approaches, social search determines the relevance of search results by considering the content created or touched by users in the social graph. Example forms of user contributions include shared bookmarks or tagging of content with descriptive labels. Currently there are more than 40 such people-powered or community-powered social search engines, including Eurekster Swiki (www.eurekster.com), Mahalo (www.mahalo.com), Wikia (answers.wikia.com/wiki/Wikianswers), and Google social search (googleblog.blogspot.com/2009/10/introducing-google-social-search-i.html). Mass collaboration systems on the Web are categorized and discussed in [7].

3. OVERVIEW

In this section, we overview the main architecture and design principles of `ClusteringWiki`. Figure 2 shows the two key modules. The *query processing module* takes a query q and a set of stored user preferences as input to produce a cluster tree T that respects the preferences. The *cluster editing module* takes a cluster tree T and a user edit e as input to create/update a set of stored user preferences. Each user editing session usually involves a series of edits. The processing-editing cycle recurs over time.

Query processing. `ClusteringWiki` takes a query q from a user u and retrieves the search results R from a data source (e.g., Google). Then, it clusters R with a default clustering algorithm (e.g., frequent phrase hierarchical) to produce an initial cluster tree T_{init}. Then, it applies P, an applicable set of stored user preferences, to T_{init} and presents a modified cluster tree T that respects P.

Note that `ClusteringWiki` performs clustering. The modification should not alter R, the input data.

If the user u is logged-in, P will be set to $P_{q,u}$, a set of preferences for q previously specified by u. In case $P_{q,u} = \emptyset$, $P_{q',u}$ will be used on condition that q' is sufficiently close to q. If the user u is not logged-in, P will be set to $P_{q,U}$, a set of aggregated preferences for q previously specified by all users. In case $P_{q,U} = \emptyset$, $P_{q',U}$ will be used on condition that q' is sufficiently close to q.

In the cluster tree T, the internal nodes, i.e., non-leaf nodes, contain cluster labels and are presented on the left-hand *label panel*. Each label is a set of keywords. The leaf nodes contain search results, and the leaf nodes for a selected label are presented on the right-hand *result panel*. A search result can appear multiple times in T. The root of T represents the query q itself and is always labeled with *All*. When it is chosen, all search results will be presented on the result panel. Labels other than *All* represent the various, possibly overlapping, sub-topics of q. When there is no ambiguity, *internal node*, *label node*, *cluster label* and *label* are used interchangeably in the paper. Similarly, *leaf node*, *result node*, *search result* and *result* are used interchangeably.

Cluster editing. If logged-in, a user u can edit the cluster tree T for query q by creating, deleting, modifying, moving or copying nodes. User edits will be validated against a set C of consistency constraints before being written to $P_{q,u}$.

The set C contains predefined constraints that are specified on, for example, the size of clusters, the height of the tree and the length of labels. These constraints exist to maintain a favorable user interface for fast and intuitive navigation. The cluster tree T is *consistent* if it satisfies all the constraints in C.

By combining preferences in $P_{q,u}$ for all users who have edited the cluster tree T for query q, we obtain $P_{q,U}$, a set of aggregated preferences for query q. We use P_u to denote the collection of clustering preferences by user u for all queries, which is a set of sets of preferences such that $\forall q, P_{q,u} \in P_u$. We also use P_U to denote the collection of aggregated preferences by all users for all queries, which is a set of sets of aggregated preferences such that $\forall q, P_{q,U} \in P_U$. P_u and P_U are maintained over time and used by `ClusteringWiki` in processing queries for the user u.

Design principles. In a search result clustering engine, there are significant uncertainties from the data to the clustering algorithm. Wiki-facilitated personalization further adds substantial complications. Simplicity should be a key principle in designing such a complex system. `ClusteringWiki` adopts a simple yet powerful *path approach*.

With this approach, a cluster tree T is decomposed into a set of root-to-leaf *paths* that serve as independent editing components. A path always starts with *All* (root) and ends with some search result (leaf). In `ClusteringWiki`, maintenance, aggregation and enforcement of user preferences are based on simple path arithmetic. Moreover, the path approach is sufficiently powerful, being able to handle the finest user preference for a cluster tree.

In particular, each edit of T can be interpreted as operations on one or more paths. There are two primitive operations on a path p, *insertion* of p and *deletion* of p. A modification of p to p' is simply a deletion of p followed by an insertion of p'.

For each user u and each query q, `ClusteringWiki` maintains a set of paths $P_{q,u}$ representing the user edits from u for query q. Each path $p \in P_{q,u}$ can be either *positive* or *negative*. A positive path p represents an insertion of p, meaning that the user prefers to have p in T. A negative path $-p$ represents a deletion of p, meaning that the user prefers not to have p in T. Two *opposite* paths p and $-p$ will cancel each other out. The paths in $P_{q,u}$ may be added from multiple editing sessions at different times.

To aggregate user preferences for query q, `ClusteringWiki` first combines the paths in all $P_{q,u}$, $u \in U$, where U is the set of users who have edited the cluster tree of q. Then, certain statistically significant paths are selected and stored in $P_{q,U}$.

Suppose in processing query q, P is identified as the applicable set of paths to enforce. `ClusteringWiki` first combines the paths in P and the paths in T_{init}, where T_{init} is the initial cluster tree. Then, it presents the combined paths as a tree, which is the cluster tree T. The combination is straightforward. For each positive $p \in P$, if $p \notin T_{init}$, add p to T_{init}. For each negative $p \in P$, if $p \in T_{init}$, remove p from T_{init}.

Reproducibility. It is easy to verify that `ClusteringWiki` has the property of reproducing edited cluster trees. In particular, after a series of user edits on T_{init} to produce T, if T_{init} remains the same in a subsequent query, exactly the same T will be produced after enforcing the stored user preferences generated from the user edits on T_{init}.

4. FRAMEWORK

In this section, we introduce the `ClusteringWiki` framework in detail. In particular, we present the algorithms for the query processing and cluster editing modules and explain their main components.

4.1 Query Processing

Algorithm 1 presents the pseudocode for the query processing algorithm of `ClusteringWiki`. In the input, P_u and P_U are used instead of $P_{q,u}$ and $P_{q,U}$ for preference transfer purposes. In processing query q, it is likely that $P_{q,u} = \emptyset$ or $P_{q,U} = \emptyset$; then some applicable $P_{q',u} \in P_u$ or $P_{q',U} \in P_U$ can be used. The creation and maintenance of such user preferences will be discussed in Section 4.2. The output of the algorithm is a consistent cluster tree T.

Retrieving search results. Line 1 retrieves a set R of search results for query q from a chosen data source. The size of R is set to 50 by default and adjustable to up to 500. The available data sources include Google and Yahoo! Search APIs among others (see Section 5 for details). `ClusteringWiki` retrieves the results via *multi-threaded parallel requests*, which are much faster than sequential requests.

The combined titles and snippets of search results retrieved from the sources are preprocessed. In order to extract phrases, we implemented our own tokenizer that identifies whether a token is a word, numeric, punctuation mark, capitalized, all caps, etc. We then remove non-textual tokens and stop words, using the stop word list from the Apache Snowball package (www.docjar.com/html/api/org/apache/lucene/analysis/ snowball/SnowballAnalyzer.java.html). The tokens are then stemmed using the Porter (tartarus.org/ martin/PorterStemmer/) algorithm and indexed as terms. For each term, document frequency and collection frequency are computed and stored. A numeric id is also assigned to each

Algorithm 1 *Query processing*

Input: q, u, C, P_u and P_U: q is a query. u is a user. C is a set of consistency constraints. P_u is a collection of preferences by user u for all queries, where $\forall q, P_{q,u} \in P_u$. P_U is a collection of aggregated preferences for all queries, where $\forall q, P_{q,U} \in P_U$.

Output: T: a consistent cluster tree for the search results of query q.

1: retrieve a set R of search results for query q;
2: cluster R to obtain an initial cluster tree T_{init};
3: $P \leftarrow \emptyset$; //P is the set of paths to be enforced on T_{init}
4: **if** (u is logged-in) **then**
5:   $q' \leftarrow Trans(q, u)$;
6:   **if** ($q' \neq NULL$) **then**
7:     $P \leftarrow P_{q',u}$; //use applicable personal preferences
8:   **end if**
9: **else**
10:   $q' \leftarrow Trans(q, U)$;
11:   **if** ($q' \neq NULL$) **then**
12:     $P \leftarrow P_{q',U}$; //use applicable aggregated preferences
13:   **end if**
14: **end if**
15: $T \leftarrow T_{init}$; //initialize T, the cluster tree to present
16: clean P; //remove $p \in P$ if its result node is not in R
17: **for each** $p \in P$
18:   **if** (p is positive) **then**
19:     $T \leftarrow T \cup \{p\}$; //add a preferred path
20:   **else**
21:     $T \leftarrow T - \{p\}$; //remove a non-preferred path
22:   **end if**
23: **end for**
24: $trim(T, C)$; //make T consistent
25: $present(T)$; //present the set of paths in T as a tree

term in the document collection in order to efficiently calculate document similarity, identify frequent phrases, etc.

Building initial tree. Line 2 builds an initial cluster tree T_{init} with a built-in clustering algorithm. `ClusteringWiki` provides 4 such algorithms: k-means flat, k-means hierarchical, frequent phrase flat and frequent phrase hierarchical. The hierarchical algorithms recursively apply their flat counterparts in a top-down manner to large clusters.

The k-means algorithms follow a strategy that generates clusters before labels. They use a simple approach to generate cluster labels from titles of search results that are the closest to cluster centers. In order to produce stable clusters, the typical randomness in k-means due to the random selection of initial cluster centers is removed. The parameter k is heuristically determined based on the size of the input.

The frequent phrase algorithms follow a strategy that generates labels before clusters. They first identify frequent phrases using a suffix tree built in linear time by Ukkonen's algorithm. Then they select labels from the frequent phrases using a greedy set cover heuristic, where at each step a frequent phrase covering the most uncovered search results is selected until the whole cluster is covered or no frequent phrases remain. Then they assign each search result r to a label L if r contains the keywords in L. Uncovered search results are added to a special cluster labeled *Other*. These algorithms are able to generate very meaningful cluster labels with a couple of heuristics. For example, a sublabel

Algorithm 2 *Trans(q, u)*

Input: q, u and P_u: q is a query. u is a user. P_u is a collection of preferences by user u for all queries, where $\forall q, P_{q,u} \in P_u$.

Output: q': a query such that $P_{q',u}$ is applicable for q.

1: **if** ($P_{q,u}$ exists) **then**
2:   return q; //u has edited the cluster tree of q
3: **else**
4:   find q' s.t. $P_{q',u} \in P_u \wedge termSim(q, q')$ is the largest;
5:   **if** $termSim(q, q') \geq \delta_{ts}$ **then** //δ_{ts} is a threshold
6:     **if** $resultSim(q, q') \geq \delta_{rs}$ **then** //δ_{rs} is a threshold
7:       $P_{q,u} \leftarrow P_{q',u}$; //copy preferences from q' to q
8:       return q';
9:     **end if**
10:   **end if**
11: **end if**
12: return $NULL$;

cannot be a subset of a superlabel, in which case the sublabel is redundant.

`ClusteringWiki` smoothly handles flat clustering by treating partitions as a special case of trees. The built-in clustering algorithms are meant to serve their basic functions. The focus of the paper is not to produce, but to modify, the initial cluster trees.

Determining applicable preferences. Lines 3 $\sim$ 14 determine P, a set of applicable paths to be enforced on T_{init}. Two cases are considered. If the user u is logged-in, P will use some set from P_u representing personal preferences of u (lines 4 $\sim$ 8). Otherwise, P will use some set from P_U representing aggregated preferences (lines 9 $\sim$ 14). The subroutine $Trans()$ determines the actual set to use if any.

The pseudocode of $Trans(q, u)$ is presented in Algorithm 2. Given a user u and a query q, it returns a query q', whose preferences stored in $P_{q',u}$ are applicable to query q. In the subroutine, two similarity measures are used. *Term similarity*, $termSim(q, q')$, is the Jaccard coefficient that compares the terms of q and q'. *Result similarity*, $resultSim(q, q')$, is the Jaccard coefficient that compares the URLs of the top k (e.g., $k = 10$) results of q and q'. This calculation requires that the URLs of the top k results for q' be stored.

To validate q', both similarity values need to pass their respective thresholds δ_{ts} and δ_{rs}. Obviously, the bigger the thresholds, the more conservative the transfer. Setting the thresholds to 1 shuts down preference transfer. Instead of thresholding, another reasonable way of validation is to provide a ranked list of similar queries and ask the user for confirmation.

The subroutine in Algorithm 2 first checks if $P_{q,u}$ exists (line 1). If it does, preference transfer is not needed and q is returned (line 2). In this case, u has already edited the cluster tree for query q and stored the preferences in $P_{q,u}$.

Otherwise, the subroutine tries to find q' such that $P_{q',u}$ is applicable (lines 4 $\sim$ 11). To do so, it first finds q' such that $P_{q',u}$ exists and $termSim(q, q')$ is the largest (line 4). Then, it continues to validate the applicability of q' by checking if $termSim(q, q')$ and $resultSim(q, q')$ have passed their respective thresholds (lines 5 *sim* 6). If so, user preferences for q' will be copied to q (line 7), and q' will be returned (line 8). Otherwise, $NULL$ will be returned (line 11), indicating no applicable preferences exist for query q.

The preference copying (line 7) is important for the correctness of ClusteringWiki. Otherwise, suppose there is a preference transfer from q' to q, where $P_{q,u} = \emptyset$ and $P_{q',u}$ has been applied on T_{init} to produce T. Then, after some editing from u, T becomes T' and the corresponding edits are stored in $P_{q,u}$. Then, this $P_{q,u}$ will be used the next time the same query q is issued by u. However, $P_{q,u}$ will not be able to bring an identical T_{init} to the expected T'. It is easy to verify that line 7 fixes the problem and ensures reproducibility.

$Trans(q, U)$ works in the same way. Preference transfer is an important component of ClusteringWiki. Cluster editing takes user effort and there are an infinite number of queries. It is essential that such user effort can be properly reused.

Enforcing applicable preferences. Back to Algorithm 1, lines 15 $\sim$ 23 enforce the paths of P on T_{init} to produce the cluster tree T. The enforcement is straightforward. First P is cleaned by removing those paths whose result nodes are not in the search result set R (line 16). Recall that ClusteringWiki performs clustering. It should not alter the input data R. Then, the positive paths in P are the ones u prefers to see in T, thus they are added to T (lines 18 $\sim$ 19). The negative paths in P are the ones u prefers not to see in T, thus they are removed from T (lines 20 $\sim$ 21). If $P = \emptyset$, there are no applicable preferences and T_{init} will not be modified.

Trimming and Presenting T. The cluster tree T must satisfy a set C of predefined constraints. Some constraints maybe violated after applying P to T_{init}. For example, adding or removing paths may result in small clusters that violate constraints on the size of clusters. In line 24, subroutine $trim(T, C)$ is responsible for making T consistent, e.g., by re-distributing the paths in the small clusters. We will discuss the constraint set C in detail in Section 4.2.

In line 25, subroutine $present(T)$ presents the set of paths in T as a cluster tree on the search interface. The labels can be expanded or collapsed. The search results for a chosen label are presented in the result panel in their original order when retrieved from the source. Relevant terms corresponding to current and ancestor labels in search results are highlighted.

Sibling cluster labels in the label panel are ordered by lexicographically comparing the lists of original ranks of their associated search results. For example, let A and D be two sibling labels as in Figure 3, where A contains P_1, P_2, P_3 and P_4 and D contains P_1 and P_5. Suppose that i in P_i indicates the original rank of P_i from the source. By comparing two lists $< 1, 2, 3, 4 >$ and $< 1, 5 >$, we put A in front of D. "Other" is a special label that is always listed at the end behind all its siblings.

Discussion. As [17] suggested, the subset of web pages visited by employees in an Enterprise is centered around the company's business objectives. Additionally, employees share a common vocabulary describing the objects and tasks encountered in day to day activities. ClusteringWiki can be even more effective in this environment as user preferences can be better aggregated and utilized.

4.2 Cluster Editing

Before explaining the algorithm handling user edits, we first introduce the essential consistency constraints for cluster trees and the primitive user edits.

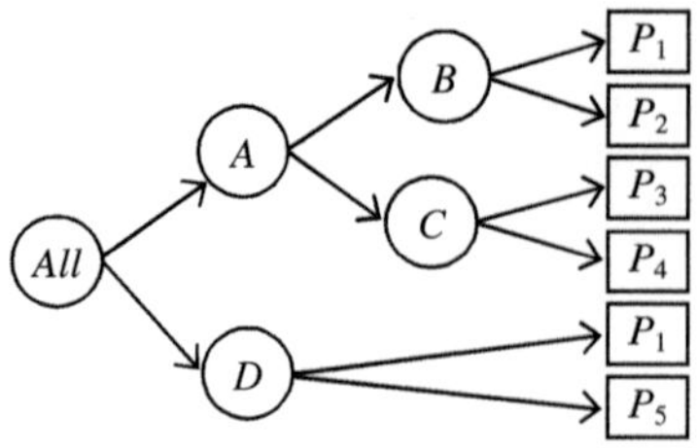

Figure 3: Example cluster tree.

Essential consistency constraints. Predefined consistency constraints exist to maintain a favorable user interface for fast and intuitive navigation. They can be specified on any structural component of the cluster tree T. In the following, we list the essential ones.

- *Path constraint*: Each path of cluster tree T must start with the root labeled *All* and end with a leaf node that is a search result. In case there are no search results returned, T is empty without paths.

- *Presence constraint*: Each initial search result must be present in T. It implies that deletion of paths should not result in absence of any search result in T.

- *Homogeneity constraint*: A label node in T must not have heterogeneous children that combine cluster labels with search results. This constraint is also used in other clustering engines such as Clusty and Carrot2.

- *Height constraint*: The height of T must be equal or less than a threshold, e.g., 4.

- *Label length constraint*: The length of each label in T must be equal or less than a threshold.

- *Branching constraint*: We call a label node a *bottom label node* if it directly connects to search results. Each non-bottom label node must have at least T_n children. Each non-special bottom label node must have at least T_m children. *Other* is a special bottom label node that may have less than T_m children. *All*, when being a bottom label, could also have less than T_m children in case there are insufficient search results. By default both T_n and T_m are set to 2 in ClusteringWiki as in Clusty.

Primitive user edits. ClusteringWiki implements the following categories of atomic primitive edits that a logged-in user can initiate in the process of tree editing. Each edit e is associated with P_e and NP_e, the set of paths to be inserted to the tree and the set of paths to be deleted from the tree after e.

- e_1: copy a label node to another non-bottom label node as its child. Note that it is allowed to copy a parent label node to a child label node.

  Example: in Figure 3, we can copy D to A. For this edit, $P_e = \{All \rightarrow A \rightarrow D \rightarrow P_1, All \rightarrow A \rightarrow D \rightarrow P_5\}$. $NP_e = \emptyset$ for any edit of this type.

Algorithm 3 *Cluster editing*

Input: q, u, T, C, $P_{q,u}$, $P_{q,U}$ and e: q is a query. u is a user. T is a cluster tree for q. C is a set of consistency constraints for T. $P_{q,u}$ is a set of paths representing the preferences by u for q. $P_{q,U}$ is a set of paths representing the aggregated preferences for q. e is an edit by u on T.

Output: updated T, $P_{q,u}$ and $P_{q,U}$

```
1: if (pre-validation fail) then
2:     return;
3: end if
4: identify Pe;
5: identify NPe;
6: if (validation fail) then
7:     return;
8: end if
9: update T;
10: add Pe as positive paths to Pq,u;
11: add NPe as negative paths to Pq,u;
12: update Pq,U;
```

- e_2: copy a result node to a bottom label node.

  Example: in Figure 3, we can copy P_3 to D, but not to A, which is not a bottom label node. For this edit, $P_e = \{All \rightarrow D \rightarrow P_3\}$. $NP_e = \emptyset$ for any edit of this type.

- e_3: modify a non-root label node.

  Example: in Figure 3, we can modify D to E. For this edit, $P_e = \{All \rightarrow E \rightarrow P_1, All \rightarrow E \rightarrow P_5\}$ and $NP_e = \{All \rightarrow D \rightarrow P_1, All \rightarrow D \rightarrow P_5\}$.

- e_4: delete a non-root node, which can be either a label node or a result node.

  Example: in Figure 3, we can delete P_5. For this edit, $NP_e = \{All \rightarrow D \rightarrow P_5\}$. $P_e = \emptyset$ for any edit of this type.

- e_5: create a label node, which can be either a non-bottom or bottom label node. In particular, recursive creation of non-bottom labels is a way to add levels to cluster trees.

  Example: in Figure 3, we can add E as parent of D. For this edit, $P_e = \{All \rightarrow E \rightarrow D \rightarrow P_1, All \rightarrow E \rightarrow D \rightarrow P_5\}$ and $NP_e = \{All \rightarrow D \rightarrow P_1, All \rightarrow D \rightarrow P_5\}$.

The editing framework results in several *favorable properties*. Firstly, the primitive user edits are such that, with a series of edits, a user can produce *any* consistent cluster tree. Secondly, since e_1 only allows a label node to be placed under a non-bottom node and e_2 only allows a result node to be placed under a bottom node, the homogeneity constraint will not be violated after any edit given the consistency of T before the edit. Thirdly, the framework uses *eager* validation, where validation is performed right after each edit, compared to *lazy* validation, where validation is performed in the end of the editing process. Eager validation is more user-friendly and less error-prone in implementation.

Note that, user editing can possibly generate *empty labels*, i.e., labels that do not contain any search results and thus not on any path. Such labels will be trimmed.

To add convenience, `ClusteringWiki` also implements several other types of edits. For example, move (instead of copy as in e_1) a label node to another non-bottom label node as its child, or move (instead of copy as in e_2) a result node to a bottom label node. Such a move edit can be considered as a copy edit followed by a delete edit.

Editing algorithm. Algorithm 3 presents the pseudocode of the cluster editing algorithm in `ClusteringWiki` for a single edit e, where e can be any type of edit from e_1 to e_4.

Lines 1 $\sim$ 3 perform pre-validation of e to see if it is in violation of consistency constraints. Violations can be caught early for certain constraints on certain edits, for example, the label length constraint on e_1 type of edits. If pre-validation fails, the algorithm returns immediately.

Otherwise, the algorithm continues with lines 4 $\sim$ 5 that identify P_e and NP_e. Then, lines 6 $\sim$ 8 perform full validation of e against C, the set of consistency constraints. If the validation fails, the algorithm returns immediately.

Otherwise, e is a valid edit and T is updated (line 9). Then, the personal user preferences are stored by adding P_e and NP_e to $P_{q,u}$ as positive paths and negative paths respectively (lines 10 $\sim$ 11). In adding these paths, the opposite paths in $P_{q,u}$ cancel each other out. In line 12, the aggregated preferences stored in $P_{q,U}$ are updated. We further discuss preference aggregation in the following.

Preference sharing. Preference sharing in `ClusteringWiki` is in line with the many social-powered search engines as a mass-collaborative way of improving search utility. In `ClusteringWiki`, U is considered as a special user and $P_{q,U}$ stores the aggregated user preferences.

In particular, we use $P^0_{q,U}$ to record the paths specified for query q by all users. Each path $p \in P^0_{q,U}$ has a *count* attribute, recording the total number of times that p appears in any $P_{q,u}$. All paths in $P^0_{q,U}$ are grouped by leaf nodes. In other words, all paths that end with the same search result are in the same group. For each group, we keep track of two *best* paths: a positive one with the most count and a negative one with the most count. We mark a best path if its count passes a predefined threshold. All the marked paths constitute $P_{q,U}$, the set of aggregated paths that are used in query processing. Note that, here `ClusteringWiki` adopts a conservative approach, making use of at most one positive path and one negative path for each search result.

Editing interface. Cluster editing in `ClusteringWiki` is primarily available through context menus attached to label and result nodes. Context menus are context aware, displaying only those operations that are valid for the selected node. For example, the *paste result* operation will not be displayed unless the selected node is a bottom label node and a result node was previously copied or cut. This effectively implements pre-validation of cluster edit operations by not allowing the user to choose invalid tasks.

Users can drag and drop a result node or cluster label in addition to cutting/copying and pasting to perform a move/copy operation. A label node will be tagged with an icon if the item being dragged can be pasted within that node. An item that is dropped outside a label node in which it could be pasted simply returns to its original location.

5. EVALUATION

`ClusteringWiki` was implemented as an AJAX-enabled Java Enterprise Edition 1.5 application. The prototype is maintained on an average PC with Intel Pentium 4 3.4 GHz CPU and 4Gb RAM running Apache Tomcat 6.

5.1 Methodology and Metrics

We performed two series of experiments: system evaluation and utility evaluation. The former focused on the correctness and efficiency of our implemented prototype. The latter, our main experiments, focused on the effectiveness of `ClusteringWiki` in improving search performance.

Data sources. Multiple data sources were used in our empirical evaluation, including Google AJAX Search API (code.google.com/apis/ajaxsearch), Yahoo! Search API (developer.yahoo.com/search/web/webSearch.html), and local Lucene indexes built on top of the New York Times Annotated Corpus [29] and several datasets from the TIPSTER (disks 1-3) and TREC (disks 4-5) collections (www.nist.gov/tac/data/data_desc.html). The Google API can retrieve a maximum of 8 results per request and a total of 64 results per query. The Yahoo! API can retrieve a maximum of 100 results per request and a total of 1000 results per query. Due to user licence agreements, the New York Times, TIPSTER and TREC datasets are not available publicly.

System evaluation methodology. For system evaluation of `ClusteringWiki`, we focused on *correctness* and *efficiency*. We tested the correctness by manually executing a number of functional and system tests designed to test every aspect of application functionality. These tests included cluster reproducibility, edit operation pre-validations, cluster editing operations, convenience features, applying preferences, preference transfer, preference aggregation, etc.

In order to have repeatable search results for same queries, we used the stable New York Times data source. We chose queries that returned at least 200 results.

We evaluated system efficiency by monitoring query processing time in various settings. In particular, we considered:

- 2 data sources: Yahoo! and New York Times
- 5 different numbers of retrieved search results: 100, 200, 300, 400, 500
- 2 types of clusterings: flat (F) and hierarchical (H)

For each of the combinations, we executed 5 queries, each twice. The queries were chosen such that at least 500 search results would be returned. For each query, we monitored 6 portions of execution that constitute the total query response time:

- Retrieving search results
- Preprocessing retrieved search results
- Initial clustering by a built-in algorithm
- Applying preferences to the initial cluster tree
- Presenting the final cluster tree
- Other (e.g., data transfer time between server and browser)

For the New York Times data source, the index was loaded into memory to simulate the server side search engine behavior. The time spent on applying preferences depends on the number of applicable stored paths. For each query, we made sure that at least half the number of retrieved results existed in a modified path, which is a practical upper-bound on the number of user edits on the clusters of a query.

Utility evaluation methodology. For utility evaluation, we focused on the *effectiveness* of `ClusteringWiki` in improving search performance, in particular, the time users spent to locate a certain number of relevant results. The experiments were conducted through a user study with 22 *paid* participants. The participants were primarily undergraduate, with a few graduate, colleage students.

We compared 4 different search result presentations:

- Ranked list (RL): search results were not clustered and presented as a traditional ranked list.
- Initial clustering (IC): search results were clustered by a default built-in algorithm (frequent phrase hierarchical).
- Personalized clustering (PC): search result clustering was personalized by a logged-in user after a series of edits, taking on average 1 and no more than 2 minutes per query.
- Aggregated clustering (AC): search result clustering was based on aggregated edits from on average 10 users.

Navigational queries seek the website or home page of a single entity that the user has in mind. The more common [4, 27] informational queries seek general information on a broad topic. The ranked list interface works fine for the former in general but is less effective for the latter, which is where clustering can be helpful [23]. In practice, a user may explore a varied number (e.g., 5 or 10) of relevant results for an informational query. Thus, we considered 2 types of informational queries. In addition, we argue that for some *deep* navigational queries where the desired page "hides" deep in a ranked list, clustering can still be helpful by skipping irrelevant results. Thus, we also considered such queries:

- R_{10}: Informational. To locate any 10 relevant results.
- R_5: Informational. To locate any 5 relevant results.
- R_1: Navigational. To locate 1 pre-specified result.

For each query type, 10 queries were executed, 5 on Google results and 5 on the AP Newswire dataset from disk 1 of the TIPSTER corpus. The AP Newswire queries were chosen from TREC topics 50-150, ensuring that they returned at least 15 relevant results within the first 50 results. For R_1 queries, the topic descriptions were modified to direct the user to a single result that is relatively low-ranked to make the queries "deep". Google queries were chosen from topics that participants were familiar with. All queries returned at least 50 results. These queries and their descriptions and narratives can be found at [1].

Each user was given 15 queries, 5 for each query type. Each query was executed 4 times for the 4 presentations being compared. Thus, in total each user executed $15 \times 4 = 60$ queries. For each execution, the user exploration effort was computed.

User effort was the metric we used to measure the search result exploration effort exerted by a user in fulfilling her information need. [19] used a similar metric under a probabilistic model instead of user study. Assuming both search results and cluster labels are scanned and examined in a top-down manner, user effort Ω can be computed as follows:

- Add 1 point to Ω for each examined search result.
- Add 0.25 point to Ω for each examined cluster label. This is because labels are much shorter than snippets.
- Add 0.25 point to Ω for each *uncertain result.* Based on our assumption, all results before a tagged relevant result are examined. However, results after the last tagged result remain uncertain. For linked list presentation, there is no uncertainty because the exploration ends at a tagged result due to the way the queries are chosen (more relevant results than needed).

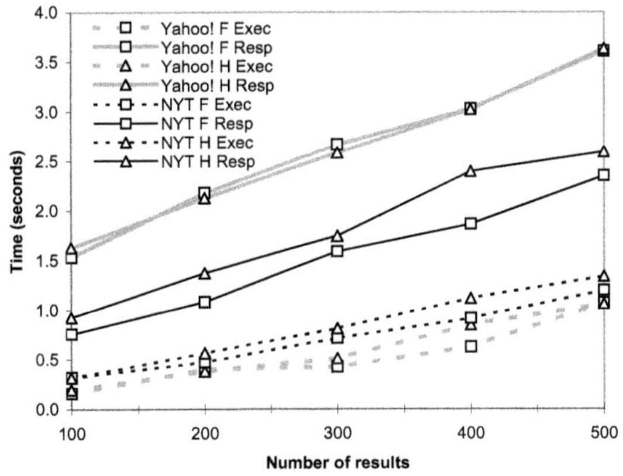

Figure 4: Efficiency evaluation.

Uncertainty could occur for results within a chosen cluster C. As an effective way of utilizing cluster labels, most users would partially examine a few results in C to evaluate the relevance of C itself. If they think C is relevant, they must have found and tagged some relevant results in C. If they think C is irrelevant, they would ignore the cluster and quickly move to the next label. Thus, each uncertain result has a probability of being examined. Based on our observation for this particular user study, we empirically used 0.25 for this probability.

5.2 System Evaluation Results

For correctness, all functional and system tests were executed successfully. A detailed description of these tests can be found at [1]. In the following, we focus on the efficiency evaluation results.

We recorded and averaged (over 10 queries) the runtime in seconds for all 6 portions of total response time. In addition, we also computed the average *total execution time*, which includes preprocessing, initial clustering, applying preferences and presenting the final tree. This is the time that our prototype is responsible for. The remaining time is irrelevant to the way our prototype is designed and implemented. While the details are reported in [1], Figure 4 shows the trends of the average total execution time (Exec in the figure) and response time (Resp) for both flat (F) and hierarchical (H) presentations over 2 sources of Yahoo! (Yahoo!) and New York Times (NYT). From the figure we can see that:

- Response and execution time trends are linear, testifying to the scalability of our prototype. In particular, for both flat and hierarchical clustering, the total execution time is about 1 second for 500 results and 0.4 second for 200 results from either source. Note that most existing clustering search engines, e.g., iBoogie (www.iboogie.com) and CarrotSearch (carrotsearch.com), cluster 100 results by default and 200 at maximum. Clusty (www.clusty.com) clusters 200 results by default and 500 at maximum.
- Hierarchical presentation (H) takes comparable times to flat presentation (F), showing that recursive generation of hierarchies does not add significant cost to efficiency.
- There is a bigger discrepancy between response and execution times for the Yahoo! data source compared to New York Times, suggesting a significant efficiency improvement by integrating our prototype with the data sources.

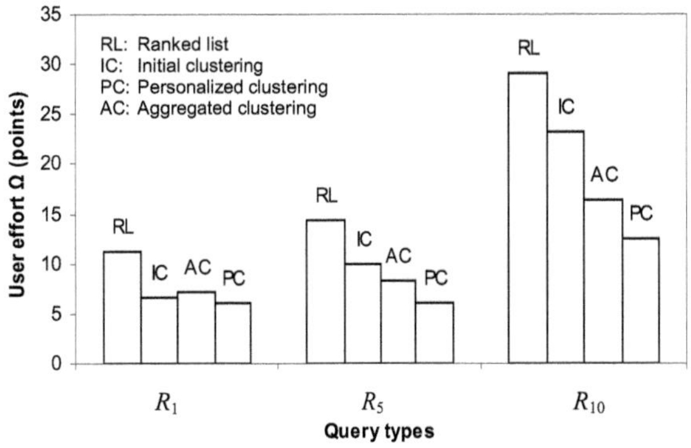

Figure 5: Utility evaluation on Google data source.

- Execution times for Yahoo! are shorter than New York Times due to the shorter titles and snippets.

In addition, we observe (and report in [1] with supporting data) that applying preferences takes less than 1/10 second in all test cases, which certifies the efficiency of our "path approach" for managing preferences. Moreover, presenting the final tree takes the majority (roughly 80%) of the total execution time, which can be improved by using alternate user interface technologies.

5.3 Utility Evaluation Results

Figure 5 shows the averaged user effort (over $22 \times 5 = 110$ queries) for each of the 4 presentations (RL, IL, PC, AC) and each of the query types (R_1, R_5, R_{10}) on the Google data source. Similar trends can be observed from the AP Newswire data source (see [1] for details). From the figure we can see that:

- Clustering saves user effort in informational and deep navigational queries, with personalized clustering the most effective, saving up to 50% of user effort.
- Aggregated clustering also significantly benefits, although it is not as effective as personalized clustering. However, it is "free" in the sense that it does not take user editing effort, and it does not require user login.

  In evaluating aggregated clustering, we made sure that the users using the aggregated clusters were not the ones who edited them.
- The effectiveness of clustering is related to how "deep" the relevant results are. The lower they are ranked, the more effective clustering is because more irrelevant results can be skipped.

The hierarchy of cluster labels plays a central role in the effectiveness of clustering search engines. From the data we have collected as well as the user feedback, we observe that:

- Cluster labels should be short and in the range of 1 to 4 terms, with 2 and 3 the best. The total levels of the hierarchy should be limited to 3 or 4.
- There are two types of cluster edits, (1) assigning search results to labels and (2) editing the hierarchy of labels. Both types are effective for personalized clustering. However, they respond differently for aggregated clustering. For type 1 edits, there is a ground truth (in a loose sense) for each assignment that users tend to agree on. Such edits are easy to aggregate and be collaboratively utilized.

For type 2 edits, it can be challenging (and a legitimate research topic) to aggregate hierarchies because many edited hierarchies can be good but in diverse ways. A good initial clustering (e.g., frequent phrase hierarchical) can alleviate the problem by reducing the diversity.

As part of the user study, we also surveyed on the effectiveness of general, personalized and aggregated clustering in helping with search result exploration. On a scale of 1 to 10 with 10 as the best, users responded with an average rating of 8.21. Most users found `ClusteringWiki` efficient and useful in reducing their search effort.

6. CONCLUSION

Search engine utility has been significantly hampered due to the ever-increasing information overload. Clustering has been considered a promising alternative to ranked lists in improving search result organization. Given the unique human factor in search result clustering, traditional automatic algorithms often fail to generate clusters and labels that are interesting and meaningful from the user's perspective. In this paper, we introduced `ClusteringWiki`, the first prototype and framework for personalized clustering, utilizing the power of direct user intervention and mass-collaboration. Through a Wiki interface, the user can edit the membership, structure and labels of clusters. Such edits can be aggregated and shared among users to improve search result organization and search engine utility.

There are many interesting directions for future work, from fundamental semantics and functionalities of the framework to convenience features, user interface and scalability. For example, in line with social browsing, social network can be utilized in preference aggregation.

7. ACKNOWLEDGMENTS

This work (LLNL-CONF-461652) was performed under the auspices of the U.S. Department of Energy by Lawrence Livermore National Laboratory under Contract DE-AC52-07NA27344. It was partially supported by the Texas Norman Hackerman Advanced Research Program under Grant No.003656-0035-2009.

8. REFERENCES

[1] D. C. Anastasiu, D. Buttler, and B. J. Gao. Clusteringwiki technical report. *dmlab.cs.txstate.edu/ClusteringWiki/pdf/cw.pdf.*

[2] S. Basu, M. Bilenko, and R. J. Mooney. A probabilistic framework for semi-supervised clustering. In *KDD*, 2004.

[3] R. Bekkerman, H. Raghavan, J. Allan, and K. Eguchi. Interactive clustering of text collections according to a user-specified criterion. In *IJCAI*, 2007.

[4] A. Broder. A taxonomy of web search. *SIGIR Forum*, 36(2):3–10, 2002.

[5] C. Carpineto, S. Osiński, G. Romano, and D. Weiss. A survey of web clustering engines. *ACM Comput. Surv.*, 41(3):1–38, 2009.

[6] D. Cohn, A. K. McCallum, and T. Hertz. *Constrained Clustering: Advances in Algorithms, Theory, and Applications*, chapter Semi-Supervised Clustering with User Feedback. Chapman and Hall/CRC, 2009.

[7] A. Doan, R. Ramakrishnan, and A. Halevy. Mass collaboration systems on the world-wide web. *Communications of the ACM*, to appear.

[8] B. S. Everitt, S. Landau, and M. Leese. *Cluster analysis.* Oxford University Press, 2001.

[9] B. J. Gao and J. Jan. Rants: a framework for rank editing and sharing in web search. In *WWW*, 2010.

[10] A. Griffiths, H. C. Luckhurst, and P. Willett. Using interdocument similarity information in document retrieval systems. *Journal of the American Society for Information Sciences*, 37(1):3–11, 1986.

[11] R. V. S. H. Halpin H. The complex dynamics of collaborative tagging. *WWW*, 2007.

[12] M. A. Hearst and J. O. Pedersen. Reexamining the cluster hypothesis: scatter/gather on retrieval results. In *SIGIR*, 1996.

[13] A. Iskold. Overview of clustering and clusty search engine. *www.readwriteweb.com/archives/overview_of_clu.php*, 2007.

[14] A. K. Jain and R. C. Dubes. *Algorithms for clustering data.* Prentice-Hall, 1988.

[15] X. Ji and W. Xu. Document clustering with prior knowledge. In *SIGIR*, 2006.

[16] M. Käki. Findex: search result categories help users when document ranking fails. In *CHI*, 2005.

[17] A. Kale, T. Burris, B. Shah, T. L. P. Venkatesan, L. Velusamy, M. Gupta, and M. Degerattu. icollaborate: harvesting value from enterprise web usage. In *SIGIR*, 2010.

[18] L. Kaufman and P. Rousseeuw. *Finding groups in data: an introduction to cluster analysis.* John Wiley & Sons, 1990.

[19] J. Koren, Y. Zhang, and X. Liu. Personalized interactive faceted search. In *WWW*, 2008.

[20] K. Kummamuru, R. Lotlikar, S. Roy, K. Singal, and R. Krishnapuram. A hierarchical monothetic document clustering algorithm for summarization and browsing search results. In *WWW*, 2004.

[21] J. Lee, S.-w. Hwang, Z. Nie, and J.-R. Wen. Query result clustering for object-level search. In *KDD*, 2009.

[22] J. MacQueen. Some methods for classification and analysis of multivariate observations. In *5th Berkeley Symposium on mathematics, Statistics and Probability*, 1967.

[23] C. D. Manning, P. Raghavan, and H. Schtze. *Introduction to Information Retrieval.* Cambridge University Press, 2008.

[24] S. Osinski and D. Weiss. A concept-driven algorithm for clustering search results. *IEEE Intelligent Systems*, 20(3):48–54, 2005.

[25] P. Pirolli, P. Schank, M. Hearst, and C. Diehl. Scatter/gather browsing communicates the topic structure of a very large text collection. In *CHI*, 1996.

[26] C. J. V. Rijsbergen. *Information Retrieval.* Butterworth-Heinemann, Newton, MA, USA, 1979.

[27] D. E. Rose and D. Levinson. Understanding user goals in web search. In *WWW*, 2004.

[28] G. Salton. *The SMART Retrieval System.* Prentice-Hall, 1971.

[29] E. Sandhaus. The New York Times Annotated Corpus. *Linguistic Data Consortium, Philadelphia*, 2008.

[30] A. Tombros, R. Villa, and C. J. Van Rijsbergen. The effectiveness of query-specific hierarchic clustering in information retrieval. *Inf. Process. Manage.*, 38(4):559–582, 2002.

[31] K. Wagstaff, C. Cardie, S. Rogers, and S. Schrödl. Constrained k-means clustering with background knowledge. In *ICML*, 2001.

[32] X. Wang and C. Zhai. Learn from web search logs to organize search results. In *SIGIR*, 2007.

[33] S. Xu, S. Bao, B. Fei, Z. Su, and Y. Yu. Exploring folksonomy for personalized search. *SIGIR*, pages 155–162, 2008.

[34] O. Zamir and O. Etzioni. Web document clustering: a feasibility demonstration. In *SIGIR*, 1998.

[35] O. Zamir and O. Etzioni. Grouper: a dynamic clustering interface to web search results. In *WWW*, 1999.

[36] H.-J. Zeng, Q.-C. He, Z. Chen, W.-Y. Ma, and J. Ma. Learning to cluster web search results. In *SIGIR*, 2004.

Using Query Log and Social Tagging to Refine Queries Based on Latent Topics*

Lidong Bing Wai Lam
Department of Systems Engineering and Engineering Management
The Chinese University of Hong Kong
Shatin, Hong Kong
{ldbing, wlam}@se.cuhk.edu.hk

Tak-Lam Wong
Department of Mathematics and Information Technology
The Hong Kong Institute of Education
Tai Po, Hong Kong
tlwong@ied.edu.hk

ABSTRACT

An important way to improve users' satisfaction in Web search is to assist them to issue more effective queries. One such approach is query refinement (reformulation), which generates new queries according to the current query issued by users. A common procedure for conducting refinement is to generate some candidate queries first, and then a scoring method is designed to assess the quality of these candidates. Currently, most of the existing methods are context based. They rely heavily on the context relation of terms in the historical queries, and cannot detect and maintain the semantic consistency of queries. In this paper, we propose a graphical model to score queries. The proposed model exploits a latent topic space, which is automatically derived from the query log, to assess the semantic dependency of terms in a query. In the graphical model, both term context dependency and topic context dependency are considered. This also makes it feasible to score some queries which do not have much available historical term context information. We also utilize social tagging data in the candidate query generation process. Based on the observation that different users may tag the same resource with different tags of similar meaning, we propose a method to mine these term pairs for new candidate query construction.

Categories and Subject Descriptors

H.3.3 [**Information Storage and Retrieval**]: Information Search and Retrieval—*Query Formulation, Search Process*

* The work described in this paper is substantially supported by grants from the Research Grant Council of the Hong Kong Special Administrative Region, China (Project Codes: CUHK4128/07 and CUHK413510) and the Direct Grant of the Faculty of Engineering, CUHK (Project Codes: 2050442 and 2050476). This work is also affiliated with the Microsoft-CUHK Joint Laboratory for Human-centric Computing and Interface Technologies.
We also acknowledge the suggestions received from Xuanhui Wang on the baseline method implementation.

CIKM'11, October 24–28, 2011, Glasgow, Scotland, UK.

General Terms

Algorithms, Experimentation

Keywords

Query Refinement, Social Tagging, Query Log Mining

1. INTRODUCTION

Extensive research works have been conducted to improve the performance of search engines by exploiting search logs [1, 11, 21, 29]. One important area is to help users issue more effective queries. There are two major directions in this research, namely, query suggestion (recommendation) and query refinement (reformulation). In query suggestion, historical queries are recommended to users according to a certain similarity measure with the current query issued by users. This suggestion can be performed based on the click graph [13, 26] or query flow graph [5, 6]. However, it cannot provide new queries which are not contained in the query log. On the other hand, in query refinement, the query log is used in a more delicate manner that the current query is refined by exploiting the term dependency information in the historical queries. The generated query may be an existing query in the query log, or a totally new query. According to the operations performed, there are three major types of refinement, namely, substitution [22, 32], expansion [3, 11, 18], and deletion [24, 36]. A common procedure of carrying out refinement is to generate some candidate queries first, and then a scoring method is used to assess the quality of these candidates.

A contextual model was proposed by investigating the context similarity of terms in historical queries [32]. Two terms in a pair with similar contexts are used to substitute each other in new query generation. Then, a context based translation model is employed to score the generated queries. Jones et al. employed hypothesis likelihood ratio to identify those highly related query phrase or term pairs in all user sessions [22]. Then, these phrase pairs are utilized to generate new queries for the input query. All the above methods make use of query log, and exploit the context information to generate term pairs and score new queries. For example, Table 1 shows top 15 output queries of an existing context based method, which is used as the comparison baseline in our experiments, for the original query "wrestling ring instructions". We can observe that the context based method has two shortcomings. First, the context based candidate term generation process is easily affected by noise when deal-

Table 1: **Top 15 results given by a context based method for original query "wrestling ring instructions". "◇" represents the unchanged original terms.**

1	◇ rings ◇	6	◇ ◇ poncho	11	◇ ◇ steps
2	championship ◇ ◇	7	◇ ◇ stitches	12	◇ ◇ instruction
3	◇ ◇ instrutions	8	◇ ◇ scarf	13	◇ ◇ manual
4	◇ ◇ instuctions	9	◇ ◇ loom	14	championships ◇ ◇
5	◇ ◇ afghans	10	◇ ◇ afghan	15	◇ blaylock ◇

ing with ambiguous terms. For example, considering the term "instructions", due to the fact that "instructions" has very diverse contexts in historical queries, a lot of noise is involved in its candidate list such as "afghans", "poncho", etc. Furthermore, typos such as "instrutions" and "instuctions" also degrade the performance when dealing with the typo-prone terms. Second, context based method cannot detect and maintain consistency of semantic meaning when scoring a new query. For example, as shown in Table 1, a good output query is "wrestling ring manual", but it is ranked as the 13th. The reason is that the scoring function highly depends on the co-occurrence of the terms in the contexts of historical queries. "championship ring" is quite popular in query log owing to NBA. Consequently, "championship ring instructions" is assigned a high score although the semantic meaning of the terms in this refined query is not consistent.

Furthermore, when an unfamiliar or rare query is issued by a user, existing context based methods cannot work well too. The definition of unfamiliar query is given as follows:

DEFINITION 1 (UNFAMILIAR QUERY). *Let $(t_1, \cdots, t_n)$ denote a particular query q with length greater than 1, i.e. $n > 1$. Let $(t_i, \cdots, t_j)$ denote a sub-sequence of q, where $1 \leq i < j \leq n$. If none of $(t_i, \cdots, t_j)$s has ever been observed before as a whole query or a sub-sequence of other queries, q is regarded as an unfamiliar query.*

The main reason for ineffective handling of unfamiliar queries by existing context based methods is that these methods mine the historical queries to obtain hints for refining the issued query. When there is no or very little related information, the performance will inevitably be affected. First, it is not easy to figure out the candidate terms to refine the query. Second, the statistical information may not be reliable to differentiate the quality of different candidate queries. One may expect that as the amount of available query log increases, the number of unfamiliar queries will decrease. We conducted an investigation on the percentage of unfamiliar queries in an existing query log used in our experiments and found out that the situation is not as optimistic as what we expect. This query log consists of queries issued to a search engine for a period of 3 months. We started with the queries of the first 2 months as historical queries on hand. At the beginning, the queries in the first day of the third month were

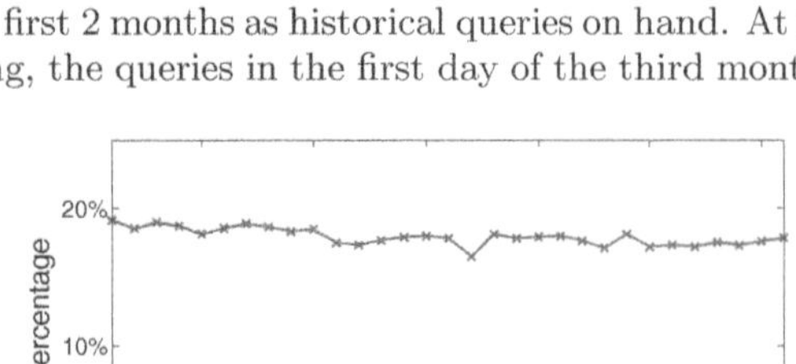

Figure 1: Percentage of unfamiliar queries.

Table 2: Top 30 tags of "http://www.dvguru.com/". The tag frequency is given on the right of each tag.

video	237	news	26	daily	13
dv	156	tech	22	blogging	13
blog	145	howto	19	audio	12
filmmaking	113	editing	17	reviews	10
digital	87	tools	16	movie	10
film	79	tips	16	digitalvideo	10
blogs	50	tv	15	entertainment	9
technology	41	movies	15	business	8
tutorial	29	software	14	cinema	7
tutorials	27	vlog	13	advice	7

used to simulate the newly issued queries, and we calculated the percentage of unfamiliar queries in that day. Then, these queries were added into historical query set so that they were treated as historical queries when we proceeded to the second day of the third month. The same statistical procedure was repeated for all the subsequent days. The statistical information is shown in Figure 1. We can see that the percentage of unfamiliar queries does not change significantly when the amount of historical queries accumulate. Thus, it shows that a certain percentage of unfamiliar queries will always be issued by users. Consequently, it poses another challenge in generating candidate terms for those unfamiliar queries due to the lack of context information. Moreover, it also causes difficulty in scoring of new queries.

In summary, the context based methods have limitations in both major tasks, namely, candidate generation and query scoring. In candidate generation, noise will be involved as exemplified in Table 1 for the terms with diverse meaning. The candidates cannot be generated properly when lacking context information for some terms. In query scoring, the context based methods cannot detect and maintain the semantic consistency of the terms in the query. Furthermore, if the query is not familiar, the scoring task becomes even harder. To tackle the problems in the first task, we propose a method to generate better candidate term pairs by considering useful information from social tagging data. Social tagging is an important application and a valuable semantic repository, and its potential in enhancing Web search performance has been studied in personalized search [7] and query suggestion [16]. Currently, millions of users are involved in some famous social tagging systems such as Delicious[1] and Flickr[2], and they tag and share their favorite online resources. For example, in Delicious data, the tag set of URL "http://www.dvguru.com/", which is a Web site for users to share their experience on digital videos, is given in Table 2. From this tag set, term pairs with similar meaning such as "film" and "movie", "tips" and "tutorial" can be easily found. This is due to the fact that different users may choose their own preferred tags to express the same concept. Therefore, if two tags co-occur frequently in different resources' tag sets, they are very likely to have closely related meaning. Moreover, users regularly maintain their own tagging data and correct some typos and inaccurate tags, so social tagging data contains less noise than query log.

To tackle the problems in the second task, we propose a graphical model which can score a query taking into account the semantic consistency of the terms in the query as well as the term context. First we discover the latent topics in the

[1] `http://www.delicious.com/`

[2] `http://www.flickr.com`

query log, and these topics are utilized to construct a latent topic sequences of the terms in a query. When we score a query with the proposed graphical model, the latent topic sequence of the query is used as hidden evidence to guide the semantic dependency assessment.

2. OVERVIEW OF OUR FRAMEWORK

As mentioned above, there are two major tasks to refine a query. The first task is to generate some candidate queries for the original query via operations such as substitution. The second task is to score the generated candidate queries, and rank them according to the predicted quality.

In the first task, we focus on query term substitution. We first determine a set of possible substitution terms for each term in the original query. These terms are utilized to substitute one or more original terms in the original query. As discussed in Section 1, the noise and the lack of sufficient context information are the major problems when using query log. To tackle these problems, we develop a method to generate better candidate term pairs by considering useful information from social tagging data. Based on the observation that terms with similar meaning are often used to tag the same resource by different users, we can extract some candidate substitution pairs. Then a filtering method is proposed with a delicately designed similarity function. This method is capable of filtering out different types of noisy pairs such as "north" and "carolina", "free" and "music".

In the second step, we propose a graphical model to score the quality of the candidate queries generated in the first step. In the proposed graphical model, the semantic consistency of the queries is considered. Two groups of variables are designed in the graphical model. One group corresponds to the terms, and the other group corresponds to the concepts of the terms. Unlike existing context based methods, we examine the query quality taking into account the semantic consistency of the consecutive terms in a latent concept space. We first derive a set of pseudo-documents from the query log data. Then these pseudo-documents are used to generate a latent concept space. The graphical model can capture the concept dependency between consecutive terms. Therefore, even when the term context information is not sufficient in the query log, it can still give reliable score by considering the semantic dependency of the consecutive terms in the latent concept space.

3. CANDIDATE TERM GENERATION

To generate candidate terms from social tagging data for query refinement, we make use of a bookmark data, namely Delicious, to illustrate our method and test the performance in the experiment. Note that the proposed method is applicable to other types of social tagging data. In this component, we first develop a method for mining term pairs from the bookmark data. After that, we consider the pseudo-context of the candidates to filter out noise.

3.1 Candidate Term Extraction

A piece of bookmark, denoted by $\mathcal{B}_{lu} = \{t_1, t_2, \cdots\}$, is a set of tags which are given by a user u to summarize the content of a URL, l such as {film, tutorial, blog} and {movie, technology, tips}. Our candidate term extraction method is based on the observation that different users may use tags with similar meaning to describe the same resource. To capture this kind of co-occurrence, we aggregate all tags from different users of the same URL together, and compose a set of distinct tags for each URL, which is denoted by $\mathcal{T}_l$.

The mutual information of two tags, t_1 and t_2, can be calculated as in Equation 1:

$$I(t_1, t_2) = \sum_{X_{t_1}, X_{t_2} \in \{0,1\}} P(X_{t_1}, X_{t_2}) \log \frac{P(X_{t_1}, X_{t_2})}{P(X_{t_1})P(X_{t_2})}, \quad (1)$$

where X_{t_i} is a binary random variable indicating whether term t_i appears in a particular tag set $\mathcal{T}_l$. For example, $P(X_{t_1} = 1, X_{t_2} = 1)$ is the proportion of the tag sets which contain t_1 and t_2 simultaneously. Because commonly used terms may be used to tag a lot of URLs such as "free" and "good". To cope with this problem, we adopt the normalized form of mutual information:

$$NMI(t_1, t_2) = \frac{I(t_1, t_2)}{[H(t_1) + H(t_2)]/2}, \quad (2)$$

where $H(t_i)$ is the entropy of t_i's distribution among all the tag sets, and calculated as in Equation 3:

$$H(t_i) = -\sum_{X_{t_i} \in \{0,1\}} P(X_{t_i}) \log P(X_{t_i}). \quad (3)$$

If $NMI(t_1, t_2)$ is greater than a threshold, the term pair t_1 and t_2 will be stored for the next stage of term filtering.

3.2 Candidate Term Filtering

The term pairs generated in the previous step may involve noise. The first kind of noise is mainly caused by noun phrases. For example, "north" is found as the top 1 candidate for "carolina", and "united" is top 1 for "states". These are obviously not good candidates for term refinement. The main reason is that the phrases, i.e. "north carolina" and "united states", are used by many users to tag URLs. Thus, the NMI values of two terms in the same phrase are large. Another kind of noise is caused by the frequently used terms. For example, "free" is found as one of the candidates for many terms such as "music", "movie", "film", etc. By manually examining the data, we find that users maintain a large amount of bookmarks for these free resources on the Web. We propose a method to filter out this undesirable candidate terms.

For each tag t, we first construct its pseudo-context in the bookmark environment, denoted by $C(t)$, which is composed of all tags that co-occur with t in at least one $\mathcal{B}_{lu}$. $cnt(t_i|C(t))$ denotes the frequency of t_i in the pseudo-context of t. It is equivalent to the co-occurrence frequency of t and t_i in all $\mathcal{B}_{lu}$s. Then the pseudo-context document of tag t, $\mathcal{D}_t$, is defined as:

$$\mathcal{D}_t \triangleq (w_1^t, w_2^t, \cdots, w_T^t), \quad (4)$$

where w_i^t is t_i's weight in $\mathcal{D}_t$, which can be computed as:

$$w_i^t = \frac{cnt(t_i|C(t))}{\sum_{t_j} cnt(t_j|C(t))} \times \log \frac{|\mathbb{D}_T|}{|\{\mathcal{D}_{t_k}|t_i \in \mathcal{D}_{t_k}\}|}, \quad (5)$$

where $\mathbb{D}_T$ denotes the set of all pseudo-context documents, and T is the vocabulary of the bookmark data. Then, we calculate a refined cosine similarity between a pair of pseudo-context documents:

$$sim(\mathcal{D}_{t_i}, \mathcal{D}_{t_j}) = \frac{\sum_{k=1}^{|T|}(w_k^{t_i} \times w_k^{t_j})(1 - \gamma(t_i, t_j|t_k))}{|\mathcal{D}_{t_i}||\mathcal{D}_{t_j}|}, \quad (6)$$

where $\gamma(t_i, t_j|t_k)$ is the relation factor between term t_i and t_j given t_k, which is calculated as:

$$\gamma(t_i, t_j|t_k) = \frac{cnt(t_i, t_j|C(t_k))}{\min\{cnt(t_i|C(t_k)), cnt(t_j|C(t_k))\}}, \quad (7)$$

where $cnt(t_i, t_j|C(t_k))$ is the number of $\mathcal{B}_{lu}$s that contain t_i, t_j and t_k simultaneously. Therefore, for the terms which co-occur with "north carolina" frequently will contribute less when calculating the similarity of $\mathcal{D}_{carolina}$ and $\mathcal{D}_{north}$. The design of $\gamma(t_i, t_j|t_k)$ is based on the following observation: one URL is seldom tagged by the same user with two terms that have similar meaning such as "film" and "movie", "car" and "automobile". According to Equation 7, the value of γ("car", "automobile"|"repair") tends to be small, while, the value of γ("carolina", "north"|"lottery") tends to be large. Consequently, the contribution of the term "repair" to the similarity between $\mathcal{D}_{car}$ and $\mathcal{D}_{automobile}$ is increased, and the contribution of the term "lottery" to the similarity between $\mathcal{D}_{carolina}$ and $\mathcal{D}_{north}$ is decreased. The refined cosine similarity can also filter out the terms which are frequently used such as "free" and "howto", because their contexts are quite diverse, and cannot have a high similarity with other specific terms' contexts.

4. GRAPHICAL MODEL BASED SCORING

In this section, we first present the graphical model and the scoring method. Then we describe the details of the model, namely, latent topic discovery from the query log, and model parameter training.

4.1 The Graphical Model

A query q is composed of a sequence of terms, which can be denoted by $q: t^1 \cdots t^n$, where the superscript indicates the position of the term, and $t^r (1 \le r \le n)$ may take any term in the vocabulary. We propose a graphical model which considers the dependency among latent semantic topics. Figure 4 depicts the design of the graphical model. The query terms, i.e. t^r, are observable and represented by filled nodes, and the latent topics, denoted by z^r, of the corresponding terms are unobservable and represented by empty nodes. The discovery of latent topics will be discussed later.

The transition probability, denoted by $P(z^{r+1}|z^r)$, between topics is considered, where z^r and z^{r+1} are the semantic topics of t^r and t^{r+1} respectively. We also make use of the probability of obtaining the term t^{r+1} given t^r and z^{r+1}, i.e. $P(t^{r+1}|z^{r+1}, t^r)$. Hence, in this model, each term depends on its latent topic and the preceding term, and each topic depends on its preceding topic. When we score a query with this graphical model, the latent topic sequence of the query is used as hidden evidence to guide the semantic consistency assessment. For queries with good semantic consistency, their corresponding topic sequences will increase the score of their quality. For these queries, the transition probability between the consecutive topics in the topic sequence is higher.

When we employ this graphical model to score a candidate query, the score of a query q can be denoted as $P(t^1 \cdots t^n)$, which is given in Equation 8:

$$P(t^{1:n}) = \sum_{z^r = z_1, 1 \le r \le n}^{z_N} P(t^{1:n}, z^{1:n}). \quad (8)$$

We marginalize over all possible latent semantic topic sequences to calculate the joint probability of generating the term in query q. Based on the structure of the designed graphical model, $P(t^{1:n}, z^{1:n})$ can be calculated as in Equation 9 by the chain rule:

$$P(t^{1:n}, z^{1:n}) = \prod_{1 \le r \le n} P(z^r|z^{r-1}) P(t^r|z^r, t^{r-1}). \quad (9)$$

When $r = 1$, $P(z^1|z^0) = P(z^1)$ and $P(t^1|z^1, t^0) = P(t^1|z^1)$.

This graphical model shares some resemblance to Hidden Markov Models (HMM). However, one major difference is that there are dependencies between neighboring terms, which capture their co-occurrence.

4.2 Scoring Algorithm

As mentioned above, the scoring function needs to concretize the latent topic sequence in the graphical model depicted in Figure 4. The possible latent topic paths compose a trellis structure, which is shown in Figure 4.1. To marginalize the joint probability $P(t^{1:n}, z^{1:n})$ (refer to Equation 9) over all possible latent topic paths, we can employ a dynamic programming method, similar to the forward algorithm. The forward variable $\alpha_r(i)$ is defined as:

$$\alpha_r(i) \triangleq P(t^{1:r}, z^r = z_i), \quad (10)$$

which is the score of the partial query $t^1 \cdots t^r$ given the topic z_i at the position r. When $r = 1$, we set $\alpha_1(i) = P(z^1 = z_i) P(t^1|z^1 = z_i, t^0)$. The recursive calculation of α is:

$$\alpha_r(i) = \left[\sum_{z_j \in Z} \alpha_{r-1}(j) P(z^r = z_i|z^{r-1} = z_j) \right] P(t^r|t^{r-1}, z_i), \quad (11)$$

where $P(z^r = z_i|z^{r-1} = z_j)$ is independent of the position r, and equal to $P(z_i|z_j)$. Finally the score of a query can be calculated by summing over all possible z_i for $\alpha_n(i)$:

$$P(t^{1:n}) = \sum_{z_i \in Z} \alpha_n(i). \quad (12)$$

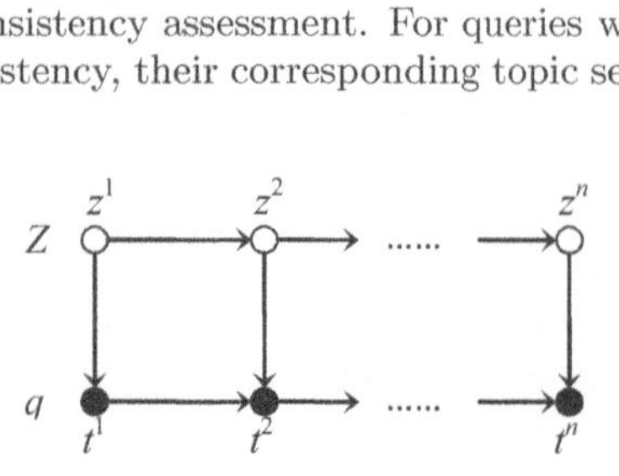

Figure 2: The graphical model for scoring a query.

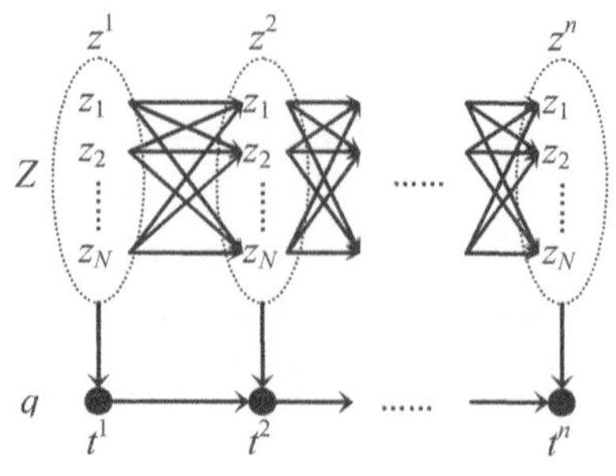

Figure 3: Trellis structure of latent topic sequences.

Therefore, to conduct the scoring, we need three kinds of model parameters, namely, $P(z_i)$, $P(z_j|z_i)$, and $P(t_l|z_j, t_k)$, which can be learned in the model training phase.

4.3 Latent Topic Analysis and Training Algorithm

The latent topics of the terms in queries are discovered from the query log. These latent sematic topics discovered are transferred to initialize the model parameters of the graphical model. Then, the historical queries are treated as training sequences to learn the model parameters.

4.3.1 Latent Topic Analysis of Query Log

A typical format of the records in query log can be represented as a triple $(query, clicked\_url, time)$. One direct way of using query log data for latent topic analysis is to treat each *clicked_url* as a single document unit. This approach will suffer from the data sparseness problem since most of URLs only involve very small number of queries. Instead of adopting such a simple strategy, we aggregate all the queries related to the same host together, and construct one pseudo-document for each host, denoted by $\mathcal{H}$. For example, the pseudo-document of "www.mapquest.com" consists of the queries such as "mapquest", "travel map", "driving direction", etc. Some general Web sites such as "en.wikipedia.org" and "www.youtube.com" are not suitable for latent topic analysis, because they involve large amount of queries which cover very diverse aspects. To tackle this problem, we first sort the host pseudo-documents in descending order according to the number of distinct query terms they have. Then, the top ranked pseudo-documents are eliminated in our latent topic discovery process.

We employ the standard Latent Dirichlet Allocation (LDA) algorithm [4] to conduct the latent semantic topic analysis on the collection of pseudo-documents. In particular, GibbsLDA[3] package is used to generate a set of latent topics $Z = \{z_1, z_2, \cdots, z_N\}$. Each topic z_i is associated with a multinomial distribution of terms, denoted by $P(t_k|z_i)$, where t_k is a term. Each t_k in a certain pseudo-document $\mathcal{H}$ is assigned a topic, denoted by $z(t_m|\mathcal{H})$ in this paper.

4.3.2 Latent Topic Transfer

We transfer the latent topics discovered above to initialize the model parameters in the beginning of training phase:

$$\hat{P}(z_i) = \frac{1}{|Z|}, \tag{13}$$

$$\hat{P}(z_j|z_i) = \frac{\exp(-D_{KL}(z_j||z_i))}{\sum_{z_k \in Z} \exp(-D_{KL}(z_k||z_i))}, \tag{14}$$

$$\hat{P}(t_l|z_j, t_k) = \frac{\hat{P}(t_k, t_l, z_j)}{\hat{P}(t_k, z_j)} = \frac{\hat{P}(t_k, t_l|z_j)}{\hat{P}(t_k|z_j)}, \tag{15}$$

where $D_{KL}(z_j||z_i) = \sum_{t_k} P(t_k|z_j) \log \frac{P(t_k|z_j)}{P(t_k|z_i)}$ is the Kullback-Leibler divergence between two distributions $P(\cdot|z_i)$ and $P(\cdot|z_j)$. When z_i and z_j are highly related topics, the value of $\hat{P}(z_j|z_i)$ is large. $\hat{P}(t_k, t_l|z_j)$ is the probability that t_k and t_l co-occur in the topic z_j, and $\hat{P}(t_k|z_j)$ is the probability of t_k in z_j.

[3] `http://gibbslda.sourceforge.net/`

$\hat{P}(t_k, t_l|z_j)$ and $\hat{P}(t_k|z_j)$ are calculated as:

$$\hat{P}(t_k, t_l|z_j) = \frac{cnt(t_k, t_l|z_j)}{\sum_m \sum_n cnt(t_m, t_n|z_j)}, \tag{16}$$

$$\hat{P}(t_k|z_j) = \frac{\sum_n cnt(t_k, t_n|z_j)}{\sum_m \sum_n cnt(t_m, t_n|z_j)}, \tag{17}$$

where $cnt(t_m, t_n|z_j)$ denotes the co-occurrence time of t_m and t_n in the topic z_j, and calculated as:

$$cnt(t_m, t_n|z_j) = \sum_{\mathcal{H}} \mathbf{1}_{\{t_m, t_n \in \mathcal{H} \ \wedge \ z(t_m|\mathcal{H}) = z(t_n|\mathcal{H}) = z_j\}}, \tag{18}$$

where $\mathbf{1}_{\{\}}$ is an indicator function, and $z(t_m|\mathcal{H})$ is the topic assigned to t_m in the pseudo-document $\mathcal{H}$, which can be obtained from the result of LDA in the previous step. Then we utilize a global language model to smooth $\hat{P}(t_l|z_j, t_k)$:

$$\tilde{P}(t_l|z_j, t_k) = \frac{cnt(t_k, t_l|z_j) + \mu_1 P(t_k)P(t_l)}{\sum_n cnt(t_k, t_n|z_j) + \mu_1 P(t_k)}, \tag{19}$$

where $P(t) = \frac{cnt(t)}{\sum_{t_i} cnt(t_i)}$ is the global probability of term t in the query log data, $cnt(t)$ denotes the frequency of t.

Note that we do not directly apply the probability $P(t_k|z_j)$ generated by LDA as $\hat{P}(t_k|z_j)$ in Equation 15. The reason is that $\hat{P}(t_l|z_j, t_k)$ should satisfy the constraint of $\sum_l \hat{P}(t_l|z_j, t_k) = 1$, and using $P(t_k|z_j)$ may violate this constraint.

4.3.3 Latent Topic Parameter Estimation

To conduct the training process, we refine the standard Baum-Welch algorithm [2]. Given a set of historical queries, we preprocess them so that the frequency of distinct queries is aggregated and collected. Since we assume that each query is independent of the others, the intermediate calculation can be illustrated with a single query. Then, the intermediate results for each single query are aggregated to obtain the final updating formulas with the similar way in [25].

For a query $q : t^1 \cdots t^n$, we define backward variable $\beta_r(i)$:

$$\beta_r(i) \triangleq P(t^{r+1:n}|z^r = z_i, t^r), \tag{20}$$

which is the score of partial query $t^{r+1} \cdots t^n$ given z^r and t^r. We define $\beta_n(i) = 1$. The recursive calculation of β is:

$$\beta_r(i) = \sum_{z_j \in Z} P(z_j|z_i) P(t^{r+1}|t^r, z_j) \beta_{r+1}(j). \tag{21}$$

Then the joint probability of a query q and $z^r = z_i$ can be derived as:

$$\begin{aligned} P(q, z^r = z_i) &= P(t^{1:r-1}, t^{r+1:n}|t^r, z^r = z_i) P(t^r, z^r = z_i) \\ &= P(t^{1:r-1}, t^r, z^r = z_i) P(t^{r+1:n}|z^r = z_i, t^r) \\ &= \alpha_r(i)\beta_r(i). \end{aligned} \tag{22}$$

Therefore, $P(q)$ can also be computed by $\sum_i \alpha_r(i)\beta_r(i)$.

Now we introduce two conditional probabilities. $P(z^r = z_i|q)$ is the probability that z^r takes the value z_i in q, which can be calculated as:

$$P(z^r = z_i|q) = \frac{\alpha_r(i)\beta_r(i)}{P(q)}. \tag{23}$$

The joint probability of $z^r = z_i$ and $z^{r+1} = z_j$ in a given q is $P(z^r = z_i, z^{r+1} = z_j|q)$:

$$P(z^r = z_i, z^{r+1} = z_j|q) = \frac{\alpha_r(i) P(z_j|z_i) P(t^{r+1}|t^r, z_j) \beta_{r+1}(j)}{P(q)}. \tag{24}$$

The next step is to aggregate the intermediate results and obtain the final updating formulas of $P'(t_l|z_j,t_k)$, $P'(z_j|z_i)$ and $P'(z_i)$. $P'(t_l|z_j,t_k)$ is designed as follows:

$$P'(t_l|z_j,t_k) = \mu_2 \frac{\sum_{q\in Q}\left(\sum_{r=1, \; s.t.\; t^r=t_k, t^{r+1}=t_l}^{n-1} P(z^{r+1}=z_j|q)F(q)\right)}{\sum_{q\in Q}\left(\sum_{r=1, \; s.t.\; t^r=t_k}^{n-1} P(z^{r+1}=z_j|q)F(q)\right)} +(1-\mu_2)\tilde{P}(t_l|z_j,t_k), \quad (25)$$

where Q is the set of training queries, and $F(q)$ is the frequency of q, μ_2 is used to control the weights of two parts, namely the initial value $\tilde{P}(t_l|z_j,t_k)$, and the newly estimated part. In this way, the value of $P'(t_l|z_j,t_k)$ does not solely depend on the queries which have sub-sequence $(t_k,\ t_l)$, a proportion of the initial $\tilde{P}(t_l|z_j,t_k)$ is also kept in $P'(t_l|z_j,t_k)$. Therefore, when a new query contains term sequence $(t_k,\ t_l)$, and no previous queries contain $(t_k,\ t_l)$, the value of $P'(t_l|z_j,t_k)$ can still be calculated relying on $\tilde{P}(t_l|z_j,t_k)$, and the score of the new query is still reliable. The updating formulas of $P'(z_j|z_i)$ and $P'(z_i)$ are straightforward and they are given as follows:

$$P'(z_j|z_i) = \frac{\sum_{q\in Q}\sum_{r=1}^{n-1} P(z^r=z_i, z^{r+1}=z_j|q)F(q)}{\sum_{q\in Q}\sum_{r=1}^{n-1} P(z^r=z_i|q)F(q)}, \quad (26)$$

$$P'(z_i) = \frac{1}{|Q|}\sum_{q\in Q} P(z^1=z_i|q)F(q), \quad (27)$$

After one iteration, new parameters, namely, $P'(t_l|z_j,t_k)$, $P'(z_j|z_i)$, and $P'(z_i)$, will be used in the next iteration. This iterative procedure will stop when a pre-defined condition is satisfied.

5. DATA PREPROCESSING AND EXPERIMENT SETUP

5.1 Data Sets and Preprocessing

The query log data used in our experiments is the AOL data [27] spanning three months from 1 March, 2006 to 31 May, 2006. The raw data is composed of queries and clicks recorded by a search engine. Since it contains a lot of noise, we first clean the raw data as done by most of the existing works. If a query contains non-alphabetical character, or is a host navigation query such as "google.com" and "www.yahoo.com", it is removed. Then, the stop words are removed from the remaining queries. We adopt a hybrid method to detect user session boundary [19]. First, consecutive queries in the same session have to share at least one term. Second, the interval between two consecutive queries should be less than 10 minutes. After sessions are detected, we remove those sessions without any clicked URL. In each session, we remove the queries which are at the end of the session and have no clicked URL. Finally we obtain 7,041,319 sessions, in which 1,276,498 are multi-query sessions. There are 4,315,124 unique queries and 673,073 distinct terms.

The data set is split into two subsets by the time stamp: the historical set and the test set. The historical set contains the first two months' log, and the test set contains the third month's log. The pseudo-documents for latent topic analysis are constructed with the historical set as mentioned in Section 4.3. If a host involves less than 5 queries, it will be eliminated. Then all pseudo-documents are ranked in descending order according to the number of distinct terms they have. In order to filter out those Web sites that are too general, we remove URLs from the top 0.1% of the pseudo-documents. Finally, 189,670 pseudo-documents are retained and fed into the latent topic discovery algorithm, where the number of topics is set to 30. In the historical set, 1,882,638 queries with at least one clicked URL are used to build the training set, which is used in the parameter estimation.

Currently, the largest existing bookmark data collection is provided by Wetzker et al. [34]. In our experiment, we use a subset of the data spanning two years, namely, 2006 and 2007. In this period, 101,485,670 bookmarks were assigned to 39,232,530 distinct URLs by 891,479 users, including 2,523,190 distinct tags. To tackle the vocabulary gap between the AOL log and bookmark data, we filter out the tags that are not contained by the query log such as "socialsoftware", "visualstudio", etc. To tackle the problem of data sparseness, we only consider the URLs which are tagged by at least five users. After this filtering, 1,910,547 URLs are collected and used in candidate term generation. And the similarity threshold value used is 0.19 when filtering the noise. The smoothing parameter value of μ_1 is 3,000 in Equation 19.

5.2 Experiment Setup

For conducting the comparison, we implement a context based term association (CTA) method proposed by Wang and Zhai [32], and follow the advice of the authors on some implementation details. This method is based on an observation that terms with similar meaning tend to co-occur with the same or similar terms in the queries. For example, both "auto" and "car" often occur with "rental", "pricing", etc. Therefore, both candidate term generation and query scoring in CTA are conducted by exploiting the association of term contexts in the historical queries. A contextual model is defined to capture context similarity, and a translation model is defined to score the quality of a candidate query. We denote the two steps of CTA, namely, candidate term generation, and query scoring, as "CTA-CAND" and "CTA-SCR" respectively. We generate the contextual and translation models for the top 100,000 terms in the historical set. Then the threshold given in [32] is applied to filter out the noise. We mainly compare the performance of our framework and CTA for query term substitution. A conservative strategy is adopted, specifically, only one term in the original query will be replaced. This is also the strategy adopted by some previous works such as [32].

Because manual evaluation of the output of query refinement methods is time-consuming and very labor intensive, we conduct an automatic evaluation by utilizing the session information of query log. In a search session, when users feel unsatisfied with the results of current query, they may refine current query and search again. After obtaining satisfactory results, they may stop searching. The importance of the terminal URL was well discussed in previous works [14, 35]. Therefore, an automatic and reliable evaluation can be conducted based on this observation. We introduce the definitions of two kinds of query as follows:

DEFINITION 2 (SATISFIED QUERY). *In a user session, the query which causes at least one URL clicked and is located in the end of the session is called a satisfied query.*

Table 3: Substitution term pairs generated by our method.

air		birthday		car		cd		children		health	
cand.	*NMI*	*cand.*	*NMI*	*cand.*	*NMI*	*cand.*	*NMI*	*cand.*	*NMI*	*cand.*	*NMI*
apollo	0.135	birthdays	0.085	cars	0.319	dvd	0.130	kids	0.207	medical	0.135
airline	0.127	greeting	0.061	auto	0.260	cds	0.081	parenting	0.136	fitness	0.131
airlines	0.113	ecards	0.059	automotive	0.176	iso	0.077	child	0.080	medicine	0.126
flights	0.105	anniversary	0.053	automobile	0.132	burning	0.071	baby	0.072	nutrition	0.124
flight	0.100	ecard	0.043	vehicle	0.082	cdrom	0.064	parents	0.053	diet	0.103
house		lotto		mail		msn		music		pc	
cand.	*NMI*	*cand.*	*NMI*	*cand.*	*NMI*	*cand.*	*NMI*	*cand.*	*NMI*	*cand.*	*NMI*
houses	0.161	lottery	0.321	email	0.267	messenger	0.219	audio	0.135	computer	0.092
housing	0.122	lotteries	0.127	webmail	0.099	im	0.115	musica	0.118	computers	0.088
realestate	0.104	loto	0.085	smtp	0.096	icq	0.105	musik	0.087	hardware	0.074
estate	0.079	powerball	0.081	gmail	0.091	aim	0.103	bands	0.076	windows	0.069
property	0.063	lotterie	0.042	spam	0.090	chat	0.074	rock	0.060	xp	0.060

Table 4: Comparison of substitution pair generation for high frequency terms.

google		yahoo		county		lyrics		school		myspace	
Our	*CTA*	*Our*	*CTA*	*Our*	*CTA*	*Our*	*CTA*	*Our*	*CTA*	*Our*	*CTA*
googlemaps	goggle	yui	msn	berks	count	songs	lyric	education	schools	facebook	space
search	yahoo	msn	aol	orange	couty	lyric	listen	college	speed	socialnetworking	xanga
seo	googl	google	google	counties	parish	song	song	schools	heels	socialnetworks	profile
gmail	satellite	pipes	aim	speedway	township	letras	lryics	teaching	scool	socialnetwork	html
maps	googles	search	voice	carfax	couny	chords	titles	university	heel	sns	premade
searchengine	gogle	searchengine	ako	alamo	conty	canciones	lyrcis	learning	scholl	friendster	glitter
googleearth	goole	messenger	yaho	hertz	dade	paroles	lyricks	educational	shool	socialsoftware	cool
map	virtual	woman	electronic	kia	coutny	tablature	lyics	teacher	fiber	profile	page
mashup	planet	engine	yhoo	armored	okeechobee	tabs	remix	students	cholesterol	social	background
adsense	msn	aim	monkey	towing	twp	songtexte	album	edu	protein	socialmedia	website
university		ebay		college		bank		city		mapquest	
Our	*CTA*	*Our*	*CTA*	*Our*	*CTA*	*Our*	*CTA*	*Our*	*CTA*	*Our*	*CTA*
college	college	auction	outboard	university	colleges	banking	bankof	cities	yankees	drivingdirections	maps
universities	univ	auctions	trolling	colleges	collage	banks	holland	urban	knicks	onlinemapping	defensive
academic	athletics	sell	general	school	colege	money	morning	urbanism	mets	navteq	drunk
uni	univeristy	selling	boat	universities	webshots	finance	guns	oklahoma	jets	sidesearch	mcnally
school	colleges	paypal	mitsubishi	schools	colleg	cash	scouts	urbanplan	ciy	teleatlas	quest
academia	unversity	ecommerce	kia	education	outreach	savings	mid	chicago	aviation	routeplanners	google
colleges	fullerton	shipping	crate	students	collge	finances	mall	newyork	ave	routefinder	petty
education	parks	marketplace	rebuilt	highered	colledge	payment	mbna	miami	cty	direcciones	aaa
edu	universtiy	sale	clock	academia	policing	account	reserve	nyc	blvd	kaardid	drinking
gradschool	prisons	sales	yamaha	edu	helpers	hsbc	latin	places	counties	strade	directions

DEFINITION 3 (UNSATISFIED QUERY). *The query which is located just ahead of the satisfied query in the same user session.*

We collect a set of unsatisfied queries used as the input, and collect their corresponding satisfied queries treated as the benchmark query set of the refinement task. Note that this requirement is only for conducting automatic evaluation, and our framework can take any query as input.

6. EXPERIMENTAL RESULTS

6.1 Candidate Term Generation

The candidate terms for 12 selected terms are given in Table 3. For each term, the top 5 candidates are given along with their NMI scores. In general, there are four kinds of relations between the terms in a substitution pair. The first kind refers to the fact that the candidates' meaning is identical with input terms' meaning such as "automotive" and "auto" for "car", "kids" for "children", "lottery" for "lotto", etc. The second kind is that the candidate terms' meaning is related to the input term's meaning, such as "dvd" for "cd", "fitness" for "health", "estate" for "house", "messenger" for "msn". etc. The third kind refers to the fact that the candidate terms have a similar property of the input terms such as "icq" and "aim" for "msn". The last kind refers to other types of strongly associated relation. In the last case, although the candidate terms do not have similar meaning or property of the inputs, the relationship between them is quite obvious. For example, "powerball" is a kind of lottery ticket, "rock" is a genre of popular music. Interestingly, two non-English terms are suggested for "music", namely, "musica" from Spanish and "musik" from Swedish, and both are correct. We can see that social tagging data can provide us some useful term pairs with similar or related meaning.

We find that when dealing with high frequency terms, CTA suggests a lot from typos. The candidates of the top 12 most frequent terms in the AOL log are given in Table 4. It can been seen that typos are recommended by CTA for 8 input terms, except for "myspace", "ebay", "bank" and "mapquest". After the filtering is performed with the threshold given in [32], the top 5 remaining candidates for "county" are "count", "couty", "couny", "conty" and "dade", and for "lyrics" are "listen", "song", "lryics", "lyrcis" and "lyics". The main reason of this observation is that their candidate generation method is context based, and the filtering method relies on the co-occurrence of two terms among different sessions. After users issue a query containing typo terms and cannot get satisfied results, they may correct it manually. But this typo is already recorded in the query log. Worse still, most of search engines can return some results even for a query with typo. So after users click any one of

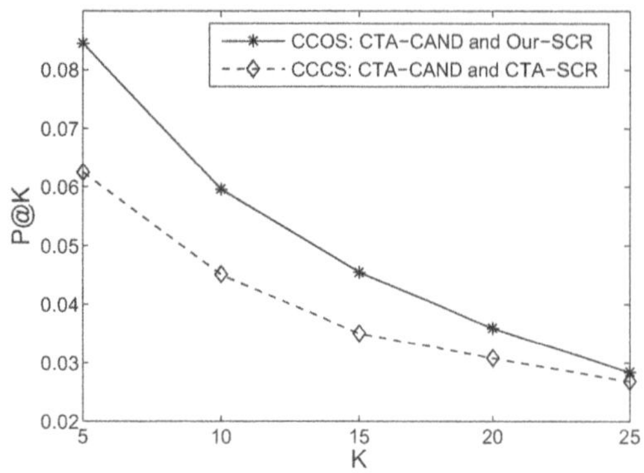

Figure 4: Comparison of scoring performance between CTA-SCR and Our-SCR.

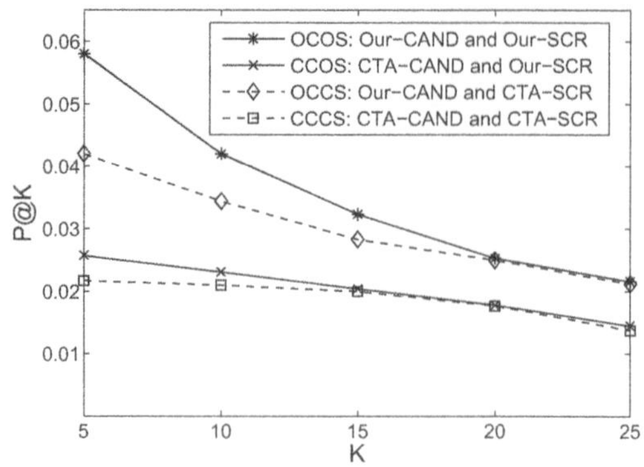

Figure 5: Refinement performance of different combinations on QS2.

the results for the query with typo, we cannot easily filter out this query. Therefore, the typo and its corresponding correct term have very similar context and often co-occur in the sessions. In contrast, our method utilizes the bookmark data, which has a better quality compared with the query log. When a user provides a typo tag, it may be corrected when the user comes back to maintain his or her bookmarks. On the other hand, the bookmark data also has its own shortcoming. A user may connect several terms as a single tag, such as "googlemaps" and "searchengine". Fortunately, it is not difficult to split this kind of tags into single terms.

6.2 Comparison of Scoring Performance

Recall that our framework contains two major components, namely, the graphical model for scoring and the candidate term generation from social tagging data, and they aim at solving different steps or tasks in query refinement. To compare the performance of query scoring between our graphical model and CTA, we randomly select 1,000 multi-query sessions from the test set of the query log, and the unsatisfied queries in these sessions are used as input of the query refinement task. This query set is named as Query Set 1 (QS1). As mentioned before, the corresponding satisfied queries in these sessions are used as the benchmark results.

The scoring component of CTA, i.e. CTA-SCR, is a term context based method, and it is designed to score the candidate query generated from the context based candidate generation method, i.e. CTA-CAND. To compare the performance of two scoring methods, namely, CTA-SCR, and our graphical model (called Our-SCR), we apply CTA-CAND to generate candidate terms from the historical query set for them. For a query q in QS1, CTA-CAND outputs a list of candidate terms for each term of q. Then, each candidate term is used to generate a candidate query. All candidate queries of q are fed into one scoring method to assess the quality. Then, according to their score, the top candidates are determined as the final output results for q.

We adopt the metrics P@K (precision at K) to evaluate the result, and K is the number of top result queries given by the model. For each method, at most 25 result queries are considered here. The performance of both models is given in Figure 4, where CCOS denotes the scoring performance of our graphical model. It can be observed that our graphical model outperforms CTA (denoted by CCCS) significantly when K is small. The P@5 value of our graphical model is 0.085, while the P@5 value of CTA is 0.062. The differences between the performances of our method and CTA are significant with significance level 0.05. The major reason for the different performance is that our graphical model scores a query taking into account the semantic consistency of the terms, which cannot be captured by the comparison baseline. Because most of the input queries have less than 25 candidate queries, both methods achieve similar P@25.

The effect of the parameter μ_2 is depicted in Figure 6. In general, a large value of μ_2 can achieve better result than a small value. Recall that we randomly generate QS1 from the test set. Commonly used queries have more chance to be selected, because they are issued many times by users. Therefore, there is more information from historical queries that can be used in scoring their candidate queries. Refer to Equation 25, a large value of μ_2 reserves small amount of initial estimation value of $\tilde{P}(t_l|z_j,t_k)$, and the value of $P'(t_l|z_j,t_k)$ depends more on the re-estimation part from the historical queries. This weight distribution is preferred when dealing with queries in QS1. If the value of $P'(t_l|z_j,t_k)$ only depends on the re-estimation part, i.e., $\mu_2 = 1.0$, the result is worse than that when we reserve some initial estimation of $\tilde{P}(t_l|z_j,t_k)$, for example, $\mu_2 = 0.7$. It shows that the initial estimation from the latent topic analysis can capture some intrinsic feature of the queries in Web search.

6.3 Performance of Unfamiliar Query Refinement

To investigate the efficacy of our candidate term generation method based on social tagging data, we select another query set from the test set in a similar way of selecting QS1, named as Query Set 2 (QS2). The only difference is that the queries in QS2 are unfamiliar, so that we can investigate whether social tagging data can help solve the problem of lacking information.

The queries in QS2 are unfamiliar, therefore, this poses some challenges in both tasks of query refinement as we discussed in Section 1. Figure 5 depicts the results of different combinations. Our-CAND denotes the candidate term generation component of our framework. It can be observed that the combination OCOS performs the best, and followed by combination OCCS. Combinations CCOS and CCCS achieve similar performance. In summary, the combinations with Our-CAND as the candidate term genera-

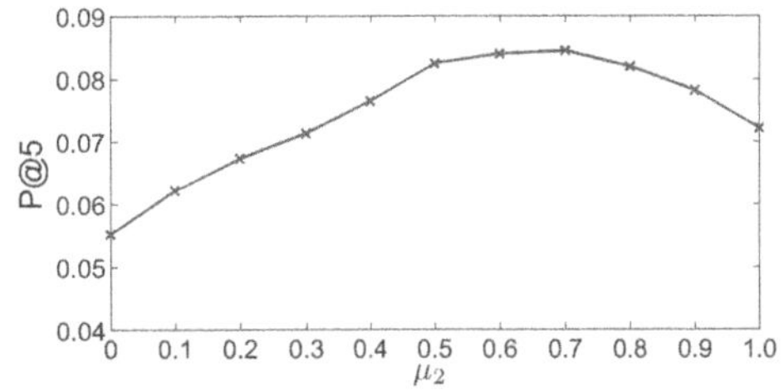

Figure 6: The effect of μ_2 under the CCOS method in the comparison of the scoring performance.

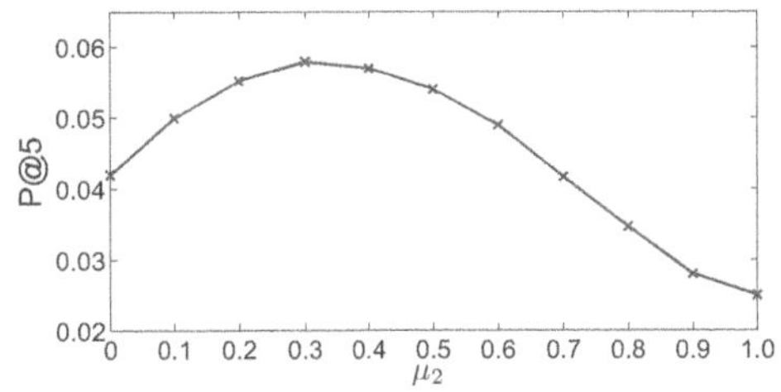

Figure 7: The effect of μ_2 under the OCOS method in unfamiliar query refinement.

tion component can perform better. This is mainly due to the lack of information for these unfamiliar query, and good candidate terms cannot be generated by CTA-CAND. Furthermore, Our-SCR performs better than CTA-SCR. Our graphical model scores the query in a latent semantic space. Therefore, even when the term context information is very sparse, Our-SCR can still achieve a reliable score.

The effect of parameter μ_2 in the combination OCOS is given in Figure 7. It can be observed that when refining the unfamiliar queries, a small value of μ_2, say 0.3, can achieve a better performance in query scoring, because a small value of μ_2 reserves larger amount of initial estimation value, i.e. $\tilde{P}(t_l|z_j, t_k)$. When the historical query information is sparse, reserving more of $\tilde{P}(t_l|z_j, t_k)$ value can offer a reliable score.

6.4 Case Study of Refined Queries

We conduct some case studies to analyze the query refinement result qualitatively. Table 5 depicts the top 5 output queries from our model for 4 input queries, namely "dutch folklore" and "racing logistics" from QS2, and "kids anger disorders" and "discount gucci eyeglasses" from QS1. To refine "dutch folklore" and "racing logistics", the main difficulty is the generation of candidate terms. For example, "folklore" is not a frequently used term in the historical query set, but in the bookmark data it is employed to tag many URLs. Our candidate generation method can figure out some very good candidate terms such as "myths", "mythology", and "legend". On the other hand, to refine "kids anger disorders", the main difficulty is to detect and maintain the semantic meaning consistency of the candidate queries. Because each term in "kids anger disorders" has tens of candidate substitution terms, the semantic consistency is not easy to maintain when generating a new query.

7. RELATED WORK

Huang et al. analyzed and evaluated different types of query refinement in the query log [20]. Except the three mentioned types, namely, substitutions, expansion, and deletions, they also investigated some other fine-grained types such as stemming [28], spelling correction [10], abbreviation expansion [33], etc. In [17], a Conditional Random Field model is proposed to conduct these fine-grained refinement operations. Chirita et al. exploited user's personal information repository such as text documents, emails and cached Web pages to implicitly personalize the query expansion for the user [9]. Sadikov et al. conducted an investigation on clustering the refinements of the same original query [30]. The clusters provide a summary of the possible diverse interests of the users who issue the same original query. Their method can also be used to achieve a better personalized query refinement. Some works investigated the effectiveness of using anchor texts in query refinement [12, 23]. They find that anchor text is also an effective resource.

In query suggestion, a commonly used method is mining the click graph [13, 26]. In [26], a sub-bipartite graph of queries and URLs is generated for a particular input query. Then the hitting time of each node is computed by performing a random walk on the subgraph. After that, the query nodes which have the top n earliest hitting time are used as the suggestions. Deng et al. constructed a query-to-query graph instead of the bipartite graph, and the random walk is conducted on the entire graph [13]. They also proposed an entropy based method to calculate the weight of the edges. Cao et al. investigated context aware query suggestion by mining query log [8]. They used a clustering method on the bipartite graph to summarize queries into concepts. Then user sessions are employed to mine the concept patterns, which can help to provide more precise suggestions.

Table 5: Some examples of query refinements.

dutch folklore	kids anger disorders
dutch literature dutch myths dutch mythology dutch legend holland folklore	kids feelings disorders kids anxiety disorders kids emotions disorders kids mental disorders teens anger disorders
racing logistics	discount gucci eyeglasses
sports logistics sport logistics racing operations race logistics playing logistics	discount gucci sunglasses discount vuitton eyeglasses discount gucci glasses discount versace eyeglasses discount chanel eyeglasses

8. CONCLUSIONS AND FUTURE WORK

In this paper, we present a framework for performing query refinement, and this framework mainly has two contributions. First, a graphical model is proposed to score candidate queries, and this model can detect and maintain the semantic consistency of terms in queries. Second, a method is presented to mine term pairs with similar meaning from social tagging data. From the experimental results, we observe that taking the semantic consistency into account can help to give a more reliable prediction of query quality. Furthermore, social tagging data can provide useful information in generating similar term pairs, which is especially important for some unfamiliar terms in previous queries.

Currently, phases are separated into single words in our framework in both latent topic analysis and term dependency estimation. One future direction is to promote our model from single word level to phrase level. Some models such as topical N-grams model [31] and phrase translation model [15] have attested the efficacy of the phrase level solution. In our current model, the score of a candidate query is independent of the current session in which the original query locates and the user who issues the original query. Therefore, another future direction is to consider more personalized or other available information in scoring queries such as the users' Web search history, existing queries in the current user session, etc.

9. REFERENCES

[1] E. Agichtein, E. Brill, and S. Dumais. Improving web search ranking by incorporating user behavior information. In *SIGIR'06*, pages 19–26, 2006.

[2] L. E. Baum, T. Petrie, G. Soules, and N. Weiss. A maximization technique occurring in the statistical analysis of probabilistic functions of markov chains. *The Annals of Math. Statist.*, 41(1):164–171, 1970.

[3] B. Billerbeck, F. Scholer, H. E. Williams, and J. Zobel. Query expansion using associated queries. In *CIKM'03*, pages 2–9, 2003.

[4] D. M. Blei, A. Y. Ng, and M. I. Jordan. Latent dirichlet allocation. *J. Mach. Learn. Res.*, 3:993–1022, 2003.

[5] P. Boldi, F. Bonchi, C. Castillo, D. Donato, A. Gionis, and S. Vigna. The query-flow graph: model and applications. In *CIKM'08*, pages 609–618, 2008.

[6] P. Boldi, F. Bonchi, C. Castillo, D. Donato, and S. Vigna. Query suggestions using query-flow graphs. In *WSCD'09*, pages 56–63, 2009.

[7] Y. Cai and Q. Li. Personalized search by tag-based user profile and resource profile in collaborative tagging systems. In *CIKM'10*, pages 969–978, 2010.

[8] H. Cao, D. Jiang, J. Pei, Q. He, Z. Liao, E. Chen, and H. Li. Context-aware query suggestion by mining click-through and session data. In *SIGKDD'08*, pages 875–883, 2008.

[9] P. A. Chirita, C. S. Firan, and W. Nejdl. Personalized query expansion for the web. In *SIGIR'07*, pages 7–14, 2007.

[10] S. Cucerzan and E. Brill. Spelling correction as an iterative process that exploits the collective knowledge of web users. In *EMNLP'04*, pages 293–300, 2004.

[11] H. Cui, J.-R. Wen, J.-Y. Nie, and W.-Y. Ma. Probabilistic query expansion using query logs. In *WWW'02*, pages 325–332, 2002.

[12] V. Dang and B. W. Croft. Query reformulation using anchor text. In *WSDM'10*, pages 41–50, 2010.

[13] H. Deng, I. King, and M. R. Lyu. Entropy-biased models for query representation on the click graph. In *SIGIR'09*, pages 339–346, 2009.

[14] D. Downey, S. Dumais, D. Liebling, and E. Horvitz. Understanding the relationship between searchers' queries and information goals. In *CIKM '08*, pages 449–458, 2008.

[15] J. Gao, X. He, and J.-Y. Nie. Clickthrough-based translation models for web search: from word models to phrase models. In *CIKM'10*, pages 1139–1148, 2010.

[16] J. Guo, X. Cheng, G. Xu, and H. Shen. A structured approach to query recommendation with social annotation data. In *CIKM'10*, pages 619–628, 2010.

[17] J. Guo, G. Xu, H. Li, and X. Cheng. A unified and discriminative model for query refinement. In *SIGIR'08*, pages 379–386, 2008.

[18] B. He and I. Ounis. Combining fields for query expansion and adaptive query expansion. *Inf. Process. Manage.*, 43:1294–1307, 2007.

[19] D. He, A. Göker, and D. J. Harper. Combining evidence for automatic web session identification. *Inf. Process. Manage.*, 38(5):727–742, 2002.

[20] J. Huang and E. N. Efthimiadis. Analyzing and evaluating query reformulation strategies in web search logs. In *CIKM'09*, pages 77–86, 2009.

[21] T. Joachims. Optimizing search engines using clickthrough data. In *SIGKDD'02*, pages 133–142, 2002.

[22] R. Jones, B. Rey, O. Madani, and W. Greiner. Generating query substitutions. In *WWW'06*, pages 387–396, 2006.

[23] R. Kraft and J. Zien. Mining anchor text for query refinement. In *WWW'04*, pages 666–674, 2004.

[24] G. Kumaran and J. Allan. Effective and efficient user interaction for long queries. In *SIGIR'08*, pages 11–18, 2008.

[25] S. E. Levinson, L. R. Rabiner, and M. M. Sondhi. An introduction to the application of the theory of probabilistic functions of markov process to automatic speech recognition. *Bell System Technical Journal*, 62(4):1035–1074, 1983.

[26] Q. Mei, D. Zhou, and K. Church. Query suggestion using hitting time. In *CIKM'08*, pages 469–478, 2008.

[27] G. Pass, A. Chowdhury, and C. Torgeson. A picture of search. In *InfoScale'06*, 2006.

[28] F. Peng, N. Ahmed, X. Li, and Y. Lu. Context sensitive stemming for web search. In *SIGIR'07*, pages 639–646, 2007.

[29] F. Radlinski and T. Joachims. Query chains: learning to rank from implicit feedback. In *SIGKDD'05*, pages 239–248, 2005.

[30] E. Sadikov, J. Madhavan, L. Wang, and A. Halevy. Clustering query refinements by user intent. In *WWW'10*, pages 841–850, 2010.

[31] X. Wang, A. McCallum, and X. Wei. Topical n-grams: Phrase and topic discovery, with an application to information retrieval. In *ICDM'07*, pages 697–702, 2007.

[32] X. Wang and C. Zhai. Mining term association patterns from search logs for effective query reformulation. In *CIKM'08*, pages 479–488, 2008.

[33] X. Wei, F. Peng, and B. Dumoulin. Analyzing web text association to disambiguate abbreviation in queries. In *SIGIR'08*, pages 751–752, 2008.

[34] R. Wetzker, C. Zimmermann, and C. Bauckhage. Analyzing social bookmarking systems: A del.icio.us cookbook. In *ECAI'08*, pages 26–30, 2008.

[35] R. W. White, M. Bilenko, and S. Cucerzan. Studying the use of popular destinations to enhance web search interaction. In *SIGIR '07*, pages 159–166, 2007.

[36] X. Xue, S. Huston, and W. B. Croft. Improving verbose queries using subset distribution. In *CIKM'10*, pages 1059–1068, 2010.

Retrieval Models for Audience Selection in Display Advertising

Sarah Tyler
Department of Computer Science
University of California at Santa Cruz
skt@soe.ucsc.edu

Sandeep Pandey, Evgeniy Gabrilovich, Vanja Josifovski
Yahoo! Research
{spandey, gabr, vanjaj}@yahoo-inc.com

ABSTRACT

Web applications often rely on user profiles of observed user actions, such as queries issued, page views, etc. In *audience selection* for display advertising, the audience that is likely to be responsive to a given ad campaign is identified via such profiles. We formalize the audience selection problem as a ranked retrieval task over an index of known users. We focus on the common case of audience selection where a small *seed set* of users who have previously responded positively to the campaign is used to identify a broader target audience. The actions of the users in the seed set are aggregated to construct a query, the query is then executed against an index of other user profiles to retrieve the highest scoring profiles, validate our approach on a real-world dataset, demonstrating the trade-offs of different user and query models and find that our approach is particularly robust for small campaigns. The proposed user modeling framework is applicable to many other applications requiring user profiles such as content suggestion and personalization.

Categories and Subject Descriptors

H.3.1 [**Information Storage and Retrieval**]: Content Analysis and Indexing

General Terms

Algorithms, Experimentation

Keywords

Retrieval models, audience selection, ad targeting

1. INTRODUCTION

"Half the money I spend on advertising is wasted; the trouble is I don't know which half."
– John Wanamaker (attributed).

CIKM'11, October 24–28, 2011, Glasgow, Scotland, UK.

Display advertising is the placement of graphical ads displayed on web pages alongside the original content. In display advertising, targeting is often performed by categorizing users into standard segments (e.g., auto, health) based on their online activities. However, such pre-defined segments might be too broad and poorly aligned with audience partitioning by the advertiser. This mismatch has led to the emergence of the current trend of *advertiser-centric* characterization of audiences. One popular approach for the advertisers is to characterize their desired audience by providing a small *seed set* of existing customers as examples for identifying additional prospective customers who are *similar* to those in the seed set, and are likely to "respond" to the advertiser's campaigns. This problem formulation is referred to as *audience selection*.

There are multiple ways to identify users similar to the seed set. One possible approach is K-Nearest Neighbors (KNN) modeling, however, KNN is less effective in very high dimensional spaces. Another possibility is to use Collaborative Filtering (CF) techniques, however, CF requires a sufficiently long history of user-item interactions. In our scenario we only have a few observations of users' prior interactions with ads, and many fewer prior purchases or conversions. Furthermore, unlike CF, where user interests are mostly stationary (e.g., a preference trend for action movies), in online advertising users' interests and needs change over time.

We formulate the audience selection problem as a *retrieval* problem. We build rich user profiles using their entire online experience and explore two retrieval approaches inspired by language modeling and vector space models. Given the seed set of positive examples (users) for the advertiser, we construct a *query*, in a way that is reminiscent of relevance feedback in IR. This query is then executed against the index of all other users (potential customers), and used to identify users for targeting the advertiser's campaign. This method allows for very efficient audience selection when searching over a large space of users.

Our setting differs from that of conventional ad-hoc IR in several interesting ways. First, natural language documents indexed by IR systems are usually fairly coherent around a single topic (or several related topics). On the other hand, users' online history are composed from numerous, often unrelated activities. Furthermore, the events we observe (e.g., Web searches, page views, ad clicks) are heterogeneous and contain varying amounts of information, hence reconciling them into a single user profile is an important research task. Additionally, users' interests evolve over time. The change in their interests can be either personal (e.g., planning a vacation), or can reflect a global trend (e.g., a popular movie). Finally, in contrast to conventional IR, which judges the relevance of retrieved documents, we focus on maximizing the conversion rate, namely, the fraction of (retrieved) users who purchase the product or service being advertised.

2. METHODOLOGY

Given the seed set of users $U = \{s_1, s_2, ...s_3\}$ who have previously converted on a given campaign, our goal is to rank other users by their conversion potential. We approach this problem within the information retrieval paradigm, developing two alternative representations for indexing users. First, we consider *language modeling* (LM), a generative model where documents are generated by a multinomial distribution estimated through maximal likelihood over a document collection. We represent users as sequences of their observed events, hence we can talk about the probability of "generating" a user by estimating the probability of observing a given event sequence. Our second approach is based on the *vector space model* (VSM), which maps documents and queries into a space defined by their features.

2.1 User representation

We represent a user by the set of events $u = \{e_1, e_2 \dots e_n\}$ she has performed over a given history span. Each event is a triplet $e_i =< type_i, int_i, c_i >$, where $type_i$ denotes the event *type*, int_i is the time *interval*, and c_i is the event *content*.

An event *type* describes the nature of the event, such as a page view, ad click, etc. An event occurs at a specific time, and events are grouped in *time intervals* of varying length, ranging from 1 day to 1 month. Time intervals span non-overlapping continuous ranges of user activity, and together cover the whole period of user activity. Different intervals can be assigned different weights, effectively "decaying" the importance of older events. Finally, the event *content* contains the observed information about the event, usually in textual or numeric form, i.e., ids of ads viewed, the text of search queries issued, etc. We employ the bag of words method for modelling content strings, like queries, using both unigrams and bigrams, as well as nodes of a topical taxonomy that represent more general text categories.

An important research question is how to reconcile different events (ie queries the user issued two weeks ago, with ad clicks from the last minute) in a single model. Each of these cues can provide a valuable signal, yet the heterogeneous nature and large volume of user activity would make a very noisy representation if all combined in a single bin. To this end, we propose to represent users as a two-dimensional *array* of models, where we build a separate model (whether a language model or a vector space model) for each combination of a time interval and event type (see Figure 1). For example, if our time intervals are week-long, we have a separate model for the user's page views each week, as well as an additional models for her search queries issued each week. Each entry of this two-dimensional array contains a single model built over the concatenation of the content of all the events of the same type observed in the given interval. We build a single user model by learning weights for the different cells of the two-dimensional array.

2.2 Language modeling for audience selection

Language modeling (LM) has been successfully applied to representing documents and queries in textual information retrieval. LMs are often favored for their competitive performance, clean formalization and probabilistic interpretation.

User model.

Language models are generative models, where each user is assigned a probability of being generated. This probability is computed by estimating the probability of the sequence of events observed for this user. With a simplifying assumption of independence between events, we can transform this probability into a product of the probabilities of individual events. In this form, the model assumes a multinomial distribution over the space of events: $p(u) = p(e_1, e_2 \dots e_n) = p(e_1)p(e_2|e_1)p(e_3|e_2e_1)\dots p(e_n|e_1e_2\dots e_{n-1}) \sim \prod_{i\in 1\dots n} p(e_i)$.

A common strategy to alleviate the independence assumption in document retrieval models is to define composite features or n-grams. Similarly, here we can define composite events that are based on commonly performed actions, e.g., submitting a query followed by browsing the top search results. While we do not present experiments with these type of features, they can be easily facilitated by our model.

We further develop this model by considering the structure of events, namely, their time interval, type, and content: $p(u) = \prod_{i\in 1\dots n} p(e_i) \sim \prod_{i\in 1\dots n}\{p(int_i)\cdot p(type_i|int_i)\cdot p(c_i|int_i, type_i)\}$.

The probability of each event is estimated using three components: (1) the probability of observing an event in the given time interval ($p(int_i)$), (2) the probability of observing in that interval an event of the given type ($p(type_i|int_i)$), and (3) the probability of observing a specific event content given the interval and the event type ($p(c_i|int_i, type_i)$).

The model is simplified by assuming that the activity of the user proceeds with constant frequency. That is, $p(int_i)$ is proportional to the length of the interval, and $\sum_{int\in T} p(int) = 1$, where T is the entire history span. A further simplification can be made by assuming that the mix of event types does not depend on the interval: $p(type|int) \sim p(type)$, that is, the ratio between the number of page views, queries and other event types stays constant. Although this assumption does not necessarily always hold, our intervals are usually fairly long (several days), hence the assumption is not violated too much in practice.

To compute $p(c_i|int_i, type_i)$, we use standard modeling techniques to generate the content of the events. The probability of the textual content of the event is generated based on the probability of individual words: $p(c_i|int_i, type_i) = \prod_{w\in c_i} p(w|int_i, type_i)$, where w stands for a word from the event content and $\sum_w p(w|int_i, type_i) = 1$. These word probabilities are estimated using the maximum-likelihood estimator over the aggregated content of all events of a given type in a given time interval. We used Laplace smoothing.

Query construction.

The query for audience selection is very different than in standard retrieval tasks. In the standard document retrieval, the query is essentially a short fragment of text. In the audience selection task the query is created from a set of seed users, and contains more events than an individual user might. To develop an adequate query representation, we build upon the work on language modeling with relevance feedback [16]. There, the query is composed by merging several documents (users in our case). Conceptually, we treat the seed set of users as relevance

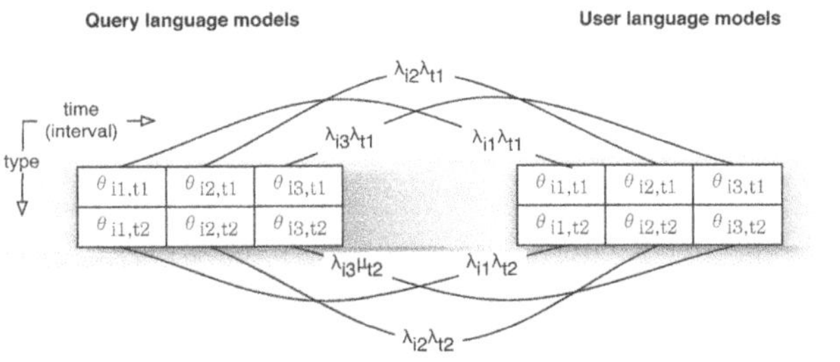

Figure 1: Component models of the user and query.

feedback from the advertiser. The query is thus calculated by finding a language model θ^q that is close to the models of the users in the seed set, but far from the other users (the collection background model) [16]: $p(w|\theta^q) = \exp(\frac{1}{1-\mu}\frac{1}{n}\sum_{i=1}^{n} log\ p(w|\theta^i) - \frac{1}{1-\mu} log\ p(w|C))$, where θ^i are the models for the users in the seed set, C is the background model composed of all other users, and μ is a parameter learned on a validation set. By subtracting the background model we are emphasizing those words/events in the query that discriminate positive users from the rest. Note that this approach is reminiscent of the Rocchio method [12].

Scoring functions.

We use two alternative LM scoring paradigms. First, as in standard language modeling, we score users based on the query likelihood — the probability of the query being generated using the user's language model: $p(q|u) \sim \prod_{w \in q} p(w|\theta^u)$, where θ^u is the language model of the user u. To compute θ^u, we separately analyze the content of events for each combination of interval and event type. More precisely, we manipulate an array of models, $\theta^u_{int,type}$. The user model is then computed as a combination of individual models for different intervals and events types (in a way that is reminiscent of the mixture language models [2, 17]): $p(w|\theta^u) = \sum_{int,type} \lambda_{int} \cdot \lambda_{type} \cdot p(w|\theta^u_{int,type})$. To make the model simpler, we opted to reduce the number of parameters and to learn one parameter for each time interval and event type (λ_{int} and λ_{type}, respectively) from the held-out validation set, instead of learning one parameter for each possible combination (i.e., $\lambda_{int,type}$). Figure 1 illustrates how the query and user models are compared when each is represented as a two-dimensional array of language models.

In the second scoring paradigm we use the model comparison approach. Drawing on the language modeling work for relevance feedback, we use KL-Divergence to compare the query and the user sub-models: $KL(\theta^u, \theta^q) = \sum_{w \in u \cup q} p(w|\theta^q) \cdot log \frac{p(w|\theta^q)}{p(w|\theta^u)}$. Note that log-likelihood is a special case of KL-divergence when the model does not use smoothing, but in our case these two represent different metrics. Here we also compare an array of models, as shown in Figure 1.

2.3 Vector space models for audience selection

Users are represented in our framework as a set of events we observed for them, where each event is a triplet of its time interval, type, and content. In essence, we first construct a meta-document by concatenating the content of all the events of the same type in the same interval. Then, we represent this meta-document as a TFIDF vector of its bag of words. Each user profile is then represented as a weighted combination of such vectors, where the weights are learned on a validation set: $\sum_{int,type} \varphi_{int} \cdot \varphi_{type} \cdot VSM_{int,type}$. Again, to make the model simpler, we reduce the number of parameters and learn one parameter for each time interval and event type (φ_{int} and φ_{type}, respectively). In order to compute $VSM_{int,type}$, we experimented with several TF and IDF formulations (Table 1), and used dot product as the distance metric to compare query and user vectors.

Query construction using the Rocchio algorithm.

We use the Rocchio approach to incorporate pseudo relevance feedback and compose the queries [12] for our vector space model. As a first approximation, we construct the query from two sets of users—the seed set of positive examples (U) who converted on this campaign, and a set of negative examples (V') sampled from the rest of the users (who did not convert on this campaign): $\vec{q} = \rho \cdot \frac{1}{|U|} \cdot \sum_{\vec{u} \in U} \vec{u} - \tau \cdot \frac{1}{|V'|} \cdot \sum_{\vec{u'} \in V' \subset \overline{U}} \vec{u'}$.

Since conversion rates are usually very low, the set of converted users is small, which leads to extreme data sparsity over a rich feature set. To this end, we also experimented with augmenting the seed set of users who converted with an additional set (U^{click}) of *pseudo-positive* users, who clicked on the ad but did not convert (a similar approach was used in [1]). The assumption behind this approach is that the users who clicked on the ad found it relevant at least to some degree, and might still convert later: $\vec{q} = \rho \cdot \frac{1}{|U|} \cdot \sum_{\vec{u} \in U} \vec{u} + \sigma \cdot \frac{1}{|U^{click}|} \cdot \sum_{\vec{u'} \in U^{click}} \vec{u'} - \tau \cdot \frac{1}{|V''|} \cdot \sum_{\vec{u''} \in V'' \subset \overline{U \bigcup U^{click}}} \vec{u''}$, where $V'' \subset \overline{U \bigcup U^{click}}$ is a subsample of negative examples.

In both formulations, values of the free parameters ρ, σ and τ are estimated on held-out validation data.

3. EXPERIMENTAL SETUP

We randomly selected 34 different display ad campaigns, which were registered on the Yahoo Advertiser Network. All these campaigns are performance-based, i.e., advertisers only pay for actual conversions. Of the 34 campaigns, some had only 30-50 conversions per week on average, while others receive many thousands of conversions every week.

User who either viewed, clicked, or converted on the ads from the three week period from 02/04/2010 to 02/24/2010 were identified. Users who converted for campaign c in the first two weeks make up our (positive) seed user set U for c (Section 2.3). The first 2 days of the final week make up the validation set for parameter tuning, and the last 5 days for the test set. In total there were more than 150K validation and 450K test instances across the 34 campaigns.

Each user's profile is constructed from four weeks online activity preceding the user's ad view. Note that while predicting a test instance, say on day t, we access user history up to day $t-1$. Hence, the method is not using any future information.

3.1 Evaluation Metric

One way to evaluate the ranked list of users produced by the different audience selection methods is to use the Receiver Operating Characteristic (ROC) curve. A ROC curve plots true positives versus false positives for different classification thresholds. The Area Under Curve (AUC) for a ROC curve is the probability that the audience selection method assigns a higher score to a random positive example than a random negative example (i.e., probability of concordance).

Term Frequency		Document Frequency		Normalization	
n (natural)	$n(d,t)$	n (no)	1	n (none)	1
r (ratio)	$\frac{n(d,t)}{\sum_{t' \in d} n(t',d)}$	t (idf)	$log(\frac{N}{df_t})$	c (cosine)	$\frac{1}{\sqrt{w_1^2+w_2^2+...+w_M^2}}$
l (log)	$1 + log(n(d,t))$	p (prob idf)	$max\{0, log(\frac{N-df_t}{df_t})\}$		
b (boolean)	$\begin{cases} 1, & \text{if n(d,t)} > 0 \\ 0, & \text{otherwise} \end{cases}$	r (PrTFIDF [7])	$\sqrt{\frac{N}{df_t}}$		

Table 1: TFIDF variants we experimented with.

So, a purely random selection method will have an area under the curve of exactly 0.5. An algorithm that achieves AUC of 0.6 can distinguish a positive user from a negative user with 60% accuracy.

4. RESULTS

We begin by evaluating Vector Space Modeling (VSM) and for Language Modeling (LM), and vary one parameter at a time to study its effect. In most cases, the effect of varying parameter values was similar for VSM and LM, suggesting that both approaches use the information in the data in a similar way; consequently, owing to lack of space we present parameter exploration results only for the VSM model.

While an AUC of 0.8 or more is common in many retrieval tasks, note that the audience selection task is inherently much more difficult than standard textual query-based retrieval. This is due in part because conversions are extremely rare and there are no true negative examples. Users who did not convert right away might still convert later. To put the sparsity into perspective, in the literature researchers have often found it to be difficult to predict clicks where the click-through rates are very small (e.g. 0.01 for certain applications) [3, 8, 11]. Conversions are usually two to three orders of magnitude rarer than clicks. Additionally, there are a multitude of activities in the user profiles that may not be relevant to the conversion.

4.1 Initial Results

For the initial vector space model we set TF to $\frac{n(d,t)}{\sum_{t' \in d} n(t',d)}$ (ratio), IDF to $max\{0, log(\frac{N-df_t}{df_t})\}$ (prob idf), without normalization. In this configuration all events were put into a single time interval and one event type (i.e., only one cell in the two-dimensional array of Figure 1). We study the effect of these parameters later. The query from the seed set was constructed using the Rocchio algorithm with weights $\rho = 1$, $\sigma = 0$, and $\tau = 1$ and dot product was used to score the users. Using this configuration, macro-averaged across all campaigns achieved an AUC of 0.65. Figure 2 shows the performance breakdown of the VSM model over individual campaigns. For some campaigns our approach does remarkably well (and achieves 0.90 AUC), while for some others the model does not perform any better than random guessing. In Section 4.6 we analyze these results and attempt to understand the variation in performance across campaigns.

For the language modeling approach, we use the query construction method as described in Section 2.2. Again, we use a single time interval and merge all the events as if they were of the same type (i.e., effectively consider one event type for this experiment). Overall, we found that the language modeling approach performed on par with the vector space one. In our experiments log-likelihood had a AOC of 0.66, better than both KL-divergence which had a ROC score of 0.63 and VSM score of 0.65.

4.2 The effect of relevance feedback

Recall from Section 2.3 that the query is constructed from the seed set of relevant users and a set of non-relevant users, with ρ and τ representing their weights in the query composition (we discuss the effect of using clicks to create pseudo-positive examples later). Figure 5 illustrates the effect of these two parameters.

Note that when $\tau = 0$, the query is being constructed using only the relevant users. Even though many retrieval systems use only positive feedback [10], in our experiments we found that negative examples can help significantly. For example, the performance goes up from 0.62 to 0.65 when the ratio $\frac{\tau}{\rho}$ is increased from 0 to 1. However, further increasing the value of $\frac{\tau}{\rho}$ causes the non-relevant users to overwhelm the relevant users, which in turn hurts the performance.

When compared on the per campaign basis, using non-relevant users leads to superior performance for most campaigns (over 80%). The increase in performance over the model from Section 2.3 is illustrated in Figure 3. Augmenting the seed set of converted users with users who clicked on ads but did not convert (which we called pseudo-positive examples) resulted in only a negligible improvement in AUC.

4.3 The effect of using time intervals

We represent the user history with a two-dimensional array of time intervals and event types. In section 2.3 we used one bucket of time, yet user histories are four weeks long in our dataset. We divide them into equi-width intervals where each interval is w days long. We vary the value of w from 1 to 28. We learn the importance weights λ_{int} for each time interval using the validation set. When width w is small, it allows us to capture finer patterns in the user history. On the other hand, by making w smaller, we reduce the amount of content in each cell of this two-dimensional array. This leads to data sparsity and worsens the individual cell-based scores computed for a user. For example, while a user and query may match reasonably well when their aggregated representation is a whole week, when compared on a daily basis they may look much less similar.

The best performance comes from $w = 28$, i.e., when the entire user history is put into one interval (Figure 6). This shows that the performance loss due to sparsity when w is decreased, outweighs the benefit of capturing finer user patterns. When $w < 28$, we found that the model learned higher weights for more recent intervals than the older ones. For example, with $w = 10$ we get the weight of 0.76 for the most recent interval, 0.19 for the second interval, and only 0.05 for the oldest one. This shows that recent activities are a better indicator of conversion likelihood, as expected.

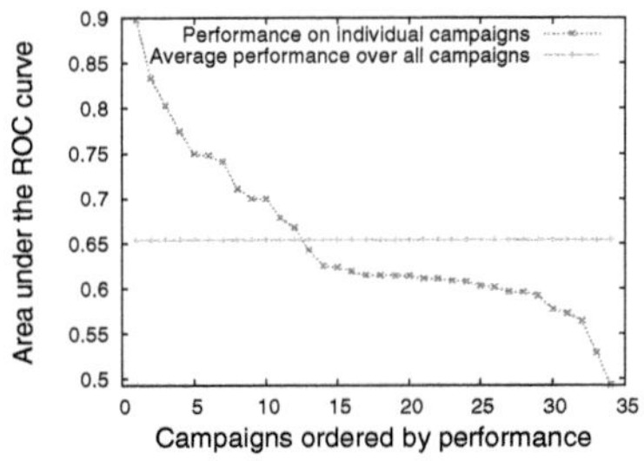

Figure 2: Performance of our VSM approach.

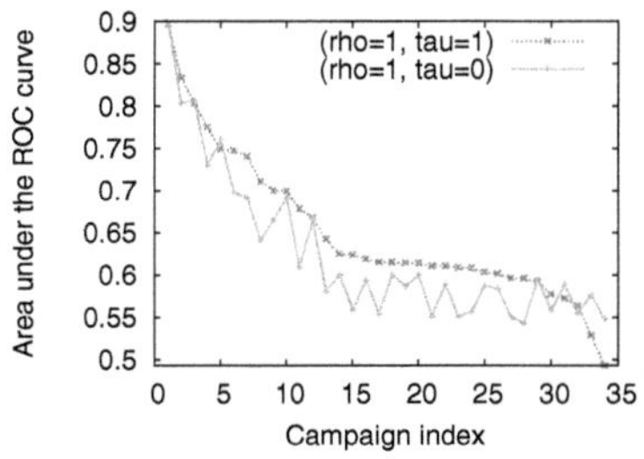

Figure 3: Using vs. not using non-relevant users.

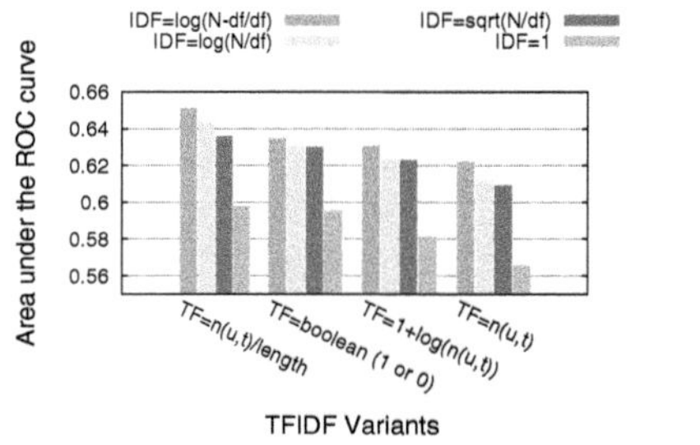

Figure 4: The effect of TFIDF variations.

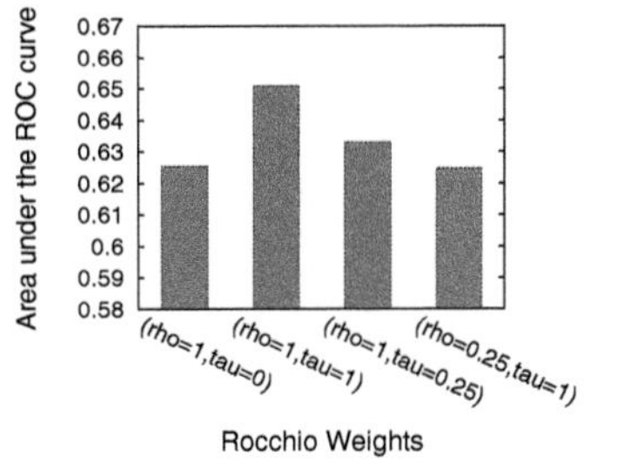

Figure 5: The effect of using non-relevant users.

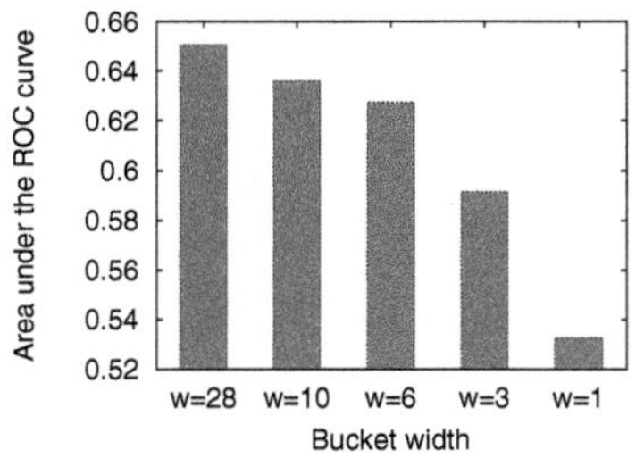

Figure 6: The effect of the time interval width.

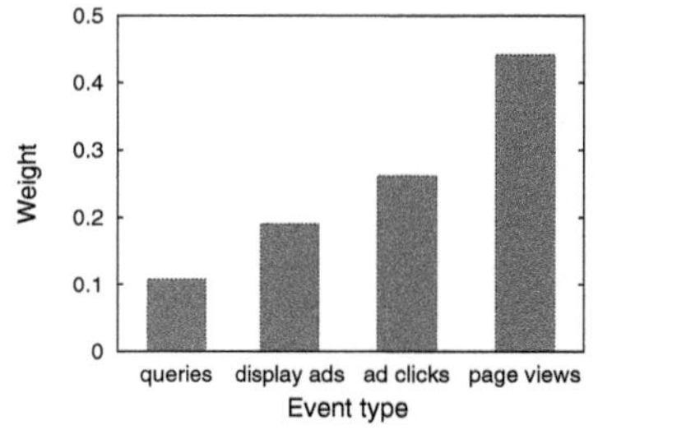

Figure 7: Weights learned for different event types.

4.4 The effect of event types

User history consists of different kinds of events (such as page views, ad clicks and the like). Instead of treating them collectively as was done in the previous experiments, each event is divided into four event types: page views, search queries, organic and sponsored result clicks, and ad views. As described in Section 2.3, we construct a separate representation for each event type, score them, and then take a weighted linear combination of these scores (where the weights for the different event types, λ_{type}, are learned using the validation set). By doing so, we achieved a marginal improvement of 0.005 in AUC over the 0.65 AUC achieved by the baseline (Section 4.1). More interestingly, we found that some event types are much more indicative of user interests than others. In Figure 7, we show the weights learned for the different event types using the validation set. Browsed page views seem to help the most in predicting conversions. Even though one might expect page views to be less predictive than other event types such as queries and clicks, in our dataset they have higher density (i.e., much more events of this type) compared to other event types.

4.5 TFIDF Variants

TFIDF weighting of features has been central to the vector space models. The success of the TFIDF weighting scheme is due to its capturing the importance of features both within the document (TF) and in the entire collection (IDF).

In traditional IR, the TF function is based on the number of occurrences of the term within the document, namely, the raw term frequency which we will denote by $n_{u,t}$. In user modeling there are multiple ways of defining $n_{u,t}$. We considered (1) number of days on which feature t appeared in the (time interval, event type) cell for user u (ie #days) and (2) number of times feature t appeared in the (time interval, event type) cell for user u (ie #occurrences). While both forms of $n_{u,t}$ perform fairly similar, the best performance comes from the #days definition of $n_{u,t}$. A likely explanation is that it captures sustained user interest in an activity for a conversion to happen. Additionally, #days is more robust, e.g., some Web pages reload automatically and can dramatically bloat the number of the occurrences, while their adverse effect on #days is significantly limited.

We evaluate four different forms of TF defined in terms of $n_{u,t}$: boolean, log, natural, and ratio and different forms of and IDF functions (see Table 1). The results are shown in Figure 4. First, we note that the rightmost bar corresponds to no TFIDF weighting, i.e., TF $=n_{u,t}$ (natural), IDF $=1$ (no). It achieves an AUC of 0.56 while our best setting achieves AUC $= 0.65$. This shows the significance of TFIDF weighting in the vector space model for users.

Among the various TF forms, TF $=\frac{n_{u,t}}{\sum_{t' \in u} n_{u,t'}}$ (ratio) is consistently the best across all forms of IDF. This is remarkable because we normally expect more active users to be more likely to convert, and vice versa. However, this TF form, normalized with respect to the total amount of user activity, shows that it is not necessarily the case. Instead, it is the user activity in a specific topic relative to her overall activity that leads to the best prediction performance.

Among the IDF variants, we found $max\{0, log(\frac{N-df_t}{df_t})\}$ (prob idf) to perform the best, with $log(\frac{N}{df_t})$ and $\sqrt{\frac{N}{df_t}}$ taking the second and third spot.

4.6 Individual Campaigns

To investigate the variation in performance over individual campaigns, we divided the campaigns into 3 sets, *large*, *medium* and *small*, where the *large* group contains the top one-third of the campaigns with the highest number of conversions, while the *small* group contains the bottom one-third. We found that our approach performs well in all three groups, in fact it does better on the medium (0.657) and small (0.673) campaigns compared to the large ones (0.624). Since most methods suffer when they are trained on fewer positive examples, this is a nice advantage of our approach, as it seems it can be applied to these tail/small campaigns, where other methods, especially discriminative ones, struggle to perform. This can also explain why our approach did not benefit much from using pseudo-positive examples based on users who clicked on the ads but did not immediately convert. These pseudo-positive examples typically prove helpful on small campaigns where there are few positive examples. However, our approach already performs well on those campaigns.

In further analysis of large campaigns we found that these campaigns are quite diverse and are thus associated with a variety of goals (ad groups, in computational advertising terminology), and thus different kinds of users convert on them. In other words, there is more heterogeneity among the seed users in these campaigns (compare to the smaller ones), and when these diverse users are combined together during the query construction process, they weaken the signal and hurt the performance of our approach.

5. RELATED WORK

Audience selection/segmentation is an important task in marketing. Since customers have diverse interests and needs, marketing strategies that target individual segments perform better than a single global strategy for the entire population [6]. In this paper we formulated the problem of audience selection in display advertising within the IR paradigm.

Our approach has similarities to user profiling and behavioral targeting based on observed past events. A commonly used approach in behavioral targeting is to infer user interests and use them to predict whether she will be interested in a product. Chen et al. [4] proposed a linear regression model to leverage user behavior for predicting ad clicks. However, learning regression models for conversions is difficult since conversions are typically several order of magnitude fewer than clicks. Another difficulty in modeling user behavior is that user interests are not always fixed, and some interests are transient, influenced by media and pop culture. Shmueli-Scheuer et al. [13] used a decay model to predict clicks to give recent features more emphasis. In their analysis of query interests, Wedig et al. [14] found that users tend to stabilize on a distribution of interests. In contrast, Liu et al. [9] found that user interests change from month to month based on their analysis of news topics and attributed this change to the task of browsing news (compare to the task of issuing queries studied by Wedig et al. [14]).

In their empirical study on understanding the potential of behavioral targeting for online advertising, Yan et al. [15] studied how ad click-through rates relate to the search queries and page views of the users who clicked on these ads. They found that users who clicked on the same ads tend to have more behavioral similarities than users who clicked on different ads. Our work builds on this hypothesis to perform audience selection, where we model user similarity using multiple sources of information, such as page views, clicks on search results, and the like, and not only ad clicks. We also focus on conversions rather than clicks. In particular, we first construct a query based on the seed set of users who converted in the past, and then execute this query against an index of user profiles. This allows us to retrieve more users who are similar to the seed set, and are therefore likely to convert in the future.

6. CONCLUSION

In this paper, we formulated the problem of audience selection as an information retrieval task, retrieving user profiles instead of documents. These profiles are constructed based on users' online actions such as browsing and searching. Unlike documents, which are often coherent units, user activity is composed of multiple events at distinct time points, each potentially having distinct intent. We then defined a formal retrieval model for the audience selection task based on language modeling and vector space modeling.

We found that both vector space and language models performed well for this task. We also found that using TFIDF feature weighting, as well as using a set of non-relevant users for Rocchio-style query expansion significantly improves performance. Although recent activity proved more important than past activity, bucketing based on time intervals degraded performance, as it led to the sparsity of data.

Acknowledgements.

We thank Fernando Diaz for his insightful comments.

7. REFERENCES

[1] A. Bagherjeiran, A. O. Hatch, and A. Ratnaparkhi. Ranking for the conversion funnel. In *SIGIR*, 2010.

[2] J. Bai, J.-Y. Nie, H. Bouchard, and G. Cao. Using query contexts in information retrieval. In *SIGIR*, 2007.

[3] D. Chakrabarti, D. Agarwal, and V. Josifovski. Contextual advertising by combining relevance with click feedback. In *WWW '08*, pages 417–426, 2008.

[4] Y. Chen, D. Pavlov, and J. F. Canny. Large-scale behavioral targeting. In *KDD '09*, 2009.

[5] M. Gonen. Receiver operating characteristic (ROC) curves. *SAS Users Group International (SUGI)*, 31:210–231, 2006.

[6] B. J. P. II. Mass customizing products and services. In *Strategy & Leadership. Vol. 21, no. 4*, 1993.

[7] T. Joachims. A probabilistic analysis of the rocchio algorithm with tfidf for text categorization. In *ICML'97*, pages 143–151, 1997.

[8] A. Lacerda, M. Cristo, M. A. Goncalves, W. Fan, N. Ziviani, and B. Ribeiro-Neto. Learning to advertise. In *SIGIR '06*, pages 549–556, 2006.

[9] J. Liu, P. Dolan, and E. R. Pedersen. Personalized news recommendation based on click behavior. In *IUI*, 2010.

[10] C. D. Manning, P. Raghavan, and H. Schuetze. *Introduction to Information Retrieval*. Cambridge University Press, 2008.

[11] M. Richardson, E. Dominowska, and R. Ragno. Predicting clicks: estimating the click-through rate for new ads. In *WWW '07*. ACM Press, 2007.

[12] J. J. Rocchio. Relevance feedback in information retrieval. In *The SMART Retrieval System: Experiments in Automatic Document Processing*. 1971.

[13] M. Shmueli-Scheuer, H. Roitman, D. Carmel, Y. Mass, and D. Konopnicki. Extracting user profiles from large scale data. In *MDAC'10*, 2010.

[14] S. Wedig and O. Madani. A large-scale analysis of query logs for assessing personalization opportunities. In *KDD '06*, pages 742–747, 2006.

[15] J. Yan, N. Liu, G. Wang, W. Zhang, Y. Jiang, and Z. Chen. How much can behavioral targeting help online advertising? In *WWW '09*, 2009.

[16] C. Zhai and J. Lafferty. Model-based feedback in the language modeling approach to information retrieval. In *CIKM '01*, pages 403–410, 2001.

[17] C. Zhai, X. Lu, X. Ling, X. He, A. Velivelli, X. Wang, H. Fang, and A. Shakery. Uiuc/musc at trec 2005 genomics track. In *TREC '05*, 2005.

A Language Model Approach to Capture Commercial Intent and Information Relevance for Sponsored Search

Lei Wang
Yahoo! Global R&D Center, Beijing
Beijing, 100083, China
wanglei@yahoo-inc.com

Mingjiang Ye
Yahoo! Global R&D Center, Beijing
Beijing, 100083, China
mye@yahoo-inc.com

Yu Zou
Yahoo! Labs
Beijing, 100083, China
yuzou@yahoo-inc.com

ABSTRACT

A fundamental task of sponsored search is how to find the best match between web search queries and textual advertisements. To address this problem, we explicitly characterize the criteria for an advertisement to be a 'good match' to a query from two aspects (it should be relevant with the query from information perspective, and it should be able to capture and satisfy the commercial intent in the query). Correspondingly, we introduce in this paper a mixture language model of two parts: a commercial model which characterizes language bias of commercial intent leveraging on users' clicks on advertisements, and an informational model which is a traditional language model with consideration of the entropy of each word to capture informational relevance. We then introduce a regularized expectation-maximization (EM) algorithm model for parameters estimation, and integrate query commercial intent into the scoring function to boost overall click efficiency.

Empirical evaluation shows that our model achieves better performance as compared to a well tuned classical language model and deliberated TFIDF-pLSI model (6% and 5% precision improvement at our operating point in production environment of 30% recall, and 5.3% and 6.3% AUC improvement), and performs superior to the KL Divergence language model for tail queries (0.5% nDCG improvement). Live traffic test shows over 2% CTR lift and 2.5% RPS lift as well.

Categories and Subject Descriptors

H.3.3 [**Information Storage and Retrieval**]: Information Search and Retrieval

General Terms

Algorithms, Measurement, Performance, Experimentation

CIKM'11, October 24–28, 2011, Glasgow, Scotland, UK.

Keywords

Online Advertising, Sponsored Search, Language Model, Commercial Intent, Relevance

1. INTRODUCTION

Sponsored search has become a $\$10B+$ business [15] in recent years. In sponsored search, most often, the advertisements are selected by 'exact match' between queries and bid phrases. This kind of intuitive methods, though are effective in general situations, do have some obvious drawbacks, such as low coverage for tail queries and not robust in precision. On the other hands, language model, a prominent IR model, though has been successfully applied to many problems and has gained superior performance, faces two challenges when applying to sponsored search: 1) *how to characterize and capture commercial intent.* In sponsored search, besides informational relevance, an equally, may be more, important objective is to identify and serve users' commercial intent which may bring in further commercial activities, and 2) *how to estimate model parameters reliably.* Advertisements are relatively short, usually just tens of words (in our work we do not take landing pages into consideration because they are usually very noisy and are not available all the time), not sufficient for model estimation.

Firstly we regard an advertisement as a 'good match' to a user query if it satisfies two criteria: 1) it is relevant with the query from information perspective, and 2) it captures and satisfies the commercial intent (if there is any) in the query. Correspondingly, from the demand perspective, we explicitly model users' intents in raising a query from two aspects, informational intent and commercial intent. For example when a user has an interest on iPad2. He may raise a query like 'iPad2 with Wi-Fi 3G' to learn some informational knowledge about features such as Wi-Fi and 3G, as well as to learn some commercial characteristics like the price and how to buy, and then leveraging on these information he may make a decision about whether to take further commercial activities.

Accordingly, from the supply perspective, a 'clever' advertiser is expected to deliberately organize his advertisements to satisfy both of the two kinds of intents concurrently to maximize the attraction of the advertisements. In this sense, we design our language model as a mixture model of an informational model and a commercial model, in which the informational model is a traditional language model with consideration of the entropy of each word for informational relevance, while the commercial model characterizes language bias of commercial intent leveraging on users' clicks on advertisements. Further more, we explicitly introduce query commercial propensity into the scoring function to boost commercial queries.

Secondly, we leverage on both local and global information to try to estimate model parameters more reliably. We first utilize global information such as query set and click logs to compute the global word importance in expressing informational intent and commercial intent respectively, and then incorporate them with local information such as term frequency to estimate the informational model and commercial model. We then introduce a regularized EM algorithm to refine the parameter estimations together with the model selection probability estimation, which integrates the global and local information better. Empirical evaluation and live traffic performance confirms the effectiveness of our model.

2. MIXTURE LANGUAGE MODEL

As illustrated in formula (1), in classical language model, we generally use a model θ which is a distribution over words to characterize a people's language habit. For documents retrieval tasks, we usually regard a document D as a sample from θ, and then use this sample to estimate a model θ_D to approximate θ (the V in formula (1) is the vocabulary of the language of the document D). Maximum likelihood estimation (MLE) is widely used in the estimation, according to which $P(w|D)$ is equal to the relative term frequency of w in D as in formula (2). We then assume that the query is generated from some language model as well, and in this sense the likelihood that the query Q is generated from θ_D can be used to score D.

$$\theta \simeq \theta_D = \{P(w|D)\}_{w \in V} \tag{1}$$

$$P(w|D) = \frac{tf(w, D)}{\sum_w tf(w, D)} \tag{2}$$

For sponsored search, we assume that a person has different language biases in expressing commercial intent and informational intent. The generation procedure for each query word then includes two steps: the user first implicitly selects a language model corresponding to his instant intent (commercial or informational), and then select a word within the selected language model. With these assumptions, we define our language model θ (or θ_D in estimation) as a Bernoulli mixture model of two multinomial models, a commercial language model θ_C and an informational language model θ_I:

$$\theta_D \simeq \theta = Bern(\theta_C, \theta_I) \tag{3}$$

In the more precise form in formula (4), α_i is the model selection probability with constrain that $\sum_{i \in \{I,C\}} \alpha_i = 1$.

$$P(w|\theta) = \sum_{i \in \{I,C\}} \alpha_i P(w|\theta_i) \tag{4}$$

The model parameters estimation and model selection probability estimation appear in the following sub sections.

2.1 Commercial Model

We use the commercial model θ_C to characterize an advertiser's language bias when he expresses commercial intent. Given a document D, intuitively θ_C can be estimated by regarding the commercial portion of D as a sample, which can be formulated as formula (5), in which C denotes '*the person is under commercial intent*' or can be equally defined as '*the commercial model θ_C is selected*', so $P(w|C, D)$ defines the words distribution of the commercial portion of D.

$$\theta_C = \{P(w|C, D)\}_{w \in V} \tag{5}$$

With this definition, challenge comes soon that it is hard to tell the commercial portion of a document from other portions, and thus we can't use MLE to estimate the model directly. Instead, we transform the formula using Bayesian method as formula (6), in which the task is transformed to compute $P(w, C|D)$.

$$P(w|C, D) = \frac{P(w, C|D)}{P(C|D)} = \frac{P(w, C|D)}{\sum_w P(w, C|D)} \tag{6}$$

Our lines of thinking to estimate $P(w, C|D)$ originate from two perspectives, global context perspective and local context perspective. We heuristically compute two estimations denoted as $P_g(w, C|D)$ and $P_l(w, C|D)$ from the two perspectives respectively, and then linearly combine them as the final estimation of $P(w, C|D)$.

2.1.1 Global Context Perspective

We estimate $P_g(w, C|D)$ as formula (7), in which $P(w|D)$ can be estimated using MLE as in formula (2), and $P(C|w, D)$ refers to '*given D as a prior sample, and suppose that a person raises a word w, the probability that w derives from the commercial intent of the person*'. As illustrated in formula (8), we make an independency assumption here that the posterior probability of a person's commercial intent given a word he has raised is a global characteristic of the word (an example of global characteristic is IDF) determined by the global context such as global query set or click feedback set, while has no relationship with the local context in which the word exists (here the local context refers to the document D). In this way, the problem is transformed to compute $P(C|w)$.

$$P_g(w, C|D) = P(w|D)P(C|w, D) \tag{7}$$

$$P(C|w, D) \simeq P(C|w) \tag{8}$$

We refer to Sandeep's work in estimating advertisability of tail queries [11] to estimate $P(C|w)$ utilizing click feedback. We make two assumptions: 1) $P(C|w)$ is uniform for (independent of) users and advertisers, and 2) each instance of click or not click on advertisements served for a query is a referendum of the commercial intent of each word in the query independently. The computation method is as formula (9), in which $c(q)$ indicates the number of times users click some advertisements after raising the query q, while $n(q)$ indicates the number of times users raise q without clicking any advertisements.

$$P(C|w) = \frac{\sum_q^{w \in q} c(q)}{\sum_q^{w \in q} (c(q) + n(q))} \tag{9}$$

2.1.2 Local Context Perspective

Another thinking line for this problem is to introduce topics as mediator as follows.

$$P_l(w, C|D) = \sum_i P(w|t_i)P(C|t_i, w)P(t_i|D) \tag{10}$$

In formula (10), $P(w|t_i)$ and $P(t_i|D)$ denotes words distribution on a topic and topics distribution on a document respectively. Both of them can be solved by pLSI [8][7] or L-DA [2] etc., and $P(C|t_i, w)$ refers to '*suppose a person issues a word w to express a topic t_i, the probability that w derives from the commercial intent of the person*'. As in formula (11), we make an independency assumption here that the posterior probability of a person's commercial intent given the word he has raised is totally decided by the local context in which the word occurs, that is the topic the person is to express using the word, but has no relationship with the global context. In this way, the problem is transformed to compute $P(C|t_i)$, which boils down to compute $P(t_i|C)$ and $P(t_i)$.

$$P(C|t_i, w) \simeq P(C|t_i) \propto \frac{P(t_i|C)}{P(t_i)} \tag{11}$$

In our implementation, we first train 1000 topics utilizing pLSI (we sample 100 million queries no matter commercial or not from an industrial search engine's query logs in one month, and use the corpus of the top 5 search result pages for each query to train the topics), and then leverage on fold-in algorithm [3] to compute $P(t_i|C)$ on a set of click-through data of query-advertisement pairs in three months and compute $P(t_i)$ on the corpus of all advertisements of the three months. Here we regard $(P(t_i|C))$ as the topics distribution on the corpus of clicked advertisements, in which an advertisement clicked i times will be counted $1 + \log i$ times in occurrence to weight its importance, while regard $P(t_i)$ as the topics distribution on corpus of all advertisements no matter shown or not.

2.2 Informational Model

Besides commercial intent, we want to capture the ordinary 'relevance' as well. Generally this can be achieved by a traditional language model such as [12]. In our work we refine the traditional language model to explicitly characterize 'relevance' from the informational perspective. We use the informational model θ_I to characterize an advertiser's language bias when he expresses informational intent. Similar with θ_C, intuitively θ_I can be estimated by regarding the informational portion of D as a sample, which can be formulated as formula (12), in which I denotes '*the person is under informational intent*' or can be equally defined as '*the informational model θ_I is selected*', and thus $P(w|I, D)$ defines the words distribution of the informational portion of D.

$$\theta_I = \{P(w|I, D)\}_{w \in V} \tag{12}$$

We make an assumption that the relative frequency of a word in the informational portion of a document can be approximated by the proportion of the quantity of information from information theory perspective, and thus we define $P(w|I, D)$ as the ratio of information content of word w in D towards the sum of information content of all words in D. In formula (13), $ic(w)$ denotes the information content of w , which equals to the term frequency of w in D (that is $tf(w, D)$) multiplies the self information of w (that is $-\log P(w)$). We first estimate $P(w)$ using MLE on a corpus of 100 million user queries sampled from an industrial search engine's query logs, and then use Bayesian smoothing to smooth it with the one estimated on a larger archive of web pages of the search engine.

$$P(w|I, D) = \frac{ic(w)}{\sum_w ic(w)} = \frac{tf(w, D)\log P(w)}{\sum_w tf(w, D)\log P(w)} \tag{13}$$

2.3 Model Selection Probability Estimation and Parameters Refinement

In this section we present a regularized EM algorithm to estimate the model selection probability and to refine the model parameters estimated in the above two subsections in the mean time.

In classical EM algorithm [5][10], we generally denote the log likelihood of a document D to be generated from a mixture model as formula (14), in which α_j denotes the model selection probability. In order to maximize $L(D)$, in E step, EM algorithm estimates the expectation of the complete likelihood denoted as $Q(\psi; \psi^o)$ in formula (15), in which ψ denotes all parameters while ψ^o denotes values of ψ estimated in the last iteration, and $z(w, j)$ here is a hidden variable which denotes the probability that w is generated from model θ_j and boils down to the form in formula (16), and $\mu(1 - \sum_j \alpha_j)$ is the Lagrange Multiplier corresponding to the constrain that $\sum_j \alpha_j = 1$. Then in M step, EM algorithm finds the values of ψ which maximize $Q(\psi; \psi^o)$, that is to find $\psi^{(o+1)} = \underset{\psi}{\text{argmax}} Q(\psi; \psi^o)$.

$$L(D) = \sum_w tf(w, D) \log \sum_j \alpha_j P(w|\theta_j) \tag{14}$$

$$\begin{aligned} Q(\psi; \psi^o) = &\sum_w tf(w, D) \sum_j z(w, j) \log(\alpha_j P(w|\theta_j)) \\ &+ \mu(1 - \sum_j \alpha_j) \end{aligned} \tag{15}$$

$$z(w, j) = P(\theta_j|w, \psi^o) = \frac{\alpha_j^o P^o(w|\theta_j)}{\sum_{i \in \{C,I\}} \alpha_i^o P^o(w|\theta_i)} \tag{16}$$

The key idea of our regularized EM algorithm is as follows: the model selection probability and the refined model parameters estimations should maximize the likelihood that the document is generated from the mixture model as much as possible, with regularization that the refined estimations should be similar with the original estimations (computed as in subsection 2.1 and 2.2) as much as possible. In this way, we expect to integrate the local information and global information better.

$$\begin{aligned} Q^R(\psi; \psi^o) = &\lambda Q(\psi; \psi^o) + (1 - \lambda) \sum_j D_{KL}(\theta_j^g \parallel \theta_j) \\ \simeq &\lambda \sum_w tf(w, D) \sum_j z(w, j) \log \alpha_j P(w|\theta_j) \\ &- (1 - \lambda) \sum_j \sum_w P(w|\theta_j^g) \log P(w|\theta_j) \\ &+ (1 - \lambda) \sum_j \sum_w P(w|\theta_j^g) \log P(w|\theta_j^g) \\ &+ \mu(\sum_j \alpha_j - 1) \\ &+ \nu \sum_j (\sum_w P(w|\theta_j) - 1) \end{aligned} \tag{17}$$

As illustrated in formula (17), in the regularized EM algorithm, we denote the original model parameters estimations got from subsections 2.1 and 2.2 as θ_C^g and θ_I^g respectively, and denote the refined parameters to be computed by regularized EM algorithm as θ_C and θ_I correspondingly. We then define the regularized expectation of complete likelihood $Q^R(\psi;\psi^o)$ for EM algorithm as a combination of two portions: 1) the expectation of complete data likelihood $Q(\psi;\psi^o)$ as in classical EM algorithm, and 2) the KL-Divergence of original estimations towards new estimations $\sum_j D_{KL}(\theta_j^g \parallel \theta_j)$. In formula (17), $\mu(\sum_j \alpha_j - 1)$ and $\nu\sum_j(\sum_w P(w|\theta_j)-1)$ are Lagrange Multipliers with respect to limitations of $\sum_j \alpha_j = 1$ and $\sum_w P(w|\theta_j) = 1$.

There are closed form solutions for the regularized EM problem as follows. The estimation of α_j remains the same as in original EM, while $P(w|\theta_j)$ reflects the influence from both the document and the original estimations. $z(w,j)$ is same as in formula (16).

$$\alpha_j = \frac{\sum_w tf(w,D)z(w,j)}{\sum_j \sum_w tf(w)z(w,j)} \tag{18}$$

$$P(w|\theta_j) = \frac{(1-\lambda)P(w|\theta_j^g) - \lambda tf(w,D)z(w,j)}{(1-\lambda) - \lambda \sum_w tf(w,D)z(w,j)} \tag{19}$$

3. COMMERCIAL QUERY BIASED SCORING FUNCTION

Generally in classical language model we utilize the query likelihood function $P(Q|\theta_D)$ to score the document, which denotes the likelihood that the query Q is generated from the language model θ_D estimated by document D.

3.1 Query Commercial Intent Integration

In sponsored search we have a special and critically important demand. We want to serve more advertisements to queries with high commercial intent than queries with low commercial intent. The benefits are double folded: 1) it improves user experience by satisfying users who need to reach advertisements to facilitate their commercial activities without bothering users who do not want to see advertisements at present, and 2) it increases the number of advertisements candidates going to the second (ranking) stage for valuable queries, which helps to increase the probability to draw users' clicks. In this sense, we integrate query commercial intent into query likelihood function.

$$P(Q,C|\theta_D) = P(Q|\theta_D)P(C|Q,\theta_D) = P(Q|\theta_D)P(C|Q) \tag{20}$$

In formula (20), C denotes '*user is under commercial intent*', and $P(Q,C|\theta_D)$ denotes '*the likelihood that a user raises a query Q from the language model estimated from D and the user is to express his commercial intent*'. Because the commercial intent is only expressed by Q, it is independent with θ_D. The method to compute $P(C|Q)$ is same with Sandeep's work of query's advertisability [11] as follows, in which $S \subseteq Q$ and $|S| \leq k$ and k is a truncating parameter to avoid biasing long queries.

$$P(C|Q) = \max_S\{1 - \Pi_{w\in S}(1 - P(C|w))\} \tag{21}$$

3.2 The Scoring Function in Practice

In practice, we use the Bayesian transformed function to score advertisements as formula (22).

$$P(D,C|Q) = \frac{P(Q,C|D)P(D)}{P(Q)} = \frac{P(Q|D)}{P(Q)}P(C|Q)P(D) \tag{22}$$

Here we interpret $P(Q|D)$ as $P(Q|\theta_D)$, which further equals to $\Pi_{w\in Q}P(w|\theta_D)^{tf(w,Q)}$ with the query words independency assumption. For words which exist in query Q without existing in D we assign to them a non-zero probability in the model θ_D as $P(w|\theta_D) = \rho P(w)$, in which $P(w)$ is the global prior probability, and ρ is a document specific parameter which equals to $\frac{\eta}{|D|+\eta}$ [14] (η is the parameter of Dirichlet smoothing that is widely used in traditional language models). With further assuming $P(Q) = \prod_{w\in Q} P(w)^{tf(w,Q)}$, we can compute $\frac{P(Q|D)}{P(Q)}$ as formula (23).

$$\begin{aligned}\frac{P(Q|D)}{P(Q)} &= \prod_{w\in Q}\left(\frac{P(w|\theta_D)}{P(w)}\right)^{tf(w,Q)} \\ &= \prod_{w\in Q \bigcap w\in D}\left(\frac{P(w|\theta_D)}{P(w)}\right)^{tf(w,Q)} \\ &\times \prod_{w\in Q \bigcap w\notin D}\left(\frac{\rho P(w)}{P(w)}\right)^{tf(w,Q)}\end{aligned} \tag{23}$$

And thus we get the final scoring function as formula (24).

$$\begin{aligned} score(D,Q) &= \log P(D,C|Q) \\ &= \sum_{w\in Q\bigcap w\in D} tf(w,Q)\log\frac{P(w|D)}{P(w)} \\ &+ \sum_{w\in Q\bigcap w\notin D} tf(w,Q)\log\rho \\ &+ \log P(C|Q) + \log P(D)\end{aligned} \tag{24}$$

4. EVALUATION

In this section we first evaluate the effectiveness of our model on editorial data set by comparing with a classical baseline language model, the TFIDF and the TFIDF-pLSI vector space model, as well as the deliberated KLD language model, and then show live traffic performance. Our evaluation dataset consists of 87690 query-ad pairs (14000 queries) manually labeled by professional editors.

4.1 Compare with Baseline Language Model

In this section we compare the performance of mixture language model with that of baseline language model. We evaluate the effectiveness of biasing query commercial intent in scoring function as well. The details are as follows.

Baseline LM: we use Hema Raghavan's refinement [14] of the classical Multinomial language model for sponsored search as baseline. In Hema's evaluation, this baseline performs considerately better than the query-rewriting method and TFIDF. In implementation we use $P(D|Q) = \frac{P(Q|D)P(D)}{P(Q)}$ as scoring function and use MLE and Dirichlet smoothing to estimate $P(w|D)$ (both unigrams and phrases from a large phrases dictionary are used). We set the smoothing factor η to be 0.5 which achieves the best performance in our dataset. $P(D)$ derives from the host trust score corresponding to the URL of the advertisements.

Mixture LM: the methods and dataset used to implement our mixture language model are the same as described in section 2 and section 3. The combination coefficient of the $P_g(w,C|D)$ in computing θ_C is 0.6. In the regularized EM algorithm, we re-scaled the $Q^R(\psi;\psi^o)$ to comparable granularity with $\sum_j D_{KL}(\theta_j^g \parallel \theta_j)$ and set λ to be 0.3. These two parameters are chosen empirically by evaluations.

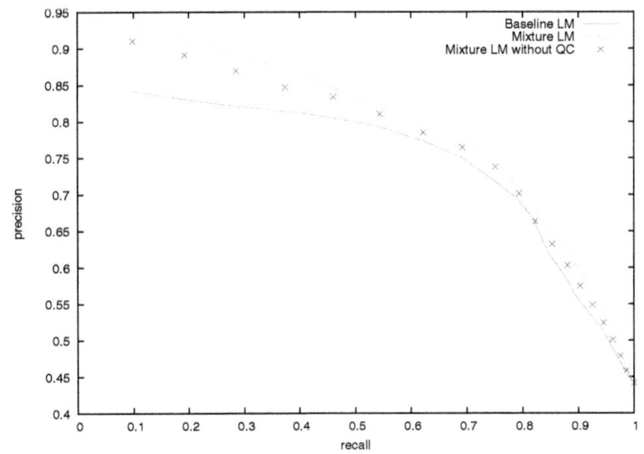

Figure 1: comparison with Baseline LM in PR.

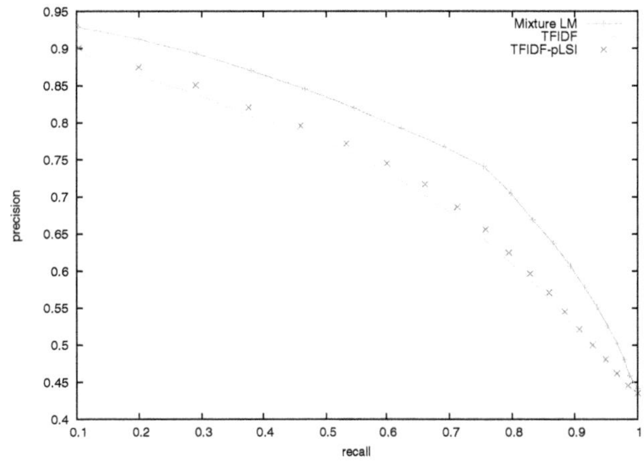

Figure 2: comparison with TFIDF and pLSI in PR.

Mixture LM without QC: the only difference with 'Mixture LM' is that we do not use the commercial queries biased scoring function but use the one same as Baseline LM.

Our Mixture LM performs better than Baseline LM. As in Figure 1, the precision improvement when recall is less than 0.4 is in range 5%-9%. At our operating point in product environment (of 0.3 recall) the precision improvement is 6%. On tail portion when recall is above 0.8 there is about 1% precision lift as well. In terms of ROC, from Table 1 we can see that the improvement in AUC is 5.3%.

Both the mixture model estimation methods and commercial query biased scoring function (QC for abbreviation) contribute to the improvement. However, they contribute in different ways. Mixture model estimation focuses on advertisements side and contributes through differentiating terms' roles in expressing people's intents, while QC focuses on query side and contributes through relatively boosting scores for high commercial intent queries which deserve more advertisements.

4.2 Compare with TF-IDF and pLSI

In this section we compare the performance of mixture language model with that of TFIDF vector space model and TFIDF-pLSI combined vector space model. Before implementing language model, we have deployed well tuned TFIDF and TFIDF-pLSI combined model in production whose performance are very promising. The details of candidates are as follows.

TFIDF: we elaborately refined the classical TFIDF model [16] for evaluation. We introduced term importance t leveraging on click feedback and tuned different weights z for different zones (title, description and bid phrases) by simulated annealing. The advertisements side feature weight for term w is then $t(1 + \log(\sum_i tf(w, zone_i)z_i)) \log idf$, and that of query side is similar. The matching score is cosine similarity. Both unigrams and phrases are used.

TFIDF-pLSI: in order to integrate semantic benefits into matching, we combined TFIDF with pLSI topic model linearly. We trained 1000 topics and utilize fold-in algorithm [8][3] to compute $P(t_i|Q)$ and $P(t_i|D)$, and then use cosine similarity for scoring. We elaborately adjusted the combination coefficient to reach the optimal performance.

Mixture LM performs superior than TFIDF and TFIDF-pLSI combination. As illustrated in Figure 2, for recall in range of 0.1 and 0.8 the precision lift is between 4% and 12%. Particularly for recall in the area we are the most interested in (near 0.3) for production deployment, the precision improvement is about 5%. In terms of ROC, from Table 1 we can see that the improvements in AUC are 6.1% and 5.0%.

The improvement on tail portion is some more significant than that on head portion. The reasons are two-folded. First, TFIDF does have good discrimination ability on head portion. Our investigation has confirmed that it performs better than Baseline LM when recall is low. The integration of term importance derived from click feedback further sharpens it's performance in this area. Second, language model is more robust. Its scores distribution is more concentrated than TFIDF. Even Baseline LM performs better TFIDF when recall is in middle and tail area. Mixture LM strengthens this advantage further.

Besides, we find that semantic match does help to improve syntactic match. Combined with pLSI, TFIDF gains about 1% precision lift in our interested recall range.

Table 2: comparison with KLD LM on nDCG

Methods	nDCG@1	nDCG@3	nDCG@5
Mixture LM	0.732	0.736	0.753
KLD LM	0.723	0.731	0.747

4.3 Compare with KLD Language Model

In evaluation, we differentiated hot and tail queries according to whether they have at least three 'relevant advertisements' in the logs of an industrial search engine in one month. An advertisement is regarded as a 'relevant advertisement' for a query if the absolute click number of the query-advertisement pair exceeds a threshold l_1 and the expected click number predicted by click modeling exceeds a threshold l_2. With these limitations, there are about 9000 queries regarded as 'hot queries' and the left 5000 queries are 'tail queries'. We use $\sum_w P(w|\theta_Q) \log P(w|\theta_D)$ for scoring. For hot queries, we integrated 'relevant advertisements' into query models estimation. The combination coefficient λ of background prior $P(w|C)$ is 0.05 in EM estimation.

We first retrieve the top n advertisements for each query from the two models and then evaluate precision and recall

Table 1: AUC values of different models

Methods	Mixture LM	Baseline LM	TFIDF	TFIDF-pLSI
AUC	0.837	0.784	0.776	0.787

on different n, which comes out that the overall precision of KLD LM is slightly better than Mixture LM, about 0.5% overall. However, as illustrated in Table 2, the performance on nDCG is opposite, in which Mixture LM is about 0.5% better than KLD LM. These results show that these two models are comparable for hot queries generally. KLD LM is somewhat better at telling the good from the bad, while Mixture LM is somewhat better at distinguishing the best from the fair. For tail queries, Mixture LM is 2%-4% better than KLD LM. Considering the overlap of advertisements in feedback collection and editorial dataset which may have boosted the performance of KLD LM and the volume of tail queries, we think Mixture LM is superior for our advertisements retrieval tasks.

4.4 Live Traffic Performance

Besides the offline evaluations, in order to compare the online performance of different models, we split the live search traffic into different 'buckets', a Baseline LM bucket, a TFIDF-pLSI bucket and a Mixture LM bucket. Users in each bucket are served by advertisements retrieved by the corresponding model in addition to other matching approaches already existing in the system such as query rewriting, advertisements expansion and so forth. As such, the CTR (click through rate) and RPS (revenue per search) of the Mixture LM bucket is 3.0% and 3.6% higher than that of TFIDF-pLSI bucket; and the improvements are 2.0% and 2.5% respectively comparing with the Baseline LM.

5. RELATED WORK

The fundamental work on advertisments selection of sponsored search mainly focus on query expansion [13] or bid term generation [15]. Besides IR technologies, some machine learning approaches are exploited as well, such as Dustin's relevance model [6] and Broder's 'learn when to advertise' model [4]. In recent years, some work pay attention to the commercial nature of online advertising, such as Pandy's work in estimating advertisability of tail queries [11] and Ashkan's work on queries' commercial intent [1].

Early work of language model mainly remain in the family of query-likelihood scoring [12]. As a generalization, the KL-divergence language model [18] which supports feedback integration through estimating a query language model is regarded as a 'state-of-the art' approach [17]. Flourishing works in query language model estimation include Zhai's mixture model feedback method [18] and Croft's relevance model [9] etc. Very recently, Raghavan [14] introduced the classical language model into searching advertising.

6. CONCLUSIONS

In this paper we focus on characterizing and capturing the relevance and commercial intent in sponsored search. We develop a mixture language model of a commercial model and an informational model for this purpose. The evaluation on both editorial data and live traffic confirm the effectiveness of our model. For future work, we are still investigating the generalization of our work to content match advertising as well as some personalization areas such as sentimental analysis and news recommendation.

7. ACKNOWLEDGMENTS

This work is sponsored by Yahoo! Global R&D Center, Beijing.

8. REFERENCES

[1] A. Ashkan and C. L. Clarke. Term-based commercial intent analysis. In *SIGIR*, pages 800–801, 2009.

[2] D. Blei, A. Ng, and M. Jordan. Latent dirichlet allocation. *J. Mach. Learn. Res*, 2:993–1022, 2003.

[3] T. Brants and F. Chen. Topic-based document segmentation with probabilistic latent semantic analysis. In *CIKM*, 2002.

[4] A. Broder, M. Ciaramita, and M. Fontoura. To swing or not to swing: learning when (not) to advertise. In *CIKM*, pages 1003–1012, 2008.

[5] A. P. Dempster and N. M. Laird. Maximum likelihood from incomplete data via the em algorithm. *Journal of Royal Statist. Soc. B*, pages 1–38, 1977.

[6] D. Hillard and S. Schroedl. Improving ad relevance in sponsored search. In *WSDM*, pages 361–369, 2010.

[7] T. Hofmann. Probabilistic latent semantic analysis. In *UAT*, 1999.

[8] T. Hofmann. Probabilistic latent semantic indexing. In *SIGIR*, pages 50–57, 1999.

[9] V. Lavrenko and W. B. Crof. Relevance-based language models. In *SIGIR*, pages 120–127, 2001.

[10] Q. Mei, D. Cai, D. Zhang, and C. Zhai. Topic modeling with network regularization. In *WWW*, 2008.

[11] S. Pandey and K. Punera. Estimating advertisability of tail queries for sponsored search. In *SIGIR*, 2010.

[12] J. M. Ponte and W. B. Croft. A language modeling approach to information retrieval. In *SIGIR*, 1998.

[13] F. Radlinski, A. Broder, and P. C. etc. Optimizing relevance and revenue in ad search: A query substitution approache. In *SIGIR*, pages 403–410, 2008.

[14] H. Raghavan and R. Iyer. Probabilistic first pass retrieval for search advertising: from theory to practice. In *CIKM*, pages 1019–1028, 2010.

[15] S. Ravi, A. Broder, and E. Gabrilovich. Automatic generation of did phrases for online advertising. In *WSDM*, pages 341–350, 2010.

[16] G. Salton and C. Buckley. Term weighting approaches in automatic text retrieval. *Information Processing and Management*, 23(5):513–523, 1998.

[17] C. Zhai. Statistical language models for information retrieval a critical review. *Foundations and Trends in Information Retrieval*, 2(3):137–213, 2008.

[18] J. Zhai and J. Lafferty. Model-based feedback in the language modeling approach to information retrieval. In *CIKM*, 2001.

Learning to Rank Audience for Behavioral Targeting in Display Ads

Jian Tang[1*], Ning Liu[2], Jun Yan[2], Yelong Shen[3*], Shaodan Guo[4*], Bin Gao[2], Shuicheng Yan[5], and Ming Zhang[1]

[1]School of EECS, Peking University, Beijing, China, {tangjian, mzhang}@net.pku.edu.cn

[2]Microsoft Research Asia, Beijing, China, {ningl, junyan, bingao}@microsoft.com

[3]Beihan University, Beijing, China, shengyelong@gmail.com

[4]Huazhong University of Science and Technology, Wuhan, China, guoshaodan@gmail.com

[5]National University of Singapore, Singapore, eleyans@nus.edu.sg

ABSTRACT

Behavioral targeting (BT), which aims to sell advertisers those behaviorally related user segments to deliver their advertisements, is facing a bottleneck in serving the rapid growth of long tail advertisers. Due to the small business nature of the tail advertisers, they generally expect to accurately reach a small group of audience, which is hard to be satisfied by classical BT solutions with large size user segments. In this paper, we propose a novel probabilistic generative model named Rank Latent Dirichlet Allocation (RANKLDA) to rank audience according to their ads click probabilities for the long tail advertisers to deliver their ads. Based on the basic assumption that *users who clicked the same group of ads will have a higher probability of sharing similar latent search topical interests*, RANKLDA combines topic discovery from users' search behaviors and learning to rank users from their ads click behaviors together. In computation, the topic learning could be enhanced by the supervised information of the rank learning and simultaneously, the rank learning could be better optimized by considering the discovered topics as features. This co-optimization scheme enhances each other iteratively. Experiments over the real click-through log of display ads in a public ad network show that the proposed RANKLDA model can effectively rank the audience for the tail advertisers.

Categories and Subject Descriptors

H.3.3 [**Information Storage and Retrieval**]: Information Search and Retrieval – retrieval models

General Terms: Algorithms, Economics, Experimentation

Keywords

User ranking, behavioral targeting, display ads

* This work was done when the first, fourth and fifth author were visiting Microsoft Research Asia.

CIKM'11, October 24-28, 2011, Glasgow, Scotland, UK.

1. INTRODUCTION

Behavioral targeting (BT) [4, 5, 9, 11] is one of the mainstream forms in online advertising. It aims to deliver the right advertisements to the right audience according to their online behaviors such as searching and browsing histories. Display advertising [12], which is one of the major ads delivery channels nowadays, generally appears on the Internet in the form of graphical ads, including text, images, logos, flashes, videos, etc. Due to the well-known semantic gap and the limited textual information involved in display ads, behavioral targeting is playing an important role in targeting the display ads to the right audience.

The classical behavioral targeting solutions [11] pre-divide users into user segments, i.e. user categories, within each of which users are assumed to share similar interests. Each segment is labeled with keywords to indicate the interests of the users in the segment. For example, a segment labeled with "car buyer" indicates the users in this segment may want to buy cars. For advertisers, they buy one or more user segments for their ads delivery based on the keyword descriptions of the user segments. Recently, with the rapid growth of online Customer to Customer (C2C) business, there is an emerging market of the long tail advertisers. These long tail advertisers have a common characteristic: they have limited budget for their ads delivery. However, even a single user segment produced by classical behavioral targeting solutions, which has little consideration to the long tail advertisers, may have a large number of users and hence it is generally too large for these advertisers, who cannot afford to reach such a large number of targeted users. Thus if only by adopting classical behavioral targeting solutions, the long tail advertisers, who consist a huge and underexplored market in display ads, cannot be satisfied. This motivates us to study the problem of user ranking (audience ranking) according to their click probabilities over the given group of ads. Then those long tail advertisers may select arbitrary number of top ranked users according to their budget for ads delivery.

The classical ranking algorithms, which calculate the relevance between display ads and users and then ranking according to the relevance score, are not applicable for the user ranking problem since the display ads contain little textual information. Instead, we propose to learn to rank users from their ads click behaviors, and it only relies on user features. Specifically, we proposed a novel generative model RankLDA for learning to rank users according to their ads click probabilities from their ads click behaviors. Based on the basic assumption that *users who clicked the same group of ads will have a higher probability of sharing similar latent search topical interests,* the RankLDA model combines the topic discovery from users' search behaviors and learning to rank users from their ads click behaviors together. By combining the two procedures together, on one hand, the topic discovery can benefit from the supervised information of rank learning, namely users' ads click behaviors; on the other hand, the discovered topics can serve as good features in the process of learning to rank users. Thus the two processes are mutually enhanced. Experiments with a real word search engine log with corresponding ads click through demonstrate the superiority of the RANKLDA model over the baselines both in audience ranking and topic discovery. Furthermore, by comparing the weights of the topics, we can understand what behaviors of users tend to lead to ads clicks in the target domain.

2. PRELIMINARIES&RELATED WORK

2.1 Behavioral Targeting in Display Ads

Behavioral targeting [4, 5, 9, 11] has attracted much research attention recently in online advertising community, especially for display advertisement. It does not rely on the contextual information of Web pages for ad delivery. Instead, it enables advertisers to target the advertisements to the right audience by leveraging users' recent online activities such as their search queries in search engines, page views in some special Websites. For example, if we observe a user often searches queries about cell phone or visits websites about cell phone, then this user may want to buy a cell phone recently and we may deliver the ads about cell phone to him.

Classical behavioral targeting methods [11] generally segment users into multiple user interest segments, within each of which users are assumed to share similar interests. Each segment is labeled with keywords and corresponds to a product domain. For example, suppose there is a user segment labeled as "car buyer", then the users are grouped into this segment because they have shown behaviors related with buying a car. Then based on the keyword descriptions of the user segments, the advertisers buy one or more user segments for their ads delivery. However, even a single user segment may have a large number of users, and those long-tail small advertisers cannot afford an entire user segment. Instead, they may only want to buy a small portion of users who are most interested in their ads. Thus this results in a user ranking problem, which ranks users according to their probabilities of interest in the target ads.

2.2 Learning to Rank

In this subsection, we briefly introduce the pairwise learning to rank methods, which will be used in our proposed algorithms and compared baselines. The general pairwise ranking criterion is to minimize the expected empirical risk, which is the average loss over the whole training pairs. In order to overcome the over fitting problem, regularization is incorporated. As a result, the general criterion for pairwise ranking methods is to minimize the following objective function:

$$min_{\boldsymbol{\eta}} L(\boldsymbol{\eta}, P) + C \parallel \boldsymbol{\eta} \parallel_2^2$$

where $L(\boldsymbol{\eta}, P)$ is the empirical risk over all the preference pairs in the training data P:

$$\mathrm{L}(\boldsymbol{\eta}, P) = \frac{1}{|P|} \sum\nolimits_{(u_i, u_j) \in P} \ell(f(\boldsymbol{\eta}, \boldsymbol{x}_i), f(\boldsymbol{\eta}, \boldsymbol{x}_j))$$

$\ell(\cdot,\cdot)$ is a loss function defined on a preference pair $(\boldsymbol{x}_i, \boldsymbol{x}_j)$, $f(\boldsymbol{\eta}, \boldsymbol{x}_i) = \boldsymbol{\eta}^T \boldsymbol{x}_i$ is the prediction function, and $\boldsymbol{\eta}$ is the corresponding feature weight vector. C is a parameter to tradeoff between minimizing empirical risk and finding a simple model, $\parallel \boldsymbol{\eta} \parallel_2$ is the ℓ_2-norm of vector $\boldsymbol{\eta}$.

2.3 Topic Models

Topic models such as Latent Dirichlet Allocation (LDA) [1] are used to extract latent semantic topics within a corpus. Most of the existing models built on LDA are unsupervised methods, which all rely on the co-occurrence of words, and don't rely on any supervised information. Recently, some models that combine the unsupervised process in LDA and supervised information together are proposed [2, 6]. In [2], Blei *et al.* proposed a supervised topic model (sLDA), in which each document is paired with a response. In sLDA, for each document, the words are generated in the same manner as that in the classic LDA, and then a response variable is generated based on the topics of the document. The goal of sLDA is to jointly discover the latent topics in documents and infer latent topics predictive of the response. The most similar work with RANKLDA model is the relational topic model (RTM) [3], which models the generation of documents and the links between them. However, RTM is a pure unsupervised model and focuses on link prediction while RANKLDA integrates supervised information from users' ads click behaviors and focuses on ranking, which is different from existing variants of LDA model.

3. LEANING TO RANK AUDIENCE WITH RANKLDA

In this section, we describe our model for learning to rank audience. We first formally formulate the audience ranking problem and then introduce a novel model, which is named Rank Latent Dirichlet Allocation (RANKLDA), for ranking users according to their probabilities of interest in the ads of the target domain.

3.1 Problem Formulation

The audience ranking problem aims to rank users according to their ads click probabilities. Specifically, we formally defined the problem as below:

Given a group of ads in the target domain and a collection of users that viewed one of these ads at least once, each user u is represented with a feature vector $\boldsymbol{x}$*, which is extracted from his search behaviors, including search queries and the titles of the clicked URLs. Audience ranking aims to rank users according to a ranking score* $f(\boldsymbol{x}) = \boldsymbol{\eta}^T \boldsymbol{x}$*, where* $\boldsymbol{\eta}$ *is the feature weight vector.*

In order to learn to rank audience, we collect training data from their ads click behaviors. Given a group of ads, if two users u_i and u_j both viewed the ads, but u_i clicked the ads and u_j did not click the ads, then u_i is generally more interested in this group of ads than u_j, and (u_i, u_j) is treated as a user preference pair. Additionally, we associate each user preference pair with a confidence score c_{ij}, which is used to measure the confidence that u_i is more interested in this group of ads than u_j, and is defined as:

$$c_{ij} = \frac{click_i}{Impres_i} * \sigma(Impres_j)$$

where $click_i$ and $Impres_i$ are the number of clicks and impressions over this group of ads respectively, $\sigma(.)$ is the logistic function $\sigma(x) = 1/(1 + \exp(-x))$.

Let U be the set of all users, C the set of click users, then the training data P can be formally defined as:

$$P = \{(u_i, u_j, c_{ij}) | u_i \in C, u_j \in U \backslash C\}$$

3.2 RANKLDA

In this subsection, we describe the proposed RANKLDA model for user ranking, which is a probabilistic generative model that jointly models topic discovery from users' search behaviors and learning to rank users from their ads click behaviors. The Notations to be used is summarized in Table 1.

Table 1. Notations to be used in RANKLDA model

Notation	Description
K	Total number of topics
M	Total number of users
α	The prior parameter for the user topic Dirichlet
$\boldsymbol{\theta}_i$	Topic distribution of user *i*
w_{in}	The n_{th} word in user *i*'s profile
z_{in}	The topic of the n_{th} word in user *i*'s profile
N_i	The total number of words in user *i*'s profile
$\boldsymbol{w}_i$	The words of user *i*'s profile
$\boldsymbol{z}_i$	The topics of user *i*'s profile
$\{\boldsymbol{\beta}_k\}$	The topics
$\boldsymbol{\eta}$	The topic weight vector
y_{ij}	Response variable between user *i* and *j*
P	The user preference pair set

3.2.1 Definition of RANKLDA

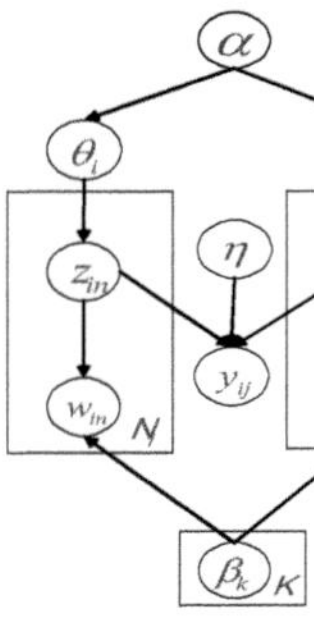

Figure 1. Graphical representation of RANKLDA

Our RANKLDA model combines topic discovery from users' search behaviors and learning to rank users from their ads click behaviors together. The intuition that combines the two processes together is that users who both clicked the same group of ads have a higher probability of sharing similar search topical interests, thus the topic discovery from users' search behaviors can benefit from their ads click behaviors; meanwhile, the learning of user ranking can also be better optimized by using the discovered topics as users' features. Specifically, the model consists of two parts: the modeling of topic discovery from users' search behaviors and the learning to rank users from their ads click behaviors. For the topic discovery, each user *i* with search profile $\boldsymbol{w}_i$ is generated as the manner in the classic LDA model [1]; for the user ranking, a response variable $y_{ij} = 1$ is generated for each user preference pair (i, j), i.e. $y_{ij} = 1$ if user *i* clicked the ads in the domain and user *j* did not. The graphical representation of RANKLDA is presented in Figure 1, and the detailed generative process is summarized as:

(1) For each user *i*,

  a. Draw a topic proportion $\boldsymbol{\theta}_i \sim Dirichlet(\alpha)$,

  b. For each word w_{in} in user *i*'s profile, $n = 1, 2, \cdots, N_i$,

  Draw a topic assignment $z_{in} \sim Multinomial(\boldsymbol{\theta}_i)$,

  Draw a word $w_{in} \sim Multinomial(\boldsymbol{\beta}_{z_{in}})$,

(2) For each user preference pair with corresponding weight $(i, j, c_{ij}) \in P$, draw a response variable $y_{ij} = 1 | \bar{\boldsymbol{z}}_i, \bar{\boldsymbol{z}}_j, \boldsymbol{\eta} \sim \text{Bernoulli}\left(\sigma(\rho_{ij})^{c_{ij}}\right)$.

where $\bar{\boldsymbol{z}}_i = 1/N_i \sum_{n=1}^{N_i} z_{in}$, $\sigma(x) = 1/(1 + \exp(-x))$ is the logistic function ,and $\rho_{ij} = \boldsymbol{\eta}^T \bar{\boldsymbol{z}}_i - \boldsymbol{\eta}^T \bar{\boldsymbol{z}}_j$.

Given model parameters $\Theta = \{\alpha, \{\boldsymbol{\beta}_k\}_{k=1}^K, \boldsymbol{\eta}\}$, the joint probability of the observed and hidden variables is:

$$P\left(\{\boldsymbol{w}_i, \boldsymbol{z}_i, \boldsymbol{\theta}_i\}_{i=1}^M, \{y_{ij}\}_{(i,j,c_{ij}) \in P} | \Theta\right)$$
$$= \prod_{i=1}^M P(\boldsymbol{\theta}_i | \alpha) \prod_{n=1}^{N_i} P(z_{in} | \boldsymbol{\theta}_i) P(w_{in} | \boldsymbol{\beta}_{z_{in}})$$
$$\times \prod_{(i,j,c_{ij}) \in P} P(y_{ij} = 1 | \bar{\boldsymbol{z}}_i, \bar{\boldsymbol{z}}_j, \boldsymbol{\eta})^{c_{ij}} \quad (1)$$

3.2.2 Model Learning

The learning process for RANKLDA is to maximize the log likelihood of the observed variables $\log P\left(\{\boldsymbol{w}_i\}_{i=1}^M, \{y_{ij}\}_{(i,j) \in P} | \Theta\right)$. In order to maximize this objective function, we adopt Expectation Maximization (EM) algorithm, which is composed of two key steps: E-step and M-step. In the E-step, we aim to calculate the posterior distribution of the latent variables. In the M-step, we aim to maximize the expectation of the log complete likelihood over the distribution calculated in E-step.

However, as its counterpart in the conventional LDA learning [1], in the E-step, the posterior distribution of latent variables is computational intractable. Thus we resort to the variational inference method, which tries to minimize the KL-divergence between the approximated and the true posterior distribution of latent variables.

Specifically, we adopt the mean-field variational inference [8], which is generally used in the classical LDA model. The mean-field variational inference forms a factorized distribution over the latent variables, which is expressed as:

$$q(\boldsymbol{\theta}, \mathbf{z} | \boldsymbol{\gamma}, \boldsymbol{\phi}) = q(\boldsymbol{\theta} | \boldsymbol{\gamma}) \prod_{n=1}^N q(z_n | \phi_n), \quad (2)$$

where $\{\boldsymbol{\gamma}, \boldsymbol{\phi}\}$ are the free parameters, and $\boldsymbol{\theta} \sim \text{Dirichlet}(\boldsymbol{\gamma})$, $z_n \sim Multinomial(\phi_n)$. So the objective is to find the optimum $\{\boldsymbol{\gamma}, \boldsymbol{\phi}\}$ such that $q(\boldsymbol{\theta}, \mathbf{z} | \boldsymbol{\gamma}, \boldsymbol{\phi})$ can be the best approximation of conditional distribution $P(\boldsymbol{\theta}, \mathbf{z} | \mathbf{w}, \Theta)$.

Based on the Jensen inequality [7], we can find a lower bound of the log likelihood. Besides, the difference between the log likelihood and the lower bound is the KL divergence between the variational posterior probability and the true posterior probability, i.e.

$$\log P\left(\{\boldsymbol{w}_i\}_{i=1}^{M}, \{y_{ij}\}_{(i,j)\in P}\right) = L(\boldsymbol{\gamma}, \boldsymbol{\phi}; \Theta) + D(q(\boldsymbol{\theta}, \mathbf{z}|\boldsymbol{\gamma}, \boldsymbol{\phi})||P(\boldsymbol{\theta}, \mathbf{z}|\mathbf{w}, \Theta)), \tag{3}$$

where $L(\gamma, \phi; \Theta)$ is the lower bound of the log likelihood and can be calculated as below:

$$L(\boldsymbol{\gamma}, \boldsymbol{\phi}; \Theta) = E_q\left[\log\left(\{\boldsymbol{w}_i, \boldsymbol{z}_i, \boldsymbol{\theta}_i\}_{i=1}^{M}, \{y_{ij}\}_{(i,j)\in P} \middle| \Theta\right)\right] = \sum_{(i,j)\in P} E_q\left[c_{ij} \log P\left(y_{ij} = 1 | \bar{\boldsymbol{z}}_i, \bar{\boldsymbol{z}}_j, \boldsymbol{\eta}\right)\right] + \sum_{i=1}^{M} E_q \log P(\boldsymbol{\theta}_i|\alpha) + \sum_{i=1}^{M} E_q \log P(\boldsymbol{z}_i|\boldsymbol{\theta}_i) + \sum_{i=1}^{M} E_q \log P(\boldsymbol{w}_i|\boldsymbol{z}_i, \{\boldsymbol{\beta}_k\}_{k=1}^{K}) - \sum_{i=1}^{M} E_q \log q(\boldsymbol{\theta}_i) - \sum_{i=1}^{M} E_q \log q(\boldsymbol{z}_i) \tag{4}$$

For the last five terms on the right-hand side of above equation, we can calculate them as the way introduced in standard LDA [1], so we only need to focus on calculating the first term, in which

$$E_q\left[c_{ij} \log P\left(y_{ij} = 1 | \bar{\boldsymbol{z}}_i, \bar{\boldsymbol{z}}_j, \boldsymbol{\eta}\right)\right] = c_{ij} E_q\left[\log \sigma\left(\boldsymbol{\eta}^T \bar{\boldsymbol{z}}_i - \boldsymbol{\eta}^T \bar{\boldsymbol{z}}_j\right)\right] \tag{5}$$

To calculate the expectation, we adopt the method introduced in [10], which uses the variational method again with the following variational bound [8]:

$$\sigma(x) \geq \sigma(\xi) \exp\left(\frac{x-\xi}{2} + g(\xi)(x^2 - \xi^2)\right), \tag{6}$$

where ξ is the free variational parameter, and $g(\xi) = (\frac{1}{2} - \sigma(\xi))/2\xi$. Then we have

$$E_q\left[\log P\left(y_{ij} = 1 | \bar{\boldsymbol{z}}_i, \bar{\boldsymbol{z}}_j, \boldsymbol{\eta}\right)\right] \geq \log \sigma(\xi) - \frac{\xi}{2} - \xi^2 g(\xi) + \frac{1}{2}\boldsymbol{\eta}^T E_q(\bar{\boldsymbol{z}}_i) - \frac{1}{2}\boldsymbol{\eta}^T E_q(\bar{\boldsymbol{z}}_j) + g(\xi) E_q(\rho_{ij}^2). \tag{7}$$

In order to minimize the KL-divergence between the variational distribution q and the true distribution p, we only need to maximize $L(\boldsymbol{\gamma}, \boldsymbol{\phi}; \Theta)$ with respect to $\{\{\xi_{ij}\}, \boldsymbol{\gamma}, \boldsymbol{\phi}\}$. We omit some derivations here and just list the final update equations:

$$\xi_{ij} = (E_q(\rho_{ij}^2))^{\frac{1}{2}}, \tag{8}$$

$$\gamma_{ik} = \alpha_k + \sum_{n=1}^{N_i} \phi_{i,n,k}. \tag{9}$$

For user i who clicked ads:

$$\phi_{i,n,k} \propto \beta_{kv} \exp\left(\sum_j c_{ij} \frac{1}{2N_i}\eta_k + c_{ij} g(\xi_{ij})\left(\frac{2\left(\boldsymbol{\eta}^T \sum_{s=1,s\neq n}^{N_i} \boldsymbol{\phi}_{-is}\right)\eta_k + (\boldsymbol{\eta}\circ\boldsymbol{\eta})_k}{N_i^2} - \frac{2(\boldsymbol{\eta}^T \sum_{t=1}^{N_j} \phi_{jt})\eta_k}{N_i N_j}\right) + \Psi(\gamma_k) - \Psi\left(\sum_{j=1}^{K} \gamma_j\right)\right)$$

$$s.t \sum_{k=1}^{K} \phi_{i,n,k} = 1. \tag{10}$$

For user j who did not click ads:

$$\phi_{j,n,k} \propto \beta_{kv} \exp\left(\sum_i c_{ij} \frac{-1}{2N_j}\eta_k + c_{ij} g(\xi_{ij})\left(\frac{2\left(\boldsymbol{\eta}^T \sum_{s=1,s\neq n}^{N_i} \boldsymbol{\phi}_{-is}\right)\eta_k + (\boldsymbol{\eta}\circ\boldsymbol{\eta})_k}{N_j^2} - \frac{2(\boldsymbol{\eta}^T \sum_{t=1}^{N_i} \phi_{jt})\eta_k}{N_i N_j}\right) + \Psi(\gamma_k) - \Psi\left(\sum_{j=1}^{K} \gamma_j\right)\right),$$

$$s.t \sum_{k=1}^{K} \phi_{j,n,k} = 1, \tag{11}$$

where $\boldsymbol{\eta} \circ \boldsymbol{\eta}$ means the element-wise product between $\boldsymbol{\eta}$ and $\boldsymbol{\eta}$.

For the learning of RANKLDA, the variational EM algorithm is adopted, the detail updating equations are summarized as below:

1. **E-step:** update the parameters $\{\{\xi_{ij}\}, \boldsymbol{\gamma}, \boldsymbol{\phi}\}$ according to equations (8), (9), (10) and (11).
2. **M-step:** update the parameters $\Theta = \{\alpha, \{\boldsymbol{\beta}_k\}_{k=1}^{K}, \boldsymbol{\eta}\}$,

Update equation for $\boldsymbol{\eta}$:

$$\boldsymbol{\eta} = -\frac{1}{4}\left(\sum_{(i,j)\in P} c_{ij} g(\xi_{ij}) E_q\left[(\bar{\boldsymbol{z}}_i - \bar{\boldsymbol{z}}_j)(\bar{\boldsymbol{z}}_i - \bar{\boldsymbol{z}}_j)^T\right]\right)^{-1} \times \sum_{(i,j)\in P} c_{ij}\left(E_q(\bar{\boldsymbol{z}}_i) - E_q(\bar{\boldsymbol{z}}_j)\right) \tag{12}$$

The updated equations for the parameters $\alpha, \{\boldsymbol{\beta}_k\}_{k=1}^{K}$ are the same as in the classic LDA [1].

3.2.3 *RANKLDA for Audience Ranking*

Given a set of users together with their search behaviors, how should we rank these users with the estimated model Θ? Firstly, for each user with profile $\mathbf{w}$, we need to estimate the topic proportion of the user. Thus we approximate the posterior distribution of latent variables $P(\boldsymbol{\theta}, \mathbf{z}|\mathbf{w}, \Theta)$ with factorized distribution $q(\boldsymbol{\theta}, \mathbf{z}|\boldsymbol{\gamma}, \boldsymbol{\phi})$ and by minimizing the KL divergence between the two distributions we can estimate the optimum $\boldsymbol{\gamma}, \boldsymbol{\phi}$. Then the ranking score $f(\mathbf{w})$ for user with profile $\mathbf{w}$ is calculated as:

$$f(\mathbf{w}) = \boldsymbol{\eta}^T E_q(\bar{\mathbf{z}}) = \frac{1}{N}\boldsymbol{\eta}^T \sum_{n=1}^{N} \phi_n \tag{13}$$

4. EXPERIMENT

In this section, we elaborate on the experiments for audience ranking. We first introduce the dataset used, and then describe the evaluation metrics. For the performance of user ranking, we compare RANKLDA with pairwise learning to rank methods with BOW features and topics discovered by LDA respectively.

4.1 Dataset

Our dataset is an integration of two data sources. One is the query log of a commercial search engine, which records the search behaviors of search engine users. The other data source is the advertisement click-through log in corresponding ad network using the display ads as the ads delivery channel. The two datasets have overlapped user IDs for us to identify the unique users. To avoid the privacy issues, only the abstract user IDs are used and no other user information such as demographic and geographic are used. In other words, the dataset contains both users' ad click information in a display ads' ad network and users' search behaviors in corresponding search engine of the ad network. The advertisements we used for research purpose are a group of ads in the "auto insurance" domain. There are 43 different ads in this group. Our dataset is preprocessed in three steps. First, we extract all the users that viewed any ads in this group at least once range from 20th to 26th of September 2010 and extract the number of clicks and impressions for each user from display ads click through log. Second, we extract the search behaviors of these users between 13th to 19th of September 2010, including search queries and the clicked URLs, from a corresponding commercial search engine query log. We filter out users that did not have any behaviors during this period. Finally, we extract the titles of all the webpages that have been clicked by these users. Through this way we get a total number of 1,935,534 unique users with 5,294,484 ad impressions in display ads and 1,912 ad clicks. Thus the average click through rate (CTR) for this group of ads is 0.036% and the ratio of user who clicked ads is 0.090%. With respect to users' search behaviors, the number of average queries and clicked URLs for each user is 6.6 and 6.1 respectively.

4.2 Evaluation Metric

The evaluation aims to measure the effect of improving average user CTR for advertisers who only buy a small part of users that are most likely to click the ads. We evaluate the performance of the improvement of users' average CTR. Firstly, based on the ranking result, we calculate the average CTR of users who are ranked in the top 20%, denoted by CTR@20%, i.e.,

$$\text{CTR@20\%} = \frac{\sum_{u \in \{u|user\ u\ ranked\ in\ top\ 20\%\}} CTR_u}{|u \in \{u|user\ u\ ranked\ in\ top\ 20\%\}|}$$

where CTR_u is the CTR of user u, which is calculated by:

$$CTR_u = \frac{Click_u + \alpha}{Impres_u + \beta}$$

and $Click_u, Impres_u$ are the number of clicks and impressions for user u respectively, and α, β are the average number of users' clicks and impressions respectively, which are the smoothing coefficients that are defined globally for all users as done in [5]. In our dataset, $\alpha = 9.88 \times 10^{-4}$ and $\beta = 2.74$. The definition of CTR@40%, CTR@60%,..,CTR@100% can be defined similarly.

In order to calculate the CTR improvement after user ranking, we compare CTR@20% with the average CTR of the whole users, i.e., CTR@100%. We define:

$$\text{Impr@20\%} = \frac{CTR@20\% - CTR@100\%}{CTR@100\%}$$

By observing the value of Impr@20%, we can see how much average user CTR can be improved if the advertisers only buy the segment of users who are ranked in top 20%.

4.3 Baselines

The pairwise learning to ranking method introduced in Section 2.2 can be used to rank users directly with any kinds of user features. We provide two kinds of user features: "bag-of-words" (BOW) and topic discovered by classic LDA with the corresponding topic weight as feature value. We summarize our baselines as below:

(1) *BOW+Pairwise ranking*: The pairwise learning to rank method with "bag-of-words" features.

(2) *Topic+Pairwise ranking*: The pairwise learning to rank method with topics discovered by classic LDA as features (with the corresponding topic weight as feature value).

4.4 Results

4.4.1 Audience Ranking

We perform five-fold cross validation over all the users in the dataset with our RANKLDA model. Figure 2 shows the average results. We can see that after user ranking, users ranked in higher positions have higher ads CTR, which proves that user ranking is effective in ranking users according to their ads click probabilities and hence can help find better small user segments.

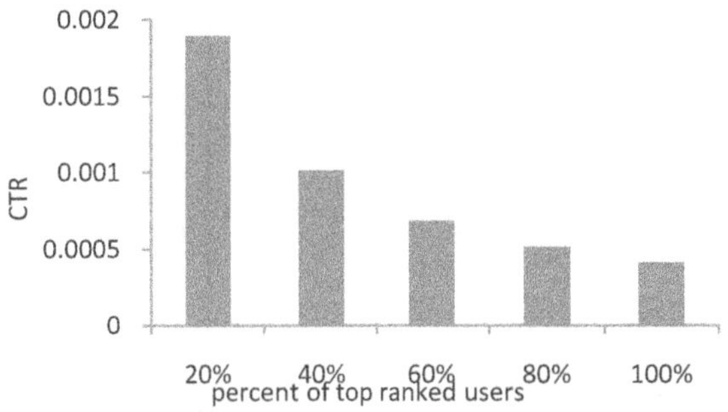

Figure 2: Average user CTR with different percent of top ranked users

Table 2 lists the result of audience ranking with Impr@20% metric. We can see that no matter how many topics we choose, the performance of RANKLDA or Topic+Pairwise ranking method is consistently better than that of BOW+Pairwise ranking. This proves that topics can serve as better features than "BOW". Furthermore, the performance of RANKLDA is much better than the *Topic+Pairwise ranking* method. As mentioned previously, RANKLDA combines the topic discovery from users' search behaviors and learning to rank users from their ads click behaviors together, and the two processes are mutually enhanced.

4.4.2 Topic Discovery

In Table 3, we compare the topics that discovered by *Topic+Pairwise ranking* and the RANKLDA model respectively. For both models, we have a weighting vector associated with the features, i.e., the topics. The weight of each topic reflects its importance in influencing users' ads click behaviors, and thus we rank the discovered topics according to their weights in descending order, and finally we choose the topics ranked in the top three positions. The discovered topics with both models in "auto insurance" domain are listed in Table 3. The topics discovered by *Topic+Pairwise ranking* are quite general, such as "car", "insurance", and "travel". On the contrary, RANKLDA integrates supervised information which are users' ads click behaviors and the topics are much more specific. For example, the topic "car insurance" is a self-contained topic discovered by RANKLDA, while the baseline method treats it as two separate topics: "car" and "insurance". The discovered topics tell us that people who pay attention to car insurance, travel, and health & kids are most likely to click the ads in "auto insurance" domain.

Table 2: The audience ranking results with Impr@20% Metric

	Impr@20%			
Model	**Topic 20**	**Topic 40**	**Topic 60**	**Topic 80**
BOW+Pairwise ranking	1.015±0.210			
Topic+Pairwise ranking	1.266±0.253	1.426±0.154	1.337±0.345	1.088±0.249
RANKLDA	**3.599±0.118**	**3.637 ± 0.176**	**3.626 ± 0.079**	**3.640±0.090**

Table 3: The discovered topics that lead to ads clicks in "auto insurance" domain

Topic+Pairwise ranking			RANKLDA		
#Topic : Car	#Topic : Healthy	#Topic : Travel	#Topic : CarInsurance	#Topic : Travel	#Topic : Healthy&Kids
chevy	houston	airline	car	los	health
car	hospital	vegas	insurance	city	medical
ford	insurance	travel	auto	travel	care
truck	center	southwest	america	coolest	child
wheel	medical	vaction	banking	town	houston
bmw	health	hotel	account	iowa	story
racing	care	flight	bmw	texas	toy
auto	saint	cheap	drive	lake	boy

5. CONCLUSIONS

In this paper, we investigated the problem of learning to rank audience for behavioral targeting in display ads. By ranking audience according to their probabilities of interest over the given ads, those small long tail advertisers can select to buy an appropriate portion of top ranked users for their ads delivery. We proposed a novel audience rank model referred to as Rank Latent Dirichlet Allocation (RANKLDA). RANKLDA well integrates the process of topic discovery from users' search behaviors and also learning to rank audience from their ads click behaviors. By the joint process, the two tasks are mutually boosted. We performed a large scale evaluation study based on a commercial search engine log and also the corresponding display ads click through log. The experimental results well demonstrated that the RANKLDA model outperforms the baselines both in audience ranking and topic discovery.

6. REFERENCES

[1] D. Blei and J. Lafferty. Latent dirichlet allocation. In *Journal of Machine Learning Research,* pages 993-1022 , 2003.

[2] D. Blei and J. Lafferty. Supervised topic models. In *Proceedings of the Twenty-First Annual Conference on Neural Information Processing Systems,* 2007.

[3] J.Chang and D. Blei. Relation topic models for document networks. *Artificial Intelligence and Statistics,* 2009.

[4] T. Chen, J. Yan, G.Xue, and Z. Cheng. Transfer learning for behavioral targeting. In *Proceedings of the 19th International Conference on World Wide Web,* pages 1077-1078, 2010.

[5] Y. Chen, D. Pavlov, and J. F.Canny. Large-Scale Behavioral Targeting. In *Proceedings of the 15th ACM SIGKDD International Conference on Knowledge Discovery and Data Mining,* pages 209-218, 2009.

[6] X. Gu, S. Yang, and H. Li. Named entity mining from click-through data using weakly supervised latent dirichlet allocation. In *Proceedings of the 15th ACM SIGKDD International Conference on Knowledge Discovery and Data Mining,* pages 267-274, 2009.

[7] M. Jordan, editor. Learning in Graphical Models. *MIT Press,* Cambridge, MA, 1999.

[8] T. Jaakkola. Variational methods for inference and estimation in graphical methods. *PhD thesis,* MIT. 1997.

[9] N. Liu, J. Yan, D. Shen, D. Chen, Z. Chen, and Y. Li. Learning to rank audience for behavioral targeting. In *Proceeding of the 33rd International ACM SIGIR Conference on Research and Development in Information Retrieval*, pages 719-720, 2010.

[10] Y. Liu, A. Niculescu-Mizil, and W. Grys. Topic-Link LDA: joint models for topic and author community. In *Proceedings of the 26th Annual International Conference on Machine Learning,* 2009.

[11] J. Yan, N. Liu, G. Wang, W. Zhang, Y. Jiang, and Z. Chen. How much can behavioral targeting help online advertising? In *Proceedings of the 18th International Conference on World Wide Web,* pages 261-270, 2009.

[12] Wikipedia. http://en.wikipedia.org/wiki/Display_advertising

Simulating Simple User Behavior for System Effectiveness Evaluation

Ben Carterette*, Evangelos Kanoulas‡, Emine Yilmaz†
carteret@cis.udel.edu, e.kanoulas@shef.ac.uk, {eminey@microsoft.com, eyilmaz@ku.edu.tr}
* Department of Computer & Information Sciences, University of Delaware, Newark, DE
‡ Information School, University of Sheffield, Sheffield, UK
† Microsoft Research, Cambridge, UK & Koc University, Istanbul, Turkey

ABSTRACT

Information retrieval effectiveness evaluation typically takes one of two forms: batch experiments based on static test collections, or lab studies measuring actual users interacting with a system. Test collection experiments are sometimes viewed as introducing too many simplifying assumptions to accurately predict the usefulness of a system to its users. As a result, there is great interest in creating test collections and measures that better model user behavior. One line of research involves developing measures that include a parameterized user model; choosing a parameter value simulates a particular type of user. We propose that these measures offer an opportunity to more accurately simulate the variance due to user behavior, and thus to analyze system effectiveness to a simulated user population. We introduce a Bayesian procedure for producing sampling distributions from click data, and show how to use statistical tools to quantify the effects of variance due to parameter selection.

Categories and Subject Descriptors: H.3.4 [Information Storage and Retrieval] Performance Evaluation

General Terms: Experimentation, Measurement

Keywords: information retrieval, test collections, evaluation, simulation, statistical analysis

1. INTRODUCTION

There are two broad classes of information retrieval system effectiveness evaluation: the *systems-based* approach, using a test collection comprising canned information needs and static relevance judgments to compute evaluation measures such as precision and recall; and *user studies*, in which actual users are observed and measured in controlled interactions with a system. Both have strengths and weaknesses. Systems-based evaluations are fast, repeatable, and relatively inexpensive (since the data can be reused many times), but they make many simplifying assumptions about tasks, relevance, and so on. User studies can answer questions about user behavior and user interaction with systems that cannot be touched by systems-based evaluation, but because there is so much variance in user populations they tend to be either expensive and difficult to analyze, or require simplifying assumptions about the system and the types of information needs and tasks it will be used for.

There is increasing interest in better modeling user needs and user interaction with an engine in systems-based effectiveness evaluations [11]. Some recent directions based on test collections include the TREC Web track's diversity task, which models different intents for a query and penalizes redundancy in the retrieved results, and the TREC Sessions track, which attempts systems-based evaluation of a sequence of query reformulations. Test collection work dovetails with the development of evaluation measures such as *rank biased precision* (RBP) that use test collections and relevance judgments but also incorporate explicit models of user behavior [12]. RBP models a user stepping down a ranked list and deciding whether to stop with probability p. The probability that a user stops at rank k is then $(1-p)^{k-1}p$, which is the geometric probability density function. RBP itself is computed as an expectation over ranks for some value of p.

These measures are typically evaluated with fixed parameter values. If we are to see them as simulating users, using fixed values is akin to a user study with just one user at one fixed point in time. Using a geometric distribution captures the idea that the user might choose different stopping points for different needs (at random in the case of RBP), but using a single parameter value cannot capture the idea that the distribution of stopping points might vary by user, or that even a single user might have a different distribution at some times. In other words, though these measures are intended to model users better, in practice they simplify the user population so much that there is little difference between them and traditional systems-based measures except that they provide a tunable weighting of ranks.

One way to think about the distinction between systems-based evaluation and user studies is in terms of the *bias-variance tradeoff*: a simpler model has less variance but more bias; a more complex model has more variance but less bias. Systems-based evaluations make many simplifying assumptions that reduce variance—allowing statistical analysis with high power to find subtle differences between systems—but increase bias, so that they may be measuring something quite different from the user experience (some

CIKM'11, October 24–28, 2011, Glasgow, Scotland, UK.

work suggests this is definitely the case [15]). By using actual users, user studies have less bias, but they have substantially more variance because users can differ in how they interact with a system in so many ways.

In this work we propose to bring systems-based evaluations slightly closer to user studies through better simulation of a population of users. We do this by evaluating system performance with model-based measures over varying parameter values. We still simplify many of the sources of variance in real users by reducing them to a parameterized probability distribution, but we have a more complex model with more sources of variance than traditional systems-based approaches.

We first present well-known measures based on user models and user simulation in Section 2. We then describe how we can use logged user interactions to inform sampling distributions for model parameters (Section 3). In Section 4, we show how we will analyze the results of a study simulating users by varying parameter values—since traditional tools like the t-test are not suitable for this. Section 5 analyzes TREC test collections by this simulation procedure.

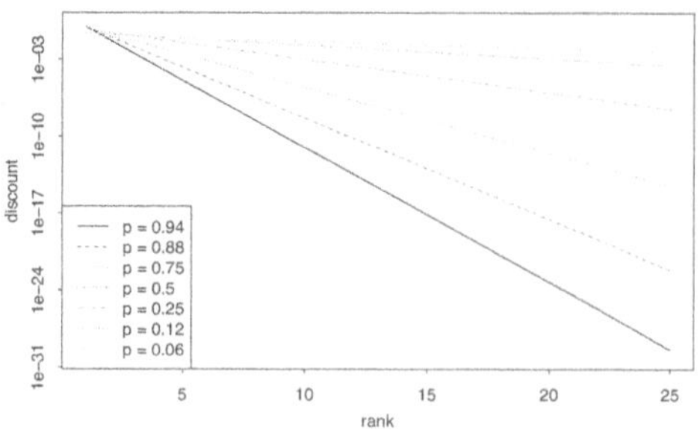

Figure 1: RBP discount $(1-p)^{k-1}p$ curves for different values of parameter p.

2. PREVIOUS WORK

Effectiveness measures based on user models nearly all take the same form: a user progresses down a ranked list one document at a time, deriving utility from relevant documents (with the relevance judgment coming from an assessor that may not be a user, as is typical in the systems-based setting), and stopping at some point modeled by a random variable. This work focuses on one such measure: *rank biased precision* (RBP). We describe that first, then briefly discuss some other similar measures as well as other approaches to selecting parameter values.

2.1 Rank biased precision

We introduced RBP [12] earlier. Its user model is that described above; it is implemented by the use of a "patience parameter" p that describes whether, at any given rank, the user decides to stop scanning results (with probability p) or to go on to the next rank (with probability $1-p$). The probability that a user ends up at rank k is then $P(k|p) = (1-p)^{k-1}p$, i.e. the probability that the user made $k-1$ decisions in a row to go to the next document followed by one decision to stop. RBP is calculated as a sum over ranks:

$$RBP = \sum_{i=1}^{n} rel_i(1-p)^{i-1}p$$

RBP has one parameter p that models user patience; p is drawn from the range $[0,1]$. In our formulation, higher values of p indicate *less* patience, i.e. greater probability of stopping early. Probability density curves for selected patience parameters are shown in Fig. 1.

2.2 Other measures and models

The most commonly-used model-based measure is *discounted cumulative gain* (DCG) [8]. DCG is typically computed as a sum over ranks 1 to k, with each document contributing a gain according to its relevance discounted by a log function of the rank.

$$DCG@k = \sum_{i=1}^{k} \frac{gain(rel_i)}{\log_b(i+b-1)}$$

The parameters that define a user are the rank cut-off k, the log base b (which can be seen as modeling patience similar to RBP), and the gain values for each grade of relevance. By varying all these parameters together we could investigate the effect of sampling from a user space.

A number of other measures and models have been proposed in recent literature. These include *expected reciprocal rank* (ERR), which uses geometric distributions with nonzero probabilities only at the ranks of relevant documents [4]; α-nDCG, which penalizes redundancy according to a parameterized model [5]; the *intent aware* family of measures, which probabilistically model a diverse set of possible intents for a query [2]; and others [14, 19, 18]. All of these have at least one free parameter. Carterette organizes them into a framework partly based on features of their user modeling distributions [3].

In this work we focus exclusively on RBP, for two reasons: first, with just one parameter it is the simplest of all measures that have been described in the literature, and therefore a good starting point for this work. Second, because it uses proper probability distributions, it is very amenable to the type of analysis we would like to do. The methods we present here can be generalized to other measures (assuming data is available); we reserve this for future investigation.

2.3 Choosing parameter values

There has been previous work on the choice of parameter value and the analysis of the effects of making different choices. Nearly every paper that proposes such a measure spends at least some time justifying the existence of the parameter, comparing the models that use it to user data, and describing a way to choose a value.

Kanoulas & Aslam investigated the choice of discount and gain function for nDCG to minimize variance in an evaluation [9]. Their goal was to take advantage of a free parameters to improve the robustness of systems-based evaluation, whereas ours is to intentionally decrease robustness in order to draw conclusions about a wider (simulated) user base.

Zhang et al. develop a model of "gaps" between the ranks of clicks in a user log and use this model to find an expected patience parameter p for RBP [20]. We will similarly model the relationship between patience and clicks, but instead of using the expected value we will use the entire distribution. Zhang et al. also looked at the sensitivity of RBP to choice of parameter value using a bounding approach [21], with the goal of showing that RBP is not sensitive to parameter selection. We actually hope RBP *is* sensitive to parameter selection, in that we would like to be able to detect differences in effectiveness between systems on the basis of how users might respond to them.

The work described above tends to treat the existence of a free parameter as a problem that needs to be addressed or solved. We view it instead as an *opportunity* to model an additional source of variance that we would not have access to without a larger user study. Instead of using one fixed value, however, we vary it in a way that is informed by user data. Through this approach we are able to evaluate systems in the presence of noise due to a simulated user. In the best case, we can learn something about systems and their utility to a user population that we could not discover with a traditional systems-based evaluation or with a single fixed parameter value.

3. USER SAMPLING DISTRIBUTIONS

We first need a way to sample parameter values in a way that simulates sampling users. To this end we introduce a Bayesian model that starts with uniform distributions and updates them based on logged user data. The advantages of a Bayesian approach are that it produces a posterior distribution from which we can sample, and that we can use it regardless of whether we have very large amounts of user data (as in web search settings) or very little data (as in many domain-specific search settings). When a lot of data is available, the posteriors will closely track the data; when little is available, we are still able to use it to model users better than having no data at all while maintaining uncertainty due to the lack of data.

3.1 Patience distribution for RBP

Our goal in this section is to develop a way to compute a posterior distribution $P(p|E)$ for RBP's patience parameter p given a uniform prior distribution $P(p)$ and user log evidence E consisting of user queries and ranks at which clicks occurred. We will do this using Bayesian methods, so we start by applying Bayes' rule:

$$P(p|E) \propto P(E|p)P(p)$$

We will need a way to model click evidence given the patience parameter p. While there are many models of clicks in the literature (e.g. [20, 6]), none that we are aware of are directly applicable to our purpose. We believe this model—and our reason for using it—is novel.

In the language of Bernoulli trials, which are used to model coin flips and other binary random variables, we can treat a click as a "success" and the absence of a click as a "failure". Counting the number of failures before the first success gives a random variable that has a geometric distribution. For a fair coin, for instance, the probability of seeing zero tails before the first head is 0.5; the probability of seeing one tail before the first head is 0.25; two tails before the first head is 0.125; and so on. Similarly, if we model clicks as geometrically distributed with patience parameter p, the probability of zero unclicked documents before the first click (that is, the probability that the first click is at rank 1) is p; the probability of one unclicked document before the first click (the probability that the first click is at rank 2) is $(1-p)p$; and so on. Thus we can model the rank of the first click with a geometric distribution.

The geometric distribution is a special case of the negative binomial distribution, which can be used to model the total number of failures before a target number of successes is reached. If there are c clicks, the negative binomial distribution parameterized by p and the target number of failures r is defined as:

$$P(c|p,r) = \binom{c+r-1}{c}(1-p)^r p^{c-1}$$

When $r = 1$, $P(c|p, r = 1)$ reduces to the geometric distribution: the probability of $c = 1$ clicks is $(1-p)$; $c = 2$ clicks is $(1-p)p$; and so on. As our user model assumes a user progressing down a ranked list and deciding whether or not to stop, we will assume that the number of failures r is equal to the rank of the last click for a search minus the total number of clicks.

Since a negative binomial distribution is parameterized by the number of failures r and the probability p, we will return to $P(p|E)$ and treat it as marginal over the number of viewed but unclicked documents (assuming that all documents above the rank of the last click were seen):

$$P(p|E) = \sum_{r=0}^{\infty} P(p|r,E)P(r|E)$$

$P(r|E)$ is the probability that some user skips r documents in a search. $P(p|r,E)$ is the posterior distribution of patience parameter values for a given number of unclicked documents, and $P(p|r,E) \propto P(E|p,r)P(p|r)$. The prior $P(p|r)$ is still uniform. We compute $P(E|p,r) = P(c|p,r)$ using the negative binomial distribution above. One way to estimate $P(p|E)$, then, is to iterate over r, for each one sampling p from a uniform distribution and then computing $P(c|p,r)$ for every search in the click log for which there were r failures. Repeating this many times produces an estimate of the posterior distribution.

3.1.1 *Fast computation*

There is a simple way to obtain $P(p|r,E)$ with just one pass over the click data in E. We will define $P(p|r)$ as having a Beta distribution parameterized by α,β. Beta distributions are defined over the range $[0,1]$. When $\alpha = \beta$, they are symmetric. When $\alpha > \beta$, they are skewed left. When $\beta > \alpha$, they are skewed right. When $\alpha = \beta = 1$, the distribution is uniform. We will write:

$$P(p|r) = Beta(p|\alpha,\beta)$$

to denote a parameter with a Beta prior. Formally,

$$Beta(p|\alpha,\beta) = \frac{p^{\alpha-1}(1-p)^{\beta-1}}{Z}$$

where Z is a normalization constant.

The Beta distribution is the *conjugate prior* of the negative binomial distribution. This means that if we start with the uniform prior, then sample from a negative binomial distribution (by looking at clicks), when we use those samples to update the prior the resulting posterior distribution is from the same family but with updated parameter values. For a negative binomial random variable parameterized by r total failures and probability p of success, if we have m distinct sampled instances and c_i is the number of successes in instance i, and if the prior of p is $Beta(\alpha,\beta)$, the posterior of p is $Beta(\alpha+\sum_{i=1}^{m} c_i, \beta+rm)$. Thus this gives us an easy way to update the distribution of p given data.

To estimate $P(p|r,E)$ from data, then, we look at all instances (searches) for which there were r unclicked doc-

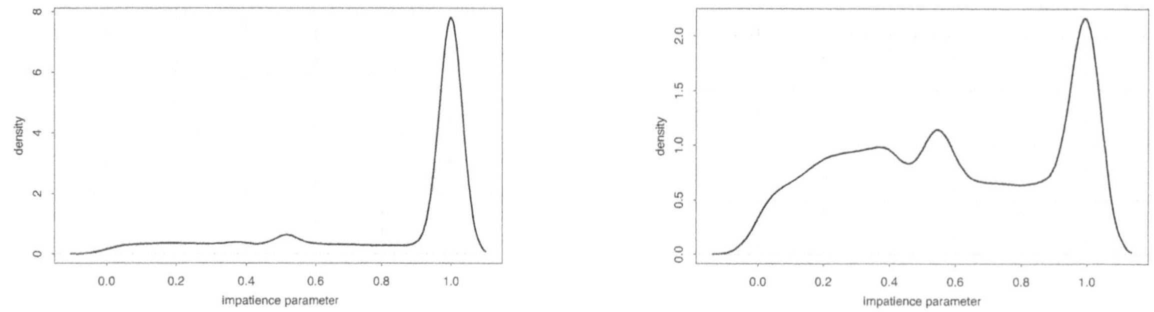

Figure 2: Empirical patience profiles for navigational (left) and informational (right) queries. Users exhibit much less patience for navigational needs, nearly always clicking only the first rank (if they click anything).

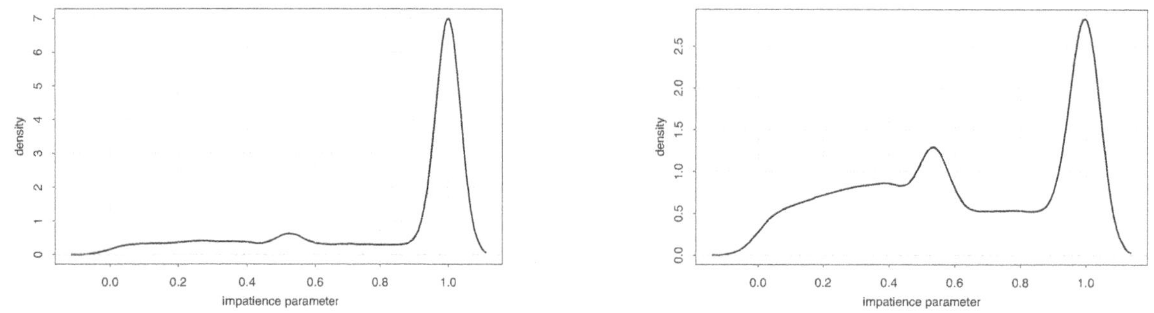

Figure 3: A second set of empirical patience profiles for navigational (left) and informational (right) queries. These are significantly different from those shown in Figure 2.

uments. For example, suppose $r = 1$ and there are m_1 searches with one unclicked document (and varying numbers of clicked documents). The posterior $P(p|r = 1, E)$ is $Beta(\alpha + \sum_{i=1}^{m_r} c_i, \beta + rm_r)$, where c_i is the number of clicks for instance i.

Therefore the full set of equations required is:

$$P(p|E) = \sum_{r=0}^{\infty} P(r|E)P(p|r, E)$$

$$P(r|E) = \frac{m_r + 1}{\sum_{i=0}^{\infty} m_i + 1}$$

$$P(p|r, E) = Beta\left(p|\alpha + \sum_{i=1}^{m_r} c_i, \beta + rm_r\right)$$

where m_r is the number of searches with r unclicked documents (estimated as the rank of the last click minus the total number of clicks), α,β are hyperparameters that we will set to 1, and c_i is the total number of clicks for the ith search with r unclicked documents. $P(r|E)$ is an empirical estimate with simple plus-one smoothing, and $P(p|r, E)$ is calculated with the Beta density function. Note that when no documents go unclicked ($r = 0$), there are two cases: either all ranks from 1 to the stopping rank were clicked, or nothing was clicked at all. These two cases are treated differently; for the former, the clicks can be used in the Beta distribution as usual, but for the latter there is no evidence with which to update priors. Thus there is a special case $P(r = 0, c = 0|E)P(p|r = 0, c = 0)$ with $P(p|r = 0, c = 0)$ modeled as a uniform distribution.

By training these distributions we obtain an empirical "patience profile". We can define this profile over all data, or over subsets of it. For instance, we could compute a patience profile for a particular user by just looking at that user's queries and clicks. We could compute a patience profile for classes of queries (such as informational and navigational) by just looking at the click data for queries in that class. Patience profiles for this case (with queries labeled "informational" or "navigational" by human assessors) are shown in Fig. 2. As expected, users exhibit much more patience for informational queries. Fig. 3 shows the same distributions learned from a different log (from the same search engine); they are similar in shape, though there are differences visible by inspection.

4. METHODS FOR ANALYSIS

Conclusions from both systems-based evaluations and user studies depend on statistical analysis of measurements on systems, topics, and (in the latter case) users. Systems-based evaluations typically use a statistical hypothesis test such as the t-test or a non-parametric alternative such as the Wilcoxon signed rank test to make an inference about the significance of the result. User studies vary tremendously in their design and analysis, but one typical approach is a Latin-squares design in which each user interacts with one or more systems on one or more topics, but never with the same topic twice. The typical statistical analysis for this design is the analysis of variance (ANOVA) or non-parametric alternatives like the Friedman test that analyze variance due to both topics and users.

The t-test and similar tests are not adequate for our goal of introducing user-model variance into a systems-based evaluation. Those tests model a topic sample as a so-called "random effect" that introduces variance to the measure, but they can only model one random effect. If we are to model users, we will have at least two random effects: the topic sample and the values of the parameters that model users. In other words, the parameters can be viewed as random variables, and we can view the selection of a value as sampling from some distribution, just as a user study would sample users from some population.

These two sources of variation are different in an important way: we generally have access to only one sample of topics and we cannot sample another set without incurring a fairly high one-time cost of relevance judging. But we can sample as many parameter values as we like; there is almost no cost to sampling them. Studying variance due to the latter is therefore somewhat easier than studying variance due to the former, and it is useful to study parameter values in isolation of topic sample variance.

4.1 Marginal distribution analysis

As we have discussed, RBP and other measures in Section 2 are typically computed by selecting one value for the parameter(s), then evaluating all systems and topics with that value. The value may be informed by data, but it usually does not reflect variability in the data. To do that, we could instead sample many values of the parameters from distributions such as those in Figure 2, compute the measure for every value, and produce a *marginal distribution* for that measure. We can compare two of these distributions to investigate the effect of variability in the user space.

For the sake of generality, we will use θ to denote a vector of parameters and $P(\theta)$ to denote a distribution over that vector. For RBP $\theta = p$ and $P(p)$ is a distribution over $[0, 1]$. Sampling from the distribution $P(p)$ simulates sampling a user that interacts with the system as described by the RBP model. Each value we sample from these distributions can be used to compute RBP for a system; over a number of samples we can create a histogram of RBP values.

In general, we can form a marginal distribution over values of a measure M parameterized by θ by averaging over parameter vectors θ:

$$P(M = m) = \int P(M = m|\theta)P(\theta)d\theta$$

where $P(M = m|\theta) = 1$ if $M = m$ for parameters θ and 0 otherwise. We can estimate the distribution by Monte Carlo simulation: sample values of θ and use them to calculate M; over many trials the distribution $P(M)$ emerges.

This basic procedure allows us to form many other marginal distributions. We can ask questions such as:

- Over all possible choices of a parameter, what is the probability that one system is better than another? (i.e. $P(M_1 > M_2)$)?
- Over all possible choices of a parameter, what is the probability that the magnitude of the difference in performance is greater than some threshold (i.e. $P(M_1 - M_2 > t)$)?
- If there are parameters such that $M_1 > M_2$ and others such that $M_2 > M_1$, what is the probability that the magnitude of the former is greater than the magnitude of the latter?
- Over all possible choices of a parameter, what is the probability that the percent difference in performance is greater than some threshold (i.e. $P(\frac{M_1 - M_2}{M_1} > t)$)?

As an example, suppose we are evaluating two systems on a single topic by RBP. The relevance of the documents retrieved by the two are:

$$S_1 = [R \quad N \quad N \quad N \quad N \quad N \quad N \quad N \quad N \quad N]$$
$$S_2 = [N \quad R \quad R \quad R \quad R \quad R \quad R \quad R \quad R \quad R]$$

Depending on the choice of parameter value, we would draw different conclusions. If $p = 0.2$, we would conclude that S_2 is more than three times better than S_1. If $p = 0.8$, we would conclude that S_2 is four times worse than S_1. For $p = 0.5$, they are about the same.

Let us instead consider their performance over the entire range $p \in (0, 1)$. For now we will assume that $P(p)$ is uniform over that range. Fig. 4 shows three RBP histograms: the first shows the two marginal distributions of RBP over p. The second shows the distribution in the difference in RBP; depending on the parameter value, there is a 50% chance that the first system will be better than the second, but when that system is better it is likely to be a greater magnitude difference than when the reverse is true. The third shows the distribution in the percent difference in RBP; while 50% of the mass is to the right of 1 (meaning S_1 is better), the values of p for which S_2 is better can result in a much greater percent difference in performance. If we believe a user is as likely to be impatient as patient, we may want to deploy S_1 just so those impatient users will see at least one relevant document.

4.2 Mixed-effect models

Marginal distribution analysis looks at variance due to the choice of parameter value. It ignores variance due to the topic sample, but this is the variance we model when we perform statistical hypothesis tests such as the t-test. Analyzing a user study with an ANOVA takes variance from both topics and users into account; we would like to use a similar approach in our analysis. Because our "users" are such simple objects, we can use more powerful tools than ANOVA. A general *mixed-effect model* (of which both ANOVA and the t-test are special cases) can incorporate arbitrary sources of evidence into an analysis [7]; in this section we show how to set up and interpret a mixed-effect model.

Specifically, we would like to model the parameter as a random effect along with the topic sample. This would take into account the idea that users may have varying patience depending on their information need and other random variables. The standard t-test/ANOVA linear model is:

$$y_{ij} = \mu + \alpha_i + \beta_j + \epsilon_{ij} \qquad (1)$$

where y_{ij} is the value of an evaluation measure calculated on topic j for system i, μ is a population effect or model intercept, α_i is the effect of system i, β_j is the effect of topic j, and ϵ_{ij} is the residual error, which subsumes system/topic interaction effects. One way to understand the topic effect is as a linear model with an intercept (but no slope) that is dependent on the topic number j; then fitting the model involves fitting both a topic model to the random topic sample as well as the overall model to the measures.

A mixed-effect model based on the ANOVA model but including an additional continuous-valued source of variance from the parameter could be expressed as:

$$y_{ijk} = \mu + \alpha_i + (\beta_j + \phi_j p_k) + (\kappa_{ij} + \gamma_{ij} p_k) + \epsilon_{ijk} \qquad (2)$$

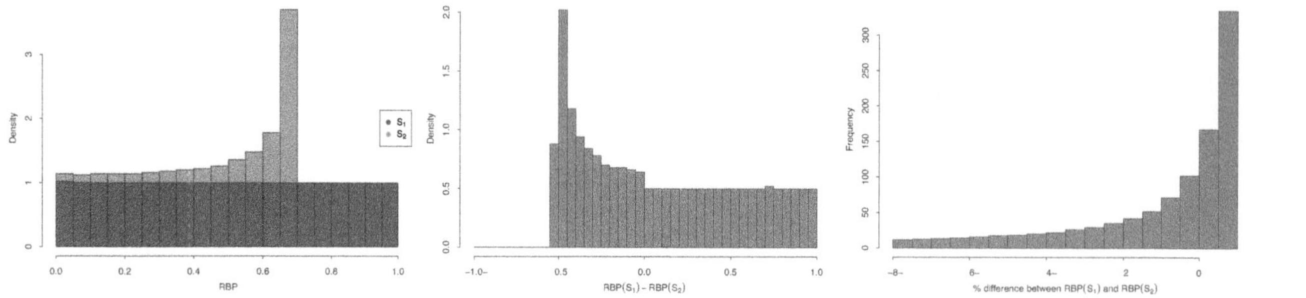

Figure 4: Distributions of RBP (left), difference in RBP (center), and percent difference in RBP (right) over uniform distributions of parameter p.

where y_{ijk} is the measure calculated on topic j, system i with parameter value p_k. In this formulation, the topic effect is itself a linear model with intercept β_j and slope ϕ_j (which vary by topic), and furthermore there is a separate system/topic interaction effect modeled as a line with intercept κ_{ij} and slope γ_{ij} (which vary by topic and system together). If topic effects dependent on p or system/topic interaction effect dependent on p wash out the system effects independent of p, we will not be able to detect a significant difference between systems.

4.2.1 *Fitting mixed-effect models*

Here we describe how to fit a mixed-effect model in the statistical programming environment R. While there are formulas that one can use, they are quite complicated and fairly non-transparent. We hope it will be more useful to show how to use a freely-available open source library to fit them and at the same time provide some intuition about the relationship between linear regression, the t-test, ANOVA, and mixed-effect models that is not immediately evident from looking at the formulas.

One can become convinced that the t-test is a special case of ANOVA, which in turn is a special case of linear regression, by the following analysis. First we obtain some data; this may be actual IR experimental data or randomly generated (which is useful for illustration). The data must be in an R data frame with one row for each system/topic pair.

```
data <- data.frame(y = rnorm(25*2),
                   system = as.factor(rep(1:2, each=25)),
                    topic = as.factor(rep(1:25, 2)))
```

This samples 50 numbers from a standard normal distribution to simulate an evaluation being performed for two systems over 25 topics each. Each sampled number is associated with a system number (1 or 2) and a topic number (from 1 to 25).

Once the data has been generated, the following procedures fit the linear model (Eq. 1) and result in equivalent inferences:

```
t.test(y ~ system, paired=T, data)
summary(aov(y ~ system + Error(topic/system), data))
summary(lm(y ~ system + topic, data))
```

The absolute value of the t statistic output by the `t.test` is equal to the square root of the F value output by the `aov` ANOVA analysis; the p-values are identical. The t statistic on the coefficient for `system2` output by the linear regression `lm` is equivalent to the t statistic from the `t.test`. These equivalencies can be observed across any two systems over n topics generated by any process. This demonstrates the utility of the linear model in analyzing evaluation results.

A mixed-effect linear model can be fit using the `lmer` function in the `lme4` package. The following is equivalent to the `t.test`, `aov`, and `lm` above:

```
lmer(y ~ system + (1|topic), data)
```

The t value for the `system2` fixed effect is again identical to the t values produced by the t-test and linear regression and to the square root of the ANOVA F value. The syntax makes a clear distinction between fixed effects and random effects, and furthermore allows much more flexibility in modeling random effects.[1]

Given that a t-test is an instance of a linear model, it is a short leap to including measure parameters in a linear model. When we have multiple measures for each system/topic pair based on using different parameter values, we fit the more complex mixed-effect linear model (Eq. 2):

```
lmer(y ~ system + (p|topic/system), data)
```

This sets up random intercepts for topics and system/topic pairs, and random slopes for both based on p as described above. This model allows us to analyze variance due to the topic sample and variance due to the choice of p within a system/topic pair.

4.2.2 *Interpreting mixed-effect models*

The output of R's `lmer` function (with two systems evaluated by RBP over 25 topics with 50 different parameter values sampled from a uniform distribution) looks like this:

```
   AIC   BIC logLik deviance REMLdev
 -6243 -6190   3130    -6271   -6261
Random effects:
 Groups       Name        Variance  Std.Dev. Corr
 system:topic (Intercept) 0.0229323 0.151434
              p           0.2788552 0.528067 -0.401
 topic        (Intercept) 0.0000000 0.000000
              p           0.1149877 0.339098   NaN
 Residual                 0.0037814 0.061493
Num obs: 2500, groups: system:topic, 50; topic: 25
```

[1]It is better to think of the random effect as being `(1|topic/system)` for congruence with `aov`'s syntax. However, because of inconsistencies in implementation, `lmer` cannot use that syntax unless there is more than one measure for each system/topic pair.

```
Fixed effects:
            Estimate Std. Error t value
(Intercept)  0.34353    0.02853  12.043
system2      0.01068    0.03949   0.271
```

Consider this output from the bottom to the top. First, as with the linear model, the `lmer` function gives a coefficient and a t-statistic for each system in the experiment in the `Fixed effects` section. We can therefore evaluate the significance of a system with variance due to both topics and modeled users. In this case the t-statistic is quite low, suggesting that the systems are not significantly different. Unfortunately it does not provide the number of degrees of freedom to use to compute a *p*-value, but as long as the design is fully nested (that is, every system evaluated on every topic with every sampled parameter value), we can use $df = n - m + 1$ where n is the number of topics and m the number of systems. Thus a p-value for the hypothesis that the second system is better is $P(t > 0.271 | df = 24) = 0.394$.

Second, the `Random effects` section gives the variance in the measure due to the parameter value in system/topic groups and topic groups. The higher this variance is, and in particular the greater it is relative to residual variance, the greater effect the selection of parameter has on the final results. In this example we can see the variance due to system/topic interaction is greater than residual variance ($0.023 > 0.004$); the variance due to parameter p within system/topic groups is much greater than residual variance ($0.279 > 0.004$); and the variance due to parameter p in topic groups is greater than residual variance ($0.115 > 0.004$). This clearly shows that the parameter is responsible for a great deal of variance in the measure separately from the system and the topic.

Finally, the first two lines give some statistics about the goodness of the model fit. These cannot easily be interpreted absolutely, but they can be interpreted relative to other models. Fitting a model without random slope due to p to the same data gives the following:

```
    AIC    BIC logLik deviance REMLdev
 -951.2 -922.1  480.6   -969.2  -961.2
```

The goodness-of-fit for the model including p is much better than the model not including p. The `anova` function tests whether the difference is significant:

```
> anova(m1, m2)
Models:
m2: y ~ system + (1 | topic/system)
m1: y ~ system + (p | topic/system)
   Df      AIC     BIC logLik Chisq Chi Df Pr(>Chisq)
m2  5   -959.2  -930.1  484.6
m1  9  -6253.2 -6200.8 3135.6  5302      4  < 2.2e-16
```

So including p in the model gives a significantly better fit (p-value $< 2.2 \times 10^{-16}$ by the χ^2 test).[2] This is not too surprising but we note the implication that changing p does not just result in constant differences in the magnitude of effectiveness difference.

[2]The goodness-of-fit statistics reported by `anova` are slightly different from those reported by `lmer`. This is because `anova` re-fits the models with a different likelihood function. In practice this does not make much difference.

dataset	task	topics	runs submitted
Terabyte 2005	ad hoc	751–800	58
Terabyte 2005	named page	601–872	42
Terabyte 2006	ad hoc	701–850	61
Terabyte 2006	named page	901–1081	43

Table 1: TREC Terabyte track data for 2005–2006.

5. EXPERIMENTAL ANALYSIS

We will analyze the application of the proposed simulation and analysis to TREC evaluation. The idea is that we simulate users who have TREC-style information needs but who vary in their patience according to the distributions shown in Fig. 2: many will stop after rank 1, but a significant fraction will go to rank 100 or deeper. The mean patience is $p = 0.83$ for navigational queries and $p = 0.59$ for informational queries.

The primary question we are interested in is this: when we perform our simulated user study and analyze results using marginal distribution analysis and mixed-effect models, do we learn anything about systems that we did not already know from purely systems-based experiments with unparameterized evaluation measures and t-tests? If not, then traditional systems-based evaluation is good enough for all intents and purposes. Otherwise, we should consider adding this approach to our evaluation toolkit.

A secondary question is whether evaluation results differ depending on the log used to learn a sampling distribution. The distributions in Figures 2 and 3, learned from two separate logs, are similar by inspection, but they are significantly different by statistical goodness-of-fit tests. Thus the question: if two different logs produce two different distributions, will we draw different conclusions about the evaluation, or are these methods robust?

5.1 Data

For this analysis we focused on evaluating two tasks: an ad hoc retrieval task (meant to model informational needs) and a named-page finding task (to model navigational needs). For this we used data from the TREC Terabyte 2005 and 2006 tracks, described in Table 1. Note that we removed 19 Terabyte 2006 ad hoc manual runs, since they were evaluated over a smaller subset of topics than the automatic runs from the same year.

Our patience profiles are derived from the query log of a commercial search engine collected in January 2009. The log consists of queries, their frequency in the log and the ranks at which clicks occurred for each query. All queries in the log have been labeled as "navigational" or "informational" by human assessors. We randomly divided the queries into two sets of training (used in Fig. 2) and testing (used in Figure 3) with approximately equal size. We form patience profiles from the navigational and informational classes separately; we sample from the navigational profile (Fig. 2, left) to evaluate the named page task and from the informational profile (Fig. 2, right) to evaluate the ad hoc task. We will use Fig. 3 to test the effect of the sampling distribution.

5.2 Marginal distribution analysis

All of our marginal distribution analysis is based on the distribution of a measure over the parameter space. For any pair of systems, we can answer any of the questions in

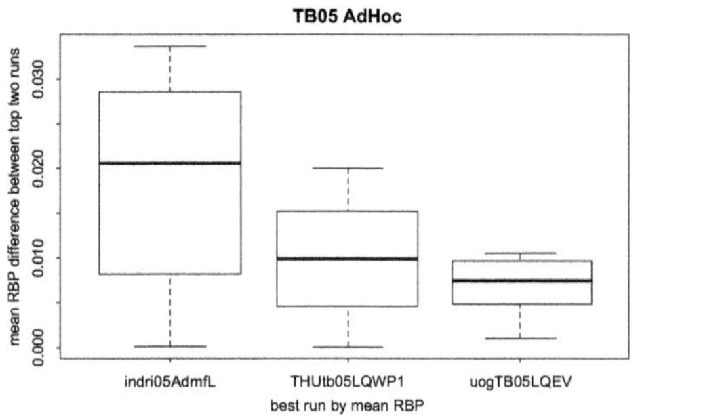

Figure 5: Depending on parameter value, the "best" ad hoc system as measured by RBP is one of these three. Boxes show the distribution of differences between each system (given that it is the best) and the second-best system.

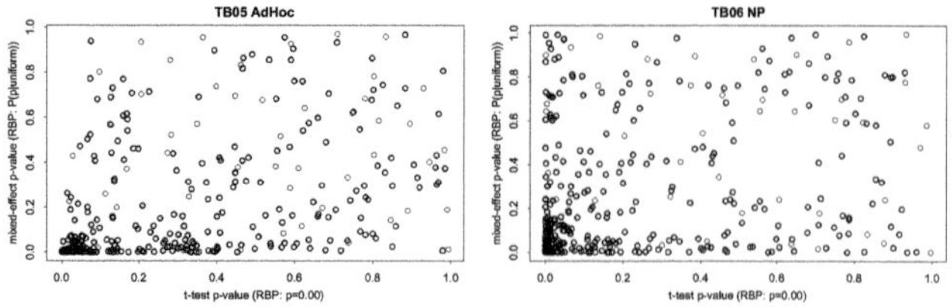

Figure 7: RBP p-values for TB05 ad hoc (left) and TB06 named page (right) from a paired two-sided t-test with a fixed parameter $p = 0.59$ or $p = 0.83$ (respectively) versus the mixed-effect model with 25 parameter values sampled from the respective distributions in Fig. 2.

Section 4.1; for analyzing a set of systems we investigate questions about orderings. To do so, we sample a parameter value, then evaluate all systems in the set with that value and rank them. Over many samples we form histograms of measurements on the rankings. We select some interesting results from our four datasets; much more analysis is possible, but space is limited.

Which system provides the best user experience? Typically the "best" system is the one with the greatest value according to some evaluation measure. But with enough variance over the user space, some users may find a different system much more useful to their particular needs. By varying parameters in a model-based measure, we may obtain a *distribution* of "best" systems, with different systems being "best" for different user classes.

When we vary RBP's patience parameter according to the informational distribution, we find that there are three different TB 2005 ad hoc systems that could claim to be best: indri05AdmfL for very patient users in roughly the range $p \in (0, 0.10]$, uogTB05LQEV for patient users in the range $p \in (0.10, 0.82]$, and THUtb05LQWP1 for impatient users—33% of the distribution—in the range $p \in (0.82, 1.00]$. indri05AdmfL has the highest mean average precision of any system, and uogTB05LQEV has the highest precision@5 of any system, but THUtb05LQWP1 is no better than third place for any of the traditional TREC evaluation measures. Thus we have already learned something new: a system that does not rank better than third place by any standard measure actually provides the best experience for a large proportion of our simulated users. It is particularly interesting that it is better for these users than the system with highest precision@5, since that is usually thought to be a good measure to model impatient users.

Fig. 5 shows the distribution of differences in mean RBP between each of the "best" systems and the second-best system for the same parameter value. When indri05AdmfL is best, the difference between it and the second-best system is relatively large, but it is only best for a very small group of users. uogTB05LQEV has a much smaller difference, though it is useful to a much larger group of users. THUtb05LQWP1 seems to strike the best balance between being useful to a wide range of users while also being likely to be substantially better than the next-best system for those users. Again, this is something that no traditional evaluation paradigm could tell us.

For TB 2006 ad hoc, there are again three systems that vie for first place: indri06AtdnD ($p \in (0, 0.17]$), uogTB06S50L ($p \in (0.17, 0.99]$), and JuruTWE ($p \in (0.99, 1.00]$). Again we have one system—uogTB06S50L—that covers most user patience profiles, and one—JuruTWE—that covers a large part of the users, including the most impatient, and that is not among the top three systems by any traditional measure. For the named page tasks, there is much more consistency; a single system is best for the vast majority of the user space.

How much does the ranking of systems change with parameter value? Besides the "best" system, we are often interested in an overall ranking of systems by some measure. As the parameter value changes, the ranking will change as well. We computed Kendall's τ rank correlation between the ranking of systems for each parameter value and the ranking by a single point parameter value ($p = 0.59$ for ad hoc; $p = 0.83$ for named page) for the same measure. Histograms of τ values are shown in Fig. 6 for both tracks (with distributions for two tasks superimposed). Both tasks have relatively stable rankings, and the distributions are similarly-shaped for both tasks. But there is enough variability—particularly in the 2005 runs—that τ frequently drops below the usual standard of 0.9 for two rankings to be "equivalent" [16]. In some cases τ can drop nearly as low as 0.5, which reflects a major difference in system ranking.

5.3 Mixed-effect model analysis

We used the mixed-effect model to test for significant differences between pairs of systems as described in Section 4.2.2. We randomly sampled 500 pairs of runs to use in experiments from each of the four settings: TB 2005 ad hoc (1,653 total pairs), TB 2006 ad hoc (1,830 total pairs), TB 2005 named page (861 total pairs), and TB 2006 named page (903 total pairs).

Fig. 7 compares p-values reported by a paired two-sided t-test for RBP (with parameter fixed according to task) to those reported by a mixed-effect model with 25 randomly sampled parameters from the distributions in Fig. 2. The left plot (for TB 2005 ad hoc) has a linear correlation of 0.55; the two tests agree about significance in 81% of the pairs. The mixed-effect model tends to find more pairs significant, with 16.2% of its pairs not significant by a t-test. The right plot (for TB 2006 named page) has a lower linear correlation of 0.38. The two tests agree about the significance of about 70% of the pairs. In this case, 17.2% of the pairs are significant by a t-test but not by the mixed-effect model.

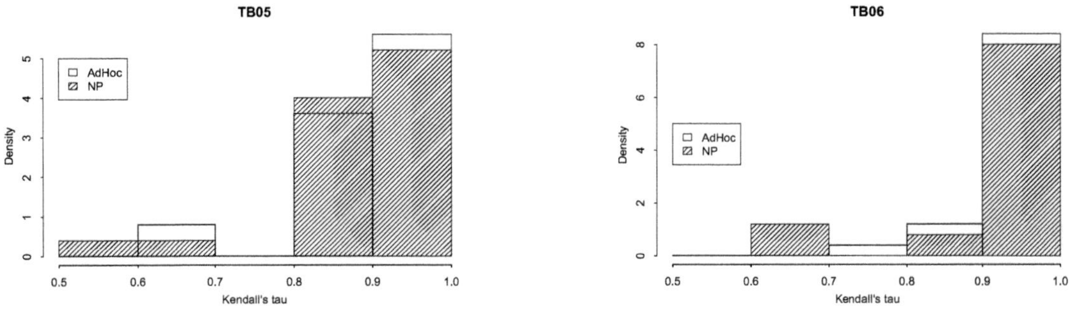

Figure 6: Histograms of Kendall's τ rank correlations for varying RBP patience parameter; Terabyte 2005 (left) and Terabyte 2006 (right) with two histograms for the two tasks. Rankings are relatively stable, but there are some substantial differences.

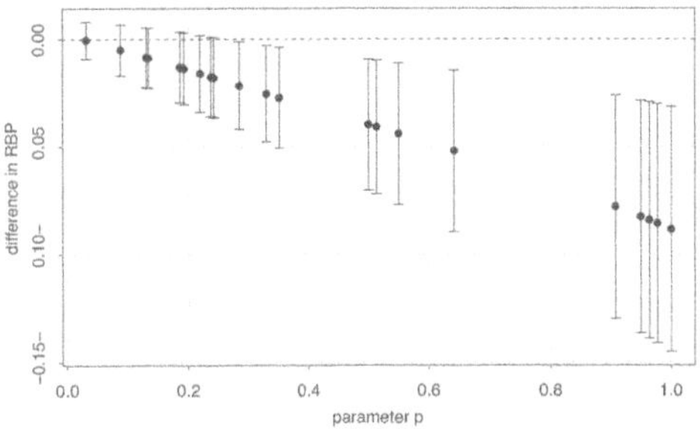

Figure 8: Mean difference and 95% c.i. for RBP for two systems over 50 parameter values sampled from the navigational distribution in Fig. 2. For any given parameter value, the systems are likely to be significantly different (by a t-test), but they are not significantly different when the space of parameters is modeled (with the mixed-effect model).

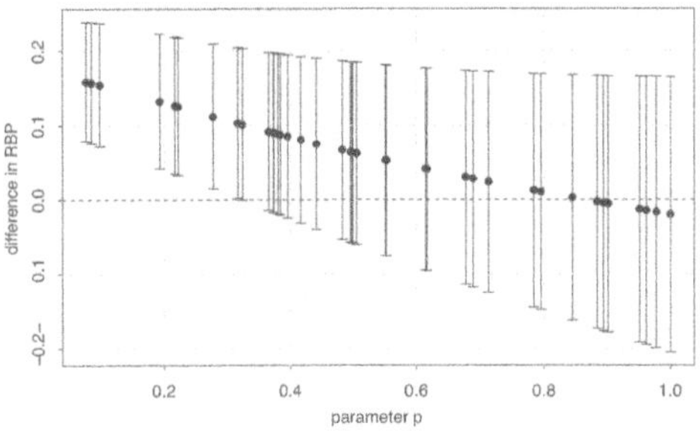

Figure 9: Mean difference and 95% c.i. for RBP for two systems over 50 parameter values sampled from the informational distribution in Fig. 2. For any given parameter value, the systems are not likely to be significantly different (by a t-test), but they are significantly different when the space of parameters is modeled (with the mixed-effect model).

The fact that the t-test and mixed-effect model agree on the majority of pairs is good: it means that we can indeed use this model and trust that it will give results that match previous experiments in general. The fact that they disagree is also interesting, as is the fact that some pairs that are not even close to the significance threshold by one method are very close by the other. These are the pairs that offer the opportunity to learn something new, so we selected some of them to try to identify causes.

Our first pair (NTUNF4 and humTN05pl from TB 2005 named page) is significant by a t-test but not by the mixed-effect model. Fig. 8 shows the difference in mean RBP over topics for each sampled p with 95% confidence intervals. Note that the difference is significant for most individual values, including the most likely in the navigational distribution. Yet these two systems are *not* significantly different by any traditional precision measure; from precision@5 to precision@1000, the t-test p-values are well above the 0.05 threshold. The mixed-effect model in this case reveals that the choice of parameter value contributes more to variability in RBP than differences between systems do.

Our second pair (TWTB05AD02 and ctfadhocaf1 from TB 2005 ad hoc) is not significant by a t-test but is significant by the mixed-effect model. Fig. 9 shows the difference in mean RBP over topics for each sampled p with 95% confidence intervals. In this case, the difference is *not* significant for values greater than about 0.33. Yet these two systems *are* significantly different by traditional IR measures, including MAP and precision@10. In this case the mixed-effect model can reveal that the selection of parameter value does not matter since the difference in system effects holds once variance due to that value is modeled.

5.4 Differences due to sampling distribution

To determine whether the sampling distribution affects the evaluation, we compared p-values from the mixed-effect model: for each pair of systems in the Terabyte 2005 ad hoc data, we calculated the p-value from a mixed-effect model based on sampling users from the distributions in Fig. 2 and the p-value from a mixed-effect model based on sampling users from those in Fig. 3.

The results are shown in Figure 10. It is clear that there is a high degree of concordance between the results of tests based on the two logs: the linear correlation is 0.97, and the two agree on 97% of the pairs (39% are not significant with both logs; 58% are significant with both logs). For the remaining 3% on which the two logs result in disagreement, the p-values are very close to the 0.05 significance boundary in both cases. From this we tentatively conclude that the log does not make a major difference.

6. CONCLUSION

We have presented a way to simulate simple user behavior for a systems-based evaluation, starting from click data and a simple model of users. We first use click data to create a distribution of parameters modeling a user that steps

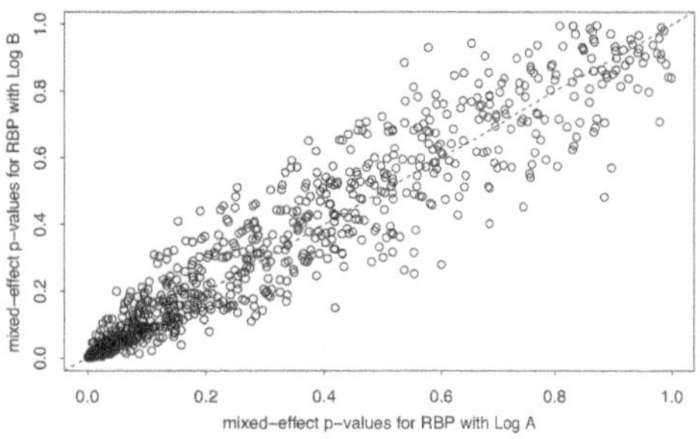

Figure 10: Comparison of p-values from mixed-effect models based on sampling users from distributions in Fig. 2 and Fig. 3. The linear correlation is 0.97.

down search results one rank at a time, deciding whether or not to stop after each one. That distribution can model a single user's behavior changing from search to search, or a wider user population. Sampling from that distribution simulates sampling users; using a value sampled from the distribution together with an evaluation measure based on a user model simulates a user interacting with a system. We demonstrated how to use this to analyze TREC runs and learn something about their potential utility to a user base.

Of course, this simulation procedure is still very far from a true user study. It offers no opportunity for serendipitous discoveries that might occur while exploring data from a user study. The "users" are highly simplified mathematical objects with no will or motivation of their own, and no ability to provide useful feedback that might inform future research directions. We do not believe that we can replace user studies; we only hope to better model the user experience in systems-based evaluations to more thoroughly explore questions of system utility to users.

In the future, we will want to use user data other than clicks, both for informing parameter sampling distributions and for building probabilistic models that measures can be based on. The more we can incorporate user data, the better we can simulate the actual user experience. This data might include dwell time, reformulations, mouse movements, and features such as those used for learning to rank [1, 13, 17]. Measures such as *expected browsing utility* (EBU) [19] and session precision [10] are starting to model much more detailed user behavior for systems effectiveness evaluation.

This work can be extended to measures such as ERR and even more complex measures such as α-nDCG. These will require more information about users—for ERR, we need relevance judgments that we can relate to clicks; for α-nDCG we need to be able to update a redundancy penalty parameter from data. But they will allow us to perform deeper simulations of varying intents, the value of redundant information, the value of better relevant documents, and so on.

Acknowledgments: Research was sponsored in part by the Army Research Laboratory under Cooperative Agreement Number W911NF-09-2-0053. The views and conclusions contained in this document are those of the authors and should not be interpreted as representing the official policies, either expressed or implied, of the Army Research Laboratory or the U.S. Government. The U.S. Government is authorized to reproduce and distribute reprints for Government purposes notwithstanding any copyright notation here on. We also gratefully acknowledge the support provided by the European Commission grant FP7-PEOPLE-2009-IIF-254562.

7. REFERENCES

[1] Eugene Agichtein, Eric Brill, and Susan Dumais. Improving web search ranking by incorporating user behavior information. In *Proceedings of SIGIR*, pages 19–26, 2006.

[2] Rakesh Agrawal, Sreenivas Gollapudi, Halan Halverson, and Samuel Ieong. Diversifying search results. In *Proceedings of WSDM*, pages 5–14, 2009.

[3] Ben Carterette. System effectiveness, user models, and user utility: A conceptual framework for investigation. In *Proceedings of SIGIR*, 2011.

[4] Olivier Chapelle, Donald Metzler, Ya Zhang, and Pierre Grinspan. Expceted reciprocal rank for graded relevance. In *Proceedings of CIKM*, 2009.

[5] Charles L. A. Clarke, Maheedhar Kolla, Gordon V. Cormack, Olga Vechtomova, Azin Ashkan, Stefan Büttcher, and Ian MacKinnon. Novelty and diversity in information retrieval evaluation. In *Proceedings of SIGIR*, pages 659–666, 2008.

[6] Georges E. Dupret and Benjamin Piwowarski. A browsing model to predict search engine click data from past observations. In *Proceedings of SIGIR*, pages 331–338, 2008.

[7] Julian J. Faraway. *Extending the Linear Model with R*. CRC Press, 2005.

[8] Kalervo Järvelin and Jaana Kekäläinen. Cumulated gain-based evaluation of IR techniques. *ACM Transactions on Information Systems*, 20(4):422–446, 2002.

[9] Evangelos Kanoulas and Javed A. Aslam. Empirical justification of the gain and discount function for nDCG. In *Proceedings of CIKM*, 2009.

[10] Evangelos Kanoulas, Ben Carterette, Paul D. Clough, and Mark Sanderson. Evaluation over multi-query sessions. In *Proceedings of SIGIR*, 2011.

[11] Evangelos Kanoulas, Paul Clough, Ben Carterette, and Mark Sanderson. Session track at trec 2010. In *Proceedings of SIGIR 2010 Workshop on Simulation of Interaction: Automated Evaluation of Interactive IR*, 2010.

[12] Alistair Moffat and Justin Zobel. Rank-biased precision for measurement of retrieval effectiveness. *ACM Trans. Inf. Syst.*, 27(1):1–27, 2008.

[13] Filip Radlinski and Thorsten Joachims. Query chains: learning to rank from implicit feedback. In *Proceedings of SIGKDD*, pages 239–248, 2005.

[14] Stephen E. Robertson, Evangelos Kanoulas, and Emine Yilmaz. Extending average precision to graded relevance judgments. In *Proceedings of SIGIR*, pages 603–610, 2010.

[15] Andrew Turpin and Falk Scholer. User performance versus precision measures for simple search tasks. In *Proceedings of SIGIR*, pages 225–231, 2006.

[16] Ellen Voorhees. Variations in relevance judgments and the measurement of retrieval effectiveness. In *Proceedings of SIGIR*, pages 315–323, 1998.

[17] Xuanhui Wang and ChengXiang Zhai. Learn from web search logs to organize search results. In *Proceedings of SIGIR*, pages 87–94, 2007.

[18] Yiming Yang and Abhimanyu Lad. Modeling expected utility of multi-session information distillation. In *Proceedings of ICTIR*, 2009.

[19] Emine Yilmaz, Milad Shokouhi, Nick Craswell, and Stephen Robertson. Expected browsing utility for web search evaluation. In *Proceedings of CIKM*, pages 1561–1564, 2010.

[20] Yuye Zhang, Laurence A. Park, and Alistair Moffat. Click-based evidence for decaying weight distributions in search effectiveness metrics. *Inf. Retr.*, 13:46–69, Feb 2010.

[21] Yuye Zhang, Laurence A. F. Park, and Alistair Moffat. Parameter sensitivity in rank-biased precision. In *Proceedings of ADCS*, 2008.

Click the Search Button and Be Happy: Evaluating Direct and Immediate Information Access

Tetsuya Sakai
Microsoft Research Asia, China
tetsuyasakai@acm.org

Makoto P. Kato
Kyoto University, Japan
kato@dl.kuis.kyoto-u.ac.jp

Young-In Song
Microsoft Research Asia, Beijing, P.R.C.
yosong@microsoft.com

ABSTRACT

We define *Direct* Information Access as a type of information access where there is no user operation such as clicking or scrolling between the user's click on the search button and the user's information acquisition; we define *Immediate* Information Access as a type of information access where the user can locate the relevant information within the system output very quickly. Hence, a *Direct and Immediate Information Access* (DIIA) system is expected to satisfy the user's information need very quickly with its very first response. We propose a nugget-based evaluation framework for DIIA, which takes nugget positions into account in order to evaluate the ability of a system to present important nuggets first and to minimise the amount of text the user has to read. To demonstrate the integrity, usefulness and limitations of our framework, we built a Japanese DIIA test collection with 60 queries and over 2,800 nuggets as well as an offset-based nugget match evaluation interface, and conducted experiments with manual and automatic runs. The results suggest our proposal is a useful complement to traditional ranked retrieval evaluation based on document relevance.

Categories and Subject Descriptors

H.3.3 [**Information Storage and Retrieval**]: Information Search and Retrieval

General Terms

Experimentation

Keywords

evaluation, information access, nugget, test collection

1. INTRODUCTION

Information Retrieval (IR) evaluation methods need to evolve together with users' needs and with IR systems. Classical IR evaluated *set retrieval* by means of *recall* and *precision*; but when the exponential growth of searchable information made *ranked retrieval* a necessity, IR evaluation turned to metrics such as *Average Precision* and *normalised Discounted Cumulative Gain* (nDCG) [10]. Furthermore, as Web search studies have revealed that user's queries are often *ambiguous* and/or *underspecified*, new evaluation metrics suitable for selectively *diversifying* search results have begun to receive attention (e.g., [6, 20]). However, all of these evaluation efforts still focus on ranked retrieval: a list of documents is presented to the user, and the user is expected to choose from the list and then read the entire Web pages that have been chosen.

In modern Web search engines used in desktop and mobile environments, providing a simple ranked list of documents to the user is becoming increasingly insufficient. A Search Engine Result Page (SERP) typically consists of several components besides a list of URLs with snippets, depending on query type. Some of these components aim to satisfy the user needs directly: for example, weather, flight status, stock prices, currency conversion, machine translation and other types of "answers" can be embedded in the SERP [5].

We define *Direct* Information Access (DIA) as a type of information access where there is no user operation such as clicking or scrolling between the user's click on the search button and the user's information acquisition. Chilton and Teeven's "answers" [5] are examples that enable DIA; Li, Huffman and Tokuda [12] have referred to successful DIA cases as "good abandonements." Moreover, we define *Immediate* Information Access (IIA) as a type of information access where the user can locate the relevant information within the system output very quickly. For example, if a system can show a query-biased summary (a search engine snippet would be a trivial example) of a retrieved Web page to the user, this system may be more effective for IIA compared to one that shows the entire contents of that page. Hence, a *Direct and Immediate Information Access* (DIIA) system is expected to satisfy the user's information need very quickly with its very first response.

Suppose that a Japanese user needs to visit a particular Japanese hospital, and he enters the name of the hospital in the query box of a DIIA system. Figure 1 shows a possible DIIA system output (This is from our manual run which we shall discuss in Section 5.1) that the present study considers. As the English translation shows, our "imaginary" DIIA system outputs the contact details and opening hours of the hospital. The Japanese text is about 140 characters and may fit a mobile phone screen size. If the DIIA system is used on a PC, then the DIIA system may be able to return more information, such as the nearest train station, car park availability and so on.

This paper proposes and validates a new methodology for evaluating textual DIIA systems that respond to a given query as shown in Figure 1. Our framework is closely related to multi-document summarisation and Question Answering (QA) evaluations, but differs in the following aspects. First, while the summarisation task treats the set of documents to be summarised as a given input to the system, our DIIA framework considers both the phases of *knowledge source selection* (i.e., finding relevant documents by means of a Web search API etc.) and *knowledge compilation* (i.e., extracting relevant pieces of information or *nuggets* [7, 15] from documents

CIKM'11, October 24–28, 2011, Glasgow, Scotland, UK.

[Japanese output]

電話 046-223-3636。fax 046-223-3630。住所 243-8551 厚木市温水 118-1。email soumu@shonan-atsugi.jp。面会時間:一般病棟月〜金 15-20 時、土日祝日 13-20 時／集中治療室(ICU) 11-11 時半 15-15 時半 19-19 時半。

[English translation]

Phone:046-223-3636. Fax:046-223-3630.Address:118-1 Nurumizu, Atsugi, 243-8551. Email:soumu@shonan-atsugi.jp. Visiting hours:general ward Mon-Fri 15-20; Sat&Holidays 13-20 / Intensive Care Unit (ICU) 11-11:30,15:30,19-19:30.

Figure 1: An example Japanese DIIA output and its translation (query: "Shonan Atsugi Hostpital").

and organising them for effective presentation for a given output screen size). Second, while traditional summarisation and QA evaluations are based on similarities with gold standards or nugget recall and precision (See Section 2.2), the DIIA task we define require the following features of a system:

- Present important nuggets first;
- Minimise the amount of text that the user has to read.

This is a Direct IA task because the system has to return a text that contain pieces of relevant information in response to a given query (instead of returning a list of URLs); it is an Immediate IA task because the above two requirements enable the user to obtain the desired information quickly.

To evaluate the aforementioned requirements of DIIA systems, we introduce a simple evaluation metric called *S-measure* which is an extension of weighted nugget recall but takes the positions of nuggets within the system output into account. To demonstrate the integrity, usefulness and limitations of our DIIA framework, we built a Japanese DIIA test collection with 60 queries and over 2,800 nuggets as well as an offset-based nugget match evaluation interface, and conducted some experiments.

Clearly, DIIA is not just about textual responses: effective DIIA systems should output visual "answers" such as maps, images and so on. These are beyond the scope of our study. Moreover, even when we restrict ourselves to textual responses, aesthetic features such as highlighting and font sizes are important in practice. Our current framework can only handle plain text. Nevertheless, we claim that our evaluation framework is a useful departure from and complement to traditional ranked list evaluation.

Section 2 describes previous work related to the present study. Section 3 proposes our new evaluation framework for the DIIA task. Section 4 describes the DIIA evaluation environment we constructed, and Section 5 reports on a set of experiments using this environment. Finally, Section 6 concludes this paper.

2. RELATED WORK

2.1 Evaluating Search

In modern IR (particularly Web search) evaluation, nDCG [10] has become a popular evaluation metric. While essentially the same idea for evaluating ranked retrieval based on graded relevance existed back in the 1960s (i.e., Pollack's *sliding ratio* [11]), the simple ideas behind nDCG are appealing: a system is rewarded with a gain value for retrieving a relevant document, and the gain values vary according to the relevance levels; each gain is *discounted* according to the rank of the retrieved relevant document; and an *ideal ranked list* is used to normalise the overall system score.

Our proposed metric for evaluating DIIA was inspired by nDCG. However, while nDCG evaluates a ranked list of items, we evaluate a textual output, which is much more problematic. It should also be noted that, while the original nDCG incorporated the notion of *user's patience* as a parameter (i.e., the logarithm base), the *de facto* standard version of nDCG [4] lacks this parameter. In contrast, our proposed metric retains a similar parameter that represents the maximum amount of text the user is expected to read, or equivalently, the maximum amount of time the user is expected to spend. In this respect, Dunlop's work [8] that explored IR evaluation by *expected search duration* is also related to our work.

Recently, methods for evaluating *search result diversification* have been proposed (e.g., [6, 20]). Among them, *α-nDCG* and *Novelty- and Rank-Biased Precision* (NRBP) [6] are somewhat related to our study, as they view both information needs and documents as sets of nuggets. However, these metrics are for evaluating ranked lists, not text.

INEX (INitiative for the Evaluation of XML retrieval) 2011 has launched the Snippet Retrieval Track[1], which is also somewhat relevant to this study as the task involves generation of a textual snippet for each retrieved document. However, the INEX task is still based on document relevance, and the snippets are regarded as a means to judge the relevance of the original documents within the traditional ranked list evaluation framework [21].

Bailey *et al.* [3] proposed a frawework for evaluating the *whole page relevance* of a SERP, which typically consists of multiple components, not all of which are textual. While their approach and our DIIA framework both attempt to go beyond ranked list evaluation, the former does not aim at producing a reusable test collection. In contrast, while our DIIA framework focusses on a single textual response, we aim to provide a nugget-based test collection that is reusable to some extent.

2.2 Evaluating Textual Output

As our DIIA task is similar to summarisation and QA evaluations in that the systems return textual responses, prior art in these areas needs to be discussed.

ROUGE is a family of evaluation metrics for evaluating summaries *automatically* [13]. While several versions of ROUGE exist, the key idea is to compare a system output with a set of gold-standard summaries in terms of *recall* (or alternatively *F-measure*), where recall is defined based on automatically-extracted textual fragments such as N-grams and longest common subsequences. *POURPRE*, an automatic evaluation metric for complex QA, is essentially F-measure computed based on unigram matches between the system output and gold-standard nuggets [14]. Also, new automatic summarisation metrics are being explored at the recent AESOP (Automatically Evaluating Summaries of Peers) task at TAC (Text Analysis Conference)[2].

The above automatic methods assume that automatic string matching between the system output and the gold standard works well. While these methods reduce the evaluation cost dramatically and work for *extractive* approaches (i.e., summaries or answers are parts of source documents), they are probably insufficient for evaluating intelligent systems that can handle consolidation of information across multiple sources, paraphrasing, textual entailment and inference. Hovy, Lin and Zhou [9] discuss some challenges in automatic matching in the context of evaluating summaries using *Basic Elements*. Indeed, we believe that, in order to quickly satisfy the user's information need with a small piece of text, systems will ultimately have to employ *abstractive* techniques. While a few approaches to incorporating paraphrase matching into automatic evaluation exist [16, 25], the premise in our study is that a system output and

[1] `https://inex.mmci.uni-saarland.de/tracks/snippet/`

[2] `http://www.nist.gov/tac/2011/Summarization/`

a list of gold-standard nuggets need to be compared *manually*, at least until we fully understand exactly what kinds of abstractive techniques are useful and reliable for the DIIA task.

The *pyramid method* [17], a recently-proposed method for manually evaluating summaries, is similar to our new proposal. The pyramid method requires multiple gold-standard summaries, from which *semantic content units* (SCUs) are extracted. Each SCU is weighted according to the number of gold-standard summaries it matches with. An assessor manually identifies SCUs within a system's summary, and the pyramid method essentially computes SCU-based weighted precision or weighted recall.

A similar method has been used for evaluating complex QA at TREC (and "squishy-list" QA at TAC) [7]. As was mentioned earlier, the TREC QA systems were required to output a set of documentID-answer pairs rather than a single text. In this evaluation methodology, gold-standard nuggets are created by a single assessor, but nugget importance is determined based on multiple assessors, who assign either *vital* or *okay* to each nugget. Nugget-based precision, weighted recall and F-measure were used for evaluation. However, the computation of precision is problematic here, because the number of "incorrect nuggets" present in a system output is difficult to define [7, 14]. Hence, an *allowance* of 100 characters per nugget match was introduced: if there are k nugget matches and if the system output length l is smaller than $100 * k$, then precision was defined as 1; otherwise precision was defined as $100 * k/l$. This evaluation method was also used for QA tasks with Asian languages at NTCIR[3], with different allowance values for different question types [15].

Unlike the pyramid methods for summarisation and QA, we aim to evaluate the system's ability to present important nuggets first and to minimise the amount of text the user has to read. Hence we take into account the *position* of each nugget match within a system output. Moreover, while the pyramid QA evaluation relies on an arbitrarily-set, fixed-length allowance for computing precision, our methodology allows nugget constructors to define *vital strings* which are used for approximating a length lowerbound for each gold-standard nugget (See Section 3). Note also that the pyramid methods discussed above are *content selection* evaluation metrics: the assumption is that *linguistic quality* evaluation is done separately [17]. Our evaluation framework is similar: S-measure is a *content ranking* evaluation metric, and does not directly consider readability aspects such as coherence and cohesiveness. The challenging problem of evaluating the readability of summaries is being tackled at the aforementioned TAC AESOP task.

2.3 DARPA GALE Distillation Evaluation

Another relevant line of research that lies more or less in between the aforementioned document retrieval paradigm and the textual output paradigm is the nugget-based evaluation effort for the DARPA GALE *distillation* program which was completed in 2010. Babko-Malaya [2] describes a systematic way to define nuggets in a bottom-up manner from a pool of system output texts. This is done prior to determining whether each nugget is relevant or not: thus, even nonrelevant parts of text need to be "nuggetised." In contrast, our nuggets are created in a top-down manner by means of manual web search. However, Babko-Malaya's approach to defining the *nugget granularity* and handling *world knowledge* may also be useful for our task: we leave this to future work.

White, Hunter and Goldsten [22] defined several nugget-based metrics for the distillation task, but they are set retrieval metrics. Allan, Carterette and Lewis proposed a character-based version of *bpref* (binary preference) to evaluate a ranked list of passages [1][4]. Yang *et al.* [24] and Yang and Lad [23] have also discussed nugget-based evaluation metrics that are similar in spirit to the aforementioned α-nDCG, but their distillation tasks are quite different from, and more complex than, our DIIA task: they consider multiple queries issued over a period of time, and multiple ranked lists of retrieved passages. On the other hand, their proposal to explicitly incorporate the user cost (of reading nonrelevant text at the end of system output) deserves attention and may be considered in our DIIA framework in the future.

[3]`http://research.nii.ac.jp/ntcir/`

3. PROPOSED FRAMEWORK

3.1 Task Definition

We first define the DIIA task as follows. Given a query input by the user, return a textual response whose length is no more than X characters (or words, or bytes), excluding white spaces and punctuation marks. We assume that some pieces of information are more important than others, and that important ones should be presented first to the user. Moreover, we expect a DIIA system to try to minimise the amount of text that the user has to read in order to satisfy his information need. Thus, a piece of relevant information near the beginning of the output text (which we call the X*-string*) will be rewarded more than the same piece of information near the end of the text. As the output length is limited, redundancy (i.e., repetition of the same information within the text) is penalised.

In this paper, we consider a Japanese DIIA task as an example, and consider $X = 140$ or 500 in Japanese characters. The former is designed to represent a mobile phone screen size; the latter roughly corresponds to top five snippets in a typical SERP, which are usually visible without scrolling in a desktop environment;

3.2 User Model and Nugget Discounting

We propose a simple evaluation framework for DIIA. First, let us assume that the human reading speed is constant. For example, it is known that the average reading speed of a Japanese person is 400-600 characters per minute. For convenience, we assume that the speed is 500 characters per minute. Our arguments can be extended to other languages, for example, by replacing the constant with 250 words per minute for English, and so on.

As we have discussed earlier, DIIA aims to present important nuggets first and to minimise the amount of text the user has to read in order to obtain the desired information. To evaluate this, we propose to conduct nugget-based evaluation following the practices of QA and summarisation communities, *and* to evaluate each system output by taking into account the *positions* of nugget matches found in it. This is in contrast to traditional QA and summarisation evaluation, where it is only the *presence* of nugget matches that matters. More specifically, we use a *discount factor* with each nugget match based on its *offset* (i.e., distance from the beginning of text), so that a nugget match near the beginning of text receives more credit than one near the end. This is analogous to how normalised discounted cumulative gain (nDCG) [10] discounts relevant documents based on document ranks. However, while the log-based discounting function of nDCG is understood as a model of the user scanning a ranked list of retrieved items from top to bottom while his patience gradually runs out, we are to model a user reading a piece of text from beginning to end. Assuming that the reading speed is constant, applying a *linear* discount to nugget matches based on the offset values is probably one sensible approach.

[4]It is known that there are more elegant and reliable ranked retrieval metrics than bpref, the simplest being the average precision defined over a *condensed list* [18].

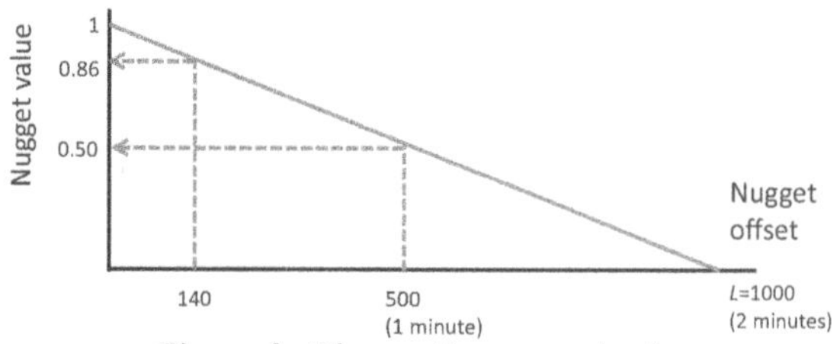

Figure 2: Discounting nugget values.

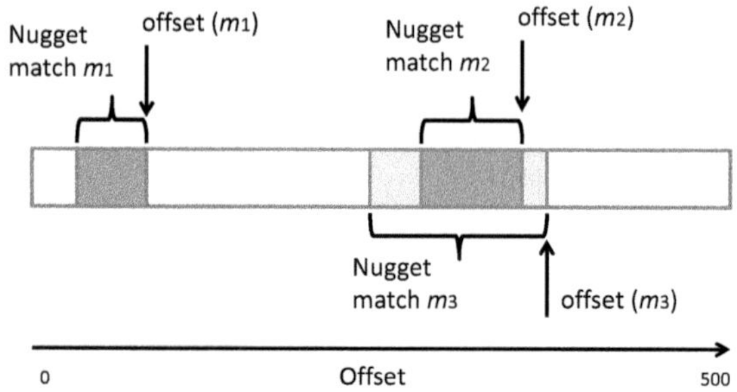

Figure 3: Nugget matches and offsets.

Let us therefore assume that the value of a nugget match decays linearly with respect to the offset. Moreover, let us assume that the value of a nugget wears out completely after (say) two minutes. This corresponds to a situation where the user cannot afford to spend more than two minutes (after pressing the search button) to gather information. For our average Japanese user, this translates to $L = 2 * 500 = 1,000$ characters.

Figure 2 shows how nugget values can be discounted in the above setting. For a *DESKTOP run* (where $X = 500$), the value of a nugget found at the very beginning of the text is 1, but that of one found at the very end is only 0.5. For a *MOBILE run* (where $X = 140$), the value of a nugget found at the very end is $1 - 140/1000$=0.86. Ideally, the parameter L should be determined based on a practical requirement.

How to define the offset of a nugget match deserves a discussion. We assume that an assessor uses an interface dedicated to evaluating an X-string by comparing it with a list of nuggets. Moreover, unlike traditional nugget-based evaluation, we assume that when the assessor identifies a nugget match, he records which part of the X-string corresponds to a nugget. As we shall describe in Section 4.3, the *nugget match area* can easily be recorded by means of a mouse drag. We thus assume that for every nugget match, we can obtain the start and end positions of the nugget match area.

Figure 3 depicts how we define the offset of a nugget match in this study. As the figure shows, we propose to use the end position of a nugget match area as the offset value, because the user probably has to read *through* the nugget match area in order to obtain the information conveyed in that nugget. Note also that, in Figure 3, there are three nugget matches, and one nugget match area subsumes another. In general, nugget match areas can overlap with one another, and also multiple nugget matches may share the same offset value, which is analogous to tied documents in IR.

Following previous work in QA and summarization, we define a nugget loosely as an atomic piece of information whose presence/absence in a text can be judged by an assessor. Moreover, we assume that we have a weight (i.e., importance) assigned to each nugget, just like *graded* relevance assessments are available in modern IR test collections. In practice, we let multiple assessors assign a grade to each nugget, and then take the sum of the grades to define *nugget weights*. An alternative approach would be to define "vital" and "okay" nuggets [7].

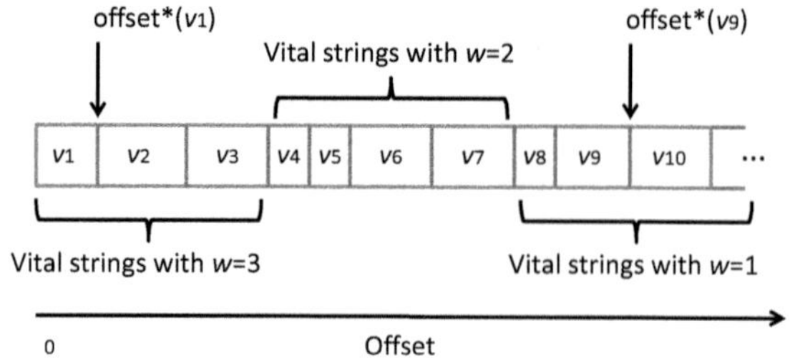

Figure 4: A pseudo minimal output composed of vital strings.

3.3 S-measure

We now formally define S-measure. Let N be a set of gold-standard nuggets constructed for a particular query, and let $M(\subseteq N)$ denote the set of *matched* nuggets, i.e., those manually identified in the X-string. For each $m \in M$, let $w(m)$ denote its nugget weight, and let $\mathit{offset}(m)$ denote its offset value. Then, by applying the aforementioned linear discounting scheme, we could evaluate an output for a DIIA task by computing:

$$\sum_{m \in M} w(m) \max(0,\ 1 - \mathit{offset}(m)/L)\ . \qquad (1)$$

As shown in Figure 2, L is the amount of text read that corresponds to the point where all information becomes useless to the user (set to 1000 in this paper). The max operator just means "ignore nuggets whose offsets are greater than L."

For evaluation with a set of queries, we should *normalise* the above metric so that it lies within the 0-1 range. In the case of IR evaluation based on nDCG, this is easily done by defining an ideal ranked list that exhaustively lists up all relevant documents in descending order of relevance levels. In our case, however, defining an ideal output is problematic, because our evaluation is based on offset-based discounting rather than rank-based one. Our proposed solution is to prepare a *vital string* $v(n)$ for each nugget n in order to approximate the minimal text length required to convey the meaning of a nugget within a textual output. For example, suppose that for query "Waseda university," we have two nuggets n_1 and n_2 representing the phone and fax numbers of this university, amongst other nuggets. That is, n_1 represents the fact: "Waseda university's phone number is YY-YYYY-YYYY" while n_2 represents the fact: "Waseda university's fax number is ZZ-ZZZZ-ZZZZ" (where X and Y represent any digit). Then we may define $v(n_1)$ and $v(n_2)$ as "YY-YYYY-YYYY" and "ZZ-ZZZZ-ZZZZ." Note that if an X-string contains "ZZ-ZZZZ-ZZZZ" but does not mention that this is a fax number, the user may not find it useful. Thus, a vital string represents a small piece of text that probably *needs* to be included in the output: it does not necessarily contain sufficient information. The idea is to provide a (possibly unreachable) length lowerbound for each nugget.

For normalising our evaluation metric, we define a *Pseudo Minimal Output* (PMO) by sorting all vital strings that correspond to all nuggets $n \in N$ for a query. The first sort key is the nugget weight $w(n)$ (larger the better), and the second sort key is the vital string length $|v(n)|$ (smaller the better). Figure 4 shows an example of PMO. Here, we assume that we have three different nugget weights $w = 3, 2, 1$, and the vital strings are sorted accordingly. Morever, within each set of nuggets with the same weight, the vital strings are sorted by length. For example, v_1 is the first vital string in this PMO because its nugget has the highest weight (namely 3) *and* v_1 is shorter than the other two vital strings with the same weight. Note that a PMO is a mere concatenation of vital strings and may completely lack cohesiveness and coherence.

For any vital string v, let $offset^*(v)$ denote its offset position within a PMO. As Figure 4 shows, we use the end position of each vital string. Then, we define *S-measure* as[5]:

$$S\text{-}measure = \frac{\sum_{m \in M} w(m) \max(0,\ 1 - offset(m)/L)}{\sum_{n \in N} w(n) \max(0,\ 1 - offset^*(v(n))/L)}$$

$$= \frac{\sum_{m \in M} w(m) \max(0,\ L - offset(m))}{\sum_{n \in N} w(n) \max(0,\ L - offset^*(v(n)))}\ . \qquad (2)$$

It is clear that as L approaches infinity and the effect of offset-based discounting is reduced, S-measure approaches the traditional *weighted nugget recall*. The novel features of S-measure when compared to existing QA and summarisation metrics for the purpose of DIIA evaluation are: (1) It takes into account the position of nugget matches; and (2) It approximates the minimal length required *for each nugget*, while traditional nugget-based precision assumes that this length is a constant (i.e., the allowance). On the other hand, the above definition implies that S-measure is not theoretically bounded above by 1: there are two reasons for this.

The first reason is that the PMO as defined above does not necesarily maximise S-measure's numerator. Suppose that we have two nuggets n_1 and n_2, such that $w(n_1) = 2, |v(n_1)| = l_1$ and $w(n_2) = 1, |v(n_2)| = l_2$. Then it is easy to show that an X-string "$v(n_2)v(n_1)$" (i.e., one that presents the vital string of the less important nugget first) may receive an S-measure greater than one if $l_1 > 2l_2$. For example, if $l_1 = 3$ and $l_2 = 1$ (i.e. the important nugget requires a much larger space than the other one), the numerator for the above X-string would be $1 * (1000 - 1) + 2 * (1000 - (1 + 3)) = 2991$. (We repeat, however, that a simple concatenation of vital strings such as "$v(n_2)v(n_1)$" may be unreadable as vital strings do not necessarily contain *sufficient* information.) On the other hand, the denominator, which represents the PMO "$v(n_1)v(n_2)$", would be $2 * (1000 - 3) + 1 * (1000 - (3 + 1)) = 2990 (< 2991)$. Despite this shortcoming, we use the nugget weight as the first sort key and the vital string length as the second sort key for defining the PMO because (a) we consider presenting important nuggets first more important than presenting short nuggets first; and (b) the above simple definition of PMO makes S-measure computationally cheap.

The second reason that S-measure can exceed one arises from the basic assumption behind *all* nugget-based evaluation methods, namely, that nuggets are independent of one another. For example, consider the aforementiond example with a phone number and a fax number of a university. Suppose that these two numbers happen to be identical, and that we have defined the vital strings as "YY-YYYY-YYYY" (10 characters, excluding "-"s) for both nuggets. Then, a PMO will require at least 20 characters in total for these two nuggets. However, an intelligent DIIA system might express these pieces of information as "phone&fax:YY-YYYY-YYYY" (19 characters, excluding "-"s and ":"), which is in fact more concise than the PMO.

We later demonstrate that this lack of a theoretical upperbound for S-measure is not a serious problem in practice. One method for preventing S-measure from exceeding one is to define very short vital strings. We will provide real examples in Section 4.2. Nevertheless, we can also formerly define a version of S-measure that is guaranteed to range between 0 and 1 as follows:

$$S\flat\text{-}measure = \min(1, S\text{-}measure)\ . \qquad (3)$$

We call this "S flat measure" because it "flattens" S-measure whenever it exceeds one.

[5]S stands for "the user Scanning a String at a constant Speed."

4. CONSTRUCTING AN EVALUATION ENVIRONMENT

To demonstrate the feasibility of our new evaluation framework, we constructed a Japanese DIIA test collection containing 60 queries and over 2,800 nuggets[6]. As DIIA systems are expected to perform both *knowledge source selection* and *knowledge compilation* (See Section 1), we allow DIIA systems to utilise any existing Web pages as their knowledge sources instead of requiring them to draw information from a closed document collection. We call this the *open knowledge source* evaluation.

Each of our nuggets is associated with a URL: this is the supporting document based on which the nugget was constructed. Thus, instead of making DIIA systems perform both knowledge source selection and knowledge compilation, we may optionally let the DIIA systems utilise the supporting URLs directly, thus isolating and evaluating the knowledge compilation component. We call this the *oracle knowledge source* evaluation.

In order to make our test collection as reusable as possible and to ensure successful matches between our gold-standard nuggets and system responses, we contructed queries that seek *established facts* rather than time-sensitive, controversial or subjective information. However, as we shall discuss in Section 4.2, even "established" facts may change over time, and some *truth maintenance* effort in the future may help prolong the life of our DIIA test collection.

4.1 Creating Queries

As we wanted our DIIA test collection to handle both DESKTOP and MOBILE situations (See Section 3.1), we referred to the work by Li, Huffman and Tokuda [12] that analysed mobile and desktop query logs from the United States, Japan and China, and identified frequent query types for potential "good abandonment" queries. They found that the query distributions over query types are quite different across the three countries: for Japan (which they considered to be a mature market in mobile search), the *LOCAL*, *QA*[7], *CELEBRITY* and *DEFINITION* query types were very popular in both mobile and desktop environments. We therefore decided to collect queries for these four query types. The *original* definitions of these query types by Li, Huffman and Tokuda were as follows:

CELEBRITY User seeks news or images of a celebrity.

LOCAL User seeks a local listing (address and/or phone number).

DEFINITION User seeks the definition of a term.

QA User seeks a short answer to a question.

While we basically followed the original definitions for the DEFINITION and QA query types, we interpreted CELEBRITY and LOCAL query types differently, as shown below:

CELEBRITY User wants to gather various facts about a celebrity: date/place of birth, real name, blood type, height, hobbies, profession, personal history, awards, publications, discography, films, TV series, favourite baseball team, favourite food etc.

LOCAL User wants to contact or visit a facility (school, shop, office, amusement park, hotel, train station etc.). Hence (s)he wants facts such as postal and email addresses, phone and fax numbers, opening hours, how to access the facility by train/bus/car, nearest stations, time required for the travel, whether the facility has a car park and its opening hours etc.

[6]We will make the test collection available through NTCIR.

[7]Li, Huffman and Tokuda [12] called it the "answers" category.

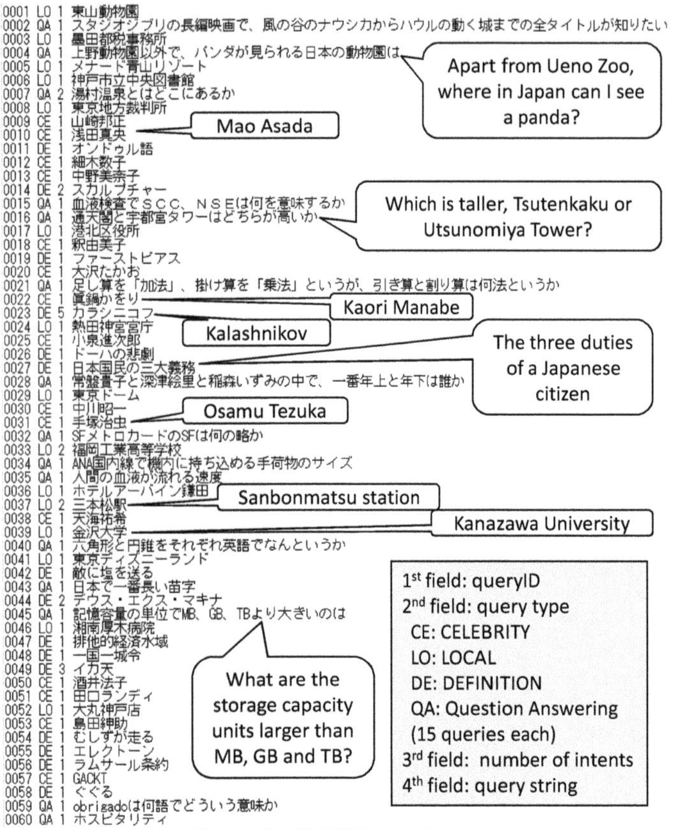

Figure 5: 60 DIIA queries.

Table 1: Number of nuggets per query type.

query type	#queries	mean	range
CELEBRITY	15	126.5	[38, 368]
LOCAL	15	30.9	[10, 125]
DEFINITION	15	26.3	[2, 174]
QA	15	5.6	[2, 26]
all	60	47.3	[2, 368]

Note that we had to replace the original definition of CELEBRITY completely to make the test collection as reusable as possible. These detailed specifications were formulated through repeated revisions during the nugget creation process.

After deciding on the four query types, we collected 15 queries for each type, thereby obtaining 60 queries in total. As we wanted to handle information needs that are as realistic as possible, we used two sets of real query data. For obtaining CELEBRITY and LOCAL queries, we used a proprietary Japanese mobile query log which covered two weeks in October 2009. It contained approximately 39,000 unique queries ranked by query frequency. From this data set, we manually selected celebrity names and local facility names while conducting trial Web searches and ensuring that good information sources exist on the Web. For obtaining DEFINITION and QA queries, we examined the Yahoo! Chiebukuro (Japanese Yahoo! Answers) data [19]. Natural language questions were manually selected from categories such as *education*, *local* and *health* categories, which we thought were more appropriate for factual information seeking than other categories such as *love*. For the DEFINITION query type, we used the look-up term as the query, while for QA, we formulated a short natural language sentence from each original question in the Yahoo! data.

Figure 5 shows the entire query set thus constructed, with some rough English translations[8]. For example, Query 0010 ("Mao Asada," a figure skater) is a CELEBRITY query. We classfied 0023 "Kalashnikov" as a DEFINITION query, as the original question in the Yahoo! data set was "What is Kalashnikov?". As the second field for this query shows, it has five different interpretations in our data: a gun inventor's name, his son's name, the gun's name, and brands called "Kalashnikov vodka" and "Kalashnikov watch." Similarly, the LOCAL query 0037 has two interpretations, as there are two train stations named "Sanbonmatsu" in Japan. We intentionally included these ambiguous queries in the set, as we believe that handling such queries in DIIA evaluation will be important just as in traditional diversified ranked list evaluation [6, 20]. However, how to explictly encourage diversification in DIIA evaluation is beyond the scope of the present study.

[8]Query 0036 is misspelt, but we did not correct it. Current Web Search APIs can actually correct the spelling automatically.

N001	3	1928年11月3日生	1928.11.03	http://tezukaosamu.net/jp/about/index.html
N002	3	出身地 大阪府	大阪	http://tezukaosamu.net/jp/about/index.html
N003	3	1989年2月9日没	1989.02.09	http://tezukaosamu.net/jp/about/index.html
N004	3	漫画家	漫画家	http://tezukaosamu.net/jp/about/index.html
N009	3	1951年 大阪大学卒業	卒業	http://tezukaosamu.net/jp/about/1950.html
N013	2	1959年 結婚	結婚	http://tezukaosamu.net/jp/about/1950.html
N014	1	妻 悦子	悦子	http://tezukaosamu.net/jp/about/1950.html
N015	3	1961年 医学博士	医学博士	http://tezukaosamu.net/jp/about/1960.html

Figure 6: Some nuggets from 0031 "Osamu Tezuka" (CELEBRITY).

4.2 Creating Nuggets

Through searching and browsing Web pages (mostly official pages or Wikipedia), the first author of this paper, who is a native Japanese speaker, created a total of 2,839 nuggets across the 60 queries. Statistics on the number of nuggets are shown in Table 1. The query with the highest number of nuggets (368) is 0031 "Osamu Tezuka" (See Figure 5), an extremely prolific cartoonist who died in 1989: about 300 nuggets correspond to comics and films that he created. A small portion of the nuggets for 0031 is shown in Figure 6: the first field is the nugget ID; the second field is the nugget grade (1, 2, or 3) assigned by the nugget creator (i.e., the first author); the third field is the *nugget semantics* in natural language, which represents an atomic piece of factual information and is used as a criterion for manually determining if a system output contains this nugget or not; the fourth field is the aforementioned *vital string* used for normalising S-measure; and the fifth field is the URL from which the nugget was extracted. Nuggets N001 and N003 say that Osamu Tezuka was born on November 3, 1928 and died on February 9, 1989, respectively; N002 says that he was born in Osaka; N004 says that he was a cartoonist; N009 and N013 say that he graduated from Osaka University in 1951 and that he got married in 1959; N014 says that his wife's name is Etsuko; and N015 says that he received a medical doctoral degree in 1961. The English translations of the corresponding vital strings would be: "Nov 3, 1928," "Osaka," "Feb 9, 1989," "cartoonist," "graduated," "married," "Etsuko" and "medical doctor."

The nugget grades assigned by the first author are subjective. For example, for 0031, all the comic book titles by Osamu Tezuka were given the grade of 1, as the first author judged that it is more important to include in the system output some basic facts about Osamu Tezuka (personal history etc.) than some of his comic titles selected from his lifetime's work. Note also that in Figure 6, the fact that he got married in 1959 (N013) is considered less important than the fact that he graduated from Osaka university in 1951 (N009). To remedy this subjectivity issue, the second author of this paper (also a native Japanese speaker) assigned his nugget grades (1, 2 or 3) independently, and the sum of these two grades were used as the final nugget weights in our experiments. The inter-assessor agreement was reasonable: 0.689 in terms of *quadratic-weighted kappa*. Note that, as in summarisation and QA evaluation, the nugget *creation* is still done by a single person.

Even though nugget creation depends on the view of a single person in our study, we devised a nugget creation policy document that can be shared by future nugget creators. An excerpt from the document is shown below:

(a) A nugget is a short factual statement such that an assessor can judge whether a given text shows or clearly implies that statement to be true.

(b) Information available on official Web pages is considered factual. Information available from other Web sources is considered factual provided that it does not contradict with the official information.

(c) Nuggets are built based on established facts as of December 31, 2010. Events that occur after this date will be ignored.

Item (b) was included based on the observation that information in official pages and that in Wikipedia are occasionally contradictory. For example, for the CELEBRITY query 0022, the official date of birth is different from the one in Wikipedia (as of December 31, 2010). In such a case, we assume that the *official* information is correct. Item (c) tries to free us from the burden of updating our nuggets indefinitely in response to future events. However, nuggets do become obsolete, sometimes unexpectedly quickly: on October 28, 2010, we finished constructing our *preliminary* nugget sets which contained a nugget representing a famous Japanese blog for the aforementioned query 0022 "Kaori Manabe" (who was once known as "Queen of Blogs"). However, to our surprise, the blog was shut down permanently on October 31, 2010! On the other hand, for the figure skater query 0010, we later had to *add* nuggets representing figure skating competitions that took place in November and December 2010. We thus re-examined all of the preliminary nugget sets and made revisions where necessary, to ensure that the final nugget sets represent facts as of December 31, 2010.

How efficient was the nugget creation process? The difficult part was devising the nugget creation policy document: deciding on what kinds of information to expect from DIIA systems in general as well as for each query type. Once this was done, the actual process of searching, browsing and collecting nuggets was not difficult. Although we did not measure the total time required for constructing the entire test collection (as the nugget creation policy writing and most of the actual nugget creation were done in parallel), we recorded the time spent for nugget creation for some typical cases. For example, it took about 68 minutes to construct 148 nuggets for a CELEBRITY query (0.46 minutes per nugget), and about 40 minutes to construct 31 nuggets for a LOCAL query (1.29 minutes per nugget). This includes the time to form nugget semantics and vital strings, to record URLs, and to decide on the first set of nugget grades as shown in Figure 6. In general, queries with many nuggets were created relatively efficiently, because they usually contained large lists (CDs released, books published, etc.) that are simple to handle. For DEFINITION and QA queries which generally have a very small number of nuggets, the time spent was typically 2-20 minutes per query. Our overall experience suggests that nugget creation for the DIIA task is just as feasible as that for QA and summarization or relevance assessments for traditional IR, provided that a clear nugget policy document and training material are given to the nugget creator. Note, however, that DIIA evaluation also requires a manual nugget match evaluation for each system, as will be described in the next section.

4.3 Nugget Match Evaluation Interface

To evaluate a system for the DIIA task, an X-string and the list of nuggets are compared manually. Figure 7 shows screenshots of the interface we have developed for this purpose. The left panel shows the X-string for a particular query. (This is an X-string from the manual DESKTOP run which will be described later). The nugget match evaluation interface can truncate each X-string into 500 (or 140) characters before evaluation. The right panel shows the list of nuggets for this query, in the PMO order (i.e., sorted first by the nugget weight and then by the vital string length). The assessor examines each nugget in turn, and decides whether it is covered by the X-string or not. If it is covered, he selects and records a nugget match area within the X-string by means of a mouse drag, as shown Figure 7 (a). In response to this user action, a Save button pops up, and the user can click on it. As a result, as shown in Figure 7 (b), the nugget match area is stored together with its start and end positions. The end position (44) is used as the offset for this nugget for computing S-measure later. The output from this interface is a list of nuggetID-offset pairs.

As was mentioned earlier, a nugget match area may overlap with or subsume another. We believe that this flexible feature is necessary for evaluating intelligent systems that go beyond extracting texts from source documents "as is". While the interface technically allows the assessor to record multiple matches per nugget, we use only the nugget match with the smallest offset (i.e., first nugget occurrence within the X-string) so that repetition is penalised when computing S-measure.

Given the output from the interface (i.e., a list of nuggetID-offset pairs), S-measure can easily be computed by automatically comparing it with the gold-standard that consists of nuggetIDs, nugget weights and the lengths of vital strings (See Eq. 2)[9]. In practice, it is probably useful to hire multiple assessors to evaluate each X-string, and to average the S-measure values across the assessors, which should serve two purposes: (a) trivial human errors (i.e., missing an existing nugget or locating a nonexistent nugget) can be detected by automatically comparing the assessment results; and (b) since recognition of nugget matches and selection of nugget match areas may vary across assessors, we can obtain more reliable results by averaging. In this study, however, only the first author performed nugget match evaluation. As the purpose of our DIIA experiments is to demonstrate the integrity, usefulness and limitations of our general approach, we argue that this is sufficient.

5. EXPERIMENTS

This section reports on a set of experiments using our DIIA test collection and S-measure. In addition to evaluating a pilot *automatic* run, we evaluated a *manual* run composed of X-strings constructed by hand for each query in order to estimate a *practical upperbound* for each query. This is because the maximum achievable S-measure value is often below one by design, as the denominator (i.e., normalisation factor) of S-measure is often unreachable by its numerator in Eq. 2. This normalisation issue arises from the fact that the Pseudo Minimal Output (PMO) is constructed using vital strings, which are probably necessary to be included in the system output, but probably not sufficient to convey the meaning of the nugget to the user. In addition, we compare the behaviour of S-measure with the traditional weighted nugget recall, which is equivalent to S-measure without offset-based discounting.

5.1 Manual Run

We devised a manual run in order to approximate S-measure values that are *actually* achievable if we have ideal information re-

[9]A software for computing S-measure is publicly available at `http://research.nii.ac.jp/ntcir/tools/ntcireval-en.html`.

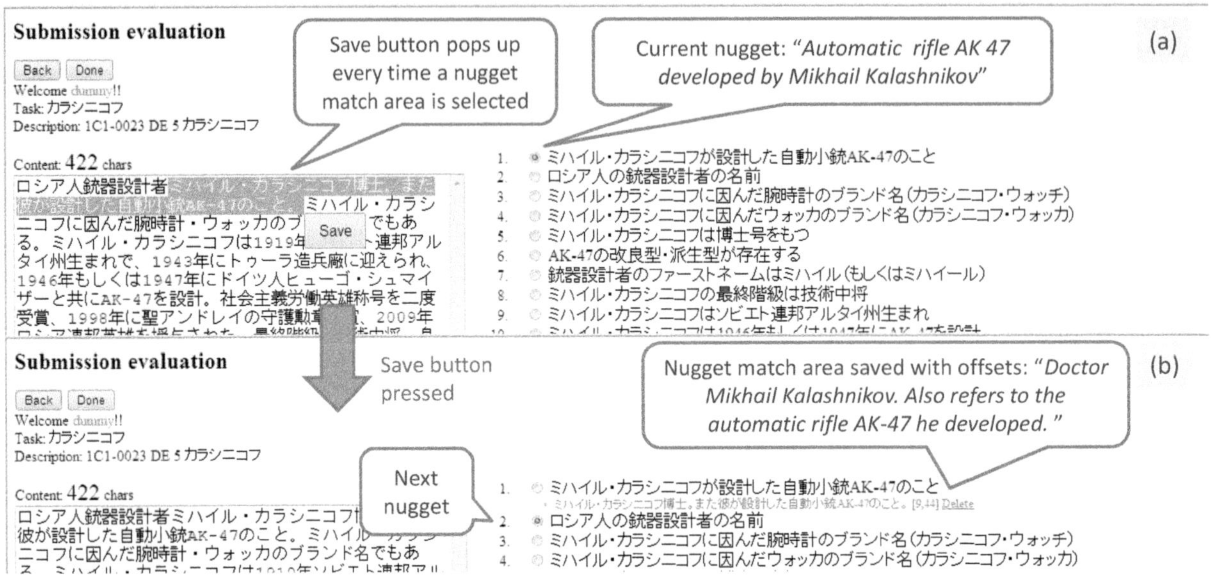

Figure 7: Nugget Match Evaluation Interface.

trieval and natural language processing techniques. Each output of the manual run is perfectly readable, in contrast to a PMO which may lack a lot of necessary information and may be defective as a natural language text.

Each X-string of our manual run was prepared as follows: the first author looked at the complete list of nuggets in the PMO order. Starting with an empty output text file, he added, for each nugget, a natural language text that concisely expresses the nugget semantics. (The text is often similar to the nugget semantics itself.) While he basically respected the original nugget order, he reordered some nuggets so that similar kinds of information are output close to each other. For example, even if a phone number is ranked at 1 and a fax number is ranked at number 5 in the PMO, he put the phone number and the fax number together in the output file (by basically respecting the rank of the first nugget). Similarly, for example, a list of book titles were output as one block even if they were spread across within the PMO, as the latter situation is not natural to the human eye. He also consolidated multiple nuggets where appropriate: recall the phone/fax number example discussed in Section 3.3. In short, he used common sense to re-arrange and merge the pieces of information conveyed in the PMO from the viewpoint of readability and conciseness. As the manual run was created by relying on the "right answers," it should be regarded as an oracle knowledge source run (See Section 4).

Figure 7 includes the first part of the X-string from our manual run for 0023 "Kalashnikov" (DEFINITION). The first sentence in this X-string means "Dr. Mikhail Kalashnikov, the Russian gun designer" and this sentence covers the second nugget "Kalashnikov is the name of a Russian gun designer" and the fifth nugget "Mikhail Kalashnikov has a Ph.D." The second sentence in the X-string means "Also refers to AK-47, the automatic rifle he designed" and this sentence covers the first nugget, "Kalashnikov means AK-47, an automatic rifle designed by Mikhail Kalashnikov."

The original manual run was created so that each X-string is around 700 characters long. Then, the nugget match evaluation interface truncated each X-string to 500 and 140 characters to produce DESKTOP and MOBILE runs, respectvely.

5.2 Automatic Run

We also generated an automatic run by assuming that the correct query types are known to the DIIA system[10]. Using the query type information and the Bing API, our automatic run adopted the simple heuristics shown in Figure 8 for each query q. Hence this is an open knowledge source run (See Section 4). Just like the manual runs, the automatic DESKTOP and MOBILE runs were created from the same 700-character run by truncation. Note that these runs are just *examples* for demonstrating the integrity of our DIIA evaluation framework.

CELEBRITY

1. Submit query "*q*", and obtain the snippet of the first retrieved URL that matches the pattern "*ja.wikipedia.org*";
2. Submit queries "*q* 公式[official]" and "*q* 名鑑[name encyclopaedia]", obtain the top-ranked snippets, and concatenate to the above.

LOCAL

Submit queries "*q* 住所[address]", "*q* 所在[location]", "*q* 電話[phone]", "*q* アクセス[access]", "*q* 時間[hour]", obtain the top-ranked snippets and concatenate.

DEFINITION

1. Submit query "*q*とは [what is *q*]" and obtain the top-ranked snippet;
2. Submit query "*q*", and obtain the snippet of the first retrieved URL that matches the pattern "*ja.wikipedia.org*". Concatenate to the above.

QA

Submit query "*q*", obtain the snippets of retrieved URLs that match the patterns "*chiebukuro.yahoo.co.jp*", "*oshiete.goo.ne.jp*", "*q.hatena.ne.jp*" and "*questionbox.jp.msn.com*", and concatenate.

Figure 8: The automatic run heuristics. (The URL pattern "ja.wikipedia.org" represents Japanese Wikipedia pages and the four URL patterns for the QA queries represent Japanese community QA sites.)

5.3 Results and Discussions

Table 2 shows the mean S-measure (in bold) and weighted nugget recall (in italics) values for our four runs (Manual/Automatic × DESKTOP/MOBILE). It can be observed that S-measure behaves similarly to weighted recall on average: the DESKTOP runs (500

[10]Another approach would be to provide the DIIA system with some training queries (which we lacked at this point), and make it determine the query type of each given query using an automatic classification technique.

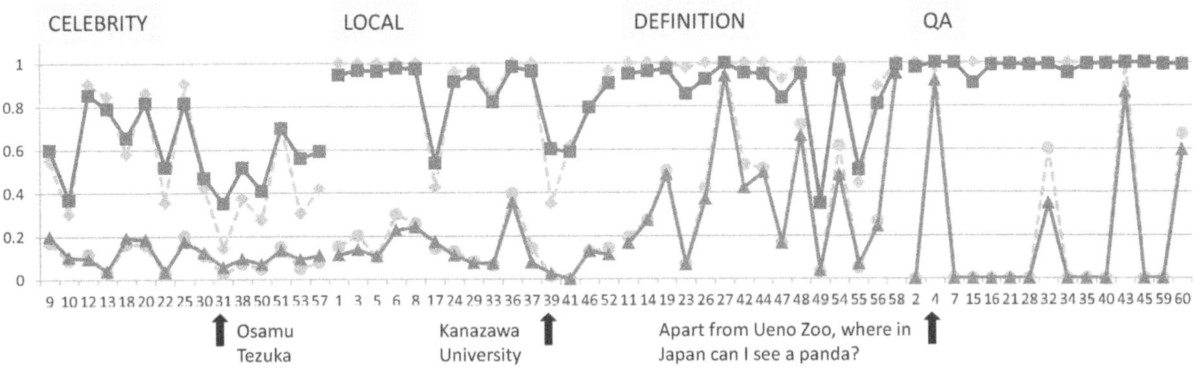

Figure 9: Per-query DESKTOP run performances: manual run S-measure / weighted recall (red solid / orange dotted lines); automatic run S-measure / weighted recall (blue solid / light blue dotted lines). The x-axis shows the query IDs.

Table 2: Manual and automatic run mean performances: S-measure (in bold) / weighted recall (in italics). D:DESKTOP; M:MOBILE.

	Manual-D	Auto-D	Manual-M	Auto-M
CELEBRITY	**.601**/*.530*	**.113**/*.099*	**.322**/*.244*	**.038**/*.032*
LOCAL	**.859**/*.861*	**.130**/*.150*	**.491**/*.460*	**.044**/*.043*
DEFINITION	**.865**/*.907*	**.388**/*.423*	**.702**/*.715*	**.294**/*.304*
QA	**.985**/*1.000*	**.182**/*.218*	**.954**/*.963*	**.079**/*.085*
all	**.828**/*.824*	**.203**/*.222*	**.617**/*.596*	**.114**/*.116*

characters) naturally outperform the corresponding MOBILE runs (140 characters); the automatic runs do better with DEFINITION queries than with others; and the manual runs substantially outperform the automatic runs, but are far from "perfect."

There two reasons why the mean S-measure across all queries does not reach one even for the manual DESKTOP run (.828). The first is simply because of the output widow size of 500: for some queries, it is simply impossible to list up all nuggets within this window, and this is exactly why the mean weighted recall is also below one (.824). The second reason is that the maximum possible S-measure value is often smaller than one.

Figure 9 visualises S-measure and weighted nugget recall for the manual and automatic DESKTOP runs per query. The performance of any DIIA DESKTOP run is expected to lie below the manual DESKTOP curves as the latter represents practical upperbounds. It can be observed, for example, that the practical upperbounds are actually 1 for the QA queries as they have few nuggets per query, while those for some CELEBRITY queries are indeed quite low, for exactly the reasons discussed above.

At the other extreme, there was exactly one query for which the S-measure only slightly *exceeded* 1, though this is not visible in Figure 9. The QA query 0004 "Apart from Ueno Zoo, where in Japan can I see a panda?" has the following four nuggets:

N001 Adventure World has pandas (vital string length = 11 for "Adventure World" in Japanese); weight = 6;

N002 Adventure World is in Wakayama prefecture (vital string length = 3 for "Wakayama" in Japanese); weight = 4;

N003 Oji Zoo has pandas (vital string length = 5 for "Oji Zoo" in Japanese); weight = 6;

N004 Oji Zoo is in Kobe city (vital string length = 2 for "Kobe" in Japanese); weight = 4.

Therefore, its PMO ranks the nuggets as <N003 N001 N004 N002> by using the weights as the first sort key and the lengths as the second sort key. Whereas, the manually composed X-string was "Oji Zoo (Kobe), Adventure World (Wakayama)" [English translation]. This covers all four nuggets, and is of the form <N003 N004 N001 N002> after removing punctuation marks etc., and it happens to outperform the PMO very slightly. As a result, the S-measure for this query was 1.001. Note that this is exactly one of the potential problems we discussed in Section 3.3. However, as was discussed earlier, this problem can be avoided by using the S♭-measure (Eq. 3) instead.

Let us now compare S-measure with weighted recall using Figure 9. It can be observed that, while S-measure generally resembles weighted recall, there are many cases where it is less than one even though weighted recall is one. This means that S-measure is more demanding for these queries. For example, see the manual DESKTOP performances for the LOCAL and DEFINITION queries. Also, for the aforementioned "panda" query 0004, our automatic DESKTOP run achieved a weighted recall of one but an S-measure of around 0.9: the first part of the X-string is shown in Figure 10. As the English translation shows, the red block in this figure covers all of the aforementioned four nuggets. However, because this X-string was automatically generated from search engine snippets, the part preceding the red block is completely irrelevant. That is, while this output achieves perfect nugget recall, it is still not satisfactory in terms of *Immediate* Information Access: the automatic run fails to minimise the amount of text that the user has to read in order to obtain the desired information. There were other similar cases in our experiments, which suggest that evaluation with S-measure will help us design our system output strategy carefully for DIIA.

Figure 10: Part of the X-string from the automatic run for Query 0004.

Finally, let us discuss a few cases where S-measure is *greater* than weighted recall. In Figure 9, the S-measure of the manual DESKTOP run is higher than the weighted recall for 0031 "Osamu Tezuka" (CELEBRITY). Recall that this is the query with the largest number of nuggets (368). The manual DESKTOP run returned only 35 nugget matches for this query (unweighted recall= 35/368 = .095). However, as the X-string basically showed the nuggets in order of importance (as this was the strategy used for creating the manual runs), the S-measure was .351, while the weighted recall was .142. Similarly, for 0039 "Kanazawa University" (LOCAL) which had 125 nuggets, the manual DESKTOP run returned 31 nugget matches, and the S-measure was .602 while the weighted recall was .348. These examples show that S-measure can reward systems that present important nuggets first, even when their nugget recall values are low.

6. CONCLUSIONS

We defined the Direct and Immediate Information Access (DIIA) task, where the system is expected to satisfy the user's need very quickly with its very first textual output, and proposed an evaluation framework for it. We proposed a simple evaluation metric called S-measure that takes the positions of nugget matches into account, and built a real DIIA test collection and an offset-based nugget match evaluation interface. Our experiments have demonstrated the integrity and usefulness of our framework. In particular, we have verified that S-measure rewards systems that reflect nugget importance, and those that return nuggets near the beginning of the output string. We also demonstrated that S-measure usually lies within the 0-1 range, and showed a simple variant of S-measure called S♭-measure which is strictly bounded above by 1.

Clearly, there are limitations to the present approach. The first is that S-measure is purely a content ranking measure, and that it does not consider linguistic quality. As we discussed in Section 2.2, this is a problem inherent in all nugget-based approaches. One possible problem with S-measure in particular is that there may be cases where presenting important information first may actually hurt readability. We thus recommend that readability evaluation be done separately for evaluating DIIA. Also, note that while S-measure penalises presentation of nonrelevant information before relevant information as in Figure 10, it does *not* explicitly penalise presentation of nonrelevant information *after* relevant information [23, 24]. This is similar to IR evaluation that treats a list of nonrelevant documents and an empty list as equally useless.

The second limitation is that we can only evaluate plain text outputs, even though real DIIA systems will probably use highlighting, different font sizes, and even non-textual presentations.

The third limitation is that, as we have observed in Section 4.2, our nuggets may become obsolete relatively quickly even though we are already restricting ourselves to retrieval of "established" facts. To address this problem, building a semi-automated *truth maintenance system* for nuggets may be useful. Such a system could periodically monitor the URLs that the current nuggets rely on (See Figure 6), and notify the test collection builder if the contents of the URLs have been revised. Note, however, that while some queries may require frequent updating, others do not: for example, many DEFINITION and QA queries do not require frequent updating, and the same goes even for some CELEBRITY queries, particularly for people who have passed away.

Despite the above limitations, we believe that our framework is a useful departure from and complement to traditional ranked retrieval evaluation. Since we explictly encourage *concise* presentations of important information, the DIIA task may foster research in abstractive text presentation methods as opposed to simple extractive ones (e.g. sentence selection). As future work, we plan to extend our DIIA experiments to other languages such as English. Our framework may also be useful to other related applications, such as search engine snippets and Bing's hover previews.

7. REFERENCES

[1] J. Allan, B. Carterette, and J. Lewis. When will information retrieval be "good enough"? In *Proceedings of ACM SIGIR 2005*, pages 433–440, 2005.

[2] O. Babko-Malaya. Annotation of nuggets and relevance in gale distillation evaluation. In *Proceedings of LREC 2008*, pages 3578–3584, 2008.

[3] P. Bailey, N. Craswell, R. W. White, L. Chen, A. Satyanarayana, and S. M. M. Tahaghoghi. Evaluating search systems using result page context. In *Proceedings of IIiX 2010*, 2010.

[4] C. Burges, T. Shaked, E. Renshaw, A. Lazier, M. Deeds, N. Hamilton, and G. Hullender. Learning to rank using gradient descent. In *Proceedings of ICML 2005*, 2005.

[5] L. B. Chilton and J. Teevan. Addressing people's information needs directly in a web search result page. In *Proceedings of ACM WWW 2011*, 2011.

[6] C. L. Clarke, N. Craswell, I. Soboroff, and A. Ashkan. A comparative analysis of cascade measures for novelty and diversity. In *Proceedings of ACM WSDM 2011*, 2011.

[7] H. T. Dang and J. Lin. Different structures for evaluating answers to complex questions: Pyramids won't topple, and neither will human assessors. In *Proceedings of ACL 2007*, pages 768–775, 2007.

[8] M. D. Dunlop. Time, relevance and interaction modelling for information retrieval. In *Proceedings of ACM SIGIR '97*, 1997.

[9] E. Hovy, C.-Y. Lin, and L. Zhou. Evaluating DUC 2005 using basic elements. In *Proceedings of DUC 2005*, 2005.

[10] K. Järvelin and J. Kekäläinen. Cumulated gain-based evaluation of IR techniques. *ACM Transactions on Information Systems*, 20(4):422–446, 2002.

[11] R. R. Korfhage. *Retrieval Effectiveness Measures*, chapter 8, pages 191–218. Wiley Computer Publishing, 1997.

[12] J. Li, S. Huffman, and A. Tokuda. Good abandonment in mobile and PC internet search. In *Proceedings of ACM SIGIR 2009*, pages 43–50, 2009.

[13] C.-Y. Lin. ROUGE: A package for automatic evaluation of summaries. In *Proceedings of the ACL 2004 Workshop on Text Summarization Branches Out*, 2004.

[14] J. Lin and D. Demner-Fushman. Methods for automatically evaluating answers to complex questions. *Information Retrieval*, 9(5):565–587, 2006.

[15] T. Mitamura, H. Shima, T. Sakai, N. Kando, T. Mori, K. Takeda, C.-Y. Lin, R. Song, C.-J. Lin, and C.-W. Lee. Overview of the NTCIR-8 ACLIA tasks: Advanced cross-lingual information access. In *Proceedings of NTCIR-8*, pages 15–24, 2010.

[16] H. Nanba, K. Hirahara, and T. Takezawa. Hiroshima city university at evaluation subtask in the NTCIR-8 patent translation task. In *Proceedings of NTCIR-8*, pages 415–419, 2010.

[17] A. Nenkova, R. Passonneau, and K. McKeown. The pyramid method: Incorporating human content selection variation in summarization evaluation. *ACM Transactions on Speech and Language Processing*, 4(2):Article 4, 2007.

[18] T. Sakai. Alternatives to bpref. In *Proceedings of ACM SIGIR 2007*, pages 71–78, 2007.

[19] T. Sakai, D. Ishikawa, N. Kando, Y. Seki, K. Kuriyama, and C.-Y. Lin. Using graded-relevance metrics for evaluating community QA answer selection. In *Proceedings of ACM WSDM 2011*, pages 187–196, 2011.

[20] T. Sakai and R. Song. Evaluating diversified search results using per-intent graded relevance. In *Proceedings of ACM SIGIR 2011*, pages 1043–1052, 2011.

[21] A. Turpin, F. Scholer, K. Järvelin, M. Wu, and J. S. Culpepper. Including summaries in system evaluation. In *Proceedings of ACM SIGIR 2009*, pages 508–515, 2009.

[22] J. V. White, D. Hunter, and J. D. Goldstein. Statistical evaluation of information distillation systems. In *Proceedings of LREC 2008*, pages 3598–3604, 2008.

[23] Y. Yang and A. Lad. Modeling expected utility of multi-session information distillation. In *Proceedings of ICTIR 2009*, pages 164–175, 2009.

[24] Y. Yang, A. Lad, N. Lao, A. Harpale, B. Kisiel, M. Rogati, J. Zhang, J. Carbonell, P. Brusilovsky, and D. He. Utility-based information distillation over temporally sequenced documents. In *Proceedings of ACM SIGIR 2007*, pages 31–38, 2007.

[25] L. Zhou, C.-Y. Lin, D. S. Munteanu, and E. Hovy. ParaEval: Using paraphrases to evaluate summaries automatically. In *Proceedings of HLT-NAACL 2006*, 2006.

Local Computation of PageRank: the Ranking Side

Marco Bressan
Department of Information Engineering
University of Padova
bressanm@dei.unipd.it

Luca Pretto
Department of Information Engineering
University of Padova
pretto@dei.unipd.it

ABSTRACT

Imagine you are a social network user who wants to search, in a list of potential candidates, for the best candidate for a job on the basis of their PageRank-induced importance ranking. Is it possible to compute this ranking for a low cost, by visiting only small subnetworks around the nodes that represent each candidate? The fundamental problem underpinning this question, i.e. computing locally the PageRank ranking of k nodes in an n-node graph, was first raised by Chen et al. (CIKM 2004) and then restated by Bar-Yossef and Mashiach (CIKM 2008). In this paper we formalize and provide the first analysis of the problem, proving that any local algorithm that computes a correct ranking must take into consideration $\Omega(\sqrt{kn})$ nodes – even when ranking the top k nodes of the graph, even if their PageRank scores are "well separated", and even if the algorithm is randomized (and we prove a stronger $\Omega(n)$ bound for deterministic algorithms). Experiments carried out on large, publicly available crawls of the web and of a social network show that also in practice the fraction of the graph to be visited to compute the ranking may be considerable, both for algorithms that are always correct and for algorithms that employ (efficient) local score approximations.

Categories and Subject Descriptors: H.3.3 [Information Storage and Retrieval]: Information Search and Retrieval; G.2.2 [Discrete Mathematics]: Graph Theory – Graph algorithms

General Terms: Theory, Algorithms, Experimentation

Keywords: IR theory: ranking, link and graph mining, web and social media search, local computation, PageRank

1. INTRODUCTION

This work tackles the problem of computing locally the ranking induced by PageRank on k target nodes of an n-node graph, studying if the correct ranking can be obtained for a low cost, i.e. by visiting only small subgraphs around those target nodes. Previous work shows that computing PageRank *scores* locally is infeasible (i.e. the cost is not bounded by polylog(n)) in the worst case; one could think, however, that the *ranking* provided by the algorithm (which is the only aspect that matters for many applications) might be obtained "more easily" than the output scores: after all, the correct ranking can be reached with scores even vastly different from the correct ones. Instead, it turns out that the ranking problem is, in a sense, as non-local as the score computation problem: in a nutshell, we prove that no deterministic algorithm exists which guarantees the correct ranking by visiting less than a number of nodes linear in the size of the input graph, and no randomized algorithm exists which guarantees the correct ranking by visiting in expectation less than a number of nodes proportional to the square root of the size of the input graph – even if only the top ranked nodes are examined and if their PageRank scores are well separated. Experimental results show that, in a large crawl of the `.it` web graph, the estimated cost of local ranking is substantially smaller than the graph size (but still very high), while in a smaller crawl of the LiveJournal friendship graph the estimated cost is an important fraction of the size of the graph and even higher than in the `.it` web graph.

This introductory section motivates our work and provides related work (Subsection 1.1), and then outlines the structure of the paper (Subsection 1.2).

1.1 Motivation and Related Work

This paper ideally builds a bridge between the research on the ranking induced by PageRank and that on the local computation of PageRank.

The first research stream arises from the consideration that PageRank [10], originally proposed as a means to infer the importance of web pages from the topological structure of the web graph, is nowadays a reference algorithm in computer science, especially for the information retrieval, knowledge management and data mining communities. Paradoxically, while its utility as a web search algorithm is decreasing in favour of new techniques such as clickthrough-based measures, its importance is still growing, due to a large number of applications in diverse fields: for instance, in web crawling [13], web spam detection [19], social network mining [20], ranking in databases [17], structural re-ranking [23], opinion mining [16], word sense disambiguation [29], credit and reputation systems [22], gene ranking [27] and bibliometrics [32]; indeed, PageRank has been rated among the top 10 algorithms in data mining [31]. This large and growing number of applications suggests to study PageRank in the abstract, considering it as a graph algorithm which accepts a graph in

CIKM'11, October 24–28, 2011, Glasgow, Scotland, UK.

input and provides a score to each node of the graph as output. While in the original web application these scores were combined with traditional text-based information retrieval scores, in most of the other applications they are directly used to *rank* the nodes of the input graph. For instance, in *web crawling*, PageRank is used to decide 'in what order a crawler should visit the URLs it has seen, in order to obtain more "important" pages first' [13]. In *bioinformatics*, modified versions of PageRank are used to rank genes in order of their "importance", offering 'an improved ranking of genes compared to pure expression change rankings' [27]. This naturally moved research towards the ranking induced by PageRank, investigating its stability under graph perturbations [8, 25], the convergence of its iterative computation [28, 30], and its dependence on damping factor variations [26, 9].

On the other hand, a vast body of research has been carried out on the local computation of PageRank scores. This research is motivated by the fact that the input graph is often accessible only for a high cost – or one may simply have access only to the local structure of the graph, without any knowledge of the full topology. The first case happens, for instance, when the input graph is too large to fit completely in one specific level of the *memory hierarchy* and must be stored in larger (and slower) levels, where (random) accesses have a significant cost [21]. The second case happens, for instance, when a *web user* can access the web graph only by querying a "link server", e.g. using the '`link:`' option provided by some search engines, or when a *social network user* has limited access to the friendship graph due to privacy settings (see [18]). In all these cases it would be useful to compute PageRank locally, i.e. exploiting only the structure of a small subgraph around the target nodes – indeed, this is the approach of [1]. To this end, [12] provides heuristics to locally approximate PageRank scores, [2] gives a well-founded local algorithm to approximate the contributions of the nodes of a graph to the PageRank score of a target node, while [3] proves the infeasibility of locally approximating the PageRank scores in the worst case, and provides lower bounds for deterministic and randomized local score approximation algorithms.

Neither theoretical nor experimental work has ever been carried out on the local computation of PageRank-induced ranking – indeed, the problem itself has never been formally defined, even if previous work [12, 3] has repeatedly suggested the need for this kind of study.

1.2 Outline of the Paper

This work formally defines the problem of locally computing PageRank-induced rankings and provides the first theoretical and experimental results on this subject. The paper is organized as follows.

Section 2 gives a short overview of the PageRank algorithm with an emphasis on the mathematical formulation which allows a local computation of the output scores.

Section 3 gives an informal introduction to the problem in hand, and proves that the reference algorithm used to locally approximate PageRank scores can not guarantee a correct ranking when visiting less than a number of nodes linear in the size of the input graph, or may even never stabilize.

Section 4 formally defines the problem of local ranking, and Section 5 provides the main theoretical results of the paper, showing that the results of Section 3 extend to *every* algorithm which attempts a local computation of PageRank-induced rankings. In short, it proves that the local computation of PageRank-induced ranking is infeasible in the worst case both for deterministic and for randomized algorithms – even if only the top ranked nodes are examined and if their PageRank scores are well separated.

Section 6 describes two experiments suggesting that the cost of local ranking in real graphs is actually high and strongly dependent on the input graph.

Section 7 discusses our results and their consequences, and states a few open problems before concluding with the bibliography.

2. PAGERANK

Let $G = (V, A)$ be an n-node graph with no dangling nodes (i.e. nodes with no outgoing arcs); if dangling nodes originally exist, the graph is preprocessed by adding to each of them outgoing arcs towards each node of the graph. An arc from u to v is interpreted as a conferral of importance from u to v. The entries of the transition probability matrix $\mathbf{M} = [m_{i,j}]$ of G are

$$m_{i,j} = \begin{cases} \frac{1}{\text{outdegree}(i)} & \text{if an arc exists from } v_i \text{ to } v_j \\ 0 & \text{otherwise} \end{cases}$$

Let the damping factor α be a real number in $[0, 1)$ and let

$$\mathbf{T} = \alpha\mathbf{M} + (1 - \alpha)\mathbf{U}$$

where $\mathbf{U}$ is a matrix whose entries equal $1/n$; $\mathbf{T}$ can be seen as the transition probability matrix of a Markov chain. The PageRank row vector $\mathbf{P} = [P(v_1), P(v_2), \ldots, P(v_n)]$ is defined as the limit probability vector of this Markov chain, and can be obtained either as the unique probability vector which is the solution of the linear system $\mathbf{P} = \mathbf{PT}$ or as the limit of the iteration $\mathbf{P}^{(n)} = \mathbf{P}^{(n-1)}\mathbf{T}$, where the starting vector $\mathbf{P}^{(0)}$ can be any probability vector. When considering a local computation of PageRank, however, none of these roads can be followed, since the entire graph structure is not available; in this case, straightforward algebraic manipulations are exploited which take to the formula:

$$\mathbf{P} = \frac{1-\alpha}{n}\mathbf{1}(\mathbf{I} - \alpha\mathbf{M})^{-1} = \frac{1-\alpha}{n}\mathbf{1}\sum_{\tau=0}^{+\infty}(\alpha\mathbf{M})^{\tau}$$

where $\mathbf{1} = [1, 1, \ldots, 1]$. This leads to the following formula to compute the PageRank score of a node v:

$$P(v) = \frac{1-\alpha}{n}\sum_{\tau=0}^{+\infty}\alpha^{\tau}\sum_{z\in G}\text{inf}_{\tau}(z, v) \qquad (1)$$

where the influence $\text{inf}_{\tau}(z, v)$ of z on v gives the probability of ending in v by following a chain of τ arcs from z. Therefore, the score of node v can be seen as the weighted sum of the influences of its ancestors at each layer τ, or as the sum of their contributions.

3. LIMITS AND PITFALLS OF THE BRUTE FORCE ALGORITHM

This section investigates the brute force algorithm, one of the simplest methods to locally approximate the PageRank score of a single node, in light of the local ranking problem. Although unlikely to be among the best local score approximation algorithms to lever on in the local ranking problem (see Section 6), the brute force is still a reference algorithm for at least two reasons. First, it is the basis of virtually any known local *score* approximation algorithm (such as those proposed in [3] and [12]) which in turn are natural bases for local *ranking* algorithms. Second, it naturally derives from the expression of PageRank given by Equation (1) that turns out to be very useful in the analysis of those algorithms. Thus it is important to understand why the brute force may fail to be the basis for a good local ranking algorithm – one that, ideally, should incur a limited cost and return a correct result. Indeed, as we shall prove after a short review, a naive brute force-based ranking algorithm may incur extremely high costs to guarantee a correct result (Theorem 1) or oscillate indefinitely between two "opposite" results (Theorem 2).

Given an n-node graph G and a target node $v \in G$, the brute force algorithm performs a breadth-first visit of the ancestors of v, querying at iteration τ all the ancestors of layer τ and cumulating their influence on v weighted by $\frac{1-\alpha}{n}\alpha^{\tau}$. After iteration ℓ, the resulting *brute force score* at layer ℓ is

$$P^{(\ell)}(v) = \frac{1-\alpha}{n}\sum_{\tau=0}^{\ell}\alpha^{\tau}\sum_{z\in G}\mathrm{inf}_{\tau}(z,v) \tag{2}$$

If graph G has no dangling nodes, $P^{(\ell)}(v)$ converges from below to the PageRank score of v as given by Equation (1). A natural way to compute the relative ranking of two target nodes u and v is then to compare their brute force scores $P^{(\ell)}(u)$ and $P^{(\ell)}(v)$ once ℓ has reached a sufficiently large threshold ℓ_0. Unfortunately, such a threshold is unknown a priori, and this may lead to a premature halt and an incorrect ranking. Indeed we prove that, for any given ℓ_0, there exist graphs where the "decisive" layer is at depth $\ell_0 + 1$ while the ranking induced by the output of the brute force algorithm at *every* iteration up to ℓ_0 is the complete reversal of the correct ranking. Before stating the result formally in the next theorem, we provide a lemma that will greatly simplify our proofs.

LEMMA 1. *Let G be a graph, $v \in G$ a dangling node, and build G' adding a self-loop (v,v) to G. Let $B(v)$ and $B'(v)$ be the brute force scores of v computed respectively on G and G'. Then $B'(v) = \frac{B(v)}{1-\alpha}$.*

PROOF. Every path from a generic node z to v in G' is the unique concatenation of a path from z to v in G and $t \geq 0$ self-loops (v,v). Conversely, every path $p : z \to v$ in G generates, for $t = 0,\ldots,\infty$, the paths from z to v in G' that are the concatenation of $p : z \to v$ and t self-loops (v,v) that damp the contribution of z by a factor α^t. Thus the expression of $B'(v)$ given by Equation (2) can be rewritten as:

$$\begin{aligned} B'(v) &= \frac{1-\alpha}{n}\sum_{\tau=0}^{\infty}\alpha^{\tau}\sum_{z\in G}\mathrm{inf}_{\tau}(z,v)\sum_{t=0}^{\infty}\alpha^{t} \\ &= \frac{1-\alpha}{n}\sum_{\tau=0}^{\infty}\alpha^{\tau}\sum_{z\in G}\mathrm{inf}_{\tau}(z,v)\frac{1}{1-\alpha} \\ &= B(v)\frac{1}{1-\alpha} \end{aligned}$$

□

Lemma 1 proves that one can compute the brute force score of a node whose only outgoing arc forms a self-loop by disregarding it at each iteration and multiplying the result by a constant factor. We can now state Theorem 1.

THEOREM 1. *For any $k \geq 2$, any $\alpha \in (0,1)$ and any $\ell_0 > 0$ there exists a graph where the ranking induced by $P^{(\ell)}$ on the top k nodes $v_1,\ldots,v_k$ is:*

$$\begin{aligned} v_1 < \ldots < v_k \quad &\text{for } \ell \leq \ell_0 \\ v_k < \ldots < v_1 \quad &\text{for } \ell > \ell_0 \end{aligned}$$

PROOF. Due to space limitations, we give a sketch of the proof exhibiting a graph G that satisfies the statement. G consists of k subgraphs $G_1,\ldots,G_k$. Subgraph G_i (Figure 1) contains node v_i and its self-loop (making the graph free of dangling nodes), $k - i + 1$ orphan nodes that have v_i as their sole child, and $\ell_0 + 1$ layers of ancestors structured as a tree of depth ℓ_0 with root node v_i and indegree d (d will be computed below) pointed by an additional $\ell_0 + 1$-th layer of im orphans (m will be computed below).

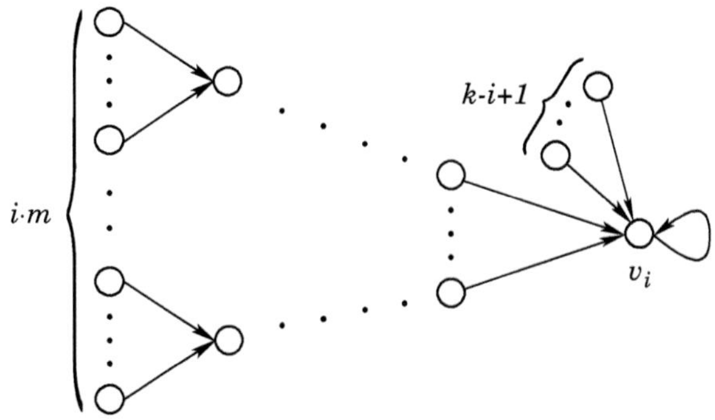

Figure 1: Subgraph G_i (Theorem 1) containing node v_i and all its ancestors up to layer $\ell_0 + 1$.

Consider v_i and v_j for $1 \leq i < j \leq k$. For $\ell \leq \ell_0$, node v_i receives the contribution of $j - i$ parents more than v_j. But for $\ell \geq \ell_0 + 1$, node v_j receives from layer $\ell_0 + 1$ the contribution of $(j - i)m$ ancestors more than v_i. Thus, intuitively, v_j receives a lower contribution from the first ℓ_0 layers but a higher contribution from layer $\ell_0 + 1$. Indeed, choosing $m > \frac{1-\alpha^{\ell_0+1}}{\alpha^{\ell_0}(1-\alpha)}$, we obtain $P^{\ell}(v_i) > P^{\ell}(v_j)$ for $\ell \leq \ell_0$ and $P^{\ell}(v_i) < P^{\ell}(v_j)$ for $\ell \geq \ell_0 + 1$.

To make $v_1,\ldots,v_k$ the top k nodes in the graph, balance the im arcs from layer $\ell_0 + 1$ so that the number of parents of any ancestor at layer ℓ_0 is at most $\lceil \frac{im}{d^{\ell_0}} \rceil$ which, for a sufficiently large d, is no more than d. Note that $v_1,\ldots,v_k$ have more than d parents and, in general, at any layer they have more ancestors (with outdegree 1, which translates to a higher contribution) than any other node in the graph – thus, they are the top k. □

By Theorem 1, for any $\ell_0 > 0$ there exist graphs where, to compute the correct relative ranking of the top k nodes, the brute force algorithm not only must take into account at least the first $\ell_0 + 1$ layers, but halting at *any* layer below ℓ_0+1 yields the *same* complete reversal of the correct ranking – a misleading "stability" condition.

Although to correctly rank the top k nodes of the graph of Theorem 1 the brute force algorithm incurs a very high cost (exponential in ℓ and linear in n), it still converges in a finite number of iterations. Unfortunately, the situation can worsen in presence of cycles that produce periodical *oscillations* in the relative ranking of nodes. The following theorem proves that in this case the number of iterations required to converge to a stable ranking may be unbounded:

THEOREM 2. *For any even integer $k > 1$ and any rational $\alpha \in (0, 1)$ there exists a graph where the ranking induced by $P^{(\ell)}$ on the top k nodes $v_1, \ldots, v_k$ satisfies, for any $i \in [1, \frac{k}{2}]$, any $j \in [\frac{k}{2}+1, k]$, and any $\ell \geq 0$:*

$$v_i = v_j \quad \text{for } \ell \equiv 0 \mod 3$$
$$v_i < v_j \quad \text{for } \ell \equiv 1 \mod 3$$
$$v_i > v_j \quad \text{for } \ell \equiv 2 \mod 3$$

PROOF. Due to space limitations, we give a sketch of the proof exhibiting a graph G that satisfies the statement. G consists of $k/2$ identical subgraphs $G_1, \ldots, G_{k/2}$. Subgraph G_i (Figure 2) contains target nodes v_i and $v_{i+k/2}$, two nodes that are the sole children of v_i and the sole parents of $v_{i+k/2}$, and a set W_i of p nodes with q children each (v_i being one of them).

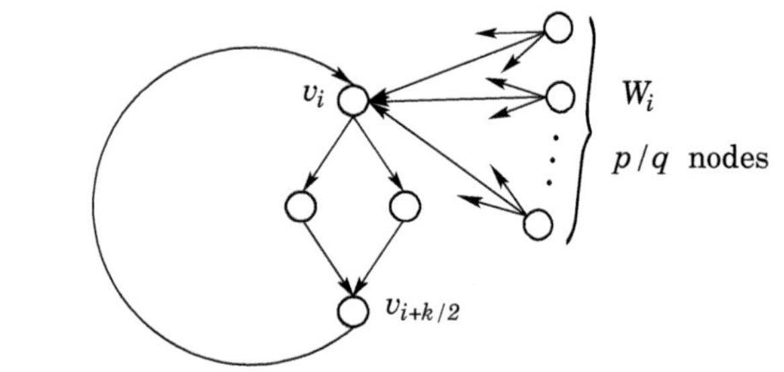

Figure 2: Subgraph G_i (Theorem 2) has a cycle that causes a perpetual oscillation in the relative ranking given by the brute force algorithm.

Intuitively, both target nodes receive the contribution of nodes in W_i, but v_i only at layers $\ell \equiv 1 \mod 3$ and $v_{i+k/2}$ only at layers $\ell \equiv 0 \mod 3$ for $\ell > 0$; this makes the relative ranking induced by their brute force scores at layer ℓ oscillate with ℓ. More formally, choose p and q such that the overall contribution of nodes in W_i is $p/q = 1/(1+\alpha)$; this is possible since α is rational by hypothesis. Plugging this value into the expressions of the brute force scores of v_i and $v_{i+k/2}$ at layer ℓ given by Equation (2), it is easy to see that $P^{(\ell)}(v_i) = P^{(\ell)}(v_j)$ for $\ell \equiv 0 \mod 3$, $P^{(\ell)}(v_i) < P^{(\ell)}(v_j)$ for $\ell \equiv 1 \mod 3$, and $P^{(\ell)}(v_i) > P^{(\ell)}(v_j)$ for $\ell \equiv 2 \mod 3$. Furthermore, the target nodes are the top k ranked in the graph, since each child of v_i has a brute force score smaller than that of both v_i and $v_{i+k/2}$ at any layer $\ell > 1$, while nodes of set W_i are orphans and thus always have the lowest brute force scores in the graph. □

By Theorem 2, there exist graphs where the relative ranking given by the brute force algorithm on the top k nodes never converges nor shows stability. Note that, depending on α, p and q, the size of the graph in Figure 2 can become arbitrarily large but also range in the tens – a situation where the brute force algorithm presents an excellent cost performance, yet its output oscillates indefinitely.

Although by Theorems 1 and 2 the brute force algorithm may in theory become impractical, other algorithms could perform better for at least three reasons. First, they could visit the ancestors of the target nodes using a strategy that includes highly-contributing ancestors earlier than the simple breadth-first does. Second, they could compute the approximate PageRank scores more accurately, for example taking into account the cycles in the graph to eliminate oscillations and include "in one shot" the total contribution of an ancestor appearing in an infinite number of layers. Third, as the number of visited nodes increases, the approximation error on the PageRank scores drops (eventually going beyond the resolution of a physical machine) and the correct ranking of the target nodes may become apparent after just a few steps, especially if their scores are not too close.

These observations raise the necessity to discuss and formally define the problem of local ranking. The next section is fully devoted to this task.

4. LOCAL RANKING OF NODES

This section formally restates the local ranking problem informally introduced in Section 1, taking into account the observations raised at the end of Section 3.

Formally, a *local algorithm* is an algorithm that has no direct access to (the arcs of) a graph G, but must instead query a *link server* for G that accepts (the ID of) a node v in input and returns (the IDs of) the parents and children of v in output. The *local ranking problem* consists in ranking a subset of nodes of a graph using only local algorithms. Since the major bottleneck of local algorithms is the communication with the link server, their cost can be defined as the number of queries performed. The cost of locally ranking two target nodes $u, v \in G$ is then the minimum cost incurred by any correct algorithm A to rank u and v.

In this paper, the local ranking problem is considered in a PageRank context. Formally, given a graph G, a damping factor α, and k *target* nodes $v_1, \ldots, v_k \in G$, the local ranking problem requires to rank the target nodes in nonincreasing order of their PageRank scores (with ties broken arbitrarily) using only local algorithms. In many applications, however, only the top PageRank scores really matter; furthermore, often only the ranking induced by well-separated scores matters – if two scores are very close to each other, they could be considered equivalent (after all, PageRank itself gives an approximate model of the reality), and they are practically indistinguishable if their difference is smaller than the resolution of a modern machine. To deal with this last issue, we modify the problem and require to rank all and only the target nodes whose relative PageRank score difference is not less than a given ϵ. Formally, given a graph G, a damping factor α, and k target nodes $v_1, \ldots, v_k \in G$, the *local ϵ-ranking problem* requires to rank each pair u, v of target nodes with $P(u)/P(v) \geq 1 + \epsilon$ in decreasing order of their PageRank scores using only local algorithms. The definitions of cost of an algorithm A and cost of local ranking given above can be ported in this context with obvious modifications.

It is thus natural to ask how high is the cost of local ϵ-ranking – even considering only the top nodes of a graph. In the next section we prove theoretical lower bounds on this cost, for both randomized and deterministic algorithms.

5. THE COST OF LOCAL RANKING

In general, locally computing the exact PageRank *score* of a single node may require a number of queries proportional to the size n of the whole graph. More surprisingly, a very high number of queries may be required even to compute an *ϵ-approximation* of the PageRank score of a single node, i.e. a value between $1 - \epsilon$ and $1 + \epsilon$ times the score itself. In particular (see [3]), to ϵ-approximate the score of a node for a reasonable constant ϵ, any deterministic local algorithm incurs a cost of $\Omega(n)$ queries in the worst case, while any randomized (with deterministic cost) Monte Carlo local algorithm with constant confidence incurs an expected cost of $\Omega(\sqrt{n})$ queries in the worst case.

It is not known, however, if the same bounds apply to the problem of locally computing the relative *ϵ-ranking* of two or more target nodes, as described in Section 4. We prove that this is indeed the case: the following Theorem 3 shows that, in the worst case, locally ranking the top k nodes of a graph requires $\Omega(\alpha\sqrt{n/\epsilon})$ queries for both Las Vegas algorithms and Monte Carlo algorithms with constant confidence, while Theorem 4 strengthens the bound to $\Omega(n)$ for deterministic algorithms.

THEOREM 3. *Choose integers $k > 1$ and $n_0 \geq 6k^3$, a damping factor $\alpha \in (0,1)$, and an $\epsilon \in \left[\frac{\alpha^2 k^2}{4n_0}, \frac{\alpha^2}{24k}\right]$. Then*

- *for any Las Vegas local algorithm A there exists a graph of size $n \in \Theta(n_0)$ where the top k nodes $v_0, \ldots, v_{k-1}$ are ϵ-separated and, to compute their relative ranking, A performs an expected $\Omega\left(\alpha\sqrt{\frac{n}{\epsilon}}\right)$ queries.*
- *for any Monte Carlo local algorithm A with constant confidence there exists a graph of size $n \in \Theta(n_0)$ where the top k nodes $v_0, \ldots, v_{k-1}$ are ϵ-separated and, to compute their relative ranking, A performs $\Omega\left(\alpha\sqrt{\frac{n}{\epsilon}}\right)$ queries.*

The proof is based on a reduction from the 1-OR problem. In this problem, the instance is a binary string $\mathbf{x}$ of length $m \geq 1$ such that either all its bits are 0, in which case the solution is 0, or exactly one is 1, in which case the solution is 1 – i.e., the solution is $\|\mathbf{x}\|$. Local algorithms for 1-OR can retrieve the value of a bit only via a *bit server*. We use Yao's principle [33] to show that the expected cost of any Las Vegas randomized local algorithm for 1-OR is at least $\frac{m}{2}$ in the worst case:

LEMMA 2. *The expected worst-case cost of any Las Vegas randomized local algorithm for 1-OR is at least $\frac{m}{2}$.*

PROOF OF LEMMA 2. Any (Las Vegas) algorithm issues a sequence of queries and stops either when it finds a 1 or every bit has been queried (every algorithm behaving differently would produce an incorrect result and/or incur unnecessary costs). Consider an input probability distribution where each of the $m+1$ possible m-bit strings (m of them contain exactly a 1, and one contains only zeros) has probability $\frac{1}{m+1}$. Whatever the sequence of queries, the probability that the j-th query returns 1 (and thus that the cost is j) is $\frac{1}{m+1}$. Therefore the expected cost is at least

$$\sum_{j=1}^{m} j\frac{1}{m+1} = \frac{m}{2}$$

By Yao's principle, this is a bound on the expected number of queries performed by any randomized Las Vegas algorithm on its worst-case input. □

PROOF OF THEOREM 3. Let A be a randomized Monte Carlo (Las Vegas) local algorithm that ranks the top k nodes of a graph performing (in expectation) S_A queries to the link server; we use A to build a randomized Monte Carlo (Las Vegas) local algorithm B that solves $k-1$ independent instances of 1-OR performing (in expectation) $S_B \leq S_A$ queries to the bit server. Lemma 2 gives a lower bound on (the expected value of) S_B, and thus on (the expected value of) S_A.

Let $\mathbf{x_1}, \ldots, \mathbf{x_{k-1}}$ be $k-1$ m-bit instances of 1-OR and b a positive integer (m and b will be computed below). We build a link server that lets A run on a graph G consisting of k disjoint subgraphs $G_0, G_1, \ldots, G_{k-1}$. For $i = 1, \ldots, k-1$, subgraph G_i (Figure 3) contains the target node v_i and its self-loop, $m+1$ nodes $u_i^0, \ldots, u_i^m$ that have v_i as their sole child, ib nodes $w_i^0, \ldots, w_i^{ib-1}$ that have u_i^0 as their sole child and, for $j = 1, \ldots, m$, kb nodes $w_i^{jkb}, \ldots, w_i^{(j+1)kb-1}$ that have u_i^j as their sole child if $\mathbf{x_i}(j) = 1$ or a self-loop if $\mathbf{x_i}(j) = 0$. Subgraph G_0 contains the reference target node v_0 and its self-loop, $m+1$ nodes $u_0^0, \ldots, u_0^m$ that have v_0 as their sole child and kb nodes $w_0^0, \ldots, w_0^{kb-1}$ whose sole child is u_0^0.

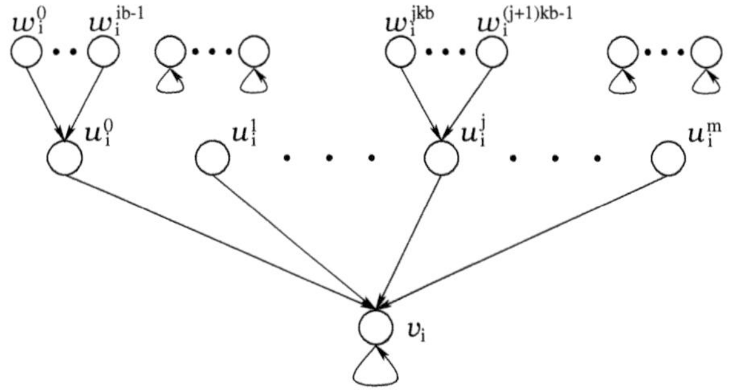

Figure 3: Subgraph G_i (Theorem 3). Node u_i^0 always has exactly ib parents; node u_i^j has kb parents if $\mathbf{x_i}(j) = 1$, else it has an associated group of kb "disconnected parents".

The link server for G is described by the following rules:

1. when queried for u_i^j with $i, j \geq 1$, it queries the bit server for $\mathbf{x_i}(j)$; if $\mathbf{x_i}(j) = 1$ then it returns v_i as the sole child and $w_i^{jkb}, \ldots, w_i^{(j+1)kb-1}$ as the parents, else it returns v_i as the sole child and no parents.
2. when queried for w_i^j with $i \geq 1$ and $j \geq kb$, it computes $j' = \lfloor \frac{j}{kb} \rfloor$ and queries the bit server for $\mathbf{x_i}(j')$; if $\mathbf{x_i}(j') = 1$ then it returns $u_i^{j'}$ as the sole child and no parents, else it returns w_i^j as the sole child and no parents.
3. otherwise, it answers without querying the bit server.

It is easy to see that this is a link server for the graph G. Given the output of algorithm A, algorithm B computes the solution of $\mathbf{x_i}$ as follows. If A ranks v_i lower than v_0, then B returns 0; if A ranks v_i higher than v_0, then it returns 1. We prove that if A ranks correctly $v_0, \ldots, v_{k-1}$ then B solves correctly the $k-1$ instances of 1-OR.

Since G has no dangling nodes, by Lemma 1 the scores of the target nodes are $\frac{1}{1-\alpha}$ times the brute force score computed on the same nodes ignoring their self-loops. Thus, according to Equation (2) these scores become:

$$P(v_0) = \tfrac{1}{n}\left(1 + \alpha(m+1) + \alpha^2 kb\right)$$
$$P(v_i) = \tfrac{1}{n}\left(1 + \alpha(m+1) + \alpha^2(i + k\|\mathbf{x_i}\|)b\right) \qquad i \geq 1$$

By hypothesis, algorithm A ranks $v_0, v_1, \ldots, v_{k-1}$; in particular, it computes the relative ranking of v_0 and v_i for $i = 1, \ldots, k-1$. But v_0 is ranked lower than v_i if and only if $k < i + k\|\mathbf{x_i}\|$, which is true if and only if $\|\mathbf{x_i}\| = 1$. Conversely, v_i is ranked lower than v_0 if and only if $i + k\|\mathbf{x_i}\| < k$, which is true if and only if $\|\mathbf{x_i}\| = 0$. Thus, if A ranks correctly $v_0, \ldots, v_{k-1}$, then B solves correctly the $k-1$ instances of 1-OR.

We now exhibit values of m and b such that G and the target nodes satisfy the thesis. In particular, choose

$$m = \left\lceil \frac{\alpha\sqrt{n_0/\epsilon}}{12k} \right\rceil \qquad \text{and} \qquad b = \left\lfloor \frac{2\sqrt{\epsilon n_0}}{\alpha k} \right\rfloor$$

It is immediate to verify that the size n of the graph is in $\Theta(mbk^2)$ which, substituting m and b, is in $\Theta(n_0)$. The hypothesis $n_0 \geq 6k^3$ guarantees also that $b \geq 1$ and $m \geq kb \geq 2$; therefore $v_0, v_1, \ldots, v_{k-1}$ are the top k nodes in the graph, since each of them has at least $m + 1 > kb$ parents and at least one grandparent – more than any other node in the graph. Furthermore, any two target nodes are ϵ-separated since one of them has the same number of parents but at least b grandparents more than the other, and thus their scores differ by $\Delta P \geq \frac{\alpha^2 b}{n}$. This value, divided by the maximum possible score of a target node (obtained for $i = k-1$ and $\|\mathbf{x_i}\| = 1$), gives a lower bound on the score separation of any two target nodes:

$$\frac{\Delta P}{P} \geq \frac{\alpha^2 b}{n} / \frac{1}{n}\left(1 + \alpha(m+1) + \alpha^2(k-1+k)b\right) \geq \frac{\alpha^2 b}{5m}$$

where the last inequality follows from $kb \leq m$ and $1 \leq m/2$. Plugging in the above values for b and m we obtain:

$$\frac{\Delta P}{P} \geq \frac{\alpha^2 b}{5m} = \frac{\alpha^2 \left\lfloor \frac{2\sqrt{\epsilon n_0}}{\alpha k} \right\rfloor}{5\left\lceil \frac{\alpha\sqrt{n_0/\epsilon}}{12k} \right\rceil} \geq \frac{\alpha^2 \frac{\sqrt{\epsilon n_0}}{\alpha k}}{5\frac{\alpha\sqrt{n_0/\epsilon}}{6k}} = \frac{6}{5}\epsilon > \epsilon$$

which proves that the target nodes are ϵ-separated.

We now compute the cost of locally ranking the target nodes $v_1, \ldots, v_k$. The link server performs at most one query to the bit server for each query performed by A, therefore $S_B \leq S_A$. If A (and thus B) is a Las Vegas algorithm, Lemma 2 gives a worst-case expected cost of at least $m/2$ bit queries for each of the $k-1$ instances solved by B, and thus $E[S_A] \geq E[S_B] \geq \frac{m}{2}(k-1) \in \Omega(mk)$. If A (and thus B) is a Monte Carlo algorithm with constant confidence (note that B is correct if A is, thus the confidence of B is equal to at least the confidence of A), a sensitivity argument for randomized algorithms with bounded error [11] gives a worst-case cost of $\Omega(m)$ bit queries for each of the $k-1$ instances, and thus $S_A \geq S_B \in \Omega(mk)$. In every case $S_A \in \Omega(mk)$ which, plugging in the above value for m and recalling that $n_0 \in \Theta(n)$, becomes:

$$S_A \in \Omega\left(\left\lceil \frac{\alpha\sqrt{n_0/\epsilon}}{12k} \right\rceil k\right) = \Omega\left(\alpha\sqrt{\frac{n}{\epsilon}}\right)$$

which concludes the proof. □

The bound for deterministic algorithms is even stronger. Intuitively, an adversarial link server can adaptively build a worst-case graph by refusing to give enough information until $\Omega(n)$ queries have been performed. More formally:

THEOREM 4. *Choose integers $k > 1$ and $n_0 \geq k^2$, a damping factor $\alpha \in (0,1)$, and an $\epsilon \leq \frac{\alpha^2}{20k}$. For any deterministic local algorithm A there exists a graph of size $n \in \Omega(n_0)$ where the top k nodes $v_0, \ldots, v_{k-1}$ are ϵ-separated and, to compute their relative ranking, A performs $\Theta(n)$ queries.*

PROOF. Let A be a deterministic local algorithm that ranks the top k nodes of a graph performing S_A queries to the link server; we exhibit an adversarial link server that lets A run on a worst-case graph G similar to that of Theorem 3 and consisting of k disjoint subgraphs $G_0, G_1, \ldots, G_{k-1}$. Let m and b be two positive integers (we compute them below). For $i = 1, \ldots, k-1$, subgraph G_i (Figure 4) contains target node v_i and its self-loop, $m+1$ nodes $u_i^0, \ldots, u_i^m$ that have v_i as their sole child, ib nodes $w_i^0, \ldots, w_i^{ib-1}$ that have u_i^0 as their sole child and kb nodes $w_i^{ib}, \ldots, w_i^{(i+k)b-1}$ that either have self-loops or, for some $1 \leq j \leq m$, have u_i^j as their sole child. Subgraph G_0 contains target node v_0 and its self-loop, $m+1$ nodes $u_0^0, \ldots, u_0^m$ that have v_0 as their sole child, and kb nodes $w_0^0, \ldots, w_0^{kb-1}$ that have u_0^0 as their sole child.

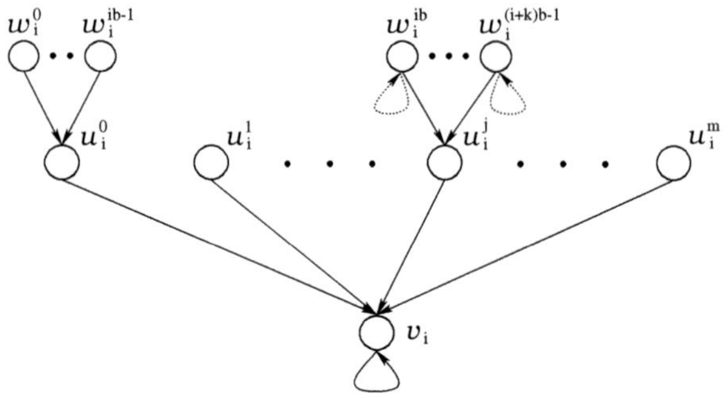

Figure 4: Subgraph G_i (Theorem 4). Node u_i^0 always has ib parents, while nodes $w_i^{ib}, \ldots, w_i^{(i+k)b-1}$ may or may not have u_i^j as their sole child.

The link server exploits the fact that the mapping of node IDs (i.e. the content of queries) to nodes in the graph is arbitrary, and forces algorithm A to query almost all the nodes before giving enough information to compute a correct ranking. Indeed, the link server follows this simple rule:

- on the first mk queries, it never maps an ID to any of the nodes $w_i^{ib}, \ldots, w_i^{(i+k)b-1}$ for $i = 1, \ldots, k-1$ or any of their children.

Note that this is a legitimate behaviour since each of the k subgraphs $G_0, \ldots, G_{k-1}$ has at least m nodes that are neither $w_i^{ib}, \ldots, w_i^{(i+k)b-1}$ nor their children.

We now exhibit values of m and b such that G and the target nodes satisfy the theorem. In particular, choose

$$m = \left\lceil \frac{n_0}{k} \right\rceil \qquad \text{and} \qquad b = \left\lfloor \frac{n_0}{k^2} \right\rfloor$$

The size of the graph, $n \in \Theta(mk + k^2 b)$, is thus in $\Theta(n_0)$. The hypothesis $n_0 \geq k^2$ guarantees that $m \geq kb$ and $b \geq 1$; thus $v_0, \ldots, v_{k-1}$ are the top k nodes in the graph, since at any layer they have more ancestors than any other node.

It remains to prove that the target nodes are ϵ-separated. Since the number of parents and grandparents of v_i is the same as in the graph of Theorem 3, and since $kb \leq m$, the difference between scores satisfies the same lower bound $\frac{\Delta P}{P} \geq \frac{\alpha^2 b}{5m}$. The substitution of b and m gives

$$\frac{\Delta P}{P} \geq \frac{\alpha^2 b}{5m} \geq \frac{\alpha^2 \lfloor \frac{n_O}{k^2} \rfloor}{5 \lceil \frac{n_O}{k} \rceil} \geq \frac{\alpha^2 \frac{n_O}{2k^2}}{5 \frac{2n_O}{k}} \geq \frac{\alpha^2}{20k} \geq \epsilon$$

which proves that the target nodes are ϵ-separated.

Note that the link server can invalidate *any* ranking of the target nodes that A should output *before* querying at least mk nodes. Indeed, suppose that A has queried less than mk nodes and consider a target node v_i such that one of its parents, u_i^j, has not been queried (one such node always exist). If A ranks v_i higher than v_0, the link server disconnects $w_i^{ib}, \ldots, w_i^{(i+k)b-1}$ from u_i^j, otherwise it connects them to u_i^j. The expression of $P(v_i)$ (see proof of Theorem 3) shows that in either case A gives an incorrect ranking. Therefore A must incur a cost of at least mk; substituting $m = \lceil \frac{n_O}{k} \rceil$ and $n_O \in \Theta(n)$, we conclude the proof:

$$S_A \geq mk = \left\lceil \frac{n_O}{k} \right\rceil k \geq n_O \in \Omega(n)$$

□

Note that, as the sizes of the graphs of Theorems 3 and 4 increase, the upper bound on the choice of ϵ falls within a small constant factor of $\frac{\alpha^2}{k}$, taking the lower bounds on the incurred costs within a small constant factor of, respectively, $\sqrt{kn}$ (increasing to n/k for $\epsilon \approx \frac{\alpha^2 k^2}{n}$) and n. Therefore, by Theorems 3 and 4 there exist graphs of size in the billions (comparable to the estimated size of the web graph) where, assuming a "standard" damping factor of 0.85, the PageRank scores of the top 10 nodes are $\approx$ 0.1-separated, which in absolute terms is *orders of magnitude* greater than the average PageRank score $\frac{1}{n}$, yet any "useful" (i.e. with a reasonable confidence level) local ϵ-ranking algorithm incurs $\approx$ 100k queries (increasing to $\approx$ 100M for $\epsilon \approx 10^{-7}$) in the randomized case and $\approx$ 1B queries in the deterministic case.

It is now clear that, at least *in theory*, a general efficient local ranking algorithm does not exist. In practice, real graphs may behave differently, and state-of-the-art algorithms may be able to exploit their properties to efficiently compute the correct ranking of the target nodes. The next section provides experimental results to investigate this issue.

6. EXPERIMENTS

This section describes two experiments, both partially levering on known score approximation algorithms ([3, 12]), aimed at estimating how far the theoretical lower bounds of Section 4 are in practice from the cost of local ranking on real graphs. Subsection 6.1 introduces the experimental setting, while Subsections 6.2 and 6.3 detail the two experiments and the results obtained.

6.1 Experimental Design

We ran the experiments on two publicly available real graphs provided by the Laboratory for Web Algorithmics, University of Milan (see [5, 7]). The first is a large snapshot (over 40M nodes and 1150M arcs) of the 2004 `.it` web domain; since the structure of the web graph is self-similar (i.e. fractal-like) [15], these experimental results naturally extend to the whole web graph. Furthermore, the `.it` graph is relatively isolated from the rest of the web because most pages are written in Italian, a language seldom used outside this domain; thus, this graph is well suited for link analysis experiments – carving it out of the web does not imply deleting many links. The second graph is a fairly large snapshot (over 5M nodes and 79M arcs) of the 2008 LiveJournal friendship graph, where nodes represent users and a directed arc from u to v means that u reputes v as a friend (the graph is not symmetric). Conferral of importance has a natural meaning in this graph, and its nature is completely different from that of the web, providing a wider experimental basis to test our theory. Furthermore, being a completely isolated graph, no arcs have been discarded by the crawling process.

Graph preprocessing deserves a special note. It is well known that PageRank treats dangling nodes as having virtual outgoing arcs towards all the nodes of the graph [24]. This makes it difficult to approximate PageRank scores locally since the influence of these virtual arcs can only be guessed – the link server provides only the *real* arcs – unless their number is known a priori, in which case the correct scores can be computed applying a scaling factor that depends only on the fraction of dangling nodes in the graph [14, 6]. Surprisingly, the literature on local score approximation always neglects this issue. However, the estimation of such fraction is beyond the scope of this paper. This led us to eliminate all the dangling nodes by repeated pruning, as done in [12]. For both graphs, this removed less than 15% of the nodes and less than 6% of the arcs.

For the sake of clarity, in both experiments we focused on ranking *pairs* of target nodes, which we sampled among the top ranked nodes of the graphs. This latter choice has two reasons. First, in most practical applications only the top scores really matter. Second, nodes with a high score are likely to have many ancestors on many layers, and therefore are the best candidates to test the worst-case lower bounds provided by theorems of Section 4. We thus computed the exact PageRank scores of all the nodes of the graphs, using 100 iterations of the power method and a "standard" value of 0.85 for α, and selected the top 10k nodes (i.e. less than the top 0.3%) from both graphs. Then we sampled 1000 pairs uniformly at random among all the pairs of nodes u, v that are $(1+\epsilon, 1+2\epsilon)$-separated, i.e. $(1+\epsilon)P(v) \leq P(u) \leq (1+2\epsilon)P(v)$, for values of ϵ ranging from $0.01 \cdot 2^0$ (scores differing by 1-2%) to $0.01 \cdot 2^8$ (scores differing by 256-512%) in doubling steps. On each sample we ran the experiments detailed in the following two subsections.

6.2 Is Ranking Local in Real Graphs?

The goal of the first experiment is to estimate a lower bound on the cost of locally ranking ϵ-separated nodes as a function of ϵ. This bound can be seen as the size of the *minimal set* of nodes that must be visited to compute correctly the relative ranking of two target nodes:

Definition 1. Let u, v be nodes of graph G and let A be a local ranking algorithm. The *minimal set* $S_A(G, u, v)$ for A contains the minimal number of nodes of G that A fetches to correctly rank u and v.

In other words, $S_A(G, u, v)$ is the (not necessarily unique) smallest set of nodes such that A correctly ranks u and v if it fetches any set $S \supseteq S_A(G, u, v)$. Clearly, a general (i.e. valid for all algorithms) lower bound on the size of $S_A(G, u, v)$ gives a lower bound on the cost of locally ϵ-ranking u and v in G. Note that, for any choice of G, u and v, there always exists an algorithm A such that $S_A(G, u, v) = \emptyset$. For example, a trivial algorithm returning a constant ranking could rank correctly some of the pairs of nodes in G; unfortunately, it would rank incorrectly all the remaining. It is therefore natural to restrict the definition to algorithms that provide a correct ranking for *any* pair of target nodes u and v of *any* possible graph G – in other words, algorithms that *solve* the ϵ-ranking problem. We further restrict to algorithms that compute approximate scores as the sum of the (known) contributions of the visited nodes on the target nodes, and thus do not overestimate the real score, similarly to existing algorithms (we conjecture that *any* algorithm that behaves differently would fail for some input G,u,v). In this case, a(n ideal) "perfect" algorithm PER would build a set $S_{PER}(G,u,v)$ containing all and only the top c contributors of the highest ranked node u for a sufficiently large c such that $\tilde{P}(u) = \sum_{z \in S_{PER}(G,u,v)} \text{contrib}(z,u) \geq P(v)$. It is easy to see that, on any superset $S \supseteq S_{PER}(G,u,v)$, algorithm PER estimates $\tilde{P}(u) \geq P(v)$ and $\tilde{P}(v) \leq P(v)$, and infers the correct ranking from the inequality $\tilde{P}(u) \geq \tilde{P}(v)$, while any set smaller than $S_{PER}(G,u,v)$ would lead to $\tilde{P}(u) < P(v)$ and to an incorrect result for some (G,u,v). Therefore the cardinality of $S_{PER}(G,u,v)$ is a lower bound to the cost of locally ranking u and v in G for any correct algorithm. Note that, since the contribution of an ancestor z is α times the average of the contributions of its children, at least one of them has a contribution not smaller than that of z. Therefore, if $S_{PER}(G,u,v)$ contains z, it also contains one of its children, and thus $S_{PER}(G,u,v)$ induces a connected graph which is in principle *reachable* by those (reasonable) algorithms that query only parents of already-queried nodes.

In practice, for each pair u,v we estimated their minimal set as follows. We collected the first 15 layers of the ancestors of u, stopping earlier if their number reached a given threshold ($0.02n$ for the `.it` graph and $0.2n$ for the LiveJournal graph). These ancestors induced a subgraph where we ran 40 iterations of the brute force algorithm with u as the target node. This yielded the contribution of each collected ancestor, which was used to sort them and build the estimated minimal set.

Figure 5 illustrates the average size of the estimated minimal sets as a function of ϵ for both graphs. As expected, this size increases as ϵ decreases – ranking weakly-separated nodes costs more than ranking well-separated ones. In the `.it` web graph, the cost of local ranking is 100 to 1000 times smaller than the size of the graph, i.e. in the order of $10^4 - 10^5$ queries, which may be intolerably high for applications that use a remote link server. Surprisingly, in the LiveJournal graph minimal sets are much larger, in spite of the significantly lower graph size (< 4.8M vs. > 37M nodes) and average degree (< 16.5 vs. > 30). Indeed, except for $\epsilon \approx 1$, the number of collected ancestors almost always reached the threshold of $0.2n$ and their contribution was not sufficient to give a correct ranking. Thus, ϵ-ranking in the LiveJournal graph is strongly non-local.

6.3 Local Ranking with Real Algorithms

The second experiment evaluates the performance of two real (returning *wrong* results in some cases) algorithms, giving an empirical upper bound on the cost of local ranking if one accepts an unavoidably positive rate of error.

We first tested the brute force (BF) algorithm, which serves more as a benchmark than as a realistic efficient method for local ranking. BF explores the ancestors of each

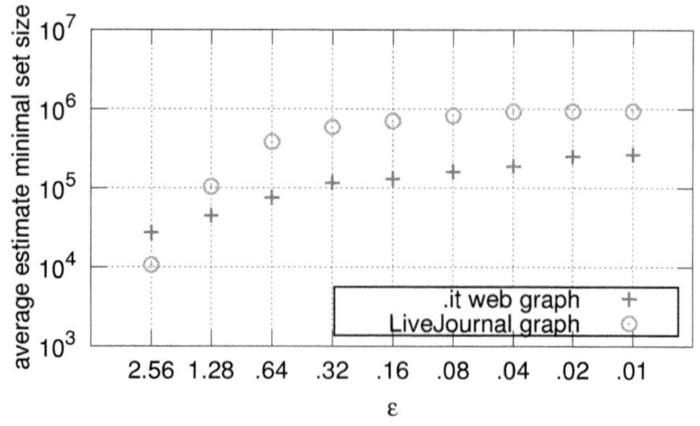

Figure 5: Average size of estimated minimal sets for $(\epsilon, 2\epsilon)$-separated nodes as a function of ϵ for the `.it` web graph and the LiveJournal graph

of the two target nodes layer by layer, computing their approximate scores according to Equation (2) and inferring their relative ranking. Figures 6.1 - 6.2 (`.it` graph) and 6.3 - 6.4 (LiveJournal graph) show respectively the average cost (number of visited nodes) and the average precision (fraction of correctly ranked node pairs), for different values of $(\epsilon, 2\epsilon)$, as a function of the number of layers visited from 0 to 25 – a limit that seems sufficient to saturate the set of visited nodes. Unsurprisingly, BF incurs overwhelmingly high costs (several million queries) in both graphs, even to guarantee a precision ≥ 0.9 only for the most separated nodes.

We then tested ImPBF, an improved version of PBF, the pruned brute force algorithm [3]. PBF is an intuitively efficient variation of the BF algorithm that, at each layer $\tau \geq 1$, visits only the nodes whose estimated contribution (over paths known at iteration τ) to the score of the target node is above a given threshold. The conjecture underpinning this heuristics is that nodes with a small contribution over paths of length $\leq \tau$ probably give a small *overall* contribution, and their parents likely do the same. Counterexamples show that sometimes this is false [4], but [12] shows that this heuristics works on real web graphs; and although other algorithms for local score approximation exist (see [12]), they have less clear theoretical backgrounds, are unrealistic (e.g. assuming to know the total number of arcs), or sometimes overestimate the true PageRank score – all assumptions not fitting our general model. We terminated PBF either when no more candidates had a sufficient estimated contribution or when it visited more than $0.1n$ nodes, which in practice is $\Theta(n)$. On the subgraph induced by the visited nodes, ImPBF runs BF for 40 iterations (while PBF typically did not visit more than 20 layers) or until the relative per-iteration increment in the estimated score drops below 0.1%. This "squeezes" most of the overall contribution out of the visited nodes, giving a more accurate score approximation.

We ran ImPBF for different contribution thresholds, ranging from 10^{-1} to 10^{-7}. Figures 6.5 - 6.6 (`.it` graph) and 6.7 - 6.8 (LiveJournal graph) show respectively the average cost and the average precision of the ImPBF algorithm as a function of the contribution threshold, for different values of $(\epsilon, 2\epsilon)$. In the `.it` web graph, ImPBF reached a precision ≥ 0.9 for $\epsilon > 0.02$ incurring a cost 2.5 to 5 times the estimated minimal set size and is thus reasonably close to the optimum. In the LiveJournal graph, ImPBF guaranteed

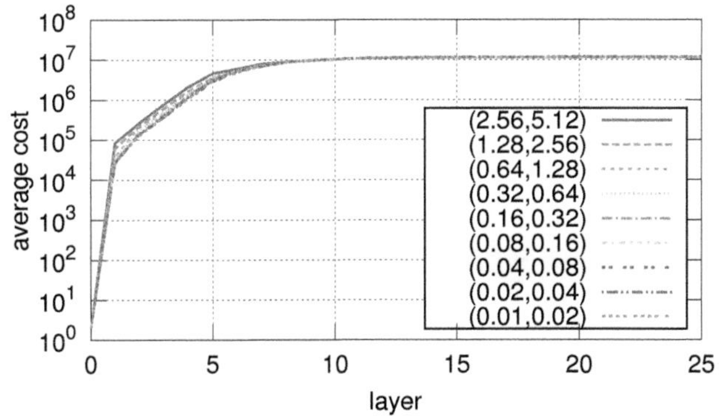

Figure 6.1: `.it` web graph, BF algorithm: average cost vs. layers visited, for different values of $(\epsilon, 2\epsilon)$

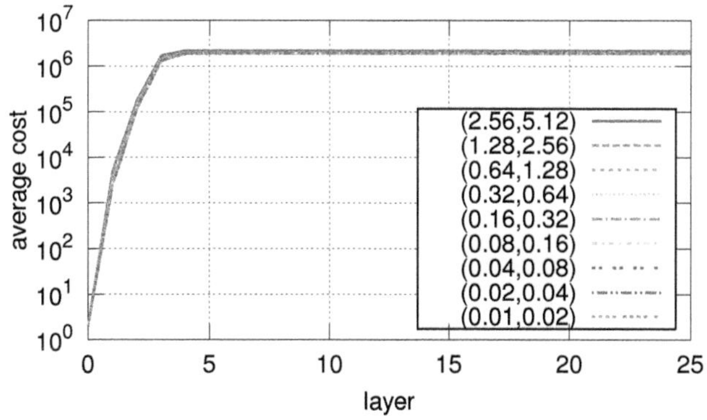

Figure 6.3: LiveJournal graph, BF algorithm: average cost vs. layers visited, for different values of $(\epsilon, 2\epsilon)$

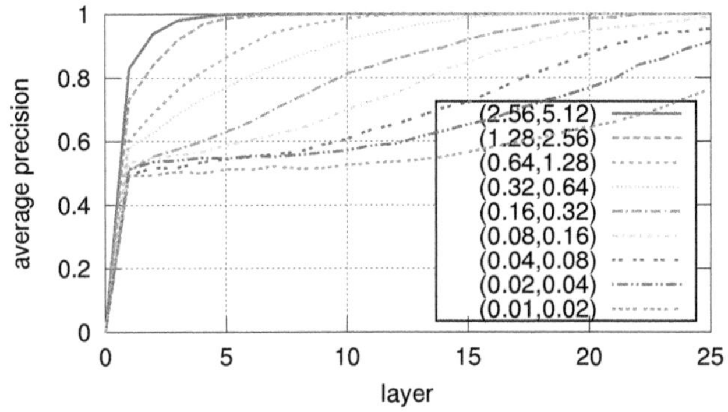

Figure 6.2: `.it` web graph, BF algorithm: average precision vs. layers visited, for different values of $(\epsilon, 2\epsilon)$

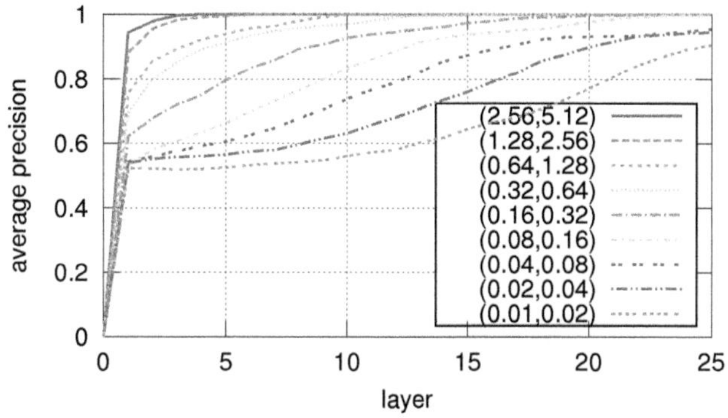

Figure 6.4: LiveJournal graph, BF algorithm: average precision vs. layers visited, for different values of $(\epsilon, 2\epsilon)$

a precision ≥ 0.9 only for $\epsilon \geq 0.64$, incurring a cost of a few thousand nodes, or ≈ 0.1 times the average estimated minimal set size. For $\epsilon < 0.64$, its precision dropped below 0.9, falling below 0.7 for $\epsilon < 0.16$, and the cost increased to a large fraction of the estimated minimal set size – confirming that ranking in this graph is strongly non-local except for extremely-separated nodes. Counterintuitively, the precision of ImPBF in the LiveJournal graph tends to decrease as the contribution threshold lowers and the cost increases. This is likely due to the saturation of the $0.1n$ cost threshold and confirms that local ranking is definitely non-trivial.

7. CONCLUSIONS

Motivated by a large and growing number of applications (such as web crawling and social network mining) that use PageRank as a pure ranking algorithm, we define and investigate the problem of computing locally the relative PageRank ranking of a set of k nodes in an n-node graph. We prove that a general, efficient local ranking algorithm does not exist: in the worst case, any correct algorithm must consider $\Omega(\sqrt{kn})$ nodes if randomized and $\Omega(n)$ nodes if deterministic, even when ranking the top k nodes in the graph and even if their scores are "well separated". We show experimentally that, in practice, real (web and social) graphs behave almost as poorly, requiring intolerably high costs both for exact algorithms and for algorithms based on state-of-the-art local score approximation algorithms.

Two questions naturally arise from our theoretical and experimental results. First, what are the topological properties of a graph that make it a hard, or instead, easy instance for local ranking? Second, how can these properties be exploited by local algorithms to compute the ranking efficiently?

8. ACKNOWLEDGEMENTS

This work was supported by Univ. Padova Strategic Proj. AACSE, by MIUR Proj. AlgoDEEP, and by PAT, FBK, and INFN Proj. Aurora-Science. We thank Massimo Melucci, Enoch Peserico, Geppino Pucci, Michele Scquizzato, Francesco Silvestri, and the anonymous reviewers for their valuable comments; Paolo Bertasi and Michele Bonazza for setting up the computing infrastructure.

9. REFERENCES

[1] B. Amento, L. Terveen, and W. Hill. Does "authority" mean quality? Predicting expert quality ratings of web documents. In *Proc. of ACM SIGIR*, pages 296–303. 2000.

[2] R. Andersen, C. Borgs, J. Chayes, J. Hopcroft, V. Mirrokni, and S.-H. Teng. Local computation of PageRank contributions. *Internet Mathematics*, 5(1–2):23–45, 2008.

[3] Z. Bar-Yossef and L.-T. Mashiach. Local approximation of PageRank and reverse PageRank. In *Proc. of ACM CIKM*, pages 279–288. 2008.

[4] Z. Bar-Yossef and L.-T. Mashiach. Local approximation of PageRank and reverse PageRank. Technical report, Israel Institute of Technology, 2008.

[5] P. Boldi, B. Codenotti, M. Santini, and S. Vigna. Ubicrawler: A scalable fully distributed web crawler. *Software: Practice & Experience*, 34(8):711–726, 2004.

[6] P. Boldi, R. Posenato, M. Santini, and S. Vigna. Traps and pitfalls of topic-biased PageRank. In *Proc. of WAW*, pages 107–116. 2006.

[7] P. Boldi and S. Vigna. The WebGraph framework I: Compression techniques. In *Proc. of WWW*, pages 595–601. 2004.

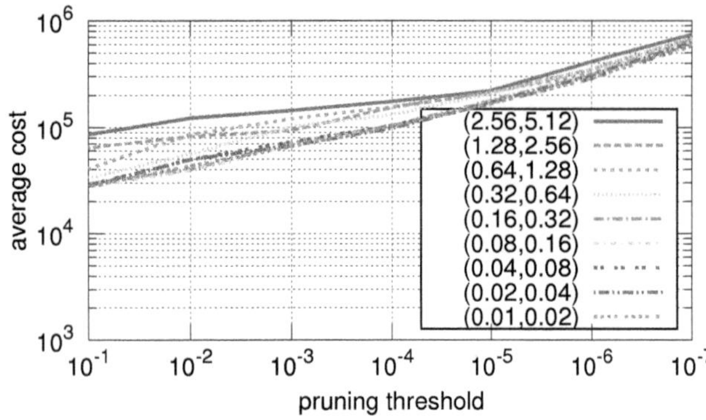

Figure 6.5: `.it` graph, ImPBF algorithm: average cost vs. contribution threshold, for different values of $(\epsilon, 2\epsilon)$

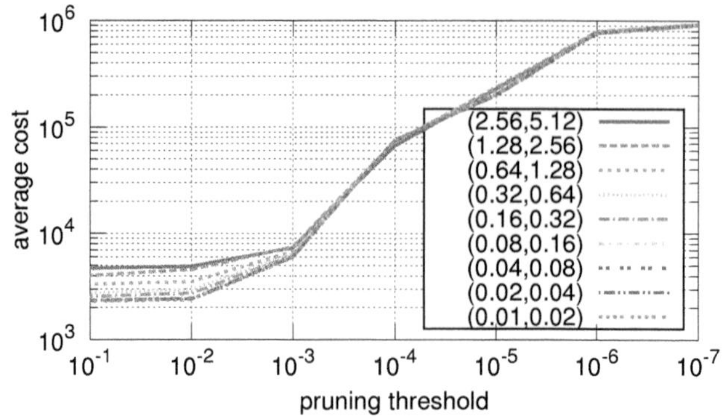

Figure 6.7: LiveJournal graph, ImPBF algorithm: avg. cost vs. contrib. threshold, for different values of $(\epsilon, 2\epsilon)$

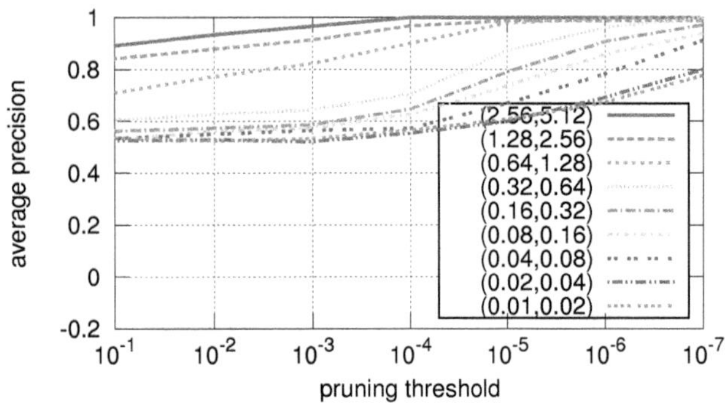

Figure 6.6: `.it` graph, ImPBF algorithm: average precision vs. contribution threshold, for different values of $(\epsilon, 2\epsilon)$

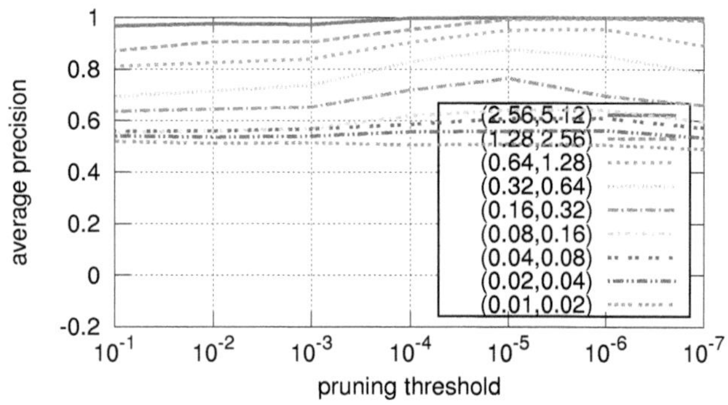

Figure 6.8: LiveJournal graph, ImPBF algorithm: avg. precision vs. contrib. threshold, for different values of $(\epsilon, 2\epsilon)$

[8] A. Borodin, G. O. Roberts, J. S. Rosenthal, and P. Tsaparas. Link analysis ranking: Algorithms, theory, and experiments. *ACM Transactions on Internet Technology*, 5(1):231–297, 2005.

[9] M. Bressan and E. Peserico. Choose the damping, choose the ranking? *Journal of Discrete Algorithms*, 8(2):199–213, 2010.

[10] S. Brin and L. Page. The anatomy of a large scale hypertextual Web search engine. In *Proc. of WWW*. 1998.

[11] H. Buhrman and R. D. Wolf. Complexity measures and decision tree complexity: A survey. *Theoretical Computer Science*, 288(1):21–43, 2002.

[12] Y.-Y. Chen, Q. Gan, and T. Suel. Local methods for estimating PageRank values. In *Proc. of ACM CIKM*, pages 381–389. 2004.

[13] J. Cho, H. Garcia-Molina, and L. Page. Efficient crawling through URL ordering. *Computer Networks*, 30(1-7):161–172, 1998.

[14] G. M. Del Corso, A. Gulli, and F. Romani. Fast PageRank Computation via a Sparse Linear System. *Internet Mathematics*, 2(3):251–273, 2005.

[15] S. Dill, R. Kumar, K. S. McCurley, S. Rajagopalan, D. Sivakumar, and A. Tomkins. Self-similarity in the web. *ACM Transactions on Internet Technology*, 2(3):205–223, 2002.

[16] A. Esuli and F. Sebastiani. PageRanking WordNet synsets: An application to opinion mining. In *Proc. of ACL*, pages 424–431. 2007.

[17] F. Geerts, H. Mannila, and E. Terzi. Relational link-based ranking. In *Proc. of VLBD*, pages 552–563. 2004.

[18] R. Gross and A. Acquisti. Information revelation and privacy in online social networks. In *Proc. of ACM WPES*, pages 71–80. 2005.

[19] Z. Gyöngyi, H. Garcia-Molina, and J. Pedersen. Combating web spam with TrustRank. In *Proc. of VLDB*, pages 576–587. 2004.

[20] J. Heidemann, M. Klier, and F. Probst. Identifying key users in online social networks: A PageRank based approach. In *Proc. of ICIS*, 2010.

[21] J. L. Hennessy and D. A. Patterson. Computer architecture: A quantitative approach. 4th ed. Morgan Kaufmann, 2007.

[22] S. D. Kamvar, M. T. Schlosser, and H. Garcia-Molina. The EigenTrust algorithm for reputation management in P2P networks. In *Proc. of WWW*, pages 508–516. 2003.

[23] O. Kurland and L. Lee. PageRank without hyperlinks: Structural re-ranking using links induced by language models. In *Proc. of ACM SIGIR*, pages 306–313. 2005.

[24] A. N. Langville and C. D. Meyer. *Google's PageRank and Beyond: The Science of Search Engine Rankings*. Princeton University Press, 2006.

[25] R. Lempel and S. Moran. Rank-stability and rank-similarity of link-based Web ranking algorithms in authority-connected graphs. *Information Retrieval*, 8:219–243, 2005.

[26] M. Melucci and L. Pretto. PageRank: When order changes. In *Proc. of ECIR*, pages 581–588. 2007.

[27] J. L. Morrison, R. Breitling, D. J. Higham, and D. R. Gilbert. GeneRank: Using search engine technology for the analysis of microarray experiments. *BMC Bioinformatics*, 6:233, 2005.

[28] E. Peserico and L. Pretto. What does it mean to converge in rank? In *Proc. of ICTIR*, pages 239–245. 2007.

[29] P. Tarau, R. Mihalcea, and E. Figa. Semantic document engineering with WordNet and PageRank. In *Proc. of ACM SAC*, pages 782–786. 2005.

[30] R. S. Wills and I. C. F. Ipsen. Ordinal ranking for Google's PageRank. *SIAM Journal on Matrix Analysis and Applications*, 30(4):1677–1696, 2009.

[31] X. Wu, V. Kumar, J. Ross Quinlan, J. Ghosh, Q. Yang, H. Motoda, G. J. McLachlan, A. Ng, B. Liu, P. S. Yu, Z.-H. Zhou, M. Steinbach, D. J. Hand, and D. Steinberg. Top 10 algorithms in data mining. *Knowledge and Information Systems*, 14(1):1–37, 2007.

[32] S. Yan and D. Lee. Toward alternative measures for ranking venues: a case of database research community. In *Proc. of ACM/IEEE JCDL*, pages 235–244. 2007.

[33] A. C.-C. Yao. Probabilistic computations: Toward a unified measure of complexity. In *Proc. of IEEE FOCS*, pages 222–227. 1977.

Prioritizing Relevance Judgments to Improve the Construction of IR Test Collections

Mehdi Hosseini[1+], Ingemar J. Cox[1+], Natasa Milic-Frayling[2*], Trevor Sweeting[1^], Vishwa Vinay[2*]

University College London[1], Microsoft Research Cambridge[2]

{m.hosseini, ingemar}@cs.ucl.ac.uk[+], trevor@stats.ucl.ac.uk[^], {natasamf,vvinay}@microsoft.com[*]

ABSTRACT

We consider the problem of optimally allocating a fixed budget to construct a test collection with associated relevance judgements, such that it can (*i*) accurately evaluate the relative performance of the participating systems, and (*ii*) generalize to new, previously unseen systems. We propose a two stage approach. For a given set of queries, we adopt the traditional pooling method and use a portion of the budget to evaluate a set of documents retrieved by the participating systems. Next, we analyze the relevance judgments to prioritize the queries and remaining pooled documents for further relevance assessments. The query prioritization is formulated as a convex optimization problem, thereby permitting efficient solution and providing a flexible framework to incorporate various constraints. Query-document pairs with the highest priority scores are evaluated using the remaining budget. We evaluate our resource optimization approach on the TREC 2004 Robust track collection. We demonstrate that our optimization techniques are cost efficient and yield a significant improvement in the reusability of the test collections.

Categories and Subject Descriptors

H.3.3 [**Information Storage and Retrieval**]: Information Search and Retrieval – *selection process*

General Terms: Performance

1. INTRODUCTION

A test collection consists of (*i*) a document collection, (*ii*) a set of test queries, and (*iii*) a set of corresponding relevance judgements. Ideally, every document in the collection would be judged relevant or non-relevant with respect to every query in the test set. In practice this is infeasible. Instead, the relevance assessments are typically obtained for a subset of documents retrieved by the set of participating IR systems. Each participating system contributes a fixed number of retrieved documents to the common pool which are then assessed for relevance by expert judges. While this approach increases the chance of identifying relevant documents, economic constraints may still prevent exhaustive judgments of all the documents in the pool.

In this paper, we consider how to prioritize query-document pairs for relevance judgments, when budget constraints preclude obtaining relevance judgments for all documents. We formulate the question as an optimization problem in which, for a given budget, we seek to identify a set of n query-document pairs that most accurately rank the participating systems and provide the best generalization to yet unseen systems.

The unique contributions of this paper are (i) explicitly incorporating a cost constraint within the optimization, (ii) formulating the optimization problem as a convex optimization, leading to computationally efficient algorithms for finding a globally optimum solution, and (iii) incorporating a *generalization constraint* based on the estimated number of un-judged relevant documents for each query.

In Section 2 we discuss related work. Particular attention is given to the work of Webber and Park [1], to which we compare our algorithm. Section 3 then provides a detailed description of our algorithm, while Section 4 describes specific implementation issues. Section 5 provides experimental results on the TREC 2004 Robust test collection. Finally, Section 6 provides a summary of our results and suggestions for future research directions.

2. RELATED WORK

Document pooling, originally proposed by Spärck-Jones and Van Rijsbergen [2] has been widely adopted for the construction of test collections. While studies showed that the number of pooled documents in the early TREC experiments was sufficient to rank the systems performance reliably, it also transpired that a considerable number of relevant documents remained undiscovered [3]. Thus, several alternative approaches have been suggested in order to judge more relevant documents, for example, Zobel [3] and Cormack et al. [4].

Webber and Park [1] estimated the bias that the uniform pooling and incomplete judgments introduce when un-judged documents are considered as non-relevant and when they are simply omitted from the computation of the performance scores. They also considered a more precise error estimation by considering a set of *common topics* and newly introduced systems for which they had full assessments. By removing the uncertainty of the un-judged documents they proposed an *adjusted estimator* that can be extrapolated to new topics and new systems. Their experiments demonstrate the effectiveness of the estimator with different sizes of common topics sets. However, they do not provide criteria for topic selection nor prioritization of new documents for relevance assessment when these are required to evaluate new systems. Research presented in this paper addresses these issues and explicitly models the query and document selection process in relation to the fixed budget constraints.

Many TREC test collections contain only 50 queries. Using a relatively small query set allows NIST to judge many documents per query and still stay within the available budget for relevance assessments. This increases the reusability of a test collection for other tasks and systems. On average about 2000 documents are judged per query. Sanderson and Zobel [5] suggested an alternative and less costly approach. They showed that if NIST evaluated systems by using a significantly larger set of queries, i.e., much larger than sets of 50 queries, and shallower pools of

CIKM'11, October 24-28, 2011, Glasgow, Scotland, UK.

candidate documents, i.e., much smaller than 100 documents per query, then the assessors' effort would be greatly reduced without compromising the accuracy of evaluation. Carterette and Smucker [6] supported this suggestion by using statistical tests. Evaluation based on a large number of queries with shallow judgments motivated a variety of approaches for selecting documents for assessments and defining evaluation metrics for partially judged result sets, such as statAP [7] or MTC [8].

Following the belief that a larger query set is desirable, the TREC 2007 Million Query track [9] was the first to include thousands of queries. The organizers made use of recent document selection methods to collect few judgments per query. However, due to the small number of documents assessed per query, the reusability of such a test collection still remains questionable [10]. This raises a fundamental question of how many and which documents should be assessed per query to achieve an optimal trade-off between the evaluation accuracy and the limited budget that is available for document assessments. In our work, we give a mathematical formulation of this problem that is tractable and extendible to include various refinements.

3. PROBLEM FORMULATION

Let $\boldsymbol{S}$ denote the population of all IR systems. Although the distribution of $\boldsymbol{S}$ is unknown, we assume that all, past, present and future systems are drawn from this distribution. This is a simplifying assumption but a good starting point for developing the mathematical model.

We are given a document corpus $\mathcal{D}$ and a set of N test queries $\boldsymbol{Q}_N = \{q_1, q_2, \dots, q_N\}$. We assume that there is a set $\boldsymbol{S_L}$ of L participating systems ($\boldsymbol{S_L} \subset \boldsymbol{S}$), each of which returns a number of retrieved documents for each of N queries. From the retrieved documents we create a *common pool* $\mathcal{P}$, ($\mathcal{P} \subset \mathcal{D}$) of documents to be used for comparative evaluation of the systems. Let Ω denote the desired budget required to build relevance judgments over the pooled documents $\mathcal{P}$. For a given budget B, that is much smaller than Ω $(B \ll \Omega)$, we seek to collect relevance judgments for a subset of query-document pairs in order to accurately evaluate the performance of the participating systems and reliably estimate the performance of yet unseen systems. We propose a two-stage process to allocate the limited budget B, which we outline next.

Stage 1. *– Acquire relevance judgments for an initial set of documents in* $\mathcal{P}$*.*
In the first stage we allocate a portion B_1 of the budget B to assess the relevance of some of the documents in the common pool $\mathcal{P}$. A number of methods have been proposed to select documents for relevance assessment, e.g. [8]. Generally, the selection methods assign a priority value w_d to each document and process them accordingly. Given a limited budget, the simplest allocation strategy is to divide the budget equally among N queries and, for each query, select a fixed number of documents with the highest priority scores. In the standard pooling technique, the documents are ranked based on the query relevance. Thus one can choose a uniform pool depth across queries to select documents to fit the available budget B_1. Therefore, the priority score w_d is 1 for documents above the cut-off rank and 0 for those below.

Stage 2. *– Selectively expand relevance judgments*
In the second stage we utilize the remaining budget, B_2 $(B = B_1 + B_2)$, to extend the pool of relevance judgments from Stage 1. The allocation of B_2 is based on a convex optimization of a cost function that seeks to (i) achieve maximum agreement with the evaluation of $\boldsymbol{S_L}$ systems using the full set of common documents $\mathcal{P}$ and ideal budget Ω, and (ii) generalize to new, unseen systems.

Before we describe in detail the method for prioritizing queries and documents, we first introduce the mathematical notation and formulation of the model.

3.1 Concepts and Notation

For the population of all IR systems $\boldsymbol{S}$, we observe the retrieval performance of each participating system over a finite set of N test queries. The performance measurements are represented in the form of a performance matrix $\boldsymbol{X}$. Each row corresponds to a system and each column to a query[1]. An entry $x_{i,j}$ in $\boldsymbol{X}$ denotes the performance score of the *i-th* system on the *j-th* query. We refer to a column of the matrix $\boldsymbol{X}$ as a *query-system vector* comprising the performance scores of all the systems for a given query. The column vector $\boldsymbol{m}$ is the average of all query-systems vectors across queries. Let μ denote the average performance of a randomly selected system in $\boldsymbol{S}$ across all the queries. If $\boldsymbol{x}$ is the system's row in the matrix $\boldsymbol{X}$, then

$$\mu = N^{-1}\boldsymbol{xe}$$

where $\boldsymbol{e} = \{1\}^{N\times 1}$ is an N-dimensional vector of 1's. By definition, the column vector $\boldsymbol{m}$ comprises system average performance μ.

We are interested in the expectation and variance of μ across all the systems. We therefore define $\boldsymbol{\alpha} \in R^{1\times N}$ to be the vector of average performance scores for an individual query across the systems. Further, let $\boldsymbol{\Sigma}$ denote the $N \times N$ covariance matrix of the N query-systems vectors. Then the expectation and the variance of μ across systems are given by [11],

$$E(\mu) = N^{-1}\boldsymbol{\alpha e}, \qquad var(\mu) = N^{-2}\boldsymbol{e}^{\boldsymbol{T}}\boldsymbol{\Sigma e}$$

More generally, the performance μ of a system can be expressed as a weighted combination of the scores $x_{i,j}$. Let $\boldsymbol{\beta} \in [0,1]^{N\times 1}$ denote the associated weight vector with real values in [0,1]. Then the weighted average is expressed as $\mu_\beta = \boldsymbol{x\beta}$ and the expectation and the variance of μ_β across systems are given by

$$E(\mu_\beta) = \boldsymbol{\alpha\beta}, \qquad var(\mu_\beta) = \boldsymbol{\beta}^{\boldsymbol{T}}\boldsymbol{\Sigma\beta}$$

We now determine $\boldsymbol{\beta}$ as priority scores of queries in order to expand relevance judgments from Stage 2 under specified conditions.

3.2 Prioritizing Query-Document Pairs

In practice, it has been shown that some documents are more effective than others in discriminating systems' performance for a given query (e.g., [8] & [12]). Similarly, some queries are more effective than others [13]. Thus, it is useful to define a query-document priority score s_{qd} as $s_{qd} = w_q \times w_d$ where w_q and w_d are weight coefficients for queries and documents, respectively. While there are many ways to prioritize documents [8], for simplicity, we adopt the uniform selection of documents across queries and focus our attention on the query prioritization.

We consider a query j as representative of the query set if its performance across systems is similar to the average performances of systems across all the test queries, i.e., the *j-th* column of $\boldsymbol{X}$ is close to the vector $\boldsymbol{m}$.

Our objective is to determine the most representative subset of queries based on several criteria. We formalize this by defining the vector $\boldsymbol{m}_\beta$ to represent the weighted average performance of

[1] For simplicity we shall denote the row and the column vector in the same manner; it will be clear from the context which operation is being performed with the vectors.

the systems across queries with query weights $\boldsymbol{\beta}$ and $\boldsymbol{m}_\beta[i] = \mu_{\beta i}$, $\{\forall i : s_i \in S\}$, the weighted average performance of the system i across queries. We introduce an objective function $f(\boldsymbol{\beta})$ to define the distance criteria between $\boldsymbol{m}_\beta$ and $\boldsymbol{m}$. In the context of IR systems evaluation, two criteria naturally present themselves: (i) the similarity in the ranking of the systems and (ii) the similarity in the absolute values of performance, i.e., $\mu_{\beta i} \approx \mu_i$.

The closeness of two rankings is usually measured using Kendall-τ. Unfortunately, using such a measure leads to computationally inefficient solutions. Consequently, we did not consider this similarity measure further. However, we do use Kendall-τ as an evaluation measure in our experiments to assess the quality of the optimization method.

3.2.1 *Performance Score Similarity*

There are many ways to characterize similarity in values between $\boldsymbol{m}_\beta$ and $\boldsymbol{m}$ such as the mean squared error and correlation. In our experiments we measure and report on correlation. Experiments with mean squared error are reported in [14].

The linear correlation measure ρ_β, between μ_β and μ is given by

$$\rho_\beta = \frac{cov\,(\mu,\ \mu_\beta)}{var(\mu)^{1/2} var(\mu_\beta)^{1/2}} = \frac{e^T \Sigma \beta}{(e^T \Sigma e)^{1/2}\,(\beta^T \Sigma \beta)^{1/2}} \qquad (2)$$

with the covariance between μ and μ_β computed as

$$cov\,(\mu, \mu_\beta) = N^{-1}\, \boldsymbol{E}\{\boldsymbol{e}^T (\boldsymbol{x} - \boldsymbol{\alpha})^T\, (\boldsymbol{x} - \boldsymbol{\alpha})\boldsymbol{\beta}\} = N^{-1}\, \boldsymbol{e}^T \boldsymbol{\Sigma \beta}$$

where $\boldsymbol{x} \in R^{1\times N}$ represent a system row in the matrix $\boldsymbol{X}$. We seek a set of $\boldsymbol{\beta}$ coefficients that maximizes ρ_β. Reordering Equation (2) gives

$$\gamma_\beta \equiv (\boldsymbol{e}^T \boldsymbol{\Sigma e})^{1/2} \rho_\beta = \frac{e^T \Sigma \beta}{(\beta^T \Sigma \beta)^{1/2}} \qquad (3)$$

Maximizing ρ_β is equivalent to maximizing γ_β since $(\boldsymbol{e}^T \boldsymbol{\Sigma e})^{\frac{1}{2}}$ is a constant. The maximum value of Equation (2) can be approximated by the minimization problem that is expressed in a quadratic programming form[2]:

$$min_\beta \quad f(\beta) = \tfrac{1}{2} \boldsymbol{\beta}^T \boldsymbol{\Sigma \beta} - \eta\, \boldsymbol{e}^T \boldsymbol{\Sigma \beta} \qquad (4)$$

where the $\eta \geq 0$ is a regularization parameter to adjust the trade-off between the quadratic part $(\boldsymbol{\beta}^T \boldsymbol{\Sigma \beta})$ and the linear part $(\boldsymbol{e}^T \boldsymbol{\Sigma \beta})$ part. In our experiments the regularization term η is set to N^{-1}. We now add constraints to arrive to the final optimization function.

3.3 Constraints

We consider two constraints. The first establishes the maximum available budget that can be used for additional judgments while the second, referred to as the *generalizability constraint*, ensures effective evaluation of new, previously unseen systems. We note that other constraints could easily be incorporated into this framework.

3.3.1 *Budget Constraint*

During Stage 2, we assume that a fixed budget B_2 is available for relevance judgments. It is natural to assume that the budget is allocated in proportion to each query's priority. We can, without loss of generality, take the query weight coefficients $\boldsymbol{\beta}$ to represent the proportion of the available budget that will be allocated to individual queries. In other words, if query j has a corresponding weight $\beta_j>0$, we will expend a proportion of the budget that is a function of β_j. Given the finite budget, we have that $\sum_{j=1}^{N} \beta_j = \frac{B_2}{\Omega - B_1}$. The number of 'active' queries, i.e., queries for which $\beta_j>0$, is then based on the optimization:

$$min_\beta\ f(\boldsymbol{\beta}) \qquad subject\ to: \begin{cases} \sum_{j=1}^{N} \beta_j = \frac{B_2}{\Omega - B_1} \\ \forall j : 0 \leq \beta_j \leq 1 \end{cases} \qquad (5)$$

3.3.2 *Generalizability Constraint*

If all the relevant documents for each query in the test collection are identified, then the test collection generalizes to any system. While we cannot guarantee that all the relevant documents are detected, it is clear that the *fewer unidentified relevant documents there are, the more generalizable the test collection is*. Thus, we define a cost function that not only minimizes the difference between $\boldsymbol{m}_\beta$ and $\boldsymbol{m}$, but also minimizes the number of un-judged relevant documents.

Let r_j be the expected number of un-judged relevant documents for query q_j. Given that we allocate $\beta_j \times (\Omega - B_1)$ of the B_2 budget to a query q_j then, at the end of the Stage 2, the number of newly judged relevant documents will be proportional to $\beta_j r_j$. Thus, the total number of relevant documents judged in Stage 2 is simply $\sum_{j=1}^{N} \beta_j r_j$, ignoring the constant of proportionality. Clearly, we want to maximize the total number of relevant documents in order to achieve maximum generalizability. Using a Lagrange multiplier λ we combine the constraint and the objective function $f(\boldsymbol{\beta})$ to obtain

$$QP = \min_\beta \left[f(\beta) - \lambda \frac{\sum_{j=1}^{N} \beta_j r_j}{\sum_{j=1}^{N} r_j} \right] \ \text{subject to:} \begin{cases} \sum_{j=1}^{N} \beta_j = \frac{B_2}{\Omega - B_1} \\ \forall j : 0 \leq \beta_j \leq 1 \end{cases} \qquad (6)$$

where $\sum_{j=1}^{N} r_j$ is added as a normalization factor to keep the first and second term in the same scale. The above optimization function is convex and we solve it using a sequential quadratic programming algorithm [16]. Section 4.2 discusses how to estimate the expected number of relevant documents r_j.

4. IMPLEMENTATION DETAILS

Before describing the experiments, we discuss a number of implementation issues. Note, however, that we cover setting of λ in Section 5.

4.1 Random Sampling of Systems

In practice, the mean vector $\boldsymbol{\alpha}$ and the covariance matrix $\boldsymbol{\Sigma}$ are unknown because the complete population of systems $\boldsymbol{S}$ is unknown. Indeed, we have no information about yet unseen systems. Instead, we have a sample of $\boldsymbol{x}_1, \ldots, \boldsymbol{x}_L$ of scores ($\boldsymbol{x}_i$ is a row of matrix $\boldsymbol{X}$) of L participating systems by which we can estimate $\boldsymbol{\alpha}$ and $\boldsymbol{\Sigma}$. Assuming that the set of participating systems is uniformly sampled from $\boldsymbol{S}$, the standard unbiased estimators of $\boldsymbol{\alpha}$ and $\boldsymbol{\Sigma}$, denoted as $\widehat{\boldsymbol{\alpha}}$ and $\widehat{\boldsymbol{\Sigma}}$, are given by

$$\widehat{\boldsymbol{\alpha}} = \overline{\boldsymbol{x}} \equiv L^{-1} \textstyle\sum_{i=1}^{L} \boldsymbol{x}_i\ , \quad \widehat{\boldsymbol{\Sigma}} = (L-1)^{-1} \textstyle\sum_{i=1}^{L} (\boldsymbol{x}_i - \widehat{\boldsymbol{\alpha}})^T (\boldsymbol{x}_i - \widehat{\boldsymbol{\alpha}})$$

If L is large and the sample of participating systems is diverse, we can get reliable estimations of $\boldsymbol{\alpha}$ and $\boldsymbol{\Sigma}$.

In practice, new systems may not be considered as drawn from a random sample. For example, over time, new systems are likely to perform better than participating systems, as system performance improves. In this case, we can use unbiased estimators for *weighted* systems to approximate $\boldsymbol{\alpha}$ and $\boldsymbol{\Sigma}$. Unfortunately, space

[2] The optimization form in Equation 3 is in *convex-fractional form* [15] and is optimized by transferring it to quadratic programming form.

limitations precludes further discussion and the interested reader is directed to [17].

4.2 Estimating the Number of Unseen Relevant Documents

It is difficult to determine whether or not all relevant documents for a query have been judged. However, the prior work of Zobel [3] suggests that some degree of estimation is possible, given an initial set of relevance judgments.

Given a set of initially judged documents, Carterette et al. [18] applied logistic regression to calculate the probability of relevance of un-judged documents. We use the same method to partition un-judged documents into relevant and non-relevant. Specifically, given an initial set of judged documents for a query, the relevance of a document d_i to query q_j is estimated by:

$$R(d_i, q_j) = \frac{1}{1 + \exp(-\boldsymbol{w}^T \boldsymbol{F})}$$

where $\boldsymbol{w}$ is the parameter vector of the model and $\boldsymbol{F}$ is a feature vector that uses the document similarity features as introduced in [18]. An un-judged document d_i, retrieved for a query q_j is labelled as relevant if the probability of relevance $R(d_i, q_j) >$ 0.5; otherwise d_i is labelled as non-relevant. Hence, the total number of relevant unseen documents for a query j is estimated by the number of un-judged documents with $R(d_i, q_j) > 0.5$.

5. EXPERIMENTAL EVALUATION

In this Section we describe a set of experiments that we conducted to evaluate the proposed *QP* method (Equation 6). Evaluations are conducted by comparing the ranking of the systems based on the full set of queries and available relevance judgments, with the ranking based on our method. The comparison uses Kendall-τ.

In the evaluation, we are particularly interested in the generalization to unseen systems. Thus we define the criteria for identifying markedly different systems. We use the *mean average reuse* (MAR) to characterize individual systems (see Section 5.3) and select those with low MAR as 'new', yet unseen systems.

Note, in order to avoid bias against any individual system, all participating systems contribute equally to the pooling of documents in both phases.

5.1 Benchmarks

We consider three baseline methods for resource allocation in comparison with our resource optimization method (*QP*):

(i) ***Uniform Allocation (UN)***, in which the available budget is uniformly allocated across queries. For example, if the budget can cover only 200 new judgments and there are 100 queries, we judge two new documents per query.

(ii) ***Random Allocation (RA)***, in which a random set of n queries is selected and the budget B_2 is uniformly allocated across the selected queries. In our experiments we use n that corresponds to the number of queries selected by our optimization method. We repeat the random query sampling for 1000 trials and report the average of the corresponding results.

(iii) ***Score Adjustment (SA)***, in which a random set of n queries is selected and the budget B_2 is uniformly allocated across the selected queries. Once the new relevance judgments are acquired, one can compare the difference between the original and new performance scores and use the average bias as a correction term for both the queries and the systems, as proposed by Webber and Park [1].

Note, the original algorithm by Webber and Park [1] assumes that relevance judgments are rendered for documents retrieved by new systems. In our context, the score adjustment is applied to the relevance judgments of documents within the common pool $\mathscr{P}$, i.e., contributed by the participating systems. We use the *SA* method in 1000 trials of random query sampling and report the average of the corresponding results.

5.2 Data Sets and Parameter Settings

Our experiments were performed using TREC 2004 Robust track. Normally, organizations participating in TREC register as *sites* and submit a number of experimental *runs* for evaluation. These runs often represent variations of the same IR system. For our purposes we consider each *run* as an individual IR system but take special care when considering IR submissions from the same site. In particular, when experiments require that we exclude some of the systems in order to treat them as 'new' systems, we hold out the entire set of runs from the same site. Furthermore, during the computation of performance metrics, we remove documents that are uniquely retrieved by the held-out systems.

The TREC 2004 Robust track consists of 249 queries, 14 sites with a total of 110 automatic runs, and 311,410 relevance judgments obtained over documents in TREC Disks 4 & 5 corpora, excluding the Congressional Record sub-collection.

Comparative evaluation of TREC runs is conducted based on the *average precision* (AP). However, since we use only a fraction of relevance judgments in Stage 1, many documents remain un-judged. Consequently, the AP scores measured for participating systems are uncertain and the performance matrix $\boldsymbol{X}$ is noisy. For that reason, in our experiments we use *infAP* rather than AP to measure systems effectiveness with respect to the initial judgments. The *infAP* scores provide a better approximation of the true AP scores [19] and, hence, a less noisy performance matrix $\boldsymbol{X}$.

5.3 Experimental Setup

In order to test the generalization and robustness of the four resource allocation methods relative to the evaluation of new systems, we first divide the TREC runs into participating systems and held-out systems. During Stage 1, we randomly select a few sites and use their corresponding runs as participating IR systems. Using the pooling technique we select the set of documents retrieved by these participating systems and compile the corresponding relevance judgments. The pool depth is adjusted to fit the budget allocated to Stage 1.

For each held-out system, and each query, we compute the *average reuse* (AR) [18] to measure the overlap between the documents retrieved by a held-out system and the judged documents. We then define the *mean average reuse* (MAR) as the average of AR values over the full set of queries. Based on the MAR values, we split the held-out systems into two groups. The first group consists of systems with high MAR across runs. This auxiliary group is evaluated with the relevance judgments obtained at Stage 1 and their performance values are added to the matrix $\boldsymbol{X}$. Note, however, that the auxiliary group does not contribute to the document pool. The second group, consisting of runs with low MAR values, forms the set of new systems.

The full experiment comprises the following steps:

1. Pick s_l percent of sites at random, these are the *held-in* sites.
2. For each query, construct the training pool of top k_0 documents using documents retrieved by the held-in runs and collect the associated relevance judgments. Compute the

performance matrix ***X***. The value of k_0 is determined based on the budget allocated to Stage 1. The budget is uniformly distributed across queries.

3. Compute the MAR for the held-out runs. Average the MAR scores across runs from the same site and produce average reuse score for each site.
4. Pick s_2 percent of sites with low MAR scores and treat their runs as *new* systems. The remaining runs, constituting the auxiliary group, are evaluated with the existing (Stage 1) relevance judgments and their performance values are added to the matrix ***X.***
5. Prioritize queries using the *QP* method, i.e., using the optimization defined in Equation 6.
6. For the *RA* and *SA* method, given that n queries are activated at step 5 (have non-zero β coefficients), randomly select a subset of n queries from the total set of N.
7. Given the budget B_2, acquire additional relevance judgments for documents pooled by participating systems in one of the four ways:
   (i) *Uniform* (*UN*): for each of the N queries, acquire relevance judgments for an additional k_1 documents, where k_1 is adjusted based on B_2.
   (ii) Random Allocation (*RA*): for a random sample of n queries acquire relevance judgments for additional k_2 documents per query, where $n \times k_2 = N \times k_1$.
   (iii) Score Adjustments (*SA*): for a random sample of n queries acquire relevance judgments for additional k_2 documents per query, where $n \times k_2 = N \times k_1$. Apply score adjustment.
   (iv) Query-Document Optimization (*QP*): order the query-document pairs and acquire relevance judgments for the $N \times k_1$ pairs with the highest priority scores.

5.3.1 Lagrange Multiplier

The *QP* formulation of the budget optimization in (6) requires the computation of the Lagrange multiplier λ. We determine λ empirically by systematic exploration of the range of values for λ, $0 \leq \lambda \leq 10$. This is performed after Stage 1 but before Stage 2.

During Stage 1, we have allocated budget B_1 and acquired the same number of relevance judgments for all queries. We then simulate the steps 1 through 7 above, where we split the budget B_1 into two parts B_1' and B_2' in the same proportion as true budget allocation B_1 and B_2. Note that during this simulation the estimated number r_j of un-judged relevant documents for a query q_j is set to the number of relevant documents identified during Stage 1, using the budget B_1 for query q_j. This ensures that at Stage 2 of the simulation to determine λ, no selected query requires more assessments than we have acquired during Stage 1. Thus, we have all the relevance judgments needed to evaluate the performance of the simulation.

For a particular value of λ within the range $0 \leq \lambda \leq 10$ we apply a 10-fold cross-validation technique. In each of the 10 iterations, 10% of participating systems are held out (these become our simulated new systems). Relevant documents that are in the initial document pool but solely retrieved by the held-out systems are removed from the pool. The *QP* method, using the reduced set of judgements, produces a set of query-document pairs. We evaluate this solution by computing the Kendall-τ of the systems' ranks with the corresponding systems' ranks using all the relevance judgments acquired using budget B_1 and Stage 1. We record the average Kendall-τ for the 10 trials. Finally, we choose the λ value with the highest average Kendall-τ.

Table 1. Result for Robust TREC 2004 runs evaluated by MAP. The first two columns report experimental parameters. The next columns report the Kendall-τ of (i) participating systems, and (ii) previously unseen systems for each resource allocation.

#	(s_1, s_2) %	(B_1, B_2) $\times 10^3$	Kendall-τ							
			participating systems				new systems			
			UN	*RA*	*SA*	*QP*	*UN*	*RA*	*SA*	*QP*
1		(2,8)		0.58	0.65	0.68		0.51	0.59	0.58
2	(10, 50)	(5,5)	0.63	0.61	0.7	0.78	0.54	0.52	0.66	0.71
3		(8,2)		0.63	0.67	0.79		0.52	0.63	0.74
4		(4,16)		0.66	0.76	0.9		0.62	0.7	0.76
5	(10, 40)	(10,10)	0.72	0.68	0.79	0.89	0.68	0.65	0.77	0.81
6		(16,4)		0.74	0.81	0.91		0.67	0.74	0.83
7		(4,16)		0.69	0.83	0.91		0.66	0.74	0.84
8	(20, 40)	(10,10)	0.79	0.75	0.82	0.89	0.8	0.67	0.8	0.9
9		(16,4)		0.77	0.83	0.91		0.7	0.81	0.91

5.4 Experimental Results

For the TREC 2004 Robust collection we report experiments using a total budget that covers either 10,000 or 20,000 relevance judgments. This is less than 7% of the collection's assessor budget of 311,410 relevance judgments.

We applied the steps 1 through 7 in Section 5.3 across 10 trials and, in each trial we randomly choose s_1 percent of sites and associated runs as participating systems. The remaining runs are evaluated for MAR and the s_2 percent of sites with the lowest MAR scores are chosen to be *new* systems. Depending on the average MAR scores, s_2 varies between 50% and 40% of the total number of sites. We report averages over the 10 trials. These experiments are repeated for 3 different values of s_1 and s_2, and 3 different budget allocations, B_1 and B_2. Table 1 summarizes the results.

We report the Kendall-τ statistic between the ranking of the systems induced by a resource allocation method and the ranking over the full set of queries and corresponding relevance judgments. We report separate Kendall-τ statistics for participating systems and for new systems, which is common in the literature and permits us to separately discuss the accuracy and generalization of the methods.

5.4.1 Experimental Results

We observe that for all 9 experimental configurations, the Kendall-τ scores of the *QP* method outperform the other three resource allocation methods. Note that the uniform allocation strategy is comparable and often better than the random allocation strategy for both the participating and the new systems. The score adjustment (*SA*) method outperforms the uniform allocation when s_1=10% (rows 1 through 6). However, when for s_1=20%, the *SA* method performs no better than the uniform allocation for new systems but remains better for participating systems. In contrast, our *QP* method yields superior results in all cases, except for configuration #1, in which the initial budget B_1 provides only 2000 relevance judgments, i.e., only 0.6% of the total judgments.

It is important to note that the *QP* method has significantly better Kendall-τ scores than the random allocation method, for both participating and new systems; an indication that the query prioritization achieved both accuracy and generalizability.

We note that increasing the number of participating systems s_1, with the same budgets B_1 and B_2, leads to a larger improvement in Kendall-τ of *new* systems' ranking than increasing the budgets, i.e., relevance assessments, and keeping the number of participating systems s_1 constant. This can be seen by comparing experimental configurations 5 & 8 or 6 & 9. These results are probably related to observations by Carterette et al. [18] that a higher diversity of participating systems results in a better ranking of new systems.

6. DISCUSSION AND FUTURE DIRECTIONS

In this paper we consider the problem of prioritizing query-document pairs for relevance assessment given a budget constraint, in order to (*i*) improve the accuracy of evaluating participating systems, and (*ii*) ensure that the test collection generalizes to new, previously unseen systems. We propose a two-stage procedure. In Stage 1, we allocate a budget B_1 uniformly across all queries, acquiring a corresponding set of relevance judgments. In Stage 2, we sue information from Stage 1 to prioritize query-document pairs and allocate a budget B_2 accordingly. While we presented a 2-stage process, our method is iterative and can be applied repeatedly to support a growing set of systems and the corresponding set of relevance assessments.

The novelty of our work is in (*i*) modeling query and document selection through explicit cost optimization, and (*ii*) formulating the problem as a convex optimization for which computationally efficient algorithms exist for identifying the optimum solution. Our experiments compare the *QP* method with, uniform, random sampling and a variant of the score adjustment method presented in [1]. They provided strong evidence that the *QP* method is (*i*) superior to the selected benchmark methods, (*ii*) exhibits good accuracy, i.e., predicts the performance of participating systems, and (*iii*) exhibits good generalization, i.e., predicts the performance of new systems.

One of the main advantages of the *QP* method is its extensibility. We can leverage research on identifying query characteristics that make queries *better* suited for use in system evaluation and formulate new components and constraints within the optimization framework. Our future work will investigate a richer set of such heuristics, aiming to produce methods for test collection construction that are efficient, in terms of required resources for relevance assessments, and effective, in terms of accuracy of systems evaluations.

Furthermore, our experiment set up can be expanded to examine the sensitivity of estimation errors such as estimating the number of un-judged relevant documents and errors in the matrix X. Finally, the full potential of the method would be realized through an effective iterative model of relevance assessment. Thus, it would be beneficial to evaluate the dynamic and real time application of the cost optimization in the context of the emerging practice of crowdsourcing relevance assessments.

REFERENCES

[1] W. Webber and L. A. F. Park, "Score Adjustment for Correction of Pooling Bias," in *Proc of the 32nd international ACM SIGIR Conference on Research and Development in Information Retrieval*, Boston 2009, pp. 444-451.

[2] K. Sparck-Jones and C. J. van Rijsbergen, "Information retrieval test collections," *Journal of Documentation*, vol. 32, no. 1, pp. 59-72, 1976.

[3] J. Zobel, "How reliable are the results of large-scale information retrieval experiments," in *Proceeding of ACM SIGIR Special Interest Group on Information Retrieval*, 1998, pp. 307-314.

[4] G. Cormack, C. Palmer, and C. Clarck, "Efficient Construction of large test collections," in *Proceeding of ACM SIGIR Special Interest Group on Information Retrieval*, 98, pp. 282-289.

[5] M. Sanderson and J. Zobel, "Information retrieval system evaluation: effort, sensitivity, and reliability," in *Proceeding of ACM SIGIR Special Interest Group on Information Retrieval*, 2005, pp. 162-169.

[6] B. Carterette and M. D. Smucker, "Hypothesis testing with incomplete relevance judgments," in *the Sixteenth ACM Conference on Information and Knowledge Management*, Lisbon, 2007, pp. 643-652.

[7] J. A. Aslam, V. Pavlu, and E. Yilmaz, "A Statistical Method for System Evaluation Using Incomplete Judgments," in *Proceeding of ACM SIGIR Special Interest Group on Information Retrieval*, 2006, pp. 541-548.

[8] B. Carterette, J. Allan, and R. Sitaraman, "Minimal test collections for retrieval evaluation," in *Proceeding of ACM SIGIR Special Interest Group on Information Retrieval*, 2006, pp. 268-275.

[9] J. Allan, J. A. Aslam, V. Pavlu, E. Kanoulas, and B. Carterette, "Overview of the TREC 2007 million query track," in *Notebook Proceedings of TREC 2007.*

[10] B. Carterette, E. Kanoulas, V. Pavlu, and H. Fang, "Reusable Test Collection Through Experimental Design," in *Proceeding of ACM SIGIR Special Interest Group on Information Retrieval*, Geneva, 2010, pp. 67-73.

[11] P. J. Huber, *Robust Statistics*, 2nd ed. Wiley, 2009.

[12] E. Yilmaz, E. Kanoulas, and J. A. Aslam, "A Simple and Efficient Sampling Method for Estimating AP and NDCG," in *Proceedings of the 31st annual international ACM SIGIR conference on Research and development in information retrieval*, 2008, pp. 603-610.

[13] J. Guiver, S. Mizzaro, and R. Stephen, "A few good topics: Experiments in topic set reduction for retrieval evauluation," *ACM Trans of Info Systems*, vol. 27, no. 4, pp. 1-26, 2009.

[14] M. Hosseini, I. Cox, N. Milic-Frayling, V. Vinay, and T. Sweeting, "Selecting a Subset of Queires for Acquisition of further Relevance Judgements," in *3rd international Conference on the Theory of Information Retrieval*, 2011, pp. 113-124.

[15] W. Dinkelbach, "On nonlinear fractional programming," *Management Science*, vol. 13, no. 7, pp. 492-498, Mar. 1967.

[16] R. W. Cottle, J.-S. Pang, and R. E. Stone, *The linear complementarity problem*. Boston, London: Academic Press Inc, 1992.

[17] M. Hosseini, I. J. Cox, T. Sweeting, N. Milic-Frayling, and V. Vinay, "Generalizing IR Test Collections through Incremental and Cost Constrained Gathering of Relevance Judgements," University College London RN/11/16, 2011.

[18] B. Carterette, E. Gabrilovich, V. Josifovski, and D. Metzler, "Measuring the Reusbility of Test Collections," in *Proceeding of ACM International conference on Web Search and Data Mining*, New York, 2010, pp. 231-240.

[19] E. Yilmaz and J. Aslam, "Estimating average precision with incomplete and imperfect judgments," in *Proceedings of the 15th ACM International Conference on Information and Knowledge Management*, 2006, pp. 102--111.

Evaluating an Associative Browsing Model for Personal Information

Jinyoung Kim, W. Bruce Croft, David A. Smith and Anton Bakalov
Department of Computer Science
University of Massachusetts Amherst
{jykim,croft,dasmith,abakalov}@cs.umass.edu

ABSTRACT

Recent studies [3] [2] suggest that associative browsing can be beneficial for personal information access. Associative browsing is intuitive for the user and complements other methods of accessing personal information, such as keyword search. In our previous work [9], we proposed an associative browsing model of personal information in which users can navigate through the space of documents and concepts (e.g., person names, events, etc.). Our approach differs from other systems in that it presented a ranked list of associations by combining multiple measures of similarity, whose weights are improved based on click feedback from the user.

In this paper, we evaluate the associative browsing model we proposed in the context of known-item finding task. We performed game-based user studies as well as a small scale instrumentation study using a prototype system that helped us to collect a large amount of usage data from the participants. Our evaluation results show that the associative browsing model can play an important role in known-item finding. We also found that the system can learn to improve suggestions for browsing with a small amount of click data.

Categories and Subject Descriptors

H.3.3 [**Information Storage and Retrieval**]: [Information Search and Retrieval]

General Terms

Algorithms

Keywords

Associative Browsing, Personal Information Management, Known-item Finding, Human Computation Game

1. INTRODUCTION

Associative browsing, the process of going through personal information by following a chain of associations, has several benefits. First of all, studies in cognitive psychology [5] [15] suggest that people remember facts primarily by associations, which explains the intuitive appeal of associative browsing. Also, Teevan et al. [14] suggest that many people tend to find information by a series of small steps (orienteering) instead of using keyword search.

Recently [9], we proposed a conceptual model of associative browsing for personal information. When keyword search fails to bring the desired item into the top results, a user can try browsing to the item by clicking on a result and following associations between that and other items. These associations are calculated based on various features, which are combined to create a ranking of associated items. This ranked list of items are presented to the user and the click from the user is used as a feedback to improve the weighting between features. The work improved on previously suggested models of associative browsing [3] [2] in that we proposed using more general measures of association (e.g. textual similarity and co-occurrence), and that we introduced the idea of click-based training of the feature weights.

In this paper, we introduce a learning framework for ranking suggestions for browsing, and evaluate the associative browsing model in the context of known-item finding, which is the most common task in personal information access [6]. The known-item finding task also has a well-defined structure with a concrete target item, which allowed us to use a novel evaluation method.

Specifically, we performed a game-based user study in which participants were asked to find a set of target documents by combining keyword search and associative browsing. The study shows that the participants often choose to use associative browsing. It also reveals insights on their known-item finding behavior.

Using the click data collected during the user study, we show that it is beneficial to combine many similarity measures for ranking browsing suggestions, and that the system can improve the quality of the ranked list with a small amount of click data. Moreover, the analysis of user's behavior during a game-based user study shows that people choose to use browsing when search results are only marginally satisfactory.

The rest of this paper is organized as follows. In the next section, we provide an overview of related work (§2). Then we introduce the associative browsing model (§3) and the learning method for ranking browsing suggestions (§4), followed by the evaluation methods based on game-based user study (§5). Finally, we present experimental results(§6).

CIKM'11, October 24–28, 2011, Glasgow, Scotland, UK.

2. RELATED WORK

Since the early days of IR, researchers have been interested in the combination of search and browsing for accessing document collections. Lucarella [11] described a system with a network of concepts and documents which provides search and browsing capability in a complementary manner. The I^3R system developed by Croft et al. [4] also assumes a scenario where documents returned by a user's initial query provide a starting point for subsequent browsing.

Kaplan et al. [8] described a navigation scheme that adapts to user behavior. Smucker et al. [13] found that similarity browsing can improve retrieval effectiveness when used as a search tool. Compared to these systems, our proposed approach is novel in that it suggests a feature representation of links between items. The weights of these links are trained using the click feedback from the user. Our model also has the notion of *concept*, which provides an extra access mechanism to documents. Finally, while they assumed that the user has already found a relevant document, we do not make such assumption here.

Human computation games [16] have recently been suggested as a method for obtaining a large amount of human annotations in a way that motivates participants. In the context of IR research, Ma et al. [12] introduced PageHunt, which is a game designed to collect web search log data by asking participants to find pages that they were shown. Recently, Kim et al. [10] developed a variant of PageHunt to collect the data for the evaluation of desktop search algorithms. This work is different in that we designed a game in which search and browsing are supported at the same time. We also analyzed session logs to gain insights into the use of the system, whereas previous work mostly used the data at the query level.

3. ASSOCIATIVE BROWSING MODEL

In this section, we briefly introduce the associative browsing model we proposed earlier [9], focusing on its application to known-item finding. At a high level, our associative browsing model is composed of information *items* and the *associations* between them. An item is a fundamental unit of our data model, which can be either the *documents* collected from many sources (e.g., desktop files, emails, calendar items), or the *concepts* (e.g., person names, events, etc.).

One distinctive part of our model is *concepts*, which denote entities and terms of interest to the user. They are similar to labels or facets in that they provide an abstract layer of organizing documents, yet they are distinctive in that they form a space of associations on their own.

Another feature of our data model is a rich link structure between items as seen in Figure 1. The associations between concepts and documents are created based on the occurrence of a concept within a document (e.g. an *email* and its *sender*). While this provides natural connections between documents and concepts, creating associations between documents and between concepts is harder, since there is no single method that gives both high coverage and precision.

Previous research solves this problem by asking the users to create associations manually, or by extracting the associations automatically between a limited set of items. In our work, we address this issue by ranking candidates for browsing using the combination of many similarity metrics. The top k items are then presented to the user as suggestions for browsing, and the system learns to improve suggestions based on the click feedback from the user. The details of ranking suggestions for browsing are provided in Section 4.

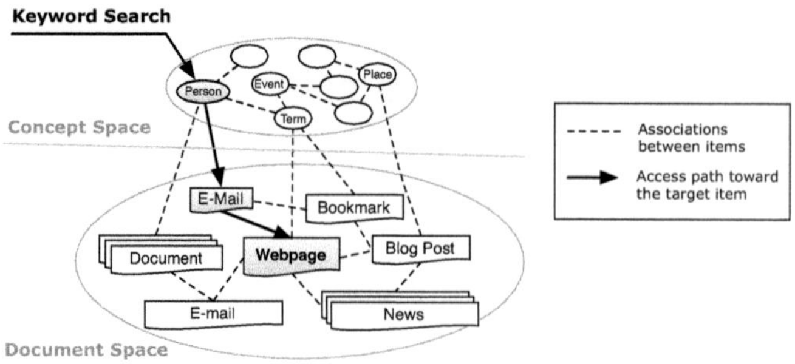

Figure 1: An illustration of how the suggested associative browsing model can be used for known-item finding.

3.1 Using the Model for Known-item Finding

There can be many use cases for this associative browsing model. For instance, such a rich network of association would be suitable for exploratory search [17] in personal information. Another common use case is known-item finding, where associative browsing can provide a back-up strategy for keyword search. In this paper, we focus on evaluating the model in the known-item finding scenario, since it is the most common task in personal information access and the well-defined structure allows us to use the evaluation methods introduced in Section 5.

Here, we provide an example on how associative browsing can be combined with keyword search for known-item finding. Imagine a user who is trying to find a webpage she has seen. Further assume that she cannot come up with a good keyword for search, yet she remembers the sender of related email. Using our model, as shown in Figure 1, the user can first use keyword search to find a relevant concept (person), and then browse into the target document (webpage) through another document (email) associated with both the concept and the target document. Here, dotted lines represent the associations between documents and concepts. Directed lines denote how a user can access the target webpage by using keyword search and associative browsing.

4. RANKING SUGGESTIONS FOR ASSOCIATIVE BROWSING

A core component of our model is the ranked list of related concepts or documents, generated by combining multiple measures of association. Another important task is finding appropriate weights for each feature.

In this section, we introduce a learning framework for creating and improving suggestions for browsing. As is the case of our data model, this learning framework is sufficiently general to be used beyond the domain of personal information. We first explain the features we used for representing the associations between two items, followed by the methods we employed to learn feature weights. Since many features are similarity measures, we will use the term *similarity* interchangeably with *association*.

4.1 Features

The following subsections describe the features we used to rank suggestions for browsing. Note that some of features are applicable only for the ranking of concepts or documents. If that is the case, then the text in brackets after the name of the feature will reflect that.

4.1.1 Term Vector Similarity

We can create a term vector for each item based on the text in the title or content fields. Since many concepts do not have any text in their content fields, we use the documents in which the concepts occur. The term vector similarity score of two items is just the cosine similarity of the corresponding term vectors.

4.1.2 Tag Overlap

Since concepts and documents have tags associated with them, we can consider two items with common tags to be similar. Given two vectors of tags, we compute the tag overlap score using the cosine similarity.

4.1.3 Temporal similarity

Intuitively, two items are deemed to be close to one another if the system indexes them or if the user creates them within a short period of time. Therefore, the closer the creation of two items is in time, the higher their temporal similarity score. We got the feature value by taking the reciprocal of the difference in creation time (in seconds).

4.1.4 String Similarity (concept)

We compute the string-level similarity by dividing the Levenshtein distance between the titles of two concepts by the square root of the product of the title lengths as follows:

4.1.5 Co-occurrence (concept)

This feature counts how many times each concept pair occurs together in the collection's documents. It captures the semantic distance between two concepts. This metric is available only for the calculation of concept similarity.

4.1.6 Occurrence (concept)

This feature counts the number of times a concept has occurred in the document collection in log scale. Although all the other features measure some kind of similarity, this metric is intended to capture the popularity of a concept, since such concepts are likely to be clicked by a user.

4.1.7 Topical Similarity (document)

This feature relies on the topic model Latent Dirichlet Allocation (LDA) [1]. LDA is a hierarchical Bayesian model, which allows us to model a text document as a mixture of topics. To measure the similarity between two documents, we calculate the cosine similarity between the distribution of topics associated with each document. This is similar to computing the similarity of term vectors, except that each document is mapped to a vector of latent topics instead of terms.

4.1.8 Path / Type Similarity (document)

Since each document has a URI, we can compute a similarity score between two documents based on the *path*. Specifically, we calculate the similarity between two path strings by counting the word-level overlaps from the beginning of the path, normalized by the number of words. Also, since each document has a *type* (e.g., email, pdf, etc.), we developed a binary feature based on whether two documents are of the same type.

4.1.9 Concept Overlap (document)

This feature is similar to tag overlap in that it considers two documents with common concepts to be similar. Unlike tags, since we can measure the strength of association between any two concepts, we can use it to measure the similarity between documents. In other words, even if two documents are linked to different sets of concepts, we can consider them to be similar if the concepts that each of them has are strongly associated.

4.2 Learning Feature Weights

One key step of our system is learning the weight of each feature. We examined two algorithms – iterative grid search and RankSVM [7]. The two learning methods used here have different characteristics. As far as the objective function is concerned, grid search simply finds the set of parameters that maximizes the target metric, whereas the goal of RankSVM is to predict the pairwise preference relation with highest accuracy. There is another aspect in which the two methods differ. While grid search uses each click as a relevance judgment, RankSVM interprets each click as a pairwise preference. We investigate the performance of the two learning methods in Section 6.1.

5. GAME-BASED EVALUATION METHOD

The method we employed for our evaluation is a game-based user study where we asked people to perform known-item finding tasks using both search and browsing capabilities. Using the data from the user study, we analyze the user's behavior in finding known-items, and evaluate the algorithms for ranking suggestions for browsing.

We call this a game because participants were competing against one another for how well they find known items. In addition to providing usage data in a controlled environment, this game-based evaluation method has advantages in terms of reusability—the whole collection and usage logs can be made public without privacy concerns.

Now we describe the design of the game-based user study. From the player's perspective, the purpose of the game is to find a target document by combining keyword search and associative browsing. We use the term 'session' to denote the process of finding each target document, and each game is composed of 10 sessions.

The sequence of interaction for each session, and the corresponding user interface is shown in Figures 2 and 3. As a starting point, the system shows two candidate documents to the users for a certain period of time, and then randomly chooses one target document. The user then combines keyword search and associative browsing to find the item. Each keyword query or click on the ranked list is considered a trial, and users are given 10 trials for each session. The score is determined by the rank position of each target document in the final rank list — the higher the position, the higher the score.

The rationale behind showing multiple target documents is to simulate the state of vague memory for the target document. For instance, if the user is shown an *email* and a *webpage* in a row and then asked to find it, he or she might get confused about the content of two documents. We assumed that this kind of confusion would be similar to the memory of a typical known-item searcher. We leave it as a future work to verify whether this kind of trick realistically simulates the state of memory for known-item finders.

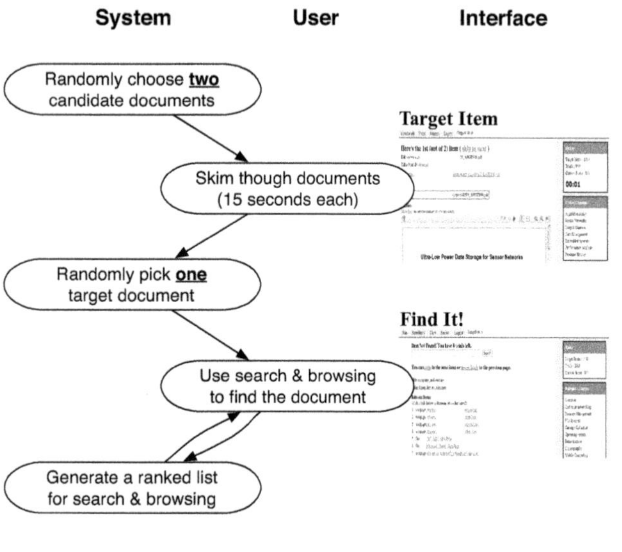

Figure 2: The sequence of interaction for each session during a game.

We ran two rounds of user studies with slightly different settings. In the first round, users were asked to find the target document using only keyword search of documents and associative browsing between documents. In other words, they did not have access to the concept space. In the second round, concepts were available for searching and browsing, thereby providing a full access to the model. We chose this two-stage design to evaluate the role of each system component and to help users gradually familiarize themselves with the system.

6. EVALUATION RESULTS

In this section we present the evaluation results. We used three document collections to evaluate the system. The first two collections are based on a preliminary study we did with two users, and we used the click data from these collections for training and evaluating ranking methods for browsing suggestions. We built the third collection, and used it to run the game-based user study. We describe the details of the collections below.

For creating the first and the second collections, two student volunteers in our department, Person 1 and Person 2, deployed the system in their machine and used it over the period of two weeks. They were encouraged to use the system for everyday information access tasks. The former contains 8,841 documents and 368 concepts and the latter contains 9,441 documents and 945 concepts. Both collections are mostly composed of emails, webpages they visited and desktop files.

As for concepts and tags, users created them as they use the system. No specific task was given to them, except that they were encouraged to use the system for their information access. At the end of data collection period, Person 1 clicked 145 times on the ranked list of concepts and 58

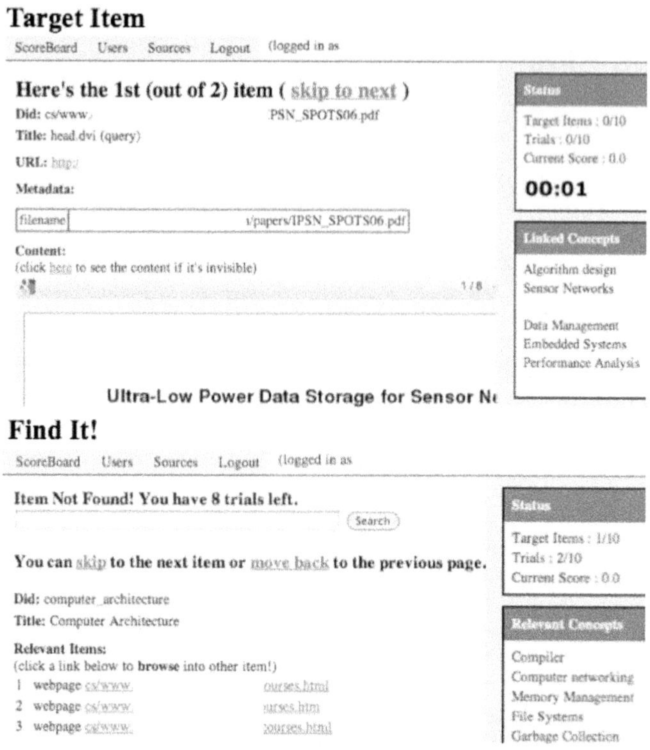

Figure 3: Game user interface. Top: a target document is being shown along with related concepts. Bottom: the user interface for finding a target document by searching and browsing.

Table 1: Number of documents, concepts, and clicks in the case of document similarity and concept similarity experiments for each of the collections we used.

	#Items		#Clicks	
	Document	Concept	Document	Concept
Person 1	8841	368	58	129
Person 2	9411	945	204	196
CS/Top1	7984	650	145	42
CS/Top5	"	"	309	220

times on the ranked list of documents. Person 2 had 196 clicks and 204 clicks on concepts and documents, respectively. We also found that only Person 2 actively created tags (56 unique tags created in total), whereas Person 1 created only a handful of tags.

The third dataset (called CS collection) contains public emails, webpages, publications and lectures crawled from the computer science department website of the authors. As for concepts, we selected the names and terms related to the computer science department and the domain of computer science in general — the name of people, lab and conferences. We also created 42 tags and assigned to each item, mostly based on its categorical information (e.g., 'student', 'professor' and 'staff' for person names).

The CS collection was created as a reasonable simulation of personal information, since we experimented with participants from our department, who had some knowledge of these documents and concepts. This collection is composed of 7,984 documents and 650 concepts.

We had 30 participants for the game-based user study within our department, who were mostly graduate students. They played 53 games in total, although some of the games were not completed (less than 10 sessions were recorded). Regarding click data, since most people contributed only a few clicks, we used the data from a user with the highest number of clicks (CS/Top1). To find the effectiveness of ranking when the click data pooled from many people, we also experimented with the aggregate data from the five users with most clicks (CS/Top5). The number of items and clicks are summarized in Table 1.

For learning methods, we used our own implementation of Iterative Grid Search and SVM^{rank} [7], which is a popular implementation of RankSVM. To facilitate the training of SVM^{rank}, each feature value was scaled to values that were approximately between 0 and 1. We also used 10-fold cross validation for training feature weights and evaluating the system.

In order to measure retrieval performance, we used the mean reciprocal rank (MRR), which is the average of the reciprocal of click positions. We also used clicks as relevance judgments, because the goal of the ranking is to show the items that the user is likely to click on the top. In other words, we wanted the ranking to adapt to user's subjective notion of relevance. In what follows, we first describe the results on the quality of the suggestions generated by the learning framework. We then present the analysis of users' behavior in known-item finding.

6.1 Evaluating Suggestions for Browsing

We present the evaluation results on the quality of browsing suggestions, with the goal of evaluating the effectiveness of click-based feature combination as well as individual feature. We compared the performance obtained when each feature was used by itself and when three combination methods were used—feature values with equal weights (*Uniform*), weights obtained with grid search (*Grid*) and with RankSVM (*SVM*), respectively. Note also that *title* and *content* are term vector similarity features, and the title and the content field was used for constructing term vectors, respectively.

Table 2 shows the concept ranking results for each feature and combination method. Regarding the single-feature results, different features turned out to be the most effective ones for each collection. Specifically, we found that *co-occurrence* is the most effective feature in Person 1's and Person 2's collection, while *occurrence* and *tag* was the best in CS/Top5 and CS/Top1, respectively. From this we can conclude that there exists a considerable variation in the value of each feature depending on the collection and the click behavior.

Among the combination methods, RankSVM performed the best for all collections except for Person 2's, where Grid Search performed the best. Another observation is that even the naive uniform combination of features produced better results than any of the ones obtained by using a feature by itself. In summary, different features perform the best for each collection, yet combination results are consistently better than singe-feature results. These results imply that feature combination is beneficial for ranking concepts for browsing.

As far as the document ranking task is concerned, Table 3 shows a slightly different trend. Term vector similarity using the *content* field is far more important than any other features in the case of Person 1 and Person 2. This makes intuitive sense because documents typically contain more textual content. This results in more accurate term vectors and subsequently better term vector similarity estimates. The best feature for the CS collection was the *topic* similarity.

In the case of combination methods, grid search performed better than any feature used by itself, while RankSVM was not as effective as it was in concept ranking. Although the performance margin between combination and single-features methods is small, given that it is hard to know which feature would work best a priori, we can conclude that feature combination should be used here as well.

For both concept and document ranking tasks, another observation is that using the click data from one user (CS/Top1) showed better performance than the one we obtained using the click data from the top five users. Since more click data usually leads to better performance, this unexpected drop in ranking quality seems to suggest that learning from the data of each user is important for improving performance. We investigate this point in the following subsection.

6.2 Analyzing How Users Find Known-items

Here we analyze user's behavior in known-item finding using the data from the game-based user study. As described in Section 5, we performed two rounds of game-style user studies in which participants were asked to find a set of randomly chosen target documents using the game interface. While each session had to be initiated by keyword search, participants had an option of browsing by clicking on a document in ranked list.

We first focus on the role of browsing in known-item finding by analyzing the portion of sessions where browsing was used, and how much of them was successful (target document found at Top 10). Table 4 presents the results. We have 290 sessions from Round 1 and 142 sessions from Round 2. The percentage of sessions during which users chose to browse as well as search is 14.5% (or 42 sessions) for Round 1 and 30.2% (or 43 sessions) for Round 2.

Although the percentage of sessions with browsing was not as high as was expected, since we envisioned the browsing as a complementary method to keyword search, what seems more important is the portion of success with browsing. Furthermore, the fact that we have more browsing in the second round seems to suggest that the concept space provided further motivation for browsing.

Table 4: The ratio of the sessions where users chose to use browsing, and the choice of browsing led to success.

Round	Total	Browsing used	Successful
1st	290	42 (14.5%)	15 (35.7%)
2nd	142	43 (30.2%)	32 (74.4%)

Let's look at the success ratio of the sessions with browsing. Out of the 42 sessions in Round 1 involving both searching and browsing, 35.7% (or 15 sessions) of them were successful, i.e., the user found the required document. For Round 2, this percentage is 74.4 (or 32 sessions). Given that users turn to browsing only when initial search is not successful, this success rate can be considered moderately high.

Also, the higher successful rate in the second round can be attributed to the presence of the concept layer. In fact, many users commented that they could find the target document using the concept as an intermediate step. Another

Table 2: Concept ranking performance (MRR) for the single-feature and combination methods. 10-fold cross-validation was used for grid search and RankSVM (SVM).

Collection	title	content	tag	time	string	cooc	occur	Uniform	Grid	SVM
Person 1	0.097	0.229	0.194	0.136	0.136	**0.241**	0.151	0.243	0.236	**0.277**
Person 2	0.037	0.350	0.403	0.221	0.310	**0.516**	0.234	0.506	**0.581**	0.509
CS/Top1	0.142	0.179	**0.289**	0.235	0.107	0.191	0.195	0.306	0.255	**0.433**
CS/Top5	0.184	0.127	0.170	0.155	0.100	0.158	**0.222**	0.293	0.301	**0.340**

Table 3: Document ranking performance (MRR) for the single-feature and combination methods. 10-fold cross-validation was used for grid search and RankSVM (SVM).

Collection	title	content	tag	time	topic	path	type	concept	Uniform	Grid	SVM
Person 1	0.392	**0.480**	0.063	0.296	0.229	0.274	0.183	0.264	0.404	**0.500**	0.494
Person 2	0.334	**0.564**	0.268	0.372	0.184	0.137	0.092	0.187	0.512	**0.592**	0.478
CS/Top1	0.074	0.097	0.065	0.114	**0.140**	0.098	0.070	**0.140**	0.109	**0.156**	0.098
CS/Top5	0.081	0.138	0.05	0.114	**0.151**	0.132	0.062	0.129	0.139	**0.150**	0.133

comment was that the process of browsing was helpful in suggesting good query words.

In summary, the analysis of user's behavior shows that users find associative browsing helpful for known-item finding, and the use of concept layer makes the interaction more effective.

7. CONCLUSIONS

In this paper, we evaluated an associative browsing model we proposed in the context of known-item finding. In ranking suggestions for browsing, we showed that the value of each association measure varies depending on the collection and on the user behavior, and that the weighted combination of individual features improves the quality of suggestions in all cases. he game-based user study also suggests that the model is useful for the known-item finding task, especially when concepts are used in addition to documents.

As far as future work is concerned, we plan to evaluate our model in a more realistic setting. Although we found initial evidence that associative browsing is helpful for the known-item finding task, a long-term study with actual users could further verify our claims. For learning methods, we are going to examine whether incorporating more features and click data leads to better performance.

8. ACKNOWLEDGEMENTS

This work was supported in part by the Center for Intelligent Information Retrieval and in part by the Central Intelligence Agency, the National Security Agency and National Science Foundation under NSF grant #IIS-0326249 . Any opinions, findings and conclusions or recommendations expressed in this material are those of the authors and do not necessarily reflect those of the sponsor.

9. REFERENCES

[1] D. M. Blei, A. Y. Ng, and M. I. Jordan. Latent dirichlet allocation. *J. Mach. Learn. Res.*, 3:993–1022, 2003.

[2] D. H. Chau, B. Myers, and A. Faulring. What to do when search fails: finding information by association. In *CHI '08*, pages 999–1008, New York, NY, USA, 2008. ACM.

[3] J. Chen, H. Guo, W. Wu, and W. Wang. imecho: an associative memory based desktop search system. In *CIKM '09*, pages 731–740, New York, NY, USA, 2009. ACM.

[4] W. B. Croft and R. H. Thompson. I^3R : A new approach to the design of document retrieval system. Technical report, Amherst, MA, USA, 1987.

[5] G. Davis and D. Thomson. Memory in context: Context in memory. England, 1988. Wiley.

[6] D. Elsweiler and I. Ruthven. Towards task-based personal information management evaluations. In *SIGIR '07*, pages 23–30, New York, NY, USA, 2007. ACM.

[7] T. Joachims. Optimizing search engines using clickthrough data. In *KDD '02*, pages 133–142, New York, NY, USA, 2002. ACM.

[8] C. Kaplan, J. Fenwick, and J. Chen. Adaptive hypertext navigation based on user goals and context. *User Modeling and User-Adapted Interaction*, 3(3):193–220, 1993.

[9] J. Kim, A. Bakalov, D. A. Smith, and W. B. Croft. Building a semantic representation for personal information. In *In Proceedings of CIKM'2010, Toronto, Ontario, Canada*, 2010.

[10] J. Kim and W. B. Croft. Ranking using multiple document types in desktop search. In *In Proceedings of SIGIR '10*, pages 50–57, New York, NY, USA, 2010. ACM.

[11] D. Lucarella. A model for hypertext-based information retrieval. pages 81–94, 1992.

[12] H. Ma, R. Chandrasekar, C. Quirk, and A. Gupta. Improving search engines using human computation games. In *CIKM*, pages 275–284, 2009.

[13] M. D. Smucker and J. Allan. Find-similar: similarity browsing as a search tool. In *SIGIR '06*, pages 461–468, New York, NY, USA, 2006. ACM.

[14] J. Teevan, C. Alvarado, M. S. Ackerman, and D. R. Karger. The perfect search engine is not enough: a study of orienteering behavior in directed search. In *CHI '04*, pages 415–422, New York, NY, USA, 2004. ACM.

[15] E. Tulving and D. Thomson. Encoding specificity and retrieval processes in episodic memory. In *Psychological Review*, pages 352–373, England, 1973.

[16] L. von Ahn and L. Dabbish. Designing games with a purpose. *Commun. ACM*, 51(8):58–67, 2008.

[17] R. W. White and R. A. Roth. *Exploratory Search: Beyond the Query-Response Paradigm.* Morgan & Claypool, 2009.

Semi-Supervised SVMs for Classification with Unknown Class Proportions and a Small Labeled Dataset

S Sathiya Keerthi
Yahoo! Labs
Santa Clara, California, U.S.A
selvarak@yahoo-inc.com

Bigyan Bhar
Indian Institute of Science
Bangalore, India
bigyan@csa.iisc.ernet.in

S Sundararajan
Yahoo! Labs
Bangalore, India
ssrajan@yahoo-inc.com

Shirish Shevade
Indian Institute of Science
Bangalore, India
shirish@csa.iisc.ernet.in

ABSTRACT

In the design of practical web page classification systems one often encounters a situation in which the labeled training set is created by choosing some examples from each class; but, the class proportions in this set are not the same as those in the test distribution to which the classifier will be actually applied. The problem is made worse when the amount of training data is also small. In this paper we explore and adapt binary SVM methods that make use of unlabeled data from the test distribution, viz., Transductive SVMs (TSVMs) and expectation regularization/constraint (ER/EC) methods to deal with this situation. We empirically show that when the labeled training data is small, TSVM designed using the class ratio tuned by minimizing the loss on the labeled set yields the best performance; its performance is good even when the deviation between the class ratios of the labeled training set and the test set is quite large. When the labeled training data is sufficiently large, an unsupervised Gaussian mixture model can be used to get a very good estimate of the class ratio in the test set; also, when this estimate is used, both TSVM and EC/ER give their best possible performance, with TSVM coming out superior. The ideas in the paper can be easily extended to multi-class SVMs and MaxEnt models.

Categories and Subject Descriptors: I.5.2 [Pattern Recognition] Design Methodology-Classifier design and evaluation

General Terms: Algorithms, Experimentation

Keywords: Transductive and Semi-supervised learning, Classification, Support Vector Machines

1. INTRODUCTION

The problem of classifying web pages into a given set of classes arises frequently in web applications. Linear classifiers such as support vector machines (SVMs) and maximum entropy (MaxEnt) models employing a rich feature representation (e.g., bag-of-words) are used successfully for this purpose. When labeling is expensive one is forced to work with a small set of labeled examples for training. In such cases a linear classifier trained using only labeled data does not give a good performance. Performance can be significantly boosted by employing semi-supervised methods that make effective use of unlabeled data, which is usually available in plenty. The transductive support vector machine (TSVM) [10] and MaxEnt models trained with expectation regularization (ER) [12] are good examples of such methods. Such semi-supervised methods assume the knowledge of auxiliary information about the underlying data such as class proportions.

The performance of semi-supervised methods such as ER and TSVM are sensitive to the class proportion values used to find their solution; see section 4.2 for a detailed empirical analysis. In many practical situations, class proportions are unknown. Often it also happens that the class proportions in the labeled training set are different from those in the actual distribution to which the classifier will be applied. A few examples of such scenarios are as follows.

- There are tens of thousands of city aggregator sites covering categories such as dining, attractions, night life etc. The content and vocabulary across these sites are very similar, but in each site the proportion of examples belonging to various classes can be quite different. So, building a separate classifier for each site is appropriate. Let us say that we are given a few global examples of dining and non-dining pages. The aim is to develop a classifier for each site to separate dining pages from others making use of unlabeled web pages in that site.

- Frequently, in classifier design, one would like to reuse labeled data from a previous run to develop a classifier for a new distribution (e.g., a new stream of news pages); the old labeled set is still good as the union of sets of samples from the individual classes, but class proportions are different.

- A user shows a few relevant and irrelevant example

CIKM'11, October 24–28, 2011, Glasgow, Scotland, UK.

web pages and asks for finding relevant pages from a fresh collection of web pages.

The main aim of this paper is to address the problem of mismatched class proportions mentioned above.

Let x denote a generic example web page and c denote a class. From a probabilistic viewpoint our problem consists of dealing with a situation in which: (i) $p(x|c)$ is same in the labeled data and the actual data of interest for all c; but, (ii) $\{p(c)\}$ is very different in the two sets. Coupled with labeled data being small the problem becomes difficult.

Note that, even if labeled data is not small, extension of methods such as TSVM and ER to deal with mismatched class proportions requires careful thought because labeled data does not have information on actual class proportions and unlabeled data has to be suitably brought in to estimate them. There have been some previous efforts to address this problem for TSVMs [7, 14]. But these methods have some basic issues: they make adhoc changes to the training process in an active self-learning mode and are not cleanly tied to a well-defined problem formulation; they significantly deviate from the TSVM formulation and hence perform quite worse than TSVMs when labeled data and the actual distribution are indeed well matched in terms of class proportions; and, they have not been demonstrated in difficult situations involving large distortions in class proportions.

In this paper we empirically analyze various issues related to the problem of mismatched class proportions, propose ways of estimating actual class proportions and demonstrate their usefulness. We only take up binary classification problems in this paper; but the ideas are quite general and they have the potential for extension to multi-class settings. Since binary classification involves only two classes (positive and negative), class proportion can be represented using a single quantity f, the fraction of positive examples.

1.1 Contributions of the paper

In a nutshell following are our main contributions, listed by order of treatment in the paper.

1. The ER method is introduced in the context of SVMs. In addition we introduce two related methods based on expectation constraints (EC) and simple threshold adjustment (SVMTh).

2. We empirically analyze all the methods (TSVM, ER, EC and SVMTh) in terms of their learning curves and their sensitivity to incorrect specification of f.

3. If labeled data has distorted class proportion (even severe), but the actual f happens to be known, we empirically show that the methods are pretty much unaffected.

4. To handle the crucial case in which the actual f is unknown we propose and empirically analyze two methods for estimating the actual f. The first estimation method is based on finding the f having the least labeled loss along a trajectory of solutions given by a method as f is varied. The second estimation method is based on fitting a mixture of two Gaussians to the output of the SVM trained using only labeled data. The first estimation method works well with TSVM and it is suited for the situation where labeled data is small while the second estimation method is powerful and works well with all semi-supervised methods when labeled data is large. Overall, TSVM combined with the two estimation methods (suitably switched depending on the amount of labeled data available) is the top performing method.

2. DESCRIPTION OF METHODS

In this section we describe all the methods that will be analyzed in this paper. These methods are meant for binary classification. Labeled data consists of l examples $\{x_i, y_i\}_{i=1}^{l}$ where the input patterns $x_i \in R^d$ are feature vectors representing web pages and the labels $y_i \in \{+1, -1\}$. Semi-supervised/transductive methods make use of unlabeled examples in addition; unlabeled data consists of u examples $\{x_i\}_{i=l+1}^{l+u}$. All the methods develop a linear classification function $w^T x$ with $\{x : w^T x > 0\}$ denoting the positive class region. Web page classification problems involve a large feature space (d is large); the input patterns are sparse, i.e., the fraction of non-zero elements in one x_i is small. Unlabeled data is always a random sample picked from the actual distribution to which the classifier will be applied; labeled data, on the other hand, may have a class proportion which is different from that in the actual distribution.

2.1 Supervised SVMs

Supervised SVMs make use of labeled data and optimize the regularized large margin loss function:

$$\min_{w} T_{\text{sup}} = \frac{\lambda}{2}\|w\|^2 + \frac{1}{l}\sum_{i=1}^{l} L(y_i, o_i) \qquad (1)$$

where $o_i = w^T x_i$. An example of the large margin loss function is the squared hinge loss $L(y, o) = \max(0, 1 - yo)^2$. Alternatively one can use the hinge loss: $L(y, o) = max(0, 1 - yo)$. All the experiments in this paper are done with the squared hinge loss. Irrespective of which loss is used there exist very efficient numerical methods [11, 13] for solving (1); the running time of these methods is linear in the number of examples.[1] On web page and text classification tasks the performance of the SVM classifier is quite steady over a large range of values of the regularization coefficient, λ. In all the experiments of the paper we use $\lambda = 1$.

2.2 Transductive SVMs

Transductive/Semi-Supervised SVMs (TSVMs) make effective use of unlabeled data to enhance the performance of SVMs. These methods perform very well on web page and text classification problems. Even with just a few labeled examples they can combine this labeled data with a large unlabeled set to attain a performance equal to that of a supervised SVM designed using a large labeled set. Through unlabeled examples many features which are even completely absent in the labeled set end up getting very good weights.

TSVMs are based on the *cluster (or, low density separation) assumption* which states that the decision boundary should not cross high density regions, but instead lie in low density regions. Joachims [10] gave the first effective TSVM formulation. A key ingredient of this formulation is that it

[1]Good software for supervised and transductive SVMs can be found in `http://svmlight.joachims.org/` and `http://vikas.sindhwani.org/svmlin.html`.

assumes f, the fraction of positive examples in the actual distribution is known and also the corresponding constraint is enforced in the formulation.[2] Joachims [10] solved the following problem in which, apart from w, the set of labels of unlabeled examples, $\{y_i\}_{i>l}$ are also variables:

$$\min_{w,\{y_i\}_{i>l}} T_{\text{sup}} + \frac{1}{u}\sum_{i>l} L(y_i, o_i) \quad s.t. \quad \frac{1}{u}\sum_{i>l}[y_i == 1] = f \tag{2}$$

where $[z]$ is 1 if z is true and 0 otherwise. Unlike (1), (2) is a not a convex minimization problem. In general, it is hard to solve. It has been pointed out [5] that the solution of (2) can get stuck in poor local minima. *Fortunately, this is not the case in linear classification problems involving large feature space, such as web page and text classification.* TSVMs are routinely used to solve applied problems [4, 3]. Alternative optimization iterations (fix w and optimize $\{y_i\}_{i>l}$, then fix $\{y_i\}_{i>l}$ and optimize w) are usually used to solve (2).

There also exist variations of the TSVM algorithm. For example the discrete variables in $\{y_i\}_{i>l}$ can be eliminated from (2) to get the following equivalent problem:

$$\min_{w} T_{\text{sup}} + \frac{1}{u}\sum_{i>l} \min\{L(1, o_i), L(-1, o_i)\} \; s.t. \; \frac{1}{u}\sum_{i>l}[o_i > 0] = f \tag{3}$$

Sigmoid smoothing or other methods can be applied to write $[o_i > 0]$ in a differentiable form. Then the solution can be approached via gradient based optimization of w. See [6, 13, 5] for methods of this kind. Most often this method yields a performance that is slightly better than (2).

2.3 Expectation Methods

Mann and McCallum [12] proposed the *Expectation Regularization (ER)* method in the context of MaxEnt models. The idea is to use expectation terms related to some domain knowledge to influence the training process. This can be easily done with SVM models too, like we do here. In our case the domain knowledge of interest is the fact that the fraction of positively classified examples in unlabeled data equals f. This fraction constraint can be used to influence the solution by including an additional regularization term in the objective function:

$$\min_{w} T_{\text{sup}} + \frac{\rho}{2}\left(\frac{1}{u}\sum_{i>l}[o_i > 0] - f\right)^2 \tag{4}$$

As mentioned earlier with respect to (3), sigmoid smoothing can be used to make the expectation regularization term to be differentiable so that gradient based numerical optimization techniques can be employed. In our implementation of ER we use $\rho = 50$ as the default value. Later we will also study the effect of varying ρ.

Note that in (4) the expectation constraint on the fraction of positive examples is only approximately enforced since it is only included as a regularizer term. If the domain knowledge says that the fraction constraint holds certainly then it may be better to force the constraint rather than adding a regularizer. This leads to a new method which we call as the *Expectation Constraints (EC)* method. The optimization problem to be solved is:

$$\min_{w} T_{\text{sup}} \quad s.t. \quad \frac{1}{u}\sum_{i>l}[o_i > 0] = f \tag{5}$$

Again, sigmoid smoothing can be used to write the fraction constraint function in a differentiable form. A suitable numerical method that can deal with equality constraints can be used to solve for w. In our implementation we use the Augmented Lagrangian method [1].

Let us introduce another expectation based baseline method that has been ignored in the literature. The method consists of taking the supervised SVM solution w (i.e., solution of (1)) and adding a threshold θ to the scoring function so that the fraction of unlabeled examples that satisfy $w^T x + \theta > 0$ equals f. The new classifier boundary is defined by $w^T x + \theta = 0$. We will refer to this method as SVMTh.

2.4 Relations between the methods

It is easy to see that ER and EC methods are closely related. In particular, when the parameter ρ in (4) is made very large then ER and EC are expected to show very similar behavior. SVMTh is quite different from EC although both methods enforce the fraction constraint; while EC tries to balance the minimization of T_{sup} with the fraction constraint, SVMTh simply adjusts the threshold to satisfy the fraction constraint without worrying about its effect on T_{sup}. If we compare (3) and (5) we see that TSVM has an extra term (loss on unlabeled data). This term turns out to be important as it helps TSVM to place the classifier boundary more precisely by making it pass through low density regions of unlabeled data; as we will see later the performance improvement due to it is large especially when the size of labeled data is small.

For MaxEnt models, Grandvalet and Bengio [9] suggested including an unlabeled loss term called *entropy regularization* that is similar in spirit to the unlabeled loss term in (3). However, their formulation does not include the fraction constraint. Mann and McCallum [12] conduct experiments to clearly point out the fact that without this constraint this method does not do well. They also show that, if the constraint is included (even as a regularizer term) then the performance is greatly enhanced.

3. DATASETS AND NOTATIONS

All the empirical analyses in this paper are done using the following five text classification datasets: `gcat`, `ccat`, `aut-avn`, `real-sim` and `earn`. The first four datasets are same as the ones used in [13]; `earn` is a binary dataset created from the *Reuters-21578* dataset[3] by taking examples in the *earn* class as positive and the remaining examples as negative. Key properties of the datasets are given in Table 1.

Each dataset is divided into three parts: labeled data, unlabeled data and test data. Unlabeled data and test data have the same class proportion; let f^{actual} denote the fraction of positive examples in test/unlabeled data. Labeled data can have a different class proportion depending on the experiment; note that the main aim of the paper is to find ways of dealing with a mismatch in class proportion between labeled data and the actual distribution. Let f^{lab} denote the fraction of positive examples in labeled data.

[2]We will refer to the constraint as the *fraction constraint*. Also, when applied in a discrete setting (e.g., the fraction constraint in (2)) it is assumed that appropriate rounding of f is allowed.

[3]`http://www.daviddlewis.com/resources/testcollections/reuters21578/`

Table 1: Properties of datasets. n : number of examples, d : data dimensionality, f^{actual} : positive class ratio.

Dataset	n	d	f^{actual}
gcat	23149	47236	0.30
ccat	23149	47236	0.46
aut-avn	71175	20707	0.65
real-sim	72309	20958	0.31
earn	9603	10783	0.30

Always f^{actual} is set to the fraction of positive examples in the original, full dataset. Given f^{lab} and the number of labeled examples, n^{lab}, we create a random division of the full dataset into test, labeled and unlabeled data as follows. First, 50% of the examples are randomly chosen in a class-stratified fashion and kept as testing data. Let $\mathcal{R}$ denote the set of remaining examples. We form labeled data by choosing $\lceil n^{lab} f^{lab} \rceil$ positive examples from $\mathcal{R}$ and $n^{lab} - \lceil n^{lab} f^{lab} \rceil$ negative examples from $\mathcal{R}$. Of the remaining examples, unlabeled data is randomly chosen to be the largest set obeying f^{actual}. Since the dataset sizes are large and n^{lab} is small, the size of unlabeled data is large and it is several times larger than n^{lab}.

Performance of the methods will be measured in terms of F score, which is the harmonic mean of precision and recall of the positive class.

To ease the understanding we use consistent notations in all the figures. The following colors will be used to denote the various methods:

- Black dotted: *LSVM* - SVM trained with labeled examples only;
- Red dotted: *FullSVM* - SVM trained using all unlabeled examples taking their labels as known;
- Blue: *TSVM* - Transductive SVM;
- Black: *SVMTh* - LSVM with threshold adjustment based on f;
- Green: *ER* - Expectation Regularization; and,
- Red: *EC* - Expectation Constraints.

In most figures f or f^{lab} is the horizontal axis. In such figures f^{actual} is shown as a vertical dotted line. In most figures the plots are averages over four random splits of a dataset into labeled, unlabeled and test data. Exceptions are Figures 3, 8, 9, and 10 where just one random split is used. In the figures *LabSize* and *LabFrac* denote, respectively, the size of labeled data, n^{lab} and the fraction of positive examples in labeled data, f^{lab}.

4. BASIC EXPERIMENTS

Before we go on to deal with differences in class proportions in labeled data and unlabeled/test data it is useful to give some basic experimental results that help understand the methods.

4.1 Learning Curves

Figure 1 shows the learning curves (variations of performance with n^{lab}) for various methods on four datasets. All methods use the value $f = f^{actual}$. TSVM gives a much

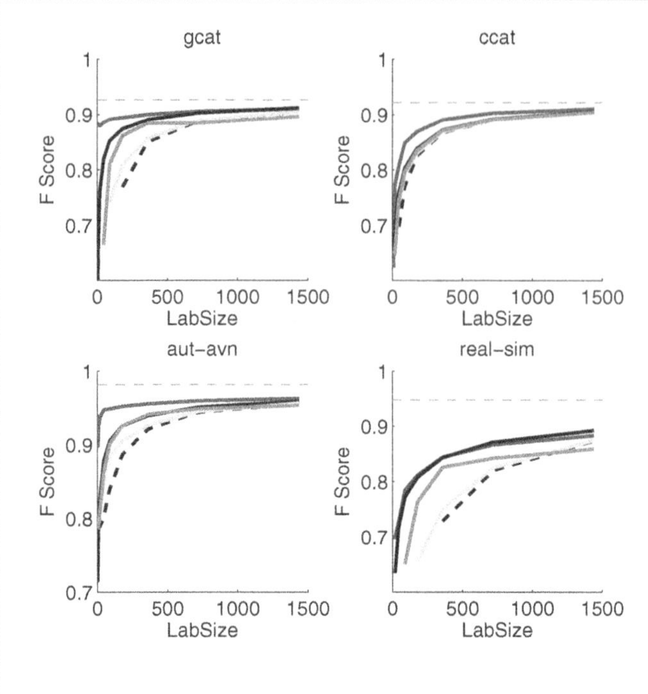

Figure 1: Learning curves for various datasets. All methods use $f = f^{actual}$.

stronger performance than other methods at small values of n^{lab}. Even at higher values of n^{lab} it is better than or competitive with others. Whenever TSVM does significantly better than SVMTh it is a clear indication of the important role played by the unlabeled loss term in (2). The magnitude of performance improvement given by TSVM over others depends on the dataset. On `gcat` and `aut-avn` TSVM is very much superior; on `ccat` it is quite better than others; and, on `real-sim` its performance matches that of SVMTh. After TSVM, SVMTh is the next best performer, followed by EC, ER and LSVM, in that order.

4.2 Sensitivity Analysis

Since our aim is to deal with situations in which f^{actual} is unknown, it is useful to understand how the performance of each method is affected when f (the value of positive class fraction used in (1)-(5)) is changed away from f^{actual}. Figure 2 describes this sensitivity for $n^{lab} = 90$ and $n^{lab} = 1440$. We chose these n^{lab} values as they represent the rising and stable parts of the learning curves for most (method, dataset) combinations.

Let us first make some observations for $n^{lab} = 90$. All methods suffer when f is too much lower/higher than f^{actual}. If f is sufficiently far from f^{actual} then the performance can degrade to be even worse than that of LSVM. The fall in performance on the lower side is sharper since recall is badly affected when f is decreased from f^{actual} and this has an adverse effect on the F score.

TSVM and SVMTh attain their peak performance at f values that are close to f^{actual}. On the other hand, ER and EC attain their best performance at f values that are quite shifted away from f^{actual}. Consistently, this shifting away from f^{actual} is such that the fraction of the minority class is larger than its actual value in the unlabeled/test distribu-

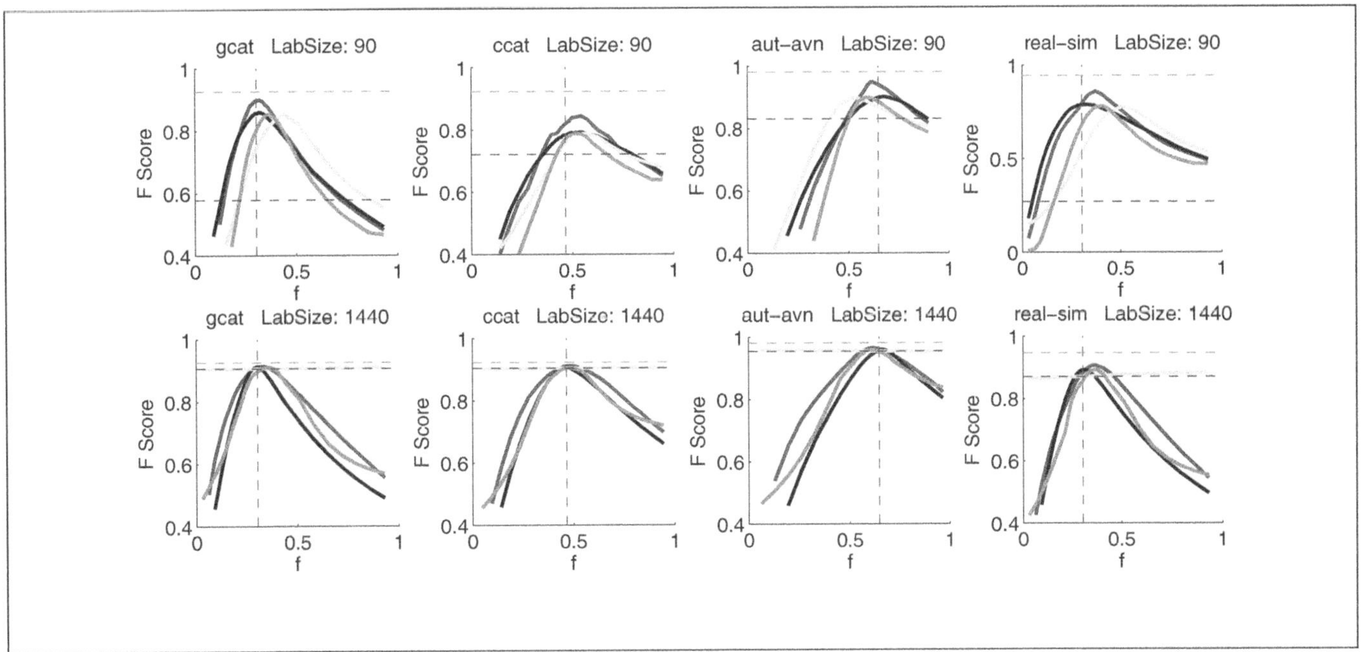

Figure 2: Sensitivity of methods with respect to f. The top row is for $n^{lab} = 90$ and the bottom row is for $n^{lab} = 1440$.

tion; in the top row of Figure 2 note the left shift of the peak for **aut-avn** and right shifts for all other datasets. This is due to two properties associated with LSVM, of which EC and ER are modifications. First, when n^{lab} is small the direction of the LSVM classifier makes a large angle with that of the ideal SVM classifier built using a large labeled training set. So the LSVM classifier boundary cuts through dense regions of the test set. Second, this cutting is more severe on the minority class examples due to lesser representation.[4] Thus, LSVM (which optimizes T_{sup}) ends up choosing a classifier boundary placement in which many test examples of the minority class are pushed to the wrong side. See the left bottom plot of Figure 8 (which comes later in the paper) to confirm this for the **gcat** dataset. Therefore, to pull the classifier towards satisfying the f^{actual} fraction and hence do well on F score, EC and ER methods need to use a value f (see (4) and (5)) that is higher (lower) than f^{actual} when the minority class is the positive (negative) class. The f value that is needed by ER to get the best F score on the test set is farther from f^{actual} than the f value needed for EC because ER only loosely enforces the f constraint. SVMTh behaves differently because it doesn't try to balance T_{sup} optimization and the fraction constraint; it simply enforces the fraction constraint in post-processing without worrying about what happens to T_{sup} in that step.

When n^{lab} is large the behavior is different. The bottom row of Figure 2 gives sensitivity for LabSize=1440. LSVM gives a very good performance since labeled data set is sufficiently large. The performance of ER is close to that of LSVM (see the green continuous and black dotted lines in the bottom row of Figure 2) because the ρ value (50) used in (4) is not strong enough to exert the fraction constraint. TSVM, SVMTh and EC suffer when f is moved well away from f^{actual} because they enforce the fraction constraint.

The observations made above imply that, for EC and ER it is a good idea to employ an f value that is different from f^{actual}, when n^{lab} is small. This observation is missing in previous works on ER [12]. If the class proportions in labeled, unlabeled, and test data are all matching and n^{lab} is not too small, it is then a good idea to use cross validation to choose f to optimize performance. If n^{lab} is not large the Leave-One-Out method can be used for cross validation. However we do not go ahead and demonstrate this in this paper since the main focus of the paper is to suggest ways of handling a mismatch between class proportions in labeled data and the actual distribution of interest.

Figure 3 gives the sensitivity plots for the **earn** dataset. The experimental setup is close to that used by Zhang and Oles [15] who used the setup to point out (wrongly) that TSVM does not work well. Zhang and Oles [15] possibly optimized the TSVM objective function in (2) without the fraction constraint. Figure 3 explains what can go wrong if that is done. From the right side plot of Figure 3 it is clear that the least value of the objective function occurs at $f = 0$ where the performance is very poor. This clearly shows the important role played by the fraction constraint in TSVM. Recall a similar comment that we made earlier at the end of subsection 2.4, with respect to MaxEnt models and entropy regularization.

5. DISTORTION IN CLASS PROPORTION

The results of section 4 concern the case in which labeled data and test/unlabeled data have the same class proportion. We now consider situations in which the class proportions in the two sets are different. Sometimes it happens that even though there is a difference in those class proportions,

[4]This can be explained as follows. Take the case where the positive class is the minority class. Since the positive class has a smaller number of loss terms (see (1)) the classifier boundary of LSVM is placed closer to the labeled examples of the positive class in order to reduce the total loss on the labeled examples of the negative class. Therefore the fraction of examples classified by LSVM as positive is less than f^{actual}.

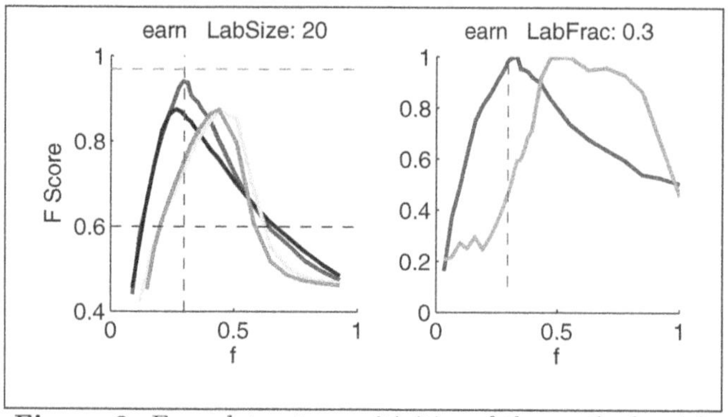

Figure 3: Earn dataset: sensitivities of the methods with respect to f with just 20 labeled examples. The left plot shows performance of various methods. The right plot shows TSVM performance (blue) and TSVM objective function in equation (2) (magenta) (both are normalized to max value of 1 to show them on the same plot). When f^{actual} is known TSVM gives an F score of 0.93.

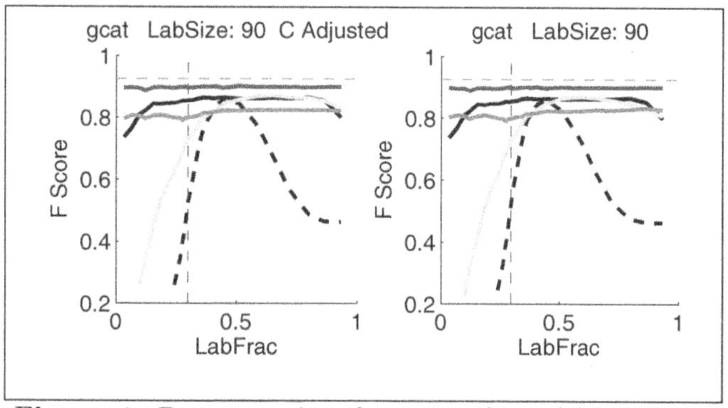

Figure 4: Demonstration that cost adjusted labeled loss does not change performance significantly.

f^{actual} may actually be known. Such knowledge helps the methods to achieve a good performance. In subsection 5.1 we take up this case. In subsection 5.2 we deal with the more difficult case in which f^{actual} is unknown.

5.1 Case 1: f^{actual} is Known

Since we know f^{actual} as well as the number of positive and negative labeled examples in the labeled set, it is appropriate to modify the SVM objective function T_{sup} so that the labeled loss term can be viewed as if it is the mean loss of labeled data picked (with replacement) from the actual distribution of interest. To do this we change T_{sup} to $T_{\text{sup}}^{\text{Adj}}$ by introducing γ, a relative weighting parameter for positive labeled examples. $T_{\text{sup}}^{\text{Adj}}$ is given by

$$T_{\text{sup}}^{\text{Adj}} = \frac{\lambda}{2}\|w\|^2 + \frac{1}{N}(\gamma \sum_{1\le i\le l, y_i=1} L(y_i, o_i) + \sum_{1\le i\le l, y_i=-1} L(y_i, o_i)) \tag{6}$$

where γ is chosen so that $\gamma\frac{f^{lab}}{(1-f^{lab})} = \frac{f^{actual}}{1-f^{actual}}$, $f^{lab} = \frac{n_p}{n_p+n_n}$, n_p and n_n are the number of positive and negative examples in labeled data, and $N = n_p\gamma + n_n$ is the normalizer chosen to make sure that the labeled loss term is the mean loss. Note that when $f^{lab} < f^{actual}$, γ is bigger than 1, and so the weight on the positive labeled examples is increased. When $f^{lab} > f^{actual}$, γ is smaller than 1. All

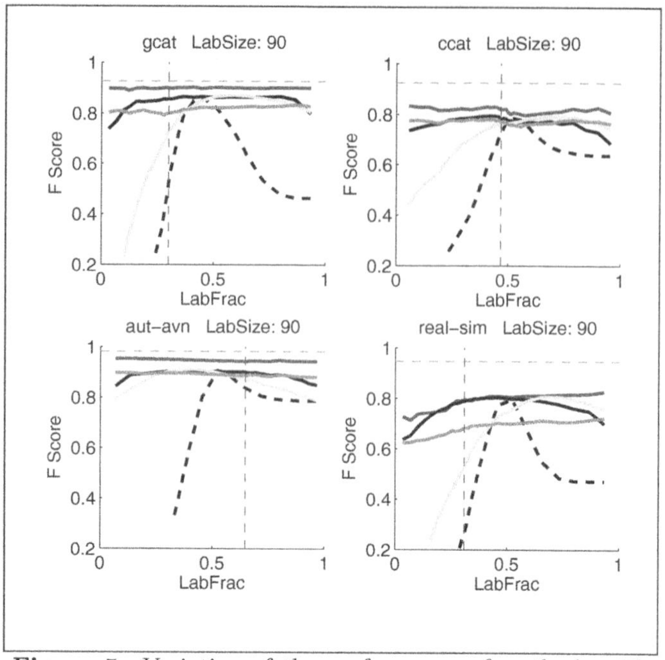

Figure 5: Variation of the performance of methods with f^{lab} (LabelFrac) when f^{actual} is known and the methods use $f = f^{actual}$.

the methods can be appropriately modified to use $T_{\text{sup}}^{\text{Adj}}$ instead of T_{sup}. However, we found that the performance of the methods are little affected when $T_{\text{sup}}^{\text{Adj}}$ is used instead of T_{sup}. Figure 4 compares the performance for one dataset, gcat. Similar behavior is seen on other datasets.

Figure 5 compares all methods on four datasets when $f = f^{actual}$ is used by the methods and f^{lab} is varied over a range of values from 0 to 1. Interestingly, TSVM, SVMTh and EC are only mildly affected by changes in f^{lab}. This is very much due to f^{actual} being known and used well by the methods via the fraction constraint with $f = f^{actual}$. On the other hand LSVM is badly affected when f^{lab} is moved away from f^{actual}. ER suffers when $f^{lab} < f^{actual}$. The penalty weight, ρ used in (4) plays a key role in ER. Figure 6 shows the performance variation for a range of ρ values. When ρ is small the performance of ER is close to that of LSVM. For large ρ its performance is close to that of EC. Both these observations are along expected lines. For different values of f^{lab} the optimal ρ is different.

5.2 Case 2: f^{actual} is Unknown

We propose and explore some methods for estimating f^{actual} in the presence of large variations in f^{lab}. Note that, even when labeled data is large, it cannot be used alone to get an estimate of f^{actual} since the class proportion in that set are distorted. We explore three methods for estimating f^{actual}. Let us refer to an estimate of f^{actual} as f_{est}^{actual}.

Estimation Method 1. Simply take f_{est}^{actual} to be the fraction of positive examples in labeled data. This is just a baseline method.

The next two methods make use of unlabeled data together with labeled data.

Estimation Method 2. Given labeled data we can solve (1) and obtain the LSVM solution w. From the good performance of SVMTh over a large range of f^{lab} values in Figure

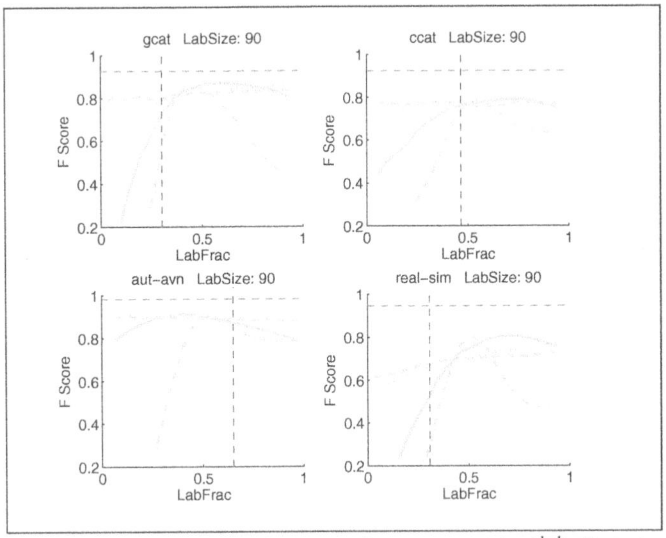

Figure 6: Variation of ER performance with f^{lab} (LabelFrac) for various ρ values. Dashdot: $\rho = 5$ (gives performance close to LSVM); Continuous: $\rho = 50$ (same as in Figure 5); Dotted: $\rho = 500$; Dashed: $\rho = 5000$. ER with $\rho \geq 500$ yields a performance close to that of EC.

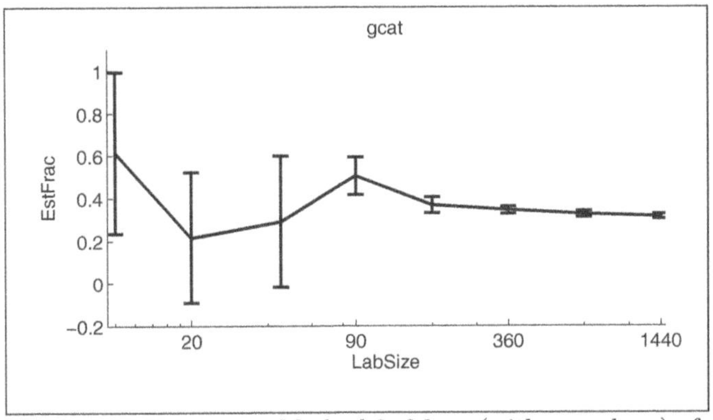

Figure 7: Estimation Method 2. Mean (with error bars) of f_{est}^{actual} versus n^{lab} for **gcat**. $f^{actual} = 0.3011$ for **gcat**.

5 we know that the classifier direction corresponding to w is good. It is appropriate to model the classifier scoring function, $o = w^T x$ applied on unlabeled data, $\{o_i = w^T x_i\}_{i>l}$ as a mixture of two Gaussians:

$$p(o_i) = \beta_1 g(o_i; \mu_1, \sigma_1) + \beta_2 g(o_i; \mu_2, \sigma_2) \quad (7)$$

where $g(\cdot; \mu_k, \sigma_k)$ is the univariate Gaussian density function with mean μ_k and standard deviation σ_k, and β_1, β_2 are (non-negative) mixing proportion values satisfying $\beta_1 + \beta_2 = 1$. By fitting this model to the data $\{o_i\}_{i>l}$ to maximize likelihood we can get the parameter values β_1, β_2, μ_1, μ_2, σ_1 and σ_2. The Gaussian with the larger μ_k represents the positive class; so, the corresponding β_k can be taken as f_{est}^{actual}, an estimate of the positive class fraction.

Figure 8 helps us understand the usefulness of this method. When the number of labeled examples is small, w, the solution of (1), makes a large angle with $w^\star$, the solution associated with the ideal SVM classifier built using a large labeled training set having the actual class proportion; so the $\{o_i = w^T x_i\}_{i>l}$ distribution is not a clean mixture of two Gaussians, and the estimate f_{est}^{actual} is also poor. On

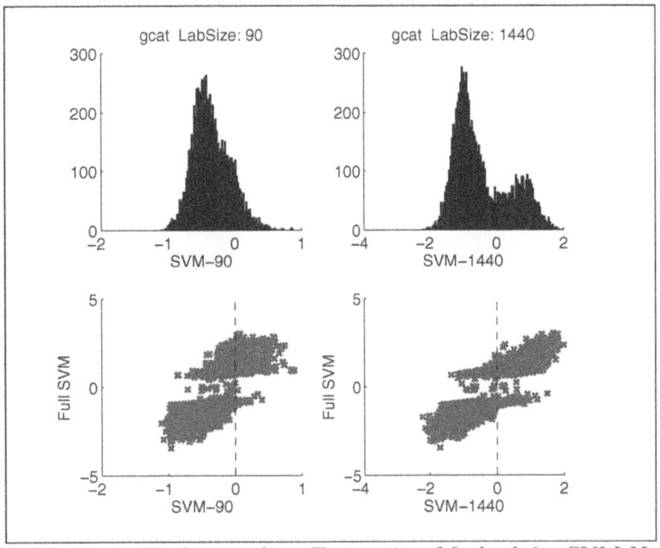

Figure 8: Understanding Estimation Method 2. SVM-N denotes LSVM output for N labeled examples and FullSVM is output of SVM corresponding to a very large labeled set.

the other hand, when the number of labeled examples is large (closer to the higher side of the learning curve) this estimation method performs much better.

Figure 7 plots the mean (with error bars) of f_{est}^{actual} (computed using 10 random splits of **gcat**) as n^{lab} is varied. Such a plot can help one decide when this estimation method is useful.

Estimation Method 3. In this method we explore to see if some property associated with the solution of a method can be used to find f_{est}^{actual}. Let us take TSVM. Figure 9 gives, for **gcat** and **ccat**, the variation of the TSVM objective function (see (2)), the Labeled Loss (the second term of T_{sup} in (1)), as well as the F score with respect to f used in (2). The behavior in other datasets is similar. Clearly the TSVM objective function is not useful for tuning f. Gärtner et al [8] suggest to minimize the TSVM objective function to tune class proportions; but Figure 9 clearly points out that it is not the right thing to do. The plots also show the goodness of minimizing the Labeled Loss as a way of obtaining f_{est}^{actual}.[5] A rough explanation for this goodness is as follows. Consider (2), the optimization problem associated with TSVM. End f values (near 0 and 1) put heavy pressure on containing all examples on one side of the classifier boundary. With such pressure Labeled Loss becomes large for such f values. Near $f = f^{actual}$ minimizing Labeled Loss, Unlabeled Loss and satisfying the fraction constraint are all consistent, so Labeled Loss achieves small values there.

We also tried the same estimation method (i.e., minimize labeled loss along the trajectory of solutions defined by varying f) on the expectation methods. But it did not work well. Figure 10 gives, for EC and **gcat** and **ccat**, the variation of labeled loss as well as the F score as a function of f. The minimizer of the labeled loss does not coincide quite well with the maximizer of F score. Similar behavior is observed

[5] To avoid confusion we note that (2) is always the optimization problem that is solved to get the TSVM solution; minimizing the Labeled Loss that we are doing here is for tuning f at a higher level treating f as a hyperparameter.

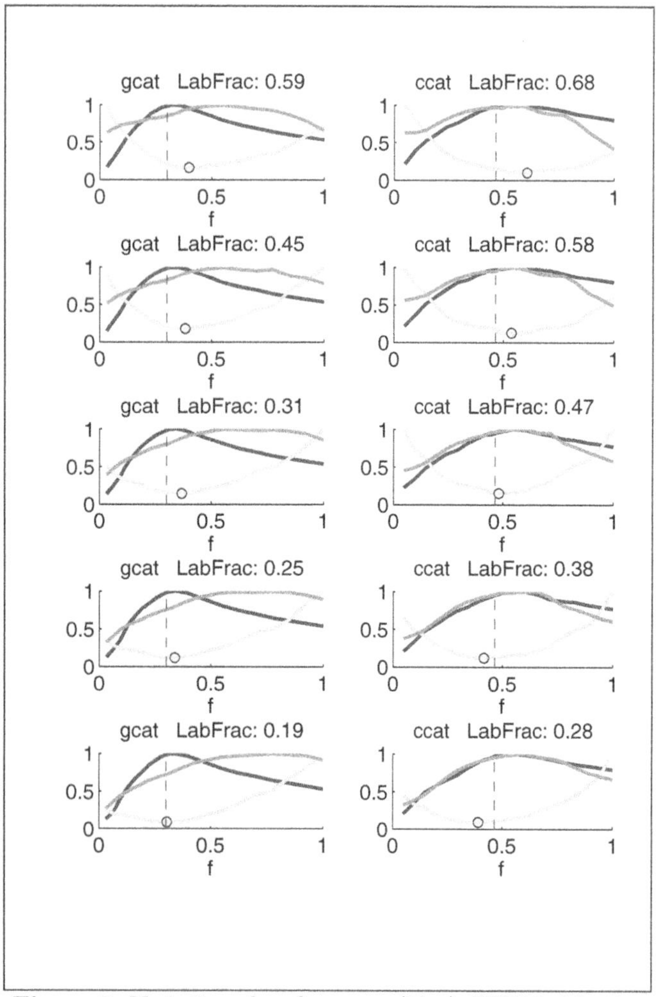

Figure 9: Variation of performance (blue), TSVM objective function in (2) (magenta) and Labeled Loss (the second term of T_{sup} in (1)) (cyan) with respect to f, for gcat and ccat. The minimizer of Labeled Loss is marked by a black circle. The rows correspond to different fraction distortions. The middle row corresponds to $f^{lab} = f^{actual}$. The bottom two rows correspond to $f^{lab} = 0.8f^{actual}$ and $f^{lab} = 0.6f^{actual}$. The top two rows correspond to $(1 - f^{lab}) = 0.8(1 - f^{actual})$ and $(1 - f^{lab}) = 0.6(1 - f^{actual})$.

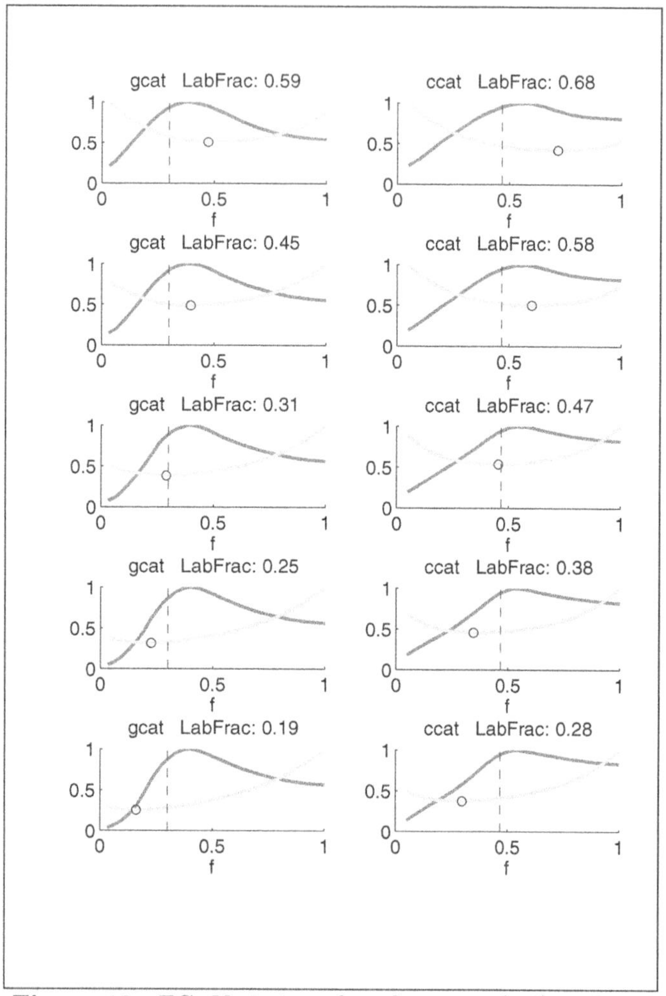

Figure 10: EC: Variation of performance (red) and Labeled Loss (the second term of T_{sup} in (1)) (cyan) with respect to f, for gcat and ccat. The minimizer of Labeled Loss is marked by a black circle. The rows correspond to different fraction distortions. The middle row corresponds to $f^{lab} = f^{actual}$. The bottom two rows correspond to $f^{lab} = 0.8f^{actual}$ and $f^{lab} = 0.6f^{actual}$. The top two rows correspond to $(1 - f^{lab}) = 0.8(1 - f^{actual})$ and $(1 - f^{lab}) = 0.6(1 - f^{actual})$.

for SVMTh and ER. For $n^{lab} = 90$ Figure 11 shows the performance of Estimation Method 3 with EC and SVMTh.

Figure 12 compares the three estimation methods as applied to TSVM. For $n^{lab} = 90$ Estimation Method 2 doesn't do even as well as Estimation Method 1. Estimation Method 3 is very good in a large range of f^{lab} values containing f^{actual}. It suffers only at extreme f^{lab} values. When n^{lab} is large, e.g., 1440, Estimation Method 2 performs very well. It is appropriate to switch between the two estimation methods depending on how large n^{lab} is. Going by what we saw in Figure 7, we can use the steadiness of f_{est}^{actual} given by Estimation Method 2 over a range of n^{lab} values to decide when to switch to it. Of course, n^{lab} has to be reasonably big to notice a clear steady pattern. Until that size is reached it is best to use Estimation Method 3.

When n^{lab} is large LSVM itself does quite well; since it is not dependent on f it becomes the preferred method for that case. Therefore, the value of a fraction estimation method should be determined by how well it performs when labeled data is small. From that viewpoint Estimation Method 3 (as applied to TSVM) is most valuable.

Of all (Method, Estimation Method) combinations (TSVM, Estimation Method 3) is the one that takes the most computing time; even for that combination, the computation time for one run on any of our five datasets is less than two minutes on a 3 GHz machine.

6. RELATED WORK

Since the first crucial paper of Joachims [10] several works (for a sample see [15, 7, 14, 6, 13, 5]) have been published extending and exploring various aspects of the first TSVM model. Of these, the works of Chen, Wang and Dong [7] and Wang and Huang [14] are the most relevant to our work since they address the problem of mismatch in class proportions. The main drawback of these methods is that they make adhoc labeling of the unlabeled examples during the training process in an active self-learning mode and are not cleanly tied to a well-defined problem formulation. Due to this they significantly deviate from the TSVM formulation and hence perform quite worse than TSVMs for the normal situation in which labeled data and the actual distribution are indeed well matched in terms of class proportions. Also, the methods have been demonstrated only in situations where LSVM itself gives decent performance, which is not true when there are large distortions in class proportions.

Mann and McCallum [12] empirically analyze ER in binary, multi-class and structured output settings in the context of MaxEnt models. ER's working and performance in SVMs and MaxEnt models are similar. Mann and McCallum [12] do a brief study of the sensitivity of ER's performance with respect to class proportions. But they only focus on the case of distortion towards uniform class proportions; in the binary case this corresponds to changing f from f^{actual} to 0.5. Unfortunately their study is done only on one multi-class dataset. As we saw in section 4.2, ER shows interesting behavior in the binary case; in fact ER improves in performance when f is moved towards 0.5. SVMTh is an important baseline method that is completely missed in [12].

There is a building literature on dealing with differences in train and test distributions referred to as *covariate shift* (see [2] for instance), but such papers introduce and analyze new formulations and do not help to modify TSVM or the expectation methods while keeping their spirit in tact.

7. CONCLUSION

The main contributions of this paper are: (i) empirical analysis of TSVM and expectation methods and their sensitivity with respect to label proportions; and, (ii) proposal and evaluation of new methods for dealing with mismatches in label proportions between labeled and test sets. We have also done preliminary experiments to verify the ideas on Least squares and MaxEnt models of binary classification and observed behavior similar to SVM loss. With some care all the ideas can also be extended to the multi-class setting. The ideas and results of this paper are mainly for web page and text classification. More work is needed to see if they hold on other types of problems.

8. REFERENCES

[1] D. P. Bertsekas and J. N. Tsitsiklis. *Parallel and Distributed Computation: Numerical Methods.* Athena Scientific, 1997.

[2] S. Bickel, M. Brückner, and T. Scheffer. Discriminative learning for differing training and test distributions. In *ICML*, pages 81–88, 2007.

[3] L. Bruzzone, M. Chi, and M. Marconcini. A novel transductive SVM for semisupervised classification of remote-sensing images. *IEEE-GRSS*, 3363–3373, 2006.

[4] O. Chapelle, B. Schölkopf, and A. Zien. *Semi-Supervised Learning.* MIT Press, 2006.

[5] O. Chapelle, V. Sindhwani, and S. S. Keerthi. Optimization techniques for semi-supervised support vector machines. *JMLR*, 9:203–233, 2008.

[6] O. Chapelle and A. Zien. Semi-supervised classification by low density separation. In *AISTATS*, pages 57–64, 2005.

[7] Y. Chen, G. Wang, and S. Dong. Learning with progressive transductive support vector machine. *Pattern Recognition Letters*, 24:1845–1855, 2003.

[8] T. Gärtner, Q. V. Le, S. Burton, A. J. Smola, and S. V. N. Vishwanathan. Large-scale multiclass transduction. In *NIPS*, 2005.

[9] Y. Grandvalet and Y. Bengio. Semi-supervised learning by entropy minimization. In *NIPS*, 2004.

[10] T. Joachims. Transductive inference for text classification using support vector machines. In *ICML*, 1999.

[11] T. Joachims. Training linear SVMs in linear time. In *KDD*, 2006.

[12] G. S. Mann and A. McCallum. Generalized expectation criteria for semi-supervised learning with weakly labeled data. *JMLR*, 11:955–984, 2010.

[13] V. Sindhwani and S. S. Keerthi. Large scale semi-supervised linear SVMs. In *SIGIR*, pages 477–484, 2006.

[14] Y. Wang and S.-T. Huang. Training TSVM with the proper number of positive samples. *Pattern Recognition Letters*, 26:2187–2194, 2005.

[15] T. Zhang and F. J. Oles. A probability analysis on the value of unlabeled data for classification problems. In *ICML*, pages 1191–1198, 2000.

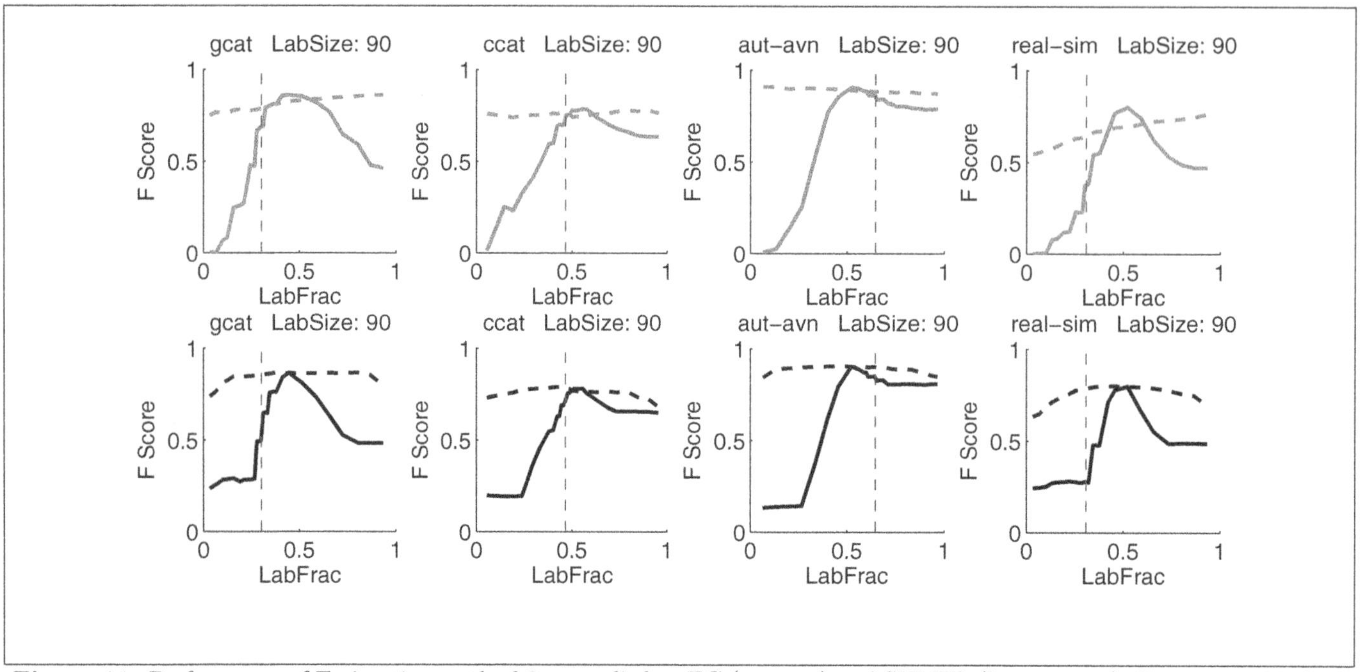

Figure 11: Performance of Estimation method 3 as applied to EC (top row) and SVMTh (bottom row). Estimation Method 3: Continuous. Dashed: Use $f = f^{actual}$ (Upper baseline)

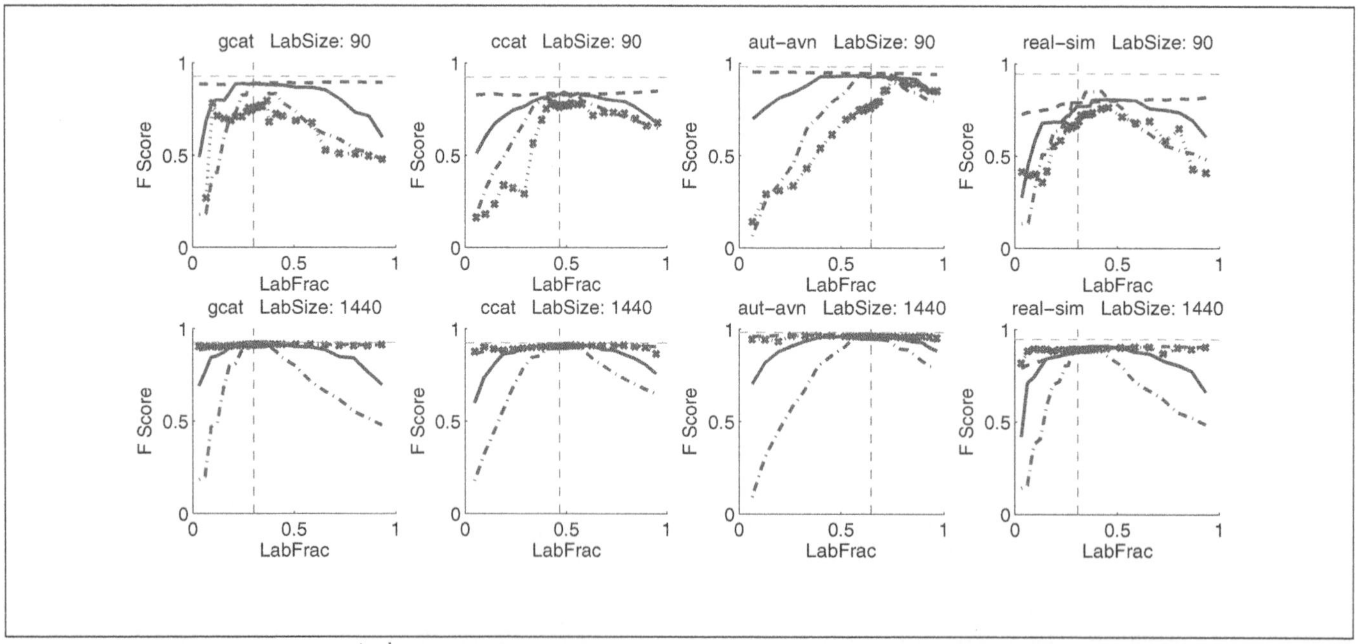

Figure 12: Comparison of f^{actual} estimation methods as applied to TSVM. Estimation Method 1: Dashdot. Estimation Method 2: Dotted with x. Estimation Method 3: Continuous. Dashed: Use $f = f^{actual}$ (Upper baseline)

A Pairwise Ranking Based Approach to Learning with Positive and Unlabeled Examples

Sundararajan Sellamanickam
Yahoo! Labs
Bangalore, India
ssrajan@yahoo-inc.com

Priyanka Garg
The Chinese University of Hong Kong
New Territories, Hong Kong
priyanka@cse.cuhk.edu.hk

Sathiya Keerthi Selvaraj
Yahoo! Labs
Santa Clara, CA
United States
selvarak@yahoo-inc.com

ABSTRACT

A large fraction of binary classification problems arising in web applications are of the type where the positive class is well defined and compact while the negative class comprises everything else in the distribution for which the classifier is developed; it is hard to represent and sample from such a broad negative class. Classifiers based only on positive and unlabeled examples reduce human annotation effort significantly by removing the burden of choosing a representative set of negative examples. Various methods have been proposed in the literature for building such classifiers. Of these, the state of the art methods are Biased SVM and Elkan & Noto's methods. While these methods often work well in practice, they are computationally expensive since hyperparameter tuning is very important, particularly when the size of labeled positive examples set is small and class imbalance is high. In this paper we propose a pairwise ranking based approach to learn from positive and unlabeled examples (LPU) and we give a theoretical justification for it. We present a pairwise RankSVM (RSVM) based method for our approach. The method is simple, efficient, and its hyperparameters are easy to tune. A detailed experimental study using several benchmark datasets shows that the proposed method gives competitive classification performance compared to the mentioned state of the art methods, while training 3-10 times faster. We also propose an efficient AUC based feature selection technique in the LPU setting and demonstrate its usefulness on the datasets. To get an idea of the goodness of the LPU methods we compare them against supervised learning (SL) methods that also make use of negative examples in training. SL methods give a slightly better performance than LPU methods when there is a rich set of negative examples; however, they are inferior when the number of negative training examples is not large enough.

Categories and Subject Descriptors: I.5.2 [Pattern Recognition] Design Methodology-Classifier design and evaluation

General Terms: Algorithms, Performance, Experimentation

Keywords: Learning with Positive and Unlabeled Examples, Pairwise Ranking, Classification, Support Vector Machines

CIKM'11, October 24–28, 2011, Glasgow, Scotland, UK.

1. INTRODUCTION

Binary classification problems arise frequently in web applications. Traditionally binary classifiers are built via supervised learning (SL) using a training set that consists of manually collected positive and negative examples. Consider, as an example, the problem of forming a classifier that determines if a page contains reviews of restaurants or not. While it is easy to sample from the positive class, i.e., collect a representative set of pages having reviews of restaurants, it is not that easy to form a representative set of negative examples. What is usually done in practice is to analyze the domain and choose 'boundary' negative examples that are truly negative but which potentially look like positive examples. For instance, in the case of the restaurant reviews example one can choose the following as (boundary) negative examples: pages that describe restaurants but do not contain reviews; and pages that only contain reviews of businesses other than restaurants. There are two problems with this approach. (1) The relative proportion of positive and negative examples in the training set may not be indicative of the corresponding proportion in the space of pages where the classifier will be deployed. (2) It is possible that other types of negative examples that are similar to positive examples are missed during the analysis. Several other interesting web applications of a similar kind can be found in [16][23].

While it is hard to choose representative negative examples, it is usually easy to form a large collection of unlabeled examples from the space of interest. Therefore it is useful to look for methods that learn from positive and unlabeled examples (LPU). The presence of positive examples in the unlabeled set and high class imbalance (ratio of positive to negative examples is small) bring in challenges in building classifiers in the LPU setting. Various approaches have been suggested in the literature [2],[8],[9],[16],[18],[19],[20],[21],[23],[24] for solving this problem. These approaches differ in the way the examples are used, the type of classifiers employed, etc.

The main aim of this paper is to propose a new approach for LPU. This approach is related to two good LPU methods, namely, Biased SVM [18] and a method recently proposed by Elkan and Noto [9]. We will refer to these methods as BSVM and EN respectively. These methods are based on building a binary classifier that separates positive examples from unlabeled examples; the above mentioned papers also provide good theoretical justifications for the proposed idea. The BSVM method has been demonstrated to work well in practice; however, 2-dimensional hyperparameter tuning using cross-validation makes it computationally expensive. In [9] the EN method was demonstrated to work well using a default hyperparameter setting on a dataset that is not imbalanced. In general, for imbalanced datasets EN also requires expensive 2-dimensional hyperparameter tuning to achieve good classifier performance. In addition, EN requires the estimation of some probabilistic quantities, which is of concern in imbalanced situations.

Our approach for LPU is based on ranking and we give a theoretical justification for this. We use the pairwise ranking method [7], [13]. The basic idea is to first build a ranking model that encourages the score of each positive example to be higher than that of each unlabeled example and then estimate a threshold parameter θ to form the final classifier. The approach is general in the sense that any pairwise ranking method can be used. In this paper we use a support vector machine (SVM) based ranking method (RSVM) proposed in [7],[12],[13] for learning, and employ the efficient RSVM solver in [7] for fast solution. The main advantage of the proposed method over BSVM and EN is that it has only one hyperparameter (C); an additional threshold parameter (θ) can also be estimated efficiently. Further, it is easy to implement using publicly available RSVM codes [5],[14]. Experimental results show that our method gives a performance that is competitive with BSVM and EN, while being 3-10 times faster than them.

A second contribution of this paper is the proposal of a new technique for doing feature selection in the LPU setting. Feature selection is useful in web classification since it helps to remove useless/redundant features and thus reduce classifier complexity. Except the recent work of Calvo et al [3], there is no other technique for feature selection in LPU that we are aware of; Calvo et al's technique is limited to discrete variables and also requires additional knowledge on the fraction of positive examples. Our feature selection method is free of such limitations, is based on computing the best AUC value possible with each feature used alone, and works effectively; for instance, an order of magnitude reduction in the number of features can be achieved using it with a loss in F Measure performance of only 2-3%.

A third useful contribution of the paper is a detailed set of experiments that shed insight on various methods in the SL and LPU settings. The paper is organized as follows. Related work is presented in adequate detail in Section 2. Section 3 describes our method in detail followed by a presentation of our AUC based feature selection technique in Section 4. The discussion of the various methods in Section 5 forms a prelude to the detailed empirical evaluation and comparison of methods given in Section 6. We conclude the paper in Section 7.

2. RELATED WORK

Various approaches have been suggested in the literature to solve the problem of positive example based learning [2],[8],[9],[16], [18],[19],[20],[24]. These approaches differ in the way the dataset is constructed and used by the methods, and by the choice of classifiers employed. In the first approach, the dataset consists of only labeled positive examples. One-class SVM [20] is one such approach and it does not use any unlabeled examples U. The classifier is built using only P. In One-class SVM, the origin is considered to be the only member of the negative class. A previous study in [17] shows that the performance of one class SVM is poor. Wu et al [22] studied one-class SVMs in detail and showed that the poor performance can partly be attributed to document representation. They empirically showed that a modified document representation helps in improving classification accuracy.

In the second approach, unlabeled examples (U) are also used along with the labeled positive examples (P). The methods that use this approach differ in the way they use the unlabeled examples. In one such class of methods, the classifier is built iteratively. For example, suppose a set of reliable negative examples $R_N^{(i)}$ is found from the unlabeled set U, say, in i-th iteration and a classifier $\mathcal{C}_i$ is built using P and $R_N^{(i)}$. Then $R_N^{(i)}$ is expanded to $R_N^{(i+1)}$ using predictions of $\mathcal{C}_i$ on $U - R_N^{(i)}$; next a classifier $\mathcal{C}_{i+1}$ is built using P and $R_N^{(i+1)}$. This procedure is repeated until some convergence criterion is met. These techniques are referred to as *2 step techniques* in [9],[18], where identifying R_N is the first step and the second step is building the standard classifier using them. Roc-SVM[17], S-EM[19], PEBL[23] and Support Vector Mapping Convergence (SVMC) [24] are some of the well known 2-step techniques with some variations.

In another class of methods, Denis et al [8] showed how the Naive Bayes algorithm can be adapted (called positive Naive Bayes (PNB)) for learning from positive and unlabeled examples. Subsequently, Calvo et al [2] enhanced the PNB algorithm and also proposed a Bayesian approach to deal with the prior probability of the positive class.

Semi-supervised learning methods can be used to solve LPU; see [21]. But these methods require a knowledge of the fraction of positive examples in the distribution.

Biased SVM (BSVM) [18] falls under another class of positive example based learners. It treats all the unlabeled examples U as negative examples; that is, $\{y_i = 1 : i \in P\}$ and $\{y_i = -1 : i \in U\}$. The SVM classifier is built by giving appropriate weights to the positive examples P and unlabeled examples U. It solves the following optimization problem:

$$\min \ \frac{1}{2}||\mathbf{w}||^2 + C_P \sum_{i \in P} \xi_i + C_U \sum_{i \in U} \xi_i \quad (1)$$
$$s.t. \ y_i(\mathbf{w}^T \mathbf{x}_i + \theta) \geq 1 - \xi_i; \xi_i \geq 0, \forall i$$

Here C_P and C_U are the weights given to the classification error on P and U respectively; $\mathbf{w}$ and θ denote the weight vector and threshold parameter of the SVM classifier; $\mathbf{x}_i$ and ξ_i denote the i-th input feature vector and slack variable respectively. Intuitively, C_P is expected to be given a higher value than C_U. This is because P is noise-free and U contains *noise* as it contains positive examples as well. Liu et al [18] showed that the BSVM method outperforms the 2-step techniques.

Elkan & Noto [9] also considered the problem of learning from positive and unlabeled examples. Let us represent each training example by $(\mathbf{x}, y, s)$ where $y \in \{-1, 1\}$ is the class label of the example and let s be a binary variable that denotes if the example is labeled ($s = 1$) or unlabeled ($s = 0$). By making the (reasonable) assumptions that (i) P is chosen by labeling randomly chosen positive examples and (ii) $p(s = 1|y = -1) = 0$ (that is, negative examples are never labeled), they derived the following useful result:

$$p(s = 1|\mathbf{x}) = Kp(y = 1|\mathbf{x}) \quad \text{where} \quad K = p(s = 1|y = 1) \quad (2)$$

Note that K is independent of $\mathbf{x}$ and so $p(s = 1|\mathbf{x})$ and $p(y = 1|\mathbf{x})$ are proportional to each other.

Using the above result Elkan & Noto [9] suggested two methods. In their first method (EN1), a first stage classifier that predicts probability of an example as *labeled* $p(s = 1|\mathbf{x})$ is learnt by treating each positive example as belonging to *labeled* class and each unlabeled example as belonging to *unlabeled* class. Now given a test example $\mathbf{x}$, $p(s = 1|\mathbf{x})$ is estimated using this classifier; then $p(y = 1|\mathbf{x})$ is estimated as: $p(y = 1|\mathbf{x}) = p(s = 1|\mathbf{x})/K$. The constant $K = p(s = 1|y = 1)$ is estimated using a validation set. In the second method (EN2), another classifier (second stage) is learnt by giving each training example a different weight using the estimated probability from the first stage classifier. EN2 is much more complex than EN1 because it involves two stages of classification. In the rest of the paper we will use EN1 to represent Elkan and Noto's method, and simply refer to it as EN.

Since the new approach that we propose for LPU in section 3 is based on ranking, it is useful to review some related work on ranking methods. Learning to rank is an important problem [1],[7],[11],[12],[13] in various applications like web search ranking, information retrieval etc. For example, in web search ranking the training data consists of a number of queries and for each query there is an associated set of returned documents. For each (query, document) pair there is a feature vector $\mathbf{x}_i, i = 1, \ldots, n$ and a relevancy judgment of how suitable the document is to the query. The aim is to build a ranking model that ranks a set of documents based on relevance scores for a given query. There are several methods known as *pointwise* methods, *pairwise* methods, etc., to address this problem. See [7] and references given there. Here we consider only the pairwise ranking method. In this method first a set of preference pairs $\mathbf{Q}$ is constructed by comparing the relevance of the documents associated with a given query. If $(i, j) \in \mathbf{Q}$ then document i is preferred over document j. A specific example is the ranking model based on SVM (RSVM) that is built by minimizing the following objective function [7]:

$$\frac{1}{2}||\mathbf{w}||^2 + C \sum_{(i,j)\in\mathbf{Q}} g(\mathbf{w}^T\mathbf{x}_i - \mathbf{w}^T\mathbf{x}_j) \quad (3)$$

where $g(\cdot)$ is a suitable loss function. Typical loss functions are $L1$ and $L2$ loss functions defined as: $g(t) = max(0, 1 - t)$ and $g(t) = max(0, 1-t)^2$. The use of the $L1$ loss leads to the method in [13]. In the next section we show how this formulation can be used to learn from the labeled positive and unlabeled examples. Other pairwise rank modeling methods like RankNet [1] and RankBoost [11] can also be used.

3. PROPOSED METHOD

Our aim is to find a classifier function $f(\mathbf{x}) = \mathbf{w}^T\mathbf{x}+\theta$ such that $f(\mathbf{x}) = 0$ represents the boundary between the positive and negative classes; we want to do this using only positive and unlabeled examples. The essence of our approach consists of two steps. First we find $\mathbf{w}$ such that, along the $\mathbf{w}^T\mathbf{x}$ score axis positive examples are placed higher than negative examples. Given the lack of negative examples, we instead work on placing the positive examples higher than the unlabeled examples and this can be achieved using a ranking method. In subsection 3.1 we borrow ideas from Elkan and Noto [9] to give a theoretical justification for this. A ranking method such as RSVM is used to form $\mathbf{w}$. In the second step we choose the threshold θ by maximizing a proxy F Measure. We give all the details associated with these steps as well as the complete design in the rest of the section.

3.1 Pairwise Ranking Based Approach

Let us begin by recalling (2). If we take two examples $\mathbf{x}_i$ and $\mathbf{x}_j$, (2) implies

$$\frac{p(y = 1|\mathbf{x}_i)}{p(y = 1|\mathbf{x}_j)} = \frac{p(s = 1|\mathbf{x}_i)}{p(s = 1|\mathbf{x}_j)} \quad (4)$$

In fact Elkan & Noto [9] make the observation that *if the classifier is only used to rank examples* $\mathbf{x}$ *according to the chance that they belong to class* $y = 1$, *then the classifier* $p(s = 1|\mathbf{x})$ *can be used directly instead of* $p(y = 1|\mathbf{x})$.

In linear classifiers such as logistic regression (where the probability function is in-built) and large margin methods such as SVM (where the probability function is formed after the classifier is designed), the probability of belonging to the positive class at a given $\mathbf{x}$ has a monotonic relationship with the scoring function $\tilde{f}(\mathbf{x}) = \mathbf{w}^T\mathbf{x}$.

For us the take away from the above two results is the following. Let P, N and U denote positive, negative and unlabeled example index sets. We are interested in building a classifier that ranks positive examples higher than negative examples, i.e., $\tilde{f}(\mathbf{x}_i) > \tilde{f}(\mathbf{x}_j)$ for all $(i, j) \in P \times N$. By the monotonic relation between $\tilde{f}(\mathbf{x})$ and $p(y = 1|\mathbf{x})$ this is same as requiring $\frac{p(y=1|\mathbf{x}_i)}{p(y=1|\mathbf{x}_j)} > 1$ for all $(i, j) \in P \times N$. By (4), this is equivalent to asking for $\frac{p(s=1|\mathbf{x}_i)}{p(s=1|\mathbf{x}_j)} > 1$ to be satisfied, and, given only P and U we can use $(i, j) \in P \times U$ to achieve this. By invoking the monotonic relation between $\tilde{f}(\mathbf{x})$ and $p(s = 1|\mathbf{x})$ we can see that building such a classifier is same as building a classifier that satisfies $\tilde{f}(\mathbf{x}_i) > \tilde{f}(\mathbf{x}_j)$ for all $(i, j) \in P \times U$.

While the above results and arguments suggest how to build a ranking model ($\tilde{f}$) in the LPU setting, we need a classifier model (f) for which we need to set a value for the threshold parameter θ. We determine this parameter using an idea given by Liu et al [19]; we will give the details in subsection 3.3.

3.2 RSVM Formulation

A ranking model based on SVM (RSVM) [7],[12],[13] is constructed by minimizing a regularized margin based pairwise loss as given in (3). Our binary classification context correspond to a simpler case of the more general ranking model given in [7] with a single query and two relevance values; the given n examples can be partitioned into two sets that define a binary classification problem: $A = \{i : \mathbf{x}_i \; is \; in \; the \; higher \; relevance \; class\}$ and $B = \{i : \mathbf{x}_i \; is \; in \; the \; lower \; relevance \; class\}$. In our context, we set $A = P$ and $B = U$; that is, the labeled positive examples belong to the higher relevance class and the unlabeled examples belong to the lower relevance class. Then from (3) we have the following objective function:

$$\frac{1}{2}||\mathbf{w}||^2 + C \sum_{(i\in P, j\in U)} g(\mathbf{w}^T\mathbf{x}_i - \mathbf{w}^T\mathbf{x}_j) \quad (5)$$

where $g(\cdot)$ is a suitable loss function and we choose $g(\cdot)$ to be the L2-loss function. One can also use L1-loss function; often there is very little difference in their performances. This objective function penalizes any violation of $\tilde{f}(\mathbf{x}_i) > \tilde{f}(\mathbf{x}_j), i \in P, j \in U$ with some margin where $\tilde{f}(\mathbf{x}) = \mathbf{w}^T\mathbf{x}$; it can be minimized using the Truncated Newton method efficiently [7]. A key aspect of this objective function is that the summation is over all pairs of examples in the sets P and U; therefore, the computational cost can be prohibitively high if done crudely. In [7] a very efficient solution to this problem is obtained with computational complexity $O(n \log n + n_{nz})$ where n and n_{nz} denote the number of training examples and number of non-zero elements in the $(|P| + |U|) \times d$ data matrix respectively. (Here d is the number of features, i.e., the dimension of $\mathbf{x}$ and $\mathbf{w}$.)

3.3 Hyperparameter, Threshold parameter Optimization

The choice of the hyperparameter C in (5) and the threshold parameter θ play important roles in the classification performance. They can be selected using standard 5-fold cross-validation (CV) technique by computing a suitable measure. In this technique we partition the sets P and U separately into 5-folds. We build five models where each model is built using one combination of 4-folds of data and then evaluated on the corresponding left-out 5th fold of data.

In traditional binary classification problems, measures like validation set accuracy and F Measure are typically used. While the accuracy is defined as the percentage of examples correctly classified, F Measure is defined as $F = \frac{2pr}{p+r}$ where p and r denote precision and recall (with respect to the positive class) respectively. Precision p is defined as: $p = \frac{TP}{TP+FP}$ and recall r is defined as: $r = \frac{TP}{|P|}$ where TP and FP denote the number of true positive and false positive examples respectively.

$\hat{F}$ Optimization Unlike standard binary classification problems, we do not have all the examples labeled; also, we have *only* positive examples. Therefore, it is not possible to find FP and hence we cannot directly use the F Measure. Simply using the accuracy measure based on the labeled positive examples is not good enough. This is because we also would like to to minimize the number of unlabeled examples getting classified as positive. This requirement is motivated by the key observation made by Liu et al [18],[19]: *"If the sample size is large enough, minimizing the number of unlabeled examples classified as positive while constraining the positive examples to be correctly classified will give a good classifier."* While using this principle as a guideline it is also necessary to be in tune with F Measure (giving appropriate importance to the positive class). The following F Measure like quantity (we call it as *proxy F Measure*) due to Lee and Liu [16][1] satisfies these requirements:

$$\hat{F} = \frac{r^2}{\hat{P}(f(\mathbf{x}) \geq 0)} \tag{6}$$

where $\hat{P}(f(\mathbf{x}) \geq \mathbf{0}) = \frac{\mathbf{TP+UP}}{\mathbf{n}}$ is the fraction of examples labeled as positive; UP (Unlabeled Positive) denote the number of unlabeled examples classified positive and $r = \frac{TP}{|P|}$ as earlier. Therefore, we can rewrite $\hat{F}$ as: $\hat{F} = \frac{TP^2}{TP+UP} \frac{n}{|P|^2}$. Since n and $|P|$ are fixed, it is seen that *the numerator maximizes the number of labeled positive examples to be correctly classified as positive and the denominator minimizes the number of unlabeled examples classified as positive.* This measure when used to optimize both C and θ in the LPU setting gives a good classifier. For a given C value we find the optimal value for the threshold parameter θ using 5-fold CV technique. The threshold value that gives the maximum average $\hat{F}$ over the 5-folds is chosen as the optimal threshold value $\theta^*(C)$. The optimal C value is chosen similarly as the one that gives the best $\hat{F}$ value. In all our experiments we used this approach to choose the hyperparameter. Finally we note that it is also possible to use other measure like AUC (Area under the ROC) [13] (to choose C) given below:

$$AUC = \frac{|(i,j) \; such \; that \; i \in P, j \in U, \mathbf{w}^T\mathbf{x}_i > \mathbf{w}^T\mathbf{x}_j|}{|P||U|} \tag{7}$$

We can estimate C by maximizing a 5-fold CV estimate of AUC; however, given that AUC is unaffected by θ, estimation of θ has to be done using an alternate measure such as $\hat{F}$.

3.4 Implementation

The algorithmic implementation of the proposed method for learning with positive and unlabeled examples (LPU) is given in algorithm 3.1. This algorithm is quite easy to implement with a wrapper module (to perform optimization of C and θ) and having the publicly available RSVM codes [5] and [14] to solve (5) as the core module. As mentioned earlier, an efficient solution to solve (5) is very useful to reduce the computational complexity. Some variations of algorithm 3.1 include using the AUC-score (7) to find the optimal C value, choice of N_f, choice of C values in $\bar{\mathbf{C}}$, etc.

[1]Lee and Liu [16] designed this measure for selecting hyperparameters; they did not use it for tuning θ.

Algorithm 3.1 Pairwise RSVM based LPU Algorithm

- Set $\bar{\mathbf{C}} = \{C_{min}, \ldots, 10^{-5}, 10^{-4}, 10^{-3}, \ldots, C_{max}\}$ and N_f=5
- Partition the dataset P and U into N_f partitions, $Q^{(i)} = (P^{(i)}, U^{(i)}), i = 1, \ldots, N_f$
- For each hyperparameter value $C \in \bar{\mathbf{C}}$
  1. Perform N_f fold CV with the $\hat{F}$ Measure (6) using the partitions $\{Q^{(i)}, i = 1, \ldots, N_f\}$
     (a) Solve (5) using any pairwise RSVM method for each split of train set $(P - P^{(i)}, U - U^{(i)})$
     (b) Compute predictions $\tilde{f}^{(i)}(\mathbf{x}_j)$, $\{j, j \in Q^{(i)}\}$
  2. Find the optimal threshold value $\theta^*(C)$ that maximizes the average $\hat{F}$ Measure (6) using the predictions
  3. Update the best C value (C^*) that maximizes the average $\hat{F}$ Measure using the predictions
- Solve (5) with the entire dataset $\{P, U\}$ with C^*
- Output: $\mathbf{w}$ and $\theta^*(C^*)$

4. FEATURE SELECTION - LPU SETTING

Feature selection is useful in web classification since it helps to remove useless/redundant features and thus reduce classifier complexity. While there have been several techniques proposed in the literature to address the problem of feature selection in the supervised learning (SL) setting, class imbalanced condition, etc (see eg., [10], [25]), little has been done in the LPU setting. We are not aware any work other than that of Calvo et al [3], who proposed a correlation based filter selection (CFS) technique which forwardly selects the features by maximizing a merit function; this function is based on the correlation between each feature and the class and on the correlation among the features. The technique has two limitations: (i) it works only on discrete data; and (ii) it requires additional information in the form of either the overall probability of positive examples or some (parameterized) beta distribution that models this probability.

Here we propose an AUC based feature selection (AUCFS) technique. It is generic in the sense that it can also be used in the supervised learning setting. It is free of the type of limitations mentioned for Calvo et al's method [3].

The AUCFS technique is a filter technique where we take each feature one by one and compute achievable AUC score using only that feature on the training set. This is done as follows. In the single feature scenario the scoring function is given by $\tilde{f}(x) = w \cdot x$ where w and x are scalar quantities. Then the AUC score is computed using (7). Further with w a scalar and $x_{i,k}$ and $x_{j,k}$ denoting k-th feature value of i-th and j-th examples, $w.x_{i,k} < w.x_{j,k}$ imply either $x_{i,k} < x_{j,k}$ or $x_{i,k} > x_{j,k}$ depending on the sign of w. Therefore only the sign of w matters and not the magnitude of w. Thus we *do not have* to find w for any individual feature. Now to take care of the sign part, we can compute two AUC scores one each by considering the actual feature value and its negated value separately. This is necessary because the values for some feature could be higher for positive class examples and lower for negative class examples, and vice-versa. Let us denote $AUC_P^{(k)}$ and $AUC_N^{(k)}$ as the AUC scores corresponding to using the k-th feature value and its negated value. Then we compute the AUC score for the k-th feature as: $AUC^{(k)} = \max(AUC_P^{(k)}, AUC_N^{(k)})$; we choose max because with appropriate sign for the weight, the maximum value can be achieved. These quantities can be computed efficiently by sorting the feature values. After doing this computation for all features, the features are ranked by sorting $AUC^{(k)}, \forall k$ in decreasing order and the required number of features are selected from the top of the list. We do not claim any optimal properties for this selection; nevertheless, we found this approach to work well in our experiments.

We note that the AUCFS technique can be applied in the SL setting also. While the procedure to compute the scores remains the same, we have $j \in N$ (negative examples) instead of $j \in U$. We feel that, compared to other feature selection metrics AUCFS has the innate ability to be less affected by differences in the distribution of positive and negative examples in the training and test sets. This needs to be tested. For the LPU setting, although it is possible to consider other measures like proxy F Measure, here we restrict our attention to AUCFS technique only. In subsection 6.5 we do experiments to demonstrate the usefulness of AUCFS.

5. DISCUSSION

A highlight of this paper is a set of experiments that shed insight into various methods in the SL and LPU settings. These experiments and the conclusions derived from them are described in section 6. In this section we discuss various practical aspects of the methods and raise questions that form a prelude to the experiments.

SL with SVM and RSVM Since SVM and RSVM (as applied to binary classification in the SL setting) form the basis for LPU methods, it is useful to understand them comparatively. Although these methods are well known we are unaware of any results that compare binary classifiers built using them under varying train/test distributions. Note that in the SL setting we have both positive and negative examples for training. Suppose our aim is to maximize F Measure. Since the loss functions associated with SVM or RSVM are not truly designed to optimize F Measure, it is useful to adjust the classifier threshold θ after the models are trained. We can use 5-fold CV based F Measure to estimate θ; the same measure can also be used to optimize the hyperparameters. Hyperparameter optimization is easier with RSVM since it involves only one hyperparameter; SVM requires two hyperparameters to *effectively* handle imbalance data. Experimental results comparing SVM and RSVM in the SL setting are given in subsection 6.2.

SL versus LPU Given that SL also has knowledge of negative examples, one expects that SL will perform better than LPU. Is this true? If so how much is the difference? Also, if the distribution of positive and negative examples in the test set differs from that in the SL train set, does SL suffer, say to the point of being even worse than LPU? One of the weaknesses of LPU is that, given the lack of negative examples, it doesn't have clear cues to set the classifier threshold θ. The proxy F Measure in (6) is what RSVM-LPU (RSVM in the LPU setting) use, but how good is it for choosing θ? These are questions worth answering, and are taken up in subsections 6.3 and 6.6.

Hyperparameter Optimization Note that there are three terms in (1); therefore, two hyperparameters will be needed under any reparametrization, unless one hyperparameter is set as *fixed constant* times the other hyperparameter. For example, we can also optimize $\frac{C_w}{2}||\mathbf{w}||^2 + \tilde{C}_P \sum_{i \in P} \xi_i + \sum_{i \in U} \xi_i$. In standard SVM, $\tilde{C}_P$=1 and equal importance is given to both positive and negative examples. However, it is important to have two hyperparameters when the class imbalance is high, which is the case in our setting with large number of unlabeled examples. Furthermore, there is some amount of noise present in the unlabeled examples (when treated as negative examples) since they can contain positive examples. Therefore, for achieving good performance, it is necessary to have two hyperparameters C_P and C_U in (1). In BSVM the unlabeled examples are treated as negative examples, and the solution is obtained by using any SVM solver as the core module and optimizing the hyperparameters C_P and C_U using the proxy F Measure(6) [18]. Two dimensional grid search to optimize the hyperparameters C_P and C_U makes BSVM computationally expensive.

In [9] where EN is proposed, there is no discussion of how the hyperparameters must be chosen; in the datasets used there, there is no class imbalance and $|P|$ is not small, and so default hyperparameters give good performance. In our experiments with EN we observed that when the percentage of positive labeled examples is small compared to the unlabeled set size, the performance loss due to the use of default hyperparameters as compared to *with hyperparameter optimization* can be quite high. Thus, like BSVM, optimizing the two hyperparameters C_P and C_U is necessary for EN too. In fact, the situation is worse with EN since it requires more parameters to be estimated. The additional parameters are: K; and the parameters in the probability model that converts the decision function score to the probability score ($p(s = 1|\mathbf{x})$). These parameters are again estimated using cross-validation. Any estimation error in these parameters compounds the performance loss. In our implementation of EN we used the proxy F Measure for selecting the hyperparameters. Since EN is a probabilistic method, probabilistic measures (e.g., likelihood) may be worth exploring.

For RSVM we have only one hyperparameter C to be optimized and this reduces the computational complexity significantly. The following two observations are also relevant here. (i) The computational complexity of solving (5) may seem higher compared to solving a standard SVM problem due to pairwise comparison in the data fitting term. However, as pointed out at the end of subsection 3.2, (5) can actually be solved efficiently. (ii) Even though RSVM needs to optimize the threshold parameter θ separately, this step is not expensive because the CV data used for C tuning is also used for tuning θ (see steps 2 and 3 of Algorithm 3.1).

The experiments of subsection 6.4 give more insight on the LPU methods.

6. EXPERIMENTS

We conducted experiments on six benchmark datasets (details are given in Table 1) to answer the following five questions: (1) In a supervised learning (SL) setting how good is RSVM when compared to SVM? (2) How does LPU compare with SL, given the expectation that SL will do much better because it has a knowledge of negative training examples? (3) In the LPU setting how do BSVM, EN and RSVM compare and, how important is hyperparameter optimization? (4) How effective is the AUC based LPU feature selection method? and (5) How good is the proxy F Measure when it comes to setting the classifier threshold correctly? In these experiments RSVM is used both in SL and LPU settings; so, to avoid confusion we will refer to RSVM in the LPU setting as RSVM-LPU and RSVM in the SL setting simply as RSVM. Throughout, classifier performance is measured in terms of F Measure. When the underlying problem is a multi-class problem (News20 and WebKB) the Macro F Measure (average of the F Measures of all One-vs-All binary classification problems) is used; for computational effort we report the average time over all these problems. While reporting training time, the time taken by the RSVM based method is considered as the reference and is taken as one unit; then the times taken by the other methods are given relative to this unit. The time is computed as the *total* training time taken by any given method

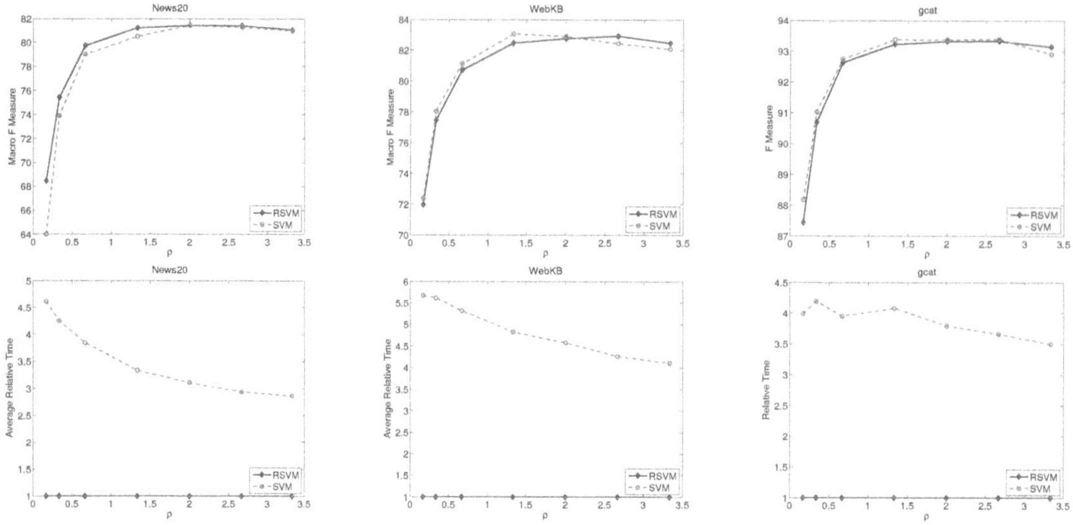

Figure 1: Macro F Measure and Training time (relative to RSVM) of RSVM and SVM on News20, WebKB and gcat for $X = 30$. ρ is as in (8).

as it searches over its grid of hyperparameter values. For each hyperparameter setting, 5-fold CV estimate of F Measure (for the SL setting) or proxy F Measure (for the LPU setting) is used. The search is done in two stages. In the first stage a coarse grid is used to narrow down the region around the optimal value. Then a finer grid search is carried out in the second stage. For BSVM and EN, the coarse grid is set to $C_U = \{0.0001, 0.001, 0.01, 0.1, 1, 10\}$ and $J = \{1, 3, 9, 27, 81, 243\}$; note that $C_P = J \cdot C_U$. In the SL setting we have C_N in place of C_U. In the case of RSVM it is set to $C = \{10^{-7}, 10^{-6}, \ldots, 10^{-2}\}$. The finer grid contained 6 values around the optimal value chosen from the coarser grid. For BSVM and EN we used *Liblinear* (`http://www.csie.ntu.edu.tw/~cjlin/liblinear`) since it uses state-of-the-art SVM solvers and is suited for text classification. We integrated the probability estimation module from libsvm [4] (`http://www.csie.ntu.edu.tw/~cjlin/libsvm`) with *Liblinear* to get the probability estimates for EN. For RSVM, we used the C implementation of [5] in our experiments. In the case of BSVM we used 5-fold CV based proxy F Measure estimate to choose the hyperparameters. In the case of EN method we used 5-fold CV based F Measure estimate since the classification problem is *labeled versus unlabeled* in the first stage (that is, estimating $p(s = 1|\mathbf{x})$). In all the experiments with random partitions average performance over 10 partitions is reported. Finally, due to space limitation we present plots only for some datasets and report observations on other datasets when some behavioral variations were observed.

6.1 Description of Datasets

The News20 [15] dataset contains text documents from 20 different newsgroups. We combined the preprocessed train and test sets obtained from [4] to form the whole dataset. Each newsgroup is used as the positive class and the rest as the negative class. This results in 20 One-vs-All binary classification problems. The WebKB [6] dataset is a web page classification problem where the web pages are collected from university websites and these web pages belong to one of 7 classes. For our experiments we considered only the classes 1, 3, 4 and 7. This is because the number of positive examples was very small (for example, to do meaningful cross-validation) for other classes. We considered 4 One-vs-All binary classification problems treating examples belonging to each of the 4 classes (1, 3, 4 and 7) as the positive class and the rest of the examples as negative class. The *adult* dataset is a binary classification problem. We combined the train and test splits of *a5a* available from [4] to form the whole dataset. The *ccat* and *gcat* datasets are binary classification problems that classify articles into corporate versus non-corporate and government versus non-government articles respectively. The classes corporate and government are top-level categories in the RCV1 training dataset. The *realsim* dataset is also a binary classification problem and is obtained from a collection of UseNet articles from four discussion groups, for simulated auto racing, simulated aviation, real autos, and real aviation [21]. The *ccat*, *gcat* and *realsim* datasets are available at `http://people.cs.uchicago.edu/~vikass/svmlin.html`; see original source details there-in. These datasets cover a wide range of problems, class imbalance and n. The construction of train/test sets are explained for each experiment below in detail.

Table 1: Datasets Description: n_+ and n_- denote the number of positive and negative examples in the overall (train+test) dataset. $u(\%)$ denotes the percentage of positive examples ($\frac{100n_+}{n_+ + n_-}$). For News20 each of the 20 classes has close to 1000 examples; so the indicated values are approximate. For the WebKB dataset the class number is indicated in parentheses.

Dataset	n_+	n_-	$u(\%)$
News20	1000	18928	5
WebKB (1)	929	6506	12.5
WebKB (3)	1124	6311	15.1
WebKB (4)	3741	3694	50.32
WebKB (7)	1641	5794	22.07
adult	6414	26147	19.70
ccat	10786	12363	46.59
gcat	6970	16179	30.11
realsim	22238	50071	30.75

6.2 RSVM versus SVM

In this experiment we compare RSVM and SVM in the SL setting. Apart from a basic comparison, the intention is to study how well these methods perform under different train and test distribution conditions; this is important for web classification because, many a times there is lack of clarity in the space of negative examples and so it is often the case that the negative examples chosen for training do not represent that space well.

Experimental Setup We evaluate the performances under different scenarios of train and test distributions. We fix the test distribution and vary the train distribution. The train and test sets are constructed as follows. First we randomly split the dataset into two sets in a 80:20 proportion, while maintaining the same class imbal-

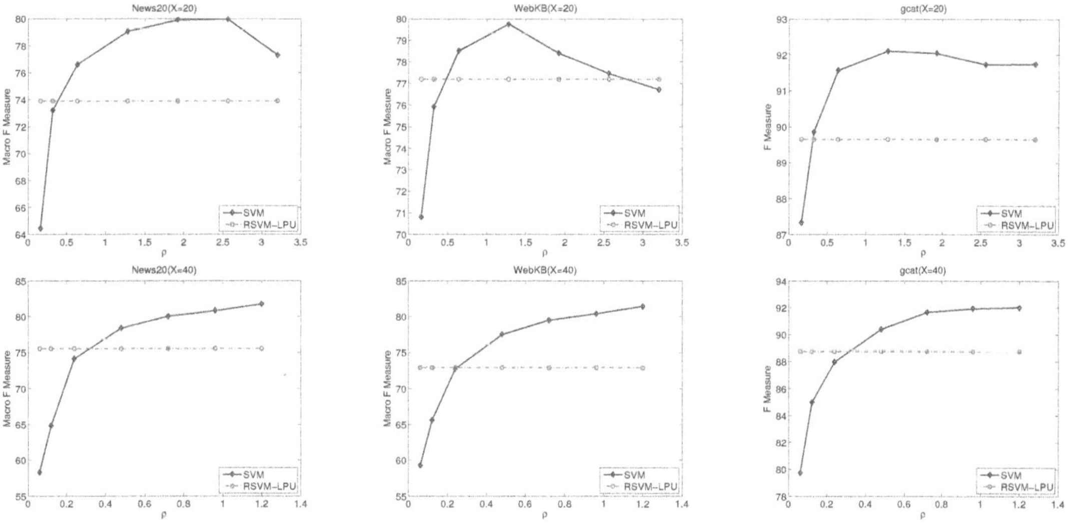

Figure 2: Macro F Measure of SVM and RSVM-LPU on News20, WebKB and gcat. ρ is as in (8). The top and bottom rows correspond to the cases, X=20 and 40 respectively.

ance ratio between the positive and negative examples in the two sets. Let us denote these sets as $\mathbf{S}$ and $\mathbf{T}$. Now keeping $\mathbf{T}$ as the test set, the train set is constructed from $\mathbf{S}$ as follows. We randomly select $X\%$ of positive examples from $\mathbf{S}$. Let us denote this set as $\mathbf{P}$. Now keeping $\mathbf{P}$ fixed, we randomly select the negative example set $\mathbf{N}$; to vary the train distribution we vary the size of $\mathbf{N}$ (denoted as $|\mathbf{N}|$). We conduct this experiment on 10 random partitions of negative examples for each size and repeat this experiment for 3 different sizes of $\mathbf{P}$ (denoted as $|\mathbf{P}|$). Since we did not find any noticeable behavioral changes for different $|\mathbf{P}|$ we report results only for one $|\mathbf{P}|$ value (corresponding to X=30). The results are given in figure 1. In the figure

$$\rho = r(\text{test})/r(\text{train}) \quad (8)$$

where $r(A)$ is the class ratio in A, i.e., the ratio of the number of positive examples and the number of negative examples in set A. Thus when the class ratios in the train and test distributions are the same we have $\rho = 1$.

Observations The F Measures of RSVM and SVM are very close. One key observation is that the performances of both the methods drop rapidly as ρ falls below 1; note that this corresponds to the situation where there are relatively lesser negative examples in the train distribution as compared to the test distribution. For very small values of ρ, we also observed that the performance of RSVM was better, particularly on the News20 and WebKB datasets as X decreased. The performances of both the methods improve for $\rho \geq 1$ (the situation where there are relatively more negative training examples) and their performances are very close. The results suggest that an insufficient number of negative training examples ($\rho < 1$) (with respect to the test set distribution) has significant impact on performance. RSVM is significantly faster (>3 times). In fact, on the adult dataset the speed-up was around 10 times; on this dataset the SVM classifier chooses a high value of C_P and C_N for some of the folds, resulting in larger training times. Note that RSVM is faster only when two hyperparameters are needed in the standard SVM (i.e., when the class imbalance is high).

6.3 Supervised Learning versus LPU

To represent SL we choose SVM since it is more well known standard; also, in section 6.2 we saw that its performance is close to that of RSVM. For LPU we choose RSVM-LPU to represent it. Our intention is to see how well RSVM-LPU performs in comparison to SVM and see if there are any specific conditions under which it even performs better.

Experimental Setup We construct the train and test sets as follows. For the LPU setting, we first randomly pick $X\%$ of positive examples from the overall dataset. Let us denote this dataset as $\mathbf{P}$. Then we split the remaining examples in 80:20 unlabeled-test set proportion. Let us denote this split as $\mathbf{U}$ and $\mathbf{T}$. The main motivation behind this construction is that the unlabeled set is collected in such a way as to represent the test set in practice. Therefore *the same class ratio is maintained in the unlabeled and test sets.* Thus $(\mathbf{P}, \mathbf{U})$ form the training set and $\mathbf{T}$ forms the test set. In the SL setting, we randomly sample negative examples $\mathbf{N}_{sl}$ from the negative example set $\mathbf{N}_u$ in $\mathbf{U}$. Thus, $(\mathbf{P}, \mathbf{N}_{sl})$ form the training set and $\mathbf{T}$ again forms the test set. We conduct this experiment on 10 random partitions for different sizes of $\mathbf{N}_{sl}$ and repeat this experiment on three different sizes of $\mathbf{P}$ (corresponding to X=20,30 and 40). The F Measure values corresponding to the cases X=20 and 40 are given in figure 2. The performance results corresponding to X=30 turned out to be closer to the case of X=40. Note that the performance in the LPU setting does not change as the ρ-axis reflects only the change in the number of negative training examples.

Observations Though unimportant for comparing RSVM-LPU and SVM, it is worth noting that different values of X correspond to test sets with different class ratios. Low values of ρ correspond to lesser number of negative examples. Interestingly, on all the datasets, RSVM-LPU performs significantly better when ρ is small. SVM improves as more negative examples are added and the performance almost stabilizes after some point when X=40. When the number of positive examples is less (X=20), there is some drop in the performance seen when large number of negative examples is added; of course the drop is not as high as the one observed when ρ is small. In general, the peak performance of SVM was observed approximately around ρ=1, which is expected since the distribution used for parameter tuning in training matches the distribution evaluated in testing. Overall, around $\rho = 1$ SVM does better than RSVM-LPU. While this improvement is significant on News20 and WebKB datasets it is not that significant (<3%) on other datasets like gcat, ccat and realsim.

6.4 Comparison of Various LPU Methods

In this section we present two sets of experiments. In the first experiment we demonstrate the need for hyperparameter optimization

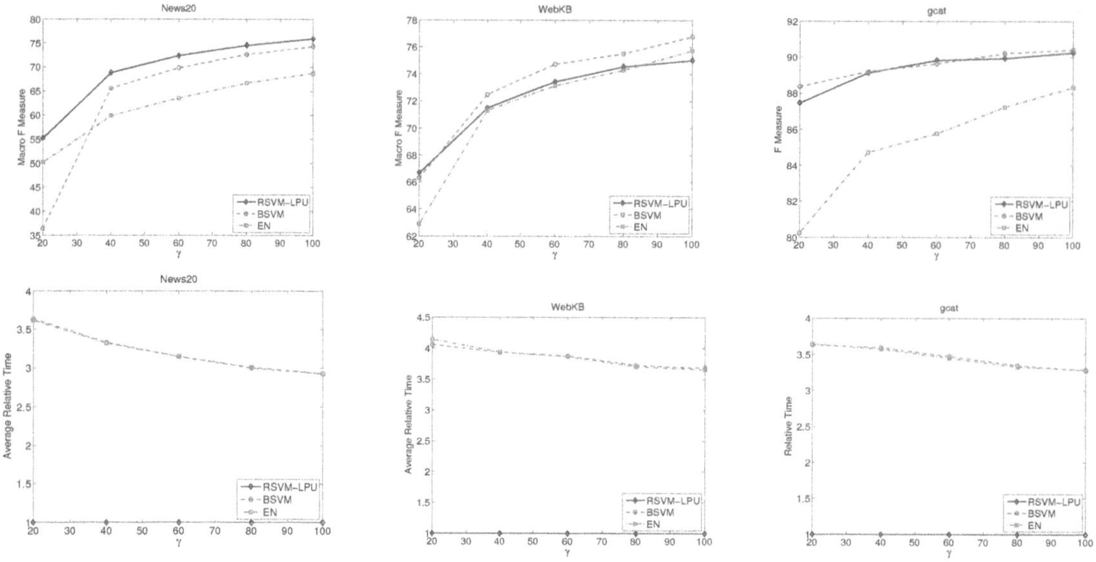

Figure 3: Macro F Measure and Training (relative) time of the LPU methods (RSVM, BSVM and EN) on News20, WebKB and gcat for X=30. γ is the percentage of positive labeled examples with reference to the available positive labeled examples $|P|$.

in LPU methods. In the second experiment we compare the performances of the proposed RSVM-LPU method with the BSVM and EN methods.

Experimental Setup The construction of the sets $\mathbf{P}$, $\mathbf{U}$ and $\mathbf{N}$ remains the same as in subsection 6.3. In this experiment we also study the performances of the LPU methods as the number of positive examples is increased. We construct the positive labeled set $\tilde{\mathbf{P}}$ by randomly sampling γ percentage of samples from $\mathbf{P}$. Thus $(\tilde{\mathbf{P}}, \mathbf{U})$ forms the training set and $\mathbf{T}$ forms the test set. Note that $|\tilde{\mathbf{P}}| = \frac{\gamma}{100}|\mathbf{P}|$ and $\gamma = 100$ corresponds to the case in subsection 6.3 (that is, $\mathbf{P} = \tilde{\mathbf{P}}$). We conducted this experiment on 10 random partitions of $\tilde{\mathbf{P}}$ and repeated this experiment for each size of $\tilde{\mathbf{P}}$. The results given in the figure are average F Measure values obtained from these partitions. We also varied $|\mathbf{P}|$ by varying $\mathbf{X}$ (corresponding to X=20,30 and 40) and since there were no changes in the behavioral patterns of methods (relative to one another) we only present the results corresponding to X=30.

Observations on Hyperparameter Optimization Hyperparameter tuning turns out to be important for all three LPU methods, viz. BSVM, EN and RSVM-LPU. We take EN to illustrate this. We conducted an experiment to study the effect of hyperparameter optimization as γ is varied. Default hyperparameter values for EN are: $C_P = 1$ and $C_U = 1$. We observed significant performance improvements (more than 10% F Measure value in several cases) with hyperparameter optimization for EN. The performance difference with and without hyperparameter optimization was more at lower values of γ (that is, when the number of labeled positive examples is low).

Observations on RSVM-LPU, BSVM and EN Methods In this experiment we performed hyperparameter optimization for all the methods. Since no specific behavioral differences were seen for different X values, we give results only for X=30; see figure 3. All the methods improve their F Measure as γ increases. At lower γ values, the F Measure values of all the methods fall relatively sharply. This is both due to the paucity in (positive) labeled examples as well as the fact that this paucity causes CV based hyperparameter tuning to become inferior.

Overall RSVM-LPU and BSVM are quite close in classifier performance. There are exceptions too: on News20 RSVM-LPU is significantly better and, on WebKB BSVM is significantly better. EN is generally inferior, sometimes quite badly (see, for example, the results in figure 3 for News20 and gcat). We believe that the inferior performance of EN is due to inaccurate estimates of both K and $p(s = 1|\mathbf{x})$, and this affects the final probability score: $p(y = 1|\mathbf{x}) = p(s = 1|\mathbf{x})/K$; refer to sections 2 and 5 for details. In general, we observed that the performance comes closer to other methods as γ increases and this happens due to improved parameter estimates.

The training times for BSVM and EN are close; RSVM-LPU is significantly faster than them. As can be seen from figure 3, the speed-up is more than 3 times; on the adult dataset it was about 10 times. On the adult dataset, the BSVM and EN methods picked large C_U as the optimal value on some of the folds, resulting in longer training time; on the other hand the RSVM-LPU method picked the hyperparameter value more consistently.

6.5 Feature Selection in the LPU Setting

We did the feature selection experiment on WebKB and News20 in both LPU and SL settings with RSVM. We note that the feature selection technique proposed by Calvo et al [3] cannot be *directly* compared with our method for the reasons explained earlier (see section 5). For reference we present results from SL setting using the proposed AUC based feature selection technique. Note that our intention here *is not to compare* AUC based feature selection method with other feature selection methods in supervised setting, a study that can be taken up separately.

Experimental Setup The experimental setup is essentially same as the one described in section 6.4. We set aside 20% of positive examples (X=20) and set $\gamma = 100$. In the SL setting we have both positive and negative labeled examples, and we set $\rho = 1$. We fixed C at $5 \cdot 10^{-4}$. We ranked the features using the AUC score of each individual feature observed in the training set as discussed in Section 4. We evaluated the Macro F Measure on the test set as a function of number of selected features. To assess the quality of features selected in the LPU setting, we can also evaluate the performance of SL classifier built with features selected in the LPU setting and compare it with the performance obtained using features selected in the SL setting. We considered the following variations of LPU-LPU, LPU-SL and SL-SL. The prefixes LPU and SL correspond to the cases where the features are selected from positive/unlabeled and positive/negative examples respectively. The suffixes LPU and

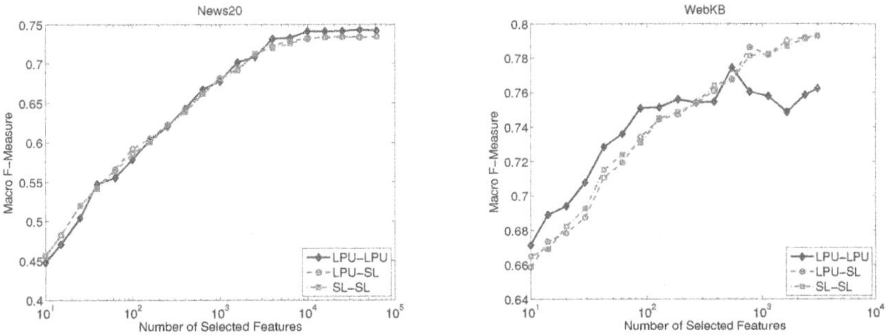

Figure 4: Macro F Measure of RSVM classifier in both SL and LPU settings with the proposed AUC based feature selection technique on News20 and WebKB. The prefixes LPU and SL correspond to the selection of features using positive/unlabeled and positive/negative examples respectively. The suffixes LPU and SL correspond to the classifier being built in the LPU and SL setting respectively.

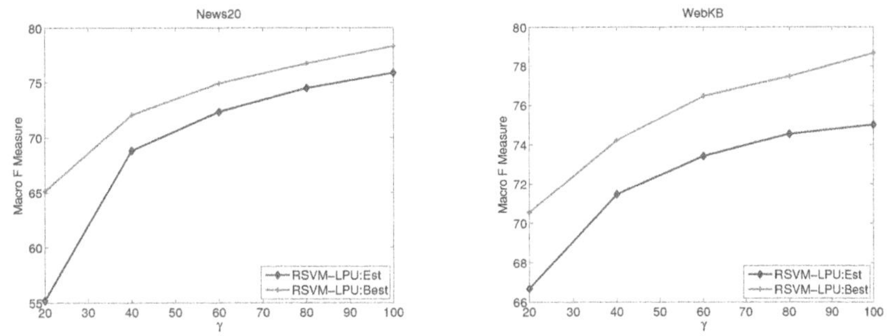

Figure 5: Macro F Measure of RSVM in LPU setting with estimated and best threshold values as a function of γ for X=30 on News20 and WebKB; definition of γ is as in the caption of Figure 3.

SL correspond to the cases where the classifier is built in the LPU and SL setting respectively.

Observations The results corresponding to these variations are shown in figure 4. On News20, the performances of all variations are very close. On WebKB, it is observed that the LPU classifier performance is slightly better than the SL classifier when the number of features is small. The SL classifier starts performing better after a sufficient number of features have been added. On both the datasets, the usefulness of the proposed technique is clearly seen: even with an order of magnitude reduction in the number of features the loss in performance is within 2-3%. Also, the SL classifier performance with LPU selected features is almost same as the performance achieved with SL selected features.

6.6 Estimated Threshold vs Best Threshold

In this experiment we compare the performances of RSVM classifier in the LPU setting with estimated and best thresholds. The experimental setup for the LPU setting remains the same as in subsection 6.4. Recall that in the LPU setting we estimate the threshold using 5-fold CV proxy F Measure. To assess the quality of the threshold estimate we compared the F Measure performances (as a function of γ) achievable by the estimated threshold and the best threshold on the test set. The results are given in figure 5. Note that the proxy F Measure estimate and hence the threshold estimate are expected to be poor at lower values of γ. This is because the number of examples available to perform 5-fold CV is very small and the proxy F Measure cannot be reliably estimated. This effect is more clearly seen in the News20 dataset as compared to the WebKB dataset. We believe this is due to the reason that the class ratio is lower in the News20 dataset as compared to the WebKB dataset. The results demonstrate that when γ is reasonably high, the performance difference is almost same and is within approximately 2-3%. Overall, the results in this subsection seem to indicate that further research to come up with a measure better than proxy F Measure for tuning threshold is worthwhile. Suppose one has a knowledge of the fraction of positive examples in the train/test distributions. How this can be effectively used to choose the threshold is worth investigating.

6.7 Summary

In this subsection we summarize the key observations from all the experiments discussed in the previous subsections.

- **RSVM vs SVM** The performances of both the methods are very close on the F Measure. RSVM is significantly faster than SVM due to easier one dimensional hyperparameter optimization than the two dimensional search needed with the SVM (when the class imbalance is high).
- **SL vs LPU** The performance of RSVM-LPU is better than SVM operating in the SL setting for small values of ρ. Overall there is performance improvement with the SL-setting around ρ=1 over the LPU setting. While this improvement is significant on News20 and WebKB it is not that significant (<3%) on other datasets.
- **Comparison of LPU Methods**
  - **Hyperparameter Optimization:** This is important for LPU methods. The performance improves a lot with hyperparameter optimization. As in the case of supervised setting optimization of hyperparameter is easier with RSVM-LPU compared to BSVM and EN.
  - **Training Time Comparison:** With hyperparameter optimization BSVM and EN take similar training time. RSVM-LPU is faster than BSVM and EN by more than 3-10 times.
  - **Performance Measures:** The performances of RSVM and BSVM are very close. While EN lags behind on some datasets at lower values of γ, it catches up as γ increases; we believe that the lagging behavior at lower γ is due to inaccurate probability estimates obtained.

- **Feature Selection:** The proposed AUC based feature selection technique in the LPU setting works quite well; an order of magnitude reduction in the number of features is achieved without significant degradation from the peak performance. The feature selection from the LPU setting as tested in the SL setting is interestingly *as good as* the features selected using supervised learning data.

- **Threshold Setting:** When γ is reasonably large the performance degradation with the estimated threshold value is typically within 2-3% of the performance obtained with the best threshold.

7. CONCLUSION

In this paper we proposed a pairwise ranking based SVM (RSVM) method to build classifier models from positive and unlabeled examples. We build a ranking model by encouraging the positive examples to score higher than the unlabeled examples. Then the final classifier is built by estimating a threshold parameter. The proposed method is fast and also easy to implement via publicly available RSVM codes. We also proposed an AUC based feature selection technique for the LPU setting and demonstrated its usefulness. We conducted comprehensive experiments with various methods in both SL and LPU settings on several benchmark datasets and made several important observations. These experiments show that RSVM-LPU is worthy of inclusion in the repertoire of good methods for solving binary classification problems in web applications.

Acknowledgments: The authors are thankful to the anonymous reviewers for their helpful comments.

8. REFERENCES

[1] C. Burges, T. Shaked, E. Renshaw, A. Lazier, M. Deeds, N. Hamilton, and G. Hullender. Learning to rank using gradient descent. In *ICML '05: Proceedings of the Twenty Second International Conference on Machine Learning*, 2005.

[2] B. Calvo, P. Larranaga, and J. A. Lozano. Learning Bayesian classifiers from positive and unlabeled examples. *Pattern Recognition Letters*, 28:2375–2384, 2007.

[3] B. Calvo, P. Larranaga, and J. A. Lozano. Feature subset selection from positive and unlabeled examples. *Pattern Recognition Letters*, 30:1027–1036, 2009.

[4] C.-C. Chang and C.-J. Lin. *LIBSVM: a library for support vector machines*, 2001. Software available at http://www.csie.ntu.edu.tw/~cjlin/libsvm.

[5] O. Chapelle. *Software for Rank SVM*. {http://olivier.chapelle.cc/primal/ranksvm.m}.

[6] O. Chapelle and S. S. Keerthi. Multi-class feature selection with support vector machines. In *Proceedings of the American Statistical Association*, 2008.

[7] O. Chapelle and S. S. Keerthi. Efficient algorithms for ranking with SVMs. *To appear in Information Retrieval Journal, Special Issue on Learning to Rank*, 2009.

[8] F. Denis, R. Gilleron, and M. Tommasi. Text classification classifiers from positive and unlabeled examples. In *The 9th International Conf. Information Processing and Management of Uncertainty in Knowledge Based Systems*, pages 1927–1934, 2002.

[9] C. Elkan and K. Noto. Learning classifiers from only positive and unlabeled data. In *KDD '08: Proceeding of the 14th ACM SIGKDD international conference on Knowledge discovery and data mining*, pages 213–220, New York, NY, USA, 2008. ACM.

[10] G. Forman. An extensive empirical study of feature selection metrics for text classification. *Journal of Machine Learning Research*, pages 1289–1306, 2003.

[11] Y. Freund, R. Iyer, R. Schapire, and Y. Singer. An efficient boosting algorithm for combining preferences. *Journal of Machine Learning Research*, 4:933–969, 2003.

[12] R. Herbrich, T. Graepel, and K. Obermayer. Large margin rank boundaries for ordinal regression. In *Advances in Large Margin Classifiers*, pages 115–132. MIT Press.

[13] T. Joachims. A support vector method for multivariate performance measures. In *ICML '05: Processing of International conference on Machine learning*, pages 377–384, New York, NY, USA, 2005. ACM.

[14] T. Joachims. Training linear SVMs in linear time. In *KDD '06: Processing of Knowledge Discovery and Data Mining*. ACM, 2006. Software available at {http://www.cs.cornell.edu/People/tj/svm_light/svm_rank.html}.

[15] K. Lang. Newsweeder: Learning to filter netnews. In *ML '95: Proceedings of the 12th International Machine Learning Conference*, pages 331–339, 1995.

[16] W. S. Lee and B. Liu. Learning with positive and unlabeled examples using weighted logistic regression. In *ICML '03: Proceedings of the Twentieth International Conference on Machine Learning*, pages 448–455, 2003.

[17] X. Li and B. Liu. Learning to classify texts using positive and unlabeled data. In *Proceedings of International Joint Conferences on Artificial Intelligence*, pages 587–594, 2003.

[18] B. Liu, Y. Dai, X. Li, W. S. Lee, and P. S. Yu. Building text classifiers using positive and unlabeled examples. In *ICDM '03: Proceedings of the Third IEEE International Conference on Data Mining*, pages 179–186. IEEE Computer Society, 2003.

[19] B. Liu, W. S. Lee, P. S. Yu, and X. Li. Partially supervised classification of text documents. In *ICML '02: Proceedings of the Nineteenth International Conference on Machine Learning*, pages 387–394, San Francisco, CA, USA, 2002. Morgan Kaufmann Publishers Inc.

[20] L. M. Manevitz, M. Yousef, N. Cristianini, J. Shawe-taylor, and B. Williamson. One-class SVMs for document classification. *Journal of Machine Learning Research*, 2:139–154, 2001.

[21] V. Sindhwani and S. S. Keerthi. Large scale semi-supervised linear SVMs. Technical report, 2006. available at http://www.keerthis.com/semisup_techreport_06.ps.

[22] X. Wu, R. K. Srihari, and Z. Zheng. Document representation for one-class SVM. In *Proceedings of European Conference on Machine Learning*, pages 489–500, 2004.

[23] H. Yu, J. Han, and K. C.-C. Chang. PEBL: Web page classification without negative examples. *IEEE Transactions on Knowledge and Data Engineering*, 16:70–81, 2004.

[24] H. Yu, C. Zhai, and J. Han. Text classification classifiers from positive and unlabeled documents. In *Proc. 12th International Conf. Information and Knowledge Management*, pages 232–239, 2003.

[25] Z. Zheng, X. Wu, and R. Srihari. Feature selection for text categorization on imbalanced data. In *ACM KDD Explorations Newsletter*, pages 80–89, 2004.

Robust Nonnegative Matrix Factorization using L21-norm

Deguang Kong
Dept. of Computer Science and Engineering, University of Texas at Arlington,
doogkong@gmail.com

Chris Ding
Dept. of Computer Science and Engineering, University of Texas at Arlington,
CHQDing@uta.edu

Heng Huang
Dept. of Computer Science and Engineering, University of Texas at Arlington,
heng@uta.edu

ABSTRACT

Nonnegative matrix factorization (NMF) is widely used in data mining and machine learning fields. However, many data contain noises and outliers. Thus a robust version of NMF is needed. In this paper, we propose a robust formulation of NMF using $L_{2,1}$ norm loss function. We also derive a computational algorithm with rigorous convergence analysis. Our robust NMF approach, (1) can handle noises and outliers; (2) provides very efficient and elegant updating rules; (3) incurs almost the same computational cost as standard NMF, thus potentially to be used in more real world application tasks. Experiments on 10 datasets show that the robust NMF provides more faithful basis factors and consistently better clustering results as compared to standard NMF.

Categories and Subject Descriptors

I.2 [**Artificial Intelligence**]: Learning; I.5.3 [**Pattern Recognition**]: Clustering

General Terms

Algorithms, Theory

Keywords

NMF, L21 norm, Robust, Clustering

1. INTRODUCTION

Nonnegative Matrix Factorization (NMF) has been popularly studied in data mining and machine learning areas since the initial work of Lee and Seung [13]. Originally proposed as a method for finding matrix factors with parts-of-whole interpretations [13], NMF has been applied to a number of different areas, e.g., environmetrics [19], chemometrics [25], pattern recognition [14], multimedia data analysis [3], text mining [20] and DNA gene expression analysis [1]. Algorithmic extensions of NMF also have been developed to accommodate a variety of objective functions [4, 7] into different data analysis problems, including classification [21] collaborative filtering [22], and constrained clustering [15, 23]. It also can be extended by making a combination with Laplacian embedding [2, 11]. One of the key features of NMF is its clustering capabilities. It was shown [5, 8] that NMF essentially solves a matrix clustering problem.

Standard NMF uses the least square error function which is well-known to be unstable w.r.t. noises and outliers [24]. However, many real data in various applications probably contain noise and outliers. Potential applications in real world drive us to consider about a robust version of NMF. For this reason, a robust NMF model is studied in this paper.

To our knowledge, a robust NMF has not been studied so far. In this paper, we propose a novel robust formulation of NMF by using $L_{2,1}$-norm loss function[1]. The proposed method is termed as "robust" because it can accommodate outliers and noises in a better way than standard one. We derive the computational algorithm and provide rigorous analysis on its convergence and correctness. More importantly, the derived solution for robust NMF has very elegantly updating rules, with nearly the same computation cost as standard NMF, and also easy for implementation. We perform experiments on 10 datasets using both robust NMF and standard NMF. On all 10 datasets, robust NMF consistently outperforms standard NMF in terms of clustering results.

The merits of our Robust NMF are in threefold.

- Robust NMF can handle outliers and noises.
- Robust NMF provides very efficient and elegant updating rules.
- Robust NMF incurs almost the same computation cost as standard NMF, convenient for applications in different contexts.

The rest of the paper is organized as follows. In section 2 we propose the robust NMF formulation using $L_{2,1}$ norm, emphasize the advantages of our approach compared with standard NMF. In section 3, we present a rigorous convergence analysis of the algorithm. In section 4, we show that the converged solution satisfies the Karush-Kuhn-Tucker condition and thus is a correct optimal solution. In section 5 we present experimental results on 10 datasets. We show convergence properties, speed, and clustering results by making comparisons with standard NMF. Finally we discuss the extension of $L_{2,1}$ NMF to L_1 NMF followed by the conclusion.

2. ROBUST NMF USING $L_{2,1}$ NORM

In this section we first revisit standard NMF, show the assumption of the Gaussian noise leads to the formulation of standard NMF

[1]Robust NMF can also be formalized as L_1-NMF. We discuss the extension to L_1-NMF in section 6. In this paper, we focus on robust NMF with $L_{2,1}$-norm.

by imposing constraints $F \geq 0,\ G \geq 0$; then we present our robust NMF formulation, show the assumption of the Laplacian noise leads to the formulation of $L_{2,1}$ NMF; next we give two illustrative examples both on toy data and real data to show the robustness and effectiveness of $L_{2,1}$ NMF; finally we present the computational algorithm for $L_{2,1}$ NMF, and highlight the main contribution of our paper.

2.1 Review on standard NMF

Given input data vectors $X = (x_1, x_2, ...x_n)$, where $x_i \in R^p$ represents a data point. Standard NMF is defined as,

$$\min_{F,G} \ \|X - FG\|_F^2, \ \ s.t. \ F \geq 0, \ G \geq 0, \tag{1}$$

where $\|X\|_F^2 = \sum_{ij} X_{ij}^2$ is the Frobenius form of a matrix. Above problem is usually solved by an iterative updating algorithm, where F and G are updated alternatively using

$$F_{jk} \Leftarrow F_{jk} \frac{(XG^T)_{jk}}{(FGG^T)_{jk}}, \tag{2}$$

$$G_{ki} \Leftarrow G_{ki} \frac{(F^T X)_{ki}}{(F^T FG)_{ki}}. \tag{3}$$

2.2 From Gaussian noise to standard NMF

In general, the input data x_i is a p-dimensional column vector contaminated by additional noise,

$$x_i = \theta_i + \varepsilon_i, \tag{4}$$

where θ_i is the unobservable true value of the observed x_i, and ε_i is the additive noise. θ_i can be viewed as a point in a k-dimensional subspace ($k < p$) such that,

$$\theta_i = F g_i, \tag{5}$$

where g_i is the projection of x_i on the subspace defined by columns of F.

Suppose the noise ε_i follows zero-mean normal distribution with standard deviation of σ, thus $x_i \sim N(\theta_i, \sigma^2)$. Usually the elements of each vector x_i in X are independent, thus the probability distribution of x_i conditioned on θ_i is,

$$p(x_i|\theta_i) \sim \exp\{-\frac{||x_i - \theta_i||^2}{2\sigma^2}\} \tag{6}$$

The data log likelihood can be written as,

$$\log \prod_{i=1}^{n} p(x_i|\theta_i) = -\frac{1}{2\sigma^2} \sum_{i=1}^{n} ||x_i - \theta_i||^2 \tag{7}$$

To maximize the data log likelihood is equivalent to minimize the term $\sum_{i=1}^{n} ||x_i - \theta_i||^2$ in Eq.(7). Thus we have Eq. (8) by substituting θ_i with Fg_i by using Eq. (5),

$$\min_{\theta_i} \sum_{i=1}^{n} ||x_i - \theta_i||^2 = \min_{F,g_i} \sum_{i=1}^{n} ||x_i - Fg_i||^2 = \min_{F,G} ||X - FG||_F^2 \tag{8}$$

where g_i is the i-th column of G. This means the assumption of i.i.d Gaussian noise model transfers the maximum likelihood problem into a standard NMF problem by imposing constraints $F \geq 0, G \geq 0$.

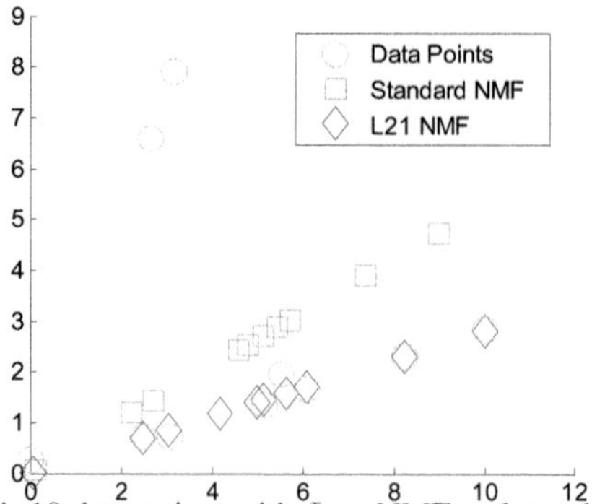

Figure 1: Fit 10 data points with $L_{2,1}$ NMF and standard NMF by using Fg_i. Two data points on upper-left are outliers.

2.3 Robust NMF using $L_{2,1}$ norm

One of the most important drawbacks of standard NMF is that it is prone to outliers. Let $X = (x_1, \cdots, x_n)$, $G = (g_1, \cdots, g_n)$. The error function of standard NMF is

$$\|X - FG\|_F^2 = \sum_{i=1}^{n} \|x_i - Fg_i\|^2 \tag{9}$$

Here the error for each data point enters the objective function as **squared** residue error in the form of $\|x_i - Fg_i\|^2$. Thus a few outliers with large errors easily dominate the objection function because of the squared errors. Note in NMF, both matrices F, G are unknown, the impact of the outliers may be more complicate than the simpler convex case. Thus it is very necessary to present robust NMF formulation and discuss its properties.

The robust formulation of the error function is

$$\|X - FG\|_{2,1} = \sum_{i=1}^{n} \sqrt{\sum_{j=1}^{p} (X - FG)_{ji}^2} = \sum_{i=1}^{n} \|x_i - Fg_i\| \tag{10}$$

In this robust formulation, the error for each data point is $\|x_i - Fg_i\|$, which is not squared, and thus the large errors due to outliers do not dominate the objective function because they are not squared.

For this reason, in this paper, we propose robust NMF ($L_{2,1}$ NMF) formulated as

$$\min_{F,G} \ \|X - FG\|_{2,1} \ \ s.t. \ F \geq 0, G \geq 0 \tag{11}$$

$L_{2,1}$ norm of a matrix A is first introduced in [9] and is defined as

$$\|A\|_{2,1} = \sum_{i=1}^{n} \sqrt{\sum_{j=1}^{p} A_{ji}^2} = \sum_{i=1}^{n} \|a_i\|. \tag{12}$$

where a_i is the ith column of A. In [9] it is called rotational invariant L_1 norm, because the column vectors a_i contribute in the form of vector Euclidean norm which is rotational invariant. $\|\cdot\|_{2,1}$ is a valid *norm* because it satisfies the 3 conditions for a norm: (1) positive scalability: $\|\alpha A\|_{2,1} = |\alpha|\|A\|_{2,1}$ where α is a real scalar; (2) triangle inequality: $\|A + B\|_{2,1} \leq \|A\|_{2,1} + \|B\|_{2,1}$; (3) existence of a zero vector: if $\|A\|_{2,1} = 0$, then $A = 0$. These 3 properties can be easily proved.

Note that in general, the $L_{2,1}$ norm of Eq.(11) is harder to solve than the least squares of the standard NMF of Eq.(1). One main contribution of our paper is to derive an efficient algorithm to solve the $L_{2,1}$ formulation of Eq.(11). We will present the algorithm in section 2.7.

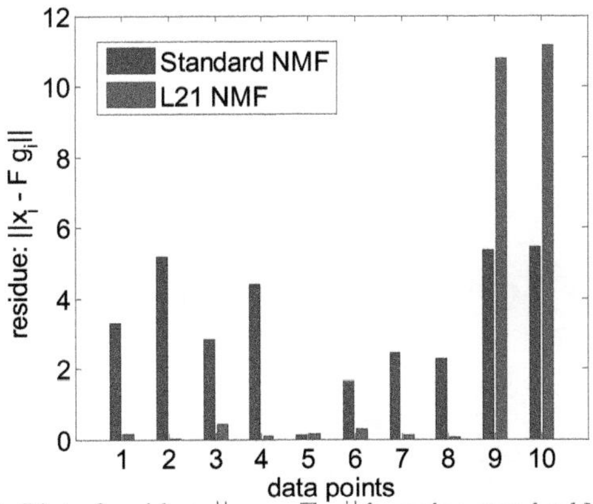

Figure 2: Plot of residue: $||x_i - Fg_i||$ by using standard NMF and $L_{2,1}$ NMF for each of 10 data points in Fig. 1. Data points #9 and #10 are outliers.

2.4 From Laplacian noise to $L_{2,1}$ NMF

Further, we show the motivation of $L_{2,1}$ NMF from probability point of view. Different from the normal distribution assumption in section 2.2, if we assume the noise ε_i follows the Laplacian distribution with zero mean, we have

$$p(x_i|\theta_i) \sim \exp\{-\frac{||x_i - \theta_i||}{\lambda}\}, \quad (13)$$

where λ is a scale parameter.

Following the strategy of maximizing the data log likelihood, we obtain,

$$\max_{\theta_i} \log \prod_{i=1}^{n} p(x_i|\theta_i) = \max_{\theta_i} -\frac{1}{\lambda}\sum_{i=1}^{n} ||x_i - \theta_i|| \quad (14)$$

To maximize the data log likelihood is equivalent to minimize the term $\sum_{i=1}^{n} ||x_i - \theta_i||$ in Eq.(14). Thus we have Eq. (15) by substituting θ_i with Fg_i,

$$\min_{\theta_i} \sum_{i=1}^{n} ||x_i - \theta_i|| = \min_{F,g_i} \sum_{i=1}^{n} ||x_i - Fg_i|| = \min_{F,G} ||X - FG||_{2,1} \quad (15)$$

This means the assumption of i.i.d Laplacian noise model transfers the maximum likelihood problem into a $L_{2,1}$ NMF problem by imposing constraints $F \geq 0, G \geq 0$.

2.5 Illustration of robust NMF on toy data

We use 2-dimensional toy data to show the robustness of $L_{2,1}$ NMF in Fig.(1). 10 original 2-dimensional data points are generated, two of which are outliers. For each data point, we use Fg_i to fit the original data point. Here we project all data into 1D subspace (i.e., $k = 1$). Both the fitting values from $L_{2,1}$ and standard NMF are shown in Fig. 1. $L_{2,1}$ NMF gives much better results while standard NMF is greatly influenced by two outliers. In Fig.(2), we also plot the residue $||x_i - Fg_i||$ corresponding to each data point of Fig.(1). Clearly, $L_{2,1}$ NMF gives much smaller errors compared with standard NMF.

2.6 Illustration of robust NMF on real data

To further illustrate the effectiveness of our $L_{2,1}$ NMF, we run $L_{2,1}$ NMF algorithm on real world data sets. Due to space limit, here we only show the results obtained from AT&T face image data set and Yale face data set in Figs. (3-4). On these two datasets, each x_i is corresponding to an image, which is linearized into a vector. The basis factor f_k in the computed $F = (f_1, f_2, ..., f_K)$ is thus an image. After NMF algorithms converge, we can reshape each f_k into its original size and show each f_i as an image.

Results on AT&T data and Yale data are shown in Fig.(3) and Fig.(4), respectively. Upper images of each row show the robust NMF results. Lower images of each row show the results of standard NMF. Better visual effects indicate better performance of the algorithm. Generally, $L_{2,1}$ NMF performs much better than standard NMF.

One example is the 6th upper image and the corresponding lower image in the top row of Fig.(3). You can see the clear differences between them. First of all, upper image is much clearer by keeping most of the pixel information. It is hard to tell "who is who" from the lower one. Next, most of the important pixels (e.g., pixels on eyes, month, nose) are preserved on upper image while some of them(e.g., eyes, month, cheek) are lost with noises of distorted pixels (e.g., anamorphic nose). Finally, compared to the particular category it comes from, the upper image resembles much more than the lower one.

Another example is images from Yale data set. See the 2nd face image in the upper part and the corresponding one in the lower part of top row of Fig.(4). The upper image is much better than the lower one. First of all, the lower image is fuzzy and shaded while the upper one is unshaded and vivid. Secondly, without any distortion and transformation, the upper image preserves most of the pixels while the lower one loses nearly half of the face pixels, and resembles more to the faces from the other categories (e.g., the 8th face in the 3rd row). Finally, the upper one is more similar to the particular category it is originated from.

From above results on real world data, we can see the superiority of robust NMF. Due to the noises and outliers existed in real data, it is reasonable for $L_{2,1}$ NMF to produce better results, which validates the effectiveness of our approach.

2.7 Computation Algorithm for $L_{2,1}$ NMF

The main contribution of this paper is to derive the following iteratively updating algorithm for Eq. (11),

$$F_{jk} \Leftarrow F_{jk} \frac{(XDG^T)_{jk}}{(FGDG^T)_{jk}} \quad (16)$$

$$G_{ki} \Leftarrow G_{ki} \frac{(F^T XD)_{ki}}{(F^T FGD)_{ki}} \quad (17)$$

where D is a diagonal matrix with the diagonal elements given by

$$D_{ii} = 1 \Big/ \sqrt{\sum_{j=1}^{p} (X - FG)_{ji}^2} = 1/||x_i - Fg_i||. \quad (18)$$

The computational algorithm for robust NMF is surprisingly simple. It has almost the same computational cost as standard NMF. It is easy to be adapted for various applications in different context. To our knowledge, this is the first study of the robust NMF with $L_{2,1}$ norm formulation.

We provide the proof of the convergence of the algorithm in section 3 and the correctness of the algorithm in section 4. We note that similar algorithmic approach has been used in $L_{2,1}$ based regression model [17] where no nonnegativity constraints are involved.

3. CONVERGENCE OF THE ALGORITHM

In this section, our main goal is to prove the convergence of the algorithm described in Theorem 1.

Figure 3: Computed $F = (f_1, \cdots f_K)$ on AT&T dataset ($K = 40$) shown as 4 rows. Upper images in each row are $L_{2,1}$ NMF results and lower images are standard NMF results.

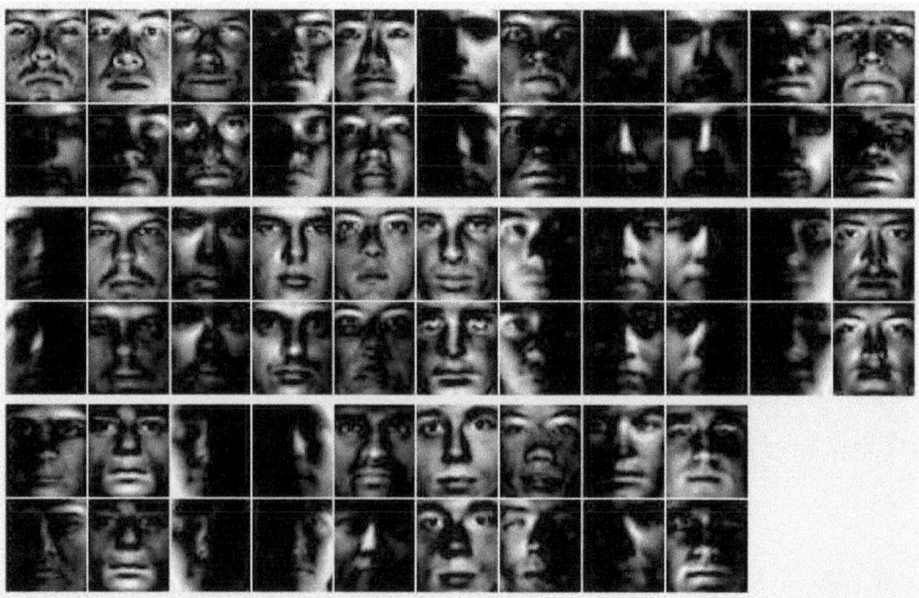

Figure 4: Computed $F = (f_1, \cdots f_K)$ on Yale dataset ($K = 31$) shown as 3 rows. Upper images in each row are $L_{2,1}$ NMF results and lower images are standard NMF results.

THEOREM 1. *(A) Updating G using the rule of Eq.(17) while fixing F, the objective function of Eq.(11) monotonically decreases. (B) Updating F using the rule of Eq.(16) while fixing G, the objective function of Eq.(11) monotonically decreases.*

We prove (A,B) separately in next two subsections.

3.1 Updating G

We focus on updating G while fixing F. The proof of Theorem 1(A) requires the following two lemmas.

LEMMA 2. *Let G^t be the old G [on the RHS of Eq.(17)] and G^{t+1} be the new G [on the LHS of Eq.(17)]. Under the updating rule of Eq.(17), the following inequation holds*

$$\begin{aligned} &Tr(X - FG^{t+1})D(X - FG^{t+1})^T \\ &\leq Tr(X - FG^t)D(X - FG^t)^T, \end{aligned} \tag{19}$$

where $D_{ii} = 1/\|x_i - Fg_i^t\|$.

The proof of Lemma 2 is given in section 3.3.

LEMMA 3. *Under the updating rule of Eq.(17), the following inequation holds*

$$\|X - FG^{t+1}\|_{2,1} - \|X - FG^t\|_{2,1} \leq \tag{20}$$

$$\begin{aligned} &\frac{1}{2}\Big[Tr(X - FG^{t+1})D(X - FG^{t+1})^T \\ &-Tr(X - FG^t)D(X - FG^t)^T\Big], \end{aligned} \tag{21}$$

where $D_{ii} = 1/\|x_i - Fg_i^t\|$.

The proof of Lemma 3 is given in section 3.4.

PROOF. (Theorem 1(A)). From Lemma 2, the value of expression inside $[\cdot]$ in Eq.(21) is negative or zero. Therefore

$$\|X - FG^{t+1}\|_{2,1} - \|X - FG^t\|_{2,1} \leq 0 \tag{22}$$

This proves that the objective function of Eq.(11) decreases monotonically. □

3.2 Updating F

We now focus on updating F while fixing G. Similarly, the proof of Theorem 1(B) also requires the following two lemmas.

LEMMA 4. *Let F^t be the old F [on the RHS of Eq.(16)] and F^{t+1} be the new F [on the LHS of Eq.(16)]. Under the updating rule of Eq.(16), the following inequation holds*

$$\begin{aligned} &Tr(X - F^{t+1}G)D(X - F^{t+1}G)^T \\ &\leq Tr(X - F^tG)D(X - F^tG)^T, \end{aligned} \tag{23}$$

where $D_{ii} = 1/\|x_i - F^tg_i\|$.

The proof of Lemma 4 is similar to the proof of Lemma 2 and thus is skipped due to space limitations.

LEMMA 5. *Under the updating rule of Eq.(16), the following inequation holds*

$$\|X - F^{t+1}G\|_{2,1} - \|X - F^tG\|_{2,1} \leq \tag{24}$$

$$\begin{aligned} &\frac{1}{2}\Big[Tr(X - F^{t+1}G)D(X - F^{t+1}G)^T \\ &-Tr(X - F^tG)D(X - F^tG)^T\Big], \end{aligned} \tag{25}$$

where $D_{ii} = 1/\|x_i - F^tg_i\|$.

The proof of Lemma 5 is similar to the proof of Lemma 3 and thus is skipped due to space limitations.

PROOF. (Theorem 1(B)). From Lemma 4, the value of expression inside $[\cdot]$ in line Eq.(25) is negative or zero. Therefore

$$\|X - F^{t+1}G\|_{2,1} - \|X - F^tG\|_{2,1} \leq 0 \tag{26}$$

This proves that the objective function of Eq.(11) decreases monotonically. □

3.3 Proof of Lemma 2

PROOF. Eq.(19) can be re-expressed as

$$J(G^{t+1}) \leq J(G^t) \tag{27}$$

where

$$J(G) = \mathrm{Tr}(X - FG)D(X - FG)^T \tag{28}$$

Lemma 2 states that under updating rule of Eq.(17), $J(G)$ monotonically decreases.

We prove Lemma 2 using the auxiliary function approach [13]. If a function satisfies

$$J(G) \leq Z(G, G'), \forall G' \tag{29}$$

$$Z(G, G) = J(G) \tag{30}$$

we say $Z(G, G')$ is an auxiliary function of $J(G)$. We define

$$G^{(t+1)} = \arg\min_G Z(G, G^{(t)}) \tag{31}$$

Then, we have

$$J(G^{(t+1)}) = Z(G^{(t+1)}, G^{(t+1)}) \leq Z(G^{(t+1)}, G^{(t)}) \leq J(G^{(t)})$$

This proves that $J(G^{(t)})$ monotonically decreases.

The key steps in the remainder of the proof are: (1) find an appropriate auxiliary function; (2) find the global maxima of the auxiliary function.

Now we show that an auxiliary function of $J(G)$ of Eq.(27) is

$$\begin{aligned} Z(G, G') = &\mathrm{Tr}(XDX^T - 2G^TF^TXD) \\ &+ \sum_{k=1}^{K}\sum_{i=1}^{n} \frac{(F^TFG'D)_{ki}G_{ki}^2}{G'_{ki}} \end{aligned} \tag{32}$$

First, $J(G)$ of Eq.(28) can be expressed as

$$J(G) = \mathrm{Tr}\left(XDX^T - 2G^TF^TXD + FGDG^TF^T\right). \tag{33}$$

We make use of the following matrix inequality [6]

$$\mathrm{Tr}\,(H^TAHB) \leq \sum_{ik}(AH'B)_{ik}\frac{H_{ik}^2}{H'_{ik}} \tag{34}$$

where A, B, H are nonnegative matrices with appropriate sizes and $A = A^T$, $B = B^T$. The equality holds when $H = H'$.

In the inequality Eq.(34), setting $A = F^TF, B = D, H = G, H' = G'$, then the 3rd term of Eq.(33) is always smaller than the 3rd term of Eq.(32). The equality holds when $G = G'$. Thus $Z(G, G')$ of Eq.(32) is an auxiliary function of $J(G)$ of Eq.(33).

Now we need to find the global minima of Eq.(32). Let $f(G) = Z(G, G')$. The gradient of $f(G)$ is

$$\frac{\partial f(G)}{\partial G_{ki}} = -2(F^TXD)_{ki} + 2\frac{(F^TFG'D)_{ki}G_{ki}}{G'_{ki}} \tag{35}$$

The 2nd order derivatives (Hessian matrix) is

$$\frac{\partial^2 f(G)}{\partial G_{ki}\partial G_{lj}} = \left(2\frac{(F^TFG'D)_{ki}}{G'_{ki}}\right)\delta_{ij}\delta_{kl}$$

Therefore, the Hessian matrix $\frac{\partial^2 f(G)}{\partial G_{ki} \partial G_{lj}}$ is semi-positive definite. This implies function $f(G)$ is a convex function and there is a unique global minima for $f(G)$.

The global minima is obtained by setting the gradient of $f(G)$ to zero and solve for G. Thus we set Eq.(35) to zero and obtain

$$G_{ki} = G'_{ki} \frac{(F^T XD)_{ki}}{(F^T FG'D)_{ki}} \tag{36}$$

Noting $G^{(t+1)} \leftarrow G$ and $G^{(t)} \leftarrow G'$, the above equation recovers the updating rule of Eq.(17). Therefore under this updating rule, the objective function $J(G)$ of Eq.(28) decreases monotonically. □

3.4 Proof of Lemma 3

PROOF. First we note that

$$\mathrm{Tr}(X - FG^t)D(X - FG^t)^T = \sum_{j=1}^{p} \sum_{i=1}^{n} (X - FG^t)^2_{ki} D_{ii} \tag{37}$$

$$= \sum_{i=1}^{n} \|x_i - Fg_i^t\|^2 D_{ii} \tag{38}$$

Similarly,

$$\mathrm{Tr}(X - FG^{t+1})D(X - FG^{t+1})^T = \sum_{i=1}^{n} \|x_i - Fg_i^{t+1}\|^2 D_{ii} \tag{39}$$

Thus the right-hand-size (RHS) of Eq.(21) becomes

$$RHS = \frac{1}{2} \sum_{i=1}^{n} \left(\|x_i - Fg_i^{t+1}\|^2 D_{ii} - \|x_i - Fg_i^t\|^2 D_{ii} \right) \tag{40}$$

$$= \frac{1}{2} \sum_{i=1}^{n} \left(\|x_i - Fg_i^{t+1}\|^2 D_{ii} - \frac{1}{D_{ii}} \right) \tag{41}$$

by using the definition $D_{ii} = 1/\|x_i - Fg_i^t\|$.

The left-hand-size (LHS) of Eq.(21) becomes

$$LHS = \sum_{i=1}^{n} \left(\|x_i - Fg_i^{t+1}\| - \|x_i - Fg_i^t\| \right) \tag{42}$$

$$= \sum_{i=1}^{n} \left(\|x_i - Fg_i^{t+1}\| - \frac{1}{D_{ii}} \right) \tag{43}$$

Therefore, we have

$$\begin{aligned} & LHS - RHS \\ &= \sum_{i=1}^{n} \left(\|x_i - Fg_i^{t+1}\| - \frac{1}{2}\|x_i - Fg_i^{t+1}\|^2 D_{ii} - \frac{1}{2D_{ii}} \right) \\ &= \sum_{i=1}^{n} \frac{D_{ii}}{2} \left(\frac{2\|x_i - Fg_i^{t+1}\|}{D_{ii}} - \|x_i - Fg_i^{t+1}\|^2 - \frac{1}{D_{ii}^2} \right) \\ &= \sum_{i=1}^{n} \frac{-D_{ii}}{2} \left(\|x_i - Fg_i^{t+1}\|^2 - 2\|x_i - Fg_i^{t+1}\| \frac{1}{D_{ii}} + \frac{1}{D_{ii}^2} \right) \\ &= \sum_{i=1}^{n} \frac{-D_{ii}}{2} \left(\|x_i - Fg_i^{t+1}\| - \frac{1}{D_{ii}} \right)^2 \\ &\le 0 \end{aligned} \tag{44}$$

This competes the proof. □

4. CORRECTNESS OF THE ALGORITHM

In previous section, we proved that the objective function decreases monotonically under updating of Eqs.(16,17). Here we prove that the converged solution is the correct optimal solution, i.e., the converged solution satisfies the Karush-Kohn-Tucker condition of the constrained optimization theory.

First we have Theorem 6 to prove the correctness of the algorithm w.r.t. F, and then we have Theorem 7 to prove the correctness of the algorithm w.r.t. G.

THEOREM 6. *At convergence, the converged solution F^* of the updating rule of Eq.(16) satisfies the KKT condition of the optimization theory.*

PROOF. The KKT condition for G with the constraints $F_{jk} \ge 0,\ j = 1 \cdots p,\ k = 1 \cdots K$, is

$$\frac{\partial J(F)}{\partial F_{jk}} F_{jk} = 0,\ \forall\, j, k \tag{45}$$

The derivative is

$$\begin{aligned} & \frac{\partial J(F)}{\partial F_{jk}} \\ &= \sum_{i=1}^{n} \frac{1}{\sqrt{\sum_{j'} (X - FG)^2_{j'i}}} \sum_{j''=1}^{p} (X - FG)_{j''i} \frac{\partial (X - FG)_{j''i}}{\partial F_{jk}} \\ &= \sum_{i=1}^{n} \frac{-1}{\sqrt{\sum_{j'} (X - FG)^2_{j'i}}} (X - FG)_{ji} G_{ki} \\ &= \sum_{i=1}^{n} -(X - FG)_{ji} G_{ki} D_{ii} \\ &= -(XDG^T)_{jk} + (FGDG^T)_{jk} \end{aligned} \tag{46}$$

Thus the KKT condition for F is

$$[-(XDG^T)_{jk} + (FGDG^T)_{jk}] F_{jk} = 0,\ \forall\, j, k \tag{47}$$

On the other hand, once F converges, according to the updating rule of Eq.(16), the converged solution F^* satisfies

$$F^*_{jk} = F^*_{jk} \frac{(XDG^T)_{jk}}{(F^* GDG^T)_{jk}} \tag{48}$$

which can be written as

$$[-(XDG^T)_{jk} + (F^* GDG^T)_{jk}] F^*_{jk} = 0, \tag{49}$$

This is identical to Eq.(47). Thus the converged solution satisfies the KKT condition. □

THEOREM 7. *At convergence, the converged solution G^* of the updating rule of Eq.(17) satisfies the KKT condition of the optimization theory.*

PROOF. The KKT condition for G with the constraints $G_{ki} \ge 0,\ k = 1 \cdots K,\ i = 1 \cdots n$, is

$$\frac{\partial J(G)}{\partial G_{ki}} G_{ki} = 0,\ \forall\, k, i \tag{50}$$

The derivative is

$$\begin{aligned}
&\frac{\partial J(F)}{\partial G_{ki}} \\
&= \sum_{i'=1}^{n} \frac{1}{\sqrt{\sum_{j'}(X-FG)_{j'i}^2}} \sum_{j=1}^{p} (X-FG)_{ji'} \frac{\partial (X-FG)_{ji'}}{\partial G_{ki}} \\
&= \sum_{i'=1}^{n} \frac{-1}{\sqrt{\sum_{j'}(X-FG)_{j'i'}^2}} \sum_{j=1}^{p} (X-FG)_{ji} F_{jk} \delta_{ii'} \\
&= -\frac{[F^T(X-FG)]_{ki}}{\sqrt{\sum_{j'}(X-FG)_{j'i}^2}} \\
&= -[F^T(X-FG)]_{ki} D_{ii} \\
&= -[F^T(X-FG)D]_{ki} \qquad (51)
\end{aligned}$$

Thus the KKT condition for G is

$$[-(F^T XD)_{ki} + (F^T FGD)_{ki}]G_{ki} = 0, \ \forall\, k, i \qquad (52)$$

On the other hand, once G converges according to the updating rule of Eq.(17), the converged solution G^* satisfies

$$G^*_{ki} \Leftarrow G^*_{ki} \frac{(F^T XD)_{ki}}{(F^T FG^* D)_{ki}} \qquad (53)$$

which can be written as

$$[-(F^T XD)_{ki} + (F^T FG^* D)_{ki}]G^*_{ki} = 0, \qquad (54)$$

This is identical to Eq.(52). Thus the converged solution G^* satisfies the KKT condition. □

5. EXPERIMENTS

In this section, we apply the proposed $L_{2,1}$ NMF clustering algorithm to compare its performance with standard NMF algorithm and k-means algorithm. Extensive experiments are made on ten well known data sets.

5.1 Dataset description

We use 6 widely used image data sets and also 4 UCI[1] data sets. Table 1 summarizes the characteristics of those data sets.

AT&T[2]. There are totally 400 images belonging to 40 different subjects. For each subject, the images are in great varieties because of different taking time with changing lighting variance and facial expressions. All the pictures are taken with dark homogeneous background. The size of each cropped image is 112x92 pixels. We resize each image to 56x46 pixels in our evaluation.

MNIST. This hand-written digits data set consists of 70,000 digital images, which are from digit "0" to "9" [12]. We centralize each image to 28x28 pixels according to the center of the mass of the pixel intensities. We random select 15 images from each class, and there are totally 150 images in our evaluation data set.

UMIST. It is a face-recognition data set frequently used in computer vision field. It is challenge to recognize the faces in this data set because the variations for the face from the same class are larger than those in other face recognition problems. Each image is cropped to 28x23 pixels. There are totally 360 images with 20 different classes.

CMU PIE. It is a face data set containing 68 subjects with 41,368 face images. In the preprocessing step, we normalize the images(in scale and direction) to keep the two eyes are aligned at the same position. Each image is resized into 32x32 pixels. In our experiment, we random select 10 images from each class with different combinations of pose, face expression and illumination condition.

Yale. It is a data set obtained from the combinations of the original and extended Yale database [10]. There are totally 38 classes (10 subjects in original database with 28 subjects in the extended database) under 576 viewing conditions (9 poses with 64 different illumination conditions). We shrink each image by a factor of 0.25 to size 48x42. We select 64 images in different illumination conditions from 31 classes, and therefore there are totally 1984 images.

Bin-alpha. This data set is composed of 1404 binary images of handwritten digits from "0" to "9" and also characters from "A" to "Z", totally 36 classes. The resolution of each image is 20x16 pixels.

For all the image data sets, we use the same original space without making any changes and also the raw gray level values as features. The other four non-image data sets German, Car, Lenses, Vehicle are randomly selected from the UCI Repository. All of them only have non-negative values as features. Robust NMF can be applied to text, web and social network datasets for various applications.

5.2 Measurement

The evaluation metrics [16, 18] we used here are clustering accuracy, normalized mutual information and purity. These measurement are widely used in the evaluation of different clustering approaches.

Clustering accuracy(ACC) is defined as,

$$ACC = \frac{\sum_{i=1}^{n} \delta(l_i, map(c_i))}{n}, \qquad (55)$$

where l_i is the true class label and c_i is the obtained cluster label of x_i, map(.) is the best mapping function, $\delta(x, y)$ is the delta function where $\delta(x, y) = 1$ if $x = y$, and $\delta(x, y) = 0$ otherwise. The mapping function map(.) matches the true class label and the obtained clustering label, where the best mapping is solved by Hungarian algorithm. A large ACC value indicates a better clustering performance.

Normalized mutual information (NMI) is used to evaluate the clustering quality from information point, and defined by normalization on the mutual information between the cluster assignments and the pre-existing input labeling of the classes. The normalization used is the average of the entropy of the cluster assignment and that of pre-existing input labeling. More formally,

$$NMI = \frac{I(S, C)}{(H(S) + H(C))/2}, \qquad (56)$$

where $C = \{c_1, c_2, ..., c_k\}$ is the pre-existing classes, $S = \{S_1, S_2, ..., S_k\}$ is a particular clustering result, $I(S, C)$ is the mutual information of clustering assignment with pre-existing class labels, and $H(S)$ is the entropy for the clustering assignment. A larger NMI valuealso indicates a better clustering solution.

Purity measures the extent to which each cluster contained data points from primarily one class. The purity of a clustering is obtained by the weighted sum of individual cluster purity values, given as,

$$Purity = \sum_{i=1}^{k} \frac{n_i}{n} P(S_i), P(S_i) = \frac{1}{n_i} \max{}_j(n_i^j). \qquad (57)$$

where S_i is a particular cluster size of n_i, n_i^j is the number of the i-th input class that were assigned to the j-th cluster. k is the number of the clusters and n is the total number of the data points. A large Purity value indicates a good clustering solution.

[1]http://archive.ics.uci.edu/ml/

[2]http://www.cl.cam.ac.uk/research/dtg/attarchive/facedatabase.html

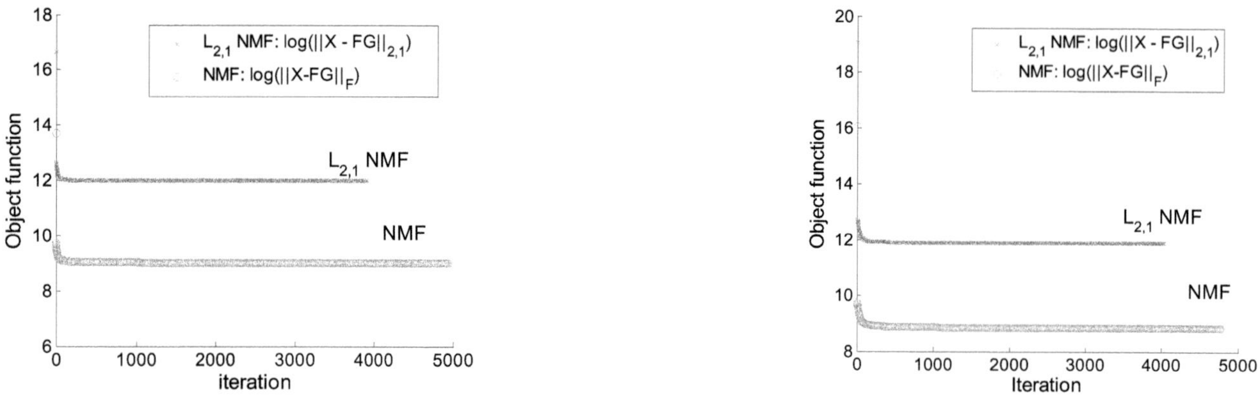

(a) UMIST (b) AT&T

Figure 5: Demonstration of the object function and the number of iterations needed before convergence of $L_{2,1}$ NMF and NMF on data sets UMIST and AT&T. The object functions we demonstrate are $log(||X - FG||_{2,1})$ and $log(||X - FG||_F)$. The convergence criteria is described in Eq. (58).

Table 1: Description of dataset

Dataset	#Size	#Dimensions	#Class
AT&T	400	2576	40
MNIST	150	784	10
CMUPIE	680	1024	68
UMIST	360	644	20
YALE	1984	2016	31
Bin-alph	1404	320	36
German	1000	20	2
Cars	392	8	3
WINE	178	13	3
Vehicle	846	18	4

Table 2: Comparison on the object functions and time cost on data sets, UMIST and AT&T. We present the normalized convergence error (NCE), i.e., $\frac{||X-FG||_{2,1}}{||X||_{2,1}}$ and $\frac{||X-FG||_F}{||X||_F}$. *Iteration* represents the time of iterations needed before converges according to the convergence criteria of Eq.(58).

Dataset	Metric	$L_{2,1}$NMF	NMF
UMIST	NCE	0.1598	0.1721
	Time(sec.)	73.6396	52.6239
	Iteration	3906	4932
AT&T	NCE	0.1185	0.1375
	Time(sec.)	121.5217	96.0741
	Iteration	4029	4783

5.3 Convergence analysis for $L_{2,1}$ NMF

We make convergence analysis on real world image data sets. We reshape each image into one vector, and then form a large matrix X, where each column is a linearized vector from an image. For example, AT&T data set has 400 images, where the size of each image is 56x46 pixels, thus X is constructed with size 2576x400. With the same input data X, we random generate the same F and G to feed into NMF model and $L_{2,1}$ NMF model. We compare the convergence properties (e.g., speed, object function values) of $L_{2,1}$ NMF with standard NMF.

We test convergence in each iteration by computing the object function values. The convergence criterion we used is

$$\frac{J_{t+1} - J_t}{J_t} < 10^{-7}, \tag{58}$$

where J_t is the object function values ($||X - FG||_F$ for NMF and $||X - FG||_{2,1}$ for robust NMF) in the t-th iteration in the convergence tests. For the fairness of comparisons, we use the non-squared object function $||X - FG||_F$ in standard NMF instead of the squared object function $||X - FG||^2$.

We implement our algorithm in Matlab 7.0. All the experiments are done on a AMD Phenom(tm) 2.80GHZ machine with 6GB memory running Windows 7. The initial object functions are computed through the random guess of F and G. Fig.(5) shows the log object functions and also the number of iterations needed for the convergence of NMF and $L_{2,1}$ NMF on the data sets UMIST and AT&T. Because data matrix X can be very large, for the convenience of demonstration, here we show the log values of the object functions, i.e., $log(||X - FG||_F)$ and $log(||X - FG||_{2,1})$.

Our experiment results show that on data set UMIST, $L_{2,1}$ NMF needs 3906 iterations before convergence while NMF needs 4932 iterations before convergence. However, the computation time cost on $L_{2,1}$ NMF is higher than NMF due to the updating rule on the diagonal matrix D. As is shown in Table 2, both on UMIST and AT&T data sets, $L_{2,1}$ NMF takes less iterations to converge than NMF, yet with more computation time.

Also, the object function of $L_{2,1}$ NMF is always larger than non-squared NMF object function due to the formulation of $L_{2,1}$ norm defined in Eq.(10). It is worth mentioning that the larger object function values do not necessarily mean the worse matrix factorization results. As is shown in Table 2, $L_{2,1}$ NMF has lower normalized convergence error compared with NMF on those two testing data, which shows the effectiveness of $L_{2,1}$ NMF.

5.4 Clustering Results

We report clustering results by making comparisons with K-means clustering and standard NMF clustering approach. For the initializations of F and G, we did not use the random generated matrices. Firstly, we use the principal component analysis to get a subspace with r-dimension. After this, k-means clustering approach is employed on the projection data to get clustering results. We use above clustering results G' to initialize $G = G' + 0.3$, and then F are

Table 3: Clustering quality comparison of $L_{2,1}$ NMF with NMF and k-means on 10 data sets.

Dataset	Metric	Approaches		
		$L_{2,1}$-NMF	NMF	k-means
AT&T	ACC	**0.6808**	0.6496	0.6519
	NMI	**0.8206**	0.7945	0.8134
	PUR	**0.7210**	0.6822	0.7021
MNIST	ACC	**0.7719**	0.7297	0.6872
	NMI	**0.7429**	0.6966	0.6788
	PUR	**0.7849**	0.7461	0.7068
UMIST	ACC	**0.5176**	0.4861	0.4744
	NMI	**0.6174**	0.5869	0.6030
	PUR	**0.5306**	0.5029	0.5185
CMUPIE	ACC	**0.4321**	0.4138	0.2227
	NMI	**0.6782**	0.6557	0.5386
	PUR	**0.4562**	0.4377	0.2429
YALE	ACC	**0.2117**	0.1950	0.0870
	NMI	**0.3114**	0.2882	0.0933
	PUR	**0.2238**	0.2082	0.0943
Bin-alpha	ACC	**0.3594**	0.3283	0.3342
	NMI	**0.5621**	0.4987	0.5072
	PUR	**0.4138**	0.3791	0.3897
German	ACC	**0.6670**	0.6431	0.6308
	NMI	**0.4621**	0.4306	0.4275
	PUR	**0.7000**	0.7000	0.7000
Cars	ACC	**0.6171**	0.5436	0.4617
	NMI	**0.4394**	0.3837	0.2989
	PUR	**0.6720**	0.6406	0.6356
WINE	ACC	**0.8764**	0.8371	0.7138
	NMI	**0.6373**	0.5619	0.4268
	PUR	**0.8764**	0.8371	0.7138
Vehicle	ACC	**0.4812**	0.4697	0.4456
	NMI	**0.3987**	0.3767	0.3429
	PUR	**0.4934**	0.4719	0.4456

obtained by computing the clustering centroid for each category. Empirically, we run k-means 10 times during initializations of G.

Clustering Analysis on Confusion Matrices. Firstly, we show the confusion matrices constructed from the clustering analysis. The diagonals of the matrices show the number of data points that are clustered into the default subject clusters. The number of data with correct clustering labels can be directly computed by summing over all the diagonals in each matrix. Due to space limit, we did not show all the confusion matrices on all data sets. Figs. (6-9) show the confusion matrices on data sets UMIST, YALE, MNIST, PIE. It is easy to see that the diagonals of confusion matrices in $L_{2,1}$ NMF are much stronger than those of standard NMF approach.

Clustering Results Analysis. Table 3 summarizes the clustering results of our approach by making comparisons with standard NMF and k-means clustering. The metrics we used here are clustering accuracy(ACC), normalized mutual information(NMI) and purity(PUR). Extensive experiments are made on 10 data sets, 6 of which are image data sets and the other 4 are from UCI data sets. The experiments can also be easily conducted on other text/web data sets. On each dataset, the clustering number is set to the real number of classes in ground truth (e.g., for data set AT&T, K = 40; for data set MNIST, K = 10). For fairness, we use the same generated F and G to compare the performance of NMF and $L_{2,1}$ NMF in each round. k-means algorithm is run 10 times to get the clustering results with the least object function values. From Table

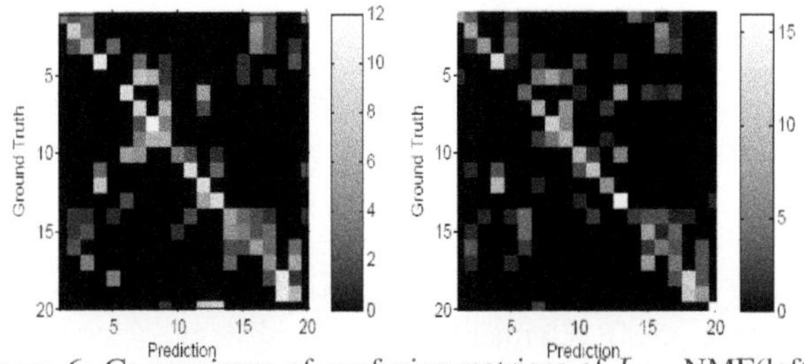

Figure 6: Comparisons of confusion matrices of $L_{2,1}$ NMF(left in each panel) and NMF(right in each panel) on dataset UMIST. Each column of a matrix represents the instances in a predicted class, and each row represents the instances in an actual class.

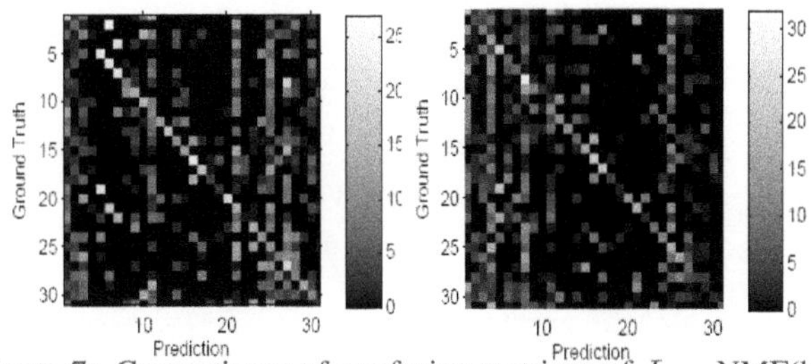

Figure 7: Comparisons of confusion matrices of $L_{2,1}$ NMF(left) and NMF(right) on dataset Yale.

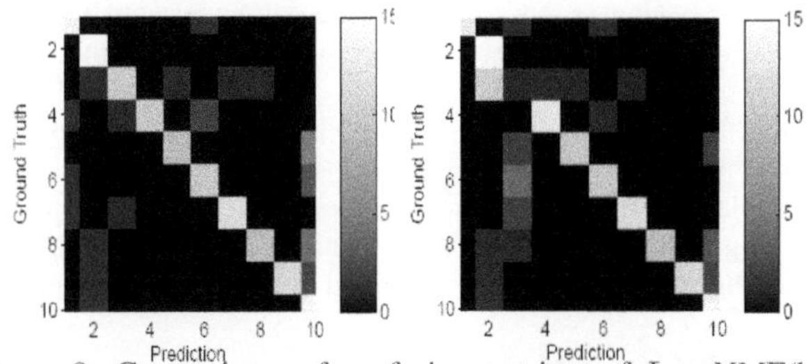

Figure 8: Comparisons of confusion matrices of $L_{2,1}$ NMF(left) and NMF(right) on dataset MNIST.

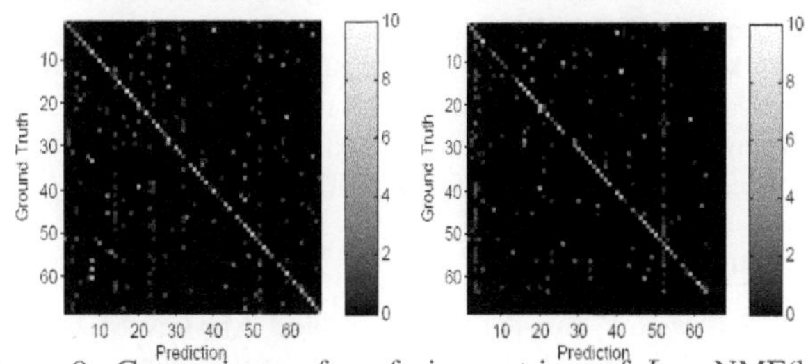

Figure 9: Comparisons of confusion matrices of $L_{2,1}$ NMF(left) and NMF(right) on dataset PIE.

3, we can see, (1). $L_{2,1}$ NMF approach performs better than standard NMF approach on all data sets. (2). $L_{2,1}$ NMF outperforms k-means clustering on all data sets.

6. EXTENSION TO L_1-NMF

Here we briefly discuss the extension of NMF to another form of robust NMF: L_1-NMF. The most robust formulation of the error function is

$$\|X - FG\|_1 = \sum_{i=1}^{n}\sum_{j=1}^{p} |(X - FG)_{ji}|. \tag{59}$$

For computational reasons, we replace $|(X - FG)_{ij}|$ by $\left((X - FG)_{ij}^2 + \epsilon^2\right)^{1/2}$. Here ϵ is set to a very small number. Thus we minimize the objective function

$$J_1 = \|X - FG\|_1 = \sum_{i=1}^{n}\sum_{j=1}^{p}((X - FG)_{ji}^2 + \epsilon^2)^{1/2}. \quad (60)$$

Formally, L_1-NMF is formulated as

$$\min_{F,G} \; J_1(F, G) \;\; s.t. \;\; F \geq 0, \; G \geq 0. \quad (61)$$

Extending our approach in deriving the computational algorithm for $L_{2,1}$-NMF, we can derive the following updating algorithms for L_1-NMF:

$$F_{jk} \Leftarrow F_{jk}\frac{[X \circ WG^T]_{jk}}{[(FG) \circ WG^T]_{jk}}, \quad (62)$$

$$G_{ki} \Leftarrow G_{ki}\frac{[F^T X \circ W]_{ki}}{[F^T (FG) \circ W]_{ki}}, \quad (63)$$

where W is a matrix given by $W_{ij} = \left((X - FG)_{ij}^2 + \epsilon^2\right)^{-1/2}$, and $\circ$ is the Hadamard product, i.e., elementwise product between two matrices. Here we assume Hadamard product has higher operator precedence over regular matrix product, i.e., $AB \circ CD = A(B \circ C)D$. Convergence property and correctness analysis can be similarly established. Details will be published in a forthcoming paper.

A striking feature of the L_1-NMF updating algorithm [Eqs.(62-63)] is its nearly-identical forms the $L_{2,1}$-NMF algorithm [Eqs.(16,17)] if we replace D by W; they are also nearly-identical to the algorithm [Eqs.(2,3)] of standard NMF. Analysis of this unified NMF algorithmic framework will be presented in the forthcoming paper.

7. CONCLUSION

In this paper, we propose a robust formulation of NMF using L21-norm. We also derive a computational algorithm with rigorous convergence analysis. Experiments on 10 datasets show that the robust NMF provides more faithful basis factors and consistently better clustering results as compared to standard NMF.

Acknowledgements. This work is partially supported by NSF-CCF-0939187, NSF-CCF-0917274, NSF-DMS-15228.

8. REFERENCES

[1] J.-P. Brunet, P. Tamayo, T. Golub, and J. Mesirov. Metagenes and molecular pattern discovery using matrix factorization. *Proc. Nat'l Academy of Sciences USA*, 102(12):4164–4169, 2004.

[2] D. Cai, X. He, X. Wu, and J. Han. Non-negative matrix factorization on manifold. In *ICDM*, pages 63–72, 2008.

[3] M. Cooper and J. Foote. Summarizing video using non-negative similarity matrix factorization. In *Proc. IEEE Workshop on Multimedia Signal Processing*, pages 25–28, 2002.

[4] I. Dhillon and S. Sra. Generalized nonnegative matrix approximations with Bregman divergences. In *Advances in Neural Information Processing Systems 17*, Cambridge, MA, 2005. MIT Press.

[5] C. Ding, X. He, and H. Simon. On the equivalence of nonnegative matrix factorization and spectral clustering. *Proc. SIAM Data Mining Conf*, 2005.

[6] C. Ding, T. Li, and M. Jordan. Convex and semi-nonnegative matrix factorizations. *IEEE Trans. Pattern Analysis and Machine Intelligence*, 2010. (LBNL Tech Report 60428, 2006).

[7] C. Ding, T. Li, and W. Peng. Nonnegative matrix factorization and probabilistic latent semantic indexing: Equivalence, chi-square statistic, and a hybrid method. *Proc. National Conf. Artificial Intelligence*, 2006.

[8] C. Ding, T. Li, W. Peng, and H. Park. Orthogonal nonnegative matrix tri-factorizations for clustering. In *Proceedings of ACM SIGKDD*, pages 126–135, 2006.

[9] C. Ding, D. Zhou, X. He, and H. Zha. R1-pca: Rotational invariant l1-norm principal component analysis for robust subspace factorization (pdf file). *Proc. Int'l Conf. Machine Learning (ICML)*, June 2006.

[10] A. S. Georghiades, P. N. Belhumeur, and D. J. Kriegman. From few to many: Illumination cone models for face recognition under variable lighting and pose. *PAMI*, 23:643–660, 2001.

[11] Q. Gu and J. Zhou. Co-clustering on manifolds. In *KDD*, pages 359–368, 2009.

[12] Y. Lecun, L. Bottou, Y. Bengio, and P. Haffner. Gradient-based learning applied to document recognition. In *Proceedings of the IEEE*, pages 2278–2324, 1998.

[13] D. D. Lee and H. S. Seung. Algorithms for non-negative matrix factorization. In *NIPS*, 2000.

[14] S. Li, X. Hou, H. Zhang, and Q. Cheng. Learning spatially localized, parts-based representation. In *CVPR*, pages 207–212, 2001.

[15] T. Li, C. Ding, and M. I. Jordan. Solving consensus and semi-supervised clustering problems using nonnegative matrix factorization. In *ICDM*, pages 577–582, 2007.

[16] F. Nie, C. H. Q. Ding, D. Luo, and H. Huang. Improved minmax cut graph clustering with nonnegative relaxation. In *ECML/PKDD*, pages 451–466, 2010.

[17] F. Nie, H. Huang, X. Cai, and C. Ding. Efficient and robust feature selection via joint l2,1-norms minimization. *NIPS*, 2010.

[18] F. Nie, D. Xu, I. W. Tsang, and C. Zhang. Spectral embedded clustering. In *IJCAI*, pages 1181–1186, 2009.

[19] P. Paatero and U. Tapper. Positive matrix factorization: A non-negative factor model with optimal utilization of error estimates of data values. *Environmetrics*, 5:111–126, 1994.

[20] V. P. Pauca, F. Shahnaz, M. Berry, and R. Plemmons. Text mining using non-negative matrix factorization. In *Proc. SIAM Int'l conf on Data Mining*, pages 452–456, 2004.

[21] F. Sha, L. K. Saul, and D. D. Lee. Multiplicative updates for nonnegative quadratic programming in support vector machines. In *Advances in Neural Information Processing Systems 15*. MIT Press, Cambridge, MA, 2003.

[22] N. Srebro, J. Rennie, and T. Jaakkola. Maximum margin matrix factorization. In *Advances in Neural Information Processing Systems*, Cambridge, MA, 2005. MIT Press.

[23] F. Wang, T. Li, and C. Zhang. Semi-supervised clustering via matrix factorization. In *SDM*, pages 1–12, 2008.

[24] N. Z. Weixiang Liu and Q. You. Nonnegative matrix factorization and its applications in pattern recognition. *Chinese Science Bulletin*, 51(1):7–18, 2006.

[25] Y.-L. Xie, P. Hopke, and P. Paatero. Positive matrix factorization applied to a curve resolution problem. *Journal of Chemometrics*, 12(6):357–364, 1999.

TAKES: A Fast Method to Select Features in the Kernel Space*

Ye Xu[1], Furao Shen[2], Wei Ping[3], and Jinxi Zhao[2]
Computer Science Department, Dartmouth College, NH, USA[1]
ye@cs.dartmouth.edu
National Key Laboratory for Novel Software Technology, Nanjing University, Nanjing, China[2]
{frshen,jxzhao}@nju.edu.cn
Department of Computer Science, University of California Irvine, CA, USA[3]
weiping.thu@gmail.com

ABSTRACT

Feature selection is an effective tool to deal with the "curse of dimensionality". To cope with the non-separable problem, feature selection in the kernel space has been investigated. However, previous study cannot adequately estimate the intrinsic dimensionality of the kernel space. Thus, it is difficult to accurately preserve the sketch of the kernel space using the learned basis, and the feature selection performance is affected. Moreover, the computing load of the algorithm reaches at least cubic with the number of training data. In this paper, we propose a fast framework to conduct feature selection in the kernel space. By designing a fast kernel subspace learning method, we automatically learn the intrinsic dimensionality and construct an orthogonal basis set of kernel space. The learned basis can accurately preserve the sketch of kernel space. Then backed by the constructed basis, we directly select features in kernel space. The whole proposed framework has a quadratic complexity with the number of training data, which is faster than existing kernel methods for feature selection. We evaluate our work under several typical datasets and find it not only preserves the sketch of the kernel space more accurately but also achieves better classification performance compared with many state-of-the-art methods.

Categories and Subject Descriptors

I.2.6 [**Learning**]: Induction; I.5.4 [**Pattern Recognition**]: Application

General Terms

Theory, Algorithm, Performance

Keywords

Feature Selection, Kernel Space, Orthogonal Subspace Learning

*This paper was done when Ye Xu was affiliated with Nanjing University.

CIKM '11 October 24–28, 2011, Glasgow, Scotland, UK.

1. INTRODUCTION

The "curse of dimensionality" is a serious problem for classification tasks involving high-dimensional data. Reducing the dimensionality is an important tool to address this problem. By reducing the dimensionality, we obtain a reduced representation of input data that is much smaller in volume, and produce the same (or almost the same) analytical result.

Generally, techniques for reducing dimensionality can be categorized into two classes, i.e., dimensionality reduction and feature selection. Some typical dimensionality reduction methods, such as Principal Component Analysis (PCA) [9], Linear Discriminant Analysis (LDA) [21], Maximum Margin Criterion (MMC) [17], Locally Linear Embedding (LLE) [24], ISOMAP[31] and their invariants [8, 38, 37, 19, 23, 39, 5], try to use transformations to convert original high-dimensional data space into lower-dimensional feature space, which have been proved to be effective. However, the high dimensionality of data sets often fails many such algorithms due to their high computational cost.

In this paper we focus on feature selection techniques. Feature selection algorithms (e.g., [15, 40, 32, 33, 29, 14, 36]) directly remove non-discriminative features in order to build robust learning models based on some certain criterions, which attract a variety of attentions [16, 28, 12, 25].

Traditional methods for reducing dimensionality may work well in linear separable problems. However, for nonlinear problems, the performance may be affected. Therefore, kernel technique is proposed to tackle this issue. Some traditional dimensionality reduction methods have been extended into kernel version [22, 30, 1] and achieve sweet results.

For feature selection methods, some works [20, 18] have been done to employ kernels to help select features in original space, which improve classification performance to some extent. However, such algorithms still select features in the original space, which can not guarantee a good performance for the nonlinear problems. Because the dimensionality of the kernel space is implicit, it is a big challenge to directly select features in the kernel space. It is no wonder that few works can handle this thorny issue.

In this paper, we propose a feature selection method in the kernel space named as Two-stage fAst Kernel fEature Selection (TAKES). In the first stage, we design a fast kernel subspace learning method to learn the intrinsic dimensionality of the kernel space, and construct an orthogonal basis. Then in the second stage, via the learned orthogonal basis, we directly select discriminative features in the kernel space using the kernel trick. In summary, the first contribution of this paper is that, we design a framework to directly select discriminative features in the kernel space. The classification performance under the selected features is better. The second contribution of our work is designing a kernel subspace learning algorithm to automatically estimate the intrinsic dimensionality of the kernel space and construct an orthogonal basis. The learned dimensionality of the kernel space is completely data-dependent and a small reconstruction cost [24] is guaranteed. Here, the reconstruction cost is a measure to evaluate whether the learned basis can accurately preserve the sketch of data [10] in the kernel space. The third contribution is the small computing load compared with other kernel methods for reducing dimensionality.

The rest of this paper is organized as follows. In section 2, we briefly discuss some related works. Our TAKES method is proposed in section 3. In section 4, we report on experimental results. Finally in Section 5, we conclude the paper.

2. RELATED WORK

Feature selection algorithms have been investigated for many years. Because obtaining an optimum set of features has been demonstrated as an NP-hard problem [35], many algorithms handle feature selection tasks by introducing weights on dimensionality to obtain approximate solutions. Such methods can be divided into several categories. Based on the assumption that the discriminative power of each feature is independent of each other, Information Gain (IG) [33] and χ^2-test [40] measure the amount of information obtained by each feature for classification and then discard those features whose discriminative powers are small. But these methods might fail when features are not independent of each other. Relief [15, 29] is another category feature selection algorithm. It estimates features according to how well their values distinguish among instances that are near each other, where smart heuristic is used. Boosting methods [32] have been used for feature selection, in which discriminative features are selected and combined into an ensemble classifier. The generalization error of boosting family algorithms [14] has been proven to be controlled by a bound in terms of a margin measure [34]. Therefore, such algorithms have better performance and wide applications [16, 28]. To improve the time complexity of boosting methods, Forward Feature Selection (FFS) [36] has been proposed. Unlike many other boosting algorithms, FFS trains weak classifiers only once, and thus is able to obtain lower time complexity (O(dN)) compared with most boosting family methods (O($dNlogN$)). Here, N is the size of the training set, and d is the number of selected features.

Our work also relates to kernel methods for feature selection [20, 18]. Most of such methods still select features in the original space, which cannot change the non-separability nature of the data. A better solution is directly selecting features in kernel space. To the best of our knowledge, [6] is the only work that selects features in the kernel space. In this work, by learning a basis for the kernel space, Relief [15] is employed to select features. However, the major shortcoming of [6] is that, the intrinsic dimensionality of the kernel space in their work is constantly set up as the size of training set. It is not accurate unless all mapped training data in the kernel space are independent of each other. However, they are not necessarily independent. Therefore, this heuristically determined dimensionality undermines the orthogonality of learned basis. In this case, the basis set cannot accurately preserve the sketch of the kernel space; the feature selection performance is influenced. Another limitation of [6] is the computing load. By employing a kernel subspace learning method such as Kernel Gram-Schmidt (KGS) or Kernel Principal Component Analysis (KPCA) [26] to construct the basis, the time complexity is at least $O(N^3)$.

In our work, we aim at selecting features in the kernel space. First we design a fast kernel subspace learning method to learn the intrinsic dimensionality of the kernel space, and construct an orthogonal basis to accurately preserve the sketch of the mapped data in the kernel space. Then with the aid of the basis, discriminative features in the kernel space are directly selected with a smaller computing load.

3. SELECT FEATURES IN THE KERNEL SPACE

Traditional feature selection methods may not work well in linearly non-separable problems. To overcome the shortcoming, in this paper, we select discriminative features directly from the kernel space instead of from the original data space.

Suppose ϕ maps input data $\boldsymbol{x} \in \mathcal{R}^D$ to a $\mathcal{H}$-dimensional kernel space:

$$\phi : \boldsymbol{x} \rightarrow [\phi_1(\boldsymbol{x}), \phi_2(\boldsymbol{x}), ...\phi_{\mathcal{H}}(\boldsymbol{x})]^\top \tag{1}$$

In order to directly select discriminative features in the kernel space, we need to know the value of $\phi_i(\boldsymbol{x})$, i.e., the ith feature of $\phi(\boldsymbol{x})$. However, in the kernel space, $\phi(\boldsymbol{x})$ and the number of features $\mathcal{H}$ are implicit. Thus it is difficult for us to achieve $\phi_i(\boldsymbol{x})$ explicitly.

To address this problem, we construct an orthogonal basis set $\{\mathbf{w_i}\} = \{\sum_{j=1}^N \hat{\alpha}_{i,j}\phi(\boldsymbol{x_j})\}$ for the kernel space, where $\{\boldsymbol{x_j}\}_{j=1}^N$ are training data, $\hat{\alpha}_i$ are the coefficient vectors, and $\hat{\alpha}_{i,j}$ is the jth component of $\hat{\alpha}_i$. Then $\phi_i(\boldsymbol{x})$ can be calculated by using the kernel trick:

$$\phi_i(\boldsymbol{x}) =< \mathbf{w_i}, \phi(\boldsymbol{x}) >= \\ \sum_{j=1}^N \hat{\alpha}_{i,j}\phi(\boldsymbol{x_j})^\top\phi(\boldsymbol{x}) = \sum_{j=1}^N \hat{\alpha}_{i,j}K(\boldsymbol{x_j}, \boldsymbol{x}) \tag{2}$$

Therefore, a key issue for feature selection in the kernel space is to properly estimate the intrinsic dimensionality and find an orthogonal basis of the kernel space, so that the mapped data in the kernel space can be accurately represented. In other words, the $\phi_i(\boldsymbol{x})$ computed by (2) can be accurate only if the sketch of the kernel space is accurately preserved by the learned basis .

The dimensionality of basis set for kernel space is the rank of mapped data set $\{\phi(\boldsymbol{x_j})\}_{j=1}^N$. This rank equals to the numerical rank of kernel matrix $\mathbf{K}$, whose entries are defined by:

$$K_{ij} =< \phi(\boldsymbol{x_i}), \phi(\boldsymbol{x_j}) >= K(\boldsymbol{x_i}, \boldsymbol{x_j}) \tag{3}$$

Computing the rank of a matrix (i.e. the intrinsic dimensionality of kernel space) is a difficult issue, which has a time complexity of $O(N^3)$ [13]. It is, however, not an ideal choice to predetermine the target dimensionality as a constant, either. If it is too small, the learned basis will have a large distinction from the kernel space. On the contrary, a too large predetermined dimensionality, as adopted by [6], renders it difficult in learning orthogonal base vectors and aggravates computing load. Take the Hilbert Matrix [7] for example:

$$H_{ij} = (\frac{1}{i+j-1}) \tag{4}$$

The $n \times n$ Hilbert matrix $H(n)$ is a positive definite symmetric matrix. It means that, theoretically speaking, the dimensionality of the space that is spanned by $H(n)$'s column vectors should be n. However, in a case study, we validate that there are only about 18 linear independent base vectors in the space spanned by $H(100)$'s 100 column vectors. If we set up the dimensionality of the space spanned by $H(100)$'s column vectors as 100, many learned base vectors of this space are numerically non-orthogonal and the too large predetermined dimensionality increases the computing load of the algorithm. Therefore, under both of the two conditions, the learned basis cannot accurately preserve the sketch of the kernel space and the performance of feature selection is undermined.

To tackle this problem, we design a fast kernel subspace learning method – Kernel Orthogonal Basis Learner (KOBL). KOBL automatically learns the intrinsic dimensionality of the kernel space, and constructs an orthogonal basis set with a small reconstruction cost [24]. Here, reconstruction cost is employed to measure the quality of the learned basis set. A small value of reconstruction cost means the learned basis set can accurately preserve the sketch of the data that are used to learn the basis, i.e., the quality of learned basis is high. By designing a stop criterion, KOBL has a time complexity of $O(dN^2)$, which outperforms many other kernel subspace learning methods such as KGS and KPCA (at least $O(N^3)$). Backed by a high quality basis learned by KOBL, our feature selection work achieves better performance. In the rest of Section 3, we give the detailed TAKES.

3.1 Learn the Intrinsic Dimensionality and Orthogonal Basis for the Kernel Space

In this part, we propose the KOBL algorithm to learn the intrinsic dimensionality of feature space and construct an orthogonal basis from the mapped training data.

At first, we initialize the data matrix $A^{(0)} = [\phi(\boldsymbol{x}_1)^{(0)}, \phi(\boldsymbol{x}_2)^{(0)}, ..., \phi(\boldsymbol{x}_N)^{(0)}]$, basis $\mathbf{M}$ of the kernel space to empty basis and its dimensionality $k = Dim(\mathbf{M}) = 0$. Therein, $\{\phi(\boldsymbol{x}_i)^{(0)}\}_{i=1}^{N}$ are mapped data in the kernel space. (In this paper, we use $\phi(\boldsymbol{x}_i)^{(0)}$ and $\phi(\boldsymbol{x}_i)$ interchangeably.)

In every iteration, we first find the $(k+1)^{th}$ pivot column as follows (Suppose the former k iterations have finished and the former k base vectors have been obtained.):

$$j = \underset{k<i\leq N}{\text{argmax}} \, \|\phi(\boldsymbol{x}_i)^{(k)}\|_2 \tag{5}$$

Here, j is the column that has the largest column norm from the $(k+1)^{th}$ column to the Nth column.

Then we interchange the pivot column j with column $k+1$, where k is the current number of the learned base vectors. After the process of column pivoting and exchange, we calculate the norm of the $(k+1)^{th}$ column vector $r_{k+1,k+1}$ by:

$$r_{k+1,k+1} = \|\phi(\boldsymbol{x}_{k+1})^{(k)}\|_2. \tag{6}$$

And we obtain the normalized potential base vector $\mathbf{w_{k+1}}$ by

$$\mathbf{w_{k+1}} = \frac{\phi(\boldsymbol{x}_{k+1})^{(k)}}{r_{k+1,k+1}}. \tag{7}$$

Here, the potential base vector means the learned base vectors that may be accepted or rejected determined by a threshold policy that is discussed later. If $\mathbf{w_{k+1}}$ is accepted, the data matrix $A^{(k)}$ is updated using orthogonal transformation as follows,

$$\phi(\boldsymbol{x}_j)^{(k+1)} \leftarrow \phi(\boldsymbol{x}_j)^{(k)} - r_{k+1,j}\mathbf{w_{k+1}}, j = k+2 : N. \tag{8}$$

Therein, $r_{k+1,j}$ can be computed by

$$r_{k+1,j} = \mathbf{w_{k+1}}^{\top}\phi(\boldsymbol{x}_j)^{(k)}, j = k+2 : N. \tag{9}$$

Now, $A^{(k+1)} = [\mathbf{w_1}, ..., \mathbf{w_{k+1}}, \phi(\boldsymbol{x}_{k+2})^{(k+1)}, ..., \phi(\boldsymbol{x}_N)^{(k+1)}]$.

On the contrary, if the threshold condition does not satisfy, we will not accept $\mathbf{w_{k+1}}$.

Note that the kernel map ϕ is unseen, and the form of basis $\{\mathbf{w_j}\}$ is implicit. Therefore, using the kernel trick described in (2), the norm of mapped data in (5) can be computed by the following equation,

$$\begin{aligned}\|\phi(\boldsymbol{x}_i)^{(k)}\|_2 &= \|\phi(\boldsymbol{x}_i)^{(0)} - \sum_{j=1}^{k}(\mathbf{w_j}^{\top}\phi(\boldsymbol{x}_i)^{(0)})\mathbf{w_j}\|_2 \\ &= \sqrt{\mathbf{K}(\boldsymbol{x}_i, \boldsymbol{x}_i) - \sum_{j=1}^{k}(\sum_{m=1}^{N}\hat{\alpha}_{j,m}\mathbf{K}(\boldsymbol{x}_i, \boldsymbol{x}_m))^2}\end{aligned} \tag{10}$$

Therein, $\hat{\alpha}_1, ..., \hat{\alpha}_k$ are the k coefficient vectors achieved in the former k iterations.

Because the norm of $\mathbf{w_{k+1}}$ is

$$\|\mathbf{w_{k+1}}\|_2 = \|\phi(\boldsymbol{x}_{k+1})^{(k)}\|_2 = \|\sum_{i=1}^{N}\alpha_{k+1,i}^{(k)}\phi(\boldsymbol{x}_i)\|_2 = \sqrt{\alpha_{k+1}^{(k)}{}^{\top}\mathbf{K}\alpha_{k+1}^{(k)}}, \tag{11}$$

we implicitly achieve the $(k+1)^{th}$ normalized base vector $\mathbf{w_{k+1}}$ by setting the $(k+1)^{th}$ coefficient vectors[1] ,

$$\hat{\alpha}_{k+1} = \alpha_{k+1}^{(k+1)} = \frac{\alpha_{k+1}^{(k)}}{\sqrt{\alpha_{k+1}^{(k)}{}^{\top}\mathbf{K}\alpha_{k+1}^{(k)}}} \tag{12}$$

Similarly, (8) is fulfilled via updating the coefficient vectors as follows,

$$\alpha_j^{(k+1)} \leftarrow \alpha_j^{(k)} - \hat{\alpha}_{k+1}\sum_{i=1}^{N}\alpha_{k+1,i}^{(k)}\mathbf{K}(\boldsymbol{x}_j, \boldsymbol{x}_i), j = k+2 : N \tag{13}$$

It deserves mentioning that most kernel subspace learning methods such as KGS, KPCA and their invariants [27] ceaselessly learn the basis until all training data are used, which suffers from heavy computing time. In KOBL, a stop criterion is designed to overcome this shortcoming. In the rest of this part, we analyze KOBL algorithm in detail.

3.1.1 *Independence Measurement and Learn Orthogonal Basis*

To learn an orthogonal basis, KOBL takes the independence between the learned base vectors and the mapped data in the kernel space into consideration. Suppose we have learned basis $\mathbf{w_1}, \mathbf{w_2}, ..., \mathbf{w_k}$ sequentially by orthogonal transformations. If a mapped data $\phi(\boldsymbol{x}_{k+1})$ is dependent on the learned basis, the corresponding computed vector $\mathbf{w_{k+1}}$ is unsuitable to be accepted. It is because that if a base vector is transformed from a pattern that has strong dependence on the learned basis, the computation error would arise and affect the numerical orthogonality of the learned basis [13]. Therefore, it is necessary to consider the independence between the learned basis and the mapped data.

Here, based on the linear dependence theorem [13], we use the projection distance of a mapped data $\phi(\boldsymbol{x}_{k+1})$ onto the current learned basis space $span\{\mathbf{w_1}, \mathbf{w_2}, ..., \mathbf{w_k}\}$ to measure the numerical independence between $\phi(\boldsymbol{x}_{k+1})$ and the learned basis for the kernel space: (Suppose we have already learned the base vectors $\mathbf{w_1}, \mathbf{w_2}, ...,$ and $\mathbf{w_k}$. The potential base vector $\mathbf{w_{k+1}}$ is currently computed by (7).)

$$\|\phi(\boldsymbol{x}_{k+1}) - span\{\mathbf{w_1}, \mathbf{w_2}, ..., \mathbf{w_k}\}\|_2 \tag{14}$$

[1] At the beginning of the algorithm, the coefficient vectors are simply initialized as the unit vectors: $\alpha_j^{(0)} = \boldsymbol{e}_j$, for $j = 1 : N$. Therein, $\boldsymbol{e}_j$ is the vector whose j^{th} component is 1 and the rest components are 0.

The distance in (14) can be rewritten in the following form:

$$\min_{\hat{\mathbf{a}}} \|\phi(\boldsymbol{x}_{k+1}) - (a_1\mathbf{w_1} + a_2\mathbf{w_2} + ... + a_k\mathbf{w_k})\|_2 \quad (15)$$

where $\hat{\mathbf{a}} = (a_1, a_2, ..., a_k)^\top$ is a coordinate vector.

We define matrix $\mathbf{W_k} = [\mathbf{w_1}, \mathbf{w_2}, ..., \mathbf{w_k}]$, thus (14) can be rewritten in the form:

$$\min_{\hat{\mathbf{a}}} \|\mathbf{W_k}\hat{\mathbf{a}} - \phi(\boldsymbol{x}_{k+1})\|_2 \quad (16)$$

The column vectors of $\mathbf{W_k}$ are orthogonal. Thereby, we can construct an orthogonal matrix $\mathbf{Q_2}$ in the following form: $\mathbf{Q_2} = [\mathbf{W_k}, \mathbf{Q_1}]$.Therein, $\mathbf{Q_2} \in \mathbb{R}^{\mathcal{H}\times\mathcal{H}}$, $\mathbf{Q_1} \in \mathbb{R}^{\mathcal{H}\times(\mathcal{H}-k)}$, and the column vectors of $\mathbf{Q_1}$ and $\mathbf{W_k}$ are orthogonal.

Since orthogonal transformation never changes the 2-norm of a vector, (16) is equal to the following expression:

$$\begin{aligned} \|\mathbf{W_k}\hat{\mathbf{a}} - \phi(\boldsymbol{x}_{k+1})\|_2 &= \|\mathbf{Q_2}^\top(\mathbf{W_k}\hat{\mathbf{a}} - \phi(\boldsymbol{x}_{k+1}))\|_2 \\ &= \| \begin{pmatrix} \hat{\mathbf{a}} \\ \mathbf{0} \end{pmatrix} - \begin{pmatrix} \mathbf{W_k}^\top\phi(\boldsymbol{x}_{k+1}) \\ \mathbf{Q_1}^\top\phi(\boldsymbol{x}_{k+1}) \end{pmatrix} \|_2 \quad (17) \end{aligned}$$

We let

$$\hat{\mathbf{a}} = \mathbf{W_k}^\top\phi(\boldsymbol{x}_{k+1}), \quad (18)$$

thereby, the value of (14) is equal to $\|\mathbf{Q_1}^\top\phi(\boldsymbol{x}_{k+1})\|_2$, i.e., the independence between the learned base vectors and $\phi(\boldsymbol{x}_{k+1})$ can be measured by the value of $\|\mathbf{Q_1}^\top\phi(\boldsymbol{x}_{k+1})\|_2$.

According to (6) and (8), it is straightforward to validate that $r_{k+1,k+1}$ is the projection distance of initial mapped data $\phi(\boldsymbol{x}_{k+1})$ onto the orthogonal complement space $span\{\mathbf{w_1}, \mathbf{w_2}, ..., \mathbf{w_k}\}^\perp$, i.e., $r_{k+1,k+1} = \|\mathbf{Q_1}^\top\phi(\boldsymbol{x}_{k+1})\|_2$. Therefore, we can determine whether to accept the computed vectors $\mathbf{w_{k+1}}$ into current basis $\mathbf{M}$ or not according to the value of $r_{k+1,k+1}$. As illustrated in Fig.1, If $r_{k+1,k+1}$ is small, it means that the mapped data $\phi(\boldsymbol{x}_{k+1})$ is nearly or even completely in the space spanned by the base vectors $span\{\mathbf{w_1}, \mathbf{w_2}, ..., \mathbf{w_k}\}$. In this case, $\phi(\boldsymbol{x}_{k+1})$ has a strong dependence on $span\{\mathbf{w_1}, \mathbf{w_2}, ..., \mathbf{w_k}\}$, and it is not reasonable to add the potential base vector $\mathbf{w_{k+1}}$ into the basis $\mathbf{M}$ since $\mathbf{w_{k+1}}$ is transformed from $\phi(\boldsymbol{x}_{k+1})$. On the contrary, when $r_{k+1,k+1}$ is large, $\phi(\boldsymbol{x}_{k+1})$ is orthogonal to $span\{\mathbf{w_1}, \mathbf{w_2}, ..., \mathbf{w_k}\}$. It means that $\phi(\boldsymbol{x}_{k+1})$ is independent of $span\{\mathbf{w_1}, \mathbf{w_2}, ..., \mathbf{w_k}\}$, and $\mathbf{w_{k+1}}$ is an ideal base vector.

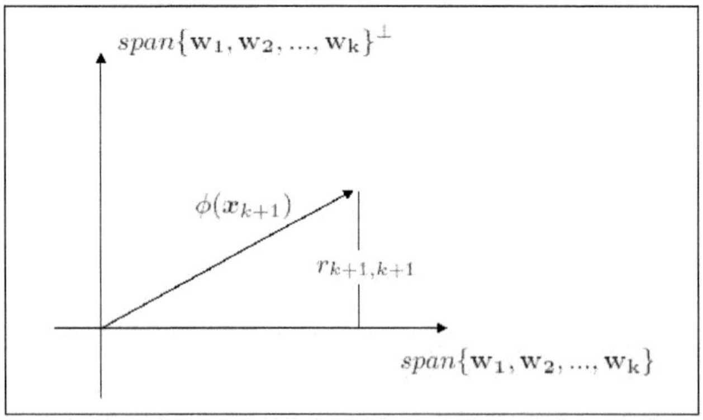

Figure 1: $\phi(\boldsymbol{x}_{k+1})$ is projected onto two orthogonal spaces: $span\{\mathbf{w_1}, \mathbf{w_2}, ..., \mathbf{w_k}\}$ and $span\{\mathbf{w_1}, \mathbf{w_2}, ..., \mathbf{w_k}\}^\perp$. The projection distance onto the space $span\{\mathbf{w_1}, \mathbf{w_2}, ..., \mathbf{w_k}\}^\perp$ is $r_{k+1,k+1}$. If $r_{k+1,k+1}$ is large, we will accept $\mathbf{w_{k+1}}$ as an ideal base vector. Otherwise we have to discard it.

3.1.2 *Learn Intrinsic Dimensionality for the Kernel Space with Small Reconstruction Cost*

As discussed above, to keep the independence of learned basis and mapped data, we make the decision of whether to accept the computed vectors $\mathbf{w_{k+1}}$ into basis according to the value of $r_{k+1,k+1}$. In KOBL, we use a threshold T to make the decision: if $r_{k+1,k+1} \geq T$, we accept the potential vector $\mathbf{w_{k+1}}$ and vice versa. The value of r_{11} is not smaller than r_{ii} for all $i > 1$. (It will be demonstrated in Theorem 2.) Therefore, for the purpose of convenient comparison, instead of $r_{k+1,k+1}$, we use $\frac{r_{k+1,k+1}}{r_{11}}$ to make the final decision.

The learned dimensionality for the kernel space equals to the number of accepted base vectors. Therefore, the value of threshold T plays an important role in estimating the intrinsic dimensionality of kernel space and affects the orthogonality of the learned basis. If the estimated dimensionality is too small, the learned basis will have a large distinction from the kernel space. On the contrary, a too large estimated dimensionality will render it difficult in learning orthogonal base vectors. Take the Hilbert Matrix [7] for example. If we simply set up the dimensionality of the space spanned by $H(100)$'s column vectors as 100, many base vectors learned are not orthogonal. Under both of the two cases, using (2) to compute $\phi_i(\boldsymbol{x})$ is not accurate, so that the performance of feature selection would be affected.

Many current subspace learning methods (e.g, KPCA and KGS) need a user to predetermine the intrinsic dimensionality for the kernel space. Although for KPCA and some KPCA based methods such as Kernel Feature Analysis [27], the intrinsic dimensionality for the kernel space can be determined based on the accumulation ratio whose lower bound comes from the tolerable approximation error, this lower bound has to be predetermined by users as parameters, which may still lead to an improper dimensionality for the kernel space. On the other hand, there are some reported schemes such as Relevant Dimension Estimation(RDE) [3, 4] that can provide an estimation for relevant dimensionality in the kernel space with respect to a supervised learning task. However, such schemes themselves suffer from heavy computational cost ($O(N^3)$) which is impractical.

In KOBL, instead of employing an user defined threshold, we aim at proposing an adaptive threshold scheme to learn the intrinsic dimensionality of kernel space without adding much extra computing burden.

Besides ensuring the orthogonality of the basis, we hope the adaptive threshold scheme to guarantee that the learned basis can preserve the sketch of the kernel space, namely, the reconstruction cost $\mathcal{E}(\mathbf{M})$ defined as follows is small.

$$\begin{aligned} \mathcal{E}(\mathbf{M}) &= \frac{1}{N}\sum_{j=1}^{N} \|\phi(\boldsymbol{x}_j) - span\{\mathbf{M}\}\|_2 \\ &= \frac{1}{N}\sum_{j=1}^{N} \|\phi(\boldsymbol{x}_j) - \sum_{i=1}^{d}(\mathbf{w_i}^\top\phi(\boldsymbol{x}_j))\mathbf{w_i}\|_2 \quad (19) \end{aligned}$$

Therein, $\mathbf{w_1}, \mathbf{w_2}, ..., \mathbf{w_d}$ are all learned base vectors in basis set $\mathbf{M}$. Moreover, we hope that the threshold T is confined between 0 and 1, so that T is comparable to $\frac{r_{k+1,k+1}}{r_{11}}$. ($\frac{r_{k+1,k+1}}{r_{11}}$ varies between 0 and 1.)

To satisfy the above constraints, we propose a self-adaptive threshold: we accept the potential base vector $\mathbf{w_{k+1}}$ if

$$\frac{r_{k+1,k+1}}{r_{11}} \geq T = f(\frac{Dim(\mathbf{M})}{N}) \quad (20)$$

Therein, $Dim(\mathbf{M})$ is the currently learned dimensionality of the kernel space, and $f(t)$ is a monotonically increasing function and $0 \leq f(t) \leq 1$ when $0 \leq t \leq 1$.

Now, in the following theorem, we show how the threshold policy defined by (20) can ensure a small reconstruction cost.

THEOREM 1. *The value of $\mathcal{E}(\mathbf{M})$ for OCA has an upper bound of $r_{11} f(\frac{Dim(\mathbf{M})}{N})$, i.e., $\mathcal{E}(\mathbf{M}) < r_{11} f(\frac{Dim(\mathbf{M})}{N})$.*

PROOF. Suppose finally we obtain d base vectors for the kernel space: $\mathbf{w_1}, \mathbf{w_2}, ..., \mathbf{w_d}$.

Therefore, for those mapped data $\phi(\boldsymbol{x}_j)$ ($j \leq d$), we have

$$\|\phi(\boldsymbol{x}_j) - span\{\mathbf{w_1}, \mathbf{w_2}, ..., \mathbf{w_d}\}\|_2 = \sqrt{\|\phi(\boldsymbol{x}_j)\|_2^2 - \sum_{i=1}^{d} (\mathbf{w_i}^\top \phi(\boldsymbol{x}_j))^2} = 0$$

As for those mapped data $\phi(\boldsymbol{x}_j)$ ($j > d$), due to the non-increasing monotonicity of r_{jj}, (which is demonstrated in Theorem 2,) we achieve the following equations,

$$\|\phi(\boldsymbol{x}_j) - span\{\mathbf{w_1}, \mathbf{w_2}, ..., \mathbf{w_d}\}\|_2 = \|\phi(\boldsymbol{x}_j) - \sum_{i=1}^{d} (\mathbf{w_i}^\top \phi(\boldsymbol{x}_j))\mathbf{w_i}\|_2 \leq r_{d+1,d+1}$$

As a result, $\mathcal{E}(\mathbf{M}) \leq \frac{1}{N}(N-d) r_{d+1,d+1}$. From (20), we know that,

$$\mathcal{E}(\mathbf{M}) < \frac{N-d}{N} r_{11} f(\frac{d}{N}) < r_{11} f(\frac{Dim(\mathbf{M})}{N})$$

which completes the proof. □

Since $f(t) \leq 1$ is a monotonically increasing function, and $Dim(\mathbf{M}) << N$, the value of $r_{11} f(\frac{Dim(\mathbf{M})}{N})$ would be small. It means the adaptive threshold technique ensures that the basis obtained by KOBL can accurately preserve the sketch of the kernel space, which meets our demand.

$N+1$ vectors of N dimensionality must be linearly dependent and non-orthogonal. The number of base vectors is always smaller than the dimensionality of input data, i.e., $Dim(\mathbf{M}) \leq N$. Therefore, the value of T is confined between 0 and 1.

We should notice that all elements in this threshold policy, namely $Dim(\mathbf{M})$, N, $r_{k+1,k+1}$, and r_{11}, are easily available and automatically updated during the learning process. It means that the threshold scheme is self-adaptive, and costs little extra computing load.

The very threshold policy helps KOBL learn the intrinsic dimensionality of the kernel space and construct an orthogonal basis with small reconstruction cost.

3.1.3 Decrease Time Complexity by Designing a Stop Criterion

Most subspace learning methods use all the data to learn the basis, which suffers from heavy computing load when the data volume is large. In KOBL, to address this problem, we propose a stop criterion based on the following theorem.

THEOREM 2. *If $j \leq k$ then $r_{jj} \geq r_{kk}$.*

PROOF. We denote the original data matrix $A^{(0)} = [\phi(\boldsymbol{x}_1)^{(0)}, \phi(\boldsymbol{x}_2)^{(0)}, ..., \phi(\boldsymbol{x}_N)^{(0)}]$, where N is the number of data. In every iteration of KOBL, the data matrix is transformed. Suppose we have learned k base vectors $\mathbf{w_1}, \mathbf{w_2}, ..., \mathbf{w_k}$ through k times iterations, then

$$A^{(k)} = [\mathbf{w_1}, ..., \mathbf{w_k}, \phi(\boldsymbol{x}_{k+1})^{(k)}, ..., \phi(\boldsymbol{x}_N)^{(k)}].$$

In the $(k+1)^{th}$ iteration of KOBL, we obtain the following equation:

$$\phi(\boldsymbol{x}_{k+1})^{(k+1)} = \mathbf{w_{k+1}} = \frac{\phi(\boldsymbol{x}_{k+1})^{(k)}}{r_{k+1,k+1}}$$

For all $j > k+1$, we have,

$$\phi(\boldsymbol{x}_j)^{(k+1)} = \phi(\boldsymbol{x}_j)^{(k)} - r_{k+1,j} \frac{\phi(\boldsymbol{x}_{k+1})^{(k)}}{r_{k+1,k+1}}$$

$\phi(\boldsymbol{x}_j)^{(k+1)}$ is orthogonal to $\mathbf{w_{k+1}}$, thus we can arrive at the following item:

$$\|\phi(\boldsymbol{x}_j)^{(k+1)}\|_2^2 = \phi(\boldsymbol{x}_j)^{(k)\top} \phi(\boldsymbol{x}_j)^{(k)} - r_{k+1,j}^2 \leq \|\phi(\boldsymbol{x}_j)^{(k)}\|_2^2$$

Due to the column pivoting scheme, we have

$$\|\phi(\boldsymbol{x}_j)^{(k)}\|_2^2 \leq \|\phi(\boldsymbol{x}_{k+1})^{(k)}\|_2^2 = r_{k+1,k+1}^2$$

for all $j > k+1$, and

$$r_{k+2,k+2} = \max_{j \geq k+2} \|\phi(\boldsymbol{x}_j)^{(k+1)}\|_2.$$

Thereby, we obtain $r_{k+1,k+1} \geq r_{k+2,k+2}$, which completes the proof. □

According to the above theorem, we develop a stop criterion in KOBL: we stop the algorithm if we arrive at the first computed vector $\mathbf{w_d}$ satisfying the following inequality:

$$\frac{r_{dd}}{r_{11}} < T = f(\frac{Dim(\mathbf{M})}{N}) \quad (21)$$

Suppose $\mathbf{w_d}$ is the first computed vector that does not satisfy the threshold condition, i.e., $\frac{r_{dd}}{r_{11}} < T$. Obviously the threshold T is monotone nondecreasing, and $\frac{r_{dd}}{r_{11}}$ is monotone nonincreasing during training, as indicated in Theorem 2. Therefore, if the integer d does not satisfy $\frac{r_{dd}}{r_{11}} \geq T$, all the integers $i > d$ do not satisfy the threshold condition, either. It means even if we use the remaining training data to learn the basis, the potential base vectors learned later ($\{\mathbf{w_i}\}_{i=d+1}^{N}$) do not meet the threshold condition and will be rejected. Thus, we don't need to continue learning the basis any more.

Based on the stop criterion (21), KOBL is able to realize a low computing complexity. Without this stop criterion, KOBL would have to process all training data; the time complexity would reach $O(N^3)$. By the stop criterion, the time complexity reduces to $O(N^2 d)$. Here, N is the size of training set, and d is number of base vectors. Usually $d << N$, thus the stop criterion saves a lot of computing time, and helps KOBL outperform those typical kernel subspace learning methods such as KGS ($O(N^3)$) and KPCA ($O(N^3 + N^2 d)$).

According to the above discussion, we give the detailed KOBL in Algorithm 1.

3.2 Kernel Forward Feature Selection (KFFS)

Backed by the orthogonal basis set constructed by KOBL, we can select discriminative features in the kernel space. During past few years, many methods [33, 15, 32, 36] have been proposed for feature selection in the original space. In our work, we extend Forward Feature Selection (FFS) to select features in the kernel space due to its smaller computing load. In this part, we show how to adjust FFS, a method that was proposed to select features in the original space [36], to directly select features in the kernel space with the assistance of the orthogonal basis set learned by KOBL.

The key issue of FFS is to train weak classifiers and store the their classification results. Here, each weak classifier is trained

1: **Input:** Data matrix $A^{(0)} = [\phi(\boldsymbol{x}_1), \phi(\boldsymbol{x}_2), ..., \phi(\boldsymbol{x}_N)]$.
2: Initialize the basis $\mathbf{M} = \emptyset$ and the coefficient vectors $\alpha_j^{(0)} = \boldsymbol{e_j}, j = 1 : N$.
3: Initialize the basis dimensionality $k = Dim(\mathbf{M}) = 0$.
4: Column pivoting: find the column j by (5).
5: Interchange column j and column $k+1$ of matrix $A^{(k)}$ if $j \neq k+1$.
6: Implicitly compute the potential base vector $\mathbf{w_{k+1}}$ by (12).
7: **if** Threshold condition (20) satisfies **then**
8: Accept $\mathbf{w_{k+1}}$ as a base vector and add it into $\mathbf{M}$.
9: Implicitly update matrix $A^{(k)}$ using (13).
10: Update basis dimensionality $k \leftarrow k+1$.
11: Goto step 4 to continue the learning process.
12: **else**
13: Stop the algorithm.
14: **end if**
15: **return** Basis $\mathbf{M}$ and $Dim(\mathbf{M})$.

Algorithm 1: Kernel Orthogonal Basis Learner

based on one feature. By the aid of the learned orthogonal basis set $\{\mathbf{w_i}\}_{i=1}^d$ of the kernel space, we obtain the ith feature of the mapped data $\phi(\boldsymbol{x_j})$ when training the weak classifiers:

$$\phi_i(\boldsymbol{x_j}) =< \mathbf{w_i}, \phi(\boldsymbol{x_j}) >= \sum_{m=1}^{N} \hat{\alpha}_{i,m} \mathbf{K}(\boldsymbol{x_m}, \boldsymbol{x_j}) \tag{22}$$

In Adaboost and its variants, many supervised methods can be used to train the weak classifiers. The most commonly used method is Nearest Neighbor Classifier, which has a time complexity of $O(N^2)$. Thus its kernel version (Kernel Nearest Neighbor Classifier) is $O(N^3)$. In our work, Kernel Least Mean Square algorithm is employed because it only costs $O(N^2 d)$ computing time.

The detailed KFFS is given in Algorithm 2.

1: **Input:** Data set $\{\phi(\boldsymbol{x}_i), y_i\}_{i=1}^N$ and basis set $\{\mathbf{w_k}\}_{k=1}^d$.
2: **for** $i = 1$ to d **do**
3: Train a weak classifier only using the ith feature of the mapped data by the aid of the orthogonal basis.
4: Store the classification result under all the training data $\phi(\boldsymbol{x_j})$ into the ith row of table $V, j = 1 : N$.
5: **end for**
6: **for** $t = 1$ to d **do**
7: Normalize the weights $c_{t,i} \leftarrow \frac{c_{t,i}}{\sum_j c_{t,j}}$.
8: **for** $i = 1$ to d **do**
9: $v' = v + V(i, :)$.
10: ϵ_i = the error rate of ensemble classifier under feature sets v'.
11: **end for**
12: $k = \text{argmin}_{1 \le i \le d} \epsilon_i$.
13: $v = v + V(k, :)$.
14: Update the weights: $c_{t+1,i} = c_{t,i}(\frac{\epsilon_k}{1-\epsilon_k})^{1-b_i}$, where $b_i = 0$ if samples $\phi(\boldsymbol{x}_i)$ is classified correctly, $b_i = 1$ otherwise.
15: Computed the weight of the selected feature by equation (23).
16: **end for**
17: **return** The weight of each feature $\{\gamma_i\}_{i=1}^d$.

Algorithm 2: Kernel Forward Feature Selection

The Kernel Forward Feature Selection (KFFS) operates as follows: first, weak classifiers are trained (step 2- step 5 of Algorithm 2). Then we select features that make the ensemble classifier have smallest error on the training set (step 6 - step 13). After the features in an ensemble are selected, we update the weights of features according to the smallest error rate ϵ_k (step 14- step 15):

$$\gamma_k = log \frac{1-\epsilon_k}{\epsilon_k} \tag{23}$$

The discriminative ability of each feature is reflected by the computed weight. The time complexity of KFFS is $O(N^2 d)$.

3.3 Summary of Algorithm

In this section, we give the detailed TAKES in Algorithm 3. In the first stage, we learn an orthogonal basis for the kernel space by KOBL. Note that the intrinsic dimensionality of the feature space can be estimated by KOBL in the first stage. Then in the second stage, with the aid the basis learned in the first stage, the discriminative features are weighted directly in the kernel space.

1: **Input:** Data $\{\boldsymbol{x}_i\}_{i=1}^N$ and label $\{y_i\}_{i=1}^N$.
2: Construct an orthogonal basis set $\{\mathbf{w_k}\}_{k=1}^d$ of the kernel space by KOBL.
3: Calculate weight $\{\gamma_k\}_{k=1}^d$ by KFFS.
4: Project the data into learned subspace with the aid of the learned weights.

Algorithm 3: TAKES

As discussed above, the time complexity of constructing basis set is $O(N^2 d)$, and KFFS is $O(N^2 d)$. Thus, the total time complexity of the proposed TAKES is $O(N^2 d)$. Therein, N is the number of training data, and d is the dimensionality of the original data. To compare with KOBL, we analyze the time complexity of some other kernel based feature selection such as *Feature Selection via KPCA* (FSKPCA) and *Feature Selection via KGS*(FSKGS)[6], and some dimensionality reduction methods such as *Kernel Discriminant Analysis*(KDA) [22] and *Generalized Discriminant Analysis*(GDA)[1]. The results are listed in Table 1.

Table 1 indicates that the proposed TAKES outperforms the only existing kernel feature selection methods FSKPCA and FSKGS [6] as far as we know. Compared with some kernel based dimensionality reduction methods, such as KDA and GDA, TAKES is encouraging to the aspects of time complexity.

4. EXPERIMENTS

To validate the effectiveness and efficiency of the proposed methods, we conduct experiments under some widely used real-world databases from [2] and [11]: Australian, Diabetes, Ionosphere, Heart, Sonar, and Thyroid. Some typical kernel methods for reducing dimensionality are compared with our TAKES. As discussed above, as far as we know, the only existing work that selects features in the kernel space is [6]. Thus, we compare our work with FSKGS and FSKPCA [6]. Kernel Discriminant Analysis (KDA), a typical kernel dimensionality reduction method, is also used to compare with our work.

4.1 Reconstruction Cost

In our work, we estimate the intrinsic dimensionality for the kernel space and construct an orthogonal basis by the proposed KOBL to conduct feature selection in the kernel space. In this part, we employ the reconstruction cost $\mathcal{E}(\mathbf{M})$ [24] to testify whether the learned basis can accurately preserve the sketch of the mapped data in the kernel space.

Table 1: Time complexity of TAKES, FSKPCA, FSKGS, KDA, and GDA

Algorithm	TAKES	FSKPCA	FSKGS	KDA	GDA
Time Complexity	$O(N^2d)$	$O(N^3+N^2d)$	$O(N^3)$	$O(N^3)$	$O(N^3+N^2d)$

Table 2: Reconstruction Cost $\mathcal{E}(\mathrm{M})$ of Each Method

Dataset	KOBL		KGS		KPCA		KDA	
	$\mathcal{E}(\mathrm{M})$	Dim	$\mathcal{E}(\mathrm{M})$	Dim	$\mathcal{E}(\mathrm{M})$	Dim	$\mathcal{E}(\mathrm{M})$	Dim
Australian	**0.044**	36	0.063	345	0.412	345	0.523	36
Diabetes	**0.062**	58	0.082	468	0.392	468	0.496	58
Heart	**0.145**	44	0.158	170	0.384	170	0.503	44
Ionosphere	0.111	69	**0.098**	281	0.383	281	0.915	69
Sonar	**0.047**	12	0.067	104	0.519	104	0.949	12
Thyroid	**0.043**	20	0.083	140	0.407	140	0.700	20

To compare with the quality of basis set constructed by our work, we use some typical kernel subspace learners such as KGS, KPCA, and KDA to compare with KOBL under some widely used databases [2, 11]. Without loss of generality, we use RBF kernel for KOBL, KGS, KPCA, and KDA respectively. It deserves noting KOBL automatically estimates the intrinsic dimensionality of the kernel space, which is listed in Table 2. But for KGS and KPCA, the dimensionality of the kernel space needs users to predetermine. For KGS and KPCA, we take the policy adopted by [6]: the target dimensionality is predetermined as the size of training set. For KDA, the target dimensionality needs users to set up as well. For the purpose of fair comparison, in KDA we set up the dimensionality for the kernel space the same as it learned by KOBL.

The results of $\mathcal{E}(\mathrm{M})$ listed in Table 2 indicate that under most conditions, KOBL achieves the smallest reconstruction cost compared with other methods. It is because for KOBL, the proper learned intrinsic dimensionality of the kernel space and the orthogonality of constructed basis guarantee that the sketch of the kernel space is accurately preserved. For KGS, the improper predetermined dimensionality for the kernel space undermines the orthogonality of basis set. KPCA achieves higher reconstruction cost than KOBL under all datasets. It demonstrates again that setting up the number of mapped data as the kernel space dimensionality adopted by [6] is unreasonable because the too large predetermined dimensionality of the kernel space renders it difficult to obtain orthogonal basis, and preserve the sketch of the data accurately. The basis set constructed by KDA is not necessary orthogonal, thus it is no wonder that its reconstruction cost is poor.

From the experiments, we can conclude that, compared with other methods, KOBL constructs the basis set with the smallest reconstruction cost. It means the learned basis set by our work can preserve the sketch of data in the kernel space accurately.

4.2 Classification Performance

In this section, we conduct experiments to validate the classification power of the proposed method. Similar to section 4.1, the six datasets, i.e., Australian, Diabetes, Ionosphere, Heart, Sonar, and Thyroid, are also used in this experiment.

4.2.1 Case Study: the Effectiveness of the Constructed Basis

In our algorithm, we design the KOBL to learn the intrinsic dimensionality and the orthogonal basis of the kernel space (i.e., the first stage), and then adopt KFFS to directly select features in the kernel space (i.e., the second stage). In this subsection, to further validate the effectiveness of the basis constructed by KOBL, we compare the classification accuracy of TAKES with another case that the feature selection stage is the same but the basis learners are different. Namely, in this case, we use KGS to learn the basis (in the first stage), and then apply KFFS to select features in the kernel space (in the second stage).

We execute the above two methods to obtain the selected features. Then we simply use 1−Kernel Nearest Neighbor Classifier (KNNC) to classify data in test sets under the selected features. We depict the classification results of each method under different databases in Fig.2. In the figures, the abscissa stands for the number of selected features and the vertical ordinate stands for the corresponding classification accuracy. It deserves noting that for the proposed TAKES, the dimensionality of the kernel space is automatically learned. In the stage of selection, we employ KFFS to weight all features according to their respective discriminative abilities. Therefore, the number of selected features for TAKES is data-dependent, and we only need to portray a point instead of a curve line to reflect the classification performance of TAKES.

Fig.2 dedicates that the classification accuracy of TAKES is better than the KGS+KFFS case under most databases. The feature selection method (in the second stage) used in the case study is the same, thus we can conclude the basis learned by KOBL is the best. It is because different from KGS, KOBL can estimate the intrinsic dimensionality for the kernel space, which ensures the sketch of the kernel space is accurately preserved by the learned orthogonal basis and the classification accuracy is good. As for the KGS+KFFS case, the heuristically predetermined target dimensionality undermines the orthogonality of the learned basis set, and leads to poorer classification performance.

4.2.2 Compared with Typical Methods

In this part, we compare the classification accurcy of TAKES with the only existing feature selection works in the kernel space [6] as far as we know: FSKGS and FSKPCA. KDA is also used to compare with TAKES.

We execute each algorithm to obtain the selected features. Then we use 1−KNNC for classification under the selected features. Meanwhile, we compute the classification accuracy that is obtained merely by KNNC without dimensionality reduction or feature selection scheme, which reflects the classification performance of all features in the kernel space. We depict the classification results in Fig.3.

Fig. 3 indicates that TAKES can obtain sound classification performance compared with other typical kernel methods for reducing dimensionality. Compared with KNNC, TAKES obtains better classification results under all datasets. It indicates that after feature selection, the selected features have better discriminative power than all features in the kernel space.

The classification accuracy of the proposed TAKES outperforms FSKGS and FSKPCA under almost all the datasets. It is because that TAKES can properly estimate the intrinsic dimensionality of the kernel space and obtain orthogonal basis. Another point worth mentioning is that, compared with the classification accuracy of

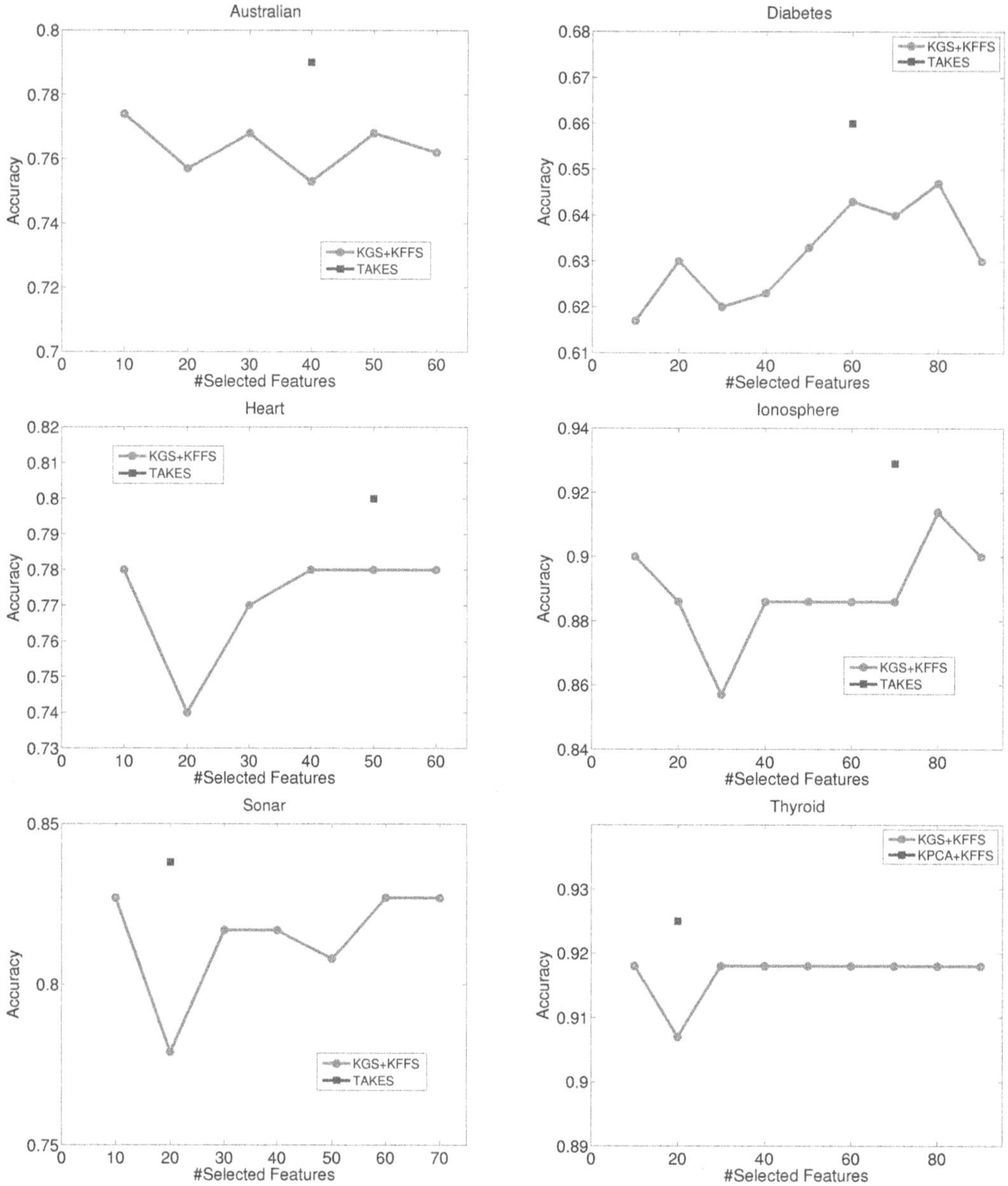

Figure 2: The classification accuracy of TAKES and KGS+KFFS under different number of selected features: the abscissa coordinate stands for the selected feature number, while the vertical coordinate stands for the corresponding classification accuracy. Noting that TAKES can learn the intrinsic dimensionality of the kernel space. Therefore, we only portray a point instead of a curve line to show the classification accuracy of TAKES.

FSKGS, KGS+KFFS (shown in the last subsection) is a little better under most datasets. (KGS+KFFS is better under the Diabetes, Heart, Ionosphere, Sonar, and Thyroid.) It demonstrates that the Kernel Forward Feature Selection (KFFS) adopted by the proposed TAKES is effective to detect discriminant features in the kernel space.

Compared to KDA, which is a kernel dimensionality reduction method that aims at obtaining a transformation matrix to convert original data into data in feature space, TAKES works better under all conditions. Although KDA improves the classification accuracy by maximizing the between-class scatter and minimizing the within-class scatter, TAKES, which directly selects discriminative features from the kernel space, is proven to be more effective.

Then considering the fact that the time complexity of TAKES is better than many typical kernel methods for reducing dimensionality, our method is promising.

5. CONCLUSION

In this paper, we propose a framework for feature selection in the kernel space. In the first stage, we design a subspace learning method KOBL to estimate the intrinsic dimensionality and construct an orthogonal basis for the kernel space. The designed subspace learning algorithm automatically learns the intrinsic dimen-

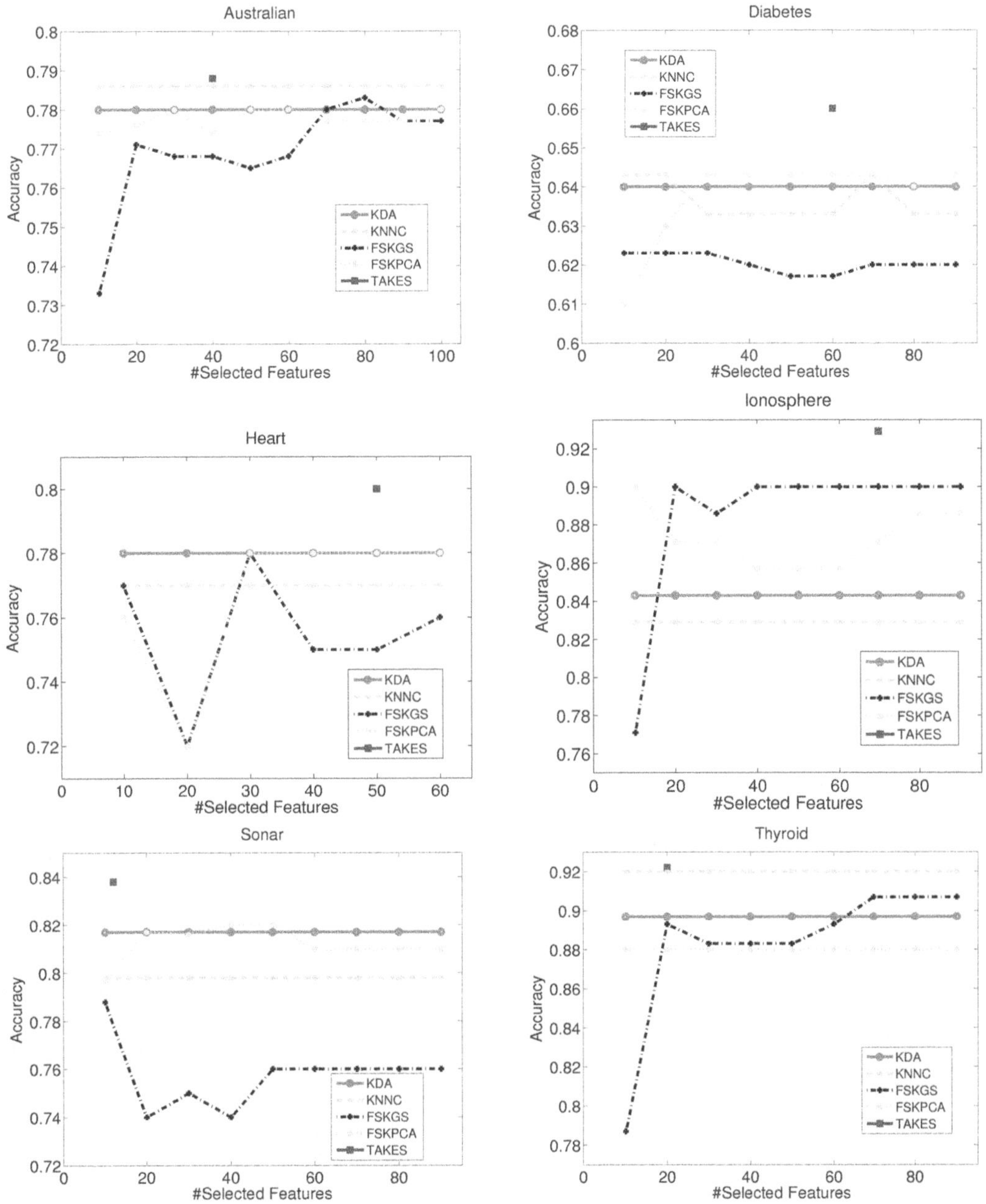

Figure 3: The classification accuracy of TAKES, FSKGS, FSKPCA, KDA, and KNNC: the abscissa coordinate stands for the number of selected features, while the vertical coordinate stands for the corresponding classification accuracy. Noting that TAKES can learn the intrinsic dimensionality of the kernel space. Therefore, different from other algorithms, we only portray a point instead of a curve line to show the classification accuracy of TAKES.

sionality of the kernel space guaranteeing that the sketch of the kernel space is accurately preserved. In the second stage, with the aid of the learned basis set, we select features directly in the kernel space. The whole procedure enjoys a smaller time complexity compared with other typical kernel methods.

In the experiments, we compare the proposed TAKES framework with FSKGS and FSKPCA (the only existing feature selection methods as far as we know), and KDA (a famous kernel dimensionality reduction method) under several typical datasets. The results dictate that the reconstruction cost and the classification performance of TAKES are the best.

6. ACKNOWLEDGEMENT

We would like to thank Shaohan Hu from UIUC and the anonymous reviewers for their invaluable inputs. This work was supported in part by the Fund of the National Natural Science Foundation of China (Grant #60975047, 60723003, 60721002), 973 Program (2010CB327903), and Jiangsu NSF grant (#BK2009080).

7. REFERENCES

[1] G. Baudat and F. Anouar. Generalized discriminant analysis using a kernel approach. *Neural Computation*, 12(10):2385–2404, 2000.

[2] C. L. Blake and C. J. Merz. UCI repository of machine learning databases. *Irvine, CA: University of California Department of Information*, 1996.

[3] M. L. Braun and J. M. Buhmann and K.-L. Muller. Denoising and Dimension Reduction in Feature Space. In *the Advances in Neural Information Processing Systems*, pages 185–192, 2006.

[4] M. L. Braun and J. M. Buhmann and K.-L. Muller. On Relevant Dimensions in Kernel Feature Spaces. *Journal of Machine Learning Research*, 9:1875–1908, 2008.

[5] D. Cai and X. He. Orthogonal locality preserving indexing. In *ACM SIGIR*, pages 3–10, 2005.

[6] B. Cao, D. Shen, J. Sun, Q. Yang, and Z. Chen. Feature selection in a kernel space. In *ICML*, pages 121–128, 2007.

[7] M. D. Choi, "Tricks or treats with the hilbert matrix," *American Mathematical Monthly*, 90:301–312, 1983.

[8] I. Dagher and R. Nachar. Face recognition using IPCA-ICA algorithm. *IEEE Trans. Pattern Analysis and Machine Intelligence*, 28(6):996–1000, 2006.

[9] P. A. Devijver and J. Kittler. *Pattern Recognition: A Statistical Approach*. Prince-Hall, 1982.

[10] W. Dong, M. Charikar, and K. Li. Asymmetric distance estimation with sketches for similarity search in high-dimensional spaces. In *ACM SIGIR*, pages 479–490, 2008.

[11] M. Duarte and Y. H. Hu. Vehicle classification in distributed sensor networks. *J. Parallel and Distributed Computing*, 64(7):826–838, 2004.

[12] X. Geng and T.-Y. Liu and T. Qin and H. Li. Feature selection for ranking. In *ACM SIGIR*, pages 407–414, 2007.

[13] G. H. Golub and C. F. V. Loan. *Matrix Computations, 3rd Edition*. Johns Hopkins University Press, 1996.

[14] H. Grabner and H. Bischof. On-line boosting and vision. In *IEEE CVPR*, pages 260–267, 2006.

[15] K. Kira and L. A. Rendell. A practical approach to feature selection. In *ICML*, pages 249–256, 1992.

[16] A. Kolcz, X. Sun, and J. Kalita. Efficient handling of high-dimensional feature spaces by randomized classifier ensembles. In *ACM SIGKDD*, pages 307–313, 2002.

[17] H. Li, T. Jiang, and K. Zhang. Efficient and robust feature extraction by maximum margin criterion. In *the Advances in Neural Information Processing Systems*, pages 97–104, 2003.

[18] Z. Liang and T. Zhao. Feature selection for linear support vector machines. In *ICPR*, pages 606–609, 2006.

[19] Y. Ma, S. Lao, E. Takikawa, and M. Kawade. Discriminant analysis in correlation similarity measure space. In *ICML*, pages 577–584, 2007.

[20] S. Martin, M. Kirby, and R. Miranda. Kernel/feature selection for support vector machines applied to materials design. In *the Symposium on Artificial Intelligence in Real Time Control*, pages 29–34, 2004.

[21] A. M. Martinez and A. C. Kak. PCA versus LDA. *IEEE Trans. Pattern Analysis and Machine Intelligence*, 23(2):228–233, 2001.

[22] S. Mika, G. Ratsch, and K. R. Muller. A mathematical programming approach to the kernel fisher algorithm. In *the Advances in Neural Information Processing Systems*, pages 591–597, 2001.

[23] W. Ping, Y. Xu, K. Ren, C.-H. Chi, and F. Shen. Non-I.I.D. Multi-Instance Dimensionality Reduction by Learning a Maximum Bag Margin Subspace. In *AAAI*, pages 551–556, 2010.

[24] S. T. Roweis and L. K. Saul. Nonlinear dimensionality reduction by locally linear embedding. *Science*, 290:2323–2326, 2000.

[25] Y. Saeys and I. Inza and P. Larranaga. A review of feature selection techniques in bioinformatics. *Bioinformatics*, 23(19):2507–2517, 2007.

[26] B. Scholkopf, A. Smola, and K. R. Muller. Nonlinear component analysis as a kernel eigenvalue problem. *Neural Computation*, 10:1299–1319, 1998.

[27] A. J. Smola and O. L. Mangasarian and B. Scholkopf. parse Kernel Feature Analysis. *Technical Report*, 1999.

[28] Y. Song, D. Zhou, J. Huang, I. G. Councill, H. Zha, and C. L. Giles. Boosting the feature space: Text classification for unstructured data on the web. In *IEEE ICDM*, pages 1064–1069, 2006.

[29] Y. Sun. Iterative relief for feature weighting: Algorithms, theories, and applications. *IEEE Trans. Pattern Analysis and Machine Intelligence*, 29(6):1035–1051, 2007.

[30] X. Tao, J. Ye, Q. Li, R. Janardan, and V. Cherkassky. Efficient kernel discriminant analysis via QR decomposition. In *the Advances in Neural Information Processing Systems*, pages 1529–1536, 2004.

[31] J. B. Tenenbaum, V. de Silva, and J. C. Langford. A global geometric framework for nonlinear dimensionality reduction. *Science*, 290:2319–2323, 2000.

[32] P. Viola and M. Jones. Rapid object detection using a boosted cascade of simple features. In *IEEE CVPR*, pages 511–518, 2001.

[33] G. Wang, F. H. Lochovsky, and Q. Yang. Feature selection with conditional mutual information maximin in text categorization. In *ACM CIKM*, pages 342–349, 2004.

[34] L. Wang, M. Sugiyama, Z. H. Zhou, and J. Feng. On the margin explanation of boosting algorithms. In *COLT*, pages 479–490, 2008.

[35] J. Weston, A. Elisseeff, and B. Scholkopf. Use of zero-norm with linear models and kernel methods. *J. Machine Learning Research*, 3:1439–1461, 2003.

[36] J. Wu, S. C. Brubaker, M. D. Mullin, and J. M. Rehg. Fast asymmetric learning for cascade face detection. *IEEE Trans. Pattern Analysis and Machine Intelligence*, 30(3):369–382, 2008.

[37] Y. Xu. Orthogonal component analysis for dimensionality reduction. *Master Thesis, Nanjing University*, 2010.

[38] Y. Xu, S. Furao, J. Zhao, and O. Hasegawa. To obtain orthogonal feature extraction using training data selection. In *ACM CIKM*, pages 1819–1822, 2009.

[39] J. Yan, B. Zhang, S. Yan, Q. Yang, H. Li, and Z. Chen. IMMC: incremental maximum margin criterion. In *ACM SIGKDD*, pages 725–730, 2004.

[40] Y. Yang and J. O. Pedersen. A comparative study on feature selection in text categorization. In *ICML*, pages 412–420, 1997.

Designing an Ensemble Classifier over Subspace Classifiers using Iterative Convergence Routine

Bhanukiran Vinzamuri
International Institute of Information Technology
Centre for Data Engineering
Andhra Pradesh, India
vinzamuri@research.iiit.ac.in

Kamalakar Karlapalem
International Institute of Information Technology
Centre for Data Engineering
Andhra Pradesh, India
kamal@iiit.ac.in

ABSTRACT

There can be multiple classifiers for a given data set. One way to generate multiple classifiers is to use subspaces of the attribute sets. In this paper, we generate subspace classifiers by an iterative convergence routine to build an ensemble classifier. Experimental evaluation covers the cases of both labelled and unlabelled (blind) data separately. We evaluate our approach on many benchmark UC Irvine datasets to assess the robustness of our approach with varying induced noise levels. We explicitly compare and present the utility of the clusterings generated for classification using several diverse clustering dissimilarity metrics. Results show that our ensemble classifier is a more robust classifier in comparison to different multi-class classification approaches.

Categories and Subject Descriptors

H.2.8 [**Database Applications**]: Data Mining

General Terms

Algorithms, Performance

Keywords

Subspace Classification, Multiple Clustering

1. INTRODUCTION

Classification and Clustering are two unique and well defined problems of data mining where the former addresses the problem of *supervised* learning and the latter deals with *unsupervised learning.* Clustering focuses on grouping points in a dataset with high intra group similarity and low intergroup similarity. One very interesting correlated problem is on exploring the role of unsupervised learning in building a superior supervised learning framework and vice-versa. This can be interpreted from the perspective of obtaining several different multiple clusterings of a dataset where each one of them contributes their knowledge inorder to build a better classifier.

Ensemble methods [6] in the field of data mining have several advantages over single clustering or classification algorithms. For example, in classification one can build different decision trees from the same dataset such that the outputs from each of them can be combined to predict the class labels effectively. In subspace classification, one can observe that the same classification algorithm applied on different independent subspaces will result in models which have different properties. This entire set of classifiers can constitute a diverse ensemble. The information provided by the predictions of the members in this diverse ensemble can be used to create a better supervised learning algorithm.

So the idea to use several subspace classification models built from clustered data for prediction in a single framework offers a new approach to this problem of supervised learning. The main steps involved in building our framework are (**i**) to exploit the interdependency between clustering and classification to get dissimilar clusterings, (**ii**) to build a *supplementary* dataset with information from the knowledge provided by the subspace classifiers and clusterings, (**iii**) to develop an ensemble classifier that works on subspace classifiers and (**iv**) to provide goodness results for subspace classifiers.

The major contributions of this work are (**i**) that we study the notion of *convergence* among the different members (classification models) as an ensemble of subspace classifiers, (**ii**) we observe the phenomenon of the existence of different types of convergence of learners for the same dataset, (**iii**) we evaluate the performance of the classifiers on the supplemented dataset.

The paper is organized as follows. Section **2** summarizes the contributions of algorithms developed in the fields of ensemble learning, multi class classification, subspace classification and evaluation of subspace clusterings. In Section **3**, we provide the algorithm and procedure involved in the description of the ensemble over subspace classifiers. This is followed by an illustrative example on the working and a discussion of our approach

Later on in Section **4** we provide an experimental setup to evaluate our approach and present the goodness results for our classifier. Finally in Section **5** we provide the conclusions derived from this work.

2. RELATED WORK

Ensemble learning [7, 4] is a field of machine learning which resulted in the development of the paradigms of multiple classifier fusion etc. The issue of combining classifiers has been explored by Kittler *et-al* [8]. ADABOOST [5] is an ensemble learner which like bagging manipulates the training examples to generate multiple hypotheses. The final

CIKM'11, October 24–28, 2011, Glasgow, Scotland, UK.
Copyright 2011 ACM 978-1-4503-0717-8/11/10 ...$10.00.

voting in ADABOOST is done using the weighted vote of the individual classifiers. RANDOMFOREST [2] is also an ensemble learner which is based on bootstrapping.

Meta clustering [3] is a method which aims at presenting several alternate clusterings to the user instead of one optimal clustering. *Multiple clustering* [11] and *Alternative view clusterings* are fields which present multiple dissimilar clusterings of a dataset. These different clusterings are obtained by using methods which project the data to a space orthogonal to the one that defines the current clusters optimally and obtain the new clusters in the projected space. So here dissimilar clusters are obtained iteratively using orthogonal transformations.

Multi class classification is another field which builds different classifiers using paradigms such as one vs all, one vs one etc. Joachim *et-al* built the Multi class SVM tool called $SVM^{multiclass}$ [13] which uses different classifier building techniques for prediction by constructing multiple hyperplanes. Several other approaches such as ADABOOST.M1 [5], Label stacking [14] and combining multiple neural networks [9] have also been proposed in the literature which exploit the knowledge of such different classifiers and combine their predictions effectively.

Assent *et-al* [1] came up with an approach to use subspace clusters for classification in noisy domains called *Subclass*. The goal of this approach was to come up with *locally* relevant attributes combinations for classification using subspace clustering information. These set of subspaces are ranked based on their interestingness. Finally, those subspaces are selected which maximize the information gain of a class label. The classes are then obtained by applying the nearest neighbor approach in classification. Our approach differs from *Subclass* as we do not use subspace clusters for classification, instead we detect subspace classifiers through an iterative convergence routine and build an ensemble of subspace classifiers.

Comparing subspace clusterings [10] is different than comparing ordinary clusterings. Patrikainen *et-al* [12] have defined Clustering error, Rand-index, Variation of Information as three distance measures for subspace clusterings. Apart from these there are several other measures which also help us compare subspace clusterings [12].

3. OUR ENSEMBLE CLASSIFIER

In Figure 1, we provide a flowchart for the supplementary dataset generation step of our ensemble over subspace classifiers approach. Initially, we start with the available real world data by clustering it in case it does not have class information (blind/unlabelled data). If the data is originally labelled we use it in it's existing form or else for the blind data we give the number of labels as the number of clusters.

This data is clustered using a clustering algorithm to create the labelled data (Lines 1-2 of Algorithm 1). On the labelled data we apply a decision tree classifier to construct a decision tree. The attributes selected by the decision tree are separated as the detected subspaces (Lines 8-9 of Algorithm 1). During each iteration we use 33% of the data as holdout to determine the accuracy of the decision tree.

After that we begin the *iterative convergence* process which creates subspaces of the dataset iteratively. This process of iterative convergence is carried on until the convergence criterion is met. As mentioned in Procedure 1, the convergence approach proceeds in a *greedy* fashion from the perspective of improving the accuracy of the decision tree (Line 6 of Procedure 1).

We maintain a threshold parameter here to specify the allowed negative deviation in accuracy for the decision tree during convergence. This process of iterative convergence is carried on until either the accuracy or attribute list of the decision tree remains unchanged. (Lines 2,4 of Procedure 1)

During each iteration a decision tree classifier model and a modified dataset D' which confines to the subspace A'' is output. The instances in D' are clustered using the *same distance function on the subspace* attribute set A'' to obtain the labelling (Line 12 of Algorithm 1).

Once the convergence criterion is met, the outputs of all the different subspace classification models and the original features are concatenated to generate a supplemented dataset of higher dimensionality. This will be explained in detail through the illustration provided later on in this section.

Procedure1:*IsConvergent*

Require: DecisionTree DT, DecisionTree DT', Threshold $Thres$.
1: flag=false
2: **if** $DT.accuracy == DT'.accuracy$ **then**
3: flag=true
4: **else if** $DT.attributes == DT'.attributes$ **then**
5: flag=true
6: **else if** $DT.accuracy - DT'.accuracy > Thres$ **then**
7: flag=true
8: **end if**
9: **return** flag

The number of rows in this supplemented dataset are equal to the number of instances in the original dataset. Each instance is a combination of the original features and the augmented dimensions of the classification labels obtained using all the convergent subspace classifiers. Once the dataset is prepared we can apply any classification algorithm on this supplemented dataset. This step captures the essence of ensemble learning in a different sense as we do not directly vote among the ensemble of subspace classifiers but transform the dataset according to the ensemble.

3.1 Discussion

In our approach, the supplemented data generation can be done using only *decision tree* algorithms (eg J48, CART). However, while evaluating the classifier performance on the supplemented dataset we can choose any classifier and get its accuracy. The essence of this algorithm lies in the fact that it *enriches* the subspace decision trees during the final stage by providing additional information. So the built ensemble classifier uses the knowledge from the original features and the predictions of subspace classification models to come up with classification boundaries.

In this paper, our approach does not address the quality of subspace clusters got instead we look at the problem of building good quality subspace classifiers. The major advantage gained here by using ensemble methods in clustering is to obtain increased stability of clustering solutions and the ability to construct *multiple* clusterings which are not at-

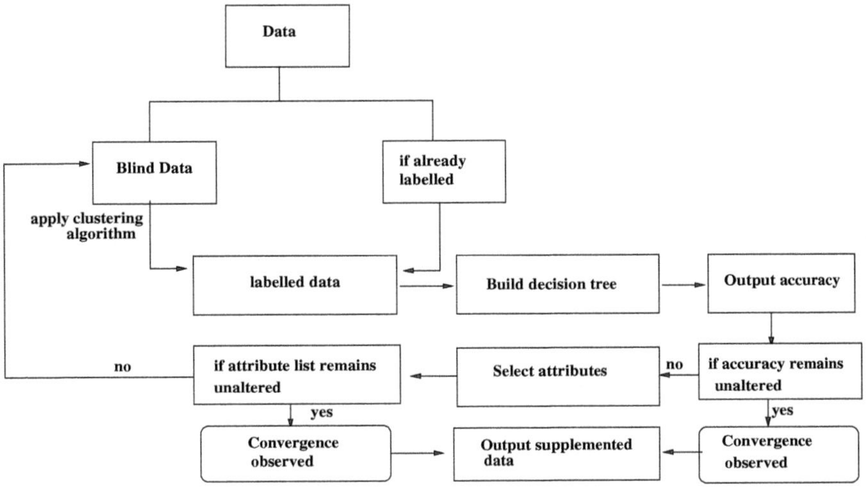

Figure 1: Data generation for the Ensemble Classifier

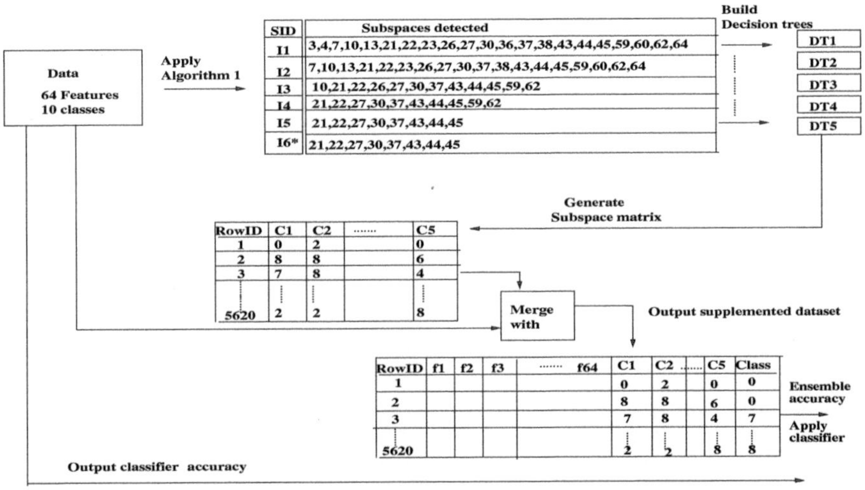

Figure 2: Illustrative example of working of our ensemble classifier

---

Algorithm 1 Data Generation for Ensemble Classifier

Require: Data D, DecisionTreeClassifier C, AttributeList A, ClusteringAlgorithm $Clus$, Threshold $Thres$

if D is not labelled **then**
  Apply $Clus$ to label D with cluster labels
end if
repeat
  Apply C on D to build a decision tree DT
  Estimate the accuracy acc of the DT
  Select the attributes $A^{'}$ of the DT
  $DT.accuracy = acc$
  $DT.attributes = A^{'}$
  Construct the subspace of attributes $A^{''} = A - A^{'}$
  Construct the modified dataset $D^{'}$ confining to the subspace $A^{''}$
  Apply $Clus$ on $D^{'}$ using the same distance function on attribute set $A^{''}$ to get clusters
  Apply C on $D^{'}$ to build a decision tree $DT^{'}$
until $IsConvergent(DT, DT^{'}, Thres)$

---

tainable by any single clustering algorithm. Evaluating the multiple clusterings is out of the scope of this paper.

3.2 Illustrative Example

In this section, we present an illustrative example of the working of our approach on a sample dataset from the UC Irvine repository (Optical Digits) which consists of 64 features, 5620 instances and 1 class with 10 labels (0-9) respectively. In this example, to represent the working we consider the data without the labels. Initially, we pass the dataset through our data generation algorithm given above in Algorithm 1. The classification algorithm used here is a *J48* Tree classifier and the clustering algorithm is **k**-means with the **k** set to 10. The **k** value is set here directly as we have *prior* knowledge from the classified Optical Digits dataset.

We begin the algorithm with the entire set of 64 attributes and continuously detect subspaces till the *convergence* criterion is met. In this example, we notice that during the 6th iteration ($I6$) the attribute list of the decision tree remains unchanged and hence the process terminates by giving 5 subspaces only. We now construct a supplemented dataset which consists of all the features of the original dataset as they occur, further for each of the 5 subspace classifiers generated using Algorithm 1 a new column is augmented to the original dataset giving the classification result.

For example if we consider the first instance in the the original data as $Inst = \{f_1, f_2, \ldots, f_{64}\}$ then the corresponding instance in the supplemented dataset would be $Inst' = \{Inst, DT_1(Inst), DT_2(Inst), \ldots, DT_5(Inst)\}$ where $DT_i(Inst)$ represents the prediction of the ith convergent subspace decision tree classifier DT_i on $Inst$.

The supplemented dataset generated for our current example through this transformation stage consists of 69 features, 5620 instances and the class. We apply our base classifier (*J48* Tree classifier) on this supplemented dataset and directly compare its accuracy to that when applied on the original data. This represents the final evaluation step in Figure 2. Our experiments in Section 4 confirm that our approach attains higher accuracy values of **0.912** and **0.877** in both the cases of labelled and blind data with respect to the J48 classifier which attains values of **0.894** and **0.863** respectively. Further results of our approach on different datasets are provided in Section 4.3.

4. EVALUATION OF OUR APPROACH

4.1 Setup

In this section, we provide the experimental setup used by us for assessing the performance of our approach. We choose the data selected from the UC Irvine repository. The clustering algorithm used by our ensemble subspace classifier is the **k**-means algorithm. The value of **k** is set as explained in the Section 3.2. The *J48* decision tree classifier is used for subspace detection and subsequent data generation. The preprocessing and data preparation is done using the Weka data mining tool. The major parts of preprocessing in our current scenario include normalization and discretization of the dataset to apply the decision tree classifier. The threshold parameter $Thres$ has been set to 0.05. We determined the value of this parameter so as to attain quicker convergence and get good subspace classifiers. Once the data generation is completed as explained in section 3 the accuracy for our ensemble over subspace classifiers is reported after a **5** fold cross validation.

4.2 Importance of the augmented attributes

In this experiment, we assess the importance of the attributes augmented to the original dataset during the data generation stage of our approach. In Figures 3 and 4, we plot the *dissimilarity* values for the clusterings derived in each iteration with respect to the original clustering/labelling of the data until convergence is observed. The dissimilarity values are important here because they provide us with an insight on how much information we gain or lose on moving from one clustering to another.

For the dataset generated using our approach, clustering dissimilarity is analogous to information gain or mutual information for the attributes used during feature selection for classification. Hence dissimilar clusters should provide more information to the classifier. The metric we use here is the **Variation in Information** (**VI**) metric for computing the clusterings dissimilarity.

Let us suppose that we want to compute the Variation in Information for two clusterings C and C' where $P(k)$ and $P'(k')$ represent random variables associated with clusterings C and C'. $H(C)$ represents the entropy associated with a clustering C. Now the mutual information between these two clusterings C and C' is computed using the equation **1**. The **VI** metric is calculated using the formula provided in equation **2**.

$$I(C, C') = \sum_{k=1}^{K} \sum_{k'=1}^{K'} P(k, k') log(P(k, k')/P(k)P'(k') \quad (1)$$

$$VI(C, C') = H(C) + H(C') - 2I(C, C') \quad (2)$$

The **VI** values are obtained by comparing the clusterings produced in each iteration with respect to the original dataset clustering/labelling until convergence is observed. The labelling for the datasets are generated either through original (labelled) or clustered blind data respectively. We plot the **VI** values on the Y-axis and the number of iterations for convergence on the X-axis for six datasets considered in Table 1.

Figure 3 represents the plots obtained by considering the datasets without and with labels respectively. One can observe from these plots that as the subspaces are detected during the process of iterative convergence their **VI** metric values are significantly higher. The **VI** values differ for the same datasets in both the cases.

We repeat the same kind of experiment again for the same six datasets using the **Rand Index** clusterings dissimilarity measure. When comparing two clusterings C and C' each pair of points comes under one of the following 4 categories labelled as $N_{11}, N_{10}, N_{01}, N_{00}$ respectively. The category N_{11} consists of point pairs that are in the same clusters in both C and C'. N_{10} consists of points that are in the same cluster C but not in C'. The definitions of N_{01} and N_{00} are similar. The **RI** value is then given by the equation below in equation 3 where $N = N_{11} + N_{10} + N_{01} + N_{00}$.

$$RI(C, C') = (N_{11} + N_{00})/N \quad (3)$$

A **RI** value of 1 between two clusterings indicates that both the clusters are identical and 0 indicates that both the clusters are exactly dissimilar. For our experiment the **RI** values are obtained by comparing each of the clusterings derived in each iteration with respect to the original labelling of the dataset until convergence. From Figure 4 one can observe that the **RI** values decreases significantly with further iterations while attaining convergence for both the cases of without and with labels. Our results using these two metrics shows that the clusterings generated are much *dissimilar* than the original labelling and will hence contribute effectively to the classifier. This also demonstrates that the augmented dimensions in the supplemented dataset add good diversity to the existing feature space which helps the classifier in finding better boundaries amongst the existing classes in the dataset.

4.3 Goodness of Our Ensemble Classifier

In Table 1, we provide the results where we compare the performance of the *J48* classifier on the supplemented dataset versus those directly obtained by applying it on the original dataset. We consider 7 datasets from the UC Irvine repository. For each dataset in Table 1, we deal with both labelled and blind (without labels) data respectively. The

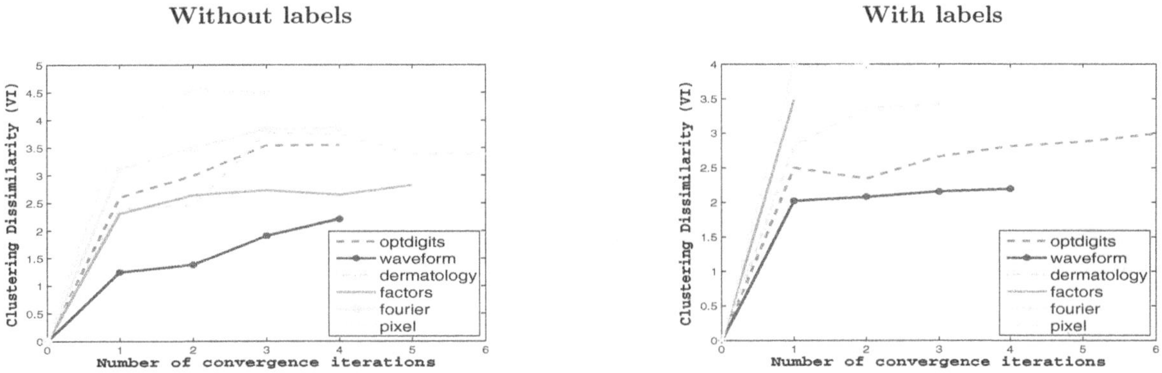

Figure 3: High VI implies more dissimilar

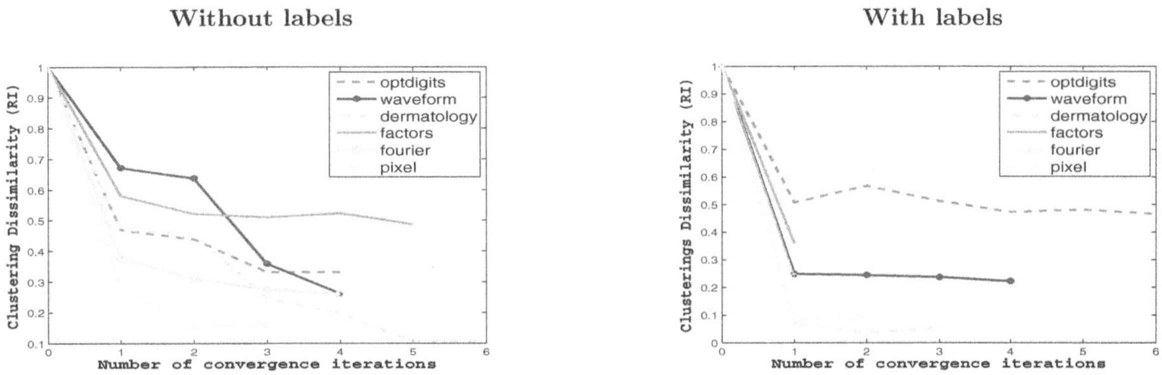

Figure 4: Low RI implies more dissimilar

number of iterations for convergence (**N.I.C**) values are reported for each dataset.

From Table 1, one can notice that in both the cases of considering either blind or labelled data the supplemented dataset yields better accuracies. In case of the labelled dataset this is observed for **five** out of **seven** cases whereas for the blind data the accuracy is better in all the cases. However, the number of iterations for convergence for the same dataset in both the cases differ. We attribute this better performance to the fact that while clustering through our iterative convergence routine we strengthen the capability of the subspace classifiers to determine the classes.

4.4 Performance with induced noise

In this subsection, we look at how our approach compares to the normal J48 classifier and other multi class classifier approaches when noise is artificially induced in the datasets. We only consider the blind/unlabelled datasets in this experiment. Hence we originally generate the clustered dataset with labels using **k**-means as mentioned in Sections 3, 3.2. Once this is done we use the AddNoise filter of Weka to add noise artificially in the datasets. The noise levels used by us for this experiment are varied from 10% to 50%.

By observing the accuracy values in Table 2 one can infer that the performance of our ensemble classifier is significantly better for low to mediocre noise levels (10%-20%) and marginally better than J48 for high noise levels around 50%. It is observed that as the artificial noise added is increased the performance of all the classifiers considered in Table 2 start deteriorating. However, our ensemble classifier maintains its robust nature and performs better than the J48 classifier. This can be attributed to the fact that the appended features in the supplemented dataset essentially provide important information to the classifier helping it form further discrete hyperplanes.

It is also observed that the stacking performs very well in the presence of high noise. In such cases the results derived from our approach are comparable and are within 10-15% of those derived from stacking. Stacking suffers from certain disadvantages associated with the increase in the number of stacked attributes appended to the dataset with increase in the class labels. In such scenarios stacking may result in the curse of dimensionality. In comparison our approach performs better than stacking for 2-class datasets and is an overall simpler approach.

5. CONCLUSIONS

In this paper, we (**i**)developed an iterative approach to get subspace classifiers (**ii**) used the supplemented dataset to generate an ensemble classifier (**iii**) showed that our ensemble classifier performs well in noisy domains. Our work can be used to generate multiple descriptions of classes in the dataset which can help the end user refine his analytics criterion. Finally, this is the first of its kind of exploratory work which explores a notion of convergence between classifiers and the role of clustering here. In our future work, we intend to study the relationship between subspace classifiers and subspace clustering and the effectiveness of differ-

Table 1: Performance of *J48* on supplemented dataset vs original dataset

Dataset	With Labels			Without Labels		
	Original	Our Ensemble Classifier	N.I.C	Original	Our Ensemble Classifier	N.I.C
Optical Digits	0.894	0.912*	7	0.863	0.877*	5
M-Feat-Factors	0.874*	0.8727	2	0.843	0.853*	6
M-Feat-Fourier	0.728	0.746*	2	0.734	0.753*	5
M-Feat-Pixels	0.78	0.869*	3	0.734	0.798*	5
Waveform	0.756	0.818*	6	0.898	0.955*	5
Dermatology	0.925	0.942*	4	0.677	0.81*	6
Pima Diabetes	0.778*	0.7707	2	0.952	0.976*	4

Table 2: Performance comparison of Our Ensemble Classifier against different classifiers with varying induced noise levels

	J48			Our Ensemble Classifier		
Dataset	**10%**	**20%**	**50%**	**10%**	**20%**	**50%**
Optical Digits	0.759	0.648	0.27	0.771	0.66	0.2706
M-Feat-Fourier	0.603	0.531	0.230	0.64	0.549	0.228
Waveform	0.762	0.614	0.382	0.784	0.626	0.39
Pima Diabetes	0.833	0.719	0.49	0.861	0.728	0.499
	ADABOOST.M1			**STACKING**		
Dataset	**10%**	**20%**	**50%**	**10%**	**20%**	**50%**
Optical Digits	0.724	0.597	0.296	0.798	0.714	0.405
M-Feat-Fourier	0.577	0.487	0.216	0.710	0.595	0.333
Waveform	0.773	0.664	0.453	0.795	0.691	0.453
Pima Diabetes	0.81	0.689	0.465	0.84	0.693	0.472

ent classifiers in designing ensemble classifiers based on our approach.

6. ACKNOWLEDGEMENTS

We would like to thank Microsoft Research India for supporting our research work.

7. REFERENCES

[1] I. Assent, R. Krieger, P. Welter, J. Herbers, and T. Seidl. Subclass: Classification of multidimensional noisy data using subspace clusters. In *Proceedings of Pacific Asia Conference on Knowledge Discovery and Data Mining , PAKDD*, pages 40–52, 2008.

[2] L. Breiman. Random forests. *Machine Learning*, 45(1):5–32, 2001.

[3] R. Caruana, M. F. Elhawary, N. Nguyen, and C. Smith. Meta clustering. In *Proceedings of International Conference on Data Mining*, pages 107–118, 2006.

[4] T. Dietterich. Ensemble methods in machine learning. In *Multiple Classifier Systems*, pages 1–15, 2000.

[5] Y. Freund and R. Schapire. Experiments with a new boosting algorithm. In *Proceedings of ICML*, pages 148–156, 1996.

[6] J. Han and M. Kamber. *Data Mining: Concepts and Techniques*. Morgan-Kaufmann, 2006.

[7] A. Jain, R. Duin, and J. Mao. Statistical pattern recognition a review. *IEEE Transactions on Pattern Analysis and Machine Intelligence*, 22(1):4–37, 2000.

[8] J. Kittler, M. Hatef, R. Duin, and J. Matas. On combining classifiers. *IEEE Transactions on Pattern Analysis and Machine Intelligence*, 20(3):226–239, 1998.

[9] R. Maclin and J. W. Shavlik. Combining the predictions of multiple classifiers: Using competitive learning to initialize neural networks. In *Proceedings of IJCAI*, pages 524–531, 1995.

[10] E. Muller, S. Gunnemann, I. Assent, and T. Seidl. Evaluating clustering in subspace projections of high dimensional data. In *Proceedings of VLDB*, pages 1270–1281, 2009.

[11] E. Muller, S. Gunnemann, I. Farber, and T. Seidl. Discovering multiple clustering solutions: Grouping objects in different views of the data. In *Tutorials at International Conference on Data Mining, ICDM*, page 1220, 2010.

[12] A. Patrikainen and M. Meila. Comparing subspace clusterings. *IEEE Transactions on Knowledge and Data Engineering*, 18(7), July 2006.

[13] I. Tsochantaridis, T. Hofmann, T. Joachims, and Y. Altun. Support vector learning for interdependent and structured output spaces. In *Proceedings of ICML*, 2004.

[14] D. Wolpert. Stacked generalization. *Neural Networks*, 5:241–259, 1992.

Bayesian Latent Variable Models for Collaborative Item Rating Prediction

Morgan Harvey[1], Mark J. Carman[2], Ian Ruthven[3] and Fabio Crestani[4]

[1]Department of Computer Science (8 AI), University of Erlangen, Germany
[2]Faculty of Informatics, Monash University, Melbourne, Australia
[3]Department of Computer Science, Strathclyde University, Glasgow, Scotland
[4]Faculty of Informatics, University of Lugano, Lugano, Switzerland

morgan.harvey@i8.informatik.uni-erlangen.de

ABSTRACT

Collaborative filtering systems based on ratings make it easier for users to find content of interest on the Web and as such they constitute an area of much research. In this paper we first present a Bayesian latent variable model for rating prediction that models ratings over each user's latent interests and also each item's latent topics. We describe a Gibbs sampling procedure that can be used to estimate its parameters and show by experiment that it is competitive with the gradient descent SVD methods commonly used in state-of-the-art systems. We then proceed to make an important and novel extension to this model, enhancing it with user-dependent and item-dependant biases to significantly improve rating estimation.

We show by experiment on a large set of real ratings data that these models are able to outperform 3 common baselines, including a very competitive and modern SVD-based model. Furthermore we illustrate other advantages of our approach beyond simply its ability to provide more accurate ratings and show that it is able to perform better on the common and important case where the user profile is short.

Categories and Subject Descriptors

H.3.3 [**Information Storage & Retrieval**]: Information Search & Retrieval

General Terms

Algorithms, Experimentation, Performance

Keywords

Recommender systems, Topic Models, User modelling

CIKM'11, October 24–28, 2011, Glasgow, Scotland, UK.

1. INTRODUCTION

The sheer number of items available in online systems can be overwhelming for users and makes finding items of interest extremely challenging. Furthermore the rapid and continual expansion of the Web makes it impossible to manually evaluate each new item to determine if it might be of interest. Content filtering systems, based on techniques from information retrieval, are designed to assist in this process by narrowing down the number of items a user has to look through in order to fulfil a particular information need. These systems rely on textual descriptions of items and seek to match these descriptions with a user's profile in order to suggest useful items. One significant issue with this content-based filtering is that for some types of items it can be extremely difficult to choose suitable descriptive terms to search for.

Another, more accurate, approach to discovering items of interest is provided by ratings-based collaborative filtering systems, which use past ratings to predict items the user may like. Such systems predict which items a given user will be interested in based on the information provided in their user profile. These profiles consist of votes or ratings for items in the system that the user has already viewed and evaluated. The profiles of other users are frequently also exploited to improve predictions for the target user.

Profiles are generally constructed explicitly from user ratings, however they may also be compiled implicitly by considering a user's purchase or bookmark history. Explicit ratings systems are commonly found on movie and music recommendation sites such as MovieLens [14] or imdb where users can give each item a rating from 0 to 5 stars. Zero indicates that the user strongly dislikes the item and five indicates that they really like the item, however any discrete set of values could be used. Implicit systems can also be used, for example in online retail stores such as Amazon [12] where users purchase items or add them to a "wish list", indicating that they are interested in that kind of item.

Given the collection of ratings provided by users, the goal is to use the data to suggest additional items or resources that a particular user may like or be interested in. This process of machine recommendation is frequently called "ratings-based collaborative filtering" or simply "collaborative filtering" and the systems themselves are often referred to as "recommender systems". Note that if a system is able to predict unknown ratings then the suggestion task can be achieved by simply ordering unrated items in descending order of their predicted rating. In doing so, such an algorithm is effectively achieving two outcomes: the "forced prediction" of whether or not a user will have a preference for an item and the "free prediction" of the expected rating itself.

In this work we focus on the problem of recommending items to users based purely on the explicit ratings they have assigned to other items in the system. We introduce 2 novel (and related) Bayesian probabilistic models designed to accurately predict ratings given the very sparse training data commonly found on e-commerce and recommendation web sites. We go on to show by experiment with a large set of real ratings data that our models are able to outperform 3 common baselines, including a very competitive and modern SVD-based model. Furthermore we illustrate a number of other advantages of our approach, beyond simply its ability to provide more accurate ratings.

The rest of the paper is structured as follows: we first discuss some relevant related work in the field of collaborative filtering and describe how the majority of modern methods approach the problem. In section 3 we describe the rating estimation problem in more detail and outline common measures for algorithm performance. In section 4 we introduce a pair of novel Bayesian models designed to decompose the problem by use of latent factors and describe how these models can be used to estimate unknown ratings. In sections 5 and 6 we describe experiments conducted with a large data set of 10 million movie ratings comparing the performance of these new models to 3 appropriate baselines and discuss the result of these experiments. Finally we offer our concluding remarks and make suggestions of possible future work building upon the results of this paper.

2. RELATED WORK

Collaborative filtering systems can be placed in the context of information retrieval by considering that in a retrieval system items are "pulled" by users through the issuing of explicit search queries. Filtering systems on the other hand are described as "push" systems since they quite literally push items at a user that is predicted he/she will like. Much early work was done in the 90s and the field has seen a resurgence of interest lately, primarily due to the Netflix prize [11]. Collaborative filtering algorithms can be generally classified into 2 distinct types: memory-based and model-based.

2.1 Memory-based CF

Early systems were memory-based and made use of the original ratings matrix to formulate predictions. Such systems follow a relatively simple 2 step process: First they identify a neighbourhood of users similar to the target user and then use an aggregate weighted summation of the neighbours' ratings for an item in order to predict the rating for the target user. These algorithms form the basis of most filtering currently performed on the Web including sites such as Amazon and CDNow and were the cornerstone of much early research in the field [7, 4]. We refer to [1] for a comprehensive description of how these methods operate. It has been speculated that their popularity is due to their relative simplicity and their inherently intuitive nature [10].

Unfortunately these simple, memory-based algorithms suffer from 2 major shortcomings. Firstly the number of items rated by most users is oftentimes small and therefore it can be difficult to choose a good neighbourhood of similar users. Once a neighbourhood is chosen only a very small number of similar users may have rated the item for which we wish to predict a rating. Secondly, these algorithms require all of the ratings data to be utilised when making a prediction and, although it is possible to maintain a cache of user similarities, this will have to be updated whenever new ratings are made. This shortcoming is perhaps the most problematic as without clever implementation, it severely restricts the potential growth of the recommendation system. This is because, over time the amount of ratings data becomes too large to allow for the efficient computation of both the neighbourhoods and the predictions themselves.

2.2 Model-based CF

These issues led to the development of the second general type of collaborative filtering algorithm: the model-based approach. In this approach we use the observed ratings to construct a model of the data and we decompose the observed ratings into a sum of biases; one for the user, one for the item and a third joint bias. Modern examples of these models frequently use some form of dimensionality reduction to uncover latent factors and to calculate the joint bias. These latent factors are constructed in a manner that best explains the training ratings and if we make the assumption that any further ratings will be drawn IID[1] from the same distribution then the model should be able to predict new ratings well.

These model-based algorithms are able to overcome many of the scalability problems associated with the earlier memory-based systems. This is particularly the case when real-time recommendations are required, which is obviously the most likely situation given the on-line nature of the systems where collaborative filtering is most often used. The most time-consuming task is the generation of the model itself, after which the task of new predictions is extremely quick due to the significant reduction in dimensionality afforded by the latent factors. With model-based systems the entire modeling operation can be completed off-line thus allowing for near-instantaneous real-time predictions as and when users need them.

Many examples of this approach, including most attempts at the Netflix prize, use gradient descent algorithms to estimate an approximation of the Singular Value Decomposition (SVD) of the original sparse ratings matrix [15]. The values computed for the SVD matrices are regularised so as to prevent over-fitting and individual biases for each user and movie are commonly added to improve prediction performance. Other techniques use probability theory to construct the models where observed ratings are assumed to arise from some latent variables which have to be estimated. In [13], Marlin represents each user as a mixture of "attitudes" with each rating being generated by selecting one of these attitudes and then selecting the rating based on the ratings distribution for that attitude. Hofmann [10] extends his earlier pLSI model to model ratings by again assuming that users have a distribution over "interests" or "attitudes" and that each rating is associated with a single interest drawn from the user's interest distribution. His work differs from that of Marlin [13] however by then assuming that there is a rating distribution for each latent interest and item pair. So the observed rating is assumed conditional on both the latent

[1]IID stands for *independently and identically distributed.*

interest of the user who rated the item and also on the item itself.

Other probabilistic approaches include [19] in which the authors introduce a novel adaptation of the EM algorithm to learn the parameters of a prediction model for personalised content-based prediction. Stern et. al. [17] instead use Expectation Propagation and Variational Message Passing to learn a model using both ratings data and content. In other recent work Chen et al. [5] compare the performance of Latent Dirichlet Allocation (LDA) [2] with association rule mining (ARM) for the purpose of community recommendation. This is a similar problem to rating prediction but instead involves the suggestion of online communities of interest rather than items. They show that LDA consistently outperforms ARM for this task, particularly when considering later recommendation. They also demonstrate that it is less likely to make extreme errors due to its Bayesian nature, certainly a useful property when recommending items.

In this paper we discuss 2 probabilistic model-based collaborative filtering algorithms that can be seen as comparable to these models and draw on similar background theory. Blei [2] in fact uses collaborative filtering as an example of a problem for which LDA could be used and shows that it is able to outperform both probabilistic LSA [9] and a simple unigram model. Our models do not use LDA itself in order to predict ratings but use its ability to extrude latent factors from sparse data as a strong basis from which to build models more suited to the task at hand. Also in this work we extend the basic ratings model by including individual biases for each user and item requiring an iterative fixed-point optimisation procedure to be interleaved with the Gibbs sampler and providing significant improvements in performance.

3. PROBLEM DEFINITION

Before proceeding any further we will formally define the problem of rating prediction and describe the format of the data we have to work with. We have a set of users of the system $\mathcal{U} = \{\mathtt{u}_1, \ldots, \mathtt{u}_U\}$, a set of items $\mathcal{M} = \{\mathtt{m}_1, \ldots, \mathtt{m}_M\}$ and a discrete set of possible ratings $\{\mathtt{1}, \ldots, \mathtt{R}\}$. Our training data is a collection of ratings given by the users to items. We can view each individual rating as a tuple: (u_i, m_i, r_i) for $i := 1 \ldots N_{train}$. For example the tuple $(u_i = 1, m_i = 1, r_i = 4)$ would indicate that user 1 had given item 1 a rating of 4. It can sometimes be convenient to visualise the complete collection of user ratings as a large and very sparse matrix R of size $U \times M$ where r_{um} would indicate the rating given by user u to item m. The prediction problem is best described by saying that we would like to "fill in" the sparse ratings matrix, extrapolating (or predicting) a rating $\hat{r}_{um}$ for every possible user-item pair from the limited data available. More practically we wish to define some function or model which will minimise the root mean squared prediction error over the test data:

$$RMSE = \sqrt{\frac{1}{N_{test}} \sum_{i=1}^{N_{test}} (r_i - \hat{r}_i)^2} \tag{1}$$

The RMSE is commonly used in statistics for measuring the difference between the set of values predicted by a model and the values actually observed from the system being modelled. It is a good measure of precision and is an unbiased estimator of the standard deviation of the predictions and is therefore a good choice of error function for collaborative filtering. We also report the Mean Absolute Error (MAE) which is simply the mean absolute difference between the predicted rating and the actual rating, over the whole test set.

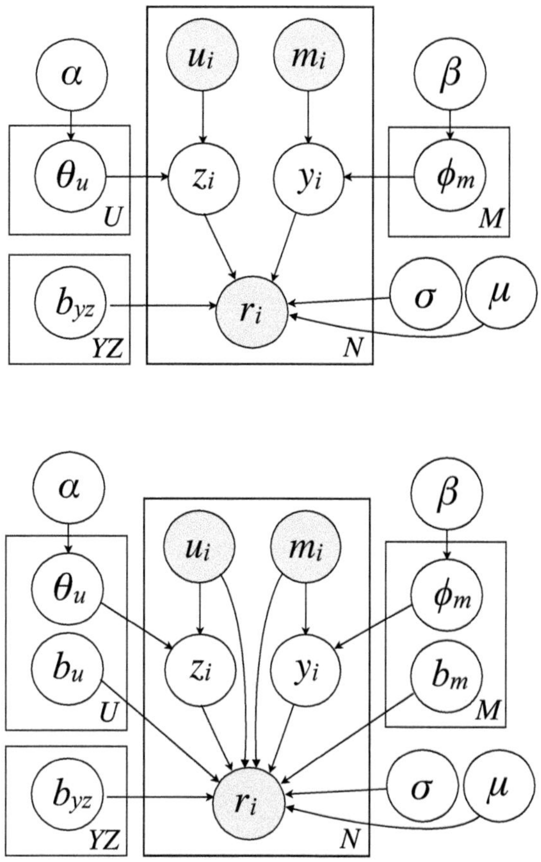

Figure 1: Latent Interest and Topic Ratings Model (LITR) where each observed change in the rating from the mean is due to both a user interest and an item topic or genre and Biased-LITR (BLITR) where it is also dependent on the bias for the user and the item.

4. LATENT INTEREST AND TOPIC RATINGS MODELS

In order to implement a new latent variable model for collaborative filtering it is necessary to choose how best to represent the latent factors and how to incorporate the ratings data, both in terms of statistical distributions. A popular modern latent variable model called Latent Dirichlet Allocation is commonly used to estimate latent variable distributions and serves as a good starting point for a new model. LDA is predominantly used to model textual data where it represents documents as random mixtures over latent topics where each topic is a distribution over the observed words in

Symbol	Description
M	number of items
U	number of users
N	number of ratings
Y	number of topics/genres
Z	number of user interests
r_i	rating at position i
m_i	item for rating at position i
u_i	user who contributed rating at position i
y_i	topic/genre allocation at position i
z_i	user interest allocation at position i
$\hat{r}_{um}$	predicted rating for user u and item m
ϕ_m	distribution over topics for item m
θ_u	distribution over interests for user u
b_m	bias due to item m
b_u	bias due to user u
b_{yz}	bias due to interest/topic pair yz
α	parameter of Dirichlet prior over Θ
β	parameter of Dirichlet prior over Φ
ρ	smoothing parameter for bias estimates
σ	standard deviation over all ratings
μ	mean rating

Table 1: List of notation for Ratings Models

the vocabulary. Each word position i in the document collection is assigned a latent random variable z_i which ranges over the latent topics.

The model possesses a number of advantageous attributes; it is fully generative meaning that it is easy to make inferences on new documents and its Bayesian nature helps to overcome the over-fitting problem present in models such as Probabilistic Latent Semantic Indexing (pLSI) [9]. Also since in LDA each document is a mixture of topics it is far more flexible than models that assume each document is only drawn from a single topic. These advantages also extend to models based on LDA with both the added flexibility and ability to easily incorporate new data being very important for our own models, as we shall discuss later. Many useful models have used LDA as a base to work from, for example the Author-Topic model [18] which models academic publications and citations. It has even been used to develop models to annotate images based on their visual features [3].

As we can see from these publications, LDA can serve as a very flexible starting point for more complex models even when those models are not just using discrete data. In the case of collaborative filtering we do not have documents and terms, but rather a collection of observed ratings from a set of users over a set of items. We must therefore significantly adapt the model to fit the problem. Since we are primarily interested in predicting ratings with the smallest possible error in aggregate it is sensible to consider models (and therefore distributions) that are continuous in nature. In doing so the predictions will not be constrained to be bound to the finite discrete values of the original ratings but will have the freedom to model the complex interactions of biases in the data at higher granularity.

4.1 Basic Generative Model

Perhaps the simplest possible prediction algorithm one could imagine would be to assign the mean rating over the training data, denoted μ (where $\hat{\mu} = \frac{1}{N}\sum_i r_i$), as a prediction to each item for every user, (i.e. $\hat{r}_{um} = \mu$). This overly simplistic model corresponds to a generative process in which each rating r_i is considered a normally distributed random variable with mean μ and standard deviation σ:

$$r_i \sim \mathcal{N}(\mu, \sigma^2) \quad (2)$$

This model makes a large number of assumptions and ignores a lot of the complexity in the data. It assumes that ratings are completely independent of both the item and user and that there are no interactions between the combinations of user and item that would affect the rating. We relax some of these assumptions and extend this model by following similar conclusions to both Hofmann [10] and Marlin [13]. That is that the change in the rating is dependent on the user and that each user can be characterised by a distribution over a small number of latent interests.

In addition, (and in contrast to previous work) we then assume that the change in rating is also equally dependent on the items, which themselves can be characterised by a distribution over a small number of latent topics. For example in the case of movies this may be more intuitively thought of as their latent genres or for general items in a web store it could be the category/ies to which they could be assigned. This conjecture leads to a more useful generative model for personalised item filtering and ranking involving three random variables: a user interest z_i, an item topic (or movie genre) y_i and a rating r_i, where only the last variable, the rating itself, is observed. Following previous work on topic models, we then assume the user-interest and item-topic variables are drawn from Multinomial distributions.[2] The same assumption could also be made regarding the ratings, as the original ratings assigned by users are indeed drawn from a discrete set. However as noted earlier, the flexibility of the model can be increased as can the granularity of its predictions, by instead modelling them as being drawn from Normal distributions. These assumptions can be summarised as follows:

$$z_i \sim Mult(\theta_{u_i}) \quad (3)$$

$$y_i \sim Mult(\phi_{m_i}) \quad (4)$$

$$r_i \sim \mathcal{N}(\mu + b_{y_i z_i}, \sigma^2) \quad (5)$$

Thus the model consists of a discrete probability distribution over interests for each user θ_u, a discrete distribution over topics for each item ϕ_m, a mean rating μ, a bias value b_{yz} for every pair of interests and topics, and a standard deviation parameter σ. A graphical model corresponding to this generative process is shown at the top of Figure 1.

The intuition for introducing the bias b_{yz} in this model is that we believe each interest and topic combination will have an effect on how the item is rated. For example in the case of movies we might expect that a user who likes romance would give a horror movie a lower than average rating, meaning that the bias b_{yz} for this interest-topic pair would be negative. Similarly if the same user was to rate a romance movie then we would expect them to give a higher

[2]The interest and topic variables are actually drawn from discrete distributions, but we use the term Multinomial in keeping with the literature.

than average rating and the bias would therefore be positive. Since these biases are calculated over the low-dimensionality latent spaces they will not be sparse and should allow the model to generalise well to unseen user-item combinations, a key objective of any collaborative filtering model.

Given suitable estimates for these parameters, we can predict the rating for a user u and item m by calculating the expected value as follows:

$$\hat{r}_{um} = \mathbb{E}[r|u,m] = \sum_{y,z} \mathbb{E}[r|y,z]P(y|m)P(z|u) \quad (6)$$

$$= \mu + \sum_{y,z} b_{yz}\phi_{y|m}\theta_{z|u} \quad (7)$$

Here $\theta_{z|u}$ and $\phi_{y|m}$ denote probability of an interest given a user and a topic given an item respectively. This model is quite intuitive. It states that the rating given by a user to an item will be the product of a user's affinity for an interest, the item's probability of belonging to a topic and the average bias for that interest-topic combination, summed over all possible combinations of interests and topics.

In this model we have associated a possibly non-zero bias with every pair of interest topic dimensions. Thus not only is a positive bias associated with "corresponding"' interests and topics (e.g. the user-interest "horror" and the movie-genre "horror") but also a possibly negative bias with "non-corresponding"' interests and topics. For instance if a user's primary interest is "horror", they may still have a positive bias towards a "thriller" while having a negative bias against a "comedy". In SVD terms this is to some extent equivalent to replacing the diagonal singular-value matrix with a matrix containing non-zero off-diagonal values. These values then allow us to model both positive and negative correlations across different factors. By defining the predictions in terms of a generative model, we can interpret and explain the parameters of the model in a way that is not possible with SVD-based prediction algorithms.

4.2 Parameter Estimation

Given vectors of latent variable assignments $\mathbf{z} = (z_1, ..., z_N)$ and $\mathbf{y} = (y_1, ..., y_N)$, we can compute estimates of both the probability of an interest given a user $\theta_{z|u}$ and a topic given an item $\phi_{y|m}$. Following principles from LDA, and in keeping with Bayesian statistics, we place symmetric Dirichlet priors on both of these distributions, resulting in the following expectations for the parameter values under their respective posterior distributions:

$$\hat{\theta}_{z|u} = \frac{N_{zu} + \alpha\frac{1}{Z}}{N_u + \alpha} \quad (8)$$

$$\hat{\phi}_{y|m} = \frac{N_{ym} + \beta\frac{1}{Y}}{N_m + \beta} \quad (9)$$

Here N_{zu}, N_{ym}, N_u and N_u are counts denoting the number of times the interest z appears (in $\mathbf{z}$) together with user u, the number of times topic y appears (in $\mathbf{y}$) with item m, and the total ratings by user u and for item m respectively. Z is the number of interests and Y is the number of topics. The hyperparameters α and β act as pseudo-counts, allowing the model to fall back on the (uniform) prior probability in the event of sparse data, which is particularly useful in this setting where sparse data is common.

In addition to estimating the distributions over interests and topics we need to estimate the bias for each interest and topic pair denoted b_{yz}. Given that we have a complete set of assignments for these latent variables for each observed r_i we can calculate an estimate of this bias as follows:

$$\hat{b}_{yz} = \frac{\sum_{i:(y_i=y)\wedge(z_i=z)}(r_i - \mu)}{N_{yz} + \rho} \quad (10)$$

Here N_{yz} denotes the number of ratings for which y and z appear together and ρ is a smoothing parameter. It is related to the variance of the zero mean Gaussian prior on b_{yz}, which keeps the model Bayesian and helps to deal with sparsity in the data.[3] We note that it would also be possible to estimate a variance parameter separately for each (y, z) pair, but we instead make the simplifying assumption that all biases have the same fixed variance.

While exact inference of latent variable models such as LITR is intractable, a number of methods of approximating the posterior distribution exist including mean field variational inference [2] and Gibbs sampling [8]. Gibbs sampling is a Markov chain Monte Carlo method where a Markov chain is constructed that converges to the target distribution of interest over a number of iterations. In Gibbs sampling the next state in the chain is reached by sampling all variables from their conditional distribution given the current values of all other variables [6].

Gibbs sampling for this model involves sampling first z_i and then y_i for each rating r_i. To sample for z_i we calculate distribution $P(z|r_i, y_i, u_i, \mu, \sigma, \mathbf{z}_{-i})$, which is conditioned on the current assignment to all interest variables except z_i. Similarly for y_i we sample from the distribution $P(y|r_i, z_i, m_i, \mu, \sigma, \mathbf{y}_{-i})$. Note that our estimates for the parameters $\theta_{z|u}$, $\phi_{y|m}$ and b_{yz} depend on the interest and topic assignments $\mathbf{z}$ and $\mathbf{y}$, so when calculating estimates using Equations 8, 9 and 10, we simply remove the ith rating from the sample. The conditional probability distributions are then estimated as follows:

$$P(z|r_i, ...) \propto p(r_i|y_i, z)P(z|u_i)$$

$$\propto \exp\left(\frac{(r_i - (\mu + b_{y_i z}))^2}{\sigma^2}\right)\frac{N_{zu} + \alpha\frac{1}{Z}}{N_u + \alpha} \quad (11)$$

$$P(y|r_i, ...) \propto p(r_i|y, z_i)P(y|m_i)$$

$$\propto \exp\left(\frac{(r_i - (\mu + b_{yz_i}))^2}{\sigma^2}\right)\frac{N_{ym} + \beta\frac{1}{Y}}{N_m + \beta} \quad (12)$$

Here $p(r|y, z)$ denotes the conditional probability density at rating r for the interest y and topic z. Since the algorithm only require estimates proportional to the true probabilities the normalising factor of the Normal distribution is not required. Therefore the first parts of Equations 11 and 12 are the unnormalised probabilities of a Normal distribution. This model provides a method of predicting ratings by considering perturbations from the mean rating over a number of latent interests and topics.

After sufficient iterations of the sampler, the Markov chain converges and the parameters of the model can then be estimated from the assignments $\mathbf{z}$ and $\mathbf{y}$ via equations 8 and 9. For increased accuracy, we average parameter estimates over consecutive samples from the Markov chain. Gibbs sampling is a preferable alternative to methods such as Expectation

[3]The value ρ is equal to the ratio of the variances of the likelihood and the prior (both Normal distributions).

Maximisation as it is able to sample from the entire posterior distribution and is therefore unlikely to get "stuck" in local maxima and does not require the use of additional machinery such as simulated annealing to get around this problem [16]. Another benefit of this technique is the ability to quickly "fold-in" new data into the model, this is particularly useful for this task as new ratings, items and users are likely to appear quite frequently. To include this new data into the model we can simply run the Gibbs sampler over the new data, holding all of the pre-existing interest and topic allocations fixed. After the sampler has converged on this new data (which usually occurs within less than 50 iterations) we can simply recalculate parameter estimates in equations 8 and 9.

4.3 Adding User and Movie Biases

As noted in section 2, the most successful models competing in the Netflix prize also estimate a bias for each user and a bias for each item as well as the bias due to the user and the item together. This is a sensible assumption as some users may naturally rate items higher than others and some may naturally choose from a lower baseline score. Similarly some items are intrinsically better than others and are therefore likely to be rated higher by all users, while items of a lesser quality will be given a lower than average score by most users. While we would expect that these biases would be at least partially accounted for by the joint biases over the reduced genre and interest spaces it is likely that users and movies that give/have unusually high or low ratings (outliers) would affect the accuracy of the biases for other users. By calculating a separate bias for each user and item separately we effectively remove these eccentricities from the ratings, giving the joint biases the freedom to deal purely with the variations caused by observing the various interest/genre pairs. The Biased-LITR model (BLITR) is therefore an extension of the model described previously to also include these biases in order to improve prediction accuracy. The graphical representation for this model is on the bottom in Figure 1.

The generative model is the same as the previous case, except that the mean of the Gaussian distribution that generates the rating r_i takes into account the user and item biases b_{u_i} and b_{m_i} as follows:

$$r_i \sim \mathcal{N}(\mu + b_{u_i} + b_{m_i} + b_{y_i z_i}, \sigma^2) \tag{13}$$

Given estimates for the parameters of this more complicated model, the predicted rating for a user u and an item m is now:

$$\hat{r}_{um} = \mathbb{E}[r|u,m] = \mu + b_u + b_m + \sum_{y,z} b_{yz}\phi_{y|m}\theta_{z|u} \tag{14}$$

Note that the prediction under this new model and the previous model can be viewed as perturbing the mean μ by a combination of biases. Both models add a bias for the likely interests and topics given the user and item pair, while the second model adds also explicit biases for the user and for the item.

Estimates for the parameters $\theta_{z|u}$ and $\phi_{y|m}$ are the same as in the previous model, while the estimate for b_{yz} must now include the effects of the extra biases as follows:

$$\hat{b}_{yz} = \frac{\sum_{i:(y_i=y)\wedge(z_i=z)}(r_i - (\mu + b_{u_i} + b_{m_i}))}{N_{yz} + \rho}$$

Furthermore we must also compute estimates for the new user and item-dependent biases. The most obvious way to compute these biases is to take the mean difference of all ratings for a given user/item from the mean rating for all users/items. However since we are also computing an implied bias (denoted b_{um}) for each user-item pair we need to include the effects of this bias in the estimations. We therefore estimate the user and item biases as follows:

$$\hat{b}_u = \frac{\sum_{i:(u_i=u)}(r_i - (\mu + b_{m_i} + b_{um_i}))}{N_u + \rho} \tag{15}$$

$$\hat{b}_m = \frac{\sum_{i:(m_i=m)}(r_i - (\mu + b_{u_i} + b_{u_i m}))}{N_m + \rho} \tag{16}$$

$$\texttt{where } b_{um} = \sum_{y,z} b_{yz}\phi_{y|m}\theta_{z|u} \tag{17}$$

We note that the Equations 15 and 16 are mutually dependent and thus an iterative fixed-point calculation is required to estimate the biases. Holding the joint b_{um} biases fixed this procedure converges very quickly and stabilises within less than ten iterations. Finally the distributions used for the Gibbs sampling routine must also be updated to include the new biases:

$$P(z|\ldots) \propto \exp(\frac{(r_i - (\mu + b_{u_i} + b_{m_i} + b_{y_i z}))^2}{\sigma^2})\theta_{z|u_i} \tag{18}$$

$$P(y|\ldots) \propto \exp(\frac{(r_i - (\mu + b_{u_i} + b_{m_i} + b_{y z_i}))^2}{\sigma^2})\phi_{y|m_i} \tag{19}$$

Since the user and item biases are not strongly dependent on the allocations of ratings to y and z we can simply estimate them after every k^{th} iteration of the Gibbs sampler and the algorithm will still converge. Not only does this speed up computation of the model but it also gives the sampler time to re-converge after changes to the user and item biases. In all the experiments performed we re-calculate these biases after every 10 Gibbs iterations.

5. EXPERIMENTS

We now discuss the experiments we performed on a large sample of ranking data from the MovieLens[4] movie rating web site, this data is freely available from the GroupLens website.[5] The data consists of 10 million ratings for 10,681 movies made by 71,567 users. The users are selected at random and have all rated at least 10 movies. Consequently the average number of ratings per user is 140 and per movie is 936. The ratings are all given on a scale of 0 to 5 stars with increments of 0.5 stars. The mean rating over all users and movies is 3.53 and the variance is 0.96.

We separated this data set into training and test sets by randomly choosing k percent of the ratings to be kept for testing and used the remaining ratings to train the models. For our experiments we set k to be 20%. Therefore the results reported in the remainder of the paper are based on

[4]http://www.movielens.org/

[5]http://grouplens.org/node/73

predictions over all of the test data, amounting to almost 2 million individual predictions.

To evaluate the relative performance of the various models we report both the RMSE, as described previously, and also the Mean Absolute Error (MAE). This is simply the mean absolute difference between the predicted rating and the actual rating over all testing examples. We report both metrics as they provide different information regarding the performance of predictions: the RMSE penalises large errors much more than small errors while the MAE penalises all errors equally relative to their size.

5.1 Baselines

In order to evaluate the utility of our new models we must choose suitable baseline methods with which to compare their performance. For this work we compare our methods to 3 baselines from CF literature:

mean-r a naïve, simple baseline which returns the mean rating as an estimate for all user-item pairs.

neighbourhood a nearest-neighbour method using Pearson correlation coefficient as the similarity metric with case amplification and significance weighting [4]. Represents earlier memory-based CF systems.

SVD a fully-regularised gradient descent SVD model with user and item biases providing a thoroughly modern and highly competitive baseline.

5.2 Parameter settings and sampling

For the LITR and BLITR models we set the concentration parameters of both α and β to 5, providing some light smoothing to the user-interest and item-topic distributions. The settings for ρ and σ were 0.5 and 0.1 respectively. The models were not particularly sensitive to parameter values, provided excessively low or high values were not chosen, i.e. applying almost no smoothing, or in the other extreme smoothing out the information from the data completely.

For the SVD method we optimised the parameter values based on performance over a small sub-sample of the test set. The values obtained in doing this are very similar to the standard best performing parameters values as described in the literature[15]. Specifically the learning rate was set to 0.002 and the 2 regularisation constants λ and $\lambda 2$ were set to 0.02 and 0.05. For the gradient descent algorithm, prediction errors on a sub-sample of the test set were observed to stabilise after approximately 30 iterations, however to ensure convergence we continued until 50 iterations had elapsed. For the neighbourhood method the number of neighbours used for the estimates was set to 100.

For sampling in the LITR models we use the Rao-Blackwellised Gibbs sampler [8]. For both models we sampled the chain for 300 iterations in total, as this appeared to consistently give good convergence in terms of model likelihood. We discarded the first 200 samples from the chain as "burn-in". The remaining 100 samples from the end of the chain were averaged to obtain the final parameter values.

6. RESULTS

The results from our experiments are summarised in table 2. We can see, somewhat unsurprisingly, that all of the methods significantly outperform the most simple choice of estimate: the mean over all ratings. The nearest-neighbour method performs well, however the more modern model-based approaches are all able to outperform it by a large margin. In testing we encountered one of the main disadvantages of memory-based approaches as prediction using the neighbourhood model took orders of magnitude longer than the model-based approaches.

In comparing the model-based approaches, we see that LITR, which does not include individual biases for each user and item, is still able to outperform the SVD method, however not by a significant margin. The more complex BLITR model on the other hand, which is able to leverage predictive power from the user and item biases as well as from the latent variable mixture of Gaussians, is able to outperform all of the other methods over both reported metrics by a statistically significant margin. In terms of MAE the BLITR model outperforms SVD by 2.7% and by 2% in terms of RMSE (paired t-test, 99% confidence, p-value = $4.5 * 10^{-05}$ and $1.2 * 10^{-05}$). Furthermore it improves upon the nearest neighbour approach by 3.8% for the MAE metric and 2.9% for the RMSE metric.

These results demonstrate the appropriateness of the LITR models to the problem of rating prediction and indicate that the generative models are able to make predictions with less error. Considering that the SVD model includes individual item and user biases it is notable that the LITR model without these additional biases is able to remain competitive. By incorporating these biases in the BLITR model we are able

Table 2: Comparison of best results from each model. For latent factor/variable models the number of latent variables is set to 50. Percentages indicate improvement over baseline.

	Prediction error		Improvement	
Model	MAE	RMSE	MAE	RMSE
μ rating	0.8516	1.0521	-	-
n'hood	0.6582	0.8481	22.7%	19.4%
SVD	0.6516	0.8401	23.5%	20.1%
LITR	0.6496	0.8384	23.7%	20.3%
BLITR	0.6334	0.8236	25.6%	21.7%

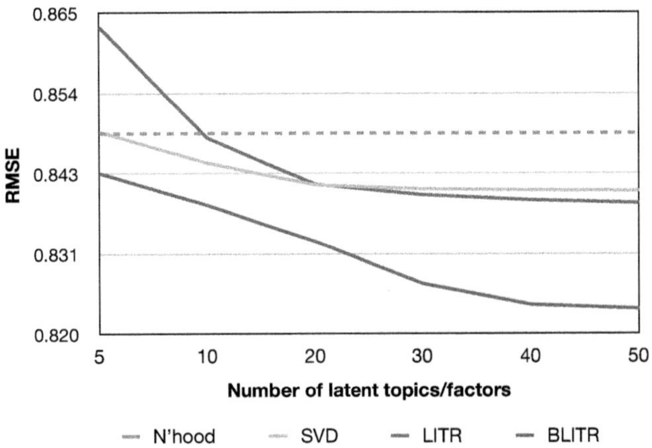

Figure 2: RMSE over different numbers of latent topics/factors.

to significantly outperform SVD, however. Thus it is clear that the inclusion of these biases into the generative process is important if we are to achieve optimal prediction results.

6.1 Varying the number of latent factors

We now look at how performance of the models vary as we increase the number of topics. By referring to the chart in Figure 2 we can see that all of the model-based approaches increase in performance as we increase the number of topics or latent factors. Notice that when the number of latent topics is set to 5 only BLITR is able to clearly outperform the memory-based nearest neighbour model, however as the number of factors is increased all of the model-based approaches begin to outperform it.

Initially the performance of the LITR model appears to be quite poor in comparison to the other latent variable models. This is because when the number of latent variables is small both SVD and BLITR can rely on user and item biases to explain the differences in ratings and thus improve their predictions while LITR cannot. As the number of factors increases we see that LITR is able to approach and then eventually exceed the performance of SVD, however it is still unable to come close to the performance of BLITR. The performance of all of the models appears to have reached a plateau by around 40 factors with any further improvements after this point being quite small.

6.2 Performance for "difficult" users

Table 3: Comparison of results over different user profile sizes.

	Prediction error (RMSE)			
#ratings/user	≤ 20	≤ 50	≤ 100	all
SVD	0.9115	0.8840	0.8692	0.8401
BLITR	0.8536	0.8435	0.8379	0.8236
#users	9,404	33,965	50,297	71,567

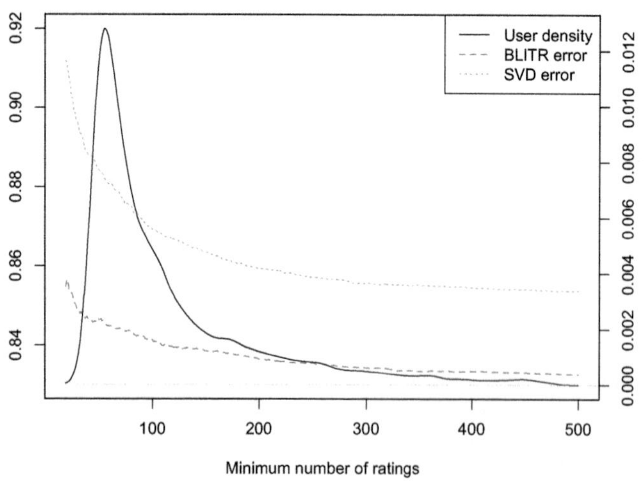

Figure 3: Prediction error and user count for varying profile sizes

As discussed earlier, an important consideration for any collaborative filtering algorithm is how well it does in the most difficult cases. This is generally users (or items) with a very small number of training ratings, for example the case of a new user or item. Analysing the data set we find that 13.4% of all users have 20 or fewer ratings and nearly half (47.5%) have 50 or fewer. We expect that these will be the users for whom the algorithms struggle the most to make accurate predictions for.

Table 3 shows how the performance of the best performing baseline and the best of the new models (SVD and BLITR) vary over different user profiles sizes. The results show that the BLITR model performs much better for smaller profiles (relative to its performance over all users) than SVD. The SVD model's performance decreases by 8.4% when dealing with small user profiles (20 or fewer ratings) whereas BLITR's performance only sees a very small decrease of 3.6%.

This result is perhaps illustrated more clearly in Figure 3, which shows the mean error over varying user profile sizes, for all users with a profile size smaller than or equal to the value on the x-axis. This is plotted for both SVD (dotted red line) and BLITR (dashed blue lines). The figure also shows on the right-hand y-axis the density of user counts over profile sizes (solid black line). We can see clearly that a large proportion of the users have a small number of ratings with very, very few having a large number. The maximum number of ratings for any user is 2876, 97% of users have fewer than 500 ratings and the minimum is 10 (this lower limit is imposed by the MovieLens web site). We can see from this plot that SVD's error for users with small profiles is quite high and that it fairly rapidly decreases as the profile size increases. On the other hand LITR has much smaller error for users with small profiles and is able to produce much smaller errors than SVD over the whole range of profile sizes.

This is an important outcome as it demonstrates that our models are able to perform much better when data is particularly sparse which is the most common case and are the situations for which we are most interested in improving performance. We speculate that this is a consequence of the Bayesian nature of the models; allowing them to cope better when there is little data available to base predictions on. It may also be because the LITR models are better at leveraging the limited information obtained from the small number of ratings that are available in these cases.

6.3 Variance of errors

The main focus of rating prediction is of course to make predictions with minimal error, however of course there will always be some error and it is not possible to always make perfect predictions. This being the case, a secondary focus is to try to ensure that when errors are made they are not too large as this can frustrate and confuse users and even a single instance of poor prediction can cause a user to lose faith in the system's abilities. Figure 4 shows a density plot of mean errors for users over the testing data made by both SVD and the BLITR model. The plot shows that the errors made by SVD have larger variance (0.065 versus 0.045 for BLITR) and also have a much thicker tail at the higher end of the errors. This means that not only are the predictions made by BLITR better in the expectation but they are also less likely to be extreme and as a result are less likely to frustrate users.

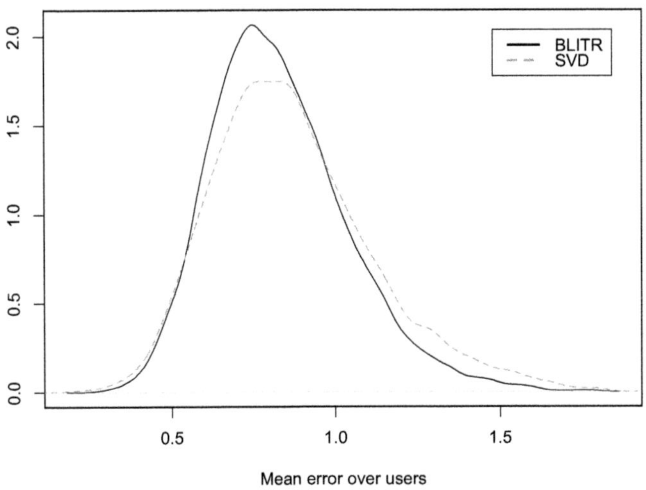

Figure 4: Density plot of mean error over all users

7. CONCLUSIONS AND FUTURE WORK

In this work we have presented two Bayesian models for collaborative rating prediction based on clustering users and items into latent interests and latent topics simultaneously. We first introduced the concept of collaborative filtering and briefly discussed related work, including both memory and model-based methods. We motivated our work by outlining the benefits of model-based collaborative filtering systems and of the Bayesian approach to data modelling. The first model predicts a user-item rating by perturbing the mean rating across items and users by the weighted summation of interest and topic biases, where the weights are the probability of the interest-topic pair given the particular user and item. The second model is an important and novel extension of the first, including user and item specific biases in the prediction.

We describe an estimation procedure for this model which alternates between Gibbs sampling of the latent variables and an iterative fixed-point estimation of the additional biases. We explain reasons why Gibbs sampling is both suitable and necessary for this task, in particular that it allows new data to be easily, quickly and accurately folded into the existing model. We motivate the use of latent topics in the model due to their flexibility and the ease of interpretation of results that they permit. We concede that the ideas of performing item recommendation using Bayesian probabilistic models and the inclusion of user and item biases are not in themselves novel. However the combination of these techniques via the interleaving of Gibbs sampling and fixed-point optimisation and the use of multinomial distributions for latent vectors for users and items and the b_{yz} matrix presents an important new contribution.

By experiment over a large, freely-available and commonly used data set of real item ratings we have shown that the models are extremely competitive, with the extended model significantly outperforming the most competitive baselines. Furthermore we investigated how well the strongest baseline and our best model performed in cases where the user profiles were very short (where the user had rated very few items). We found that our model is able to cope far better than the SVD baseline in these cases which is an important result as such cases are both common and an area where improvement in performance is most useful. Lastly, analysis of the residual errors showed that BLITR's errors had much smaller variance than those of SVD and as such is much less likely to generate extremely erroneous predictions which could frustrate and confuse users.

This work opens up many potential opportunities for future research by taking advantage of the modular structure of the models to provide a framework for various extensions. Here we make a number of suggestions for future work:

- The models could be extended to include more information such as the time when each rating was made. It is likely that this would yield good improvements to the predictive power of the models as it did for participants in the Netflix prize.
- Improvements could be made to the fit of the models by estimating the variances of the various Gaussian mixture components separately, rather than using a fixed value. This may serve to improve the accuracy of predictions made.
- As noted earlier in the paper we calculate a point estimate for the user and item biases. The Bayesian ideology could be taken further by instead treating these as random variables with their own priors and calculating a posterior for them in order to obtain a more principled, and potentially more accurate, estimate.
- To leverage the tag data provided about the movie in the latest release of the MovieLens data set to make up for some of the sparsity in the ratings data. It may be possible to use this information to create an informative prior over $P(y|m)$, replacing the uniform prior we currently use.

8. REFERENCES

[1] G. Adomavicius and A. Tuzhilin. Toward the next generation of recommender systems: A survey of the state-of-the-art and possible extensions. *Knowledge and Data Engineering, IEEE Transactions on*, 17(6):734–749, 2005.

[2] D. Blei, A. Ng, and M. Jordan. Latent dirichlet allocation. *Journal of Machine Learning Research*, (3):993–1022, 2003.

[3] D. M. Blei and M. I. Jordan. Modeling annotated data. In *SIGIR '03: Proceedings of the 26th annual international ACM SIGIR conference on Research and development in informaion retrieval*, pages 127–134, New York, NY, USA, 2003. ACM.

[4] J. S. Breese, D. Heckerman, and C. Kadie. Empirical analysis of predictive algorithms for collaborative filtering. In *Proceedings of the14th Annual Conference on Uncertainty in Artificial Intelligence (UAI98)*, pages 43–52, 1998.

[5] Wen Y. Chen, Jon C. Chu, Junyi Luan, Hongjie Bai, Yi Wang, and Edward Y. Chang. Collaborative filtering for orkut communities: discovery of user latent behavior. In *Proceedings of the 18th international conference on World wide web*, WWW '09, pages 681–690, New York, NY, USA, 2009. ACM.

[6] Andrew Gelman, John B. Carlin, Hal S. Stern, and Donald B. Rubin. *Bayesian Data Analysis*. London: Chapman and Hall, 2004.

[7] D. Goldberg, D. Nichols, B. M. Oki, and D. Terry. Using collaborative filtering to weave an information tapestry. *Communications of the ACM*, 35:61–70, 1992.

[8] T. Griffiths and M. Steyvers. Finding scientific topics. *National Academy of Science*, 2004.

[9] T. Hofmann. Unsupervised learning by probabilistic latent semantic analysis. *Machine Learning*, 42(1/2):177–196, 2001.

[10] T. Hofmann. Latent semantic models for collaborative filtering. *ACM Trans. Inf. Syst.*, 22(1):89–115, January 2004.

[11] Yehuda Koren. Factorization meets the neighborhood: a multifaceted collaborative filtering model. In *KDD '08: Proceeding of the 14th ACM SIGKDD international conference on Knowledge discovery and data mining*, pages 426–434, New York, NY, USA, 2008. ACM.

[12] G. Linden, B. Smith, and J. York. Amazon.com recommendations: Item-to-item collaborative filtering. *IEEE Internet Computing Jan/Feb*, 2003.

[13] B. Marlin. Modeling user rating profiles for collaborative filtering. In *NIPS17*, 2003.

[14] B. N. Miller, I. Albert, S. K. Lam, J. A. Konstan, and J. Riedl. Movielens unplugged: Experiences with an occasionally connected recommender system. In *Proceedings of ACM 2003 Conference on Intelligent User Interfaces (IUI'03)*, 2003.

[15] A. Paterek. Improving regularized singular value decomposition for collaborative filtering. In *KDDCup.07*, 2007.

[16] A. F. M. Smith and G. O. Roberts. Bayesian computation via the gibbs sampler and related markov chain monte-carlo methods (with discussion). In *Journal of the Royal Statistical Society*, volume 55, pages 3–23, 1993.

[17] David H. Stern, Ralf Herbrich, and Thore Graepel. Matchbox: large scale online bayesian recommendations. In *Proceedings of the 18th international conference on World wide web*, WWW '09, pages 111–120, New York, NY, USA, 2009. ACM.

[18] Mark Steyvers, Padhraic Smyth, Michal R. Zvi, and Thomas Griffiths. Probabilistic author-topic models for information discovery. In *KDD '04: Proceedings of the tenth ACM SIGKDD international conference on Knowledge discovery and data mining*, pages 306–315, New York, NY, USA, 2004. ACM.

[19] Yi Zhang and Jonathan Koren. Efficient bayesian hierarchical user modeling for recommendation system. In *SIGIR '07: Proceedings of the 30th annual international ACM SIGIR conference on Research and development in information retrieval*, pages 47–54, New York, NY, USA, 2007. ACM.

Timing When to Buy

Rakesh Agrawal
Search Labs
Microsoft Research
rakesha@microsoft.com

Samuel Ieong
Search Labs
Microsoft Research
saieong@microsoft.com

Raja Velu*
School of Management
Syracuse University
rpvelu@syr.edu

ABSTRACT

Most e-commerce sites to-date have focused on helping consumers decide what to buy and where to buy. We study the complementary question of helping consumers decide *when* to buy, focusing on consumer durables. We introduce a utility-based model for evaluating different approaches to this question. We focus on how best to make use of forecasts in making recommendations, and propose three natural strategies. We establish a relationship between these strategies, and show that one of them is optimal. We conduct a large-scale experimental study to test the performance and robustness of these strategies. Across a wide range of conditions, the best strategy obtains 90% of the maximum possible gains.

Categories and Subject Descriptors

J.4 [**Social and Behavioral Sciences**]: Economics; F.2.0 [**Analysis of Algorithms and Problem Complexity**]: General

General Terms

Economics, Algorithms, Experimentation

Keywords

Recommendation, Automated Shopping

1. INTRODUCTION

In recent times, there has been tremendous growth in the amount of commerce conducted over the Web. The yearly retail e-commerce sales in U.S. alone are estimated to have topped $100 Billion. Nearly seven out of ten consumers say that the Internet has become important in providing them with information to help them make buying decisions and that they are likely to shop online before making an offline purchase [11]. Thus the Internet has started to play a crucial role in the decision making process of the consumers irrespective of whether they buy online or offline.

Various e-commerce sites exist to help consumers make purchasing decisions. Some websites provide product reviews to help consumers decide what to buy among similar products. Others compare prices across different retailers to help consumers decide where to buy the product. However, few sites exist to help consumers decide *when to buy*.

In this paper, we study the design of decision aids that help consumers decide the timing of the purchase of durable products such as household appliances and electronic goods. Such decision aids are important as consumer durables are typically expensive, and consumers experience remorse when they find out they could have bought the products at lower prices had they waited a little longer [6].

Certain websites advice consumers about potential price changes in the domain of airfare (`bing.com/travel`, formerly *farecast* [9]) and event tickets (`seatgeek.com`). There is a crucial difference between the domain of tickets and the domain of durable goods which we study in this paper. While both problems have to deal with the uncertainty of future prices, in the case of a durable product, there is a cost associated with waiting to buy the product due to loss of use, which has to be factored into the decision. Thus, while recommending when to buy a ticket is driven solely by potential price changes, recommending when to buy a consumer durable requires a more in-depth modeling of the utility to the consumer.

In order to make good recommendations, we must first be able to predict potential price changes. In [1], we compared and evaluated different forecasting methods incorporating prices, sales volume, seasonality, and competition for predicting prices in consumer durables. We found that methods that use both the current price level and the recent price changes can generally predict product prices well. In this paper, we set out to answer the following questions:

- What is a formal framework for modeling a recommendation system that advices consumers when to buy? How do we measure the performance of such a system and compare alternatives?
- How can we best take advantage of forecasts in coming up with recommendations to the users?
- How much utility can these approaches create for users under realistic settings?

We address the first question by proposing a utility-driven model that captures the trade-off a prospective consumer

*Work done while author was visiting Search Labs.

CIKM'11, October 24–28, 2011, Glasgow, Scotland, UK.

has to make when faced with the decision of when to buy, namely between potential price drops and the loss in utility due to waiting. An essential feature of the formulation is the *sequential* nature of the recommendations, inspired by Markov decision processes. We address the second question by introducing three natural strategies for recommendations treating forecasts as blackboxes. We conduct a theoretical analysis to compare these strategies, and establish optimality for one of them. We address the last question by conducting an empirical analysis that measures the potential gains users make by following the recommendations. The analysis provides a foundation for building a system that helps forward-looking consumers make more informed decisions.

1.1 Road Map

The rest of the paper is organized as follows. We begin with a discussion of related work in Section 2. We introduce a formal model for the recommendation problem by proposing a model of utility of the consumers in Section 3. We then describe three recommendation strategies in Section 4 and analyze them in Section 5. In Section 6, we present a large-scale experiment using prices in the electronic goods category that quantifies the gains to the consumers from using our system. We discuss the implication of this study and future research directions in Section 7.

2. RELATED WORK

The decision between present and future consumption has been studied in economics as the *intertemporal choice* problem. In his seminal work *Theory of Interest*, Fisher proposed that such trade-off should be captured by means of discounting [10]. More recent marketing studies on forward-looking consumer behavior has also been based on discounting, including [21] that estimates the discount rates for different types of products, and [18] that compares different forms of discounting. Inspired by these studies, we propose to model the loss of utility due to waiting by means of discounting. However, while these past proposals attempt to explain consumer behavior through discounting, we are interested in helping consumers that discount future consumption to make the best timing decision.

Our formulation of the problem of when to buy a consumer durable is related to optimal stopping problems studied in probability theory [5]. To our knowledge, no past work has proposed a framework for analyzing this decision using optimal stopping, which we believe provide a natural formulation that allows us to compare different approaches in a formal and rigorous way. One important distinction in our work, in contrast to prior work on optimal stopping, is that the distributions of the random variables are not assumed to be known; rather, their distributions are observed through forecasting algorithms that may be inaccurate.

There have been a number of studies in the marketing literature on the pricing of consumer durables [16, 19]. Price evolutions are often modeled from the product life-cycle point of view, where price changes are linked to stages of the life of a product. Dino applied this model for electronic products at a category level and the model fits well [7]. The methodology has also been extended to incorporating demand models [8]. These prior works suggest that prices for consumer durables follow definite patterns. See [3, 14] for surveys of forecasting methods.

Traditionally, recommender systems focus on suggesting to users items that they may like [15]. Recommendations may be made based on items that similar users like [20], similar items that a user likes [17], or hybrid methods that combine the two [4]. While our work is also about making recommendations to users, the recommendations are about when an item should be purchased. The recommendation is different in nature and is not amenable to a solution by existing techniques.

3. SYSTEM DESIGN

In this section, we present the design of our system. We first propose a formal framework for analyzing the problem of timing the purchase of consumer durables based on utility theory. We then describe how such a system may be implemented as part of a shopping service.

3.1 Model

Consider a consumer who has selected a particular product to buy, and is deciding whether to buy the product right away or wait for its price to drop. We treat time as discrete, and denote the latest time until the consumer would wait as time T, which we call the consumer's *decision horizon.*

The problem of *timing when to buy* is to decide the time index τ within consumer's decision horizon at which she should buy the product. It is a *sequential decision problem*—at each time step s, she decides whether to buy the product or wait. If she chooses to wait, she will face another decision at the next time step. The problem repeats itself until she buys the product.

The consumer has a *value* θ for the product, which measures the benefit she expects to derive from owning and using the product. In deciding whether to buy now or wait, the consumer faces a trade-off between starting to derive the benefit right away and the loss due to potential price drops in the future. This *intertemporal trade-off* is commonly modeled by *discounting* the value of the product if it is purchased in the future [18, 21]. We denote the discount rate of the consumer by δ $(0 < \delta \leq 1)$, and take it to be time-invariant within the consumer's decision horizon. If a consumer decides to buy the product at time t, she derives a utility of $\theta\delta^t$. The quantities T, θ, and δ are specific to the consumer of a given product, and may vary for different consumers and products.

Let the prices of the product from start uptil time T be $(p_0, p_1, \ldots, p_T)$, which we call the *price path* $\mathbf{p}$ of the product. The consumer first gets interested in buying the product at time t. For the purpose of this paper, we assume $t = 0$. This is without loss of generality since the prices before time t cannot change the utility of the consumer, which we define momentarily. At time s, the prices up to time s are called the *history*, $\mathbf{h}_s = (p_0, p_1, \ldots, p_s)$, and prices after s are called the *future prices*, $\mathbf{f}_s = (p_{s+1}, \ldots, p_T)$. We sometimes write $\mathbf{p}$ as $(\mathbf{h}_s, \mathbf{f}_s)$.

Given a price path, a value, and a discount rate, the utility of the consumer if she buys the product at time s equals

$$u(s, \mathbf{p}, \theta, \delta) = \theta\delta^s - p_s \ . \quad (1)$$

If a consumer possesses a crystal ball that informs her of the price path of the product $\mathbf{p}$, deciding when to buy is a simple matter of selecting the time t that maximizes the utility $u(t, \mathbf{p}, \theta, \delta)$. Unfortunately, at time s, the consumer has only access to the history $\mathbf{h}_s$, and has to make a decision without the full knowledge of $\mathbf{p}$.

The role of a forecasting algorithm is to make use of the history of a product to forecast its future prices in order to help the consumer make a more informed decision.

Definition 1. A *forecasting algorithm* F maps a history $\mathbf{h}_s$ to a distribution over future prices $\mathbf{f}_s$. We denote by E the distribution over future prices predicted by the forecasting algorithm. We also write E as $F(\mathbf{h}_s)$.

Using the forecasts over future prices, a *recommendation strategy* makes a recommendation to buy or to wait taking into account the consumer parameters.

Definition 2. A *recommendation strategy* r maps a history $\mathbf{h}_s$, a distribution E over future prices, a value θ of the product, and a discount rate δ to $\{0, 1\}$, where 0 is a recommendation to wait and 1 is that to buy.

As the latest time the consumer will wait before buying the product is time T, we require that $r(\mathbf{h}_T, E, \theta, \delta) = 1$ for any distribution E.

We refer to the pair (F, r) as a *buy-or-wait recommendation system*, or *system* when the context is clear. Given a system (F, r), a price path $\mathbf{p}$, and a discount rate δ, we can determine when a consumer following its advice will buy the product.

Definition 3. Given price path $\mathbf{p}$, value θ of the product, discount rate δ, and system (F, r), the *purchase time* τ is defined as

$$\tau(\mathbf{p}, \theta, \delta, F, r) = \min_{0 \le s \le T} \{s : r(\mathbf{h}_s, F(\mathbf{h}_s), \theta, \delta) = 1\} ,$$

i.e., this is the first time index the system recommends the consumer to buy.

Manufacturers actively manage their revenue through product pricing, and hence product prices often change according to some planned schedule, albeit with uncertainty due to supply, demand, and competition [7, 19]. This results in a distribution over price paths. We use D to denote this true distribution over price paths. The success of a system can be measured in terms of the expected utility the system generates for the consumer, where expectation is taken with respect to the distribution D over price paths.

Definition 4. Given distribution D over price paths, value θ of the product, discount rate δ, the *performance* η of system (F, r) for a given consumer equals

$$\eta(F, r, D, \theta, \delta) = \mathbb{E}_D\Big[u\big(\tau(\mathbf{p}, \theta, \delta, F, r), \mathbf{p}, \theta, \delta\big)\Big] , \quad (2)$$

i.e., the expected utility to a consumer who follows the advice of system (F, r) over the distribution D of price paths.

Putting it together, our problem can be stated as

Problem Definition. Given a set of price paths sampled according to distribution D, value θ of the product, and discount rate δ, select a system (F, r) that maximizes performance $\eta(F, r, D, \theta, \delta)$.

3.2 Integration With Shopping Services

We envision the recommendation system for helping users to decide when to buy to be integrated as an alert service to existing product search portals. When a user issues a query for a product, a price chart will be displayed to the user to help her understand the historical evolution of the prices for the product. If the user is interested in buying the product, additional information related to the user choices, such as the decision horizon, the value for the product, and the discount rate, will be elicited from the user. The elicitation process can be based on techniques described in [12, 21]. The service will then monitor changes in the product prices, and alert the user when the system recommends buying the product.

4. RECOMMENDATION STRATEGIES

In this section, we present three recommendation strategies as well as techniques for implementing them. These strategies take as input a consumer's value for a product θ, her discount rate δ for the product, and the distribution E of future prices forecasted by algorithm F at time s taking into account the price history $\mathbf{h}_s$. They output 0 if the recommendation at time s is to wait and 1 if it is to buy. These strategies differ in how they estimate the utility of waiting.

4.1 Expected Utility Strategy

A natural recommendation strategy is to choose to wait if there exists a future time for which the expected utility is greater than zero. It can be formally stated as follows.

Definition 5. The *Expected Utility Strategy*, EUS$(\mathbf{h}_s, E, \theta, \delta)$, outputs 1 (buy) if for all t, $s < t \le T$, the expected utility buying at time t is no better than the expected utility from buying at time s. That is, it outputs 1 if

$$\begin{aligned}\max_{s<t\le T} \mathbb{E}_E[u(t, (\mathbf{h}_s, \mathbf{f}_s), \theta, \delta)] &\le \mathbb{E}_E[u(s, (\mathbf{h}_s, \mathbf{f}_s), \theta, \delta)] \\ &= (\theta\delta^s - p_s) , \end{aligned} \quad (3)$$

and 0 (wait) otherwise.

EUS is an easy strategy to implement. First, the RHS is a fixed quantity. To evaluate the LHS of Eq (3), by linearity of expectation,

$$\max_{s<t\le T} \mathbb{E}_E[u(t, (\mathbf{h}_s, \mathbf{f}_s), \theta, \delta)] = \max_{s<t\le T} \Big(\theta\delta^t - \mathbb{E}_E[p_t]\Big) . \quad (4)$$

The expensive part of the computation involves computing the expected price at time t according to the distribution E. For many distributions (e.g. normal distribution and uniform distribution), this value can be computed efficiently by evaluating a closed-form formula. In general, it can be computed through sampling and taking the sample average.

Example 1. We give an example of how EUS is evaluated. Suppose that $s = 0$, $p_0 = 100$, $\theta = 100$, $\delta = 1$, $T = 2$, and E, the distribution of future prices $\{p_1, p_2\}$, is given as

$$E(\{105, 105\}) = 0.25 \qquad E(\{105, 95\}) = 0.25$$
$$E(\{95, 105\}) = 0.25 \qquad E(\{95, 95\}) = 0.25 .$$

The RHS of Eq (3) equals $(100 - 100) = 0$. The LHS equals

$$\begin{aligned}\max_{0<t\le 2} \mathbb{E}_E[u(t, \mathbf{p}, 100, 1)] &= \max_{0<t\le 2} (100 - \mathbb{E}_E[p_t]) \\ &= \max_{0<t\le 2} (100 - 100) = 0 .\end{aligned}$$

Hence, EUS recommends to buy. □

4.2 Sample Path Strategy

Another natural recommendation strategy, motivated by options pricing theory [13], is to generate and evaluate sample price paths according to the forecasted distribution. If, in expectation, there exists a future time for which the expected utility is greater than the utility of buying the product now along the path, it recommends to wait. It can be formally stated as follows.

Definition 6. The *Sample Path Strategy*, $\text{SPS}(\mathbf{h}_s, E, \theta, \delta)$, outputs 1 if the expected maximum utility of buying at some future time t, $s < t \leq T$, is no better than the expected utility of buying at time s, i.e.,

$$\mathbb{E}_E[\max_{s<t\leq T} u(t, (\mathbf{h}_s, \mathbf{f}_s), \theta, \delta)] \leq (\theta\delta^s - p_s) \ , \qquad (5)$$

and outputs 0 otherwise.

The difference between EUS and SPS is the order in which expectation and maximization is taken. Whereas under EUS, expectation is taken separately over each time index, and the time index with the highest utility is selected, under SPS, expectation of the highest utility along an entire price path is taken. Their values could be different for some distribution E. We explore this further in Section 5.

To implement SPS, one needs to evaluate the LHS of Eq (5). Unlike EUS, the value of the LHS of Eq (5) depends on the joint distribution of future prices $\mathbf{f}_s$, since the expectation is taken over price paths, and hence does not lend itself to the same decomposition as in Eq (4). A parsimonious approach to implement this strategy is to sample a set of price paths and evaluate the maximum on each price path, and estimate the expectation by averaging the sampled values.

Example 1 (cont'd). Under the same setting, we give an example of how SPS is evaluated. The RHS remains unchanged. The LHS of Eq (5) equals

$$\mathbb{E}_E[\max_{0<t\leq 2} u(t, \mathbf{p}, 100, 1)] = 0.25(100 - 105) + 0.25(100 - 95)$$
$$+ 0.25(100 - 95) + 0.25(100 - 95) = 2.5 \ .$$

Hence, SPS recommends to wait. □

4.3 Self Application Strategy

The final recommendation strategy we consider is defined recursively through self application. It makes a buy recommendation if the expected utility obtained from waiting at time s and following itself thereafter is no larger than that of buying the product at time s. In other words, the strategy estimates the expected utility of waiting by computing how much utility it would gain if it follows its own recommendation starting from time $(s+1)$, i.e., applies itself at time $(s+1)$, and compares the expected utility to that of buying at time s.

To give a formal definition of the strategy, we introduce a notation for conditioning the present forecast with new prices. Suppose that the present forecast over future prices $\mathbf{f}_s$ is E. If the price at time $(s+1)$ equals p_{s+1}, then the *updated* forecast over future prices $\mathbf{f}_{s+1}$, denoted by $E|p_{s+1}$, is a distribution over $\mathbf{f}_{s+1}$ that satisfies

$$\mathbb{P}_{E|p_{s+1}}(\mathbf{f}_{s+1}) = \mathbb{P}_E((p_{s+1}, \mathbf{f}_{s+1}) \mid p_{s+1}) \ ,$$

i.e., for any future prices $\mathbf{f}_{s+1}$, the probability of the future prices according to $E|p_{s+1}$ equals the probability according to E conditioned on the price at time $(s+1)$ being p_{s+1}.[1]

Definition 7. The *Self Application Strategy*, $\text{SAS}(\mathbf{h}_s, E, \theta, \delta)$, outputs 1 if and only if the expected utility obtained from waiting at time s and following SAS thereafter is no larger than the expected utility of buying at time s, i.e.,

$$\mathbb{E}_E[w(p_{s+1}, |\mathbf{h}_s| + 1, E|p_{s+1}, \theta, \delta)] \leq (\theta\delta^s - p_s) \ , \qquad (6)$$

where $w(p, t, E, \theta, \delta)$ is defined as the utility obtained from following the recommendations of SAS after having waited for the first $(t-1)$ time steps. It can be written recursively as the maximum between the utility of buying the product at time t, or waiting at time t and following SAS thereafter,

$$w(p, t, E, \theta, \delta) = \max \begin{cases} \theta\delta^t - p \\ \mathbb{E}_E[w(p_{t+1}, t+1, E|p_{t+1}, \theta, \delta)] \end{cases} \qquad (7)$$

and for time $t = T$,

$$w(p, T, E, \theta, \delta) = \theta\delta^T - p \ . \qquad (8)$$

Remark 1. SAS depends on history $\mathbf{h}_s$ only through the current price p_s and the length of the history $|\mathbf{h}_s|$. We separate these factors in the recursion to highlight how they evolve. This dependence relationship is also true for EUS and SPS. We make use of this relationship in Section 5.

Like SPS, SAS can be implemented by sampling and estimating the expectations via sample averages. However, a direct sampling algorithm will run in time exponential in T due to its recursive nature. This is because each evaluation of $w(p, t, E, \theta, \delta)$ according to Eq (7) requires evaluating an expectation that calls the function w with different arguments. If k samples are drawn for estimating the expectation by sample average, a total of $O(k^{T-s})$ number of evaluations of Eq (8) will be needed.

Based on experiments reported in [1], autoregressive model of order 1 is often a good fit for product prices. Under this model, prices follow a *Markov process*, i.e., the distribution of future prices $\mathbf{f}_s$ depend only on the price p_s but not the prices before. In this case, we can speed up the computation exponentially by *backward induction*.

Starting from time T, we draw k samples, and evaluate the utility of buying at time T. We then compute the value of waiting till time $(T-1)$ by using these values in evaluating the expectations, and taking the maximum according to Eq (7). We proceed backwards in time until we reach time s. A formal description is given in Algorithm 1.

The algorithm depends on two auxiliary functions. The function $\text{SAMPLE}(E, t)$ draws a price *uniformly at random* from the domain of prices at time t under distribution E. The function $\text{PROB}(E, t, p, p')$ evaluates the transition probability from price p to price p' at time t according to the distribution E. Prices are drawn uniformly at random from their domains to avoid factoring in the probabilities twice, as the samples are subsequently weighted by the transition probabilities. Lines 1 and 2 estimate the expectations needed in Eqs (6) and (7) by sample averages (v/s).

[1]More formally, $\mathbb{P}_E$ is a measure over the elements $\mathbf{f}_s$, and $\mathbb{P}_{E|p_{s+1}}$ is a measure over the elements $\mathbf{f}_{s+1}$. For any event e measurable over the σ-field generated by $\mathbf{f}_{s+1}$, $\mathbb{P}_{E|p_{s+1}}(e) = \mathbb{P}_E(e|p_{s+1})$. For exposition, we simplify the statement and state the results as if the distribution is discrete.

Algorithm 1: SAS Evaluation by Backward Induction

Input : History $\mathbf{h}_s$; Dist. E; Discount rate δ; Value θ
Output: LHS of Eq (6), $\mathbb{E}_E[w(p_{s+1}, s+1, E|p_{s+1}, \theta, \delta)]$
Params: Samples per time step, k

/* The array entry $p[t,i]$ stores the i-th sampled price for time t, and the array entry $w[t,i]$ stores the value estimated for $w(p[t,i], t, E|p[t,i], \theta, \delta)$. SAMPLE and PROB are two auxiliary functions that samples uniformly at random from the domain of E and evaluates transition probabilities according to E. */

for $i \leftarrow 1$ **to** k **do**
  $p[T,i] \leftarrow$ SAMPLE(E,T)
  $w[T,i] \leftarrow \theta\delta^T - p[T,i]$
end
for $t \leftarrow (T-1)$ **downto** $(s+1)$ **do**
  for $i \leftarrow 1$ **to** k **do**
    $p[t,i] \leftarrow$ SAMPLE(E,t)
    $v \leftarrow \sum_{j=1}^{k}$ PROB$(E, t, p[t,i], p[t+1,j]) \times w[t+1,j]$
    $s \leftarrow \sum_{j=1}^{k}$ PROB$(E, t, p[t,i], p[t+1,j])$
    $w[t,i] \leftarrow \max\{\theta\delta^t - p_t, v/s\}$
  end
end
$v \leftarrow \sum_{j=1}^{k}$ PROB$(E, s+1, p_s, p[s+1,j]) \times w[s+1,j]$
$s \leftarrow \sum_{j=1}^{k}$ PROB$(E, s+1, p_s, p[s+1,j])$
return v/s

Algorithm 1 produces an unbiased estimate of the LHS of Eq (6) when prices follow a Markov process, since the probability of transitioning from price p_t to p_{t+1} is independent of prices $p_{t'}$ for $t' < t$. Hence, for price paths $\mathbf{p}$ and $\mathbf{p}'$, $E|(p_s, p_{s+1}, \ldots, p_t)$ equals $E|(p'_s, p'_{s+1}, \ldots, p'_t)$ if $p_t = p'_t$.

The running time of the algorithm is $O(k^2T)$, since each computation of $w[t,i]$ requires a summation over k terms, which is computed once for each of the k samples per time step, and there are T time steps. Though the time is polynomial in k and T, the algorithm implicitly considers an exponential number of price paths $\mathbf{p}$, as the final expectation takes into account each combination of prices $p[t,i]$ from every time index t and i from 1 to k.

Example 1 (cont'd). Under the same setting, we give an example of how SAS is evaluated. The RHS remains unchanged. The LHS of Eq (6) equals

$$\mathbb{E}_E[w(p_1, 1, E|p_1, 100, 1)] = \mathbb{E}_E[\max\{100 - p_1, \mathbb{E}_{E|p_1}[100 - p_2]\}]$$
$$= \mathbb{E}_E[\max\{100 - p_1, 0\}] = 0.5(5) + 0.5(0) = 2.5 \ .$$

Hence, SAS recommends to wait. □

5. ANALYSIS

We now analyze the strategies presented in Section 4. First, we study whether the recommendations made by the three strategies are related. Second, we consider an idealized situation where the forecasting algorithm is perfect, and determine which of the strategies works best. For exposition, we present the results as if the distributions are discrete. The statements can be made formal for continuous distributions.

5.1 Relationship Among the Strategies

Without loss of generality, we take $s = 0$. When the decision is between buying now or the next period, i.e., $T = 1$, all three strategies makes the same recommendation.

Theorem 1. *When $T = 1$, for any distribution E, value θ, and discount rate δ, EUS, SPS, and SAS make the same recommendation.*

Proof. When $T = 1$, the decision is between buying at time 0 and at time 1. It is clear from Eq (3), (5), and (6) that the RHS of the three strategies are equal. The LHS of Eqs (3), (5), and (6) are also equal, since for discrete t, if $0 < t \leq 1$, $t = 1$. Hence, the LHS are all equal to

$$\mathbb{E}_E[u(1, (p_0, p_1), \theta, \delta)] = \mathbb{E}_E[\theta\delta - p_1] \ . \qquad \square$$

When $T \geq 2$, the strategies may make different recommendations. Nonetheless, the recommendations are related, and we can show that SPS is more optimistic about the value of waiting than SAS, and SAS is more optimistic about the value of waiting than EUS.

Theorem 2. *For any history $\mathbf{h}_t$, distribution E, value θ, and discount rate δ, if EUS recommends to wait, then SAS will also recommend to wait. If SAS recommends to wait, then SPS will also recommend to wait.*

To prove this theorem, note that the recommendations made by these strategies are determined by the values of the LHS of Eqs (3), (5), and (6). These values can be interpreted as the values of waiting estimated by the strategies. Let $v_{\mathrm{EUS}}(\mathbf{h}_s, E, \theta, \delta)$, $v_{\mathrm{SPS}}(\mathbf{h}_s, E, \theta, \delta)$, and $v_{\mathrm{SAS}}(\mathbf{h}_s, E, \theta, \delta)$ denote the respective LHS of the strategies for history $\mathbf{h}_s$. We claim that for all history $\mathbf{h}_s$,

$$v_{\mathrm{EUS}}(\mathbf{h}_s, E, \theta, \delta) \leq v_{\mathrm{SAS}}(\mathbf{h}_s, E, \theta, \delta) \leq v_{\mathrm{SPS}}(\mathbf{h}_s, E, \theta, \delta) \ . \quad (9)$$

Let $v_{buy}(\mathbf{h}_s, \theta, \delta)$ denote the value of the RHS of the strategies for history $\mathbf{h}_s$. If the claim is true, then if EUS recommends to wait, so will SAS, since $v_{\mathrm{SAS}}(\mathbf{h}_s, E, \theta, \delta) \geq v_{\mathrm{EUS}}(\mathbf{h}_s, E, \theta, \delta) \geq v_{buy}(\mathbf{h}_s, \theta, \delta)$. Similarly, if SAS recommends to wait, so will SPS, since $v_{\mathrm{SPS}}(\mathbf{h}_s, E, \theta, \delta) \geq v_{\mathrm{SAS}}(\mathbf{h}_s, E, \theta, \delta) \geq v_{buy}(\mathbf{h}_s, \theta, \delta)$.

To show the claim, we examine the order in which the expectation and the maximum is taken under the three strategies. The relationship between EUS and SPS can be easily established by Jensen's Inequality. The difficulty is with SAS. The proof makes use of an inductive argument and Jensen's inequality to establish the desired relationship, and can be found in the full paper [2].

Recall that Remark 1 states that the three strategies depend on history $\mathbf{h}_s$ only through the current price p_s, and its length $|\mathbf{h}_s|$. Further, the value of waiting does not depend on the current price p_s. Henceforth, we rewrite the function $v_{\mathrm{EUS}}(\mathbf{h}_s, E, \theta, \delta)$ as $v_{\mathrm{EUS}}(s, E, \theta, \delta)$, and likewise for SPS and SAS.

5.2 Performance Under Perfect Forecasts

We now consider the performances of the three strategies when the forecasting algorithm is *perfect*, which informally means that the forecasted distribution coincides with the true distribution D. Note that it does *not* mean that the price path itself is known with certainty. While it is not possible to design a forecasting algorithm that is perfect, this analysis helps us to isolate the difference in performance that is solely explained by the choice of recommendation strategy. It also helps to develop insights as to why some of the strategies may fail to make the best recommendation despite very good forecasts.

We first define a property of forecasting algorithm about how current forecasts are related to future ones.

Definition 8. A forecasting algorithm F is *consistent* if for all histories $\mathbf{h}_s$ and $\mathbf{h}_t$ where $\mathbf{h}_t$ includes $\mathbf{h}_s$ as its first s prices, i.e., $\mathbf{h}_t = (\mathbf{h}_s, p_{s+1}, \ldots, p_t)$, $F(\mathbf{h}_t)$ produces a distribution identical to the *conditional* distribution induced by $F(\mathbf{h}_s)$, i.e., for all $\mathbf{f}_t$,

$$\mathbb{P}_{F(\mathbf{h}_t)}(\mathbf{f}_t) = \mathbb{P}_{F(\mathbf{h}_s)|(p_{s+1},\ldots,p_t)}(\mathbf{f}_t) \ .$$

Intuitively speaking, a consistent forecasting algorithm is one where there are "no surprises" when it updates its forecast. Given the current forecast, when a new price arrives, one just needs to condition on the latest observation to obtain the updated forecast.

A consistent forecasting algorithm is related to a collection of distributions over price paths. Consider a consistent forecasting algorithm F. Given any history $\mathbf{h}_t$, it produces a distribution $F(\mathbf{h}_t)$ over the price paths $\mathbf{f}_t$, which by consistency equals $F(p_0)|(p_1, \ldots, p_t)$. Therefore, it can be viewed as a collection of distributions of price paths indexed by p_0. Conversely, given a distribution E of price paths $\mathbf{f}_t$, it can be turned into a forecasting algorithm for $\mathbf{f}_{t+1}$, such that given any price p_t, it produces a conditional distribution over $\mathbf{f}_{t+1}$. This duality between distributions and consistent forecasting algorithms will be exploited further in this section. For semantic clarity, we denote the forecasting algorithm for prices $\mathbf{f}_{t+1}$ induced by distribution E over price paths $\mathbf{f}_t$ as $[E]$.

A forecasting algorithm F is perfect for distribution of price paths D when F and D are "interchangeable".

Definition 9. A forecasting algorithm F is *perfect* for distribution of price paths D if F is consistent, and $F(\mathbf{h}_0)$ produces the same distribution as D conditional on p_0, i.e., for all price paths $\mathbf{p}$,

$$\mathbb{P}_{F(p_0)}(\mathbf{f}_0) = \mathbb{P}_D((p_0, \mathbf{f}_0) \mid p_0) \ .$$

Another way to interpret a perfect forecasting algorithm is that $[D]$ gives the same forecasts for any p_0 as F. Note that if F is perfect, by property of consistency, for all history $\mathbf{h}_t$,

$$\mathbb{P}_{F(\mathbf{h}_t)}(\mathbf{f}_t) = \mathbb{P}_D((\mathbf{h}_t, \mathbf{f}_t) \mid \mathbf{h}_t) \ .$$

Hence, other than not knowing the distribution of the first price p_0, F has as much information as D.

We now consider the performance of the three strategies under perfect forecasts. We start with an example that shows that EUS is not optimal.

Example 2 (Suboptimality of EUS). Suppose that $s = 0$, $p_0 = 100$, $\theta = 100$, $\delta = 1$, $T = 2$. Let the true distribution D of price paths be

$$D(\{100, 105, 105\}) = 0.25 \quad D(\{100, 105, 95\}) = 0.25$$
$$D(\{100, 95, 105\}) = 0.25 \quad D(\{100, 95, 95\}) = 0.25 \ .$$

This setup is identical to Example 1, and assume that $E = F(\{100\})$ in Example 1 is a perfect forecast for D. We have shown that

$$v_{\text{EUS}}(0, F(\{100\}), 100, 1) = 0$$
$$v_{\text{SPS}}(0, F(\{100\}), 100, 1) = 2.5$$
$$v_{\text{SAS}}(0, F(\{100\}), 100, 1) = 2.5$$

and EUS will recommend to buy at time 0, whereas SPS and SAS will recommend to wait. One can verify that waiting is better, since there is a 0.5 chance that the price will drop to 95 at time 1, at which point the consumer can buy and earn a utility of 5, and if the price goes to 105 at time 1, the consumer can choose to wait and earn an expected utility of 0 from buying at time 2. □

This example reveals a weakness in the estimation procedure used in EUS, namely that it fails to take into account the sequential nature of the decisions to be made. Even though waiting and buying at the next time step may earn zero utility in expectation, one may be able to choose differently depending on the outcome at the next time step. Hence EUS may systematically underestimate the value of waiting.

Our next example shows that SPS is not optimal either.

Example 3 (Suboptimality of SPS). Consider the same setup as Example 2, but with a change to the true distribution D of price paths

$$D(\{100, 110, 125\}) = 0.25 \quad D(\{100, 110, 95\}) = 0.25$$
$$D(\{100, 95, 125\}) = 0.25 \quad D(\{100, 95, 95\}) = 0.25 \ .$$

Under a perfect forecast, the value of the three strategies are:

$$v_{\text{EUS}}(0, F(\{100\}, 100, 1) = \max\{100 - 102.5, 100 - 110\} = -2.5$$
$$v_{\text{SPS}}(0, F(\{100\}, 100, 1) = 0.25(100 - 110) + 0.25(100 - 95) + 0.25(100 - 95) + 0.25(100 - 95) = 1.25$$
$$v_{\text{SAS}}(0, F(\{100\}, 100, 1) = 0.5(\max\{100 - 95, 100 - 115\}) + 0.5(\max\{100 - 110, 100 - 110\}) = -1.25 \ .$$

Now, SPS will recommend to wait at time 0, whereas EUS and SAS will recommend to buy. In this case, buying is better than waiting at time 0. If one waits, at time 1, if $p_1 = 95$, one can at most gain a utility of 5 by buying at time 1. But if $p_1 = 110$, then both waiting and buying at time 1 lead to an expected utility of -10. Combining the two, it is better to buy at time 0. □

This example reveals a weakness in SPS, namely that it assumes it can pick out the best time to buy as if the price path is known. In the above example, it assumes that if the price path is $\{100, 110, 125\}$, it will buy at time 1; but if the price path is $\{100, 110, 95\}$, it will buy at time 2. This is an inconsistent choice, since the price histories at time 1 in both cases are identical. As a result, SPS overestimates the value of waiting.

Remark 2. In Example 3, all three strategies produce different estimated values for waiting. Hence, there exists distributions for which the inequality in Eq (9) holds strictly.

Through these two examples, we observe that SAS accounts for the sequential nature of the decision problem, and ensures consistency in the choices through self application. It turns out that these are the key properties for a recommendation strategy to be optimal in expectation.

Theorem 3. *For any distribution of price paths D, value θ, discount rate δ, if the forecasting algorithm F is perfect, there does not exist a recommendation strategy r that has higher performance than SAS, i.e., for all strategies r, $\eta(F, r, D, \theta, \delta) \leq \eta(F, SAS, D, \theta, \delta)$.*

The key to establishing this theorem is that the value SAS estimated for waiting precisely measures the performance it will obtain if it decides to wait. This is provided by the following "Lemma". We put this lemma in quotes because the statement of the Lemma is not sufficiently formal. A formal statement of the Lemma involves some subtlety, and is presented in the full paper.

"Lemma." *For any δ, θ, $\mathbf{h}_s$ for $s \in [0, T)$,*

$$v_{\text{SAS}}(s, F(\mathbf{h}_s), \theta, \delta) = P([F(\mathbf{h}_s)], \text{SAS}, F(\mathbf{h}_s), \theta, \delta) \ .$$

Using this lemma, we can establish using an inductive argument that SAS is optimal in expectation. The proof is similar in spirit to the optimality proof of using dynamic programming (Bellman equations) to solve Markov decision processes, but with added subtlety due to the semantic differences between a forecasting algorithm and a distribution. The proof can be found in the full paper [2].

5.3 Implications

We have established two theoretical results. The first relates the recommendations made by the three strategies, and holds for *any* forecasting algorithm. Theorem 1 shows that the choice of recommendation strategies does not matter when the decision horizon is over a single period. Theorem 2 establishes a relationship useful for post-hoc analysis of empirical performances. For example, if we observe that SPS outperforms EUS, we can infer that the system under EUS is erring on the side of making too many buy recommendations, as for any data set and forecasting algorithm, the set of situations where EUS makes a buy recommendation is a superset of ones for SPS.

The second result shows that when forecasts are perfect, SAS is the optimal recommendation strategy. We believe that SAS continues to be the best strategy when forecasts are imperfect, although we cannot directly establish its optimality theoretically, as a poor recommendation may be either due to the strategy or the forecasts. We address this question by means of experiments in the next section.

6. EXPERIMENTS

We now conduct an experimental study to evaluate the performance of the three proposed recommendation strategies. The objective of this study is to quantify the performances under realistic settings of price changes and forecasting errors. It also complements the theoretical analysis, which shows the optimality of SAS, by quantifying the differences in performances among EUS, SPS, and SAS.

6.1 Setup

To generate realistic distribution of price paths, we analyzed price changes in four categories of electronic products—Televisions, Digital cameras, Camcorders, and Printers. The data was obtained for prices between January 2005 and September 2008 from NPD, a firm that tracks prices registered at major retail stores. We found that the average price decrease per time period for these products was about 3.5%, with a standard deviation of about 5%. We generate synthetic data based on these statistics, and systematically vary different factors to measure the performances of the strategies under different settings.

We consider a family of distributions to model the price paths of these products based on how persistent are unexpected price changes, which we call *shocks*. Formally, suppose that the average decrease per time period is μ, we define the shock at time t as the difference between the actual price p_t and the expected price $p_0\mu^t$. We select a parameter $\alpha \in [0, 1]$ that controls *shock persistence*. In more detail, from time period t to time period $(t+1)$, the change in prices is sampled from a normal distribution $N(\mu, \sigma)$. Let p_t and q_t denote the price and the shock in time period t. The price p_{t+1} in time period $(t+1)$ equals

$$p_{t+1} = d(p_t - (1 - \alpha)q_t)$$

where d is sampled from $N(\mu, \sigma)$.

Shock persistence is important as it models whether product prices exhibit definite patterns. When its value is low, the prices follow definite paths; when its value is high, the prices appear random. At the extremes, when $\alpha = 0$, shocks are *transient* and do not carry over from one time period to the next. This setting gives rise to a distribution where the prices of one period is independent of another, since the price p_{t+1} at time period $(t+1)$ depends on $(p_t - q_t) = p_0\mu^t$, a quantity that is independent of p_t. It can be shown that the price at time period t is sampled from $N(p_0\mu^t, p_0\mu^{t-1}\sigma)$. In contrast, when $\alpha = 1$, shocks are *persistent* and affect all future prices. This gives rise to a distribution of price path that resembles random walks, since the price p_{t+1} at time period $(t+1)$ depends on p_t, the sampled price of time period t.

The first decision starts at time 0 (i.e. $s = 0$), and the decision horizon T of the consumer is selected to be between four and eight time periods, which we believe is a reasonable timeframe for purchasing consumer durables. The discount rate δ is selected to be between 95.5% and 97.5%, and is comparable to the study of [21], after adjusting for technological improvements. Finally, the value of the product θ is selected to be a multiple ρ of the initial price p_0, i.e.,$\theta = \rho p_0$. We vary ρ between 1.0 and 1.1, our best guess on when a user starts to be interested in purchasing the product.

To evaluate the effect of imperfect forecasting algorithms on the performances of the strategies, we introduce two parameters, err_μ and err_σ, that control the accuracy of the estimated mean and that of the estimated standard deviation of the forecasts. We assume that the forecasting algorithm correctly identifies the level of shock persistence, but may make (normally-distributed) errors in estimating the parameters to the distribution. For example, with $\mu = 3.5\%$, it estimates the mean to be μ', where μ' is sampled from the distribution $N(\mu, \text{err}_\mu)$. Likewise, a mistake may be made in estimating the standard deviation. Based on our price prediction experiments conducted in [1], values of err_μ around 3% and err_σ around 1% are consistent with the errors made by the best forecasting algorithms we evaluated.

The simulation parameters are summarized in Table 1, where we give the default choices for these parameters along with their minimum and maximum values in our sensitivity analysis. In the subsequent experiments, we vary one parameter at a time between its minimum and maximum values to understand its impact on the performances. For

Parameter	Default	Min	Max
μ (mean price decrease)	3.5%	2.5%	4.5%
σ (stdev. of price decrease)	5%	3%	6%
α (shock persistence)	0	0	1
T (decision horizon)	6	4	8
δ (discount rate)	96.5%	95.5%	97.5%
ρ (ratio of init. value to price)	1.05	1.00	1.10
err_μ (stdev. of estimated μ)	0%	0%	4%
err_σ (stdev. of estimated σ)	0%	0.5%	2%

Table 1: Summary of simulation parameters.

each combination of parameters, we sampled 100 price paths according to the true distribution, and for each path, evaluated each strategy 100 times on the path to obtain its average performance. For imperfect forecasting algorithms, the estimated mean and the estimated standard deviation are sampled once for each run.

In reporting the results, we present the *relative* performances. This is done by normalizing the performance of a strategy by that of an *omniscient* strategy that knows all the prices on the price path and selects the optimal time to buy. The omniscient strategy is not constrained to make the same choice for the same price history. Thus, its value constitutes an upper bound on the utility that can be gained on each path. As it requires knowing the price path in advance, its performance is unachievable in practice. Nonetheless, it helps us to gauge how close to optimal we can achieve. We also report the performance of always buying at time 0 as a baseline. Since relative performance is scale-free and does not depend on p_0, p_0 is not varied in the experiments.

6.2 Perfect Forecasts with Transient Shocks

In the first set of experiments, we focus on the case where the forecasting algorithm is perfect and shocks are transient. While we already know from the theoretical analysis that SAS is optimal for this setting, the experiments serve two important purposes. First, they serve to quantify the differences in performances between SAS and the other two strategies. Second, they identify factors that influence the performances of these strategies.

The performances with a sensitivity analysis on each of the five variables are shown in Figure 1. Key findings are

(1) Across all conditions, all three strategies outperform the baseline of always buying at time 0. The performances of SAS and SPS are consistently higher than that of EUS. In 70% of the settings, SAS and SPS achieves about 90% of the maximum possible savings. The differences in performances are statistically significant under a *paired t-tests* with p-values < 0.001 for all but one cases. Despite the visual similarity, SAS outperforms SPS in all of the cases.

(2) In most of the cases, EUS recommends buying at time 0, hence its performance overlaps with the baseline. The cases where the recommendations are different are when $\mu > (1-\delta)$ (Figures 1(a) and (d)).

(3) As Figures 1(a) and (d) show, varying μ and δ leads to almost identical results. This is because μ and $(1-\delta)$ are closely related. Generally speaking, when $\mu > (1-\delta)$, it is better to wait, since prices are dropping faster than utility loss due to discounting; conversely, when $\mu < (1-\delta)$, it is better to buy. However, when the standard deviation of the decrease is high, one could gain by waiting due to

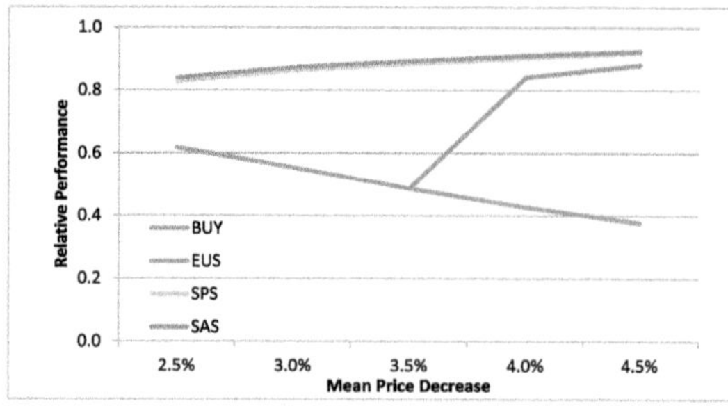

(a) Relative performance vs. μ

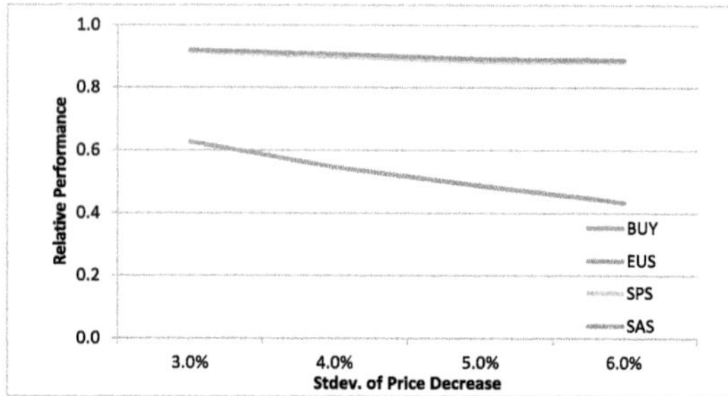

(b) Relative performance vs. σ

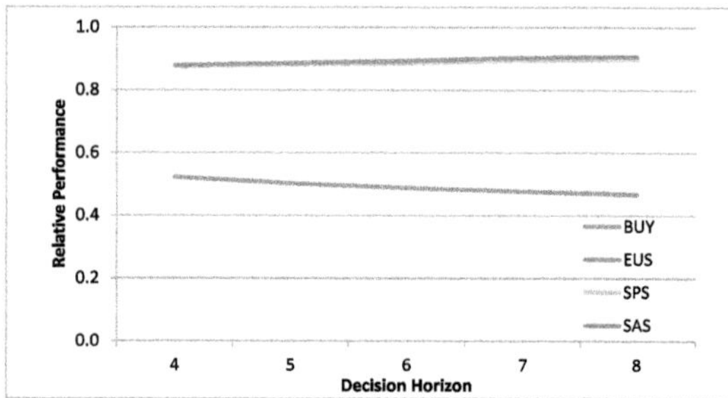

(c) Relative performance vs. T

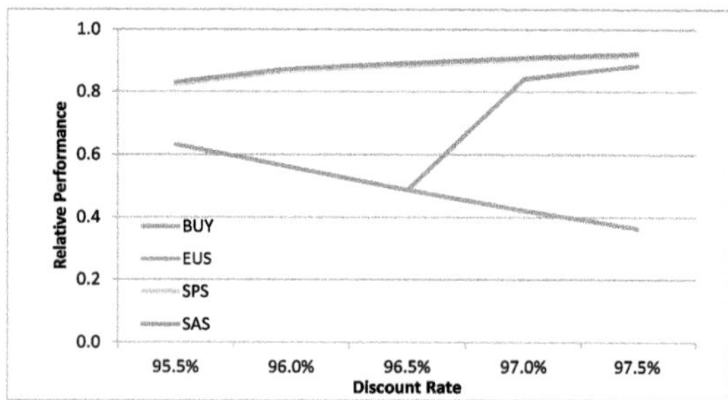

(d) Relative performance vs. δ

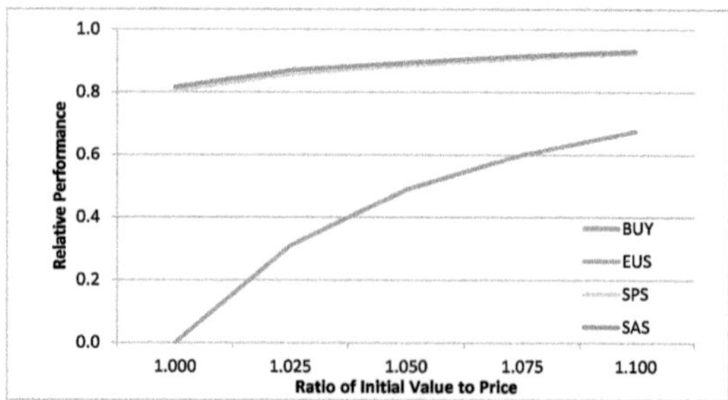

(e) Relative performance vs. ρ

Figure 1: Relative performances under different simulation parameters

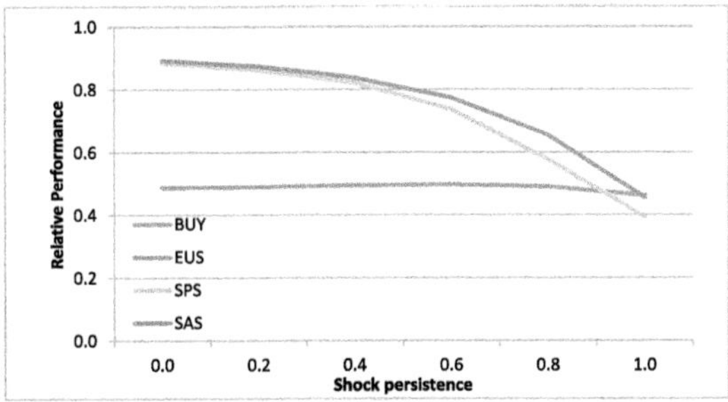

Figure 2: Relative perf. vs. shock persistence

price fluctuations even when μ is smaller than $(1-\delta)$. Both SAS and SPS (correctly) recommend waiting in such cases, leading to large outperformance compared to EUS.

(4) As Figure 1(b) shows, as the standard deviation of the price decrease (σ) increases, the relative performance of EUS decreases, highlighting the importance of considering more than just the expected utility. The performances of SAS and SPS keep pace with that of the omniscient strategy.

(5) As Figure 1(c) shows, the relative performances are almost constant across different decision horizons (T). This suggests that T is not a critical factor in the simulation.

(6) As Figure 1(e) shows, the relative performances improve as the ratio of initial value to price (ρ) increases. The shape of the curve is concave (downwards) due to the following reason. As ρ increases, the absolute performances for all strategies increases due to the larger difference between $\theta(= \rho p_0)$ and p_0. On the other hand, the expected utility obtained from timing the purchase better, which applies to SAS, SPS, and the omniscient strategy, grows at a much slower pace. Hence, the curves are shaped concave downwards.

In summary, in the majority of the experimental conditions, SAS performs within 90% of the maximum utility that can only be obtained knowing the entire price path. A consumer following SAS does better than the baseline of always buying by about 40% of the maximum utility on average.

6.3 Perfect Forecasts with Persistent Shocks

The next set of experiments evaluates the relative performances of the strategies under different shock persistence level (α). We single out the shock persistence as a separate experiment since its level has a profound impact on the behavior of the price paths. As mentioned, at $\alpha = 0$, shocks are transient and the distribution is independent from time period to time period; at $\alpha = 1$, the distribution of price paths resembles that of a random walk. The results are presented in Figure 2.

We observe that SAS outperforms the other two strategies. However, its relative performance decreases as α increases. This is because as the distribution of price paths becomes more like that of a random walk, timing the purchase without knowledge of the price path becomes difficult. For an increasing fraction of the price paths, the price shocks stay either positive or negative over the entire path. While uptil $\alpha = 0.8$, a strategy may yield a positive expected utility by recommending to wait at time 0, as α increases, a larger fraction of the gains are offset by losses on price paths for which the price shocks stay positive throughout. On the other hand, since the omniscient strategy makes it choices knowing the price paths, it can selectively wait on ones for which waiting yields positive expected utilities, and buy on ones where waiting would have yielded negative expected utilities. These together lead the relative performances of SAS to become lower as α increases.

Note that as α increases, SPS performs worse and worse, and this is one of few cases where we can separate visually the relative performances of SAS and SPS. The problem here is that under a random-walk like price path, SPS will systematically overestimate the value of waiting as highlighted in Example 3, leading to its recommending the user to wait when it is not advisable to do so. Hence its relative performance deteriorates faster than SAS as α increases.

Based on the marketing literature surveyed in Section 2, we believe that the price evolution of durable products exhibit definite patterns and do *not* resemble random walks. Thus, the regime in which our system operates is likely to have small α. Nonetheless, these experiments highlight the importance of this assumption. The shock persistence levels determine how well we can do for a given category of products.

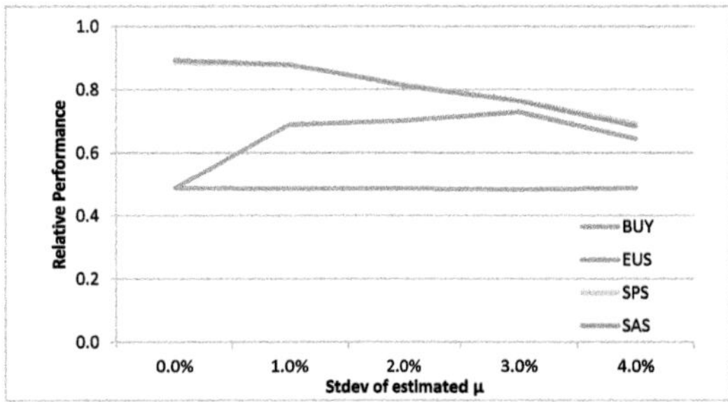

(a) Relative performance vs. err_μ

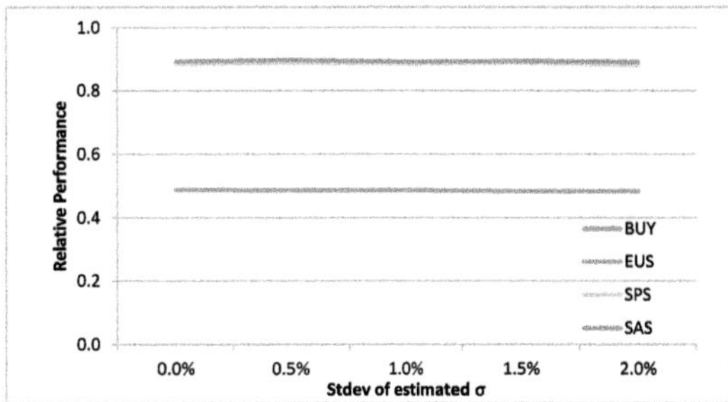

(b) Relative performance vs. err_σ

Figure 3: Relative perf. under imperfect forecasts

6.4 Imperfect Forecasts

The final set of experiments evaluates the relative performances of the strategies under imperfect forecasting algorithms. The degree of imperfection is measured by the size of the errors in estimating the mean and the standard deviation of the distribution. These experiments help to quantify the true performances of the system, as forecasting algorithms in real application do make errors. Our parameters are chosen to reflect realistic levels of errors as measured by related experiments conducted in [1]. The results under transient shocks are presented in Figure 3. We observe similar trends for persistent shocks.

The results depend on what kind of errors is made. When

errors involve estimating the means of the price decreases, both SAS and SPS perform worse than when forecasts are perfect, and their performances get worse as the errors get larger. On the other hand, the performance of EUS *improves* for small errors. This is because at the default parameter values, $\mu = (1 - \delta) = 3.5\%$, EUS will always recommend to buy at time 0. When there are errors in the estimated mean μ', some fraction of the time EUS will recommend to wait at time 0 when μ' happens to be large. EUS earns higher expected utilities for such cases, resulting in higher relative performance of EUS. However, for large errors, the noise takes over and the performance of EUS decreases.

In contrast, when errors involve estimating the standard deviation of the price decreases, all three strategies perform almost identically as if the forecasts are perfect. We found that the recommendations made by the strategies were the same as the ones made under perfect forecasts in many cases. This suggests that the strategies are tolerant to this form of estimation errors.

7. CONCLUDING REMARKS

We addressed the question of how to design a system that helps forward-looking consumers decide *when* to buy durable products. We proposed a utility-based framework that discounts the value of the product if its purchase is deferred and incorporates the savings accruing from the potential drop in the price of the product. Rather than designing forecasting algorithms for which a rich body of work already exists, we focused on developing recommendation strategies that employ forecasting algorithms as blackboxes. We devised three strategies as well as techniques for implementing them. These strategies differ in how they estimate the value of waiting. The Expected Utility Strategy (EUS) recommends a buy only if the maximum expected utility from buying the product in future is no better than the expected utility from buying it now. The Sample Path Strategy (SPS) recommends a buy only if the expected maximum utility of buying at some future time is no better than the expected utility of buying the product now. The difference between EUS and SPS is the order in which expectation and maximization is taken. Whereas under EUS, expectation is taken separately over each time index, and the time index with the highest utility is selected, expectation of the highest utility along an entire price path is taken under SPS. The Self Application Strategy (SAS) makes a buy recommendation only if the expected utility obtained from waiting now and following the strategy thereafter is no better than the expected utility of buying now.

We conducted a theoretical analysis of these strategies, and showed that the recommendations made by the three strategies are related—when SPS recommends to buy, so will SAS; when SAS recommends to buy, so will EUS. This is due to the estimated value of waiting is related through an inequality. We also established that SAS is optimal when the forecasts are perfect. We conducted an extensive experimental study to measure their performances both when forecasts are perfect and imperfect, and under different assumptions about the persistence of price shocks. The model parameters were derived from real data obtained from a data provider for durable goods. Based on the experimental study, we conclude that the optimal strategy SAS can improve the utility of consumers under most conditions. The improvements are especially significant when the standard deviations of price changes are high, or when the value the consumer placed on the product is close to the initial price. The present work complements our past study of price prediction for consumer durables [1]. Together they suggest that across a wide range of conditions, the proposed system can deliver significant savings to prospective users.

This work opens up several research directions. First, it is a challenging and interesting problem to establish an approximation bound on the proposed SAS evaluation (Algorithm 1). Second, we have assumed that the user has already selected which product to buy. A natural extension is when a user is interested in one of a few products (e.g., different models of TVs), and needs to decide which one to purchase as a function of time. Another question is how to improve user experience of product search through ranking functions that factor in whether it is a good time to buy the product.

8. REFERENCES

[1] R. Agrawal, S. Ieong, and R. Velu. Ameliorating buyer's remorse. In *Proc. KDD*, 2011.

[2] R. Agrawal, S. Ieong, and R. Velu. Timing when to buy. Technical Report MSR-TR-2011-97, Microsoft Research, 2011.

[3] G. Box, G. M. Jenkins, and G. Reinsel. *Time Series Analysis: Forecasting and Control.* Prentice Hall, 1994.

[4] R. Burke. Hybrid recommender systems: Survey and experiments. *User Model. & User-Adapted Inter.*, 12(4), 2002.

[5] Y. S. Chow, H. Robbins, and S. D. *Great Expectations: The Theory of Optimal Stopping.* Houghton Mifflin Co, 1971.

[6] W. H. Cummings and M. Venkatesan. Cognitive dissonance and consumer behavior: A review of the evidence. In M. J. Schlinger, editor, *Advances in Consumer Research Volume 2*, pages 21–32. Association for Conusmer Research, 1975.

[7] R. N. Dino. Forecasting the price evolution of new electronic products. *J. Forecasting*, 4:39–60, 1985.

[8] R. J. Dolan and A. P. Jeuland. Experience curves and dnamic demand models: Implications for optimal pricing strategies. *J. Marketing*, 45:52–62, 1981.

[9] O. Etzioni, R. Tuchinda, C. A. Knoblock, and A. Yates. To buy or not to buy: mining airfare data to minimize ticket purchase price. In *Proc. KDD*, pages 119–128, 2003.

[10] I. Fisher. *Theory of Interest.* Augustus M. Kelly, 1930.

[11] G. Fulgoni. State of the U.S. retail economy in Q2 2009. Technical report, Comscore, August 2009.

[12] C. Gonzales and P. Perny. GAI networks for utility elicitation. In *Proc. 9th Int. Conf. Principles of Knowledge Representation and Reasoning*, 2004.

[13] J. C. Hull. *Options, Futures, and Other Derivatives.* Prentice Hall, 5th edition, 2002.

[14] R. J. Hyndman, A. B. Koehler, J. K. Ord, and R. D. Snyder. *Forecasting with Exponential Smoothing.* Springer, 2008.

[15] D. Jannach, M. Zanker, A. Felfering, and G. Friedrich. *Recommender Systems: An Introduction.* Cambridge University Press, 2010.

[16] S. S. Oren. Comments on "pricing research in marketing: The state of the art". *J. Business*, 57:61–64, 1984.

[17] P. Pazzani and D. Billsus. Content-based recommendation systems. In *The Adaptive Web*, 2007.

[18] D. Prelec and G. Loewenstein. Beyond time discounting. *Marketing Letters*, 8:97–108, 1997.

[19] V. R. Rao. Pricing research in marketing: The state of the art. *J. Business*, 57:39–60, 1984.

[20] B. Sarwar, G. Karypis, J. Konstan, and J. Reidl. Item-based collaborative filtering recommendation algorithms. In *WWW*, 2001.

[21] R. S. Winer. Discounting and its impact on durables buying decision. *Marketing Letters*, 8:109–118, 1997.

Assisting Web Search Users by Destination Reachability

Chi-Hoon Lee*
Nokia Research Center
Palo Alto
CA, USA
chihoon.lee@nokia.com

Alpa Jain
Yahoo! Labs
701 First Ave. Sunnyvale
CA, USA
alpa@yahoo-inc.com

Larry Lai
Yahoo! Labs
701 First Ave. Sunnyvale
CA, USA
larrylai@yahoo-inc.com

ABSTRACT

Search engine users are increasingly performing complex tasks based on the simple keyword-in document-out paradigm. To assist users in accomplishing their tasks effectively, search engines provide query recommendations based on the user's current query. These are suggestions for follow-up queries given the user-provided query. A large number of techniques have been proposed in the past on mining such query recommendations which include past user sessions (e.g., sequence of queries within a specified window of time) to identify most frequently occurring pairs, using click-through graphs (e.g., a bipartite graph of queries and the urls on which users clicked) and rank these suggestions using some form of frequency counts from the past query logs. Given the limited number of queries that are offered (typically 5) it is important to effectively rank them. In this paper, we present a novel approach to ranking query recommendations which not only consider relevance to the original query but also take into account *efficiency* of a query at accomplishing a user search task at hand. We formalize the notion of *query efficiency* and show how our objective function effectively captures this as determined by a human study and eliminates biases introduced by click-through based metrics. To compute this objective function, we present a pseudo-supervised learning technique where no explicit human experts are required to label samples. In addition, our techniques effectively characterize preferred url destinations and project each query into a higher dimension space where each sub-spaces represents user intent using these characteristics. Finally, we present an extensive evaluation of our proposed methods against production systems and show our method to increase task completion efficiency by 15%.

*Chi-Hoon Lee participated in the work during his tenure at Yahoo! Labs.

CIKM'11, October 24–28, 2011, Glasgow, Scotland, UK.

Categories and Subject Descriptors

H.3.3 [**Information Search and Retrieval**]: Query formulation; H.3.5 [**Online Information Services**]: Web-based services

General Terms

Algorithms, Design

Keywords

Query Log mining, Query Recommendation, Search Assist Metric

1. INTRODUCTION

Search engines are continuously looking into ways to improve user search experience and reduce user efforts in formulating their search tasks. One such user assistance method is *query suggestions* or *query recommendations* where search users are provided a suggestion for follow-up query based on a query they input. Query recommendation is a fundamental tool in helping users complete their search task. Almost all state-of-the art search engines provide query recommendations which largely focuses on providing as suggestion queries that are relevant to the user query. For instance, when a user submits the query 'alamo,' the search engine may suggest 'alamo discount coupons', 'hertz' or 'thrifty'.

Traditionally, studies on query recommendation have been largely focused on identifying sources or candidates for query suggestions. While relevance to original query is important, these approaches have not yet considered the *efficiency* of a suggestion in helping users to arrive at their desired destination, as the following example shows.

EXAMPLE 1.1. *Consider the query q = 'plenty of fish' for which candidates for query recommendations after mining query log sessions are: s1 = 'plenty of fish pof' s2 = 'plenty of fish login' and s3 = 'plenty of fish dating site' ranked in the order of relevance based on frequency. Interestingly, in our dataset we observed that sometimes relevant suggestions can 'slow down' users by competing with search results and can lead to in-efficient search sessions. Specifically, user search query logs reveal that after submitting the query 'plenty of fish' users arrive to the desired destination url* `www.plentyoffish.com` *but via several alternative paths. Figure 1 shows these alternative paths as edges between node q representing the query, node u representing the url, and s_i representing query suggestions $s1, s2, s3$. As seen in the figure, sometimes users click on the desired search result after*

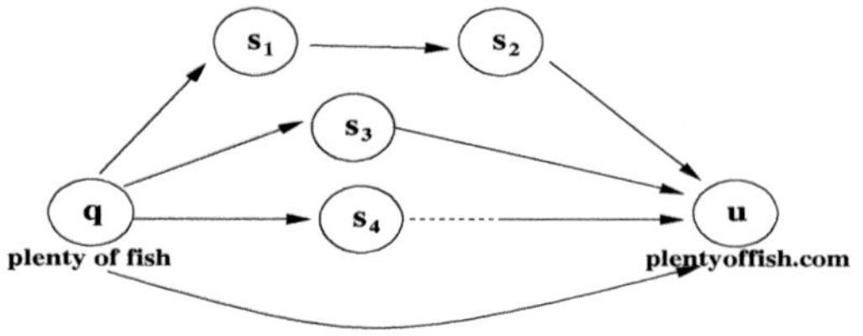

Figure 1: An example of paths from query to destination URL which include algorithmic path as well as reformulated paths via recommended suggestions.

submitting the query, whereas sometimes users follow the query recommendations and after multiple clicks on query suggestions arrive at the desired destination.

As illustrated by the above example, sometime users end up using query recommendations as 'steps' towards their desired destination until they arrive at a suggestion that is highly indicative of their intent or the typical intent associated with the destination. For instance, users may consider 'facebook login page' as a suggestion associated with their daily facebook activity as opposed to 'facebook' even if search results for both suggestions contain the desired result. We hypothesize that an effective query recommendations approach should reduce such alternatives that compete with the search results and distract users.

Effectively ranking query recommendations presents several open challenges. First, commonly used user-feedback-based relevance metrics, e.g., click-through rate, prove to be insufficient and a biased estimator. The examples above illustrates how often users may click multiple query recommendations to arrive to their destination but unfortunately these clicks are not indicative of relevance or utility to search tasks; instead these are *distractive* clicks. Second, query logs typically consist of rich information for head queries and relatively sparser information for tail queries. However, query recommendations should be effectively produced for as many queries as possible. Finally, a search engine processes millions of queries on a daily basis and thus the ranking mechanism should not be computationally prohibitive.

Until now, the choice of query suggestions is largely based on relevance to original query and the impact of this choice on the efficiency of arriving at a destination page was ignored. However, considering the impact of suggestion efficiency is critical and with this in mind we propose a novel query suggestion ranking objective based on the efficiency with which a suggestion leads to the desired destination, i.e., url, and reduces alternatives that compete with the search results. For this, we first analyze past user query logs to understand the importance of efficiency and capture this by proposing a novel metric, called PGL for query q and suggestion s. We assert the effectiveness of our efficiency-based metric by conducting a first user-study. As we will see, this metric appropriately captures the efficiency in destination reachability but is computationally expensive and at times prohibitive at Web search scale. However, this analysis allows us to postulate necessary data requirements for characterizing the efficiency of query suggestions. Using these, we provide techniques to estimate the efficiency of a query suggestion conditioned on the user-provided query. In summary, the contributions of this paper are:

- We formalize and present a first analysis of query recommendation efficiency.
- We establish the effectiveness of efficiency as a ranking objective and present techniques to estimate this objective.
- We present an extensive evaluation of our proposed techniques and ranking objectives on real-world data sets and user-studies.

The rest of the paper is organized as follows: First, we present a detailed search logs analysis which forms the basis of our efficiency metric (Section 2). Then, we show how this metric can be computed for large scale query volumes observed by commercial search engine (Section 3). Finally, we present a detailed experimental evaluation (Section 4) and discuss related work (Section 5).

2. DESTINATION REACHABILITY

A critical goal for search engines is to help users in efficiently arriving at their destinations as quickly as possible.

2.1 Search Logs Analysis

As a first step towards building effective ranking algorithms for query recommendations, we performed an in-depth analysis of the past user query logs. Specifically, we 'sliced' the query logs to focus on the sequence of events that occur between users issuing a query to the search engine and reaching a *destination page* that meets the users needs. The problem of characterizing a destination page is an active research area and several methods have been proposed in the past [22, 7]. Without loss of generality, we used a simple destination page classifier based on the *landing page dwell time*, which is the total time a user spends on a webpage after clicking on one of the search results page. Intuitively, short dwell time could indicate that the page does not meet user's needs and similarly, long dwell time indicates vice versa. In our experiments, we learned a threshold for the dwell time based on a user-study and set it to 100s. The details of this user-study are out of the scope of this paper but in brief, experienced annotators were asked to judge the quality of landing pages and these annotations were used to examine the page dwell time and pick a threshold based on precision and recall metrics. Applying this threshold allows us to efficiently process millions of queries in the logs, however, other methods proposed in the literature can also be applied to this task.

Given this set of queries along with their destination pages, we denote the sequence of search events in between as a *search path* or simply *path*. Figure 1 shows one such *query-destination* graph. An interesting observation was made on analyzing these search paths. There were two types of search paths: (a) *algorithmic paths*, where users simply clicked on the search results directly, and (b) *reformulated paths*, where users reformulated their queries either by clicking on suggestions offered by the search engine or by themselves. An example algorithmic path would be (1: query='amazon', 2: url=`www.amazon.com`) where the query was 'amazon' and the user consumed `www.amazon.com` as their destination. The number (e.g., 1 and 2) preceding the colon symbol denotes the sequence number of observed search events. An example of reformulated path would be (1:query='amazon', 2:query='amazon kindle', 3:url=`kindle.amazon.com`) where the first query 'amazon' was reformulated to 'amazon kindle' before the destination page was consumed. This indicates that oftentimes query recommendations compete with search results in that users parse the query recommendations (instead of the search results), click on the recommendations and spend relatively more time in arriving to their destinations. This could be due to several reasons: first, oftentimes recommendations are placed in high-visibility regions (e.g., north of search results or south of search results before users click on the Next search page); second, some suggestions add additional context to the original query and may appear more promising even though the search results page may be near identical; third, users simply use these recommendations as milestones towards their search goals.

To gain further insights, we traced the timestamps for each search event and computed the *path time* defined as:

DEFINITION 2.1. **[Search path time]** *The* search path time *is the difference in timestamps for the first query event and last destination page event. Path times measure the overall time users spent in search before they arrive at their destination page.* □

We compared the algorithmic path time and reformulation path time and observed that for a large fraction of queries there exist reformation paths with shorter path times than algorithmic path times. This could be the case when reformulations can bring about the destination page at a higher rank position and thus easily visible to the user. Ideally, we would like to minimize the search path time for each queries and therefore surface query reformulations that are likely to reduce the search path time. Specifically, we characterize *query suggestion efficiency* as:

DEFINITION 2.2. **[Suggestion efficiency]** *Given a query suggestion, its* efficiency *is defined as the inverse of the search path time if a user were to accept this suggestion.* □

Our goal now is to rank query recommendations based on their efficiency and thus helping in arriving at their destination pages quickly. For this, we show we can characterize suggestion efficiency based on the query-destination graphs such as that in Figure 1.

2.2 Characterizing Suggestion Efficiency

Given a query-destination graph, we characterize the efficiency of each suggestion on a reformulated path using a novel metric called *path gain-loss (PGL)*. For a suggestion s, we mine the graph to estimate the amount of *gain* and *loss* in efficiency that will be introduced by s. Specifically, the process to compute the PGL of a suggestion s given an initial query, denoted as *pgl(q,s)* is shown in Algorithm 1. We split the search paths on the graph into the set P_a of algorithmic paths and the set P_s of all reformulated paths that 'visited' suggestion s. For each set P_a and P_s, we compute their median search path times, denoted m and $\mu(s)$, respectively. We then apply two-sample $t-$ test to μ_a and $\mu(s)$ with the null hypothesis H_0 that both means are equal. When the null hypothesis is accepted, we conclude that using suggestion s does not bring obvious gains or losses in the search path time. If otherwise, we use m, median search time for algorithmic paths, as an approximate time an average search user takes to arrive to the destination page. For each path $p \in P_s$ (eg., $q \to s_3 \to u$ from Figure 1), we further derive the gain $G(q, s, d, p)$ and loss $L(q, s, d, p)$ as follows:

$$G(q, s, d, p) = \begin{cases} 1 & \text{if } m \succ t_p; \\ 0 & \text{if } t_p \succ m. \end{cases}$$

```
Input: Search Logs
Extract all competitive path sets , reformulated R and
algorithmic A.
R = p|first_query(p) = q, last_url(p) = u, s ∈ p
A = p|first_query(p) = q, last_url(p) = u, s ∈ p
for each competitive sets R and A do
  Compute average search time μR, μA
  Apply t-test on the following hypotheses:
  H0: μR = μA
  if H0 rejected then
    Compute medium time m of A
    for each path p and its path time t in R do
      if t <m then
        increase gain by 1
      else
        increase loss by 1
      end if
    end for
  end if
end for
Compute PGL by Equation 1
Output: PGL(q,s)
```

Algorithm 1: PGL of suggestion s for query q.

$$L(q, s, d, p) = \begin{cases} 1 & \text{if } t_p \succ m; \\ 0 & \text{if } m \succ t_p. \end{cases}$$

where $m \succ t_p$ indicates that m is longer than t_p and t_p denotes the search time for path p. We would report gain if the reformulated path time t_p is shorter than the median algorithmic path time m. Finally, we aggregate the $G(q, s, d, p)$ and $L(q, s, d, p)$ values for each query-destination graph that contains s and begins with the same query q but may lead to different destination urls (i.e., d). Formally,

$$PGL = \frac{\sum_{(d,p)} G(q, s, d, p) + \alpha}{\sum_{(d,p)} G(q, s, d, p) + \sum_{(d,p)} L(q, s, d, p) + \alpha + \beta} \tag{1}$$

where $G_(q, s, d, p)$ and $L(q, s, d, p)$ are the gain and loss statistics for each reformulated path, s, over the query-destination graph (q, d). In this equation, we aggregate across all reformulated paths (i.e., p) and destination urls to derive a PGL value for a pair of q and s. The smoothing parameters, α and β, deal with corner cases where the denominator is zero. Without loss of generality, we set both of them as 10 in our experiments. The *pgl(q,s)* values ranges from 0 to 1 with a value close to 1 indicates that suggestion s tends to reduce the search path time. Alternatively, PGL can be used to compute the overall quality of the suggestion set by aggregating *pgl(q,s_i)* for all suggestions s_i to identify poor query recommendation cases.

With the PGL metric, we also attempt to address an inherent bias introduced by CTR (click-through rate) of suggestions. CTR is a commonly used suggestion quality metric which ranks suggestions based on the click-through rates observed in the query logs. As discussed in the Introduction (see Example 1), oftentimes, suggestions compete with the search results and users may click on these suggestions to either arrive at a similar SERP or to further click on other suggestions. Such suggestions extend a user's search session without contributing any new information, but can be ranked high if only CTR was considered. PGL on the other hand, only merits suggestions that are likely to bring users to their desired destinations faster.

As we will see in our experiments, PGL effectively captures suggestion efficiency and ranking suggestions by PGL generates shorter search sessions. However, in practice deriving *pgl(q,s)* for each query and its suggestion can prove to be prohibitively expensive. In particular, given a query q and suggestion s for which we want to derive *pgl(q,s)*, we need to examine *all* search paths (algorithmic and reformulated via s) across *all users* that issued query q for *all destination pages*. Building query-destination graphs for each observed query q over terabytes of query logs is prohibitively expensive. To address this challenge and build a ranking algorithm amenable to production, we propose a novel method to estimate *pgl(q,s)* for each suggestion s without exhaustively building each query-destination graph. Before discussing our estimation techniques, we give an overview of our suggestion ranking algorithm that incorporates both efficiency and relevance of a suggestion.

2.3 Suggestion Ranking with Efficiency: An Overview

While PGL captures the efficiency of a suggestion, *relevance* of the suggestion to the original user query cannot be ignored. To incorporate both efficiency and relevance into suggestion recommendation, we follow a two-phase approach:

1. Given a query q, identify a set S of candidate suggestions relevant to q.
2. For each suggestion $s \in S$, assign an efficiency score.
3. Rank suggestions in S by their efficiency scores.

In Step 1, to identify a candidate set of relevant suggestions we mine search query logs sent to a major search engine for a period of approximately two years. The mining process constructs pairs of (q, s) where q is a query and s is a highly correlated query which can be offered as a suggestion. The mining process to generate these pairs is as follows: Given raw query logs data, we first identify a *user session* which is a sequence of queries issued within a time window of ten minutes. Typically, a user session consists of queries of a single intent[1] and therefore, queries $q_1, q_2, \cdots, q_n$ issued within a query session could be considered as highly-correlated queries. However, due to the high level of noise in the query logs, several filters and proprietary algorithms are applied to these 'raw' query-suggestion pairs to filter out low quality suggestions. For instance, queries that were issued by a robot, or had low responses on SERP, or had no meaningful SERP. We aggregate each pair to compute an association score $C(q, s)$.

A simple approach deriving $C(q, s)$ is to identify queries with high reformulation probability $p(s|q)$ as suggestions. This can simply be measured over the frequency counts in the session logs:

$$p(s|q) = \frac{f(s,q)}{f(q)}$$

where $f(s, q)$ is the frequency that these two queries are issued by the same user within a session. The problem with using reformulation probability as the merit for suggestion candidate generation is that a query that is not dependent on q might have a high reformulation probability just because of its high marginal probability. To account for this, one can use point-wise mutual information (PMI) instead,

$$PMI(s,q) \approx log\left(\frac{f(s,q)}{f(q)f(s)}\right)$$

where $f(s)$ and $f(q)$ are individual marginal counts[2]. The difference is that PMI normalizes the reformulation probability by a factor of $f(s)$; hence, it measures the dependency of these two queries. One weakness of PMI is that it might become very unstable for pairs of rare queries. As $f(q)$ and $f(s)$ get low, even a single coincidental co-occurrence might lead to a high PMI value. To account for this, we use a variant of PMI, namely, the log-likelihood ratio (LLR) instead [15]. We present further details of this algorithm is Section 4.1. A key advantage of this approach is that it is highly scalable when processing hundreds of terabyte log data, where each log record contains approximately 300 number of fields, using a grid computing technology such as Hadoop [10]. Specifically, we use Map/Reduce and Pig to process query logs.

For Step 2, we could rank each suggestion $s \in S$ by their *pgl(q,s)* but due to the reasons discussed above we compute ePGL, an estimate of the *pgl(q,s)* which we discuss next. In summary, given query q, our goal is to rank suggestions in S and select top k out of S, which is formalized as

$$T = \underset{\{s_1 \dots s_k\} \subseteq S}{\arg\max} \sum_{i=1}^{k} epgl(q, s_i),$$

where $ePGL$ is a scoring function with two input parameter queries q and s which is a suggestion candidate (typically, k is 5 or 12).

3. ESTIMATING PGL VALUES

So far, we presented a novel metric *pgl(q,s)* to score a suggestion candidate s by its efficiency in arriving at a destination page. We are now interested in building an estimator for PGL that is computationally feasible. We formulate the problem of estimating PGL as a "pseudo-supervised" learning problem which does not require explicit label samples. In our paper, our targets are generated by real search engine users' responses, not by professional annotators who might miss real users' intents with their own biases.

A fundamental observation in deriving *pgl(q,s)* is that efficient suggestions (i.e., suggestions with high PGL scores) tend to be those that have led to clicks on search results (instead of clicks on other query suggestions). Therefore, a straightforward estimator would be to examine the relation between the fraction of clicks generated after accepting suggestion s that were SERP clicks. Figure 2 shows the relation between PGL values and the fraction of SERP clicks per suggestions for our test set of 6000 suggestions (see Section 4.1 for details). Unfortunately, these two quantities are unrelated and thus this naive approach of click fraction is insufficient since it does not incorporate the quality of the suggestion in terms of its SERP.

3.1 Feature Representation

A critical point captured by PGL scores is also that the search result pages of efficient suggestions are substantially

[1]Note that this assumption has been empirically proven to be effective to serve 500 millions users per month.

[2]Without losing any generality, we approximate PMI by omitting term N from the nominator within log, which is the query and suggestion size from the query logs.

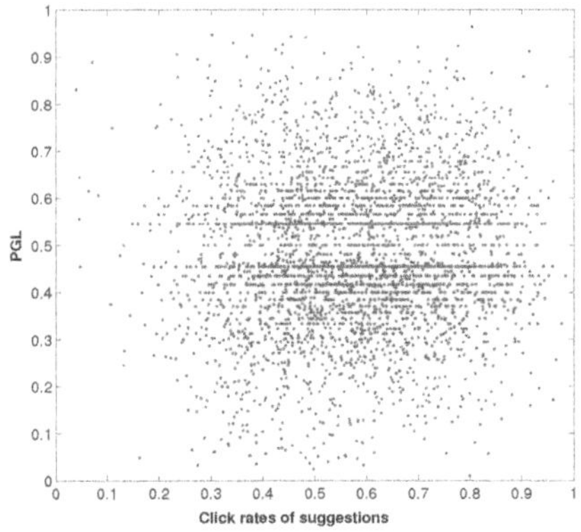

Figure 2: Relation between PGL values and fraction of SERP clicks per suggestion clicks.

different from the original query (e.g., the last 'hop' on the query-destination graph). Given a query q and a suggestion candidate s, we could capture difference in SERP by examining the top-k results for both q and s. To capture this, we could examine the top-k results generated by q and s but this is naturally not feasible due to the query-per-second limitations of search engines. However, we can mine the query logs to reconstruct the SERP for both q and s. In particular, we use the clicked urls data for each query as a surrogate for the SERP and preferred destinations for a query, with the click frequency as an indicator of the rank position. To this end, we can compute a measure of similarity (or its dual diversity) to assign a score to s with respect to q. The rest of this section presents our estimator which represents a query q and suggestion s using information from clicked-urls and computes a similarity $Sim(q, s)$ between q and s. Later in Section 3.2 we discuss the relation between $Sim(q, s)$ and $pgl(q,s)$ values.

Our feature space to estimate PGL, which mines the clicked-urls data, projects queries into a higher dimension based on the url destination preferences of users for these queries. Several researchers have studied the problem of understanding destination preferences of a query, namely understanding the intent of the query based on the graph structural information [4, 13, 5], lexical characteristics and query log statistics [15, 23]. In this work, we exploit a new source of information – the contextual information encoded in the URLs that users clicked as derived from the query logs. The idea here is the oftentimes users design and structure their web pages to reflect the intent or action associated with the page and thus url strings act as a short summary of its contents. Table 1 shows some examples of queries and the urls that users clicked on. Intuitively, the tokens of a url string capture the intrinsic user intents and in turn the diversity between SERPs.

Given a query q and set $U = \{u_1, u_2, \cdots, u_n\}$ of clicked urls from the search logs, we construct a query-click-graph as shown in Figure 3. query q is generalized to n connectivities of urls, which is represented as vector $\mathbf{q} = (f_{w_1}, f_{w_2}, \ldots, f_{w_k})^T$, where

$$f_{w_k} = \sum_{i=1}^{n} N(w_k, S(u_i)) = c_i * I(w_k \in S(u_i)) \qquad (2)$$

which is a weight of connectivity between q and url $u_i \in U$ with their associated click counts c_i when word w_i is in bag of words $S(u_i)$ created from url u_i. $I(E)$ is an indicator

Query	URL
Vitamin C	http://lpi.oregonstate.edu/infocenter/vitamins/vitaminC
python	http://en.wikipedia.org/wiki/Python_(programming_language)
rome	http://wikitravel.org/en/Rome

Table 1: Examples of URL strings as summary of contents

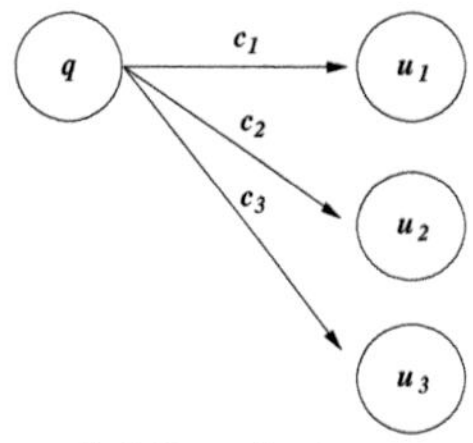

Figure 3: Connectivities between query q and its clicked-urls u_i. Query q has connections with urls $\{u_i\}_{i=1}^{3}$ and each connectivity i is associated with click counts c_i used as an association weight.

function: it returns 1, when E is true. A word w_i is the minimum unit of terms from a url string, which determines a dimension in higher feature space[3] of q. A weight that measures the association between q and u_i is represented by its clicks from the query logs.

Given the feature vector representations $\mathbf{q}$ and $\mathbf{s}$ of q and suggestion candidate s, respectively, we compute similarity in SERPs as a product of two vectors and a $d \times d$ matrix $\mathbf{M}$ that determines importance of each feature dimension, expressed as

$$Sim(q, s) = \mathbf{q}^T \mathbf{M} \mathbf{s} \qquad (3)$$

Much research has addressed to improve the effectiveness of a score $Sim(q, s)$ such as learning matrix $\mathbf{M}$ [2, 12] and an approximation of a row matrix of $\mathbf{q}$ to discover latent structure [6, 11]. However, most of the work involves polynomial computations (e.g., inverse of a matrix), which is extremely challenging in dealing with large scale of data such as a commercial search engine. Instead of learning matrix $\mathbf{M}$, we assume the matrix as a diagonal (e.g., unit) matrix, which reduces Equation (3) to cosine similarity in our feature space. As we will see the characteristics of PGL (its efficiency is strongly correlated with destination diversity), allow for our feature representation to be a good candidate as a predictor variable in estimating PGL.

3.2 Fitting an Estimator

Figure 4 illustrates the correlations between scores generated from Equation (3) and PGL. Each data point in Figure 4 plots pair of (score, PGL) values for two queries. As claimed from the previous section, the graph shows correlations: as our scores in X-axis approach to 1, PGLs values in Y-axis decreases. This strongly supports the utility of our score as an estimator of PGL. Note that the red curve in Figure 4 is a quadratic fit. Using this fit, we simply tested the quality of the quadratic fit. Basically, we convert a PGL value for pair (q, s) to 0 when they are less than 0.5. Otherwise 1. Here, s is a suggestion of q. Having 0 for pair (q, s) indicates that s is not a good suggestions since its efficiency has produced more loss paths, while 1 for a good suggestion. Accuracy of the quadratic fit is plotted in Figure 5. Red colored points indicate true positive (TP), where the es-

[3]Note that the sparseness of the feature space can be further discussed using low rank approximation.

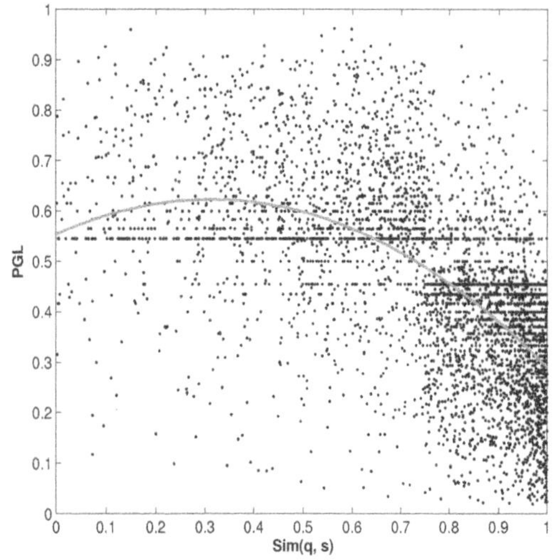

Figure 4: Correlation between $Sim(q, s)$ scores from Equation (3) (X-axis) and PGL (Y-axis). Each point in the plot is generated from a pair of two queries (q, s) (note that s can be considered as a suggestion of query q.) The red curve from the plot is a quadratic regression fit to estimate PGL with inputs of score from Equation(3).

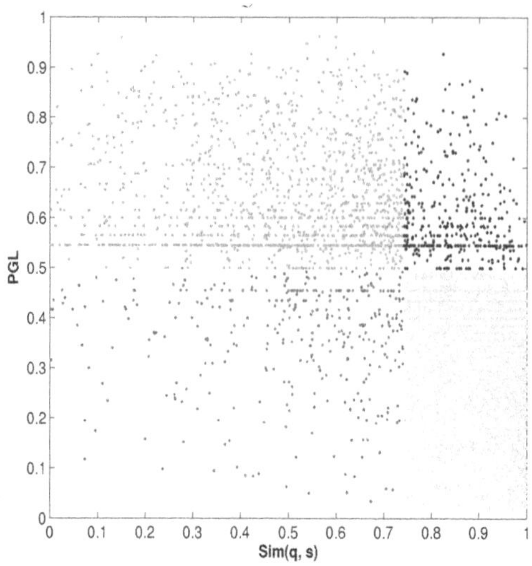

Figure 5: Performance of a quadratic estimator to PGL values mapped to {0, 1} and $ePGL$. Colors red, black, blue, and green correspond to true positive, false negative, false positive, and true negative, respectively.

timates and PGL agree that suggestions from the pairs are good ones. The green colored points indicate true negative, where both of the estimates and PGL consider the suggestions are not useful to users queries. Blues are for false positive (FP) and blacks false negative. Based on the fit, the precision is 0.8127, derived from TP/(TP+FP), which is the ratio to correctly classifies items into a target class.

As an alternative, we also trained a Classification And Regression Tree (CART) [3], which is a non-parametric decision tree learning algorithm, specifically using classification trees. This allows to learn a non linear decision boundary as opposed to the result from the previous quadratic fit. Although CART is one of the state-of-art in predictive models, it requires users' input to start with such as the minimum number of data samples per node. We have used a held-out set to tune the parameter to avoid over-fitting. Figure 6(a) shows that the testing errors (Blue curve) are increased by increasing the model complexity (ie., reducing the number of minimum samples per nodes (X-axis)), as opposed to training errors (Red curve) are decreased. In this exercise, it is obvious to observe the over-fitting due to our single predictor variable.

To compare accuracy between the quadratic fitting with a tree approach, we randomly select 6000 samples and split them into training and testing data as 60% and 40%, respectively with 100 iterations. Overall, a tree (an example shown in Figure 6(b)) shows better accuracy: 0.832 (tree) vs. 0.824 (quadratic fit), although the difference is marginal. When our $Sim(q, s)$ is between 0.1965 and 0.6665 in Figure 6(b), it corresponds to high utility w.r.t. PGL. This is aligned with PGL's characteristic to penalize suggestions that compete with algo results of query due to possibility of redundant paths to a same destination. It in turn implicitly favors suggestions that diversifies query's reachability. In addition, it is interesting to observe that low scores from Equation (3) are estimated as high utility w.r.t. PGL, although the low score itself from Equation (3) implies that q and s are orthogonally projected onto the feature space. However, this is a critical characteristic in understanding PGL since some suggestions that are not contextually related to a query could be good candidates to lead users to enhanced experiences (eg., suggestion "Sears" would be a good candidate for query "Fry's electronics".) This insight is in turn captured by estimators using scores from Equation (3) with projection on our feature representation.

4. EXPERIMENTS

We now present our experimental evaluation. We present our experimental settings in Section 4.1. Next, we establish the effectiveness of PGL as an effective metric at improving user interaction with a search engine in Section 4.2. Finally, we evaluate our estimation techniques for PGL in Section 4.3.

4.1 Experimental Settings

Data collection. We processed a fully anonymized set of query logs of a major search engine for a period of about two years to generate pairs (q, s) where q is a query for which s is a relevant suggestion. Each pair is given an association score based on their co-occurrence and relevance strength as discussed in Section 2.3. Of these, we used a random sample of 55K queries from the first three months of 2011 for our search log analysis presented in Section 2.2. Table 2 shows the distribution of the number of suggestions per query.

Compared methods. To the best of our knowledge, we are not aware of any other method on ranking suggestions by their efficiency. However, as a strong baseline we use the suggestion recommendation system of a major search engine. We denote this method as BN. We implement our ranking algorithm discussed in Section 2.3 and denote that method

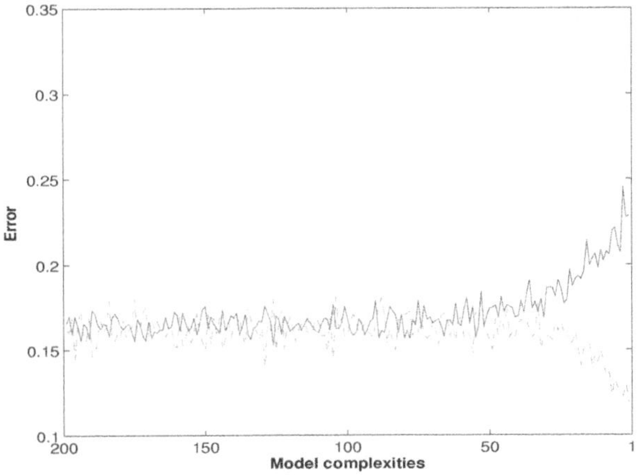

(a) By increasing model complexity the training errors (Red curve) decreased, while the testing errors (Blue curve) increased. Errors are in Y-axis. Model complexities in X-axis are increased by decreasing minimum number of samples in a splitting node. As the model complexity moves to the right side, the min number of data sample for a node to split gets smaller.

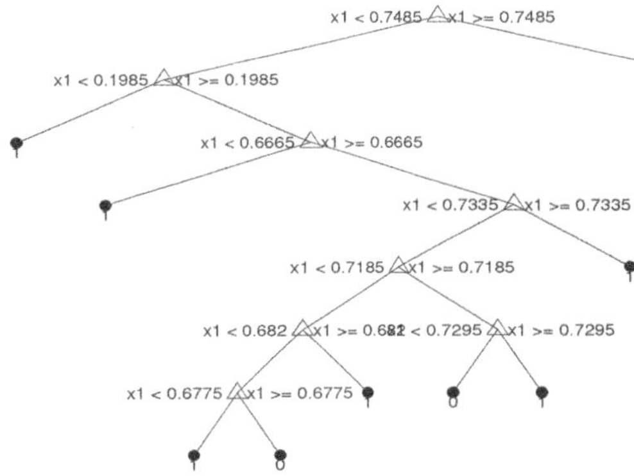

(b) An example of a learned tree showing non-linearity decision boundary. Precision of this decision tree is 0.8363. It is important to note that when x1 (ie., our $Sim(q, s)$) is between 0.1965 and 0.6665, it corresponds to high utility w.r.t. PGL, by being classified as 1. This is aligned with PGL's characteristic that favors a lateral move type of suggestions yielding high PGL values.

Figure 6: Learning a tree to estimate PGL

Nr. of suggestions	Nr. of queries
1	1507054
2	474183
3	247258
4	167168
5	127604
6	101864
7	86177
8	82136
9	117595
10	241345
11	10165
12	78530

Table 2: Distribution of number of suggestions.

as ePGL. In particular, for Step 2, we build an estimator for ePGL using the quadratic regression method discussed in Section 4.3 over a training set of 6000 (q, s) query-suggestion pairs randomly sampled from the query set.

Evaluation method. To examine the effectiveness of our proposed metric, PGL, we ran a bucket test over live search traffic. To evaluate ePGL, we performed two types of tests: (a) an *offline* test which involved a team of professional annotators that were asked to judge the overall quality of the suggestions produced by a suggestion algorithm, the details of which were hidden from the annotator; (b) an *online* test which involved live search traffic. We present the details of these studies shortly in the next sections.

Evaluation metrics. For experiments involving live search traffic, we evaluated the performance of a suggestion recommendation system using a variety of proprietary "user-engagement" metrics. When necessary we will provide the intuition behind these metrics but leave out complete details of these metrics due to Intellectual Properties.

4.2 Effectiveness of our PGL Metric

We start our evaluation by examining the effectiveness of our PGL metric. A particularly important challenge here is collecting the "ground-truth." Manually building ground-truth sets of evaluating the quality of suggestions is unfeasible due to the following reasons: first, we would require queries that span across all quantiles of query frequencies (i.e., head as well as tail queries) and the annotators would need to have some background information about these topics which can be impractical; second, manual annotators often introduce a bias similar to that introduce by suggestion CTR, e.g., 'facebook login' is considered a good suggestion candidate for the query 'facebook' although it can introduce inefficiency in the search task.

We tested PGL using *on-line* tests (i.e., bucket tests on live search traffic). Specifically, we generated two mutually exclusive groups or buckets of search users. In one bucket, we presented our baseline suggestion algorithm `BN`. For the other bucket, we presented our test suggestion algorithm denoted `PGL-OVR`. As discussed earlier, computing PGL values for every suggestion is unfeasible therefore to implement `PGL-OVR`, we generated a 'blacklist' of suggestions for each query. For this, we mined three months of query logs and generated 600K unique query-destination graphs and computed PGL values for each suggestion in these graphs. All suggestions with $pgl(q,s)$ values below or equal 0.3 were added to the blacklist and at runtime, suggestions that belong to the blacklist were not shown to the users. The blacklist consisted of 18 thousand suggestions.

To avoid position bias, we placed suggestions in two sections on the search result page, (a) **Nqs**, north of the search results, (b) **Sqs**, south of the search results. Table 3 shows the various search performance metrics for both algorithms where the improvements by `PGL-OVR` were statistically significant. As seen in the table, using `PGL-OVR`, the rate at which users are submitting manually reformulated queries (i.e., when suggestions are not useful to them), and the rate

Metric	Baseline	PGL-OVR
Manual retry	15,188	**-0.39%**
SERP clicks	66,885	**0.30%**
Abandonment rate	7,116	-0.248%
Ads	11,661	0.07%
Time (sec)	10.16	**-0.39%**

Table 3: PGL-OVR's relative percentage changes over baseline.

Configuration	Loss	Gain	PGL
	Nqs		
Baseline	43,943	40,823	48.2%
PGL	29,163	33,134	**53.2%**
	Sqs		
Baseline	1,253	2,592	67.3%
PGL	997	2,311	**70.2%**

Table 4: Per-algorithm PGL values

at which users are abandoning the results decrease. Further, we also see an increase in SERP clicks and interestingly an increase in the advertisements displayed. This happens mostly due to the fact that PGL promotes suggestions that bring about diverse search result pages. Finally, we also show the average search path time (see Section 2.2) and using PGL-OVR, reduces the search path time as expected. Next, we examine the gain and loss values (see Section 2.2 for both **Nqs** and **Sqs**; see Table 4. As we can see, the PGL utility improved about 9.3% for **Nqs** suggestions and 4.3% for **Sqs** suggestions; both improvements are statistically significant. In summary, through tables 3 and 4, PGL correlates well with user experience and quicker search sessions.

4.3 Effectiveness of ePGL Estimation

We now present our evaluation of ePGL which is two-fold: Offline evaluation (Section 4.3.1) and Online evaluation (Section 4.3.2).

4.3.1 Offline Evaluation

For our offline experiments, we conducted a user study which consisted of five professional search engine quality evaluators experienced in assessing the quality of query suggestions. We randomly selected 1500 queries and selected top-k suggestions generated by both BN and ePGL, and presented them to evaluators. Evaluators were asked to compare both suggestions 'side-by-side' and provide a judgment on which side was preferred. In order to avoid a position bias that could be driven by a presentation for results, we randomly swapping a side of each result per query. Judgments were split into: left/right side is much better, left/right side is better, left/right side is slightly better, both are equal. The judgement criteria was to consider 1) poor ranking of suggestions (ie., highly relevant suggestions are ranked higher than non-relevant suggestions); 2) suggestions redundant to queries are included in a result set. (e.g., suggestion "yahoo mail login" is not a good candidate for query "yahoo mail signin"); 3) a suggestion set is disambiguated enough to cover uncertain query intents. As an example, Figure 7 shows suggestions produced by BN (left) and ePGL (right) for query "python". BN produces a single suggestion where

Figure 7: Ranked list of suggestions produced by BN (left) and ePGL (right) for query 'python.'

ePGL delivers suggestions that cover a variety of SERPs, namely, programming language or a snake. Finally, Table 5 summarizes the grade distributions highlighting strong editorial preferences of ePGL's ranking over BN's one. According to the comments from the evaluators, ePGL's ranking improves ranking quality itself as well as reduces redundancy with queries.

Grades	Percentages
BN much better	0.20%
BN better	6.79%
BN slightly better	21.36%
BN and ePGL same	23.85%
ePGL much better	0.60%
ePGL better	**12.48%**
ePGL slightly better	**34.73%**

Table 5: Preferences for BN and ePGL gathered from a user study.

4.3.2 Online Evaluation

Evaluations of our online experiments are based on two different families of performance metrics: *suggestion-level* metrics and *search engine result page, SERP-level* metrics. Suggestion-level metrics examine whether users utilize query recommendations and if they are assisting in reducing users' querying efforts; similarly, SERP-level metrics examine if users are arriving at their desired destinations and their interaction with SERP. Table 6 shows results for these metrics and shows the relative percentage difference between BN and ePGL. As seen in the table, CTR on suggestions, which captures total click counts for displayed suggestion, was improved by 43% when using ePGL, and Drop rate, which captures cases where users click on a suggestion but do not click on the SERP, decreases by -0.24%. Direct retry rate, which captures the case of users manually reformulating their queries (since query suggestions are not useful) decreased by -0.074%. On SERP, the CTR increased by 0.25% and good click rate, which captures the case where users are arriving at their desired destination after a SERP click, increased by 0.19%. Overall, using ePGL improves the quality of query suggestions by surfacing suggestions that capture users diverse needs and helping them arrive at their destination pages quickly.

To highlight the difference between ePGL and BN, Table 7 shows examples of suggestions provided for two queries in the online test setting. We pick as examples two queries with different typical intents and show how ePGL can produce interesting results for both cases. The query 'advance auto parts store' has a strong navigational intent to its authority url, **http:**//shop.advanceautoparts.com with emphasis on finding locations of the store. Our ePGL method effectively captures the utility based on the feature that explores the destination reachability, and thus it ranks 'store locator'

Metric	Relative Percentage change
CTR on suggestion	**43%**
Dropped rate	-0.024%
CTR on SERP	**0.25%**
Good click rate	**0.19%**
Direct retry rate	-0.074%

Table 6: Relative percentage change comparing users' responses from ePGL with BN. Bolded statistics indicate statistical significance at level $p < 0.05$

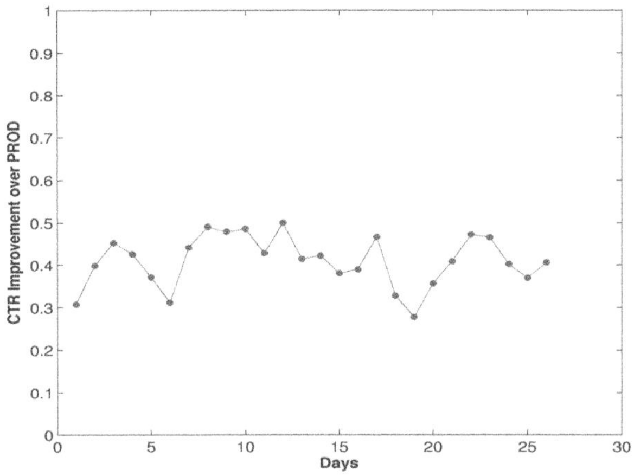

Figure 8: Daily ratio of click rates. A positive click rate in Y-axis for each day in X-axis indicates suggestions by ePGL attracts more users' attentions than ones by BN at statistically significance level $p < 0.05$.

suggestion to the top, which helps users efficiently find their destination. In addition, we also take an example for an intent of information exploration, which shows how ePGL effectively ranks suggestions when the destination of an intent typically does not have an authority. For query 'world's oldest cat' in Table 7, more relevant suggestions are shifted to higher ranks in ePGL: that is, suggestion 'world's oldest cat creme puff' directly leads users to destinations that provide relevant information for the world's oldest cat, whose name is Creme Puff. In addition, suggestion 'how old is the world's oldest cat' lets users find a specific answer strongly associated with the query. Figure 8 visualizes ratio on the daily clicks of suggestions to highlight robustness of ePGL over BN. Overall, suggestions delivered by ePGL show significantly (at statistically significant level $p < 0.05$) much higher attentions than ones to BN.

Finally, we also perform a post-mortem analysis on the query logs for this online traffic and compare BN and ePGL using PGL. As expected, users experiences from ePGL show significant improvement ($\approx$ **15.07%**) over ones from BN: that is, PGL value from ePGL is **0.84** and **0.73** from BN. We focus on subset of paths from PGL to see how many of suggestions degrades efficiency for destination reachability due to the algorithmic competing. Specifically, we count paths between a query and users' destinations. If a destination is presented on SERP by a query offering a suggestion leading to the same destination would delay reachability. Therefore, the less number these incidents are, the more efficient users' search experiences are. For ePGL, there are 8.3% of total

Query: advance auto parts store	
BN	ePGL
auto parts	advance auto parts store locator
auto parts store	auto zone auto parts
advance auto parts store locations	auto zone locations
discount auto parts	autozone
advance auto parts store locator	carquest auto parts

Query: World's oldest cat	
BN	ePGL
world's oldest cat guinness	world's oldest cat guinness
world's oldest cat dogs	world's oldest cat creme puff
world's oldest cat 2009	world's oldest cat dogs
world's oldest cat creme puff	world's oldest cat 2009
world's oldest dog	how old is the world's oldest cat

Table 7: Top 5 Suggestions using BN and ePGL.

paths ($\approx 50K$) that were delayed by suggestions while BN has 9.6%.

4.4 Evaluation Summary

In summary, we observed that using PGL, even in the form of a blacklist of suggestions, can greatly improve the quality of interaction users have with a search engine. Furthermore, our estimator ePGL effectively captures the merits of PGL and shows improvements for performance metrics related to user engagement on the query recommendations as well as the search results page.

5. RELATED WORK

Ranking query suggestions: Many research has been working to improve the quality of suggestion by exploring ranking objective functions. Mei et al. [16] constructed a bipartite-graph between query and clicked urls with a random walk by "hitting time" that estimates the expected first time to reach to a node. The lower from a query to a suggestion the hitting time is, the higher the suggestion is ranked. Several differences from our work are; 1) Mei's ranking only considers the clicks between queries and urls, and thus intents implied from ulrs are not well incorporated; 2) their graph construction is a query dependent, where incremental query processing is computationally challenging.; 3) there is no clear way to distinguish if click on a url are good or an accidental ones. Dang and Croft [20] discussed a ranking objective for suggestion recommendation. However, their work did not explicitly consider the associations between queries and suggestions, and often miss users' intents.

Providing query suggestions: Several past research efforts have built methods to generate suggestions for follow-up queries. Typically, these methods mine observed queries and developed similarity measures: in [8] association rules are used to mine query recommendations from queries in individual users' search sessions which are defined as fixed length periods of interaction. [23] builds a graph representation of the of the sequential search queries and combines it with a content based similarity method to account for the sparsity of the query logs. These methods simply mine query reformulations from observed queries. Other methods leverage the click information, as well. In [17], a query similarity measure is developed based on term-weight vector space representations of the queries and clicked URLs. Query term and click pattern overlap is used in [21] to develop query similarity measures in order to cluster user queries. Random walks on query-click graph is used by [4]. Slightly differently,

Markov Random Field models are used over the query-click graph to generate bid terms in [9].

Earlier methods of generating alternative queries also included query expansion by pseudo-relevance feedback where additional query terms are obtained from the documents retrieved by the original query. These terms are used to expand the original query to retrieve more specific documents [18, 1, 14, 15, 19].

Our work complements the above line of work in that we are interested in ranking suggestions with the goal of helping users reach their end goals efficiently.

6. DISCUSSION

This paper introduced a novel performance objective for query recommendation systems employed by search engines. Our proposed metric, PGL, examines the likelihood of a suggestion competing with a search result page and in turn delaying the users in arriving at their destination, and captures the efficiency of a query suggestion. We establish the effectiveness of this metric over a real-world setting and show how accounting for efficiency improves search user experience. We present a highly scalable algorithm to estimate PGL values that handle the large volume of queries processed by a commercial search engine. Our experiments show that our estimation technique correctly predicts the PGL values and also improves the search session quality of users.

Our work in the paper has so far only established the foundations of this area, and many interesting research problems remain open. First, while PGL captures the efficiency with which a user will arrive at their destination *post* clicking a suggestion, we still need to account for the efficiency with which a user will click on the suggestion *pre* suggestion click. Specifically, suggestions carry an inherent click appeal which also needs to be modeled which remains future work. Second, we would like to study the case of queries where no effective suggestions can be provided. For instance, navigational queries such as 'cnn' or 'citibank' often result in a direct SERP click and make the case of no-query recommendations. Third, we plan on extending our estimation technique to incorporate an 'explore-exploit' model which observes how users interact with a suggestion over a period of time or over a fixed number of views. After exploring a suggestion for fixed window, we can identify suggestions that failed to generate any interest from the search users. This could be either due to poor suggestion or a simple temporal drift in the interesting topic pertaining the query.

7. ACKNOWLEDGMENTS

We appreciate anonymous reviewers' comments that were valuable in improving the quality of this paper. We also thank the editorial team at Yahoo! Inc. for their insightful comments.

8. REFERENCES

[1] P. Anick. Using terminological feedback for web search refinement: a log-based study. In *SIGIR '03*, 2003.

[2] F. R. Bach and M. I. Jordan. Learning spectral clustering. In S. Thrun, L. Saul, and B. Schölkopf, editors, *Advances in Neural Information Processing Systems 16*. MIT Press, Cambridge, MA, 2004.

[3] L. Breiman et al. *Classification and Regression Trees*. Chapman & Hall, New York, 1984.

[4] N. Craswell and M. Szummer. Random walks on the click graph. In *SIGIR '07*, 2007.

[5] H. Cui, J.-R. Wen, J.-Y. Nie, and W.-Y. Ma. Query expansion by mining user logs. *IEEE Transaction On Knowledge and Data Engineering*, 15(4):829–839, 2003.

[6] S. Deerwester, S. T. Dumais, G. W. Furnas, T. K. Landauer, and R. Harshman. Indexing by latent semantic analysis. *Journal Of The American Society For Information Science*, 41(6):391–407, 1990.

[7] D. Downey, S. Dumais, D. Liebling, and E. Horvitz. Understanding the relationship between searchers' queries and information goals. In *CIKM '08: Proceeding of the 17th ACM conference on Information and knowledge management*, pages 449–458, New York, NY, USA, 2008. ACM.

[8] B. M. Fonseca, P. B. Golgher, E. S. de Moura, and N. Ziviani. Using association rules to discover search engines related queries. In *LA-WEB '03*, 2003.

[9] A. Fuxman, P. Tsaparas, K. Achan, and R. Agrawal. Using the wisdom of the crowds for keyword generation. In *WWW '08*, 2008.

[10] Hadoop. `http://hadoop.apache.org/`, 2009.

[11] T. Hofmann. Probabilistic latent semantic indexing. In *Proceedings of the 22nd annual international ACM SIGIR conference on Research and development in information retrieval*, SIGIR '99, pages 50–57, New York, NY, USA, 1999. ACM.

[12] T. Hofmann. Learning the similarity of documents: An information-geometric approach to document retrieval and categorization, 2000.

[13] Y. M. Idan Szpektor, Aristides Gionis. Improving recommendation for long-tail queries via templates. In *WWW '11*, 2011.

[14] R. Jones and D. C. Fain. Query word deletion prediction. In *SIGIR '03*, 2003.

[15] R. Jones, B. Rey, O. Madani, and W. Greiner. Generating query substitutions. In *WWW '06*, 2006.

[16] Q. Mei, D. Zhou, and K. Church. Query suggestion using hitting time. In *CIKM '08*, 2008.

[17] C. H. Ricardo Baeza-Yates and M. Mendoza. Query recommendation using query logs in search engines. In *Trends in Database Technology - EDBT 2004 Workshops*, 2005.

[18] I. Ruthven. Re-examining the potential effectiveness of interactive query expansion. In *SIGIR '03*, 2003.

[19] E. Terra and C. L. Clarke. Scoring missing terms in information retrieval tasks. In *CIKM '04*, 2004.

[20] M. B. Van Dang and W. B. Croft. Learning to rank query reformulations. In *SIGIR '10*, 2010.

[21] J.-R. Wen, J.-Y. Nie, and H.-J. Zhang. Clustering user queries of a search engine. In *WWW '01*, 2001.

[22] R. W. White, M. Bilenko, and S. Cucerzan. Studying the use of popular destinations to enhance web search interaction. In *Proceedings of the 30th Annual International ACM SIGIR Conference on Research and Development in Information Retrieval (SIGIR-2007)*, pages 159–166, 2007.

[23] Z. Zhang and O. Nasraoui. Mining search engine query logs for query recommendation. In *WWW '06*, 2006.

Modeling Personalized Email Prioritization: Classification-based and Regression-based Approaches

Shinjae Yoo
Computational Science Center
Brookhaven National Lab.
Upton, NY, USA
sjyoo@bnl.gov

Yiming Yang
Language Technologies Inst.
Carnegie Mellon University
Pittsburgh, PA, USA
yiming@cs.cmu.edu

Jaime Carbonell
Language Technologies Inst.
Carnegie Mellon University
Pittsburgh, PA, USA
jgc@cs.cmu.edu

ABSTRACT

Email overload, even after spam filtering, presents a serious productivity challenge for busy professionals and executives. One solution is automated prioritization of incoming emails to ensure the most important are read and processed quickly, while others are processed later as/if time permits in declining priority levels. This paper presents a study of machine learning approaches to email prioritization into discrete levels, comparing ordinal regression versus classifier cascades. Given the ordinal nature of discrete email priority levels, SVM ordinal regression would be expected to perform well, but surprisingly a cascade of SVM classifiers significantly outperforms ordinal regression for email prioritization. In contrast, SVM regression performs well – better than classifiers – on selected UCI data sets. This unexpected performance inversion is analyzed and results are presented, providing core functionality for email prioritization systems.

Categories and Subject Descriptors

I.7.m [**Computing Methodologies**]: Document and Text Processing—*Miscellaneous*; I.5.4 [**Computing Methodologies**]: Pattern Recognition—*Applications*

General Terms

Algorithms, Experimentation, Human Factors

1. INTRODUCTION

Email overload is an endemic problem, especially for the busiest and most productive professionals, managers and executives, and trends indicate aggravation rather than alleviation of the problem. Spira and Goldes report that a typical worker receives 200 non-spam email messages per day [21] and managers receive increasing numbers as their responsibilities broaden. NSF program managers, for instance, report 500 to 1000 non-spam emails per day. Productivity is compromised by constantly reading email streams loaded with low-priority announcements and acknowledgments, or alternatively by not reading email frequently and ignoring high-priority urgent emails. Hence, a partial solution is to develop automated email prioritization software, whose output would be binning incoming email streams into discrete priority levels, enabling the time-challenged user to query only the highest priority emails frequently, and lower priorities in declining order if and when she has the time to do so.

An additional major challenge is that unlike spam filtering, where the vast majority of email users would agree on what constitutes spam, e.g. Viagra commercials and penny-stock scams, non-spam email prioritization is very much user dependent. A patient receiving an email from her physician with the latest lab test results may be of crucial importance to her. But the same email sent back to the lab acknowledging receipt of the test results would be considered much less important by the lab technician. Hence, we need to mine each user's email data and solicit priority judgments in order to build personalized email prioritization systems. Given privacy issues and personalized priority preferences, data mining and priority elicitation is best done in massively distributed environments, replicating the process of each user, e.g. on a cloud or at the client side. This paper explores two different machine learning approaches to personalized email prioritization (PEP).

Although there has been significant and successful work in spam filtering, past progress on directly addressing PEP has been frustratingly slow. There are two main reasons: (1) privacy issues making it difficult to share open data sets of personal email, and (2) personalization entailing per-user data sparsity of priority-labeled emails. With respect to the first issue, possibly none of us would make our entire mailbox openly available to researchers; nor would email providers such as Google or Yahoo do likewise with their clients' email, for good reason. Due to the lack of personal priority labels, we could not use Enron corpus for PEP [11], which has been widely used as an email research benchmark dataset. Although Google recently started email prioritization service, they have not released the details of their models and the prioritization service has only two levels, whether it is important or not. In a nutshell, there are no publicly available dataset with very personal priority labels. To make progress on PEP, there is no other way except privately collecting PEP datasets from each individual subject, entails strict IRB (Institutional Review Board) supervision. It is an expensive and time consuming process, but we collected a modest dataset for our research. We should note, however, that once a PEP system is developed and proved

CIKM'11, October 24–28, 2011, Glasgow, Scotland, UK.

effective, no data sharing is required for its widespread application, since it trains on each user's emails and priority judgments, without cross-talk. The latter issue – limited priority judgments per user – requires us to investigate machine learning methods with a degree of robustness and suggests future work in active learning.

This paper addresses how to model and predict personal email priority. Specifically, we systematically analyze the effect of (1) multiple importance levels (ordinal regression) [23] and (2) personalization of email priority, using a five level Likert scale [14]. We investigate two machine learning approaches (1) ordinal regression, primarily SVM-based, and (2) classification-based, primarily a cascade of SVM classifiers. Intuitively, regression-based approaches look promising and appear to be natural choice for personalized email prioritization. To our best knowledge, there are only a handful of previous research efforts after the first mention of email overload in 1982 [3] and there have been no conclusive results on how to model personal priority. In 1999, Horvitz et al. [8] built an email alerting system which used Support Vector Machines to classify newly arrived email messages into two categories, i.e., high or low in terms of utility. In contrast to Horvitz et al., Hasegawa and Ohara [7] chose the alternate approach, using linear regression [13] but only looked at two priority levels, high and low. Recently Yoo et al. [23] applied classifiers in five-level priority prediction, presenting a basis for the present work. In summary, there have been no systematic comparisons between classification-based and regression-based approaches in terms of email priority modeling. Also there was no consideration of personalization except in Yoo et al., which serves as an initial basis for the present work.

The main contribution of this paper is a thorough comparison of ordinal regression versus classifier cascades as the underlying machine learning engine for PEP. We present the first thorough and systematic study with both regression-based approaches and classification-based approaches (including our new approaches) addressing the PEP problem based on personal importance judgments of multiple users and further analyzing on ordinal regression benchmark dataset for general performance and synthetic dataset for controlled study. Especially for personalized email prioritization, we extended the dataset of Yoo et. al. [23] from seven to 19 subjects. Specifically, our contributions in this paper include:

1. We summarized and analyzed the advantages, disadvantages and their assumptions of the regression-based approaches and classification-based approaches with the perspective of personalized email prioritization and general ordinal regression problems in Section 2 and 3.

2. Based on our analysis, we propose new approach to handle personalized ordinal regression problems in Section 3. Our proposed models take advantages of both classification-based approaches and regression-based approaches. It is based on how to model more flexible models like classification based approaches and yet we want to take advantages of partial ordinal relations if there are.

3. We evaluate two approaches with our proposed methods in three different dataset: personalized email prioritization dataset, ordinal regression benchmark dataset [2] and synthetic dataset (Section 4). The PEP dataset strongly favors classification-based approaches but ordinal regression benchmark dataset follows the underlying assumption of SVOR, and performs better on those data sets (by an 8% to 16% margin). Using an additional synthetic dataset, we can control the environment to allows us to tell which method is better under given conditions

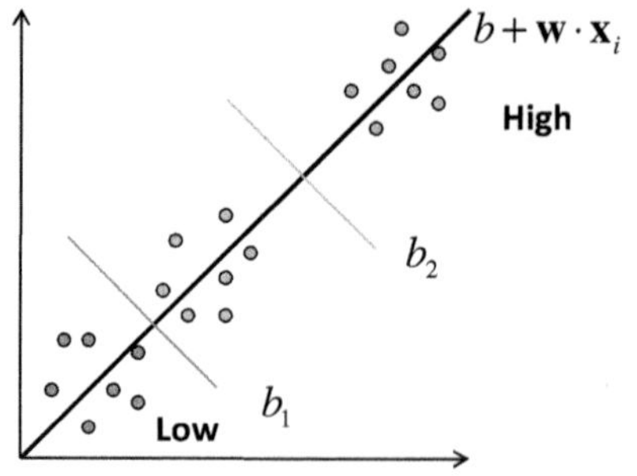

Figure 1: Three ordinal levels with a regression model and two separating thresholds

2. REGRESSION-BASED APPROACHES

2.1 Pure Regressions

The natural choice to handle ordinal response variables such as priority levels, survey answers or movie preference ratings is an ordinal regression model. After applying standard regression such as linear regression [13] or support vector regression [4], we may map the response variable to certain ordered discrete values, such as priority levels. For instance, SVR (Support Vector Regression) optimizes the following conditions:

$$\min_{\mathbf{w},b,\xi,\xi^*} \frac{1}{2}\|\mathbf{w}\|^2 + C\sum_{i=1}^{n}(\xi_i + \xi_i^*) \quad (1)$$

subject to

$$\begin{aligned}(\mathbf{w}\cdot\mathbf{x}_i - b) - y_i &\le \varepsilon + \xi_i, \xi_i \ge 0, \forall i\\ (\mathbf{w}\cdot\mathbf{x}_i - b) - y_i &\ge -\varepsilon - \xi_i^*, \xi_i^* \ge 0, \forall i\end{aligned} \quad (2)$$

where $\mathbf{w} \in R^d$ is a row weight vector and $\mathbf{x}_i \in R^d$ is a column vector for the input, ε is the margin for regression, ξ_i and ξ_i^* are slack variables, C is a regularization parameter and b is the intercept of a regression model. In case of prediction, we pick the closest level l from the predicted score of $\mathbf{w}\cdot\mathbf{x}_i - b$.

There are two important assumptions we need to address when we model ordinal regression problems by using the pure regression models. The first assumption is that one weight vector $\mathbf{w}$ defines the whole ordinal relations among different levels from Equation 1. As shown in Figure 1, the decision hyperplanes are parallel to each other and orthogonal to the weight vector $\mathbf{w}$. We call it *one model assumption* because there is only one weight vector $\mathbf{w}$ compared to multiple weight vectors of classification-based approaches. Since it is biased to have only one model or parallel decision hyperplanes, it is economical and it could be less sensitive to the noisy data than multiple models as shown in Figure 2 where we have three hyperplanes and they are not parallel. Since PEP (Personalized Email Prioritization) has to handle

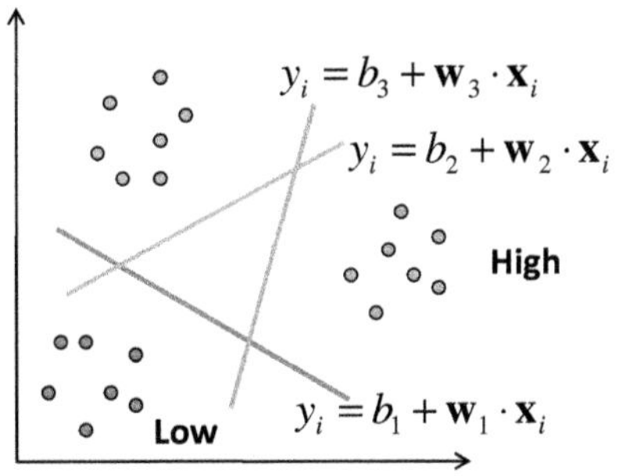

Figure 2: Three ordinal classes with three hyperplanes (OVA)

limited amount of training data, it would be attractive to have only one model to represent whole priority relations. However, if the assumption does not hold, the performance of regression models may not be guaranteed. In other words, the decision hyperplanes may not be parallel. In practice, PEP has to handle personalized priorities and the user defined priority is not necessarily satisfying this assumption. If a priority is based on a task or topic, then it could be closer to classification than regression.

The second underlying assumption is that the pure regression approaches assume *the fixed equal distance* between adjacent ordinal levels. This assumption could be less critical than *one model assumption* but it is still affecting the accuracy of prediction because regression models predict to the closest level. For instance, the difference between *important* and *very important* could be smaller than the difference between *neutral* and *important.*

2.2 Ordinal Regressions

Rather than modeling an ordinal regression problem through the pure regression, we may explicitly model ordinal regression. Ordinal regression models drop the second assumption, *the fixed equal distance* between adjacent levels. Therefore, it provides multiple thresholds which tell us the predicted priority levels as shown in Figure 1, although it still learns one regression weight vector $\mathbf{w}$. These thresholds allow us to have different distances among different levels. For example, Support Vector Ordinal Regression (SVOR) [2] learns a model weight vector $\mathbf{w}$ and $r-1$ thresholds when we have r priority levels.

More specifically, SVOR optimizes the following conditions:

$$\min_{\mathbf{w},b,\xi,\xi^*} \frac{1}{2}\|\mathbf{w}\|^2 + C\sum_{j=1}^{r-1}\sum_{i=1}^{n_j}\left(\xi_i^j + \xi_i^{*j}\right) \tag{3}$$

subject to

$$\begin{aligned}(\mathbf{w}\cdot\mathbf{x}_\mathrm{i}^\mathrm{j} - b_j) &\le -1 + \xi_i^j, \xi_i^j \ge 0, \forall i,j\\ (\mathbf{w}\cdot\mathbf{x}_\mathrm{i}^\mathrm{j} - b_{j-1}) &\ge 1 - \xi_i^{*j}, \xi_i^{*j} \ge 0, \forall i,j\\ b_{j-1} &\le b_j, \mathrm{for} j = 2,\cdots,r-1.\end{aligned} \tag{4}$$

where n_j is the number of training emails which belong to priority level j, b_j is the threshold for j or lower level threshold, and $\mathbf{x}_\mathrm{i}^\mathrm{j}$ is j^{th} priority level email. The formulation of SVOR is quite similar to SVR but SVOR has $r-1$ thresholds, b_j, compared to only one intercept b of SVR.

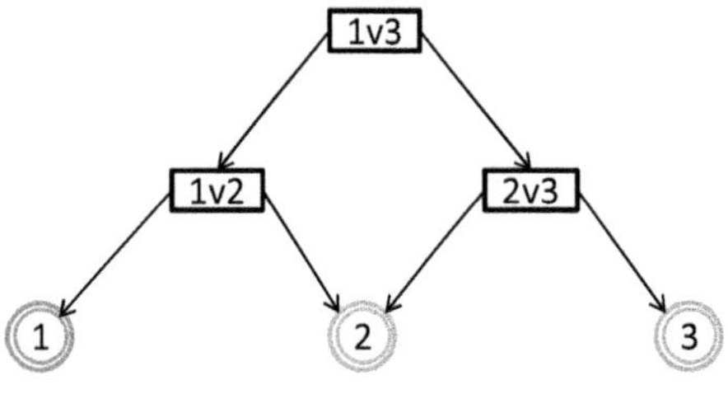

Figure 3: Decision DAG (Directed Acyclic Graph) for One vs. One multi-class classification. The rectangular represents a OVO classifier and the double circle shows the final decision. When testing a decision node, take the left child if the left-hand class is more probable than the right-hand class.

3. CLASSIFICATION-BASED MODELS

3.1 Multi-class Classification

We can drop *one model assumption* by treating the ordinal regression problem as multi-class classification problems and thus we may have multiple models for each priority level. Multi-class classification provides the most flexible model but there are no predefined relations among different priority levels. Although there are numerous ways to build multi-class classifiers from binary classifiers, we focus on three popular approaches: OVA (One vs. All), OVO (One vs. One), and DAGSVM [18].

One vs. All (OVA), also known as One vs. Rest (OVR), is the most common way to handle the multi-class classification problem, Figure 2. OVA treats remaining classes as negatives and thus we need r models if we have r priority levels. When testing, we choose the most confident priority level as our prediction.

One vs. One (OVO), also known as all pairs, build all possible pairs of binary classifiers [9, 15] such as (1 vs. 2), (1 vs. 3), ..., ($r-1$ vs. r). When testing, each classifier votes and the majority class will be the predicted class. Although One vs. One (OVO) classification requires $r\cdot(r-1)/2$ classifiers, each classifier has less amount of training examples than OVA classifiers and thus overall training time is reduced [9].

Instead of majority voting, we may use decision DAG (Directed Acyclic Graph) during testing as shown in Figure 3. We call it DAG instead of DAGSVM [18] because we may apply it to different classifiers instead of just SVM. DAG is faster than OVO during prediction because it requires only $r-1$ test. Although Plattet et al. [18] reported the order of classes from DAG did not affect final results, we sorted the order of priority levels as shown in Figure 3.

3.2 Order Based DAG

Although regression models make use of priority relations, their models are not flexible due to *one model assumption.* It could be critical for personalized email prioritization because each person might have different assumption about the priority levels. Multi-class classification provides flexibility because they allow multiple models among the different priority levels. However, they ignore the ordinal relations among the priority levels. Therefore, we propose models which have both the flexibility of multi-class classification models and the ordinal relations of regression models.

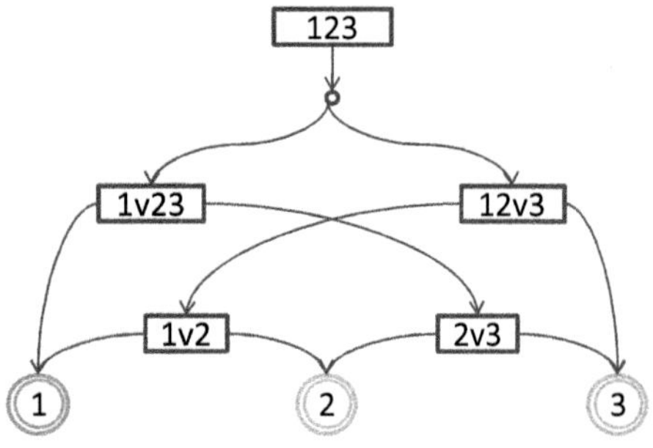

Figure 4: Decision DAG (Directed Acyclic Graph) for three level Order-Based (OB) classification. The rectangular represents a OB classifier and the double circle shows the final decision. When testing a decision node, take the left child if the left-hand class is more probable than the right-hand class.

Rather than directly predicting each priority level, we may use the order information for guiding better specific cases. Figure 4 shows the decision directed acyclic graph (DAG) for Order-Based (OB) classification models. When there are multiple paths available from top nodes to leaf nodes, any path may guide to the correct decision as long as each node's decision is correct. Since there are multiple choices available, we can always choose the **most confident** decision node among candidate decision nodes, OB-MC or we may do **majority voting**, OB-MV. For instance, when we have three priority levels, we can start from both "12 vs 3" and "1 vs 23" of Figure 4. For a testing email x_i, suppose that an SVM classifier trained "12" as positive and "3" as negative training classes (12 vs 3) and the classifier predicted 0.7 but SVM trained with "1" as positive and "23" as negative training labels (1 vs 23) and predicted -0.9. In case of OB-MC, we follow "1 vs 23" decision path because -0.9 is more confident than 0.7 and the next decision node is "2v3" instead of "1" due to the negative prediction score. OB-MV test all possible paths and then majority voting will determine which one is our final decision. If there are even votes, we may test even votes results using one vs remaining even vote node classification. For instance, "12 vs 3" predicted "1" for final decision but "1 vs 23" ended up with "3". Then we choose the better one out of "1 vs 3".

Order-Based approaches have multiple flexible models as classification-based models but they also have model bias to the order of priority levels as regression-based models, resulted in robust modeling to the noisy data. If the priority levels have no relations (perfect for classification) or satisfy ordinal regression assumption (perfect for regression), our proposed order-based approaches may not be able to outperform than these two extreme approaches. However, if users have set any form of partial ordinal relations, then our proposed models have a potential to improve the prediction accuracy.

When we apply r level prioritizer, the total number of basic classifier is $\sum_{k=1}^{r}(r-k+1)\cdot(k-1)$. The classification models listed above can be paired with any kinds of classification algorithm and we tested SVMs and Regularized Logistic Regression depending on dataset.

Table 1: Collected Dataset

User	# of emails	# of train	# of test
1	1750	150	1600
2	503	150	353
3	519	150	469
4	989	150	839
5	275	150	125
6	279	150	129
7	234	150	84
8	899	150	749
9	408	150	258
10	404	150	254
11	282	150	132
12	863	150	713
13	758	150	608
14	476	150	326
15	2989	150	2839
16	569	150	419
17	816	150	666
18	582	150	432
19	1126	150	1076
Avg	774.8	150	624.8

Table 2: PEP Evaluation results with p-values

# of tr	Base(b) MAE	SVOR(o) MAE	SVOR(o) p-val(b)	OB-MV MAE	OB-MV p-val(b)	p-va
30	1.1560	1.1340	0.3576	**0.9980**	* 0.0148	* 0.0
60	1.1560	1.0736	0.1362	**0.9185**	* 0.0010	* 0.0
90	1.1560	1.0459	0.0844	**0.8837**	* 0.0004	* 0.0
120	1.1560	1.0441	0.0746	**0.8791**	* 0.0003	* 0.0
150	1.1560	1.0480	0.0902	**0.8689**	* 0.0002	* 0.0

(a) Macro MAE Results

# of tr	Base(b) MAE	SVOR(o) MAE	SVOR(o) p-val(b)	OB-MV MAE	OB-MV p-val(b)	p-va
30	1.0887	1.0992	* 0.0000	**0.9700**	* 0.0000	* 0.(
60	1.0887	1.0647	* 0.0000	**0.8597**	* 0.0000	* 0.(
90	1.0887	1.0406	* 0.0000	**0.8140**	* 0.0000	* 0.(
120	1.0887	1.0278	* 0.0000	**0.8083**	* 0.0000	* 0.(
150	1.0887	1.0259	* 0.0000	**0.7907**	* 0.0000	* 0.(

(b) Micro MAE Results

4. EXPERIMENTS AND ANALYSIS

We evaluated the regression-based approaches and classification-based approaches on three different datasets.

4.1 Personalized Email Prioritization

4.1.1 *Dataset and Preprocessing*

We extended the personalized email prioritization datasets of Yoo et al. [23] from 7 experimental subjects to 19 experimental subjects using our developed Thunderbird Add-ons. The original datasets were collected from Carnegie Mellon University but we recruited additional subjects from local churches and universities. We finally collected data from two faculties, six staff members, ten students, two pastors and one job seeker. We asked the subject to label at least 400 non-spam emails during one month period and suggested labeling 800 non-spam emails (or equivalently labeling 40 emails per day). We applied five importance levels (not important at all, not important, neutral, important, and very

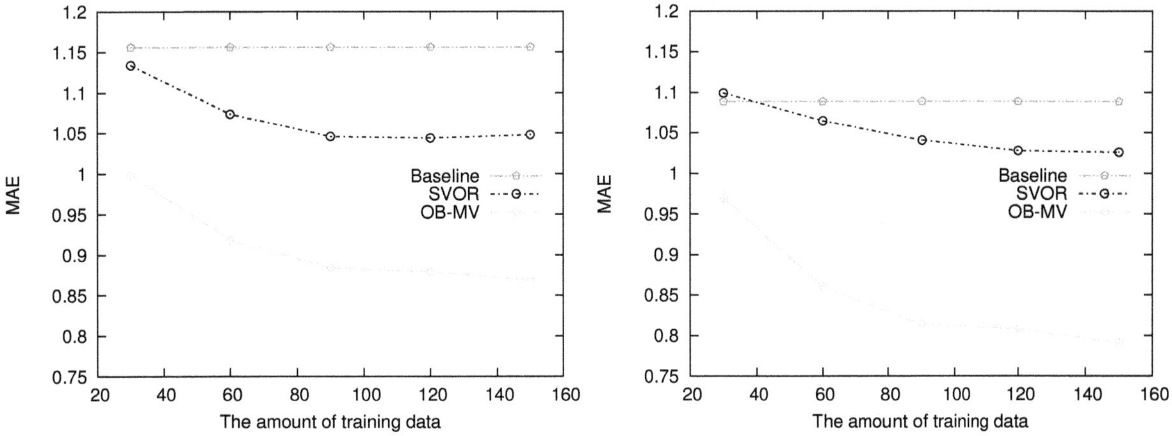

(a) Macro MAE (b) Micro MAE

Figure 5: Macro and Micro Average MAE Learning Curves with Baseline, SVOR and OB-MV

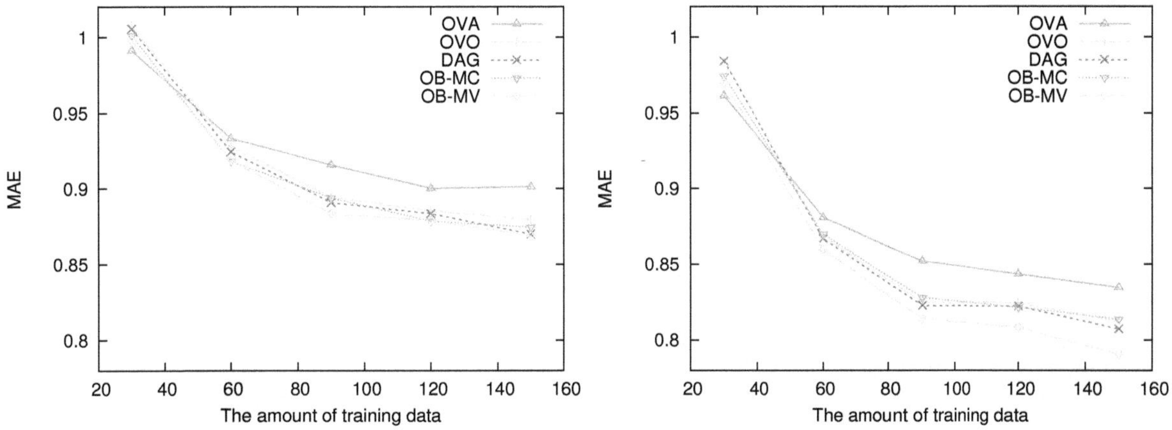

(a) Macro MAE (b) Micro MAE

Figure 6: Macro and Micro Average MAE Learning Curves Among Classification-based Approaches.

important). Table 1 shows the summary statistics of the final collected emails with labels. We split the first 150 email messages as training and the rest as testing based on the timestamp of email messages. If we did not reserve the first 150 email messages as training, then we could build prioritization models from future data and it would not be realistic.

We applied the email address canonicalization [23]. Then we preprocessed email messages by tokenization but we did not remove stop words or apply stemming. The basic features were the tokens in the sections of from, to, and cc address, title, and body text of email messages. We used *ltc* term weighting to construct a document vector per message.

Since we want to show improvement on limited amount of training data through learning curves, we randomly shuffled 150 training examples ten times and choose every 30 training email increments from 30 emails to 150 emails.

4.1.2 Estimation Models

For classification-based approaches, we used linear SVM classifiers for our base classifiers. Each classifier took the vector representation of each message as its input, and produces a score with respect to a specific importance level. We used the SVM^{light} software package and tuned the margin parameter C in the range from 10^{-3} to 10^{3} with ten-fold cross validation of training data.

For regression-based approaches, we tested only SVOR with implicit constraints [2] with linear kernel. We tested explicit constraints SVOR and other non-linear kernels but they showed worse results than implicit constraints SVOR with linear kernels. Again we only tuned regularization parameters with the same ranges of SVM classifiers.

Our baseline always predict priority level 3 out of 5 levels, which is the most common priority level on our data collection and which minimizes MAE.

4.1.3 Evaluation Metric

We use MAE (Mean Absolute Error) as the main evaluation metric, which is standard in evaluating systems that produce multi-level discrete predictions. MAE is defined as:

$$MAE = \frac{1}{N}\sum_{i=1}^{N}|y_i - \hat{y}_i| \qquad (5)$$

where N is the number of messages in the test set, y_i is true priority level and $\hat{y}_i$ is predicted priority level. Since we have five levels of importance, the MAE scores range from zero (the best possible) to four (the worst possible). There are two conventional ways to compute the performance average over multiple users. One way is pooling the test instances from all users to obtain a joint test set, and computing the MAE on the pool. This way has been called *micro-averaged* MAE. The other way is to compute the MAE on the test instances of each user and then take the average of the per-user MAE values. This way has been called as *macro-averaged* MAE. The former gives each instance an equal weight, and is possibly dominated by the system's performance on the data of a user who has the largest test set. The latter gives each user an equal weight instead. Both methods can be informative; therefore we present the evaluation results in both metrics.

We also applied a paired t-test on macro-averaged MAE and Wilcoxon signed rank test on micro-averaged MAE.

4.1.4 Results and Analysis

First of all, surprisingly, the state-of-the-art regression-based approach, SVOR, showed significantly worse performance than the performance of classification based approach, OB-MV, shown in Figure 5 and Table 2. The performance gap is not only significant but also it is statistically significant regardless of the types of significance test. It is evident that SVOR performance among machine learning models suggested that *one model assumption* did not hold on personalized email prioritization.

Second, we could validate the machine learning approaches significantly improve over baseline. In other words, we could make use of machine learning approach to improve the prediction performance of personal importance.

Third, among the classification methods, the evaluation results show that there are not many distinctions among classification based methods on Figure 6. However, OVA showed the worst performance except 30 trainings and others did notably better. Also our proposed order based approaches, especially OB-MV, showed the overall best performances among the classification approaches and the difference was statistically significant. We conjecture that order based approaches could take advantages of the partial order relations. Between DAG and OVO, DAG showed significantly better statistically but it was on limited ranges.

Suppose that we might have very limited amount of training data (less than 30 messages) and we might not be sure about *one model assumption*, we might use OVA. However, we may want to try order-based DAGs when we have more emails available. If we have to choose from popular classification-based approaches, then DAGs are a good choice given enough amount of training email messages.

4.2 Benchmark Experiments

4.2.1 Dataset and Experimental Setups

Our next research question was whether our proposed order-based approaches would work well or not on a benchmark dataset. Therefore, we tested order-based approaches along with other approaches to ordinal regression benchmark datasets generated from UCI dataset [1][1]. [1] used two collections of datasets but we tested only one of them because the size of the other collection was too small to test different training set size. The datasets were normalized to be zero mean and unit variance for each feature. The response variable was split into 10 ordinal levels using equal-size binning. Note that this procedure will satisfy ordinal regression assumption but does not guarantee fixed equal distance assumption. We randomly selected training from 25 instances to 300 instances by 25 increments and then tested on the remaining. The training and testing splits were repeated 100 times independently. Table 3 summarizes datasets and their statistics.

For classification-based approaches, we could not use SVM classifiers as our base classifiers due to the slow speed of SVM classifiers and thus we used Regularized Logistic Regression [22] due to its convergence properties and comparable accuracies and we got similar performance with regularized logistic regression performance compared to SVM classifier on benchmark datasets and [13] reported both of them showed similar performance. Again we tuned regularization parameter λ from 10^{-8} to 10^{-1}. We applied the same SVOR settings as in personalized email prioritization.

[1]http://www.gatsby.ucl.ac.uk/ chuwei/ordinalregression.html

Table 3: UCI Ordinal Regression Benchmark Dataset Statistics

Data Sets	Features	Instances
Bank Domains(1)	8	8192
Bank Domains(2)	32	8192
Computer Activities(1)	12	8192
Computer Activities(2)	21	8192
California Housing	8	15640
Census Domains(1)	8	16784
Census Domains(2)	16	16784

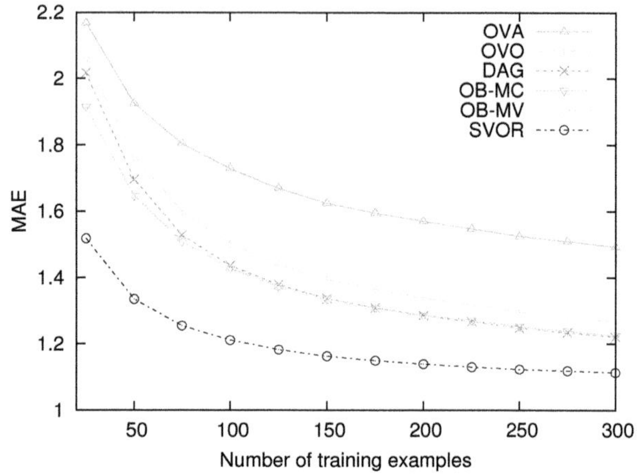

Figure 7: UCI 7 Dataset Average MAE Results

4.2.2 Results and Analysis

On the contrary to personalized email prioritization datasets, we got quite different results from UCI benchmark datasets, shown in Figure 7. First of all, SVOR showed the best performance regardless of training sizes and datasets and OVA showed the worst performance in most cases. As we observed in personalized email prioritization datasets, DAG is better than OVO. Order-Based DAGs showed better performance than DAG but the improvement is limited to the limited training size. With the limited amount of training data, order information was more helpful but with enough training data, DAG performance is similar to OB-DAG. The main

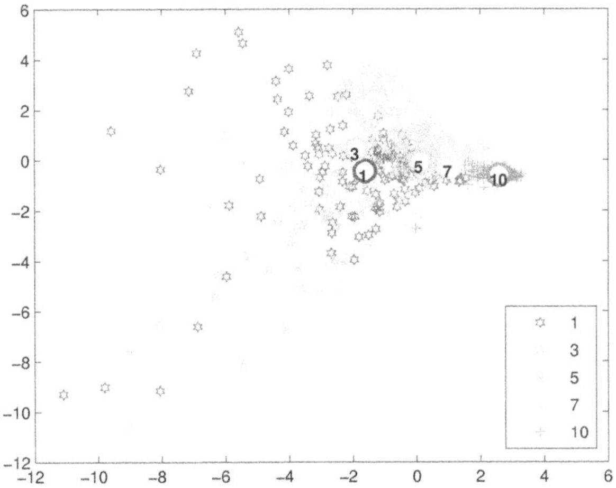

(a) PCA projection with Centroids

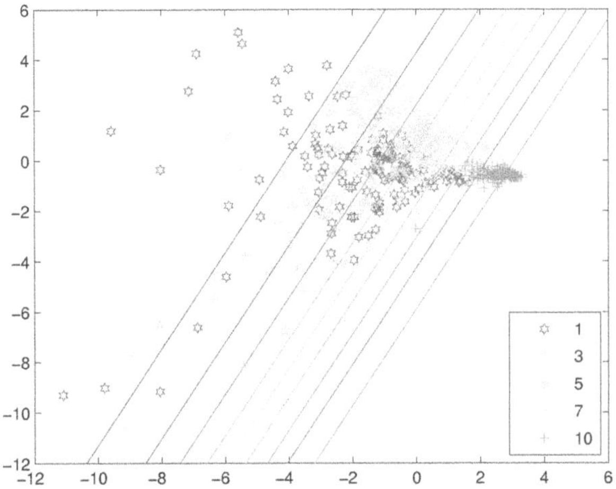

(b) PCA projection with Ordinal Regression Decision Hyperplanes

Figure 8: Computer Activities (2) on two the most correlated reduced dimensions with the response levels. The drawn lines are threshold for each ordinal levels and the fixed equal distance assumption do not hold here. Ordinal regression thresholds well captured different levels except level 1.

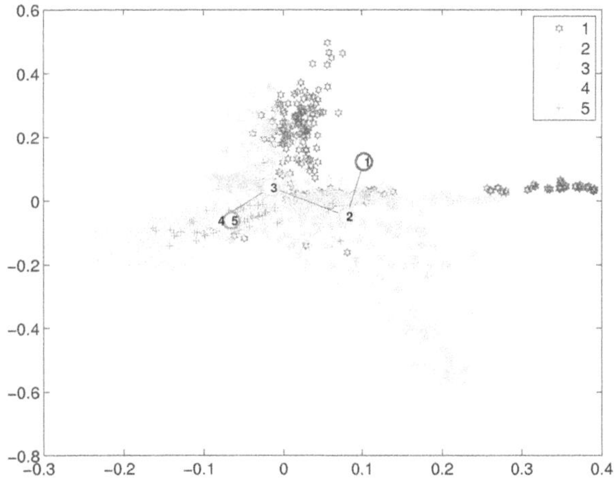

(a) PCA projection with Centroids

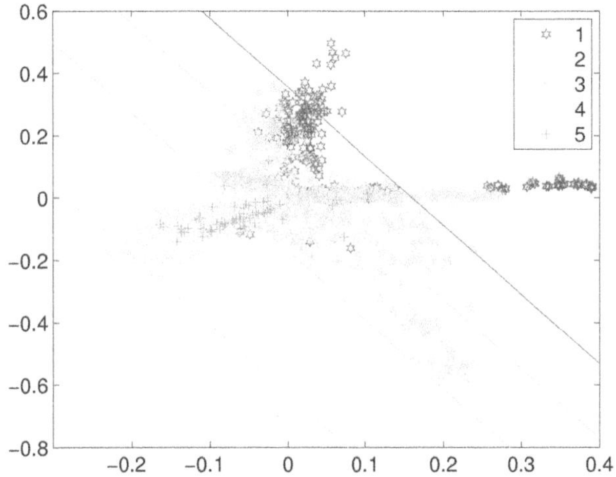

(b) PCA projection with Ordinal Regression Decision Hyperplanes

Figure 9: One user of email prioritization datasets was projected on two most correlated reduced direction with the response levels. The drawn lines are threshold for each ordinal levels. Ordinal regression thresholds captured different levels to some degree but it was not as good as CPU Activity (2).

difference between personalized email prioritization datasets and UCI datasets is whether the datasets satisfy *one model assumption* or not, discussed in the rest of Experiments Section.

4.3 Principle Component Analysis

However, it was not clear why SVOR outperformed on certain datasets but it did not outperform on the email prioritization datasets. To answer this question, we used Principal Component Analysis (PCA), which is one of the most popular dimensionality reduction approaches. We projected Email Prioritization and UCI datasets onto the two most correlated reduced dimensions with the ordinal response variable by using Pearson Correlation Coefficients. Note that this projection should be the best projection for regression based approach. We also learned decision hyperplanes of SVOR models from the projected two dimensional datasets and drew decision hyperplanes in Figure 8 and 9.

Among seven ordinal regression benchmark datasets, we focused on the Computer Activities (2) dataset because the dataset well characterized ordinal regression conditions and with the same reason, we chose one user from email prioritization datasets. We observed the data distribution looks quite different. First, the centroids of Computer Activities (2) on Figure 8(a) were well aligned as a linear line according to the ordinal levels (except level 1), resulted in good alignment with SVOR decision hyperplanes compared to email prioritization datasets where the centroids were not well aligned as the linear line, so that we had better distribution for classification decision hyperplanes. We would like to point out that there were still partial ordinal relations from email prioritization datasets, which confirmed why our proposed order-based approaches worked better than other classification approaches.

In summary, this analysis tells us whether the dataset follows *one model assumption* or not. Computer Activities (2)

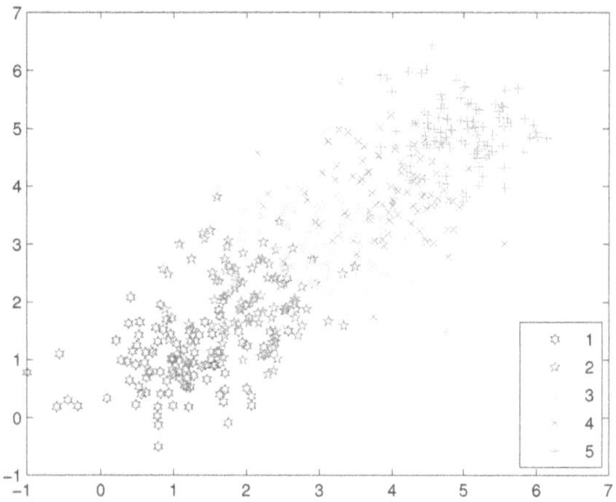

(a) Linearly Aligned Centroids on $y = x$

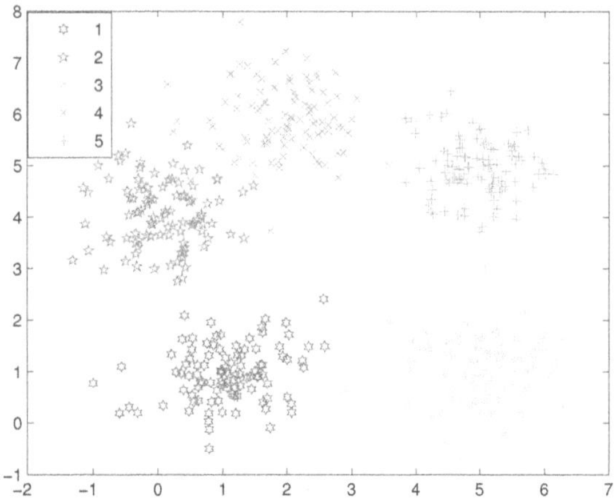

(b) Star-shaped Centroids

Figure 10: Two synthetic data generation conditions (Linear and Star)

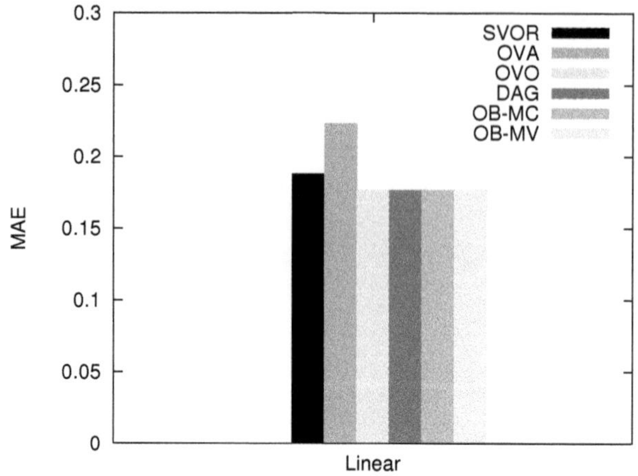

(a) Linear Results

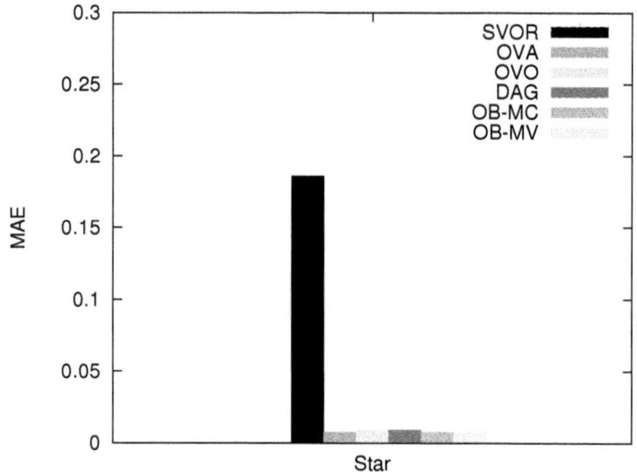

(b) Star Results

Figure 11: Experiment results of two synthetic data conditions

follows *one model assumption* pretty well, so that regression-based approaches outperformed classification based approaches. However the tested email prioritization dataset seemed not well fitted with *one model assumption*, which resulted in better classification performance.

4.4 Synthetic Experiments

4.4.1 Dataset and Experimental Setups

Although we reflected the correlations between reduced dimensions and the response variable on PCA, our two dimensional PCA analysis may not be perfect. Through our synthetic analysis experiments, we present that what we discovered is still valid on the controlled study.

We generated two dimensional Gaussian data distributions with the centroids on (1,1), (2,2), (3,3), (4,4) and (5,5) as shown in Figure 10(a). Note that it satisfies *one model assumption* and *fixed equal distance assumption* perfectly. To control the linearity of the centroid distribution, we shifted centroids from (2,2) to (0,4), from (4,4) to (2,6) and from (3,3) to (5,1), shown in Figure 10(b), which does not satisfy two regression assumptions. We repeated the above procedures 100 times independently and reported the average results. We apply the same evaluation strategy of UCI ordinal regression benchmark datasets to this synthetic datasets.

4.4.2 Results and Analysis

First of all, with linearly aligned centroids, SVOR did not show the better performance. However, SVOR showed better performance than OVA approaches. All classification approaches except OVA showed better performance than SVOR. But with more difficult cases (high signal-to-noise ratio), we observed SVOR showed better results than any other classification-based approaches, which was omitted due to limited space.

When the centroids are not linearly aligned, classification based approaches showed significantly better results than SVOR. Therefore, to be the best condition for SVOR, noisy and linearly aligned centroids are required, which is favorable for *one model assumption*.

4.5 Discussion

Although we presented only two simulation conditions for our synthetic data experiments, we could not test all possible conditions such as diverse training set size, different levels of ordinality, the skewed size distribution of different priority levels or different kinds of deviation conditions. However, we present here the most interesting results, which may not be the best but we believe it still delivers what we would like to show in this paper.

One would wonder why we did not try other kinds of regression-based approaches such as Support Vector Regression [4], Gaussian Process Ordinal Regression (GPOR) [1] or classification approaches such as Half-against-half [12]. What we chose are state-of-the-art or the most popular approaches and we believe they will have representative characteristics. For instance, suppose that GPOR was slightly better than SVOR but it would not change our main observations.

Non-linear classifiers or additional features could improve each individual approach performance but they could not change our main observation too. For instance, our test results on personalized email prioritization showed that non-linear SVOR showed severely worse results than linear-SVOR but OVA classification results were slightly improved and again overall observation was not changed.

Due to the difficulties of data collection procedures and limited data availability, our collected dataset could not reveal long-term relations such as topic or priority drifting over time here. It is an interesting topic to be investigated.

5. RELATED WORK

Pang and Lee [17] tried both OVA classification and Support Vector Regression approaches in sentiment ordinal regression problem but they also applied a simple form of re-ranking to the output of classifiers or regressions. They reported regression approaches were better for four levels but three levels preferred OVA classification and the re-ranking showed consistent improvements. Unfortunately they evaluated on only four users of Internet movie reviews and as we pointed out OVA is worst choice for classification and SVOR is better than SVR [2] due to fixed equal distance assumption. Therefore, it is hard to generalize their observation but applying re-ranking to ordinal regression might have potential to improve ordinal regressions.

Frank and Hall [6] tried to model cumulative odds of general ordinal regression by decision tree classifiers. We believe it was the first approach to handle ordinal regression problems by using classification-based approaches. However, when we tested this on our personal email prioritization datasets, it showed quite poor performance and most predictions directed to the highest or lowest priority due to its strong bias of this model assumption. Therefore, we did not include this as one of our baseline approaches.

Qin et al. [19] share the same line of thought with ours in ranking approaches. They tried multiple models instead of only one model in ranking algorithm. They also observed that ranking dataset is not satisfying one model assumption and proposed a model based on multiple models and how to aggregate multiple model results.

There are some works which utilize decision tree structures [10, 12, 5, 20, 16]. Since there are so many ways to build tree structures, most of them, [10, 12, 5, 16] utilize a form of clustering algorithms at each level. Most of them start from one root node and split it into two classes and keep splitting until there are only two classes left. However, their main concern is scalability or speeding up of multi-class classification instead of robustness of classification. In our proposed order based DAGs, we tried all possible decision paths at each level and resulted in more robust estimation with the assumption of ordinality of classification data.

6. CONCLUSIONS

Personalized email prioritization requires effective mapping from a high-dimensional input feature space to ordinal output variables. We presented a comparative study of two types of supervised learning approaches: ordinal regression-based and classification-based approaches, including a classifier cascade. Our conceptual analysis and empirical evaluations show that the effectiveness of ordinal-regression based methods crucially depend on the separability of priority classes by parallel hyperplanes, which may be too restrictive for personalized email prioritization. Classification-based methods, on the other hand, offer more general and robust solutions when complex decision boundaries are needed because they allow multiple non-parallel hyperplanes as decision functions. With the proposed OB-MV and OB-MC schemes, we effectively combine the outputs of different binary classifiers into email priority predictions, yielding significant improvements over the results of SVOR, a state-of-the-art method among ordinal-regression based approaches. Our experiments with synthetic datasets and ordinal-regression benchmark datasets further support our conclusions, and provide additional insights regarding when regression-based methods work better and when classification-based methods work better.

7. REFERENCES

[1] W. Chu and Z. Ghahramani. Gaussian processes for ordinal regression. *Journal of Machine Learning Research*, 6:1019–1041, 2005.

[2] W. Chu and S. S. Keerthi. New approaches to support vector ordinal regression. In L. D. Raedt and S. Wrobel, editors, *Machine Learning, Proceedings of the Twenty-Second International Conference (ICML 2005), Bonn, Germany, August 7-11, 2005*, volume 119 of *ACM International Conference Proceeding Series*, pages 145–152. ACM, 2005.

[3] P. J. Denning. ACM President's letter: Electronic junk. *Communications of the ACM*, 25(3):163–165, 1982.

[4] H. Drucker, C. J. C. Burges, L. Kaufman, A. J. Smola, and V. Vapnik. Support vector regression machines. In M. Mozer, M. I. Jordan, and T. Petsche, editors, *NIPS*, pages 155–161. MIT Press, 1996.

[5] B. Fei and J. Liu. Binary tree of svm: a new fast multiclass training and classification algorithm. *IEEE Transactions on Neural Networks*, 17(3):696–704, 2006.

[6] E. Frank and M. Hall. A simple approach to ordinal classification. In *EMCL '01: Proceedings of the 12th European Conference on Machine Learning*, pages 145–156, London, UK, 2001. Springer-Verlag.

[7] T. Hasegawa and H. Ohara. Automatic priority assignment to E-mail messages based on information extraction and user's action history. In R. Loganantharaj and G. Palm, editors, *Intelligent Problem Solving, Methodologies and Approaches, 13th International Conference on Industrial and Engineering Applications of Artificial Intelligence and Expert Systems, IEA/AIE 2000, New Orleans,*

Louisiana, USA, June 19-22, 2000, Proceedings, volume 1821 of *Lecture Notes in Computer Science*, pages 573–582. Springer, 2000.

[8] E. Horvitz, A. Jacobs, and D. Hovel. Attention-sensitive alerting. In K. B. Laskey and H. Prade, editors, *UAI '99: Proceedings of the Fifteenth Conference on Uncertainty in Artificial Intelligence, Stockholm, Sweden, July 30-August 1, 1999*, pages 305–313. Morgan Kaufmann, 1999.

[9] C.-W. Hsu and C.-J. Lin. A comparison of methods for multi-class support vector machines. *IEEE Transactions on Neural Networks*, 13:415–425, 2002.

[10] J. Kittler and F. Roli, editors. *Multiple Classifier Systems, Second International Workshop, MCS 2001 Cambridge, UK, July 2-4, 2001, Proceedings*, volume 2096 of *Lecture Notes in Computer Science*. Springer, 2001.

[11] B. Klimt and Y. Yang. The Enron corpus: A new dataset for email classification research. In J.-F. Boulicaut, F. Esposito, F. Giannotti, and D. Pedreschi, editors, *Machine Learning: ECML 2004, 15th European Conference on Machine Learning, Pisa, Italy, September 20-24, 2004, Proceedings*, volume 3201 of *Lecture Notes in Computer Science*, pages 217–226. Springer, 2004.

[12] H. Lei and V. Govindaraju. Half-against-half multi-class support vector machines. In N. C. Oza, R. Polikar, J. Kittler, and F. Roli, editors, *Multiple Classifier Systems*, volume 3541 of *Lecture Notes in Computer Science*, pages 156–164. Springer, 2005.

[13] F. Li and Y. Yang. A loss function analysis for classification methods in text categorization. In *Proceedings of ICML-03, 20th International Conference on Machine Learning*, Washington, DC, 2003. Morgan Kaufmann Publishers, San Francisco, US.

[14] R. Likert. A technique for the measurement of attitudes. *Archives of Psychology*, 140:1–55, 1932.

[15] Y. Liu, Y. Yang, and J. G. Carbonell. Boosting to correct inductive bias in text classification. In *CIKM*, pages 348–355. ACM, 2002.

[16] G. Madzarov, D. Gjorgjevikj, and I. Chorbev. A multi-class svm classifier utilizing binary decision tree. *Informatica*, 33(2):233–241, 2009.

[17] B. Pang and L. Lee. Seeing stars: Exploiting class relationships for sentiment categorization with respect to rating scales. In *ACL*. The Association for Computer Linguistics, 2005.

[18] J. C. Platt, N. Cristianini, and S. J. Taylor. Large margin DAGs for multiclass classification. In S. A. Solla, T. K. Leen, and K. R. Müller, editors, *Advances in Neural Information Processing Systems*, volume 12. MIT Press, 2000.

[19] T. Qin, X.-D. Zhang, D.-S. Wang, T.-Y. Liu, W. Lai, and H. Li. Ranking with multiple hyperplanes. In W. Kraaij, A. P. de Vries, C. L. A. Clarke, N. Fuhr, and N. Kando, editors, *SIGIR*, pages 279–286. ACM, 2007.

[20] A. Ramanan, S. Suppharangsan, and M. Niranjan. Unbalanced decision trees for multi-class classification. In *International Conference on Industrial and Information Systems, 2007. ICIIS 2007.*, pages 291–294, Aug. 2007.

[21] J. B. Spira and D. M. Goldes. Information overload: We have met the enemy and he is us, 2007. Basex Inc.

[22] Y. Yang, S. Yoo, J. Zhang, and B. Kisiel. Robustness of adaptive filtering methods in a cross-benchmark evaluation. In R. A. Baeza-Yates, N. Ziviani, G. Marchionini, A. Moffat, and J. Tait, editors, *SIGIR*, pages 98–105. ACM, 2005.

[23] S. Yoo, Y. Yang, F. Lin, and I.-C. Moon. Mining social networks for personalized email prioritization. In J. F. E. IV, F. Fogelman-Soulié, P. A. Flach, and M. J. Zaki, editors, *KDD*, pages 967–976. ACM, 2009.

8. ACKNOWLEDGMENT

This work is supported in parts by the Defense Advanced Research Project Agency (DARPA) under contract NBCHD03001 by the National Science Foundation (NSF) under grant IIS_070468 and by Department of Energy under contract DE-AC02-98CH10886. Any opinions, findings, conclusions or recommendations expressed in this material are those of the authors and do not necessarily reflect the views of the sponsors.

Diversification and Refinement in Collaborative Filtering Recommender *

Rubi Boim Tova Milo Slava Novgorodov
School of Computer Science
Tel-Aviv University
{boim,milo,slavanov}@post.tau.ac.il

ABSTRACT

This paper considers a popular class of recommender systems that are based on Collaborative Filtering (CF) and proposes a novel technique for diversifying the recommendations that they give to users. Items are clustered based on a unique notion of *priority-medoids* that provides a natural balance between the need to present highly ranked items vs. highly diverse ones. Our solution estimates items diversity by comparing the rankings that different users gave to the items, thereby enabling diversification even in common scenarios where no semantic information on the items is available. It also provides a natural zoom-in mechanism to focus on items (clusters) of interest and recommending diversified similar items. We present DiRec , a plug-in that implements the above concepts and allows CF Recommender systems to diversify their recommendations. We illustrate the operation of DiRec in the context of a movie recommendation system and present a thorough experimental study that demonstrates the effectiveness of our recommendation diversification technique and its superiority over previous solutions.

Categories and Subject Descriptors: H.2.8 [Database Applications]: Data mining

General Terms: Algorithms, Experimentation

Keywords: diversification, refinement, recommendations, CF

1. INTRODUCTION

Online shopping has grown rapidly over the past few years. Besides the convenience of shopping directly from one's home, an important advantage of e-commerce is the great variety of items that online stores offer. However, with such a large number of items, it becomes harder for vendors to determine which items are more relevant for a given user and, given the limited size of the screen, which of these possibly relevant items should be presented first.

Much research has been devoted recently to the development of *Recommender systems*[2]. These systems predict the rating (e.g., a grade on a scale of 1 to 5) that a user would assign to an unseen item, and consider items with a high predicted rating to be relevant. But, which of these highly rated items should be presented first to the user? A naive solution would be to simply sort the items by their estimated rating and present the top-k that fit onto the screen. This however may result in an over-specialized items list. For example, suppose that a user is interested in movie recommendations. Assume that only 5 movies may fit onto the screen and that the top-5 ranked movies, for this user, all happen to be Star Wars sequels. While the given user may indeed like this series, a more *diverse* and wider view of the highly ranked movies may be desirable. For instance one that includes a Star Wars movie, but also other movies like Star Trek or E.T., with the access to more Star Wars sequels enabled via a "more of that" zoom-in button.

This papers aims to provide precisely such diversification and zoom-in facilities. Specifically, we focus here on a popular class of recommender systems that is based of Collaborative Filtering (CF), in which user ratings to items based on previous ratings of (similar) items by (similar) users[15]. A first question that needs to be addressed when designing such a diversification mechanism is how to measure the similarity/diversity of two given items. Previous proposals are often based on the assumption that some semantic information on items (e.g. the genre of the movie, the director, the actors) is given. CF recommender systems, however, typically *do not carry such semantic information* [2]. But even if they had, a problem is that it is not always clear how to define item diversity based on a given semantic information [20]. For example, some movies of the same director/leading actor may indeed be similar, whereas others may not. To overcome this difficulty, we follow the CF approach [15, 17] and instead of relying on semantic information, determine items similarity (and correspondingly diversity) based solely on ratings that previous users gave to the items. Intuitively, each item here is viewed as a vector of ratings, with vector distance (measured, e.g., by cosine, L^i distance, or Pearson correlation coefficient) used as measure of similarity/diversity.

A second important challenge is the need to balance, when choosing items, between two possibly conflicting objectives: presenting highest ranked items vs. choosing highly diverse ones. Some previous works attempted to resolve this by assigning a weight to each objective and selecting an items set that maximizes the weighted sum[9]; others used thresholds to bound the allowed similarity between items and the drop in rank [16]. But the difficult question always is *which weights or thresholds to choose*?. Indeed, a manual tuning of weights/thresholds (e.g. by experimentation) for a given data set is not only time consuming but is also no longer effective when the data changes [9]. To solve this problem we propose here a novel approach that *avoids the use of weights/thresholds altogether*. We introduce the notion of *priority-medoids*, an adaptation of the classical notion of *medoids*[11] to a context where items have pri-

*This work was partly supported by the EU project Mancoosi, by the Israel Science Foundation and by the US-Israel Binational Science Foundation.

CIKM'11, October 24–28, 2011, Glasgow, Scotland, UK.

orities (ratings). *Priority-medoids* (to be defined formally in the sequel) allow for natural clustering of items and the selection of cluster representatives that balance rank and diversity. The clustering further allows the realization of an intuitive "zoom-in" mechanism, where users can focus on specific items on the screen and view similar recommended items. Priority-medoids sub-clustering is then be used, recursively, to diversify their presentation (and to allow further zooming-in).

To best of our knowledge, the only other previous algorithm without weights/threshold is Algorithm Greedy of [16], which does not support zoom-in. The tradeoff between ranking and diversity is hard-coded in the algorithm without any declarative notion of optimality. An advantage of a declarative definition is that it is not tied to a particular algorithm and thus allows for formal analysis and optimization. While we show that identifying the optimal priority-medoids is NP-hard, we present an efficient (ptime) heuristic based on *priority cover-trees*, a particular sub-class of cover-trees [4] that proves to be extremely effective in this context. Our experiments show that the representatives chosen by our algorithms, with no need for weights tuning whatsoever, are as good and sometimes even superior to those obtained even with optimally-tuned weights of previous algorithms. We further present an optimization technique that exploits the properties of our algorithm for an efficient realization of the above mentioned "zoom-in" mechanism.

DiRec . To demonstrate the effectiveness of our approach, we implemented the above solution in the DiRec prototype system. DiRec is designed as a plug-in that can be deployed on CF-based recommender systems, and was demonstrated in [7]. [7] provides a high-level description of the system, while the current paper presents the underlying model and algorithms.

Related Work. As explained above, a recommendations list that consists of the items with top-k predicted ratings may suffer from over specialization. Indeed, [19] evaluated the diversity of top-k items generated by traditional CF algorithms and showed it to be fairly low. Several algorithms that attempt to diversify the recommendation were proposed in the literature (see [9] for a survey). They fall generally into two classes: *greedy heuristics*, where the recommendation list is constructed "one-by-one" by maximizing a given distance function at each step (e.g. [10, 20, 16]), and *interchange (Swap) heuristics*, where an initial list is first constructed and then refined by a series of actions (e.g. [17, 16]). But common to most is the use of *predefined weights or thresholds* to determine the balances between ranking and diversity or to bound the allowed similarity between items and the drop in rank [10, 20, 17, 18]. While the selected weights/thresholds clearly affects the performance of the algorithms, their precise choice is left open in all the works we are aware of. Such use of weights/thresholds is problematic since their manual tuning (e.g. by experimentation) for a given data set is not only time consuming but is also no longer effective when the data changes [9]. As explained above, our solution employs, instead, priority medoids, to declaratively capture the desired balance. This is in contrast to [16] where the tradeoff is hard-coded in the algorithm. It further has the advantage of allowing for a natural (and optimizable) zoom-in mechanism.

The importance of results diversification has been recognized also in the context of database queries [8, 14, 12]. For example, [8] proposes a notion of diversity over structured query results which are post-processed and organized in a decision tree to help users navigate them; [14] uses attributes content to group tuples in a meaningful way that allows for convenient data exploration. This line of works however relays heavily on the *structured data content*. But such structured (semantic) information is *not available* in CF Recommender systems. Our work alleviates this problem by adopting the CF approach and relying on CF (dis)similarity measures rather than semantic ones.

The most relevant to our work, although also targeted to structured databases, is [12], where the authors used the notion of classical medoids (approximated by classical cover-trees) to select representatives for the query results and to zoom in on similar answers. While our work was inspired by [12], a key difference is that [12] *completely ignores tuples rating/priority*. We will see that our use of *priority* medoids and, resp., *priority* cover-trees, over the classical ones, prove to be extremely effective and greatly improves that generated recommendations.

Contributions. The technical contributions of this paper can be summarized as follows:

- We introduce the novel notion of priority-medoids as a tool for selecting item representatives. Our approach naturally balances the rating and the diversity of the recommended items and is applicable even in the absence of semantic information (as often is the case is CF recommender systems).
- We show that finding optimal priority-medoids is NP-hard and provide an alternative effective heuristic based on priority cover-trees.
- We exploit the properties of our algorithm to design an efficient, incremental zoom-in mechanism that allows to focus on individual items, identify their neighborhood (similar) items and select appropriate representatives for them.
- We demonstrates the superiority of our solution relative to previous algorithms as well as its efficiency.

The paper is organized as follows. Section 2 presents priority-medoids. Section 3 then explains how they are approximated and how item representatives are selected. Section 4 describes the zoom-in mechanism,and our experiments are described in Section 5 . Finally, we conclude in Section 6. For space constraints, some details of the algorithms and the experiments are omitted and can be found in the full version of the paper [6].

2. PRIORITY-MEDOIDS

We start by providing the needed background and notation for Collaborative Filtering (CF). We then consider the problem of balancing the ratings and the diversity of the recommended items and define priority-medoids.

2.1 Collaborative Filtering

Common CF algorithms are *item-based*, consisting of two main steps: (1) choosing for each item a *neighborhood* of similar items, and (2) predicting the rating that a user u will give to an item i using some aggregation function on the actual ratings, gave by u, to the items within the neighborhood of i [15]. Symmetric *user-based* variants also exist but are less frequently used [15]. A key ingredient in the algorithm is thus the estimation of similarity between two items. Intuitively, each item is viewed as a vector of ratings in a multi-dimensional speace, where each dimension corresponds to a given user, (recording her rating of that item). The distance between item vectors is then used as a measure for the items similarity. In principle, any distance measure can be employed here (e.g. Cosine or L^i distance) but Pearson's correlation coefficient [13] seems to be the preferred choice in most major systems. The basic intuition behind Pearson's measure is to give a high similarity score for two items that tend to be rated the same by many users. In the reminder of this paper we use $rate(u, i)$ do denote the predicted

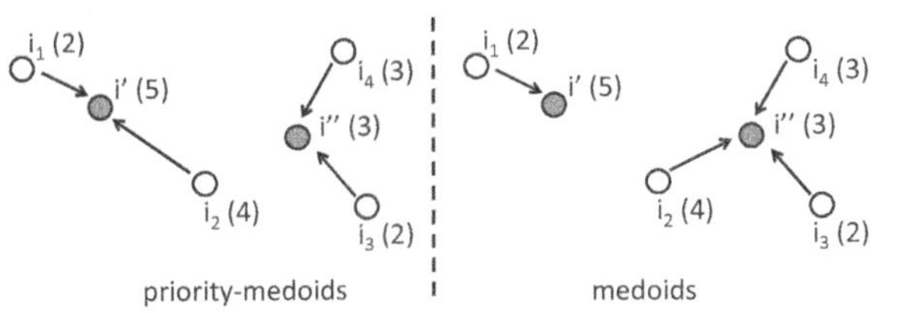

Figure 1: Priority-medoid vs. standard medoid

rating of a user u to item i. When u is known from the context we omit it and simply write $rate(i)$. We use $dist(i, j)$ to denote the distance between items i and j. W.l.o.g. we assume below that distance values are in the range of $[0, 1]$. (When this is not the case one may naturally map the values to this range). The smaller the distance is, the more similar (and less diverse) are the items.

2.2 Balancing Rating and Distance

We can now describe our main problem: given a set I of items and a size k, where the former holds the most relevant items for a given user (as decided by the given CF recommender system) and the latter denotes the number of items fitted onto the screen, we need to choose the subset $I_k \subseteq I$ (of size k) that will be presented to the user. A naive solution simply selects the top-k items with the highest $rate()$ values, namely the ones who maximize the sum $\sum_{i \in I_k} rate(i)$. This however may result in an over-specialized subset, as described in the Introduction. Thus, we should consider the diversity of the items as well, which may be analogically measured by the sum $\sum_{i,j \in I_k} dist(i, j)$. As these are two opposing measures, one needs to provide a good balance between the two. Additionally, this subset should also provide a good coverage for the entire set I, which intuitively can be viewed as a classic clustering problem, where we need to minimize the distances between the items in I and the "center" of the cluster they belong to.

Our solution, as mentioned in the Introduction, is based on the notion of *priority-medoids*, an adaptation of the classical notion of medoids to this context. To explain this, let us first briefly (and informally) recall what standard medoids are. Consider a set I of items split into k disjoint subsets, referred to as clusters. The *medoid* of a given cluster (also called the cluster's representative) is an element in the cluster s.t. the sum of the distances from it to the other items in the cluster is minimal. Other variants that consider e.g. the average, min or max distance, also exist [11]. This sum is called the cluster's weight. The classical goal is to find a clustering that minimize the overall sum of cluster weights. Note that, given a set $I_k \subseteq I$ of k items in I, the minimal-weight clustering for which the I_k items serve as representatives (medoids), is one where each item $i \in I$ is associated (clustered) with the element in I_k that is closest to it. Thus to find the best clustering one essentially needs to identify the best I_k set.

In our context we are interested in representatives with high rating. Priority-medoids therefore add the requirement that the representatives are the ones having *highest rating* in their corresponding clusters. Thus, when considering a set I_k of priority-medoids, the clusters it forms are different than the ones formed when considering standard medoids.

More formally, consider a subset $I_k \subseteq I$ of size k of items, s.t. I_k contains, among others, an item having the highest rating in I. We will explain below why having such an item in I_k is important. For an element $i \in I$, we denote by $rep(i)$ the item within I_k satisfying the following two constraints:

- the rating of $rep(i)$ is greater or equal to that of i
- among all items in I_k satisfying the above, $rep(i)$ is the closest to i, namely there is no other $j \in I_k$ with $dist(i, j) < dist(i, rep(i))$.

The items with the same representative $rep(i)$ form a cluster, and thus I_k yields a clustering formation for the items of I. We refer to the items in I_k as the *priority-medoids* of their corresponding clusters. Note that the fact that the highest rated element in I is a member of I_k guarantees that all elements in I indeed have a cluster to which they may belong.

EXAMPLE 2.1. *The example in Figure 1 illustrates the difference between the cluster formation in regular medoids and that of priority-medoids. Assume that $k = 2$ and that the set I_k consists of the two items i' and i''. Also assume that the euclidian distance between items describes their similarity. The number in parenthesis, next to each item, describes its rating. On the right (resp. left) hand side we see the clusters formed when the items in I_k are treated as regular (resp. priority-) medoids. The arrows outgoing the elements $i_1 - i_4$ point to their cluster representative. On the right hand side (regular medoids) items i_2,i_3 and i_4 are clustered with i'', as they are closer to it than to i'. i_1 is clustered with i'. In contrast, on the left hand side (priority-medoids), the clustering formation is different as the item ratings are now also being considered. Specifically, since the rating of i'' is lower than that of i_2, i_2 is clustered with (and represented by) i', that has higher rating, even though it is slightly further.*

The quality of the obtained clustering (and thereby the quality of the set I_k of priority-medoids that yielded the clustering), is measured, as before, by the distance of the items to the corresponding cluster representatives, namely by $\Sigma_{i \in I} dist(i, rep(i))$. When I is known from the context, we use a simplified notation and denote this sum by $weight(I_k)$. As for standard medoids, the lower the weight, the better the clustering (and the set I_k of priority-medoids) is. We are thus interested in a set I_k with minimal $weight(I_k)$. However, we point out that there may be several sets with the same minimal weight, in which case we break the tie by choosing the one where rating values are lexicographically higher.

For example, assume $k = 3$ and we have two sets $I_3 = \{i_1, i_2, i_3\}$, $I'_3 = \{i'_1, i'_2, i'_3\}$, where $weight(I_3) = weight(I'_3)$. If the rating values of the three elements in I_3 (resp. I'_3), sorted in decreasing order are $5, 4, 1$, (resp. $5, 3, 2$) then we choose I_3 over I'_3. (An alternative could be to prefer, e.g., item sets with higher average/sum of rating). Ties may still occur when distinct items have the same rating, in which case we break it arbitrarily.

We can show that identifying the best priority-medoids is NP-hard (proof is omitted). We thus use a heuristic, based on *priority cover-trees* - an adaptation of the classical cover-trees [4] to our context. We explain this next.

3. PRIORITY COVER-TREE

A cover-tree is a data structure originally designed to speed up a nearest neighbor search [4]. The use of cover-trees as a tool for selecting (regular) medoids was recently proposed in [12], in the context of diversification of query results. A key difference from the present work is that *item ratings were not taken into consideration*. We next show that a fairly simple modification to the algorithm of [12] allows to account for such ratings and thereby gradely improve the quality of the generated recommendations.

A conventional cover-tree can be thought of as a hierarchy of levels, where each node corresponds to a specific item, and each level is a "cover" for the level beneath it. (The root is at level zero, its children at level one, and so on). Each node in the tree is associated with an item in I. An item can be associated with multiple nodes but can appear at most once in every level l. A conventional cover-tree obeys, for all levels, the first three invariants below. In our algorithms we use a special sub-class of these trees, which we call *priority* cover-trees, that further obey the *forth invariant*.

1. (Nesting) If a node is associated with an item i, then one of its children must also be associated with i.
2. (Separation) All nodes at level l are at least $\frac{1}{2^l}$ far from one another.
3. (Covering) Each node at level l is within distance $\frac{1}{2^l}$ to its children in level $l+1$.
4. (Priority) Each node has a rating higher or equal to that of any of its children.

An example for such a tree can be found in [6]. Next, we explain the role that invariant 4 plays in our algorithms for constructing priority-cover trees and for selecting items representatives, based on the constructed tree.

3.1 Construction

We first recall the conventional algorithm for cover-tree construction [4], then explain the needed modifications.

Given a set I of items, the standard algorithm first selects one item, arbitrarily, to serve as the root of the tree. Then it inserts the other items, iteratively, one by one (again in an arbitrary order), into the tree using an `Insert Single Item` function. For each item, the function finds the upper-most level into which the given item can be inserted, in a recursive fashion. Intuitively, it traverse the tree top-down, level-by-level, where at each step it maintains a set of nodes which can act as possible ancestors for the given item. These nodes are the ones whose descendants may potentially preserve the first three cover-tree invariants describe above. The given item is finally added once the algorithm reaches a point in the tree where all these invariants hold.

Now, to construct our *priority* cover-tree, only two simply changes to this algorithm are required:

- *Ordered Insertion.* In the conventional cover-tree construction algorithm, items are inserted in an arbitrary order. Instead, our algorithm first sorts the items w.r.t their ratings, then inserts them in descending order.
- *Tight Insertion.* In the original algorithm, at the point when the algorithm finally inserts the given item into the tree, it may have several candidate nodes that may act as the item's parent. As any node in this set is a 'legal' parent (in the sense that the invariants will be preserved), the original algorithm chooses among them arbitrary. In contrast, our refined algorithm always prefers the node with the smallest $dist()$ measure to the inserted items.

For space constraints the full details of the algorithm, as well as its correctness proof, are deferred to [6]. We only note here that ordered insertion suffices to guarantee Invariant 4. Tight insertion, on the other hand, is not mandatory for the correctness of the construction. However it will prove useful later, when considering recommendations refinement (zoom-in). We discuss this issue in more detail in Section 4.

3.2 Representative Selection

We next explain how the constructed priority cover-tree is used to select item representatives. We use below the following notations. Given a node n in the tree and an integer $l \geq 0$, we say that n is at level l in the tree, if the distance between n and the root of the tree (counted by the number of edges on the path between them) is l. We use C_l to denote the set of nodes at level l.

The pseudo-code of the algorithm is given in [6] and we sketch below the key ideas. Consider a set I of items which the CF recommender determined as most relevant for a given user. As explained above, the k items that we want to present to users are the priority-medoids of I. To find such a subset, with low weight, we use the priority cover-tree of I as follows: Starting from the tree root, we search for the first level l within the tree that includes at least k nodes, namely where $|C_{l-1}| < k$ and $|C_l| \geq k$. We then choose our k representatives from within C_l. Recall that due to the structure of the priority cover-tree the nodes in C_i are at least $\frac{1}{2^l}$ far from one another and have rating higher than their descendants. If C_l contains exactly k nodes, then we simply choose these nodes for representatives and we are done. Otherwise, we need to select a subset of size k. To select good representatives, we use the tree structure: Recall the *nesting* property of the tree, which implies that $C_{l-1} \subseteq C_l$. Moreover, because of the hierarchical structure of the tree, the nodes (items) within C_{l-1} have rating $\geq$ than those in C_l and are pairwise further apart from each other than from the remaining nodes. Thus, we first select the nodes (items) in C_{l-1}, then add the remaining $k - |C_{l-1}|$ from within $C_l - C_{l-1}$. We consider in our implementation and experiments three alternative methods for choosing these additional elements:

- *Max-rating* - the elements having the maximal ratings,
- *Max-diversity* - the elements that are farthest from the previously chosen elements, and
- *Max-coverage* - the elements having the maximal number of descendants.

Note that, during the tree construction, we can easily record the number of descendants each node has, and use this information for the implementation of the Max-coverage variant. Thus, all three options are equivalent in terms of computational effort. They may differ however, as we shall see later, in the quality of the generated representatives set.

4. RECOMMENDATION REFINEMENT

Alongside each item (representative) i that is presented on the screen, DiRec offers a "more of that" zoom-in button that allows the user to view further related items.

One possible approach for identifying such items in I is to select the ones whose distance from i (as measured by the $dist()$ function) is below a certain threshold. However, as it is never obvious which threshold should one choose, we take, instead, an alternative approach based on the following intuition: when a user clicks on a specific item i, she not only signals her interest in item's i family but also signals that i interests her more than the other $k-1$ presented representatives. Recalling the clustering formation generated by the presented representatives (priority-medoids), we determine the items in the cluster represented by i as relevant, denoting this set by $relevant(i)$.

Here again, the set $relevant(i)$ often contains more items than could fit on the screen and a subset needs to be chosen, to be presented to the user.

A straightforward approach to choose k representatives for $relevant(i)$ is to build a priority cover-tree for the set, then use it to select representatives, as described above. Rather than doing so, we employ instead an optimized, significantly more efficient, algorithm that is based on the following observation: In the priority cover-tree previously constructed for I, most of the elements in $relevant(i)$ already appear in subtree rooted at i. Indeed, the *tight Insertion* used in to the construction algorithm (Section 3.1) was employed precisely to increase the number of such elements. We thus use this subtree as a basis for the construction of the priority cover-tree of $relevant(i)$. Note however that the subtree may not include all the members of $relevant(i)$ and also it might include some redundant elements that are not members of $relevant(i)$. Full details of the algorithm is available at [6].

5. EXPERIMENTS

We have implemented the above algorithms in DiRec [7], a plug-in that allows CF Recommender systems to diversify the recommendations that they present to users. We used DiRec in a variety of settings to evaluate the described algorithms by (1) a user study, (2) empirical evaluations, (3) performance measures and (4) refinement process. Due to space constraints, we present in this paper the results only for (2) and a short summary for (1). Nevertheless, the full description of all experiments are available at [6] for the intrigue readers.

Experiments setting. In our experiments, DiRec was employed on top of a CF-based recommender system (C2F [5]). For estimating item similarity, C2F (and thus DiRec) uses Pearson's correlation coefficient [13]. We used a natural linear inverse mapping to compute items distance out of their Pearson correlation value: $dist(i, j) = (1 - Pearson(i, j))/2$. The experiments were preformed on an Intel quad-core machine (Q9400) with 2.66 GHz CPUs, (using only a single core of the CPU), 4GB memory and windows XP x64 edition. As data, we used a real-life data set from the cinema domain, provided by Netflix [3], which contains over 100 million distinct raw movie ratings (such as 1 to 5 "stars"), by almost 500,000 users, and no semantic information on the movies.

Algorithms. Our algorithm for representatives selection first constructs a priority cover tree, then chooses representatives out of this tree. We consider the three variants of this choice: Max-rating, Max-diversity and Max-coverage, denoted below *PCT-R*, *PCT-D* and *PCT-C*, respectively. (PCT stands for Priority Cover-Tree). As we have mentioned, our use of *priority* cover-tree, instead of the classical cover-tree of [12], allows to take items rating into consideration. To illustrate the resulting improvement in the quality of the generated recommendations we had also implemented the cover-tree algorithm of [12], denoted below *CT*.

Recall that previous works typically use semantic information, to diversify items, and predefined weights/thresholds, to balance between rating and diversity. Since no sematic information is available in our context, one can employ here only algorithms that operate without it. We have implemented the state of the art such algorithms from [16] (*Greedy* and *Swap*) and compared them to ours. Note that Algorithm Swap, like all other previous works (except for Algorithm Greedy), use predefined thresholds to balance rating and diversity. We had thus first optimized the thresholds ([6]) and had our algorithms compete against these optimized versions. The results for *Greedy* and *Swap* were similar and we thus show below only those of *Swap*. (Interested readers can find a brief description of the algorithm in [6]).

Finally, as a base line, we had also implemented the two "extreme case" algorithms, *optR* (for Optimal Rating), which operated like a standard CF algorithm, selecting the k items having highest rating and ignoring diversity, and *optD* (for Optimal Diversity), which ignores the rating of items and selects k items whose pairwise distance values is the highest. [1]

[1]Note that *optD* require solving an NP-hard problem [9]. Its EXP-time algorithm iterates over all subsets of size k to find the best one. In our experiments this became infeasible for items sets of size $\geq$ 100, and we thus show results for them only up to that size.

User Study. To assess the quality of the item sets that DiRec generates (and thereby the quality of our algorithms), we ran a set of experiments with 50 volunteers who were asked to evaluate the quality of the presented movie recommendations. Due to space constrains, we only note the final results of the experiment (for a full description see [6]). Algorithm *PCT-R* got the highest results, with *PCT-C*, *Swap* and *PCT-D* not so far behind. Not surprisingly, these four algorithms got much higher results than *optR*, *optD* and *CT*, as they consider both the relevance and the diversity of the items (while the others focus solely on one property). While the grade difference between *PCT-R* and *Greedy* is smaller, recall that the former has further the advantage of supporting a natural zoom-in mechanism.

5.1 Empirical Evaluation

To better understand the results and how the *PCT* algorithms (and the preferred *PCT-R* in particular) balance ranking and diversity, we run a second set of experiments over the Netflix data where we analyzed the quality the item sets generated by all the algorithms, in terms of their rating and diversity. In each set of experiments reported below we randomly chose a set of 1000 users from the Netflix data set and run the experiment for each of them. The results presented here are the average of all 1000 users. (The variance was less that 5%). We ran all experiments for varying size I of item candidates returned by the CF-system (I ranging from 10 to 1000) and varying number k of representative items selects out of them (k ranging from 3 to 20). The results were generally independent of the number k of selected representative. Thus, except when stated otherwise, we present below a representative sample for $k = 5$, the common number of recommendations given by typical recommender systems. For a generated set I_k of representatives, we evaluated its quality w.r.t to the following measures.

Rating. We measure the relevance of the suggested set of item I_k to the current user by the sum of the element ratings, i.e. $rating(I_k) = \sum_{i \in I_k} rate(i)$. (Higher value means better results).

Diversity. In the absence of semantic information, the diversity of the items in I_k may be measured by the pairwise-distances of the items, namely $diversity(I_k) = \sum_{i,j \in I_k} dist(i, j)$. (Here too, higher value means better results).

Although our algorithms do not require semantic information, it is interesting to examine the actual semantic diversity of the selected items. To get a sense of this, we extracted for each movie information from the Internet Movie Databases IMDb [1] and used it to determine, for each movie, to which of series it belongs (if any). We also extracted the movie's genre (action, drama, etc.). For diversification, it is intuitively preferable not to have multiple movie sequels in the set presented to the user, and to have movies from different genres. We quantify this as follows.

- We denote below by $sequel(i)$ the series to which an item (movie) i belongs. We count the number of distinct series to which the movies in I_k belong and divide this by k, the number of movies in I_k. Namely, $sequelDivers(I_k) = \frac{|\{sequel(i)|i \in I_k\}|}{k}$. Observe that $sequelDivers$ is a number in the range of $(0:1]$. Higher values reflect higher diversity, hence better result.

- We assume some total order (e.g. lexicographical) on the possible move genres and denote by $genres(i)$ a boolean vector that records the (possibly multiple) genres of the movie i. (A value 1 in entry j means that the movie i belongs to genre i). To measure diversity we consider the pairwise dis-

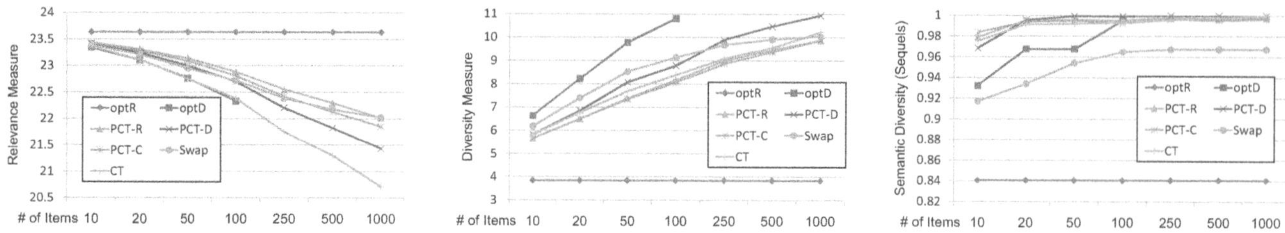

Figure 2: (a) Rating measure **(b) Distance-based diversity** **(b) Semantic (sequel) diversity**

	Rating	Distance-based diversity	Sequel diversity
PCT-D	-	+	=
PCT-C	-	=	=
Swap	-	+	-
CT	- -	=	=
optR	++	- -	- -
optD	- -	++	-

Table 1: Summary of the results (relative PCT-C)

tances (by the Cosine measure) between the vectors. Then, $genreDivers(I_k) = 1 - average\{cosine(genres(i), genres(j)) \mid i, j \in I_k\}$. Here again $genreDivers$ is a number in the range of $(0 : 1]$ with higher values reflecting higher diversity.

Figure 2 shows the values for the relevance, distance-based diversity, and sequel-based diversity, for the various algorithms, for varying sizes of item sets I. The results for genre-based diversity are similar to those of sequel-based one and are thus omitted for space constraints. The figure depicts these values, for the sets computed by the seven algorithms mentioned before: *PCT-R*, *PCT-D*, *PCD-C*, *Swap* (with its tuned threshold), *CT*, *optR* and *optD*. *k* here equals 5 and the size of the set *I* ranges from 10 to 1000.[2]

Recall that higher values here mean better results. Diversity generally increases when *I* grows, as there are more items to choose from; Rating decreases, as more diverse but lower ranked items are chosen. Table 1 provides a summary of the graphs in Figure 2 that highlights how the various algorithms perform (for the various measures) relative to *PCT-R*, and helps to explain why users may have found its results superior. For an algorithm *A* and measure M, an "+" (resp. "++") entry indicates that Algorithm *A* generally performed slightly (significantly) better than *PCT-R* in measure M. Similarly, "−" (resp. "−−") indicates that *A* performed slightly (significantly) worse than *PCT-R* in M. An "=" entry indicates similar performance.

As expected *optR* have the highest rating value and lowest diversity. Analogously, *optD* has lowest rating value and highest distance-based diversity. *CT* too has lowest rating value as it ignores item ranks. An interesting point to observe is that although some algorithms (and in particular *optD*) achieve better distance-based diversity than *PCT-R*, no algorithm achieves better sequel diversity. This discrepancy occurs, intuitively, because *optD* tries to maximize the *total sum* of distances without considering the (minimal) distance between two individual representatives (and thus may select two sequels in the same set). For a concrete example see [6]. The same phenomenon occurs more generally in many real life cases and explains why *PCT-R* is not handicapped by its non optimal distance diversity. Indeed, its sequel diversity is close to 1 (meaning that, as desired, the result contains no sequels) and we can see that no other algorithm was able to achieve better semantic (sequel) diversity. Furthermore, among the algorithms that achieve sequel diversity equal to that of *PCT-R*, it is the one with highest rating score, which can explain why its recommendations were more favorable than the rest.

[2]Recall that *optD* became infeasible for items sets of size greater than 100, and we thus show results for them only up to that size.

6. CONCLUSION

The DiRec plug-in presented in this paper allows CF recommender systems to diversify the recommendations that they present to users. It is based on a novel notion of priority-medoids that declaratively balances the rating and the diversity of the recommended items. We introduced priority cover-trees as a tool for efficient selection of item representatives. Our solution further allows for an effective realization of a natural "zoom-in" mechanism, presenting to users similar yet diversified items. Our experiments demonstrated the effectiveness of our recommendation diversification technique and its superiority over previous proposals.

DiRec provides an effective solution in common scenarios where semantic information is unavailable. Combining our ratings-based (quantitative) approach with a semantic (qualitative) one, when such semantic data is available, is an intriguing future research direction.

7. REFERENCES

[1] Imdb interface. *http://www.imdb.com/interfaces/*.
[2] G. Adomavicius and A. Tuzhilin. Towards the next generation of recommender systems. *IEEE TKDE*, 2005.
[3] J. Bennet and S. Lanning. The netflix prize. *KDD Cup*, 2007.
[4] A. Beygelzimer, S. Kakade, and J. Langford. Cover trees for nearest neighbor. *ICML*, 2006.
[5] R. Boim, H. Kaplan, T. Milo, and R. Rubinfeld. Improved recommendations via (more) collaboration. *WebDB*, 2010.
[6] R. Boim, T. Milo, and S. Novgorodov. Diversification and refinement in collaborative filtering recommender (full version). *http://www.cs.tau.ac.il/boim/publications/cikm11-full.pdf*.
[7] R. Boim, T. Milo, and S. Novgorodov. Direc: Diversified recommendations for semantic-less collaborative filtering. *ICDE*, 2011.
[8] Z. Chen and T. Li. Addressing diverse user preferences in sql-query-result navigation. *SIGMOD*, 2007.
[9] M. Drosou and E. Pitoura. Search result diversification. *SIGMOD Record*, 2010.
[10] S. Gollapudi and A. Sharma. An axiomatic approach for result diversification. *WWW*, 2009.
[11] L. Kaufman and P. Rousseeuw. Finding groups in data: An introduction to cluster analysis. *Wiley's Series in Probability and Statistics*, 1990.
[12] B. Liu and H. Jagadish. Using trees to depict a forest. *VLDB*, 2009.
[13] J. L. Rodgers and W. A. Nicewander. Thirteen ways to look at the correlation coefficient. *The American Statistician*, 1988.
[14] J. Stoyanovich, S. Amer-Yahia, and T. Milo. Making interval-based clustering rank-aware. *to appear in EDBT*, 2011.
[15] X. Su and T. Khoshgoftaar. A survey of collaborative filtering techniques. *Advances in Artificial Intelligence*, 2009.
[16] C. Yu, L. Lakshmanan, and S. Amer-Yahia. It takes variety to make a world: Diversification in recommender systems. *EDBT*, 2009.
[17] C. Yu, L. Lakshmanan, and S. Amer-Yahia. Recommendation diversification using explanations. *ICDE*, 2009.
[18] M. Zhang and N. Hurley. Avoiding monotony: Improving the diversity of recommendation lists. *RecSys*, 2008.
[19] M. Zhang and N. Hurley. Evaluating the diversity of top-n recommendations. *ICTAI*, 2009.
[20] C.-N. Ziegler, S. M. McNee, J. A. Konstan, and G. Lausen. Improving recommendation lists through topic diversification. *WWW*, 2005.

Emerging Topic Detection using Dictionary Learning

Shiva Prasad Kasiviswanathan
IBM T.J. Watson Research
kasivisw@gmail.com

Prem Melville
IBM T.J. Watson Research
pmelvil@us.ibm.com

Arindam Banerjee
University of Minnesota
banerjee@cs.umn.edu

Vikas Sindhwani
IBM T.J. Watson Research
vsindhw@us.ibm.com

ABSTRACT

Streaming user-generated content in the form of blogs, microblogs, forums, and multimedia sharing sites, provides a rich source of data from which invaluable information and insights maybe gleaned. Given the vast volume of such social media data being continually generated, one of the challenges is to automatically tease apart the emerging topics of discussion from the constant background chatter. Such emerging topics can be identified by the appearance of multiple posts on a unique subject matter, which is distinct from previous online discourse. We address the problem of identifying emerging topics through the use of dictionary learning. We propose a two stage approach respectively based on detection and clustering of novel user-generated content. We derive a scalable approach by using the alternating directions method to solve the resulting optimization problems. Empirical results show that our proposed approach is more effective than several baselines in detecting emerging topics in traditional news story and newsgroup data. We also demonstrate the practical application to social media analysis, based on a study on streaming data from Twitter.

Categories and Subject Descriptors

H.0 [**Information Systems**]: General

General Terms

Algorithms, Design, Performance

1. INTRODUCTION

The wide-spread popularity of social media, such as blogs and Twitter, has made it the focal point of online discussion and breaking news. Given the speed at which such user-generated content is produced, news flashes often occur on social media before they appear in traditional media outlets. Twitter, in particular, has been at the forefront of updates on disasters, such as earthquakes, on the 2009 post-election protests in Iran, and even on news of celebrity deaths [29]. Identifying such trending topics is of great interest beyond just reporting news, with applications to marketing, disease control, national security and many more. The business case for marketing and PR is particularly compelling, given that 19% of all tweets [16] and 32% of blog posts [26] talk about products or brands. Businesses need to be aware of what consumers, in general, are saying about their products; especially since any emerging negative information or opinions are best dealt with promptly.

Motivated by this need, we focus on the task of automatically detecting emerging topics, hot topics, or buzz from streams of documents/posts. For a subject to be considered an emerging topic, it must have *support*, in that it must appear from multiple sources; and it must be *novel*, in that it should be different from topics that have been, or are already, popular and well-known. Several current techniques that can be applied to address this problem, do not adequately meet both these criteria.

One possible approach to identifying emerging topics in document streams is to take all new posts and identify sets of posts that are similar. Extensive research in the area of document clustering and topic modeling with Latent Dirichlet Allocation [5], Probabilistic Latent Semantic Analysis [15], and Non-negative Matrix Factorizations [20] can be brought to bear here. Although clustering and topic modeling techniques (including, the dynamic ones) can find sets of posts expressing cohesive patterns of discussion, they are not guaranteed to identify clusters that are also novel or informative compared to previously appearing topics.

An alternative approach is to use techniques that have been developed for First Story Detection (FSD) [2], in the context of Topic Detection and Tracking (TDT) for traditional news streams. While seemingly related, FSD is only focused on detecting when a document discusses a previously unseen event. While first story detection by itself is very valuable for broadcast news, given the low signal-to-noise ratio in social media, it is less effective. In the space of social media, many posts that may be considered as "first stories" solely because they are very different from previous posts, may actually be of little value, e.g., the fact that *intlevg* on Twitter is eating "honey roasted peanuts for lunch", may be of little interest to the population at large.

For successful emerging topic detection, we need to identify several recent posts that are both similar to each other, and are dissimilar to previous posts. In this paper, we propose an approach based on sparse coding, in which data vectors are modeled as sparse linear combinations of basis elements. A stream of documents (where each document is modeled a vector $\mathbf{x} \in \mathbb{R}^m$) can be used to learn a *dictionary* ($A \in \mathbb{R}^{m \times k}$) of k *atoms*, such that the documents can be *approximately* represented by a linear combination of a *few* atoms. If a new document cannot be represented with low error as a sparse linear combination of these atoms, it is a good indicator of novelty of the document. Novel document, thus identified, are used to learn a new dictionary of novel topics. This new dictionary is

CIKM'11, October 24–28, 2011, Glasgow, Scotland, UK.

then used to cluster similar novel posts together, which we identify as the emerging topic clusters.

We validated our approach on several datasets from broadcast news, news groups, and Twitter. Empirical results show that our approach is more effective at detecting emerging topics in terms of precision and recall, than an approach based on first story detection followed by clustering of the first stories detected, and other variations. This paper makes the following main contributions:

(1) We formulate the task of detecting novel signals in streaming datasets as a sparse signal representation problem. A signal is represented with a sparse code over an existing dictionary along with a sparse error term. A novel signal is detected based on the lack of sparsity in such a representation. While our main application is emerging topic detection on streaming text, our methodology applies more broadly to other domains.

(2) Our objective function is a combination of the ℓ_1-norms of a sparse error (robust reconstruction) and a sparse code, i.e., $\|\mathbf{e}\|_1 + \lambda\|\mathbf{x}\|_1$ (for the signal $\mathbf{y} = A\mathbf{x}+\mathbf{e}$), which appears well suited for sparse high-dimensional datasets such as those that arise in text applications. Additionally, we have non-negativity constraints on the sparse code ($\mathbf{x}$) and dictionary (A), to maintain interpretability. Such a natural formulation combining sparsity, robustness, and non-negativity appears novel and highly appropriate for the task.

(3) Most algorithms for dictionary learning are iterative batch procedures, that operate on the entire training set, which is not feasible for very large and dynamic data. We present an online algorithm which computes the sparse coding for each data point only once, instead of an iterative batch update scheme. As a result, our approach is very scalable and well-suited for streaming data, such as from social media.

(4) We use a new practical alternating direction method (ADM) to solve various optimization problems appearing in our formulation, that may be of independent interest. ADM has recently gathered significant attention in the Machine Learning community due to its wide applicability to a range of learning problems with complex objective functions [6].

(5) We introduce a new dictionary learning based text clustering algorithm which, in our setting, outperforms the widely used Spherical K-Means [12] algorithm for clustering novel documents. The new algorithm is more generally applicable, and inherits the scalability of dictionary learning methods.

Notation. We use $[n]$ to denote the set $\{1, \ldots, n\}$. Vectors are always column vectors and are denoted by boldface letters. For a scalar $r \in \mathbb{R}$, let $\text{sign}(r)$ denote the sign of r and $\text{soft}(r, T) = \text{sign}(r) \cdot \max\{|r| - T, 0\}$. The operator soft is extended to a matrix by applying it to every entry in the matrix. For arbitrary real matrices the standard inner product is defined as $\langle A, B \rangle = Tr(A^\top B)$, and the (squared) *Frobenius* matrix norm $\|A\|_{\text{fro}}^2 = \langle A, A \rangle$ is the sum of all squared entries of the matrix. We use s.t. as an abbreviation for subject to.

2. BACKGROUND WORK

Sparse error recovery has found success in applications such as image and speech processing [7], computer vision and pattern recognition [23]. One of most successful (and relevant to this paper) applications is in robust face recognition [36, 35]. It is known that a well-aligned frontal face image under different lighting and expression lies close to a special low-dimensional linear subspace spanned by the training samples from the same subject [4]. This observation has led to face recognition to be cast as a *sparse representation* problem where the objective is to recover a high-dimensional sparse signal $\mathbf{x} \in \mathbb{R}^k$ from a highly compressed linear measurement $\mathbf{y} = A\mathbf{x} + \mathbf{e} \in \mathbb{R}^m$ (where $\mathbf{e}$ is an unknown error vector) [35]. In recent work, Wright *et al.* [36] proposed to estimate $\mathbf{w} = [\mathbf{x}, \mathbf{e}]$ jointly as the sparsest solution to the extended equation: $\min_{\mathbf{w}} \|\mathbf{w}\|_1$ s.t. $\mathbf{y} = [A, \mathbb{I}]\mathbf{w}$, where $\mathbb{I}$ is the identity matrix. They show this formulation performs exceedingly well for robust face recognition. For example, they show that this ℓ_1-minimization enables almost perfect recognition even if more than 60% pixels of the query image are severely corrupted. In a later paper, Wright and Ma [35] provided theoretical justification for this ℓ_1-minimization formulation. We use a similar formulation to construct a sparse representation (see Section 4). One crucial difference between our approach and that advocated by Wright *et al.* is that our matrix A does not contain all the documents, but is a *compact* representative dictionary of the documents seen before. This makes our approach more scalable.

Dictionary learning falls into a general category of techniques known as *matrix factorization*. In this paper, we additionally enforce non-negativity constraint on the factor matrices and such factorizations have been widely studied as *non-negative matrix factorization* (NMF) [20]. Most NMF formulations deal with squared loss [20, 22] . Several papers have considered ℓ_1-regularized matrix factorizations with applications to topic models in text, e.g., [17, 39] but with an ℓ_2-loss function. Similar to our loss function (6), Ke and Kanade [19] consider an ℓ_1-loss function for non-negative matrix factorization, but do not impose sparsity in the factors. In their paper, Ke and Kanade [19] gave a simple alternative convex programming approach for solving non-negative matrix factorization with ℓ_1-loss. Another framework with closely related goals is that of Robust PCA [8] where a decomposition of a matrix is sought in terms of a low-rank component with small nuclear norm and sparse errors. However, the repeated need to solve linear/quadratic programs or SVD in these approaches not scalable to large matrices. Our use of the alternating directions method allows us to scale-up to large matrices that are typically encountered in the text domain. For a review of ADMs and their suitability to a variety of large scale learning problems, we point the reader to [6]. To the best of our knowledge, our approach is the first to propose a scalable algorithm for ℓ_1-regularized dictionary learning with robust ℓ_1-reconstruction error with an application in temporal topic analysis of streaming documents.

3. TASK DEFINITION

In order to represent documents in our data stream, we will use the conventional vector space model with TF-IDF (Term Frequency-Inverse Document Frequency) term-weighting [24]. Additionally, each document has a timestamp that indicates when the document arrives. The timestamp could be at the granularity of our liking, e.g., it could be the day or the exact time the document arrives. As new documents come in and new terms are identified, our vocabulary set increases, but for simplicity, we are going to work with a global vocabulary space containing m terms that is independent of t. The extension to the case where the vocabulary set increases with t is quite simple, and just requires adjusting the size of the matrices by zero-padding.

Let $\{P_t \in \mathbb{R}^{m \times n_t}, t = 1, 2, \ldots\}$ denote a sequence of streaming matrices, where P_t represents the sparse term-document matrix whose unit ℓ_1-normalized columns are the documents with timestamp t and n_t is the number of documents with timestamp t. Analogous to P_t, we also define $P_{\leq t}$ which is constructed by using all

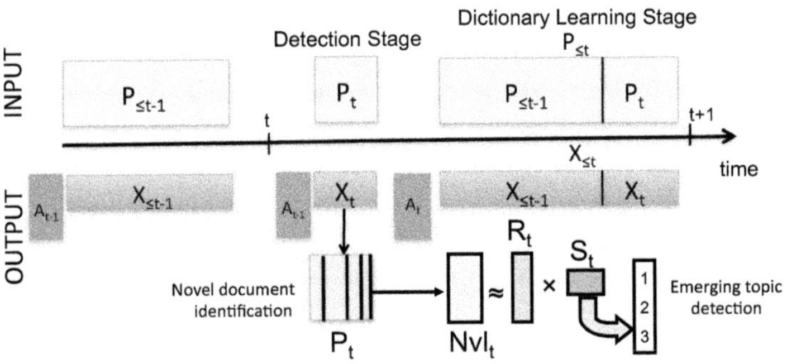

Figure 1: Schematic of our framework: At each timestep, we solve a sparse coding/dictionary learning problem with ℓ_1 reconstruction error and ℓ_1 regularization. The reconstruction error is used to identify novel documents which are again clustered using our framework to report emerging topics.

documents whose timestamp is $\le t$. Let $n_{\le t}$ be the number of documents with timestamp $\le t$, then $P_{\le t} \in \mathbb{R}^{m \times n_{\le t}}$. Informally, the goal of *emerging topic detection* is to identify sets of documents in P_t that are similar to each other and are dissimilar to documents in $P_{\le t-1}$.

4. OUR FORMULATION

We split the task of emerging topic detection into two sub-tasks: (1) Identifying the novel documents (Nvl_t) from P_t (novel documents are those that belong to any of the emerging topics at time t), and (2) Clustering the novel documents. We use dictionary learning to solve both these sub-tasks (see Figure 1).

4.1 Identifying Novel Documents

Let $A_{t-1} \in \mathbb{R}^{m \times k}$ represent the dictionary matrix after time $t-1$; where dictionary A_{t-1} is a compact summary representation of all the documents in $P_{\le t-1}$. Each column of A_{t-1} is called a *basis vector* or *atom*. The exact construction of the dictionary is described later, but ideally we want the dictionary to have a set of representative atoms for each of the old topics. With such a representative dictionary, documents from old topics can be represented as a linear combination of the atoms corresponding to that topic.

Given a new document vector $\mathbf{y}$ with timestamp t, we see if $\mathbf{y}$ could be represented as a sparse linear combination of the columns of A_{t-1}. The sparsest representation is the solution of

$$\min_{\mathbf{x}} \|\mathbf{x}\|_0 \text{ s.t. } \mathbf{y} = A_{t-1}\mathbf{x}, \mathbf{x} \ge 0, \tag{1}$$

where $\|\cdot\|_0$ is the ℓ_0-norm, counting the non-zero entries of a vector. However, in the general case, solving (1) is NP-hard and also hard to approximate [3]. Recently, a series of papers (see [9, 13] and references therein) have shown that under some favorable conditions one could obtain the solution to (1) by solving the following

$$\min_{\mathbf{x}} \|\mathbf{x}\|_1 \text{ s.t. } \mathbf{y} = A_{t-1}\mathbf{x}, \mathbf{x} \ge 0. \tag{2}$$

In essence, (2) can be viewed as a convex relaxation of (1). We will work with the ℓ_1-norm based convex relaxation in the sequel.

In most practical situations, (2) is not applicable because it may not be possible to represent $\mathbf{y}$ as $A_{t-1}\mathbf{x}$, e.g., if $\mathbf{y}$ has new words which are absent (i.e., have no support) in A_{t-1}. In such cases, one could represent $\mathbf{y} = A_{t-1}\mathbf{x} + \mathbf{e}$ where $\mathbf{e}$ is an unknown noise vector. Normally, if one considers a specific topic over time, typically a small set of new words get introduced in the discussion, e.g., if the topic is a sporting event like the Olympics, with time the discussion shifts to different athletes or events. The error vector $\mathbf{e}$ captures these terms. Since there are few such new words, the vector $\mathbf{e}$ is sparse. However, these terms do get used with much higher frequency within few documents than one might expect from the overall statistics of the corpus. So even though $\mathbf{e}$ is sparse it has some large, impulsive values. A natural relaxation to (2) for handling noise is $\min_{\mathbf{x}} \|\mathbf{x}\|_1$ s.t. $\|\mathbf{y} - A_{t-1}\mathbf{x}\|_2 \le \delta, \mathbf{x} \ge 0$. The above problem (generally without the non-negativity constraint) is commonly known as the *constraint basis pursuit denoising problem* [10] and its variant

$$\min_{\mathbf{x}} \|\mathbf{y} - A_{t-1}\mathbf{x}\|_2^2 + \lambda\|\mathbf{x}\|_1 \text{ s.t. } \mathbf{x} \ge 0, \tag{3}$$

is referred to as the unconstrained basis pursuit denoising problem, also known as the Lasso [31]. Here, $\delta, \lambda > 0$ are parameters. The formulation (3) naturally takes into account both the reconstruction error (with the $\|\mathbf{y} - A_{t-1}\mathbf{x}\|_2^2$ term) and the complexity of the sparse decomposition (with the $\|\mathbf{x}\|_1$ term).

In the presence of isotopic Gaussian noise the ℓ_2-penalty on $\mathbf{e} = \mathbf{y} - A_{t-1}\mathbf{x}$ gives the best approximation of $\mathbf{x}$ [36, 37, 38]. However, for text documents (and in most other real scenarios), the noise vector $\mathbf{e}$ rarely satisfies the Gaussian assumption, and some of its coefficients contain large, impulsive values. In such scenarios, the ℓ_2-penalty of (3) may give an extremely bad approximation of $\mathbf{x}$ [37, 27]. However, in such real-world scenarios recent results [19, 36, 38, 35] have shown that imposing an ℓ_1-reconstruction error gives a more robust and better approximation of $\mathbf{x}$. We refer readers to these papers to get a more detailed exposition of the advantages of ℓ_1 over ℓ_2-reconstruction error. The basic intuition is that the ability of ℓ_1-penalty to recover the true solution $\mathbf{x}$ is independent of the magnitude of the $\mathbf{e}$, and depends only on the signs of $\mathbf{e}$ and the relative geometry of the column space of A and the unit ℓ_1 ball [36].

We use the following ℓ_1-formulation to recover $\mathbf{x}$

$$\min_{\mathbf{x}} \|\mathbf{y} - A_{t-1}\mathbf{x}\|_1 + \lambda\|\mathbf{x}\|_1 \text{ s.t. } \mathbf{x} \ge 0. \tag{4}$$

It is well-known that unlike (3) where squared ℓ_2-norm is used on the error, the ℓ_1-reconstruction error makes (4) an exact penalty method in the sense that it reduces to (2) when $\lambda > 0$ is less than some threshold [38]. Additionally, Yang *et al.* [38] claim that even without impulsive noise the ℓ_1-reconstruction error does not harm the solution quality as long as the data does not contain a large amount of Gaussian noise.

Given a new document $\mathbf{y}$ with timestamp of t and a dictionary A_{t-1}, we solve (4) to determine whether $\mathbf{y}$ is *novel* (with respect to dictionary A_{t-1}) or not. If the objective value of (4) is "small," then $\mathbf{y}$ is well-reconstructed by a linear combination of some basis vectors in A_{t-1}. We mark such documents as *non-novel* and discard them. Now, if the objective value is "large," then $\mathbf{y}$ has no good reconstruction among the basis vectors of the previous topics, thus suggesting novelty of $\mathbf{y}$. We add such documents to the set Nvl_t. Note that all documents are normalized to unit ℓ_1 length, and hence the objective values are in the same scale. The performance of this algorithm depends on the "quality" of the dictionary. We now describe our dictionary learning formulation.

4.2 Dictionary Learning

For simplicity of explanation, we assume that the dictionary is of fixed size $\mathbb{R}^{m \times k}$ (independent of t). Classic dictionary learning techniques [28, 1, 21] consider a finite training set of signals $S = [\mathbf{s}_1, \ldots, \mathbf{s}_n] \in \mathbb{R}^{m \times n}$ and optimize the empirical cost function $\sum_{i=1}^{n} l(\mathbf{s}_i, A)$, where $A \in \mathbb{R}^{m \times k}$ is the dictionary and $l(\cdot, \cdot)$

is a loss function such that $l(\mathbf{s}, A)$ should be small if A is "good" at representing the signal $\mathbf{s}$ in a sparse fashion. The value k is referred to as the size of the dictionary. A typical choice of the loss function is the Lasso-style objective

$$l(\mathbf{s}, A) = \min_{\mathbf{x}} \|\mathbf{s} - A\mathbf{x}\|_2^2 + \lambda\|\mathbf{x}\|_1. \quad (5)$$

However, as we mentioned above in the absence of Gaussian noise using ℓ_1-loss on the error improves the estimation, therefore, we use the following loss function $l(\mathbf{s}, A) = \min_{\mathbf{x}} \|\mathbf{s} - A\mathbf{x}\|_1 + \lambda\|\mathbf{x}\|_1$. Additionally, we want dictionary A and $\mathbf{x}$'s to contain non-negative entries. Therefore, the problem of dictionary learning becomes

$$\min_{\mathbf{x}_i, A} \sum_{i=1}^{n} \|\mathbf{s}_i - A\mathbf{x}_i\|_1 + \lambda\|\mathbf{x}_i\|_1 \text{ s.t. } A \geq 0, \mathbf{x}_i \geq 0 \,\forall i \in [n].$$

In our setting at time t, we want to update the dictionary so that it forms a compact summary representation of all the documents in $P_{\leq t}$. Let $P_{\leq t} = [\mathbf{p}_1, \dots, \mathbf{p}_{n_{\leq t}}] \in \mathbb{R}^{m \times n_{\leq t}}$. We learn a dictionary for time t by minimizing

$$\min_{\mathbf{x}_i, A} \sum_{i=1}^{n_{\leq t}} \|\mathbf{p}_i - A\mathbf{x}_i\|_1 + \lambda\|\mathbf{x}_i\|_1 \text{ s.t. } A \geq 0, \mathbf{x}_i \geq 0 \;\forall i \in [n_{\leq t}].$$

Equivalently this could be written as minimizing the following function over (X, A):

$$f(X, A) = \|P_{\leq t} - AX\|_1 + \lambda\|X\|_1 \text{ s.t. } A, X \geq 0. \quad (6)$$

Since we are factorizing $P_{\leq t}$ into two non-negative matrices, Equation (6) (without the $\lambda\|X\|_1$ term) is referred to as ℓ_1-loss non-negative factorization problem [20]. The optimization problem (6) is in general non-convex. But if one of the variables, either A or X is known, the objective function with respect to the other variable becomes a convex function (in fact, a linear function) and the global solution to (6) can be found. This iterative alternative minimization is the core idea behind most algorithms for dictionary learning [28, 1, 21]. However, these algorithms access the whole of the dataset in each iteration, and therefore, these algorithms cannot efficiently deal with large datasets. To overcome this problem, we use an online version of dictionary learning, where we update only A and use X obtained from previous stages of the algorithm (see Section 5).

4.3 Novel Documents to Emerging Topics

We now describe our procedure for going from novel documents to emerging topics. The idea is to again use dictionary learning. Given as input a set of (novel) documents and the number of topics (k_1) to be generated, we use a suitable modification of (6) to do detect emerging topics. The idea is as follows: If Nvl_t represents the set of novel documents, we learn a dictionary with k_1 atoms, where each atom corresponds to an emerging topic. In other words, we minimize the following function over (R, S):

$$f(R, S) = \|\text{Nvl}_t - RS\|_1 + \lambda\|S\|_1 \text{ s.t. } R, S \geq 0, \quad (7)$$

where $R \in \mathbb{R}^{m \times k_1}$ is the dictionary matrix of term-topic association and $S \in \mathbb{R}^{k_1 \times |\text{Nvl}_t|}$ is the matrix of topic-document association. The distribution of terms in each column of R is the latent representation of the k_1 emerging topics in the data. In order to present these topics in a meaningful way to users, we represent each topic by the most relevant documents to the topic. We do this by assigning each document to the atom in which it has the most dominant representation as given by the matrix S. This gives a clustering of novel documents into emerging topics.

5. OUR ALGORITHM

We present in this section our algorithm for detecting emerging topics. Our main procedure is summarized in Algorithm NVLCLUST. The algorithm alternates between a "detection stage" and a "dictionary learning stage." The detection stage at time t gets as input the dictionary A_{t-1} and P_t, and for each document $\mathbf{p}_j$ in P_t computes the best representation of $\mathbf{p}_j$ in terms of A_{t-1} by solving (4) (where $\mathbf{y}$ is replaced by $\mathbf{p}_j$). It is quite easy to transform (4) into a linear program. However, in our experiments the linear programming approach turned out to be quite slow (even when using commercial solvers like CPLEX). To speedup our algorithm, we use the alternating directions method (also known in the literature as alternating directions method of multipliers) [11, 38]. We explain this approach in Section 6. We classify a document $\mathbf{p}_j$ as novel if the objective value of (4) is above some chosen threshold ζ. Let $\text{Nvl}_t \subseteq P_t$ be the set of document that are marked as novel at time t. The set of novel documents is then passed as input to Algorithm DICTCLUST which does clustering of these documents as explained in Section 4.3. Since, the size of Nvl_t is typically small, we solve it using a simple iterative batch procedure, alternatively fixing R, S and updating the other using the method of alternating directions.

We perform the dictionary learning stage in an online fashion. Online dictionary learning was recently introduced by Mairal *et al.* [22] who showed that it provides a scalable approach for handling large dynamic datasets. They consider an ℓ_2-loss function and show that their online algorithm converges to the minimum objective value in the stochastic case. Our online dictionary learning framework has similar structure to that of Mairal *et al.*, although we focus on ℓ_1-loss. In the online setting, instead of (6), we update the dictionary by minimizing the following function over A:

$$f_X(A) = \|P_{\leq t} - AX_{\leq t}\|_1 + \lambda\|X_{\leq t}\|_1 \text{ s.t. } A \geq 0, \quad (8)$$

where $X_{\leq t} = [\mathbf{x}_1, \dots, \mathbf{x}_{n_{\leq t}}]$ are computed during the previous detection stages. Notice that $\min_{A \geq 0} f_X(A)$ is an upper bound on $\min_{A,X \geq 0} f(X, A)$ (as we only optimize over A in $f_X(A)$). However, unlike $f(X, A)$ (which is not convex), minimizing $f_X(A)$ is a convex program (in fact, it can be re-cast as a linear program). For efficiency purposes, we use the method of alternating directions to compute $f_X(A)$ (see Section 6). The matrix A that minimizes the right hand side of (8) is the new dictionary A_t.

Remark. Our framework allows for several variations. By default, the optimization of A is initialized using A_{t-1} and therefore the number of topics tracked by the system is static. Alternatively, the set of emerging topics as discovered by the procedure described in Section 4.3 may also be explicitly injected as columns (in addition to A_{t-1}) in the initialization of A. In this case, the number of topics tracked steadily grows. A guided process may also be possible where a user scans the list of emerging topics and selectively introduces topics of interest in the dictionary. For simplicity, in this paper we use the default variation.

6. ALTERNATING DIRECTIONS METHOD

To speedup the algorithms NVLCLUST and DICTCLUST, we use the method of alternating directions to solve the various optimization problems. The reader is referred to [38, 6] and references therein for details and historical development of the alternating direction method (ADM). We start with a brief review of the general framework of ADM from [38]. Let $p(\mathbf{x}) : \mathbb{R}^a \to \mathbb{R}$ and $q(\mathbf{y}) : \mathbb{R}^b \to \mathbb{R}$ be convex functions, $F \in \mathbb{R}^{c \times a}$, $G \in \mathbb{R}^{c \times b}$, and

ADM EQUATIONS FOR SOLVING (10)
Input: $A_{t-1} \in \mathbb{R}^{m\times k}, \mathbf{p}_j \in \mathbb{R}^m, \lambda, \beta, \tau, \gamma > 0$
1. $\mathbf{x}_{(1)} \leftarrow 0, \mathbf{e}_{(1)} \leftarrow 0, \rho_{(1)} \leftarrow 0$
2. **for** $i = 1, 2, \ldots$, *convergence* **do**
a) $\mathbf{e}_{(i+1)} \leftarrow \text{soft}(\mathbf{p}_j - A_{t-1}\mathbf{x}_{(i)} + \rho_{(i)}/\beta, 1/\beta)$
b) $\mathbf{g}_{(i)} \leftarrow A_{t-1}^{\top}(A_{t-1}\mathbf{x}_{(i)} + \mathbf{e}_{(i+1)} - \mathbf{p}_j - \rho_{(i)}/\beta)$
c) $\mathbf{x}_{(i+1)} \leftarrow \max\{\mathbf{x}_{(i)} - \tau\mathbf{g}_{(i)} - (\lambda\tau)/\beta, 0\}$
d) $\rho_{(i+1)} \leftarrow \rho_{(i)} + \gamma\beta(\mathbf{p}_j - A_{t-1}\mathbf{x}_{(i+1)} - \mathbf{e}_{(i+1)})$

ADM EQUATIONS FOR SOLVING (8)
Input: $A_{t-1} \in \mathbb{R}^{m\times k}, P_{\leq t} \in \mathbb{R}^{m\times n_{\leq t}}, X_{\leq t} \in \mathbb{R}^{m\times n_{\leq t}}, \beta, \tau, \gamma > 0$
1. $A_{(1)} \leftarrow A_{t-1}, \Gamma_{(1)} \leftarrow P_{\leq t} - A_{t-1}X_{\leq t}, \Delta_{(1)} \leftarrow 0$
2. **for** $i = 1, 2, \ldots$, *convergence* **do**
a) $\Gamma_{(i+1)} \leftarrow \text{soft}(P_{\leq t} - A_{(i)}X_{\leq t} + \Delta_{(i)}/\beta, 1/\beta)$
b) $G_{(i)} \leftarrow (A_{(i)}X_{\leq t} + \Gamma_{(i+1)} - P_{\leq t} - \Delta_{(i)}/\beta)X_{\leq t}^{\top}$
c) $A_{(i+1)} \leftarrow \max\{A_{(i)} - \tau G_{(i)}, 0\}$
d) $\Delta_{(i+1)} \leftarrow \Delta_{(i)} + \gamma\beta(P_{\leq t} - A_{(i+1)}X_{\leq t} - \Gamma_{(i+1)})$

Figure 2: ADM equations for detection and dictionary learning stages. The operator soft along with other notations are defined at the end of the Section 1.

ALGORITHM NVLCLUST: NOVEL TOPIC CLUSTERING

Input: $P_t = [\mathbf{p}_1, \ldots, \mathbf{p}_{n_t}] \in \mathbb{R}^{m\times n_t}, A_{t-1} \in \mathbb{R}^{m\times k}, \lambda, \zeta \in \mathbb{R}$
Detection stage:
1. $\text{Nvl}_t \leftarrow \emptyset$
2. **for each** $\mathbf{p}_j \in P_t$ **do**
 a) $\mathbf{x}_j = \text{argmin}_{\mathbf{x}\geq 0} \|\mathbf{p}_j - A_{t-1}\mathbf{x}\|_1 + \lambda\|\mathbf{x}\|_1$
 b) **if** $\|\mathbf{p}_j - A_{t-1}\mathbf{x}_j\|_1 + \lambda\|\mathbf{x}_j\|_1 > \zeta$ **then**
 $\text{Nvl}_t = \text{Nvl}_t \cup \{\mathbf{p}_j\}$
3. Invoke Algorithm DICTCLUST on Nvl_t

Dictionary Learning stage:
4. $X_{\leq t} \leftarrow [X_{\leq t-1} \mid \mathbf{x}_1, \ldots, \mathbf{x}_{n_t}]$
5. $P_{\leq t} \leftarrow [P_{\leq t-1} \mid \mathbf{p}_1, \ldots, \mathbf{p}_{n_t}]$
6. $A_t = \text{argmin}_{A\geq 0} \|P_{\leq t} - AX_{\leq t}\|_1 + \lambda\|X_{\leq t}\|_1$

ALGORITHM DICTCLUST: DICTIONARY-BASED CLUSTERING

Input: Matrix of documents $\text{Nvl}_t, \lambda \in \mathbb{R}, k_1 \in \mathbb{R}$
1. $R_t, S_t = \text{argmin}_{R\geq 0, S\geq 0} \|\text{Nvl}_t - RS\|_1 + \lambda\|S\|_1$
2. let $S_t = [\mathbf{s}_1, \ldots, \mathbf{s}_{|\text{Nvl}_t|}]$ where each $\mathbf{s}_j \in \mathbb{R}^{k_1}$
3. **for each** document $\mathbf{p}_j \in \text{Nvl}_t$ **do**
 a) $l = \text{argmax}_j\{\mathbf{s}_j\}$
 b) assign document $\mathbf{p}_j$ to topic l

$\mathbf{z} \in \mathbb{R}^c$. Consider the following optimization problem

$$\min_{\mathbf{x},\mathbf{y}} p(\mathbf{x}) + q(\mathbf{y}) \text{ s.t. } F\mathbf{x} + G\mathbf{y} = \mathbf{z}, \qquad (9)$$

where the variable vectors $\mathbf{x}$ and $\mathbf{y}$ are separate in the objective, and coupled only in the constraint. The augmented Lagrangian for the above problem is given by

$$\mathcal{L}(\mathbf{x}, \mathbf{y}, \rho) = p(\mathbf{x}) + q(\mathbf{y}) + \rho^{\top}(\mathbf{z} - F\mathbf{x} - G\mathbf{y}) + \frac{\beta}{2}\|\mathbf{z} - F\mathbf{x} - G\mathbf{y}\|_2^2,$$

where $\rho \in \mathbb{R}^c$ is the Lagrangian multiplier and $\beta > 0$ is a penalty parameter.

ADM utilizes the separability form of (9) and replaces the joint minimization over $\mathbf{x}$ and $\mathbf{y}$ with two simpler problems. The ADM first minimizes $\mathcal{L}$ over $\mathbf{x}$, then over $\mathbf{y}$, and then applies a proximal minimization step with respect to the Lagrange multiplier ρ. In the ith iteration of the ADM procedure, given $(\mathbf{x}_{(i)}, \mathbf{y}_{(i)}, \rho_{(i)})$[1], we obtain $(\mathbf{x}_{(i+1)}, \mathbf{y}_{(i+1)}, \rho_{(i+1)})$ as follows

$$\begin{cases} \mathbf{x}_{(i+1)} \leftarrow \text{argmin}_{\mathbf{x}} \mathcal{L}(\mathbf{x}, \mathbf{y}_{(i)}, \rho_{(i)}), \\ \mathbf{y}_{(i+1)} \leftarrow \text{argmin}_{\mathbf{y}} \mathcal{L}(\mathbf{x}_{(i+1)}, \mathbf{y}, \rho_{(i)}), \\ \rho_{(i+1)} \leftarrow \rho_{(i)} + \gamma\beta(\mathbf{z} - F\mathbf{x}_{(i+1)} - G\mathbf{y}_{(i+1)}). \end{cases}$$

Here, $\gamma > 0$ is a constant. The ADM procedure has been proved to converge to the global optimal solution under quite broad conditions [11]. We now apply ADM to the various optimization problems encountered in Algorithms NVLCLUST and DICTCLUST. The ADM procedure stops when the relative change in the objective function is less than a given constant. In practice few iterations are needed to reach good results. Due to lack of space all proofs are omitted and can be found in the full version of the paper.

ADM for Detection Stage. Let $\mathbb{R}_+$ be the set of positive real numbers. In the detection stage of Algorithm NVLCLUST for each document $\mathbf{p}_j$, we solve the following program

$$\min_{\mathbf{x}\in\mathbb{R}^k} \|\mathbf{p}_j - A_{t-1}\mathbf{x}\|_1 + \lambda\|\mathbf{x}\|_1 \text{ s.t. } \mathbf{x} \geq 0. \qquad (10)$$

This can be written equivalently as

$$\min_{\mathbf{x}\in\mathbb{R}_+^k, \mathbf{e}\in\mathbb{R}^m} \|\mathbf{e}\|_1 + \lambda\|\mathbf{x}\|_1 \text{ s.t. } \mathbf{e} = \mathbf{p}_j - A_{t-1}\mathbf{x}. \qquad (11)$$

Then the augmented Lagrangian form of (11) is

$$\mathcal{L}(\mathbf{x}, \mathbf{e}, \rho) = \min_{\mathbf{x}\in\mathbb{R}_+^k, \mathbf{e}\in\mathbb{R}^m} \|\mathbf{e}\|_1 + \lambda\|\mathbf{x}\|_1$$
$$+ \rho^{\top}(\mathbf{p}_j - A_{t-1}\mathbf{x} - \mathbf{e}) + (\beta/2)\|\mathbf{p}_j - A_{t-1}\mathbf{x} - \mathbf{e}\|_2^2. \qquad (12)$$

We now apply ADM to the above Lagrangian. Let us assume that we have $(\mathbf{x}_{(i)}, \mathbf{e}_{(i)}, \rho_{(i)})$, we construct $(\mathbf{x}_{(i+1)}, \mathbf{e}_{(i+1)}, \rho_{(i+1)})$ as follows. First, for a fixed $\mathbf{x}_{(i)}$ and $\rho_{(i)}$, we update $\mathbf{e}$ by solving

$$\min_{\mathbf{e}} \|\mathbf{e}\|_1 + \rho_{(i)}^{\top}(\mathbf{p}_j - A_{t-1}\mathbf{x}_{(i)} - \mathbf{e}) + \frac{\beta}{2}\|\mathbf{p}_j - A_{t-1}\mathbf{x}_{(i)} - \mathbf{e}\|_2^2.$$

LEMMA 6.1. *The minimum value of the above optimization is attained by setting* $\mathbf{e} = \textit{soft}(\mathbf{p}_j - A_{t-1}\mathbf{x}_{(i)} + \rho_{(i)}/\beta, 1/\beta)$.

The above lemma gives the derivation for $\mathbf{e}_{(i+1)}$. Now, for a fixed $\mathbf{e}_{(i+1)}$ and $\rho_{(i)}$ a simple manipulation shows that we can obtain $\mathbf{x}$ that minimizes (12) by solving the following

$$\min_{\mathbf{x}\in\mathbb{R}_+^k} \lambda\|\mathbf{x}\|_1 + (\beta/2)\|\mathbf{p}_j - A_{t-1}\mathbf{x} - \mathbf{e}_{(i+1)} + \rho_{(i)}/\beta\|_2^2. \qquad (13)$$

[1]The subscript (i) denotes the ith iteration of the ADM procedure.

However, instead of solving (13) exactly, we approximate it by

$$\min_{\mathbf{x}\in\mathbb{R}^k_+} \lambda\|\mathbf{x}\|_1 + \beta\left(\mathbf{g}_{(i)}^\top(\mathbf{x}-\mathbf{x}_{(i)}) + (1/2\tau)\|\mathbf{x}-\mathbf{x}_{(i)}\|_2^2\right), \quad (14)$$

where $\tau > 0$ is a proximal parameter and

$$\mathbf{g}_{(i)} = \frac{\partial}{\partial \mathbf{x}}\|\mathbf{p}_j - A_{t-1}\mathbf{x} - \mathbf{e}_{(i+1)} + \rho_{(i)}/\beta\|_2^2 \text{ at } \mathbf{x} = \mathbf{x}_{(i)}$$
$$= A_{t-1}^\top(A_{t-1}\mathbf{x}_{(i)} + \mathbf{e}_{(i+1)} - \mathbf{p}_j - \rho_{(i)}/\beta).$$

The above approach belongs to the class of proximal gradient methods in optimization [33, 38]. We use it in the context of a composite function with a smooth and a non-smooth part, where the gradient is computed only based on the smooth part [33].

LEMMA 6.2. *The minimum value of* (14) *is attained by setting* $\mathbf{x} = \max\{\mathbf{x}_{(i)} - \tau\mathbf{g}_{(i)} - (\lambda\tau)/\beta, 0\}$.

The above lemma gives the derivation for $\mathbf{x}_{(i+1)}$. Now given fixed $\mathbf{x}_{(i+1)}$ and $\mathbf{e}_{(i+1)}$, we update multiplier ρ as $\rho_{(i+1)} = \rho_{(i)} + \gamma\beta(\mathbf{p}_j - A_{t-1}\mathbf{x}_{(i+1)} - \mathbf{e}_{(i+1)})$. The update equations are summarized in Figure 2. The following theorem shows the convergence of the ADM.

THEOREM 6.3. *Let* $\tau, \gamma > 0$ *satisfy* $\tau\lambda_{\max}(A) + \gamma < 2$, *where* $\lambda_{\max}(A)$ *is the maximum singular value of* A. *For any fixed* $\beta > 0$, *the sequence* $\{(\mathbf{e}_{(i)}, \mathbf{x}_{(i)}, \rho_{(i)})\}$ *generated by Figure 2 from any starting* $\{(\mathbf{e}_{(1)}, \mathbf{x}_{(1)}, \rho_{(1)})\}$ *converges to* $\{(\tilde{\mathbf{e}}, \tilde{\mathbf{x}}, \tilde{\rho})\}$ *where* $\tilde{\mathbf{e}}, \tilde{\mathbf{x}}$ *is the optimum solution to* (11).

ADM for Dictionary Learning Stage. In the dictionary learning stage, we solve (8) which can be rewritten as

$$\min_{A,\Gamma} \|\Gamma\|_1 + \lambda\|X_{\leq t}\|_1 \text{ s.t. } \Gamma = P_{\leq t} - AX_{\leq t}, A \geq 0.$$

Since $\|X_{\leq t}\|_1$ is a constant term in the objective, we can ignore that term and look at the following optimization problem

$$\min_{A,\Gamma} \|\Gamma\|_1 \text{ s.t. } \Gamma = P_{\leq t} - AX_{\leq t}, A \geq 0. \quad (15)$$

The augmented Lagrangian form of (15) is

$$\mathcal{L}(A,\Gamma,\Delta) = \min_{A\in\mathbb{R}^{m\times k}_+, \Gamma\in\mathbb{R}^{m\times n}} \|\Gamma\|_1 \quad (16)$$
$$+ \langle\Delta, P_{\leq t} - AX_{\leq t} - \Gamma\rangle + (\beta/2)\|P_{\leq t} - AX_{\leq t} - \Gamma\|_{\text{fro}}^2,$$

where $\Delta \in \mathbb{R}^{m\times n}$ is a multiplier and $\beta > 0$ is a penalty parameter. The ADM equations for this stage are a generalization (matrix version) of the ADM equations derived for the detection stage. Figure 2 summarizes these equations. We use A_{t-1} as warm restart for computing A_t. Similar to Theorem 6.3 one can also show the convergence of these ADM equations.

ADM for Algorithm DICTCLUST. We now derive the ADM equations for solving (7). We solve (7) by doing an alternative minimization over R and S.

$$R^{(j)} = \text{argmin}_{R\geq 0}\|\text{Nvl}_t - RS^{(j-1)}\|_1 + \lambda\|S^{(j-1)}\|_1, \quad (17)$$

$$S^{(j)} = \text{argmin}_{S\geq 0}\|\text{Nvl}_t - R^{(j)}S\|_1 + \lambda\|S\|_1. \quad (18)$$

We use ADM to solve both (17) and (18). The derivation of the ADM equations are quite similar to that done for detection and dictionary learning stages, so we summarize the results in Figure 3.

Remark about Parallelization. The optimization problems encountered in detection stage, dictionary learning stage, and Algorithm DICTCLUST can all be trivially parallelized. For detection stage, we could invoke ADM for each $\mathbf{p}_j \in P_t$ in parallel. For, the dictionary learning stage, we can rewrite the $\|P_{\leq t} - AX_{\leq t}\|_1$ as $\sum_{i=1}^m \|P_{\leq t}(i) - A(i)X_{\leq t}\|_1$ where $P_{\leq t}(i)$ and $A(i)$ are the ith rows in $P_{\leq t}$ and A, respectively. Since the terms in the summation are independent of each other, we can solve them in parallel using a modification of the ADM equations used for the detection stage. The right hand side of Figure 2 is a matrix version of this parallel optimization over rows of A. A similar idea also works for alternative minimization used in Algorithm DICTCLUST.

7. EMPIRICAL EVALUATION

In this section, we first empirically evaluate our approach on publicly-available labeled datasets from news streams and newsgroups. We then present a study of our approach applied to Twitter data from a PR campaign.

7.1 Evaluation Metrics

For the purpose of evaluation, we assume that documents in the corpus have been identified with a set of topics. For simplicity, we assume that each document is tagged with a single, most dominant topic that it associates with which we refer to as the *true topic* for that document.

We use variations of standard IR measures like pairwise precision, recall, and F1 score [24]. Given P_t, the set of documents arriving at time t, let $\text{TNvl}_t \subseteq P_t$ be the set of true novel documents in P_t (i.e., TNvl_t contains documents belonging to true emerging topic clusters). Let $\mathcal{C}_t$ be the set of system generated emerging topic clusters at time t, and let $\mathcal{T}_t$ be the true emerging topic clusters at time t. Note that clusters in $\mathcal{T}_t$ are formed over documents in TNvl_t, whereas the clusters in $\mathcal{C}_t$ are formed over documents in $\text{Nvl}_t \subseteq P_t$, and TNvl_t may not be equal to Nvl_t.

We define our evaluation metrics over the novel documents. Pairwise precision (Prec_{nvl}) is the number of pairs of documents that are in the same cluster in both $\mathcal{T}_t$ and $\mathcal{C}_t$ divided by the number of pairs of documents that are in the same cluster in $\mathcal{C}_t$. Pairwise recall (Rec_{nvl}) is the number of pairs of documents that are in the same cluster in both $\mathcal{T}_t$ and $\mathcal{C}_t$ divided by the number of pairs of documents that are in the same cluster in $\mathcal{T}_t$. Pairwise F1 (F1_{nvl}) is the harmonic mean of Prec_{nvl} and Rec_{nvl}. The following example illustrates these definitions. Let $P_t = \{p_1, p_2, \ldots, p_9\}$, $\text{TNvl}_t = \{p_3, p_4, p_5\}$, and $\text{Nvl}_t = \{p_3, p_4, p_5, p_6, p_7\}$. Let $\mathcal{T}_t = \{(p_3, p_4, p_5)\}$ (i.e., $\mathcal{T}_t$ contains one cluster made up of p_3, p_4, p_5), and $\mathcal{C}_t = \{(p_3, p_4, p_6), (p_5, p_7)\}$. Then,

$$\text{Prec}_{\text{nvl}} = \frac{|\{(p_3, p_4)\}|}{|\{(p_3, p_4), (p_3, p_6), (p_4, p_6), (p_5, p_7)\}|} = \frac{1}{4}$$
$$\text{Rec}_{\text{nvl}} = \frac{|\{(p_3, p_4)\}|}{|\{(p_3, p_4), (p_3, p_5), (p_4, p_5)\}|} = \frac{1}{3}$$

7.2 Baseline Approaches

We compare the performance of our algorithm against three alternative approaches we created, which are based on combining nearest neighbor (NN) and K-Means algorithms with dictionary learning. We describe these baselines below:

NN-KM: To detect novel documents, we use the nearest neighbor approach used by the UMass FSD system [2], which is one of the best performing system for this task [29]. As in the UMass system, we use cosine distance as a similarity measure and a TF-IDF weighted document representation. Every document in P_t whose cosine distance to its nearest neighbor in $P_{\leq t-1}$ is below some η is marked as novel. We build on this algorithm to get a baseline for emerging topic detection, by running a K-Means clustering with cosine distance (a.k.a. Spherical K-Means) on the doc-

ADM EQUATIONS FOR (17)	ADM EQUATIONS FOR (18)
Input: $S^{(j-1)} \in \mathbb{R}^{k_1 \times \lvert\text{Nvl}_t\rvert}, \text{Nvl}_t \in \mathbb{R}^{m \times \lvert\text{Nvl}_t\rvert}, \beta, \tau, \gamma > 0$	**Input:** $R^{(j)} \in \mathbb{R}^{m \times k_1}, \text{Nvl}_t \in \mathbb{R}^{m \times \lvert\text{Nvl}_t\rvert}, \lambda, \beta, \tau, \gamma > 0$
1. $R^{(j)}_{(1)} \leftarrow R^{(j-1)}, \Gamma_{(1)} \leftarrow \text{Nvl}_t - R^{(j-1)}S^{(j-1)}, \Delta_{(1)} \leftarrow 0$	1. $S^{(j)}_{(1)} \leftarrow S^{(j-1)}, \Gamma_{(1)} \leftarrow \text{Nvl}_t - R^{(j)}S^{(j-1)}, \Delta_{(1)} \leftarrow 0$
2. **for** $i = 1, 2, \ldots,$*convergence* **do**	2. **for** $i = 1, 2, \ldots,$*convergence* **do**
a) $\Gamma_{(i+1)} \leftarrow \text{soft}(\text{Nvl}_t - R^{(j)}_{(i)}S^{(j-1)} + \Delta_{(i)}/\beta, 1/\beta)$	a) $\Gamma_{(i+1)} \leftarrow \text{soft}(\text{Nvl}_t - R^{(j)}S^{(j)}_{(i)} + \Delta_{(i)}/\beta, 1/\beta)$
b) $G_{(i)} \leftarrow (R^{(j)}_{(i)}S^{(j-1)} + \Gamma_{(i+1)} - \text{Nvl}_t - \Delta_{(i)}/\beta)S^{\top}_{(j-1)}$	b) $G_{(i)} \leftarrow R^{(j)^{\top}}(R^{(j)}S^{(j)}_{(i)} + \Gamma_{(i+1)} - \text{Nvl}_t - \Delta_{(i)}/\beta)$
c) $R^{(j)}_{(i+1)} \leftarrow \max\{R^{(j)}_{(i)} - \tau G_{(i)}, 0\}$	c) $S^{(j)}_{(i+1)} \leftarrow \max\{S^{(j)}_{(i)} - \tau G_{(i)} - (\lambda\tau)/\beta, 0\}$
d) $\Delta_{(i+1)} \leftarrow \Delta_{(i)} + \gamma\beta(\text{Nvl}_t - R^{(j)}_{(i+1)}S^{(j-1)} - \Gamma_{(i+1)})$	d) $\Delta_{(i+1)} \leftarrow \Delta_{(i)} + \gamma\beta(\text{Nvl}_t - R^{(j)}S^{(j)}_{(i+1)} - \Gamma_{(i+1)})$

Figure 3: ADM equations for dictionary learning used in Algorithm DICTCLUST.

Phase	No. of old clusters	No. of docs from old clusters	No. of new clusters	No. of docs from new clusters	F1_{nvl} (our)	F1_{nvl} (NN-KM)	F1_{nvl} (DICT-KM)	F1_{nvl} (NN-DICT)
TDT2 Corpus								
1	18	1390	2	63	0.868	0.694	0.781	0.859
2	20	2256	6	139	0.349	0.324	0.364	0.338
3	26	669	3	45	0.784	0.650	0.730	0.721
4	29	2526	1	140	0.163	0.130	0.146	0.155
Avg.					**0.541**	**0.450**	**0.505**	**0.518**
20 NewsGroup Corpus								
1	6	572	2	783	0.652	0.555	0.630	0.626
2	8	769	2	991	0.586	0.536	0.561	0.519
3	10	964	2	1182	0.655	0.579	0.673	0.654
4	12	1160	2	1366	0.667	0.566	0.620	0.588
5	14	1359	2	1565	0.696	0.576	0.679	0.583
6	16	1552	2	1412	0.731	0.565	0.599	0.681
7	18	1713	2	1714	0.705	0.561	0.598	0.613
Avg.					**0.670**	**0.563**	**0.623**	**0.610**

Table 1: Results for TDT2 and 20 Newsgroups corpora. We set $k = 100$. The F1_{nvl} value reported is the maximum F1_{nvl} obtained for each phase by varying ζ, η in the interval $[0, 1]$. In Phase 0 of TDT2 corpus 2166 documents from 18 clusters and in Phase 0 of 20 Newsgroups corpus 1718 documents from 6 clusters are used to initialize the dictionary, respectively.

uments marked novel. We use Spherical K-Means, as it is a well-established approach to clustering high-dimensional text data [12].

DICT-KM: The second baseline is a modification of our dictionary based scheme. We use a dictionary learning approach to detect novel documents (this can be done by invoking Algorithm NVL-CLUST without Step 3) and then run a Spherical K-Means clustering on these novel documents to create emerging topic clusters.

NN-DICT: The third baseline is also a modification of our dictionary based scheme. We first use the nearest neighbor approach (explained above) to detect novel documents and then run Algorithm DICTCLUST on these novel documents to create emerging topic clusters.

We implemented all the algorithms in Matlab. In all our experiments $k = 100$ and $\lambda = 1/100$. We noticed that varying these parameters does affect the evaluation metrics (e.g., increasing the dictionary sizes leads to better scores, but comes at a cost of increased running times). However, due to space constraints, we postpone a discussion of these results to the full version of this paper. The parameters of ADM are fixed as $\beta = 10$, $\tau = 1/50$, and $\gamma = 1.618$ (these are chosen in consultation with [38] and Theorem 6.3 for faster convergence).

7.3 TDT2 and 20 Newsgroups Datasets

We use two standard labeled datasets to evaluate the performance of our proposed algorithm. We start by describing these datasets and our experimental setup.

Our first dataset is the NIST topic detection and tracking (TDT2) corpus[2] which consists of news stories in the first half of 1998. For our evaluation, we use a set of 9,394 documents represented over 19,528 terms and spread over 27 weeks. These documents are partitioned into 30 human-labeled topics. We introduce the documents from the 27 weeks in 5 different phases. In the zeroth phase, we introduce all the documents between weeks 1 to 5 and these documents are used for initializing the dictionary A_0. We do so by running Algorithm NVLCLUST (without the Step 3) in an offline fashion (as in we alternate between the detection stage and dictionary learning stage for each document). In the first phase, we introduce all the documents between weeks 6 to 7 and run Algorithm NVLCLUST on these documents with dictionary A_0. In the second phase, we introduce all the documents between weeks 8 to 13 and run Algorithm NVLCLUST on these documents with dictionary A_1 (outputted by the first phase). We repeat the same steps for the third phase (between weeks 14 to 17) and fourth phase (between weeks 18 to 27). The reason for choosing such asymmetric time intervals is to make sure that at least one new topic cluster gets introduced in each phase.

As our second dataset we use the 20 Newsgroups corpus[3]. The corpus contains 18,774 articles distributed among 20 clusters where each cluster is a Usenet group. For our experiments, we use a vo-

[2]http://www.itl.nist.gov/iad/mig/tests/tdt/1998/

[3]http://people.csail.mit.edu/jrennie/20Newsgroups/

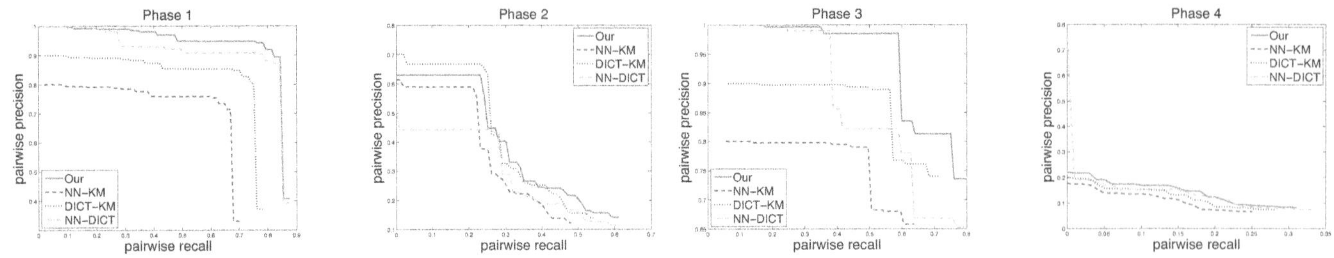

Figure 4: Interpolated pairwise precision-recall curves for TDT2, obtained by varying ζ and η between $[0.05, 0.15]$.

cabulary of 10,000 terms selected based on frequency. We do a set of controlled experiments on this corpus. Again, we introduce the documents in phases. Documents within each cluster are temporally ordered, and we use this temporal ordering to introduce the documents. At the end of Phase $i - 1$, we have documents from some (old) clusters, and in Phase i we introduce a mixture of documents, some coming from these old clusters and some belonging to new clusters; and see how well our algorithm performs in detecting these new clusters. We begin Phase 0 with documents sampled from 6 randomly chosen clusters. In each subsequent phase, we introduce documents from 2 new clusters. The numbers of documents from added at each phase are presented in Table 1.

For our baselines with K-Means clustering, we run the algorithm 8 times (with random initialization for centroids) and take the best result. For each phase, we set both k_1 (number of topics to be generated by Algorithm DICTCLUST) and K (number of clusters to be generated by K-Means) to be equal to 10. We vary the threshold $0 \leq \zeta \leq 1$ to find the threshold where $\mathrm{F1}_{\mathrm{nvl}}$ is maximized for our algorithm (similarly, for the DICT-KM algorithm with threshold ζ, and for the NN-KM and NN-DICT algorithms with threshold η).

Table 1 presents the maximum $\mathrm{F1}_{\mathrm{nvl}}$ for both datasets (obtained by varying ζ, η). Our algorithm always outperforms all the three baselines. For TDT2, our algorithm gives on average 16.9% improvement in $\mathrm{F1}_{\mathrm{nvl}}$ score over the NN-KM, 6.7% improvement over DICT-KM, and 4.3% improvement over NN-DICT. For 20 Newsgroups, we notice on average 16.0% improvement over NN-KM, 7.0% improvement over DICT-KM, and 9.0% improvement over NN-DICT. While the results shows that we get a big improvement over NN-KM, the improvements over DICT-KM and NN-DICT are only moderate. Since, both DICT-KM and NN-DICT use in parts our dictionary learning algorithm, the results suggest that using dictionary learning could lead to an improvement in the $\mathrm{F1}_{\mathrm{nvl}}$ score over just using nearest neighbor/clustering techniques. Furthermore, our algorithm consistently outperforms DICT-KM, and NN-DICT consistently outperforms NN-KM, indicating that a dictionary-based clustering scheme results in better clustering than Spherical K-Means.

Note that, the $\mathrm{F1}_{\mathrm{nvl}}$ scores are lower than what one would encounter in "typical clustering" applications. Intuitively, this happens because we evaluate these metrics only over the novel documents, which are far fewer in number than the documents from the old clusters; and each missed document (from $\mathrm{TNvl}_t \setminus \mathrm{Nvl}_t$) affects $\mathrm{Rec}_{\mathrm{nvl}}$ combinatorially because of the pairwise mistakes that they lead to (similarly, each wrongly added document from $\mathrm{Nvl}_t \setminus \mathrm{TNvl}_t$ severely affects $\mathrm{Prec}_{\mathrm{nvl}}$).

In Figure 4, we present interpolated (pairwise) precision-recall curves [24] for the TDT2 dataset, obtained by varying the threshold ζ, η. We see that the precision-recall curve of our algorithm mostly dominates the curves of the baseline algorithms, which illustrates the superiority of our algorithm over different operating points. The curves for the 20 Newsgroups corpus are similar and are omitted for lack of space.

7.4 Novel Document Detection Evaluation

The performance of our approach relies on first, accurately identifying novel documents, and then appropriately clustering these document. Results in the previous section show that we do well in the overall task of emerging topic detection, but in order to get a better understanding of the strengths of our approach, we investigate performance on the sub-task of novel document detection. Given a set of documents, this task is to classify each document as either novel (positive) or non-novel (negative). True labeling is created by labeling the documents from any of the emerging topic clusters as positive, and the documents from any of the existing true topics as negative. For evaluating this classification task, we use Area Under Curve (AUC) of the ROC curve [24]. As a baseline, we use the NN approach explained in Section 7.2. As mentioned earlier, this NN approach is one of the best performing systems for FSD, a task that is very similar to novel document detection.

The results, presented in Table 2, show that for this sub-task our dictionary-based approach and the NN approach have almost the same performance. Even though the AUCs are near identical, the sets of documents that the two approaches mark as novel are quite different. This is evidenced by the superior performance of our approach over NN-DICT, which uses the same approach for the second sub-task of clustering novel documents into emerging topics (see Table 1). In summary, while our dictionary-based approach is picking novel documents with the same accuracy as NN, it is more likely to pick documents from the same emerging topic.

	TDT2		**20 Newsgroups**	
Phase	*Our*	*NN*	*Our*	*NN*
1	0.982	0.982	0.941	0.942
2	0.926	0.933	0.941	0.942
3	0.976	0.961	0.880	0.880
4	0.844	0.850	0.898	0.902
5			0.915	0.917
6			0.917	0.921
7			0.919	0.920
Avg.	**0.932**	**0.932**	**0.916**	**0.918**

Table 2: Performance, in AUC, on novel document detection.

7.5 Watson Jeopardy Twitter Data

In Section 7.3, we evaluated our approach on labeled benchmark data sets. Here, we analyze how well our approach performs in practice, when applied to Twitter data. In particular, we look at the Twitter discussion around IBM's Watson DeepQA system.[4] In February 2011, the Watson DeepQA system participated on the

[4]http://www.ibm.com/watson

Jeopardy! game-show, competing against humans; and the event was televised over 3 days: Feb 14, 15, and 16. We used Twitter's search API to collect all tweets relevant to the participation of Watson in Jeopardy! from Feb 1 – 16; where tweets were judged relevant by keyword and pattern filters. We used a sample set of 8,434 tweets from Feb 1 – 14, to initialize our dictionary. Then, we tested our system on detecting emerging topics on a sample of 5,199 tweets from Feb 16. The entire corpus of tweets had a vocabulary of size 1,139, after removing common stop words.

We give as input to Algorithm NVLCLUST the learned dictionary and the tweets of Feb 16. Instead of presenting the entire range of parameter values, here we pick $k_1 = 15$ and $\zeta = 0.5$ to illustrate the clusters identified at a particular setting. From the topic clusters outputted by our algorithm, in Table 3, we present three selected ones. These clusters were manually inspected to identify the dominant topic in them. Note that, these three topics are emerging, as the date of their occurrence is Feb 15 or later, whereas we learn our initial dictionary only on tweets till Feb 14.

The fourth and fifth columns in Table 3 show the size of the novel clusters detected, and the number of tweets that were judged, by a human annotator, to be relevant to the identified dominant topic in these clusters. The sixth column shows the top keywords for each topic. These are selected by looking at the atoms corresponding to these topics in the dictionary matrix produced by Algorithm DICT-CLUST and by picking the top 3 words on which these atoms have the largest mass. The first selected cluster contains tweets on Watson's Final Jeopardy mistake on Feb 15th, which subsequently received much media coverage. The second and third selected clusters contain tweets related to two influential news articles on Feb 16. Note that, large fractions of tweets in these clusters are relevant to the dominant topic, indicating high coherence of the identified clusters. Table 4 presents three sample tweets from each of the three topics; which illustrates that our approach can cluster together tweets that are clearly on the same topic, even if syntactically quite different. Being able to automatically comb through tens of thousands, and potentially millions, of documents, to identify such emerging topics of discussion amongst consumers is of significant value to PR and marketing efforts.

8. RELATED WORK

Several existing approaches to identify *hot topics* or *trends* in social media are based on the frequency of mentions of terms, such as Twitscoop.com, Trendistic.com, Twopular.com, and trends on Twitter.com. While high frequency of terms may be a good indicator of popularity, it does not necessarily identify new or emerging trends. Instead, comparing the *relative* frequency of occurrence of terms and phrases in the current time period to the occurrences in the past, is likely to identify more topical phrases. Tomokiyo and Hurst [32] propose such an approach for extracting key-phrases based on statistical language models, which they apply to 20 Newsgroups data. Similarly, Cataldi *et al.* [25] present an approach in which they identify emergent keywords, which have been extensively used in a given time period, but not in previous ones. They find words that frequently co-occur with each emergent word, and report these together as emerging topics. Glass *et al.* [14] go a step further, from emerging words to tracking emerging *memes* – "distinctive phrases which propagate relatively unchanged." Their work focuses on building models to predict which memes will spread widely. Our work differs from the above approaches by going beyond unigrams and n-grams, to identifying novel clusters of similar documents, which provides a richer characterization of topics. Furthermore, we distinguish emerging, novel topics from merely popular or well-known ones.

9. CONCLUSION

User-generated content is increasingly playing a pivotal role as the source for breaking news and developments, as well as shaping opinions on a variety of matters ranging from products to policies. In this paper, we presented a dictionary learning based framework for detecting emerging topics in social media and related streams. The dictionary learning formulation naturally combines ideas from robustness, sparsity, and non-negative matrix factorization for analysis of streaming text. The overall framework was divided into two stages—first, determining novel documents in the stream, and subsequently identifying cluster structure among the novel documents. The objective functions in each stage were optimized using the alternating directions method, which can be easily parallelized for further scalability. Empirical evaluation on a variety of datasets illustrate the effectiveness of the proposed framework.

One can envision several directions for future work based on the proposed framework. While the current work uses fixed sized dictionaries, using adaptive dictionaries whose size changes based on the set of active or emerging topics may be more desirable in certain applications. While learning the dictionary A_t, the current work uses the entire historical data $P_{\leq t}$. A fully online version which only maintains sufficient statistics of historical data may be more scalable for real world streams. Further, from an optimization perspective, one may be able to use accelerated gradient descent and related proximal methods [33] to further speed up the alternating directions method. Finally, while the focus of the current work was on detecting emerging topics in text streams, similar ideas can be developed for other domains (such as healthcare, climate sciences) where detection of novel signal streams is of interest.

Acknowledgments

We would like to thank Richard Lawrence for many fruitful discussions. We would also like to thank Estepan Meliksetian and Phaneendra Divakaruni for collecting the Jeopardy Twitter dataset. This research is continuing through participation in the Anomaly Detection at Multiple Scales (ADAMS) program sponsored by the U.S. Defense Advanced Research Projects Agency (DARPA) under Agreement Number W911NF-11-C-0200. AB was supported in part by NSF CAREER award IIS-0953274, and NSF grants IIS-1029711, IIS-0916750, and IIS-0812183.

10. REFERENCES

[1] M. Aharon, M. Elad, and A. Bruckstein. The K-SVD: An Algorithm for Designing Overcomplete Dictionaries for Sparse Representation. *IEEE TSP*, 54(11):4311–4322, 2006.

[2] J. Allan. *Topic Detection and Tracking: Event-based Information Organization*. Springer, 2002.

[3] E. Amaldi and V. Kann. On the Approximability of Minimizing Nonzero Variables or Unsatisfied Relations in Linear Systems. *Elsevier TCS*, 209(1-2):237–260, 1998.

[4] R. Basri and D. Jacobs. Lambertian Reflectance and Linear Subspaces. *IEEE TPAMI*, pages 218–233, 2003.

[5] D. Blei, A. Ng, and M. Jordan. Latent Dirichlet Allocation. *JMLR*, 3:993–1022, 2003.

[6] S. Boyd, N. Parikh, E. Chu, B. Peleato, and J. Eckstein. Distributed Optimization and Statistical Learning via the Alternating Direction Method of Multipliers. *Foundations and Trends in Machine Learning*, 2011.

[7] A. Bruckstein, D. Donoho, and M. Elad. From Sparse Solutions of Systems of Equations to Sparse Modeling of Signals and Images. *SIAM review*, 51(1):34–81, 2009.

Id	*Topic/Event*	*Date of Occurrence*	*Size of Detected Cluster*	*Tweets Relevant to Topic in the Cluster*	*Top Topic Keywords*
1	Watson's Final Jeopardy Mistake [34]	Feb 15, 2011	118	118	trebek, toronto, check
2	News Article [30]	Feb 16, 2011	110	82	people, amazed, google
3	News Article [18]	Feb 16, 2011	100	70	speed, creators, advantage

Table 3: Emerging Topics on Feb 16, 2011 in Watson Jeopardy Twitter Archive.

Id	*Sample Tweets from each of the 3 Emerging Topics shown in Table 3*
1	Watson on Jeopardy! Day Two: The Confusion Over an Airport Clue US Cities: Its largest airport was named for a WWII hero; its 2nd for a WWII battle. IBM Watson: What is Toronto Why Watson answered Toronto to "Its largest airport was named for a World War II hero; its second largest, for...
2	Search Engine Land: Could Google Play Jeopardy Like IBM's Watson? SEO::: Could Google Play Jeopardy Like IBM's Watson?: Like many people, I was amazed to watch IBM's Watson super... Could Google Play Jeopardy Like IBM's Watson?: Like many people, I was amazed to watch IBM's Watson supercompute...
3	Arstechnica: Creators: Watson has no speed advantage as it crushes humans in Jeopardy New on ArsTechnica Creators: Watson has no speed advantage as it crushes humans in Jeopardy ... Technology Creators: Watson has no speed advantage as it crushes humans in Jeopardy

Table 4: Some tweets from the 3 emerging topics detected on Feb 16, 2011. We omit the tiny urls appearing in the tweets.

[8] E. Candes, X. Li, Y. Ma, and J. Wright. Robust Principal Component Analysis. abs/0912.3599, 2009.

[9] E. Candes and P. Randall. Highly Robust Error Correction by Convex Programming. *IEEE TIT*, 54(7):2829–2840, 2008.

[10] S. Chen, D. Donoho, and M. Saunders. Atomic Decomposition by Basis Pursuit. *SIAM SISC*, 20(1), 1999.

[11] P. Combettes and J. Pesquet. Proximal Splitting Methods in Signal Processing. Arxiv preprint arXiv:0912.3522, 2009.

[12] I. S. Dhillon and D. S. Modha. Concept Decompositions for Large Sparse Text Data using Clustering. *Machine Learning*, 42(1):143–175, 2001.

[13] D. Donoho. For most Large Underdetermined Systems of Equations, the Minimal L1-norm Near-solution Approximates the Sparsest Near-solution. *Communications on Pure and Applied Mathematics*, 59(7):907–934, 2006.

[14] K. Glass and R. Colbaugh. Toward Emerging Topic Detection for Business Intelligence: Predictive Analysis of Meme Dynamics. *CoRR*, 2010.

[15] T. Hofmann. Probabilistic Latent Semantic Analysis. In *UAI*, pages 289–296, 1999.

[16] B. J. Jansen, M. Zhang, K. Sobel, and A. Chowdury. Twitter Power: Tweets as Electronic Word of Mouth. *J. Am. Soc. Inf. Sci. Technol.*, 60, 2009.

[17] R. Jennaton, J. Mairal, G. Obozinsky, , and F. Bach. Proximal Methods for Sparse Hierarchical Dictionary Learning. *ICML*, pages 487–494, 2010.

[18] C. Johnston. Creators: Watson has no speed advantage as it crushes humans in Jeopardy. http://bit.ly/fmfmwz.

[19] Q. Ke and T. Kanade. Robust L1 Norm Factorization in the Presence of Outliers and Missing Data by Alternative Convex Programming. In *CVPR*, pages 739–746, 2005.

[20] D. Lee and H. Seung. Learning the Parts of Objects by Non-negative Matrix Factorization. *Nature*, 1999.

[21] H. Lee, A. Battle, R. Raina, and A. Ng. Efficient Sparse Coding Algorithms. *NIPS*, 19:801–808, 2007.

[22] J. Mairal, F. Bach, J. Ponce, and G. Sapiro. Online Learning for Matrix Factorization and Sparse Coding. *JMLR*, 2010.

[23] J. Mairal, F. Bach, J. Ponce, G. Sapiro, and A. Zisserman. Discriminative Learned Dictionaries for Local Image Analysis. In *CVPR*, pages 1–8, 2008.

[24] C. Manning, P. Raghavan, and H. Schütze. *Introduction to Information Retrieval*. Cambridge University Press, 2008.

[25] C. Mario, D. C. Luigi, and S. Claudio. Emerging Topic Detection on Twitter based on Temporal and Social Terms Evaluation. In *IWMDM*, pages 1–10, 2010.

[26] P. Melville, V. Sindhwani, and R. Lawrence. Social Media Analytics: Channeling the Power of the Blogosphere for Marketing Insight. In *Proc. of the WIN*, 2009.

[27] K. Min, Z. Zhang, J. Wright, and Y. Ma. Decomposing Background Topics from Keywords by Principal Component Pursuit. In *CIKM*, pages 269–278, 2010.

[28] B. Olshausen and D. Field. Sparse Coding with an Overcomplete Basis Set: A Strategy Employed by V1? *Vision Research*, 37(23):3311–3325, 1997.

[29] S. Petrović, M. Osborne, and V. Lavrenko. Streaming First Story Detection with Application to Twitter. In *ACL*, 2010.

[30] D. Sullivan. Could Google Play Jeopardy Like IBMs Watson? http://selnd.com/hL5kvY.

[31] R. Tibshirani. Regression Shrinkage and Selection via the Lasso. *JRSS*, 58(1):267–288, 1996.

[32] T. Tomokiyo and M. Hurst. A Language Model approach to Keyphrase Extraction. In *ACL Workshop on Multi-word Expressions*, pages 33–40, 2003.

[33] P. Tseng. Aprroximation Accuracy, Gradient Methods, and Error Bound for Structured Convex Optimization. *Mathematical Programming, Series B*, 125:263–295, 2010.

[34] Wikipedia. Watson (computer). http://bit.ly/mTwstz.

[35] J. Wright and Y. Ma. Dense Error Correction Via L1-Minimization. *IEEE TIT*, 56(7):3540–3560, 2010.

[36] J. Wright, A. Yang, A. Ganesh, S. Sastry, and Y. Ma. Robust Face Recognition via Sparse Representation. *IEEE TPAMI*, 2008.

[37] A. Y. Yang, S. S. Sastry, A. Ganesh, and Y. Ma. Fast L1-minimization Algorithms and an Application in Robust Face Recognition: A Review. In *ICIP*, 2010.

[38] J. Yang and Y. Zhang. Alternating Direction Algorithms for L1-Problems in Compressive Sensing. Arxiv, 2009.

[39] Y. Zhang, A. d'Aspremont, and L. E. Ghaoui. *SparsePCA: Convex Relaxations, Algorithms and Applications*. Springer, 2010.

Focusing on Novelty: A Crawling Strategy to Build Diverse Language Models

Luciano Barbosa
AT&T Labs – Research
180 Park Ave
Florham Park, NJ 07932
lbarbosa@research.att.com

Srinivas Bangalore
AT&T Labs – Research
180 Park Ave
Florham Park, NJ 07932
srini@research.att.com

ABSTRACT

Word prediction performed by language models has an important role in many tasks as e.g. word sense disambiguation, speech recognition, hand-writing recognition, query spelling and query segmentation. Recent research has exploited the textual content of the Web to create language models. In this paper, we propose a new focused crawling strategy to collect Web pages that focuses on novelty in order to create diverse language models. In each crawling cycle, the crawler tries to fill the gaps present in the current language model built from previous cycles, by avoiding visiting pages whose vocabulary is already well represented in the model. It relies on an information theoretic measure to identify these gaps and then learns link patterns to pages in these regions in order to guide its visitation policy. To handle constantly evolving domains, a key feature of our crawler approach is its ability to adjust its focus as the crawl progresses. We evaluate our approach in two different scenarios in which our solution can be useful. First, we demonstrate that our approach produces more effective language models than the ones created by a baseline crawler in the context of a speech recognition task of broadcast news. In fact, in some cases, our crawler was able to obtain similar results to the baseline by crawling only 12.5% of the pages collected by the latter. Secondly, since in the news domain avoiding well-represented content might lead to novelty, i.e. up-to-date pages, we show that our diversity-based crawler can also be helpful to guide the crawler for the most recent content in the news. The results show that our approach was able to obtain on average 50% more up-to-date pages than the baseline crawler.

Categories and Subject Descriptors

H.3.3 [**Information Search and Retrieval**]: Search process.

General Terms

Algorithms, Design, Experimentation.

Keywords

Web Crawling, Language Modeling, Novelty, Perplexity.

1. INTRODUCTION

Web is an invaluable data repository. The text data on the Web has been harnessed for tasks as diverse as named entity recognition [25], word sense disambiguation [23] and machine translation [17] in natural language processing; search and question answering [18] in information retrieval; and pronunciation modeling and language modeling in speech recognition [19].

What makes the text on the Web so attractive for these applications? Apart from the sheer size of the textual repository, Web text is compelling for two main reasons. First, Web text in general is *diverse* and not limited to a particular domain. This aspect is particularly important as language technologies are beginning to cope with ever increasing need to handle open domain input in tasks such as search, question-answering, and language translation. Second, and perhaps more important, is that the Web text from sources, such as news websites, blogs, microblogs and others, is *dynamic*, and tracks the current news and popular events.

For these reasons, recent research has exploited the textual content of the Web to create models for natural language tools, in particular, language models [14, 21]. Typically, language models are built on a training corpus of sentences with the assumption that the distribution of n-grams in the training set is the same as the distribution of n-grams in the task context where the language model would be used. This assumption, also called as the *independent and identically distributed (iid)* assumption, is reasonable for tasks which are domain limited and where the target data does not change over time. However, in open domain applications such as question-answering, broadcast news speech recognition, where the input to the models change based on the current events, the *iid* assumption results in a mismatch between the training and target contexts. This mismatch can be interpreted as holes or gaps in the training data. To address this issue, language models are typically transformed to match the target distributions using adaptation techniques [5].

In this paper, we handle this mismatch problem in a different way. To fill the gaps present in the language model, we design techniques to collect Web text whose vocabulary is not well represented in the model, producing a more diverse language model. Unlike a traditional static-corpus driven method where models trained on static corpora would soon be outdated due to the changing profiles of the input, Web text based models can potentially be continuously updated to keep them from becoming stale.

Previous approaches [21, 6] have mined sentences from Web text to increase the corpus of a language model. Their primarily goal is to collect data most similar to the domain of interest. It is to be expected that with the increase in size of the training data from this kind of content a language model would be more *specialized* to the domain of interest. Along similar lines, regular focused crawling also aims to gather Web pages in a well-defined topic [8, 11]. Topics are defined using a few example documents and the task of the crawler is to increase the coverage of pages in the defined topic.

In contrast to these previous approaches, we want to *unfocus* the crawler on previous collected data, from which the language model had originated, and crawl for regions of novelty with respect to the language model. The crawler identifies these regions by using an information theoretic measure, and then guides its visitation policy based on the patterns of links in these regions. To handle constantly evolving domains, wherein new events appear constantly, an important feature of our crawler is its ability to adjust its focus as the crawl progresses, to be able to reflect in its policy the most current state of its environment. In summary, the main contributions of this work are:

- A novel crawling strategy that is tightly coupled with the goal of creating diverse language models by filling in the gaps in the current language model;
- The usage of an information theoretic measure to guide the crawling policy instead of using regular supervised learning techniques [8];
- The combination of techniques from different research communities – NLP, Machine Learning, Information Theory and Information Retrieval – to address the important problem of creating a corpus for language models.

The remainder of the paper is organized as follows. In Section 2, we introduce concepts of a language model and explain the need for diversification of a language model. We present in detail the main components that compose our crawling in Section 3 and present experimental results in Section 4. We review related work in Section 5 and conclude in Section 6.

2. LANGUAGE MODELS

Many speech and language applications need a mechanism to rank sentences according to their well-formedness based on the grammar of a language. However, designing such a ranking function has eluded us despite many years of research. Instead, the likelihood of a sentence (denoted as $P(W)$, where W is a sentence) in a corpus of text is used an approximation for grammatically, with the assumption that grammatically well-formed sentences occur more often than ungrammatical ones. However, due to sparseness concerns, the probability of the joint event $W = w_1, w_2, \ldots, w_m$ is approximated using an independence assumption as shown in Equation 2, also known as an n-gram model.

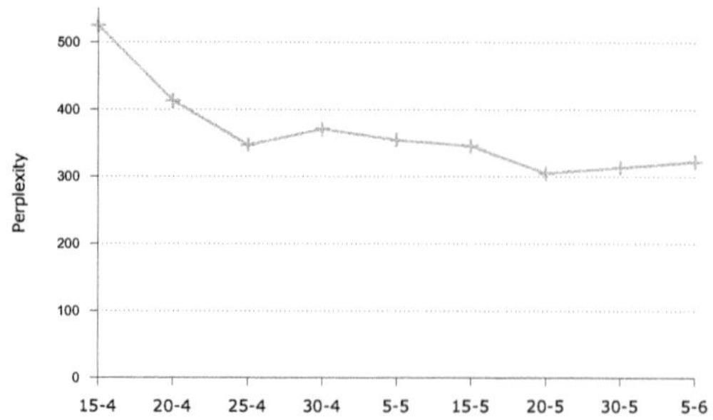

Figure 1: The perplexity of a news story from May 20, 2010 over language models from news Websites ranging from mid April to beginning of June 2010.

$$P(W) = \prod_{i=1}^{m} P(w_i|w_1, \ldots, w_{i-n+1}) \quad (1)$$

$$\approx \prod_{i=1}^{m} P(w_i|w_{i-1}, \ldots, w_{i-n+1}) \quad (2)$$

The individual probabilities in the product are computed using maximum likelihood estimation from a corpus of word sequences, and when a given n-gram is not observed in the corpus, then its probability is estimated using a lower order $n-1$ gram.

Besides evaluating the effectiveness of a language model in the context of a task, such as machine translation or speech recognition, a metric that is commonly used to compare language models that is independent of the task is called *Perplexity*. As seen in Equation 2, an n-gram model can be viewed as a model for predicting the nth word given the preceding $n-1$ words of history. Low perplexity implies a better fit of the model for the word sequence. Perplexity of a language model P on an m-word sequence W is defined as in Equation 3.

$$Perplexity(P, W) = P(W)^{-\frac{1}{m}} \quad (3)$$

$$= \sqrt[m]{\prod_{i=1}^{m} \frac{1}{P(w_i|w_{i-1}, \ldots, w_{i-n+1})}} \quad (4)$$

To give a better intuition about perplexity and how perplexity can be associated to time, we show how the perplexity of a fixed page evolves over different language models built over time. Figure 1 presents the perplexity of a news article from May 20th, 2010 over language models created from news Websites between April 15th and June 6th [1]. As it can be seen, the closer the language model is to the story, the smaller the perplexity. In fact, the lowest value is on the day that the story was released. The perplexity starts to increase again afterwards. Our assumption is that the vocabulary of pages that have high perplexity over a language model represent the gaps on it. In Section 3, we explain how we exploit this to create our diversity crawler.

3. CRAWLING FOR DIVERSITY

Our primary goal in this work is to create a crawling strategy that prioritizes diversity. In order to do so, the crawler searches for Web regions where the vocabulary of the pages is poorly covered by previous crawls. Thus, the current

[1]The news article was not used the model of May 20th.

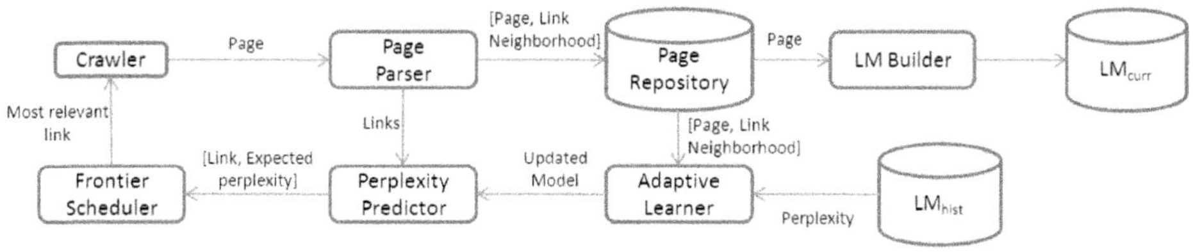

Figure 2: Architecture of the Diversity Crawler.

crawl will be guided based on the language model created from previous crawls. Our assumption is that pages whose vocabulary is well-covered on the language model contain some common patterns in their links. These patterns will then guide the link visitation of the current crawl to avoid collecting similar pages.

Figure 2 presents the architecture of our crawler. Let LM_{hist} represent the language model from previous crawls and LM_{curr} the language model to be created from the current crawl. The crawler uses the *Perplexity Predictor* to guide its visitation policy by predicting the expected perplexity with respect to LM_{hist} of a page given its link. This prediction is sent to the *Frontier Scheduler* that then decides the next link to be visited by the crawler. The downloaded pages are stored in the *Page Repository* which are used by the *LM Builder* to create the new language model, LM_{curr}. In the next cycle, LM_{curr} replaces LM_{hist}. Since the language model changes every cycle, the crawler needs to adapt its visitation policy accordingly. This is done by the *Adaptive Learner*. It creates a new model for the Perplexity Predictor as the crawl progresses based on LM_{hist} and on the pages/links collected in the current crawl. In the remainder of this section, we describe in detail these core components of the system.

3.1 Perplexity Predictor

As we mentioned before, to create diverse language models, the crawler should focus on novel regions for LM_{hist}. We model them as regions that contain pages with high perplexity values over LM_{hist}. To guide the crawler visitation policy to these regions, the crawler relies on the links to pages in these regions, similar to previous focused crawlers [7, 20]. But, in contrast with these approaches, which try to focus the crawler on a particular topic, we aim to *de-emphasize* the pages previously covered, since our objective is to increase the diversity of the language model.

Formally, let $P = p_1, \ldots, p_{|P|}$ be the pool of $|P|$ pages and $N = n_1, \ldots, n_{|P|}$ be the neighborhoods of the links pointing to these pages. The link neighborhood is composed of the words in the anchor of the link, around it (10 words before and after the anchor) and in its URL. Ideally, we would like to visit a set, **VP**, with the k-best pages with the highest perplexity according to LM_{hist}, as shown in Equation 5. However, this involves crawling all the pages and evaluating the perplexity of the text on each page which is an expensive operation. We instead would like to estimate the perplexity of the text on a page *without* crawling it.

$$\mathbf{VP} = argmax_{p_i}^{(k)} Perplexity(LM_{hist}, p_i) \qquad (5)$$

In order to do so, we assume that the text in the neighborhood of the link that points to the page has some predictive power about the perplexity of the page. Our assumption here is that the link neighborhood contains information that indicates the content of the page. This indication can be at different levels. There might be links that contain no indication of the page's content, when its link neighborhood is empty or just contains non-descriptive words; a broad indication, for instance, a URL that contains the term "sports" probably has content about sports in its body but just inspecting it, it is not clear which topic within sports that page is talking about; or a more descriptive indication of the page's content, for instance, a URL with the string "yankees-clinch-playoff-berth-beat-blue-jays" indicates that its content is about the baseball teams Yankees and Blue Jays, and their participation in playoffs.

Now, the problem of estimating the perplexity of a page based on the neighborhood of a page is a regression problem with the text features of the neighborhood serving as the independent variables. However, since we are not interested in the exact perplexity value but just in a shallow approximation of the real value for the crawling schedule, and to reduce learning time [16] (learning is performed on the fly), we aggregated links with similar perplexity values in the same class. To discretize the perplexity values, we use the equal-frequency binning approach, since we want to avoid the problem of having unbalanced training data [22], and set the number of bins equal to 3 (we empirically tried other values but obtained poorer results). As the overall distribution of perplexity values changes over time, its distribution within each bin also changes.

To give a better intuition about the distribution of perplexity values in this task, in Figure 3, we plot the distribution of the perplexity of pages from a random crawl of 100,000 pages at time t_1 from a set of news sites over a language model created in a previous day (LM_0) composed by 100,000 pages collected using the same strategy on these sites. As one can see, the perplexity is skewed towards small values: for 40% of the pages, it is between 0 and 100, and the higher the perplexity value, the smaller the number of pages. As one would expect, and we show in Section 4, this distribution varies over time, skewing more towards small values, which makes the problem of finding high-perplexity pages much harder.

Thus, given the text neighborhood n_i, the Perplexity Predictor classifies n_i into a particular perplexity class c using the features (ϕ) computed from the text of the neighborhood as shown in Equation 6.

$$c_i^* = argmax_c \;\; P(c|\phi(n_i)) \qquad (6)$$

We tried three different algorithms which are widely used in text classification: [2] Naïve Bayes, Suppport Vector Machines (SVM) and Maximum Entropy (MaxEnt). From the t_1 crawl used in the previously presented perplexity distribution experiment, we prepared the training data by randomly

[2]We use the data mining software Weka to build the classifiers [13].

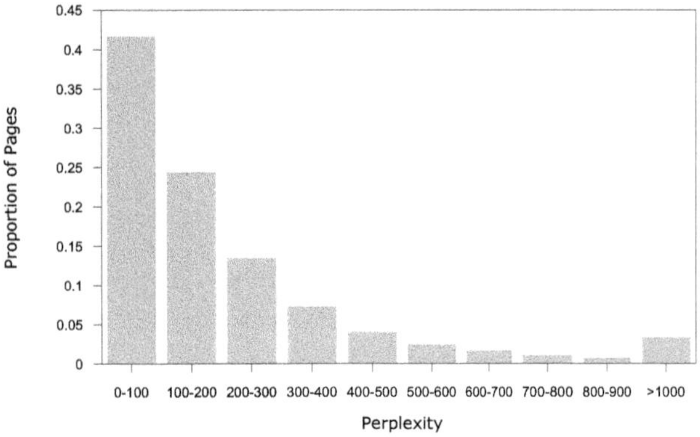

Figure 3: Distribution of perplexity values obtained by pages from a random crawl over a language model created in a previous day.

Algorithm	Accuracy	F-measure for High
Naïve Bayes	0.48	0.45
SVM	0.57	0.616
MaxEnt	0.57	0.613

Table 1: Overall accuracy and F-measure over the high-perplexity class obtained by the 3 classifier algorithms over the test set.

selecting 48,000 links and a different set of 12,000 links as testing set and, using the LM_0 from the same experiment, we calculated the perplexity of their respective pages. We binned the perplexity values for the training and test pages and trained the different classifiers and evaluated them on the test set.

Table 1 presents the accuracy over the three perplexity classes (Low, Medium, High) and F-measure over the class that corresponds to the highest expected perplexity values (High), which is the one we are most interested in, since the links in this class might point to pages that can diversify the language model. The best results in terms of accuracy were obtained by SVM and MaxEnt classifiers. SVM performed slightly better than MaxEnt for F-measure. For this reason, we selected SVM as the algorithm for the Perplexity Predictor.

To verify whether the Perplexity Predictor based crawler performs a better job than a random crawler, we set up two crawls: a random crawler and a crawler guided by the Perplexity Predictor. Figure 4 shows the percentage of pages for different values of perplexity obtained using LM_0. Whereas 40% of the pages collected by the random crawler is between 0-100, only 30% within this range was collected by the perplexity crawler. Moreover, the perplexity crawler was able to collect a much higher proportion of pages with perplexity greater than 200: 45% versus 35%. Overall, the average perplexity value of the pages obtained by the perplexity crawler was much higher than the one obtained by the random crawler: 361 versus 255. These numbers indicate that Perplexity Predictor is in fact able to focus the crawler on Web regions that contain high-perplexity pages.

One of the reasons of the effectiveness of Perplexity Predictor is its ability to capture the link patterns of stale pages from Web site sections whose vocabulary is similar across sites as, e.g., login, subscription and obituary pages. To give a concrete example of this, we looked at the distribution of *login*, "contact us" and *subscription* pages over the perplexity

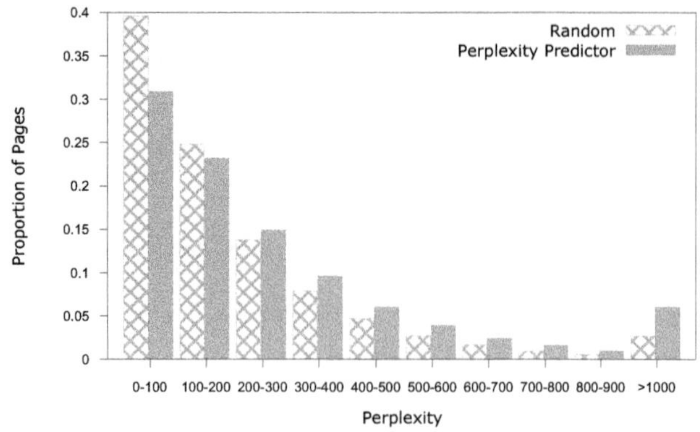

Figure 4: Comparison of perplexity values obtained by pages crawled using the Perplexity Predictor and a random approach.

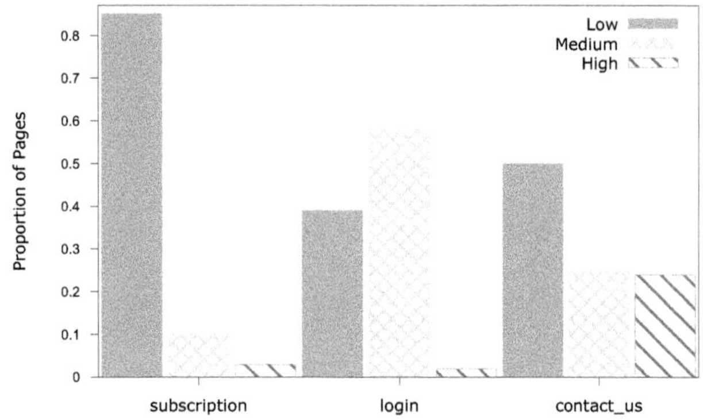

Figure 5: Proportion of login, subscription and "contact us" pages in the 3 different perplexity classes.

classes. More specifically, we selected for each class (Low, Medium, High), 3,500 links classified by the Perplexity Predictor and plotted, in Figure 5, the proportion of links of such pages in each set. The numbers show that most of the links to these pages were classified as having low perplexity, which is the result we would expect. In fact, looking at features with high information gain in this classification task, patterns in the links as login, log, sign, obituary have high values of information gain.

3.2 Frontier Scheduler

Having identified the links to crawl using the Perplexity Predictor module, the role of the Frontier Scheduler is to schedule the next link to be visited by the crawler. The schedule for visitation is defined based on expected perplexity of the links available in the frontier and on other visitation policies, for example, to avoid hitting a same Web server in a short period of time.

The Frontier Scheduler is implemented as a set of N queues, where each queue corresponds to a Perplexity Predictor class. Within a queue, links are ordered based on their likelihood of belonging to the class associated with the queue. The queue from the highest perplexity class contains more elements than the other ones. In our experiments the proportion of the queue sizes was 1 (low), 2 (medium), 10 (high).

As the accuracy of the Perplexity Predictor is far from perfect and also to avoid some possible bias contained in the links that might hurt the diversity of the crawl, the crawling frontier is updated in batches. When the crawler

Algorithm 1 *LM Builder*

1: **Input:** N, $predictorLM$, $webPages$, $devSet$
{N: number of language models to be merged,
$predictorLM$: LM used for the Perplexity Predictor in the current crawl,
$webPages$: Web pages from current crawl,
$devSet$: development set.}
2: $sents = ParsePages(webPages)$
{Parse the Web pages into sentences.}
3: $lm = CreateLM(sents)$
{Create LM from sentences.}
4: $currentLM = CombineLMs(predictorLM, lm, devSet)$
{Combine LMs used by the $predictorLM$ and the current LM.}
5: $predictorLM = SelectLMs(devSet, N)$
{Select the best N LMs from the pool of previous LMs and combine them.}
6: **Output:** $predictorLM$, $currentLM$

starts, all seeds are placed in the highest perplexity queue. At each step, the crawler selects the link with the highest estimated perplexity from the first nonempty queue. When a page is downloaded, its links are extracted and added to a separate persistent frontier according to the prediction of the Perplexity Predictor. Only when the queues in the crawling frontier become empty, the crawler loads the queues from the persistent frontier.

3.3 LM Builder

After the crawler finishes its cycle, the LM Builder creates a language model from the crawled pages, as we show in Algorithm 1. First, it parses the Web pages downloaded by the crawler in the Page Repository into sentences. It does this by breaking the documents based on the HTML tags that correspond to the newline characters: "p","dt","dd","tr", "li", "br" and all header tags ("h1","h2", etc). After removing all of the HTML tags, pieces of text located between these special tokens are considered to be sentences. All the punctuation and special characters are also removed.

The next step is to create a language model from these sentences. We build trigram models from these sentences for all the experiments presented in this paper. The trigram model is built using a language modeling toolkit [12], with Katz back-off scheme for the n-grams not observed in the training corpus. The resulting model is represented as a weighted finite-state acceptor which is used for evaluating the perplexity of a given input sentence.

The resulting language model is then merged with the previous ones, created in previous cycles. The ideal scenario would be if one could merge an infinite number of LMs. But in practice, we need to limit the total number of LMs to be merged. First, because the higher the number of models, the longer is the merging process. This is an issue because we want to provide up-to-date LM to be used for the word prediction. Second, because the higher the number of models, the longer the perplexity computation, since its calculation time is dependent on the size of the LM. The crawler needs to calculate on the fly the perplexity of the pages just crawled in order to guide its policy according to the current LM (see Section 3.4). Large perplexity calculation times lead the online learning to be prohibitive. Due to all of that, we have to limit the number of models to be merged. A simple approach would be to consider only the n previous models to merge. This, however, does not work well for our approach because language models from the past have influence in how language models are built in present. Thus, for instance, the language model from the first cycle has a greater influence over data in many cycles ahead than LMs built without this dependency.

Our solution to that is to limit the total number of LMs to merge by choosing the k most suitable LMs from the pool of previous LMs. Given a set of language models $LM = \{LM_1, \ldots, LM_n\}$, the objective is to provide a weighted interpolation of the language model as shown in Equation 7. The weights in this equation are estimated using a Expectation-Maximization algorithm so as to minimize the perplexity of a tuning set of sentences.

$$LM_{merged} = \sum_{i=1}^{n} w_i * LM_i \quad (7)$$

The set of k selected LMs is merged using a development set to set their weights ($predictorLM$) and used by the crawler for the next crawl cycle. After the next cycle, the LM generated from the crawl is added to $predictorLM$ using interpolation creating the LM for the current word prediction ($currentLM$). Finally, a new $predictorLM$ is created from the current pool of LMs for the next cycle.

3.4 Adaptive Learner

Previously, in Section 3.3, we mentioned that after every crawl a language model, the $predictorLM$, is built to guide the crawler policy in the next crawling cycle. This is primarily done by updating the Perplexity Predictor according to the new $predictorLM$. Recalling that the Perplexity Predictor matches patterns in the links to pages (link neighborhood) with perplexity values from a language model, the task is to obtain from the current crawl this information: link neighborhood -> perplexity. An important point here is, since we want to deal with dynamic environments with new events (patterns) constantly arising, the patterns of the links used by the Perplexity Predictor need to be up-to-date. That is the reason why we need to use the patterns in the links of the current crawl and, as a result, the Adaptive Learner process needs to be performed on the fly. The task of updating the Perplexity Predictor is performed by the Adaptive Learner. It works as follows. Initially, the crawler starts with a random link visitation policy, since it does not know a good strategy to follow for the new language model, $predictorLM$. After a specified number of crawled pages, a learning iteration is performed by collecting, for each page p, the link neighborhood of the links that point to p, and the perplexity of p over $predictorLM$. A training data is produced as a result of this process and then, a new Perplexity Predictor is created (see Section 3.1), updating the crawler's link policy. As the last step, the Adaptive Learner updates the values of expected perplexity of the current links in the frontier based on the new Perplexity Predictor. The Adaptive Learner is invoked periodically, when the crawler visits a pre-determined number of pages.

4. EXPERIMENTAL EVALUATION

In this section, we assess our crawling strategy to build diverse language models. We chose to perform this evaluation in the news domain. Looking for novelty is an important requirement in this domain since new content is constantly being generated. We measure the performance of our approach in two different tasks. First, in the context of an automatic speech recognition (ASR) task of broadcast news. Secondly, in the context of crawling up-to-date news content, since in the news domain avoiding well-collected content from the past might lead to novelty.

4.1 Experimental Setup

Data. We compiled a list of 4,874 news Web sites, and used Web pages crawled from them to compose the language models' corpus. Since we aim to create generic language models, we tried to cover a great variety of Web sites – local, national and international news – as well as news from different topics: business, sports, technology, student life etc.

Crawler and Language Model Strategies. We executed two different crawling strategies to create the corpus for the language models:

- Baseline Crawler: to the best of our knowledge there is no preivous crawling strategy to handle the problem we are addressing in this paper. However, a reasonable approach to obtain diverse content is to randomly select the next link to be visited by the crawler in order to avoid been trapped in a particular region/content. This is the strategy implemented by the baseline. Thus, from the corpus generated by this crawler, we composed the language models in two different ways: a single language model from the current crawl, which we denote as *Basline Crawler (Single)* in the remaining of this section; and a language model created by the combination of the LM of the current crawl with previous LMs generated by this crawler (see Section 3.3), termed as *Basline Crawler(Merged)*;
- Diversity Crawler: This is our approach that uses perplexity to guide the crawler's policy. As we mentioned in Section 3.4, the crawler starts with a random policy. The learning iteration to create and update the Perplexity Predictor, performed by the Adaptive Learner, runs when the crawler collects 15,000, 30,000 and 50,000 pages. Similar to the baseline crawler, we created two different language model compositions: a single language model from the current crawl – *Diversity Crawler (Single)*; and a combination of the current LM with previous LMs produced by this crawler – *Diversity Crawler (Merged)*.

Each crawling cycle is one day long. Thus, the two crawlers were executed every day during 23 days. Each crawler collected a total of 100,000 pages, generating a corpus of about 8 million sentences, on average. Initially, a random crawl was performed to create the initial LM (day 0), and was used by the Diversity Crawler to define its policy in the next cycles. To interpolate the language models, we use a window of eight days. The models chosen to compose from this window is based on the methodology discussed in Section 3.3.

The development set used to set the interpolated weights has to reflect the current news stories, otherwise it would give higher weights to a model built in the past that do not have much influence in the present. Our assumption is that the root pages from the news Web sites usually contain the most up-to-date information in the site and a good summary of the current main stories. For this reason, the development set used is a subset of the initial pages of the news sites. This sample is not used in the corpus that create the language model.

Evaluation in the ASR task. There are two main metrics used to evaluate the performance of language models in the context of an ASR system: word-error rate (WER) and perplexity. WER measures the number of substitutions, deletions and insertions between the actual output of an ASR system with respect to a reference transcript. To use it, it is necessary to build a full speech recognition system, which invloves other components than the LM such as an acoustic model and a pronunciation model. As a result of that, computing the WER is very expensive and it does not isolate the contribution of the language model. The perplexity of a reference transcript over a language model, on the other hand, can be easily calculated and does not dependent on the other components, only the language model itself. Furthermore, previous work has showed there is a strong correlation between perplexity and WER for in-domain data [15, 9], i.e., when the language model data and the speech task are in the same domain, which is the case in this experiment, as we show later in this section.

Based on that, in this evaluation, we measure the perplexity of the daily language models from news sites over reference audio transcripts from broadcast news in the same day[3]. For this purpose, we collected daily transcripts of TV and radio programs from three Web sources:

- CNN[4]: cnn.com provides an archive of transcripts of their TV shows as well as of some CNN international and HLN programs;
- NPR[5]: NPR makes available an API that can be used to retrieve audio and transcripts for their main programs. These programs cover a broad range of topics: politics, economy, sports etc. We were able to obtain transcripts from 8 programs;
- Livedash[6]: Livedash.com is a website in which the user can search over the transcripts of TV shows as well as read the actual transcripts of these shows. From this source, we obtained transcripts from a total of 21 programs in different topics such as sports (e.g. ESPN), business (e.g. CNBC) and general news (e.g. MSNBC, Fox News).

As our goal is to build broad-domain language models, we tried to cover as many different transcripts as possible to evaluate the approaches. It must be noted that, as some programs are aired only on weekdays and others only on weekends, the total number of transcripts available may vary over time.

Evaluation in the news crawling task. Regarding the news crawling task, we want to verify, besides generating diverse language models, whether our strategy is also useful to collect fresh pages in the news domain. More specifically, we are interested in assessing how many up-to-date pages

[3]The language models built from news sites each day in this experiment contain on average 97% of the words in the daily transcripts, which means that we can consider we are dealing with in-domain data.

[4]CNN transcripts: http://archives.cnn.com/TRANSCRIPTS/

[5]NPR API: http://www.npr.org/api/index.php

[6]Livedash: http://www.livedash.com/

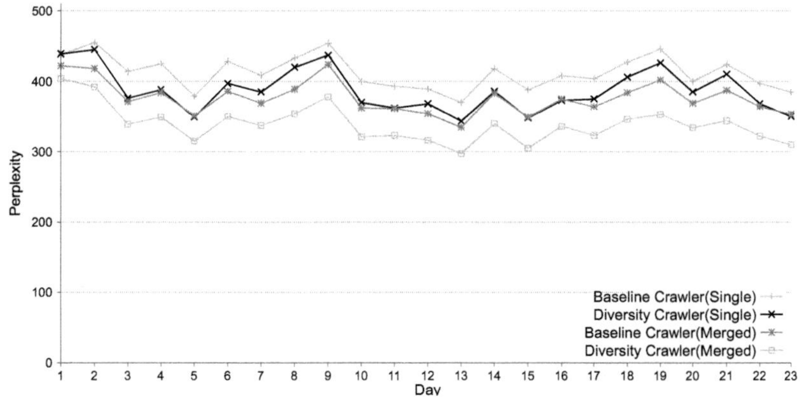

Figure 6: Perplexity obtained by the 4 language model configurations over the transcripts.

from the news sites were collected daily by each crawler. One possible way to calculate that is to look at the HTTP Last-Modified header of these pages. However most of the sites do not provide such field. Instead, we counted the number of pages collected by each crawler whose URL indicates the page was posted in the current day. Patterns as <year>/<month>/<day>, <year>-<month>-<day> and <year><month><day> were used for this purpose. Although this is an understimation of the actual number of up-to-date pages, since some of them might not have any indication of posting date in their URL, we believe it is a reasonable measure to compare the different approaches.

4.2 Assessing the Diversity Crawler

First, we present results regarding the ASR task. Figure 6 presents the perplexity obtained by the 4 different LM configurations over the daily transcripts. The first thing to note is that the Diversity Crawler(Merged) got the lowest perplexity values on all days of the experiment, followed by Baseline Crawler(Merged), Diversity Crawler(Single) and Baseline Crawler(Single). These numbers confirm that our crawling approach combined with the model merging is in fact effective in building more fresh and diverse language models. In addition to that, the Diversity Crawler(Single) outperforms the Baseline Crawler(Single) in all days. This means that, by only using the LM of the day's crawl, our crawler was able to detect more novelty on the LM than the Baseline Crawler. It does so by avoiding pages whose vocabulary already appeared in the past, or is not useful for the day's news as, for instance, stale pages in the websites (e.g. "contact us", "about" etc, see Section 3.1). Another interesting result from these numbers is that the Diversity Crawler(Single), which only uses the current LM produced by the Diversity Crawler, had a performance close to the Baseline Crawler (Merged) and, on some days, almost the same (e.g. 3, 15 and 23). Recall that the Baseline Crawler (Merged) uses around 800,000 pages in its corpus whereas Diversity Crawler(Single) only 100,000. In terms of numbers of tokens contained in the LM, the LM of Diversity Crawler(Single) is usually less than half of the Baseline Crawler (Merged).

With regard to the changing behavior of these configurations over time, they present similar trends, as shown in Figure 6. These trends are mostly influenced by the performance of the LM of the day. Initially, the difference of performance between Diversity Crawler (Merged) and Baseline

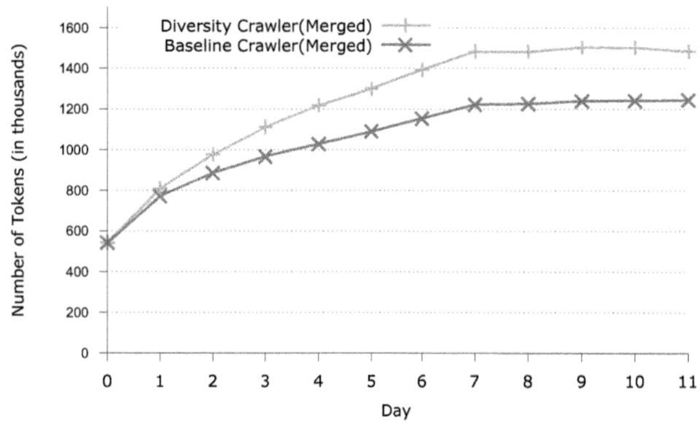

Figure 7: Size of the language model generated from the merging for the first 12 days of the experiment.

Crawler (Merged) increases for the first eight days, which is the size of the window of the model merging. This occurs because on each day, the Diversity Crawler generates a much fresher and more diverse LM. This can clearly be seen by looking at the size of the LMs produced by each crawling strategy with merging. Figure 7 depicts the number of tokens that composes the merged LMs each day for the first twelve days (after this period their size did not change much). At the beginning, both approaches started from the same LM, i.e., the language model created on the first day by running a Baseline Crawler. However, on each day, the Diversity Crawler (Merged) obtained many more new tokens than the Baseline Crawler. Since both approaches crawled the same number of pages, this increased difference of LM's sizes suggests that the vocabulary of the pages collected by the Baseline Crawler has a greater overlap with previous crawls than for the Diversity Crawler. This confirms that the Diversity Crawler is in fact able to produce more diverse language models. For the days 7-10, the number of LMs are fixed to eight, the difference of LMs' sizes fluctuates within a small interval, since their sizes did not change much. An interesting observation from these numbers is that an LM created by the Baseline Crawler (Merged) with eight models (e.g., day 7) has similar size than an LM with only five models (e.g. day 4) created by the Diversity Crawler(Merged).

News Crawling Task. Figure 8 presents the total number of up-to-date pages collected daily by each crawling strategy. The Diversity Crawler outperforms the baseline in all days of the experiment. On average, it collected 50% more up-to-

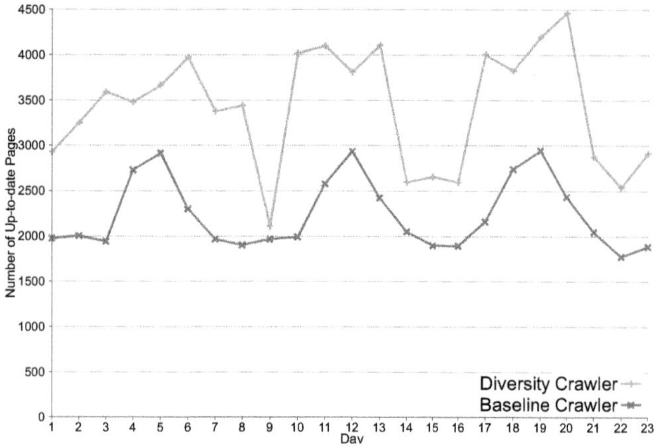

Figure 8: Number of up-to-date pages collected by each crawler.

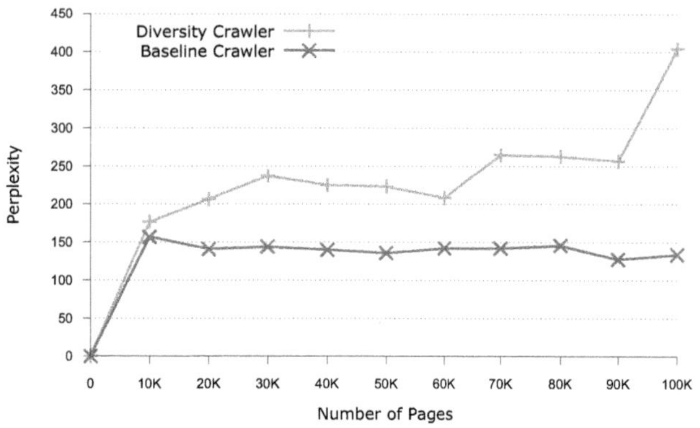

Figure 9: Average perplexity obtained by the Diversity and Baseline Crawlers during a crawling cycle.

date pages than the baseline and, in some days (day 10, for instance), almost twice more. These numbers confirm that in the news domain, focusing on the gaps of language models created from previous crawls lead the crawler to explore regions of more novelty where there are more up-to-date pages. An additional observation from Figure 8 is the occurence of a weekly cycle of fresh content. This is clearer for the Baseline Crawler, although the Diversity Crawler presents a similar trend. Peaks were at days 5,12 and 19, which were Wednesdays in our experiment, and after these days there was a decay in the number of up-to-date pages towards the weekend.

Performance within Cycles. To illustrate the behavior of the Diversity Crawler during each crawling cycle and to show the dynamic nature of the newscasts, we look now at numbers about its performance within cycles. Figure 9 depicts the perplexity of the pages collected by the Diversity Crawler and Baseline Crawler during the crawl of day 1. The perplexities of these pages were calculated over the LM of day 0 (LM_{hist}), and their values were averaged in intervals of 10,000 pages (0-10k, 10k-20k etc). As our goal is to obtain as diverse set of pages as possible in relation to the LM_{hist}, the higher the number of high-perplexity pages that were collected, the better is the performance of the crawling approach, since the crawler is filling more gaps in the LM. These numbers show that the Diversity Crawler outperforms the Baseline Crawler throughout the entire cycle. Moreover, the Diversity Crawler improves its performance

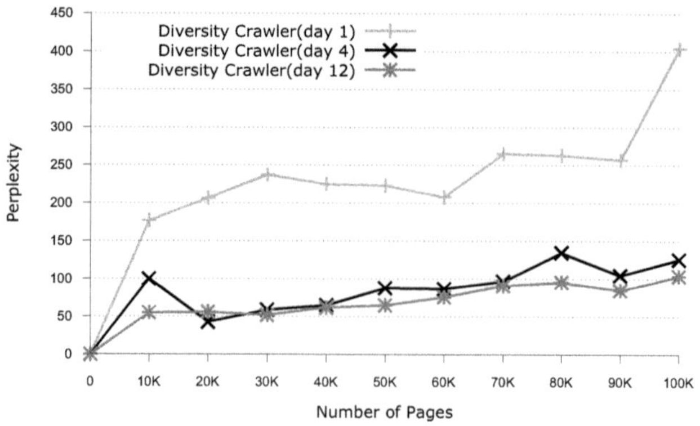

Figure 10: Average perplexity obtained by the crawler during three different crawling cycles.

over time, mainly because its Adaptive Learner component is able to learn on the fly the patterns of the links to high-perplexity pages, whereas the performance of the Baseline Crawler remains almost constant.

Fewer Gaps over Time. As the Diversity Crawler fills the gaps in the language model in each new crawling cycle, fewer gaps remain to be filled which makes the problem of finding new gaps even harder. To illustrate this, we plotted, in Figure 11, the overall distribution of the perplexity over the corresponding LM_{hist} from pages collected by the Diversity Crawler in the first three days of our experiment. As one can see, the distribution of the perplexity becomes more and more skewed towards pages with low perplexity making the problem of finding high-perplexity pages harder. This is reflected in the overall crawler's performance during each cycle. Figure 10 shows the performance over time of the Diversity Crawlers at three different days: 1, 4, 12. It is clear that the crawler from the first day obtained many more high-perplexity pages than the later ones. It is worth noting that in all three crawls the Diversity Crawler's performance improves over time. Again, this occurs because of the online learning component of the crawler, which is able to learn patterns in the links to the pages in the LM gaps.

Interpolation Weights. As a final point, we present some details about the weights assigned to different models by interpolation (Section 3.3). Figure 12 shows these weights for the Baseline and Diversity Crawlers in the first eight days of our experiment. Both curves indicate a decay factor over time, as we would expect given that we are dealing with time-sensitive data. However, the weights assigned to the more recent models in the Baseline Crawler are much higher than the ones assigned to the models created by the Diversity Crawler. Furthermore, the first LM in the Diversity Crawler interpolation has the third highest weights among the other models in this mixture, whereas in the Baseline Crawler interpolation the first LM has the lowest weight. These weights reflect the strategy used by each crawler to collect the data. As the Diversity Crawler's visitation policy of the current crawl is influenced by previous LMs, complimentary in some sense, these LMs have a higher influence over the current data and, consequently, have higher weights than the ones created by the Baseline Crawler, which produces independent LMs. Recall that these weights are assigned by interpolation based on the development set that we provide (a sample of the initial pages of the Websites, see Section 1). The exponential decay of weights indicates that this development set in fact contains up-to-date data.

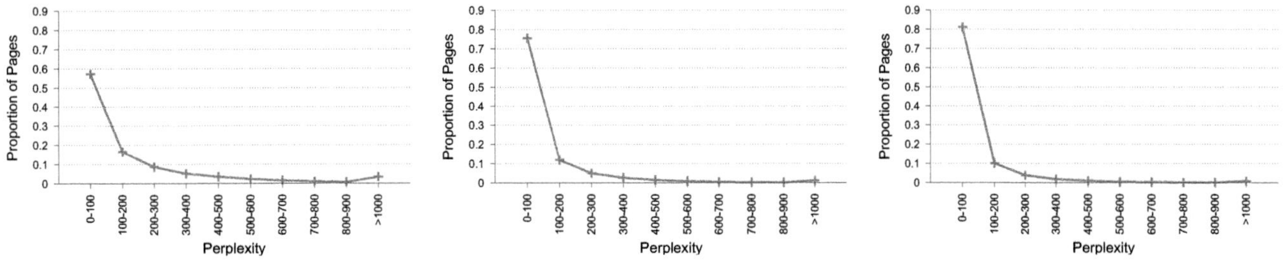

(a) Day 1 (b) Day 2 (c) Day 3

Figure 11: Evolution of the perplexity distribution.

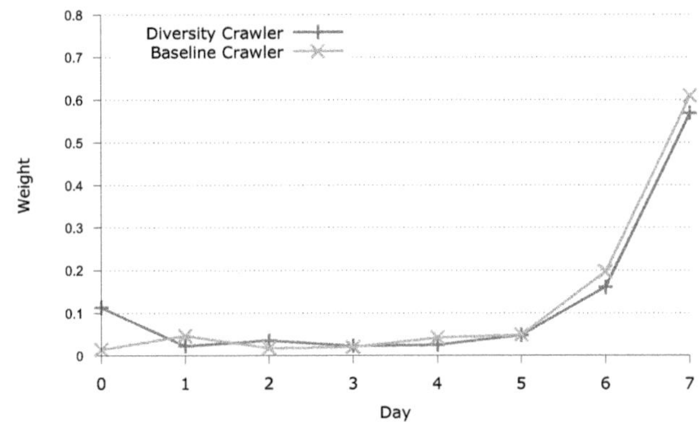

Figure 12: Weights assigned by the merging process to the language models created by the Diversity and Baseline Crawlers for the first eight days of the experiment.

5. RELATED WORK

This work applies focused crawler techniques to the well-known NLP problem of building language models. In this section, we discuss previous approaches in these two areas related to ours.

5.1 Focused Crawling

There is a vast literature in the area of focused crawlers [11, 8, 7, 20, 1, 4, 3]. Their primarily goal is to collect Web pages in a well-defined topic. For instance, Chakrabarti et al. [7] look for Web pages in domains such as astronomy, linux, cancer etc; Barbosa and Freire [4] propose a crawling approach that tries to locate Web forms in domains as airfare, hotel, cars etc. In direct contrast with these previous approaches, our goal in this work is to build a broad-domain language model by avoiding crawling pages which are well represented in previous crawls. Although we have different goals, we use similar strategies. We exploit patterns in the links, anchors and around the links, similar to [20, 7], to guide the crawler towards regions with pages with high perplexity, and use online learning to change the crawling policy according to some feedback about the "quality" of the pages currently crawled [1, 7]. Online learning is specially important in very dynamic scenarios, since a policy used in a previous crawling cycle might not have the same effect in the current one.

5.2 Language Modeling

Huan et al. [14] presented a very extensive study of language models built from a Web crawl for three particular problems: query spelling, query bracketing and query segmentation. They showed, for instance, that the anchor language model is more similar to the queries (lower perplexity) than the body of the page and also obtained the best performance in almost all the presented scenarios for these three tasks. This work is complementary to ours. It motivates the usage of language models for IR tasks whereas ours presents a solution to produce better language models.

Sarikaya et al. [21] proposed a query-based method to collect Web data to build a language model for spoken dialog domains in combination with a in-domain LM, created from dialogs in the domain. The queries are generated from utterances of dialogs and the resulting pages are cleaned by selecting the sentences in these pages more similar to sentences in the domain. Their experiments, in the financial transaction domain, showed there is a great reduction in the word error rate by adding the Web LM. Our approach also tries to build LMs from the Web to help in the problem of word prediction. The approach of using queries to build LMs works well in well-defined and focused domains as the one used in their paper (financial transactions). However, when the goal is to build LMs for more general purposes, a more scalable approach needs to be used as the one we propose in this paper, since there is a limit for the numbers of queries that can be issued to a search engine.

There are other methods that are more focused on the process of building the language model from Web data and/or time-sensitive data. For instance, Wang and Li [24] introduced a method that adapts the LM as chunks of data are available, as in the scenario of Web crawling. Another work [10] proposed techniques to build general-purpose language models by partitioning the data into mixture components giving different weights for these components and by taking into account the recency of the words (recent words have a higher probability of appearing in the future). Along the same lines, [26] also tries to use term recency to build the language models. We performed something similar in terms of word recency when we combine the language models since the weights of the language models are set based on a development set from very up-to-date pages.

6. CONCLUSIONS

We have presented in this paper a crawling strategy that collects a corpus from which diverse language models are generated for the open domain of newscasts. Instead of focusing on a particular domain as regular focused crawlers, our crawler tries to diversify the language model by detecting Web regions whose vocabulary is not well represented in the model (gaps in the model). It does so by identifying high-perplexity pages. The crawler then learns patterns of links to high-perplexity pages in order to guide its link visitation policy. In addition to that, as the newscast environment is so dynamic, the crawler uses an online learning component to adapt its policy according to the current state of the environment. We have shown in the experimental evaluation that the Diversity Crawler is able in fact to create more diverse language models than a baseline crawler, and because the crawler is able to fill in the language model's gaps, the problem of finding gaps becomes even harder after some crawling cycles.

It is important to point out that, although the framework that we present in this paper was applied for building diverse language models, it can also be employed by any kind of domain in which diversity in the data is a key component. For instance, regular Web crawlers might apply the crawling technique proposed in this paper to schedule its visitation policy in order to increase the diversity of the search engine index, which would be very helpful, for example, to improve diversity in search results [2].

7. REFERENCES

[1] C. C. Aggarwal, F. Al-Garawi, and P. S. Yu. Intelligent crawling on the world wide web with arbitrary predicates. In *WWW*, pages 96–105, 2001.

[2] R. Agrawal, S. Gollapudi, A. Halverson, and S. Ieong. Diversifying search results. In *Proceedings of the Second ACM International Conference on Web Search and Data Mining*, pages 5–14, 2009.

[3] D. Ahlers and S. Boll. Adaptive geospatially focused crawling. In *Proceeding of the 18th ACM conference on Information and knowledge management*, pages 445–454, 2009.

[4] L. Barbosa and J. Freire. An adaptive crawler for locating hidden-web entry points. In *WWW*, pages 441–450, 2007.

[5] J. Bellegarda. Statistical language model adaptation: review and perspectives. *Speech Communication*, 42(1):93–108, 2004.

[6] I. Bulyko, M. Ostendorf, M. Siu, T. Ng, A. Stolcke, and Ö. Çetin. Web resources for language modeling in conversational speech recognition. *ACM Transactions on Speech and Language Processing (TSLP)*, 5(1):1, 2007.

[7] S. Chakrabarti, K. Punera, and M. Subramanyam. Accelerated focused crawling through online relevance feedback. In *WWW*, pages 148–159, 2002.

[8] S. Chakrabarti, M. van den Berg, and B. Dom. Focused crawling: A new approach to topic-specific web resource discovery. *Computer Networks*, 31(11-16):1623–1640, 1999.

[9] S. Chen, D. Beeferman, and R. Rosenfeld. Evaluation metrics for language models. In *DARPA Broadcast News Transcription and Understanding Workshop*, pages 275–280. Citeseer, 1998.

[10] P. Clarkson and A. Robinson. Language model adaptation using mixtures and an exponentially decaying cache. In *Acoustics, Speech, and Signal Processing, 1997. ICASSP-97., 1997 IEEE International Conference on*, volume 2, pages 799–802. IEEE, 1997.

[11] M. Diligenti, F. Coetzee, S. Lawrence, C. L. Giles, and M. Gori. Focused Crawling Using Context Graphs. In *VLDB*, pages 527–534, 2000.

[12] V. Goffin, C. Allauzen, E. Bocchieri, D. Hakkani-Tur, A. Ljolje, S. Parthasarathy, M. Rahim, G. Riccardi, and M. Saraclar. The AT&T Watson speech recognizer. In *Proceedings of ICASSP*, pages 1033–1036, 2005.

[13] M. Hall, E. Frank, G. Holmes, B. Pfahringer, P. Reutemann, and I. Witten. The WEKA data mining software: An update. *ACM SIGKDD Explorations Newsletter*, 11(1):10–18, 2009.

[14] J. Huang, J. Gao, J. Miao, X. Li, K. Wang, F. Behr, and C. Giles. Exploring web scale language models for search query processing. In *Proceedings of the 19th international conference on World wide web*, pages 451–460. ACM, 2010.

[15] R. Iyer, M. Ostendorf, and M. Meteer. Analyzing and predicting language model improvements. In *Automatic Speech Recognition and Understanding, 1997. Proceedings., 1997 IEEE Workshop on*, pages 254–261. IEEE, 1997.

[16] R. Jin, Y. Breitbart, and C. Muoh. Data discretization unification. *Knowledge and Information Systems*, 19(1):1–29, 2009.

[17] P. Koehn. Europarl: A parallel corpus for statistical machine translation. In *MT summit*, volume 5. Citeseer, 2005.

[18] C. Kwok, O. Etzioni, and D. Weld. Scaling question answering to the Web. *ACM Transactions on Information Systems (TOIS)*, 19(3):242–262, 2001.

[19] C. Munteanu, G. Penn, and R. Baecker. Web-based language modelling for automatic lecture transcription. In *Proceedings of 8th Annual Conference of the International Speech Communication Association*, pages 2353–2356, 2007.

[20] J. Rennie and A. McCallum. Using Reinforcement Learning to Spider the Web Efficiently. In *ICML*, pages 335–343, 1999.

[21] R. Sarikaya, A. Gravano, and Y. Gao. Rapid language model development using external resources for new spoken dialog domains. In *IEEE International Conference on Acoustics, Speech and Signal Processing*, pages 573–576, 2005.

[22] C. Seiffert, T. Khoshgoftaar, J. Van Hulse, and A. Napolitano. Building useful models from imbalanced data with sampling and boosting. In *Proc. 21st Annual FLAIRS Conference*, pages 306–311, 2008.

[23] C. Stokoe, M. Oakes, and J. Tait. Word sense disambiguation in information retrieval revisited. In *Proceedings of the 26th annual international ACM SIGIR conference on Research and development in informaion retrieval*, pages 159–166. ACM, 2003.

[24] K. Wang and X. Li. Efficacy of a constantly adaptive language modeling technique for web-scale applications. In *IEEE International Conference on Acoustics, Speech and Signal Processing*, pages 4733–4736, 2009.

[25] C. Whitelaw, A. Kehlenbeck, N. Petrovic, and L. Ungar. Web-scale named entity recognition. In *Proceeding of the 17th ACM Conference on information and Knowledge Management*, pages 123–132. ACM, 2008.

[26] D. Zhang, J. Lu, R. Mao, and J. Nie. Time-Sensitive Language Modelling for Online Term Recurrence Prediction. *Advances in Information Retrieval Theory*, pages 128–138, 2010.

Natural Event Summarization

Yexi Jiang
School of Computer Science
Florida International University
Miami, FL, 33199, USA
yjian004@cs.fiu.edu

Chang-Shing Perng
IBM T.J Watson Research Center
Hawthorne, NY, 10532, USA
perng@us.ibm.com

Tao Li
School of Computer Science
Florida International University
Miami, FL, 33199, USA
taoli@cs.fiu.edu

ABSTRACT

Event mining is a useful way to understand computer system behaviors. The focus of recent works on event mining has been shifted to event summarization from discovering frequent patterns. Event summarization seeks to provide a comprehensible explanation of the event sequence on certain aspects. Previous methods have several limitations such as ignoring temporal information, generating the same set of boundaries for all event patterns, and providing a summary which is difficult for human to understand.

In this paper, we propose a novel framework called *natural event summarization* that summarizes an event sequence using inter-arrival histograms to capture the temporal relationship among events. Our framework uses the minimum description length principle to guide the process in order to balance between accuracy and brevity. Also, we use multi-resolution analysis for pruning the problem space. We demonstrate how the principles can be applied to generate summaries with periodic patterns and correlation patterns in the framework. Experimental results on synthetic and real data show our method is capable of producing usable event summary, robust to noises, and scalable.

Categories and Subject Descriptors: H.2.8 [Database Management]: Database Applications-Data Mining

General Terms: Algorithms, Experimentation, Performance

Keywords: Event Summarization, Minimum Description Length, Wavelet Transformation

1. INTRODUCTION

Many system applications produce and process temporal events (i.e., event sequences with associated time-stamps), for example, system logs, HTTP requests, database queries, network traffic data, etc. These events capture system states and activities over time, and mining historical event data is a useful way to understand and optimize system behaviors. By examining event patterns, system administrators can set up event and incident management rules to eliminate or mitigate IT risks. It has become a standard way to manage large scale distributed systems in IT companies like IBM [13] and HP [3].

Most existing event mining research efforts focus on episodes mining or frequency pattern discovering [2, 16, 19]. These methods simply output a number of patterns that are independent to each other, so they fail to provide a brief and comprehensible event summary revealing the big picture that the dataset embodies. Obtaining insights from the huge number of patterns remains to be a daunting task for practitioners.

Instead of discovering frequent patterns, recent works on event mining have been focused on event summarization, namely how to concisely summarize temporal events [14, 15, 25]. Current state-of-art event summarization techniques are based on sequence segmentation where an event sequence is first split into disjoint segments and patterns are then generated to describe events in each segment. Kiernan and Terzi [14, 15] model the set segmentation problem as an optimization problem that balances between the shortness of the local models for each segment (i.e., the summary) and the accuracy of data description. Their method reveals the local patterns of the sequence but fails to provide the inter-segment relationships. Based on their work, [25] provides a more sophisticated method that not only describes the patterns in each segment but also learns a Hidden Markov Model (HMM) to characterize the global relationships among the segments.

1.1 A Motivating Example

EXAMPLE 1. *Figure 1 shows an event sequence containing 4 event types, where event type A denotes "an event created by an antivirus process", event type B denotes "the firewall asks for the access privilege", event type C denotes "a port was listed as an exception", event type D denotes "the firewall operation mode has been changed". The approach presented in [25] segments the sequence into 4 segments based on the frequency changes of the events. For each segment, the approach further clusters the event types according to the frequency of each event type. Finally, an HMM is used to describe the transactions between intervals.*

The result of [25] can produce a comprehensive summary for the input sequence. However, these frequency-based methods have several limitations: (1) They only focus on the frequency changes of event types across adjacent segments and ignore the temporal information among event types within a segment. As a result, the generated summary

CIKM'11, October 24–28, 2011, Glasgow, Scotland, UK.

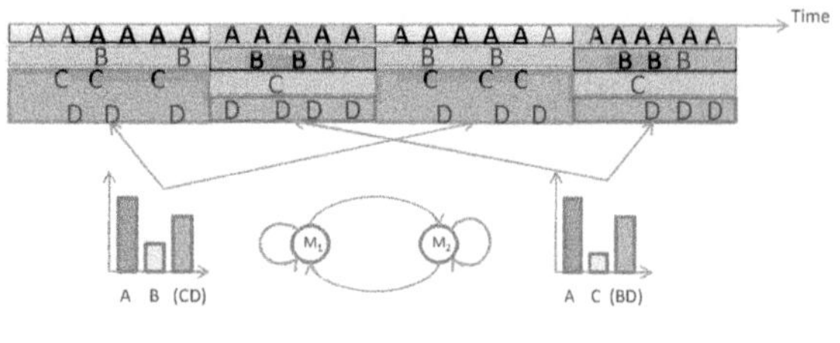

Figure 1: A motivating example. Event type A denotes "an event generated by antivirus monitor", event type B denotes "firewall asks for the access privilege", event type C denotes "a port was listed as an exception", event type D denotes "firewall operation mode has been changed".

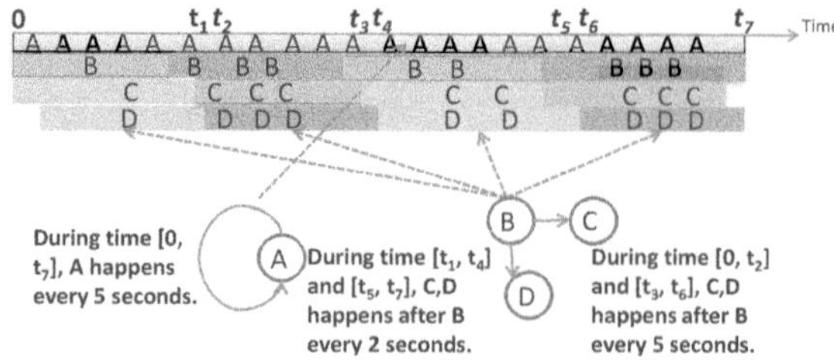

Figure 2: Output summary of our proposed approach.

fails to capture the temporal dynamics of event patterns. (2) They generate the same number of event patterns with the same boundaries for all event types. The unified pattern boundary requirement is impractical since different event types can have different underlying generating mechanisms. Consider in a distributed system, events may come from thousands of hosts that are not related to each other, forcing global segmentation means a simple event episode can be split to many segments because other events do not occur uniformly during the period; this yields a large number of small segments that may unnecessarily inflate the event summary. Having different boundaries for different event types could improve the event pattern identification and lead to better summaries. (3) Their generated summary (e.g., event distributions or HMMs) is difficult for system administrators to understand and take actions.

1.2 Our approach

In this paper, to address the above limitations, we take a novel approach called ***natural event summarization*** **(*NES*** *for short)* which first uses inter-arrival histograms to capture temporal relationships among same-type and different-type events, then finds a set of disjoint histograms to summarize the input event sequence based on minimum description length principle (MDL) [12], and finally represents the generated summary using event relationship networks. Using inter-arrival histograms allows for different boundaries for different event types. Moreover, inter-arrival histograms provide a conducive way to describe two main types of event patterns: the *periodic patterns* and the *correlation patterns*. These patterns capture the temporal dynamics of event sequences and can be used to generate the summaries. Many action rules can be derived almost directly from the generated summary. Figure 2 shows the output summary generated by our natural event summarization for Example 1. In the example event sequence, events of type C, D always appear after B for a short delay in both the second and fourth segments. Similarly, events of type C, D always appear after B for a long delay in both the first and third segments, Therefore, two correlation patterns: $B \to C, B \to D$ are identified. The change of periods implies that there may exist ill-configuration of the firewall. For events of type A, they appear regularly throughout the whole sequence, so all the instances of event type A belong to only one segment. Since event type A is the antivirus monitoring process event, its stable period shows that the antivirus process works normally. Note that in this paper we only consider pairwise correlations for events, since they are critical in understanding system behaviors. Discovering of correlation among three or more event types (two or more events trigger one event) is quite time-consuming and is one of our future works.

The framework of natural event summarization is shown in Figure 3. Our framework is based on inter-arrival histograms which capture the distribution of time intervals between events. These histograms provide a concise way to describe periodic patterns (of the same event type) and correlation patterns (of different event types). In this paper, we only focus on summarization on the aspect of temporal patterns of the events, since such information tells most of the story of the running status of the system.

The event summarization problem is formulated as finding a set of disjoint inter-arrival histograms, each representing a certain periodic pattern or correlation pattern, to approximate the original input sequence using MDL. MDL is an elegant theory to naturally balance the accurateness and the conciseness of the summarization information.

Although MDL has been used in previous event summarization methods for encoding the event segments, it is used here for encoding the inter-arrival histograms and for identifying the set of disjoint histograms for summarization. The problem of finding a set of disjoint histograms can be solved optimally in polynomial time by seeking a shortest path from the histogram graph that represents the temporal relations among histograms. To improve the efficiency of event summarization, we also explore an efficient alternative by using the multi-resolution property of wavelet transformation to reduce the size of the histogram graph. The final summary of our natural event summarization can be described as an easy-to-understand event relationship network (ERN) where many actionable rules are readily available.

In summary, our contributions are: (1) We propose a systematic and generic framework for natural event summarization using *inter-arrival histograms*. Through natural event summarization, an event sequence is decomposed into many disjoint subsets and well-fitted models (such as periodic patterns and correlation patterns) are used to describe each subset. Inter-arrival histograms demonstrate clear event patterns and capture temporal dynamics of events. To the best of our knowledge, this is the first work of using inter-arrival histograms for event summarization. (2) We formulate the event summarization problem as *finding the optimal combination of event patterns using MDL principle.* The usage of MDL principle automatically balances the complexity and the accuracy of summarization and makes our framework parameter free. (3) We present the *encoding scheme* for histograms and cast the summarization problem as seeking a shortest path from the histogram graph. (4) We also propose a *boundary pruning algorithm* that greatly accelerates

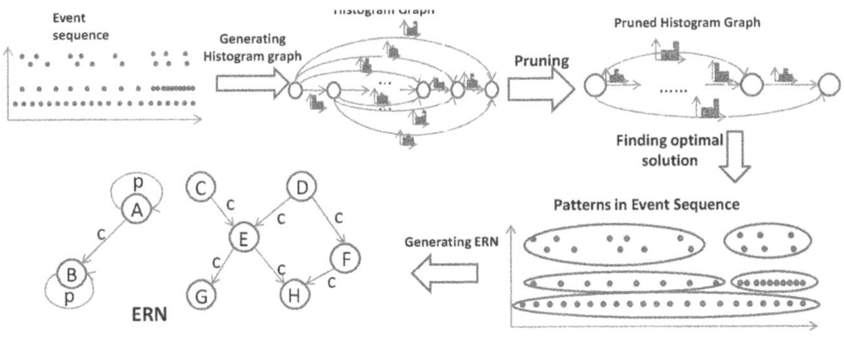

Figure 3: The framework of natural event summarization

the event summarization process by taking advantage of the multi-resolution property of wavelet transformation.

The rest of this paper is organized as follows. We present the interval histogram model for event summarization and its encoding scheme in Section 2 and 3 respectively. In Section 4, we introduce the algorithm of finding the best summarization solution. Then in Section 5, we present the segments boundary pruning algorithm that greatly improves the efficiency of our framework. In Section 6, we present our experiment evaluation. Finally, we discuss the related work in Section 7 and conclude in Section 8.

2. INTERVAL HISTOGRAMS

An event sequence D comprises of a series of event instances in the form of (e, t) ordered by their timestamps: $D = (< t_1, e_1 >, \cdots, < t_n, e_n >)$, where t_i is a timestamp and e_i is the type of the event. Each instance belongs to one of the m types $\mathcal{E} = \{e_1, \cdots, e_m\}$. We first describe the inter-arrival histograms used in our framework to represent the inter-arrival distribution of time interval between events.

Given two event types x and y, let S be the subsequence of D that only contains events of types x and y. Suppose S is split into k disjoint segments $S = (S_1, S_2, ...S_i, ..., S_k)$. We use an interval histogram (or inter-arrival histogram) $h_{xy}(S_i)$ to capture the distribution of time interval between events of type x and type y in S_i. Specifically, the bin $h_{xy}(S_i)[b]$ is the total number of intervals whose length is b. Let $next(t, y)$ denote the timestamp of the *first* type y event that occurs after t in S_i.

DEFINITION 1. ***Inter-arrival histogram:***

$$h_{xy}(S_i)[b] = |\{i|e_i = x, next(t_i, y) - t_i = b\}|.$$

where t_i denotes the timestamp of e_i.

If $x \neq y$, then the inter-arrival histograms capture the time intervals for the events of different types; for the case of $x = y$, they capture the time intervals of events of the same type. Given an interval histogram, we can use a standard histogram to approximate it. The standard histogram is formally defined with definition 2.

DEFINITION 2. ***Standard Histogram** is a special kind of interval histogram with one or two non-empty bin and all these non-empty bins have the same value $\frac{\#intervals}{n_{non}}$, where $\#intervals$ indicates the number of intervals and n_{non} indicates the number of non-empty bins. We use $\bar{h}_{xy}(S_i)$ to denote the corresponding standard histogram of $h_{xy}(S_i)$.*

Note that the two types of event relationships: *periodic patterns* and *correlation patters* can be easily described using standard histograms. The *periodic patterns* and *correlation patters* is formally defined in definition 3.

DEFINITION 3. ***Periodic pattern and Correlation pattern:** A pattern is a 5-tuple (t_s, t_e, x, y, P), where (1) t_s and t_e denotes the start position and end position of the event sequence described by the pattern respectively. (2) x and y denote the types of events involved in the pattern, (3) P contains the periodic parameters. The pattern can contain 1 or 2 period parameters, which indicate the inter-arrival value between event x and y. Moreover, if $x = y$, this pattern is a **periodic pattern**, otherwise, it is a **correlation pattern**.*

Example 2 provides a detailed illustration about how to utilize standard histogram and periodic/correlation patterns to summarize a given event sequence.

EXAMPLE 2. *Given an event sequence D, the timestamps for e_a, e_b and the related subsequences are listed in Table 1 (S for event type a, b is the same as D). There is only one segment in S and there exists a periodic pattern for e_a and a correlation pattern between e_a and e_b. The segment are described by inter-arrival histograms $h_{aa}(S)$ and $h_{ab}(S)$ in Figure 4 and are approximated by two standard histograms in Figure 5.*

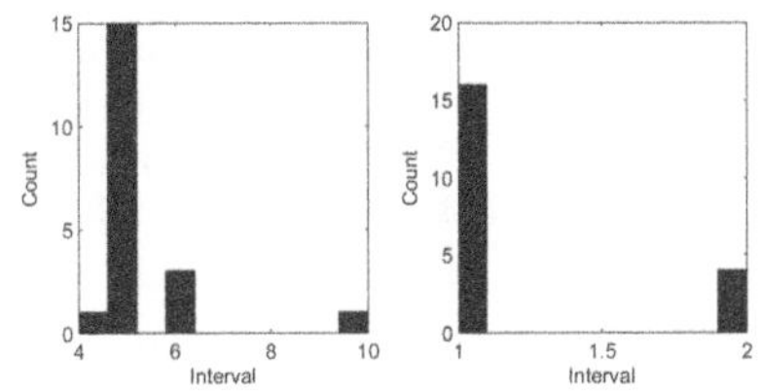

Figure 4: (a) inter-arrival histogram $h_{aa}(S)$; (b) inter-arrival histogram $h_{ab}(S)$.

Table 1: Occurrence of two events

Event type	Occurrence timestamp
a	5,11,16,21,26,30,35,41,46,51,61,66,71,76,81,86,92,97,102,107
b	6,12,17,22,28,31,36,43,47,52,63,67,72,77,82,87,93,99,103,108
S for $h_{aa}(S)$	The same as a
S for $h_{ab}(S)$	5,6,11,12,16,17,...,102,103,107,108

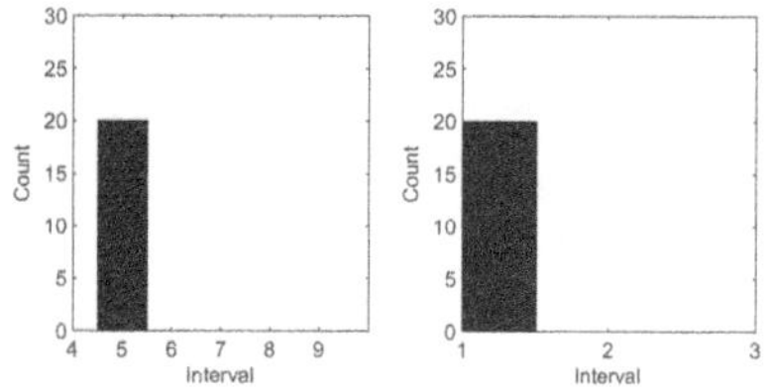

Figure 5: (a) standard histogram that best approximate $h_{aa}(S)$; (b) standard histogram that best approximate $h_{ab}(S)$.

It is obvious that the histograms demonstrate clear patterns. However, the total number of different histograms can be large for datasets with many events. The 2 histograms shown in Figure 4 and their corresponding standard histograms in Figure 5 are just one of many possible histogram combinations that depict the event relationships/patterns hidden in Example 2. For example, we can use two histograms to respectively depict the first and the second half of e_a. Hence one challenge is how to find the most suitable combination of histograms to describe the event sequence. In our framework, we use MDL principle to find out the best set of disjoint segments and the corresponding standard histograms to summarize the event sequence.

3. SUMMARIZATION USING MDL

In this section, we propose an information theoretic method to describe the histogram, i.e., encoding the histogram in *bits*. [22] proposed an encoding scheme for histograms with fixed number of bins and fixed number of bin elements (the total value of all bins). However, for the histograms used in event summarization, neither the number of bins and the number of bin elements is fixed beforehand. To the best of our knowledge, there is no encoding scheme that can be directly used in our scenario. Based on such situation, we first describe the scheme for encoding standard histograms (e.g., periodic patterns and correlation patterns). Then given an inter-arrival histogram, we show how it can be approximated using standard histograms. Finally, we formulate our event summarization problem. It should also be pointed out that, although MDL has been used in event summarization for encoding the event segments [14, 25], our work is the first one that uses MDL to encode the inter-arrival histograms and to identify the set of disjoint histograms for summarization.

3.1 Encoding Standard Histograms

Given an event subsequence S of event types x and y with disjoint segments $S = (S_1, S_2, ...S_i, ..., S_k)$, to encode a standard histogram $\bar{h}_{xy}(S_i)$, the following four components need to be encoded. These components are necessary and enough to describe the histogram.

Event type depicted by the histogram. Each histogram should be associated with one or two event types depending on the type of the relationship it depicts. Given the set of event types $\mathcal{E}$, it is enough to use $L(m) = \log|\mathcal{E}|$ bits to represent each event type.

Boundaries of S_i. The relationship depicted by an interval histogram has two boundaries indicating where the corresponding segment is. Each boundary requires $L(b) = \log|S|$ bits to encode its information.

Information of non-empty bins in the histogram. This piece of information can be encoded using

$$L(bin) = \log\delta + \log i_{max} + \log|S| + \sum_{i=1}^{n_{non}} \log i_{max} + \sum_{i=1}^{n_{non}} \log|S_i|.$$

The coding length consists of five terms. The first term uses $\log\delta$ bits to encode the largest interval i_{max} in S_i, where δ denotes the allowed largest interval. In our framework it is set as the number of seconds in one day. The second term uses $\log i_{max}$ bits to encode the number of non-empty bins n_{non}. The third term uses $\log|S|$ bits to encode the length of S_i. The fourth and fifth terms encode all the indices (1 to i_max) and the number of elements contained in the n_{non} bins respectively.

Putting them all together, the bits needed for encoding a standard histogram $\bar{h}_{xy}(S_i)$ is

$$L(\bar{h}_{xy}(S_i)) = L(m) + L(b) + L(bin). \quad (1)$$

3.2 Encoding Interval Histograms

Given an inter-arrival histogram $h_{xy}(S_i)$, we want to measure how well it can be represented by event patterns, or equivalently, how well it can be approximated by standard histograms.

Histogram distance. Histogram distance describes how much information is needed to depict the *necessary bin element movements* defined in [6] to transform $\bar{h}(S_i)$ into $h(S_i)$ (To make notations uncluttered, we drop the subscripts xy and they should be clear from the context.). The code length of the distance can be calculated as:

$$L(h[S_i]|\bar{h}[S_i]) = \sum_{i \in Non} |be_i - bs_i| \log i_{max}, \quad (2)$$

where Non is the union of the indices sets of non-empty bins in both histograms, be_i and bs_i denote the value (number of elements) of bin i in $h[S_i]$ and $\bar{h}[S_i]$ respectively. For each element at bin i, we can assign a new bin index to indicate where it should be moved. Equation 2 measures the bits of information needed by summing up the elements in unmatched bins.

In summary, the amount of information required to describe an inter-arrival histogram $h(S_i)$ using an event pattern $\bar{h}(S_i)$ equals to the summation of the code length for $\bar{h}(S_i)$ and the distance between $h(S_i)$ and $\bar{h}(S_i)$. Since there may be multiple standard histograms, we define the code length for an interval histogram $h(S_i)$ as follows:

$$L(h(S_i)) = argmin_{\bar{h}(S_i) \in \bar{H}(S_i)} L(\bar{h}(S_i) + L(h(S_i)|\bar{h}(S_i)), \quad (3)$$

where $\bar{H}(S_i)$ is the set of all possible standard histograms on S_i.

3.3 Problem Statement

Given an event sequence D, for each subsequence S containing event types x and y, the minimum coding length $L(S)$ for S is defined as

$$L(S) = \arg\min_{\{S_1, S_2, ..., S_k\}} \sum_i L(h(S_i)). \quad (4)$$

Since the boundaries for different subsequences are independent, then the minimum description length for the input event sequence D is

$$L(D) = \sum_{S \in D} L(S). \quad (5)$$

Hence the event summarization problem is to *find the best set of segments* $\{S_1, S_2, ..., S_k\}$ *as well as the best approximated standard histograms to achieve the minimum description length.*

4. THE NES ALGORITHM

In this section, we first introduce a heuristic algorithm that can find the best set of segments of S in polynomial time. Then we present the method of generating ERN using the event patterns.

4.1 Finding the best segmentation

The problem of finding the best set of segments can be easily reduced to the problem of finding a shortest path from the generated histogram graph G. The histogram graph G is generated as follows:

1. Given S, let n_{xy} be the number of inter-arrivals between event x and y (x, y can be the same type) in S, generate n_{xy} vertices and label them with the positions of each x (1 to n_{xy}).
2. Add $edge(a, b)$ from vertex $v[a]$ to vertex $v[b]$ for each vertex pair $v[a], v[b]$, where $1 \leq a < b \leq n_{xy}$. Assign the weight of each $edge(a, b)$ as $L(h(S_i))$, where S_i starts at position a and ends at b. Note that to compute $L(h(S_i))$, we need to find the best standard histogram $\bar{h}(S_i)$ for $h(S_i)$ in the sense that $L(h(S_i))$ is minimized (as shown in Eq.(3). This can be done using a greedy strategy. Given $h(S_i)$, we can sort the bins in decreasing order based on their values. Then iteratively perform the following two steps: (1) generating $\bar{h}(S_i)$ using the top i bins, and (2) computing $L(h(S_i))$. (3) increase i by 1. The iteration continues till $L(h(S_i))$ begins to increases. The $\bar{h}(S_i)$ corresponding to the minimum description length $L(h(S_i))$ is often referred as the best standard histogram for $h(S_i)$.

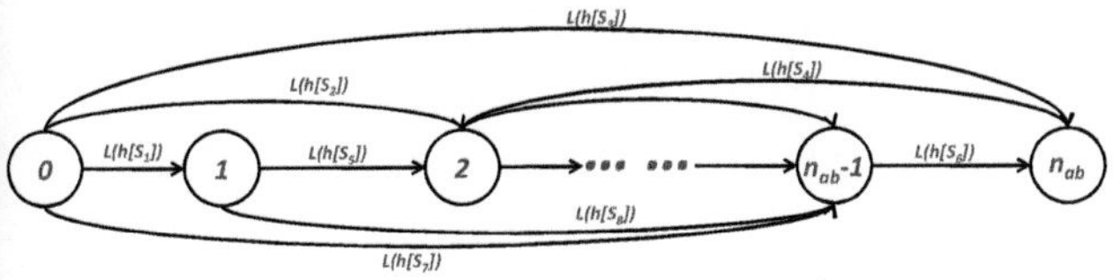

Figure 6: An example histogram graph

After generating the histogram graph, we can use the classical shortest path algorithm (e.g., *Dijkstra* algorithm) to output the vertices on the shortest path from $v[1]$ to $v[n_{xy}]$. Figure 6 shows an example histogram graph and Algorithm 1 illustrates the *summarization* process of our natural event summarization framework (*NES* for short). In line 4, the algorithm generates a set of event subsequences from D, there are m subsequences for the same event type (i.e., $x = y$) and $m^2 - m$ subsequences for different event types (i.e., $x \neq y$). Line 6 generates the directed acyclic histogram graph for each subsequence S and uses *Dijkstra* algorithm to find the shortest path $P = (v[i_1], v[i_2], ..., v[i_p])$. The best segmentation solution contains the segments $< v[i_1], v[i_2] >$, $< v[i_2], v[i_3] >, ..., < v[i_p - 1], v[i_p] >$. Line 8 and 9 represent each segment using the best fitted event patterns (i.e., the best standard histograms), and put them into the set $\mathcal{R}$.

Algorithm 1 The NES Algorithm

1. **input:** event sequence D.
2. **output:** all relationships $\mathcal{R}$.
3. Identify m from S, relationship set $\mathcal{R} \leftarrow \emptyset$;
4. Separate D into a set of S;
5. **for all** S **do**
6.   Generate directed graph G;
7.   Use **Dijkstra**(G) to find shortest path P;
8.   Generate relationships R from P;
9. $\mathcal{R} \leftarrow \mathcal{R} \bigcup R$;
10. **end for**
11. **return** $\mathcal{R}$;

For each histogram graph G, *Dijkstra* algorithm requires $O(|E| + |V| \log |V|) = O(|S|^2)$ time. Therefore, the total running time is $O((m + m(m-1))|S|^2) = O(|D|^2)$.

4.2 Generating summarization graph

Although the set of event patterns can be described in text, we show that they can be used to construct an easy-to-understand event relationship network (ERN) [26] which produces a concise yet expressive representation of the event summary. ERN is a graph model that represents the relationship between event types. The procedure for building ERN is straightforward: it first generates the vertices for each event type involved in any event patterns, and then adds edges for event patterns and stores necessary information (e.g., segmentation, periods and time intervals) onto the edges.

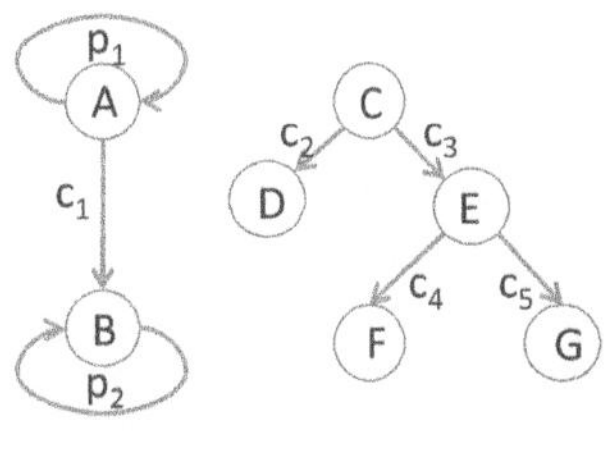

Figure 7: An example ERN graph.

Figure 7 shows an example ERN graph. It contains two periodic patterns: $A \xrightarrow{p_1} A$, $B \xrightarrow{p_2} B$ and five correlation patterns: $A \xrightarrow{c_1} B$, $C \xrightarrow{c_2} D$, $C \xrightarrow{c_3} E$, $E \xrightarrow{c_4} F$, $E \xrightarrow{c_5} G$. For simplicity, the ranges of segments are ignored.

5. EFFICIENCY IMPROVEMENT

The NES algorithm described in Section 4 finds the best segmentation by checking all positions in S, which is computational intensive. In fact, given an event subsequence S, boundaries should only locate at positions where inter-arrival times change rapidly, because segmentation at smooth places would waste encoding bitsj. Based on this observation, we propose an effective pruning algorithm which is able to prune a large part of boundaries that are unlikely to be the boundaries of segments. This algorithm greatly accelerates the summarization process by reducing the size of the histogram graph. By utilizing the multi-resolution analysis (MRA) of wavelet transformation, the pruning can be done in linear time in the worst case.

5.1 Preprocessing

For ease of pruning, some preprocessing steps are needed. Given an event subsequence S, we preprocess it as follows:

1. *Obtaining inter-arrival sequences*: given $S = (< e, t_1 >, \cdots, < e, t_{|S|} >)$, transform it into inter-arrival sequence $V = (t_2 - t_1, t_3 - t_2, \cdots, t_{|S|} - t_{|S|-1})$;
2. *Padding*: Append 0's to the tail of sequence until the length of interval sequence equals to a power of 2;
3. *Transforming*: Use *Haar* [4] wavelet as the the wavelet function and apply fast wavelet transformation (FWT) on V to obtain the transformation result W.

The resulting W contanis the wavelet coefficients of the inter-arrival sequence, which is the input of our pruning algorithm.

5.2 Pruning unlikely Boundaries

Due to the multi-resolution analysis (MRA) property of wavelet transformation, the deviation of inter-arrivals in V can be viewed from W at different resolutions. Since wavelet transformation captures both the resolution and the location information, for each $W[i]$, we can quickly locate the corresponding segment in V. For example, if $|V| = 1024$, the elements $W[1]$ and $W[2]$ contain the averaging information and the diff information of the highest resolution (in this example, resolution 1024) of original series respectively. The elements $W[3]$ and $W[4]$ contain the information of V at resolution 512. Specifically, $W[3]$ corresponds to the first half of V and $W[4]$ corresponds to the second half of V.

By taking advantage of such a property, our pruning algorithm identifies the inter-arrival deviation in a top-down manner. The basic idea of algorithm is as follows: it checks the element $W[i]$, starting from $i = 2$, which contains the deviation of inter-arrival for the whole sequence V. There are three possible cases:

Case I: If $W[i]$ is small, it means the corresponding subsequence in V for $W[i]$ is smooth enough and segmentation is not needed. In this case, the algorithm records the boundaries of the segment, and then stops.

Case II: If $W[i]$ is large, it means the deviation of inter-arrivals in the corresponding subsequence in V is too large. In this case, the subsequence needs to be split into two halves and the algorithm needs to perform recursively.

Case III: If $W[i]$ records the deviation of inter-arrivals at the lowest resolution, the algorithm just records the start and end boundaries and returns.

Algorithm 2 provides the pseudocode for *BoundaryPruning*. The parameter *level* (initialized as $\log|W|$) denotes the current level of resolution that the algorithm checks, and i denotes the current position in transformed result W (i.e. $W[i]$) to be checked. The algorithm calculates the corresponding threshold as $\frac{W[1]}{2^{\log|W|-level}}$, which reflects the average deviation of inter-arrival at resolution 2^{level} and changes dynamically according to the *level*.

Example 3 uses a small dataset to illustrate how the pruning algorithm works.

Algorithm 2 Algorithm of *BoundaryPruning*

input: $W, level, i$.
output: Boundary set B after pruning.
Set $B \leftarrow \emptyset$;
$threshold \leftarrow \frac{W[1]}{2^{\log|W|-level}}$;
$spectrum \leftarrow W[i]$;
if $spectrum < threshold$ or reaches to the lowest resolution **then**
  Add corresponding boundaries to B;
else
  $i_1 = 2i - 1, i_2 = 2i$;
  $B_1 \leftarrow$ BoundaryPruning($W, level - 1, i_1$);
  $B_2 \leftarrow$ BoundaryPruning($W, level - 1, i_2$);
  $B \leftarrow B \cup B_1 \cup B_2$
end if
return B;

EXAMPLE 3. *An input inter-arrival sequence V is shown in Figure 8. The algorithm starts from the highest resolution. It finds that $W[2] = 3$ is too large, so the whole inter-arrival sequence cannot be segmented with only one segment. At a lower resolution, the algorithm finds that $W[4]$ is small enough, so the corresponding subsequence $< 2, 1, 2, 1, 2, 1, 3, 1 >$ can be considered as one segment. For the element $W[3] = -2$ representing the first half of V, it is still too large and the corresponding subsequence $< 1, 1, 1, 1, 1, 3, 1, 1 >$ cannot be considered as only one segment. Hence the algorithm drills down to a lower resolution to do the same check task. Finally, the algorithm divides V into 5 segments, and 6 boundaries are recorded and the remaining 11 boundaries are pruned. Figure 9 shows the effect of BoundaryPruning in reducing the size of the histogram graph.*

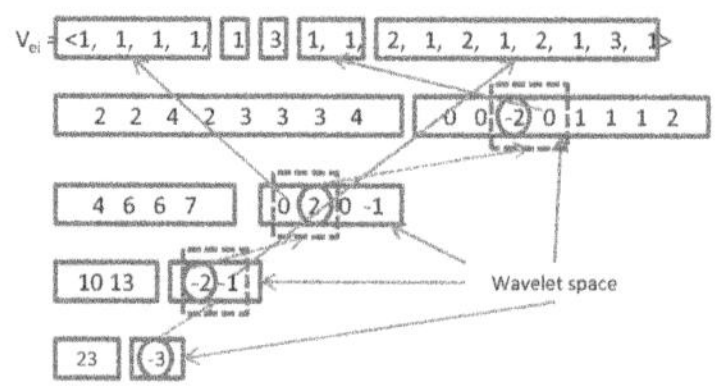

Figure 8: Segments information in wavelet spectrum sequence.

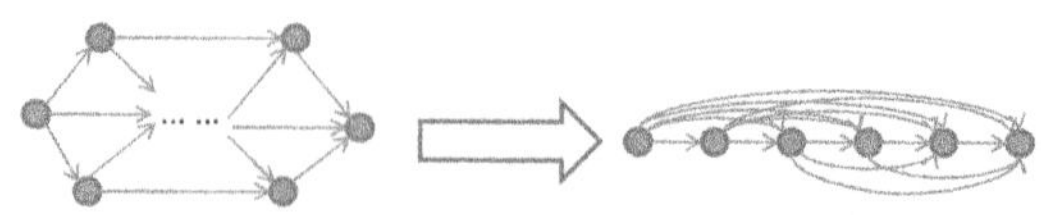

Figure 9: Before pruning, the histogram graph contains 17 vertices and 136 edges, after pruning, the histogram graph contains only 6 vertices and 14 edges.

The pruning algorithm only scans W once. In general cases, the algorithm does not need to check all the elements in W. If the inter-arrival sequence is smooth enough, the algorithm would stop checking at a high resolution. Only in the worst case, the algorithm has to check every elements in W. Since $|W| = |V| = |S| - 1$, the algorithm runs in $o(|S|)$ for the average case and $O(|S|)$ in the worst case.

6. EXPERIMENTAL EVALUATION

In order to investigate the effectiveness and efficiency of our proposed approach, we design two sets of experiments to evaluate our algorithm on both synthetic and real datasets. There are two reasons that we evaluate our algorithm on synthetic data:

1. There is no ground-truth summarization result for real world data, thus there is no way to evaluate the summarization result if we directly run our algorithm on real world data.

2. The real world event sequence is generated automatically by the operating system, there is no way to precisely control the size of the dataset. We cannot just pick a subset of the real world sequence with a fixed size, since it may destroy a lot of hidden patterns.

With synthetic data, we can freely set the parameters of dataset such as the number of patterns of each type, the location of each patterns, the level of noise, and the size of dataset. Since we know the ground-truth of the synthetic data, we are able to investigate the capabilities as well as limitations of our algorithm by comparing its output with the ground-truth.

Our tasks in synthetic data experiments part are trying to answer the following answers: (1) Can our event summarization framework indeed discover the hidden relationships from the event sequence and effectively summarize them? (2) Is our framework efficient in handling event summarization task? (3) Is the approximation algorithm precise enough that covers most of the relationships comparing with the optimal counterpart?

For the real world data experiments part, there are two tasks: (1) Does our algorithm find out any useful patterns from the real world data? (2) Is the summarization result more meaningful and friendly than the counterparts?

6.1 Experimental Setup

The whole framework along with the experiments code is implemented in Java 1.6. All the experiments are conducted on a machine with Intel Core2 CPU @2.83GHz, 2G main memory and running on Windows XP SP2. We use the open source library JWave[1] for wavelet transformation and Jung[2] for ERN visualization.

We preprocess the datasets by transforming all event instances into a predefined format $inst =< event\_type, date, time, source, category, event\_ID >$. Since different event types generated by different programs may share the same event_ID in some systems like Windows series operating system, it is not enough to distinguish the events just by their ID. We map each distinct tuple $< event\_type, source, category, event\_ID >$ as unique event type e.

6.2 Experiments on Synthetic Data

We generate several groups of synthetic datasets to evaluate our approach, each group consists a set of datasets generated by changing a particular parameter and fixing the remains. The meaning of each parameter is listed in Table 2. For each dataset, we intentionally plant some relationships/patterns and add the noise indicated by noise level [3] to simulate the real scenario.

[1]http://code.google.com/p/jwave/

[2]http://jung.sourceforge.net/

Table 2: Parameters and their meanings

Parameter	Description
n	Number of events in sequence.
m	Number of event types.
n_p	Number of periodic patterns.
n_c	Number of correlation patterns.
r_{noise}	Degree of noise.
l	Number of events in one pattern.

We use *NES-Prune* to represent summarization with *BoundaryPruning*, *NES* to represent summarization without *BoundaryPruning*.

Accuracy of the approaches. The first goal of experiments on synthetic data is to check whether our approach can really discover the correct hidden patterns from the data. We generate 5 datasets by fixing $n = 15000, m = 150, n_p = 50, n_c = 50, l = 100$ and iterate the noise levels from 0.1 to 0.5 with an increment of 0.1. Fore each dataset, we generated 50 periodic and 50 correlation patterns respectively with distinct period parameters and distinct event types. Then we randomly order these patterns to build the synthetic dataset. Table 3 shows the result of how many planted patterns are found via *NES* and *NES-Prune* respectively. In this table, NES_p and NES_c denote the proportion of planted periodic and correlation patterns found by *NES*, $NESP_p$ and $NESP_c$ denote those found by *NES-Prune*.

Table 3: Accuracy for synthetic datasets, $n = 15000, m = 150, n_p = 50, n_c = 50, l = 100$

No.	NES_p	NES_c	$NESP_p$	$NESP_c$
1	48/50	48/50	48/50	48/50
2	48/50	48/50	46/50	48/50
3	46/50	48/50	46/50	48/50
4	41/50	45/50	40/50	45/50
5	10/50	11/50	9/50	11/50

From the result, we observe that both *NES* and *NES-Prune* can discover most of the relationships. We only count the relationships that with the exact same event type, the exact periodical parameters and more than 95% overlap with the ground-truth patterns we plant in, so the criterion is quite demanding.

Compression ratio. We evaluate the quality of event summarization by compression ratio CR with the formula used in [15]: $CR(A) = \frac{L(A)}{L(direct)}$, where A is an algorithm, $L(A)$ denotes the code length achieved by A and $L(direct)$ denotes the code length of directly encoding the event sequence.

Figure 10 shows the compression ratio of our two algorithms as a function of *noiselevel*. For this experiment, we use the same datasets of the accuracy experiments. As expected, *CR* increases as the *noiselevel* increases. It is reasonable because more extra bits are required to describe the noise.

The proportion of planted patterns in the datasets is another factor that affects *CR*. We define the proportion of

[3]We set the noise levels as the probability of inter-arrival deviation, e.g, if noise level is 0.2, then with the probability of 20% the inter-arrival time will be shifted by a random value.

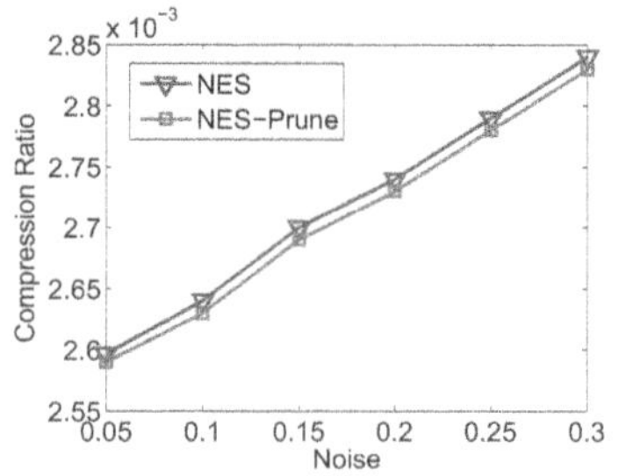

Figure 10: CR vs. noise, $n = 15000, m = 150, n_p = 50, n_c = 50, l = 100$

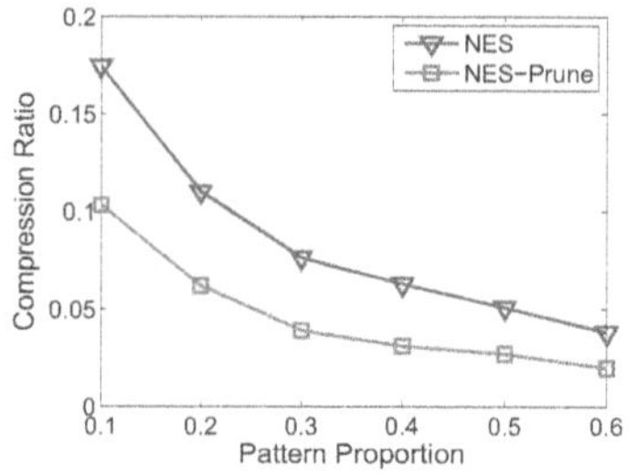

Figure 11: CR vs. Proportion of Pattern, $n = 5000, m = 50, l = 100, noise\ level = 0.1$

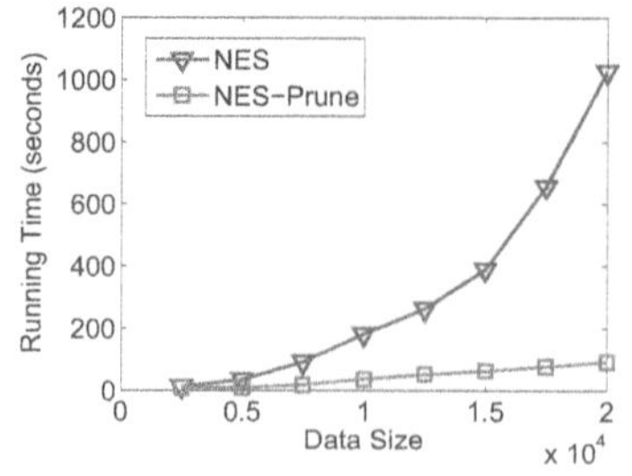

Figure 12: Scalability of *NES* and *NES-Prune*, $m = 60, l = 100, noise\ level = 0.1$

patterns as $\frac{|Patterns|}{|S|}$, where $|Patterns|$ denotes the number of events belonging to the injected patterns. We run the experiment on 6 datasets by fixing $n = 5000, m = 50, l = 100, noiselevel = 0.1$ and ranging the proportion of patters from 10% to 60% with an increment of 10%. Figure 11 shows that *CR* decreases as the pattern proportion increases. The result is straightforward because as the proportion of patterns increases, more events can be well fitted by event patterns, which results in shorter description length for the event sequence.

It should be pointed out that our *NES* summarizes an event sequence from different aspects simultaneously using event patterns with the goal of providing natural, interpretable and comprehensive summaries. It is quite possible that some events may belong to multiple correlation patterns and their coding length might be counted multiple times. So *CR* might not be the criterion to measure the quantity of summarization for our approach. This phenomenon also explains why *NES* leads to longer code lengths than *NES-Prune*.

Performance and scalability. We generate 8 datasets by fixing $m = 100, n_c = 0, noiselevel = 0.1$ to evaluate the scalability of our approach. The length of event sequence for the datasets ranges from 2500 to 20000 with an increment of 2500, and n_p is set proportional to the length of sequence. Figure 12 shows the scalability results. As expected, *NES-Prune* runs much faster than *NES* and it shows better scalability, since *BoundaryPruning* prunes a large number of boundary candidates.

The number of event type m is an important factor that affects the running time, we use 6 datasets to do the evaluation by fixing $n = 4096, n_c = 0, noise\ level = 0.1$ and set m from 4 to 128 with an increment of a power of 2. Figure 13(a) shows that as m increases, the running time of *NES* decreases but the running time of *NES-Prune* increases. This is because the running time of *NES* procedure is $O(|D|^2) = O(m^2|S|^2)$. Since $S \gg m$ in general cases, for *NES*, the running time is dominated by $|S|$. By fixing n, the average length of S decreases as m increases, therefore the running time of *NES* decreases. For *NES-Prune*, since the input is pruned, the average length of S does not affect running time. Hence, the running time is dominated by m and would increase as m increases,

The proportion of patterns is another important factor that affects the running time. We generate 8 datasets by fixing $n = 5000, m = 50, l = 100, noiselevel = 0.1$ and ranging the proportion of patterns from 10% to 80%. Figure 13(b) shows that as the proportion of patterns increases, the running time of *NES-Prune* decreases, but the running time of *NES* is independent of the proportion of patterns. This is because as the proportion of patterns increases, more boundaries are removed using *BoundaryPruning*. And without *BoundaryPruning*, the size of input for *NES* is independent of the proportion of patterns.

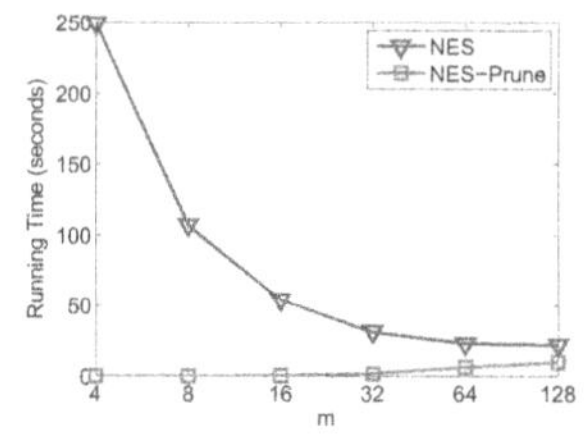

(a) Running time vs. m, $n = 4096, noiselevel = 0.1$

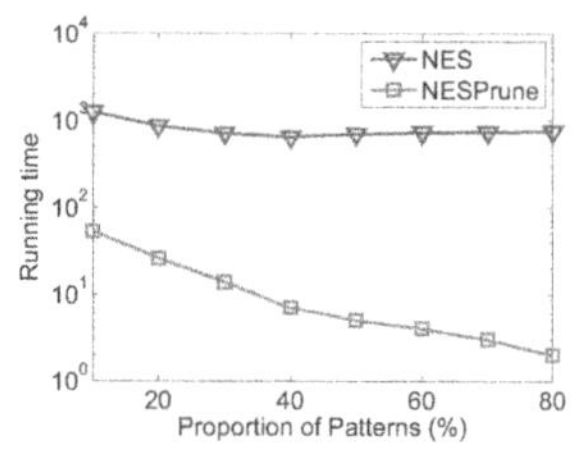

(b) Running time vs. Proportion of Patterns, $n = 5000, m = 50, l = 100, noiselevel = 0.1$

Figure 13: Running Time Analysis

6.3 Experiments on Real Data

In order to explore whether our framework can really help system administrators, we test our approach with real log datasets recorded in Windows event viewer.

The real datasets consist of **application log**, **security log** and **system log**. The detailed information of the three datasets with their running times and compression ratios are listed in Table 4.

Our methods show a significant improvement over previous approaches. The algorithm in [15] needs more than a thousand seconds to find the optimal summarization solution while our methods just need 1/10 of the time. Due to inherent difficulty of event summarization, our methods are still not efficient enough. Further improvement in efficiency is needed and this is one of our future works.

Note that our algorithm utilize MDL to summarize the event sequence on the aspect of period pattern and correlation pattern, we successfully compressed the pattern information to just several percent of the original amount without loss any information.

Our algorithm finds and summarizes a lot of interesting event relationships. For example in system log, we find event <35, W32Time> occurs every 3600 seconds. This event type is a well known periodic event that synchronizes the computer time with the remote server. We also find that there

Table 4: Experiments with real datasets

	application	security	system
Period	09/10-02/11	11/10-12/10	09/10-02/11
Time range (secs)	12,005,616	2,073,055	12,000,559
Event instances	5634	21850	3935
Event types	100	17	50
Running Time (secs)			
NES	173	3102	108
NES-Prune	22	56	4
Compression Ratio $CR(A)$			
NES	0.0597	0.0312	0.0454
NES-Prune	0.0531	0.0216	0.0464

exist correlation relationships among the event types <6005, eventlog>, <6006, eventlog>, and <6009, eventlog>. The description on EventID.NET[1] verifies that such results are meaningful. Moreover, we find several important relationships from security log and application log. Figure 14 shows the whole ERN graph for the security log which includes 15 vertices and 36 edges. In this figure, the labels of vertices denote the event types and the labels on edges denote the relationships in form of $C[param1, param2]$, where C or P denotes the type of relationship and $param1, param2$ denote the time interval parameter of the relationship.

6.4 Application of Event Summarization

ERNs like the one shown in Figure 14 are immediately useful for managing computer systems. A system administrator can devise automatic event handling for each pattern type. For example, in the context of security monitoring, periodic event patterns with a short period like the one formed by event type 861 is usually caused by a malicious or ill-configured program that attempts to exploit security holes. Once such a pattern is identified, a security response process should be triggered. A correlation pattern usually represents an episode of an evolving problem going through various phases. One can devise proactive event-condition-action rules to prevent serious incidents from happening.

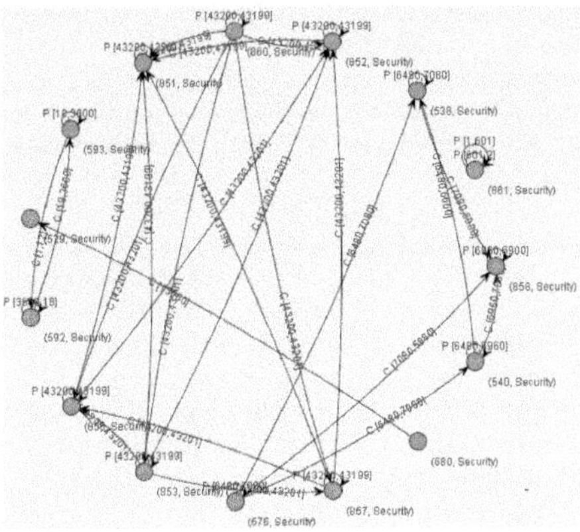

Figure 14: ERN for security log

Moreover, after we applying clique finding algorithm [5] to find all the cliques of this ERN by ignoring the directions, we further find larger patterns by combining the pairwise patterns. There are 4 sets of event groups found: Firewall related events (6 types), network access events (4 types), process management events (2 types) and antivirus monitoring events (1 type). The detailed information for discovered cliques are listed in Table 5.

[1]http://www.eventid.net

7. RELATED WORK

Event Summarization. Event Summarization is a relatively new research area that combines the area of data mining and computer systems. It can be deemed as an extension of frequent itemset mining [1, 7] and frequent episode mining [9, 16, 20, 21]. These frequent pattern mining techniques can reveal some interesting patterns by identifying the correlations of discrete events and are the building blocks of event summarization. Event summarization has attracted a lot of research attention recently [14, 15, 25, 24]. Peng et al. [24] proposed an approach to find the patterns in the event logs by measuring inter-arrivals of the events. Kiernan et al. [14, 15] proposed a summarization method by segmenting the event sequence according to the frequency changes of events. Based on the work of Kiernan, Wang et al. [25] further improved the summary by proposing a Hidden Markov Model to describe the transition of states among sequence segments. However, since they are either too general or too hard to be understood by data mining outsider, none of the results provided by these works are helpful enough for the system administrators.

Minimum Description Length. Minimum Description Length Principle (MDL) [12] is a general method for inductive inference. It is effective for generalization, data compression, and de-noising. In data mining community, it has been successfully used for temporal pattern mining [7], clustering [29], graph mining [10], trajectory outlier detection [17] and social network analysis [30]. Although MDL has been used in event summarization for encoding the event segments [14, 25], our method is the first one that uses MDL to encode the inter-arrival histograms and to identify the set of disjoint histograms for summarization.

Wavelet Transformation. Wavelet transformation is a useful tool for dividing up data, functions, or operators into different frequency components and then studies each component with a resolution matched to its scale [11, 18]. It has been widely used in many data mining tasks such as clustering [28], similarity search [27] and visualization [23]. The most relevant application to event summarization is wavelet-based time-series analysis [8, 27] where wavelet tools are used to measure the similarity of time-series in a global perspective. used in event summarization. In this paper, we use wavelet transformation as a subroutine to find the possible boundaries of the patterns hidden in an event sequence. We rely on its multi-resolution property to improve the efficiency of our approach.

8. CONCLUSION AND FUTURE WORK

In this paper, we propose a framework called *natural event summarization* and an algorithmic solution to the problem of summarizing event sequences that are generated by system logger. Our framework summarizes the event sequence from the perspective of depicting the event patterns by capturing the temporal relationships among same-type and different-type of events. The framework finds the best set of disjoint histograms to summarize the input event sequence based on MDL. Moreover, to improve the efficiency, we present a heuristic boundary pruning algorithm to prune

Table 5: Cliques of event relationships and their interpretations

Size	Event Types	Interpretation (After matching clique back to original ERN)
6	(851, security), (860, security) (852, security), (850, security) (853, security), (857, security)	This clique is related to the firewall actions. At first, event 860 (The windows firewall has switched the active policy profile) is triggered, then the other five types are triggered by 860.
4	(576, security) , (540, security) (538, security), (858, security)	This clique is related to the operation of network accessing. At first, event 76 (Special privileges assigned to new logon) is triggered, then event 540 (Logon successful) is triggered, and then event type 538 (User logoff) and 858 (Unknown) happens afterward.
2	(592, security), (593, security)	This clique is related to the creation and destroy of process. Event type 593 (A new process has been created) and type 593 (A process has exited) occur alternatively.
1	(861, security)	This clique is related to the actions of firewall. Event type 861 (The windows firewall has detected an application listening for incoming traffic) appears periodically. This is because the antivirus scanner installed on this machine continuously monitors the ports.

the unlikely boundaries and reduce the size of the histogram graph. Finally, we use ERN to present the final event summary in a more interpretable way.

There are several directions for the future work. Firstly, there is still a long way to go for the efficiency improvement. Secondly, one limitation of our current solution is the fixed time interval across time. In the future, we should also consider the pseudo temporal patterns for summarization. Moreover, many of the event logs in modern distributed systems are in form of streams, but our current event summarization is designed based on the static event log. One immediate goal is to design a new framework that is able to handle stream event sequences. Finally, we plan to build a whole event summarization system, which includes modules like event log structure extraction module, event summarization module, summarization postprocess module and summarization visualization module.

Acknowledgements

The work is partially supported by NSF CAREER grant IIS-0546280.

9. REFERENCES

[1] R. Agrawal, H. Mannila, R. Srikant, H. Toivonen, and A.I. Verkamo. *Fast Discovery of Association Rules*, pages 307–328. AAAI/MIT Press, 1996.

[2] R. Agrawal and R. Srikant. Mining sequential patterns. In *ICDE*, 1995.

[3] M. Aharon, G. Barash, I. Cohen, and E. Mordechai. One graph is worth a thousand logs: Uncovering hidden structures in massive system event logs. In *PKDD*, 2009.

[4] Haar A.Zur. Theorie der orghogonalen funktionensysteme. *Mathematische*, 69:pp331–371, 1910.

[5] C. Bron and J. Kerbosch. Algorithm 457: finding all cliques of an undirected graph. *Communications of the ACM*, 16:575–577, 1973.

[6] S. Cha and S.N. Srihari. On measuring the distance between histograms. *Pattern Recognition*, 35:1355–1370, 2002.

[7] S. Chakrabarti, S. Sarawagi, and B. Dom. Mining surprising patterns using temporal description length. In *VLDB*, 1998.

[8] K. Chan and A. Fu. Efficient time series matching by wavelets. In *ICDE*, 1999.

[9] D. Chudova and P. Smyth. Pattern discovery in sequences under a markov assumption. In *KDD*, 2002.

[10] D.J. Cook and L.B. Holder. Substructure discovery using minimum description length and background knowledge. *Journal of Artificial Intelligence Research*, 1:231–255, 1994.

[11] I. Daubechies. *Ten Lectures on Wavelets*. Captital City Press, 1992.

[12] P.D. Grunwald. *The Minimum Description Length Principle*. MIT Press, 2007.

[13] J.L. Hellerstein, S. Ma, S. M. Weiss, R. Vilalta, and C. Apte. Predictive algorithms in the management of computer systems. *IBM Systems Journal*, 4, 2002.

[14] J. Kiernan and E. Terzi. Constructing comprehensive summaries of large event sequences. In *KDD*, 2008.

[15] J. Kiernan and E. Terzi. Constructing comprehensive summaries of large event sequences. *ACM Transactions on Knowledge Discovery from Data*, 3:1–31, 2009.

[16] S. Laxman and K.P. Unnikrishnan P.S. Sastryand. Discovering frequent episodes and learning hidden markov models: A formal connection. *IEEE Transactions on Knowledge and Data Engineering*, 17:1505–1517, 2005.

[17] J.G. Lee, J. Han, and X. Li. Trajectory outlier detection: A partition-and-detect framework. In *ICDE*, 2008.

[18] T. Li, Q. Li, S. Zhu, and M. Ogihara. A survey on wavelet applications in data mining. *ACM SIGKDD Explorations*, 4:pp49–68, 2002.

[19] T. Li, F. Liang, S. Ma, and W. Peng. An integrated framework on mining logs files for computing system management. In *KDD*, 2005.

[20] S. Ma and J.L. Hellerstein. Mining partially periodic event patterns with unknown periods. In *ICDE*, 2001.

[21] H. Mannila and M. Salmenkivi. Finding simple intensive description from event sequence data. In *KDD*, 2001.

[22] S. Marsland, C. J. Twining, and C.J. Taylor. A minimum description length objective function for groupwise non-rigid image registration. In *Image and Vision Computing*, 2008.

[23] N.E. Miller, P.C. Wong, M. Brewster, and H. Foote. Topic islands - a wavelet-based text visualization system. In *IEEE Visualization*, 1998.

[24] W. Peng, C. Perng, T. Li, and H. Wang. Event summarization for system management. In *KDD*, 2008.

[25] W. Peng, H. Wang, M. Liu, and W. Wang. An algorithmic approach to event summarization. In *SIGMOD*, 2010.

[26] C. Perng, D. Thoenen, G. Grabarnik, S. Ma, and J. Hellerstein. Data-driven validation, completion and construction of event relationship networks. In *KDD*, 2003.

[27] I. Popivanov and R.J. Miller. Similarity search over time-series data using wavelets. In *ICDE*, 2002.

[28] G. Sheikholeslami, S. Chartterjee, and Aidong Zhang. Wavecluster: a wavelet-based clustering approach for spatial data in very large databases. *VLDB Journal*, 8, 2000.

[29] R.S. Wallace and T. Kanade. Finding natural clusters having minimum description length. In *Pattern Recognition*, 1990.

[30] K. Xu, C. Tang, C. Li, Y. Jiang, and R. Tang. An mdl approach to efficiently discover communities in bipartite network. In *DASFAA*, 2010.

Transferring Topical Knowledge from Auxiliary Long Texts for Short Text Clustering

Ou Jin*
Shanghai Jiao Tong University
800 Dongchuan Road
Shanghai, China
kingohm@apex.sjtu.edu.cn

Nathan N. Liu
Hong Kong University of Science and Technology
Clear Water Bay, Hong Kong
nliu@cse.ust.hk

Kai Zhao
NEC Labs China
Beijing, China
zhao_kai@nec.cn

Yong Yu
Shanghai Jiao Tong University
800 Dongchuan Road
Shanghai, China
yyu@apex.sjtu.edu.cn

Qiang Yang
Hong Kong University of Science and Technology
Clear Water Bay, Hong Kong
qyang@cse.ust.hk

ABSTRACT

With the rapid growth of social Web applications such as Twitter and online advertisements, the task of understanding short texts is becoming more and more important. Most traditional text mining techniques are designed to handle long text documents. For short text messages, many of the existing techniques are not effective due to the sparseness of text representations. To understand short messages, we observe that it is often possible to find topically related long texts, which can be utilized as the auxiliary data when mining the target short texts data. In this article, we present a novel approach to cluster short text messages via transfer learning from auxiliary long text data. We show that while some previous works for enhancing short text clustering with related long texts exist, most of them ignore the semantic and topical inconsistencies between the target and auxiliary data and may hurt the clustering performance on the short texts. To accommodate the possible inconsistencies between source and target data, we propose a novel topic model - Dual Latent Dirichlet Allocation (DLDA) model, which jointly learns two sets of topics on short and long texts and couples the topic parameters to cope with the potential inconsistencies between data sets. We demonstrate through large-scale clustering experiments on both advertisements and Twitter data that we can obtain superior performance over several state-of-art techniques for clustering short text documents.

*Part of this work was done while the first author was a visiting student in Hong Kong University of Science Technology.

CIKM'11, October 24–28, 2011, Glasgow, Scotland, UK.

Categories and Subject Descriptors

H.3.3 [**Information Storage and retrieval**]: Information Search and Retrieval—*Clustering*; I.2.6 [**Artificial Intelligence**]: Learning; I.2.7 [**Artificial Intelligence**]: Natural Language Processing—*Text analysis*

General Terms

Algorithms, Experimentation

Keywords

Short Text, Statistical Generative Models, Unsupervised Learning

1. INTRODUCTION

Short texts play an important role in various emerging Web applications such as online advertisements and micro-blogging. Sponsored search and display advertisements as commonly found on search result pages or general web pages can usually accommodate just a few keywords or sentences. Similarly, the popular micro-blogging service Twitter restricts the message length to be less than 140 characters. Effective techniques for mining short texts are crucial to these application domains. While many successful text mining techniques have been developed in the past, they have only been designed for and tested on traditional long text corpus such as blogs or newswires. Directly applying these methods on short texts often leads to poor results [12]. Compared with long texts, short text mining has to address two inherent difficulties caused by their highly sparse representations: the lack of sufficient word co-occurrence information and the lack of context information in the text.

To alleviate the sparseness of short texts, a common approach is to conduct "pseudo relevance feedback" in order to enrich the original short text corpus with an additional set of *auxiliary data* consisting of semantically related long texts. This can be achieved by sending the input short texts as queries to a search engine to retrieve a set of most relevant results [18]. Another popular method is to match short texts with topics learned from general knowledge repositories such as Wikipedia or ODP [12, 11]. Once the auxiliary data or auxiliary topic is obtained, the data or topics are often directly combined with the original short texts, which are then processed by some traditional text mining models.

While the pseudo relevance feedback based data augmentation approach is a promising approach, one should note that such a process is an inherently noisy operation and there is a risk that certain portion of the auxiliary data may in fact be semantically unrelated to the original short texts. Similarly, the unrelated or noisy auxiliary topics may also bring negative result. Therefore, naively combining the short texts with semantically unrelated long texts or topics could hurt the performance on the short texts. The problem can become even more serious for unsupervised learning on short texts as there is no labeling information to guide the selection of auxiliary data and auxiliary topics.

In this paper, we study the problem of enhancing short text clustering by incorporating auxiliary long texts. We propose a class of topic model - Dual Latent Dirichlet Allocation (DLDA), which jointly learns a set of *target topics* on the short texts and another set of *auxiliary topics* on the long texts while carefully modeling the attribution to each type of topics when generating documents. In particular, we design and compare two mechanisms for DLDA to accommodate domain inconsistencies between the two data sets: (1) using two asymmetric priors on the topic mixing proportions to control the relative importance of different topic classes for generating short and long texts (2) introducing a latent binary switch variable to control whether each document should be generated using target or auxiliary topics. Our DLDA model allows topical structure to be shared in a more flexible manner between the collections of short and long texts and could therefore lead to more robust performance improvement when the auxiliary long texts are only partially related to the input short texts. Clustering experiments on two real world data sets consisting of textual advertisements and twitter messages demonstrated consistent improvements over existing methods for short text clustering, especially when there are many irrelevant documents in the auxiliary data set.

2. RELATED WORK

2.1 Mining Short Text

Due to its importance in popular web applications such as Twitter, short text mining has attracted growing interests in recent years. Hong et al. [4] compared different schemes to train standard topic model on tweets from Twitter. Sriram et al. [19] compared some features for classification to conquer the problem coming with the short of tweets. Mihalcea et al. [8] proposed to measure the similarity of short text snippets by using both corpus-based and knowledge-based measures when acquiring words similarity. Sahami et al. [18] present a novel similarity measure for short text snippets, which utilizes search engines to provide additional context for the given short text, just like query expansion techniques. This similarity measure can also be proven to be a kernel. [21] improved Sahami's work by involving a learning process to make the measure more appropriate for the target corpus. Phan et al. [12, 11] proposed to convert additional knowledge base to topics to improve the representation of the short texts. The knowledge base is crawled with selected seeds from several topics to avoid noise. Hu et al. [5] proposed a three level framework to utilize both the knowledge from Wikipedia and WordNet. Most of these works focus on how to acquire auxiliary data in order to enrich short text. They generally make the implicit assumption that the auxiliary data are semantically related to the input short texts, which is hardly true in practice due to the noisy nature of the pseudo relevance feedback operation.

2.2 Transfer Learning

A closely related area with our work is that of transfer learning [15] which studies how to transfer knowledge from one related auxiliary domain to the target domain to help the learning task on target domain. However, most existing works in this area focused on supervised [20] or semi-supervised setting [14], whereas we need to solve the problem in a totally unsupervised fashion. A similar setting has been considered by Dai et al. [1], who proposed a co-clustering based solution to enhance clustering on target domain data with the help of an auxiliary data set. However, the model is not designed for handling short texts. Moreover, it makes a strong assumption that the word co-clusters are completely shared between the two domains, which, as we will be shown, is much less effective than our much flexible DLDA model.

3. DUAL LATENT DIRICHLET ALLOCATION (DLDA)

Due to its high dimensional yet extremely sparse representations, clustering short texts directly based on the bag of words representation can be very ineffective as we would demonstrate in the experiments. In this section, we develop a topic modeling based approach to discover some low dimensional structure that can more effectively capture the semantic relationships between documents. Directly learning topic models on short text is much harder than on traditional long text. For this reason, [12, 11] proposed to train topic models on a collection long text in the same domain and then make inference on short text to help the learning task on short texts. However, in highly dynamic domains like Twitter where novel topics and trends constantly emerge, it is not always possible to find strongly related long texts via a search engine or a static knowledge base such as Wikipedia. Furthermore, for application domains like advertisement, short texts and long texts are often used for very different purposes. As a result, they may adopt quite distinct language styles. For example, when merchants advertise a product using short banner Ads, the content often emphasizes on the credibility and price aspects. At the same time, in a Web page for selling the product, merchants may focus more on the branding and product features. Similarly, when comparing Twitter messages and Blog articles posted by the same authors, one can also note significant differences in their content as well as language styles.

In the presence of such inconsistencies between short texts and auxiliary long texts, it would be unreasonable to assume that the topical structure of the two domains is completely identical, as done in several previous works [12, 11, 20]. In this section, we describe a better solution to the problem by designing a novel topic model, referred to as the Dual Latent Dirichlet Allocation (DLDA), which can distinguish between consistent and inconsistent topical structures across domains when learning topics from short texts with an additional set of auxiliary long texts. In the following sections, we first review the basic LDA model and several related ex-

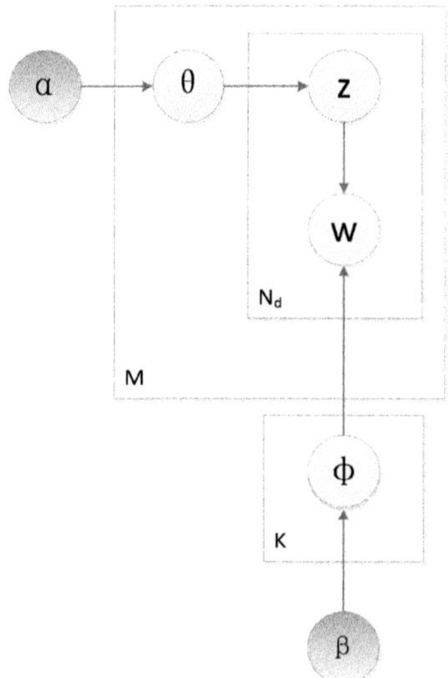

Figure 1: Graphical representation of LDA

tensions, and then put forward the α-DLDA and γ-DLDA models, which extend the LDA model to cope with domain differences based on two different mechanisms.

3.1 Task Setting and Background

Let $\mathcal{W}^{tar} = \{\vec{w}_m^{tar}\}_{m=1}^{M^{tar}}$ denote the set of short texts from the target domain (i.e., domain of interests), which are to be clustered, and let $\mathcal{W}^{aux} = \{\vec{w}_m^{aux}\}_{m=1}^{M^{aux}}$ denote a set of auxiliary documents consisting of long texts. The auxiliary data set could be extracted from general knowledge base, such as Wikipedia, or extracted from some documents relevant to the target short texts. In this work, we attempt to transfer the topical knowledge from the auxiliary long texts to help with the unsupervised learning task on target short texts. Any long texts that are topically related to the target short texts can be used as auxiliary data.

3.2 Latent Dirichlet Allocation and Extensions

A common approach to dealing with data with high dimensional sparse representation is dimensionality reduction, which has a rich history and literature. A recent trend in dimensionality reduction is the use of probabilistic models. In particular, Latent Dirichlet Allocation (LDA) is a Bayesian probabilistic graphical model, which models each document as a mixture of underlying topics and generates each word from one topic. The generation process of a document is described in Table 1, which corresponds to a graphical model as shown in Figure 1. A document $\vec{w}_d = \{w_{d,n}\}_{n=1}^{N_d}$ is associated a document under a specific multinomial distribution $Mult(\vec{\theta}_d)$ that determines the mixing proportion of different topics within the document. Then, topic assignment for each word is performed by sampling a particular topic $z_{d,n}$ from a multinomial distribution $Mult(\vec{\theta}_d)$. Finally, a particular word $w_{d,n}$ is generated by sampling from a multinomial distribution $Mult(\vec{\varphi}_{d,n})$ over the words in the corpus.

The LDA model is entirely unsupervised, whereas in many applications one cannot expect to have additional knowledge such as class labels, tags, etc. To incorporate such side information so as to arm the LDA model with class labels, several extensions of LDA have been proposed by imposing various

Table 1: The generation process of LDA

- For each topic $z \in \{1, \dots, K\}$, draw a multinomial distribution over terms, $\phi_z \sim Dir(\beta)$.
- For each document $d \in \{1, \dots, M\}$
  - Draw a multinomial distribution over topics, $\theta_d \sim Dir(\alpha)$
  - For each word $w_{d,n}$ in document d :
    - draw a topic $z_{d,n} \sim Multinomial(\theta_d)$
    - draw a word $w_{d,n} \sim Multinomial(\phi_{z_{d,n}})$.

constraints on the document-specific topic-mixing proportions $\vec{\theta}_d$. In the DiscLDA model [7], additional supervisory information in the form of document labels is utilized by learning a class-label dependent linear transformation of $\vec{\theta}_d$ with some discriminative criterion.

Similarly, to handle documents annotated with multiple tags such as social bookmarks, the Labeled LDA model [17] learns a topic for each tag and restricts that each document be generated using only those topics corresponding to the set of tags associated with the document. This is achieved by setting a document-specific hyper-parameter vector $\vec{\alpha}_d$. The model was later successfully applied on a large collection of twitter messages annotated with hashtags to map the short messages into different categories [16]. Note that although both [16] and our work attempt to apply topic model for characterizing short text document collections, the focus of our works and their objectives are quite different. [16] studies the utility of hashtags, whereas our work is motivated by the use of additional auxiliary long text documents. In practice, both tags and auxiliary long texts are potential data sources that can be exploited. We believe the two approaches are indeed complementary to each other.

3.3 α-DLDA

Two key ideas are exploited in our work in the DLDA model for coping with domain inconsistencies:

1. We can model two separate sets of topics for auxiliary data and target data. This approach captures the major themes within the two data sets, respectively. Distinguishing auxiliary topics from target topics allows irrelevant or inconsistent topical knowledge in the auxiliary data to be filtered out.

2. We can also use different generative process for auxiliary and target documents, respectively, so that the model favors generating a document using the topics that belongs to its domain.

To realize the first idea, we can simply split the topics in a LDA model into two groups. In particular, we assume that there are K^{tar} topics with parameters $\{\phi_1^{tar}, ..., \phi_{K^{tar}}^{tar}\}$ in the target domain and K^{aux} topics with parameters $\{\phi_1^{aux}, ..., \phi_{K^{aux}}^{aux}\}$ in the auxiliary domain.

To realize the second idea, a simple idea is to properly set the hyper-parameter vector $\vec{\alpha}$, which determines the prior distribution for the document specific mixing proportions

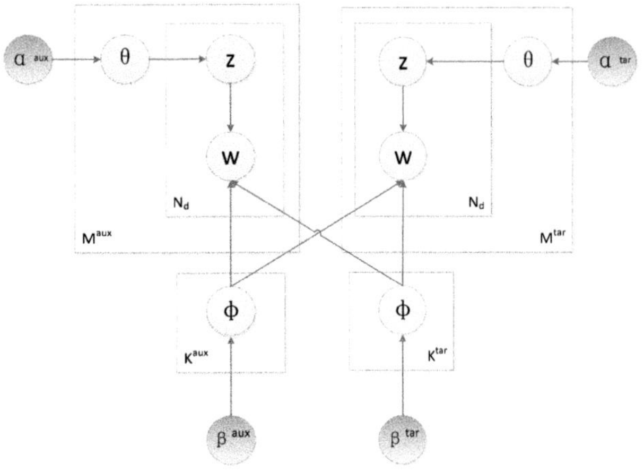

Figure 2: Graphical representation of α-DLDA

$\vec{\theta}$. Traditionally, without any prior knowledge, the entries of $\vec{\alpha}$ are often assumed to be all equal to some small positive value, which corresponds to having no preferences over particular topics. To make the model generate target documents using target topics more often, we can make the entries of $\vec{\alpha}$ correspond to the target topics to be greater than those corresponding to auxiliary topics. The same idea can be applied to designate another asymmetric Dirichlet prior for generating the topic mixing proportions for auxiliary documents. This leads to having two separate asymmetric Dirichlet distributions with parameters

$$\vec{\alpha}^{tar} = [\alpha^{tar}_{aux}, \ldots, \alpha^{tar}_{aux}, \alpha^{tar}_{tar}, \ldots, \alpha^{tar}_{tar}]$$

and

$$\vec{\alpha}^{aux} = [\alpha^{aux}_{aux}, \ldots, \alpha^{aux}_{aux}, \alpha^{aux}_{tar}, \ldots, \alpha^{aux}_{tar}]$$

respectively, which corresponds to the generative process depicted in Figure 2. We refer to this particular variation of DLDA model based on modifying the α parameters as the α-DLDA model. Note that the inference and learning algorithms of the basic LDA model can be easily applied to α-DLDA model, which does not change the model structure but only imposes certain settings of the hyperparameters.

3.4 γ-DLDA

The α-DLDA model uses asymmetric Dirichlet prior to control the relative importance of target versus auxiliary topics when generating a document. However, the asymmetric Dirichlet prior is imposed on all the documents from each domain. In this section, we develop the γ-DLDA model, which constrains that each document be generated using either auxiliary or target topics. This introduces a document-dependent binary-switch variable to be used for choosing between the two types of topics when generating the document. This new mechanism allows the model to automatically capture whether a document should be more related to the target or auxiliary domain.

More specifically, under the γ-DLDA model, each document is associated with (1) a binomial distribution over auxiliary topics versus target topics π_d with Beta prior $\gamma^c = [\gamma^c_{aux}, \gamma^c_{tar}]$ for each corpus $c \in \{aux, tar\}$, and (2) two multinomial distribution over auxiliary topics and target topics $\theta^{aux}, \theta^{tar}$ separately, with a symmetric Dirichlet prior α.

Table 2: The generation process of DLDA

- For each target topic $z \in \{1, \ldots, K^{tar}\}$, draw a multinomial distribution over terms, $\phi^{tar}_z \sim Dir(\beta^{tar})$.
- For each auxiliary topic $z \in \{1, \ldots, K^{aux}\}$, draw a multinomial distribution over terms, $\phi^{aux}_z \sim Dir(\beta^{aux})$.
- For each corpus $c \in \{aux, tar\}$
  - For each document $d \in \{1, \ldots, M^c\}$
    - Draw a multinomial distribution over target topics, $\theta^{tar}_d \sim Dir(\alpha^{tar})$
    - Draw a multinomial distribution over auxiliary topics, $\theta^{aux}_d \sim Dir(\alpha^{aux})$
    - Draw a binomial distribution over target topics versus auxiliary topics, $\pi_d \sim Beta(\gamma^c)$
    - For each word $w_{d,n}$ in document d :
      - Draw a binary switch $x_{d,n} \sim Binomial(\pi_d)$
      - if $x_{d,n} = tar$, draw a target topic $z_{d,n} \sim Multinomial(\theta^{tar}_d)$
      - if $x_{d,n} = aux$, draw a auxiliary topic $z_{d,n} \sim Multinomial(\theta^{aux}_d)$
      - draw a word $w_{d,n} \sim Multinomial(\phi^{x_{d,n}}_{z_{d,n}})$.

The generative process is shown below, and a graphical representation of the model is shown in Figure 3.

The Beta prior parameterized by γ^c can be used to capture the prior belief on the consistency between the two domains. Here we constrain that $\gamma^{aux}_{aux} > \gamma^{aux}_{tar}$ and $\gamma^{tar}_{tar} > \gamma^{tar}_{aux}$, in order to ensure that the auxiliary topics and target topics focus more modeling the documents in their respective corpus.

3.4.1 *Parameter Estimation with Gibbs Sampling*

From the generative graphical model, we can write the joint distribution of all known and hidden variables given the hyper parameters:

$$p(\vec{w}^c_m, \vec{z}, \vec{x}, \vec{\theta}, \vec{\pi}, \Phi | \vec{\alpha}, \vec{\beta}, \vec{\gamma}^c) \quad (1)$$

$$= \prod_{n=1}^{N_m} p(w^{aux}_{m,n} | \vec{\varphi}_{z^x_{m,n}}) p(x_{m,n} | \vec{\pi}) p(z_{m,n} | \vec{\theta}_m) \quad (2)$$

$$\cdot\, p(\vec{\theta}_m | \vec{\alpha}) \cdot p(\vec{\pi} | \vec{\gamma}^c) \cdot p(\Phi | \vec{\beta}) \quad (3)$$

The likelihood of a document $\vec{w}$ can be obtained by integrating out $\vec{\theta}, \vec{\pi}, \Phi$ and summing over $z^x_{m,n}$:

$$p(\vec{w}^c | \vec{\alpha}, \vec{\beta}, \vec{\gamma}^c) = \int\int\int p(\vec{\theta}_m | \vec{\alpha}) p(\vec{\pi}_m | \vec{\gamma}^c) p(\Phi | \vec{\beta}) \quad (4)$$

$$\cdot \prod_{n=1}^{N_m} p(w_{m,n} | \vec{\theta}_m, \vec{\pi}, \Phi) d\Phi d\vec{\theta}_m d\vec{\pi}_m \quad (5)$$

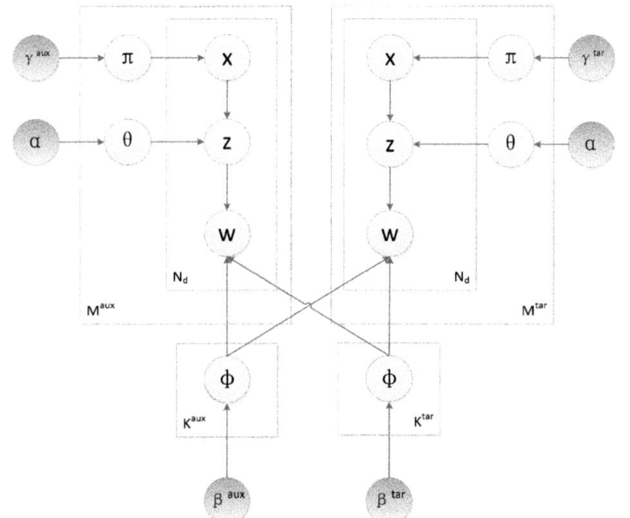

Figure 3: Graphical representation of the proposed γ-DLDA model

Finally, the likelihood of the whole data set under the model is $\mathcal{W} = \{\vec{w}_m^{aux}\}_{m=1}^{M^{aux}} \cup \{\vec{w}_m^{tar}\}_{m=1}^{M^{tar}}$ is

$$p(\mathcal{W}|\vec{\alpha}, \vec{\beta}, \vec{\gamma}) \tag{6}$$

$$= \prod_{m=1}^{M^{aux}} p(\vec{w}_m^{aux}|\vec{\alpha}, \vec{\beta}, \vec{\gamma}^{aux}) \cdot \prod_{m=1}^{M^{tar}} p(\vec{w}_m^{tar}|\vec{\alpha}, \vec{\beta}, \vec{\gamma}^{tar}) \tag{7}$$

To estimate the parameters, we need to estimate the latent variables conditioned on the observed variables; i.e. $p(\mathbf{x}, \mathbf{z}|\mathbf{w}, \alpha, \beta, \gamma)$, where $\mathbf{x}$, $\mathbf{z}$ are vectors of assignments of auxiliary/target topics binary switches and topics for all the words, respectively. We perform approximate inference using Gibbs sampling, a type of Markov Chain Monte Carlo (MCMC) algorithm, with the following updating formulas.

For auxiliary topics $z \in \{1, \ldots, K^{aux}\}$,

$$p(x_i = x, z_i = z|w_i = w, \mathbf{x}_{\neg\mathbf{i}}, \mathbf{z}_{\neg\mathbf{i}}, \mathbf{w}_{\neg\mathbf{i}}, \alpha, \beta, \gamma) \tag{8}$$

$$\propto \frac{n_{w,\neg i}^{aux,z} + \alpha}{\sum_{v=1}^{V} (n_{v,\neg i}^{aux,z} + \alpha_v)} \cdot \frac{n_{d,\neg i}^{aux,z} + \beta}{\sum_{k=1}^{K^{aux}} (n_{k,\neg i}^{aux,z} + \beta_k)} \tag{9}$$

$$\cdot (n_{d,x,\neg i}^{aux} + \gamma_x^{c_i}) \tag{10}$$

For target topics $z \in \{1, \ldots, K^{tar}\}$,

$$p(x_i = x, z_i = z|w_i = w, \mathbf{x}_{\neg\mathbf{i}}, \mathbf{z}_{\neg\mathbf{i}}, \mathbf{w}_{\neg\mathbf{i}}, \alpha, \beta, \gamma) \tag{11}$$

$$\propto \frac{n_{w,\neg i}^{tar,z} + \alpha}{\sum_{v=1}^{V} n_{(v,\neg i}^{tar,z} + \alpha_v)} \cdot \frac{n_{d,\neg i}^{tar,z} + \beta}{\sum_{k=1}^{K^{tar}} (n_{k,\neg i}^{aux,z} + \beta_k)} \tag{12}$$

$$\cdot (n_{d,x,\neg i}^{tar} + \gamma_x^{c_i}) \tag{13}$$

where $n_{w,\neg i}^{aux,z}$ is the number of times the term w is assigned to an auxiliary topic z. Similarly, $n_{w,\neg i}^{tar,z}$ is the count of w for a target topic z. $n_{d,\neg i}^{aux,z}$ is the number of times a word in document d is assigned to a topic z, while $n_{d,\neg i}^{tar,z}$ is for target topic, $n_{d,x,\neg i}^{aux}$ and $n_{d,x,\neg i}^{tar}$ denote the number of times a word is assigned to auxiliary and to target topics, respectively. c_i denotes the corpus (aux, tar) which the current document is drawn from. For all the counts, subscript $\neg i$ indicates that the i-th word is excluded from the computation.

After the Gibbs sampler reaches a burn-in state, we can then harvest samples and count the word assignments in order to estimate the parameters:

$$\theta_{d,z}^x \propto n_d^{x,z} + \alpha^x \tag{14}$$

$$\phi_{z,w}^x \propto \theta_w^{x,z} + \beta^x \tag{15}$$

Table 3: The statistical information of the two corpus

	Short Text		Long Text	
	words/doc	docs	words/doc	docs
ADs	29.06	182209	560.40	99737
TWEETs	9.71	24047	1106.79	4482

3.5 Clustering with Hidden Topics

After estimating the model parameters and inferring the parameters for new documents, we can represent each document d by θ_d as:

$$f_d = \left[\frac{\theta_{d,1}^{aux}}{S_1^{aux}}, \ldots, \frac{\theta_{d,K^{aux}}^{aux}}{S_{K^{aux}}^{aux}}, \frac{\theta_{d,1}^{tar}}{S_1^{tar}}, \ldots, \frac{\theta_{d,K^{tar}}^{tar}}{S_{K^{tar}}^{tar}} \right]$$

where $S_j^x = \sum_i \theta_{i,j}^x, x \in \{aux, tar\}$. We normalize the scale of each feature in order to reduce the importance of some topics that are overly general, such as a topic that represents the functional words and common language. Such topics tend to occur in most documents, but they lack the discriminative power.

Another important issue is that we should collect sufficient samples of θ in the sampling. Because the texts are short, the result in one sample may vary much, while the average of multi samples will produce a more robust result. This process may be affected by the *label switching* problem caused by the MCMC algorithm. But, in practice, we find that this is not a serious problem.

After having the topic based representations for the short text documents, we can apply the traditional clustering methods on them. Since these features have already involved the knowledge from the auxiliary data, clustering on the new representation may achieve better results, as we will demonstrate in the experiments.

4. EXPERIMENTAL RESULTS

4.1 Data Set

In order to evaluate our algorithm DLDA, we conduct experiments on two real data sets, a collection of advertisements (ADs) from an online consumer to consumer (C2C) shopping Web site and a collection of tweets (TWEETs) from Twitter.

The short texts in the ADs data set are a collection of text-based display advertisements crawled from an e-commerce Web site of a commercial company. To obtain the auxiliary long texts, we randomly crawled some product web pages listed on the e-commerce site's home page. Each advertisement has been labeled with 42 classes according to the product taxonomy used by the site. To create the TWEETs data set, we crawled 197,535 tweets from 405 Twitter users' time line. We then filter out 24,047 tweets (12.1%) with hashtags (i.e. semantic annotations added by the author of a tweet). In these tweets, there are 4,282 tweets (17.8%) containing URLs, we therefore crawled the content of the referenced URLs to form the set of auxiliary long texts. Some statistics of these two data sets are shown in the Table 3, from which we can see that the short texts in each data set contain a very small fraction of the number of words in the corresponding long texts. Moreover, the short texts in the TWEETs data set contain very few words on average and are much shorter in length when compared with the ADs data set.

We performed standard data preprocessing including stopword removal on the raw text. For the TWEETs data, we filter out the non-semantic symbols such as mentions of user names (@user), shorted URLs, etc. We also extract hashtags (#tag) from the text, since we rely on the hashtags as the semantic labeling information for evaluating the clustering quality.

It should be noted that our model does not require any correspondence structures between the short texts and the long texts, such as those indicating which tweet contains which URL. This type of correspondence is also not available at all in the ADs data set. The short and long texts in both data sets are of very different nature and are only topically related. The crawled Web pages in the ADs data set may not necessarily contain any information related to the products mentioned in the advertisements. Similarly, in the TWEET's data set, the referenced URLs are often news articles and blogs written by the users themselves, whereas the tweet messages are mostly the users' subjective comments. Thus, the tweets and the web pages are very likely about the same topics, though the style of the languages can be quite different.

4.2 Evaluation Criteria

In the experiments on the ADs data, we used *Entropy*, *Purity* and *Normalized Mutual Information (NMI)* as the evaluation criterion. Purity is a simple and transparent evaluation measure, which can help us understand the quality of the clustering result directly. Entropy and NMI can be information-theoretically interpreted. NMI allows us to trade off the quality of the clustering against the number of clusters, which the Purity measure cannot achieve. The larger the Purity and NMI values are, the higher the quality of the clustering is. Similarly, a smaller entropy means better performance.

Due to the lack of ground truth of the TWEET's data, we use the hashtags contained in the tweets as their hidden-meaning indicator. Since a lot of tweets are assigned more than one hashtags, we propose to employ *Davies-Bouldin Validity Index* (DBI) [2] calculated on the hashtags as the evaluation criterion. DBI is a function of the ratio of the sum of within-cluster scatter to between-cluster separation, which is defined as:

$$DBI = \frac{1}{n}\sum_{i=1}^{n} \max_{i \neq j} \left\{ \frac{S_n(Q_i) + S_n(Q_j)}{S(Q_i, Q_j)} \right\}$$

where n is the number of clusters, Q_x is the centroid of cluster x, $S_n(Q_x)$ is the average distance from all elements in cluster x to centroid Q_x, and $S(Q_i, Q_j)$ is the distance between centroids c_i and c_j. Here we use the Euclidian distance as the distance measure for both functions $S_n(\cdot)$ and $S(\cdot,\cdot)$. Since the algorithms that produce clusters with low intra-cluster distances (high intra-cluster similarity) and high inter-cluster distances (low inter-cluster similarity) will have a low Davies-Bouldin index, the clustering algorithm that produces a collection of clusters with the smallest DBI is considered the best algorithm based on this criterion.

Table 4: The performance of all the evaluation methods on ADs

	Purity	Entropy	NMI
Direct	0.280	0.681	0.215
LDA-short	0.305	0.650	0.250
LDA-long	0.360	0.599	0.310
LDA-both	0.362	0.594	0.315
STC	0.320	0.636	0.259
α-DLDA	0.383	0.578	0.336
γ-DLDA	**0.392**	**0.553**	**0.364**

4.3 Baseline Methods and Implementation Details

We compare our DLDA with the following methods:

Direct Direct clustering method without incorporating auxiliary data. We use CLUTO [1] with the TF-IDF representation.

LDA-short Learning a LDA from short texts and directly clustering with the θ learned.

LDA-long Learning a LDA from long texts and then apply to short text, which is proposed in [12]. We use GibbsLDA++ [2], the implementation mentioned in the paper.

LDA-both Learning a LDA from the combined collection of long texts and short texts as proposed in [20].

Self-Taught Clustering (STC) This is a state of the art unsupervised transfer learning method [1], which exploits an additional set of unlabeled auxiliary data for clustering target data. It does co-clustering [3] on both data sets simultaneously and uses shared word-clusters to bridge the two domains.

For LDA-short, LDA-long, LDA-both and our DLDA model, we first build the topic based representations of the short texts following the procedures described in Section 3.3, and then use CLUTO to obtain the document clusters.

For each application of the LDA-based algorithm, we repeat the step for five times and compute mean. We tune each algorithm to its best parameter setting. For the experiments on the ADs data, we set the cluster number to 42, since the data set is labeled with 42 classes. For the experiments on the TWEET's data, we set the cluster number to 50.

4.4 Result

The experimental results on two corpuses are shown in Table 4 and Table 5, respectively. As expected, our methods

[1]CLUTO:`http://glaros.dtc.umn.edu/gkhome/views/cluto/`

[2]GibbsLDA++:`http://gibbslda.sourceforge.net/`

[3]Co-clustering:`http://www.cse.ust.hk/TL/index.html`

Table 5: **The performance in DBI of all the evaluation methods on TWEETs**

	DBI
Direct	18.270
LDA-short	15.002
LDA-long	14.249
LDA-both	13.960
STC	13.342
α-DLDA	12.485
γ-DLDA	**11.748**

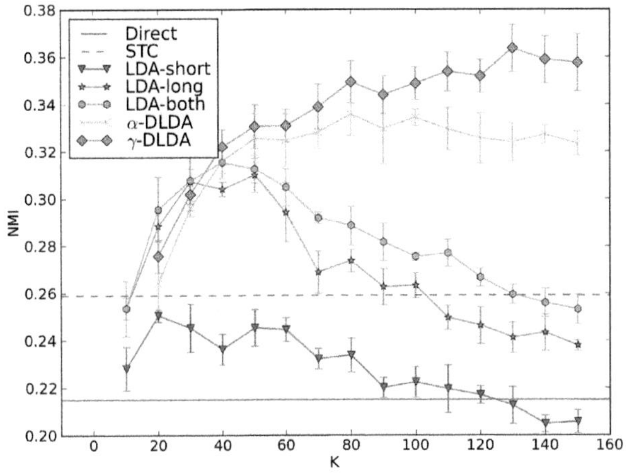

Figure 4: The performance of all the algorithms on ADs with different K

α-DLDA and γ-DLDA clearly outperformed all the other baseline methods on both data sets. Due to the high dimensionality and sparseness of the representations in short texts, directly clustering the short texts gave the poorest performance. LDA-short outperformed Direct on both data sets, which demonstrates the benefit of using topic based low dimensional representation for the short texts.

All methods that utilized auxiliary long texts can be observed to significantly outperform both the Direct and LDA-short, which clearly shows the value of transferring knowledge from auxiliary long texts. Interestingly, the LDA-long model, which ignores all the short texts, performs better than LDA-short. We believe that this is because learning topic models on short texts is inherently much more difficult.

Both variations of the proposed DLDA model consistently beat the LDA-both and STC algorithms. LDA-both does not distinguish the target domain from the auxiliary domain, and can suffer from domain inconsistencies as a result. The STC model distinguishes target and auxiliary domains, but lacks a document-level mechanism for determining if a document is more related to the target or the auxiliary domain. The empirical results confirm that the DLDA can effectively address these difficulties.

Finally, when comparing α-DLDA with γ-DLDA, we see that α-DLDA treats the documents in each set uniformly. However, for γ-DLDA, the document-dependent binary-switch

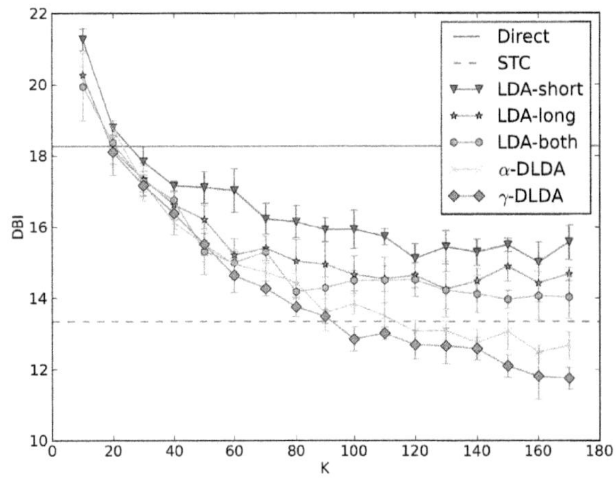

Figure 5: The performance of all the algorithms on TWEETs with different K

variables may only help select those auxiliary long texts that are related to the target domain. This document level mechanism gives γ-DLDA an extra flexibility over α-DLDA, which can lead to the observed superior performance.

4.5 Influence of the Parameters and Auxiliary Data

We conduct additional experiments to show the influence of the parameters and auxiliary data. These experiments are done on the ADs corpus with NMI as the evaluation metric. Due the stochastic nature of the algorithm, we repeat each algorithm for 5 times and report the mean as well as standard deviation values.

Hyperparameters.

In [3] parameters are set as $\alpha = 50/K$ and $\beta = 0.01$. In our work, we set $\gamma_{tar}^{aux} = \gamma_{aux}^{tar} = \gamma_{small}$ and $\gamma_{tar}^{tar} = \gamma_{aux}^{aux} = \gamma_{big}$, where $\gamma_{small} < \gamma_{big}$. Since the model is not very sensitive to this prior, we use $\gamma_{small} = 0.2$ and $\gamma_{big} = 0.5$ in the experiments.

For α-DLDA, we rely on the setting of α prior to constrain the topic selection. We have four parameters α_{aux}^{tar}, α_{tar}^{tar}, α_{aux}^{aux}, α_{tar}^{aux} to be tuned. We set $\alpha_{aux}^{aux} = 50/K$ and vary the other three in $\{0, 0.01, 0.05, 50/K\}$.

Topic Numbers.

The performance of all the LDA-based algorithms on different topic numbers is shown in the Figure 4 and 5 ,for both the ADs and TWEETs data sets. For α-DLDA and γ-DLDA, $K = K^{aux} + K^{tar}$ represents the overall complexity of the model. With the same K, the computational complexities of these LDA-based methods are nearly the same.

From these results, we can find that the method without any additional information is poor, while the other algorithms achieve much better performance. Those topic models with small-sized topics have similar performance, but perform much differently when the number of topics is large. The method that treats auxiliary data and target data dif-

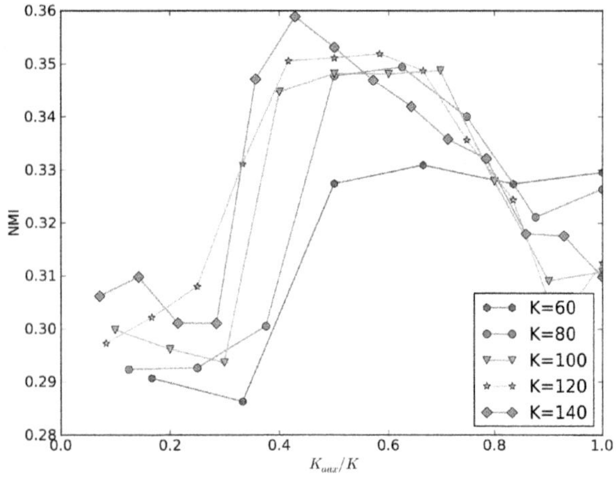

Figure 6: The influence of different K^{aux} and $K^{aux} + K^{tar}$ for γ-DLDA

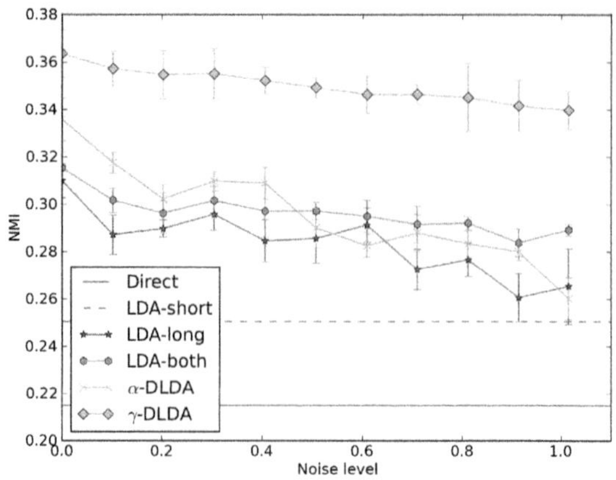

Figure 8: The influence of irrelevant data in auxiliary data

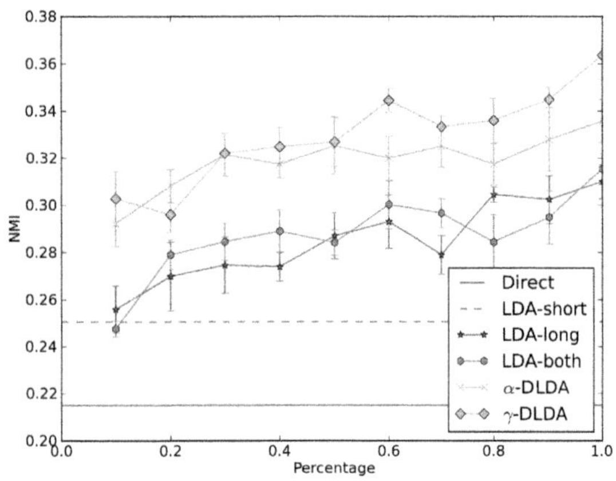

Figure 7: The influence of the number of auxiliary data used

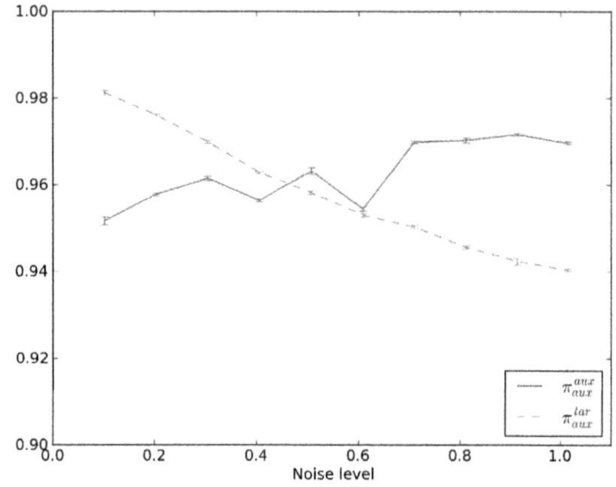

Figure 9: The variation of π with irrelevant data in auxiliary data

ferently can handle a larger number of topics with better result.

We also examine different K^{aux} for γ-DLDA. The result is shown in the Figure 6. For a set of K values ranging between 60 and 140 , we plot the model performances as K^{aux} goes from 10 to K. The value of K controls the overall complexity of the topic model, whereas tuning K^{aux} allows us to enforce different degrees of topics shared among the target and auxiliary data. Given a fixed K, reducing K^{aux} is equivalent to enforcing more shared topics between the two domains, whereas increasing K^{aux} allows more auxiliary domain-dependent information to be captured by the auxiliary topics. From Figure 6, we can clearly see that the optimal performance is achieved with neither very small nor very large K^{aux} values, which shows the important tradeoff between topic-sharing and domain inconsistencies.

Auxiliary Data.

The amount of auxiliary data involved in the learning process also influences the result. In the second set of experiments, we examine such an influence by varying the amount of auxiliary data used for training from 10% to 100%. The result is shown in the Figure 7. We can see that even with a small amount of auxiliary data, the performances of α-DLDA and γ-DLDA are already much better than the other methods. Furthermore, increasing the amount of auxiliary data can lead to consistent improvement. With more flexibility, γ-DLDA begins to perform better when more auxiliary data is involved.

Irrelevant Data.

We also compare the robustness of our algorithms α-DLDA and γ-DLDA with the other two topic model based methods: LDA-long and LDA-both. In this experiment, the auxiliary data is mixed with some documents that are randomly selected from a general knowledge base. There are certainly a lot of useful documents in the general knowledge base that share topics with our target documents. But without any filtering, much more irrelevant data can be included. These documents are not strongly related to the target data and can be considered as noise in the auxiliary data. We control the noise level by inserting different number of irrelevant documents into the auxiliary data. The performance of different models under different noise levels is shown in the Figure 8. The results of LDA-long and LDA-both are not very stable when more irrelevant documents are added to the auxiliary data whereas our method γ-DLDA achieved stable performances with different amounts of noise. This proves that, by explicitly considering domain inconsistency, we can effectively improve the robustness of short text clustering with auxiliary long texts.

When dealing with the auxiliary documents without noise, there is no huge difference between γ-DLDA and α-DLDA. In Figure 8, we found that simply treating the documents uniformly will suffer a lot of trouble. Manually adjusting the α priors can lighten this problem, but it requires much human effort. Without carefully tuning the α priors, the performance can drop dramatically.

The result of γ-DLDA can also be explained by the following analysis. We calculate the π when mixing the irrelevant data. The π is calculated by

$$\pi_{d,x}^c \propto n_{d,x}^c + \gamma_x^c.$$

Then the average value of π for auxiliary documents and target documents are calculated separately, as shown in Figure 9. With more irrelevant data, the model automatically adjusts the relevance between target documents and auxiliary topics. This adaptability helps the model escape from using many irrelevant topics.

5. CONCLUSIONS AND FUTURE WORK

In this paper, we presented a type of novel topic model for enhancing short text clustering by incorporating auxiliary long texts. The model jointly learns two sets of latent topics on short and long texts. When considering the difference between the topics of the auxiliary and target data, our method can robustly improve the result of clustering on target data, even when there are a lot of irrelevant documents in auxiliary data. The experimental result shows that DLDA can outperform many state-of-the-art methods. This helps validate that, by considering the difference between auxiliary data and target data, the clustering quality on short text can be improved.

In the future, we wish to evaluate other forms of domain difference criteria between data sets, and evaluate their performance when knowledge transfer is conducted between the data. We will also consider other forms of topic models to enable more effective learning.

6. ACKNOWLEDGEMENT

We thank the support of Hong Kong RGC project 621010, and Projects of International Cooperation and Exchanges National Natural Science Foundation of China 60931160445.

7. REFERENCES

[1] W. Dai, Q. Yang, G.-R. Xue, and Y. Yu. Self-taught clustering. In *Proceedings of the 25th international conference on Machine learning*, ICML '08, pages 200–207. ACM, 2008.

[2] D. L. Davies and D. W. Bouldin. A Cluster Separation Measure. *IEEE Transactions on Pattern Analysis and Machine Intelligence*, PAMI-1(2):224–227, April 1979.

[3] T. L. Griffiths and M. Steyvers. Finding scientific topics. *Proceedings of the National Academy of Sciences of the United States of America*, 101:5228–5235, April 2004.

[4] L. Hong and B. Davison. Empirical study of topic modeling in twitter. *1st Workshop on Social Media Analytics*, 2010.

[5] X. Hu, N. Sun, C. Zhang, and T.-S. Chua. Exploiting internal and external semantics for the clustering of short texts using world knowledge. In *Proceeding of the 18th ACM conference on Information and knowledge management*, CIKM '09, pages 919–928. ACM, 2009.

[6] X. Hu, X. Zhang, C. Lu, E. K. Park, and X. Zhou. Exploiting wikipedia as external knowledge for document clustering. In *Proceedings of the 15th ACM SIGKDD international conference on Knowledge discovery and data mining*, KDD '09, pages 389–396. ACM, 2009.

[7] S. Lacoste-Julien, F. Sha, and M. I. Jordan. Disclda: Discriminative learning for dimensionality reduction and classification. In *NIPS*, 2008.

[8] R. Mihalcea, C. Corley, and C. Strapparava. Corpus-based and knowledge-based measures of text semantic similarity. In *Proceedings of the 21st national conference on Artificial intelligence - Volume 1*, pages 775–780. AAAI Press, 2006.

[9] C.-T. Nguyen, X.-H. Phan, S. Horiguchi, T.-T. Nguyen, and Q.-T. Ha. Web search clustering and labeling with hidden topics. *ACM Transactions on Asian Language Information Processing*, 8:12:1–12:40, August 2009.

[10] S. J. Pan and Q. Yang. A survey on transfer learning. *IEEE Transactions on Knowledge and Data Engineering*, 22:1345–1359, October 2010.

[11] X.-H. Phan, C.-T. Nguyen, D.-T. Le, L.-M. Nguyen, S. Horiguchi, and Q.-T. Ha. A hidden topic-based framework towards building applications with short web documents. *IEEE Transactions on Knowledge and Data Engineering*, 99, 2010.

[12] X.-H. Phan, L.-M. Nguyen, and S. Horiguchi. Learning to classify short and sparse text & web with hidden topics from large-scale data collections. In *Proceeding of the 17th international conference on World Wide Web*, WWW '08, pages 91–100. ACM, 2008.

[13] X. Quan, G. Liu, Z. Lu, X. Ni, and L. Wenyin. Short text similarity based on probabilistic topics. *Knowledge and Information Systems*, 25:473–491, December 2010.

[14] R. Raina, A. Battle, H. Lee, B. Packer, and A. Y. Ng. Self-taught learning: transfer learning from unlabeled data. In *Proceedings of the 24th international conference on Machine learning*, ICML '07, pages 759–766. ACM, 2007.

[15] R. Raina, A. Y. Ng, and D. Koller. Constructing informative priors using transfer learning. In *ICML '06*, pages 713–720, New York, NY, USA, 2006. ACM.

[16] D. Ramage, S. Dumais, and D. Liebling.

Characterizing microblogs with topic models. In *ICWSM*, 2010.

[17] D. Ramage, D. Hall, R. Nallapati, and C. D. Manning. Labeled lda: a supervised topic model for credit attribution in multi-labeled corpora. In *Proceedings of the 2009 Conference on Empirical Methods in Natural Language Processing: Volume 1 - Volume 1*, EMNLP '09, pages 248–256, Stroudsburg, PA, USA, 2009. Association for Computational Linguistics.

[18] M. Sahami and T. D. Heilman. A web-based kernel function for measuring the similarity of short text snippets. In *Proceedings of the 15th international conference on World Wide Web*, WWW '06, pages 377–386. ACM, 2006.

[19] B. Sriram, D. Fuhry, E. Demir, H. Ferhatosmanoglu, and M. Demirbas. Short text classification in twitter to improve information filtering. In *Proceeding of the 33rd international ACM SIGIR conference on Research and development in information retrieval*, SIGIR '10, pages 841–842. ACM, 2010.

[20] G.-R. Xue, W. Dai, Q. Yang, and Y. Yu. Topic-bridged plsa for cross-domain text classification. In *Proceedings of the 31st annual international ACM SIGIR conference on Research and development in information retrieval*, SIGIR '08, pages 627–634. ACM, 2008.

[21] W.-T. Yih and C. Meek. Improving similarity measures for short segments of text. In *Proceedings of the 22nd national conference on Artificial intelligence - Volume 2*, pages 1489–1494. AAAI Press, 2007.

LogSig: Generating System Events from Raw Textual Logs

Liang Tang
School of Computer Science
Florida International University
11200 S.W. 8th Street
Miami, Florida, 33199
U.S.A
ltang002@cs.fiu.edu

Tao Li
School of Computer Science
Florida International University
11200 S.W. 8th Street
Miami, Florida, 33199
U.S.A
taoli@cs.fiu.edu

Chang-Shing Perng
IBM T.J. Watson Research Center
19 Skyline Drive
Hawthorne, NY, 10532
U.S.A
perng@us.ibm.com

ABSTRACT

Modern computing systems generate large amounts of log data. System administrators or domain experts utilize the log data to understand and optimize system behaviors. Most system logs are raw textual and unstructured. One main fundamental challenge in automated log analysis is the generation of system events from raw textual logs. Log messages are relatively short text messages but may have a large vocabulary, which often result in poor performance when applying traditional text clustering techniques to the log data. Other related methods have various limitations and only work well for some particular system logs. In this paper, we propose a message signature based algorithm `logSig` to generate system events from textual log messages. By searching the most representative message signatures, `logSig` categorizes log messages into a set of event types. `logSig` can handle various types of log data, and is able to incorporate human's domain knowledge to achieve a high performance. We conduct experiments on five real system log data. Experiments show that `logSig` outperforms other alternative algorithms in terms of the overall performance.

Categories and Subject Descriptors

I.5.4 [**Pattern Recognition**]: Applications; H.4.m [**Information Systems Applications**]: Miscellaneous; G.2.3 [**Discrete Mathematics**]: Applications

General Terms

Algorithms, Experimentation

Keywords

Event generation, Message signature, System logs

1. INTRODUCTION

Modern computing systems generate large amounts of log data. The log data describes the status of each component and records system internal operations, such as the starting and stopping of services, detection of network connections, software configuration modifications, and execution errors. System administrators or domain experts utilize the log data to understand and optimize system behaviors.

Most system logs are raw textual and unstructured. There are two challenges in analyzing system log data. The first challenge is transforming raw textual logs into system events. The number of distinct events observed can be very large and also grows rapidly due to the large vocabulary size as well as various parameters in log generation [6]. Once raw textual logs are transformed into events, the second challenge is to develop efficient algorithms to analyze or summarize the patterns from events. A lot of studies investigate the second challenge and develop many algorithms to mine system events [22] [30] [13] [15] [10] [20] [29] [14]. In this paper, we focus on the first challenge. The traditional solution to the first challenge is to develop a specialized log parser for a particular system. However, it requires users fully understand all kinds of log messages from the system. In practice, this is time-consuming, if not impossible given the complexity of current computing systems. In addition, a specialized log parser is not universal and does not work well for other types of systems.

Recent studies [6] [18] [26] apply data clustering techniques to automatically partition log messages into different groups. Each message group represents a particular type of events. Due to the short length and large vocabulary size of log messages [24], traditional data clustering methods based on the *bag-of-word* model cannot perform well when applied to the log message data. Therefore, new clustering methods have been introduced to utilize both the format and the structure information of log data [6] [18] [26]. However, these methods only work well for strictly formatted/structured logs and their performances heavily rely on the format/structure features of the log messages. To address these limitations, this paper proposes a message signature based algorithm `logSig` to generate system events from raw textual logs. It can handle various types of log data, and is able to incorporate human's domain knowledge to achieve a high performance.

CIKM'11, October 24–28, 2011, Glasgow, Scotland, UK.

1.1 Motivation

Each log message consists of a sequence of terms. Some of the terms are variables or parameters for a system event, such as the host name, the user name, IP address and so on. Other terms are plain text words describing semantic information of the event. For example, three sample log messages of the Hadoop system [3] describing one type of events about the IPC (Inter-Process Communication) subsystem are listed below:

```
1.  2011-01-26 13:02:28,335 INFO org.apache.hadoop.ipc.
Server:  IPC Server Responder:  starting;

2.  2011-01-27 09:24:17,057 INFO org.apache.hadoop.ipc.
Server:  IPC Server listener on 9000:  starting;

3.  2011-01-27 23:46:21,883 INFO org.apache.hadoop.ipc.
Server:  IPC Server handler 1 on 9000:  starting.
```

The three messages contain many different words(or terms), such as the date, the hours, the handler name, and the port number. People can identify them as the same event type because they share a common subsequence: "*INFO: org.apache.hadoop.ipc.Server: IPC Server:starting*". Let's consider how the three log messages are generated by the system. The Java source code for generating them is described below:

```
logger = Logger.getLogger("org.apache.hadoop.ipc.Server");
logger.info("IPC Server "+handlerName+":  starting");
```

where `logger` is the log producer for the IPC subsystem. Using different parameters, such as `handlerName`, the code can output different log messages. But the subsequence "*INFO: org.apache.hadoop.ipc.Server: IPC Server : starting*" is fixed in the source code. It will never change unless the source code has been modified.

Therefore, the fixed subsequence can be viewed as a **signature** for an event type. In other words, we can check the signatures to identify the event type of a log message. Other parameter terms in the log message should be ignored, since messages of the same event type can have different parameter terms. Note that some parameters, such as the `handlerName` in this example, consist of different numbers of terms. Consequently, the position of a message signature may vary in different log messages. Hence, the string matching similarity proposed in [6] would mismatch some terms. Another method `IPLoM` proposed in [18] also fails to partition log messages using the term count since the length of `handlerName` is not fixed and three log messages have different numbers of terms.

Given an arbitrary log message, we do not know in advance which item is of its signature, or which term is its parameter. That is the key challenge we aim to address in this paper.

1.2 Contributions

In this paper, we first describe the drawbacks of traditional text clustering techniques for event generation from log messages. We show that, it is difficult for the *bag-of-word* model to accurately partition log messages. We also analyze that, the string kernel based approach would be inefficient when the log vocabulary size is large. In addition, we discuss some limitations of related approaches proposed in previous literatures.

Then, we propose `logSig` algorithm to generate system events from textual log messages. `logSig` algorithm tries to find k message signatures to match all given messages as much as possible, where k is specified by the user. We conduct experiments on five real system log data. Experiments show that `logSig` outperforms other alternative algorithms in terms of the overall performance.

The rest of the paper is organized as follows: Section 2 describes the related work about system event generation from textual logs. Then, we formulate the problem of the system events generation in Section 3. In Section 4, we present an overview of the `logSig` algorithm. Section 5 discusses some detailed implementation issues. Section 6 proposes two approaches for incorporating the domain knowledge to improve the accuracy of the `logSig` algorithm. In Section 7, we present the experimental studies on five real system log data. Finally, Section 8 concludes our paper and discusses the future work.

2. RELATED WORK

It has been shown in [24] that log messages are relatively short text messages but could have a large vocabulary size. This characteristic often leads to a poor performance when using the bag-of-words model in text mining on log data. The reason is that, each single log message has only a few terms, but the vocabulary size is very large. Hence, the vector space established on sets of terms would be very sparse. The string kernel can be used to extract deep semantic information (e.g., the order of terms) to improve the performance of the clustering algorithm. It maps a string to a high dimensional vector to represent all possible term orders. However, because of the large vocabulary size, the dimensionality of the transformed space would be very high. Although the kernel trick does not have to explicitly create those high dimensional vectors, clustering algorithms would still be influenced by the high dimensionality due to the *Curse of Dimensionality* [25].

The related work about the log data analysis can be broadly summarized into two categories. One category is on system event generation from raw log data [6] [9] [18] [26] and the other category is on analyzing patterns from system events [22] [30] [13] [15] [10] [29] [14]. Our work in this paper belongs to the first category. A word matching similarity measurement is introduced in [6] for clustering the log messages. One problem is that, if most terms of a log message are parameter terms, then this type of log messages may not have many matched common words. This method is denoted as `StringMatch` in this paper. [18] develops a 4-steps partitioning method `IPLoM` for clustering the log messages based on inherent characteristics of the log format. However, the method can only be useful for strictly formatted log data. The `logSig` algorithm proposed in this paper can handle various types of log data without much prior knowledge about the log format.

3. PROBLEM FORMULATION

The goal of this paper is to identify the event type of each log message according to a set of message signatures. Given a log message and a set of signatures, we need a metric to determine which signature best matches this log message. Therefore, we propose the *Match Score* metric first.

Notations: Let $\mathcal{D}$ be a set of log messages, $\mathcal{D} = \{X_1, ..., X_N\}$, where X_i is the ith log message, $i = 1, 2, ..., N$. Each X_i is a sequence of terms, i.e., $X_i = w_{i_1} w_{i_2} .... w_{i_{n_i}}$. A message signature S is also a sequence of terms $S = w_{j_1} w_{j_2} .... w_{j_n}$.

Given a sequence $X = w_1 w_2 ... w_n$ and a term w_i, $w_i \in X$

indicates w_i is a term in X. $X - \{w_i\}$ denotes a subsequence $w_1...w_{i-1}w_{i+1}...w_n$. $|X|$ denotes the length of the sequence X. $LCS(X, S)$ denotes the *Longest Common Subsequence* between two sequences X and S.

DEFINITION 1. ***(Match Score)*** *Given a log message X_i and a message signature S, the* match score *is computed by the function below:*

$$\begin{aligned} match(X_i, S) &= |LCS(X_i, S)| - (|S| - |LCS(X_i, S)|) \\ &= 2|LCS(X_i, S)| - |S|. \end{aligned}$$

Intuitively, $|LCS(X_i, S)|$ is the number of terms in X_i matched with S. $|S| - |LCS(X_i, S)|$ is the number of terms in X_i not matched with S. $match(X_i, S)$ is the number of matched terms minus the number of not-matched terms. We illustrate this by a simple example below:

EXAMPLE 1. *A log messages $X = abcdef$ and a message signature $S = axcey$. The longest common subsequence $LCS(X, S) = ace$. The matched terms are "a","c","e", shown*

Table 1: Example of Match Score

X	a	b	c	d	e	f
S	<u>a</u>	x	<u>c</u>		<u>e</u>	y

by underline words in Table 1. "x" and "y" in S are not matched with any term in X. Hence, $match(X, S) = |ace| - |xy| = 1$.

Note that this score can be negative. $match(X_i, S)$ is used to measure the degree of the log message X_i owning the signature S. If two log messages X_i and X_j have the same signature S, then we regard X_i and X_j as of the same event type. The longest common subsequence matching is a widely used similarity metric in biological data analysis [7] [19], such as RNA sequences.

3.1 Problem Statement

If all message signatures S_1, S_2,...,S_k are known, identifying the event type of each log message in $\mathcal{D}$ is straightforward. But we don't know any message signature at the beginning. Therefore, we should partition log messages and find their message signatures simultaneously. The optimal result is that, within each partition, every log message matches its signature as much as possible. This problem is formulated below.

PROBLEM 1. *Given a set of log messages $\mathcal{D}$ and an integer k, find k message signatures $\mathcal{S} = \{S_1, ..., S_k\}$ and a k-partition C_1,...,C_k of $\mathcal{D}$ to maximize*

$$J(\mathcal{S}, \mathcal{D}) = \sum_{i=1}^{k} \sum_{X_j \in C_i} match(X_j, S_i).$$

The objective function $J(\mathcal{S}, \mathcal{D})$ is the summation of all match scores. It is similar to the k-means clustering problem. The choice of k depends on the user's domain knowledge to the system logs. If there is no domain knowledge, we can borrow the idea from the method finding k for k-means [11], which plots clustering results with k. We can also display generated message signatures for $k = 2, 3, ..$ until the results can be approved by experts.

Comparing with k-means clustering problem
Problem 1 is similar to the classic k-means clustering problem, since a message signature can be regarded as the representative of a cluster. People may ask the following questions: *Why we propose the match function to find the optimal partition? Why not use the LCS as the similarity function to do k-means clustering?* The answer for the two questions is that, our goal is not to find good clusters of log messages, but to find the message signatures of all types of log messages. K-means can ensure every two messages in one cluster share a subsequence. However, it cannot guarantee that there exists a common subsequence shared by all (or most) messages in one cluster. We illustrate this by the following example.

EXAMPLE 2. *There are three log messages X_1: "abcdef, X_2: "abghij" and X_3: "xyghef". Clearly, $LCS(X_1, X_2)=2$, $LCS(X_2, X_3)=2$, and $LCS(X_1, X_3)=2$. However, there is no common subsequence that exists among all X_1, X_2 and X_3. In our case, it means there is no message signature to describe all three log messages. Hence, it is hard to believe that they are generated by the same log message template.*

3.2 Problem Analysis

Problem 1 is an NP-hard problem, even if $k = 1$. When $k = 1$, we can reduce the *Multiple Longest Common Subsequence* problem to the Problem 1. The *Multiple Longest Common Subsequence* problem is a known NP-hard [17].

LEMMA 1. *Problem 1 is an NP-hard problem when $k = 1$.*

Proof: Let $\mathcal{D} = \{X_1, ..., X_N\}$. When $k = 1$, $\mathcal{S} = \{S_1\}$. Construct another set of N sequences $\mathcal{Y} = \{Y_1, ..., Y_N\}$, in which each term is unique in both $\mathcal{D}$ and $\mathcal{Y}$. Let $\mathcal{D}' = \mathcal{D} \cup \mathcal{Y}$,

$$J(\mathcal{S}, \mathcal{D}') = \textstyle\sum_{X_j \in \mathcal{D}} match(X_j, S_1) + \sum_{Y_l \in \mathcal{Y}} match(Y_l, S_1)$$

Let S_1^* be the optimal message signature for $\mathcal{D}'$, i.e.,

$$S_1^* = \arg\max_{S_1} J(\{S_1\}, \mathcal{D}').$$

Then, the longest common subsequence of X_1,...,X_N must be an optimal solution S_1^*. This can be proved by contradiction as follows. Let S_{lcs} be the longest common subsequence of X_1,...,X_N. Note that S_{lcs} may be an empty sequence if there is no common subsequence among all messages.
Case 1: If there exists a term $w_i \in S_1^*$, but $w_i \notin S_{lcs}$. Since $w_i \notin S_{lcs}$, w_i is not matched with at least one message in X_1,...,X_N. Moreover, Y_1,...,Y_N are composed by unique terms, so w_i cannot be matched with any of them. In $\mathcal{D}'$, the number of messages not matching w_i is at least $N + 1$, which is greater than the number of messages matching w_i. Therefore,

$$J(\{S_1^* - \{w_i\}\}, \mathcal{D}') > J(\{S_1^*\}, \mathcal{D}'),$$

which contradicts with $S_1^* = \arg\max_{S_1} J(\{S_1\}, \mathcal{D}')$.
Case 2: If there exists a term $w_i \in S_{lcs}$, but $w_i \notin S_1^*$. Since $w_i \in S_{lcs}$, X_1,...,X_N all match w_i. The total number of messages that match w_i in $\mathcal{D}'$ is N. Then, there are N remaining messages not matching w_i: Y_1,...,Y_N. Therefore,

$$J(\{S_{lcs}\}, \mathcal{D}') = J(\{S_1^*\}, \mathcal{D}'),$$

which indicates S_{lcs} is also an optimal solution to maximize objective function J on $\mathcal{D}'$.

To sum up the two cases above, if there is a polynomial time-complexity solution to find the optimal solution S_1^* in $\mathcal{D}'$, the *Multiple Longest Common Subsequence problem* for X_1,...,X_N can be solved in polynomial time as well. However, *Multiple Longest Common Subsequence problem* is an NP-hard problem [17].

LEMMA 2. *If when $k = n$ Problem 1 is NP-hard, then when $k = n+1$ Problem 1 is NP-hard, where n is a positive integer.*

Proof-Sketch: This can be proved by contradiction. We can construct a message Y whose term set has no overlap to the term set of messages in $\mathcal{D}$ in a linear time. Suppose the optimal solution for $k = n$ and $\mathcal{D}$ is $\mathcal{C} = \{C_1, ..., C_k\}$, then the optimal solution for $k = n + 1$ and $\mathcal{D} \cup \{Y\}$ should be $\mathcal{C}' = \{C_1, ..., C_k, \{Y\}\}$. If there is a polynomial time solution for Problem 1 when $k = n + 1$, we could solve Problem 1 when $k = n$ in polynomial time.

4. ALGORITHM OVERVIEW

In this section, we first present an approximated version of Problem 1 and then present our `logSig` algorithm. `logSig` algorithm consists of three steps. The first step is to separate every log message into several pairs of terms. The second step is to find k groups of log messages using *local search* strategy such that each group share common pairs as many as possible. The last step is to construct message signatures based on identified common pairs for each message group.

4.1 Term Pair Generation

The first step of `logSig` algorithm is converting each log message into a set of term pairs. For example, there is a log message collected from FileZilla [2] client:

```
2010-05-02 11:34:06 Command:  mkdir ".indexes"
```

We extract each pairwise of terms and preserve the order of two terms. Then, the converted pairs are as follows:

```
{2010-05-02,11:34:06}, {2010-05-02,Command:},
{2010-05-02, mkdir}, {2010-05-02, ".indexes" }
{11:34:06,Command:}, {11:34:06,mkdir},
{11:34:06,".indexes"}, {Command:,mkdir},
{Command:,".indexes"}, {mkdir,".indexes"}
```

The converted term pairs preserve the order information of message terms. On the other hand, the computation on the discrete term pairs is easier than a sequence. A similar idea was proposed in string kernel [16] for text classification. Their output is a high dimensional vector, and our output is a set of pairs.

4.2 Log Messages Partition

The second step is to partition log messages into k groups based on converted term pairs.

4.2.1 The Approximated Version of Problem 1

Notations: Let X be a log message, $R(X)$ denotes the set of term pairs converted from X, and $|R(X)|$ denotes the number of term pairs in $R(X)$.

PROBLEM 2. *Given a set of log messages $\mathcal{D}$ and an integer k, find a k-partition $\mathcal{C} = \{C_1, ..., C_k\}$ of $\mathcal{D}$ to maximize objective function $F(\mathcal{C}, \mathcal{D})$:*

$$F(\mathcal{C}, \mathcal{D}) = \sum_{i=1}^{k} |\bigcap_{X_j \in C_i} R(X_j)|.$$

Object function $F(\mathcal{C}, \mathcal{D})$ is the total number of common pairs over all groups. Intuitively, if a group has more common pairs, it is more likely to have a longer common subsequence. Then, the match score of that group would be higher. Therefore, maximizing function F is approximately maximizing J in Problem 1. Lemma 4 shows the average lower bound for this approximation.

LEMMA 3. *Given a message group C, it has n common term pairs, then the length of the longest common subsequence of messages in C is at least $\lceil\sqrt{2n}\rceil$.*

Proof-sketch: Let l be the length of a longest common subsequence of messages in C. Let $T(l)$ be the number of term pairs that generated by that longest common subsequence. Since each term pair has two terms, this sequence can generate at most $\binom{l}{2}$ pairs. Hence, $T(l) \leq \binom{l}{2} = l(l-1)/2$. Note that each term pair of the longest common subsequence is a common term pair in C. Now, we already know $T(l) = n$, so $T(l) = n \leq l(l-1)/2$. Then, we have $l \geq \lceil\sqrt{2n}\rceil$.

LEMMA 4. *Given a set of log messages $\mathcal{D}$ and a k-partition $\mathcal{C} = \{C_1, ..., C_k\}$ of $\mathcal{D}$, if $F(\mathcal{C}, \mathcal{D}) \geq y$, y is a constant, we can find a set of message signatures $\mathcal{S}$ such that on average:*

$$J(\mathcal{S}, \mathcal{D}) \geq |\mathcal{D}| \cdot \lceil\sqrt{\frac{2y}{k}}\rceil$$

Proof-sketch: Since $F(\mathcal{C}, \mathcal{D}) \geq y$, on average, each group has at least y/k common pairs. Then for each group, by Lemma 3, the length of the longest common subsequence must be at least $\lceil\sqrt{\frac{2y}{k}}\rceil$. If we choose this longest common subsequence as the message signature, each log message can match at least $\lceil\sqrt{\frac{2y}{k}}\rceil$ terms of the signature. As a result, the match score of each log message is at least $\lceil\sqrt{\frac{2y}{k}}\rceil$. $\mathcal{D}$ has $|\mathcal{D}|$ messages. Then, we have the total match score $J(\mathcal{S}, \mathcal{D}) \geq |\mathcal{D}| \cdot \lceil\sqrt{\frac{2y}{k}}\rceil$ on average.

Lemma 4 shows that, maximizing the $F(\mathcal{C}, \mathcal{D})$ is approximately maximizing the original objective function $J(\mathcal{S}, \mathcal{D})$. But $F(\mathcal{C}, \mathcal{D})$ is easier to optimize because it deals with discrete pairs.

4.2.2 Local Search

The `logSig` algorithm applies the *local search* strategy to solve Problem 2. It iteratively moves one message to another message group to increase the objective function as large as possible. However, unlike the classic *local search* optimization method, the movement is not explicitly determined by objective function $F(\cdot)$. The reason is that, the value of $F(\cdot)$ may only be updated after a bunch of movements, not just after every single movement. We illustrate this by the following example.

EXAMPLE 3. *Message set $\mathcal{D}$ is composed of 100 "`ab`" and 100 "`cd`". Now we have 2-partition $\mathcal{C} = \{C_1, C_2\}$. Each message group has 50% of each message type as shown in Table 2. The optimal 2-partition is C_1 has 100 "`ab`" and C_2 has 100 "`cd`", or in the reverse way. However, beginning with current C_1 and C_2, $F(\mathcal{C}, \mathcal{D})$ is always 0 until we move 50 "`ab`" from C_2 to C_1, or move 50 "`cd`" from C_1 to C_2. Hence, for first 50 movements, $F(\mathcal{C}, \mathcal{D})$ cannot guide the local search because no matter what movement you choose, it is always 0.*

Table 2: Example of two message groups

term pair \ group	C_1	C_2
"ab"	50	50
"cd"	50	50

Therefore, $F(\cdot)$ is not proper to guide the movement in the local search. The decision of every movement should consider the *potential* value of the objective function, rather than the immediate value. So we develop the *potential function* to guide the local search instead.

Notations: Given a message group C, $R(C)$ denotes the union set of term pairs from messages of C. For a term pair $r \in R(C)$, $N(r, C)$ denotes the number of messages in C which contains r. $p(r, C) = N(r, C)/|C|$ is the portion of messages in C having r .

DEFINITION 2. *Given a message group C, the potential of C is defined as $\phi(C)$,*

$$\phi(C) = \sum_{r \in R(C)} N(r, C)[p(r, C)]^2.$$

The potential value indicates the overall "purity" of term pairs in C. $\phi(C)$ is maximized when every term pair is contained by every message in the group. In that case, for each r, $N(r, C) = |C|$, $\phi(C) = |C| \cdot |R(C)|$. It also means all term pairs are common pairs shared by every log message. $\phi(C)$ is minimized when each term pair in $R(C)$ is only contained by one message in C. In that case, for each r, $N(r, C) = 1$, $|R(C)| = |C|$, $\phi(C) = 1/|C|$.

DEFINITION 3. *Given a k-partition $\mathcal{C} = \{C_1, ..., C_k\}$ of a message set $\mathcal{D}$, the overall potential of $\mathcal{D}$ is defined as $\Phi(\mathcal{D})$,*

$$\Phi(\mathcal{D}) = \sum_{i=1}^{k} \phi(C_i),$$

where $\phi(C_i)$ is the potential of C_i, $i = 1, ..., k$.

Connection between Φ and F:
Objective function F computes the total number of common term pairs in each group. Both Φ and F are maximized when each term pair is a common term in its corresponding message group. Let's consider the average case.

LEMMA 5. *Given a set of log messages $\mathcal{D}$ and a k-partition $\mathcal{C} = \{C_1, ..., C_k\}$ of $\mathcal{D}$, if $F(\mathcal{C}, \mathcal{D}) \geq y$, y is a constant, then in the average case, $\Phi(\mathcal{D}) \geq y \cdot |\mathcal{D}|/k$.*

Proof-sketch: Since $F(\mathcal{C}, \mathcal{D}) \geq y$, there are at least y common term pairs distributed in message groups. For each common term pair r_i, let C_i be its corresponding group. On average, $|C_i| = |\mathcal{D}|/k$. Note that the common pair r_i appears in every message of C_i, so $N(r_i, C_i) = |C_i| = |\mathcal{D}|/k$ and $p(r_i, C_i) = 1$. There are at least y common term pairs, by Definition 2, we have $\Phi(\mathcal{D}) \geq y \cdot |\mathcal{D}|/k$.

Lemma 5 implies, in the average case, if we try to increase the value of F to be at least y, we have to increase the overall potential Φ to be at least $y \cdot |\mathcal{D}|/k$. As for the local search algorithm, we mentioned that Φ is easier to optimize than F.

Let $\Delta_{i \underrightarrow{X} j}\Phi(\mathcal{D})$ denote the increase of $\Phi(\mathcal{D})$ by moving $X \in \mathcal{D}$ from group C_i into group C_j, $i, j = 1, ..., k$, $i \neq j$. Then, by Definition 3,

$$\begin{aligned} \Delta_{i \underrightarrow{X} j}\Phi(\mathcal{D}) &= [\phi(C_j \cup \{X\}) - \phi(C_j)] \\ &\quad -[\phi(C_i) - \phi(C_i - \{X\})], \end{aligned}$$

where $\phi(C_j \cup \{X\}) - \phi(C_j)$ is the potential increase brought by inserting X to C_j, $\phi(C_i) - \phi(C_i - \{X\})$ is the potential loss brought by removing X from C_i. Algorithm 1 is the pseudocode of the local search algorithm in `logSig`. Basically, it iteratively updates every log message's group according to $\Delta_{i \underrightarrow{X} j}\Phi(\mathcal{D})$ to increase $\Phi(\mathcal{D})$ until no more update operation can be done.

Algorithm 1 `logSig_localsearch` $(\mathcal{D}, k)$

Parameter: $\mathcal{D}$: log messages set; k: the number of groups to partition;
Result: $\mathcal{C}$: log message partition;

```
C ← RandomSeeds(k)
C' ← ∅ // Last iteration's partition
Create a map G to store message's group index
for C_i ∈ C do
    for X_j ∈ C_i do
        G[X_j] ← i
    end for
end for
while C ≠ C' do
    C' ← C
    for X_j ∈ D do
        i ← G[X_j]
        j* = arg max_{j=1,..,k} Δ_{i X_j} Φ(D)
        if i ≠ j* then
            C_i ← C_i − {X_j}
            C_j* ← C_j* ∪ {X_j}
            G[X_j] ← j*
        end if
    end for
end while
return C
```

Why choose this Potential Function?
Given a message group C, let $g(r) = N(r, C)[p(r, C)]^2$, then $\phi(C) = \sum_{r \in R(C)} g(r)$. Since we have to consider all term pairs in C, we define $\phi(C)$ as the sum of all $g(r)$. As for $g(r)$, it should be a convex function. Figure 1 shows a curve of $g(r)$ by varying the number of messages having r, i.e., $N(r, C)$. The reason for why $g(r)$ is convex is that, we hope

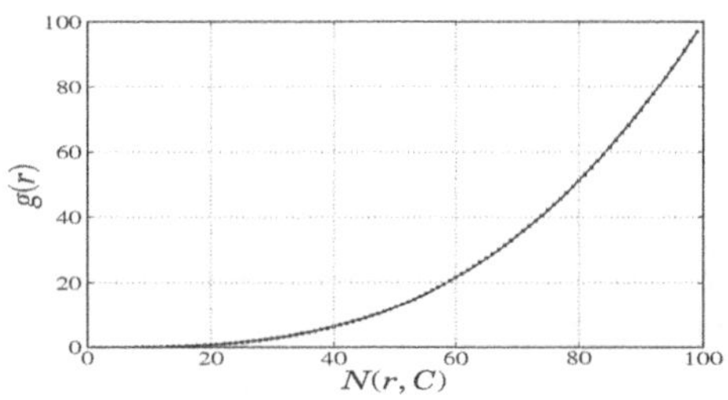

Figure 1: Function $g(r)$, $|C| = 100$

to give larger awards to r when r is about to being a common term pair. That is because, if $N(r, C)$ is large, then r is more likely to be a common term pair. Only when r becomes a common term pair, it can increase $F(\cdot)$. In other words, r has more potential to increase the value of objective function $F(\cdot)$, so the algorithm should pay more attention to r first.

In the experimental section, we will empirically compare the effectiveness of our proposed potential function Φ with the objective function function F in the local search.

4.3 Message Signature Construction

The final step of `logSig` algorithm is to construct the message signature for each message group. Recall that a message signature is a sequence of terms that has a high match score to every message in the corresponding group. So it could be constructed by highly frequent term pairs identified in the second step.

LEMMA 6. *Let S be an optimal message signature for a message group C, the occurrence number of every term $w_j \in S$ must be equal or greater than $\lfloor |C|/2 \rfloor$.*

The proof of Lemma 6 is similar to the proof of Lemma 1. If there exists a term $w'_j \in S$ only appearing in less than $\lfloor |C|/2 \rfloor$ messages, we can have: $J(\{S - \{w'_j\}\}, C) > J(\{S\}, C)$, then S is worse than $S - \{w'_j\}$. Thus, S is not optimal.

Lemma 6 indicates that we only need to care about those terms which appear in at least one half of the messages in a group. By scanning every message in a group, we could obtain the optimal sequence of those terms. Since log messages are usually very short, there are only a few term whose occurrence number is equal or greater than $\lfloor |C|/2 \rfloor$. Therefore, there are not many candidate sequences generated by those terms. We enumerate each one of them and select the best one to be the message signature.

5. ALGORITHM IMPLEMENTATION

In this section, we discuss some detailed issues about the implementation of the `logSig` algorithm.

Term Pair Histogram

To efficiently compute the potential value of each message group $C_i \in \mathcal{C}$, a histogram is maintained for each group. The histogram is implemented by a hash table, whose key is a term pair and the value is the number of messages containing that term pair in the group. Then, for a term pair r, $c(r, C_i)$ and $p(r, C_i)$ can be obtained in a constant time complexity.

Approximately Computing $\Delta\Phi(\mathcal{D})$

The straightforward way to compute $\Delta_{i\underrightarrow{X}j}\Phi(\mathcal{D})$ is enumerating all term pairs in C_i and C_j. The computation cost of finding the maximum $\Delta_{i\underrightarrow{X}j}\Phi(\mathcal{D})$ is $O(\sum_{l=1}^{k} |R(C_l)|)$, which is the total number of term pairs in the entire data set. In log data, this number is even tens of times greater than $|\mathcal{D}|$. Hence, this computation cost is not affordable for each single log message.

Our approximated solution is to consider the change of $N(r, C)$, for each $r \in R(X)$. The reason is that, $|C|$ is large. The impact to $|C|$ by inserting or removing one message could be ignored comparing to the impact to $N(r, C)$. $|C)| \approx |C|+1 \approx |C|-1$. So $|C|$ can be treated as a constant in one exchange operation in *local search*. Then,

$$\frac{\partial\phi(C)}{\partial N(r,C)} = \frac{\partial[[N(r,C)]^3/|C|^2]}{\partial N(r,C)} = \frac{3[N(r,C)]^2}{|C|^2} = 3[p(r,C)]^2.$$

$$\Delta_{i\underrightarrow{X}j}\Phi(\mathcal{D}) \approx 3 \cdot \sum_{r \in R(X)} [[p(r, C_j)]^2 - [p(r, C_i)]^2].$$

By utilizing the histograms, $p(r, C_j)$ and $p(r, C_i)$ can be obtained in a constant time. Hence, for each log message $X \in \mathcal{D}$, the time complexity of finding the largest $\Delta_{i\underrightarrow{X}j}\Phi(\mathcal{D})$ is at most $O(k \cdot |R(X)|)$. Although $\Delta_{i\underrightarrow{X}j}\Phi(\mathcal{D})$ is would underestimate the actual change of $\Phi(\mathcal{D})$, it can save a lot of computation cost.

5.1 Algorithm Analysis

Convergence and Local Optima

In the local search algorithm, exchanging messages' groups only increases the overall potential $\Phi(\mathcal{D})$. There is no operation to decrease the overall potential. $\Phi(\mathcal{D})$ is not infinite, which is less than or equal to $|R(D)| \cdot |D|$. Therefore, the local search algorithm would converge.

Similar to other local search based optimization algorithms, `logSig` may converge into a local optima as well. However, `logSig`'s potential function provides a more reliable heuristic to guide the optimization process. It is much less likely to stop at a local optima.

Time Complexity and Space Complexity

The time complexity of converting log messages into term pairs is $O(|D| \cdot L^2)$, where L is the maximum length of log messages. For every $X_j \in D$, $L^2 \geq |R(X_j)|$. For the local search, each iteration goes through every message. So the time complexity of an iteration is $O(k \cdot L^2 \cdot |D|)$. Let t be the number of iterations, so the time complexity of the local search is $O(t \cdot k \cdot L^2 \cdot |D|)$. Our experiments shows that t is usually 3 to 12 for most system log data.

The space cost of the algorithm is mainly determined by the term pair histograms created for every message group. The total space complexity is the total number of term pairs, $O(|R(\mathcal{D})|)$.

6. INCORPORATING DOMAIN KNOWLEDGE

In real world applications, analyzing system behaviors mainly relies on the generated system events, so the event generation algorithm should be reliable. Current approaches for grouping log messages into different event types are totally unsupervised. In practice, for most sorts of logs (e.g., Hadoop system logs), there are some domain knowledge about a fixed catalog of Java exceptions. In addition, the log generation mechanisms implicitly create some associations between the terminologies and the situations. Incorporating domain knowledge into the clustering process could improve the performance of event generation. In this section, we present two approaches for incorporating domain knowledge to improve the accuracy of `logSig` algorithm.

6.1 Term Feature Layer

Some terms or words in log messages share some common features which can help our algorithm identify the log message type. The features are domain knowledge from human experts. For example, "2011-02-01" and "2011-01-02" are different terms, but they are both *dates*; "192.168.0.12" and "202.119.23.10" are different terms, but they are both *IP addresses*.

`logSig` algorithm allows users to provide a list of features. Each feature is described by a regular expression. An additional feature layer is built to incorporate those features for representing log messages. The feature layer is created by regular expression matching. For example, we have following regular expressions [1]:

```
Timestamp:  \d{4}-\d{2}-\d{2} \d{2}:\d{2}:\d{2}
FilePath:   "(\w|\\)+"
```

Then, we could scan the log message X_1 to create the feature layer Y_1 as shown in Table 3. The feature layer Y_1 contains more semantic information. It can gather similar terms and reduce noisy terms. In addition, regular expression is easy for domain experts to write. Using a sophisticated regular language toolkit, a feature layer can be built efficiently.

Table 3: Example of Feature Layer

X_1	2010-05-02	11:34:06	Command:	mkdir	".indexes"
Y_1	*Timestamp*		Command:	mkdir	*FilePath*

[1]The grammar of regular expressions is defined by Java Regular Library

6.2 Constraints on Message Signature

In reality, domain experts usually identify the event type of a log message by scanning keywords or phrases. For example, as for SFTP/FTP logs, they would be sensitive to those phrases: "`Command`", "`No such file`", "`Error`", "`Transfer failed`" and so on. Those sensitive phrases should be included in the generated message signature to express system events. On the other hand, domain experts also know that some trivial phrases should be ignored, such as the message IDs and the timestamps. Those trivial phrases should not be included in any message signature. To sum up, those knowledge can be transferred as constraints on message signatures. Those constraints can help the event generation algorithm to improve its accuracy. Unlike traditional constraints in semi-supervised clustering, such as *Must-Link* or *Cannot-Link* [28], our constraints are placed in the subsequences (or phrases) of messages, not on the messages themselves.

Constraint-based `logSig` Algorithm

To incorporate constraints on message phrases, Problem 1 can be revised as follows:

PROBLEM 3. *Given a set of log messages $\mathcal{D}$, a set of sensitive phrases $\mathcal{P}_S$ and trivial phrases $\mathcal{P}_T$, find k message signatures $\mathcal{S} = \{S_1, ..., S_k\}$ with a k-partition C_1,...,C_k of $\mathcal{D}$ to maximize:*

$$J'(\mathcal{S}, \mathcal{D}, \mathcal{P}_S, \mathcal{P}_T) = \lambda \sum_{i=1}^{k} \sum_{X_j \in C_i} match(X_j, S_i) +$$

$$(1-\lambda)\sum_{i=1}^{k}[\sum_{P_s \in \mathcal{P}_S} match(P_s, S_i) - \sum_{P_s \in \mathcal{P}_T} match(P_t, S_i)],$$

where λ is a user-defined parameter between 0 and 1.

The revised optimization problem can be solved by constraint-based `logSig` Algorithm. The basic idea of constraint-based `logSig` is to increase the weight of term pairs in $R(\mathcal{P}_S)$ and decrease the weight of term pairs in $R(\mathcal{P}_T)$. Let w_r denote the weight of pair r. The only revised part in `logSig` algorithm is $\Delta_{i\underset{\rightarrow}{X}j}\Phi(\mathcal{D})$. By multiplying the weight w_r, it becomes:

$$\Delta_{i\underset{\rightarrow}{X}j}\Phi(\mathcal{D}) \approx 3 \sum_{r \in R(X)} [[p(r, C_j)]^2 - [p(r, C_i)]^2] \cdot w_r,$$

and

$$w_r = \begin{cases} 1.0, & r \notin R(\mathcal{P}_S), r \notin R(\mathcal{P}_T) \\ \lambda', & r \in R(\mathcal{P}_S), r \notin R(\mathcal{P}_T) \\ 1/\lambda', & r \notin R(\mathcal{P}_S), r \in R(\mathcal{P}_T) \end{cases},$$

where $\lambda' \geq 1$ is a user-defined parameter that can be approximately derived from the original parameter λ. λ' is utilized to increase(and decrease) the importance of term pairs in sensitive phrases(and trivial phrases). The choice of λ' depends on users' confidence in those sensitive phrases and trivial phrases. In experiments, we let $\lambda' = 10.0$. We show the performances of the algorithm when varying λ' from 0.0 to 20.0 and explain why we choose 10 in the experimental section.

7. EVALUATION

7.1 Experimental Platforms

We implement our algorithm and other comparative algorithms in Java 1.6 platform. Table 5 summarizes our experimental enviroment.

Table 5: Experimental Machine

OS	CPU	bits	Memory	JVM Heap Size
Linux 2.6.18	Intel Xeon(R) @ 2.5GHz, 8 core	64	16G	12G

7.2 Data Collection

We collect log data from 5 different real systems, which are summarized in Table 6. Logs of FileZilla [2], PVFS2 [4] Apache [1] and Hadoop [3] are collected from the server machines/systems in the computer lab of a research center. Log data of ThunderBird [5] is collected from a supercomputer in Sandia National Lab. The true categories of log messages are obtained by specialized log parsers. For instance, FillZilla's log messages are categorized into 4 types: "*Command*", "*Status*", "*Response*", "*Error*". Apache error log messages are categorized by the error type: "*Permission denied*", "*File not exist*" and so on.

Table 6: Summary of Collected System Logs

System	Description	#Messages	#Terms Per Message	#Category
FileZilla	SFTP/FTP Client	22,421	7 to 15	4
ThunderBird	Supercomputer	3,248,239	15 to 30	12
PVFS2	Parallel File System	95,496	2 to 20	11
Apache Error	Web Server	236,055	10 to 20	6
Hadoop	Parallel Computing Platform	2,479	15 to 30	11

The vocabulary size is an important characteristic of log data. Figure 2 exhibits the vocabulary sizes of the 5 different logs along with the data size. It can be seen that some vocabulary size could become very large if the data size is large.

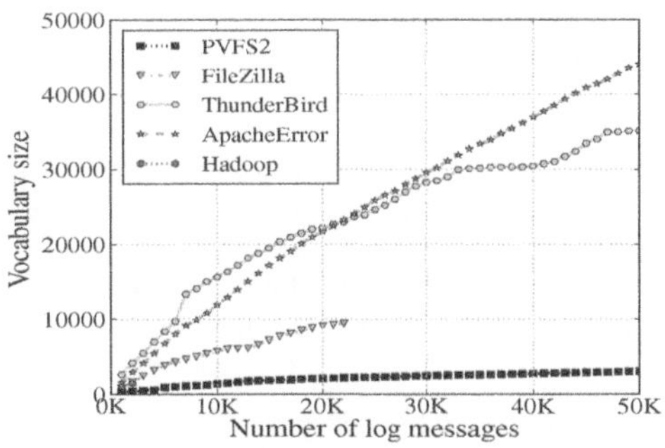

Figure 2: Vocabulary size

7.3 Comparative Algorithms

We compare our algorithm with 7 alternative algorithms in this experiment. Those algorithms are described in Table 7. 6 of them are unsupervised algorithms which only look at the terms of log messages. 3 of them are semi-supervised algorithms which are able to incorporate the domain knowledge. `IPLoM` [18] and `StringMatch` [6] are two methods proposed in recent related literatures . `VectorModel` [23], `Jaccard` [25], `StringKernel` [16] are traditional methods for text clustering. `VectorModel` and `semi-StringKernel` are implemented by k-means clustering algorithm [25]. `Jaccard` and `StringMatch` are implemented by k-medoid algorithm [12], since they cannot compute the centroid point of a cluster. As for `Jaccard`, the Jaccard similarity is obtained by a hash table to accelerate the computation. `VectorModel` and `StringKernel` use *Sparse Vector* [23] to reduce the computation and space costs.

Table 4: Average F-Measure Comparison

Algorithm \ Log Data	FileZilla	PVFS2	ThunderBird	Apache Error	Hadoop
`Jaccard`	0.3794	0.4072	0.6503	0.7866	0.5088
`VectorModel`	0.4443	0.5243	0.4963	0.7575	0.3506
`IPLoM`	0.2415	0.2993	**0.8881**	0.7409	0.2015
`StringMatch`	0.5639	0.4774	0.6663	0.7932	0.4840
`StringKernel`$_{0.8}$	0.4462	0.3894	0.6416	0.8810	0.3103
`StringKernel`$_{0.5}$	0.4716	0.4345	0.7361	**0.9616**	0.3963
`StringKernel`$_{0.3}$	0.4139	0.6189	0.8321	0.9291	0.4256
`logSig`	**0.6949**	**0.7179**	0.7882	0.9521	**0.7658**
`semi-Jaccard`	0.8283	0.4017	0.7222	0.7415	0.4997
`semi-StringKernel`$_{0.8}$	0.8951	0.6471	0.7657	0.8645	0.7162
`semi-StringKernel`$_{0.5}$	0.7920	0.4245	0.7466	**0.8991**	0.7461
`semi-StringKernel`$_{0.3}$	0.8325	0.7925	0.7113	0.8537	0.6259
`semi-logSig`	**1.0000**	**0.8009**	**0.8547**	0.7707	**0.9531**

Table 7: Summary of comparative algorithms

Algorithm	Description
`VectorModel`	Vector space model proposed in information retreival
`Jaccard`	Jaccard similarity based k-medoid algorithm
`StringKernel`	String kernel based k-means algorithm
`IPLoM`	Iterative partition method proposed in [18]
`StringMatch`	String matching method proposed in [6]
`logSig`	Message signature based method proposed in this paper
`semi-logSig`	`logSig` incorporating domain knowledge
`semi-StringKernel`	Weighted string kernel based k-means
`semi-Jaccard`	Weighted Jaccard similarity based k-medoid

`semi-logSig`, `semi-StringKernel` and `semi-Jaccard` are semi-supervised versions of `logSig`, `StringKernel` and `Jaccard` respectively. To make a fair comparison, all those semi-supervised algorithms incorporate the **same** domain knowledge offered by users. Specifically, the 3 algorithms run on the same transformed feature layer, and the same sensitive phrases $\mathcal{P}_S$ and trivial phrases $\mathcal{P}_T$. Obviously, the choices of features, $\mathcal{P}_S$ and $\mathcal{P}_T$ have a huge impact to the performances of semi-supervised algorithms. But we only compare a semi-supervised algorithm with other semi-supervised algorithms. Hence, they are compared under the same choice of features, $\mathcal{P}_S$ and $\mathcal{P}_T$. The approaches for those 3 algorithms to incorporate with features, $\mathcal{P}_S$ and $\mathcal{P}_T$ are described as follows:

Feature Layer: Replacing every log message by the transformed sequence of terms with features.

$\mathcal{P}_S$ and $\mathcal{P}_T$: As for `semi-StringKernel`, replacing Euclidean distance by Mahalanobis distance [8]:

$$D_M(x, y) = \sqrt{(x-y)^T M (x-y)}.$$

where matrix M is constructed according to term pairs $\mathcal{P}_S$, $\mathcal{P}_T$ and λ'. As for `semi-Jaccard`, for each term, multiply a weight λ' (or $1/\lambda'$) if this term appears in $\mathcal{P}_S$ (or $\mathcal{P}_T$).

`Jaccard`, `StringMatch` and `semi-Jaccard` algorithms apply classic k-medoid algorithm for message clustering. The time complexity of k-medoid algorithm is very high: $O(tn^2)$ [27], where t is the number of iterations, n is the number of log messages. As a result, those 3 algorithms are not capable of handling large log data. Therefore, for the accuracy comparison, we split our log files into smaller files by time frame, and conduct the experiments on the small log data. The amounts of log messages, features, term pairs in $\mathcal{P}_S$ and $\mathcal{P}_T$ are summarized in Table 8. In Section 7.5, larger logs are used to test the scalability.

Table 8: Summary of small log data

Measure	#Message	#Feature	$\lvert R(\mathcal{P})_S \rvert$	$\lvert R(\mathcal{P})_T \rvert$
FileZilla	8555	10	4	4
ThunderBird	5000	10	11	9
PVFS2	12570	10	10	1
Apache Error	5000	2	4	2
Hadoop	2479	2	7	3

7.4 Quality of Generated Events

7.4.1 *Average F-Measure*

Table 4 shows the accuracy comparison of generated system events by different algorithms. The accuracy is evaluated by F-measure (F1 score) [23], which is a traditional metric combining *precision* and *recall*. Since the results of k-medoid, k-means and `logSig` depend on the initial random seeds, we run each algorithm for **10 times**, and put the average F-measures into Table 4. From this table, it can be seen that `StringKernel` and `logSig` outperform other algorithms in terms of the overall performance.

`Jaccard` and `VectorModel` apply the *bag-of-word* model, which ignores the order information about terms. Log messages are usually short, so the information from the bag-of-word model is very limited. In addition, different log messages have many identical terms, such as *date*, *username*. That's the reason why the two methods cannot achieve high F-measures. `IPLoM` performs well in ThunderBird log data, but poorly in other log data. The reason is that, the first step of `IPLoM` is to partition log message by the term count. One type of log message may have different numbers of terms. For instance, in FileZilla logs, the length of *Command* messages depends on the type of SFTP/FTP command in the message. But for ThunderBird, most event types are strictly associated with one message format. Therefore, `IPLoM` could easily achieve the highest score.

Due to the *Curse of dimensionality* [25], k-means based `StringKernel` is not easy to converge in a high dimensional space. Figure 2 shows that, 50K ThunderBird log messages contain over 30K distinct terms. As a result, the transformed space has over $(30K)^2 = 900M$ dimensions. It is quite sparse for 50K data points.

7.4.2 *Message Signatures*

Generated message signatures are used as descriptors for system events, so that users can understand the meanings of those events. Due to the space limit, we cannot list all

Table 9: Message Signatures

System Log	Message Signature	Associated Category
FileZilla	*Date Hours Number Number* Status: ...	Status
	Date Hours Number Number Response: *Number*	Response
	Date Hours Number Number Command:	Command
	Date Hours Number Number Error: File transfer failed	Error
Apache Error	*Timestamp* (13) Permission denied: /home/bear-005/users/xxx/public_html/ke/.htaccess pcfg_openfile: unable to check htaccess file ensure it is readable	Permission denied
	Timestamp Error [client] File does not exist: /opt/website/sites/users.cs.fiu.edu/ data/favicon.ico	File does not exist
	Timestamp Error [client 66.249.65.4] suexec *policy* violation: see suexec log for more details	Policy violation
	Timestamp /home/hpdrc-demo/sdbtools/public_html/hpdrc2/.htaccess: AuthName takes one argument The *Authentication* realm (e.g. "Members Only")	Authentication
	Timestamp Error [client] 2010-04-01 using	N/A
	Timestamp Error [client]	N/A

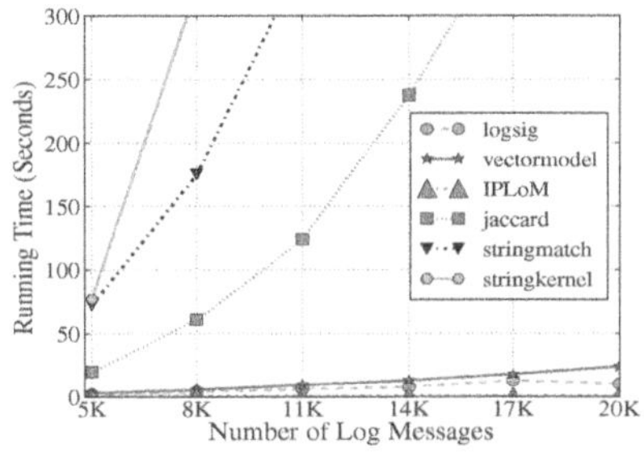

Figure 3: Average Running Time for FileZilla logs

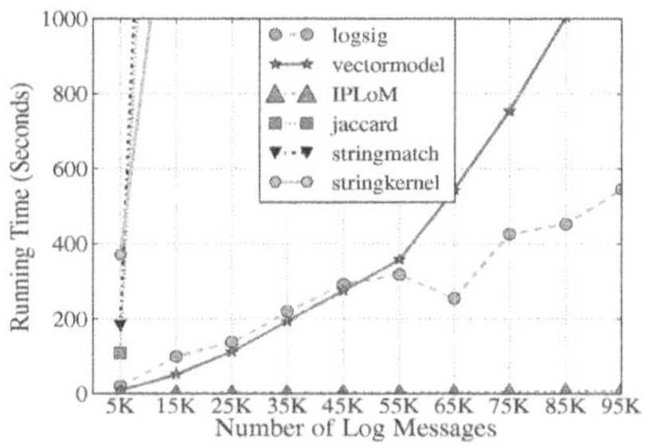

Figure 4: Average Running Time for ThunderBird logs

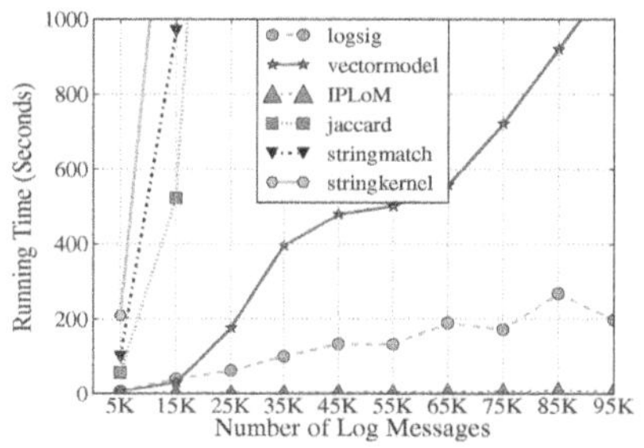

Figure 5: Average Running Time for Apache logs

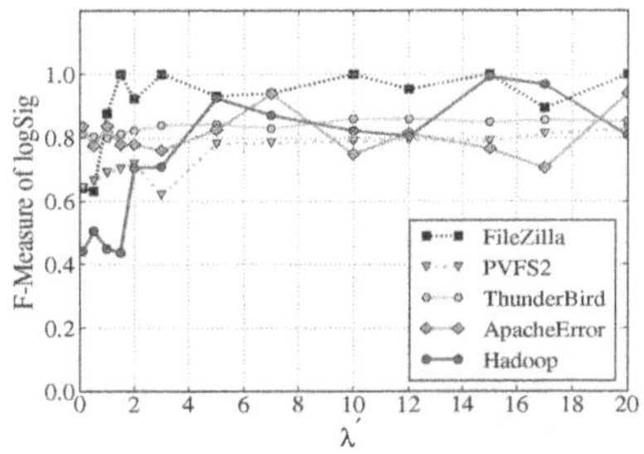

Figure 6: Varying parameter λ'

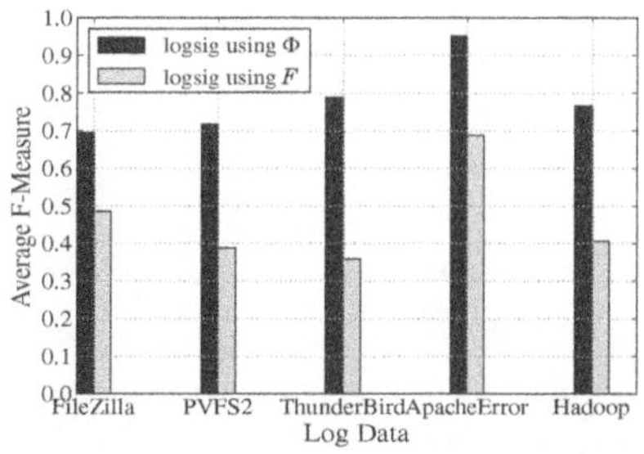

Figure 7: Effectiveness of Potential Function

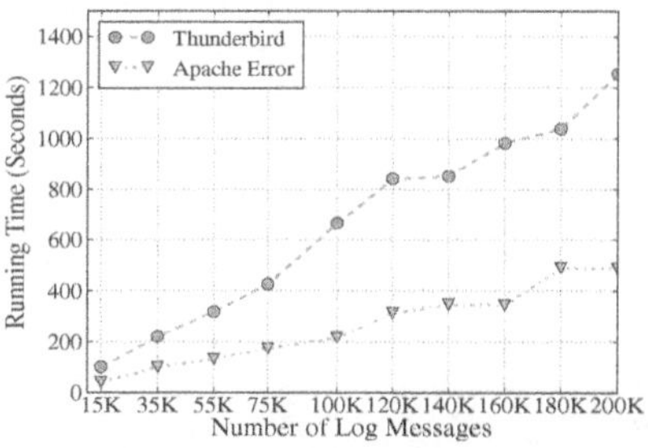

Figure 8: Scalability of logSig

message signatures. Table 9 shows generated signatures of FileZilla and Apache Error by **semi-logSig**, in which features are indicated by *italic words.*

As for FileZilla log, each message signature corresponds to a message category, so that the F-measure of FileZilla could achieve 1.0. But for Apache Error log, Only 4 message signatures are associated with corresponding categories. The other 2 signatures are generated by two ill-partitioned message groups. They cannot be associates with any category of Apache Error logs. As a result, their "Associated Category" in Table 9 are "N/A". Therefore, the overall F-measure on Apache error log in Table 4 is only 0.7707.

7.4.3 Parameter Setting

All those algorithms have the parameter k, which is the number of events to create. We let k be the actual number of message categories. String kernel method has an additional parameter λ, which is the decay factor of a pair of terms. We use $\texttt{StringKernel}_\lambda$ to denote the string kernel method using decay factor λ. In our experiments, we set up string kernel algorithms using three different decay factors: $\texttt{StringKernel}_{0.8}$, $\texttt{StringKernel}_{0.5}$ and $\texttt{StringKernel}_{0.3}$.

As for the parameter λ' of our algorithm **logSig**, we set $\lambda' = 10$ based on the experimental result shown by Figure 6. For each value of λ', we run the algorithm for **10 times**, and plot the average F-measure in this figure. It can be seen that, the performance becomes stable when λ' is greater than 4.

7.4.4 Effectiveness of Potential Function

To evaluate the effectiveness of the potential function Φ, we compare our proposed **logSig** algorithm with another **logSig** algorithm which uses the objective function F to guide its local search. Figure 7 shows the average F-measures of the two algorithms on each data set. Clearly, our proposed potential function Φ is more effective than F in all data sets. In addition, we find **logSig** algorithm using F always converges within 2 or 3 iterations. In other words, F is more likely to stop at a local optima in the local search. The reason for this has been discussed in Section 4.2.2.

7.5 Scalability

Scalability is an important factor for log analysis algorithms. Many high performance computing systems generate more than 1Mbytes log messages per second [21]. Figure 3, Figure 4 and Figure 5 show the average running time comparison for all algorithms on the data sets with different sizes. We run each algorithm 3 times and plot the average running times. `IPLoM` is the fastest algorithm. The running times of other algorithms depend on the number of iterations. Clearly, k-medoid based algorithms are not capable of handling large log data. Moreover, `StringKernel` is not efficient even though we use *Sparse Vector* to implement the computation of its kernel functions. We keep track of its running process, and find out the low speed convergence is mainly due to the high dimensionality.

Figure 8 shows the scalability of `logSig` algorithm on ThunderBird logs and Apache Error logs. Its actual running time is approximated linear with the log data size.

8. CONCLUSION AND FUTURE WORK

In this paper, we show the drawbacks of traditional methods and previous log message analyzing methods. To address the limitations of existing methods, we propose `logSig`, a message signature based method for events creation from system log messages. `logSig` utilizes the common subsequence information of messages to partition and describe the events generated from log messages.

As for the future work, we will integrate the structural learning techniques into our framework to capture the structural information of log messages. We hope those structures could improve the performance of the `logSig` algorithm.

Acknowledgement

The work is supported in part by NSF grants IIS-0546280 and HRD-0833093.

9. REFERENCES

[1] Apache HTTP Server : An Open-Source HTTP Web Server. `http://httpd.apache.org/`.

[2] FileZilla: An open-source and free FTP/SFTP solution. `http://filezilla-project.org`.

[3] Hadoop : An Open-Source MapReduce computing platform. `http://hadoop.apache.org/`.

[4] PVFS2 : The state-of-the-art parallel I/O and high performance virtual file system. `http://pvfs.org`.

[5] ThunderBird: A supercomputer in Sandia National Laboratories. `http://www.cs.sandia.gov/~jrstear/logs/`.

[6] M. Aharon, G. Barash, I. Cohen, and E. Mordechai. One graph is worth a thousand logs: Uncovering hidden structures in massive system event logs. In *Proceedings of ECML/PKDD*, pages 227–243, Bled, Slovenia, September 2009.

[7] S. Bereg, M. Kubica, T. Walen, and B. Zhu. RNA multiple structural alignment with longest common subsequences. *Journal of Combinatorial Optimization*, 13(2):179–188, 2007.

[8] M. Bilenko, S. Basu, and R. J. Mooney. Integrating constraints and metric learning in semi-supervised clustering. In *Proceedings of ICML*, Alberta, Canada, July 2004.

[9] K. Fisher, D. Walker, and K. Q. Zhu. Incremental learning of system log formats. *SIGOPS Oper. Syst. Rev.*, 44(1):85–90, 2010.

[10] J. Gao, G. Jiang, H. Chen, and J. Han. Modeling probabilistic measurement correlations for problem determination in large-scale distributed systems. In *Proceedings of the 29th International Conference on Distributed Computing Systems (ICDCS'09)*, pages 623–630, 2009.

[11] G. Hamerly and C. Elkan. Learning the k in k-means. In *Proceedings of NIPS*, Vancouver, British Columbia, Canada, December 2003.

[12] J. Han, M. Kamber, and J. Pei. *Data Mining: Concepts and Techniques, 2ed.* Morgan Kaufmann, 2005.

[13] J. L. Hellerstein, S. Ma, and C.-S. Perng. Discovering actionable patterns in event data. *IBM Systems Journal*, 43(3):475–493, 2002.

[14] J. Kiernan and E. Terzi. Constructing comprehensive summaries of large event sequences. In *Proceedings of ACM KDD*, pages 417–425, Las Vegas, Nevada, USA, August 2008.

[15] T. Li, F. Liang, S. Ma, and W. Peng. An integrated framework on mining logs files for computing system management. In *Proceedings of ACM KDD*, pages 776–781, Chicago, Illinois, USA, August 2005.

[16] H. Lodhi, C. Saunders, J. Shawe-Taylor, N. Cristianini, and C. Watkins. Text classification using string kernels. *The Journal of Machine Learning Research*, 2:419–444, March 2002.

[17] D. Maier. The complexity of some problems on subsequences and supersequences. *Journal of the ACM*, 25:322–336, April 1978.

[18] A. Makanju, A. N. Zincir-Heywood, and E. E. Milios. Clustering event logs using iterative partitioning. In *Proceedings of ACM KDD*, pages 1255–1264, Paris, France, June 2009.

[19] K. Ning, H. K. Ng, and H. W. Leong. Finding patterns in biological sequences by longest common subsequencesand shortest common supersequences. In *Proceedings of BIBE*, pages 53–60, Arlington, Virginia, USA, 2006.

[20] A. J. Oliner, A. Aiken, and J. Stearley. Alert detection in system logs. In *Proccedings of ICDM*, pages 959–964, Pisa, Italy, December 2008.

[21] A. J. Oliner and J. Stearley:. What supercomputers say: A study of five system logs. In *Proceedings of DSN 2007*, pages 575–584, Edinburgh, UK, June 2007.

[22] W. Peng, C. Perng, T. Li, and H. Wang. Event summarization for system management. In *Proceedings of ACM KDD*, pages 1028–1032, San Jose, California, USA, August 2007.

[23] G. Salton and M. McGill. *Introduction to Modern Information Retrieval.* McGraw-Hill, 1984.

[24] J. Stearley. Towards informatic analysis of syslogs. In *Proceedings of IEEE International Conference on Cluster Computing*, pages 309–318, San Diego, California, USA, September 2004.

[25] P.-N. Tan, M. Steinbach, and V. Kumar. *Introduction to Data Mining.* Addison Wesley, 2005.

[26] L. Tang and T. Li. LogTree: A framework for generating system events from raw textual logs. In *Proceedings of ICDM*, pages 491–500, Sydney, Australia, December 2010.

[27] S. Theodoridis and r. e. Konstantinos Koutroumbas. *Pattern Recognition.* Academic Press, 2006.

[28] K. Wagstaff, C. Cardie, S. Rogers, and S. Schrodl:. Constrained k-means clustering with background knowledge. In *Proceedings of ICML*, pages 577–584, June 2001.

[29] P. Wang, H. Wang, M. Liu, and W. Wang. An algorithmic approach to event summarization. In *Proceedings of ACM SIGMOD*, pages 183–194, Indianapolis, Indiana, USA, June 2010.

[30] W. Xu, L. Huang, A. Fox, D. A. Patterson, and M. I. Jordan. Mining console logs for large-scale system problem detection. In *SysML*, San Diego, CA, USA, December 2008.

Coupling or Decoupling for KNN Search on Road Networks? A Hybrid Framework on User Query Patterns

Ying-Ju Chen† and Kun-Ta Chuang‡ and Ming-Syan Chen†*
Department of Electrical Engineering, National Taiwan University†
Department of Computer Science and Information Engineering, National Cheng Kung University‡
Research Center for Information Technology Innovation, Academia Sinica*
yjchen@arbor.ee.ntu.edu.tw, ktchuang@mail.ncku.edu.tw, mschen@cc.ee.ntu.edu.tw

ABSTRACT

We explore in this paper a new KNN algorithm, called the SQUARE algorithm, for searching spatial objects on road networks. Recent works in the literature discussed the necessity to support object updates for promising location-based services. Among them, the decoupling spatial search algorithms, which separate the handle of the network traversal and the object lookup, has been recognized as the most effective approach to cut the maintenance overhead from updates. However, the queue-based network traversal needs to be performed from scratch for each KNN query until the KNN objects are exactly identified, indicating that the query complexity is in proportion to the number of visited network nodes. The query efficiency is concerned for online LBS applications since they only allow lightweight operations for minimizing the query latency. To improve the query scalability while supporting data updates, SQUARE constructs the network index similar to the way used in decoupling models, and meanwhile exploit the coupling idea to maintain the KNN information relative to hot regions in the network index. The hot region denotes the area with frequent queries discovered in the query history. Inspired from the prevalently observed 80-20 rule, SQUARE can maximize the query throughput by returning KNN results in the quasi-constant time for 80% queries that are roughly issued within 20% area (hot regions). As validated in our experimental results, SQUARE outperforms previous works and achieves the significant performance improvement without sacrifice on the maintenance overhead for object updates.

Keywords

KNN query, Spatial databases

Categories and Subject Descriptors

H.2.8 [Database Applications]: Spatial databases and GIS

General Terms

Algorithms, Management

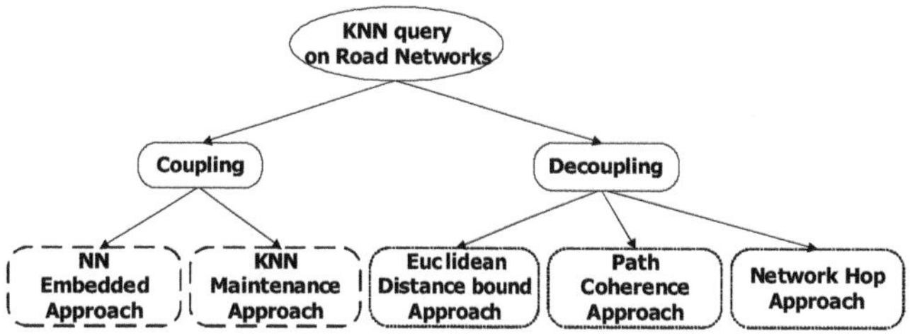

Figure 1: Categorization of previous studies on Location Dependent Spatial Queries.

1. INTRODUCTION

As the number of mobile users is growing at rapid pace, Location-Based services (LBS) are becoming an area of increasing interests in recent years. Among them, the Location Dependent Spatial Queries (LDSQ for short), especially the most recognized LDSQ for searching k-nearest neighbors (KNN), has been deemed as an essential means to the success of LBS applications [17]. Research advances in the literature particularly concentrate on the consideration of user trajectories in road networks, which allows users seeking nearby objects in the metric of the network distance or the traveling time. An example of such LDSQ may like "Q: find five hotels with the shortest walking distance from the conference venue."

To achieve KNN queries on road networks, numerous approaches have been explored [4][11][12][17][18]. Formally, these prior works can be classified into two major categories according to their manners of associating two basic operations in processing LDSQ, namely, network traversal and object lookup [12]. The first category, as shown in Figure 1, is named as the "Coupling" approach, which indicates that the object information is intrinsically embedded in the network index structure. For example, the Distance Index algorithm [4] precomputes the distance signatures for all network nodes, where the distance signatures encode the information of paths towards individual objects. As such, the KNN result can be efficiently obtained by merely looking relative signatures. Clearly, since paths to objects can be precomputed and sophisticatedly indexed in such coupling methodologies, the required searching steps for some specific queries could be minimized, achieving the high efficiency for LDSQ.

Recent LBS applications call for the need of supporting data updates such as the insertion of new activities, the deletion of expired information, and the movement of on-going events. Unfortunately, aforementioned coupling techniques inevitably incur the prohibitively expensive maintenance overhead in such requirements due to the tight association between the initial network topology and the object location [18]. The research direction thus turns to explore the alternative "Decoupling" methodologies [12][17][18], i.e., the second category in Figure 1. Essentially, the construction of network index in this kind of algorithms is orthogonal to the object locations. This property allows object updates in LDSQ applications without a significant performance sacrifice for the index reconstruction. Note that due to the lacks of object information in the network structure, the major concern in the decoupling model is how to avoid the blind node-by-node network expansion until KNN objects are identified [12][18], as the way of the traditional Dijkstra's algorithm [2].

The ROAD framework is the state-of-the-art decoupling framework for LDSQ [12], which explored a level-wise network structure, called the Rnet hierarchy, to facilitate cutting the overhead of the network expansion. Specifically, ROAD partitions the whole road network into a set of disjointed regional sub-networks, denoted as Rnets, in a pre-computing stage. Without taking the object distribution into consideration, the network partitioning procedure mainly follows the criterion that the interconnection between Rnets could be minimized. Each Rnet is equipped with two essential functionalities for LDSQ: (1) check the object repository and answer whether the Rnet contains objects of interest; and (2) return all shortcuts, i.e., shortest paths between two border nodes of the Rnet, in the constant time, where a border is a network node connecting with nodes in another Rnet. Suppose that a Rnet does not contain candidate objects of a KNN query, indicating that this Rnet can be logically viewed as a single node with outside edges equal to its set of shortcuts. The thorough network traversal within the Rnet can be bypassed and substituted by the set of shortcuts, thus leading to the better efficiency in comparison with the blind network expansion. More importantly, supporting object updates is straightforward in the ROAD framework. Only the lightweight update operation in the object database is required, showing the robustness of decoupling models against the update effect.

However, the query latency still needs the further improvement in current decoupling algorithms such as ROAD. The queue-based network traversal for verifying candidate KNN objects is necessary for each query. Clearly, the more network traversals and object lookups are involved, the larger the query processing overhead is incurred. The query efficiency cannot be guaranteed close to the constant time, indicating its performance concern for online LBS applications.

Therefore, we in this paper further explore the solution to support data updates while also minimizing the query overhead. Note that as compared to coupling approaches, decoupling approaches is capable of supporting data updates without the need of the index reconstruction. However, using the decoupling concept inevitably compromises the chance to minimize the query overhead by referring to the object distribution. As thus, we consider to combine advantages of both models in this paper. A hybrid framework, called the SQUARE algorithm (stands for Spatial Query with User-pattern awAREness), is proposed in this paper. Specifically, SQUARE builds the network hierarchy with borders and shortcuts which is used in the decoupling model ROAD. But the construction of the network index will further consider the query patterns to identify the hot regions with frequent queries in the history. For these specific partitions, we follow the coupling concept to embed the related KNN information in the network index. In light of the famous 80-20 rule [10], we can expect that 80% queries will be roughly issued within 20% area, i.e., these hot regions with frequent queries. SQUARE is devised with the capability to return KNN results of the majority of queries, i.e., queries issued within these hot regions, in the quasi-constant time, thus leading to the higher throughput as compared to previous works. In addition, same as decoupling models, SQUARE has the advantage to avoid the network reconstruction with respect to data updates. SQUARE requires another maintenance overhead to ensure that the maintained KNN information is up-to-date. With the help of some filtering strategies, the maintenance overhead of SQUARE will be inexpensive and comparable to that of the decoupling models.

The contributions of this work can be summarized as follows: (1) While previous works generally need to initiate an expensive queue-based network search for every query without the bounded time cost, we consider a solution which can answer the majority of queries in the quasi-constant time. (2) SQUARE is the first paper considering the query pattern into the object search on road networks. Utilizing the 80-20 behavior shown in query patterns can facilitate the query processing. (3) We have devised in SQUARE good filtering properties and criteria to execute KNN recalculation while data are updated. As such, SQUARE is capable of handling data updates with affordable maintenance overhead. (4) The result demonstrates that, instead of only providing the flexibility of striking a compromise between the update support and the query efficiency, SQUARE can both achieve high query performance and low update cost, showing its prominent advantages to be the capability of online LBS applications.

The rest of this paper is organized as follows. Section 2 gives preliminaries including related works and the problem description. In Section 3, we describe the design of the SQUARE algorithm. Section 4 discusses the handle for data updates. The experimental results are shown in Section 5. Finally, this paper concludes with Section 6.

2. PRELIMINARIES

We present related works in Section 2.1 and formalize the discussed problem in Section 2.2. Note that we focus on KNN queries in the metric of network distance. For the orthogonal problem to retrieve KNN objects in the Euclidean space, interested readers can refer to [19][20] for details.

2.1 Related Works

In recent years, a considerable number of studies have been proposed to retrieve KNN objects on road networks [1][6][11][17]. Among them, the INE (incremental network expansion) algorithm first exposes the issue and extends the Dijkstra's algorithm to search KNN objects by gradually expanding the network space, and check if the objects associated to the visited network nodes belong to the KNN result [17]. The procedure of network expansions is terminated while all KNN objects are identified. To further improve the query efficiency, a heuristic alternative is also devised in [17] to prune the unnecessary expansion of the search space according to the Euclidean lower bound properties, which state that the Euclidean distance is the lower bound of the network distance. However, the blind node-by-node query expansion in INE will inevitably face the performance issue in a huge spatial network.

Recent works thus moved to the direction of using some precomputed structures to facilitate the search of KNN objects [1][4][5][11]. Note that two major operations are generally involved in processing the KNN search, namely network traversal and object lookup. The operation of network traversal is used to visit network nodes according to network proximity, and object lookup is used to discover objects located in traversed network nodes and checks if the objects match the search criteria. Essentially, previous precomputation based approaches can be categorized as coupling approaches and decoupling approaches according to their manners to associate network traversal and object lookup. We individually discuss these two approaches below

Coupling Approaches: Intrinsically, the coupling approaches embed the object information in the index for network traversals. As shown in Figure 1, the coupling approaches can be further categorized as NN-embedded approaches and KNN maintenance approaches. In general, the NN-embedded methods embed the information of the nearest object for each network node in the network index, such as VN^3 [11], UNICONS [1], and SPIE [5]. Specifically, the VN^3 algorithm [11] generates network Voronoi polygons (NVP) for each object such that the object is the nearest neighbor for all network nodes inside the NVP. The KNN objects can be quickly obtained by checking NVPs around the NVP that the query is issued. The UNICONS algorithm [1] obtains KNN objects by precomputing nearest objects for some condensed points, where condensed points are nodes with large fanouts. When the network search reaches a condensed point, the precomputed NN lists can be retrieved directly to reduce the search space. In the SPIE algorithm [5], a network reduction approach is used to reduce the road network to a set of interconnected trees. The nearest object for each node in the tree is then precomputed. In this method, the KNN objects can be obtained by traversing the tree without using the network expansion like the Dijkstra's algorithm.

Distance Index [4] is one of KNN maintenance approaches. It precomputes distance signatures for all network nodes. The distance signatures encode the information of all paths from each node towards individual objects. Therefore, the KNN results can be efficiently obtained by decoding the relative signatures. Moreover, a cache based query algorithm is discussed in [7], which utilizes the LRU cache-replacement to maintain previous KNN results for future queries.

However, the coupling model is infeasible to support data updates for web-based LBS applications. Note that the network index is built based on the object locations. The update of objects will make the initial index invalid for KNN queries, and the reconstruction of the network index inevitably incurs the expensive maintenance overhead.

Decoupling Approaches: Recently, the object search on road networks turns to use decoupling approaches, which generally do not consider the object distribution while constructing the network index. Such a property enables the decoupling approach to support data updates without the need of the index reconstruction. Basically, the aforementioned INE approach is a kind of decoupling algorithms, i.e., the Euclidean distance bound approach as shown in Figure 1. In addition, the distance browsing algorithm exploits the phenomenon of path coherence to maintain the shortest paths between all nodes [18]. A non-incremental best-first algorithm is then used to retrieve KNN without blind network traversals. However, as discussed in [12], this method pays for the expensive precomputation overhead for all-pair shortest paths. In addition, the KNN search in this work still needs a node-by-node fashion until KNN objects are identified.

The ROAD algorithm is the state-of-the-art decoupling framework [12], which exploits the network hop concept to avoid blind node-by-node expansions for KNN queries. In ROAD, the whole road network is initially partitioned into a set of disjointed regional sub-networks, called Rnets. The network partitioning procedure follows the criterion that the interconnection between Rnets could be minimized. Afterward, the set of borders in each Rnet is identified, where a border is a network node connecting with nodes in another Rnet. In the meanwhile the shortest paths of all pairs of borders within a Rnet, called as shortcuts, are precomputed and maintained. While a KNN query is issued, operations of the network expansion within a Rnet can be skipped and completely substituted by shortcuts if no required object is located within the Rnet. Essentially, the search space pruning in the ROAD algorithm is specifically favorable to the huge network with the relatively small set of objects. While objects are densely distributed in the network, such as the case of restaurants in the metropolis, all KNN objects are likely to locate within the Rnet of the query or its neighbor Rnet. The search space will not be effectively reduced by the hop across Rnets. In worse cases, ROAD is degenerated to the INE algorithm without valid space pruning.

2.2 Problem Formulation

We introduce the notations and definitions used hereafter and then formalize the problem. Suppose that a road network is modeled as a graph G consisting of a pair (N, E), where N is a set of nodes, and E is a set of edges connecting the nodes. A node $n \in N$ represents a road junction or a starting/ending point of a road segment, and an edge $e = (u, v) \in E$ represents a road segment that connects node u and node v. The weight of the edge, denoted by $|(u, v)|$, is the travel distance of the road segment. Let a path $p = (p_1, p_2, ..., p_l)$ exist in G, which is a list of connected edges $(p_i, p_{i+1}) \in E$ for $1 \leq i \leq l-1$. The weight of this path is defined as the sum of the weights of its constituent edges, i.e., $|p| = \sum_{i=1}^{l-1} |(p_i, p_{i+1})|$. Note that it is likely to have more than one path between two network nodes u and v. In this model, the shortest path is used to represent the network distance between two nodes u and v, which is denoted by $d_N(u, v)$ (here the suffix symbol N means that the distance is the network distance). The Euclidean distance between u and v is notated as $d_E(u, v)$ correspondingly.

Consider a set of data objects $O = \{o_1, o_2, ..., o_m\}$ in G, where each object contains the information of its location and its active time period. Note that the time information of objects is requisite in the model of supporting data updates. For simplicity, we present the model based on the static objects in Section 2 and Section 3. The update and time issues will be discussed in Section 4. Specifically, we can logically transform the location of the object o_i to be the location of node v plus $d_E(v, o_i)$, where $d_E(v, o_i)$ denotes the Euclidean distance between v and o_i, and v is the nearest

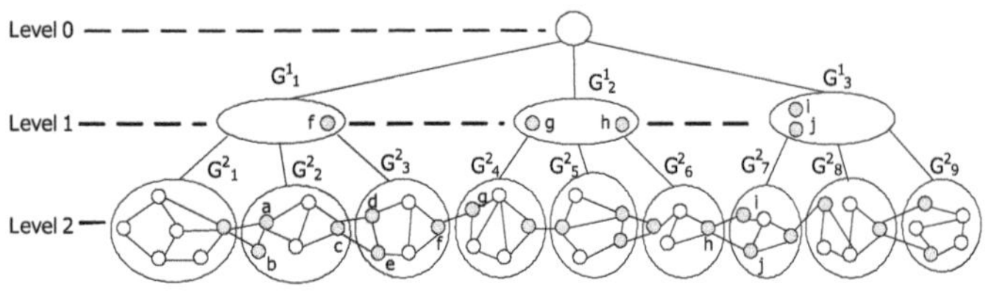

Figure 2: An example graph hierarchy.

node of o_i. Therefore, the location of the object o_i can be represented as $loc(o_i) =< v,\ d_E(v, o_i) >$. Without loss of generality, we can associate the node v for o_i in the object repository.

The spatial query q_j for KNN objects consists of two parameters k and $loc(q_j)$, where k is the number of nearest objects to discover and $loc(q_j)$ denotes the location of q_j. Similar to the handle of object locations, $loc(q_j)$ can also be transformed to $loc(q_j) =< v,\ d_E(v, q_j) >$, where v is the nearest node of q_j. For ease of exposition, we simply assume the query q_j is issued in the node v. It is a matter of implementation to precisely calculate the distance by further checking $d_E(v, q_j)$.

Inspired by the ROAD algorithm [12], we also consider to build the network index as a form of the graph hierarchy, which can benefit to prune the search space hierarchically. Here we first give the definitions of subgraphs and the graph partitioning below.

Definition 1 (Subgraph): Let a subgraph $G_s = (N_s,\ E_s)$ be a subset of road network G, where $N_s \subset N$ and $E_s = \{(u, v)|u, v \in N_s \wedge (u, v) \in E\}$.

Definition 2 (Graph partitioning): A graph $G = (N, E)$ can be partitioned into a set of disjointed subgraphs $\{G_1 = (N_1, E_1), G_2 = (N_2, E_2), ..., G_k = (N_k, E_k)\}$. The general definition for the graph partition is stated as follows.

1) $N_1 \cup ... \cup N_k = N$, and $N_i \cap N_j = \emptyset$ for $1 \leq i, j \leq k,\ i \neq j$.
2) $E_i = \{(u, v)|u \in N_i, v \in N_i\}$, and $E_1 \cup E_2 \cup ... \cup E_k \subset E$.
3) $E_B = \{(u, v)|u \in N_i, v \in N_j$, where $i \neq j\}$, and $E_B \subset E$
4) $E_1 \cup E_2 \cup ... \cup E_k \cup E_B = E$

Several graph-partitioning methods have been proposed to achieve graph partitioning [8][9]. The general criterion used in these graph partitioning methods is to separate the graph into subsets of roughly the same size and the connections between the subgraphs are as minimal as possible.

Formally, by recursively applying the graph-partitioning algorithm in a top-down manner, we can generate the graph hierarchy. Two parameters, i.e., l and p, are thus considered when constructing the graph hierarchy, where l denotes the number of levels in the hierarchy, and p denotes the partition factor. Initially, the graph hierarchy is constructed by setting the whole graph as the root. We then apply the graph partitioning algorithm to segment the parent graphs/subgraphs to p smaller child subgraphs recursively. An example of the graph hierarchy with $l = 2, p = 3$ is shown in Figure 2. The root level, i.e., level 0 in Figure 2, represents the entire network graph. Three subgraphs in level 1 are generated by partitioning the entire graph in level 0. Each of the subgraphs in the level 1 is further divided into three smaller subgraphs in level 2.

We state below the important concept of borders and shortcuts, which are used in the graph hierarchy to efficiently prune the search expansion in the subgraph.

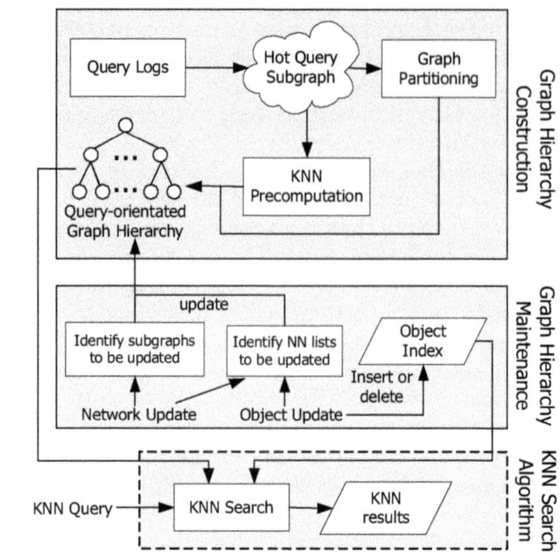

Figure 3: The overview of the SQUARE framework.

Definition 3 (Borders): In a subgraph $G_s = (N_s,\ E_s)$, the set of border nodes V_b is a subset of N_s, where $V_b = \{u|u \in N_s \wedge \exists(u,v) \notin E_s, v \notin N_s\}$.

Definition 4 (ShortCuts): For a subgraph $G_s = (N_s,\ E_s)$ with the border set V_b, the shortest path between two borders v_i and v_j is referred to as shortcut $s_{i,j}$, i.e., $s_{i,j} = d_N(v_i, v_j)$. Shortcuts in G_s is thus defined as $SP(G_s) = \{s_{i,j}|v_i \in V_b \wedge v_j \in V_b\}$.

Consider the example in Figure 2. The subgraph G_2^2 contains three borders, i.e., a, b, and c. In addition, the subgraph G_2^1 in level 1 contains two borders g and h, which connect G_2^2 to other subgraphs G_3^2 and G_7^2. Note that the borders and shortcuts in each subgraph can be identified and calculated after the network partitioning is completed. As discussed in [12], we can traverse the graph hierarchy and utilize the shortcuts to skip the network expansion in the subgraph. We roughly present the concept in the following example. The formal discussion can be found in [12].

Example 1: Consider the graph in Figure 2. Suppose an object is located in G_7^2 and a query is issued at G_3^2. A priority queue is initiated for the network traversal. The search is gradually expanded until reaching the border node f of G_3^2. In generally, the KNN search needs 3 hops for G_4^2, G_5^2, and G_6^2 before reaching G_7^2. But since we can check the parent subgraph G_2^1 and find it does not contain objects, the shortcut between g and h in G_2^1 can be used to substitute for the full network expansion in G_2^1. Finally, one hop is sufficient for searching toward G_7^2. Clearly, the KNN search can be achieved by checking only a partial nodes in G_3^2 and G_7^2.

Based on the foregoing, our objective to search KNN objects on road networks can be further transformed to search objects on the graph hierarchy. In Section 3, we will discuss how to embed the KNN information in the graph hierarchy for further improving the KNN search efficiency.

3. THE SQUARE FRAMEWORK

In this paper, we explore a new framework for KNN spatial queries, called the SQUARE framework. SQUARE stands for Spatial Query with User-pattern awAREness, indicating that we take the user query history into consideration. The overview of the framework is illustrated in Figure 3. Three major components are included in the frameworks, namely (1) graph hierarchy construction; (2) graph hierarchy maintenance, and (3) the KNN search functionality. We describe the graph hierarchy construction and the KNN search in this section. The graph hierarchy maintenance will be discussed in Section 4.

3.1 User-Pattern-Aware Subgraph

Since the first observation of the power-law relationship in [21], the skewness phenomenon has been successively discovered in many real data [3]. The phenomenon is also famous as the name "80-20 rule" [10]. The existence of the 80-20 rule has been identified and applied to geographic applications [16], which stated that 80% data are roughly located within less than 20% area[1]. Inspired by such a nature of geographic data, we apply the query history to identify so-called hot query subgraphs which contain frequent queries in the history.

Definition 5 (Hot Query Subgraph): Given the frequency threshold θ and the maximum node number within a hot query subgraph α, we have the hot query subgraph $G_h = (N_h, E_h) \in G_s$, where $N_h = \{u | f_u \geq \theta\}$, $E_h = \{(u,v) | u,v \in N_h\}$, $|N_h| \leq \alpha$, and f_u is the number of queries issued in u.

For ease of exposition, the hot query subgraph is abbreviated as HQgraph in the sequel. It is expected that the majority of future queries will issue within all discovered HQgraph. Essentially, we can precompute the KNN results for all network nodes in HQgraph. For cases that objects are not updated, the answer for queries issued within a HQ-graph can be straightforwardly returned, resulting in high throughput and constant-time query efficiency. Note that such a solution is generally used in coupling models. However, when objects are inserted or deleted frequently, the overhead to maintain up-to-date KNN data is computationally expensive. Even worse, nearby nodes are likely to have similar KNN data [18]. The information redundancy inevitably incurs the unnecessary storage cost.

To provide the flexibility of striking a compromise between the query efficiency and the maintenance overhead, only KNN information of borders in HQgraph are precomputed and maintained in the SQUARE framework. For cases that queries are issued in the interior node of a HQgraph, Lemma 1 shows the property to conduct their KNN results.

Lemma 1: Suppose that we have a HQgraph G_h with the border set $V_b = \{v_1, v_2, ..v_p\}$ and a query q issued in node u in the HQgraph, where $u \notin V_b$. The KNN result of q is the subset of the union set of $K_1, K_2, ..., K_p, O_h$, where K_i is the KNN result of the border v_i and O_h is the set of objects located in G_h.

Proof: (Proof by Contradiction) Assume o_i belongs to KNN objects of q, and $o_i \notin \{K_1 \cup K_2 \cup ... \cup K_p \cup O_h\}$. The network distance between o_i and q is $d_N(v_b, q)$. Let v_b be the border which has minimum $d_N(v_b, q) + d_N(v_b, o_i)$. According to the shortcut property, we have $d_N(v_b, q) = d_N(v_b, q) + d_N(v_b, o_i)$. In addition, since o_i does not belong to the KNN result of v_b, we have $d_N(v_b, q) + d_N(v_b, o_{b_j}) < d_N(v_b, q)$, where o_{b_j} is one of the KNN result of v_b for $1 \leq j \leq k$. Note that we have $d_N(o_{b_j}, q) \leq d_N(v_b, q) + d_N(v_b, o_{b_j})$, leading that $d_N(o_{b_j}, q) < d_N(v_b, q)$ for $1 \leq j \leq k$. Since the number of o_{b_j} is k, it is not possible to include o_i into the KNN set of q and thus contradicts our assumption. Q.E.D.

[1]The skewness phenomenon can also be found in many public websites for geographic data. For example: http://www.cs.fsu.edu/~lifeifei/SpatialDataset.htm

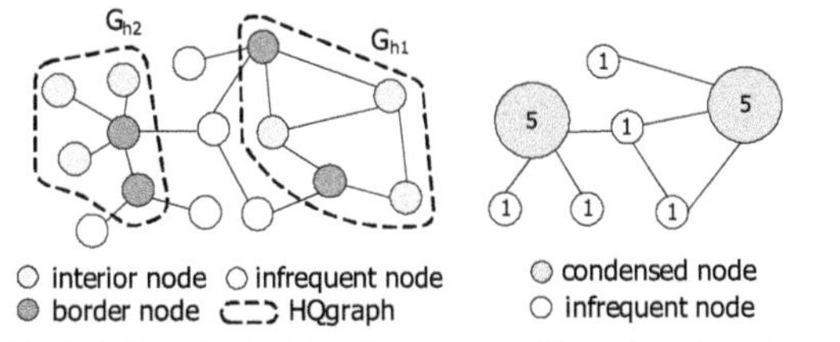

(a) illustration of hot query subgraphs (b) condensed graph

Figure 4: Examples of Hot Query subgraphs and condensed graphs.

```
Procedure: HQgraph_construction():
  Input:
    The graph, i.e., G;
    The query logs, i.e., Q;
    The frequency threshold θ;
    The size of hot query subgraph, i.e., δ;
  Output:
    A set of hot query subgraphs, i.e., HQ;
  process Q, and calculate the query freq. of each node in G;
  let S = {n1, n2, ...} be nodes with freq. higher than θ;
  HQ = ∅
  while S is not empty
      u := a node randomly selected from S
      sg := ∅
      queue := {u}
      while queue is not empty
          v := dequeue(queue)
          for each neighbor d of v
              if d ∈ S
                  if sg.size > δ
                      HQ := HQ ∪ sg;
                      sg := ∅;
                  sg.N := sg.N ∪ d;
                  sg.E := sg.E ∪ (v, d);
                  queue = queue ∪ d;
          remove v from S;
      HQ := HQ ∪ sg;
  return HQ;
```

In light of Lemma 1, for a query issued in the interior node of a HQgraph G_h, we could return the KNN result by traversing nodes in G_h plus the KNN data of borders in G_h. While the size of G_h is relatively smaller than the size of general subgraphs, using HQgraph can help to achieve the quasi-constant query efficiency. We defer the discussion on the maximum number of network nodes in a HQgraph to Section 4.

An illustrative example of HQgraphs is given in Figure 4(a), which contains two HQgraphs G_{h1} and G_{h2}. For G_{h1}, we need to precompute the KNN objects of two border nodes. The other three interior nodes in G_{h1} can utilize the KNN results of borders instead of precomputing their own KNN objects.

The procedure to find hot query subgraphs is outlined in Procedure HQgraph_construction. There are three algorithm inputs: the graph G, the query logs Q, the frequency threshold θ and the maximum number of nodes in a HQ-graphs δ. Initially, the query frequency of each node in G is calculated by checking Q. We can obtain the node set S

where the query frequency of the node is higher than θ. To generate a hot query subgraph, we start by randomly removing a node u from S, and execute network expansion from u. Each unvisited neighbor node d of u is checked whether it is an element of S or not. If d also belongs to S, we add d into the same subgraph, and insert d to the queue while also removing d from S. The first element of the queue is iteratively popped up and checked until the queue is empty. After the HQgraph is identified, a node from S is randomly selected again to find other hot query subgraphs until the S is empty.

3.2 User-Pattern-Aware Hierarchy

Here we present the construction of User-Pattern-Aware graph hierarchy, called the UPA hierarchy, by integrating HQgraph into the general graph hierarchy discussed in Section 2. Specifically, to ensure the integrity of the HQgraph, each HQgraph is treated as a predetermined leaf subgraph. For partitioning the graph into the intermediate level, the HQgraph can be logically condensed to a node with the number of fanouts equal to its number of borders. Note that graph partitioning methods [8][9] generally include two criteria to separate the graph: (1) generating subgraphs of roughly the same node size and (2) the connections between the subgraphs are as minimal as possible. To smoothly incorporate the handle of HQgraphs into general graph partitioning models, we can specifically process the HQgraph as the single node with the number of nodes equal to the node size in the HQgraph.

```
Procedure: UPA_hierarchy_construction():
  Input:
    The graph, i.e., G;
    The set of hot query subgraphs, i.e., HQ;
    The hierarchy level, i.e., ℓ;
    The partition factor, i.e., p;
  Output:
    The UPA hierarchy, i.e, UPA;
 1. generate a condensed graph G' of G according to HQ;
 2. S := {G'}
 3. for (i = 1; i <= ℓ; i++)
 4.      SG := ∅;
 5.      for each member m in S
 6.           if ((i = ℓ)&&(m has k condensed nodes)) then
 7.                SG := SG ∪ {n_1, ..., n_k, m − (n_1 ∪ ... ∪ n_k)};
 8.           else
 9.                partition m into p subgraphs by METIS;
10.                SG := SG ∪ {sg_1, sg_2, ..., sg_p};
11.      S := SG;
12. for each member m in S;
13.      if (m is a condensed node)
14.           replace m with its corresponding HQgraph;
15.           calculate KNN of borders;
16.      calculate shortcuts of borders;
17. set the subgraphs in S as the leaf nodes in UPA;
18. for (j = ℓ − 1; j > 0; j − −)
19.      calculate shortcuts of subgraphs in level j
20.      create a tree node for each subgraphs in level j;
21.      each node records its borders and shortcuts;
22.      insert nodes to UPA;
23. return UPA
```

As such, we can apply the well-known graph partitioning method to construct the UPA hierarchy in a top-down manner. Note that several graph-partitioning methods have been proposed to achieve graph partitioning [8][9]. In this work, we adopt the METIS framework [8], which implements a multilevel graph partitioning algorithm and has been shown to have the partitioning quality better than the traditional Kernighan-Lin algorithm [9].

We outline the construction in UPA_hierarchy_construction. In the first step, the graph G is transformed to a condensed graph $G\prime$. The graph in Figure 4(b) is an example of the condensed graph transforming from the graph in Figure 4(a). The HQgraph is represented as a weighted node with the weight equal to the number of nodes in this HQgraph. The weights of other nodes in the condensed graph are set as 1. Afterward, the condensed graph $G\prime$ is partitioned into p subgraphs by utilizing the METIS algorithm. The partitioning procedure is repeated for level 0 to level $\ell - 1$. Note that in the leaf level ℓ, each HQgraph is already a predetermined graph set. Suppose that there are i HQgraphs involved in a subgraph of level $\ell - 1$, the complement of HQgraphs is used to generate $p - i$ leaf subgraphs.

```
Procedure: knn_search():
  Input:
    The UPA hierarchy, i.e, UPA;
    The object index, i.e., OI;
    The number of NNs, i.e., k;
    The query point, i.e., q;
  Output:
    The NN results, i.e, ANS;
 1. create a queue Q and enqueue (q, 0) onto Q;
 2. ANS := ∅;
 3. while (Q is not empty and |ANS| < k )
 4.      dequeue an element from Q into (v, v.dist);
 5.      if (v is marked) continue;
 6.      while (small_dist < v.dist and |ANS| < k )
          // small_dist is the smallest distance of object in C
 7.           dequeue an element from C into (o, o.dist);
 8.           if (o ∩ ANS ≠ ∅) continue;
 9.           ANS := ANS ∪ {o};
10.      if (|ANS| = k) break;
11.      if (v is a border node) then
12.           if (v has pre-computed NNs) then
13.                for each NN a
14.                     enqueue (a, a.dist + v.dist) onto C;
15.           else
16.                S := FindSubgrah(v,UPA);
17.                while (S is not empty)
18.                     for each subgraph s ∈ S
19.                          remove s from S;
20.                          if (not HaveObjects(s,OI) and
                                not HaveHQ(s,UPA)) then
21.                               for each shortcut < v, w > of s
22.                                    put (w, d_N(v, w) + v.dist) in Q;
23.                          else if (s has child subgraphs) then
24.                               S := S∪ChildSubgraph(UPA,s,v);
25.                          else
26.                               for each (u, v) that belongs to s
27.                                    put (u, |(u, v)| + v.dist) in Q;
28.      else // v is not a border node
29.           if ( HaveObjects(v,OI))
30.                for each attached object o
31.                     enqueue (o, o.d + v.dist) onto C;
32.           for each edge (u, v)
33.                enqueue (u, |(u, v)| + v.dist) onto Q;
34.      mark v;
35. while (|ANS| < k and C is not empty)
36.      dequeue an element from C into (o, o.dist);
37.      if (o ∩ Ans ≠ ∅) continue;
38.      ANS := ANS ∪ {o};
39. return ANS;
```

In the final step, shortcuts and KNN results of border nodes in all HQgraphs are computed. For other leaf subgraphs, only border and their shortcuts are calculated. Following the same approach discussed in the ROAD algorithm, the borders and shortcuts of intermediate subgraphs can be determined by referring shortcuts of their child subgraphs without the need of traversing the corresponding graph.

Note that another major component in the SQUARE framework is the object repository, i.e., the object index shown in Figure 3. Essentially, the Association Directory structure proposed in the ROAD algorithm [12] can be directly applied in SQUARE. Interested readers can refer to [12] for such an object index structure used to decouple the association between the network graph and the object locations.

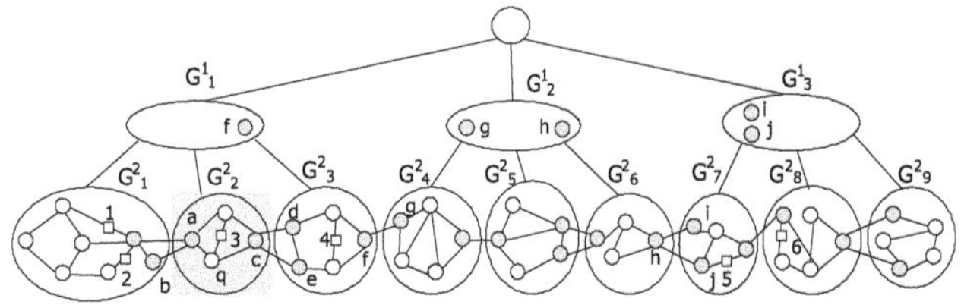

Figure 5: Example of the UPA Hierarchy with HQgraph G_2^2.

3.3 KNN Search in UPA Hierarchy

In this section, we present how to achieve the KNN search by traversing the UPA hierarchy. Specifically, the KNN search can be categorized into two search scenarios: (1) queries issued in a HQgraph, and (2) queries issued in a non-HQgraph. Queries issued in HQgraph: Two situations can be further considered. First, for the query issued in a border of HQgraph, we can return the KNN result in the constant time since it is maintained. Second, for queries issued in the interior node of the HQgraph, we apply the traditional Dijkstra's algorithm to obtain the shortest paths to borders and to objects in the HQgraph. In light of Lemma 1, we use a priority queue to sort the network distances of objects in the HQgraph and KNN objects of borders. Finally, the top-k objects are returned as the KNN results.
Queries issued in non-HQgraph: For such situations, the KNN search is similar to the search in the ROAD algorithm. But we can further improve the search efficiency by exploiting the information embedded in HQgraphs. Specifically, when the network traversal reaches a border of a HQgraph, the insertion of the border to the search queue can be replaced as the insertion of its KNN objects to the queue, thus further reducing the search spaces.

The procedure of the KNN search is outlined in the procedure knn_search. There are four algorithm inputs: the UPA hierarchy UPA, the object index OI, the number of KNN objects k, and the query point q. The knn_search procedure will return the KNN result, i.e. ANS. Q and C are priority queues. In Q, the element $(v, v.dist)$ represents a node and its distance from the query point. Similarly, the element $(o, o.dist)$ in C represents an object and its distance from the query point. The elements in Q and C are sorted by the distances in the ascending order. The dequeuing operation will remove an element from Q or C that has the smallest distance. The procedure begins by enqueuing $(q, 0)$ onto Q. An element $(v, v.dist)$ is dequeued repeatedly from Q until Q is empty or top-k objects are identified. After an element is dequeued, three operations are executed: (1) Check the dequeued node if it is visited. If the dequeued node is visited, further network expansion from the node is not necessary. The search procedure continues dequeuing the next element from Q. (2) Dequeue objects from C. The element is dequeued from C continuously until the element in C with the distance is larger than the distance of node v or the size of ANS is larger than k. These elements dequeued from C belong to KNN objects and are inserted to the set ANS. (3) Enqueue candidate objects retrieved from v into C and enqueue following nodes that should be explored from v into Q. If the node v is a border of a HQgraph, its KNN objects are enqueued into C. Otherwise, nodes that should be explored from v are enqueued into Q.

In the KNN search, we use FindSubgraph(v,UPA) to identify the highest subgraph which contains node v as its border. In addition, HaveObjects(s,OI) and HaveHQ(s,UPA) will check OI and UPA if the subgraph s contains objects and HQgraphs. If no object and no HQgraph are included in s, each border on the another side of shortcuts of v are enqueued into Q. When the subgraphs in the leaf level are checked, all nodes connecting to v are enqueued into Q. If v is not a border, the attached objects of v are enqueued into C, and the connecting nodes of v are enqueued into Q. Finally, the process is terminated when the size of ANS is k.
Example 2: As shown in Figure 5, the UPA hierarchy contains a HQgraph G_2^2. Suppose a query q is issued in G_2^2 to find KNN with $k = 3$. The precomputed KNN results of the border a are $\{o_3, o_2, o_1\}$, where $d_N(a, o_3) = 5$, $d_N(a, o_2) = 7$, $d_N(a, o) = 8$. The precomputed KNN of border c are $\{o_3, o_4, o_2\}$, where $d_N(c, o_3) = 6$, $d_N(c, o_4) = 13$, $d_N(c, o_2) = 15$. We first calculate the network distance between q and the object in G_2^2, i.e., $d_N(q, o_3) = 2$. The network distances between q and borders a and c are also computed in the same network expansion procedure, and get $d_N(q, a) = 3$, $d_N(q, c) = 5$. Then, we can derive $d_N(q, o_3 : a) = 8$, $d_N(q, o_2 : a) = 10$, $d_N(q, o_1 : a) = 11$, $d_N(q, o_3 : c) = 11$, $d_N(q, o_4 : c) = 18$, and $d_N(q, o_2 : c) = 20$, where $d_N(u, v : m)$ denotes the network distance between node u and v passing through node m. Finally, we can obtain the candidate objects of q sorting by their network distances, i.e., $\{o_3, o_2, o_1, o_4\}$ and the corresponding travel distances $\{2, 10, 11, 18\}$. The KNN of q are $\{o_3, o_2, o_1\}$. Clearly, as compared to the ROAD algorithm, the network expansions in G_1^2 and G_3^2 can be fully omitted. The query time can be bounded with respect to the size of G_2^2, which is in general small and controlled by the parameter α. In cases of queries issued in node a or c in G_2^2, we can straightforwardly return their KNN without invoking the network expansion procedure, thus showing the search efficiency of SQUARE. Note that for queries issued within other leaf subgraph, the search process is as same as that in ROAD, which is stated in Example 1 in Section 2.

4. MAINTENANCE FOR DATA UPDATES

In this section, we discuss the maintenance issue when data or the road network are updated. Note that updates may affect the correctness of the precomputed information. The general goal is to identify the minimum set of information which requires recomputation. In the SQUARE framework, the precomputed data include KNN results of borders in HQgraphs and the shortcuts between borders in each subgraph. The procedure to maintain shortcuts due to network

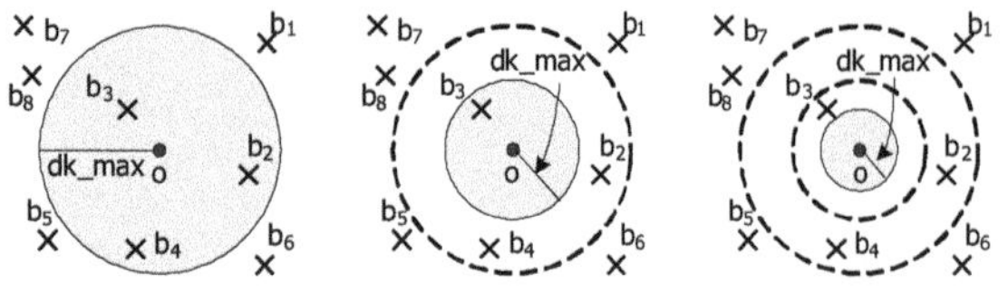

Figure 6: Example of filtering insert-check candidates by Remark 2.

update is as same as the procedure discussed in the ROAD algorithm.

4.1 KNN Update for Object Insertion

When an object is inserted, it is necessary to recalculate some precomputed KNN to ensure the KNN data are update-to-date. Intuitively, we can calculate the distances between the new object and all borders in HQgraphs. Suppose that $d_k(b_i)$ is the distance between a border b_i in a HQ-graph and its kth nearest object. If the distance between b_i and the new object is smaller than $d_k(b_i)$, the KNN objects of b_i need to be updated by removing the kth nearest object and adding the new object. However, checking updates for all borders is time-consuming, indicating the impracticability of the naive method especially in web-based LBS applications with frequent updates.

We thus propose a novel filtering method that utilizes the Euclidean lower-bound property [17] to avoid checking unnecessary borders. Consider the example of an object o and a border b_i. According to the Euclidean lower-bound property, the Euclidean distance $d_E(o, b_i)$ is smaller than $d_N(o, b_i)$. Therefore, if $d_E(o, b_i) > d_k(b_i)$, $d_N(o, b_i)$ will be larger than $d_k(b_i)$, indicating that o does not belong to KNN results of b_i. The precomputed KNN results of b_i remain valid. In contrast, if $d_E(o, b_i) \leq d_k(b_i)$, it is likely to have $d_N(o, b_i)$ smaller than or equal to $d_k(b_i)$. In such cases, we have to verify their KNN results with respect to the object insertion. Based on the foregoing, we describe Remark 1 below that help to filter unnecessary border check.

Remark 1: Let $\{b_1, b_2, ..., b_n\}$ be the set of borders in HQ-graphs and o is a newly inserted object. Suppose $dk\_max = \max_{b_i}(d_k(b_i))$. Let "insert-check candidates" C be the set of borders whose KNN results may be altered. We have $C = \{b_i | d_E(o, b_i) \leq dk\_max\}$.

Specifically, to identify insert-check candidates, we maintain the global dk_max in the SQUARE framework, which can be calculated after the initial construction of the UPA hierarchy. While a data insertion happens, the global dk_max can be used to identify the insert-checking candidates. More importantly, we can extend Remark 1 to be a multiple filtering strategy for further reducing the set of insert-check candidates.

Remark 2: Let $C = \{b_1, b_2, ..., b_n\}$ be the insert-check candidates which is identified by the global dk_max. We remove from C for the border with $d_E(o, b_i) = dk\_max$, and insert the border into the set of "must-check candidates". Afterward, we can further use the $dk\_max' = \max_{b_i}(d_k(b_i))$, for $b_i \subset C$, to reduce the insert-check candidates. That is $C' = \{b_i | d_E(o, b_i) \leq dk\_max'\}$. The border in C' with $d_E(o, b_i) = dk\_max'$ will be removed from C' and insert into must-check candidates. The iteration can be repeated until insert-check candidates are reduced to a empty set. Finally, only the border in must-check candidates needs to check if its KNN result is changed.

Figure 6 shows an example to illustrate the multiple filtering strategy in Remark 2. In the example, the object o is the newly inserted object and there are 8 border nodes included. Suppose $d_k(b_1) = 12$, $d_k(b_2) = 9$, $d_k(b_3) = 5$, $d_k(b_4) = 15$, $d_k(b_5) = 5$, $d_k(b_6) = 13$, $d_k(b_7) = 11$, $d_k(b_8) = 10$, and the Euclidean distance $d_E(b_1, o) = 18$, $d_E(b_2, o) = 13$, $d_E(b_3, o) = 8$, $d_E(b_4, o) = 11$, $d_E(b_5, o) = 17$, $d_E(b_6, o) = 19$, $d_E(b_7, o) = 20$, $d_E(b_8, o) = 18$. In this case, the global $dk\_max = 15$ and the first-step insert-check candidates are those borders located within the shadow area in Figure 6(a), i.e. $C = \{b_2, b_3, b_4\}$. Since in C, b_4 has $d_k(b_i) = dk\_max$, b_4 is removed from C and included into the must-check candidate $M = \{b_4\}$. In the second step, $dk\_max = 9$, which equals to $d_k(b_2)$. As shown in Figure 6(b), only b_3 is located in the shadow area and $d_k(b_3) \neq dk\_max$. Therefore, the set of must-check candidates is unchanged. Now $C = \{b_3\}$ and $dk\_max = 5$ for the third step. As shown in Figure 6(c), no border is located in the shadow area, leading to the empty set of C. The filtering process is thus terminated. Finally, we only need to check the shortest path related to the border in M, i.e., b_4.

4.2 KNN Update for Object Deletion

The maintenance operation for the object deletion is relatively simple as compared to the object insertion. Specifically, each object maintains the set of borders which involve the object as the KNN result. For deleting objects with the empty set of affected borders, the object deletion will not invoke any KNN recalculation. On the other hand, the deletion will invoke KNN recalculation for the affected borders.

Note that the nature of data skewness will make the number of HQgraphs is much smaller than the number of leaf subgraphs. Moreover, reducing the number of borders in HQgraphs is the goal of graph partitioning methods. We generally have a small set of borders with precomputed KNN, indicating that the number of KNN recalculation from the deletion is small and the overhead is acceptable.

5. PERFORMANCE STUDIES

In this section, we evaluate the performance of SQUARE by checking (1) index overhead (2) KNN query performance, and (3) update overhead. We used three real road networks: CA, NA, and SF, obtained from [14][15]. These datasets are widely utilized to evaluate the query performance [13]. Specifically, CA represents California road network containing 21,048 nodes and 21,693 edges. NA represents road network of North America with 175,813 nodes and 179,179 edges. SF represents San Francisco road network with 174,956 nodes and 223,001 edges. The simulation was implemented by Java1.5 in Windows 7, and experiments are executed on 2.4GHz Core 2 CPU and 4GB RAM. Note that we synthetically identify the total number of nodes belonging to HQgraph as 800 in all experiments. The value of δ is fixed by making the ratio (node number in a HQ-graph over node number in a leaf subgraph) be 0.2. We also implement INE [17] and ROAD [13] for the comparison.

5.1 Index Overhead

We first evaluate the index size and the construction time of all three approaches under different networks. Because

Network	Memory Usage (KB)		Construction Time (second)	
	ROAD	SQUARE	ROAD	SQUARE
CA	8907	8956 (0.55%)	39.192	39.581 (0.99%)
NA	74293	74343 (0.07%)	374.227	376.955 (0.73%)
SF	105106	105188 (0.08%)	760.59	768.183 (1%)

(a) various networks

k	Memory Usage (KB)		Construction Time (second)	
	UPA Hierarchy	HQgraph with KNN	UPA Hierarchy	HQgraph with KNN
1	8907	36 (0.4%)	28.89	0.26 (0.89%)
5		56 (0.62%)		0.4 (1.37%)
10		69 (0.77%)		0.62 (2.1%)
15		88 (0.98%)		0.71 (2.4%)
20		105 (1.17%)		0.86 (2.89%)

(b) various k on SQUARE index

Figure 7: Evaluation of the index overhead

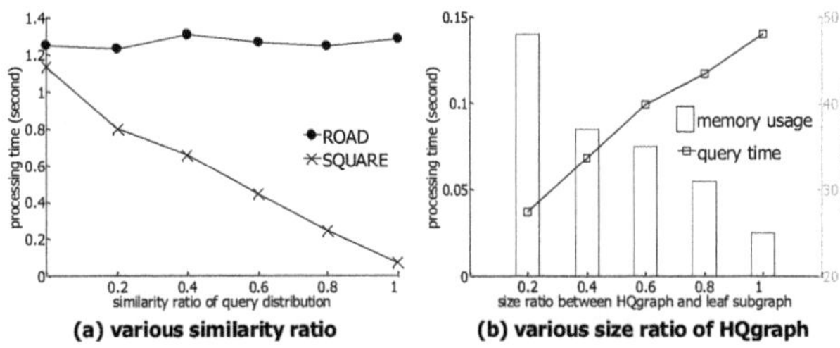

Figure 8: Evaluation of varying parameters in SQUARE.

the index overhead of INE is relatively smaller than other two methods, we only compare the results of ROAD and SQUARE. Figure 7(a) reveals the results with respect to the memory usage and the construction time in three data sets. We also show the cardinality ratios. In column 3, the ratio means the difference in memory usage between SQUARE and ROAD over the memory usage of ROAD. In column 4, the ratio represents the difference in index construction time between SQUARE and ROAD over the index construction time of ROAD. As shown, the memory usage and construction time increase as the size of road networks increases. Note that the numbers of nodes in NA and SF are similar and the road network of SF is more complicated. More memory and time are required to construct the index structure in the SF case. We can also observe that the extra overhead of SQUARE is relatively small as compared to ROAD. SQUARE only requires small resources to keep additional information which can facilitate the KNN search.

Figure 7(b) shows the effect of varying k on the index size and construction time of SQUARE. The cardinality ratios (i.e., the memory usage of HQgraph over the memory usage of UPA hierarchy, and the construction time of HQgraph over the construction time of UPA hierarchy) are specified in columns 3 and 5. We first observe that the memory usage and index construction increase as k increases. The increase is caused by the precomputed KNN in HQgraph. Moreover, we can find that the overhead of precomputed KNN is affordable even when k is large. The experimental results on the index overhead demonstrate that the overhead of the index in the SQUARE framework is acceptable.

5.2 KNN Query Performance

Before evaluating the query performance of all approaches, we first discuss the parameter settings in SQUARE. In Figure 8(a), we show the query processing time in terms of varying the similarity ratio of query distribution in the evaluated query sequence. The similarity ratio is the number of queries issued at HQgraphs over the total number of queries in the query sequence. One means all queries are issued at HQgraphs, whereas zero means all queries are issued at non-HQgraphs. To compare the performance of SQUARE and ROAD, we apply the same query sequence to these two approaches. As expected, the query processing time significantly decreases when the similarity ratio increases in SQUARE. Clearly, the figure illustrates that if the distribution of following queries is close to that in the history query logs, the query performance of SQUARE is extremely efficient as compared to ROAD. Note that ROAD does not take the object distribution into consideration during the index construction, thus leading to the query performance orthogonal to the query behavior.

We then examine the effect of different maximum sizes of HQgraphs, and the result is shown in Figure 8(b). The size of leaf subgraphs for CA is close to 80. In the figure, the cardinality ratio in x-axis is the size of a HQgraph over the size of leaf subgraph, which varies from 0.2 to 1. The experimental results show that smaller HQgraphs has better performance while needs more memory storage.

We conduct experiments to evaluate the query performance of three algorithms over various k, various number of objects and various networks, respectively. The results are shown in Figure 9. We run the experiments on 1000 queries that are randomly generated and show the total query time in terms of CPU processing time. In Figure 9(a), the value of k varies from 1 to 30. It can be clearly found that, SQUARE outperforms ROAD and INE for various k setting, thus demonstrating its effectiveness of using precomputed KNN in HQgraphs. Figure 9(b) shows the results by varying object number from 50 to 900. As expected, SQUARE has the better performance. It is noted that we can observe that when the object number is larger than 300, INE outperforms ROAD. The reason is that the search space pruning in ROAD is decreased as the object number increases, since many subgraphs contain objects. In worse cases that each subgraph contains objects, the network traversal in ROAD is similar to INE, but ROAD needs extra traversal in the graph hierarchy. In contrast, queries in HQgraphs can be answered in the quasi-constant time in SQUARE, which is orthogonal to the impact of object counts, thus showing the robustness of SQUARE. We also show the query time on various networks in Figure 9(c). For better comparison, we construct the graph hierarchy of NA and SF networks by setting partition level to 5 and 6 to obtain almost equal size of leaf subgraphs as that generated in the CA network. INE has the worse performance as expected. In the SF data set, which contains extremely many edges, the cost of query processing time is high without the use of search space pruning. The experiment demonstrates the efficiency of search space pruning of ROAD and SQUARE in large networks. Node that SQUARE still has the better efficiency, showing the feasibility of HQgraphs in various network topologies.

5.3 Update Overhead

In this section, we measure the maintenance overhead caused by object update over different number of updates. We execute 1000 random queries and the number of object updates varies from 200 up to 1000 to observe the processing time of the query system, where the updates contain object insertion and object deletion. In Figure 10(a) the processing time of query time plus update time are shown. Although

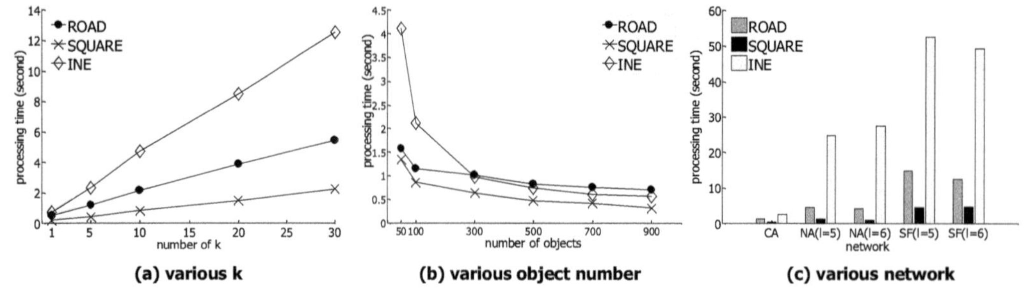

Figure 9: Evaluation of KNN query performance

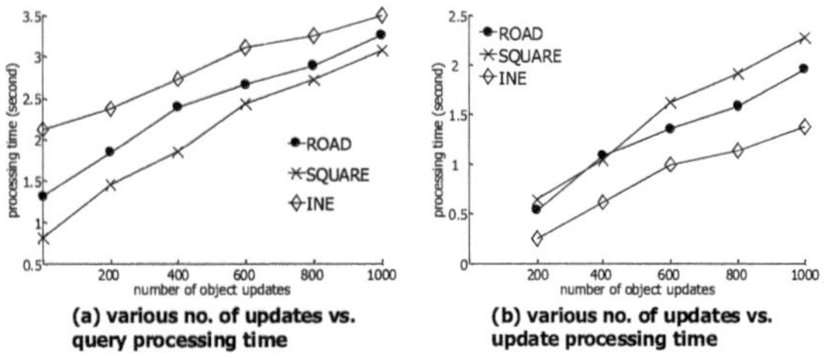

Figure 10: Evaluation of object update.

SQUARE pays for more time for updates, the processing time is still better to that of ROAD. In Figure 10(b), we show the update overhead as the number of updates increases. The update cost of SQUARE is still similar and comparable to that of ROAD. This demonstrates the efficiency of SQUARE while the objects are updated frequently.

6. CONCLUSIONS

We discussed in this paper an efficient search algorithm for KNN objects on road networks. The SQUARE algorithm is the first work considering the query patterns. Specifically, SQUARE is devised based on the well-known power-law phenomenon, which states that 80% queries will be roughly issued within 20% regions, i.e., hot query regions. As such, SQUARE especially maintains the KNN information relative to hot query regions which contain frequent queries, and queries issued within such regions can be answered in the quasi-constant time. In addition to its high query efficiency, the SQUARE algorithm can also handle the issue of data updates. The maintenance overhead is comparable to that of the state-of-the-art algorithm. As validated by our empirical studies, SQUARE can efficiently obtain the update-to-date KNN set, showing its prominent advantage of being an component of online LBS applications.

7. ACKNOWLEDGEMENTS

This paper was supported in part by National Science Council of Taiwan under Contract NSC 97-2221-E-002-172-MY3.

8. REFERENCES

[1] H.-J. Cho and C.-W. Chung. An Efficient and Scalable Approach to CNN Queries in a Road Network. Proc. of VLDB, 2005.

[2] E. W. Dijkstra. A note on two problems in connexion with graphs. NUMERISCHE MATHEMATIK, 1959.

[3] C. Faloutsos. Next Generation Data Mining Tools: Power Laws and Self-similarity for Graphs, Streams and Traditional Data. ECML, 2003.

[4] H. Hu, D. L. Lee, and V. C. S. Lee. Distance Indexing on Road Networks. Proc. of VLDB, 2006.

[5] H. Hu, D. L. Lee, and J. Xu. Fast Nearest Neighbor Search on Road Networks. Proc. of EDBT, 2006.

[6] X. Huang, C.S. Jensen, and S. Saltenis. The Island Approach to Nearest Neighbor Querying in Spatial Networks. Proc. of SSTD, 2005.

[7] X. Huang, C.S. Jensen, and S. Saltenis. Multiple k Nearest Neighbor Query Processing in Spatial Network Databases. Proc. of ADBIS, 2006.

[8] G. Karypis and V. Kumar. A Fast and Highly Quality Multilevel Scheme for Partitioning Irregular Graphs. SIAM Journal on Scientific Computing, 1999.

[9] B. Kernighan and S. Lin. An Efficient Heuristic Procedure for Partitioning Graphs. Bell Systems Technical Journal, 1970.

[10] R. Koch. The 80/20 Principle: The Secret of Achieving More With Less. Nicholas Brealey Publishing, 1998.

[11] M. Kolahdouzan and C. Shahabi. Voronoi-based k Nearest Neighbor Search for Spatial Network Databases. Proc. of VLDB, 2004.

[12] K. C.K. Lee, W.-C. Lee, B. Zheng, and Y. Tian. ROAD: A New Spatial Object Search Framework for Road Networks. IEEE Trans. on Know. and Data Engineering, 2010.

[13] Ken C.K. Lee, W.-C. Lee, and B. Zheng. Fast Object Search on Road Networks. Proc. of EDBT, 2009.

[14] F. Li. Real Datasets for Spatial Databases: Road Networks and Points of Interest. http://www.cs.fsu.edu/ lifeifei/SpatialDataset.htm.

[15] F. Li, D. Cheng, M. Hadjieleftheriou, G. Kollios, and S. Teng. On Trip Planning Queries in Spatial Databases. SSTD, 2005.

[16] C. R. Palmer and C. Faloutsos. Density Biased Sampling: An Improved Method for Data Mining and Clustering. Proc. of SIGMOD, 2000.

[17] D. Papadias, J. Zhang, N. Mamoulis, and Y. Tao. Query Processing in Spatial Network Databases. Proc. of VLDB, 2003.

[18] H. Samet, J. Sankaranarayanan, and H. Alborzi. Scalable Network Distance Browsing in Spatial Databases. Proc. of the ACM SIGMOD, 2008.

[19] Z. Song and N. Roussopoulos. K-Nearest Neighbor Search for Moving Query Point. Proc. of SSTD, 2001.

[20] J. Zhang, M. Zhu, D. Papadias, Y. Tao, and D. L. Lee. Location-based Spatial Queries. Proc. of the ACM SIGMOD, 2003.

[21] G.K. Zipf. Human Behavior and the Principle of Least Effort. Addison-Wesley Press, 1949.

Toward Traffic-Driven Location-Based Web Search

Zhiyuan Cheng, James Caverlee, Krishna Y. Kamath, and Kyumin Lee
Department of Computer Science and Engineering
Texas A&M University
College Station, TX, USA
(zcheng, caverlee, kykamath, kyumin)@cse.tamu.edu

ABSTRACT

The emergence of location sharing services is rapidly accelerating the convergence of our online and offline activities. In one direction, Foursquare, Google Latitude, Facebook Places, and related services are enriching real-world venues with the social and semantic connections among online users. In analogy to how clickstreams have been successfully incorporated into traditional web ranking based on content and link analysis, we propose to mine traffic patterns revealed through location sharing services to augment traditional location-based search. Concretely, we study location-based traffic patterns revealed through location sharing services and find that these traffic patterns can identify semantically related locations. Based on this observation, we propose and evaluate a traffic-driven location clustering algorithm that can group semantically related locations with high confidence. Through experimental study of 12 million locations from Foursquare, we extend this result through supervised location categorization, wherein traffic patterns can be used to accurately predict the semantic category of uncategorized locations. Based on these results, we show how traffic-driven semantic organization of locations may be naturally incorporated into location-based web search.

Categories and Subject Descriptors

H.2.8 [**Database Management**]: Database Application—*Data mining*; H.3.3 [**Information Storage and Retrieval**]: Information Search and Retrieval; J.4 [**Computer Application**]: Social and Behavioral Sciences

General Terms

Algorithms, Experimentation

Keywords

Location-based search, traffic pattern, checkin, spatio-temporal data mining

1. INTRODUCTION

After the explosive growth of on-line social networks like Facebook and Twitter, we are beginning to see a similar rise in location sharing services. These services – like Foursquare, Google Latitude, Facebook Places, among many others – allow users to voluntarily annotate the real world with "checkins" indicating the specific time that a user was at a particular location, often through a smartphone application. In the aggregate, these checkins – along with other user-generated descriptors supported by these services like tags, ratings, and comments – have resulted in billions of explicit "geo-semantic" markers that link people, places, and their activities. As these services continue to grow, there are great opportunities for extremely granular temporal and spatial mining of human mobility, as well as new mobile+location-based services, augmented traffic forecasting, and urban planning.

In this paper, we propose one direction in which location-sharing services may have strong impact – in augmenting traditional location-based web search. Location-based web search (also known as local search) has drawn intensive attention in both industry (Google Maps, Yelp, Yahoo! Local, and Yellow Pages), and the academic community (e.g., [2, 6, 17]). Nearly all the current location-based search systems typically provide rankings for nearby venues based on a user's query and current location. For example, a local search for "coffee" may return a map and an associated ranked list of nearby coffee shops and coffee bean wholesalers. Some of the factors that location-based search engines use for ranking venues in response to a query include: (i) the distance between the user and the target venue; (ii) category analysis of venues (e.g., to group all coffeeshops in a pre-processing step); (iii) the overall ratings for the venue (which are often available for commercial places of business like restaurants); (iv) query and click popularity of the venue's associated web page (e.g., Starbucks may be considered more popular from its web presence than a local coffee shop); (v) reputation of the location via PageRank-style link analysis of the web graph; and (vi) content-based relevance between the query and the location's description (e.g., via information retrieval similarity between the query and a summary of the venue on Yelp or the content from a location's web presence).

In many ways analogous to how clickstreams [11, 26, 5] have been successfully incorporated into traditional search systems based on content similarity [20] and link analysis [12] by connecting real-world user actions (clicks) to relevance, this paper proposes that the *temporal dynamics embedded in the checkins* from location sharing services have great potential to augment traditional location-based search systems by connecting real-world actions (checkins) to relevance. To illustrate:

- Mike wants to make a reservation for a tennis court on Saturday afternoon so that he can teach his son to play tennis without being disturbed by nearby players. Hence, a local search for "tennis courts" could be augmented with the temporal dynamics mined from location-sharing services to indicate which courts are at off-peak times in terms of player traffic.
- Tina and her friends are going to celebrate their graduation on a Thursday evening and are looking for late-night hot spots. Which local bars are at-peak in terms of traffic? Or will be peaking by the time Tina and her friends arrive?
- John plays a lot of basketball. He usually goes to Williams Park during Wednesday early evening, and Saturday afternoon, which are both free time for him and peak times for other players to get together and play basketball. Suppose John moves to a new neighborhood and wants to find places nearby that have similar traffic patterns, so that he can meet new friends there and play basketball. A traffic-driven location-based search can also easily handle this kind of queries by returning semantically correlated venues with similar traffic patterns.

In all three cases, factors traditionally considered for location-based web search – like distance, overall venue reputation and popularity – are less important than fine-grained temporal dynamics of the traffic patterns of the target venues. Hence, there is an opportunity to augment these traditional approaches with real-world user actions revealed through location sharing services.

In this paper, we propose to study the potential and viability of mining traffic patterns revealed through location sharing services to augment traditional location-based search. As a first step, we propose to model each venue by a *traffic pattern* – essentially a frequency function corresponding to each venue. Two essential and open questions are (i) whether such a model, as compared to traditional content-based and popularity-based models of location-based search, encodes semantically meaningful information; and (ii) whether there is wide enough coverage of location sharing services to support large-scale application of traffic patterns to location-based search. With these questions in mind, this paper makes the following contributions:

- First, we present in this paper a large-scale study of every venue in Foursquare, totaling 12 million unique venues annotated by users of Foursquare via checkins. Based on this study, we propose and evaluate a *traffic pattern*-based model of venues through an investigation of the location-based traffic patterns mined from 22 million checkins from Foursquare and other location sharing services.
- Second, we propose a measure of semantic correlation across venues for organizing venues according to the traffic patterns revealed through location sharing services. Based on this measure, we propose and evaluate a traffic-driven location clustering algorithm that can group semantically related locations with a best-effort performance of F1-Measure 0.675, and Purity 0.764, a critical function for a location-based search engine.
- Third, we observe significant sparsity of checkin data for venues on the "long tail", and so we propose and evaluate a traffic pattern-driven approach for supervised location categorization, wherein traffic patterns can be used to accurately predict the semantic category of uncategorized locations with a F1-Measure of almost 0.8.
- Finally, based on these results, we show how traffic-driven semantic organization of locations may be naturally incorporated into location-based web search through two example scenarios.

2. RELATED WORK

Increasing focus has been put on location sharing services in recent years. Ye et al. [28] proposed friend-based collaborative filtering algorithms to recommend locations utilizing a dataset scraped from Foursquare; Lindqvist et al. [15] analyzed how and why people use location sharing services; Cheng et al. [3] explored human mobility patterns and factors that affect the mobility patterns based on a sampled dataset from location sharing services; and Noulas et al. [18] analyzed user checkin dynamics, and user activities in location sharing services. Compared to these previous studies, this paper focuses on analyzing the temporal traffic patterns revealed from location sharing services and how the traffic patterns can be utilized to enhance traditional location-based search.

Several studies have analyzed the temporal dynamics of on-line social networks and other web corpuses. Golder et al. [10] explored the temporal dynamics associated with on-line social tagging activities. Researchers in [13] studied how queries, their associated documents, and the query intent change over time by analyzing query log data. Temporal evidence was incorporated into models of semantic relatedness for words in [19]. Yang et al. [27] proposed a clustering algorithm that groups temporal patterns associated with online content, and studied how the popularity of the content grows and fades over time. A temporal correlation measure was introduced and applied to study semantic similarity between queries by Chien et al. [4].

Related to our temporal model of traffic patterns, in terms of time series data analysis, Fu [8] provides comprehensive summary on the existing time series data mining literature including representation, indexing, similarity measure, segmentation, visualization and mining. A numerosity reduction component was proposed by Xi et al. [25] and proved to speed up the best performing classifier of one-nearest-neighbor with Dynamic Time Warping (DTW). [14] provided a survey for techniques in time-series data clustering, and corresponding evaluation metrics.

Location-based web search has drawn intensive attention in both industry (Google Maps, Yelp, Yahoo! Local, and Yellow Pages), and the academic community. Early research efforts (e.g., [2, 6, 17]) mainly focused on the extraction of geographic information from page content and structure. Several studies [9, 1, 21] showed that more than one fifth of the queries in general web search systems were geographical relevant queries. Geotagging and gazeteers have been widely used in [16, 22, 23] to augment location-based web search. Watters and Amoudi [24] proposed a method to assign location coordinates to URLs, and a corresponding framework for location-based ranking of search results.

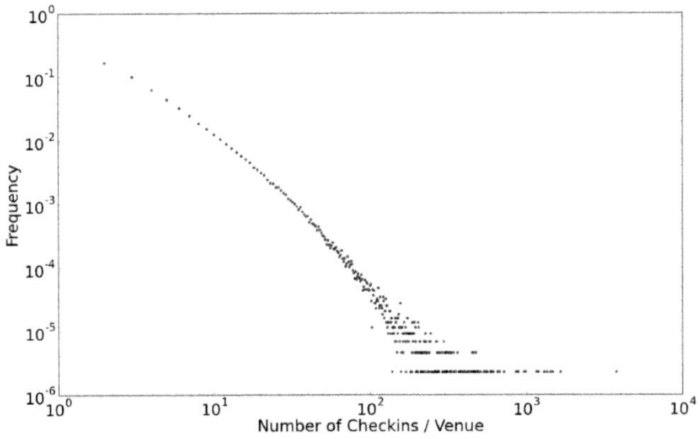

Figure 1: Distribution of # of Checkins Per Venue

3. LOCATION SHARING SERVICES

In this section, we introduce the location sharing service data, present our sampling strategy, and provide a characterization of the venue data collected from Foursquare.

3.1 Sampling Checkin Data

To start with, firstly we need a set of checkins. While Foursquare, Facebook Places, and other related location sharing services are rich resources, all restrict access to a user's immediate social circle and hence are unavailable for public sampling. Hence, we adopt a data collection technique that relies on sampling location sharing status updates from the public Twitter feed. While users of location sharing services in general and the subset who choose to advertise their location via Twitter may not be a representative sample, these status updates are inherently public (mitigating concerns over privacy violations that would arise from mining services like Facebook Places) and offer a rich vein of checkin data. Specifically, we monitor Twitter's public streaming API and search API from October 2010 to January 2011, and collected a set of more than 22 million checkins. Worth mentioning, our data is available on-line at link.

Each checkin contains a fine-granularity location (latitude and longitude) and a timestamp. More than 62% (~14 million) of the checkins are associated with a venue, and in total 603,796 venues are referenced. Note that since each venue has on average only ~23 checkins (with a skewed distribution, where some venues are heavily "checked in" to, but the majority have only a handful of checkins as plotted in Figure 1), we aggregate all checkins for venues based on the venue name (e.g., grouping all instances of "Starbucks") for the analysis in the rest of the paper. Venues in the set may be associated with varying degrees of spatial granularity based on the bounding box linked to the venue – from country to province / state to city to district and finally to points-of-interest. In this paper, we mainly focus on the checkins corresponding with the 515,862 point-of-interest venues, each of which is finely geo-labeled with a latitude and longitude.

3.2 Crawling Foursquare Venues

Each venue posted to Twitter has a corresponding "venue page" hosted by Foursquare. To retrieve more information about the venues, we crawled the entire Foursquare-sphere, resulting in nearly 20 million "venue pages" in HTML format. Based on our best-effort parser, we successfully parse 12,677,314 html pages of venues. Specifically, each venue is stored as the tuple *venue(venueID) = {venueID, name, latitude, longitude, address, city, region, postal_code, categories, tags}* An example tuple of a venue is: *venue(877) = {877, "once upon a tart", 40.7267, -74.0019, "135 sullivan st", "new york", "ny", 10012, "sandwiches, salad, bakery", "salads, roast pork sandwich, strawberry lemonade ginger iced tea, tarts, desserts"}*.

Table 1: Distribution of Venue Categories

Category	Percentage	# of Venues
Home, Work and Other	31.7%	2,457,172
Food	24.3%	1,886,875
Shop	17.1%	1,329,185
Travel Spot	7.0%	541,482
Great Outdoors	6.4%	493,635
Nightlife Spot	5.7%	438,400
Arts & Entertainment	4.3%	334,700
College & University	3.5%	271,825

3.2.1 *Venue Characterization*

Among the 12 million venues, 56.4% (i.e., 7,147,755) of the venues are voluntarily assigned by users of Foursquare at least a single category. And there are 7,753,274 occurrences of 833 unique categories identified in the dataset. Based on Foursquare's 3-level categorization system, we group the 833 categories into 8 coarse groups: Arts & Entertainment, College & University, Food, Great Outdoors, Home, Work and Other, Nightlife Spot, Shop, and Travel Spot. The distribution of the eight categories is listed in Table 1. Among the categorized venues, the category of Home, Work and Other presents almost one third (31.7%) of the venues. Venues in the category of Food (24.3%) and the category of Shop (17.1%) are also popular. The other five categories (Travel Spot, Great Outdoors, Nightlife Spot, Arts & Entertainment, and College & University) possess similar percentages (around 5% for each) in the dataset.

Besides the category information for venues, about 7.8% (i.e., 989,281) of the venues are labeled with at least a single tag. The tags are user-generated keywords posted by users of the location sharing service. Based on inspection, tags typically contain information such as category of the venue (e.g., coffee, food, and bar); items provided by the venue (e.g., burgers, flu shot, and long island iced tea); features of the venue (e.g., free wifi, 24 hrs, and pet friendly); location of the venue (e.g., houston downtown, bridge street); and users' comments for the venue (e.g., awesome, good deal, and great food). Each of the tagged venues is assigned with an average of 3.37 tags. Different from the categorization system, the tagging feature in Foursquare gives users more freedom to generate appropriate tags. In total, we find 615,457 unique tags that are collectively used a total of 3,329,641 times across all venues.

Together, these user-assigned tags and the top-level categories provide descriptive information about specific venues and provide clues to study the semantic correlation between venues. Recall that one of the key pre-processing steps in location-based search is category analysis of venues – to group together semantically-related venues – but in isolation we can see that the category assignments are fairly sparse (56%) and at a coarse-level; similarly, the tag information is even sparses (8% of all venues), and both tags and categories provide only *descriptive* information about the venues. Our goal in the rest of the paper is to consider the traffic-driven temporal patterns revealed through checkins to augment this semantic grouping based on the real-world behaviors of users of these services.

4. EXPLORING SEMANTIC CORRELATION BETWEEN VENUES

In this and the following two sections, we begin an exploration of the temporal dynamics of venues as revealed through location sharing services. Given the large-scale checkin data, we propose to model venues through traffic-based patterns and seek to answer the following questions:

- Can we measure semantic correlation between venues based on associated traffic patterns?
- Can we cluster venues into semantically correlated groups based on traffic patterns?
- Can we use traffic patterns to accurately predict the semantic category for uncategorized locations?

We begin in this section by defining a traffic pattern and its frequency function. We discuss metrics to measure semantic similarity between traffic patterns, and we apply the temporal correlation measure to quantify the semantic relatedness between traffic patterns. Based on this initial study, we identify semantically correlated groups of venues based on measuring the pairwise temporal correlation between the venues' associated traffic patterns.

4.1 Modeling Venues

A **Traffic Pattern** (T Pattern) T for a venue over n time units is defined as the temporal dynamic of checkins during the time period. It can be measured by its **Frequency Function** F_T formally defined as $F_T = (f_{t_1}, f_{t_2}, ..., f_{t_n})$, in which f_{t_i} is the frequency for time unit t_i over the whole series of T. More specifically, for each venue, we generate a daily mean traffic pattern and a weekly mean traffic pattern given the timestamps of checkins in the venue. The **Daily (Mean) Traffic Pattern** contains 24 time units in which each of the time unit represents an hour in a day. Similarly, the **Weekly (Mean) Traffic Pattern** contains 70 time units in which each unit represents one tenth of a day. Examples of daily traffic pattern and weekly traffic pattern for Walmart are plotted in Figure 2 and Figure 3 respectively. The daily t pattern shows that customers tend to go shopping in Walmart in the afternoon and early evening, and the weekly t pattern indicates that there is a bigger crowd at Walmart over the weekends than on weekdays.

4.2 Temporal Similarity Measures

Given a traffic pattern for a venue, can we identify related venues based solely on this pattern? This is an important step for semantically grouping venues for improved location-based search. But perhaps traffic patterns do not vary much from venue to venue, meaning that traffic patterns could have only limited impact.

The most straightforward similarity measures for time-series data are Euclidean Distance [7] and its variants based on the common $L_p - norms$ (L_1 – Manhattan Distance, and L_2 – Euclidean Distance). These metrics can be easily implemented and are surprisingly competitive with other complex measures with a large training set. However, these distance measures are sensitive to noise and misalignments

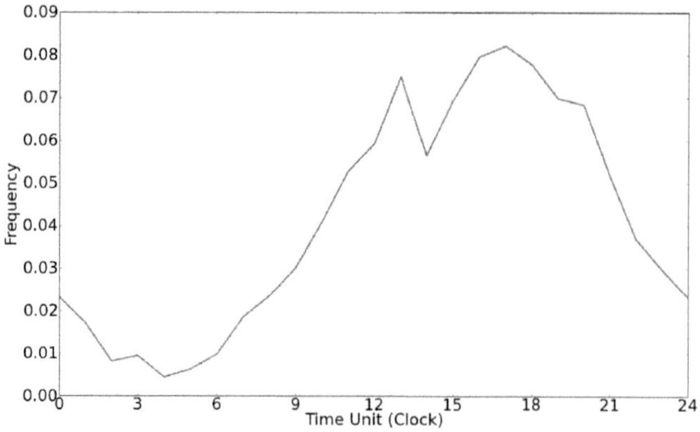

Figure 2: Daily Traffic Pattern for Walmart

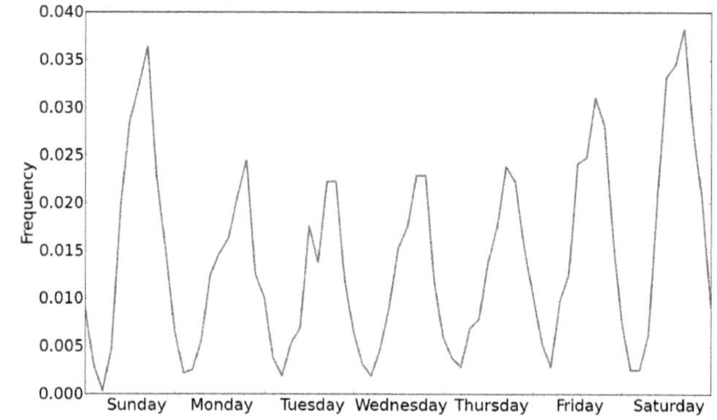

Figure 3: Weekly Traffic Pattern for Walmart

in time. Another effective temporal correlation measure is a temporally-grounded variation of the correlation coefficient. Given two traffic patterns Tp, Tq and their frequency functions F_{Tp} and F_{Tq}, the temporal correlation $T_{Corr}(F_{Tp}, F_{Tq})$ between the two traffic patterns Tp and Tq is:

$$T_{Corr}(F_{Tp}, F_{Tq}) = \frac{1}{n}\sum_i \left(\frac{f_{tp_i} - \mu(F_{Tp})}{\sigma(F_{Tp})}\right)\left(\frac{f_{tq_i} - \mu(F_{Tq})}{\sigma(F_{Tq})}\right)$$

where $\mu(F_{Tp})$, $\mu(F_{Tp})$ are the mean frequencies, and $\sigma(F_{Tp})$, $\sigma(F_{Tq})$ are the standard deviations for the two traffic patterns Tp and Tq. A version of this same metric was shown to be effective by Chien et al. [4] for measuring the similarity of search engine queries by comparing their frequency functions.

4.3 Mining Semantic Correlation between Venues

To study the semantic correlation between venues based on their traffic patterns, we sample a set of 271 venues from the checkins dataset with a criteria of at least 100 branches and 100 checkins to ensure the density of the traffic patterns. For each of the 271 venues, we retrieve both a mean daily traffic pattern and a mean weekly traffic pattern to capture their traffic. Then, we calculate the pairwise temporal similarity for all the pairs in the 271 venues set. After sorting the pairs of venues based on the descending order of temporal correlation measure, we find quite a few interesting pairs of venues that have obvious semantic correlation. Using the results for calculations based on daily mean traffic patterns only, we show the top-10 similar pairs of venues in Table 2. Each pair of venues in the table has obvious se-

Table 2: Top Pairs with Highest Temporal Correlation

Pair of Venues	Correlation
Target – Borders	0.949
Walgreens – CVS Pharmacy	0.947
Panda Express – Five Guys Burgers and Fries	0.947
Pizza Hut – California Pizza Kitchen	0.947
Chipotle – Five Guys Burgers and Fries	0.946
Staples – Apple Store	0.946
Target – Barnes & Noble	0.946
Subway – Jason's Deli	0.945
Chili's – Ruby Tuesday	0.944
Starbucks – Caribou Coffee	0.944

mantic correlation: both "Walgreens" and "CVS Pharmacy" are 24 hour pharmacy stores; both "Subway" and "Jason's Deli" are chain fast food restaurants; and both "Starbucks" and "Caribou Coffee" are coffee shops. The results listed in the table clearly indicate that the traffic pattern of a venue reveals its semantic category, and the temporal correlation between traffic patterns of two venues can help measure the semantic relatedness between venues.

Having all pairwise temporal similarities between venues, we are also interested to see whether we can find inherent groups of venues that belong to the same semantic category. For example, do all the coffee shops have similar temporal traffic patterns? We model the venues and temporal similarities as vertices and weights for edges in a graph. An edge between two vertices (venues) exists when the temporal correlation between traffic patterns of the two venues exceeds a pre-defined threshold. In this way, a graph modeling the semantic relationship between venues is generated. Instead of focusing on the whole graph itself, we are more interested in the strong connected components in the graph, which are potential candidates for semantic categories of venues.

As an example, when we set the pre-defined threshold for minimum temporal similarity as 0.93, a graph with 68 vertices, and 12 strong connected components is generated. Six example components are plotted in Figure 4. One component (plotted in Figure 4(a)) contains "Jason's Deli", "McAlister's Deli", "Qdoba Mexican Grill", "Subway", and "Zaxby's" which are all chain restaurants. The traffic patterns of the "steakhouse" component is displayed in Figure 4(b). Both the sub restaurants and the steakhouses have two peaks (lunch time and dinner time), though the frequencies differ dramatically. The major crowd arrives at sandwich shops at noon to grab lunch, while many more people choose to have steaks for dinner rather than lunch. Similar comparisons are plotted in Figure 4(c) and Figure 4(d), in which traffic patterns for the component of coffee shops and ice cream shops are featured respectively. People buy coffee in the early morning, and the busyness for the coffee shops gradually decreases during the day. However, people tend to have ice cream in the afternoon, and the ice cream shops are especially crowded in the early evening after dinner. Figure 4(e) and Figure 4(f) plot the components corresponding to office supply stores, and to a component of book store and pharmacies. Both the components have quite similar traffic patterns, and traffic patterns for book stores and pharmacies decrease from their peaks slower than the traffic patterns for the group of office supply stores. The other strong connected components are also highly semantically connected: there is a group of pizza restaurants, a group of juice shops, a group of chained family restaurants, and two groups of fast food restaurants. All the examples validate our hypothesis that measuring temporal correlation between traffic patterns can identify groups of venues that are semantically connected.

5. CLUSTERING VENUES

Motivated by the results shown in last section, a natural step to utilize the traffic patterns is to group the venues into similar categories. For example, clustering the traffic patterns may lead to clusters of categorized groups of venues, such as "coffee shops", "steakhouses", "hotels", and "gyms". Specifically, in this section, we apply several different clustering methods and different similarity metrics to cluster the venues based on features of traffic patterns.

5.1 Methods

The graph modeling method we used in mining the semantically group of venues is one way to cluster the venues. However, it heavily relies on the value of the pre-defined correlation threshold, and it is difficult to control the number of strong connected components by tuning the threshold. Thus, in this section, we apply K-means and EM clustering algorithm for grouping the venues given their traffic patterns. We apply features of daily traffic pattern, weekly traffic pattern, and daily + weekly traffic pattern respectively in clustering the venues. We also explore using the tags for the venues to group the venues into semantically correlated categories.

5.2 Experimental Setup

To evaluate the clustering results, a ground truth category is retrieved for each of the venues from the venues dataset collected from Foursquare. For K-means algorithm, we apply Euclidean Distance, Manhattan Distance, and Temporal Distance. Worth mentioning, the temporal correlation discussed earlier ranges between -1 and 1, with higher values indicating higher correlation. Since clustering requires a distance measure, we rescale the temporal correlation to define a metric **Temporal Distance**, where $T_{Dist} = 1.0 - \frac{T_{Corr}+1}{2}$. This temporal distance ranges between 0 and 1, with larger values indicating less similarity (greater distance). In evaluating the results for the clustering, we use the F1-Measure and Purity, which are both standard metrics to evaluate the quality of a clustering. Specifically, F1-Measure balances both the precision and recall of clustering. Purity measures the ratio of the total number of correctly clustered venues over the total number of venues.

Additionally, four test sets are generated to evaluate the clusters based on the criteria of minimum number of checkins (500+, 300+, 200+, and 100+) for each venue. Venues with more checkins are expected to have denser traffic patterns, and thus contain stronger indication of semantic information. The four test sets include 148, 242, 383, 585 venues respectively. For each venue, two feature sets are generated: traffic patterns, and vector space models generated from tags. For the traffic patterns, we use daily traffic pattern, weekly traffic pattern, and daily plus weekly traffic pattern respectively. For the vector space models, we retrieve tags for the venues from the venue dataset, and generate features of tf, idf, and tf-idf values for the tags respectively. To normalize the features, we apply L2 normalization on both vectors of traffic patterns and for the vector space model. In the four testsets, only venues of the categories "Food", "Shop", "Home, Work, and Other", and "Travel Spot" (among the eight categories in categorization

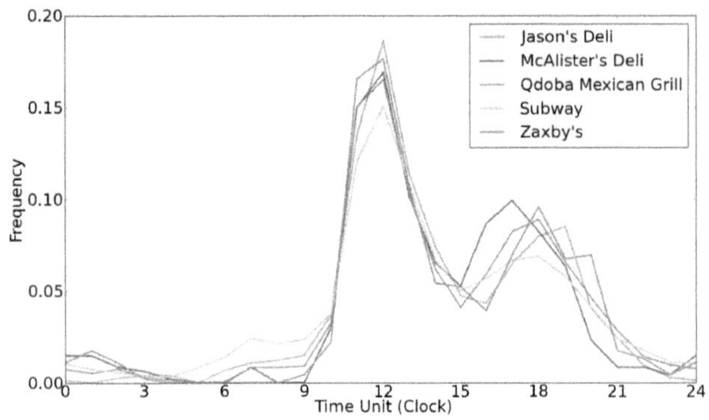

(a) Comparison between T Patterns of "Sub" Shops

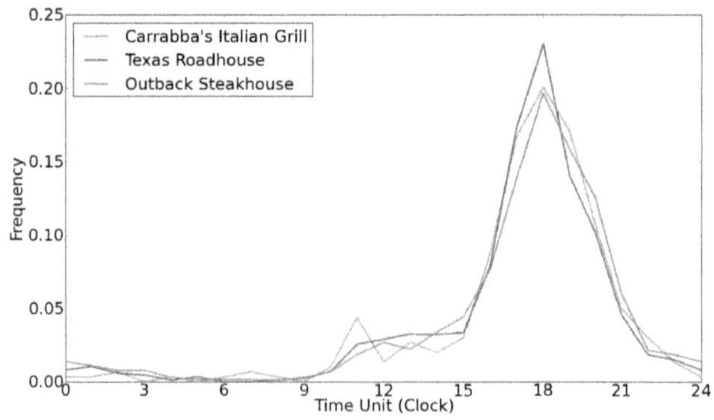

(b) Comparison between T Patterns of "Steakhouses"

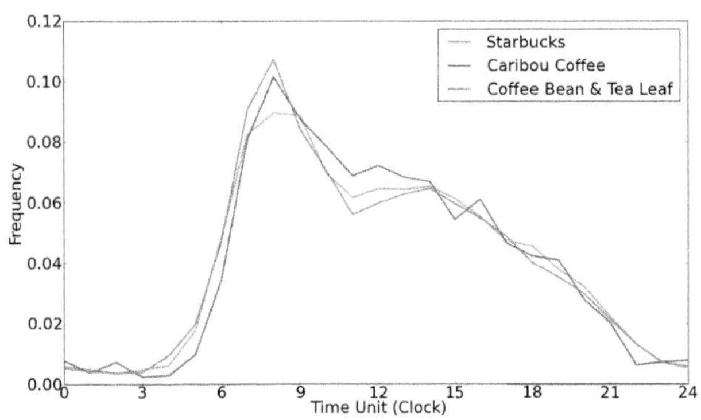

(c) Comparison between T Patterns of "Coffee" Shops

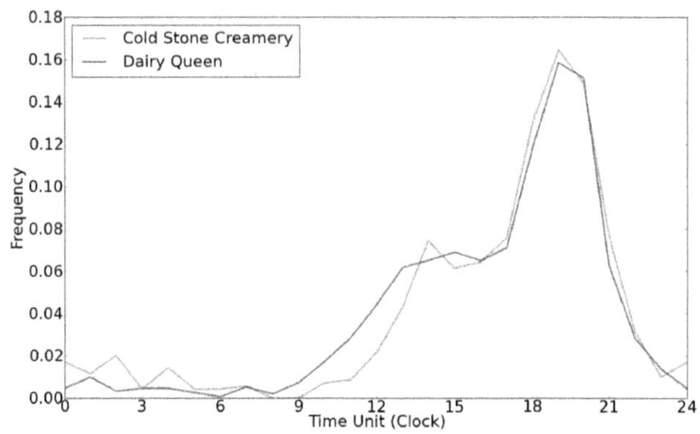

(d) Comparison between T Patterns of "Ice Cream" Shops

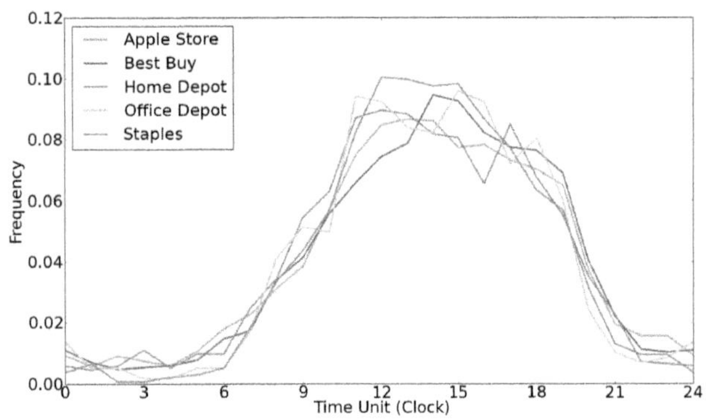

(e) Comparison between T Patterns of "Office Supply Stores"

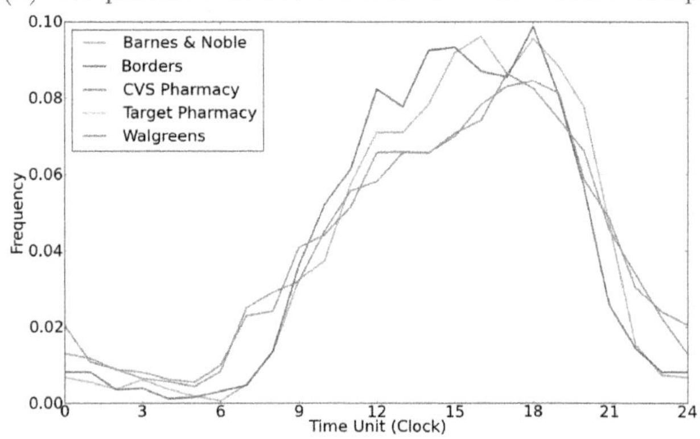

(f) Comparison between T Patterns of "Book Stores and Pharmacies"

Figure 4: Comparisons between T Patterns in Different Strong Connected Groups

system of Foursquare) have sufficient checkins. Thus, in both K-means and EM algorithm, we pre-specify the number of clusters to be 4.

5.3 Experimental Results

Clustering with the Traffic Patterns:
Results for K-means and EM algorithms evaluated by F1-Measure and Purity using the four test sets are listed in Table 3. In most of the cases, clustering with the daily traffic pattern itself performs the best. Combining both daily and weekly traffic patterns performs better than using weekly traffic pattern alone. Among combination of method and metric, K-means plus Temporal Distance performs the best with a significant increase (around 15% to 20% increase) over K-means with the other two metrics, as well as the EM algorithm. K-means with Manhattan Distance performs better than K-means with Euclidean Distance. And they both outperform the EM algorithm when the venues have the sufficient checkins. However EM algorithms performs competitively when the venues have fewer checkins.

The best performing methods and their results are extracted from Table 3 and plotted in Figure 5. As we can see from Figure 5, generally, test sets with denser traffic patterns reach better performance in F1-Measure, and Purity. Results for the dataset with least checkins suffer from lack of sufficient data in traffic patterns. We also observe that the dataset with the most checkins do not reach the best performance. This is partly due to the lack of number of venues (only 2) in the category of travel spots.

Clustering with the Vector Space Models: As men-

Table 3: Results for Traffic Pattern Clustering

Dataset	Features	Daily T Pattern		Weekly T Pattern		Daily + Weekly T Pattern	
	Method / Metric	F1-Measure	Purity	F1-Measure	Purity	F1-Measure	Purity
500+ Checkins Dataset	K-means + Euclidean	0.495	0.595	0.419	0.534	0.412	0.520
	K-means + Manhattan	0.502	0.608	0.442	0.554	0.451	0.574
	K-means + T Distance	0.539	0.608	0.603	**0.689**	**0.608**	0.635
	EM	0.424	0.541	0.43	0.554	0.416	0.534
300+ Checkins Dataset	K-means + Euclidean	0.427	0.504	0.465	0.533	0.466	0.562
	K-means + Manhattan	0.502	0.566	0.435	0.533	0.476	0.583
	K-means + T Distance	**0.675**	**0.764**	0.586	0.674	0.616	0.698
	EM	0.465	0.537	0.467	0.579	0.47	0.562
200+ Checkins Dataset	K-means + Euclidean	0.416	0.483	0.463	0.441	0.456	0.535
	K-means + Manhattan	0.498	0.527	0.446	0.504	0.477	0.548
	K-means + T Distance	**0.671**	**0.700**	0.566	0.621	0.527	0.585
	EM	0.482	0.512	0.412	0.452	0.408	0.446
100+ Checkins Dataset	K-means + Euclidean	0.415	0.525	0.435	0.535	0.427	0.444
	K-means + Manhattan	0.437	0.535	0.406	0.504	0.437	0.515
	K-means + T Distance	0.571	0.667	0.552	0.658	**0.599**	**0.706**
	EM	0.477	0.568	0.403	0.487	0.464	0.405

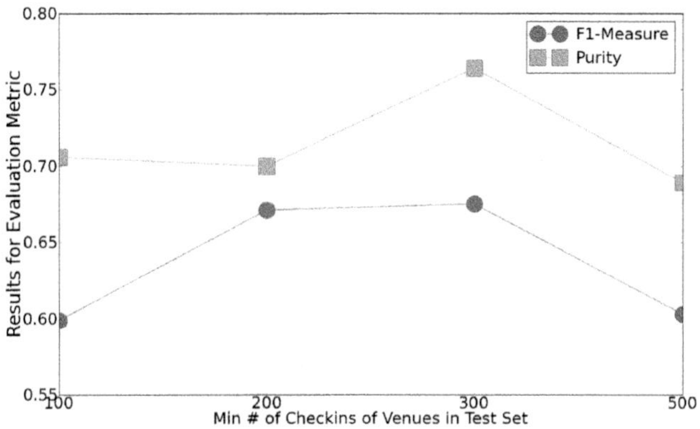

Figure 5: Comparison of Best Results over Different Test Sets

tioned, we retrieve tags for the venues in the four test sets from the venue dataset collected from Foursquare. We apply the same clustering methods using the features of vector space models (tf, idf, tf-idf) modeled from the tags respectively. However, for different methods over different training sets, all the venues tend to converge to a single large cluster, primarily due to the sparseness of the tags in the datasets.

Together, these results show that modeling venues by traffic patterns and using temporal correlation to measure venue similarity are viable alternatives to traditional content-based clustering methods.

6. SUPERVISED VENUE CATEGORIZATION

While clustering of venues by traffic-based temporal correlation can provide a foundation for organizing venues for improved location-based search, there is still the challenge of sparsity for venues on the "long tail". Hence, in this section, we propose and evaluate a traffic pattern-driven approach for supervised location categorization, wherein traffic patterns can be used to accurately predict the semantic category of uncategorized locations. Given a set of venues with known category labels, and their corresponding traffic patterns, are we able to train classifiers with the labeled set to categorize incoming venues with their corresponding traffic patterns? As in our study of clustering, we also consider an alternative tag-based model as a point-of-comparison.

6.1 Training Set and 10-Fold Cross Validation

The training set contains a set of the 271 most popular venues which all have at least 100 branches and over 100 checkins in the checkins dataset. As mentioned earlier, we retrieve the ground-truth labels for the venues from Foursquare venue data. The 271 venues are grouped into four categories (all belong to the category system mentioned before): Food; Home, Work & Other; Shop; and Travel Spot. We adopt the same two set of features as in the clustering work: traffic pattern (including daily traffic pattern weekly traffic pattern, and daily plus weekly traffic patterns), and vector space models (tf, idf, and tf-idf values) for tags associated to the venues.

We apply the features in training classifiers of Naive Bayes, 1NN (we iterate k from 1 to 5 for kNN, and 1NN always perform the best, so we fix k to 1 in the following experiments), AdaBoostM1, and SimpleCart. We also apply L2 normalization on both vectors of traffic patterns and for the vector space model. To evaluate the effectiveness of the classifiers, we use 10-fold cross validation and the F1-Measure.

Traffic Pattern Features:

Results for traffic pattern features are plotted in Figure 6. Using either daily traffic pattern or the weekly traffic pattern displays a strong indication of the category of the venue, reaching an F1-Measure higher than 0.8 with 1NN classifier. The other three classifiers – Naive Bayes, AdaBoostM1, and Simple Cart – seem incompatible with the time series data. Combining both daily traffic pattern and weekly traffic pattern gives a boost of 6.5% for Simple Cart, 1.7% for 1NN, and 0.6% for Naive Bayes. Overall, the 1NN classifier still performs best with an F1-Measure of 0.820 slightly above AdaBoostM1 and SimpleCart with a best F1-Measure of 0.819. These results agree with the observations in Xi et al.'s work [25] that 1NN classifier has excellent performance in time-series classification.

Vector Space Model Features:

Traditionally, an alternative way to categorize locations is using the social tags associated with the locations. As in the clustering approach, we again apply the vector space model features using tf, idf, and tf-idf respectively. Results in Figure 7 significantly differ from the results shown in Figure 6: for both tf and tf-idf, Naive Bayes, AdaBoostM1, and SimpleCart perform much better than 1NN, which verifies our previous assumption that those classifiers work well

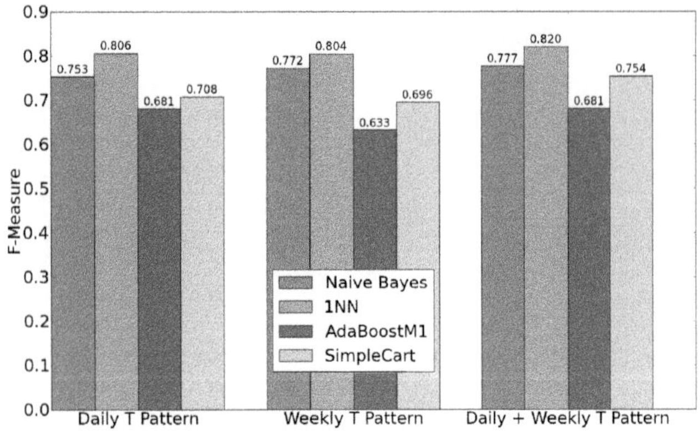

Figure 6: 10-Fold Cross Validation of 271 Venues Classification With T Patterns

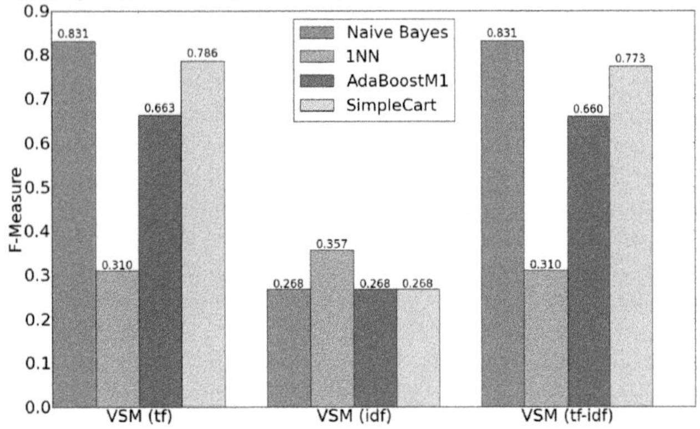

Figure 7: 10-Fold Cross Validation of 271 Venues Classification With Vector Space Models

with text-driven features. Classifiers trained by tf or tf-idf models significantly outperform ones trained by idf models. Furthermore, classifiers trained by tf-idf and tf have very similar results, which shows that enriching with the idf information could not help classify the venues. Besides, the best result for the vector space model based classifiers performs a little better (1.3%) than the best result for traffic pattern based classifiers.

Combination of the Two Sets of Features:

To answer the question of whether enriching information from tags could help facilitate venue categorization, we train classifiers on both sets of features (each set of features are normalized independently with L2-normalization before being merged). Unexpectedly, the results using both sets of features (daily + weekly t pattern, and tf-idf vector models) perform similar or even a little bit worse than the best performing classifiers trained by either set of features (results listed in Table 4). We attribute this drop in performance to the inclusion of possibly unhelpful countervailing features (94 temporal features, and 10,324 vector space model features). Thus, we apply feature selection to reduce the number of features by filtering irrelevant and redundant features.

Feature Selection:

We apply the standard Chi-Square feature selection method to reduce the number of vector space model features from 10,324 to 358 by filtering insignificant and redundant features. All traffic pattern features are considered significant

Table 4: 10-Fold Cross Validation of 271 Venues Classification With Traffic Pattern and Vector Space Models

Metric	Naive Bayes	1NN	AdaBoostM1	SimpleCart
F1-Measure	0.831	0.59	0.66	0.753

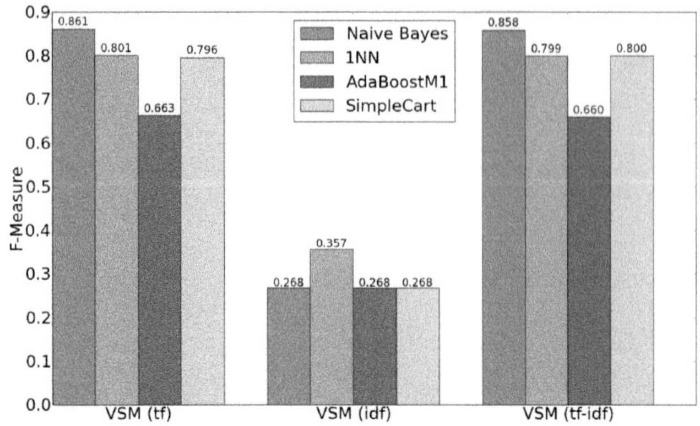

Figure 8: 10-Fold Cross Validation of 271 Venues Classification With Vector Space Models + Feature Selection

Table 5: 10-Fold Cross Validation of 271 Venues Classification With Traffic Pattern and Vector Space Model + Feature Selection

Metric	Naive Bayes	1NN	AdaBoostM1	SimpleCart
F1-Measure	0.866	0.765	0.66	0.75

by Chi-Square and so remain for the following classification experiments. Thus, we get exactly same results for traffic patterns comparing to results in Figure 6. The results for vector space model features are displayed in Figure 8. Comparing to the results without feature selection, classifiers trained by idf features, AdaboostM1 trained by tf features, and tf-idf features still perform the same. 1NN classifier trained with tf features and tf-idf features outperform with an almost 158.4% increase over the previous results. Besides, Naive Bayes classifiers trained with tf features and tf-idf features also have a 3.2% increase in their performance; as well as the Simple Cart with over 1% increase. The best performing classifier so far becomes Naive Bayes, which reaches a F1-Measure of 0.861.

Feature selection also shows its effectiveness when we train the classifiers using both the traffic pattern features and vector space model features. Comparing to results in Table 4, results in Table 5 show increase of performance for 1NN (29.7%), and Naive Bayes (4.2%).

6.2 Evaluation on Test Set

Based on the 10-fold cross validation on the training set, we only use 1NN as the classifier to classify venues based on the feature of traffic patterns. The test set of venues are generated based on the criteria of at least 10 branches with certain number of checkins above a pre-defined threshold. We set the threshold as 10, 30, 50, 100, 200, 300, and 500 respectively, and the corresponding number of venues in the test sets are listed in Table 6. As we can see from the table, with a relaxed criteria of only 10 checkins and above, the test set contains 1,392 venues, and with a strict criteria of

Table 6: Number of Venues in Test Sets

Min # of Checkins	10	30	50	100	200	300	500
# of Venues	1392	983	695	353	142	60	21

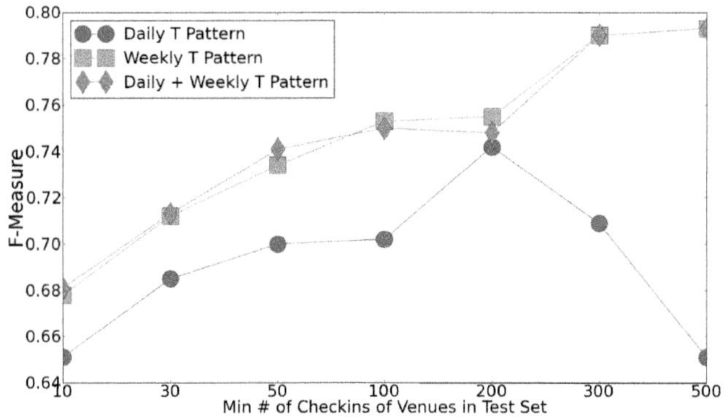

Figure 9: Evaluation of 1NN Trained by Traffic Patterns on Test Sets

500 checkins and above, the test set only contains 21 venues. Note that the test sets are disjoint with the training set.

We train the 1NN classifier on the training set using daily traffic pattern, weekly traffic pattern, and daily plus weekly traffic patterns respectively, and evaluate test sets with corresponding features. The results for the classification are plotted in Figure 9 (each tick in x axis represents a test set). As we can see in the figure, with more checkins required for a venue in a test set, the results get better for the classifier trained by daily traffic pattern, and it reaches its peak with an F1-Measure of 0.742. However, it gets worse performance for the tests requiring at least 300 checkins and 500 checkins. This is probably caused by the lack of venues in the two test sets, and a small number of mis-classified venues can significantly affect the results. For the classifier trained by weekly traffic pattern and daily plus weekly traffic pattern, the results generally get better with test sets which only contain venues with dense traffic patterns. With weekly traffic pattern features, the classifier works much better overall than the one trained by daily traffic patterns. The classifier trained by daily plus weekly traffic patterns works slightly better than the one trained by weekly traffic patterns with test sets with relaxed condition, falls behind a little bit for test set 100, and test set 200, and finally catches up for test set 300 and test 500. In the figure, we can see that with only 50 or more checkins input per venue, the 1NN classifier can reach a F1-Measure almost 0.75, which shows its good performance in venue categorization.

7. AUGMENTING LOCATION-BASED SEARCH

So far, we have seen that the traffic patterns for venues revealed through location sharing services contain rich information about the venues' semantic category. And we have successfully taken advantage of these traffic patterns for both unsupervised semantic group clustering and supervised venue categorization. In this section, we show how we can incorporate venues' traffic patterns and their category information into traditional location-based web search.

Answering Queries for Traffic:

Traffic patterns and category information for venues can

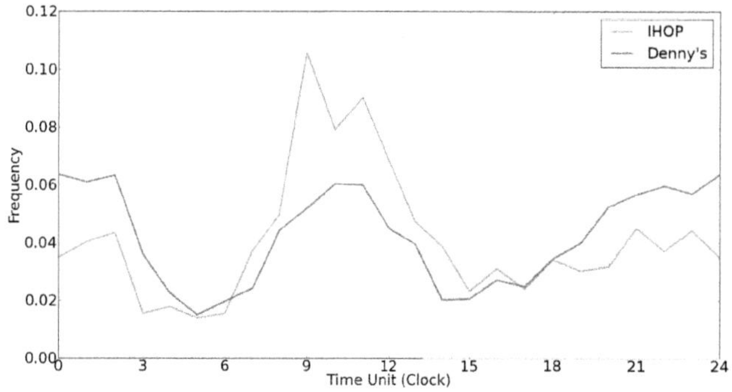

(a) T Patterns for IHOP and Denny's

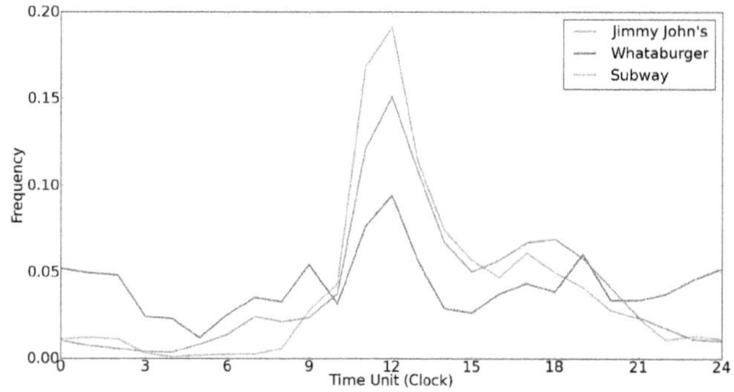

(b) T Patterns for Jimmy John's, Whataburger, and Subway

(c) T Pattern for Jack Astor's Bar & Grill

Figure 10: Traffic Patterns for Venues Off-Peak between 5-7 PM

be easily incorporated into traditional location-based search to answer the information need for traffic. One scenario for answering the traffic-driven query is: Karen is searching for a restaurant which is off-peak during dinner time between 5 - 7 PM, so that she can enjoy the quiet environment talking with her friends. Knowing the traffic patterns and category for venues, the system could easily retrieve the venues nearby in the category of food, and rank the results by the descending order of busyness. Example results are plotted in Figure 10. For example, Karen can choose IHOP and Denny's where the crowd usually come in the early morning, lunch time, and late in the evening; she can also go to fast food venues like Jimmy Johns, and Chipotle which are crowded in during lunch time; besides, Karen can also choose grill & bars which are more popular in late evening like Jack Astor's Bar & Grill.

Location Recommendation based on Traffic:

Another potential application is recommendation of venues having similar traffic patterns. For example, Jerry plays a

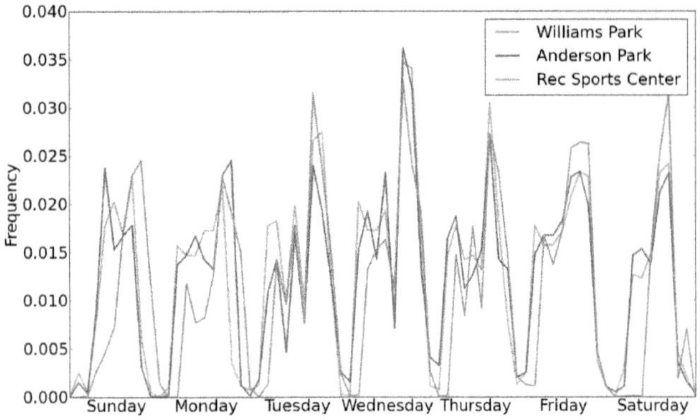

Figure 11: Example Showing Venue Recommendation based On T Pattern

lot of basketball, and tennis. He usually goes to the Williams Park during Wednesday early evening, and Saturday afternoon, which are both free time for him and peak times for guys to get-together and play basketball and tennis. Recently, he moves to a new neighborhood, and wants to find places nearby that have similar traffic patterns, so that he can meet new friends there and play some basketball or tennis. A traffic-driven location-based search can also easily handle this kind of queries. Given the name of the venue, the system calculates temporal similarity between traffic patterns of the venue and other venues in the same category (or in other categories as well), and return the locations with the highest temporal similarities. The example results are plotted in Figure 11, which shows the comparison of traffic patterns of Williams Park and two similar nearby venues Anderson Park and Rec Sports Center.

8. CONCLUSION

In this paper, we propose to mine traffic patterns revealed through location sharing services to augment traditional location-based search. Strong indication of semantic information are found in the traffic patterns generated from 22 million checkins from location sharing services. Then, we take advantage of the traffic patterns and successfully cluster venues into semantically correlated groups, and categorize incoming venues based on the associated traffic dynamics. Based on the results, we also provide two examples to show how traffic-driven semantic organization of locations may be naturally incorporated into traditional location-based search.

9. REFERENCES

[1] S. Asadi, C. Chang, X. Zhou, and J. Diederich. Searching the world wide web for local services and facilities: A review on the patterns of location-based queries. In *Advances in Web-Age Information Management: 6th International Conference*, WAIM '05, 2005.

[2] O. Buyukkokten, J. Cho, H. Garcia-Molina, L. Gravano, and N. Shivakumar. Exploiting geographical location information of web pages. In *Proceedings of the ACM SIGMOD Workshop on the Web and Databases*, 1999.

[3] Z. Cheng, J. Caverlee, and K. Lee. Exploring millions of footprints in location sharing services. In *ICWSM 2011.*

[4] S. Chien and N. Immorlica. Semantic similarity between search engine queries using temporal correlation. In *WWW 2005.*

[5] M. Ciaramita, V. Murdock, and V. Plachouras. Online learning from click data for sponsored search. In *WWW 2008.*

[6] J. Ding, L. Gravano, and N. Shivakumar. Computing Geographical Scopes of Web Resources. In *VLDB 2000.*

[7] C. Faloutsos, M. Ranganathan, and Y. Manolopoulos. Fast subsequence matching in time-series databases. In *SIGMOD 1994.*

[8] T.-c. Fu. A review on time series data mining. *Engineering Applications of Artificial Intelligence*, 24, 2011.

[9] Q. Gan, J. Attenberg, A. Markowetz, and T. Suel. Analysis of geographic queries in a search engine log. In *Proceedings of the first international workshop on Location and the web*, LOCWEB '08, 2008.

[10] S. A. Golder, D. M. Wilkinson, and B. A. Huberman. Rhythms of social interaction: Messaging within a massive online network. In *Proceedings of the Third Communities and Technologies Conference*, 2007.

[11] T. Joachims. Optimizing search engines using clickthrough data. In *SIGKDD 2002.*

[12] J. M. Kleinberg. Authoritative sources in a hyperlinked environment. *Journal of the ACM*, 46, 1999.

[13] A. Kulkarni, J. Teevan, K. Svore, and S. Dumais. Understanding temporal query dynamics. In *WSDM 2011.*

[14] W. T. Liao. Clustering of time series dataâĂŤa survey. *Pattern Recognition*, 38(11), 2005.

[15] J. Lindqvist, J. Cranshaw, J. Wiese, J. Hong, and J. Zimmerman. I'm the mayor of my house: Examining why people use foursquare - a social-driven location sharing application. In *SIGCHI 2011.*

[16] A. Markowetz, Y.-Y. Chen, T. Suel, X. Long, and B. Seeger. Design and implementation of a geographic search engine. In *Proceedings of the ACM SIGMOD Workshop on the Web and Databases*, 2005.

[17] K. S. McCurley. Geospatial mapping and navigation of the web. In *WWW 2001.*

[18] A. Noulas, S. Scellato, C. Mascolo, and M. Pontil. An empirical study of geographic user activity patterns in foursquare. In *ICWSM 2011.*

[19] K. Radinsky, E. Agichtein, E. Gabrilovich, and S. Markovitch. A word at a time: Computing word relatedness using temporal semantic analysis. In *WWW 2011.*

[20] G. Salton and C. Buckley. Term-weighting approaches in automatic text retrieval. In *Information Processing and Management*, volume 24, 1988.

[21] M. Sanderson and J. Kohler. Analyzing geographic queries. In *SIGIR 2004.*

[22] O. Uryupina. Semi-supervised learning of geographical gazetteers from the internet. In *Proceedings of the HLT-NAACL Workshop on the Analysis of Geographic References*, 2003.

[23] C. Wang, X. Xie, L. Wang, Y. Lu, and W.-Y. Ma. Detecting geographic locations from web resources. In *GIR '05: Proceedings of the 2005 workshop on Geographic information retrieval*, 2005.

[24] C. Watters and G. Amoudi. GeoSearcher: location-based ranking of search engine results. *Journal of the American Society for Information Science and Technology (JASIST)*, 54(2):140–151, 2003.

[25] X. Xi, E. Keogh, C. Shelton, and L. Wei. Fast time series classification using numerosity reduction. In *ICML 2006.*

[26] G.-R. Xue, H.-J. Zeng, Z. Chen, Y. Yu, W.-Y. Ma, W. Xi, and W. Fan. Optimizing web search using web click-through data. In *CIKM 2004.*

[27] J. Yang and J. Leskovec. Patterns of temporal variation in online media. In *WSDM 2011.*

[28] M. Ye, P. Yin, and W. C. Lee. Location recommendation for location-based social networks. In *Proceedings of the 18th SIGSPATIAL International Conference on Advances in Geographic Information Systems*, 2010.

CLUES: A Unified Framework Supporting Interactive Exploration of Density-Based Clusters in Streams

Di Yang, Zhenyu Guo, Elke A. Rundensteiner, and Matthew O. Ward
Worcester Polytechnic Institute
100 Institute Road, Worcester, MA, USA
diyang, zyguo, rundenst, matt@cs.wpi.com

ABSTRACT

Although various mining algorithms have been proposed in the literature to efficiently compute clusters, few strides have been made to date in helping analysts to interactively explore such patterns in the stream context. We present a framework called CLUES to both computationally and visually support the process of real-time mining of density-based clusters. CLUES is composed of three major components. First, as foundation of CLUES, we develop an evolution model of density-based clusters in data streams that captures the complete spectrum of cluster evolution types across streaming windows. Second, to equip CLUES with the capability of efficiently tracking cluster evolution, we design a novel algorithm to piggy-back the evolution tracking process into the underlying cluster detection process. Third, CLUES organizes the detected clusters and their evolution interrelationships into a multi-dimensional pattern space – presenting clusters at different time horizons and across different abstraction levels. It provides a rich set of visualization and interaction techniques to allow the analyst to explore this multi-dimensional pattern space in real-time. Our experimental evaluation, including performance studies and a user study, using real streams from ground group movement monitoring and from stock transaction domains confirm both the efficiency and effectiveness of our proposed CLUES framework.

Categories and Subject Descriptors

H.4 [**Information Systems Applications**]: Miscellaneous

General Terms

Algorithms, Management, Performance

Keywords

Density-Based Cluster, Evolution, Stream, Visualization

1. INTRODUCTION

The discovery of complex patterns such as clusters, outliers, and associations from huge volumes of streaming data has been recognized as critical for numerous domains, ranging from financial analysis to moving object monitoring. Such applications built upon high-speed data streams not only expect a stream processing system to computationally detect patterns in a highly efficient manner, but also require it to provide an exploratory platform that helps the analysts to interact with and thus comprehend both the detected patterns and their interrelationships. For example, in traffic monitoring applications, an analyst does not only need to know the major traffic congestions (clusters) just detected in the traffic streams, but also needs to keep track of how these clusters evolve over time. During routine monitoring, the analyst may monitor the clusters at a highly abstract level, such as whether new patterns formed recently or whether an earlier cluster now has split into several smaller ones. A closer exploration may be necessary in some circumstances. For example, a cluster that is growing quickly in size but not moving in position may indicate a traffic congestion or even an accident. The analyst then needs to zoom into that particular cluster to study the cluster structure (how vehicles are distributed in the cluster) and obtain information on the individual vehicles needing help. Obviously, using the traditional console or file output to simply report the clusters as tuples associated with cluster identifications would be of limited use, because the analysts can hardly comprehend such high volume data presented in plain text in real time.

To better support complex pattern mining in the streaming environments poses the following requirements: **1)** pattern evolution semantics as foundation are neccessary to characterize pattern changes over time in the streams; **2)** efficient pattern and evolution computation methods have to be designed to handle high input rate streams; **3)** appropriate visualization techniques must effectively convey the detected patterns and their interrelationships; and **4)** most importantly, all these critical components above need to be well integrated into a unified framework, which provides analysts an efficient and easy-to-use exploration platform.

Target Query Semantics. We support mining of density-based clusters [13, 14] in *sliding stream windows*. For this query semantics, arbitrarily shaped clusters are continuously detected within the most recent portion of the stream that fall into the query window. The traffic congestion monitoring task discussed above is an example that requires such query semantics. This is because the traffic congestions can be in any shape, and position information being valid for only a certain period of time necessitates cluster formation based on the most recent positions of the vehicles. Other applications that can be served by such query semantics include detecting intensive-transaction areas in most recent stock trades, and identifying malicious attacks in current network traffic.

1.1 Analysis of State-of-the-Art

While mining of streaming data has been studied for various pattern types [2, 9, 7], little attention has been paid to date for design of holistic frameworks that support the overall mining process

CIKM'11, October 24–28, 2011, Glasgow, Scotland, UK.

for density-based clusters in sliding windows. First, an evolution model that effectively characterizes the changes of density-based cluster structures over time is needed. Reporting the changes of patterns in data streams [1, 2, 5, 6, 10, 17] has long been recognized as important. The previous efforts of clustering streaming data [2, 5, 6, 10, 17] assume that the streaming clusters are sphere-shaped and can be expressed using accumulative statistics. They use a "subtraction" function to calculate the difference between the statistics of clusters identified at different time points. However, these techniques usually do not deal with cluster changes caused by cluster membership transformations of individual objects, such as split and merge. Also they either cannot handle clusters with arbitrary shapes or with sliding window semantics, and thus do not meet the requirements of the applications mentioned earlier.

To our knowledge, no evolution semantics specific to density-based clusters in streaming environment have been presented so far in the literature. [17] is perhaps the closest research effort to us in terms of designing cluster evolution model. It presents a cluster change model, MONIC, to track cluster transactions. However, this model is neither designed for the streaming environment nor specifically for density-based clusters. In particular, in streaming window semantics, as object expirations and arrivals happen within a single window slide process, an evolution model needs to handle the composite effect caused by both of them in a single transaction (see section 3). While [17] provides evolution semantics for covering losing (expiration) or gaining (arrivals) cluster members separately, it does not offer semantics covering the situations in which both happen together. Second, to handle potentially high speed input streams, the cluster changes have to be detected and conveyed in a highly efficient manner. For density-based clusters, monitoring the changes of their complex cluster structures in streaming environment is particularly challenging. However, [17] provides neither efficient computational methods nor visualization and interaction techniques to allow analysts to quickly identify and understand the cluster changes in real time.

Second, to track cluster evolution across sliding windows, an efficient computational method needs to be designed. Existing algorithms for detecting density-based clusters in streams [8, 9] do not meet the requirements of our target applications, because they neither identify the individual members in the clusters nor enforce the sliding window semantics for the clustering process. [20], the only algorithm we are aware of that detects density-based clusters in sliding windows, suffers from dramatically increasing demands on system resources when the ratio between the window size and the slide size of the query window increases. We characterize this problem in depth in Section 4. More importantly, none of these clustering algorithms support evolution tracking for density-based clusters, which is one of the key focuses of this work.

Third, appropriate visualizations are needed to display the clusters as well as their evolution. Previous research focuses on visualizing time series data [15, 19], data associated with timestamps in static datasets. In such context, no issues of data arrival speed nor continuous updates of streams arise. Also, although visualization tools [11, 18] have been developed to present cluster structures in static environments, none of them tackle visualization and real-time visual interaction support for monitoring clusters and their evolution in the stream context.

1.2 Proposed Solution

In this work, we present a unified CLUster Evolution in Stream analysis framework, CLUES, to both computationally and visually support cluster mining in data streams.

First, we design the first *evolution semantics* for density-based clusters over sliding windows, deployed to model cluster evolutions in the CLUES framework. We address the following two key challenges. 1) Our proposed semantics not only cover statistical changes of individual clusters, such as the size or the centroid changes, but also classify structural cluster changes that involve multiple clusters, including splitting and merging of clusters. Such semantics are shown to effectively describe the changes of clusters over time in our user study. 2) Our proposed evolution semantics are efficiently computable. This is critical for real time applications, because a system conducting expensive clustering processes can hardly bear any additional computational burden.

Second, a novel algorithm is proposed to serve as the computational component of CLUES. It does not only efficiently extract clusters from sliding windows, but more importantly to also track cluster changes based on our proposed evolution semantics. This algorithm uses a compact hierarchical structure to incrementally store and update the progressive clusters and their evolution interrelationships. Our experimental study (Section 6) demonstrates that our proposed algorithm is not only on average 300% times faster than the state-of-the-art detection technique [20], but also consumes significantly (on average 60%) less memory space. In addition, this algorithm only consumes a very modest amount (less than 10%) of extra system resources to conduct evolution tracking along with the clustering process.

Finally, CLUES organizes the detected clusters and their evolution information into a multi-dimensional pattern space, with one dimension representing the cluster changes over time and the other representing clusters in different abstraction levels. We have designed a rich set of visualization and interaction techniques to enable analysts to easily navigate through the proposed pattern space by reviewing, monitoring, and even predicting cluster changes over time at different levels of abstraction. Our user study in Section 6 shows that our system can effectively improve both the efficiency and accuracy of human analysts for tracking cluster evolution compared to the alternative strategies.

2. PRELIMINARIES

We now introduce the concept of density-based clusters [13, 14]. We use the term "data point" to refer to a multi-dimensional tuple in the data stream. Density-based cluster detection uses a range threshold $\theta^{range} \geq 0$ to define the *neighborship* between any two data points. For two data points p_i and p_j, if the distance between them is no larger than θ^{range}, p_i and p_j are said to be neighbors. We use the function $NumNeigh(p_i, \theta^{range})$ to denote the number of neighbors a data point p_i has, given the θ^{range} threshold.

Definition 2.1. ***Density-Based Cluster:*** *Given θ^{range} and a count threshold θ^{count}, a data point p_i with $NumNeigh(p_i, \theta^{range}) \geq \theta^{count}$ is defined as a core point. Otherwise, if p_i is a neighbor of any core point, p_i is an edge point. p_i is a noise point if it is neither a core point nor an edge point. Two core points c_0 and c_n are connected, if they are neighbors of each other, or there exists a sequence of core points $p_0, p_1, ...p_{n-1}, c_n$, where for any i with $0 \leq i \leq n-1$, each pair of core points p_i and p_{i+1} are neighbors of each other. Finally, a density-based cluster is defined as a maximum group of "connected core points" and the edge points attached to them. Any pair of core points within a cluster are "connected". Figure 2 shows an example of a density-based cluster composed of 11 core points (black) and 2 edge points (grey) in window W_0.*

We focus on periodic sliding window semantics as proposed in *Countinuous Query Language* [3] and widely used in the literature [4, 20]. These proposed semantics can be either time-based or count-based. In both cases, each query has a query window W with with a fixed window size win and a fixed slide size $slide$ (either a time interval or a tuple count). The query window covers the most recent portion of the stream quantified by the window size win, say the latest 10K tuples (count-based) or the tuples coming into the system within the last 10 minutes. When a certain amount of time has elapsed (time-based) or a certain number of tuples have arrived (count-based), the query window slides (moves forward) by the slide size $slide$. During each window slide, old tuples expire from the query window, while new tuples arrive and fall into the query window. Such query semantics periodically extract patterns based on all tuples falling into the query window.

3. EVOLUTION MODEL OF CLUSTERS

In this section, we propose the first evolution model that models the semantics of density-based clusters changes over sliding windows. The proposed evolution semantics is defined between any two adjacent sliding windows upon a data stream, say W_n and W_{n+1}. The process of sliding a query window can be divided into two phases, namely purging the expired and then adding the new data points. Our evolution semantics covers not only the cluster changes caused by each of these two phases in isolation, but also by both of them together. We call the cluster changes caused by either of these two phases, *single-step evolution*, and those caused by both of them, *multiple-step evolution*.

Model for Single-Step Evolution. Our single-step evolution semantics covers seven change types. Given two cluster sets Clu_set1 and Clu_set2 identified in W_n and W_{n+1} respectively, the change types of single-step evolution are:

birth: If a cluster C_i in Clu_set2 does not include any core point members from any cluster C_j in Clu_set1, we define this as the *birth* of a new cluster C_i in Clu_set2.

termination: If none of the core point members of a cluster C_i in Clu_set1 appear in any cluster C_j in Clu_set2, we define this as the *termination* of C_i.

split: A cluster C_i in Clu_set1 *splits*, if its non-expired core point members now belong to at least two different clusters in Clu_set2.

merge: Clusters C_i, C_{i+1}... C_{i+n} in Clu_set1 *merge*, if all their core point members remaining in W_{n+1} now belong to a single cluster C_j in Clu_set2.

preserve/shrink/expand: A cluster C_i in Clu_set1 *preserves/ shrinks/expands*, if no *termination*, *split* or *merge* has happened to it, and its size doesn't change/decrease/increase significantly in Clu_set2 respectively. Here the definition of "significance" can be controlled by an adjustable threshold θ^{sig}, which denotes a percentage of the original cluster size of C_i in W_n.

These seven change types describe all possible cluster changes from one window to the next if considering either tuple expirations or tuple insertions only.

Lemma 3.1. *For any density-based cluster set Clu_set identified in a window W_n, the seven change types above cover all potential cluster changes that can be caused by either inserting or deleting data points from W_n.*

Here we give an intuitive explanation for Lemma 3.1. When inserting new tuples into W_n, these tuples can only either join the existing clusters or fall into non-cluster areas in W_n. **1)** When new tuples join existing clusters, they can only cause either ***preservation*** or ***expansion*** of individual clusters, depending on whether the number of new members each cluster gains is significant or not, or ***merge*** of several clusters, when new tuples build connections between existing clusters. **2)** When new tuples fall into non-cluster areas, they can only cause either the **birth** of new clusters (as density reaches the threshold) or no cluster changes (as they become new noise). Thus, insertion of new data points into W_n can only cause ***birth***, ***merge***, ***expansion*** or ***preservation*** of the existing clusters in Clu_set.

Second, when data points are deleted from W_n, they can either be members of existing clusters in Clu_set or belong to non-cluster areas (noises). **1)** Deleting cluster members from existing clusters can only cause ***shrinkage*** or ***preservation*** of clusters, depending on whether the number of members each cluster loses is significant or not, ***termination*** of clusters, when the whole cluster structure is deleted or collapsed after losing members, or ***split*** of the clusters, when the connections between subparts of an existing cluster are broken but at least two subparts still constitute smaller clusters. **2)** Deleting noises causes no cluster changes. Thus, deleting data points from W_n can only cause ***shrinkage*** or ***preservation***, ***termination*** or ***split*** of clusters

This shows that the seven single-step change types cover all potential cluster changes that can be caused by either inserting or deleting tuples from W_n.

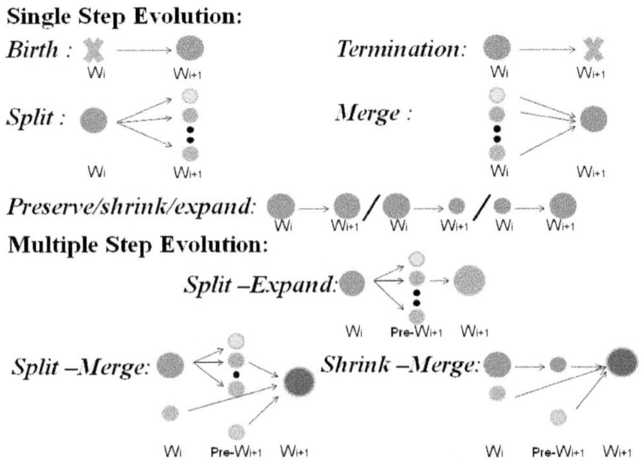

Figure 1: Depiction of Evolution Semantics

Model for Multi-Step Evolution. We now consider change types caused by the combination of both inserting and deleting data points from W_n. For example, given two clusters C_i and C_j both in W_n, two subparts of C_i, say C_{i_sub1} and C_{i_sub2}, and two subparts of cluster C_j, say C_{j_sub1} and C_{j_sub2}, C_{i_sub1} and C_{j_sub1} may belong to a new cluster C_k in W_{n+1}, while C_{i_sub2} and C_{j_sub2} may belong to another new cluster C_l in W_{n+1}.

To cover such more complex cases, we define the notion of multi-step evolution as a composition of two single-step evolutions to express cluster changes caused by first deleting all expired tuples and then inserting new tuples.

split-expand: In W_{n+1}, new cluster C_i formed by splitting of cluster C_j in W_n has, in addition, gained more members.

split-merge: In W_{n+1}, new cluster C_i formed by splitting of a cluster C_j in W_n merges with other clusters from W_n.

shrink-merge: In W_{n+1}, cluster C_i in W_n shrinks in size and then merges with other clusters from W_n.

Theorem 3.1. *For any density-based cluster set Clu_set identified in a query window W_i, the seven single-step evolution types and the three multiple-step evolution types cover all potential cluster changes caused by window sliding.*

We give an intuitive explanation of Theorem 3.1 below. Each

phase of the window sliding process, namely deleting expired and inserting new tuples, can only cause four types of single-step evolution (Lemma 3.1). Among these single-step evolution types, ***termination*** and ***birth*** are non-composable single step evolutions. This is because a cluster already terminated cannot participate in any further evolution, and a cluster just born cannot have any evolution before its birth. Thus nine (3×3) possible combinations remain. Among them, six of these combinations composed by two single-step evolution types regarding cluster size changes only, namely ***preservation***, ***shrinkage*** and ***expansion***, can be collapsed into single-step evolution again. For example, ***shrinkage*** and then ***expansion*** will be classified as ***preservation***, ***shrinkage*** or ***expansion***, depending on the specific size change of the cluster. So, the only three real multi-step evolution types remaining are the ones we listed above. In conclusion, our proposed evolution semantics (demonstrated in Figure 1) cover all possible cluster changes caused by window slides.

4. A NOVEL CLUSTERING STRATEGY SUPPORTING EVOLUTION TRACKING

We now design an algorithm that not only significantly improve the performance of the state-of-the-art techniques in terms of clustering, but more importantly supports tracking of cluster evolution based on our proposed evolution semantics (Section 3).

4.1 Proposed Stream Clustering Algorithm

As both analytically and experimentally shown in [20], detecting clusters from scratch at each window is prohibitively expensive. [20] also demonstrates that Incremental DBSCAN [13], which was designed to handle a single insertion or deletion to density-based clusters in data warehouse, does not scale well to handle large numbers of updates in each stream window. Thus, designing an efficient incremental computation method is critical for cluster detection.

For incremental clustering, one key challenge is to efficiently maintain cluster memberships of cluster member tuples over time. The expiration of data points may cause complex cluster changes, such as splitting, which may require cluster membership relabeling of all the remaining cluster members from scratch. Thus, discounting the effect of expired points from the detected clusters can be computationally very expensive.

To address this problem, we exploit the property of sliding window semantics and apply the general concept of "predicted view" [4, 20] as described below. Since sliding windows tend to partially overlap ($slide < win$) [3], some data points falling into the window W_i will also participate in some of the windows right after W_i. Based on the knowledge about data points in the current window and the slide size, we can pre-determine which subsets of the current data points will participate in certain future windows. Figure 2 shows "predicted views" for four future windows. In particular, 16 data points, namely p_1 to p_{16} (each depicted as circles, and the number in the circle representing its time stamp), fall into the current window W_0 and 14 of them (p_1 to p_{13}) form a single cluster. By analyzing the slide size (equal to 4) and the time stamps on each point, we know that data points p_{13} to p_{16} will also participate in three future windows, namely W_1 to W_3. While data points p_9 to p_{12} and data points p_5 to p_8 can only participate in two and one future windows respectively.

By using this concept, we can avoid the computational effort needed for discounting the effect of expiring data points. The idea is to pre-generate "partial clusters" for future windows based on the data points in the current window that are known to participate in the respective future windows. Using the same example shown in

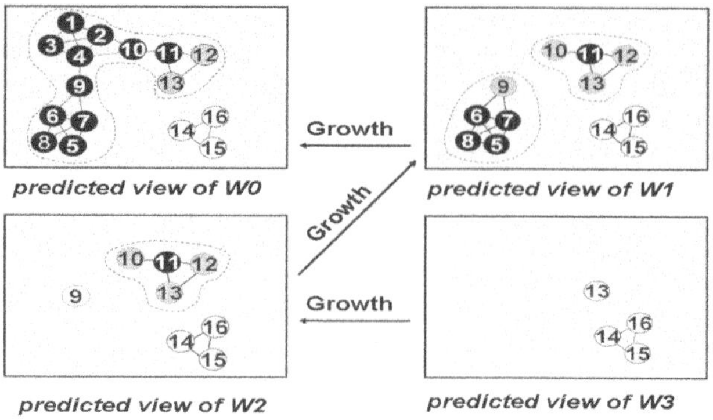

Figure 2: Predicted views of four consecutive windows at time of W_0 (slide size = 4 tuples)

Figure 2, the 12 data points in W_0 that are known to participate in W_1, namely p_5 to p_{16}, will form two clusters in W_1, without considering the new objects that later may come into W_1.

When the window slides, we simply update the pre-generated clusters in the "predicted views" by inserting the new data points into them. No effort for handling expiration of data points is needed, because these views were generated without considering these to-be-expired data points. Note all the cluster changes caused by insertion of additional data points, namely birth of new clusters or expansion or merge of existing clusters, are incrementally maintainable. They are computationally much cheaper than handling expiration-related changes, which may require recomputation from scratch. Figure 3 demonstrates the updated clusters at the time of W_1 after the window slides from W_0 to W_1. The two clusters in W_1 (pre-generated at time of W_0) actually merge into one after the new data points p_{17} to p_{20} arrive.

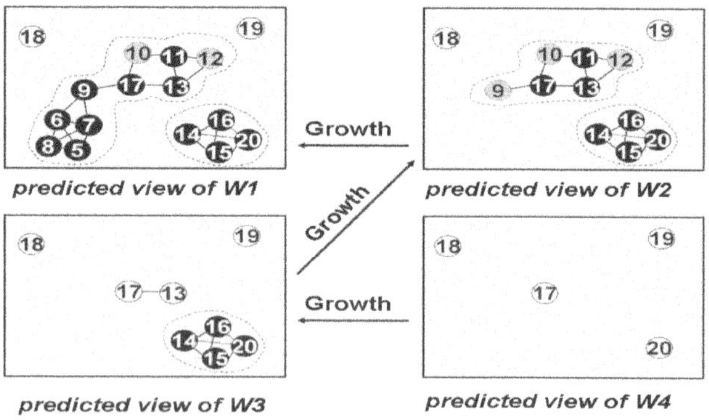

Figure 3: Updated predicted views of four consecutive windows at time of W_1 (slide size = 4 tuples)

Independent View Maintenance. As a straightforward application of the predicted view concept, the "pre-generated" clusters in each future window can be maintained independently. In particular, one can represent and thus update the "pre-generated" clusters in these views independently when the window slides. However, the demands of this approach on both CPU and memory resources increase linearly as the number of predicted views to be maintained increases. More specifically, for a clustering query Q_i, the number of predicted views to be maintained equals $\lceil \frac{Q_i.win}{Q_i.slide} \rceil$. For example, given a query Q_i with $Q_i.win$=10000(s) and $Q_i.slide$=10(s), this approach must maintain 1000 independent "predicted views". Clearly, this represents a heavy burden in terms of both memory and CPU resources. Figure 8 (left part) shows an example of the independent storage for the predicted views depicted in Figure 2. Here, information for representing cluster structures is repeatedly stored even if unchanged across predicted views. More importantly, as the clusters in different windows are treated independently, it does not facilitate cluster evolution tracking, which is based on interrelationships between cluster sets identified in adjacent windows. Extra-N [20], the only algorithm in the literature conducting density-based clustering in sliding windows, suffers from both of these shortcomings.

Integrated View Maintenance. To overcome these shortcomings, we now propose our new clustering algorithm based on an Integrated predicted WINdow maintenance strategy, called IWIN. IWIN exploits the interrelationships among the "pre-generated" cluster structures in a sequence of future windows to compress them into one single compact structure. This integrated storage mechanism enables efficient maintenance of a sequence of predicted views.

We first exploit the notion of **"growth"** between any two density-based cluster sets.

Definition 4.1. *If Clu_Set2 is a "growth" of Clu_Set1, any two data points that belong to the same cluster in Clu_Set1 will also belong to a single cluster in Clu_Set2.*

Figures 4 and 5 demonstrate an example of two cluster sets between which the "growth property" holds. The white circles represent the data points belonging to both cluster sets, while the black ones represent those belonging to Clu_Set2 only. As demonstrated in Figures 4 and 5 also, ***birth*** of "new" clusters, ***expansion*** and ***merge*** are the only three possible cluster changes between any two cluster sets between which the "growth property" holds (see Section 3 for definitions for those change types).

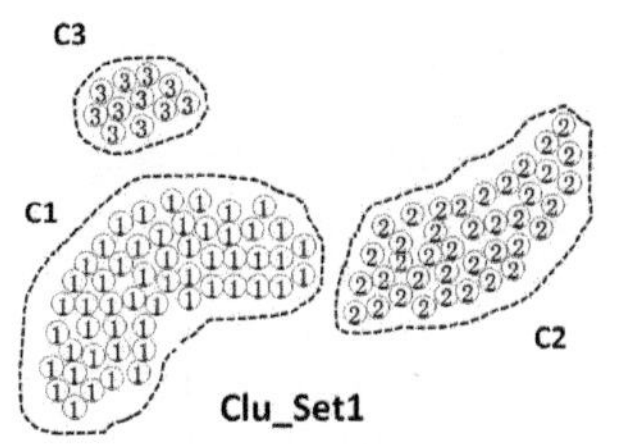

Figure 4: Cluster Set 1 containing 3 clusters

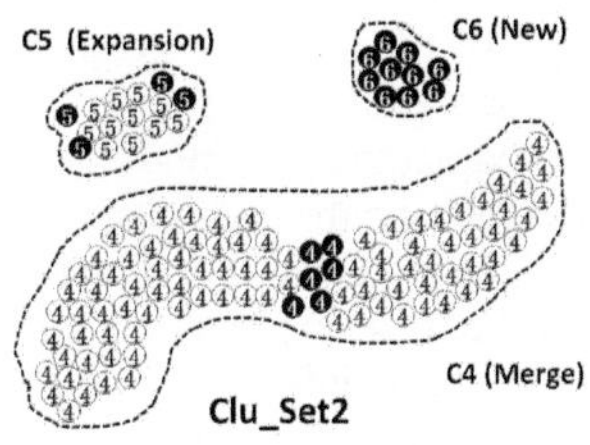

Figure 5: Cluster Set 2 containing 3 clusters

If the growth property transitively holds among a sequence of cluster sets, a **Hierarchical Cluster Structure** can be built to incrementally store the clusters in these cluster sets. The key idea of such a hierarchical cluster membership structure is to incrementally store the cluster "growth information" from one cluster set to another. Figures 6 and 7 respectively give examples of independent and hierarchical cluster membership structures built for the two cluster sets shown in Figures 4 and 5.

As shown in Figure 6, if we store the clusters in these two cluster sets independently, each cluster member (white squares) belonging to both clusters has to store two cluster memberships, one for each cluster set. However, if we store them in the hierarchical cluster structure (Figure 7), we no longer need to repeatedly store the cluster memberships for these "shared" cluster members. Instead, we simply store cluster memberships for each cluster member belonging to Clu_Set1, and then store the cluster growth informa-

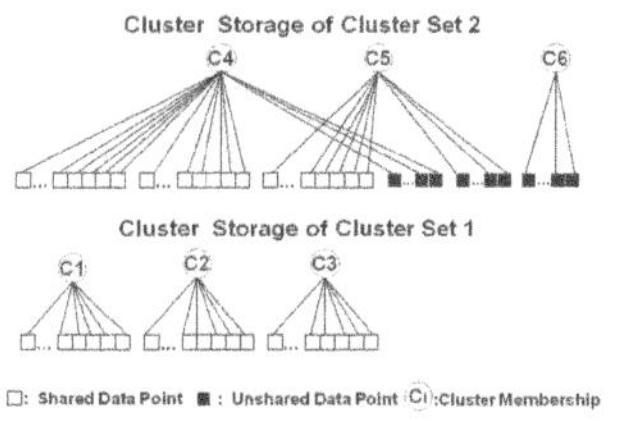

Figure 6: Independent Cluster Storage for Cluster Sets 1 and 2

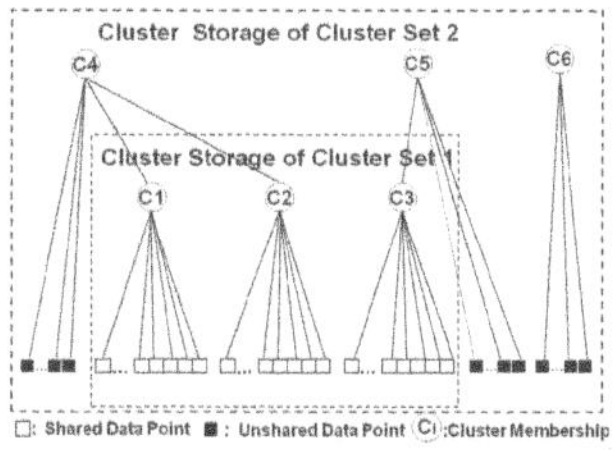

Figure 7: Hierarchical Cluster Storage for Cluster Sets 1 and 2

tion from Clu_Set1 to Clu_Set2. Such growth information is based on the **granularity of clusters** rather than the granularity of individual tuples. In particular, we correlate each cluster C_i in Clu_Set1 with the "grown clusters" in Clu_Set2 that contain C_i.

Such hierarchical cluster structure does not only saves the memory space, but will also allow us to incrementally tracking cluster evolution. Now we explore the insights from this hierarchical cluster structure to design the IWIN algorithm. We first make the observation that, at any given time T with W_n being the current window, the pre-generated cluster set in a future W_{n+i} is always a **growth** of that identified in the predicted view of W_{n+i+1}. The intuitive explanation for this observation is that a cluster set in an earlier window W_{n+i} can be considered as formed by adding data points to the cluster set in the later window W_{n+i+1} (data points expire in the opposite direction). Put differently, adding data points to a cluster set can only cause "growth" of it.

Given the growth property holds among pre-generated cluster sets in any pair of adjacent future windows, we now design an integrated structure to maintain the pre-generated cluster structures in adjacent windows. We call it the ***Integrated Representation of Predicted Views (IntView)***. For any window W_n, $IntView\_W_n$ is an integrated data structure that represents the predicted views of W_n, W_{n+1} ... W_{n+i}, where W_{n+i} is the last window that any current data point in W_n will participate in before its expiration. The right part of Figure 8 gives an example of $IntView\_W_0$ representing the "predicted views" of W_0, W_1, W_2 and W_3 at the time of W_0 (Figure 2), with the left part depicting independent representation. By using the *IntView* structure, IWIN realizes incremental storage of pre-generated clusters for future windows, reducing the memory utilization.

Since the clusters in different "predicted views" are now correlated in $IntView$ ("grow" from one to the next) , we design an update method that is able to incrementally update the pre-generated clusters in all future windows in one single pass. More specifically, for each new data point, the update process to $IntView\_W_n$ starts from the predicted window with the largest window number (the lowest level in the $IntView$ hierarchy). It then incrementally updates other windows in decreasing order of window numbers (in the higher levels of $IntView$). When updating the clusters in a window W_{n+i}, a new data point p_{new} communicates with its neighbors in this window only. If p_{new} causes a merge of two clusters C_i and C_j in W_{n+i}, and C_i and C_j are subparts of two different clusters C_n and C_m in the earlier window(s), it propagates the "growth information", namely merge C_n and C_m, as well. This assures that all the cluster "growth" in W_{n+i} will be "known" by the upper level windows. Thus, p_{new} never needs to re-communicate with the data points stored in W_{n+i} when updating the upper level windows. The pseudo-code of the IWIN algorithm is listed in Figure 9.

In conclusion, the upper bound of the memory consumption for

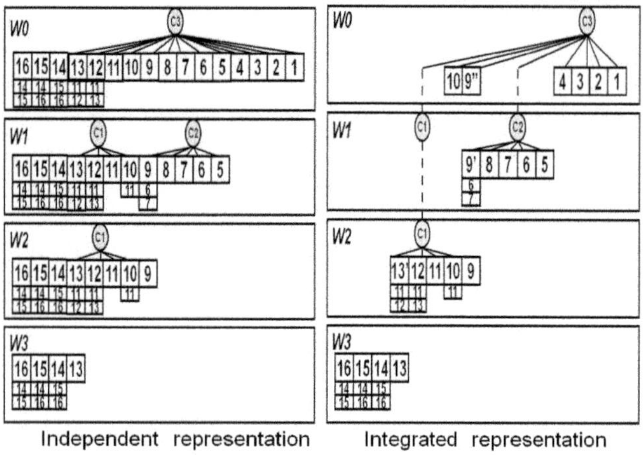

Figure 8: Independent vs. Integrated Representation of Predicted Views

```
pi: a data point.  pnew: a new data point.
pi.T:pi's time stamp.
clu_mem:cluster membership.   Wi : predicted window.
W.Tend/start : ending/starting time of W.
PV :predicted view. Wi.PV :PV built for Wi.
PV.neighbors: neighbors distributed to PV.
evo optional: optional, for evolution maintenance only
 IWIN (θ^range, θ^cnt, win, slide)
 1  For each new data point pnew
 2    if pnew.T > Woldest.Tend
(2.1) PregenerateEvolution(Evo,sig); //(evo optional)
 3      Purge the oldest Wi
 4    load pnew into index
 5    neighbors:=RangeQuerySearch(pnew, θ^range)
 6    UpdateIntView (pnew, neighbors)
 7    if pnew.T == Toutput
 8      Output();
 9      add new window Wnewest to IntView
 10     Toutput = Toutput + slide

 UpdateIntView (p, neighbors)
 1  For each predicted window Wi (from Wnewest)
 2    UpdatePredictedView(p, Wi.PV);
(2.1)If Wi = Woldest (evo optional)
(2.2)   UpdateEvolution(p,Evo) (evo optional)

 UpdatePredictView (p, PV)
 1 p.neighborcount = PV.neighbors.size();
 2 For i:=1 to PV.neighbors.size()
 3     PV.neighbors[i].neighborcount + +;
 4     if PV.neighbors[i] becomes a new core
 5         HandleNewCore(PV.neighbors[i]);
 6 if p.neighborcount ≥ Qi.θ^cnt
 7     HandleNewCore(p, PV);

 HandleNewCore(p, PV)
 1 p.type = core;
 2 p.clu_mem=new clu_mem ;
 3 For i:=1 to PV.neighbors.size()
 4     if PV.neighbors[i].type == core
 5         Merge PV.neighbors[i]. and p. clu_mem;
 6     if PV.neighbors[i].type == noise
 7         PV.neighbors[i].type := edge;
 8         PV.neighbors[i].clu_mem := p.clu_mem;
```

Figure 9: The *IWIN* Algorithm

IWIN is now independent of the number of predicted views to be maintained, while that for the state-of-the-art technique [20] increases linearly with the number of predicted views. Computationally, at each window, IWIN only requires a single pass through the new data points, each communicating with its neighbors once, while Extra-N requires each new data point to communicate with each of its neighbors in all windows in which they both will participate.

4.2 Evolution Tracking Procedures

Next we discuss how IWIN incrementally determines the evolution of clusters at each window slide. Our key insight here is that this evolution semantics computation can be piggy-backed with the process of IWIN's cluster structure maintenance. Generally, the computation for evolution semantics is composed of two steps. First, before each window slide, when the view of the current window is still available, information about "predicted evolution" will be extracted based on the relationship between the current view and the predicted view of the next window. Second, after each window slide, when new data points arrive, an evolution update process will be carried out along with the cluster structure update to compute the impact of each new data point on the cluster evolution. Now we further explain the proposed techniques for these two steps.

Step 1: Extract Predicted Evolution Relationships. The key idea here is that using $IntView$ techniques the single-step evolutions caused by purging are already known before the window slides. In particular, since our proposed IWIN algorithm uses the hierarchical structure $IntView$ to incrementally store the clusters identified in the current window and those pre-generated for later windows, the cluster changes caused by the expiration of data points are already captured in our structure.

Using the earlier example in Figure 2, at W_0, the only cluster identified in this window is "predicted" to be split after purging the to-be-expired data points in the next window W_1. This information is already captured in the $IntView$ structure depicted on the right of Figure 8. Namely, this cluster is associated with two pre-generated clusters in W_1. So, before each window slide (purge), we extract the predicted evolution based on the view of the current window and the predicted view for the next window.

Such predicted evolution reflects future cluster changes after purging the to-be-expired data points. Although subsequent arrivals of new data points may *expand* or *merge* these pre-generated clusters or cause *birth* of new clusters, it is guaranteed that the pre-generated clusters will never *terminate*, *shrink* or *split* with the arrival of new data points. In other words, any two data points predicted to be in the same cluster are guaranteed to remain in the same cluster. This is important for applications in which the life span and stability of clusters needs to be analyzed.

Step 2: Update Evolution Relationships. We incrementally maintain the evolution relationships between clusters in adjacent windows at the arrival of each new data point. Since the new data points may only cause growth related changes, this maintenance process of the evolution semantics is fairly straightforward. We simply keep track of which type of cluster change is caused by the insertion of each new data point. Since such effort is anyway needed for cluster computation itself, the only extra effort here is to record the accumulative cluster changes caused by incoming tuples.

In general, this evolution tracking is an incorporated but optional part of our IWIN algorithm. It can be activated during the IWIN clustering process by simply calling the two functions, namely $PregenerateEvolution()$ and $UpdateEvolution(p, Evo)$, shown in Figure 11. Where these two functions are called in IWIN algorithm are shown in Figure 9.

5. MULTI-DIMENSIONAL PATTERN SPACE AND VISUALIZATION

We now describe our proposed pattern space of CLUES framework, which organizes the detected patterns and their evolution in an intuitively accessible and understandable fashion. Our current system supports a two dimensional pattern space with dimensions representing the change over time and across different abstraction levels (Figure 10).

5.1 Past, Present and Future Views

Along the time dimension, our pattern space provides a sequence of views representing the clusters identified in the different portions of the data stream over time. More specifically, each view in the pattern space is a snapshot of the clusters identified in a single window. Those views are organized in the order of their recentness, and thus systematically reflect the *past*, the *present* and the predicted *future* of clusters identified in the stream.

Evo: Evolution Semantics Maintained.
W_{cur}: current window (W_{oldest} on IntView).
W_{next}: the window after W_{cur}.
W_{cur-p}: current window before inserting p.
W_{last}: the (expired) window before W_{cur}.
C_i: a cluster. $W_i.C_a$ a cluster in W_i.
$DistClu(W_i, D)$: distinct clusters in W_i to which data points in dataset D belong to .

```
PregenerateEvolution()
For each W_cur.C_i
  If |DistClu(W_next, C_i)| == 0
    add [W_cur.C_i terminates] to Evo;
  If |DistClu(W_next, C_i)| == 1
    C_a.clu_mem = C_i.clu_men;
                      (C_a ∈ DistClu(W_next, C_i))
    If |W_cur.C_i| − |W_next.C_a| > sig
      add [W_cur.C_i shrinks] to Evo;
    Else add [W_cur.C_i remains] to Evo;
  If DistClu(W_next, C_i)| > 1
    For each C_a ∈ DistClu(W_next, C_i)
      add [W_cur.C_i splits into W_next.C_a] to Evo;

UpdateEvolution(p,Evo)
If p is a new core
  If |DistClu(W_cur−p, p.neighbors)| == 0
    add [W_cur.C_new birth] to Evo;
  If |DistClu(W_cur−p, p.neighbors)| == 1
    If |W_last.C_i| − |W_cur.C_i| ≤ sig (p ∈ C_i)
      remove [W_cur.C_i shrinks] from Evo if any;
    If |W_cur.C_i| − |W_last.C_i| > sig
      add [W_cur.C_i expands] to Evo;
  If |DistClu(W_cur−p, p.neighbors)| > 1
    If DistClu(W_cur−p, p.neighbors) covers
      all clusters split from W_last.Clu_i
      remove all [W_last.Clu_i split into ...] from Evo;
    add [DistClu(W_cur−p, p.neighbors) merge
      Clu_new] into Evo;
Else If p belongs to any C_i
  If |W_last.C_i| − |W_cur.C_i| ≤ sig
    remove [W_cur.C_i shinks] from Evo if any;
  If |W_cur.C_i| − |W_last.C_i| > sig
    add [W_cur.C_i expands] to Evo;
```

Figure 11: IWIN Functions for Tracking Evolution

Two important characteristics distinguish our pattern space from simply lining up the clusters identified in previous windows. First, we depict the cluster evolution interrelationships between the clusters from one window to the next. For example, our system can tell the analyst that a cluster identified in the current window has been formed by a "merge" of two clusters in the previous window, or reversely, two clusters identified in the current window are the results of the "splitting" of a previous cluster. Second, besides the views presenting the clusters identified in the previous and current windows, our system depicts a sequence of views for the near future, each presenting the clusters that are predicted to appear in a subsequent future window. As in the past and the present views, these future views are also "linked" by lineage information, indicating that users can track the potential evolution of clusters over multiple views. For example, a future view generated by our system may indicate that a cluster identified in the current window may split into several smaller clusters or totally disappear in the next window. Although future views are predictions and thus may differ from actual clusters identified later, it is guaranteed that the "predicted" clusters will never shrink, split, or disappear (see Section 3).

Generally, by navigating along the time dimension, analysts can 1) monitor the cluster in the current window, 2) review the cluster evolution in the recent past, and 3) study the prediction of cluster evolution in the near future.

5.2 Tuple vs. Pattern Level Cluster Views

The second dimension in the pattern space represents changes of the abstraction levels, namely tuple vs. pattern level.

In the *pattern level views*, each cluster in a window is abstracted as a single object. Visually, our system presents each cluster using a colored circle. Two important characteristics of a cluster, namely its size (population) and its position, are conveyed by its radius and relative position in the view. More specifically, the radius of each circle is increased as the size of the corresponding cluster increases. We also layout the clusters by mapping their centroids into a single dimension (vertical axis in Figure 10) based on their positions in the data space. Other statistical properties about each cluster, such as density, can be retrieved for any cluster by moving the mouse over it.

The pattern level cluster views also explicitly depict the cluster evolution across windows. First, in each window, a color mapping mechanism is used to preserve the lineage of the identified clusters. For example, if a cluster identified in W_{n+1} is defined to be the "same" cluster as one identified in W_n, we use the same color to present both of them in these two adjacent windows. The specific color mapping is driven by our cluster evolution semantics discussed in Section 3.

Second, we propose to customize the "river metaphor" technique [15], initially designed to visualize frequency changes, to express the evolution of clusters. In particular, the derivation of each cluster from the last window is presented by the "river" (links) between them. For a given cluster C_i in W_{n+1}, if it is considered to be (partially) derived from a cluster C_j in W_n, our system draws a "river" between C_i and C_j. In addition, the volume of each river (width of each link) represents the number of cluster members the cluster in the later window inherits from the previous window. The larger the volume of a river, the more cluster members the clusters in the two windows share.

Tuple level cluster views present specific information about the members of identified clusters. Visually, cluster members are mapped to a two dimensional display. The members of a cluster C_i are all presented in the same color associated with C_i, which is consistent with the color used in the cluster level view. Our system allows analysts to study the characteristics of any individual cluster in depth by zooming into it. For the zoomed-in clusters, we provide a general color mapping mechanism, including hue, saturation, and lightness variations, to express useful information about the cluster

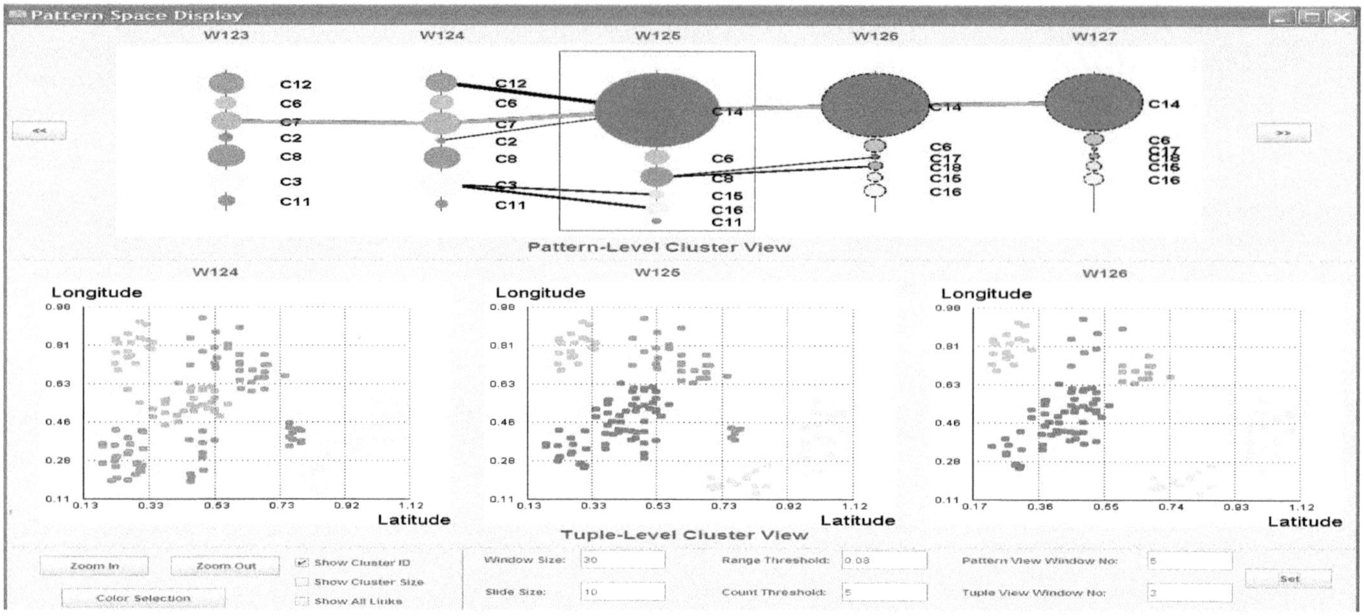

Figure 10: A screen shot of visualized pattern space.

members, such as their "freshness" or "object type (core object or not)". Analysts can retrieve detailed information about a tuple, including its lineage across the windows, by a mouse click on it. A screen shot of our system about a zoomed-in view for a cluster at tuple level view is shown in Figure 12.

Generally, by navigating along the abstraction dimension, analysts can 1) examine the summary information for the clusters in each window; and 2) zoom into a specific cluster to retrieve information on individual members.

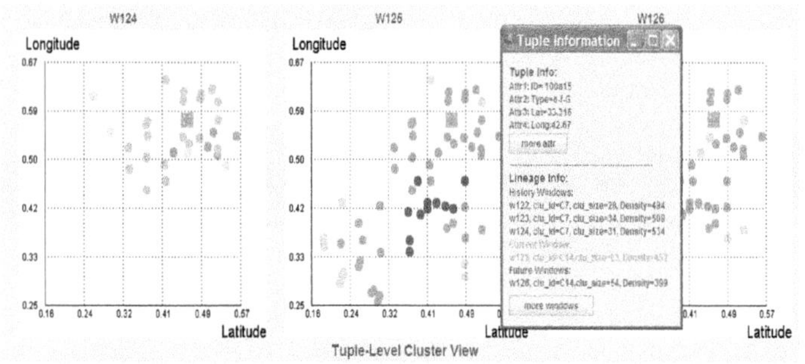

Figure 12: Zoomed-In View for A Single Cluster.

6. EXPERIMENTAL EVALUATION

We conducted our experiments on a Dell desktop with an Intel Core2 2.2GHz processor and 3GB memory, which runs Windows 7 professional operating system. We implemented the algorithms in VC++ 7.0.

Real Datasets. We used two streaming datasets in our experiments. The first dataset, GMTI (Ground Moving Target Indicator) [12], records the real-time information on moving objects gathered by 24 different ground stations or aircraft over 6 hours. It has around 100,000 records regarding the information on vehicles and helicopters (speed ranging from 0-200 mph) moving in a certain geographic region. The second real dataset we use is the Stock Trading Traces data (STT) from [16], which has one million transaction records throughout the trading hours of a day. In our experiment, we detect clusters based on targets' latitude and longitude in GMTI and transactions' price, volume and time in STT.

6.1 Performance Evaluation

Evaluation of IWIN Algorithm. We experimentally verified the correctness of IWIN by comparing the cluster sets identified by it with those identified by two alternative algorithms from the literature, namely Extra-N [20] and Incremental DBSCAN [13]. In all our test cases the cluster sets identified by IWIN were identical with those identified by Extra-N and Incremental DBSCAN.

We then compared the performance of IWIN (without evolution tracking) with the two alternatives mentioned above. Based on our analysis in Section 4, Extra-N is expected to suffer from scalability issues when the number of predicted views maintained increases. This arises when the ratio between the window size and slide size increases. Also, as reported in [20], Incremental DBSCAN has scalability problems when the number of data points expiring at each window slide is large. Thus, one goal of our experiment was to evaluate the performance of the three competitor algorithms when handling queries with different query windows. In particular, we first used all three algorithms to cluster the GMTI data using a fixed window size 5K, while varying the slide size from 0.25K to 2.5K, implying that 5 to 50 percent of data points will be expired at each window slide in different testing cases. We set θ^{range} equal to 0.02 and θ^{cnt} equal to 5, respectively. To evaluate the performance for each algorithm in term of both CPU and memory utilization, we measured two major performance metrics: 1) the average processing time for each data point, and 2) the memory footprint to store the progressive clusters.

As shown in C1 of Figure 13, the CPU time consumed by IWIN was significantly lower than in both alternatives in all the test cases. The CPU time of all three algorithms increased as the ratio between the slide size and the window size increases. For Extra-N and IWIN, this is because the number of predicted views they need to maintain increases. However, such increase is quite modest for IWIN, while dramatic (almost linear) for Extra-N. This matches our analysis in Section 4, as IWIN used an integrated maintenance strategy for multiple predicted views, while Extra-N maintains them independently. For Incremental DBSCAN, as it always maintains each individual update (a single addition or removal of a data point) independently, such increase in CPU time is mainly caused by more frequent output. However, since such single-update-oriented optimization does not scale to handle large numbers of data points expiring at each window, its performance is significantly worse than that of the other two competitors.

For memory consumption, as shown in C2 of Figure 13, IWIN uses much less memory compared with Extra-N, especially for smaller slide sizes. Incremental DBSCAN, which uses a simple cluster maintenance strategy, consumes even less memory in many test cases. However, because of its significantly worse performance in CPU time, its overall performance was deemed worse than IWIN.

We also have conducted a series of experiments showing the performance of the competitor algorithms when handling data with different characteristics. As discussed in [20], one of the most important factors that affects the performance of density-based clustering algorithms is the Average Number of Neighbors (ANN) each data point has in each window. ANN is indicated as a percentage of the window size. So, we utilize a query with the same parameter settings as the previous experiment but a fixed slide size equal to 5K. We use a synthetic cluster generator as described in [20] to control ANN to vary from 1% to 20%. Experimental results in C3 and C4 of Figure 13 show that the superiority of IWIN is not affected by changes to ANN of the input data.

In conclusion, IWIN is on average 3 times faster in all our test cases than Extra-N, the best state-of-the-art technique, while using 60% less memory space. Put differently, we have a win-win selection in terms of gains in both CPU and memory resources.

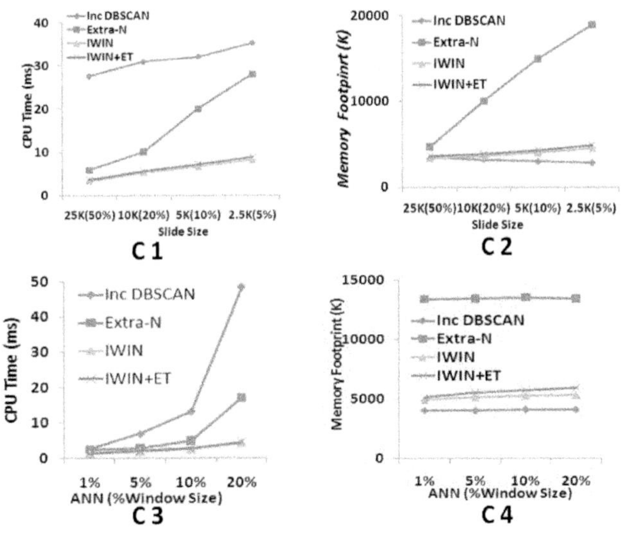

Figure 13: CPU (C1) and memory (C2) comparison when handling queries with different slide sizes. CPU (C3) and memory (C4) comparison when handling streams with different ANN

Evaluation for Evolution Semantics Computation. In the previous test cases, we also evaluate the performance of our IWIN algorithm when evolution tracking is activated ("IWIN+ET"). As shown in all charts in Figure 13, the overhead caused by the computation of the evolution semantics was modest, if not negligible, compared to the maintenance of clusters. In particular, both the CPU and memory utilization caused by semantics computation were always less than 10% of those used for cluster maintenance in all our test cases. On average, only 6% overhead on CPU and 4% overhead on memory are caused by computing evolution in all our test cases. This is expected, because in our proposed method, this evolution computation process is naturally embedded and thus elegantly piggy-bagged by the clustering process.

6.2 User Study for Evolution Tracking

To show that our system effectively helps analysts to track cluster evolution in streams, we conducted a user study based on the STT data. We invited fifteen users (Users 1 - 15), all students from a college, to monitor the transaction pattern changes in stock trades using our proposed system and state-of-the-art techniques. In particular, the users were asked to identify the evolution of intensive-transaction areas (clusters formed based on transaction price, volume and time) with the support of three different exploration systems. **1)** The traditional console view (state-of-the-art technique). **2)** The tuple-level view of our system. **3)** Our full-fledged system with both tuple- and pattern-level views. All three systems used the same cluster detection and evolution tracking logic based on our semantics. The console view showed the statistics of clusters in each window and individual tuples by text. It conveyed cluster evolution using a consistent cluster identification mechanism, namely the clusters detected in different windows were given the same cluster identification, if they were considered to be the same cluster by our evolution semantics. The other two systems displayed the clusters and their evolution as we described in Section 5.

We randomly picked twelve time periods in the STT stream, each covering four successive windows. The monitoring tasks for each user were to identify cluster changes from one window to the next in each of these twelve time periods. We call them Tasks 1 to 12, and put them into three task groups (A, B and C), each covering four tasks. For Task Group A, Users 1 - 5 used the console view, while Users 6 - 10 and Users 11 -15 used the tuple-level view and the full-fledged system respectively. For Task Group B, Users 1 - 5 used the tuple-level view, while Users 6 - 10 and Users 11 - 15 used the full-fledged system and the console view respectively. For Task Group C, Users 1 - 5 used our full-fledged system, while Users 6 - 10 and Users 11 - 15 used the console view and the tuple-level view respectively. The specific task assignment is also shown in Table 1. In this task assignment, no "pre-knowledge" problem will rise, as each of the users was only asked to finish particular task once.

	Console View	Tuple-Level View	Full-Fledged System
Users 1- 5	Task Group A (task 1-4)	Task Group B (task 5-8)	Task Group C (task 9-12)
Users 6-10	Task Group C (task 9-12)	Task Group A (task 1-4)	Task Group B (task 5-8)
Users 11-15	Task Group B (task 5-8)	Task Group C (task 9-12)	Task Group A (task 1-4)

Table 1: Task Assignment for User Study.

We measured both the efficiency and accuracy of the users finishing the monitoring tasks. We asked each user to report all pattern changes they observed in each task. For efficiency, we measured the time consumed by each user for each task. For accuracy, we measured the "correctness rate" of each user's report, namely the number of correct pattern changes reported by the user divided by the total number of pattern changes within each task (acquired by pre-analysis of the stream). Figures 14 and 15 depicted the average time consumed and the average accuracy of users for finishing each task within three task groups when supported by different exploration techniques.

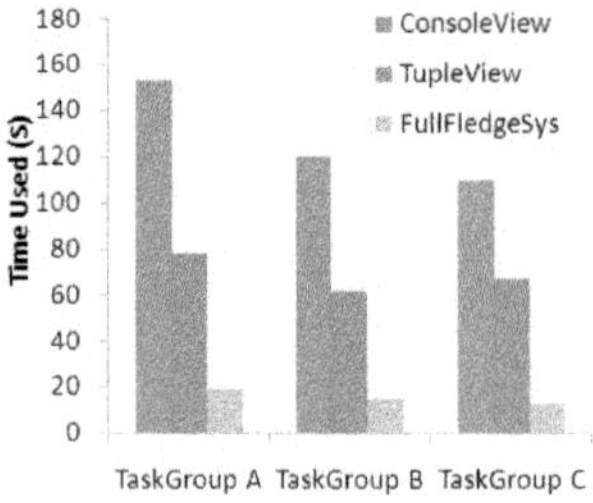

Figure 14: Comparison of Users' Efficiency

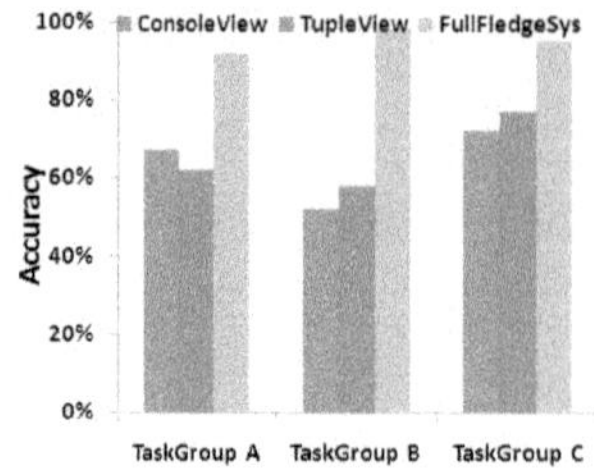

Figure 15: Compassion of Users' Accuracy

As shown in Figure 14, for the same tasks, the users used much less time when supported by our full-fledged system (10-20 sec for each task), while they needed a significantly longer time using the tuple-level view (60-80 sec) and the console view (110-160 sec). This is because both the console and tuple view do not provide any intuitive mechanism for users to identify the pattern changes. Users needed to learn about the relationships among clusters by analyzing the specific cluster members shown in either the text or the tuple level visualization. This was clearly time-consuming. While our full-fledged system provides an intuitive pattern-level view that allows analysts to quickly observe the cluster evolution.

Accuracy-wise, the performance of users was similar when using the console and tuple views ($52 - 70\%$). By analyzing the specific evolution types identified by the users, we observed that although the users could easily identify single-cluster evolution (preservation, expansion and shrinkage) using these two methods, they had difficulties in identifying the evolutions involving multiple clusters, such as splits and merges. In particular, by using the console or tuple view, only 25 and 32 % of such evolution types respectively were correctly identified by the users. This is because although these two methods are able to convey the size changes of single clusters, they lack effective mechanisms to express complex relationships among multiple clusters. In contrast, our full-fledged system intuitively conveys all evolution types. Thus, users were able to correctly identify almost all the cluster evolutions (92% on average) using our full-fledged system. In conclusion, our proposed solution is shown to help human analysts to track cluster evolution in the streams in an accurate and efficient manner.

7. CONCLUSION AND FUTURE WORK

In this work, we present a unified framework CLUES supporting interactive exploration of density-based clusters in streaming windows. As a foundation, we designed the first comprehensive model for classifying the evolution of density-based clusters in sliding windows. At the back-end, a new density-based clustering algorithm over sliding windows is introduced to efficiently compute not only clusters in isolated windows but also their evolution across windows. At the front-end, new visualization and interaction techniques were developed to effectively convey the detected clusters to the analysts. Our performance studies and user studies confirm the efficiency and effectiveness of our system for tracking clusters in data streams, respectively.

As future work, based on the platform built in this work, we will extend our study to more evolution models for clusters and also other pattern types, including allowing users to customize the models based on their own applications. At the visualization end, domain experts will be invited to help us design more customized visualization and interaction technics, which will provide functionalities specifically needed by some critical application domains.

8. REFERENCES

[1] C. C. Aggarwal. A framework for change diagnosis of data streams. In *SIGMOD*, pages 575–586, 2003.

[2] C. C. Aggarwal, J. Han, J. Wang, and P. S. Yu. A framework for clustering evolving data streams. In *VLDB*, pages 81–92, 2003.

[3] A. Arasu, S. Babu, and J. Widom. The cql continuous query language: semantic foundations and query execution. *VLDB J.*, 15(2):121–142, 2006.

[4] A. Arasu and J. Widom. Resource sharing in continuous sliding-window aggregates. In *VLDB*, pages 336–347, 2004.

[5] B. Babcock, M. Datar, R. Motwani, and L. O'Callaghan. Maintaining variance and k-medians over data stream windows. In *PODS*, pages 234–243, 2003.

[6] J. Beringer and E. Hüllermeier. Online clustering of parallel data streams. *Data Knowl. Eng.*, 58(2):180–204, 2006.

[7] A. Bifet and R. Gavaldà. Mining adaptively frequent closed unlabeled rooted trees in data streams. In *KDD*, pages 34–42, 2008.

[8] F. Cao, M. Ester, W. Qian, and A. Zhou. Density-based clustering over an evolving data stream with noise. In *SDM*, 2006.

[9] Y. Chen and L. Tu. Density-based clustering for real-time stream data. In *KDD*, pages 133–142, 2007.

[10] B.-R. Dai, J.-W. Huang, M.-Y. Yeh, and M.-S. Chen. Adaptive clustering for multiple evolving streams. *IEEE Trans. Knowl. Data Eng.*, 2006.

[11] Denny, G. J. Williams, and P. Christen. Redsom: Relative density visualization of temporal changes in cluster structures using self-organizing maps. In *ICDM*, pages 173–182, 2008.

[12] J. N. Entzminger, C. A. Fowler, and W. J. Kenneally. Jointstars and gmti: Past, present and future. *IEEE Trans on Aero and Elec Sys*, 35(2):748–762, april 1999.

[13] M. Ester, H. Kriegel, J. Sander, M. Wimmer, and X. Xu. Incremental clustering for mining in a data warehousing environment. In *VLDB*, 1998.

[14] M. Ester, H.-P. Kriegel, J. Sander, and X. Xu. A density-based algorithm for discovering clusters in large spatial databases with noise. In *KDD*, pages 226–231, 1996.

[15] S. Havre, E. Hetzler, P. Whitney, and L. Nowell. ThemeRiver: Visualizing thematic changes in large document collections. *IEEE Transactions on Visualization and Computer Graphics*, 8(1):9–20, January 2002.

[16] I. INETATS. Stock trade traces. http://www.inetats.com/.

[17] M. Spiliopoulou, I. Ntoutsi, Y. Theodoridis, and R. Schult. Monic: modeling and monitoring cluster transitions. In *KDD*, pages 706–711, 2006.

[18] A. K. H. Tung, X. Xu, and B. C. Ooi. Curler: Finding and visualizing nonlinear correlated clusters. In *SIGMOD*, pages 467–478, 2005.

[19] M. Wattenberg. Baby names, visualization, and social data analysis. *Proc. IEEE Symp. Information Visualization*, pages 1–7, 2005.

[20] D. Yang, E. A. Rundensteiner, and M. O. Ward. Neighbor-based pattern detection for windows over streaming data. In *EDBT*, pages 529–540, 2009.

e-NSP: Efficient Negative Sequential Pattern Mining Based on Identified Positive Patterns Without Database Rescanning

Xiangjun Dong
School of Information
Shandong Polytechnic University, Jinan, China
dxj@spu.edu.cn

Zhigang Zheng, Longbing Cao
QCIS, AAI
University of Technology, Sydney, Australia
{zgzheng,lbcao}@it.uts.edu.au

Yanchang Zhao
Centrelink
Australia
yanchang.zhao@centrelink.gov.au

Chengqi Zhang
QCIS
University of Technology, Sydney, Australia
chengqi@it.uts.edu.au

Jinjiu Li
QCIS, AAI
University of Technology, Sydney, Australia
jinjiu.li@eng.uts.edu.au

Wei Wei, Yuming Ou
QCIS, AAI
University of Technology, Sydney, Australia
{wwei,yuming}@it.uts.edu.au

ABSTRACT

Mining Negative Sequential Patterns (NSP) is much more challenging than mining Positive Sequential Patterns (PSP) due to the high computational complexity and huge search space required in calculating Negative Sequential Candidates (NSC). Very few approaches are available for mining NSP, which mainly rely on re-scanning databases after identifying PSP. As a result, they are very inefficient. In this paper, we propose an efficient algorithm for mining NSP, called e-NSP, which mines for NSP by only involving the identified PSP, without re-scanning databases. First, negative containment is defined to determine whether or not a data sequence contains a negative sequence. Second, an efficient approach is proposed to convert the negative containment problem to a positive containment problem. The supports of NSC are then calculated based only on the corresponding PSP. Finally, a simple but efficient approach is proposed to generate NSC. With e-NSP, mining NSP does not require additional database scans, and the existing PSP mining algorithms can be integrated into e-NSP to mine for NSP efficiently. e-NSP is compared with two currently available NSP mining algorithms on 14 synthetic and real-life datasets. Intensive experiments show that e-NSP takes as little as 3% of the runtime of the baseline approaches and is applicable for efficient mining of NSP in large datasets.

Categories and Subject Descriptors

H.2.8 [**Data-base Applications**]: Data Mining

General Terms

Algorithms, Performance, Experimentation

Keywords

Negative Sequential Pattern, Sequence Mining, Negative Containment

1. INTRODUCTION

Negative sequential patterns (NSP) refer to sequences with non-occurring items. For instance, assume p_1=<a b c X> is a positive sequential pattern (PSP); p_2=<a b $\neg c$ Y> is a NSP. It is increasingly recognized [5][10] that such NSP, composed of both occurring and non-occurring items, can play an irreplaceable role in deeply understanding and tackling many business applications, such as the associations between treatment services and illnesses, and the detection of high impact occurring (positive behaviors) and non-occurring behavior (negative behaviors) sequences [3, 2], which cannot be handled by mining PSP only. NSP cannot be described or discovered by classic PSP mining algorithms such as GSP, SPADE, PrefixSpan and SPAM. NSP mining has seen only very limited progress in recent years [6][5][10][11], and all existing methods are very inefficient in mining NSP. This is because NSP is much more difficult to mine than PSP, in particular because of two intrinsic complexities.

High computational complexity. The existing methods calculate the support of negative sequential candidates (NSC) by additionally scanning the database after identifying PSP. This leads to additional costs and results in low efficiency in NSP mining.

Large NSC search space. The existing approaches generate k-size NSC by conducting a joining operation on (k-1)-size NSP. This leads to a huge number of NSC [6][5][7][10], which makes it difficult to search for meaningful outputs. Further, NSC does not satisfy the anti-monotony principle [10]. It is a challenge to prune the large proportion of meaningless and unnecessary NSC, and it is therefore important to develop efficient approaches for generating a limited number of truly useful NSC.

To address the above critical challenges in NSP mining and make NSP mining workable in handling real-life applications, this paper proposes a novel and efficient NSP mining approach called *e-NSP*. The main idea is as follows. To avoid additional database scanning, we convert the negative containment problem to a positive containment problem. The NSC supports are then calculated by only using a NSC's corresponding PSP information. In this way, there is no need to re-scan the database after discovering PSP. To the best of our knowledge, this is the first approach to conduct efficient NSP mining by involving PSP only, without rescanning the database. e-NSP provides a new and promising strategy for efficient NSP mining which is workable in large datasets.

The remainder of the paper is organized as follows. Section 2 discusses the related work. In Section 3, we formalize the problem of mining PSP and NSP. The e-NSP algorithm is detailed in Section 4. Section 5 presents the experiment results, which are followed by conclusions and future work in Section 6.

2. RELATED WORK

Very limited research is available in the literature on mining NSP. [10] proposes a negative version of GSP algorithm NegGSP to mine for NSP. [5] proposes a PNSP approach for mining positive and negative sequential patterns in the form of $<(abc)\ \neg(de)\ (ijk)>$. [6] only handles NSP with the last element as negative. [11] proposes a genetic algorithm for mining NSP. [9] proposes an approach to mining event-oriented negative sequential rules. [7] identifies NSP in the form of $(\neg a,b)$, $(a,\neg b)$ and $(\neg a,\neg b)$, which is similar to [9]. The above approaches either re-scan the database or do not directly address NSP mining. In addition, different researchers present inconsistent definitions and explanations about the basic concept of negative containment [4]. [5] considers that data sequence $ds=<d\ c>$ cannot contain $<\neg(ab)\ c\ \neg d>$, $<\neg c\ d>$,and $<c\ \neg d>$,while [10] allows that *ds* contains them.

3. PROBLEM STATEMENT

In association rule mining, a non-occurring item is called a *negative item* and an occurring item is called a *positive item* [8]. This tradition is followed in NSP mining. Those sequences consisting of at least one negative item are called *negative sequences*. Sequential pattern mining (as it is usually called) mainly focuses on occurring items, namely *positive sequences* [6][5][7][10]. The sequences in source data are called *data sequences*.

3.1 Positive Sequential Patterns - PSP

Let $I = \{i_1, i_2, \ldots, i_n\}$ be a set of *items*. An *itemset* is a subset of I. A *sequence* is an ordered list of itemsets. A sequence s is denoted by $<s_1\ s_2 \ldots s_l>$, where $s_j \subseteq I\ (1 \leqslant j \leqslant l)$. s_j is also called an *element* of the sequence, and denoted as $(x_1x_2\ldots x_m)$, where x_k is an item, $x_k \in I\ (1 \leqslant k \leqslant m)$. For simplicity, the brackets are omitted if an element only has one item, i.e., element (x) is coded x. An item can occur at most once in an element, but can appear multiple times in different elements of a sequence.

The *length* of sequence s, denoted as *length(s)*, is the total number of items in all elements in s. s is a k-length sequence if $length(s)=k$. The *size* of sequence s, denoted as $size(s)$, is the total number of elements in s. s is a k-size sequence if $size(s)=k$.

Sequence $s_\alpha=<\alpha_1\ \alpha_2 \ldots \alpha_n>$ is called a *sub-sequence* of sequence $s_\beta=<\beta_1\ \beta_2 \ldots \beta_m>$ and s_β is a *super-sequence* of s_α, denoted as $s_\alpha \subseteq s_\beta$, if there exists $1 \leqslant j_1 < j_2 < \ldots < j_n \leqslant m$ such that $\alpha_1 \subseteq \beta_{j_1}$, $\alpha_2 \subseteq \beta_{j_2}$, ..., $\alpha_n \subseteq \beta_{j_n}$. We also say that s_β contains s_α.

A *sequence database D* is a set of tuples $<sid,ds>$, where *sid* is the *sequence_id* and *ds* is the *data sequence*. The number of tuples in D is denoted as $|D|$. The set of tuples containing sequence s is denoted as $\{<s>\}$. The support of s, denoted as $sup(s)$, is the number of $\{<s>\}$, i.e., $sup(s)=|\{<s>\}|=|\{<sid,ds>, <sid,ds> \in D \wedge (s \subseteq ds)\}|$. *min_sup* is a minimum support threshold which is predefined by users. Sequence s is called a frequent *(positive) sequential pattern* if $sup(s) \geqslant min\_sup$.

3.2 Negative Sequential Patterns - NSP

In real applications, the number of negative sequences is large, and many of them are not meaningful. In order to reduce the number of NSC and discover meaningful NSP efficiently, constraints must be added to negative sequences [9][11][5][10][6]. This paper also refers to the constraints in these existing papers. The only difference is that we mine NSP only from frequent PSP. The reason is that PSP is most useful for users to make decisions so far.

In order to formalize the constraints, we provide a definition as following.

Definition 1. Positive Partner

The positive partner of a negative element $\neg e$ is e, denoted as $p(\neg e)$, i.e., $p(\neg e)=e$. The positive partner of positive element e is e itself, i.e., $p(e)=e$. The positive partner of a negative sequence $ns=<s_1\ldots s_k>$ is to change all negative elements in ns to their positive partners, denoted as $p(ns)$, i.e., $p(ns)=\{<s'_1\ldots s'_k> \mid s'_i=p(s_i),\ s_i \in ns\}$. For example, $p(<\neg(ab)\ c\ \neg d>)=<(ab)\ c\ d>$.

Constraint 1. Frequency constraint. This paper only focuses on the negative sequences ns whose positive partner is frequent, i.e., $sup(p(ns)) \geqslant min\_sup$. While [5] and [10] only require the positive partner of each element in ns is frequent.

Constraint 2. Format constraint. Continuous negative elements in a NSC are not allowed. For example, $<\neg(ab)\ \neg c\ d>$ is not allowed. This constraint is same as [5][10].

Constraint 3. Element negative constraint. The minimum negative unit in a NSC is an element [10]. For example, $<(\neg ab)\ c\ d>$ does not satisfy this constraint, $<\neg(ab)\ c\ \neg d>$ does.

In this paper, we assume that a negative sequence implicitly satisfies the above three constraints.

Because of constraint 3, the definition of sub-sequence in positive sequence is not suitable for that in negative sequence. Now we formally redefine it by the definitions of element-id set and order preserving sequence. *Element id* is the order number of an element in a sequence. Given a sequence $s=<s_1\ s_2 \ldots s_m>$, $id(s_i)=i$ is the element id of element s_i. *Element-id set* $EidS_s$ of s is the set that includes all elements and their ids in s, i.e., $EidS_s=\{(s_i, id(s_i)) \mid s_i \in s\}=\{(s_1,1), (s_2,2), \ldots, (s_m,m)\}\ (1 \leqslant i \leqslant m)$. The set including all positive/negative element-ids is called *positive/negative element-id set* of s, denoted as $EidS_s^+$, $EidS_s^-$ respectively.

For any subset $EidS'_s=\{(\alpha_1,id_1), (\alpha_2,id_2), \ldots, (\alpha_p,id_p)\}$ $(1<p \leqslant m)$ of $EidS_s$, $\alpha=<\alpha_1\ \alpha_2 \ldots \alpha_p>$, if $\forall\ \alpha_i,\ \alpha_{i+1} \in \alpha$

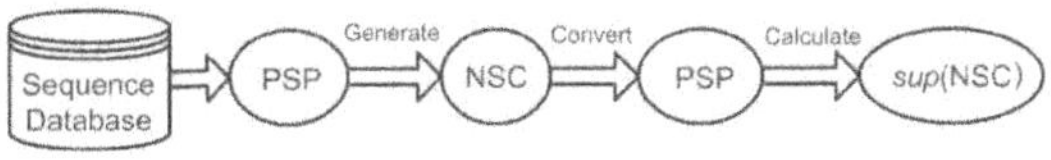

Figure 1: Framework of e-NSP

$(1 \leqslant i < p)$, there exist $id_i < id_{i+1}$, then α is called an *order-preserving sequence* of $EidS'_s$, denoted as $\alpha = OPS(EidS'_s)$.

Sequence s_α is called a *sub-sequence* of negative sequence s_β, and s_β is a *super-sequence* of s_α, if $\forall EidS'_{s_\beta}$, $EidS'_{s_\beta}$ is subset of $EidS_{s_\beta}$, $s_\alpha = OPS(EidS'_{s_\beta})$, denoted as $s_\alpha \subseteq s_\beta$. If s_α is a negative sequence, it is required to satisfy Constraint 2. Specially, the sub-sequence containing all positive elements, $OPS(EidS^+_s)$ is called the *Maximum Positive Sub-sequence* of s, denoted as $MPS(s)$.

Example 1. Given $s=<\neg(ab)\ c\ d>$, $EidS^+=\{(c,2), (d,3)\}$, $MPS(s)=<c\ d>$, $OPS(\{(c,2),(\neg(ab),1)\})=<\neg(ab)\ c>$ is a sub-sequence of s.

Definition 2. Negative Sequential Pattern (NSP)

A negative sequence s is a negative sequential pattern (NSP) if its support is not less than the threshold *min_sup*.

4. E-NSP ALGORITHM

Figure 1 shows the framework and working mechanism of e-NSP. First, it mines all PSP by traditional PSP mining algorithm, then it generates NSC based on PSP, after that, it calculates supports of NSC by converting them to calculating support of corresponding PSP.

4.1 Negative Containment

Because a sub-sequence (e.g., $s_1=<d>$) may occur more than one times in its super-sequence (e.g., $s_2=<a\ (bc)\ d\ (cde)>$), we need to know the positions that s_2 contains s_1 from left and right sides of s_2. It is very important to our Negative Containment Definition. Therefore we give the following definition.

Definition 3. First Sub-sequence Ending Position / Last Sub-sequence Beginning Position

Given a data sequence $ds=<d_1\ d_2 \ldots d_t>$ and a positive sequence α, (1) if $\exists p\ (1<p\leqslant t)$, $\alpha \subseteq <d_1 \ldots d_p> \wedge \alpha \nsubseteq <d_1 \ldots d_{p-1}>$, then p is called the *First Sub-sequence Ending Position*, denoted as $FSE(\alpha,ds)$; if $\alpha \subseteq <d_1>$ then $FSE(\alpha,ds)=1$; (2) if $\exists q\ (1\leqslant q<t)$, $\alpha \subseteq <d_q \ldots d_t> \wedge \alpha \nsubseteq <d_{q+1} \ldots d_t>$, then q is called the *Last Sub-sequence Beginning Position*, denoted as $LSB(\alpha,ds)$; if $\alpha \subseteq <d_t>$ then $LSB(\alpha,ds)=t$; (3) if $\alpha \nsubseteq ds$, then $FSE(\alpha,ds)=0$, $LSB(\alpha,ds)=0$.

Example 2. Given $ds=<a\ (bc)\ d\ (cde)>$. $FSE(<a>,ds)=1$, $FSE(<c>,ds)=2$, $FSE(<c\ d>,ds)=3$, $LSB(<a>,ds)=1$, $LSB(<c>,ds)=4$, $LSB(<c\ d>,ds)=2$, $LSB(<(cd)>,ds)=4$.

Our definition of a data sequence containing a negative sequence is as follows. We use *n-neg-size* to denote a negative sequene containing n negative elements.

Definition 4. Negative Containment Definition

Let $ds=<d_1\ d_2 \ldots d_t>$ be a data sequence, $ns=<s_1\ s_2 \ldots s_m>$ be an *m-size* and *n-neg-size* negative sequence, (1) if $m>2t+1$, then *ds does not contain ns*; (2) if $m=1$ and $n=1$, then *ds contains ns* when $p(ns) \nsubseteq ds$; (3) otherwise, *ds contains ns* if, $\forall (s_i, id(s_i)) \in EidS^-_{ns}\ (1\leqslant i \leqslant m)$, one of the following three holds:

(a) $(lsb=1)$ or $(lsb>1) \wedge p(s_1) \nsubseteq <d_1 \ldots d_{lsb-1}>$, when $i=1$,

(b) $(fse=t)$ or $(0<fse<t) \wedge p(s_m) \nsubseteq <d_{fse+1} \ldots d_t>$, when $i=m$,

(c) $(fse>0 \wedge lsb=fse+1)$ or $(fse>0 \wedge lsb>fse+1) \wedge p(s_i) \nsubseteq <d_{fse+1} \ldots d_{lsb-1}>$, when $1<i<m$,

where $fse=FSE(MPS(<s_1\ s_2 \ldots s_{i-1}>),ds)$, $lsb=LSB(MPS(<s_{i+1} \ldots s_m>),ds)$.

Example 3. Given $ds=<a\ (bc)\ d\ (cde)>$, we have

(1) $ns=<\neg a\ c>$. $EidS^-_{ns}=\{(\neg a,1)\}$. ds does not contain ns. $lsb=4>0$, but $p(s_1)=<a> \subseteq <d_1 \ldots d_3>=<a\ (bc)\ d>$ (Case a).

(2) $ns=<\neg a\ a\ c>$. $EidS^-_{ns}=\{(\neg a,1)\}$. ds contains ns because $lsb=1$ (Case a).

(3) $ns=<(ab)\ \neg(cd)>$. $EidS^-_{ns}=\{(\neg(cd),2)\}$. ds does not contain ns because $fse=0$ (Case b).

(4) $ns=<(de)\ \neg(cd)>$. $EidS^-_{ns}=\{(\neg(cd),2)\}$. ds contains ns because $fse=4 (t=4)$(Case b).

(5) $ns=<a\ \neg d\ d\ \neg d>$. $EidS^-_{ns}=\{(\neg d,2), (\neg d,4)\}$. ds does not contain ns. For $(\neg d,2)$, $fse=1$, $lsb=4$, but $p(\neg d) \subseteq <d_2 \ldots d_3>=<(bc)\ d>$ (Case c). If one negative element does not satisfy the condition, we do not need to consider other negative elements.

(6) $ns=<a\ \neg b\ b\ \neg a\ (cde)>$. $EidS^-_{ns}=\{(\neg b,2), (\neg a,4)\}$. ds contains ns. For $(\neg b,1)$, $fse=1$, $lsb=2$, $fse>0 \wedge lsb=fse+1$ (Case c); For $(\neg a,4)$, $fse=2$, $lsb=4$, $p(\neg a) \nsubseteq <d_3>=<d>$ (Case c).

4.2 Negative Conversion

In order to convert negative containment problems to positive containment problems, we need to define a special sub-sequence as follows.

Definition 5. 1-neg-size Maximum Sub-sequence

For a negative sequence ns, its sub-sequence that includes $MPS(ns)$ and one negative element e is called a *1-neg-size* maximum sub-sequence, denoted as $1\text{-}negMS=OPS(EidS^+_{ns}, e)$, where $e \in EidS^-_{ns}$. The sub-sequence set including all 1-neg-size maximum sub-sequences of ns is called 1-neg-size maximum sub-sequence set, denoted as $1\text{-}negMSS_{ns}$, $1\text{-}negMSS_{ns}=\{OPS(EidS^+_{ns},e) |\ \forall\ e \in EidS^-_{ns}\}$.

Corollary 1. Negative Conversion Strategy

Given a data sequence $ds=<d_1\ d_2 \ldots d_t>$, and $ns=<s_1\ s_2 \ldots s_m>$, which is an *m-size* and *n-neg-size* negative sequence, the negative containment definition can be converted as follows: data sequence ds contains negative sequence ns if and only if the two conditions hold: (1) $MPS(ns) \subseteq ds$; and (2) $\forall\ 1\text{-}negMS \in 1\text{-}negMSS_{ns}$, $p(1\text{-}negMS) \nsubseteq ds$.

Example 4. Given $ds=<a\ (bc)\ d\ (cde)>$, 1) if $ns=<a\ \neg d\ d\ \neg d>$, $1\text{-}negMSS_{ns}=\{<a\ \neg d\ d>, <a\ d\ \neg d>\}$, then ds does not contain ns because $p(<a\ \neg d\ d>)=<a\ d\ d> \subseteq ds$; 2) if $ns'=<a\ \neg b\ b\ \neg a\ (cde)>$, $1\text{-}negMSS'_{ns}=\{<a\ \neg b\ b\ (cde)>, <a\ b\ \neg a\ (cde)>\}$, then ds contains ns because $MPS(ns)=<a\ b\ (cde)> \subseteq ds \wedge p(<a\ \neg b\ b\ (cde)>) \nsubseteq ds \wedge p(<a\ b\ \neg a\ (cde)>) \nsubseteq ds$.

Corollary 1 proves that the problem of whether a data sequence contains a negative sequence is equivalent to the problem of whether the data sequence does not contain its corresponding positive sequences. The proof of Corollary 1 is omitted here because of limited space.

4.3 Support of Negative Sequence

Corollary 2.

Given a *m-size* and *n-neg-size* negative sequence ns, for $\forall 1\text{-}negMS_i \in 1\text{-}negMSS_{ns}\ (1\leqslant i \leqslant n)$, the support of ns in sequence database D is:

$$sup(ns) = |\{ns\}| = |\{MPS(ns)\} - \cup_{i=1}^{n}\{p(1\text{-}negMS_i)\}| \quad (1)$$

This can be easily derived from Corollary 1. Because $\cup_{i=1}^{n}\{p(1\text{-}negMS_i)\} \subseteq \{MPS(ns)\}$, equation 1 can be rewritten as:

$$sup(ns) = |\{MPS(ns)\}| - |\cup_{i=1}^{n}\{p(1\text{-}negMS_i)\}|$$

$$= sup(MPS(ns)) - |\cup_{i=1}^{n}\{p(1 - negMS_i)\}| \qquad (2)$$

Example 5. $sup(<\neg a\ (bc)\ d\ \neg(cde)>) = sup(<(bc)\ d>) - |\{<a\ (bc)\ d>\} \cup \{<(bc)\ d\ (cde)>\}|$;

If ns only contains a negative element

$$sup(ns) = sup(MPS(ns)) - sup(p(ns)) \qquad (3)$$

Example 6. $sup(<(ab)\ \neg c\ d>) = sup(<(ab)\ d>) - sup(<(ab)\ c\ d>)$

In particular, for negative sequence $<\neg e>$,

$$sup(<\neg e>) = |D| - sup(<e>) \qquad (4)$$

From equation 2 we can see that $sup(ns)$ can be easily calculated if we know $sup(MPS(ns))$ and $|\cup_{i=1}^{n}\{p(1\text{-}negMS_i)\}|$. According to Constraint (1) and the negative candidate generation approach discussed in Section 4.4, $MPS(ns)$ and $p(1\text{-}negMS_i)$ are frequent. So $sup(MPS(ns))$ can be easily obtained by traditional algorithms.

Now the problem is how to calculate $|\cup_{i=1}^{n}\{p(1\text{-}negMS_i)\}|$. Our approach is as follows.

We use a data structure, which is called e-NSP data structure, like Table 2 to store the corresponding data, including PSP, support and $\{sid\}$ (containing all ids of the tuples that contain corresponding PSP). These data are stored in a hash table to identify PSP efficiently. In order to calculate the union set efficiently, we propose two other optimization methods as follows: (1) When we calculate support of a N-SC, we also utilize a hash table to accelerate search speed. Compared with the performance using common array, the search speed with hash table is far more efficient. (2) We assume that all data in Table 2 are stored in main memory. This is feasible in practice since the mainstream memory can reach gigabytes and above. We do not record the *sid* of 1-size PSP because the equations do not need to calculate the union set of those *sid* of 1-size PSP.

4.4 Negative Sequential Candidates Generation

The basic idea of generating a negative sequential candidate is to change any non-contiguous elements (not items) in a PSP to their negative ones.

Definition 6. e-NSP Candidate Generation

For a k-size PSP, its NSC are generated by changing any m non-contiguous element(s) to its (their) negative one(s), $m=1,2,\ldots,\lceil k/2 \rceil$, where $\lceil k/2 \rceil$ is a minimum integer that is not less than $k/2$.

Example 7. The NSC based on $<(ab)\ c\ d>$ include:

$m=1$, $<\neg(ab)\ c\ d>, <(ab)\ \neg c\ d>, <(ab)\ c\ \neg d>$;

$m=2$, $<\neg(ab)\ c\ \neg d>$.

Obviously, for all PSP in a sequence database, we can generate all NSC that satisfy the three constraints, as described in Section 3.2.

4.5 Algorithm Pseudocode

The e-NSP algorithm, as shown in Algorithm 1, is proposed to mine for NSP using only identified PSP.

Algorithm 1: e-NSP Algorithm

```
Input: Sequence Dataset D and min_sup;
Output: NSP;
PSP = minePSP();
HashTable PSPHash = CreatePSPHashTable(PSP);
For (each psp in PSP){
  NSC = e-NSP_Candidate_Generation(psp);
  For (each nsc in NSC){
    if (nsc.size==1 && nsc.neg_size==1) {
      nsc.support = |D| - p(nsc).support;
    } else if (nsc.size>1 && nsc.neg_size==1){
      nsc.support = MPS(nsc).support - p(nsc).support;
    } else {
      1-negMSS_nsc = {1-negMS_i | 1<=i<=nsc.neg_size};
      HashTable cHash = new HashTable();
      For (i=1; i<=nsc.neg_size; i++) {
        For (each sid in p(1-negMS_i).sidSet) {
          If (sid.hashcode NOT IN cHash)
            cHash.put(sid.hashcode(),sid);
          nsc.support=MPS(nsc).support - cHash.size();
      }
      If (nsc.support > min_sup) NSP.add(nsc);
}}}}
return NSP;
```

Table 1: Example Data Set

Sid	Data Sequence
10	$<a\ b\ c>$
20	$<a\ (ab)>$
30	$<(ae)\ (ab)\ c>$
40	$<a\ a>$
50	$<d>$

Table 2: Example Result - Positive Patterns

PSP	Support	{sid}
$<a>$	4	-
$<b>$	3	-
$<c>$	2	-
$<a\ a>$	3	{20,30,40}
$<a\ b>$	3	{10,20,30}
$<a\ c>$	2	{10,30}
$<b\ c>$	2	{10,30}
$<(ab)>$	2	-
$<a\ b\ c>$	2	{10,30}
$<a\ (ab)>$	2	{20,30}

4.6 An Example

The sequence database is shown in Table 1 [5]. The process is as follows.

(1) Mine PSP using one of the well-known algorithms, such as GSP, and fill in the e-NSP data structures, which are shown as Table 2.

(2) Use the e-NSP Candidate Generation method to generate all NSC.

(3) Use Equations 2-4 to calculate the support of these NSC. The results are shown in Table 3, and the resulting NSP are marked in bold.

From this example, we can see that $<a\ c>$ and $<a\ \neg c>$, $<a\ (ab)>$ and $<a\ \neg(ab)>$ are frequent patterns, but clearly not all of them can be used to make decisions because they may be misleading. How to select the meaningful and workable patterns is one of our ongoing tasks.

Table 3: Example Result - NSC and Support (min_sup=2)

PSP	NSC	Related PSP	Sup
<a>	<¬a>	<a>	1
<b>	<¬b>	<b>	**2**
<c>	<¬c>	<c>	**3**
<a a>	<¬a a>	<a>, <a a>	1
	<a ¬a>	<a>, <a a>	1
<a b>	<¬a b>	<b>, <a b>	0
	<a ¬b>	<a>, <a b>	1
<a c>	<¬a c>	<c>, <a c>	0
	<a ¬c>	<a>, <a c>	**2**
<b c>	<¬b c>	<c>, <b c>	0
	<b ¬c>	<b>, <b c>	1
<(ab)>	**<¬(ab)>**	<(ab)>	**3**
<a (ab)>	<¬a (ab)>	<(ab)>, <a (ab)>	0
	<a ¬(ab)>	<a>, <a (ab)>	**2**
<a b c>	<¬a b c>	<b c>, <a b c>	0
	<a ¬b c>	<a c>, <a b c>	0
	<a b ¬c>	<a b>, <a b c>	1
	<¬a b ¬c>	<b>, <a b>, <b c>	0

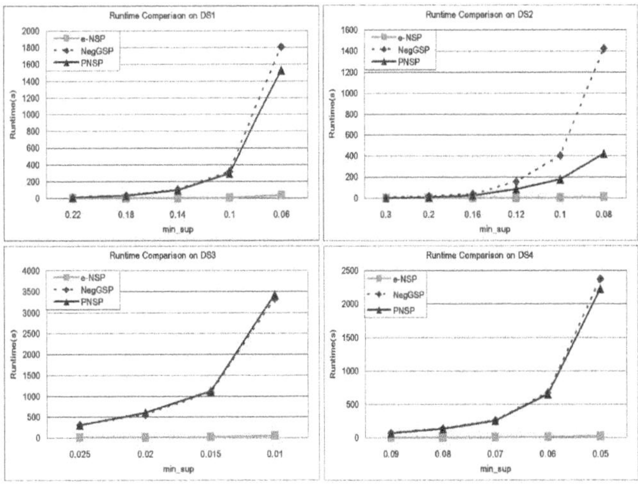

Figure 2: Runtime Comparison

5. EXPERIMENTS AND EVALUATION

We conduct experiments on 14 synthetic and real datasets to compare the efficiency of e-NSP with two baseline approaches PNSP [5] and NegGSP [10]. We select PNSP and NegGSP because they are the only available algorithms that are comparable to our algorithm. To compare their performance, we adapt PSNP and NegGSP to follow the same definitions and constraints as stated in Section 3. In the comparison, all positive patterns are identified by GSP. NSP are further mined by e-NSP, PNSP and NegGSP. We conduct intensive experiments to compare the difference between three algorithms in terms of computational costs on different data sizes and data characteristics.

All algorithms are implemented in Java in a PC with Intel Core 2 CPU of 2.9GHz, 2GB memory and Windows XP Professional SP2.

5.1 Data Sets

To describe and observe the impact of data characteristics on algorithm performance, we use following data factors: *C*, *T*, *S*, *I*, *DB* and *N*, which are defined to describe characteristics of sequence data [1].

C: Average number of elements per sequence; *T*: Average number of items per element; *S*: Average length of maximal potentially large sequences; *I*: Average size of items per element in maximal potentially large sequences; *DB*: Number of sequences (= size of Database); and *N*: Number of items.

Four source datasets are used for the experiments. They include both real data and synthetic datasets generated by IBM data generator [1]. By partitioning the data, we obtain 14 datasets in total.

Dataset 1 (DS1), C8_T4_S6_I6_DB100k_N100. We further adjust *DS*1 to generate 10 additional datasets, labelled as $DS1.x$ ($x = 1, \ldots, 10$).

Dataset 2 (DS2), C10_T8_S20_I10_DB10k_N0.2k.

Dataset 3 (DS3) is from UCI Datasets. There are 989,818 records. The average number of elements in a sequence is 4, and each element only has one item.

Dataset 4 (DS4) is real-application data from financial service industry. It contains 5,269 customers/sequences. The average number of elements in a sequence is 21. The minimum number of elements in a sequence is 1, and the maximum number is 144.

5.2 Computational Cost

The runtime of mining NSP by the three approaches is shown in Figure 2. e-NSP takes mostly less than 3% of the runtime of PNSP and NegGSP on all datasets. For example, e-NSP spends 2.7% to 1.6% runtime of PNSP on *DS*3 when *min_sup* decreased from 0.025 to 0.01. When *min_sup* is reduced to 0.01, PNSP and NegGSP take around one hour, but e-NSP takes less than one minute, because e-NSP only needs to "calculate" NSP support based on the *sid* sets of corresponding positive patterns, while PNSP and NegGSP have to re-scan the whole dataset.

The results on the maximum length and number of negative patterns are shown in Figure 3. It is difficult to draw a reliable conclusion from them, because the characteristics of the datasets are not comparable. Therefore, we conduct a dataset characteristics analysis in following section.

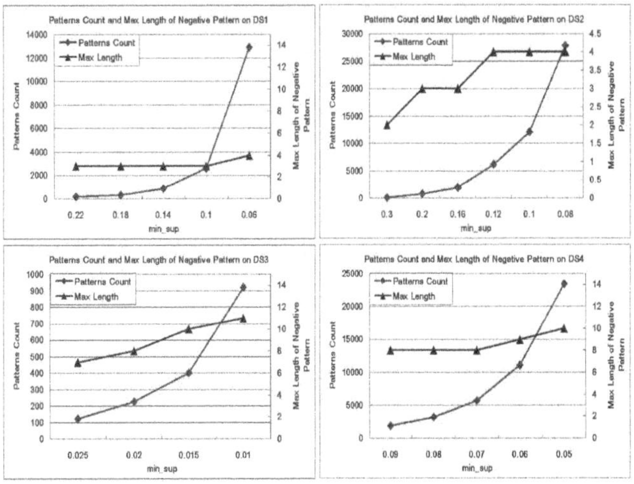

Figure 3: Maximum Length and Number of Negative Patterns

Table 4: Dataset Characteristics Analysis Result

ID	Dataset Characteristics	min sup	NGSP (t_1,s)	PNSP (t_2,s)	eNSP (t_3,s)	t_3/t_2
DS1	C8T4S6I6.DB10k.N100	0.04	1451.7	638.2	14.94	2.3%
		0.06	241.4	163.1	4.16	2.5%
		0.08	78.9	61.9	1.53	2.5%
DS1.1	**C4**T4S6I6.DB10k.N100	0.01	517.5	208.4	1.08	0.5%
		0.015	130.4	64.5	0.33	0.5%
		0.02	48.0	28.4	0.16	0.5%
DS1.2	**C12**T4S6I6.DB10k.N100	0.14	229.0	191.9	7.99	4.2%
		0.16	127.6	109.5	4.49	4.1%
		0.18	73.8	66.9	2.53	3.8%
DS1.3	C8**T8**S6I6.DB10k.N100	0.22	130.8	118.5	5.22	4.4%
		0.24	83.7	76.5	3.19	4.2%
		0.26	55.9	52.8	2.14	4.1%
DS1.4	C8**T12**S6I6.DB10k.N100	0.3	1205.2	969.3	57.55	5.9%
		0.4	133.2	123.5	6.75	5.5%
		0.5	23.6	23.0	1.06	4.6%
DS1.5	C8T4**S12**I6.DB10k.N100	0.04	1130.0	478.6	12.22	2.6%
		0.06	187.0	124.7	3.39	2.7%
		0.08	61.2	47.5	1.23	2.6%
DS1.6	C8T4**S18**I6.DB10k.N100	0.04	297.1	157.4	3.47	2.2%
		0.06	64.2	45.5	0.97	2.1%
		0.08	23.5	19.0	0.36	1.9%
DS1.7	C8T4S6**I10**.DB10k.N100	0.06	690.2	395.1	7.33	1.9%
		0.07	334.7	227.5	4.23	1.9%
		0.08	188.1	138.0	2.63	1.9%
DS1.8	C8T4S6**I14**.DB10k.N100	0.08	983.9	630.8	8.88	1.4%
		0.1	320.5	248.9	3.63	1.5%
		0.12	141.8	112.7	1.61	1.4%
DS1.9	C8T4S6I6.DB10k.**N200**	0.03	378.2	98.4	0.59	0.6%
		0.04	101.8	43.1	0.17	0.4%
		0.05	39.5	23.3	0.06	0.3%
DS1.10	C8T4S6I6.DB10k.**N400**	0.015	823.0	97.4	0.08	0.1%
		0.02	197.3	42.0	0.03	0.1%
		0.025	99.8	20.6	0.02	0.1%

5.3 Dataset Characteristics Analysis

We analyze the dataset characteristics in terms of the above defined data factors to see the impact of the data factors (see Section 5.1) on the performance of e-NSP, compared to PNSP and NegGSP. We generate various types of synthetic datasets with different distributions. Dataset *DS1* is extended to ten different datasets by tuning each factor, as shown in Table 4. For example, dataset *DS1.1*(C4T4S6I6. DB10k.N100) is different to *DS1*(C8T4S6I6.DB10k.N100) on C factor, which means they have different average numbers of elements in a sequence. We mark the difference by underlining the distinct factor for each dataset in Table 4.

In Table 4, *t1*, *t2* and *t3* represent the runtime of NegGSP, PNSP and e-NSP correspondingly. We use *t3/t2* to show e-NSP's performance compared with PNSP. From the results (see Table 4), we can say that factors C, T and N seriously affect the performance of e-NSP, and factors S and I do not greatly affect it. When factor C is low, such as *DS1.1*, e-NSP works better than on datasets with big C, such as *DS1* and *DS1.2*. Similar results hold for T, such as *DS1* with small T, compared with *DS1.3* and *DS1.4* with big T. When N is high, such as in *DS1.9* and *DS1.10*, e-NSP works better than that with small N, such as in *DS1*.

6. CONCLUSIONS AND FUTURE WORK

Mining NSP is very challenging due to the large search space of negative candidates. Current NSP techniques rely on re-scaning databases after identifying positive patterns. This has been shown to be very inefficient, and little progress has been made in NSP mining. We have proposed a simple but very efficient NSP mining algorithm: e-NSP. e-NSP is based on a formal and consistent concept, negative containment, which defines how a data sequence contains a negative sequence. e-NSP encloses a negative conversion strategy to convert the problem of whether a data sequence contains a negative sequence to the problem of whether the data sequence contains some of the corresponding positive sequences. Supports of NSC are then calculated based only on the corresponding PSP. Finally, a simple but efficient approach has been proposed to generate NSC. e-NSP has been tested on both synthetic and real-world datasets and compared with existing NSP mining algorithms. The experimental results and comparisons on 14 datasets from data characteristics perspectives have clearly shown that e-NSP is much more efficient than existing approaches. e-NSP offers a new strategy for efficiently mining large scale NSP.

We are currently working on effective approaches to select the most meaningful patterns, and the application of negative sequence mining on complex behavior analysis.

Acknowledgment

This work was supported by Projects of International Cooperation Training for Shandong Province Higher Educational Excellent Backbone Teacher, Shandong Provincial Natural Science Foundation, China (No.ZR2011FM028), and by Australian Research Council Grants (DP1096218, DP0988016, LP100200774, LP0989721).

7. REFERENCES

[1] R. Agrawal and R. Srikant. Mining sequential patterns. In *ICDE' 95*, pages 3–14, 1995.

[2] L. Cao. In-depth behavior understanding and use: the behavior informatics approach. *Information Science*, 180:3067–3085, 2010.

[3] L. Cao, Y. Zhao, and C. Zhang. Mining impact-targeted activity patterns in imbalanced data. *IEEE TKDE*, 20:1053–1066, 2008.

[4] X. Dong, L. Zhao, X. Han, and H. Jiang. Comparisons of several definitions about negative containment. In *ICCNT' 11*, pages 553–556, 2011.

[5] S.-C. Hsueh, M.-Y. Lin, and C.-L. Chen. Mining negative sequential patterns for e-commerce recommendations. In *APSCC '08. IEEE*, pages 1213–1218, 2008.

[6] N. P. Lin, H.-J. Chen, and W.-H. Hao. Mining negative sequential patterns. In *WSEAS' 07*, pages 654–658, 2007.

[7] W.-M. Ouyang and Q.-H. Huang. Mining negative sequential patterns in transaction databases. In *ICMLC' 07*, volume 2, pages 830–834, 2007.

[8] X. Wu, C. Zhang, and S. Zhang. Efficient mining of both positive and negative association rules. *ACM Trans. Inf. Syst.*, 22:381–405, July 2004.

[9] Y. Zhao, H. Zhang, L. Cao, C. Zhang, and H. Bohlscheid. Mining both positive and negative impact-oriented sequential rules from transactional data. In *PAKDD' 09*, volume 5476, pages 656–663. 2009.

[10] Z. Zheng, Y. Zhao, Z. Zuo, and L. Cao. Negative-gsp: An efficient method for mining negative sequential patterns. In *Data Mining and Analytics*, volume 101, pages 63–67. 2009.

[11] Z. Zheng, Y. Zhao, Z. Zuo, and L. Cao. An efficient ga-based algorithm for mining negative sequential patterns. In *PAKDD' 10*, volume 6118, pages 262–273. 2010.

Optimising Ontology Stream Reasoning with Truth Maintenance System *

Yuan Ren
Department of Computing Science
University of Aberdeen, Aberdeen
AB24 3UE, UK
y.ren@abdn.ac.uk

Jeff Z. Pan
Department of Computing Science
University of Aberdeen, Aberdeen
AB24 3UE, UK
jeff.z.pan@abdn.ac.uk

ABSTRACT

So far researchers in the Description Logics / Ontology communities mainly consider ontology reasoning services for static ontologies. The rapid development of the Semantic Web and its emerging data ask for reasoning technologies for dynamic knowledge streams. Existing work on stream reasoning is focused on lightweight languages such as RDF and RDFS. In this paper, we introduce the notion of Ontology Stream Management System (OSMS) and present a stream-reasoning approach based on Truth Maintenance System (TMS). We present optimised $\mathcal{EL}^{++}$ algorithm to reduce memory consumption. Our evaluations show that the optimisation improves TMS-enabled $\mathcal{EL}^{++}$ reasoning to deal with relatively large volumes of data and update efficiently.

Categories and Subject Descriptors

I.2.3 [**Artificial Intelligence**]: Deduction and Theorem Proving—*Inference engines*

General Terms

Algorithms

Keywords

Ontology, Stream Reasoning, Truth Maintenance System

1. INTRODUCTION

Ontologies are the knowledge infrastructures of the Semantic Web and many intelligent systems. The standard Web Ontology Language OWL is based on the Description Logics (DLs). So far researchers in the DL/ Ontology communities mainly consider ontology reasoning services for static ontologies. However, in real world data and knowledge is usually subject to change. Parsia et. al. [12] described several typical scenarios such as ontology editing, web service matchmaking, sensor networks and mobile semantic web [11]. Considering the following running example:

EXAMPLE 1. *Given the schedule of a conference and researchers' personal information and activities, such as who is attending which events, a knowledge management system would be able to collect data and provide recommendations, in real time.*

In this paper, we assume such data has been extracted and formalised, and focus on the data processing and reasoning aspect. Due to the real-time nature of these user generated information and ongoing events, it is adequate to consider them as data streams.

There have been many works regarding **querying streaming data** on the semantic web. A. Bolles et al. [7] proposed an extension of SPARQL to process data streams. Similarly, C-SPARQL [5], another extension of SPARQL can continuously query from a RDF knowledge base. More related work focus on **continuously and incrementally updating and materialising ontological knowledge bases**. R. Volz et al. [14] adopted the Delete and Re-derive (DRed) algorithm [9] from traditional data stream management systems and proposed a declarative variant of it. When change occurs, the "stream reasoner" first overestimates the consequences of the deletion, then "cash-back" the over-deleted consequences that can be derived by other facts, and finally adds new entailments that are derived from the new facts. Further optimisation was proposed [6] with an additional assumption that the time window of stream is fixed and known to the stream reasoner. The relation between a consequence and a time point can be maintained so that when the time comes, the stream reasoner expires corresponding consequences. In their evaluation, this approach outperforms a naive approach with up to 13% of RDF triples changed, which is better than the 3% limit of [14]. However, these approaches are still limited to relatively simple languages such as RDF, RDFS. The optimisation also requires a known fixed time window. Otherwise, the optimisation can not work. This also means deleting axioms in real-time is not allowed. For example, if data collected from different sources make the ontology inconsistent, such inconsistency can not be actively resolved by removing conflicting knowledge.

In this paper, we introduce the notion of ontology stream management system (OSMS). We present an ontology stream reasoning approach by applying Truth Maintenance Systems (TMS [8]) for OSMS. A TMS maintains not only reasoning results, but also intermediate results and the deduction relations among them. Thus on the one hand, impacted results of removed knowledge can be retrieved without prior knowledge of fixed time window. On the other hand, further inference can be carried on from the intermediate results, instead of the original asserted knowledge. Both will significantly increase the efficiency of stream reasoning to facilitate real-time response. However, TMS has a well-known disadvantage of excessive memory consumption. To address this issue, we present an optimised algorithm for $\mathcal{EL}^{++}$, the logic underpinning OWL 2 EL, by reducing the number of unnecessary intermediate

*This paper is an extension of [13], an earlier work presented in a workshop.

CIKM'11, October 24–28, 2011, Glasgow, Scotland, UK.

results. Our evaluation shows that our approach can outperform naive re-computation with relatively large volumes of knowledge base (up to 30000 axioms) and updates (up to 10%).

2. BACKGROUND

A signature $\Sigma = (\mathcal{CN}, \mathcal{RN}, \mathcal{IN})$ consists of three disjoint sets $\mathcal{CN}$, $\mathcal{RN}$, $\mathcal{IN}$, where $\mathcal{CN}$ is the set of atomic concepts, $\mathcal{RN}$ is the set of atomic roles and $\mathcal{IN}$ is the set of individuals. Given a signature, $\top$ the top concept, $\bot$ the bottom concept, A an atomic concept, a an individual, r an atomic role, $\mathcal{EL}^{++}$ concept expressions C, D can be composed with the following constructs:

$$\top \mid \bot \mid A \mid C \sqcap D \mid \exists r.C \mid \{a\}$$

We slightly abuse the notion of atomic concepts to include also $\top$, $\bot$ and nominals (i.e. concepts of form $\{a\}$). Given a knowledge base $\mathbf{K}$, we use $CN_{\mathbf{K}}$, $RN_{\mathbf{K}}$, $IN_{\mathbf{K}}$ to denote the set of atomic concepts, atomic roles and individuals in $\mathbf{K}$, respectively.

A DL ontology $\mathcal{O} =< \mathcal{T}, \mathcal{A} >$ is composed of a TBox $\mathcal{T}$ and an ABox $\mathcal{A}$. A TBox is a set of concept and role axioms. $\mathcal{EL}^{++}$ supports general concept inclusion axioms (GCIs, e.g. $C \sqsubseteq D$) and role inclusion axioms (RIs, e.g. $r \sqsubseteq s$, $r_1 \circ \cdots \circ r_n \sqsubseteq s$). If $C \sqsubseteq D$ and $D \sqsubseteq C$, we write $C \equiv D$. An ABox is a set of concept assertion axioms, e.g. $a : C$, role assertion axioms, e.g. $(a, b) : R$, and individual equality axioms, e.g. $a = b$, and individual inequality axioms, e.g. $a \neq b$.

EXAMPLE 2. *Here are some simple $\mathcal{EL}^{++}$ ontologies: Ontology $\mathcal{O}$: $\{$ $ActiveTalk \sqsubseteq \exists in.Session$, $hasTopic \circ interest \sqsubseteq recommend$, $\exists recommend.\{David\} \sqsubseteq Talk4Dave$, $ActiveTalk \sqcap Talk4Dave \sqsubseteq TargetTalk$, $(ontology, Daivd) : interest$, $(talk1, ontology) : hasTopic$, $(talk2, ontology) : hasTopic$, $\}$ specifies that an* ActiveTalk *must be presented in some* Session*; A talk can be recommended to someone if the talk has topic that interests the person; A talk is for David if it can be recommended to David and such a talk will be a $TargetTalk$ if it is active; It also says that David is interested in ontology. There are two talks $talk1$ and $talk2$ that have topic about ontology.*

$\mathcal{O}(0) = \{talk0 : ActiveTalk\}$ *shows that talk0 is an $ActiveTalk$.*
$\mathcal{O}(1) = \{talk1 : ActiveTalk\}$ *shows that talk1 is an $ActiveTalk$.*
$\mathcal{O}(2) = \{talk2 : ActiveTalk\}$ *shows that talk2 is an $ActiveTalk$.*

If an axiom α can be derived from an ontology $\mathcal{O}$, we say that α is entailed by $\mathcal{O}$, denoted by $\mathcal{O} \models \alpha$. α is an entailment of $\mathcal{O}$. For an ontology $\mathcal{O}$ and its entailment α, a set of axioms $J_{\mathcal{O}}(\alpha) \subseteq \mathcal{O}$ is a justification of α *iff* $J_{\mathcal{O}}(\alpha) \models \alpha$ and $J' \not\models \alpha$ for all $J' \subset J_{\mathcal{O}}(\alpha)$. For $\mathcal{EL}^{++}$, a single justification can be computed in PTIME [4].

Franz Baader et. al. [1] presents a completion-based algorithm to classify an $\mathcal{EL}^{++}$ TBox. Given an $\mathcal{EL}^{++}$ TBox $\mathcal{T}$, it can be *normalised* in linear time [3] into a **normal form** TBox $\mathcal{T}'$ in which all axioms are in one of the following forms, where $A_i \in \mathcal{CN}_{\mathcal{T}'}$ and $r_i \in \mathcal{RN}_{\mathcal{T}'}$, by introducing fresh atomic concepts and roles:

$$\begin{array}{rclrcl} A_1 & \sqsubseteq & A_2, & A_1 & \sqsubseteq & \exists r.A_2, \\ A_1 \sqcap \cdots \sqcap A_n & \sqsubseteq & A_{n+1}, & \exists r.A_1 & \sqsubseteq & A_2, \\ r_1 \circ r_2 & \sqsubseteq & r_3, & r_1 & \sqsubseteq & r_2. \end{array}$$

For any two $A, B \in \mathcal{CN}_{\mathcal{T}}$, $\mathcal{T} \models A \sqsubseteq B$ iff $\mathcal{T}' \models A \sqsubseteq B$ [2]. Given a normalised $\mathcal{EL}^{++}$ TBox $\mathcal{T}$, the algorithm uses a set of completion rules (Table 1, in **R6** $X \leadsto_R A$ iff there exists $C_1, \ldots, C_k \in \mathcal{CN}_{\mathcal{T}}$ s.t. $C_1 = X$ or $C_1 = \{b\}$, $C_j \sqsubseteq \exists r_j.C_{j+1}$ for some $r_j \in \mathcal{RN}_{\mathcal{T}}$ ($1 \leq j \leq k$) and $C_k = A$) to compute, for each two $A, B \in \mathcal{CN}_{\mathcal{T}}$, entailed subsumption $\mathcal{T} \models A \sqsubseteq B$.

Reasoning with rules **R1-R8** is PTIME-Complete [2]. ABox reasoning can also be reduced to TBox reasoning with these rules [2].

Table 1: $\mathcal{EL}^{++}$ TBox completion rules (no datatypes)

R1	If $X \sqsubseteq A$, $A \sqsubseteq B$ then $X \sqsubseteq B$
R2	If $X \sqsubseteq A_1, \ldots, A_n$, $A_1 \sqcap \cdots \sqcap A_n \sqsubseteq B$ then $X \sqsubseteq B$
R3	If $X \sqsubseteq A$, $A \sqsubseteq \exists r.B$ then $X \sqsubseteq \exists r.B$
R4	If $X \sqsubseteq \exists r.A$, $A \sqsubseteq A'$, $\exists r.A' \sqsubseteq B$ then $X \sqsubseteq B$
R5	If $X \sqsubseteq \exists r.A$, $A \sqsubseteq \bot$ then $X \sqsubseteq \bot$
R6	If $X, A \sqsubseteq \{a\}$, $X \leadsto_R A$ then $X \sqsubseteq A$
R7	If $X \sqsubseteq \exists r.A$, $r \sqsubseteq s$ then $X \sqsubseteq \exists s.A$
R8	If $X \sqsubseteq \exists r_1.A$, $A \sqsubseteq \exists r_2.B$, $r_1 \circ r_2 \sqsubseteq r_3$, then $X \sqsubseteq \exists r_3.B$

Alternatively, we can internalize ABox axioms into TBox axioms as follows to perform reasoning. In the rest of the paper, we always internalize ABox into TBox.

$$\begin{array}{rclrcl} a : C & \leadsto & \{a\} \sqsubseteq C & (a, b) : r & \leadsto & \{a\} \sqsubseteq \exists r.\{b\} \\ a \doteq b & \leadsto & \{a\} \equiv \{b\} & a \dot{\neq} b & \leadsto & \{a\} \sqcap \{b\} \sqsubseteq \bot \end{array}$$

3. ONTOLOGY STREAM MANAGEMENT SYSTEMS

In this section, we introduce the notion of ontology stream management systems (OSMS). A typical ontology stream management system is illustrated in Fig. 1. It can retrieve certain information

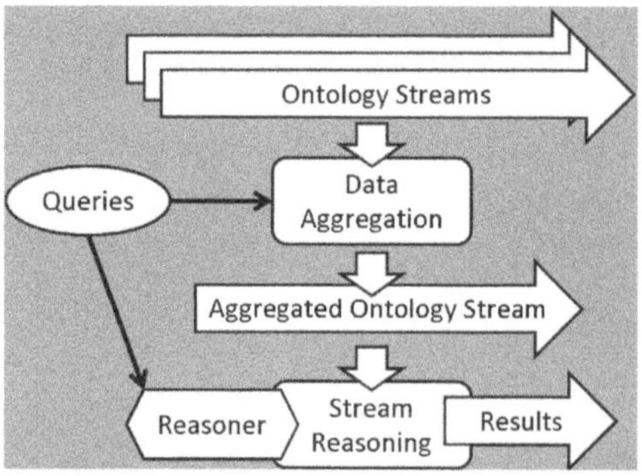

Figure 1: Ontology Stream Management System

from streams. **Data Aggregation** is the type of retrieval that does not require reasoning. For example, in the above stream, we can ask which takes are active. This type of retrieval has been widely addressed by, e.g., the C-SPARQL proposals. **Stream Reasoning** requires reasoning to be performed on the stream to yield correct answers. Their output are streams of results.

In stream reasoning [6] a streaming RDF knowledge base is defined as a set of pairs (α, t) where each RDF triple α is associated with a timestamp t. By grouping triples of the same timestamp t we have the ontology at time point t. Such a versioning idea resembles the concept of *Linear Version Space* (LVS) [10], which is a sequence of ontologies $S = (\mathcal{O}_0, \mathcal{O}_1, \ldots, \mathcal{O}_n)$. We recast these concepts and present a unified definition:

DEFINITION 1. ***(Discrete Ontology Stream)*** *An discrete ontology stream $\mathcal{O}_m^n$ from point of time m to point of time n is a sequence of ontologies $\mathcal{O}_m^n(t_0), \mathcal{O}_m^n(t_1), \ldots, \mathcal{O}_m^n(t_x)$ where $t_0 = m \leq t_1 \leq \cdots \leq t_x = n$. $\mathcal{O}_m^n(t_i)$ is called a* snapshot *at t_i.*

For conciseness, in the rest of the paper we use the name *ontology stream* or *stream* for short. We also assume that a stream always starts from time point 0 and is updated at each following integer time point, i.e. $\mathcal{O}_0^n = \mathcal{O}_0^n(0), \mathcal{O}_0^n(1), \ldots \mathcal{O}_0^n(n)$. A change from

$\mathcal{O}_0^n(i)$ to $\mathcal{O}_0^n(i+1)$ is an update. When a "new" update occurs, the stream is consequently updated from $\mathcal{O}_0^n$ to $\mathcal{O}_0^{n+1}$. It's important to note that the updates are not necessarily known to stream reasoners in advance. That means any axiom can be added into, or removed from the changing ontology at any time.

From Example 2 we construct a stream $\mathcal{O}_0^1 = \mathcal{O} \cup \mathcal{O}(0), \mathcal{O} \cup \mathcal{O}(1)$. The stream is illustrated in Fig. 2. We assume all ABox axioms have been internalised. This stream specifies that the feature of $ActiveTalk$, the role chain of $recommend$, the condition of $Talk4Dave$ and $TargetTalk$, $David$'s interest on $ontology$, and the topics of the two talks preserve from time point 0 to 1. $talk0$ is active in time point 0 and $talk1$ is active in time point 1.

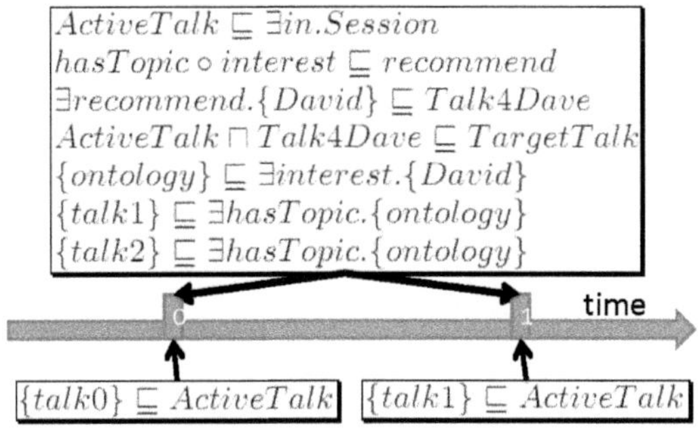

Figure 2: Example Stream

In this paper, we focus on such stream reasoning services. More formally, for a stream $\mathcal{O}_0^n$ and a reasoning problem Q, applications usually ask for reasoning results of Q on snapshot $\mathcal{O}_0^n(i)$, denoted by $Ans(\mathcal{O}_0^n(i), Q)$. For example, with the information in Fig. 2, we can ask for all ongoing talks that are interesting to David, which can be regarded as Q =*retrieving instances of* $TargetTalk$. Such a request can be simply fulfilled by applying the completion rules on the snapshots. By manual checking we know that $Ans(\mathcal{O}_0^1(0), Q) = \emptyset$ and $Ans(\mathcal{O}_0^1(1), Q) = \{talk1 : TargetTalk\}$. If we update $\mathcal{O}_0^1$ to $\mathcal{O}_0^2$ with $\mathcal{O}_0^2(2) = \mathcal{O} \cup \mathcal{O}(2)$. A new talk $talk2$ is being presented at time point 3 (Fig. 3). Now David wants to know, what is $Ans(\mathcal{O}_0^2(0), Q)$, given the results of $Ans(\mathcal{O}_0^1(0), Q)$?

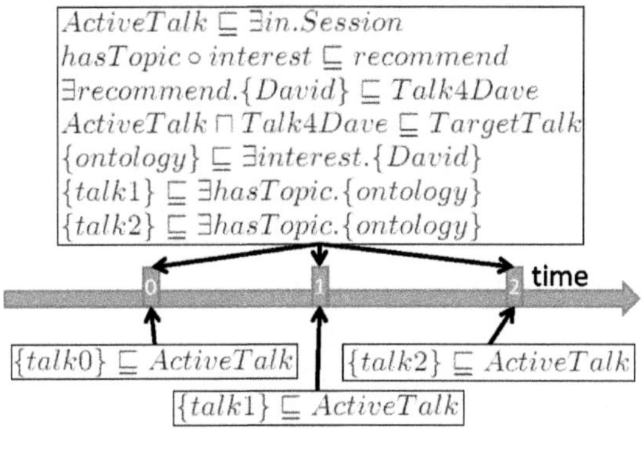

Figure 3: Updated Stream

We can directly compute the new results on $\mathcal{O}_0^2(2)$. We call this approach the *naive approach*. This approach is not efficient because the time of computing the new results is determined by the entire ontology, instead of the changed part. Even if the change is very small, the updating of results can take very long time if the ontology is big. More interestingly, people would like to compute results on the latest snapshot based on results on the previous snapshot, so that partial results can be reused without re-computation.

As we mentioned in the last section, existing work is limited to relatively simple languages and have certain restrictions. In the next sections, we propose a truth maintenance system-based approach for $\mathcal{EL}^{++}$ and which requires no fixed time window.

4. STREAM REASONING WITH TMS

In this section, we present how to provide stream reasoning in OSMS. Different from the naive approach, which re-compute everything from scratch, we propose to maintain the (intermediate) results and their inferencing relations, so that when updating, entailments affected or not affected by the removed axioms can be easily distinguished and intermediate results can be re-used. Such maintenance can be realised by a Truth Maintenance System (TMS [8]).

A TMS maintains both beliefs and their dependencies in the form of a dependency network, in which nodes are beliefs and edges are the inference steps from which the nodes are derived.

DEFINITION 2. ***(Truth Maintenance System)*** *Given an ontology* $\mathcal{O}$, *a TMS* $G_\mathcal{O} = \langle N_\mathcal{O}, E_\mathcal{O}\rangle$ *of* $\mathcal{O}$ *is a directed graph such that (1)* $\mathcal{O} \subseteq N_\mathcal{O}$*; (2)*$N_\mathcal{O} \subseteq \{\alpha | \mathcal{O} \models \alpha\}$*; (3) for any* $\alpha \in N_\mathcal{O}$, $\{\beta | (\beta, \alpha) \in E_\mathcal{O}\}$ *is a minimal set of axioms that entails* α.

The 3rd property is important such that if all inbound nodes of an entailment are preserved, then the entailment is preserved. Otherwise the entailment should be removed unless a different set of axioms can entail it.

It is obvious that a node can have multiple inbound edges if the entailment is derived from multiple other entailments. Tautology axioms do not have any inbound edges. Asserted axioms only have inbound edges from themselves. It is also apparent that an ontology can have multiple or even infinite TMSes, depending on how many entailments are preserved. For example, applying **R1-8** in Table 1, a TMS of $\mathcal{O}_0^1(1)$ from our running example is illustrated in Fig. 4.

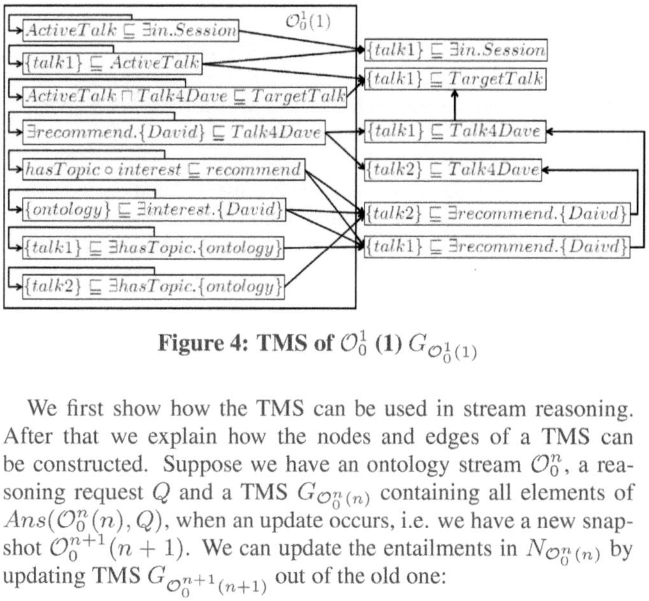

Figure 4: TMS of $\mathcal{O}_0^1$ (1) $G_{\mathcal{O}_0^1(1)}$

We first show how the TMS can be used in stream reasoning. After that we explain how the nodes and edges of a TMS can be constructed. Suppose we have an ontology stream $\mathcal{O}_0^n$, a reasoning request Q and a TMS $G_{\mathcal{O}_0^n(n)}$ containing all elements of $Ans(\mathcal{O}_0^n(n), Q)$, when an update occurs, i.e. we have a new snapshot $\mathcal{O}_0^{n+1}(n+1)$. We can update the entailments in $N_{\mathcal{O}_0^n(n)}$ by updating TMS $G_{\mathcal{O}_0^{n+1}(n+1)}$ out of the old one:

1. Initialise $G_{\mathcal{O}_0^{n+1}(n+1)} = G_{\mathcal{O}_0^n(n)}$;
2. Remove all the erased axioms and their reachable nodes from $N_{\mathcal{O}_0^{n+1}(n+1)}$. The erased TMS of our example is illustrated in Fig. 5, where the red node and edges are removed;
3. Add all new axioms in $\mathcal{O}_0^{n+1}(n+1)$ to $N_{\mathcal{O}_0^{n+1}(n+1)}$;

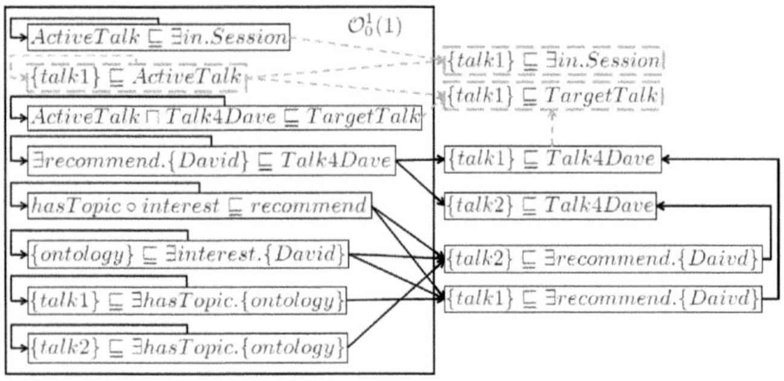

Figure 5: Erased TMS of $\mathcal{O}_0^1$ (1)

4. Check which new result of $Ans(\mathcal{O}_0^{n+1}(n+1), Q)$ can be entailed and add corresponding nodes and edges to $G_{\mathcal{O}_0^{n+1}(n+1)}$. In our example, new results $\{talk2\} \sqsubseteq \exists in.Session$, $\{talk2\} \sqsubseteq Talk4Dave$ and $\{talk2\} \sqsubseteq TargetTalk$ should be added.

As a example, applying the above procedure on our example $\mathcal{O}_0^2(2)$ will produce the following new TMS (Fig. 6). In this TMS the green nodes and edges are newly added while the others are preserved from $G_{\mathcal{O}_0^1(1)}$.

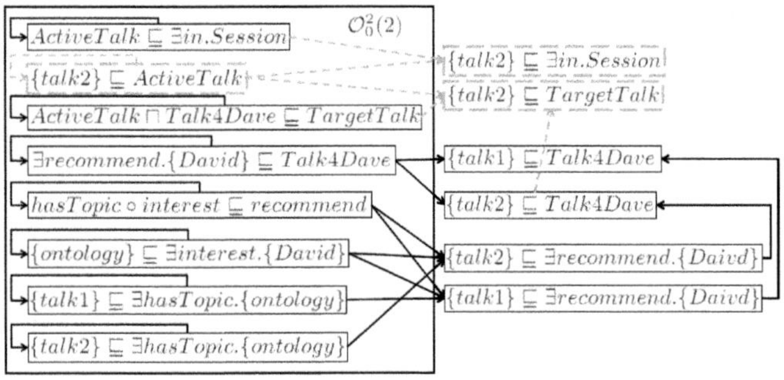

Figure 6: TMS of $\mathcal{O}_0^2$ (2) $G_{\mathcal{O}_0^2(2)}$

As we can see, the answer to David's question has been updated after the updating of ongoing events in the conference. During this procedure, intermediate results $\{talk2\} \sqsubseteq \exists recommend.\{Daivd\}$ and $\{talk2\} \sqsubseteq Talk4Dave$ have been preserved and reused to infer the new results, without being re-computed.

The way in which a TMS is constructed has significant impact on its structure and performance. A most straightforward way is to directly connect reasoning results with their justifications. However this approach contradicts with the intention of stream reasoning as it omits all intermediate results. This leads to potentially redundant computation of justifications and potentially redundant edges. For example, if $\alpha, \beta \in Ans(\mathcal{O}, Q)$ and $\mathcal{O} \models \beta$ only if $\mathcal{O} \models \alpha$, then α is needed to entail β and $J_{\mathcal{O}}(\alpha) \subseteq J_{\mathcal{O}}(\beta)$. Obviously, when computing $J_{\mathcal{O}}(\beta)$, the $J_{\mathcal{O}}(\alpha)$ should be computed at the same time, and all edges from axioms in $J_{\mathcal{O}}(\alpha)$ to β can be replaceable by a single edge from α to β.

To overcome the above drawbacks and improve efficiency, one can also develop a glass-box approach. The basic idea is to capture all the run-time states of a reasoner. For example, whenever a new belief is entailed from the ontology, we include it as a node of the TMS and connect it with the beliefs or assumptions we use to entail it, which should also be included as nodes if not included in previous reasoning steps. If an assumption is made, we include this assumption as a new node into the TMS. If it is withdrawn, we remove this assumption. All nodes derived from it, and all corresponding edges, should also be removed, etc. In this approach, the construction of the TMS does not affect the termination, soundness, completeness of the original reasoning algorithms. It does not change the reasoning results. These are all because the TMS does not interfere with the reasoning procedure. It does not require additional reasoning, and can be performed on-the-fly with reasoning.

Due to the fact that the completion-based algorithm of $\mathcal{EL}^{++}$ uses entailments as antecedents and consequents of rules, and requires no assumption in reasoning, it naturally fit with the construction of a TMS. And the glass-box approach for a completion-based algorithm can be described by the following algorithm **A-1**:

Algorithm A-1:
$GlassboxTMS(\mathcal{O}, Q)$
INPUT: an ontology $\mathcal{O}$, a reasoning request Q
OUTPUT: a directed graph $G = \langle N_{\mathcal{O}}, E_{\mathcal{O}} \rangle$

1: $N_{\mathcal{O}} := \mathcal{O}$, $E_{\mathcal{O}} := \{(\alpha, \alpha) | \alpha \in \mathcal{O}\}$
2: **while** a rule $R = \bigwedge_{i=1,2,\ldots,n} \alpha_i \rightarrow \bigwedge_{j=1,2,\ldots,m} \beta_j$ is executed for Q **do**
3: $\quad N_{\mathcal{O}} := N_{\mathcal{O}} \cup \bigcup_{j=1,2,\ldots,m} \{\beta_j\}$
4: $\quad E_{\mathcal{O}} := E_{\mathcal{O}} \cup \bigcup_{i=1,2,\ldots,n, j=1,2,\ldots,m} \{(\alpha_i, \beta_j)\}$
5: **return** $\langle N_{\mathcal{O}}, E_{\mathcal{O}} \rangle$

It is not difficult to show that the constructed directed graph is a TMS of $\mathcal{O}$ containing all results in $Ans(\mathcal{O}, Q)$:

THEOREM 1. *For an ontology $\mathcal{O}$ and a reasoning request Q, $GlassboxTMS(\mathcal{O}, Q) = \langle N_{\mathcal{O}}, E_{\mathcal{O}} \rangle$ as computed by **A-1** is a TMS of $\mathcal{O}$ and $Ans(\mathcal{O}, Q) \subseteq N_{\mathcal{O}}$.*

TMS can thus be constructed and updated. First of all, given an $\mathcal{EL}^{++}$ ontology $\mathcal{O} = (\mathcal{T}, \mathcal{A})$, we internalize it into $\mathcal{O}' = (\mathcal{T}', \emptyset)$ and we initialise a TMS $G = \langle N_{\mathcal{T}'}, E_{\mathcal{T}'} \rangle$ as $N_{\mathcal{T}'} = \mathcal{T}'$ and $E_{\mathcal{T}'} = \{(\alpha, \beta) | \alpha \in \mathcal{A}, \beta \in \mathcal{T}'$ and β is internalised from $\alpha\} \cup \{(\alpha, \alpha) | \alpha \in \mathcal{T} \cup \mathcal{A}\}$. Then we normalise the TBox $\mathcal{T}'$ into its normal form $\mathcal{T}''$. Meanwhile we extend the TMS as $N_{\mathcal{T}'} = \mathcal{T}''$ and $E_{\mathcal{T}'} := E_{\mathcal{T}'} \sqsubseteq \{(\alpha, \beta) | \alpha \in \mathcal{T}', \beta \in \mathcal{T}''$ and β is normalised from $\alpha\}$. Then in reasoning, we apply completion rules to add new entailments into $\mathcal{T}''$, which is also the node set of the TMS. At the same time, we add edges between all antecedents and consequent into $E_{\mathcal{T}'}$. For example, for **R1**, we have $E_{\mathcal{T}'} := E_{\mathcal{T}'} \cup \{(X \sqsubseteq A, X \sqsubseteq B), (A \sqsubseteq B, X \sqsubseteq B)\}$. For **R5**, we have $E_{\mathcal{T}'} := E_{\mathcal{T}'} \cup \{(X \sqsubseteq \exists r.A, X \sqsubseteq \bot), (A \sqsubseteq \bot, X \sqsubseteq \bot)\}$

When no rule can be executed, the reasoning terminates and the TMS is constructed. When the TMS is updated from $\mathcal{O}_0^n$ (n) to $\mathcal{O}_0^{n+1}$ (n+1), the same procedure is applied on the previous TMS.

5. OPTIMISING TMS IN $\mathcal{EL}^{++}$

Although completion-based algorithms are suitable for stream reasoning with TMS. They could still unnecessarily consume some time and memory if not all intermediate results are contributing to answering the reasoning request. Taking $\mathcal{EL}^{++}$ algorithm as an example, it performs the **Classification** of a TBox by computing results of form $A \sqsubseteq B$ and $A \sqsubseteq \exists r.B$. The former is useful when computing the concept hierarchies of the ontology, or retrieving the types of individuals (in form of $\{x\} \sqsubseteq A$), while the later is of less use in such scenarios. For example, in Fig. 4 and Fig. 6, we can see that inference results $\{talk1\} \sqsubseteq \exists in.Session$ and $\{talk2\} \sqsubseteq \exists in.Session$ are not needed.

In order to address this issue, we further optimise completion-based algorithms. The key point is, instead of directly performing the forward-chaining reasoning procedure and apply all executable rules, we develop some backward-chaining control mechanism to determine which intermediate results will *NOT* be useful and thus they are not needed to be computed.

As we can see from Table 1, the intermediate results of the form $A \sqsubseteq \exists r.B$ are involved in the following rules:

1. **R3**, **R7** and **R8** use them to generate results of the same form.
2. **R4** and **R6** use them to generate new results of form $A \sqsubseteq B$.

This means that, all results of form $A \sqsubseteq \exists r.B$ will eventually contribute to inference of results of form $A \sqsubseteq B$ through **R4** and **R6**. If we know which axioms of form $A \sqsubseteq \exists r.B$ will (not) be used in **R4** and **R6**, we can inductively know which of them will (not) be used in the entire reasoning process to compute all results of form $A \sqsubseteq B$, without even executing any rule. Apparently, this is related to the role r in the entailment.

Given an internalised and normalised $\mathcal{EL}^{++}$ TBox $\mathcal{T}$, we assume that all role subsumption closures have been pre-computed [1]. We analyse the roles as follows:

In **R4:** If $X \sqsubseteq \exists r.A$, $A \sqsubseteq A'$, $\exists r.A' \sqsubseteq B$ then $X \sqsubseteq B$. It is obvious that antecedents of form $X \sqsubseteq \exists r.A$ is worth entailed only if there is some $\exists r.A' \sqsubseteq B \in \mathcal{T}$. Note that the later will not be computed from any rule and can only exist in the original TBox. Therefore for a role r, if there is no axiom of form $\exists r.A' \sqsubseteq B \in \mathcal{T}$, all results of form $X \sqsubseteq \exists r.A$ will not be useful in **R4**.

In **R6:** If $X, A \sqsubseteq \{a\}$, $X \leadsto_R A$ then $X \sqsubseteq A$. It is obvious that antecedent axioms of form $C_j \sqsubseteq \exists r_j.C_{j+1}$ is worth entailed only if there is some $X \sqsubseteq \{a\}$ entailed, which eventually requires there being some $\{a\}$ appearing on the RHS (Right Hand Side) of some GCI. Therefore, if there is no nominal $\{a\}$ on the RHS of any GCI, all results of form $X \sqsubseteq \exists r.A$ will not be used in **R6**.

From the above analysis, we define the classification-relevant roles as follows:

DEFINITION 3. ***(Classification-relevant role)*** *Given a normalised $\mathcal{EL}^{++}$ TBox $\mathcal{T}$, a role r is classification relevant (C-R for short) if r is on the LHS (left hand side) of some GCI, or there exists some GCI whose RHS (right hand side) is a nominal, or r is on the LHS of some RI whose RHS is a C-R role.*

The first two conditions correspond to **R4** and **R6**, respectively. The last condition corresponds to **R7** and **R8**. According to this definition, in our example, roles $hasTopic$, $interest$, $recommend$ are C-R, and role in is not. All C-R roles can be identified in polynomial time. They control which entailment $A \sqsubseteq \exists r.B$ will be useful in classification:

THEOREM 2. *When classifying an $\mathcal{EL}^{++}$ TBox $\mathcal{T}$ with **R1-8**, an entailed $A \sqsubseteq \exists r.B$ will contribute to execution of **R4** or **R6** only if r is a C-R role.*

In classification of an $\mathcal{EL}^{++}$ TBox, we computes intermediate results of form $A \sqsubseteq \exists r.B$ only if r is C-R. Thus the corresponding **R3**, **R7** and **R8** should be revised as follows:

- **R3'**: If $X \sqsubseteq A$, $A \sqsubseteq \exists r.B$ and r is C-R, then $X \sqsubseteq \exists r.B$;
- **R7'**: If $X \sqsubseteq \exists r.A$, r is C-R, $r \sqsubseteq s$ then $X \sqsubseteq \exists s.A$
- **R8'**: If $X \sqsubseteq \exists r_1.A$, $A \sqsubseteq \exists r_2.B$, $r_1 \circ r_2 \sqsubseteq r_3$, r_3 is C-R, then $X \sqsubseteq \exists r_3.B$

Such an optimisation is not only applicable on TMS construction. It is a generic optimisation on $\mathcal{EL}^{++}$ classification algorithm and preserves soundness and completeness of classification:

THEOREM 3. *For any normalised $\mathcal{EL}^{++}$ TBox $\mathcal{T}$, $A \sqsubseteq B$ can be inferred by **R1-8** iff $A \sqsubseteq B$ can be inferred by **R1-2, R3', R4-6, R7'-8'**.*

When constructing TMS with a glass-box approach, the TMS enjoys the same optimisation. The construction of TMS will follow the same rule as before. The fact that some role r is C-R is not necessary to be maintained as a node. For example, the optimised TMS of $\mathcal{O}_0^1$ (1) is illustrated in the Fig. 7:

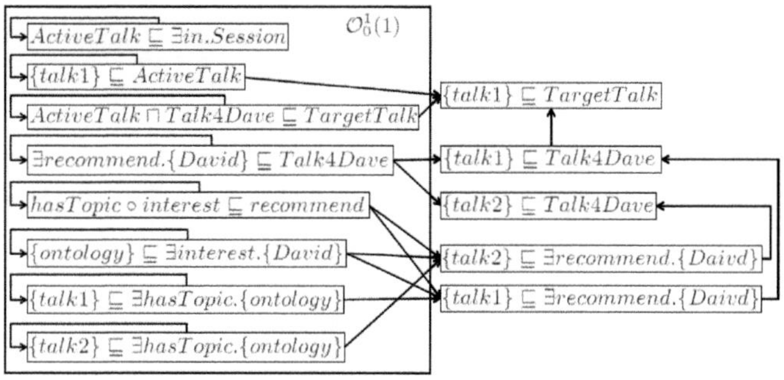

Figure 7: Optimised TMS of $\mathcal{O}_0^1$ (1)

Such modifications will help eliminate unnecessary intermediate results and will not require additional reasoning. Therefore it should improve both the efficiency and scalability.

6. EXPERIMENTAL EVALUATION

We implemented the proposed approach and optimisations in our TrOWL [1] reasoner. We perform experiments to evaluate whether the optimisation presented in Sec.5 can improve the efficiency of TMS-enabled reasoning and reduce memory consumption, and furthermore how does such an optimised TMS-enabled $\mathcal{EL}^{++}$ stream reasoner perform in reality. Therefore, we first evaluate the optimisation, then the stream reasoning. All experiments were conducted in an environment of 64-bit Windows 7 Enterprise with 1.60 GHz CPU and 3G RAM allocated to JVM 1.6.0.07.

In this optimisation evaluation, our test cases are two ontologies generated from the Galen ontology [2]. Both of them are $\mathcal{EL}^{++}$ ontologies. The stats of these two ontologies are summarized in Table 2. Although they don't contain ABox, the optimisation evaluated here will have the similar effects on ABoxes.

In this evaluation we perform ontology classification to retrieve entailed subsumptions between all pairs of atomic concepts. For each of the ontologies, we classify it with two TMS-enabled $\mathcal{EL}^{++}$ reasoners. The one without optimisation implemented is called **TMS**. And the one with optimisation implemented is called **TMS-Opt**. For each reasoner, we measure the time used to classify the ontology. Due to the difficulty of precise measurements of the memory consumption, we calculate the number of intermediate results of the form $A \sqsubseteq \exists r.B$ for each reasoner. For **TMS-Opt** we further calculate the number of C-R roles. The results of our evaluation is shown in Table 2.

From results we can see that in both ontologies, not all roles are necessary for classification. With **TMS-Opt**, the number of unnecessary intermediate results ($\#Ext.$) is significantly reduced. In NotGalen$^-$, only 15.3% is computed. In FullGalen$^-$ only 39.8% is computed. With less unintended and unnecessary inference, the efficiency is improved (24% in NotGalen$^-$ and 44% in FullGalen$^-$). Also, the memory consumption of maintaining such inference should also be significantly reduced.

With the positive results on TMS optimisations, we evaluate its performance in stream reasoning. Due to the lack of stream reason-

[1] http://trowl.eu

[2] http://www.opengalen.org/

Table 2: Evaluation of optimisation. $|\mathcal{CN}|$, $|\mathcal{RN}|$, $\#GCI$ and $\#RI$ are numbers of atomic concepts, atomic roles, GCIs and RIs, respectively. $\#Sub.$ is the number of entailed atomic concept subsumptions. t is classification time (in seconds). $\#Ext.$ is the number of entailed intermediate results $A \sqsubseteq \exists r.B$. $\#C - R$ is the number of classification-relevant roles.

Ontology	$\lvert\mathcal{CN}\rvert$	$\lvert\mathcal{RN}\rvert$	$\#GCI$	$\#RI$	$\#Sub.$	TMS		TMS-Opt		
						t	$\#Ext.$	t	$\#Ext.$	$\#C - R$
NotGalen$^-$	2748	413	4348	442	30682	1,843	73156	1.407	11294	245
FullGalen$^-$	23141	950	37482	1015	475211	45.741	1687552	25.572	671595	749

ing benchmark, we generated our test data from the FullGalen$^-$ ontology and simulated streams. We randomly partition the ontology into 45 sub-ontologies of same size. We call them $\mathbf{K}_0, \mathbf{K}_1, \ldots, \mathbf{K}_{44}$. We construct an ontology stream $\mathcal{O}_0^{10}$ in a way that $\mathcal{O}_0^{10}(i) = \bigcup_{j=i,\ldots,i+34} \mathbf{K}_j$. Therefore for each $i = 0, \ldots, 9$, $\mathcal{O}_0^{10}(i+1) = \mathcal{O}_0^{10}(i) \setminus \mathbf{K}_i \cup \mathbf{K}_{i+35}$. Now we create a stream with 10 updates. In each update, 2.9% of the ontology is changed. Each snapshot contains about 30000 axioms. Each update changes about 855 axioms. For each snapshot $\mathcal{O}_0^{10}(i)$, we perform classification to compute the subsumption between all atomic concepts. The reasoner does not know which axioms will be updated in advance. We accomplish such a reasoning task with both the naive approach (re-do reasoning on $\mathcal{O}_0^{10}(i)$ from scratch) and the **TMS-Opt**. We record the time of both approaches to evaluate the effectiveness of the **TMS-Opt**. The results are summarised in the following table (Table 3).

Table 3: Evaluation Results. t_0 shows the time for the initial ontology. $Max(t_i)$, $Min(t_i)$ and $Ave(t_i)$ show the maximal, minimal and average time for the updated ontologies, respectively. Time unit is second.

Approach	t_0	$Max(t_i)$	$Min(t_i)$	$Ave(t_i)$
Naive	4.119	3.323	2.625	3.125
TMS-Opt	5.492	2.543	1.482	1.856

From the table we can see that, **TMS-Opt** took more time to classify the original ontology due to the construction of TMS. But in updating, **TMS-Opt** was significantly faster.

It is interesting to see how many percentages of the ontology can be updated while the TMS stream reasoning approach remains faster than the naive approach. To answer this question, we further increase to size of update to 3.33%, 5% and 10% of the original ontology, respectively. We perform classification on such ontology streams and calculate the relative time as $(Ave(t_i)_{Naive} - Ave(t_i)_{\textbf{TMS-Opt}})/Ave(t_i)_{Naive}$. Our experiments and calculation yield 75.1%, 86.0% and 96.5% relative time for the above relative size of updates, respectively. From these results, we can see that although TMS gradually loses its efficiency advantage to Naive approach when the relative volume of update increases, it still pays off when about 10% of ontology is changed. This figure is better than the maintenance program approach [14] and comparable to the fixed-window approach [6]. Considering the higher expressive power and difficulty of the test ontology FullGalen$^-$ and its large volume, our evaluation justifies the usability of our approach.

7. CONCLUSION

In this paper, we introduce Ontology Stream Management Systems (OSMS). We focus on how to provide stream reasoning services based on TMS for OSMS. We chose $\mathcal{EL}^{++}$, the logic underpinning the tractable OWL 2 EL language and developed a classification-relevant role optimisation for $\mathcal{EL}^{++}$ by controlling the kind of intermediate results that should be inferred. Evaluation on real world ontologies shows that our approach and optimisation work nicely in practice with relatively large volume of knowledge base and update. In the future, we would like to investigate stream reasoning in complete OWL 2 EL, QL and RL profiles, and even OWL 2 DL, as well as related optimisations.

Acknowledgement: This work is partially funded by the RCUK dot.rural and the EU K-Drive projects.

8. REFERENCES

[1] F. Baader, S. Brandt, and C. Lutz. Pushing the $\mathcal{EL}$ Envelope. In *Proceedings IJCAI-05*, 2005.

[2] F. Baader, S. Brandt, and C. Lutz. Pushing the EL Envelope Further. In K. Clark and P. F. Patel-Schneider, editors, *In OWLED-2008*, 2008.

[3] F. Baader, C. Lutz, and B. Suntisrivaraporn. Is Tractable Reasoning in Extensions of the Description Logic EL Useful in Practice? In *Proceedings of the 2005 International Workshop on Methods for Modalities (M4M-05)*, 2005.

[4] F. Baader and B. Suntisrivaraporn. Debugging SNOMED CT using axiom pinpointing in the description logic $\mathcal{EL}^+$. In *Proceedings of the 3rd Knowledge Representation in Medicine (KR-MED'08): Representing and Sharing Knowledge Using SNOMED*, volume 410 of *CEUR-WS*, 2008.

[5] D. F. Barbieri, D. Braga, S. Ceri, E. D. Valle, and M. Grossniklaus. C-sparql: Sparql for continuous querying. In *WWW2009*, 2009.

[6] D. F. Barbieri, D. Braga, S. Ceri, E. D. Valle, and M. Grossniklaus. Incremental reasoning on streams and rich background knowledge. In *ESWC2010*, 2010.

[7] A. Bolles, M. Grawunder, and J. Jacobi. Streaming sparql extending sparql to process data streams. In *ESWC08*, 2008.

[8] J. Doyle. A truth maintenance system. *Artificial Intelligence*, 12:231–272, 1979.

[9] A. Gupta, I. S. Mumick, and V. S. Subrahmanian. Maintaining views incrementally. In *SIGMOD '93*, 1993.

[10] Z. Huang and H. Stuckenschmidt. Reasoning with multi-version ontologies: A temporal logic approach. In *In Proceeding of ISWC2005*, 2005.

[11] M. Luther and S. Bohm. Situation-Aware Mobility: An Application for Stream Reasoning. In *in Proc. of 1st International Workshop on Stream Reasoning (SR2009)*, 2009.

[12] B. Parsia, C. Halaschek-wiener, and E. Sirin. E.s.: Towards incremental reasoning through updates. In *in OWL DL. In: Proc. WWW-2006. (2006)*, 2006.

[13] Y. Ren, J. Z. Pan, and Y. Zhao. Towards Scalable Reasoning on Ontology Streams via Syntactic Approximation. In *the Proc. of IWOD2010*, 2010.

[14] R. Volz, S. Staab, and B. Motik. Incemently maintaining materializations of ontologies stored in logic databases. *In Journal of Data Semantics II, LNCS, Vol 3360*, 2:1–34, 2005.

Harvesting Facts from Textual Web Sources by Constrained Label Propagation

Yafang Wang, Bin Yang, Lizhen Qu, Marc Spaniol and Gerhard Weikum
Max-Planck-Institut für Informatik
Saarbrücken, Germany
{ywang|byang|lqu|mspaniol|weikum}@mpi-inf.mpg.de

ABSTRACT

There have been major advances on automatically constructing large knowledge bases by extracting relational facts from Web and text sources. However, the world is dynamic: periodic events like sports competitions need to be interpreted with their respective timepoints, and facts such as coaching a sports team, holding political or business positions, and even marriages do not hold forever and should be augmented by their respective timespans. This paper addresses the problem of automatically harvesting temporal facts with such extended time-awareness. We employ pattern-based gathering techniques for fact candidates and construct a weighted pattern-candidate graph. Our key contribution is a system called PRAVDA based on a new kind of label propagation algorithm with a judiciously designed loss function, which iteratively processes the graph to label good temporal facts for a given set of target relations. Our experiments with online news and Wikipedia articles demonstrate the accuracy of this method.

Categories and Subject Descriptors

H.1.0 [**Information Systems**]: Models and Principles—*General*

General Terms

Algorithms, Design, Experimentation

Keywords

Knowledge Harvesting, Label Propagation, Temporal Facts

1. INTRODUCTION

1.1 Motivation

Who were the teammates of the legendary Argentinian player Diego Maradona? How often has the pop singer Madonna been married, and to whom? Questions like these often arise from the information needs of Internet users, but are not supported by keyword-based search engines. Instead, answering them requires an understanding of entities and relationships embedded in Web contents, or even better, a knowledge base that contains facts about people, organizations, locations, etc. In the last few years, such knowledge bases have indeed been built and made publicly accessible, for example: *DBpedia* [1], *YAGO* [17], *TextRunner* [9], *ReadTheWeb* [6], the commercial knowledge portals *freebase.com* and *trueknowledge.com*, the computational knowledge engine *wolframalpha.com*, the entity search engine *entitycube.research.microsoft.com*, and others. Most of these have been automatically compiled, either by integrating structured sources (e.g., geospecies.org, geonames.org, world factbook, etc.), by harvesting semi-structured sources such as Wikipedia info boxes, lists, and categories, or by information extraction from Web pages. Some of them involve a substantial amount of manual curation for quality assurance. Moreover, there is a strong momentum towards semantically inter-linking many knowledge sources into the *Linked Data* cloud [10], see *linkeddata.org*.

CIKM'11, October 24–28, 2011, Glasgow, Scotland, UK.

However, the world is highly dynamic and nothing lasts forever! Knowledge evolves over time, and many facts are fairly ephemeral, e.g., winners of sports competitions, and occasionally even CEOs and spouses. In addition, many information needs by advanced users require *temporal knowledge*. For example, consider the following variations of the above example questions: Who were the team mates of Diego Maradona during the 1990 FIFA World Cup? When did Madonna get married, when did she get divorced? None of these questions are supported by existing knowledge bases. The problem that we tackle in this paper is to automatically distil, from news articles and biography-style texts such as Wikipedia, *temporal facts* for a given set of relations. By this we mean instances of the relations with additional time annotations that denote the validity point or span of a relational fact. For example, for the *winsAward* relation between people and awards, we want to augment facts with the time points of the respective events; and for the *worksForClub* relation between athletes and sports clubs, we would add the timespan during which the fact holds. This can be seen as a specific task of extracting ternary relations, which is much harder than the usual information extraction issues considered in prior work.

1.2 Contribution

Our system called PRAVDA (label PRopagated fAct extraction on Very large DAta) gathers fact candidates and distills facts with their temporal extent based on a new form of *label propagation (LP)*. This is a family of graph-based semi-supervised learning methods, applied to (in our setting) a similarity graph of fact candidates and textual patterns. LP algorithms start with a small number of manually labelled seeds, correct facts in our case, and spread labels to neighbors based on a *graph regularized objective function* which we aim to minimize. The outcome is an assignment of labels to nodes which can be interpreted as a per-node probability distribution over labels. In our scenario, the labels denote relations to which the fact in a correspondingly labelled node belongs.

We adopt the specific algorithm of [18], coined MAD (Modified Adsorption), with an objective function that combines the quadratic loss between initial labels (from seeds) and estimated labels of vertices with a data-induced graph regularizer and an L2 regularizer.

The graph regularizer is also known as the un-normalized graph Laplacian, which penalizes changes of labels between vertices that are close. We develop substantial extensions, and show how to judiciously construct a suitable graph structure and objective function. Notably, we consider inclusion constraints between different relation labels for the same node in the graph. For example, we may exploit that a relation like *joinsClub* (with time points) is a sub-relation of *worksForClub* (with time spans).

Research on temporal fact extraction is still in its infancy: prior work is scarce and has major limitations. [23] showed how to extract temporal facts from Wikipedia infoboxes and lists, but can handle only semi-structured input and does not carry over to textual sources. [27] and [11] used an elaborated learning machinery to tap into temporal statements in text, but are computationally expensive and reliant on extensive training data. In contrast, our method is much more efficient and requires only minimal supervision. NLP research (e.g., [21, 5]) has also looked into temporal phrases, but has focused on detecting events (e.g., "her birthday"), relative expressions (e.g., "last Sunday"), and time-order relations (before, after, during, etc.). These basic tasks are still far from actual fact extraction. LP algorithms have been applied to knowledge-harvesting problems, but only to the simpler task of acquiring taxonomic relations between entities and classes (instanceOf) and among classes (subclassOf), see most notably the work of [19]. For harvesting arbitrary types of binary relations and especially for ternary relations with time points or time spans, we need a very different graph construction and loss function, and we have extended the MAD algorithm to consider also inclusion constraints (i.e., subsumptions) among relations.

In summary, this paper makes the following contributions:

- a new model for distilling temporal facts from text sources like news or biographies,
- an algorithm for extended label propagation with consideration of inclusion constraints,
- experimental studies, comparing the extraction of base facts (without time) against a state-of-the-art baseline [13], and demonstrating the effectiveness of harvesting temporal facts for a variety of relations from the domains of soccer and celebrities.

2. FRAMEWORK & SYSTEM OVERVIEW

This section gives a brief overview on the relation types we harvest and the system architecture. In particular, we introduce the distinction between *base* (without temporality) and *temporal relations* (including temporality).

2.1 Relation Types

We distinguish between *base* and *temporal relations*. *Base relations* indicate the relationships between two entities without any temporal information. A base relation R_b is commonly described with a type signature, $sig(R_b) = (TYPE_1, TYPE_2)$, meaning that the relation R_b only holds its semantic meaning for two entities whose types are $TYPE_1$ and $TYPE_2$, respectively. A base relation contains a set of base facts. Each base fact is in the form of (e_i, e_j), where e_i and e_j indicate two entities whose types are consistent with the corresponding base relation's type signature. For example, *worksForClub* is a base relation with signature (*PERSON*, *CLUB*). The base fact `(Lionel_Messi, FC_Barcelona)` holds for the *worksForClub* relation, where `Lionel_Messi` is a *PERSON* entity and `FC_Barcelona` is a *CLUB* entity.

Temporal relations indicate the relationships between two entities at specific time points or during particular time spans. Similar to base relations, a temporal relation is always associated with a type signature indicating the pertinent entity types. A temporal relation contains a set of temporal facts in the form of $(e_i, e_j)@t_k$, where e_i and e_j are two entities with pertinent types, and t_k indicates a temporal mention (either a time point or a time span). For example, *joinsClubTemp* is a temporal relation with type signature (*PERSON*, *CLUB*). The temporal fact `(David_Beckham, Real_Madrid)@2005` holds for the *joinsClubTemp* relation, indicating that `David_Beckham` joined `Real_Madrid` in 2005.

2.2 System Architecture

Figure 1 gives an overview of our system for fact harvesting from Web sources. The system consists of four components: *candidate gathering*, *pattern analysis*, *graph construction*, and *label propagation*. The components are invoked in four phases.

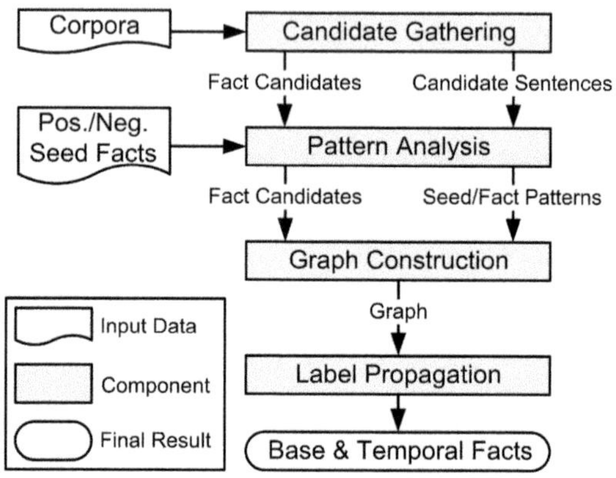

Figure 1: System Overview

1. *Candidate Gathering*: This phase serves to collect potentially relevant sentences. A sentence is interesting if it contains entities in relevant types for a target relation of interest. We employ a test for the potential presence of a base fact in a sentence, by checking for the existence of two noun phrases (denoting two entities) in the same sentence. In addition, we test for the existence of a temporal expression (currently only explicit date) in the sentence, thus producing raw input also for temporal fact candidates.
2. *Pattern Analysis*: Based on a (small, manually crafted) set of seed facts for a particular relation (either base or temporal), seed patterns in the form of sets of word-level n-grams are extracted from the interesting sentences. For each target relation that we aim to extract, a statistical prior is then computed based on how strongly fact candidates have evidence in the form of seed patterns. This will be discussed in Section 3.2.
3. *Graph Construction*: To facilitate the knowledge harvesting procedure, the fact candidates and pattern candidates are represented as vertices of a graph. Edges represent the evidence connection between a pattern and a fact candidate, as well as the similarity between two patterns. The graph construction is presented in Section 3.3.
4. *Label Propagation*: Finally, a graph-based semi-supervised learning method is employed to harvest both base facts and temporal facts. To this end, we have developed an extended label propagation algorithm (cf. Section 4 for details).

3. PATTERNS & GRAPH MODEL

In this section, we first describe our candidate gathering approach, raising surface (text) strings to entities. Then, we introduce our pattern analysis method, which is based on "basic", "seed" and "fact" patterns. Basic patterns are (entity) type-aware word-level n-grams of surface strings. Based on statistical analytics, those patterns yielding in high quality results for a certain relation become seed patterns. Fact patterns are finally derived from sentences where the similarity of an observed basic pattern and seed patterns exceeds a pre-defined threshold. Finally, we will explain the underlying (pattern-candidate) graph model between patterns and candidate sentences. To facilitate the following discussions, we use bold capital letters to indicate matrices, and normal lower-case letters to indicate scalar values.

3.1 Candidate Gathering

Our approach is driven by target relations for which we would like to gather instances. The set of relations of interest is denoted as $\mathcal{R}$={R_1, R_2, ..., R_m}. Each is associated with a type signature and is either a base relation or a temporal relation. $Type(\mathcal{R})$ contains all possible entity types in the type signatures of the relations in $\mathcal{R}$.

We assume that there exists a knowledge base with typed entities which contains the individual entities whose types are in $Type(\mathcal{R})$. In this paper, we consider relations of interest from the domains of soccer and celebrities, and use YAGO [17] as knowledge base. The YAGO knowledge base contains almost all the pertinent entities harvested from Wikipedia, such as persons (both sports people and celebrities), clubs, locations, awards, universities, and even a large fraction of people's spouses. YAGO also provides us with a fairly complete dictionary of surface names for entities, including abbreviations (e.g., "ManU" for the entity `Manchester_United`). Thus, detecting mentions of entities in an input text is straightforward.

We consider a textual corpus $\mathcal{C}$, e.g., a set of Wikipedia articles, news articles, or Web pages, as input for candidate gathering. The corpus is pre-processed to generate meaningful segments. In this paper, we consider sentence-level segments: the corpus is decomposed into a set of sentences where each sentence is a sequence of tokens.

Given a sentence, an entity recognition and disambiguation module first checks whether at least two entities (and a temporal mention for temporal relations) are mentioned in the same sentence. This is primarily based on YAGO's "means" relation, where a string means an entity (e.g., "ManU" meaning `Manchester_United`). The entity recognition engine works in four stages:

1. Based on a sliding window technique "interesting" strings are extracted. A text string becomes interesting when it matches the subject of a YAGO fact with the means relation. That means, the string can be mapped to at least one YAGO entity.
2. Entities that can be mapped unambiguously (by plain string matching between the textual input and the means relation of YAGO) are identified. These entities serve as "ground-truth entities" for the following disambiguation steps.
3. The "ground-truth entities" and Wikipedia anchor links are used to build a graph for disambiguation. The graph consists of edges between those (entity-) nodes where mutual anchor links among pages exist. For each "interesting string" it is now checked if an entity exists that is directly linked with a single "ground-truth entity". If more than two links to "ground-truth entities" exist, the analyzed entity becomes - due to its strong relation to this context a "ground-truth" entity, too.
4. Disambiguation of each "interesting" string to a single (highest ranked) entity based on a distance function applied to the before constructed graph.

We then check whether the entity types are compatible with the type signature of some target relation R_m. If so, a candidate fact is generated, and the sentence is added to the set of interesting sentences. For example, the sentence "`David_Beckham` played for `Real_Madrid` and `LA_Galaxy`" will create the candidate facts (`David_Beckham`, `Real_Madrid`) and (`David_Beckham`, `LA_Galaxy`), but <u>not</u> (`Real_Madrid`, `LA_Galaxy`) as there is no relation of interest between two entities of type *CLUB*.

3.2 Pattern Analysis

3.2.1 Basic Patterns

Our notion of patterns builds upon the prior work of [13], where sets of word-level n-grams from sentences are used as patterns. We extend this approach by exploiting the type signatures of the target relations for which we perform fact harvesting.

Consider a fact candidate (e_i, e_j) and its corresponding candidate sentence, written in the form $x\ e_i\ y\ e_j\ z$ where x, y and z are surface string surrounding the entities. We consider the *context surface string* y as an (initial) indicator of the relationship with fact (e_i, e_j). For example, we observe a fact candidate (`David_Beckham`, `LA_Galaxy`) in the sentence s = "`David_Beckham` finally moved from Real_Madrid before his recent joining `LA_Galaxy` in 2007.", the context surface string "finally moved from Real_Madrid before his recent joining" is the evidence for the *joinsClubTemp* relationship between `David_Beckham` and `LA_Galaxy`.

Context surface strings are usually long and over specific. It is extremely rare to observe other entity pairs sharing exactly the same context surface strings. To overcome this problem, we generalize the pattern representation. One possible solution is to adopt word level n-grams to represent patterns. Before generating the n-grams, we first do compression and lifting on context surface strings.

In order to avoid getting misguided by problems induced from natural language processing, we convert each surface string into a *compressed surface string*. These contain only - preserving their original order - nouns, verbs, and prepositions after stop words removal based on Wikipedia's "List of English Stop Words"[1]. Nouns, verbs and prepositions are identified by LingPipe Part-of-Speech tagger[2]. All verbs are transformed into present tense based on the verb dictionary provided by Assert (Automatic Statistical SEmantic Role Tagger)[3]. Nouns are stemmed with PlingStemmer[4].

The compressed surface strings are further generalized by considering the set of types that constitute the type signatures of our target relations. This is done by replacing entities by their types (e.g. *PERSON*, *CITY*, *CLUB*, and *DATE*). Thus, the corresponding *lifted surface string* of sentence s is {"move from *CLUB* before join"}. For a lifted surface string, we generate word-level n-grams as its *basic pattern* (with n typically set to 2). For example, the basic pattern of s w.r.t. the entity pair (`David_Beckham`, `LA_Galaxy`) is denoted as $BP(s$, `David_Beckham`, `LA_Galaxy`$)$ = ("move from", "from *CLUB*", "*CLUB* before", "before join").

3.2.2 Seed Patterns

Given a set of positive and negative samples for the facts in a specific relation, we are able to measure how good a pattern is for a particular relation. The best patterns are then regarded as *seed patterns* for this relation. The overall procedure of identifying seed patterns for a specific relation is similar to [13].

A positive seed fact (e_i, e_j) (or (e_i, e_j)@t_k) for a base relation R_b (or a temporal relation R_t), is a valid fact of the relation R_b (or R_t). A negative seed fact (e_i, e_j) (or (e_i, e_j)@t_k) for R_b (or R_t) is an entity pair (with temporal mention) that is not a fact of R_b (or

[1] *http://en.wikipedia.org/wiki/Stop_words*

[2] *http://alias-i.com/lingpipe/web/demo-pos.html*

[3] *http://cemantix.org/assert.html*

[4] *http://www.mpi-inf.mpg.de/yago-naga/javatools/*

R_t). $PF(R_i)$ and $NF(R_i)$ denote the manually crafted positive and negative seed facts for R_i.

For each base relation R_b we identify the sentences that contain two entities from a positive seed in $PF(R_i)$ and the sentences that contain two entities from a negative seed in $NF(R_i)$. These sentences are collected into the sets $PS(R_b)$ and $NS(R_b)$, respectively. Analogously, for each temporal relation R_t, the positive sentences are those that contain both entities and the temporal expression (date) of a positive seed, and the negative sentences are those that contain a negative seed. The sets of positive and negative sentences are denoted as $PS(R_t)$ and $NS(R_t)$, respectively.

Given a relation $R_i \in \mathcal{R}$, a candidate sentence s with lifted surface string $L(s)$ containing a basic pattern p, support and confidence are defined as follows:

$$supp(p, R_i) = |\{s \in PS(R_i) | p \subseteq L(s)\}|$$

$$conf(p, R_i) = \frac{|\{s \in PS(R_i) | p \subseteq L(s)\}|}{|\{s \in PS(R_i) \cup NS(R_i) | p \subseteq L(s)\}|}$$

The support value captures the frequency of a pattern in conjunction with positive seed facts, whereas the confidence value denotes the ratio of a pattern co-occurring with positive seed facts versus negative seed facts. If $supp(p, R_i)$ is above predefined thresholds, the basic pattern p is considered as a *seed pattern* of R_i. $SP(R_i)$ denotes the set of all seed patterns for R_i. In our experiment, we vary the threshold of support in different settings.

3.2.3 *Fact Patterns*

Given a candidate sentence $s = x\ e_i\ y\ e_j\ z$, the *fact pattern* of the sentence w.r.t. the entity pair (e_i, e_j) is defined as:

$$(\mathit{TYPE}_1, \mathit{TYPE}_2, BP(s, e_i, e_j)) \tag{1}$$

TYPE_1 and TYPE_2 are the types of e_i and e_j, respectively. $BP(s, e_i, e_j)$ is a basic pattern of sentence s w.r.t. the entity pair (e_i, e_j). In addition, a fact pattern is associated with a weight vector that contains the weights of the fact patterns with regard to the target relations of interest: $(w(BP(s, e_i, e_j), R_1), w(BP(s, e_i, e_j), R_2), \ldots, w(BP(s, e_i, e_j), R_m))$.

Given a relation R_k, if its type signature is the same as the fact pattern's type signature, the weight is defined by Equation (2):

$$weight(BP(s, e_i, e_j), R_k) = \max_{p \in SP(R_k)} (sim(BP(s, e_i, e_j), p) \times conf(p, R_k)) \tag{2}$$

where the similarity between the basic pattern $BP(s)$ and a pattern p in the seed patterns of R_i is defined based on the Jaccard coefficient with regard to n-grams q:

$$sim(BP(s, e_i, e_j), p) = \frac{|\{q \in BP(s, e_i, e_j) \cap q \in p\}|}{|\{q \in BP(s, e_i, e_j) \cup q \in p\}|}$$

3.3 Graph Model

A weighted undirected graph $G(V, E, \mathbf{W})$ is employed to facilitate the knowledge harvesting, where V is the set of vertices, E is the set of edges, and $\mathbf{W}$ is the weight matrix (i.e., an entry $\mathbf{W}_{ij}$ indicating the similarity of the corresponding vertices v_i and v_j).

We divide the set of vertices into two subsets: *fact candidate vertices* (V_F) and *fact pattern vertices* (V_P), where $V_F \cap V_P = \emptyset$ and $V = V_F \cup V_P$. A vertex in V_F corresponds to a fact candidate, i.e., either a base fact (e_i, e_j) or a temporal fact $(e_i, e_j)@t_k$. A vertex in V_P corresponds to a fact pattern in the form of $(\mathit{TYPE}_1, \mathit{TYPE}_2, p)$, as defined in formula (1), where p indicates a basic pattern.

Edges between a fact candidate vertex and a fact pattern vertex: An edge between a fact candidate vertex v_f and a fact pattern vertex v_p is generated, if there is a candidate sentence containing both. Intuitively, more candidate sentences provide higher support for the fact candidate v_f held in the relation v_p. Let $S(v_f, v_p)$ be the set of candidate sentences, then the weight of the edge (v_f, v_p) is defined and normalized as $1 - e^{(-1)*\beta*|S(v_f, v_p)|}$, where $\beta \in (0, 1]$. The parameter β smoothens similarity values by reducing the impact of outliers with undesirable high cardinality such as spam.

Edges between two fact pattern vertices: If two fact patterns are similar, their corresponding vertices are connected by an edge with a similarity-based weight. The intuition is that similar patterns often indicate the same relation. Two fact pattern vertices v_{p_i} and v_{p_j} are considered dissimilar (similarity is zero) if their corresponding type signatures are inconsistent (i.e., $v_{p_i}.\mathit{TYPE}_1 \neq v_{p_j}.\mathit{TYPE}_1$ or v.v.). If their type signatures are consistent, the edgeweight is defined by the similarity of the basic patterns $v_{p_i}.p$ and $v_{p_j}.p$ as follows:

1. If the two patterns share the same verb and preposition, the similarity between them is the distance-weighted Jaccard similarity. If the two patterns differ in their verbs or prepositions, then the similarity is set to zero.
2. If one pattern contains a verb and the other one does not, the similarity between them is zero.
3. If neither of them contains a verb, the similarity is the distance-weighted Jaccard similarity.

The distance-weight of an n-gram in a basic pattern is defined based on its position in the sentence. The closer the n-gram appears to the target entity, the higher the weight. This way, we can effectively deal with relatively long patterns. For instance in the example graph in Figure 2, although the two patterns V_{P2} and V_{P3} share the n-gram "move from", its weight in V_{P3} is very low, thus resulting in a very low similarity between the two patterns.

4. LABEL PROPAGATION ALGORITHM

After constructing the graph of fact candidates and fact patterns, a semi-supervised label propagation algorithm is applied to extract the relations that hold between fact candidates. The idea of label propagation is that the labeling of vertices (here the possible relations) is propagated to nearby vertices via weighted edges until convergence. In this process, the vertices linked by highly weighted edges are more likely to have the same labels, because the weights of edges represent the vertex similarities. All vertices are treated uniformly, regardless of whether they represent fact candidates or fact patterns.

Suppose the graph contains n vertices, consisting of fc fact candidate and fp fact pattern vertices, where $|V| = n$, $|V_F| = fc$, $|V_P| = fp$, and $n = fc + fp$. In addition, there are $m + 1$ labels. The first m labels correspond to the m relations in the set $\mathcal{R}$ of target relations, plus a "none" label (denoting no or an unknown relation). In the following, we will use labels and relations interchangeably.

The matrix $\mathbf{Y} \in \mathbb{R}_{+}^{n \times (m+1)}$ denotes the graph's initial label assignment. The vector $\mathbf{Y}_{i*}$ denotes the ith row of matrix $\mathbf{Y}$, with each element $\mathbf{Y}_{ik} \in [0, 1]$ indicating vertex v_i's confidence score for label k, where $k \in \{1, 2, ..., m + 1\}$. The ℓth column of matrix $\mathbf{Y}$ is denoted by vector $\mathbf{Y}_{*\ell}$.

When a fact candidate vertex v_i corresponds to a positive seed fact of relation R_k, the vertex is labelled as R_k with confidence 1, i.e., $\mathbf{Y}_{ik} = 1$. A fact pattern vertex v_j is labelled as R_k with confidence 1 (namely $\mathbf{Y}_{jk} = 1$), if its weight for a seed pattern of relation R_k (evaluated by Equation 2) is greater than a pre-specified threshold value γ. Note that if v_j has a strong weight (greater than γ) with the seed patterns of more than one relation, all the corresponding relations are labelled. All other entries in $\mathbf{Y}$ are initially set to 0.

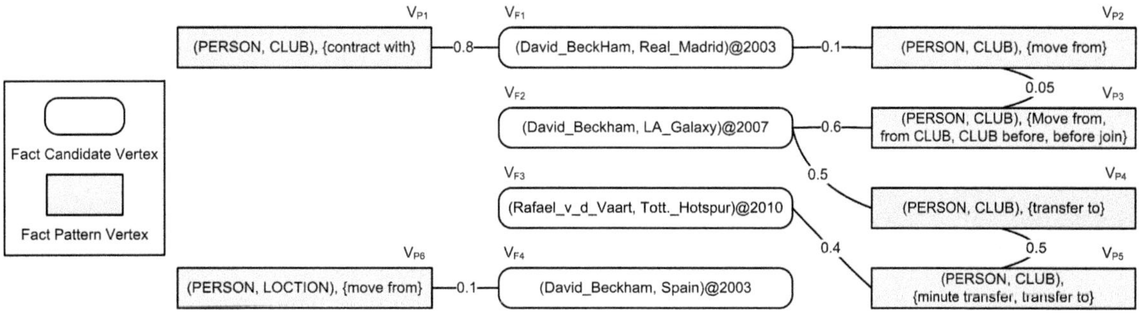

Figure 2: An Example Graph

When the label propagation process finishes, each vertex is associated with a vector indicating the estimated labels. We use matrix $\widehat{\mathbf{Y}} \in \mathbb{R}_{+}^{n\times(m+1)}$ to indicate the estimated labels for all vertices. Note that the matrix $\widehat{\mathbf{Y}}$ has exactly the same ordering of vertices and labels as $\mathbf{Y}$. Finally, for each vertex, the labels with sufficiently high confidence scores are selected.

4.1 Basic Objective Function

As shown in [18], the process of label propagation is realized by minimizing the following objective function:

$$\mathcal{L}(\widehat{\mathbf{Y}}) = \sum_{\ell} \Big[(\mathbf{Y}_{*\ell} - \widehat{\mathbf{Y}}_{*\ell})^T \mathbf{S}^{\ell} (\mathbf{Y}_{*\ell} - \widehat{\mathbf{Y}}_{*\ell}) + \mu_1 \widehat{\mathbf{Y}}_{*\ell}^T \mathbf{L} \widehat{\mathbf{Y}}_{*\ell} + \mu_2 \| \widehat{\mathbf{Y}}_{*\ell} - \mathbf{R}_{*\ell} \|_2 \Big] \quad (3)$$

where $\mathbf{Y}_{*\ell}$ and $\widehat{\mathbf{Y}}_{*\ell}$ denote the ℓth column vector of the initial assignment matrix $\mathbf{Y}$ and estimated label matrix $\widehat{\mathbf{Y}}$, respectively.

The intuition of keeping estimated labels centred around initial labels is realized by the first term of the objective function (3), which is the quadratic loss that measures the discrepancies between the initial labels and the estimated labels. In the original MAD algorithm of [18], the diagonal matrix $\mathbf{S}^{\ell}$ is identical for every label, with p_i^{inj} on the main diagonal for labeled vertices and 0 for unlabeled ones, where p_i^{inj} is set to be proportional to vertex v_i's degree. Since the initially labelled fact pattern vertices may be noisy, the corresponding elements on the main diagonal of $\mathbf{S}^{\ell}$ should also be able to control the confidences on the label. Assuming that we are considering label ℓ and v_i is a fact pattern vertex, we represent the confidences on the label ℓ by multiplying p_i^{inj} with the vertex v_i's fact-pattern weight on label ℓ (evaluated by Equation 2).

The label spreading effect is achieved by the unnormalized graph Laplacian matrix $\mathbf{L}$, which smoothes label similarities between linked vertices based on edge weights. This property becomes clearer when $\mu_1 \widehat{\mathbf{Y}}_{*\ell}^T \mathbf{L} \widehat{\mathbf{Y}}_{*\ell}$ is rewritten as

$$\mu_1 \widehat{\mathbf{Y}}_{*\ell}^T \mathbf{L} \widehat{\mathbf{Y}}_{*\ell} = \mu_1 \frac{1}{2} \sum_{i,j} \mathbf{Z}_{ij} (\widehat{\mathbf{Y}}_{i\ell} - \widehat{\mathbf{Y}}_{j\ell})^2 \quad (4)$$

where $\mathbf{Z}_{ij} = \mathbf{W}_{ij} \times p_i^{cont} + \mathbf{W}_{ji} \times p_j^{cont}$ and $\mathbf{W}_{ij}$ is the edge weight between vertices v_i and v_j. Following [18], we set p_i^{cont} to be inversely proportional to vertex v_i's degree. The hyper-parameter μ_1 controls the influence of the graph Laplacian. In order to minimize the function, similarities of labels between vertex pairs linked with high edge-weight are enforced, while different labels are tolerated for those vertex pairs with low edge-weights.

The last term in the objective function (3) can be regarded as a combination of an L2 regularizer for the m relations of interest and a loss function for the "none" label. $\mathbf{R}_{*\ell}$ is the ℓth column of the abandon matrix $\mathbf{R} \in \mathbb{R}_{+}^{n\times(m+1)}$. Specifically, $\mathbf{R}_{*\ell}$ is a zero-valued column vector for every $\ell \in \{1, 2, ..., m\}$, which works exactly as an L2 regularizer for the estimated labels of the m relations of interest to avoid over-fitting to their seed labels. However, the vector of the last label $(m+1)$ is $\mathbf{R}_{*(m+1)} = (p_1^{abnd}, p_2^{abnd}, ... p_n^{abnd})^T$, where p_i^{abnd} is set to 1-p_i^{inj}-p_i^{cont} like in the original MAD algorithm [18]. The hyper-parameter μ_2 adjusts the degree of regularization and the trust in the "none" relation.

Since we only change the diagonal matrices $\mathbf{S}_{\ell}$, the objective function can still be solved by the optimization algorithm of MAD [18].

4.2 Incorporating Inclusion Constraints

Sometimes, a relation R_i implies another relation R_j, meaning that a valid fact of R_i should also be a valid fact of R_j. In such a case, there is an inclusion constraint (subsumption) that R_i implies R_j. For example, the relation *isCapitalOf* between cities and countries implies the *isCityOf* relation. Inclusion dependencies arise in specific forms for temporal relations, that is, between events and their implied lasting relations, and also between base relations and their temporal counterparts. For example, the event relation *joinsClubTemp* implies *worksForClubTemp* and the base relation *worksForClub*. The temporal fact *joinsClubTemp* `(David_Beckham, Real_Madrid)` @2003 also implies the temporal fact *worksForClubTemp* `(David_Beckham, Real_Madrid)` @2003, which in turn implies the base fact *worksForClub* `(David_Beckham, Real_Madrid)`.

Inclusion constraints provide an additional asset: it can generate (or reinforce) the evidence of a fact by observing another fact of a different relation. Thus, if relation ℓ implies relation ℓ', it suggests for a fact candidate v_m having label ℓ, that the estimated confidence value $\widehat{\mathbf{Y}}_{m\ell'}$ should be greater or equal than the estimated confidence value $\widehat{\mathbf{Y}}_{m\ell}$. For instance, if a fact candidate v_m is estimated as *joinsClubTemp*, its estimated labels should satisfy the following constraint $\widehat{\mathbf{Y}}_{m(worksForClubTemp)} \geq \widehat{\mathbf{Y}}_{m(joinsClubTemp)}$. In the following, we will show how to incorporate inclusion constraints into an extended label propagation framework.

4.2.1 Objective Function with Inclusion Constraints

We first introduce some notations. The matrix $\mathbf{C} \in \mathbb{R}_{+}^{m\times m}$ records the inclusion dependencies between different relations of interest. Specifically, if relation ℓ implies relation ℓ', we set $\mathbf{C}_{\ell'\ell} = 1$. Given a label ℓ, $imply(\ell)$ denotes the labels that imply ℓ and $implied(\ell)$ those labels that are implied by ℓ.

We introduce a new objective function, described in equation (5), to incorporate inclusion constraints between different relations:

$$\mathcal{L}(\widehat{\mathbf{Y}}) = \sum_{\ell} \Big[(\mathbf{Y}_{*\ell} - \widehat{\mathbf{Y}}_{*\ell})^T \mathbf{S}_{\ell} (\mathbf{Y}_{*\ell} - \widehat{\mathbf{Y}}_{*\ell}) + \mu_1 \widehat{\mathbf{Y}}_{*\ell}^T \mathbf{L} \widehat{\mathbf{Y}}_{*\ell}$$

$$+ \mu_2 \|\widehat{\mathbf{Y}}_{*\ell} - \mathbf{R}_{*\ell}\|_2 + \mu_3 \sum_v \sum_{k \neq \ell} \mathbf{C}_{\ell k} \mathbf{Y}_{vk} (\widehat{\mathbf{Y}}_{v\ell} - \widehat{\mathbf{Y}}_{vk})^2 \Big]$$

$$s.t.\ \widehat{\mathbf{Y}}_{v\ell'} \geq \widehat{\mathbf{Y}}_{v\ell},\ \ v \in V,\ \ell' \in implied(\ell) \tag{5}$$

The last term in Equation (5) serves to smoothen the estimated labels which satisfy the inclusion constraints. Note that only vertices containing initial labels are smoothed. In contrast to the MADDL algorithm [18], which assumes all correlations among classes to be symmetric, our approach does not assume symmetry of correlations. For example, assume that *joinsClubTemp* implies *worksForClubTemp* and the fact candidate `(David_Beckham, Real_Madrid)` @2003 holds for *joinsClubTemp* with high probability (e.g. 0.9), but has low probability for the *worksForClubTemp* relation (e.g. 0.1). This is undesirable and should be smoothed, as *joinsClubTemp* implies *worksForClubTemp*. Therefore, the objective function (5) will pull the estimated value for *worksForClubTemp* closer to the value for *joinsClubTemp* by reducing the labels' differences. On the contrary, if the same fact candidate holds for *worksForClubTemp* with high probability (e.g., 0.9), but has low probability for the *joinsClubTemp* (e.g., 0.1), the objective function (5) will not pull the estimated value for the *joinsClubTemp*.

4.2.2 Optimization Problem Solution

In the Appendix, we proove that adding inclusion constraints does not change the *convexity* of the objective function in Equation (3). The convex optimization problem is solved by *cyclic coordinate descent* [3]. The algorithm iterates through each coordinate of $\widehat{\mathbf{Y}}$, and solves sequentially the following sub-problems until it converges:

$$\min_{\widehat{\mathbf{Y}}_{v\ell}} \mathcal{L}(\widehat{\mathbf{Y}})\ \ s.t.\ lb \leq \widehat{\mathbf{Y}}_{v\ell} \leq ub \tag{6}$$

where lb and ub are the lower and upper bounds of $\widehat{\mathbf{Y}}_{v\ell}$, respectively.

In each sub-problem, all variables of $\widehat{\mathbf{Y}}_{v\ell}$ except the one at the current coordinate are fixed. So this technique optimizes the objective function by solving a sequence of single-variable optimization problems. Because the problem is a weighted sum of quadratic functions, there is a closed-form solution for each sub-problem. For coordinate $\widehat{\mathbf{Y}}_{v\ell}$, we set the first partial derivative with respect to $\widehat{\mathbf{Y}}_{v\ell}$ to zero. Thus, the optimum in the absence of constraints is:

$$\widehat{\mathbf{Y}}_{v\ell} = \frac{\mathbf{S}_{\ell vv}\mathbf{Y}_{v\ell} + \mu_1 \sum_i \mathbf{Z}_{vi}\widehat{\mathbf{Y}}_{i\ell} + \mu_2 \mathbf{R}_{v\ell} + \mu_3 \sum_{k\neq\ell} \theta \widehat{\mathbf{Y}}_{vk}}{\mathbf{S}_{\ell vv} + \mu_1 \sum_i \mathbf{Z}_{vi} + \mu_2 + \mu_3 \sum_{k \neq \ell} \theta}$$

$$\theta = (\mathbf{C}_{\ell k} + \mathbf{C}_{k\ell})\mathbf{Y}_{vk} \tag{7}$$

From the inclusion constraints we can infer a lower (lb) and an upper bound (ub) for the solution. Specifically, if $imply(\ell)$ is not empty, $lb = \max_{\ell' \in imply(\ell)} \widehat{\mathbf{Y}}_{v\ell'}$, otherwise $lb = 0$; if $implied(\ell)$ is not empty, $ub = \min_{\ell' \in implied(\ell)} \widehat{\mathbf{Y}}_{v\ell'}$, otherwise $ub = 1$. For example, the lower bound of *worksForClubTemp* is the maximum of *joinsClubTemp* and *leavesClubTemp*, with the upper bound 1. Similarly, the upper bound of *joinsClubTemp*/*leavesClubTemp* is the value on *worksForClubTemp*, with the lower bound 0. The final optimum is computed by $\max(\min(\widehat{\mathbf{Y}}_{v\ell}, ub), lb)$ to ensure that the optimal solution satisfies the inclusion constraints.

We refer to this algorithm as *ICMAD* (Inclusion-Constraints-aware MAD). The complete method is shown in Algorithm 1. Compared to the original MAD method, the lower and upper bounds are checked after each label update.

Algorithm 1 ICMAD Algorithm.

Input: Graph: $G = (V, E)$,
Matrices $\mathbf{S}^\ell$ for each $\ell \in [1...m+1]$,
Matrix $\mathbf{Z}$ derived from the graph Laplacian,
Abandon matrix $\mathbf{R}$,
Initial labels matrix $\mathbf{Y}$,
Inclusion constraint weight matrix $\mathbf{C}$
Output: Estimated labels matrix $\widehat{\mathbf{Y}}$

```
Ŷ ← Y;
repeat
  for each v ∈ V do
    for each ℓ ∈ [1, ...m + 1] do
      // Evaluation based on Equation (7);
      numerator ← S^ℓ_vv Y_vℓ + μ1 Σ_i Z_vi Ŷ_iℓ + μ2 R_vℓ +
                  μ3 Σ_{k≠ℓ} (C_ℓk + C_kℓ) Y_vk Ŷ_vk;
      denominator ← S^ℓ_vv + μ1 Σ_i Z_vi + μ2 +
                  μ3 Σ_{k≠ℓ} (C_ℓk + C_kℓ) Y_vk;
      Ŷ_vℓ ← numerator / denominator;
      for each k ∈ [1, ...m] ∧ k ≠ ℓ do
        // Lower and upper bounds checking;
        if C_ℓk > 0 ∧ Ŷ_vℓ < Y_vk then Ŷ_vℓ ← Y_vk;
        if C_kℓ > 0 ∧ Ŷ_vℓ > Y_vk then Ŷ_vℓ ← Y_vk;
      end for
    end for
  end for
until converged
```

4.3 Combining Base and Temporal Graphs

The above *ICMAD* algorithm can be applied to either base or temporal facts and their patterns. So far, however, these would be two separate instantiations of the same algorithm. In this subsection, we discuss how to combine the two settings for enhanced output.

For base relations, seed patterns may be noisy, especially when positive seeds (entity pairs) hold for multiple relations. For example, a person may be born and may die in the same place, so both relations *isBornIn* and *hasDiedIn* have similar seed patterns, which is undesired. However, the corresponding temporal relations are better distinguishable, as - usually - people do not die on the same date (or same year) they are born. Thus, by combining base and temporal graph, the seed patterns from the temporal graph can help to counter ("correct") noisy patterns in the base graph.

The pattern nodes in the temporal graph are actually a subset of those in the base graph. Thus, we can unify both graphs by sharing all pattern nodes and conceptually connecting the fact candidate nodes from base and temporal graph with their respective patterns. A new objective function is described in Equation (8), where matrix $\mathbf{G} \in \mathbb{R}_+^{p_b \times p_t}$ records the relationship of the same pattern nodes in base and temporal graph. p_b and p_t are the number of pattern nodes in base and temporal graph. If a pattern node v_i in the base graph is exactly the same as the pattern node v_j in the temporal graph, then we assign $\mathbf{G}_{ij}$ to 1. Otherwise, $\mathbf{G}_{ij}$ is set to 0.

Suppose $\mathbf{Y} = \begin{pmatrix} \mathbf{Y_b} & 0 \\ 0 & \mathbf{Y_t} \end{pmatrix}$, where $\mathbf{Y_b}$ and $\mathbf{Y_t}$ indicate the initial label matrices of base and temporal graph, respectively. Likewise, $\widehat{\mathbf{Y}} = \begin{pmatrix} \widehat{\mathbf{Y_b}} & 0 \\ 0 & \widehat{\mathbf{Y_t}} \end{pmatrix}$, where $\widehat{\mathbf{Y_b}}$ and $\widehat{\mathbf{Y_t}}$ indicate the estimated label matrices of base and temporal graph, respectively. $\mathbf{S}^\ell$ and $\mathbf{L}$ can also be re-written analogously. On this basis, we define Equation (8) as the new objective function as follows:

$$\mathcal{L}(\widehat{\mathbf{Y}}) = \sum_\ell \Big[(\mathbf{Y}_{*\ell} - \widehat{\mathbf{Y}}_{*\ell})^T \mathbf{S}^\ell (\mathbf{Y}_{*\ell} - \widehat{\mathbf{Y}}_{*\ell}) + \mu_1 \widehat{\mathbf{Y}}_{*\ell}^T \mathbf{L} \widehat{\mathbf{Y}}_{*\ell}$$

$$+ \mu_2 \|\widehat{\mathbf{Y}}_{*\ell} - \mathbf{R}_{*\ell}\|_2 + \mu_3 \sum_v \sum_{k \neq \ell} \mathbf{C}_{\ell k} \mathbf{Y}_{vk} (\widehat{\mathbf{Y}}_{v\ell} - \widehat{\mathbf{Y}}_{vk})^2$$

$$+ \mu_4 \sum_{v,u} \mathbf{G}_{vu} (\widehat{\mathbf{Y}_{\mathbf{b}}}_{v\ell} - \widehat{\mathbf{Y}_{\mathbf{t}}}_{u\ell''})^2 \Big]$$

$$s.t.\ \widehat{\mathbf{Y}}_{v\ell'} \geq \widehat{\mathbf{Y}}_{v\ell},\ \ v \in V,\ \ell' \in implied(\ell) \tag{8}$$

Base Relations	Temporal Relations	Type Signatures
isBornIn	*isBornInTemp*	(*PERSON*, *CITY*)
hasDiedIn	*hasDiedInTemp*	(*PERSON*, *CITY*)
worksForClub	*worksForClubTemp*	(*PERSON*, *CLUB*)
	joinsClubTemp	(*PERSON*, *CLUB*)
	leavesClubTemp	(*PERSON*, *CLUB*)
isMarriedTo	*isMarriedToTemp*	(*PERSON*, *PERSON*)
	getsMarriedWithTemp	(*PERSON*, *PERSON*)
	getsDivorcedFromTemp	(*PERSON*, *PERSON*)
	winsAwardTemp	(*PERSON*, *AWARD*)

Table 1: Relations of Interest

where label ℓ'' is the corresponding temporal relation of base label ℓ (e.g., ℓ for *worksForClub* with ℓ'' for *worksForClubTemp*).

The new objective function shown in Equation (8) keeps the same form as Equation (5). Therefore, it is still solvable by cyclic coordinate descent.

5. EXPERIMENTS

All methods used in this paper are implemented in Java using Sun JDK 1.6. We then detect and disambiguate entities based on the Stanford named entity recognizer[5] and YAGO's "means" relation as oulined in Section 3.1. Temporal mentions are identified by regular expressions (currently yearly granularity). The actual label propagation algorithm is based on the Junto library [18].

Experiments have been conducted on a workstation with two Intel Xeon 2.40GHz, 4-Core CPUs, and 40GB memory. Except parameters $\beta = 0.05$ and $\gamma = 0.5$, all the other hyper parameters used in our experiments are manually tuned on a separate dataset.

5.1 Experimental Setup

Data Sets: Our methods have been evaluated against two corpora from the soccer and celebrity domain. In the soccer domain, we selected more than 23.000 soccer players' Wikipedia articles. In addition, we retrieved around 110.000 on-line news articles (e.g., BBC, Yahoo! news, ESPN, etc.) by searching for players contained in the "FIFA 100 list"[6]. Likewise, the celebrity corpus has been populated with more than 88.000 news articles of persons mentioned in the "Forbes 100 list"[7] in addition to their Wikipedia articles.

Relations of Interest: In the current experiments, we are interested in four base relations and nine temporal relations. The relations and their type signatures are summarized in Table 1. It is worth mentioning that temporal relations (highlighted in grey) such as *isBornInTemp* or *hasDiedInTemp* are "extensions" of their corresponding base relations *isBornIn* resp. *hasDiedIn* by temporal information for the identified event (e.g. birth, death, etc.).

Seed Selection: For each relation positive and negative seed facts have been manually selected. Facts with prominent entities are chosen as seed facts due to their frequency. Thus, k co-occurring entities are chosen as seed facts for each relation type signature.

For example, when selecting seed facts for the *worksForClub* relation, we compute the co-occurrence statistics (eventually supported by keyword filtering) of *PERSON* and *CLUB* entities based on the same sentence. Starting with the highest ranked entity pair, we manually check in Wikipedia if the relation of interest is satisfied. If approved, it becomes a positive seed fact, otherwise a negative.

Performance Metrics: Baseline for our experiments is the state-of-the-art PROSPERA system [13]. We evaluate both approaches in terms of precision correctness of the extracted facts. Due to the size of the corpus, evaluation of recall is impossible. Precision estimates are based on sampling (50 facts per relation) with a human evaluation against ground truth information in Wikipedia.

Sample Output: For the relations of interest we generate patterns and (temporal) facts. Table 2 depicts randomly chosen results from both corpora. Results for temporal facts are marked in grey.

Relation	Pattern	Fact
joinsClubTemp	join *LEAGUE* side	(David_Beckham, Los_Angeles_Galaxy)@2007
leavesClubTemp	transfer from	(Thierry_Henry, Juventus_F.C.)@1999
getsMarriedWithTemp	marry	(Demi_Moore, Ashton_Kutcher)@2005
getsDivorcedFromTemp	divorce	(Jennifer_Aniston, Brad_Pitt)@2005
worksForClub	to join at	(Michael_Owen, Real_Madrid_C.F.)
isMarriedTo	husband	(Hillary_Rodham_Clinton, Bill_Clinton)

Table 2: Patterns and Facts extracted for Relations of Interest

5.2 Results on Base Fact Extraction

We first compare base fact extraction with PROSPERA and PRAVDA. The support threshold in pattern analysis is $supp(p, R_i) = 10$ with 100 positive and 10 negative seed facts for each relation.

	PRAVDA		PROSPERA	
Relation	# Facts	Precision	# Facts	Precision
worksForClub	12.724	88%	4.536	82%
isBornIn	3.629	88%	2.426	90%
hasDiedIn	183	90%	55	93%
isMarriedTo	428	74%	147	90%

Table 3: Base Fact Extraction (100 positive, 10 negative seeds)

Table 3 summarizes the results of this experiment. As one can see both approaches achieve comparable precision. However, PRAVDA clearly outperforms PROSPERA with respect to the number of extracted facts. The reason for this major gain can be explained with LP's propagation of the labels' confidence scores from one node to another. This results in confidence propagation among very similar, but less frequently occuring patterns ("be born in" and "born in"). Of course, this comes with the risk of inducing more noise, which becomes apparent for more complex relations such as *isMarriedTo*. The explanation for this "misbehavior" is simple: a prominent couple will be frequently mentioned in the media in completely different contexts (e.g. when dating, talking, visiting, etc.), thus, propagating high confidence to less useful labels, too.

In order to quantify the impact of the number of seed facts, we now evaluate the performance of two base relations (*worksForClub* and *isMarriedTo*) for varying numbers of positive seed facts while keeping the number of negative seeds fixed with 10. We vary them from 10, 20, 50 to 100 by simultaneously adopting the support $supp(p, R_i)$ used in pattern analysis to 4, 6, 8 and 10 respectively.

[5] *http://www-nlp.stanford.edu/software/CRF-NER.shtml*

[6] *http://en.wikipedia.org/wiki/FIFA_100*

[7] *http://www.forbes.com/lists/2010/53/celeb-100-10_The-Celebrity-100.html*

		PRAVDA		PROSPERA	
	# Pos. Seeds	# Facts	Precision	# Fact	Precision
worksForClub	10	4.882	84%	2.202	86%
	20	8.381	82%	3.358	86%
	50	10.826	82%	4.321	84%
	100	12.724	88%	4.536	82%
isMarriedTo	10	388	74%	16	0%
	20	391	64%	123	88%
	50	391	78%	159	82%
	100	428	74%	147	90%

Table 4: Impact of Varying the Number of Positive Seed Facts

Table 4 summarizes the results on the impact of varying the number of positive seed facts. PRAVDA extracts far more facts than PROSPERA, particularly if the number of positive seeds is low. Both approaches achieve similar precision quality throughout the experiments (except for PROSPERA for the *isMarriedTo* relation with 10 positive seeds given). It can again be recognized that PRAVDA is slightly prone to generate more noise, particularly when the relation of interest is more complex. As an exapmle of the *isMarriedTo* relation, please consider the following text from our corpus:

> "The Scottish News of the World has published photographs which it claims show how Sir Paul McCartney is secretly dating Hollywood actress Rosanna Arquette - the virtual double of his estranged wife Heather Mills."

Since we do not use a dependency parser for efficiency reasons, there is no evidence that the two entities `Rosanna Arquette` and `Heather Mills` are not directly connected. Consequently, the surface string pattern "wife" links `Rosanna Arquette` with `Heather Mills` and identifies them (incorrectly) as a couple.

5.3 Results on Temporal Fact Extraction with Inclusion Constraints

In the following we will present the results of our methods on temporal fact extraction with inclusion constraints (yearly granularity). Since PROSPERA is not geared for harvesting temporal facts, we only report the performance of our method. We evaluate inclusion constraints for two relations:

- *joinsClubTemp* and *leavesClubTemp* imply *worksForClubTemp*
- *getsMarriedWithTemp* and *getsDivorcedFromTemp* imply *isMarriedToTemp*

The results are depicted in Table 5 (10 positive and negative seed facts for the first seven relations) with a special highlighting in dark grey of the relations *worksForClubTemp* and *isMarriedToTemp*. Without giving any seed facts to the *worksForClubTemp* and *isMarriedToTemp* relations, inclusion constraint are successfully applied to extract facts for the two relations.

We see that results with respect to the number of extracted facts and precision are not so good as for base fact extraction. This is not surprising for at least three reasons. First, our extraction currently operates on the sentence level, meaning that entity pair and temporal expression have to be in the very same sentence. Second, we are currently able to detect only explicit temporal expressions. Third, associating temporal expressions to the appropriate relation and/or entity/ies is sometimes complex for human, too.

Extraction of facts for the *leavesClubTemp* and *joinsClubTemp* relations are particularly difficult. Usually media coverage starts a long time before the actual transfer actually occurs. Consequently, this induces a lot of noise to the *leavesClubTemp* relation. In addition, both before mentioned relations are - of course - affected by unsupported rumors, which are common to sport news coverage.

Relation	# P/N Seeds	# Facts	Precision
isBornInTemp	10/10	3.471	82%
hasDiedInTemp	10/10	65	88%
winsAwardTemp	10/10	243	84%
joinsClubTemp	10/10	1.871	80%
leavesClubTemp	10/10	235	71%
getsMarriedWithTemp	10/10	76	78%
getsDivorcedFromTemp	10/10	13	71%
worksForClubTemp	0/0	2.086	86%
isMarriedToTemp	0/0	88	80%

Table 5: Temporal Fact Extraction with Inclusion Constraints

5.4 Joint Base and Temporal Fact Extraction

In the following we now investigate the results of joint base and temporal fact extraction. In contrast to the experiments before, we now combine the base and temporal graphs and extract the facts simultaneously. Table 6 compares the joint approach with the separate (for base facts resp. temporal facts) ones. For the sake of clarity, results of temporal fact extraction have been highlighted in grey. Experiments have been conducted with 10 positive/negative seed facts per base relation and 5 positive/negative seed facts per temporal relation (except *worksForClubTemp* and *isMarriedToTemp* in order to evaluate the impact of inclusion constraints).

As we can see from Table 6, particularly base fact extraction benefits from the joint apporach, while temporal fact extraction remains more or less unchanged. It is worth mentioning that the *worksForClub* relation increases a lot in terms of number of extracted facts as well as slightly with respect to precision. Even more, the number of extracted facts as well as the precision for the *worksForClub* relation is higher than its separate "counterpart", which is the 20-seed baseline compared with 10 seeds for *worksForClub* + 5 seeds for *joinsClubTemp* + 5 seeds for *leavesClubTemp* in the joint approach.

Finally, we study the impact of inclusions constraints on the joint approach. From the results in Table 7 we can see that inclusion constraints play an important role in the joint extraction approach. Both base relations (*worksForClub* and *isMarriedTo*) benefit from their inclusion, while precision slightly decreases for *worksForClub*. Accuracy for temporal relations (colored in grey) remains almost unchanged. Please note that no facts have been discovered for *worksForClubTemp* and *isMarriedToTemp* (indicated in dark grey in Table 7) as they have been extracted via inclusion constraints, only.

6. RELATED WORK

Relation extraction aims at detecting and classifying semantic relationships between entities typically from text. Many machine learning methods have been exploited to address this task. Supervised learning methods, such as [8, 29] suffer from a large amount of manually labelled training data. Semi-supervised methods (e.g. [28]) require less labelled data, and particularly [7] first attempted to apply label propagation for relation extraction. Recently distant supervision for relation extraction(e.g. [12, 26]) became popular. Instead of using a labelled corpus, the input of distant supervision

	Joint		Separate	
Relation	**# Facts**	**Precision**	**# Facts**	**Precision**
worksForClub	10.467	84%	4.882	84%
isBornIn	3.139	92%	368	96%
worksForClubTemp	2.761	84%	2.032	88%
isBornInTemp	3.184	84%	3.297	85%

Table 6: Comparison of Joint and Separate Fact Extraction

	W/ Constraints		W/O Constraints	
Relation	**# Facts**	**Precision**	**# Facts**	**Precision**
worksForClub	10.467	84%	5.657	90%
isMarriedTo	413	64%	480	64%
worksForClubTemp	2.761	84%	0	NA
isMarriedToTemp	98	82%	0	NA
joinsClubTemp	1.788	82%	1.840	82%
leavesClubTemp	249	64%	273	66%
getsMarriedWithTemp	73	77%	73	77%
getsDivorcedFromTemp	13	78%	13	73%

Table 7: Joint Extraction With and Without Constraints

only requires an existing knowledge base. These advances in information extraction and the success of knowledge communities like Wikipedia have enabled the largely automated construction of fairly comprehensive knowledge bases such as *DBpedia* [1], *YAGO* [17], *freebase.com*, *trueknowledge.com*, the TextRunner project [9, 24], the StatSnowball project [30], and others. None of these knowledge bases has a temporal dimension. They are all designed for time-invariant knowledge and built as snapshots in time. For example, while several of them know that people can have multiple spouses, none of them can capture the time intervals for the various marriages. Birth and death dates of people are available, though, as they can be extracted at the level of base-facts such as `Diego_Maradona bornOn 30-October-1960`. This is much simpler than the kind of temporal facts that tackled in this paper.

Temporal knowledge as a first-class citizen in knowledge bases has been addressed solely by a few prior papers: [27], [23], and [11]. [27] focuses on extracting business-related temporal facts such as terms of CEOs. It uses an NLP machinery, with deep parsing of every sentence, and machine-learning methods for classifiers for specifically interesting relations. It workes reasonably well, but is computationally expensive, requires extensive training, and cannot be easily generalized to other relations. [23] focuses on extracting relevant timepoints and intervals from semistructured data in Wikipedia: dates in category names, lists, tables, infoboxes. However, there is no support for processing free text. [11] uses training data with fine-grained annotations to learn an inference model based on Markov Logic. This involves using consistency constraints on the relative ordering of events. This machinery is computationally expensive and cannot easily be scaled up.

The NLP community has event extraction tasks in its SemEval workshop series [20], using representations such as TimeML and reference corpora such as Timebank [5]. The TARSQI toolkit [21] provides a suite of techniques for detecting events and temporal expressions, based on a dictionary of time-related adverbial phrases and regular-expression matching. [25] use a small set of seeds to learn pattern rules for various complex relations, such as joining (leaving) a job. The algorithm works on parsed input data, which requires preprocessing by a dependency parser. Moreover, temporal mentions associated with these relations are not considered.

Temporal facts or temporal information are also considered in other fields. For instance, [22] focuses on logics-based querying over uncertain temporal facts, but does not address the extraction and temporal fact harvesting process. There is also recent awareness of temporal IR: ranking of search results for keyword queries with temporal phrases [4, 14].

Label propagation belongs to a family of graph-based semi-supervised learning methods. The first LP method [31] assumed that initial labels are fully correct. This assumption is inappropriate for our setting, as the seed patterns are not fully correct, but only associated with a confidence value. The Adsorption algorithm [2] copes with noisy initial labels, and is successfully used in video recommendation. The MAD algorithm [18] optimizes the Adsorption algorithm. The MADDL algorithm [18] incorporates possible dependencies on different labels into the optimization function. However, these dependencies must be symmetric, in contrast to the asymetric inclusion constraints in our work. In a recent survey [19], MAD is regarded as the most effective label propagation algorithm across various data sets and experimental conditions. The nature of label propagation, which can be iteratively approximated by the Jacobi method, makes it nicely scalable [2]. For example, [15] describes a scalable implementation of label propagation on MapReduce to deal with Web-scale graphs.

7. CONCLUSIONS & OUTLOOK

This paper introduced a unified framework for harvesting base facts and temporal facts from textual Web sources. Our experimental results with news articles and Wikipedia pages demonstrate the viability and high accuracy of our approach. Moreover, for the base-facts case, we have shown much higher recall over one of the best state-of-the-art baselines, while achieving similar precision. We believe that extended forms of constrained label propagation, as developed in this paper, are a very promising alternative to prior methods like Max-Sat reasoning or sampling over Markov-Logic models or factor graphs.

Our extended LP method is nicely geared for scale-out on distributed platforms. So far, however, our experiments were at a scale where we did not need to utilize this property. Our future work aims at experiments with Web-scale datasets (e.g., the TREC ClueWeb corpus), and will explore the scalability behavior of our method.

Acknowledgements

This work is supported by the 7th Framework IST programme of the European Union through the focused research project (STREP) on Longitudinal Analytics of Web Archive data (LAWA) under contract no. 258105.

8. REFERENCES

[1] S. Auer, C. Bizer, G. Kobilarov, J. Lehmann, R. Cyganiak, and Z. G. Ives. Dbpedia: A nucleus for a web of open data. In *ISWC/ASWC*, pages 722–735, 2007.

[2] S. Baluja, R. Seth, D. Sivakumar, Y. Jing, J. Yagnik, S. Kumar, D. Ravichandran, and M. Aly. Video suggestion and discovery for youtube: taking random walks through the view graph. In *WWW*, pages 895–904, 2008.

[3] M. S. Bazaraa, H. D. Sherali, and C. M. Shetty. Nonlinear programming: theory and algorithms. 1993.

[4] K. Berberich, S. J. Bedathur, O. Alonso, and G. Weikum. A language modeling approach for temporal information needs. In *ECIR*, pages 13–25, 2010.

[5] B. Boguraev, J. Pustejovsky, R. K. Ando, and M. Verhagen. Timebank evolution as a community resource for timeml parsing. *Language Resources and Evaluation*, pages 91–115, 2007.

[6] A. Carlson, J. Betteridge, B. Kisiel, B. Settles, E. R. H. Jr., and T. M. Mitchell. Toward an architecture for never-ending language learning. In *AAAI*, pages 1306–1313, 2010.

[7] J. Chen, D.-H. Ji, C. L. Tan, and Z.-Y. Niu. Relation extraction using label propagation based semi-supervised learning. In *ACL*, 2006.

[8] A. Culotta and J. S. Sorensen. Dependency tree kernels for relation extraction. In *ACL*, pages 423–429, 2004.

[9] O. Etzioni, M. Banko, S. Soderland, and D. S. Weld. Open information extraction from the web. *Commun. ACM*, 51(12):68–74, 2008.

[10] T. Heath and C. Bizer. *Linked Data: Evolving the Web into a Global Data Space*. Morgan & Claypool, 2011.

[11] X. Ling and D. S. Weld. Temporal information extraction. In *AAAI*, 2010.

[12] M. Mintz, S. Bills, R. Snow, and D. Jurafsky. Distant supervision for relation extraction without labeled data. In *ACL/AFNLP*, pages 1003–1011, 2009.

[13] N. Nakashole, M. Theobald, and G. Weikum. Scalable knowledge harvesting with high precision and high recall. In *WSDM*, pages 227–236, 2011.

[14] M. Pasca. Towards temporal web search. In *SAC*, pages 1117–1121, 2008.

[15] D. Rao and D. Yarowsky. Ranking and semi-supervised classification on large scale graphs using map-reduce. In *Graph-based Methods for Natural Language Processing*, pages 58–65, 2009.

[16] C. E. Rasmussen. Gaussian processes for machine learning. MIT Press, 2006.

[17] F. M. Suchanek, G. Kasneci, and G. Weikum. Yago: a core of semantic knowledge. In *WWW*, pages 697–706. ACM, 2007.

[18] P. P. Talukdar and K. Crammer. New regularized algorithms for transductive learning. In *ECML/PKDD (2)*, pages 442–457, 2009.

[19] P. P. Talukdar and F. Pereira. Experiments in graph-based semi-supervised learning methods for class-instance acquisition. In *ACL*, pages 1473–1481, 2010.

[20] M. Verhagen, R. Gaizauskas, F. Schilder, M. Hepple, J. Moszkowicz, and J. Pustejovsky. The tempeval challenge: identifying temporal relations in text. *Language Resources and Evaluation*, 43:161–179, 2009.

[21] M. Verhagen, I. Mani, R. Sauri, J. Littman, R. Knippen, S. B. Jang, A. Rumshisky, J. Phillips, and J. Pustejovsky. Automating temporal annotation with tarsqi. In *ACL*, 2005.

[22] Y. Wang, M. Yahya, and M. Theobald. Time-aware reasoning in uncertain knowledge bases. In *MUD*, pages 51–65, 2010.

[23] Y. Wang, M. Zhu, L. Qu, M. Spaniol, and G. Weikum. Timely yago: harvesting, querying, and visualizing temporal knowledge from wikipedia. In *EDBT*, pages 697–700, 2010.

[24] F. Wu and D. S. Weld. Automatically refining the wikipedia infobox ontology. In *WWW*, pages 635–644, 2008.

[25] F. Xu, H. Uszkoreit, and H. Li. A seed-driven bottom-up machine learning framework for extracting relations of various complexity. In *ACL*, 2007.

[26] L. Yao, S. Riedel, and A. McCallum. Collective cross-document relation extraction without labelled data. In *EMNLP*, pages 1013–1023, 2010.

[27] Q. Zhang, F. Suchanek, and G. Weikum. TOB: Timely ontologies for business relations. In *WebDB*.

[28] Z. Zhang. Weakly-supervised relation classification for information extraction. In *CIKM*, pages 581–588, 2004.

[29] G. Zhou, M. Zhang, D.-H. Ji, and Q. Zhu. Tree kernel-based relation extraction with context-sensitive structured parse tree information. In *EMNLP-CoNLL*, pages 728–736, 2007.

[30] J. Zhu, Z. Nie, X. Liu, B. Zhang, and J.-R. Wen. Statsnowball: a statistical approach to extracting entity relationships. In *WWW*, pages 101–110, 2009.

[31] X. Zhu, Z. Ghahramani, and J. D. Lafferty. Semi-supervised learning using gaussian fields and harmonic functions. In *ICML*, pages 912–919, 2003.

Appendix

Convexity Proof

We show that the function 5 is convex, following the convention of [16], we rewrite the estimated labels of $\widehat{\mathbf{Y}}$ into a vector $\widehat{\mathbf{y}}$ with length $n \times (m+1)$.

$$\widehat{\mathbf{y}} = (\widehat{\mathbf{Y}}_{11}, ..., \widehat{\mathbf{Y}}_{n1}, \widehat{\mathbf{Y}}_{12}, ..., \widehat{\mathbf{Y}}_{n2}, ..., \widehat{\mathbf{Y}}_{1(m+1)}, ..., \widehat{\mathbf{Y}}_{n(m+1)})^T \tag{9}$$

In the same way, the initial label assignment matrix $\mathbf{Y}$ can be converted into a vector $\mathbf{y}$. Following the same idea, the graph Laplacian $\mathbf{L}$ is block diagonal with the matrices $\mathbf{L_1}, ..., \mathbf{L_{m+1}}$. In our case, $\mathbf{L_i} = \mathbf{L}$.

$$\begin{bmatrix} \mathbf{L_1} & & & \\ & \mathbf{L_2} & & \\ & & \cdots & \\ & & & \mathbf{L_{m+1}} \end{bmatrix}. \tag{10}$$

And the diagonal matrix $\mathbf{S}$ is represented analogously.

$$\begin{bmatrix} \mathbf{S_1} & & & \\ & \mathbf{S_2} & & \\ & & \cdots & \\ & & & \mathbf{S_{m+1}} \end{bmatrix}. \tag{11}$$

Then the matrix $\hat{\mathbf{C}}$ implied by inclusion constraints has the same form as the unnormalized graph Laplacian, which is $\hat{\mathbf{C}} = \mathbf{D}^{\hat{\mathbf{C}}} - \mathbf{W}^{\hat{\mathbf{C}}}$. The elements ${\mathbf{W}^{\hat{\mathbf{C}}}}_{v^{\ell} v^{\ell'}}$ and ${\mathbf{W}^{\hat{\mathbf{C}}}}_{v^{\ell'} v^{\ell}}$ of affinity matrix $\mathbf{W}^{\hat{\mathbf{C}}}$ have the same positive weights $\mathbf{C}_{\ell\ell'} \cdot \mathbf{Y}_{v\ell'}$, if an inclusion constraint between labels ℓ and ℓ' is included. The remaining entries of $\mathbf{W}^{\hat{\mathbf{C}}}$ are zeros. Then the degree matrix $\mathbf{D}^{\hat{\mathbf{C}}}$ is a diagonal matrix with ${\mathbf{D}^{\hat{\mathbf{C}}}}_{ii} = \sum_j {\mathbf{W}^{\hat{\mathbf{C}}}}_{ij}$.

With the new formulation of the problem, the optimization problem including inclusion constraints takes the form

$$\min_{\widehat{\mathbf{y}}} \Big[(\widehat{\mathbf{y}} - \mathbf{y})^T \mathbf{S} (\widehat{\mathbf{y}} - \mathbf{y}) + \mu_1 \widehat{\mathbf{y}}^T \mathbf{L} \widehat{\mathbf{y}} + \mu_2 (\widehat{\mathbf{y}} - \mathbf{r})^T \mathbf{I} (\widehat{\mathbf{y}} - \mathbf{r}) + \mu_3 \widehat{\mathbf{y}}^T \hat{\mathbf{C}} \widehat{\mathbf{y}} \Big] \quad s.t. \ \widehat{y_v^l} \geq \widehat{y_v^{l'}}$$

The Hessian matrix of the objective function with respect to $\widehat{\mathbf{y}}$ is

$$\mathbf{S} + \mu_1 \mathbf{L} + \mu_2 \mathbf{I} + \mu_3 \hat{\mathbf{C}} \tag{12}$$

which is positive definite if $\mu_2 > 0$ ($\hat{\mathbf{C}}$ is positive semi-definite following the same reason as for the unnormalized graph Laplacian). Finally, as the feasible region is defined by linear constraints, the optimization problem is convex.

Towards A Top-Down and Bottom-up Bidirectional Approach to Joint Information Extraction*

Xiaofeng Yu† Irwin King†§ Michael R. Lyu†

†Computer Science & Engineering Dept.
The Chinese University of Hong Kong
{xfyu,king,lyu}@cse.cuhk.edu.hk

§AT&T Labs Research
201 Mission St. Ste 200, San Francisco, CA
irwin@research.att.com

ABSTRACT

Most high-level information extraction (IE) consists of compound and aggregated subtasks. Such IE problems are generally challenging and they have generated increasing interest recently. We investigate two representative IE tasks: (1) entity identification and relation extraction from Wikipedia, and (2) citation matching, and we formally define joint optimization of information extraction. We propose a joint paradigm integrating three factors – segmentation, relation, and segmentation-relation joint factors, to solve all relevant subtasks simultaneously. This modeling offers a natural formalism for exploiting bidirectional rich dependencies and interactions between relevant subtasks to capture mutual benefits. Since exact parameter estimation is prohibitively intractable, we present a general, highly-coupled learning algorithm based on variational expectation maximization (VEM) to perform parameter estimation approximately in a top-down and bottom-up manner, such that information can flow bidirectionally and mutual benefits from different subtasks can be well exploited. In this algorithm, both segmentation and relation are optimized iteratively and collaboratively using hypotheses from each other. We conducted extensive experiments using two real-world datasets to demonstrate the promise of our approach.

Categories and Subject Descriptors

I.5.1 [**Pattern Recognition**]: Models—*Statistical*; H.2.8 [**Database Management**]: Database Applications—*Data mining*; I.2.7 [**Artificial Intelligence**]: Natural Language Processing—*Text analysis*

General Terms

Algorithms, Experimentation

*This work is supported by two grants from the Research Grants Council of the Hong Kong SAR, China (Project No. CUHK 413210 and Project No. CUHK 415410).

CIKM'11, October 24–28, 2011, Glasgow, Scotland, UK.

Keywords

Factor graphs, top-down and bottom-up bidirectional learning, variational inference, joint information extraction

1. INTRODUCTION

Information extraction (IE) aiming at extracting structured information from text or semi-structured sources plays an important role for a wide variety of applications and it has been investigated for decades. Among such IE tasks, high-level IE problems consisting of compound subtasks have become increasingly popular and they present new challenges to research communities. Typically, two key subtasks are *segmentation* which identifies candidate records (e.g., word segmentation, chunking and entity recognition), and *relation* discovery which discovers certain relations between different records (e.g., entity resolution, relation extraction and social relation mining) [23].

The most common and simplest approach to performing compound IE tasks is to use 1-best or K-best pipeline architecture: components are run independently in some order, and there is no feedback from later components to earlier ones [2, 3]. This approach is feed-forward, which is only top-down or bottom-up integrated, and mutual interactions between different components cannot be exploited. Errors cascade and accumulate, and a once-made error can hardly be corrected in the pipeline. Due to this reason, the end-to-end performance is often hampered and upper-bounded.

Ideally, we would like to advocate *joint* information extraction, which is to solve all relevant subtasks in information extraction jointly, that is, all relevant IE subtasks are optimized simultaneously and decisions of them are made together in a single coherent manner. Joint IE aims to handle multiple hypotheses and uncertainty information and to predict many variables at once such that subtasks can aid each other to boost the performance [6, 12, 29, 24, 15, 10, 26, 25]. This is usually very challenging, and often increases the model complexity. It is typically intractable to run a joint model and they sometimes can hurt the performance, since they increase the number of paths to propagate errors. Due to these difficulties, research on building joint approaches is still in the infancy stage.

Recently, a significant amount of work has shown the feasibility and effectiveness of discriminatively-trained probabilistic graphical models for a variety of IE tasks [18, 20]. The superiority of graphical model is its ability to represent a large number of random variables as a family of probability distributions that factorize according to an underlying graph, and it can capture complex dependencies between

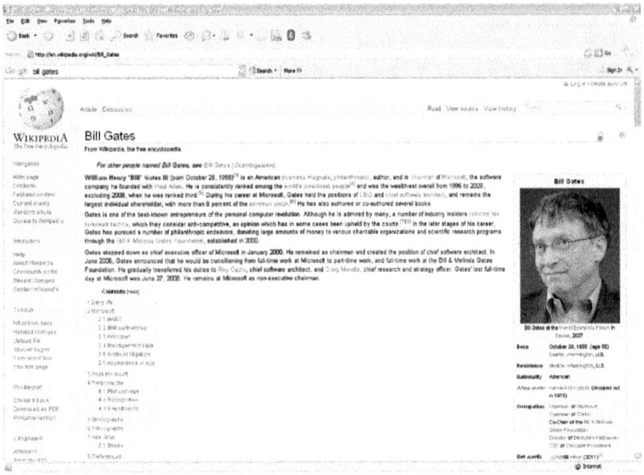

Figure 1: A snapshot of the encyclopedic article about Bill Gates in Wikipedia.

variables. This progress has begun to make the joint learning approach possible. While a number of previous researchers have taken steps toward this direction, there are still various shortcomings: high computational complexity [19], the number of uncertain hypotheses is severely limited [6, 2], the subtasks are only loosely coupled [27], or the approach is feed-forward or top-down integrated and it only allows information to flow in one direction [30].

Exploring bidirectional information and rich interdependencies between relevant subtasks is intuitively appealing. In the following, we use examples from two real-world datasets in our experiments to show the disadvantages of the pipeline architecture and the necessarity of top-down and bottom-up modeling, and to demonstrate the merits of our approach.

1.1 Motivating Examples

1.1.1 Entity Identification and Relation Extraction From Wikipedia

For compound, aggregated IE problems, the availability of robust, flexible, and accurate systems is highly desirable. Wikipedia[1] is the world's largest free online encyclopedia, representing the outcome of a continuous collaborative effort of a large number of volunteer contributors. We investigate the task of identifying entities (e.g., *person*, *location*, and *organization* names) and extracting semantic relationships (e.g., *member_of* and *associate*) between entity pairs in English encyclopedic articles from Wikipedia. For example, Figure 1 gives a snapshot of Wikipedia Web page about the person *Bill Gates*. The basic document is an article, which mainly defines and describes an entity (e.g., *Bill Gates*). This document mentions some other entities (e.g., *Microsoft*, *Paul Allen*, *Seattle*, etc) related to the entity *Bill Gates*. As an illustrative example, consider the following text excerpted from our dataset:

> *George W. Bush was elected President in 2000 as the Republican candidate.*

Clearly, our task consists of two subtasks. First, for entity identification, we need to recognize the entities (both the boundaries and types of them): the *person* name *George W. Bush*, the *year 2000* and the *organization Republican*. Second, for relation extraction, we should extract the *executive* relation between *George W. Bush* and *Republican*. However, the pipeline approach in our experiments cannot extract the *executive* relation between *George W. Bush* and *Republican*, since the *organization* name *Republican* is incorrectly labeled as *miscellaneous* in entity identification stage, and the later relation extraction stage consuming this result also produces erroneous output. From the bottom-up viewpoint, knowing that *Republican* is an *organization* is helpful for the *executive* relation discovery between this entity and the *person George W. Bush*. From the top-down viewpoint, the *executive* relation is a strong evidence indicating a *person* name *George W. Bush* and an *organization Republican*. Modeling top-down and bottom-up simultaneously can therefore explore interdependencies between multiple subtasks, and allow information to flow in both directions to exploit mutual benefits.

1.1.2 Citation Matching

Citation matching requires extracting bibliographic records (e.g., *author*, *title*, and *venue* fields) from citation lists in technical papers (segmentation), and then identifying duplicate records to find the citations referring to the same paper (entity resolution). Citation strings may have different citation styles, different abbreviations, and typographical errors. Correct coreference of a messy citation with a clean citation provides the opportunity for an alignment between these two citations to help the model correctly segment the messy one. Also, coreference between two citations can be assessed more accurately if we can compare well-segmented *title* fields and *venue* fields. Given the following two citations from the Cora database:

> *Hu, Y. & Kibler, D Generation of Attributes for Learning Algorithms, in Proceeding of the 13th National Conference on Artificial Intelligence, p806-811, 1996.*
>
> *Hu, Y., and Kibler, D., Generation of Attributes for Learning Algorithms, Proceedings of the Thirteenth National Conference on Artificial Intelligence (AAAI96), p.806-811, 1996.*

In the second citation, the *author* field *Hu, Y., and Kibler, D.* and the *title* field *Generation of Attributes for Learning Algorithms* are clearly separated by a comma, and extracting them is fairly straightforward. However, in the first one, there is no clear author-title boundary, and correctly pinpointing it seems very difficult. Large quantities of labeled training data and an extensive lexicon could help, but they are very expensive to obtain, and even available they are far from a guarantee of success. However, if we notice that the two citations are coreferent and the *title* of the second one begins with the substring "*Generation of Attributes for*", we can hypothesize that the *title* of the first one also begins with this substring, allowing us to correctly segment it.

To summarize, what appears to be necessary is a mechanism to consistently integrate top-down and bottom-up processing in a bidirectional manner such that segmentation and entity resolution can aid each other to boost the performance of citation matching. In the following, we summarize our major contributions to show that our approach meets these requirements.

[1]http://www.wikipedia.org/

1.2 Our Contributions

Inspired by the above motivation and to address the problems such as brittle accumulation of errors in pipeline systems, in this paper we propose a general, strongly-coupled, and bidirectional paradigm, based on conditionally-trained factor graphs for both top-down and bottom-up modeling, to attack the problem of joint information extraction. More specifically, we summarize our major contributions of this paper as follows:

- First, we formally define joint optimization of information extraction. We propose a discriminative framework in which the segmentation-relation joint factor connects bidirectionally with the segmentation and relation factors. This modeling offers a natural formalism for exploiting rich dependencies and interactions between relevant subtasks to capture mutual benefits. It also has several advantages over previous probabilistic graphical models.

- Second, since exact parameter estimation in this model is too expensive, we propose a highly-coupled learning algorithm based on variational expectation maximization (VEM) to perform parameter estimation approximately in a top-down and bottom-up manner, which allows information to flow in both directions and explores mutual benefits from relevant subtasks. Both segmentation and relation are optimized collaboratively to boost the performance. This algorithm is guaranteed to converge in finding the maximum a posteriori (MAP) assignments for model parameters.

- Third, we perform extensive experiments on two important IE tasks, namely, entity identification and relationship extraction from Wikipedia's encyclopedic articles, and citation matching. Our model significantly outperforms state-of-the-art pipeline, integrated and joint models. Some interesting issues, such as the effect of joint factors on performance and efficiency of our approach, are also discussed and analyzed.

2. PROBLEM FORMULATION

Let $\mathbf{x} = \{x_1, x_2, \ldots, x_p\}$ be an observation sequence containing p tokens. Let $\mathbf{s} = \{s_1, s_2, \ldots, s_q\}$ be a segmentation assignment of observation sequence $\mathbf{x}$. Each segment s_i is a triple $s_i = \{\alpha_i, \beta_i, y_i\}$, where α_i is a start position, β_i is an end position, and $y_i (y_i \in \mathcal{Y})$ is the label assigned to all tokens of this segment. It is reasonable to assume that segments have positive lengths, and the segment s_i satisfies $0 \leq \alpha_i < \beta_i \leq p$ and $\alpha_{i+1} = \beta_i + 1$. $\mathbf{s}$ essentially models entity candidates, and each segment s_i can be an entity or a non-entity. Without loss of generality, let e_m and e_n $(e_m, e_n \in \mathbf{s})$ be two arbitrary entities in the sequence $\mathbf{x}$, and r_{mn} be the relation assignment between them. $\mathbf{r}$ is the set of relation assignments of all entity pairs in sequence $\mathbf{x}$. $\mathbf{r}$ allows a variety of relations and dependencies, and it is built upon the segmentation $\mathbf{s}$ which models entity candidates. Note that the definitions of $\mathbf{s}$ and $\mathbf{r}$ are general and therefore can be applied to a variety of IE tasks. For example, e_m and e_n can be entity candidates from segments or entire observation sequences. r_{mn} can be a semantic relation (e.g., *employer*) between entity candidates or the boolean coreference variable indicating whether or not two sequences (e.g., paper citations) are referring to each other. r_{mn} can also be an author community or a *friendship* relation in a social Web.

Based on the preliminaries and notations, we define the concepts of segmentation and relation discovery as follows.

DEFINITION 1. ***(Segmentation)***. *Given an observation sequence $\boldsymbol{x}$, segmentation is the task of assigning segments $\boldsymbol{s}$ to $\boldsymbol{x}$ such that $\boldsymbol{s}^* = \arg\max_{\boldsymbol{s}} P(\boldsymbol{s}|\boldsymbol{x})$.*

DEFINITION 2. ***(Relation Discovery)***. *For a segmentation $\boldsymbol{s}$ of sequence $\boldsymbol{x}$, relation discovery is the process of extracting and discovering relation $\boldsymbol{r}$ between pairs of entity candidates from $\boldsymbol{s}$ such that $\boldsymbol{r}^* = \arg\max_{\boldsymbol{r}} P(\boldsymbol{r}|\boldsymbol{s}, \boldsymbol{x})$.*

Let $\mathbf{y} = \{\mathbf{r}, \mathbf{s}\}$ be the pair of segmentation $\mathbf{s}$ and relation $\mathbf{r}$. $\mathbf{y}$ must satisfy the condition that both the assignments of the segments and the assignments of the relations of segments are maximized simultaneously. We now formally define the problem of joint information extraction as follows.

DEFINITION 3. ***(Joint Optimization of Information Extraction)***. *Given an observation sequence $\boldsymbol{x}$, the goal of joint information extraction is to find the assignment $\boldsymbol{y}^* = \{\boldsymbol{r}^*, \boldsymbol{s}^*\}$ that has the maximum a posteriori (MAP) probability*

$$\boldsymbol{y}^* = \arg\max_{\boldsymbol{y}} P(\boldsymbol{y}|\boldsymbol{x}), \tag{1}$$

where $\boldsymbol{r}^*$ and $\boldsymbol{s}^*$ denote the most likely relation assignment and segmentation assignment, respectively.

Note that this definition is different from pipeline models which perform segmentation and relation in sequential order without capturing interactions between them. This problem is more challenging, and offers new opportunities for information extraction.

3. MODEL

Following the notations in Section 2, we define a joint conditional distribution based on discriminatively-trained factor graphs. Let $\mathcal{G}$ be a factor graph [7] defining a probability distribution over a set of output variables $\mathbf{o}$ conditioned on observation sequences $\mathbf{x}$. $\{\Phi_i\}$ is a set of factors in $\mathcal{G}$, where each factor is defined as the exponential family of an inner product over sufficient statistics $\{f_{ik}(\mathbf{x}_i, \mathbf{o}_i)\}$ and corresponding parameters θ_{ik} as $\Phi_i = \exp\{\sum_k \theta_{ik} f_{ik}(\mathbf{x}_i, \mathbf{o}_i)\}$ [8, 18]. Using parameter tying, the nature of our modeling enables us to partition the factors of $\mathcal{G}$ into three groups, namely the segmentation factor, the relation factor, and the segmentation-relation joint factor. Each factor is a clique template whose parameters are tied. In the following we describe these factors in detail. As we will see, this modeling offers a natural formalism for exploiting top-down and bottom-up bidirectional dependencies and interactions between relevant subtasks to capture mutual benefits, as well as a great flexibility to incorporate a large collection of arbitrary, overlapping and nonindependent features.

Segmentation factor. The segmentation factor $\phi_S(i, \mathbf{s}, \mathbf{x})$ models segmentations $\mathbf{s}$ in $\mathbf{x}$. We assume that $\phi_S(i, \mathbf{s}, \mathbf{x})$ factorizes according to a set of feature functions $g_k(i, \mathbf{s}, \mathbf{x})$ and a corresponding set of real-valued weights λ_k as

$$\phi_S(i, \mathbf{s}, \mathbf{x}) = \exp\left(\sum_{k=1}^{K} \lambda_k g_k(i, \mathbf{s}, \mathbf{x})\right), \tag{2}$$

where K is the number of feature functions. To effectively capture properties of segmentation, we relax the first-order

Markov assumption to semi-Markov [14] such that each segment feature function $g_k(\cdot)$ depends on the current segment s_i, the previous segment s_{i-1}, and the whole observation sequence $\mathbf{x}$, that is, $g_k(i, \mathbf{s}, \mathbf{x}) = g_k(s_{i-1}, s_i, \mathbf{x}) = g_k(y_{i-1}, y_i, \alpha_i, \beta_i, \mathbf{x})$. In addition, transitions within a segment can be non-Markovian.

Relation factor. The relation factor $\phi_R(e_m, e_n, r_{mn})$ models relations r_{mn} $r_{mn} \in \mathbf{r}$ between all possible entity candidate pairs (e_m, e_n), $e_m, e_n \in \mathbf{s}, m \neq n$ in observation sequence $\mathbf{x}$. Similar to the segmentation factor, the relation factor is written as

$$\phi_R(e_m, e_n, r_{mn}) = \exp\left(\sum_{w=1}^{W} \xi_w f_w(e_m, e_n, r_{mn})\right), \qquad (3)$$

where W is the number of features, $f_w(e_m, e_n, r_{mn})$ are feature functions, and ξ_w are corresponding weights. The factor $\phi_R(e_m, e_n, r_{mn})$ represents dependencies (e.g., long-distance dependencies, relation transitivity, etc.) between any two entity candidates e_m and e_n. For example, if the same entity is mentioned more than once in an observation sequence, all occurrences probably have the same relation to another entity. Using the relation factor $\phi_R(e_m, e_n, r_{mn})$, evidences for the same entity segments (or entity candidates) to another entity are shared among all their occurrences within the observation sequence.

Segmentation-relation joint factor. Both of segmentation and relation factors are *local*, since they do not take into account dependencies between relevant subtasks. We propose a *global* factor, the segmentation-relation joint factor, to capture both segmentation-to-relation (bottom-up) and relation-to-segmentation (top-down) dependencies. This joint factor $\phi_{\text{SRJ}}(\mathbf{s}, \mathbf{r}, \mathbf{x})$ involves both segmentation and relation hypotheses as its input. It captures the rich and complex interactions between segmentations and relations bidirectionally, which is defined as

$$\phi_{\text{SRJ}}(\mathbf{s}, \mathbf{r}, \mathbf{x}) = \exp\left(\sum_{t=1}^{T} \eta_t q_t(s_{i-1}, s_i, \mathbf{r}, \mathbf{x}) + \sum_{t=1}^{T} \gamma_t h_t(e_m, e_n, r_{mn}, \mathbf{s}, \mathbf{x})\right). \qquad (4)$$

The newly introduced feature function $q_t(s_{i-1}, s_i, \mathbf{r}, \mathbf{x})$ exploits relation-to-segmentation (top-down) dependencies, which uses relation hypotheses $\mathbf{r}$ between different segments for segmentation of observation sequence $\mathbf{x}$. Intuitively, knowing the relation between two entity segments is very helpful for segmentation and entity identification. For example, the *employment* relation can only exist between an *organization* and a *person*, and cannot exist between an *organization* and a *location*, or a *location* and a *person*). On the other hand, the function $h_t(e_m, e_n, r_{mn}, \mathbf{s}, \mathbf{x})$ captures segmentation-to-relation (bottom-up) interactions, which uses segmentation information $\mathbf{s}$ for relation discovery. For example, if two segments are labeled as a *location* and a *person*, the semantic relation between them can be *birth_place* or *visited*, but cannot be *employment*. η_t and γ_t are the corresponding real-valued weights for $q_t(\cdot)$ and $h_t(\cdot)$, respectively, and T is the number of features. Notably, this joint factor captures bidirectional interactions and mutual benefits between segmentations and relations. Such dependencies are crucial and modeling them often leads to improved performance.

According to the celebrated Hammersley-Clifford theorem, the joint conditional distribution $P(\mathbf{y}|\mathbf{x}) = P(\{\mathbf{r}, \mathbf{s}\}|\mathbf{x})$ is factorized as a product of potential functions over cliques in the graph $\mathcal{G}$ as the form of an exponential family:

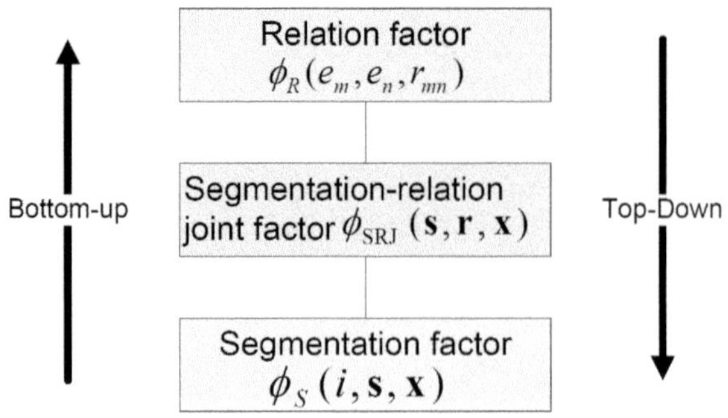

Figure 2: Graphical representation of the proposed model consisting of a bidirectional structure. The segmentation-relation joint factor enables both top-down and bottom-up connections with relation and segmentation factors to explore tight dependencies and mutual benefits for multiple subtasks.

$$P(\mathbf{y}|\mathbf{x}) = \frac{1}{Z(\mathbf{x})}\left(\prod_{i=1}^{|\mathbf{s}|} \phi_S(i, \mathbf{s}, \mathbf{x})\right)\left(\prod_{m,n}^{M} \phi_R(e_m, e_m, r_{mn})\right)\left(\prod_{i=1}^{|\mathbf{s}|}\prod_{m,n}^{M} \phi_{\text{SRJ}}(\mathbf{s}, \mathbf{r}, \mathbf{x})\right), \qquad (5)$$

where M is the number of arbitrary entity segments in the observation sequence $\mathbf{x}$, $|\mathbf{s}|$ is the number of segments of $\mathbf{x}$, and $Z(\mathbf{x}) = \sum_{\mathbf{y}} \prod_{i=1}^{|\mathbf{s}|} \phi_S(i, \mathbf{s}, \mathbf{x}) \prod_{m,n}^{M} \phi_R(e_m, e_m, r_{mn}) \prod_{i=1}^{|\mathbf{s}|} \prod_{m,n}^{M} \phi_{\text{SRJ}}(\mathbf{s}, \mathbf{r}, \mathbf{x})$ is the normalization factor of our model.

In summary, our model consists of three sub-structures: (1) a semi-Markov chain on the segmentations $\mathbf{s}$ conditioned on the observation sequences $\mathbf{x}$, represented by $\phi_S(i, \mathbf{s}, \mathbf{x})$; (2) potential $\phi_R(e_m, e_n, r_{mn})$ measuring dependencies and relations r_{mn} between two arbitrary entity candidates e_m and e_n from segmentations $\mathbf{s}$; and (3) a fully-connected graph exploiting tight dependencies between segmentations $\mathbf{s}$ and relations $\mathbf{r}$, represented by $\phi_{\text{SRJ}}(\mathbf{s}, \mathbf{r}, \mathbf{x})$. It is particularly notable that our model has a dynamic graphical structure. Since the segments (entity candidates) from the semi-Markov chains are dynamically changed, the structure of relation factor will change correspondingly given different segmentations. Moreover, different structures of the relation factor will also have influence on segmentations. This is different from the conventional semi-CRFs [14].

While some special cases of CRFs are of particular interest, several major elements make our model different. We emphasize on the differences and advantages of our model against others. Most importantly, our model captures bidirectional top-down and bottom-up dependencies between multiple subtasks for joint IE problems. Linear-chain CRFs [8] and semi-CRFs [14] can only perform single IE tasks such as sequence labeling, which lack the ability to capture long-distance dependencies and to represent complex interactions between multiple subtasks. Skip-chain CRFs [17] introduce skip edges to model long-distance dependencies to handle the label consistency problem in single sequence labeling and extraction. 2D CRFs [28] are two-dimensional conditional random fields incorporating the two-dimensional neighborhood dependencies in Web pages, and the graphical representation of this model is a 2D grid. Hierarchical CRFs [9] are a class of CRFs with hierarchical tree structure. Our proposed model, on the other hand, has a distinct graphical structure from 2D and hierarchical CRFs. By modeling both segmentations $\mathbf{s}$ and relations $\mathbf{r}$ simultaneously in a single coherent framework, this paradigm offers a natural way for joint information extraction, avoiding the problems such as error propagation occurred in pipeline approaches. Furthermore, this modeling has several advantages over previous probabilistic graphical models, including the employment of semi-Markov chains for efficient segmentation and labeling, the representation of long-range dependencies between different segments, and the capture of rich and complex interactions between relevant subtasks to exploit mutual benefits.

4. TOP-DOWN AND BOTTOM-UP LEARNING

Given independent and identically distributed (i.i.d.) training data $\mathcal{D} = \{\mathbf{x}^i, \mathbf{y}^i\}_{i=1}^{N}$, where $\mathbf{x}^i$ is the i-th sequence instance, and $\mathbf{y}^i = \{\mathbf{r}^i, \mathbf{s}^i\}$ is the corresponding segmentation and relation assignments. The objective of parameter estimation is to estimate the whole set of model's parameters $\Theta = \{\{\lambda_k\}_{k=1}^{K}, \{\xi_w\}_{w=1}^{W}, \{\eta_t\}_{t=1}^{T}, \{\gamma_t\}_{t=1}^{T}\}$. Under the i.i.d. assumption, we ignore the summation operator $\sum_{i=1}^{N}$ in the log-likelihood during the following equations and derivations. We would like to maximize the log-likelihood of the observation given the data:

$$\mathcal{L}(\Theta) = \log P_\Theta(\mathbf{x}) = \log \sum_{\mathbf{s},\mathbf{r}} P_\Theta(\mathbf{s}, \mathbf{r}, \mathbf{x}). \qquad (6)$$

The above function does not have a closed-form solution because of the marginalization taking place within the logarithm. Working directly with this function is typically precluded by the need to compute the normalization factor $Z(\mathbf{x})$, which is intractable in our model. We exploit variational approximation methods [5, 20] that offer guarantees in the form of a lower bound on the marginal probabilities. This family of approaches aims to minimize the Kullback-Leibler (KL) divergence between an approximated distribution Q and the target distribution $P_\Theta(\mathbf{s},\mathbf{r}|\mathbf{x})$ by finding the best distribution Q from some family of distributions for which an inference is feasible. The variational inference method provides a fast, deterministic approximation to otherwise unattainable posteriors. Also its convergence time is independent of dimensionality [20].

Let $Q_\nu(\mathbf{s},\mathbf{r}|\mathbf{x})$ be the variational distribution which serves as an approximation of the target distribution $P_\Theta(\mathbf{s},\mathbf{r}|\mathbf{x})$. According to the mean-field variational theory [5, 21, 4], the optimal solution is the distribution that has the minimum KL divergence between two distributions Q and P. Based on Jensen's inequality we have

$$\mathcal{L}(\Theta) = \log \sum_{\mathbf{s},\mathbf{r}} Q_\nu(\mathbf{s},\mathbf{r}|\mathbf{x}) \frac{P_\Theta(\mathbf{s},\mathbf{r},\mathbf{x})}{Q_\nu(\mathbf{s},\mathbf{r}|\mathbf{x})}$$

$$\geq \sum_{\mathbf{s},\mathbf{r}} Q_\nu(\mathbf{s},\mathbf{r}|\mathbf{x}) \log \frac{P_\Theta(\mathbf{s},\mathbf{r},\mathbf{x})}{Q_\nu(\mathbf{s},\mathbf{r}|\mathbf{x})} = KL(Q_\nu(\mathbf{s},\mathbf{r}|\mathbf{x})||P_\Theta(\mathbf{s},\mathbf{r},\mathbf{x})). \qquad (7)$$

As can be seen, Equation 7 is the same as maximizing a lower bound on the log-marginal probability $P_\Theta(\mathbf{x})$, with equality when $Q_\nu(\mathbf{s},\mathbf{r}|\mathbf{x}) = P_\Theta(\mathbf{s},\mathbf{r}|\mathbf{x})$. It is easy to obtain the following formulation:

$$\log P_\Theta(\mathbf{x}) - KL(Q_\nu(\mathbf{s},\mathbf{r}|\mathbf{x})||P_\Theta(\mathbf{s},\mathbf{r}|\mathbf{x})) = KL(Q_\nu(\mathbf{s},\mathbf{r}|\mathbf{x})||P_\Theta(\mathbf{s},\mathbf{r},\mathbf{x})). \qquad (8)$$

According to Equations 7 and 8, optimizing a variational bound on the observed data is equivalent to minimizing the KL divergence between $P_\Theta(\mathbf{s},\mathbf{r}|\mathbf{x})$ and $Q_\nu(\mathbf{s},\mathbf{r}|\mathbf{x})$. This is equivalent to minimizing the KL divergence between the distribution $Q_\nu(\mathbf{s},\mathbf{r}|\mathbf{x})$ and the distribution $P_\Theta(\mathbf{s},\mathbf{r},\mathbf{x})$. Given the non-negativity property of the KL divergence, the cost function we work is

$$\begin{aligned}\mathscr{L} &= KL(Q_\nu(\mathbf{s},\mathbf{r}|\mathbf{x})||P_\Theta(\mathbf{s},\mathbf{r},\mathbf{x})) \\ &= \sum_{\mathbf{s},\mathbf{r}} Q_\nu(\mathbf{s},\mathbf{r}|\mathbf{x}) \Big[-\log Q_\nu(\mathbf{s},\mathbf{r}|\mathbf{x}) + \log P_\Theta(\mathbf{s},\mathbf{r},\mathbf{x}) \Big] \qquad (9) \\ &= \mathbb{H}(Q_\nu) + \mathbb{E}_{Q_\nu}\Big\{ \log P_\Theta(\mathbf{s},\mathbf{r},\mathbf{x}) \Big\} \qquad (10) \\ &\leq \mathcal{L}(\Theta), \qquad (11)\end{aligned}$$

where $\mathbb{H}(Q_\nu) = -\sum_{\mathbf{s},\mathbf{r}} Q_\nu(\mathbf{s},\mathbf{r}|\mathbf{x}) \log Q_\nu(\mathbf{s},\mathbf{r}|\mathbf{x})$ is the entropy of the variational distribution, and $\mathbb{E}_{Q_\nu}\Big\{ \log P_\Theta(\mathbf{s},\mathbf{r},\mathbf{x}) \Big\} = \sum_{\mathbf{s},\mathbf{r}} Q_\nu(\mathbf{s},\mathbf{r}|\mathbf{x}) \log P_\Theta(\mathbf{s},\mathbf{r},\mathbf{x})$ is the expectation with respect to $Q_\nu(\mathbf{s},\mathbf{r}|\mathbf{x})$. Notice that the cost $\mathscr{L}$ balances two competing goals: assign values to variables $\mathbf{r}$ and $\mathbf{s}$ with high probability under $P_\Theta(\mathbf{s},\mathbf{r},\mathbf{x})$ (the second term), but at the same time be as less committed as possible (the entropy term). Clearly, $\mathscr{L}$ is the lower bound of the log-likelihood $\mathcal{L}(\Theta)$. Thus by maximizing $\mathscr{L}$ we will always recover the log-likelihood of the data $\mathscr{L}^* = \log P_\Theta(\mathbf{x}) - 0$.

For efficient learning, it is critical that the variational family of distributions Q_ν has a tractable form [5, 4]. In the following, we use $Q_\nu(\mathbf{s},\mathbf{r})$ to denote $Q_\nu(\mathbf{s},\mathbf{r}|\mathbf{x})$. According to the mean-field variational theory, we assume that $Q_\nu(\mathbf{s},\mathbf{r})$ forms a factorized distribution; that is, the variables are independent and the joint distribution is a product of single variable marginal probabilities as

$$Q_\nu(\mathbf{s},\mathbf{r}) = Q_\nu(\mathbf{y}) = \prod_{i \in V_s} Q_{\nu i}(s_i) \prod_{j \in V_r} Q_{\nu j}(r_j), \qquad (12)$$

where $\mathbf{s} = \{s_i\}_{i \in V_s}$ and $\mathbf{r} = \{r_j\}_{j \in V_r}$. Let $P_\Theta(\mathbf{s},\mathbf{r},\mathbf{x})$ factorize into a product of pairwise potentials depending only on the variables associated with each undirected edge as $P_\Theta(\mathbf{s},\mathbf{r},\mathbf{x}) = \prod_{e \in E} \Psi(\mathbf{s}_e, \mathbf{r}_e, \mathbf{x}_e)$. Mean-field inference algorithms exploit this additional factorization structure. Note that we absorb the normalization constant into one of the potentials. The cost function $\mathscr{L}$ reduces to a sum of the following terms as

$$\begin{aligned}\mathscr{L} &= \mathbb{H}(Q_\nu) + \mathbb{E}_{Q_\nu}\Big\{ \log P_\Theta(\mathbf{s},\mathbf{r},\mathbf{x}) \Big\} \\ &= \mathbb{H}(Q_\nu) + \mathbb{E}_{Q_\nu}\Big\{ \log \prod_{e \in E} \Psi(\mathbf{s}_e, \mathbf{r}_e, \mathbf{x}_e) \Big\} \qquad (13) \\ &= \sum_{i \in V_s} \mathbb{H}(Q_{\nu i}) + \sum_{j \in V_r} \mathbb{H}(Q_{\nu j}) + \sum_{e \in E} \sum_{\mathbf{y}_{e \cap V}} \\ &\quad Q_\nu(\mathbf{y}_{e \cap V}) \log \Psi(\mathbf{s}_e, \mathbf{r}_e, \mathbf{x}_e), \qquad (14)\end{aligned}$$

where $Q_\nu(\mathbf{y}_{e \cap V})$ is the variational marginal probability over variables $\mathbf{y} = \{\mathbf{r}, \mathbf{s}\}$ associated with edge e and $V_s \cup V_r = V$.

To optimize the function $\mathscr{L}$, let $\mathbb{E}_{Q_\nu}\{\cdot|y_k\}$ $k \in V$ be the conditional expectation with respect to Q_ν. We provide a more explicit illustration and the feasibility of evaluating $\mathbb{E}_{Q_\nu}\{\cdot|y_k\}$ in the updates as

$$\begin{aligned}&\mathbb{E}_{Q_\nu}\{\log P_\Theta(\mathbf{s},\mathbf{r},\mathbf{x})|y_k\}\\ &= \sum_{\{y_i\}_{i\in V\backslash k}} \Big[\prod_{i\in V\backslash k} Q_{\nu i}(y_i)\Big] \log P_\Theta(\mathbf{s},\mathbf{r},\mathbf{x}) \quad (15)\\ &= \sum_{e\in E} \sum_{\mathbf{y}_{e\cap\{V\backslash k\}}\mathbf{y}_{V\backslash k}} Q_\nu(\mathbf{y}_{e\cap\{V\backslash k\}}) \log \Psi(\mathbf{s}_e,\mathbf{r}_e,\mathbf{x}_e), \quad (16)\end{aligned}$$

where $V\backslash k$ is the set of variables other than k and $Q_{\nu i}(y_i) = Q_{\nu i}(s_i)Q_{\nu i}(r_i)$. Note that the expectation specifically does not depend on the variational marginal $Q_{\nu k}(\cdot)$ over y_k. The result is a function of the conditional variable y_k.

To update the kth variational marginal, we view $\mathscr{L}$ as a function of $Q_{\nu k}(\cdot)$ while keeping other marginals fixed. We treat the entropy terms $\mathbb{H}(Q_\nu)$ corresponding to remaining marginals as fixed and appeal to the linearity of expectation $\mathbb{E}_{Q_\nu}\{\cdot\} = \sum_{y_k} Q_{\nu k}(y_k)\mathbb{E}_{Q_\nu}\{\cdot|y_k\}$ to obtain

$$\begin{aligned}\mathscr{L} &= \mathbb{H}(Q_{\nu k}(y_k))\\ &+ \sum_{y_k} Q_{\nu k}(y_k)\mathbb{E}_{Q_\nu}\{\log P_\Theta(\mathbf{s},\mathbf{r},\mathbf{x})|y_k\} + \text{const}, \quad (17)\end{aligned}$$

where the dependence of $\mathscr{L}$ on the marginal $Q_{\nu k}(y_k)$ is explicit. It is easy to verify via straightforward calculation that maximizing this cost function with respect to the marginal $Q_{\nu k}(y_k)$ yields the following mean field equations for all k as:

$$Q_{\nu k}(y_k) \leftarrow \frac{1}{Z_k} \exp\Big\{\mathbb{E}_{Q_\nu}\{\log P_\Theta(\mathbf{s},\mathbf{r},\mathbf{x})|y_k\}\Big\} \quad (18)$$

$$Z_k \leftarrow \sum_{y_k} \exp\Big\{\mathbb{E}_{Q_\nu}\{\log P_\Theta(\mathbf{s},\mathbf{r},\mathbf{x})|y_k\}\Big\} \quad (19)$$

Obviously, $Q_{\nu k}(y_k)$ is in the form of the exponential family. This property considerably simplifies the complexity and facilitates the computation. Recall that $Q_\nu(\mathbf{s},\mathbf{r}) = Q_\nu(\mathbf{s})Q_\nu(\mathbf{r}) = \prod_{i\in V_s} Q_{\nu i}(s_i)\prod_{j\in V_r} Q_{\nu j}(r_j)$ (Equation 12), we further assume $Q_\nu(\mathbf{s})$ to be of the form $\frac{1}{Z_{Q_\nu(\mathbf{s})}}\prod_{i\in V_s}\phi_i(\mu_i)$ and $Q_\nu(\mathbf{r})$ to be $\frac{1}{Z_{Q_\nu(\mathbf{r})}}\prod_{j\in V_r}\phi_j(\omega_j)$. $Z_{Q_\nu(\mathbf{s})}$ and $Z_{Q_\nu(\mathbf{r})}$ are two local normalization factors. Here, we introduce two variational parameters $\mu = \{\mu_i\}_{i\in V_s}$ and $\omega = \{\omega_j\}_{j\in V_r}$, where μ and ω are associated with segmentation and relation, respectively, and we rewrite $\mathscr{L}$ as $\mathscr{L}(\mu,\omega)$.

We propose a bidirectional learning algorithm based on variational expectation maximization (VEM) to optimize the variational parameters μ and ω efficiently in a collaborative manner such that they can benefit from each other. For example, if we have trained segmentation parameter μ, its decision can guide the learning for relation parameter ω. As shown in Algorithm 1, we summarize the whole parameter estimation procedure as follows: in the E-step, we maximize the variational distributions $Q_{\nu k}(y_k)$, which is accomplished by computing $\mathbb{E}_{Q_\nu}\{\log P_\Theta(\mathbf{s},\mathbf{r},\mathbf{x})|y_k\}$ based on Equations 15 and 16, and by updating $Q_{\nu k}(y_k)$ based on Equations 18 and 19. After we calculate the cost function $\mathscr{L}(\mu,\omega)$ based on Equation 17, we perform bottom-up learning to optimize the relation parameter ω using the hypotheses from segmentations. Here we keep the segmentation parameter μ fixed. In the M-step, we perform top-down learning to optimize the segmentation parameter μ using hypotheses from relations while keeping $Q_{\nu k}(y_k)$ fixed. Such iterative optimization allows information to flow bidirectionally to boost

Algorithm 1: The variational expectation maximization (VEM) algorithm for bidirectional top-down and bottom-up learning

Input: A set of pairwise potentials $\Psi(\mathbf{s}_e,\mathbf{r}_e,\mathbf{x}_e)$ defining $\log P_\Theta(\mathbf{s},\mathbf{r},\mathbf{x})$, initial potentials for $Q_\nu(\mathbf{s})$ and $Q_\nu(\mathbf{r})$.
Output: Optimized variational parameters μ^* and ω^* for segmentation $\mathbf{s}$ and relation $\mathbf{r}$.
while *equilibrium states or a threshold number of iterations are not reached* **do**
  E-step:
  repeat
    Compute $\mathbb{E}_{Q_\nu}\{\log P_\Theta(\mathbf{s},\mathbf{r},\mathbf{x})|y_k\}$ based on Equation 15 and 16,
    Update $Q_{\nu k}(y_k)$ based on Equation 18 and 19,
    Compute $\mathscr{L}(\mu,\omega)$ based on Equation 17.
    `// Bottom-up learning`
    $\omega^{i+1} = \arg\max_\omega \mathscr{L}(\mu^i,\omega)$.
  until *converge*;
  M-step:
  repeat
    `// Top-down learning`
    $\mu^{i+1} = \arg\max_\mu \mathscr{L}(\mu,\omega^i)$.
  until *converge*;
end
return μ^* *and* ω^*

both the segmentation and relation performance. This two-step max-max algorithm leads to a monotonically increasing cost function $\mathscr{L}(\mu,\omega)$ and log-likelihood of data. Consequently, it is guaranteed to converge to an equilibrium state of the KL divergence between Q and P among all distributions Q of the given form $Q_\nu(\mathbf{s}) = \frac{1}{Z_{Q_\nu(\mathbf{s})}}\prod_{i\in V_s}\phi_i(\mu_i)$ and $Q_\nu(\mathbf{r}) = \frac{1}{Z_{Q_\nu(\mathbf{r})}}\prod_{j\in V_r}\phi_j(\omega_j)$. This shows that the algorithm is theoretically sound and correct. Moreover, the variational formulation remains applicable even when we can no longer handle $\log P_\Theta(\mathbf{s},\mathbf{r},\mathbf{x})$, this is superior to the conventional EM algorithm.

4.1 Complexity Analysis

We now investigate and analyze the computational complexity of Algorithm 1. Suppose $|V|$ is the number of segmentation and relation variables, and d is the number of distinct values each variable (either $\mathbf{s}$ or $\mathbf{r}$) may take. In Equation 17, the evaluation of the first summation term $\mathbb{H}(Q_{\nu k}(y_k))$ takes $O(|V|d)$. For computing $\mathbb{E}_{Q_\nu}\{\log P_\Theta(\mathbf{s},\mathbf{r},\mathbf{x})|y_k$ in the second term of Equation 17, $e\cap\{V\backslash k\}$ is either an empty set or a single node associated with edge e, where each expectation involves at most two variables and there are $|E|$ edges, thus the complexity will be at most $O(|E|d^2)$. For Algorithm 1, suppose the iteration number is $\mathbb{I}$, then the overall computational complexity is $O((|V|d + |E|d^2)\mathbb{I})$.

4.2 Inference

Ideally, the objective of inference is to find the most likely segmentation assignment $\mathbf{s}^*$ and the corresponding most likely relation assignment $\mathbf{r}^*$, that is, to find $\mathbf{y}^* = \arg\max_{\mathbf{y}} P(\mathbf{s},\mathbf{r}|\mathbf{x})$ such that both of them are optimized simultaneously. Unfortunately, exact inference to this problem is generally intractable, since the search space is the Cartesian product

Table 1: Comparative performance of our model, the CRF+CRF, Single MLN, and DCRF models for entity identification from Wikipedia.

Entities	CRF+CRF			Single MLN			DCRF			Our model		
	P	R	F_1	P	R	F_1	P	R	F_1	P	R	F_1
person	75.33	83.22	79.08	75.94	83.93	79.74	75.96	83.82	79.70	82.91	84.26	**83.58**
location	77.03	69.45	73.04	77.42	70.13	73.59	77.68	70.13	73.71	82.95	81.44	**82.19**
organization	53.78	47.76	50.59	54.11	47.06	50.34	54.55	46.98	50.48	72.43	63.69	**67.78**
date	98.54	97.53	**98.03**	97.79	95.68	96.72	97.98	95.22	96.58	98.90	96.24	97.55
year	97.14	99.10	98.11	98.06	99.12	98.59	98.12	99.09	**98.60**	97.36	99.55	98.44
time	60.00	20.33	30.37	50.00	15.38	23.53	50.00	25.33	33.63	100.0	33.00	**49.62**
number	98.88	60.33	74.94	100.0	66.07	79.57	100.0	70.00	**82.35**	100.0	65.52	79.17
miscellaneous	77.42	80.56	78.96	79.81	84.14	**81.92**	79.81	83.14	81.44	81.50	82.16	81.83
Overall	89.55	88.70	89.12	90.45	90.45	90.45	90.98	90.37	90.67	94.06	93.95	**93.97**

of all possible segmentation and relation assignments. Consequently, approximate inference becomes an inevitable alternative. At the equilibrium state of Algorithm 1, variational distributions $Q_\nu(\mathbf{s})$ and $Q_\nu(\mathbf{r})$ are obtained such that $Q_\nu(\mathbf{s}, \mathbf{r}) = Q_\nu(\mathbf{s})Q_\nu(\mathbf{r})$ is an equilibrium state of the KL divergence $KL(Q||P)$. Such kind of inference is straightforward, since the maximum a posterior (MAP) segmentation assignment **s** is constructed from the optimized variational parameter μ^*, and the MAP or most likely relation assignment **r** is found from the variational parameter ω^*.

Table 2: Comparative performance of different models for relation extraction from Wikipedia.

Method	Accuracy	Precision	Recall	F-measure
CRF+CRF	93.72	70.40	57.85	63.51
Single MLN	93.96	68.54	61.75	64.97
DCRF	93.90	69.30	60.22	64.44
Our model	96.92	72.85	64.25	**68.28**

Table 3: Performance comparison with other top-performing systems on relation extraction.

System	Precision	Recall	F-measure
Culotta et al. [1]	75.53	61.69	67.91
Nguyen et al. [11]	29.07	53.86	37.76
Yu et al. [27]	72.80	59.80	65.66
Our model	72.85	64.25	**68.28**

5. EXPERIMENTS

5.1 Entity Identification and Relation Extraction

5.1.1 *Data and Methodology*

Our dataset consists of 1,127 paragraphs from 441 pages from the online encyclopedic articles in Wikipedia. The labeled 7,740 entities are classified into 8 categories, yielding 1,243 *person*, 1,085 *location*, 875 *organization*, 641 *date*, 1,495 *year*, 38 *time*, 59 *number*, and 2,304 *miscellaneous* names. This dataset also contains 4,701 relation instances and 53 labeled relation types, and the 10 most frequent relation types are *job_title*, *visited*, *birth_place*, *associate*, *birth_year*, *member_of*, *birth_day*, *opus*, *death_year*, and *death_day*. The 8 entity categories and 53 relation types are label sets for entity identification and relation extraction in our model. All experiments were performed on the Linux platform, with a 3.2GHz Pentium 4 CPU and 4 GB of memory.

Accurate entities enable features that are naturally expected to be useful to boost relation extraction. A wide range of rich, overlapping features can be exploited in our model. These features include contextual features, part-of-speech tags, morphological features, entity-level dictionary features, and clue word features. Feature conjunctions are also used. In leveraging relation extraction to improve entity identification, we employ a combination of syntactic, entity, keyword, semantic, and Wikipedia characteristic features. More importantly, our model introduces joint factors to capture both top-down and bottom-up dependencies, and function $q_t(\cdot)$ uses relation hypotheses and $h_t(\cdot)$ uses segmentation hypotheses as features. These features capture deep dependencies between entities and relations, and they are natural and effective in enhancing the performance.

We perform four-fold cross-validation on this dataset, and take the average performance. For performance evaluation, we use the standard measures of Precision (P), Recall (R), and $F_{\beta=1}$ ($F_{\beta=1}$ is the harmonic mean of P and R and $F_{\beta=1} = \frac{2PR}{P+R}$) for both entity identification and relation extraction. We compare our approach with one pipeline model **CRF+CRF**, one integrated model **Single MLN**, and one joint model **DCRF**. **CRF+CRF** employs one linear-chain CRFs [8] for entity recognition, and another linear-chain CRF for relation prediction. **Single MLN** performs joint inference for both subtasks in a single Markov logic network (MLN) [12], which is a highly expressive language for first-order logic and can conduct relational learning between entity pairs. **DCRF** [19] is a factorial CRF applied to jointly solve the two subtasks. All these models exploit standard parameter learning and inference algorithms in our experiments. To avoid over-fitting, penalization techniques on likelihood are also performed.

5.1.2 *Experimental Results and Discussions*

Table 1 shows the performance of entity identification and Table 2 shows the overall performance of relation extraction[2] of different models, respectively. For relation extraction in Table 2, we also recorded the token-wise labeling accuracy. Our model substantially outperforms all baseline models on F-measure for both entity identification and relation extraction, and it is statistically significantly better (p-value < 0.05 with a 95% confidence interval) according to McNemar's paired tests. The pipeline model **CRF+CRF** suffers from pipeline inherent inferiority such as brittle accumulation of errors. For example, this model cannot correctly extract relations between mis-recognized entities. As discussed, it performs entity identification and relation extraction independently without considering the mutual correlations between them, leading to reduced performance. By modeling interactions between two subtasks, boosted performance can be achieved, as illustrated by the integrated model **Single MLN** and the joint model **DCRF**. The **Single MLN** model captures dependencies between entities and relations via first-order logic; however, limitations of first-order logic

[2]Due to space limitation, we only present the overall performance, and omit the performance on 53 relation types.

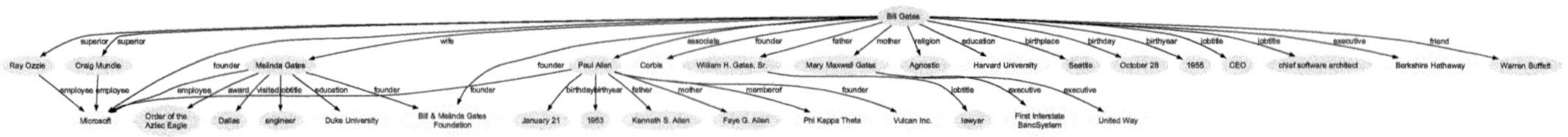

Figure 3: An example of identified entities and extracted semantic relationships from Wikipedia's encyclopedic article about *Bill Gates* by using our model. The major person name *Bill Gates* is in pink and other person names are in green color. Organizations are in yellow and locations are in blue, and other types of entities are in gray. Semantic relations between entities are also labeled.

make it difficult to specify a relation factor that utilizes the uncertain output of segmentation [15, 22]. Joint inference in **Single MLN** is only weakly coupled and does not enforce transitivity, since the logic formulas only examine pairs of consecutive labels, not whole fields. As can be seen, our model achieves stronger interactions between two subtasks, which is strongly coupled and bidirectional. The **DCRF** model applies loopy belief propagation (LBP) for approximate learning and inference, which is inherently unstable and may cause convergence problems. Consequently, training a **DCRF** model with unobserved nodes (hidden variables) makes this approach difficult to optimize. Figure 3 illustrates an example of identified entities and extracted semantic relationships from Wikipedia's encyclopedic article about *Bill Gates* by employing our model. As can be seen, different entity types are in different colors, and the relations between them are also linked and labeled. Interestingly, these results are versatile for a variety of applications, such as Web data mining, social network analysis and mining, etc.

A large number of engineered systems were developed for identifying relations of interest. Table 3 compares our results with some recently published results on the same dataset. Notably, our approach outperforms previous ones given that we deal with a fairly more challenging problem involving both entity identification and relation extraction. Similar to [13], these systems assume that the golden-standard entities are already known or extracted from text without errors, and they only perform relation extraction (due to this reason, we only compare the performance on relation extraction.). Unfortunately, such assumption is not valid in practice. As a result, our model is more applicable to real-world IE tasks.

5.1.3 *Effect of Joint Factors on Performance*

We investigate the nature and effectiveness of segmentation-relation joint factors and Figure 4 demonstrates their feasibility in our modeling. It shows that the joint factors consistently enhance precision, recall, and F-measure for both entity identification and relation extraction subtasks. For example, the joint factors significantly improve the overall F-measure by 2.65% for entity identification. Our approach demonstrates its merits by using joint factors to explore bidirectional tight interactions between segmentations and relations and by optimizing them collaboratively in a top-down and bottom-up manner, resulting in improved performance.

5.1.4 *Efficiency*

Table 4 summarizes the efficiency of different models. The pipeline **CRF+CRF** takes the least time for learning, due to its simple pipeline architecture. Compared to **Single MLN**, the running time of our model is only increased slightly, which is reasonable to apply to real IE problems. It is particularly notable that our model takes much less time than the joint model **DCRF**. Specifically, our model is over an order of magnitude (approximately 17.5 times) faster than **DCRF** for running. When the graph has large tree-width as in our case, the LBP algorithm in **DCRF** is inefficient and slow to converge.

Table 4: Efficiency comparison of different models on learning time (min.) and inference time (min.).

Method	Learning time	Inference time
CRF+CRF	15.30	0.20
Single MLN	35.95	2.67
DCRF	677.67	0.33
Our model	39.83	0.30

5.2 Citation Matching

5.2.1 *Data and Methodology*

We apply the Cora dataset to evaluate our approach. This dataset contains 1295 citations and 134 clusters (sets of citations that refer to the same paper), and each citation has three fields – *author*, *title*, and *venue*. We run three-fold cross-validation on this dataset. Segmentation is evaluated by P, R, and F_1. For entity resolution, we measure both pairwise P, R, F_1 and cluster recall. Cluster recall is the fraction of clusters that are correctly output by the system after taking transitive closure from pairwise decisions.

A wide range of rich features can be exploited in our model. For segmentation, these features largely consider field-level similarity using a number of string and token-based comparison metrics (e.g., string edit distance, tf-idf over tokens and n-grams, etc.). We also include feature conjunctions, specialized features for *author* and *title* matching, and global features based on distance metrics for entire citations. In leveraging coreference to improve segmentation, we employ a combination of local (e.g., contextual and morphological), layout, lexicon membership features.

For performance comparison, the **CRF+CRF** model applies first CRF for segmentation, and another CRF for entity resolution (which views resolution as a pairwise classification problem). For the **Single MLN** model, we follow [12] to design it, engaging features mentioned above. Moreover, we also compare the performance of our model with some recently published results on the same dataset.

5.2.2 *Experimental Results and Discussions*

Our comparative results are shown in Table 5 and Table 6, demonstrating the promise of our approach with significant improvements on both segmentation and coreference compared with the three baseline models **CRF+CRF**, **Single MLN**, **DCRF**, and other previously published results.

Table 5 shows the improvements on F-measure for segmentation, where we list both the overall performance and

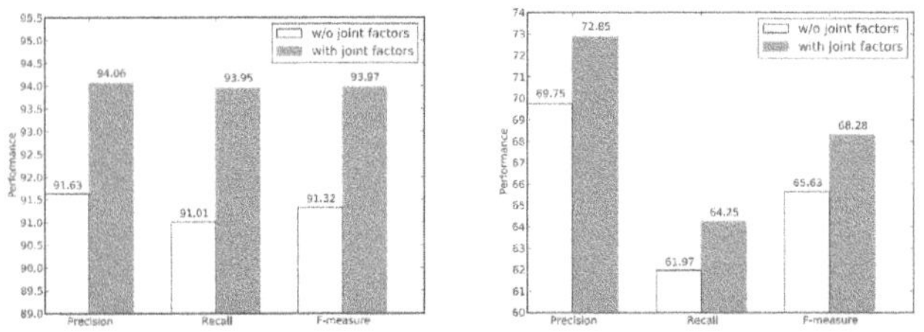

Figure 4: Performance comparison of joint factors on entity identification (left) and relation extraction (right) from Wikipedia.

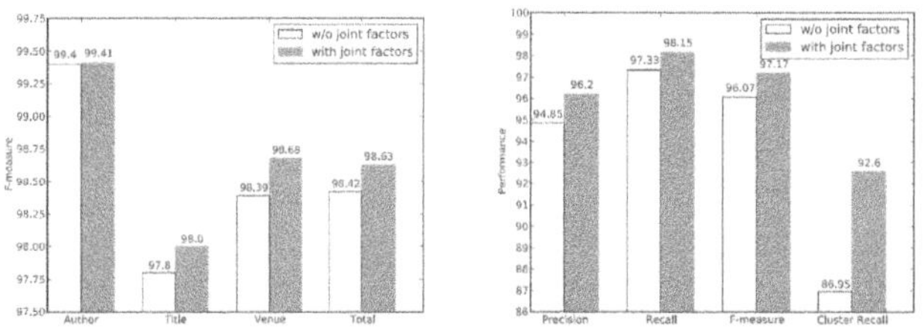

Figure 5: Performance comparison of joint factors on segmentation (left) and entity resolution (right) in citation matching.

Table 5: Comparative performance of different models for segmentation in citation matching.

Method	Author	Title	Venue	Total
Isolated MLN [12]	99.30	97.30	98.20	98.20
Single MLN [12]	99.50	97.60	98.30	98.40
CRF+CRF	98.77	97.02	97.56	97.66
Single MLN	99.39	97.79	98.36	98.41
DCRF	99.40	97.82	98.45	98.47
Our model	99.41	98.00	98.68	**98.63**

the performance on the three fields. Our model outperforms earlier results such as **Isolated MLN** [12] and **Single MLN** [12]. Compared to the three baseline models, the relative error reduction (RER) is 41.45%, 13.84% and 11.68%, respectively. Note that the difference between our **Single MLN** model and the one in [12] is that we engage different features. Table 6 compares the performance of entity resolution for different models on both metrics of F_1 and cluster recall. Our model, which concurrently solves the citation matching task, easily outperforms previously published results in [16] and [12]. It also outperforms the three baseline models by 3.30%, 1.15%, and 0.88% in pairwise F_1. Even though the **Single MLN** model in [12] captures interactions between segmentation and coreference, it is only a weak interaction. Since the logic formulae in [12] only examine pairs of consecutive labels but not whole fields – failing to utilize information from predicted field range and non-consecutive words in the field. As can be seen, our model is highly-coupled and achieves stronger interaction between multiple subtasks. Importantly, Table 6 shows that our approach allows cluster recall to improve substantially, resulting in an improvement of up to 6.83% compared to **DCRF** model. This is particularly notable given that cluster recall is more strict than the pairwise F_1 metric.

5.2.3 Effect of Joint Factors on Performance

Figure 5 illustrates the benefits of the joint factors in our modeling for citation matching. This figure demonstrates the bidirectionality of joint factors using segmentation to aid coreference and vice versa, which is highly coupled and information can flow in both directions to capture mutual benefits and strong interactions between segmentation and resolution. Compared to the pairwise F-measure, the cluster recall is boosted substantially (up to 5.65%) by joint factors. This is particularly interesting as it shows that exploiting joint factors is much more accurate under the strict metric.

5.2.4 Efficiency

Table 7 lists the running times (for both training and inference) for **CRF+CRF**, **Single MLN**, **DCRF**, and our

Table 6: Comparative performance of different models for entity resolution in citation matching.

Method	P	R	F_1	Cluster Recall
Fellegi-Sunter [16]	78.00	97.70	86.70	62.70
Single MLN [12]	94.30	97.00	95.60	78.10
CRF+CRF	93.10	94.65	93.87	76.32
Single MLN	94.84	97.22	96.02	85.15
DCRF	94.92	97.69	96.29	85.77
Our model	96.20	98.15	**97.17**	**92.60**

model (we cannot compare it with the models in [16] and [12] since experimental settings are different). The running time of our model is reasonably slower than that of the pipeline model **CRF+CRF**, and comparable to that of **Single MLN**, illustrating the efficiency of our approach. However, the **DCRF** model takes 458.83 minutes to converge, which is very slow. This disadvantage limits the ability of **DCRF** for real-world IE problems to a large extent.

6. RELATED WORK

Some work has been dedicated to improving the pipeline architecture [2, 3]. Finkel et al.[2] modeled pipelines as Bayesian networks, with each low level task corresponding to a variable in the network. This architecture has the drawback that it only allows information to flow in one direction. Hollingshead and Roark [3] proposed pipeline iteration, using output from later stages of a pipeline to constrain earlier stages of the same pipeline, but it lacks the ability to model internal tight dependencies between stages. However, all these approaches suffer from inherent problems such as brittle accumulation of errors caused by their pipeline architecture.

Integrated and joint models exploring mutual benefits on different subtasks have shown great promise, where several closely related approaches have been proposed. Recently, Zhu et al. [30] proposed an integrated probabilistic approach to Web page understanding. Nevertheless, this model is feed-forward or top-down integrated and it only allows information to flow in one direction. Ko et al. [6] proposed a joint answer ranking framework based on probabilistic graphical models for question answering. However, they employed N-best list for inference procedure which is a restricted approximation for the full distribution of large-output components. Thus, the number of uncertain hypotheses in their framework is severely limited. Yu et al.[27] integrated two sub-models, semi-CRFs and MLNs, together, but they are only loosely coupled in that the parameter estimation is performed separately and the inference information can only flow in one direction, which is similar to [2]. Luo et al. [10]

Table 7: **Efficiency comparison of different models on learning time (min.) and inference time (min.).**

Method	Learning time	Inference time
CRF+CRF	10.33	0.17
Single MLN	23.80	1.85
DCRF	458.83	0.30
Our model	26.67	0.25

combined Web classification and Web IE based on the CRF model. However, since it was defined according to the DOM tree structure for Web pages, this model cannot be applied to more general tasks that we are investigating.

Furthermore, Poon and Domingos [12] performed joint inference in a single MLN to citation matching, and Sutton et al.[19] proposed dynamic CRFs to jointly solve part-of-speech tagging and NP chunking tasks. As shown in our experiments, limitations of first-order logic make the model in [12] only loosely coupled. On the other hand, the dynamic CRF model in [19] includes complex graphical structure and high computational complexity, which may cause convergence problems. Our proposed model is highly coupled and bidirectional, and considerably outperforms both of them.

7. CONCLUSION AND FUTURE WORK

We presented a strongly-coupled, bidirectional approach to the problem of joint information extraction. We introduced joint factors to capture top-down and bottom-up bidirectional tight correlations and dependencies between subtasks, and we proposed a learning algorithm based on VEM to perform parameter estimation approximately in a top-down and bottom-up manner. This algorithm allows information to flow in both directions and explores mutual benefits from multiple subtasks. Experimental results on two real-world datasets exhibit that our model significantly outperforms recent state-of-the-art pipeline, integrated and joint models while also running much faster than the joint models. Several interesting issues, such as the effect of joint factors on performance and the efficiency of our approach are analyzed and discussed as well. This approach allows extensive further investigation, both for parameter learning and inference. We also plan to apply and test our model to other real-world IE applications.

8. REFERENCES

[1] A. Culotta, A. McCallum, and J. Betz. Integrating probabilistic extraction models and data mining to discover relations and patterns in text. In *Proceedings of HLT/NAACL-06*, pages 296–303, New York, 2006.

[2] J. R. Finkel, C. D. Manning, and A. Y. Ng. Solving the problem of cascading errors: Approximate Bayesian inference for linguistic annotation pipelines. In *Proceedings of EMNLP-06*, pages 618–626, Sydney, Australia, 2006.

[3] K. Hollingshead and B. Roark. Pipeline iteration. In *Proceedings of ACL-07*, pages 952–959, Prague, Czech Republic, 2007.

[4] T. S. Jaakkola. Tutorial on variational approximation methods. In *Advanced Mean Field Methods: Theory and Practice*, pages 129–159. MIT Press, 2000.

[5] M. I. Jordan, Z. Ghahramani, T. S. Jaakkola, and L. K. Saul. An introduction to variational methods for graphical methods. *Machine Learning*, 37:183–233, 1999.

[6] J. Ko, L. Si, and E. Nyberg. A probabilistic graphical model for joint answer ranking in question answering. In *Proceedings of SIGIR-07*, pages 343–350, Amsterdam, The Netherlands, 2007.

[7] F. R. Kschischang, B. J. Frey, and H.-A. Loeliger. Factor graphs and the sum-product algorithm. *IEEE Transactions on Information Theory*, 47(2):498–519, 2001.

[8] J. Lafferty, A. McCallum, and F. Pereira. Conditional random fields: Probabilistic models for segmenting and labeling sequence data. In *Proceedings of ICML-01*, pages 282–289, 2001.

[9] L. Liao, D. Fox, and H. Kautz. Extracting places and activities from GPS traces using hierarchical conditional random fields. *International Journal of Robotics Research*, 26:119–134, 2007.

[10] P. Luo, F. Lin, Y. Xiong, Y. Zhao, and Z. Shi. Towards combining Web classification and Web information extraction: a case study. In *Proceedings of KDD-09*, pages 1235–1244, Paris, France, 2009.

[11] D. P. T. Nguyen, Y. Matsuo, and M. Ishizuka. Relation extraction from Wikipedia using subtree mining. In *Proceedings of AAAI-07*, pages 1414–1420, Vancouver, British Columbia, Canada, 2007.

[12] H. Poon and P. Domingos. Joint inference in information extraction. In *Proceedings of AAAI-07*, pages 913–918, Vancouver, British Columbia, Canada, 2007.

[13] F. Reichartz, H. Korte, and G. Paass. Semantic relation extraction with kernels over typed dependency trees. In *Proceedings of KDD-10*, pages 773–782, New York, 2010.

[14] S. Sarawagi and W. W. Cohen. Semi-Markov conditional random fields for information extraction. In *Proceedings of NIPS-04*, 2004.

[15] S. Singh, K. Schultz, and A. Mccallum. Bi-directional joint inference for entity resolution and segmentation using imperatively-defined factor graphs. In *Proceedings of ECML/PKDD-09*, pages 414–429, Bled, Slovenia, 2009.

[16] P. Singla and P. Domingos. Entity resolution with Markov logic. In *Proceedings of ICDM-06*, pages 572–582, 2006.

[17] C. Sutton and A. Mccallum. Collective segmentation and labeling of distant entities in information extraction. In *Proceedings of ICML Workshop on Statistical Relational Learning and Its Connections to Other Fields*, 2004.

[18] C. Sutton and A. McCallum. An introduction to conditional random fields for relational learning. In L. Getoor and B. Taskar, editors, *Introduction to Statistical Relational Learning*. MIT Press, 2006.

[19] C. Sutton, A. McCallum, and K. Rohanimanesh. Dynamic conditional random fields: Factorized probabilistic models for labeling and segmenting sequence data. *Journal of Machine Learning Research*, 8:693–723, 2007.

[20] M. J. Wainwright and M. I. Jordan. Graphical models, exponential families, and variational inference. *Foundations and Trends in Machine Learning*, 1:1–305, 2008.

[21] W. Wiegerinck. Variational approximations between mean field theory and the junction tree algorithm. In *Proceedings of UAI-2000*, pages 626–633, San Francisco, CA, 2000.

[22] K. Yoshikawa, S. Riedel, M. Asahara, and Y. Matsumoto. Jointly identifying temporal relations with Markov logic. In *Proceedings of ACL-09*, pages 405–413, Suntec, Singapore, 2009.

[23] X. Yu. Chinese named entity recognition with cascaded hybrid model. In *Proceedings of HLT/NAACL-07*, pages 197–200, Rochester, New York, 2007.

[24] X. Yu and W. Lam. An integrated probabilistic and logic approach to encyclopedia relation extraction with multiple features. In *Proceedings of COLING-08*, pages 1065–1072, Manchester, United Kingdom, 2008.

[25] X. Yu and W. Lam. Bidirectional integration of pipeline models. In *Proceedings of AAAI-10*, pages 1045–1050, Atlanta, Georgia, USA, 2010.

[26] X. Yu and W. Lam. Jointly identifying entities and extracting relations in encyclopedia text via a graphical model approach. In *Proceedings of COLING-10*, pages 1399–1407, Beijing, China, 2010.

[27] X. Yu, W. Lam, and B. Chen. An integrated discriminative probabilistic approach to information extraction. In *Proceedings of CIKM-09*, pages 325–334, Hong Kong, China, 2009.

[28] J. Zhu, Z. Nie, J.-R. Wen, B. Zhang, and W.-Y. Ma. 2D conditional random fields for Web information extraction. In *Proceedings of ICML-05*, pages 1044–1051, Bonn, Germany, 2005.

[29] J. Zhu, Z. Nie, B. Zhang, and J.-R. Wen. Dynamic hierarchical Markov random fields for integrated Web data extraction. *Journal of Machine Learning Research*, 9:1583–1614, 2008.

[30] J. Zhu, B. Zhang, Z. Nie, J.-R. Wen, and H.-W. Hon. Webpage understanding: an integrated approach. In *Proceedings of KDD-07*, pages 903–912, San Jose, California, USA, 2007.

From Names to Entities using Thematic Context Distance

Anja Pilz
Fraunhofer IAIS
Schloss Birlinghoven
Sankt Augustin, Germany
anja.pilz@iais.fraunhofer.de

Gerhard Paaß
Fraunhofer IAIS
Schloss Birlinghoven
Sankt Augustin, Germany
gerhard.paass@iais.fraunhofer.de

ABSTRACT

Name ambiguity arises from the polysemy of names and causes uncertainty about the true identity of entities referenced in unstructured text. This is a major problem in areas like information retrieval or knowledge management, for example when searching for a specific entity or updating an existing knowledge base.

We approach this problem of named entity disambiguation (NED) using thematic information derived from Latent Dirichlet Allocation (LDA) to compare the entity mention's context with candidate entities in Wikipedia represented by their respective articles. We evaluate various distances over topic distributions in a supervised classification setting to find the best suited candidate entity, which is either covered in Wikipedia or unknown. We compare our approach to a state of the art method and show that it achieves significantly better results in predictive performance, regarding both entities covered in Wikipedia as well as uncovered entities.

We show that our approach is in general language independent as we obtain equally good results for named entity disambiguation using the English, the German and the French Wikipedia.

Categories and Subject Descriptors

I.2.7 [**Natural Language Processing**]: Text analysis; I.5.2 [**Design Methodology**]: Classifier design and evaluation, Feature evaluation and selection; H.3.3 [**Information Search and Retrieval**]: Information Search and Retrieval

General Terms

Algorithms, Experimentation

Keywords

named entities, named entity disambiguation, topic modeling, named entity resolution, classification

CIKM'11, October 24–28, 2011, Glasgow, Scotland, UK.

1. INTRODUCTION

Recently several analysts have estimated that more than 70%-80% of all data in organizations is unstructured information [24]. The enrichment of knowledge bases from unstructured text can hence gain from reliable information extraction methods. Among those are text mining techniques, such as entity recognition, relation extraction or entity disambiguation.

Named entity recognition identifies name phrases in a text as named entities by labeling the words with type labels, such as person or location. Subsequently *named entity disambiguation* (NED) or *name disambiguation* aims to assign a *name mention* in a text to the underlying *real-world entity*, e.g., to a unique entity description. This is a critical step in the construction of semantic knowledge bases from unstructured text, because it enables entity-based retrieval instead of keyword search.

It is well known that names are not unique. The name mention *John Taylor*, for example, can denote a South Carolina governor, an athlete, a racing driver, a jazz musician, a bass guitarist and so on. Note that the last two entities also have a similar artistic profession (both are musicians), which makes their distinction even more difficult. Additionally, polysemy of names spans across entity types. The term *Bush*, for example, may be used to refer to a large number of persons, a shrub, to undeveloped landscape, to a number of locations, brands, as well as to two rock bands.

The effects resulting from name ambiguity can easily be seen when carrying out web searches or retrieving articles from an archive of newspaper texts. For example, the top ten hits of a Google search for the string *John Taylor* contain ten different entities, among them a professor, a jazz guitarist, and a college. It may be clear to a human that these mentions do not refer to the same real-world entity. However, it is difficult to draw this conclusion automatically, for example using natural language processing techniques.

Miller and Charles observed that words with similar meanings are often used in similar contexts [17]. Hence, most approaches to name disambiguation estimate the identity of a name mention by comparing the words in the neighborhood of the mention with the words in the descriptions of real-world entities. While the comparison of (bag-of-) word vectors for NED is quite successful [1, 8, 5, 7] it is not robust if different words with a similar meaning are used in the neighborhood of a name mention and the corresponding descriptions of the real-world entity.

Figure 1 depicts examples for some contexts mentioning the names *Taylor* and *John Taylor*. Consider for example T2

T1 (John Taylor (bass guitarist)):
*Duran Duran was chosen to do the song after bassist **John Taylor** (a lifelong Bond fan) approached producer Cubby Broccoli at a party, and somewhat drunkenly asked "When are you going to get someone decent to do one of your theme songs?"*

T2 (John Taylor (poet)):
*Thames watermen played an important part in the very early movements that ultimately led to the creation of modern trade unionism in the United Kingdom, most notably in the writings of pamphleteer **John Taylor** (1580-1653) and later with the use of petitions or "petitions of grievances" in particular the petitions supporting the curtailment of the growth of hackney coaches in the 17th century.*

T3 (John Taylor (poet)):
*In 1630, **John Taylor**, a poet wrote "At Bow, the Thursday after Pentecost, There is a fair of green geese ready rost, Where, as a goose is ever dog cheap there, The sauce is over somewhat sharp and deare".*

T4 (Elizabeth Taylor):
*Critical reaction to the film was mostly negative, with much being made of **Taylor's** wildly fluctuating weight from scene to scene.*

Figure 1: Context examples for the name *Taylor* referring to three different entities (extracted from Wikipedia).

and T3: while the thematic information is similar, the overlap of common terms is very low, even though both contexts refer to the same person. A pure word comparison could not detect that *pampleteer* and *poet* are thematically related to a topic such as *writing*. Additionally, disambiguation approaches that are based on word comparisons are also often unable to reason on previously unseen attributes (e.g., new terms), and thus are likely to suffer from a lower recall for new data.

There have been several approaches to overcome the problem of synonymy. Srinivasan et al., for example, generate probable words according to a topic model of a document [19]. In this paper, instead of representing topics by some words, we used topic model probabilities directly to describe the document content that a name mention appears in. This is motivated by the idea that topic models automatically disambiguate terms based on the co-occurrences with other terms. If LDA is trained on a sufficiently large corpus, most words of a new document will already be present in the LDA model. Thus, we assume that in a new document we can infer a topic probability distribution with sufficient quality, which may be used to assess semantic similarity to Wikipedia articles.

Our approach is able to assign name mentions in new documents to unseen entity descriptions (Wikipedia articles). The topic models may be applied to new documents as well as to new Wikipedia articles and yield useful semantic characterizations even if some words are not covered by the topic model. Hence it is not necessary to train the topic model with all Wikipedia articles as long as a sufficiently large sample is used.

As topic models do not require labeled training data, the approach presented in this paper can be applied to any language as long as unique descriptions of named entities are available (currently Wikipedia is available in 269 languages). To demonstrate that our approach is in general language independent, we apply the proposed method to the English, the German, and the French version of Wikipedia, the currently three largest versions. We also show that we achieve quite similar performance figures for all three languages.

In the next section we describe prior work in name disambiguation, which is also often referred to as entity resolution or as record linkage in the field of databases. Then we outline the properties of Wikipedia as a reference for unique named entities (Sec. 3) and the construction of a disambiguated dataset of corresponding entity mentions (Sec. 3.1). Next, we describe the classification approach used in this paper (Sec. 4). Subsequently, we give a short overview of LDA (Sec. 5) and outline the different topic distances used for thematic context comparison (Sec. 5.3). Then we present the experimental setup and discuss the obtained results (Sec. 6).

2. RELATED WORK

2.1 Problem Description

In this work, we study the task of name disambiguation using Wikipedia as a knowledge base with describing contexts. Given a *name mention* m with surrounding text $T(m)$, we want to assign this mention to the corresponding true entity $e(m)$ described by a Wikipedia article. By matching the surface forms of names (e.g., first and last name) m we get a set of *candidate entities* or candidate articles $\mathcal{E}(m) = \{e_1, \ldots, e_{|\mathcal{E}|}\}$ from Wikipedia, such that for all $e_j \in \mathcal{E}(m)$ we have $m = name(e_j)$ in the case of an exact name match or $m \subset name(e_j)$ in the case of a partial name match. We denote the Wikipedia text around entity e_j as $T(e_j)$. The task is to select one of the entities in $\mathcal{E}(m)$ as the correct entity ($e(m) = e_j$) or to decide that $e(m)$ is *not covered* by Wikipedia ($e(m) \notin \mathcal{E}(m)$).

2.2 Prior Work on Name Disambiguation

Name disambiguation is closely related to the task of word sense disambiguation, which aims at resolving the ambiguity of words in a text. Both rely on the assumption that the meaning of a mention is strongly dependent on the context it appears in [17]. However, studies in the fields of word sense disambiguation and entity resolution do often not assume the presence of a reference knowledge base.

One of the first studies in the field of name disambiguation is that of Bagga and Baldwing [1]. They propose to create context vectors for each target name mention m, where each vector contains exactly the words that occur within a fixed-sized window around the ambiguous name. To cluster contexts referring to different entities, the authors measure the similarity among these vectors by the cosine measure. This algorithm was extended to a large corpus by Dill et al. [8].

Chen and Martin [6] combined lexical context features and extracted information in a vector space model: non-stop words appearing within a fixed window around any mention m of the entity, noun phrases in the sentences containing the ambiguous name, and named entities (persons other than the ambiguous name, organizations, etc.) in the entire document. The authors reported better performance compared to previously published results.

The outputs of relation extractors or named entity recognizers are certainly useful features for name disambiguation, but unfortunately they cannot be used out of the box for other languages, such as German or French. Creating such modules is often a laborious task, as it can require annotated training data or rely on language specific characteristics, such as capitalization and word order. For example, the German language has a free word order and a different capitalization scheme. Thus, both entity recognizers as well as relation extraction methods can be harder to construct. Because we wanted to apply our approach simultaneously to different languages without extensive manual annotation, we did not use these features.

To describe an entity [19] use a bag of features similar to [6]. Additionally, the authors employ entity profiles that combine attributes of the entity (links from the entity to a value), relations (to or from another entity), and events that this entity is involved in. As a third feature the authors estimate a topic model with 50 topics and determined the top 10 words with highest probability for the document according to the topic model. Disambiguation is then performed via single-link hierarchical agglomerative clustering. Experiments show an improvement over the results presented in [6]. Srinivasan et al. generate words according to a topic model and then add these to the respective feature vector to overcome the synonymity problem [19]. In contrast, our approach relies on the overall topic probability distribution of a document, thus using a completely different feature vector representation based on topic clusters instead of words.

Other approaches use relation evidence for entity resolution. Bhattacharya and Getoor [2] resolve ambiguity in the context of citations, considering the mutual relations between authors, paper titles, paper categories, and conference venues. For example, we may conclude that the names *R. Srikant* and *Ramakrishnan Srikant* refer to the same person, because both denote a coauthor of another author. Bhattacharya and Getoor argue that the joint resolution of the identity of authors, papers, etc. leads to a better result than considering each type seperately.

Similarly, Hassel et al. [9] disambiguate researcher names in citations by exploiting relational information contained in an ontology derived from the DBLP database. Attributes, such as affiliations, topics of interests, or collaborators are extracted from the ontology and matched against the text surrounding a name occurrence. The results of the match are then combined in a linear scoring function that ranks all possible senses of the name of interest. The scoring function is trained on a set of disambiguated name queries that are automatically extracted from Wikipedia articles. The method is also able to detect when a name denotes an entity that is not covered in Wikipedia.

Both of the last mentioned approaches require relational information, for example provided by a relation extraction system or a well-maintained ontology. However, this relational information is currently not available for arbitrary persons and in multiple languages. Therefore we did not include these features into our analysis.

Cucerzan [7] presents a large-scale system for the recognition and semantic disambiguation of named entities based on information extracted from Wikipedia and Web search results. The system uses co-reference analysis to associate different surface forms of a name in a text, e.g., *George W. Bush* and *Bush*. Again, context words are combined with Wikipedia categories to describe entities. The proposed method then assigns entities by maximizing the non-normalized scalar products for the contexts of entities and name phrases.

Bunescu and Pasca [5] disambiguate entities using a Ranking SVM [12], which generates a ranked list of plausible entities for a given context $T(m)$ of the target name mention m. Features are words in a window around m in combination with Wikipedia categories of the articles describing the corresponding real-world entities. To apply this method for uncategorized knowledge bases, one has to estimate classifiers to predict the Wikipedia categories for the text $T(m)$, which requires a considerable effort, especially if needed for several languages.

As we find the problem formulation in [5] most similar to ours, we re-implemented this method (outlined in Section 4.2.2) and use it as a baseline for comparison with our approach. Similar to our work, the reference corpus is extracted from Wikipedia (for details, see Section 3.1).

3. WIKIPEDIA AS A KNOWLEDGE RESOURCE

In the last years, Wikipedia[1] has received much attention in the scientific community. Many projects and scientific studies build upon this free, constantly updated repository of world knowledge. Due to its sheer size, however, handling this semi-structured knowledge resource for data mining or information retrieval purposes is a challenge.

Most of the textual content in Wikipedia is stored in articles. The English, German and French versions currently contain about 3.6 million, 1.2 million, and 1.0 million articles respectively. About 15% of its articles describe biographies and persons and 14% of the articles cover geography and places [13].

Each article in Wikipedia is uniquely identified through its title, which is typically the most common name of the described subject. Ambiguous names are further qualified with additional terms, for example affiliations or professions, e.g., *Jason Taylor (athlete)*, *Jason Taylor (jazz)*, or *Jason Taylor (racing driver)*.

Articles usually hold information focused on one specific concept or entity, describing it in a concise but comprehensive way. The information is substantiated and enhanced by many links to other articles and citations using external documents. In the following we consider the Wikipedia article as the definition of the real-world entity it refers to.

Additionally, each Wikipedia article is labeled with one or more categories. These categories can represent content topics but also more general attributes, such as gender in the case of persons or the founding year in case of organizations. Aside from very general categories there exist very specific categories that apply to only very few articles. In our version of the English Wikipedia, which was downloaded on 15th January 2011, we found 600k different categories.

Relations between articles (entities) are expressed by links. When referring to an entity or concept with an existing article page, contributing authors are supposed to link at least the first mention of the related entity to its corresponding article. Inspired by [5] we exploit Wikipedia's internal link structure to generate an automatically disambiguated dataset of entity mentions, which is described in Section 3.1.

[1] `http://www.wikipedia.org`

3.1 Generation of a disambiguated dataset from Wikipedia

To create a disambiguated training dataset, we assume the correctness of links in Wikipedia, and extract all articles referencing an entity of interest. As the link provides the true entity, this results in a set of disambiguated entity mentions.

Note that this corpus is not really a gold-standard dataset, as the linking is done by different Wikipedia contributors and thus depends on their individual taste. Sometimes links are rather conceptional links, i.e., link to a thematically related article, and do not mean identity. For example, the term *client* can be linked to the article *Lawyer*. Unfortunately, we are not aware of other publicly available benchmark datasets (with links to Wikipedia), especially for German and French. Still, we assume that the model evaluated on this dataset can generalize to other corpora.

In the following, we use the definitions of Section 2.1. Let $L(e_j)$ be the set of Wikipedia articles containing a mention m which is linked to a different article describing e_j. The articles $T(m)$ in $L(e_j)$ are also called *query documents*. Note that a pair $(T(m), T(e_j))$ with $T(m) \in L(e_j)$ can be used to train the relation between the entity e_j and its mention m. As we observed rather few articles without ingoing links we get positive examples for nearly all entities e_j in Wikipedia. Negative examples may be constructed by relating an entity e_j to a mention m not referring to it, i.e., $e(m) \neq e_j$.

Following [5] this set of disambiguated queries can be used for the training as well as the evaluation of a disambiguation model.

To construct such a disambiguated training data set, we first selected a set of entities e_j for which referencing documents (e.g., links in other articles) are to be found. Here, we consider persons and other entities with ambiguous names. As we did not focus on Wikipedia's category hierarchy, we use YAGO [20] to determine articles referencing persons. YAGO is build jointly over Wikipedia and WordNet and endows Wikipedia articles with attributes, such as person, group, location, etc.. Each entity article, which is ambiguous, i.e., whose surface name corresponds to more than one Wikipedia article, is added to the entity dataset A.

Next we define a dataset Q containing the mentions corresponding to A. Note that there are articles with more than 1000 incoming links while other articles have only one incoming link. To balance this inequality we added at most ten randomly selected referencing documents from $L(e_j)$ as examples to Q, also storing a reference to the the linked entity e_j. This restriction allows a better balanced model over all entities in A. Otherwise, we would run in danger to introduce a bias towards frequently referenced entities. We ignored references outgoing from documents in A, such that $Q \cap A = \emptyset$.

As the text $T(m)$ corresponding to a mention m we used the complete Wikipedia article containing m as this yields better results than just using a small window around m. We experimented with different context width configurations and found that an additional boost on the local context can improve disambiguation performance (see 5.3.1).

We apply the same configuration for English, German and French, remove stop words from respective lists and use the stemmed word forms obtained by the Snowball algorithm [18] (again for the respective language).

4. NAME DISAMBIGUATION AS A CLASSIFICATION PROBLEM

Ignoring the possibility of different spellings of the name of an entity, we consider an entity e_j only as a candidate for some name mention m, if its title matches the name mention in the query document. The assignment to one of the candidate entities in $\mathcal{E}(m) = \{e_1, \ldots, e_{|\mathcal{E}|}\}$ can be considered as a multi-class classification problem, with each e_j one distinctive class. Note that with increasing number of entities this classification problem rapidly becomes intractable, if we would want to learn one model per name (or per entity).

As an alternative, we can formulate this task as a binary classification problem, deciding if $e(m) = e$ or $e(m) \neq e$. Following [12], we create the classifier input using groups of feature vectors $\{\vec{\phi}(m, e_j)\}_{e_j \in \mathcal{E}(m)}$, where each $\vec{\phi}(m, e_j)$ is a feature vector describing the pair (m, e_j). To each $\vec{\phi}(m, e_j)$ we assign a label y

$$y(\vec{\phi}(m, e_j)) = \begin{cases} +1, & \text{if } e(m) = e_j \\ -1, & \text{else.} \end{cases} \quad (1)$$

For at most one e_j we get a positive label. In the special case that $e(m)$ is an uncovered entity and $e(m) \notin \mathcal{E}(m)$, none of the describing feature vectors $\vec{\phi}(m, e_j)$ receives a positive label.

This binary classification problem can be tackled with many different classifiers. We use the SVM^{Light}[2] implementation by Thorsten Joachims [11] as learning framework employing different kernels. This classifier has shown excellent performance in many text mining problems. It is trained with the feature vectors $\vec{\phi}(m, e_j)$ constructed from Wikipedia.

For a new mention $\tilde{m}$ we can construct new feature vectors $\vec{\phi}(\tilde{m}, e_j)$ for $e_j \in \mathcal{E}(\tilde{m})$. Subsequently, the estimated SVM is applied to all $\vec{\phi}(\tilde{m}, e_j)$. Then the entity which receives the highest score is selected as the best match. Note that it is possible that two entities come from a very similar field (i.e., two politicians may be member of the same party). Then it is likely that both entities receive high scores for a given name mention m. The difference between the scores of the best and the second best match can be used as an indicator of the uncertainty of the decision.

4.1 Revealing uncovered Entities

As already discussed, there are millions of entities not present in Wikipedia, many of them appearing for example in the local parts of a news paper. To account for this, we simulate non-covered entities similar to [5]. In particular, we remove the Wikipedia article and consequently all provided information for a fixed fraction of entities e_j. Consequently all mentions m previously linked to these e_j now correspond to an entity not covered in Wikipedia and all training examples get assigned to class $y = -1$. During the application of the estimated SVM to new data, we consider a mention m as *uncovered*, if the model predicts no score higher than the threshold 0 for any of the candidates $\vec{\phi}(\tilde{m}, e_j)$:

$$\forall_{e_j \in \mathcal{E}(\tilde{m})} \hat{y}(\vec{\phi}(\tilde{m}, e_j)) \leq 0. \quad (2)$$

Note that for future work it would also be possible to fine tune this threshold on a validation set. Alternatively, [5]

[2]The SVM^{Light} package is available at `http://svmlight.joachims.org/`

have shown that using a linear kernel, this threshold can be learned automatically from the weight of an indicative feature.

4.2 Baseline attributes for name disambiguation

We compare our proposed method to previous approaches to the task of name disambiguation and describe these attributes in the following.

4.2.1 Cosine Similarity

Cosine similarity was used by [1] as one of the first approaches to assess the similarity between two documents. [5] and [7] both evaluated experimentally a ranking function based on the cosine similarity between the text of the query document $T(m)$ and the text of the entity's article $T(e)$. Specifically, this denotes cosine similarity as

$$\phi_{cos} = \cos(T(m), T(e)) = \frac{V(T(m))}{||V(T(m))||}\frac{V(T(e))}{||V(T(e))||}. \quad (3)$$

Here $V(T(m))$ is the standard vector space model of $T(m)$, where each component corresponds to a term in the vocabulary and each entry to the word count in the respective context.

In the formulation in Eq. 3, cosine similarity is an unweighted but normalized summation over common words (terms appearing both in the query document and the article text). The larger this number the more similar are $T(m)$ and $T(e)$ and hence the more similar are the entities denoted.

Measuring the similarity between contexts in this way has one major drawback: if alternative terms for one concept are used in $T(m)$ and $T(e)$, the similarity will be low even if the contexts denote the same entity. Additionally, entities in similar context will be difficult to distinguish using such an aggregated measure.

We use the feature ϕ_{cos} as a baseline feature in the feature vectors $\vec{\phi}(m, e_j)$ in all of the following experiments, as it evaluates directly matching words in the contexts of e_j and m.

4.2.2 Word-Category Pairs

Bunescu and Pasca ([5]) used the categories of Wikipedia articles as particularly indicative features, to learn the magnitude of semantic correlations between words w and categories c. In particular, the authors assume that common words are indicative, and create the following feature vector representation:

$$\phi_{wc}(m, e) = \begin{cases} 1, & \text{if } w \in T(m) \cap T(e) \text{ and } c \in c(e) \\ 0, & \text{else.} \end{cases} \quad (4)$$

In this approach, $T(m)$ is reduced to a context window of width 25 around the entity mention.

Here, the maximal dimension of $\vec{\phi}_{wc}$ is restricted by $|W| \times |C|$, where $|W|$ is the number of all possible words and $|C|$ the number of all possible categories.

We re-implement this approach using the Ranking SVM included in SVM^{Light} (and denote it as $Bun06$ in the following), with the slight modification that we use only directly assigned categories, instead of analyzing the category hierarchy to extract top-level categories. Note that analyzing Wikipedia's category hierarchy is not a trivial task, as we can encounter loops and other inconsistencies.

In this paper we present an approach that is applicable for different languages and does not rely on category information.

5. THEMATIC CONTEXT DISTANCE FOR NAME DISAMBIGUATION

5.1 Latent Dirichlet Allocation

LDA recently achieved very much attention in a growing number of research fields, ranging from text analysis to computer vision. One very attractive point of LDA is that it effectively generates low-dimensional representations from sparse high-dimensional data, representing documents by a low-dimensional vector of *topics*. In this section, we briefly review the most important aspects of Latent Dirichlet Allocation, for more details the interested reader is referred to [4] and references therein.

LDA is a Bayesian probabilistic model that describes document corpora in a fully generatively way [4]. It assumes a fixed number K of underlying topics in a document collection D, where each document d is a mixture of topics t_i. According to LDA, the observable variables, i.e., the words in a document, are generated as follows: First, for each document d, document-specific topic proportions θ_d are drawn according to $\theta_d \sim Dir(\alpha)$. The parameter α is the concentration parameter of the Dirichlet prior, which is a convenient conjugate to the multinomial distribution. Then for each word i in d a topic z_{di} is randomly chosen according to $z_{di} \sim Mult(\theta_d)$. Finally the observed word w_{di} is randomly drawn from the distribution of the selected topic, $w_{di} \sim Mult(\beta_{z_{di}})$. This overall topic distribution is assumed to be drawn randomly beforehand from a Dirichlet distribution $\beta_k \sim Dir(\eta)$, where *beta* is the prior vector on the per-topic word distribution.

The nature and influence of the priors α and β has been studied for example by Wallach et al. [22]. We use the Mallet implementation [16], which automatically optimizes the prior α according to the underlying collection.

The resulting word distributions $p(w_n|z_n, \beta)$ for each topic have high probabilities for words that often co-occur in documents. Topic models alleviate two main problems arising in natural language processing: synonymy and polysemy. Synonymy refers to the case where two different words (say car and automobile) have the same meaning. Synonyms usually will co-occur in similar contexts and hence belong to similar topics. Polysemy, on the other hand, refers to the case where a term, such as plant, has multiple meanings (industrial plant, biological plant). Depending on the context at hand (e.g., the document is mostly about industry or biology) different topics will be assigned to the word plant.

5.2 Topic based entity representation

We build topic models for each the languages treated in this paper. We extracted 100k random documents from the respective versions of the English, French, and German Wikipedia and use them as training documents for LDA. Most of these documents describe persons. We use the trained models to infer the probability of a topic t_i for each word w in an article d. The average probability of topic t_i for document d is the average of the probabilities of topic t_i for each word w in d. These yield topic distributions both for the query document with name mention m as well as the candidate articles e and define new attributes for both documents:

- $\mathbf{P}(e) = (p_1(e), \ldots, p_K(e))$: the probability distribution of K topics in the article text $T(e)$
- $\mathbf{P}(m) = (p_1(m), \ldots, p_K(m))$: the probability distribution of K topics in the query text $T(m)$.

The distributions $\mathbf{P}(e)$ and $\mathbf{P}(m)$ and functions thereof may be used as features in $\vec{\phi}(m, e_j)$, as they are able to represent the proportions of semantically similar words.

Table 1 shows exemplary topics for Wikipedia articles with name *John Taylor* together with the titles (stemmed terms) for topics generated by Mallet[3]. For each topic t_i, the associated probability $p(t_i)$ is the probability of the given topic for the respective article text. For example, the most prominent topic (t_{80}) derived for the athlete *John Taylor* describes his sportive success in the Olympic Games. The topic with lower probability ($p(t_{135})$ is only about 10%) can be interpreted as an indicator for his nationality. We see that most articles can be described sufficiently by one or two topic clusters which is a good example for the dimensionality reduction provided by LDA. One phenomenon in LDA is that depending on the document length the mixture of topics varies. While in very short documents we often find one very prominent topic (for example the racing driver), longer documents have a higher variety (e.g., the article describing the bass guitarist is the longest one in this example).

5.3 Comparing Thematic Distances

For each mention-entity pair (m, e_j) we compare the topic distribution $\mathbf{P}(m)$ of the query document containing m with the distributions $\mathbf{P}(e_j)$ for the candidates $e_j \in \mathcal{E}(m)$ computed over the corresponding article texts $T(e_j)$.

One of the simplest ways to compare the topic probabilities is a concatenation of the respective probabilities:

$$\phi_{TC} = \{p_1(m), ..., p_K(m), p_1(e), ..., p_K(e)\} \in R^{2K}. \quad (5)$$

Hence each of the probabilities is used as a separate feature and the classifier has the task to evaluate the differences.

Alternatively, we may compute distance terms between corresponding topic probabilities directly. There are a number of distance measures for probability distributions that propose different weighting factors. Instead of just summing differences in probability values to a scalar difference value we use the difference terms separately as features. Then the classifier can evaluate correlations between these terms/features to improve performance.

The symmetric Kullback-Leibler divergence[14] or relative entropy is very popular in the topic model literature:

$$\phi_{sKLD}(m, e)_i = \frac{1}{2}\left(p_i(m) \log \frac{p_i(m)}{p_i(e)} + p_i(e) \log \frac{p_i(e)}{p_i(m)}\right). \quad (6)$$

Here we use the symmetric version as the $T(e)$ and $T(m)$ are interchangeable with respect to similarity. Each term $\phi_{sKLD}(m, e)_i$ can be used as a scalar feature in $\vec{\phi}(m, e_j)$.

The Jensen-Shannon distance [15], is derived from the Kullback-Leibler divergence and adds an additional factor

[3]The topics are taken from a model over a subset of Wikipedia with $K = 200$, $|D| = 100k$.

Table 2: F1 (micro) performance for name disambiguation using different topic distance representations and kernel types

distance representation	linear	kernel type quadratic	RBF
Hellinger ϕ_{HD}	0.9248	0.9286	0.9256
Jensen-Shannon ϕ_{JSD}	0.9236	0.9249	0.9231
sym. Kullback-Leibler ϕ_{sKLD}	0.9278	**0.9328**	0.9096
topic concatenation ϕ_{TC}	0.8899	0.9107	0.9109

to (6):

$$\phi_{JSD}(m, e)_i = \frac{1}{2}\left(p_i(m) \log \frac{p_i(m)}{r} + p_i(e) \log \frac{p_i(e)}{r}\right), \quad (7)$$

where $r = 0.5(p_i(m) + p_i(e))$.

The Hellinger distance [3] is another alternative measure for the similarity of probability distributions:

$$\phi_{HD}(m, e)_i = \left(\sqrt{p_i(m)} - \sqrt{p_i(e)}\right)^2. \quad (8)$$

The maximum distance 1 is achieved when $p_i(m)$ assigns probability zero to every set to which $p_i(e)$ assigns a positive probability, and vice versa.

Except for ϕ_{TC} all feature representations yield a maximum dimension of $\phi_{(\cdot)} \in R^K$, with K the number of topics.

We ignore topic indices if both $p_i(m)$ and $p_i(e)$ are less than 0.01. This is based on the assumption that we don't need to spend modeling effort for uninfluential topics. Note that this has the side effect that the overall number of non-sparse features will be rather low, which speeds up the kernel computation.

We evaluated all of the above distances using five-fold cross-validation on a small dataset (similar to $Q1$, see Table 3) with different kernels using SVM^{Light} standard parameters to find the most appropriate distance and kernel for the task at hand.

As depicted in Table 2, using ϕ_{TC} yields the weakest results with a linear kernel. A linear kernel can not model the interactions between the topics for e and m. Better results can be achieved using a quadratic or an RBF kernel. The Hellinger distance also improves results over the Jensen-Shannon distance (significantly with $p < 0.05$ only for the quadratic kernel). To summarize, we find that basically all of the above distances yield similar results, which we assume is based on their similar origin. Still, even though the superiority of the symmetric Kullback-Leibler distance is not striking, we found it to be significant with $p < 0.05$ for the linear kernel and $p < 0.06$ for the quadratic kernel. Thus, we used this distance for all the experiments described in Section 6.

5.3.1 *Influence of the context width*

Both [1] and [5] observed that the direct context around an entity mention often contains most of the disambiguating information. Thus, we performed some initial experiments to evaluate the optimal context width. We found that reducing the context window to the 25 left and 25 right tokens around the entity mention (as done by [5], and also reported for the corresponding experiments here), yields a slight decrease in predictive performance for our approach. We be-

Table 1: Topics for entities with name *John Taylor* (excerpt) with associated probability value

disambiguation term	i	$p(t_i)$	Important words (titles) of the topics
South Carolina governor	109	0.3805	unit state, state senat, lieuten governor, hous repres, elect governor, ...
	120	0.2477	north carolina, south carolina, unit state, west virginia, civil war, ...
athlete	80	0.4190	summer olymp, gold medal, world record, silver medal, world championship, ...
	135	0.1047	unit state, rhode island, baltimor maryland, new hampshir, georg washington, ...
racing driver	129	0.7407	grand prix, race driver, motor race, formula, race team, sport car, ...
jazz	141	0.5781	jazz musician, big band, new york, duke ellington, jazz band, ...
bass guitarist	18	0.2964	rock band, solo album, play guitar, band member, rock roll, ...
	70	0.1594	album releas, studio album, debut album, record label, music video, ...

lieve that the reason behind this is that the inferred topic distributions are less smooth and thus also less reliable.

Thus, we propose to use the complete document of the entity mention m with an additional boost on the local context. We found that a context window of [10,10] around the mention yields the best result. The terms from this window are added five times to the overall tokens of the query document m. We found that this overweighting of the local context increases the performance significantly ($p < 0.05$) in comparison to the unboosted version. Hence, we use the local boosting for all of the following experiments based on topic information.

5.3.2 *LDA parameters*

In preliminary experiments, we also evaluated topic models with different values of K for the task of entity disambiguation. That is, we varied the number of topics clusters K from 50 to 500 on the same training corpus and found no major difference in the predictive performance when increasing the number of topics above 200.

Note that the Mallet implementation of LDA automatically optimizes the α parameter, such that topic models with the same number of topics but different initial values for α yield the same (or very similar) performance. For all topic models we used $\beta = 0.01$ as prior on the word-topic distribution.

6. EXPERIMENTAL EVALUATION

The approach proposed in this paper using symmetric Kullback-Leibler distance over topic distributions is denoted as *sKLD*. We compare our approach to [5] on the English version of Wikipedia. In the respective tables, we refer to this method as *Bun06*.

We first describe the employed datasets, the properties of the different data sets are summarized in Table 3.

6.1 Datasets

6.1.1 *English Wikipedia*

The first dataset, denoted Q_1, constitutes of references for a random selection of persons[4] with an ambiguous name. The reference dataset A contains 6213 different entities, from which we randomly selected each fifth entity as an uncovered entity. After the removal of these uncovered entities, we have a ratio of 1242 uncovered vs. 4971 covered entities. We then extracted 16582 queries with 2.06 candidates each (e.g., we build 34197 feature vectors).

Note that in application data, for example news articles, entities are often referenced merely by the surname, which makes their distinction even more difficult. To account for this difficulty, we create an additional dataset denoted Q_2, in which we allow candidates on partial name matches as well. In contrast to the other datasets, a candidate is selected if the surface name is also partially contained in the candidate's title (without disambiguation term). For example, the surface name *Jones* can match *Bruce Jones*, *Adam Jones*, *Catherine Zeta-Jones*, but also *Jones Soda* or *Jones, Oklahoma*. This way we get more than 26 candidates per query mention and thus a highly ambiguous data set with more than 400k feature vectors representing all possible (name, entity)-pairs. Uncovered entities are modeled as above.

Table 3: Statistics on the disambiguation datasets for different languages. $|A|$ is the size of the reference data set, $|Q|$ the size of the query dataset.

	$\|A\|$	$\|Q\|$	avg. ambiguity level
English Q_1	6213	16582	2.06
English Q_2	10734	15410	26.76
German	22211	4442	2.91
French	7201	1440	1.88

6.1.2 *German and French Wikipedia*

To show that our approach is in general language independent, we also report results for disambiguation using the German and the French Wikipedia. For the German version, we extracted 22211 articles (again persons[5] with ambiguous names), and 44332 query documents referencing the respective entities. 4442 of the available entities were modeled as default entities. Here, we had in average 2.91 candidates per query, resulting in 129091 feature vector instances.

For the French version, we extracted 7201 articles (again persons with ambiguous names), and 15149 query documents. 1440 of the entities were modeled as default entities. Here, we had in average 1.88 candidates per query, resulting in 28430 instances.

For both datasets, we trained a topic model with 200 topics on a random selection of articles from the respective version of Wikipedia. We used the same preprocessing tech-

[4]The information that an article refers to a person is extracted from YAGO.

[5]We used language links from the English version to extract persons in other languages.

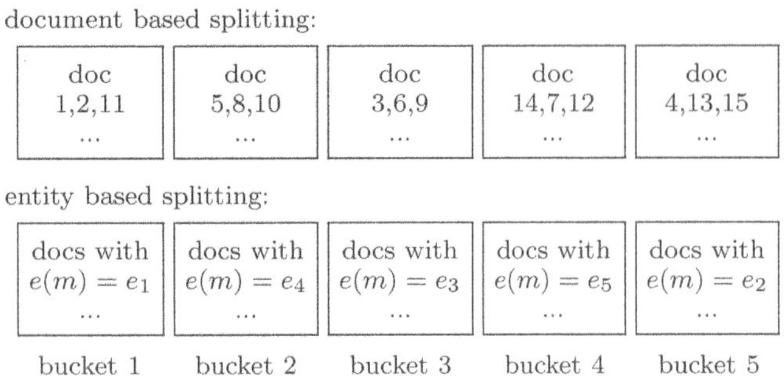

Figure 2: Exemplary document and entity based splitting for cross-validation

niques as for the English version, adapting only the stop word lists and the language of the employed stemmer.

6.2 Results

We report results obtained on five-fold cross-validations for each of the datasets. Additionally, we propose two splitting strategies for cross-validation: one based on documents, one based on the identity of the referenced entities.

The two splitting policies are depicted in Figure 2 for an exemplary set of documents and entities. The document based splitting (upper part of Figure 2) is analogous to the standard procedure for cross-validation, documents (examples) are distributed i.i.d. over the buckets. The entity based splitting (lower part of Figure 2), in contrast, considers the true entities denoted in the query documents, and creates a splitting over the overall entity set.

Even though this can result in unbalanced bucket sizes (note that the number of query documents per entity varies and uncovered entities all fall into one bucket), this strategy allows for additional interpretation of the model's ability to generalize, as the testing instances only contain previously unseen entities (together with context). The intuition behind the entity based splitting is that with new documents new entities described by previously unseen terms may appear. Previously unseen terms constitute new features that can not be considered by a trained SVM model based only on words.

We use several performance indicators for evaluation that are commonly used in classification scenarios. We report on micro and macro performance (for more details see [23]), to asses both document and class (entity) based performance. Macro measurements constitute the averaged Precision (P), Recall (R) and F1-measure (F1) per entity. This is often used when the number of instances is unbalanced over the classes. In contrast, the formulation of micro performance computes the averaged Precision, Recall and F1 per document.

6.2.1 *Results on dataset Q1*

In Table 4 we report results for Q_1 using a linear as well as quadratic kernel for the topic based approach. As shown in Table 2 the RBF-kernel did not perform better, so we omitted experiments using this kernel. To emphasize the performance for uncovered entities, we report the accuracy for these mentions separately.

In the entity based splitting, the baseline *Bun*06 approach completely failed to predict uncovered entities. As uncovered entities are observed only in one fold, *Bun06* never got the chance to learn the appropriate decision threshold. Hence, we observe a rather low recall in micro performance, while in the macro performance the correct predictions for covered entities compensate this. In contrast, in the document based splitting (where a threshold could be learned), the method achieved an accuracy of 70.74% for uncovered entities.

We observe that using thematic context distance measured by symmetric Kullback-Leibler distance (*sKLD*) yields better results in the prediction of uncovered entities for both splitting policies, even though we did not learn an adapted threshold $\neq 0$. Considering macro performance, both *sKLD* approaches, using either a quadratic or a linear kernel, show significantly better results ($p < 0.001$) compared to the baseline approach. Thus, our method increases recall and precision simultaneously in the disambiguation across all entities. The increase in recall compared to the baseline approach is significant in all experiments (document/entity split).

We found that even though we achieve higher precision as well, the improvement is only significant in the document based splitting. The entity based splitting has a higher variance, which is both an effect of the differing bucket sizes as well as the distribution of uncovered entities.

Note that although the entity based splitting seems difficult, the precision of all approaches is higher compared to the document based splitting. The document based splitting has to treat the difficult uncovered entities in each fold, resulting in a lower precision but also a lower variance compared to the entity splitting.

Table 4 also shows the averaged SVM's computation time (cpu-sec). These learning times are relative fractions, where 1 indicates the shortest time and all others are multiples. For example, a topic model with 200 topics and a quadratic kernel requires a more than ten times longer computation time than a model with the same number of topics but a linear kernel.

Comparing the explicit increase in learning time to the rather low increase in performance when using a quadratic kernel instead of a linear one (92.33% vs. 91.90% F1 in the entity splitting, resp. 90.44% vs. 88.28% F1 in the document splitting), we chose to use the linear kernel in the remainder of the experiments. Note that *sKLD* using a linear kernel is also about four times faster than *Bun06*.

6.2.2 *Results on dataset Q2*

Especially for the highly ambiguous dataset Q_2 an SVM training run using a quadratic kernel is computationally expensive. Table 5 shows the results for this dataset using a linear kernel. Even though we increased the SVM's cost ratio for false negative predictions (as we have many more negative than positive examples), *Bun06* does not achieve satisfying results for this dataset as the F-measure is always below 22%. We believe that this is because the approach is more focussed on the disambiguation of persons, while in this dataset many other entities (or entity types) appear. In contrast, our approach keeps up the good performance reported for the smaller corpus. Even though precision and recall are notably lower, we conclude that the proposed thematic context distance is a very good measure for the disambiguation of name phrases. We suspect that for larger datasets a more sensitive topic model (i.e., with more topics over more documents) might be needed. Recent approaches

Table 4: Results for name disambiguation on the dataset Q1

		entity based splitting						document based splitting					
method		micro perf.	*p-val.*	macro perf.	*p-val.*	Accuracy uncov.	cpu sec.	micro perf.	*p-val.*	macro perf.	*p-val.*	Accuracy uncov.	cpu sec.
Bun06[5]	F1	0.7990		0.8286		0.0000	3.91	0.8730		0.8658		0.7074	4.89
	P	0.9563		0.9043				0.9056		0.8800			
	R	0.6937		0.8027				0.8427		0.8704			
sKLD	F1	0.9233	0.06	0.9152	0.00	0.6926	15.21	0.9044	0.00	0.9061	0.00	0.787	13.77
quadratic	P	0.9813	0.31	0.9516	0.00			0.9238	0.00	0.9177	0.00		
kernel	R	0.8720	0.03	0.8995	0.00			0.8859	0.00	0.9094	0.00		
sKLD	F1	0.9190	0.09	0.9079	0.00	0.7455	1.00	0.8828	0.03	0.8856	0.00	0.7862	1.00
linear	P	0.9821	0.28	0.9517	0.00			0.9012	0.13	0.9022	0.00		
kernel	R	0.8636	0.05	0.8874	0.00			0.8651	0.01	0.8862	0.00		

Table 5: Results for name disambiguation on the dataset Q2

method	splitting type	perf.	F1	P	R
Bun06	by entity	micro	0.2299	0.9454	0.1722
		macro	0.2083	0.2612	0.1906
	by document	micro	0.1595	0.1600	0.1589
		macro	0.0661	0.0737	0.0629
sKLD	by entity	micro	**0.8752**	0.9733	0.7965
		macro	0.8557	0.9051	0.8346
	by document	micro	**0.8354**	0.8964	0.7822
		macro	0.8315	0.8414	0.8346

Table 6: Name disambiguation using thematic context distance *sKLD* on the German dataset

splitting type	perf.	F1	P	R	std. F1
by entity	micro	0.8796	0.9748	0.8015	0.0462
	macro	0.8491	0.9022	0.8279	0.0055
by document	micro	0.8292	0.8681	0.7937	0.0049
	macro	0.8275	0.8442	0.8288	0.0053

to speed up LDA on very large corpora (for example [10] or [21]) provide a useful tool to be explored.

6.2.3 *Results on German and French datasets*

Tables 6 and 7 show results for the disambiguation model using the German and the French dataset. In either scenario, the obtained F1-measure is well above 80%, with low derivation, which is a promising result. We find that although we did not spend additional efforts on the specific characteristics of these languages, we can very accurately assign name phrases to the corresponding articles.

On the relatively small French dataset, we also evaluated the quadratic kernel and found that performance could be increased mostly in the document splitting setting, by up to 3% in F-measure.

As LDA is a language independent method, these results are not surprising but nevertheless new: we have shown that the same approach to measure thematic context distance works for various source languages and yields very good results. Note that apart from training the LDA model, which is unsupervised, no other language specific adaptations needed to be made.

Table 7: Name disambiguation using thematic context distance *sKLD* on the French dataset

splitting type	perf.	F1	P	R	std. F1
by entity	micro	0.8801	0.9748	0.8025	0.0449
	macro	0.8486	0.9034	0.8268	0.0087
by document	micro	0.8378	0.8755	0.8032	0.0045
	macro	0.8314	0.8493	0.8348	0.0064

7. CONCLUSION

In this paper we approach the problem of name ambiguity using thematic distances over describing documents. We compare our approach to a state of the art method that exploits word-category information extracted from Wikipedia. Our approach relies on semantic topics provided by LDA and is thus able to exploit more information than other, rather restrictive, word-matching methods. We significantly improve the assignment of name mentions to the underlying articles in Wikipedia. We also treat names that are not covered by an article in Wikipedia and show that our method can handle this problem very accurately, superior to the baseline approach. This is a crucial aspect: When we retrieve information for a known entity, we don't want to assign false facts to it.

In future work we will apply the proposed method to the automatic updating of knowledge bases, which is a very interesting line of research. It opens the possibility to automatically generate articles in Wikipedia for entities that are currently not covered.

Acknowledgements

The work presented here was funded by the German Federal Ministry of Economy and Technology (BMWi) under the THESEUS project. We would like to thank the reviewers for their constructive comments and suggestions on this paper.

8. REFERENCES

[1] A. Bagga and B. Baldwin. Entity-based cross-document coreferencing using the vector space model. In *Proc. of COLING-ACL*, pages 79–85, San Francisco, California, 1998.

[2] I. Bhattacharya and L. Getoor. Relational clustering for multi-type entity resolution. In *Proceedings of the*

4th international workshop on Multi-relational mining, MRDM '05, pages 3–12, 2005.

[3] D. Blei and J. Lafferty. Topic models. In A. Srivastava and M. Saham, editors, *Text Mining: Theory and Applications.* Taylor and Francis, 2009.

[4] D. M. Blei, A. Y. Ng, and M. I. Jordan. Latent dirichlet allocation. *Journal of Machine Learning Research*, 3:993–1022, 2003.

[5] R. C. Bunescu and M. Pasca. Using encyclopedic knowledge for named entity disambiguation. In *Proceedings of EACL*, pages 9–16, 2006.

[6] Y. Chen and J. Martin. Towards robust unsupervised personal name disambiguation. In *Proc. EMNLP-CoNLL*, pages 190–198, 2007.

[7] S. Cucerzan. Large-scale named entity disambiguation based on wikipedia data. In *Proceedings of the Joint Conference on EMNLP and CoNLL*, pages 708–716, 2007.

[8] S. Dill, N. Eiron, D. Gibson, D. Gruhl, R. Guha, A. Jhingran, T. Kanungo, S. Rajagopalan, A. Tomkins, J. A. Tomlin, and J. Y. Zien. Semtag and seeker: bootstrapping the semantic web via automated semantic annotation. In *Proceedings of the 12th international conference on World Wide Web*, WWW '03, pages 178–186. ACM, 2003.

[9] J. Hassel, B. Aleman-Meza, and I. B. Arpinar. Ontology-driven automatic entity disambiguation in unstructured text. *Lecture Notes in Computer Science (LNCS)*, pages 44–57, 2006.

[10] M. Hoffman, D. M. Blei, and F. Bach. Online learning for latent dirichlet allocation. In *Proceedings of NIPS*, 2010.

[11] T. Joachims. *Learning to Classify Text Using Support Vector Machines - Methods, Theory and Algorithms.* Kluwer/Springer, 2002.

[12] T. Joachims. Optimizing search engines using clickthrough data. In *Eighth ACM SIGKDD International Conference on Knowledge Discovery and Data Mining (KDD-2002)*, 2002.

[13] A. Kittur, E. H. Chi, and B. Suh. What's in wikipedia? mapping topics and conflict using socially annotated category structure. In *Proceedings of CHI '09*, pages 1509–1512, 2009.

[14] S. Kullback and R. A. Leibler. On information and sufficiency. *Annals of Mathematical Statistics*, 22(1):49–86, 1951.

[15] J. Lin. Divergence measures based on the shannon entropy. *IEEE Transactions on Information Theory*, 37(1):145–151, 1991.

[16] A. McCallum. Mallet: A machine learning for language toolkit. http://mallet.cs.umass.edu, 2002.

[17] G. Miller and W. Charles. Contextual correlates of semantic similarity. *Language and Cognitive Processes* 6(1):1–28, 1991.

[18] M. F. Porter. Snowball: A language for stemming algorithms. Published online, October 2001.

[19] H. Srinivasan, J. Chen, and R. Srihari. Cross document person name disambiguation using entity profiles. In *Proceedings of the Text Analysis Conference (TAC) Workshop*, 2009.

[20] F. Suchanek, G. Kasneci, and G. Weikum. Yago - a large ontology from wikipedia and wordnet. *Elsevier Journal of Web Semantics*, 6(3):203–217, 2008.

[21] M. Wahabzada, K. Kersting, C. Bauckhage, and A. Pilz. More influence means less work: Fast latent dirichlet allocation by influence scheduling. Poster paper in CIKM, 2011.

[22] H. Wallach, D. Mimno, and A. McCallum. Rethinking lda: Why priors matter. In *Proceedings of the 23rd Annual Conference on Neural Information Processing Systems*, 2009.

[23] Y. Yang. An evaluation of statistical approaches to text categorization. *Information Retrieval*, 1(1–2):69–90, 1999.

[24] N. Yuhanna. Today's challenge in government: What to do with unstructured information and why doing nothing isn't an option. Technical report, Forrester Research, 2010.

Learning Conditional Random Fields with Latent Sparse Features for Acronym Expansion Finding

Jie Liu
College of Information Technical Science
Nankai University
Tianjin, China
jliu@nankai.edu.cn

Jimeng Chen
College of Information Technical Science
Nankai University
Tianjin, China
jeanchen@mail.nankai.edu.cn

Yi Zhang
School of Engineering
UC, Santa Cruz
Santa Cruz, CA, USA
yiz@soe.ucsc.edu

Yalou Huang
College of Software
Nankai University
Tianjin, China
huangyl@nankai.edu.cn

ABSTRACT

The ever increasing usage of acronyms in many kinds of documents, including web pages, is becoming an obstacle for average readers. This paper studies the task of finding expansions in documents for a given set of acronyms. We cast the expansion finding problem as a sequence labeling task and adapt Conditional Random Fields (CRF) to solve it. While adapting CRFs, we enhance the performance from two aspects. First, we introduce nonlinear hidden layers to learn better representations of the input data. Second, we design simple and effective features. We create a hand labeled evaluation data based on Wikipedia.org and web crawling. We evaluate the effectiveness of several algorithms in solving the expansion finding problem. The experimental results demonstrate that the new method achieves performs better than Support Vector Machine and standard Conditional Random Fields.

Categories and Subject Descriptors

H.3.3 [**Information Storage and Retrieval**]: Information Search and Retrieval-Information filtering.

General Terms

Algorithms

Keywords

Text mining, sequence labeling, expansion finding

1. INTRODUCTION

People often use acronyms to avoid using long phrases repeatedly. For example, 'ROM' is often used to refer to 'Read Only Memory';'HIV' is often used instead of 'Human Immunodeficiency Virus'. Using abbreviations or acronyms can simplify our writing and reading, since the same amount of information is conveyed with less words to process. However, acronyms in documents also introduce challenges for the readers who do not have the necessary domain-specific knowledge to understand the acronyms. The need to establish a database of acronyms is becoming an important task. However, manually collecting open domain acronyms and the corresponding explanations is difficult and costly.

The existing methods for automatically building dictionaries of acronyms fall into two categories: pattern-matching methods and supervised learning methods. The pattern-matching methods [1] [2] often fail, because the ways of constructing acronyms varies a lot from case to case, which makes it very difficult to design rules or patterns to achieve high precision and recall. On the other hand, the supervised learning methods [3] [4] that can learn the patterns automatically from a large corpus have shown the advantages over pattern-matching methods. However, the supervised learning models used so far can not automatically capture the sequential information well.

In this paper we focus on the acronym search problem: finding the corresponding expansions given acronyms as queries. This solves the major challenge when building an acronym dictionary. It can also be used as an acronym expansion search engine, which could be useful in practice (education, training, etc.) and is not well studied.

Specifically, the main contribution of this paper is threefold. First, we formulate the expansion finding problem as a sequence labeling task and use Conditional Random Fields (CRF) [5] to solve it. Compared with the previous supervised learning approach [4], the CRF takes the context and structure information into account, which is very important for the expansion finding problem. This problem is a structured prediction task to recognize a sequence of tokens which construct a corresponding expansion from a sentence. Second, in order to deal with the complex nonlinear data, we propose to use a neural network and CRF hybrid model that we call SNCRF (Sparse Neural Conditional Random Fields), since the proposed CRF model learns sparse latent features for the expansion finding task. Third, we design simple and

Query: *NBA*
Sentence: *The National Basketball Association is a professional basketball league.*

The	*National*	*Basketball*	*Association*	*is*	*a*	*professional*	*basketball*	*league*
O	B	I	I	O	O	O	O	O

Figure 1: An example tagging of a training sentence for the linear-chain CRF. The label 'B' stands for 'Beginning of an expansion', 'I' stands for 'Inside of an expansion', and 'O' stands for 'Others'.

effective features and label schemes for this novel sequence labeling task. We test our model on a real dataset collected from Wikipedia. Experimental results indicate that the proposed approach performs better than the state-of-the-art solutions.

2. RELATED WORK

Existing methods for automatic acronym search can be classified into two categories: pattern-matching techniques and machine learning-based methods.

The acronym finding systems based on pattern-matching methods, such as AFP (Acronym Finding Program) [1] and TLA (Three Letter Acronym) [2], rely heavily on expert a priori knowledge and require much human effort on designing and tuning the rules and patterns. Another recent work [6] uses similar methods to design complex patterns and rules to extract acronyms and expansions in texts.

Machine learning methods require less expert design effort and learn from labeled training data automatically. Chang et al. [3] proposed a supervised learning method to extract acronyms and expansions in biomedical literature. Nadeau and Turney [7] present a machine learning approach that uses weak constraints to reduce the search space of the acronym and the expansion candidates. Xu and Huang use SVM to search an acronym and its expansions [4].

CRFs can model the interactions between labels and learn the structures and dynamics of sequence data. The CRF [5] model and related models have achieved state-of-the-art performance in many structured prediction tasks, such as Natural Language Processing , bioinformatics, and computer vision, etc. To handle the complexity and nonlinearity of the data, Lafferty et al. [8] present a kernelized version of a linear CRF to enable nonlinear mapping. Liu et al. [9] proposed a deep CRF which can learn high level latent features. A similar model that combines neural network with CRF was proposed by Peng etc.[10] .

3. PROPOSED METHOD

Considering the problem of expansion finding in text given acronym queries, this section first analyzes the characteristic of the problem. Then the CRF modeling approach, including the details of nonlinear CRFs with latent sparse feature learning, is described.

3.1 Expansion Identification as a Sequence Labeling Problem

The task of expansion identification, which is also called expansion finding, is to recognize tokens that constitute the long original form of a given acronym. For example, when the system is given an acronym query 'NBA', it tries to find a sequence of words 'National Basketball Association' in the sentences. This task is much related to the more general sequence labeling tasks.

We propose to model the structure of a sequence rather than modeling merely the label for each token. Thus, the task can be formalized as a sequence labeling problem: given an acronym query q and a sentence consisting of token sequence $\mathbf{x} = (x_1, ..., x_n)$, determine the optimal sequence of token label names $\mathbf{y} = (y_1, ..., y_n)$ of all possible sequences. With the predicted label sequence y, we can identify whether there is an expansion for the acronym term q; and which subsequence of the sentence is the corresponding expansion.

Furthermore, we adapt the label scheme which is widely used for sequence labeling tasks in natural language processing. For example, the NP chunking tasks usually represent a chunk (e.g., NP) with two labels, the beginning (e.g., B-NP) and inside (e.g., I-NP) of a chunk [11]. We use 'B', 'I' and 'O' to represent 'Beginning of expansion', 'Inside of expansion', and 'Others', respectively. An example of the BIO labeling method is shown in Figure 1.

3.2 Conditional Random Fields

The CRF models have been very successful in many sequence labeling tasks. By modeling conditional probability $P(\mathbf{y}|\mathbf{x})$ rather than joint probability $P(\mathbf{y}, \mathbf{x})$, the discriminative models are believed to be better than generative models for supervised labeling tasks [12]. In addition, the CRF models allow arbitrary, non-independent features on the observation sequence x, because the probability of a transition between labels may depend on the past and future observations. For the CRF model in the expansion finding problem, we want to learn a mapping from an observation sequence $\mathbf{x} = \{x_1, x_2, ..., x_T\}$ to a label sequence $\mathbf{y} = \{y_1, y_2, ..., y_T\}$. Each observation x_t is represented by a feature vector $\phi(x_t) \in R^d$ that is computed from the pair of the tth token and the given acronym.

A linear chain CRF model for the expansion finding problem defines a conditional probability of $\mathbf{y}$ as

$$P(\mathbf{y}|\mathbf{x};\theta) = \frac{1}{Z(\mathbf{x};\theta)} \exp\left\{\theta^\top F(\mathbf{y},\mathbf{x})\right\} \quad (1)$$

where $F(\mathbf{y}, \mathbf{x})$ denotes a global feature vector for input observation sequence $\mathbf{x}$ and output sequence $\mathbf{y}$,

$$F(\mathbf{y},\mathbf{x}) = \sum_t f(\mathbf{y},\mathbf{x},t), \quad (2)$$

and $\mathbf{x}_t = \{x_i | i = t-\frac{Q-1}{2}, \cdots, t+\frac{Q-1}{2}\}$ is a segment of length Q centered at t of $\mathbf{x}$. $Z(\mathbf{x};\theta)$ is a normalization factor over all the possible states of $\mathbf{y}'$ of length $|\mathbf{x}|$ defined as

$$Z(\mathbf{x};\theta) = \sum_{\mathbf{y}'} \exp\left\{\theta^T \cdot F(\mathbf{y}', \mathbf{x})\right\}, \quad (3)$$

the function $f(\mathbf{y}, \mathbf{x}, t)$ computes a set of features for input sequence $\mathbf{x}$ and $\mathbf{y}$ at position t, and θ is a vector of linear weights.

Typically, given a set of training example $\mathcal{D} = \{\mathbf{x}^{(n)}, \mathbf{y}^{(n)}\}_{n=1}^N$, where $x_t^{(n)} \in \mathcal{X}$ and $y_t^{(n)} \in \mathcal{Y}$, the linear weights can be estimated by maximizing the penalized log-likelihood with respect to the conditional probability

$$\max_\theta \left\{\sum_{n=1}^N \log P(\mathbf{y}^{(n)}|\mathbf{x}^{(n)};\theta)\right\} \quad (4)$$

There are efficient exact inference algorithms for linear chains CRFs such as the Viterbi algorithm [13] and belief propagation algorithms [14].

3.3 CRF with Latent Sparse Features

Motivated by [9, 10], we want to make the CRF models have the ability to learn features. To do so, we introduce a nonlinear transformation layer to compute the hidden representation of input observation vectors. Here the hidden representation can be seen as powerful features learned from input data.

Consider a sequence of observations $\mathbf{x} = \{x^{(n)}\}_{i=1}^N$ and labels $\mathbf{y} = \{y^{(n)}\}_{i=1}^N$. Let $y_t \in y = \{1, \cdots, C\}$, we use $c_t = [\mathbb{I}_{n=y_t}]_{n=1}^N$ to encode y_t, e.g., if $y_t = 2$ and $C = 4$, then $c_t = [0, 1, 0, 0]^T$, we define our nonlinear-chain CRF as

$$P(\mathbf{y}|\mathbf{x};\theta,\alpha) = \frac{1}{Z(\mathbf{x};\theta)} \exp\left\{\sum_t \theta^\top F(\mathbf{y}, \phi(\mathbf{x}_t;\alpha), t)\right\} \quad (5)$$

where the global feature function is defined as

$$F(\mathbf{y}, \phi(\mathbf{x}_t;\alpha)) = \sum_t f(\mathbf{y}, \phi(\mathbf{x}_t;\alpha), t), \quad (6)$$

$\phi(x_i;\alpha)$ is a nonlinear feature extractor $x \rightarrow \mathbb{R}^M$ with parameter α, and parameter vector $\Gamma = (\theta, \alpha)$. In its simplest form, $\phi(\mathbf{x}_t;\alpha)$ is a $Q \times M$ vector by concatenating $\{\phi(x_i;\alpha)|x_i \in (x)_t\}$. There are many other ways to enrich the model, for example, by defining higher-order features $c_{t-1} \otimes c_t \otimes \phi(\mathbf{x}_t;\alpha)$.

The proposed model (5) is like a multi-layer neural network (NN), which generally optimizes the classifier and hidden-layer features simultaneously. Our model puts a CRF upon $\phi(x_i;\alpha)$ that amounts to a hidden layer. In fact, our implementation $\phi(x_i;\alpha)$ itself is a neural network

$$\phi_i(x_i;\alpha) = \varrho\left(\sum_{k=1}^H \omega_{i,k}^\phi h_k(x) + b_i^\phi\right),$$
$$h_k(x) = \varrho\left(\sum_{j=1}^D \omega_{k,j}^h x_j + b_k^h\right) \quad (7)$$

where $i = 1, \ldots, M$, ϱ is a non-linear (tanh) transfer function, and the parameters α include all the weights ω and bias term b. Therefore, the overall SNCRF hybrid contains two nonlinear hidden layers and one structured-output layer.

The model (5) not only learns the linear parameters, i.e., θ, but also optimizes the features by tuning the transformation parameter α in transformation function ϕ. This capacity of learning features is important, especially when the task is complex.

We use the following objective function to learn the parameters Γ^*:

$$L(\Gamma) = \sum_n^N \log P(\mathbf{y}^{(n)}|\mathbf{x}^{(n)}) - \mu \sum_n^N |\phi(\mathbf{x}_t^{(n)};\alpha)| - \frac{1}{2\delta^2}||\Gamma||^2. \quad (8)$$

The first term in Eq. 8 is the conditional log-likelihood of the training data. The second term constrains the latent feature to be sparse using $L1$ norm, where μ is used to control the weight for its contribution of the learning. In our implementation μ is fixed to 1. The third term is the log of a Gaussian prior with variance δ^2, i.e., $P(\Gamma) \sim \exp(\frac{1}{2\delta^2}||\Gamma||^2)$.

With the sparsity regularization, only a tiny fraction of the hidden units are active in relation to a given stimulus. Plenty of research shows that sparse features could improve the model performance [15] [16]. We adapt the methods in [9] to compute the gradients. Then gradient ascent is used to search for the optimal parameter values, $\Gamma^* = \arg\max_\Gamma L(\Gamma)$. Although the proposed model is non-convex, the experimental results show that it can achieve good performance in practice. In our experiments, we performed gradient ascent with the BFGS optimization technique.

3.4 Feature Functions

In this study, we investigate multiple alternative feature functions and explore different combinations.

In the traditional CRF models, there are usually two kinds of feature functions which are state functions and transition feature functions, respectively. A state function computes the features on individual vertex, and a transition function compute the features on an edge on the graph. In our study, we design one type of state feature function and two types of transition functions.

The state functions depend on the dependency of a vertex given a single label. The state function has the form

$$F^v(\mathbf{x}_i, \mathbf{y}_i) = \sum_t f^v(\phi(x_t), y_t) \quad (9)$$

where $\phi(x_t)$ is the feature vector for x_t. For a standard CRF, $\phi(x_t)$ is the raw input vector, and for SNCRF, $\phi(x_t)$ is the output of multiple hidden layers. Assuming ϕ_t has dimension d, we have $|\mathcal{Y}| \times d$ state functions.

The transition functions depend on pairs of labels of adjacent vertices. The first transition function is defined as:

$$F^e(\mathbf{x}_i, \mathbf{y}_i) = \sum_t f^e(y_{t-1}, y_t), \quad (10)$$

where

$$f^e(y_{t-1}, y_t) = \begin{cases} 1 \text{ if } y_{j-1} = y \text{ and } y_j = y' \\ 0 \text{ otherwise} \end{cases} \quad (11)$$

There are $|\mathcal{Y}| \times |\mathcal{Y}|$ transition functions and each corresponds to a hidden state variable pair (y, y').

In addition to the above two widely used feature functions, we also introduce another function that considers both the vertex and edge information simultaneously

$$F^{ve}(\mathbf{x}_i, \mathbf{y}_i) = \sum_t f^{ve}(\phi(x_t), y_{t-1}, y_t) \quad (12)$$

Table 1: Orthographical features

Feature Name	Regular expression
ALLCAPS	[A-Z]+
INITCAP	^[A-Z].*
CAPMIX	.*[A-Z][a-z].*|.*[a-z][A-Z].*
HAS DASH	.*-.*
PUNCTUATION	[,.;?!-+]

The number of this type is $|\mathcal{Y}| \times |\mathcal{Y}| \times d$. In the experiments, we will show that the third feature function can boost the model performance by a large margin.

3.5 Inference

Given the model parameters $\Lambda = \{\theta, \alpha\}$, prediction of a new test sequence $\mathbf{x}$ is to estimate the most probable label sequence $\mathbf{y}^*$ that maximizes our conditional model:

$$\mathbf{y}^* = \arg\max_{\mathbf{y}} P(\mathbf{y}|\mathbf{x}, \Lambda). \tag{13}$$

In this study, belief propagation is used to compute the marginal probability $P(y_i = a|\mathbf{x}, \Lambda)$ for each possible state $a \in \mathcal{Y}$. Then the predicted label y_i^* is the one associated with the maximum sum of marginal probabilities.

3.6 Features

In order to capture various information that might be useful for acronym expansion recognition, we design three kinds of features to be used by CRFs.

Orthographical features: Orthographical features describe the structure of the target token (i.e. word to be labeled) without considering the query (i.e. acronym). For example, whether it contains both upper and lower case letters, whether it contains digits and whether it contains special characters. These features are important, because people often use some orthographical information to emphasize the tokens of expansions. We list the orthographical features in Table 1.

Token-query features: Token-query features describe the relationships between the target token and the given acronym query. For example, whether the first character of the token occurs in the given acronym, whether the token contains an upper case letter that occurs in the acronym.

Context feature: The neighbor tokens are important indicators of a target token's category. We identify a context window of size= 3, which includes the target token, the token right before the target token and the token right after the token. We extract the same orthographical features and token-query features for each token in the context window. Specifically, we also extract the context token-query features: (1) whether the initial letter $Init_{t-1}$ of the token at position $t-1$ appears in the acronym and the initial letter $Init_t$ of the token at position t appears in the acronym after the letter $Init_{t-1}$, (2) whether the initial letter $Init_t$ of the token at position t appears in the acronym and the initial letter $Init_{t+1}$ of the next token appears in the acronym after the letter $Init_t$, (3) whether the capitalized letter Cap_{t-1} of the token at position $t-1$ appears in the acronym and the capitalized letter Cap_t of the current token appears in the acronym after the letter Cap_{t-1}, (4) the capitalized letter Cap_t of the token at position t appears in the acronym and the capitalized letter Cap_{t+1} of the next token appears in the acronym after the letter Cap_t.

4. EXPERIMENTS

4.1 Evaluation Corpus

An evaluation data set is created based on Wikipedia.org in which there are a large amount of acronyms and corresponding definitions, a.k.a., expansions. It is common for an expansion to appear without the corresponding acronym nearby.

A random set of acronyms are selected as queries, and possible relevant pages are crawled using them as seeds. After some pre-processing, such as removing the html tags and segmenting the text into sentences, we manually labeled the corpus. This results a data set containing 255 unique acronyms, 1,372 distinct expansions, 6,185 expansion sentences, and 108,830 words. The average length of an acronym is 4.02 letters. It is worth to note that one acronym may have multiple expansions. On average, an acronym has 5.2 distinct expansions, and each expansion contains 3.11 words. The average sentence length is 17.6 words.

4.2 Evaluation Criteria

Various approaches for acronym expansion identification are evaluated from two aspects. One is the performance measurements per token, which tell how well the model classifies each token in the sequence. The other is the measurement per expansion.

Precision, recall and F1 scores are used to evaluate the performance per token. However, the data is very unbalanced, as a dominating majority of tokens have label 'O'. Instead of the average performance measurements over all categories, the precision $PrecPerToken_i$, recall $PrecPerToken_i$ and F1 $PrecPerToken_i$ on each category $y_i \in \{\text{B, I, O}\}$ are reported, so that the reported measures are not all overwhelmed by tokens with label 'O'.

We define A_i as number of correctly labeled tokens of class y_i, B_i as the number of false negative tokens of class y_i, C_i as the number of false positive tokens of class y_i, D_i as the number of true negative tokens of class y_i, and $A_i + B_i + C_i + D_i$ is the total number of tokens. The definitions are:

$$PrecPerToken_i = \frac{A_i}{A_i + C_i} \tag{14}$$

$$ReclPerToken_i = \frac{A_i}{A_i + B_i} \tag{15}$$

$$F1PerToken_i = 2\frac{PrecPerToken_i \cdot ReclPerToken_i}{PrecPerToken_i + ReclPerToken_i} \tag{16}$$

We realize the dataset created is not a random sample of the whole web, and thus the the recall on the evaluation data set is biased. However, we expect that it is highly correlated with the true recall and can be used to compare different methods.

The accuracy per token is also used in this paper:

$$AccPerToken_i = \frac{A_i + C_i}{A_i + B_i + C_i + D_i} \tag{17}$$

To estimate the performance per expansion, we first find each predicted expansion, which corresponds to a label sequence that begins with 'B' and ends right before the next

'O'. If the expansion is exactly right, a correct expansion is found. The precision, recall and F1 per expansion are defined as follows:

$$PrecPerExpan = \frac{\#\text{ of correct expansions found}}{\text{total }\#\text{ of expansions found}}, \quad (18)$$

$$ReclPerExpan = \frac{\#\text{ of correct expansions found}}{\text{total }\#\text{ of expansions in corpus}}, \quad (19)$$

$$F1PerExpan = 2\frac{PrecPerExpan \cdot ReclPerExpan}{PrecPerExpan + ReclPerExpan}. \quad (20)$$

4.3 Baseline Models

To verify the effectiveness of our proposed model for the expansion finding problem, we compare it with several baseline methods, using five-fold cross-validation. The baseline methods can be categorized into two classes, i.e. sequence models such as CRF, SNCRF, and non-sequence models, linear SVM and kernel SVM which are trained on token-based samples. Moreover, the methods can be orthogonally classified as linear models, namely CRF and SVM, and nonlinear models for the others. Each method is tuned with window size $Q = 1, 3, 5$ (Q is the size of windows described after equation (1)).

For the non-sequence models, linear SVM and kernel SVM, the training set is decomposed into token-based samples. The penalty parameter C is tuned with values $10^k, k = -3..3$. There are two parameters to be tuned: the penalty parameter C and the RBF kernel parameter γ. Both the parameters of kernel SVM are also tuned with values $10^k, k = -3..3$.

For the sequence models, we train the standard linear-chain CRFs and nonlinear-chain SNCRFs. A regularizer is added to avoid overfitting during training. The regularization parameter is tuned with values $10^k, k = -3..3$. Moreover, we also specify the architecture of the hidden layers for the SNCRF model. In our experiment, we use one hidden layer, and the number of hidden nodes is enumerated in the set {5,10,15,20,25}.

The sequence models are evaluated under two configurations according to the different combinations of alternative feature functions. For the first configuration, only feature types F^v and F^e are used. The corresponding models are denoted as $\text{CRF}^{v,e}/\text{SNCRF}^{v,e}$. For the second configuration, the other transition feature functions F^{ve} were added. The corresponding models are denoted as $\text{CRF}^{v,e,ve}$ and $\text{SNCRF}^{v,e,ve}$, respectively.

4.4 Results

Figure 2 shows that label 'O' is predicted more accurately than label 'B' and 'I' by each method in all evaluation measures, which is because the data is unbalanced. The number of the tokens with label 'O' is approximately fifteen times of that of tokens with label 'B' and eight times of that of tokens with label 'I'.

For the first configuration for sequence model, $\text{SNCRF}^{v,e}$ performs better than the linear sequence model $\text{CRF}^{v,e}$. The linear SVM model and $\text{CRF}^{v,e}$ model produces similar performance. The reason may be that the SVM and CRF have orthogonal ability in classification. The SVM has better generalization by maximizing the margin, while the CRF can take advantage of the sequence structure information of the data. Compared to the linear models, both the nonlinear models, kernel SVM and $\text{SNCRF}^{v,e}$, performs better than the linear counterparts, namely linear SVM and $\text{CRF}^{v,e}$. Moreover, SNCRF which is a nonlinear sequence model achieves the best performance including kernel SVM in all evaluation measures.

Table 2: Experimental results per expansion

Method	Precision	Recall	F1
Linear SVM	0.6742	0.7523	0.7106
Kernel SVM	0.6971	0.7311	0.7121
$\text{CRF}^{v,e}$	0.7486	0.7114	0.7284
$\text{SNCRF}^{v,e}$	0.8072	0.8386	0.8218
$\text{CRF}^{v,e,ve}$	0.8353	0.8720	0.8532
$\text{SNCRF}^{v,e,ve}$	0.8429	0.9170	0.8784

The second configuration for sequence model, $\text{CRF}^{v,e,ve}$ and $\text{SNCRF}^{v,e,ve}$ outperform those of the first configuration. We can see from Figure 2 that they achieve higher precision and recall. As a result, the F1 score of the sequence models with second configuration is much better than those of the first configuration, which implies that introducing the feature function of F^{ve} provide positive effect for the sequence models. It is more important to note that the proposed $\text{SNCRF}^{v,e,ve}$ achieves the best performance on all the three measurements.

Figure 3 gives the accuracy per token, which demonstrates consistent comparison results with Figure 2.

Table 2 shows the performance per expansion, which more directly and precisely reflect the actual effectiveness of each model. From Table 2 we have following observations: (1) the linear and nonlinear sequence models, CRF and SNCR-F, outperform the counterpart non-sequence models SVM and kernel SVM respectively, (2) the nonlinear sequence model SNCRF further improves the performance of CRF , (3) the sequence with second configuration achieves better performance than those of the first configuration, and $\text{SNCRF}^{v,e,ve}$ achieves the best performance on the result of per expansion. We also conduct statistical significance tests (t-test) on the improvements achieved by $\text{SNCRF}^{v,e,ve}$ over the other comparison models. The results indicate that all the improvements are statistically significant (p-value< 0.05).

The experimental results demonstrate that the nonlinear sequence model $\text{SNCRF}^{v,e,ve}$ fits for the acronym expansion recognition task better than the other state-of-the-art compared models.

5. CONCLUSION

This paper studies the problem of expansion finding given an acronym. We formulate this task as a sequence labeling task based on the analysis of the problem characteristic. We propose to use a nonlinear sequence model, SNCRF model, for the problem of acronym expansion finding. Furthermore, effective feature functions and features for expansion finding are described in this paper. The experimental results on real data collected from wikipedia.org demonstrate that the proposed approach outperforms the state-of-the-art algorithms with a large margin.

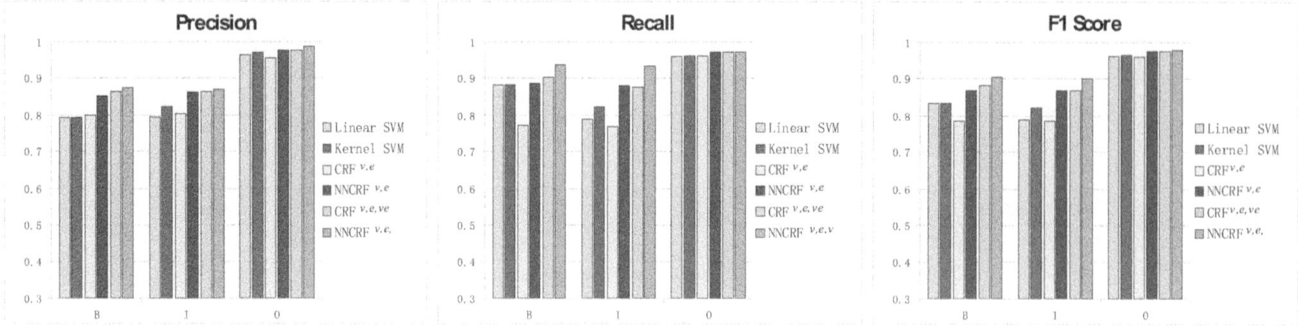

(a) (b) (c)

Figure 2: The results on per label. (a)Precision. (b)Recall. (c)F1 value.

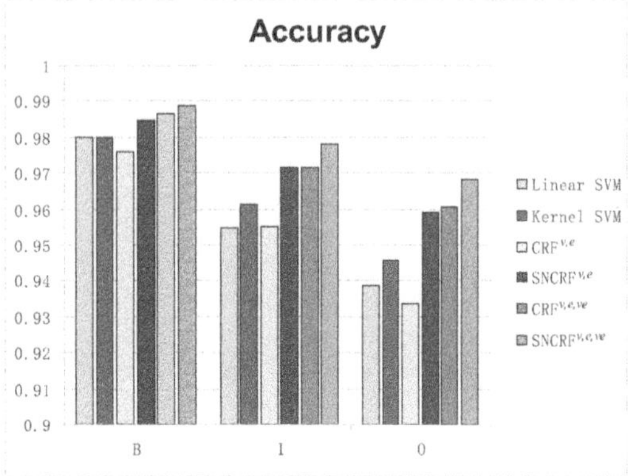

Figure 3: Accuracy per token.

6. ACKNOWLEDGEMENT

The authors would like to thank Aaron Michelony for valuable feedback about the manuscript. This research is supported by the Fundamental Research Foundation for the Central Universities under Grant No.65010571 and the Ph.D. Programs Foundation of Ministry of High Education of China under Grant No.20100031110096.

7. REFERENCES

[1] Kazem Taghva and Jeff Gilbreth. Recognizing acronyms and their definitions. *IJDAR*, 1(4):191–198, 1999.

[2] Stuart Yeates. Automatic extraction of acronyms from text. In *New Zealand Computer Science Research Students' Conference*, pages 117–124, 1999.

[3] Jeffrey T. Chang, Hinrich SchÃÂijtze, and Russ B. Altman. Creating an online dictionary of abbreviations from MEDLINE. *Journal of the American Medical Informatics Association*, 9(6):612–620, November 2002.

[4] Jun Xu and Yalou Huang. Using svm to extract acronyms from text. *Soft Computing*, pages 369–373, 2007.

[5] John Lafferty, Andrew Mccallum, and Fernando Pereira. Conditional random fields: Probabilistic models for segmenting and labeling sequence data. In *ICML*, pages 282–289, 2001.

[6] Mathieu Roche and Violaine Prince. Managing the acronym/expansion identification process for text-mining applications. *Int. J. Software and Informatics*, pages 163–179, 2008.

[7] David Nadeau and Peter D. Turney. A supervised learning approach to acronym identification. In *In 8th Canadian Conference on Artificial Intelligence (AI 2005) (LNAI 3501)*, pages 319–329, 2005.

[8] John Lafferty, Xiaojin Zhu, and Yan Liu. Kernel conditional random fields: representation and clique selection. In *ICML*, 2004.

[9] Jie Liu, Kai Yu, Yi Zhang, and Yalou Huang. Training conditional random fields using transfer learning for gesture recognition. In *ICDM '10: Proceedings of the 10th international conference on Data Ming*, Sydney, Australia, 2010.

[10] Jian Peng, Liefeng Bo, and Jinbo Xu. Conditional neural fields. In Y. Bengio, D. Schuurmans, J. Lafferty, C. K. I. Williams, and A. Culotta, editors, *Advances in Neural Information Processing Systems 22*, pages 1419–1427. 2009.

[11] Lance Ramshaw and Mitch Marcus. Text chunking using Transformation-Based learning. In David Yarovsky and Kenneth Church, editors, *Proceedings of the Third Workshop on Very Large Corpora*, pages 82–94, Somerset, New Jersey, 1995. Association for Computational Linguistics.

[12] Vladimir N. Vapnik. *The Nature of Statistical Learning Theory (Information Science and Statistics)*. Springer, November 1999.

[13] L. R. Rabiner. A tutorial on hidden markov models and selected applications in speech recognition. *Proceedings of the IEEE*, 77(2):257–286, 1989.

[14] Ben Tasker, Abbeel Pieter, and Daphne Koller. Discriminative probabilistic models for relational data. In *Proceedings of the 18th Annual Conference on Uncertainty in Artificial Intelligence (UAI-02)*, pages 485–49. Morgan Kaufmann, 2002.

[15] Bruno A. Olshausen and David J. Field. Emergence of simple-cell receptive field properties by learning a sparse code for natural images. *Nature*, 381(6583):607–609, June 1996.

[16] Chaitanya Ekanadham. Sparse deep belief net model for visual area v2. In *Advances in Neural Information Processing Systems 20*. MIT Press, 2008.

Accounting for Data Dependencies within a Hierarchical Dirichlet Process Mixture Model

Dongwoo Kim
KAIST
Department of Computer Science
dw.kim@kaist.ac.kr

Alice Oh
KAIST
Department of Computer Science
alice.oh@kaist.edu

ABSTRACT

We propose a hierarchical nonparametric topic model, based on the hierarchical Dirichlet process (HDP), that accounts for dependencies among the data. The HDP mixture models are useful for discovering an unknown semantic structure (i.e., topics) from a set of unstructured data such as a corpus of documents. For simplicity, HDP makes an exchangeability assumption that any permutation of the data points would result in the same joint probability of the data being generated. This exchangeability assumption poses a problem for some domains where there are clear and strong dependencies among the data. A model that allows for non-exchangeability of data can capture these dependencies and assign higher probabilities to clusters that account for data dependencies, for example, inferring topics that reflect the temporal patterns of the data. Our model incorporates the distance dependent Chinese restaurant process (ddCRP), which clusters data with an inherent bias toward clusters of data points that are near to one another, into a hierarchical construction analogous to the HDP, and we call this new prior the distance dependent Chinese restaurant franchise (ddCRF). When tested with temporal datasets, the ddCRF mixture model shows clear improvements in data fit compared to the HDP in terms of heldout likelihood and complexity. The resulting set of topics shows the sequential emergence and disappearance patterns of topics.

Categories and Subject Descriptors

G.3 [**Probability and Statistics**]: Nonparametric statistics; H.3.3 [**Information Search and Retrieval**]: Clustering, Text Mining

General Terms

Algorithms, Experimentation

Keywords

Latent Topic Modeling, Bayesian Nonparametric Models

1. INTRODUCTION

A probabilistic topic model seeks to discover a hidden structure referred to as "topics" from an unannotated set of data. The assumptions of the LDA (latent Dirichlet allocation) family, a popular topic model initially developed for modeling text, is that a topic is represented by a multinomial over the vocabulary, each document is generated from a set of topics, and each word token in the document is assigned to a specific topic. This topic modeling problem is an example of the grouped clustering problem where the data are composed of a set of groups, each data point within a group is assigned to a latent cluster, and these latent clusters are shared across the groups. When applied to text, each document corresponds to a group, each word token within the document corresponds to each data point, a topic corresponds to a latent cluster, and these topics are shared across all the documents in the corpus. The nonparametric extension of the LDA, called the HDP-LDA for Hierarchical Dirichlet process [12], is widely used for the grouped clustering problem, and numerous variants of the HDP have been applied to text modeling [17], sound source modeling [5], activity recognition [6], and computational biology [11]. The nonparametric nature of the HDP means the model can be fitted without specifying the number of clusters a priori because the model infers an appropriate number of clusters.

The HDP assumes that data are exchangeable, and when applied to text, this means that the word tokens, as well as the documents, can be permuted in any way without affecting the outcome of the model. For some applications, the exchangeability assumption is appropriate, but in some other applications, it is an overly simplifying assumption. In discovering topics from text, the exchangeability assumption would result in topic assignments without considering the ordering of the documents in the corpus. This poses a problem for many corpora such as the corpus of conference proceedings where there are clear temporal patterns of documents and topics. For example, when analyzing conference proceedings, "collaborative filtering" came to be a major research topic around the year 1999, and so the documents before the year 1999 are unlikely to be generated from that topic. However, a model that assumes exchangeability of data does not distinguish the temporal index of the documents and would allow older documents to be assigned to the new topic.

We propose a new model, the distance dependent Chinese restaurant franchise (ddCRF), which takes the concept of the distance dependent Chinese restaurant process (ddCRP) [1] into a hierarchical construction of the HDP. In the ddCRP, the random assignments of the data points to the clusters depend on the distances between the data points, and this allows the ddCRP to result in a better fit than the Chinese restaurant process (CRP), a metaphor of the Dirichlet process (DP) prior with the usual exchangeability assumption. By incorporating this idea into the HDP, we are able to construct a new model that performs better on the topic modeling task than the HDP on a sequential dataset. We show this by testing the ddCRF on the task of topic modeling using four datasets of conference proceedings. The ddCRF outperforms the HDP on measures of heldout likelihood and complexity, and the ddCRF is also able to discover interesting temporal patterns of topics.

This paper is organized in the following structure. Section 2 describes how we build in data dependence into the CRF to make our model, the ddCRF. Section 3 demonstrates the posterior inference procedure for the ddCRF. Section 4 presents the modeling performance of ddCRF by inferring the topics of four different time-varying corpora of conference proceedings. Finally, Section 5 summarizes this work and discusses directions for future work.

2. DISTANCE DEPENDENT CHINESE RESTAURANT FRANCHISE

We propose a new model, the distance-dependent Chinese restaurant franchise (ddCRF) by adopting the concept of the distance dependent Chinese restaurant process (ddCRP) into the CRF, to account for dependencies among data. We preserve the notation of ddCRF as described in the original CRF paper [12]. In this section, we show how the ddCRP can be integrated into the CRF.

2.1 Table-Based Distance Dependent CRP

Blei and Frazier [1] introduced the customer-based distance dependent Chinese restaurant process (ddCRP) where, instead of customers being assigned to tables, they are assigned to other customers or not assigned to anyone. The probability of a new customer being assigned to other customers is proportional to the distances between the new customer and the other customers. Explicit table assignments do not occur in the customer-based CRP, but the connected components of customers implicitly exhibit a clustering property.

This customer-based ddCRP can be reverted to a table-based ddCRP by summing over the distances to each of the customers within the same connected component. Let K be an imaginary number of tables, which would be the same as the number of connected components of customers, and z_i denote the index of the imaginary table of the ith customer. Let D denote the set of all distance measurement between customers, d_{ij} denote the distance between customer i and j, and f denote the decay function which takes a distance as its parameter. The probability of each table for the ith customer is specified as follows:

$$\begin{aligned} p(z_i = k \mid D, z_{1:(i-1)}, \gamma) &= \frac{\sum_{z_j=k} f(d_{ij})}{\gamma + \sum_{j \neq i} f(d_{ij})} \\ p(z_i = K+1 \mid D, z_{1:(i-1)}, \gamma) &= \frac{\gamma}{\gamma + \sum_{j \neq i} f(d_{ij})}. \end{aligned}$$

In general, the decay function mediates how the distances among customers affect the resulting distribution over partitions. We consider two decay functions: the *exponential decay* $f(d_{ij}) = e^{-d_{ij}/a}$, and the *logistic decay* $f(d_{ij}) = exp(-d_{ij} + a)/(1 + exp(-d_{ij} + a))$, where a is a decay parameter.

By setting the right combination of the type of decay function and the distance measure, we obtain the special case of sequential CRPs. When we define the distance measure such that $d_{ij} = \infty$ for those $j > i$, using either the logistic or the exponential decay function brings $f(\infty) = 0$, and this results in a sequential CRP.

The partition probability over customers can be computed in the customer-based ddCRP simply as defined in [1]. In the table-based ddCRP, however, to compute the partition probability over customers, we must consider all combinations of table assignments, and the number of combinations increases factorially as the number of customers increases. If we make the assumption of sequential non-exchangeability of data such that the model would be the sequential ddCRP, the partition probability can be computed by

$$p(z_{1:N} \mid D, f, \gamma) = \prod_{i=1}^{N} \left(\frac{\mathbf{1}[z_i = K_{i-1}+1]\gamma}{\sum_{j<i} f(d_{ij}) + \gamma} + \frac{\mathbf{1}[z_i \neq K_{i-1}+1] \sum_{z_j=z_i, j<i} f(d_{ij})}{\sum_{j<i} f(d_{ij}) + \gamma} \right), \quad (1)$$

where K_i is the number of allocated tables until the ith customer sits at a table.

Although this commitment to a table-based ddCRP would mean we cannot take advantage of the sampling efficiency of the customer-based ddCRP [1], we propose the table-based distance dependent CRP and use it for the rest of this paper. We do so because in the hierarchical model presented in the next section, it is relatively easy to implement and compute the conditional posterior probabilities.

2.2 CRF to ddCRF

The Chinese restaurant franchise is designed as an approach to the problem of model-based clustering of grouped data. The CRF assumes that the data are exchangeable, but this assumption does not take into account inherent dependencies among data points in some corpora. In order to capture such dependencies, we can incorporate the key idea of ddCRP, which takes into account the non-exchangeability of data, into the CRF. There are three ways to do that.

1. We can model the first (menu) level CRP as a ddCRP. The intuition behind this approach is that the selection of a menu could be influenced by nearby restaurants. If there is a famous menu in a specific region, menus in the other restaurants may be affected by that menu. In this case, however, customers in the restaurants do not exhibit dependences with other customers in the same restaurant.

2. We can model the second (customer) level CRP as a ddCRP. The intuition behind this approach is that the selection of a table by a customer could be affected by other customers already sitting at the tables, but the selection of menu at each table is not affected by menus in the other restaurants.

3. We can model both first and second levels of CRP as ddCRP. By replacing both levels of CRP with ddCRP, we can combine both of the approaches above.

In the rest of this paper we only consider the first approach. Although we only implement and test the first approach, the other two approaches can be implemented in a straightforward way. For the task of topic modeling of a text corpus, replacing the first level CRP by ddCRP indicates that the topic allocation within a document can be influenced by the topics of other documents that are close to the document. Replacing the second level CRP by ddCRP is also interesting, especially for an application such as object recognition in images where the locations and spatial distances of pixels within one image should be considered [16].

The conditional distribution of the ddCRF follows directly from the conditional distribution of the CRF, only we need to consider the decay function and the distances between data points for the ddCRF. Let ϕ_k is an atom drawn from based distribution H, ψ_{jt} is drawn from first level CRP which is a menu of tth table at jth restaurant, and θ_{ij} is drawn from second level CRP which is a ith customer of jth restaurant. In the case where the first level of CRP is replaced by ddCRP, the conditional distribution of second level θ_{ji} only depends on the other Θ. However, the conditional distribution of the first level ψ_{jt} must be computed by considering the distances with other Ψ, hence we have:

$$\begin{aligned}&\psi_{jt} \mid \psi_{11}, \psi_{12}, ..., \psi_{21}, ..., \psi_{j,t-1}, \gamma, H \\ &\sim \sum_{k=1}^{K} \frac{\sum_{j't' \neq jt, k_{j't'}=k} f(d_{j't',jt})}{\sum_{j't' \neq jt} f(d_{j't',jt}) + \gamma} \delta(\phi_k) \\ &\quad + \frac{\gamma}{\sum_{j't' \neq jt} f(d_{j't',jt}) + \gamma} H.\end{aligned}$$

The distance $d_{j't',jt}$ between tables ψ_{jt} and $\psi_{j't'}$ must be carefully defined because it mediates the conditional distribution of ψ_{jt}. It is possible to treat each table in each restaurant to have its own location, or to treat all tables in the same restaurant to share the same location so the distance would be zero between tables at the same restaurant, i.e., $d_{jt',jt} = 0$.

3. POSTERIOR INFERENCE

In this section, we describe a Gibbs sampling method for the ddCRF mixture model. Several posterior approximation techniques including MCMC [12] and variational inference techniques [13] are introduced for the CRF mixture and its related Bayesian non-parametric mixture models.

3.1 Posterior Sampling in the ddCRF Mixture

Let us recall the variables of interest. x_{ji} is the ith data point in the jth group, t_{ji} is an indicator variable for the table index of x_{ji}, k_{jt} is an indicator variable of the menu index of the tth table at jth restaurant, and n_{jtk} is the number of data points at tth table in jth restaurant with dish k. We use dot to represent a marginal sum, and a superscript to denote the counts or indicators of variable excluding the one specified by the superscript.

The sampling process is used in order to infer about $\boldsymbol{t}$ and $\boldsymbol{k}$ based on the observed data set $\boldsymbol{x}$. Before computing the posterior probabilities of these variables, we need to compute the probability of data point x_{ji} given all other variables. We let H denote the prior distribution over probability of data points, and ϕ_k is drawn from this distribution with probability $p(\phi_k|\eta)$ with hyperparameter η, then each data point belonging to this latent cluster has a probability $p(\cdot|\phi_k)$. Therefore, the conditional density of data x_{ji} given all other variables under mixture component k is computed as:

$$\begin{aligned}p(x_{ji}|\boldsymbol{x}^{-ji}, \boldsymbol{t}, \boldsymbol{k}) &= \frac{p(x_{ji}, \boldsymbol{x}^{-ji}|\boldsymbol{t}, \boldsymbol{k})}{p(\boldsymbol{x}^{-ji}|\boldsymbol{t}, \boldsymbol{k})} \\ &= \frac{\int p(x_{ji}|\phi_k) \prod_{j'i' \neq ji, z_{j'i'}=k} p(x_{j'i'}|\phi_k) p(\phi_k|\eta) d\phi_k}{\int \prod_{j'i' \neq ji, z_{j'i'}=k} p(x_{j'i'}|\phi_k) p(\phi_k|\eta) d\phi_k}.\end{aligned}$$

This equation can be further simplified if we use a conjugate prior H. If we use a dirichlet multinomial conjugacy on H, this equation can be further simplified as follows:

$$p(x_{ji}|\boldsymbol{x}^{-ji}, \boldsymbol{t}, \boldsymbol{k}) = \frac{\sum_{j'i' \neq ji} 1[x_{j'i'} = x_{ji}] + \eta}{\sum_{j'i' \neq ji} 1[k_{j't_{j'i'}} = k_{jt_{ji}}] + K \cdot \eta}.$$

Sampling $\boldsymbol{t}$ Now we show the conditional probability of t_{ji} given other variables by bringing the Chinese restaurant franchise metaphor. The probability of t_{ji} is proportional to the number of customers sitting at the table t times the probability of data point x_{ji} arising from the table.

$$\begin{aligned}&p(t_{ji} = t|\boldsymbol{t}^{-ji}, \boldsymbol{k}, \boldsymbol{x}) \\ &\propto \begin{cases} n_{jt}^{-ji} \cdot p(x_{ji}|\boldsymbol{x}^{-ji}, \boldsymbol{t}^{-ji}, t_{ji} = t, \boldsymbol{k}) \\ \qquad (t \text{ is used before}) \\ \alpha \cdot p(x_{ji}|\boldsymbol{x}^{-ji}, \boldsymbol{t}^{-ji}, t_{ji} = t^{\text{new}}, \boldsymbol{k}) \\ \qquad (\text{new } t), \end{cases}\end{aligned} \tag{2}$$

where the probability of the data point x_{ji} drawn from a new table can be calculated by marginalizing over the latent cluster k,

$$\begin{aligned}&p(x_{ji} \mid \boldsymbol{x}^{-ji}, \boldsymbol{t}^{-ji}, t_{ji} = t^{\text{new}}, \boldsymbol{k}) \\ &= \sum_{k=1}^{K} \frac{\sum_{j't' \neq jt, k_{j't'}=k} f(d_{j't',jt})}{\sum_{j't' \neq jt} f(d_{j't',jt}) + \gamma} \\ &\times p(x_{ji}|\boldsymbol{x}^{-ji}, \boldsymbol{t}^{-ji}, t_{ji} = t^{\text{new}}, \boldsymbol{k}, k_{jt^{\text{new}}} = k) \\ &+ \frac{\gamma}{\sum_{j't' \neq jt} f(d_{j't',jt}) + \gamma} \\ &\times p(x_{ji}|\boldsymbol{x}^{-ji}, \boldsymbol{t}^{-ji}, t_{ji} = t^{\text{new}}, \boldsymbol{k}, k_{jt^{\text{new}}} = k^{\text{new}}).\end{aligned} \tag{3}$$

Sampling $\boldsymbol{k}$ If t_{ji} is drawn from the second term of Equation 2 then we have to draw $k_{jt^{new}}$ for the new table from the following distribution.

$$\begin{aligned}&p(k_{jt^{\text{new}}} = k|\boldsymbol{x}, \boldsymbol{t}, \boldsymbol{k}^{-jt}) \\ &\propto \begin{cases} \sum_{j't' \neq jt, k_{j't'}=k} f(d_{j't',jt}) \\ \times p(x_{ji}|\boldsymbol{x}^{-ji}, \boldsymbol{t}^{-ji}, t_{ji} = t^{\text{new}}, \boldsymbol{k}, k_{jt^{\text{new}}} = k) \\ \qquad (k \text{ is used before}) \\ \gamma \cdot p(x_{ji}|\boldsymbol{x}^{-ji}, \boldsymbol{t}^{-ji}, t_{ji} = t^{\text{new}}, \boldsymbol{k}, k_{jt^{\text{new}}} = k^{\text{new}}) \\ \qquad (\text{new } k). \end{cases}\end{aligned}$$

We use the same computation as in Equation 3 (omitting the common denominator), but we present this again to clarify the sampling procedure. We can also sample k_{jt} by excluding all data items in table jt, and this sampling of new k_{jt} changes the component membership of all data items in table jt.

3.2 Sampling Hyperparameters

To improve our model, we place a prior for first and second level concentration parameters γ and α, as used in the original CRF. Sampling α is done in the same way as [12], so we

Table 1: **Dataset statistics of four conference proceedings.**

Conference	Period	# of articles	# of unique terms	# of tokens
NIPS	1988-1999	1,740	6,455	450K
SIGIR	1978-2010	1,838	1,988	106K
SIGMOD	1978-2010	2,311	2,745	165K
SIGGRAPH	1974-1991	783	2,381	53K

discuss here how to sample γ. We note that the probability of γ is conditionally independent of customer assignments $\boldsymbol{t}$ given dish assignments $\boldsymbol{k}$. From this fact, the probability of γ is

$$p(\gamma|\boldsymbol{k}) \propto p(\boldsymbol{k}|\gamma)p(\gamma),$$

where $p(\gamma)$ is the prior on the concentration parameter γ. As we derived in Equation 1, $p(\boldsymbol{k}|\gamma)$ can be computed in a sequential setup. Therefore, γ can be sampled from its posterior distribution.

$$p(\boldsymbol{k}|\gamma)$$
$$= \prod_{i}^{N} \frac{\mathbf{1}[k_i = K_{i-1}+1]\gamma + \mathbf{1}[k_i \neq K_{i-1}+1]\sum_{k_j=k_i, j<i} f(d_{ij})}{\gamma + \sum_{j<i} f(d_{ij})}$$
$$\propto \gamma^K \left[\prod_{i}^{N}\left(\alpha + \sum_{j<i} f(d_{ij})\right)\right]^{-1}$$

where K_i is the number of allocated tables until the ith customer in the sequential setup. To sample from the continuous variable we use Griddy-Gibbs method in [8]. This method evaluates the probabilities on a finite set of points, approximates the inverse cdf $p(\gamma|\boldsymbol{k})$ using these points, and samples from the approximated inverse cdf.

4. EMPIRICAL STUDY

We now describe the experiments to evaluate the performance of the ddCRF on four different text datasets and show how the ddCRF compares against the HDP. The datasets for the experiments include conferences, SIGIR, SIGMOD, SIGGRAPH abstracts, collected through the ACM digital library,[1] and the NIPS article dataset[2]. These four conferences have long histories, their proceedings are published over 20 years, and like many academic publications, their main topics have shifted through time. The detailed statistics of the four datasets we used in the experiments are in Table 1.

4.1 Experimental Setup

We modeled these datasets using the ddCRF to capture the topic changes within a conference though time. We removed stop words, terms that occurred less than 10 times in NIPS, SIGIR and SIGMOD, and terms that occurred less than 5 times in SIGGRAPH.

We trained the HDP mixture model, the ddCRF mixture model, and the latent Dirichlet allocation(LDA) [2] with these datasets and compared their results. Each of the results are averaged over 20 runs. All models used for the evaluation used a symmetric Dirichlet distribution with parameter of 0.5 for the prior H over topic distribution. It is possible to sample the Dirichlet parameter over H, but in that case, the number of topics increases too much [15], and it is not efficient in practice, so we just leave it as a constant. The concentration parameters α and γ were given vague gamma priors with the scale parameter of 1 and the shape parameter of 1.

[1]http://portal.acm.org/

[2]http://www.cs.utoronto.ca/~sroweis/nips

4.2 Comparison to HDP

We compare the ddCRF with the HDP using two metrics, heldout likelihood and complexity. We also compare the discovered topics from the two models for a qualitative analysis.

Heldout Likelihood: Heldout likelihood is widely used in the topic modeling community to compare how well the trained model explains the heldout data (cf. [9, 14, 12]). A better model will give rise to a higher likelihood of heldout documents on average.

$$\text{Heldout likelihood} = \mathit{log}\ p(W|M_{\text{train}}),$$

where M_{train} denotes the model already trained by a training data, and W denotes the heldout data. To calculate the heldout likelihood we used the last 10% of documents for testing and 90% of documents for training.

Figure 1 shows the heldout likelihood of the datasets. For all datasets the ddCRF shows better heldout likelihood than the HDP regardless of the decay parameter and the decay function.[4] The results exhibit that the heldout likelihood gets lower when the decay parameter increases on average. Therefore our model inferences more time sensitive topics with lower decay parameters.

Complexity: Bayesian nonparametrics and the related methods are often used as an alternative of the model selection and integrate over all complexities of a model. If there are two or more models that produce similar results in terms of heldout likelihood, the less complex model is preferred. To measure the complexity of models, we compute a complexity of each model, as defined in [15]. From the posterior topic assignment of the Gibbs sample, we compute the complexity as follows:

$$\text{Complexity} = K + \sum_k \sum_d \mathbf{1}[(\sum_n \mathbf{1}[z_{d,n} = k]) > 0],$$

where K is the number of allocated topics. This measure considers how many topics are used to explain each document and sum it through the entire corpus. A lower complexity indicates that the model uses fewer topics to represent the corpus, and a higher complexity indicates that the model decomposes the data into many dimensions.

Figure 2 shows the model complexities for the four different datasets. The average complexities of the ddCRF are better than the HDP in all cases except the SIGMOD dataset.

[4]We also compared the results with LDA, and it showed that ddCRF outperforms LDA with the same number of topics.

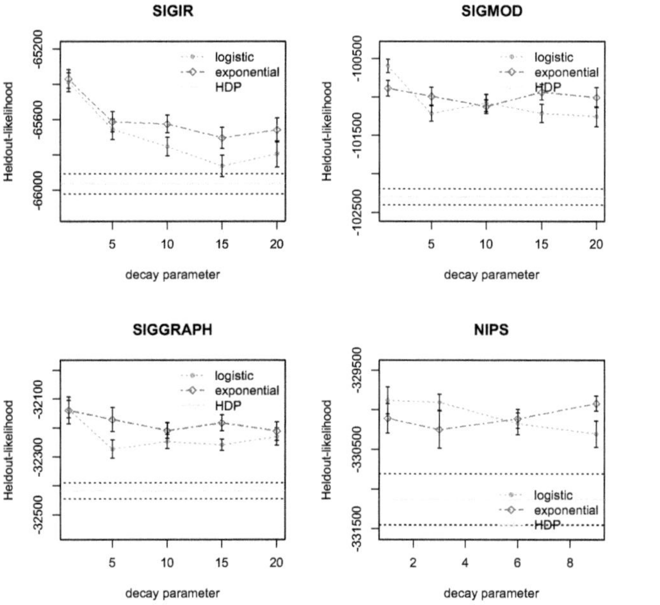

Figure 1: Heldout-Likelihood. Higher is better. The ddCRF outperforms the HDP regardless of the decay function for all datasets.

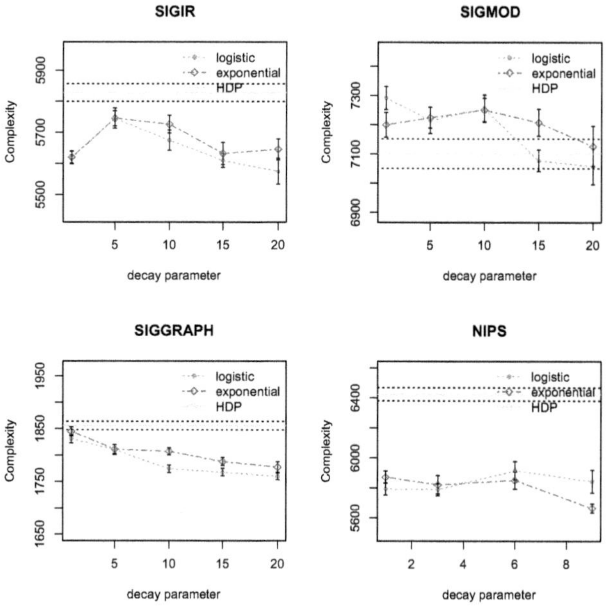

Figure 2: Model complexity where lower values indicate that better (simpler) models were learned. The ddCRF exhibits lower complexity than the HDP for all datasets except for the SIGMOD dataset.

Emergence and disappearance of topics: One strength of our model is that the model imposes a sequential assumption to the first level CRP, and it disallows a word to be assigned to a topic that first appears at a later point in the dataset. Therefore the posterior topic assignment explicitly shows when the topic first appears.

The emergence of topics, combined with the topic trends over time, shows the strength of the ddCRP to model the sequential non-exchangeability of data. To measure the topic trends over time, we define topic *intensity* computed from the posterior sample assignment. At each time slice t, the intensity of topic k is computed by the number of terms assigned to a topic k over the total number of terms at time slice t.

We choose two topics from the SIGIR dataset based on the training results of the ddCRF and look for the most similar topics from the results of the HDP, similarity measured in terms of JS divergence. Figure 3 shows the intensity of those four topics over time. The figures on the left show the topics and their intensities as found by the HDP, and the figures on the right show the topics and their intensities as found by the ddCRF. The topics on the top are about "collaborative filtering", and the topics on the bottom are about "spam filtering". The "spam filtering" topic, which emerged with the rapid growth of email spams, was found by the ddCRF around the year 2000, but the similar topic found by the HDP seems to be a mix of a topic related to spam filtering and another topic related to news articles. The spam filtering topic in fact became a major topic in the SIGIR conference in 2000, and the HDP did not capture this phenomenon well. Similarly, for the "collaborative filtering" topic which became a major research topic in the year 2000, the ddCRF correctly identified the emergence of the topic, whereas the HDP was unable to do so.

We also found interesting patterns of topic emergences from the SIGMOD corpus as shown in Figure 4. The ddCRF identified the "web search" topic emerging around 1994 and the "xml" related topic emerging around 2000. When we modeled the same dataset using the HDP, however, these two topics seem to mix together into one topic.

While the emergence of new topics is simple to identify, the disappearance of topics cannot be explicitly captured from the posterior assignment. With certain decay function and parameter, however, we can deduce when the topic disappeared. An example of a topic that disappears is "File structure and record" in the SIGIR corpus, which last appeared in the year 1988.

5. SUMMARY AND FUTURE WORK

We introduced the distance dependent Chinese restaurant franchise, a hierarchical Bayesian nonparametric model that accounts for dependencies among data. By generalizing the widely used HDP to assume non-exchangeability of data, our model captures temporal patterns in sequential data much better than the existing topic models, HDP and LDA.

One property of the ddCRF that distingishes from the previos attempts is that it can accomodate spatial dependencies in addition to the temporal dependencies. We only considered temporal dependencies here, but modeling spatial dependencies will be the most promising future application of our model. Further, applications of the probabilistic topic model are not restricted to analyzing a document corpus. One of the advantages of the probabilistic topic modeling framework is the flexibility to extend the basic LDA and HDP models. These variants are widely applied to diverse fields[10, 4, 3, 7]. Our model can also be applied to various types of data to uncover other meaningful structure from

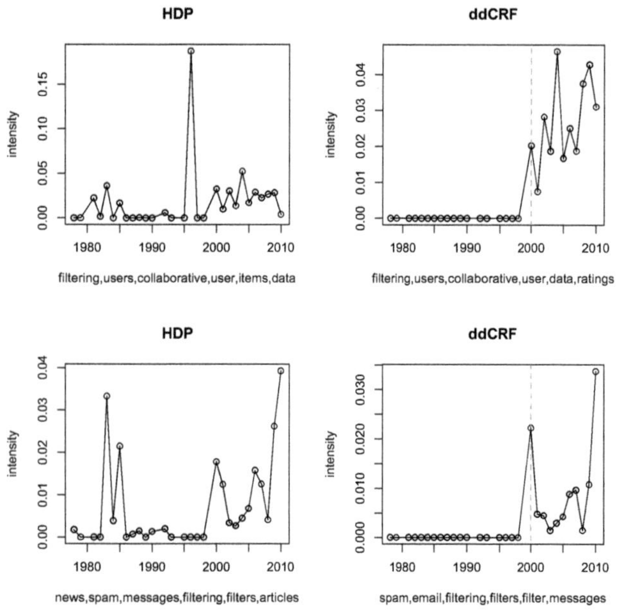

Figure 3: Topic proportions over time identified by the HDP and the ddCRF from the SIGIR corpus. The words beneath the x-axis are the top probability words in each of the topics. As the dotted (red) lines in the ddCRF figures show, the ddCRF clearly captures when the topics first emerged.

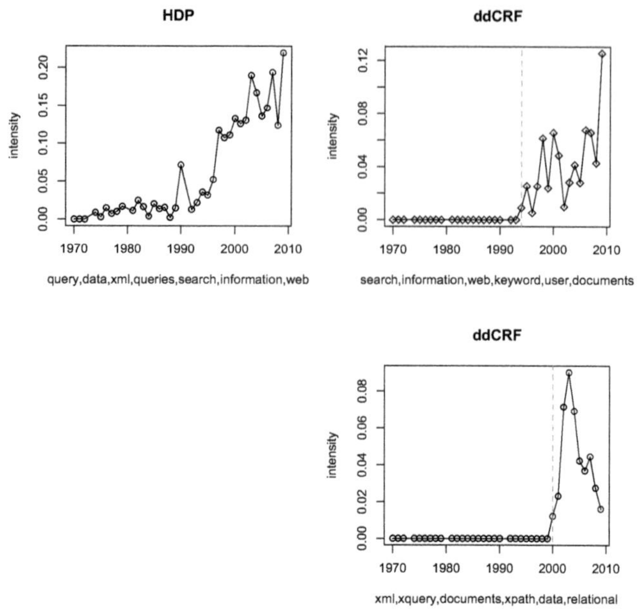

Figure 4: Topic proportions over time identified from the SIGMOD. As the dotted (red) lines in the figures show, the ddCRF captures the emergences of topics about "web search" in 1994 and "xml" in 2000.

data. More specifically, we plan to explore spatial dependencies in modeling of images and spatiotemporal dependencies in geo-tagged data (e.g, tweets). . Further, we can explore other approximation inference methods such as a variational method.

6. ACKNOWLEDGEMENTS

This research was supported by Basic Science Research Program through the National Research Foundation of Korea (NRF) funded by the Ministry of Education, Science and Tehcnology (2010-0025706).

7. REFERENCES

[1] D. Blei and P. Frazier. Distance dependent chinese restaurant processes. *ICML*, 2010.

[2] D. Blei, A. Ng, and M. Jordan. Latent dirichlet allocation. *The Journal of Machine Learning Research*, pages 993–1022, Jan 2003.

[3] L. Dietz, S. Bickel, and T. Scheffer. Unsupervised prediction of citation influences. *ICML*, 2007.

[4] T. L. Griffiths, M. Steyvers, D. M. Blei, and J. B. Tenenbaum. Integrating topics and syntax. *NIPS*, 2005.

[5] M. Hoffman, D. Blei, and P. Cook. Finding latent sources in recorded music with a shift-invariant hdp. *DAFx*, 2009.

[6] D. Hu, X. Zhang, J. Yin, V. Zheng, and Q. Yang. Abnormal activity recognition based on hdp-hmm models. *International Joint Conferences on Artificial Intelligence*, 2009.

[7] C. Lin and Y. He. Joint sentiment/topic model for sentiment analysis. *CIKM*, 2009.

[8] C. Ritter and M. Tanner. Facilitating the gibbs sampler: The gibbs stopper and the griddy-gibbs sampler. *Journal of the American Statistical Association*, 87(419):pp. 861–868, 1992.

[9] M. Rosen-Zvi, T. Griffiths, M. Steyvers, and P. Smyth. The author-topic model for authors and documents. *UAI*, 2004.

[10] R. Socher, S. Gershman, A. Perotte, and P. Sederberg. A bayesian analysis of dynamics in free recall. *NIPS*, 2009.

[11] K. Sohn and E. Xing. A hierarchical dirichlet process mixture model for haplotype reconstruction from multi-population data. *Annals of Applied Statistics*, 3(2):791–821, 2009.

[12] Y. Teh, M. Jordan, M. Beal, and D. Blei. Hierarchical dirichlet processes. *Journal of the American Statistical Association*, Jan 2006.

[13] Y. Teh, K. Kurihara, and M. Welling. Collapsed variational inference for HDP. *NIPS*, 20, 2008.

[14] H. Wallach, D. Mimno, and A. McCallum. Rethinking LDA: Why Priors Matter. *NIPS*, 2009.

[15] C. Wang and D. Blei. Decoupling sparsity and smoothness in the discrete hierarchical dirichlet process. *NIPS*, 2010.

[16] X. Wang and E. Grimson. Spatial latent dirichlet allocation. *NIPS*, 2007.

[17] J. Zhang, Y. Song, C. Zhang, and S. Liu. Evolutionary hierarchical dirichlet processes for multiple correlated time-varying corpora. *KDD*, 2010.

Summarizing Web Forum Threads based on a Latent Topic Propagation Process

Zhaochun Ren[1], Jun Ma[1], Shuaiqiang Wang[2] and Yang Liu[1]
School of Computer Science and Technology
[1]Shandong University, [2]Shandong University of Finance
Jinan, China
{zhc.ren, shqiang.wang}@gmail.com, {majun, yangliu}@sdu.edu.cn

ABSTRACT

With an increasingly amount of information in web forums, quick comprehension of threads in web forums has become a challenging research problem. To handle this issue, this paper investigates the task of Web Forum Thread Summarization (WFTS), aiming to give a brief statement of each thread that involving multiple dynamic topics. When applied to the task of WFTS, traditional summarization methods are cramped by topic dependencies, topic drifting and text sparseness. Consequently, we explore an unsupervised topic propagation model in this paper, the Post Propagation Model (PPM), to burst through these problems by simultaneously modeling the semantics and the reply relationship existing in each thread. Each post in PPM is considered as a mixture of topics, and a product of Dirichlet distributions in previous posts is employed to model each topic dependencies during the asynchronous discussion. Based on this model, the task of WFTS is accomplished by extracting most significant sentences in a thread. The experimental results on two different forum data sets show that WFTS based on the PPM outperforms several state-of-the-art summarization methods in terms of ROUGE metrics.

Categories and Subject Descriptors

H.3.1 [**Content Analysis and Indexing**]: abstracting methods; H.3.3 [**Information Search and Retrieval**]: Information filtering; I.2.6 [**Artificial Intelligence**]: Learning

General Terms

Algorithms, Experimentation

Keywords

Web Forums, Thread Comprehension, Summarization, Topic Modeling

1. INTRODUCTION

Web forum is an online portal for open threads on specific issues. For each thread, a user makes an initial post and others express their opinions by replying to some previous ones. In web forums, people participate in threaded discussions to deliver knowledge and ask questions. Unfortunately, they have to face ascending amount of redundant thread information when browsing web forums. Generally, people often read only few posts ranked ahead in a thread with large posts quantities, whereas this scanning style only reflects incomplete views of the conversation. Hence with an increase of the thread volume, the requirement for summarizing each thread to help human comprehension is becoming more and more urgent. Intuitively, a smooth transition from multi-document summarization to web forums seems to be reasonable. However, as complicated and dynamic topics exist in each ongoing thread, traditional multi-document summarization methods fail to capture the following three characteristics that are crucial to summarize the content of one thread, especially in those ones with large quantities of posts:

Topic Dependencies. Thread is a kind of asynchronous conversation based on temporal topic dependencies among posts. When one thread participant A replies to another post's author B, we consider a topic dependency has been built from user B to user A. Yet there are other factors in reality, it is believed that the reply relations among posts dominant the topic dependencies [8].

Topic Drifting. A conversation always results in various subtopics. As the post conversation progresses, the semantic divergence among these subtopics will be widened.

Text Sparseness. Most posts are composed of short and elliptical messages. As short texts do not provide sufficient term co-occurrence information, traditional text representation methods, such as "tf-idf", have several limitations when directly applied to the mining tasks [5].

In this paper, we investigate the task of Web Forum Thread Summarization (WFTS), aiming to generate a compressed version of a given thread delivering the majority of topics adequately. To handle the three challenges, tracking those dynamic topics existing in each thread has become a significant work to generate the summarization. In recent years, topic models has attracted much attention to the topic discovery and tracking in complicated structural data [6, 9, 13, 1, 14]. This paper explores a novel topic model, called Posts Propagation Model (PPM) [11], that takes account of *topic dependencies*, *topic drifting* and *text sparseness* during the thread modeling process.

Illuminated by the Dirichlet-tree distribution [2], PPM connects topic dependencies based on reply-relations so that topic distributions depend on the product of parameters of its modified structural ancestors. Based on probabilistic distributions derived from the PPM, we accomplish WFTS task by extracting significant sentences to generate the summarization. Topic-sensitive markov random walks(MRW) and mutual reinforcement between posts and sentences is employed for sentence scoring process.

CIKM'11, October 24–28, 2011, Glasgow, Scotland, UK.

The rest of this paper is organized as follows: Our problem formulation is demonstrated in section 2. The Model (PPM) is demonstrated in section 3. In section 4 PPM-based WFTS is detailed. Section 5 presents and discusses the experiments and results, and section 6 concludes the paper.

2. PROBLEM FORMULATION

In this section, we discuss the summarization problem in detail and then present the definition of the WFTS task. First, we introduce some basic concepts in web forums:

DEFINITION 1 (POST). *A post is a user-submitted message containing the content and the time it was submitted. A group of related posts constitute into one thread, where all posts appear as boxes one after another. Except for the root post in one thread, each post is submitted to "reply" one of its previous post in the thread.*

DEFINITION 2 (THREAD). *A thread is a collection of posts, usually displayed from oldest to latest. One thread begins with a root post that may contain questions or news, and is followed by a series of non-root posts, each of which replies to one of its previous posts in the same thread.*

As mentioned in previous section, ascending amount of redundant thread in web forums make the quick comprehension become more and more difficult for participants. Based on this structure in web forums, we investigate the problem of quick comprehension of one forum's thread with multiple posts. An intuitive way to help people understand the thread rapidly is to generate a brief and understandable summary for all posts in the ongoing thread. Therefore, this paper handles the Web Forum Thread Summarization (WFTS) task that extracts sentences from the thread to generate a summary. To formally define our problem, we give the definition of the task of Web Forum Thread Summarization(WFTS):

DEFINITION 3 (WEB FORUM THREAD SUMMARIZATION). *For one thread with $|S|$ sentences $\{s_1, s_2, ..., s_{|S|}\}$, the task of Web Forum Thread Summarization(WFTS) aims to generate a brief statement of the whole thread by extracting Lim significant sentences from all posts, where Lim is a threshold of the summary size.*

An intuitive way to solve WFTS task is just transfer traditional document-summarization methods to the WFTS task. However, existence of multiple dynamic topics and the short-text nature in each post obstruct this transformation process. As we have mentioned previously, *topic dependencies*, *topic drifting* and *text sparseness* are three main challenges in WFTS process. To handle the three challenges, using a dynamic way to track all topics seems to be a reasonable solution. Thus, in this paper we employ a dynamic topic model, efficient in track topics among complicated documents, to model each thread in web forums.

3. THREAD TOPIC MODELING

Based on the reply relations among posts, we extract the reply-relation tree (RRT) structure to represent each thread, intuitively.

DEFINITION 4 (REPLY-RELATION TREE). *The built-in structure of a thread can be represented by a tree (r, V, E), where r is the root post and V refers to the set of posts in the thread. $\forall u, v \in V$, $\langle u, v\rangle \in E$ iff post v replies post u.*

For our modeling task, thread in web forums is a kind of ongoing document. If we handle all posts as a whole collection, every time to generate the summary would have to re-train the whole model. Thus a trade-off agglomeration process [7] is employed here to merge those short posts submitted close in time. At last, RRT$= (r, V, E)$ is transformed into a graph structure as RRG(reply-relation graph)$= (s, \widehat{V}, \widehat{E})$, which is defined below.

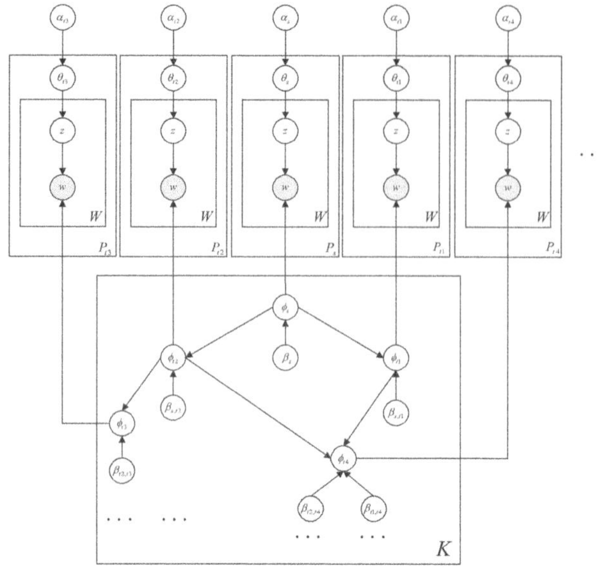

Figure 1: Graph model representation for Posts Propagation

DEFINITION 5 (REPLY-RELATION GRAPH). *A RRG$= (s, \widehat{V}, \widehat{E})$is a directed network derived from a RRT$= (r, V, E)$, where s is a source node with in-degree is 0 and $r \in s$. $\widehat{V}$ and $\widehat{E}$ are the node set and edge set of RRG respectively. $\forall t \in \widehat{V}$, $note(t)$ denotes a nodes subset of V, such that, all nodes of $note(t)$ were reduced into the node in $\widehat{V}$ and labeled by t. Edge $\langle t_i, t_j\rangle \in \widehat{E}$ iff $\exists u \in t_i, \exists v \in t_j, \langle u, v\rangle \in E$ in RRT$= (r, V, E)$.*

Given the RRG$= (s, \widehat{V}, \widehat{E})$ after the agglomeration, we primarily define the following notations for each thread.

- One thread has been separated into $\left|\widehat{V}\right|$ discrete post collections
- All post collections cover the same vocabulary **W**
- All post collections share the same topic number K
- Each post collection $note(t)$ contains $|P_t|$ posts.

As we all know, the *topic dependencies* and the *topic drifting* both come with reply-relations among nodes in RRG. Thus for node t (not the source node) in RRG$= (s, \widehat{V}, \widehat{E})$, a reasonable assumption is derived that there are some semantic dependencies between t and all its predecessors in paths from t to s. Illuminated by the Dirichlet-tree distribution [2], we calculate the *topic dependencies* in node t using a product of Dirichlet distributions placed over the probabilities of each internal node on each path from source node to t. We denote this calculation as PoD process.

Given RRG$= (s, \widehat{V}, \widehat{E})$, for $note(t), t \in \widehat{V}$, dependencies ϕ_t is generated from a product of Dirichlet distribution over t's predecessors. Let $\beta_{t,t'}$ be the edge weight from node t to one of its successors t', which characterizes the contact between t and t'. E_t is the set of edges included in any path from the source node s to

t. To generate $\phi_t \sim PoD(\{\beta_{c,d}, \phi_c, \phi_d\}_{(c,d)\in E_t})$, we first draws the posterior PoD values for t's predecessors; then ϕ_t is derived from the product of posterior parameters of each edge.

To reduce another influence of the *text sparseness*, background semantic similarities is added to the PPM modeling process. As mentioned earlier, participants usually use different terms to describe the same topic. Intuitively, it will be helpful to integrate several semantic similarities into the calculation of topic dependencies. For the vocabulary in a thread, we establish a $W \times \kappa$ similarity matrix $\mathfrak{W}_{sim}$ where each row corresponds to a similarity vector including semantic similarities from κ most similar words. We obtain the semantic similarity $sim(w, w')$ between word w and w', from the WordNet:Similarity tool[1]. Thus for post collection t we rewrite the parameter $\phi_{z,t}$ over topic z:

$$\prod_{(c,d)\in E_t} \frac{\Gamma(\sum_w \Delta_{z,c,d,w})}{\prod_w \Gamma(\Delta_{z,c,d,w})} \prod_w \phi_{z,t,w}^{\sum_{(c,d)\in E_t} \Delta_{z,c,d,w}-1} \quad (1)$$

$$\Delta_{z,c,d,w} = \sum_{w'}^{\kappa} sim(w,w')\beta_{z,c,d}\widehat{\phi}_{z,c,w'}\widehat{\phi}_{z,d,w'} \quad (2)$$

Thus the calculation of PoD with $\{\beta_{c,d}, \phi_c, \phi_d\}_{(c,d)\in E_t}$ has been introduced in Equation 1. Given RRG= $(s, \widehat{V}, \widehat{E})$ after the posts agglomeration, the generative process for each post collection $note(t)$ in the PPM is as follows:

1. For the vocabulary, establish the similarity matrix $\mathfrak{W}_{sim}$
2. For each topic $z, 1 \le z \le K$: Draw

   $\phi_{z,t} \sim PoD(\{\beta_{c,d}, \phi_c, \phi_d\}_{(c,d)\in E_t}, \mathfrak{W}_{sim})$
3. For each post $p, p \in note(t)$:
   - Draw $\theta_{p,t} \sim Dir(\alpha_t)$
   - For each term index $i, 1 \le i \le W$
     - Draw $z_{i,p,t} \sim Mult(\theta_p)$
     - Draw $w_{i,p,t} \sim Mult(\phi_{z_{i,p,t},t})$

Figure 2 shows a graph model representation of the PPM, where shaded and unshaded nodes indicate observed and latent variables, respectively. For each $note(t)$ in RRG= $(s, \widehat{V}, \widehat{E})$ the posterior distribution is intractable because of the unknown relation between ϕ_t and θ_t. To find an approximate inference method, we use the Gibbs EM algorithm [12] for inference that optimizes the edge parameters $\{\beta_{c,d}\}_{(c,d)\in E_t}$ and the Dirichlet prior α_t during each sampling iteration.

4. THREAD SUMMARIZATION

For each post collection $note(t)$ in RRG= $(s, \widehat{V}, \widehat{E})$, there are two parametric matrix Θ_t and Φ_t after Gibbs EM sampling, which reflect the topic-post distribution and the word-topic distribution, respectively. *i.e* $P(z|p) = \theta_{z,p}; P(w|z_t) = \phi_{z,t,w}$. Based on these distributions, a naive summarization method is proposed as the basic algorithm. Then we introduce the markov random walk(MRW) strategy and the mutual reinforcement effect between posts and sentences to our WFTS process.

[1]http://www.cogs.susx.ac.uk/users/drh21

4.1 Basic Algorithm

We can calculate the probability of each topic by summing and normalizing mixture components over topics for all of posts in the thread. By assuming that each post's generation is assigned the same probability, we have:

$$P(z) = \sum_p P(z|p)P(p) = \sum_p \frac{P(z|p)}{|V|} \quad (3)$$

where $|V|$ is the amount of all posts. Equation (3) actually indicates the synthetic salience of topic z all over the dynamic conversation. Meanwhile, we assume that each sentence is generated by a mixture of topics. Thus given sentence s_j, we have:

$$P(s_j) = \sum_z P(s_j|z)P(z) = \prod_{w\in s_j} \sum_z P(w|z)^{n(w)}P(z) \quad (4)$$

where $P(z)$ is derived from Equation (3), and $n(w)$ reflects the term-frequency of w in sentence s_j. Based on Equation (4), each sentence's probability in the thread is assigned. We rank the sentences by the value of probabilities from Equation (4).

4.2 Topic-sensitive Random Walks

The basic algorithm is a little unrealistic that each post's generation is assigned the same probability $1/|V|$. Illuminated by the idea of the Topic-sensitive PageRank [4], we utilize a new WFTS method with the markov random walks(MRW), where each sentence is scored by the "votes" from other sentences based on an complete weighted undirected graph.

Formally, let $G_S = (S, E_S)$ be the complete undirected graph with S nodes and E_S edges, where there are $|S|$ sentences in the thread and each edge $(s_i, s_j) \in E_S$ has an affinity weight that reflects the similarity between sentence s_i and $s_j, i \neq j$. After topic modeling, each sentence s has the topical feature vector $D_{s,z} = \{P(w|z,s)\}_{w=1}^{W}$, that:

$$P(w|z,s) = \begin{cases} \phi_{z,t,w} & w \in s \\ sim(w,w') \cdot \phi_{z,t,w} & w' \in s \\ 0 & else \end{cases} \quad (5)$$

where we utilize the $\mathfrak{W}_{sim}$ to reduce the sparsity when $sim(w, w') \in \mathfrak{W}_{w'}$. Using the Jensen-Shannon Divergence between $D_{s_i,z}$ and $D_{s_j,z}$, the topical divergence is given:

$$Di_{JS}(s_i, s_j, z) = \frac{1}{2}\left(KL(D_{s_i,z} \| M) + KL(D_{s_j,z} \| M)\right) \quad (6)$$

where M is the average of the two probability vectors, $KL(D \| M)$ is the Kullback-Leibler Divergence.The divergence is transformed into similarity measure by:

$$sim(s_i, s_j) = \frac{1}{K} \sum_z 10^{-\delta Di_{JS}(s_i,s_j,z)} \quad (7)$$

So we have the affinity matrix SIM for all S sentences, $SIM_{i,j} = sim(s_i, s_j)$. After the row-normalization for SIM, transition probability matrix $\widehat{SIM}$ is built that each row $\left\|\widehat{SIM}_i\right\|_1 = 1$. Adding smoothing vector $1/|S|$, salience score $Sco(s_j)$ for each sentence s_j is deduced by:

$$Sco(s_i) = \mu \sum_{i\neq j} \widehat{sim}(s_i, s_j) \cdot Sco(s_j) + \frac{(1-\mu)}{|S|} \quad (8)$$

where μ is the damping factor usually set to 0.85 as in PageRank algorithm. The salience score vector Sco for all sentences are set to 1 at the iteration beginning. Usually the convergence of the iteration algorithm is achieved when the difference between the scores computed at two successive iterations for any sentences falls below a given threshold. Sentences are ranked according to their salience scores converged in Sco.

4.3 Post's Influence to Summarization

All of the naive scoring and the MRW-based scoring ignore the effect of the posts to sentences' salience. Intuitively, a post is important if (1) it includes the important sentences; (2) it associates to other important posts. On the other hand, a sentence is important if (1) it appears in an important post; (2) it associates to the other important sentences. Thereby, mutual reinforcement(MR) [16, 15] between sentences and posts is employed to calculate the salience of sentences based on the MRW-based scoring procedure.

Let Pco denote salience scores for all posts in the thread, we construct the salience score vector $Rco = [Pco, Sco]^T$ for the MR framework. Each post p can be represented in the form of: (1) a vector of post-topic distributions $D_p = \{P(z|p)\}_{z=1}^{K}$; (2) a $K \times W$ matrix KW where item $KW_{i,j}$ denotes the topic-word distribution $P(w_j|z_i,p)$. $P(w_j|z_i,p)$ is defined similarly from Equation (5). The first representation is used for the post to post affinity calculation whereas the second is used for the affinities between posts and sentences. In the MR framework, the key problem is to construct the blocking matrix PSM including the affinities among objects (sentences and posts).

$$PSM = \begin{bmatrix} PIM & PS \\ SP & SIM \end{bmatrix} \tag{9}$$

where PIM denotes the post-post affinity matrix. Item $PIM_{i,j}$ reflects the similarity measure between post p_i and post p_j:

$$\begin{aligned} PIM_{i,j} &= sim(p_i, p_j) = 10^{-\delta Di_{JS}(p_i,p_j)} \\ Di_{JS}(p_i,p_j) &= \frac{1}{2}\left(KL(D_{p_i}\|M) + KL(D_{p_j}\|M)\right) \end{aligned} \tag{10}$$

Meanwhile, both affinity matrices PS and its transposed matrix of SP reflect the similarities between posts and sentences. For each item (i,j) in PS, we have:

$$PS_{i,j} = sim(p_i, s_j) = \frac{1}{K}\sum_{z} 10^{-\delta Di_{JS}(p_i,s_j,z)} \tag{11}$$

After the row-normalization for the block matrix PSM, the ranking of posts and sentences can be iteratively derived from the MR framework by:

$$\overrightarrow{Rco}^{(k+1)} = \mu PSM \cdot \overrightarrow{Rco}^{(k)} + \frac{(1-\mu)}{|V+S|} \tag{12}$$

The ranking process of the Equation (12) is the same way with the Equation (8) in section 4.2. After achieving the convergence of the iteration, both posts and sentences in the thread have been ranked by the salience scores Rco.

For summary extraction, we establish a greedy algorithm to detect the semantic orthogonality among summary sentences. Given selected sentences set S_s and the current candidate sentence s in one step of extraction, s will not be selected unless the maximal semantic similarity between s and S_s, calculated by Equation (7), is below one threshold.

5. EXPERIMENT DESIGN

5.1 Data Set and Evaluation Metric

A new data set is opt to be created because there is no existing benchmark data set for evaluating the WFTS task. In this paper, Apple Discussion[2] and Slashdot[3] are used as our data sources. We obtained threads from our two data sources with the limitation that each thread has no less than 5 posts. To evaluate our summary method performances with different thread volume, we classify threads into 4 different thread volume intervals. Since 15 posts constitute one web page in Apple Discussion, we set intervals as $[5,15]$, $[16,30]$, $[31,45]$ and $[46,\infty]$, with the limitation that the amount of threads in each interval is equal. 100 threads (50 from Apple and 50 from Slashdot) on each interval are crawled respectively.

To generate the evaluation references, 4 human assessors were asked to summarize the content individually. The final evaluation score for a WFTS strategy is on average of all scores using each referenced summary. We use ROUGE toolkit[4] to measure our proposed WFTS methods. ROUGE-1 (Recall against unigram), ROUGE-2 (Recall against bigram), and ROUGE-L (Recall against longest common subsequence) are chosen for the WFTS performance measure. In the ROUGE settings we use Porter Stemming algorithm to stem the words to their root form.

5.2 Experimental Results

5.2.1 *Strategy Selection*

In section 3, we agglomerate posts from RRT= (r, V, E) structure into RRG= $(s, \widehat{V}, \widehat{E})$ structure. To identify how this strategy enhance the summarization performance by reducing the *text sparseness* during the PPM process, we compare the results of the PPM-based WFTS using posts agglomeration with the one that ignores the posts agglomeration. Based on the PPM, we denote PPM-S as the basic algorithm in section 4.1, PPM-ST as the topic-sensitive MRW-based method in section 4.2, and PPM-STP as the MR-based ranking method using mutual reinforcement in section 4.3. These methods are measured in terms of ROUGE metrics for 200 summary length when stop-words are kept.

Table 2 presents us performances with and without the posts agglomeration. We can find for each WFTS algorithm the results after merging posts outperform results without posts agglomeration. The difference is obvious so that it is easy to conclude the posts agglomeration is worthwhile even though this may generate a little information loss for reply-relations. As shown in Table 2, both PPM-STP and PPM-ST are able to produce better results than PPM-S that seems a little naive for WFTS calculation. However, the tradeoff between the low complexity cost and competitive ROUGE performances make PPM-S still valuable in practice.

5.2.2 *Overall Performance*

Several baselines, including both methods using other topic models and some effective algorithms in the field of document summarization [3, 17, 10], are introduced for comparison. Among the topic models, we choose **Latent Dirichlet Allocation** (LDA) and **Dynamic Mixture Models** (DMMs) as comparisons. All we proposed WFTS algorithms in section 4 are based on topic models, thus we compare different performances between the PPM and these models using the MR-based WFTS algorithm in section 4.3.

---

[2]http://discussions.info.apple.com
[3]http://slashdot.org
[4]version 1.5.5 is used here

Table 1: Overall summarization results in terms of ROUGE

Stop-word Kept								
Length	Constraint Set	PPM-STP	DMMs	LDA	HIERSUM	ST-C	MEAD	NIST-B
200	ROUGE-1	**0.4695**	0.4629	0.4606	0.4516	0.4176	0.4172	0.3753
	ROUGE-2	**0.1742**	0.1712	0.1701	0.1714	0.1339	0.1384	0.1021
	ROUGE-L	**0.4134**	0.4119	0.4062	0.4074	0.3723	0.3661	0.3338
400	ROUGE-1	**0.5133**	0.5012	0.4907	0.5006	0.4623	0.4556	0.4372
	ROUGE-2	**0.2266**	0.2156	0.2027	0.2069	0.1882	0.1891	0.1584
	ROUGE-L	**0.4653**	0.4517	0.4426	0.4462	0.4271	0.4055	0.3983
Stop-word Removed								
Length	Constraint Set	PPM-STP	DMMs	LDA	HIERSUM	ST-C	MEAD	NIST-B
200	ROUGE-1	**0.3605**	0.3587	0.3422	0.3581	0.323	0.3256	0.3017
	ROUGE-2	**0.1682**	0.1634	0.1574	0.1602	0.1486	0.1489	0.1269
	ROUGE-L	**0.3214**	0.3206	0.3103	0.3126	0.2925	0.2901	0.2767
400	ROUGE-1	**0.4112**	0.3918	0.3871	0.3910	0.3742	0.3667	0.3591
	ROUGE-2	**0.2053**	0.1916	0.1914	0.2015	0.1804	0.1833	0.1665
	ROUGE-L	**0.3641**	0.3472	0.3378	0.3511	0.3297	0.3172	0.3082

Table 2: Post-merging's influence for WFTS

WFTS Algorithms	ROUGE-1	ROUGE-2	ROUGE-L
Without Post-Merging			
PPM-S	0.4072	0.1622	0.3587
PPM-ST	0.4175	0.1648	0.3604
PPM-STP	0.4282	0.1681	0.3821
After Post-Merging			
PPM-S	0.4582	0.1731	0.4052
PPM-ST	0.4594	0.1741	0.4082
PPM-STP	**0.4695**	**0.1742**	**0.4134**

For all 400 threads, we calculate results of all baselines in terms of ROUGE-1, ROUGE-2 and ROUGE-L using 2 methods, keeping stop-words and removing stop-words. For each method, we evaluated performances for 200 and 400 length summary. As shown in Table 1, PPM-STP results in obvious improvements over the others: For 200 length summary, PPM-STP achieves an increase of 1.9%, 2.4% and 1.8% over LDA in terms of ROUGE-1, ROUGE-2 and ROUGE-L respectively. For 400 length summary, PPM-STP gives an increase of 4.6%, 11.8% and 5.1% over LDA when stop-words are kept. We further compare PPM with the WFTS using DMMs. By and large, for 200 length summary PPM-STP offers relative performance improvements of 1.4%, 1.8% and 0.4%, respectively, in the ROUGE-1, ROUGE-2 and ROUGE-L measures as compared to the DMMs; while the relative improvements are 2.4%, 5.1% and 3.0% in the same measurements for 400 length summary case. Thus although only slight improvement happens when the summarization length is relatively small, dissimilarities between PPM and DMMs rises with the increase of the summary length. A natural explanation to the fact is Dynamic Mixture Models (DMMs) cannot capture reply-relations existing in each thread.

5.2.3 *Impact of Thread Volume to Results*

To precisely illustrate the performances for various thread volume, the impact of the thread volume is evaluated in Figure 7 by comparisons of WFTS performances on each interval respectively. In Figure 7, (a) and (b) illustrate the ROUGE-1 and ROUGE-2 scores for 200 length summary whereas (c) and (d) reflect the ROUGE metrics for 400 length summary. In Figure 7(a) and (c), PPM, DMMs and LDA have similar performances in terms of ROUGE-1 when posts number ≤ 15. However, with the increase of thread volume, ROUGE-1 from the LDA and DMMs decreases rapidly while the PPM keep relatively stable. Shown by Figure 7(b) and (d), PPM has obviously better performance in terms of ROUGE-2 than others for each interval. All these improvements reflect the effectiveness for the thread summarization task to capture the reply-relations in each thread.

5.2.4 *Impact of the Factor κ to Results*

In section 3, given each thread's vacabulary W we establish a $W \times \kappa$ matrix including the background semantic similarities between each word and its top κ most similar words. The larger κ, the more dependencies for one word propagated from other similar words. Figure 8 (a) to (c) shows the ROUGE-1, ROUGE-2 and ROUGE-L curves for different WFTS strategies under the PPM, respectively. As shown in Figure 8, when κ is greater than 1, better performances are observed for both PPM-based strategies. This can suggest that semantic similarities among words improve the performance of each PPM-based WFTS strategy. Meanwhile, we can observe that each metrics (ROUGE-1, ROUGE-2 and ROUGE-L) keeps on increasing till the κ comes to 6, after that value curves for the PPM-based methods begin to decline.

6. CONCLUSION

In this paper, we propose the task of Web Forum Thread Summarization (WFTS) to help people understand the thread in web forums rapidly. Web Forum Thread Summarization works by extracting a group of sentences from all posts in one thread to constitute the summary. Based on a hierarchical Bayesian model that track all dynamic topics through the threaded discussion, we employ the markov random walk strategy and the mutual reinforcement to the sentence scoring progressively. Final summary is generated from a greedy sentence extraction process that keep the semantics orthogonality. In experiments, we establish our data set from popular web forums and verify the effectiveness of our WFTS strategies, which give us remarkable performances comparing with other effective baselines.

7. ACKNOWLEDGEMENT

This work is supported by the Natural Science Foundation of China (60970047, 60903108), IIFSDU (2009TB016) and the Natural Science Foundation of Shandong Province (Y2008G19).

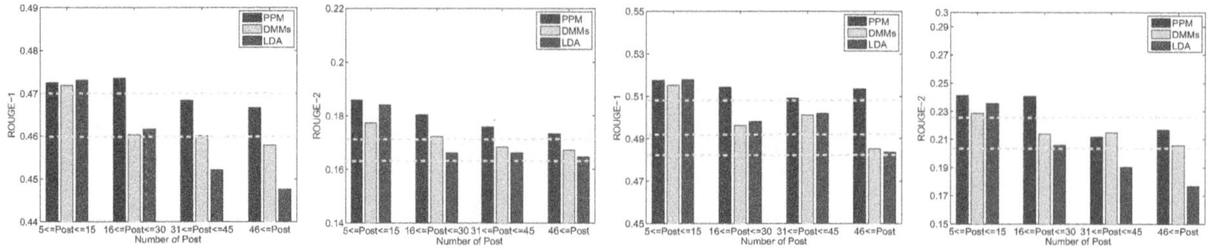

(a) ROUGE-1, Length=200 (b) ROUGE-2, Length=200 (c) ROUGE-1, Length=400 (d) ROUGE-2, Length=400

Figure 2: Performances of methods using topic models on 4 volume intervals in terms of ROUGE metrics

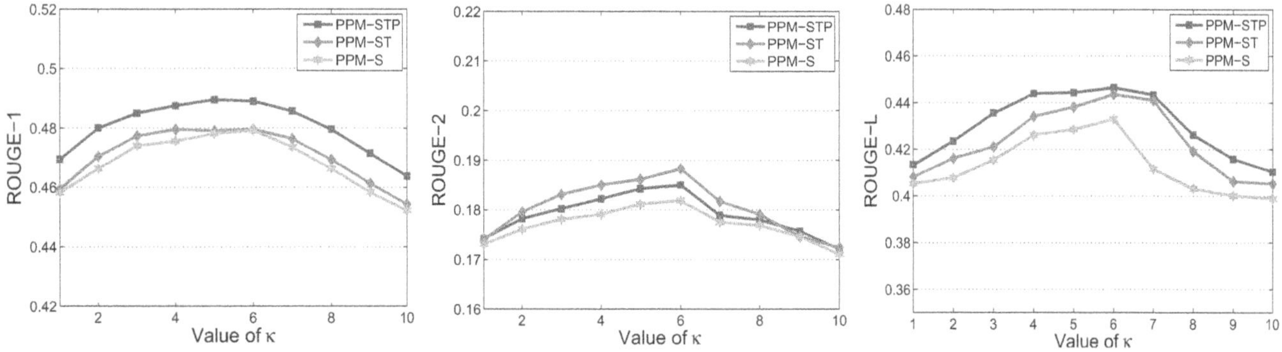

(a) ROUGE-1 (b) ROUGE-2 (c) ROUGE-L

Figure 3: Impact of κ in terms of ROUGE metrics for 200 length summary

8. REFERENCES

[1] D. Blei and J. Lafferty. Dynamic topic models. In *ICML*, 2006.

[2] S. Dennis. On the hyper-Dirichlet type 1 and hyper-Liouville distributions. *Communications in Statistics-Theory and Methods*, 1991.

[3] A. Haghighi and L. Vanderwende. Exploring content models for multi-document summarization. In *HLT-ACL*, 2009.

[4] T. Haveliwala. Topic-sensitive pagerank: A context-sensitive ranking algorithm for web search. *IEEE Transactions on Knowledge and Data Engineering*, 2003.

[5] X. Hu, N. Sun, C. Zhang, and T. Chua. Exploiting internal and external semantics for the clustering of short texts using world knowledge. In *CIKM*, 2009.

[6] T. Iwata, S. Watanabe, T. Yamada, and N. Ueda. Topic tracking model for analyzing consumer purchase behavior. In *IJCAI*, 2009.

[7] A. Jain, M. Murty, and P. Flynn. Data clustering: a review. *ACM computing surveys*, 1999.

[8] C. Lin, J. Yang, R. Cai, X. Wang, and W. Wang. Simultaneously modeling semantics and structure of threaded discussions: a sparse coding approach and its applications. In *SIGIR*, 2009.

[9] Y. Liu, A. Niculescu-Mizil, and W. Gryc. Topic-link LDA: joint models of topic and author community. In *ICML*, 2009.

[10] D. Radev, H. Jing, M. Sty, and D. Tam. Centroid-based summarization of multiple documents. *Information Processing & Management*, 2004.

[11] Z. Ren, J. Ma, G. Wang, C. Cui, and X. Han. Dynamically modeling semantic dependencies in web forum threads. In *WI-IAT*, 2011.

[12] H. Wallach. Topic modeling: beyond bag-of-words. In *ICML*, 2006.

[13] C. Wang, D. Blei, and D. Heckerman. Continuous time dynamic topic models. In *UAI*, 2008.

[14] X. Wang and A. McCallum. Topics over time: a non-markov continuous-time model of topical trends. In *SIGKDD*, 2006.

[15] F. Wei, W. Li, Q. Lu, and Y. He. Query-sensitive mutual reinforcement chain and its application in query-oriented multi-document summarization. In *SIGIR*, 2008.

[16] H. Zha. Generic summarization and keyphrase extraction using mutual reinforcement principle and sentence clustering. In *SIGIR*, 2002.

[17] L. Zhou and E. Hovy. Digesting virtual geek culture: The summarization of technical internet relay chats. In *ACL*, 2005.

Cloning for Privacy Protection in Multiple Independent Data Publications

Muzammil M. Baig, Jiuyong Li, Jixue Liu
School of Computer and Information Science
University of South Australia, Mawson Lakes, SA. 5095 Australia
{muzammil.baig, jiuyong.li, jixue.liu}@unisa.edu.au

Hua Wang
Department of Maths and Computing
University of Southern Queensland, Toowoomba, Queensland, 4350 Australia.
wang@usq.edu.au

ABSTRACT

Data anonymization has become a major technique in privacy preserving data publishing. Many methods have been proposed to anonymize one dataset and a series of datasets of a data owner. However, no method has been proposed for the anonymization of data of multiple independent data publications. A data owner publishes a dataset, which contains overlapping population with other datasets published by other independent data owners. In this paper we analyze the privacy risk in the such scenario and vulnerability of partitioned based anonymization methods. We show that no partitioned based anonymization methods can protect privacy in arbitrary data distributions, and identify a case that the privacy can be protected in the scenario. We propose a new generalization principle ϵ-cloning to protect privacy for multiple independent data publications. We also develop an effective algorithm to achieve the ϵ-cloning. We experimentally show that the proposed algorithm anonymizes data to satisfy the privacy requirement and preserves good data utility.

Categories and Subject Descriptors

H.2.0 [**Database Management**]: General

General Terms

Security, Integrity, Protection

1. INTRODUCTION

Private individual-specific information such as customer data, employee data etc. are maintained and shared for various purposes. The advantages of such sharing are well documented but in the recent past several instances of data privacy breaches [2], due to data sharing, have resulted in financial and reputational losses for enterprises. Partition-based privacy preserving data publishing techniques address this problem by anonymizing data such that individual privacy is preserved when data is shared or released. The basic idea behind these techniques is *one-in-crowd* which guarantees that an individual cannot be distinguished from a minimum number of other people. Partition-based anonymization techniques are widely discussed in literature and well known schemes include k-anonymity [25], (α,k)-anonymity [28], ℓ-diversity [20], t-closeness [19] and anatomy [32]. Existing partition-based techniques focus on one-time publication [25, 20], multiple views of the same data [35, 34]; and the series of datasets by single data owner [29, 10, 31]. Multiple data publications are restricted to single owner, and does not support privacy preserving data publications of overlapping records by multiple publishers. Ganta et al. [11] firstly identified the privacy breach of overlapping population within multiple published datasets, and called this privacy breach *composition attack*. However, the solution of [11] supports only *interactive setting* (where only data statistics and/or query results are released), and is inapplicable for *non-interactive setting* (where the data is published after anonymization). Privacy preserving data anonymization against known and unknown overlapping population remains an open problem. To the best of our knowledge no solution exists for these scenarios.

	Hospital-1	Hospital-2	Hospital-3
Nancy	•	•	
David	•		•
Eliza		•	•

Figure 1: Full overlapping scenario among three hospitals

Before we illustrate the problem, firstly let us consider patient overlapping scenario of three hospitals in Figure 1. There are three overlapping patients i.e. Nancy, David and Eliza. Nancy has visited Hospitals 1 and 2, Eliza, has visited the Hospitals 2 and 3 and David has visited the Hospitals 1 and 3. All hospitals independently anonymize their datasets and are unaware of their overlapping records with other hospitals.

Table 1(a) is the original data of Hospital-1, which has three type of attributes. *Identifier attributes* can directly identify individuals, such as Name, SSN etc. They should be removed in a published dataset. *Quasi identifier (QI) attributes* could indirectly lead to the identification of individuals in a dataset, such as Age, Zipcode and Sex etc. They are normally generalized so that no individuals are identifiable in a generalized dataset. The *Sensitive attribute* contains the private information about the individuals that needs to be protected such as Disease, Income etc. There is another type of attribute called *non-sensitive attribute*, which do not fall under aforementioned types but is useful for some data analysis. In our case, we do not consider them since they are unrelated to

CIKM'11, October 24–28, 2011, Glasgow, Scotland, UK.

Table 1: Hospital-1

(a) Original Table

<Marry, 15, F> C
<Vince, 18, M> C
<Rabi, 25, F> D
<Nana, 30, F> D
<Nancy, 50, F>D
<Bob, 23, M> G
<Steve, 40, M> G
<David, 15, M>J
<Paul, 35, M> J

(b) 4-anonymous release

Age	Sex	Disease
15 – 40	M	C (1) G (2) J (2)
15 – 50	F	C (1) D (3)

(c) Privacy clone release

Age	Sex	Disease
15 – 50	*	J (2) G (2) C (2) D (3)

(d) ϵ-clone release with micro-statistics

Age	Sex	Disease
~19 15 – 25	M (2) F (2)	C (1) D (1) G (1) J (1)
~35 18 – 50	M (3) F (2)	C (1) D (2) G (1) J (1)

Table 2: Hospital-2

(a) Original Table

<Alex, 15, M > A
<Mary, 22, F > A
<Tom, 38, M > A
<Linda, 10, F> D
<Khan, 18, M> D
<Nancy, 50, F> D
<Andy, 25, M> G
<Eliza, 30, F> G
<Maxi, 45, F> G
<Hussy, 23, M> J
<Tina, 35, F> J
<Paul, 35, M> J

(b) 6-anonymous release

Age	Sex	Disease
10 – 38	M	A (2) D (1) G (1) J (2)
10 – 50	F	A (1) D (2) G (2) J (1)

(c) Privacy clone release

Age	Sex	Disease
10 – 50	*	D (3) J (3) A (3) G (3)

(d) ϵ-clone release with micro-statistics

Age	Sex	Disease
~19 19 – 23 (2)	M (4) F (2)	A (2) D (2) G (1) J (1)
10 – 25		
~39 35 – 39 (2)	M (2) F (4)	A (1) D (1) G (2) J (2)
30 – 50		

data anonymization. A *generalized* table is considered privacy preserved, if it satisfies a privacy requirement, such as k-anonymity [25], (α,k)-anonymity [28], ℓ-diversity [20], t-closeness [19] etc. Hospital-1 releases Table 1(b) as a 4-*anonymous* and 2-*diverse* version of the original Table 1(a). 4-anonymity means that values in the quasi-identifier have at least 4 identical copies. So one could not be distinguished from other 3 records. Such a group is called an *equivalence class* (formal definition in Section 4). 2-diversity means that each of such a group has at least 2 distinct values in the sensitive attribute. So the sensitive value of each individual could not be inferred with a high confidence.

2. PROBLEM DESCRIPTION AND MOTIVATION

All existing partition-based privacy preserving data publishing techniques, such as [20, 32, 33, 19, 22, 6, 16, 26, 14, 30] focus on forming equivalence classes (also called partitions or QI groups) based upon some generalization principles. To illustrate the problem, let us assume that Hospital-2 releases Table 2(b) as a 6-anonymous and 3-diverse version of the original Table 2(a) and Hospital-3 releases Table 3(b) as 4-anonymous and 3-diverse version of the original Table 3(a). The Nancy's equivalence class in Table 1(b) (Hospital-1's anonymous release) and in Table 2(b) (Hospital-2's anonymous release) has only 1 common sensitive value i.e. $\{D\}$. So an adversary knowing the QIs of Nancy (50 years old female) and the fact she has visited two hospitals can derive her sensitive value from both tables. Such utilization of more than one individually anonymized datasets to infer the privacy of overlapping individual(s) is called a 'composition attack' [11]. Using the composition attack adversary can get the diseases of David and Eliza in Tables 1(b), 3(b) and Tables 2(b), 3(b) respectively.

Individually all three anonymous datasets, Table 1(b), Table 2(b) and Table 3(b) pose low privacy risk but collectively compromise the privacy of overlapping patients due to the composition attack [11, 3]. In other words independently anonymized datasets do not retain the privacy properties under the composition attack. Note that there are other possible generalized tables of original tables too. However, they suffer the same type of privacy disclosures.

Our method proposed in this paper leads to the publication of Table 1(d), 2(d) and 3(c). Specifically, each equivalence class of these tables contains all the sensitive values of its respective original dataset. Moreover, unlike a definite QI range (as done in previous releases of these tables), each equivalence class of Table 1(d), 2(d) and 3(c) has *micro-statistics* values (to be discussed in detail in Section 6). The purpose of releasing such statistics is for better privacy preserving and retaining statistical properties.

Let adversary now attempt to infer the diseases of Nancy, David and Eliza from Table 1(d), 2(d) and 3(c). The adversary can locate that the equivalence classes of Nancy has 3, and David/Eliza have 2 sensitive values common i.e. $\{D,G,J\}$ and $\{G,J\}$ respectively. Therefore adversary cannot get a specific disease that Nancy, David or Eliza has contracted.

One straightforward approach that can tackle the composition attack is trivial sanitizer [4] which simply suppresses all quasi-identifiers (QIs) or all sensitive attributes and publish all *non-sensitive* attributes intact. In our case, such sanitization makes data less useful since all information of QIs and sensitive value is lost. Our motivation is to achieve privacy against composition attack and also to maintain, as much as possible, the high data utility of anonymous releases.

Table 3: Hospital-3

(a) Original Table

	Name	Age	Sex	Marital Status	Disease
David	t_1	**15**	**M**	**Never-married**	**J**
	t_2	18	F	Never-married	J
	t_3	25	M	CIV-spouse	J
	t_4	35	F	AF-spouse	J
	t_5	38	M	Divorced	J
	t_6	10	M	Never-married	B
	t_7	18	M	Never-married	B
	t_8	20	M	Never-married	B
	t_9	25	F	Never-married	B
	t_{10}	30	F	Separated	B
	t_{11}	35	F	Divorced	B
	t_{12}	45	M	Separated	B
	t_{13}	20	M	AF-spouse	G
Eliza	t_{14}	**30**	**F**	**CIV-spouse**	**G**
	t_{15}	40	F	CIV-spouse	G
	t_{16}	10	F	Never-married	L
	t_{17}	17	F	Never-married	L
	t_{18}	22	M	Separated	L
	t_{19}	28	F	Widowed	L

(b) 4-anonymous release

Age	Sex	Marital Status	Disease
10 – 18	*	Never-married	B (2) J (2) L (1)
17 – 25	*	*	B (2) J (1) L (1)
20 – 40	*	*	B (1) G (2) L (1)
25 – 28	*	*	B (1) J (2) L (1)

(c) ϵ-clone release with micro-statistics

Age	Sex	Marital Status	Disease
~15 14 – 16 (1)	M (3)	AF-spouse (1) Never-married (2)	G (1) J (2) B (2) L (1)
~21 19 – 21 (1)	M (2) F (1)	Never-married (2) CIV-spouse (1)	
10 – 20			
~22 18 – 22 (1)	M (1) F (2)	CIV-spouse (1) Never-married (2)	G (1) J (2) B (2) L (1)
~27 25 – 27 (1)	M (1) F (2)	Separated (1) AF-spouse (1) Never-married (1)	
18 – 35			
~38 37 – 39 (1)	M (1) F (2)	CIV-spouse (1) Divorced (2)	G (1) J (2) B (2) L (1)
~29 28 – 28 (1)	F (2) * (1)	Widowed (1) * (1) Separated (1)	
28 – 40			

3. CONTRIBUTIONS

The problem of overlapping data publications is not resolvable by the methods of sequential data publishing, such as [29, 31, 10] and multiple views of the same dataset [34, 35]. Both, sequential data and multiple view, deals with two overlapping data publications of the same data owner. The data owner *knows* the previously released data/view(s) of the dataset and *uses* these data/view(s) during the anonymization process of the next publication. In our scenario of multiple publications, a publisher is *unaware* of other datasets that have overlapping records with it. Therefore, methods of sequential and multiple view data publication are inapplicable to multiple independent data publications. The sequential/multiple views inference is between the two different releases of same location; whereas the composition attack works between the independent releases of mutually unknown locations.

Firstly, In this paper we analyze the privacy risk in multiple independent data publications situations and vulnerability of partition based anonymization methods in such an environment. We show that no partition based anonymization methods can protect privacy in arbitrary data distributions, and identify a case that the privacy can be protected in.

Secondly, this paper proposes a multiple data publications model to protect a dataset from the composition attack when different locations independently release the anonymous data of overlapping population. The core of our solution is the integration of two novel concepts: *ϵ-cloning* and *micro-statistics based anonymization.* The former is a new model, whose satisfaction ensures the association of a tuple with all sensitive values of data; hence providing the maximum privacy protection. The latter is an anonymization technique that facilitates the implementation of ϵ-cloning.

4. BASIC DEFINITIONS

Let P be a dataset maintained by a publisher. There are n other publishers which have overlapping subset with P. We assume that all n publishers and their published datasets are unknown to the publisher of P. Each published dataset Q_i^* ($i \in 1,2,3, \ldots, n$) is independently anonymized from its original dataset Q_i.

We classify the columns of P and Q_i into three types (already explained in Section 1): **(i)** an identifier attribute A^{id}, which is the primary key of P and Q_i, **(ii)** the d quasi-identifier (QI) attributes $A_1^{qi}, A_2^{qi}, \ldots, A_d^{qi}$, and **(iii)** a sensitive attribute S. The QI attributes can be either numerical or categorical. For each tuple $t \in P$, $t[A]$ denotes its value on attribute A.

Definition 1 (Generalized QI group / Equivalence class) *For anonymous dataset P^*, an equivalence class (E) is set of the tuples in P^* with the same values in QI attributes. Each equivalence class is assigned an ID A^g.*

For a tuple $t \in P^*$; we refer $t.E$ as the **hosting equivalence class** of the tuple t in P^*. When the publisher P releases P^*, the adversary can use P^* and any Q_i^* to intrude the privacy of overlapping subset by the composition attack. To formalize the attack, we first introduce a notation $O(P^*, Q_i^*)$.

Definition 2 (Overlapping set) *Let publisher P releases P^*, anonymous version of P, for each independent release Q_i^* ($i \in 1,2,3 \ldots, n$) the overlapping set $O(P^*, Q_i^*)$ contains all those tuples in P^* and Q_i^* such that:*

$$O(P^*, Q_i^*) = \bigcup_{i=1}^{n} (P^* \cap Q_i^*) \;\; (i \in 1, 2, 3 \ldots, n)$$

Each tuple in $O(P^*, Q_i^*)$ is an intersection (to be explained) of two corresponding tuples $t_i \in Q_i^*$ and $t \in P^*$; which satisfy the following requirements:

1. *$t[S] = t_i[S]$; both tuples have the same sensitive value*
2. *$\forall_j : t[A_j^{qi}] \cap t_i[A_j^{qi}] \neq \emptyset$; t and t_i have overlapping value intervals in every QI attribute.*

For two value intervals (or values), the intersection returns the overlapping range of two intervals. For example, for age QI intervals (15–25) $\cap$ (20–30) = (20–25). For categorical QI values in generalization taxonomies, the intersection returns the most specific QI value of two QI values if the one is a generalization of another otherwise returns $\emptyset$. For example, for sex QI values ($* \cap male = male$), ($* \cap female = female$) and ($female \cap male = \emptyset$); '$*$' corresponds to the most generalized QI value in any generalization hierarchy. In sex QI generalization hierarchy, '$*$' presents both $male$ and $female$.

Assume that a tuple t occurs in two generalized tables P^* and Q_i^*. As per Definition 2, tuple $t \in O(P^*, Q_i^*)$ and it has two corresponding tuples; each in P^* and Q_i^*. The probability for inferring the sensitive value of overlapping tuple t from tables P^* and Q_i^* is $\text{prob}(t[S] \mid (P^*, Q_i^*))$:

$$\text{prob}\left(t[S] | (P^*, Q_i^*)\right) = \text{prob}\left(t[S] | O(P^*, Q_i^*)\right) \quad (1)$$

Equation (1) reveals the reason of the failure of partition based generalization schemes like k-anonymity [25] , ℓ-diversity [20], t-closeness [19] etc. for the composition attack . After proper anonymization, the corresponding generalized tuples of overlapping tuple t are protected in each of P^* and Q_i^*. However, composition attack inference has nothing to do with their respective individual probabilities in P^* and Q_i^*. Composition attack inference is only determined by their overlapping set $O(P^*, Q_i^*)$. An overlapping set $O(P^*, Q_i^*)$ may not satisfy either generalization scheme of individual anonymized datasets. In the worst case:

$$\text{prob}\left(t[S] | O(P^*, Q_i^*)\right) = 1 \quad (2)$$

The worst case (2) occurs when only one record in $O(P^*, Q_i^*)$ matches overlapping tuple t or all tuples have the same sensitive value.

Example 1. Let t = <Nancy, 50, F, D> and Q_1^* and P^* as Table 1(b) and 2(b) respectively. The overlapping set $O(P^*, Q_1^*)$ contains the tuple <15–50, F, D>. So the probability for inferring the true sensitive value of Nancy from tables Q_1^* and P^* is $\text{prob}\left(t[S] \mid O(P^*, Q_1^*)\right) = 1$. All matching records in $O(P^*, Q_1^*)$ have the same sensitive value.

5. PRIVACY PRESERVING IN MULTIPLE INDEPENDENT PUBLISHING

In the previous section, we have shown that the privacy of an individual in the overlapping dataset can be inferred with 100% accuracy. Now we discuss when we can prevent such inference and how to do it.

We start with the inference of the probabilities of sensitive values shared by two different datasets with overlapping **QI** values. Let S be a set of all possible sensitive values of two datasets D_1 and D_2. Let $f_{D_1}(s)$ be the frequency of sensitive values in dataset D_1 and $f_{D_2}(s)$ for D_2. Note when a sensitive value, say s_j, is not present in a dataset, for example D_1, $f_{D_1}(s_j) = 0$.

The probability for inferring $s_i \in C$ from both datasets based on their sensitive values distribution is given as the following. Note that $\alpha = \frac{|D_1|}{|D_2|}$ and $|D_1|$ and $|D_2|$ are sizes of datasets D_1 and D_2 respectively. Let us assume that $|D_1| \leq |D_2|$ (we can swap the datasets if otherwise) and $0 < \alpha \leq 1$.

$$\begin{aligned}\text{prob}(s_i|(D_1, D_2)) &= \text{prob}(s_i|O(D_1, D_2)) \\ &= \frac{\min(f_{D_1}(s_i) \cdot |D_1|, f_{D_2}(s_i) \cdot |D_2|)}{\sum_{r=1}^{|S|} \min(f_{D_1}(s_r) \cdot |D_1|, f_{D_2}(s_r) \cdot |D_2|)} \\ &= \frac{\min(\alpha f_{D_1}(s_i), f_{D_2}(s_i))}{\sum_{r=1}^{|S|} \min(\alpha f_{D_1}(s_r), f_{D_2}(s_r))} \quad (3)\end{aligned}$$

The probability for inferring an overlapping sensitive value from two overlapping datasets relies on **1)** the number of overlapping sensitive values, **2)** their frequencies, especially in the smaller dataset of two datasets. In other words, it depends on what have been remained in the intersection. Next, we show how to use equation (3) in the following example.

Example 2. Let D_1 be Table 1(c) and D_2 be Table 2(c). $S = \{A, C, D, G, J\}$. We infer Nancy's sensitive value knowing her record is in both datasets. The sensitive values in $O = \{D(3), G(2), J(2)\}$ where the numbers in parentheses are counts. $\text{prob}(D \mid O(D_1, D_2)) = 3/(3 + 2 + 2) = 3/7$.

If we use the distributional information to infer the probability, we use the following table.

frequency	A	C	D	G	J
$\|D_1\| = 9$	0	2/9	1/3	2/9	2/9
$\|D_2\| = 12$	1/4	0	1/4	1/4	1/4

We obtain $\text{prob}(s = D|(D_1, D_2))$:

$$= \frac{(3/4) * (1/3)}{(3/4) * (1/3) + (3/4) * (2/9) + (3/4) * (2/9)} = 3/7$$

Now we present the objective of privacy preservation in multiple independent publications in the following.

$$\forall i : \text{prob}(s_i|(D_1, D_2)) - \max(\text{prob}(s_i|D_1), \text{prob}(s_i|D_2)) < \theta \quad (4)$$

$\text{prob}(s_i|D_1)$ and $\text{prob}(s_i|D_2)$ are the confidences of the adversary inferring the sensitive value s_i individually from two published datasets D_1 and D_2 respectively. θ is a small positive number. Let us recall what an adversary knows. Based on the background knowledge and the quasi-identifier values, an adversary knows that the victim's record is in both datasets D_1 and D_2. $\max(\text{prob}(s_i \mid D_1), \text{prob}(s_i \mid D_2))$ means the maximum probability that the adversary would know the sensitive value from the two published datasets individually. The objective (4) is to bound the improvement of the confidence of the adversary (caused by the composition attack) by θ. If $\theta = 0$, then the adversary gets no advantage by using two datasets collectively. $\text{prob}(s_i|D_1)$ and $\text{prob}(s_i|D_2)$ can be estimated as $f_{D_1}(s_i)$ and $f_{D_2}(s_i)$ if two datasets have been anonymized properly.

Now, we discuss when objective (4) can be achieved. We firstly study how difference in sensitive value distributions in D_1 and D_2 affect the inference probability. Let us fix $\alpha = 1$.

$$\text{prob}(s_i|(D_1, D_2)) = \frac{\min(f_{D_1}(s_i), f_{D_2}(s_i))}{\sum_{r=1}^{|S|} \min(f_{D_1}(s_r), f_{D_2}(s_r))} \quad (5)$$

Let $\beta = \frac{1}{\sum_{r=1}^{|S|} \min(f_{D_1}(s_r), f_{D_2}(s_r))}$. When distributions of sensitive values in both D_1 and D_2 are similar, $\beta \approx 1$. When the distributions are significantly different, β is a large number.

Example 3. Let $S = \{s_1, s_2, s_3, s_4, s_5\}$, datasets D_1 and D_2 contain some of the sensitive values of S. We give some distributions of sensitive values in D_1 and D_2 and their corresponding β values as the following.

frequency	s_1	s_2	s_3	s_4	s_5
D_1	0.1	0.2	0.3	0.4	0
D_2	0.1	0.2	0.3	0.4	0

$\beta = 1.$

frequency	s_1	s_2	s_3	s_4	s_5
D_1	0.1	0.2	0.3	0.4	0
D_2	0	0.2	0.3	0.4	0.1

$\beta = 1.11$

frequency	s_1	s_2	s_3	s_4	s_5
D_1	0.1	0.2	0.3	0.4	0
D_2	0	0.1	0.2	0.3	0.4

$\beta = 1.67$

In an ideal situation when $\beta = 1$, the overlapping dataset does not reveal more privacy of an overlapping individual than each individual dataset does. Therefore, the privacy of overlapping individuals in multiple datasets is preserved.

In the worst situation, when β is a large number, distributions of two datasets are almost distinct and have very little overlap. In such situation, $\text{prob}(s_i|(D_1, D_2)) \approx 1$ and an adversary can obtain the probability of an overlapping sensitive value with the nearly certain confidence using just the distribution information.

From the above examples, we see that distributions dominate the inference probability in the composition attack. Thus, we have the following observation.

Observation 1 *There is not a general solution for the composition attack for any distribution of two datasets.*

PROOF. Given a dataset D_1 with a distribution. We can always find a distribution of another dataset D_2 so that β is a large number. As a result, $\text{prob}(s_i|(D_1, D_2)) \approx 1$, and the objective (4) will be dissatisfied for some i's. □

For example, in the worst case, the privacy will be revealed just based on distributional information of two datasets, such as two datasets have only a single sensitive value in common. Such a disclosure does not even need QI information.

In the following, we consider a solution in a restricted form. We firstly define the *closed community*. In a closed community, the dataset of each data owner (i.e hospital in our case) is drawn from the same population and their data distributions are similar. In our words, $\beta \approx 1$. For example, different hospitals take different sets of patients, but in most cases, the disease distributions of the hospitals are similar. There are some exceptions that the distributions of some specialized hospitals are different from those of general hospitals. However, in such exceptions, the knowledge of a patient visiting a specialized hospital gives an adversary large chance for guessing the disease anyway. Let us assume that a number of general hospitals plan to publish their datasets independently in anonymized form (for research purposes etc.) and want to ensure privacy against the composition attack. So, a solution in the assumption of the closed community, where hospitals have similar distributions, is still useful.

In the following discussions, we assume that $\beta \approx 1$ for a solution in a closed community. When $\beta \approx 1$, α does not make much difference because both distributions are similar. An ideal solution can be achieved if sensitive values in every equivalence class of P^* and Q_i^* has the same distribution as of P and Q_i respectively. To formalize such best solution scenario, we introduce the following concept.

Definition 3 (Clone equivalence class) *Given the distribution of sensitive values of dataset P as $f(S)$. An equivalence class $E \subset P^*$ is called a clone equivalence class if it has all the sensitive values S and the distribution of sensitive values in E is the same as $f(S)$.*

Example 4. A clone equivalence class of Table 2(a) is Table 2(c). Apparently, the utility of this clone equivalence class is low. Table 2(d) has two clone equivalence classes generalized by our *micro-statistics method* (to be discussed later).

Observation 2 (Property of clone equivalence classes) *Let all equivalence classes of anonymized datasets P^* and Q_i^* be clone equivalence classes. The objective* (4) *can be achieved when $\theta \geq \max\big(\beta \min(\text{prob}(s_j \mid P^*), \text{prob}(s_j \mid Q_i^*)) - \max(\text{prob}(s_j \mid P^*), \text{prob}(s_j \mid Q_i^*))\big)$ for all $j \in 1,2,3,\ldots, |S|$.*

PROOF. If all the equivalence classes of anonymized datasets P^* and Q_i^* are clone equivalence classes (Definition 3), the probability for inferencing a sensitive value in an equivalence class is the same as that for inferencing the sensitive value in whole dataset. Therefore, we can replace D_1 and D_2 with P^* and Q_i^* in equations (3) and (4) and the lower bound of θ is obtained. □

Since $\max(\text{prob}(s_i|P^*), \text{prob}(s_i|Q_i^*)) \geq \min(\text{prob}(s_i|P^*), \text{prob}(s_i|Q_i^*))$ and $\beta \approx 1$, the θ can be very small.

Clone equivalence classes are ideal but inappropriate for real world situations. We may lose a lot of utility if we require datasets to be anonymized to such an ideal situation (as we see in Tables 1(c) and 2(c)). We need a practical goal. We relax the requirement of clone equivalence classes as the following ϵ-clone equivalence classes.

Definition 4 (ϵ-clone equivalence class) *Given the distribution of sensitive values of dataset P as $f(S)$. An equivalence class $E \subset P^*$ is called ϵ-clone if it has all the sensitive values S and for every sensitive value in S, the difference of probabilities of the sensitive value in P and in E is bound by a small number ϵ. More specifically, $|\text{prob}(s_i|P) - \text{prob}(s_i|E)| \leq \epsilon$.*

The magnitude of ϵ is determined by the data distribution of a dataset. We will analyze the upper bound of the ϵ in Section 6.2 after the algorithm is presented. Finally, we present the problem of creating ϵ-clone equivalence classes.

Definition 5 (ϵ-clone publication) *The objective of privacy preserving ϵ-clone publication is to compute such anonymous P^* that each equivalence class E in P^* is ϵ-clone equivalence class and retains as much information in anonymous P^* as possible.*

The requirement of ϵ-clone equivalence class looks like t-closeness [19]. However, they are different in the following way. The t-closeness bounds the total difference of the distribution between an equivalence class and the dataset, but ϵ-cloning bounds the frequency difference of each sensitive value of an equivalence class and the dataset. When the overall difference is bounded in two distributions (like in t-closeness), the frequency differences of a sensitive value between dataset and an equivalence class can still be large. Therefore, t-closeness [19] is also vulnerable to the composition attack as shown in [11].

6. MICRO-STATISTICS BASED ANONYMIZATION

There is a practical problem for anonymizing a table to comply with ϵ-clone publication. The size of an ϵ-clone equivalence class can be big when the distribution of sensitive values is skewed. The generalization of such a large equivalence class makes a dataset useless, as we saw in Table 1(c) and 2(c) where most QI values have been suppressed. In this section, we will introduce a *micro-statistic* technique to make such a super equivalence class more useful than the generalization.

6.1 Phases

We aim at achieving two intuitive goals. First, each equivalence class has all the sensitive values of the anonymized dataset. Second, we attempt to reduce, as much as possible, the frequency difference for each sensitive value between original dataset and the equivalence class i.e. ϵ. We do not pre-specify ϵ but adaptively find it out in the process of anonymization. The detail discussion on ϵ is given in Section 6.2.

6.1.1 Division

This phase divides all the tuples of P into $|S|$ ($|S|$ is the number of distinct sensitive values in P) sub-datasets i.e. $W_1, W_2, \ldots, W_{|S|}$, such that each sub-dataset contains only the tuples with same sensitive value. In the end of this phase, we calculate the frequency of each sub-dataset $f(W_j)$ in original dataset P. This phase is different from the *bucket partition* phase of [5] because [5] starts out with buckets of more than one *closely related* distinct sensitive values in one bucket but we strictly allocate only one sensitive value to each sub-dataset.

As an example, we consider Table 3(a) as P, $u = 4$ because P (Table 3(a)) has 4 distinct sensitive values i.e, $\{J,B,G,L\}$. We create 4 sub-datasets i.e. $W_1(J)$, $W_2(B)$, $W_3(G)$, $W_4(L)$. We calculate the ratio of each sub-dataset to the whole dataset; for example the sensitive value J has 5 tuples and its ratio in Table 2(a) is 0.26.

6.1.2 Assignment

First, we create b empty equivalence classes (E_1, E_2, E_3 ..., E_b); where $b = \min(|W_j|)$, i.e. the sub-dataset with the minimum tuples. We call such sub-dataset as the *key sub-dataset*, denoted as W^{κ}. Next, we decide how many tuples to be assigned to each empty equivalence class E_r ($r = 1, 2, 3, \ldots, b$).

The assignment algorithm takes the $|S|$ sub-datasets, already created in the division phase, and calculates a separate γ_j value for each sub-dataset; γ_j is the number of tuples to be assigned to each equivalence class E_r from each sub-dataset W_j. To calculate the γ_j, we first make a temporary calculation of $\eta_j = \frac{|W_j|}{b}$. Where b is the number of equivalence classes created earlier in this phase i.e. $b = |W^{\kappa}|$. Now we calculate γ_j for *j-th* sub-dataset as:

$$\gamma_j = round(\eta_j) \tag{6}$$

Where *round* is a function that returns the nearest integer from η_j. For example, $round(2.3) = 2$, $round(2.8) = 3$ and $round(2) = 2$. In an ideal situation, the $\gamma_j = \eta_j$. Such ideal situation exists for all sub-datasets of Table 2(a). If η_j is not an integer then there is a *deficiency* of some tuples in W_j; there are not enough tuples in W_j that can equally be allocated to all b equivalence classes. In such case, we need to handle this *deficiency* by suppressing/adding $\hbar_j$ tuples from/to sub-dataset W_j, where:

$$\hbar_j = \begin{cases} (\gamma_j * b) - |W_j| & \text{if } (\eta_j - \lfloor \eta_j \rfloor) > 0.5 \\ |W_j| - (\gamma_j * b) & \text{if } (\eta_j - \lfloor \eta_j \rfloor) < 0.5 \end{cases} \tag{7}$$

We *add* $\hbar_j$ counterfeited tuples to sub-dataset W_j if deficiency ($\eta_j - \lfloor \eta_j \rfloor$) > 0.5 because in such case suppression will cause more utility lost. The counterfeit tuples only has sensitive value s_i in sub-dataset W_j and all QIs have '$*$' values. In other case, we *suppress* the $\hbar$ tuples from sub-dataset W_j if deficiency ($\eta_j - \lfloor \eta_j \rfloor$) < 0.5 because in such case counterfeit tuples will cause more utility lost. If $(\eta_j - \lfloor \eta_j \rfloor) = 0.50$ then suppress and counterfeit equal number of sub-datasets.

Once γ_j information is ready for all sub-datasets, the assignment algorithm selects a sub-dataset W_j and calculates the *Distortion* (a distance metric) [18] of first ρ ($\gamma_j \leq \rho \leq |W_j|$) tuples with equivalence class E_r. Next, out of ρ tuples it assigns γ_j *closest* (defined in next paragraph) tuples to equivalence class E_r. This process is repeated for all equivalence classes. The ρ is a parameter, called *distortion control*, to improve the performance of the assignment algorithm and it restricts the calculation of *Distortion* to the first ρ tuples of the sub-dataset, instead of calculating distortion for all tuples of the sub-dataset.

Now we explain the *closest* tuples in detail. Alongside complying with the ϵ-clone publication objective (Definition 5), we also

---

Algorithm 1 *Micro-Statistic based Anonymization*

Input:

P ▷ Input dataset to be anonymized
k ▷ Input parameter for k-anonymity
ρ ▷ Input parameter, a trade-off for efficiency and quality
λ ▷ Input parameter to be utilized in *Micro-Statistics* phase

Output:

P^* ▷ Anonymized dataset

```
Create w (w = P/|S|) empty sub-datasets W[ ] ▷ Division phase
Populate sub-datasets W[ ], each sub-dataset has tuples with
  same sensitive value in P ▷ Division phase
b = min(|W[j]|)(j ∈ 1,2,3,...,|W[ ]|) ▷ Get number of
  tuples in key sub-dataset
Create b empty equivalence classes E[ ] ▷ Assignment phase
γ[j] = round(|W[j]|/b) ▷ get γ for each sub-dataset
for j ← 1, |W| do ▷ Access all sub-datasets one-by-one
    for r ← 1, |E| do ▷ Access all equivalence classes
        Calculate Distortion Distance for first ρ tuples of W[j]
  with E[r]
        E[r] = γ[j] of ρ in W[j] ▷ out of ρ tuples in W[j],
  assign γ[j] tuples with minimum distortion to E[r]
    end for
end for
Merge/divide equivalence classes in E[ ] by requirement k
Generate 'micro-statistics' for each equivalence class in E[ ]
  using input parameter λ ▷ Micro-Statistics phase
Combine all E[ ] to form P* ▷ Anonymized dataset created
```

---

need to make sure that anonymous dataset P^* maintains a reasonable utility and it has been done through putting *closest* tuples of each sub-dataset W_j into an equivalence class E_r. We use *Distortion* [18] to measure the closeness between a tuple t and equivalence class E_r. The distortion is the sum of the generalization steps in the generalization hierarchies if t is assigned to E_r. Still, the problem of forming equivalence classes with the minimum distortions is similar to other optimal k-anonymity problems [1, 23]. So, we *randomly* pick ρ tuples from each sub-dataset W_j and calculate the *Distortion* for each of ρ tuples with an equivalence class E_r. We assign that tuple t out of ρ tuples to an equivalence class E_r that has the minimum distortion with it. Due to the space constraint, we omit the calculation details of distortion and readers are referred to the original paper [18] for further details.

In the running example where we assume Table 3(a) as P, the $b = |W_3(G)|$ i.e. 3 and we create 3 empty equivalence classes. We have already created 4 sub-datasets in division phase. For all four sub-datasets, the $\gamma_1(J) = 2$, $\gamma_2(B) = 2$, $\gamma_3(G) = 1$, $\gamma_4(L) = 1$ and deficiency values ($\eta_j - \lfloor \eta_j \rfloor$) are 0.66, 0.33, 0, 0.33 respectively. We need to add 1 counterfeit tuple in $W_1(J)$ and need to suppress 1 tuple from sub-datasets $W_2(B)$ and $W_4(L)$. In the assignment phase, we do not suppress any tuple and once the ($\gamma_j * b$) closest tuples are assigned to b equivalence classes; we suppress the remaining ($|W_j| - (\gamma_j * b)$) tuples in the sub-dataset W_j.

Assignment operation accesses each sub-dataset and assigns 'closest' γ_j tuples of each sub-dataset W_j to each of three equivalence classes.

6.1.3 Micro-Statistics.

In the beginning of this phase, we suppress any remaining tuples in all sub-datasets and divide/merge or leave intact each equivalence class as per the input parameter k from k-anonymity [25]. We divide the QIs of any equivalence class into sub-equivalence classes if $|E_r| > k$ or merge an equivalence class with some another one if $|E_r| < k$. We only divide the QIs into sub-equivalence classes and leave the sensitive values intact because we have to maintain the association of each tuple of sub-equivalence class with all the sensitive values of the equivalence class. We merge those equivalence classes that have minimum distortion with each other.

Next, we calculate the *micro-statistics* for all QIs within each sub/equivalence class. We have two types of QIs i.e. categorical and numerical. For categorical QI, we include the number of distinct QI values in each sub-equivalence class. For numerical QI, first we calculate the 'average' of QI values within sub/equivalence class and next select an indicative range that covers λ QI values of the same sub/equivalence class; where $\lambda \leq k$ and is an input parameter. Algorithm 1 formally presents the anonymization operation.

In our running example, we have two remaining tuples t_{12} = <45, M, Separated> in $W_2(B)$ and t_{18} = <22, M, Separated> in $W_4(L)$; we suppress these tuples first. Now, we consider $k = 3$ and $\lambda = 1$ and divide each equivalence class into two sub-equivalence classes, each of 3 tuples. As last step, we generate the micro-statistics for all the sub-equivalence classes. We have 3 QIs, the Age is numerical whereas Sex and $Marital\ Status$ are categorical. We replace the Age QI values in all sub-equivalence classes with the average Age of each sub-equivalence class and also include an indicative range that covers 1 ($\lambda = 1$) Age value nearest to the average value in each sub-equivalence class. For Sex and $Marital\ Status$ QIs, we put the number of all distinct QI values in all sub-equivalence classes. The result is Table 3(c).

The Table 2(a) is case of equivalence class merger. Ideally, there should be 3 equivalence classes (having 4 tuples each) but we assume $k = 6$ for Table 2(a); so one equivalence class is split and merged into others two.

6.2 Discussion

The ϵ-clone equivalence classes formed by our algorithm makes use of *micro-statistics* instead of *local recoding* [17] and *global recoding* [25] generalization schemes often adopted in literature. We employ the micro-statistics scheme because it provides high degree of privacy and utility in anonymous dataset (shown in experiments of Section 7). The concept of ϵ-cloning can also be implemented by local/global-recoding generalization. Although it will result in same privacy guarantee but with lower utility (shown in Tables 1(c), 2(c)).

Now, we discuss the effectiveness of our scheme (micro-statistics based anonymization) in achieving the ϵ-clone publication. The major concern of the ϵ-clone publication is the magnitude of ϵ. We aim at the maximum possible value of ϵ in our scheme. A large ϵ means high distribution difference between the original and the anonymized dataset.

We now compute the maximum value of ϵ, for all distinct sensitive values $s_1, s_2, \ldots, s_u$ of a dataset P. As dataset P has u distinct sensitive values so there will be u sensitive sub-datasets as $W_1, W_2, \ldots, W_u$. We also assume the ratio of these u sub-datasets as: $f(W_1) \leq f(W_2) \leq \ldots \leq f(W_u)$. As the ratio $f(W_1)$ of sensitive value s_1 is the smallest, the sub-dataset W_1 will be the 'key sub-dataset' and the number of initial empty equivalence classes $b = |W_1|$ (i.e. the number of tuples in key sub-dataset). In an ideal situation, if $\hbar_j = 0$ ($j = 2, 3, \ldots, n$) for all n sub-datasets (it occurs when $\gamma_j = \eta_j$ in (6)) then $\epsilon_j = 0$ for all sub-datasets. In other case, where $\hbar_j > 0$ (i.e. $\gamma_j \neq \eta_j$), we need to *distort* the sub-dataset(s) by suppressing and/or adding counterfeiting $\hbar_j$ tuples. In such case, we need to find the upper bound of the ϵ_j. We denote such maximum value of ϵ_j as $\epsilon_j^{\max}$.

Table 4: Attribute domain size

Attribute	Age	Sex	Education	Birth Place	Occupation	Income
Domain Size	79	2	17	57	50	50

We consider the worst case and assume that, excluding the key sub-dataset W_1, for all other sub-datasets $\gamma_j \neq \eta_j$ and $(\eta_j - \lfloor \eta_j \rfloor) = 0.50$. Now we need to compute the $\hbar_j$ suppress and counterfeit tuples for equal number of sub-datasets. The values of $\hbar_j$ are calculated as per (7) and in any case the maximum number of distorted (suppressed and/or counterfeit) tuples, denoted as $\hbar_j^{\max}$, are:

$$\hbar_j^{\max} \leq |W^{\kappa}|/2 \tag{8}$$

The W^{κ} is the key sub-dataset (W_1 in our case). So as per (8), the maximum number of distorted (suppress and/or counterfeit) tuples in any sub-dataset are not more than the half number of the tuples in the key sub-dataset. Now if the property (8) holds for all sub-datasets then following property will also hold for any sub-dataset W_j:

$$\epsilon_j^{\max} = f(W^{\kappa})/2 \tag{9}$$

Now for any dataset P having at least two distinct sensitive values, the frequency of key sub-dataset to get the worst case scenario $(\eta - \lfloor \eta \rfloor) = 0.50$ for the non-key sub-dataset is $f(W^{\kappa}) = 0.40$. We have to suppress/counterfeit $(0.40/2 * |P|)$ tuples from/to the non-key sub-dataset. Even in such extreme case, the $\epsilon_j^{\max} < 0.2$. If we have 3 sensitive values the $\epsilon_j^{\max} = 0.125$. In real life datasets, we have moderate number of distinct sensitive values; causing even lower $\epsilon_j^{\max}$. For Table 3(c) the $\epsilon_j^{\max}$ is 0.07. If we have 10 sensitive values, $\epsilon_j^{\max} = 0.03$.

ϵ-cloning is also not vulnerable to other privacy threats like [27, 15]. The minimality attack [27] exploits the *minimum generalization* required for anonymization and it cannot be successful on our scheme due to incorporation of *micro-statistics* instead of (local or global) generalization. Adversary cannot get the exact QIs range for any equivalence class from its micro-statistics and adversary's confidence remains split about the inclusion of a tuple in an equivalence class or not. The deFinett attack [15] can be successful when the frequency difference of a sensitive value between original and anonymous dataset is 'large'; which is not in the case of ϵ-clone equivalence classes because each ϵ-clone equivalence class has all the sensitive values of the original dataset with a small ϵ threshold. So, adversary gets very little information from ϵ-cloned dataset after deFinett attack [15].

7. EXPERIMENTS

Experiments are performed on a machine running a 2.4 Ghz CPU with 3 Giga-byte memory. We deploy two real world datasets OCC and SAL from United States census data downloadable from http://ipums.org. Both contain 600k tuples and each tuple contains the information of an American adult. OCC includes four QI attributes, age, sex, $education$, $birth\ place$, and a sensitive attribute $occupation$. SAL contains the same set of QI attributes, but different sensitive attribute $income$. All columns, except age, are discrete and the sizes of their domains are given in Table 4.

We create five disjoint sub-datasets Q_i^{occ} (Q_i^{sal}) ($i \in 1, \ldots, 5$) from $OCC(SAL)$. It suffices to clarify the generation and generalization of Q_i^{occ}, since the same method is applied for Q_i^{sal}. We assign 100k tuples to each sub-dataset Q_i^{occ}. The remaining 100k tuples initiates an overlap pool. All sub-datasets and overlapping pool have same set of sensitive values.

We randomly select specific *overlapping tuples* from overlap pool and insert them to each Q_i^{occ}. The overlapping tuples control the overlap rate. We insert overlapping tuples of 20k, 40k, 60k, 80k, 100k to each of five sub-datasets to create 5 groups of sub-datasets each with the size of 120k, 140k, 160k, 180k and 200k. In each group, five sub-datasets have the same size and the same overlapping rate. We refer to the five sub-datasets in each group Q_i^{occ} (Q_i^{sal}) as independent publishers. We do experiments on five separate publishers for OCC and SAL, and repeat the experiments for five different overlapping rates and sizes.

7.1 Failure of Conventional Generalization

In the first set of experiments, we show that the existing generalization methods lead to severe privacy disclosure in independent data publications. The findings were also observed previously in [11, 3]. We increase the overlapping tuples from 20k to 100k and adopt the algorithm in [16] to compute ℓ-diverse [20] versions Q_1^{occ*}, Q_2^{occ*}, ..., Q_n^{occ*}. Then, we identify all the overlapping tuples that appear in any Q_i^{occ*} and whose sensitive values will definitely be revealed (called *privacy risk* tuples) using any another sub-dataset. These privacy risk tuples are extracted using Definition 2; where we use Q_1^{occ*} as P^* and all other 4 sub-datasets are treated as Q_i^*. In Fig. 2(a), we plot the maximum number of privacy risk tuples in any sub-dataset as a function of ℓ. We repeat this process by increasing ℓ from 2 to 10. The ℓ-diversity [20] fails to support independent publications of overlapping data, because it results in a large number of privacy risk tuples. Although fewer privacy risk tuples exist as ℓ increases, privacy risk tuples still cannot be completely prevented with larger ℓ.

As all sub-datasets Q_i^{x*} ($x = occ$ or sal) and overlap pool have the same set of sensitive values (Table 4) so ϵ-cloning preserves the privacy because an ϵ-cloning the overlapping set contains most sensitive values and privacy compromise does not occur. We repeat these experiments on sub-datasets Q_i^{sal} and the results are illustrated in Fig. 2(b), confirming the same observations.

7.2 ϵ-Cloning Evaluation

In following experiments, we examine the effectiveness of ϵ-cloning. We invoke the micro-statistics based anonymization on $Q_1^x, Q_2^x, \ldots, Q_5^x$ ($x = occ$ or sal) to compute generalized versions $Q_1^{x*}, Q_2^{x*}, \ldots, Q_5^{x*}$. Each Q_i^{x*} is characterized by overlapping tuples and distortion control parameter ρ (ρ from Section 6.1.2). We use 20% of dataset size as ρ, unless otherwise mentioned.

We cannot benchmark our experiments with existing partition-based generalization schemes i.e. k-anonymity [25], ℓ-diversity [20], t-closeness [19] etc. because all of these schemes are prone to composition attack [11, 3].

7.2.1 Number of Distorted Tuples

Our algorithm needs to suppress and/or counterfeit some tuples in the Assignment phase. We demonstrate that only a small number of distorted tuples (both suppressed and counterfeited) are needed to enforce ϵ-cloning. In Fig. 3(a), we vary the dataset size from 120k to 200k and measure the number of distorted tuples in OCC (SAL). The number of distorted tuples increases along with dataset size because higher dataset size requires more tuples in each equivalence class for assignment; resulting possibility of more distortion. The maximum number of distorted tuples are only 579(607) for dataset size of 200k in OCC (SAL).

In Fig. 3(b), we show the percentage of distorted tuples in OCC

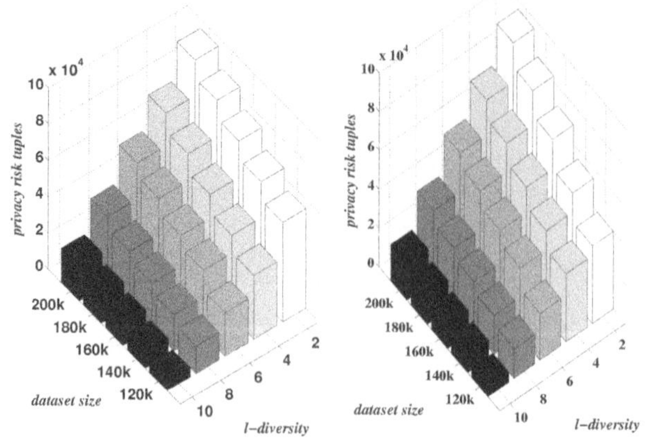

(a) OCC (b) SAL

Figure 2: Successful composition attacks with various overlapping tuples and ℓ-diversitity

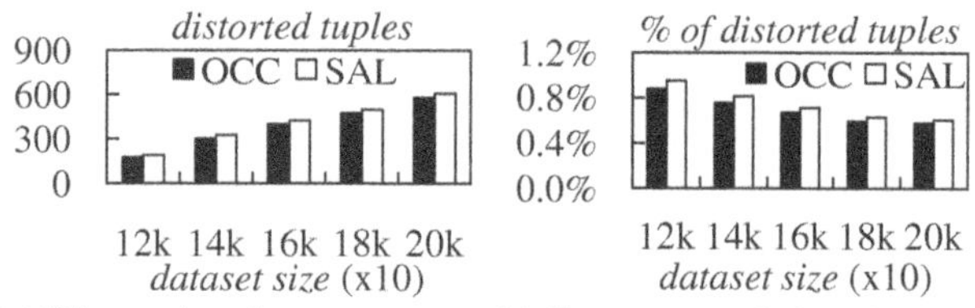

(a) Distorted tuples vs. dataset size (b) Percentage of distortion vs. dataset size

Figure 3: Average and percentage of distorted (suppressed and counterfeited) tuples in OCC and SAL with various dataset sizes and overlapping rates

(SAL) versus the dataset size. The percentage decreases as dataset size increases. As a result, that micro-statistics based anonymization can utilize more tuples. As dataset size increases, the total number of distorted tuples also increases (Fig 3(a)) but overall the percentage of distorted tuples with dataset size decreases (Fig 3(b)). In any case the percentage of distorted tuples is less than 1% of dataset size.

7.2.2 Utility of the Published Data.

In the following set of experiments, we will use Q_i^{x*} ($x = occ$ or sal) to answer queries about the original sub-dataset Q_i^x. We use aggregate queries, since they are the basic operation for numerous data mining tasks (e.g., decision tree learning, association rule mining, etc.). Specifically, each query has the form:

SELECT COUNT (*) FROM Q_i^{x*} WHERE $pred(t[A_1^{qi}]$ AND ... AND $t[A_4^{qi}]$ AND $t[S])$

The Q_i^{x*} is the sub-dataset generalized using ϵ-cloning, ($t[A_1^{qi}]$, ..., $t[A_4^{qi}]$) denote the four QI attributes, and $t[S]$ is the sensitive attribute $occupation$ ($income$). For each attribute A, the condition $pred(A)$ has the form $A \in \delta$. Here δ is a query parameter called *selection range*, and has length $|A| * \delta$, where $|A|$ is the domain size of attribute A (see Table 4). A larger result is returned with higher δ. Our workload consists of 10000 queries with same sub-dataset Q_i^{x*} and sensitive value $t[S]$.

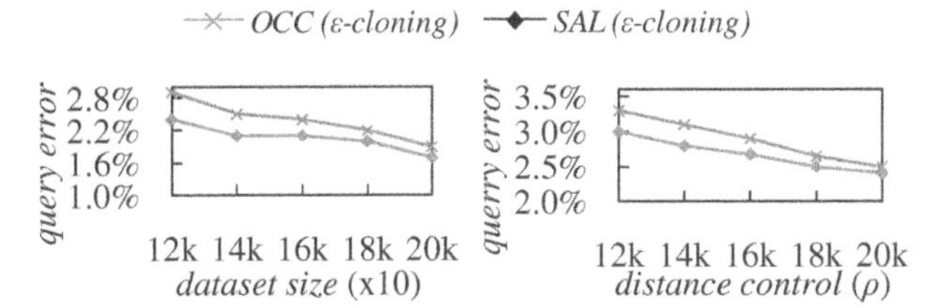

(a) Median relative error vs. dataset size, ($\delta = 25\%$)

(b) Median relative error vs. ρ (dataset size = 120k, $\delta = 25\%$)

Figure 4: Query error with fixed query selection range (δ) and increasing dataset size and increasing distance control parameter (ρ)

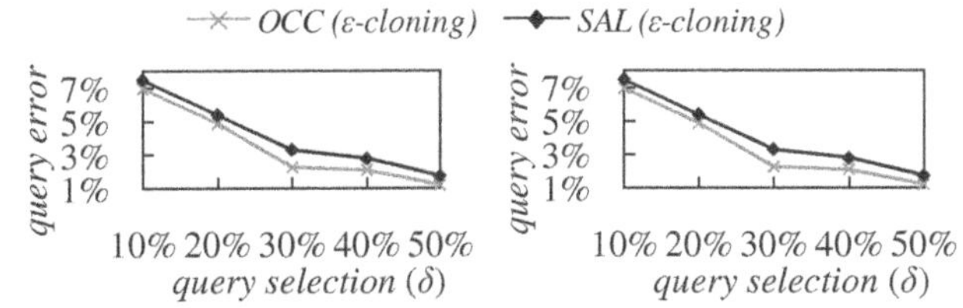

(a) Workload error vs. δ (dataset size = 120k)

(b) Workload error vs. δ (dataset size = 200k)

Figure 5: Average workload error with increasing query selection range (δ) and increasing dataset size

Given a query, we obtain its actual result R_{act} from the original sub-dataset Q_i^x, and compute an estimated answer R_{est} from its ϵ-clone generalized version Q_i^{x*}. The relative error of a query equals $|R_{act} - R_{est}|/R_{act}$. We measure the workload error as the median relative error of all the queries of all sub-datasets.

Fig. 4(a), plots the workload error as a function of dataset size for OCC and SAL respectively. In all experiments, the median error is at most 2.5%. In the experiments of Fig. 4(b), we set dataset size to 120k and measure the workload error as the function of distortion control parameter ρ. The error decreases (accuracy improves) with ρ because higher ρ results the more search in finding the closest tuple during the assignment phase. Our experiments show that error does not vary significantly with dataset size, and is not very sensitive to the distortion control parameter ρ.

In the experiments of Fig. 5, we set dataset size to 120k and 200k (i.e. minimum and maximum values of dataset in Fig. 3) and study workload error in Q_i^{x*} ($x = occ$ or sal) as the function of query selection range δ. The accuracy improves i.e. workload error decreases with increase in δ. This is expected because higher δ leads to larger query results, whereas, in general, aggregate analysis is effective for sizable queries.

7.2.3 Computation Overhead.

The last experiment evaluates the efficiency of our micro-statistics based generalization algorithm. In Fig. 6(a), we measure the average time of computing a generalized sub-dataset Q_i^{occ*} (Q_i^{sal*}) as function of dataset size. The cost is more expensive when dataset size is higher, because the algorithm needs to process more tuples in a dataset. In Fig. 6(b), we fix dataset size to 120k, and get the computation time as a function of distortion control parameter ρ. The overhead increases as ρ increases, since a larger ρ results the involvement of more tuples in finding the closest tuple during the assignment phase. In comparison Figure 6(b) and Figure 4(b), we see that ρ controls a trade off between the efficiency and utility.

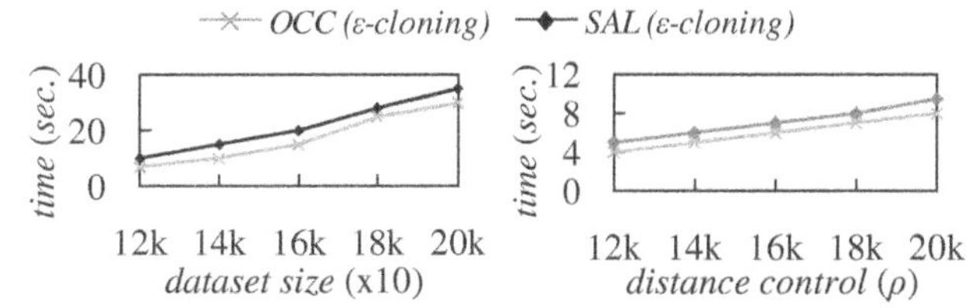

(a) Computation time vs. dataset size

(b) Computation time vs. ρ (dataset size = 120k)

Figure 6: Computation overhead with increasing dataset size and increasing distance control parameter (ρ)

8. RELATED WORK

It is important to point out that the partition-based schemes in the literature were not designed to be used in contexts where independent releases of overlapping population are available from different locations. Thus, essentially the composition attack is not a flaw in these schemes, but rather it directs the community's attention to an important direction of research.

There has already been made substantial progress in privacy preserving data publishing. One line has focused on taking into account other, known releases, such as previous publications by the same organization (called sequential, serial or incremental releases) [29, 31, 10] and multiple views of the same dataset [34, 35]. Another line has considered incorporating knowledge from partitioned views to group individuals [34]. In our case, each publisher is independent and unaware from the dataset of other publisher(s).

Some other works have sought to model unknown background knowledge of adversary [22, 6]. Martin et al. [22] and Chen et al. [6] provide complexity measures for an adversary's side information (roughly, they measure the size of the smallest formula within a CNF-like class that can encode the side information). Both works design schemes that provably resist attacks based on side information whose complexity is below a given threshold. A hypothetical discussion of the same problem is in [11], driving concepts from differential privacy [7, 9]. Differential privacy guarantees that the attacker should not be able to distinguish between two possibilities, i.e. a specific person's record is in or not in a statistical database, thus preserving the privacy. Most relevant to this paper are works that elaborate the privacy risk due to the anonymous data release of overlapping population by multiple locations [21, 13, 12]. All of these incorporate the *co-ordinated model*; where all locations communicate with each other to calculate the privacy risk of overlapping population and subsequently release dataset that is *k-linkable* i.e. each overlapping record is minimum linked to *k* records in each release.

Independent and asynchronous release by multiple locations (and hence composition attacks) fall outside the models proposed by these works. The sequential release models do not fit because they assume the multiple synchronous releases from the single location. In this paper, we deal with the case when there are multiple independent publishers. The complexity-based measures do not fit because independent releases appear to have complexity that is linear in the size of the datasets. The differential privacy is ideally suitable for interactive-setting (where there is no public release of anonymous data) and solution purposed in [11] lacks the actual implementation and test results. Moreover recent test results show that no differently private algorithm can have meaningful utility unless the privacy requirement is very low [8, 24]. The co-ordinated model also does not satisfy our requirement because we are dealing with a non co-ordinated scenario where each location independently anonymizes its data without having any communication with other location(s).

9. CONCLUSION

Existing data publishing and serial data publishing methods do not support multiple independent data publication by different publishers where there are overlapping individual records. This paper has developed ϵ-cloning model to prevent an adversary from using independent data releases of multiple data owners to infer sensitive information of overlapping individuals. We have provided an efficient algorithm for computing anonymized dataset to achieve ϵ-cloning. We experimentally showed that the anonymized data adequately protects privacy and yet supports effective data analysis.

10. ACKNOWLEDGEMENT

The authors would like to thank the anonymous reviewers for their constructive suggestions. This research has been supported by ARC Discovery grants DP0774450 and DP110103142.

11. REFERENCES

[1] AGGARWAL, G., FEDER, T., KENTHAPADI, K., MOTWANI, R., PANIGRAHY, R., THOMAS, D., AND ZHU, A. Anonymizing tables. In *ICDT'05* (2005), pp. 246–258.

[2] AGRAWAL, R., KIERNAN, J., SRIKANT, R., AND XU, Y. Hippocratic databases. VLDB '02, pp. 143–154.

[3] BAIG, M. M., AND JIUYONG LI, JIXUE LIU, H. W. Studying genotype-phenotype attack on k-anonymized medical and genomic data. *AusDM* (2009), 159–166.

[4] BRICKELL, J., AND SHMATIKOV, V. The cost of privacy: destruction of data-mining utility in anonymized data publishing. KDD '08, pp. 70–78.

[5] CAO, J., KARRAS, P., KALNIS, P., AND TAN, K.-L. Sabre: a sensitive attribute bucketization and redistribution framework for t-closeness. *JVLDB 20* (2011), 59–81.

[6] CHEN, B.-C., LEFEVRE, K., AND RAMAKRISHNAN, R. Privacy skyline: privacy with multidimensional adversarial knowledge. VLDB '07, pp. 770–781.

[7] DWORK, C. Differential privacy. In *ICALP* (2006), pp. 1–12.

[8] DWORK, C., MCSHERRY, F., NISSIM, K., AND SMITH, A. Calibrating noise to sensitivity in private data analysis. 3rd Theory of Cryptography Conference, Springer, pp. 265–284.

[9] FRIEDMAN, A., AND SCHUSTER, A. Data mining with differential privacy. KDD'10, ACM, pp. 493–502.

[10] FUNG, B. C. M., WANG, K., FU, A. W.-C., AND PEI, J. Anonymity for continuous data publishing. EDBT '08, pp. 264–275.

[11] GANTA, S. R., KASIVISWANATHAN, S. P., AND SMITH, A. Composition attacks and auxiliary information in data privacy. KDD'08, pp. 265–273.

[12] JIANG, W., AND CLIFTON, C. Privacy-preserving distributed k-anonymity. In *Data and Applications Security XIX* (2005), vol. 3654 of *LNCS*, Springer, pp. 924–924.

[13] JIANG, W., AND CLIFTON, C. A secure distributed framework for achieving k-anonymity. *JVLDB 15* (2006), 316–333.

[14] JIN, X., ZHANG, M., ZHANG, N., AND DAS, G. Versatile publishing for privacy preservation. KDD '10, pp. 353–362.

[15] KIFER, D. Attacks on privacy and definetti's theorem. SIGMOD'09, pp. 127–138.

[16] LEFEVRE, K., DEWITT, D. J., AND RAMAKRISHNAN, R. Mondrian multidimensional k-anonymity. ICDE'06, pp. 25–.

[17] LEFEVRE, K., DEWITT, D. J., AND RAMAKRISHNAN, R. Incognito: efficient full-domain k-anonymity. SIGMOD'05, pp. 49–60.

[18] LI, J., WONG, R. C.-W., FU, A. W.-C., AND PEI, J. Anonymization by local recoding in data with attribute hierarchical taxonomies. *TKDE 20* (2008), 1181–1194.

[19] LI, N., LI, T., AND VENKATASUBRAMANIAN, S. t-closeness: Privacy beyond k-anonymity and ℓ-diversity. ICDE'07, pp. 106–115.

[20] MACHANAVAJJHALA, A., KIFER, D., GEHRKE, J., AND VENKITASUBRAMANIAM, M. ℓ-diversity: Privacy beyond k-anonymity. *TKDD* (2007).

[21] MALIN, B. k-unlinkability: A privacy protection model for distributed data. *DKE 64*, 1 (2008), 294–311.

[22] MARTIN, D., KIFER, D., MACHANAVAJJHALA, A., GEHRKE, J., AND HALPERN, J. Worst-case background knowledge for privacy-preserving data publishing. ICDE'07, pp. 126 –135.

[23] MEYERSON, A., AND WILLIAMS, R. On the complexity of optimal k-anonymity. PODS '04, ACM, pp. 223–228.

[24] MURALIDHAR, K., AND SARATHY, R. Does differential privacy protect terry gross' privacy? In *Privacy in Statistical Databases*, vol. 6344 of *LNCS*. Springer, 2011, pp. 200–209.

[25] SWEENEY, L. k-anonymity: a model for protecting privacy. *Int. J. Uncertain. Fuzziness Knowl.-Based Syst.* (2002), 557–570.

[26] TAO, Y., XIAO, X., LI, J., AND ZHANG, D. On anti-corruption privacy preserving publication. ICDE'08, pp. 725 –734.

[27] WONG, R. C.-W., FU, A. W.-C., WANG, K., AND PEI, J. Minimality attack in privacy preserving data publishing. VLDB'07, pp. 543–554.

[28] WONG, R. C.-W., LI, J., FU, A. W.-C., AND WANG, K. (α, k)-anonymity: an enhanced k-anonymity model for privacy preserving data publishing. 754–759.

[29] WONG, R.-W., FU, A.-C., LIU, J., WANG, K., AND XU, Y. Global privacy guarantee in serial data publishing. ICDE'10, pp. 956–959.

[30] WONG, W. K., MAMOULIS, N., AND CHEUNG, D. W. L. Non-homogeneous generalization in privacy preserving data publishing. SIGMOD'10, pp. 747–758.

[31] XIAO, X., AND TAO, Y. m-invariance: towards privacy preserving re-publication of dynamic datasets. SIGMOD '07, pp. 689–700.

[32] XIAO, X., AND TAO, Y. Anatomy: simple and effective privacy preservation. VLDB'06, pp. 139–150.

[33] XIAO, X., AND TAO, Y. Personalized privacy preservation. SIGMOD'06, pp. 229–240.

[34] YANG, B., NAKAGAWA, H., SATO, I., AND SAKUMA, J. Collusion-resistant privacy-preserving data mining. KDD'10, pp. 483–492.

[35] YAO, C., WANG, X. S., AND JAJODIA, S. Checking for k-anonymity violation by views. VLDB '05, pp. 910–921.

Privacy-Aware Querying over Sensitive Trajectory Data

Nikos Pelekis
Department of Statistics and Insurance Science
University of Piraeus, Greece
npelekis@unipi.gr

Aris Gkoulalas-Divanis
Information Analytics Lab
IBM Research–Zurich
Rüschlikon, Switzerland
agd@zurich.ibm.com

Marios Vodas
Department of Informatics
University of Piraeus
Piraeus, Greece
mvodas@gmail.com

Despina Kopanaki
Department of Informatics
University of Piraeus
Piraeus, Greece
dkopanak@unipi.gr

Yannis Theodoridis
Department of Informatics
University of Piraeus
Piraeus, Greece
ytheod@unipi.gr

ABSTRACT

Existing approaches for privacy-aware mobility data sharing aim at publishing an anonymized version of the mobility dataset, operating under the assumption that most of the information in the original dataset can be disclosed without causing any privacy violations. In this paper, we assume that the majority of the information that exists in the mobility dataset must remain private and the data has to stay in-house to the hosting organization. To facilitate privacy-aware sharing of the mobility data we develop a trajectory query engine that allows subscribed users to gain restricted access to the database to accomplish various analysis tasks. The proposed engine (i) audits queries for trajectory data to block potential attacks to user privacy, (ii) supports range, distance, and k-nearest neighbors spatial and spatiotemporal queries, and (iii) preserves user anonymity in answers to queries by (a) augmenting the real trajectories with a set of carefully crafted, realistic fake trajectories, and (b) ensuring that no user-specific sensitive locations are reported as part of the returned trajectories.

Categories and Subject Descriptors

K.4.1 [**Computers and Society**]: Public Policy Issues—*privacy*; H.2.8 [**Database Management**]: Database Applications—*Spatial databases and GIS*

General Terms

Algorithms, Design, Experimentation

Keywords

Privacy-aware query engine, mobility data, anonymity, trajectory database

CIKM'11, October 24–28, 2011, Glasgow, Scotland, UK.

1. INTRODUCTION

The advances in mobile devices, positioning technologies and spatiotemporal database research, have made possible the tracking of mobile devices at a high accuracy, while supporting the efficient storage of mobility data in databases. From this perspective, we have nowadays the means to collect, store and process mobility data of an unprecedented quantity, quality and timeliness. As ubiquitous computing pervades our society, user mobility data represents a very useful but also sensitive source of information. On one hand, the movement traces of the users can aid traffic engineers, city managers and environmentalists towards decision making in a wide spectrum of applications, such as urban planning, traffic engineering and environmental pollution. On the other hand, the disclosure of mobility data to untrusted parties may jeopardize the privacy of the users whose movement is recorded, leading the way to abuse scenarios such as user tailing and profiling. As it becomes evident, the sharing of user mobility data for analysis purposes has to be done only after the data has been protected against potential privacy breaches.

Recently, several methodologies have been proposed to enable privacy-preserving mobility data sharing. Existing approaches, such as [1,7,8,11,17], aim at publishing an anonymous counterpart of the original dataset in which adversaries can no longer match the recorded movement of each user to the real identity of the user. A common assumption that is implicitly made in these approaches is that most of the information that is stored in the original dataset can be disclosed without causing any privacy violations. In this paper, we refrain from this assumption as it can be proven unrealistic in certain data sharing scenarios. Instead, we employ a more conservative approach to privacy by assuming that the majority of the information that is captured in the mobility dataset must remain private and that *the data has to stay in-house to the hosting organization.* Our assumption is primarily based on the following arguments:

- The data owner may be reluctant to publish the entire mobility dataset, or conformance to certain business regulations may require that the dataset resides in-house to the hosting organization.

- Mobility datasets can typically support many types of data analysis. In order for the anonymous dataset to be useful in practical applications, it is necessary that the anonymization approach can offer specific utility guarantees and this, in turn, requires knowledge of the intended workload. When the data resides in-house, the privacy preservation algorithms can support many types of data analysis (which may be unknown apriori) by guaranteeing at the same time the privacy of the users, whose information is recorded in the dataset.

- Data sharing policies may change from time to time and new types of privacy attacks to mobility data may be identified, yielding previously released data unprotected. In such events, it is crucial for the data owner to have knowledge of the sensitive information that was leaked, as well as be capable of safeguarding the data based on the new evidence. When the data resides in-house, the privacy-aware query engine can be updated to conform to the new policies and block new types of attack. Additionally, the auditing of queries allows the data owner to have knowledge about the extent of the data leakage by examining the history of user queries to the database.

Data sharing scenario: A data holder, such as a telecom operator or a governmental agency, collects movement information for a community of people. The raw movement data, capturing the location of each individual in the course of time, is processed to generate user trajectories that are subsequently stored in a database. Apart from the analysis that this data undergoes within the premises of the hosting organization, we assume that at least part of the data has to be made available to external, possibly untrusted, parties for querying and analysis purposes. As is evident, direct publishing of this information, even if the data is first deprived from any explicit identifiers, would severely compromise the privacy of the individuals whose movement is recorded in the database. This is due to the fact that malevolent end-users could potentially link the published trajectories to sensitive locations of the individuals (such as their houses), thus identify the users. To ensure privacy-aware sharing of in-house mobility data, a mechanism is necessary to control the information that is made available to external parties when they query the database, so that only nonsensitive information leaves the premises of the hosting organization.

In this paper, we realize and extend the basic design principles that were discussed in [6] by introducing HERMES++, a novel query engine for sensitive trajectory data that allows subscribed end-users to gain restricted access to the database to accomplish various analysis tasks. HERMES++ can shield the trajectory database from potential attacks to user privacy, while supporting popular queries for mobility data analysis, such as range queries, distance queries and nearest neighbors queries. Similarly to [6], HERMES++ operates by retrieving real user trajectories from the database and mixing them with carefully crafted fake trajectories in order to reduce the confidence of attackers regarding the real trajectories in the query result. However, unlike the privacy-engine that was described in [6], HERMES++ achieves to (a) audit end-user queries and effectively block an extended set of attacks to user privacy, securing the database against user identification, sensitive location tracking, and sequential tracking attacks, (b) generate smooth and more realistic fake trajectories that preserve the trend of the original data and use them to augment the real ones in returned answers to queries, and (c) ensure that no sensitive locations that would lead to user identification are reported as part of the returned trajectories. The latter goal is achieved by modifying parts of the trajectories that are close to sensitive locations, such as the houses of the users.
Our work makes the following contributions:

- It improves the design principles of [6] and proposes a full-fledged system that supports privacy-aware sharing of in-house mobility data.
- The proposed fake generation algorithm uses a sophisticated approach to generate smooth, realistic fake trajectories that respect the general trend of the real trajectories in the query result. By preserving the trends of the real trajectories when generating fakes, our framework minimizes the impact of the privacy mechanism to the outcome of the mobility data analysis.
- The proposed auditing mechanism can effectively identify and block a range of potential attacks that could lead to user identification or tracking.

The rest of this paper is organized as follows. Section 2 surveys the related work. In Section 3, we present the types of attacks to user privacy that are blocked by the privacy-aware query engine. Section 4 discusses in detail the auditing and the fake trajectory generation algorithms that are implemented as part of the query engine to support its functionality, while Section 5 sheds light on implementation issues of the engine. In Section 6, we experimentally evaluate the proposed framework demonstrating its effectiveness towards blocking attacks to user privacy, while generating realistic fake trajectories. Section 7 concludes this work.

2. RELATED WORK

Privacy-preserving data publishing has been the focus of attention of the database community for almost three decades. The research in this domain has progressed along two main directions: *providing on-site, restricted access to in-house data* and *providing off-site publication of sanitized data*. In the first category, methodologies have been proposed for disclosure control in statistical databases [2]. These approaches support only count and/or sum queries, since no other information can be made available to the inquirer.

The second direction in privacy-preserving data publishing collects methodologies that provide off-site publication of sanitized data. Several methodologies have been proposed to support different data types and analysis tasks [1,10,11,15–17]. Since our approach aims at concealing sensitive trajectory information, in the following we focus our attention on approaches that protect sensitive mobility data.

Hoh and Gruteser [7] present a data perturbation algorithm that is based on path crossing. The approach identifies when two nonintersecting trajectories that belong to different users are "sufficiently" close to each other in the original dataset and generates a fake crossing of these trajectories in the sanitized counterpart to prevent adversaries from tracking a complete user's trajectory.

Terrovitis and Mamoulis [17] consider datasets that depict user movement in the form of sequences of places that each user has visited, set out in the order of visit. They propose an anonymization approach that suppresses selected places from user trajectories to protect users from adversaries who hold projections of the data on specific sets of places.

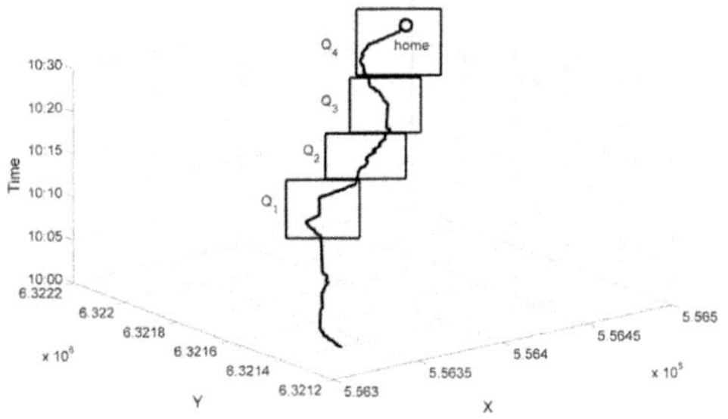

Figure 1: The sensitive location tracking and the sequential tracking attacks to user privacy

Nergiz, et al. [11] also rely on the sequential nature of mobility data and propose a coarsening strategy to generate a sanitized dataset that consists of K-anonymous [15, 16] sequences. The algorithm consolidates the trajectories of the original dataset into clusters of K and then anonymizes the trajectories in each cluster.

Abul, et al. [1] propose a K-anonymity approach that relies on the inherent uncertainty that exists with respect to the whereabouts of the users in historical datasets representing user mobility. The anonymity algorithm identifies trajectories that lie close to each other in time, employs space translation and generates clusters of at least K trajectories. Each cluster of K trajectories forms an anonymity region and the co-clustered trajectories can be released.

The most related work to ours is the study of Gkoulalas-Divanis and Verykios [6], which describes the design principles of a query engine that protects user privacy by generating fake trajectories. The idea behind [6], and also behind this work, is that malevolent users who query the trajectory database should not be able to discover (with high confidence) any real trajectories that are returned as part of the answer set of their queries, while they can use the returned data to support their analytic tasks. A shortcoming of [6] is that the time dimension was not explicitly handled in the overall design. Moreover, the interpolation technique that was proposed for the generation of the fake trajectories was applied on pairs of real trajectories and thus could fail to account for the actual trend in the query region, while also leading to the generation of non-smooth fake trajectories. The current proposal fully implements the proposed privacy engine and, to our knowledge, is the first to introduce a Moving Object Database Engine (MOD) with privacy-preservation functionality.

3. PRIVACY ATTACKS

HERMES++ can effectively protect the privacy of the users by blocking three types of attacks that malevolent users may try to pursue in the original database:

- **User identification attack**: In this attack the identity of the user can be exposed by ad hoc queries involving overlapping spatiotemporal regions.
- **Sensitive location tracking attack**: In this attack the malevolent user tries to map-match one or more locations in a user trajectory to known locations that can effectively expose the identity of the user (e.g., the address of a house or a betting office). We call such locations *sensitive* for the user as they should not be disclosed to the attackers.
- **Sequential tracking attack**: In this attack the user is tracked down through his trajectory by a set of focused queries on regions that are near to each other, in terms of space and time. The attacker can "follow" the user and learn the places that he has visited.

The user identification attack is possible when the query engine answers a query involving a spatial (or spatiotemporal) region and then another, more specific query, involving part of this region. In this case, the attacker can breach the enforced privacy model by identifying fake trajectories which, in turn, increases his confidence regarding the real trajectories in the system. To block this attack, we use auditing to track the queries initiated by each end-user in the system and deny answering overlapping queries.

The sensitive location tracking attack allows malevolent users to distinguish real trajectories from fakes, learn sensitive locations that real users have visited, and (possibly) reveal the identity of these users. To block these attacks, we protect the starting and the ending location of trajectories, as well as any other (owner-specified) location in the course of the user trajectory that can be considered as *sensitive* for the user. As an example of this type of attack, assume a query that involves region Q_4, shown in Figure 1. Since in this region the trajectory has its end point to a sensitive location, the attacker can map-match this location and reveal the user's identity. The attack can succeed even if fake trajectories are generated in this region because the probability of a fake trajectory having an end point to a sensitive location is low, while this is very common for real users. To block the sensitive location tracking attack, our auditing approach identifies sensitive locations of trajectories that appear in the query window and proceeds to dislocate them so that the sensitive location is not disclosed.

Last, in the sequential tracking attack an attacker attempts to "follow" a user trajectory in the system by using a set of focused queries involving spatiotemporal regions that are adjacent to each other. To block this attack, the proposed auditing algorithm takes the necessary measures to smoothly continue the movement of fake trajectories from neighboring regions (returned as part of previous queries of the user) to the current region, so as to prohibit attackers from distinguishing the fake trajectories from the real ones.

4. ALGORITHMS

In the following sections we present the algorithms that deliver the functionality of HERMES++. Section 4.1 describes the algorithm that we designed for the generation of realistic fake trajectories. In Section 4.2, we present the auditing technique that is used to audit user queries and preserve the privacy in the answers to the queries.

4.1 Fake trajectory generation

The proposed fake trajectory generation algorithm has the ability to produce trajectories that follow the trend of the input set of real trajectories, thus minimize the potential of privacy breaches when query results are released to the end-users. This algorithm plays a central role in our privacy-aware query engine. When a user poses a query to the database, the engine provides the answer only if at least

Algorithm 1 Fake Trajectory Generation

```
1: function FAKE-GEN(line segments S_i, minimum number of points
   MinLns, smoothing parameter γ, time step of sampling rate
   Timestep, MBB(t_MBBmin, t_MBBmax), d_min, d_max, l_min, l_max,
   l_avg, avgU_min, avgU_max)
2:     fake_trajectory ← RTG(S_i, MinLns, γ)
3:     calculate initial timestamp t_0 of the fake trajectory
4:     t_max ← t_0 + |fake_trajectory| * Timestep
5:     if (t_max > t_MBBmax) then
6:         repeat
7:             Douglas_Peucker (fake_trajectory, f)
8:             f ← f/2
9:             t_max ← t_0 + |fake_trajectory| * Timestep
10:        until (t_max < t_MBBmax)
11:        if (l_max > 2 * l_avg) then
12:            l_max ← random(l_avg, 2 * l_avg)
13:        else
14:            l_max ← l_avg * random(1, l_max/l_avg)
15:    for each (p_i ∈ fake_trajectory) do
16:        set timestamps of initial and final point of p_i
17:        calculate speed U_i of p_i
18:        if (U_i < avgU_min or U_i > avgU_max) then
19:            repeat
20:                l ← random(l_min, l_max)
21:                calculate new speed U_i of p_i
22:            until (U_min < U_i < U_max)
23:        calculate angle φi
24:        define coords of new ending point based on l
25:        map match p_i
26:    return fake_trajectory
```

L real user trajectories exist in the area. The lower bound L in the number of users is a simple way to prevent answering queries whose original result set is very small (e.g., a range query in a region with very few trajectories), as in this case the generated fake trajectories may fail to capture the trend of the real trajectories. Prior to releasing any real trajectory, an approach is employed (*see* Section 4.2) to protect any sensitive locations in the trajectory that could be used by malevolent end-users to identify the corresponding user. To produce the answer set for the query, the engine generates N fake trajectories, where N is an owner-specified threshold. The proposed algorithm has the ability to produce fake trajectories for different types of queries, such as range, nearest neighbor and distance queries, while it is used by our auditing mechanism (Section 4.2) to handle different types of attacks from malevolent users.

Unlike the simple fake generation approach of [6], the fake trajectory generation algorithm that we propose in this work is based on the idea of the *Representative Trajectory Generation* (*RTG* for short) algorithm, introduced by Lee et al. in [9]. The main idea of this algorithm is that the resulting representative trajectory describes the overall movement of a set of directed segments, produced after the partitioning of a set of trajectories. The partitioned trajectories (i.e., directed segments) are clustered according to a distance function taking into account the parallel, perpendicular and angle distance of the segments. The outcome of the *RTG* algorithm, applied on each cluster, produces a smooth (more or less) linear trajectory that best describes the corresponding cluster. However, similarly to [6], the *RTG* algorithm also fails to consider the temporal dimension of the generated trajectory. As a result, our proposed fake trajectory generation algorithm has to transform the *RTG* output by appropriately integrating the time dimension into the fake trajectory generation process.

Algorithm 1 provides the details of our fake trajectory generation approach. The algorithm takes as input a set of line segments S_i resulting from a set of trajectories which form the answer to a user query. In the first step (line 2), the representative trajectory is produced based on this set of line segments of trajectories. For simplicity reasons, in Figure 2 we depict segments as consecutive parts of trajectories; however, in the general case, they could be disconnected and independent segments that are filtered in a way that all move towards (more or less) the same direction. This is because the *RTG* algorithm assumes that all segments follow the same directional pattern. In the sequel, the *RTG* algorithm sweeps a rotated vertical line according to the average direction vector towards the major axis, counting the number of line segments that are either the starting or the ending point of a line segment. If the resulted number is equal to or greater than a threshold *MinLns*, the algorithm calculates the average coordinate of those points and assigns the average into the set of representative trajectory; otherwise, it proceeds to the next point. To avoid segments that are too close to each other, a smoothing parameter γ is utilized. The final outcome of this step is the trajectory with the dotted line shown in Figure 2.

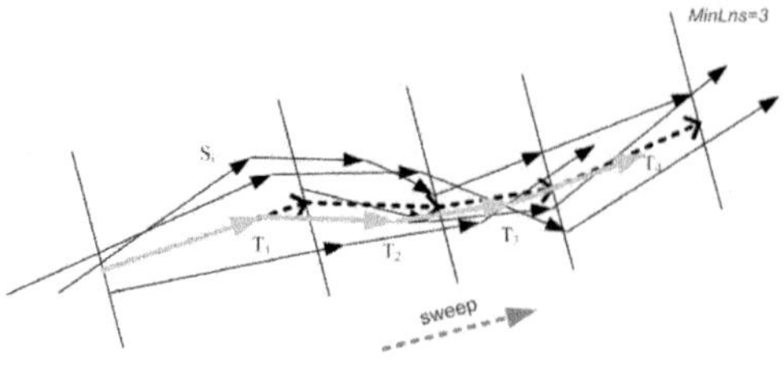

Figure 2: Generating a fake trajectory based on the representative trajectory of a set of line segments

After calculating the representative trajectory (line 2), the algorithm inserts the time dimension to each line segment and performs additional computations to adjust it and make it more plausible. In detail, we examine and require for a realistic length and speed for the 3D segments of the fake trajectory. If these measures get unusual values then an adversary may be able to identify which trajectory is the fake one. In Figure 2, the grey solid line depicts the final fake trajectory after assigning the time dimension to the segments and adjusting them to be more realistic. In order to achieve this, the algorithm takes as parameter the spatiotemporal *Minimum Bounding Box* (MBB), which is set by the auditing mechanism and may be either the MBB of the user's query parameter (in the case of range queries), or the MBB that is formed by the whole trajectories whose parts belong to the results of user's query. An additional set of input parameters that is provided by the auditing mechanism corresponds to statistical computations regarding $d_{min}, d_{max}, l_{min}, l_{max}$, which are the minimum and maximum trajectories' duration and segments' length, respectively, and $avgU_{min}, avgU_{max}, l_{avg}$, which are the average minimum and maximum speed, as well as, the average length of the segments, respectively. The *Timestep* parameter is the duration of a line segment and is considered to be constant indicating that the moving object transmits its location update at regular temporal intervals. The outcome of the algorithm is a set of line segments forming a trajectory, which are stored in the array *fake_trajectory*.

Having calculated the set of line segments, the algorithm computes the initial timestamp t_0 that the fake trajectory will start at (line 3). The initial timestamp is defined as $t_0 = t_{MBBmin} +$ random(0,SP), where $SP = (t_{max} - t_{min}) - random(d_{min}, d_{max})$ corresponds to a value used to ensure that time t_0 of the first point of the fake trajectory will not be placed near t_{MBBmax}. Moreover, the maximum timestamp of the fake trajectory should not exceed t_{MBBmax}, otherwise it will differ from the real trajectories. In order to ensure this, the maximum timestamp t_{max} of the fake trajectory is calculated (line 4) as a function of the initial timestamp t_0 and the duration of the fake trajectory (i.e., $|fake\_trajectory| * \ Timestep$). If ($t_{max} > t_{MBBmax}$) then a line simplification procedure is applied to reduce the number of line segments (lines 6-10). *Douglas-Peucker* (line 6) [5] is an algorithm that compresses the generated segments by using a polyline representation and a parameter f that corresponds to a distance threshold, defined as a percentage of the trajectory's length. The compression procedure is repeated until ($t_{max} < t_{MBBmax}$) and in each iteration the parameter f is halved.

Having calculated the initial timestamp, the algorithm adjusts the maximum length l_{max} of the segments that have been generated (lines 11-14) in order to manipulate long segments that will lead to the generation of non-realistic fake trajectories. Specifically, if l_{max} is greater than twice the average length l_{avg}, then l_{max} is being recalculated as a random value between l_{avg} and the twice of l_{avg}. Otherwise, the algorithm sets l_{max} randomly between l_{avg} and l_{max}. Then, the algorithm enters a loop (line 15) and assigns the time dimension to each line segment of the fake trajectory. The initial timestamp t_0 of the first line segment has been calculated in previous steps. The timestamp of the ending point of this segment equals to t_0 increased by the sampling rate's duration, i.e., is equal to $t_0 + \ Timestep$. The ending timestamp of the initial segment will be the starting timestamp of the next segment. Generally, for each line segment it holds that $t_{i+1} = t_i + \ Timestep$, where $0 \leq i < |fake\_trajectory|$.

After assigning the time dimension to the current segment p_i (line 16), the algorithm proceeds to calculate the speed U_i for each segment p_i (line 17) and checks if it lies within $avgU_{min}$ and $avgU_{max}$ (lines 18-22). If it is outside this range, the algorithm calculates a random segment length l, between l_{min} and l_{max}, such that the speed U_i of the specific segment is within the limits. As a final step, the coordinates of the new ending point are identified based on the length of segment l that was calculated before (lines 23-24).

Depending on the direction of the segment and its angle ϕ_i with the x-axis, the fake trajectory generation algorithm calculates the new coordinates (x_{t+1}, y_{t+1}). The angle ϕ_i is given by $\phi_i = \text{atan2}(y_{t+1} - y_t, x_{t+1} - x_t)$, while the new coordinates (x_{t+1}, y_{t+1}) are calculated as:$x_{t+1} = x_t + l * cos(\phi)$ and $y_{t+1} = y_t + l * sin(\phi)$, where l is the length of the line segment. In the case that trajectory data are related to an underlying road network, the fake trajectory generation algorithm map matches the generated fake trajectory with the specific road network by employing a map matching algorithm (line 25) [3]. This functionality of the algorithm can lead to a more realistic representation of the fake trajectory and thus disincline adversaries from identifying real users. After calculating the new coordinates the algorithm proceeds to the next segment and the procedure continues until all line segments are examined. Finally, the generated fake trajectory is returned (line 26). Figure 3 demonstrates the outcome of the *Fake-Gen* algorithm (green trajectory) with respect to the *RTG* algorithm (red trajectory), when applied to a set of trajectories (i.e. blue trajectories). Obviously, the result of *Fake-Gen* produces a more realistic representation of the trend of the real trajectories.

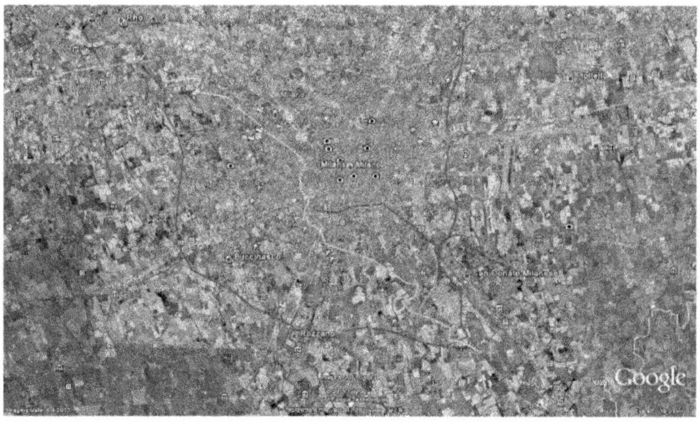

Figure 3: The outcome of *Fake-Gen* (green trajectory) w.r.t. the *RTG* algorithm (red trajectory) when applied on a set of trajectories (shown in blue)

4.2 Query auditing

Algorithm 2 presents our query auditing approach for shielding the database against malevolent queries. When a new query is submitted to the engine, the auditing algorithm first examines if this query involves an area that (partially) overlaps with that of a previous query, submitted by the same end-user. If this is the case, then it denies servicing the query (lines 2-3) to block a potential user identification attack. If the previous test is negative, the auditing mechanism executes the actual query of the user and retrieves the result set (line 4). In order to prohibit the identification of an individual by an adversary that is able to link sensitive locations that are visited by a user (e.g., the home of the user) with trajectories that belong to the specific query, we propose the *Hide Sensitive Location Algorithm* (line 5). This algorithm takes as input a set of sensitive locations SL, a set of trajectories T and the MBB formed by user's query. Initially, the algorithm selects all sensitive locations SL' that lie inside the MBB (line 2 of Algorithm 3). For each trajectory of the given set T, it defines those sensitive locations, SL'_i, that correspond to the current trajectory (lines 3-4). For every sensitive location, $SL'_{i,j}$, it examines if fake sub-trajectories that hide the sensitive locations have been previously computed for this trajectory and retrieves them from *History* (lines 5-7). Otherwise, it computes a new synthetic (fake) trajectory that is then stored for future reference (lines 9-14).

The procedure that is followed by Algorithm 2 to generate and update the synthetic sub-trajectory is based on a variant of the GSTD trajectory synthesizer, called GSTD*, proposed in [13]. GSTD* produces trajectories following complex mobility patterns based on a given distribution of spatiotemporal focal points, to be visited by each trajectory in a specific order. The general idea behind the generator is to use the focal points so as to attract each trajectory's movement. When a particular trajectory has reached the area around a focal point, having at the same time completed the respective temporal predicate, the generation algorithm changes the attracting point to the next focal point in the list, and so on, until no focal points are left unvisited.

The idea of hiding sensitive locations of a trajectory by misplacing its route is illustrated in Figure 4. The algorithm discovers the intersection points of the trajectory with a circle that is formed around a sensitive location by taking as radius the distance between the sensitive location from a point where the object would have been moved after a certain period of time tw (i.e., tw is a temporal window), if it was moving with its current speed. The idea is to use these intersection points as the focal points in GSTD* (line 9) (see the filled gray circles in Figure 4). If the number of focal points is greater than two (i.e. the object enters and/or leaves the circle more than two times), the algorithm utilizes the first (entering) and the last (leaving) one. In case where the sensitive location is either the initial or the ending point causing the creation of only one focal point, the algorithm randomly selects another random focal point in the perimeter of the circle (line 10-11). After determining focal points it produces a synthetic (fake) trajectory by applying GSTD* between the two chosen focal points as illustrated in the figure with the dotted line (line 12). The algorithm returns the set of trajectories that does no longer contains sensitive locations (line 15).

Having protected the sensitive locations of the trajectories in the querying region, Algorithm 2 commands the generation of the necessary fake trajectories for this region (lines 12-22). To generate the requested number of fake trajectories, the algorithm calculates a set of basic statistics (line 12) that are needed by the fake trajectory generation approach (Algorithm 1), while trying to find trajectories that follow more or less the same direction in the query region (lines 13-21). Specifically, a step dir_{step} (in degrees) is randomly selected (line 14) in the rage of $(0, dir_{step_{max}})$, with $dir_{step_{max}}$ being an input parameter that defines the size of an angular range used to divide the Cartesian plane. As illustrated in Figure 5, the algorithm selects those segments from the real trajectories that belong to the range (dir_{min}, dir_{max}) (see the solid lines in the figure), which are set by randomly assigning dir_{min} and then setting dir_{max} equal to $dir_{min} + dir_{step}$. Subsequently, it calls Algorithm 1 on these segments and passes the query window to create one new fake trajectory. The same process is repeated for the next range of directions, which leads to the generation of another fake trajectory, until the 360° are exceeded. Then, the algorithm selects a new dir_{step} and repeats the same process, until the requested number of fake trajectories are generated (line 22). Note that the filtering approach on the directional property of the segments guarantees that the fake generation algorithm will produce nice representative trajectories of the query result, as it acts as a simple clustering methodology on the overall set of available segments.

After generating the fake trajectories, Algorithm 2 takes the necessary measures to protect the privacy of the users whose movement is depicted in the query window by smoothly continuing the movement of the fake trajectories from neighboring regions, returned as part of previous queries posed by the end-user, to the current one. Specifically, the algorithm examines if the query posed by the end-user has a nearby query made by the same end-user in the past, which does not exceed a spatial s_{thr} and a temporal t_{thr} threshold. In case that the query has only one such neighbor, the algorithm performs a one-by-one matching (line 24) between the fake trajectories of MBB and MBB_{hist} (i.e. the nearby query saved in *History*). In detail, it first finds the MBB with the minimum number of fake trajectories and then it randomly matches each one of them with fakes from the other query, by producing pairs P_i of fake trajectories. For each pair, it examines if MBB touches MBB_{hist} or if they are apart. In the first case, illustrated in Figure 6, a space time translation is performed to connect the two fake trajectories. The fake trajectory is transferred in the x and y axes, if necessary. Then, the algorithm checks the time dimension to assure there is no temporal gap. If such a gap exists, the algorithm recalculates the timestamp of each point of the fake trajectory. In the second case (see Figure 7), where a spatial and/or a temporal gap exists between MBB and MBB_{hist}, Algorithm 2 generates a connection-trajectory (see the dotted lines) between them by using the GSTD* algorithm [13]. Focal points are the ending point of the one trajectory with the starting point of its matching trajectory in P_i. After generating the fake trajectories, the algorithm applies the hiding process of the sensitive locations also for these trajectories (line 32), to conceal the fact that they are fakes.

The trajectory auditing algorithm (i.e., *TrajAuditor*), as presented in Algorithm 2, covers the cases of range and distance queries. The same algorithm can be minimally adapted to support k-nearest neighbors queries. In the case of k-nearest neighbors queries, the end-user has to provide as parameters the value of k, the trajectory for which he or she searches its k nearest neighbors, and a temporal period which is a sub-period of the trajectory's lifespan. Moreover, the MBB window in a k nearest neighbors query refers to the MBB of the trajectories that form the result of this query. Thus, to support such queries, Algorithm 2 has to be modified so that in lines 12 (17), where statistics (MBB parameter for Algorithm 1) for the generation of the fake trajectories are computed, the window will be the MBB of all real trajectories in the query result.

As a last remark, we need to point out that Algorithm 2 commands the generation of the necessary number of fake trajectories based on the parts of the real trajectories that appear inside the query window. An alternative approach (henceforth called *TrajFaker*) would be to generate wide fake trajectories that exceed the limits of the window the user submitted. In this case, auditing would still be applicable but not forced, contrary to the case of Algorithm 2. The alternative strategy differs from that of Algorithm 2 in the following steps. When a user executes a query, the new approach finds the trajectories that are contained in the specific spatiotemporal window (or the k nearest neighbors in case of such queries) and then retrieves the whole trajectories and not the parts of them that lie inside the window. Subsequently, it generates fake trajectories by employing Algorithm 1 on the whole trajectories. Each generated fake trajectory is examined to see whether it crosses the spatiotemporal window of the query and, if so, it is included to the returning set. Otherwise, the trajectory is discarded and the same process is repeated. All generated fake trajectories are stored in order to participate to the generation of other fake trajectories. Finally, there are no privacy threats with respect to sequential tracking as before, since the generated fake trajectories are based on the whole trajectories and not parts of them, and are stored. If an adversary tries to exe-

Algorithm 2 Query Auditing Algorithm

```
function TrajAuditor(user's query MBB, number of generated fake trajectories N, lower bound threshold L, spatial threshold s_thr, temporal threshold t_thr, maximum direction step dir_stepmax, set of sensitive locations SL, temporal window tw, MinLns, γ, Timestep)
    if (CheckHistory(User has posed an overlapping query w.r.t. MBB) = true) then
        Privacy threat: Overlapping queries
    TR ← SpatioTemporalRangeQuery(MBB)
    TR ← HideSensitiveLocations(SL, TR, MBB, tw)
    if (CheckHistory(User has posed in the past a nearby query w.r.t. s_thr, t_thr) = true) then
        Privacy threat: Sequential tracking attack
    else
        if (|TR| ≤ L) then
            Privacy threat: Lower bound threshold violation
        else
            CalculateStatistics(d_min, d_max, l_min, l_max, l_avg, avgU_min, avgU_max)
            repeat
                dir_step ← random(0, dir_stepmax)
                dir_min ← random(0, 360); dir_max = dir_min + dir_step
                repeat
                    S_i ← FILTER_BY_DIRECTION(dir_min, dir_max, TR)
                    FT ← FT ∪ FAKE_GEN(S_i, MinLns, γ, Timestep, MBB, Statistics)
                    dir_min ← dir_min + dir_step
                    dir_max ← dir_max + dir_step
                until (dir_max > 360)
            until (|FT| = N)
    Retrieve from History all fakes FT_hist from a nearby query of the user w.r.t. s_thr, t_thr
    P_match ← MinRandomMax(FT, FT_hist)
    for each pair (P_i(T_j, T_k) ∈ P_match) do
        if (MBB touches a historic query of the user) then
            SPACE_TIME_TRANSLATION(P_i)
        else
            focal_points ← (T_j_end, T_k_start)
            GSTD*(focal_points)
            Update in FT the fake trajectory that corresponds to P_i
    FT ← HideSensitiveLocations(SL, FT, MBB, tw)
    UpdateHistory
    return (TR ∪ FT)
```

Algorithm 3 Hide Sensitive Locations Algorithm

```
function HideSensitiveLocations(set of sensitive locations SL, set of trajectories T, user's query MBB, temporal window tw)
    SL' ← SL inside MBB
    for each (T_i ∈ T) do
        SL'_i ← select the subset of SL' that corresponds to T_i
        for each (sensitive location of T_i, SL'_i,j ∈ SL'_i) do
            if (a fake sub-trajectory has been computed in the past for this SL'_i,j) then
                Retrieve the fake sub-trajectory from History and update T_i
            else
                focal_points ← Intersection(T_i, buffer(SL'_i,j, tw))
                if (|focal_points| = 1) then
                    focal_points ← AddRandomPointOnSurface(buffer(T_i, tw))
                Produce a synthetic/fake trajectory by applying GSTD* between first and last focal_points
                Update the part of T_i with the synthetic/fake sub-trajectory
                UpdateHistory
    return (T)
```

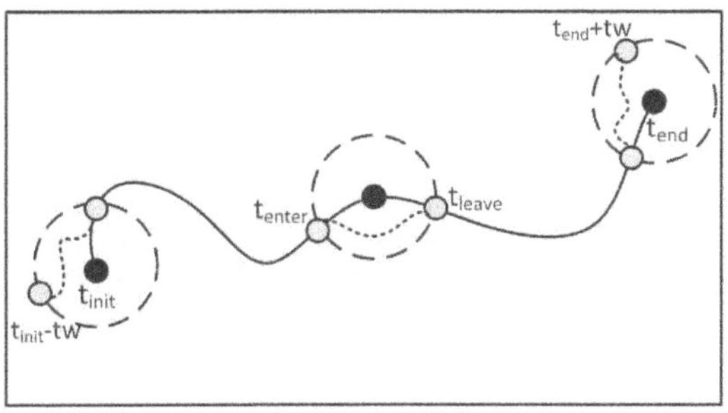

Figure 4: Protecting the sensitive locations of user trajectories

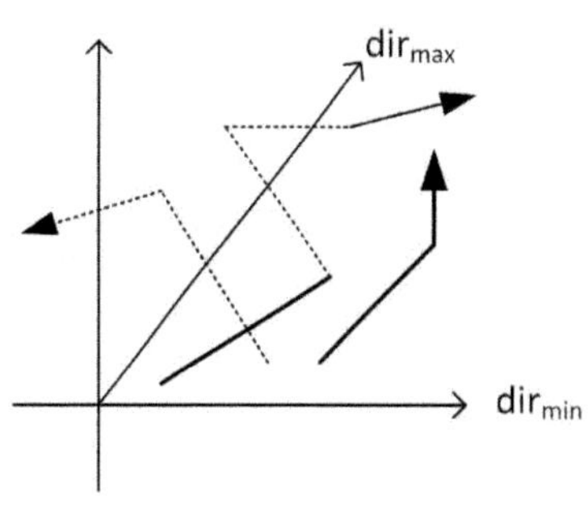

Figure 5: Selecting segments from real trajectories

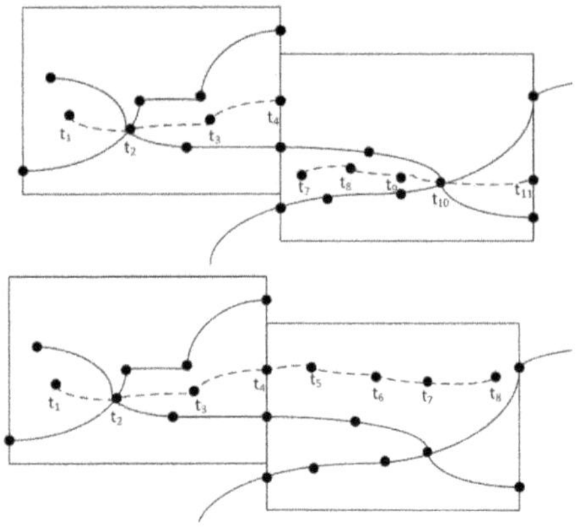

Figure 6: Prohibiting sequential tracking (Case I)

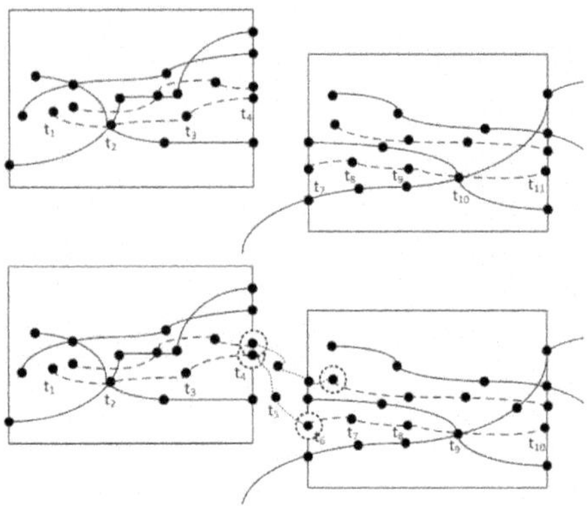

Figure 7: Prohibiting sequential tracking (Case II)

cute overlapping or sequential queries, the fakes will appear in all of these queries' answers.

5. SYSTEM IMPLEMENTATION

HERMES++ has been designed as a system extension of the HERMES query engine [12], which in turn was developed as an extension that provides trajectory functionality to Oracle's Object-Relational DBMS (ORDBMS). HERMES++ exploits on the trajectory storage functionality and the spatiotemporal query processing capabilities of HERMES for providing anonymous queries to users. More specifically, HERMES defines a trajectory data type and a collection of operations as an Oracle data cartridge, which is further enhanced by a special trajectory preserving access method, namely the TB-tree [14]. HERMES++ directly utilizes this functionality at the ORDBMS level to store real and fake trajectories, as well as any historic information of all the users' queries (and the corresponding responses), in order to avoid different types of tracking attacks (e.g., sequential tracking). It succeeds so by an embedded auditing module which invokes the HERMES's queries and the fake trajectory generator algorithm. The whole framework is build at the ORDBMS level, which means that HERMES++'s users have the ability to pose their queries through a PL/SQL interface. As such, from an architectural point of view, HERMES++ acts as a wrapper over the HERMES query engine and not as a secure middleware. Figure 8 illustrates HERMES++ architectural framework.

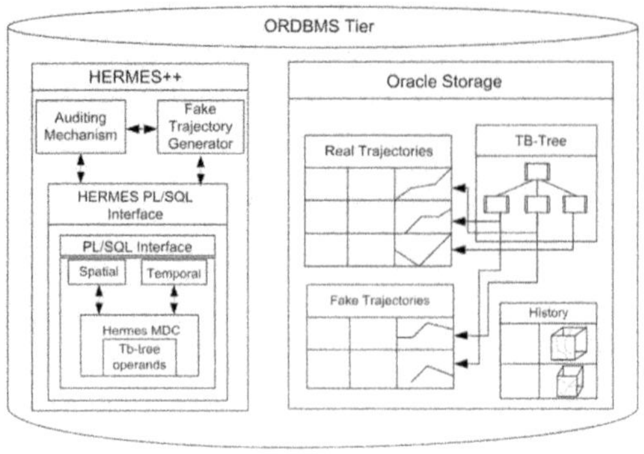

Figure 8: HERMES++ system architecture

6. EXPERIMENTAL EVALUATION

In this section, we experimentally evaluate the proposed privacy-aware query engine to assess its effectiveness in protecting user privacy when answering queries. To evaluate the distortion that is caused by the query engine to the database due to the generation of fake trajectories, we consider that the data owner *requires that at least K trajectories are returned to the end-users in response to their queries*, for all different types of supported queries. Parameter K is similar to using a variable N threshold for the generation of fake trajectories; it's purpose is to provide insight on the performance of the query engine when the number of generated fake trajectories is dynamically changing. To assess the efficiency of the proposed auditing methodology, we compute the time lag in the responses to the end-users' queries. We report experiments over a synthetic dataset, which was generated using Brinkhoff's network-based generator for moving objects [4]. The dataset contains 4495 trajectories, all living in a temporal period of 800 timestamps. A location update is performed in successive timestamps that are 5 minutes far from each other. The dataset has been generated over the road network of Oldenburg (Germany). It contains 153163 points, the radius area containing all trajectories is 17889.6, the maximum length of a trajectory is 668 and the average distance between consecutive points is 697.9.

For each query type that is supported by our query engine, we evaluated our methodology by measuring the database distortion that is defined as the percentage of the generated fake trajectories with respect to the size of the database. For each experiment, we created 1000 random queries. For range queries (and distance queries, which are handled as range queries with the distance threshold being the measure for determining the range size), we randomly selected different sizes, locations and time durations, while for k nearest neighbors queries we randomly selected the query trajectory and the temporal period (sub-period of the query trajectory's lifespan) for different values of k. For k nearest neighbors queries the corresponding MBB was set to $0.1 * d$, where d is the length of the maximum side of the MBB of the whole dataset. This implies that a trajectory is not included in the k nearest neighbors if its distance is greater than $0.1 * d$. We use this approach to exclude results sets that cover a disproportionally large MBB that will have as an effect the creation of many fakes. In all cases, we have set the $MinLns$ parameter to 2, the γ smoothing parameter to 5m, and the $Timestep$ to the sampling rate of the dataset.

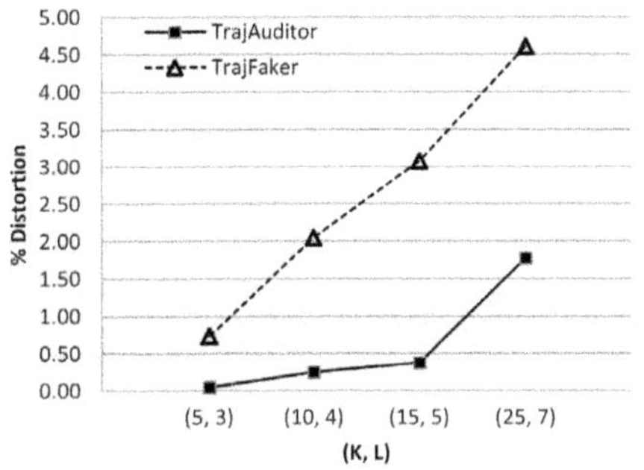

Figure 9: Distortion by range queries w.r.t. K, L

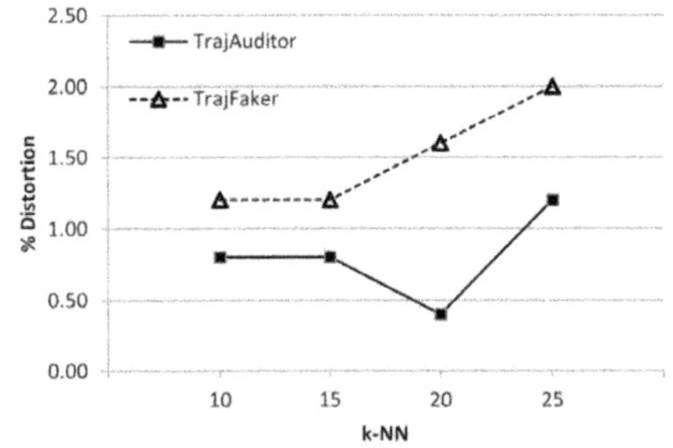

Figure 10: Distortion by kNN queries w.r.t k ($K = 5$)

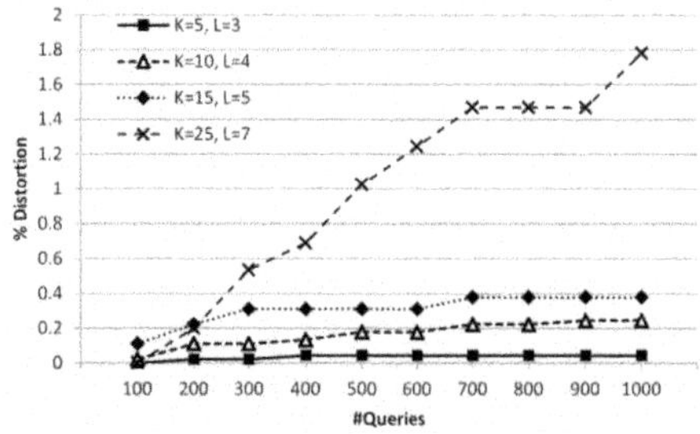

Figure 11: Distortion over time w.r.t. the value of K **-** ***TrajAuditor***

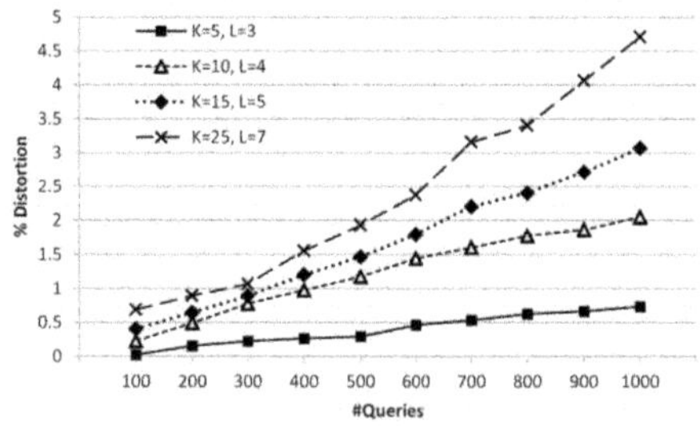

Figure 12: Distortion over time w.r.t. the value of K **-** ***TrajFaker***

Moreover, we have set the spatial (temporal) threshold s_{thr} (t_{thr}) to $0.001*d$, respectively, while the maximum direction step $dir_{step_{max}}$ was set to $45°$.

Figure 9 illustrates the distortion of the database for spatiotemporal range queries for both proposed approaches. Specifically, the figure shows the percentage of the generated fake trajectories for different value-pairs of K and L. Note that we slightly increase the L bound analogously with the increase of the K threshold. Clearly, the overall distortion of the database even for large thresholds of K (w.r.t the size of the database) is very low. Moreover, the *TrajAuditor* results in less distortion for small values of K, while for larger values the relative rate of distortion w.r.t. *TrajFaker* is decreased. This is rational, as for larger K thresholds the *TrajFaker* will produce less fakes, but longer, which have been generated in preceding queries. Intuitively, the fakes are less in this case as the algorithm re-uses parts of the long fakes produced by other queries.

In Figure 10 we repeat the same experiment for kNN queries but this time we keep the K threshold stable to 5 and scale the number of k nearest neighbors. As expected, again the results present the same pattern. In the sequel and due to space limitations, we omit further presentation regarding k nearest neighbors queries as they do not allow different conclusions from those of range queries.

Figures 11 and 12 show the distortion in the database for *TrajAuditor* and *TrajFaker* (respectively) at any given time. The distortion is plotted with respect to the users' queries (in temporal order, but still in random sizes and locations), for different values of K. As expected, lower values of K result in a smaller distortion of the database, since less fakes are generated. Furthermore, for any value of K the curve is increasing, however, for the case of *TrajAuditor* it is convex, which means that there is some time instance at which the fakes in the dataset suffice to answer a reasonable amount of user queries, without the need of generating additional fakes. On the other hand, in the case of *TrajFaker*, the curve is monotonously increasing, but note that in this case we have not applied any of the auditing mechanisms, so we respond to any user query by generating fakes. Despite this the distortion remains at low levels, lower than 5%, even for $K = 25$. The reason that the database distortion is low, relies on the re-use of the fake trajectories across different users' queries. An additional qualitative advantage of the *TrajFaker* is that fake trajectories in this case are more realistic, as they are produced by whole, real trajectories and not portions whose size depend on the query size.

Next, we conducted experiments over range queries of varying volumes (i.e. multiples of the whole space-time). The queries are clustered in ten equally sized groups. Each group contains randomly selected queries of the same volume. Figure 13 depicts the distortion in the database when applying randomly 1000 queries using *TrajFaker*. Notice the decrease in database distortion as the size of the queries increases. This is because large queries will not be forced to generate more fakes, since some of the fakes will have already been created by small queries that produce long fakes.

Figure 14 presents the number of query rejections (denials) of the *TrajAuditor* for different values of K, and L. The upward convex trend of the curves is due to the fact that as the volume of the queries increases it is more probable to lead to sequential tracking attacks. We note that larger K values result in less query rejections. This is justified by the simultaneous increase of the L bound. A larger lower bound L results in more query denials. More such

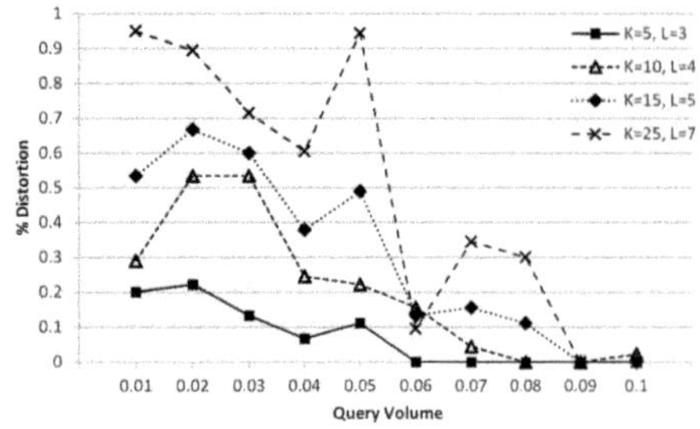

Figure 13: Distortion vs. query size w.r.t. the value of K - *TrajFaker*

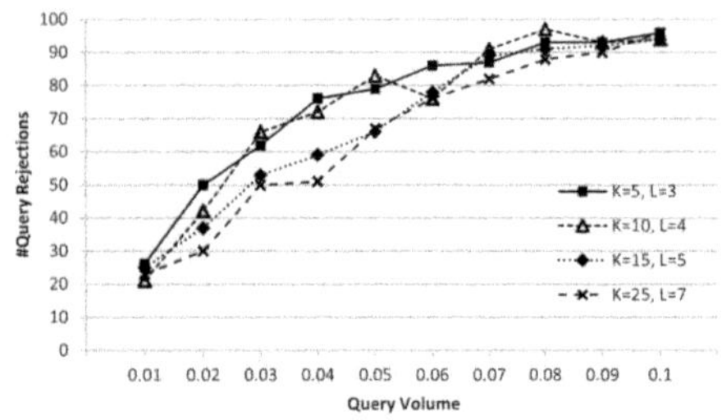

Figure 14: Query rejections vs. query size w.r.t. K

rejections mean fewer MBBs to be stored in history, which means fewer rejections due to sequential tracking attacks.

Last, we study the efficiency of the auditing mechanism. Figure 15 presents the average time over all 1000 queries of how much does *TrajAuditor* (*TrajFaker*) delay the response to the user's query. As expected, *TrajAuditor* presents larger time lags, while both approaches show a superlinear behavior due to the generation of fakes.

7. CONCLUSION

In this paper we presented HERMES++, a privacy-aware query engine that enables the remote analysis of user mobility data. HERMES++ supports a variety of popular spatial and spatiotemporal queries and uses auditing and fake trajectory generation techniques to identify and block, respectively, potential attacks to user privacy. Through experimental evaluation, we demonstrated the effectiveness of our approach to protect the privacy of the users, while minimally distorting the mobility dataset.

Acknowledgments

Research partially supported by the FP7 ICT/FET Project MODAP (Mobility, Data Mining, and Privacy) funded by the European Union. URL: www.modap.org.

8. REFERENCES

[1] O. Abul, , F. Bonchi, and M. Nanni. Never walk alone: Uncertainty for anonymity in moving objects databases. In *ICDE*, pages 376–385, 2008.

[2] N. R. Adam and J. C. Worthmann. Security-control methods for statistical databases: A comparative study. *ACM Computing Surveys*, 21(4):515–556, 1989.

[3] S. Brakatsoulas, D. Pfoser, R. Salas, and C. Wenk. On map-matching vehicle tracking data. In *VLDB*, pages 853–864, 2005.

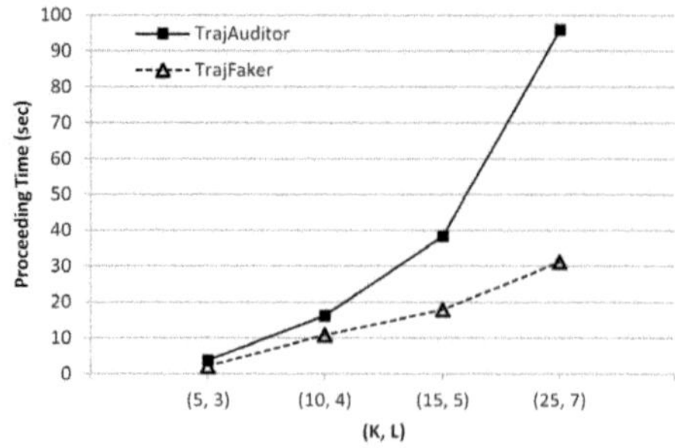

Figure 15: Time lag w.r.t the value of K

[4] T. Brinkhoff. A framework for generating network-based moving objects. *Geoinformatica*, 6(2):153–180, 2002.

[5] D. Douglas and T. Peucker. Algorithms for the reduction of the number of points required to represent a digitized line or its caricature. *Canadian Cartographer*, 10(2):112–122, 1973.

[6] A. Gkoulalas-Divanis and V. S. Verykios. A privacy-aware trajectory tracking query engine. *SIGKDD Explorations*, 10(1):40–49, 2008.

[7] B. Hoh and M. Gruteser. Protecting location privacy through path confusion. In *SECURECOMM*, pages 194–205, 2005.

[8] B. Hoh, M. Gruteser, H. Xiong, and A. Alrabady. Preserving privacy in GPS traces via uncertainty-aware path cloaking. In *CCS*, pages 161–171, 2007.

[9] J.-G. Lee, J. Han, and K.-Y. Whang. Trajectory clustering: A partition-and-group framework. In *SIGMOD*, pages 593–604, 2007.

[10] K. LeFevre, D. DeWitt, and R. Ramakrishnan. Mondrian multidimensional k-anonymity. In *ICDE*, page 25, 2006.

[11] M. E. Nergiz, M. Atzori, and Y. Saygin. Towards trajectory anonymization: A generalization-based approach. In *ACM GIS Workshop on Security and Privacy in GIS and LBS*, pages 1–10, 2008.

[12] N. Pelekis, E. Frentzos, N. Giatrakos, and Y. Theodoridis. HERMES: Aggregative LBS via a trajectory DB engine. In *SIGMOD*, pages 1255–1258, 2008.

[13] N. Pelekis, I. Kopanakis, E. E. Kotsifakos, E. Frentzos, and Y. Theodoridis. Clustering uncertain trajectories. *KAIS*. to appear.

[14] D. Pfoser, C. S. Jensen, and Y. Theodoridis. Novel approaches to the indexing of moving object trajectories. In *VLDB*, pages 395–406, 2000.

[15] P. Samarati. Protecting respondents' identities in microdata release. *TKDE*, 13(6):1010–1027, 2001.

[16] L. Sweeney. $\mathcal{K}$-anonymity: A model for protecting privacy. *International Journal on Uncertainty, Fuzziness and Knowledge Based Systems*, 10(5):557–570, 2002.

[17] M. Terrovitis and N. Mamoulis. Privacy preservation in the publication of trajectories. In *MDM*, pages 65–72, 2008.

Privacy-Preserving Indexing for eHealth Information Networks

Yuzhe Tang, Ting Wang, Ling Liu, Shicong Meng, and Balaji Palanisamy
College of Computing, Georgia Institute of Technology
Atlanta, GA 30332, USA
yztang@gatech.edu, {twang, lingliu, smeng, balaji}@cc.gatech.edu

ABSTRACT

The past few years have witnessed an increasing demand for the next generation health information networks (e.g., NHIN[1]), which hold the promise of supporting large-scale information sharing across a network formed by autonomous healthcare providers. One fundamental capability of such information network is to support efficient, privacy-preserving (for both users and providers) search over the distributed, access controlled healthcare documents. In this paper we focus on addressing the privacy concerns of content providers; that is, the search should not reveal the specific association between contents and providers (a.k.a. content privacy). We propose SS-PPI, a novel privacy-preserving index abstraction, which, in conjunction of distributed access control-enforced search protocols, provides theoretically guaranteed protection of content privacy. Compared with existing proposals (e.g., flipping privacy-preserving index[2]), our solution highlights with a series of distinct features: (a) it incorporates access control policies in the privacy-preserving index, which improves both search efficiency and attack resilience; (b) it employs a fast index construction protocol via a novel use of the secrete-sharing scheme in a fully distributed manner (without trusted third party), requiring only constant (typically two) round of communication; (c) it provides information-theoretic security against colluding adversaries during index construction as well as query answering. We conduct both formal analysis and experimental evaluation of SS-PPI and show that it outperforms the state-of-the-art solutions in terms of both privacy protection and execution efficiency.

Categories and Subject Descriptors: D.4.6 [Security and Protection]: Access controls H.3.1 [Content Analysis and Indexing]: Indexing methods H.3.3 [Information Search and Retrieval]: Search process

General Terms: Security Algorithm

Keywords: Privacy preserving protocol, keyword search, distributed indexing

1. INTRODUCTION

Many healthcare providers, payers, and pharmaceutical companies have increased their use of eHealth solutions to manage health-related information and to automate administrative and clinical functions. We are witnessing an increasing demand for the next generation health information networks, which hold the promise of providing large-scale information sharing over distributed, access controlled content across a network of healthcare providers. A representative example is the work currently under way to construct the Nationwide Health Information Network (NHIN) [1] that supports information sharing among more than 20 federal agencies, along with numerous private hospitals and doctors' offices. A fundamental capability of such information network is to provide privacy-preserving search over distributed, access controlled content.

More specifically, individual healthcare providers typically enforce strict regulations over the healthcare information for a number of reasons, such as patients' privacy requirements, conflicting economic interests, and federal administration; meanwhile, the capability of efficiently identifying and retrieving relevant content across healthcare administrative boundaries is crucial for the healthcare information network to improve care quality, emergency response, and diagnosis accuracy. This poses the question of how to facilitate effective search while minimally revealing which providers possess which content (i.e., content privacy).

A naive approach to achieve privacy-aware search is query broadcasting: each query is forwarded to all the participating providers; those providers with matched content may then contact the querier directly. Content privacy is best preserved in this manner, since no sensitive information is required to route the query. However, such global-scale probing is not scalable with respect to the number of providers, in terms of both communication bandwidth and query latency. In the case of selective queries that most providers do not have matched content, broadcasting results in huge waste of communication and computation resources.

Alternative is to use a centralized index server (in implementation which can be readily replicated) that holds an indexing structure to facilitate the query routing. Query efficiency and scalability is attained for each query is only re-directed to providers which are bound to have matched contents. However, to construct the indexing structure, which is publicly accessible, typically requires providers to fully expose their content possession information. In this sense, the centralized index server must be trusted by all participating providers in its behavior. In healthcare applications, however, not only the enormous trust is impractical for providers with conflicting interests, but also the centralized architecture is vulnerable to security attacks and suffers from single point of failure.

The first Privacy Preserving Index (PPI) was proposed in [2] to strike a balance between privacy preservation and search efficiency. We refer to this approach as flipping PPI. It leverages an abstraction of group-wise index, by which providers are organized into a set of disjoint *privacy groups*.[1] Content privacy is preserved in the sense that providers in the same group are indistinguishable. Query dissemination is performed at the granularity of privacy group. Within a privacy group, a given query is forwarded either to all providers or to none of them, depending on whether there exists (at least) one provider with matched content. Flipping PPI is known to suffer from index construction inefficiency, due to the large number of rounds of PPI computation, and is vulnerable to colluding attacks.

[1]We use "privacy group" and "group" interchangeably when no confusion occurs.

CIKM'11, October 24–28, 2011, Glasgow, Scotland, UK.

In sum, we argue that existing privacy preserving index and search protocols suffer from the following drawbacks:

- **Ineffectiveness**: Flipping PPI is ineffective on making trade-off between privacy preservation and search efficiency. In the case that a considerable number of providers possess content matching the query, the flipping PPI approach essentially degrades to query broadcasting which as aforementioned suffers from scalability in terms of search performance. We elaborate on this in the start of Section 3.1.

- **Inefficient index construction**: Efficient construction of group-wise index is crucial for indexing frequently updated content. Existing schemes suffer from either complexity of computation by using secure multiparty computation [9], or excessive privacy leakage by using tailored algorithms. Flipping PPI [2] employs a randomized and iterative algorithm that is neither time-efficient nor privacy preserving. To build index, flipping PPI needs to run multiple rounds (typically above 20 rounds); in each round a sequential scan ($O(n)$ time complexity where n is group size) is required. Flipping PPI's index construction protocol also features weak privacy preservation, since it is vulnerable to colluding attacks with even two collaborators.

- **Role-insensitivity**: Existing PPI approaches are either role insensitive or preserve no privacy in terms of provider's access control policy. Typically, a fully trusted index server is required to conduct user authentication, which is not scalable or practical [23]. Queries are redirected to the same set of providers regardless of the role of the querier in the access control policy. We argue that this role insensitivity may lead to both query routing inefficiency and privacy leakage. Consider a querier having access rights to a very limited set of providers poses a query for a common term. PPI returns a large set of providers that possess this term, yet a handful of which are accessible to the querier, yielding unnecessary query overhead. In contrast, a querier is directed to a group from which she gets negative results from $n-1$ providers but does not have access to the remaining one. The querier can then ensure the last provider must hold the term in question, leading to privacy leakage.

In this paper, we propose the concept of *role-sensitive PPI* and a secure protocol for fast construction of PPI based on the primitives of secret sharing. We entitle this concrete implementation of our role-sensitive PPI as SS-PPI. Given a query in conjunction with the role of the querier, our *role-sensitive PPI* returns the groups of providers that potentially hold the content that matches the search term for this role. Both privacy preserving and search efficiency are attained on a finer-granularity level. Since our PPI abstraction is defined on fine granularity (role sensitive), we preserve content privacy as well as *access policy privacy* at the same time. This new type of privacy protects the sensitive information in provider-defined access rules, such as to which role provider p has granted access. To the best of our knowledge, this paper is the first one addressing the privacy of access policy in the PPI framework. Technically, our index construction protocol (SS-PPI) makes a novel use of secret sharing without requiring third party involved, which comparing to existing secret-sharing schemes sees better scalability. It is efficient in the sense that all "secret shares[2]" are constructed in a distributed, parallel manner with constant complexity of computation and communication. In particular, it finishes in 2 stages, each expected to take 1 time unit (for reasonable setting of group size n, like $1k$). More importantly, our SS-PPI protocol achieves information-theoretic security against colluding attacks. For less than $2c-2$ adversaries in the network, any provider's privacy is not leaked , where c is a system parameter.

[2]Packets and shares are used interchangeably in the following paper.

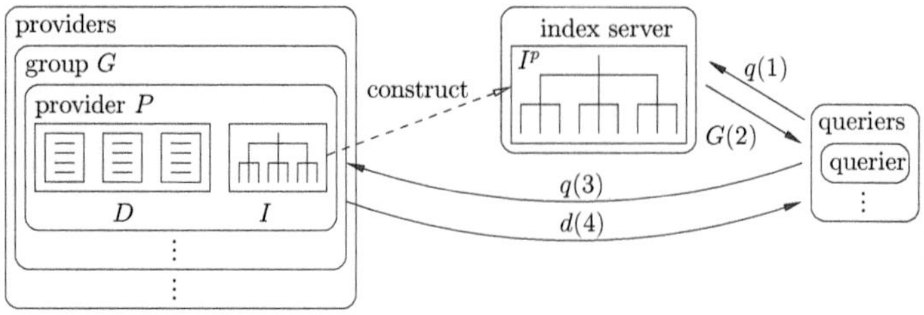

Figure 1: Multi-source information search and retrieval.

The remaining of this paper is organized as follows. Section 2 presents the overview of our system, and Section 3 elaborates privacy-aware index construction protocol. Security analysis is given in Section 4. Experimental results are shown in Section 5. Finally, Section 6 surveys related work and Section 7 concludes this paper.

2. OVERVIEW

In this section, we formally describe the system architecture, our role-sensitive PPI and then overview the secret-sharing based protocol for index construction.

2.1 Architecture of Role-sensitive PPI

We first give an overview of our targeted multi-source information sharing infrastructure, as shown in Figure 1. The infrastructure mainly involves three entities, including a set of autonomous information providers, an index server, and a set of queriers (or users who consume the information)[3].

Each provider holds at its depository a set of documents and has self-specified privacy requirements and regulations. The set of information providers jointly provide information search for users. And each provider itself is responsible for search processing (at a finer granularity) and data retrieval. This way, each provider is able to determine the disclosure of information to the corresponding querier at its discretion. Specifically, provider p possesses a depository of private documents, $D(p)$, on which a role-based access control policy is enforced. We assume that each document d can be described by a set of content descriptors (CD), denoted by $T(d)$ [6] (e.g., keywords), from a finite set of CDs T. Provider p can summarizes its local data and access policy by bitmap $b(p)$, where each column is associated with a role o and each row with a content descriptor or term t. The cell at column o and row t is a bit, with 1 meaning provider p has one or more documents matched to term t and accessible to subject role with o, and 0 otherwise. The bitmap $b(p)$ is intended for being published to the index server. Also, each provider optionally maintains a local indexing structure I regarding its documents to facilitate local search and access enforcement.

A querier searches information by issuing queries and presenting her roles. A query q is represented by a set of CDs, denoted by $T(q)$ and querier's roles $O(q)$. Document d satisfies query q if $T(q) \subseteq T(d)$ and d is accessible to certain role in $O(q)$. From the local bitmap's point of view, provider p can answer query q if for every row in $T(q)$, there are at least one cell that is 1 for all columns in $O(q)$. In the framework, a query is successfully answered if *all* the information providers that possess documents satisfying the query receive the query. It is at the discretion of the corresponding information providers to enforce access to the relevant documents (retrieval), which may involve further steps such as charge negotiation. In this paper, we focus on the phase of information search.

Overall, a query q can be answered in the following steps, as shown in Figure 1. The querier sends query q consisting of $T(q)$ and $O(q)$ to the index server, (step (1)), which by looking up the public privacy preserving index I_p returns the identity information of the corresponding providers G (step (2)). The querier then issues q to these providers (step (3)), who at their discretion contact the querier and provide access of documents d that satisfy q (step (4)).

[3]Following, we use "querier" and "user" interchangeably.

2.2 Privacy Goal in Role-sensitive PPI

In a typical PPI system, there are privacy of various information needed to be protected, including content privacy, *policy privacy* and query privacy, among many others. While query privacy, which involves with searcher's identity being kept from disclosure, can be protected by anonymity protocols (e.g. [20, 18, 17]), content privacy and policy privacy are the ones we primarily address in this paper. Following flipping PPI [2], we define content privacy as below,

Definition *Given provider p and term t, content privacy is defined to be information about provider p's possession of certain document containing sensitive term t. Content privacy is leaked when one party without access to provider p can claim with certainty if provider p possesses term t.*

In addition to content privacy, we identify the access policy privacy in generic PPI systems, since our published index is fine-grained and incorporates the access policy information in it. The formal definition is introduced as follows,

Definition *Given provider p and role o, access policy privacy is defined to be the information about p has granted access to o on certain document that provider p holds. Policy privacy is leaked when one party without access to privoder p can claim with certainty if provider p grants access to users with role o.*

In our architecture, a querier is expected to report her true role, but also allowed for falsely reported roles, namely the one she is not associated with. No authentication or access control are enforced, on our public, untrusted index server. Our role-sensitive PPI is well-designed that querier reporting true role obtains a list of providers that cover full set of query answers, and that querier falsely reporting her roles receives a somewhat meaningless list of providers from which she can't deduce any sensitive knowledge in terms of content privacy and policy privacy.

2.3 Index Construction Protocol

Motivated by the deficits of existing solutions in facing large-scale multi-source information sharing infrastructures, we propose SS-PPI, a novel indexing scheme that supports information network comprising thousands of content providers, and provides theoretical guarantees on both possession privacy protection and execution efficiency.

The framework of SS-PPI mainly consists of two phases, index construction and query answering. The former further processes in three major components, group formation, group aggregation and global index construction.

- *Grouping*. SS-PPI organizes providers into privacy groups. In this paper, we adopt the strategy of random grouping based on universal hashing [2].

- *Secure group aggregation*. Within each privacy group, a summarization structure is built in a privacy-preserving manner that indexes the content possession by group members. Instead of using the generic circuit computing [9], SS-PPI constructs this aggregation by an extended secrete sharing scheme [19], which endows our solution with both scalability and attack-resilience. Our analysis and experiments show that the scheme can achieve information-theoretic privacy of a provider even when multiple providers within the group are compromised.

- *Privacy-aware global index construction*. The global index is constructed efficiently by merging the set of group aggregations. SS-PPI adopts a distributed scheme that not only amortizes the trust on a single third party, but also supports localized, incremental index update.

3. PRIVACY-PRESERVING INDEX CONSTRUCTION

In this section, we present in detail the phase of privacy-preserving index construction in SS-PPI. It entails three main components; group formation, secure group aggregation, and global index construction.

3.1 Random Group Formation

Group formation is the process that organizes providers into different privacy groups. In the design of a good formation strategy that strike a balance between search efficiency and privacy preserving, group term selectivity is critical. Group term selectivity refers to the ratios of providers in a group that possesses the term to the group size. The less group-wise selective a term is, the harder an adversary can pinpoint a provider that possesses a specific term, thus better privacy preserving. On the other hand, less group term selectivity implies queries are forwarded to more providers with no answer, thus more bandwidth overheads. For a given group size, the goal of group formation is to make all indexed terms reach an expected values in group selectivity.

We follow in this paper the conventional approach, that is, random grouping (e.g. [2]), which randomly assigns providers to groups. Group size is a critical factor to utility and privacy preserving of published index. When group size is configured to be too big, it could easily make the group-wise index degrade to query broadcasting. Consider a group of size n and a term with global selectivity q, the probability for a group to be negative (i.e., no providers in it having the term) is $(1-q)^n$. This value quickly approaches 0 as n grows, regardless of value of q. For example, when $q = 0.5, n = 10$, the value is 0.1%, and when $n = 20$, the negative probability becomes 10^{-6}, implying all groups are positive ones and query broadcasting is thus required. On the other hand, when group size n is configured to be too small, privacy could easily be leaked since the possibility for providers in one group to all be positive is q^n which is fairly large for small n. As shown in experiment part, we empirically set the value of group size and show its effectiveness.

3.2 Secure Group Aggregation: Design Rationale

After the privacy groups are formed, one needs to aggregate the group-wise term-possession index. The technical goal is to protect individuals' privacy during the process in which group-wise index is formed. That is, one can not guess with confidence higher than what final aggregated index discloses. In particular, we address two technical goals,

- We firstly address privacy preserving in the presence of colluding attacks. Our privacy goal can be guaranteed, if the total number of colluders is bounded below a certain threshold.

- We secondly address performance in terms of both bandwidth and time. Our designs aims at best performance as long as privacy is not sacrificed.

With regards to the above goals, existing protocols show flaws in a way or two. One conventional scheme is flipping PPI's iterative randomized algorithm. However, it is time-inefficient; it requires to run multiple iterations before the final group index reaches certain level of accuracy. This problem is compounded when group-wise index is frequently updated, resulting in prohibitively high cost for re-constructing the indexing structure. More importantly, its publishing process is vulnerable to colluding attacks, specially in the case of an innocent provider ending up with its predecessor and successor both being malicious. Another possible technique can be used is the generic secure multi-party computation [6] which consumes considerable computation overheads.

3.3 Secure Group Aggregation: The Algorithms

Inspired by the observation above, we propose a secret-sharing based scheme for fast and secure index construction. Our novel secure group aggregation scheme is based on an extended secrete sharing protocol [19], which achieves constant communication cost in group aggregation and provides strong privacy protection. Within each group, group aggregation collects the statistics of the possession of providers in the group with respect to each query term and access role. We assume that the providers have already been grouped and placed into in group-wise overlay. Without loss of generality, we consider a specific group comprising a set of providers $p_0, p_1, \ldots, p_{n-1}$, each holding a private value $v_i \in \{0,1\} = \mathbb{Z}_2$, called *sub-secret*, corresponding to a specific term and access role[4]. The output, called *super-value* v, is the number of providers with $v_i = 1$, that is,

$$v = \sum_{i=0}^{n-1} v_i \tag{1}$$

where the super-value v can span from 0 to n. Our protocol computes the super-value accurately and securely. Each involved provider works in four stages: generates sub-packets for sub-secret, distributes sub-packets, computes super-packets from received sub-packets, and aggregates the super-packets to form super-value. Next, we discuss the four stages in details.

3.3.1 *Generating sub-packets*

In this stage, each provider p_i splits its sub-secret v_i into c sub-packets $u_{i,j}$, such that their modulo sum equals v_i, formally,

$$v_i = f(u_{i,0}, u_{i,1}, \ldots, u_{i,c-1}) = \sum_{j=0}^{c-1} u_{i,j} \mod q \tag{2}$$

where q is the modulus with $q \gg n$, and each sub-packet $u_{i,j}$ is defined on the packet domain $\mathbb{Z}_q$. The packet-generating process generates a (c,c)-secret packets; that is, given any less than c sub-packets, the sub-secret v_i is still completely undeterminable. A set of implementations are available to generate the sub-packets[5]. In this paper, we select the simplest one: randomly and independently pick the first $c-1$ sub-packets $u_{i,j}$'s (for $j = \{0, \ldots, c-2\}$), and let the last one be $u_{i,c} = (v_i - \sum_{j=1}^{c-1} u_{i,j}) \mod q$. In Appendix, we prove this is a (c,c)-secret sharing in Theorem A.1.

3.3.2 *Distributing sub-packets*

We assume that the providers in a group are structured into a ring-like overlay, as illustrated in Fig. 2. In the overlay, each provider p_i has $c-1$ neighbors in the clockwise direction, $p_{h(i,1)}, \ldots, p_{h(i,j)}, \ldots, p_{h(i,c-1)}$, where $h(i,j)$ denotes the index of the j-th neighbor of p_i. A bi-directional secure channel is set up on each neighboring connection. Provider p_i also has $c-1$ neighbors in the counter-clockwise direction, $p_{h'(i,1)}, \ldots, p_{h'(i,j)}, \ldots, p_{h'(i,c-1)}$, where $h'(i,j)$ denotes the index of the provider whose j-th clockwise neighbor is p_i, that is, $h(h'(i,j),j) = i$. In total, each provider knows $2c-2$ neighbors in the group, and unaware of the rest's positions. In particular, the 0-th neighbor of p_i is itself, i.e., $h(i,0) = i$. A variety of instantiations of $h(\cdot,\cdot)$ are possible. At this point, for simplicity, we assume $h_1(i,j) = i + j \mod n$, that is, p_i take the nearest-$(c-1)$ providers to be its neighbors. For instance, in Fig. 2, p_0 knows p_1, p_2, p_6, p_7 and no more; p_0 knows p_6 because mutual communications are required when p_6 is to set up a secure channel with p_0.

Provider p_i proceeds to distributing the sub-packets to its neighbors: $u_{i,j}$ will be sent to $p_{h(i,j)}$. In particular, since $h(i,0) = i$, the first sub-packet $u_{i,0}$ is always kept locally on p_i. During this stage, all communication are through the secure channels; that is, they are encrypted and authenticated. Messages from different providers are sent asynchronously and in parallel, and thus consuming $O(1)$ time-unit.

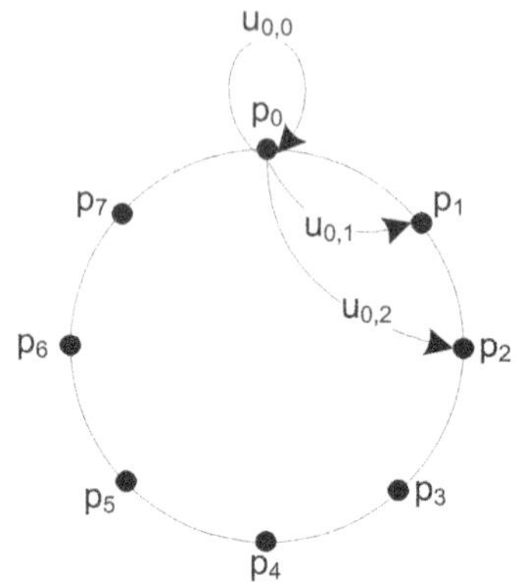

Figure 2: Overlay of secret packet distribution (with $c = 3, n = 8$)

3.3.3 *Computing super-packets*

While sending out sub-packets, providers also receive sub-packets from other providers. Specifically, p_i receives from its previous neighbor p_{i-j} sub-packet $u_{i-j,j}$, where $1 \leq j \leq c-1$. p_i then sum them up, together with its local sub-packet $u_{i,0}$, to get the super-packet u_i,

$$u_i = \sum_{j=0}^{c-1} u_{i-j,j} \mod q \tag{3}$$

Thus, $u_{i,0} = (u_i - \sum_{j=1}^{c-1} u_{i,j}) \mod q$. Combining it with Equation 2, we get,

$$\begin{aligned} v_i &= (u_i - \sum_{j=1}^{c-1} u_{i-j,j} + \sum_{j=1}^{c-1} u_{i,j}) \mod q \\ &= f'(u_i, u_{i-c+1,c-1}, \ldots, u_{i-1,1}, u_{i,1}, \ldots, u_{i,c-2}, u_{i,c-1}) \end{aligned} \tag{4}$$

Interestingly, Equation 4 defines a $(2c-1, 2c-1)$ secret sharing scheme, as will be proved in Theorem 4.1. It implies that even with $2c-2$ packets, the secret value v_i is still completely undeterminable. Note that each input sub-packet in Equation 4 corresponds to a distinct remote provider, e.g., $u_{i-c+1,c-1}$ is received from p_{i-c+1}, u_{i+1} is sent to p_{i+1}, and so on. When the group size n is large, e.g., containing at least $2c-1$ or $2c-2$ providers (depending on how u_i is aggregated, as below), our protocol is resilient to collusion attacks of up to $2c-2$ or $2c-3$ malicious providers in the group.

3.3.4 *Aggregating super-packets*

In the last stage, super-packets from all providers are aggregated to form super-value $u = (u_0 + u_1 + \cdots + u_{n-1}) \mod q$. In our implementation, we adopt the most time-efficient one: every provider p_i sends u_i to a special provider, say p_0 which is then responsible for summing up all u_i's. The final results u will be sent to index server as part of the privacy preserving index. The whole process is sketched in Algorithm 1.

---

[4]As will be discussed later, the aggregation process of v_i for different terms and roles can be combined together and related messages can be piggybacked.

[5]For example, Shamir's secret sharing[19] is a possible way to generate $u_{i,j}$ in the form of Equation 2. Specifically, for sub-secret v_i, we randomly generate a polynomial $g_i(x)$, s.t. $g_i(0) = v_i$. Also there are c input values x_j's ($j \in \{0, 1, \ldots, c-1\}$) that are globally-agreed on. Applying x_j on g_i, we have $y_{i,j} = g_i(x_j)$. Applying Lagrange Interpolation, $v_i = g_i(0) = \sum_{j=0}^{c-1} \mathbb{L}_{i,j}(0) \cdot y_{i,j}$. By picking $u_{i,j} = \mathbb{L}_{i,j}(0) \cdot y_{i,j}$, we get equation 2 (without modulo operation, though).

Algorithm 1 index-construction(provider p_i, sub-secret v_i)

```
{Generating sub-packets}
for all j ∈ [0, c − 2] do
    u_{i,j} ← random number in Z_q
u_{i,c−1} ← (v_i − Σ_{j=1}^{c−1} u_{i,j})  mod q
{Distributing sub-packets}
for all j ∈ [1, c − 1] do
    p_i sends u_{i,j} to provider p_{i+j}
{Computing super-packets}
for all j ∈ [1, c − 1] do
    p_i receives u_{i−j,j} from provider p_{i−j}
u_i ← (u_{i−c+1,c−1} + u_{i−c+2,c−2} + ··· + u_{i−1,1} + u_{i,0})  mod q
{Aggregating super-packets}
p_i send u_i to p_0 (p_0 will then sum up all received super-packets)
```

Example. Consider four providers with security parameter $q = 5, c = 3$. In the first round, every provider p_i starts with splitting her sub-secret v_i into $c = 3$ sub-packets. For instance, on p_1, $v_1 = 0 = (2 + 3 + 0) \mod 5$, where the first two numbers are randomly distributed in domain $\mathbb{Z}_q = \{0, 1, 2, 3, 4\}$. Then, p_1 sends out the sub-packets, e.g., 0 to p_3, 3 to p_2, but 2 kept locally. At the same time, p_1 receives sub-packets from other providers, e.g., 0 from p_3 and 1 from p_4. Then p_1 sums up all these sub-packets to get the super-packet $u_1 = (0 + 1 + 2) \mod 5 = 3$. Other providers work in a similar manner, and they further send all super-packets to p_1. At the end, p_1 sums up all super-packets $(3 + 0 + 2 + 2) \mod 5 = 2$.

(q=5,c=3)	p_1	p_2	p_3	p_4
v_i	0	1	1	0
$u_{i,3}$	0	4	0	3
$u_{i,2}$	3	3	2	1
$u_{i,1}$	2	4	4	1
$u_{i-2,3}$	0	3	0	4
$u_{i-1,2}$	1	3	3	2
$u_{i,1}$	2	4	4	1
$u_i=\sum u_{i-j+1,j}$	3	0	2	2
v	2			

Figure 3: Secret Sharing-based Index Construction Example

3.4 Analysis of Protocol Correctness and Complexity

Our protocol outputs the correct value of v, namely, $u = v$, as below,

$$\begin{aligned} u &= \sum_{l=0}^{n-1} u_l \mod q = (\sum_{l=0}^{n-1}\sum_{j=0}^{c-1} u_{l-j,j} \mod q) \mod q \\ &= (\sum_{j=0}^{c-1}\sum_{l=0}^{n-1} u_{l-j,j}) \mod q = (\sum_{j=0}^{c-1}\sum_{i=-j}^{n-1-j} u_{i,j}) \mod q \\ &= (\sum_{j=0}^{c-1}\sum_{i=0}^{n-1} u_{i,j}) mod q = (\sum_{i=0}^{n-1}\sum_{j=0}^{c-1} u_{i,j} \mod q) \mod q \\ &= \sum_{i=0}^{n-1} v_i \mod q = \sum_{i=0}^{n-1} v_i = v \end{aligned} \tag{5}$$

The last step is due to that $q \gg n$, and $v \in \{0, 1, \ldots, n\}$. Hence, in the final public index, for each provider having $v_i = 1$, the group will have aggregated sum $v \geq 1$, thus being present in the posting list. Completeness can be attained. Besides, we use posting-list intersection for multi-keyword query processing, thus query consistency is achieved; that is, the results of multiple-keyword query equals the intersection of all results of multiple single-keyword queries. In short, our protocol is correct.

Efficiency of our protocol can be analyzed in two aspects: the time latency and bandwidth overhead. Stage 1 of our protocol requires $n \cdot c$ messages to be sent, and can finish within O(1) time-unit due to parallelism. The actual latency depends on the slowest provider in the network. In this stage, the bandwidth overhead also implies the costs of setting up secure channels. For second stage, the basic aggregation protocol can finish within $O(1)$ time and with n messages.

Overall, the above protocol runs for one single term and one access role. To build PPI for multiple terms and access roles, it runs multiple single-term protocols, independently with each other. Specifically, the aggregation process carries a set of bitmaps or vectors, each vector corresponding to a role and each vector bit summarizing the possession information regarding to an indexed term. Sending and merging different bits or vectors can be piggybacked in the same messages and packets the same secure channel. By this way, time latency stays unchanged with growing number of indexed terms and roles.

3.5 Global Index Construction

The group-wise indices are not ready for direct use by the index server to route queries, since they may, to some extent, violate the content privacy of participating providers. It happens when a majority number of providers in a group hold a (set of) specific term(s), which makes it possible for the adversary to identify the content possession of these providers with high confidence. Therefore, we need enforce another layer of protection before the global index is published. We achieve this by adjusting and merging group-wise indices to quantitatively meet providers' privacy needs. In the following, we will introduce a group merging process. This process is optional in our system, because it may requires a partially trusted coordinator. However, after merging, privacy preserving can attain certain quality as system/providers want. It is noteworthy here that security of the coordinator can be strengthened by making it periodically offline [13].

3.5.1 *Group-wise Index Adjustment*

The goal of our adjusting/merging process is to guarantee each group g has positive providers with respect to each term lower than a threshold $q \cdot n(g)$, where $n(g)$ is group size and q is a predefined privacy parameter. We consider a centralized coordinator which collects the group-wise indices and merges them to address the participating providers' privacy in a best-effort manner. For example, for term t, coordinator will find the group with the most positive providers g and the one with the least positive providers g'[6]. If g contains more positive providers than the threshold, the coordinator merges g with g' such that the percentage of positive providers $\frac{v(t,g)+v(t,g')}{n(g)+n(g')}$ drops in the merged group, where $v(t, g)$ denotes the percentage of positive providers regarding to term t. If the merged percentage is still too big, that is, bigger than q, the merging process continues to merge with the group currently with smallest $\frac{v(t,g)}{n(g)}$. The whole process stops when the merged percentage drops below q.[7]. For multiple terms, we define a metric $\alpha(g)$ for group g,

$$\alpha(g) = \sum_{t \in ST} v(t, g) - q \cdot n(g) \tag{6}$$

[6]We address the global meta-information, like the number of positive providers, can be leaked since it does not disclose any information on which provider is positive.

[7]The stop condition must be met in certain iteration, for we assume the threshold q is bigger than global term selectivity. It is a reasonable restriction, since otherwise even query broadcasting can't make all group-wise percentage of positive providers be smaller than term selectivity.

where ST is the subset of terms that are privacy-sensitive, defined by providers. For multiple terms, in each iteration, we try to merge group g with lowest $\alpha(g)$, and the rest similarly runs. In practice, in case that there is no trusted coordinator, one can omit this process and privacy preserving is attained in a best effort way.

3.5.2 Global Rank-aware Index Construction

The group-wise index of each group is combined into a single global index. A naïve way is to let each group send her index to the centralized index server and to combine locally there. In this scheme, the percentage of positive providers in each group is then known by the index server, which however is sensitive information. In order to avoid this privacy breach, we adopt the privacy-preserving protocol [22] to output posting index ordered by positive percentage but without publishing the percentages. To further save the query processing costs, one can only publish Top-K groups with most positive providers, where K is a system parameter. Depending on the value of K, this strategy makes a trade-off between query performance and result recall. For example, small K can result in more efficient query processing, but not more effective. That is, query recall may be harmed, since certain results appear in bottom of the ordered posting lists. In practice, K should be set according to users' demands on result quality and system resource budget.

3.5.3 Index Updates

In real systems, data may be frequently updated and new providers may come and leave. A naive way to handle this update is to rebuild our privacy preserving index from scratch every time an update occurs. For index update efficiency, we adopt an incremental, batch-oriented update approach. Whenever there are t providers that newly join or locally updates their index, we re-run the index construction protocol among the updated providers. Thus, updates can not be tied to any specific provider out of t. In addition, since we add noise and do not disclose exact value of term selectivity (as discussed in Section 4.2.4), content privacy in update is preserved.

4. PROTOCOL SECURITY ANALYSIS

In our system, privacy leakage consists of two parts, one $P1$ is during index construction and the other $P2$ after index gets published. For $P1$, in our protocol for index construction, there are four kinds of information; the "super-value" v, the "super-packets" u_l, the "sub-packets" $u_{i,j}$ and "sub-secret" v_i. The super-value v is the final result and is made publicly known. Out of the four, only "sub-secret" v_i's is the private information to protect.

4.1 Privacy Model

4.1.1 Privacy Adversaries

For security analysis, we start with adversaries of different roles with different capabilities. Adversaries could be providers, network eavesdroppers, searchers and even the index server. However, to make a system function correctly, one needs to assume minimal level of trusts. For instance, providers and the index server in our network are assumed to be semi-honest, implying they follow our protocol specification, but may attempt to learn additional information by analyzing the transcript of messages received during the execution[15]. More specifically, providers will follow the secret-sharing based index construction protocol and index server will perform work for query answering, like posting list intersections. A network eavesdropper could passively log the messages under her surveillance. She can have the global power to monitor all messages coming through the network or the local power to monitor messages sent out by a particular providers. A searcher could pose queries to the index server in the wish to obtain sensitive information. Overall, an adversary in our model can assume multiple roles, like she could be one of participating providers and can pose queries to index server at the same time. Or multiple adversaries can collude to gain more knowledge.

For privacy $P1$, providers can obtain more information than other roles, since all messages are encrypted in our network and only providers can see the content/payload of the network messages.

4.1.2 Privacy Metric

Recall that content privacy and policy privacy are addressed in this paper. The degree of privacy preservation is quantitatively measured by the probability with which an adversary's claim on sensitive knowledge fails. The actual claim differs for different types of privacy, as defined above. The probability is equal to the percentage of false positive providers in the result list, which is used as privacy metric in our system. For instance, in the result list of 10 providers, if they all possess a sensitive term t, content privacy is definitely leaked. Because for any provider p in the list, adversary can claim p possess term t in question and such claim is true with 100% probability. On the other hand, when there are 5 false positive providers in the list, in the case that adversary randomly pick a provider to perform attack, the probability for her claim to fail is at least half (50%). In this paper, we choose the "Probable Innocence"[2, 18]) as our main quantitative privacy goal, in which the false positive rate should be higher than one half 0.5.

4.1.3 Attack Model

Our general attack model involves that a security role (e.g., a provider) observing certain messages from other parties makes claim on sensitive knowledge that breaches privacy. We consider attack to breach both privacy $P1$ and privacy $P2$. 1) For privacy $P1$, we consider both attacker as a single provider and attackers as colluding providers. We assume that a single provider observing the messages from its neighbors always claim its neighbor has the term (even she can only see the sub-packets). Providers in collusion can observe multiple messages from a single innocent provider. If number of such messages is $2c-1$, colluding providers can see all sub-packets of a secret value and thus be able to reconstruct the sub-secret value. If the reconstructed secret value equals 1, providers claim the innocent provider has the term, otherwise, the innocent provider do not have the term. 2) For privacy $P2$, we assume searchers/index server search for term t and claim any provider in the result list has documents of term t.

4.2 Privacy Characteristic

We analyze privacy characteristic of our protocol against different roles. Our protocol achieves privacy preserving in many situations, like against network eavesdroppers and single semi-honest provider. There are also certain scenarios in which privacy could be possibly leaked, as the two cases stated in our attack model. In this section, we analyze privacy preserving of $P1$ against eavesdroppers, single provider and colluding providers. For privacy $P2$, we will conduct privacy evaluation by experiments.

4.2.1 Network Eavesdropper

For eavesdroppers, our protocol achieves privacy preserving mainly by encrypted communication; All communications in our protocol are authenticated and encrypted. Eavesdroppers seeing a series of cyphertext can not have any knowledge about its content and thus can't make any informed claims. Secure channels[13] guarantees eavesdroppers themselves can not obtain the cryptographic keys.

4.2.2 Single Semi-honest Provider

In the presence of semi-honest providers, our protocol achieves information-theoretic security.[8] A single provider p_i can only see at most one sub-packet/share out of totally $2c-1$ sub-packets of one sensitive sub-secret from other provider $p_{i'}$. The fact that $f'(\cdot)$ is a $(2c-1, 2c-1)$ secret sharing scheme, as proved by Theorem4.1, yields the information-theoretic security. Thus, adversary obtaining one piece/packet learn no information on the value of v_i at all and can not even make informed claim.

[8]Unlike cryptographic security as in secure channel case, information-theoretic security does not rely on any assumptions of computation theory and is less computation-intensive.

THEOREM 4.1. *If $f(\cdot)$ is a (c, c) secret sharing scheme with packets on domain $\mathbb{Z}_q$, $f'(\cdot)$ is a $(2c-1, 2c-1)$ secret sharing scheme on $\mathbb{Z}_q$, too. Specifically,*

- ***Recoverability**: Given $2c-1$ packets (j, y_j)'s where*

$$y_j = \begin{cases} u_{i+j,-j} & \text{if } j \in \{-c+1, \ldots, -1\}, \\ u_i & \text{if } j = 0, \\ u_{i,j} & \text{if } j \in \{1, \ldots, c-1\}. \end{cases}$$

the secret v_i can be easily reconstructed.

- ***Secrecy**: Given any $2c-2$ or fewer packets, one can learn nothing about value of v_i, in the sense that the conditional distribution given the known packets is the same to the prior distribution,*

$$\forall x \in \mathbb{Z}_q, prob(v_i = x) = prob(v_i = x | \forall j \in I, (j, y_j))$$

where I is any set with $2c-2$ or less elements in $\{-c+1, -c+2, \ldots, 0, \ldots, c-1\}$.

PROOF. The first condition is directly implied by Equation 4. For the second condition, we take the worst case in consideration, that is, when there are $2c-2$ packets available to adversary. Let $(j', y_{j'})$ denote the only missing packet. We consider two cases: Case 1), $j' \geq 0$. In this case, we can use Equation 3 to reconstruct the value $u_{i,0}$, that is, $u_{i,0} = (y_0 - y_{-c+1} - \cdots - y_{-1}) \mod q$. Then for (c, c) secret sharing scheme f, we have all c packets determined, except for $u_{i,j'}$. By the definition of (c, c) secret sharing, the value $v_i = f(\cdot)$ is completely undetermined. Case 2), $j' \leq 0$. We can determine all $c-1$ packets $u_{i,j}$ for $j \in \{1, 2, \ldots, c-1\}$, and we turn to prove that $u_{i,0} \equiv (y_0 - y_{-c+1} - \cdots - y_{-1}) \mod q$ is completely undetermined given one packet $(j', y_{j'})$ is missing. We further consider two cases, if $j' = 0$, we have $u_{i,0} - y_{j'} \equiv (-y_{-c+1} - \cdots - y_{-1}) \mod q$; otherwise, we have $u_{i,0} + y_{j'} \equiv (y_0 - y_{-c+1} - \cdots - y_{j'-1} - y_{j'+1} - \cdots - y_{-1}) \mod q$. In both cases, the RHS of the equation is completely determined, while LHS, in the form $u_{i,0} \pm y_{j'}$, is not. Applying lemma 4.2, we can see that the distribution of $u_{i,0}$ is fully unaffected by the given knowledge of $u_{i,0} \pm y_{j'}$ (but not $y_{j'}$). Thus, $u_{i,0}$ is completely undetermined. Note $v_i = f(u_{i,0}, u_{i,1}, \ldots, u_{i,c-1})$ is a (c, c) secret sharing scheme, thus the secret v_i is completely undetermined. □

LEMMA 4.2. *Random variable a, b are natural numbers in domain $\mathbb{Z}_q$. Their values are independently chosen and uniformly distributed in $\mathbb{Z}_q$. Then $\forall x, y \in \mathbb{Z}_q$, we have*

$$prob(a = x) = prob(a = x | (a \pm b) \mod q = y) = \frac{1}{q} \quad (7)$$

Proof of Lemma 4.2 can be found in Appendix.

4.2.3 Semi-honest Providers in Collusion

Our protocol is resistent to providers in collusion. In specific, 1) when collusion is of no more than $2c-3$ providers, attackers can't gain any information on v_i $\forall i \in \{1, \ldots, n\}$, as in the single provider case. Hence, our protocol retains the information-theoretic security. 2) When there are more than $2c-3$ colluding providers, privacy could be possibly leaked. In this section, we analyze the possibility and argue it's very unlikely for such breach to occur.

Note sub-packets of a single sub-secret v_i are distributed to at least $2c-2$ providers, which are the $2c-2$ consecutive neighbors of provider p_i. When these nearest-$(2c-2)$ providers happen to form a collusion, then privacy regarding sub-secret v_i is definitely leaked. [9] However, we argue the likehood for collusion of this kind to occur is fairly low. Besides, even in this case, only one sub-secret is disclosed, while other sub-secrets' privacy is still guaranteed. Note in our protocol group members are randomly ordered in ring-like overlay and they follow this protocol specification (since they are semi-honest). The probability for a honest provider to be surrounded by $2c-2$ adversaries is,

$$h = \frac{P^m_{2c-2}}{P^{n-1}_{2c-2}} = \frac{m!(n-2c+1)!}{(n-1)!(m-2c+2)!} \quad (8)$$

m is the total number of colluding providers in the network. As can be seen, the probability is very low for moderate value of c. For example, when $m = \frac{n}{2}$, the probability is $h < (\frac{1}{2})^{2c-2}$, which quickly approaches 0 for large n.

In practice, the number of colluding adversaries is usually small. For example, as discovered in a peer-to-peer measurement study [14], most collusions are of two or three mutually colluding nodes. Thus, by setting c at relatively small value (e.g., 5), it suffices to make our SS-PPI secure against colluding attacks.

4.2.4 Index Server aware of Term Selectivity

Our protocol discloses group-wise term selectivity in the published index, rendering privacy $P2$ vulnerable. With this information, index server can make informed decision on picking up the right group and term (if any) and perform security attacks successfully. To overcome this vulnerability in our system, we propose an enhanced version of SS-PPI which preserves privacy $P2$ and still achieves efficiency in performance. In specific, we add noises to the term-wise bit before group aggregation starts. For term t and a possession bit v, the provider generate another number v' in $\{0, 1, \ldots, b\}$ to do aggregation, as follows,

$$v' = \begin{cases} rand(b) \text{ in } \{1, 2, \ldots, b\} & \text{if v=1} \\ 0 & \text{if } v = 0. \end{cases}$$

Now the sum of v' does not necessarily equal the number of positive providers in each group. By this means, privacy can be further preserved, at expenses of extra inaccuracy of ranking between groups in the public index. Parameter b controls the trade-off between meta-data privacy and ranking accuracy. With this approach, the selectivity observed to be high could end up being small ones. In this sense, we prevent an adversary from picking up the term with high selectivity.

5. EXPERIMENTAL EVALUATION

In this section, we evaluate our SS-PPI, mainly by simulations. The evaluation is based on the comparison to previous work, flipping PPI[2]. Throughout the experiments, we mainly use synthetic dataset which consists of 10^5 providers, which are further mapped to 1000 groups. Groups are disjoint and are configured with an expected group size, that is, $10^5/10^3 = 100$. We also used a peer-to-peer dataset[16], which is developed based on the TREC WT10g web test collection, a 10 gigabyte, 1.69 million document subset of the VLC2 collection[11]. In our default setting, we run each experiments 20 times and report the averaged results.

5.1 Correctness

In the first set of experiments, we evaluate the PPI's correctness. For SS-PPI, the correctness is measured by the probability that the aggregated result equals number of positive providers in a group, that is, $\sum_0^{n-1} v_i$; for flipping PPI, it's measured by that for logical OR of v_i's. In the first experiment, we vary the number of rounds and fix term selectivity being 0.1, the results are shown in 4a; then, we test the protocol with terms of different selectivity and fixing the rounds to be 10, results shown in 4b. In general, SS-PPI achieves 100% accuracy, while flipping PPI doesn't. For small number of rounds and selective terms, flipping PPI incurs relatively high inaccuracy and uncertainty. It becomes more accurate as the number of rounds goes up. However, this improvement comes at the expenses of more severe privacy leakage, more bandwidth consumption and longer time duration, as will be shown.

[9] Here, we exclude the trivial case that p_i is itself in collusion, because then v_i can be known locally from p_i.

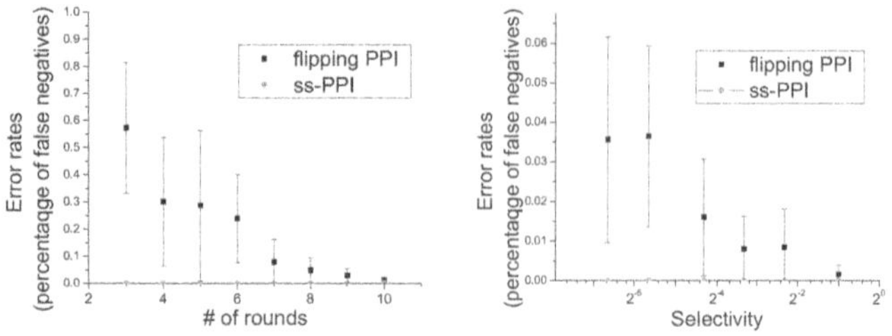

(a) Varying number of rounds (b) Varying term selectivity

Figure 4: Search correctness

5.2 Privacy Preserving

This set of experiments evaluate the level of privacy preservation of our SS-PPI. We mainly follow our security analysis to conduct experiments, in which two types of privacy are considered, including index construction privacy $P1$ and published privacy $P2$.

5.2.1 *Preserving Index Construction Privacy $P1$ against Colluding Attacks*

Our simulation for evaluation of privacy preserving against collaborating adversaries is based on Equation 8. flipping PPI can be modeled with $c = 1$ and in our SS-PPI, c ranges from 3 to 18. We have done two experiments; the one is with varying the number of colluding adversaries and fixed group size of 100, the other with varying group size, and the adversaries accounting for 20% of the group. We evaluate the probability of specific positioning of adversaries that leaks privacy. The results are plotted in Figure 5. In general, flipping PPI incurs the highest privacy breach; its leaking probability is an order of magnitude higher than that of SS-PPI, even with small c. As c grows up, the improvement of SS-PPI's privacy preserving against flipping PPI becomes significant. In Figure 5b, the privacy breach generally become more severe, as there are more adversaries. When all providers in a group are malicious, the probability of privacy breach becomes 100%, for all protocols. When there are limited adversaries (which is more likely the case in real world), SS-PPI achieves much better privacy preserving comparing to flipping PPI. As can be observed, there exist a threshold on number of adversaries under which SS-PPI's leaking probability is 0. For example, in the plot, the curve for SS-PPI-18 shows up only when adversaries are more than 35. This is more obvious in Figure 5a. By contrast, flipping PPI is vulnerable to collaborating attacks in all experiment settings. In Figure 5a, we can also see SS-PPI slightly increase privacy leaking probability until certain converging value as group size goes up, while flipping PPI stays constant. Note the probability (y axis) is plotted in log scale, differences between two protocols are significant.

In previous experiment, we consider privacy leakage of one innocent provider. Here, we move forward to study the multiple-provider case. Given a number of colluding adversaries, we measure the number of innocent providers being attacked. Let $a(l)$ denote the minimum number of colluding adversaries required to hack l providers' private information. By analysis model in Section 4, SS-PPI has,

$$a_{SS-PPI}(l) = (c-1)(l+1) \quad (9)$$

For l and c large enough, the above equation must meet $(c-1)(l+1) + l \leq n$, or $l \leq \frac{n+1}{c} - 1$. For flipping PPI, $c = 2$ and we have,

$$a_{flipping}(l) = l + 1 \quad (10)$$

Comparing to flipping PPI, our SS-PPI has higher requirement on the number of colluding adversaries, thus less likely to leak privacy.

5.2.2 *Preserving Privacy $P2$ against Searchers*

In this experiment, we evaluate property of privacy preserving of random grouping. We considered two cases, the common term case and the rare term case. For each case, we measure the true positive rates (i.e., the group-wise selectivity or how many providers in a group do possess the term) under different group sizes. The results are shown in Fig. 6. To visualize the degree of preserving privacy $P2$, we ranked groups based on true positive rates, decently. The maximal level of true positive ratios is critical to the overall degree of privacy preserving, thus being of interests to us. As can be seen from the results, the smaller the group size is, the more non-uniform the distribution of true positive rates is. For instance, the maximal true positive rate for group size of 10 is 0.6 for common terms of selectivity 0.2, while for group size configured to be 100, the maximal true positive rate is around 0.3. In this sense, larger group size leads to more privacy preserving. Comparing rare terms and common terms, grouping with common terms could end up with every group having non-zero true positive rate, implying query broadcast, which is not the case for those rare terms.

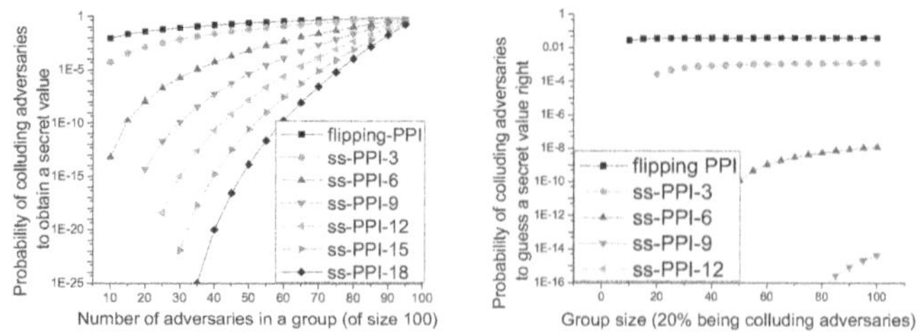

(a) Varying number of adversaries (b) Varying group size

Figure 5: Privacy preserving against collaboration of adversaries

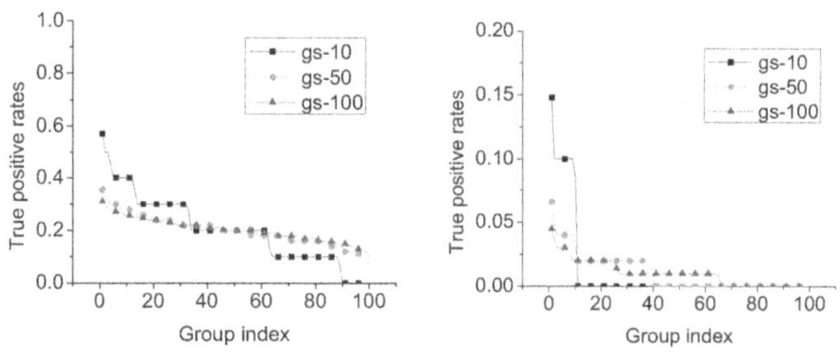

(a) Common terms (b) Rare terms

Figure 6: Preserving privacy $P2$ of random grouping

5.3 Performance of Group Aggregation

We evaluate the performance of SS-PPI by simulation. Specifically, we use two distributions on round-trip times (RTTs) to emulate the message delays, that is, gaussian distribution with deviation being 1 and mean being 3, and the distribution modeled from real network traces [12]. In the latter case, about 35% of the messages have RTT $< 50ms$, 60% with RTT $< 100ms$, 25% with RTT $> 200ms$, and the rest are in seconds. For fair comparison, we set $r = c$ (by which the bandwidth costs of SS-PPI are equal to those of flipping PPI). The simulation results are shown in Fig. 7, from which we can see that SS-PPI achieves much better performance in terms of scalability (especially in the large groups). We explain the results based on time-complexity analysis. For SS-PPI, the bandwidth costs are $n \cdot c$ and latency is $max(hop_{i,j})$ for $\forall i \in [0, n-1], j \in [i+1, i+c-1]$. For flipping PPI, the latency is $r \cdot \sum_{i=0}^{n-1} hop_{i,i+1}$ and bandwidth costs are $n \cdot r$ (in terms of number of messages transmitted). When $c = r$, latency of flipping PPI is $O(n \cdot r)$ while that of SS-PPI is $O(1)$.

5.4 Query Processing Costs

The query processing costs are measured by the number of providers

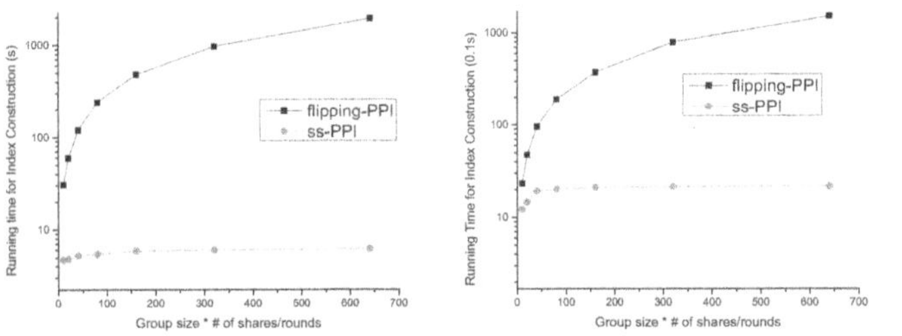

(a) On network with RTT of gaussian distribution (b) On network with RTT modeled from real trace data [12]

Figure 7: Time-efficiency of SS-PPI

returned from the index server for a single query. In this experiment, we focus on single-term queries, in which term is randomly picked from index dictionary. We vary the group size from 2 to 1000 and plot the results in Figure 8. Overall, the query costs grow up as the group size increases. For group size bigger than 50, the percentage of providers that need to check by queriers quickly approaches to 100%, implying our index deteriorates to query broadcasting in this setting, which conforms to our previous experimental and analysis result.

We further study the relationship between search recall and search costs. Experiments are conducted in the both cases of common terms and rare terms. Common term is with selectivity 0.1 while rare term with selectivity 0.004, as they can be picked from the peer-to-peer text dataset[16]. Different value of group sizes are picked for experiments. With results illustrated in Fig. 9, we can see that search costs approximately grow in linear to search recall. For 100% recall, search for common terms always require query broadcasting, while search for rare terms only need multicast to the partial set of providers. In rare term case, the search costs are sensitive to the group size; a big group size generally results in more search costs.

The set of experiments give us implication to properly set the value of group sizes. Finding an appropriate value for group size is tricky, because as aforementioned, too big a group size could lead to query broadcast which hurts scalability and performance, while too small a group size deteriorates the level of privacy preserving. From the experiment results, rules of thumb are to set group size to 50, by which only terms with selectivity bigger than 0.01 will ends up with query broadcast (from Fig. 8) and maximal true positive rate for common terms (e.g., with selectivity 0.2) is less than 0.4 (note in this case, the false positive rate is smaller than 0.5, thus meeting the privacy requirement of "Probable Innocence"[2, 18]).

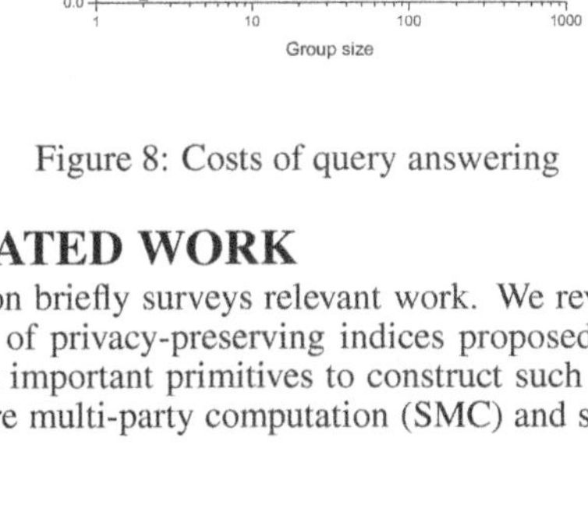

Figure 8: Costs of query answering

6. RELATED WORK

This section briefly surveys relevant work. We review different architectures of privacy-preserving indices proposed in literature, compare two important primitives to construct such architectures, namely secure multi-party computation (SMC) and secret sharing,

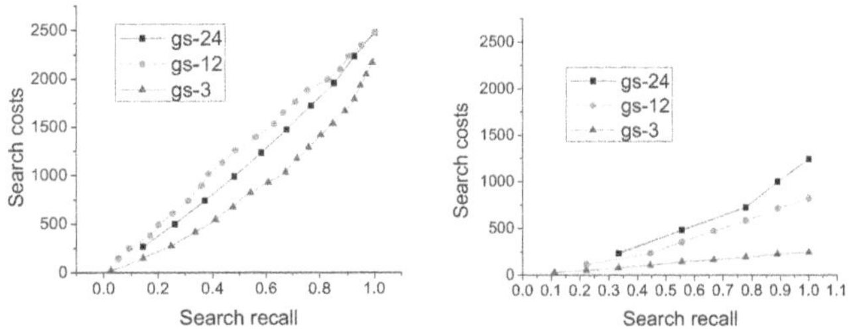

(a) Common terms (b) Rare terms

Figure 9: Search costs in number of providers contacted

and finally discuss other privacy issues in information sharing infrastructures.

6.1 Indexing on Untrusted Servers

The work [2] paved the way for public privacy preserving index from multiple content providers. It randomly organizes providers into disjoint privacy groups; it employs an iterative, randomized algorithm to form group-wise indexing structure, which is further used to direct queries. Comparing to our protocol, this solution suffers three major drawbacks. First, the random grouping strategy makes privacy groups tend to have all terms, and query processing ends up broadcasting. Second, the probabilistic index construction scheme take arbitrary rounds before convergency, leading to unacceptable running time. Third, index construction leaks considerable privacy and is vulnerable to colluding attacks.

Zerber [23] is based on multiple servers with certain amounts of trusts. Zerber distributes inverted index over n servers by using a k-out-of-n secret sharing scheme. During query time, a searcher has to be authenticated and authorized by at least k servers. Then after issuing masked queries individually, searcher obtains shares of matched posting entries from each server, and proceeds to composite the secrets, including indexed terms, document id and relevances. The scheme performs client-side intersection of positing lists, which seriously slow down query performance for large scale dataset (in terms of large number of documents), multiple-keyword queries and searcher with broader accesses. Overall, the amount of trusts assumed on index servers may become unacceptable, since it relies on servers to do authentication and authorization. In particular, access policy privacy is seriously leaked in the sense that any single malicious server cloud disclose such privacy.

Union query dissemination trees (or UQDT) [6] is a distributed privacy preserving index; the indexes are organized as multiple trees, which share the same set of leaf nodes, each corresponding to a disjoint privacy group of publishers/providers. In essence, each QDT can be viewed as a hierarchy of group-wise index at different granularity, and privacy preserving (defined in publisher k-anonymity) is attained in a similar group-wise way. To form the finest group at leaf level, a generic secure multi-party computation [9] is adopted, which however is inefficient and unscalable to thousands of providers. Different QDT's are responsible for different (disjoint) subset of index terms; The multiple-QDT architecture is intended for better load balance and higher throughput, as compared to single UQDT with global set of indexed terms. Specifically, the same physical nodes are intelligently positioned at different levels of different QDT, so overall load is balanced.

6.2 SMC and Secret Sharing

Secure multiparty computation (or SMC) [10] refers to the problem in which multiple parties, each holding a private input, collectively perform a computation without disclosing information more than the output reveals. Many operations in privacy-aware applications [7] can be deemed as secure multiparty computation, including the group-wise index aggregation in our problem. Secret sharing is one primitive for SMC problems. In particular, a generic secret sharing scheme splits a secret into multiple shares, only more than a certain mount of which can reconstruct the secret. Many secret sharing schemes [19] are additive homomorphic [3]. Our protocol takes advantages of this nice property and applies in privacy preserving index construction. Comparing to other primitives for secure multiparty computation, secret sharing is advantageous; it attains information-theoretic security, robust against colluding attacks. More importantly, secret sharing has been shown to significantly outperform those generic SMC protocols in execution efficiency [5, 4]. Secret sharing has been applied in various contexts, for example, database query processing [8], information aggregation [5] and keyword searches[23]. The above approaches put the computation of secret shares onto multiple third parties while index construction in our SS-PPI involves no third party, which sees better scalability.[10] Other work [21] uses similar secret-sharing protocol to preserve privacy in data mining. However, their way to distribute shares incurs load imbalance and hurts performance.

7. CONCLUSION

In this paper, we propose SS-PPI, an efficient and strong privacy preserving index over multiple content sources. Specifically, SS-PPI adopts a new architecture of PPI, namely role-sensitive PPI, that takes into account role access information and achieves better search performance. We also identify a new type of potential privacy leakage in this architecture, that is, access policy privacy. Further, we propose a secret sharing based approach for efficient and secure construction of public index, from multiple content providers. Comparing to previous work, SS-PPI makes a better balance between privacy preserving and search performance. Our protocol is secure against colluding adversaries and achieves information-theoretic privacy preserving. We also conduct extensive analysis and experiments that show advantages of SS-PPI in terms of query performance and security properties.

Acknowledgements

The authors would like to thank the anonymous reviewers. This work is partially supported by grants from NSF CISE NetSE, NSF CyberTrust, an IBM SUR grant, an IBM faculty award, and a grant from Intel Research Council.

8. REFERENCES

[1] Nhin: http://www.hhs.gov/healthit/healthnetwork.

[2] M. Bawa, R. J. Bayardo, Jr, R. Agrawal, and J. Vaidya. Privacy-preserving indexing of documents on the network. *The VLDB Journal*, 18(4), 2009.

[3] J. C. Benaloh. Secret sharing homomorphisms: Keeping shares of a secret sharing. In *CRYPTO*, pages 251–260, 1986.

[4] D. Bogdanov, S. Laur, and J. Willemson. Sharemind: A framework for fast privacy-preserving computations. In *ESORICS*, pages 192–206, 2008.

[5] M. Burkhart, M. Strasser, and X. A. Dimitropoulos. Sepia: Security through private information aggregation. In *USENIX Security*, 2010.

[6] E. Curtmola, A. Deutsch, K. K. Ramakrishnan, and D. Srivastava. Load-balanced query dissemination in privacy-aware online communities. In *SIGMOD*, 2010.

[7] W. Du and M. J. Atallah. Secure multi-party computation problems and their applications: a review and open problems. In *NSPW*, pages 13–22, 2001.

[8] F. Emekçi, D. Agrawal, A. E. Abbadi, and A. Gulbeden. Privacy preserving query processing using third parties. In *ICDE*, page 27, 2006.

[9] O. Goldreich, S. Micali, and A. Wigderson. How to play any mental game. In *STOC*, 1987.

[10] S. Goldwasser. Multi-party computations: Past and present. In *PODC*, pages 1–6, 1997.

[11] D. Hawking. Overview of the trec-9 web track. In *TREC*, 2000.

[12] H. Jiang and C. Dovrolis. Passive estimation of tcp round-trip times. *Computer Communication Review*, 32(3):75–88, 2002.

[13] B. W. Lampson, M. Abadi, M. Burrows, and E. Wobber. Authentication in distributed systems: Theory and practice. *ACM Trans. Comput. Syst.*, 10(4):265–310, 1992.

[14] Q. Lian, Z. Zhang, M. Yang, B. Y. Zhao, Y. Dai, and X. Li. An empirical study of collusion behavior in the maze p2p file-sharing system. In *ICDCS*, 2007.

[15] Y. Lindell and B. Pinkas. Privacy preserving data mining. *J. Cryptology*, 15(3):177–206, 2002.

[10] It implies the more providers participate in the network, the more secure we will end up with, because adversaries now need to compromise all providers to obtain all secrets.

[16] J. Lu and J. P. Callan. Content-based retrieval in hybrid peer-to-peer networks. In *CIKM*, pages 199–206, 2003.

[17] H. Pang, X. Ding, and X. Xiao. Embellishing text search queries to protect user privacy. In *VLDB*, 2010.

[18] M. K. Reiter and A. D. Rubin. Crowds: Anonymity for web transactions. *ACM Trans. Inf. Syst. Secur.*, 1(1):66–92, 1998.

[19] A. Shamir. How to share a secret. *Commun. ACM*, 22(11):612–613, 1979.

[20] M. Srivatsa and L. Liu. Securing publish-subscribe overlay services with eventguard. In *CCS*, 2005.

[21] S. Urabe, J. Wang, E. Kodama, and T. Takata. A high collusion-resistant approach to distributed privacy-preserving data mining. In *Parallel and Distributed Computing and Networks*, pages 307–312, 2007.

[22] L. Xiong, S. Chitti, and L. Liu. Topk queries across multiple private databases. In *ICDCS*, pages 145–154, 2005.

[23] S. Zerr, E. Demidova, D. Olmedilla, W. Nejdl, M. Winslett, and S. Mitra. Zerber: r-confidential indexing for distributed documents. In *EDBT*, pages 287–298, 2008.

APPENDIX

A. PROOF OF THEOREM

THEOREM A.1. *Suppose packets are defined on $\mathbb{Z}_{q'}$ and secrets on $\mathbb{Z}_q$. If $q' = k \cdot q$ (where k is an integer) and the first $c-1$ packets are chosen randomly and independently, $f(\cdot)$ defined by Equation 2 is a (c, c) secret sharing scheme. Formally,*

***Recoverability**: Given c sub-packets $u_{i,j}$ with $j \in \mathbb{Z}_q$, the secret v_i can be easily reconstructed.*

***Secrecy**: Given $c-1$ or fewer sub-packets, the secret v_i is completely undetermined, in the sense that each possible value on sub-secret domain is equally likely for v_i.*

$$\forall x \in \mathbb{Z}_{q'}, \quad prob(v_i = x) = prob(v_i = x | \forall j \in I, u_{i,j} = y_j) = \frac{1}{q'}$$

where I is any set of $2c-2$ or less elements in $\{-c+1, \ldots, 0, \ldots, c-1\}$.

PROOF. We consider the worst case, that is, when $2c-2$ $u_{i,j}$ are known in priori and there is only one packet variable that is unknown. Denote the unknown variable and the sum of the known variables by u_x and v_i', respectively. Then, $v_i = v_i' + u_x \mod q$. For any value $v_i = x$ in $\mathbb{Z}_q$ and fixed v_i', there is exactly k values in $\mathbb{Z}_{q'}$, subject to $v_i = v_i' + u_x \mod q$. And it's easy to see for different x, the set of these k values are disjoint (essentially, forming an equivalence class). The probability for $v_i = x$ is then the probability for u_x to fall in the equivalence classes corresponding to x. Since u_x is unknown and uniformly distributed, probability for $v_i = x$ stays the same, even when $2c-2$ $u_{i,j}$ is known in advance. The theorem holds.

B. PROOF OF LEMMA

Lemma 6.2 Random variable a, b are natural numbers in domain $\mathbb{Z}_q$. Their values are independently chosen and uniformly distributed in $\mathbb{Z}_q$. Then $\forall x, y \in \mathbb{Z}_q$,

$$prob(a = x) = prob(a = x | (a \pm b) \mod q = y) = \frac{1}{q} \tag{11}$$

PROOF.

$$\begin{aligned} & prob((a \pm b) \mod q = y | a = x) \\ & = prob(b = (y \mp x) \mod q | a = x) \\ & = prob(b = (y \mp x) \mod q) = \frac{1}{q} \end{aligned}$$

The derivation is due to the fact that variable a and b are mutually independent.

$$\begin{aligned} & prob(a = x | (a \pm b) \mod q = y) \\ & = \frac{prob(a = x \wedge (a \pm b) \mod q = y)}{prob((a \pm b) \mod q = y)} \\ & = \frac{prob(a = x) \cdot prob((a \pm b) \mod q = y | a = x)}{prob((a \pm b) \mod q = y)} \\ & = \frac{prob(a = x) \cdot prob(b = (y \mp x) \mod q | a = x)}{\sum_{x'=1}^{q} prob(b = (y \mp x') \mod q | a = x') \cdot prob(a = x')} \end{aligned}$$

Because a,b are independent random variables, so $\forall x'$, $prob(b = (y \mp x') \mod q | a = x') = prob(b = (y \mp x') \mod q) = \frac{1}{q}$. And since $prob(a = x') = \frac{1}{q}$, we have

$$\begin{aligned} & prob(a = x | (a \pm b) \mod q = y) \\ & = \frac{\frac{1}{q} \cdot \frac{1}{q}}{\sum_{x'=1}^{q} \frac{1}{q} \cdot \frac{1}{q}} = \frac{1}{q} \\ & = prob(a = x) \end{aligned}$$

Recommendation in the End-to-End Encrypted Domain

Jyh-Ren Shieh
Graduate Institute of Networking and Multimedia
National Taiwan University
Taipei, 10617, Taiwan, ROC
jerry@cmlab.csie.ntu.edu.tw

Ching-Yung Lin
IBM T. J. Watson Research Center
Hawthorne, New York
NY 10532
USA
chingyung@us.ibm.com

Ja-Ling Wu
Graduate Institute of Networking and Multimedia & Department of CS
National Taiwan University
Taipei, 10617, Taiwan, ROC
wjl@cmlab.csie.ntu.edu.tw

ABSTRACT

In recommendation systems, a central host typically requires access to user profiles in order to generate useful recommendations. This access, however, undermines user privacy; the more information is revealed to the host, the more the user's privacy is compromised. In this paper, we propose a novel end-to-end encrypted recommendation mechanism which encrypts sensitive private data at the user end, without ever exposing plaintext private data to the host server. Unlike previously proposed privacy-preserving recommendation mechanisms, the data in this proposed system are lossless – a pivotal feature to many applications, e.g., in health informatics, business analytics, cyber security, etc. We achieve this goal by developing encrypted-domain polynomial ring homomorphism cryptographic algorithms to compute similarity of encrypted scores on the server, so that collaborative recommendations can be computed in the encryption domain and only an authorized person can decrypt the exact results. We also propose a novel key management system to make sure private information retrieval and recommendation computations can be executed in the encrypted domain in practice. Our experiments show that the proposed scheme offers robust security and lossless accurate recommendation, as well as high efficiency. Our preliminary results show the recommendation accuracy is 21% better than the existing statistical lossy privacy-preserving mechanisms based on random perturbation and user profile distribution. This new approach can potentially be applied to various data mining and cloud computing environments and significantly alleviates the privacy concerns of users.

Categories and Subject Descriptors

H.3.3 [Information Search and Retrieval]: Information Filtering;

General Terms

Algorithms, Design, Security, Experimentation.

Keywords

Recommender Systems, Personalization, Privacy.

1. INTRODUCTION

Users can be overwhelmed by the huge number of choices available on the Internet. Recommendation systems are widely used to narrow down their choices, for items of any type: books, movies, sports, restaurants, tourist destinations, online news, etc. User profiles such as age range, gender, and location, as well as web activity history such as search keywords and click-through sequences all can be used to find dating prospects over the Internet. The widely-used collaborative recommendation systems rely on the similarity of user tastes: if two users have similar preferences for certain items, one user will probably be interested in the items that the other is interested in. Thus, the more information each user gives to the recommender system about his interests, the more meaningful the recommendations will be.

A recommendation system creates user profiles by collecting information about user preferences for different items. The preferences of a user in the past can facilitate the prediction of other matching information that might also be of interest to the user in the future. In order to recommend items to users, a recommendation host must access the user's profiles, which contain various person-identifiable information. These profiles are usually stored in the host repositories. Currently, users of any recommendation system must allow the host access to the complete contents of their profiles and trust (or, in most cases, just hope) that the host company and the server administrators will keep this information private.

Allowing "plaintext" information, which is readable by the server, leads to many thorny privacy issues. First, if a user's real identity is known to the host, the host can associate the user's personal profile, which contains his private information, to his real identity. This is an obvious privacy breach, considering that although using the service, the user does not want the link between his real identity and his profile to be revealed. This threat becomes more obvious when users reveal sensitive personal data, such as age, height, weight, sexual orientation, and religion. Second, even if the real identity of a user is not known to the server, it can attempt to de-anonymize the user's identity by correlating the information contained in the user's profile and information obtained from other related databases. Third, hosts may collect personal information about their users and resell it to various vendors for sales and marketing to gain significant financial benefits. Today, there is much such user data to be had. However, user data is vulnerable to criminals; it can affect one's reputation, business operations, etc. From a privacy perspective, it is obvious that hiding personal information from the host is a good thing. To do so, an end-to-end encrypted recommendation computing system such as that proposed in this paper is probably the best solution. It leaves private information in each individual's possession, while allowing the server to conduct recommendation computations in the encrypted domain without knowing the original plaintext profiles.

CIKM'11, October 24–28, 2011, Glasgow, Scotland, UK.

Several techniques have been proposed to preserve user privacy in recommendation systems. The three main categories for privacy preservation in recommendation systems are user score perturbation, cryptographic approaches, and distributed storage of user profiles. Randomized perturbation [1][2] techniques have been used to preserve privacy in collaborative recommendations. In this approach, user data are modified by adding random noise in order to prevent the central server from deriving the actual user rating. However, the added noise prevents the server from being able to estimate the actual values for similarity measurements; moreover, additional security flaws are caused by small user space sizes. Canny [3][4] proposed a community-based cryptographic privacy-preserving collaborative filtering method. A community of users can compute a public "aggregate" of their data without disclosing any individual user's data. This aggregation allows personalized referrals to be computed by members of the community. A partially homomorphic encryption like RSA [5] is employed to allow sums of encrypted vectors to be computed and decrypted without exposing individual data, but this approach still has accuracy problems. Thus both randomized perturbation and cryptography-based aggregate computation entail a compromise between recommendation accuracy and personal data security. The third option is to store user profiles locally and run the recommendation system in a distributed manner by revealing partial information, without relying on a centralized server [8]–[12]. In this case, although servers only know partial information, eventually, an end-to-end service provider may still be able to assemble the information from each individual server which knows part of the information. For instance, dividing my personal information into 10 pieces and telling 10 different people does not really protect my privacy.

Our contributions are as follows. In this paper, we first propose a novel system solution for privacy-preserving recommendations in which we do not require several customers to be online simultaneously, nor do we introduce random perturbations. Second, we conduct encrypted-domain addition and multiplication operations based on polynomial rings, so that we can generate the same collaborative filtering results as that obtained from the plaintext data. Third, we propose a ring homomorphic encryption algorithm which makes the encrypted-domain recommendation calculations highly computationally efficient, a key step toward making encrypted-domain recommendations feasible. As our approach is based on lossless number theory, recommendation results are the same as recommendations made based on plaintext data. This solves the many drawbacks described above, and is the goal of this paper.

The rest of this paper is organized as follows. We review related work in Section 2. In Section 3, we describe in detail our privacy-preserving system, including how to handle the key management of collaborative recommendation and how to compute the user-to-user similarity entirely in the encryption domain. In Section 4 we analyze the security, efficiency, and accuracy of the proposed system, and in Section 5 we conclude and suggest directions for future work.

2. RELATED WORKS

2.1 Randomized Perturbation

In the randomized perturbation scheme, each user disguises his or her personal data and then sends it to a central place (the data collector) such that the data collector cannot derive the user's actual private information. This scheme should still be able to allow the data collector to conduct collaborative filtering using the disguised data. Polat and Du [1][2] proposed a technique in which user ratings are modified by adding random noise to them in order to prevent the central server from deriving the actual user ratings. The challenge is to find a perturbation algorithm that imposes the smallest error on the recommendation process. Users enjoy a high level of privacy if the server is not able to estimate the actual ratings that they assigned to the items. However, the perturbed list of items rated by the users is revealed, regardless of the perturbation level. This overlooks the fact that keeping the connection between users and items is more crucial (in order to preserve users' privacy) than disguising the ratings assigned to those connections. Also, revealing the places visited by the users to the server enables it to track users over space and time, whether they liked those places or not.

2.2 Homomorphic cryptography

Recommendation schemes based on partially homomorphic cryptography as proposed by Canny et al. [3][4] require user participation in the distributed system, which may not reflect real-world usage such as cloud computing. Recently, in cryptography, Gentry et al. proposed a breakthrough fully homomorphic encryption scheme using lattice-based cryptography that supports computation in the encrypted domain [6][7]. To the best of our knowledge, we are not aware of any prior work applying such a fully homomorphic scheme to recommendation applications (or, perhaps, any data mining application). In practice, their scheme may need substantial improvements in order to be used in practical applications, because the ciphertext size and computation time increase sharply as one increases the security level. Their constructions are limited to evaluating low-degree polynomials over encrypted data. Moreover, the scheme allows only single bit operations, and even that is computationally prohibitive. Also, the scheme does not offer a practical key management solution where all of the users share the same public key for a full homomorphic encryption application.

2.3 User Profile Distribution

Another option is to store user profiles locally and to run the recommender system in a distributed manner, without relying on any server. Miller et al. [8] proposed transmitting only the similarity measures over the network and keeping users' profiles secret on their sides to preserve privacy. Berkovsky et al. [9] proposed a distributed P2P system to avoid storing users' profiles on a single server. Although these methods eliminate the main source of threat against users' privacy, they require high cooperation among users to generate meaningful recommendations. Every user pays the price of using this method, regardless of his interest in protecting privacy. Lathia et al. [10] proposed a concordance measure to estimate the similarity between two users in a distributed system without revealing their actual profiles to each other. Lathia's method demands that users trust each other to estimate their similarity is hardly feasible in a recommendation system based on thousands of users [11][12].

2.4 Collaborative Recommendation

The most common form of collaborative recommendation is the neighborhood-based approach, which works by computing the similarity between all pairs of users; predictions are made by aggregating ratings of the target item by the user's neighbors or the user's ratings of items that are neighbors of the target item. Algorithms within these families differ in the definition of similarity and the formulation of neighborhoods. Finding a particular consumer's neighborhood with similar tastes or interests and quantifying the strength of similarity are the most crucial steps for making a collaborative recommendation. Recently, algorithms based on a weighted user-item bipartite-graph soft clustering [15] [16] have been proposed which yield higher accuracies than classical collaborative filtering approaches. This serves as the kernel of our collaborative recommendation system.

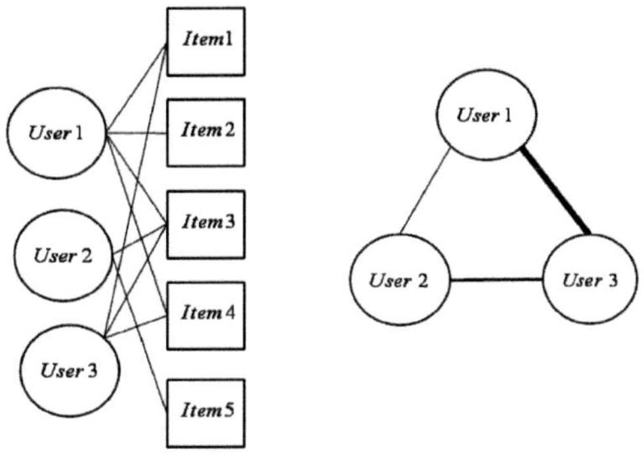

(a) (b)

Figure 1. Illustration of soft communities: (a) the bipartite graph representing user-to-item relations, and (b) the induced user cluster affinities.

We summarize the relationship among users, items, and the corresponding item scores, $\mathbb{E}_{\mathrm{ui}}$, using the bipartite graph $\mathbb{G}(\mathbb{U}_{\mathrm{usr}}, \mathbb{I}_{\mathrm{item}}, \mathbb{E}_{\mathrm{ui}})$ shown in Figure 1 (a). In the graph, the nodes at the left denote the groups of n users, the nodes at the right denote the m items, and user groups and item objects are connected by edges associated with corresponding weighting scores. The corresponding user affinities are shown in Figure 1 (b). As pre-scribed, let $\mathbb{G}(\mathbb{U}_{\mathrm{usr}}, \mathbb{I}_{\mathrm{item}}, \mathbb{E}_{\mathrm{ui}})$ denote a bipartite graph, where $\mathbb{U}_{\mathrm{usr}} = \{\mathrm{u}_{\mathrm{usr}}^{i}\}_{i=1}^{n}$ and $\mathbb{I}_{\mathrm{item}} = \{\mathrm{i}_{\mathrm{item}}^{k}\}_{k=1}^{m}$ are two disjoint vertex sets and $\mathbb{E}_{\mathrm{ui}}$ denote all the edges that connect $\mathbb{U}_{\mathrm{usr}}$ and $\mathbb{I}_{\mathrm{item}}$. Let $\mathbb{E}_{\mathrm{ui}} = \{\mathrm{e}_{\mathrm{ui}}^{ik}\}$ denote the $n \times m$ adjacency matrix with $\mathrm{e}_{\mathrm{ui}}^{ik} \geq 0$ being the the corresponding item score between $\mathrm{u}_{\mathrm{usr}}^{i}$ and $\mathrm{i}_{\mathrm{item}}^{i}$. The bipartite graph induces a similarity between $\mathrm{u}_{\mathrm{usr}}^{a}$ and $\mathrm{u}_{\mathrm{usr}}^{j}$, that is,

$$\mathrm{SIM}(\mathrm{u}_{\mathrm{usr}}^{a}, \mathrm{u}_{\mathrm{usr}}^{k}) = \sum_{i=1}^{m} \frac{\mathrm{e}_{\mathrm{ui}}^{ai}\mathrm{e}_{\mathrm{ui}}^{ki}}{\lambda_i} = \left(\mathrm{E}_{\mathrm{UI}} \Lambda^{-1} \mathrm{E}_{\mathrm{UI}}{}^{\mathrm{T}}\right)_{ak,} \tag{1}$$

where $\Lambda = \mathrm{diag}(\lambda_1, \cdots, \lambda_m)$, and $\lambda_k = \sum_{i=1}^{m} \mathrm{e}_{\mathrm{ui}}^{ik}$ denotes the degree of the vertex $\mathrm{u}_{\mathrm{usr}}^{i} \in \mathbb{U}_{\mathrm{usr}}$. Equation (1) can be interpreted from the perspective of Markov random walks on graphs. $\mathrm{SIM}(\mathrm{u}_{\mathrm{usr}}^{a}, \mathrm{u}_{\mathrm{usr}}^{k})$ is essentially a quantity proportional to the stationary probability of the direct transition between $\mathrm{u}_{\mathrm{usr}}^{a}$ and $\mathrm{u}_{\mathrm{usr}}^{k}$. However, this shows only the similarity between users. To measure the similarity of the whole group, we have the following matrix formulation:

$$\mathrm{SIM} = \mathrm{W} \Lambda \mathrm{W}^{\mathrm{T}}, \tag{2}$$

where $\mathrm{W} \in Z_{n \times m}^{+}$ is a non-negative $n \times m$ matrix. For the components of this matrix, one column corresponds to one user and one row to one item, i.e., $\mathrm{w}_{\mathrm{ui}}^{ai}$ is the score of item $\mathrm{i}_{\mathrm{item}}^{i}$ rated by user $\mathrm{u}_{\mathrm{usr}}^{a}$. Λ is an $m \times n$ non-negative diagonal matrix within which λ_k indicates the user's level of participation.

It is well-known that such collaborative filtering can be realized by the calculation of user-to-user similarity so as to recommend items to users on the basis of the past history of the most similar users.

3. PRIVACY-PRESERVING RECOMMENDATION SYSTEM

3.1 Encrypted-Domain Recommendation System

3.1.1 One possible use case

We use the following example to describe our privacy-preserving encrypted-domain recommendation system. In health informatics, patient privacy must be carefully protected. Therefore, after seeing the doctor, the patient encrypts the more sensitive parts of his or her own medical record – for instance, psychological treatments, infertility treatments, or cosmetic procedures – and then transmits them to the server at the hospital or insurance company via a secure channel. Thus sensitive data stored in the central database is totally encrypted. When another doctor diagnoses a new patient, in order to find the most appropriate treatment, he or she looks for similar patients with similar symptoms in the encrypted database to see how other doctors diagnosed them, and then takes this into account to give their own patient the best treatment. Figure 2 illustrates our privacy-preserving recommendation scheme for this particular case.

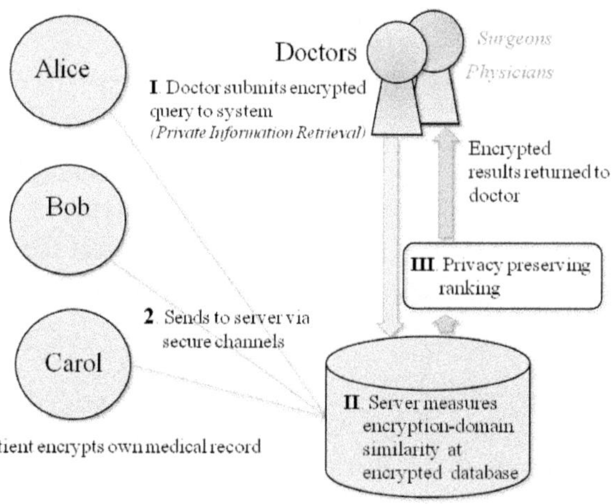

Figure 2. Privacy-preserving recommendation scheme.

3.1.2 System Structure

In order to achieve the above functions, our system requires three encryption mechanisms. The first one is the ring homomorphic encryption. To ensure privacy, the patient should encrypt his or her own data. The goal is that every patient's sensitive medical records are encrypted and that similarity measurements on this data are evaluated in the encryption domain. Thus, ring homomorphic encryption provides the first tier of data protection, allowing for computing multiplication and addition in the encryption domain and inducing these two operations for the underlying plaintext. Homomorphic key distribution is conducted at the key manager server. Thus, when the inspection data is obtained at the clinic, the key management server delivers the homomorphic key to the patients, who encrypt their own private medical information and send it to the hospital database server via a secure channel.

The channel between the parties, such as from the user to the server, may be vulnerable to eavesdropping and malicious attacks, including man-meet-in-the-middle and replay. Also, to ensure the confidentiality of medical records, we must hide the identity of the patients. Thus, another important issue is how to send these medical records in a way that preserves the patient's privacy and anonymity. Ring homomorphic encryption calculation alone cannot ensure information security. Thus, we here apply the second tier of communication security mechanisms using the improved Diffie-Hellman-based protocols, which enable us to securely send the patient's encrypted data to the server. Also, instead of using digital signatures, our scheme hides patient identities by using a hash function. Effective key generation and management is critical for a complete, end-to-end encrypted domain recommendation system. The key for the secure channel by our improved Diffie-Hellman-based protocol is based on the secret sharing principle. Hence the session key is obtained by the two communication parties.

When the doctor submits an encrypted request to the server to calculate the similarity of private information, the similarity measure is calculated in the encryption domain. Therefore, the server needs not be trusted since it knows nothing about the real medical information. Our homomorphic encryption and private information retrieval procedures are illustrated in Figure 3.

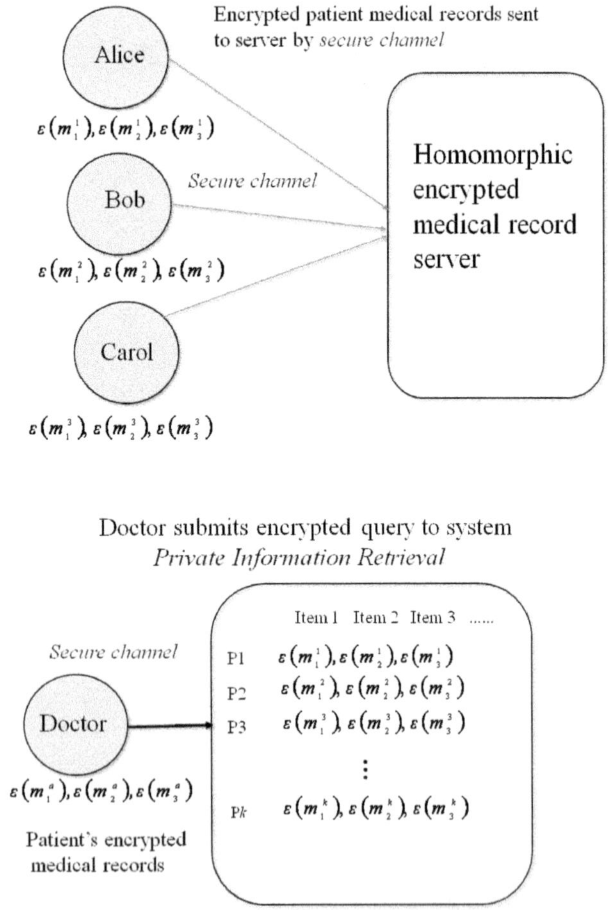

Figure 3. Homomorphic encryption and private information retrieval via end-to-end secure channel.

After the encryption-domain similarity measurement is completed, the doctor provides order-preserving encryption keys to the server database. The third-tier order-preserving encryption is applied to transform these encryption similarity results, which are then sent to the proxy for ranking. Thus, even if the proxy has the homomorphic private key to decrypt the transformed similarity results, it still is limited to calculating rankings, and has no way of knowing the real similarity value. The case ranked most similar to the information is then returned in encrypted form to the doctor, who can use his or her private key to participate the order-preserving data encryption. In this way the doctor takes into account the treatment for similar patients when deciding on the best treatment for the current patient, as shown in Figure 4.

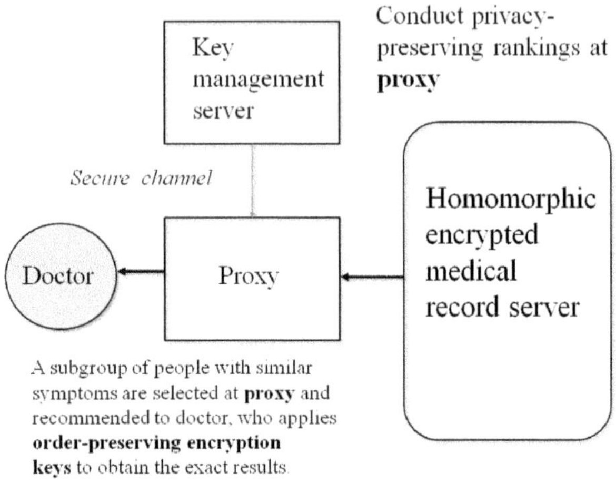

Figure 4. Order preserving encryption and encrypted similarity ranking.

3.2 Ring Homomorphic Encryption

Homomorphic encryption is a form of encryption where a specific algebraic operation performed on the plaintext is equivalent to another (possibly different) algebraic operation performed on the ciphertext. The commonly used RSA code is only homomorphic with respect to multiplication. Given public key (N, k), x is encrypted as $x^k \bmod N$. Since $(x^k \, mod \, N) \cdot (y^k \, mod \, N) = (xy)^k mod \, N$, it follows that the encrypted form of xy is the product of the codes for x and y. Hence we can correctly multiply two encrypted numbers without ever knowing what the numbers were, and obtain a lossless result.

Multiplication-only homomorphic cryptosystems such as RSA are not enough for end-to-end encrypted-domain recommendation. For this task fully homomorphic encryption is required. The utility of fully homomorphic encryption has been long recognized. However, it was not considered feasible until 2009, when Gentry et al. [6] proposed the first fully homomorphic encryption scheme based on lattice-based cryptography. The scheme is limited to evaluating low-degree polynomials over encrypted data, and thus a modified bootstrable scheme was applied to improve its efficiency [7]. One obstacle of these methods is that the key operations are based on one binary bit [6][7].

We propose an efficient ring homomorphic encryption system based on polynomial rings which directly calculates integers in the encrypted domain, and is thus more efficient for tasks such as collaborative filtering based recommendations. A ring homomorphism is a function between two rings which respects the operations of addition and multiplication. With ring homomorphic encryption, you submit an encrypted copy of all your private data and get back an encrypted copy of the actual scalar matching result you are looking for, without revealing any of your private data. A ring homomorphism function, in our scheme, is a function between two polynomial rings with respect to the operations of addition and multiplication. More precisely, if R and S are polynomial rings, then a ring homomorphism is a function $\phi\colon R \rightarrow S$ such that

$$\phi(x+y) = \phi(x) + \phi(y) \text{ and } \quad (3)$$

$$\phi(x \times y) = \phi(x) \times \phi(y) \quad (4)$$

3.3 Encrypted Domain Operations

We need to derive encrypted-domain calculations, including both multiplications and additions. In (2), we have $\mathrm{SIM} = \mathrm{W}\Lambda\mathrm{W}^{\mathrm{T}}$, where $\mathrm{W} \in \mathrm{Z}^{+}_{\mathrm{n}\times\mathrm{m}}$ is a non-negative matrix and its entry component represents the weighting of the relationship between each user and each item. To preserve user privacy we must define a method for measuring similarity in the encryption domain. Based on equations (1) and (2), we have

$$\mathcal{E}(\mathrm{SIM}(\mathrm{u}^{a}_{\mathrm{usr}}, \mathrm{u}^{k}_{\mathrm{usr}})) = \sum_{i} \frac{\varepsilon(m^{a}_{i}) \cdot \varepsilon(m^{k}_{i})}{\sum_{k}\sum_{a} \varepsilon(m^{a}_{i}) \cdot \varepsilon(m^{k}_{i})}$$

$$\approx \textstyle\sum_{i} \varepsilon(m^{a}_{i}) \cdot \varepsilon(m^{k}_{i}), \quad (5)$$

where $\varepsilon(.)$ stands for the ring homomorphic encryption algorithms and m^{a}_{i} denotes the weight of the relationship between user a and item i, which is the simplified notation for $\mathrm{w}^{ai}_{\mathrm{ui}}$ used in Equations (2) for describing the graph model.

For all users and items we also have, in matrix form, the soft clustering formulation for a group of people in the encryption domain as follows:

$$\mathcal{E}(\mathrm{SIM}) = \mathcal{E}(\mathrm{W}\Lambda\mathrm{W}^{\mathrm{T}}) = \mathcal{E}(\mathrm{W})\mathcal{E}(\Lambda)\mathcal{E}(\mathrm{W}^{\mathrm{T}}), \quad (6)$$

where Λ is an $m \times n$ non-negative diagonal matrix with λ_k indicating how often a user participates in a given activity. We propose polynomial ring homomorphism, which is described in this section also with details in Section 4, to realize equation (4) in practice. After the server-side encrypted-domain computation, the encrypted recommendation results are returned to each user, again via a secure channel, with which the authorized user can decrypt the results using his or her private key. Thus from the user side to the server, and then back to the user side, all the user's information is encrypted, transferred, and computed in the encrypted domain. The encrypted-domain computation is based on the polynomial ring homomorphism. In this section, we derive a new ring homomorphism based on the concept of lattice-based cryptosystems [14].

Lattice-based cryptographic schemes hold great promise even against quantum computers, as they boast very strong security proofs based on worst-case hardness, relatively efficient implementations, and great simplicity. Compared to modular exponentiation (RSA) as well as repeated squaring and doubling (ECC), lattice-based polynomial ring homomorphic encryption provides not only strong encryption-domain summation and multiplication, but also boasts $O(N^2)$ performance or even $O(NlogN)$ when applying FFT. Note that both RSA and ECC are of complexity $O(N^3)$. This is because polynomial ring convolution operations are faster than the other approaches. Moreover, the cryptosystem uses the polynomial ring $P[N] = \mathrm{Z}[x] / (x^N - 1)$ and $\mathrm{P}_q[N] = \mathrm{Z}_q[N]/(x^N - 1)$, where N is positive prime, Z denotes the ring of integers, and Z_q is the integer modulo q. Therefore the encryption capability associated with the polynomial ring $\mathrm{P}_q[N]$ is Z^N_q. For example, if modulo q is 17 and the degree N is 7, the total representation plaintext number can reach 17^7. Thus the throughput of the proposed encryption scheme is far greater than Gentry et al's single-bit representation with only 2^1 options. This shows that our system lends itself to real-world implementations.

As shown in Figure 5, a lattice is a regular array of points in space: note that we can connect the dots to form parallelograms. The lattice may be described by giving basis vectors that span such a parallelogram. The closest vector problem (CVP) is that given point P, it is difficult to find the point Q in the lattice that is closest to P without knowing L, the basis of the lattice.

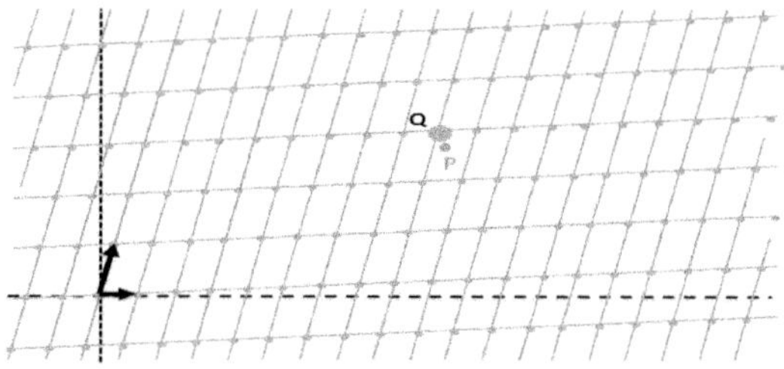

Figure 5. Example of lattice-based cryptography, where Q is the encrypted point of P, and the basis of the lattice

3.4 Lattice-Based Polynomial Ring Homomorphic Encryptions

In this section we describe the encryption and decryption scheme. User-side encryption is conducted as follows.

Score mapping to polynomial rings. Alice transfers the integer score for a item to a polynomial. For example, 3 is mapped to $x+1$, 5 is mapped to x^2+1, and 11 to x^3+x+1. This approach in effect spreads an integer over several coefficients of a polynomial. This idea is the basis for the secrecy, efficiency, and encryption-domain operation of our proposed approaches.

Parameter settings. Three positive integral parameters (N, p, q) are chosen for the key generation which satisfy the following conditions: (1) N is prime; (2) p and q are chosen such that they are relatively prime to each other, i.e., $gcd(N, q) = gcd(p, q) = 1$. The values of (N, p, q) can be known to the public.

Polynomials chosen. There are four sets of polynomials $\mathcal{L}_f$, $\mathcal{L}_g$, $\mathcal{L}_r$, and $\mathcal{L}_m$ respectively defined in the polynomial ring $R[x] \triangleq \mathrm{Z}[x] / (x^N - 1)$. The coefficients of these polynomials are constrained by the choice of parameter p, i.e. all the operations are defined in the polynomial ring $\mathrm{R}_p[x] \triangleq \mathrm{Z}_p[x]/(x^N - 1)$, which is equivalent to the operations defined by taking modulo $(x^N - 1)$ on polynomials and modulo p on polynomial coefficients simultaneously.

Key generation. Homomorphic key generation is a crucial part of an encryption scheme. In our scheme, the key is embedded in the coefficient of the polynomials as follows.

We first define

$$T(d_1, d_2) = \left\{ \begin{matrix} f(x)\text{: the set of trinary polynomials, in which } d_1 \text{ coefficients} \\ \text{of } f(x) = 1 \text{ and } d_2 \text{ coefficients of } f(x) = -1 \end{matrix} \right\}.$$

Since $f(x)$ is a trinary polynomial, the system chooses a $f(x) \in T(d+1, d)$ as his or her private key which is used to decrypt the encrypted-domain recommendation result. Alice then randomly selects a polynomial $f(x) \in \mathcal{L}_f$ such that $f(x)$ has an inverse both in modulo p and modulo q, i.e., the inverses exist in both $R_p[x] = Z_p[x]/(x^N - 1)$ and $R_q[x] = Z_q[x]/(x^N - 1)$.

That is, the system can compute the two inverses of $f(x)$, $F_p(x)$, and $F_q(x)$, respectively in $R_p[x]$ and $R_q[x]$ as

$$f(x)F_p(x) \equiv 1 \bmod R_p[x] \quad \text{and} \qquad (7-\text{a})$$

$$f(x)F_q(x) \equiv 1 \bmod R_q[x]. \qquad (7-\text{b})$$

Then Alice randomly selects a trinary polynomial $g(x) \in \mathcal{L}_g$ in which $g(x) \in T(d, d)$ and then computes

$$h(x) = F_q(x)g(x) \bmod R_q[x] \qquad (8)$$

Alice uses the polynomial $h(x)$ as her public key, and $f(x)$ and $F_q(x)$ becomes her private key for decryption [15].

Centered lift coefficients. Alice keeps each coefficient of the plaintext score polynomial $m_i^a(x)$ within the range $\left(-\frac{p}{2n}, \frac{p}{2n}\right]$ to ensure correct encryption and decryption, maintaining the one-to-one and onto property between the plaintext and the cipher text, where n is the number of plaintexts we are going to encrypt and p is the modulo we have chosen. It is well known that if we take integers 2 modulo 7, we can express 2 as $-12, -5, 2, 9, 16$ and so on. Now, we define the centered lift operation (CLO) to restrict the coefficients to be centered around 0. That is, every coefficient $m_i^a(j)$ of $m_i^a(x)$ satisfies $-\frac{p}{2n} < m_i^a(j) \leq \frac{p}{2n}$, where $0 \leq j \leq n$. After applying CLO, the representation for each of the coefficient is unique. As an example, if we choose p=4 and n=1, then $-\frac{4}{2} < m_i^a(j) \leq \frac{4}{2}$. That is, the centered lifted version of the plaintext score polynomial $m_i^a(x) = 3x^5 + 6x^4 + 7x^2 - 3x - 15$ is $CLO_{4,1}\{m_i^a(x)\} = -x^5 + 2x^4 - x^2 + x + 1$.

Encryption. Alice encrypts her score for item i (denoted as $m_i^a(x)$) using the public key $h(x)$ and the randomly blinding key $r_i^a(x)$ as

$$\boldsymbol{e_i^a(x)} = \left(pr_i^a(x)h(x) + m_i^a(x)\right) \bmod R_q[x] \qquad (9)$$

to make each cipher as unique as if a one-time pad were applied. Likewise, she encrypts her score for item l (denote as $m_l^a(x)$) using the public key $h(x)$ and the blinding key $r_l^a(x)$ as

$$e_l^a(x) = \left(pr_l^a(x)h(x) + m_l^a(x)\right) \bmod R_q[x]. \qquad (10)$$

As each group of attendees encrypts their own scores for each item using different randomly chosen blinding keys $r(x) \in \mathcal{L}_r$ and their corresponding public keys $h(x)$, in general, the encryption of participant k's score polynomial $m_i^k(x)$ to item i is

$$\boldsymbol{e_i^k(x)} = (pr_i^k(x)h(x) + m_i^k(x)) \bmod R_q[x] \qquad (11)$$

When the server receives the encrypted scores $e_i^a(x)$ and $e_i^k(x)$, it can only multiply the encrypted scores, yielding

$$e_i^a(x)e_i^k(x) \bmod R_q[x] =$$

$$\left(\left(pr_i^a(x)h(x) + m_i^a(x)\right)\left(pr_i^k(x)h(x) + m_i^k(x)\right)\right) \bmod R_q[x] =$$
$$(p^2 r_i^a(x)r_i^k(x)h(x)^2 + ph(x)\left(r_i^a(x)m_i^k(x) + r_i^k(x)m_i^a(x)\right) +$$
$$\boldsymbol{m_i^a(x)m_i^k(x)}) \bmod R_q[x]. \qquad (12)$$

As we can see in the formula, although the encrypted $m_i^a(x)$ and $m_i^k(x)$ corresponding to $e_i^a(x)$ and $e_i^k(x)$ are multiplied, the plaintext score multiplication $\boldsymbol{m_i^a(x)m_i^k(x)}$ still remains a separate term in Equation (12). Therefore, although the multiplication of $e_i^a(x)$ and $e_i^k(x)$ is performed in the encryption domain, it still induces multiplication of the underlying plaintext $\boldsymbol{m_i^a(x)m_i^k(x)}$, which is the exact, lossless multiplication score of the plaintext, to which is no perturbed noise or distribution. The homomorphic private key owner decrypts the $e_i^a(x)e_i^k(x)$ at the owner side. When the owner receives the encrypted product $e_i^a(x)e_i^k(x)$ from the server, he or she applies the first private key $f(x)^2$ and proceeds as follows:

$$f(x)^2 e_i^a(x)e_i^k(x) \bmod R_q[x] = f(x)^2\left(p^2 r_i^a(x)r_i^k(x)\boldsymbol{h(x)^2} +\right.$$
$$ph(x)(r_i^a(x)m_i^k(x) + r_i^k(x)m_i^a(x)) +$$
$$\left.m_i^a(x)m_i^k(x)\right) \bmod R_q[x] \text{it which is addedwere} \qquad (13)$$

Since $h(x) = F_q(x)g(x) \bmod R_q[x]$, we have

$$h(x)^2 = F_q(x)^2 g(x)^2 \bmod R_q[x] \qquad (14)$$

Since$f(x)^2 F_q(x)^2 \equiv 1 \bmod R_q[x]$, $f(x)^2$ deduces $\boldsymbol{F_q(x)^2}$ but keeps $\boldsymbol{g(x)^2}$ intact.

After the private key owner applies $f(x)^2$ over $R_q[x]$, we have

$$\alpha \equiv f(x)^2 e_i^a(x)e_i^k(x) \bmod R_q[x] = (p^2 r_i^a(x)r_i^k(x)\, \boldsymbol{g(x)^2} +$$
$$pf(x)g(x)\left(r_i^a(x)m_i^k(x) + r_i^k(x)m_i^a(x)\right) +$$
$$f(x)^2 m_i^a(x)m_i^k(x)) \bmod R_q[x]. \qquad (15)$$

Correct encryption and decryption needs to maintain the isomorphism, i.e., one-to-one and onto, between plaintexts and ciphertexts, where the coefficients of α should fall within the interval $-\frac{q}{2}$ to $\frac{q}{2}$. The first criterion is that the range of modulo q is bounded from modulo p, and the second is the number of coefficients of $f(x)$ equals to 1 and -1, respectively. If we select appropriate values for multiplication modulo p as well as d, the number of the coefficients equals 1 in the trinary polynomial $f(x)$, $g(x)$ and the homomorphic private key, and then applies the second private key $F_p(x)^2$ and takes operations modulo p as

$$(F_p(x)^2(\boldsymbol{p^2 r_i^a(x)r_i^k(x)\, g(x)^2}$$
$$+\, \boldsymbol{pf(x)g(x)\left(r_i^a(x)m_i^k(x) + r_i^k(x)m_i^a(x)\right)}$$
$$+\, (\boldsymbol{F_p(x)^2 f(x)^2} m_i^a(x)m_i^k(x)) \bmod R_q[x] (\bmod p).$$

As both terms $(\boldsymbol{p^2 r_i^a(x)r_i^k(x)\, g(x)^2})$ and $\boldsymbol{pf(x)g(x)\left(r_i^a(x)m_i^k(x) + r_i^k(x)m_i^a(x)\right)}$ are divisible by p, these two terms are zeroed out. The remaining term becomes $\boldsymbol{m_i^a(x)m_i^k(x)}$ since $\boldsymbol{f(x)^2 F_q(x)^2 \equiv 1}$. We show that $e_i^a(x)e_i^k(x)$ can be decrypted at the user side to get the real weight $\boldsymbol{m_i^a(x)m_i^k(x)}$. Let us use the encryption-domain scalar product $\boldsymbol{m_1^a m_1^k + m_2^a m_2^k + m_3^a m_3^k = 3 \times 7 + 5 \times 6 + 10 \times 1 = 61}$ as an example.

Taking N= 7, p = 29, and q = 491531,

$f(x) = x^5 - x^4 - x^2 + x + 1$, $g(x) = -x^6 + x^3 + x^2 - 1$, the inverse $F_p(x)$ of $f(x)$ modulo p is $F_p(x) = 7x^6 + 6x^5 + 22x^4 + 10x^3 + 24x^2 + 4x + 15$ and the inverse $F_q(x)$ of $f(x)$ modulo q is $F_q(x) = 359995x^6 + 214612x^5 + 477685x^4 + 48461x^3 + 76153x^2 + 470762x + 318457$.

The public key $h(x)$ is $h(x) = F_q(x)g(x) \bmod R_q[x] = 339225 + 41538x^5 + 346149x^4 + 263073x^3 + 62307x^2 + 27692x + 394609$.

Plaintext scores given from* Users *A and K

$m_1^a = \boldsymbol{3}$, $m_1^a(x) = x + 1$, $\qquad m_1^k = \boldsymbol{7}$, $m_1^k(x) = x^2 + x + 1$

$m_2^a = \mathbf{5},\ m_2^a(x) = x^2 + 1,$ $\quad m_2^k = \mathbf{6},\ m_2^k(x) = x^2 + x$

$m_3^a = \mathbf{10},\ m_3^k(x) = x^3 + x,$ $\quad m_3^k = \mathbf{1},\ m_3^k(x) = 1$

The random blinding keys for the encryption of each score are as follows:

$r_1^a(x) = x^3 + x^2 - x - 1,\quad r_1^k(x) = -x^4 - x^2 + x + 1$

$r_2^a(x) = -x^6 + x^3 - x + 1,\ r_2^k(x) = x^6 + x^5 - x^3 - 1$

$r_3^a(x) = x^6 + x^5 - x^4 - x,\ r_3^k(x) = x^5 - x^4 - x^3 + 1$

Encryption

$$e_1^a(x) = 235408x^6 + 159221x^5 + 179994x^4 + 353054x^3 + 484568x^2 + 269992x + 283889$$

$$e_1^k(x) = 179965x^6 + 353083x^5 + 484626x^4 + 270020x^3 + 283860x^2 + 235380x + 159193$$

$$e_2^a(x) = 394600x^6 + 339244x^5 + 41546x^4 + 346120x^3 + 263058x^2 + 62319x + 27708$$

$$e_2^k(x) = 186928x^6 + 83034x^5 + 200738x^4 + 34641x^3 + 124639x^2 + 55386x + 297698$$

$$e_3^a(x) = 387666x^6 + 117646x^5 + 325376x^4 + 90027x^3 + 422307x^2 + 242314x + 380790$$

$$e_3^k(x) = 221511x^6 + 207672x^5 + 256152x^4 + 332339x^3 + 311566x^2 + 138448x + 6906$$

Similarity measurement in the encryption domain

$$(e_1^a(x)e_1^k(x) + e_2^a(x)e_2^k(x) + e_3^a(x)e_3^a(x))\ mod\ R_q[x] = 464241x^6 + 345580x^5 + 79051x^4 + 9314x^3 + 130865x^2 + 131419x + 314135$$

Decryption

$$\alpha \equiv (\boldsymbol{f(x)}^2(e_1^a(x)e_1^k(x) + e_2^a(x)e_2^k(x) + e_3^a(x)e_3^a(x)))mod\ R_q[x] = 468645x^6 + 475249x^5 + 1531x^4 + 18383x^3 + 23015x^2 + 8623x + 479159$$

Centered lift coefficients

$$\alpha = -22886x^6 - 16282x^5 + 1531x^4 + 18383x^3 + 23015x^2 + 8623x - 12372$$

$$\boldsymbol{F_p(x)}^2((-22886x^6 - 16282x^5 + 1531x^4 + 18383x^3 + 23015x^2 + 8623x - 12372)\ mod\ R_q[x])\ \boldsymbol{mod\ p} = x^4 + 3x^3 + 3x^2 + 4x + 1$$

We then recover the **exact** plaintext similarity measurement results.

$$\mathbf{x^4 + 3x^3 + 3x^2 + 4x + 1 = 1 \times 2^4 + 3 \times 2^3 + 3 \times 2^2 + 4 \times 2^1 + 1 = 61}$$

In the general case $\sum_{i=1}^{n}(e_i^a(x)e_i^k(x))\ mod\ R_q[x]$, the criteria of $\frac{q}{2n} > Q_n$, $Q_n = 8p^2d^3 + \frac{4}{n}p^2d^2(2d+1) + \frac{p}{2n}(2d+1)^2$ must be held.

We have thus demonstrated the complete procedure of ring homomorphic encryption-domain similarity measurement. Note that in this paper, our focus is to fundamentally solve the system, key management, and algorithmic challenges of recommendations in the end-to-end encrypted domain. Therefore, we omit the detailed cryptographic proofs of the ring polynomial homomorphism, which is outside the scope of this paper.

3.5 Order-Preserving Encryption Ranking

3.5.1 Concept and scheme

We here present an order-preserving encryption scheme for data which allows any comparison operation to be directly applied on the encrypted data. Figure 4 shows the use of this order-preserving encryption ranking proxy in the overall system. In the original proxyless scenario, when the encryption-domain computation is completed, the server sends back the encrypted weights to the proxy, which decrypts the results using a homomorphic private key. In the original scenario, only the doctor can decrypt the results. Therefore, in order to identify the most similar patient, the server must conduct pairwise encrypted-domain similarity measures between the patient and all other people in the database and then return all the encrypted measurements to the doctor. We derive an order-preserving encryption ranking that makes use of a proxy. As this result is protected by the doctor with order-preserving encryption, the proxy does not know the actual similarity measurement results, as this would allow access to private patient data. Thus the proxy is allowed only to see rankings and not the similarity measurements. This is an important aspect, because the proxy needs to know the rankings of the patients and thus only return the most relevant ones to the doctor. Without this order-preserving encryption ranking procedure, the server would be required to return to the doctor all pairwise similarity measurements, which are not known by the server.

It sends the ranking results to the doctor via a secure channel, after which the doctor uses his or her order-preserving private key to decipher the real measurement results. We have thus shown that a scalar product-based algorithm can be implemented in the encryption domain, which in turn shows that a privacy-preserving collaborative recommendation system can be realized accordingly.

3.5.2 Implementation

Order-preserving encryption ranking is accomplished as follows: after the server implemented the encryption-domain similarity measurement stated in Section 3.4, if it were to directly carry out ranking, the proxy might be able to obtain the actual similarity measure values, which would be a breach of the patient's privacy. Thus we apply order-preserving encryption at the server to rescale the actual similarity measurement value with the order-preserving encryption secret key provided by the doctor. The encrypted similarity measurement is then

$$\mathrm{e}(\mathrm{W}_{op}^{ak}) = \mathrm{e}(pk_{op}^1).\,\mathrm{e}(\mathrm{W}^{ak}) + \mathrm{e}(pk_{op}^2), \tag{17}$$

where $\mathrm{e}(pk_{op}^1)$ and $\mathrm{e}(pk_{op}^2)$ are the order-preserving encryption keys provided by the doctor. $\mathrm{e}(\mathrm{W}^{ak})$ is the original encryption-domain similarity measurement results, and $e(\mathrm{W}_{op}^{ak})$ is the similarity measurement results after applying order-preserving encryption. This idea is derived from the affine transform function

$$y = \mathrm{A}x + b. \tag{18}$$

In the finite-dimensional case, each affine transformation is given by a matrix A and a vector b. This transformation satisfies the following two properties: (1) the collinearity relation between points; i.e., points which lie on a line continue to be collinear after the transformation. (2) The ratios of distances along a line; i.e., for distinct collinear points p_1, p_2, and p_3 the ratio $|p_2 - p_1|/|p_3 - p_2|$ is preserved. With this property we can encrypt the real similarity result but still preserve the order of the underlying similarity scores for comparison. After proxy ranking, the group of patients the doctor is looking for is sent to the doctor via a secure channel. The doctor then decrypts this data to gain access to the reference information that he or she needs.

3.6 Secure Channel between Parties

3.6.1 Secure channel

The spirit of our end-to-end encryption domain recommendation is that after getting the information from the patient in the clinic, e.g., the client, the information is encrypted and sent to the server to measure similarity in the encryption domain and then sent to the proxy for ranking, also in the encryption domain. The most correlated patient's clinical information is sent to the doctor so as to assist the doctor in deciding on an effective treatment. Secure channels are required for every connections involved, e.g., client to server, server to proxy, and proxy to doctor.

3.6.2 Diffie-Hellman-based Protocols

The Diffie–Hellman key exchange protocols allow two parties that have no prior knowledge of each other to establish a shared secret key jointly over an insecure communications channel to provide end-to-end security. This key can then be used to encrypt subsequent communications using a symmetric key cipher. As shown in figure 6, we adopted Diffie-Hellman-based protocols because it offers the following advantages: first, it provides anonymity: our proposed protocols use hash functions instead of digital signatures to confirm identities. In our scheme, a user does not need to sign for his or her private data as this would compromise the user's identity. Second, due to the nature of this protocol, our scheme is protected from man-meet-in-the-middle and replay attacks. Moreover, our scheme is effective and simple, since we adopt a uniform data format and because the hash function is more efficient than the use of digital signatures.

3.6.3 Protocol implementation

In the Diffie-Hellman key protocol, Alice and Bob agree on a public g that generates multiplicative group G. They then select random values r_a and r_b, respectably, in the range between 1 and the order of G, and Alice calculates $t_a = g^{r_a}$ and Bob calculates $t_b = g^{r_b}$, after which they exchange these values. Due to the group homomorphic property, the shared secret key S_{AB} can be generated as $S_{AB} = {t_b}^{r_a} = {t_a}^{r_b}$. In thus doing, Alice and Bob agree on, but do not confirm, the key. We use the hash function $H(.)$ and message authentication code with key k denoted as $MAC_k(.)$ with challenge with response nounces N_A and N_B encrypted using public keys $E_A(.)$ and $E_B(.)$ to prevent compromising the key agreement information.

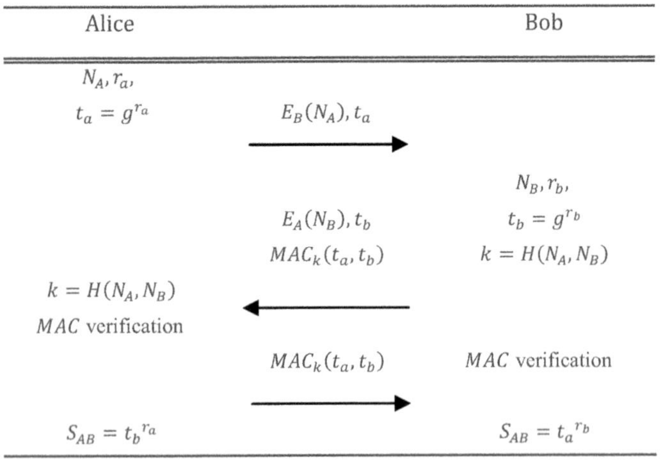

Figure 6. The protocol uses hashes and the MAC function to provide anonymity and identify confirmation.

4. EXPERIMENTS

4.1 Experiment Setting

To demonstrate end-to-end encrypted domain recommendation, we implemented the proposed algorithms as a prototype system using Microsoft Windows 7 (32-bit) operation system, an Intel Core 2 Quad CPU, and 2 GB RAM. We also used this system to evaluate our system security, recommendation accuracy, and system performance.

4.2 Data Sets

In our experiments, we use the Jester and Book-Crossing datasets to evaluate the accuracy of the encrypted-domain recommender. We used the recommendation algorithm described in Section 2, and then compared the results with those from the proposed privacy-preserving collaborative recommendation scheme. We also compared our approaches with randomized perturbation [2] based on the same traditional recommendation method. The Jester dataset is a web-based joke recommendation system, developed at the University of California, Berkeley, collected between April 1999 and May 2003, this database has 4.1 million continuous ratings (from +10 to −10) of 100 jokes from 73,421 users. The Book-Crossing dataset has been mined by Cai-Nicolas Ziegler, DBIS Freiburg, and includes 1,149,780 integer ratings (from 0 to 10) of 271,379 books from 278,858 users.

4.3 Efficiency Comparison

Compared with the standard recommendation system, our system requires a longer running time. This is because we execute end-to-end encryption to secure user information and calculate similarities and ranks in the encryption domain. This is reflected in figure 7, which illustrates the roles that more users and stronger encryption play in increasing runtimes. However, as shown in Section 4, in our privacy information retrieval system, encryption can be done in advance; decryption is a process separate from encryption. Hence in the figure we isolate the running times for the encryption-domain and non-privacy-preserving similarity measurements. These indicate that the difference is limited.

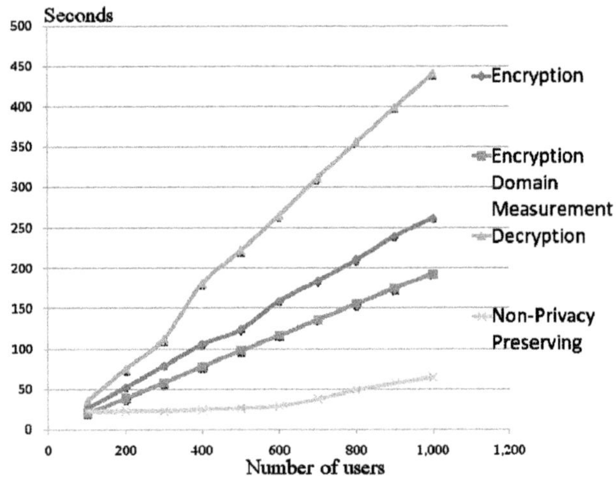

Figure 7. Efficiency comparison between a standard non-privacy preserving recommendation system and the proposed system.

4.4 Accuracy Comparison

Since our approaches are based on number theory with ring homomorphic encryption, our lossless privacy-preserving recommendation scheme provides exactly the same results as the standard non-privacy-preserving recommendation. This is in notable contrast to statistics-based approaches to privacy-preserving recommendation: such approaches yield only approximate results.

4.4.1 Evaluation criteria

We evaluate the system accuracy using the most common criterion: mean absolute error (MAE). This quantity is used to measure how close forecasts or predictions are to the actual outcomes. The mean absolute error is given by

$$MAE = \frac{1}{n}\sum_{i=1}^{n}|f_i - y_i| = \frac{1}{n}\sum_{i=1}^{n} e_i. \quad (19)$$

We compare MAE as the accuracy for our privacy-preserving approach with that for the non-privacy preserving approach.

4.4.2 Evaluation results

We also compare the results of the random perturbation and user profile distribution approaches. In terms of accuracy, that is, MAE, we compare the results of clustering on the original data with the clustering results for the privacy-preserving approach. Since our approaches are based on ring homomorphism number theory, we obtain exact the same operation values as the unencrypted values, in contrast to the random perturbation and user profile distribution approaches, both of which modify the statististical characteristics of the original values to protect the user's privacy. As shown in Figure 8, in contrast to our approaches, these two methods do not result in higher accuracy.

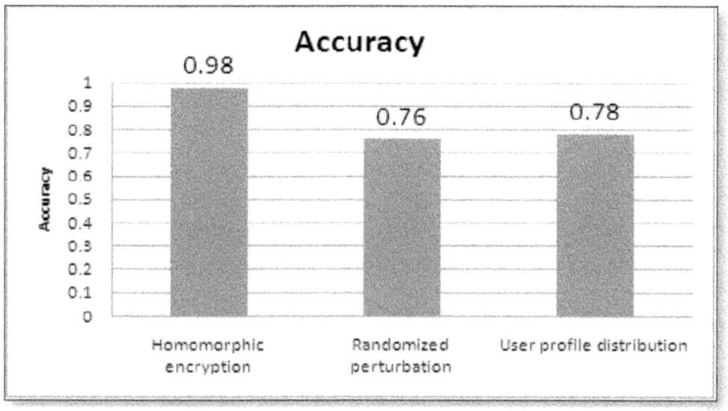

Figure 8. Comparison with the average accuracy of other approaches of privacy-preserving recommendation.

4.4.3 Accuracy effective by user data

In prior work on statistics-based privacy-preserving recommendation systems [2], if there is little user data, or if the data is randomly distributed, recommendation results suffer dramatically. For our system, since we calculate the Euclidean metric in the encryption domain, we have no such limitation.

4.5 Security Comparisons

4.5.1 End-to-end encryption principle for private information retrieval

One serious problem with other privacy-preserving recommendation systems is that users do not encrypt their own data but instead must trust other potentially un-trusted parties to encrypt the data for them. Thus, besides lacking encryption during some parts of the procedure, user privacy is left in the hands of a third party. In comparison, our system provides a level of security that other systems do not provide. Since we implement an end-to-end encryption security environment, it creates a security domain amongst the user's terminal, the service provider, and the database. In Table 1, we compare the recommendation schemes for the other two kinds of privacy-preserving systems.

4.5.2 Encryption algorithm security

As one of post-quantum cryptosystems, our proposed lattice-based encrypted algorithm is stronger than any other lightweight based encryption [1][2][3]. The measurement of the hardness of the system is similar to that of a public key cryptosystem which is usually judged by the most effective known attacks against it. The corresponding most effective known attack is the meet-in-the-middle and the lattice reduction algorithms. When compared to our approach, the randomized perturbation privacy-preserving scheme has the following security problems. First, the privacy is not sufficiently protected, because in order to obtain more accurate recommendation results their systems must fit the perturbation random numbers to a Gaussian distribution with zero mean. This limits their encryption strength. Whereas big plaintext scores and relatively small amounts of random noise render such privacy preservation useless, larger amplitude noise vectors to mask the original data lower prediction accuracy. The second problem is that the system is vulnerable to chosen plaintext attacks. A malicious user who submits scores of zero may be able to compromise the system's random perturbation number. The third security concern is that this approach requires the revealing of extra information to maintain the accuracy of the random perturbation scalar product.

For privacy preservation via factor analysis for user profile distribution, which involves a secure computation technique using partially homomorphic encryptions, user scores are stored as encrypted vectors and aggregates of the data are provided in the public domain. This approach requires users to seek out recommendations explicitly. The partially homomorphic encryptions of this approach, such as RSA and ECC, allow for homomorphic computation of only one operation (either addition or multiplication) on plaintext. Therefore, the similarity measurements it yields are not as accurate as those yielded with our ring homomorphic algorithm, which supports both addition and multiplication in the encryption domain. We compare the security of various privacy-preserving recommendation approaches in table 1.

Table 1. Comparison with the security other approaches

	Our approach	Randomized perturbation	User profile distribution
Vulnerable to attack	No	Yes	Yes
Trusted third party	No	Yes	Yes
Accuracy	High	Medium	Medium
Security	High	Fair	Fair
End-to-end encryption	Yes	No	No

4.4 Accuracy Comparison

Since our approaches are based on number theory with ring homomorphic encryption, our lossless privacy-preserving recommendation scheme provides exactly the same results as the standard non-privacy-preserving recommendation. This is in notable contrast to statistics-based approaches to privacy-preserving recommendation: such approaches yield only approximate results.

4.4.1 Evaluation criteria

We evaluate the system accuracy using the most common criterion: mean absolute error (MAE). This quantity is used to $d_2 \approx N/3$. This will yield stronger security.

4.6 Computation Cost and Complexity

4.6.1 Running time

Experiments indicate that our decryption process requires more computation time, due to our squaring of the private key. However, as our system is based on polynomial rings, the main speed improvements can be made by optimizing polynomial ring operations. The most time-consuming operation is ring inversion. As shown in the experiments, the key part of arithmetic is the ring multiplication operation. Our implementation uses a naive multiplication algorithm. The encryption and decryption performance of our implementation could be improved by implementing a better multiplication algorithm and optimizing it. In a newer version of our system, we pre-calculate the square operation and use a table lookup to retrieve the private key to reduce decryption key generation time.

4.6.2 Real system implementation

We ran a series of tests and extrapolated the data in a conservative manner. A system that works well in practice must get a lot of details right, including security and scalability, respect to the operations on plaintext data. Since the criteria and parameters are more complicated than those for the standard NTRU systems [17], the performance of our system differs from theirs. To make our message space the same as that of the standard NTRU, our system would have to use a larger p and q, which would require more computation time. However, since the operation is done on $R[x] = Z[x]/(x^N - 1)$, which is limited to evaluating low-degree polynomials over indecipherable encrypted data. Our simulation using the data in Section 4.2 shows each recommendation takes, in average, 1.7 min for 200 users, which is fast enough for some applications e.g. the healthcare informatics scenario mentioned in Section 3.1.

5. CONCLUSION

To the best of our knowledge, we are the first team to propose an end-to-end encrypted domain recommender system which fully protects privacy without the drawback of adding noise or partially revealing information. Our key management protocol and the ring homomorphism mechanism are the key to make a real recommendation work. Our solution makes it possible for servers to collect private data from users without compromising privacy. Our experiments have shown that our solution is accurate, effective, and highly secure. We see a potential advantage in using such an approach for various privacy-preserving mining tasks in people's daily activities. In contrast to the randomized perturbation scheme which adds randomized perturbation to real data, thus yielding only approximate results, our system provides exact measurements. Instead of storing user profiles in a distributed manner, our approach meets the criteria of a centralized scheme, which would work well for cloud computing. Moreover, we provide an effective cryptosystem with ring homomorphism which we have proven not only secure but also practical and implementable as compared to ideal lattice-based approaches, which only allow one bit operation. In the future, we will study how these kinds of operations can be extended to techniques such as singular value decomposition in the encryption domain for other privacy-preserving data mining tasks.

6. REFERENCES

[1] Polat, H. and Du, W. 2006. Privacy-Preserving Collaborative Filtering on Vertically Partitioned Data. PAKDD 2005: 651-658.

[2] Polat, H. and Du, W. 2006. Achieving private recommendations using randomized response techniques. PAKDD 2006. LNCS (LNAI), vol. 3918, 9-12. Springer, Heidelberg.

[3] Canny, J. 2002. Collaborative filtering with privacy. In *proceedings of the IEEE Symposium on Security and Privacy* (Oakland, CA, SA, May, 2002) 45-57.

[4] Canny, J. 2002. Collaborative filtering with privacy via factor analysis. In *proceedings of the 25th Annual International ACM SIGIR Conference on Research and Development in Information Retrieval* (Tampere, Finland, August, 2002) 238-245.

[5] Rivest, R. L., Shamir, A., and Adleman, L. 1978. A method for obtaining digital signatures and public-key cryptosystems, Commun. ACM 21, 120-126.

[6] Gentry, C. 2009. Fully Homomorphic Encryption Using Ideal Lattices. ACM 41, 169-178.

[7] van Dijk, M., Gentry, C., Halevi, S., and Vaikuntanathan, V. 2010. Fully homomorphic encryption over integer. In *proceedings of* 29th Annual International Conference on the Theory and Applications of Cryptographic Techniques.

[8] Miller, B. N., Konstan, J. A., and Riedl, J. 2004. Pocketlens: Toward a personal recommender system. *ACM Trans. Inf. Syst.* 22, 3 (2004).

[9] Berkovsky, S., Eytani, Y., Kuflik, T., and Ricci, F. 2007. Enhancing privacy and preserving accuracy of a distributed collaborative filtering. In *proceedings of ACM RecSys* (2007).

[10] Lathia, N., Hailes, S., and Capra, L. 2007. Private distributed collaborative filtering using estimated concordance measures. In *proceedings of ACM RecSys* (2007).

[11] Miller, B. N., Konstan, J. A., and Riedl, J. 2004. Pocketlens: Toward a personal recommender system. *ACM Trans. Inf. Syst.* 22, 3 (2004).

[12] Luo, B. and Hancock, E. R. 2001. Structural graph matching using the em algorithm and singular value decomposition. *IEEE Trans. Pattern Anal. Mach.* (2001).

[13] NIST, 2006. Recommendation for Pair-Wise Key Establishment Schemes Using Discrete Logarithm Cryptography *Special Publication 800-56A* (2006).

[14] Regev, O. 2006. Lattice-based cryptography. In *Advances in cryptology* (CRYPTO), 131-141, (2006).

[15] Yu, K., Yu, S., and Tresp, V. 2005. Soft Clustering on Graphs. In *Advances in Neural Information Processing Systems.*

[16] Sarwar, B., Karypis, G., Konstan, J., and Riedl, J. 2001. Item-based collaborative filtering recommendation algorithms. In *proceedings of the 10th International World Wide Web Conference* (2001).

[17] Hoffstein, J., Pipher, J., and Silverman, J. H. 1998. NTRU, A Ring-Based Public Key Cryptosystem (ANTS III), LNCS 1423, Springer-Verlag, Berlin, 267-288.

Privacy Preservation by Independent Component Analysis and Variance Control

Chih-Ming Hsu†, Ming-Syan Chen†‡
†Electrical Engineering Department, National Taiwan University, Taipei, Taiwan
‡Research Center for Information Technology Innovation, Academia Sinica, Taipei, Taiwan
ming@arbor.ee.ntu.edu.tw, mschen@citi.sinica.edu.tw

ABSTRACT

The primary objective of privacy preservation is to protect an individual's confidential information in released data sets. In recent years, several simulation-based approaches for privacy preservation have been proposed. The idea is to generate a synthetic data set with the constraint that the probability distribution is as close as possible to that of the original set. In this paper, we propose two frameworks for simulation-based privacy preservation of multivariate numerical data. The first framework, called PRIMP (PRivacy preserving by Independent coMPonents), is based on independent component analysis (ICA). It is shown empirically that PRIMP outperforms other simulation-based approaches in terms of Spearman's rank correlation and Kendall's tau correlation. The second approach proposed is a hybrid method that combines PRIMP and Cholesky's decomposition technique. It is shown empirically that the hybrid method preserves the covariance matrix of the original data exactly. The method also resolves the problem of generating good seeds for the Cholesky-based approach. Although the empirical results show that the hybrid approach is not always better than the PRIMP in terms of Spearman's rank correlation and Kendall's tau correlation, in theory, the risk of information leakage under the hybrid approach is much less than that under PRIMP.

Categories and Subject Descriptors: H.2.8 [Database Management]: Database Applications – Data Mining
General Terms: Algorithms.
Keywords: Privacy Preservation, Independent Component Analysis, Cholesky's Decomposition.

1. INTRODUCTION

Protecting an individual's confidential information in multivariate numerical data has attracted a great deal of attention in recent years. The most relevant works are those based on perturbation techniques, which can be classified into two categories. The first consist of random data perturbation [1] [2] and random rotation perturbation [3], which disguise sensitive data by distorting the structure of the data. The second category generates a new synthetic data set that preserves certain statistical requirements.

CIKM'11, October 24–28, 2011, Glasgow, Scotland, UK.

Simulated-based approaches release a synthetic data set for public use. Synthetic data is sufficiently different to the original data, but it retains the statistical characteristics of the original data as much as possible. Liew et al. proposed a simulation-based scheme, called data distortion by probability distribution, which generates a synthetic data set by randomly drawing from the underlying distribution of the original data set [17]. Because the distribution of the original data set is invalid, in the first step, the Komlogorov-Smirnov test [22] is used to identify the underlying density function of the original data set from some pre-determined set and estimate the parameters of the function. In this framework, the candidates for the density function of the original data set should be empirically selected by the user in advance. Because of the tremendous number of possible data distributions, in most cases, we can not find a suitable density function in the pre-determined set to fit the data. Furthermore, the synthetic data generated by the Liew et al. proposed technique does not preserve the internal relationships among the attributes of a multivariate data set, because the process of identifying the underlying density function deals with each attribute separately. Consequently, synthetic data generated based on the probability distribution leads to high information loss in many cases. In contrast, Dandekar et al. [6] used the Latin Hypercube Sampling (LHS) technique to generate synthetic data for privacy preserving. It maintains Spearman's rank correlation structure of the original data.

Mateo-Sanz proposed another simulated-based approach based on Cholesky's decomposition of the covariance matrix of sensitive data. The major advantage of this approach is that Pearson's covariance matrix is preserved exactly in the synthetic data set. However, as shown in Figure 1, the major problem with the Cholesky-based approach is that the quality of the synthetic data set depends on that of the generated seeds. Figure 1(a) is the scatter plot of some generated seeds G, while Figure 1(b) shows the original data set X and the synthetic data generated by the Cholesky-based approach from G. In this example, the synthetic data set clearly misrepresents the probability distribution of the original data set X. Observably, the joint distribution of the synthetic data set is sensitive to the generated seeds G. Essentially, the spread shape of the synthetic data shall imitate the spread shape of the generated seeds. Since the distribution of X is invalid, generating good seeds could be very difficult if the Cholesky-based approach is used for privacy preserving. How to develop good seeds for the Cholesky-based approach still is an open problem.

In summary, existing simulation-based approaches only

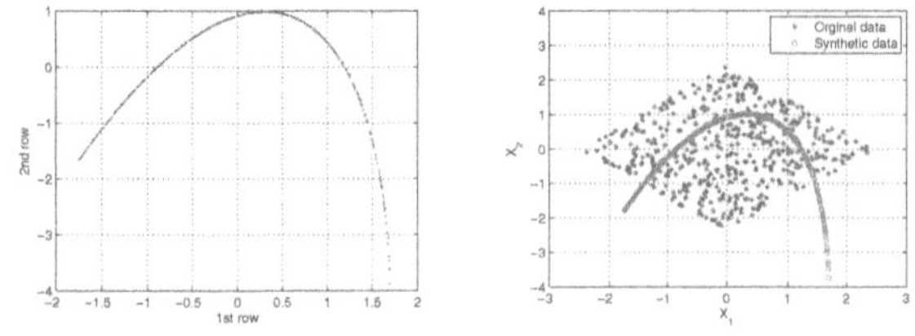

(a) The scatter plot of a (2×500) generated seeds with identity covariance for the Cholesky-based approach

(b) The scatter plot of the original confidential data set and the synthetic data generated by the Cholesky-based approach

Figure 1: An example of the Cholesky-based approach.

preserve some specific statistics of the original data set. Explicitly, synthetic data generated by these simulated-based approaches can not provide analytical validity. In [5], the author asked: Why not directly publish the statistics one wants to preserve directly, rather than release a synthetic data set? To remedy the data utility problem in these approaches, we propose two simulation-based frameworks using independent component analysis (ICA).

2. PRIVACY PRESERVATION WITH SYNTHETIC DATA

In this section, we introduce the simulation-based privacy preserving framework PRIMP for multivariate numerical data sets.

We assume that users must be given access to released data without restrictions [21]. The goal of privacy preservation is to provide released data that has analytical validity, but does not disclose confidential information about individuals. The *analytical validity* represents the extent to which analyzing the synthetic data provides similar results to those obtained by analyzing the original data [21]. Simulation-based privacy preservation generates a synthetic data set that preserves the statistical characteristics of the original data set for release to the public. If the synthetic data is sufficiently different from the original data, then the privacy of the original data is said to be preserved.

Let X be an original sensitive data set, with n records and d attributes. For ease of exposition, X can be viewed as a $d \times n$ matrix whose columns and rows represent, respectively, a record and the collection of samples for an attribute of X. For $j = 1, 2, \cdots, n$, we assume that the jth column of X (,i.e. $X(j)$) is sampled from some unknown random vector $\mathbf{X} = (\mathbf{X_1}, \mathbf{X_2}, \cdots, \mathbf{X_d})^T$. In fact, we have no information about the probability distribution of $\mathbf{X}$ except for the data set X. We know that all the statistical characteristics of any data set are determined by its probability distribution. Therefore, the simulation-based approach to database privacy preservation involves generating a synthetic data set $\hat{X}$ with the same joint distributions as the original sensitive data set X. Explicitly, our purpose is to design an effective and efficient simulating schema based only on the observed data. A list of symbols used throughout this paper is given in Table 1.

Table 1: List of symbols.

Notation	Definition
X	The d-dimensional sensitive set
$\hat{X}$	The disguised synthetic data set of X
S	The m-dimensional source signal data set estimated by ICA, $m \leq d$
n	The number of records of X
$\mathbf{g}$	The mixing function of the ICA model: $X = \mathbf{g}(S)$
$\mathbf{g}^{-1}$	The unmixing function of the ICA model: $X = \mathbf{g}(S)$ satisfies $S = \mathbf{g}^{-1}(X)$
M^T	The transpose of the data matrix M
M_i	The ith row of the data matrix M, i.e., the samples of ith attribute of M
$M(j)$	The jth column of the data matrix M, i.e., the jth record of M
$E[M_i]$	The sample expectation of the ith row of matrix M
$var(M_i)$	The sample variance of the ith row of matrix M
$cov(M)$	The (Pearson's) covariance matrix of the M
I_m	An $m \times m$ identity matrix

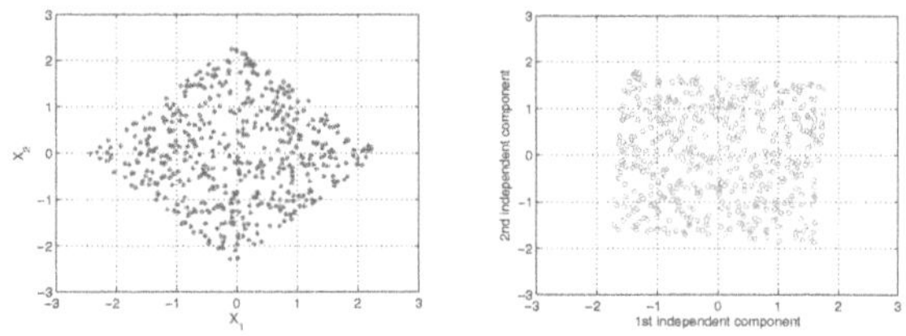

(a) Observed data

(b) Source signals

Figure 2: (a) The scatter plot of the observed data X. (b) The scatter plot of the independent source signals estimated by using the FastICA algorithm.

2.1 Independent Component Analysis

Here, we introduce some basic concepts of independent component analysis (ICA). A detailed study of ICA can be found in [14]. ICA defines a generative model for observed multivariate data. The model's data variables are assumed to be linear or nonlinear mixtures of some unknown *independent* latent variables, and the mixing system is also unknown [14]. The latent variables are called *independent components* or *source signals*. Let x be a d-dimensional observation. Explicitly, ICA is a problem of recovering a latent random vector s from observations of unknown m-variate $(m \leq d)$ functions of that vector. The latent vector s is assumed to be sampled from some unknown random vector, i.e., source signals, whose elements are *mutually independent*. Formally, we can write the relationship of the observed data x and the realization of the source signals s in a general form

$$x = \mathbf{g}(s), \tag{1}$$

where $\mathbf{g} : R^m \rightarrow R^d$ is an unknown real-value d-component vector function. Given n independent, identically distributed observations $\{X(1), X(2), \cdots, X(n)\}$, ICA tries to find an inverse mapping $\mathbf{g}^{-1} : R^d \rightarrow R^m$, which estimates of n realizations of the source signals by

$$S(t) = \mathbf{g}^{-1}(X(t)) \tag{2}$$

for any particular $X(t)$, $t = 1, 2, \cdots, n$. The functions $\mathbf{g}$ and $\mathbf{g}^{-1}$ are called a *mixing function* and an *unmixing function*, respectively.

Example 1: Consider the scenario of a 2-dimensional data set X with attributes X_1 and X_2, as shown in Figure 2(a). Clearly, the attributes X_1 and X_2 of X are not independent; thus, it is difficult to predict the value of one attribute from the value of the other. It is also very difficult to generate a synthetic data set to preserve the joint distribution of X based on the sampled data set only [9].

We use FastICA[1] to estimate the source signals and the mixing matrix. The joint distribution of the *independent* source signals is shown in Figure 2(b). Clearly, the joint distribution of the source signals is uniform on a square, so the joint probability density of the signals is simply the product of their marginal probability densities. Hence, we can use a re-sampling technique or LHS to generate a synthetic data set with the joint distribution as the source signals. Furthermore, we can use the mixing matrix and the synthetic data generated from the source signals to obtain a synthetic data set of X, which preserves the distribution of X. □

The above results show that the "independence" property of the source signals estimated by ICA simplifies the problem of generating a synthetic data set based on sampled (or observed) data only. In addition, in terms of the re-identification disclosure risk[2], it is better to distort or transform the data structure in the independent component space, rather than in the original data set.

2.2 ICA-based Approach for Privacy Preservation

In this section, we describe how ICA can be extended to a new application for privacy preservation. We assume that the normalized sensitive data set X satisfies the ICA model, as in Equation (1).

The outline of PRIMP is given in Table 2. Whitening is useful as a preprocessing step in ICA [14]. Because whitening is essentially decorrelation followed by scaling, the technique of principle component analysis is often used [14], but it is not advisable to use a covariance matrix to find the principle components when the attributes' variances are very different [15]. So, normalization can reduce the complexity and improve the quality of ICA substantially [14]. Therefore, the first step of PRIMP normalizes the original data set.

As mentioned earlier, how to generate a multivariate synthetic data set with the same distribution of input is still an open question. Because of the tremendous number of internal relationships among attributes, generating a synthetic data set that preserves all the statistical characteristics of a multivariate data set without distribution information is almost impossible [9]. However, if the attributes of the input are mutually independent, generating a synthetic data set based solely on the sampled data set becomes straightforward.

The proposed approach views the sensitive data set generated by an unknown function of some latent independent random process. Explicitly, we assume that the normalized data set $\tilde{X}$ belonging to the sensitive data set X satisfies the equation $\tilde{X} = \mathbf{g}(S)$, where S is the latent independent random process. Under this assumption, we gain two important insights for designing a simulation-based privacy preserving technique. First, for privacy preservation, we can transform the source signals obtained by ICA into protected data by some distortion technique. Hence, we hide any clue about the distortion technique in the source signals to prevent a hacker accessing the sensitive data. (Note that most existing distortion techniques disguise the sensitive attributes in original data. Consequently, clues about adapted distortion techniques can be obtained by comparing the difference between the released data and the original data [2][13][16].) Second, the "independence" property of source signals simplifies the problem of generating a synthetic data for source signals. If the attributes of the original data set are mutually independent, we can apply a re-sampling technique, such as bootstrap [8], or LHS [19] to individual attributes to generate the synthetic data. In theory, the inter-relationships and statistical characteristics among attributes should be well maintained by such re-sampling techniques, because we do not need to consider the inter-relationships of attributes. In other words, using the ICA technique to generate a synthetic data set for the original data set requires little effort. In PRIMP, we randomly shuffle the realizations[3] of the estimated source signals to preserve privacy. Because of the "independence" property, the shuffled source signals preserve the overall statistical characteristics of the original source signals.

Table 2: The PRIMP algorithm.

Algorithm: PRIMP(X, m)

Inputs: X (d-dimensional data set),
m (the dimensions of source signals, the default value is d, $m \leq d$)

Output: $\hat{X}$ (d-dimensional synthetic data set)

1. **Normalization.** For each $j = 1, 2, \cdots, d$, we normalize the projected data X_j of the jth attribute of X to give $\tilde{X}_j$ with $E[\tilde{X}_j] = 0$ and $var(\tilde{X}_j) = 1$.
2. **Decoupling.** Use ICA to estimate the source signals $S = (S_1, S_2, \cdots, S_m)^T$ and the mixing function $\mathbf{g}$ of the normalized data set $\tilde{X} = (\tilde{X}_1, \tilde{X}_2, \cdots, \tilde{X}_d)^T$.
3. **Permutation.** For each $j = 1, 2, \cdots, m$, we randomly permutate the independent component S_j to obtain $\tilde{S}_j$.
4. **Coupling.** Compute $\hat{X} = \left(\hat{X}(1), \hat{X}(2), \cdots, \hat{X}(n)\right)$, where $\hat{X}(j) = \mathbf{g}(\tilde{S}(j))$ $(j = 1, 2, \cdots, n)$.
5. **Rescaling.** For each $j = 1, 2, \cdots, d$, $\hat{X}_j = \hat{X}_j \times \sqrt{var(X_j)} + E[X_j]$.

We mix the the shuffled source signals by mixing function, as shown in Equation (1), to obtain the (normalized) synthetic data set $\hat{X}$. Therefore, the statistical characteristics of the (normalized) synthetic data set can approximate the (normalized) original data set X. The quality of the synthetic data in terms of its data utility depends on the approximation of independence determined by ICA. Note that, the first step of PRIMP normalizes the original data set. Consequently, adjusting the synthetic data to preserve the mean and variance of each attribute of X is the final step of PRIMP.

Example 2: Recall the data set X in Example 1. Figure 3(a) shows the scatter plot of the synthetic data generated

[1] FastICA is one of the widely used algorithms for performing linear ICA. The fundamental mathematical background and implementation techniques of it can be found in [14]. The free FastICA package can be downloaded from http://www.cis.hut.fi/projects/ica/fastica.

[2] The re-identification disclosure risk is the risk of disclosing a one-to-one relationship between the synthetic data set and the original data set [7].

[3] The term "realizations" of a random variable means some experiment outcomes (or observations) according to its probability distribution.

by PRIMP. Because the assumption of multivariate normal distribution for the original data set is made by some privacy preserving techniques [13] [20], we generate a multivariate normal data set with the same mean and covariance structure as X, as shown in Figure 3(b). Figures 3(c) and 3(d) present the scatter plots of the synthetic data sets generated by the LHS-based and Cholesky-based approaches, respectively. As the figures show, all the sets misrepresent the joint distribution of the original data X, except for the set generated by PRIMP. □

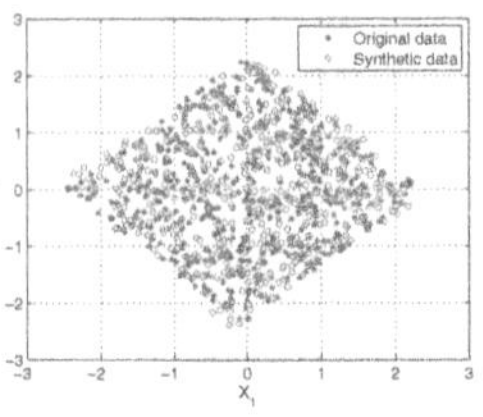

(a) PRIMP

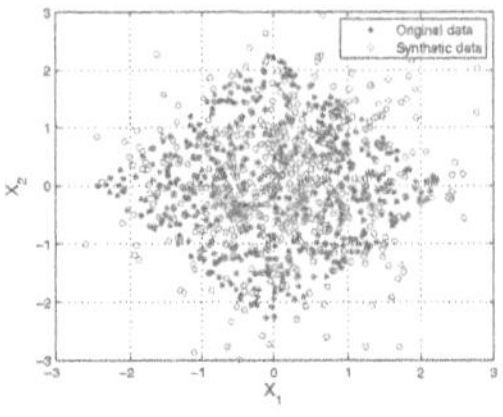

(b) Multivariate normal assumption

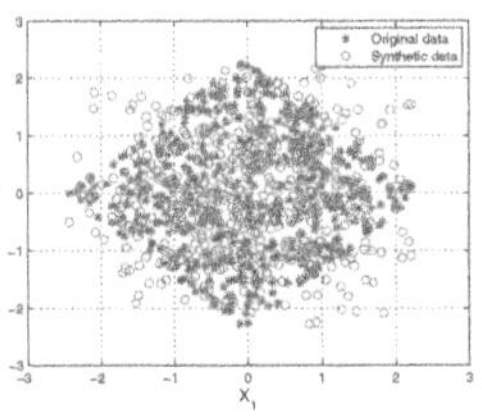

(c) LHS-based

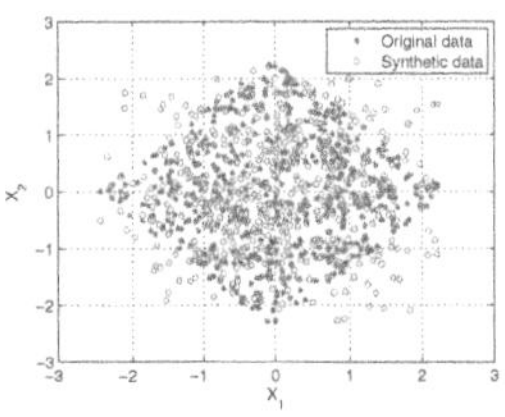

(d) Cholesky-based

Figure 3: The synthetic data sets for the data set X in Example 1.

3. A HYBRID PRIMP AND CHOLESKY-BASED APPROACH FOR PRIVACY PRESERVATION

In this section, we develop a hybrid privacy preserving method that combines PRIMP and the Cholesky-based approach [18]. The fundamental concept of the Cholesky-based privacy preserving technique is based on the following theorem.

THEOREM 1. *Let X be any d-dimensional data set and G be any $d \times n$ matrix whose Pearson's covariance matrix is equal to the identity matrix. Then, the covariance matrix of LG should be the same as that of X, where L is a lower triangular matrix by the equation $cov(X) = LL^T$ using Cholesky's decomposition.*

From Theorem 1, we can generate a $d \times n$ random matrix G whose Pearson's covariance matrix is equal to the identity matrix, where n and d are the size of the synthetic data set and the dimensions of the sensitive data set X, respectively. Therefore, the synthetic data set should be obtained by $\hat{X} = LG$, where L is a lower triangular matrix derived by the equation $C = LL^T$ using Cholesky's decomposition and C is the Pearson covariance matrix of X. By Theorem 1, the covariance matrix and correlation matrix of X are preserved exactly in the synthetic data set $\hat{X}$. We call the random matrix G the *seeds* of Cholesky-based privacy preservation.

Table 3: The hybrid PRIMP and Cholesky-based approach for privacy preservation.

Algorithm: The hybrid approach for privacy preservation

Inputs: X (d-dimensional data set),
m (the dimensions of source signals, the default value is d, $m \leq d$)

Output: $\hat{X}$ (d-dimensional synthetic data set)

(Use PRIMP to generate seeds)

1. Use PRIMP to generate a $d \times n$ synthetic data G.
2. Adjust the matrix G such that its covariance matrix is I_d. (G is used as the seeds of the Cholesky-based approach)

(Use the Cholesky-based approach)

3. Compute $C = cov(X)$.
4. Use Cholesky's decomposition on C to obtain $C = LL^T$, where L is a lower triangular matrix.
5. Obtain the synthetic data $\hat{X} = LG$.
6. Adjust the mean of each attribute of the synthetic data by $\hat{X}_j = \hat{X}_j + E[X_j]$, for $j = 1, 2, \cdots, d$.

As mentioned above, in terms of data utility, the performance of the Cholesky's approach depends on the generated seeds G. For example, as shown in Figures 1 and 3(d), the distributions of synthetic data sets are different significantly from those of the original data. Consequently, the synthetic data can not provide analytical valid. For example, in these cases, the data's extreme statistics and the range of each attribute differ significantly from those of the original data. Unfortunately, how to generate good seeds for the Cholesky-based approach is still an open question.

The probability distribution of synthetic data generated by PRIMP can successfully approximate the probability distribution of the original data. However, in terms of preserving the covariance structure, the Cholesky-based method outperforms all existing simulation-based approaches. Following the above observations, we use the Cholesky-based technique to modify the covariance structure of the synthetic data generated by PRIMP for covariance matrix preservation. In the other words, because the output of PRIMP can satisfactorily preserve the distribution of the original data, we use PRIMP in the construction process to generate seeds for the Cholesky-based approach. As such, the hybrid PRIMP and Cholesky-based approach can preserve the distribution and the covariance matrix of a sensitive data set. The stages of the hybrid approach are the same as those of PRIMP, except for the rescaling procedure, which uses the Cholesky-based approach to refine the covariance structure of the synthetic data. The resulting, synthetic data preserves the covariance and correlation structures of the original data exactly like the Cholesky-based approach. It also solves the problem of how to generate good seeds for the Cholesky-based approach. The outline of the hybrid approach is summarized in Table 3.

Example 3: Again, we consider the data set X in Example 1. Figure 4 shows the scatter plots of the synthetic data generated by the hybrid method. Because PRIMP can preserve the distribution, the outputs of the hybrid method approximate the distribution of the original data sufficiently. □

4. EXPERIMENT EVALUATIONS

To assess the performance of PRIMP and the hybrid approach in terms of data utility, we conducted a series of experiments on both artificial and real data sets. We compared the information loss in the synthetic data sets produced by PRIMP with the synthetic data sets produced by

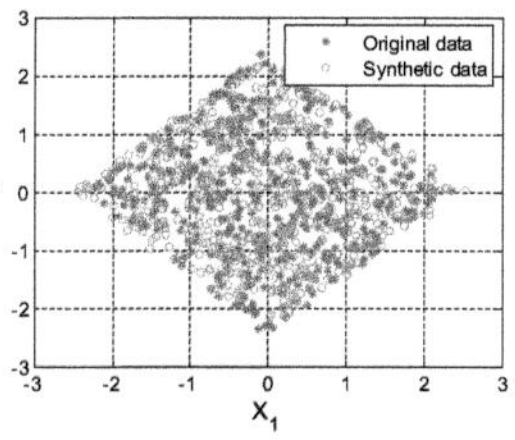

Figure 4: The synthetic data set generated by the hybrid approach for the data set X in Example 1.

the following privacy preserving approaches: the LHS-based approach, the Cholesky-based approach, the hybrid PRIMP and Cholesky-based approach, and sampling under the multivariate normal assumption (MN).

Table 4 summarizes the data sets used in our experiments. Data set 1 was derived from the American Housing Survey of the U. S. Census Bureau using the DataFerrett system[4]. Data sets 2 and 3 were used in [20] and [21], respectively[5]. Data sets 3 to 10 were downloaded from the UCI Machine Learning Database [10]. Data set 11, downloaded from the web site of the Computational Aspects of Statistical Confidentiality (CASC) project[6], was also used in [18], [7], and [11]. Note that, in this paper, our proposed method focuses on multivariate numerical data sets. Therefore, we removed the non-numerical attributes of the above data sets.

As noted in [14] (page 152), for linear ICA model, the independent source signals must have non-Gaussian distributions; at most, one of the independent components can have a Gaussian distribution. To evaluate the effect of the non-Gaussian assumption, we generate the following artificial data set as Data set 12, $X = (X_1, X_2, X_3)^T$. For $i = 1, 2, 3, \cdots, 2000$,

$$\begin{aligned} x_{1,i} &= s_{1,i} + 3s_{2,i} + 3s_{3,i} \\ x_{2,i} &= 4s_{1,i} + 4s_{2,i} + 6s_{3,i} \\ x_{3,i} &= 12s_{1,i} + 13s_{2,i} + 17s_{3,i}, \end{aligned} \tag{3}$$

where $x_{i,j}$ is the j-th element of X_i, $s_{1,i}$ and $s_{2,i}$ are randomly sampled from a univariate Gaussian distribution with mean 0 and variance 1, and $s_{3,i}$ is randomly sampled uniformly from $(0, 1)$.

The generated source signals $S_j = (s_{j,1}, \cdots, s_{j,2000})$, $j = 1, 2, 3$, are mutually independent. Clearly, the model (3) violates the non-Gaussian restriction of the linear ICA model.

Here, we use three well-known measures of bivariate relationships: Pearson's correlation matrix, Spearman's rank correlation matrix, and Kendall's tau to evaluate the information loss of privacy preserving algorithms. Let $X_i = (x_{i1}, x_{i2}, \cdots, x_{i,n})$ and $X_j = (x_{j1}, x_{j2}, \cdots, x_{j,n})$ be the observations of the ith and jth attributes of data set X, respectively. The ijth element of (Pearson's) correlation matrix, (Spearman's) rank correlation matrix, and Kendall's Tau can be computed as follows ([4], chapter 3):

$$\text{Correlation: } \frac{\sum_{k=1}^{n}(x_{i,k} - \bar{x_i})(x_{j,k} - \bar{x_i})}{\sqrt{\sum_{k=1}^{n}(x_{i,k} - \bar{x_i})^2 \sum_{k=1}^{n}(x_{j,k} - \bar{x_j})^2}}, \tag{4}$$

[4]The DataFerrett system can be downloaded from http://dataferrett.census.gov/.

[5]Data set 2 and Data set 3 can be downloaded from http://gatton.uky.edu/faculty/muralidhar/maskingpapers/.

[6]Data set 11 can be downloaded from http://neon.vb.cbs.nl/casc/testsets.html.

Table 4: The data sets used in our experiments.

Index	Name of Database	# Records	# Attributes
1	American Housing Survey	20000	9
2	Bank Database	50000	5
3	Data Shuffling	50000	3
4	Iris Plant Database	150	4
5	Ecoli Database	336	5
6	Ionosphere Database	351	32
7	Housing Database	351	32
8	Pima Indians Diabetes Database	768	8
9	Yeast Database	1484	6
10	New diagnostic database	569	30
11	ACAS	1080	13
12	Simulated	2000	3

$$\text{Rank correlation: } 1 - 6\frac{\sum_{k=1}^{n}(R_{i,k} - R_{j,k})^2}{n(n^2-1)}, \tag{5}$$

$$\text{Kendall's tau: } \frac{2}{n(n-1)} \sum_{k=1}^{n} \sum_{l>k} sgn\left((x_{i,k} - x_{i,l})(x_{j,k} - x_{j,l})\right), \tag{6}$$

where $\bar{x_i} = \sum_{k=1}^{n} x_{i,k}/n$; $R_{i,k}$ is the rank of $x_{i,k}$ in $\{x_{i,j}; j = 1 \cdots, n\}$ in ascending order; and $sgn(\cdot)$ is the sign function, defined as $sgn(x) = 1$ if $x \geq 0$ or $sgn(x) = -1$ if $x < 0$, for $i = 1, 2, \cdots, d$, $k = 1, 2, \cdots, n$.

Let C and $\hat{C}(P)$ denote, respectively, the matrix of bivariate relationship measurements for the original data set and the synthetic data set generated by algorithm P. The *relative bias* of C for algorithm P is defined as:

$$\frac{2}{m^2+m} \sum_{i=1}^{m} \sum_{j=i}^{m} \frac{|\hat{C}_{ij}(P) - C_{ij}|}{|C_{ij}|},$$

where C_{ij} and $\hat{C}_{ij}(P)$ denote, respectively, the elements of C and $\hat{C}$ in the ith row and jth column. A smaller relative bias implies better preservation of the bivariate structure C. That is, a lower relative bias represents less information loss by the statistic C.

In our experiments, we use FastICA to evaluate the information loss of PRIMP. The elements of the seeds of the Cholesky-based approach were generated from a uniform distribution over $(0, 1)$. Then, the Gram-Schmidt process [12] was applied to transform the covariance matrix of the generated seeds into an identity matrix. We also set the number of source signals to be the same as the dimensions of the input (,i.e. $m = d$). Because the scales of the attributes vary, we normalize all of the data sets in the pre-processing stage to prevent the side effect encountered by attributes with differing variances significantly. The empirical results of 100 trials are summarized in Table 5.

As expected, the Cholesky-based approach preserves the correlation structure of the original data set exactly. However, the probability distribution of the synthetic data generated by the Cholesky-based approach depends on the seeds generated; thus, the output of the approach does not always preserve the distribution of the original data successfully, as shown in Figure 3(d). Compared to the relative biases of Spearman's rank correlation matrix and Kendall's Tau, the performance of PRIMP is better than those approaches in most cases. Even though data set 12 violates the non-Gaussian restriction of the linear ICA model, PRIMP outperforms the other approaches.

Although the results show that the hybrid approach is not always better than PRIMP for Spearman's rank correlation

Table 5: The approach which has the minimum average relative bias among PRIMP, the multivariate normal assumption, the LHS-based approach, the Cholesky-based approach, and the hybrid method.

Index	Correlation	Rank correlation	Kendall's tau
1	Cholesky-based	PRIMP	PRIMP
2	Cholesky-based	PRIMP	PRIMP
3	Cholesky-based	PRIMP	Hybrid
4	Cholesky-based	PRIMP	Hybrid
5	Cholesky-based	Hybrid	Hybrid
6	Hybrid	LHS-based	PRIMP
7	Cholesky-based	Hybrid	PRIMP
8	Cholesky-based	Hybrid	PRIMP
9	Cholesky-based	PRIMP	PRIMP
10	Cholesky-based	Cholesky-based	PRIMP
11	Cholesky-based	PRIMP	PRIMP
12	Hybrid	Hybrid	Hybrid

Table 6: The average relative biases of correlation matrix based on the hybrid method and Cholesky-based approach over 100 trials.

Index	Hybrid	Cholesky-based
1	6.432×10^{-17}	4.406×10^{-17}
2	9.280×10^{-17}	4.937×10^{-17}
3	4.693×10^{-17}	5.124×10^{-17}
4	3.382×10^{-18}	3.250×10^{-18}
5	8.232×10^{-18}	3.704×10^{-18}
6	2.468×10^{-17}	9.552×10^{-17}
7	3.143×10^{-17}	1.079×10^{-17}
8	1.501×10^{-17}	1.007×10^{-17}
9	1.525×10^{-17}	7.393×10^{-18}
10	3.257×10^{-16}	1.072×10^{-17}
11	2.379×10^{-4}	1.035×10^{-17}
12	5.530×10^{-18}	8.279×10^{-18}

matrix and Kendall's tau matrix, like Cholesky-based approach, it can exactly preserve the covariance matrix of the original data as shown in Table 6. In the other words, the hybrid method significantly outperforms PRIMP in terms of preserving the correlation matrix. Also, it solves the problem of generating seeds for the Cholesky-based approach. Furthermore, in theory, the leakage risk of the hybrid approach is less than that of PRIMP. Therefore, it is also useful for privacy preserving.

5. CONCLUSION

We have proposed two new simulation-based privacy preserving frameworks for multivariate numerical data sets. The first is called PRIMP (PRivacy preserving by Independent coMPonents). It is shown empirically that the synthetic data set generated by PRIMP can preserve more statistical characteristics of the original data set than previous approaches. We have also proposed a hybrid method that combines PRIMP and the Cholesky-based approach for privacy preservation. The proposed method resolves the problem of generating good seeds for the Cholesky-based approach. Although the empirical results show that the hybrid approach is not always better than PRIMP in terms of Spearman's rank correlation matrix and Kendall's tau matrix for preserving privacy, like the Cholesky-based approach, it can preserve the covariance matrix of the original data exactly. Finally, in theory, the leakage risk of the hybrid approach is less than that of PRIMP. Overall, it is also useful for privacy preservation.

6. ACKNOWLEDGMENTS

The work was supported in part by the National Science Council of Taiwan, R.O.C., under Contracts NSC97-2221-E-002-172-MY3.

7. REFERENCES

[1] N. R. Adam and J. C. Worthmann. Security-control methods for statistical databases: a comparative study. *ACM Computing Surveys*, 21(4):515–556, 1989.

[2] R. Agrawal and R. Srikant. Privacy-preserving data mining. In *Proceedings of the 2000 ACM SIGMOD international conference on Management of data*, pages 439–450, New York, NY, USA, 2000. ACM Press.

[3] K. Chen and L. Liu. Privacy preserving data classification with rotation perturbation. In *ICDM*, pages 589–592, 2005.

[4] U. Cherubini, E. Luciano, and W. Vecchiato. *Copula Methods in Fiance.* Wiley, 2004.

[5] G. Crises. Synthetic microdata generation for database privacy protection. Technical Report CRIREP-04-2004, The CRISES research group, 2004.

[6] R. A. Dandekar, M. Cohen, and N. Kirkendall. Sensitive micro data protection using latin hypercube sampling technique. In *Inference Control in Statistical Databases, From Theory to Practice*, pages 117–125, London, UK, 2002. Springer-Verlag.

[7] R. A. Dandekar, J. Domingo-Ferrer, and F. Sebé. Lhs-based hybrid microdata vs rank swapping and microaggregation for numeric microdata protection. In *Inference Control in Statistical Databases, From Theory to Practice.*

[8] A. C. Davison and D. V. Hinkley. *Bootstrap Methods and Their Application.* Cambridge University Press, 1997.

[9] L. Devroye. *Non-Uniform Random Variate Generation.* Springer-Verlag, 1986.

[10] C. B. D.J. Newman, S. Hettich and C. Merz. UCI repository of machine learning databases, 1998.

[11] J. Domingo-Ferrer and V. Torra. A quantitative comparison of disclosure control methods for microdata. In *confidentiality, Disclosure and Data Access: Theory and Practical Applications for Statistical Agencies*, pages 111–134. North-Holland, 2001.

[12] R. A. Horn and C. R. Johnson. *Matrix Analysis.* Cambridge University Press, 1985.

[13] Z. Huang, W. Du, and B. Chen. Deriving private information from randomized data. In *Proceedings of the 2005 ACM SIGMOD international conference on Management of data*, pages 37–48, New York, NY, USA, 2005. ACM Press.

[14] A. Hyvärinen, J. Karhunen, and E. Oja. *Independent Component Analysis.* John Wiley & Sons, 2001.

[15] I. T. Jollife. *Principle Component Analysis.* Springer-Verlag, New York, 2 edition, 2002.

[16] H. Kargupta, S. Datta, Q. Wang, and K. Sivakumar. On the privacy preserving properties of random data perturbation techniques. In *Proceedings of the Third IEEE International Conference on Data Mining*, pages 19–22, Washington, DC, USA, 2003. IEEE Computer Society.

[17] C. K. Liew, U. J. Choi, and C. J. Liew. A data distortion by probability distribution. *ACM Transactions Database Systems*, 10(3):395–411, 1985.

[18] J. M. Mateo-Sanz, A. Martínez-Ballesté, and J. Domingo-Ferrer. Fast generation of accurate synthetic microdata. In *Privacy in Statistical Databases*, pages 298–306, 2004.

[19] M. D. McKay, R. J. Beckman, and W. J. Conover. A comparison of three methods for selecting values of input variables in the analysis of output from a computer code. *Technometrics*, 21(2):239–245, 1979.

[20] K. Muralidhar and R. Sarathy. Security of random data perturbation methods. *ACM Transactions Database Systems*, 24(4):487–493, 1999.

[21] K. Muralidhar and R. Sarathy. Data shuffling - a new masking approach for numerical data. *Management Science*, 52(5):658–670, 2006.

[22] G. G. Roussas. *A Course in Mathematical Statistics.* Academic Press, 1997.

Author Index

www.ingramcontent.com/pod-product-compliance
Ingram Content Group UK Ltd.
Pitfield, Milton Keynes, MK11 3LW, UK
UKHW051454290926
15471UKWH00008B/1200

9 781450 313544